India

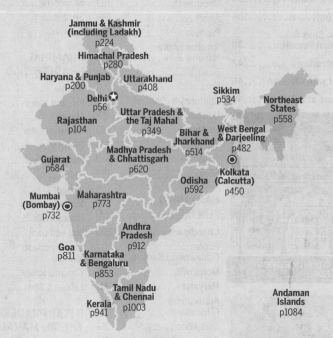

Jammu & Kashmir
(including Ladakh)
p224

Himachal Pradesh
p280

Haryana & Punjab
p200

Uttarakhand
p408

Delhi ★
p56

Sikkim
p534

Northeast
States
p558

Rajasthan
p104

Uttar Pradesh &
the Taj Mahal
p349

Bihar &
Jharkhand
p514

West Bengal
& Darjeeling
p482

Gujarat
p684

Madhya Pradesh
& Chhattisgarh
p620

Kolkata
(Calcutta)
p450

Odisha
p592

Mumbai
(Bombay) ◉
p732

Maharashtra
p773

Andhra
Pradesh
p912

Goa
p811

Karnataka
& Bengaluru
p853

Tamil Nadu
& Chennai
p1003

Kerala
p941

Andaman
Islands
p1084

THIS EDITION WRITTEN AND RESEARCHED BY

Sarina Singh

Michael Benanav, Joe Bindloss, Lindsay Brown, Mark Elliott,
Paul Harding, Trent Holden, Amy Karafin, Anirban Mahapatra, Bradley
Mayhew, Daniel McCrohan, Kate Morgan, John Noble, Kevin Raub

Contents

NIKADA / GETTY IMAGES ©

CITY PALACE, JAIPUR
P109

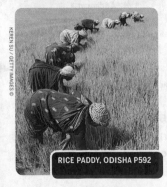

KEREN SU / GETTY IMAGES ©

RICE PADDY, ODISHA P592

Contents

ON THE ROAD

Contents

SPECIAL FEATURES

Welcome to India

India bristles with a mind-stirring mix of landscapes and cultural traditions. Your journey through this intoxicating country will blaze in your memory long after you've left its shores.

The Great Outdoors

From the soaring snow-dusted mountains of the far north to the steamy sun-washed beaches of the deep south, India's dramatic terrain is breathtaking. Along with abundant natural beauties, exquisitely carved temples rise majestically out of pancake-flat deserts and crumbling old fortresses peer over plunging ravines. Aficionados of the great outdoors can scout for big jungle cats on wildlife safaris, paddle in the shimmering waters of one of many beautiful beaches, take blood-pumping treks high in the Himalaya, or simply inhale pine-scented air on meditative forest walks.

Food, Glorious Food

Brace yourself – you're about to take one of the wildest culinary trips of your travelling life. Here you'll fry, simmer, sizzle, knead, roast and flip across a deliciously diverse repertoire of dishes. The hungry traveller can look forward to a tasty smorgasbord of regionally distinct creations, each with their own traditional preparation techniques and presentation styles – from the competing flavours of masterfully marinated meats and thalis to the simple splendour of vegetarian curries and deep-sea delights.

Expect the Unexpected

India loves to toss up the unexpected. This can be challenging, particularly for the first-time visitor: the poverty is confronting, Indian bureaucracy can be exasperating and the crush of humanity may turn the simplest task into a frazzling epic. Even veteran travellers find their nerves frayed at some point; yet this is all part of the India experience. With an ability to inspire, frustrate, thrill and confound all at once, adopting a 'go with the flow' attitude is wise if you wish to retain your sanity. Love it or loathe it – and most travellers see-saw between the two – to embrace India's unpredictability is to embrace its soul.

Simply Soul Stirring

Spirituality is the common thread that weaves its way through the vast and complex tapestry that is contemporary India. The multitude of sacred sites and time-honoured rituals are testament to the country's long, colourful and sometimes tumultuous religious history. And then there are the festivals! India hosts some of the world's most spectacular devotional celebrations – from formidable city parades celebrating auspicious events on the religious calendar to simple harvest fairs that pay homage to a locally worshipped deity.

Why I Love India

by Sarina Singh, Author

The moment I start to think I'm right on the precipice of unravelling one of its deep mysteries, India has an uncanny way of reminding me that it would take more than just a few lifetimes to do so. Indeed, demystifying India is a perpetual work in progress. And that is precisely what makes the country so deeply addictive for me. The constant exploration. The playful unpredictability. And knowing that, just when it's least expected, you can find yourself up close and personal with moments that have the power to alter the way you view the world and your place in it.

For more about our authors, see page 1248

Above: Decorated elephant with rider, Elephant Festival (p105), Jaipur

India

Delhi
Architectural splendour and a 400-year-old bazaar (p56)

Agra
Home to the iconic Taj Mahal (p351)

Khajuraho
Sensuous sculptures wrap handsome temples (p633)

Himalayan Mountains
Starkly beautiful mountainscapes (p534)

Darjeeling
Quintessential hill station, famed for its tea (p494)

Varanasi
Intense spirituality by the Ganges River (p388)

Amritsar
Sikhism's deeply revered Golden Temple (p212)

Jaisalmer
Formidable fort and desert camel safaris (p183)

ELEVATION

6000m
5000m
4000m
3000m
2000m
1000m
0

External boundaries shown reflect the requirements of the Government of India. Some boundaries may not be those recognised by neighbouring countries. Lonely Planet always tries to show on maps where travellers may need to cross a boundary (and present documentation) irrespective of any dispute.

0 — 500 km
0 — 250 miles

TAJIKISTAN

Dushanbe

AFGHANISTAN

Kabul

Islamabad

PAKISTAN

Under Administration of Pakistan

Jammu & Kashmir

Srinagar

Kargil

K2 (Godwin Austin) (8611m)

Leh

Padum

Ladakh

Zanskar

Kishtwar

Under Administration of China

CHINA
TIBET

Lhasa

Gyantse

Thimphu Valley

Thimphu

BHUTAN

Gangtok

Sikkim

Mt Everest (8848m)

Darjeeling

Siliguri

Jaldapara Wildlife Sanctuary

Guwahati

Shillong

Meghalaya

BANGLADESH

Dhaka

Agartala

Aizawl

Manipur

Imphal

Kohima

Nagaland

Kaziranga National Park

Dibrugarh

Itanagar

Arunachal Pradesh

Great Himalayan Range

Jammu

Pathankot

Dalhousie

Dharamsala

Manali

Kullu

Shimla

Himachal Pradesh

Dehra Dun

Haridwar

Nainital

Uttarakhand

Nanda Devi (7816m)

Annapurna (8090m)

NEPAL

Kathmandu

Gorakhpur

Bihar

Muzaffarpur

Patna

Gaya

Bodhgaya

Jharkhand

West Bengal

Shantiniketan

Attari

Amritsar

Firozpur

Bathinda

Punjab

Chandigarh

Haryana

Churu

Hansi

Corbett Tiger Reserve

Delhi

Mathura

Agra

Gwalior

Jhansi

Shivpuri

Khajuraho

Satna

Madhya Pradesh

Bareilly

Lucknow

Ayodhya

Allahabad (Tirth Raj)

Prayag

Varanasi

Ganges

Yamuna

Uttar Pradesh

Kanpur

Keoladeo Ghana National Park

Jaipur

Ranthambhore National Park

Ajmer

Bundi

Kota

Chittorgarh (Chittor)

Udaipur

Mt Abu

Rajasthan

Bikaner

Jodhpur

Barmer

Jaisalmer

Great Thar Desert

Great Rann of Kutch

Gujarat

Ajanta Caves
Ancient caves along a horseshoe-shaped cliff (p788)

Hampi
Ruins peppered amid enigmatic boulders (p896)

Mumbai
India's cosmopolitan capital of cool (p732)

Goan Beaches
Golden sands nuzzle the Arabian Sea (p811)

Keralan Backwaters
Palm-fringed rivers, lakes and lagoons (p966)

MYANMAR (BURMA)

Andaman Sea

Nicobar Islands

Andaman Islands

Port Blair

Bay of Bengal

SRI LANKA

Gulf of Mannar

INDIAN OCEAN

Arabian Sea

Lakshadweep Sea

Tripura

Mizoram

Ranchi

Kolkata (Calcutta)

Kharagpur

Digha

Balasore

Paradip

Cuttack

Konark

Puri

Berharrpur

Simlipal National Park

Jamshedpur

Chhattisgarh

Odisha (Orissa)

Bhubaneswar

Bheemunipatnam

Visakhapatnam

Kakinada

Machilipatnam

Raipur

Bilaspur

Sambalpur

Ranipur

Jhaial

Dindori

Bhopal

Kanha National Park

Seoni

Nagpur

Maharashtra

Watangal

Hyderabad

Andhra Pradesh

Vijayawada

Ongole

Chennai (Madras)

Mamallapuram

Puducherry (Pondicherry)

Chidambaram

Trichy (Tiruchirappalli)

Vellore

Chittoor

Nandi Hills

Bengaluru (Bangalore)

Hampi

Hospet

Gadag

Karnataka

Belgaum

Hubli

Bijapur

Sholapur

Sanchi

Raisen

Watanpur

Aurangabad

Ajanta

Upper Godavari Valley

Pune

Nasik

Kalyan

Mumbai (Bombay)

Mahabaleshwar

Konkan Hills

Panaji (Panjim)

Goa

Mangalore

Thalasseri (Tellicherry)

Kozhikode (Calicut)

Lakshadweep Islands

Kochi (Cochin)

Kerala

Kollam

Kovalam

Kanyakumari

Thiruvananthapuram (Trivandrum)

Periyar Wildlife Sanctuary

Coimbatore

Ooty (Udhagamandalam)

Mysore

Hassan

Madurai

Rameswaram

Tamil Nadu

Western Ghats

Eastern Ghats

Colombo

Gandhinagar

Ahmedabad

Ratlam

Ujjain

Dewas

Indore

Mandu

Khandwa

Vadodara (Baroda)

Surat

Dhule

Jalgaon

Daman

Dahanu

Diu

Bhavnagar

Rajkot

Junagadh

Sasan Gir Wildlife Sanctuary

Porbandar

Dwarka

Jamnagar

Bhuj

Little Rann Wildlife Sanctuary

Porbandar Coast

Sunderbans Tiger Reserve

India's
Top 17

Dreamy Hampi

1 The surreal boulderscape of Hampi (p896) was once the glorious and cosmopolitan Vijayanagar, capital of a powerful Hindu empire. Still glorious in ruins, its temples and royal structures combine sublimely with the terrain: giant rocks balance on skinny pedestals near an ancient elephant garage; temples tuck into crevices between boulders; and wicker coracles float by rice paddies and bathing buffaloes near a gargantuan bathtub for a queen. Watching the sunset cast a rosy glow over the dreamy landscape, you might just forget what planet you're on.

Taj Mahal

2 Don't let fears of tour buses or touts or hordes of visitors get you thinking you can skip Agra's Taj Mahal (p354) – you can't. Even on a crowded, hot day, this world wonder is still the 'Crown of Palaces', a monument to love whose very walls seem to resound with the Emperor Shah Jahan's adoration of his beloved Mumtaz Mahal, the 'Gem of the Palace'. The marble mausoleum – inlaid with calligraphy, precious and semiprecious stones and intricate flower designs representing eternal paradise – is the world's most poetic parting.

1

DOZIER MARC / GETTY IMAGES ©

ANDREW PARKINSON / GETTY IMAGES ©

SARAVANAN ALAGARSAMY / GETTY IMAGES ©

Cuppa in a Hill Station

3 The valleys, deserts and palm-lined beaches are all well and good, but it can get hot down there. India's princes and British colonials long used cool mountain towns like Darjeeling (p494) as refuges from the heat, and today the hill stations still have lush forests and crisp mountain air. So curl up under a blanket with a steaming cup of local tea and watch mountain birds swooping over misty hillsides, moody clouds passing over undulating hills of bulbous tea trees and village kids running through mountain fog and wildflowers.

Tea estate, Darjeeling

Safaris

4 You have to be lucky to spot a tiger or a leopard in India, but it can be done. Even if you don't see any, you'll enjoy wandering one of India's many forest wildlife reserves on the back of an elephant, observing deer, peacocks and langur monkeys while birds and butterflies flit overhead. Or just forget the tigers and elephants and go for camels: desert safaris around Jaisalmer (p188) and Bikaner (p195) involve riding atop the tall, goofy animals and camping out among dunes under star-packed skies.

Bengal tiger

Backwaters of Kerala

5 It's unusual to find a place as gorgeous as Kerala's backwaters (p966): 900km of interconnected rivers, lakes and lagoons lined with tropical flora. And if you do, there likely won't be a way to experience it that's as peaceful and intimate as a few days on a teak-and-palm-thatch houseboat. Float along the water – maybe as the sun sets behind the palms, maybe while eating to-die-for Keralan seafood, maybe as you fall asleep under a twinkling sky – and forget about life on land for a while.

Himalayan Mountains & Monasteries

6 Up north, where the air is cool and crisp, quaint hill stations give way to snow-topped peaks. Here, the cultural influences came not via coasts but via mountain passes. Tibetan Buddhism thrives, and multilayered monasteries emerge from the forest or steep cliffs as vividly and poetically as the sun rises over golden Khangchendzonga (p551). Prayer flags blow in the wind, the sound of monks chanting reverberates in meditation halls, and locals bring offerings, all in the shadow of the mighty Himalaya.

Amritsar's Golden Temple

7 The Sikhs' holiest of shrines, the Golden Temple (p212) is a magical place. Seeming to float atop a glistening pool named for the 'nectar of immortality', the temple is a gorgeous structure, made even more so by its extreme goldness (the lotus-shaped dome is gilded in the real thing). Even when crowded with pilgrims, the temple is peaceful, with birds singing outside and the sacred waters gently lapping against the godly abode.

Delhi

8 India's capital (p56) has had several incarnations over the last few thousand years, which partly explains why there's so much going on here. The big lures are the atmospheric ruins on every corner (the remains of seven historical cities) and the crumbling splendour of Old Delhi with the majestic Jama Masjid, Red Fort and other monuments of the historic Mughal capital. Plus, brilliant museums, spectacular food and Chandni Chowk – a 400-year-old bazaar designed by Shah Jahan's daughter, Jahanara. Red Fort (p61)

Goan Beaches

9 There might be no better place in the world to be lazy than on one of Goa's spectacular beaches (p811). With palm-tree groves on one side of the white sands and gently lapping waves on the other, the best of the beaches live up to your image of a tropical paradise. But it's not an undiscovered one: the sands are also peppered with fellow travellers and beach-shack restaurants. Goa's treasures are for social creatures and fans of creature comforts who like their seafood fresh and their holidays easy. Palolem (p849)

8

9

Mumbai's Architectural Visions

10 Mumbai (p732) has always absorbed everything in its midst and made it its own. The architectural result is a heady mix of buildings with countless influences. The art deco and modern towers give the city its cool, but it's the eclectic Victorian-era structures – the neo-Gothic, Indo-Saracenic and Gothic hodgepodge – that have come to define Mumbai. All those spires, gables, arches and onion domes, set off by palm trees and banyans, are fitting ornaments for this city. Chhatrapati Shivaji Terminus (Victoria Terminus; p737)

Neighbourhood Markets

11 Shopaholics: be careful not to lose control. Those with no interest in shopping: get in touch with your consumerist side. India's markets have something you want, guaranteed (though you may not have known it), with a fun haggle to go with it. The range of Technicolor saris, glittering gold and silver bling, mounds of rainbow vermilion, aromatic fresh spices, stainless-steel head massagers, bangles and bobby pins, motorcycle bumper stickers, heaping piles of fruit, Bollywood-star-silkscreened pajamas, and marigold and coconut offerings is, well, astounding.

Jaisalmer's Desert Mirage

12 Rising like a sandcastle from the deserts of Rajasthan, the 'Land of Kings', Jaisalmer's 12th-century citadel (p186) looks more like something from a dream than reality. The enormous golden sandstone fort, with its crenellated ramparts and undulating towers, is a fantastical structure, even while camouflaged against the desert sand. Inside, an ornate royal palace, fairytale *havelis* (traditional residences), intricately carved Jain temples and narrow lanes conspire to create the world's best place to get lost. Jaisalmer Fort (p186)

Riding the Rails

13 India's quintessential journey is still the long train ride. Domestic flights are increasingly common, but as the train's 25 million daily passengers will tell you, you can't watch the Indian landscape change from dry valley to mountain forest to lime-green rice paddies on a plane. The train's also where you can hang out with families and other domestic travellers, learning about Indian culture the old-fashioned way – over a cup of tea, to the rhythm of the rails.
Nilgiri Mountain Railway (p1082)

Sexy Khajuraho

14 Some say that the sensuous carvings on Khajuraho's temples (p633) depict the Kama Sutra, or Tantric practices for initiates; others, that they're educational models for children or allegories for the faithful. But pretty much everyone agrees that they're naughty and fun. Want to see a nine-person orgy? Men getting it on with horses? Hot nymphs? Khajuraho's your chance. Once the titillation passes, you'll notice that the carving and architecture of these thousand-year-old temples are exquisite, and the magical feeling of being in 11th-century India pleasantly absorbing.
Kandariya-Mahadev (p633)

Streets Alive

15 At first it might be overwhelming – dust will get in your eyes, honking in your ears, people in your way – but you'll adjust. And when you do, you'll find insanely good food being fried in carts, trucks painted with baroque designs, flower garlands sold by friendly vendors, cars, rickshaws and bicycles dancing together to a rhythm only they can hear, people speaking several of India's 1500-plus languages and, of course, cows – those sweet, stubborn animals that Gandhi called the 'mother to millions of Indian mankind'.

Caves of Ajanta

16 They may have been ascetics, but the 2nd-century-BC monks who created the Ajanta caves (p788) had an eye for the dramatic. The 30 rock-cut forest grottoes punctuate the side of a horseshoe-shaped cliff, and originally had individual staircases leading down to the river. The architecture and towering stupas made these caves inspiring places in which to meditate and live, but the real bling came centuries later, in the form of exquisite carvings and paintings depicting the Buddha's former lives. Renunciation of the worldly life was never so sophisticated.

Holy Varanasi

17 Everyone in Varanasi (p388) seems to be dying or praying or hustling or cremating someone or swimming or laundering or washing buffaloes in the city's sewage-saturated Ganges. The goddess river will clean away your sins and help you escape from that tedious life-and-death cycle – and Varanasi is the place to take a sacred (and exceedingly dirty) dip. So take a deep breath, put on a big smile for the ever-present touts, go to the holy water and get your karma in order.

16

17

Need to Know

For more information, see Survival Guide (p1173)

Currency
Indian Rupees (₹)

Languages
Hindi and English

Visas
Most people travel using a six-month tourist visa, which is valid from the date of issue, not the date you arrive in India.

Money
ATMs in most large towns; carry cash or travellers cheques as back-up. MasterCard and Visa are the most widely accepted credit cards.

Mobile Phones
Roaming connections are excellent in urban areas, poor in the countryside and Himalaya. Local prepaid SIMs are widely available but security checks are complex and time-consuming and it may take days to get connected.

Time
Indian Standard Time (GMT/UTC plus 5½ hours)

When to Go

Leh
GO Jul–Sep

Delhi
GO Nov–Mar

Kolkata (Calcutta)
GO Nov–Mar

Mumbai (Bombay)
GO Nov–Feb

Bengaluru (Bangalore)
GO Nov–Mar

- Desert, dry climate
- Mild to hot summers, cold winters
- Tropical climate, rain year-round
- Tropical climate, wet & dry seasons
- Warm to hot summers, mild winters

Low Season
(Apr–Jun)

➡ April is hot; May and June are scorching. Competitive hotel prices.

➡ From June, the monsoon sweeps from south to north, bringing draining humidity.

➡ Beat the heat (but not the crowds) in the cool hills.

Shoulder
(Jul–Nov)

➡ Passes to Ladakh and the high Himalaya open from July to September.

➡ Monsoon rain-showers persist through to September.

➡ The southeast coast and southern Kerala see heavy rain from October to early December.

High Season
(Dec–Mar)

➡ Pleasant weather – warm days, cool nights. Peak tourists. Peak prices.

➡ December and January bring chilly nights in the north.

➡ Temperatures climb steadily from February.

Useful Websites

Lonely Planet (www.lonely planet.com/india) Destination information, the Thorn Tree Travel Forum and more.

Incredible India (www. incredibleindia.org) Official India tourism site.

Templenet (www.templenet .com) Temple talk.

Rediff News (www.rediff.com/ news) Portal for India-wide news.

World Newspapers (www. world-newspapers.com/india .html) Links to India's English-language publications.

Important Numbers

From outside India, dial your international access code, India's country code (☏00) then the number (minus '0', only used when dialling domestically).

Country code	☏91
International access code	☏00
Ambulance	☏102
Fire	☏101
Police	☏100

Exchange Rates

Australia	A$1	₹57
Canada	C$1	₹54
Euro zone	€1	₹71
Japan	¥100	₹55
New Zealand	NZ$1	₹47
UK	UK£1	₹84
US	US$1	₹55

For current exchange rates see www.xe.com

Daily Costs

Budget: Less than ₹2000

➡ Dorm bed: ₹100–200

➡ Double room in a budget hotel: ₹300–700

➡ All-you-can-eat thalis (plate meals): ₹120–300

➡ Bus & train tickets: ₹300–500

Midrange: ₹2000–7000

➡ Double hotel room: ₹800–4000

➡ Meals in midrange restaurants: ₹400–1500

➡ Admission to historic sights and museums: ₹100–1000

➡ Local taxis/autorickshaws: ₹200–500

Top End: More than ₹7000

➡ Deluxe hotel room: ₹4000–20,000

➡ Meals at superior restaurants: ₹1000–4000

➡ First-class train travel: ₹800–8000

➡ Renting a car and driver: ₹1000 upwards per day

Opening Hours

Business hours are year-round for banks, offices and restaurants; many sights keep summer and winter opening hours.

Banks 9am–5pm Monday to Friday, 9am–2pm Saturday (some banks close at 3pm Monday to Friday)

Restaurants lunch noon–3pm, dinner 7pm–10pm or 11pm

Bars & Clubs noon–1am or later

Shops 10am–7pm or 8pm, some closed Sunday

Markets 10am–7pm in major cities, usually with one closed day; rural markets may be once weekly, from early morning to lunchtime

Arriving in India

Indira Gandhi International Airport (Delhi; p144) Prepaid taxis cost ₹350 to ₹800 to the centre; express buses run every 20 minutes; airport express metro trains (5.15am to 11.30pm) link up with the metro system.

Chhatrapati Shivaji International Airport (Mumbai; p769) Prepaid taxis to Colaba, Fort and Marine Dr cost ₹650/750 (non-AC/AC). Expect to pay ₹395 to ₹495 to southern neighbourhoods.

Chennai International Airport (Chennai; p1020) Suburban trains to central Chennai run several times hourly from 4am to midnight from Tirusulam station at the airport. Prepaid taxis cost ₹380 to ₹515.

Getting Around

Transport in India is frequent and inexpensive, though not always fast. Consider domestic flights or sleeper trains as an alternative to long, uncomfortable bus rides.

Air Flights to most major centres and state capitals; cheap flights with budget airlines.

Train Frequent services to most destinations; inexpensive tickets available even on sleeper trains.

Bus Buses go everywhere; some destinations are served 24 hours but longer routes may have just one or two buses a day (typically early morning or afternoon/evening).

For much more on **getting around**, see p1195

If You Like...

Forts & Palaces

India's history is riddled with tales of conquest and domination: guys trying to get or keep the region's many literal and figurative jewels – and then enjoying them.

Rajasthan Jaisalmer, Jodhpur and Amber are rightly the most popular forts; Udaipur palace is surreally romantic. (p104)

Maharashtra The land of Shivaji has defensive masterpieces like Daulatabad (p784), camouflaged on a hilltop, and Janjira (p794), an island fortress.

Hyderabad The rugged Golconda Fort complements the many ethereal palaces of the City of Pearls. (p917)

Delhi It's been a strategic city for a few millennia, with a number of forts to show for it. (p61)

Ladakh Leh (p230) and Stok (p246) Palaces, resembling mini versions of Tibet's Potala Palace, are memorable if relatively empty.

Grand Temples & Monasteries

No one does temples like India – from psychedelic Technicolor Hindu towers to silently grand Buddhist cave temples and Amritsar's gold-plated fairy-tale Sikh shrine.

Tamil Nadu A temple wonderland, with towering, fantastical structures that climb to the sky in busy rainbows of sculpted deities. (p1003)

Golden Temple The queen of Sikh temples rises like a shining gem over a pool in Amritsar. (p212)

Rajasthan Jain temples at Jaisalmer, Ranakpur and Mt Abu are the stone-architecture equivalent of princesses draped in piles of jewellery. (p104)

Khajuraho Exquisite carvings of deities, spirits, musicians, regular people, mythological beasts – and lots of sex. (p633)

Tawang Gompa The world's second-largest Buddhist monastery, in Arunachal Pradesh, is set against snowy peaks. (p577)

Ajanta & Ellora Ancient, vast, sculpted caves. Because monks like beautiful sculpture, too. (p788 & p785)

Ancient Ruins

You don't get to be a 5000-year-old civilisation without having lots of atmospheric ruins around. So many cultures and empires have left their marks here, making for easy time travel.

Hampi Rosy-hued temples and palaces of the mighty capital of Vijayanagar are scattered among otherworldly looking boulders and hilltops. (p897)

Mandu Many of the tombs, palaces, monuments and mosques on Mandu's 20-sq-km green plateau are among India's finest Afghan architecture. (p668)

Nalanda This 1600-year-old university once enrolled 10,000 monks and students. Its monasteries, temples and stupas are still elegant in ruins. (p530)

Delhi Conquered and rebuilt again over the past 3000 years, Delhi has a high ruin density. (p60)

IF YOU LIKE... MOTORCYCLING

The mountain pass between Manali and Ladakh or Spiti may be the most spectacular motorcycle ride of your life. (p315)

City Sophistication

City people here had attained high planes of sophistication when culture was

just a glimmer in the West's eye. India's cities have great arts scenes, excellent restaurants and heaps of style.

Mumbai Mumbai has it all: fashion, film stars, incredible restaurants, glamorous lounges and (along with Delhi) the country's best art galleries. (p732)

Delhi This urban sophisticate has historic attractions, exceedingly good shopping, museums, street food and fine dining. (p56)

Kolkata Long known for its poetic and political tendencies, Kolkata also has fabulous colonial-era architecture and a lively arts scene. (p450)

Hyderabad The ancient architecture of several excessively wealthy dynasties sits across town from excellent dining, nightlife and shopping. (p915)

Bazaars

Indian megamalls may be popping up like monsoon frogs, but the age-old bazaar – with its crowds and spices, garbage and flowers, altars and underwear – is still where it's at.

Old Delhi The Mughal-era bazaars sell pretty much everything, while Chandni Chowk has some of India's best street food. (p95)

Goa Tourist flea markets are huge on the north coast, while Panaji (Panjim) and Margao bazaars make for excellent wandering. (p837)

Mumbai The megalopolis's old, characterful markets are handily themed: Mangaldas (fabric), Zaveri (jewellery), Crawford (produce) and Chor (random antique things). (p767)

Mysore Devaraja Market is about 125 years old and filled with about 125 million flowers, fruits and vegetables. (p870)

(Top) Dried rose petals on a rooftop, Chandni Chowk area (p66), Delhi
(Bottom) Golden Temple (p212), Amritsar

Beaches

India's coastlines are diverse and gorgeous, with lots of personality. Several Goan and Keralan beaches are downright paradisiacal, while elsewhere, the shoreline is more tinselled, with strolling and snack carts.

Kerala Kovalam and Varkala, with their crescent-shaped white-sand beaches, palm trees, lighthouse (Kovalam) and dramatic cliffs (Varkala), are a vision. (p954)

Goa Even when overrun with travellers, they're still lovely somehow. Vagator and Palolem are two of the prettiest. (p849)

Havelock Island In the Andaman Islands, one of the world's prettiest beaches has clear, aquamarine water lapping against white powder. (p1093)

East Coast Puri (p605) and Visakhapatnam (p933) are more fun than precious: think esplanades, balloon-wallahs and extended families eating candy floss.

Gokarna Originally for Goa overflow, Gokarna's beaches are cosy, beautiful and part of a sacred ancient village (p894)

Hill Stations

India is blessed with lots of warm sunshine and lots of hills to escape from it. Royalty and colonials of old laid the foundations for today's hill-station resort culture.

Tamil Nadu Tamil hill stations in the Western Ghats have lush, misty pine forests, tea planta-

tions, waterfalls, gorgeous vistas and colonial bungalows. (p1067)

Uttarakhand Mussoorie (p415) has Raj-era architecture, Himalayan views and walking trails galore; Nainital (p440) has those, too, plus a gigantic volcanic lake.

Munnar Kerala's not-too-touristy hill station is all rolling tea and spice plantations, unusual birds and dreamy mist. (p973)

Matheran This weekend retreat for Mumbaikars is scenic and car-free; it's also reached by narrow-gauge toy train. (p796)

Boat Tours

India has such a diverse collection of waterways that the cruising possibilities are endless. From canoes to steamships to houseboats, there are lots of ways to experience India's aquatic side.

Kerala Languorous drifting on the backwaters around Alappuzha (Alleppey), canoe tours from Kollam and bamboo-raft tours in Periyar Wildlife Sanctuary. (p969)

Andaman Islands See mangroves, rainforest and reefs with 50 types of coral at Mahatma Gandhi Marine National Park. (p1093)

Uttar Pradesh Navigate UP's chaotic holiness with dawn tours of Varanasi's ghats and sacred river cruises in Chitrakut, Mathura and Allahabad. (p349)

Assam Four- to 10-night steamboat cruises are offered along the mighty Brahmaputra River as it meanders through the Northeast. (p563)

Traveller Enclaves

Sometimes you don't want to explore exciting sights. Sometimes you just want to find travel partners, exchange stories and discuss strange bowel events.

Hampi The stunning beauty of Hampi's landscape and architecture makes everyone want to stay for a while. (p896)

Palolem Goa is one big traveller enclave, but Palolem is its current epicentre, with a gorgeous beach and cheap sleeps. (p849)

Yoga Centres Rishikesh (p424), Mysore (p869) and Pune (p799) all have major international yoga centres – and concomitant hang-outs.

Sudder St The accommodation on Kolkata's tourist lane is grungy but great for meeting fellow Mother Teresa volunteers. (p466)

Dharamsala Because who doesn't want to be near the Dalai Lama? (p318)

Arts & Crafts

Practically every place has its own tradition of devotional painting, silk weaving, camel-hide decorating, mirrored embroidering, silver-inlaid-gunmetal bangle-making, or other art you won't find elsewhere.

Odisha Indians like bling – always have – and silver's an old favourite. Odisha's *tarakasi*, a kind of filigree work, is stunning. (p592)

Gujarat & Rajasthan India's textile traditions are legion. Gujarati (p684) and Rajasthani (p104) villages specialise in embroidery with tiny mirrors: like jewellery for your clothes.

Bihar Folk paintings known as Mithila (or Madhubani) colourfully depict village scenes. The

---

IF YOU LIKE... CYCLING

Go for a peaceful roll around the ruins of Bidar Fort and nearby Bahmani tombs. (p910)

Travelling the backwaters (p966), near Alappuzha (Alleppey)

style is ancient but looks surprisingly contemporary. (p514)

Andhra Pradesh The intricate lines of *kalamkari* fabric are hand-drawn with a bamboo stick dipped in jaggery water. (p940)

Tamil Nadu The Tamil tradition of sculpting bronze figures of Nataraja, the cosmic dancer, is about 1000 years old. (p1003)

Mountains & Trekking

India has several beautiful mountain ranges that would be knockouts anywhere else. But here, there's only one range that matters: the Himalaya. The only question is how to approach it.

Ladakh The trekking and the views are excellent in the 'land of high passes', whose landscape resembles the moon. (p229)

Lahaul & Spiti Green Lahaul and dryer, more rugged Spiti are separated from the rest of Himachal Pradesh by seasonal mountain passes. (p339)

Arunachal Pradesh This off-the-beaten-track 'land of dawn-lit mountains' is all forest, hills and peaks on the Tibetan border. (p572)

Darjeeling Take the Singalila Ridge Trek for incredible views of the mighty Himalaya. (p494)

Sikkim See Khangchendzonga, the world's third-highest mountain, in the early morning from Pelling or on treks to Goecha La and Dzongri. (p556)

Wildlife Safaris

India's tigers and leopards do come out sometimes, but its elephants, antelope, bison, one-horned rhinos and deer are much more extroverted. Trips are usually by jeep or elephant.

Madhya Pradesh & Chhattisgarh This is tiger country, and tiger-spotting safaris are offered in several national parks. (p626)

Assam Kaziranga National Park is the world's rhinoceros capital. Seeing them involves an hour's ride on a lumbering elephant. (p567)

Kerala Wayanad Wildlife Sanctuary is one of the few places where you have a good chance of spotting wild elephants. (p996)

Gujarat The only wild Asiatic lions, along with 300 species of birds, live in the Sasan Gir Wildlife Sanctuary. (p713)

Karnataka Bandipur National Park, at the southern end of the Western Ghats, has 36 shy tigers, plus leopards and sloth bears. (p880)

Month By Month

TOP EVENTS

Carnival, January or February

Trekking, May to June and September to October

Ganesh Chaturthi, August or September

Navratri & Dussehra, September or October

Diwali, October or November

January

Post-monsoon cool lingers throughout the country, with downright cold in the mountains. Pleasant weather and several festivals make it a popular time to travel (book ahead!), while Delhi hosts big Republic Day celebrations.

◉ Free India

Republic Day commemorates the founding of the Republic of India on 26 January 1950; the biggest celebrations are in Delhi, which holds a huge military parade along Rajpath, and the Beating of the Retreat ceremony three days later.

🪁 Kite Festival

Sankranti, the Hindu festival marking the sun's passage into Capricorn, is celebrated in many ways across India – from banana-giving to holy dips in the Ganges to cockfights. But it's the mass kite-flying in Gujarat, Andhra Pradesh, Uttar Pradesh and Maharashtra that steal the show.

🪁 Southern Harvest

The Tamil festival of Pongal, equivalent to Sankranti, marks the end of the harvest season. Families prepare pots of *pongal* (a mixture of rice, sugar, dhal and milk), symbolic of prosperity and abundance, then feed them to decorated and adorned cows.

◉ Celebrating Saraswati

On Vasant Panchami, Hindus dress in yellow and place books, musical instruments and other educational objects in front of idols of Saraswati, the goddess of learning, to receive her blessing. The holiday may fall in February.

🪁 The Prophet Mohammed's Birthday

The Islamic festival of Eid-Milad-un-Nabi celebrates the birth of the Prophet Mohammed with prayers and processions, especially in Jammu and Kashmir. It falls around 13 January in 2014, 3 January in 2015 and 26 December in 2016.

February

The weather is comfortable in most nonmountainous areas, with summer heat starting to percolate in the south (up to Maharashtra and West Bengal). It's still peak travel season; sunbathing and skiing are still on.

LUNAR CALENDAR

Many festivals follow the Indian lunar calendar (a complex system based on astrology) or the Islamic calendar (which falls about 11 days earlier each year), and therefore change annually relative to the Gregorian calendar. Contact local tourist offices for exact festival dates.

✥ Tibetan New Year

Losar is celebrated by Tantric Buddhists all over India – particularly in Himachal Pradesh, Sikkim, Ladakh and Zanskar – for 15 days. Losar is usually in February or March, though dates can vary between regions.

◉ Shivaratri

This day of Hindu fasting recalls the *tandava* (cosmic victory dance) of Lord Shiva. Temple processions are followed by the chanting of mantras and anointing of linga (phallic images of Shiva). Shivaratri can also fall in March.

✥ Carnival in Goa

The four-day party kicking off Lent is particularly big in Goa. Sabado Gordo, Fat Saturday, starts it off with elaborate parades, and the revelry continues with street parties, concerts and general merrymaking.

March

The last month of the travel season, March is full-on hot in most of the country, with rains starting in the Northeast. Wildlife is easier to spot as animals come out to find water.

✥ Holi

One of North India's most ecstatic festivals; Hindus celebrate the beginning of spring according to the lunar calendar, in February or March, by throwing coloured water and *gulal* (powder) at anyone within range. Bonfires the night before symbolise the demise of demoness Holika.

(Dates: 17 March 2014; 6 March 2015; 23 March 2016.)

✥ Wildlife-Watching

When the weather warms up, water sources dry out and animals venture into the open to find refreshment: your chance to spot elephants, deer and, if you're lucky, tigers and leopards. See p1165 and visit www.sanctuaryasia.com for detailed info.

✥ Rama's Birthday

During Ramanavami, which lasts anywhere from one to nine days, Hindus celebrate Rama's birth with processions, music, fasting and feasting, enactments of scenes from the Ramayana and, at some temples, ceremonial weddings of Rama and Sita idols.

April

The heat has officially arrived in most places, which means you can get deals and avoid tourist crowds. The Northeast, meanwhile, is wet, but it's peak time for visiting Sikkim and upland West Bengal.

✥ Mahavir's Birthday

In April or March, Mahavir Jayanti commemorates the birth of Jainism's 24th and most important *tirthankar* (teacher and enlightened being). Temples are decorated and visited, Mahavir statues are given ritual baths, processions are held and offerings are given to the poor.

May

In most of the country it's hot. Really hot. Festivals slow down as humidity builds up in anticipation of the rain. Hill stations are hopping, though, and in the mountains it's premonsoon trekking season.

✥ Buddha's Birthday

Commemorating the Buddha's birth, nirvana (enlightenment) and parinirvana (total liberation from the cycle of existence, or passing away), Buddha Jayanti is quiet but moving: devotees dress simply, eat vegetarian food, listen to dharma talks and visit monasteries or temples.

✥ Northern Trekking

May and June, the months preceding the rains in the northern mountains, are good times for trekking, with sunshine and temperate weather. Consider Himachal Pradesh, Uttarakhand, and Jammu & Kashmir.

June

June's not a popular travel month in India, unless you're trekking up north. The rainy season, or premonsoon extreme heat, has started just about everywhere else.

✥ Odisha's Festival of Chariots

During Rath Yatra (Car Festival), effigies of Lord Jagannath (Vishnu incarnated as lord of the world) and his siblings are carried through towns on massive chariots, most famously in Puri, Odisha (Orissa; p593). Millions come to see them. (Dates: 19 June 2014; 18 July 2015; 6 July 2016.)

✸✸ Ramadan (Ramazan)

Thirty days of dawn-to-dusk fasting mark the ninth month of the Islamic calendar. Muslims traditionally turn their attention to God, with a focus on prayer and purification. Ramadan begins around 28 June 2014, 18 June 2015 and 6 June 2016.

July

It's really raining almost everywhere, with many remote roads being washed out. Consider visiting Ladakh, where the weather's surprisingly fine, or do a rainy-season meditation retreat, an ancient Indian tradition.

✸✸ Brothers & Sisters

On Raksha Bandhan (Narial Purnima), girls fix amulets known as *rakhis* to the wrists of brothers and close male friends to protect them in the coming year. Brothers reciprocate with gifts and promises to take care of their sisters.

August

It's still high monsoon season, but it's prime time in Ladakh. Some travellers love tropical areas, like Kerala or Goa, this time of year: the jungles are lush,

(Top) Revellers at the Holi festival (p25)

(Bottom) Traditional floor designs using powder during Diwali (p28)

green and glistening in the rain.

Snake Festival

The Hindu festival Naag Panchami is dedicated to Ananta, the serpent upon whose coils Vishnu rested between universes. Women return to their family homes and fast, while serpents are venerated as totems against flooding and other evils. Falls in July or August. (Dates: 1 August 2014; 19 August 2015; 7 August 2016.)

Pilgrimage, Size: Extra-Large

There are several versions of the huge Hindu pilgrimage, Kumbh Mela, held every few years, but all involve mass devotion – mass as in tens of millions of people. The next ritual group bathings are in Nasik (August/September 2015) and Ujjain (April/May 2016).

Independence Day

This public holiday on 15 August marks the anniversary of India's independence from Britain in 1947. Celebrations include flag-hoisting ceremonies (the biggest one is in Delhi), parades and patriotic cultural programs.

Celebrating the Buddha's Teaching

Drupka Teshi commemorates Siddhartha Gautama's first teaching, in which he explained the Four Noble Truths to disciples in Sarnath. Celebrations are big in Sikkim. The festival may also fall in July.

Krishna's Birthday

Janmastami celebrations can last a week in Krishna's birthplace, Mathura (p372); elsewhere the festivities range from fasting to *puja* (prayers) and offering sweets, to drawing elaborate *rangoli* (rice-paste designs) outside the home. Janmastami is held in August/September. (Dates: 17 August 2014; 5 September 2015; 25 August 2016.)

Parsi New Year

Parsis celebrate Pateti, the Zoroastrian new year, especially in Mumbai. Houses are cleaned and decorated with flowers and *rangoli*, the family dresses up and eats special fish dishes and sweets, and offerings are made at the Fire Temple.

Eid al-Fitr

Muslims celebrate the end of Ramadan with three days of festivities. Prayers, shopping, gift-giving and, for women and girls, *mehndi* (henna designs) may all be part of the celebrations.

September

The rain begins to ease up (with temperatures still relatively high), with places like Rajasthan all but finished with the monsoon. The second trekking season begins midmonth in the Himalaya and runs through October.

Ganesh's Birthday

In August or September Hindus celebrate Ganesh Chaturthi, the birth of the elephant-headed god, with verve, particularly in Mumbai (p732). Clay idols of Ganesh are paraded through the streets before being ceremonially immersed in rivers, tanks (reservoirs) or the sea. (Dates: 29 August to 8 September 2014; 17 to 27 September 2015; 5 to 15 September 2016.)

October

Some showers aside, this is when India starts to get its travel mojo on. October, aka shoulder season, brings festivals, mostly good weather with reasonably comfy temperatures, and lots of post-rain greenery and lushness.

Gandhi's Birthday

The national holiday of Gandhi Jayanti is a solemn celebration of Mohandas Gandhi's birth, on 2 October, with prayer meetings at his cremation site in Delhi, Raj Ghat (p67).

Water, Water Everywhere

Water bodies are full up after the rains, making for spectacularly gushing white-water falls. This is also the season for rafting in some areas; visit www.indiarafting.com.

Navratri

The Hindu 'Festival of Nine Nights' leading up to Dussehra celebrates the goddess Durga in all her incarnations. Festivities, in September or October, are particularly vibrant in West Bengal, Gujarat and Maharashtra; in Kolkata (p461), Durga images are ritually immersed in rivers and tanks.

Dussehra

Colourful Dussehra celebrates the victory of the Hindu god Rama over the demon-king Ravana and the triumph of good over evil. Dussehra is big in Kullu (p303), where effigies of Ravana are ritually burned, and Mysore (p875), which hosts one of India's grandest parades. (Dates: 4 October 2014; 22 October 2015; 11 October 2016.)

Diwali (Festival of Lights)

In the lunar month of Kartika, in October or November, Hindus celebrate Diwali (Deepavali) for five days, giving gifts, lighting fireworks, and burning butter and oil lamps (or hanging lanterns) to lead Lord Rama home from exile. One of India's prettiest festivals. (Dates: 23 October 2014; 11 November 2015; 30 October 2016.)

Eid al-Adha

Muslims commemorate Ibrahim's readiness to sacrifice his son to God by slaughtering a goat or sheep and sharing it with family, the community and the poor. (Dates: 14 October 2013; 4 October 2014; 3 September 2015.)

November

The climate is blissful in most places, but the southern monsoon is sweeping Tamil Nadu and Kerala.

Guru Nanak's Birthday

Nanak Jayanti, birthday of Guru Nanak, founder of Sikhism, is celebrated with prayer, *kirtan* (devotional singing) and processions for three days, especially in Punjab and Haryana. The festival may also be held on 14 April, possibly Nanak's actual 1469 birth date.

Muharram

During this month of grieving and remembrance, Shiite Muslims commemorate the martyrdom of the Prophet Mohammed's grandson Imam, an event known as Ashura, with beautiful processions. It begins around 4 November (2013), 25 October (2014) and 13 October (2015).

December

December is peak tourist season for a reason: the weather's glorious (except for the chilly mountains), the humidity's low, the

mood is festive and the beaches are sublime.

Weddings

Marriage season peaks in December, and you may see a *baraat* (bridegroom's procession), replete with white horse and fireworks, on your travels. Across the country, loud music and spectacular parties are the way they roll, with brides in *mehndi* and pure gold.

Birding

Many of India's 1000-plus bird species perform their winter migration from November to January or February, and excellent birdwatching spots are peppered across the country; www.birding.in is an excellent resource.

Camel Treks in Rajasthan

The cool winter (November to February) is the time to mount a camel and ride through Rajasthan's sands. See the Thar Desert from a whole new perspective: observe gazelles, cook dinner over an open fire and camp out in the dunes.

Itineraries

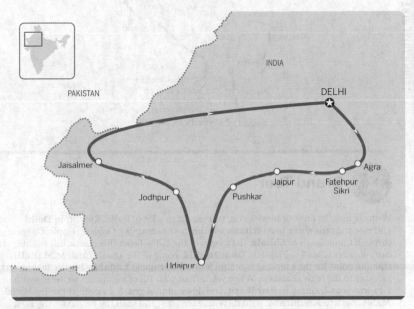

2 WEEKS Golden Triangle & Rajasthan

A tourist trail with genuine highlights to make up for the crowds, the Golden Triangle of Delhi, Agra and Jaipur combines some of India's top sights.

Kick off in **Delhi**, touring the must-sees – the Mughal-era Red Fort and Jama Masjid, and the magnificent Qutb Minar. Next, catch a train to **Agra** and gaze on the glory of the Taj Mahal, the world's most extravagant monument to love. Explore Agra Fort and devote a day to nearby **Fatehpur Sikri**, a mesmerising Mughal city. Continue on to **Jaipur**, and devote several days to the dusty bazaars and myriad monuments of the Pink City. Essential stops include the City Palace and Amber Fort.

Loop back to Delhi, or travel on to **Pushkar** for a few days of roaming around lakeside temples. Next, devote several days to graceful **Udaipur** and a lavish dinner at the hotel on the lake. Next visit Kumbhalgarh and the temple at Ranakpur, en route to **Jodhpur**. Soak up the colours of the Blue City from the battlements of magnificent Mehrangarh Fort. Spend the last few days in fortified **Jaisalmer** and indulge your *Arabian Nights* fantasies on a camel safari through the dunes. Finally, loop back to Delhi, with one last detour to the Qutb Minar, for a final dose of imperial splendour.

 Grand Tour

With six months on your tourist visa, you can fit in a lot of India. Kick off in **Delhi** and ride the rails north to **Amritsar**, to admire the gleaming Golden Temple. Connect through Chandigarh to **Shimla**, the Queen of the Hills. From this classic hill station you can roam northwest to Buddhist **Dharamsala**, home of the Dalai Lama, or **Manali**, starting point for the gruelling overland journey to rugged **Ladakh** (July to September), gateway to the high Himalaya. When you've had your fill of mountain air, head south for some yoga-training in **Rishikesh**, and descend to **Agra**, for a peek at the Taj Mahal. Amble south to **Khajuraho**, with its risque temples, and scan the jungle for tigers in **Bandhavgarh National Park**. Continue to the holy city of **Varanasi** for a boat trip along the sacred Ganges.

Take time for detours as you wander east to **Kolkata** (Calcutta), bustling capital of West Bengal. Swing north as far as **Darjeeling** or **Sikkim** for sweeping Himalayan views, then drift down the coast to the temple towns of **Konark** and **Puri** in Odisha (Orissa). Consider a flight to transport you south to **Chennai** (Madras) for a dose of southern spice.

As you loop around the bottom of India, essential stops include **Mamallapuram** (Mahabalipuram), for temple carvings; **Puducherry** (Pondicherry), for colonial quaintness; and **Madurai**, for deity-encrusted temple towers. Allow a few days to kick back on **Kerala's beaches**, then swing inland to nostalgic **Mysore** to see how maharajas lived.

Continuing north, head to **Hampi**, where temples and ruined cities are strewn amongst the boulders, then get a second dose of beach life on the coast of **Goa**. Onward to **Mumbai** (Bombay), fast-paced capital of the West Coast; take in a Bollywood movie, then admire the glory of the cave paintings and carvings at **Ajanta** and **Ellora**.

To finish, heed the call of the desert in Rajasthan and complete the coloured-city triple – pink (**Jaipur**), blue (**Jodhpur**) and white (**Udaipur**). There might just be time to detour to the fascinating temples and nature reserves of **Gujarat**, before closing the circle with a last train ride to Delhi.

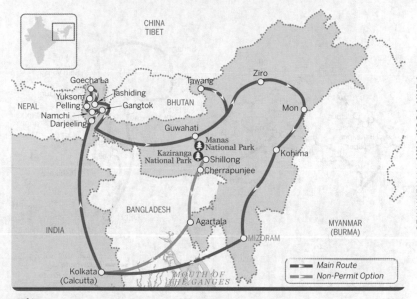

Sikkim & the Northeast States

1 MONTH

Surprisingly few people explore Sikkim and the Northeast States. Kept from prying eyes by insurgencies and permit restrictions, India's last frontier is slowly opening up to the outside world. From Kolkata, you can swing north to Darjeeling, get a full dose of Himalayan vistas in Sikkim then enter the fascinating world of India's hill tribes. Advance planning is essential – permits are mandatory and there are security risks to consider.

Starting in **Kolkata**, make your first stop **Darjeeling** – here you can sample India's finest teas and pick up a permit for Sikkim, one of India's most serene quarters. **Gangtok**, the Sikkimese capital, is the starting point for jeep rides to a string of historic, dramatic Buddhist temples. Veer to **Namchi** to see the giant statues of Shiva and Padmasambhava, and to **Pelling** for inspiring views of the white-peaked Khangchendzonga and the beautiful Pemayangtse Gompa, ringed by gardens and monks' cottages. Take the week-long trek from **Yuksom** to **Goecha La**, a 4940m pass with incredible views, then exit Sikkim via **Tashiding**, with more wonderful views and another stunning gompa, before travelling to Siliguri for the journey east.

In **Guwahati**, the Assamese capital, arrange tours and permits for the Northeast States: the remote areas of Arunachal Pradesh, Nagaland, Mizoram and Manipur. If you can't get a permit, try this loop: from Guwahati, head to **Manas National Park** and **Kaziranga National Park** to spot rare wildlife. Detour to sleepy **Shillong**, and the waterfalls and incredible living root bridges of **Cherrapunjee**. From **Agartala**, capital of Tripura, return to Kolkata by air or overland through Bangladesh.

With the right permits, head from Guwahati to Arunachal Pradesh to pay your respects at the stunning Buddhist monastery at **Tawang**, or the tribal villages near **Ziro**, where the elders have dramatic facial tattoos and piercings. A Nagaland permit opens up fascinating tribal villages around **Mon**, rugged countryside dotted by traditional longhouses and remote settlements, and the capital **Kohima**, with its WWII relics. Manipur permits are rarely granted, but there's a fair chance of encountering Mizo culture in **Mizoram**, before you fly back to Kolkata.

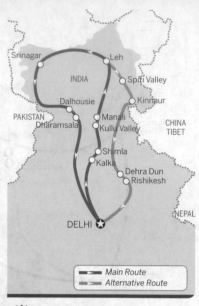

Main Route
Alternative Route

 Central Temples

3 WEEKS

Visit some of India's most spiritual places on this temple-hopping trip around the central plains. Start in the chaotic but cultured city of **Kolkata**, then swap the big-city bustle for the peace of **Bodhgaya**, where the Buddha attained enlightenment. Roll across the plains to **Sarnath**, where the Buddha first taught the dharma.

Hinduism replaces Buddhism as you approach the sacred city of **Varanasi**. Meditate on the banks of the River Ganges, then ramble to **Khajuraho**, where Hindu temples drip with erotic carvings. Head southwest to **Sanchi**, where Emperor Ashoka first embraced Buddhism, then zip through Bhopal to Jalgaon, jumping-off point for the carving-filled **Ajanta caves**.

Next, detour into Rajasthan; stop off in whimsical **Udaipur**, with its lakes and palaces, then explore the extraordinary Jain temples of **Ranakpur** or **Mt Abu**. Continue to pilgrim-crammed **Pushkar**, then make a trip to nearby **Ajmer**, one of India's most holy Islamic sites. Take a final stop in atmospheric **Jaipur**, then end the trip in **Delhi**, with its magnificent Islamic ruins.

 Northern Mountains

4 WEEKS

This mountainous loop takes in some of India's most spectacular views. Start by riding the rails from **Delhi** to **Kalka**, to board the narrow-gauge train to colonial-era **Shimla**. Spend a day or two rambling around the hills, then join the traveller pilgrimage north to the **Kullu Valley** for adventurous mountain activities.

From the hill resort of **Manali**, embark on the epic, two-day journey to **Leh** in Ladakh (July to September), to hike to dramatic Buddhist monasteries and trek-king peaks. For a short loop, continue from Leh to Kargil and on to Kashmir (checking first that is safe to travel). Stay on a **Srinagar** houseboat, then loop through Jammu to elegant **Dalhousie**, and soak up Buddhist culture in nearby **Dharamsala**, before returning to Delhi.

With more time to spare, head southeast from Leh into the dramatic **Spiti Valley**, where ancient monasteries blend into the arid landscape. Ride the rattletrap bus to rugged **Kinnaur**, with its plunging land-scapes, and make stops in **Dehra Dun** and **Rishikesh** to soak up some Hindu culture, before finishing in Delhi.

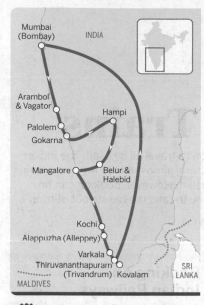

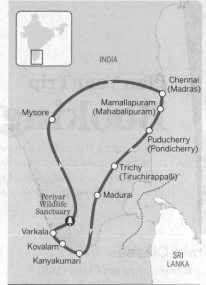

 Southern Beaches

2 WEEKS

This trip gambols to some of India's finest beaches and charismatic coastal towns. Start at **Mumbai** and sample *bhelpuri* (crisp noodle salad) on the sand at Chowpatty Beach. Cruise to the stunning rock-cut temples on Elephanta Island, then travel south by train to beach-blessed Goa.

Enjoy the best of the sand at **Arambol**, **Vagator** and **Palolem**, then continue along the coast to the sacred town of **Gokarna**. Now change the pace entirely; head inland to **Hampi**, with its serene Vijayanagar ruins, and witness the zenith of medieval stone-carving in the Hoysala temples of **Belur** and **Halebid**. Return by train to **Mangalore** to sample spectacular seafood, then chug south to melting-pot **Kochi**, which draws influences from as far afield as China and the Middle East.

Cruise Kerala's languorous backwaters from **Alappuzha** (Alleppey), before dipping your toes in the warm waters around beach resorts **Varkala** or **Kovalam**. Make your last stop **Thiruvananthapuram** (Trivandrum), home to fascinating, often-overlooked museums, before closing the loop with the flight back to Mumbai.

 The Southern Tip

3 WEEKS

Chennai (Madras) is the capital of the south, and the easiest starting point for exploring India's steamy southern tip. Time your trip to avoid the monsoon – the sunniest skies are from October to February. Kick off sampling incendiary thalis in **Chennai**, then surround yourself with intricate temple carvings in **Mamallapuram** (Mahabalipuram), one-time home of the Pallava kings. Next, head for the decadent grace of French-flavoured **Puducherry**, then leave the coast behind and head inland to the temple-towns of Tamil Nadu: essential stops include boulder-covered **Trichy** (Tiruchirappalli), and **Madurai**, with its soaring, deity-covered *gopurams* (temple towers). From here, it's easy to zip down to **Kanyakumari**, the southernmost point of India. Time to unwind: kick back on the coast at sand-dusted **Kovalam** and **Varkala**, then trade the sand for jungle fronds in steamy **Periyar Wildlife Sanctuary**, home to tigers and herds of wild elephants. En route back to Chennai visit colourful **Mysore**, with its outrageous maharaja's palace and giant stone Nandi (bull statue). Bingo – a neat circuit, stringing together the jewels of the south.

Plan Your Trip
Booking Trains

In India, riding the rails is a reason to travel all by itself. The Indian rail network goes almost everywhere, almost all the time, and trains have seats to suit every size of wallet. However, booking can be quite an undertaking – book online to take the hassle out of train travel.

Train Classes

Air-Conditioned 1st Class (1AC)
The most expensive class, with two- or four-berth compartments with locking doors and meals included.

Air-Conditioned 2-Tier (2AC)
Two-tier berths arranged in groups of four and two in an open-plan carriage. Bunks convert to seats by day and there are curtains, offering some privacy.

Air-Conditioned 3-Tier (3AC)
Three-tier berths arranged in groups of six in an open-plan carriage with no curtains; popular with Indian families.

AC Executive Chair
Comfortable, reclining chairs and plenty of space; usually on Shatabdi express trains.

AC Chair
Similar to the Executive Chair carriage but with less-fancy seating.

Sleeper Class
Open-plan carriages with three-tier bunks and no AC; the open windows afford great views.

Unreserved 2nd Class
Wooden or plastic seats and a lot of people – but cheap!

Booking on Indian Railways

Bookings open 90 days before departure and seats fill up quickly – reserve at least a week ahead where possible. Trains and seats come in a variety of classes, from the crush of unreserved class to the air-conditioned luxury of 1st class. Sleeper trains offer the chance to travel huge distances for not much more than the price of a midrange hotel room. Express and mail trains form the mainstay of Indian rail travel. Not all classes are available on every train, but most long-distance services have general (2nd-class) compartments with unreserved seating and more comfortable reserved compartments, usually with the option of sleeper berths for overnight journeys. Shatabdi express trains are same-day services with seating only; Rajdhani express trains are long-distance overnight services between Delhi and state capitals with a choice of 1AC, 2AC, 3AC and 2nd class. More expensive sleeper categories provide bedding. In all classes, a padlock and a length of chain are useful for securing your luggage to baggage racks.

Booking Online

When booking online, it pays to know the details of your journey – particularly station names, train numbers, days of operation and available classes. Start by visiting

RAILWAY RAZZLE DAZZLE

You can live like a maharaja on one of India's luxury train tours, with on-board accommodation, tours, admission fees and meals included in the ticket price.

➡ **Palace on Wheels** (www.palaceonwheels.net) Eight- to 10-day luxury tours of Rajasthan, departing from Delhi. Trains run on fixed dates from September to April; the fares per person per night start at US$601/458/417 (in a single/double/triple cabin). Try to book 10 months in advance.

➡ **Royal Rajasthan on Wheels** (www.royalrajasthanonwheels.com) Runs lavish one-week trips October to March, starting/finishing in Delhi. Fares per person per night start from US$1600 (super deluxe suites) and US$825/590 (single/twin occupancy deluxe suites).

➡ **Deccan Odyssey** (www.deccan-odyssey-india.com) Seven nights covering the main tourist spots of Maharashtra and Goa. From October to March, fares per person per night start at US$650/500/425 for single/double/triple occupancy (US$500/390/315 in September and April).

➡ **Golden Chariot** (www.thegoldenchariot.co.in) Tours the south in style from October to March, starting in Bengaluru (Bangalore); eight-day/seven-night trips visiting Karnataka and Goa, or Tamil Nadu and Kerala. Rates per person per night start at US$754/545/440 for single/double/triple occupancy.

➡ **Mahaparinirvan Express** (aka Duddhist Circuit Special; www.railtourismindia.com) Running September to March to Buddhist sites over eight days, starting in Delhi, with overnight stays in hotels. Rates start from US$160/120/110 per person per night in 1AC/2AC/3AC class. Additional charges apply for single occupancy of hotel rooms.

http://erail.in – the search engine will bring up a list of all trains running between your chosen destinations, along with information on classes and fares. Step two is to register for an account with IRCTC (www.irctc.co.in), the government-run ticket booking service. This is required even if you plan to use a private ticket agency. Registration is a complex process, involving passwords, emails, scans of your passport and texts to your mobile phone. The ever-helpful Man in Seat 61 (www.seat61.com/India.htm) has a detailed guide to all the steps. Once registered, you can use a credit card to book travel on specific trains, either directly with IRCTC, or with private agencies. You'll be issued with an e-ticket, which you must print out ready to present alongside your passport and booking reference once you board the train. Note that the railway reservation system is only open from 1.30am to 11.30pm (IST) every day. Booking in country is a notoriously convoluted process, but you can avoid the hassle by booking online. Recommended agencies for bookings:

IRCTC (www.irctc.co.in) Government site offering bookings for regular trains and luxury tourist trains; only American Express cards for international ticketing.

Cleartrip (www.cleartrip.com) Reliable private agency; accepts international credit cards.

Make My Trip (www.makemytrip.com) Reputable private agency; accepts international cards.

Yatra (www.yatra.com) Books flights and trains; accepts international cards.

Reservations

You must make a reservation for all chaircar, sleeper, 1AC, 2AC and 3AC carriages. No reservations are required for general (2nd-class) compartments. Book well ahead for overnight journeys or travel during holidays and festivals. Waiting till the day of travel to book is not recommended.

Train Passes

IndRail passes permit unlimited rail travel for a fixed period, ranging from one day to 90 days, but offer limited savings and you must still make reservations. Prices start at US$19/43/95 (sleeper/2AC, 3AC and chair car/AC first class) for 24 hours. The easiest way to book these is through the IndRail pass agency in your home country – click on the Passenger Info/Tourist Information link on www.indianrailways.gov.in/railwayboard for further details.

Plan Your Trip
Trekking

India has world-class trekking opportunities, particularly in the Himalaya, where staggering snow-clad peaks, traditional tribal villages, sacred Hindu sites, ancient Buddhist monasteries and blazing fields of wildflowers are just some of the features that create extraordinary alpine experiences. Hit the trails for easy half-day jaunts or strenuous multiweek expeditions.

Best Treks

The Himalaya

Jammu & Kashmir The high, dry and rugged ranges rising in Ladakh boast a bounty of unforgettable treks, including routes through the popular Markha Valley and wildly beautiful Zanskar region (p229).

Himachal Pradesh Alpine bliss is easily accessible, including on treks from McLeod Ganj to Bharmour (p324), between the Parvati and Pin Valleys (p302), and on the Buddhist-infused Homestay Trail in the Spiti region (p343).

Uttarakhand Immerse yourself in pristine scenery on the Kauri Pass, Milam Glacier and Har-ki-Dun treks (p434) or join throngs of pilgrims en route to sacred religious sites, such as Kedarnath Temple (p432) or Hem Kund (p436).

Sikkim Gape at Khangchendzonga (8598m), the world's third-highest mountain, on the Goecha La trek (p556).

South India

Karnataka Explore the serene hills and forests of Kodagu (p882).

Kerala Check out tigers, elephants and boar in Periyar Wildlife Sanctuary (p969).

Tamil Nadu The hill station Ooty (Udhagamandalam) is popular for relaxing forest hikes (p1078).

Trail Tips

With a commercial trekking industry that's far less developed than in neighbouring Nepal, many places still feel wild and relatively unspoiled.

Trekking rest houses or village homestays can be found on a handful of well-established routes, but in many places you may have to haul a tent, stove and sleeping bag. Fortunately, you can usually hire porters or pack animals to do the schlepping for you. If you opt to go with a trekking company, some gear will probably be supplied. Specify *everything* that's included before you sign up, and get it in writing if possible. Wherever you go, make sure you have any permits you may need.

Acute Mountain Sickness is a serious risk on trails over 3000m (p1209).

Route Planning

Most trekkers head for trails with established routes – and there is a long list of possibilities. On the popular pilgrims' trails it's nearly impossible to get lost, but less-travelled tracks can fork or vanish altogether, so hiring a local guide can be wise.

High-quality maps of the Indian Himalaya are difficult to buy in-country. You can find some online that are good enough for planning and even navigating (if you're experienced at reading them). For Ladakh, pricey 1:300,000 scale maps can be bought in Leh.

Lonely Planet's detailed *Trekking in the Indian Himalaya* is a great resource for planning and following trekking routes.

Packing

➡ Bring gear and clothing that's appropriate for the conditions you expect to encounter.

➡ On well-established trails heavy hiking boots are overkill, but on remote mountain tracks they can be lifesavers.

➡ First-aid and water-purification supplies are often essential.

➡ Raingear is a must, and warm layers are crucial for comfort at altitude.

➡ Remember sunscreen!

Trekking Ethics

➡ As anywhere, follow low-impact trekking protocols (you know the mantra – leave only footprints, take only photographs – see www.nols.edu/lnt/principles.shtml for more details).

➡ In India it's important to cook over stoves, since local people rely on limited fuelwood sources for their own sustenance.

➡ People live throughout the Indian Himalaya; even in remote spots, you may encounter a shepherd camp (beware of their dogs).

➡ Respect local cultural sensibilities by dressing modestly; asking permission before snapping photos; remembering that while local hospitality may be endless, their food supply might not be; and refraining from giving gifts to children.

PEAK BAGGING

Mountaineers need permission from the Indian Mountaineering Foundation (www.indmount.org) in Delhi to climb most peaks over 6000m. Expedition fees start at US$1000 and rise with the height of the peak and number of people on your team. Fortunately, quite a few high summits don't require these exorbitant climbing fees, particularly in Ladakh, Lahaul, Spiti and Sikkim. For example, the four-day ascent of Stok Kangri (6120m;p234) is one of the most popular treks in India, providing an affordable but rewarding taste of high-altitude mountaineering.

MOST ADVENTUROUS TREKS

Only an intrepid few hike the tough terrain in the isolated, northeast mountain state of Arunachal Pradesh. One of the top spots to check out is Namdapha National Park (p572), which is bogglingly rich in biodiversity.

When To Go

With India's diverse variety of terrain and altitudes, there's no single time throughout the country that's best for trekking; seasonal conditions vary greatly depending on what region you're in. Here's an overview of what you can expect, when:

May–June Before the monsoon hits; this is a good time for mountain trekking. Trails to holy Hindu sites can be packed with pilgrims. In the lowlands this season can be ridiculously hot.

Mid-July–mid-September This is monsoon season, so trekking in the wrong place can range from uncomfortable to deadly. Jungle trails can be forbiddingly muddy, while in many parts of the Himalaya cloudbursts cause massive landslides. Meanwhile, peaks are obscured by thick clouds, greatly diminishing the rewards trekkers seek for their efforts. The best places to trek during this time are Ladakh and Spiti, which generally stay pretty dry. The one place worth braving the rain is Uttarakhand's famous Valley of Flowers National Park (p436), which draws most of its visitors during the rainy season, when its dazzling botanical carpet spreads most vibrantly across the valley floor.

Mid-September–late October Once the monsoons clear out, searing blue skies usually bless the Himalaya. While nights at high altitude may dip below freezing, days are usually sunny and warm. Facilities and services (and some roads) in many mountain regions close for winter in October or November, so if you hope to trek then, check in advance to see what will be open.

December–March The most comfortable season to trek in South India. Winter is also prime time to tackle the frozen Chadar Trek (p263) in the Zanskar region of Ladakh.

April Head for the hill stations (which are at the middle altitudes), as it's ripping hot down low and usually still snow-packed up high.

Plan Your Trip
Yoga, Spas & Spiritual Pursuits

Birthplace of at least three of the world's great religions, India offers a profound spiritual journey for those so inclined. Even sceptical travellers can enjoy the benefits of trips to spas and yoga centres.

What to Choose

Ashrams

India has hundreds of ashrams – places of communal living established around the philosophies of a guru (a spiritual guide or teacher).

Ayurveda

Ayurveda is the ancient science of Indian herbal medicine and holistic healing, based on natural plant extracts, massage and therapies to treat body and mind.

Buddhist Meditation

Many centres in Buddhist areas offer training in *vipassana* (mindfulness meditation) and Buddhist philosophy; many require a vow of silence and abstinence from tobacco, alcohol and sex.

Spa Treatments

India's spas offer an enticing mix of international therapies and local techniques based on ancient ayurvedic traditions.

Yoga

Yoga's roots lay firmly in India and you'll find hundreds of schools to suit all levels.

Ayurveda

Ayurveda – Indian herbal medicine – aims to restore balance in the body through two main techniques: *panchakarma* (internal purification) and herbal massage. Centres all over India offer ayurvedic treatments, from *abhyangam* (whole body massage with herbal oils) to *shirodhara* (where warm oil is dribbled onto the forehead from a hanging bowl); the use of enemas is likely to appeal to serious converts only. Here are some recommended centres.

Goa

➤ **Ayurvedic Natural Health Centre** (p830; Saligao) A reputable school with professional courses and treatments.

Gujarat

➤ **International Center for Ayurvedic Studies** (p722; Jamnagar) Offers ayurvedic therapy and courses in yoga and naturopathy.

Karnataka

➤ **Ayurvedagram** (p861; Bengaluru) Varied treatments in a garden setting.

➤ **Soukya** (p861; Bengaluru) Excellent programs in ayurvedic therapy and yoga.

➤ **Indus Valley Ayurvedic Centre** (p874; Mysore) Therapies from ancient scriptures.

➡ **Swaasthya** (p874; Mysore) Traditional therapies and residential retreats.

➡ **SwaSwara** (p895; Gokarna) Resort combining therapies and artistic pursuits.

Himachal Pradesh

Amchi (Tibetan traditional medicine) is closely linked to ayurveda, and places a similar focus on whole-body well-being and herbal treatments.

➡ **Tibetan Medical & Astrological Institute** (p321) The primary authority on Tibetan medicine and offers treatments in McLeod Ganj, Leh and other Buddhist centres.

Kerala

➡ **Eden Garden** (p954; Varkala) Offers single treatments and packages.

➡ **Santhigiri Ayurveda Centre** (p959; Kollam) Seven- to 21-day packages and day treatments.

➡ **Ayur Dar** (p981; Kochi) One- to three-week treatments on Vypeen Island.

Tamil Nadu

➡ **Ayurveda Holistic Healing Centre** (p1039; Puducherry) Has treatments and courses in yoga, ayurveda and varma.

Uttar Pradesh

➡ **Swasthya Vardhak** (p393; Varanasi) Reputable ayurvedic consultations and treatment.

Yoga

You can practise yoga almost everywhere in India, from Goan beach resorts to mountain retreats in the Himalaya. Note that some centres are only open to experienced practitioners – seek recommendations from other travellers, and visit several to find one that suits your needs and ability.

Recommended centres are listed here, but you can also study yoga in Delhi; Kolkata; Anjuna, Palolem and Arambol in Goa; Vashisht and McLeod Ganj in Himachal Pradesh; and Pushkar, Udaipur and Jaipur in Rajasthan.

Andaman Islands

➡ **People Tree** (p1097; Havelock Island) Offers yoga and meditation retreats in tropical surroundings.

Bihar

Munger in Bihar is a major centre for the study of Satyananda yoga, invented by the famous guru Satyananda Saraswati.

➡ **Bihar School of Yoga** (☎06344-222430; www.yogavision.net; Munger Fort; Munger) Has long-term courses in yogic studies and the gurukul lifestyle.

Goa

➡ **Himalaya Yoga Valley** (p840; Mandrem) Popular training school with an international focus.

Karnataka

Mysore was the birthplace of *ashtanga* yoga, popularised by K Pattabhi Jois in the 1940s, and the city has numerous centres offering courses (see p876).

Kerala

Thiruvananthapuram (Trivandrum), Varkala and Kochi (Cochin) are popular places for yoga.

➡ **Sivananda Yoga Vedanta Dhanwantari Ashram** (p950; Trivandrum) Renowned for two-week (and longer) hatha yoga courses.

Madhya Pradesh & Chhattisgarh

➡ **Yogi Sudarshan Dwiveda** (p641; Khajuraho) Tuition from a revered local yogi.

➡ **Amar Mahal** (p631; Orchha) Yoga training in luxury surroundings.

➡ **Orchha Resort** (p629; Orchha) Daily classes and ayurvedic treatments.

Maharashtra

➡ **Kaivalyadhama Yoga Hospital** (p798; Lonavla) Offers yogic healing – a combination of yoga and naturopathic therapies.

➡ **Ramamani Iyengar Memorial Yoga Institute** (p802; Pune) Advanced Iyengar yoga courses (for experienced practitioners only).

Mumbai

➜ **Yoga Institute** (p749) Has daily classes as well as longer-term residential programs.

Tamil Nadu

➜ **International Centre for Yoga Education & Research** (p1039; Puducherry) Offers three-week introductory courses and advanced training.

Uttarkhand

Rishikesh (p424) and Haridwar (p419) have numerous yoga centres and ashrams offering yoga training, with courses from beginner level all the way to advanced techniques.

Buddhist Meditation

Whether you want an introduction to Buddhism or are seeking something more profound, there are courses and retreats on offer in Buddhist regions across India. McLeod Ganj is the main centre for the study of Tibetan Buddhism; public teachings are given by the Dalai Lama and 17th Karmapa at certain times of year – visit www.dalailama.com/teachings/schedule for the schedule. We recommend the following centres.

Andhra Pradesh

Numerous centres in AP offer courses in the Burmese-style *vipassana* tradition, including in Hyderabad (p921), Vijayawada (p938) and Nagarjuna Sagar (p932).

Bihar

There are several options in the birthplace of Buddhist teaching.

➜ **Tergar Monastery** (p526; Bodhgaya) Introductory courses in Tibetan Buddhism.

➜ **Bodhgaya Vipassana Meditation Centre** (p526; Bodhgaya) Intensive 10-day *vipassana* courses year-round.

➜ **International Meditation Centre** (p526; Bodhgaya) Informal courses; three-day commitment preferred.

Himachal Pradesh

➜ **Library of Tibetan Works & Archives** (p325; McLeod Ganj) Serious Buddhist philosophy courses.

➜ **Vipassana Meditation Centre** (p325; McLeod Ganj) Offers strict 10-day retreats.

➜ **Tushita Meditation Centre** (p325; McLeod Ganj) Basic and advanced courses on Buddhist philosophy and meditation.

Jammu & Kashmir

➜ **Mahabodhi Centre** (p233; Leh) Classes and three- or 10-day courses in *vipassana* meditation.

➜ **Open Ladakh** (p234; Stok) Courses in meditation and yoga.

Maharashtra

➜ **Vipassana International Academy** (p780; Igatpuri) Offers 10-day courses in the Burmese tradition of *vipassana* meditation free of charge.

Mumbai

➜ **Global Pagoda** (p744; Gorai Island) Has one- to 10-day *vipassana* courses.

Spa Treatments

There are spas all over India, from accessible spas in big-city shopping centres to indulgence in opulent five-star hotels. Be cautious of dodgy one-on-one massages by private (often unqualified) operators, particularly in tourist towns – seek recommendations from fellow travellers and trust your instincts. Here is just a sprinkling of recommended options.

Delhi

➜ **Amatra Spa** (p76) A luxury-defining spa at the swanky Ashok Hotel.

Goa

➜ **Nilaya Hermitage** (p832; Arpora) Enjoy maximum indulgence at this famous celebrity-hangout.

Karnataka

➡ **Emerge Spa** (p874; near Mysore) Offers pampering treatments based on ayurveda and other Asian traditions.

Kolkata

➡ **Vedic Village** (p487; near Kolkata) Is touted to have the finest medical spa in the country.

Madhya Pradesh & Chhattisgarh

Many of the state's luxury hotels have opulent spas.

➡ **Jiva Spa** (Map p624; Usha Kiran Palace, Gwalior; massage treatments from ₹3450; ⊙8am-8pm) Massages, scrubs and wraps in beautiful surrounds.

➡ **Amar Mahal** (p631; Orchha) Spa treatments in a lavish setting.

Uttar Pradesh

➡ **Aarna Spa** (p393; Varanasi) Offers pampering treatments, including ayurveda and aromatherapy.

Uttarakhand

➡ **Haveli Hari Ganga** (p421; Haridwar) An ayurvedic health spa overlooking the Ganges.

Ashrams

Many ashrams (literally 'places of striving') have made a name for themselves – both within India and abroad – thanks to their charismatic gurus, and some tread a fine line between spiritual community and personality cult. Many gurus have amassed vast fortunes collected from devotees, and others have been accused of sexually exploiting their followers. Always check the reputation of any ashram before enrolling in a program.

Most ashrams offer courses of study, typically with elements of philosophy and yoga or meditation, and visitors are usually required to adhere to strict rules, which may include a dress code, a daily regimen of yoga or meditation, and charitable work at social projects run by the ashram. Make sure you're willing to abide by the rules before committing.

A donation is appropriate to cover the expenses of your food, accommodation and the running costs of the ashram. The following are some of India's most famous ashrams.

Kerala

➡ **Matha Amrithanandamayi Mission** (p961; Amrithapuri) Famed for its female guru Amma, 'The Hugging Mother'.

Kolkata

➡ **Belur Math** (p462) The sprawling headquarters of the Ramakrishna Mission, founded by Swami Vivekananda

Maharashtra

➡ **Brahmavidya Mandir Ashram** (p793; Sevagram) Established by Gandhi's disciple Vinoba Bhave.

➡ **Sevagram Ashram** (p793; Sevagram) The famous ashram founded by Gandhi.

➡ **Osho Meditation Resort** (p802; Pune) Follows the sometimes controversial teachings of Osho.

Tamil Nadu

➡ **Sri Aurobindo Ashram** (p1037; Puducherry) Founded by the famous Sri Aurobindo.

➡ **Isha Yoga Center** (p1074; Coimbatore) Offers residential courses and retreats.

➡ **Sri Ramana Ashram** (p1035; Tiruvannamalai) Long-established ashram of Sri Ramana Maharsh.

Plan Your Trip

Volunteering

For all India's beauty, rich culture and history, its poverty and hardship are unavoidable facts of life. Many travellers feel motivated to help, and charities and aid organisations across the country welcome committed volunteers. Here's a guide to help you start making a difference.

How to Volunteer

Choosing an Organisation

Consider how your skills will benefit the people you are trying to help, and choose an organisation that can specifically benefit from your abilities.

Time Required

Think realistically about how much time you can devote to a project. You're more likely to be of help if you commit for at least a month, ideally more.

Money

Giving your time for free is only part of the story; most organisations expect volunteers to cover their accommodation, food and transport.

Working 9 to 5

Make sure you understand what you are signing up for; many organisations expect volunteers to work full time, five days a week.

Transparency

Ensure that the organisation you choose is reputable and transparent about how it spends its money. Where possible, get feedback from former volunteers.

Aid Programs in India

India faces considerable challenges and there are numerous opportunities for volunteers. It may be possible to find a placement after you arrive, but charities and nongovernment organisations (NGOs) prefer volunteers who have applied in advance and been approved for the kind of work involved. **Ethical Volunteering** (www.ethicalvolunteering.org) provides useful guidelines for choosing an ethical sending agency.

As well as international organisations, local charities and NGOs often have opportunities, though it can be harder to assess the work that these organisations are doing. For listings of local agencies, check www.indianngos.com or contact the Delhi-based **Concern India Foundation** (Map p78; ☑011-26210998; www. concernindiafoundation.org; A-52 Amar Colony, Lajpat Nagar IV, Delhi). The Delhi magazine *First City* (www.firstcitydelhi.com) also has listings.

The following programs are just some of many that may have opportunities for volunteers; contact them in advance to arrange a placement.

Caregiving

If you have medical experience, there are numerous opportunities to provide health care and support for the most vulnerable in Indian society.

Delhi

➜ **Missionaries of Charity** (☎011-65731435; www.motherteresa.org; 1 Magazine Rd) Based in Kolkata (Calcutta); also offers volunteer opportunities in Delhi.

Kolkata

➜ **Missionaries of Charity** (p455) Mother Teresa's charity (Mother Teresa's Motherhouse) places volunteers in hospitals and homes for impoverished children and adults.

➜ **Calcutta Rescue** (p465) Placements for medical and health professionals in Kolkata and other parts of West Bengal.

Madhya Pradesh & Chhattisgarh

➜ **Sambhavna Trust** (☎0755-2730914; www.bhopal.org; Berasia Rd, Bafna Colony; Bhopal) Accepts volunteers to help long-term victims of the 1984 disaster.

Maharashtra

➜ **Sadhana Village** (☎020-25380792; www.sadhana-village.org; 1 Lokmanya Colony, Priyankit, Pune) A residence for disabled adults, has a minimum commitment of two months for volunteers.

Community

Many community volunteer projects provide health care and education to villages.

Bihar & Jharkhand

➜ **Root Institute for Wisdom Culture** (p526; Bodhgaya) Occasional placements to train local health workers.

➜ **Village Experience Program** (☎0631-2227922; www.peoplefirstindia.net; People First Educational Charitable Trust, Averill Centre, Gaya to Dhobi Rd, Bodhgaya) Volunteer placements in July and August, working in village schools and with street children.

Delhi

➜ **Hope Project** (p81) Broad-based community work in the basti (slum) of Nizamuddin.

Karnataka

➜ **Kishkinda Trust** (p902; Hampi) Volunteers assist with sustainable community development.

➜ **Equations** (☎080-25457607; www.equitabletourism.org; 415, 2nd C Cross, 4th Main Rd, OMBR Layout, Banaswadi Post, Bengaluru) Volunteers assist with sustainable tourism initiatives.

Madhya Pradesh & Chhattisgarh

➜ **Friends of Orchha** (p632; Orchha) Offers volunteer placements to help improve the livelihoods of rural villagers.

West Bengal

➜ **Human Wave** (☎033-26854904; www.humanwaveindia.org; Mankundu) Short-term placements on community development and health schemes around West Bengal.

➜ **Makaibari Tea Estate** (p494; Kurseong) Volunteers assist with primary school teaching, health work and organic farming.

Teaching

Many Buddhist schools need teachers of English for long-term placements; enquire locally in Sikkim, Himachal Pradesh, West Bengal and Ladakh. Experience preferred.

Himachal Pradesh

➜ **Himalayan Buddhist Cultural School** (☎01902-251845; palkithakur@yahoo.com; Manali) Placements for experienced teachers lasting six months or more.

➜ **Kullu Project** (☎94181-02083; www.kulluproject.web.officelive.com; Kullu) Arranges volunteers to work with schools and orphanages in the Kullu Valley.

➜ **Learning & Ideas for Tibet** (p324; McLeod Ganj) Volunteer placements teaching skills to Tibetan refugees.

➜ **Tibet Hope Center** (p324; McLeod Ganj) Teaching placements with the Tibetan community.

➜ **VolunteerTibet** (p324; McLeod Ganj) Arranges placements assisting Tibetan refugees in Dharamsala.

Jammu & Kashmir

➜ **Druk White Lotus School** (p247; Shey) A Buddhist monastery school in Ladakh with long-term placements for teachers of English.

West Bengal & Darjeeling

➜ **Hayden Hall** (p504; Darjeeling) Offers minimum two- to three-month opportunities for volunteers with medical, teaching and business experience.

Working with Children

The following charities provide support for disadvantaged children.

Delhi

→ **Salaam Baalak Trust** (Map p83; ☎011-23681803; www.salaambaalaktrust.com; Chandiwalan, Main Bazaar, Paharganj) Volunteer English teachers, doctors and computer experts provide education and support for street children.

Goa

→ **Mango Tree Goa** (p827; Mapusa) Opportunities for volunteer nurses and teaching assistants to help impoverished children.

→ **El Shaddai** (p827; Assagao) Placements helping impoverished and homeless children; one-month minimum commitment.

Himachal Pradesh

→ **Tibetan Children's Village** (p322; Dharamsala) Placements for volunteer teachers on a project for refugee children.

→ **Jamyang Foundation** (p343; Kaza) Arranges placements in schools in the Spiti Valley.

→ **Rogpa** (p324; McLeod Ganj) Volunteers provide childcare for Tibetan families.

Mumbai

→ **Child Rights & You** (p749) Volunteers can assist with campaigns to raise funds for projects around India; six-week minimum commitment.

→ **Vatsalya Foundation** (p749) Long- and short-term opportunities teaching and running sports activities for street children.

Tamil Nadu

→ **RIDE** (p1032; Rural Institute for Development Education; Kanchipuram) Volunteer teachers and support staff help rural communities and children rescued from forced labour.

Uttar Pradesh

→ **Learn for Life Society** (p393; Varanasi) Volunteer opportunities at a small school for disadvantaged children.

→ **Kiran** (p393; Varanasi) Minimum five-month commitment working with village children.

Working with Women

The following charities work to empower and educate women.

Delhi

→ **Apne Aap Women Worldwide** (www.apneaap.org) Provides education and livelihood training for trafficked women.

Rajasthan

→ **Sambhali Trust** (Map p176; ☎0291-2512385; www.sambhali-trust.org; c/o Durag Niwas Guest House, 1st Old Public Park, Raika Bagh, Jodhpur) Volunteers teach and help organise workshops for disadvantaged women.

AGENCIES OVERSEAS

There are so many international volunteering agencies, it can be bewildering trying to assess which ones are reputable. Agencies offering the chance to do whatever you want, wherever you want, are almost always tailoring projects to the volunteer rather than finding the right volunteer for the work that needs to be done. Look for projects that will derive real benefits from your skills. To find sending agencies in your area, read Lonely Planet's *Volunteer: a Traveller's Guide*, the *Big Trip* and the *Career Break Book*, or try one of the following.

Himalayan Education Lifeline Programme (HELP; www.help-education.org) British-based charity organising placements for volunteer teachers at schools in Sikkim.

Indicorps (www.indicorps.org) Matches volunteers to projects across India, particularly in social development.

Jamyang Foundation (www.jamyang.org) Arranges volunteer placements for experienced teachers in Zanskar and Himachal Pradesh.

Mondo Challenge (www.mondochallenge.org) Program with placements for volunteers in West Bengal hill towns.

Voluntary Service Overseas (VSO; www.vso.org.uk) British organisation offering long-term professional placements in India and worldwide.

Environment & Conservation

These charities focus on environmental education and sustainable development.

Andaman Islands

➡ **ANET** (p1093; North Wandoor) Volunteers assist with environmental activities from field projects to general maintenance.

Himachal Pradesh

➡ **Ecosphere** (p343; Kaza) Volunteers (two-week commitment required) live in homestays and work on eco-friendly construction projects.

Jammu & Kashmir

➡ **International Society for Ecology & Culture** (www.isec.org.uk; Leh) One-month placements on rural farms to promote sustainable agriculture.

➡ **Ladakh Ecological Development Group** (✆01982-253221; www.ledeg.org; Ecology Centre, Leh) Placements in environmental education and sustainable development.

Maharashtra

➡ **Nimbkar Agricultural Research Institute** (✆02166-222396; www.nariphaltan.org; Phaltan-Lonand Rd, Tambmal, Phaltan) Offers internships in sustainable agriculture lasting two to six months for agriculture, engineering and science graduates.

Tamil Nadu

➡ **Keystone Foundation** (p1075; Kotagiri) Offers occasional opportunities to help improve environmental conditions, working with indigenous communities.

Uttarakhand

➡ **Eco Development Committee** (p436; Ghangaria) Runs conservation projects between June and September in the Valley of Flowers.

Working with Animals

From stray dogs to rescued reptiles, opportunities for animal lovers are plentiful.

Andhra Pradesh

➡ **Blue Cross of Hyderabad** (p921; Hyderabad) A shelter with over 1000 animals; volunteers help care for shelter animals or work in the office.

Goa

➡ **International Animal Rescue** (p847; Assagao) Volunteers needed to assist vets and tend to sick strays.

➡ **Animal Rescue Centre** (p847; Chapolim) Animal welfare group also has volunteer opportunities.

Mumbai

➡ **Welfare of Stray Dogs** (p749; Mumbai) Volunteers can work with the animals, manage stores or educate kids in school programs.

Rajasthan

➡ **Animal Aid Unlimited** (✆9784005989, 9950531639; www.animalaidunlimited.com; Badi Village, Udaipur) accepts volunteers to help injured, abandoned or stray animals.

Tamil Nadu

➡ **Madras Crocodile Bank** (p1024; Vadanemmeli) A reptile conservation centre with openings for volunteers (minimum two weeks).

Heritage & Restoration

Those with architecture and building skills should look at the following.

Jammu & Kashmir

➡ **Tibet Heritage Fund** (www.tibetheritage fund.org; Leh) Openings for volunteers with experience in art restoration or architecture to help preserve traditional buildings.

➡ **Csomas Room** (p264; Zanskar) Volunteers restore and preserve traditional architecture in Zanskar.

Madhya Pradesh & Chhattisgarh

➡ **Saathi** (✆242852, 9425259152; saathibastar@yahoo.co.in; Kondagaon; training & daily board ₹500, weekly materials ₹500) Volunteers with design experience help train tribal people in handicraft production.

Rajasthan

➡ **Haveli Nadine Le Prince** (p138; Shekhawati) Has opportunities to assist the running of this historic *haveli* home.

Tamil Nadu

➡ **ArcHeS** (p1057; Karaikkudi) Aims to preserve the architectural and cultural heritage of Chettinadu; openings for historians, geographers and architects.

Plan Your Trip

Travel With Children

Fascinating and thrilling; India can be every bit as exciting for children as it is for their wide-eyed parents. The scents, sights and sounds of India will inspire and challenge young enquiring minds, and with careful preparation and vigilance, a lifetime of vivid memories can be sown.

Best Regions for Kids

Rajasthan

Vibrant festivals, medieval forts, fairy-tale palaces, camel rides across desert dunes and a well-oiled tourist infrastructure for hassle-free travel.

Goa

Palm-fringed, white-sand beaches and inexpensive exotic food; an ideal choice for family holidays, whatever the budget.

Uttar Pradesh

The picture-perfect Taj Mahal and the nearby abandoned city of Fatehpur Sikri will set young imaginations ablaze.

Kerala

Houseboat adventures, surf beaches, Arabian Sea sunsets, snake boat races, ayurvedic massage and elephant festivals; from the Ghats down to the coast Kerala offers action and relaxation.

Himachal Pradesh

Pony rides around colonial-era hill stations, trekking, zorbing and rafting in Manali; explore Buddhism in McLeod Ganj.

India for Kids

In many respects, travel with children in India can be a delight, and warm welcomes are frequent. Locals will thrill at taking a photograph or two beside your bouncing baby. But while all this is fabulous for outgoing children it may prove tiring, or even disconcerting to younger kids and those with more retiring dispositions.

As a parent on the road in India, the key is to stay alert to your children's needs and to remain firm in fulfilling them, even if you feel you may offend a well-meaning local by doing so. The attention your children will inevitably receive is almost always good natured; kids are the centre of life in many Indian households, and your own will be treated just the same. Hotels will almost always come up with an extra bed or two, and restaurants with a familiar meal.

Children's Highlights

Best Story-book Splendours

➡ **Jaisalmer** Revel in *Arabian Nights* grandeur in Jaisalmer's centuries-old fort on the edge of the Thar Desert.

➜ **Delhi** See the famous Red Fort spotlit while listening to the booming voice of a storyteller at the sound-and-light show.

➜ **Hampi** Explore the boulder-strewn shores of the Tungabhadra River (crossable by coracle), enjoy Hampi's magical ancient ruins, and stop for a tasty dosa at the riverside Mango Tree.

➜ **Ranthambhore National Park** Step into a *Jungle Book* world of abandoned palaces now home to a monkey kingdom and hop aboard a jeep to scout for Shere Khan.

➜ **Udaipur** Explore impossibly romantic palaces, take a horse riding excursion, and spoil your children rotten with a stay at the glorious Taj Lake Palace.

➜ **Orchha** Wander the crumbling palaces and battlements of little-known Orchha, not far from the rather more adult-oriented attractions of Khajuraho.

Best Natural Encounters

➜ **Tiger Parks, Madhya Pradesh** Delve deep into the jungle or roam the plains at the tiger parks of Kanha, Pench or Bandhavgarh. You might not see a tiger, but there's plenty of other wildlife worth spotting.

➜ **Birds, Rajasthan** Cycle along the tree-shaded levee banks of Keoladeo Ghana National Park to spot countless migratory birds, resplendent in bright breeding plumage.

➜ **Dolphins, Goa** Splash out on a dolphin-spotting boat trip from almost any Goan beach to see them cavorting among the waves.

➜ **Hill Station Monkeys** Head up to Shimla (Himachal Pradesh) or Matheran (Maharashtra) for close encounters with cheeky monkeys. Be cautious – these feisty simians can be aggressive and are known to bite and grab food from unsuspecting visitors.

Fun Forms of Transport

➜ **Autorickshaw, Old Delhi** Hurtle at top speed to create a scene worthy of Indiana Jones in the colourful, congested, incredibly atmospheric alleyways off Old Delhi's Chandni Chowk.

➜ **Toy Train, Darjeeling** Ride the huffing, puffing steam toy train between Kurseong and Darjeeling, past colourful mountain villages and gushing waterfalls.

➜ **Hand-pulled rickshaw, Matheran** A narrow-gauge diesel toy train takes visitors most of the way up to this cute, monkey-infested hill station, after which your children can choose to continue to the village on horseback or in a hand-pulled rickshaw.

➜ **Houseboat, Alappuzha** Hop on a houseboat to luxuriously cruise Kerala's beautiful backwaters. If you happen to hit town on the second Saturday in August, take the kids along to see the spectacular Nehru Trophy Snake Boat Race.

Best Beaches

➜ **Palolem, Goa** Hole up in a beachfront palm-thatched hut and watch your kids cavort at beautiful Palolem beach, featuring the shallowest, safest waters in Goa.

➜ **Patnem, Goa** Just up the leafy lane from Palolem, quieter Patnem draws scores of long-stayers with children to its nice sand beach and cool, calm, child-friendly beach restaurants.

➜ **Havelock Island** Splash about in the shallows at languid Havelock Island, part of the Andaman Island chain, where, for older children, there's spectacular diving on offer.

Planning

Before You Go

➜ Look at climate charts; choose your dates to avoid the extremes of temperature that may put younger children at risk.

➜ Visit your doctor to discuss vaccinations, health advisories and other heath-related issues involving your children well in advance of travel.

➜ For more tips on travel in India, and first-hand accounts of travels in the country, pick up Lonely Planet's *Travel with Children* or visit the Thorn Tree Forum at lonelyplanet.com.

What to Pack

You can get all these items in many parts of India too, but often prices are at a premium and brands may not be those you recognise.

➜ For babies or toddlers: disposable or washable nappies, nappy rash cream (Calendula cream works well against heat rash too), extra bottles, a good stock of wet wipes, infant formula and canned, bottled or rehydratable food.

➜ A fold-up baby bed or the lightest possible travel cot you can find (companies such as

KidCo make excellent pop-up tent-style beds), since hotel cots may prove precarious. A stroller, though, is optional, as there are few places with pavements even enough to use it successfully.

➡ A few less-precious toys that won't be mourned if lost or damaged.

➡ A swimming jacket, life jacket or water wings for the sea or pool.

➡ Good sturdy footwear (for older kids).

➡ Child-friendly insect repellent, hats and sun lotion – these are a must.

Eating

➡ You may have to work hard to find something to satisfy sensitive childhood palates, but if you're travelling in the more family-friendly regions of India, such as Rajasthan, Himachal Pradesh, Goa, Kerala or the big cities, you'll find it easier to feed your brood. Here you will find familiar Western dishes in abundance.

➡ While on the road, easy portable snacks such as bananas, samosas, *puri* (puffy dough pockets) and packaged biscuits (Parle G brand are a perennial hit) are available.

➡ Adventurous eaters and vegetarian children will delight in *paneer* (unfermented cheese) dishes, simple dhals (mild lentil curries), creamy kormas, buttered naans (tandoori breads), pilaus (rice dishes) and Tibetan *momos* (steamed or fried dumplings).

➡ Few children, no matter how culinarily unadventurous, can resist the finger food fun of a vast South Indian dosa (paper-thin lentil-flour pancake) served up for breakfast.

Accommodation

➡ India offers up such an array of accommodation options – from beach huts to heritage boutiques to five-star fantasies – that you're bound to find something that will appeal to the whole family.

➡ The swish upmarket hotels are almost always child-friendly, but so are many upper midrange hotels, whose staff will usually rustle up an extra mattress or two; some places won't mind cramming several children into a regular-sized double room along with their parents.

➡ The very best five-stars come equipped with children's pools, games rooms and even children's clubs, while an occasional night with a warm bubble bath, room service, macaroni cheese and the Disney channel will revive even the most disgruntled young traveller's spirits.

On the Road

➡ Travel in India, be it by taxi, bus, train or air, can be arduous for the whole family. Concepts such as clean public toilets, changing rooms and safe playgrounds are rare in much of the country. Public transport is often extremely overcrowded so plan fun, easy days to follow longer bus or train rides.

➡ Pack plenty of diversions (iPads or laptops with a stock of downloaded movies make invaluable travel companions, as do the good old-fashioned story books, cheap toys and games widely available across India).

➡ If you are hiring a car and driver – a sensible and flexible option – and you require safety capsules, child restraints or booster seats, you will need to make this absolutely clear to the hiring company as early as possible. Don't expect to find these items readily available. And don't be afraid to tell your driver to slow down and drive responsibly.

Health

➡ The availability of a decent standard of health care varies widely in India. Talk to your doctor at home about where you will be travelling to get advice on vaccinations and what to include in your first-aid kit.

➡ Access to health care is certainly better in traveller-frequented parts of the country where it's almost always easy to track down a doctor at short notice (most hotels will be able to recommend a reliable one).

➡ Prescriptions are quickly and cheaply filled over the counter at numerous pharmacies, often congregating near hospitals.

➡ Diarrhoea can be very serious in young children; seek medical help if it is persistent or accompanied by fever; rehydration is essential. Heat rash, skin complaints such as impetigo, insect bites or stings can be treated with the help of a well-equipped first-aid kit.

Regions at a Glance

Delhi

Cuisine
Shopping
Ruins

India's Dining Table

Delhi is a feast for the tastebuds; sample cutting-edge Indian fusion cuisine in five-star hotels, or munch on fresh-from-the-fire *Dilli-ka-Chaat* (Delhi's delectable street food).

Beguiling Bazaars

All of India's riches sparkle in Delhi's bazaars and emporiums. Take your pick from intricately wrought handicrafts, modern designer boutiques, quirky bookshops, and music shops piled high with Indian classical instruments.

Lost Empires

The ruins of seven imperial cities are scattered around the Delhi suburbs; wander in and out of centuries of history at the Red Fort, Humayun's tomb, Hauz Khas, Qutb Minar, Mehrauli, the Lodi gardens and a dozen other sites across the city.

p56

Rajasthan

Palaces & Forts
Arts & Crafts
Wildlife

Fabulous Forts

The signature attraction of Rajasthan is the architectural legacy left behind by its maharajas. An incredible collection of forts, palaces and gardens are strewn across its mountains and deserts.

Able Artisans

From exquisite miniature paintings and jewellery fit for royalty to camel-hide shoes, traditional puppets and block-printed fabrics, Rajasthan has arts and crafts to suit any shopping list.

Wildlife Wonders

There's more to Rajasthan than desert sand – the state's former royal hunting reservations are now protected national parks, where you might get lucky and spot tigers, crocodiles, monkeys and exotic birdlife.

p104

Haryana & Punjab

Architecture
Borders
Cuisine

Awesome Architecture

Amritsar is the setting for the stunning Golden Temple. Surrounding towns are dotted with the palaces and follies erected by flamboyant maharajas, while Chandigarh is a 1950s modernist sculpture on a massive scale.

Border Bravado

Not many national borders are tourist attractions. The Attari–Wagah Border crossing is the setting for a fabulous piece of pomp and ceremony, where border guards from India and Pakistan compete to out-do each other with high-steps and chest-thrusting.

Flavours of Punjab

You'll eat well here, in the home of butter chicken, basmati rice, and the wonders from the tandoor (clay oven).

p200

Jammu & Kashmir

Landscapes
Trekking
Religion

Himalayan Heights

From the alpine terrain of Kashmir to the high-altitude deserts of Ladakh and Zanskar, be humbled by the awesome scale of nature. Dotted around this rugged territory are monasteries and villages that almost vanish into the craggy landscape.

Cultural Trails

Dramatic high-altitude hikes through Buddhist villages, made fascinating by overnight stops in traditional Ladakhi and Kashmiri farmsteads.

Spiritual Smorgasbord

Murmured mantras fill Ladakh's gompas, Hindu pilgrims converge on Amarnath's ice lingam and Sufi spirituality suffuses Srinagar where, some believe, you'll find the grave of Jesus Christ.

p224

Himachal Pradesh

Religion
Adventure
Hill Stations

Momos & Mantras

Some 80,000 Tibetan exiles have joined the Dalai Lama in exile at Dharamsala, creating a mini Tibet; more ancient Buddhist monasteries with centuries-old murals are dotted along the Lahaul and Spiti Valleys.

Mountain Thrills

Himachal's mountains offer the best combination of awe and accessibility anywhere in India. Trekking routes criss-cross the state, and rock climbing, rafting, mountain biking, skiing, snowboarding and paragliding are all on the menu.

Hit the Hills

Complete with colonial bungalows, mountain viewpoints and the country retreats of maharajas, hill stations like Dalhousie and Shimla seem to float in a vanished, Raj-era summer.

p280

Uttar Pradesh & the Taj Mahal

Architecture
Religion
Ghats

Not just the Taj

The Taj Mahal is one of the wonders of the world, but the state's architectural treasure trove boasts plenty more besides: check out the ancient monuments in Lucknow, Allahabad and Fatehpur Sikri.

Holy Hubs

India's great religions come together in Uttar Pradesh. The state boasts ancient Islamic cities, two of Buddhism's most sacred pilgrimage centres, and two of the seven sacred cities of Hinduism.

Sacred Waters

The mighty river Ganges and its tributaries flow across UP, lined with holy ghats (ceremonial steps). Watch the intense spiritual activity on the banks in Allahabad, Chitrakut and Varanasi.

p349

Uttarakhand

Trekking
Yoga
Wildlife

Pilgrim Trails

The *char dham* – four sacred Hindu temples – are just one option for trekkers in this rugged mountain state. Take your pick from sacred lakes, remote glaciers and rolling alpine meadows on the shoulders of Himalayan giants.

Yoga Retreats

Head to Rishikesh and Haridwar for a spiritual tune-up; there are dozens of yoga centres where you can learn breathing, stretching and mind-clearing from yoga masters by the clear waters of the River Ganges.

Big Game

Seek tigers, leopards and wild elephants in the steamy jungles of Corbett Tiger Reserve and the forests of Rajaji National Park. Snow leopards and sloth bears roam in northern national parks, like Gangotri and Valley of Flowers.

p408

Kolkata (Calcutta)

Culture
Cuisine
Architecture

Colonial Contrasts

Calcutta was once the British Indian capital, but with its chaotic street-life, spiritual leanings, and cultured attitude, modern-day Kolkata is resolutely Indian.

Sublime Seafood

Eating seafood in some parts of the country can be a recipe for disaster; but in Kolkata, fresh fish and prawns are central to a rich, delicious cuisine, renowned across the subcontinent.

Relics of the Raj

The British filled their colonial capital with grand monuments; Kolkata's streets are crowded with stately civic buildings and monumental office blocks that set the mould for India's legendary bureaucracy.

p450

West Bengal & Darjeeling

Hill Stations
Tigers
Hotels

Raj Relics

Darjeeling is the quintessential Indian hill station, studded with colonial-era buildings recalling faded ghosts of the Raj. Oh, and there are also spectacular Himalayan views.

Earn your Stripes

Where better to spot an awesome Royal Bengal tiger than its eponymous habitat? Nearly 300 big cats roam the waterlogged wonderland of the Sunderbans Tiger Reserve.

Hotels with Heritage

Historic accommodation is West Bengal's stock in trade; choose from faded Raj-era cottages, grand colonial residences and elegant tea estates, where you can sip fine teas or G&Ts on the terrace.

p482

Bihar & Jharkhand

Religion
Ruins
Wildlife

Powerful Pilgrimages

Buddhist pilgrims from across the world flock to Bodhgaya, where Siddhartha Gautama, the historical Buddha, attained enlightenment beneath a bodhi tree.

Learned Relics

Dating back to the 5th century, the Unesco-listed ruins of the ancient Nalanda university are just one of many early Buddhist relics scattered around Rajgir and Bodhgaya.

Elephants on Parade

Jharkhand's Betla (Palamau) National Park is one of the easiest places to peer at pachyderms; even if encounters are elusive, an overnight stay amid its bamboo thickets and forest groves is blissfully serene.

p514

Sikkim

Views
Monasteries
Treks

Misty Vistas

Sikkim's curtain wall of Himalayan peaks guarantees epic views, whether up close and personal on dramatic Himalayan treks, or from a comfortable distance in green, Alpine-style valleys.

Majestic & Monastic

This former Buddhist kingdom is dotted with Tibetan-style monasteries, where maroon-robed monks chant mantras in front of gilded Buddha statues and prayer flags flutter serenely in the breezes that blow down from the Himalaya.

Breathless Trails

Khangchendzonga draws trekkers like bears to Himalayan honey. The must-trek trail is the ascent to the Goecha La, which offers front-row views over the world's third-highest peak.

p534

Northeast States

Tribes
Wildlife
Adventure

Tribal Tapestry

From former head-hunting Naga tribes to delicately tattooed and pierced Apatani women, the Northeast is India's tribal heartland; culturally, this is one of the most fascinating places in Asia.

Run with Rhinos

The one-horned Indian rhino is just one glamorous character on a roll-call of exotic animals that can be seen in the Northeast's magnificent national parks, which feature some of the highest biodiversity in India.

Off-trail Adventures

Get truly off the beaten track on this remote frontier, where India, Tibet and Southeast Asia collide. The region is slowly opening its doors to the outside world; there are trails here that have yet to see a foreign traveller footprint.

p558

Odisha

Temples
Tribes
Wildlife

Top Temples

Odisha (Orissa) once boasted temples in the thousands; those that survive tell a captivating tale of vanished kingdoms whose rulers spared no expense in their veneration of the divine.

Adivasi Experiences

The tribal markets of Onkadelli and Chatikona offer fascinating opportunities to mingle with Adivasi tribes who staunchly cling to a fiercely traditional way of life.

Jungles with Bite

Odisha is a playground for nature lovers: here are tiger reserves, crocodile-filled mangrove forests and coastal wetlands with throngs of exotic birdlife.

p592

Madhya Pradesh & Chhattisgarh

Tigers
Temples
Adventure

Prowling the Plains

Madhya Pradesh is the king of the jungle when it comes to tiger parks; Bandhavgarh offers the best chances of spotting a *sher* (tiger), but plenty of wildlife-spotters see stripes in the forests of Kanha.

Terrific Temples

The raunchy relief work on the World Heritage–listed Khajuraho temples is just the start; visit Orchha, Maheshwar, Omkareshwar and Ujjain for more temple-tastic treats.

Thrills & Spills

Madhya Pradesh will suit outdoor adventurers down to the ground, and up into the sky, and down the rivers. Take your pick from rafting, trekking, paragliding, mountain biking...

p620

Gujarat

Wildlife
Crafts
Treks

Endangered Encounters

In Gujarat's national parks and wildlife sanctuaries, you can see Asia's only wild lions, India's only wild asses, plus antelopes, gazelles and rare and spectacular birds.

Sequined Splendour

Gujarati embroiderers, weavers, printers and dyers produce some of the most colourful, intricate clothing and textiles in India; markets in the western region of Kachchh (Kutch) are a mosaic of mirrored spangles.

Sacred Peaks

In this predominantly flat state, mountains act as spiritual magnets; join Hindu and Jain pilgrims on treks up stunning, temple-topped peaks such as Shatrunjaya, Girnar Hill and Pavagadh.

p684

Mumbai (Bombay)

Architecture
Cuisine
Nightlife

Architecture

Thank the British (and Indian stone-masons) for Mumbai's colonial era architecture; tops are the Chhatrapati Shivaji Terminus, the High Court and the University of Mumbai.

Divine Dinners

Flavours from all over India mingle in Mumbai – sample hot and sour *dhansak* (curried lentil stew) in Parsi canteens, munch on *bhelpuri* (crisp noodle salad) on Chowpatty Beach, or sit down to a globe-trotting feast in an five-star hotel eatery.

Bollywood Beats

With the world's most prolific film industry, Mumbaikars are unapologetically party people. Keep an eye out for Bollywood stars as you dance till dawn in sleek bars and neon-filled nightclubs with beautiful people.

p732

Maharashtra

Caves
Beaches
Wine

Caves as Galleries

The World Heritage–listed caves at Ajanta and Ellora hide exquisite cave paintings and rock sculptures dating back to India's golden ages.

Secret Sands

Strung out along Maharashtra's Konkan Coast are some of the most secluded beaches in India, custom-made for romantics and adventurers.

Tasty Tipples

Nasik, the *grand cru* of India's up-and-coming wine industry, boasts vineyards that blend California-style new world attitude with Indian atmosphere.

p773

Goa

Beaches
Cuisine
Architecture

Super Sands

So beautiful, they're almost a cliché, Goa's beaches have undeniably been discovered, but with the surf breaking over your toes and palm fronds swaying overhead, it doesn't seem to matter.

Colonial-era Cookpot

Goa has fresh-off-the-boat seafood and chefs who blend cooking tricks and ingredients from India and Portugal to create a fabulous interplay of flavours.

A Catholic Legacy

When the Portuguese decamped from Goa in 1961, they left behind a grand colonial-era legacy: mansions in Quepem and Chandor, shop-houses in Panaji, stately basilicas in Old Goa and villas scattered along the coastline.

p811

Karnataka & Bengaluru

Temples
Parks
Cuisine

Temple Extravagance

From the Hoysala beauties at Belur, Halebid and Somnathpur to the towering Virupaksha Temple in Hampi and delicate shrines in Gokarna and Udupi, the temples of Karnataka overflow with carved embellishments.

Pristine Reserves

Draped in tropical vines, the Nilgiri Biosphere Reserve boasts some of the most pristine forests in India. Seek abundant wildlife in national parks such as Bandipur and Nagarhole.

Cuisine

Start off with a delectable Udupi vegetarian thali, then move on to some fiery Mangalorean seafood, washing it all down with fresh draught Kingfisher in beer-town Bengaluru.

p853

Andhra Pradesh

Religion
Cuisine
Beaches

Soulful Sites

Hindu pilgrims flock to Tirumala's Venkateshwara Temple; Buddhists contemplate amid the ruins of once-flourishing monastic centres; and in monument-crammed Hyderabad, Muslims recall the heyday of Islamic India.

Brilliant Biryanis

Biryani is a local obsession. The similarly famous Hyderabadi *haleem* (mutton stew with pounded spiced wheat) has been patented so that it can't be served unless it meets local quality standards.

Coastal Exuberance

Beach tourism in Andhra Pradesh is geared towards the domestic market, lending a unique and festive atmosphere to its seaside resorts. Visakhapatnam has the most gorgeous stretch of coastline.

p912

Kerala

Backwaters
Cuisine
Wildlife

Serene Waterways

Behind the beaches, the inlets and lakes of Kerala's backwaters spread far inland; exploring this waterlogged world by houseboat or canoe is one of India's most relaxing pleasures.

Fire & Spice

Delicious, delicate dishes flavoured with coconut, chilli and myriad spices – the Keralan kitchen is a melting pot of international cultural influences and local ingredients.

Wildlife

Kerala has been dealt a fine hand of wildlife-filled national parks, where, amid lush mountain landscapes, you can spot wild elephants, tigers, leopards and other native Indian species.

p941

Tamil Nadu & Chennai

Temples
Hill Stations
Hotels

Towering Temples

The amazing architecture, daily rituals and colourful festivals of Tamil Nadu's Hindu temples draw pilgrims from around India. Major temples are topped by soaring *gopurams* (gateway towers) and intricately carved *mandapas* (pavilions).

Cool Escapes

The hill stations of the Westerns Ghats offer cool weather, animated festivals, cosy colonial-era guesthouses with open fires, and the chance to hike to gorgeous viewpoints looking out over the plains.

Heritage Hotels

Elegant spots to lay your head include the picturesque townhouses of Puducherry's French Quarter, grand old palace hotels in the hills, and the Chettiar mansions of the south.

p1003

Andaman Islands

Diving
Beaches
Tribes

Undersea Adventures

Explore underwater jungles of coral teeming with tropical fish in jewel-bright colours. India's prime diving destination has easy dips for first-timers and challenging drift dives for veterans.

Superior Sands

If you're searching for that picture-postcard beach, or kilometres of deserted coastline, the Andamans boast some of the most unspoiled beaches in India.

Island Culture

An anthropologist's dream, the Andamans are home to dozens of fascinating tribal groups; most reside on outlying islands, which tourists are prohibited from visiting, but even the major islands offer a beguiling blend of of South Asian and Southeast Asian cultures.

p1084

On the Road

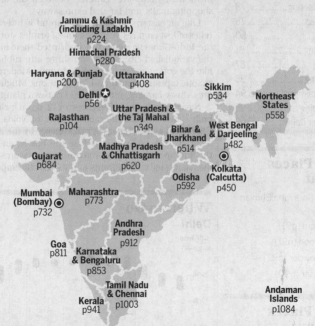

Delhi

Includes ➡

Best Places to Eat

➡ Hotel Saravana Bhavan (p89)

➡ Bukhara (p91)

➡ Monsoon (p91)

➡ Gunpowder (p92)

➡ Alkauser (p90)

Best Places to Stay

➡ Imperial (p84)

➡ Devna (p85)

➡ Manor (p87)

➡ Claridges (p85)

➡ Hotel Amax Inn (p82)

Why Go?

Mystery, magic, mayhem. Welcome to Delhi, City of Djinns, and 16.7 million people, where the ruins of Mughal forts and medieval bazaars are scattered between the office blocks, shopping malls, and tangled expressways.

Like an eastern Rome, India's capital is littered with the relics of lost empires. A succession of armies stormed across the Indo-Gangetic plain and imprinted their identity onto the vanquished city, before vanishing into rubble and ruin like the conquerors who preceded them. Modern Delhi is a chaotic tapestry of medieval fortifications, Mughal mausoleums, dusty bazaars, and colonial-era town planning.

Navigating Delhi's seven cities (or 12, if you include British-built New Delhi and the satellite cities of Noida, Faridabad, Ghaziabad and Gurgaon) is made easier by the metro. With a smart card, you can minimise the hassle, and maximise the time spent in the city's magnificent museums and monuments, its stellar restaurants and its eclectic emporiums.

When to Go
Delhi

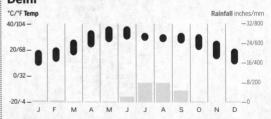

Oct–Mar Delhi at its best – warm, not hot, with clear skies, but morning fog can play havoc with flight schedules.

May–Aug The months to avoid – hot, humid and uncomfortable.

Jun–Sep Monsoon season sees high temperatures and regular rain – a sticky combination.

Top Tips

➡ Ensure your taxi or autorickshaw driver takes you where to want to go, rather than a hotel, souvenir shop or unscrupulous travel agent masquerading as a tourist office.

➡ Be dubious of chatty young men who hang around touristy spots claiming to be students wanting to improve their English – the conversation is usually the preamble to a scam.

➡ Don't believe the helpful gents who try to direct you to a 'tourist office' around Connaught Place. There is only one Government of India tourist office, at 88 Janpath.

➡ Carry small denomination bills (below ₹50), as rickshaw drivers rarely have change.

➡ Ignore touts who surreptitiously dirty your shoe and offer to clean it at a price.

DON'T MISS

Wandering the medieval bazaars of **Old Delhi**, where whole streets are devoted to the sale of kites, tin pots, wrapping paper, saris, fancy brocade and pretty much anything else you could imagine.

Top Festivals

To confirm dates contact India Tourism Delhi (p99).

➡ **Republic Day** (☺26 Jan; Rajpath, p69) Displays of national pride and a spectacular military parade.

➡ **Beating of the Retreat** (☺29 Jan; Rajpath, p69) More military pageantry to mark the end of the Republic Day celebrations.

➡ **Independence Day** (☺15 Aug; Red Fort, p61) India celebrates Independence from Britain and the prime minister addresses the nation from the Red Fort.

➡ **Dussehra** (Durga Puja; ☺Sep/Oct; citywide) Hindus celebrate the victory of good over evil with parades of colourful effigies.

➡ **Qutb Festival** (☺Oct/Nov; Qutb Minar, p102) Several days of Sufi singing and classical music and dance performances at Qutb Minar.

➡ **Diwali** (☺Nov/Dec; citywide) Fireworks across the city for the festival of light.

➡ **Delhi International Arts Festival** (☺Dec; citywide) Three weeks of exhibitions, performing arts, film, literature and culinary events.

MAIN POINTS OF ENTRY

➡ Indira Gandhi International Airport

➡ New Delhi, Old Delhi and Nizamuddin train stations

➡ Kashmere Gate, Anand Vihar and Sarai Kale Khan bus terminals.

Fast Facts

➡ **Population**: 16.7 million

➡ **Area**: 1483 sq km

➡ **Area code**: ☎011

➡ **Main languages**: Hindi, English, Urdu & Punjabi

➡ **Sleeping prices**: $ below ₹1000, $$ ₹1000 to ₹5000, $$$ above ₹5000

Planning Your Trip

Best to book accommodation ahead – see the website hotels.lonelyplanet.com – and call your hotel to confirm the day before you arrive. Book train tickets for longer journeys at least a week ahead.

Resources

➡ **Delhi Tourism** (http://delhitourism.nic.in) Free advertising city maps are widely available; for street-by-street detail, seek out the excellent 245-page *Eicher City Map* (₹340)

➡ **Lonely Planet** (www.lonelyplanet.com/india/delhi) For planning advice, author recommendations, traveller reviews and insider tips

Delhi Highlights

1 Visit Mughals at home in the **Red Fort** (p61), the sandstone palace of the last emperors of Delhi

2 Be wowed by the architectural perfection of **Humayun's Tomb** (p68), inspiration for the Taj Mahal

3 Stand at the base of the magnificent **Qutb Minar** (p102), then plunge into the overgrown ruins of neighbouring **Mehrauli Archaeological Park** (p103)

4 Lose yourself in the maze-like **bazaars** (p60) of Old Delhi

5 Experience a living piece of Islamic history, at the atmospheric **Hazrat Nizam-ud-din Dargah** (p68)

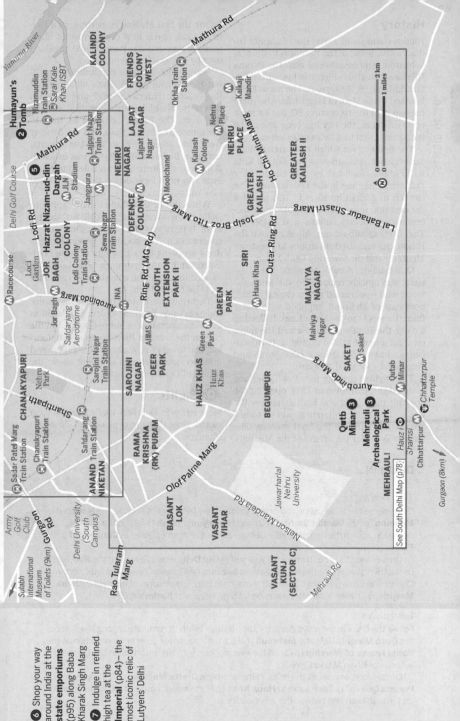

6 Shop your way around India at the **state emporiums** (p95) along Baba Kharak Singh Marg

7 Indulge in refined high tea at the **Imperial** (p84) – the most iconic relic of Lutyens' Delhi

History

Hindus claim Delhi as the site of ancient Indraprastha, home of the Pandavas in the Mahabharata, and excavations near the Purana Qila have revealed evidence of human habitation dating back 3000 years. The name Delhi is linked to the Maurya king Dhilu, who ruled the region in the 1st century BC, but for most of its existence, the city has been known by the names given to it by its conquerors.

The first city for which clear archaeological evidence remains was Lal Kot, or Qila Rai Pithora, founded by the Hindu king Prithviraj Chauhan in the 12th century. The city fell to Afghan invaders in 1191, and for the next 600 years, Delhi was ruled by a succession of Muslim sultans and emperors. The first, Qutub-ud-din Aibak, razed the Hindu city and used its stones to construct Mehrauli and the towering Qtub Minar.

Qutub-ud-din Aibak's 'Mamluk' (Slave) dynasty was quickly replaced by the Khilji dynasty, who constructed a new capital at Siri, northeast of Mehrauli, supplied with water from the royal tank at Hauz Khas. Following a coup, the Tughlaq sultans seized the reins, creating a new fortified capital at Tughlaqabad, and two more cities – Jahanpurah and Ferozabad – for good measure.

The Tughlaq dynasty fell after Tamerlane stormed through town in 1398, opening the door for the Sayyid and Lodi dynasties, the last of the Delhi sultanates, whose tombs are scattered around the Lodi gardens. The scene was set for the arrival of the Mughals.

Babur, the first Mughal emperor, seized Delhi in 1526, and a new capital rose at Shergarh (the present-day Purana Qila), presided over by his son, Humayun.

Frantic city building continued throughout the Mughal period. Shah Jahan gained the Peacock Throne in 1627 and raised a new city, Shahjahanabad, centred on the Red Fort. The Mughal city fell in 1739, to the rampaging Nadir Shah, and the dynasty went into steep decline. The last Mughal emperor, Badahur Shah Zafar, was exiled to Burma by the British for his role in the 1857 First War of Independence; there were some new rulers in town.

When the British shifted their capital to Delhi from increasingly rebellious Calcutta in 1911, it was time for another bout of construction. The architect Edwin Lutyens drew up plans for a new city of wide boulevards and stately administrative buildings to accommodate the colonial government – New Delhi was born.

Delhi has faced numerous challenges since Independence, from the violence of Partition to the assassination of Indira Gandhi, but the city on the Yamuna River continues to flourish, and another new city of skyscrapers and designer apartments is climbing above the rubble of Delhi's lost empires.

◉ Sights

Most sights in Delhi are easily accessible via metro. Note that many places are closed on Monday.

DELHI IN...

Two Days

Give yourself time adjust on day one at calmer New Delhi sights such as the **National Museum** (p69), **Gandhi Smriti** (p70) and **Humayun's Tomb** (p68). In the evening, celebrate your arrival in delectable Delhi in one of the posh eateries at **Connaught Place** (p89).

On day two, it's time to immerse yourself in **Old Delhi**. Ramble around the **Red Fort** (p61), then plunge into the action-packed **bazaars** (Ⓜ Chandni Chowk) around Chandni Chowk and Chawri Bazaar. Survey the mayhem from the minaret of the mighty **Jama Masjid** (p67), then feast afterwards on sizzling kebabs at **Karim's** (p87).

Four Days

Follow the Delhi in two-days itinerary, then detour south to ruminate among the ruins of the **Qutb Minar** (p102) and **Mehrauli** (p103), then pause for quiet contemplation at the **Bahai House of Worship** (p73). In the evening, sup with the smart set in the bars and eateries of **Khan Market** (p90).

On day four, wonder at the relics in the laid-back **Crafts Museum** (p72) and nearby **Purana Qila** (p71). Then head to **Hauz Khas** (p73) to wander around this historic tank and mausoleum and browse the arty boutiques.

Old Delhi

Sprawling around the Red Fort, medieval-era Old Delhi is a constant barrage of noise, colour and smells that bombard the senses.

★ Red Fort
FORT

(Map p64; Indian/foreigner ₹10/250, video ₹25, combined museum ticket ₹5, audio tour in Hindi/English ₹60/100; ⊙9am-6pm Tue-Sun; Ⓜ Chandni Chowk) Converted to a barracks by the British, this massive fort is a sandstone carcass of its former self, but it still conjures up memories of the splendour of Mughal Delhi. Protected by a dramatic 18m-high wall, the marble and sandstone monuments here were constructed at the peak of the dynasty's power, when the empire was flush with gold and precious stones. Shah Jahan founded the fortress between 1638 and 1648 to protect his new capital city of Shahjahanabad, but he never took up full residence, after his disloyal son, Aurangzeb, imprisoned him in Agra Fort. The last Mughal emperor of Delhi, Bahadur Shah Zafar, was flushed from the Red Fort in 1857 and exiled to Burma for his role in the First War of Independence. The new conquerors cleared out most of the buildings inside the fortress walls and replaced them with ugly barrack blocks for the colonial army. The ticket for foreigners covers the museums inside the fort. The audio tour is worthwhile to bring the site to life.

➡ Lahore Gate

(Map p64) The main gate to the fort looks towards Lahore in Pakistan, the second most important city in the Mughal empire. During the struggle for Independence, nationalists promised to raise the Indian flag over the gate, an ambition that became a reality on 15 August 1947. Immediately beyond the gate is the regal Chatta Chowk (Covered Bazaar; Map p64), which once sold silk and jewels, but now mainly sells souvenirs. At the eastern end of the bazaar, the arched Naubat Khana (Drum House; Map p64) once accommodated royal musicians and served as a parking lot for royal horses and elephants. Upstairs is the Indian War Memorial Museum (Map p64; ⊙8am-5pm Tue-Sun), with a fearsome-looking collection of historic weaponry.

A short stroll north, housed in a colonial block, the Museum on India's Struggle for Freedom (Map p64; ⊙9am-5pm Tue-Sun) tells the story of the Independence struggle using paintings, busts and dioramas. If you walk on through the dilapidated barracks, you'll reach a deserted *baoli* (step well) and a causeway leading to the Salimgarh (Map p64; ⊙10am-5pm Tue-Sun), a fortress built by Salim Shah Suri in 1546; it's still occupied by the Indian army, but you can visit the ruined mosque.

➡ Diwan-i-Am

(Map p64) Beyond the Naubat Khana, a monumental arcade of sandstone columns marks the entrance to the 'hall of public audiences', where the emperor greeted guests and dignitaries from a pietra-dura covered balcony.

➡ Diwan-i-Khas

(Map p64) Those in favour with the emperor, or conquered rivals begging for peace, were admitted to the white marble hall of private audiences. This delicate, wedding cake–like pavilion features some outstanding carving and inlay work. The legendary gold and jewel-studded Peacock Throne was looted from the pavilion by Nadir Shah in 1739.

South of the Diwan-i-Khas is the dainty Khas Mahal (Map p64), containing the emperor's private apartments, and shielded from prying eyes by lace-like carved marble screens. An artificial stream, the *nahr-i-bihisht* (river of paradise) once flowed through the apartments to the adjacent Rang Mahal (Palace of Colour; Map p64), home to the emperor's chief wife. The exterior of the palace was once lavishly painted; inside is an elegant lotus-shaped fountain.

➡ Mumtaz Mahal

(Map p64) South of the Rang Mahal, this pavilion once contained the quarters for other women of the royal household. Today, it houses the Museum of Archaeology (⊙9am-5pm Tue-Sun), with royal vestments, miniature paintings, astrolabes, Mughal scrolls and a shirt inscribed with verses from the Quran to protect the emperor from assassins.

➡ Royal Baths & Moti Masjid

North of the Diwan-i-Khas are the royal hammams (baths; Map p64), which once contained a sauna and hot baths for the royal family, and the Moti Masjid (Pearl Mosque; Map p64), an elegant private place of worship for the emperor. The outer walls align with the fort walls, while the inner walls are slightly askew to correctly align with Mecca. Both are closed to visitors, but you can peer through the screen windows.

Shahi Burj
HISTORIC BUILDING

(Map p64) North of the Royal Baths is the Shahi Burj, a three-storey octagonal tower,

(Continues on page 66)

Red Fort

HIGHLIGHTS

The main entrance to the Red Fort is through Lahore Gate **1** – the bastion in front of it was built by Aurangzeb for increased security. You can still see bullet marks from 1857 on the gate.

Walk through the Chatta Chowk (Covered Bazaar), which once sold silks and jewellery to the nobility; beyond it lies Naubat Khana **2**, a russet-red building, which houses Hathi Pol (Elephant Gate), so called because visitors used to dismount from their elephants or horses here as a sign of respect. From here it's straight on to the Diwan-i-Am **3**, the Hall of Public Audiences. Behind this are the private palaces, the Khas Mahal **4** and the Diwan-i-Khas **5**. Entry to this Hall of Private Audiences, the fort's most expensive building, was only permitted to the officials of state. Nearby is the Moti Masjid (Pearl Mosque) **6** and south is the Mumtaz Mahal **7**, housing the Museum of Archaeology, or you can head north, where the Red Fort gardens are dotted by palatial pavilions and old British barracks. Here you'll find the *baoli* **8**, a spookily deserted water tank. Another five minutes' walk – across a road, then a railway bridge – brings you to the island fortress of Salimgarh **9**.

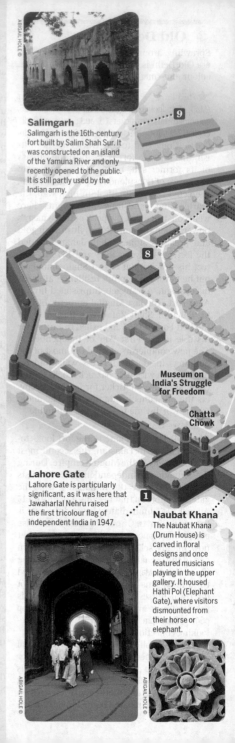

Salimgarh
Salimgarh is the 16th-century fort built by Salim Shah Sur. It was constructed on an island of the Yamuna River and only recently opened to the public. It is still partly used by the Indian army.

Museum on India's Struggle for Freedom

Chatta Chowk

Lahore Gate
Lahore Gate is particularly significant, as it was here that Jawaharlal Nehru raised the first tricolour flag of independent India in 1947.

Naubat Khana
The Naubat Khana (Drum House) is carved in floral designs and once featured musicians playing in the upper gallery. It housed Hathi Pol (Elephant Gate), where visitors dismounted from their horse or elephant.

TOP TIPS

➡ **To avoid crowds**, get here early or late in the day; avoid weekends and public holidays.

➡ **An atmospheric way** to see the Red Fort is by night; you can visit after dark if you attend the nightly Sound-&-Light Show.

Baoli

The Red Fort step well is seldom visited and is a hauntingly deserted place, even more so when you consider its chambers were used as cells by the British from August 1942.

Moti Masjid

The Moti Masjid (Pearl Mosque) was built by Aurangzeb in 1662 for his personal use. The domes were originally covered in copper, but the copper was removed and sold by the British.

Diwan-i-Khas

This was the most expensive building in the fort, consisting of white marble decorated with inlay work of cornelian and other stones. The screens overlooking what was once the river (now the ring road) were filled with coloured glass.

Baidon Pavilion

Zafar Mahal

Hammam

5

Rang Mahal

6

Mumtaz Mahal

7

4

3

2

Pit Stop

To refuel, head to Paratha Gali Wali, a food-stall-lined lane off Chandni Chowk noted for its many varieties of freshly made *paratha* (traditional flat bread)

← NORTH

Delhi Gate

Diwan-i-Am

These red sandstone columns were once covered in shell plaster, as polished and smooth as ivory, and in hot weather heavy red curtains were hung around the columns to block out the sun. It's believed the panels behind the marble throne were created by Florentine jeweller Austin de Bordeaux.

Khas Mahal

Most spectacular in the Emperor's private apartments is a beautiful marble screen at the northern end of the rooms; the 'Scales of Justice' are carved above it, suspended over a crescent, surrounded by stars and clouds.

Old Delhi

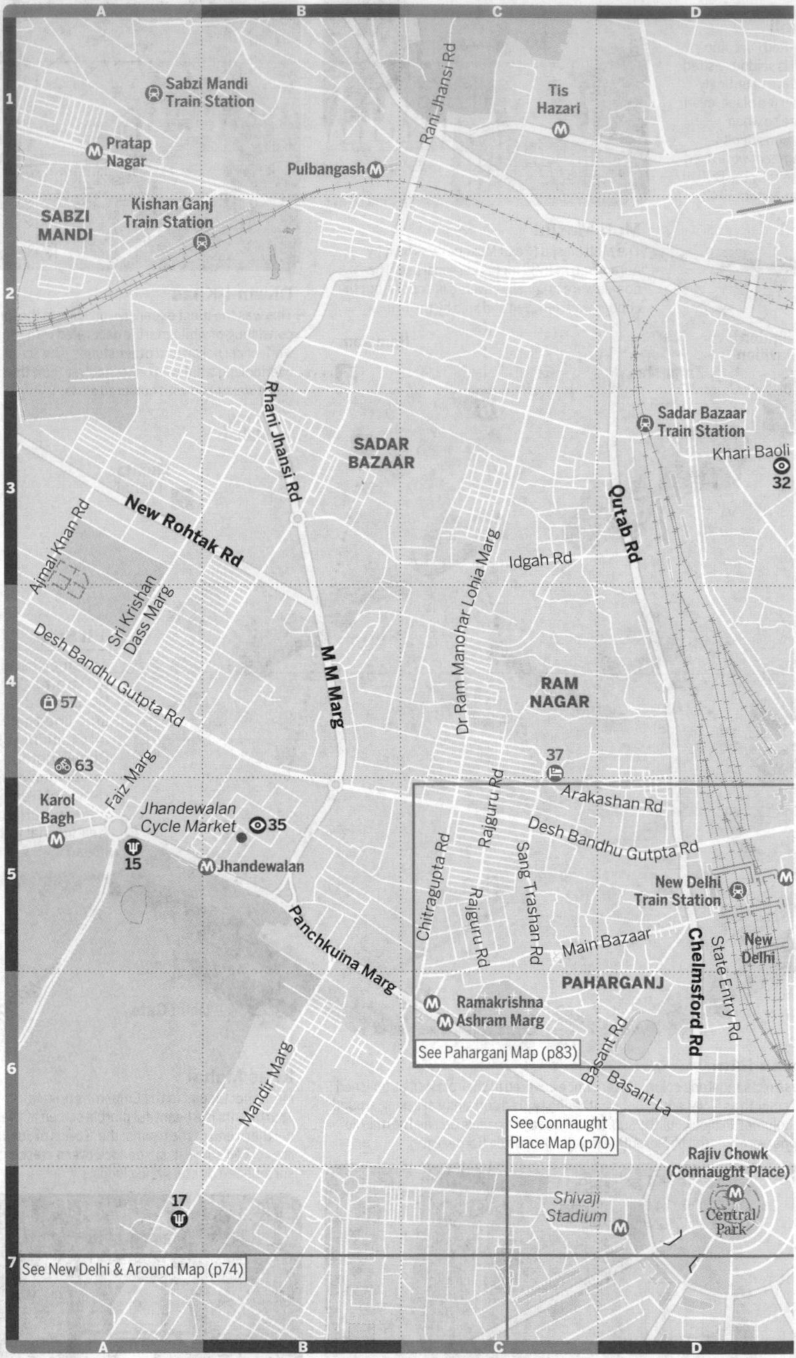

Sabzi Mandi Train Station

Pratap Nagar

Pulbangash

Tis Hazari

Kishan Ganj Train Station

SABZI MANDI

Rani Jhansi Rd

Sadar Bazaar Train Station

Khari Baoli

32

SADAR BAZAAR

Rhani Jhansi Rd

New Rohtak Rd

Qutab Rd

Ajmal Khan Rd

Sri Krishan Dass Marg

Desh Bandhu Gutpta Rd

Idgah Rd

Dr Ram Manohar Lohia Marg

M M Marg

RAM NAGAR

57

63

37

Karol Bagh

Faiz Marg

Jhandewalan Cycle Market

35

Arakashan Rd

Desh Bandhu Gutpta Rd

15

Jhandewalan

Chitragupta Rd

Rajguru Rd

Rajguru Rd

Sang Trashan Rd

New Delhi Train Station

New Delhi

Panchkuina Marg

Main Bazaar

Chelmsford Rd

State Entry Rd

PAHARGANJ

Ramakrishna Ashram Marg

Basant Rd

See Paharganj Map (p83)

Mandir Marg

B. Basant La

See Connaught Place Map (p70)

Rajiv Chowk (Connaught Place)

Shivaji Stadium

Central Park

17

See New Delhi & Around Map (p74)

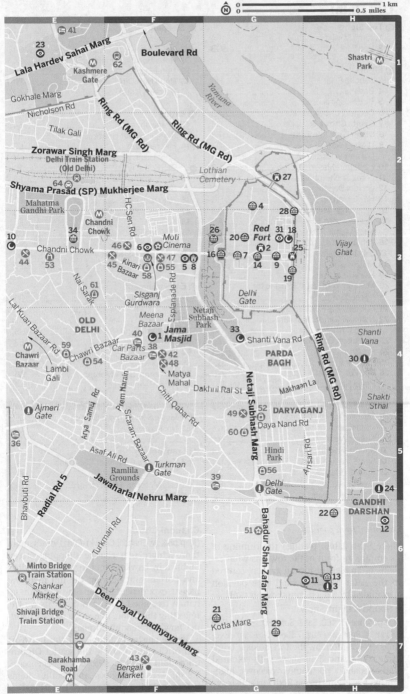

0 — 1 km
0 — 0.5 miles

Shastri Park

Lala Hardev Sahai Marg

23

41

Boulevard Rd

62
Kashmere Gate

Gokhale Marg
Nicholson Rd
Tilak Gali

Ring Rd (MG Rd)

Ring Rd (MG Rd)

Yamuna River

Zorawar Singh Marg
Delhi Train Station (Old Delhi)

Shyama Prasad (SP) Mukherjee Marg

64

Mahatma Gandhi Park

Chandni Chowk

10

34

44
53
Chandni Chowk

HC Sen Rd

Moti Cinema

46
6

45
Kinari Bazaar
58

47
55
5 8

Lothian Cemetery

27

4
28

26
20
Red Fort
31 18

16
7
2
25

14
9
19

Nai Sarak

61

Sisganj Gurdwara

Esplanade Rd

OLD DELHI

Meena Bazaar

Jama Masjid

Delhi Gate

Netaji Subhash Park

Vijay Ghat

Lal Kuan Bazaar Rd

59
Chawri Bazaar

40
1

33
Shanti Vana Rd

Shanti Vana

Chawri Bazaar

54
Lambi Gali

Car Parts Bazaar

38
42
48
Matya Mahal

PARDA BAGH

30

Shakti Sthal

Ajmeri Gate

36

Arya Samaj Rd

Prem Narain

Sitaram Bazaar

Chitli Qabar Rd

Dakhni Rai St

Netaji Subhash Marg

Makhaan La

Asaf Ali Rd
Ramlila Grounds

Turkman Gate

49
52
DARYAGANJ
Daya Nand Rd

60

Ansari Rd

Jawaharlal Nehru Marg

39

Hindi Park

56
Delhi Gate

24

GANDHI DARSHAN

22

12

Radial Rd 5

Bhavbuti Rd

Turkman Rd

51

Bahadur Shah Zafar Marg

Minto Bridge Train Station
Shankar Market

Deen Dayal Upadhyaya Marg

11
13
3

Shivaji Bridge Train Station

50

Barakhamba Road

43
Bengali Market

21
Kotla Marg

29

Old Delhi

Top Sights

1	Jama Masjid	F4
2	Red Fort	G3

Sights

3	Ashoka Pillar	H6
4	Baoli	G2
5	Bird Hospital	F3
6	Chandni Chowk	F3
7	Chatta Chowk	G3
8	Digambara Jain Temple	F3
9	Diwan-i-Am	G3
	Diwan-i-Khas	(see 25)
10	Fatehpuri Masjid	E3
11	Feroz Shah Kotla	H6
12	Gandhi Darshan	H6
13	Hawa Mahal	H6
14	Indian War Memorial Museum	G3
15	Jhandewalan Hanuman Temple	A5
	Khas Mahal	(see 25)
16	Lahore Gate	G3
17	Lakshmi Narayan Temple	A7
18	Moti Masjid	G3
19	Mumtaz Mahal	G3
20	Museum on India's Struggle for Freedom	G3
21	National Bal Bhavan	G7
22	National Gandhi Museum	H6
	Naubat Khana	(see 14)
23	Nicholson Cemetery	E1
24	Raj Ghat	H5
25	Rang Mahal	G3
26	Red Fort Ticket Kiosk	G3
	Royal Baths	(see 18)
27	Salimgarh	G2
28	Shahi Burj	G3
29	Shankar's International Dolls Museum	G7
30	Shanti Vana	H4
31	Sound & Light Show	G3
32	Spice Market	D3
33	Sunehri Masjid	G4
34	Town Hall	E3
35	Videocon Tower	B5

Sleeping

36	Ginger	E5
37	Hotel Amax Inn	C4
38	Hotel Bombay Orient	F4
39	Hotel Broadway	G5
40	Hotel New City Palace	F4
41	Maidens Hotel	E1

Eating

42	Al-Jawahar	F4
43	Bengali Sweet House	F7
44	Bikanervala	E3
	Chor Bizarre	(see 39)
	Gali Kababiyan	(see 48)
45	Gali Paratha Wali	F3
	Ghantewala	(see 45)
46	Haldiram's	F3
47	Jalebiwala	F3
48	Karim's	F4
49	Moti Mahal	G5

Drinking & Nightlife

50	24/7	E7

Entertainment

51	Dances of India	G6

Shopping

52	Aap Ki Pasand (San Cha)	G5
53	Ballimaran	E3
54	Chawri Bazaar	E4
55	Dariba Kalan	F3
56	Daryaganj Book Market	G5
57	Karol Bagh Market	A4
58	Kinari Bazaar	F3
59	Lal Kuan Main Bazaar	E4
60	Musical Instrument Shops	G5
61	Nai Sarak	E3

Transport

62	Kashmere Gate Inter State Bus Terminal	F1
63	Lalli Motorbike Exports	A4
64	Pre-paid Autorickshaws	E2

(Continued from page 61)

where Shah Jahan planned the running of his empire. In front of the tower is what remains of an elegant formal garden, centred on the Zafar Mahal, a sandstone pavilion surrounded by a deep, empty water tank.

➡ **Sound & Light Show**

(Map p64; Tue-Fri ₹60, Sat & Sun ₹80; in English 8.30pm & 9pm May-Aug, 7.30pm Nov-Jan) Evenings except Monday, the fort holds a bombastic sound and light show, with coloured spotlights and a portentous voiceover, highlighting key events in the Red Fort's history.

Chandni Chowk AREA

(Map p64; M Chandni Chowk) Old Delhi's main thoroughfare is a chaotic shopping street, mobbed by hawkers, motorcycles, stray dogs and porters and offering the full medieval bazaar experience. In the time of Shah Jahan, a tree-lined canal ran down its centre, reflecting the moon, hence the name Chandni Chowk, or 'moonlight place'.

In the cluster of temples at the Red Fort end of Chandni Chowk, the scarlet **Digambara Jain Temple** (Map p64; 6am-noon & 6-9pm) – remove shoes and leather items before entering – contains a fascinating

bird hospital (Map p64; donations appreciated; ☺10am-5pm) established to further the Jain principle of preserving all life. Only vegetarian birds are admitted, though predators are treated as outpatients. Nearby, the 18th-century **Sisganj Gurdwara** (Map p64) marks the the the martyrdom site of the ninth Sikh guru, Tegh Bahadur, executed by Aurangzeb in 1675 for resisting conversion to Islam. The western end of Chandni Chowk is bookended by the mid-17th-century **Fatehpuri Masjid** (Map p64), named after one of Shah Jahan's wives; it offers a moment of tranquility after the craziness of Chandni Chowk.

Small green buses shuttle between Digambara Jain Temple and Fatehpuri Masjid (₹5).

★ **Jama Masjid** MOSQUE
(Map p64; camera or video ₹300, tower ₹100; ☺non-Muslims 8am-½hr before dusk, minaret 9am-5.30pm; Ⓜ Chawri Bazaar) Towering over Old Delhi, the 'Friday Mosque' was Shah Jahan's final architectural opus, built between 1644 and 1658. India's largest mosque has room for 25,000 of the faithful in its central courtyard, and it remains an animated place of worship. Perfectly proportioned, the mosque is crowned by three onion domes, constructed of alternating vertical strips of red sandstone and white marble, and guarded by towering 40m-high minarets.

For an extra charge you can climb the narrow southern minaret (notices say that unaccompanied women are not permitted) for mesmerising views over the jumbled rooftops of the old city, with tiny paper kites flitting over the cityscape. On a clear day, you can see one of the key features of Lutyens' design for New Delhi – the Jama Masjid, Connaught Place and Sansad Bhavan (Parliament House) are in a direct line.

Entry is through gate 1 or 3 – remove your shoes at the top of the stairs. Women are asked to wear the scarves and robes provided. You'll be expected to pay the camera fee, even if the only camera is inside your mobile phone, and additional requests for money are not unheard of.

Raj Ghat MONUMENT
(Map p64; ☺6am-6pm) South of the Red Fort, on the banks of the Yamuna River, a simple black-marble platform marks the spot where Mahatma Gandhi was cremated following his assassination in 1948. It's a thought-provoking spot, inscribed with what are said to have been Gandi's final words, 'Hai Ram' (Oh, God). Across Kisan Ghat Rd is the

Gandhi Darshan (Map p64; Kisan Ghat Rd; ☺10am-5pm Mon-Sat) FREE, a huge pavilion displaying photos relating to the Mahatma.

Jawaharlal Nehru, the first Indian prime minister, was cremated just to the north, at **Shanti Vana** (Forest of Peace; Map p64), in 1964. The cremation sites of Nehru's daughter, Indira Gandhi, and grandsons Sanjay and Rajiv are lined up along the riverbank in their own memorial parks.

National Gandhi Museum MUSEUM
(Map p64; ✆23311793; ☺9.30am-5.30pm Tue-Sun & 2nd Sun of month) FREE A small but moving museum displaying historic photos and some of Gandhi's spinning wheels and personal effects.

Feroz Shah Kotla HISTORIC SITE
(Map p64; Bahadur Shah Zafar Marg; Indian/foreigner ₹5/100, video ₹25; ☺dawn dusk; Ⓜ Pragati Maidan) Ferozabad, the fifth city of Delhi, was built by Feroz Shah in 1354 as a replacement for Tughlaqabad. Ringed by crumbling fortifications are a huge mosque, a *baoli* (step well), and the pyramid-like **Hawa Mahal** (Map p64), topped by a 13m-high sandstone **Ashoka Pillar** (Map p64) inscribed with Ashoka's edicts. There's an otherworldly atmosphere to the ruins, which are still an active place of worship – on Thursday afternoons, crowds gather to light candles and incense and leave bowls of milk to appease Delhi's djinns (invisible spirits). Shoes should be removed when entering the mosque and Hawa Mahal.

**Shankar's International
Dolls Museum** MUSEUM
(Map p64; ✆23316970; www.childrensbooktrust.com; Nehru House, Bahadur Shah Zafar Marg; adult/child ₹17/6; ☺10am-6pm Tue-Sun) From tacky Spanish bullfighting figurines to graceful Japanese geisha dolls, this cutesy but engaging museum has 6500 dolls from 85 countries, from Brazil to Japan.

National Bal Bhavan MUSEUM
(Map p64; www.nationalbalbhavan.nic.in; Kotla Rd; adult/child ₹5/free; ☺9am-5.30pm Tue-Sat) Delhi's museum for children is a disorderly affair, with a toy train, animal enclosures, an exhibition on astrology and astronomy, and some delightful mini-dioramas showing key events in Indian history.

Nicholson Cemetery CEMETERY
(Map p64; ☺8am-6pm, 9am-5pm winter; Ⓜ Kashmere Gate) FREE Close to Kashmere Gate, this forgotten cemetery is the last resting

place for hundreds of Delhi's colonial-era residents, many of whom died tragically in childhood. One famous resident is Brigadier General John Nicholson, who died from injuries sustainedp while storming Delhi during the 1857 First War of Independence. At the time he was hailed as the 'Hero of Delhi', but author William Dalrymple described him as an 'imperial psychopath'. If you ride the metro to nearby Pulbangash, you can see the British-erected **Mutiny Memorial** and an **Ashoka Pillar**, transported here by Feroz Shah (on Rani Jhansi Rd).

Coronation Durbar Site   MONUMENT
(Shanti Swaroop Tyagi Marg; Ⓜ Model Town) FREE In a desolate field, north of Old Delhi, an obelisk marks the site where King George V was declared emperor of India in 1911, and where the great *durbars* (fairs) were held to honour India's British overlords in 1877 and 1903. Take an autorickshaw from Model Town metro station.

Lakshmi Narayan Temple   HINDU TEMPLE
(Birla Mandir; Map p64; Mandir Marg; ◷ 6am-9pm; Ⓜ Ramakrishna Ashram Marg) West of Connaught Place, the rather overwrought, Orissan-style Lakshmi Narayan Temple was erected by the wealthy industrialist BD Birla. Gandhi inaugurated the complex in 1938 as a temple for all castes; a sign on the gate says, 'Everyone is Welcome'.

⊙ Connaught Place Area

Connaught Place   AREA
(Map p70; Ⓜ Rajiv Chowk) New Delhi's colonial heart is Connaught Place, named after George V's paternal uncle. Its white, colonnaded streets radiate out from the central circle of Rajiv Chowk, lined with swanky stores and restaurants. The outer circle (divided into blocks G to N) is technically called Connaught Circus, and the inner circle (divided into blocks A to F) is Connaught Place, but locals call the whole area 'CP'. Almost every visitor to Delhi comes here, which partly explains the rampant touts.

Jantar Mantar   HISTORIC SITE
(Map p70; Sansad Marg; Indian/foreigner ₹5/100, video ₹25; ◷ 9am-dusk; Ⓜ Patel Chowk) The most eccentric of Delhi's historic sites, Jantar Mantar (equivalent to 'abracadabra' in Hindi) looks like an enormous abstract sculpture, but this odd collection of curving geometric buildings has a purpose – the monuments are carefully calibrated to mon-

itor the movement of the stars and planets. Maharaja Jai Singh II constructed the observatory in 1725 – it's an extremely popular place to pose for a portrait.

Agrasen ki Baoli   MONUMENT
(Map p70; Hailey Rd; ◷ dawn-dusk; Ⓜ Barakhamba Rd) A remarkable thing to discover among the office towers southeast of Connaught Place, this atmospheric step-well was erected in the 14th century; 103 steps descend to the bottom, flanked by arched niches.

⊙ New Delhi & Around

★ **Humayun's Tomb**   HISTORIC BUILDING
(Map p74; Indian/foreigner ₹10/250, video ₹25; ◷ dawn-dusk; Ⓜ JLN Stadium) The most perfectly proportioned and captivating of Delhi's mausoleums, Humayun's tomb seems to float above the gardens that surround it. Built in the mid-16th century by Haji Begum, the Persian-born senior wife of the Mughal emperor Humayun, the tomb brings together Persian and Mughal elements, creating a template that strongly influenced the Taj Mahal.

The arched facade is inlaid with bands of white marble and red sandstone, and the building follows strict rules of Islamic geometry, with an emphasis on the number eight. Alive with green parakeets, the surrounding gardens contain the tombs of the emperor's favourite barber and Haji Begum. This was where the last Mughal emperor, Bahadur Shah Zafar, took refuge before being captured and exiled by the British in 1857.

To the right as you enter the complex, **Isa Khan's tomb** (Map p74) is a fine example of Lodi-era architecture, constructed in the 16th century. Further south is the monumental **Khan-i-Khanan's tomb** (Map p74; Indian/foreigner ₹5/100; ◷ dawn-dusk), plundered in Mughal times to build Safdarjang's tomb.

★ **Hazrat Nizam-ud-din Dargah**   SACRED SITE
(Map p74; off Lodi Rd; ◷ 24hr; Ⓜ JLN Stadium) FREE Hidden away in a tangle of bazaars selling rose petals, *attars* (perfumes) and offerings, the marble shrine of the Muslim Sufi saint, Nizam-ud-din Auliya, offers a window through the centuries. Brightly painted, full of music and crowded with devotees, this is how Delhi's historic tombs and shrines must once have been. The ascetic Nizam-ud-din died in 1325 at the ripe old age of 92, and his mausoleum became a point of pilgrimage for Muslims from across the empire.

Other tombs in the compound include the graves of Jahanara (daughter of Shah Jahan), and the renowned Urdu poet, Amir Khusru. It's one of Delhi's most extraordinary pleasures to take a seat on the marble floor and listen to Sufis singing rousing *qawwali* (devotional hymns) at sunset. Scattered around the surrounding alleyways are more tombs and a huge *baoli* (step well). Entry is free, but visitors may be asked to make a donation.

Rajpath
AREA

(Ⓜ Khan Market) The focal point of Edwin Lutyens' plan for New Delhi was Rajpath (Kingsway), a grand parade linking India Gate to the offices of the Indian government. Constructed between 1914 and 1931, these grand civic buildings were intended to spell out in stone the might of the British empire – just 16 years later, the British were out on their ear and Indian politicians were pacing the corridors of power.

Shielded by a wrought-iron fence at the western end of Rajpath, the 340-room **Rashtrapati Bhavan** (President's House; Map p74; ☏ 23012960; dmsp@rb.nic.in; ◷ 9.30-11.30am & 2.30-4pm Mon, Wed, Fri & Sat), is the official residence of the president of India, and former home to the British viceroy. Mountbatten, India's last viceroy, was said to have employed 418 gardeners to care for the Mughal-style **gardens** – they can be visited during the annual opening from mid-February to mid-March (free admission, no cameras, 10am to 5pm daily) and at other times with advance permission; bring your passport.

Rashtrapati Bhavan is flanked by the mirror-image, dome-crowned **North Secretariat** (Map p74) and **South Secretariat** (Map p74), housing government ministries. The Indian parliament meets nearby in the **Sansad Bhavan** (Parliament House; Map p74), a circular, colonnaded edifice at the end of Sansad Marg.

At Rajpath's eastern end, and constantly thronged by tourists, is **India Gate** (Map p74). This 42m-high stone memorial arch, designed by Lutyens, pays tribute to around 90,000 Indian army soldiers who died in WWI, the Northwest Frontier operations, and the 1919 Anglo-Afghan War.

National Museum
MUSEUM

(Map p74; ☏ 23019272; www.nationalmuseumindia.gov.in; Janpath; Indian/foreigner ₹10/300, audio guide English, French or German ₹400, Hindi audio guide ₹150, camera Indian/foreigner ₹20/300; ◷ 10am-5pm Tue-Sun; Ⓜ Central Secretariat) Offering a compelling snapshot of India's last 5000 years, this splendid museum is perfect for a rainy day and not so large that it overwhelms. Exhibits include rare relics from the Harappan Civilisation, antiquities from the Silk Route, a mesmerising collection of miniature paintings (look out for the hand-painted playing cards), woodcarvings, textiles, statues, musical instruments, and an

---

DELHI'S MIGHTY MEN

Wander the districts north of Kashmere Gate in Old Delhi and you may notice a disproportionately high number of muscular men. No, it's not your imagination; this dusty quarter is the favoured stomping ground for Delhi's traditional mud wrestlers. *Kushti*, or *pehlwani*, is a full-contact martial art, fusing elements of yoga and philosophy with combat and intense physical training.

Young men enrol at *akharas* (training centres) in their early teens, and follow a strict regimen of daily exercise, climbing ropes hand over hand, lifting weights and hauling logs to build up the necessary muscle bulk for this intensely physical sport. Even diet and lifestyle is strictly controlled; sex, tobacco and alcohol are forbidden, and wrestlers live together in rustic accommodation under the supervision of a coach who doubles as spiritual guide.

Bouts take place on freshly tilled earth, adding an extra element of grit to proceedings. As with other types of wrestling, the aim is to pin your opponent to the ground, but fights often continue until one wrestler submits or collapses from exhaustion. At regional championships, wrestlers compete for golden *gadas* (ceremonial clubs), a tribute to the favoured weapon of Hanuman, patron deity of wrestling.

Most *akharas* welcome spectators at the daily dawn and dusk training sessions, so long as this doesn't interfere with training. Seek permission first to avoid offending these muscle-bound gents – the blog http://kushtiwrestling.blogspot.com is a good introduction to the sport and the main *akharas*.

Connaught Place

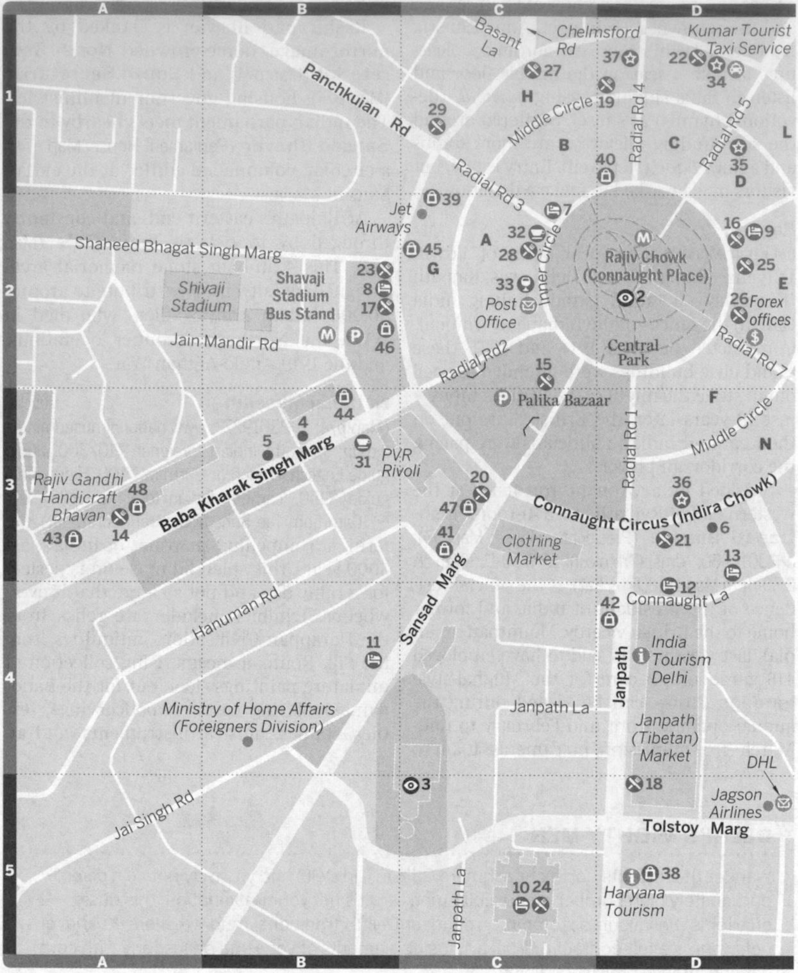

Basant
La
Chelmsford Rd
Kumar Tourist
Taxi Service
Panchkuian Rd
27
37
22
34
29
H
Middle Circle
19
Radial Rd 4
C
Radial Rd 5
B
40
35
L
D
Radial Rd 3
Jet
Airways
39
7
16
9
45
A
32
28
Rajiv Chowk
(Connaught Place)
25
Shaheed Bhagat Singh Marg
Shivaji
Stadium
Shavaji
Stadium
Bus Stand
23
8
17
46
G
33
Post
Office
2
26 Forex
offices
E
Central
Park
Jain Mandir Rd
Radial Rd2
15
Radial Rd 7
Rajiv Gandhi
Handicraft
Bhavan
5
4
44
31
PVR
Rivoli
Palika Bazaar
F
Radial Rd 1
Middle Circle
N
43 14
48
Baba Kharak Singh Marg
20
47
Connaught Circus (Indira Chowk)
36
21
6
41
Clothing
Market
13
Hanuman Rd
Sansad Marg
42
12
Connaught La
11
Janpath
India
Tourism
Delhi
Ministry of Home Affairs
(Foreigners Division)
Janpath La
Janpath
(Tibetan)
Market
DHL
3
18
Jagson
Airlines
Jai Singh Rd
Tolstoy Marg
Janpath La
38
10 24
Haryana
Tourism

---

armoury with gruesomely practical weapons and a suit of armour for an elephant.

Allow at least two hours, preferably half a day. Bring identification to obtain an audio guide. Video cameras are prohibited. Next door is the **Archaeological Survey of India** (Map p74; ☑ 23019108; asi.nic.in; Janpath; ⊙ 9.30am-1pm & 2-6pm Mon-Fri) which stocks publications about India's main archaeological sites.

National Gallery of Modern Art ART GALLERY (Map p74; ☑ 23382835; http://ngmaindia.gov.in; Jaipur House; Indian/foreigner ₹10/150; ⊙10am-5pm Tue-Sun; Ⓜ Khan Market) Delhi's flagship art gallery displays a remarkable collection of paint-

ings, from colonial-era landscapes and 'Company Paintings', created by Indian artists to suit their new British rulers, to the primitive-inspired artworks of Nobel Prize–winner Rabindranath Tagore. Photography prohibited.

Gandhi Smriti MUSEUM (Map p74; ☑ 23012843; 5 Tees January Marg; camera free, video prohibited; ⊙10am-5pm Tue-Sun, closed every 2nd Sat of month; Ⓜ Racecourse) FREE This poignant memorial is where Mahatma Gandhi was shot dead by a Hindu zealot on 30 January 1948, after campaigning against intercommunal violence. Con-

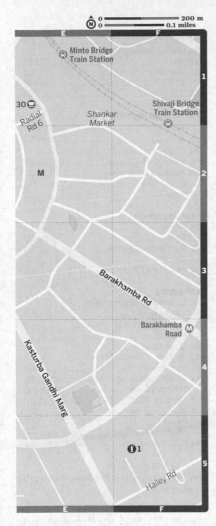

Indira Gandhi Memorial Museum MUSEUM

(Map p74; ☑ 23010094; 1 Safdarjang Rd; ⊙ 9.30am-4.45pm Tue-Sun; Ⓜ Racecourse) **FREE** The former residence of Indira Gandhi is now a moving museum, displaying her personal effects (including her Rubik's cube) and, more tragically, the blood-stained sari she was wearing when she was assassinated in 1984 in reprisal for the storming of the Golden Temple in Amritsar. Many rooms are preserved in state, offering a fascinating window onto the elegant lives of Delhi's political elite. An exhibit at the rear charts the similarly truncated life of Indira's son, Rajiv, assassinated in 1991. In the garden, an enclosed crystal pathway marks Indira Gandhi's final footsteps.

Nehru Memorial Museum & Planetarium MUSEUM

(Map p74; ☑ 23016734; www.nehrumemorial.com; Teen Murti Rd; ⊙ 8am-5.15pm Tue-Sun; Ⓜ Udyog Bhawan) **FREE** Stately Teen Murti Bhavan was the official residence of Jawaharlal Nehru (India's first prime minister), and before that, the official residence of the British commander-in-chief. Appropriately, the interior now contains an encyclopaedic museum detailing India's struggle for Independence, using photographs, letters, newspaper cuttings and items belonging to the former prime minister. In the grounds is an old-fashioned **planetarium** (☑ 23014504; http://nehruplanetarium.org; 45min show ₹50; ⊙ Hindi 1.30pm & 4pm, English 11.30am & 3pm).

Purana Qila FORT

(Old Fort; Map p74; ☑ 24353178; Mathura Rd; Indian/foreigner ₹5/100, video ₹25, sound & light show ₹80; ⊙ dawn-dusk; Ⓜ Pragati Maidan) With its towering walls and dramatic gateways, Purana Qila conjures up images of conquest and combat. The fortress was constructed by Afghan ruler Sher Shah (1538–45), who briefly seized control of Delhi from the emperor Humayun, and the monumental gatehouse opens onto a peaceful garden studded with ancient monuments. The graceful octagonal, red-sandstone **Sher Mandal** was used by Humayun as a library; it was a fall down the stairs of the library that ended his reign, and life, in 1556. Just beyond is the **Qila-i-Kuhran Mosque** (Mosque of Sher Shah), with intricate patterns of inlaid marble and standstone.

Across busy Mathura Rd are more relics from the city of Shergarh, including the **Khairul Manazil** (Map p74) mosque, still used by local Muslims, A popular **boating lake** has been created from the former moat, with

crete footsteps lead to the spot where Gandhi died, marked by a small pavilion. The adjacent house, where the Mahatma spent his last 144 days, contains rooms preserved as Gandhi left them, plus photographs, paintings and dioramas depicting scenes from Gandhi's life, set in boxes like 1950s TVs. Upstairs is the interpretative exhibition **Eternal Gandhi**, with abstract sculptures, curious video displays and sound installations. In the room where Gandhi lodged, you can see his meagre possessions – not much more than a walking stick, spectacles, a spinning wheel and a pair of *chappals* (sandals).

Connaught Place

pedaloes for hire. There's a sound and light show (in English 8.30pm, 9pm May to August, 7.30pm November to January) at the fort every evening.

Crafts Museum MUSEUM
(Map p74; ☑ 23371641; Bhairon Marg; ☉ 10am-5pm Tue-Sun; Ⓜ Pragati Maidan) **FREE** Set up like a traditional village, this captivating museum aims to preserve the traditional crafts of India, from handloom weaving to Mithila wall painting. Highlights include an enormous carved temple *rath* (chariot), a mock-up of a Gujarati *haveli* (house) and a shrine made from giant terracotta figures. Look out for the magnificent cloth painting of the Islamic heaven and hell, with a tiny European being tortured by snakes, centipedes and scorpions. In the rear courtyard, artisans demonstrate their skills and sell their products. Photography is only allowed with prior permission.

National Zoological Gardens ZOO
(Map p74; ☑ 24359825; http://nzpnewdelhi.gov.in; Mathura Rd; Indian/foreigner ₹10/100, video ₹100; ☉ 9am-4.30pm Sat-Thu Apr-Sep, to 4pm Oct-Mar; Ⓜ Pragati Maidan) Popular with families and couples, India's biggest zoo is set in 86 hectares. In fact, the grounds are so extensive you may have trouble finding the animals. Kept in reasonably considerate conditions are lions, tigers, elephants, hippos, rhinos, spectacular birds and monkeys who periodically take leave of their enclosures.

Lodi Gardens PARK
(Map p74; Lodi Rd; ☉ 6am-8pm Oct-Mar, 5am-8pm Apr-Sep; Ⓜ Khan Market/Jor Bagh) **FREE** This peaceful park is Delhi's favourite escape, pop-

ular with everyone from power-walking politicians to amorous teens. The gardens are dotted with the crumbling tombs of Sayyid and Lodi rulers, including the impressive 15th-century **Bara Gumbad tomb** (Map p74) and mosque, and the strikingly different tombs of **Mohammed Shah** (Map p74) and **Sikander Lodi** (Map p74). It's a haven for birds and butterflies but mobbed by picnickers on Sundays.

Safdarjang's Tomb
HISTORIC BUILDING

(Map p74; Aurobindo Marg; Indian/foreigner ₹5/100, video ₹25; ⊙ dawn-dusk; Ⓜ Jor Bagh) Built by the Nawab of Avadh for his father, Safdarjang, this grandiose mid-18th-century tomb was erected during the final throes of the Mughal empire. With its intricate and slightly overwrought detailing, the tomb is often described as the 'last flicker in the lamp of Mughal architecture'.

Tibet House
MUSEUM

(Map p74; ☑ 24611515; 1 Lodi Rd; admission ₹10; ⊙ 9am-1pm & 2-5.30pm Mon Fri; Ⓜ JLN Stadium) Tibet House has a small museum displaying sacred manuscripts, votive carvings and historic *thangkas* (Tibetan paintings on cloth), brought out of Tibet following the Chinese occupation. Photography prohibited.

Nehru Park
PARK

(Map p74; Vinay Marg; ⊙ 5am-8pm Apr-Sep, 6am-8pm Oct-Mar; Ⓜ Racecourse) **FREE** On the edge of the Diplomatic Quarter, this green and pleasant park is a calm place to unwind away from the hubbub. In the centre is a statue of Lenin, revealing India's political sympathies during the Cold War.

Gurdwara Bangla Sahib
SIKH TEMPLE

(Map p74; Ashoka Rd; ⊙ 4am-9pm; Ⓜ Patel Chowk) **FREE** Topped by golden domes, this handsome white-marble gurdwara was constructed at the site where the eighth Sikh guru, Harkrishan Dev, stayed before his death in 1664. Despite his tender years, the six-year-old guru tended to victims of Delhi's cholera and smallpox epidemic, and the waters of the gurdwara tank are said to have healing powers. Sikh pilgrims flock here at all hours, and devotional songs waft over the compound, adding to the contemplative mood.

National Museum of Natural History
MUSEUM

(Map p74; www.nmnh.nic.in; Barakhamba Rd; ⊙ 10am-5pm Tue-Sun; Ⓜ Barakhamba Road) **FREE** You can while away a peaceful hour at Delhi's under-appeciated natural history museum, amid dinosaur bones and slightly time-worn stuffed animals.

National Rail Museum
MUSEUM

(Map p74; ☑ 26881816; Service Rd, Chanakyapuri; adult/child ₹20/10, video ₹100; ⊙ 9.30am-5.30pm Tue-Sun) Trainspotters and kids will adore this museum, with its decaying collection of old steam locos and carriages. Among the venerable bogies are the former Viceregal Dining Car and the Maharaja of Mysore's rolling saloon. The indoor gallery displays Indian Railways memorabilia, including the skull of an elephant that charged the *UP Mail* in 1894. A toy train (adult/child ₹20/10) chuffs around the grounds.

⊙ South Delhi

Hauz Khas
AREA

(Map p78; Ⓜ Green Park) Hauz Khas takes its name from the vast royal tank built by Sultan Allauddin Khilji in the 13th century to provide water for Siri Fort. Thronged by birds and fringed by parkland, the lake is fronted by the ruins of Firoz Shah's 14th-century madrasa (religious school) and **tomb** (Map p78), with a magnificent calligraphy-covered incised plaster ceiling.

The ruins have become a popular hangout for Delhi students, who come here to enjoy some unchaperoned time with the opposite sex. To reach the lake shore, cut through the adjacent **Deer Park** (daylight hours), which has more ruined tombs, a well-stocked deer enclosure and a popular drumming circle that meets every second Saturday.

Surrounding the ruins, Hauz Khas village (p97) is one of Delhi's artiest enclaves, filled with upmarket boutiques, hip bars and restaurants and quirky curio shops. There are numerous **Lodi-era tombs** scattered along the access road to Hauz Khas Village, and in nearby Green Park – just take a stroll and see what you discover.

Bahai House of Worship
TEMPLE

(Lotus Temple; Map p78; ☑ 26444029; www.bahaihouseofworship.in; Kalkaji; ⊙ 9am-7pm Tue-Sun, to 6pm winter; ☎; Ⓜ Kalkaji Mandir) Designed by Iranian-Canadian architect Fariburz Sahba in 1986, Delhi's Bahai temple is a wonderful place to enjoy silence – a rare experience in Delhi. Styled after a lotus flower, with 27 immaculate white-marble petals, the temple was created to bring faiths together; visitors are invited to pray or meditate silently according to their own beliefs. The attached visitor centre tells the story of the Bahai faith. Note that photography is prohibited inside the temple. Nearby is Delhi's flamboyant

DELHI SIGHTS

See Old Delhi Map (p64)

Park St

New Delhi
General
Post Office

Baba Kharak
Singh Marg

7

32

41

Pusa
Hill
Forest

68

Talkatora
Gardens

Talkatora Rd

Red Cross
Rd

Upper Ridge Rd

Southern
Ridge
Forest

PRESIDENT'S
ESTATE

North Ave

25

Central Secretariat

21

Buddha
Jayanti
Smarak Park

Delhi
Polo
Club

Mughal
Gardens

23

27

Vijay
Chowk

Udyog
Bhawan

Krishna
Menon Marg

Willingdon Cres

South Ave

Mahavir
Jayanti Park

Kautilya Marg

42

79

Teen Murti Rd

19

Teen
Murti Rd

Rajaji Marg

Akbar Rd

9

Sardar Patel Marg

DIPLOMATIC
ENCLAVE

40

Teen Murti Rd

Racecourse Rd

Sadar Patel
Marg
Train Station

Manas Rd

Panchsheel Marg

66

29

Kamal Ataturk Rd

36

Chandragupta Marg

81

70

63

74

77

61

CHANAKYAPURI

Nyaya Marg

Safdarjang Rd

Chanakyapuri
Train Station

69

67

71

20

Nehru
Park

Golf
Course

24

64

Niti Marg

78

80

65

76

Satya Marg

73

Vinay Marg

Safdarjang
Aerodrome

Ring Rd (MG. Rd)

Shantipath

17

Service Rd

Safdarjang
Train Station

Sarojini Nagar
Train Station

Africa Ave

ANAND
NIKETAN

Baba Balaknath
Mandir Marg

Rao Tularam Marg

See South Delhi Map (p78)

RAMA
KRISHNA (RK)
PURAM

SAROJINI
NAGAR

LAKSHMIBAI
NAGAR

ISKCON temple, operated by the Hare
Krishna movement.

Chhatarpur Mandir
TEMPLE
(Map p58; ☎ 26802360; www.chhattarpurman-
dir.org; Main Chhatarpur Road; ⊙ 4am-midnight;

Ⓜ Chhatarpur) FREE India's second largest
temple (after Akshardham), the Shri Adya
Katyayani Shakti Peeth Mandir is dedicated to the goddess Katyayani (one of the
nine forms of Parvati). There are dozens of
shrines with towering South Indian *gop-*

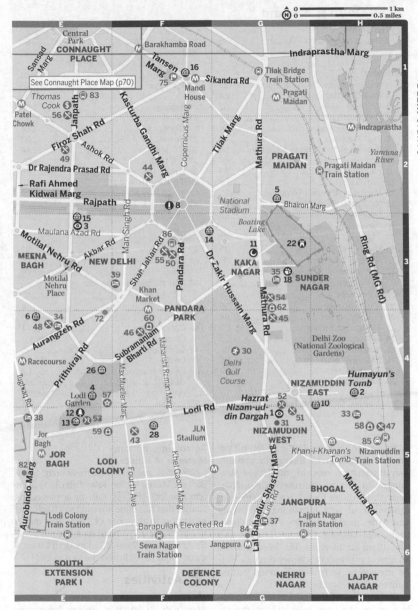

urams (temple towers), and an enormous statue of Hanuman stands guard over the compound. Weekdays tend to be fairly sedate, but the complex gets crowded at weekends, and during the Navratri celebrations in September/October.

◉ Other Areas

Akshardham Temple
TEMPLE

(Map p58; ☏ 22016688; www.akshardham.com; National Hwy 24, Noida turning; admission free,

New Delhi & Around

exhibitions ₹170, fountains ₹30; ⊘ 9.30am-6.30pm Tue-Sun; Ⓜ Akshardham) Rising dramatically over the eastern suburbs, the Hindu Swaminarayan Group's controversially ostentatious Akshardham Temple is a wedding-cake confection of salmon-coloured sandstone and white marble, drawing elements from traditional Orissan, Gujarati, Mughal and Rajasthani architecture. The interior offers an almost psychedelic journey through Hindu mythology, with 20,000 carved deities, saints and mythical beings.

Surrounding this spiritual showpiece is a series of Disneyesque exhibitions, including a boat ride through 10,000 years of Indian history, animatronics telling stories from the life of Swaminarayan, and musical fountains. Allow at least half a day to do it justice (weekdays are less crowded).

Sulabh International
Museum of Toilets   MUSEUM
(☑ 25031518; www.sulabhtoiletmuseum.org; Sulabh Complex, Mahavir Enclave, Palam Dabri Rd; ⊘ 10am-5pm Mon-Sat) ✐ FREE Run by a pioneering charity that has done amazing work bringing sanitation to the poor of Delhi, this quirky museum displays toilet-related paraphernalia dating from 2500 BC to modern times. A guided tour (free) brings the loos to life.

🏃 Activities

★ **Amatrra Spa**   SPA
(Map p74; ☑ 24122921; www.amatrraspa.com; Ashok Hotel, Chanakyapuri; ⊘ 9am-10pm; Ⓜ Racecourse) Amatrra is where the A-list come to be pampered. There's a cover charge of ₹1000 for nonguests; treatments range from conventional massages to ayurvedic treatments such as *njavarakizhi* (massage with bundles of heated rice; ₹4800 per hour).

Aura
SPA

(Map p74; ☏ 8800821206; www.aurathaispa.com; Middle Lane, Khan Market; ⊙10am-9pm; Ⓜ Khan Market) Glitzy spa offering Thai-inspired massages and treatments; a one-hour massage costs ₹2100, or ₹2450 with aromatherapy oils. There are numerous branches, including at the **Basant Lok Community Centre** (Map p78; Basant Lok Community Centre) and **Green Park** (Map p78; Green Park).

Delhi Golf Club
GOLF

(Map p74; ☏ 24307100; www.delhigolfclub.org; Dr Zakir Hussain Marg; 18 holes weekdays/weekends US$50/70; ⊙dawn-dusk; Ⓜ Khan Market) Founded in 1931, with beautiful fairways, peacocks and Mughal pavilions; weekends are busy.

Kerala Ayurveda
AYURVEDA

(Map p78; ☏ 41754888; www.keralaayurveda.biz; E-2 Green Park Extn; ⊙8am-8.30pm; Ⓜ Green Park) A reputable ayuverdic centre, offering a full range of treatments, from *sarvang ksheer-*dhara (massage with butter milk) to *sirodhara* (warm oil poured on the forehead). Treatments start from ₹1300 per hour.

Floriana Chandan Sparsh
SPA

(Map p78; ☏ 40587983; www.chandansparsh. com; M-24 Greater Kailash II; ⊙9am-9pm) A top-of-the-range spa offering everything from manicures and pedicures to massage (from ₹1000 for an hour).

Jaypee Vasant Continental Hotel
SWIMMING

(Map p78; ☏ 26148800; Basant Lok Community Centre, Vasant Vihar; per person ₹1675; ⊙9am-6pm) Escape the summer heat at this five-star hotel pool.

Siri Fort Sports Complex
SWIMMING

(Map p78; ☏ 26496657; off August Kranti Marg; nonmember day fee ₹120; ⊙7-11am & 3-8pm Tue-Sun ; Ⓜ Green Park) Facilities for every imaginable sport, including an Olympic-sized swimming pool and a toddler pool.

South Delhi

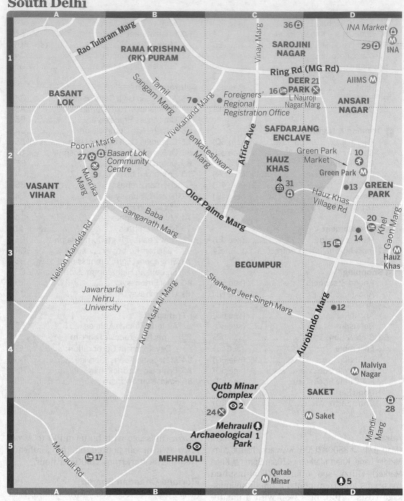

🏃 Volunteering

There plenty of ways to assist Delhi's less fortunate residents. The Salaam Balaak Trust (p81) in Paharganj and the Hope Project (p81) in Nizamuddin often have openings for volunteers – contact them directly for opportunities. Mother Teresa's Missionaries of Charity run projects in Delhi which may accept volunteers – contact the Kolkata office (p465) for information.

🍴 Courses

Tannie Baig   COOKING
(Map p78; ☑ 9899555704; tanniebaig13@gmail.com; 2hr class ₹3200; Ⓜ Hauz Khas) Recommended two-hour cooking lessons (the fee covers up to five participants) run by food writer Tannie Baig, who runs the Treetops (p85) guesthouse (guests get 50% discount).

Parul Puri   COOKING
(Map p74; ☑ 9810793322; www.parigold.com; K-11 Jangpura Extn; 2hr class ₹1200; Ⓜ Jangpura) Parul Puri at K-One One runs two-hour classes

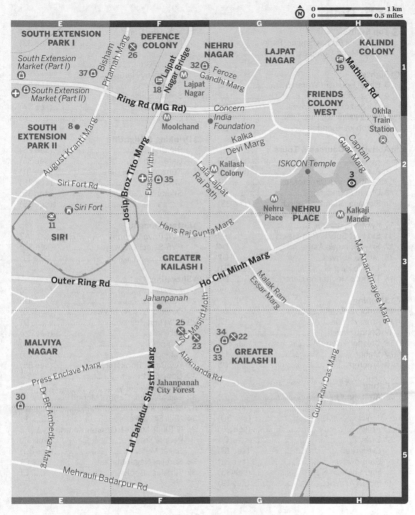

with a focus on cuisine from North India regions; book at least two days in advance.

Central Hindi Directorate LANGUAGE
(Map p78; ☑26178454; http://hindinidesha laya.nic.in; West Block VII, RK Puram; 60hr course ₹6000) Runs certificate and diploma courses in Hindi; the basic course lasts 60 hours with three classes a week.

Dhyan Foundation MEDITATION, YOGA
(Map p78; ☑26253374; www.dhyanfoundation. com; A-80 South Extension II) Various yoga and meditation sessions at a spiritually led centre in South Extension II.

Morarji Desai National Institute of Yoga MEDITATION, YOGA
(Map p74; ☑23730417; www.yogamdniy.nic.in; 68 Ashoka Rd; M Patel Chowk) Offers one-year diploma courses that include pranayama and hatha yoga, and meditation.

Sri Aurobindo Ashram MEDITATION, YOGA
(Map p78; ☑26567863; www.sriaurobindoashram. net; Aurobindo Marg; M Hauz Khas) Yoga and meditation for serious practioners rather than hobbyists.

South Delhi

Studio Abhyas MEDITATION, YOGA
(Map p78; ☑ 26962757; www.abhyastrust.org; F-27 Green Park; Ⓜ Green Park) Yoga classes, meditation classes, and Vedic chanting in a comfortable suburban home. Prior experience preferred.

Tushita Meditation Centre MEDITATION
(Map p78; ☑ 26513400; mahayanadelhi@gmail.com; 9 Padmini Enclave, Hauz Khas; Ⓜ Hauz Khas) Tibetan/Buddhist meditation sessions – call or email them for details. Donations are appropriate.

Tours

Tours are a good way to see Delhi without being overwhelmed, but avoid Monday when many sites are shut. Admission fees and camera/video charges aren't included in tour prices below, and rates are per person. Book several days in advance. For a bespoke tour, India Tourism Delhi can arrange multilingual, government-approved guides.

★**DelhiByCycle** CYCLING
(☑ 9811723720; www.delhibycycle.com; tour ₹1600; ⊙ 6.30-10am) Run by a Dutch journalist, this is a fantastic way to see Delhi. Tours focus

on specific neighbourhoods – Old Delhi, New Delhi, Nizamuddin and Lodi Rd, and the banks of the Yamuna. The price includes chai and a Mughal breakfast.

Salaam Balaak Trust
WALKING

(Map p83; ☎ 23584164; www.salaambaalaktrust.com; Gali Chandiwali, Paharganj; suggested donation ₹200; Ⓜ Ramakrishna Ashram Marg) This charitable organisation offers two-hour 'street walks' guided by former street children, who will show you first-hand what life is like for Delhi's homeless youngsters. The fees help the Trust assist children on the streets.

Hope Project
WALKING

(Map p74; ☎ 24353006; www.hopeprojectindia.org; 127 Hazrat Nizamuddin; 90min walk ₹200) This charity runs 90-minute walks around the *basti* (slum) of Nizamuddin, providing some challenging insights into the lives of some of Delhi's most neglected citizens. The fee supports the Hope Project's work. Wear modest clothing.

Delhi Tourism & Transport Development Corporation
BUS TOURS

(DTTDC; Map p70; http://delhitourism.nic.in; Baba Kharak Singh Marg; ⊙ 7am-9pm; Ⓜ Rajiv Chowk) Offers zip-around bus tours (AC ₹310) of New Delhi (9am to 1.30pm) and Old Delhi (2.15pm to 5.45pm) visiting all the big sights. It also runs the air-conditioned Ho Ho (Hop-on, Hop-off) Dilli Dekho bus service, which buzzes around the major sights every 30 minutes from 8am to 8pm (Indian/foreigner ₹300/600, two-day ticket ₹500/1000) – buy tickets from the booth (Map p70) near the office. It also runs slightly rushed tours to Agra, Jaipur and Haridwar.

Old Delhi Walks
WALKING

(☎ 24641304; www.intachdelhichapter.org; tour ₹50) Intach runs a walking tour (approximately two hours) every weekend with an expert guide, exploring different areas, such as Chandhi Chowk, Nizamuddin, Hauz Khas, and Mehrauli. Custom walks can be arranged. Book ahead via the website.

Delhi Transport Corporation Tours
TOUR

(Map p70; ☎ 23752774; www.dtc.nic.in; Scindia House; tour ₹200; ⊙ Tue-Sun; Ⓜ Rajiv Chowk) Inexpensive full-day air-con bus tours to the top sights from Connaught Place, leaving 9.15am and returning at 5.45pm.

🛏 Sleeping

Delhi is well stocked with places to stay, though prices have risen steeply in recent years – the days of ₹100 rooms are long gone. It's wise to book in advance, as popular places can fill up in a flash, leaving new arrivals easy prey for commission sharks. Call or email ahead to confirm your booking 24 hours before you arrive. Most hotels offer pick-up from the airport with advance notice. Homestays are becoming an attractive alternative to hotels. For details of government-approved places contact India Tourism Delhi, or check www.incredibleindianhomes.com and www.mahindrahomestays.com.

Hotels with a minimum tariff of ₹1000 charge luxury tax (10% at the time of research) and service tax (7.42% at the time of research), and some also add a service charge (up to 10%). Room rates in this chapter include taxes; all rooms have private bathrooms unless otherwise stated. Most hotels have a noon checkout and luggage storage is usually possible.

🛏 Old Delhi

Most hotels in the old town see few foreign visitors.

Hotel New City Palace
HOTEL $

(Map p64; ☎ 23279548; www.hotelnewcitypalace.in; 726 Jama Masjid; r ₹500-800; ❄; Ⓜ Chawri Bazaar) A palace it's not, but this maze-like hotel has an amazing location overlooking the Jama Masjid. Some rooms have windows and views; the bathrooms could do with a good scrub, but staff are friendly.

Hotel Bombay Orient
HOTEL $$

(Map p64; ☎ 43101717; Matya Mahal; s/d/tr ₹650/990/1300; ❄; Ⓜ Chawri Bazaar) Reached through a doorway off the busy bazaar leading south from the Jama Masjid, this place is better than most, and bookings are recommended. Rooms are clean and tidy, but ask to see a few before you commit.

Hotel Broadway
HOTEL $$

(Map p64; ☎ 43663600; www.hotelbroadwaydelhi.com; 4/15 Asaf Ali Rd; s/d incl breakfast ₹3060/5000; ❄@; Ⓜ New Delhi) A surprising find in a commercial part of the old city, Broadway is smarter inside than out. Some rooms have old-fashioned wood panelling while others have been elegantly kitted out by French designer Catherine Lévy. For refreshments, head to the curio-filled Chor Bizarre restaurant or the atmospheric 'Thugs' bar upstairs.

Ginger
HOTEL $$

(Map p64; ☎1800 209 3333; www.gingerhotels.com; Rail Yatri Niwas; d/tw/q ₹1527/1703/1880; ❄@🛜; Ⓜ New Delhi) Behind the depots on the east side of New Delhi railway station, this transit hotel offers better than expected rooms that are handy for transit stops. There's a net centre and 24-hour restaurant.

Maidens Hotel
HOTEL $$$

(Map p64; ☎23975464; www.maidenshotel.com; 7 Sham Nath Marg; r from ₹9980; ❄@🛜⛲; Ⓜ Civil Lines) Set in immaculate gardens, Maidens is a graceful wedding cake of a hotel, built in 1903. Lutyens stayed here while supervising the building of New Delhi, and the enormous high-ceilinged rooms still have a certain colonial-era charm. There are two restaurants, a pool and a bar.

🛏 Paharganj & Around

With bumper-to-bumper budget hotels and a deserved reputation for hassle and dodgy characters, Paharganj isn't everyone's cup of chai. However, it's extremely convenient for New Delhi railway station and it's a great place to plug into the traveller grapevine. Note that many rooms here are sun-starved, grimy cells and prices have been shooting up recently, without any accompanying increase in standards. There are better rooms for not much more on nearby Arakashan Rd.

Be warned that street noise can be diabolical – keep ear plugs handy. Ask to see a few rooms before you decide. Because of the pedestrian congestion, taxi-wallahs may be reluctant to take you right to the doorstep of your hotel, but you can walk to everywhere from New Delhi railway station or metro or the Ramakrishna Ashram Marg metro stop. To avoid commission scams when you first arrive, ask rickshaws to drop you at Chhe Tooti Chowk and complete your journey on foot.

★ Hotel Amax Inn
HOTEL $

(Map p64; ☎23543813; www.hotelamax.com; 8145/6 Arakashan Rd; s/d from ₹750/850; ❄@🛜) Set back from chaotic Arakashan Rd, the Amax offers fairly standard budget rooms, but the friendly staff run the place with the globe-trotting traveller in mind. The rooftop terrace is a great spot to swap travel stories and there's wi-fi in reception.

Hotel Namaskar
HOTEL $

(Map p83; ☎23583456; www.namaskarhotel.com; 917 Chandiwalan, Main Bazaar; r ₹400-650, with AC ₹650.; ❄🛜) Up the alleyway opposite Dayal Boot House, this old favourite is run by two amiable brothers. It's not the Ritz, but the simple rooms are usually freshly painted and the colour scheme will tickle you pink. Car hire can be arranged, and wi-fi is available.

Cottage Yes Please
HOTEL $

(Map p83; ☎23562300; www.cottageyesplease.com; 1843 Laxmi Narayan St; d from ₹950; ❄@) One street north of Main Bazaar, this calm, comfortable place offers a selection of agreeable, chintzy rooms, linked by a maze of Escher-like stairways. Rooms have TVs and fridges, and the decor runs to wood panelling and stained glass.

Vivek Hotel
HOTEL $

(Map p83; ☎46470555; www.vivekhotel.com; 1534-1550 Main Bazaar; s/d from ₹550/650; ❄@) A multistorey favourite with a good range of rooms – all are reasonably priced and reasonably clean, and more expensive rooms have a small window with a view.

Hare Rama Guest House
GUESTHOUSE $

(Map p83; ☎47343333; Main Bazaar; s/d from ₹400/500; ❄) You get what you pay for here, but you don't have to pay very much. Fan-cooled rooms are basic and only a few have exterior-facing windows.

Hotel Rak International
HOTEL $

(Map p83; ☎23562478; www.hotelrakinternational.com; off Main Bazaar; s/d ₹550-650, with AC ₹800/900; ❄) Tucked off the main bazaar and overlooking a scruffy courtyard, the modest rooms at this popular hotel have marble floors and bathrooms, chintzy built-in beds, and...windows!

Ajay Guest House
GUESTHOUSE $$

(Map p83; ☎23583125; www.ajayguesthouse.com; 5084 Main Bazaar; s/d ₹800/1000; ❄@🛜) Ajay is more promising than it appears from its alleyway entrance. Rooms are bright and welcoming, if gaudy, with geometric wall panelling and occasionally outlandish colour schemes.

Metropolis Tourist Home
HOTEL $$

(Map p83; ☎23561794; www.metropolistourist home.com; 1634-5 Main Bazaar; r from ₹2000; ❄@🛜; Ⓜ Ramakrishna Ashram Marg) A recent refurb has raised standards at the Metropolis. A slightly haphazard lobby gives way to sleek rooms with mood lighting and tasteful fabrics. The rooftop restaurant is one of the best in Paharganj.

Paharganj

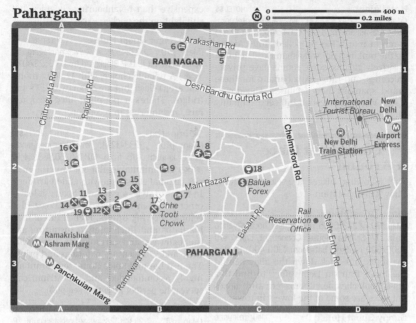

Paharganj

⊕ Activities, Courses & Tours
1	Salaam Baalak Trust	B2
	Salaam Balaak Trust	(see 8)

⬤ Sleeping
2	Ajay Guest House	B2
3	Cottage Yes Please	A2
4	Hare Rama Guest House	B2
5	Hotel Ajanta	C1
6	Hotel Grand Godwin	B1
7	Hotel Hari Piorko	B2
8	Hotel Namaskar	B2
9	Hotel Rak International	B2
10	Jyoti Mahal Guesthouse	B2
11	Metropolis Tourist Home	A2

	Vivek Hotel	(see 15)

⊗ Eating
12	Khosla Café	A2
13	Madan Café	A2
14	Malhotra	A2
	Metropolis Restaurant & Bar	(see 11)
15	Sam's Café	B2
16	Sita Ram Dewan Chand	A2
17	Tadka	B2

⊕ Drinking & Nightlife
18	Gem	C2
	Metropolis Restaurant & Bar	(see 11)
19	My Bar	A2

Jyoti Mahal Guesthouse   GUESTHOUSE $$
(Map p83; ☏ 23580523; www.jyotimahal.net;
2488-2490 Nalwa St; s/d ₹2000/2500; ❉@🛜)
Crammed full of Rajasthani carvings and
antiques, Jyoti feels like a traditional *haveli*
home. Arranged around a central atrium,
rooms have handmade furniture, marble
floors and four-poster beds.

Hotel Hari Piorko   HOTEL $$
(Map p83; ☏ 23587999; www.hotelharipiorko
delhi.com; 4775 Main Bazaar; d from ₹1394, tr/q
₹2090/2450; ❉@) A bit of a chintz-fest, this
eccentric hotel even has fish tanks in some

of the rooms. Nevertheless, rooms are clean,
there's room to move in the bathrooms and
you can dine on the terrace or up on the roof.

Hotel Grand Godwin   HOTEL $$
(Map p83; ☏ 23546891; www.godwinhotels.com;
8502/41 Arakashan Rd; s/d incl breakfast from
₹2114/2348; ❉@🛜; Ⓜ New Delhi) Located
north of Main Bazaar on the hotel strip of
Arakashan Rd, the Grand Godwin is firmly
midrange, and the glitzy feel of the lobby ex-
tends to the smart rooms. Run by the same
owners, the nearby Godwin Deluxe offers
similar facilities for similar prices.

Hotel Ajanta
HOTEL $$

(Map p83; ☎ 42350000; www.ajantahotel.com; 8647 Arakashan Rd; d/ste ₹2642/4697; ❄ @ ☎) A recent refurb has propelled Hotel Ajanta up the rankings on Arakashan Rd. The hotel positively gleams, some rooms have private balconies, and rates are a bargain for these brand spanking new facilities. The downstairs Vagabond restaurant serves quality Mughlai food.

🛏 Connaught Place & Around

The following places are close to Rajiv Chowk metro station.

Ringo Guest House
GUESTHOUSE $

(Map p70; ☎ 23310605; ringo_guest_house@yahoo.co.in; 17 Scindia House, Connaught Lane; s/d ₹500/600, r without bathroom ₹300-400) Dodge the touts and duck down the alley behind the India Tourism Delhi office to find this old-school cheapie. Rooms are tiny boxes but rates are some of the lowest in town.

Sunny Guest House
GUESTHOUSE $

(Map p70; ☎ 23312909; sunnyguesthouse1234@hotmail.com; 152 Scindia House, Connaught Lane; r without bathroom ₹400-600, with bathroom ₹800) Sunny Guest House is fractionally more expensive than neighbouring cheapies, but still light on the pocket; expect no frills.

Prem Sagar Guest House
GUESTHOUSE $$

(Map p70; ☎ 23345263; www.premsagarguesthouse.com; 1st fl, 11 P-Block; s/d from ₹3523/4110; ❄ @) A reliable choice, with 12 snug rooms that aren't flash, but are clean, with TVs and fridges. There's a pot-plant-filled rear terrace, and internet in reception.

★ Imperial
HOTEL $$$

(Map p70; ☎ 23341234; www.theimperialindia.com; Janpath; s/d from ₹18,166/20,868; ❄ @ ☎ ❄) The inimitable, Raj-era Imperial marries colonial classicism with gilded art deco. In terms of style, service and luxury, it leaves other hotels in the cold. Rooms boast high ceilings, flowing drapes, French linen, marble baths and finely crafted furniture, and the hallways and atriums are lined with 18th- and 19th-century paintings and prints. The 1911 bar and Spice Route restaurant are highly recommended, and the Atrium cafe serves the perfect high tea (see p93).

Hotel Alka
HOTEL $$$

(Map p70; ☎ 23344328; www.hotelalka.com; P-Block; s/d from ₹4110/5500; ❄ @ ☎) Alka's standard rooms are a little cramped and overpriced but more money buys more pizzazz, including grrrroovy leopard-skin pattern trim. There's a good vegetarian restaurant.

Park
HOTEL $$$

(Map p70; ☎ 23743000; www.theparkhotels.com; 15 Parliament St; s/d from ₹12,779/13,996; ❄ @ ☎ ❄) Conran-designed, with lots of modern flair, the Park boasts stylish, business-like rooms, a spa, smart eateries and a great poolside bar.

Hotel Palace Heights
HOTEL $$$

(Map p70; ☎ 43582610; www.hotelpalaceheights.com; 26-28 D-Block; s/d ₹7632/8219; ❄ @ ☎) This boutique hotel is cool enough to wear shades, offering sleek rooms with gleaming white linen, black lampshades and caramel and amber tones. There's an excellent restaurant, Zäffrän (p90), and 24-hour room service.

Corus
HOTEL $$$

(Map p70; ☎ 43652222; www.hotelcorus.com; 49 B-Block; s/d from ₹7045/7632; ❄ @ ☎) As well as a prime location, you get spotless tiled floors and dazzling white sheets at the Corus. More money gets you more floor space. There's an attractive restaurant, Bonsai, with a white-pebbled courtyard.

DELHI'S LITTLE LHASA

Home to Delhi's refugee Tibetan population, Majnu-ka-Tila is a long way from the centre, but good for the little Lhasa vibe. This mellow enclave is packed with travel agents, cyber cafes and trinket vendors, and you'll rub shoulders with maroon-clad Buddhist monks, local Tibetans and rather a lot of beggars. To get here, take the metro to Vidhan Sabha, then take a rickshaw to the enclave on KB Hedgewar Marg.

Clean, friendly and well-cared for **Wongdhen House** (☎ 23816689; 2wongdhenhouse@gmail.com; 15-A New Tibetan Colony; r ₹700-750, without bathroom ₹450; ❄), this is the pick of the Majnu-ka-Tila bunch. Rooms are simple but homey, the rooftop has views over the Yamuna and the restaurant rustles up everything from shredded chicken with chilli to momos.

West Delhi

Master Guest House GUESTHOUSE $$
(☏28741089; www.master-guesthouse.com; R-500 New Rajendra Nagar; s/d incl breakfast from ₹3250/4250; ❄@☎; Ⓜ Rajendra Place) Somewhat out of the way, but handy for the metro, this smart suburban home has three tastefully furnished rooms with spotless bathrooms. There's a leafy rooftop terrace.

Bajaj Indian Home Stay GUESTHOUSE $$$
(☏25736509; www.indianhomestay.com; 8A/34 WEA Karol Bagh; s/d/tr incl breakfast ₹4700/5900/7200; ❄@☎; Ⓜ Karol Bagh) More of a hotel than a homestay, this highly professional place has 10 agreeably decorated rooms. The tariff includes complimentary tea and coffee, local telephone calls and airport transfers. There's an attractive rooftop restaurant.

Shanti Home HOTEL $$$
(☏41573366; www.shantihome.com; A-1/300 Janakpuri; s/d incl breakfast from ₹8500/9500; ❄@☎; Ⓜ Janakpuri West) Off the tourist radar in West Delhi, this delightful small hotel is close to the metro and offers beautifully decorated rooms, inspired by Indian cities, and an excellent rooftop restaurant.

New Delhi

Youth Hostel HOSTEL $
(Map p74; ☏26116285; www.yhaindia.org; 5 Nyaya Marg, Chanakyapuri; dm/d ₹275/800, with AC ₹500/1400; ❄@) The dormitory and rooms here are clean, basic and institutional but benefit from a quiet location (by Delhi standards). The obligatory one-month temporary YHA membership costs ₹30.

YWCA Blue Triangle Family Hostel HOSTEL $$
(Map p74; ☏23360133; www.ywcaofdelhi.org; Ashoka Rd; dm ₹760, s/d incl breakfast from ₹1582/2752; ❄@; Ⓜ Patel Chowk) Despite having an institutional vibe and hint of eau de mothball, this Y (men and women) is central and has reasonable rooms for the price. Obligatory one-month membership costs ₹50.

Taj Mahal Hotel HOTEL $$$
(Map p74; ☏23026162; www.tajhotels.com; 1 Mansingh Rd; s/d ₹24,071/28,181; ❄@☎☀) The Taj pulls out all the stops, with a lobby full of Indian artworks and painted Mughal domes, lavish restaurants and a pool surrounded by manicured gardens. The luxuriously appointed rooms have all the five-star frills.

Claridges HOTEL $$$
(Map p74; ☏39555000; www.claridges.com; 12 Aurangzeb Rd; r from ₹18,584; ❄@☎☀) Surrounded by green lawns and gracious colonial-era bungalows, Claridges is an elegant choice. Rooms are decked out in colonial deco style; facilites are luxurious, including three fine-dining restaurants, a pool and a coffeeshop on the lawn.

ITC Maurya HOTEL $$$
(Map p74; ☏26112233; www.itchotels.incom; Sardar Patel Marg; s/d ₹15,852/17,613; ❄@☎☀) In the diplomatic enclave, the stylish ITC Maurya offers lavish rooms with every imaginable creature comfort, and service to match. Hobnob with Delhi's movers and shakers at the hotel restaurants, including the famous Bukhara (p91).

Lutyens Bungalow GUESTHOUSE $$$
(Map p74; ☏24611341; www.lutyensbungalow.co.in; 39 Prithviraj Rd; s/d incl breakfast from ₹5000/6500; ❄@☎☀; Ⓜ Racecourse) This great rambling house is an atmospheric green oasis, and perfect located for exploring New Delhi. The garden is great – lawns, flowers and fluttering parrots – but rooms are a little stuffy and overpriced. However, it's a good place to stay with kids.

South Delhi

Treetops GUESTHOUSE $$
(Map p78; ☏9899555704; tanniebaug13@gmail.com; R-8b Hauz Khas Enclave; r incl breakfast ₹2500-3500; ❄@☎; Ⓜ Hauz Khas) The elegant home of a charming and hospitable couple, journalist Murad Baig and food writer Tannie, Treetops offers lovely large rooms opening onto a leafy roof terrace overlooking the park. It's minutes from the metro, and Tannie gives cookery lessons. Evening meals are available.

K-One One GUESTHOUSE $$
(Map p74; ☏43592583; www.parigold.com; K-11 Jangpura Extn; s/d incl breakfast ₹4000/4500; ❄@☎; Ⓜ Jangpura) Set in a tidy and peaceful enclave, and handy for the metro, this family-run guesthouse offers four en-suite rooms painted in jewel-bright hues, and there's a roof terrace dotted with pot plants. The owner runs the Parul Puri cooking classes.

★**Devna** GUESTHOUSE $$$
(Map p74; ☏41507176; www.tensundernagar.com; 10 Sunder Nagar; d ₹4500-5500; ❄@☎) Fronted by a pretty courtyard garden, and

DELHI

Delhi Metro Map

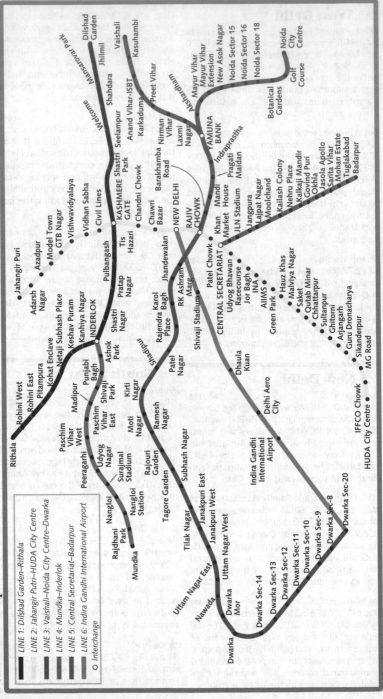

LINE 1: Dilshad Garden–Rithala
LINE 2: Jahangir Putri–HUDA City Centre
LINE 3: Vaishali–Noida City Centre–Dwarka
LINE 4: Mundka–Inderlok
LINE 5: Central Secretariat–Badarpur
LINE 6: Indira Gandhi International Airport
○ Interchange

run with panache by the charming Atul and Devna, this one of Delhi's most charismatic guesthouses. The walls are lined with photos of maharajas and works of art (yes, those are original Jamini Roys) and the rooms are decked out with quirky antiques. The upstairs rooms front onto tiny terraces.

★ Manor   HOTEL $$$
(Map p78; ☎ 26925151; www.themanordelhi.com; 77 Friends Colony West; d incl breakfast from ₹8760; ❋ @) A more intimate alternative to Delhi's five-star chains, this 16-room boutique hotel oozes privacy and elegance. Set amid lush lawns off Mathura Rd, the Manor offers the kind of designer touches normally found in the homes of Bollywood stars. There's a colonial air to the opulent rooms and the restaurant, Indian Accent (p92), is one of Delhi's finest.

Bnineteen   GUESTHOUSE $$$
(Map p74; ☎ 41825500; www.bnineteen.com; B-19 Nizamuddin East; d incl breakfast from ₹8500; ❋ @) Located in posh and peaceful Nizamuddin East, with views over Humayun's Tomb from the rooftop, this gorgeous place shows an architect's touch. Rooms are modern and refined, and there is a state-of-the-art shared kitchen on each floor.

Amarya Villa   GUESTHOUSE $$$
(Map p78; ☎ 41759267; www.amaryagroup.com; a-2/20 Safdarjang Enclave; s/d ₹4725/5203; ❋ @ ☎; Ⓜ Hauz Khas) The European owners of Amarya Villa have created a stylish haven straight out of an interior-design magazine. It's boutique all the way, with scattered artefacts, lavish fabrics and colour themes for every room. The same owners run the similarly chic Amarya Haveli (Map p78; ☎ 41759268; P5 Hauz Khas; Ⓜ Lajpat Nagar) in Hauz Khas, with similar prices (same contact details).

Colonel's Retreat   GUESTHOUSE $$$
(Map p78; ☎ 9999720024; D-418, Defence Colony; s/d incl breakfast from ₹4300/4800; ❋ @ ☎; Ⓜ Lajpat Nagar) With four immaculate rooms, livened up with hand-painted details, this agreeable guesthouse offers a taste of the affluent suburbs. It's quiet and tucked away but handy for the metro.

🛏 Airport Area

New Delhi Bed & Breakfast   HOMESTAY $$
(☎ 26894812; www.newdelhibedandbreakfast.com; C8/8225 Vasant Kunj; s/d ₹3000/3500; ❋ @) Renu Dayal's welcoming homestay has two cosy double rooms (one en suite) in her elegant house in a leafy enclave, only 10 minutes' drive from the airport.

Inn at Delhi   HOMESTAY $$
(☎ 24113234; www.innatdelhi.com; C-34 Anand Niketan; r ₹3500-6000; ❋ @ ☎) Between the city and the airport, this cosy suburban residence is a good choice for single women. Your hosts are a professional couple, rooms are spacious but human in scale and some thought has gone into the decor.

Chhoti Haveli   HOMESTAY $$
(Map p78; ☎ 26124880; http://chhotihaveli.com; A1006, Pocket A, Vasant Kunj; s/d ₹3300/3800; ❋ @ ☎) Set in a block of low-rise apartments, in a quiet, leafy area near the airport, this well-kept place offers tastefully decorated rooms. Potted plants and scattered petals on the doorstep show a personal touch.

Radisson Blu Plaza   HOTEL $$$
(☎ 26779191; www.radissonblu.com; National Hwy 8; s/d from ₹10,624/11,804; ❋ @ ☎ ⊠) Airport-facing Radisson is your typical business-class hotel. But oh, what a joy to lie down on soft linen and orthopaedic beds after a long-haul flight. On-site are Chinese, Indian and Italian restaurants.

✗ Eating

Delhi is a foodie paradise, and locals graze throughout the day, whether munching the city's famous *dilli ki chaat* (street-food snacks and salads) at stalls in the old town, or sitting down to indulgent feasts at Delhi's fine-dining restaurants. Midrange and upmarket restaurants charge a service tax of around 10%; drinks taxes can suck a further 20% (alcoholic) or 12.5% (nonalcoholic) from your money belt. Taxes haven't been included unless indicated. Many restaurants also levy a 10% service charge, in lieu of a tip. Telephone numbers have been provided for restaurants where reservations are recommended.

✗ Old Delhi

★ Karim's   MUGHLAI $
(Map p64; Gali Kababyan; mains ₹37-340; ⊙ 7am-midnight; Ⓜ Chawri Bazaar) Just off the lane leading south from the Jama Masjid, Karim's has been delighting carnivores since 1913. The menu is dominated by meaty Mughlai treats such as mutton *burrah* (marinated chops), *seekh* kebabs and tandoori chicken.

There's a **branch** (Map p74; Nizamuddin West) in Nizamuddin West.

★ Jalebiwala
SWEETS $

(Map p64; Dariba Corner, Chandni Chowk; jalebis per 100g ₹25; ⊘8.30am-9.45pm; Ⓜ Chandni Chowk) Century-old Jalebiwala does Delhi's – if not India's – finest *jalebis* (deep-fried, syrupy fried dough), so pig out and worry about the calories tomorrow.

Haldiram's
FAST FOOD $

(Map p64; 1454/2 Chandni Chowk; mains ₹55-160; ⊘10am-10.30pm; Ⓜ Chandni Chowk) This clean, bright cafeteria cum sweet shop is a popular stop for its top-notch dosas, idli and thalis, and it also sells delectable *namkin* (savouries) and *mithai* (sweets) to eat on the hoof. There's a popular **branch** (Map p70; Ⓜ Rajiv Chowk) on Connaught Place.

Bikanervala
FAST FOOD $

(Map p64; 382 Chandni Chowk; snacks ₹60-140; ⊘8am-10.30pm; Ⓜ Chandni Chowk) This bright little canteen offers tasty snacks such as *paratha* (stuffed bread) and *channa bhatura* (spicy chickpeas with fried puffed bread). There's a handy **branch** (Map p70) among the state emporiums on Baba Kharak Singh Marg.

Gali Paratha Wali
STREET FOOD $

(Map p64; Gali Paratha Wali; parathas ₹15-35; ⊘7am-11pm; Ⓜ Chandni Chowk) Head to this foodstall-lined lane off Chandni Chowk for delectable *parathas* fresh off the *tawa* (hotplate). Choose from a spectacular array of stuffings, from green chilli and paneer to lemon and banana.

Ghantewala
SWEETS $

(Map p64; 1862A Chandni Chowk; mithai per 100g from ₹20; ⊘8am-10pm; Ⓜ Chandni Chowk) Delhi's most famous sweetery, 'the bell ringer' has been churning out *mithai* (Indian sweets) since 1790. Try some *sohan halwa* (ghee-dipped gram flour biscuits).

Al-Jawahar
MUGHLAI $$

(Map p64; Matya Mahal; mains ₹100-275; ⊘7am-midnight; Ⓜ Chawri Bazaar) South of the Jama Masjid, Al-Jawahar serves up tasty Mughlai cuisine at formica tables in an orderly dining room. Kebabs and mutton curries dominate the menu, but they also do good butter chicken and kormas.

Chor Bizarre
KASHMIRI $$

(Map p64; ☏23273821; Hotel Broadway, 4/15 Asaf Ali Rd; mains ₹305-500; ⊘7.30-10.30am, noon-3.30pm & 7.30-11.30pm; Ⓜ New Delhi) A dimly lit cavern, filled with antiques and bric-a-brac, Chor Bizarre (meaning 'thieves market') offers delicious and authentic Kashmiri cuisine, including *wazwan*, the traditional Kashmiri feast. It offers an old-town walking tour combined with lunch for ₹1800.

Moti Mahal
MUGHLAI $$

(Map p64; ☏23273661; 3704 Netaji Subhash Marg; mains ₹200-380; ⊘11am-midnight) The original, much-copied Moti Mahal has been open for six generations – the food is much more impressive than the faded surroundings. Delhi-ites rate the place for its superior butter chicken and *dhal makhani*. There's live *qawwali* (Islamic devotional singing) Wednesday to Monday (8pm to midnight).

✗ Paharganj & West Delhi

Paharganj's restaurants are a reflection of the globe-trotting backpackers who eat here. As well as Indian staples, you'll find everything from banana pancakes to pizzas, Mexican wraps and Israeli falafel...all of which can taste remarkably similar to the Indian staples. Come for low prices and the traveller hubbub, rather than gourmet dining. There are more cheap eats in the bazaars at Karol Bagh. The following are all close to the Ramakrishna Ashram Marg or Karol Bagh metro stations.

Madan Café
MULTICUISINE $

(Map p83; Main Bazaar; mains ₹20-100; ⊘8am-10pm) Cheap but certainly cheerful, this hole-in-the-wall cafe is a popular spot to sit and watch the human traffic. Facing is the similar **Khosla Café** (Map p83).

Sita Ram Dewan Chand
INDIAN $

(Map p83; 2243 Chuna Mandi; dishes ₹38; ⊘8am-6pm) A family-run hole-in-the-wall, serving inexpensive portions of just one dish – *chole bhature* (spicy chickpeas), accompanied by delicious, freshly made, puffy, fried bread.

Bikanervala Angan
FAST FOOD $

(82 Arya Samaj Rd, Karol Bagh; mains ₹60-125; ⊘8am-midnight; Ⓜ Karol Bagh) From the Bikanervala stable, this small but buzzing Karol Bagh canteen is a useful pitstop for South Indian treats, fast food and snacks.

Roshan di Kulfi
ICE CREAM $

(Ajmal Khan Rd, Karol Bagh; kulfi ₹75; ⊘8.30am-9.30pm; Ⓜ Karol Bagh) A Karol Bagh institution for its scrumptious special *pista badam kulfi* (frozen milk dessert with pistachio, almond and cardamom).

Metropolis Restaurant & Bar MULTICUISINE $$

(Map p83; Metropolis Tourist Home, Main Bazaar; mains ₹150-400; ⊗11am-11pm) On the rooftop at Metropolis Tourist Home, this energetic travellers' haunt is a cut above the competition. Enjoy a cold beer and tasty tandoori chicken while you share your first impressions of Delhi with other new arrivals.

Tadka INDIAN $$

(Map p83; 4986 Ram Dwara Rd; mains ₹100-150; ⊗9am-10.30pm) Named for everyone's favourite dhal, Tadka serves up tasty paneer dishes and other veggie treats to an appreciative clientele of vegetarians and meat-avoiders.

Sam's Café MULTICUISINE $$

(Map p83; Vivek Hotel, 1534-1550 Main Bazaar; mains ₹90-190; ⊗8am-11.30pm) With a pokey downstairs dining room and a much more inviting rooftop terrace, this traveller stalwart is a calm oasis where you can relax with a book while enjoying inexpensive backpacker fare.

Malhotra MULTICUISINE $$

(Map p83; 1833 Laxmi Narayan St; mains ₹75-250; ⊗7am-11pm) One street back from the Main Bazaar chaos, Malhotra is smarter than most, with a good menu of set breakfasts, burgers, Indian standards and spirited attempts at continental dishes.

✕ Connaught Place

The following eateries are all close to the Rajiv Chowk metro stop.

★ Hotel Saravana Bhavan SOUTH INDIAN $

(Map p70; 15-P Block; mains ₹65-165; ⊗8am-10pm) Delhi's best thali (₹165) is served up in unassuming surroundings – a simple Tamil canteen on the edge of Connaught Place. There are queues every meal time to sample the splendid array of richly spiced veg curries, dips, breads and condiments that make it onto every thali plate. There's a second branch (Map p70; 46 Janpath) on Janpath.

Sagar Ratna SOUTH INDIAN $

(Map p70; 15-K Block; dishes ₹45-150; ⊗8am-11pm) Another dosa dreamland, with expertly prepared dosas, idlis, uttapams (savoury rice pancakes) and other southern goodies, plus thalis. There's a branch (Map p78) in the Defence Colony Market.

Nizam's Kathi Kabab FAST FOOD $

(Map p70; 5 H-Block; kebabs ₹70-330; ⊗11.30am-10.45pm) This takeaway eatery creates masterful kebabs, biryani and kati rolls (kebabs wrapped in a hot paratha). It's always busy with meat-loving hoards.

Rajdhani INDIAN $$

(Map p70; ☎43501200; 1/90 P-Block; thalis ₹125-249; ⊗11am-4pm & 7-11pm) This pristine, nicely decorated two-level place serves up excellent-value vegetarian Gujarati and Rajasthani thalis with plenty of side dishes.

Bengali Sweet House SOUTH INDIAN $

(Map p64; 27-37 Bengali Market; snacks & dishes ₹40-150; ⊗8am-11pm) East of CP, Bengali Market is famous for its sweets and chaat (try the golgappas – stuffed miniature puris), but this Delhi landmark is also good for inexpensive dosas and thalis.

Wenger's BAKERY $

(Map p70; 16 A-Block; snacks ₹30-90; ⊗10.45am-7.45pm) Legendary Wenger's has been baking since 1926; come for cakes, sandwiches, biscuits, savoury patties and other snacks to eat on the trot.

Nirula's ICE CREAM $

(Map p70; 14 K-Block Connaught Place; ice cream from ₹50; ⊗10am-midnight) A decades-old ice-cream parlour serving a rainbow of flavours, from workaday strawberry to exotic badam pista (almond and pistachio with cardamom).

Pind Balluchi INDIAN $$

(Map p70; Regal Bldg, Sansad Marg; mains ₹170-300; ⊗noon-11pm) A high-kitsch 'village restaurant' that cooks up reasonably priced and tasty Mughlai standards. The inexpensive drinks menu is a big hit with Delhi students.

Kwality INDIAN $$

(Map p70; ☎23742352; 7 Regal Bldg; mains ₹200-350; ⊗noon-11pm) Charmingly old-school (even the waiters look like they've been here since the Raj), Kwality is family-style all the way, with homey dishes from a familiar Mughlai menu, including excellent channa bhatura (chickpeas with fried bread).

Véda INDIAN $$$

(Map p70; ☎41513535; 27 H-Block; mains ₹300-700; ⊗12.30-11.30pm) Fashion designer Rohit Baal created Véda's sumptuous interior, a dark boudoir with swirling neo-Murano chandeliers and shimmering mirror mosaics. The menu puts a modern spin on classic

Mughlai dishes and chefs make liberal use of fresh herbs and spices. It's great for a date.

Swagath
SOUTH INDIAN $$$

(Map p74; ✉ 23366761; Janpath Hotel, Janpath; mains ₹375-1145; ⊙ noon-11.45pm; 🛜; Ⓜ Lajpat Nagar) Serving supremely scrumptious Indian seafood (especially crab, prawns, lobster and fish), Swagath will take you on a culinary tour through the fishing villages of south India. There are several branches, including in the **Defence Colony Market** (Map p78; Ⓜ Lajpat Nagar) and **M Block Market** (Map p78).

Spice Route
ASIAN $$$

(Map p70; ✉ 23341234; Imperial Hotel, Janpath; mains ₹500-2050) It took seven years to create the extravagant interior at Spice Route, with its murals, temple columns and wood carvings. The menu spans South India, Sri Lanka and Southeast Asia, and the food offers substance to match the style. Reservations recommended.

Zãffrãn
MUGHLAI $$$

(Map p70; ✉ 43582610; 26-28 D-Block, Hotel Palace Heights; mains ₹435-500; ⊙ 11am-3.30pm & 7-11pm) An excellent restaurant serving topnotch Mughlai cuisine and designed to feel like a bamboo-shuttered terrace.

United Coffee House
MULTICUISINE $$$

(Map p70; ✉ 23416075; 15 E-Block; mains ₹250-490; ⊙ 10am-11pm) Not a coffeeshop, but an upscale restaurant, with an old-world dining room full of characters who look as elderly as the fixtures and fittings. The menu covers everything from pizza to butter chicken.

Chinese
CHINESE $$$

(Map p70; ✉ 65398888; 14/15 F-Block; mains ₹300-1200; ⊙ 11am-11pm) Popular with Chinese diplomats, Chinese serves up authentic Hunanese cuisine in a wow-factor calligraphy-decorated interior.

Zen
CHINESE $$$

(Map p70; ✉ 23357444; 25 B-Block; mains ₹189-635; ⊙ 11am-11pm) A high-ceilinged place with walls quilted like a Chanel handbag, Zen offers a more authentic take on Chinese cuisine than most Delhi eateries. Look out for dishes such as claypot tofu and spicy shredded lamb among the familiar standards.

Tao
ASIAN $$$

(Map p70; ✉ 43582666; 8 E-Block; mains ₹245-695; ⊙ 11am-11pm) Connaught Place businessmen rate Tao for its dim sum, Japanese, Thai

and Chinese cuisine. Good for sushi, bean curd and fixed-price business lunches (veg/nonveg ₹375/395).

Embassy
INDIAN $$$

(Map p70; ✉ 23416434; 11 D-Block; mains ₹315-500; ⊙ noon-11pm) A long-established family favourite, gracious and old-fashioned, serving Indian and continental creations.

✗ New Delhi & Around

To dine in style, head to Delhi's upmarket hotels or the posh enclaves around Khan Market, Lodi Rd and Mathura Rd. Shoppers at Khan Market will be spoilt for choice.

Lodi Colony Kebab Stands
STREET FOOD $

(Map p74; Hazrat Nizam-ud-din Dargah; kebabs from ₹50; ⊙ noon-11pm) The alley in front of Hazrat Nizam-ud-din Dargah becomes a hive of activity every evening as devotees leave the shrine in search of sustenance. Canteenstyle kebab houses cook up lip-smacking beef, mutton and chicken kebabs at bargain prices, with biryani and roti as filling side orders.

Andhra Pradesh Bhawan Canteen
SOUTH INDIAN $

(Map p74; 1 Ashoka Rd; breakfast ₹55, thalis ₹100; ⊙ 8-10.30am, noon-3pm & 7.30-10pm; Ⓜ Patel Chowk) A hallowed bargain, the canteen at the Andhra Pradesh state house serves cheap and delicious unlimited South Indian thalis to a seemingly unlimited stream of patrons. Come on Sunday for the Hyderabadi biryani (₹150).

Nathu's
SOUTH INDIAN $

(Map p74; Sunder Nagar Market; dishes & snacks ₹27-160; ⊙ 7am-11pm) A much-loved sweeterie serving up yummy *chaat* (Indian-style salad) and filling thalis. Upstairs is Navanda's, with a broad menu of veg and nonveg Indian and Chinese treats.

Comesum
FAST FOOD $

(Map p74; Nizamuddin Train Station; dishes ₹50-150; ⊙ 24hr) Fast food, from dosas to *kadhai* curries, served in double-quick time at all hours. There are branches at all the main train stations, but the biggest and best is at Nizamuddin.

★ Alkauser
STREET FOOD $$

(Map p74; www.alkausermughlaifood.com; Kautilya Marg; kebabs from ₹110; ⊙ 6-10.30pm) The family behind this hole-in-the-wall takeaway earned their stripes cooking kebabs for the Nawabs of Lucknow in the 1890s. The house speciality is the *kakori* kebab, a pâté-smooth combination of lamb and spices, but other treats include biryani (cooked *dum puhkt* style in a *handi* pot sealed with pastry), and perfectly prepared lamb *burra* (marinated chops) and *murg malai tikka* (chicken marinated with spices and paneer). There are several **branches** (Map p78), including one in the Safdarjang Enclave market.

Cafe Kitchen
MULTICUISINE $$

(Map p74; ☎41757960; Khan Market; mains ₹199-399; ⏱10.30am-11.45pm) A buzzing small cafe offering an informal alternative to the glam eateries. The menu trots from Italy (pasta) to Thailand (pad thai) to England (fish and chips).

Khan Chacha
FAST FOOD $$

(Map p74; Khan Market; snacks ₹130-210; ⏱noon-11pm) A simple eatery serving lip-smacking roti-wrapped mutton, chicken and paneer kebabs to a youthful crowd who appreciate the moderate prices and no-fuss attitude.

All American Diner
FAST FOOD $$

(Map p74; India Habitat Centre, Lodi Rd; mains ₹125-455; ⏱7am-midnight; Ⓜ JLN Stadium) American 1950s nostalgia, transported to the arty enclave of the Indian Habitat Centre. Come for malt shakes, burgers and stomach stretching American breakfasts.

★ Bukhara
INDIAN $$$

(Map p74; ☎26112233; ITC Maurya, Sardar Patel Marg; mains ₹1475-2550; ⏱12.30-2.45pm & 7-11.45pm) Widely considered Delhi's best restaurant, this glam hotel eatery serves Northwest Frontier–style cuisine at low tables, with delectable kebabs that you won't find in cheaper kebab houses. Reservations are essential.

★ Eau de Monsoon
INDIAN $$$

(Map p74; ☎23710101; Le Meridien, Janpath; mains ₹1200-2495; ⏱12.30-3pm & 7-11.30pm; Ⓜ Patel Chowk) Behind waterfall windows, the Meridien's top restaurant works magic with the globally-sourced ingredients. The fusion menu runs to morel mushroom and pea curry and lobster combined with char-grilled prawns. Smart dress is the way to go.

Dhaba
PUNJABI $$$

(Map p74; ☎39555000; The Claridges, 12 Aurangzeb Rd; thalis veg/nonveg ₹1495/1795; ⏱12.30-2.30pm & 7-11.30pm) Set in the ritzy Claridges hotel, Dhaba offers a posh take on Punjabi highway cuisine in a room that looks like a Punjabi highway (there's even half a Tata truck on the wall).

Lodi Garden Restaurant
MEDITERRANEAN $$$

(Map p74; ☎24652808; Lodi Rd; mains ₹395-895; ⏱12.30pm-12.45am; Ⓜ Jor Bagh) Set in a funky garden with lanterns dangling from the trees and tables in curtained pavilions and wooden carts, this is the most romantic dinner spot in New Delhi. Although not quite as impressive as the surroundings, the menu traverses Europe and the Middle East, and cocktails (from ₹400) are two-for-one from 4pm to 6.30pm. The Sunday brunch (₹1699) always pulls in a crowd.

Mamagoto
ASIAN FUSION $$$

(Map p74; ☎45166060; Middle Lane, Khan Market; mains ₹195-500; ⏱12.30pm-11.30am) The name means 'to play with food' in Japanese, and the kidult theme extends to the manga art on the walls. The eclectic menu spans Japan, China and Southeast Asia – including some authentically spicy hawker-style Thai food.

Amici
ITALIAN $$$

(Map p74; ☎43587191; 47 Khan Market; pizzas ₹300-400; ⏱11am-11pm) Calm and unpretentious, Amici actually pays some attention to the way they make pizzas in Italy. There are branches in the **Select Citywalk Mall** (Map p78; Saket), **Defence Colony Market** (Map p78) and **Hauz Khas Village** (Map p78).

Sidewok
ASIAN FUSION $$$

(Map p74; ☎46068122; 45 Khan Market; mains ₹175-1395; ⏱noon-11.30pm) All dark timber and Asian minimalism, Sidewok dishes up woksizzling Asian cuisine, from Japanese tempura to Thai red curry. There's a **branch** (Map p70) at Connaught Place.

Pandara Market
INDIAN $$$

(Map p74; Pandara Rd; mains ₹150-500; ⏱noon-1am; Ⓜ Khan Market) Less a market than a strip of upmarket restaurants, this is a good option for night owls – most eateries here are open to 1am or later. Prices, standards and atmosphere are very similar along the strip. For quality Mughlai and North Indian food, try **Gulati** (Map p74; Pandara Market; mains ₹150-500; ⏱noon-1am), **Havemore** (Map p74; Pandara Market; mains ₹160-390; ⏱noon-2am), **Pindi** (Map p74; Pandara Market; mains ₹150-500; ⏱noon-midnight), or the surpisingly glitzy **Chicken Inn** (Map p74; Pandara Market; mains ₹150-500; ⏱noon-1am). For Indian-style Chinese and Thai food, head to **Ichiban** (Map p74; Pandara Market; Mains 150-500; ☺noon-12.30am).

Baci
ITALIAN $$$

(Map p74; ☑41507445; Sunder Nagar Market; mains ₹360-700; ☺11am-1am) A top choice for a romantic dinner, Baci serves Italian cuisine and freshly ground coffee in cosmopolitan surroundings, to a soundtrack of smooth jazz crooning.

South Delhi

South Delhi's best eateries are tucked away in the southern suburbs of Hauz Khas, Greater Kailash II, Saket, Vasant Vihar and further afield.

Evergreen
FAST FOOD $

(Map p78; S29-30 Green Park Market; mains ₹65-210; ☺8am-10.30pm; Ⓜ Green Park) Part cafe, part sweet shop, Evergreen has been keeping punters happy since 1963 with its veg snacks, *chaat*, thalis and dosas.

★ Gunpowder
SOUTH INDIAN $$

(Map p78; ☑26535700; 3rd fl, 22 Hauz Khas Village; mains ₹100-400; ☺noon-3pm & 7.30-11pm Tue-Sun; Ⓜ Green Park) Tucked away on the 3rd floor at the end of the last alley in Hauz Khas, Gunpowder serves up Keralan treats like toddy-shop *meen* (fish) curry, sweet-and-sour pumpkin and blistering stir-fried buffalo with coconut and chilli. It's small and informal; bookings are advised.

Not Just Parathas
INDIAN $$

(Map p78; 84 M-Block, Great Kailash II; dishes ₹64-395; ☺noon-midnight) They don't just serve *parathas*, they serve 120 types of *parathas*! Try them stuffed with kebabs, veg curries, shredded chicken and untold other fillings.

★ Olive
MEDITERRANEAN $$$

(Map p78; ☑29574443; One Style Mile, Mehrauli; tasting lunch menu from ₹495, dinner mains from ₹575; ☺noon-12pm; Ⓜ Qutab Minar) Uberchic Olive creates a little piece of the Mediterranean in the suburbs. The *haveli* setting, combined with beach-house colours, is unlike anywhere else in Delhi. Come for inventive Mediterranean dishes – asparagus and walnut pizza, seasonal vegetables in filo pastry – as tasty as the clientele.

★ Indian Accent
INDIAN $$$

(Map p78; ☑26925151; Manor, 77 Friends Colony; tasting menu veg/non-veg ₹2375/2575) Overlooking lush lawns at the Manor hotel, this exclusive restaurant serves inspired modern Indian cuisine. Familiar and unfamiliar ingredients are thrown together in surprising combinations – try the silken tofu with quinoa pulao and goji berry curry.

Diva
ITALIAN $$$

(Map p78; ☑29215673; M8-M-Block, Greater Kailash II; mains ₹490-1100; ☺12.30-3pm & 7.30-11.30pm) Chef Ritu Dalmia's *molto chic* Italian restaurant is an intimate space on two levels, with starched tablecloths, plate-glass windows, a sophisticated modern-Italian menu, and a proper wood-fired oven.

Hao Shi Nian Nian
CHINESE $$$

(Map p78; ☑47748888; M25 M-Block, Greater Kailash II; mains ₹350-1180; ☺11.30am-3.30pm & 6.30-11.30pm) Cool as ice, Hao Shi Nian Nian oozes sophistication. This is fine dining for grown ups, with starched table cloths and a menu of fiery Sichuan stir-fries, Thai curries, dim sum and sushi.

Mainland China
CHINESE $$$

(Map p78; ☑29222123; 4 Local Shopping Centre, LSC Masjid Moth, Greater Kailash II; mains ₹495-850) Delhi's most glamorous Chinese restaurant, attracting well-heeled families from the burbs. Sample superior dim sum, noodles and seafood in full-flavoured sauces, surrounded by golden deities.

Smokehouse Grill
MULTICUISINE $$$

(Map p78; ☑41435531; 2 VIPPS Center, LSC Masjid Moth, Greater Kailash II; mains ₹600-800; ☺7.30pm-12.30am) An uberhip hang-out, showcasing surprising smoked ingredients in a European fusion menu (try the John Dory with smoked chilli). DJs spin on Friday and Saturday nights.

Punjab Grill
MUGHLAI $$$

(Map p78; ☑41572977; Select Citywalk, Saket; Mains ₹420-1200; ☺11am-11.30pm; Ⓜ Malviya Nagar) Don't be put off by the shopping-mall setting. This sleek eatery offers superior Mughlai food – kebabs, *kadhai* (metal pot) curries and unleavened breads – in classy surroundings. Take your pick from the gleaming dining room or the open-air terrace.

Punjabi by Nature
PUNJABI $$$

(Map p78; ☑46117000; Basant Lok Community Centre, Vasant Vihar; mains ₹525-1995; ☺12.30pm-1am) Adorned with murals of men in turbans, this place offers ravishingly delicious Punjabi food. As well as perfectly prepared roadhouse standards, look out for fusion treats such as salmon tikka and tandoori lamb chops.

Drinking

Whether it's cappuccino and pastries for breakfast, or beer and bites in the evening, Delhi has plenty of spots to wet your whistle.

Cafes

Chain coffeeshops abound – Café Coffee Day is the most prolific (you'll rarely have to walk more than a hundred yards to find a branch), but there are also abundant branches of Costa and Barista, particularly around Connaught Place.

Café Turtle   CAFE
(Map p74; Full Circle Bookstore, Khan Market; M Khan Market) Allied to the Full Circle bookshop, this boho cafe ticks all the boxes when you're in the mood for coffee, cakes and calm reading space. There are branches in **N-Block Market** (Map p78; N-Block, Greater Kailash Part I) and **Nizamuddin East** (Map p74; Nizamuddin East).

Latitude 28°   CAFE
(Map p74; Good Earth, Khan Market; ⊙11.30am-11pm; M Khan Market) Above the bijou Good Earth homewares store, this is Khan Market's prettiest cafe, with sparkly chandeliers and stenciled walls. Run by the team behind Diva, and oh so popular with ladies who lunch.

Kunzum Travel Cafe   CAFE
(Map p78; www.kunzum.com; Hauz Khas Village; ⊙11am-7.30pm Tue-Sun; ☎; M Green Park) Run by the team of travel writers behind the informative *Delhi 101* guidebook, Kunzum has a pay-what-you-like policy for the self-service French-press coffee and tea. There's free wi-fi and travel books and magazines to browse. It also runs heritage walks.

Big Chill   CAFE
(Map p74; Khan Market; ⊙noon-11.30pm; M Khan Market) There are two branches of this film-poster-lined cafe at Khan market, packed with chattering Delhi-ites. The menu is a telephone directory of continental and Indian dishes. There's a branch in the **DLF Place** (Map p78) mall in Saket.

L'Opera   CAFE
(Map p74; Khan Market; ⊙9.30am-10pm; M Khan Market) The French pastries at this cute Khan Market bakery are so authentic they even have a branch in the French embassy. Come for rainbow macaroons, fruit tarts, and cream-filled fancies. There are just a few stools for seating.

Indian Coffee House   CAFE
(Map p70; Mohan Singh Place, Baba Kharak Singh Marg; ⊙9am-9pm; M Rajiv Chowk) Stuck-in-time Indian Coffee House looks poised to go under, but the roof terrace is a popular hangout thanks to the staggeringly cheap menu of snacks (₹9 to ₹40) and South Indian coffee (₹14).

Costa   CAFE
(Map p70; L-Block, Connaught Place; ⊙9am-11pm; M Rajiv Chowk) Arguably the best of the coffee chains; the Connaught Place branch offers a thoroughly Westernised escape from the noise and tumult.

Keventer's Milkshakes   CAFE
(Map p70; 17 A-Block, Connaught Place; milkshakes ₹50-80; ⊙9am-11pm; M Rajiv Chowk) If you want to find the best cheap treats, follow the teenagers. Keventer's has a cult following for its legendary milkshakes, slurped on the pavement in front of the stand.

Bars

Nightlife in Delhi is fairly low-key, but a party mood prevails from Wednesday to Saturday night. A smart-casual dress code (no shorts, vests or flip-flops) applies at most places. Taxes can pack a nasty punch (alcoholic 20%, nonalcoholic 12.5%); taxes aren't included here unless stated. Most bars have two-for-one happy hours from around noon till 8pm.

1911   BAR
(Map p70; Imperial Hotel, Janpath; drinks from ₹650; ⊙6am-1am; M Rajiv Chowk) The elegant bar at the Imperial is the ultimate neocolonial extravagance. Sip perfectly prepared cocktails in front of murals of cavorting maharajas.

Q'BA   BAR
(Map p70; ☎45173333; 1st fl, 42 E-Block; ⊙noon-1am; M Rajiv Chowk) Connaught Place's swishest watering hole has a Q-shaped bar, sultry lighting and sumptuous leather upholstery. Upstairs is for fine dining and there's a cool

DELHI DRINKING

HIGH TEA AT THE IMPERIAL

Raise your pinkie finger! High tea at the Imperial (p84) is perhaps the most refined way to while away an afternoon in Delhi. Sip tea from bone-china cups and pluck dainty sandwiches and cakes from tiered stands, while discussing the latest goings-on in Shimla and Dalhousie. High tea is served in the Atrium from 3pm to 6pm daily (weekday/weekend ₹750/1050). For ₹2500, you can add a 1½ hour tour of the Imperial's fantastic collection of Indian and colonial art.

roof terrace, a great place to spend a sticky summer evening.

Nero
BAR

(Map p74; Le Meridien, Janpath; ⊙11am-1am; Ⓜ Patel Chowk) A sleek black box inside the sleek Le Meridien hotel, this watering hole oozes style. Dress to impress and bring a full wallet.

Urban Pind
BAR

(Map p78; 4 N-Block, Greater Kailash I; ⊙1pm-1am) Serving up three floors of soft sofas, saucy mock-Khajuraho carvings, and DJ beats, Urban Pind is sexy and proud. DJs play nightly – come on Tuesday for Salsa night, or Thursday for drinks deals. The same owners run the similarly glam **Urban Cafe** (Map p74; ✆43597127; Middle Lane, Khan Market; ⊙11pm-1am) in Khan Market.

Aqua
BAR

(Map p70; Park Hotel, 15 Parliament St; ⊙11am-midnight; Ⓜ Rajiv Chowk) Aqua offers well-heeled patrons the chance to see and be seen beside the pool at the Park Hotel. The curtained day beds are the perfect place to unwind after visiting Jantar Mantar or shopping in Connaught Place.

Shalom
BAR

(Map p78; www.shalomexperience.com; 18-N Block Market, Greater Kailash I; ⊙11am-1am) This lounge-bar and restaurant, with wooden furniture and moody lighting, is one of the doyennes of the Delhi bar scene. As well as wine, beers, cocktails and nightly DJs, there's top-notch Mediterranean fare.

Rodeo
BAR

(Map p70; ✆23713780; 12 A-Block; ⊙11am-1am; Ⓜ Rajiv Chowk) In the mood for tequila, saddle barstools and staff in cowboy hats? Then easygoing Rodeo is for you, partner. There's live country music on Thursdays.

Mocha
BAR

(Map p78; ✆46588445; www.mocha.co.in; 28A Defence Colony Market) Originally a sheesha bar, Mocha has weathered the smoking ban by reinventing itself as a laid-back bar and coffeeshop, with comfy chairs, chill-out tunes and an all-day happy hour.

Metropolis Restaurant & Bar
BAR

(Map p83; Metropolis Tourist Home, Main Bazaar, Paharganj; ⊙7am-11pm; Ⓜ Ramakrishna Ashram Marg) This hotel's rooftop restaurant is the most salubrious choice on Paharganj's Main Bazaar – perfect for when you want to escape the chaos at street level.

My Bar
BAR

(Map p83; Main Bazaar, Paharganj; ⊙10am-12.30pm; Ⓜ Ramakrishna Ashram Marg) A dark and dingy bar where the main charm is the cheap beer and the chance to hang out with other backpackers.

Gem
BAR

(Map p83; 1050 Main Bazaar, Paharganj; ⊙9am-midnight; Ⓜ Ramakrishna Ashram Marg) In this dark, wood-panelled dive, large bottles of beer cost from ₹120. The upstairs area has more atmosphere.

24/7
BAR

(Map p64; Lalit Hotel, Maharaja Rajit Singh Marg; ⊙24hr; Ⓜ Barakhamba Rd) The 24-hour lobby bar at the Lalit Hotel is the perfect spot for a welcome-to-Delhi drink after a long flight.

☆ Entertainment

To access Delhi's dynamic arts scene, check local listings. October and March are the 'season', with shows and concerts (often free) happening nightly.

Music & Cultural Performances

TLR
LIVE MUSIC

(Map p78; www.tlrcafe.com; Hauz Khas Village; ⊙noon-1am; Ⓜ Green Park) Delhi's prime boho hang-out, TLR (The Living Room) more than justifies the trek to Hauz Khas. Come for groovy people, live music, jam sessions, DJ sets and other streetwise events from 9pm most evenings.

Blues
LIVE MUSIC

(Map p70; 18 N-Block, Connaught Place; ⊙noon-1am; Ⓜ Rajiv Chowk) A dark den with reasonably priced beers and random photos of rock stars on its brick walls. It's a lively, snob-free zone with a live band daily from 6.30pm.

@Live
LIVE MUSIC

(Map p70; 12 K-Block, Connaught Place; entry free; ⊙noon-1am; Ⓜ Rajiv Chowk) Fun and informal, @Live has a cool gimmick: a live jukebox. The band plays from 8.30pm, and punters pick the track listing from a song menu that runs from cheesy 1960s hits to modern-day boy-band pop.

Attic
CULTURAL PROGRAM

(Map p70; ✆23746050; www.theatticdelhi.org; 36 Regal Bdg, Sansad Marg; Ⓜ Rajiv Chowk) Small arts space, with regular free classical concerts, film screenings, cultural talks, and 'food meditation' (where participants eat in silence and then analyse the meal – sessions cost ₹150 and should be booked in advance).

Habitat World
CULTURAL PROGRAM
(Map p74; ☑43663333; www.habitatworld.com; India Habitat Centre, Lodi Rd; Ⓜ Jor Bagh) Temporary art shows at the Visual Arts Gallery, and plays and arty performances in the public courtyards.

Dances of India
DANCE
(Map p64; ☑26234689; Parsi Anjuman Hall, Bahadur Shah Zafar Marg; show ₹400; ⊘6.45pm; Ⓜ Chawri Bazaar) A one-hour performance of regional dances that includes Bharata Natyam (Tamil dance), Kathakali, bhangra and Manipuri.

India International Centre
CULTURAL PROGRAM
(Map p74; ☑24619431; www.iccdelhi.nic.in; 40 Max Mueller Marg; Ⓜ Khan Market) This cultural centre holds regular free exhibitions, talks and cultural performances.

Cinemas

Big Cinemas Odeon
CINEMA
(Map p70; www.bigcinemas.com/in; 23-D Block; Ⓜ Rajiv Chowk) A smart modern cinema screening Bollywood blockbusters and Hollywood hits.

PVR Plaza Cinema
CINEMA
(Map p70; www.pvrcinemas.com; H-Block, Connaught Place; Ⓜ Rajiv Chowk) Glossy chain cinema, screening the latest Bollywood releases and high-profile Hollywood imports. There are branches on **Baba Kharak Singh Marg**, in the **Basant Lok Community Centre** (Map p78; Vasant Vihar) and Saket's **Select Citywalk mall** (Map p78; www.pvrcinemas.com; Saket).

🔒 Shopping

Away from government-run emporiums and other fixed-price shops, haggle like you mean it. Many taxi and autorickshaw drivers earn commissions (via your inflated purchase price) by taking travellers to dubious, overpriced emporiums – don't fall for it.

🔒 Old Delhi

As well as the following shops and markets, it's worth browsing the myriad **music shops** (Map p64; Netaji Subhash Marg; ⊘Mon-Sat) along Netaji Subhash Marg for sitars, tabla sets and other beautifully crafted Indian instruments.

Main Bazaar
HANDICRAFTS, CLOTHING
(Paharganj; ⊘10am-9pm Tue-Sun; Ⓜ Ramakrisha Ashram Marg) The backpacker-oriented bazaar that runs through Paharganj is lined with shops and stalls selling everything from incense and hippy kaftans to religious stickers and cloth printing blocks. Haggle with purpose. The market officially closes on Monday, but most stores stay open.

Aap Ki Pasand (San Cha)
FOOD & DRINK
(Map p64; 15 Netaji Subhash Marg; ⊘9.30am-7pm Mon-Sat) An elegant tea shop selling a full range of Indian teas, from Darjeeling and Assam to Nilgiri and Kangra. You can try before you buy, and teas come lovingly packaged in drawstring bags.

Karol Bagh Market
MARKET
(Map p64; 10am-7pm Tue-Sun; Ⓜ Karol Bagh) This brash middle-class market shimmers with all things sparkly, from dressy *lehanga choli* (skirt-and-blouse sets) to princess-style shoes, spices, fruit and nuts packed in shiny paper and chrome motorcycle parts.

🔒 Connaught Place

★ State Emporiums
HANDICRAFTS, CLOTHING
(Map p70; Baba Kharak Singh Marg; ⊘11am-7pm Mon-Sat; Ⓜ Rajiv Chowk) Strung out along Baba Kharak Sing Marg are the official emporiums of the different Indian states, showcasing state-produced goods and handicrafts. Shopping here is like taking a tour around India – top stops include Kashmir, for papier mâché and carpets, Rajasthan, for miniature paintings and puppets, Uttar Pradesh for marble inlaywork, Karnataka for sandalwood sculptures, Tamil Nadu for metal statues and Odisha for stone carvings.

★ Kamala
HANDICRAFTS
(Map p70; Baba Kharak Singh Marg; ⊘10am-7pm Mon-Sat; Ⓜ Rajiv Chowk) Upscale crafts and curios, designed with real panache, from the Crafts Council of India.

Central Cottage Industries Emporium
HANDICRAFTS
(Map p70; ☑23326790; Janpath; ⊘10am-7pm; Ⓜ Rajiv Chowk) This government-run, fixed-price multilevel Aladdin's cave of India-wide handicrafts is a great place to browse. Prices are higher than in the state emporiums, but the selection of woodcarvings, jewellery, pottery, papier mâché, *jootis*, brassware, textiles, beauty products and miniature paintings is superb.

Khadi Gramodyog Bhawan
CLOTHING
(Map p70; Baba Kharak Singh Marg; ⊘10am-7.45pm Mon-Sat; Ⓜ Rajiv Chowk) Well known for its excellent *khadi* (homespun cloth), including good-value shawls, plus handmade

OLD DELHI'S BAZAARS

Old Delhi's bazaars are a head-spinning assault on the senses: an aromatic barrage of incense, spices, car fumes, body odour and worse, with a constant soundtrack of shouts, barks, music and car horns. This is less retail therapy, more heightened reality. The best time to come is midmorning, when you actually move through the streets.

Whole districts here are devoted to individual items. **Chandni Chowk** (Map p70; Old Delhi; ⊘10am-7pm Mon-Sat; Ⓜ Chandni Chowk) is all clothing, electronics and break-as-soon-as-you-buy-them novelties. For silver jewellery, head for **Dariba Kalan** (Map p64), the alley near the Sisganj Gurdwara. Off this lane, the **Kinari Bazaar** (Map p64) (literally 'trimmings market') is famous for *zardozi* (gold embroidery), temple trim, and wedding turbans. Running south from the old Town Hall, **Nai Sarak** (Map p64) is lined with stalls selling saris, shawls, chiffon and *lehanga*, while nearby **Ballimaran** (Map p64) has sequinned slippers and fancy, curly-toed jootis.

Beside the Fatehpuri Masjid, on Khari Baoli, is the nose-numbing **Spice Market** (Gadodia Market; Map p64; Khari Baoli), ablaze with piles of scarlet-red chillis, knobbly ginger and turmeric roots, peppercorns, cumin, coriander seed, cardamoms, dried fruit and nuts. For gorgeous wrapping paper and wedding cards, head to **Chawri Bazaar** (Map p64), leading west from the Jama Masjid. For steel cookpots and cheap-as-chapattis paper kites, continue northwest to **Lal Kuan Main Bazaar** (Map p64).

---

paper, incense, spices, henna and lovely natural soaps.

Janpath & Tibetan Markets   HANDICRAFTS
(Map p70; Janpath; ⊘10.30am-7.30pm Mon-Sat; Ⓜ Rajiv Chowk) These twin markets sell the usual trinkets: shimmering mirrorwork embroidery, colourful shawls, Tibetan bric-a-brac, brass oms, and dangly earrings. There are some good finds if you rummage through the junk. Haggle hard.

Shop   CLOTHING, HOMEWARES
(Map p70; 10 Regal Bldg, Sansad Marg; ⊘9.30am-7pm Mon-Sat; Ⓜ Rajiv Chowk) Lovely homewares and clothes (including children's clothes) from all over India in a chic boutique with fixed prices.

People Tree   HANDICRAFTS, CLOTHING
(Map p70; Regal Bldg, Sansad Marg; ⊘10.30am-7pm Mon-Sat; Ⓜ Rajiv Chowk) Teeny tiny People Tree sells cool T-shirts with funky Indian designs and urban attitude, as well as bags, jewellery and books. There's a **branch** (Map p78) in Hauz Khas village.

Fabindia   CLOTHING, HOMEWARES
(Map p70; www.fabindia.com; 28 B-Block, Connaught Place; ⊘11am-8pm) Sells readymade clothes in funky Indian fabrics, from elegant kurtas and dupattas to Western-style shirts, plus stylish homewares. There are branches in **Green Park** (Map p78), **Khan Market** (Map p74), **N-Block Market** (Map p78; Greater Kailash I) and **Select Citywalk** (Map p78) in Saket.

Godin Music   MUSIC
(Map p70; Regal Bldg, Sansad Marg; ⊘10.30am-7.30pm Mon-Sat; Ⓜ Rajiv Chowk) Fine musical instruments, from guitars to sitars, displayed in a thoroughly modern showroom.

M Ram & Sons   CLOTHING
(Map p70; ☑ 23416558; 21 E-Block, Connaught Place; ⊘10.30am-8pm Mon-Sat; Ⓜ Rajiv Chowk) A popular Delhi tailor, offering suits from ₹8000 (including material). Tailoring is possible in 24 hours.

Marques & Co   MUSIC
(Map p70; 14 G-Block, Connaught Place; ⊘10.30am-6pm Mon-Sat; Ⓜ Rajiv Chowk) This vintage music shop (since 1918) sells guitars, tabla sets, harmonicas, and sheet music, in stuck-in-time glass cabinets.

New Delhi

Good Earth   HOMEWARES
(Map p74; www.goodearth.in; 9 ABC Khan Market; ⊘11.30am-8.30pm; Ⓜ Khan Market) Wanting to furnish your designer apartment? Look no further than Good Earth, Delhi's most chichi homewares store. The see-and-be-seen Latitude 28° cafe is upstairs. There are branches in the **Santushti Shopping Complex** (Map p74) and **Select Citywalk** (Map p78) in Saket.

Full Circle Bookstore   BOOKS
(Map p74; www.fullcirclebooks.com; 23 Khan Market; ⊘9.30am-9.30pm; Ⓜ Khan Market) Delhi's most welcoming bookstore, with racks of

specialist books on the city, plus intriguing novels and kids' books. Relaxing Café Turtle is upstairs. There are branches in **N-Block Market** (Map p78; N-Block Market, Greater Kailash I) and **Nizamuddin East** (Map p74).

Khan Market
MARKET

(Map p74; ⊙10.30am-8pm Mon-Sat; Ⓜ Khan Market) Favoured by expats and Delhi's elite, the boutiques in this enclave are devoted to fashion, books and homewares. For handmade paper, check out **Anand Stationers** (Map p74), or try **Mehra Bros** (Map p74) for cool papier mâché ornaments and Christmas decorations. Literature lovers should head to Full Circle Bookstore and **Bahrisons** (Map p74). For ethnic-inspired fashions and homeware, hit Fabindia, Anokhi and Good Earth, and for elegantly packaged ayurvedic remedies, browse **Kama** (Map p74).

Anokhi
CLOTHING

(Map p74; www.anokhi.com; 32 Khan Market; ⊙10am-8pm; Ⓜ Khan Market) Anokhi specialises in blockprint clothes and homewares, showcasing traditional designs with a modern design sensibility. There are branches in the **Santushti Shopping Complex** (Map p74), **N Block Market** (Map p78; N-Block, Greater Kailash I) and **Nizamuddin East** (Map p74).

Sunder Nagar Market
HANDICRAFTS

(Map p74; ⊙10.30am-7.30pm Mon-Sat) Just south of Purana Qila, this genteel enclave specialises in Indian and Nepali handicrafts, replica 'antiques', furniture and glass doorknobs. There are numerous stores to browse, plus two outstanding tea shops, selling fine Indian teas.

Santushti
Shopping Complex
HOMEWARES, CLOTHING

(Map p74; Santushti Enclave; ⊙10am-7pm Mon-Sat; Ⓜ Racecourse) Diplomats frequent this exclusive complex facing the Ashok Hotel. Housed inside little pavilions are such stores as Anokhi, Good Earth and Indian designer clothes-store **Ensemble** (Map p74).

Timeless Books
BOOKS

(Map p78; ☏ 46056198; www.timelessbooks. in; 1882 Jagram Mandir Lane, South Extension I; ⊙10am-8pm; Ⓜ Moolchand) Hard to find amid the narrow bazaars of Kotla Mubarakpur, Timeless resembles a private library, where you can sit in comfy chairs and leaf through quality coffee-table books. Call ahead for directions.

Nalli Silk Sarees
CLOTHING

(Map p78; 12-M Block Market, Greater Kailash II; ⊙10am-8.30pm Wed-Mon) This multistorey emporium is a kaleidoscope of shimmering silk; saris range from ₹1900 to ₹35,000. There's a **branch** (Map p70) on Connaught Place.

C Lal & Sons
HANDICRAFTS

(Map p74; 9/172 Jor Bagh Market; ⊙10.30am-7.30pm; Ⓜ Jor Bagh) After sightseeing at Safdarjang's tomb, drop into Mr Lal's 'curiosity shop' for cute Christmas-tree decorations, papier mâché and carvings.

🏠 South Delhi

Hauz Khas Village
HANDICRAFTS, CLOTHING

(Map p78; ⊙11am-7pm Mon-Sat; Ⓜ Green Park) The tight alleyways of this arty little enclave are crammed with boutiques selling designer Indian-clothing, handicrafts, handmade furniture and old Bollywood movie posters. Vendors come and go, so wander along the lanes and see what you can discover.

Saket Malls
SHOPPING CENTRE

(Map p78; Press Enclave Marg, Saket; ⊙10am-11pm; Ⓜ Malviya Nagar) Delhi's glitziest malls are lined up along Press Enclave Marg in Saket. Here you'll find the full AC shopping experience: chain stores, chain eateries, chain bars and soft play for kids. Glitzy **Select Citywalk** has a PVR cinema, branches of FabIndia and Good Earth, and lots of big-name eateries. **DLF Place** has more of same, including a branch of **Bahrisons** (Map p78) bookstore, while nearby **MGF Metropolitan** has several showy bars.

Dilli Haat
HANDICRAFTS

(Map p78; Aurobindo Marg; admission ₹20; ⊙10.30am-10pm; Ⓜ INA) Located opposite the

---

OFF THE BEATEN TRACK

MIGHTY MONKEY

While visiting the markets at Karol Bagh, it's worth making a detour to the surreal **Jhandewalan Hanuman temple** (Map p64; Link Rd, Jhandewalan; ⊙dawn-dusk; Ⓜ Jhandewalan) near Jhandewalan metro station. As well as a 34m-high Hanuman statue that soars above the train tracks, you can follow passageways through the mouths of demons to a series of atmospheric, deity-filled chambers.

colourful INA Market, this open-air food-and-crafts market sells regional handicrafts. You pay an entry fee to browse the stalls, but there are some gorgeous bits and pieces on offer; bargain hard.

N-Block Market, Greater Kailash I   MARKET
(Map p78; Greater Kailash I; ⊘10.30am-8pm Wed-Mon) More swanky boutiques and posh eateries, including popular branches of Fabindia, Anokhi and Full Circle Bookstore, complete with a Café Turtle.

Sarojini Nagar Market   CLOTHING
(Map p78; ⊘11am-8pm Tue-Sun; Ⓜ INA) Rummage around here for cut-price Western-style clothes, with minor faults or blemishes, at bargain prices.

Lajpat Nagar Central Market   MARKET
(Map p78; Lajpat Nagar Part II; ⊘11am-8pm Tue-Sun; Ⓜ Lajpat Nagar) Join bargain-hunting locals on the prowl for household goods, jewellery and high-street fashions.

ⓘ Information

DANGERS & ANNOYANCES

Shop & Hotel Touts Taxi-wallahs at the international airport and around tourist areas frequently act as touts for hotels, claiming that your chosen hotel is full, poor value, overbooked, dangerous, burned down or closed, or that there are riots in Delhi, as part of a ruse to steer you to a hotel where they'll get a commission. Insist on being taken to where you want to go – making a show of writing down the registration plate number may help. Drivers at Connaught Place run a similar scam for private souvenir emporiums.

Travel Agent Touts Many travel agencies in Delhi claim to be tourist offices, even branding themselves with official tourist agency logos. There is only one tourist office – at 88 Janpath – and any other 'tourist office' is just a travel agency. Should you legitimately need the services of a travel agent, ask for a list of recommended agents from the bona-fide tourist office. We wary of booking a multistop trip out of Delhi, particularly to Kashmir. Travellers are often hit for extra charges, or find out the class of travel and accommodation is less than they paid for.

Train Station Touts Touts at New Delhi train station endeavour to steer travellers away from the legitimate International Tourist Bureau (on level 1 in the main building on the Paharganj side) and into private travel agencies where they earn a commission. Don't believe any claims about the station booking office until you have seen it with your own eyes.

INTERNET ACCESS

Most hotels offer internet access (often with wi-fi), but internet cafes can be found everywhere, including in Khan Market, Paharganj and Connaught Place. Rates start at ₹35 per hour.

MEDIA

To check out what's on, pick up monthly magazine *First City* (₹50) or trendy *Time Out Delhi* (₹50). A cheaper option is the weekly calendar pamphlet *Delhi Diary* (₹10).

MEDICAL SERVICES

Pharmacies are found on most shopping streets and in most suburban markets. Reputable hospitals:
All India Institute of Medical Sciences (IIMS; Map p78; ☑26588500; www.aiims.edu; Ansari Nagar; Ⓜ AIIMS)
Apollo Hospital (☑26925858; www.apollo-hospdelhi.com; Mathura Rd, Sarita Vihar)
Dr Ram Manohar Lohia Hospital (Map p74; ☑23365525; www.rmlh.nic.in; Baba Kharak Singh Marg; Ⓜ Patel Chowk)
East West Medical Centre (Map p78; ☑24690429; www.eastwestrescue.com; B-28 Greater Kailash Part I)

MONEY

There are banks with ATMs everywhere you look in Delhi. Forex offices are concentrated along Main Bazaar in Paharganj and around Connaught Place, particularly along Radial Rd 7. Travel agents and moneychangers offer international money transfers.
Baluja Forex (Map p83; 4596 Main Bazaar, Paharganj; ⊘9am-7.30pm; Ⓜ New Delhi)
Thomas Cook (Map p74; Hotel Janpath, Janpath; ⊘9.30am-7pm Mon-Sat; Ⓜ Patel Chowk)

POST & TELEPHONE

Delhi has tons of telephone kiosks where you can make cheap local, interstate and international calls. Look for the 'STD ISD PCO' signs.

There are post offices all over Delhi that can handle letters and parcels (most with packing services nearby). Poste restante is available at the New Delhi **general post office** (Map p74; ☑23364111; Gole Dakhana, Baba Kharak Singh Marg; ⊘10am-1pm & 1.30-4pm Mon-Sat); address mail to GPO, New Delhi – 110001.
DHL (Map p70; ☑23737587; Tolstoy Marg, Mercantile Bldg, ground fl; ⊘8am-8pm Mon-Sat; Ⓜ Rajiv Chowk) Organises international air freight.
Post Office (Map p70; 6 A-Block, Connaught Place; ⊘8am-7pm Mon-Sat)

TOURIST INFORMATION

The only official tourist information centre is India Tourism Delhi. Ignore touts who (falsely) claim to be associated with this office. Most states around India have their own regional tourist offices in Delhi – ask at India Tourism Delhi for contact details.

India Tourism Delhi (Government of India; Map p70; ✆23320008, 23320005; www.incredibleindia.org; 88 Janpath; ⏰9am-6pm Mon-Fri, to 2pm Sat; Ⓜ Rajiv Chowk) A useful source of advice on Delhi, getting out of Delhi, and visiting surrounding states. Has a free Delhi map and brochures, and publishes a list of recommended agencies and B&Bs. Come here to report tourism-related complaints.

❶ Getting There & Away

Delhi's airport can be prone to thick fog in December and January (often disrupting airline schedules) – it's wise to allow a day between connecting flights during this period.

AIR

Indira Gandhi International Airport (✆0124-3376000; www.newdelhiairport.in) is about 14km southwest of the centre. International and domestic flights use the gleaming new Terminal 3. Ageing Terminal 1 is reserved for low-cost carriers. Free shuttle buses run between the two terminals every 20 minutes.

The arrivals hall at Terminal 3 has 24-hour forex, ATMs, prepaid taxi and car hire counters, tourist information, bookshops, cafes and a **Premium Lounge** (✆61233922; 3hr s/d ₹2348/3522) with short-stay rooms.

Airlines advise checking in three hours before international flights and one hour before domestic flights. At check-in, be sure to collect tags for all your carry-on bags and make sure these are stamped by security.

For comprehensive details of domestic routes, pick up *Excel's Timetable of Air Services Within India* (₹55) from news-stands. Note that prices fluctuate and seats can be much cheaper if you book online with low-cost carriers.

Air India/Indian Airlines (Map p74; ✆24622220; www.airindia.in; Aurobindo Marg; ⏰9.30am-5.30pm) Also has an office at Safdarjung Airport.

Jagson Airlines (Map p70; ✆23721593; Vandana Bldg, 11 Tolstoy Marg; ⏰10am-6pm Mon-Sat)

Jet Airways (Map p70; ✆39893333; www.jetairways.com; 11/12 G-Block, Connaught Place; ⏰9am-6pm Mon-Sat) Also has info on JetKonnect flights.

Spicejet (✆1800 1803333; www.spicejet.com)

BUS

Most travellers enter and leave Delhi by train, but buses are a useful option if the trains are booked.

Services to destinations north and west of Delhi leave from the **Kashmere Gate Inter State Bus Terminal** (ISBT; Map p64; ✆23860290) in Old Delhi, accessible by metro. For buses to destinations east of Delhi, including Dehra Dun, Haridwar and Rishikesh, head to the **Anand Vihar ISBT** in the eastern suburbs, accessible on the blue Metro line. Services to destinations south of Delhi leave from the **Sarai Kale Khan ISBT** (Map p58) on the ring road near Nizamuddin train station.

All the bus stands are chaotic so arrive at least 30 minutes ahead of your departure time. You can avoid the hassle by paying a little more for private deluxe buses that leave from locations in central Delhi – enquire at travel agencies or your hotel for details.

Considering the traffic situation at either end, the train is your best bet for Agra. **Himachal Pradesh Tourism Development Corporation** (HPTDC; Map p74) runs a bus for Dharamsala (₹1100, 12 hours) from Chanderlok House on Janpath. For Rishikesh, the luxury Royal Cruiser

BUSES FROM DELHI

DESTINATION	ONE-WAY FARE (₹)	BUS STAND	DURATION (HR)	DEPARTURES
Amritsar	365-842	Kashmere Gate	10	hourly 6am-9.30pm
Chandigarh	187-510	Kashmere Gate	5	every 30min 6am-2am
Dehra Dun	224-638	Anand Vihar	7	hourly 5.30am-midnight
Dharamsala	420-1037	Kashmere Gate	12	6.30am, hourly 5.30-11pm
Haridwar	171-542	Anand Vihar	6	hourly 5am-11pm
Jaipur	196-655	Kashmere Gate	6	hourly 24hr
Manali	535-1162	Kashmere Gate	15	6.40am, 7.45am & 11.30am, hourly 3.45-10pm
Shimla	381-799	Kashmere Gate	10	5am & 12.30pm, hourly 4.50-10.30pm

leaves from the Anand Vihar ISBT at 10am, 9pm and 11pm daily (₹643, six hours). Rajasthan Tourism runs deluxe buses from **Bikaner House** (Map p74; ☏ 23381884; www.rtdc.com; Bikaner House, Pandara Rd), near India Gate, to the following destinations:

Ajmer (Volvo ₹923, nine hours, one daily)

Jaipur (super deluxe/Volvo ₹500/780, six hours, hourly)

Jodhpur (super deluxe/Volvo ₹965/1256, 11 hours, two daily)

Udaipur (Volvo ₹1375, 15 hours, one daily)

State bus companies operating out of Delhi:

Delhi Transport Corporation (☏ 23865181; http://dtc.nic.in)

Haryana Roadways (☏ 23861262; http://har trans.gov.in)

MAJOR TRAINS FROM DELHI

DESTINATION	TRAIN NO & NAME	FARE (₹)	DURATION (HR)	FREQUENCY	DEPARTURES & TRAIN STATION
Agra	12280 Taj Exp	74/273 (A)	3	1 daily	7.10am NZM
	12002 Bhopal Shatabdi	384/805 (B)	2	1 daily	6.15am NDLS
Amritsar	12013/12031 Shatabdi Exp	591/1305 (B)	6	2 daily	7.20am/ 4.30pm NDLS
Bengaluru	12430 Bangalore Rajdhani	2173/3215/ 5510 (C)	34	4 weekly	8.50pm NZM
Chennai	12434 Chennai Rajdhani	2152/3150/ 5380 (C)	28	2 weekly	4pm NZM
	12622 Tamil Nadu Exp	528/1482/ 2375 (D)	33	1 daily	10.30pm NDLS
Goa (Madgaon)	12432 Trivandrum Rajdhani	1991/2960/ 5075 (C)	26	2 weekly	11am NZM
Haridwar	12017 Dehradun Shatabdi	451/960 (B)	4½	1 daily	6.50am NDLS
Jaipur	12958 ADI Swama Jayanti Rajdani	617/835/1400 (C)	5	1 daily	7.55pm NDLS
	12916 Ashram Exp	175/450/655 (D)	6	1 daily	3.20pm DLI
	12015 Ajmer Shatabdi	482/1040 (B)	4½	6 weekly	6.05am NDLS
Kalka (for Shimla)	12011 Kalka Shatabdi	482/1040 (B)	4½	1 daily	7.40am NDLS
Khajuraho	12448 UP Sampark Kranti Exp	269/728/ 1085 (D)	10½	1 daily except Wed	8.15pm NZM
Lucknow	12004 Lucknow Swran Shatabdi	726/1615 (B)	6½	1 daily	6.15am NDLS
Mumbai	12952 Mumbai Rajdhani	1550/2270/ 3870 (C)	16	1 daily	4.30pm NDLS
	12954 August Kranti Rajdani	1550/2270/ 3870 (C)	17½	1 daily	4.55pm NZM
Udaipur	12963 Mewar Exp	305/831/ 1245 (D)	12½	1 daily	7.05pm NZM
Varanasi	12560 Shivganga Exp	306/836/ 1255 (D)	13	1 daily	6.55pm NDLS

Train stations: NDLS – New Delhi, DLI – Old Delhi, NZM – Hazrat Nizamuddin
Fares: (A) 2nd class/chair car; (B) chair car/1st-class AC; (C) 3AC/2AC/1st-class AC; (D) sleeper/3AC/2AC

Himachal Road Transport Corporation
(📞23868694; http://hrtc.gov.in)

Punjab Roadways (📞23867842; www.punbus online.com)

Rajasthan State Road Transport Corporation
(📞23864470; http://rsrtc.rajasthan.gov.in)

Uttar Pradesh State Road Transport Corporation (📞23235367; www.upsrtac.com)

TRAIN

There are three main stations in Delhi – (Old) Delhi train station (aka Delhi Junction) in Old Delhi, New Delhi train station near Paharganj, and Hazrat Nizamuddin train station, south of Sunder Nagar. Make sure you know which station your train leaves from.

There are two options for foreign travellers – brave the queues at the main **reservation office** (Chelmsford Rd; ⏰8am-8pm Mon-Sat, to 2pm Sun), or visit the helpful **International Tourist Bureau** (Map p83; 📞23405156; 1st fl, New Delhi train station, ⏰8am-8pm Mon-Sat, to 2pm Sun) on the 1st floor in the main building at New Delhi railway station. Do not believe anyone who tells you it has shifted, closed or burnt down!

When making reservations here, you can pay in foreign currency, in travellers cheques (Thomas Cook cheques in US dollars, euros or pounds sterling, Amex cheques in US dollars and euros, or Barclays cheques in US dollars) or in rupees, backed up by money-exchange certificates (or ATM receipts). Bring your passport.

When you arrive, complete a reservation form, and queue to check availability, before paying for your booking at the relevant counter. This is the best place to get last-minute quota-seat bookings to popular destinations, but the queues can be outrageous.

If you prefer to brave the standard reservation office, check the details for your journey (including the train number) in advance on the **Indian Railways website** (www.indianrail.gov.in) or **Erail** (http:\\erail.in), or in the invaluable publication *Trains at a Glance* (₹45), available at news-stands. You'll need to fill out a reservation form and queue (after 7pm is the quietest time to book).

ℹ Getting Around

The metro system has transformed getting around the city, making it incredibly easy to whizz out to the remotest suburbs. Keep small change handy for rickshaw fares.

TO/FROM THE AIRPORT

International flights often arrive at ghastly hours, so it pays to book a hotel in advance and notify staff of your arrival time. Organised city transport runs to/from Terminal 3; a free shuttle bus runs every 20 minutes between Terminal 3 and Terminal 1.

Pre-arranged Pick-ups Hotels offer pre-arranged airport pick-up, but you'll pay extra to cover the airport parking fee (up to ₹140) and ₹80 charge to enter the arrivals hall. To avoid the entry fee, drivers may wait outside Gates 4 to 6.

Metro The **Airport Express line** (www.delhiair portexpress.com) runs every 13 minutes from 5.15am to 11.30pm, completing the journey from Terminal 3 to New Delhi train station in around 40 minutes (₹150); though, there are plans to reduce this journey time.

Bus Air-conditioned buses run from outside Terminal 3 to Kashmere Gate ISBT every 20 minutes, via the Red Fort, LNJP Hospital, New Delhi Station Gate 2, Connaught Place, Parliament St and Ashoka Rd (₹50).

Taxi In front of the arrivals buildings at Terminal 3 and Terminal 1 are **Delhi Traffic Police Pre-paid Taxi counters** (📞23010101; www.delhitraf ficpolice.nic.in) offering fixed-price taxi services. You'll pay about ₹350 to New or Old Delhi, and ₹450 to the southern suburbs, plus a 25% surcharge between 11pm and 5am. Insist that the driver takes you to your chosen destination and only surrender your voucher when you arrive.

You can also book a prepaid taxi at the Megacabs (p102) counter outside the arrivals building at both the international and domestic terminals. It costs ₹600 to ₹700 to the centre, but you get a cleaner car with air-con.

AUTORICKSHAW & TAXI

Local taxis (recognisable by their black and yellow livery) and autorickshaws have meters but these are effectively ornamental as most drivers refuse to use them. Delhi Traffic Police runs a network of pre-paid autorickshaw booths (see www.delhitrafficpolice.nic.in/prepaid-booths. htm) where you can pay a fixed fare, including 24-hour stands at the New Delhi, Old Delhi and Nizamuddin train stations; elsewhere, you'll need to negotiate a fare before you set off.

Fares are invariably elevated for foreigners so haggle hard, and if the fare sounds too outrageous, find another cab. For an autorickshaw ride from Connaught Place, expect to pay around ₹30 to Paharganj, ₹40 to India Gate, ₹60 to the Red Fort, ₹70 to Humayun's Tomb and ₹100 to Hauz Khas. The website www.taxiautofare.com can provide suggested fares for other journeys.

Taxis typically charge twice the autorickshaw fare. Note that fares may vary as fuel prices go up and down. From 11pm to 5am there's a 25% surcharge for autorickshaws and taxis.

CAR

Numerous operators will rent out a car with a driver, or you can negotiate directly with taxi drivers at taxi stands around the city. Note that some taxis can only operate inside the city limits, or in certain surrounding states. For a day of local sightseeing, there is normally an eight-hour, 80km limit – anything over this costs extra. The following companies get positive reports from travellers.

Kumar Tourist Taxi Service (Map p70; ☑ 23415930; www.kumarindiatours.com; 14/1 K-Block, Connaught Place; ⊙ 9am-9pm) Rates are among Delhi's lowest – a day of Delhi sightseeing costs from ₹1000 (the eight hours and 80km limit applies).

Metropole Tourist Service (Map p74; ☑ 24310313; www.metrovista.co.in; 224 Defence Colony Flyover Market; ⊙ 7am-7pm) Under the Defence Flyover Bridge (on the Jangpura side).

BICYCLE

There are cycle tours (p80), but bike hire has never taken off in Delhi. To buy your own bike, head to the **Jhandewalan Cycle Market** (Map p64), near Videocon Tower at Jhandewalan.

BUS

With the arrival of the metro, travellers rarely use Delhi's public buses, but the red air-con buses are comfortable and there are several useful routes, including the Airport Express bus and Bus GL-23, which connects the Kashmere Gate and Anand Vihar bus stations. Fares range from ₹15 to ₹25.

CYCLE-RICKSHAW

Cycle-rickshaws are useful for navigating Old Delhi and the suburbs, but are banned from many parts of New Delhi, including Connaught Place, and from the clogged main artery of Chandni Chowk. Negotiate a fare before you set off – expect to pay about ₹30 for the trip from Paharganj to Connaught Place.

METRO

Delhi's magnificent **metro** (☑ 23417910; www.delhimetrorail.com) is fast and efficient, with signs and arrival/departure announcements in Hindi and English. Trains run from around 6am to 11pm and the first carriage in the direction of travel is reserved for women only. Note that trains can get insanely busy at peak commuting times (around 9am to 10am and 5pm to 6pm) – avoid travelling with luggage during rush hour if at all possible.

Tokens (₹8 to ₹30) are sold at metro stations; there are also one-/three-day (₹150/300) 'tourist cards' for unlimited short-distance travel; and a Smart Card (₹100, with ₹50 refundable when you return it), which can be recharged for amounts from ₹50 to ₹800 – fares are 10% cheaper than paying by token.

Because of security concerns, all bags are x-rayed and passengers must pass through an airport-style scanner.

MOTORCYCLE

Karol Bagh market is the place to go to buy or rent a motorcycle.

Lalli Motorbike Exports (Map p64; ☑ 28750869; http://lallisingh.com; 1740-A/55 Hari Singh Nalwa St, Abdul Aziz Rd) Run by the knowledgeable Lalli Singh, this place sells and rents out Enfields and parts, and buyers get a crash course in running and maintaining these lovable but temperamental machines.

RADIOCAB

You'll need a local mobile number to order a radiocab, or ask a shop or hotel to assist. These air-conditioned cars are clean, efficient, and use reliable meters, charging ₹20 at flagfall then ₹20 per km.

Some reliable companies:

Easycabs (☑ 43434343; www.easycabs.com)
Megacabs (☑ 41414141; www.megacabs.com)
Quickcabs (☑ 45333333; www.quickcabs.in)

Greater Delhi

★ **Qutb Minar Complex** HISTORIC SITE
(Map p78; ☑ 26643856; Indian/foreigner ₹10/250, video ₹25, decorative light show Indian/foreigner ₹20/250, audio guide ₹100; ⊙ dawn-dusk; Ⓜ Qutab Minar) In a city awash with ancient ruins, the Qutb Minar complex is something special. The first monuments here were erected by the sultans of Mehrauli, and subsequent rulers expanded on their work, hiring the finest craftsmen and artisans to create an exclamation mark in stone to record the triumph of Muslim rule. The Qutb Festival of Indian classical music and dance takes place here every November/December. To reach the complex, take the metro to Qutab Minar station, then take an autorickshaw for the 1km to the ruins. Bags should be left in the cloakroom.

The complex is studded with ruined tombs and monuments. Ala-ud-din's sprawling **madrasa** and **tomb** stands in ruins at the rear of the complex, while Altamish is entombed in a magnificent sandstone and marble **mausoleum** almost completely covered in Islamic calligraphy.

➡ Qutb Minar

The Qutb Minar complex is dominated by the spectalclular Qutb Minar, a soaring Afghan-style victory tower and minaret, erected by sultan Qutb-ud-din in 1193 to proclaim his supremacy over the vanquished Hindu rulers of Qila Rai Pithora. Ringed by intricately carved standstone bands bearing verses from the Quran, the tower stands nearly 73m high and tapers from a 15m-diameter base to a mere 2.5m at the top.

The tower has five distinct storeys with projecting balconies, but Qutb-ud-din only completed the first level before being unfortunately impaled on his saddle while playing polo. His successors completed the job, and kept up the work of restoration and maintenance through the centuries.

➡ Quwwat-ul-Islam Masjid

At the foot of the Qutb Minar stands the first mosque to be built in India, known as the Might of Islam Mosque, intended to be a physical symbol of the triumph of Islam. An inscription over the east gate states that it was built with materials obtained from demolishing '27 idolatrous temples'. As well as intricate carvings that show a clear fusion of Islamic and pre-Islamic styles, the walls of the mosque are studded with sun disks, *shikharas* and other recognisable pieces of Hindu and Jain masonry.

Altamish, Qutb-ud-din's son-in-law, expanded the original mosque with a cloistered court between 1210 and 1220, and Ala-ud-din's added the exquisite marble and sandstone **Alai Darwaza gatehouse** in 1310. Nearby is the dainty tomb of the Turkic saint Imam Zamin, erected in the Lodi era.

➡ Iron Pillar

Standing in the courtyard of the Quwwat-ul-Islam mosque is a 7m-high iron pillar that vastly predates the surrounding monuments. A six-line Sanskrit inscription indicates that it was initially erected outside a Vishnu temple, possibly in Bihar, in memory of Chandragupta II, who ruled from AD 375 to 413. What the inscription does not tell is how it was made – scientists have never discovered how the iron, which has not rusted after 1600 years, could be cast using the technology of the time.

➡ Alai Minar

When the Sultan Ala-ud-din made additions to the Qutb Minar complex in the 14th century, he also conceived an ambitious plan to erect a second tower of victory, exactly like the Qutb Minar, but twice as high! Construction got as far as the first level before the sultan died; none of his successors saw fit to bankroll this extravagant piece of showboating. The 27m-high plinth can be seen just north of the Qutb Minar.

★ **Mehrauli Archaeological Park**   HISTORIC PARK

(Map p78; ⊘dawn-dusk; Ⓜ Qutab Minar) FREE

Bordering the Qutb Minar complex, but overlooked by most of the tourist hordes, the Mehrauli Archaeological Park preserves some of the most atmospheric relics of the second city of Delhi.

Scattered around a forest park that spills into a chaotic *bustee* (slum) are the ruins of dozens of tombs and palace buildings and several colonial follies. The most impressive structure is the **Jamali Khamali** mosque, attached to the tomb of the Sufi poet Jamali. Ask the caretaker to open the doors so you can see the intricate incised plaster ceiling. Nearby are the **Rajon ki Baoli**, a majestic 16th-century step-well with a monumental flight of steps, and the time-ravaged **tombs** of Balban and Quli Khan.

Southwest of the Archaeological Park is a complex of ruined tombs and summer palaces, constructed in the late Mughal period around the **Haus i Shamsi** tank (off Mehrauli–Gurgaon road). An empty space between two of the tombs was intended for the last king of Delhi, Bahadur Shah Zafar, who died in exile in Burma (Myanmar) in 1862.

Garden of the 5 Senses   PARK

(Map p78; ☑ 29536401; Westend Marg, off Mehrauli–Badarpur road; admission ₹20; ⊘9am-6pm; Ⓜ Saket) This relaxing garden is filled with intriguing contemporary sculptures, formal gardens, dangling wind chimes and lily ponds. There are several upmarket restaurants and bars close to Gate 3. To get here, take an autorickshaw or walk from Saket metro station.

Tughlaqabad   FORT

(Indian/foreigner ₹5/100, video ₹25; ⊘8.30am-5.30pm; Ⓜ Tughlaqabad) This mammoth stronghold, the third city of Delhi, was built by sultan Ghiyas-ud-din Tughlaq in the 14th century. For its construction, the king poached workers from the Sufi saint Nizam-ud-din, who issued a curse that Tughlaqabad would be inhabited only by shepherds. This was indeed the case – today, goats are as common as human visitors among the crumbling, vegetation-choked ruins. The sultan resides through the centuries in a sandstone mausoleum, separated from his fallen city by a busy highway. To get here, take an autorickshaw from the Tughlaqabad metro station (₹80).

Rajasthan

Best for
Forts & Palaces

➡ Jaisalmer (p186)

➡ Jodhpur (p174)

➡ Bundi (p149)

➡ Chittorgarh (p154)

➡ Udaipur (p158)

Best Off the
Beaten Track

➡ Kumbhalgarh (p168)

➡ Nawalgarh (p133)

➡ Osian (p182)

➡ Chittorgarh (p153)

➡ Deeg (p130)

Why Go?

It is said there is more history in Rajasthan than the rest of India put together. Welcome to the Land of the Kings; a fabled realm of maharajas and their majestic forts and lavish palaces. India is littered with splendid ruined bastions, but nowhere will you find fortresses quite as magnificent as those here; rising up imperiously from the desert landscape like fairy-tale mirages of a bygone era.

As enchanting as they are, though, there is more to this most royal of regions than its seemingly timeless architectural wonders. This is also a land of sand dunes and jungle, of camel trains and wild tigers, of glittering jewels, vivid colours and vibrant culture. There are enough festivals here to fill a calendar (and an artist's palette), and the shopping and cuisine are nothing short of spectacular. In truth, Rajasthan just about has it all; it is the must-see state of this must-see country; brimming with startling, thought-provoking and, ultimately, unforgettable attractions.

When to Go
Jaipur

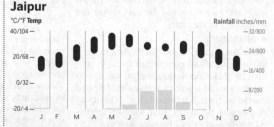

Oct Ranthambhore National Park reopens for tiger safaris.	**Oct/Nov** Don't miss the Pushkar Camel Festival, featuring camels (of course) and culture.	**Mar** Jaipur's famous Elephant Festival precedes the typically boisterous Holi celebrations.

Food

As with the rest of the north, Mughal-influenced curries and smoky tandoori food are extremely popular, but there are a few favourites with a regional twist that are worth hunting down. *Kachori* is a round-shaped, masala-dhal-filled, samosa-like package that hits the spot for a street snack. A favourite Rajasthani meal is *gatta,* gram-flour dumplings cooked in a yoghurt sauce. For refreshment you can't go past a thick and creamy *makhania* (saffron-flavoured) lassi, or a light, fragrant *kheer* (rice pudding).

DON'T MISS

In Jaipur, the **City Palace** is at the centre of a cluster of top sights, including the fascinating **Jantar Mantar**, **Hawa Mahal** and **Iswari Minar Swarga Sal**. But the stand-out attraction in the Jaipur area is **Amber Fort**. If you are a real fort connoisseur, though, you need to make the long trek west for the best of them all: the spectacular, mirage-like desert fortress that is **Jaisalmer Fort**. Running a close second is Jodhpur's imposing rock-like fortress, **Mehrangarh**, whilst more off-the-beaten-track forts worth hunting down include the remote **Kumbhalgarh** and the utterly enormous **Chittorgarh**. Nature lovers shouldn't miss the birdlife at **Keoladeo Ghana National Park** nor the very real chance of spotting a tiger at **Ranthambhore National Park**, while romantics will soon fall in love with the lake city of **Udaipur**.

Top State Festivals

⇒ **Desert Festival** (⊘Feb; Jaisalmer, p183) A chance for moustache twirlers to compete in the Mr Desert contest.

⇒ **Elephant Festival** (⊘Mar; Jaipur, p108) Parades, polo and human-versus-elephant tugs-of-war.

⇒ **Gangaur** (⊘Mar/Apr; statewide) A festival honouring Shiva and Parvati's love, celebrated with fervour in Jaipur.

⇒ **Mewar Festival** (⊘Mar/Apr; Udaipur, p157) Udaipur's version of Gangaur, with free cultural events and a colourful procession down to the lake.

⇒ **Teej** (⊘Aug; Jaipur, p108, & Bundi, p149) Honours the arrival of the monsoon, and Shiva and Parvati's marriage.

⇒ **Dussehra Mela** (⊘Oct; Kota, p152) Commemorates Rama's victory over Ravana (the demon king of Lanka). It's a spectacular time to visit Kota – the huge fair features 22m-tall firecracker-stuffed effigies.

⇒ **Marwar Festival** (⊘Oct; Jodhpur, p174, & Osian, p182) Celebrates Rajasthani heroes through music and dance; one day is held in Jodhpur, the other in Osian.

⇒ **Pushkar Camel Fair** (⊘Oct/Nov; Pushkar, p144) The most famous festival in the state; it's a massive congregation of camels, horses and cattle, traders, pilgrims and tourists.

MAIN POINTS OF ENTRY

Jaipur International Airport, Jaipur train station, Jaipur main bus station.

RAJASTHAN

Fast Facts

⇒ **Population** 68.6 million

⇒ **Area** 342,239 sq km

⇒ **Capital**Jaipur

⇒ **Main languages** Hindi and Rajasthani

⇒ **Sleeping prices**: **$** below ₹500, **$$** ₹500 to ₹1500, **$$$** above ₹1500

⇒ **Eating prices**: **$** below ₹150, **$$** ₹150 to ₹300, **$$$** above ₹300

Top Tips

⇒ Carry small denominations (below ₹50) as drivers often lack small change

⇒ Use prepaid autorickshaw booths outside large train stations to avoid the tiresome rickshaw hustle.

⇒ For shorter train journeys, when tickets are sold out, just buy an unreserved 'general ticket' and pile into second class.

Resources

⇒ **Festivals of India** (www.festivalsofindia.in)

⇒ **Incredible India** (www.incredibleindia.org)

⇒ **Rajasthan Tourism** (www.rajasthantourism.gov.in)

Rajasthan Highlights

1 Gaze wistfully at the magical, mirage-like sandstone fort at **Jaisalmer** (p186), before crossing the desert on a camel

2 Kick back in the pastel-hued pilgrimage town of **Pushkar** (p141)

3 Spot a tiger in the jungle then explore the clifftop fortress at **Ranthambhore National Park** (p147)

4 Listen to the Blue City's secrets from the soaring ramparts of Jodhpur's dramatic fortress, **Mehrangarh** (p174)

5 Indulge in the romance of **Udaipur** (p157), with its gorgeous lake vistas and labyrinthine palace

6 Wander through the colourful bazaars of the **Pink City** (p109) in the chaotic capital, Jaipur, before visiting the marvelous **Amber Fort** (p124)

7 Fall for the laidback charms and backpacker vibe of hassle-free **Bundi** (p149)

8 Admire the forgotten towns and crumbling frescoed *havelis* of **Shekhawati** (p133)

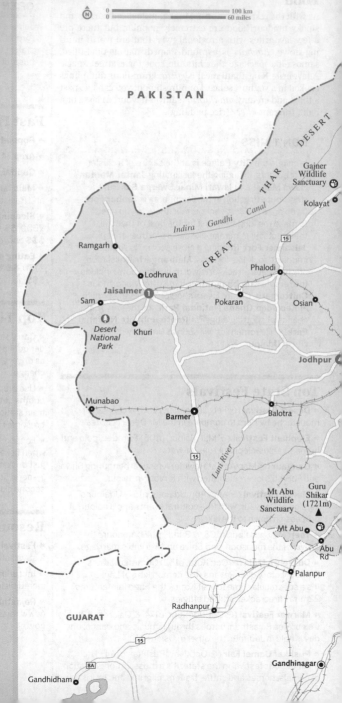

History

Rajasthan is home to the Rajputs, warrior clans who claim to originate from the sun, moon and fire, and who have controlled this part of India for more than 1000 years. While they forged marriages of convenience and temporary alliances, pride and independence were always paramount; consequently much of their energy was spent squabbling among themselves. The resultant weakness eventually led to the Rajputs becoming vassals of the Mughal empire.

Nevertheless, the Rajputs' bravery and sense of honour were unparalleled. Rajput warriors would fight against all odds and, when no hope was left, chivalry demanded *jauhar* (ritual mass suicide). The men donned saffron robes and rode out to face the enemy (and certain death), while the women and children perished in the flames of a funeral pyre. It's not surprising that Mughal emperors had such difficulty controlling this part of their empire.

With the Mughal empire declining, the Rajputs gradually clawed back independence – at least until the British arrived. As the British Raj inexorably expanded, most Rajput states allied with the British, which allowed them to continue as independent states, subject to certain political and economic constraints.

These alliances proved to be the beginning of the end for the Rajput rulers. Consumption took over from chivalry so that, by the early 20th century, many of the maharajas spent much of their time travelling the world with scores of retainers, playing polo and occupying entire floors of expensive hotels. While it suited the British to indulge them, the maharajas' profligacy was economically and socially detrimental. When India gained its independence, Rajasthan had one of the subcontinent's lowest rates of life expectancy and literacy.

At Independence, India's ruling Congress Party was forced to make a deal with the nominally independent Rajput states to secure their agreement to join the new India. The rulers were allowed to keep their titles and their property holdings, and they were paid an annual stipend commensurate with their status. It couldn't last forever, though, and in the early 1970s Indira Gandhi abolished the titles and the stipends, and severely sequestered rulers' property rights.

In their absence Rajasthan has made headway, but the state remains poor. The strength of tradition means that women have a particularly tough time in rural areas. Literacy stood at 67% in 2011 (males 81%, females 53%, a massive rise from 18% in 1961 and 39% in 1991), although it's still the third-lowest in India, while the gender gap remains India's widest.

EASTERN RAJASTHAN

Jaipur

📞0141 / POP 3.0 MILLION

Jaipur, Rajasthan's capital, is an enthralling historical city and the gateway to India's most flamboyant state.

The city's colourful, chaotic streets ebb and flow with a heady brew of old and new. Careering buses dodge dawdling camels, leisurely cycle-rickshaws frustrate swarms of motorbikes, and everywhere buzzing autorickshaws watch for easy prey. In the midst of this mayhem, the splendours of Jaipur's majestic past are islands of relative calm evoking a different pace and another world. At the city's heart, the City Palace continues to house the former royal family, while the Jantar Mantar (the royal observatory) maintains a heavenly aspect, and the honeycomb Hawa Mahal gazes on the bazaar below. And just out of sight, in the arid hill country surrounding the city, is the fairytale grandeur of Amber Fort, Jaipur's star attraction.

History

Jaipur is named after its founder, the great warrior-astronomer Jai Singh II (1688–1744), who came to power at age 11 after the death of his father, Maharaja Bishan Singh. Jai Singh could trace his lineage back to the Rajput clan of Kachhwahas, who consolidated their power in the 12th century. Their capital was at Amber (pronounced amer), about 11km northeast of present-day Jaipur, where they built the impressive Amber Fort.

The kingdom grew wealthier and wealthier, and this, plus the need to accommodate the burgeoning population and a paucity of water at the old capital at Amber, prompted the maharaja in 1727 to commence work on a new city – Jaipur.

Northern India's first planned city, it was a collaborative effort using his vision and the impressive expertise of his chief architect, Vidyadhar Bhattacharya. Jai Singh's grounding in the sciences is reflected in the precise symmetry of the new city. In 1876 Maharaja Ram Singh had the entire Old City painted pink (traditionally the colour of hospitality) to welcome the Prince of Wales (later King Edward VII). Today all residents of the Old City are compelled by law to preserve the pink facade.

◉ Sights

Consider buying a **composite ticket** (Indian/foreigner/foreign student ₹50/300/150), which gives you entry to Amber Fort, Central Museum, Jantar Mantar, Hawa Mahal and Narhargarh, and is valid for two days from time of purchase.

◉ Old City (Pink City)

The Old City (known as the Pink City by some) is partially encircled by a crenellated wall punctuated at intervals by grand gateways. The major gates are Chandpol (*pol* means 'gate'), Ajmeri Gate and Sanganeri Gate. Avenues divide the Old City into neat rectangles, each specialising in certain crafts, as ordained in the ancient Hindu texts *Shilpa-Shastra*. The main bazaars in the Old City include Johari Bazaar, Tripolia Bazaar, Bapu Bazaar and Chandpol Bazaar.

City Palace   PALACE
(Indian/foreigner incl camera ₹75/300, video camera ₹200, audio guide ₹80, human guide from ₹300, Chandra Mahal tour ₹2500; ⊙ 9.30am-5pm) A complex of courtyards, gardens and buildings, the impressive City Palace is right in the centre of the Old City. The outer wall was built by Jai Singh, but within it the palace has been enlarged and adapted over the centuries. Despite the gradual development, the whole is a striking blend of Rajasthani and Mughal architecture.

The price of admission also gets you in to Jaigarh Fort (the fort above Amber Fort, 10km from town), a deal that is valid for two days.

➡ **Mubarak Mahal**

Entering through Virendra Pol, you'll see the Mubarak Mahal (Welcome Palace), built in the late 19th century for Maharaja Madho Singh II as a reception centre for visiting dignitaries. Its multi-arched, colonnaded construction was cooked up in an Islamic, Rajput and European stylistic stew by the architect Sir Swinton Jacob. It now forms part of the **Maharaja Sawai Mansingh II**

Museum, containing a collection of royal costumes and superb shawls, including Kashmiri *pashmina* (wool shawls). One remarkable exhibit is Sawai Madho Singh I's capacious clothing. It's said he was a cuddly 2m tall, 1.2m wide and 250kg.

➡ **Diwan-i-Khas (Sarvatobhadra)**

Set between the Armoury and the Diwan-i-Am art gallery is an open courtyard known in Sanskrit as Sarvatobhadra. At its centre is a pink-and-white, marble-paved gallery that was used as the Diwan-i-Khas (Hall of Private Audience), where the maharajas would consult their ministers. Here you can see two enormous silver vessels, 1.6m tall and reputedly the largest silver objects in the world; Maharaja Madho Singh II, as a devout Hindu, used these vessels to take holy Ganges water to England.

➡ **Diwan-i-Am**

Within the lavish Diwan-i-Am (Hall of Public Audience) is an **art gallery**. Exhibits include a copy of the entire *Bhagavad Gita* handwritten in tiny script, and miniature copies of other holy Hindu scriptures, which were small enough to be easily hidden in the event that Mughal zealot Aurangzeb tried to destroy the sacred texts.

➡ **The Armoury**

The Anand Mahal Sileg Khana – the Maharani's Palace – houses the Armoury, which has one of the best collections of weapons in the country. Many of the ceremonial weapons are elegantly engraved and inlaid, belying their grisly purpose.

➡ **Pitam Niwas Chowk & Chandra Mahal**

Located towards the palace's inner courtyard is Pitam Niwas Chowk, with four glorious gates that represent the seasons. The **Peacock Gate** depicts autumn, with zigzagging patterns and peacock motifs – around the doorway are five beautiful repeated peacock bas reliefs in all their feathered glory.

Beyond this *chowk* (square) is the private palace, the Chandra Mahal, which is still the residence of the descendants of the royal family and where you can take a 45-minute guided **tour** (₹2500) of select areas.

Jantar Mantar   HISTORIC SITE
(Indian/foreigner ₹40/200, audio guide ₹150, human guide ₹200; ⊙ 9am-4.30pm) Adjacent to the City Palace is Jantar Mantar, an observatory begun by Jai Singh in 1728 that resembles a collection of bizarre sculptures. The name is derived from the Sanskrit *yanta mantr,* meaning 'instrument of calculation',

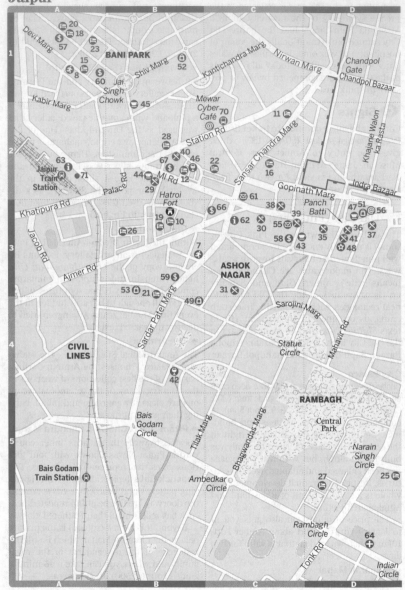

and in 2010 it was added to India's list of Unesco World Heritage Sites.

Jai Singh liked astronomy even more than he liked war and town planning. Before constructing the observatory he sent scholars abroad to study foreign constructs. He built five observatories in total, and this is the largest and best preserved (it was restored in 1901). Others are in Delhi, Varanasi and Ujjain. No traces of the fifth, the Mathura observatory, remain.

honeycombed hive that rises a dizzying five storeys. It was constructed in 1799 by Maharaja Sawai Pratap Singh to enable ladies of the royal household to watch the life and processions of the city. The top offers stunning views over Jantar Mantar and the City Palace one way, and over Siredeori Bazaar the other.

There's also a small **museum** (Sat-Thu) with miniature paintings and some rich relics, such as ceremonial armour, which help evoke the royal past.

Entrance to the Hawa Mahal is from the back of the complex. To get here, return to the roundabout on your left as you face the Hawa Mahal, turn right and then take the first right again through an archway.

New City

By the mid-19th century it became obvious that the well-planned city was bulging at the seams. During the reign of Maharaja Ram Singh (1835–80) the seams ruptured and the city burst out beyond its walls. The maharaja commissioned the landscaping of the Ram Niwas Public Gardens, on Jawaharlal Nehru (J Nehru) Rd, and the uproarious splendour of Albert Hall, built in honour of the Prince of Wales' 1876 visit, which now houses the Central Museum.

Central Museum   MUSEUM
(Albert Hall; Indian/foreigner ₹20/150, audio guide Hindi/English ₹90/124; ⊙9.30am-5pm) The museum is housed in the spectacularly florid Albert Hall, south of the Old City. It was designed by Sir Swinton Jacob, and combines elements of English and North Indian architecture. The grand old building hosts an eclectic array of tribal dress, clay models of yogis in various positions, dioramas, puppets, sculptures, miniature paintings, carpets, musical instruments and even an Egyptian mummy.

SRC Museum of Indology   MUSEUM
(24 Gangwell Park, Prachyavidya Path; Indian/foreigner incl guide ₹40/100; ⊙8am-6pm) This ramshackle, dusty treasure trove is an extraordinary private collection. It contains folk-art objects and other pieces – there's everything from a manuscript written by Aurangzeb and a 200-year-old mirrorwork swing from Bikaner to a glass bed (for a short queen). The museum is signposted off J Nehru Rd, south of the Central Museum.

Hawa Mahal   HISTORIC BUILDING
(Indian/foreigner incl camera ₹10/50, audio guide Hindi/English ₹80/110, human guide ₹200; ⊙9am-5pm) Jaipur's most distinctive landmark, the Hawa Mahal, or Palace of the Winds, is an extraordinary, pink-sandstone, delicately

Jaipur

◉ City Edge

Nahargarh
FORT

(Tiger Fort; Indian/foreigner ₹10/30; ⊘10am-5pm) Built in 1734 and extended in 1868, this sturdy fort overlooks the city from a sheer ridge to the north. The views are glorious – it's a great sunset spot, and there's a **terrace restaurant** (⊘4am-10pm) on a rampart at the far end that's perfect for a beer. Cute **Durgh Cafe** (⊘8am-10pm), in a courtyard within the palace building, also does food and booze. The best way to visit is to walk or take a cycle-rickshaw (₹50 from MI Rd) to the end of Nahargarh Fort Rd, then climb the steep winding path to the top (20 minutes). To drive, you have to detour via the Amber area in a circuitous 20km round trip.

Royal Gaitor
HISTORIC SITE

(Gatore ki Chhatryan; Indian/foreigner ₹20/30; ⊘9am-5pm) The royal cenotaphs, just outside the city walls, beneath Nahargarh, are an appropriately restful place to visit and feel remarkably undiscovered. The stone monuments are beautifully and intricately carved. Maharajas Pratap Singh, Madho Singh II and Jai Singh II, among others, are honoured here. Jai Singh II has the most impressive marble cenotaph, with a dome supported by 20 carved pillars.

The **cenotaphs of the maharanis of Jaipur** (Maharani ki Chhatri; Amber Rd; Indian/foreigner ₹20/30; ⊘9am-5pm) are also worth a visit. They lie between Jaipur and Amber, opposite the Holiday Inn.

🏃 Activities

Several hotels will let you use their pool for a daily fee; the pick of the bunch is the beautiful garden pool at **Narain Niwas Palace Hotel** (nonguests ₹200), beside which is **Orra Spa** (☏2563448; massage treatments from ₹800; ⊘9am-7pm).

Kerala Ayurveda Kendra
AYURVEDA

(☏4006060; www.keralaayurvedakendra.com; D-259 Devi Marg, Bani Park; ⊘9am-9pm) Small, understated yet professionally-run ayurvedic treatment centre. Ordinary massages (full-body from ₹500) are excellent value. Treatments also include *sirodhara* (where a thin stream of oil is poured continuously over your forehead; from ₹1200) and *pizhichil* (where your body is drenched in litres of oil before being fully massaged; from ₹1400).

DON'T MISS

HEAVEN-PIERCING MINARET

Looking down over Tripolia Bazaar, near the City Palace, is the unusual **Iswari Minar Swarga Sal** (Heaven Piercing Minaret; admission ₹20; ⊘9am-4.30pm). This 35m-tall tower was erected by Jai Singh's son Iswari, who later ignominiously killed himself by snake bite (in the Chandra Mahal) rather than face the advancing Maratha army – 21 wives and concubines then did the necessary noble thing and committed *jauhar* (ritual mass suicide by immolation) on his funeral pyre. You can spiral to the top of the minaret for excellent views over the Old City. The entrance is around the back of the row of shops fronting Chandpol Bazaar – take the alley 50m west of the minaret along Chandpol Bazaar or go via the Atishpol entrance to the City Palace compound, 150m east of the minaret.

Kerala Ayurveda
AYURVEDA

(☏4022422; www.keralaayurveda.biz; 52 Dhuleswar Bagh, Sadar Patel Marg; ⊘9am-8pm) More upmarket than others, but still friendly and good value, with back massages from ₹800. It also does synchronised massages with a steam bath for couples (₹1300 per person). They sell oils and therapy treatments, and offer consultations (₹150) with an ayurvedic-trained doctor (every day at 5.30pm).

🎓 Courses

Sakshi
BLOCK PRINTING

(☏2731862; Laxmi Colony, Sanganer Village; half-/full-day ₹1500/3000 per person; ⊘10am-5pm) You can do block-printing courses in nearby Sanganer village (p125).

Maharaja Sawai Mansingh Sangeet Mahavidyalaya
MUSIC, DANCE

(☏9829789790, 93141292155; www.msmsmv.com; Chandni Chowk, City Palace) Lessons in traditional Indian music and dance are available at this well-established outfit near Jantar Mantar.

☞ Tours

RTDC
SIGHTSEEING

(☏2200778; tours@rtdc.in; RTDC tourist information bureau, Platform 1, Jaipur train station; half-/full-day tours ₹250/300; ⊘8am-6.30pm Mon-Sat)

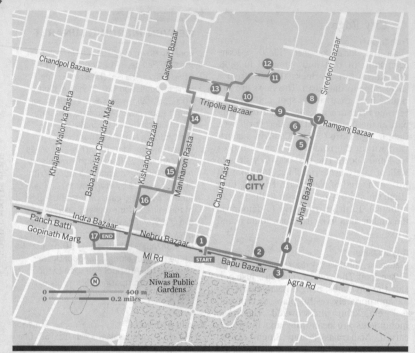

City Walk
Pink City

START NEW GATE
END INDIAN COFFEE HOUSE
LENGTH 3 KM; TWO TO THREE HOURS

Entering the Old City from **1 New Gate**, turn right inside the city wall into **2 Bapu Bazaar**. Brightly coloured bolts of fabric, *jootis* (traditional shoes) and aromatic perfumes make the street a favourite for Jaipur's women. At the end of Bapu Bazaar you'll come to **3 Sanganeri Gate**. Turn left into **4 Johari Bazaar**, the jewellery market, where you will find jewellers, goldsmiths and also artisans doing highly glazed *meenakari* (enamelling), a speciality of Jaipur.

Continuing north, walk past **5 Jama Masjid**, with its tall minarets, then duck through an archway (between Nos 145 and 146) that leads into a bustling half-covered alleyway, sparkling with the sequined shawls and saris. Turn right at the end for more colourful **6 sari stalls**. Return the way you came, turning left to reach **7 Badi Chaupar**. Take a quick look at the spectacular **8 Hawa Mahal** (p111) before walking

west along **9 Tripolia Bazaar**, leading to **10 Tripolia Gate**. This is the main entrance to **11 Jantar Mantar** (p109) and the **12 City Palace** (p109), but only the maharaja's family may enter here. The public entrance is via the less-ostentatious Atishpol (Stable Gate), a little further along.

Further west is **13 Iswari Minar Swarga Sal** (p113), which is well worth climbing for the city views (enter from the back). Cross the road here and duck into **14 Maniharon ka Rasta** (between Nos 349 and 350), an alleyway specialising in colourful *lac* (resin) bangles.

Walking south, clothes and crockery stores appear as the lane becomes less touristy. Look out for the green-painted, but rundown **15 haveli** opposite shop No 1129, before turning right through a narrow tunnel, and eventually popping out onto Kishanpol Bazaar. Turn left and walk past a collection of small **16 kite shops** before ending your tour with a well-earned break at the simple but charming **17 Indian Coffee House** (p117), just outside the Old City walls.

Rajasthan Tourism Development Corporation (RTDC) offers tours of Jaipur and its surrounds. The full-day tours (9am to 6pm) take in all the major sights (including Amber Fort), with a lunch break at Nahargarh. The lunch break can be as late as 3pm, so have a big breakfast. Rushed half-day tours (8am to 1pm, 11.30am to 4.30pm and 1.30pm to 6.30pm) still include Amber Fort. Some travellers recommend these as you avoid the long lunch break. Fees don't include admission charges. Tours include a shopping stop.

The **Pink City by Night tour** (₹375; 6.30pm to 10.30pm) explores several well-known sights, again including Amber Fort, and includes dinner at Nahargarh fort.

Tours depart from the tourist office at the train station; the company also picks up and takes bookings from the RTDC Hotel Teej, RTDC Hotel Gangaur and the Tourist Information Bureau at the main bus stand.

🛌 Sleeping

Prepare yourself to be besieged by autorickshaw and taxi drivers when you arrive by train or bus. If you refuse to go to their choice of hotel, many will either snub you or double the fare. To avoid this annoyance, go straight to the prepaid autorickshaw and taxi stands at the bus and train stations. Even better, many hotels will pick you up if you ring ahead.

From May to September, most midrange and top-end hotels offer bargain rates, dropping prices by 25% to 50%.

🛏 Around MI Road

★ **Hotel Pearl Palace** HOTEL $
(☑2373700, 9414066311; www.hotelpearlpalace.com; Hari Kishan Somani Marg, Hathroi Fort; dm ₹175, r ₹400-1250; ✸@🛜) Great-value Pearl Palace continues to set the standard for budget digs in Jaipur. There's quite a range of rooms to choose from – small, large, shared bath, private bath, dorms, some balconied, some with air-con or fan cooled, but all are thoughtfully decorated and spotlessly clean. Congenial hosts Mr and Mrs Singh offer all manner of services including free pick-up from bus and train stations (8am to 11pm only), moneychanging and travel advice. The rooftop restaurant is also excellent. The only disappointment is that wi-fi isn't free (₹150 per day), but this place is rightfully popular. Advance booking highly recommended.

HOT-AIR BALLOONING

For something a little bit special, consider treating yourself to a sunrise balloon ride above Amber Fort with India's leading hot-air balloon company, **Sky Waltz** (☑9717295801; www.skywaltz.com; US$240). Run by Aussie expat Paul Macpherson, and with a team of highly experienced foreign pilots, Sky Waltz offers spectacular early-morning balloon flights over the fort and surrounding countryside.

The package includes pick-up from your hotel in Jaipur (at around 6am), tea, coffee and cookies, watching the balloon inflation, the flight itself and drop off at your hotel afterwards. The whole thing lasts around three hours, including the one-hour flight.

Balloon-flight season is September to March.

Tony Guest House GUESTHOUSE $
(☑9928871717; tonyguesthouse@yahoo.com; 11 Station Road; s ₹200, d ₹250-350, with attached bathroom ₹400; @) A friendly choice for backpackers on a very tight budget, Tony's is well set up for travellers, with a rooftop garden, honest travel advice, internet (₹20 per hour) and free-flowing chai. Rooms are extremely basic, some with plywood partition walls, and only one has a private bathroom (with cold water only). The common shower is hot, though.

Jwala Niketan GUESTHOUSE $
(☑5108303; jwala_niketan@yahoo.com; C-6 Motilal Atal Marg; s ₹200-400, d ₹300-500, with AC s/d ₹700/800; ✸) Neat and tidy, family-run guesthouse with a charming manager and basic but perfectly adequate rooms, some with balconies. No internet.

Karni Niwas GUESTHOUSE $$
(☑2365433; www.hotelkarniniwas.com; C-5 Motilal Atal Marg; non-AC/AC from ₹700/850; ✸@🛜) Very welcoming and trustworthy management running a simple but comfortable guesthouse with large, clean rooms. There's no restaurant, but there is an all-day menu, and tables and chairs are dotted around the place, in alcoves and on shaded balconies and terraces, so there are plenty of nice spots to eat and drink. Free pick-up from the train or bus station is available. Free wi-fi throughout.

Atithi Guest House
GUESTHOUSE $$

(☏2378679; atithijaipur@hotmail.com; 1 Park House Scheme Rd; s/d from ₹750/850, with AC ₹1300/1400; ✲@☎) With slightly less character than its rivals, this spotlessly clean hotel can feel a little sterile, but it's the perfect antidote to Jaipur's dusty streets. It's central but peaceful, and the service is friendly and helpful. There's an immaculate kitchen and restaurant (guests only), and you can also dine on the very pleasant rooftop terrace. Wi-fi is ₹75 per day.

Hotel Arya Niwas
HOTEL $$

(☏4073456; www.aryaniwas.com; Sansar Chandra Marg; r from ₹1050, s/d with AC from ₹1150/1600; ✲@☎) Housed in a nicely renovated mansion hidden behind a scruffy four-storey block, this is a popular travellers' haunt, with a travel desk, bookshop, yoga lessons (₹100) and good-value massage treatments (from ₹350). The clean rooms face an inner courtyard and vary in layout and size so check out a few. It's a little drab in general, but there's a certain charm, not least because of the extensive colonial-style terrace overlooking a soothing expanse of lawn in front of the hotel's excellent Chitra Cafe.

All Seasons Homestay
HOMESTAY $$

(☏9460387055; www.allseasonshomestayjaipur.com; 63 Hathroi Fort; s ₹1150-1550, d ₹1250-1650) Ranjana and her husband Dinesh run this welcoming homestay in their lovely garden bungalow on a quiet back street behind deserted Hathroi Fort. There are only four guestrooms but each is lovingly cared for and one or two have basic kitchen facilities. There's a pleasant lawn area, home-cooked meals and free internet.

Karan's Guest House
GUESTHOUSE $$

(☏9828284433; www.karans.info; D-6 Shiv Heera Path; r ₹1190) Sweet family-run guesthouse (although the family lives down the road) in a quiet residential part of town, but not too far from all the restaurants on MI Rd. Rooms are very spacious and homely and come with air-con, TV and hot-water showers. No internet and no restaurant, although breakfast is provided.

Pearl Palace Heritage
HOTEL $$$

(☏2375242, 9414066311; www.pearlpalaceheritage.com; 54 Gopal Bari, Lane 2; r ₹2000-2500; ✲@☎) The second hotel for the successful Pearl Palace team is a more upmarket, heritage-style property. As we've come to expect from Mr Singh, the attention to detail is fabulous, with privately commissioned hand-carved panels in the corridors and hand-painted murals in the rooms, which are wonderfully spacious and individually themed (Jaisalmer, Kutch, Indus etc). Each room has its own computer plus free wi-fi, tea/coffee makers, wall-mounted TV and beautifully designed bathrooms.

Alsisar Haveli
HERITAGE HOTEL $$$

(☏2368290; www.alsisar.com; Sansar Chandra Marg; s/d from ₹4680/6160; ✲@☎☀) Beautifully renovated 19th-century *haveli* (this one really is a genuine *haveli*, unlike many namesakes) with immaculate high-ceilinged rooms, elegant Rajput arches and antique furnishings. If you can't afford to stay here, sample its atmosphere by coming for a dip in the lovely garden pool (nonguests ₹250 per hour).

🛏 Bani Park

Upmarket Bani Park is a relatively peaceful area (away from the main roads, at least), about 2km west of the Old City (₹50 in a cycle rickshaw).

Hotel Anuraag Villa
HOTEL $$

(☏2201679; www.anuraagvilla.com; D249 Devi Marg; s ₹600-1850, d ₹790-1850; ✲@☎) This quiet and comfortable option has no-fuss, spacious rooms and a large tree-shaded lawn where you can find some quiet respite from the hassles of sightseeing. It has a recommended restaurant with garden seating and open kitchen. Staff members are efficient and helpful.

Madhuban
HOTEL $$$

(☏2200033; www.madhuban.net; D237 Behari Marg; s/d from ₹1800/2000; ✲@☎☀) Elegant Madhuban has cute and cosy rooms with attractive wood furniture, and although they are small for the price, this is a comfortable stay. The pool is tiny (OK for a quick plunge, though), but the restaurant is good, and you can sometimes eat out on the lawn. Free wi-fi and pick-up from the bus or train station.

Jas Vilas
GUESTHOUSE $$$

(☏2204638; www.jasvilas.com; C9 Sawai Jai Singh Hwy; s/d ₹3700/4000; ✲@☎☀) This small but impressive hotel was built in 1950 and is still run by the same charming family. It offers 11 spacious rooms, most of which face the sparkling courtyard pool. Three garden-facing rooms are wheelchair accessible. In addition to the relaxing courtyard and lawn, there's a cosy dining room. Management will help with all onward travel planning.

Hotel Meghniwas GUESTHOUSE **$$$**
(✆ 4060100; www.meghniwas.com; C9 Sawai Jai Singh Hwy; r from ₹3500; ✳ @ ≋) Next door to Jas Vilas, this very similar guesthouse has a nicer garden pool (nonguests ₹250), but rooms are not the same quality.

🛏 Old City

Hotel Kailash HOTEL **$**
(✆ 2577372; Johari Bazaar; s/d ₹425/475, without bathroom ₹340/360) Everything about this hotel is tiny; from the tiniest of entrances – literally just a small doorway between two shops – to the narrow staircase leading up to reception (also tiny), and on into the very small rooms, which come with TVs and are surprisingly clean given the prices. Not much English spoken, but foreigners are given a friendly welcome. No wi-fi. No espresso machine. No airs and graces.

Ganpati Vishram Guesthouse GUESTHOUSE **$**
(✆ 9314203050; Chandpol Bazaar; r ₹350-600) Secreted away above shops on Chandpol Bazaar, next to the seemingly forgotten Dina 300-year-old Nadh Temple, this very basic guesthouse is set around an old, bare courtyard. Rooms are simple, but the tiled floors keep them cool and clean. Cold showers only, but hot-water buckets (₹10) can be provided. To find reception, climb the narrow staircase beside shop No 197.

Haveli Kalwara HERITAGE GUESTHOUSE **$$**
(✆ 2315736, 7737903825; neetiraj@hotmail.com; off Indra Bazaar; s/d ₹600/800, with AC ₹900/1200) In the heart of the old-city action, but set back from the main bazaar in a quiet side alley, this rundown but charming guesthouse has eight huge spartan rooms with ensuite bathrooms and shared terraces you can sit out on. No restaurant, but staff can provide tea and snacks. Walk down the alley between shops No 94 and 95, turn left at the end, then right.

🛏 Rambagh Environs

Nana-ki-Haveli HERITAGE HOTEL **$$$**
(✆ 2615502; www.nanakihaveli.com; off Moti Dungri Marg, Fateh Tiba; r ₹1800-3000; ✳ @) This tucked-away, tranquil, 100-year-old family home has attractive, comfortable rooms decorated with traditional flourishes (dis-

creet wall painting, wooden furniture) and is hosted by a lovely family.

Narain Niwas Palace Hotel HERITAGE HOTEL **$$$**
(✆ 2561291; www.hotelnarainniwas.com; Narain Singh Rd; r incl breakfast from ₹7400; ✳ @ 🛜 ≋) Built in 1928 by General Amar Singh, this genuine heritage hotel has a wonderful ramshackle splendour. There's a lavish dining room with liveried staff, an old-fashioned verandah on which to drink tea, and antiques galore. The high-ceilinged rooms are varyingly atmospheric and the bathrooms also vary greatly – so inspect before committing. The large secluded garden pool (nonguests ₹200) is heavenly, as is the spa, and the sprawling gardens come complete with wandering peacocks. The restaurant (7.30am to 10.30pm; mains ₹150 to ₹300) and bar (3pm to 11pm) are also open to nonguests. Wi-fi costs ₹500 a day!

Rambagh Palace HERITAGE HOTEL **$$$**
(✆ 2211919; www.tajhotels.com; Bhawan Singh Marg; r from ₹27,500; ✳ @ 🛜 ≋) This splendid palace was once the Jaipur pad of Maharaja Man Singh II and, until recently, his glamorous wife Gayatri Devi. Veiled in 19 hectares of gardens, there are fantastic views across the immaculate lawns, and the rooms and facilities are top notch. Nonguests are only made to feel welcome if they dress to impress and flash the cash. Minimum spend in the bar for nonguests: ₹1500 per person. In the restaurants: ₹2500.

 Eating

✗ Around MI Road

Indian Coffee House SOUTH INDIAN **$**
(MI Rd; mains ₹20-45; ◷ 8am-9.30pm) Jaipur's tucked-away branch of the South Indian institution, this 50-year-old, fan-cooled coffee house not only does the cheapest filter coffee in town (₹12), it also whips up a selection of tasty dishes – dosa (wafer-thin savoury crepes), *uttapam* (thick savoury rice pancake), *idli* (spongy round fermented rice cake) and *vada* (doughnut-shaped deep-fried lentil cake) – as well as toast, omelettes and sandwiches. A great spot for a cheap breakfast or lunch.

Old Green Tandoori Dhaba DHABA **$**
(off MI Rd; mains ₹50-200; ◷ 10am-midnight) Slightly larger, cleaner and more popular than the very similar Green Tandoori Dhaba next door, Old Green Tandoori Dhaba has

been serving locals since 1985 and is still an atmospheric, down-to-earth, roadside eating experience. Its open-sided structure allows you to see your paneer kebabs or chicken tandoori being grilled on the barbecue out front, while you work your way through the simple but tasty curries on the main menu. Does half portions. No alcohol.

Old Takeaway The Kebab Shop   KEBABS $
(151 MI Road; kebabs ₹80-120; ⊙ 6-11pm) One of a few similarly named road-side kebab shops that open up each evening on this stretch of MI Road. This one (at No 151) is the original (so we're told) and the best (we agree). It knocks up outstanding tandoori kebabs, including paneer sheesh, mutton sheesh and the mouthwatering tandoori chicken. Pull up a stool and tuck in.

The Doors   INDIAN $
(Khandaka Mansion, by Raj Mandir Cinema; mains ₹50-100, thalis ₹65-85; ⊙ 7am-10pm) Excellent-value local favourite with a range of tasty vegetarian dishes including South Indian and thalis (until 4pm). Our particular favourite is the *paneer do pyaza*, with its thick onion sauce; perfect for being mopped up by the rotis, which here are as thick and textured as naan bread, but only ₹5 each! They do half-portions too, making this ideal for solo travellers. The restaurant is behind the McDonald's to the left of Raj Mandir Cinema, as you're looking at the cinema. No alcohol.

Rawat Kachori   SWEETS $
(Station Rd; kachori ₹20, lassis ₹25; ⊙ 6am-10pm) Head to this exceedingly popular place for great Indian sweets (₹10 each, or ₹120 to ₹300 per kg), cooling, creamy lassi (yoghurt drink) and its signature kachori (spicy, round-shaped vegetable samosas).

Chitra Cafe   CAFE $
(Hotel Arya Niwas, Sansar Chandra Marg; mains ₹40-110; ⊙ 7am-9.45pm) Hotel Arya Niwas' charming Chitra Cafe conjures up images of a bygone colonial era, with its rattan tables and chairs scattered along a covered terrace overlooking the hotel's cooling front lawn. It's great value too, especially if you plump for the thali (₹125). Also does home-made cakes and cookies, plus shakes and safe-to-eat ice creams.

Baskin Robbins   SWEETS $
(Sanjay Marg; ice creams from ₹50; ⊙ noon-11.30pm) Safe-to-eat ice creams from the dependable international chain.

Peacock Rooftop Restaurant   MULTICUISINE $$
(☑ 2373700; Hari Kishan Somani Marg, Hotel Pearl Palace; mains ₹70-180; ⊙ 7am-11pm) Hotel Pearl Palace's pride and joy, Peacock is one of the best hotel rooftop restaurants you'll find. The traveller-friendly atmosphere is relaxed, the view towards Hathroi Fort is romantic and the beer is ice cold. Most importantly, though, the food is mouthwatering. A number of world cuisines are on offer; all are prepared well, but it's the Indian dishes that truly hit the spot, particularly the tandoori kebabs. They also do fresh juices, filter coffee and breakfast croissants.

Handi Restaurant   NORTH INDIAN $$
(MI Rd; mains ₹140-300; ⊙ noon-3.30pm & 6-11pm) The Indian food here is as good as at any top restaurant in town, but the atmosphere is far less stuffy. Popular with local families, Handi is decked out like a large traditional village eatery, with a dried-mud floor, bamboo-lined walls and wicker roofing. It offers scrumptious tandoori and barbecued dishes as well as rich Mughlai curries. In the evenings it sets up a smoky kebab stall at the entrance to the restaurant. No beer here.

Moti Mahal Delux   NORTH INDIAN $$
(☑ 4017733; MI Rd; mains ₹170-300; ⊙ 11am-11pm) The original Moti Mahal opened in Peshawar (in modern-day Pakistan), pre-partition, but there are now branches all across India delivering its renowned butter chicken to the masses. The kebabs here are fabulously succulent, and they do a mean *pista kulfi* (pistachio-flavoured sweet similar to ice cream). Beer (from ₹115) and wine (from ₹250) available.

Four Seasons   VEGETARIAN $$
(☑ 2374600; Bhagat Singh Marg; mains ₹130-180; ⊙ 11am-5pm & 7-11pm) One of Jaipur's best vegetarian restaurants, this is a vastly popular place on two levels, with a glass wall to the kitchens. There's a great range of dishes on offer, including tasty Rajasthani specialities, South Indian dosas and a selection of pizzas. No alcohol.

Natraj   VEGETARIAN $$
(☑ 2375804; MI Rd; mains ₹150-250; ⊙ 9am-11pm) This classy but low-key vegetarian place has been going since the 1960s and has an extensive menu featuring North Indian, Continental and Chinese cuisine. There's a good selection of thalis and South Indian food –

the *dosa paper masala* is delicious – as well as Indian sweets. No alcohol.

Copper Chimney
INDIAN $$

(☑2372275; MI Rd, Maya Mansions; mains ₹150-400; ☺noon-3.30pm & 6.30-11pm) Copper Chimney is casual, almost elegant, and definitely welcoming, with the requisite waiter army and a fridge of cold beer (from ₹100). It offers excellent veg and nonveg Indian cuisine, including aromatic Rajasthani specials. There is also Continental and Chinese food and a small selection of Indian wine, but the curry and beer combos are hard to beat.

Niro's
INDIAN $$$

(☑2374493; MI Rd; mains ₹200-500; ☺10am-11pm) Established in 1949, Niro's is a long-standing favourite on MI Rd. It's very plush these days – and has prices to match – but the quality of food is as good as ever; with plenty of Rajasthani specialities amongst its extensive Indian menu. Also does some Chinese and international cuisine, but the Indian dishes are definitely the pick. Beer from ₹160.

Little Italy
ITALIAN $$$

(☑4022444; Prithviraj Marg, 3rd fl, KK Square; mains ₹300-500; ☺noon-11pm) Arguably the best Italian restaurant in town, Little Italy is part of a small national chain that offers excellent vegetarian pasta, risotto and wood-fired pizzas in cool, contemporary surroundings. The menu is extensive and includes some Mexican items and first-rate Italian desserts. Also has a decent wine list.

✕ Old City

Ganesh Restaurant
VEGETARIAN $

(Nehru Bazaar; mains ₹60-120; ☺9am-11.30pm) This no-nonsense, pocket-sized rooftop restaurant has a fantastic location on the top of the Old City wall near New Gate. The cook is in a pit on one side of the wall, so you can check out your great-value vegetarian food as it's being prepared. There's an easy-to-miss signpost, but it's up a narrow staircase beside shop No 10.

LMB
VEGETARIAN $$

(☑2560845; Johari Bazaar; mains ₹150-250; ☺8am-11pm) Laxmi Misthan Bhandar (LMB) is an upmarket *sattvik* (vegetarian) restaurant in the Old City that's been going strong since 1954. A welcoming air-conditioned refuge from frenzied Johari Bazaar, LMB is a bit of an institution with its singular decor, attentive waiters and extensive sweet counter. It's also very popular with tourists these days. The Rajasthan thali is excellent, as is its signature *kulfa*, a fusion of *kulfi* and *falooda* with dry fruits and saffron.

🍷 Drinking

★Lassiwala
CAFE

(MI Rd; ☺7.30am till sold out) This famous, much-imitated lassi institution is a simple place that whips up fabulous, creamy lassis in a clay cup (small/large ₹17/34). Get here early to avoid disappointment; they usually sell out by 4pm. Will the real Lassiwala please stand up? Imitators abound, it's the one that says 'Shop 312' and 'Since 1944', directly next to an alleyway.

100% Rock
BAR

(Hotel Shikha, Yudhishthir Marg, C-Scheme; beer from ₹160; ☺10am-11.30pm) Attached to, but separate from Hotel Shikha (and formerly known as TC Bar), this is the closest thing there is to a beer garden in Jaipur, with plenty of outdoor seating as well as air-conditioned side rooms and a clubby main room with a small dance floor. Two-for-one beer offers are common, making this popular with local youngsters.

Brewberry's
CAFE

(G-2 Fortune Heights, opp ICICI Bank; coffee from ₹40; ☺8am-midnight) Modern wi-fi-enabled cafe with fresh coffee and a good mix of Indian and Western food and snacks. Has some patio seating.

Café Coffee Day
CAFE

(MI Rd, Country Inn Hotel; coffee ₹60-90; ☺10am-10pm) Dependable, air-conditioned branch of India's most popular coffee-shop chain. There's another one on the way to Bani Park.

Hotel Sangam Bar
BAR

(Hotel Sangam, Motilal Atal Marg; beer from ₹75, shots from ₹30; ☺9am-11pm) Low-lit basement bar serving beer, spirits and a few Indian dishes and snacks. The beer and wine shop next door sells big bottles of Kingfisher for ₹100.

☆ Entertainment

Jaipur isn't a big late-night party town, although many hotels put on some sort of evening music, dance or puppet show. English-language films are occasionally screened at some cinemas in Jaipur – check the cinemas and local press for details.

Raj Mandir Cinema
CINEMA

(☏2379372; Baghwandas Marg; admission ₹60-150; ☺reservations 10am-6pm, screenings 12.30pm, 3.30pm, 6.30pm & 9.30pm) Just off MI Rd, Raj Mandir is *the* place to go to see a Hindi film in India. This opulent cinema looks like a huge pink cream cake, with a meringue auditorium and a foyer somewhere between a temple and Disneyland. Bookings can be made one hour to seven days in advance at window Nos 9 and 10 (10am to 6pm) – this is your best chance of securing a seat, although forget it in the early days of a new release. Alternatively, sharpen your elbows and join the queue when the current booking office opens 45 minutes before screening. Avoid the very cheapest tickets, which are very close to the screen.

Chokhi Dhani
THEME PARK

(☏2225001; Tonk Rd; adult/child aged 3-9 ₹450/350, incl Rajasthani thali ₹650/400; ☺6pm-11pm) Chokhi Dhani, meaning 'special village', is a mock Rajasthani village 20km south of Jaipur, and is a fun place to take the kids. There are open-air restaurants, where you can enjoy a tasty Rajasthani thali, and there's a bevy of traditional entertainment – dancers, acrobats, snack stalls – as well as adventure park–like activities for kids to swing on, slide down and hide in. A return taxi from Jaipur, including waiting time, is about ₹600.

🔒 Shopping

Jaipur is a shopper's paradise. Commercial buyers come here from all over the world to stock up on the amazing range of jewellery, gems, artefacts and crafts that arrive from all over Rajasthan. You'll have to bargain hard – shops have seen too many cash-rich, time-poor tourists, particularly around major tourist centres such as the City Palace and Hawa Mahal.

Most of the larger shops can pack and send your parcels home for you, although it may be slightly cheaper if you do it yourself.

The city is still loosely divided into traditional artisans quarters. The Pink City Walking Tour (p114) will take you through some of these.

Bapu Bazaar is lined with saris and fabrics, and is a good place to buy trinkets.

Johari Bazaar and **Siredeori Bazaar** are where many jewellery shops are concentrated, selling gold, silver and highly glazed enamelwork known as *meenakari*, a Jaipur speciality. You may also find better deals for fabrics with the cotton merchants of Johari Bazaar.

Kishanpol Bazaar is famous for textiles, particularly *bandhani* (tie-dye). **Nehru Bazaar** also sells fabric, as well as jootis, trinkets and perfume. MI Rd is another good place to buy jootis. The best place for bangles is Maniharon ka Rasta, near the Shree Sanjay Sharma Museum.

Plenty of factories and showrooms are strung along the length of Amber Rd, between Zorawar Singh Gate and the Holiday Inn, to catch the tourist traffic. Here you'll find huge emporiums selling block prints, blue pottery, carpets and antiques. These shops are used to bus loads swinging in to blow their cash, so you'll need to wear your bargaining hat.

Rickshaw-wallahs, hotels and travel agents will be getting a hefty cut from any shop they steer you towards. Many unwary visitors get talked into buying things for resale at inflated prices, especially gems. Beware of these get-rich-quick scams.

Kripal Kumbh
HANDICRAFTS

(☏2201127; B18A Shiv Marg; ☺9.30am-6pm Mon-Sat) This tiny showroom in a private home is a great place to buy Jaipur's famous blue pottery produced by the late Mr Kripal Singh, his family and his students. Most pieces cost between ₹250 and ₹500.

Khadi Ghar
CLOTHING, HANDICRAFTS

(MI Rd; ☺10am-7.30pm Mon-Sat) The best of a handful of *khadi* shops in Jaipur, this branch sells good quality ready-made clothing from the homespun *khadi* fabric, famously endorsed by Gandhi, as well as a small selection of handicrafts. Prices are fixed and pressure to buy is minimal.

★ Mojari
CLOTHING

(Shiv Heera Marg; shoes ₹500-750; ☺10am-6.30pm Mon-Sat) Named after the traditional decorated shoes of Rajasthan, Mojari is a UN-supported project that helps rural leatherworkers, traditionally among the poorest members of society. There is a small range of wonderful handmade footwear on display (and loads more out the back), including embroidered, appliquéd and open-toed shoes, mules and sandals. There's a particularly good choice for women, and there's a small selection of handmade leather bags and purses too.

Anokhi   CLOTHING, TEXTILES
(www.anokhi.com; 2nd fl, C-11, Prithviraj Marg, KK Square; ⏰9.30am-8pm Mon-Sat, 11am-7pm Sun) A classy, upmarket boutique that sells stunning high-quality textiles such as block-printed fabrics, tablecloths, bed covers, cosmetic bags and scarves, as well as a range of well-designed, beautifully made clothing that combines Indian and Western influences. There's a wonderful little cafe on the premises too, and an excellent bookshop in the same building.

The Silver Shop   JEWELLERY
(Hari Kishan Somani Marg, Hotel Pearl Palace; ⏰6-10pm) A trusted jewellery shop on the rooftop of Hotel Pearl Palace, offering a money-back guarantee on all items.

ⓘ Information

INTERNET ACCESS
Internet cafes are thin on the ground, but almost all hotels and guesthouses provide internet access (sometimes for a daily fee), and usually wi-fi too.

Dhoom Cyber Café (off MI Rd; per hr ₹30; ⏰8.30am-8.30pm) Down a lane off MI Road, through an arch.

Mewar Cyber Café (Station Rd; per hr ₹25; ⏰7am-11pm) Near the main bus stand.

MEDICAL SERVICES
Most hotels can arrange a doctor on-site.

Santokba Durlabhji Memorial Hospital (SDMH) (☎2566251; www.sdmh.in; Bhawan Singh Marg) Private hospital, with 24hr emergency department, helpful staff and clear bilingual signage. Consultancy fee ₹400.

Sawai Mansingh Hospital (SMS Hospital) (☎2518222, 2518597; Sawai Ram Singh Rd) State-run, but part of Soni Hospitals group (www.sonihospitals.com). Before 3pm, outpatients go to the CT & MRI Centre. After 3pm, go to the adjacent Emergency Department.

MONEY
There are plenty of places to change money, including numerous hotels and masses of ATMs (especially around MI Road), most of which accept foreign cards.

Thomas Cook (☎2360940; MI Rd, Jaipur Towers; ⏰9.30am-6pm) Changes cash and travellers cheques (Amex only) and does advances on credit cards.

POST
DHL Express (☎2361159; www.dhl.co.in; G8 Geeta Enclave, Vinobha Marg; ⏰10am-8pm) Head office is just off MI Rd. Look for the sub-branch on MI Rd (next to Standard Chartered Bank) then walk down the lane beside it. For parcels, the first 500g is expensive (eg ₹3334 to the UK), but each 500g after that is cheap (less than ₹500). All packaging is included in the price. Credit cards and cash are accepted.

Main Post Office (☎2368740; MI Rd; ⏰8am-7.45pm Mon-Fri, 10am-5.45pm Sat) Cost-effective and efficient (though the back-and-forth can infuriate). Parcel-packing wallahs in the foyer must first pack, stitch and wax seal your parcel for a fee (₹50 to ₹100 per small package) before you can then send it. As a guide, a 950g parcel cost us ₹600 to send to the UK.

TOURIST INFORMATION
The Tourism Assistance Force (police) is stationed at the train and bus stations, the airport and at Jaipur's major tourist sights.

RTDC Tourist Reception Centre (www.rajasthantourism.gov.in) Main branch(☎5155137; Room 21, former RTDC Tourist Hotel; ⏰9.30am-6pm Mon-Fri); Airport (☎2722647); Amber Fort (☎2530264; Amber Fort); Jaipur train station (☑2200778; Platform 1; ⏱24hr); main bus station (☑5064102; Platform 3; ⏱10am-5pm Mon-Fri) Has free maps and brochures on Jaipur and Rajasthan, organises city tours, private taxis and government-registered guides.

ℹ Getting There & Away

AIR

Air India (☑2743500, airport 2721333; www. airindia.com; Tonk Rd, Nehru Place) To Delhi and Mumbai daily.

IndiGo (☑2743500, 5119993; www.goindigo. in; airport) To Mumbai, Kolkata, Ahmedabad, Bengaluru and Hyderabad.

Jet Airways (☑1800 225522, 2725025; www. jetairways.com; airport; ⏱5.30am-9pm) To Delhi, Mumbai, Chennai, Chandigarh, Indore, Raipur and Hyderabad.

BUS

Rajasthan State Road Transport Corporation (RSRTC) buses all leave from the **main bus stand** (Station Rd), where there's a left-luggage 'cloakroom' (₹10 per bag for 24 hours), as well as a prepaid autorickshaw stand.

Ordinary buses are known as 'express' buses, but there are also 'deluxe' buses (coaches really, but still called buses; usually with air-con but not always), these vary a lot but are generally much more expensive and comfortable than ordinary express buses. Deluxe buses leave from Platform 3, tucked away in the right-hand corner of the bus station. Unlike ordinary express buses seats on them can be booked in advance from the **reservation office** (☑5116032) here.

With the exception of those going to Delhi (half-hourly), deluxe buses are much less frequent than ordinary buses.

CAR

Most hotels can arrange car and driver hire. Or else go to the RTDC Tourist Reception Centre (p121) at the train station. They have a list of prices for different types of vehicles. At the time of research it was ₹7 to ₹12 per kilometre, depending on the type of car, with a minimum rental rate equivalent to 250km per day. Also expect to pay a ₹150 overnight charge, and note, you will have to pay for the driver to return to Jaipur even if you aren't.

MOTORCYCLE

Hire, buy or fix a Royal Enfield Bullet (and lesser motorbikes) at **Rajasthan Auto Centre** (☑2568074, 9829188064; www.royalenfield-salim.com; Sanjay Bazaar, Sanganeri Gate; ⏱10am-8pm Mon-Sat, 10am-2pm Sun), the cleanest little motorcycle workshop in India, run by the affable Mr Salim. To hire a 350cc Bullet costs ₹500 per day (including helmet) within

Jaipur; outside ₹600. No deposit required; just show and photocopy your passport, visa and driving licence. You can buy second-hand Enfields here too (₹40,000 to ₹50,000).

TRAIN

The efficient **railway reservation office** (☑135; ⏱8am-9pm Mon-Sat, 8am-2pm Sun) is to your left as you enter Jaipur train station. It's open for advance reservations only (more than five hours before departure). Join the queue for 'Freedom Fighters and Foreign Tourists' (counter 769).

For same-day travel, buy your ticket at the northern end of the train station on Platform 1, window 10 (⏱ closed 6-6.30am, 2-2.30pm & 10-10.30pm). The railway inquiries number is ☑131.

Station facilities on Platform 1 include an RTDC tourist information bureau, Tourism Assistance Force (police), a cloakroom for left luggage (₹10 per bag per 24 hours), retiring rooms (s/d ₹225/450, with air-con from ₹750), restaurants and air-conditioned waiting rooms for those with 1st class and 2AC train tickets.

Nine daily trains go to **Delhi** (1am, 2.50am, 4.40am, 5am, 6am, 8.45am, 4.30pm, 5.50pm and 11.15pm), plus others on selected days. The 6am double-decker does the trip in 4½ hours, others take five to six.

Three daily trains leave for **Agra** (6.15am, 3pm and 5.10pm), taking 4½ hours. Second-class seats cost ₹82.

Three go to **Bikaner** (3pm, 9.15pm and 12.50am), taking six, seven and eight hours respectively. Sleeper tickets cost ₹200 to ₹240.

Four go to **Jodhpur** (11.35am, 5pm, 11.45pm and 12.15am), taking five to six hours.

Three go to **Udaipur** (6.45am, 2pm and 10.30pm), in seven to eight hours.

Four go to **Ahmedabad** (4.25am, 9am, 8.35pm and 12.35am). The 12.35am is quickest (9 hours), others take 11 to 13 hours. Sleepers cost around ₹250.

For **Pushkar**, 11 daily trains make the two-hour trip to Ajmer, plus many more on selected days so you rarely wait more than an hour. Unreserved 'general' tickets cost ₹42.

For **Ranthambhore**, six daily trains go to Sawai Madhopur (5.45am, 11.05am, 2.10pm, 5.25pm, 5.35pm and 11.30pm), plus plenty more on selected days. Unreserved 'general' tickets for the two-hour trip cost ₹50.

Only one train (11.45pm) goes to **Jaisalmer**.

ℹ Getting Around

TO/FROM THE AIRPORT

There are no bus services from the airport, which is 12km southeast of the city, although a

metro line was under construction at the time of research (it won't open for some time, though). An autorickshaw/taxi costs at least ₹200/400. There's a prepaid taxi booth inside the airport.

AUTORICKSHAW
There are prepaid autorickshaw stands at the bus and train stations. Rates are fixed by the government, which means you don't have to haggle. Keep hold of your docket, though, until

TRANSPORT FROM JAIPUR

Main Buses from Jaipur

DESTINATION	FARE (₹)	DURATION (HR)	FREQUENCY (OF NON-AC SERVICES)
Agra	179, AC 392	5½	half-hourly, 24 hours
Ajmer	120, AC 204	2½	every 10 minutes, 24 hours
Bharatpur	165	4½	half-hourly, 24 hours
Bikaner	241	8	half-hourly until 6pm
Bundi	154, AC 230	5	half-hourly until midnight
Chittorgarh	230, AC 300-570	7	half-hourly until 10pm
Delhi	210, AC 425-750	5½	half-hourly, 24 hours
Jaisalmer	AC 1073	15	1 daily (midnight)
Jhunjhunu	131	5	half-hourly
Jodhpur	262, AC 583	7	hourly, 24 hours
Kota	181, AC 245	5	half-hourly until 11pm
Mt Abu	372	13	1 daily (9.30am)
Nawalgarh	107	4	hourly, 5am-4.30pm
Pushkar (direct)	120	3	6 daily (6.45am, 7.10am, 9.20am, 1pm, 8.40pm, 11.15pm)
Sawai Madhopur	132, AC 180	6	5 daily (6am, 6.15am, 6.40am, 2.30pm, AC 5.30pm)
Udaipur	275, AC 702	10	every 45 minutes, 4am-noon (AC 9.30pm & 11pm)

Major Trains from Jaipur

DESTINATION	TRAIN	DEPARTURE TIME	ARRIVAL TIME	FARE (₹)
Agra (Cantonment)	19666 Udaipur-Kurj Exp	6.15am	11am	135/362 (A)
Ahmedabad	12958 Ahmedabad SJ Rajdhani Exp	12.35am	9.35am	923/1335 (B)
Ajmer	12195 Intercity Express	9.40am	11.45am	65/230 (C)
Bikaner	12307 Howrah-Jodhpur Exp	12.15am	8am	198/521 (A)
Delhi (New Delhi)	12016 Ajmer Shatabdi	5.50pm	10.40pm	555/1150 (E)
Delhi (S Rohilla)	12985 Dee Double Decker	6am	10.30am	360 (D)
Jaisalmer	14659 Delhi-Jaisalmer Exp	11.45pm	11am	252/703 (A)
Jodhpur	12307 Howrah-Jodhpur Exp	12.15am	6am	178/459 (A)
Sawai Madhopur	12466 Intercity Exp	11.05am	1.15pm	65/140/230 (F)
Udaipur	19665 Kurj-Udaipur Exp	10.30pm	6.10am	194/533 (A)

Fares: (A) sleeper/3AC, (B) 3AC/2AC, (C) 2nd-class seat/AC chair, (D) AC chair, (E) AC chair/1AC, (F) 2nd-class seat/sleeper/AC chair

you reach your destination. Your driver won't get paid without it.

In other cases you should be prepared to bargain hard. Expect to pay at least ₹50 from the train or bus station to the Old City.

CYCLE-RICKSHAW
Slightly cheaper than autorickshaws, but not much (about ₹40 from train station to Old City). Always agree on a fare beforehand, but don't forget to tip – it's a tough job in the Rajasthani heat, this one.

TAXI
There are unmetered taxis available which will require negotiating a fare, or you can try **Mericar** (☏ 4188888; www.mericar.in; flagfall incl 2km ₹50, afterwards per km ₹13, 25% night surcharge 10pm-5am). It's a 24-hour service and taxis can also be hired for sightseeing for four-/six-/eight-hour blocks, costing ₹650/1000/1300.

Around Jaipur

Amber

The formidable, magnificent, honey-hued fort of Amber (pronounced Amer), an ethereal example of Rajput architecture, rises from a rocky mountainside about 11km northeast of Jaipur, and is the city's must-see sight.

Amber was the former capital of Jaipur state and was built by the Kachhwaha Rajputs, who hailed from Gwalior, in present-day Madhya Pradesh, where they reigned for over 800 years. They financed construction of the fort with war booty, which was begun in 1592 by Maharaja Man Singh, the Rajput commander of Akbar's army. It was later extended and completed by the Jai Singhs before they moved to Jaipur on the plains below.

◉ Sights

Amber Fort   FORT
(Indian/foreigner ₹25/200, guide ₹200, audio guide Hindi/other ₹100/150; ⊙ 8am-6pm, last entry 5.30pm) This magnificent fort is made up largely of a royal palace, built from pale yellow and pink sandstone and white marble, and divided into four main sections, each with its own courtyard.

You can trudge up to the fort from the road in about 10 minutes (cold drinks are available at the top). However, riding up on **elephant back** (⊙ 7.30am-noon & 3.30-5.30pm,

₹900 one way per 2 passengers) is very popular. A return jeep to the top and back costs ₹300 for five passengers, including one hour waiting time.

If you walk or ride an elephant you will enter Amber Fort through **Suraj Pol** (Sun Gate), which leads to the **Jaleb Chowk** (Main Courtyard), where returning armies would display their war booty to the populace – women could view this area from the veiled windows of the palace. The ticket office is directly across the courtyard from Suraj Pol. If you arrive by car you will enter through **Chand Pol** (Moon Gate) on the opposite side of Jaleb Chowk. Hiring a guide or grabbing an audio guide is highly recommended as there are very few signs and many blind alleys.

From Jaleb Chowk, an imposing stairway leads up to the main palace, but first it's worth taking the steps just to the right, which lead to the small **Siladevi Temple** (⊙ 6am-noon & 4-8pm, photography prohibited). Every day from the 16th century until 1980 (when the government banned the practice), a goat was sacrificed here.

Heading back to the main stairway will take you up to the second courtyard and the **Diwan-i-Am** (Hall of Public Audience), which has a double row of columns, each topped by a capital in the shape of an elephant, and latticed galleries above.

The maharaja's apartments are located around the third courtyard – you enter through the fabulous **Ganesh Pol**, decorated with mosaics and sculptures. The **Jai Mandir** (Hall of Victory) is noted for its inlaid panels and multimirrored ceiling. Carved marble relief panels around the hall are fascinatingly delicate and quirky, depicting cartoon-like insects and sinuous flowers.

Opposite the Jai Mandir is the **Sukh Niwas** (Hall of Pleasure), with an ivory-inlaid sandalwood door and a channel that once carried cooling water right through the room. From the Jai Mandir you can enjoy fine views from the palace ramparts over picturesque **Maota Lake** below.

The **zenana** (women's quarters) surrounds the fourth courtyard. The rooms were designed so that the maharaja could embark on his nocturnal visits to his wives' and concubines' respective chambers without the others knowing, as the chambers are independent but open onto a common corridor.

Jaigarh FORT

(Indian/foreigner ₹35/85, camera/video ₹50/200, car ₹50, Hindi/English guide ₹100/150; ⊙9am-5pm) A scrubby green hill – Cheel ka Teela (Mound of Eagles) – rising above Amber, is topped by the imposing fortress of Jaigarh. This massive fort was planned by Jai Singh I, but what you see today dates from the reign of Jai Singh II. Punctuated by whimsically hatted lookout towers, the fort was never captured and is a splendid example of grand 18th-century defences without the palatial frills that are found in many other Rajput forts. It has water reservoirs, residential areas, a puppet theatre and the world's largest wheeled cannon, Jaya Vana.

The fort is a steep uphill walk (about 1km) beyond Amber Fort (up to the left as you face Amber Fort from the main road) and offers great views from the Diwa Burj watchtower.

Admission is free if you have a ticket to Jaipur's City Palace that is less than two days' old.

Anokhi Museum of Hand Printing MUSEUM

(Anokhi Haveli, Kheri Gate; child/adult ₹15/30, camera/video ₹50/150; ⊙10.30am-4.30pm Tue-Sat, 11am-4.30pm Sun, closed 1 May-15 Jul) Just below Amber Fort, in the village of Amber, is this interesting museum that documents the art of hand-block printing and runs hands-on demonstrations. Take the first left into the village and keep walking until you see the blue painted sign telling you to turn right, then keep following that road until it ends at Kheri Gate. The museum is just inside the gate on your right.

🛏 Sleeping & Eating

The decidedly untouristy village of Amber, with its colourful food market and scattering of temples and palace ruins, makes a low-key alternative to hectic Jaipur as a possible place to stay.

Close to Warahi Gate, the oldest surviving gateway in Amber, is **Amber Bhavan** (☑9829066268; r ₹500-700), a simple but friendly guesthouse with spacious rooms and charming owners. From Amber Fort, keep walking downhill along the main road past the village and you'll soon see it on your right. Look out for two signs; one saying 'A Hostel for Students' and another saying 'Grambharati Samiti'.

For something more comfortable, try the gorgeous French-run **Mosaics Guesthouse** (☑2530031, 8875430000; www.mosaic-sguesthouse.com; Siyaram Ki Doongri, Amber; s/d incl breakfast ₹3200/3500; ❄@🔊), with four lovely rooms and a roof terrace with beautiful fort views. Meals cost a set-price ₹500. It's about 1km past the fort. Keep going along the main road towards Kunda Village, then, just before you reach the Delhi Hwy, turn sharp right towards Narad Ka Bagh, then turn immediately right to Siyaram Ki Doongri.

❶ Getting There & Away

There are frequent buses to Amber from near the Hawa Mahal in Jaipur (non-AC/AC ₹10/20, 15 minutes). They drop you opposite where you start your climb up to the entrance of Amber Fort. The elephant rides and jeeps start 100m further down the hill from the bus drop-off.

An autorickshaw/taxi will cost at least ₹200/600 for the return trip. RTDC city tours include Amber Fort.

Sanganer

The large village of Sanganer, on the outskirts of Jaipur, near the airport, has a **ruined palace**, a group of **Jain temples** with

---

A DAY WITH THE ELEPHANTS

The hugely popular elephant rides up to the entrance at Amber Fort are fine for a quick bit of fun, but if you want to spend some quality time with elephants and their handlers, treat yourself to an afternoon with **Elefantastic** (☑8094253150; www.elefantastic.in; 90 Chandra Mahal Colony, Delhi Rd, Amber; 'day with the elephants' afternoon package per person ₹5100).

Set up by Rahul, a former elephant rider, this new, well-run company looks after around 24 elephants at their stables, 2km northeast of Amber Fort. Their 'day with the elephants' package gives you the opportunity to meet, feed, ride, wash and even swim with elephants. It's a particularly incredible experience for young children, who can come along for a negligible price if they are accompanied by paying adults.

The standard package is an afternoon thing, and includes a late-afternoon Rajasthani meal at a family home. You can stay the night too, allowing you to join in with the elephants' early-morning routines.

fine carvings (to which entry is restricted) and two ruined **tripolias** (triple gateways). However, the main reason to visit is to see its handmade paper and block-printing shops, workshops and factories (most shops can be found on or just off the main drag, Stadium Rd), where you can see the products being made by hand.

You can also walk down towards the river-bank to see the enormous, brightly coloured fabrics drying in the sun as they hang on huge racks.

For block-printed fabrics and blue pottery there are a number of shops, including **Sakshi** (☑ 2731862, 978344440; hement_78@yahoo.com; Laxmi Colony; ⏱ shop 8.30am-8.30pm, factory 9am-6pm). You can see a small block-printing workshop here, and even try your hand at block printing. It also runs courses in block printing and blue pottery. Nearby **Salim's Paper** (☑ 2730222; www.handmadepaper.com; Gramodyog Rd, Sanganer; ⏱ 9am-5pm) is the largest handmade paper factory in India and conducts free factory tours.

ℹ Getting There & Away

Local buses leave from near Ajmeri Gate in Jaipur for Sanganer every few minutes (₹10, one hour). You'll be dropped at a large junction. Turn right here, under the overpass, and keep walking for about 1km. Sanganer Village is just after you cross the river. Sakshi is on the main road on your right. Salim's Paper is 500m down a lane beside Saini Mishthan Bhander sweet shop, which you'll see on your right before you reach Sakshi.

Bharatpur

☑ 05644 / POP 252,000

Bharatpur is famous for its Unesco-listed Keoladeo Ghana National Park, a wetland and significant bird sanctuary, which can be explored by bicycle. Apart from the sanctuary, Bharatpur has a few historical vestiges, though it would not be worth making the journey for these alone.

The bird sanctuary lies 2km to the south-east of the town centre.

◉ Sights & Activities

Nonguests can use the small **swimming pool** at Hotel Pratap Palace.

Lohagarh FORT

The still-inhabited, 18th-century Lohagarh, or Iron Fort, was so named because of its sturdy defences. Despite being somewhat

forlorn and derelict it is still impressive, and sits at the centre of the town, surrounded by a moat. There's a north entrance, at **Austdhatu (Eight-Metal) Gate** – apparently the spikes on the gate are made of eight different metals – and a south entrance, at **Lohiya Gate**.

Maharaja Suraj Mahl, constructor of the fort and founder of Bharatpur, built two towers, the **Jawahar Burj** and the **Fateh Burj**, within the ramparts to commemorate his victories over the Mughals and the British. The fort also contains three much-decayed palaces within its precincts.

One of the palaces, centred on a tranquil courtyard, houses a seemingly forgotten **museum** (Indian/foreigner ₹10/50, camera/video ₹10/20, no photography inside museum; ⏱ 9.45am-5.15pm Tue-Sun). Upstairs is a rather ragtag display of royal artefacts, including weaponry. More impressive is the Jain sculpture gallery, which includes some beautiful 7th- to 10th-century pieces (which were temporarily on display outside in the courtyard at the time of research because of renovations). The most spectacular feature of the museum, though, is the palace's original *hammam* (bathhouse), which retains some fine carvings and frescoes.

🛏 Sleeping & Eating

There are tons of sleeping options near the park (suiting all budgets), either on the stretch of the highway beside Birder's Inn or on the dirt track that the Falcon Guest House is on. So don't worry if everything reviewed here is full.

Almost all guesthouses have restaurants, which are open to nonguests too, and even those without a proper bar can sort you out with a cold beer if you ask.

Shagun Guest House GUESTHOUSE $
(☑ 9828687488; rajeevshagun@hotmail.com; d ₹110, s/d without bathroom ₹80/90) Well off the tourist trail, this unusual tree-shaded courtyard guesthouse, hidden away in a quiet corner of the old town, is extremely basic, and has only four rooms, but it comes with bags of character. It's run by the very friendly Rajeev and his young family, who live in an adjacent property. Rajeev speaks excellent English and is a keen environmental campaigner who knows everything about the bird sanctuary and the old fort. If you're entering the old town from the direction of the park, turn right after walking through Muttra Gate then look out for the guest-

Bharatpur

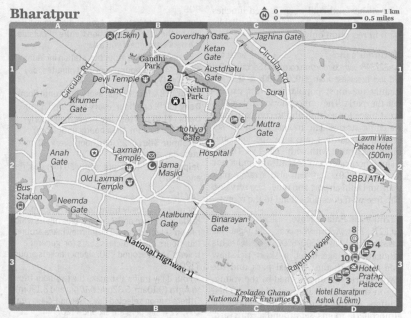

house name written on a wall in green paint and directing you down an alley to your left.

**Spoonbill
Rooms & Restaurant**   GUESTHOUSE **$**
(☎ 223571; www.hotelspoonbill.com; Gori Shankur Colony; s ₹200-500, d ₹300-600; ❄) The original Spoonbill, this place has been catering to budget travellers for more than 20 years. Rooms are simple but neat and tidy, and those on the 2nd floor have plenty of natural light. Some rooms have hot showers. Some don't. The home-cooked food (mains ₹50 to ₹150) is tasty, with curd from the family cow and Rajasthani delicacies, such as *churma* (sugar, cheese and dried fruit fried in butter), the royal dish of Rajasthan. There's sometimes a campfire in winter.

Falcon Guest House   GUESTHOUSE **$$**
(☎ 223815; falconguesthouse@hotmail.com; Gori Shankur Colony; s/d from ₹300/600, with AC from ₹1200; ❄ @) A lovely, welcoming and homely guesthouse run by the affable Mrs Rajni Singh. Her husband, Tej, is an ornithologist and is happy to answer any bird-related questions. Flavoursome home-cooked food is served in the **garden restaurant** (mains ₹60-150). Rooms, meanwhile, are cozy, clean, well-furnished and come with balconies; some shared, some private. Rates increase

slightly during colder months because of heating costs.

Hotel Sunbird   HOTEL **$$**
(☎ 225701; www.hotelsunbird.com; Bird Sanctuary Rd; s/d from ₹800/1100, with AC from ₹1980/2330; ❄) Another well-run and popular place next door to Birder's Inn. Rooms are clean and comfortable, and there's an appealing **garden bar and restaurant** (◎ 10am-3pm & 6.30-10.30pm; mains ₹100-200) with a good range of

tasty dishes and cold beer. Packed lunches and guided tours for the park are available. Wi-fi in reception only.

★ Birder's Inn   HOTEL $$$

(☑ 227346; www.birdersinn.com; Bird Sanctuary Rd; s/d incl breakfast from ₹1950/2400; ❋ @ ⦿ ≋) Rightly the most popular base for exploring the park. The atmospheric garden is a great place for a drink and to compare bird-watching stories. The rooms, which are set around the garden, are airy, spacious and nicely decorated with with LCD TVs. There's a small pool, a decent **restaurant** and a **bar** (beer from ₹200). Staff can also arrange pick up from Delhi airport and other taxi services. The free wi-fi does not extend to the rooms.

Laxmi Vilas Palace Hotel   HERITAGE HOTEL $$$

(☑ 223523; www.laxmivilas.com; Old Agra Rd, Kakaji-ki-Kothi; s/d ₹5500/6500; ❋ @ ≋) This exquisite heritage hotel, a short rickshaw ride from both the national park and the town centre, was once owned by the younger son of Maharaja Jaswant Singh. Arched ceilings and heavy old furniture make for atmospheric rooms, set around a courtyard. And the pool is gorgeous. Hotel rates do not include breakfast (₹300), lunch (₹600) or dinner (₹750).

❶ Information

Perch Forex & Travels (New Civil Lines; ◷ 7am-10pm) Fast-connection internet cafe (per hour ₹40) that also changes money and offers travel-agency services.

Tourist Reception Centre (☑ 222542; ◷ 9am-5pm) Opposite where Agra-to-Jaipur buses drop off passengers; hands out free maps of Bharatpur. Off to one side of the building is a handy **train ticket reservation office** (◷ 9am-2pm Mon-Sat).

❶ Getting There & Away

For **car hire** to onward destinations, ask at Birder's Inn or at the Tourist Reception Centre.

BUS

Buses running between Agra and Jaipur will drop you by the Tourist Reception Centre or outside the park entrance if you ask.

Buses from Bharatpur bus station include:
Agra (₹45, 1½ hours, every 30 minutes, day and night)
Alwar (₹87, four hours, every hour until 8pm)
Deeg (₹29, one hour, every hour until 8pm)
Delhi (₹145 to ₹165, five hours, half-hourly from 6am to 7pm, then hourly until 11pm)
Fatehpur Sikri (₹25, one hour, every 30 minutes, day and night)
Jaipur (₹146, 4½ hours, every 30 minutes, day and night)

TRAIN

There are four daily trains to **Delhi** (6.15am, 8.10am, 9.25am and 3.04pm), plus others which run on selected days. The journey takes around four hours. Second-class seats (or 'general tickets') cost around ₹50; sleeper tickets around ₹120.

Four daily trains also make the two-hour trip to **Agra** (9.10am, 5.32pm, 8.10pm and 8.19pm). Others run on selected days. Second-class seats cost ₹24; sleepers are around ₹120.

Daily trains go to **Jaipur** at 6.10am, 7.16am, 5.05pm, 7pm, 8.48pm and 9.15pm). The journey takes three to four hours. Second-class seats cost around ₹50; sleeper tickets around ₹120.

For **Ranthambhore National Park**, six trains run daily to Sawai Madhopur (8.25am, 10.30am, 3.50pm, 5.40pm, 7.42pm, 9.42pm). It takes two to three hours. Second-class seats cost ₹87; sleepers cost ₹140. These trains all continue to **Kota** (four hours) from where you can catch buses to **Bundi**.

❶ Getting Around

A cycle-rickshaw from the bus station to the park entrance is around ₹20; and shouldn't be much more than ₹30 to any of the hotels. Add an extra ₹10 on top of that for a trip from the train station.

MAJOR TRAINS FROM BHARATPUR

DESTINATION	TRAIN	DEPARTURE TIME	ARRIVAL TIME	FARE (₹)
Agra Cantonment	19666 Udz-Kurj Exp	9.10am	11am	120/610 (A)
Delhi (Hazrat Nizamuddin)	12059 Kota-Jan Shatabdi	9.25am	12.30pm	82/ 275 (B)
Jaipur	12036 AF-JP Shatabdi	5.05pm	7.50pm	363/ 770 (C)
Sawai Madhopur	12904 Golden Temple Mail	10.30am	1.01pm	140/640 (A)

Fares: (A) sleeper/2AC, (B) 2nd-class/AC chair, (C) AC chair/1AC

Keoladeo Ghana National Park

This famous bird sanctuary and **national park** (Indian/foreigner ₹55/400, video ₹400; ☺6am-6pm Apr-Sep, 6.30am-5pm Oct-Mar) has long been recognised as one of the world's most important bird breeding and feeding grounds. In a good monsoon season over one-third of the park can be submerged, hosting over 360 species within its 29 sq km. The marshland patchwork is a wintering area for aquatic birds, including visitors from Afghanistan, Turkmenistan, China and Siberia.

Keoladeo originated as a royal hunting reserve in the 1850s. It continued to supply the maharajas' tables with fresh game until as late as 1965. In 1982 Keoladeo was declared a national park and it was listed as a World Heritage Site in 1985.

Local campaigners have voiced concern in recent years at the increase in forest clearing to make way for small, tourist-related development, such as the carpark to your right as you enter the park. You'll notice that much of the park is no longer tree-shaded. They are also calling for a 2km 'no-construction zone' outside the park boundary. The current limit is 500m.

Visiting the Park

The best time to visit is from October to February, when you will see many migratory birds.

Admission (₹400; sunrise to sunset) entitles you to one entrance per day. Guides cost ₹100 per hour. One narrow road (no motorised vehicles are permitted past checkpoint 2) runs through the park, but a number of tracks and pathways fan out from it and thread their way between the shallow wetlands. Generally speaking, the further away from the main gate you go, the more interesting the scenery, and the more varied the wildlife becomes.

Only the government-authorised cycle-rickshaws (recognisable by the yellow license plate) are allowed beyond checkpoint 2. You don't pay an admission fee for the drivers, but they charge ₹70 per hour. Some are very knowledgable. However, these cycle-rickshaws can only travel along the park's larger tracks.

An excellent way to see the park is by hiring a bike/mountain bike (₹25/40 per six hours) at the park entrance. Having a bike is a wonderfully quiet way to travel, and allows you to avoid bottlenecks and take in the serenity on your own. However, we recommend that lone female travellers who wish to cycle do so with a guide (who will cycle alongside you), as we have had more than one report of lone women being harassed by young men inside the park in recent years.

You get a small map with your entrance ticket, although the park isn't big so it's difficult to get lost.

Alwar

📞 0144 / POP 315,000

Alwar is perhaps the oldest of the Rajasthani kingdoms, forming part of the Matsya territories of Viratnagar in 1500 BC. It became known again in the 18th century under Pratap Singh, who pushed back the rulers of Jaipur to the south and the Jats of Bharatpur to the east, and who successfully resisted the Marathas. It was one of the first Rajput states to ally itself with the fledgling British empire, although British interference in Alwar's internal affairs meant that this partnership was not always amicable.

Alwar is the nearest town to **Sariska Tiger Reserve**, and has a ruined fort and a rambling palace with an above-average museum hidden inside it. The town has relatively few tourists so there's a refreshing lack of hassle here.

⊙ Sights

Bala Qila

FORT

This imposing fort, with its 5km-long ramparts, stands 300m above the city, its fortifications hugging the steep incline. Predating the time of Pratap Singh, it's one of the few forts in Rajasthan built before the rise of the Mughals, who used it as a base for attacking Ranthambhore. Now mostly in ruins, the fort houses a radio transmitter station and can only be entered with permission from the superintendent of police. To get this, you need to visit the **Police Control Room** (☺24hr) near the bus station; turn right out of the bus station and it's on your left. It's a 2km uphill slog to the fort (turn right out of the palace), or around 7km by road. Expect to pay at least ₹100 to ₹200 in an autorickshaw.

WORTH A TRIP

SURAJ MAHL'S PALACE, DEEG

Deeg is a small, rarely visited, dusty tumult of a town. At its centre stands an incongruously glorious palace edged by stately formal gardens. **Suraj Mahl's Palace** (Indian/foreigner ₹5/100; ⏱ 9.30am-5.30pm Sat-Thu) is one of India's most beautiful and carefully proportioned palace complexes. Pick up a free leaflet with a small map on it at the entrance and note that photography is not permitted in some of the *bhavans* (buildings).

Built in a mixture of Rajput and Mughal architectural styles, the 18th-century **Gopal Bhavan** is fronted by imposing arches to take full advantage of the early-morning light. Downstairs is a lower storey that becomes submerged during the monsoon as the water level of the adjacent tank, **Gopal Sagar**, rises. This *bhavan* was used by the maharajas until the early 1950s, and contains many original furnishings, including faded sofas, huge *punkas* (cloth fans suspended from the ceiling) that are more than 200 years old, chaise longues, a stuffed tiger, elephant-foot stands and fine porcelain from China and France. Upstairs is an unusual marble dining table – a stretched oval-shaped affair raised just 20cm off the floor. Guests would sit around the edge, while food was served from the centre. In the maharaja's bedroom is an enormous bed with silver legs.

The **Keshav Bhavan** (Summer or Monsoon Pavilion) is a single-storey edifice with five arches along each side, which sits beside the complex's other large tank, **Rup Sagar**. Tiny jets once sprayed water from the archways of this *bhavan* and metal balls would rumble around in a water channel imitating monsoon thunder. Deeg's massive walls (which are up to 28m high) and 12 vast bastions, some with their cannons still in place, are also worth exploring. You can walk up to the top of the walls from the palace.

Other *bhavans* (in various states of renovation) include the marble **Suraj Bhavan**, reportedly taken from Delhi and reassembled here, **Kishan Bhavan**, which acted as a conference hall and whose back garden was the elephant stables, and **Nand Bhavan**, which isn't always open.

Food options in town are limited, so bring a picnic and have a peaceful lunch in the palace grounds.

The guy at the palace entrance will let you leave your bags in the ticket office free of charge if you smile sweetly. Don't leave valuables. He can also sell you a brochure (₹20) with a more detailed history and map of the complex than the free leaflet you get.

Deeg is about 36km north of Bharatpur, and is an easy day trip (lucky, because there's nowhere good to stay) from Bharatpur or Alwar by bus. Frequent buses run to and from Alwar (₹64, 2½ hours, until 8pm) and Bharatpur (₹29, one hour, until 9pm). From the bus stand, turn left and follow the road round to the right for about 400m to the palace entrance, known as **Singh Pol**.

City Palace Complex HISTORIC BUILDING
Below the fort sprawls the colourful and convoluted City Palace, or Vinay Vilas Mahal, with massive gates and a tank reflecting a symmetrical series of ghats and pavilions. Today, most of the palace is occupied by government offices, overflowing with piles of dusty papers and soiled by pigeon droppings and splats of *paan* (betel-nut chewing tobacco).

Hidden within the City Palace is the excellent **Alwar Museum** (Indian/foreigner ₹25/50, ⏱10am-5pm Tue-Sun). Its eclectic exhibits evoke the extravagance of the maharajas' lifestyle: stunning weapons, stuffed Scottish pheasants, royal ivory slippers, erotic miniatures, royal vestments, a solid silver table and stone sculptures, such as an 11th-century sculpture of Vishnu. It's on the top floor.

The palace complex is about 1km from the bus station; turn left out of the station, then right and immediately left at the nearby staggered junction before following the road round to the right and up towards the palace entrance.

**Cenotaph of Maharaja
Bakhtawar Singh** HISTORIC BUILDING
This double-storey edifice, resting on a platform of sandstone, was built in 1815 by Maharaja Vinay Singh in memory of his father. To gain access to the cenotaph, take the steps to the far left when facing the palace. The cenotaph is also known as the Chhatri of Moosi Rani, after one of the mistresses of

Bakhtawar Singh who performed *sati* (self-immolation) on his funeral pyre – after this act she was promoted to wifely status.

🛏 Sleeping & Eating

Hotel Sumangal   HOTEL $
(☎9413057900; Bus Stand Rd; s/d ₹200/400) One of a handful of very basic cheapies near the bus stand, Sumangal is a little on the grubby side (you'll want to use your own sleeping sheet), and has tap-and-bucket showers only, but it's kept neat and tidy and management is welcoming. Turn right out of the bus stand and it's on your right after 100m.

Hotel Aravali   HOTEL $$
(☎2332883; www.hotelaravali.co.in; Nehru Rd; s/d from ₹800/1000, with AC from ₹1400/1600; ❄🛜🏊) Ideal if you arrive by train, Aravali is a long-standing, well-run hotel with large, clean, well-furnished rooms that have bedside reading lamps, cute whitewashed table and chairs, and big bathrooms with hot-water showers. There's a summer-only pool and some garden seating. Has a decent restaurant (mains ₹100 to ₹200) and a bar (beers from ₹75). Free wi-fi, but breakfast is only included with the AC rooms. Turn left out of the train station and it's about 200m down the road on the right.

Alwar Hotel   GUESTHOUSE $$$
(☎2700012; www.alwarhotel.com; 25-26 Manu Rd; s/d incl breakfast ₹1750/2500; ❄@🛜) A 1950s home converted into a lovely little guesthouse, Alwar is a peaceful place to stay with spacious, comfortable, well renovated rooms, a neatly manicured garden and a good restaurant. The affable owner can be helpful with general information and sightseeing advice, and can help arrange trips to Sariska. Free wi-fi. Turn right out of the bus station then take the first proper turning on your right (about 300m). Alwar is about 400m down this road on your left.

⭐ Prem Pavitra Bhojnalaya   INDIAN $
(near Hope Circle; mains ₹40-70; ⊙10.30am-4pm & 6.30pm-10pm) An institution in Alwar, this low-key restaurant has been going since 1957. It is in the heart of the old town and serves fresh, tasty pure veg food – try the delicious *aloo parathas* (bread stuffed with spicy potato) and *palak paneer* (unfermented cheese cubes in spinach puree). The chapatis here are top drawer and the *special*

kheer (rice cakes smothered in yoghurt and honey) is worth every one of its 48 rupees. Turn right out of the bus station, take the first left (towards Hope Circle) and it's on your left after 100m.

Angeethi   MULTICUISINE $
(Manu Rd, Alwar Hotel; mains ₹75-200; ⊙Tue-Sun) Alwar Hotel's restaurant serves decent Indian, Continental and Chinese food; the South Indian selection is particularly good. It's slightly gloomy in the restaurant but you can eat in the pleasant garden.

ℹ Information

There's a handful of **ATMs** on your right if you turn right out of the bus station, including one at the State Bank of Bikaner & Jaipur (SBBJ), which also changes money and travellers cheques. If you continue past this bank and take the first proper turning on the right, you'll find an **internet cafe** (per hr ₹20; ⊙10am-9pm) on your right.

Tourist Reception Centre (☎2347348; Nehru Rd; ⊙10am-5pm Mon-Sat) Near the train station, this helpful office gives out a useful map of the town and can help arrange homestays in Alwar (₹500 to ₹1500). Turn left out of the train station and it's on your right, just before Hotel Aravali.

ℹ Getting There & Around

A cycle rickshaw between the bus and train stations costs ₹30. Look out for the new shared taxis that ply fixed routes around town. They come in the form of white minvans and have the word 'Vahini' printed on their side doors. One handy route goes past Hotel Aravali, the Tourist Reception Centre and the train station before continuing on to the bus station and terminating a short walk from Vinay Vilas Mahal (the palace complex). It costs ₹10 per person.

BUS

Buses to Alwar from Delhi (₹139, four hours) leave regularly from Sarai Kale Khan bus station, which is next to Hazrat Nizamuddin train station.

Services from Alwar bus station include:

Bharatpur (₹87, four hours, every hour from 5am to 8.30pm)

Deeg (₹58, 2½ hours, every hour from 5am to 8.30pm)

Delhi (₹134, four hours, every 20 minutes from 5am to 9pm)

Jaipur (₹120, four hours, half-hourly from 6am to 10.30pm)

Sariska (₹25, one hour, half-hourly from 6am to 10.30pm)

TRAIN

There are six daily trains to **Delhi** (6.40am, 7.14am, 11am, 3.40pm, 6.39pm and 7.34pm). It takes three to four hours. Second-class seats cost ₹47; sleepers around ₹140. Most go to (Old) Delhi train station.

It's also three to four hours to **Jaipur** from here. There are seven daily trains (5.05am, 7.13am, 8.40am, 2.15pm, 2.52pm, 6.03pm and 8.52pm). Prices are almost identical to those for Delhi.

Sariska Tiger Reserve

☏ 0144

Enclosed within the dramatic, shadowy folds of the Aravallis, **Sariska Tiger Reserve** (Indian/foreigner ₹60/450, vehicle ₹250; ☑ ticket sales 7am-3.30pm Oct-Mar, 6.30am-4pm Apr-Sep, park closes at sunset) is a tangle of remnant semideciduous jungle and craggy canyons sheltering streams and greenery. It covers 866 sq km (including a core area of 498 sq km), and is home to peacocks, monkeys, sambars, nilgais, chitals, wild boars, jackals and a handful of tigers.

Although Project Tiger has been in charge of the sanctuary since 1979, there has been a dramatic failure to protect tigers here.

In 2005 it was revealed that there were no longer any tigers left in the park. Since then, some tigers have been relocated from nearby Ranthambhore, and cubs have even been born, although some experts are sceptical as to whether or not the relocation program will work in the long run.

Tigers aside, Sariska is a fascinating sanctuary. Unlike most national parks, it usually opens year-round. The best time to spot wildlife is November to March.

◉ Sights

Besides wildlife, Sariska has some fine sights within the park or around its peripheries that are well worth seeking out. If you take a longer tour, you can ask to visit one or more of these. A couple of them are also accessible by public bus.

Kankwari Fort   FORT

Deep inside the sanctuary, this imposing small jungle fort, 22km away from Sariska, offers amazing views over the plains of the park, dotted with red mud-brick villages. A four- to five-hour jeep safari (one to five passengers plus guide) to Kankwari Fort from the Forest Reception Office near the

---

SARISKA'S TIGER TROUBLES

Sariska Tiger Reserve took centre stage in one of India's most publicised wildlife dramas. In 2005 an Indian journalist broke the news that the tiger population here had been eliminated, a report that was later confirmed officially after an emergency census was carried out.

An inquiry into the crisis recommended fundamental management changes before tigers be reintroduced to the reserve. Extra funding was proposed to cover relocation of villages within the park as well as increasing the protection force. But action on the recommendations has been slow and incomplete despite extensive media coverage and a high level of concern in India.

Nevertheless, a pair of tigers from Ranthambhore National Park were moved by helicopter to Sariska in 2008. By 2010, five tigers had been transferred. However, in November 2010 the male of the original pair was found dead in suspicious circumstances. Later it was confirmed that it had been poisoned. Authorities pointed the finger at local villagers, who are not supportive of the reintroduction. The underlying problem – the inevitable battle between India's poorest and ever-expanding village populace with the rare and phenomenally valuable wildlife on their doorstep – remains largely unresolved despite official plans to relocate and reimburse villagers. At the time of research, though, 25 of the 28 villages within the park h ad yet to be relocated.

In early 2012 the first cubs were sighted, and plans to relocate another three tigers from Ranthambhore were at an advanced stage at the time of research. That would bring the total number of tigers in Sariska to 10.

Only time will tell if this reintroduction is successful – another concern is that many of the reintroduced tigers are closely related. As things stand, Sariska remains a sad indictment of tiger conservation in India, from the top government officials down to the underpaid forest guards.

reserve entrance costs ₹1600, plus guide fee (₹150).

Bhangarh
HISTORIC SITE

Around 55km from Sariska, beyond the inner park sanctuary and out in open countryside, is this deserted, well-preserved and notoriously haunted city. Founded in 1631 by Madho Singh, it had 10,000 dwellings, but was suddenly deserted about 300 years ago for reasons that remain mysterious.

Bhangarh can be reached by a bus that runs twice daily through the sanctuary (₹35) to nearby Golaka village. Check what time the bus returns, otherwise you risk getting stranded.

⟲ Tours

Private cars, including taxis, are limited to sealed roads. The best way to visit the park is by 4WD gypsy (open-topped, takes six passengers), which can explore off the main tracks. Gypsy safaris start at the park entrance. Each passenger pays ₹450 for park entrance, then shares the gypsy costs (₹1260 per vehicle) with the other passengers. Guides are also available (₹250 per vehicle).

Bookings can be made at the **Forest Reception Office** (☑ 2841333; Jaipur Rd), directly opposite the Hotel Sariska Palace, which is where buses will drop you.

🛏 Sleeping & Eating

Alwar Bagh
HOTEL $$$

(☑ 2945151412; www.alwarbagh.com; r from ₹3999; ❋ ☒) This is a very peaceful option located in the village of Dhawala, between Alwar (14km) and Sariska (19km). They can arrange pick-up and drop-off from Alwar, and can also arrange Sariska safaris. The bright heritage-style hotel boasts traditional decor, spotless rooms and romantic tents, an organic orchard, a garden restaurant (breakfast/lunch/dinner ₹250/400/500) and a gorgeous swimming pool (₹150; open 6am to 7pm). You pass the hotel (on your right) on the bus from Alwar to Sariska.

Sariska Tiger Heaven
HOTEL $$$

(☑ 224815; www.sariskatigerheaven.com; s/d with full board ₹5500/6500; ❋ ☒) Run by wildlife expert Dinesh Durani, this place offers isolated luxury lodgings about 3km west of the bus stop at Thanagazi village (free pick-up is on offer). Rooms are set in stone-and-tile cottages and have big beds and windowed alcoves. Staff can arrange jeeps and guides to the park and pick-up from Jaipur (₹1200).

RTDC Hotel Tiger Den
HOTEL $$$

(☑ 2841342; s/d incl breakfast & lunch or dinner ₹1600/2250, with AC ₹2100/2900; ❋) Hotel Tiger Den is a quasi-Soviet block, backed by a rambling garden. Accommodation and meals are drab, but the rooms have balconies and occupy a pleasant setting close to the reserve entrance. Bring a mosquito net or repellent.

ℹ Getting There & Away

Sariska is 35km from Alwar, a convenient town from which to approach the reserve. There are frequent buses from Alwar (₹25, one hour) and on to Jaipur (₹100). Buses stop in front of the Forest Reception Office. The park entrance and Hotel Tiger Den are both a short walk beyond here (in the direction of Jaipur), on your left.

Shekhawati

Far less visited than other parts of Rajasthan, the Shekhawati region is most famous for its extraordinary painted *havelis* (traditional, ornately decorated residences which enclose one or more courtyards), highlighted with dazzling, often whimsical, murals. Part of the region's appeal and mystique is due to these works of art being found in tiny towns, connected to each other by single-track roads that run through lonely, arid countryside. Today it seems curious that such care, attention and money was lavished on these out-of-the-way houses, but from the 14th century onwards Shekhawati's towns were important trading posts on the caravan routes from Gujarati ports.

What makes the artwork on Shekhawati's *havelis* so fascinating is the manner in which their artists combined traditional subjects, such as mythology, religious scenes and images of the family, with contemporary concerns, including brand-new inventions and accounts of current events, many of which these isolated painters rendered straight from their imagination.

Nawalgarh

☑ 01594 / POP 60,000

Nawalgarh is a small nontouristy town almost at the very centre of the region, and makes a great base for exploring. It boasts several fine *havelis*, a colourful, mostly

Shekhawati

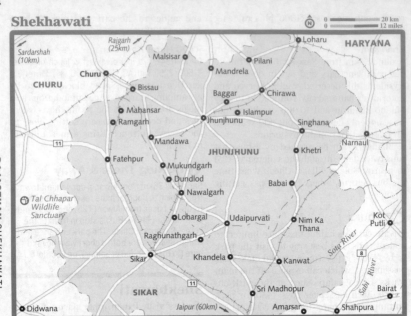

pedestrianised bazaar and some excellent accommodation options.

◉ Sights

Dr Ramnath A
Podar Haveli Museum　　　MUSEUM
(www.podarhavelimuseum.org; admission ₹100, camera ₹30; ⊙8.30am-6.30pm) Built in 1902 on the eastern side of town, and known locally simply as 'Podar Haveli', this is one of the region's few buildings to have been thoroughly restored. The paintings of this *haveli* are defined in strong colours, and are the most vivid murals in town, although purists point to the fact that they have been repainted rather than cleaned and restored. On the ground floor are several galleries on Rajasthani culture, including examples of different schools of Rajasthani painting, turbans, tablas and polystyrene forts.

Morarka Haveli Museum　　　MUSEUM
(admission ₹50; ⊙8am-7pm) This museum has well-presented original paintings, preserved for decades behind doorways blocked with cement. The inner courtyard hosts some gorgeous Ramayana scenes; look out for the slightly incongruous image of Jesus on the top storey, beneath the eaves in the courtyard's southeast corner. Turn left out

of Podar Haveli, then first right and it's on your right.

Bhagton ki Choti Haveli　　　HISTORIC BUILDING
(admission ₹50) On the external west wall here is a locomotive and a steamship. Above them, elephant-bodied *gopis* (milk maids) dance. Adjacent to this, women dance during Holi festival. Inside you'll find a host of other murals, including one strange picture (in a room on the west side) of a European-looking man with a cane and pipe, and a small dog on his shoulder. To get here, turn left out of Moraka Haveli, take the first right, then left, then first right again and it's on your left.

⚡ Activities & Tours

Ramesh Jangid at Apani Dhani and his son Rajesh at Ramesh Jangid's Tourist Pension are keen to promote sustainable rural tourism. They organise guided **hiking trips** (two to three days from ₹1750 per person), guided **camel-cart rides** (half-day ₹1400) to outlying villages and guided **tours by car** (full-day from ₹800 per person) to other towns in the region. They also arrange workshops with local craftspeople for **tie-dying** and **bangle-making** (per person ₹300) as well as **cookery classes**.

🛏 Sleeping & Eating

DS Bungalow GUESTHOUSE $
(☑ 9983168916; s ₹350-450, d ₹400-500) Next door to Shekhawati Guesthouse, this simple place is run by a friendly, down-to-earth couple and has small air-cooled rooms and tasty home cooking.

★ Apani Dhani GUESTHOUSE $$
(☑ 222239; www.apanidhani.com; s/d from ₹750/1450) 🖉 This award-winning ecotourism venture is a delightful and relaxing place. Rooms are in traditional, cosy mud-hut bungalows, enhanced by thatched roofs and comfortable beds, around a bougainvillea-shaded courtyard. It's on the west side of the Jaipur road. Multilingual Ramesh Jangid runs the show and 5% of the room tariff goes to community projects. Turn right out of the main bus stand, take the first left and it's on your left after about 500m.

★ Ramesh Jangid's Tourist Pension GUESTHOUSE $$
(☑ 224060; www.touristpension.com; s/d/tr from ₹800/1050/1350; @ 🛜) 🖉 This lovely courtyard guesthouse, run by Ramesh's son Rajesh and his family, offers clean accommodation in spacious, well-decorated rooms with big beds. Delicious vegetarian meals (lunch/dinner ₹250/350), made with organic ingredients, are available (breakfast is free), as are safe-to-drink water refills. There's solar heating, recycling bins, an internet terminal, and wi-fi stretches into the rooms. Turn right out of the main bus stand, take

the second left (by the water tower) then the second left again (after about 1km). Then take the first right (signposted), then the first left and it's on your left.

Shekhawati Guesthouse GUESTHOUSE $$
(☑ 224658; www.shekhawatiguesthouse.com; s/d/tr ₹500/600/800, cottages s/d/tr ₹ 800/1000/1400; ❄ @ 🛜) This friendly guesthouse is more like a homestay run by a very friendly couple. There are six rooms in the main building plus five atmospheric, thatch-roofed, mud-walled cottages in the garden. The restaurant has received awards for its delicious organic food and we heartily recommend the *kheer* (rice pudding). It's 4km east of the bus stand (₹60 by taxi). Pick-up from the bus or train station can be arranged, as can cooking lessons. It's about 600m walk from the Morarka and Podar Havelis (turn right out of Morarka Haveli and keep going).

ℹ Getting There & Away

BUS
The main bus stand is little more than a dusty car park accessed through a large yellow double-arched gateway. Frequent services run to **Jaipur** (₹107, 3½ hours, every 15 minutes), **Jhunjhunu** (₹31, 1 hour) and **Mandawa** (₹25, 45 minutes).

Jhunjhunu

☑ 01592 / POP 131,000
Shekhawati's most important commercial centre has a different atmosphere from the smaller towns, with lots of traffic,

---

SHEKHAWATI'S OUTDOOR GALLERIES

In the 18th and 19th centuries, shrewd Marwari merchants lived frugally and far from home while earning money in India's new commercial centres. They sent the bulk of their vast fortunes back to their families in Shekhawati to construct grand *havelis* (traditional, ornately decorated mansions) to show their neighbours how well they were doing and to compensate their families for their long absences. Merchants competed with one another to build ever more grand edifices – homes, temples, step-wells – which were richly decorated, both inside and out, with painted murals.

The artists responsible for these acres of decoration largely belonged to the caste of *kumhars* (potters) and were both the builders and painters of the *havelis*. Known as *chajeras* (masons), many were commissioned from beyond Shekhawati – particularly from Jaipur, where they had been employed to decorate the new capital's palaces – and others flooded in from further afield to offer their skills. Soon, there was a cross-pollination of ideas and techniques, with local artists learning from the new arrivals.

Haveli walls were frequently painted by the *chajeras* from the ground to the eaves. Often the paintings mix depictions of the gods and their lives with everyday scenes featuring modern inventions, such as trains and aeroplanes, even though these artists themselves had never seen them. Hence, Krishna and Radha are seen in flying motorcars and Europeans can be observed inflating hot-air balloons by blowing into them.

concrete and the hustle and bustle that befits the district's headquarters. It does, though, have some appealing *havelis* and a colourful bazaar.

◉ Sights

Rani Sati Temple
HINDU TEMPLE

(admission free; ⊘ 4am-10pm) The enormous, multistorey Rani Sati Temple is notorious for commemorating an act of *sati* (self-immolation) by a merchant's wife (after whom the temple is named) in 1595. It's fronted by two courtyards, around which 300 rooms offer shelter to pilgrims. The main hall, in the far courtyard, is made of marble with elaborate silver repoussé work before the inner sanctum. There's a tile-and-mirror mosaic on the ceiling and a relief frieze on one wall depicts the story of Rani Sati. It's a pleasant 10-minute walk north of the private bus stand. Turn left out of the bus stand, take the first left then keep asking for *Rani Sati Mandir*.

Modi Haveli
HISTORIC BUILDING

(Nehru Bazaar) On the north side of Nehru Bazaar is Mohanlal Ishwardas Modi Haveli, known simply as Modi Haveli, which dates from 1896 and which contains some delightful frescoes. A train runs merrily across the front façade. Above the entrance to the outer courtyard are scenes from the life of Krishna. On a smaller, adjacent arch are British imperial figures, including monarchs and robed judges. Facing them are Indian rulers, including maharajas and nawabs. Around the archway, between the inner and outer courtyards, there are some glass-covered portrait miniatures, along with some fine mirror-and-glass tilework. The Modi family, which own a number of *haveli* in Jhunjhunu, now lives in Mumbai (Bombay) and Kolkata (Calcutta), so the building is looked after by caretakers, who will expect a small tip for showing you round. To get here, turn right out of the private bus stand and keep walking until you reach a small floodlit roundabout (this is Gandhi Chowk). Continue straight into bustling Nehru Bazaar, then take the first right.

⨝ Sleeping & Eating

If you get stuck, there's a bunch of cheap hotels near the main bus stand.

Hotel Jamuna Resort
HOTEL $$

(☑ 512696; www.hoteljamunaresort.com; r from ₹1200; ❋ @ 🛜 🌊) A popular place for those on guided tours of the region (there's plenty of parking here), Hotel Jamuna Resort has all that you need. Rooms in the older wing are either vibrantly painted with murals or decorated with traditional mirrorwork, while the rooms in the new wing are modern and airy. Some rooms face onto a small garden, which has restaurant seating and is a pleasant spot for a beer (there's a separate bar too). There's also an inviting pool (non-guests ₹50) and the food from the **restaurant** (mains ₹95-150; ⊘ 7am-10pm) is excellent, although the set breakfasts are stingy. Note, the free wi-fi doesn't always work. It's a 20-minute walk from the private bus stand. Turn left out of the bus stand, left at the end of the road and it's on your right.

Hotel Shiv Shekhawati
HOTEL $$

(☑ 232651; www.shivshekhawati.com; Khemi Shakti Rd; s/d from ₹800/1000; ❋ @) With the same owners as Jamuna Resort, this is a more basic option (although not much cheaper). Rooms are large and spartan, and there's a boarding-school feel to the empty corridors, but the manager is friendly and gives out free maps of the town to guests. No internet or food, but you're not far from the restaurant or bar at Jamuna Resort or the sweet and snack stalls in Nehru Bazaar. To get here, turn left out of the private bus stand and it's on your left after 400m.

ⓘ Getting There & Away

There are two bus stands: the **main bus stand** and the **private bus stand**. Both have similar services and prices, but the government-run buses from the main bus stand run much more frequently. A shared autorickshaw between the two bus stands costs ₹7 per person. A private autorickshaw is ₹50.

Services from the main bus stand:

Bikaner (₹164, five to six hours, hourly)

Delhi (₹140, five to six hours, hourly)

Fatehpur (₹34, one hour, half-hourly)

Jaipur (₹130, four hours, half-hourly)

Mandawa (₹17, one hour, half-hourly)

Nawalgarh (₹31, one hour, half-hourly)

Mandawa

☑ 01592 / POP 20,700

Of all the towns in the Shekhawati region, Mandawa is the one best set up for tourists, with plenty of places to stay and some decent restaurants. It's a little too touristy for some (the attention you get from young would-be guides can become tiresome), but this small 18th-century settlement is still a pleasant base for your *haveli* explorations.

There is only one main drag, with narrow lanes fanning off it. The easy-to-find Hotel Mandawa Haveli is halfway along this street and makes a handy point of reference. Most buses drop passengers off on the main drag as well as by the bus stand.

Binsidhar Newatia Haveli (now the State Bank of Bikaner & Jaipur) has curious paintings on its outer eastern wall – a boy using a phone, a European woman in a chauffeur-driven car, and the Wright brothers in flight. From Hotel Mandawa Haveli, turn left and walk under Sonathia Gate to reach the *haveli* on your right. Other *havelis* worth seeking out include **Murmia Haveli** and the nearby **Goenka havelis** (the wealthy Goenka family own a number of homes here). To reach these, continue past Binsidhar Newatia Haveli, bear right then left and you'll see them on your left and right.

🛏 Sleeping & Eating

There are at least half a dozen *haveli* hotels here, either on or near the main drag. Rooms in them range from ₹1200 to ₹4000. Mandawa is small so wandering around town to find a room is relatively easy.

Hotel Shekhawati   HOTEL $
(📱9314698079; www.hotelshekwati.com; r ₹400-1800; 🅿@🛜) The best budget choice in town is run by a retired bank manager and his son (who's also a registered tourist guide). Bright, comically bawdy murals painted by artistic former guests give the rooms a splash of colour. OK meals (and bottles of beer) are served on the peaceful rooftop, and competitively priced camel, horse and jeep tours can also be arranged. Internet is ₹50 per hour; wi-fi ₹40. From Hotel Mandawa Haveli, walk away from Sonathia Gate, over the mini roundabout, then take the second narrow lane on your right. Hotel Shekhawati is on your left after 200m.

Hotel Mandawa Haveli   HERITAGE HOTEL $$$
(📱223088; www.hotelmandawa.com; s/d from ₹1750/2200; 🅿) Set in a glorious, restored 19th-century *haveli* with rooms surrounding a painted courtyard, this is one of the nicest places to stay. The cheapest rooms are small, but still lovingly decorated. There's a good rooftop restaurant (set meals ₹325 to ₹400; beer available), shaded garden seating, wi-fi throughout, massage treatments

(from ₹800) and camel-cart tours of the surrounding countryside (₹450).

Monica Rooftop Restaurant   INDIAN $$
(mains ₹100-300; ⊙8am-9pm) This delightful rooftop restaurant sits on top of a small but charming courtyard residence, which you have to walk through as you climb the stairs. It's signposted down an alleyway beside the half-abandoned Mandawa Fort, which in turn is signposted from the main drag, on the other side of Sonathia Gate from Hotel Mandawa Haveli.

Bungli Restaurant   INDIAN $$
(Goenka Chowk; mains ₹130-300; ⊙5am-10pm) A popular open-air travellers' eatery near the bus stand, Bungli serves piping-hot tandoori and cold beer (from ₹160). Early risers can have an Indian breakfast and a yoga class for a total of ₹450. Turn left out of Hotel Mandawa Haveli, bear right at the end of the road and Bungli is in front of you on the left.

ℹ Getting There & Away

The main bus stand, sometimes called Bikaner bus stand, has frequent services (roughly half-hourly), including those listed below. Note, there is also a separate Nawalgarh bus stand, just off the main drag, with services to Nawalgarh only. Both bus stands are so small they are unrecognisable as bus stands unless a bus is waiting at them. Look for the chai stalls that cluster beside them and you should have the right spot. The main bus stand is at one end of the main drag, on your left as the road bears right. It's a few hundred metres walk from Hotel Mandawa Haveli (turn left out of the hotel).
Bikaner (₹100, four hours)
Fatehpur (₹20, 30 minutes)
Jhunjhunu (₹17, 1 hour)
Nawalgarh (₹25, 45 minutes)

Fatehpur

📱 01571 / POP 89,000
Established in 1451 as a capital for nawabs (Muslim ruling princes), Fatehpur was their stronghold for centuries before it was taken over by the Shekhawati Rajputs in the 18th century. It's a busy little town, with plenty of *havelis*, many in a sad state of disrepair, but with a few notable exceptions.

Apart from the magnificent Haveli Nadine Le Prince, other sights include the nearby **Jagannath Singhania Haveli**; the **Mahavir Prasad Goenka Haveli** (often locked, but with superb paintings); **Geori Shankar Haveli**, with mirrored mosaics on the antechamber ceiling; and **Harikrishnan Das Sarogi Haveli**, with a colourful facade and iron lacework.

◉ Sights

Haveli Nadine Le Prince   HISTORIC BUILDING
(🔗233024; www.cultural-centre.com; admission incl guided tour ₹200; ⊙9am-6pm) This 1802 *haveli* has been restored to its former glory by French artist Nadine Le Prince and is now one of the most exquisite *havelis* you can visit in the Shekhawati region. Nadine is only here for part of the year, but often enlists foreign volunteers to help manage the building and conduct the detailed guided tours. There's a **cafe** of sorts (drinks and snacks ₹30 to ₹70) secreted away in a dusty side courtyard, and some of the rooms have been converted into small, but beautifully decorated **guest rooms** (s/d ₹1400/2500). The office isn't always staffed so it's sometimes best to reserve a room through the website rather than trying to phone. Usually, though, you can just turn up and bag a vacant room. The *haveli* is around 2km north of the two main bus stands, down a lane off the main road. Turn right out of the bus stands, and the turning will eventually be on your right, or hop into a shared autorickshaw (₹5 to ₹10).

❶ Getting There & Around

Confusingly, there are three bus stands. The main bus stand is known as Chatriya bus stand and is on Fatehpur's main road. Baori Gate bus stand is 300m north of here, on the same main road. If you turn down the side road beside Baori Gate bus stand, walk 200m then bear left, you'll reach the small Jhunjhunu bus stand.

Services from Chatriya bus stand include: **Bikaner** (₹131, 3½ hours, hourly), **Jaipur** (₹117, 3½ hours, half-hourly) and **Delhi** (₹250, seven hours, 8am, 11am then half-hourly 5pm to 10pm).

Services from Baori Gate bus stand include **Nawalgarh** (₹30, one hour, hourly), while services from the Jhunjhunu bus stand include **Jhunjhunu** (₹34, one hour, frequent) and **Mandawa** (₹20, 30 minutes, frequent).

Ajmer

🔗0145 / POP 542,000

Ajmer is a bustling chaotic city, 13km from the traveller haven of Pushkar. It skirts the tranquil lake of Ana Sagar, and is itself ringed by the rugged Aravalli Hills. Ajmer is Rajasthan's most important site in terms of Islamic history and heritage. It contains one of India's prime Muslim pilgrimage sites – the shrine of Khwaja Muin-ud-din Chishti – and contains some fine examples of early Islamic architecture. It's also a significant centre for the Jain religion. Most travellers, however, use the city as a stepping stone to Pushkar, a supremely sacred town to Hindus, and a former hippy hang-out. Ajmer is an easy half-day trip from Pushkar.

◉ Sights

**Dargah of Khwaja
Muin-ud-din Chishti**   ISLAMIC SHRINE
(www.dargahajmer.com;   ⊙5am-9pm winter, 4am-9pm summer) This is the tomb of a Sufi saint, Khwaja Muin-ud-din Chishti, who came to Ajmer from Persia in 1192 and died here in 1236. The tomb gained its significance during the time of the Mughals – many emperors added to the buildings here. Construction of the shrine was completed by Humayun, and the gate was added by the Nizam of Hyderabad. Akbar used to make the pilgrimage to the dargah from Agra every year.

You have to cover your head in certain parts of the shrine, so remember to take a scarf or cap – there are plenty for sale at the colourful bazaar leading to the dargah, along with floral offerings and delicious toffees.

The main entrance is through **Nizam Gate** (1915). Inside, the green and white mosque, **Akbari Masjid**, was constructed in 1571 and is now an Arabic and Persian school for religious education. The next gate is called the Nakkarkhana because it has two large *nakkharas* (drums) fixed above it.

A third gate, **Buland Darwaza** (16th century) leads into the dargah courtyard. Flanking the entrance of the courtyard are the *degs* (large iron cauldrons), one donated by Akbar in 1567, the other by Jehangir in 1631, for offerings for the poor.

Inside this courtyard, the saint's domed tomb is surrounded by a silver platform. Pilgrims believe that the saint's spirit will intercede on their behalf in matters of illness, business or personal problems, so the notes and holy string attached to the railings around are thanks or requests.

Pilgrims and Sufis come from all over the world on the anniversary of the saint's death, the Urs, in the seventh month of the lunar calendar, Jyaistha.

Bags must be left in the cloakroom (₹10 each, with camera ₹20) outside the main en-

Ajmer

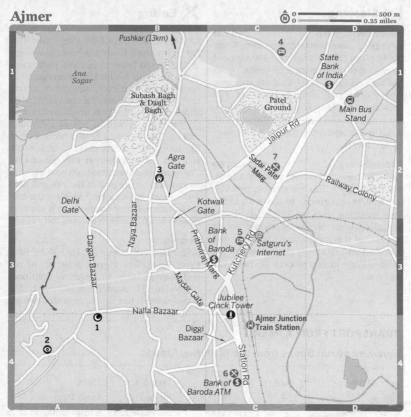

trance. Shoes should be placed in racks just inside the entrance.

Dhai-din-ka-Jhonpra   HISTORIC SITE
Beyond the dargah, on the town outskirts, are the ruins of the Dhai-din-ka-Jhonpra (Two-and-a-Half-Day Building) mosque. According to legend, construction in 1153 took 2½ days. Others say it was named after a festival lasting 2½ days. It was built as a Sanskrit college, but in 1198 Mohammed of Ghori seized Ajmer and converted the building into a mosque by adding a seven-arched wall covered with Islamic calligraphy in front of the pillared hall.

It's a beautiful piece of architecture, with soaring domes, pillars and a lovely arched screen, largely built from pieces of Jain and Hindu temples.

Nasiyan (Red) Temple   JAIN TEMPLE
(Prithviraj Marg; admission ₹10; ⊙ 8.30am-5.30pm)
This impressive temple was built in 1865. It's

also known as the Golden Temple, due to its double-storey temple hall being filled with a huge golden diorama depicting the Jain concept of the ancient world.

🛏 Sleeping

Haveli Heritage Inn
HOTEL **$$**

(📞 2621607; www.haveliheritageinn.com; Kutchery Rd; r from ₹875; ❄) Set in a 140-year-old *haveli,* this welcoming city-centre oasis has high-ceilinged rooms that are spacious, simply decorated, air-cooled and set well back from the busy road. There's a pleasant courtyard and the hotel is infused with a family atmosphere, complete with home-cooked meals.

Badnor House
GUESTHOUSE **$$$**

(📞 2627579; www.badnorhouse.com; d incl breakfast ₹2800; ❄📶) This guesthouse provides an excellent opportunity to stay with locals. Your charming hosts live in a colonial-style bungalow, while the guest rooms are at one end of the garden and are large, well furnished and spotlessly clean. You can get online using a mobile modem the hosts can lend you.

🍴 Eating

Mango Masala
INDIAN **$**

(📞 01452422100; Sadar Patel Marg; mains ₹80-190; ⊙9am-11pm) Easily the best place to eat in Ajmer, and better than most restaurants in Pushkar, this laidback three-in-one affair houses a family-friendly vegetarian restaurant, a curry house serving tandoori sizzlers and a coffee stall which brews fresh coffee (₹25 to ₹69) as well as selling cakes and cookies. There's also a proper pizza oven in the backyard, serving decent pizza which you can eat in either of the restaurants. The vegetarian restaurant (on your right as you walk in) is the pick of the two and does some excellent-value mini meals – the *malai kofta* and butter naan combo is about as close to lunchtime perfection as you can get.

Honeydew
MULTICUISINE **$$**

(📞 2622498; Station Rd; mains ₹120-300; ⊙9am-11pm) This offers a great selection of veg and nonveg Indian, Chinese and Continental food in a pleasant, clean, but overly dim atmosphere. It has long been one of Ajmer's

---

TRANSPORT FROM AJMER

Government-run Buses from the Main Bus Stand

DESTINATION	FARE (₹)	DURATION (HR)	FREQUENCY	TIMES
Bikaner	198	8	half-hourly	4am-9.45pm
Bundi	137	5	every 15 minutes	6.30am-9pm
Chittorgarh	147	5	half-hourly	6am-8pm
Delhi	375	9	hourly	6am-11pm
Jaipur	110	2½	every 10 minutes	day & night
Jodhpur	151	6	half-hourly	6am-8pm
Pushkar	10-12	½	every 10 minutes	5am-9pm
Udaipur	210	8	hourly	5.30am-midnight

Major Trains from Ajmer Junction

DESTINATION	TRAIN	DEPARTURE TIME	ARRIVAL TIME	FARE (₹)
Agra (Agra Fort)	12988 Ajmer-SDAH Exp	12.50pm	7.25pm	196/ 511 (A)
Delhi (New Delhi)	12016 Ajmer Shatabdi	3.45pm	10.40pm	669/ 1420 (B)
Delhi (New Delhi)	12957 Swarna J Raj Exp	12.55am	7.30am	684/ 980/ 1670 (C)
Jaipur	12991 Udaipur-Jaipur Exp	11.30am	1.35pm	50/ 230/ 325 (D)
Jodhpur	54802 Ajmer-Jodhpur Fast Passenger	2.30pm	7.40pm	88/ 362 (E)
Udaipur	09721 Jaipur-Udaipur SF SPL	8.55am	1.45pm	81/ 349 (F)

Fares: (A) sleeper/3AC, (B) AC chair/1AC, (C) 3AC/2AC/1AC, (D) 2nd-class/AC chair/1st-class, (E) sleeper/3AC, (F) 2nd-class/AC chair

best, and is the restaurant of choice for Mayo College students' midterm treat. The ice cream, milkshakes and floats will keep you cool.

ℹ️ Information

The **Tourist Reception Centre** (☺ 9am-6pm Mon-Fri), at the train station, has free maps of Ajmer and Pushkar.

Bank of Baroda (Prithviraj Marg) Changes travellers cheques and does credit-card advances.

Bank of Baroda ATM (Station Rd) By the entrance to Honeydew restaurant.

Satguru's Internet (60-61 Kutchery Rd; per hr ₹20; ☺ 9am-10pm) Opposite Haveli Heritage Inn.

State Bank of India Near the bus stand. Changes travellers cheques and foreign currency and has an ATM.

ℹ️ Getting There & Away

BUS

The table shows a sample of government-run buses leaving from the main bus stand in Ajmer. In addition to these, there are less-frequent 'deluxe' coach services running to major destinations such as Delhi and Jaipur. There is a 24hr cloakroom at the bus stand (per bag per day ₹10).

TRAIN

Seven trains run daily to **Delhi** (6.10am, 11.05am, 2.15pm, 3.45pm, 8.50pm, 10.45pm and 12.55am) and take around eight hours. Second-class seats cost around ₹108; sleepers ₹196.

The above Delhi trains all stop at **Jaipur** too. In addition, there are a further six daily trains to Jaipur (6.55am, 11.30am, 12.50pm, 3pm, 4.35pm and 7.15pm). The journey takes less than three hours. An unreserved 'general ticket' (2nd-class seat) costs ₹40 to ₹50; sleepers ₹120; AC chairs ₹230.

There are four daily trains for the five-hour journey to **Udaipur** (8.55am, 4.10pm, 12.50am and 2.10am).

Only one direct train goes to **Jodhpur** (2.30pm, 5 hours), while two go to **Agra Fort** (12.50pm and 3pm, 6½ hours, sleeper ₹196).

The quickest of two or three daily trains to **Mumbai** leaves Ajmer at 4.40pm and takes around 16 hours. Sleepers cost around ₹350.

There are three reasonably timed daily trains to **Chittorgarh** (1.25pm, 4.10pm and 8.40pm). They take three to four hours. Second-class seats cost around ₹60; sleepers ₹120.

For **Mount Abu**, three reasonably-timed trains run daily to Abu Road (6.50am, 11.25am and 4.40pm) and take five to six hours. Sleepers cost ₹155.

Pushkar

 0145 POP 15,000

Pushkar has a magnetism all of its own, and is quite unlike anywhere else in Rajasthan. It's a prominent Hindu pilgrimage town and devout Hindus should visit at least once in their lifetime. The town curls around a holy lake, said to have appeared when Brahma dropped a lotus flower. It also has one of the world's few Brahma temples. With 52 bathing ghats and 400 milky-blue temples, the town often hums with *pujas* (prayers) generating an episodic soundtrack of chanting, drums and gongs, and devotional songs.

The result is a muddle of religious and tourist scenes. The main street is one long bazaar, selling anything to tickle a traveller's fancy, from hippy-chic tie-dye to didgeridoos. Despite the commercialism and banana pancakes, the town remains enchantingly small and authentically mystic.

Pushkar is only 11km from Ajmer but separated from it by Nag Pahar, the Snake Mountain.

⊙ Sights

Temples   HINDU TEMPLE

Pushkar boasts hundreds of temples, though few are particularly ancient as they were mostly desecrated by Aurangzeb and subsequently rebuilt.

➡ **Brahma Temple**

(☺ 5.30am-1.30pm & 3pm-9pm) Most famous is the Brahma Temple, said to be one of the few such temples in the world as a result of a curse by Brahma's consort, Saraswati. The temple is marked by a red spire, and over the entrance gateway is the *hans* (goose symbol) of Brahma. Inside, the floor and walls are engraved with dedications to the dead.

➡ **Saraswati Temple**

The one-hour trek up to the hilltop Saraswati Temple overlooking the lake offers fantastic views at any time of day, but this is a particularly good spot for sunset.

➡ **Pap Mochani (Gayatri) Temple**

The sunrise views over town from the closer Pap Mochani (Gayatri) Temple are also well worth the 30-minute climb. Walk up through the small **Kali Temple** from the back of the main bus stand.

Pushkar

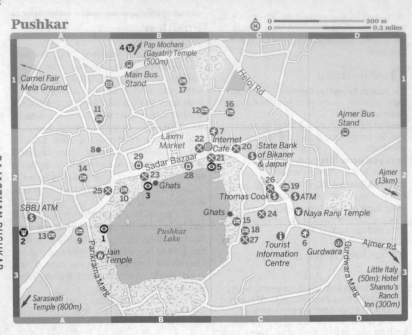

Pushkar

◎ Sights
1 Brahma Ghat	A3
2 Brahma Temple	A3
3 Gandhi (Gau) Ghat	B2
4 Kali Temple	B1
5 Varah Ghat	C2

☸ Activities, Courses & Tours
Cooking Bahar	(see 8)
6 Government Homeopathic Hospital	C3
7 Roshi Hiralal Verma	C2
8 Saraswati Music School	A2

⬚ Sleeping
9 Alka Guest House	A3
10 Bharatpur Palace	B2
11 Hotel Everest	A1
12 Hotel Kanhaia Haveli	B1
13 Hotel Navaratan Palace	A3
14 Hotel Paramount Palace	A2
15 Hotel Pushkar Palace	C2
16 Inn Seventh Heaven	C1
17 Milkman Guesthouse	B1
18 Pushkar Inn's Hotel	C3
19 Shri Shyam Krishna Guesthouse	C2

✕ Eating
20 Baba Rooftop Restaurant	C2
21 Falafel wrap stalls	C2
22 Honey & Spice	B2
23 LMB Hotel & GR Restaurant	B2
24 Om Shiva Garden Restaurant	C2
25 Out of the Blue	A2
26 Shri Vankatesh	C2
Sixth Sense	(see 16)
27 Sunset Café	C3

⬚ Shopping
28 Khadi Gramodhyog	B2
29 Lala International	B2

Ghats
GHAT

Fifty-two bathing ghats surround the lake, where pilgrims bathe in the sacred waters. If you wish to join them, do it with respect. Remember, this is a holy place: remove your shoes, and don't smoke, kid around or take photographs.

Some ghats have particular importance: Vishnu appeared at **Varah Ghat** in the form of a boar, Brahma bathed at **Brahma Ghat**, and Gandhi's ashes were sprinkled at **Gandhi Ghat** (formerly Gau Ghat).

🏃 Activities

Nonguests can use the pool at Hotel Navaratan Palace (₹100), although, bizarrely, swim times are segregated. Foreigners can swim from noon to 5pm. Indians are allowed to swim only in the morning, and then again after 5pm.

Shannu's Riding School HORSE RIDING
(☏ 2772043; www.shannus.weebly.com; Panch Kund Marg; ride/lessons per hr ₹400) French-Canadian and long-time Pushkar resident Marc Dansereau can organise riding lessons and horse safaris on his graceful Marwari steeds. You can stay here too.

Government
Homeopathic Hospital AYURVEDIC
(☏ 9413094664; Ajmer Rd; ⊙ 9am-1pm) For a totally noncommercial massage-treatment experience, try the ayurvedic department at the small and basic Government Homeopathic Hospital. A one-hour full-body massage costs ₹450. For an extra ₹50 you get a steam bath afterwards. A half-hour *sirodhara* treatment (where medicated oil is poured continuously onto your forehead) costs ₹400.

Roshi Hiralal Verma REIKI, YOGA
(☏ 9829895906) For reiki, yoga and shiatsu, Mr Hiralal Verma is based at the Ambika Guesthouse. Costs depend on the duration and type of session.

🍃 Courses

Saraswati Music School MUSIC
(☏ 2773124, Birju 9828297784; Mainon Ka Chowk) Teaches classical tabla (drums), sitar, flute, singing and *kathak* (classical dance). Contact Birju, who's been playing for around 20 years, and charges from ₹250 per hour, plus ₹700/1000 for the teaching book/CD you need to buy in order to participate. He also sells instruments (sitar/tabla from ₹8000/5000). Dance classes start from ₹300 per hour.

Cooking Bahar COOKING
(☏ 2773124; www.cookingbahar.com; Mainon Ka Chowk) Part of the Saraswati Music School family, Deepa conducts three-hour cooking classes that cover three vegetarian courses.

☞ Tours
Camel Safaris
Plenty of people in Pushkar offer short **camel rides** (around ₹200 per hour), which are a good way to explore the starkly beautiful landscape – a mixture of desert and the rocky hills – around town. Sunset rides are most popular. It's best to ask at your hotel. Inn Seventh Heaven is reliable.

For longer camel treks, prices start at around ₹500 per person per day for a group of four. You can head out to Jodhpur (five to six days) or even Jaisalmer (10 to 12 days). Numerous operators line Ajmer Rd, but note, these places are less professional than the operators we recommend in Jaisalmer and Bikaner.

🛏 Sleeping

At the time of the camel fair prices multiply enormously and it's essential to book several weeks ahead. Temporary luxury tented accommodation, which can be booked online, springs up at this time. Check out www.jodhanaheritage.com or www.hotelpushkarpalace.com.

Shri Shyam
Krishna Guesthouse GUESTHOUSE $
(☏ 2772461; skguesthouse@yahoo.com; Sadar Bazaar; s/d ₹300/500, without bathroom ₹150/350; 🖨) Housed in a lovely old blue-washed building, and sharing lawns and gardens with a still-active Krishna temple, this sprawling guesthouse has ashram austerity and genuinely friendly management, and makes a great budget choice for families. Some of the cheaper rooms are cell-like, and there's only hot water in the private bathrooms, but all rooms share the simple, authentic ambience.

Pushkar Inn's Hotel HOTEL $
(☏ 2772010; hotelpushkarinns@yahoo.com; Pushkar Lake; r ₹800, without bathroom ₹200, with AC ₹1500; ❄🖨) A charming little hotel set around a series of lush gardens with well-tended lawns, papaya trees and plenty of peace and tranquillity. Rooms themselves are fairly basic but clean, and some open out onto a front lawn with lake views. The air-conditioned rooms have a TV. The bathroomless cheapies fill up quickly. The family who owns this place also runs the excellent Sunset Café next door, while the garden restaurant Alpine Pizzeria is within the hotel grounds.

Hotel Everest HOTEL $
(☏ 2773417; www.pushkarhoteleverest.com; r ₹200-600, with AC ₹850; ❄@🖨) This welcoming budget hotel is secreted in the quiet

PUSHKAR CAMEL FAIR

Come the month of Kartika, the eighth lunar month of the Hindu calendar and one of the holiest, Thar camel drivers spruce up their ships of the desert and start the long walk to Pushkar in time for Kartik Purnima (Full Moon). Each year around 200,000 people converge here, bringing with them some 50,000 camels, horses and cattle. The place becomes an extraordinary swirl of colour, sound and movement, thronging with musicians, mystics, tourists, traders, animals, devotees and camera crews.

Trading begins a week before the official fair (a good time to arrive to see the serious business), but by the time the RTDC *mela* (fair) starts, business takes a back seat and the bizarre sidelines (snake charmers, children balancing on poles etc) jostle onto centre stage. Even the cultural program is bizarre: moustache contests, turban-tying contests or seeing how many people can balance on a camel.

It's hard to believe, but this seething mass is all just a sideshow. Kartik Purnima is when Hindu pilgrims come to bathe in Pushkar's sacred waters. The religious event builds in tandem with the camel fair in a wild, magical crescendo of incense, chanting and processions to dousing day, the last night of the fair, when thousands of devotees wash away their sins and set candles afloat on the holy lake.

Although fantastical, mystical and a one-off, it must be said that it's also crowded, touristy, noisy (light sleepers should bring earplugs) and tacky. Those affected by dust and/or animal hair should bring appropriate medication. However, it's a grand epic, and not to be missed if you're anywhere within camel-spitting distance.

It usually takes place in October or November and because dates can change the following are indicative only:

➡ 2013: 9 to 17 November

➡ 2014: 30 Oct to 6 November

➡ 2015: 18 to 25 November

---

laneways north of Sadar Bazaar. Rooms vary in size, but are colourful and spotless, and the beds are comfortable. The roof is a pleasant retreat for meals or relaxation.

Bharatpur Palace　　　　　　　HOTEL $
(☎2772320; bharatpurpalace_pushkar@yahoo.co.in; r ₹300-600; ✱) Lovely location overlooking the lake, and although very few of the rooms have a lake view there are plenty of common seating areas that do. Basic, but friendly.

Hotel Paramount Palace　　　　HOTEL $
(☎2772428; www.pushkar-paramount.com; r ₹200-1000; 🛜) Perched on one of the highest points in town, and overlooking an old temple, this welcoming hotel has excellent views over the town and lake (and lots of stairs). The rooms vary widely. The best ones (106, 108, 109) have lovely balconies, stained glass and are good value; smaller rooms can be dingy. Staff are laidback, there's wi-fi throughout and a dizzyingly magical rooftop restaurant.

Milkman Guesthouse　　　　GUESTHOUSE $
(☎2773452; vinodmilkman@hotmail.com; dm/r without bathroom ₹100/250, r ₹300-700; ✱@🛜) A cosy guesthouse in a backstreet location, the friendly Milkman has brightly painted rooms with plenty of character, as well as a 2nd-floor cafe and a 3rd-floor garden lawn.

Alka Guest House　　　　　GUESTHOUSE $
(☎2773082, 9782642546; Brahm Chowk, Badi Basti; s/d ₹300/400) Run by a welcoming but quiet family, Alka has rooms overlooking a large, tree-shaded courtyard. Each is small and basic but neat and tidy, and they come with unusual dressing areas that lend more space. Common bathrooms only, but showers are always hot.

★ Inn Seventh Heaven　　HERITAGE HOTEL $$
(☎5105455; www.inn-seventh-heaven.com; Chotti Basti; r ₹950-2800; ✱@🛜) You enter this lovingly converted *haveli* through heavy wooden doors into an incense-perfumed courtyard, centred with a marble fountain. There are 12 individually decorated rooms

on three levels, with traditionally crafted furniture and comfortable beds. On the roof you'll find the excellent Sixth Sense restaurant as well as sofas and swing chairs for relaxing with a book. Early booking (two-night minimum, no credit cards) is recommended.

Hotel Shannu's Ranch Inn
GUESTHOUSE $$

(☎2772043; www.shannus.weebly.com; Panch Kund Marg; s/d ₹500/600) Especially for horse lovers but not exclusively so, this relaxed, family-run hotel is a 10-minute walk from the lake. Rustic, brick-walled rooms with white-tiled bathrooms share a garden with the horse stables housing Marc Dansereau's beloved Marwari horses. Marc, a French-Canadian who has been in India for almost 30 years, is a self-confessed hippy, a wonderfully laid-back guy and great to hang out with. Horse riding and home-cooked meals are available. To get here, walk along Ajmer Rd, away from the lake, and take the second right after the large gurdwara (Sikh temple), then fork left at Little Italy restaurant; Shannu's will be on your left.

Hotel Kanhaia Haveli
HOTEL $$

(☎2772146; www.pushkarhotelkanhaia.com; Chotti Basti; r ₹300-1750; ❄@⬤) With a vast range of rooms, from cheap budget digs to smart air-conditioned doubles and suites, you are sure to find a room and price that suits at this converted courtyard hotel. As you spend more the rooms get bigger and lighter with more windows and even balconies.

Hotel Navaratan Palace
HOTEL $$

(☎2772145; www.pushkarnavaratanpalace.co.in; s/d from ₹400/500, with AC ₹700/800; ❄⬤) Slightly characterless but well-run hotel with simple clean rooms and a lovely enclosed garden with swimming pool. Note the hotel's strange decision to segregate pool users so that foreigners (noon to 5pm) and Indians (9.30am to 11.30am and 5.30pm to 7pm) cannot swim together.

Hotel Pushkar Palace
HERITAGE HOTEL $$$

(☎2772001; www.hotelpushkarpalace.com; r incl breakfast ₹7000; ❄@) Once belonging to the Maharaja of Kishangarh, this top-end hotel boasts a romantic lakeside setting. Beautifully appointed rooms have carved wooden furniture and separate dressing areas leading into exquisite bathrooms. Rooms open onto a shared verandah which overlooks the central garden and has views of the lake. No

internet and no swimming pool, but rooms do have coffee makers and flat-screen TVs. Expect 40% discounts when it's quiet.

✖ Eating

Almost all accommodation in Pushkar has its own cafe-restaurant, open to nonguests and often located on a rooftop.

★ Honey & Spice
MULTICUISINE $

(Laxmi Market off Sadar Bazaar; mains ₹90-150; ⏱7.30am-6.45pm) 🍃 This unassuming cafe-restaurant is pretty much unique in Pushkar, with its emphasis on super-healthy food rather than lake views. It's tucked away behind shops on Sadar Bazaar so that nothing can distract you from the fabulous menu, which is small but outstanding. Offerings such as 'exotic stir fry in ginger and honey sauce' share space with a selection of imaginative salads, pastas, juices and herbal teas. There are vegan options too and the breakfast menu – brown toasts, fresh fruits, porridge, muesli – is equally healthy, while the fresh coffee (from ₹50) includes blends infused with spices such as cardamon and cinnamon.

Sunset Café
MULTICUISINE $

(mains ₹75-200; ⏱7.30am-midnight; 📶) Right on the eastern ghats, this cafe has uninterrupted lake views. It offers the usual traveller menu, including well-priced Indian dishes, pizza and pasta, plus there's a German bakery serving OK cakes. As the name suggests, the lakeshore setting is perfect at sunset, but this is also a pleasant spot for breakfast (espresso ₹60).

Shri Vankatesh
DHABA $

(Chooti Basti; mains ₹40-90; ⏱9am-10pm) If you're sick of pizza, pasta and espresso, head to this no-nonsense local favourite and tuck into some dhal, paneer or kofta, before mopping up the sauce with freshly baked chapatis and washing it all down with some good chai (₹10). The thalis (₹60 to ₹100) are good value too, and there's some upstairs seating overlooking the street. Not much English spoken, but has an English menu.

Om Shiva Garden Restaurant
MULTICUISINE $

(☎5105045; mains ₹70-170; ⏱7.30am-late) This traveller stalwart continues to satisfy with its well-priced Indian dishes, wood-fired pizzas and decent sandwiches. The shaded garden setting is cool and peaceful and there's fresh coffee too.

Falafel Wrap Stalls MIDDLE EASTERN $
(wraps ₹60-120; ☺7.30am-10.30pm) Perfect for quelling a sudden attack of the munchies, and a big hit with Israeli travellers, these two adjacent roadside falafel joints knock up a choice selection of filling falafel-and-hummus wraps. Eat them on stools on the side of the road or devour them back at your hotel room.

LMB Hotel & GR Restaurant DHABA $
(Sadar Bazaar; meals ₹70; ☺10am-9pm) Established in 1921, this local favourite has a ground-floor sweet shop selling snacks such as kachori (round-shaped spicy pasties; ₹10) and an upstairs restaurant that serves just one thing; a ₹70-thali that includes two vegetable curries, dhal, rice, chapati and curd.

★Out of the Blue ITALIAN $$
(mains ₹100-200; ☺8am-11pm; 🐾) Arguably the best restaurant in Pushkar, Out of the Blue does decent Indian, Israeli and even Tibetan dishes, but it's the Italian food that steals the show, with excellent thin-crust pizzas sharing the menu with some delicious pasta options. It also does the best coffee in town (from ₹40), making this a smart choice for breakfast too.

★Sixth Sense MULTICUISINE $$
(Inn Seventh Heaven; mains ₹120-200; ☺8.30am-4pm & 6-10pm; 🐾) This chilled rooftop restaurant is a great place to head even if you didn't score a room in its popular hotel. Seasonal Indian vegetables and rice, vegetable sizzlers, pasta and pizzas are all excellent, as are the filter coffee and fresh juice blends. Its ambience is immediately relaxing and the pulley apparatus that delivers the delicious food from the ground-floor kitchen is enthralling.

Baba Rooftop Restaurant MULTICUISINE $$
(☎2772858; mains ₹90-180; ☺8.30am-11pm) The food is similar to that at many other traveller-friendly restaurants in Pushkar (pizza, pasta, burgers, Indian, Israeli) – tasty, but nothing to write home about. But the location, looking down onto a bustling street market, and across at the lake and mountains, sets this place apart. There's a free pool table one floor down, and you can even snag a bottle of beer (₹150) if you ask discreetly.

🛍 Shopping

Pushkar's Sadar Bazaar is lined with enchanting little shops and is a good place for picking up gifts. Many of the vibrant textiles come from the Barmer district south of Jaisalmer. There's plenty of silver and beaded jewellery catering to foreign tastes, and some old tribal pieces, too.

Lala International CLOTHING
(Sadar Bazaar; ☺9.30am-8pm) Brilliantly colourful women's clothing. Modern designs, but Indian in theme. Dresses and skirts start from around ₹500. Prices are clearly labelled and fixed.

Khadi Gramodhyog CLOTHING
(Sadar Bazaar, Pushkar Lake; ☺10am-6pm Mon-Sat) Small fixed-price *khadi* shop selling traditional hand-woven shirts, scarves, shawls and men's kurta-pyjamas.

ℹ Information

Foreign-friendly ATMs and unofficial money-changers are dotted around Sadar Bazaar. The Sadar Bazaar branch of **State Bank of Bikaner & Jaipur** (SBBJ; ☺10am-4pm Mon-Fri, to 12.30pm Sat) changes cash and travellers cheques, as does **Thomas Cook** (☺9.30am-6.30pm Mon-Sat), also on Sadar Bazaar.

BUS SERVICES FROM PUSHKAR'S MAIN BUS STAND

DESTINATION	FARE (₹)	DURATION (HR)	FREQUENCY
Ajmer	12	½	every 10 minutes
Bundi	137	6	11am
Delhi	seat/sleeper 350/450	10½	5pm, 7.30pm & 8.30pm
Jaipur	150	4	9.30am-4pm frequent
Jaisalmer	seat/sleeper 450/550	10½	9pm & 10pm
Jodhpur	250	5	7am & 8.30am
Udaipur	250	6	8am

Internet cafes are sprinkled around the lanes, and tend to charge ₹30 per hour. Most guesthouses and many restaurants and cafes have free wi-fi these days.

Internet Cafe (Sadar Bazaar) Handy internet cafe near Honey & Spice cafe.

Post Office (off Heloj Rd; ☉9.30am-5pm)

Tourist Information Centre (☑01452772040; ☉10am-5pm) In the grounds of Hotel Sarovar; staff will give out a free map.

DANGERS & ANNOYANCES

Priests – some genuine, some not – will approach you near the ghats and offer to do a *puja* (prayer) for which you'll receive a 'Pushkar passport' (a red ribbon around your wrist). Others proffer flowers (to avoid trouble, don't take any flowers you are offered). Some of these priests genuinely live off the donations of others and this is a tradition that goes back centuries. Others can be pushy and aggressive. Walk away if you feel bullied and be aware that you may be pressured into making a donation later on, even if the ribbons and flowers are at first given to you for free.

During the camel fair, Pushkar is besieged by pickpockets working the crowded bazaars. Take extra care at this time.

Fortunately, there is very little motorised traffic in Pushkar's lanes, making it a pleasurable place to explore at leisure – but do watch out for stray motorbikes.

❶ Getting There & Away

Pushkar's tiny train station is so badly connected it's not worth bothering with. Use Ajmer Junction train station instead.

Frequent buses to/from Ajmer (₹10 to ₹12, 30 minutes, every 10 minutes) use Pushkar's dedicated Ajmer bus stand, although Ajmer buses also leave from the main bus stand.

Be careful to check that your bus is direct, many services from Pushkar aren't. And note, even if they are direct buses they may well stop for some time in Ajmer, meaning it's often quicker to go to Ajmer first and then catch another bus from there.

❶ Getting Around

There are no autorickshaws, but it's a breeze to get around on foot. If you want to explore the surrounding countryside, you could try hiring a scooter (₹200 per day) from one of the many places round town. For something more susbstantial, try **Shreeram Enfield Gairej** (☉9.30am-7.30pm) on Ajmer Rd. They hire Enfield Bullets for ₹500 per day (₹50,000 deposit) and sell them from ₹55,000.

Ranthambhore National Park

☑ 07462

This famous national park, open from 1 October to 30 June, is the best place to spot wild tigers in Rajasthan. Comprising 1334 sq km of wild jungle scrub hemmed in by rocky ridges, at its centre is the 10th-century Ranthambhore Fort. Scattered around the fort are ancient temples and mosques, hunting pavilions, crocodile-filled lakes and vine-covered *chhatris* (burial tombs). The park was a maharajas' hunting ground until 1970, a curious 15 years after it had become a sanctuary.

Seeing a tiger (there were 28 at last count) is partly a matter of luck; leave time for two or three safaris to improve your chances. But remember there's plenty of other wildlife to see including more than 300 species of birds.

It's 10km from Sawai Madhopur (the gateway town for Ranthambhore) to the first gate of the park, and another 3km to the main gate and Ranthambhore Fort. There's a bunch of cheap (and rather grotty) hotels near Sawai Madhopur train station, but the nicest accommodation is stretched out along Ranthambhore Rd, which eventually leads to the park.

It's ₹50 to ₹100 for an auto from the train station to Ranthambhore Rd, depending on where you get off. Many hotels, though, will pick you up from the train station for free if you call ahead.

If you want to walk, turn left out of the train station and follow the road up to the overpass (200m). Turn left and cross the bridge over the railway line to reach a roundabout (200m), known as Hammir Circle. Turn right here to reach the **Safari Booking Office** (1.5km). But turn left to reach all the accommodation reviewed here. We've mentioned in each review how far accommodation is from Hammir Circle.

◉ Sights & Activities

Safaris take place in the early morning and late afternoon, starting between 6am and 7am, and between 2pm and 3pm, depending on the time of year. Each safari lasts for around three hours. The mornings can be exceptionally chilly in the open vehicles, so bring warm clothes.

The best option is to travel by **gypsy** (six-person open-topped jeep; price per safari per person Indian/foreigner ₹528/927).

RAJASTHAN RANTHAMBHORE NATIONAL PARK

You still have a good chance of seeing a tiger from a **canter** (20-seater open-topped truck; Indian/foreigner ₹400/800), though sometimes other passengers can be rowdy.

Be aware that the rules for booking safaris (and prices) are prone to change. At the time of research, hotels and agents could no longer book you onto a safari. You either had to book online through the park's official website (www.rajasthanwildlife.com), which we highly recommend you do, or go in person to the **Safari Booking Office**, which was inconveniently located 1.5km from Hammir Circle, in the opposite direction to the park from the accommodation on Ranthambhore Rd. You couldn't book safaris in person in advance of the day you wanted to do the safari (you could only do that online). And to be sure of bagging a seat in a vehicle, you needed to start queuing at least an hour (if not two) before the safaris were due to begin, meaning a *very* early start for morning safaris!

To visit the magical 10th-century **Ranthambhore Fort** (admission free; ⏱ 6am-6pm) on the cheap, join the locals who go there to visit the temple dedicated to Ganesh. Shared jeeps (₹30 to ₹40 per person) go from the train station to the park entrance – say 'national park' and they'll know what you want. From there, other shared jeeps (₹20 per person) shuttle to and from the fort, which is inside the park.

🛏 Sleeping

Hotel Aditya Resort HOTEL $
(📱9414728468; www.adityaresort.com; Ranthambhore Rd; r ₹300-650; ❋ @) Friendly and good value, this place has a mixed bag of rooms, some with private bathrooms, some without. But all are clean and tidy, and there's a small rooftop restaurant (mains ₹50 to ₹100). About 2km from Hammir Circle, just past Hotel Tiger Safari Resort.

Asha Guest House HOTEL $
(📱9414910019; Ranthambhore Rd; r ₹400; ❋) Small hotel above a corner shop. Clean rooms have tiled flooring, TV and small en suite bathrooms. About 1km from Hammir Circle. No internet. No restaurant.

★ Hotel Tiger Safari Resort HOTEL $$
(📱221137; www.tigersafariresort.com; Ranthambhore Rd; r ₹1300-1800; ❋ @ 🛜 🏊) All-in, this is the best-value option. Rooms are clean, comfortable and spacious and come with cable TV, hot-water showers and free wi-fi.

There's a decent restaurant, a well-tended garden, a lovely little swimming pool and it's run by management who are knowledgable, honest and friendly. About 2km from Hammir Circle.

Vatika Resort HOTEL $$$
(📱222457; www.ranthambhorevatikaresort.com; Ranthambhore Rd; r ₹1800, incl breakfast/all meals ₹2250/3000; ❋ @ 🛜) Lovely little guesthouse with simple but immaculate rooms, each with terrace seating overlooking a beautifully tended, flower-filled garden. It's about 1km beyond the main strip of accommodation on Ranthambhore Rd (although still 5km before the park's main gate) so much quieter than elsewhere. About 3km from Hammir Circle.

Ranthambhore Bagh HOTEL $$$
(📱221728; www.ranthambhore.com; Ranthambhore Rd; r/tent ₹3522/4041, incl meals ₹5626/6141; ❋ @ 🛜) This has more of a safari-camp feel to it than other places on Ranthambhore Rd, with tents dotted around a forested garden as well as well-appointed rooms in the main building. There's no pool, but the gardens have swings and a slide, making this a solid choice for young families. About 2.5km from Hammir Circle.

✖ Eating & Drinking

All the accommodation we've listed does food, except Asha Guest House. Most can get you a bottle of beer if you ask.

Manisha Restaurant DHABA $
(Ranthambhore Rd; mains ₹50-100; ⏱ 7am-3.30pm & 5-9.30pm) Streetside shack serving cheap Indian nosh to customers perched on plastic chairs. A friendly, no-nonsense alternative to all the hotel restaurants. About 2km from Hammir Circle, on the right just before Hotel Tiger Safari Resort.

ℹ Information

There's an **ATM** just by Hammir Circle, as well as others by the train station.

Safari Booking Office (www.rajasthanwildlife.com) From Hammir Circle it's 1.5km. Turn right at the circle and office will eventually be on your right. It's ₹50 to ₹70 in an autorickshaw from accommodation on Ranthambhore Rd.

Tiger Track Internet (per hr ₹60; ⏱ 7am-10pm) It's 1½km from Hammir Circle, on the left before you reach Hotel Tiger Safari Resort.

Tourist Office (⏱ 9.30am-6pm Mon-Fri) At the train station; has a free map of the area.

Getting There & Away

BUS

There are very few direct buses to anywhere of interest so it's always preferable to take the train. Three direct buses leave for **Bundi** (6am, 6.45am & 2pm, ₹93, five hours) from the Tonk bus stand (take the second left out of the train station and the bus stand is on your right after the petrol station).

TRAIN

Trains run almost hourly to **Kota** (from where you can catch buses to **Bundi**). It takes less than two hours. Just buy an unreserved 'general ticket' (₹44) and pile in.

There are five daily trains to **Jaipur** (5.50am, 9.45am, 10.40am, 2.35pm and 6.55pm), although plenty of others run on selected days so you rarely have to wait more than an hour. The journey takes two hours. Unreserved 2nd-class seats cost ₹50; sleepers cost ₹140.

Five trains run daily to **Delhi** (6.28am, 7.05am, 12.30pm, 9.15pm and 11.02pm). Journey times vary. They arrive at 10.55am, 12.30pm, 6.35pm, 5.25am and 4.30am respectively. Sleeper/3AC tickets cost around ₹190/490.

Two daily trains go to **Agra**. The 13238 Kota-PNBE Express to Agra Cantonment leaves at 4.47pm, arrives at 11.05pm and costs ₹144 for a sleeper. The 59811 Haldighati Passenger leaves at 11.25pm, arrives at 6am and costs ₹85 for a sleeper.

For **Keoladeo Ghana National Park**, four daily trains go to **Bharatpur** (7.05am, 12.30pm, 4.47pm and 9.15pm). They take 2½ hours; 2nd-class seats/sleepers ₹87/140.

Only one direct train goes to **Udaipur**; the 12963 Mewar Express. It leaves at 11.50pm, arrives at 7.20am and costs ₹201/529 for a sleeper/3AC ticket.

SOUTHERN RAJASTHAN

Bundi

☎ 0747 / POP 102,000

A captivating town with narrow lanes of Brahmin-blue houses, lakes, hills, bazaars and a temple at every turn, Bundi is dominated by a fantastical palace of faded-parchment cupolas and loggias rising from the hillside above the town. Though an increasingly popular traveller hang-out, Bundi attracts nothing like the tourist crowds of places like Jaipur or Udaipur, nor are its streets choked with noisy, polluting vehicles or dense throngs of people. Few places in Rajasthan retain so much of the magical atmosphere of centuries past.

Bundi came into its own in the 12th century when a group of Chauhan nobles from Ajmer were pushed south by Mohammed of Ghori, they wrested the Bundi area from the Mina and Bhil tribes and made Bundi the capital of their kingdom, known as Hadoti.

◉ Sights

There are plenty of interesting villages to explore in the Bundi region. Akoda (a merchant's village) and Thikardha (with potteries) are both within cycling distance, around 6km north of town.

Bundi Palace   PALACE

(Garh Palace; Indian/foreigner ₹10/100, camera/video ₹50/100; ⊙8am-5pm) This extraordinary, partly decaying edifice – described by Kipling as 'the work of goblins rather than of men' – almost seems to grow out of the rock of the hillside it stands on. Though large sections are still closed up and left to the bats, the rooms that are open hold a series of fabulous, fading turquoise-and-gold murals that are the palace's chief treasure. The palace was constructed in the reign of Rao Raja Ratan Ji Heruled (Ratan Singh; 1607–31) and added to by his successors.

If you are going up to Taragarh as well as the palace, get tickets for both at the **palace entrance**. Once inside the palace's Hathi Pol (Elephant Gate), climb the stairs to the Ratan Daulat or Diwan-e-Aam, a hall of public audience with a white marble coronation throne. You then pass into the Chhatra Mahal, added by Rao Raja Chhatra Shabji in 1644, with some fine but rather weathered murals. Stairs lead up to the Phool Mahal (1607), whose murals include an immense royal procession, and then the Badal Mahal (Cloud Palace; also 1607), with Bundi's very best murals, including a wonderful Chinese-inspired ceiling, divided into petal shapes and decorated with peacocks and Krishnas.

Within the complex is the **Chitrasala**, a small 18th-century palace built by Rao Ummed Singh. To find it, exit through Bundi Palace's Elephant Gate and walk round the corner uphill. Above the palace's garden courtyard are several rooms covered in beautiful paintings. There are some great Krishna images, including a detail of him sitting up a tree playing the flute after stealing the clothes of the *gopis* (milkmaids). The back room to the right is the Sheesh Mahal, badly damaged but still featuring

Bundi

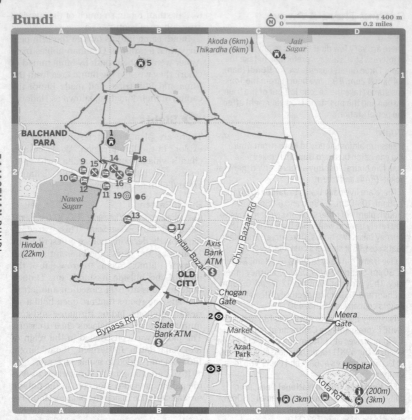

some beautiful inlaid glass, while in the front room there's an image of 18th-century Bundi itself.

Taragarh
FORT
(Star Fort; Indian/foreigner ₹10/100, camera/video ₹50/100; ⊘8am-5pm) This ramshackle, partly overgrown 14th-century fort, on the hilltop above the palace, is great to ramble around – but take a stick to battle the overgrown vegetation, help the knees on the steep climb and provide confidence when surrounded by testosterone-charged macaques. To reach it, just continue on the path up behind the Chitrasala.

Baoris
NOTABLE BUILDINGS
Bundi has around 60 beautiful *baori*s (stepwells), some right in the town centre. The majesty of many of them is unfortunately diminished by their lack of water today – a result of declining groundwater levels – and by the rubbish that collects in them which

no one bothers to clean up. The most impressive, **Raniji-ki-Baori** (Queen's Step-Well), is 46m deep and decorated with sinuous carvings, including the avatars of Lord Vishnu. The **Nagar Sagar Kund** is a pair of matching step-wells just outside the old city's Chogan Gate.

Sukh Mahal
PALACE
(⊘10am-5pm) About 2km north of the centre, the stately Sukh Mahal is a small palace, where Rudyard Kipling once stayed and wrote part of *Kim*. It's on the edge of the beautiful Jait Sagar, a picturesque 1.5km-long lake, flanked by hills.

Bhimlat Waterfall
WATERFALL
The impressive Bhimlat Waterfall is about 35km from Bundi. There's a temple at the top and a large natural pool you can swim in at the bottom. It's about ₹500 to ₹600 return in an autorickshaw.

Bundi

☞ Tours & Activities

Kukki's World   TOURS
(☏9828404527; www.kukkiworld.com; ⊙8.30am-
5pm) Passionate amateur archaeologist OP
'Kukki' Sharma conducts tours of the surrounding countryside, showing visitors the
numerous prehistoric rock paintings he has
found over the years, and swinging by the
odd tribal village en route. If you're on your
own, Kukki will take you on the back of his
motorbike at no extra cost. If you are in a
group of two or more, you'll need to hire a
car (about ₹1000 for a full day). Kukki has
a 'pay whatever you feel is fair' fee system.
As a guideline, other guides in Rajasthan
charge between ₹500 and ₹800 per day.

🛏 Sleeping

Haveli Elephant Stable   HERITAGE GUESTHOUSE $
(☏9928154064; rajnandini1979@gmail.com; r
₹250-350) This basic but unique guesthouse
used to house 15 royal elephants, but is now
a shanty home-from-home for backpackers with a sense of history. The six rooms
are simple affairs, with concrete walls and
floors (but 20ft-high ceilings!) and only one

has hot water in its attached bathroom. But
your hosts Raj and Neema are wonderfully
welcoming (as well as being good cooks)
and the huge garden – dotted with elephant
tether stones – is a great place to hang out.

Haveli Uma Megh   GUESTHOUSE $
(☏2442191; haveliumamegh@yahoo.com; r without
bathroom ₹200-350, r ₹400-650) Wonderfully
charming, albeit somewhat dilapidated,
this welcoming guesthouse has some pokey
rooms, but others that are bright and breezy
with lake views. The large well-kept lakeside
garden is perfect for food, tea or just lazing
around in.

RN Haveli   GUESTHOUSE $
(☏2443278,   9784486854;   rnhavelibundi@ya-
hoo.co.in; Rawle ka Chowk; s/d without bathroom
₹200/300, s/d ₹400/500, with AC ₹700/800;
❄) This old, slightly rundown house, with
a cute garden where you eat your meals, has
reasonably well-decorated rooms and delicious home cooking. A sound budget choice.

★**Haveli Braj Bhushanjee** HERITAGE HOTEL $$
(☏2442322; www.kiplingsbundi.com; r ₹750-4500;
❄🛜) This rambling, authentic, 200-year-old
haveli is run by the very helpful and knowl-
edgable Braj Bhushanjee family, descend-
ants of the former prime ministers of Bundi.
It's an enchanting place with original stone
interiors (plenty of low doorways), splendid
rooftop views, beautiful and well-preserved
murals, and all sorts of other historic and
valuable artefacts. The terrific range of ac-
commodation includes some lovely, recently
modernised rooms that are still in tradi-
tional style.

Haveli Katkoun   GUESTHOUSE $$
(☏2444311; http://havelikatkoun.free.fr; s from
₹350, d ₹500-1800; ❄) A reasonably modern
courtyard home that's been turned into a
friendly family guesthouse with spotless
rooms, hot-water showers and some palace
views.

Kasera Heritage View   GUESTHOUSE $$
(☏2444679; www.kaseraheritageview.com; s/d
from ₹500/700; ❄@🛜) Friendly, welcoming
guesthouse with bright, spacious, spotlessly
clean rooms, a rooftop cafe with sweeping
views and wi-fi throughout. Its nearby sister
property, **Kasera Paradise**, has similar ac-
commodation options (although rooms are
slightly gloomier) and is topped by the excel-
lent restaurant **Out of the Blue**.

Nawal Sagar Palace　HERITAGE HOTEL **$$$**
(2447050; www.nawalsagarpalace.com; r ₹1500-3000) This 300-year-old former royal residence, once home to the ladies of the court, has a beautiful location, with buildings, including a **restaurant** (mains ₹80-200), overlooking a grassy lawn, which in turn overlooks the lake. Rooms are huge, with some interesting old furniture (including enormous beds) and artwork, and some have lake views. There's no TV or internet and the atmosphere is far from homely, but there's a certain historical charm that's hard not to fall for.

Eating & Drinking

Tom & Jerry　MULTICUISINE **$**
(₹80-150; ☺8am-10pm; 🛜) A friendly, laid-back rooftop restaurant with Indian vegetarian dishes plus pasta and pizza.

Rainbow Cafe　MULTICUISINE **$**
(mains ₹100-150; ☺7am-11pm; 🛜) Bohemian ambience with chillout tunes, floor-cushion seating and two types of special (bhang) lassi. Located up on the roof to one side of the town's West Gate and caged off from marauding macaques with a bamboo trellis.

Out of the Blue　ITALIAN **$$**
(mains ₹130-220; ☺8am-10.30pm; 🛜) Following in the footsteps of the successful original branch in Pushkar, Bundi's Out of the Blue also offers excellent Italian pizza and homemade pasta as well as the best coffee in town (₹40 to ₹70).

Bundi's Coffee Comforts　CAFE
(coffee ₹40-80, tea ₹35-45; ☺9am-9pm) Hard to believe it now, but there was a time when this roadside cafe was the only place in Bundi with fresh coffee. It still does a number of coffee brews plus a range of teas, although for the real deal in Indian chai, sneak across to the simple tea stall next door (chai ₹10 to ₹20).

🛈 Information

There's an Axis Bank ATM on Sadar Bazar and a State Bank ATM west of Azad Park.

Roshan Tour & Travel (☺8am-10pm) An internet cafe (per hr ₹40), money-changer, bicycle-rental place (per day ₹80) and transport-ticket seller all rolled into one.

Tourist Office (2443697; Kota Rd; ☺9.30am-6pm Mon-Fri) This very helpful office has bus and train schedules, and offers free maps and helpful advice on most practical questions you can ask.

🛈 Getting There & Away

BUS
For Ranthambhore, it's usually quicker to catch a bus to Kota, then hop on a train to Sawai Madhopur.

Direct services from Bundi bus stand:
Ajmer (₹14, four hours, every 15 minutes from 5am to 11pm)
Jaipur (₹154, five hours, every 15 minutes from 5am to 1am)
Kota (₹27 to ₹29, one hour, every 15 minutes from 6am to 10pm)
Pushkar (₹150, 4½ hours, 8am)
Sawai Madhopur (₹93, four to five hours, 7.45am, noon and 2pm)
Udaipur (₹200, 6 hours, 7.15am, 9am and 11.15am)

TRAIN
There are no daily trains to Jaipur, Ajmer or Jodhpur. It's better to take a bus, or to catch a train from Kota or Chittorgarh.

Two trains travel daily to **Chittorgarh**. The 7.20am takes 3½ hours; the 9.38am takes 2½ hours. Sleepers cost ₹80 and ₹120 respectively.

Two daily trains also go to **Delhi** (Hazrat Nizamuddin). The 5.35pm takes 12 hours; the 10.42pm takes just eight hours. Sleepers cost ₹192 and ₹232 respectively.

Only one daily train goes to **Agra** (Agra Fort); the 59811 Haldighati Passenger (sleeper ₹109, 5.50pm, 12 hours).

And only one train goes daily to **Udaipur**; the 12963 Mewar Express (sleeper/3AC ₹157/398, 2.04am, five hours).

🛈 Getting Around

An autorickshaw to/from the train station costs ₹50 to ₹70, ₹70 to ₹100 at night.

Kota

0744 / POP 1,000,000

An easy day trip from Bundi, Kota is an industrial and commercial town on Rajasthan's only permanent river. You can take boat trips on the river here, but it's only really worth visiting Kota for its palace, which is, admittedly, quite spectacular.

⦿ Sights

City Palace & Fort　PALACE, FORT
The fort and the palace within it make up one of the largest such complexes in Rajasthan. This was the royal residence and centre of power, housing the Kota princedom's treasury, courts, arsenal, armed forces

and state offices. Some of its buildings are now used as schools. The **City Palace** (Indian/foreigner ₹20/150, camera/video ₹50/100; ⏰10am-4.30pm), entered through a gateway topped by rampant elephants, contains the excellent **Rao Madho Singh Museum**, where you'll find all the stuff necessary for a respectable Raj existence – silver furniture, an old-fashioned ice-cream maker, and ingenious, beautiful weapons. The oldest part of the palace dates from 1624. Downstairs is a durbar (royal audience) hall with beautiful mirror work, while the elegant, small-scale apartments upstairs contain exquisite, beautifully preserved paintings, particularly the hunting scenes for which Kota is renowned.

It's around ₹30 to ₹40 in an autorickshaw from the bus stand, and at least ₹60 from the train station.

ⓘ Information

Tourist Reception Centre (☎2327695; RTDC Hotel Chambal; ⏰9 30am-6pm Mon-Sat) Handy for its free map of the town. Turn left out of the bus stand, right at the second roundabout and it's on your right.

ⓘ Getting There & Away

BUS
Services from the main bus stand include:
Ajmer (₹165, four to five hours, half-hourly from 4.15am to 11.45pm)
Bundi (₹27 to ₹29, every 15 minutes from 6am to 10pm)
Chittorgarh (₹150, four hours, half-hourly from 5am to 7.30pm)
Jaipur (₹181, five hours, half-hourly from 4am to 11.45pm)
Pushkar (₹200, four to five hours, 7am and 11.15pm)

Udaipur (₹250, six to seven hours, hourly from 5am to 7.30pm)

TRAIN
For **Ranthambhore**, seven trains run daily to Sawai Madhopur (5.25am, 5.55am, 8am, 8.50am, 11.15am, 12.35pm and 2.50pm); many more run on selected days so you rarely have to wait more than an hour. The journey takes one to two hours. An unreserved 'general ticket' costs ₹44.

Likewise, trains run almost hourly to **Delhi** (sleepers ₹220, five to eight hours).

Five trains run daily to **Jaipur** (8am, 8.50am, 12.35pm, 2.55pm and 11.45pm), but again there are many others on selected days so you rarely have to wait long. It takes about four hours. Unreserved 'general ticket' seats cost around ₹70; sleepers around ₹150.

Three daily trains go to **Chittorgarh** (1.25am, 6.25am and 9am) and take three to four hours. Sleepers cost ₹80 to ₹120.

Six fast trains (around 14 hours) go daily to **Mumbai** (2.35pm, 5.35pm, 9.15pm, 9.55pm, 11.25pm and 11.45pm). Sleepers cost around ₹340.

ⓘ Getting Around

Minibuses and shared autorickshaws link the train station and central bus stand (₹6 to ₹10 per person). A private autorickshaw costs around ₹30.

Chittorgarh (Chittor)

☑ 01472 / POP 153,000

Chittorgarh, the fort (garh) at Chittor, is the largest fort complex in India, and a fascinating place to explore. It rises from the plains like a huge rock island, nearly 6km long and surrounded on all sides by 150m-plus cliffs. Its history epitomises Rajput romanticism, chivalry and tragedy, and it holds a special

MAJOR TRAINS FROM KOTA

DESTINATION	TRAIN	DEPARTURE TIME	ARRIVAL TIME	FARE (₹)
Chittorgarh	29020 Dehradun Express	9am	12.05pm	120/610 (A)
Delhi (Nizamuddin)	12964 Mewar Express	11.55pm	6.30am (next day)	220/582 (A)
Jaipur	12465 Ranthambhore Express	12.35pm	4.45pm	71/153 (B)
Mumbai	12956 JP-BCT Superfast	5.35pm	7.40am (next day)	349/931 (A)
Sawai Madhopur	12903 Golden Temple Mail	11.15am	12.25pm	44/140 (C)

Fares: (A) sleeper/3AC, (B) 2nd-class seat/sleeper, (C) sleeper/2A

Chittorgarh (Chittor)

place in the hearts of many Rajputs. Three times (in 1303, 1535 and 1568) Chittorgarh was under attack from a more powerful enemy; each time, its people chose death before dishonour, performing *jauhar*. The men donned saffron martyrs' robes and rode out from the fort to certain death, while the women and children immolated themselves on huge funeral pyres. After the last of the three sackings, Rana Udai Singh II fled to Udaipur, where he established a new capital for Mewar. In 1616, Jehangir returned Chittor to the Rajputs. There was no attempt at resettlement, though it was restored in 1905.

◉ Sights

Chittorgarh Fort   FORT
(Indian/foreigner ₹5/100, sound & light show Indian/foreigner ₹75/200; ☉ sunrise-sunset, Sound & Light Show sunset) A zigzag ascent of more than 1km starts at **Padal Pol** and leads

through six outer gateways to the main gate on the western side, **Ram Pol** (the former back entrance). Inside Ram Pol is a still-occupied village that takes up a small north-western part of the fort. You can enter the fort here, via the village, without having to pass the ticket office at the official entrance. To get to the ticket office, though, turn right after Ram Pol. The rest of the plateau is deserted except for the wonderful palaces, towers and temples that remain from its heyday, with the addition of a few more recent temples. A loop road runs around the plateau, which has a deer park at the southern end.

➜ Rana Kumbha Palace
Past the ticket office, you arrive almost immediately at this ruined palace group, which takes its name from the 15th-century ruler who renovated and added to earlier palaces on this site. The complex includes elephant and horse stables and a Shiva temple. Across from the palace is the **Sringar Chowri Tem-**

Chittorgarh (Chittor)

ple, a Jain temple built by Rana Kumbha's treasurer in 1448 and adorned with attractive, intricate carvings of elephants, musicians and deities. Just past here is **Badi Pol**, the gateway through which you pass to access the rest of the fort.

➡ **Meera & Kumbha Shyam Temples**

Both these temples southeast of the Rana Kumbha Palace were built by Rana Kumbha in the ornate Indo-Aryan style, with classic, tall *sikharas* (spires). The Meera Temple, the smaller of the two, is now associated with the mystic-poetess Meerabai, a 16th-century Mewar royal who was poisoned by her brother-in-law but survived due to the blessings of Krishna. The Kumbha Shyam Temple is dedicated to Vishnu and its carved panels illustrate 15th-century Mewar life.

➡ **Tower of Victory**

The glorious Tower of Victory (Jaya Stambha), symbol of Chittorgarh, was erected by Rana Kumbha in the 1440s, probably to commemorate a victory over Mahmud Khilji of Malwa. Dedicated to Vishnu, it rises 37m in nine exquisitely carved storeys, and you can climb the 157 narrow stairs (the interior is also carved) to the 8th floor, from where there's a good view of the area.

Below the tower, to the southwest, is the **Mahasati** area where there are many *sati* (widow suicide by immolation) stones – this was the royal cremation ground and was also where 13,000 women committed *jauhar* in 1535. The **Sammidheshwar Temple**, built in the 6th century and restored in 1427, is nearby. Notable among its intricate carving is a Trimurti (Three-Faced) figure of Shiva.

➡ **Gaumukh Reservoir**

Walk down beyond the Sammidheshwar Temple and at the edge of the cliff is a deep tank, the Gaumukh Reservoir, where you can feed the fish. The reservoir takes its name from a spring that feeds the tank from a *gaumukh* (cow's mouth) carved into the cliffside.

➡ **Padmini's Palace**

Continuing south, you reach the **Kalika Mata Temple** (across from Padmini's Palace, Fort), an 8th-century sun temple damaged during the first sacking of Chittorgarh and then converted to a temple for the goddess Kali in the 14th century. Padmini's Palace stands about 250m further south, beside a small lake with a central pavilion. Legend relates that, as Padmini sat in this pavilion, Ala-ud-din Khilji saw her reflection in mirrors from the palace, and this glimpse convinced him to destroy Chittorgarh in order to possess her.

➡ **Surajpol & Tower of Fame**

Surajpol, on the fort's east side, was the main gate and offers fantastic views across the empty plains. A little further north, the 24m-high Tower of Fame (Kirtti Stambha) is older (dating from 1301) and smaller than the Tower of Victory. Built by a Jain merchant, the tower is dedicated to Adinath, the first Jain *tirthankar* (one of the 24 revered Jain teachers), and is decorated with naked figures of various other *tirthankars*, indicating that it is a monument of the Digambara (sky-clad) order. Next door is a 14th-century Jain temple.

⌂ Sleeping & Eating

If you fancy a beer with your meal, head to the restaurant at Hotel Pratap Palace.

Hotel Bhagwati   HOTEL **$**

(☑ 246226; City Rd; s ₹200-300, d ₹300-400, s/d with AC ₹550/650) The best of Chittorgarh's budget bunch, Bhagwati has more charm than its rivals. Rooms surround an open-air inner courtyard and are simple but kept clean, and come with TV and a bathroom with squat toilet.

Hotel Pratap Palace — HOTEL $$
(☎240099; www.hotelpratappalacechittaurgarh. com; r without/with AC ₹1250/1850; ❄ @) The Pratap's rooms are smart, spacious and clean, and come with cute bay-window seating. Staff members are helpful and there's a good **restaurant** (mains ₹150-250; ☺7am-10.30pm) with tables spilling out into a pleasant garden. They have wi-fi in the lobby, and even a bar (beer ₹250). The only downside is the location – a long trek from the fort (although admittedly handy for the train station).

★Padmini Haveli — HERITAGE HOTEL $$$
(☎241251, 94141410090; www.thepadminihaveli. com; Annapoorna Temple Rd, Shah Chowk, Chittorgarh Fort; r incl breakfast ₹3200; ❄ @ 🛜) Housed in a 90-year-old converted school, and the only nonpilgrim accommodation within the fort itself, this fabulous guesthouse was designed by a Swiss couple, but is now run locally. Stylish but understated rooms come with spotless, granite-clad bathrooms, and are dotted around open-air courtyards in a design that makes wonderful use of limited space. There's home-cooked vegetarian meals (in fact, you can just drop by for lunch; ₹400), rooftop views, bicycle rental (per day ₹100) and free wi-fi throughout. The staff (who speak French and English) can act as guides for your exploration of the fort (per three-hour tour ₹500). The village location is charming too. After walking through Ram Pol on your way up to the fort, take the lane at the far left-hand corner of the small square, then take the first left (just after the lane bears round to the right). Walk a short way down here then take the second right (just before a tall pink build-

ing) and look for a whitewashed building with a chunky wooden door as its entrance. There's no number and no name, but if you ask locals for 'haveli' they'll point you in the right direction.

Chokhi Dhani
Garden Family Restaurant — DHABA $
(Bundi Rd; mains ₹50-130; ☺11am-10pm) Fan-cooled roadside *dhaba* with extra seating in the backyard. Does a range of good-value vegetarian dishes including South Indian and thalis.

Saffire Garden Restaurant — MULTICUISINE $$
(City Rd; mains ₹100-150; ☺8am-10pm) Sit at tables on the small, tree-shaded lawn or inside the air-conditioned room at the back, and tuck into a variety of standard but tasty-enough Indian and Chinese dishes. Saffire is located behind – and shares its grounds with – Hotel Vishal, a decent budget hotel (rooms from ₹500) which, annoyingly, tends not to accept foreigners.

ⓘ Information
You can access an ATM and change money at the **SBBJ** (Bhilwara Rd), and there's an ATM at **SBI** (Bundi Rd).

Mahavir Cyber Cafe (Collectorate Circle; per hr ₹25; ☺9am-10pm)

Tourist Reception Centre (☎241089; Station Rd; ☺10am-1.30pm & 2-5pm Mon-Sat) Friendly and helpful, with a town map and brochure to give out.

ⓘ Getting There & Away
BUS
There are no direct buses to Bundi. Services from Chittorgarh include:

Ajmer (₹149, four hours, hourly from 7am to 3pm)

MAJOR TRAINS FROM CHITTORGARH

DESTINATION	TRAIN	DEPARTURE TIME	ARRIVAL TIME	FARE (₹)
Ajmer	12991 Udaipur-Jaipur Exp	8.42am	11.25pm	75/273/395 (A)
Bundi	29019 NMH-Kota Exp	2.55pm	5.33pm	120/610 (B)
Delhi (Nizamuddin)	12964 Mewat Exp	8.50pm	6.30am	274/742 (C)
Jaipur	12991 Udaipur-Jaipur Exp	8.42am	1.25pm	102/374/565 (A)
Sawai Madhopur	29019 NMH-Kota Exp	2.55pm	9.10pm	146/610 (B)
Udaipur	19329 Udaipur City Exp	4.35pm	7pm	120/244 (C)

Fares: (A) 2nd-class seat/AC chair/1st-class seat, (B) sleeper/2AC, (C) sleeper/3AC

Jaipur (₹226-243, seven hours, every 90 minutes from 7.15am to 10pm)

Kota (₹150, four hours, hourly from 5.15am to 6.45pm)

Pushkar (₹159, four to five hours, 10am)

Udaipur (₹90, 2½ hours, half-hourly from 6am to 10pm)

TRAIN

Three trains run daily to **Bundi** (2pm, 2.55pm and 8.50pm). They take 3½, 2½ and 2 hours respectively. Sleepers cost ₹120.

Five daily trains make the two-hour trip to **Udaipur** (4.10am, 5.05am, 5.33am, 4.35pm and 7.25pm). Unreserved 'general tickets' cost around ₹45; sleepers around ₹120.

Three trains make the 5½-hour trip to **Jaipur** daily (8.42am, 12.35am and 2.45am). Sleepers cost around ₹160.

Three trains also make the three-hour trip to **Ajmer** daily (8.42am, 10.10am and 7.30pm). Sleepers cost around ₹160. Unreserved 2nd-class seats cost ₹60.

Two fast trains go to **Delhi** (7.30pm and 8.50pm), arriving at 5.10am and 6.30am respectively.

For **Ranthambhore**, three trains (varying greatly in speed) travel daily to Sawai Madhopur (2pm, 2.55pm and 8.50pm). They take nine, six and four hours respectively. Sleepers cost around ₹150.

ⓘ Getting Around

A full tour of the fort by autorickshaw should cost around ₹300 return. You can arrange this yourself in town. Hotel Pratap Palace gives jeep tours of the fort for ₹600.

Udaipur

♪ 0294 / POP 451,000

Beside shimmering Lake Pichola, with the ochre and purple ridges of the wooded Aravalli Hills stretching away in every direction, Udaipur has a romantic setting unmatched in Rajasthan and arguably in all India. Fantastical palaces, temples, *havelis* and countless narrow, crooked, colourful streets add the human counterpoint to the city's natural charms. Its tag of 'the most romantic spot on the continent of India' was first applied in 1829 by Colonel James Tod, the East India Company's first Political Agent in the region. Today the romance is wearing ever so slightly thin as Udaipur strains to exploit this reputation for tourist rupees. In the parts of the city nearest the lake, almost every building is a hotel, shop, restaurant, travel agent – or

all four rolled into one – and noisy, dirty traffic clogs some of the streets that were made for people and donkeys.

Take a step back from the hustle, however, and Udaipur still has its magic, not just in its marvellous palaces and monuments but in its matchless setting, the tranquillity of boat rides on the lake, the bustle of its ancient bazaars, the quaint old-world feel of its better hotels, its tempting shops and lovely surrounding countryside, which can be explored on foot, by bike or on horseback.

Udaipur was founded in 1568 by Maharana Udai Singh II following the final sacking of Chittorgarh by the Mughal emperor Akbar. This new capital of Mewar had a much less vulnerable location than Chittorgarh. Mewar still had to contend with repeated invasions by the Mughals and, later, the Marathas, until British intervention in the early 19th century. This resulted in a treaty that protected Udaipur from invaders while allowing Mewar's rulers to remain effectively all-powerful in internal affairs. The ex-royal family remains influential and in recent decades has been the driving force behind the rise of Udaipur as a tourist destination.

⊙ Sights

Lake Pichola LAKE

(boat rides adult/child 10am-2pm ₹200/100, 3-5pm ₹500/250; ⊙ boat rides 10am-5pm) Limpid and large, Lake Pichola reflects the cool grey-blue mountains on its rippling mirror-like surface. It was enlarged by Maharana Udai Singh II, following his foundation of the city, by flooding Picholi village, which gave the lake its name. The lake is now 4km long and 3km wide, but remains shallow and dries up completely in severe droughts. The City Palace complex, including the gardens at its south end, extends nearly 1km along the lake's eastern shore.

Boat rides leave roughly hourly from Rameshwar Ghat, within the City Palace complex (note, you have to pay ₹25 to enter). The trips make a stop at Jagmandir Island, where you can stay for as long as you like before taking any boat back. Take your own drinks and snacks, though, because those sold on the island are extortionately expensive. You can also take 30-minute boat rides from **Lal Ghat** (₹200 per person; ⊙ 9.30am and 5pm), without the need to enter the City Palace complex.

RAJASTHAN UDAIPUR

Udaipur

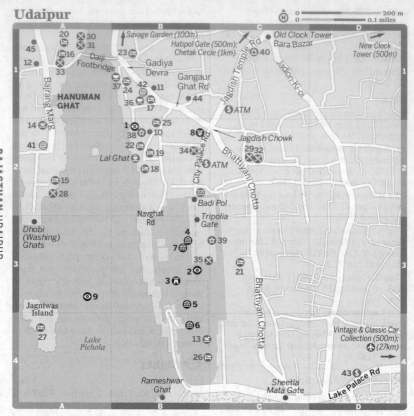

➤ Jagniwas Island

The world-famous Lake Palace hotel island of Jagniwas is about 15,000 sq m in size, entirely covered by the opulent palace built by Maharana Jagat Singh II in 1754. Once the royal summer palace, it was greatly extended and converted into the **Lake Palace hotel** in the 1960s by Maharana Bhagwat Singh, and it is now in the hands of the Indian-owned Taj hotel group. One of the world's top luxury hotels, with gleaming courtyards, lotus ponds and a pool shaded by a mango tree, it has been largely responsible for putting Udaipur on the international tourist map. You may also remember it from that classic Bond film, *Octopussy*, along with the Shiv Niwas Palace and the Monsoon Palace. Sadly, the Taj Lake Palace doesn't welcome casual visitors.

➤ Jagmandir Island

The palace on Jagmandir Island, about 800m south of Jagniwas, was built by Ma-harana Karan Singh in 1620, added to by his successor Maharana Jagat Singh, and then changed very little until the last few years when it was partly converted into another (smaller) hotel. When lit up at night it has more romantic sparkle to it than the Lake Palace. With its entrance flanked by a row of enormous stone elephants, the island has an ornate 17th-century tower, the Gol Mahal, carved from bluestone and containing a small exhibit on Jagmandir's history, plus a garden and lovely views across the lake. As well as the seven hotel rooms, the island has a restaurant, bar and spa, which are open to visitors.

City Palace
PALACE

(www.eternalmewar.in; adult/child ₹25/15, not charged if visiting City Palace Museum; ⊙ 7am–11pm) Surmounted by balconies, towers and cupolas towering over the lake, the imposing City Palace is Rajasthan's largest palace, with a facade 244m long and 30.4m high.

Udaipur

Construction was begun by Maharana Udai Singh II, the city's founder, and it later became a conglomeration of structures built and extended by various maharanas, though it still manages to retain a surprising uniformity of design.

Most people enter the complex at **Badi Pol** (Great Gate; 1615) at the north end, but you can also enter at **Sheetla Mata Gate** to the south. Tickets for the City Palace Museum are sold at both entrances. Note, you must pay the ₹25 City Palace entrance ticket in order to pass south through **Chandra Chowk Gate**, en route to the Crystal Gallery or Rameshwar Ghat for the boat rides, even if you have a City Palace Museum ticket.

Inside Badi Pol, eight arches on the left commemorate the eight times maharanas were weighed here and their weight in gold or silver distributed to the lucky locals. You then pass through the three-arched **Tripolia Gate** (1711) into a large courtyard, **Manek Chowk**. Spot the tiger-catching cage, which worked rather like an oversized mousetrap, and the smaller one for leopards.

City Palace Museum　　　　MUSEUM
(adult/child ₹100/50, camera or video ₹200, audio guide ₹225, human guide ₹250; ◷ 9.30am-5.30pm, last entry 4.30pm) The main part of the palace is open as the City Palace Museum, with rooms extravagantly decorated with mirrors, tiles and paintings, and housing a large, varied collection of artefacts. It's entered from **Ganesh Chowk**, which you reach from Manek Chowk.

The City Palace Museum begins with the **Rai Angan** (Royal Courtyard), the very spot where Udai Singh met the sage who told him to build a city here. Rooms along one side contain historical paintings, including several of the Battle of Haldighati (1576), in which Mewar forces under Maharana Pratap, one of the great Rajput heroes, gallantly fought the army of Mughal emperor Akbar to a stalemate. As you move through the palace, highlights include the **Baadi Mahal** (1699), where a pretty central garden gives fine views over the city. **Kishan (Krishna) Vilas** has a remarkable collection of miniatures from the time of Maharana Bhim Singh (1778–1828). The story goes that Bhim Singh's daughter Krishna Kumari drank a fatal cup of poison here to solve the dilemma of rival princely suitors from Jaipur and Jodhpur who were both threatening to invade Mewar if she didn't marry them. The **Surya Choupad** boasts a huge, ornamental sun – the symbol of the sun-descended Mewar dynasty – and opens into **Mor Chowk** (Peacock Courtyard) with its lovely mosaics of peacocks, the favourite Rajasthani bird. The south end of the museum comprises the **Zenana Mahal**, the royal ladies' quarters built in the 17th century. It now contains a long picture gallery with lots of royal hunting scenes. The Zenana Mahal's central courtyard, **Laxmi Chowk**, contains a beautiful white pavilion and a stable of howdahs, palanquins and other people carriers.

Crystal Gallery
GALLERY

(adult/child incl compulsory audio guide ₹500/300, plus ₹25 City Palace ticket; ⏰9am-7pm) The Crystal Gallery houses rare crystal that Maharana Sajjan Singh ordered from F&C Osler & Co in England in 1877. The maharana died before it arrived, and all the items stayed forgotten and packed up in boxes for 110 years. The extraordinary, extravagant

---

ANIMAL AID UNLIMITED

This spacious **animal refuge** (☎9950531639, 9352511435; www.animalaidunlimited.com) treats around 200 street animals a day (mainly dogs, donkeys and cows) and answers more than 3000 emergency rescue calls a year. The refuge welcomes volunteers and visitors: make contact in advance to fix a time between 9am and 5pm any day. It's in Badi village, 7km northwest of Udaipur: a round trip by autorickshaw, including waiting time, costs around ₹250. Call Animal Aid Unlimited if you see an injured or ill street animal in Udaipur.

---

collection includes crystal chairs, sofas, tables and even beds. Below, and included on the same admission ticket – along with tea or a soft drink in the Gallery Restaurant – is the grand **Durbar Hall**, one of India's largest and most lavish royal reception halls, with some of the country's biggest chandeliers. Tickets are available at Badi Pol, at Chandra Chowk Gate or at the Crystal Gallery entrance.

Government Museum
MUSEUM

(Indian/foreigner ₹5/50; ⏰9.45am-5.15pm Tue-Sun) Right beside the entrance to the City Palace Museum, this small, quirky museum has a splendid collection of jewel-like miniature paintings of the Mewar school and a turban that belonged to Shah Jahan, creator of the Taj Mahal. Stranger exhibits include a stuffed monkey holding a lamp.

Jagdish Temple
HINDU TEMPLE

(⏰5.30am-2pm & 4-10pm) Entered by a steep, elephant-flanked flight of steps 150m north of the City Palace's Badi Pol entrance, this busy Indo-Aryan temple was built by Maharana Jagat Singh in 1651. The wonderfully carved main structure enshrines a black stone image of Vishnu as Jagannath, Lord of the Universe; there's a brass image of the Garuda (Vishnu's man-bird vehicle) in a shrine facing the main structure.

Bagore-ki-Haveli
NOTABLE BUILDING

(admission ₹30; ⏰10am-5pm) This gracious 18th-century *haveli,* set on the water's edge in the Gangaur Ghat area, was built by a Mewar prime minister and has been carefully restored. There are 138 rooms set around courtyards on three levels, some arranged to evoke the period during which the house was inhabited, and others housing cultural displays, including – intriguingly enough – the world's biggest turban. The *haveli* also houses an interesting art gallery, featuring contemporary and folk art, and an eclectic selection of world-famous monuments lovingly carved out of polystyrene.

Sajjan Garh (Monsoon Palace)
PALACE

Perched on top of a distant mountain like a fairy-tale castle, this melancholy, neglected late 19th-century palace was constructed by Maharana Sajjan Singh. Originally an astronomical centre, it became a monsoon palace and hunting lodge. Now government owned, it's in a sadly dilapidated state. However, visitors stream up here for the marvellous views, particularly at sunset. It's 5km west of the old city as the crow flies, about 9km by the winding road. At the foot of the hill you enter the 5-sq-km **Sajjan Garh Wildlife Sanctuary** (Indian/foreigner ₹20/160, car ₹60, camera/video free/₹200). A good way to visit is with the daily sunset excursion in a minivan driven by an enterprising **taxi driver** (📞 9784400120) who picks up tourists at the entrance to Bagore-ki-Haveli every day at 5pm. The round trip costs ₹200 per person, including waiting time. His minivan has 'Monsoon Palace-Sajjangarh Fort' written across the front of it. You have to pay the ₹160-sanctuary fee yourself as you enter the park. Alternatively, take an autorickshaw (₹200 including waiting time) to the sanctuary gate, which they are not allowed to pass. Taxis then ferry people the final 4km up to the palace for about ₹100 per person.

Vintage & Classic Car Collection MUSEUM (Lake Palace Rd, Garden Hotel; admission ₹150, incl lunch or dinner ₹250; ⊙ 9am-9pm) The maharanas' car collection makes a fascinating diversion, both for what it tells about their elite lifestyle and for the vintage vehicles themselves. Housed in the former state garage are 22 splendid vehicles, including a seven-seat 1938 Cadillac complete with purdah system, the beautiful 1934 Rolls-Royce Phantom used in *Octopussy* and the Cadillac convertible that whisked Queen Elizabeth II to the airport in 1961. If you enjoy an unlimited vegetarian thali (and let's face it, who doesn't?), the combined museum-and-meal ticket is a very good option (lunch 11.30am to 3pm, dinner 7.30pm to 10pm). It's a 10-minute walk east along Lake Palace Rd (bear to the right at the staggered junction).

🏃 Activities

Horse Riding

The wooded hills, villages and lakes around Udaipur make lovely riding country. Several operators offer horse rides from a couple of hours to multi-day safaris. Expect to pay about ₹900 for a half-day ride, including lunch or snacks and transport to/from your hotel.

Krishna Ranch HORSE RIDING (📞 9828059505; www.krishnaranch.com; full-day incl lunch ₹1200) A Dutch-Indian company specialising in guided horse safaris (but also does guided walks) through the beautiful countryside around Udaipur. The ranch, where accommodation is also available

(single/double including meals and pick-up ₹1500/2500), is near Badi village, around 7km from town. Can also be contacted through Kumbha Palace guesthouse.

Massage

Ayurvedic Body Care AYURVEDA (📞 2413816; www.ayurvedicbodycare.com; 38 Lal Ghat; ⊙ 10am-8pm) A small and popular old-city operation offering ayurvedic massage at reasonable prices, including a 15-minute head, back or foot massage (₹250) and a 50-minute full-body massage (₹750). It also has ayurvedic products such as oils, moisturisers, shampoos and soaps for sale.

Walking

The horse-riding specialists at Krishna Ranch also offer guided hikes through the same beautiful countryside, passing through small tribal villages en route. Multi-day hikes can be arranged too.

Millets of Mewar CITY WALKS (📞 8890419048; www.milletsofmewar.com) Management at the excellent restaurant Millets of Mewar also help organise 2½-hour city walking tours where you can meet local artisans who live and work in Udaipur. Tours, which should be booked a day in advance, start from the restaurant at 10am.

Swimming

Several hotels allow nonguests to use their pools, including **Karohi Haveli** (₹200) and **Udai Kothi** (₹300), which has the only rooftop pool in town.

🍴 Courses

Cooking

Apart from organising city walks, the restaurant Millets of Mewar also runs cooking classes (₹500); choose any five dishes from their wonderful menu and staff will teach you how to cook them.

Queen Cafe COOKING (📞 2430875, 9783786028; 14 Bajrang Marg, Hanuman Ghat; 2/4hr class ₹900/1500; ⊙ 8.30am) Learn how to make Indian tea, flat breads, rice and four types of curries with the affable Meenu; owner, chef and busy mum at this homely little eatery. Class sizes: two to five people.

Music

Prem Musical Instruments MUSIC (📞 2430599; 28 Gadiya Devra; per hr ₹400; ⊙ 10.30am-6pm) Suresh Kumar Prajapati is a successful local musician who gives sitar, tabla and flute lessons. He also sells and repairs instruments (sitars from ₹8500) and can arrange performances. You can buy signed CDs of his performances for around ₹300.

Painting

Hotel Krishna Niwas PAINTING
(☑ 2420163; www.hotelkrishnaniwas.com; 35 Lal Ghat; 2hr class ₹850; ⊙ 11am-7pm) Jairaj Soni is a renowned artist who teaches miniature and classical painting. You can buy miniature paintings here too.

Ashoka Arts PAINTING
(Hotel Gangaur Palace; per hr ₹150) Here you can learn the basics of classic miniature painting.

✹ Festivals & Events

In March or April the procession-heavy **Mewar Festival** is Udaipur's own version of the springtime Gangaur festival, with free cultural programs.

🛏 Sleeping

Accommodation clusters where most people want to stay – close to the lake, especially on its eastern side near Lal Ghat. This area is a tangle of streets and lanes (some quiet, some busy and noisy), close to the City Palace and Jagdish Temple. It's Udaipur's tourist epicentre and the streets are strung not just with lodgings but also with tourist-oriented eateries and shops whose owners will be doing their best to tempt you in.

Directly across the water from Lal Ghat, Hanuman Ghat has a slightly more local vibe and often better views. It's much more hassle-free, though you're certainly not out of the tourist zone.

To bypass rickshaw drivers looking for commissions from hotels, use the prepaid autorickshaw stand outside the train station. If you're heading for the Lal Ghat area to find accommodation, you can avoid discussions about individual lodgings by taking a autorickshaw to the nearby Jagdish Temple (about ₹40 from the main bus stand), then walking.

🛏 Lal Ghat Area

Lal Ghat Guest House GUESTHOUSE $
(☑ 2525301; www.lalghat.com; 33 Lal Ghat; dm ₹150, r without/with bathroom from ₹200/600; ✷ @ 🛜) This mellow guesthouse by the lake

has been run by the same family since 1982 and was one of the first to open in Udaipur. It's still an excellent budget choice, with an amazing variety of older and newer rooms. Most rooms have lake views and those in the older part of the building (17th century) have plenty of character, although some are pretty basic. There's a small kitchen for self-caterers, wi-fi in some areas and the shaded central courtyard is a pleasant space.

Nukkad Guest House GUESTHOUSE $
(☑ 2411403; nukkad_raju@yahoo.com; 56 Ganesh Ghati; r ₹300-500, s/d without bathroom ₹100/200; @ 🛜) Always busy with travellers, Nukkad has a relaxed atmosphere and a sociable, breezy upstairs restaurant with good Indian and international dishes (mains ₹60 to ₹85). Your hosts Raju and Kala are helpful, and you can join afternoon cooking classes and morning yoga sessions without stepping out the door. Rooms are simple, fan-cooled, clean and decent value; there's plenty of hot water and many rooms have cushioned window seats. Wi-fi wasn't working when we were here, but should be available.

Jheel Palace Guest House GUESTHOUSE $$
(☑ 2421352; www.jheelguesthouse.com; 56 Gangaur Ghat; r ₹1000-3000; ✷ 🛜) Right on the lake edge (when the lake is full), Jheel Palace has three nice rooms with little balconies and four-poster beds, and three more ordinary ones. All are small but well kept. Staff are accommodating and hands-off, and there's a good Brahmin pure veg **rooftop restaurant** (mains ₹95-125, no beer). To one side of the the lobby, and right beside the water's edge, is **Jheel's Ginger Coffee Bar** (coffee ₹50-100; ⊙ 8am-8pm), which has free wi-fi and does excellent coffee. Across the street, **Old Jheel Guest House** has three budget rooms (₹300, ₹400 and ₹500) which are clean and comfortable, if a little spartan.

Hotel Gangaur Palace HERITAGE HOTEL $$
(☑ 2422303; www.ashokahaveli.com; Gadiya Devra; s ₹400-2000, d ₹500-2500; ✷ @ 🛜) This elaborate and faded 250-year-old *haveli* is set around a stone-pillared courtyard, with a wide assortment of rooms on several floors. It's gradually moving upmarket and rooms range from windowless with flaking paint to bright and recently decorated with lake views. The hotel also boasts an in-house palm reader, an art school, the good Cafe Namaste and a rooftop restaurant. Wi-fi reaches to some rooms.

Poonam Haveli
HOTEL **$$**

(2410303; www.hotelpoonamhaveli.com; 39 Lal Ghat; r ₹800-1800; ✳@🖥) A fairly modern place decked out in traditional style, friendly Poonam has 16 spacious, spotlessly clean rooms with big beds and spare but tasteful decor, plus pleasant sitting areas. None of the rooms enjoys lake views, but the rooftop restaurant does, and boasts 'real Italian' pizzas among the usual Indian and traveller fare. The ground-floor cafe **Bon Appetite** (⊙8am-10pm) does filter coffee (from ₹60) and cakes. Wi-fi throughout.

★ Jagat Niwas
Palace Hotel
HERITAGE HOTEL **$$$**

(2420133; www.jagatniwaspalace.com; 23-25 Lal Ghat; non-lake facing ₹1850-2950, lake facing ₹3250-4250 ; ✳@🖥) This leading Lal Ghat hotel set in two converted lakeside *havelis* takes the location cake. The lake-view rooms are charming, with carved wooden furniture, cushioned window seats and pretty prints. Non-lake-facing rooms are almost as comfortable and attractive, and considerably cheaper. The building is full of character with lots of attractive sitting areas, terraces and courtyards, and it makes the most of its position with a picture-perfect rooftop restaurant. Wi-fi in lobby only.

Kankarwa Haveli
HERITAGE HOTEL **$$$**

(2411457; www.kankarwahaveli.com; 26 Lal Ghat; r incl breakfast ₹3000-5000; ✳@🖥) This is one of Udaipur's few hotels that is a genuine old *haveli*. It's right by the lake, and the white-washed rooms, set around a courtyard, have a lovely simplicity with splashes of colour. They are very small for the price, but have bags of character and the pricier ones look right onto Lake Pichola. Wi-fi in ground-floor courtyard only.

Jaiwana Haveli
HOTEL **$$$**

(2411103; www.jaiwanahaveli.com; 14 Lal Ghat; s/d ₹1690/2250; ✳@🖥) Professionally run by two helpful, efficient brothers, this smart hotel has spotless, unfussy rooms with good beds, some decorated with attractive block-printed fabrics. Book corner room 11, 21 or 31 for views. Wi-fi throughout.

🛏 Hanuman Ghat Area

★ Dream Heaven
GUESTHOUSE **$**

(2431038; www.dreamheaven.co.in; r ₹200-1000; ✳@🖥) The best-value digs in Udaipur, Dream Heaven has a fabulous location (the views from the rooftop restaurant are sublime), simple but well-looked-after rooms and a friendly manager who is very helpful without being too keen to please. Deservedly popular. Wi-fi only on rooftop and upper rooms.

Karohi Haveli
HERITAGE HOTEL **$$$**

(2430026; www.karohihaveli.com; r from ₹3500; ✳@🖥🖥) A beautifully renovated, three-storey 19th-century *haveli* with tastefully-decorated rooms off a cool central marble courtyard. Quiet but welcoming. Has a rooftop restaurant, bar, garden lawn with lake views, lovely pool (nonguests ₹200) and wi-fi throughout.

Amet Haveli
HERITAGE HOTEL **$$$**

(2431085; www.amethaveliudaipur.com; s/d ₹4800/5700; ✳@🖥) This 350-year-old heritage building on the lake shore has delightful rooms with cushioned window seats and coloured glass with little shutters. They're set around a pretty little courtyard and pond. Splurge on one with a balcony or giant bathtub. One of Udaipur's most romantic restaurants, Ambrai, is part of the hotel. A swimming pool was under construction at the time of research.

🛏 City Palace Area

Kumbha Palace
GUESTHOUSE **$$**

(2422702, 9828059505; www.hotelkumbhapalace.com; 104 Bhattiyani Chotta; s/d ₹500/550, with AC ₹900; ✳@🖥) This wonderfully peaceful place, tucked up a quiet alley off Bhattiyani Chotta, is run by the same couple behind the excellent horse-riding company at Krishna Ranch. This property overlooks a lush lawn which is shaded by a section of the huge City Palace wall and is a lovely place to relax. The 10 rooms are simple but comfortable (just one has air-con), and the restaurant knows how to satisfy homesick travellers. Wi-fi throughout.

★ Taj Lake Palace
HERITAGE HOTEL **$$$**

(2428800; www.tajhotels.com; r from ₹40,000; ✳@🖥🖥) The icon of Udaipur, this romantic white-marble palace seemingly floating on the lake is extraordinary, with open-air courtyards, lotus ponds and a small, mango-tree-shaded pool. Rooms are hung with breezy silks and filled with carved furniture. Service is superb. Access is by boat from the hotel's own jetty in the City Palace gardens. Rates can vary a lot with season and demand: check the website.

Shiv Niwas Palace Hotel   HERITAGE HOTEL $$$
(☑2528016; www.eternalmewar.in; City Palace Complex; r from ₹15,000; ❄@🛜≋) This hotel, in the former palace guest quarters, has opulent common areas like its pool courtyard, bar and lovely lawn garden with a 30m-long royal procession mural. Some of the suites are truly palatial, filled with fountains and silver, but the standard rooms are not great value. Go for a suite, or just come for a drink (beer from ₹475), meal (mains ₹500 to ₹1000), or swim in the gorgeous marble **pool** (nonguests ₹300; ⊙9am-6pm). Rates drop dramatically from April to September.

🛏 Further Afield

⭐**Krishna Ranch**   COTTAGES $$
(☑3291478, 9602192902; www.krishnaranch.com; s/d incl meals ₹1500/2500) 🌿 This delightful countryside retreat has five cottages set around the grounds of a small farm. Each comes with attached bathroom (with solar-heated hot-water shower), tasteful decor and farm views. All meals are included in the price and are prepared using organic produce grown on the farm. It's an ideal base for the hikes and horse treks which the management – a Dutch-Indian couple – organises from here, although you don't have to sign up for the treks to stay. The ranch is 7km from town, near the village of Badi, but there's free pick-up from Udaipur.

🍴 Eating

Udaipur has scores of sun-kissed rooftop cafes, many with mesmerising lake views but often with uninspired multicuisine fare. Fortunately there's also a healthy number of places putting a bit more thought into their food; beer is plentiful.

🍴 Lal Ghat Area

Lotus Cafe   MULTICUISINE $
(15 Bhattiyani Chotta; dishes ₹50-150; ⊙9am-10.30pm) Run by an Australian-Indian couple, this funky little restaurant produces fabulous chicken dishes (predominantly Indian, including some Rajasthani specialities), plus salads, baked potatoes and plenty of vegetarian fare. It's ideal for meeting and greeting other travellers, with a mezzanine to loll about on and cool background sounds. The management's latest venture, a multicuisine rooftop restaurant called

Hinglish, was about to open two doors up from here when we last visited.

Jagat Niwas Palace Hotel   INDIAN $$
(☑2420133; 23-25 Lal Ghat; mains ₹150-375; ⊙7-10am, noon-3pm & 6-10pm) A classy rooftop restaurant with superb lake views, delicious Indian cuisine and good service. Choose from an extensive selection of rich curries (tempered for Western tastes) – mutton, chicken, fish, veg – as well as the tandoori classics. There's a tempting cocktail menu (from ₹255) and the beer (from ₹165) is icy. It's wise to book ahead for dinner.

O'Zen Restaurant   MULTICUISINE $$
(mains ₹100-300; ⊙8.30am-11pm) A trendy new addition to City Palace Rd, this stylish first-floor restaurant-cafe does a range of Indian curries plus Italian pizza and pasta. It's bright and modern, does good coffee (₹50 to ₹70), beer (₹180), has free wi-fi and some interesting views of the street below.

Savage Garden   MEDITERRANEAN $$
(☑2425440; 22 Inside Chandpol; mains ₹190-320; ⊙11am-11pm) Has a winning line in soups, chicken and homemade pasta dishes with assorted sauces, though portions aren't huge. There are some Middle Eastern influences too. The setting is atmospheric, in a 250-year-old *haveli* with indigo walls, bowls of flowers and tables in alcoves or a pleasant courtyard.

🍴 Hanuman Ghat Area

⭐**Millets of Mewar**   INDIAN $
(www.milletsofmewar.com; Hanuman Ghat; ₹80-140; ⊙8.30am-10.30pm; 🛜) 🌿 Our favourite restaurant in Udaipur, this place not only does the healthiest food in town, but its dishes are also super tasty and fabulous value for money. Local millet is used where possible instead of less environmentally sound wheat and rice, there are vegan options, gluten-free dishes, fresh salads, and juices and herbal teas. There are multigrain sandwiches and millet pizzas, but also regular curries, Indian street-food snacks, pasta and even pancakes. The coffee is deliciously unhealthy, and there's ice cream and chocolate pudding to go with the millet cookies on the unusual desert menu. The manager is young, friendly and laidback, and organises cookery classes and guided city walks.

Jasmin
MULTICUISINE $

(mains ₹60-90; ☻8.30am-11pm) Tasty vegetarian dishes are cooked up here in a lovely, quiet, open-air spot looking out on the quaint Daiji footbridge. There are plenty of Indian options, and some original variations on the usual multicuisine theme including Korean and Israeli dishes. The ambience is super-relaxed and service is friendly. Next door the **Little Prince** (mains ₹80-130) has the same setting and a very similar menu with slightly higher prices.

Queen Cafe
INDIAN $

(14 Bajrang Marg; mains ₹60-75; ☻8am-10pm) This friendly, pocket-sized eatery, on the ground floor of the family home of ace chef Meenu, serves up fabulous home-style Indian vegetarian dishes. Try the pumpkin curry with mint and coconut, and the Kashmir pulao with fruit, vegies and coconut. Don't pass on the chocolate desserts either! Meenu also runs cookery classes from here.

★ Ambrai
NORTH INDIAN $$

(☑2431085; Amet Haveli hotel; mains ₹250-400; ☻12.30-3pm & 7.30-10.30pm) The cuisine at this scenic restaurant – at lake-shore level, looking across to the Lake Palace Hotel, Lal Ghat and the City Palace – does justice to its fabulous position. Highly atmospheric at night, Ambrai feels like a French park, with its wrought-iron furniture, dusty ground and large shady trees, and there's a terrific bar to complement the dining. Call ahead to reserve a table by the water's edge.

🍴 City Palace

Note, you have to pay the ₹25 City Palace entrance fee to access the following.

Paantya Restaurant
INDIAN $$$

(☑2528016; Shiv Niwas Palace Hotel; mains ₹500-1000; ☻noon-3pm & 7-10.30pm) Most captivating in the evening, this semiformal restaurant in the ritzy Shiv Niwas Palace has indoor seating, but if the weather's warm enough it's best in the open-air courtyard by the pool. Indian classical music is performed nightly, and the food is great. For local flavour try the very tasty *laal maas dhungar,* a Rajasthani spiced and smoked mutton dish. A beer will set you back a cool ₹475.

Palki Khana
ITALIAN $$$

(City Palace; mains ₹300-500; ☻9am-6pm) This informal terrace restaurant is the most popular place to refuel during a tour of the City Palace complex. Located centrally in the large open courtyard beside the entrance to the museum, it does mostly Italian dishes as well as good-quality wine, beer (from ₹350) and coffee (₹110 to ₹150). Note, drinks are half price between 4.30pm and 5.30pm.

🍷 Drinking

Most guesthouses have a roof terrace serving up cold Kingfishers with views over the lazy waters of Lake Pichola. Particularly worth considering are **Jagat Niwas Palace Hotel** and **Dream Heaven**. For a drink beside the water's edge, try **Jasmin** restaurant or its equally shanty neighbour **Little Prince**. For something more upmarket, head to **Ambrai** restaurant.

Cafe Edelweiss
CAFF

(73 Gangaur Ghat Rd; coffee from ₹50; ☻8.30am-8pm; ☎) The Savage Garden restaurant folks run this itsy piece of Europe that appeals to homesick and discerning travellers with its baked snacks (sticky cinnamon rolls, squidgy blueberry chocolate cake, apple strudel) and good strong coffee.

Cafe Namaste
CAFE

(coffee ₹40-70; ☻7am-10pm) A European-themed street-side cafe on the ground floor of Gangaur Palace Hotel that delivers the goods with scrumptious muffins, apple pies, cinnamon rolls, brownies and particularly good chocolate cake. The pride and joy, though, is the shiny silver espresso machine, which squirts out some fine cups of coffee.

Jheel's Ginger Coffee Bar
CAFE

(Jheel Guest House; coffee ₹50-100; ☻8am-8pm; ☎) Small but slick air-conditioned cafe by the water's edge on the ground floor of Jheel Palace Guest House. Large windows afford good lake views, and the coffee is excellent. Also does a range of cakes and snacks. Note, you can take your coffee up to the open-air rooftop restaurant if you like, but there's no alcohol served here.

Panera Bar
BAR

(Shiv Niwas Palace Hotel; beer from ₹475, shots from ₹250; ☻11.30am-10pm) Sink into plush sofas surrounded by huge mirrors, royal portraits and beautiful paintwork, or sit out by the pool, and be served like a maharaja.

Anand Bar
BAR

(Ambrai Restaurant, Amet Haveli Hotel; beer from ₹150; ☻11.30am-10.30pm) The fabulous lakeside restaurant Ambrai, at Amet Haveli hotel, doubles up as a terrace bar, and is a classy place for a predinner drink. You can grab a small bottle of Kingfisher for ₹150, but there are also cocktails (from ₹375) and a reasonable wine list (from ₹450 per glass).

☆ Entertainment

Dharohar   DANCE, PUPPETRY
(☑2523858; Bagore-ki-Haveli; admission Indian/foreigner ₹60/100, camera ₹100; ☺7-8pm) The beautiful Bagore-ki-Haveli hosts the best (and most convenient) opportunity to see Rajasthani folk dancing, with nightly one-hour shows of colourful, energetic Mewari, Bhil and western Rajasthani dances, as well as some traditional Rajasthani puppetry.

**Mewar Sound &
Light Show**   CULTURAL PROGRAM
(Manek Chowk, City Palace; lower/upper seating English show ₹150/400, Hindi show ₹100/200; ☺7pm Sep-Feb, 7.30pm Mar-Apr, 8pm May-Aug) Fifteen centuries of intriguing Mewar history are squeezed into one atmospheric hour of commentary and light switching – in English from September to April, in Hindi other months.

🛍 Shopping

Tourist-oriented shops – selling miniature paintings, wood carvings, silver, bangles and other jewellery, traditional shoes, spices, leather-bound handmade-paper notebooks, ornate knives, camel-bone boxes and a large variety of textiles – line the streets radiating from Jagdish Chowk. Bargain hard.

Udaipur is known for its local crafts, particularly its miniature paintings in the Rajput-Mughal style. To find out more, ask at the art workshop at Hotel Krishna Niwas.

Sadhna   CLOTHING
(☑2454655; www.sadhna.org; Jagdish Temple Rd; ☺10am-7pm) 🖉 This is the outlet for Seva Mandir, an NGO set up in 1969 to help rural women. The small shop sells attractive fixed-price textiles, including women's clothing, bags and shawls, plus a small range of jewellery. Profits go to the artisans and towards community development work.

ℹ Information

EMERGENCY
Police (☑2414600, 100) There are police posts at Surajpol, Hatipol and Delhi Gates.

INTERNET ACCESS
There are plenty of internet cafes, particularly around Lal Ghat, but also around Hanuman Ghat, where you can get online for around ₹30 per hour. Many places double as travel agencies, bookshops, art shops etc.

MEDICAL SERVICES
GBH American Hospital (☑24hr enquiries 2426000, emergency 9352304050; www.gbhamericanhospital.com; Meera Girls College Rd, 101 Kothi Bagh, Bhatt Ji Ki Bari) Modern, reader-recommended private hospital with 24-hour emergency service, about 2km northeast of the Lal Ghat area.

MONEY
Annoyingly, the ATMs near Jagdish Chowk are often out of service. If so, keep walking north-east, beyond the Old Clock Tower, and you'll find some more. There are lots of unofficial money-changers around Lal Ghat.

Thomas Cook (Lake Palace Rd; ☺9.30am-6.30pm Mon-Sat) Changes cash, travellers cheques and gives cash advances on credit cards.

POST
Post Office (City Palace Rd; ☺10am-4pm Mon-Sat) This handy branch is beside the City Palace's Badi Pol ticket office. It's tiny, but sends parcels abroad, does packaging and has practically no queues.

ℹ Getting There & Away

AIR
Air India (☑2410999, airport office 2655453; www.airindia.com; Saheli Rd, 222/16 Mumal Towers) Flies to Mumbai and Delhi daily.

Jet Airways (☑5134000; www.jetairways.com; airport) Flies direct to Delhi and Mumbai daily.

BUS
Private bus tickets can be bought at any one of the many travel agencies lining the road leading from Jagdish Temple to Daiji Footbridge.

The main bus stand is 1.5km east of the City Palace. Turn left at the end of Lake Palace Rd, take the first right then cross the main road at the end, just after passing through the crumbling old Surajpol Gate. It's ₹30 to ₹40 in an autorickshaw.

If arriving by bus, turn left out of the bus stand, cross the main road, walk through Surajpol Gate then turn left at the end of the road before taking the first right into Lake Palace Rd.

See the table for a selection of services leaving from the main bus stand.

TRAIN

The train station is about 2.5km southeast of the City Palace, and 1km directly south of the main bus stand. An autorickshaw between the train station and Jagdish Chowk should cost around ₹50. There's a prepaid autorickshaw stand at the station, though, so use that when you arrive.

There are no direct trains to Abu Road, Jodhpur or Jaisalmer.

For **Pushkar**, four daily trains make the five-hour journey to Ajmer (6.15am, 2.15pm, 5.20pm and 10.20pm). An unreserved 'general ticket' costs around ₹80.

Five daily trains make the two-hour trip to **Chittorgarh** (6.15am, 5.20pm, 6.15pm, 8.35pm and 10.20pm). An unreserved 'general ticket' costs around ₹45.

Three trains run daily to **Jaipur** (6.15am, 2.15pm and 10.20pm), taking around seven hours.

Two daily trains (5.20pm and 6.15pm) make the 12-hour trip to **Delhi**.

Only one train runs daily to **Bundi** (6.15pm). Likewise, only one daily train runs to **Agra** (10.20pm).

🛈 Getting Around

TO/FROM THE AIRPORT

The airport is 25km east of town. A prepaid taxi to the Lal Ghat area costs ₹400.

BICYCLE & MOTORCYCLE

Some guesthouses can arrange bicycles to rent. **Lakeside Cycle Tourism** (per hour/day ₹15/100; ⊙ 8am-9.30pm) is a small bicycle-rental outfit near Hanuman Ghat.

Bicycle, scooters and motorbikes (including Enfield Bullets) can be rented from **Heera Cycle Store** (⊙ 7.30am-9pm), just off Gangaur Ghat Rd. Costs per day are ₹50/350/400/500 for bicycles/scooters/motorbikes/Enfields with a deposit of ₹1500/10,000/10,000/25,000 or your passport. You'll also need your driving licence.

TRANSPORT FROM UDAIPUR

Major Buses from Udaipur

DESTINATION	FARE (₹)	DURATION (HR)	FREQUENCY & TIMES
Ahmedabad	200	5	hourly, 5am-10pm
Ajmer	215	7	hourly, 6am-9.30pm
Bundi	200	6	5.30am, 8am & 9.30am
Chittorgarh	90	2½	every 30 minutes, 5.30am-11.30pm
Delhi	550	15	11am, 3.30pm, 4pm & 11.30pm
Jaipur	330	9	hourly, 4am-9.30pm
Jodhpur	210	6 8	hourly, 5.30am-10pm
Kota	230	7	half-hourly, 6am-10.30pm
Mt Abu (Abu Road)	230	4	hourly, 5.30am-5.15pm
Mt Abu (direct)	230	4½	5am

Major Trains from Udaipur

DESTINATION	TRAIN	DEPARTURE TIME	ARRIVAL TIME	FARE (₹)
Agra (Cantonment)	19666 Udaipur-Kur Exp	10.20pm	11am	267/748 (A)
Ajmer	09722 Udaipur-Jaipur SF SPL	2.15pm	7.10pm	96/349 (B)
Bundi	12964 Mewar Exp	6.15pm	10.40pm	157/398 (A)
Chittorgarh	12982 Chetak Exp	5.20pm	7.10pm	140/275 (A)
Delhi (Nizamuddin)	12964 Mewar Exp	6.15pm	6.30am	305/831 (A)
Jaipur	19666 Udaipur-Kurj Exp	10.20pm	6am	194/533 (A)

Fares: (A) sleeper/3AC, (B) 2nd-class seat/AC chair

TAXI

Most hotels, guesthouses and travel agencies (many of which are on the road leading down to the lake from Jagdish Temple) can organise you a car and driver to just about anywhere you want. As an example, a return day trip to Ranakpur and Kumbhalgarh will cost you around ₹1500 per vehicle.

Around Udaipur

Kumbhalgarh

📞 02954

About 80km north of Udaipur, **Kumbhalgarh** (Indian/foreigner ₹5/100; ⊙ 9am-6pm) is a fantastic remote fort, fulfilling romantic expectations and vividly summoning up the chivalrous, warlike Rajput era. One of the many forts built by Rana Kumbha (r 1433–68), under whom Mewar reached its greatest extents, the isolated fort is perched 1100m above sea level, with endless views melting into the blue distance. And the journey to the fort, along twisting roads through the Aravalli Hills, is a highlight in itself.

Kumbhalgarh was the most important Mewar fort after Chittorgarh, and the rulers, sensibly, used to retreat here in times of danger. Not surprisingly, Kumbhalgarh was only taken once in its entire history. Even then, it took the combined armies of Amer, Marwar and Mughal emperor Akbar to breach its strong defences, and they only managed to hang onto it for two days.

The fort's thick walls stretch for about 10km to 12km; they're wide enough in some places for eight horses to ride abreast and it's possible to walk a complete circuit on top of the wall in around four hours. They enclose around 360 intact and ruined temples, some of which date back to the Mauryan period in the 2nd century BC, as well as palaces, gardens, step-wells and 700 cannon bunkers.

Note, if you're staying here and want to make an early start on your hike around the wall, you can still get into the fort before 9am, although no one will be around to sell you a ticket.

There's a **Light & Sound Show** (₹200) at the fort every evening at 6.30pm.

The large and rugged Kumbhalgarh Wildlife Sanctuary can be visited from Kumbhalgarh. Ask at the Aodhi hotel about organising jeep, horse or walking trips in the sanctuary.

🛏 Sleeping & Eating

Lucky Restaurant and Guest House   GUESTHOUSE $

(📞 9783828309; huts/tents/rooms ₹200/300/300) Located 200m up the approach road to the fort (so about 1.5km from the fort itself), and set down from the road amongst rice paddies and surrounding farmland, this shanty guesthouse is about as basic as it gets, but it's a magical spot. There are five simple rooms, a couple of tents and two thatched huts on wooden stilts that are just about big enough for a double mattress. It's shared bathrooms only and hot water by the bucket, but the rural setting is hard to beat and the friendly manager keeps you well fed and ensures a constant flow of chai.

Aodhi   HOTEL $$$

(📞 8003722333, 242341; www.eternalmewar.in; Kumbhalgarh; r from ₹7200; ❄ @ 🛜 🐾) On the main road about 100m before the start of the approach road to the fort, and just under 2km from the fort itself, is this luxurious

---

KUMBHALGARH WILDLIFE SANCTUARY

Ranakpur is a great base for exploring the hilly, densely forested **Kumbhalgarh Wildlife Sanctuary** (Indian/foreigner ₹20/160, jeep or car ₹130, camera/video free/₹400, guide per day ₹200; ⊙ dawn-dusk), which extends over some 600 sq km to the northeast and southwest. It's known for its leopards and wolves, although the chances of spotting antelopes, gazelles, deer and possible sloth bears are higher, especially from March to June. You will certainly see some of the sanctuary's 200-plus bird species. Some of the best safaris and treks are offered (to guests and nonguests) by Shivika Lake Hotel: options include jeep safaris (per person ₹700 to ₹1200), day-long forest walks (₹750), a guided round trip to Kumbhalgarh (bus there, hike back; ₹650) and even overnight camping trips.

Note, there is a ticket office for the sanctuary right beside where the bus drops you off for the Jain temples, but the nearest of the sanctuary's four entrances is 2km beyond here, near Shivika Lake Hotel.

and blissfully tranquil hotel with an inviting pool, rambling gardens and winter campfires. The spacious rooms in stone buildings all boast their own palm-thatched terraces, balconies or pavilions, and assorted wildlife and botanical art and photos. Nonguests can dine in the restaurant (lunch/dinner ₹850/1100), where good standard Indian fare is the pick of the options on offer, have a drink in the cosy Chowpal Bar, or swim in the pool (₹400). Room rates plummet from April to September.

ℹ Getting There & Away

From Udaipur's main bus stand, catch a Ranakpur-bound bus as far as Saira (₹57, 2¼ hours, at least hourly), a tiny crossroads town where you can change for a bus to Kumbhalgarh (₹30, 1 hour, hourly). That bus, which will be bound for Kelwara, will drop you at the start of the approach road to the fort, leaving you with a pleasant 1.5km walk to the entrance gate.

The accommodation we list is within walking distance from the bus drop-off.

The last bus back to Saira swings by at 5.30pm (and is always absolutely jam-packed with villagers). The last bus from Saira back to Udaipur leaves at around 8pm.

To get to Ranakpur from Kumbhalgarh, head first to Saira then change for Ranakpur (₹14, 40 minutes, at least hourly).

A day-long round trip in a private car from Udaipur to Kumbhalgarh and Ranakpur will cost around ₹1500 per car

Ranakpur

☑ 02934

At the foot of a remote, steep, wooded escarpment of the Aravalli Hills, **Ranakpur** (camera/video ₹100/300; ☺ Jains 6am-7pm, non-Jains noon-5pm) is one of India's biggest and most important Jain temple complexes. It's 75km northwest of Udaipur (and an easy day trip), and 12km west of Kumbhalgarh as the crow flies (although 50km by road, via Saira). The main temple, the **Chaumukha Mandir** (Four-Faced Temple), is dedicated to Adinath, the first Jain *tirthankar* (depicted in the many Buddha-like images in the temple), and was built in the 15th century in milk-white marble. An incredible feat of Jain devotion, this is a complicated series of 29 halls, 80 domes and 1444 individually engraved pillars. The interior is covered in knotted, lovingly wrought carving, and has a calming sense of space and harmony. Shoes, cigarettes and leather articles must be left at the entrance; menstruating women are asked not to enter.

Also exquisitely carved and well worth inspecting are two other Jain temples, dedicated to **Neminath** (22nd *tirthankar*) and **Parasnath** (23rd *tirthankar*), both within the complex, and a nearby **Sun Temple**. About 1km from the main complex is the **Amba Mata Temple**.

Buses from Udaipur and Saira will drop you by the entrance to the temple complex, before continuing past Shivika Lake Hotel (2km), and then going on to Jodhpur.

🛏 Sleeping & Eating

Shivika Lake Hotel   GUESTHOUSE $$
(☑ 9799118573, 285078; www.shivikalakehotel.com; r ₹600-1600, tent ₹1200; ✳ @ ⊠) Less than 2km beyond the temple complex, Shivika is a welcoming, rustic, family-run guesthouse that provides free pick-ups to and from the bus drop-off at the temples. You can stay in small, cosy rooms amid leafy gardens or safari-style tents. Beautiful Nalwania Lake is a short scramble up a pathway from the guesthouse. There's a swimming pool beside the lake, as well as a sprinkling of tables and chairs where guests can eat breakfast. Boat trips on the lake are also available. The menu (mains ₹100 to ₹150) is mostly Indian and very tasty.

Ranakpur Hill Resort   HOTEL $$$
(☑ 286411; www.ranakpurhillresort.com; Ranakpur Rd; s/d from ₹2000/2500; ✳ @ ⊠) About 3km beyond the temple complex, this well-run hotel has a lovely pool in grassy gardens, around which are attractive, air-conditioned rooms sporting marble floors, stained glass and floral wall paintings.

ℹ Getting There & Away

There are direct buses to Ranakpur from the main bus stands in both Udaipur (₹70, three hours, hourly) and Jodhpur (₹109, four to five hours). You'll be dropped outside the temple complex unless you state otherwise. Return buses start drying up at around 7.30pm.

Mt Abu

☑ 02974 / POP 30,000 / ELEV 1200M

Rajasthan's only hill station sits amongst green forests on the state's highest mountain at the southwestern end of the Aravalli Range, close to the Gujarat border. Quite unlike anywhere else in Rajasthan, Mt Abu

Mt Abu

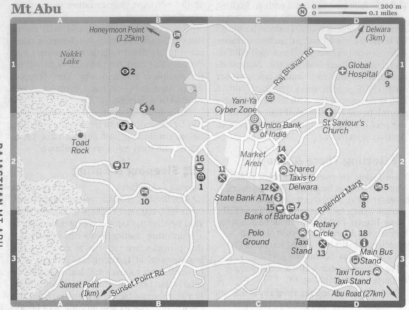

Mt Abu

⊙ Sights
1	World Renewal Spiritual Museum B2
	Brahma Kumaris Peace Hall &
	Museum .... (see 1)
2	Nakki Lake B1
3	Raghunath Temple B2

⊕ Activities, Courses & Tours
4	Boat Rental B1
	Mt Abu Treks ....(see 6)

⊜ Sleeping
5	Connaught House D2
6	Hotel Lake Palace B1
7	Hotel Samrat C2
8	Kishangarh House D2
9	Mushkil Aasan D1

10	Shri Ganesh Hotel B2

⊗ Eating
11	Arbuda C2
12	Chacha Cafe C2
13	Kanak Dining Hall D3
14	Sher-e-Punjab Hotel C2

⊜ Drinking & Nightlife
15	Cafe Coffee Day C2
16	Cafe Shikibo B2
17	Polo Bar B2

ⓘ Information
	Railway Reservation Centre ....(see 18)
18	Tourist Reception Centre D3

provides Rajasthanis, Gujaratis and a steady flow of foreign tourists with respite from scorching temperatures and arid beige terrain elsewhere. It's a particular hit with honeymooners and middle-class families from Gujarat.

Mt Abu town sits towards the southwestern end of the plateau-like upper part of the mountain, which stretches about 19km from end to end and 6km from east to west. The town is surrounded by the flora- and fauna-rich, 289-sq-km Mt Abu Wildlife Sanctuary, which extends over most of the mountain from an altitude of 300m upwards.

The mountain is of great spiritual importance for both Hindus and Jains and has more than 80 temples and shrines, most notably the exquisite Jain temples at Delwara, built between 400 and 1000 years ago.

Try to avoid arriving in Diwali (October or November) or the two weeks following, when prices soar and the place is packed. Mt

Abu also gets pretty busy from mid-May to mid-June, before the monsoon. This is when the Summer Festival hits town, with music, fireworks and boat races. In the cooler months, you will find everyone wrapped up in shawls and hats; pack something woolly to avoid winter chills in poorly heated hotel rooms.

Sights & Activities

Nakki Lake
LAKE

Scenic Nakki Lake, the town's focus, is one of its biggest attractions. It's so named because, according to legend, it was scooped out by a god using his *nakh* (nails). Some Hindus thus consider it a holy lake. It's a pleasant 45-minute stroll around the perimeter – the lake is surrounded by hills, parks and strange rock formations. The best known, **Toad Rock**, looks like a toad about to hop into the lake. The 14th-century **Raghunath Temple** (☉dawn-dusk) stands near the lake's south shore. **Boating** (₹110-450 per boat, 30min) is also popular.

Sunset Point
VIEWPOINT

Sunset Point is a popular place to watch the brilliant setting sun. Hordes stroll out here every evening to catch the end of the day, the food stalls and all the usual jolly hill-station entertainment.

Brahma Kumaris
Peace Hall & Museum
MEDITATION, MUSEUM

The white-clad people you'll see around town are either armed forces or members of the **Brahma Kumaris World Spiritual University** (www.bkwsu.com), a worldwide organisation whose headquarters are here in Mt Abu. The university's **Universal Peace Hall** (Om Shanti Bhawan; ☉8am-6pm), is just north of Nakki Lake. Free 30-minute tours are available, including an introduction to the Brahma Kumaris philosophy. The organisation also runs the small **World Renewal Spiritual Museum** (admission free; ☉8am-8pm) in the town centre.

☞ Tours

The RSRTC runs full-day (₹85) and half-day (₹30) bus tours of Mt Abu's main sights, leaving from the bus stand at 9.30am and 1pm respectively, and returning at around 6pm. A full-day taxi tour costs ₹150. Admission, camera fees and the ₹20 guide fee are extra. Buy tickets for the bus tour at the main bus stand, and tickets for the taxi tour at the nearby taxi stand.

🛏 Sleeping

Room rates can double or worse during the peak seasons – mid-May to mid-June, Diwali and Christmas/New Year – but generous discounts are often available at other times in midrange and top-end places. If you have to come here at Diwali, you'll need to book way ahead and you won't be able to move for crowds. Most hotels have an ungenerous 9am checkout time.

Shri Ganesh Hotel
HOTEL **$**

(☎237292; lalit_ganesh@yahoo.co.in; dm ₹150 200, without bathroom ₹100, s ₹300, d ₹400 1200; @) Deservedly the most popular budget spot, Shri Ganesh is well set up for travellers, with an inexpensive cafe, a small internet room

---

TREKKING AROUND MT ABU

Getting off the well-worn tourist trail and out into the forests and hills of Mt Abu is a revelation. This is a world of isolated shrines and lakes, weird rock formations, fantastic panoramas, Adivasis (tribal people), orchids, wild fruits, plants used in ayurvedic medicine, sloth bears, langurs, 150 bird species and even the occasional leopard. For safety reasons, it's highly recommended you take a guide. Foreign tourists have been injured by wild animals here in the past, and a lone Israeli tourist was murdered while hiking here in 2008.

Mt Abu–born Mahendra Dan ('Charles') of **Mt Abu Treks** (☎9414154854; www.mount-abu-treks.blogspot.com; Hotel Lake Palace) is a passionate and knowledgable nature lover who leads excellent tailor-made treks ranging from three or four hours close to Mt Abu (₹500 per person) to day-long (₹1000 per person) or overnight treks (₹2000 per person) to Adivasi villages. There's a two-person minimum, and on some routes wildlife-sanctuary entrance fees (Indian/foreigner ₹20/160) and/or transport costs (₹300 to ₹2500 for a car drop-off and pick-up) have to be paid too.

Either call Charles directly, or ask for him at Hotel Lake Palace.

DELWARA TEMPLES

These remarkable **Jain temples** (☉ Jains 6am-6pm, non-Jains noon-6pm) are Mt Abu's outstanding attraction and feature some of India's finest temple decorations. They predate the town of Mt Abu by many centuries and were built when this site was just a remote mountain fastness. It's said that the artisans were paid according to the amount of dust they collected, encouraging them to carve ever more intricately. Whatever their inducement, there are two temples here in which the marble work is dizzyingly intense.

The older of the two is the **Vimal Vasahi**, on which work, financed by a Gujarati chief minister named Vimal, began in 1031. Dedicated to the first *tirthankar*, Adinath, it took 1500 masons and 1200 labourers 14 years to build, and allegedly cost ₹185.3 million. Outside the entrance is the **House of Elephants**, featuring a procession of stone elephants marching to the temple, some of which were damaged long ago by marauding Mughals. Inside, a forest of beautifully carved pillars surrounds the central shrine, which holds an image of Adinath himself.

The **Luna Vasahi Temple** is dedicated to Neminath, the 22nd *tirthankar*, and was built in 1230 by the brothers Tejpal and Vastupal for a mere ₹125.3 million. Like Vimal, the brothers were both Gujarati government ministers. The marble carving here took 2500 workers 15 years to create, and its most notable feature is its intricacy and delicacy, which is so fine that, in places, the marble becomes almost transparent. It's difficult to believe that this huge lace-like filigree started life as a solid block of marble.

As at other Jain temples, leather articles (belts as well as shoes), cameras and mobile phones have to be left at the entrance. Menstruating women are asked not to enter.

Delwara is about 3km north of Mt Abu town centre: you can walk here in less than an hour, or hop aboard a shared taxi (₹10 per person) from up the street opposite Chacha Cafe. A taxi all to yourself should be ₹50, or ₹150 round trip with one hour's waiting. There are tea and snack stalls by the entrance to the temples.

and plenty of helpful travel information. Rooms are well used but colourful and clean and have TV and hot-water showers (from 6am to 10am only). Some have squat toilets; some sit-down versions. Daily forest walks and cooking lessons are on offer.

★**Mushkil Aasan** GUESTHOUSE $$
(☎ 235150, 9429409660; ccrrps@yahoo.com; s/d/q ₹1100/1200/1800) Cute colonial-style guesthouse run by a welcoming family and set in a beautifully maintained, tree-shaded garden, which receives daily visits from a passing troop of langurs. Nine homely rooms include three 'family rooms' that can sleep four people. There are home-cooked meals, but no internet access.

Hotel Samrat HOTEL $$
(☎ 238453; samrat.hotel@yahoo.in; r from ₹1200; ❄) Modest, unassuming hotel with clean, well turned-out rooms that come with TV, comfortable beds and views of the polo ground. No internet.

Connaught House HERITAGE HOTEL $$$
(☎ 235439; www.welcomheritagehotels.com; Rajendra Marg; r incl breakfast ₹6700; ❄ @) A charmingly stuck-in-time colonial bungalow that looks like an English cottage, with lots of sepia photographs, dark wood, angled ceilings and a gorgeous shady garden. The management are a bit keen to please, but that does mean you can fish for discounts.

Kishangarh House HERITAGE HOTEL $$$
(☎ 238092; www.royalkishangarh.com; Rajendra Marg; cottage/room ₹3000/4500; ❄ ☎) The former summer residence of the maharaja of Kishangarh is now a low-key, but enchanting heritage hotel. The rooms in the main building are big with extravagantly high ceilings. The cottage rooms at the back are smaller but cosy. There is a delightful sun-filled drawing room and the lovely terraced gardens are devotedly tended.

Hotel Lake Palace HOTEL $$$
(☎ 237154; http://savshantihotels.com; r incl breakfast ₹2100-2700; ❄ ☎) Spacious and family-friendly, Hotel Lake Palace has an attractive lakeside location and a well-tended lawn with a small children's play area. Rooms are simple, uncluttered, bright and clean. All have air-con and some have semiprivate lake-view terrace areas. Rooftop restaurant.

✗ Eating

Sher-e-Punjab Hotel PUNJABI $
(mains ₹75-130; ⏰10am-4pm & 7-11pm) This place in the market area has bargain Punjabi food and is very popular. Has plenty of regular veg curries that won't stretch the budget, plus tandoori chicken.

Chacha Cafe MULTICUISINE $
(mains ₹60-160; ☎) A very neat, bright eatery with red-check tablecloths and welcome air-con. The presentable fare includes dosa (particularly good), pizza, vegetarian burgers, cashew curry and biryani. Wi-fi is ₹50 per hour.

Kanak Dining Hall INDIAN $
(Gujarati/Punjabi thali ₹60/130; ⏰8.30am-3.30pm & 7-11pm) The excellent all-you-can-eat thalis (₹140 to ₹170) are contenders for Mt Abu's best meals; there's seating indoors in the busy dining hall or outside under a canopy.

Arbuda INDIAN $$
(Arbuda Circle; mains ₹100-150; ⏰7am-10.30pm) This busy restaurant is set on a sweeping open terrace filled with chrome chairs and overlooking the street. It's popular for its Gujarati, Punjabi and South Indian food.

🍷 Drinking

Polo Bar BAR
(Jaipur House; ⏰8am-10pm) The heritage hotel, Jaipur House, has a fabulous hilltop location, but it's overpriced, so come here instead for a beer (from ₹180) or a cocktail (from ₹200). Make sure you sit out on the roof terrace – the views over the town and the lake are stunning. You can eat here too (mains ₹160 to ₹300).

Cafe Shikibo CAFE
(coffee from ₹60; ⏰9am-10pm) Cool, comfortable, modern cafe with fresh coffee, free wifi, sandwiches and chips.

ⓘ MT ABU PRECAUTIONS

Unless you are in a group, it is very unwise to visit Sunset Point or Honeymoon Point any time other than sunset when lots of people will be around. It is also unwise to wander off the streets alone – for example along some of the town's surrounding paths shown on Tourist Reception Centre maps. Muggings, wild-animal attacks and even a murder have happened in recent years to foreign tourists who have ignored these precautions.

Cafe Coffee Day CAFE
(Rotary Circle; coffee from ₹60; ⏰9am-11pm) Abu's branch of India's most popular caffeine-supply chain. There's another **branch** on Collectorate Rd.

ⓘ Information

There are State Bank ATMs on Raj Bhavan Rd, opposite Hotel Samrat and outside the Tourist Reception Centre, and a Bank of Baroda ATM on Lake Rd.

Union Bank of India (Main Market; ⏰10am-3pm Mon-Fri, 10am-12.30pm Sat) The only bank changing travellers cheques and currency.

Yani-Ya Cyber Zone (Raj Bhavan Rd; internet per hr ₹30; ⏰9am-10pm) Has wi-fi too.

Global Hospital (☎238847)

ⓘ Getting There & Away

Access to Mt Abu is by a dramatic 28km-long road that winds its way up thickly forested hillsides from the town of Abu Road, where the nearest train station is. Some buses from other cities go all the way up to Mt Abu, others only go as far as Abu Road. Buses (₹29, one hour) run between Abu Road and Mt Abu half-hourly from about 6am to 7pm. A taxi from Abu Road to Mt Abu is ₹300 by day or ₹400 by night.

RAJASTHAN MT ABU

SELECTED TRAINS FROM ABU ROAD

DESTINATION	TRAIN	DEPARTURE TIME	ARRIVAL TIME	FARE (₹)
Ahmedabad	19224 Jammu Tawi-Ahmedabad Express	10.57am	3pm	120/308 (A)
Delhi (New Delhi)	12957 Swarna J Raj Express	8.54pm	7.30am	1068/1530 (B)
Jaipur	19707 Aravalli Express	10.02am	6.55pm	194/533 (A)
Jodhpur	19223 Ahmedabad-Jammu Tawi Express	3.22pm	8pm	143/385 (A)
Mumbai	19708 Aravalli Express	5.10pm	6.35am	264/740 (A)

Fares: (A) sleeper/3AC, (B) 3AC/2AC

There's a charge of ₹10 for each person (including bus passengers) and car as you enter Mt Abu.

BUS

Services from Mt Abu bus stand include:

Ahmedabad (₹150, seven hours, hourly from 6am to 9pm)

Jaipur (seat/sleeper ₹718/768, 11 hours, 6.30pm)

Jodhpur (₹224, six hours, 6.45am, 8.30am and 12.30pm)

Udaipur (₹153 to ₹160, 4½ hours, 8am, 9.15am, 1pm and 4.30pm)

TRAIN

Abu Road station is on the line between Delhi and Mumbai via Ahmedabad. An autorickshaw from Abu Road train station to Abu Road bus stand costs ₹10. Mt Abu has a **railway reservation centre** (☉ 8am-2pm Mon-Sat) above the tourist office.

Around Mt Abu

Guru Shikhar

At the northeast end of the Mt Abu plateau, 17km by the winding road from the town, rises 1722m-high Guru Shikhar, Rajasthan's highest point. A road goes almost all the way to the summit and the **Atri Rishi Temple**, complete with a priest and fantastic, huge views. A popular spot, it's a highlight of the RSRTC tour. If you decide to go it alone, a jeep will cost at least ₹500 return.

WESTERN RAJASTHAN

Jodhpur

🖉 0291 / POP 1 MILLION

Mighty Mehrangarh, the muscular fort that towers over the Blue City of Jodhpur, is a magnificent spectacle and an architectural masterpiece. Around Mehrangarh's base, the old city, a jumble of Brahmin-blue cubes, stretches out to the 10km-long, 16th-century city wall. The 'Blue City' really is blue! Inside is a tangle of winding, glittering, medieval streets, which never seem to lead where you expect them to, scented by incense, roses and sewers, with shops and bazaars selling everything from trumpets and temple decorations to snuff and saris. Traditionally, blue

signified the home of a Brahmin, but non-Brahmins have got in on the act too. As well as glowing with a mysterious light, the blue tint is thought to repel insects.

Modern Jodhpur stretches well beyond the city walls, but it's the immediacy and buzz of the old Blue City and the larger-than-life fort that capture travellers' imaginations. This crowded, hectic zone is also Jodhpur's main tourist area, and it often seems you can't speak to anyone without them trying to sell you something. Areas of the old city further west, such as Navchokiya, are just as atmospheric, with far less hustling.

History

Driven from their homeland of Kannauj, east of Agra, by Afghans serving Mohammed of Ghori, the Rathore Rajputs fled west around AD 1200 to the region around Pali, 70km southeast of Jodhpur. They prospered to such a degree that in 1381 they managed to oust the Pratiharas of Mandore, 9km north of present-day Jodhpur. In 1459 the Rathore leader Rao Jodha chose a nearby rocky ridge as the site for a new fortress of staggering proportions, Mehrangarh, around which grew Jodha's city: Jodhpur.

Jodhpur lay on the vital trade route between Delhi and Gujarat. The Rathore kingdom grew on the profits of sandalwood, opium, dates and copper, and controlled a large area which became cheerily known as Marwar (the Land of Death) due to its harsh topography and climate. It stretched as far west as what's now the India–Pakistan border area, and bordered with Mewar (Udaipur) in the south, Jaisalmer in the northwest, Bikaner in the north and Jaipur and Ajmer in the east.

👁 Sights & Activities

Mehrangarh FORT

(www.mehrangarh.org; museum admission ₹300/250, camera/video ₹100/200, guide ₹200; ☉ 9am-5pm) Rising perpendicular and impregnable from a rocky hill that itself stands 120m above Jodhpur's skyline, Mehrangarh is one of the most magnificent forts in India. The battlements are 6m to 36m high, and as the building materials were chiselled from the rock on which the fort stands, the structure merges with its base. Still run by the Jodhpur royal family, Mehrangarh is packed with history and legend.

Mehrangarh's main entrance, at the northeast gate, **Jai Pol**, is a 300m walk up from Hill View Guest House in the old city. Or you can take a winding 5km autorickshaw ride (around ₹100). The audio tour, included with the museum ticket, is in multiple languages and requires a deposit of passport, credit/debit card or ₹2000. You don't need a ticket to enter the fort itself, only the museum section.

Jai Pol was built by Maharaja Man Singh in 1808 following his defeat of invading forces from Jaipur. Past the museum ticket office and a small cafe, the 16th-century **Dodh Kangra Pol** was an external gate before Jai Pol was built, and still bears the scars of 1808 cannonball hits. Through here, the main route heads up to the left (down to the right is the way to **Chokhelao Bagh** gardens and the fort's back entrance at **Fateh Pol**), through the 16th-century **Imritia Pol** and then **Loha Pol**, the fort's original entrance, with iron spikes to deter enemy elephants. Just inside the gate are two sets of small handprints, the *sati* (self-immolation) marks of royal widows who threw themselves on their maharajas' funeral pyres – the last to do so were widows of Maharaja Man Singh in 1843.

Past Loha Pol you'll find a restaurant and **Suraj Pol**, which gives access to the **museum**. Once you've visited the museum, continue on from here to the panoramic **ramparts**, which are lined with impressive antique artillery.

➡ **Museum**

This beautiful network of stone-latticed courtyards and halls, formerly the fort's palace, is a superb example of Rajput architecture, so finely carved that it often looks more like sandalwood than sandstone.

The galleries around **Shringar Chowk** (Anointment Courtyard) display India's best collection of elephant howdahs and Jodhpur's royal palanquin collection.

One of the two galleries off **Daulat Khana Chowk** displays textiles, paintings, manuscripts, headgear and the curved sword of the Mughal emperor Akbar; the other gallery is the armoury. Upstairs is a **gallery of miniature paintings** from the sophisticated Marwar school and the beautiful 18th-century **Phul Mahal** (Flower Palace), with 19th-century wall paintings depicting the 36 moods of classical ragas as well as royal portraits; the artist took 10 years to create them using a curious concoction of gold leaf, glue and cow's urine.

Takhat Vilas was the bedchamber of Maharaja Takhat Singh (r 1843–73), who had just 30 maharanis and numerous concubines. Its beautiful ceiling is covered with Christmas baubles. You then enter the extensive zenana, whose lovely latticed windows (from which the women could watch the goings-on in the courtyards) are said to feature over 250 different designs. Here you'll find the **Cradle Gallery**, exhibiting the elaborate cradles of infant princes, and the 17th-century **Moti Mahal** (Pearl Palace), which was the palace's main durbar hall for official meetings and receptions, with gorgeously colourful stained glass.

➡ **Flying Fox**

This 45-minute circuit of six **zip lines** (www.flyingfox.asia; ₹1400; ☉9.30am, 10.30am, 11.30am, 2.30pm, 3.30pm, 4.30pm) flies back and forth over walls, bastions and lakes on the north side of Mehrangarh. Safety standards are good and 'awesome' is the verdict of most who dare.

Jaswant Thada HISTORIC BUILDING
(Indian/foreigner ₹15/30, camera/video ₹25/50; ☉9am-5pm) This milky-white marble memorial to Maharaja Jaswant Singh II, sitting above a small lake, within walking distance of Mehrangarh, is an array of whimsical domes. It's a welcome, peaceful spot after the hubbub of the city, and the views across to the fort and over the city are superb. Built in 1899, the cenotaph has some beautiful *jalis* (carved marble lattice screens) and is hung with portraits of Rathore rulers going back to the 13th century.

Clock Tower MONUMENT
The century-old clock tower is an old-city landmark surrounded by the vibrant sounds, sights and smells of Sardar Market, which is marked by triple gateways at its north and south ends. The narrow, winding lanes of the old city spread out in all directions from here. Westward, you plunge into the old city's commercial heart, with crowded alleys and bazaars selling vegetables, spices, sweets, silver and handicrafts.

Umaid Bhawan Palace PALACE
(museum Indian/foreigner ₹25/60; ☉museum 9am-5pm) Consider taking an autorickshaw (about ₹50) to this hilltop palace, 3km southeast of the old city. The current royal incumbent, Gaj Singh II (known as Bapji), still lives in part of the building. Built in 1929, the 365-room edifice was designed by

Jodhpur

Jai Pol

Jaswant Thada (500m)

Museum Ticket Office

Chokelao Bagh

3

MAKRANA MOHALLA

Museum

4

2

8 28

11

7

Gulab Sagar

Fateh Pol

NAVCHOKIYA

10

9

18 24

15

Chamundaji Temple

13

21

22

14

Manak Chowk

Om Forex

26

1

12

Sardar Market

25

State Bank ATM

Tambaku Bazar

27

Kapda Bazar

Moti Chowk

State Bank ATM

16

Nai Sarak

Sojati Gate

17

Mohanpura Overbridge

Station Rd

Ratanada Rd

Ranchodji Temple

6

Booking Office

Mahadev Travels

19

Ratanada Rd

20

Jodhpur Train Station

Jalori Gate

Jain Travels

Circuit House Road (600m); Ratanada (2km); (4km)

MG Hospital Rd

the British architect Henry Lanchester for Maharaja Umaid Singh. It took more than 3000 workers 15 years to complete, at a cost of around ₹11 million. The building is mortarless, and incorporates 100 wagon loads of Makrana marble and Burmese teak in the interior. Apparently its construction began as a royal job-creation program during a time of severe drought. Much of the building has been turned into a suitably grand hotel (www.tajhotels.com).

Casual visitors are not welcome at either the royal residence or the hotel, but you can visit the museum, housed in one side of the building. It includes photos showing the elegant art deco design of the palace interior, plus an eccentric collection of elaborate clocks. Don't miss the maharaja's highly polished classic cars, displayed in front of the museum, by the entrance gate.

To walk here, first go to the Tourist Reception Centre to pick up a map, then cross the nearby railway footbridge, walk straight ahead, turn left at the roundabout and keep following the road round to the left, past Rani Handicrafts and Ajay Art Emporium, before turning right just after Monarch Garments.

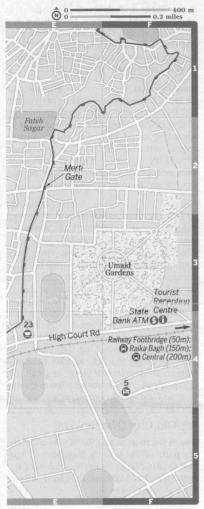

Jodhpur

◎ Sights
1	Clock Tower	C2
2	Mehrangarh	B1

◎ Activities, Courses & Tours
3	Flying Fox	B1
	Sambhali Trust	(see 5)

🛏 Sleeping
4	Cosy Guest House	A1
5	Durag Niwas Guest House	F4
6	Govind Hotel	C5
7	Hare Krishna Guest House	C1
	Haveli Inn Pal	(see 9)
8	Krishna Prakash Heritage Haveli	C1
9	Pal Haveli	C2
10	Pushp Paying Guest House	C2
11	Raas	C1
12	Shahi Guest House	B2
13	Shivam Paying Guest House	C2
14	Singhvi's Haveli	A2
15	Veggie Guest House	A2

⊗ Eating
16	Darbar	D3
17	Priya Restaurant	D4
	Indique	(see 9)
18	Jhankar Choti Haveli	C2
19	Kalinga Restaurant	C5
20	Mid Town	C5
21	Omelette Shop	D2
22	Vicky Chouhan Omelettes	C2

◎ Drinking & Nightlife
	18 Century Bar	(see 9)
23	Café Coffee Day	E4
24	Cafe Sheesh Mahal	C2
25	Shri Mishrilal Hotel	D2

🛍 Shopping
26	Krishna Book Depot	D2
27	MV Spices	D2
28	Sambhali Boutique	C1

✵ Festivals & Events

In September or October Jodhpur hosts the colourful **Marwar Festival**, which includes polo and a camel tattoo.

🛏 Sleeping

The old city has something like 100 guesthouses, most of which scramble for your custom as soon as you get within breathing distance of Sardar Market.

If a rickshaw rider or friendly local is clamouring to take you to a particular guesthouse or hotel, it's probably because he is aiming to receive a commission from them. There's a growing anticommission movement among hoteliers here, but many still pay touts, or your rickshaw/taxi driver an absurd 50% of what you pay for your room. Don't believe drivers or strangers on the street who tell you the place you want has closed, is full, is under repair, is far from the centre etc.

Many lodgings can organise a pick-up from the train station or bus stops, even at night, if you call ahead. Otherwise, for most places in the old city you can avoid nonsense by getting dropped at the clock tower and walking from there.

Old City

Shivam Paying Guest House GUESTHOUSE $
(☑ 2610688; www.shivamguesthouse.com; r ₹200-800; ❄) Decent, hassle-free budget guesthouse run by honest management. Has cosy rooms, (very) steep staircases and a lovely little rooftop restaurant with free wi-fi.

Pushp Paying Guest House GUESTHOUSE $
(☑ 2648494; sonukash2003@yahoo.co.in; Manak Chowk, Pipli-ki-Gali, Naya Bass; r ₹200-600; ❄ @ 🛜) A small guesthouse with a warm and friendly welcome and five clean, colourful rooms with windows and wi-fi. Dramatic fort views from the rooftop restaurant.

Hare Krishna Guest House GUESTHOUSE $
(☑ 2635307; www.harekrishnaguesthouse.net; r ₹200-800) This is another old house that has been extended upwards and squeezes in rooms and stairs wherever possible. The range of rooms is impressive – from the cave-like cheapie to the spacious fort-view rooms. Friendly staff, free wi-fi and, of course, a rooftop restaurant.

**Krishna Prakash
Heritage Haveli** HERITAGE HOTEL $$
(☑ 2633448; www.kpheritage.net; Nayabas; r incl breakfast ₹1000-4000; ❄ @ 🛏) This multi-level 1902 *haveli* right under the fort walls is good value and a peaceful choice. It has prettily painted furniture, murals and old family portraits, and rooms are well proportioned; the deluxe ones are a bit more spruced up, generally a bit bigger, and set on the upper floors, so airier. There's a small covered swimming pool and a relaxing terrace restaurant.

Shahi Guest House HERITAGE GUESTHOUSE $$
(☑ 2623802; www.shahiguesthouse.net; Gandhi St, City Police; r ₹1500-2750; ❄ 🛜) Shahi is an interesting guesthouse developed from a 350-year-old zenana. There's lots of cool stone, and narrow walkways surrounding a petite courtyard. The six rooms are individual and spacious yet cosy, and Anu and her family, who run the place, are charming. There is a delightful rooftop restaurant with fort views.

Pal Haveli HERITAGE HOTEL $$$
(☑ 3293328; www.palhaveli.com; Gulab Sagar; r incl breakfast ₹3500-8500; ❄ @ 🛜) This stunning *haveli*, the best and most attractive in the old city, was built by the Thakur of Pal in 1847. There are 21 charming, spacious rooms, mostly large and elaborately decorated in traditional heritage style, surrounding a cool central courtyard. The family still lives here and can show you its small museum. Three restaurants serve excellent food, including rooftop Indique with its fine views.

Haveli Inn Pal HERITAGE HOTEL $$$
(☑ 2612519; www.haveliinnpal.com; r incl breakfast ₹2050-2550; ❄ @ 🛜) The smaller, 12-room sibling of Pal Haveli. It's accessed through the same grand entrance, but is located around to the right in one wing of the grand *haveli*. It's a simpler heritage experience, with comfortable rooms and lake or fort views from the more expensive ones.

Raas BOUTIQUE HOTEL $$$
(☑ 2636455; www.raasjodhpur.com; Tunvarji-ka-Jhalra; incl breakfast r ₹17,000-21,000; ❄ @ 🛜 🏊) Developed from a 19th-century city mansion, Jodhpur's first contemporary-style boutique hotel is a splendid retreat of clean, uncluttered style, hidden behind a big castle-like gateway. If you fancy a change from the heritage aesthetic that prevails in Rajasthan's top-end hotels, Raas' clean, uncluttered style and subtle lighting are just the ticket. The red-stone-and-terrazzo rooms are not massive, but they come with plenty of luxury touches and have balconies with great Mehrangarh views or small private gardens. The terrace restaurant (mains ₹400 to ₹800) is also a classy affair.

Old City (Navchokiya)

One of the most atmospheric yet least touristy parts of the old city, Navchokiya's narrow, twisting lanes lie in the shadow of the western end of Mehrangarh, which you can enter at Fateh Pol gate.

Cosy Guest House GUESTHOUSE $
(☑ 2612066, 9829023390; cosyguesthouse@gmail.com; Chuna Ki Choki, Navchokiya; r ₹350-850, without bathroom ₹250; @ 🛜) A friendly place in an enchanting location, this 500-year-old glowing blue house has several levels of higgledy-piggledy rooftops and a mix of rooms, some monastic, others comfortable. Ask for Navchokiya Rd, from where the guesthouse is signposted, or call genial Mr Joshi.

Veggie Guest House GUESTHOUSE $
(☑ 2611010; Ramdevji-ka-Chowk, Navchokiya; r ₹400-800; ❄ @) Run by a welcoming elderly couple, this quiet but large family courtyard

home has simple rooms that are spartan, but neat and tidy. Each has a hot-water shower. Some have TV and air-con. Home-cooked meals are available, as is internet (₹40 per hour). No wi-fi.

★ **Singhvi's Haveli**   HERITAGE GUESTHOUSE $$
(☑ 2624293; www.singhvihaveli.com; Ramdevji-ka-Chowk, Navchokiya; r ₹400-2400; ❄@🛜) This red-sandstone, family-run, 500-year-old *haveli* is an understated gem. Run by two friendly brothers, Singhvi's has 13 individual rooms, ranging from the simple to the magnificent Maharani Suite with 10 windows and a fort view. The relaxing and romantic vegetarian restaurant is decorated with sari curtains and floor cushions, and the interior lounge is a delight.

🛏 Train Station Area

Govind Hotel   HOTEL $$
(☑ 2622758; www.govindhotel.com; Station Rd; r ₹600-2000; ❄@🛜) Well set up for travellers, with helpful management, an internet cafe and conveniently close to the train station. All rooms are clean and tiled, with fairly smart bathrooms. There's a rooftop restaurant and **coffee shop** (⊙7am-10pm) with excellent espresso and cakes and free wi-fi.

🛏 South of the Old City

Durag Niwas Guest House   GUESTHOUSE $
(☑2512385; www.durag-niwas.com; 1st Old Public Park Lane; r ₹400-600, with AC ₹1000-1400; ❄)
🍽 A warm, friendly and well-established family guesthouse set away from the hustle of the old city. It has good home-cooked food, a cute interior courtyard, a cushion-floored, sari-curtained area on the roof for relaxing, and honest, helpful staff. Management also offers cultural tours – including half-day Bishnoi Village tours – and the opportunity to do volunteer work with the women's empowerment NGO, **Sambhali Trust** (www.sambhali-trust.org). To get here, cross the railway footbridge near Raika Bagh train station then take the second right. Note, don't confuse this place with the next-door Durag Villas Guesthouse, another colourful place.

✕ Eating

As well as the places reviewed here, remember that most guesthouses have restaurants (usually on the roof, with a fort view).

Darbar   DHABA $
(133 Nai Sadak; mains ₹40-100; ⊙8am-10.30pm) Pocket-sized roadside *dhaba* with Rajasthani specialities leading the way on a tiny but tasty menu. The *daal bati* (wheat balls dipped in dhal) is a particular favourite, and usually eaten with the *churma* (coarsely-ground wheat crushed and cooked with ghee and sugar). We also enjoyed the *shahi masala paneer* curry; mop up the sauce with some *tawa roti*.

Jhankar Choti Haveli   MULTICUISINE $
(mains ₹90-150; ⊙8am-10pm; 🛜) Stone walls, big cane chairs, prettily painted woodwork and whirring fans set the scene at this front-garden travellers' favourite. It serves up Rajasthani specialities as part of its pure veg Indian menu (the owners are Jain, so no eggs or alcohol either). It has fresh coffee for breakfast and there's candlelit seating on the rooftop come evening.

Omelette Stalls   CAFE $
(Sardar Market) On your right and left as you leave Sadar Market through its northern gate, these two omelette stalls compete for the attentions of passing travellers by knocking up seemingly endless numbers and varieties of delicious omelettes. Some folks swear that **Omelette Shop** (omelettes from ₹25; ⊙10am-10pm) is the better of two. Others wouldn't dream of going anywhere but **Vicky Chouhan Omelettes** (omelettes from ₹20; ⊙8.30am-8pm). In truth, they both do a decent job, and are both run by characters worth spending a few minutes with.

Priya Restaurant   DHABA $
(181-182 Nai Sarak; mains ₹50-73; ⊙7am-midnight) Open late, and always busy, this clean, brightly lit, street-facing *dhaba* has a certain cheerful clamour, and serves up reliable North and South Indian cuisine. The thalis (₹89) are good and the *chaat* (savoury snacks) are popular.

Kalinga Restaurant   INDIAN $$
(off Station Rd; mains ₹130-300; ⊙8am-11pm) This smart restaurant near Jodhpur train station has air-con, a well-stocked bar (beer from ₹130), and tasty veg and nonveg North Indian tandooris and curries, including a selection of kebabs. Try the *lal maans*, a mouthwatering Rajasthani mutton curry.

Mid Town   INDIAN $$
(off Station Rd; mains ₹100-150; ⊙7am-10.30pm) This clean, air-conditioned place does great

vegetarian food, including some Rajasthani specialities, and some particular to Jodhpur, such as *chakki-ka-sagh* (wheat dumpling cooked in rich gravy), *bajara-ki-roti pachkuta* (*bajara* wheat roti with local dry vegetables) and kabuli (vegetables with rice, milk, bread and fruit). It also serves beer (from ₹188). It's right beside Kalinga Restaurant.

★ **Indique**   INDIAN $$$
(📞3293328; Pal Haveli; mains ₹250-350) This candlelit rooftop restaurant at the Pal Haveli hotel is the perfect place for a romantic dinner. Even murky Gulab Sagar glistens at night and the views to the fort, clock tower and Umaid Bhawan are superb. The food covers traditional tandoori, biryanis and North Indian curries, and you won't be disappointed by the old favourites – butter chicken and rogan josh. Has a full drinks menu too (beer from ₹200).

🍷 **Drinking**

Coffee drinkers will enjoy the precious beans and espresso machines at the deliciously air-conditioned **Cafe Sheesh Mahal** (Pal Haveli; coffee from ₹80; ⊘9am-9pm), which also has free wi-fi. Plenty of rooptop restaurants do real coffee too, with varying results. For a reliable dose of double-shot espresso, there's a branch of **Café Coffee Day** (High Court Rd, Ansal Plaza; coffee from ₹50; ⊘10am-11pm) in the shopping mall on High Court Rd.

Shri Mishrilal Hotel   CAFE
(Sardar Market; lassi ₹30; ⊘8.30am-10pm) Just inside the southern gate of Sardar Market, this place has been going since 1927 and although it looks nothing fancy it whips up the most superb creamy *makhania* lassis; the best you're likely to try anywhere on

your travels. Also does tasty kachori (₹30) and other Indian snacks.

18 Century Bar   BAR
(Pal Haveli; beer from ₹200; ⊘11am-5pm) Pal Haveli's delightful hotel bar, halfway up the stairs to the rooftop restaurant Indique, is replete with horse-saddle stools and enough heritage paraphernalia to have you ordering pink gins. It closes at 5pm, after which you can continue ordering drinks on the rooftop until the restaurant closes.

🛍 **Shopping**

Plenty of Rajasthani handicrafts are available, with shops selling textiles and other wares clustered around Sardar Market and along Nai Sarak (you'll need to bargain hard).

Jodhpur is famous for antiques, with a concentration of showrooms along Palace Rd, 2km southeast of the centre (cross the railway footbridge just before Raika Bagh train station, walk straight on, then turn left at the roundabout). These warehouse-sized shops are fascinating to wander around, but they're well known to foreign antique dealers, so you'll be hard-pressed to find any bargains. Also remember that the trade in antique architectural fixtures may be contributing to the desecration of India's cultural heritage (beautiful old *havelis* are often ripped apart for their doors and window frames). Restrictions apply to the export of Indian items more than 100 years old. However, most of these showrooms deal in antique reproductions, and can make a piece of antique-style furniture and ship it home for you. The best bets for quality replica antiques are **Ajay Art Emporium** (Palace Rd; ⊘10am-7pm) or **Rani Handicrafts** (www.ranihandicrafts.com; Palace Rd; ⊘10am-7pm), which also have more portable and often

---

JODHPUR'S JODHPURS

A fashion staple for self-respecting horsey people all around the world, jodhpurs are riding breeches – usually of a pale cream colour – that are loose above the knee and tapered from knee to ankle. It's said that Sir Pratap Singh, a legendary Jodhpur statesman, soldier and horseman, originally designed the breeches for his polo team, the Jodhpur Lancers. When he led the team on a tour of England in 1897, the design caught on in London and then spread around the world.

If you fancy taking home an authentic pair from the city they originated in, head to **Monarch Garments** (📞9352353768; www.monarch-garments.com; A-13 Umaid Bhawan Palace Rd; ⊘10.30am-8.45pm), opposite the approach road leading up to Umaid Bhawan Palace, where you can buy ready-made jodhpurs or have a pair tailored for you within two days. Prices start at ₹3500 for cotton, ₹5500 for linen.

less expensive items than furniture, such as textiles, carvings and silverware.

MV Spices
FOOD & DRINK

(www.mvspices.com; ⊗9am-9pm) The most famous and reputable spice shop in Jodhpur (and believe us, there are lots of pretenders!), MV Spices has several small branches around town (including a stall outside the entrance to the fort) that are run by the seven daughters of the founder of the original stall. It will cost around ₹80 to ₹100 for 100g bags of spices, and the owners will email you recipes so you can use your spices correctly when you get home.

Sambhali Boutique
CLOTHING, ACCESSORIES

(⊗10am-8pm Mon-Sat, noon-8pm Sun) ✔ This small but interesting fixed-price shop sells colourful clothes and handicrafts made by women who have learned craft skills with the Sambhali Trust.

Krishna Book Depot
BOOKS

(Sardar Market; ⊗10.30am-7.30pm) Upstairs is an Aladdin's Den of new and used books, piled high in no apparent order; great fun for browsing. Downstairs is filled with handicrafts.

ⓘ Information

There are foreign-friendly ATMs dotted around the city. We've marked some on our map. There are very few in the old city, though, one exception being near Shahi Guest House. Internet cafes charge around ₹30 to ₹40 per hour. Again, they're dotted around town, especially in the old city.

Main Post Office (Station Rd; ⊗9am-4pm Mon-Fri, 9am-3pm Sat, stamp sales only 10am-3pm Sun)

Om Forex (Sardar Market; internet per hr ₹30; ⊗9am-10pm) Internet place which also exchanges currency and travellers cheques.

Police (Sardar Market; ⊗24hr) Small police post inside the market's north gate.

Tourist Reception Centre (☑2545083; High Court Rd; ⊗9am-6pm Mon-Fri) Offers a free city map and willingly answers questions.

ⓘ Getting There & Away

AIR

Jet Airways (☑2515551; www.jetairways.com; airport) and **Air India** (☑2510758, airport office 2512617; www.airindia.com; 2 West Patel Nagar, Circuit House Rd, airport) both fly daily to Delhi and Mumbai. To find the Air India office, walk along Ratanada Rd then turn left.

BUS

Government-run buses leave from **Central Bus Stand** (Raika Bagh), directly opposite Raika Bagh train station. Walk east along High Court Rd, then turn right under the small tunnel. Services include:

Bikaner (₹182, 5½ hours, frequent from 5am to 7pm)

Jaipur (₹252, 7 hours, frequent from 4am to midnight)

Jaisalmer (₹193, 5½ hours, frequent from 6.30am to 7pm)

Mt Abu (Abu Road) (₹191, 7½ hours, 11am and noon)

Osian (₹47, 1½ hours, half-hourly until 10pm)

Pushkar (₹143, 5 hours, 7.15am, 9.15am, 10am, 3.30pm and 8.30pm)

Rohet (₹32, 1 hour, every 15 minutes)

Udaipur (₹209, 7 hours, frequent from 5.30am to 10.30pm)

For private buses, you can book through your hotel, although it's cheaper to deal directly with the bus operators on the road in front of Jodhpur train station. **Jain Travels** (☑2633831; www.jaintravels.com; ⊗7am-11pm) is reliable, as is **Mahadev Travels** (☑2633927; Station Rd; ⊗7am-10pm) opposite them. Buses leave from bus stands out of town, but the operator should provide you with free transport (usually a shared autorickshaw) from their ticket office. Example services through Jain Travels are as follows:

Ajmer (₹220, 5 hours, 7am, 11am, 1.30pm, 2pm, 10pm and 11pm)

Bikaner (₹200, 5 hours, 5am, 6am, 9am, 4pm, 5pm, 10pm and 11pm)

Delhi (seat only) (₹400, 12 hours, 6pm)

Jaipur (₹220, 7 hours, 7am, 11am, 1.30pm, 2pm, 10pm and 11pm)

Jaisalmer (₹230, 5½ hours, hourly from 7am-10pm)

Mt Abu (direct; seat/sleeper) (₹250/400, 7½ hours, 9.30pm)

Mumbai (seat only) (₹200 to ₹300, 19 hours, 2pm)

TAXI

You can organise taxis for intercity trips (or longer) through most accommodation places, or deal directly with drivers. There's a taxi stand outside Jodhpur train station. Expect to pay around ₹9 per kilometre (for a comfortable Toyota Innova; less for a smaller car such as a Tata Indica). The driver will charge at least ₹100 for overnight stops and will charge for his return journey.

TRAIN

The computerised **booking office** (Station Rd; ⊗8am-8pm Mon-Sat, 8am-1.45pm Sun) is 300m northeast of Jodhpur train station. Trains

BORDER CROSSING – TO/FROM PAKISTAN

For Karachi (Pakistan), the 14889 Thar Express, alias the Jodhpur–Munabao Link Express, leaves Bhagat Ki Kothi station, 4km south of the Jodhpur Train Station, at 1am on Saturdays only, reaching Munabao on the India–Pakistan border at 7am. There you undergo lengthy border procedures before continuing to Karachi (assuming you have a Pakistan visa) in a Pakistani train, arriving about 2am on Sunday. Accommodation is 2nd-class and sleeper only, with a total sleeper fare of around ₹400 from Jodhpur to Karachi. In the other direction the Pakistani train leaves Karachi at about 11pm on Friday, and Indian train 14890 leaves Munabao at 7pm on Saturday, reaching Jodhpur at 11.50pm.

to and from Bikaner also stop at Raika Bagh Train Station.

Two daily trains make the six-hour trip to **Jaisalmer** (5.10am and 11.45pm).

Four daily trains go to **Bikaner** (10am, 10.45am, 2pm and 8.15pm). Most take 5½ hours, although the 2pm takes more than seven.

Five daily trains go to **Jaipur** (6.10am, 9.45am, 8pm, 8.30pm and 11pm) in five to six hours.

Two daily trains go to **Delhi** (8pm and 11pm), arriving at 6.25am and 11.10am respectively.

Two also go to **Mumbai** (3pm and 6.45pm), arriving at 9.40am and 11.35am respectively.

For **Mount Abu**, three daily trains go to Abu Road (6am, 3pm and 6.45pm) in 4½ hours. Sleepers cost around ₹150.

For **Pushkar**, only one train per day goes to Ajmer (7am).

There are no direct trains to **Udaipur**.

ⓘ Getting Around

TO & FROM THE AIRPORT

The airport is 5km south of the city centre; at least ₹100/200 by auto/taxi.

AUTORICKSHAW

Autorickshaws between the clock tower area and the train stations or central bus stand should be about ₹20 to ₹30.

Around Jodhpur

The mainly arid countryside around Jodhpur is dotted with surprising lakes, isolated forts and palaces, and intriguing villages. It's home to a clutch of fine heritage hotels where you can enjoy the slower pace of rural life.

Osian

This ancient Thar Desert town, 65km north of Jodhpur, was an important trading centre between the 8th and 12th centuries. It was dominated by the Jains, whose wealth left a legacy of exquisitely sculptured, well-preserved temples. The **Mahavira Temple** (Indian/foreigner free/₹10, camera/video ₹50/100; ◷ 6am-8.30pm) surrounds an image of the 24th *tirthankar* (great teacher), formed from sand and milk. **Sachiya Mata Temple** (◷ 6am-7.15pm) is an impressive walled complex where both Hindus and Jains worship.

Prakash Bhanu Sharma, a personable Brahmin priest, has an echoing **guesthouse** (☏ 02922274331, 9414440479; s/d without bathroom ₹250/300), geared towards pilgrims, opposite the Mahavira Temple.

Gemar Singh (☏ 9460585154; www.hacra. org), a native of Bhikamkor village northwest of Osian, arranges camel safaris, homestays, camping, desert walks and jeep trips in the deserts around Osian and their Rajput and Bishnoi villages. His trips receive

MAJOR TRAINS FROM JODHPUR

DESTINATION	TRAIN	DEPARTURE TIME	ARRIVAL TIME	FARE (₹; SLEEPER/3AC)
Ajmer	54801 Jodhpur-Ajmer Fast Passenger	7am	12.40pm	88/362
Bikaner	14708 Ranakpur Exp	10am	3.35pm	146/394
Delhi	12462 Mandor Exp	8pm	6.25am	272/734
Jaipur	14854 Marudhar Exp	9.45am	3.30pm	158/428
Jaisalmer	14810 Jodhpur-Jaisalmer Exp	11.45pm	5.30am	155/419
Mumbai	14707 Ranakpur Exp	3pm	9.40am	323/912

rave reviews. The cost is around ₹1000 per person per day (minimum two people). Pickup from Osian bus station, or from Jodhpur, can be arranged.

There are frequent buses from Jodhpur to Osian. Trains between Jodhpur and Jaisalmer also stop here. A return taxi from Jodhpur costs about ₹1200.

Southern Villages

A number of traditional villages are strung along and off the Pali road southeast of Jodhpur. Most hotels and guesthouses in Jodhpur offer tours to these villages, often called Bishnoi village safaris. The Bishnoi are a Hindu sect who follow the 500-year-old teachings of Guru Jambheshwar, who emphasised the importance of protecting the environment long before it was popular to do so. Many visitors are surprised by the density – and fearlessness – of wildlife such as blackbuck, bluebulls (nilgai), chinkara gazelles and desert fox around the Bishnoi villages. The Bishnoi hold all animal life sacred. The 1730 sacrifice of 363 villagers to protect khejri trees is commemorated in September at Khejadali village, where there is a memorial to the victims fronted by a small grove of khejri trees.

Bishnoi village tours tend to last four hours in total and cost around ₹600 to ₹800 per person. We recommend those arranged by Durag Niwas Guest House, but loads of other places do them.

Rohet

Rohet Garh (☏ 02936-268231; www.rohetgarh. com; s/d ₹5000/6000; ✻ @ ☎ ☳), in Rohet village, 40km south of Jodhpur on the Pali road, is one of the area's most appealing heritage hotels. This 350-year-old, lovingly tended manor has masses of character and a tranquil atmosphere, which obviously helped Bruce Chatwin when he wrote *The Songlines* here, and William Dalrymple when he began *City of Djinns* in the same room, No 15. Rohet Garh has a gorgeous colonnaded pool, charming green gardens, great food (breakfast/lunch/dinner ₹500/600/700) and lovely, individual rooms. It also possesses a stable of fine Marwari horses and organises rides, from two-hour evening trots (₹2000) to six-day countryside treks, sleeping in luxury tents. The quirky **Om Bana Temple** is a short bus ride from here.

A taxi here will cost around ₹800 from Jodhpur. There are also frequent buses; once here, turn right out of Rohet's tiny bus stand, take the first right and keep walking for about 1km.

Jaisalmer

☏ 02992 / POP 78,000

The fort of Jaisalmer is a breathtaking sight: a massive sandcastle rising from the sandy plains like a mirage from a bygone era. No place better evokes exotic camel-train trade routes and desert mystery. Ninety-nine bastions encircle the fort's still-inhabited twisting lanes. Inside are shops swaddled in bright embroideries, a royal palace and numerous businesses looking for your tourist rupee. Despite the commercialism it's hard not to be enchanted by this desert citadel. Beneath the ramparts, particularly to the north, the narrow streets of the old city conceal magnificent *havelis,* all carved from the same golden-honey sandstone as the fort – hence Jaisalmer's designation as the Golden City.

A city that has come back almost from the dead in the past half-century, Jaisalmer may be remote but it's certainly not forgotten – indeed it's one of Rajasthan's biggest tourist destinations, and few people come here without climbing onto a camel in the

---

THE MOTORCYCLE TEMPLE

One of the strangest temples in all India stands beside a main road, 8km south of Rohet. The deity at **Om Bana Temple** is a garland-decked Enfield Bullet motorcycle, known as Bullet Baba. The story goes that local villager Om Bana died at this spot in the 1980s when his motorbike skidded into a tree. The bike was taken to the local police station, but then mysteriously twice made its own way back to the tree, and travellers along the road started seeing visions of Om Bana – inevitably leading to the machine's deification.

Buses from Jodhpur to Rohet (₹32, one hour) should continue on to Om Bana, but check with the driver. Otherwise, you can hop on almost any passing bus from Rohet (₹10).

Jaisalmer

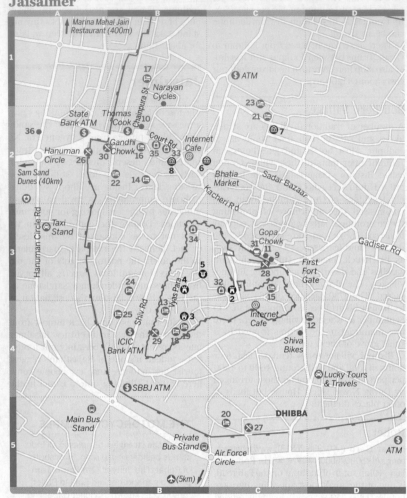

surrounding Thar Desert. Competition to get *your* bum into a camel saddle can be fierce, with some operators adopting unpleasant hard-sell tactics. Generally speaking, though, this is a much more laidback, hassle-free place to stay than the likes of Jaipur or Jodhpur.

Jaisalmer celebrates its desert culture in January or February each year with the action-packed **Desert Festival**, featuring camel races, camel polo, folk music, snake charmers, turban-tying contests and the famous Mr Desert competition. Many events take place at the Sam sand dunes.

History

Jaisalmer was founded way back in 1156 by a leader of the Bhati Rajput clan named Jaisal. The Bhatis, who trace their lineage back to Krishna, ruled right through to Independence in 1947.

The city's early centuries were tempestuous, partly because its rulers relied on looting for want of other income, but by the 16th century Jaisalmer was prospering from its strategic position on the camel-train routes between India and Central Asia. It eventually established cordial relations

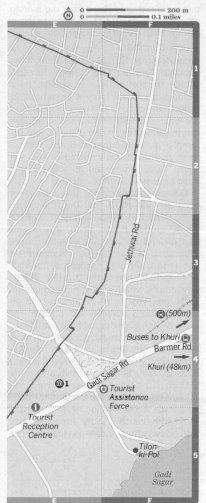

Jaisalmer

◎ Sights

◆ Activities, Courses & Tours

🛏 Sleeping

✕ Eating

🍷 Drinking & Nightlife

🛍 Shopping

ℹ Transport

with the Mughal empire. Maharawal Sabal Singh, in the mid-17th century, expanded the Jaisalmer princedom to its greatest extents by annexing areas that now fall within the administrative districts of Bikaner and Jodhpur.

Under British rule the rise of sea trade (especially through Mumbai) and railways saw Jaisalmer's importance and population decline. Partition in 1947, with the cutting of trade routes to Pakistan, seemingly sealed the city's fate. But the 1965 and 1971 wars between India and Pakistan gave Jaisalmer new strategic importance, and since the 1960s the Indira Gandhi Canal to the north has brought revitalising water to the desert.

Today tourism and the area's many military installations are the pillars of the city's economy.

⊙ Sights

Jaisalmer Fort
FORT

Founded in 1156 by the Rajput ruler Jaisal and reinforced by subsequent rulers, **Jaisalmer Fort** was the focus of a number of battles between the Bhatis, the Mughals of Delhi and the Rathores of Jodhpur. You enter the fort from its east side, near Gopa Chowk, and pass through four massive gates on the zigzagging route to the upper part. The fourth gate opens into a square, Dashera Chowk, where Jaisalmer Fort's uniqueness becomes apparent: this is a living fort, with about 3000 people residing within its walls. It's honeycombed with narrow, winding lanes which are lined with houses and temples – along with a large number of handicraft shops, guesthouses, restaurants and massage/beauty parlours.

➡ **Fort Palace**

(Indian/foreigner incl compulsory audio guide ₹50/300, camera/video ₹100/200; ⊙8am-6pm Apr-Oct, 9am-6pm Nov-Mar) Towering over the fort's main square, and partly built on top of the Hawa Pol (the fourth fort gate), is the former rulers' elegant seven-storey palace. The 1½-hour audio-guide tour, available in six languages, is included in your ticket price (whether you want it or not). It's worthwhile, but you must deposit ₹2000 or an official form of photo ID to get it. Highlights include the mirrored and painted Rang Mahal (the bedroom of the 18th-century ruler Mulraj II), a gallery of finely wrought 15th-century sculptures donated to the rulers by the builders of the fort's temples, and the spectacular 360-degree views from the rooftop. One room contains an intriguing display of stamps from the former Rajput states.

➡ **Jain Temples**

(Indian/foreigner ₹30/150, camera ₹50; ⊙Chandraprabhu 7am-1pm, other temples 11am-1pm) Within the fort walls is a mazelike, interconnecting treasure trove of seven beautiful yellow-sandstone Jain temples dating from the 15th and 16th centuries. The intricate carving almost rivals that of the marble Jain temples in Ranakpur and Mt Abu, and has an extraordinary quality because of the soft, warm stone. Shoes and all leather items must be removed before entering.

Chandraprabhu is the first temple you come to, and you'll find the ticket stand here. Dedicated to the eighth *tirthankar,* whose symbol is the moon, it was built in 1509 and features fine sculpture in the *mandapa,* whose intensely sculpted pillars form a series of *toranas.* To the right of Chandraprabhu is the tranquil **Rikhabdev** temple, with fine sculptures around the walls, protected by glass cabinets, and pillars beautifully sculpted with *apsaras* and gods. Behind Chandraprabhu is **Parasnath**, which you enter through a beautifully carved *torana* culminating in an image of the Jain *tirthankar* at its apex. A door to the south leads to small **Shitalnath**, dedicated to the 10th *tirthankar,* whose image is composed of eight precious metals. A door in the north wall leads to the enchanting, dim chamber of **Sambhavanth** – in the front courtyard, Jain priests grind sandalwood in mortars for

---

A CASTLE BUILT ON SAND

A decade ago the whole structure of Jaisalmer Fort was in danger of being undermined by water leakage from its antique drainage system. The main problem: material progress, in the form of piped water for the fort's inhabitants. Three of the ancient bastions had collapsed and parts of the fort palace were leaning at an alarming rate.

Since then, British-based **Jaisalmer in Jeopardy** (www.jaisalmer-in-jeopardy.org) and several Indian organisations, including the **Indian National Trust for Art & Cultural Heritage** (INTACH; www.intach.org), have raised funds and carried out much-needed conservation works to save the fort. Most important has been the renewal of the fort's drainage system and repaving of the streets, as well as repair works inside the fort palace.

Things have improved, although some conservationists still believe the fort's structure is in danger, and there are calls for the fort's inhabitants, and those who work in the fort, to be forced to leave. The fort's current population has been established since the 1960s; before then, the fort's inhabitants numbered in the few hundreds; made up mostly of royal family and their workers, plus monks and priests connected to the fort's temples. Visitors should be aware of the fort's fragile nature and conserve resources, especially water, as much as possible. Accommodation outside the fort is available.

devotional use. Steps lead down to the **Gyan Bhandar**, a fascinating, tiny, underground library founded in 1500, which houses priceless ancient illustrated manuscripts. The remaining two temples, **Shantinath** and **Kunthunath**, were built in 1536 and feature plenty of sensual carving. Note, the restrictive visiting times are for non-Jains. The temples are open all day for worshippers.

➡ Laxminarayan Temple

The Hindu Laxminarayan Temple, in the centre of the fort, is simpler than the Jain temples and has a brightly decorated dome. Devotees offer grain, which is distributed before the temple. The inner sanctum has a repoussé silver architrave around its entrance, and a heavily garlanded image enshrined within.

Havelis

Inside the fort but outside it, too (especially in the streets to the north), Jaisalmer is replete with the fairy-tale architecture of *havelis* – gorgeously carved stone doorways, *jali* (carved lattice) screens, balconies and turrets.

Patwa-ki-Haveli   HISTORIC BUILDING
(Indian/foreigner ₹20/50; ◷10am-5pm) The biggest fish in the *haveli* pond is Patwa-ki-Haveli, which towers over a narrow lane, its intricate stonework like honey-coloured lace. It is divided into five sections and was built between 1800 and 1860 by five Jain brothers who made their fortunes in brocade and jewellery. It's most impressive from the outside, though the first of the five sections is open as the privately owned **Kothari's Patwa-ki-Haveli Museum** (Indian/foreigner ₹50/150, camera/video ₹50/70), which richly evokes 19th-century life. Touts in the lane outside can be a pain here.

Nathmal-ki-Haveli   HISTORIC BUILDING
(◷8am-7pm) This late-19th-century *haveli* also used to be a prime minister's house and is still partly inhabited. It also contains some tourist shops. It has an extraordinary exterior, dripping with carvings, and the 1st floor has some beautiful paintings using 1.5kg of gold. A doorway is surrounded by 19th-century British postcards and there's a picture of Queen Victoria. The left and right wings were the work of two brothers, whose competitive spirits apparently produced this virtuoso work – the two sides are similar, but not identical.

Museums

Desert Cultural Centre & Museum   MUSEUM
(Indian/foreigner ₹20/50, camera/video ₹20/50, puppet shows Indian/foreigner ₹30/50, camera/video ₹20/50, combined museum-show ticket ₹70; ◷9am-8pm, puppet shows 6.30pm, 7.30pm) Next to the Tourist Reception Centre, this interesting little museum has material on the history of Rajasthan's different princely states, and exhibits on traditional Rajasthani culture. Features include Rajasthani music (with video), textiles and a *phad* scroll painting. It also hosts nightly half-hour **puppet shows** with English commentary.

Thar Heritage Museum   MUSEUM
(off Court Rd; admission ₹40) This privately run museum near Gandhi Chowk has an intriguing assortment of Jaisalmer area artefacts. It's brought alive by the guided tour you'll probably get from its founder, local historian and folklorist LN Khatri. Opening hours are variable, but if it's closed, you should find Mr Khatri at his shop, Desert Handicrafts Emporium, nearby on Court Rd.

👉 Tours

The Tourist Reception Centre runs a handful of tours, including sunset tours to the Sam sand dunes (₹200 per person, minimum four people). Add ₹100 if you'd like a short camel ride too.

🛏 Sleeping

Staying in the fort is the most atmospheric and romantic choice, but be aware of the pressure tourism is exerting on the fort's infrastructure. Outside the fort, the lanes to the north are more atmospheric than the recently renovated lanes west of Shiv Rd, or the wider, more exposed roads south of the fort. You'll get massive discounts between April and August, when Jaisalmer is hellishly hot.

🛏 Outside the Fort

Residency Centre Point   GUESTHOUSE $
(☎252883, 9414760421; residency_guesthouse@ yahoo.com; Kumbhara Para; r ₹450; @) Near to Patwa-ki-Haveli, this friendly, family-run guesthouse has five clean, spacious doubles in a lovely 250-year-old building. Rooms vary in size – budget in price but midrange in quality. The rooftop restaurant has superb fort views and offers home-cooked food.

JAISALMER CAMEL SAFARIS

Trekking around by camel is the most evocative and fun way to sample Thar Desert life. Don't expect dune seas, however – the Thar is mostly arid scrubland sprinkled with villages and wind turbines, with occasional dune areas popping out here and there. You will often come across fields of millet, and children herding flocks of sheep or goats whose neck-bells tinkle in the desert silence – a welcome change after the sound of belching camels.

Most trips now include jeep rides to get you to less frequented areas. The camel riding is then done in two-hour batches, one before lunch, one after. It's hardly camel *trekking*, but it's a lot of fun nevertheless. A cheaper alternative to arranging things in Jaisalmer is to base yourself in the small village of Khuri (p193), 48km southwest, where similar camel rides are available but where you're already in the desert when you start.

Before You Go

Competition between safari organisers is cut-throat and standards vary. Most hotels and guesthouses are very happy to organise a camel safari for you. While many provide a good service, some may cut corners and take you for the kind of ride you didn't have in mind. A few low-budget hotels in particular exert considerable pressure on guests to take 'their' safari. Others specifically claim 'no safari hassle'.

You can also organise a safari directly with one of the several reputable specialist agencies in Jaisalmer. Since these agencies depend exclusively on safari business it's particularly in their interest to satisfy their clients. It's a good idea to talk to other travellers and ask two or three operators what they're offering.

A one-night safari, leaving Jaisalmer in the afternoon and returning the next morning, with a night on some dunes, is a minimum to get a feel for the experience: you'll probably get 1½ to two hours of riding each day. You can trek for several days or weeks if you wish. The longer you ride, the more you'll gain understanding of the desert's villages, oases, wildlife and people.

The best-known dunes, at Sam (40km west of Jaisalmer), are always crowded in the evening and are more of a carnival than a back-to-nature experience. The dunes near Khuri are also quite busy at sunset, but quiet the rest of the time. Operators all sell trips now to 'nontouristy' and 'off the beaten track' areas. Ironically, this has made Khuri quieter again, although Sam still hums with day-tripper activity.

With jeep transfers included, typical rates are between ₹1100 and ₹1700 per person for a one-day-one-night trip (leaving one morning, and returning the next). This should include meals, mineral water and blankets, and sometimes a thin mattress. Check that there will be one camel for each rider. You can pay for greater levels of comfort (eg tents, better food), but always get it all down in writing.

You should get a cheaper rate (₹900 to ₹1500 per person) if you leave Jaisalmer in the afternoon and return the following morning. A quick sunset ride in the dunes at Sam costs around ₹550 per person, including jeep transfer. At the other end of the scale, you can arrange for a 20-day trek to Bikaner. Expect to pay between ₹1000 and 2000 per person per day for long, multiday trips, depending on the level of support facilities (jeeps, camel carts, etc).

Roop Mahal HOTEL **$**
(☏251700; www.hotelroopmahal.com; r ₹300-1500) Clean spacious rooms in a new buidling, trustworthy management, fort views from the rooftop restaurant (mains ₹80 to ₹180) and free wi-fi throughout. A solid budget choice, but with some fancier rooms too.

Hotel Renuka HOTEL **$**
(☏252757; hotelrenuka@rediffmail.com; Chainpura St; r ₹250-650, with AC ₹800; ❄@) Spread over three floors, Renuka has squeaky clean

rooms – the best have balconies, private bathrooms and air-con. It's been warmly accommodating guests since 1988, so management knows its stuff. The roof terrace has great fort views and a good restaurant.

Hotel Tokyo Palace HOTEL **$**
(☏255483; www.tokyopalace.net; Dhibba Para; dm ₹150, s ₹300-1200, d ₹500-2000; ❄@🌐≋) Well-run by honest, traveller-friendly management, this new place has clean mid-

What to Take

Women should consider wearing a sports bra, as a trotting camel is a bumpy ride. A wide-brimmed hat (or *Lawrence of Arabia* turban), long trousers, long-sleeved shirt, insect repellent, toilet paper (don't forget to burn it after use), torch, sunscreen, water bottle (with a strap) and some cash (tip the camel men, if nothing else) are also recommended. It can get cold at night, so if you have a sleeping bag bring it along, even if you're told that lots of blankets will be supplied. During summer, rain is not unheard of, so come prepared.

Which Safari?

➡ **Sahara Travels** (☑ 252609; www.saharatravelsjaisalmer.com; Gopa Chowk) Now run by the son of the late LN Bissa (aka Mr Desert), a real Jaisalmer character who sadly died in 2012, this place is still very professional and transparent. Trips are to 'nontouristy' areas only. Prices for an overnight trip (9am to 11am the next day): ₹1400 per person, all inclusive.

➡ **Trotters** (☑ 9828929974; www.trotterscamelsafarijaisalmer.com; ⊘ 5.30am-7.30pm) Run by 'Del Boy' – who else? – this company is also run transparently, with a clear price list in the office showing everything on offer. Does trips to 'nontouristy' areas as well as cheaper jaunts to Sam or Khuri. Prices for an overnight trip (8am to 10am the next day): ₹1100 to ₹1200 per person, all inclusive.

➡ **Thar Desert Tours** (☑ 255656; www.tharcamelsafarijaisalmer.com; Gandhi Chowk; ⊘ 8.30am 7.30pm) Located at Gandhi Chowk, this well-run operator charges ₹950 per person per day, adjusting prices accordingly depending on trip times. They are slightly pricier than Sahara or Trotters, but we also receive good feedback about them. Their system is for customers to pay 80% up front. There are several other options, including hotel-organised safaris. Note that recommendations here should not be a substitute for doing your own research. Whichever agency you go for, insist that all rubbish is carried back to Jaisalmer.

In the Desert

Camping out at night, huddling around a tiny fire beneath the stars and listening to the camel drivers' songs, is magical.

There's always a long lunch stop during the hottest part of the day. At resting points the camels are unsaddled and hobbled; they'll often have a roll in the sand before limping away to browse on nearby shrubs, while the camel drivers brew chai or prepare food.

Take care of your possessions, particularly on the return journey. Any complaints you do have should be reported, either to the **Superintendent of Police** (☑ 252233), the Tourist Reception Centre, or the intermittently staffed Tourist Assistance Force posts inside the First Fort Gate and on the Gadi Sagar access road.

The camel drivers will expect a tip or gift at the end of the trip; don't neglect to give them one.

range rooms as well as plenty of budget options, including separate dorms for men and women in the basement. Wi-fi only extends to some rooms and although it does have a pool, it is tiny.

Dylan Cafe & Guesthouse GUESTHOUSE $
(☑ 9828561818; dylancafe.guesthouse@yahoo.in; r ₹200-350; @ 🛜) Dirt cheap digs for young backpackers who like to chillout or party or both. Rooms are acceptable, but most of your time will be spent drinking and smoking with the young owners on the rooftop. Free wi-fi. Fresh coffee.

Desert Moon GUESTHOUSE $$
(☑ 250116, 9414149350; www.desertmoonguesthouse.com; Achalvansi Colony; s ₹500-800, d ₹800-1200; ❄ @ 🛜) Run by Lois (a New Zealander who's been living in Jaisalmer for more than 12 years) and her Rajasthani husband, Chanesar, this smart guesthouse,

a 10-minute walk from Gandhi Chowk, enjoys a wonderfully peaceful location beneath the royal *chhatri*. Rooms are cool, clean and comfortable, and the rooftop vegetarian restaurant has fort and *chhatri* views. It's ₹50 to ₹60 in an auto from the train station, but there's free pick-up if you call ahead. If you're walking here, head north from Hanuman Circle until you reach Marina Mahal Jain Restaurant (500m) on your left. Desert Moon is down a track about 100m behind this restaurant.

Shahi Palace
HOTEL $$

(🖉 255920; www.shahipalacehotel.com; off Shiv Rd; r ₹550-2050; ❄@🛜) A modern building in traditional style with some lovely carved sandstone, Shahi has attractive rooms, though a limited number have natural light. The multicuisine rooftop restaurant (mains ₹80 to ₹200) is also decent. Reasonably popular, but there are plenty of spillover rooms in their nearby sister properties **Star Haveli** and **Oasis Haveli**.

KB Lodge
HOTEL $$$

(🖉 253833; www.killabhawan.com; Patwa Haveli; r ₹1800, with AC ₹2500; ❄🛜) Under the same management as the luxury Hotel Killa Bhawan, KB Lodge has more of a guesthouse feel to it, with just five stylish rooms in a small building overlooking the plaza behind Patwa Haveli. There's wi-fi throughout and the pleasant rooftop restaurant, KB Cafe, has delightful views of the old town and the fort.

Hotel Nachana Haveli
HERITAGE HOTEL $$$

(🖉 252110; www.nachanahaveli.com; Gandhi Chowk; s/d ₹3150/3500; ❄@) This 280-year-old royal *haveli*, set around three courtyards – one with a tinkling fountain – is a fascinating hotel. The raw sandstone rooms have arched stone ceilings and the ambience of a medieval castle. They are sumptuously and romantically decorated, though some lack much natural light.

1st Gate
HOTEL $$$

(🖉 8696008365; www.1stgate.in; r incl breakfast ₹6500; ❄@🛜) Italian-designed and super slick, this newcomer is Jaisalmer's most sophisticated modern hotel and it is beautiful throughout. The location lends it one of the most dramatic fort views in town, especially from its split-level open-air restaurant-cafe. Rooms are immaculate and the food (Italian and Indian) and coffee are top notch. Wi-fi throughout. No pool.

Mandir Palace Hotel
HERITAGE HOTEL $$$

(🖉 252788; www.mandirpalace.com; Gandhi Chowk; s/d ₹6000/7000; ❄@🛜❄) Jaisalmer's erstwhile royal family still lives in this sprawling 18th-century palace just inside the town walls. Some rooms are full of character, the newer ones less so. Staff can be distant.

🏰 In the Fort

Hotel Siddhartha
HOTEL $

(🖉 253614; hotelsiddhartha@gmail.com; r ₹400-800; @🛜) Just past the Jain temples, little Siddhartha has well-kept, tile-floored rooms, plus one lovely stone-walled room that hasn't been renovated.

Desert Boy's Guest House
HERITAGE HOTEL $$

(🖉 253091; www.desertboysguesthouse.com; ₹500-3000) Has 15 beautifully decorated rooms. The cheaper ones have interior windows, but others have sweeping desert views. Rooms are bright and colourful, bathrooms are modern and the place is littered with antique-looking furniture. Wi-fi in some areas only. Restaurant has great views.

Hotel Suraj
HERITAGE GUESTHOUSE $$

(🖉 251623; www.hotelsurajjaisalmer.webs.com; r ₹850-1550) Enchanting family-run guesthouse with four unique rooms that come with cute alcoves, side rooms, stone floors, stone pillars and even faded old paintings on some of the stone walls. Bathrooms are very basic, but have hot-water showers. Two rooms have good views. The same family that lives here runs the small but modern Hotel Suraj Vilas opposite (r ₹500 to ₹1000).

Hotel Killa Bhawan
HERITAGE HOTEL $$$

(🖉 251204; www.killabhawan.com; 445 Kotri Para; r incl breakfast ₹6500-11,000; ❄@🛜) A mini-labyrinth of a place combining three old houses set right on the fort walls. French-owned and designed, it has vividly coloured rooms, attractive little sitting areas and all sorts of intriguing arts and crafts. Rooms are small for the prices, but are decorated exquisitely. No restaurant, but tea, coffee and breakfast are all included.

🍴 Eating

Chandan Shree Restaurant
PUNJABI $

(near Hanuman Circle; mains ₹50-130; ⏱7am-11pm) Very popular local favourite and a great spot for South Indian breakfasts. The speciality, though, is Punjabi vegetarian. Also does thalis. No booze.

Sun Set Palace
MULTICUISINE $

(Fort; mains ₹90-200) This restaurant has floor cushions and low tables on an airy terrace on the fort's west side. Pretty good vegetarian Indian dishes are prepared, as well as Chinese and Italian options. Beer available.

Desert Boy's Dhani
INDIAN $$

(mains ₹100-135; ☉11am-4pm & 7-11pm) An unusual walled-garden restaurant where tables are spread around a large stone-paved courtyard with a big tree. Rajasthani music and dance is performed from 8pm to 10pm most nights, and it's a very pleasant place to eat excellent, good-value Rajasthani and other Indian veg dishes. Does beer too (from ₹200).

Jaisal Italy
ITALIAN $$

(First Fort Gate; mains ₹120-200; ☉8.30am-10.30pm; 🛜) Though it's run by the same family as Lassi Shop, you won't have to worry about bhang-laced pizzas. Instead you'll find superb all-veg bruschetta, antipasti, pasta, pizza, salad and desserts, plus Spanish omelettes, served in an exotically decorated indoor restaurant (cosy in winter, deliciously air-conditioned in summer) or on a delightful terrace with cinematic views atop the lower fort walls. Fresh coffee. Free wi-fi.

Trio
MULITCUISINE $$

(☎252733; Gandhi Chowk; mains ₹100-190) Under a tented roof atop the wall of the Mandir Palace, this long-running restaurant does Indian (including some Rajasthani specialities), Chinese and Continental. The thalis, biryanis and tandoori items are all excellent, and the restaurant has a lot more atmosphere than most places in town. Musicians play in the evening and there's a partial fort view.

Saffron
MULTICUISINE $$

(Gandhi Chowk; mains ₹100-300) This romantic open-air restaurant, on the spacious roof terrace of Hotel Nachana Haveli, has candle-lit tables overlooking a fountain courtyard below. The Indian food – including tandoori kebabs – is hard to beat, though the Italian comes a close second. Has a range of beers (small bottle ₹160) and a wine list.

1st Gate
ITALIAN $$$

(mains ₹150-300; ☉7am-11pm; 🛜) A small but excellent menu of authentic Italian dishes as well as some delicious Indian food served on a split-level, open-air terrace with dramatic fort views. Also does good strong Italian coffee (₹100 to ₹150) as well as some fine wines.

 Shopping

Jaisalmer is famous for stunning embroidery, bedspreads, mirror-work wall hangings, oil lamps, stonework and antiques. Watch out when buying silver items: the metal is sometimes adulterated with bronze.

Hari Om Jewellers
HANDICRAFTS

(Chougan Para, Fort; ☉10am-8.30pm) This family of silversmiths makes beautiful, delicate silver rings and bracelets featuring world landmarks and Hindu gods. Asking prices for rings start at ₹1800 (at a rate of ₹300 per day's work).

Jaisalmer Handloom
HANDICRAFTS

(www.jaisalmerhandloom.com; Court Rd; ☉9am-10pm) Has a big array of bedspreads, tapestries, clothing (ready made and custommade, including silk) and other textiles, made by its own workers and others, and doesn't belabour you with too much of a hard sell.

Desert Handicrafts Emporium
HANDICRAFTS

(Court Rd; ☉9.30am-9.30pm) With some unusual jewellery, paintings and all sorts of textiles and other knick-knacks, this is one of

---

AN EXTRA-SPECIAL LASSI SHOP

Jaisalmer's, if not India's, most famous bhang-lassi shop is a simple, pocket-sized place now called **Lassi Shop** (Gopa Chowk; normal lassi ₹25-60, bhang lassi ₹50-120; ☉9.30am-10.30pm), but it has been running under various guises since the late '70s. It does a huge range of normal lassis (yoghurt drinks), but can add bhang (cannabis buds and leaves mixed into a paste with milk, ghee and spices) to any of them, which transforms them into so-called 'special lassis', and doubles their price. They also do a range of bhang-laced cookies (₹500 to ₹700 for 10) for travellers to take on their camel safaris. Bhang is perfectly legal here, but be aware that it doesn't agree with everyone so if you're not used to this sort of thing, go easy on it (or avoid it altogether). It can be very strong.

the most original and intriguing of the numerous craft shops around town.

Bellissima HANDICRAFTS
(Fort; ☺8am-9pm) Small shop selling beautiful patchworks, embroidery, paintings, bags, rugs, cushion covers and all types of Rajasthani art. Proceeds assist underprivileged women from surrounding villages, including those who have divorced or been widowed.

ℹ Information

INTERNET ACCESS
There are several internet cafes scattered around town. Typical cost is ₹40 per hour.

MONEY
Foreign-friendly ATMs are dotted round town, although none are inside the fort.

Thomas Cook (Gandhi Chowk; ☺9.30am-7pm Mon-Sat, 10am-5pm Sun) A reliable moneychanger, changing travellers cheques and cash, and providing credit- and debit-card advances.

TOURIST INFORMATION
Tourist Reception Centre (☎252406; Gadi Sagar Rd; ☺9.30am-6pm) Friendly office with a free map of town, and basic sand-dune tours.

TRAVEL AGENCIES
Hanuman Travels (☎9413362367)
Swagat Travels (☎252557)

ℹ Getting There & Away

BUS
Government-run buses leave from the **main bus stand**. Services are very limited, though. One daily air-conditioned coach goes to **Delhi** (₹1750, 15 to 17 hours, 5pm) via **Jodhpur** (₹512), **Ajmer** (₹800) and **Jaipur** (₹1060), but it's reclining seats only.

There are, though, daily services to **Jodhpur** (₹197, 5½ hours) on an ordinary bus at 6.30am, 8am, 9am, 10.30am, 1pm and 4pm.

A number of private bus companies have tickets offices at Hanuman Circle. Hanuman Travels and Swagat Travels are typical. The buses themselves leave from the **private bus stand**. Typical services include the following:

Bikaner (₹180 to ₹200, three to four daily)
Jaipur (₹350 to ₹400, 11 hours, two or three daily)
Jodhpur (₹180 to ₹200, five hours, half-hourly from 6am to 10pm)
Pushkar (₹350 to ₹400, nine hours, two or three daily)
Udaipur (₹350, one or two daily)

TAXI
One-way taxis should cost from around ₹3000 to Jodhpur, ₹4000 to Bikaner or ₹6000 to Udaipur. There's a **taxi rank** south of Hanuman Circle, or try **Lucky Tours & Travels** (☎251818), behind Hotel Maru Palace. They sometimes have cheaper 'returning taxis' available.

TRAIN
Three daily trains go to **Jodhpur** (8am, 5.15pm and 11.30pm). They take eight, five and six hours respectively. Unreserved 'general tickets' cost ₹50 to ₹75.

Two daily trains go to **Bikaner** (10.30am and 10.40pm) in around six hours; unreserved 'general' seats cost around ₹75, reserved sleepers around ₹160. One daily train goes to **Delhi** (5.15pm, 18 hours) via **Jaipur** (12 hours).

ℹ Getting Around

AUTORICKSHAW
Around ₹30 from the train station to Gandhi Chowk.

BICYCLE
A number of places hire bicycles, including **Narayan Cycles** (near Gandhi Chowk; per hr/day ₹10/60; ☺8am-7pm).

CAR & MOTORCYCLE
It's possible to hire taxis or jeeps from the stand near Hanuman Circle Rd. To Khuri or the Sam sand dunes expect to pay ₹800 to ₹1000 one way.

Shiva Bikes (scooter/motorbike per day ₹300/400; ☺8am-9pm) is a licenced hire place with adequate motorbikes and scooters for exploring town and nearby sights (helmets and area maps included).

MAJOR TRAINS FROM JAISALMER

DESTINATION	TRAIN	DEPARTURE TIME	ARRIVAL TIME	FARE (₹)
Bikaner	14701 Jaisalmer-Bikaner Exp	10.40pm	4.35am	158 (A)
Delhi (Old Delhi)	14660 Jaisalmer-Delhi Exp	5.15pm	11.10am	317/862 (B)
Jaipur	14660 Jaisalmer-Delhi Exp	5.15pm	5.08am	252/703 (B)
Jodhpur	14809 Jaisalmer-Jodhpur Exp	11.30pm	5.15am	155/419 (B)

Fares: (A) sleeper, (B) sleeper/3AC

ℹ ARRIVAL IN JAISALMER

Touts work the buses heading to Jaisalmer from Jodhpur, hoping to steer travellers to guesthouses or hotels in Jaisalmer where they will get a commission. On arrival in Jaisalmer, most buses are surrounded by a swarm of touts baying for your attention. If an autorickshaw driver has a sign with the name of the accommodation you want, by all means take the free ride offered (after checking that it is free). Otherwise, don't believe anyone who offers to take you 'anywhere you like' for just a few rupees, and do take with a fistful of salt any claims that the hotel you want is 'full', 'closed' or 'no good any more'.

Also be very wary of offers of rooms for ₹100 or similar absurd rates. Places offering such prices are almost certainly in the camel-safari hard-sell game and their objective is to get you out of the room and on to a camel as fast as possible. If you don't take up their safari offers, the room price may suddenly increase or you might be told there isn't a room available any more.

Touts are less prevalent on the trains, but the same clamour for your custom ensues outside the station once you have arrived.

Around Jaisalmer

Sam Sand Dunes

The silky **Sam sand dunes** (admission vehicle/camel ₹50/80), 41km west of Jaisalmer along a good sealed road (maintained by the Indian army), are one of the most popular excursions from the city. The band of dunes is about 2km long and is undeniably one of the most picturesque in the region. Some camel safaris camp here, but many more people just roll in for sunset – to be chased across the sands by dressed up dancing children and tenacious camel owners offering short rides. Plenty more people stay overnight in one of the couple of dozen tent resorts near the dunes. All in all the place acquires something of a carnival atmosphere from late afternoon till the next morning, making it somewhere to avoid if you're after a solitary desert sunset experience.

If you're organising your own camel ride on the spot, expect to pay ₹200 to ₹300 for a one-hour sunset ride, but beware of tricks from camel men such as demanding more money en route.

Khuri

📞 03014

The village of Khuri, 48km southwest of Jaisalmer, makes a lovely base for exploring the desert. There's quite an extensive dune area about 2km away, attracting its fair share of sunset visitors, but it's very quiet the rest of the time. There are a couple of smallish 'resorts' on the approach into the village, and the village itself has a couple of low-key guesthouses where you can stay in tranquillity in a traditional-style hut with clay-and-dung walls and thatched roof, and venture out on interesting camel trips in the relatively remote and empty surrounding area.

Khuri is within the **Desert National Park** which stretches over 3162 sq km southwest of Jaisalmer to protect part of the Thar ecosystem, including wildlife such as the desert fox, desert cat, chinkara gazelle, nilgai or bluebull (a large antelope), and some unusual bird life including the endangered great Indian bustard.

If you just want a quick camel ride on the sand dunes, expect to pay around ₹100 per person.

🍴 Sleeping & Eating

★ **Badal House** HOMESTAY $
(📞 8107339097; per person incl full board r or hut ₹300) Run by the charming Badal Singh, this simple but spotlessly clean family home in the centre of the village has basic but clean mud-walled, thatch-roofed huts and equally spotless rooms off two small yards. There's one shared bathroom, good home cooking and a very warm welcome. Prices include three meals a day. Mr Singh can also arrange overnight camel trips (₹550 per person), although he doesn't pressure you into taking them. From the bus drop-off, turn left up the main village road then left again at the signpost (200m).

Arjun Family
GUESTHOUSE $

(☎ 274132; arjunguesthouse@yahoo.co.in; per person incl full board huts/r ₹150/200) A couple of doors from Badal House, this is another family offering clean budget lodgings and camel rides, although they tout the buses to get you here.

Hotel Pansari Palace
HOTEL $$$

(☎ 9784480781; www.hotelpansaripalace.com; r ₹2500) Opposite Badal House, this new two-storey heritage-style hotel is an eyesore in the village, but has comfortable air-con rooms with hot-water showers.

ⓘ Getting There & Away

You can catch local buses from Jaisalmer to Khuri (₹30, one hour) from a road just off Gadi Sagar Rd. Walking from Jaisalmer Fort towards the train station, take the second right after the tourist office, then wait by the tree on the left, with the small shrine beside it. Buses pass here at around 10am, 11.30am, 3.30pm and 4pm.

Return buses from Khuri to Jaisalmer leave roughly at 8am, 9am, 10.30am, 11.30am and 2.30pm.

Bikaner

☎ 0151 / POP 530,000

Bikaner is a vibrant, dust-swirling desert town with a fabulous desert fort and an energising outpost feel. It's less dominated by tourism than many other Rajasthan cities, though it has plenty of hotels and a busy camel-safari scene, which attracts travellers looking to avoid the Jaisalmer hustle.

Around the full moon in January or very late December, Bikaner celebrates its three-day Camel Festival, with one day of events at the Karni Singh Stadium and two days out at Ladera, 45km northeast of the city.

History

The city was founded in 1488 by Rao Bika, a son of Rao Jodha, Jodhpur's founder, though the two Rathore ruling houses later had a serious falling out over who had the right to keep the family heirlooms. Bikaner grew quickly as a staging post on the great caravan trade routes from the late 16th century onwards, and flourished under a friendly relationship with the Mughals, but declined as the Mughals did in the 18th century. By the 19th century the area was markedly backward, but managed to turn its fortunes around by hiring out camels to the British during the Afghan War. In 1886 it was the first desert princely state to install electricity.

Sights

Junagarh
FORT

(Indian/foreigner ₹30/200, video ₹100, audio guide incl camera ₹250; ⊙ 10am-5.30pm, last entry 4.30pm) This most impressive fort was constructed between 1589 and 1593 by Raja Rai Singh, ruler of Bikaner and a general in the army of the Mughal Emperor Akbar. You enter through the Karan Prole gate on the east side and pass through three more gates before the ticket office for the palace-museum.

The admission price includes a group tour in Hindi and/or English with an official guide. The one-hour tours leave every 15 to 20 minutes. The audio guide (requiring an identity document as a deposit), is available in English, French, German and Hindi, is very informative and allows you to visit at a more leisurely pace.

The beautifully decorated Karan Mahal was the palace's Diwan-i-Am (Hall of Public Audience), built in the 17th and 18th centuries. Anup Mahal Chowk has lovely carved *jarokhas* (balcony-windows) and *jali* screens, and was commissioned in the late 17th century by Maharaja Anup Mahal. Rooms off here include the sumptuous Anup Mahal, a hall of private audience with walls lacquered in red and gold, and the Badal Mahal (Cloud Palace), whose walls are beautifully painted with blue cloud motifs and red and gold lightning.

The Gaj Mandir, the suite of Maharaja Gaj Singh (r 1745–87) and his two top wives, is a fantastic symphony of gold paint, colourful murals, sandalwood, ivory, mirrors, niches and stained glass. From here you head up to the palace roof to enjoy the views and then down eventually to the superb Ganga Durbar Hall of 1896, with its pink stone walls covered in fascinating relief carvings. You then move into Maharaja Ganga Singh's office and finally the Vikram Vilas Durbar Hall, where pride of place goes to a WWI De Havilland DH-9 biplane bomber.

Old City
AREA

The old city still has a medieval feel despite the motorbikes and autorickshaws. A labyrinth of narrow, winding streets, it conceals a number of fine *havelis*, some up to 300 years old. The best known are the Rampuria Havelis, owned by the same family and scattered around the lanes, although the carvings and frescoes on the hard-to-find Poonam Chand

Kothari Haveli are even more attractive. There are a couple of notable Jain temples, the 15th-century **Bhandasar Temple** being the oldest and most important. Next door, Bikaner's most revered Hindu temple, **Laxmi Nath**, hums with activity during its morning and evening *aarti* (prayers). **Spice stalls** also dot the lanes; head for **Bada Bazar**. Look out too for the large wooden double-bed-sized community tables dotted around the streets. Originally placed around the city so that bhang-smoking locals had somewhere to hang out, they are used mostly for card games these days. If you come early in the morning you may see women panning for silver in the open sewers at the side of the lanes, looking for discarded slivers of silver that have been washed away from old-city workshops. It all makes for a fascinating wander, during which we guarantee you will get lost at least once.

The old city is encircled by a 7km, 18th-century wall, punctuated by five gates. The main entrance from the city centre is the triple-arched **Kothe Gate**. There are great old-city views from the top of Bhandasar Temple, just inside the southern wall.

Gouri, a friendly and honest local man, who runs the small old-city guesthouse Shanti House, conducts informal, but highly recommended **guided tours of the old city** (per person per hr ₹30).

🛏 Sleeping

Shanti House GUESTHOUSE $
(☑ 2543306; inoldcity@yahoo.com; New Well, near City Kotwali; dm ₹80, r ₹250-400, with AC ₹700; ❄ @ 🖥) This tiny old-city building with a narrow staircase and four simple rooms is a lovely budget option on account of its welcoming hosts. Gouri, who doubles as an unofficial old-city tour guide, and his wife will soon make you feel part of their young family by dishing out home-cooked meals, plenty of chai and trustworthy travel tips. Rooms are basic – squat toilets, bucket hot water – but lovingly looked after with some nice wall paintings and bedspreads. And the bustle of old Bikaner is at your doorstep. Gouri can also help you rent bicycles (per day ₹20) or mopeds (per day ₹200) to get

BIKANER SAFARIS

Bikaner is an excellent alternative to Jaisalmer's camel-safari scene and is increasingly popular with travellers. There are fewer people running safaris here, so the hassle factor is quite low. Camel trips tend to focus on desert villages and the interesting wildlife.

Three days and two nights is a common camel-safari duration, but half-day, one-day and short overnight trips are all possible. If you're after a serious camel trek, go for a cross-country trip to Jaisalmer (two weeks) or Kichan (about six days), famous for its concentration of large, graceful demoiselle cranes from September to March.

Typical prices are around ₹1200 to ₹1800 per person per day, including overnight camping with tents, mattresses, blankets, meals, mineral water, one camel per person, a camel cart to carry the gear (and sometimes tired riders), and a guide in addition to the camel men. Many trips start at Raisar, about 8km east of Bikaner, or Deshnok, 30km south, so start and end with a jeep trip to and from Bikaner.

The standout operator in terms of quality, reliability and transparency of what's on offer is Vijay Singh Rathore, aka **Camel Man** (☑ 2231244, 9829217331; www.camelman.com; Jaipur Rd, Vijay Guest House; half-/full-/multi-day trips per person from ₹700/1000/1200 per day, one day-one night per person ₹1600). Contact him through his website or at his lovely family guesthouse, Vijay Guest House, 4km out of town. Also popular and long-established is **Vino Desert Safari** (☑ 2270445, 9414139245; www.vinodesertsafari.com; Vino Paying Guest House; one day-one night per person ₹1800, multi-day treks per person ₹1500-2000), run by Vinod Bhojak, who runs Vino Paying Guest House. There's a touch of the salesman about Vinod, but his tours are professional. You can also arrange higher-end camel safaris through Bikaner's more expensive hotels. Try Bhairon Vilas or Bhanwar Niwas. For something a little different, **Vinayak Desert Safari** (☑ 2202634, 9414430948; www.vinayakdesertsafari.com; Vinayak Guest House; half-day jeep safari per person ₹500, full- or multi-day jeep safaris per person ₹900-2000) is run by wildlife expert Jitu Solanki. He takes people on fascinating jeep safaris around the vast surrounding desert scrubland – although camel rides can be arranged too – and focuses on desert mammals, reptiles and birds. He also runs the quiet family guesthouse, Vinayak Guest House.

Bikaner

around on, and will pick you up from the station if you call ahead.

Hotel Marudhar Heritage HOTEL $
(☎ 2522524; hmheritage2000@hotmail.com; Ganga Shahar Rd; s/d from ₹400/500; ❋ @) Friendly, well-run and good-value option a short walk from the train station. There are plain and comfortable rooms with TV to suit most budgets, and the *haveli*-style inner court-yard design is pleasing. There's wi-fi in the lobby, hot-water showers in all rooms and 24-hour checkout.

Vijay Guest House GUESTHOUSE $
(☎ 2231244, 9829217331; www.camelman.com; Jaipur Rd; r ₹400-800, with AC ₹1200; ❋) About 4km east of the centre, this is a home away from home with spacious, light-filled rooms and a friendly family. Owner Vijay is a camel expert and a recommended safari operator. This is an ideal base for taking a safari, with good home-cooked meals (breakfast/lunch

or dinner ₹100/200), which you can eat in-side or in the garden. As well as camel trips, they offer free pick-up and drop-off from the train and bus stations, and jeep outings to Deshnok and other sights around Bikaner. It's ₹10/30 in a shared/private autorickshaw between here and the train station.

Vinayak Guest House GUESTHOUSE $
(☎ 2202634, 9414430948; vinayakguesthouse@ gmail.com; r ₹150-400, s without bathroom ₹100; ❋ @ 🛜) A short walk north of the fort, this small guesthouse offers six varied and clean rooms in a quiet family home with a lit-tle garden. On offer are free pick-up, good home-cooked food, cooking lessons and bi-cycle rental (per day ₹25). The owner also runs Vinayak Desert Safari, which runs rec-ommended desert-wildlife jeep tours.

Vino Paying Guest House GUESTHOUSE $
(☎ 2270445, 9414139245; www.vinodesertsafari .com; Ganga Shahar; s ₹200-250, d ₹350-400;

Bikaner

@ ✉) This guesthouse is in a family home 3km south of the main train station. It's a cosy choice and is the base of one of Bikaner's best-known camel-safari operations. It's good value, the family is welcoming and there's home-cooked food available. It's opposite Gopeshwar Temple; free pick-up from the main train station.

Hotel Jaswant Bhawan   HOTEL **$$**
(☏ 2548848, 9001554746; www.hoteljaswantbhawan.com; s/d ₹800/1000; ✳ @) You'll get a lovely welcome at this peaceful, unassuming 200-year-old family home, which has been been converted into a simple but elegant guesthouse. Rooms are large, bright and spotlessly clean and come with family photographs and quality furniture. The pleasant garden contains a vegetable patch and a chicken coop. It's just outside the back entrance of the train station.

Bhairon Vilas   HERITAGE HOTEL **$$$**
(☏ 2544751, 9928312283; http://hotelbhaironvilas.tripod.com; r from ₹2000; ✳ @ ☎) This delightful hotel on the west side of the fort is run by a former Bikaner prime minister's great-grandson. Rooms are mostly large and are eclectically decorated with antiques, gold-threaded curtains and old family photographs (some of the wiring and fittings seem to be of the same vintage). The restaurant and quirky bar both have outdoor seating in the well-kept gardens. Fish for discounts when it's quiet. You can sometimes get rooms for around half price.

Bhanwar Niwas   HERITAGE HOTEL **$$$**
(☏ 2529323; www.bhanwarniwas.com; Rampuria St; r ₹4500; ✳ @) Charming rather than luxurious, this fine hotel has been developed out of the beautiful 1927 Rampuria Haveli – a gem in the old city, 300m southwest of the City Kotwali police station. It has 26 individual, spacious and delightfully decorated rooms, featuring stencil-painted wallpaper, marble or mosaic floors, and antique furnishings. Comfortable common rooms drip with antiques and are arranged around a large internal courtyard, which doubles as a venue for cultural events. Nonguests can eat dinner here (from 7.30pm to 9.30pm) for a set ₹600 per person.

✖ Eating

All the hotels and guesthouses we cover also serve food.

Chhotu Motu Joshi   CAFE **$**
(Station Rd; snacks & sweets ₹10-30; ⊙ 7am-10pm) A hidden gem near the train station, this no-nonsense local favourite not only does Bikaner's best lassi (small/large ₹15/25), it also knocks up very tasty *kachori samosa* (two for ₹20) plus lip-smackingly delicious Bengali sweets such as spongy *rasgulla* (three for ₹10) or syrupy *gulab jamun* (four for ₹30). It's also a good spot for breakfast *puri* (₹6 each) and vegetable *danamethi* (an unusual Rajasthani speciality with a fenugreek sauce; ₹25). Not much English spoken, but there's an English menu chalked on the wall behind the counter.

Heeralal's   MULTICUISINE **$**
(Station Rd; mains ₹50-150; ⊙ 7.30am-10.30pm) This bright and popular 1st-floor restaurant serves up pretty good Indian dishes, plus a few Chinese dishes and pizzas, amid large banks of plastic flowers. The ground floor is more of a canteen and is popular for South Indian breakfasts, lunchtime thalis and its range of *chaat* (spicy snacks; ₹25 to ₹60).

Laxmi Hotel DHABA $

(Station Rd; mains ₹50-90, thalis ₹60-100; ⊙ 8am-10pm) One of a number of simple roadside *dhabas* near the train station, Laxmi is open to the street and dishes up tasty, fresh vegetarian thalis. You can see the roti being flipped in front of you.

Garden Café CAFE $

(off KEM Rd; dishes ₹50-100; ⊙ 8am-8pm) Previously the excellent Pause Café, this one-time travellers' hang-out, housed in part of a 160-year-old building, has changed names and management and is more rundown these days. It still boasts a nice garden setting, though. Food is simple – toast, salads, rice, dhal – but tasty enough for the price. Coffee is instant only, but the lassis are good. A warning: camel-safari operators tout for business here and can be annoying if all you're after is a cup of tea.

★ Gallops INDIAN $$

(mains ₹200-400; ⊙ 10am-10pm) This modernish cafe-restaurant, known as 'Glops' to rickshaw-wallahs, is close to the Junagarh entrance and has walls adorned with old photographs of royal polo matches. There are snacks such as pizzas, pakoras and sandwiches, but it's the good range of delicious Indian curries that stands out, plus the cold beer (₹250) and espresso coffee (₹100). You can cool off in the air-conditioned interior or sit outside on the large patio.

Bhanwar Niwas INDIAN $$$

(☑ 2529323; Rampuria St; set dinner ₹600; ⊙ 7.30-9.30pm) A splendid place to eat, this beautiful hotel welcomes nonguests to its veg dining hall for dinner (reservations essential). You can have a drink beforehand in the courtyard.

🍷 Drinking

Gallops restaurant is also a pleasant spot for a beer.

Bhairon Vilas BAR

(beer ₹175; ⊙ 6.30-10.30pm) Like something off the set of *The Addams Family*, this ec-centric hotel bar is full of nooks and crannies, moody lighting and quirky heritage decor. The manager is young, friendly and chatty, and there's outdoor seating too, on a well-kept lawn. The menu extends to whiskey, rum and vodka as well as beer and wine.

Heeralal Hotel BAR

(beer small/large ₹90/150; ⊙ noon-10.30pm) Dark and seedy-looking, low-lit basement bar with well-priced beers and spirits.

ℹ️ Information

You'll find a number of ATMs outside the main train station. The State Bank of Bikaner & Jaipur changes cash and travellers cheques.
Agarwal Internet (per hr ₹25; ⊙ 10am-10pm) Fast connection. Has Skype facilities.
Main Post Office (⊙ 9am-4pm Mon-Fri, 9am-2pm Sat) Near Bhairon Vilas hotel.

ℹ️ Getting There & Away

BUS

There's a private bus stand outside the south wall of Junagarh with similar services (albeit slightly more expensive and less frequent) to the government-run services from the main bus stand, which is 2km directly north of the fort (autorickshaw ₹20).

Services from the main bus stand include the following. Note, for Jaisalmer, you must change at Pokaran.
Delhi (₹333, 11 hours, 4.15am, 7am, 7.45am, 8.30am, 9.15am and 6.30pm)
Deshnok (₹25, one hour, half-hourly until 5.30pm)
Fatehpur (₹130, 3½ hours, half-hourly until 5.45pm)
Jaipur (₹238, 7 hours, half-hourly until 5.45pm)
Jhunjhunu (₹200, five hours, 4.15am, 7am, 7.45am, 8.30am, 9.15am and 6.30pm)
Jodhpur (₹181, five hours, half-hourly until 5.30pm)
Pokaran (₹167, five hours, hourly until 2.30pm)
Pushkar (₹186, six hours, half-hourly until 6pm)

MAJOR TRAINS FROM BIKANER JUNCTION

DESTINATION	TRAIN	DEPARTURE TIME	ARRIVAL TIME	FARE (₹; SLEEPER/3AC)
Delhi (S Rohilla)	12458 Bikaner-Dee SF Exp	11pm	6.20am	220/582
Jodhpur	14887 KLK-BME Exp	11.05am	3.45pm	146/394
Jaipur	09733 HMH-Kota Special	11pm	5.30am	178/496

DON'T MISS

THE TEMPLE OF RATS

The extraordinary **Karni Mata Temple** (camera/video ₹20/50; ☉4am-10pm) at Desh-nok, 30km south of Bikaner, is one of India's weirder attractions. Its resident mass of holy rodents is not for the squeamish, but most visitors to Bikaner brave the potential for ankle-nipping and put a half-day trip here on their itinerary.

Karni Mata lived in the 14th century and performed many miracles during her life-time. When her youngest son, Lakhan, drowned, she ordered Yama, the god of death, to bring him back to life. Yama said he was unable to do so, but that Karni Mata, as an incarnation of Durga, could restore Lakhan's life. This she did, decreeing that members of her family would no longer die but would be reincarnated as *kabas* (rats). Around 600 families in Deshnok claim to be descendants of Karni Mata and that they will be reincar-nated as *kabas*.

The temple isn't, in fact, swarming with rats, but there are a lot of them here, espe-cially in nooks and crannies and in areas where priests and pilgrims leave out food for them. And you do have to take your shoes off to enter the temple.

You can find food and drinks for yourself at the numerous snack stalls outside.

There are frequent buses here from Bikaner's main bus stand. A return autorickshaw from Bikaner with a one-hour wait costs ₹350.

TRAIN

The main train station is Bikaner Junction, with a **computerised reservations office** (☉8am-10pm Mon-Sat, 8am-2pm Sun) in a separate build-ing just east of the main station building. A couple of other useful services go from Lalgarh station in the north of the city (₹50 in an autorickshaw).

For **Jaisalmer**, an evening train with reserved ticketing options runs only on Tuesdays (sleeper ₹178, 5 hours, 6.30pm) from Bikaner Junction. On all other days there is only a morning train with unreservable seats. It leaves from Lalgarh station at 7.20am and takes around six hours. The desert views are superb and there are al-ways plenty of seats. Turn up 30 minutes or so before departure, buy an unreserved 'general ticket' (₹76) and climb aboard.

Four daily trains go to **Jodhpur** (12.35am, 6.15am, 9.30am and 11.05am) in around five hours.

Three daily trains go to **Delhi** (9.15am, 7.45pm and 11pm). They usually take seven to eight hours, although the 7.45pm takes more than 11 hours.

Three daily trains go to **Jaipur** (6am, 6.45pm and 11pm) in around 6½ hours.

There are no direct trains to Ajmer for **Pushkar**.

Around Bikaner

National Research Centre on Camels

The **National Research Centre on Cam-els** (☎01512230183; Indian/foreigner ₹20/50, camera ₹30, rides ₹30; ☉2-6pm) is 8km southeast of central Bikaner. While here you can visit baby camels, go for a short ride and look around the small museum. There are about 400 camels, of three dif-ferent breeds. Guides are available for ₹50-plus. There's an on-site Camel Milk Parlour dishing out small plastic bags of camel milk (₹5) for you to sample through a straw. Camel grazing time is 3pm to 6pm and is the best time to come. The round trip, including half an hour waiting time, is around ₹150/300 for an autorickshaw/taxi. You could also consider cycling or riding a moped out here.

Haryana & Punjab

Best Places to Eat

➡ Ghazal (p208)

➡ Punjab Grill (p208)

➡ Thai Chi (p218)

➡ Brothers' Dhaba (p217)

➡ Crystal Restaurant (p218)

Best Places to Stay

➡ Grand Hotel (p216)

➡ Hotel Aquamarine (p207)

➡ Mrs Bhandari's Guest House (p216)

➡ Hotel Satyadeep (p205)

➡ Baradari Palace (p223)

Why Go?

Northwest of Delhi, the states of Haryana and Punjab were carved from the Indian half of Punjab in the aftermath of Partition. Since then, Punjab has gone from strength to strength as the homeland of India's Sikh community, while Haryana has emerged as a dynamic hub for business and industry. Studded with gleaming gurdwaras (Sikh temples) – including the famous Golden Temple at Amritsar – Punjab has become an essential stop on the traveller circuit. Haryana is more of a touristic mystery, best known for its modernist capital, Chandigarh, brainchild of Swiss architect Le Corbusier. The hinterland around these two hubs is dotted with fascinating, rarely visited towns that tell a story of battling empires and playboy maharajas.

Punjab and Haryana are united by their love of food. This is the region that gave the world tandoori chicken, *tadka dal* (fried yellow lentils) and butter chicken, the prototype for chicken tikka masala.

When to Go
Chandigarh

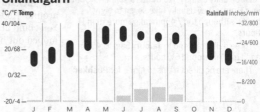

Mar Three days of Sikh celebrations for Holla Mohalla at Anandpur Sahib.

April Punjab's largest festival, Baisakhi, marks the Sikh New Year and the founding of the Khalsa.

Dec Diwali brings fireworks fun to cities across the region.

Food

Punjab is the home of nutty, long-grain basmati rice and the myriad delights to emerge from the tandoor (clay oven). Must-try Punjabi dishes include *kulcha* (fried bread), keema naan (flat-bread stuffed with mince), *dhal makhani* (black lentils and red kidney beans with cream and butter), tandoori chicken, butter chicken and, in winter, Amritsari fried fish.

DON'T MISS

Circumambulate the serene **Golden Temple** in Amritsar and join the crowds of devotees in the *langar* (refectory) – a humbling introduction to the Sikh principles of equality and hospitality.

Top State Festivals

➡ **Kila Raipur Sports Festival** (Rural Olympics; ☻Feb; Kila Raipur, p220, near Ludhiana) Three days of bullock-cart races, kabaddi, strongman contests, folk dancing and more.

➡ **Surajkund Crafts Mela** (☻1-15 Feb; Surajkund, p212) Visiting artisans demonstrate and sell colourful handicrafts, with accompanying cultural performances.

➡ **Holla Mohalla** (☻Mar; Anandpur Sahib, p221) Sikhs celebrate the foundation of the Khalsa (Sikh brotherhood) with martial-arts demonstrations and battle re-enactments.

➡ **Baisakhi** (☻Apr 13-14; statewide) Sikhs head to gurdwaras to celebrate the Sikh New Year.

➡ **Gita Jayanti** (☻Nov/Dec; Kurukshetra, p211) One week of cultural events for the anniversary of the Bhagavad Gita.

➡ **Pinjore Heritage Festival** (☻Dec; Pinjore Gardens, near Chandigarh, p210) Three-day cultural festival with music and dance performances, handicrafts and food stalls.

➡ **Harballabh Sangeet Sammelan** (☻late Dec; Jalandhar, p220) The 130-year-old music festival showcasing Indian classical music; four days.

MAIN POINTS OF ENTRY

Most visitors fly into Chandigarh International Airport or Sri Guru Ram Dass Jee International Airport in Amritsar.

Fast Facts

➡ **Population**: 25.4 million (Haryana), 27.7 million (Punjab)

➡ **Area**: 44,212 sq km (Haryana), 50,362 sq km (Punjab)

➡ **Capital**: Chandigarh

➡ **Main languages:** Hindi (Haryana), Punjabi (Punjab)

➡ **Sleeping prices**: $ below ₹1000, $$ ₹1000 to ₹5000, $$$ above ₹5000

Top Tip

Make time to detour to some of Punjab's smaller towns: Kurukshetra for Hindu mythology, Anandpur Sahib for Sikh history, or Patiala and Kapurthala for fading memories of the princely states.

Resources

➡ **Punjab Tourism** (www.punjabtourism.gov.in)

➡ **Haryana Tourism** (www.haryanatourism.gov.in)

➡ **Haryana Online** (www.haryana-online.com)

➡ **Chandigarh Tourism** (www.chandigarhtourism.gov.in)

➡ **CITCO** (www.citcochandigarh.gov.in)

➡ **Chandigarh Administration** (www.chandigarh.nic.in)

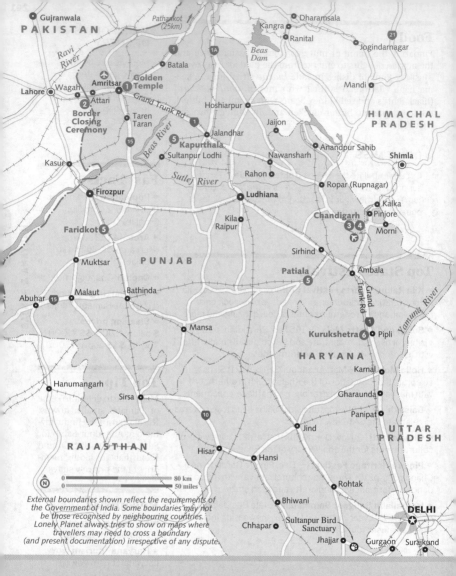

Haryana & Punjab Highlights

1 Feel the energy of absolute belief in Amritsar's spectacular **Golden Temple** (p212), Sikhism's holiest site

2 Watch the theatrical battle for supremacy between Indian and Pakistani border guards at Attari-Wagah's **border-closing ceremony** (p219)

3 Tumble into an alternative reality in Chandigarh's fascinating **Nek Chand Rock Garden** (p203)

4 Feast on the delights of the Punjabi kitchen in the upscale restaurants of **Chandigarh** (p207), Le Corbusier's modernist metropolis

5 Glimpse faded memories of once-mighty maharajas in sleepy **Patiala** (p222), **Faridkot** (p221) and **Kapurthala** (p221)

6 Get closer to Krishna at **Kurukshetra** (p211), where the deity delivered the Bhagavad Gita

CHANDIGARH

📞 0172 / POP 1,055,700

The joint capital of Punjab and Haryana, Chandigarh is officially a Union Territory controlled by the central government. Travellers are more interested in its history as the first planned city of independent India. When the Swiss architect Le Corbusier was commissioned in 1950, he conceived a people-oriented city of sweeping boulevards, lakes and gardens and grand civic buildings, executed in his favourite material, reinforced concrete.

So Chandigarh came into being; turn the clocks forward 60 years and the parks, monuments and civic squares are still there, albeit aged by decades of tropical rain. Whether Le Corbusier achieved his goal of a city for the people is open to debate – the ostentatious prosperity of Chandigarh's wealthier inhabitants stands in stark contrast to the poverty of its poorer residents, who eke out an existence begging in Chandigarh's neon-lit shopping precincts.

For travellers, Chandigarh is a place to see India as it would like to be seen – prosperous, comfortable and cosmopolitan – and to explore the city-sized modernist sculpture created by Le Corbusier. This is also the best place to eat, drink and shop in Punjab and Haryana.

Each sector of the city is self-contained and pedestrian-friendly, but marooned from neighbouring sectors by busy multi-lane highways. Most visitors concentrate their attention on Sector 17 (for shops and restaurants), Sector 22 (for hotels) and Sector 9 (for museums and galleries). Buses depart from Sectors 17 and 43; the train station is 7km southeast of the centre.

⊙ Sights & Activities

★ **Capital Complex** NOTABLE BUILDINGS

In Sector 1 – the epicentre of Le Corbusier's planned city – the imposing concrete **High Court**, **Secretariat** and **Vidhan Sabha** (Legislative Assembly) are shared by the states of Punjab and Haryana. All three are classic pieces of 1950s architecture from the proto-brutalist school, with bold geometric lines and vast sweeps of moulded concrete.

Visits inside the High Court can be arranged from Monday to Friday with prior permission from the Chandigarh Tourism booth in Sector 17; bring your passport. You can walk around to see Le Corbusier's unmistakably mid-century **Open Hand sculpture**, the city's official emblem, signifying that the people of Chandigarh are always 'open to give, open to receive'.

On the approach road to the High Court, the interesting **High Court Museum** (⊙10am-5pm Mon-Sat) **FREE** displays assorted memorabilia including original Le Corbusier sketches, a signed copy of the Indian constitution and the handcuffs worn by Nathuram Godse, Mahatma Gandhi's assassin.

★ **Nek Chand Rock Garden** GARDEN

(www.nekchand.com; adult/child ₹20/5; ⊙9am-6pm Oct-Mar, to 7pm Apr-Sep) Entering this 25-acre sculpture garden is like falling down a rabbit hole into the labyrinthine interior of one man's imagination. Transport official Nek Chand created this surreal fantasy from concrete and recycled junk, working at night to keep his eccentric masterpiece from the prying eyes of the city authorities. Materials used in the construction of the garden range from concrete and steel drums to light switches, broken bathroom sinks and bicycle frames. Highlights include a legion of dancing girls made from broken glass bangles and a graceful arcade of towering arches with dangling rope swings (you may have to queue for a ride). See also Junk Art Genius (p207).

Museums & Galleries

If you buy a ticket for the Government Museum & Art Gallery, Chandigarh Architecture Museum or Natural History Museum, it also covers entry to the other two museums.

Government
Museum & Art Gallery ART GALLERY

(📞2740261; Sector 10-C; admission ₹10, camera ₹5; ⊙10am-4.40pm Tue-Sun) You'll find a wide collection of artworks and treasures at this impressive state museum, including trippy paintings of the Himalaya by Russian artist Nicholas Roerich, elegant carvings from the Buddhist Ghandara civilisation, *phulkari* (embroidery work) and Sobha Singh's much-reproduced portrait of Guru Gobind Singh.

Chandigarh Architecture Museum MUSEUM

(City Museum; 📞2743626; Sector 10-C; admission ₹10, camera ₹5; ⊙10am-4.40pm Tue-Sun) Using photos, letters, models, newspaper reports

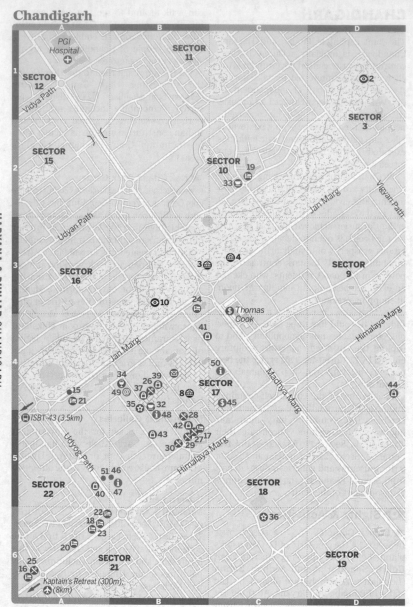

and architectural drawings, this museum tells the story of Chandigarh's planning and development, including the abandoned first plan for Chandigarh by Albert Mayer and Matthew Nowicki.

Natural History Museum MUSEUM
(☏2740261; Sector 10-C; admission ₹10, camera ₹5; ☺10am-4.40pm Tue-Sun) The National History Museum has fossils, model dinos, exquisite hand-embroidered pictures

One for fans of architecture and design, this fascinating museum displays documents, sketches and photos of Le Corbusier, along with fascinating letters revealing the politics behind the project, including one from Jawaharlal Nehru to the Chief Minister of Punjab which states, 'I do hope that you will not overrule Corbusier. His opinion is of value.'

National Gallery of Portraits ART GALLERY
(☑ 2720261; Sector 17-B; ⊙ 10am-5pm Tue-Sun, free guided tour 11am & 3pm) FREE Located behind the State Library, with photos and paintings illustrating key players and events in the struggle for independence.

Parks & Gardens
In line with Le Corbusier's vision of a garden city, Chandigarh is dotted with public parks. Most interesting are the **Rose Garden** (Sector 16; ⊙ 5am-9pm Apr-Sep, 6am-8pm Oct-Mar), with over 1500 rose varieties, and the **Bougainvillea Garden** (Sector 3; ⊙ 8am-5pm), with a thought-provoking memorial to Indian soldiers killed in cross-border conflicts since Independence.

Sukhna Lake LAKE
(paddle boats 2-seaters per 30min ₹50; ⊙ artificial lake 8am-10pm, paddle boats 8.30am-5.30pm) Fulfilling the leisure objective of Le Corbusier's masterplan, this landmark artificial lake is a popular rest and recreation stop for Chandigarh families, with ornamental gardens, a children's fairground, places to eat and drink and pedaloes for rent.

☞ Tours
The city corporation runs a double-decker **tourist bus** (☑ 2703839, 4644484; ticket ₹50; ⊙ 10am-1.30pm & 2.30-5.30pm) leaving from outside the Hotel Shivalikview (buy ticket from conductor). There are two half-day trips daily, visiting the Rose Garden, Government Museum & Art Gallery, Nek Chand Rock Garden and Sukhna Lake.

🛏 Sleeping
Chandigarh hotels are costly and fairly pedestrian – book ahead to secure a budget bed here. To stay with a family, contact the Chandigarh Tourism office for details of its Bed & Breakfast scheme (rooms from ₹1000).

Hotel Satyadeep HOTEL $$
(☑ 2703103; hddeepsdeep@yahoo.com; SCO 1102-3, Sector 22-B; s/d from ₹1100/1200; ✱ @)

of birds and a diorama with a caveman using an electric torch to illuminate his cave art!

Le Corbusier Centre MUSEUM
(☑ 2777071; www.lecorbusiercentrechd.org; Madhya Marg, Sector 19-B; ⊙ 10am-6pm Tue-Sun) FREE

Chandigarh

Upstairs from the Sai sweetshop, this is the most traveller-friendly budget option in town. Run by courteous Sai Baba devotees, it offers simple but well-kept rooms with TV. It's a sound choice for solo women.

Hotel Divyadeep HOTEL **$$**
(☑ 2705191; hddeepsdeep@yahoo.com; SCO 1090-1, Sector 22-B; s/d from ₹1100/1200; ✸) Attended by friendly staff, Divyadeep has simple, homey rooms and is a thoroughly wholesome option, close to ISBT-17. It's above the Bhoj vegetarian restaurant.

Hotel Sunbeam HOTEL **$$**
(☑ 2708100; www.hotelsunbeam.com; Udyog Path, Sector 22-B; s/d from ₹2628/3114; ✸) Rooms at this comfortable midranger look a bit dated, but overall the Sunbeam offers a good deal for the price. There's a coffee shop and a hotel restaurant and bar that you won't mind spending time in.

Hotel City Heart Premium HOTEL **$$**
(☑ 2724203; www.cityhearthotels.com; SCO 202-4, Sector 17-C; s/d incl breakfast ₹2891/3337; ✸@☎) A reasonable and, as the name suggests, central hotel that is better than it

looks at street level. The chintzy, spacious rooms have low ceilings but clean floors and the location is perfect for shopaholics and gourmands. Ask about discounts.

Kaptain's Retreat
HOTEL $$

(☎ 4661111; kaptainsretreat@hotmail.com; Sector 35-B; s/d ₹3220/3777, ste s/d ₹4111/4668; ❄ @) Owned by cricketing icon Kapil Dev, this small boutique hotel is crammed with cricket paraphernalia, including signed cricket bats and photos of famous batsmen. The inviting rooms have interesting lighting and furniture and carved stone sinks.

Piccadily Hotel
HOTEL $$$

(☎ 2707571; www.thepiccadily.com; Himalaya Marg, Sector 22-B; s/d from ₹4290/5404; ❄ @ 🛜) This old-fashioned but appealing three-star property offers complimentary breakfast. Tasteful rooms come with flatscreen TVs, minibars, tea-and-coffee-making facilities and satiny bed-covers. You won't have to travel far for a decent meal – Pomodoro serves good Italian food, and Currys serves, well, take a guess.

★ Hotel Aquamarine
HOTEL $$$

(☎ 5014000; www.hotelaquamarine.com; Himalaya Marg, Sector 22-C; s/d from ₹4457/5014, ste ₹10,595; ❄ @ 🛜) A proper boutique hotel, shielded from the road by a leafy terrace and full of luscious fabrics and framed artworks. It's worth upgrading to a suite for the glass-walled showers and enveloping divans. There's a restaurant and coffeeshop.

Taj Chandigarh
HOTEL $$$

(☎ 6613000; www.tajhotels.com; Sector 17-A; s/d from ₹12,256/13,370; ❄ @ 🛜 ⛱) Not as grand as some Taj properties, but still luxurious, with flawless service and rooms with floor-to-ceiling windows, minibars, flatscreen TVs, electronic safes and all the other mod-cons you'd expect at this price. There are several restaurants, the Lava Bar, a spa and a 24-hour business centre.

Hotel Shivalikview
HOTEL $$$

(☎ 4672222; www.citcochandigarh.com/shivalikview; Sector 17-E; s/d incl breakfast & dinner ₹5348/6128; ❄ @ 🛜) A huge, midrange hotel with unexciting but comfortable rooms, some of which have that Shivalik Hills view. A major restoration in 2012 has raised standards – for our money, the smaller standard rooms are cosier than the vast deluxe rooms. Rates include complimentary dinner at the Bazm restaurant, or try the rooftop Chinese restaurant, Yangtse.

Hotel Mountview
HOTEL $$$

(☎ 4671111; www.citcochandigarh.com/mountview; Sector 10-B; s/d incl breakfast from ₹8914/10,028; ❄ @ 🛜 ⛱) Rooms are tasteful and well appointed at this Haryana Tourism–run hotel which makes the most of its garden setting. The best rooms have views of the green grounds or the even greener Shivalik Hills. There's a health club, several restaurants (including a 24-hour cafe) and a relaxing terrace bar.

Eating

The hungry traveller is well catered for in Chandigarh, with a growing selection of fine-dining restaurants supplementing the abundant fast-food joints. Sectors 17 and 26 are foodie central. Telephone numbers are given for places where reservations are advisable.

HARYANA & PUNJAB CHANDIGARH

JUNK ART GENIUS

Surprising as it may seem, Chandigarh's most popular tourist attraction was never intended for public display. When road inspector Nek Chand Saini, a recently arrived refugee from the Pakistani Punjab, started building his surreal rock garden using recycled materials left over from the construction of Le Corbusier's model city, it was just a hobby. The hobby soon became an obsession. Working in secret, mostly at night, on a patch of waste ground, Chand unleashed legions of pottery mosaic animals and armies of broken bangle dancing girls. Cast concrete canyons appeared from nowhere; cascading waterfalls burst forth from the jungle. Chand's efforts were finally discovered by a government survey crew 15 years after work began, and came perilously close to being demolished; fortunately, the city council saw the cultural merits of the rock garden, and Chand was granted a government salary and his own work crew to complete the project. Today, the gardens cover more than 25 acres, with nearly 5000 figures of humans, animals and mythical beasties. For more on the Nek Chand story, visit www.nekchand.com.

Sagar Ratna
SOUTH INDIAN $

(SCO 47, Sector 17-E; mains ₹90-180; ⊙ 8am-11pm) A swankier-than-average branch of this reliable all-veg chain, serving first-rate dosas (thin rice-flour pancakes) and satiating, good-value thalis (all-you-can-eat meals).

Sai Sweets
SWEETS $

(SCO 1102-3, Sector 22-B; sweets & snacks ₹12-50; ⊙ 7.30am-8.30pm) A clean and wholesome sweet shop below Hotel Satyadeep, serving tasty *mithai* (Indian sweets) and more substantial veg snacks – the *channa bhatura* (Indian fried bread with spiced chickpeas) makes a good breakfast.

Aroma
MULTICUISINE $

(Off Himalaya Marg, Sector 22-C; mains ₹50-150; ⊙ 7am-3am) Open till late, this bustling concoction of fast-food joints includes a Café Coffee Day and franchises selling cakes, ice cream, South Indian dosas, Chinese snacks and Western-style fast food. Seating is shared; how they keep track of your order and bill is a mystery.

★ Ghazal
MULTICUISINE $$

(☑ 2704448; SCO 189-91, Sector 17-C; meals ₹175-395; ⊙ 11.30am-11.30pm) A Chandigarh stalwart and still going strong, Ghazal has a dignified air and a fine menu of Mughlai classics, plus Continental and Chinese dishes. The veg jalfrezi is a fiery sensation. At the back of the restaurant, a suited bartender guards a long line of imported single malts.

Mehfil
MULTICUISINE $$

(☑ 2703539; SCO 183-5, Sector 17-C; mains ₹180-380; ⊙ 11am-11pm) More elegant fine dining! Mehfil serves Indian, Chinese and Continental food in sophisticated surroundings. Come for the *romali roti* kebab rolls, *murg tawa* (Punjabi-style chicken) and *methi murg* (chicken with fenugreek).

Bhoj
INDIAN $$

(SCO 1090-1, Sector 22-B; standard/choti thali ₹170/130; ⊙ 7.30am-10.30pm) A travellers' favourite, this cosy haven run by Sai Baba devotees serves a house thali with artfully spiced curries that changes throughout the day. Thalis come large or *choti* (small).

Yangtse
CHINESE $$

(☑ 4672222; Hotel Shivalikview, Sector 17-E; mains ₹150-400; ⊙ 12.30-3pm & 7.30-11.30pm) Offering panoramic views from its lofty heights, the ritzy rooftop restaurant at the Hotel Shivalikview offers superior Indian-style Chinese food, with lots of noodle and tofu dishes.

Hot Millions
MULTICUISINE $$

(☑ 2723222; SCO 73-4, Sector 17-D; snacks from ₹50-200, mains upstairs ₹250-495; ⊙ 11am-11pm) Set in shopping central, serving fastfood downstairs and posh sit-down meals upstairs (accessed through a door on the side of the block). Locals rate the all-you-can-eat salad bar (veg/nonveg ₹345/385) served upstairs. There are branches all over town, including near Ghazal restaurant.

Tehal Singh's Chicken
MUGHLAI $$

(SCO 1121, Sector 22-B; Mains ₹50-360; ⊙ noon-midnight) Competing for business with the almost identical Singh's Chicken next door, Tehal Singh's cooks up fast-food chicken kebabs and curries, served with paper-thin *romali roti*, prepared with a showbiz flourish in front of the restaurant.

★ Punjab Grill
MUGHLAI $$$

(☑ 4029444; SCO 122-3 Sector 17-C; mains ₹425-1200; ⊙ 11am-4pm & 7-11pm) Warm tones of ivory and gold create an imperial air at this stylish restaurant in Sector 17, the brainchild of food writer Jiggs Kalra. Chefs work wonders with the tandoor – perfectly spiced duck and prawns join more familiar meats in the clay oven.

Swagath
INDIAN $$$

(☑ 5000444; SCO 128, Sector 26; mains ₹220-575; ⊙ 11am-midnight) One of a string of swanky restaurants along Madhya Marg in Sector 26, specialising in Mangalorean and Chettinad seafood – from prawns, squid and crab to fish *gassi* (coconut-based curry).

Pomodoro
ITALIAN $$$

(☑ 2707571; Piccadily Hotel, Sector 22-B; mains ₹275-450; ⊙ 11.30am-3.30pm & 7pm-midnight) This inviting basement restaurant serves hearty Italian food for grown ups and wine is available by the glass (from ₹250). Stick to the pizzas made with local ingredients; more exotic toppings may not be quite what you're used to.

🍷 Drinking & Nightlife

Chandigarh's abundant wine and liquor stores turn into pavement bars every evening, but there are plenty of more salubrious watering holes. Women are less likely to get hassled if they're with a male companion.

Oriental Lounge
BAR

(SCO 6, Sector 26; ⊙ 11am-11.30pm) Below AB's Hotel, this Buddha-filled lounge-bar is a civilised spot to slow the pace. Think mood lighting, imaginative cocktails and an international menu of spirits and beers.

Barista Crème
CAFE

(1st fl, SCO 63-4, Sector 17; snacks ₹130-250; ☺8am-11pm) This chain coffee shop is a handy retreat from the orgy of consumerism in Sector 17. As well as the miracle bean, you can sample cakes, sandwiches and Continental snacks.

Lava Bar
BAR

(Taj Chandigarh Hotel, Sector 17-A; ☺11am-11.30pm) With lava lamps and a retro vibe, this chic hotel bar offers a truly globetrotting drinks list. There's a DJ from 7pm Wednesday to Saturday.

Java Dave's
CAFE

(Sector 10-D; snacks from ₹55; ☺9.30am-11.30pm) Opposite Hotel Mountview, this is the place to come for authentic coffee, imported beers (including Leffe and Hoegaarden) and fruit-flavoured teas.

Piccadily Blue Ice
BAR

(☑2703338; SCO 7, Sector 17-E; mains ₹175-750; ☺11am-midnight) A slick, sleek, split-level resto-bar that appeals to smartly dressed drinkers.

☆ Entertainment

For a cultured night out, **Tagore Theatre** (☑4347714; Sector 18-B) hosts music, dance and theatrical performances. The latest Bollywood releases are screened at the central **Neelam Cinema** (☑2703600; Sector 17-D).

🔒 Shopping

The pedestrianised centre of Sector 17 is a cathedral to consumerism, where well-heeled locals come to stock up on the latest brands. For camera accessories and supplies, visit the stores on Udyog Path, opposite ISBT-17. For books, browse the **bookshops** on the plaza in Sector 17-D.

Fabindia
CLOTHING

(www.fabindia.com; SCO 50-1, Sector 17-A; ☺10.30am-8.30pm) Gorgeous garments (Indian-meets-Western style) and homewares.

Anokhi
CLOTHING

(www.anokhi.com; SCF 5, Sector 7-C, Inner Market; ☺10.30am-7pm Mon-Sat) Beautiful block-printed textiles.

Khadi India
CLOTHING

(SCO 28, Sector 17-E; ☺10am-7pm Mon-Sat) Homespun textiles and herbal beauty products, supporting small community producers. There's also a branch near the Ghazal restaurant (p208).

Phulkari
HANDICRAFTS

(SCO 27, Sector 17-E; ☺10.30am-8pm Mon-Sat) A Government of Punjab emporium with everything from inlaid wooden tables to *jootis* (traditional slip-in shoes).

1469
SOUVENIRS

(SCO 81, Sector 17-D; ☺10.30am-9pm) The place to come for amusing message T-shirts with a Punjabi twist.

Suvasa
CLOTHING

(Inner Market, Sector 8-B; ☺10.30am-7.30pm, from 11am Sun) Quality block-printed fabrics, from bags to *salwar kameez* (traditional tunic and trouser suits).

ℹ Information

INTERNET ACCESS

Each of the central sectors has an internet cafe.
E-Net (2nd fl, SCO-12, Sector 17-E; per 30min ₹20; ☺10.30am-7.30pm) Photo ID required.

LEFT LUGGAGE

Bus station luggage office (Sector 17; per day ₹5-20; ☺24hr) For locked bags only.

MEDICAL SERVICES

PGI Hospital (☑2747589; www.pgimer.nic.in; Post Graduate Institute, Sector 12-A)
Silver Oaks Hospital (☑2211303; www.silveroakshospital.com; Phase 9, Sector 63, Mohali)

MONEY

Most sectors have ATMs; banks are concentrated around **Bank Square** in Sector 17-B.
Thomas Cook (☑6610904; SCO 28-30, Sector 9-D; ☺10am-6pm Mon-Fri, to 4pm Sat) Foreign exchange (cash and cheques) and international money transfers.

POST

Main post office (☑2702170; Sector 17; ☺9am-7pm Mon-Sat)

TOURIST INFORMATION

Bookstands sell Vardhman's better-than-average *Chandigarh Tourist & Road Map* (₹25).
Chandigarh Tourism (☑2703839; 1st fl, ISBT-17; ☺9am-5pm) Has brochures, can arrange permission for visits to the High Court and rents out bicycles (₹100 per day). It operates a

booth in the main shopping precinct in Sector 17, open the same hours.

Haryana Tourism (☑2702955; www.haryanatourism.gov.in; SCO 17-19, Sector 17-B; ⊙9am-5pm Mon-Fri)

Himachal Tourism (☑2708569; 1st fl, ISBT-17; ⊙10am-5pm Mon-Sat, closed 2nd Sat of month)

Uttar Pradesh & Uttarakhand (Uttaranchal) Tourism (☑2707649; 2nd fl, ISBT-17; ⊙10am-5pm Mon-Sat, closed 2nd Sat of month)

ⓘ Getting There & Away

AIR

About 9km southeast of the centre, Chandigarh airport is being expanded to accommodate international flights. Air-con bus 201 runs from both bus stations to the airport from 7.30am to 6pm (₹15), or take an autorickshaw for ₹100 or a taxi for ₹350 to ₹500. The following airlines have daily flights to Delhi (from ₹2700 one way) and Mumbai (from ₹4300 one way).

Air India (Indian Airlines) (☑Toll free 1800 1801407; www.airindia.in; SCD 162-4, Sector 34-A; ☎)

Jet Airways (☑5075674; www.jetairways.com; airport)

Spicejet (☑Toll free 1800 1803333; www.spicejet.com)

BUS

Chandigarh has two Inter State Bus Terminals (ISBT) – one in **Sector 17** and one in **Sector 43**. Numerous red air-con buses run between the two terminals.

From ISBT-17, buses run to Kurukshetra (₹75, two hours), Delhi (non-AC/AC ₹190/345-510), Haridwar (₹170, five hours) and Jaipur (ordinary/Volvo ₹400/1169, 12 hours).

From ISBT-43, buses run frequently to the following destinations:

Amritsar (₹201 to ₹400, five hours)

Anandpur Sahib (₹99, two hours)

Dehra Dun (₹170, five hours)

Dharamsala (₹240 to ₹540, eight hours)

Jammu (₹300, eight hours)

Manali (₹335 to ₹545, eleven hours)

Pathankot (₹220 to ₹268, five hours)

Patiala (₹57, two hours)

Sirhind (₹39, two hours)

TRAIN

The station is 7km southeast of the city centre, but there's a handy **reservation office** (☑2720242; ⊙8am-8pm Mon-Sat, to 2pm Sun) on the 1st floor of ISBT-17. Prepaid autorickshaws from ISBT-17 to the train station cost around ₹100.

Several fast trains connect New Delhi and Chandigarh daily: the most convenient service is the twice-daily Kalka Shatabdi Express (AC chair/1AC ₹451/960, 3½ hours). Half a dozen trains (including the preceding) go to Kalka (AC chair/1AC ₹218/465, 35 minutes), where narrow-gauge trains rattle up through the hills to Shimla.

ⓘ Getting Around

The Chandigarh Tourism office hires out bicycles (₹100 per eight hours, ₹500 refundable deposit); bicycles are also available at Sukhna Lake for the same rates.

Cycle-rickshaws are useful for travelling short distances in town (and avoiding busy highway crossings). Expect to pay ₹30 to ₹50 for a short hop.

There's a **prepaid autorickshaw stand** at ISBT-17; sample fares: ISBT-43 (₹27), train station (₹65), airport (₹100).

Each sector has a taxi stand; you'll pay ₹1000 to ₹1300 for a day trip (eight hours and an 80km limit) and around ₹500 to the airport. Two reputable radio taxi companies are **Indus Cab** (☑4646464) and **Mega Cab** (☑4141414).

AROUND CHANDIGARH

Pinjore (Yadavindra) Gardens

These extensively restored 17th-century Mughal-era walled **gardens** (☑01733-230759; admission ₹20; ⊙7am-10pm) are built on seven levels with water features (that sometimes work) and serene views of the Shivalik Hills. Nearby is the **Bhima Devi Museum** (⊙10am-5pm) **FREE**, containing the remains of an ornate Hindu temple that was torn down when the gardens were originally constructed.

For refreshment, there's a **food court** on the fourth level – with, incongruously, a bar – or you can sip and sup in more salubrious surroundings at the **restaurant** (Pinjore Gardens; mains ₹70-300; ⊙10am-7pm) in the Rang Mahal pavilion. Come in December for regional delicacies and cultural performances as part of the Pinjore Heritage Festival.

Should you fancy an overnight stay, there are pleasant rooms with Mughal-style flourishes at the **Budgerigar Motel** (☑01733-231877; r from ₹2227; ❄), immediately outside the walls to the gardens.

To get here from Chandigarh, catch a bus from ISBT-43 (₹30, one hour, frequent) or rent a taxi (₹1500 return with waiting time).

Morni Hills

Perched at 1220m, Haryana's only hill station is set amid monkey-filled forests on a spur running west from the Shivalik Hills. Here you'll find a handful of rustic resorts and **Tikka Tal**, a pretty lake with boats for rent (from ₹120 per half-hour). Just before the lake, the cute **H&J Hills 'n' Thrills** (☑01733-201150; Tikka Tal; adult/child ₹50/30; ☺8am-6pm) amusement park will probably fail to live up to its promise to provide the 'adventure of a lifetime'.

About 1km before Morni village, the **Mountain Quail Tourist Resort** (☑01733-250166; r ₹1226-2227) is run by Haryana Tourism and has simple, neat rooms with hilltop views and a multicuisine restaurant and bar. On the lakeshore at Tikka Tal, Haryana Tourism's **Tikkar Taal Complex** (☑01733-250166; Tikka Tal; dm non-AC/AC ₹200/400, cabins ₹1671) has a simple restaurant, dormitories and cabins.

There are daily buses from Chandigarh to Morni (₹30, two hours), from where infrequent minibuses run to Tikka Tal (₹10). A day trip by taxi from Chandigarh will cost around ₹2000.

HARYANA

Bordering India's burgeoning capital, Haryana was the setting for pivotal events in the conquest of northern India, but its sights see few foreign visitors. For local information, contact Haryana Tourism in Chandigarh (p210) or **Delhi** (☑011-23324910; www.haryanatourism.gov.in; Chanderlok Bldg, 36 Janpath; ☺9am-5pm Mon-Fri, to 1pm Sat).

Kurukshetra (Thanesar)

☑ 01744 / POP 964200

According to Hindu legend, Kurukshetra (Thanesar in ancient times) was where Brahma created the universe, and where Krishna delivered his Bhagavad Gita sermon before the 18-day Mahabharata battle, an event commemorated by the **Gita Jayanti** (☺Nov/Dec) festival in November/December. Accordingly, the town is mobbed by pilgrims and sadhus, who vastly outnumber the few foreign visitors. Kurukshetra is an easy stop between Delhi and Chandigarh; for local info see http://kurukshetra.nic.in.

⊙ Sights

The focus of attention at Kurukshetra is the sacred **Bhramasarovar**, India's largest ceremonial tank. According to Hindu holy texts, the ghat-flanked tank was created by Lord Brahma. Sadhus crowd the ghats, and the **ashrams** beside the tank display dioramas of scenes from the Hindu epics and walk-through models of sacred sites.

Nearby is the **Kurukshetra Panorama & Science Centre** (Pehowa Rd; admission ₹20, camera ₹20; ☺10am-5.30pm), where an airbrushed sky flares behind vultures picking at severed heads in a gory diorama of the Mahabharata battle. The ground floor has interactive science exhibits (that actually work!) for kids. Next to the Panorama is the **Sri Krishna Museum** (Pehowa Rd; admission ₹30; ☺10am-5pm), with an impressive collection of sculptures, carvings and paintings, and a multimedia exhibition with dioramas, giant statues, surreal sounds and a walkthrough maze.

About 2.3km northwest of the Sri Krishna Museum is the impressive **mausoleum** of the Sufi mystic Shelkh Chaheli, who provided spiritual guidance for the Mughal prince Dara Shikoh. Behind the brick and sandstone tomb, and pre-dating it by more than a thousand years, is a raised mound known as **Harsh Ka Tilla**, where you can view excavated ruins from historical Thanesar.

About 6km west of Kurukshetra is **Jyotisar**, with an ancient banyan tree said to mark the site where Krishna delivered the Bhagavad Gita. There's a one-hour sound-and-light show at 7pm (₹20, not Monday); confirm that the show is operating before traipsing out here.

🛏 Sleeping

Neelkanthi Krishna Dham Yatri Niwas (☑291615; Pehowa Rd; r ₹1671-2786; ❄) offers the best accommodation, with charmless but spacious and clean rooms.

❶ Getting There & Away

Buses between Chandigarh and Delhi stop at Pipli on the national highway, about 5km outside Kurukshetra; shared autos and local buses offer shuttle services to the centre (₹10).

Surajkund

Some 30km south of downtown Delhi, Surajkund is named after the 10th-century **sun pool** built by Raja Surajpal, leader of the sun-worshipping Tomars. The village is mobbed for the annual two-week **Surajkund Crafts Mela** (Surajkund; ⊙1–15 Feb) in February (contact Haryana Tourism for information) but sees few visitors at other times.

Should you wish to stay over, there are several hotels. If you must have a pool, head to **Hotel Rajhans** (☑0129-2512318; rajhans@hry.nic.in; Surjkund; r ₹3343, ste from ₹4457; ✿ ▧) or the sumptuous and costly **Claridges** (☑0129-4190000; www.claridges.com; Shooting Range Rd; r from ₹13,151; ✿ @ ▧ ▧). Midrange options are **Hermitage** (☑0129-2512314; r with/without AC from ₹2000/1671; ✿) and the better **Sunbird Motel** (☑0129-2512312; r from ₹2227, ste from ₹4457; ✿).

Special buses run to Surajkund during the mela; contact Haryana Tourism (p211) for information. At other times, local buses run from Badarpur, accessible from Delhi by metro. A day trip from Delhi by taxi costs around ₹1000.

Sultanpur Bird Sanctuary

About 46km southwest of Delhi, this 145-hectare **sanctuary** (Indian/foreigner ₹5/40, camera/video ₹25/500; ⊙6.30am-6pm Apr-Sep, to 4.30pm Oct-Mar) plays host to over 250 resident and migratory bird species, including painted storks and demoiselle cranes. The best season to view feathered visitors is October to March. Haryana Tourism runs a **tourist complex** (☑0124-2015670; r with/without AC ₹2136/1611; ✿) with passable rooms. Public transport is limited – from Delhi, it's easier to hire a taxi for a day trip (around ₹1500).

PUNJAB

Forged from the Indian half of Punjab province after Partition, Punjab is the homeland of India's Sikh population. To catch Punjab in carnival mood, come for the annual Baisakhi Festival in April, celebrating the Sikh new year. For tourist information, contact Punjab Tourism (p219) in Amritsar.

Amritsar

☑0183 / 1.13 MILLION

Founded in 1577 by the fourth Sikh guru, Ram Das, Amritsar is home to Sikhism's holiest shrine, the spectacular Golden Temple, one of India's most serene and humbling sights. Alas, the same can't be said for the hyperactive streets surrounding the temple – few places can compete with Amritsar when it comes to congestion, air pollution and traffic noise.

Amritsar is divided in two by a tangle of railway lines. The old city, containing the Golden Temple and other historic sights and bounded by 12 medieval gates, is southeast of the railway lines. This is a fascinating area to explore, with a capillary network of narrow bazaars that seems to float between the centuries.

To the north of the railway lines, 'modern' Amritsar has grown up in haphazard fashion around a scattering of colonial-era boulevards. Gleaming malls and upmarket hotels stand testament to the prosperity of the city, but the hectic traffic makes this area hard to love at street level. Crossing between the old and new cities is best done by rickshaw or autorickshaw.

⊙ Sights & Activities

★ **Golden Temple**   SIKH TEMPLE
(☑information office 2553954; ⊙dawn-around 10pm, information office 8am-7pm) The legendary Golden Temple is actually just a small part of this huge gurdwara complex, known to Sikhs as Harmandir Sahib (or Darbar Sahib).

Spiritually, the focus of attention is the tank that surrounds the gleaming central shrine – the **Amrit Sarovar** (Pool of Nectar), from which Amritsar takes its name, excavated by the fourth guru Ram Das in 1577. Ringed by a marble walkway, the tank is said to have healing powers, and pilgrims come from across the world to bathe in the sacred waters.

Floating at the end of a long causeway, the Golden Temple itself is a mesmerising blend of Hindu and Islamic architectural styles, with an elegant marble lower level adorned with flower and animal motifs in pietra dura (marble inlay work, as seen on the Taj Mahal). Above this rises a shimmering second level, encased in engraved gold panels, and topped by a dome gilded with 750kg of gold. In the gleaming inner sanctum (photos prohibited), priests and musicians keep up a continuous

Amritsar

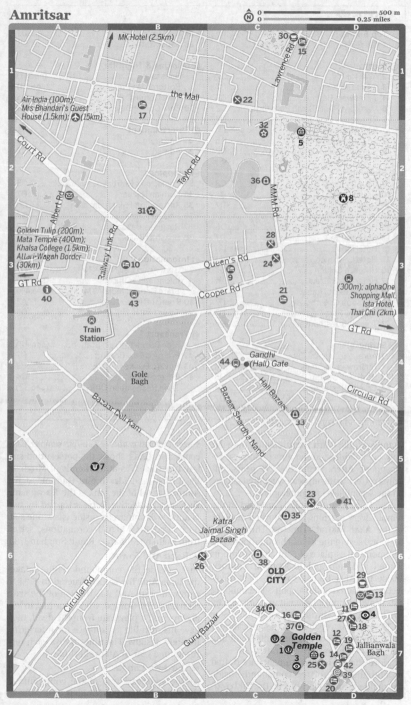

0   500 m
0   0.25 miles

MK Hotel (2.5km)

the Mall

Lawrence Rd

30
15

22

17

32
5

36

8

Air India (100m);
Mrs Bhandari's Guest
House (1.5km); (15km)

Court Rd

31

MMM Rd

Golden Tulip (200m);
Mata Temple (400m);
Khalsa College (1.5km);
Atari-Wagah Border
(30km)

Albert Rd

Railway Link Rd

Taylor Rd

28

24

Queen's Rd

9

GT Rd

40

10

43

Cooper Rd

21

(300m); alphaOne
Shopping Mall;
Ista Hotel;
Thai Chi (2km)

GT Rd

Train
Station

Gole
Bagh

Bazaar Dull Kam

44

Gandhi
(Hall) Gate

Hall Bazaar

Circular Rd

33

7

Bazaar Shardha Nand

23

41

35

Katra
Jaimal Singh
Bazaar

Circular Rd

26

38

OLD
CITY

29

13

34

16

11

27

4

18

37

12

19

34

Guru Bazaar

2

Golden
Temple

6

14

Jallianwala
Bagh

1

3

25

42

39

20

Amritsar

Top Sights
1 Golden Temple ... C7

Sights
2 Akal Takhat ... C7
3 Amrit Sarovar ... C7
4 Jallianwala Bagh ... D7
5 Maharaja Ranjit Singh Panorama ... C2
6 Ramgarhia Bunga ... D7
Sikh Museum ... (see 37)
7 Sri Durgiana Temple ... A5
8 Summer Palace (Ram Bagh) ... D2

Sleeping
9 Country Inn & Suites ... C3
10 Grand Hotel ... B3
11 Hotel City Heart ... D7
12 Hotel CJ International ... D7
13 Hotel Golden Tower ... D6
14 Hotel Grace ... D7
Hotel Indus ... (see 12)
15 Hotel Lawrence ... C1
16 Hotel Le Golden ... C7
17 Hotel Ritz Plaza ... B1
18 Lucky Guest House ... D7
19 MK Sood Guesthouse ... D7
20 Sri Guru Ram Das Niwas ... D7
21 Tourist Guesthouse ... C3

Eating
22 Aurah ... C1
Bharawan da Dhaba ... (see 23)
23 Brothers' Dhaba ... D5
24 Crystal Restaurant ... C3
25 Guru-Ka-Langar ... D7
26 Kesar Da Dhaba ... B6
27 Neelam's ... D7
28 Sagar Ratna ... C3

Drinking & Nightlife
Barista ... (see 11)
Bottoms Up Pub ... (see 10)
29 Café Coffee Day ... D6
30 Café Coffee Day ... C1

Entertainment
31 Aaanaam ... B2
32 Adarsh ... C2

Shopping
33 Booklovers Retreat ... C5
34 Kathian Bazaar ... C7
35 Katra Jaimal Singh Bazaar ... C6
36 Phulkari ... C2
37 Religious Bazaar ... C7
38 Shashtri Bazaar ... C6

Information
39 Guru Arjun Dev Niwas Net Cafe ... D7
Information Office ... (see 37)
State Bank of India ATM ... (see 40)
40 Tourist Office ... A3
41 Town Hall ... D5

Transport
Free Buses to Train Station ... (see 42)
42 Pre-paid Taxi Booth ... D7
43 Private Buses ... B3
44 Private Buses ... C4
Train Reservation Office ... (see 37)

chant from the Guru Granth Sahib, the Sikh holy book, adding to the already intense atmosphere. After paying their respects, pilgrims retreat to the intricately painted gallery on the second level to contemplate.

The Guru Granth Sahib is installed in the temple every morning and returned at night to the **Akal Takhat** (Timeless Throne), the temporal seat of the Khalsa brotherhood. The ceremony takes place at 5am and 9.40pm in winter, and 4am and 10.30pm in summer. Inside the Akal Takhat, you can view a collection of sacred Sikh weapons. The building was heavily damaged when it was stormed by the Indian army during Operation Blue Star in 1984; it was repaired by the government but Sikhs refused to use the tainted building and rebuilt the tower from scratch.

More shrines and monuments are dotted around the edge of the compound. Inside the main entrance clock tower, the **Sikh Museum** (admission free; 7am-7pm summer, 8am-6pm winter) FREE shows the persecution suffered by the Sikhs at the hands of Mughals, the British and Mrs Indira Gandhi. At the southeast end of the tank is the **Ramgarhia Bunga**, a protective fortress topped by two Islamic-style minarets; inside is a stone slab once used for Mughal coronations, seized from Delhi by Maharaja Ranjit Singh in 1783.

➡ Baba Atal Tower

Just outside the compound is the octagonal Baba Atal Tower, constructed in 1784 to commemorate Atal Rai, the son of the sixth Sikh guru Har Gobind, who according to legend revived a playmate from the dead, then gave his own life as penance for interfering in God's designs. The nine storeys each represent one year of Atal's short life.

➡ Guru-Ka-Langar

At the southeast end of the compound is the Guru-Ka-Langar (Golden Temple), an enormous dining room where an estimated 60,000 to 80,000 pilgrims a day come to eat after praying at the Golden Temple. There's no charge to eat here, but a donation is appropriate and help with the staggering pile of washing up is always appreciated! Catering to everyone from paupers to millionaires, it's a humbling demonstration of the Sikh principle of hospitality.

Jallianwala Bagh   HISTORIC SITE
(Golden Temple Rd; ⊙ 6am-9pm summer, 7am-8pm winter) Reached through a gatehouse on the road to the Golden Temple, this poignant park commemorates the 1500 Indians killed or wounded when a British officer ordered his soldiers to shoot on unarmed protesters in 1919. Some of the bullet holes are still visible in the walls, as is the well into which hundreds desperately leapt to avoid the bullets. There's an eternal (24-hour) flame of remembrance, an exhibition telling the stories of victims, and a Matryrs' Gallery, with portraits of Independence heroes. A sound-and-light show takes place daily at 6pm.

Sri Durgiana Temple   HINDU TEMPLE
(Gobindgarh Rd; ⊙ dawn-dusk) Dedicated to the goddess Durga, this 16th-century temple is a Hindu version of the Golden Temple. Surrounded by a holy water tank, it's often called the Silver Temple because of its exquisitely engraved silver doors. Soothing bhajans (devotional songs) are sung here just after the temple opens and just before it closes.

Maharaja Ranjit Singh Panorama   MUSEUM
(Ram Bagh; admission ₹10; ⊙ 9am-5pm Tue-Sun) Within the grounds of the Ram Bagh park, this extraordinary panorama is dedicated to Maharaja Ranjit Singh, the 'Lion of Punjab' (1780–1839), who founded the Sikh empire, wresting large areas of northwest India from the Mughals. A vast diorama depicts the maharaja's greatest battles, complete with booming battle cries and other sound effects. Cameras and shoes are not permitted inside. Nearby is the maharaja's **summer palace**, which is slowly being restored to accommodate the city's collection of Ranjit Singh memorabilia.

Mata Temple   HINDU TEMPLE
(Rani-ka-Bagh, Model Town; ⊙ dawn-dusk) Credited with fertility-improving powers, this labyrinthine Hindu temple commemorates the bespectacled 20th-century female saint Lal Devi. From the main hall, a narrow series of stairways and passages winds past mirrored mosaics, fairground-style carvings, and untold deity statues to a semi-submerged mock-up of the Vasihno Devi cave temple.

Khalsa College   HISTORIC BUILDING
(www.khalsacollegeamritsar.org; GT Rd; ⊙ Daylight hours) **FREE** This vast, sprawling castle of a college was founded in 1890 to educate the cream of Punjabi society; it's a glorious example of the Indo-Saracenic style.

☞ Tours

The Grand Hotel runs good-value day tours of the main sights (₹350) and night tours to the Attari–Wagah border-closing ceremony, Mata Temple and Golden Temple from ₹580 per person.

The tourist office (p219) runs two-hour Heritage Walks (Indian/foreigner ₹25/75) starting from the old Town Hall at 8am daily (9am December to February). The tour visits gurdwaras, bazaars and historic buildings.

🛏 Sleeping

Most of Amritsar's budget digs suffer from deafening traffic noise – bring earplugs!

Sri Guru Ram Das Niwas   REST HOUSE $
(dm free but donations appropriate, r with/without AC ₹/500/300; 🕭 @) Inexpensive rooms are available in the *niwas* (pilgrim hostels) at the southeast end of the temple compound. Foreigners are generally accommodated in the dorm at Sri Guru Ram Das Niwas, or in rooms in other buildings – check in at the Guru Arjan Dev Niwas to see what is available. Staying here is a fascinating experience but rooms and dorms are basic, with

> **ℹ GOLDEN TEMPLE ETIQUETTE**
>
> Before entering the compound, remove your shoes and socks (there are *chappal* (sandal) stands at the entrances), wash your feet in the shallow footbaths and cover your head; scarves can be borrowed (no charge) or hawkers sell souvenir scarves for ₹10. Tobacco and alcohol are strictly prohibited. If you want to sit beside the tank, sit cross-legged and do not dangle your feet in the water. Photography is only permitted from the walkway surrounding the pool. There's an information office near the main entrance.

THE JALLIANWALA BAGH MASSACRE

Following the introduction of the Rowlatt Act (1919), which gave British authorities the power to imprison Indians suspected of sedition without trial, Amritsar became a focal point for the Independence movement. After a series of *hartals* (strikes) in which many protesters and three British bank managers were killed, Brigadier-General Reginald Dyer was called upon to restore order to the city.

On 13 April 1919 (Baisakhi Day), over 5000 Indian protesters gathered in Jallianwala Bagh, an open courtyard surrounded by high walls. Under orders to make an example of the protesters, Dyer arrived with 150 troops and ordered his soldiers to open fire. When the barrage of bullets ceased, nearly 400 protesters were dead and 1500 wounded, including many women and children.

Dyer's action was supported by the British establishment but described as 'a savage and inappropriate folly' by Sir Edwin Montagu, the secretary of state for India. It galvanised Indian nationalism – Gandhi responded with a program of civil disobedience, announcing that 'cooperation in any shape or form with this satanic government is sinful'.

Reginald Dyer died in retirement in England in 1927; Sir Michael O'Dwyer, governor of the Punjab at the time of the massacre, was assassinated by the Sikh revolutionary Udham Singh in London in 1940. Richard Attenborough's acclaimed film *Gandhi* dramatically re-enacts the events at Jallianwala Bagh.

shared bathrooms, and there's a three-day maximum stay.

MK Sood Guesthouse
HOTEL $$

(☎ 5093376; Bharam Bhutta Bazaar; r from ₹1000; ❄) Small, quaint and clean, this place benefits from a quieter location than most old-city hotels. Rooms all have air-con but some are better than others so ask to see a few before deciding.

Hotel Grace
HOTEL $$

(☎ 2559355; www.hotelgrace.net; 35 Bharam Butta Bazaar; r with/without AC from ₹1800/1200; ❄@🖙) This modest hotel has a real mix of rooms – the best are at the front, with natural light – but all come with TV, and partial Golden Temple views are to be had from the rooftop. Ask about discounts.

Lucky Guest House
HOTEL $

(☎ 2542175; Mahna Singh Rd; r with/without AC from ₹800/450; ❄) The basic rooms are a bit pokey here, but the location is good. Not all rooms have an outside window, so ask to see a few.

Tourist Guesthouse
GUESTHOUSE $

(☎ 2553830; bubblesgoolry@yahoo.com; 1355 GT Rd; dm/s/d ₹175/250/450; @) A rare cheap option, this backpacker stalwart offers pocket-friendly prices and humble rooms with high ceilings and fans, in a rather isolated location under a flyover (which may not appeal to solo women). There's a traveller-oriented restaurant.

★ Grand Hotel
HOTEL $$

(☎ 2562424; www.hotelgrand.in; Queen's Rd; r from ₹1426; ❄@🖙) Across the road from the train station, but far from grungy, the Grand is the top choice for budget travellers. Rooms are spacious, if not exactly grand, and the hotel has a recommended restaurant with seating overlooking the courtyard garden. Drop into the genuinely inviting bar – the cheerfully named Bottoms Up. The owner runs recommended tours.

★ Mrs Bhandari's Guest House
GUESTHOUSE $$

(☎ 2228509; http://bhandari_guesthouse.tripod.com; 10 Cantonment; camping per person ₹200, s/d from ₹1846/2316, with AC ₹2424/2886; ❄@🖙❄) Founded by the much-missed Mrs Bhandari (1906–2007), this friendly guesthouse is set in spacious grounds in the Amritsar cantonment, about 2km from the centre. The sprawling rooms have a hint of colonial-era bungalow about them, but the welcome is warm, and overlanders can set up camp in the gardens (₹100 per vehicle, plus camping fees). Pick-up is free from the train station and meals are available (breakfast/lunch/dinner ₹330/475/575).

Hotel City Heart
HOTEL $$

(☎ 2554511; www.hotelcityheartamritsar.com; opposite Jallianwala Bagh; r from ₹2035; ❄@🖙) City Heart is a sophisticated choice, close to the attractions of the old city. As well as a branch of coffee chain **Barista** (snacks from ₹40), the hotel offers neat, well-thought-out rooms that offer welcome respite from the bustle outside.

Hotel Indus
HOTEL $$

(☑ 2535900; www.hotelindus.com; 211-13 Sri Hamandir Sahib Marg; r from ₹1846; ✳@?) The dramatic million-dollar view of the Golden Temple from the rooftop is reason enough to stay at this modern-style hotel. Rooms are compact but comfy – book well ahead to secure one of the two rooms with temple vistas!

Hotel Golden Tower
HOTEL $$

(☑ 2534446; www.hotelgoldentower.com; Phawara Chowk; r from ₹1550; ✳@?) More glam outside than in, this is a reasonable choice in a good location. Sparsely decorated but clean rooms come with TV and fridge.

Hotel CJ International
HOTEL $$

(☑ 2543478; www.cjhotel.net; r from ₹2250; ✳@?) The rooms are blandly comfortable and the staff can be brusque, but the draw is the hotel's proximity to the Golden Temple (book one of the five temple-facing rooms on level three).

Hotel Le Golden
HOTEL $$

(☑ 2558800; www.hotellegolden.com; r from ₹1962; ✳@?) This reasonably upmarket choice is right on the doorstep of the Golden Temple. The more expensive rooms are better value than the pokey standard rooms and there's a good veg restaurant on the roof with views.

Hotel Lawrence
HOTEL $$

(☑ 2400105; www.lawrenceamritsar.com; 6 Lawrence Rd; s/d incl breakfast ₹3116/4040; ✳@?) Reached by a lift from a shopping centre, this marble-lined midranger floats above the bustle of Lawrence Rd, with enormous rooms that feel airy and modern. There's a coffee shop and a multicuisine restaurant.

Hotel Ritz Plaza
HOTEL $$

(☑ 2562836; www.ritzhotel.in; 45 the Mall; s/d incl breakfast ₹4040/5425, ste s/d ₹5656/6579; ✳@?≋) Popular with business travellers and set in an area of upscale shopping malls, the Ritz offers creature comforts and some respite from the traffic noise. Rooms are smarter than the hallways, with big beds and big TVs.

★ Country Inn & Suites
HOTEL $$$

(☑ 5050555; www.countryinns.com; Queen's Rd; s/d from ₹5445/6655, ste ₹10,285; ✳@?≋) A scent of lemongrass wafts around the lobby of this sleek new addition to the Amritsar skyline. Rooms are stylish and comfortable; the suites with water-spouting spa baths for two are positively opulent. The rooftop pool is a great place to watch the sunset.

Golden Tulip
HOTEL $$$

(☑ 5069991; www.goldentulipamritsar.com; 8 GT Rd, Model Town; s/d incl breakfast ₹4617/5771; ✳@?≋) Thoroughly international, the Golden Tulip – formerly the Grand Legacy – offers top-class facilities and excellent value for money. The modern, tasteful rooms have almost five-star mod cons, and there's a good restaurant, a bar, a coffee shop and a gym. Ask about discounts.

Ista Hotel
HOTEL $$$

(☑ 2708888; www.istahotels.com; GT Rd; r/ste from ₹6002/13,851; ✳@?≋) Amritsar's only five-star hotel sits beside the futuristic alphaOne mall, 3km east of the bus terminus. Inside, everything is cool, calm and refined, with a gorgeous pool, a spa, two swish restaurants and compact but stylish rooms that might make you forget you are in India.

✗ Eating

Amritsar is famous for its *dhabas* (snack bars) serving such Punjabi treats as *kulcha* (filled parathas) and 'Amritsari' fish (deep-fried fish with lemon, chilli, garlic and ginger). Hotels and restaurants in the Golden Temple area don't serve alcohol.

★ Brothers' Dhaba
PUNJABI ¢

(Town Hall Chowk; dishes ₹45-145; ⊘7.30am-12.30pm) This fast and friendly *dhaba* serves Amritsar's tastiest *kulcha* (Punjabi-style *parathas* with herbs, potato and pomegranate seeds that explode in the mouth as tiny explosions of sweetness).

★ Kesar Da Dhaba
PUNJABI $

(Chowk Passian; dishes ₹10-190; ⊘11am-11pm) Devilishly hard to find (ask for directions in the old city), this takeaway and *dhaba* serves delicious *paratha* thalis (₹140 to ₹190) and silver-leaf topped *firni* (ground-rice pudding).

Bharawan da Dhaba
PUNJABI $

(Town Hall Chowk; dishes ₹40-140; ⊘8am-midnight) This Amritsar institution has been serving up tasty *kulcha* and other Punjabi treats since 1912.

Sagar Ratna
SOUTH INDIAN $

(Queen's Rd; mains ₹70-145; ⊘9am-11pm) An easygoing South Indian veg chain with thirst-busting fresh lime sodas, wafer-crisp dosas and other South Indian treats.

Neelam's
MULTICUISINE $

(Bazaar Jallianwala; mains ₹50-190; ⊙9am-11pm) Not far from the Golden Temple, this tiny two-tone eatery is a convenient spot to re-charge your batteries over a pizza, dosa or backpacker breakfast.

Crystal Restaurant
MULTICUISINE $$

(📞2225555; Crystal Chowk; mains ₹250-410; ⊙11am-11.30pm) This ground-floor restau-rant has a fin de siècle air, with mirror-lined walls and ornate stucco trim. The multicui-sine menu is dominated by Mughlai favour-ites – the house speciality is delicious *mugh tawa frontier* (morsels of chicken in a dense onion gravy). Upstairs is the **Crystal Res-taurant Plaza**, run by a rival branch of the same family and serving the same menu in more modern surroundings.

Aurah
MULTICUISINE $$

(📞5017021; Hotel Blue Moon, the Mall; mains ₹189-529; ⊙12.30-3.30pm & 7.30-11.30pm) Elegant, airy and bright, Aurah offers a real retreat from the city chaos. It's a big hit with ladies who lunch and the menu runs from Thai and Chinese treats to the homey-sounding tri-pepper bake.

★Thai Chi
ASIAN $$$

(📞2708888; Ista Hotel, GT Rd; mains 325-1150; ⊙7.30-11.30pm Wed-Mon) A strong contender for the title of Amritsar's best restaurant, serving upmarket Chinese and Thai food in upmarket surroundings. Dishes are expertly spiced, but dress to impress and make reser-vations for dinner.

Drinking & Nightlife

Café Coffee Day
CAFE

(Golden Temple Rd; snacks from ₹45) This ubiq-uitous espresso coffee chain serves savoury and sweet munchies and decent coffee. Other branches are on **Lawrence Rd** (snacks from ₹35) and inside the **alphaOne shop-ping mall**.

Bottoms Up Pub
BAR

(Grand Hotel, Queen's Rd; ⊙11am-11pm) The congenial bar at the Grand serves icy cold, glycerine-free, draught Kingfisher beer (₹80) and delicious meals from the hotel kitchen.

Entertainment

The **Aaanam** (📞2210949; Taylor Rd) and **Adarsh** (📞2565249; MMM Rd) cinemas screen Hindi movies; for international blockbust-ers, head to **Fun Cinemas** (📞9212235050; alphaOne Mall, GT Rd) in the alphaOne mall.

🔒 Shopping

Wandering around the winding alleys of the old-city bazaars is a head-spinning assault on the senses. Modern stores are concen-trated in the malls along Lawrence Rd and the mall.

Phulkari
HANDICRAFTS

(MM Malviya Rd; ⊙10.30am-7.30pm Mon-Sat) State government emporium, selling inlaid wood carvings, small tables and jootis.

Fabindia
CLOTHING, HOMEWARES

(📞2503102; www.fabindia.com; SCO 30, Ranjit Ave; ⊙11am-8pm) Contemporary-meets-tradition-al Indian clothing and homewares.

Booklovers Retreat
BOOKS

(Hall Bazaar; ⊙9am-8pm Mon-Sat) Old-school bookshop full of interesting tomes.

EXPLORING AMRITSAR'S BAZAARS

The Golden Temple sits on the edge of a mesmerising maze of market streets, where any and everything can be found, from ceremonial swords to wedding gowns. Start your explorations at the main entrance to the Golden Temple, where **religious stalls** are piled high with kirpan (daggers), khanda (Sikh symbol) medallions and other Sikh paraphernalia. Stroll northwest to the end of the temple compound and duck into the **Kathian Bazaar** for blankets, stationery, tin pots and bangles. A right turn onto Guru Bazaar Rd will lead you past shops full of glittery womenswear to the **Shashtri Ba-zaar**, where dupattas give way to fancy woollen shawls. At the end of the bazaar, turn right and continue past a string of food and fruit stalls to frenetic **Katra Jaimal Singh Bazaar**, crammed with tailors and fashion stores. One more right turn onto the main road will take you to the town hall, where Brothers' Dhaba and Bharawan da Dhaba offer well-earned sustenance.

BATTLE OF POMP & CEREMONY

Every afternoon, just before sunset, members of the Indian and Pakistani military meet at the border post between Attari and Wagah (p220) to engage in a 30-minute display of military showmanship that verges on pure theatre. Officially, the purpose of the ceremony is to lower the national flag and formally close the border for the night, but what actually occurs is a bizarre mix of formal marching, flag-folding, chest beating, forceful stomping and almost comical high-stepping, as the two sides try to outdo each other in pomp and circumstance. The oiled moustaches and over-the-top dress uniforms (with fan-like flourishes atop each turban) only add to the theatrical mood.

While the participants treat the ceremony with absolute seriousness, the crowds who gather to watch from the grandstands on either side of the border come for the carnival mood. During the build-up to the ceremony, spontaneous anthem chanting, rapturous rounds of applause and Bollywood-style dancing in the street are de rigueur. Then a roar goes up from the crowd as the first soldier from each side marches furiously towards the border, to begin the first round of who-can-high-step-the-highest. It's all highly nationalistic, but considering the tense relations between the two countries, remarkably good-natured.

The ceremony starts at around 4.15pm in winter and about 5.15pm in summer, and spectators are channelled into the appropriate stands (foreign tourists are allowed to sit in the second-best seats, just behind the VIPs) – bring your passport. Taxis and buses from Amritsar drop you off about 1km before the border post; cameras are permitted but bags, large and small, are banned (lockers are available on the road to the border).

alphaOne SHOPPING CENTRE
(GT Rd; ⊙10am-10pm) A Western-style shopping mall with international brands, including the swanky homewares store **India House**.

Information

INTERNET ACCESS

Wi-fi is widely available at Amritsar hotels.
Guru Arjun Dev Niwas Net Cafe (Guru Arjun Dev Niwas; per hour ₹25; ⊙24hr) Handy net cafe in the gurdwara complex.

MEDICAL SERVICES

Fortis Escorts Hospital (☑9915133330; www.fortishealthcare.com; Majitha Verka Bypass)

MONEY

Amritsar has an ever-mushrooming supply of ATMs, including one at the train station. Banks with foreign-exchange facilities are scattered along the mall and Queen's Rd.
HDFC (Golden Temple branch; ⊙9.30am-3.30pm Mon-Fri, to 12.30pm Sat) Exchanges travellers cheques and currencies; has an ATM.

POST

Main post office (☑2566032; Court Rd; ⊙9am-3pm Mon-Fri, to 2pm Sat)
Post office (Phawara Chowk; ⊙9am-5pm Mon-Fri, to 1pm Sat)

TOURIST INFORMATION

Tourist office (☑2402452; www.punjabtourism.gov.in; train station exit, Queen's Rd; ⊙9am-5pm Tue-Sun) Has brochures and free maps covering Punjab and Amritsar.

Getting There & Away

AIR

About 11km northwest of the centre, Amritsar's Sri Guru Ram Dass Jee International Airport services domestic and international flights. One-way flights to Delhi/Mumbai cost around ₹3150/6170.
Air India/Indian Airlines (☑2213392; www.airindia.in; 39a Court Rd; ⊙10am-5pm Mon-Sat)
Jet Airways (☑3209847; www.jetairways.com; airport)
Spicejet (☑1800 1803333; www.spicejet.com)

BUS

Private bus companies operate from near **Gandhi Gate** and from **Cooper Rd**, near the train station. Air-con buses run to Delhi (₹350 to ₹700, 10 hours), Chandigarh (₹400, four hours), Jammu (₹200 to ₹250, six hours) and Jaipur (₹600 to ₹700, 13 hours).

The main **Inter State Bus Terminal (ISBT)** is on GT Rd about 2km north of the Golden Temple, near Mahan Singh Gate. There is at least one daily bus to Chamba (₹215, six hours), Dharamsala (₹193, six hours), and Manali (₹456, 14 hours).

BORDER CROSSING – ATTARI–WAGAH (PAKISTAN)

Because of the tense relations between India and Pakistan, few foreigners cross the border between Attari and Wagah. However, plenty of people come to watch the curious border-closing ceremony every evening (p219).

The border is 30km west of Amritsar; buses run to Attari (₹28), but you'll have to walk the last 2km to the border. For the border ceremony, most people arrange a taxi with their hotel in Amritsar (around ₹600), but you can also charter a taxi (₹800), or take a shared taxi from near the southeast gate of the Golden Temple (₹100). You'll need to leave about two hours before the ceremony starts.

Border Hours
Officially, the border is open from 10am to 3.30pm daily, but confirm that the border is open at all before you leave Amritsar. Arrive at least an hour before the border closes.

Foreign Exchange
There's a tiny **State Bank of India** (⊙10am-5pm Mon-Sat) branch at the border, but it's wiser to change money in Amritsar.

Onward Transport
From Wagah (Pakistan) there are buses and taxis to Lahore, 30km away.

Sleeping
Transport to Amritsar and Lahore is fast and frequent, so there's no need to stay at the border.

Visas
Visas are theoretically available at the Pakistani embassy in Delhi; however, it is almost always easier to obtain a Pakistani visa in your home country.

Frequent buses serve the following destinations:
Pathankot (₹87, three hours)
Faridkot (₹97, three hours)
Patiala (₹203, five hours)
Chandigarh (non-AC/AC ₹201/400, four hours)
Jammu (₹151, six hours)
Delhi (non-AC/AC ₹365/846, 10 hours)

TRAIN
Apart from the train station, there's a less busy **train reservation office** (⊙8am-8pm, to 2pm Sun) at the Golden Temple.

The fastest train to Delhi is the twice-daily Shatabdi Express (chair car/executive ₹591/1305, 5¾ hours). Trains leave Amritsar at 5am and 4.55pm; from New Delhi railway station, trains leave at 7.20am and 4.30pm.

The daily Amritsar–Howrah Mail links Amritsar with Varanasi (sleeper/3AC/2AC ₹363/1028/1600, 22 hours) and Howrah (₹481/1370/2190, 37 hours).

⊙ Getting Around

Free (and jam-packed) yellow minibuses run from the train station and the bus stand to the Golden Temple from 4.30am to 9.30pm.

Otherwise, from the train station to the Golden Temple, a rickshaw/autorickshaw will cost around ₹50/70 but you'll have to haggle like fury for a fair price. Taxis loiter around at the station, or there's a **pre-paid booth** (☏9888561615) at the southeast entrance to the Golden Temple. To the airport, an autorickshaw costs ₹200 and a taxi ₹450 to ₹600.

Northern Punjab

Northern Punjab is dominated by industrial towns and fortresses erected to resist besieging armies from the west. Heading south from Amritsar, **Ludhiana** is a fairly charmless industrial hub and the headquarters of Hero Cycles. The main reason to visit is the **Kila Raipur Sports Festival** (Rural Olympics; Kila Raipur, near Ludhiana; ⊙Feb), known as the 'rural Olympics', held every February.

Further northwest, **Jalandhar** is a similar industrial centre. Little evidence remains of its ancient history, but the town resounds with Indian classical music during the **Harballabh Sangeet Sammelan** (www.harballabh.org; ⊙late Dec) every December.

Pathankot

POP 148,500

The dusty frontier town of Pathankot is a transport hub for the neighbouring states of Himachal Pradesh and Jammu & Kashmir, but there's little to make you linger. There's a **Himachal Tourism** (☑ 0186-2220316; ☺ 10am-5pm Mon-Sat) booth at Pathankot Junction station. In the centre, **Hotel Venice** (☑ 0186-2225061; www.venicehotelindia.com; Dhangu Rd; r from ₹1660; ❄) has the best accommodation and a restaurant, coffee lounge and bar.

From Pathankot Junction station (also on Gurdaspur Rd), there are express trains for Amritsar (sleeper/3AC/2AC ₹120/244/610, three hours); trains also run along the narrow-gauge line to Kangra (seat ₹22, 4½ hours. From Chakki Bank station, 2km south of the centre, trains run frequently to Jammu (₹120/218/610, three hours) and Delhi (sleeper/3AC/2AC ₹226/598/885, 11 hours). A few services to these destinations also run from Pathankot Junction.

From the bus station on Gurdaspur Rd, buses leave in the morning and evening for Dharamsala (₹105, 3½ hours). There are also frequent services to the following places:

Amritsar (₹87, 2½ hours)
Chamba (₹130, 4½ hours)
Chandigarh (₹219 to ₹268, six hours)
Dalhousie (₹85, 3½ hours)
Delhi (ordinary/Volvo ₹400/920, 11 hours)
Jammu (₹72, three hours)
Manali (₹370, 11 hours)

Kapurthala

Once the capital of a wealthy independent state, Kapurthala is a fascinating place. The resident maharaja, Jagatjit Singh, was a travel junkie; he married Spanish flamenco dancer Anita Delgado and constructed numerous buildings inspired by his travels. The **Jagatjit Palace** (now the exclusive Sainik School) was modelled on Versailles, while the **Moorish Mosque** copies the Grand Mosque in Marrakech. Other buildings of note include the British-style **Jagatjit Club** and **Jubilee Hall**, the **Shalimar Gardens** (containing the cenotaphs of the Kapurthala dynasty), and the handsome Indo-Saracenic **court house**.

Decent rooms and meals are available at the **Hotel Taj Regency** (☑ 01822-239881; Jalandhar Rd; r from ₹999; ❄) near the bus stand. Buses run to Amritsar (₹56, 2½ hours), or change at Jalandhar (from Kapurthala ₹18, 30 minutes).

Eastern Punjab

Sights in eastern Punjab are best visited from Chandigarh.

Anandpur Sahib

☑ 01887 / POP 17,000

The second most important pilgrimage site for Sikhs after the Golden Temple, Anandpur Sahib was founded in 1664 by the ninth Sikh guru, Tegh Bahadur, shortly before he was beheaded by the Mughal emperor Aurangzeb. To resist the persecution of the Sikhs, his son, Guru Gobind Singh, founded the Khalsa (Sikh brotherhood) here in 1699, an event celebrated during the **Holla Mohalla** (☺ Mar) festival every March.

◉ Sights

The largest and most dramatic gurdwara is the **Kesgarh Sahib** on the main highway. It marks the spot where the Khalsa was inaugurated, and enshrines an armoury of sacred Sikh weapons. Nearby, hidden in the bazaars of the old town, is the smaller **Sis Ganj** gurdwara, marking the spot where

---

OFF THE BEATEN TRACK

FARIDKOT

West of Ludhiana, Faridkot was the capital of another vanished Sikh state. Today, peacocks stalk the faded battlements of the once mighty **Qila Mubarak**, ancestral home of the maharajas of Faridkot. Nearby are an enclosed market square, the pastel-green **Memorial Library**, and the **Tilla Baba Farid Ji**, sacred to the 13th-century Sufi poet Baba Sheikh Farid, whose poems were an inspiration for Guru Nanak, founder of Sikhism. The current residence of the maharajas of Faridkot, **Raj Mahal**, stands behind a pastel wall on the Mall. A one-hour bus ride (₹48) south, **Bathinda** has a monumental fort offering grand views over the town bazaars.

The best accommodation option is the **Hotel Trump Plaza** (☑ 9216800789; Kotkapura Rd; r from ₹1331), which also has a decent restaurant. Buses run to Amritsar (₹97, three hours). Chandigarh (₹180, four hours) and Patiala (₹150, two hours).

Guru Tegh Bahadur's head was cremated after it was recovered from Delhi.

Behind the Kesgarh Sahib, a broad paved path climbs the hillside to the **Anandpur Sahib fort**, which affords glorious views over a sea of gurdwara domes. Below the fort is the striking five-petal form (inspired by the five warrior-saints in the Khalsa) of the **Khalsa Heritage Complex** (Virasat-e-Khalsa; ⊙9.30am-4pm Tue-Sun) FREE. One of the Punjab's most impressive buildings, this fascinating museum complex uses elaborate murals and friezes to bring Sikh history to life.

🛏 Sleeping & Eating

The many gurdwaras in Anandpur Sahib provide accommodation and meals (donations are appropriate), though they are often full with pilgrims.

Above the road linking Kesgarh Sahib to the fort, **Hotel Paramount Residency** (☑01887-233619; Academy Rd; r ₹600, with AC ₹1000) has austere, spartan rooms but a good location close to the Khalsa Heritage Complex.

ℹ Getting There & Away

The bus and train stations are 300m apart on the main road outside town. Buses leave frequently for Chandigarh (₹99, two hours), Amritsar (₹175, 4½ hours) and Patiala (₹106, three hours).

The overnight Delhi–Una Himachal Express train connects Delhi with Anandpur Sahib (sleeper/3AC/2AC ₹164/346/665, eight hours, daily). Local passenger trains run to Chandigarh.

Patiala
☑ 0175 / POP 405,200

Punjab's best-kept secret, Patiala was once the capital of an independent Sikh state, ruled by an extravagant family of maharajas. As the Mughal empire declined, the rulers of Patiala curried favour with the British and filled their city with lavish palaces and follies. Family fortunes have declined and the grand monuments are crumbling, but the old city, ringed by 10 historic gates, is swooningly atmospheric. In January/February, the skies above Patiala burst into life for the **Basant** kite festival.

⊙ Sights

Patiala's sights are dotted around the maze-like streets of the old town, south of the bus stand.

Qila Mubarak   FORT
(Arms gallery 10; ⊙10.15am-4.45pm Tue-Sun) The ancestral home of the maharajas of Patiala, this richly ornamented but fading fort is an *Arabian Nights* fantasy of soaring buttresses and latticed balconies. Visitors can walk between the inner and outer walls, surrounded by crumbling masonry and flocks of emerald-green parakeets. Inside the 1859 Durbar Hall is a wonderful collection of royal weaponry, outrageous chandeliers and other treasures rescued from the decaying palaces.

Other Sights
Follow the road leading south from Qila Mubarak and you will pass the monumen-

---

A MARTIAL ORDER

Sikhs are famous for their courage in battle, but the Sikh religion took up arms out of necessity. In 1606, the fifth Sikh guru, Guru Arjan Dev, was executed by the Mughal emperor Jahangir for refusing to convert to Islam, marking the beginning of centuries of persecution.

When Guru Tegh Bahadur, the ninth guru, was executed by Aurangzeb in 1675, his son Guru Gobind Singh summoned the Sikh congregation to Anandpur Sahib and called for five volunteers who were brave enough to lay down their lives for the Sikh religion. One by one, five Sikh warriors entered the guru's tent, and each time, the guru emerged with fresh blood dripping from his sword.

Then the guru revealed his master stroke – the five volunteers stepped out into the sunlight unharmed, and their courage and belief became a model for all Sikhs to follow. So was born the Khalsa brotherhood, the order of warrior saints to which most Sikhs subscribe.

Over the coming centuries, the brotherhood would find its courage put repeatedly to the test. During the Chhota Ghallughara (Lesser Massacre) of 1746 and the Wadda Ghallughara (Great Massacre) of 1762, up to a third of the Sikh population died at the hands of Mughal and Afghan forces.

tal gateway to the **Shahi Samadhan**, where dainty marble cenotaphs pay homage to generations of Patiala royalty.

Continue along the same road and bear left by the Samania Gate to reach Mohindra College Rd and the twin towers of the **Mohindra College**, a former palace converted into a private school.

A short stroll further south, the **Netaji Subhas National Institute of Sports** (Old Moti Bagh; ◎9.30am-5pm Tue-Sun) `FREE` occupies a wing of the vast Moti Bagh palace, constructed by Maharaja Narendra Singh in 1847. The museum contains exhibits on Indian sporting heroes, including Punjabi sprinter Milkha Singh, 'the Flying Sikh'.

Bordering the palace compound is yet another palace, the totally over-the-top **Sheesh Mahal** (Sheesh Mahal Rd; admission ₹10; ◎10.30am 5pm Tue Sun), graced by two wedding-cake towers and an ornamental suspension bridge. Inside the lavishly decorated interior is a gallery displaying royal treasures.

A short walk north of the bus stand, the **Dukh Niwaran Gurdwara** is credited with healing powers thanks to a miraculous cure carried out by the ninth Sikh guru, Tegh Bahadur, in 1672.

🛌 Sleeping & Eating

Hotel Narain Continental   HOTEL **$$**
(☎2227122; www.hotelnarain.com; Mall; r from ₹1866; ❄) Old-fashioned but comfortable, this is a reasonably luxe option in a handy location near but not too close to the bus stand. Rooms have carved bedsteads and stone tiling, and there's a good multicuisine restaurant.

Baradari Palace   HERITAGE HOTEL **$$$**
(☎2304433; www.neemranahotels.com; Baradari Gardens; s/d incl breakfast ₹3900/5571; ❄) Built as a garden palace for Maharaja Rajinder Singh, this nostalgic heritage hotel is Punjab's most graceful place to stay. The artfully restored rooms have room to swing a Bengal tiger, and the terraces overlook elegant gardens. Rates are discounted by 20% from May to August.

Gopal's   SOUTH INDIAN **$**
(Phowara Chowk; mains ₹40-200; ◎8am-11pm) This smart sweetshop has a canteen-style

A PATIALA PEG

Patiala's most famous invention dates back to a tent-pegging contest – where tent pegs are speared from the ground from a moving horse – between the viceroy of India and the sports-mad maharaja of Patiala. Desperate to win and fearful of the wrath of their maharaja, the Patiala team invited the British team to drinks the night before, serving double-sized measures (or pegs) of whisky to their guests. Come morning, smaller tent pegs were provided for the British riders; when the defeated and hung-over colonials complained that the contest was rigged, the maharaja quipped that in Patiala, famous for its hospitality, the pegs (of whisky) were always larger than elsewhere!

restaurant upstairs that serves tastebud-tingling South Indian vegetarian treats.

❶ Getting There & Away

Frequent buses run between Patiala and Chandigarh (₹57 to ₹130, two hours), Amritsar (₹137 to ₹241, 2½ hours) and Sirhind (₹28, one hour).

Sirhind
POP 73,800

Any easy day trip from Chandigarh, Sirhind (pronounced 'seer-hand') is famous for the **Gurdwara Fatehgarh Sahib**, which commemorates the 1704 martyrdom of the two youngest sons of the 10th Sikh guru, Gobind Singh, entombed alive by the Mughals for refusing to convert to Islam. The gurdwara hosts the three-day **Shaheedi Jor Mela** held every December.

Sirhind has several forlorn relics from Mughal times. The **Rauza Sharif**, mausoleum of Sufi saint Shaikh Ahmad Faruqi Sirhindi, draws pilgrims during the **Urs festival** in August. Down a lane closer to the bus stand, the dilapidated **Ram Khas Bagh** was once a grand Mughal garden with an enormous *baoli* (step well).

Buses connect Sirhind with Patiala (₹30, one hour) and Chandigarh (₹39, 1½ hours).

Jammu & Kashmir (including Ladakh)

Includes ➡

Best Buddhist Monasteries

➡ Yungdrung Gompa (p260)

➡ Thekchhok Gompa (p247)

➡ Thiksey Gompa (p247)

➡ Karsha Gompa (p264)

➡ Diskit Gompa (p252)

Best Mountain Scenery

➡ Pangong Tso (p255)

➡ Dal Lake (p267)

➡ Turtuk and the Shyok Valley (p253)

➡ Leh–Manali road (p248)

Why Go?

Welcome to three incredibly different worlds in one state. For most foreigners, J&K's greatest attractions are the Himalayan lands of Ladakh and Zanskar, with their disarmingly friendly Tibetan Buddhist people, timeless monasteries, arid canyons and soaring snow-topped mountains. But neither area is easily accessible, especially outside midsummer.

Hordes of domestic visitors make pilgrimages to temples around Hindu Jammu and love Muslim Kashmir for its cool summer air and alpine scenery. Srinagar's romantic houseboat accommodation is another drawcard. However, political volatility remains a concern. Disputes over Kashmir caused three 20th-century wars, and intercommunal strife still breaks out sporadically. Always check the security situation before travelling to Jammu or Srinagar but, even if things look dodgy there, you can expect Ladakh to be as meditatively calm as ever.

When to Go
Leh

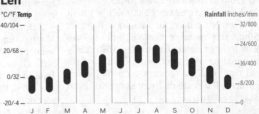

Jun & Sep Ideal for Srinagar and Sonamarg; roads to Ladakh can be blocked.

Jul & Aug Perfect for Ladakh; Pahalgam overflows with pilgrims; rain drenches Jammu.

Winter Skiing at Gulmarg. Ladakh, only accessible by air, has festivals but no tourists.

Food

A full traditional Kashmiri *wazwan* (feast) can have dozens of courses, notably mutton-based dishes such as *goshtaba* (pounded mutton balls in saffron-yoghurt curry), *tabak maaz* (fried lamb's ribs) and rogan josh (rich, vividly red-coloured mutton curry). Kashmiri chefs also serve deliciously aromatic cheese-based curries and seasonal *nadir* (lotus stems) typically served in *yakhni* (a curd-based sauce made mildly minty with fennel). Kashmiri *kahwa* is a luxurious golden tea flavoured with saffron, cinnamon and crushed almonds.

Ladakh's Tibetan favourites include salt-tea, *momos* (savoury dumplings wrapped ravioli-style in thin pasta) and *thukpa* (noodle soup) though a more genuinely Ladakhi dish is *skyu,* pieces of flat barley 'gnocchi' in a vegetable stew. Ladakh's barley-beer, *chhang*, is available at rural homestays but not for general sale.

DON'T MISS

Buddhist **Ladakh** (p228) is India at its most beguilingly human and scenically stunning, a rugged high-altitude desert softened with Tibetan temples, irrigated paddies and mesmerising mountain lakes. Come in summer when the rest of sweltering India is drenched in monsoons. But allow ample contingency time for acclimatisation, cancelled planes and roads that can suffer lengthy closures caused by landslides.

Top State Festivals

Hindu festivals are celebrated in Jammu, Muslim ones in the Kashmir Valley and Buddhist temple festivals abound in Ladakh and Zanskar.

➡ **Dosmoche** (☻Feb-early Mar; Leh, p230, Diskit, p252, Likir, p256) Buddhist New Year is celebrated with masked dances; effigies representing the evil spirits of the old year are burnt or cast into the desert.

➡ **Matho Nagrang** (☻Feb-Mar; Matho,p246) Monastery oracles perform blindfolded acrobatics and ritual mutilations.

➡ **Amarnath Yatra** (☻Jul-mid-Aug; Amarnath, p266) Hindu pilgrims' mountain trek to Amarnath.

➡ **Ladakh Festival** (☻1-15 Sep; www.reachladakh. com/festival_dates.htm; Leh, p235) Events include a carnivalesque opening parade, Buddhist dances, polo, music and archery.

➡ **Losar** (☻Dec; Ladakh & Zanskar) Tibetan New Year is celebrated two months earlier in Ladakh.

MAIN POINTS OF ENTRY

Srinagar, Jammu and Leh have commercial airports. Jammu has the only major railhead. By road, Ladakh is only accessible in summer over tortuous mountain roads from Srinagar and Manali.

Fast Facts

➡ **Population**: 10.1 million

➡ **Area**: 222,236 sq km

➡ **Capitals**: Srinagar (summer), Jammu (winter), Leh (Ladakh)

➡ **Main languages:** Kashmiri, Urdu, Ladakhi, Balti

➡ **Sleeping prices**: $ below ₹1000, $$ ₹1000 to ₹5000, $$$ above ₹5000

Top Tip

Check the security situation before heading to the Kashmir Valley. Even if troubles return to Srinagar, don't be deterred from visiting ever-calm Ladakh.

Resources

➡ **News** (www.greater kashmir.com, www.daily excelsior.com, www.kashmir times.com, www.kashmir herald.com/main.php)

➡ **Traveller Forum** (www. indiamike.com/india/ jammu-and-kashmir-f30)

➡ **Tourism** (www.jktourism. org)

➡ **Kashmir Conflicts** (http: //blankonthemap.free.fr/1_ accueil/map.php?code=1015)

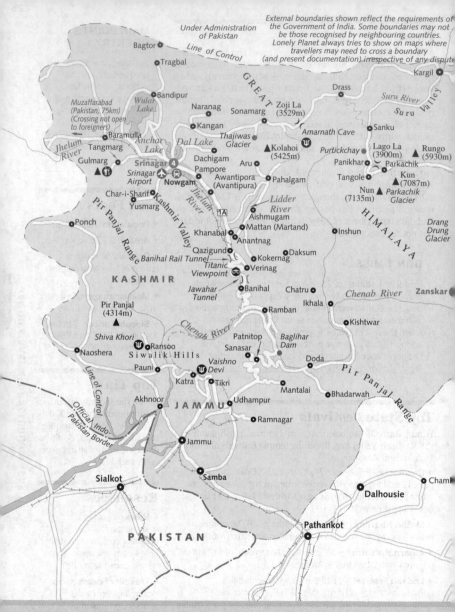

Jammu & Kashmir Highlights

1 Murmur meditative mantras in the mural-decked gompas (Tibetan Buddhist monasteries) of the **Indus Valley**, such as at Thiksey (p247)

2 Escape India's humid summer heat in entrancing **Leh** (p230), a low-key traveller hub with dusty medieval backstreets, a Potala-style palace and a deep sense of ecological awareness

3 Experience the stark magnificence of **Ladakh** (p228) or **Zanskar** (p263)

on an unforgettable high-altitude trek

4 Enjoy an amusingly caricatured British Raj–type experience relaxing on a deluxe Dal Lake houseboat in **Srinagar** (p267)

5 Gawp at the mountain-valley scenery backing surreally blue **Pangong Tso** (p255) or the splendid **Nubra Valley** (p250)

LADAKH

Spectacularly jagged, arid mountains enfold this magical, Buddhist ex-kingdom. Picture-perfect gompas dramatically crown rocky outcrops amid whitewashed stupas (Buddhist religious monuments) and meditational *mani* walls (Tibetan stone walls with sacred inscriptions) with mantra-inscribed pebbles. Colourful fluttering prayer flags spread their spiritual messages metaphorically with the mountain breeze. Prayer wheels spun clockwise release merit-making mantras. Gompa interiors are colourfully awash with murals and statuary of numerous bodhisattvas.

Ladakh's remarkably well-balanced traditional society has much to teach the West in terms of ecological awareness. While most Ladakhis are cash poor, traditional mud-brick homesteads are large, comfortable and self-sufficient in fuel and dairy products, organic vegetables and barley used to make *tsampa* (roast barley flour) and chhang. Such self-sufficiency is an incredible achievement given the short growing season and very limited arable land in this upland desert, where precious water supplies must be laboriously channelled from glacier-melt mountain streams.

History

Ladakh's (now-deposed) royal family traces its dynasty back 39 generations to AD 975. They took the name Namgyal (Victorious) in 1470 when their progenitor Lhachen Bhagan, ruling from Basgo, conquered a competing Ladakhi kingdom based at Leh/Shey. Although Ladakh had been culturally 'Tibetanised' in the 9th century, Buddhism originally arrived in an Indian form that's visible in ancient temple craftsmanship at Alchi. Over time, however, different Buddhist sects struggled for prominence, with the Tibetan Gelukpa order eventually becoming the ma-

TREKKING IN LADAKH & ZANSKAR

Bargain value, thrillingly scenic treks can take you into magical roadless villages, through craggy gorges and across dazzlingly stark mountain passes.

Seasons

The main season is essentially July and August, but in the Markha and Sham areas routes can be feasible from May to early October. Late August is preferred for certain routes with river crossings due to lower water levels. In February you could attempt the challenging **Chadar ice-trek** (p263).

Preparation

Most trekking routes start at around 3500m, often climbing above 5000m, so proper acclimatisation is essential to avoid Acute Mountain Sickness (AMS). You could acclimatise with 'baby' treks or by adding extra (if less interesting) days to the core treks, for instance starting from Lamayuru, Spituk or Martselang rather than Hinju/Photoksar, Zingchen or Shang Sumdo. Book a jeep transfer from your finishing point or choose to end up somewhere with public transport (eg Stok).

Horse Treks

At these altitudes carrying heavy packs is much more exhausting than many anticipate, so consider engaging packhorses (the accompanying horseman can often double as a guide) or do a 'homestay trek'. Agencies will happily arrange all-inclusive packages with horses, guides, food and (often old) camping gear starting from around ₹3500 per person per day. If you're self-sufficient (tent, food) and patient, it's often possible to find your own horseman from ₹400 per horse per day, but you'll generally need to engage at least three horses, and pay for any extra days needed for them to return to base (often Spituk) or to their next starting point. Prices rise considerably during harvest season (August).

Homestay Treks

Rural homestays (www.himalayan-homestays.com) and/or parachute cafes now provide simple lodging along many (though not all) popular trekking routes, reducing or negating the need to carry significant supplies and camping gear. For ₹500 per person per day you get simple meals, generally eaten with the family in their traditional kitchen where pots and pans are proudly displayed above the Aga-style winter stove. Mud-brick rooms generally have rugs and blankets for bedding, some have solar-battery electric lamps. Given the lack of telephones, 'bookings' are not generally possible, and smaller villages do occasionally run out of space,

jority philosophy after its introduction in the 14th century by Tibetan pilgrim Tsongkhapa (who left a curious relic at Spituk).

Ladakh's greatest king, Sengge Namgyal (r 1616–42) gained riches by plundering gold reserves from western Tibet and re-established a capital at Leh. Ladakh remained an independent kingdom until the 1840s when the Namgyals lost power and the region was annexed by the Jammu maharajas.

Since Independence, Ladakh has been ruled as a (now semi-autonomous) subdistrict of J&K. That's a culturally odd situation for this 'little Tibet', which is one of the last undisturbed Tantric Buddhist societies on earth. Tourism was first permitted in 1974 but, while globalised economics and climate change have certainly caused many problems, including dangerous population shifts, the traditional lifestyle has proved unexpectedly robust, and locally relevant technologies,

such as solar energy and Trombe walls, are starting to improve rural living standards.

Climate

Ladakh's short tourist season (July to early September) typically sees pleasantly mild T-shirt weather by day, with slightly crisp, occasionally chilly nights. However, on higher treks night-time temperatures can dip below –5°C even in midsummer. By September snow is likely on higher ground although major passes usually stay open until October. In winter temperatures can fall below –20°C. Access roads and much of the tourist infrastructure closes. Ladakh's crystal-blue skies enjoy sunshine for an average of 300 days a year, but storms can brew suddenly. Although rare, heavy rain can cause devastating mudslides, as happened in August 2010 when such cloudbursts killed around 200 people.

but bigger Rumbak and the Sham villages can generally take all comers. An experienced local guide (₹1200 per day), helpful with security, route-finding and social interactions, can be engaged with a few days' notice through **Hemis National Park Guide Service** (Map p236; ✓9622999424; hemis_npark@yahoo.co.in; 1st fl, unit 11, Hemis Complex, Leh; ⊙10am-7pm).

Which Trek?

Popular options:

DAYS	ROUTE	HOMESTAYS	HIGH PASSES	SEE
2	Zingchen-Rumbak-Stok	plenty	4900m	p248
2	Hinju-Sumdho Chinmu-Sumdha Do	limited	4950m	p259
2-4	Itchar-Phuktal-Itchar	limited	no	p264
3+	Chiling-Skiu (Markha Valley)-Yurutse/Rumbak-Zingchen	yes	4920m	p256
5+	Chiling-Kaya-Markha-Hankar Nimaling-Shang Sumdo	yes (or tent-camp)	5030m	p256
5 (8)	(Rumtse)-Tso Khar-Korzok	no	4 (7)	p255
6 (8)	(Padum)-Itchar-Phuktal-Ramjak (Darcha)	some days	5090m	p264
5 (9)	(Lamayuru-Honupatta)-Photoksar-Lingshet-Hanumil-(Padum)	most days	5050m	p260

For something relatively easy, Zingchen–Rumbak–Yurutse–Zingchen makes a great one- or two-day sampler from Leh. Markha Valley routes before Nimaling have no passes to cross and Sham 'treks' are little more than road walks between attractive old villages.

To make the Markha Valley trek more adventurous, it's possible (with guides and horses) to continue from Hankar into the Kharnak nomad area around Dat, returning to Leh by jeep via the Manali road.

Further Information

➜ Lonely Planet's *Trekking in the Indian Himalaya*

➜ Trailblazer's *Trekking in Ladakh*

➜ www.myhimalayas.com/travelogues/ladakh.htm

JAMMU & KASHMIR (INCLUDING LADAKH) LADAKH

Language

Though they use the same script, the Tibetan and Ladakhi languages are significantly different. The wonderfully all-purpose word *jule* (pronounced '*joo*-lay') means 'hello', 'goodbye', 'please' and 'thanks'. To the greeting *khamzang*, simply reply *khamzang*. *Zhimpo-rak* means 'it's delicious'. Rebecca Norman's excellent *Getting Started in Ladakhi* (₹200) has more phrases and useful cultural tips.

Activities

In summer Ladakh is an adventure playground for outdoor types. Thanks to Leh's vast range of agents, making arrangements is very easy for climbing, rafting, high-altitude trekking (see p234) or jeep tours.

Leh

📞 01982 / POP 28,640 / ELEV 3520M

Few places in India are at once so traveller-friendly and yet so enchanting and hassle-free as mountain-framed Leh. Dotted with stupas and crumbling mud-brick houses, the Old Town is dominated by a dagger of steep rocky ridge topped by an imposing Tibetan-style palace and fort. Beneath, the bustling bazaar area is draped in a thick veneer of tour agencies, souvenir shops and pizza restaurants, but a web of lanes quickly fans out into a green suburban patchwork of irrigated barley fields. Here, gushing streams and narrow footpaths link traditionally styled Ladakhi buildings with flat roofs, sturdy walls and ornate wooden window frames. Leh's a place that's all too easy to fall in love with, but take things easy on arrival. The altitude means that most visitors initially suffer mild headaches and breathlessness. To prevent this becoming full-blown Acute Mountain Sickness (AMS), drink plenty of ginger tea and avoid strenuous exertion at first. Climbing Palace Ridge or Shanti Stupa on your first two days in Leh is unwise unless you're already altitude acclimatised. Similarly, it's wise to wait before trekking or taking jeep excursions over high passes (to Nubra or Pangong).

◎ Sights

◎ Central Leh

★ Leh Palace   PALACE
(Map p236; Indian/foreigner ₹5/100; ⊙8am-6.30pm) Bearing a passing similarity to the Potala Palace in Lhasa (Tibet), this nine-storey dun-coloured palace took shape under 17th-century king Sengge Namgyal. Essentially it has been unoccupied since the Ladakhi royals were stripped of power and shuffled off to Stok in 1846. Today the very sturdy walls are mostly unadorned, but it's gently thrilling to weave your way through the maze of dark corridors, hidden stairways and makeshift ladders to reach the rooftop for great views across the city. You can seek out the small palace prayer room and a one-room exhibition showing photos of J&K monument restoration.

Interesting structures ranged around the palace's base include the prominent **Namgyal Stupa** (Map p236), the 1430 **Chamba Lhakhang** (Map p236) with medieval mural fragments between the inner and outer walls, and the colourfully muralled **Chandazik Gompa** (Chenrezi Lhakhang; Map p236; admission ₹20; ⊙7am-6pm) celebrating the full pantheon of 1000 Buddhas (of which 996 have yet to be born).

★ Tsemo Fort   CASTLE, RUIN
(Map p236; admission ₹20; ⊙dawn-dusk) Visible from virtually everywhere in Leh, the 16th-century Tsemo (Victory) Fort is a defining landmark that crowns the top of Palace Ridge. Up close, it's surprisingly small and the shattered walls contain little more than flapping prayer flags, but scrambling around them provides a precarious frisson. Directly beneath, **Tsemo Gompa** (Map p236; admission ₹20) consists of two little 15th-century temple buildings, one enshrining an 8m-tall gold-faced Maitreya. An alternative concreted path descends to a collection of stupas near Hotel Chubi.

REACHING LADAKH

Be aware that the two beautiful but arduous road routes into Ladakh (from Manali or Srinagar) close altogether from October or November until May, leaving flights into Leh as the only option. See websites www.leh.nic.in or http://vistet.wordpress.com to check road status and allow at least a couple of spare days in case of delays. Zanskar is essentially cut off altogether in winter except by ice-trek.

Central Asian Museum — MUSEUM
(Map p236; www.tibetheritagefund.org/pages/projects/ladakh/central-asian-museum.php) New but styled as a tapered four-storey stone tower, the building's design is loosely based on a mansion in Lhasa and exited across a fortress-style drawbridge. The four relatively limited exhibition spaces will trace the history of trade between Ladakh, Tibet and Baltistan. The museum is hidden in a courtyard opposite **Datun Sahib** (Map p236; www.shridatunsahib.com), a sacred tree supposedly planted in 1517 by a Sikh mystic, though others claim it grew magically from the walking staff of Staksang Raspa, guru to Ladakh's great king, Sengge Namgyal.

Old Town — AREA
Beside Datun Sahib or behind Leh's fanciful **Jama Masjid** (Map p236) (Sunni men's mosque), winding alleys and stairways burrow between and beneath a series of old mud brick Ladakhi houses and eroded old chortens (stupas). The alleys themselves are a large part of the attraction, but some individual buildings have been particularly well restored, notably the 17th-century **Munshi Mansion**, once the residence of the Ladakhi royal secretary and now housing the **Lamo Arts Centre** (Map p236; 251554; www.lamo.org.in; 11am-3pm Mon-Sat).

Informative small-group walking tours (per person ₹300; tours at 10am Monday to Friday) dawdle around the Old Town for three hours visiting restored historical buildings. Start from Lala's Art Cafe (p242) where you should book ahead.

Chowkhang Gompa — BUDDHIST TEMPLE
(Map p236) Hidden in a large courtyard behind Main Bazaar, the small, 20th-century Chowkhang Gompa has a gilt-roofed prayer room strung with hundreds of prayer flags. It's the headquarters of the Ladakh Buddhist Association.

◉ Greater Leh

Sankar — AREA
As you wander north, Leh's rural qualities and the impressive mountain setting become swiftly apparent. Captivating footpaths follow the remarkable network of canal streams, with a relatively accessible yet captivating area around little **Sankar Gompa** (Map p232; admission ₹30). Then, for memorable views, continue around 1km uphill to the laudable **Donkey Sanctuary**

LADAKH PERMITS

You'll need an inner line permit (valid seven days, not extendable) to visit Nubra Valley, Pangong Tso, Dha-Hanu, Tso Moriri and the Upper Indus (beyond Upshi).

Though processed by the DCO (Polo Ground; closed Sunday), foreigners' permit applications must be made through travel agencies. Apply by 2pm the day before travel (or on Saturday for Monday departures). You'll typically pay ₹400 to ₹500, ie ₹20 per day, and ₹220 for ecological and health taxes plus agency commission. This includes multiple photocopies of your documents (passport, visa, permit) to give to police checkpoints en route, but making extra copies can prove wise. Technically at least two people must apply together, but agencies can fudge this for individual travellers

---

(☎9419658777; www.donkeysanctuary.in; Korean Temple Rd) or the nearby 11th-century **Tisuru Stupa** (Tisuru Rd), a bulky, partly restored mud-brick ruin that looks like a half-built ziggurat (stepped pyramid).

Shanti Stupa — BUDDHIST, VIEWPOINT
(Map p232) Built in 1991 by Japanese monks to promote world peace, this large hilltop stupa has brightly coloured reliefs on its mid levels and is topped by a spired white hemisphere. The greatest attraction is the stunning view of Leh. Ideally, make the breathless 15-minute climb when golden afternoon light still illuminates the city but the steps up from Changspa are already bathed in cooling shadow.

Gomang Stupa — BUDDHIST SITE
(Map p232) This 9th-century stupa rises in concentric serrated layers flanked by ancient Buddhist rock carvings and numerous chortens. Its peaceful, shady setting is a refreshingly spiritual escape from the tourist-centric developments of surrounding Changspa.

Nezer Latho — VIEWPOINT, SACRED SITE
(Map p232) This mysterious whitewashed cube is the shrine of Leh's guardian deity. It sits atop a rocky outcrop offering superb 360-degree views over the city through colourful strings of prayer flags, a five-minute climb from Hotel Dragon.

Leh

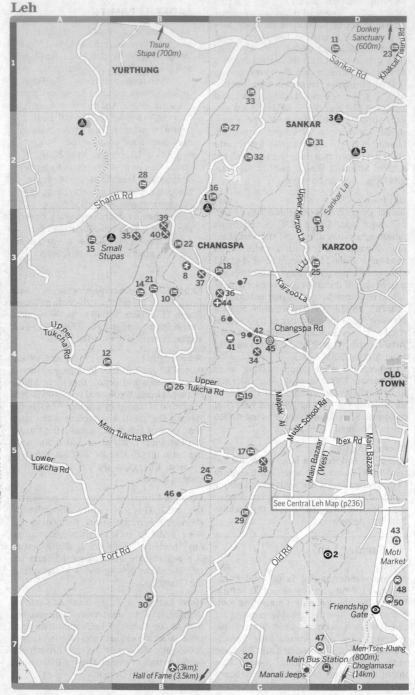

See Central Leh Map (p236)

JAMMU & KASHMIR (INCLUDING LADAKH) LEH

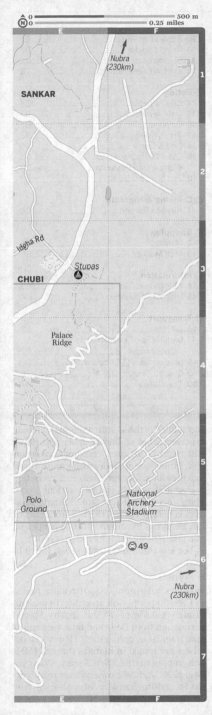

◉ Out of Town

Spituk Gompa BUDDHIST MONASTERY
(admission ₹30) Founded in the late 14th century as See-Thub (Exemplary) Monastery, impressive Spituk Gompa is incongruously perched overlooking the southern end of Leh's airport runway, around 5km from town. Multiple mud-brick buildings tumble merrily down a steep hillock towards Spituk village on the Indus riverbank. The courtyard below the gilt-roofed Skudung Lhakhang leads to a colourful Dukhang (prayer hall) containing a yellow-hatted statue of Tsongkhapa (1357–1419) who spread Gelukpa Buddhism. A Buddha statue across the same room supposedly incorporates a very odd relic: Tsongkhapa's nosebleed.

On the very top of the gompa hill is a three-tiered *latho* (spirit shrine) and the small **Palden Lama temple** (◔7am-6.30pm) hiding veiled Hindu-style deities and festival masks in an intimate rear section.

Hall of Fame MUSEUM
(Leh-Spituk Hwy Km428; Indian/foreigner/camera ₹10/50/50; ◔9am-1pm & 2-7pm Apr-Oct, to 5pm Nov-Mar) This well-presented museum mostly commemorates the various high-altitude battles fought with Pakistan during the 20th century, but there's also a 3D relief map of Ladakh and two rooms featuring local culture and nature.

🏃 Activities, Courses & Tours

Cycling

For an exhilarating yet effortless excursion take a jeep ride up to Khardung La (the 'world's highest road-pass') and let gravity bring you back down. The potholes of the uppermost 15km (above South Pullu army camp) mean you won't whizz down too fast, but the last 25km to Leh are well paved. Packages based on four riders cost around ₹1000 per person and include bike hire and a support vehicle. Permit costs extra. Book through **Summer Holidays** (Map p236; ☑9906985822; www.mtbladakh.com; Zangsti Rd) or **Himalayan Bikers** (Map p232; ☑250937; www.himalayan-biker.com; Changspa). Both also rent mountain bikes (per day ₹450 to ₹700) and can organise guided bike rides.

Meditation & Yoga

Mahabodhi Centre YOGA, MEDITATION
(Map p232; ☑9622995460; www.mahabodhi-ladakh.org; Changspa Lane) Daily, except Sundays, there are meditation sessions (by donation)

Leh

at 7.30am and 8.30am, then yoga classes (₹250) at 9am, 3pm and 4.30pm. Three-day residential courses in *vipassana* meditation (₹3000) are held at their Choglamsar Centre (approximately 1km north of Km464.2) as are Sunday 'introduction-to-meditation' sessions (₹500 including bus transfer from Leh).

Open Ladakh   MEDITATION
(Map p236; ☑ 9906981026; www.openladakh.com) Weekend *vipassana* residential retreats in Stok and occasional meditation treks.

Mountaineering
Ladakh has over 100 climbable peaks above 6000m, many rarely, if ever, scaled. Numerous agencies can arrange packages while **Venture Equipment** (Map p236) and other Changspa outfits rent climbing gear.

A popular destination is Stok Kangri/Kanglha-jhal (6121m), the triangular snow-capped peak usually visible straight across the valley from Leh. As a 'trekking peak' it's accessible to those with minimal climbing experience, but scaling its uppermost slopes still requires ice axes, crampons, considerable fitness and a guide, with groups roped together for safety. Pre-climb acclimatisation is essential as AMS can be a serious worry. Many agencies offer Stok Kangri packages generally taking five days from Stok or Zingchen, costing around ₹15,000 per person in a group of six (permits and gear extra).

For less vigourous climbing, see Gravit.In (p243).

➡ **Permits**

Peak fees range from US$50 (trekking peaks) to US$500 per person according to peak altitude. Peaks over 7000m require special permission from Delhi and thus the permits take months of preparation. However, most others are issued in minutes through IMF's Leh representative, **Sri Sonam Wangyal** (Map p236; ☑ 252992; www.indmount.org; Changspa Rd; ⊙10am-5pm Mon-Sat), who was the youngest man to scale Mt Everest back in

1965. His house-office is tucked incongruously into the Mentokling Restaurant yard. You'll need six photocopies of your passport/visa plus details of your guide. Agencies can apply on your behalf.

Rafting & Kayaking

In summer, numerous agencies offer daily rafting excursions through glorious canyon scenery. Experienced paddlers can follow in a kayak for around 50% extra. Prepare to get very wet. There are two main routes: Phey to Nimmu, grade II (beginners), typically costs ₹1200 to ₹1700; and Chiling to Nimmu, grade III, tougher, ₹1500 to ₹2000. Prices include equipment and lunch but bring extra drinking water. Once or twice a year group expeditions descend the Zanskar River from Zangla to Nimmu (three days' rafting, three days' travel). Reliable companies include **Rimo** (Map p236; ✓253348; www.rimoriverexpeditions.com; Zangsti Rd) and **Splash Adventures** (Map p236; ✓254870; www.splashladakh.com; Zangsti Rd), which also has a Changspa branch (Map p232; ✓9419880984; www.splashladakh.com; Changspa Rd).

To mix things up, **Luna Ladakh** (Map p236; ✓251800; www.lunaladakh.com; Zangsti Rd) puts together relatively inexpensive mountain-bike/trekking/rafting packages at ₹4000 to ₹6000 per person for four days. These cover Leh, Spituk, Rumbak, Chiling and Nimmu, and include meals, fees, equipment, accommodation and transport.

Trekking & Jeep Safaris

Countless agencies offer trekking packages and jeep tours. Few seem systematically bad but many are very inconsistent. If you haven't booked, a deciding factor is often simply which agent happens to have a group leaving on the day you need. Ask fellow travellers for recent recommendations.

For multiday jeep hires, agencies can put together a fare-sharing group, organising permits, vehicle and driver. Five per jeep is optimal for comfort versus expense. The most popular excursions are Pangong Tso or the Nubra/Shyok Valleys. Book at least 24 hours ahead.

Ladakhi Women's Travel Company   TREKKING
(Map p236; ✓257973, 9469158137; www.ladakhiwomenstravel.com; 1st fl, unit 14, Hemis Complex; ⏰10am-6pm) Small, highly reputed female-run operation specialising in Markha and Sham homestay trek packages. Male customers accepted only if group includes women.

Wild East Adventure   TREKKING
(Map p236; ✓250505; www.wildeastadventure.com; Hemis Complex) Long-established specialist for tailor-made treks using only their own guides. Helpful and obliging.

Shayok Tours & Travels   SAFARIS, TREKKING
(Map p236; ✓9419342346, 9419888902; shayoktravels@rediffmail.com; Changspa Rd) Frank, trustworthy and helpful. Can organise inner line permits for travellers on motorbikes.

Snowfield Tours & Travels   JEEP SAFARIS
(Map p236; ✓9469723819; Hemis Complex, Upper Tukcha Rd) Small outfit, but their driver Sharif is among the best in town.

Yama Adventures   TREKKING
(Map p232; ✓250833; www.yamatreks.com; Changspa Rd) Consistent recommendations.

Skywalker   TREKKING
(Map p236; ✓255165; www.skywalkertravel.com; Raku Complex, Fort Rd) Eco-aware homestay treks and yoga tours are specialities.

✦ Festivals & Events

Ladakh Festival   CULTURAL
(Leh; ⏰1-15 Sep) Unrepentantly touristy but entertaining cycle of events including a carnivalesque opening parade, Buddhist dances, polo, music and archery.

⛏ Sleeping

Leh has hundreds of guesthouses and around 70 hotels with dozens more under construction/reconstruction. Room standards can vary significantly within each property so, when possible, look before you book. Better guesthouses (around ₹900) are often preferable to lacklustre ₹3000 hotels with their ill-fitting carpets, saggy beds and faux veneer panelling. Hot water is typically provided either morning or evening (sometimes both) using wood-fired boilers. Geysers are likely to be more common and power cuts less frequent once the Alchi hydropower dam comes online. Many guesthouses will provide towels on request. Toilet paper (rarely provided) should *not* be flushed: use the plastic bin.

In winter most accommodation closes: those guesthouses that stay open often charge around ₹100 extra for heating, possibly offering only bucket water since pipes freeze.

Within the old city area choice is very limited and barking dogs can disturb light sleepers. Many good options lie close to busy

Central Leh

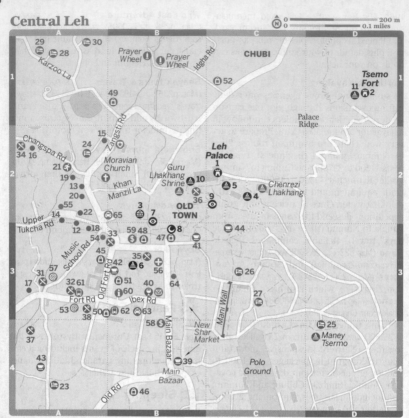

Fort Rd and Changspa Rd, conveniently full of internet cafes, travel agencies and tourist shops. Karzoo and the Tukcha roads are quieter, without shops or restaurants. Staying out as far out as Sankar or Yurthung feels very rural but it's a fairly long, dark walk home from town. Noisy Old Rd's package tour places tend to be poor value.

🛏 Central Leh

Palace View Guest House   GUESTHOUSE **$**
(Map p236; ☏96229645422; palace.view@hotmail.com; d from ₹450-700, without bathroom ₹250-300) One of Leh's original guesthouses (opened 1975), this friendly, fine-value family place is progressively upgrading its rooms with new bathrooms and plans a rooftop cafe to make the most of superb views across Palace Ridge. Ladakhi dinners available if you order by 5pm. Open year-round.

Zik Zik   GUESTHOUSE **$**
(Map p236; ☏255821; Karzoo Lane; d without/with bathroom ₹400/700; 🛜) Handily central yet with a rural feel, the best rooms are light and airy. There's a dining room offering home-cooked meals (₹70) and a big garden albeit slightly dusty from the car-park area. Friendly family owners. Wi-fi ₹50 per hour.

Travellers' House   GUESTHOUSE **$**
(Map p236; ☏250419; thetravellershouse@gmail. com; Karzoo Lane; d ₹700) Striking a great quality-price balance, the eight well-kept, no-nonsense guest rooms come with geyser-equipped bathrooms and face the attractive traditional house where the friendly, English-speaking family owners live. Sneak up onto the roof for great castle views.

Saser   GUESTHOUSE **$**
(Map p236; ☏250162, 9596967447; Karzoo Lane; d lower/upper ₹600/800) The lower rooms are bland, but upstairs rooms have wooden

Central Leh

beams, framed photos and a balcony facing the castle across the sweet little central lawn. Small library of English books in the breakfast room.

Namgyal Guest House GUESTHOUSE $
(Map p236; ☏ 9906973364; d ₹600, r without bathroom ₹200-500) In a cube of traditional old buildings, the cheaper rooms are simple but recently repainted and share three bathrooms with a geyser and seatless toilets. The newer en-suite rooms have varnished log ceilings and decent bathrooms, and many have views of Stok Kangri and the Maney Tsermo stupas. Friendly female owners.

Old Ladakh Guest House GUESTHOUSE $
(Map p236; ☏ 252951; www.littletibetladakh.com; d ₹500-600, s/d without bathroom ₹300/350) With distinctive crimson timbers, Old Ladakh has a central courtyard, traditional kitchen and breakfast room, and phenomenal rooftop

view. Downstairs rooms are dingily claustrophobic; others are bright if worn.

Kang-Lha-Chen — HOTEL $$

(Map p236; ☑ 252144, 202289; www.hotelkanglha chen.com; Zangsti; s/d ₹2000/2800; ☎) Brilliantly central yet set back from the road in ample greenery, this long-standing favourite of small tour groups has upgraded its rooms with good new mattresses, wood-effect hard floors and marble bathrooms. Tasteful Tibetan touches add interest and there's a delightful sitting room designed like a traditional Ladakhi kitchen.

Greater Leh

All of the following are within 20 minutes' walk of Old Leh, most far closer.

Solpon — GUESTHOUSE $

(Map p232; ☑ 253067; tsewangsolpon@yahoo.com; Upper Changspa; d ₹700-1000, without bathroom ₹300-400) The simplest rooms have clean vinyl floors, chairs and lump-free beds plus geyser-heated water in shared bathrooms. The new section with attached bathrooms is almost hotel standard, and some larger rooms (notably number 18) have great views. There's a vegetable patch and small garden sitting area. Excellent value.

Nurboo Guest House — GUESTHOUSE $

(Map p232; ☑ 9906988963; r without bathroom ₹300-350) Simple family place serenaded by the sound of rushing water and with great mountain views from the rooftop and upper corner rooms.

Gangs-Shun — HOMESTAY $

(Map p232; ☑ 252603, 9858060706; http://tiny.cc/GangsShun; Upper Tukcha Rd; d ₹1000; @) Seven very well appointed guest rooms of significantly variable sizes in the family home of a gregarious local doctor who is keen to encourage cultural exchange. Room 3 has a super balcony, room 1 is family-sized. Solar lamps and water heaters, free filter-water, lawn-seating and a vegetable garden add to the mix.

Lak Rook Guest House — GUESTHOUSE $

(Map p232; ☑ 252987, 9419177870; Sankar; r without bathroom ₹300-600) 🍃 This cult traveller favourite is a large, ramshackle Ladakhi farmhouse almost lost amid the flowers and fruit trees of its organic vegetable garden. It scores on atmosphere and eco-awareness more than comfort – the solar shower room is outside, Ladakhi toilets are available and mattresses are thin and sometimes lumpy. The two best rooms share a dedicated bathroom with geyser.

Gyalson — GUESTHOUSE $

(Map p232; ☑ 9622951748; gyalsean@yahoo.com; Changspa; d ₹600-700, f ₹800) Four spick-and-span new en-suite rooms in a new but semi-traditional family bungalow just behind the Wonderland restaurant.

Oriental Guesthouse — HOTEL, GUESTHOUSE $$

(Map p232; ☑ 253153; www.oriental-ladakh.com; Shanti Rd; r ₹600-1950, without bathroom ₹250; ☺ year-round; @) This self-contained 70-room complex on the edge of Changspa uses solar heating, has a lobby-library with internet, a central lawn and both traditional and modern glass-fronted kitchens, the latter serving a full-scale restaurant in an alluring Tibetan-styled lounge-dining room. Rooms range from very basic through fair-value ₹600 doubles to relatively elegant newer (single/double ₹1600/1950) versions with soft-on-hard double mattresses and sparkling bath-

---

LEH ECO-AWARENESS

Water is precious – those streams you see cascading beside virtually every lane aren't a sign of plenty but an elaborate network of irrigation that keeps Leh from reverting to dusty mountain desert. Anything you can do to save water is a positive step, such as reduced showering and using traditional Ladakhi long-drop toilets. These recycle human waste into compost, but don't put anything nonbiodegradeable down the hole: whatever goes in will end up on the farmer's field in a year or two.

To save Leh from vanishing under a sea of plastic bottles, refills of pressure-boiled, purified water are provided by environmental organisations **Dzomsa** (Map p236; ☑ 01982 250699; water refill ₹7) and LEDeG (p243). Both provide recycling and disposal services, and Dzomsa also offers ecofriendly laundry services and, like **Ladag Apricot Store** (Map p236; ☺ 9am-6pm), sells locally sourced foods including apricots and *tsestalulu* (sea buckthorn) juice as an alternative to imported chocolate and packaged soft drinks.

rooms with patterned tiles, towels and toilet paper provided. Room sizes and views vary.

Chow Guest House GUESTHOUSE $

(Map p232; ☑ 252399; d ₹600, without bathroom ₹300) Sparkling clean, airy budget rooms with good mattresses and log ceilings in two new but unobtrusive buildings set in a flower-filled walled garden down a narrow path from Changspa Rd. Family run. Partial mountain views.

Norzin Holiday Home GUESTHOUSE $

(Map p232; ☑ 252022; norzinholidays@gmail. com; Upper Tukcha Rd; r without/with bathroom ₹800/1000; ☎) Unusually well-kept local home with traditional design but modern interiors. Great views from the roof terrace, garden seating and a grape-vine dominating the glassed-in verandah. Free drinking water refills, wi fi ₹60 per hour, adorable family.

Haldupa Guest House GUESTHOUSE $

(Map p232; ☑ 251374; Upper Tukcha Rd; r without/with TV ₹700/1000, without bathroom ₹200-400) A handful of cheaper rooms (with shared squat toilets) are inside the wonderfully authentic original house, home to an utterly enchanting local family. The rest are compact but brand new, with decent bathrooms and log roofs in a separate block facing the garden.

Goba GUESTHOUSE $

(Map p232; ☑ 253670; Goba Alley; r ₹500-800, without bathroom ₹150-500) There's a great sense of traveller camaraderie in the traditional main house, topped with prayer room and lovely rooftop panoramas. Airy, simple rooms include two with wraparound-view windows. The more neutral hotel-style block has functional en-suite rooms. The garden is a veritable field from which homegrown organic vegetables form the mainstay of family-cooked meals (book ahead).

Ganzing Villina GUESTHOUSE $

(Map p232; ☑ 9419219416; Sankar Lane; d ₹600-800) New family bungalow set in small, peaceful gardens with fair-sized rooms, wicker seats and solar-powered bathrooms.

Tsetan Guest House GUESTHOUSE $

(Map p232; ☑ 250510; tsetan_n@yahoo.com; Upper Changspa; d ₹800, r without bathroom ₹200-500) Politely enthusiastic Tsetan plies guests with endless mint tea and encourages the friendly interactions that make for a memorable stay. Most rooms are very simple, two new en suites are very attractive and bathrooms have geysers.

Kunzang Guest House HOMESTAY $

(Map p232; ☑ 9906999817; kunzangguesthouse@ yahoo.in; s/d without bathroom from ₹150/300) An absolute archetype of a classic Ladakhi house down to the rooftop shrine, with simple accommodation ranging from small boxes to sunny corner rooms. Four newer options are under construction in the large field garden. Upper terrace seats.

Gomang Guest House GUESTHOUSE $

(Map p232; ☑ 252657; Old Karzoo; r without bathroom ₹350-400) Wobbly stairways link simple rooms sharing bathrooms. The main plus is that some rooms and two small communal sitting areas overlook Gomang Stupa. Hot water in buckets.

★ Deskit Villa GUESTHOUSE, HOTEL $$

(Map p232; ☑ 253498, 9419178998; bobzang-shamshu@yahoo.com; Sankar; s/d incl breakfast guesthouse ₹1200/1500, hotel ₹3000/3500) All the warmth of a genuine Ladakhi family welcome without compromising on professional standards of comfort. Bright, spacious rooms come with towels, solar showers and toilet paper even in the guesthouse section. The eight-room hotel section has some of the most comfortable beds in Leh and a stupendous rooftop panorama.

Royal Ladakh HOTEL $$

(Map p232; ☑ 251646; www.hotelroyalladakh.com; Upper Karzoo Lane; s/d ₹3300/2520; ☎) Behind the whitewashed facade and traditionally carved wooden window frames lies a stylishly appointed hotel with fine linen, flat-screen TVs and oodles of space. Bathrooms have a hint of 1960s-retro style and get hot water morning and evening. From the manicured lawn, inspiring views encompass Stok Kangri, Tsemo Fort and the Peace Pagoda. Wi-fi costs ₹1000 per stay.

Lotus Hotel HOTEL $$

(Map p232; ☑ 253129; http://lotushotel.in; Karzoo; s/d/ste ₹3666/3792/4930; ☎) The flower-filled gardens and lawn give an immediate appeal to this venerable older hotel whose architecture oozes local style and colour. Comfortable rooms now have shiny parquet floors, bathrooms come with toilet paper and 24-hour hot water. Wi-fi costs ₹90 per hour.

Alpine Villa HOTEL $$

(Map p236; ☑ 251837; www.alpinevilla.co.in; Chulung Lane; s/d ₹2820/2916; ☎) Like an Escher sketch, Alpine Villa rises in a series of stairways and marble-floored open balconies from which wicker chairs tempt loungers to gaze towards Stok Kangri. The reception and dining room burst with Tibetan colour, and the rooms are well appointed, with flat-screen TVs, carved window frames and wood-effect floors. Free wi-fi.

Gawaling International
HOTEL $$
(Map p232; ☑ 253252; www.hotelgawaling.com; s/d ₹3300/3850; ☺ Apr-Oct; @ ☎) Rooms are better maintained than at many other Leh hotels, with parquet floors and good bathrooms with partially solar-heated water. All but eight rooms have a balcony (huge in corner rooms) facing attractively rural scenery, and the whole complex is serenaded by a flowing river. Wi-fi and internet are free. Road access from Upper Tukcha Rd.

Grand Willow
HOTEL $$
(Map p232; ☑ 251835, 9419178242; www.grandwillowladakh.com; Fort Rd; s/d/ste ₹2000/2800/4500) A good choice for striking neo-traditional design and fair value for money if you want to be in the heart of the shopping area.

Lha-Ri-Mo
HOTEL $$
(Map p232; ☑ 252101; lharimo@yahoo.com; Fort Rd; s/d ₹2001/2760) Magenta window frames stacked upon whitewashed walls and all the Tibetan interior decor creates a magical monastery-like impression whose delight is amplified by the lovely enclosed lawn garden. Sadly, guest rooms aren't of quite the same standard, some having spongy beds and ill-fitting carpets.

Poplar Eco-Resort
ECORESORT $$
(Map p232; ☑ 253518; www.eprleh.com; Shenam Rd; s/d ₹2002/2772) Lost in the birdsong of an overgrown garden, amid apple, apricot and poplar trees, a series of well-spaced, tiled bungalow-cottages each contain two rooms sharing a verandah with wicker chairs. The setting is better than the slightly dated decor, but the attached bathrooms are clean and offer all-day hot water. Most food and juice served is sourced from their organic garden.

Ladakh Residency
HOTEL $$$
(Map p232; ☑ 254111; www.ladakhresidency.com; Changspa Rd; s/d/ste ₹4235/5445/7260; ☎) This relatively large, layered collage of wooden balconies and marble floors has proper king-size beds, suave bathrooms with decent toiletries and Stok Kangri views from many

balconies. It's one of very few wheelchair-friendly buildings in Ladakh. Decorated with Roerich prints.

Hotel Grand Dragon
HOTEL $$$
(Map p232; ☑ 250786; www.thegranddragonladakh.com; Old Rd, Shenam; s/d/ste ₹7150/8250/12,600; ☺ year-round; @ ☎) Leh's only really international-standard hotel, the Grand Dragon is professionally appointed, with functioning lift, fitting carpets and an art-bedecked marble-floored foyer. Rooms have excellent beds, a safe and minibar. The location is less impressive, away from shops down a busy road and with an ugly foreground to the mountain views. Wi-fi costs ₹300 per hour.

⛺ Out of Town

★ Hidden North Guest House
RURAL GUESTHOUSE $
(☑ 226007; www.hiddennorth.com; Phyang Tsakma; campsite/site & tent hire ₹130/180, r ₹800, without bathroom ₹300-600) On a rocky viewpoint perch in upper Phyang, young Ladakhi-Italian family owners have created a delightfully relaxing getaway for those wanting something even lower key than Leh. Panoramic views encompass a spiky mountain horizon and Phyang's large, recently restored gompa. Meals, climbing gear and guided treks are available. Pretty Phyang village is an emerald splash of tree-hemmed barley fields layered for miles in the next valley west from Leh, but has no other tourist facilities.

Lha-Ri-Sa Resort
HOTEL $$
(☑ 252423; www.ladakh-lharisa.com; s/d/ste ₹2800/3380/6000) Strikingly designed, the soaring atrium is held aloft on temple-like pillars. Raised walkways between apple trees link large, high-ceilinged rooms with 1940s-retro walnut furniture. This is arguably Leh's best hotel, but it's 3km south of town via unpleasantly busy major roads so you'll need wheels. There's ample parking.

✗ Eating

Traveller cafes abound, with Israeli and Chinese options supplementing curries, banana pancakes, tandoori pizzas and Tibetan favourites (notably *momos*). Curiously, few restaurants offer true Ladakhi food – try Old Town Cafe or request such dishes at family guesthouses. Many eateries, including Changspa's numerous garden restaurants, close from mid-September to early July, their owners often decamping to Goa.

Central Leh

The vast majority of visitor-centred dining is along Changspa Rd and Fort Rd, plus around Main Bazaar where there's also a fair sprinkling of dingy local dives stretching east from the main mosque.

Multicuisine eateries often have book-thick menus ranging across almost any imaginable style. On Main Bazaar's north side several places have palace and city views, perhaps most impressively from Master Chef, though few places here are very impressive foodwise.

The best garden and rooftop restaurants along/between Changspa Rd and Fort Rd generally serve more appetising fare. Self-caterers can buy fresh produce from the **vegetable market** (Map p236; Old Fort Rd) or from traditionally dressed street-vendor ladies along Main Bazaar. Fresh-baked *shirmal* (bread rounds; ₹4) are sold hot from traditional wood-fired tandoori bakeries on the road that fronts the Central Asian Museum.

Norlakh
TIBETAN $
(Map p236; Main Bazaar; mains ₹55-100, rice ₹35) The best of several bazaar-area options with mildly trendy decor touches and great pure-veg Tibetan food. Try the cheese-and-spinach *momos* or special *gyathuk* (a rich noodle soup). It's upstairs and easy to miss, hidden behind a willow tree almost opposite Ladakh Bookshop.

Gesmo
MULTICUISINE $
(Map p236; Fort Rd; mains ₹80-150) This age-old traveller haunt has been unchanged so long that its bag-lamps and chequerboard ceilings now seem almost like novel retro design features. Good-value meals range from curries and cakes to yak-cheese pizza.

Old Town Cafe
LADAKHI $
(Map p236; Lonpo House, Palace Area; mains ₹30-90, tea ₹10; ⊙9am-7pm) Hidden in the historic Lonpo House, in the shadow of Leh Palace, this is a rare opportunity to taste genuine Ladakhi fare in an equally genuine 17th-century kitchen room. Mainstays include *skyu*, barley soup and *paba* (pea-and-barley meal) that you dunk in *tangtur* (boiled vegetables in curd). Very slow service.

Dolphin Bakery
MULTICUISINE $
(Map p236; Malpak Alley; mains ₹70-180) Cakes and snack meals served in the open air at a simple triangle of a tree-shaded, stream-side terrace.

★Chopsticks
ASIAN $$
(Map p236; Raku Complex, Fort Rd; mains ₹110-190, rice ₹60; ⊙noon-10pm) This stylish pan-Asian restaurant knocks spots off most of the competition in tems of both style and flavour. Their 'Wonderwok' stir-fries, *momos* and Thai green curry are all excellent and prices are very fair, given the high quality of service. The outdoor terrace is raised above the melee of Fort Rd.

Penguin Garden
MULTICUISINE $$
(Map p236; Chulung Lane; mains ₹80-200, beer ₹140) Sit beneath the apricot trees and listen to the gushing stream at this slightly hidden but constantly popular garden restaurant. If the fresh-cooked tandoori chicken has run out (typical by early evening) there is still a world of cuisines to explore. Manali trout is occasionally available for ₹400 if you dare. Snappy if casual service.

Summer Harvest
MULTICUISINE $$
(Map p236; Fort Rd; mains ₹88-187, Kashmiri meals ₹132-253, rice ₹44) Tourist favourite with pseudo-traditional lacquered-wood columns and dangling mod-Chinese lamps. If you trust the menu's spice-factor notation, their continental breakfast will give you a chilli hit.

Il Forno
RESTAURANT, BAR $$
(Map p236; Zangsti Rd; pizzas ₹170-260) At several rooftop restaurants above Main Bazaar, the town views and (sometimes cold) beer are the main attractions, though here the thin-crust, wood-oven pizzas (₹170 to ₹260) are pretty good too.

Changspa

Calabria
MULTICUISINE $
(Map p232; Changspa Rd; mains ₹60-190, rice ₹40) The decor wins no prizes but the vegetarian Indian and Chinese fare is consistently excellent, sensibly priced and obligingly served. Pastries and real espressos (₹30) are available, electricity willing.

Grill & Curry
MULTICUISINE $
(Map p232; Fort Rd; meals ₹90-180, rice ₹50) An unexpectedly perfect view of the palace and castle are the surprise attraction at this oddly sloping rooftop restaurant. The speciality is tandoori chicken but it also produces some bizarre Ladakhi-Mexican creations and much more besides.

Wonderland Restaurant
MULTICUISINE **$**

(Map p232; Changspa Rd; meals ₹70-190, rice ₹30) The brick-thick menu is a veritable dictionary of cuisines covering virtually all bases. The rooftop offers indoor and outdoor seating, limited views and respite from traffic noise. Prices are reasonable. Real coffee served.

Cross Road
MULTICUISINE **$$**

(Map p232; Changspa Rd; meals ₹100-190) One of the best-value rooftop restaurants. Many of the wide-ranging menu items are fully garnished meals. Covered, uncovered and indoor seating with tables or floor-mat areas create a range of ambiences.

Otsal Restaurant
MULTICUISINE **$**

(Map p232; Changspa Rd; mains ₹40-90, pizza ₹90-130; ⊚) Serenaded by a gurgling stream, this pleasant backpacker retreat includes rooftop seating plus a vibrantly green and scarlet room of lanterns, floor mats and colourful Tibetan tables. Scrumptious choco-banana pie; wi-fi per hour ₹60.

La Pizzeria
MULTICUISINE **$$**

(Map p236; Changspa Rd; mains & pizzas ₹170-330) Candles, lanterns, vermillion walls and a central fire pit create a warmly underlit appeal to complement super-thin-crust pizzas, curries, pastas and some imaginative creations, including a delicious, multi-textured eggplant stack (aubergine, crispy-fried zucchini, olives, mushroom, yak cheese, rocket).

Café Jeevan
MULTICUISINE **$$**

(Map p232; Booklovers Retreat; Changspa Rd; meals ₹110-185, rice ₹55) Despite the comparatively sophisticated appearance, prices aren't significantly higher than most standard traveller hang-outs. A glass-sided kitchen turns out high-quality vegetarian meals in a wide range of cuisines, including some of Leh's best pizza, and the relaxing covered roof terrace catches sunset rays.

★ Bon Appetit
MULTICUISINE **$$$**

(Map p232; ☏ 251533; mains ₹190-380; ⊚11am-late) Hidden down unlikely footpaths, Leh's most imaginative restaurant is a stylish exercise in Ladakhi minimalist architecture and offers a wide panorama of the southern mountains. A limited but thoroughly scrumptious selection of artistically prepared dishes includes sublime cashew chicken in pesto sauce along with succulent tandoori grills. Don't confuse it with the 'Bon Appetit' beside Dolphin Bakery. Cocktails available after 7pm.

Drinking

Bon Appetit pours a mean mojito (₹230). Virtually nowhere else will you find alcoholic drinks on the menu, and during 2012 there was a crackdown on unlicensed beer sales, but it's still worth asking the waiter at garden and rooftop restaurants. For takeaway booze (but not wine), the handy **Indus Wine Shop** (Map p236; Ibex Rd; beer ₹85; ⊚10am-1pm & 3-9pm) opens daily except on the 8th, 15th and last days of the Tibetan calendar.

There is much debate as to who serves Leh's best real coffee. Contenders include Open Hand, Yama, Desert Rain and Lala's, though our vote is – perhaps oddly – Cyber Station, an internet place with a wonderful Brazilian brew.

★ Lala's Art Cafe
CAFE

(Map p236; www.tibetheritagefund.org/pages/projects/ladakh/lala-s-cafe.php; Old Town; ⊚9.30am-7.30pm) This tiny, brilliantly restored mud-brick Old Town house has trip-you-up stone steps and an open roof terrace serving Italian coffee (₹35), scrumptious quiche slices (₹60), cake of the day and, for the more adventurous, DIY Tibetan tea-sets. Check out the ancient carved steles downstairs.

Nirvana Garden
CAFE

(Map p232; Changspa Rd; ⊚noon-late) Slightly hidden away, this open-air chill-out has adobe-style low walls separating cushioned ground spaces, there's an open fire on colder evenings and, after the mountain views have faded into darkness, you might well find musicians jamming informally. Good lassis and a wide range of meals but no alcohol.

Zoya Cafe
CAFE

(Map p236; Old Town; tea ₹10-30, cake ₹50; ⊚10am-7.30pm) Handy as a landmark when climbing to the palace or as a tea-stop when returning. Entry is disconcertingly through a typical local home, but the 360-degree rooftop views are unparalleled anywhere in Leh.

Desert Rain
CAFE

(Map p236; New Shar Market; tea/espresso from ₹10/40; ⊚9.30am-8.30pm Mon-Sat) Colour-splash walls and a choice of floor-carpet, sofa or chair seating offer a relaxed respite from the bazaar's bustle. Coffee is made using a genuine espresso machine and there's a selection of (predominantly Christian) books to read.

Gravit.In
CAFE

(Map p236; Raku Complex, Fort Rd; beverages ₹29-90; ⊙11am-10pm Mon-Sat, 6-10pm Sun) Much of the cafe floor is heavily padded and walls are dotted with holds, as the main attraction here is climbing practice (per hour ₹50). On Sunday afternoons there are climbing excursions to real rocks.

Leh Cafe
CAFE

(Map p236; Old Fort Rd; mains ₹70-180) Leh's best mango lassi (₹60).

Open Hand
CAFE

(Map p236; www.openhand.in; Alpine Lane; ⊙9am-7pm) Gift shop and cafe with rough, minimalist seating in a central yet peaceful vegetable garden. Good smoothies (₹90) and coffee, disappointing food.

Shopping

Leh is a paradise for souvenir shopping. Dozens of colourful little shops, street vendors and **Tibetan Refugee Markets** (Map p236) sell wide selections of *thangkas* (cloth paintings), Ladakhi hats, 'antiques' and heavy turquoise jewellery, as well as Kashmiri shawls and Nepali, Tibetan and Chinese knick-knacks. Several bookshops are well stocked with postcards, novels, spiritual works and books on Ladakh, Kashmir and Tibet.

LEDeG
HANDICRAFTS

(Ladakh Ecological Development Group; Map p236; www.ledeg.org; ⊙9.30am-6pm Mon-Sat) Locally produced crafts and clothes (see www.himalayanhandicrafts.org).

Ladakh Bookshop
BOOKS

(Map p236; Main Bazaar; ⊙10am-10.30pm) Hidden upstairs near the State Bank of India ATM, this very well stocked bookshop publishes locally relevant works and stocks Olizane's indispensible *Ladakh Trekking Maps* (₹1300 per sheet).

Harish
MUSIC

(Map p232; Changspa Rd) Sells local and Western musical instruments.

Women's Alliance
HANDICRAFTS

(Map p236; www.womensallianceladakh.org; ⊙10am-4pm Mon-Sat) Sells postcards, calendars, handicrafts and Ladakhi clothing. Profits assist women's projects.

J&K Government Arts Emporium
HANDICRAFTS

(Map p236; Central Mosque Arcade; ⊙10am-7.30pm) Fixed-price Kashmiri souvenirs including papier-mâché boxes from ₹50, and embroidered cushion covers from ₹170.

Gol Market
MARKET

(Map p236; ⊙9am-5.30pm) A good first place to look for prosaic items of cheap clothing plus bags and limited camping supplies.

Moti Market
MARKET

(Map p232) Bigger than Gol market but less central.

Book Worm
BOOKS

(Map p236; Old Fort Rd) Buys and sells second-hand books.

🛈 Information

Noticeboards all over town have adverts for tours, treks and activities. Indiamike's online forum (www.indiamike.com/india/ladakh-and-zanskar-f31) is very active with Ladakh travellers.

Numerous internet cafes charging ₹90 per hour are found along Changspa Lane, Main Bazaar and Fort Road around Dolphin Bakery. Connection speeds vary randomly and power cuts can prove annoying. Some hotels offer wi-fi but many charge extra and coverage rarely stretches beyond the lobby.

Numerous moneychangers are on Changspa Rd and Main Bazaar. Very few ATMs and none anywhere else in Ladakh until Kargil.

Central post office (Map p236; Main Bazaar; ⊙10am-8pm)

Cyber Station (Map p236; Fort Rd; internet per hr ₹90, coffee ₹40; ⊙9am-11pm) Hidden upstairs opposite HPTDC. Great coffee.

Het Ram Vinay Kumar Pharmacy (Map p236; ☑252160; Main Bazaar; ⊙9.30am-8pm) Dispenses antibiotics and other essential medicines.

J&K Forex (Map p236; 1st fl, Himalaya Complex, Main Bazaar; ⊙10.30am-4pm Mon-Fri, to 1pm Sat) Good exchange rates, better still for travellers cheques. ATM on Ibex Rd.

Men-Tsee-Khang (www.men-tsee-khang.org; museum section ₹5; ⊙8.30am-1pm & 2-5.30pm Mon-Fri, plus 1st & 3rd Sat) Amchi (Tibetan herbal medicine) consultations with no appointment required; 800m south of the bus station.

KLR Oxygen Bar (Map p232; KC Garden Restaurant; per min ₹20; ⊙11am-11pm) Breathe pure oxygen to relieve altitude sickness, or just for the buzz.

Tourist office (Map p236; ☑253462; Ibex Rd; ⊙10am-4pm Mon-Sat) General info, listings and very approximate maps.

Ultimate Adventures (Map p232; Changspa Rd) Fast internet, new computers.

ℹ Getting There & Away

AIR

Flights are dramatically scenic, but can be cancelled at short notice. Although flying into Leh means you're likely to suffer mild altitude problems on arrival, the Delhi–Manali–Leh drive is arguably worse, as you'll cross passes over 5000m. Flying to Leh is the only way to reach Ladakh once roads close in winter.

Air India (Map p232; ✆252076; Fort Rd; ⏱10am-1pm & 2-4.30pm Mon-Sat) Flies Leh–Delhi (₹13,600), via Srinagar (₹4600 to ₹8854, Wednesday) or via Jammu (₹4600 to ₹9553, Monday and Friday). Fly to Jammu for Dharamsala.

Jet Airways (Map p236; ✆255444; Main Bazaar; ⏱10am-1.30pm & 2-4pm) Flies Leh–Delhi twice daily May to August, and five times weekly off season.

GoAir (Map p236; ✆250999; Main Bazaar; ⏱10am-5pm) Flies Leh–Delhi (Saturday, Tuesday and Thursday), with additional summer services via Srinagar and Jammu.

BUSES FROM LEH'S MAIN BUS STATION

DESTINATION	FARE (₹)	DURATION	DEPARTURES
Alchi	80	3hr	8am, 4pm (return 7.30am, 3pm)
Chemrey	35	1½hr	use Shakti buses
Chiling	70	2½hr	9am Wed & Sun (return 1pm)
Chiktan (A)	213	8hr	8am Tue, Fri, Sun (return Wed, Sat, Mon)
Chushul (B)	239		6.30am Wed direct; Sat or Sun via Merak
Dha (A)	189	7hr	9am both directions; not Friday
Diskit/Hunder (B)	151	6hr	6am Sat (return Sun)
Hanle (B)	280		6.30am Sat
Hemis	50	2hr	3.30pm (return 7am)
Hemis Shukpachan (A)	101	4hr	2pm (return 8.30am) via Yangthang
Kargil (B)	460	10h	5am, 2pm
Keylong	475	17hr	4.30am
Khalsi (A)	115	4hr	3pm each way
Lamayuru	150	5hr	use Chiktan or Srinagar buses
Likir Gompa	65	2hr	4pm (return 6.30am)
Matho	25	40min	9am, 2pm, 5pm
Pangong Tso (B)	196	8hr	6.30am Sat, Sun
Phyang	25	40min	7am, 8am, 9am, 3pm, 4pm
Rumtse (A)	94	3hr	4pm, alternate days
Shakti	40	1¾hr	8.15am, 2pm, then half-hourly till 4.30pm (return frequent 7-9am, 12.30pm, 3.30pm)
Shang Sumdo	50	3hr	3pm (return 8am)
Shey	15	25min	use Thiksey or Shakti buses
Spituk	10	15min	1 or 2 hourly till 7pm
Srinagar (B)	920-1300	19hr	2pm
Stakna	30	40min	Thiksey buses terminate nearby
Stok	20	30min	8am, 2pm, 4.30pm (return 9am, 3pm, 5.30pm)
Thiksey	25	30min	half-hourly 8am-6pm, last return 5pm
Tia (A)	85	4½hr	noon
Timishgan (A)	78	4hr	11am (return 8am)
Turtuk (B)	242	10hr	6am Sat (return Sun)
Wanla/Phanjila (A)	135	5hr	8.30am Sun (return Mon)

Fares: (A) LBOC Bus (✆252792), (B) J&K SRTC (✆252085), other minibus (✆253262)

BUS

The **main bus station** (Map p232) is 700m south of the town centre. The shortest walk to get there from town uses a toilet-scented footpath starting opposite Hotel Grand Dragon. Alternatively, cut through the Kigu-Tak stepped bazaar from Friendship Gate.

MOTORCYCLE

Several companies along Music School Rd and Main Bazaar (west) hire Enfield Bullet motorcycles at around ₹900/4500 per day/week before bargaining. Double-check insurance and fittings. Carry spare fuel: Ladakh's only petrol stations are at Leh, Choglamsar, Serthi (Km440.5, near Karu), Diskit, Spituk, Phyang junction, Khaltse, Mulbekh and Kargil. Even those don't always have anything to sell.

SHARED JEEP

Shared through-jeeps to Manali (back/middle ₹1400/1500, 18 to 25 hours) typically depart around midnight, to Kargil (per seat/vehicle ₹600/4500, eight hours) around 7am, and Srinagar (front/back seats ₹1500/1300, 15 hours) around 5pm. Vehicles congregate in the bus station. Go one day ahead to check out cars and drivers, then book your place, directly, via an agency or through the **Ladakh Taxi Operators Cooperative** (Map p232; ☎ 252723; ☺ 7am-7.30pm). The latter is hidden on the 1st floor of the building on the bus station's north side: go upstairs beside a butcher's shop then take the fourth door along the balcony ledge. For Diskit (Nubra) departures are from the *zabakhana* (abattoir), early mornings, usually without booking.

TAXI & CHARTER JEEPS

Published in an annually updated booklet, fares are the same for taxi-vans and Sumo charter jeeps, though jeep prices are around 10% more for higher class vehicles. Rates include reasonable stopping time en route for photos/visits. Longer waits are charged (₹192/900/1800 per hour/half-day/full day); extra overnight stops add ₹350. Unplanned diversions from the agreed route can cause unexpected difficulties so plan carefully. Check whether aircon usage is included – if not you could officially be charged ₹5 per kilometre extra if the driver turns it on.

Indus Valley Monastery villages make interesting day trips. Engage a driver at one of Leh's three main taxi-van stands or add sights as extra stops to longer jeep tours.

Jeep Tours For multiday jeep hire, agencies can put together a fare-sharing group, organising permits, vehicle and driver. Five per jeep is optimal for comfort versus expense. The most popular excursions are Pangong Tso or the Nubra/Shyok Valleys. Book at least 24 hours ahead.

TRAIN

There's no railway. Some agencies, plus a cash-only **train booking room** (☺ 8am-6pm) at Trishul Army Camp near the airport, sell all India train tickets. Check the train number required before going.

❶ Getting Around

TO & FROM AIRPORT

The airport (Km430, Leh–Spituk highway) is 4km south of the centre. Taxi transfers cost ₹150/190 to central Leh/Changspa. Passing public minibuses to town cost only ₹5 but are usually packed.

TAXI

Leh's little micro-van taxis charge from ₹75 per hop. Flagging down rides rarely works; go to a taxi stand to make arrangements. Taxi and charter jeep services from Leh include the following destinations:

DESTINATION	ONE WAY (₹)	RETURN (₹)
Alchi	1609	2092
Basgo	991	1287
Chiling	2138	2768
Hemis	1932	2509
Kargil	5698	7928
Keylong*	14,420	18,876
Lamayuru	3121	4036
Likir	1362	1770
Manali (1 day)*	15,192	
Manali (2 days)*	16,992	
Matho	802	1043
Nimmu	892	1159
Phey	396	515
Phyang	618	803
Shang Sumdo	1422	1885
Shey	338	439
Spituk	246	322
Srinagar*	12317	18,881
Stakna	831	1079
Stok Palace	459	595
Sumur*	4574	5945
Thiksey	535	694
Wanla	3100	4029
Zingchen	892	1159

* using upper class jeep

Note: combining destinations reduces the total price, eg Leh–Stok–Matho–Stakna–Hemis–Leh costs ₹2001.

JAMMU & KASHMIR (INCLUDING LADAKH) LEH

Around Leh – South & East

☏ 01982

To visit Stok and Matho and then return to Leh via Thiksey and Shey, you'll need a vehicle that's small enough to cross the narrow Stakna Bridge. To make a full day trip these destinations could be combined with Hemis and Chemrey. Alternatively visit a selection as part of a trip to Pangong, Tso Moriri or Nubra via Wari La.

Stok

Ladakh's former royal family now keeps a low profile, dividing its time between a private mansion in Manali and the stately **Stok Palace** (admission ₹50; ⊙ 8am-1pm & 2-7pm May-Oct). Vaguely potala-like and with colourful window frames, the three-storey palace is undoubtedly photogenic despite a giant telecommunication tower that looms directly behind. Inside, the handful of rooms that are opened to visitors display family treasures, including the queen's ancient turquoise-and-gold *yub-jhur* (crown) and a sword that the king's oracle managed to bend into a knot, Uri Geller-style. A delightful bonus is the palace's **cafe** (tea ₹15, sandwiches ₹30) with open terrace seating that enjoys spectacular views.

Across from the palace, a short alley leads to the 350-year-old **Stok Abagon** (☏ 9906988325; suggested donation ₹20), the decrepit former home of the royal physician. Calling its unlit old kitchen and storeroom a 'museum' is a serious overstatement, but the fun of a visit is simply getting in and meeting the wizened old lady key-keeper. Bring a torch.

Stok's peaceful main lane winds up past whitewashed farmhouses, crumbling old stupas and, after 1.4km, bypasses the modest **Stok Gompa**, where royal oracles make predictions about the future during Stok's important **Guru Tse-Chu festival** (⊙ Feb/Mar). Another kilometre south, buses from Leh terminate at a pair of simple food shacks known as the trekking point. Ten minutes' walk upstream from here on the path towards Rumbak, the village's last house is the misnamed **Hotel Kangri** (☏ 9797457008; per person incl full-board ₹500), a very authentic homestay with wall murals and a full-blown Ladakhi kitchen.

Along the main road, about 200m north of the trekking point, **Yarsta Guest House** (☏ 9906987272, 9622964623; s/d ₹600/1100) is set in a garden amid poplar trees. Two top-floor rooms with beds and plenty of windows share a clean, tiled bathroom.

Around 2km north of the palace beside the Leh road, isolated **Hotel Skittsal** (☏ 242051, 9622999970; www.skittsal.com; s/d ₹2300/2800) has a neo-traditional facade and giant Buddha seated in the garden. There are lovely valley views but corridors are straight from *The Shining*, decor is sparse and rooms have old sheets and carpets. It's overpriced at rack rates.

Matho

Sakya-Buddhist **Matho Gompa** (☏ 246085; admission ₹50; ⊙ 9am-6pm) is perched on a colourfully stratified ridge above Matho village. Incomparable views from here encompass a vast swathe of the mountain-backed Indus Valley, from emerald-green patchwork fields to areas of sandy desert. The monastery itself is attractive, but most of the early-15th-century structure has been replaced and the top-floor museum is only one room. A *thangka* restoration workshop opens sporadically. During the monastery's famous **Matho Nagrang festival** (Matho; ⊙ Feb-Mar), a pair of monk-oracles performs daring physical challenges while effectively blindfolded by mop-wigs, 'seeing' only through the fearsome 'eyes' painted on their chests. They also engage in ritual acts of self-mutilation and make predictions for the coming year.

The Stok–Matho road needs resurfacing.

Stakna

Small but visually impressive, the 1618 **Stakna Gompa** (admission ₹30; ⊙ 8am-7pm) crowns a rocky outcrop that rises like an apparition out of the Indus Valley floor. Off the gompa's small central courtyard, four rooms with vivid new tantric murals can be visited. Behind the main prayer hall, sub-shrines retain 400-year-old sandalwood statues, original frescoes and statuettes of the Bhutanese lamas who founded the monastery. From the Leh–Thiksey bus terminus (Km449), the complex is 1.7km away (less on foot), crossing the Indus on a narrow suspension bridge decked with prayer flags then climbing a winding access road.

Shey

Once one of Ladakh's royal capitals, Shey is an attractive, pond-dappled oasis from which rises a central dry rocky ridge, inscribed with roadside **Buddha carvings** (Km459). Along the rising ridge-top, a series of **fortress ruins** bracket the three-storey, 17th-century **Naropa Royal Palace** whose wholesale reconstruction is nearing completion. The palace **temple** (admission ₹20; ⊙ 8am-6pm) contains a highly revered 7.5m-tall gilded-copper Buddha, originally installed in 1645. The upper door opens to his inscrutably smirking face.

For the most photogenic views of Shey's palace ridge, walk part way along the access track to the delightful **Besthang Guest House** (☑ 267556; r without bathroom ₹300), one of Ladakh's best value homestays.

Experienced teachers are in demand for volunteer work at the local, architecturally innovative, ecofriendly **Druk White Lotus School** (www.dwls.org).

Thiksey

Glorious **Thiksey Gompa** (☑ 267011; www.thiksey-monastery.org; admission ₹30, video ₹100; ⊙ 6am-1pm & 1.30-6pm, festival Oct/Nov) is one of Ladakh's biggest and most recognisable monasteries. Covering a large rocky outcrop with layered Tibetan-style buildings, it's a veritable monastic village incorporating shops, a school, restaurant and hotel. The main gompa starts with a prayer chamber containing a 14m high Buddha whose expression is simultaneously peaceful, smirking and vaguely menacing. Smaller but much more obviously ancient is the **Gonkhang** (Protectors' Temple) and little rooftop library. A **museum** hidden away beneath the monastery restaurant displays well-labelled tantric artefacts, including a wine vessel made from a human skull. Notice the 10 weapons symbolically used to combat evil spirits.

Over 40 monks gather for morning chanted prayers, lasting around two hours from 6am. It's a fascinating ceremony and visitors are welcome, but it's so popular that tourists often outnumber worshippers.

Pedestrian access is a steep climb from near Km455. By car it's a 1.5km loop starting from Km454.2 where monastery-run **Chamba Hotel** (☑ 267385; d ₹600 & 1500) has a restaurant with Ladakhi-style decor that makes a popular breakfast stop. The best rooms are unexpectedly plush, with geyser-heated water. Simple courtyard rooms have en-suite squat toilets.

The monastery itself also has some **guest rooms** (☑ 9622952486; tw without bathroom ₹500-600) beneath the gompa museum.

Hemis

The 1672 **Hemis gompa** (www.drukpa-hemis.org; admission ₹100; ⊙ 8am-1pm & 2-6pm) is the spiritual centre of Ladakh's Drukpa Buddhists. Documents supposedly found here were used to support Jesus-in-India conspiracists' notion that Christ visited Kashmir.

The complex is hidden in a high sharp valley behind curtains of craggy red rocks that look especially dramatic when the mountains behind are misty with low cloud. The main monastery's rectilinear exterior lacks the vertically stacked perfection of Chemrey or Thiksey, but inside the fine central courtyard has plenty of colourfully detailed timbers, the main prayer hall has wobbly four-storey pillars, and the garish 8m-high statue of Padmasambhava has hypnotic boggle eyes. The monastery's extensive **museum** has some very precious religious treasures mixed in with spurious tiger skins, skull vessels, swords, a bra-shaped wooden cup case and a stuffed 'vulture pup'. Escape the tourist hordes by arriving early and exploring the atmospheric upper, rear shrines and hiking the lovely stream path beyond the big new school construction site for peace and great mountain views.

The annual **Tse-Chu festival** (⊙ Jul) sees three days of masked dances, and every 12th year (next in 2016) the festival culminates in the unfurling of Hemis' famous three-storey-high, pearl-encrusted *thangka*.

The winding 7km road from Karu passes a pair of astonishingly long *mani* walls.

Chemrey & Takthog

Spectacularly viewed across barley fields and buckthorn bushes, Chemrey village is dominated by the beautifully proportioned **Thekchhok Gompa** (⊙ 8am-5pm, festival Nov) covering a steep hillock with a maze of pathways and Tibetan buildings. Above the appealingly wobbly 17th-century prayer hall, the Lama Lhakhang has murals blackened to semi-invisibility by butter-lamp smoke. On the penultimate floor the Guru Lhakhang has contrastingly vivid colours and a 3m-high golden Padmasambhava statue encrusted with turquoise ornamentation.

LEH–MANALI

Utterly beautiful but exhaustingly spine-jangling, this is a ride you won't forget. And many prefer to fly one way (to/from Delhi) rather than doing it twice. The Upshi–Keylong section crosses four passes over 4900m, and then there's the infamously unpredictable Rohtang Pass before Manali. Although the road is 'normally' open from June to late September, unseasonable snow or major landslides can close it for days (or weeks). BCM (www.bcmtouring.com) and LAHDC (http://leh.nic.in) report the road's current status. When the road is open, there are several choices.

Transport Options

Bus The cheapest options are J&K SRTC buses (ordinary/deluxe ₹585/850, two days) or HRTC buses that run to Keylong (₹513, 12 hours) both departing Leh's main bus station around 4.30am. Marginally more comfortable HPTDC buses (without/with accommodation ₹1500/2000, two days) leave every second day at 5am from outside J&K Bank (Ibex Rd). They must be booked at **HPTDC** (Map p236; ☑ 9622374300; Fort Rd; ⏲ 10am-1.30pm & 2.30-7pm), upstairs opposite Iceland Travel. The included accommodation is in rather cold tents at Keylong.

Shared jeeps and agency minibuses They claim to take around 17 hours, but 22 to 26 hours is more typical. To get more space and improved photo ops, consider hiring your own jeep with one or more overnight stops. The agency tariff is over ₹15,000, but rates offered informally by drivers at the bus station for one-/two-/three-day hires to Manali were around ₹8500/9000/10,500 by Qualis jeep, and ₹10,000/12,000/13,000 in a smart new Inova.

Driving If driving yourself, beware of vehicle permit rules for the Rohtang La pass (see p340). There's no petrol station for 365km between Karu and Tandi (8km south of Keylong).

Route Highlights

The Manali road heads south at **Upshi** (Km425) via **Miru** (Km410), a pretty village with a shattered fortress and numerous stupas. Beyond is a beautiful, narrow valley edged with serrated vertical mineral strata in alternating layers of vivid red purple and ferrous green. A millennium ago, **Gya** (Km398) was the capital of King Gyapacho's upper Ladakhi monarchy before he joined forces with Tibetan Prince Skiddeyimagon (who shifted the power

The monastery access lane starts from near Km8 on the Karu–Pangong road. At Km10.4, a paved side lane passes through Shakti, a spread-out village of gently terraced fields, waterlogged meadows and dry-stone walls. The lane skirts Shakti's shattered stone **fortress ruins** (also visible from the main Pangong road above) and after nearly 5km, passes beside **Takthog (Dakthok) Gompa** (donation appropriate; ⏲ festival Jul), the region's only Nyingmapa monastery. The name Takthog ('stone roof') refers to a pair of small but highly revered cave-shrines in which the great sage Padmasambhava supposedly meditated during the 8th century. These smoke-blackened prayer chambers now form part of the monastery's attractive older section, directly opposite the tin-roofed **Tourist Bungalow** (s/d ₹300/500) where four simple rooms have en-suite squat toilets and share a kitchen.

Around Leh – Trekking Villages

Zingchen

For treks, the pretty two-house oasis of Zingchen (Zinchan, Jingchian) makes a much better starting point than Spituk village, as the first 10km of the Spituk–Zingchen road is a sun-blistered masochistic slog. A Leh–Zingchen taxi ride (₹1300) should allow stops at Spituk Gompa and at photogenic spots in the monumentally stark canyonlands that start 6km before Zingchen.

Zingchen has a homestay, campsite and parachute cafe. There's no bus but, with a little patience, hitching a (paid) ride back to Leh is often possible with vehicles that arrive to drop off trekkers.

centre to Shey). Today it's a small, picturesque village across the river from which a steep 15-minute hike leads up to the 1000-year-old castle ruin now partly occupied by a loveable little gompa. **Rumtse** (Km394), with its handful of homestays and camping spots, is the last green oasis and there are no further villages for 250km, just tiny seasonal camp-settlements. Numerous hairpins climb to **Taglang La** (Km364), which at 5328m is claimed to be the world's second-highest road pass (after Khardung La). Further south the wide Moray Plains are edged with smooth peaks. At Km287, 10km beyond Pang, the road rises through a memorable, spiky-edged canyon before crossing **Lachung La** (5035m) and **Nakeela La** (4915m), descending the 21 switchbacks of the **Gata Loops** and trundling through two very photogenic valleys featuring Cappadocia-style erosion formations.

Southbound Advantages

If doing the trip southbound you'll be better acclimatised for high-altitude sleeps (Pang or Sarchu); you could visit Tso Moriri en route; and, if there's a major landslide on the Rohtang Pass, you could 'escape' by walking two hours down to Mahri, a group of cafes jammed with day-trip tourist traffic from Manali.

Which Overnight Stop(s)?

Overnighting in **Sarchu** handily breaks the journey into two roughly equal sections, but the altitude (around 4000m) can cause problems. Note that there are essentially two Sarchus. Km222 has a set of cheap parachute tent-cafes and a liquor store. Isolated on an attractive plateau at Km216-214 are half a dozen much more upmarket luxury tent camps used by tour groups and some private minibus operators.

Keylong, **Jispa** (Km138-139, three hotels) and **Gemur** (Km134) offer more comfortable accommodation at significantly lower altitudes, but Leh–Keylong is a very long day's ride (around 14/17 hours by jeep/bus).

To make a three-day ride you might add **Pang** (4634m) to a Keylong stop. However Pang's parachute cafes (bed space ₹200) are very basic and the unacclimatised might need Pang army camp's free oxygen if altitude sickness hits.

Other parachute cafes are available at Km343, Km270, **Bharatpur** (Km197), **Zingzingbar** (Km174), Km159.5 and **Darcha Bridge** (Km143).

Rumbak & Yurutse

Roadless Rumbak (4050m) is a magical village with a high proportion of closely packed traditional homes, almost all of which offer homestay beds. It's around a three-hour riverside hike from Zingchen. The route is mostly easy to follow given a decent map: where in doubt, follow donkey droppings and cross any bridge you see. At a lone summer parachute cafe take the left valley (half an hour) to Rumbak, or continue for one hour to Yurutse (4200m), an eerie one-house hamlet/homestay flanked by little stupas. Yurutse has a dribbling, drinkable spring and enjoys a perfectly framed view of Stok Kangri (6121m) through a cleft valley opposite.

Next day from Yurutse, you could trek across the 4920m Ganda La in around six hours to Shingo village (two farms, both homestays), possibly continuing three hours further to Kaya/Skiu in the Markha Valley. Alternatively from Rumbak, a similarly strenuous trek crosses the equally high Stok La (Namling La) pass and reaches Stok in around seven hours (turn left and descend at the second mini-pass). If there's cloud on either pass definitely do not hike without a guide.

Markha Valley

Very well trodden tracks between diffuse roadless villages make this Ladakh's most popular trekking area. There are fort ruins at Markha and Hankar and several seasonal parachute cafes. Homestays (₹500 per person including food) exist in virtually every settlement and if you're hiking across the Kongmaru La (5050m) towards Shang Sumdo without camping gear, there are tent-spaces at Nimaling (₹700). From Nimaling allow nine hours of walking to Shang Sumdo via Chokdo (seven hours). Both places

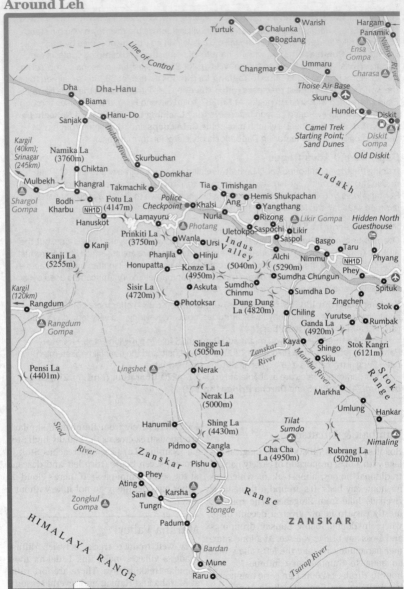

have homestays and there's an 8am bus to Leh from Shang Sumdo. Allow at least five days for the Chiling–Nimaling–Shang Sumdo loop, including transport to/from Leh. Or simply explore the valley out-and-back from Chiling.

Nubra Valley

☏ 01980

The deep valleys of the Shyok and Nubra Rivers offer tremendous yet accessible scenery (permit required) with green oa-

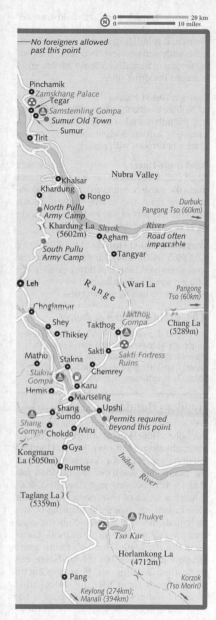

Ensa Gompa; ₹9466 to ₹10,326 with Turtuk. While it's possible to do all that in two days, lengthy view stops are the main attraction so taking a third day is recommended.

Almost all visitors go out and back via Khardung but there are two possible alternatives. The narrow road across the very remote **Wari La** is now mostly asphalted and allows a loop returning via pretty **Tangyar** to Takthog. Until late August, some fords can prove tough to cross so drivers are often reluctant to come this way. A second possibility is the road linking Khalsar to Durbuk and thus to Pangong Tso. While we know of at least one cyclist who succeeded in taking that route, there is some doubt as to its legality for foreigners and it has been impassably washed out on several occasions.

Khardung La

ELEV 5602M

Zigzagging up a stark bare-rock mountain from Leh, it takes around 1½ hours to reach 5602m **Khardung La** (Km39), disputably claimed to be the world's highest motorable pass. Celebrate by sipping a cuppa at the pass-top canteen, buy T-shirts at the souvenir shop or, if your altitude acclimatisation allows, get dizzy clambering five minutes to a viewpoint through a chaos of prayer flags and boulders. Beyond Khardung La, the road descends northbound past the **Tsolding Buddha Park** (Km50.5), a misnomer for a high-altitude pond around which you'll often find Himalayan marmots and grazing dzo (cow-yak half-breed). Permits are checked at South and North Pallu Army Camps (Km24 and Km53).

Khardung

The yak-herding village of Khardung (Km71) is a diffuse shelf of barley fields and scattered Ladakhi buildings set within a jaw-dropping bowl of arid crags, giant tiger-paw bluffs and the distantly glimpsed teeth of snow-covered mountains. Catering to numerous jeep-tour transit folks, several tiny roadside shop-cafes dish up delicious dhal while the **Maitreya Midway Garden Restaurant** (curries ₹70-120, rice/buffet ₹30/200; ⊙11am-3pm) offers a far wider range of dishes and a pretty meadow setting. **Cho Guest House** (☏9469628669; per person incl half-board ₹400; ⊙May-Sep) offers mattresses on the floor of a large room with en-suite squat toilet. Guests dine in the traditional kitchen.

sis villages surrounded by thrillingly stark scree slopes, boulder fields and harsh arid mountains. Visiting from Leh by chartered jeep, including Panamik, Diskit, Hunder and everything in between, costs ₹7624 to ₹8317 per vehicle; ₹8064 to ₹8797 if you add

NUBRA NAMES

Note that on many maps, the names for several western Nubra settlements don't correspond at all with local reality.

On maps	Local usage
Thoise village	Terchey
Khar	Skuru
Yaglung	Changmar
Biadango	Bogdang

Beyond Khardung, the road descends through Grand Canyon scenery towards the impressively wide Shyok Valley, where soaring red-brown cliff-mountains rise from the gleaming grey-white sand of the floodplain.

Diskit

ELEV 3144M

Schizophrenic Diskit has two very different centres. Nubra's biggest settlement, Central Diskit, is a comparatively unattractive place by Ladakh's very high standards, but it has the area's bus/taxi stand, internet cafes, a useful bazaar, a tourist reception centre and the region's only petrol pump (1km north towards Hunder). Following the bazaar east then swinging right past the Spangla Guesthouse and Hotel Stendel you'll find an altogether softer Diskit that leads 1.5km to an area of stupas, a big *mani* wall, and a crumbling old Ladakhi Mansion before rejoining the main road just beyond Sunrise Guest House. Above this 'Old Diskit' a 2km spaghetti of hairpins winds up to the 17th-century **Diskit Gompa** (admission ₹30; ⊙7am-1pm & 2-7pm), a brilliant jumble of Tibetan-style box buildings piled higgledy-piggledy up a steep rocky peak that ends in a toe-curlingly vertical chasm. On the lap of the guardian deity statue, the human scalp is supposedly that of a Mongol warrior who mysteriously dropped dead when attempting to sieze the monastery. The entry fee includes access to a gigantic (32m) full-colour **Statue of Chamba** (Maitreya-Buddha) on an intermediate hill, formally inaugurated by the Dalai Lama in July 2010.

🛏 Sleeping & Eating

There are six hotels and eight guesthouses.

Sunrise Guest House   GUESTHOUSE $
(☑220011; r ₹500, without bathroom s/d/tr ₹200/250/300; ⊙year-round) Reached through a 'tunnel stupa', this old traveller stalwart has cheap if slightly dusty older rooms and is building six new en-suite ones, some with gompa-view balconies. Interesting setting in a small sunflower garden amid scattered Buddhist ruins.

Spangla Guest House   GUESTHOUSE $
(☑220058; d without bathroom ₹300-350) Central, friendly female-run guesthouse with a small tidy garden. Simple older-style rooms share a bathroom with geyser.

Sand Dune Hotel   GUESTHOUSE $
(☑220022; r ₹600-1100) Shaded by apricot trees, the garden courtyard makes a pleasant oasis from the nearby bazaar. Rooms vary considerably in size and style but all are well kept and the family is friendly.

Lhasthang Guest House   HOTEL $
(☑220165, 9469176104) Directly beneath the gompa turn-off, this sparkling-clean place with geysers and Buddha roof-views is being rebuilt and is due to reopen soon.

ℹ Getting There & Away

Leh-bound shared jeeps (₹350, 4½ hours) leave frequently between 6am and 9am. From Leh, these start near the *zabakhana*. Buses to Diskit depart from virtually every main Nubra village before 7am, returning from Diskit after lunch.

Hunder (Hundur)

Lost in greenery and closely backed by soaring valley cliffs, Hunder village is a popular overnight stop 10km from Diskit. Hunder's big draw, especially for domestic visitors, is the chance for **Bactrian camel rides** (per 15min/hr ₹150/500, one way to Diskit ₹600-800) through a series of photogenic sand dunes. Host camels are reputedly offspring of animals that plied the Ladakh–Xinjiang caravans up until the closure of the India–China border in the 1940s. Hunder's dunes aren't exactly Sahara-sized but the landscape can prove disorientating so, if attempting to walk through them back to Diskit, bring plenty of water, stick relatively near to the road and beware following dead-end camel tracks into impenetrable thorn thickets.

The camel mounting point is around 600m southeast of the army camp. That's nearly 3km from old Hunder where a precarious little ridgetop **fort ruin** rises above the main road near the expanding little **gompa**.

🛏 Sleeping & Eating

Hunder has nearly 20 garden guesthouses, mostly clumped into two loose groupings around 1.4km apart, with Himalayan and Snow Leopard lying in between. The first, lower group (Karma Inn, Olgok, Ldumra Oasis) is around 1km north of the army camp. The second forms Hunder's vague 'centre' where the village lane turns a right angle beside Jamshed Guesthouse. About 200m further there's a small grocery shop on the paved side lane that runs to the Ibex and Goba guesthouses. Ibex, Olgok and Ldumra Oasis are pleasant if unremarkable new bungalow guesthouses each offering a handful of en-suite rooms at ₹600. At least seven overpriced 'luxury' camps charge ₹3000 to ₹4000 full-board for bedded tents.

Arrange meals with your accommodation or eat at the **Himalayan Guest House** (thali ₹150-300, curries ₹70-150, rice ₹40), which also attempts pasta and sandwiches.

Goba Guest House
GUESTHOUSE $

(☑ 221083; d ₹800, without bathroom ₹300-600) Choose upper options especially rooms 8 (₹800) and 9 (₹600), rose-fronted with wraparound windows and a shared view terrace. Around the attractive garden some rooms are cheap and dark, others bright and brand new. Obliging staff, soothing setting.

Himalayan Guest House
GUESTHOUSE $

(☑ 221131; d/tr ₹550/600, without bathroom ₹250/300) Tucked into a warren of village footpaths, rooms have geysers, there's a garden sitting area and a bamboo kitchen shack (mains ₹70-150, thalis ₹150-300, rice ₹40) that turns out a comparatively wide range of meals – open to nonguest diners.

Snow Leopard Guest House
GUESTHOUSE $

(☑ 221097, 9469176759; r old-block/new-block/ with TV ₹800/1000/1200) The extensive central garden is one of the most colourful festivals of flowers you'll see. Rooms come with geyser bathrooms, most have new box-spring beds and the cheapest old-block versions have a little more character than the rest.

Karma Inn Hotel
HOTEL $$

(☑ 200123, 9419612342; www.hotelkarmainn.com; s/d/tr ₹2430/3200/4265; ⊙ May-Sep) Hunder's expanded 'real' hotel has 21 comparatively smart rooms with big bathrooms and good firm beds. Each has either balcony or bay-window seating overlooking a panorama of mountains across the hotel lawns.

Turtuk

It's easy to run out of superlatives as you drive along the turbulent Shyok Valley towards Turtuk, 80km beyond Hunder. Scenically magnificent the whole way apart from a few military installations, the grand raw-rock valley briefly narrows near tiny Changmar after which the few green splashes of village change culturally and linguistically from Buddhist–Ladakhi to Muslim–Balti. Visitors can expect considerable attention at Bogdang whose main village ledge is up a steep stairway from its western edge – leading to stone terracing, a touchingly naive-painted mosque and a small waterfall with miniature water mill. Here and in Turtuk, summer sees locals busy carting huge bundles of barley on their backs when Turtuk's two-layer fields are partly shaded by apricot trees. The upper half has unforgettable views across the patchwork of wheat and barley fields towards the serrated high peaks of Pakistan, whose front line is only 7km away. Indeed Turtuk itself was in Pakistan until the 1971 war. Though culturally Muslim, the village has a couple of small, historic gompas to seek out and an old 'royal' house.

🛏 Sleeping & Eating

To find the best of Turtuk's nine guesthouses/homestays, and indeed to explore any of the roadless upper village, drive through the lower village signing in at the checkpoint, then continue past two bedded tent camps and Ashoor Shop/Guesthouse before crossing the river and turning immediately left. Park beside the beautifully located if utterly unsophisticated **Selmo Restaurant** (instant noodles ₹20; ⊙ 7am-7pm), cross the suspension footbridge across a cascading mountain brook and walk west. Alternatively, follow steep paths and stairways from signs on the lower road.

Kharmang Guest House
GUESTHOUSE $

(☑ 248104; s/d without bathroom ₹600/700) New in July 2012, Turtuk's most appealing option has five neat rooms sharing two good bathrooms, a convivial communal sitting area and an unadorned rooftop whose 360-degree panoramic view is among the best you'll find.

Rangyul Guest House
GUESTHOUSE $

(☑ 248206, 248016; d/tr without bathroom ₹500/700) Hospitable, informative and speaking great English, Hossein Beig has so far finished four of a planned 12 rooms, ranged around a central two-table dining room where you can sample typical Balti dishes (mains ₹60 to ₹80). Tree shaded (so somewhat dark), the unmarked house is in the central knot of tunnel-passage alleys close to the village swimming pond.

Maha Guest House
GUESTHOUSE $

(☏ 248040; mahaturtuk@gmail.com; d without/with bathroom ₹600/1200, half-board ₹1300/2800) Turtuk's original guesthouse is the only one to have en-suite bathrooms.

Kashmiri Homestay
HOMESTAY $

(☏ 248117; dm incl half-board ₹300) Basic but cheap and authentic, this ramshackle concrete bungalow has six thin mat-on-floor bed spaces plus three beds in a tent outside. It's half swallowed by hollyhocks and overgrown vegetables in the middle of the upper fields. Notes in Hebrew and English plead with guests to respect local Muslim behavioural codes. Outside squat toilet.

❶ Getting There & Away

Buses leave Turtuk at 6am for Diskit (₹90, 3½ hours) on a surprisingly well-paved road, returning to Diskit at 2.30pm. On Sunday the bus continues to Leh. Bring at least four permit photocopies heading westbound. Diskit–Turtuk by charter jeep costs ₹2735/3556 one way/return.

Sumur, Tegar & Panamik

The Nubra River proper descends towards the Shyok from the heavily disputed Siachen Glacier, the world's highest battleground (between India and Pakistan) following what is reputedly one of Ladakh's most spectacular mountain valleys. However, standard Nubra permits currently prevent foreigners seeing this, stopping any venture beyond Hargam Bridge. That's just after diffuse Panamik (Km44) with its pitifully underwhelming hot spring. If you're stuck with very rare, overloaded public transport it isn't really worth coming this way. But by jeep, fine scenery justifies driving at least as far as Tegar (Tiger) village where the three-storey shell of **Zamskhang Palace** (unguarded) sits above the eerie rubble of Nubra's former royal citadel (Km25). Hidden within Tegar village **Zimskang Museum** (donation ₹50) is an unmarked historic house found by descending a path alongside chortens and *mani* wall from the ancient little Manekhang Gompa/

Angchunk Restaurant to the last unmarked wooden door on left. Some 1.5km above the palace, where Tegar and Sumur back lanes merge, there are lovely panoramas from the parking area at colourful, extensively rebuilt **Samstemling Gompa** (donation appropriate; ⊙ 6am-6pm).

🛏 Sleeping & Eating

Panamik has six budget guesthouses/homestays. Tegar has two midrange hotels while neighbouring Sumur has five guesthouses and six 'luxury' tent camps. Most guesthouses arrange simple meals (₹90 to ₹150) and allow camping (₹100) in their gardens. The only other dining option is a pair of uninspired cafes at Sumur junction.

Namgyal Guesthouse
GUESTHOUSE $

(☏ 223505, 9419887505; Sumur Link Rd Km0.9, Sumur; d ₹1000, without bathroom ₹300-400; ⊙ year-round) This attractive two-storey building has large rooms with clean tiled bathrooms but hard beds. The best have tree-tickled mountain views across the well-tended rose garden. Friendly family owners, garden seating.

K,Sar Guesthouse
GUESTHOUSE $

(☏ 9469291358; Sumur Link Rd Km0.6, Sumur; d ₹500, d/q without bathroom ₹300/400) Four fair-priced rooms in a bungalow with traditional windows and a delightfully overgrown garden field from which to contemplate the snow-capped peaks.

Choron Pa Homestay
$

(☏ 247011; Main Rd Km43.8, Panami; d ₹500, without bathroom ₹400) Simple but large loveable rooms, great rooftop views and hot-spring showers piped from the source.

Yarab Tso
HOTEL $$

(☏ 200167, 9419342231; www.hotelyarabtso.com; Main Rd Km24.5, Tegar; d ₹2500, full board ₹3700) This impressive traditional-style building with a wonderful Ladakhi-style sitting room is set in farm-size grounds. Standards among the 13 en-suite guest rooms vary significantly. The hotel might close when there are no bookings.

☆ Entertainment

A culture show (₹150 per person, minimum four) with six or seven dancer-singers can be arranged in Tegar by calling ☏ 9469613265 (no English) a day or two ahead.

Pangong Tso

Permits are required to visit Pangong Tso. Stretching around 150km (with the eastern third in China) this mesmerising lake's palette of vivid blues can't fail to impress, contrasting surreally with the colourful mineral swirls of starkly arid, snow-brushed mountains that surround it. Apart from three tiny villages and Lukung's gaggle of tent restaurants, the scene is striking for its utter lack of habitation along shores that look almost Carribbean at the sand spit 'Shooting Point' film set for 2009 Bollywood hit *The Three Idiots*. There's little to do at the lakeside except soak up the atmosphere, but the jeep safari from Leh is a joy in itself – scenically magnificent and constantly varied with serrated peaks, trickling streams, horse meadows, reflective ponds, drifting sands and a 5289m pass. However, it's tiring, and doing the return in one day is masochism. It's vastly more pleasurable to stay at least one night in Spangmik or Man, 10km beyond. Driving another 10km on unpaved lakeside trails to end-of-the-world Merak is fascinating and even more beautiful, but crossing some of the fords can be rather nail-biting in late afternoon when water levels rise.

🛏 Sleeping & Eating

The situation is evolving incredibly fast, but for now the area has no phone or internet connection so bookings aren't possible except by joining fixed agency tours. It's usually fine to just arrive and pick a place you fancy. Few guests stay more than one night so there's almost always a vacancy if you arrive by early afternoon, but don't leave it too late.

🛏 Spangmik

In pretty Spangmik, each of the dozen houses is a basic homestay charging around ₹200 per person for crammed bed spaces. Our favourite remains the homely, hospitable Gongma at the top of the village, though Nomadic Homestay is handier for the lakeshore. Nearly 20 summer **tent camps** (d incl full board ₹3000-4000) mar many formerly picturesque, dry-stone-walled meadows. Nine fancy new pine family-sized cottages with wide lake views are under construction 2km west of Spangmik.

🛏 Man

So far Man has two tent camps and five basic homestays, including the photogenic but exceedingly basic **Parkha** (dm ₹150-300) near the waterside along the Merak track. Man's **Pangong Sarai Tent Camp** (incl full board ₹3000) forms a barleyfield arc with swooning lake views, though the bathrooms could be neater.

🛏 Merak

At least three houses including the small Amchi clinic offer homestays, but the place can feel spookily deserted.

ℹ Getting There & Away

One-/two-day jeep tours from Leh cost ₹6811/8108 (per comfortable vehicle) to Spangmik, or ₹7867/9636 to Merak. Permits cost extra. If you ask when booking it'll cost little more to add side trips to Chemrey and Thaktog. And do request a stop at the colourful rock-cleft gompa 2km beyond Tangtse, a town where you'll probably stop for lunch anyway while buying the ₹10 Pangong 'ticket'. We suggest making these stops on the way back so that outbound you get a wider choice of accommodation.

Foreigners may not continue to Chushul or fabled Hanle.

Tso Moriri Loop

ELEV 4595M

Permits are required to visit this area. Tso Moriri and Tso Khar are giant high-altitude lakes whose biggest touristic advantage is that they can be combined into a two- or three-day jeep-tour loop. However, though very attractive, the scenery doesn't quite have the splendour of the shorter, cheaper Pangong excursion. The most interesting time to visit tatty little **Korzok** (Tso Moriri's only settlement) is during the 10-day period when Chang Pa nomads move their camps close to the main road and dress traditionally to welcome the annual arrival of the local Rinpoche (Buddhist priest). Consider bringing your own sleeping bag when staying at one of Korzok's seven very simple homestays/guesthouses. Relatively good choices are **Mentok Guest House** (d ₹300-500) and **Crane Homestay** (d ₹300-500), both with shared sit-down toilets and views from the better rooms. The best value of three 'luxury' tent camps on the streamside meadow beneath the Korzok gompa is **Yak Camp** (☎9469457025; yakcamp ladakh@gmail.com; tent ₹1000-2600) where some tents have inside bathroom facilities. Yak's owner, Tsering, is currently building a modest hotel. Tent camps offer meal plans but it's usually vastly cheaper to eat meals (around ₹70) at one of the three central house-restaurants.

Ornithologists seeking rare black-necked cranes have a chance of spotting some around Tso Kar lake. Three mating pairs customarily breed within binocular range of the lonely little **Tsokar Resort** (☎9906262242, 9469450295; tsokarresort@yahoo.in; s/d/tent 1800/2200/2100) whose four decent en-suite guesthouse rooms have sit-down toilets. The simple restaurant has birdwatching books. It's 500m outside Thukye (summer/winter population 250/6) which is less village than gompa-topped labyrinth of stone-walled sheep pens, used as a winter retreat for Chang Pa nomads. Thukye is 17km down a bouncy new asphalted lane from the Manali–Leh highway at Km340.

❶ Getting There & Away

Korzok buses (₹240) leave Leh at 6.30am on the 10th, 20th and 30th of each month, returning next morning. No buses to Thukye.

A two-day jeep charter looping Leh–Korzok–Thukye and returning to Leh across Taglang La costs ₹11,243. A three-day, one-way excursion continuing south to Keylong/Manali (₹21,438/25,157) after Thukye is only possible southbound since necessary permits must be issued in Leh. Attractive villages between Upshi and Mahe Bridge include Likche (Km69), Himya and much bigger Chumathang whose gompa (with panoramic views) requires a 2km detour.

Leh to Kargil

Nimmu to Chiling

For a feast of stark, colourful geology, turn off the Leh–Nimmu road at Km400 then take the riverside ledge road up the deep Zanskar River canyon. The remarkable scenery is mostly the preserve of rafting groups or trekkers shuttling to/from the Markha Valley but it's worth considering adding the 30km each-way detour to Chiling to a Leh–Basgo–Alchi taxi trip or en route by private vehicle to Lamayuru.

At Km19, the tiny hamlet of **Sumdha Do** offers a tea stop, just behind which is the loveable **Tashi Khangsar** (per person ₹500)

homestay – handy for those trekking in from Wanla or Hinju.

At first glance tiny Chiling also seems limited to a teahouse plus the boxy shop-cafe Kongma Restaurant (Km28.6; magi ₹30) where departing trekkers should pay the Hemis National Park fee (₹20 per day). But the village proper is a fascinating place, set on a fertile green plateau, more easily accessed from a low-profile path starting at Km27.9. Seven families here offer homestays. Chiling village was founded by the families of Nepali copper artisens. They originally arrived in Ladakh to build Shey Palace's classic Buddha statue and never went home. The handicraft continues, though today typical products are roughly turned-out heart-shaped spoons (around ₹200). The best-known smiths include Ishay Namgyal at Yokmapa Homestay and Ringchen Paldan behind Chikpa Homestay. Both have photogenically antiquated little forges in the most timeless area of old mud-brick buildings and giant trees, backed by serrated dry peaks.

If trekking into the Markha Valley, continue 4km further south. Just before the river confluence you'll probably need help from the nearby teahouse staff to cross the Zanskar River on a dangling-basket ropeway contraption.

Basgo

Rising above the village on a surreal collection of eroded earthen pinnacles are remnant stubs of once-great citadel walls, along with a largely derelict mud-walled **palace**, dating from when Basgo was a capital of lower Ladakh. It's worth coming just for the surreal views, but you can also visit the site's two highest buildings – two splendid one-room **temples** (per temple ₹30), each containing a two-storey seated Maitreya statue.

Likir

Surveying a grand section of mountain ridge, Likir has two distinct sections. **Likir Gompa** (☉8am-1pm & 2-6pm) very photogenically covers a hillside with archetypal Ladakhi buildings, around 5km off the Leh–Kargil road. Though founded in 1065, the monastery's current incarnation originated in the 15th century. The first prayer hall to the right on entry has seats allocated for both the Dalai Lama and his brother, Likir's honorary head lama. After two more colourful prayer halls you climb to the crammed, one-room museum (admission ₹20). The gompa is backed by a giant 20th-century Maitreya statue whose golden paint gleams dazzlingly in the sunshine.

For great photos of the gompa complex framed between barley fields and old chortens, descend for 10 minutes on the rocky footpath signed to the Old Likir Guesthouse.

Directly above the gompa are two homestay-guesthouses in traditional homesteads, each including breakfast and dinner in a wonderfully authentic Ladakhi dining room. **Chhuma Guest House** (✔9622983265; per person ₹300) has the better views and the squat toilet is inside. The **Monastery School** (www.likirmonasteryschool.org; r by donation) opposite the gompa entrance has four decent new guest rooms and operates a simple open-air restaurant (open from 6.30am to 9pm)

There are seven more accommodation choices 4km south in Likir village. By far the fanciest is **Hotel Lhukhil** (✔227137; www.hotellhukhil.com; d rack-rate/walk-in ₹2800/1200) designed vaguely like a Chinese temple, with dragons and painted wall motifs as well as en-suite bathrooms and mountain views from most rooms. There's oodles of outdoor sitting space, though some rooms smell a little drainlike. Almost opposite on the same hidden lane, **Lotos Guest House** (✔9419579194; per person incl meals ₹350) is the newest and neatest Likir homestay, but the toilet is in the yard. **Smalan Guest House** (✔9469462361; d without/with bathroom ₹300/400, per person incl meals ₹600) has four acceptable rooms tucked behind one of the three main-street grocery windows.

The cheapest option is **Norboo Lagams Chow Guest House** (✔227145; s/d without bathroom ₹200/300) with four neat but claustrophobic boxy rooms hidden at the back of a farm garden off the central asphalted road. The only toilet is in the traditional house behind which is an ornate Ladaki kitchen-dining room.

Buses (₹60) leave the gompa for Leh at 7.30am, and return from Leh at 4pm.

Sham

✔ 01982

A few kilometres north of the main NH1D, the parallel 'Sham' route links several picturesque Ladakhi villages between Likir and Timishgan. The stark arid scenery here reaches some grand Nevada-style crescendos and the route is used as a homestay 'baby trek' by walkers who don't want to cross major passes. Daily bus connections mean you could do any one-day section then give up as you please. However, there's minimal shade so hike early before the sun is high. Only Hemis Shukpachan to Ang is roadless, though guides can help you find routes that keep largely off the black-top. Altitude-wise the route is easier walked westbound.

YANGTHANG

In timeless little Yangthang, sturdy old houses fit together, forming an architecturally cohesive square around a tiny shrine. Set in barley fields backed by a jagged horizon of saw-toothed mountains, the village has four traditional if basic **homestays** (per person ₹300) with floor mattresses and meals included. **Padma Guest House** (✔08991-922129) has fine views, its corner dorm room overlooking the chasm that descends steeply to Rizong, a two-hour hike when the trail hasn't been washed away.

HEMIS SHUKPACHAN

Central Hemis Shukpachan is a curiously medieval little knot of houses clustered around a central rocky hillock. Around 1km beyond at the village's northwest edge is a famous grove of ancient juniper trees beside the footpath leading towards Ang/Timishgan (around four hours' walk). There are nearly a dozen widely scattered guesthouses and homestays all charging between ₹500 and ₹750 per person including full board. Hidden amid the central knot of monastic footpaths, TT Nyamgal's **Toro Guesthouse** (✔240021, 9469361560; tt_namgail@rediffmail.com; per person incl full board ₹600) is friendly and has a convivial little communal balcony area. The large, traditional **Sgangzur Guesthouse** (✔240035; per person incl full board ₹600) has only two guest rooms but the front one with four carpet-toppped mats has the best views in town. The access path starts close to the juniper grove.

Hemis Shukpachan is 10km west of Yangthang by a painfully bumpy jeep track.

TIMISHGAN, ANG & TIA

The former co-capital of 14th-century lower Ladakh, Timishgan (Tingmosgan, Temisgam) sits at the centre of a very large, green Y-shaped valley stretching several kilometres to Ang (northeast) and Tia (northwest). It was here in 1864 that Ladakh signed treaties with Tibet allowing for formalised trade missions.

JAMMU & KASHMIR (INCLUDING LADAKH) LEH TO KARGIL

The mostly contemporary main **monastery** sits on a high, central rocky crag climbed by a large remnant section of fortress curtain wall. There are two more small gompas in Tia, which has an architecturally interesting central core. Central Timishgan and especially parts of Ang have several fine old traditional Ladakhi houses. Around 1km northeast of Timishgan's central junction, the traditionally designed **Namra Hotel** (☑ 229033, 9419178324; namrahotel@gmail.com; s/d/deluxe ₹1600/2200/2450) is an unexpected oasis of comfort to soothe arriving trekkers. Set in relaxing parasol-decked gardens, attractive common areas have bench seats and photos of local scenes. Rooms err heavily towards the fake wooden-veneer look, but beds are comfortable and bathrooms have such miraculous luxuries as hot showers and toilet paper.

Around 10 **homestays** (per person incl full board ₹600) are available. The majority are in Ang, but a great choice if you can find it is the unsigned **MagpaPa** (☑ 229031; s/d/deluxe ₹1600/2200/2450) with warm shower and sitdown WC. It's the newly whitewashed house just after the chorten following the double hairpin bendeast of Namra Hotel.

The cheapest option is **Dolker Guesthouse** (☑ 229042; d ₹400, incl full board ₹800) at the base of the village towards Nurla.

Alchi

This rural village has become a regional tourism magnet thanks to the famous **Chhoskhor Temple Complex** (foreigner/Indian ₹50/20; ⊘ 8am-1pm & 2-6pm), founded in the 11th century by 'Great Translator' Lotsava Ringchen Zangpo. From outside, the small complex looks relatively uninteresting but original interior murals are considered the crowning glory of Ladakh's Indo-Tibetan art. Visits (no photography allowed) start with **Sumrtsek Temple** fronted by a wooden porch whose carving style is very much Indian rather than Tibetan. Inside, murals cover all three levels with hundreds of little Buddhas. The heads of oversized wooden statues of Maitreya, Manjushri and Avalokitesvara burst through to the inaccessible upper storey. Next along, **Vairocana Temple** is impressive for its mandalas: as antique murals in the rear chamber, as contemporary exercises in coloured sand at the front. In the **Lotsa Temple**, Lotsava Ringchen Zangpo himself appears as the slightly reptilian figure to the left behind the central Buddha

cabinet. Beneath him, a row of comical-faced figures underline the importance of taking nothing too seriously. The **Manjushri Temple** enshrines a joyfully colourful four-sided statue of Manjushri (Buddha of Wisdom). The compex is reached by an obvious pedestrian lane lined by guesthouses, souvenir peddlers and a 'German' bakery-restaurant. There are a dozen accommodation options.

Alchi Resort (☑ 9419218636; www.alchiresort.tripod.com; r rack-rate/walk-in ₹4700/2000) is a collection of two-room whitewashed cottages ranged around a narrow but attractive walled garden with central gazebo. Nepali fabrics enliven the interiors which have super-clean bathrooms.

The friendly, colourful **Choksor Guest House** (☑ 9419826363; r ₹400-800) is Alchi's best budget deal. Complete with shrine room and open roof terrace, it's set in a flower garden 800m back towards Leh from central Alchi. Next door the once-grand Lonpo House was formerly home to the Ladakhi king's local tax collector.

Central Alchi is 4km down a dead-end spur lane that leaves the Leh–Kargil road at Km370.

Uletokpo & Rizong

For rural Ladakh's most upmarket accommodation, choose the deluxe cottages at **Ule Ethnic Resort** (☑ 227208; http://uleresort.com; s/d ₹4860/5304) with stylishly modern solar-heated bathrooms in a clifftop orchard garden, high above a river bend. The cheaper 'canvas cottages' (tent-hut mongrels) are far less impressive. An erosion-prone 6km side lane from Uletokpo village dead-ends at the photogenic 19th-century **Rizong Gompa** (admission by donation; ⊘ 7am-1pm & 1.30-6pm), stepped handsomely up an amphitheatre of rocky cliff. A steep, sometimes treacherous footpath continues from there up to Yangthang.

Khalsi

Possibly useful as a transit point, comparatively bustling Khalsi (Km337) has shops, PCO phone booths, two basic restaurant-hotels (doubles ₹500) and several other eateries, including relatively convivial **Samyas Garden Restaurant** (mains ₹70-100, rice ₹50). The town has two taxis charging around ₹900 to Lamayuru or Phanjila, if available at all. Hitching westbound, it's generally easier to start from the checkpoint 2km west.

Dha-Hanu

Foreigners with prearranged permits (apply in Leh) may travel as far as Dha on the lovely Indus Valley road that becomes increasingly dramatic as you continue northwest from Khalsi. Just before reaching the walnut-growing village of **Domkhar** (Km15) look across the river for fine views of terraced **Takmachik**. Picturesque **Skurbuchan** village is topped by a rickety gompa fort overlooking the Indus canyon. Scattered ancient **petroglyphs** are inscribed on brown, time-polished roadside rocks, for example at Km54.8.

Accessed by a 10-minute walk up an easily missed footpath from Km61, **Dha** (population 250) is all stone walls, tomato gardens and dappled light filtered through apricot fronds. Culturally it is a notable centre of the Brokpa people (aka Drokpa or Dard), a unique ethno-religious community sometimes speculated to have been descended from Alexander the Great's invasion force... or even a lost tribe of Israel. Though outnumbered these days by 'one pen' kids, a few Brokpa people still wear pearly button ear decorations and traditional hats, with older women tying their hair in long multistranded braids reminiscent of knotted dreadlocks.

Simple, raggety **Skyabapa Guest House** (☑ 9469535269; dm/d ₹150/400, breakfast/dinner ₹70/90) has age-greyed sheets and shared outside squat toilets, but a great feature is the open-air dining area shaded by a vast grapevine that thrives in Dha's unexpectedly warm microclimate. Friendly owners make their own organic wine.

Across the bridge at Km55.9, Muslim **Sanjak** is a gaggle of basic shop-houses serving tea and instant noodles. The road towards Kargil from here passes a dramatic 16th-century **castle ruin** above the roadside in **Chiktan**.

Dha-Hanu, Sanjak and Chiktan can be added to a Leh–Kargil multistop jeep trip, but only westbound as the permits must be issued in Leh. Foreigners may not use the Dha–Battalik–Kargil road.

Yapola Valley

Several classic villages that could previously only be visited on foot or horseback have recently become accessible with new (if sometimes washed-out) jeep roads. Far less touristed than the Indus Valley towns, villages here are small and 'unspoilt', and all have delightful if spartan homestays in traditional Ladakhi houses. The scenery can be jaw-dropping.

WANLA & PHANJILA

A knife-edge ridge rising above Wanla is topped by the tiny, medieval **Wanla Gompa** (www.achiassociation.org; admission ₹20; ☺ dawn-dusk), flanked by tower remnants of a now-destroyed 14th-century fortress. The monastery's carved porch is reminiscent of Alchi's and its spookily dark prayer chamber contains three large statues backed by ancient smoke-blackened murals and naive statuettes. Monks in a hut chamber nearby keep the key.

Wanla's best homestay is the wantonly hidden **Rongstak Guest House** (☑ 9949175757; d ₹700, per person incl meals ₹750) accessed on foot through trees and gardens from the Lamayuru road at the north edge of the village. Five new rooftop rooms share a good bathroom with sit-down toilet, plus an unparalleled view of the castle-gompa's derriere and a wide mountain horizon.

Wanla has two central campsites and there are two more at Tarchit, 2km south, plus a camp-restaurant-homestay at Phanjila, a tiny junction hamlet 4km further south.

HINJU

This attractive ribbon of traditional village follows a 1km curl of barley fields and culminates in a small gompa flanked by olde-worlde Ladakhi houses. One of these is **Gyasltson Yoma Homestay** (☑ 9622975800; per person incl meals ₹500), our favourite of over a dozen simple, utterly authentic homestay options. The local kitchen is a photogenic delight, the small front guest room has windows on three sides and the room behind has the unique advantage of an en-suite bathroom with sit-down flush toilet. Many homestays can arrange horses for the two-/three-day trek to Sumdha Do/Chiling, crossing the 4950m Konze La (strenuous) for breathtaking views then sleeping at Sumdho Chinmu.

Hinju is 9km by steep jeep track from Phanjila through a long dusty valley.

URSI

Rarely visited Ursi is the destination for an off-beat mountain hike from Alchi. It's a close-packed hamlet with breathtaking views of serrated peaks to the south, including the rocky beak of Mt Mirutse. Unsigned **Stanzin Norboo Homestay** (per person incl full board ₹500) is the first house on the left on the jeep track that climbs 7km from Phanjila up a series of hairpin bends.

YAPOLA GORGE & HONUPATTA

Driving the 12km from Phanjila to Honupatta, it's tempting to burst with superlatives, especially as you traverse the spectacular Yapola Gorge, one of India's least-recognised scenic wonders. Incredibly, you can often have its soaring sides, spiky mountain vistas and colourful geological pyrotechnics virtually all to yourself. The closely clumped village of Honupatta has two seasonal parachute cafes and six basic homestays (₹500 including full board). Sonam Rigzen's traditional house is behind the big prayer wheel in the village core.

TOWARDS ZANSKAR

Scenery remains glorious as you drive south of Honupatta, traverse the 4720m Sisir La and descend to Photoksar. This used to be the trekking route to Zanskar, but with road building rapidly progressing it's likely that jeeps will be able to drive as far as the fabled Lingshet Gompa by the time you read this.

Lamayuru

🕾 01982 / ELEV 3390M

Set among mountain-backed badlands, low-paced Lamayuru is one of Ladakh's most memorable villages and an ideal place to break the Kargil–Leh journey. Picturesque homes huddle around a crumbling hilltop that's pitted with caves and topped by the ultra-photogenic **Yungdrung Gompa** (admission ₹50). Behind glass within the gompa's main prayer hall is a tiny cave in which 11th-century mystic Naropa (AD 1016–1100) meditated. Before that, legend claims, this whole area had been the bottom of a deep lake whose waters receded miraculously thanks to the powerful prayers of Buddhist saint Arahat Nimagung. Sculpted by time into curiously draped shapes, the sands of that former lake bed now form 'moonland' landscapes beside the new Leh road around 1km east of town.

New roads to Wanla, Hinju and Photoksar (soon Lingshet) challenge Lamayuru's traditional role as a trekking trailhead, but if you're reliant on public transport, Lamayuru still makes a good starting point for classic hiking routes to Chiling or Zanskar, with packhorses or donkeys (₹300 to ₹400 per day) sporadically available for hire.

🛏 Sleeping & Eating

Lamayuru only gets electricity from 7.30pm to 11pm.

Tharpaling Guest House GUESTHOUSE $
(🕾 224516, 9419343917; d without bathroom ₹300, half-board ₹500) Ever-smiling matriarch Tsiring Yandol gives this roadside place a jolly family feel, serving communal dinners in a dining room that's new but with traditional-style painted motifs. Pick one of the three upper front rooms.

Singey Homestay HOMESTAY $
(🕾 224509, 9419854809; d ₹400, without bathroom ₹250) This genuine local family home with simple but clean rooms and gompa views from the rooftop is very central, tucked away behind Dragon Guest House.

Lion's Den GUESTHOUSE $
(🕾 224542, 9419321296; liondenhouse@gmail.com; d ₹600, without bathroom ₹400-500) At the very edge of town towards Leh, the best bet here is en-suite corner room 101 with views of the 'moonland' erosion zone.

Hotel Moonland HOTEL $$
(🕾 224576, 9419888508; d ₹1000-1200) Lamayuru's best hotel is set in a pretty garden at the first hairpin, 400m beyond the bus stop. Rooms offer little in terms of decor, but tiled bathrooms have hot showers and the agreeable restaurant has postcard-perfect views back across barley fields towards the monastery complex. Dinner buffet ₹250, beer available.

Dragon Guest House GUESTHOUSE $$
(🕾 224501, 9469294037; d ₹1200, without bathroom ₹400-500; @) Four fresh en-suite rooms come with geyser-equipped private bathrooms, while simpler rooms are a decent size with new mattresses; across the yard the family maintains a traditional Ladakhi kitchen. The pleasant garden restaurant serves nonguests and, uniquely, internet is available, per hour ₹50.

ℹ Getting There & Away

Buses stop only briefly in passing, and times can be plus or minus an hour.
Kargil 9am.
Leh 8.30am and 9.30am daily, plus around 11am five days a week.
Shargol via Mulbekh 1.30pm Monday and Friday.
Srinagar 6.30pm.

Lamayuru to Kargil

From Lamayuru, the NH1D road zigzags up towards iguanodon-back spires that tower impressively over the Fotu La (4147m). At Km281 a 12km spur road leads to Kanji with its small but very historic **Chuchik-Zhal Temple** (www.achiassociation.org). After **Hansukot** (Heniskot; Km282), with its tourist bungalow and vague fortress ruins, a comparatively wide, fertile valley extends as far as **Khangral** (Km268) where passports are checked beside the Chiktan–Dha turn-off. The NH1D then crosses the Namika La (3760m) and descends into the glorious Wakha Valley continuing to Kargil via Mulbekh and Shargol. **Mulbekh** is best known for an 8m-high rock-carved **Maitreya-Buddha relief** that's over 1000 years old. Its lower half is shielded from view by the tiny **Chamba Gompa** (Km243.2; admission ₹20). Mulbekh is overlooked by the impregnable site of King Tashi Namgyal's 18th-century **castle**, high high above. Burnt during an 1835 raid, only two tower stubs remain but the site sports a small gompa and symphonic views across the green valley to the highly sculpted rocky mountains behind. The 2.8km spaghetti of a narrow access lane starts 100m west of Chamba Gompa. Mulbekh has five simple guesthouses, including the traditionally styled Karzoo homestay behind the post office.

Little **Shargol Gompa** is built memorably into a cliff-face, and appears to float above the village. Inside, its minuscule prayer chamber is lit by a single flickering butter lamp. To access the gompa from the NH1, cross the bridge at Km235.5, continue 1.6km to the baby power station and walk 10 minutes steeply uphill, climb a ladder then squeeze through the sole monk's kitchen. If he's in residence...

KARGIL & ZANSKAR

Ladakh's less visited 'second half' comprises remote, sparsely populated Buddhist Zanskar and the slightly greener Suru Valley, where villagers predominantly follow Shia Islam, as they do in the regional capital, Kargil (Km204). The scenery reaches some truly majestic mountain climaxes.

Kargil

☑ 01985 / POP 10,700 / ELEV 2817M

Most travellers only stop in Ladakh's second 'city' to change transport between Leh and Srinagar or Zanskar. After the calm and charm of Buddhist Ladakh, Muslim Kargil feels grimy and mildly hassled, though the feeling's only relative. Slow-motion internet cafes (per hour ₹80) and a single ATM are conveniently found within the three central blocks along bustling Main Bazaar (aka Imam Khomeini Chowk, Khumani Chowk). Tucked between the main bus stand and the river via an easily missed passage, the Kafka-esque **Tourist reception centre** (☑ 232721; ◷ 10.30am-4pm Mon-Sat) rents a handful of antiquated but survivable cheap rooms (doubles ₹200). Most other accommodation seems almost as unkempt while being disgracefully overpriced compared to Leh, even after bargaining a typical 30% discount.

Hotel D'Zojila (☑ 232227; hotel_dzojila@yahoo.co.in; r ₹1400-2700) nearly 2km upstream from the centre has one block of sparkling, well-appointed new rooms aimed primarily at tour groups. Across the busy road the main block is inconsistent, with rooms ranging from acceptable if kitschily panelled to sorry old boxes with blistering paintwork.

The best central option is the unusually tidy new block of the **Hotel Greenland** (☑ 232324; greenlandkargi@gmail.com; r old/new ₹1200/2000) where most fittings work, the showers are hot and the big TVs have countless channels.

Guesthouses charging under ₹1200 mostly range from grimy to unsavoury, and you might be advised to use a mat and your own bedding. Best of the cheaper bunch are the newer rooftop rooms of **Paradise Guest House** (☑ 204167, 9419186386; Hospital Rd; d ₹700-1200, without bathroom ₹500) opposite the hospital.

The best of several ho-hum eateries along Main Bazaar is **Shangrila Restaurant** (mains ₹70-180, rice ₹40), strewn with plastic flowers. Its menu features several veg options, though few are actually available.

❶ Getting There & Away

The jeep stand (Hospital Rd) and bus station are one block apart, linked via a narrow alley of butchers' and barbers' shops. Both are a short distance off Main Bazaar towards the river. The minibus station is 300m further west. Kargil's only operative petrol pump is 2.5km up the Leh road from the main river bridge (nearest alternatives at Kangan and Wakha).

Leh Buses (₹350, 10 hours) depart at 4.30am, driving via Mulbekh (1½ hours) and Lamayuru (around five hours). Shared jeeps (₹830) typically leave around 7am.

Mulbekh Minibuses (₹45) at 2pm and 3pm, returning next morning.

Srinagar Road building means traffic over the hair-raising Zoji La pass is currently one way. Till it finishes, buses (₹350, 10 hours) depart at 10.30pm and most share taxis (₹750, seven hours) leave at night. Road conditions permitting, it's worth hiring your own taxi (₹5215) to experience the beautiful, occasionally nail-biting scenery.

Suru Valley The 11.30am Parkachik and 1.30pm Panikhar J&K SRTC buses start from behind the back wall of the main bus station. Space is limited so pre-purchase tickets (from 7.30am). The 7am Panikhar bus (₹71) departs from outside the post office on Main Bazaar. A one-/two-day return jeep charter to Parkachik costs ₹3536/5300.

Zanskar Irregular Leh–Kargil–Padum buses are usually full on arrival in Kargil. Shared taxis (₹850) depart before dawn if at all. Officially organised through the central **Jeep Drivers' Cooperative** (☑232079), the charter jeeps to Padum (₹10,500, 14 hours) charge an extra ₹1800 to overnight en route at Rangdum or Parkachik (recommended). Drivers need Zanskar-endorsed permits.

Suru Valley

Were there a few more tourist facilities, this 'valley of flowers' could be a bigger attraction than better-known Zanskar to which it is the main access route. Green, semi-alpine Muslim villages are dotted among wide valleys with fabulous snow-topped mountainscapes that are most spectacularly surveyed from the excellent-value **J&K Tourist Bungalows** (d/dm ₹200/50) at Parkachik. A steep but satisfying day trek crosses the 3900m Lago La to Parkachik from the Panikhar bypass road. Lonely Purtickchay Tourist Bungalow has views of spiky, ever snow-capped Nun (7135m) and Kun (7087m). The tourist bungalows in Sanku and Panikhar are less impressive and the one at Tangole was closed when we visited, but Kangee near Panikhar has the valley's first private guesthouse, the friendly two-room **Suru Valley Guesthouse** (☑9469016630; www.nunkuneco adventure.com; small/large d without bathroom ₹400/500). Each tourist bungalow's *chowkidar* (caretaker) can rustle up extremely

basic dinners, and Sanku has very simple tea-stall shop, but that's about it so you'd be well advised to bring your own supplies if planning to explore.

Buses to Kargil leave Panikhar at 5am and 11am, and Parkachik at 7am. Taxis aren't available and, for Zanskar, onward transport is generally limited to highly uncertain hitch-hiking.

Zanskar

The greatest attraction of Zanskar, a majestically rugged, mountain-hemmed Ladakhi-Buddhist valley, is simply getting there, preferably on a trek. While days can be scorching hot, come prepared for very cold nights even in summer. Until the Wanla–Honuatta–Lingshet road is extended to Hanumil, the only motorable road in is from Kargil via the glorious Suru Valley, which becomes a very rough but dramatic glacier-dodging lane to isolated Buddhist Rangdum then crosses the 4401m Pensi La.

Rangdum

POP 280 / ELEV 3670M

Wind-scoured Rangdum makes a handy overnight break on the 12-hour Kargil–Padum jeep ride. Its 20 or so low-rise buildings look as though they were dropped randomly onto the remarkably wild, big-sky valley whose meandering streams are backed to the west by a parade of gigantic snaggle-tooth mountains. The **J&K Tourism Bungalow** (d ₹300) has four good-value en-suite rooms, albeit with neither water nor electricity beyond the solar-battery lighting. If it's full, ask at one of the five weatherbeaten tea stalls for a 'local room' (ie homestay, ₹300 to ₹500).

Isolated **Rangdum Gompa** (admission ₹50), 5km further east, looks like a tiny floating island backed by an arid pastiche of oddly contorted strata. Above a stream at the foot of the gompa, summer-only **Nun-Kun Delux Camp** (☑1982252153; www.zanskartrek. com; s/d ₹1500/2300, full board ₹3000/3500) has bedded tents sharing outside bathrooms.

Padum

☑01983 / POP 1500 / ELEV 3505M

Zanskar's dusty little capital has an impressive mountain backdrop but lacks much architectural character. Within a block of the central crossroads you'll find the bus/share-taxi stand, phone offices, an internet cafe, a **tourist office** (☑245017; ☺10am-4pm Mon-Sat) and the majority of Padum's dozen hotel-guesthouses. The main road then straggles 700m south past a sizeable 1991 mosque to the crumbling little 'old town' and a hillock of stupas and water-eroded boulders. More traditional **Pibiting** village, 2km north, has a small gompa dwarfed by a large hilltop stupa topped with a beacon lamp.

🏃 Activities

Zanskar's top activity is trekking. Although road building is steadily proceeding, walking remains a popular way to reach the Yapola Valley (north) or Ramjak (south) for connections to Keylong. Tents and provisions are needed for some sections and guides/horses can sometimes be organised on the spot. Ask around, at your guesthouse or via agencies such as **Zanskar Trek** (☑245136; www.zanskar-trek.in) or **Blue Yak** (www.blueyak-zanskar.com) along the road to the mosque. To avoid hiking within the stark, sun-blasted Padum Valley you could give the horses two days' head start, then drive out to the Hanumil/Durdong trailheads for Lingshet/Darcha respectively.

🛏 Sleeping & Eating

Most hotels close from late October to June, except when booked for winter trekking groups. A simple camping ground faces the tourist office, which has an acceptable **Tourist Bungalow** (d ₹200).

Hotel Ibex　　　　　　　GUESTHOUSE $
(☑245214; ibexpadumzanskar@gmail.com; d ₹800-1000) Rooms are aging a little but the Ibex's large sheltered garden courtyard is a peaceful oasis, and the restaurant a great place to meet fellow travellers. Neater but pricier

and with less atmosphere are the nearby Kailash Hotel and newer Zambala Hotel, a block towards Pibiting.

Padma Linga Guest House & Camping　　　GUESTHOUSE $
(☑9419888017, 9419533004; d ₹600) Brand new in 2012, three of four rooms have great views and are far smarter than you'd guess from the bare concrete-brick exterior. It's eight minutes' walk above the heliport, just far enough to feel peacefully semirural.

Phukthal Guest House　　　GUESTHOUSE $
(☑245226; r ₹450-500) Eight tidy rooms with very small en-suite bathrooms (bucket showers) and an appealing dining room above a shop in Old Padum.

Mont-Blanc Guest House　　　HOMESTAY $
(☑9469239376; r ₹450, without bathroom ₹350; 🐾) Friendly place with four traditionally furnished rooms just set back from the main road at a large prayer wheel 200m before the mosque.

Ga-Skyit (Gyaki)　　　RESTAURANT $
(☑245010; mains ₹90-190, rice ₹70) Upstairs near the main junction, Padum's best-appointed eatery attempts various cuisines and has some good-looking if slightly dark guest rooms below (single/double ₹2000/2300).

ℹ Information

Marq Cyber Cafe (internet/Skype per min ₹2/5; ☺9am-9pm)

ℹ Getting There & Away

Until the Wanla–Lingshet–Padum–Ranjak–Darcha road is finished, transport options will remain very limited, and available in summer only.

JAMMU & KASHMIR (INCLUDING LADAKH) ZANSKAR

ZANSKAR IN WINTER

In winter, snow cuts Zanskar's tenuous transport links altogether. Yet in late February, Zanskar's teachers and school kids returning from their winter break manage to walk in from Chiling following an ancient seasonal trade trail that essentially follows the frozen Zanskar River – often on the ice, crossing side streams on precarious snow bridges and camping in caves en route. This hazardous 'Chadar Trek' is likely to die out altogether once the Lingshet–Hanumil road is connected, but till then it attracts a handful of hardy winter hiking groups every year (safer in January when the ice is most stable). Never attempt this alone. While there are no high-altitude stages, you'll need serious winter kit and an experienced local guide who can 'read' the ice. Some hardy locals claim they can walk the route in around three days with minimal sleep or baggage, but trekking groups typically take roughly double that in each direction.

Every two or three days a Leh-bound bus departs Padum at around 3.30am, stopping for the night in Kargil (₹475) before continuing.

By jeep, Padum to Kargil costs ₹9000 to ₹11,000 per vehicle. Taxi-union rules don't allow Kargil–Padum–Kargil return trips. Alternatively head to Parkachik by jeep (₹7600) then continue by bus. Other one-way/return rates from Padum:

Karsha ₹800/1100

Pidmo Bridge ₹2700/3200

Rangdum ₹7000/9000.

North of Padum

SANI

At Sani, beside the Kargil road, Zanskar's oldest gompa is a small, two-storey prayer hall ringed by a tunnelled cloister and a whitewashed stone wall studded with stupas.

KARSHA

At the far side of a wide, sun-blasted plain around two hours' walk from Padum, **Karsha Gompa** is Zanskar's largest Buddhist monastery. Dating back to at least the 10th century, it's a jumble of whitewashed blocks rising almost vertically up a red rock mountain cliff. Concrete steps lead to the monastery's upper cloister and prayer hall with its cracked old murals and wobbly wooden columns. It's a great vantage point from which to survey Karsha's old-fashioned homes, barley fields and threshing circles worked by dzo. Three homestay-style 'guesthouses' all come with shared squat toilets.

ZANGLA

For a fine half-day excursion from Padum, drive to Zangla admiring the curled, contorted geological strata that are especially striking above Rinam and Shilingskit villages. A trip highlight is **Stongde Gompa** crowning a bird's-eye perch some 300m above the valley, 12km from Padum. The entrance to Zangla is guarded by a small hilltop **fortress-palace ruin**. See http://csomasroom.kibu.hu/en/join for details about volunteering to help with the restoration. At the far end of the village there's a small, friendly Buddhist **nunnery**. The road that will one day reach Lingshet already continues past Hanumil into some spectacular canyonlands.

South of Padum

The road south from Padum passes **Bardan Gompa**, spectacularly set on a rocky outcrop above the valley. Appealing little **Raru** village has two tiny eateries and a very basic homestay. The jeep road ends near Dorzong (Durdong) just beyond the rock-perched village of **Itchar** (aka Khor). Both have homestays.

PHUKTAL & THE DARCHA TREK

One of Zanskar's most photogenic monasteries, **Phuktal Gompa** is built up against a cliff face beneath a gaping cave entrance. It contains a sacred spring and some 700-year-old murals in the Alchi style. The monastery guesthouse, a fair distance beneath the gompa, has five rooms with real beds and even a shower.

Trekking to Phuktal from Dorzong is possible in one long day, but better in two or more. The southbank trail has its easiest crossing back across the river at Purne (has homestay).

Rather than returning to Padum, many trekking groups continue towards Darcha on the Manali road (around four days). You'll need proper gear and a guide to cross the 5090m Shingo La, but from Ramjak a bus reportedly now runs to Keylong.

THE KASHMIR VALLEY

Deep within seemingly endless layers of alpine peaks, the 140km-long Kashmir Valley opens up as a wide upland bowl of lakes and orchards. Traditionally fabled as a paradise of tranquility but divided after Indian Independence, Kashmir spent the later 20th century oscillating between violent upheavals and periods as an idyllic summer getaway. Tin-roofed villages guard terraced paddy fields delineated by apple groves and pin-straight poplars. Proudly independent-minded Kashmiris mostly follow a Sufi-based Islamic faith, worshipping in distinctive box-shaped mosques. Many Kashmiris have startlingly green eyes, and in winter they keep warm by clutching a kangri (wicker fire-pot holder) beneath their flowing grey-brown pheran (woollen capes).

History

Geologists and Hindu mystics agree that the Kashmir Valley was once a vast lake. Where they disagree is whether it was drained by a post–Ice Age earthquake or by Lord Vishnu and friends as a ploy to kill a lake demon.

JAMMU & KASHMIR (INCLUDING LADAKH) THE KASHMIR VALLEY

In the 3rd century BC the Hindu kingdom of Kashmir became a major centre of Buddhist learning under Emperor Ashoka. In the 13th and 14th centuries, Islam arrived through the inspiration of peaceable Sufi mystics. Later some Muslim rulers, such as Sultan Sikandar 'Butshikan' (r 1389–1413), set about the destruction of Hindu temples and Buddhist monasteries. However, others such as the great Zain-ul-Abidin (r 1423–74) encouraged such religious and cultural tolerance that medieval visitors reported finding it hard to tell Hindus and Muslims apart. Mughal emperors including Akbar (1556–1605), whose troops took Kashmir in 1586, saw Kashmir as their Xanadu and developed a series of extravagant gardens around Srinagar.

When the British arrived in India, Jammu and Kashmir were a loose affiliation of independent kingdoms, nominally controlled by the Sikh rulers of Jammu. In 1846, after the British had defeated the Sikhs, they handed Kashmir to Maharaja Gulab Singh in return for a yearly tribute of six shawls, 12 goats and a horse. Singh's autocratic Hindu-Dogra dynasty ruled until Independence, showing an infamous disregard for the welfare of the Muslim majority. Many citizens were little better than slaves, liable for service as unpaid porters or labourers at the whim of local landowners.

Partition & Conflict

As Partition approached in 1947, although the majority of J&K's population was Muslim, the (jailed) popular leader of the predominantly Islamic opposition favoured joining India. Hindu Maharaja Hari Singh favoured Kashmiri independence but failed to make a definitive decision. Finally, to force the issue, Pashtun tribesmen, backed by the new government in Pakistan, attempted to grab the state by force, setting off the first India–Pakistan war. The invaders were pushed out of the Kashmir Valley but Pakistan retained control of Baltistan, Muzaffarabad and the valley's main access routes. Kashmir has remained divided ever since along a tenuous UN-demarcated border, known as the Line of Control. A proposed referendum to let Kashmir's people decide (for Pakistan or India) never materialised and Pakistan invaded again in 1965, triggering another protracted conflict.

Although most Indian Kashmiris would prefer to be independent of both India *and*

SAFETY IN KASHMIR

Kashmir's difficult 20th-century history and the delicate relationship between nationalist Muslims and Jammu Hindus creates a cauldron of intercommunal tensions contained or exacerbated (according to one's viewpoint) by a very visible Indian army presence. When things are calm, Kashmir is probably safer than most places in India. Be aware that cycles of unrest, stone-throwing and curfews can erupt remarkably rapidly. Use common sense, avoid public demonstrations and military installations and consult a wide range of resources to get a feel of the situation before arriving, starting with your country's government travel advisory website.

Pakistan, the conflict became a cause célèbre for pro-Pakistani Islamic radicals. A militant fringe turned to armed rebellion in the later 1980s. Kashmir was placed under direct rule from Delhi in 1990, and for several bloody years massacres and bomb attacks were countered by brutal counter-insurgency tactics from the Indian armed forces. Significant human-rights abuses were reported on both sides.

After the brief Indo-Pakistan 'Kargil War' of 1999, a ceasefire and increasing autonomy for Kashmir was matched by a significant reduction in tensions. Coordinating relief after the tragic 2005 earthquake also helped bring the Indian and Pakistani governments a little closer. Militant attacks dwindled and domestic tourism blossomed. New disturbances in 2008 (over an arcane land dispute at Amarnath) and 2010 (after the shooting of juvenile stone-throwers) each caused months of strikes, violence, curfews and the closing of the Jammu–Srinagar road. But the valley has been relatively calm since 2011, causing another big resurgence of Indian tourism. In late 2012, the UK withdrew its long-standing travel advisory against visiting certain parts of Kashmir.

At the time of research there was a new bout of cross-border firing on the Line of Control that resulted in Pakistani and Indian soldier casualties, with both sides claiming the other as responsible for these ceasefire violations.

JAMMU & KASHMIR (INCLUDING LADAKH) THE KASHMIR VALLEY

Sonamarg

📋 0194 / POP 800 (SUMMER ONLY) / ELEV 2800M

Set in a Sound-of-Music alpine valley, seasonal Sonamarg (Km85) is a possible trekking base and commonly used as a meal-stop before/after crossing the nerve-racking 3529m **Zoji La** pass between Kargil and Srinagar. Big business here is catering for *yatra*-hike pilgrims en route to Amarnath's holy ice lingam via Baltal Camp, a summer-only mayhem of tents around 15km east.

In contrast to the beautiful surroundings, Sonamarg is a disappointingly scrappy series of mostly jerry-built box restaurants, almost all offering small, poorly maintained guest rooms that typically cost ₹2000 to ₹4000 in high season but can be bargained to as little as ₹700 once the *yatra* (pilgrimage) is over.

There's a smaller selection of somewhat better hotels around 2km west of town. Best of these remains the **Hotel Snowland** (📞 2417262; Srinagar-Kargil Rd Km83; rack-rate s/d/super-deluxe/ste ₹3300/4400/5500/6600; 📶) where all but the cheapest rooms combine traditional *khatamband* (carved wooden panelling) ceilings, carved bedsteads and impressive modern bathrooms.

Opposite this secondary hotel strip are a pair of grassy ridges behind which domestic tourists often get their first taste of snow by walking, driving (taxis cost ₹800 to ₹1500 return, 7km) or pony-riding towards the Thajiwas Glacier. Between the two ridges is a simple half-timbered **J&K Tourist Bungalow** (📞 9419464574; dm/cottage ₹200/3000), bookable through the tourist office in central Sonamarg town.

In relatively peaceful isolation, 2km east of Sonamarg, the half-timbered **International Youth Hostel** (📞 9419707307; iyhssonmarg@gmail.com; Srinagar-Kargil Rd Km86.3; dm/q ₹550/2400) opened in late 2011 with giant, super-airy dorms, snooker and table-tennis rooms and a unexpectedly well-equipped weight-training gym. Zorbing (from ₹200) and rafting (from ₹350) are organised.

For Srinagar, very slow buses depart at 7.30am, 9.30am and 12.30pm (₹100, four hours); shared/private jeeps (2½ hours) cost ₹150/2000. Change in Kangan for Naranag. Eastbound buses are often full by the time they reach Sonamarg, so for Kargil consider returning to Srinagar to get a seat or chartering a taxi/jeep (₹5000, six hours).

Naranag & Lake Gangabal

Relatively unspoilt Naranag sits within a grand pine valley with a heavily pounding river and a remarkable pair of huge 8th-century **Shiva temple ruins** (unfenced). Beyond are the rudimentary log cabins used seasonally by seminomadic Gujar people. Before, the main village has four guesthouses and at least two homestays, most in a deplorable state of disarray. The best option is relatively new **Gulshan Lodge** (📞 9858375734; r ₹500-1000), whose en-suite bathrooms could smell sweeter but do have geysers. It's at the first bridge, 800m before the temples. The mid-summer trek to beautiful Lake Gangabal follows a side stream near Naranag's one restaurant ('Hotel' Dhat), taking around seven hours up (gaining around 1200m altitude) and four hours back. That means that in fine weather it is possible in one very long day without the vastly expensive donkey-tent-guide packages sold to unwitting travellers in Srinagar. To get here from Srinagar first take a Sumo or bus from Batmalu bus station to Kangan. Packed-

---

AMARNATH

Far from the nearest road, in a mountain **cave** (🕐 accessible 25 Jun-2 Aug) at Amarnath, a natural stone lingam becomes opalescently encrusted with ice and is believed to wax and wane with the phases of the moon. Seen as symbolising Lord Shiva, it's the destination for a vastly popular summer *yatra* (Hindu pilgrimage). Joining the chaotic swarm is an unforgettable experience and the route is very beautiful, but it's certainly not a peaceful or meditative country hike. All prospective *yatri* (pilgrims, hikers) must sign up through **SASB** (www.shriamarnathjishrine.com), be suitably equipped for potentially subzero conditions and be ready for intrusive security: both blizzards and Kashmiri militants have killed pilgrims in the past.

There are two approach routes. From Pahalgam it's a 16km taxi ride to Chandanwari, then a 36km, three-day hike. Alternatively, from the vast Baltal Camp near Sonamarg, Amarnath is just 14km away. Wealthier pilgrims complete that journey by pony, helicopter or *dandy* (palanquin).

full buses from Kangan to Naranag run the last 16km around twice hourly.

Srinagar

📞 0194 / POP 988,000 / ELEV 1730M

Indulgent houseboats, historic gardens, distinctive Kashmiri wooden mosques and a mild summer climate combine to make Srinagar one of India's top domestic tourist attractions. Except, that is, when intercommunal tensions paralyse the city with strikes and curfews (see p265). Srinagar's three main areas converge around Dalgate, where the southwestern nose of Dal Lake passes through a lock. Northwest lies the Old City, chaotic in normal times but largely out-of-bounds during curfews. The busy commercial centre is southwest around Lal Chowk. The city's greatest drawcard is placid Dal Lake, which stretches in a southwestern channel towards the city centre, paralleled by the hotel-lined Boulevard from which a colourful array of houseboats form a particularly colourful scene. This area usually remains free of trouble even during the worst disturbances, as do the famous Mughal gardens, strung out over several kilometres further east around the lake.

For a visual portrait of Dal Lake life, watch the prize-winning 2012 movie *Valley of Saints*.

👁 Sights

Whether you sleep on one of its wonderful time-warp houseboats or just stroll along the Boulevard savouring the sunset, beautifully serene **Dal Lake** is likely to be your main memory of Srinagar. Mirror-flat waters beautifully reflect the misty peaks of the Pir Panjal mountains while gaily painted *shikaras* glide by. These are gondolalike boats, hand-powered with heart-shaped paddles and used to transport goods to market, children to school, and visitors on explorative tours of the lake's floating communities. Nehru Park jetty is a good starting point for visiting the early-morning **floating vegetable market** though you might consider pre-booking a boatman, as otherwise few will be waiting at dawn. Canal-like passages link all the way to Nagin Lake.

👁 Old City

When visiting mosques, follow normal Islamic formalities (dress modestly, remove shoes) and ask permission before entering or taking interior photos. Women will usually be expected to cover their hair and use a separate entrance.

⭐**Khanqah Shah-i-Hamadan** MOSQUE
(Khanqah-e-Muala; Khawaja Bazaar area) This distinctively spired 1730s Muslim meeting hall is one of Srinagar's most beautiful, with both frontage and interiors covered in papier-mâché reliefs and elaborately coloured *khatamband*. Non-Muslim visitors can peek through the door but may not enter. The building stands on the site of one of Kashmir's first mosques, founded by Persian saint Mir Sayed Ali Hamadani who arrived in 1372, one of 700 refugees fleeing Timur's (Tamerlane's) conquest of Iran. He is said to have converted 37,000 people to Sufi Islam, and it's likely that his retinue introduced Kashmiris to the Persian art of fine carpet-making. The saint is buried in what's now Tajikistan.

Badshah Tomb ARCHITECTURE
(donation appropriate; ⊘ 9am-6pm) Looking more Bulgarian than Kashmiri, the multi-domed 15th-century brick tomb of King Zeinalabdin's mother was built on the plinth of a much older former Buddhist temple. It's within an ancient graveyard hidden in a maze of copperware, spice and cloth vendors' shops. The tomb's domes form part of the classic view of Old Town Srinagar when looking north from the new Zeinalabdin Bridge, with the city's oldest wooden bridge as foreground.

Jama Masjid MOSQUE
(Nowhatta) Looking like a movie set for a Central Asian castle, this mighty 1672 mosque forms a quadrangle around a large fountain garden courtyard with monumental brick gatehouses marking each of the four cardinal directions. There's room for thousands of devotees between the 378 roof-support columns, each fashioned from the trunk of a single deodar tree.

Naqshband Sahib SACRED SITE
(Khanyar Chowk area) This beautifully proportioned but uncoloured 17th-century shrine was built in Himachal Pradesh style with alternating layers of wood and brick to dissipate the force of earthquakes.

Rozabal SACRED SITE
(Ziyarat Hazrati Youza Asouph) At the north end of a triangular patch of grass from the

Srinagar

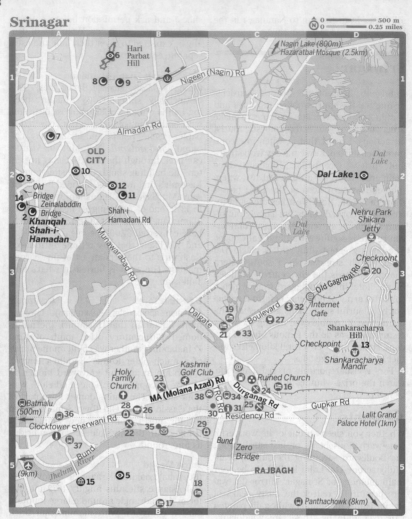

tragically fire-ravaged **Pir Dastgir Sahib** (⊘ 4am-10pm) Sufi shrine is the small green Rozabal shrine. Visually it's utterly insignificant. Yet a highly controversial theory claims that the shrine's crypt holds the grave of Jesus Christ. Tourists are actively discouraged from approaching, but the mere existence of this little place might inspire you to read more deeply about the fascinating subject of Jesus' historical career.

Hari Parbat Hill   HILL
The imposing 18th-century **Hari Parbat Fort** is visible from virtually anywhere in

Srinagar but closed to the public, for military use. It crowns a prominent hill that Hindus believe was originally the island from which Vishnu and Sharika (Durga) defeated Jalodbhava, Kashmir's mythical lake demon. On the hill's mid-slopes, Muslims pay homage at the large **Makhdoom Sahib Shrine**, reached by beggar-lined steps that pass the ruined 1649 stone mosque of Akhund Mullah Shah. The steps start a few hundred metres beyond the scant remains of Srinagar's Old City walls (built by Akbar in the 1590s) and the large **Chetipacha Gurdwara**.

Srinagar

◉ Top Sights
1	Dal Lake	D2
2	Khanqah Shah-i-Hamadan	A2

◉ Sights
3	Badshah Tomb	A2
4	Chetipacha Gurdwara	B1
5	Government Silk Weaving Factory	B5
	Hari Parbat Fort	(see 6)
6	Hari Parbat Hill	B1
7	Jama Masjid	A2
8	Makhdoom Sahib Shrine	A1
9	Mosque of Akhund Mulla Shah	B1
10	Naqshband Sahib	A2
11	Pir Dastgir Sahib	B2
12	Rozabal	B2
13	Shankaracharya Hill	D4
14	Sitoun Mosque	A2
15	Sri Pratap Singh Museum	A5

🛏 Sleeping
16	City Forest	C4
17	Comrade Inn	B5
18	Green Acre	B5
19	Hotel Akbar	C3
20	Hotel Swiss	D3
	Noor Guest House	(see 21)
21	New Zeenath Guest House	C4

⊗ Eating
22	Ahdoo's	B5
23	Coffea Arabica	B4
24	Krishna Vaishno Dhaba	C4
25	Solomon's Barbeque	C4

⊖ Drinking & Nightlife
26	Cafe Robusta	B4
27	Wine Shops	C3

⊕ Shopping
28	Gulshan Books	B4
29	Kashmir Government Arts Emporium	B5

⊕ Information
30	Houseboat Owners Association	C4
31	Tourism Reception Centre	C4
32	Transcorp International	C3

⊕ Transport
33	Air India	C4
34	J&K SRTC Bus Station	C4
35	Jet Airways	B5
36	Lal Chowk City Minibus Stand	A4
37	Shared Jeeps & Private Minibuses to Jammu	A5
38	Tourist Taxi Stand 1	C4

JAMMU & KASHMIR (INCLUDING LADAKH) SRINAGAR

◉ Central Srinagar

Sri Pratap Singh Museum   MUSEUM
(🕿 2312859; http://spsmuseum.org; Indian/foreigner ₹10/50; ◉ 10.30am-4.30pm Tue-Sun) This richly endowed historical museum features Mughal papier-mâché work, 4th-century tiles, 8th-century gods, stuffed birds, mammoth bones, weaponry and traditional Kashmiri costumes, all within the touchingly unkempt 1872 Lalmandi Palace of Maharajah Pratap Singh. It's accessed from central Srinagar by a footbridge across the Jhelum River then by shimmying through frightening coils of razor wire. Bring ID. A new exhibition hall is nearing completion.

Government Silk Weaving Factory   SILK WORKSHOP
(◉ 10am-5.30pm Mon-Sat) Founded in 1938 and virtually unchanged since, the antiquated machinery still turns out 7000m of silk cloth each month. Visits end at an emporium but with no sales pressure.

◉ Around Dal Lake

Shankaracharya Hill   VIEWPOINT, SACRED SITE
(◉ 7.30am-5pm) Thickly forested Shankaracharya Hill is topped by a small Shiva temple built from hefty blocks of visibly ancient grey stone. Previously known as Takht-i-Sulaiman (Throne of Solomon), it's now named after a sage who reached enlightenment here in AD 750, but signs date the octagonal structure as 5th century and the site is even older. Some claim, controversially, that a previous temple here was once renovated by Jesus and St Thomas. Access is by a winding 5.5km road from Nehru Park (₹150 return by autorickshaw). Walking is considered ill-advised given the population of wild bears. From road's end the temple is five minutes up a stairway from a police checkpoint where you must leave phones and cameras before reaching the panoramic views of Srinagar and Dal Lake.

Parks & Gardens
Srinagar's famous gardens date back to the Mughal era. Most have a fundamentally

similar design with terraced lawns, fountain pools and carefully manicured flowerbeds interspersed with *chinar* (Kashmir's national tree), pavilions and mock fortress facades.

Built for Nur Jahan by her husband Jehangir, **Shalimar Bagh** (adult/child ₹10/5; ◷9am-dusk), 10km beyond Nehru Park, is the most famous garden. However, **Nishat Bagh** (adult/child ₹10/5; ◷9am-dusk Sat-Thu) is more immediately impressive, with steeper terracing and a lake-facing panorama (7.5km from Nehru Park). **Pari Mahal** (◷dawn-dusk) is set amid palace ruins high above the lakeshore. The ensemble looks intriguing when floodlit at night and viewed from afar. By day, the long, steep autorickshaw ride is worthwhile more for the lake views than for the gardens themselves. Bring ID for serious police checks on your way. En route you'll pass the petite **Cheshmashahi Garden** (adult/child ₹10/5; ◷8am-8pm) and the extensive, less formal **Botanical Garden** (adult/child ₹10/5; ◷8am-dusk Sat-Thu) behind which a 12-hectare **Tulip Garden** (◷Mar-Apr) blooms in March.

Hazratbal Mosque   MOSQUE

Backing onto Dal Lake several kilometres north of the Old City, Srinagar's main university area extends around the large, white-domed Hazratbal Mosque. This 20th-century building enshrines Kashmir's holiest relic, the Moi-e-Muqqadas, supposedly a beard hair of the Prophet Mohammed. The hair's brief December 1963 disappearance nearly sparked a civil war.

🛏 Sleeping

Staying on a houseboat is one of the city's main attractions, but when first arriving you might prefer to sleep at least the first night or two in a hotel while carefully selecting a suitable boat. While hotel choice is enormous, many rely primarily on noisy, self-catering groups of domestic tourists, especially during Indian holidays (notably April, June and October). Others have subcontracted to the army. A useful string of lower midrange options are dotted along Old Gagribal Rd and around Dalgate. Srinagar's most deluxe option, **Vivanta Dal View** (www.vivantabytaj.com/Dal-View-Srinagar/Overview.html), is out of town on a hill beyond the picturesque Botanical Garden.

New Zeenath Guest House   GUESTHOUSE $

(☑2474070; www.newzeenath.com; off Dalgate; r ₹400-800) Compact, but sparklingly clean

with new tile-floored rooms above a doctors' clinic along with slightly older versions tucked behind a paved central yard.

Noor Guest House   GUESTHOUSE $

(☑2450872; yulabshakeel@yahoo.in; off Dalgate; d ₹400-500, without bathroom ₹250-500) Cheaper rooms are in a creaky but characterful old wooden house, and newer ones have thin hardboard divider walls, but the family owners are kind and there's bike rental available.

Hotel Swiss   GUESTHOUSE $$

(☑2472766; www.swisshotelkashmir.com; Old Gagribal Rd; foreigners d ₹600-1200, Indians ₹1200-2500; @) The Swiss is one of the friendliest family guesthouses in India. It's not showy but has reliably good-value budget accommodation and the new block has hotel-standard rooms at walk-in prices that are significantly discounted for foreigners (online rates are far higher). There's a peaceful lawn, free and fast wi-fi, and lots of informed opinion from the tirelessly helpful Sufi-spiritual manager. The area stays calm during curfews.

Hotel Akbar   HOTEL $$

(☑2500507; http://hotelakbar.com; d ₹3000-4500, ste ₹6500; 🛜) Trump cards are the manicured garden with trellises of blooming vines and the quiet yet central lakeside location.

Green Acre   FAMILY HOTEL $$

(☑2313848; Rajbagh; s ₹2500-6000, d ₹3000-7500; ❄) The main house is a 1940s late-raj mansion set in the most glorious rose garden and lawns. Rooms are almost all large and well appointed especially in the newer rear block. The main 1940s Raj-era mansion is a mixed bag with lots of varnished dark wood, and elements of period furniture in some, though others are a little plain. The 1st-floor common balcony is the perfect reading perch.

Comrade Inn   HOTEL $$$

(☑2459001; www.comradeinn.com; Rajbagh; s/d ₹6700/7200; ❄) Well-trained staff lead you through corridors tastefully decked out in modern art to fully equipped new rooms with excellent box-spring beds, crisp cotton sheets, rainforest showers, fridge, kettle and stylish lighting. Back-up power supply, lift and AC in lobby.

Lalit Grand Palace Hotel   HERITAGE HOTEL $$$

(☑2501001; www.thelalit.com; r ₹14,000-16,000, ste ₹20,000-27,000) Vast period suites in the Maharaja's 1910 palace and a wing of (slightly) cheaper new rooms are all beauti-

HOUSEBOATS

Srinagar's signature houseboats first appeared in colonial times, because the British were prohibited from owning land. Most houseboats you'll see are less than 40 years old, but the best deluxe ones are still palatial, with chandeliers, carved walnut panels, *khatamband* (facetted wood panelling) ceilings and chintzy sitting rooms redolent of the 1930s Raj era. Category A boats are comfy but less grand. Lower categories often lack interior sitting areas. Category D boats hopefully stay afloat. Better houseboats typically have three double bedrooms; when the political climate drives tourists away you're likely to get the whole boat to yourself, chef and all.

Choosing from 1400 boats is challenging. Some owners are super-friendly families, others are crooks – ask fellow travellers for recent first-hand recommendations. For most visitors, staying on a houseboat is a relaxing Srinagar highlight. But others report feeling cheated, being virtually held hostage ('kidnapped' passport, external dangers exaggerated, etc), or suffering inappropriate advances from houseboat staff.

Houseboat Tips

➡ Don't prepurchase houseboat packages and *never book in Delhi*.

➡ Thoroughly check out houseboats in person before agreeing to or paying anything.

➡ Get a clear, possibly written, agreement stating what the fees cover.

➡ Don't be pressured into giving 'charity' donations or signing up for overpriced treks.

➡ Beware of isolated houseboats or those with a less friendly feel.

➡ Don't leave valuables unattended.

➡ Don't leave your passport with the boat owner.

➡ Tell a friend or trusted hotelier where you're staying.

➡ Sleep on shore when first arriving in Srinagar so you can check out possibilities calmly.

➡ Trust your instincts.

Choosing the Area

The boats facing the Boulevard offer a good variety close together, so you can visit a wide selection by *shikara* (gondolalike boat) before choosing. Just drop into the ones that take your fancy (the boatman may nudge you towards those that give him better commission). Their proximity to shore makes it relatively easy to hail a *shikara* should you need to 'escape'.

A second row of boats directly behind in golden Dal Lake is still easily accessible but quieter, with sunset views. Houseboats further out offer beguiling solitude but leave you prey to pressures from owners. Nagin Lake houseboats also suffer somewhat from isolation but there are many good options. In almost any location, visits from *shikara*-borne souvenir sellers are an unavoidable irritation.

Prices

Officially prices are 'set' by the **Houseboat Owners Association** (☑ 2450326; www. houseboatowners.org; TRC Rd; ⊗ 10am-5pm Mon-Sat) varying between ₹600/900 (category D) and ₹3150/4800 (deluxe) for a double room including half-board. However, when occupancy is low you might pay only a fraction of that.

Always double-check what's included and how much: food and drink (Only dhal and rice? Is tea extra? Second helpings charged extra?); heating (usually ₹400 extra); *shikara* transfers and/or use of a canoe (Once or unlimited?). Ideally, get this in writing and check the price of extras.

fully set above hectares of manicured lawns. The Durbar Hall features royal portraits and one of the world's largest handmade carpets. Sumptuous. Big internet discounts are possible.

City Forest BOUTIQUE HOTEL **$$$**
(☑ 2500314; www.royalkhazir.com; s/d/ste ₹8500/ 9500/12,000; ❄ 🖥) Oddly hidden up a steep, narrow lane, City Forest provides all the elegant amenities you'd hope for in a classy

JESUS IN KASHMIR?

To many, the theory sounds crackpot or even blasphemous, but several authors have claimed that Jesus' 'lost years' (between his youth and the start of his ministry when he was 30) were spent in India where Buddhism moulded his ideas. This theory gained a lot of publicity in the 1890s when Russian traveller/spy Nicolas Notovitch 'discovered' supposedly corroborating documents at Hemis Gompa (Ladakh), described in his book *Unknown Life of Jesus Christ*. The Hemis documents have since gone missing.

The Quran (surah 4, verses 156–157) suggests that Jesus' death on the cross was a 'grievous calumny' and that 'they slew him not'. Khwaja Nazir Ahmad's *Jesus in Heaven & Earth* further postulates that Jesus (as Isa, Yuz Asaf or Youza Asouph) retired to Kashmir post-crucifixion and was buried in Srinagar. Holger Kersten's *Jesus Lived in India*, widely sold in Indian traveller bookshops, agrees and even gives a floor plan of that tomb at Rozabal in Srinagar. The roughly four-million-strong Ahmadiyya sect (who consider themselves Muslim but are not recognised as such by some Islamic communities) also subscribe to the idea of Jesus dying in Kashmir (www.alislam.org/topics/jesus), seeing Christ's mortality as underlining his role as a human prophet.

boutique hotel along with quirky touches including toilets disguised as wooden trunks. The open-fronted lobby sports Tim Burton-esque high-backed chairs and there's an excellent rooftop restaurant that serves a wide range of cuisines and has a tree-screened city view. Small outside swimming pool.

Eating

Inexpensive *dhaba* (snack bar) restaurants are dotted along the Boulevard. For tikka tandoori snacks or meals (half/whole chicken ₹170/320, mutton tube ₹80) stroll along Khayam St, a block north of Dalgate.

Krishna Vaishno Dhaba VEGETARIAN $
(Durganag Rd; mains ₹32-65, rice ₹38; ⊘8am-10.30pm) The 'original' Srinagar *dhaba*, Krishna Vaishno serves tasty, inexpensive pre-cooked vegetarian meals, dosas and South Indian breakfasts.

Ahdoo's KASHMIRI $$
(☑ 2472593; Residency Rd; mains ₹280-350, rice ₹70; ⊘9am-11pm) This longstanding middle-class restaurant with speedy service and pewter finger bowls is a sedate venue for tasting Kashmiri delicacies. For those that don't want lamb, there's also a range of Chinese and vegetarian choices. There's a tree-shaded terrace section outside and a bakery downstairs.

Coffea Arabica MULTICUISINE $$
(MA Rd; meals ₹160-350; ⊘9am-10.30pm) Behind a half-timbered facade, this spacious modern eatery features movie images and has various individually designed serving stations (Arabic, Chinese, Italian, coffee-and-cake) plus a little bookshop. Trout (₹500) available on occasions.

Solomon's Barbeque MULTICUISINE $$
(Durganag Rd; mains ₹60-275; ⊘3pm-9pm) Solomon's Barbeque offers seasonal tandoori trout at ₹275. It's one of three fast-food-style places clumped in front of Hotel Akbar Residency along with Chaatzz and Café Coffee Day.

🍷 Drinking

Srinagar's Muslim mores mean that alcohol isn't served in restaurants and there are just a tiny handful of bars, mostly in upmarket hotels.

Cafe Robusta CAFE
(MA Rd; coffee ₹42-90; ⊘9.30am-9.30pm; 🛜) Srinagar's hip young set sip a selection of coffees or share sundaes and smoothies in a pseudo-Western upstairs lounge with chess and wi-fi (per hour ₹50) available.

Dar Bar BAR
(cocktails ₹690; ⊘9am-10.30pm) Even if you can't afford to stay at the Lalit Grand Palace Hotel, consider sipping a drink at its little bar or, better still, on the hotel's glorious lawns with indulgent views towards Dal Lake. Add 30% tax to menu prices.

Wine Shops WINE SHOP
(Heemal Hotel Shopping Complex, Boulevard; ⊘10am-8pm Sat-Thu, closed during Ramadan) These shops are rare takeaway outlets for alcoholic beverages.

🛍 Shopping

The Boulevard has several emporia flogging Kashmiri souvenirs, including elegantly painted papier-mâché boxes and carved walnut woodwork, plus cashmere and pashmina shawls, originally popularised in Europe by Napoleon's wife Josephine. Saffron, cricket bats and dried fruits are widely sold around Lal Chowk. Carpet-selling 'factories' line the road to Shalimar Bagh targeting tour groups. Unless you know how to assess carpet values, consider erring instead towards much cheaper chain-stitched *gabbas* (Kashmiri rugs with appliqué) or floral *namdas* (felted wool carpets). Be aware that your guide, driver or even hotelier may be getting hefty commissions unless you show up without 'help'.

Kashmir Government Arts Emporium HANDICRAFTS
(📞2452783; Bund; ⏰10am-5.30pm Mon-Sat) A veritable museum of Kashmiri crafts at marked, fixed prices in the century-old half-timbered former British Residency Building (restored 2004).

Gulshan Books BOOKS
(www.gulshanbooks.net; Residency Rd; ⏰9.30am-8.30pm Mon-Sat) Stocks a wide selection of English-language books including plenty on Kashmiri history and politics.

ℹ Information

ATMs are widespread, especially on Residency Rd. Beware of freelance moneychangers offering improbably good rates – you're likely to get forged banknotes.

Internet cafe (Old Gagribal Rd; per hr ₹30; ⏰9am-11pm)

Tourism reception centre (📞2456291; www.jktourism.org; ⏰24hr) With perseverance you might actually find answers to your questions.

Transcorp International (Boulevard; ⏰9.30am-6pm Mon-Sat) Half-hidden between hotels Sunshine and Dal View, this money-changer offers good cash rates.

ℹ Getting There & Away

AIR

Arrival Forms ask the name of your hotel. Any random hotel will do. Don't be bullied into believing that you HAVE to go to the place you wrote. You don't.

Departure Srinagar's new airport is 1.2km behind a high-security barrier where there can be long queues for baggage and body screening. You'll need to show an air ticket (or e-ticket confirmation print-out) to get through so don't come to the airport hoping to buy a ticket on departure. Allow at least two hours' leeway.

Airlines

Air India (📞2450247; www.airindia.in; Boulevard) Delhi, Jammu, Leh

GoAir (www.goair.in) Delhi, Jammu (Leh in summer)

IndiGo (www.goindigo.in) Delhi, Jammu, Mumbai

Jet Airways (📞2480801; Residency Rd) Delhi, Jammu

SpiceJet (www.spicejet.com) Delhi, Jammu, Amritsar

BUS

J&K SRTC bus station (📞2455107) has buses to Jammu (class B/A/18-seater bus ₹230/321/445, 10 hours) at 7.30am and Leh (class B/A ₹919/1300, two days) at 8am via Kargil (₹475/650, 10 hours). If there's sufficient demand, day-return excursion buses run to the mountain 'resorts' Sonamarg (₹325, 87km northeast), Gulmarg (₹310, 52km west), Pahalgam (₹325, 100km southeast) and Yousmarg (₹310, 55km southwest), all departing between 7.30am and 8.30am. Book one day ahead.

The giant Batmalu bus station, west of centre, has services thrice daily to Sonamarg and frequent Sumos to Tangmarg for Gulmarg. Panthachowk bus station, 8km south of the centre, has various buses to Pampore and Anantnag (change for Pahalgam).

Two private buses to Kargil (₹350) leave before 5am from Kaksarai near SMHS hospital in Karam Nagar (western Srinagar).

JEEP

From **Tourist Taxi Stand 1** (Residency Rd) there are shared jeeps to Leh (per person ₹1800, 6am) and Jammu (per person/vehicle ₹600/4200, 6.30am to 9am). The well-paved Srinagar–Jammu road has many scenic points and snow is cleared year-round, but it's also exceedingly busy – a thundering conveyer belt of trucks and army convoys jams up entirely during *hartals* (strikes) and when landslides block the passes. Be prepared to fly at such times. Kargil shared jeeps (per person/car ₹700/5300) depart around 7am from both Kaksarai and from Tourist Taxi Stand 1. Dozens of stands offer jeep rental. Return prices include Pahalgam (₹2616), Sonamarg (₹2452) and Gulmarg (₹1635). Your hotel might offer better deals.

TRAIN

Local services only. The Banihal–Qazigund–Anantnag–Srinagar (Nowgam)–Baramulla line is already built. The planned connection to Katra and Jammu should be finished by around 2017 via the world's highest rail bridge.

ℹ️ Getting Around

Autorickshaws cost ₹40 for short hops, ₹200 per hour for tours. Don't rely on being able to find an autorickshaw or boatman after 9.30pm.

Airport taxis cost ₹550.

Shikaras charge ₹20 for the shortest houseboat-to-shore hops or ₹200 to ₹300 for longer excursions.

Minibuses are overcrowded with destination boards only in Urdu. Useful routes include Lal Chowk–Hazratbal and Lal Chowk–Shalimar Bagh via Dal Lake's south bank and Nishat Bagh.

Around Srinagar

Gulmarg

📋 01954 / ELEV 2730M

Pine-fringed Gulmarg is the nearest India gets to a ski resort. It's not so much a town as a twisting 4km-long loop of road ringing the undulating 'Meadow of Flowers' after which it's named. The meadow is given some visual focus by the demure 1890s Anglican **Church of St Mary's** sitting on a lonely hillock, accessed off the dead-end road linking historic **Gulmarg Golf Club** (📋 9906866941; clubhouse admission ₹5, 9 holes/18 holes/driving range/club rental ₹1200/1800/500/500) to the 1965 neo-colonialstyle **Hotel Highlands Park** (www.hotelhighlandspark.com). However, the main reason to come to Gulmarg is to venture up through the backing stands of mature pines towards the bald ridge of **Mt Afarwat**. This can be done on foot or with ponies (₹300 per hour) but is easiest using the two-stage **gondola cable car** (www.gulmarggondola.com; cable car 1st/2nd stage ₹300/500, day-pass ₹700/1200; ⏰ 9am-3pm, lower stage till 4pm) that whisks you to 3747m for outstanding clear-day views, reputedly encompassing Nanga Parbat (the world's ninth-highest mountain, across in Pakistan). Booking online can save long queues in peak season (May and June), but service is cancelled in bad weather (or during civil unrest) and getting a refund can prove annoying. The gondola's base-station is around 1km west of the bus stand.

Gulmarg offers over 40 accommodation choices. In July, musty, ageing rooms average ₹2000, newer ones over ₹5000 a night. Prices dip around 20% in winter and can fall massively during troubles in Srinagar and in less popular months (notably September). For skiers and hikers the most convenient accom-modation is on the rise just north of the gondola where you'll find the following options.

Falak Hut   HOTEL $$
(📋 9596226630, 9469780697; r ₹1500-2000) In an unpretentious but well-kept old chalet, Gulmarg's best-value budget rooms share a common lounge and kitchen and are relatively well appointed for the price. The two downstairs have en-suite bathrooms. The same company manages the more dated **Shanu Hut** (r ₹1200-1500) behind Hotel Pine Palace.

Heevan Retreat   HOTEL $$$
(📋 254455; www.ahadhotelsandresorts.com; s/d/ste ₹5000/6500/8000, dinner buffet ₹550) Several new hotels are under construction but for now the Heevan remains head and shoulders above most competition. Fresh pine interiors are inlaid with crewel embroidery panels, there's a well-kept lawn and an enticing lounge with rocking chairs.

ℹ️ Getting There & Away

Shared jeeps run from Srinagar's Batmalu Bus Station to Tangmarg (₹60) where you change for the last 13km to Gulmarg (₹30) up a series of hairpins through the splendid pine forest. Hiring a private day-return jeep from Srinagar to Gulmarg costs ₹1635 per vehicle. All transport usually has to park around 1km short of the gondola: good business for the horsemen.

Yousmarg

Around 50km south of Srinagar, Yousmarg is a pine-framed grassy hilltop meadow where, according to some versions of the Jesus-in-Kashmir theory (p272), Christ spent some of his post-cruxifiction 'retirement'. Pleasantly rural without particular grandeur, the site is popular with noisy weekend picnickers and is now being touted for development as a major climbing, sports and pony-trekking base. However, when we visited midweek we were the only tourists. Apart from two rather dismal ₹1000 private guesthouses, accommodation is so far limited to the widely scattered large cottages of the **YDA Tourist Complex** (📋 9797044827; www.yda.co.in; dm/d ₹200/1000, 2-/3-room cottages ₹6000/7000). One of these has a great-value dormitory, a maybe-open restaurant (mains ₹55 to ₹185) and a pony-rental service (around ₹900 to beauty-spot Sang-i-Safed).

The tour complex is 4km past a toll booth on a bumpy, 8.5km part-paved road from Char-i-Sharif. That's a sprawling hilltop pil-

SKIING AT GULMARG

In season (mid-December to mid-March) Gulmarg is famed among serious skiers for its high-altitude powder. Apart from beginners' drag-lifts on the meadow, ski access is by the gondola cable car. The basin enfolding the gondola is patrolled and blasted for avalanche prevention, but the vast majority of other couloirs and forest tracks descending from the 10km-long ridge are unsecured so it's essential to check conditions carefully. Gulmarg Avalanche Centre (http://gulmargavalanche.org) gives detailed snow and safety updates throughout the season, and its resources section lists contacts for approved ski guides (per day ₹2000) – highly advised for Gulmarg first timers. Associated outfit **Gulmarg Snow Safety** (http://gulmargsnowsafety.com) runs half- and full-day guided skis, and Australia-based **Bills Trips** (www.billstrips.com) offers complete packages.

Quality ski-gear can be hired from **Kashmir Alpine** (☏254638; www.kashmiralpine. com) outside Hotel Highlands Park and from the **Indian Institute of Skiing and Mountaineering** (☏214037; www.iismgulmarg.com) which also offers great-value ski packages for Indian nationals.

Après-ski bars at Hotels Pine Palace, Alpine Ridge and Highlands Park only serve alcohol in the winter season. It is possible to ski down through the forest all the way to Tangmarg where there are more hotels.

grimage town celebrating Kashmir's 'patron saint' Sheikh Nuraddin-Wali (1377–1440). His shrine is covered by a vast new mosque with nine storey minaret, which replaced a previous structure that burnt down during a 1995 battle.

South of Srinagar

The following could be easily visited as part of a one-day jeep trip to Pahalgam from where you could continue (another day) by bus to Jammu.

Pampore & Sangam

Straggling between Km279 and Km281 at Srinagar's southern limits, dusty Pampore is India's saffron capital. In October the violet crocuses, whose yellow stamens produce the saffron, bloom colourfully around Km276, but in summer you'll see nothing but dusty fields. Between Km255 and Km257, Sangam specialises in cricket bats sold from countless roadside stores.

Awantipora (Avantipura)

Beside the Jammu highway in Awantipora, 30km south of Srinagar, lies the ruin of 9th-century **Avantiswamin Temple** (Indian/foreigner ₹5/100; ☉dawn-dusk). The stone blocks are massive with numerous column bases, but most carvings have long been defaced. The essentially similar but even less complete **Avantisvara Shiva Temple** (Km226.9) can be visited on the same ticket.

Mattan (Martand)

The Lidder Valley towards Pahalgam branches off the Jammu road at Khanabal/Anantnag, a place that is infamous as a trouble spot at times of unrest. Around 9km towards Pahalgam, many visitors stop to visit the large Shiva temple in Mattan, but most miss Mattan's vastly more interesting 8th-century **Sun Temple** (admission free; ☉dawn-dusk). Though ruined, the site feels more complete than Awantipora and retains much of an arcade of Doric columns that create an almost Mediterranean impression. The surrounding gardens are pretty and peaceful. From Mattan, follow 'Kehrbal' signs, climbing 1.5km up short hairpins towards Achabal then veering left for another 1km.

Aishmugam

At Km23 of the Anantnag–Pahalgam road, a 500m lane followed by a sweaty beggar-plagued stairway leads up to a hilltop shrine complex devoted to 15th-century Sufi holy man Zainalabddin Wali. The main section is within a heavily adorned cave worn smooth by adoring hands. Expect queues on Fridays.

Pahalgam

POP 6000 / ELEV 2740M

Surrounded by high peaks, the Lidder and Seshnag Rivers tumble down picturesque, deep-cut mountain valleys covered with giant conifers. The surrounding mountains contain many beauty spots and over 20 lakes to which countless guides and horsemen are more than keen to take you for a ride. The most popular hike of all is the multi-day *yatra* to Amarnath. The main accommodation centre is the sprawling low-rise resort town of Pahalgam, with over 230 hotels and guesthouses, several manicured parks, temples for different religions and a super mountain-ringed **golf course** (9-/18-holes US$24/32, club rental ₹700; ⊘ 6am-6pm). **Rafting** (per person ₹350; ⊘10am-6pm) a 2.5km stretch of the Lidder is possible from a point 12km west of Pahalgam (taxi ₹500) once a group of six or more people has assembled.

For a short, easy unguided walk, heading up the very pretty Lidder Valley towards Aru gets you fairly rapidly away from the worst of the pilgrim crowds. Given around three hours, horsemen will be more than happy to take you on a standard roadless circuit to a lake, viewpoint and upland meadow for ₹750. Guesthouses are likely to encourage you to go for longer treks that take you well into the glorious alpine scenery. While the landscapes are undoubtedly lovely, prices tend to be far higher than for equivalent hikes in Ladakh so, if your time is limited, think carefully as to which area suits you better.

🛏 Sleeping & Eating

Accommodation prices fluctuate up to 600%, peaking during the Amarnath *yatra* season. Choice is vast, though most places close in winter. Guesthouses stretch almost 4km along Pahalgam's long main road, but few are recommendable. Better options tend to be set close to the river, especially along the rougher lane that follows the river beside the back of the golf course to the 'second bridge' near the Laripura bus stand.

Brown Palace   GUESTHOUSE $$
(🖉 243255; www.brownpalace.in; r ₹2000-2500, without bathroom ₹300-700) Fronted with bark and wooden shingles, this old-fashioned traveller haunt has rooms with lots of varnished dark hardboard/wood that are about the best value options in Pahalgam. Decorated with roots and horns, the dining room looks out across the lawn and there's a small library of English-language books.

Himalaya House   GUESTHOUSE $$
(🖉 243072; www.himalayafunandtours.com; ₹2000-4500) Directly across the quiet laneway from the Hotel Pine Spring, this spick-and-span place feels like a homely guesthouse, but most of the rooms have been rebuilt and upgraded to hotel standard. There are cheaper versions in the roof and in a second house across the way, but all share a delightful, large lawn garden that forms an island in a pretty section of river.

Hotel Pine Spring   BOUTIQUE HOTEL $$$
(🖉 243386; www.hotelpinespring.com; s/d/ste ₹5000/5500/7000, winter ₹3300/3600/4800) Stylish new design hotel with raked, open lounge-lobby areas, dried floral displays and high-quality fittings. Nice lawn and big view terrace (undergoing reconstruction).

Log Inn   COFFEEHOUSE, VEGETARIAN $$
(www.pahalgamhotel.com; veg mains from ₹110, espresso ₹56) Cakes, good coffee and vegetarian meals served in a timber cabin cafe where barrel seats are backed in sheepskin. Next door the co-owned **Troutbeat** (fish meals ₹390-530) has similar decor but serves fish meals. Both front the venerable 1931 Pahalgam Hotel in the upper bazaar area.

ℹ Information

Tourist office (⊘8am-8pm, 9am-6pm during Ramadan) ATM outside.

ℹ Getting There & Away

Local buses from Anantnag (₹30, one hour) drive right through Pahalgam village to Laripora bus stand. However, shared jeeps and J&KSTRC buses stop in central Pahalgam behind the tourist office. Most days, buses depart at 7.30am to Jammu (₹190) and 4.30pm to Srinagar (₹180). In *yatra* time there are many supplementary services.

Union rules mean that only local taxis are allowed to drive to Aru (₹550, 12km from the donkey stables) and Chandawari (₹600) – 16km from Laripora.

SOUTHERN JAMMU & KASHMIR

The state's predominantly Hindu southern region swelters at the edge of the plains, with Jammu forming the rail hub and winter capital. *Yatri* (pilgrims) flood to Katra (April–June and October–December) and transit Jammu en route to Amarnath (July), but foreign visitors are rare.

Jammu

📞 0191 / POP 612,000 / ELEV 327M

Although Hindu Jammu dubs itself the 'city of temples', few of these are historically compulsive, and for western tourists there's little pressing need to hang around longer than necessary to make transport connections to Amritsar, Srinagar or Dharamsala.

Half a dozen widely spaced minor sights are included in a three- to four-hour sightseeing package offered by some autorickshaw drivers (₹350 to ₹450) including the glitteringly colourful Krishna and Shiva caves of **Gupawala Mandir** (Pinkho Rd), the large but squat 19th-century **Bahu Fort** and the garish **Har-ki-Paori Mandir**, a family of giant concrete gods in a modern, Disneyesque style. Driver Tarsem (📞9469238028) speaks decent English.

Mubarak Mandi
HINDU TEMPLE

If you have time to kill, the most intriguing sight is the large, touchingly decrepit Mubarak Mandi, which was once the palace complex of Jammu's 19th-century royalty. The Durba Hall is one part that remains accessible, as the **Dogra Art Gallery** (foreigner/Indian ₹50/10; ⊙10am-5pm Tue-Sun), a museum featuring bronzes, armaments, instruments, 9th-century carvings and Kushan coins.

Amar Mahal
PALACE

(www.karansingh.com/amml; foreigner/Indian ₹100/20; ⊙9am-1pm & 2-6pm Tue-Sun, to 5pm Apr-Sep) In the 20th century the Maharajas moved further up the ridge to a very European brick mansion, the Amar Mahal with its token castle-style tower. Rather than paying the entry fee to see the rajas' canopied gold throne, you might prefer to observe the scene over a cocktail (₹250) at the refreshingly air-conditioned Polo Lounge bar of the Hari Niwas Palace Hotel, which shares the same manicured cliff-top lawns.

Raghunath Mandir
HINDU TEMPLE

(Raghunath Bazaar; by donations; ⊙6am-9.30pm) The large, 19th-century Raghunath Mandir marks the heart of the older city and features several pavilions containing thousands of what look like grey pebbles set in concrete. In fact, these are saligrams (ammonite fossils) symbolically representing the myriad deities of the Hindu pantheon. Requests for donations are almost as plentiful. You'll be asked to deposit bags, cameras, phones and even pens before entering.

🛏 Sleeping

Hotels are spread all over town but Vaishno Devi pilgrims fill virtually every bed during peak *yatra* periods. Basic budget options are plentiful around Vinaik Bazaar (a block southeast of the bus station) but names such as Hotel Touch Wood give a premonition of their chancy nature. If booking online, be aware that many 'Jammu' hotels listed are actually 45km away in Katra.

Green View Hotel
GUESTHOUSE $

(📞2573906; 69 Chand Nagar; r ₹150-900; ❄) Quieter, friendlier and more accustomed to foreigners than most Vinaik Bazaar options, the best air-con rooms here are small but freshly re-tiled. It's hidden at the end of an unprepossessing dead-end side lane east of Jewel Chowk.

Ashoka New Diamond
HOTEL $$

(📞2576737; Rani Mandir; s/d ₹1290/1890; ❄) Large and relatively smart rooms are good value – at least while they remain brand new. However, the entrance and corridors feel unfinished and most rooms are windowless, so are likely to be susceptible to damp in the longer term.

Hotel Samrat
HOTEL $$

(📞2547402; s/d from ₹1810/1980; ❄@) The neatest of numerous options as you leave the bus station, the 30-room Samrat has lashings of marble and Chagall prints on wooden backboards. The best rooms are relatively plush, with new sofas, fitted wardrobes and flat-screen TVs.

Fortune Riviera
HOTEL $$$

(📞2561415; www.fortunehotels.in; Gulab Singh Marg; s/d from ₹4950/5280; ❄@🛜) Jammu's most stylish address includes a glass elevator in the four-storey atrium, a variety of artistically conceived bed posts and the most businesslike approach to hotel service. Wi-fi costs ₹200/500 per hour/day.

🍴 Eating & Drinking

Between Jewel Chowk and Vinaik Bazaar are several inexpensive *dhabas*, a fast-food place, wine shops and two bars. City Square Mall has Domino's Pizza, Barista Coffee and three other air-conditioned restaurants.

Jammu

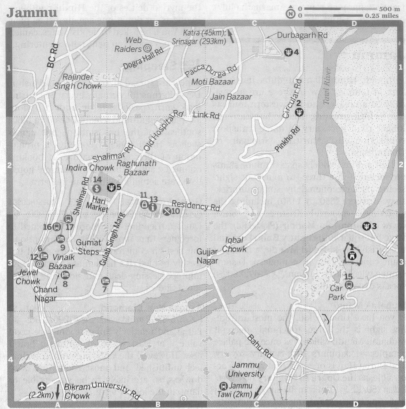

JAMMU & KASHMIR (INCLUDING LADAKH) JAMMU

Residency Rd has a wide range of options from cheap fish barbecues (near Raghunath Mandir) and air-con vegetarian restaurants to ever-reliable Café Coffee Day opposite KC Plaza.

Falak   INDIAN $$
(☏2520770; www.kcresidency.com; 7th fl, KC Residency Hotel, Residency Rd; mains veg/nonveg/fish ₹260/265/490, rice ₹155; ☺12.30-10.45pm) This revolving restaurant serves superb pan-Indian cuisine and offers 360-degree views of the crowded Jammu townscape. Although views are best before sunset, the floor only starts spinning after 7.30pm.

ⓘ Information

Cyber Point (Jewel Chowk; per hr ₹20; ☺9am-10pm) Tiny but cheap central internet access.
J&K Tourism (☏2548172; www.jktdc.org; Residency Rd; ☺8am-8pm Mon-Sat) Refreshingly air-conditioned reception centre. Just west is a

well-presented government arts emporium and an English-language bookshop.
State Bank of India (Hari Market; ☺10am-4pm Mon-Fri) Exchanges currency and travellers cheques. Has an ATM.

ⓘ Getting There & Away

AIR

Air India (☏2456086; www.indianairlines.in; J&K Tourism complex; ☺10am-4.45pm Mon-Sat) Delhi, Srinagar, Leh
GoAir (www.goair.in) Delhi, Srinagar, Leh, Mumbai
IndiGo (www.goindigo.in) Delhi, Srinagar
Jet Airways (www.jetairways.com) Delhi, Srinagar
SpiceJet (www.spicejet.com) Delhi, Srinagar, Jaipur, Hyderabad

BUS & JEEP

Private buses and shared jeeps depart from a chaotic **strip** in the shadow of the BC Rd (NH1A

Jammu

⊙ **Sights**
1	Bahu Fort	D3
	Dogra Art Gallery	(see 4)
2	Gupawala Mandir	C1
3	Har-ki-Paori Mandir	D3
4	Mubarak Mandi	C1
5	Raghunath Mandir	B2

🛏 **Sleeping**
6	Ashoka New Diamond	A3
7	Fortune Riviera	A3
8	Green View Hotel	A3
9	Hotel Samrat	A3

🍴 **Eating**
10	Falak	B2

🛍 **Shopping**
	J&K Government Arts Emporium	(see 11)
11	Jay Kay Bookhouse	B2

ℹ **Information**
12	Cyber Point	A3
13	J&K Tourism	B2
14	State Bank of India	A2

ℹ **Transport**
	Jet Airways	(see 7)
15	Matador 108 Terminus	D3
16	Private Buses & Shared Jeeps	A3
17	Public Bus Station	A3

Hwy) overpass. Public buses use the big, rotting concrete **bus station** complex immediately east. Destinations:

Amritsar Up to 30 buses daily (₹145, six hours) via Pathankot in Punjab (₹71, 2½ hours).

Chamba Bus (₹195, seven hours, 8.05am).

Chandigarh Private buses (₹600) depart around 9.30pm. Change in Chandigarh for Manali.

Dalhousie Bus (₹185, six hours, 8am).

Delhi Public buses 13 times daily (₹390, 13 hours) plus many private services leaving between 5pm and 10.30pm (seat/sleeper ₹500/800, luxury AC ₹700/900).

Dharamsala Direct bus at 8.30am (₹200, six hours) or take an Amritsar service and change at Pathankot. Taxis cost around ₹4800.

Katra Buses, minibuses and taxis depart very regularly from both bus and train stations.

Srinagar Buses run daily departing at 7am (class B/A/18-seater bus ₹230/321/445, 10 hours).

Shared/chartered jeeps (from ₹400/3000) depart from early morning till around 11am and late in the evening from both bus and train stations. Some operators will charge less if they think they can sell you a houseboat package. Beware!

TRAIN

Jammu Tawi, Jammu's main train station, is well south of the river, 5km from the bus station.

Agra Rourkela Express (18810) departing 2.30pm (sleeper/3AC/2AC ₹307/864/1320) is slower (18 hours) but arrives at a more sociable hour than the daytime Malwa (12920, from ₹158).

Amritsar Muri Express (18110) departs at 2.30pm (₹124, four hours).

Delhi Uttar Sampark Kranti Express (12446) departs at 8.10pm arriving at 6.10am (sleeper/3AC/2AC ₹261/705/1045).

The new northbound railway currently reaches Udhampur but should continue to Katra by 2014 and Srinagar around 2017, crossing the Chenab River on the world's tallest rail bridge.

ℹ Getting Around

Turn left on exiting the airport grounds on a busy road – local taxis (₹200 to Jewel Chowk) wait in the forecourt of the Durga Filling Station.

From town to the airport pay around ₹120 for an autorickshaw or ₹10 for a 'Satwari'-bound minibus.

Short autorickshaw hops cost ₹40, train station to bus station ₹120.

Overloaded minibuses and curiously stretched 'Matadors' charge ₹10 per hop; route 117 links bus and train stations, 108 to the fort.

Around Jammu

Accessed by foot, palanquin or helicopter from nearby Katra, the latter-day **Vaishno Devi Shrine** (www.maavaishnodevi.org) is one of India's busiest pilgrim sites. It attracts millions of domestic visitors but its appeal is hard to understand for most non-Hindus.

Southwest of Udhampur, Ramnagar has a recently restored historic palace but it hardly justifies the long journey. Be aware that Ramnagar station is around 30km from Ramnagar.

Between Udhampur and Srinagar, the road winds up a vertical kilometre into mature coniferous woodlands where, between Kud and Patnitop lies a sprinkling of resort hotels.

JAMMU & KASHMIR (INCLUDING LADAKH) AROUND JAMMU

Himachal Pradesh

Why Go?

With spectacular peaks and gorgeous river valleys, Himachal is India's outdoor adventure playground. From trekking and climbing to rafting, paragliding and skiing, if it can be done in the mountains, it can be done here. Yet Himachal offers much more than just a quick fix of alpine adrenaline.

Across the state, traditional Himachali culture flourishes amid Himalayan landscapes. Villages perched on staggering slopes enchant with fairy tale wood-and-stone architecture and the easygoing grace of the people who live there. Elsewhere, hill stations appeal with colonial-era charm, while groovy backpacker magnets lure with their blissed-out vibe and mountain trails.

In many places, you might think you've stumbled into Tibet. But the ancient Buddhist monasteries, troves of Buddhist arts, and the home-away-from-home of the Dalai Lama are just another part of the essence of Himachal.

Best Places to Stay

➡ Chonor House (p326)

➡ Norling Guest House (p331)

➡ Orchard Hut (p338)

Best Off the Beaten Track

➡ Nako(p347)

➡ Lhalung Monastery (p346)

➡ Chitkul (p295)

When to Go
Manali

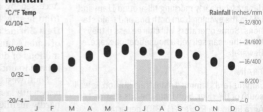

Jan/Feb Tibetan New Year is celebrated across Himachal.

May–Jun & mid-Sep–Oct Outside the monsoon season is perfect for trekking; plenty of festivals in October.

Nov–Apr Great for skiers, but snow blocks the high passes to the Lahaul and Spiti Valleys.

Food

Himachal is the best place in India to get a taste of authentic Tibetan cuisine. *Momos* (steamed or fried dumplings), *thukpa* (noodle soup) and *thenthuk* (noodle squares) are found virtually everywhere. Tasty and cheap, these dishes hit the spot when you're not in the mood for curry.

Carnivores enjoy traditional Himachali food, which frequently features chicken or fresh trout from the region's streams. Most vegetarian specialities are flavourful dhal-based concoctions, often mixed with yogurt, *paneer* (unfermented cheese made from milk curd) or potatoes. Himachal is also known for producing India's finest apples, harvested in autumn.

DON'T MISS

McLeod Ganj isn't called 'Little Lhasa' just because it's the seat of the Tibetan government-in-exile; it's infused with a living blend of ancient and contemporary Tibetan culture, from arts to religion to food. It's the perfect place to volunteer with the refugee community, study Tibetan or simply learn how to make Tibetan *momos*.

Further east, Himachal's stretch of the **Great Himalayan Circuit** crosses towering mountain passes as it traverses the spectacular **Lahaul** and **Spiti Valleys**. In a remote land of rugged, elemental beauty, you'll find countless trekking opportunities beside some of the highest villages and Buddhist monasteries on Earth. A favourite gateway to this region is **Manali**, Himachal's outdoor adventure capital, with activities from the relaxed (walking) to the intense (mountaineering or heli-skiing) to the absurd (zorbing).

Top State Festivals

➡ **Losar** (⊙ Jan/Feb; McLeod Ganj, p320, Spiti, p342) Tibetan New Year is celebrated with processions, music and dancing, and masked performances by monks in Buddhist monasteries.

➡ **Ladarcha Fair** (⊙ Aug; Kaza, p343) An ancient trade fair celebrated in Spiti, these days with Buddhist dances, mountain sports and bustling rural markets.

➡ **Phulech Festival** (⊙ Sep/Oct; Kalpa, p296, Sangla, p294) Villagers throughout Kinnaur fill temple courtyards with flowers; oracles perform sacrifices and make predictions for the coming year.

➡ **Dussehra** (⊙ Oct; Kullu, p303) An intense celebration of the defeat of the demon Ravana, with a huge parade led by a chariot-bound god.

➡ **International Himalayan Festival** (⊙ 10-12 Dec; McLeod Ganj, p320) Celebrating the Dalai Lama's Nobel Peace Prize, this festival promotes peace and cultural understanding with Buddhist dances and music.

MAIN POINTS OF ENTRY

Shimla, Dharamsala and towns in the Kullu Valley are connected to Delhi by direct buses, while Shimla and Pathankot (in the Punjab) offer the nearest rail links. A long and wild road connects Manali to Leh, in Ladakh.

Fast Facts

➡ **Population**: 6.9 million
➡ **Area**: 55,673 sq km
➡ **Capital**: Shimla
➡ **Main languages**: Hindi, Pahari, Punjabi
➡ **Sleeping prices**: **$** below ₹1000, **$$** ₹1000 to ₹2500, **$$$** above ₹2500

Top Tip

If travelling between the Spiti and Kinnaur Valleys, foreigners must obtain an easy-to-get Inner Line Permit in Kaza (see boxed text, p344), Rekong Peo (p295) or Shimla (boxed text, p290). Solo travellers will find it easiest in Kaza.

Resources

➡ **Himachal Pradesh Tourism Development Corporation** (www.hptdc.nic.in/bus.htm)
➡ **Himachal Road Transport** Corporation (www.hrtc.gov.in)
➡ **Himachal Tourism** (www.hptdc.gov.in)
➡ **Himachal Tourist Guide** (www.himachaltouristguide.com)

HIMACHAL PRADESH

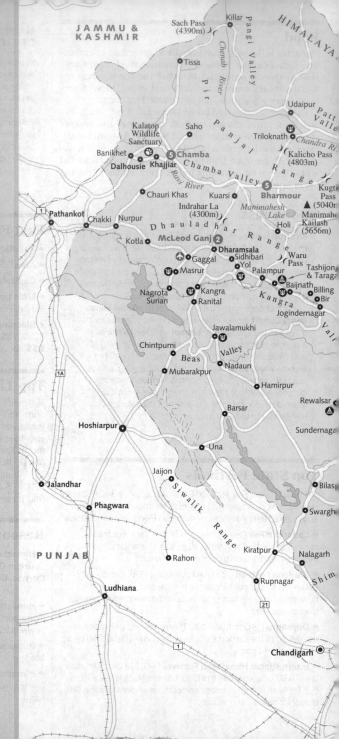

Himachal Pradesh Highlights

1 Take the toy train up to **Shimla** (p284), one of India's favourite hill stations

2 Earn karma credits by volunteering with the Tibetan refugees of **McLeod Ganj** (p320)

3 Ski, trek, climb, paraglide or raft in the backpacker playground of **Manali** (p306)

4 Chill out in the **Parvati Valley** (p300) and trek to the mountain village of **Malana** (p300)

5 Get off the tourist trail and visit centuries-old temples in **Chamba** (p336) and **Bharmour** (p339)

6 Cross the high mountain passes to the spectacular monasteries of **Tabo** (p346) and **Dhankar** (p345) in the remote Spiti Valley

7 Visit **Kalpa** (p296) or **Chitkul** (p295), charming villages with awesome Himalayan views in the upper Kinnaur Valley

History

Ancient trade routes dominate the history of Himachal Pradesh. Large parts of northern Himachal were conquered by Tibet in the 10th century, and Buddhist culture still dominates the mountain deserts of Lahaul and Spiti. The more accessible areas in the south of the state were divvied up between a host of rajas, ranas and *thakurs* (noblemen), creating a patchwork of tiny states, with Kangra, Kullu and Chamba at the top. Sikh rajas came to dominate the region by the early 19th century, signing treaties with the British to consolidate their power.

During the 19th century the British started creating little bits of England in the hills of Shimla, Dalhousie and Dharamsala. Shimla later became the British Raj's summer capital, and narrow-gauge railways were pushed through to Shimla and the Kangra Valley. The British slowly extended their influence until most of the region was under Shimla's control.

The state of Himachal Pradesh was formed after Independence in 1948, liberating many villages from the feudal system. In 1966 the districts administered from Punjab – including Kangra, Kullu, Lahaul and Spiti – were added and full statehood was achieved in 1971. Initially neglected by central government, Himachal has reinvented itself as the powerhouse of India, with huge hydroelectric plants providing power for half the country.

Climate

Himachal is a land of extremes, with some of the rainiest spots in India (around McLeod Ganj) as well as some of the driest (the Spiti Valley). When monsoons drench much of the state from mid-July to mid-September, landslides can block roads for hours or days, so plan on facing delays. From November to April, many mountainous areas, including the Manali–Leh road, are closed by snow, while others are just very cold! The best weather seasons statewide are May to mid-July and mid-September to early November.

ⓘ Getting There & Away

Along with the main points of entry, you can reach Shimla by toy train from Kalka and ride the old metre-gauge rail lines from Pathankot to Jogindarnagar.

ⓘ Getting Around

Steel your nerves – and your stomach – as rattletrap buses captained by drivers with Formula One fantasies hurtle over the narrow, twisting mountain roads that connect towns throughout the state. For local sightseeing, or the freedom to stop off at sights en route between towns, it often makes sense for couples or groups to hire a taxi for the day.

EASTERN HIMACHAL PRADESH

Eastern Himachal Pradesh is dominated by Shimla, the state capital, and the mountainous district of Kinnaur, which spreads east to the Tibetan border then loops north to Spiti, on one of Asia's great road trips. The official district website is http://hpshimla.nic.in.

Shimla

📞 0177 / POP 170,000 / ELEV 2205M

Strung out along a 12km ridge, Shimla is today an engaging blend of hill town and holiday resort. Indian vacationers stroll the Mall, while the lower bazaars flow with local life and with shops selling hardware, stationery, fabric and spices. Many of the hand-painted signs in the market are so retro they look like they haven't been changed since the 'Britishers' left. With cars banned from the main part of town, walking anywhere is very pleasant – even when huffing and puffing uphill.

Shimla sprawls for miles, but the official centre of town is Scandal Point. From here, the flat open area known as the Ridge stretches east to Christ Church, where trails lead uphill through forest towards the Jakhu Temple. A jagged line of snow-covered peaks is clearly visible from April to June, and in October and November. There are some particularly rewarding forested walks in this eastern part of Shimla.

The long, winding, pedestrian-only Mall runs west and east along the spine of the hill. South of here, the maze-like alleys of the bazaar cascade downhill steeply to the main Cart Rd, which has the train station, the old bus terminal and taxi stands. A passenger lift provides a quick route between the eastern Mall and Cart Rd.

Expect a stiff walk to your hotel. Porters will carry your luggage uphill for ₹80 to ₹100 but most double as touts, and hotels will increase your room tariff to cover their commission.

History

Until the British arrived, there was nothing at Shimla but a sleepy forest glade known as Shyamala (a local name for Kali – the Hindu goddess who is the destroyer of evil). Then a Scottish civil servant named Charles Kennedy built a summer home in Shimla in 1822 and nothing was ever the same again. By 1864 Shimla had developed into the official summer capital of the Raj, from where British bureaucrats ruled over a quarter of the world. Every summer until 1939, the entire government of India fled here from the sweltering heat of the plains, bringing with them hundreds of muleloads of files, forms and other paraphenalia of government.

When the Kalka–Shimla railway line was constructed in 1903, Shimla's status as India's premier hill station was assured. The city was even briefly the capital of Punjab until the map was redrawn in 1966.

At its height, Shimla became a 'centre of empire' and 'a place of philandering and frivolity', home to 'the cad, the card, the fortune-hunter and the flirt'. To this day the town carries echoes of Curzon, Kitchener and Kipling, all of whom spent many years living and working in Shimla. Kipling, in fact, used Shimla as a backdrop to parts of *Kim* and also *Plain Tales from the Hills*, a collection of short stories mostly written in Shimla.

◎ Sights & Activities

Jakhu Temple   HINDU TEMPLE
Shimla's most famous temple is dedicated to the Hindu monkey god Hanuman; it's therefore appropriate that hundreds of rhesus macaques loiter around, harassing devotees for *prasad* (temple-blessed food offerings). Set atop a hill awash in devotional music, the temple houses a small shrine surrounded by funky relief murals of Hanuman performing feats from the Ramayana. Nearby a newly built 33m-high statue of Hanuman towers over the town. The dining hall serves delicious all-you-can-eat plates of dhal, rice and *sabzi* (vegetables) from 10am to 4pm, so time your visit with meal time (for a donation). Getting here involves a

steep 30-minute hike from the east end of the Ridge. Primate alert: the monkeys on this route can be a menace, so bring a walking stick to discourage them. Taxis charge around ₹350 return.

Himachal State Museum   MUSEUM
(Indian/foreigner ₹10/50, camera/video ₹100/1500; ◎10am-5pm Tue-Sun) About 2.5km west of Scandal Point and a stiff walk up to the telecommunications mast, the state museum is home to an impressive collection of miniatures from Kangra and Rajasthan, as well as Chamba-style *rumal* embroideries, coins and jewellery, temple carvings, and the obligatory display of weapons.

★Viceregal Lodge   HISTORIC BUILDING
(Indian/foreigner ₹30/65, cameras ₹20; ◎9.15am-1pm & 2-5pm, to 7pm May-Jul, tours every 30min from 10.15am) Built as an official residence in 1888 for the British viceroys, the Viceregal Lodge looks like a cross between Harry Potter's Hogwarts School and the Tower of London. Every brick used in its construction was hauled up here by mule. Today it houses the Indian Institute of Advanced Study, but you can take a guided tour of the buildings. The easily missed photo gallery behind the ticket office is worth a visit.

Opposite the lodge entrance is the glum **Himalayan Bird Park** (admission ₹5; ◎10am-5pm), where you can see the iridescent monal pheasant, Himachal's state bird, among others.

The lodge is a 4.5km walk west from Scandal Point along the Mall; the path to the left of the Himachal State Museum entrance leads there in five minutes via Peterhof Hotel (itself a former viceregal residence).

Christ Church   CHURCH
(☑2652953; the Ridge; ◎10.30am-1pm & 2.15-5.30pm, services in English 9am Sun) This very English church dominates the top of the ridge and is the second-oldest church in northern India (the oldest is in Ambala in Haryana). Built between 1844 and 1857, it contains some moving Raj-era memorials and fine stained glass.

Gaiety Theatre   HISTORIC BUILDING
(☑2650173; www.gaiety.in; the Mall; admission ₹25, camera ₹25; ◎11am-1.30pm & 2-6pm Tue-Sun) This newly refurbished Victorian theatre (1877), modelled on the Garrick in London, reopened recently after a five-year restoration. Mr Gautam gives excellent guided

Shimla

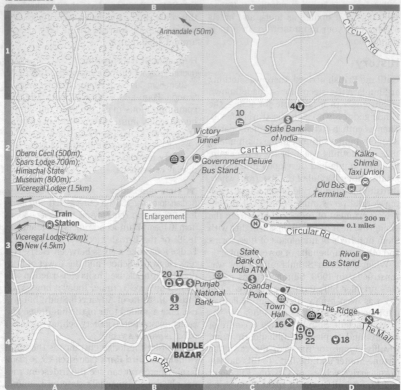

backstage tours through the bowels of the building, explaining its history as you appreciate the view from the Viceroy's private box. Local amateur dramatic clubs still give occasional performances on the Burmese teak stage.

Historic Buildings
HISTORIC BUILDING

The Ridge is lined with grand examples of British architecture, including the **Town Hall**, oddly reminiscent of the mansion in Hammer Horror films, and the mock-Tudor folly housing the post office (1883). At the west end of the Mall is the grand neo-Gothic **Gorton Castle**, formerly the government secretariat and now the Offices of the Accountant General. Above Shimla on the way to the Jakhu Temple, you can peek through the gates of **Rothney Castle**, former home of Allan Octavian Hume, which housed Asia's largest collection of stuffed birds during the 19th century.

Shimla Heritage Museum
GALLERY

(⊘11am-6pm Wed-Sun) **FREE** This gallery in the old United Services Club (1862) has some historic B&W photos of old Shimla, and helpful staff, though it's not a must-see. A new museum is planned here over the coming years.

Kali Bari Mandir
HINDU TEMPLE

About 1km west of the Ridge, on the hillside above the Mall, is the Bengali hut-style Kali Bari Mandir, enshrining an image of Kali as Shyamala. There are good views of Shimla from here.

Walking
WALKING

About 4km northwest of Scandal Point is **The Glen**, a former playground of British colonialists, selected for its similarity to the Scottish highlands. The road here passes through the flat green meadow at **Annandale**, once the site of the gymkhana club

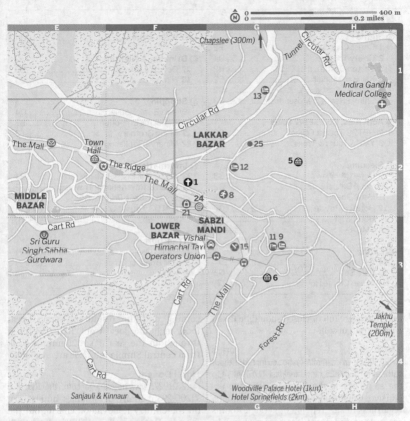

0 — 400 m
0 — 0.2 miles

Chapslee (300m)

Circular Rd
Tunnel

Indira Gandhi
Medical College

Circular Rd

13

The Mall

Town
Hall

The Ridge

LAKKAR
BAZAR

25

5

The Mall

12

MIDDLE
BAZAR

The Mall

1

24

8

21

Cart Rd

LOWER
BAZAR

SABZI
MANDI

Sri Guru
Singh Sabha
Gurdwara

Vishal
Himachal Taxi
Operators Union

15

11 9

Cart Rd

The Mall

6

Forest Rd

Jakhu
Temple
(200m)

Cart Rd

Sanjauli & Kinnaur

Woodville Palace Hotel (1km);
Hotel Springfields (2km)

and a famous racecourse, and still a popular venue for cricket and polo matches. The army runs the show here now, including a small army museum. The walk down here is pleasant but you should prebook a taxi for the return uphill slog.

There's an interesting temple of Kamna Devi and excellent views at **Prospect Hill**, about 4km west of Shimla and accessible from walking paths at the entrance to the Viceregal Lodge complex. About 2km further away on the Shimla–Kalka railway line, **Summer Hill** has pleasant, shady walks. Pretty **Chadwick Falls** are 2km further west, best visited just after the monsoon.

YMCA Tours & Treks   OUTDOOR ADVENTURE
(✆ 9857102657; www.himalayansites.com; the Ridge, Shimla YMCA) The affable and knowledgeable Anil Kumar runs day trips around Shimla as well as treks throughout Himachal and Uttarakhand.

☞ Tours

The **HPTDC tourist office** (Himachal Pradesh Tourist Development Corporation; www.hptdc.gov.in; Scandal Point; ◎ 9am-8pm, to 7pm mid-Jul–Sep & Dec-Mar) organises daily sightseeing bus tours to Narkanda, Chail and Narkanda, if there are enough passengers. The tours leave from the Rivoli bus stand at around 10.30am. Seats cost ₹250 to ₹290. Contact the office for current itineraries.

The taxi unions also offer one-day sightseeing tours to Kufri, Naldehra, Fagu and Mashobra (₹1000), and to Mashobra, Naldehra and Tattapani (₹1250).

🛏 Sleeping

Hotels in Shimla charge steep rates during the peak tourist season (April to June, October and Christmas). At all other times, ask about discounts of up to 40%. In winter, heating can usually be provided for an extra charge. Touts abound in Shimla – claims

Shimla

that hotels are full or closed should be taken with a grain of salt.

YMCA
HOTEL $

(☏2650021; ymcashimla@yahoo.co.in; s/d without bathroom ₹550/825, r incl breakfast ₹1761; @) Up the steps beside the Ritz Cineplex, the expansive, bright-red YMCA takes all comers, regardless of age, religion or gender. Rooms are neat and pleasant (the corner rooms in particular have great views), with immaculate shared bathrooms, and there's a nice sunset terrace and sun room, with an internet cafe and lockers for valuables. Rooms with bathroom offer poorer value. Book ahead April to July.

Hotel City View
HOTEL $

(☏2811666; jagdishthakur80@gmail.com; r ₹600-1400) This friendly place has a variety of well-kept rooms, the best of which are at the front and have bright views. The top floor has a pleasant shared terrace and there are discounts for singles, making this solid value for Shimla. It's next to the Deogar Hotel.

★ Spars Lodge
GUESTHOUSE $$

(☏2657908; Museum Rd; s/d ₹990/1400, ste from ₹1990; @) On the little road up to the Himachal State Museum, Spars is a budget place with an inviting, homey feel. It's bright, clean and airy with a lovely sunny dining room upstairs. The owners are welcoming and the restaurant serves great food, including local trout. Rates are fixed throughout the year. It's a 25-minute walk from central Shimla but taxis are available.

Hotel Doegar
HOTEL $$

(☏2811927; www.hoteldoegar.com; the Ridge; d ₹1200-2936) Many of Shimla's hotels turn on the chintzy honeymoon charm, but the friendly Doegar pulls out all the stops, with kinky mirrored ceilings and harem-style curtains. Beyond this, it's a decent midrange option, especially in shoulder season when discounts of 40% are standard. Rooms are small but vary a lot, so check out a selection. Expect to spend your time on the roof terrace with its unbeatable views of Shimla. It's a stiff 10-minute uphill walk from the lift.

Hotel Le Royale
HOTEL $$

(☏2651002; www.hotelleroyaleshimla.com; Jakhu Rd; r ₹1808-3850) Perched on the track up to Jakhu Temple, this modern hotel has plenty of charm, with fresh, bright and tastefully furnished rooms and great views. It's close to the Ridge but tucked away enough to feel private. The on-site Green Leaf restaurant is excellent.

Hotel White
HOTEL $$

(☏2656136; www.hotelwhitesimla.com; Lakkar Bazar; r ₹1320-1815, ste from ₹1980) Northeast of Scandal Point through the bustling bazaar, this place is well run and sensibly priced – rates are fixed all year. No two rooms are the same, but all are clean and comfortable and the better ones have terrace or balcony views. The huge suites are perfect for families.

Hotel Dalziel   HOTEL $$
(☑2652691; www.dalzielhotel.com; d from ₹715-4110) The historic 180-year-old Hotel Dalziel was being gutted and renovated at the time of research and you can expect a substantial price leap when it reopens. Well located at the west end of the Mall, the old building – a former colonial bungalow – has a lodge-like inner lounge, and there are cheaper and grimmer economy rooms in a lower block.

★Hotel Springfields   HERITAGE HOTEL $$$
(☑2621297; www.ushalexushotels.com; Chotta Shimla; r ₹4697; ❄🔲) Built for the wife of the raja of Sheikhapura and featuring charming drawing rooms, a lounge bar and immaculately trimmed lawns, Springfields is a perfect combination of colonial-era charm and mod cons that won't break the bank. It's just below Cart Rd in Chotta Shimla, a pleasant 30-minute walk or ₹200 taxi ride from Shimla centre. Off-season discounts are negotiable. The best of the bright and spacious rooms are upstairs.

Woodville Palace Hotel   HERITAGE HOTEL $$$
(☑2623919; www.woodvillehotel.com; Raj Bhawan Rd; d ₹4227-7045) Built in 1938 by the raja of Jubbal for his bride Princess Leila, this slightly doddering mansion has the requisite tiger heads but also some lovely art-deco touches. Choose between slightly tired, old-style rooms in the main building or modern deluxe rooms in a seperate block. Heavy discounts are standard. Non-guests can pop in for a drink on the lawn or at the bar with its autographed photos of Hollywood stars collected by the socialite princess Brindi Devi.

Chapslee   HERITAGE HOTEL $$$
(☑2802542; www.chapslee.com; s/d with full board ₹9775/13,075, ste from ₹17,800; ❄) For the full Raj treatment, the outrageously ostentatious former home of Raja Charanjit Singh of Kapurthala is perched atop Elysium Hill, on the northern outskirts of Shimla. The exclusive mountain retreat is crammed with chandeliers, tapestries, Afghan carpets, big-game trophies, Mughal ceramics, baroque furniture and pieces of Victoriana. There are just five sumptuous bedrooms, all with completely original fittings, plus a library, card room, sun lounge, tennis courts and – of course – a croquet lawn.

Oberoi Cecil   HOTEL $$$
(☑2804848; www.oberoicecil.com; the Mall, Chaura Maidan; d with breakfast ₹12,095, ste from ₹25,750; ❄@🔲❄) Along the Mall about 2km west of Scandal Point, this grand high-rise is Shimla's glitziest five-star hotel. Colonial-era grandeur outside gives way to modern, wood-clad luxury within, and the cavernous central atrium/bar is particularly impressive. For the quietest rooms, opt for the Tudor wing.

🍴 Eating

Befitting a holiday town and state capital, Shimla has plenty of places to eat, especially along the Mall and the Ridge. As well as the formal restaurants, there are dozens of Indian fast-food places in Middle Bazar serving samosas, potato cakes, *channa puri* (spiced chickpeas and puffed fried bread) and other snacks. Unless otherwise stated, the following eateries are open from 10am to 10pm.

★Indian Coffee House   CAFE $
(the Mall; dishes ₹20-40; ⊙8am-8.30pm) A Shimla institution, the Indian Coffee House is like an old boys' club with its ageing booths, uniformed waiters and blackboard menu. It's the most atmospheric place in town for breakfast, cheap *dosas* and coffee (don't even ask for tea!), though it's more about the experience than the food.

Wake & Bake   INTERNATIONAL $$
(34/2 the Mall; mains ₹70-190; ⊙10.30am-9.30pm) This hip and fresh cafe is a breath of fresh air in stuffy Shimla, serving up espresso, pizza by the slice and excellent crepes. It has a tiny terrace reached through an even tinier hole in the roof. It's right above Interwebs.

Cafe Sol   MULTICUISINE $$
(the Mall; dishes ₹140-400; ⊙11am-10.30pm) Easily missed in the hangar-style atrium on the roof of Hotel Combermere but entered straight off the Mall, Sol serves tasty plates of Mexican, Italian and Mediterranean food, and has the best cake selection in Shimla, plus espresso. If you need a break from curry,

HIMACHAL PRADESH SHIMLA

INNER LINE PERMITS IN SHIMLA

Permits for travel from Rekong Peo to Tabo in Spiti are issued by the office of the **Additional District Magistrate** (ADM; ☎2657005; ⊙10am-1.30pm & 2-4pm Mon-Fri, until 2pm Sat, closed 2nd Sat each month), in the Collectorate Building, which is down a couple of flights of steps from the Mall about 200m west of Scandal Point. Bring a copy of your passport identity and visa pages to the Sangam Centre in the Collectorate to get an application form and have your photo taken, then take the form to the ADM office. Permits (₹300) are usually issued within 30 minutes, but be ready for a Kafka-esque runaround. Permits are only given to groups of two or more, so solo travellers will have to connect with another traveller or get their permit in Kaza, where restrictions are looser.

this is your best bet for a risk-free Greek salad. Take the lift down to the cleanest toilets in Shimla.

Ashiana INDIAN $$
(The Ridge; dishes ₹75-180; ⊙9am-10pm) In a fanciful circular building on the Ridge, this is an almost elegant restaurant and a good people-watching spot, with a delightful sunny terrace. As well as tasty Indian dishes there are sizzlers, dosas, Chinese and a few Thai favourites. In Ashiana's basement, Goofa serves the same food, from the same kitchen, for 25% less. You don't get the views but at night, who cares?

Cecil Restaurant MULTICUISINE $$$
(☎2804848; the Mall, Chaura Maidan; mains ₹700-1000) For a formal night out, look no further than the colonial-era elegance of the Cecil Restaurant at the Oberoi. The à la carte menu is strong on Indian and Thai curries and there are sumptuous buffets when a group is in town. Book ahead.

Drinking

Himani's BAR
(the Mall; mains ₹100-225, beer ₹150; ⊙9am-10pm) The neon and marble decor is straight out of the 1980s, but Himani's is a decent place for a casual drink or plate of chicken tikka. The lower floors are smoky and

male-dominated but the top-floor terrace overlooking the Mall is perfect on a sunny afternoon.

Devico's Bar BAR
(the Mall; ⊙10am-10pm) Head upstairs above Café Coffee Day for a beer or cocktail in this casual bar with couches, chairs and stools.

Shopping

Local holidaymakers head to the bustling Lakkar Bazar to haggle for wood and handloom souvenirs, but Middle Bazar, on the way down to the bus station, is more interesting. You can buy everything here from tin pots and peacock feathers to henna kits and bangles. Fruit and veg are sold at the heaving Sabzi Mandi at the eastern end near the Mall.

Himachal Emporium HANDICRAFTS
(☎2011234; www.himcrafts.com; the Mall; ⊙10am-1pm, 2.30-7.30pm Mon-Sat) Kangra silks, Kinnauri shawls and other Himachal souvenirs are sold here.

Asia Book House BOOKS
(the Mall; ⊙10am-8.30pm) English-language titles including novels and travel literature.

Minerva Bookshop BOOKS
(☎2803078; the Mall; ⊙10.30am-8pm) Good for novels, maps and books on Himachal Pradesh.

Maria Brothers BOOKS
(78A the Mall; ⊙11am-2pm & 5-8pm Mon-Sat) Seemingly lifted from a scene from *Kim*, Maria Bros is one of India's great antiquarian booksellers. The dusty bookshelves are packed with Himalayan travelogues, maps and engravings at prices aimed firmly at collectors.

ℹ Information

Laws exist banning plastic bags, littering, smoking and spitting in public places; police can hit offenders with a ₹200 fine.

EMERGENCY
Indira Gandhi Medical College (☎2803073; Circular Rd; ⊙24hr)
Tourist police (☎2812344; Scandal Point)

INTERNET ACCESS
Asian & International Travels (the Mall; per hr ₹30; ⊙9am-9.30pm) Cramped place on the Mall.

Interwebs (the Mall; per hr ₹30, wi-fi ₹60; ⊙10am-10pm) One of two internet cafes next to each other, and a rare wi-fi hot spot.

MONEY

If you're heading out to Kinnaur, Spiti and La-haul, stock up on rupees in Shimla. Numerous 24-hour ATMs are dotted around Scandal Point and the Mall.

Punjab National Bank (the Mall; ⊙10am-2pm & 3-4pm Mon-Fri, 10am-2pm Sat) Changes major currencies in cash and travellers cheques.

State Bank of India (the Mall; ⊙10am-2pm & 3-4pm Mon-Fri) West of Scandal Point; changes cash and travellers cheques and has an ATM opposite.

POST

Main Post Office (the Ridge) Deals with parcels. There are several suboffices west along the Mall.

TOURIST INFORMATION

HPTDC Tourist Office (Himachal Pradesh Tourist Development Corporation; ☑2652561; www.hptdc.gov.in; Scandal Point; ⊙9am-8pm, to 7pm mid-Jul–Sep & Dec-Mar) Helpful for advice, brochures and booking HPTDC buses, hotels and tours, along with a railway booking window and bus ticket booth next door.

TRAVEL AGENCIES

Great Escape Routes (☑6533037; www.greatescaperoutes.com; 6 Andi Bhavan, Jakhu; ☎) Specialises in trekking and adventure tours around the state, including some local hikes that overnight in homestays. Can put you in touch with local mountain bike guides and has an internet cafe with wi-fi. Contact Nitin.

ⓘ Getting There & Away

AIR

At the time of research there were no flights to Jubbarhatti airport, 23km south of Shimla, though seasonal services to Delhi should resume at some point.

BUS

HPTDC and private travel agencies offer over-night deluxe Volvo buses to Delhi (₹880, nine hours), plus morning and evening buses to Manali (₹500, nine hours) in season (April to June, October and November). They depart from the **government deluxe bus stand** near Victory Tunnel. There are also four Himachal Road Transport Corporation (HRTC) Volvo buses to Delhi (₹785, nine hours) each day, along with three AC deluxe (₹550) and three semideluxe (₹312) rides. Deluxe/semideluxe buses head to Manali (₹455/325, 10 hours) in the morning and evening. All HRTC buses leave from the **new bus station**, 5km outside Shimla (a taxi here costs ₹200 to ₹300). Make reservations at the **HRTC booth** (⊙11am-2pm & 3-6.30pm) next to the HPTDC Tourist Office at Scandal Point.

Frequent buses to Chail (₹50, 2½ hours), Naldehra (₹25, one hour) and Tattapani (₹50, 2½ hours) leave from the small **Rivoli bus stand** (Lakkar Bazar), north of the Ridge.

For more bus details, see p292.

TAXI

The **Kalka-Shimla Taxi Union** (☑2658225) has its stand near the old bus terminal, while **Vishal Himachal Taxi Operators Union** (☑2805164) operates from the bottom of the passenger lift. Taxis from the train station/old bus terminal to the passenger lift costs ₹150/100.

TRAIN

One of the little joys of Shimla is getting to or from it by the narrow-gauge toy train from Kalka, just north of Chandigarh. Although the steam trains are long gone, it's a scenic four- to six-hour trip, passing through 103 tunnels as it winds up through the hills. Tiny Shimla train station is 1.5km west of Scandal Point on Cart Rd – about a 15-minute uphill walk.

Ordinary trains (1st/2nd class ₹189/16, 5½ hours) run downhill to Kalka at 2.25pm, 4.25pm and 6.15pm, returning at 4am, 5.10am and 6am. Additional high-season services run at 9.25am and 3.50pm, returning at 7am and 12.45pm. To travel in style, catch the posh Shivalik Express at 5.40pm (returning at 5.30am; ₹280 with meals, 4¾ hours).

The easiest way to or from Delhi is on the Himalayan Queen Express, whose fares cost ₹167 (chair car) to Kalka, plus an additional ₹284/75 (chair car/2nd class) on to Delhi. An alternative is to connect with the 5.45pm Kalka Shatabdi to Delhi (4¼ hours).

There's a **rail booking office** (⊙9am-1pm & 2-4pm Mon-Sat) next to the HPTDC tourist office on the Ridge, or you can book at the train station.

ⓘ Getting Around

The only way to get around central Shimla is on foot. Fortunately, there's a two-part **lift** (per

TIMINGS FOR HIMALAYAN QUEEN EXPRESS

DEPART	ARRIVE/DEPART KALKA	ARRIVE	TRAIN NOS
Shimla 10.30am	4.10pm/4.50pm	Delhi 10.40pm	52456 & 14096
Delhi 5.45am	11.10am/12.10pm	Shimla 5.20pm	14095 & 52455

person ₹8; ⏱ 8am-10pm, till 9pm Jul-Sep) connecting the east end of the Mall with Cart Rd. Taxis from the train station to the bottom of the lift cost about ₹150.

Around Shimla

Shimla to Tattapani

Stunning **Wildflower Hall** (www.oberoihotels.com; r from ₹26,000, 50% discount off-season), former home of Lord Kitchener and a one-time weekend retreat for harassed Viceroys, is about 10km north of Shimla and is *the* place for classic afternoon tea on the terrace (₹650 for two; smart casual dress code).

A couple of kilometres further on, the small village of **Mashobra** has a simple colonial church and some pleasant walks among the deodar (cedar) trees.

About 15km north of Mashobra, **Naldehra** is famous chiefly for the **Naldehra Golf Course** (☑ 0177-2747656; www.naldehragolf.com; green fees Indian/foreigner ₹250/500, club hire ₹250; ⏱ 7am-6pm Apr-Oct), established in 1905 by British viceroy Lord Curzon (who loved the place so much he named his daughter after it). Set among tall cedars – some of which stand directly between the tee and green – it's a challenging course. Hire a caddy or you won't know where you're going. Ponies can be hired for treks along the ridge and there are pine-scented walks.

At the golf course, the HPTDC **Hotel Golf Glade** (☑ 0177-2747809; d from ₹2310) of-fers tatty hotel rooms and slightly less tatty cottages on a pretty wooded slope beside the road. A one-way taxi from Shimla costs around ₹800.

Tattapani

☑ 01907 / ELEV 656M

About 30km below Naldehra, on the banks of the Sutlej River, tiny Tattapani (Hot Water) is known for its steaming **sulphurous springs**, which spill out onto a sandy river beach. Legal action has temporarily halted construction on a planned dam which will eventually submerge the springs if completed.

The village has several **temples** linked to the cult of Rishi Jamdagam, and you can walk to sacred **Shiva caves** and former **palaces**. Ask directions locally or at New Spring View Guest House.

If you've come for the waters, your only option is the spa at the fancy new **Hotel Hot Spring** (☑ 230736; www.hotelhotspring.com; r ₹3500-6000; ❄), where nonguests can soak in the tubs and pools (₹350). Alternative accommodation is at the nearby **New Spring View Guest House** (☑ 9816341911; www.newspringview.com; r without/with AC ₹1000/1500; ❄), which has spacious rooms looking down to the river at tree-top level, and a good inexpensive restaurant.

Buses leave from Tattapani to Shimla every hour or so, or take a taxi for around ₹1300.

BUSES FROM SHIMLA

DESTINATION	FARE (₹)	DURATION (HR)	FREQUENCY
Chamba	405-433	14	four daily
Chandigarh	130-206	four	every 15 minutes
Dehra Dun	250	nine	three daily
Delhi	317/558 (ordinary/deluxe)	nine	hourly
Dharamsala	275/415 (ordinary/deluxe)	10	five daily
Haridwar	300	10	five daily
Kullu	250-385	8½	five daily
Manali	295-455	10	five daily
Mandi	165	six	hourly
Rampur	150	five	hourly
Rekong Peo	265	10	hourly
Sangla	270	10	7.30am
Sarahan	170	eight	three daily

OFF THE BEATEN TRACK AROUND SHIMLA

One little-visited destination easily accessible from Shimla is the mellow Pabbar Valley, running northeast towards Kinnaur. Set in rolling fields at the mouth of the valley, the 8th-century Kinnauri-style Durga temple at **Hatkoti** is worth a visit, especially when Shaivite pilgrims convene during the Chaitra Navratra and Asvin Navratra festivals in April and October. Pilgrims' quarters are available at the temple or you can stay at the HPTDC **Hotel Chanshal** (☑240661; rohru@hptdc.in; dm ₹150, d ₹1265, with AC ₹1495-1725; ✳), 10km north of Hatkoti towards Rohru. From Hatkoti, day trip out to **Jubbal**, 12km west, which has a fanciful slate-roofed palace built by the former Rana of Jubbal.

South of Shimla, the hilltop village of **Chail** lays claim to the world's highest cricket ground, a 3km walk from town. As well as forest strolls, there's a wildlife park abundant with deer and birds. Stay at **Hotel Pineview** (☑248349; r from ₹330) or the HPTDC-run **Palace Hotel** (☑248141; palace@hptdc.in; d ₹2530-9775; ✳), a former maharaja's pad and luxurious in a Raj-era way.

In the extreme southeast corner of Himachal Pradesh and virtually on the Uttarakhand state line, **Paonta Sahib** is famous as the one-time home of Guru Gobind Singh, the 10th Sikh guru. The sprawling **Paonta Sahib Gurdwara** is set on banks of the Yamuna River where Gobind Singh got off his horse. You can eat at the gurdwara and stay in its guest rooms (for a donation), or head for the nearby **Hotel Yamuna** (☑222341; paonta@hptdc.in; d ₹770-990, with AC ₹1540-2420; ✳) which could use a paint job but has very friendly management. There are hourly morning buses to Shimla (₹200, seven hours) and plenty of services to Dehra Dun (₹50, two hours).

Kinnaur Valley

The old Hindustan–Tibet Hwy, built by the British as a potential invasion route into Tibet, runs northeast from Shimla through the Kinnaur Valley, providing access to mountain villages with slate-roofed temples, vast apple orchards, and some of eastern Himachal's grandest views. The Kinnauris are proud Aryan people who mainly survive from farming and apple growing. You can recognise Kinnauris all over India by their green felt *basheri* hats.

To truly appreciate Kinnaur, you have to leave the main road, much of which is currently scarred by the multiple dam projects that are turning the powerful Sutlej River into a massive generator. With an easy-to-obtain inner line permit you can travel onwards to the high-altitude mountain deserts of the Spiti Valley.

For much of the year, Kinnaur is a relaxed rural retreat, but that all changes during the Durga Puja holiday in September/October when Bengali holidaymakers flood into Kinnaur from the plains. Simultaneously, the annual apple harvest lures hundreds of fruit wholesalers from right across India. At this time it can be hard to find a room in popular spots such as Kalpa and the Sangla Valley.

For more information on the Kinnaur Valley, visit the local government website at http://hpkinnaur.nic.in.

Rampur

☑ 01782 / 1005M

The gateway to Kinnaur, this bustling bazaar town was once the capital of the Bushahr rajas. Today, Rampur is mainly a place to change buses, but if you have a few minutes check out the delightful, terraced and turreted **Padam Palace**, built in 1925 for the maharaja of Bushahr; only the garden is open to visitors. It's just beside the bus stand.

The huge **Lavi Fair** is held yearly in the second week of November, attracting traders and pilgrims from remote villages.

🛏 Sleeping & Eating

Rampur isn't the ideal spot to stay overnight in Kinnaur, but there is cheap lodging if you get stuck.

Hotel Satluj View   HOTEL **$**

(☑233924; r ₹550-660, ste ₹1100) Just behind the temple across the road from the bus stand and down a flight of stairs, cheap rooms here at Hotel Satluj View are dingy holes, while the more expensive ones are clean and pleasant, with big windows overlooking the rushing river. The restaurant (mains ₹80 to ₹250) is the best place to eat near the bus stand.

Hotel Bushehar Regency HOTEL $$
(☑234103; d ₹1380-1840, with AC ₹2415-3220; ❄) This standard HPTDC property on the western edge of Rampur has spacious rooms and a decent restaurant.

ℹ Getting There & Away

Rampur's bus station is 2km east of town but almost everyone jumps on a through bus at the chaotic bus stand in the centre of town. There are frequent services to Rekong Peo (₹100, five hours) and Shimla (₹150, five hours). Buses to Sarahan (₹45, two hours) leave every two hours. Three daily buses run to Sangla (₹105, five hours).

Sarahan

☑ 01782 / ELEV 1920M

The former summer capital of the Bushahr kingdom, Sarahan is dominated by the fabulous **Bhimakali Temple** (⊙7am-8pm), built from layers of stone and timber to absorb the force of earthquakes. There are two towers here, one recently rebuilt after the 12th-century original collapsed, and a newer tower from the 1920s (on the left) containing a highly revered shrine to Bhimakali (the local version of Kali) beneath a beautiful silver-filigree canopy.

There are some strict entry rules. Male visitors must wear a cap (which can be borrowed inside the temple), shoes must be removed, smoking is banned, and cameras and leather goods like belts and wallets must be left with the guards. Behind the temple is a small display of ancient ceremonial horns, lamps and weaponry, and across the courtyard is the squat **Lankra Vir Temple**, where human sacrifices were carried out right up to the 18th century. The tradition lives on in a tamer form in the Astomi ritual during October's Dussehra celebration, when a menagerie of animals is sacrificed to Bhimakali, including goats, chickens and buffalo.

The grounds of the flamboyant **Shanti Kung Palace** (1917), a summer retreat built by the last maharaja of Bushahr, are worth a visit, just behind the Bhimakali Temple.

🛏 Sleeping & Eating

Apart from the temple guesthouse, all hotels offer significant discounts during the off-season months of August and December to March.

Temple Guesthouse HOTEL $
(☑274248; dm ₹70, r ₹250-450) The obvious place to stay is within the ancient temple precinct itself. Unlike most temple accommodation, rooms here are far from gloomy and austere. The upper-storey rooms in particular are bright, spacious and airy, with hot water.

Hotel Trehan's HOTEL $
(☑9816687605; pawanshashi51@gmail.com; r ₹660-1100) Run by a friendly family, rooms here have ornate ceilings, big windows and chintzy tapestries of Indian epics that give the place a touch of character. Shared terraces have great views over the valley.

Sherma Sweets INDIAN $
(thali ₹50) This local *dhaba* (snack bar) in the bazaar below the Bhimakali Temple has no English sign, but serves up fresh, tasty and excellent vegetarian thalis.

Hotel Srikhand MULTICUISINE $
(☑274234; mains ₹70-150, beer ₹150) The classiest place for a civilised dinner, or to savour a beer on the terrace while enjoying panoramic views over the valley, is this HPTDC hotel. Rooms (₹1725 to ₹3450) are available but somewhat overpriced.

ℹ Getting There & Away

Direct buses run to Shimla from Sarahan (₹220, eight hours) at 8am and noon, or take a bus to Rampur (₹50, two hours) and change there. From early morning to late afternoon, there is a frequent service to Rampur and Jeori (₹20, 45 minutes), from where you can catch buses to other destinations at the junction on the main road . The last bus from Jeori up to Sarahan leaves around 7.20pm, or take a taxi for ₹350.

Sangla

☑ 01786 / ELEV 2680M

The Sangla, or Baspa, Valley is a deeply carved cleft between burly mountain slopes, where evergreen forests rise to alpine meadows that are crowned by snowy summits. Villages here, especially further up the valley, feature houses and temples built in traditional Kinnauri wood-and-stone-style. The area is best avoided during the busy

Dussehra (Durga Puja) season, when it's overrun by Indian vacationers. The hair-raising road to the valley begins at Karcham on the Rekong Peo–Shimla Hwy, passing the gushing outflow pipes from a big hydro-electric plant.

The largest settlement in the valley, Sangla village is no longer worth a specific visit but you might find yourself staying overnight here if you can't find transport. Clinging to a rocky spur 2km (20 minutes walk) above Sangla, the village of **Kamru** was the former capital of the kingdom of Bushahr and still boasts the tower-style **Kamakhya Devi Fort**, the former home of the *thakurs* (noblemen) of Bushahr (shoes and leather items should be removed and heads must be covered).

🛏 Sleeping & Eating

Sangla centre has several identical 'Tibetan restaurants' centred on the Ashiana Cafe, all serving *momos* (Tibetan dumplings), *thukpa* (noodle soup) and chow mein.

Baspa Guesthouse   HOTEL $
(☑ 9816385065; d ₹440-550) Run by a genial Kinnauri family, centrally located Baspa is convenient for buses and offers a wide range of rooms, some pine-clad, some with verandahs, so look at a few.

Sangla Resort   GUESTHOUSE $
(☑ 242201; d ₹660-990) Two minutes' uphill from the bridge near the town centre, this is one of Sangla's most appealing places. Rooms in the main stone chalet are spotless, and the shared terrace and balconies have great views over the surrounding garden and orchards.

ℹ Getting There & Away

Buses run at 6.30am, noon and 5.30pm to Rampur (₹100, five hours) and there are several daily buses to Rekong Peo (₹50, three hours), the last at 4pm. Local buses run up the valley to Chitkul (₹30, 1½ hours) at around noon and 5pm. Buses run to Shimla (₹250, 11 hours) at 6.30am and 5.30pm.

Share jeeps can take you up to Chitkul (₹40, one hour) or down to Karcham (₹45, 1½ hours), on the main Shimla–Rekong Peo bus route. Taxis cost ₹1000 to Rekong and ₹1600 to Sarahan.

Around the Sangla Valley

Further up the valley from Sangla are the smaller villages of **Rakcham** (3050m), 14km

from Sangla, and **Chitkul** (3450m) another 10km up the road. The last stop on the old trade route to Tibet and at the junction of several trekking routes, Chitkul is easily the most scenic settlement along the Sangla and an increasingly popular stop for backpackers. The charming hamlet consists entirely of traditional Kinnauri-style wooden houses topped with slate roofs, and there is a large temple dedicated to the local god Mathi. Pleasant walks lead up the hillside behind town for great views, or head upriver 3km to the Indo-Tibet Border Post (foreigners are not allowed further) for full-on views of Rani Khanda peak. Chitkul is where the three-day trekking trail circumambulating Kinner Kailash descends into the Sangla Valley.

The best of the increasing number of guesthouses is the **Kinner Heights** (☑ 9805628801; r ₹400-700, without bathroom ₹150-200), whose owner Baabhe can give tips and supply guides for local hikes. Other decent options include the simple **Thakur Guest House** (r ₹250-300), and more up-market **Shahensha Resort** (☑ 244279; r ₹1000-1800), the latter aimed squarely at Bengali tourists and offering 50% discounts out of season.

Buses leave Chitkul for Rekong Peo (₹80, 3½ hours) at 6am, 6.45am and 1.30pm, and for Rampur (₹150) at 10.15am and noon, all going through Sangla (₹35, one hour).

Rekong Peo

☑ 01786 / ELEV 2290M
Rekong Peo is the main administrative and commercial centre for Kinnaur and an important transport hub, but the main reason to visit is as a stepping stone to the pretty village of Kalpa, or to obtain a permit for onward travel to upper Kinnaur and Spiti. A steep walk above town near the radio mast is the **Kinnaur Kalachakra Celestial Palace** (Mahabodhi Gompa), with a 10m-high statue of Sakyamuni and great views across to Kinner Kailash (6050m) and Jorkanden (6473m) peaks.

Known to locals as 'Peo', the town is spread out along a looping road about 10km above the Hindustan–Tibet Hwy. Most hotels are in the main bazaar below the bus stand. There is nowhere to change money, but the State Bank of India ATM in the main bazaar accepts international cards.

The **Tourist Information Centre** (☏ 222897; ☺ 10am-1pm & 2-5pm Mon-Sat, closed 2nd Sat of month) below the bazaar has a rail reservation office. The private travel agency here offers internet access (per hour ₹60) and helps arrange inner line permits for onward travel to upper Kinnaur and Spiti. The office issues permits (₹350) within a few hours. It's best to show up as early in the day as possible. You'll need copies of your passport identity and visa pages. The agency can help solo travellers hook up with someone else for paperwork purposes only, since the powers-that-be prefer groups of two or more. All travellers on the permit need to go in person to be photographed.

📖 Sleeping & Eating

Ridang Hotel
HOTEL $

(☏ 9816820767; d ₹450-1500) The best of a grotty bunch of hotels lining the main bazaar, Ridang has a range of acceptable rooms with TV and there's also a good ground-floor restaurant.

Little Chef's Restaurant
MULTICUISINE $

(mains ₹90-180; ☺ 8am-10pm) The sunny rooftop here is easily the best place to eat, with a good range of Indian and Chinese dishes such as Kinnauri-style *rajma* (kidney beans). Internet (₹60 per hour) is generally available.

❶ Getting There & Away

The bus stand is 2km uphill from the main bazaar by road or 500m by the steps that start next to the police compound at the top of ITBP Rd.

Buses run roughly hourly to Shimla (₹270, 10 hours), via Jeori (for Sarahan; ₹90, four hours). The 6am and 1.30pm departures are deluxe services (₹400). To Sangla (₹50, 2½ hours) or Chitkul (₹80, 4½ hours) there are direct buses at 9.30am, noon and 4pm or you can take any bus heading south and change at Karcham (₹25, one hour).

For Spiti, there's a 6.30am bus to Kaza (₹257, 11 hours) via Nako (₹125, five hours) and Tabo (₹200, nine hours). A second bus leaves for Tabo at 4pm, and another heads to Nako at 12.30pm. You need an inner line permit to travel this route.

Local buses run hourly from the roundabout in the main bazaar to Kalpa (₹10, 30 minutes), or you can take a taxi (₹350/500 to lower/upper Kalpa). Taxis charge ₹2000 to Sangla and ₹5000 to Shimla or Kaza.

Kalpa
☏ 01786 / ELEV 2960M

Reached by a winding road 7km above Rekong Peo, Kalpa is a little gem of a village. Majestic views of the Kinner Kailash massif grab your eyeballs and don't let go. There are several simple guesthouses in the village, plus a growing number of modern hotels on the ridge a 10-minute walk above town. For an ambitious day hike ask locals about the four-hour trail to the meadows of Chakkha Khanda.

According to legend, Kalpa was the winter home of Shiva, and there are some impressive Kinnauri-style temples in the ornately carved **Narayan-Nagini** temple complex, just below the colourful **Samdrup Choeling Gompa**. In September/October, villagers pile wildflowers in temple courtyards in the centre of the village as part of the annual Phulech Festival.

📖 Sleeping

The following hotels are booked solid during the two-week Durga Puja holiday season in September or October. At other times discounts of 20% to 50% are common. All the hotels have decent restaurants.

Hotel Blue Lotus
HOTEL $

(☏ 226001; r ₹500-1000) Hard to beat for its sheer convenience, 100m from the bus stand, rooms at this friendly, concrete place are priced by floor rather than facilities. The wide, sunny terrace faces directly across to the mountains – ideal for a breakfast or just hanging out in a state of Himalayan-inspired bliss.

Hotel Rollingrang
HOTEL $

(☏ 9816473746; d ₹400-700) Up in a peaceful spot on the hillside above the village, next to the HPTDC hotel, rooms here are spacious and sparkling clean, and the best ones have balconies with perfect mountain views. It's particularly good value in the low season.

Hotel Kinner Villa
HOTEL $$

(☏ 226006; www.kinnervilla.com; r ₹2114-2936) Reached via a 1km walk or drive through orchards and farmland beyond the village, Kinner Villa is a rural retreat, though somewhat overpriced. Only some rooms have mountain views, but there's a lovely terrace and a good restaurant serving delicious fresh apple juice.

ⓘ Getting There & Away

Buses run throughout the day between Kalpa and Rekong Peo (₹10, 30 minutes), or you can take a taxi or walk – follow the well-worn stepped path rather than the winding road. Of the three daily departures for Shimla, the 6.30am service is the most useful. For the Sangla Valley, catch the Chitkul Express direct from Kalpa at around 8.30am, stopping in Sangla (₹60, three hours) and Chitkul (₹90, five hours). More buses run from Rekong Peo.

CENTRAL HIMACHAL PRADESH

Central Himachal is dominated by the Kullu and Parvati Valleys – famous for the production of woollen shawls and charas. The area is popular with hippies, honeymooners, trekkers and adrenaline junkies, and is home to Manali, one of the state's main travel centres. This is also the main route northwards, and many people continue from Manali over Rohtang La (3978m) to Lahaul, Spiti and Ladakh.

For more information on Kullu district, see the websites www.kullu.net and http://hpkullu.nic.in.

Mandi

☑ 01905 / POP 27,400 / ELEV 800M

Formerly a trading stop on the salt route to Tibet, the rambunctious bazaar town of Mandi is the gateway to the Kullu Valley and the junction of the main roads from Kullu, Shimla and Dharamsala. It's no tourist town, and it feels more Punjabi than Himalayan, with a large Sikh community and sticky air reminiscent of the plains. Sprawling around the confluence of the Beas and Suketi Khad rivers, the town is dotted with ancient Shaivite temples – at least 81, according to official figures – and you can have fun tracking them down in the fascinating backstreet bazaars, before heading on to the more serene environment of Rewalsar.

Mandi is centred on a sunken shopping complex called Indira Market, with terraced steps on the north side leading to the Raj Mahal Palace. The bus stand is 500m east of town across the Suketi Khad, a ₹30 autorickshaw ride away.

⊙ Sights & Activities

Bhutnath Mandir   HINDU TEMPLE

At the entrance to the bazaar, 100m west of Indira Market, this rather garish temple actually dates from the 16th century and is the focal point for the animated Shivaratri Festival in February, honouring Lord Shiva.

River Temples   HINDU TEMPLES

If you follow Bhutnath Bazar from the Bhutnath Mandir to the Beas River you'll find the colourful **Ekardash Rudra Mandir**, the British-built Victoria Bridge, some cremation ghats and a collection of carved stone *sikharas*. Most impressive of these are the corncob-style **Panch Bahktar** and

OFF THE BEATEN TRACK: MANDI TO KULLU

Explorers and those with their own transport can find plenty to entertain them en route to Kullu. Hidden away in the high pastures between Mandi and Bajaura is scenic **Prashar Lake** (2730m), home to the striking, pagoda-style **Prashara Temple**, built in the 14th century in honour of the sage Prashar Rishi. Enquire at Mandi bus station about the early morning bus to Prashar (₹56, three hours), otherwise the lake is an 8km uphill hike from the village of Kandi on the Mandi–Bajaura road. A return taxi from Mandi costs ₹2000.

Southeast of Mandi is the little-visited **Banjar Valley**, offering peaceful walks and trips to unspoiled villages. The town of **Banjar** has a few simple hotels, and you can hike the steep 6km to the village of **Chaini** to see one of the tallest temple towers in Himachal: damaged by an earthquake in 1905 but still impressive at seven storeys. About 5km before the 3223m Jalori Pass are the faint ruins of **Raghupur Fort** at Shoja meadows.

Finally, back on the main road 15km south of Kullu, near the village of Bajaura, stop off at the **Bisheshwar (Bishweshwar) Mahadev Temple**, the largest stone temple in the Kullu Valley. Built in the 8th century AD and intricately carved, the temple is a larger version of the classic hut-style *sikharas* (Hindu temples) seen all over the Kullu Valley.

Triloknath mandirs, facing each other across the Beas, 200m east of the ghats.

🛏 Sleeping & Eating

The budget hotels facing Indira Market suffer from extreme road noise so get a room at the back if possible.

Evening Plaza Hotel   HOTEL $
(☏ 225123; d ₹440-660, with AC ₹1100-1320; ❄) Right on the main square, this is reliable value offering acceptable rooms with TVs. Front-facing rooms are best but the noisiest. If it's full try the similar **Hotel Shiva** (☏ 224211; r ₹440-770) a couple of doors down.

⭐ **Raj Mahal Palace Hotel**   HERITAGE HOTEL $$
(☏ 222401; www.rajmahalpalace.com; r with AC ₹1144-2277, ste ₹3036-3960; ❄) Mandi's most romantic hotel, this refurbished heritage place occupies part of the palace of Mandi's royal family. The rooms are bright, cosy and clean, some with the air of a colonial hunting lodge, others with a modern chalet design. Book in advance. The deliciously peaceful Garden Restaurant here (mains ₹120 to ₹250) is the best in town, with a choice of indoor and outdoor dining.

ℹ Information

There are international ATMs at the State Bank of India and HDFC around the market square.

The **Kapoor Cyber Cafe** (per hr ₹40; ⏱10am-9pm Mon-Sat) is on the ground floor of the Indira Market.

ℹ Getting There & Away

Local buses run frequently to Rewalsar (₹25, one hour) until late afternoon from the taxi stand on the north side of Indira Market. Other buses leave from the main bus station 500m east of town. If there are no direct services to Dharamsala, head to Palampur or Gaggal and change there.

Taxis at the bus station charge ₹1200 to Kullu.

Rewalsar Lake

☏ 01905 / ELEV 1350M

Hidden in the hills 24km southwest of Mandi, the sacred lake of Rewalsar is revered by Buddhists, Hindus and Sikhs. Tibetan Buddhists know the lake as Tso-Pema (Lotus Lake) and believe it was created when the king of Mandi tried to burn alive the Indian guru Padmasambhava, to prevent his daughter Mandarava running off with the long-haired Tantric master.

Today the lake is home to the ochre-red Tibetan-style **Drikung Kagyu Gompa**, with its academy of Buddhist studies and a large, central Sakyamuni statue. Moving clockwise around the prayer flag-strewn lake, you pass a lakeshore shrine to Padmasambhava and then the **Tso-Pema Ogyen Heruka Nyingmapa Gompa**, with artful murals and atmospheric afternoon and morning *pujas* (offerings or prayers). A short detour uphill from the lake is the towering white **Zigar Drukpa Kagyud Institute**, with outsized statues of tantric protectors. A five-minute climb up steps from here takes you to a dramatic 12m-high **statue of Padmasambhava**, which towers over the lake to offer grand views.

Continuing clockwise around the lake you pass a couple of **Hindu temples** dedicated to the sage Rishi Lomas (who was forced to do penance here as a dedication to Shiva) and arrive at lakeshore ghats, where hundreds of fish practically jump out of the water to get to the puffed rice being thrown in by pilgrims. One the far side of the lake is the gold-domed gurdwara (Sikh temple)

BUSES FROM MANDI

DESTINATION	FARE(₹)	DURATION (HR)	FREQUENCY
Bhuntar	70	2	half-hourly airport
Delhi	410/550/884 (ordinary/ semideluxe/deluxe)	12	10 daily
Dharamsala	152	6	6 daily
Kullu	85	2½	half-hourly
Manali	130	4	half-hourly
Shimla	165	6	hourly until 1pm

built in honour of Guru Gobind Singh in the 1930s.

The other main pilgrim site is the **Padmasambhava Cave**, high above the lake on the ridge, where Padmasambhava allegedly meditated. Take a taxi here (₹400) or jump on one of the five daily buses to the Naina Devi Temple (₹20) and get off 1km before the temple.

Rewalsar is an easy day trip from Mandi but it's also a pleasant place to stay overnight and a much more serene choice than Mandi.

🛏 Sleeping & Eating

Hotel Lotus Lake   HOTEL $
(☏240239; hlotuslake@yahoo.com; r ₹450-650, ste ₹700) Facing the lake, this modern place is Buddhist-run, and the bright rooms, with TV and hot water, are good value. The best upper-floor rooms have lake views.

Drikung Kagyu Gompa Guesthouse   HOTEL $
(☏9816735264; www.dk-petsek.org; r without/with bathroom ₹150/250) Several of Rewalsar's monasteries have guesthouses but this is probably the best, offering a shared terrace with peaceful lake views. Nicer rooms in the attached Namkhaling block are available to long-term visitors (₹500 to ₹700 per night). There are several cafes popular with visiting Western Buddhists. **Ema Ho Coffee Shop** (drinks & snacks ₹30-50), at the entrance to the Drikung Kagyu Gompa, helps support the monastery through its sale of coffees, teas and fresh-baked pastries. **Kora Community Cafe** (meals ₹40-80), near Hotel Lotus Lake, is good for coffee, breakfasts and veg thali (₹130).

ℹ Getting There & Away

Frequent buses shuttle between Rewalsar and Mandi (₹25, one hour) until around 6pm. A taxi from Mandi costs ₹600/850 one way/return.

Bhuntar

☏ 01902
Bhuntar is useful only as the main airport for the Kullu Valley and as the junction town for transport to the beautiful Parvati Valley. Most travellers merely pass through on the road to or from Manali or Kasol, or stay at Kullu, 10km up the road.

Bhuntar has a State Bank of India ATM, which is the last place you're able to get cash with plastic if you're headed to the Parvati Valley.

🛏 Sleeping & Eating

If you're catching an early morning flight, the best hotel and restaurant in town is the **Malabar Hotel** (☏266199; www.hotelmalabarkullu.com; opposite airport; r ₹1292-2231). There's a collection of budget places centred on the **Hotel Amit** (☏265123; ◷d ₹550-1550; ﹡), with its decent restaurant, and the next-door **Hotel Sunbeam** (☏265790; d ₹450-650).

ℹ Getting There & Away

AIR
The airport is next to the bus stand. No flights were operating at the time of research, though Air India should eventually resume summer flights from Delhi.

BUS
There are frequent services to Manali (₹60, three hours, last bus 10pm), Kullu (₹13, 30 minutes) and Mandi (₹68, two hours). Buses to other destinations pass through three hours after leaving Manali. For the Parvati Valley, there are services every half-hour until 6pm to Manikaran (₹40, 1½

hours) via Kasol (₹35, 1¼ hours) and Jari (₹25, one hour). The taxi stand is next to the bus stand.

Parvati Valley

☑ 01902

The Parvati River rises from the highway at Bhuntar to the hot springs at Manikaran and beyond, and the sublime surrounding valley is a popular traveller hang-out. Over the years the Parvati Valley has developed a well-deserved reputation for its wild and cultivated crops of charas – as well as its natural beauty. A couple of villages along the river have been transformed into hippie hang-outs, offering cheap accommodation, international food and a nonstop reggae soundtrack to crowds of dreadlocked and pierced travellers. There are some excellent treks in the area – including to the intriguing mountain village of Malana, over the Chandrakani Pass to Naggar, or across the Pin-Parvati Pass to Spiti. For safety reasons, solo trekking is not recommended. See also the boxed text on p299.

Jari & Malana

About halfway along the Parvati Valley, **Jari** consists of two parts: a bustling highway bazaar and the peaceful hillside hamlet of Mateura Jari above it, which is where most travellers head for, despite the steep 15-minute uphill hike to get there.

Jari is the starting point for the trip to the traditional mountain village of **Malana**. Malana was once an isolated collection of traditional wood and stone houses, but about half of them burned in a fire in 2008 and some have been replaced by cinderblock boxes. The villagers have their own unique caste system and, while Hindu, each February they perform a Muslim ritual, slaughtering and eating a sheep.

Visitors no longer need to wait on the outskirts of the village to be invited in, but once inside you must obey a litany of esoteric rules or face minimum fines of ₹1000. For example, it's forbidden to touch any of the villagers or their belongings, including homes, temples or buildings – they want nothing soiled by the spiritually impure hands of low-caste or non-Hindus. To get the most out of the cultural experience and avoid breaking any rules, it's worthwhile to visit with a knowledgeable guide.

There are a half-dozen guesthouses above the village proper, run by outsiders, where foreigners are welcome to stay overnight for around ₹200. A taxi (₹1000 one-way from Jari) can take you to the end of the road at Nerang, from where it's a one-hour walk up to the village. Carry your passport as you must show it to security at the hydroelectric plant. Adventurers can continue from Malana over the Rashol Pass to Kasol (17km), staying overnight in a homestay in Rashol en route. Trekkers with camping equipment can hike from Naggar over the Chandrakani Pass in two days.

For guide services to Malana or for trekking anywhere in the Parvati Valley, contact **Negi's Himalayan Adventure** (☑ 276319; www.negis-himalayan-adventure.com) in Jari. Owner Chhape Negi is head of the area's mountain rescue team, so he's as reliable as it gets. He also runs a free private museum at his house in the village of Chowki, across the river from Jari, and also offers midrange accommodation there at the excellent **Negi's Nest** (☑ 9418281894; Chowki; r ₹1500-2500).

Most guesthouses are a steep 1km walk above Jari through cornfields to the beautifully serene hamlet of Mateura Jari – follow the guesthouse signs from the main road. None have private bathrooms.

The first place you come to in Mateura Jari is the large and welcoming **Village Guest House** (☑ 9805190051; r ₹100-200). Just uphill, near some ornate wooden temples, are the laid-back **Chandra Place Guesthouse** (☑ 9805969606; r ₹100) with an awesome covered porch with blissful views, and **Rooftop Family House** (☑ 275434; r ₹100), both offering a pleasant, villagey vibe. You'll find more homestays in Punthal, 1km further.

Buses from Bhuntar to Manikaran stop in Jari (₹25, one hour). A one-way taxi between Bhuntar and Jari is around ₹550.

Kasol

☑ 01902

Spread out along the lovely Parvati River and with mountain views to the northeast, Kasol is the main traveller hang-out in the valley. It's a small village, but overrun with reggae bars, bakeries, internet cafes and cheap guesthouses catering to a largely hippie/Israeli crowd, You'll either love it or loathe it. Still, it's an easy base from which to explore the forested valley or just chill out. The village is divided into Old Kasol on the Bhuntar side of the bridge, and New Kasol on the Manikaran side.

Parvati & Kullu Valleys

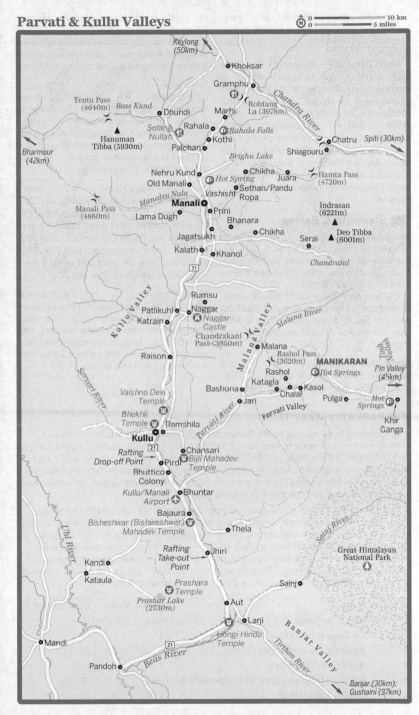

Kasol has plenty of internet cafes charging ₹40 per hour, and several travel agents who will happily change cash and travellers cheques.

From Kasol, it's a demanding four-hour walk uphill to the mountain village of **Rashol**, where there are a couple of basic guesthouses. For an easier 90-minute stroll from Kasol, cross the bridge over the Parvati River and walk downstream to **Chalal** and **Katagla** villages, both of which offer a laid-back accommodation alternative to Kasol. Recross the river at Katagla to catch a passing bus back to Kasol (₹7). More remote footpaths continue from Katagla to Chowki.

🛏 Sleeping & Eating

Accommodation rates are at their highest between March and August, with substantial discounts in September and October. Many guesthouses close down for winter from November to March.

Old and New Kasol have loads of traveller restaurants serving cakes and identical traveller fare – Moon Dance Cafe & German Bakery and Bhoj Restaurant are good choices.

Alpine Guest House　　　　HOTEL **$**
(☑273710; alpinehimachal@gmail.com; d ₹600-1000, q ₹800) One of the better places in town, this sturdy brick-and-timber place is set among pine trees next to the river in Old Kasol. Lawns and terraces provide space for swapping travel stories, and spacious rooms bask in the natural sounds of river and forest.

Taji Place　　　　HOTEL **$**
(☑9816461684; d without/with bathroom ₹250/550, cottage ₹850) A big pink house in a sweet litttle meadow down by the river, a short walk from New Kasol, Taji has a range of tidy rooms and a couple of well-equipped cottages in the spacious garden, plus a private hot spring (₹2 per minute).

Panchali Holiday Home　　　　HOTEL **$**
(☑273195; www.panchaliholidayhome.com; r ₹550-1200; 🛜) Set back from the main road, this friendly modern hotel doesn't have a ton of character but the rooms are clean and comfortable. Front rooms have nice balconies, and some have an extra bed perfect for a child. Rates double in June and July.

The Evergreen　　　　MULTICUISINE **$$**
(mains ₹90-150) Currently our favourite place for its excellent chicken *sipoodim* (barbeque) served with chips and hummus, plus sizzlers, pizza, lasagne and good Israeli and vegetarian specials. Bring a book for the outdoor seating and lounge area.

PIN-PARVATI VALLEY TREK

Only accessible from late June to late September (with September the best month), this strenuous but rewarding six- to nine-day wilderness trek crosses the snow-bound Pin-Parvati Pass (5319m) to the Pin Valley in Spiti. There's no accommodation en route so you'll have to be self-sufficient or go with a trekking agency. Organised treks are relatively pricey because your crew (often Nepali) needs to be transported back to their starting point. Sometimes two sets of porters are required, handing over loads near the pass.

The trail starts at Pulga, across the river from Barshani and accessible by bus or taxi. From Pulga, the route ascends through forest and pasture, past the Khir Ganga hot springs to Thakur Khan. Two more days through an arid alpine zone takes you to High Camp for an overnight stop before attempting the pass. A challenging tramp over snow and scree will take you up to the ridge, then down into the Pin Valley. The final stage easily could be broken up to allow for two days hiking through the Pin Valley National Park to the village of Mudh, which has accommodation and a daily bus connection to Kaza.

STAGE	ROUTE	DURATION (HR)	DISTANCE (KM)
1	Pulga to Khir Ganga	4-5	10
2	Khir Ganga to Thakur Khan	6	15
3	Thakur Khan to Mantalai Lake	7	16
4	Mantalai Lake to High Camp	4	12
5	High Camp to Pin Valley Camp via Pin-Parvati Pass	5-6	12
6	Pin Valley Camp to Mudh	8	20

Little Italy ITALIAN **$$**
(mains ₹130-180) Pizzas and pasta dishes
are better than average at this 1st-floor
restaurant, and you can get a decent Keralan
coffee or cold beer.

ℹ Getting There & Away

Buses from Bhuntar to Manikaran pass through
Kasol (₹25, one hour). Fares at the taxi stand
near the bridge in Kasol include Manikaran
(₹100), Jari (₹200), Bhuntar (₹600), Kullu
(₹800) and Manali (₹1600).

Manikaran

☑ 01902 / ELEV 1737M

With steam continually rising from its enor-
mous riverside temple, Manikaran is famous
for its hot springs and is an important place
of pilgrimage for Sikhs and Hindus. The
name means 'Jewel from the Ear' – according
to local legend, a giant snake stole ear-
rings from the goddess Parvati while she
was bathing, then snorted them out into
the ground, which released the hot springs.
The water emerging from the ground is hot
enough to boil rice (as high as 94°C) and it
has to be cooled with river water for bath-
ing. Locals claim it can cure everything from
rheumatism to bronchitis.

◉ Sights & Activities

The town is centred on the enormous multi-
storey **Sri Guru Nanak Ji Gurdwara**, which
was built in 1940 and lurks behind a veil of
steam on the north side of the river. It's half-
temple, half-spa, with bathing pools and a
'hot cave' steam room below. The shrine in-
side is revered by both Hindus and Sikh pil-
grims, so remove your shoes and cover your
head if you want to enter.

There are baths at the temple with sepa-
rate facilities for men and women, as well
as a nicer open-air pool (men only) on the
south side of the river opposite the gurd-
wara. Bring a costume, towel and flip-flops.

The village also has several temples, in-
cluding the recently restored stone hut–style
Raghunath Mandir, and the ornate wooden
Naina Devi Temple. Keep an eye out for
pots of rice and bags of potatoes boiling in
the vents, fumaroles and springs around the
village and gurdwara.

🛏 Sleeping & Eating

Manikaran is an easy half-day trip from Ka-
sol, but there are several guesthouses if you
wish to stay overnight. Most hotels are on
the north side of the river in the main vil-
lage, reached by a suspension bridge from
the bus stand. Note that alcohol is banned
on the gurdwara side of the river.

Fateh Paying Guesthouse GUESTHOUSE **$**
(☑ 9816894968; r ₹200; ❄) Signposted down
an alley in the old part of the village, this
big blue house has just five simple but pleas-
ant rooms, with welcoming owners and a
hot-spring pool (₹1 per minute). The sunny
rooftop terrace is set among the pitched
slate roofs of the old village.

Padha Family Guest House HOTEL **$**
(☑ 8894643410; d ₹150-300; ❄) In the colour-
ful, kitschy bazaar surrounding the gurd-
wara, this budget place has a range of simple
rooms set around a lemon-tree courtyard.
The mattresses are hard but the balcony
river views are great if you can snag one.
Downstairs is a good restaurant (mains ₹90
to ₹200) and a square plunge pool fed by hot
spring water.

Country Charm Hotel HOTEL **$**
(☑ 9805683677; d ₹550-990) On the south
side of the river near the bus stand, Country
Charm has views across to the village and
gurdwara. Rooms are comfortable and the
upstairs balconies practically hang out over
the river. The midpriced rooms offer the best
value.

Holy Palace Restaurant MULTICUISINE **$**
(mains ₹70-150; ◷ 8am-10pm) Travellers and
pilgrims are lured here by the red booths
and a broad menu of dosas, pizza and In-
dian food. It's in the bazaar but there's no
English sign.

ℹ Getting There & Away

Buses run at least hourly between Manikaran
and Bhuntar (₹35, 1½ hours), via Kasol (₹5, 15
minutes). For Manali, change in Kullu or Bhuntar.
Day trips by taxi can be arranged in Manali
(₹1600) or Kullu (₹1300).

From Manikaran, taxis charge ₹100 to Kasol,
₹900 to Bhuntar, ₹1000 to Kullu and ₹1700 to
Manali.

Kullu

☑ 01902 / POP 18,300 / ELEV 1220M

Kullu is the administrative capital of the
Kullu Valley and marks the beginning of
the ascent to Manali. Although there's not a

SHOPPING FOR SHAWLS

The Kullu Valley is famous for its traditional shawls, and the highway between Bhuntar and Manali is lined with scores of shops, showrooms and emporiums. The shawls are woven on wooden hand-looms using wool from sheep, pashmina goats or angora rabbits. This is one of the main industries in the Kullu Valley and it provides an income for thousands of local women, many of whom have organised themselves into shawl-weaving cooperatives.

For high quality without the hard sell, head to the nearest branch of **Bhuttico** (www.bhutticoshawls.com), the Bhutti Weavers' Cooperative, which has showrooms in Manali, Kullu and Bhuntar, and a **factory showroom** (☎01902-252196; ⏰9am-5pm Mon-Sat) at Bhuttico Colony, 8km south of Kullu. Established in 1944 by a group of village women, Bhuttico charges fixed prices, so it's a good place to gauge price and quality. Expect to pay upwards of ₹460 for lambswool, from ₹1400 for angora, ₹3300/6000 for blend/pure pashmina blend and ₹6800 for the exquisitely embroidered shawls worn by village women.

great deal of interest in the town itself, the bustling bazaar town makes a gritty change from the hippie holiday resorts found elsewhere in the valley.

In October, Kullu hosts one of the largest and loudest Dussehra festivals in India. Over 200 idols are paraded into town from surrounding temples, led by a huge *rath* (chariot) holding the statue of Lord Raghunath from the Raghunath Temple. Simultaneously, a weeklong carnival and market is held on the *maidan* (parade ground), with entertainment such as acrobats and musicians. With some 30,000 devotees hitting town, accommodation is scarce, but it's an easy day trip from Manali or even Kasol.

Kullu is divided in two by the Sarvari River. The southern part of town has the taxi stand, tourist office and most restaurants and hotels. The bus station and Raghunath Temple are north of the river – take the shortcut down through the bazaar below the Hotel Shobla International.

◉ Sights & Activities

Raghunath Temple HINDU TEMPLE
(⏰11.30am-5.30pm) The pre-eminent temple in Kullu is the Raghunath Temple, which enshrines a revered idol that's paraded through town during Dussehra. To get there, take the steps leading uphill opposite the bus station, veer right and look for the gateway, past the imposing **Raja Rupi**, the former palace of the rajas of Kullu.

Bhekhali Temple HINDU TEMPLE
There are several important temples in the surrounding hills, accessible by taxi or local

bus. About 3km from Kullu, high on the hillside in the village of Bhekhali, the Bhekali Temple (Jagannathi Devi Temple) offers an impressive vista over the valley. A return taxi here costs ₹500, and buses run here at 9am and 2pm from the bus station.

Bijli Mahadev Temple HINDU TEMPLE
Reached via a 3km hike from Chansari, 11km southeast of Kullu on the east bank of the Beas, the hilltop temple of Bijli Mahadev is surmounted by a 20m wooden pole that attracts divine blessings in the form of lightning. (The temple is also known as Bijleshwar Mahadev, but don't confuse this with the Bisheshwar Mahadev Temple in Bajaura.) The surge of power shatters the stone Shiva lingam inside the temple, which is then glued back together with butter. A return taxi costs ₹1100. A noon bus runs from the bus station (₹20) or head 2km northeast to Ramshila and look for a shared taxi there.

☞ Tours

The **Kullu Taxi Operators' Union** (☎222332; www.kullutaxiunion.com) at the taxi stand offers sightseeing day tours to four local temples for around ₹1100, or to Prashar Lake for ₹2400.

🛏 Sleeping

Hotel Vikrant HOTEL $
(☎222756; d ₹350-750) Tricky to find, down an alley behind the HPTDC office, Vikrant is a backpacker-friendly place with a friendly vibe. Wood panelling and shared balconies give rooms a simple charm. Upper floors are

bigger and brighter, but all have TVs and hot showers.

Hotel Aaditya HOTEL **$**

(☎224263; www.hotelaaditya.com; d ₹440-880) Just across the footbridge from the bus station, Aaditya tries harder than most in this price range, with friendly service, quality mattresses and oddly fancy bathroom fixtures. The best are the top-floor rooms with balconies overlooking the river.

Hotel Shobla International HOTEL **$$**

(☎224263; www.shoblainternational.com; r ₹1772-2583, ste ₹3229-4520; ❀) The best of Kullu's business hotels, this modern place near the bazaar has clean rooms, and there's a good restaurant and bar. Standard rooms offer the best value since they come with balconies and a view. Expect discounts of 30%.

✗ Eating

There are good restaurants at both the Hotel Shobla International (mains ₹150 to ₹250) and the Hotel Aaditya.

Hot Spice MULTICUISINE **$**

(mains ₹80-110) For bargain-priced Indian thalis and good breakfasts, head for this pleasant open-air cafe near the tourist office.

ℹ Information

The **HPTDC tourist office** (☎222349; ◷10am-5pm), near the taxi stand on the maidan, can book seats on deluxe HPTDC buses from Manali to Delhi and (in season) Shimla.

The main post office is uphill from the taxi stand. The State Bank of India has ATMs south of the maidan and in the bazaar.

ℹ Getting There & Away

AIR

The airport for Kullu is 10km south at Bhuntar.

BUS

On the north side of the Sarvari River, the bus station has services every 15 minutes to Bhuntar (₹13, 30 minutes), Manali (₹45, 90 minutes) and Mandi (₹82, 2½ hours), plus five buses a day to Naggar (₹24, one hour). For Manikaran (₹60, three hours) take one of the frequent private buses or take a bus to Bhuntar and change. Buses from Manali to destinations outside the Kullu Valley arrive in Kullu about 1½ hours after departure.

TAXI

Sample one-way fares include Manikaran (₹900), Naggar (₹600) and Jari (₹700).

Naggar

☎01902 / ELEV 1760M

Centred on imposing Naggar Castle, the slumbering village of Naggar was the capital of Kullu for 1500 years and remains perhaps the nicest village in the Kullu Valley. Russian painter and explorer Nikolai Roerich liked it so much he settled here in the early 20th century. The village lies on the east bank road between Kullu and Manali, about 1km above the road. Although an easy day trip from Manali, there are good guesthouses and restaurants around the castle.

◉ Sights & Activities

Naggar Castle HISTORIC BUILDING

(foreigner ₹15; ◷museum 9am-7pm) Built by the Sikh rajas of Kullu in 1460, this beautiful fort is a fine example of the alternating stone and timber style of Himachali architecture. It was converted into a hotel in 1978 when the last raja fell on hard times. There's a tiny one-room **museum** downstairs, and the **Jagtipath Temple** in the courtyard houses a slab of stone said to have been carried here by wild bees. The best way to experience the castle is to stay here.

Roerich Gallery &
Urusvati Museum MUSEUM

(☎248290; www.roerichtrust.org; adult/child combined ticket ₹50/20, camera/video ₹25/60; ◷10am-1pm & 1.30-6pm Tue-Sun, to 5pm Nov-Mar) About 2km above the castle is the **Roerich Gallery**, the former home of eccentric Russian painter, spiritualist, Inner Asian explorer and possible spy, Nikolai Roerich, who died in Naggar in 1947. The lower floors display some of Roerich's surreally colourful landscapes, while the upper floors preserve the artist's private rooms. Don't miss the 1930 Dodge car hidden around the side. Roerich was the brains behind the Roerich Pact, a treaty signed by more than 60 countries guaranteeing the preservation of cultural monuments around the world.

A five-minute walk uphill from the gallery is the **Urusvati Himalayan Folk & Art Museum** (admission with the gallery ticket), which houses ethnological artefacts and photos from the early days of the Himalayan Research Institute.

Temples HINDU TEMPLES

Heading down the track beside the castle, you'll pass the handsome 11th-century

HIMACHAL PRADESH NAGGAR

Vishnu Mandir, covered in ornate carvings. Downhill past the tiny post office is the Gauri Shankar Temple, dedicated to Shiva and surrounded by smaller temples devoted to Narayan.

Just below the Roerich Gallery is the pagodalike Tripura Sundari Devi Temple, surrounded by carved wooden outbuildings. High up on the ridge above Naggar, the Murlidhar Krishna Temple is reached by a woodland path beyond the Roerich Gallery.

Trekking   TREKKING

Naggar is the starting point for the excellent three-day trek to Malana village and Jari via the 3650m Chandrakani Pass, accessible between May and October. Ravi Sharma at Poonam Mountain Lodge (☏ 9418149827; www.poonammountain.in), beside Naggar Castle, is an experienced operator who can organise this trek, including a three-day extension to a glacier view above Malana and day hikes to a waterfall above Janna village, as well as other regional treks. Treks cost US$50 to US$70 per person per day and jeep safaris cost around US$50 per day.

🛏 Sleeping & Eating

Chander Lok Guesthouse   GUESTHOUSE $

(☏ 248213; d ₹250-350) The rooms in this family-run guesthouse are clean and pleasant but the best thing is the outdoor garden, which opens up into a charming 1500-year-old stone temple shrine. Only the downstairs rooms have piped hot water. Simple vegetarian food is possible. It's a five-minute walk below the castle in Chanalti village.

Alliance Guesthouse   GUESTHOUSE $

(☏ 9817097033; www.alliancenaggar.com; r ₹250-1000, ste ₹1200-1800; @ 🛜) Halfway between the castle and the Roerich Museum, this friendly French-run place has a wide range of well-kept rooms, from shared-bathroom cheapies to duplex suites perfect for families. A lot of thought has gone into this place, with nice touches including a kettle in the rooms, and there's a library, laundry service, restaurant and plenty of sitting areas; everything that you could want.

Soham's Chateau de Naggar   GUESTHOUSE $

(☏ 248271; www.chateaudenaggar.com; Castle Rd; r ₹660-880) The eight rooms here have a boutiquey feel, with cosy wooden floors, Tibetan carpets and balconies that overlook the valley. The top-floor restaurant offers great food (mains ₹75 to ₹200) and views. A tip: the top-floor rooms suffer from the continual scrape of restaurant chairs, making the lower-floor rooms better value. It's on the road leading up to the castle.

Castle Hotel   HERITAGE HOTEL $$$

(☏ 248316; www.hptdc.gov.in; d ₹1610-4945) The most atmospheric accommodation in town is the castle itself. Wood and stone corridors open onto a wide variety of rooms, some original and decked out in colonial-era finery, others completely refurbished. The views from valley-side rooms are superb. Even if the hotel isn't within your budget, there's an affordable restaurant with a terrace overlooking the valley.

ℹ Getting There & Away

Local buses run hourly or so between Manali and lower Naggar until 6pm (₹25, one hour). An autorickshaw up to the castle from the main road costs ₹50. A return taxi from Manali to Naggar costs ₹700.

Manali

☏ 01902 / POP 4400 / ELEV 2050M

With super views of the Dhauladhar and Pir Panjal Ranges, and with mountain adventures beckoning from all directions, Manali is a year-round magnet for tourists. Backpackers come to hang out in the hippy villages around the main town; adventure tourists come for trekking, paragliding, rafting and skiing; and Indian honeymoon couples or families come for the cool mountain air and their first taste of snow on a day trip to Rohtang La.

As the main jumping-off point for Ladakh, Spiti and Lahaul (between June and October), it makes sense to unwind here for a few days before continuing the long journey into the mountains. Most travellers stay in the villages of Vashisht or Old Manali, which have a laid-back vibe and plenty of services, but close for winter from sometime in October to May.

◉ Sights & Activities

Hadimba Temple   HINDU TEMPLE

(Map p308) Also known as the Dhungri Temple, this ancient wood and stone mandir was erected in 1553. Pilgrims come here from across India to honour Hadimba, the wife of Bhima from the Mahabharata. The

HIMACHAL PRADESH MANALI

walls of the temple are covered in wood-carvings of dancers, and horns of bulls and ibex adorn the walls. Grisly animal sacrifices are carried out in May for the three-day Dhungri Mela. Ghatotkach, the son of Hadimba and Bhima, is worshipped in the form of a sacred tree near the temple. Villagers make offerings of knives, goat horns, and tin effigies of animals, people and houses.

Hadimba is a 20-minute walk northwest of Manali, or you can take an autorickshaw (₹50).

Buddhist Monasteries   BUDDHIST TEMPLES

There's a small Tibetan community just south of the town centre. The **Himalayan Nyingmapa Buddhist Temple** (Map p312; ◷6am-6pm) contains a two-storey statue of Sakyamuni, the historical Buddha.

Just west of here is the more traditional **Panden Ngari Gompa** (Map p312; ◷6am-6pm), with an atmospheric juniper-scented prayer room crammed with statues of bodhisattvas, revered lamas and Buddhist deities. Chat with the Tibetan refugees over a bowl of *thukpa* noodles in the attached teashop.

Old Manali   AREA

About 2.5km north of the Mall on the far side of the Manalsu Nala stream, Old Manali still has some of the feel of an Indian mountain village once you get past the core backpacker zone. There are some remarkable old houses of wood and stone, and the towering **Manu Maharishi Temple** (Map p308) is built on the site where the Noah-like Manu meditated after surviving the great flood. A trail to Solang Nullah (11km) runs north from here through the village of Goshal (2km).

Nature Parks   PARKS

A towering grove of magnificent deodars (cedars) on the banks of the Beas has been set aside as a lovely **nature park** (Map p308; admission ₹5; ◷9am-7pm), with a small aviary of Himalayan birds, including the monal pheasant, Himachal's state bird. South of the centre is the similar **Van Vihar Park** (Map p312; admission ₹10; ◷8am-7pm, to 5pm winter)

☞ Tours

In high season, the HPTDC offers day tours by bus to the Rohtang La (₹290), to Manikaran and the Parvati Valley (₹330) and to Naggar and Solang Nullah (₹240), if there

CHARAS

Over the years, many tourists have been lured here by the famous Manali charas, which is seriously potent stuff. Though in Old Manali it's smoked fairly openly, it's still illegal and local police do arrest people for possession (or hit them for bribes). See also the boxed text on p299.

are enough takers. Private travel agencies offer similar bus tours.

The **Him-Anchal Taxi Operators Union** (Map p312; ☎252120; the Mall) has fixed-price tours, including to Rohtang La (₹1900), Solang Nullah (₹600) and Naggar (₹650).

☞ Adventure Tour Operators

The following places are reliable and well established and can arrange treks, tours and adventure activities.

Antrek Tours & Travel   OUTDOOR ADVENTURE
(Map p312; ☎252292; www.antrek.co.in; 1 Rambagh, the Mall) Good for trekking and skiing, and runs the tent camps at Sarchu on the road to Ladakh

Himalayan Adventurers   OUTDOOR ADVENTURE
(Map p312; ☎252750; www.himalayanadventurers-india.com; 44 the Mall) Trekking, skiing, mountain biking and mountaineering.

Himalayan Extreme Center   OUTDOOR ADVENTURE
(Map p308; ☎9816174164; www.himalayan-extreme-center.com) With offices in Old Manali and Vashisht, this Swiss-run place is your one-stop shop for almost any adventure activity.

North Face Adventure Tours   OUTDOOR ADVENTURE
(Map p312; ☎254041; www.northfaceindia.com; the Mall) Organises treks throughout the region.

Tiger Eye Adventure   OUTDOOR ADVENTURE
(Map p308; ☎252718; www.tigereyeadventure.com; Old Manali) Good for transport to Leh.

🛏 Sleeping

Manali has plenty of good-value accommodation, especially outside the peak seasons of May to July and Christmas. Peak season rates are listed here but discounts of up to

Manali & Vashisht

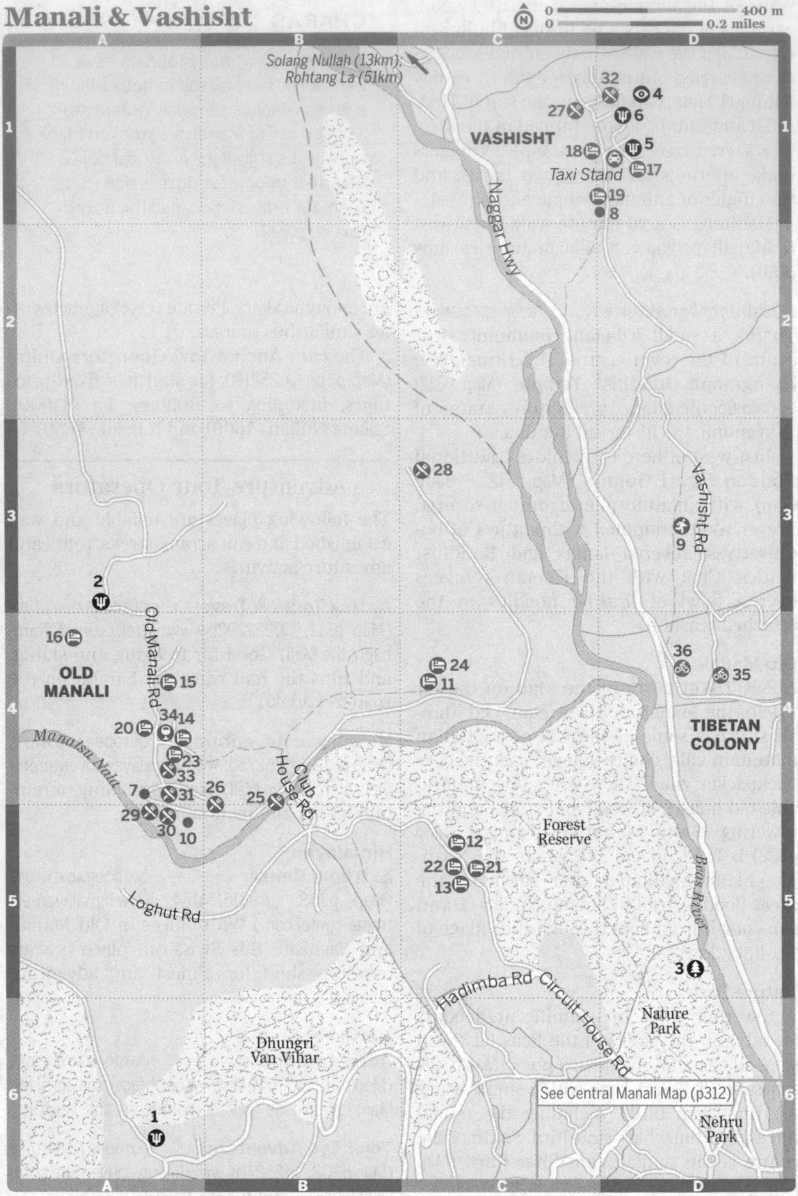

N

0 — 400 m
0 — 0.2 miles

Solang Nullah (13km);
Rohtang La (51km)

VASHISHT

32
4
27
6
18
5
Taxi Stand
17
19
8

Naggar Hwy

Vashisht Rd

28

9

2

16

**OLD
MANALI**

Old Manali Rd

15

24
11

36
35

**TIBETAN
COLONY**

20
34 14
23
33
Manalsu Nala
7
31
26
29
30 10
25

Club House Rd

12
22
21
13

Forest
Reserve

Beas River

Loghut Rd

Hadimba Rd
Circuit House Rd

3

Nature
Park

Dhungri
Van Vihar

See Central Manali Map (p312)

Nehru
Park

1

HIMACHAL PRADESH MANALI

50% are standard at other times, especially at top-end places. Heating is rare in budget places so be prepared to dive under a blanket to stay warm.

Few backpackers choose to stay in central Manali unless they're planning to catch an early bus – the best budget places, by far, are a short distance north in the villages of Old Manali and Vashisht. Manali's best upmarket hotels are found along Circuit House Rd, heading uphill to Old Manali.

Manali & Vashisht

🛏 Manali

Pushpak Hotel
HOTEL $

(Map p312; ☎253656; d ₹330-550) Down an alley opposite the bus station (and accessed through a restaurant), this is the best budget place on the Mall. The roadside rooms have a balcony and great light but are noisier; the ₹400 rooms towards the back are quieter. All have carpets, TV and hot water.

Sunshine Guest House
HERITAGE HOTEL $$

(Map p308; ☎252320; Circuit House Rd; r ₹1500) This ramshackle and rambling Raj-era mansion was due to be renovated in 2013, so you can expect the charming but neglected rooms to go upscale. Enormous suites with fireplaces, odd changing rooms and giant bathrooms may be a bit draughty, but the balconies, dining room and overgrown garden are full of colonial-era charm.

Johnson Hotel
HOTEL $$$

(Map p312; ☎253764; www.johnsonhotel.in; Circuit House Rd; d ₹3757; ❄@🏵) One of several places named in honour of the Raj-era landowner Jimmy Johnson. This is a classy wood-and-stone hotel that has nine snug rooms, a century-old lodge and lovely gardens, as well as an excellent garden restaurant (p313). Everything's in immaculate shape, making this one worth the price.

Negi's Hotel Mayflower
HOTEL $$$

(Map p308; ☎252104; http://mayflowermanali.com; Club House Rd; r ₹3523; ❄@🏵) Mayflower is a stately Swiss-style wooden lodge with cascading balconies and stylish wood-panelled rooms, some with open fireplaces. The porch rockers and gardens are a good place to relax in the afternoon sun, though it's a bit close to the road.

Baikunth Magnolia
HERITAGE HOTEL $$$

(Map p308; ☎250118; www.baikunth.com; Circuit House Rd; r ₹6106; 🏵) The Baikunth Magnolia is yet another gorgeous old heritage property, surrounded by pleasant gardens and decked out with over-stuffed couches, old prints on the walls an atmospheric bar and modern rooms, most of which have private balconies.

Johnson Lodge
HOTEL $$$

(Map p312; ☎251523; www.johnsonslodge.com; Circuit House Rd; d ₹4697, cottage ₹8807; ❄@) Built in wood and timber in the traditional Himachal style, but slick and contemporary inside, with a modern sports bar, the

OUTDOOR ACTIVITIES IN MANALI

Manali is the adventure sports capital of Himachal Pradesh, and all sorts of outdoor activities can be organised through tour operators in town.

Fishing

The rivers of the Kullu and Parvati Valleys are rich in trout and mahseer. The season runs from March to June and October to November, and rods and tackle can be hired from agencies in Manali; daily fishing licences from the Tourism Office cost ₹100. Top spots include the upper tributaries of the Beas and Parvati Rivers at Kasol.

Mountain Biking

Though you may think that the steep slopes around Manali would have some prime mountain biking, you'll probably have to take a car to most tracks that are worth riding. Agencies offer bike hire for ₹500 to ₹850 per day (and can give current info on routes) or you can organise tours to Ladakh, Spiti and Lahaul. One audacious day trip is the freewheeling descent from the Rohtang La – buses and taxis can transport you and your bike to the pass. **Himalayan Extreme Center** (Map p308; 9816174164; www.himalayan-extreme-center.com; Manalsu Nala) offers this, as well as a day's ride to Naggar and Kullu.

Mountaineering

Mountaineering training can be arranged through the **Directorate of Mountaineering & Allied Sports** (250337; www.adventurehimalaya.org), in Aleo, 3km south of Manali. Basic eight-day mountaineering and rock climbing courses run between May and October for ₹3400/13,000 (Indian/foreigner), including food, accommodation, guides and training. The course covers essential trekking techniques and a series of local ascents. Local agencies can arrange expeditions to Hanuman Tibba (5930m) and Deo Tibba (6001m).

Paragliding

Paragliding is popular at Solang Nullah and at Gulaba (below the Rohtang Pass) from April to October. Short flights start at ₹700 for a two-minute flight, but adventure-tour operators can organise longer flights from surrounding take-off points for ₹1500 to ₹2500.

Rafting

White-water rafting trips on the Beas River start from Pirdi, 3km downriver from Kullu. There is 14km of Grade II and III white water between Pirdi and the take-out point at Jhiri; trips cost around between ₹350 and ₹550 per person, depending on the duration. Book through travel agents or directly at Pirdi. May to July and late September are the best times.

---

towering Johnson Lodge boasts bright, rooms that are starting to show some wear, as well as luxurious two- and three-bedroom cottages. Sunny grounds and a spa are bonuses and they are open to discounts.

Banon Resorts　　　　　　HOTEL **$$$**
(Map p308; 253026; www.banonresortsmanali.com; d ₹7045, cottages from ₹21,136; ✳ 🌐) This quiet, luxury hotel is a little slicker than its competition. Centrally heated rooms in the main hotel are spacious but surprisingly plain, while the two-bedroom cottages are the last word in luxurious peace and privacy. The slate-floor balconies and restaurant terrace overlooking a garden provide the charm.

Old Manali

★ **Veer Guest House**　　　　GUESTHOUSE **$**
(Map p308; 252710; veerguesthouse@hotmail.com; r ₹440-1100, ste 1760-2350; @) Set in a pretty garden, long-running Veer is one of Old Manali's best-value hotels. Rooms in the quaint lime-green old block with wood-plank flooring have plenty of character, while new rooms at the front are bright and slick, with TVs and private balconies. There's a great little restaurant and an internet cafe.

Tourist Nest Guest House　　GUESTHOUSE **$**
(Map p308; 252383; touristnest@gmail.com; r ₹400-500; 🌐) In the heart of old Manali, this place has clean, tiled, well-kept rooms

Rock Climbing

The cliffs at Solang, Aleo and Vashisht have a good range of bolted and traditional routes ranging from French 6a to 6c (British 5a to 6a). Himalayan Extreme Center (p307) in Vashisht offers day trips for ₹1500/900 per full/half-day, including all equipment. Independent climbers should bring a selection of slings, nuts and cams (particularly in the smaller sizes) and a 30m or 60m rope.

Skiing & Snowboarding

From January to March, the village of Solang Nullah transforms into Himachal's main ski and snowboarding resort. Skiing and showboarding equipment can be hired through tour operators in Manali or hotels in Solang Nullah for ₹1000 per day. Year-round high-altitude skiing expeditions and snowshoe treks can be arranged on virgin powder (experienced skiers only) through Himalayan Extreme Center for around ₹2500 per day (trips last three to five days). Costly heli-skiing trips to high-altitude powder can be arranged through **Himalayan Heli Adventures** (✆9816025899; www.himachal.com).

Walking & Trekking

Manali is a popular starting point for organised mountain treks. Most agencies offer multi-day treks for around ₹2500 per day, all-inclusive. Popular options include Beas Kund (three days), the Pin-Parvati Trek from the Parvati Valley to Spiti (eight days) and the Hamta Pass (4270m) to Lahaul (four to five days).

Plenty of shorter walks are possible from Manali, though the usual rules on safe trekking apply – tell someone where you are going and never walk alone. The 13km hike up the western side of the Beas River to Solang Nullah is a pleasing alternative to the bus, or you can trek 6km to the snowline above Lama Dugh meadow along the Manalsu Nala stream.

Zorbing

During summer, the ski slope at Solang Nullah is a popular place for zorbing – basically, rolling downhill inside a giant inflatable ball. You can make arrangements in Manali or in Solang Nullah – expect to pay ₹300 for a roll down the hill.

Other Activities

Other activities available in the area include horse riding (₹1000 per day) and canyoning (₹2400 per day). Quad-bike rides around Solang Nullah cost ₹500 for a quick 4km round or ₹1500 per hour. Short hot-air balloon rides are sometimes organised from Solang Nullah during summer.

HIMACHAL PRADESH MANALI

with private balconies and some of the best rates around. The top-floor suites sleep four.

Drifters' Inn HOTEL $
(Map p308; ✆9805033127; www.driftersinn.in; Old Manali Rd; r ₹660-1174, ste ₹1409; @ ☎) The hipness of the ground-floor restaurant doesn't quite extend into the bland rooms but it's a spotless place with outdoor terraces on every floor. The loungey restaurant has great breakfasts, good espresso and imaginative beverages such as a seabuckthorn fizz.

Mountain Dew Guesthouse HOTEL $
(Map p308; ✆9816446366; d ₹300-400; ☎) This yellow three-storey hotel has good-sized rooms and nice balconies with an on-site coffee shop, though the quality of the mat-

tresses varies. It's one of the best-value places in Old Manali.

Apple View Guest House GUESTHOUSE $
(Map p308; ✆253899; www.appleviewmanali.com; r without bathroom ₹200; ☎) Up a pathway behind the HPTDC Club House, this delightful village guesthouse is set on a peaceful garden plot among apple orchards. The eight rooms are simple but well cared for, and the upstairs patio is perfect for hanging out. If it's full, try the not-quite-as-nice **Up Country Lodge** (Map p129; ✆252257; d ₹300-400) next door.

Himalayan Country House GUESTHOUSE $$
(Map p308; ✆252294; www.himalayancountryhouse.com; r ₹880-1761; ☎) Hidden at the end of the road in Old Manali, this four-storey

Central Manali

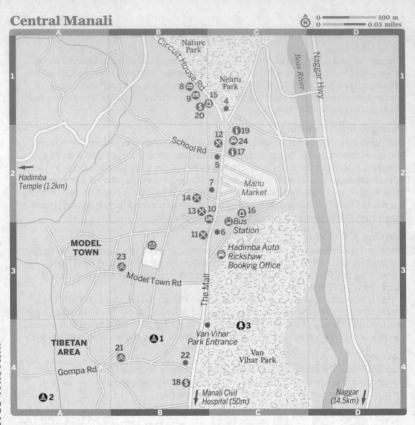

Central Manali

stone and timber hotel overlooks the slate roofs of village homes with excellent views across to the mountains. It's nicely designed, with traditional carved doors and shared balconies, but it's a bit overpriced if you don't finnagle a discount. Room rates rise with the floor but the actual rooms are the same.

Dragon Guest House HOTEL $$

(Map p308; ☏252290; www.dragontreks.com; Old Manali; r ₹550-1409, ste from ₹3288; ❇@☎) Dragon has a beautiful stone-and-wood facade and an orchard out front. All rooms are comfortable, though the better rooms are in the Swiss-chalet-style upper floors. There's a great restaurant, an internet cafe, and a reliable travel agency for treks and tours.

✗ Eating

Manali has some fine Indian and international restaurants, and there are lots of cheap travellers' cafes in Old Manali and Vashisht. Most restaurants serve trout sourced from local farms.

✗ Manali

Manali Sweets SWEETS $

(Map p312; snacks from ₹10; ⊗7am-10.30pm) Manali's favourite local *dhaba* (snack bar) serves an endless stream of hot chai, sweets and snacks. Depending on the weather, warm up with a spicy *channa samosa* (veg samosa with chickpeas) or cool down with a chilled *ras malai* (cream-cheese ball in pistachio milk).

★ Mayur INDIAN, MULTICUISINE $$

(Map p312; Mission Rd; dishes ₹90-210; ⊗9am-11pm) Locals rate Mayur highly for its well-prepared North and South Indian specialities. The decor downstairs is solidly old-school and classy, with impeccable uniformed waiters, while the upstairs is bright and contemporary. The Indian dishes are excellent and there are some refreshingly unusual Continental dishes including ratatouille, fish in coconut milk, and liver with onions and tomato.

Chopsticks ASIAN $$

(Map p312; the Mall; dishes ₹150-270; ⊗7.30am-10.30pm) The most popular traveller choice in the Manali town centre, this intimate Tibetan-Chinese-Japanese place has Tibetan lutes on the walls and serves good *momos* and *gyoza* (their Japanese equivalent),

plus some sushi and lots of Chinese dishes. Cold beers and fruit wines also served.

Khyber MULTICUISINE $$

(Map p312; the Mall; dishes ₹80-280; ⊗8am-11pm) Upstairs by the main junction, this darkened bar and restaurant is central Manali's best place for a cold beer or bottle of cider. The food is also good – the speciality is meat-heavy Punjabi and Afghani cuisine but there's also Chinese, Continental, and tandoori trout. Drinks are reasonably priced, and the booths are a good place to huddle.

Johnson's Cafe CONTINENTAL $$$

(Map p312; Circuit House Rd; dishes ₹180-400; ⊗8am-10.30pm) The restaurant at Johnson Hotel is one of the best in town for European food, with specialities such as lamb and mint gravy, ravioli with blue-cheese sauce, and fig-and-apple crumble. The restaurant-bar is cosy but the garden terrace is the place to be, especially during afternoon happy hours (2pm to 10pm).

✗ Old Manali

There are numerous garden restaurants serving all the usual suspects – pizzas, *momos*, banana pancakes, apple pie – from early morning to late evening. All these places close by November. Popular backpacker restaurants include **Shiva Garden Cafe** (Map p308; Old Manali Rd; dishes ₹80-150) and **Blue Elephant Cafe** (Map p308; Old Manali Rd; dishes ₹80-150) near the river, both serving decent traveller fare.

★ Dylan's Toasted & Roasted CAFE $

(Map p308; www.dylanscoffee.com; coffee ₹50-100; ⊗10am-8pm Mon-Sat) Manali's mellowest hang-out, this hole-in-the-wall coffeeshop serves the best espresso in town, cinnamon tea, hearty breakfasts and wicked desserts including chocolate-chip cookies and their version of 'Hello to the Queen' – a local speciality of ice cream and fried banana chunks on a bed of broken biscuits. DVDs are shown in an adjoining room.

People MULTICUISINE $$

(Map p308; mains ₹120-190) One of the best backpacker places, serving up solid versions of Thai curry, pizza, Israeli dishes, fresh vegie salads and even sushi rolls topped with grilled trout. The Russian owner's roots are showing in the blinis and *sirniki* fritters with condensed milk. Get creative with the supplied crayons and paper table cloth and your artistic expression will go up on the wall.

Pizza Olive   ITALIAN $$
(Map p308; pizzas ₹170-190; ⊙9am-10pm) The aromas wafting from the pizza oven give this place an authentic Italian feel, and the pizzas and pasta dishes don't disappoint. You can eat in the sleek modern interior or out in the garden.

★**La Plage**   FRENCH $$$
(Map p308; ☑9805340977; mains ₹280-450; ⊙noon-4pm & 7.30-10pm Tue-Sun) Head and shoulders above every other restaurant in town, dinner here is like being invited to the hip Paris apartment of your much, much cooler friend. Classic French standards such as liver pâté are joined by pumpkin ravioli and desserts including lime mousse and a chocolate thali selection, while the breakfasts are for serious aficionados. It's 1km from the old Manali bridge in an apple orchard, but call in advance and they'll pick you up in a customised tuk-tuk.

Lazy Dog Lounge   MULTICUISINE $$$
(Map p308; mains ₹140-350; 🛜) Slick restaurant-bar overlooking the river and featuring big plates of fresh and flavourful international food that's steps above typical backpacker fare. Sit on chairs, benches or floor cushions in a space that's classy yet earthy, or relax in the outdoor garden if the music is too bad (it often is). The food ranges from trout cakes to Thai rice bowls and Indian thalis, and the beer and wine lists are as good as you'll get in the mountains.

 Drinking

Restaurants double as bars to form the centre of nightlife in Manali, and most serve alcohol. Himachal's bounteous orchards produce huge quantities of apples, pears, plums and apricots, some of which are fermented locally and made into alcoholic cider, perry (pear cider) and a wide range of strong fruit wines. In Manali town, the best places for a beer or fruit wine are Khyber (p313) and Chopsticks (p313). The upmarket Johnson Hotel (p309), Johnson Lodge (p309) and Banon Resorts (p310) also have good bars.

In Old Manali, **The Hangout** (Map p308) is popular for its outdoor firepits, though most traveller cafes serve beer.

 Shopping

Manali is crammed with shops selling souvenirs from Himachal, Tibet and Ladakh. **Tibet Art Collections** (Map p312; ☑252974; NAC Market) has a good selection, with a sister shop across the alley focussing on Ladakhi amulets, jewellery, bowls and teapots. **Tibet Emporium** (Map p312; ☑252431; the Mall) stocks Tibetan knick-knacks and funky T-shirts.

Shawls are sold all over Manali. A good place to start is at the cooperative **Bhuttico** (Map p312; ☑260079; the Mall; ⊙9am-8pm), which charges fair, fixed prices and has another store located in Manu Market.

HAMTA PASS TREK

Easily accessible from Manali, this four- or five-day camping trek crosses the 4270m Hamta Pass over the Pir Panjal. The trailhead is the village of Prini, accessible by bus on the Manali–Naggar road.

From Prini, the route climbs through pine forests to Sethan, then open meadows to Chikha. A waterfall campground gives time to acclimatise before reaching the foot of the pass at Juara. The climb to the pass is steep and tiring but there are sublime snow-peak views from the top. On the descent, you can possibly push on to Chatru or break the journey with a riverside camp at Shiagouru. From Chatru, road transport runs north to Ladakh, east to Spiti and south to Manali.

STAGE	ROUTE	DURATION (HR)	DISTANCE (KM)
1	Prini to Sethan/Pandu Ropa	5-6	8
2	Sethan/Pandu Ropa to Juara	4-5	10
3	Juara to Shiagouru via Hamta Pass	7-8	10
4	Shiagouru to Chatru	3-4	8

ℹ Information

Banks in Manali don't offer foreign exchange but there are private moneychangers, and the State Bank of India has three international ATMs – the one at the bank branch south of the pedestrian mall has shorter queues. If you are heading north to Ladakh, Lahaul or Spiti, change some extra money here.

HPTDC Tourist Office (Map p312; ☑ 252116; the Mall; ⊙7am-8pm, 9am-5pm winter) Can book HPTDC buses and hotels.

Manali Civil Hospital (☑ 253385) Just south of town.

Manali Sub-post Office (Map p312; Model Town; ⊙10am-5pm Mon-Fri, 10am-1pm Sat) Come before 2pm for parcels.

Tourist Office (Map p312; ☑ 253531; the Mall; ⊙8am-9pm, 10am-5pm Mon-Sat in winter) Helpful for brochures and local information. You can book train tickets at the railway booking office (8am-1.30pm Mon-Sat) next door.

Trans Corp Forex (Map p312; the Mall; ⊙10am-7pm) Changes cash and cheques.

ℹ Getting There & Away

AIR

Manali's closest airport is 50km south at Bhuntar.

BUS

Government-run HRTC (www.hrtc.gov.in) buses are sold at the **bus station** (Map p312). Luxury buses are run by the HPTDC and private operators. Tickets can be bought from their offices or from travel agencies thronging the Mall.

Delhi The most comfortable options for Delhi are the daily HPTDC buses; the AC Volvo coach leaves at 5.30pm (₹1220, 14 hours). Private travel agencies run similar overnight services starting at around ₹900. Government buses run regularly from the bus stand till mid-afternoon; the fare to Delhi is ₹512/880/1131 (ordinary/AC deluxe/AC Volvo). Deluxe buses depart at 5.45pm and 5.50pm; AC Volvos depart at 4pm.

Kullu & Parvati Valleys Buses go to Kullu every 30 minutes (₹45, 1½ hours), continuing to Mandi (₹130, four hours) via the airport at Bhuntar (₹60, two hours). Regular local services run to Naggar (₹25, one hour) from 6am to 6pm. For the Parvati Valley, change at Bhuntar.

Lahaul & Spiti Rohtang La, between Manali and Keylong, is normally open from June to late October, and the Kunzum La, between Manali and Spiti, is open from July to mid-October (exact dates depend on snow conditions). A tunnel under the Rohtang La is scheduled to open in 2015, opening up Lahaul to year-round visits. In season, there are regular buses to Keylong between 4am and 2pm (₹130, six hours). Shared jeeps to Keylong can sometimes be found near the bus stand for ₹300 per seat. For Spiti, buses leave most days for Kaza (₹250, 10 hours) at around 5am.

Leh From 15 July to 15 September, daily government (₹650, 2pm) and HPTDC (₹2000, 11am) buses make the bone-shaking ascent to Leh in two exhausting but spectacular days, with an overnight stop at Keylong. Private buses run a little later, to around mid-October, and stop at either Keylong or a tent camp at Sarchu. Bring snacks and warm clothing; be alert to the symptoms of Acute Mountain Sickness.

Other Destinations In season, HPTDC runs a daily bus to Shimla (₹500, nine hours) at 8.30am and there are also early morning and evening government buses (₹305 to ₹440). Private coaches run to Dharamsala/McLeod Ganj (₹450, 10 hours).

TAXI

The **Him-Anchal Taxi Operators Union** (Map p312; ☑ 252120; the Mall) has share minibuses to Leh (₹1600, 14 hours) at 2am from July to mid-October; book a day in advance. In season, travel agents can usually help organise share jeeps for around ₹2000 per seat. For early morning share jeeps to Kaza (₹800 per seat), enquire the day before at the **Kiran Hotel** (Map p312; ☑ 253066) in the south of Manali, as this is where drivers from Spiti hang out.

Other one-way fares:

DESTINATION	FARE (₹)
Bhuntar airport	1100
Dharamsala	4000
Kaza	6000-8000
Keylong	4500
Kullu	800 (950 via Naggar)
Leh	16,000
Manikaran	1400
Naggar	550
Solang Nullah	800

ℹ Getting Around

Autorickshaws run to Old Manali and Vashisht for ₹50. If you can't find one in the street, head to the **Hadimba Auto Rickshaw Booking Office** (Map p312; ☑ 253366; the Mall).

Many people tackle the mountain passes to Ladakh or Spiti on bought or rented bikes. The **Enfield Club** (Map p308; ☑ 251094; Vashisht Rd), by the turn-off to Vashisht, does Enfield repairs and sells secondhand machines.

Several places rent out motorbikes, but make sure the price includes third-party insurance. Expect to pay ₹1200/1500 per day for a 350/500cc Enfield, down to ₹500 for a 150cc

Pulsar. Reliable rental places include the following:

Anu Auto Works (Map p308; 9816163378; Vashisht Rd)

Himalayan Inder Motors (Map p312; 9816113973; Gompa Rd)

Life Adventure Tours (Map p312; 253825; Model Town Rd, Diamond Hotel)

Around Manali

Vashisht

01902

About 3km north of Manali on the slopes east of the Beas River, Vashisht village is a quieter version of Old Manali and a popular travellers' hang-out. Indian tourists mostly come here to bathe in the hot springs and tour the temples, while foreign tourists largely come here for the cheap accommodation, chilled atmosphere and charas. Most guesthouses close down for the winter from late October.

There are some interesting traditional wood and stone houses with ornate carving and a number of typically Himachali temples in the middle of the village. Vashisht is far more compact than Old Manali, with travel agencies, moneychangers, traveller restaurants and internet cafes lining the single street, all within a few minutes' walk of each other.

⊙ Sights & Activities

Vashisht Mandir   HINDU TEMPLE
(Map p308; ⊙5am-9pm) Dedicated to the sage Vashisht, the ancient stone Vashisht Mandir has **public baths** (admission free; ⊙5am-9pm) with separate areas for men and women, or there are open-air baths just uphill. The hotsprings area is always busy with locals doing their laundry or washing dishes. Nearby are similar temples to Shiva and Rama, and there's a second Vashisht Mandir at the back of the village, built in the two-storey Kinnauri style.

Shri Hari Yoga Ashram   YOGA
(Map p308) Along the walking track down to the Beas, this orange-roofed ashram offers daily yoga classes for beginners at 10am, and advanced classes at 8am and 4.30pm (₹100 to ₹150).

⋐ Sleeping

Most places close from late October to April. Prices listed here can double in the peak season (April to June, September and October). There are many more guesthouses and homestays hidden in the village alleys.

★**Hotel Dharma**   HOTEL $
(Map p308; 252354; www.hoteldharmamanali. com; r ₹250-1760; @) Up a steep path above the Rama Temple, this huge and ever-expanding place has rooms in all budgets, and the hike up is rewarded with the best valley views from any hotel on either side of the Beas River. The older wing has basic but clean rooms that get more expensive as you get higher, while the pricier new section has spacious deluxe rooms with TVs, hot water and balconies.

Hotel Surabhi   HOTEL $
(Map p308; 252796; www.surabhihotel.com; d ₹880-1150) One of several big modern places on the main road but facing out over the valley, Surabhi is good value. Old-fashioned but

---

TIBETAN MEDICINE

Traditional Tibetan medicine is a centuries-old holistic healing practice and a popular treatment for all kinds of minor and persistent ailments. There are several clinics around McLeod Ganj, including the **Men-Tsee-Khang Branch Clinic** (Map p322; 221484; Tipa Rd; ⊙9am-1pm & 2-5pm Mon-Sat, closed 2nd & 4th Sat each month) and **Dr Lobsang Khangkar Memorial Clinic** (Map p322; 220811; ⊙9am-noon & 2-5pm Mon-Sat), near the post office.

The most popular *amchi* (Tibetan doctor) in McLeod Ganj is the former physician to the Dalai Lama, **Dr Yeshi Dhonden** (Map p322; ⊙8am-1pm), whose tiny clinic is squirreled away off Jogibara Rd, down an alley past Ashoka Restaurant. No appointment is necessary: you arrive at 8am and collect a token and approximate consultation time. You come back with a sample of urine, which, along with a quick examination, is all the doctor needs to prescribe the appropriate herbal pills. Many locals and expats swear by his treatments.

For an insight into traditional Tibetan medicine, visit the Tibetan Medical & Astrological Institute (p321); note this is a different location from the Men-Tsee-Khang Clinic mentioned above.

spacious, and clean rooms have balconies with great mountain and river views, and all have TVs and hot water. This is one place where you don't really need to spring for the more expensive rooms.

Hotel Valley of Gods   HOTEL $$
(Map p308; ☑ 253455; www.valleyofgods.com; r ₹2350; @) Four years in the making, this impressive stone and wood building has bright, spacious rooms with fine balconies overlooking the valley. Corner rooms come with a fireplace. It's owned by the ground-floor travel agency and has an internet cafe.

✗ Eating

Vashisht has several good traveller cafes and hotel restaurants. Most close down for the winter by November.

Rainbow Cafe   MULTICUISINE $$
(Map p308; mains ₹80-150; ⊘ 8am-10pm) Most people end up at this rooftop Vashisht institution at the end of an evening. Come here for decent traveller fare – breakfast, *momos*, yak cheese pasta, pizzas and thalis, as well as cold beers and an endless reggae soundtrack. There's an internet cafe downstairs.

World Peace Cafe   MULTICUISINE $$
(Map p308; mains ₹80-160; ⊘ 8am-10pm) On the rooftop at Hotel Surbhi, this popular choice has cushions on the floor, a menu of Italian, Mexican and Israeli food, and views across to the Dhaulardhar range from a huge patio. If you play an instrument, bring it to the open jams on Wednesday and Sunday nights.

Fuji Restaurant   JAPANESE $$
(Map p308; sushi ₹120-170; ⊘ 8am-10pm Mon-Sat; ☎) On the rooftop of Negi's Paying Guest-

house, in the central square, this surprisingly authentic Japanese veg place specialises in rice bowls, udon noodles and miso soup.

ℹ Getting There & Away

Autorickshaws charge ₹50 for the journey between Vashisht and Manali; don't rely on being able to get a lift in either direction later than 7pm. On foot it's about 30 minutes; take the trail near the Himalayan Extreme Center past the Shri Hari Yoga Ashram and down to the banks of the Beas River. Coming uphill, the trail begins about 200m north of the Vashisht turn-off.

Solang Nullah
☑ 01902

About 13km north of Manali, Solang Nullah is Himachal's favourite winter ski resort. From January to March, skiers and snowboarders can enjoy 1.5km of alpine-style runs, taking a brand new gondola up to 3200m. With the impressive backdrop of snowcapped Friendship Peak, it's also a year-round 'beauty spot',

---

LET'S DRINK TO A PLASTIC-FREE PLANET

Plastic bags are banned in Himachal Pradesh, but bottles are not. Do your bit for the local environment by refilling your drinking water bottle for around ₹5 at one of a dozen filtered-water stations around McLeod Ganj. The most obvious ones are at Lha, the Green Shop, Green Hotel, Common Ground Cafe and Khana Nirvana restaurant, though a map of all locations is available at the Clean Upper Dharamsala Project (p329).

MEETING THE DALAI LAMA

Meeting face to face with the Dalai Lama is a lifelong dream for many travellers and certainly for Buddhists, but private audiences are rarely granted. Put simply, the Dalai Lama is too busy with spiritual duties to meet everyone who comes to Dharamsala. Tibetan refugees are automatically guaranteed an audience, but travellers must make do with the occasional public teachings held at the Tsuglagkhang during the monsoon (July/August), after Losar (Tibetan New Year) in February/March and on other occasions, depending on his schedule. For annual schedules and just about everything you need to know about His Holiness, check out www.dalailama.com. To attend, you have to register with your passport and two passport photographs, at the Branch Security Office (Map p322; ☑ 221560; Bhagsu Rd; ⊘ 9am-1pm & 2-5pm Mon-Sat, closed 2nd & 4th Sat each month). Sign up a few days before the teaching begins for the best chance of getting in. To get the most out of the teachings bring a cushion and rent a radio and headset for simultaneous translation.

BUSES FROM DHARAMSALA

DESTINATION	FARE (₹)	DURATION (HR)	FREQUENCY
Amritsar	180	7	5am
Chamba	210	8	5 daily
Dalhousie	160	6	8.30am & 12.15pm
Dehra Dun	425/595 (ordinary/deluxe)	13	3pm & 9pm
Delhi	445	12	5am, 7am, 6.40pm & 8.15pm
Gaggal	13	30min	frequently
Jawalamukhi	60	1½	hourly
Kangra	20	1	frequently
Kullu	245	9	4 daily
Manali	290	10	morning & evening
Mandi	150	6	5 daily
Palampur	40	2	frequently
Pathankot	105	3½	hourly
Shimla	280-430	10	6 daily (morning & evening)

with a carnival-like atmosphere in summer. The surrounding hills are good for walking – the **Shiva temple** 3km above the village is a popular destination.

if you want to stay, try **Hotel Iceland** (☑ 256008; www.icelandsolang.com; r ₹1000-3000), a genuine ski lodge with great rooms, equipment rental, restaurant and bar.

In summer, buses to Solang Nullah (₹15, one hour) leave Manali's bus station at 8am and 2pm, heading back immediately on arrival. Snow may make the road impassable in January and February, which usually means taking a jeep or walking the 3km from the village of Palchan on the highway.

WESTERN HIMACHAL PRADESH

Western Himachal Pradesh is most famous as the home of the Tibetan government in exile, near Dharamsala, but consider travelling further afield to the fascinating Chamba Valley. The official website for Kangra district is http://hpkangra.nic.in, while the official Chamba Valley site is http://hp-chamba.nic.in.

Dharamsala

☑ 01892 / POP 30,700 / ELEV 1219M

Dharamsala is best known as the home of the Dalai Lama, but the grubby market town where the buses pull in is actually Lower Dharamsala. The Tibetan government in exile is based just uphill in Gangchen Kyishong, and travellers make a beeline further uphill to the busy little traveller town of McLeod Ganj, also known as Upper Dharamsala. The bus station, a small museum and the bustling Kotwali Bazar can be found in Dharamsala, but otherwise it's just a place to change transport on your way to McLeod.

The **State Bank of India** (Map p319; ⊙ 10am-4pm Mon-Fri, to 1pm Sat) accepts travellers cheques, changes cash and has an ATM. It's just south of the museum.

◉ Sights

★ **Museum of Kangra Art**   MUSEUM
(Map p319; Indian/foreigner ₹10/50; ⊙ 10am-5pm Tue-Sun) The Museum of Kangra Art near the bus station displays some fine miniature paintings from the Kangra school, along with temple carvings, fabrics and embroidery, weapons and palanquins belonging to local rajas.

⛏ Sleeping & Eating

There are a few sleeping options if you have an early, bus but you are generally better off lodging in McLeod Ganj and catching an early morning taxi.

Kashmir House   HERITAGE HOTEL $$
(Map p319; ☑ 224212; d ₹1643-2580) A short hike up the hill towards Gangchen Kyishong, this well-run HPTDC hotel built in 1928 once belonged to the maharaja of Jammu and Kashmir and packs plenty of charm.

Dharamsala

Dharamsala

◉ Top Sights
1 Museum of Kangra Art......................A5

◉ Sights
2 Church of St John in the
   Wilderness...A1
Cultural Museum.......................(see 4)
Men-Tsee-Khang Museum.........(see 5)
3 Namgyal Gompa...............................B3
Nechung Gompa........................(see 4)
4 Secretariat of the Tibetan
   Government in Exile.......................B4
5 Tibetan Medical & Astrological
   Institute (Men-Tsee-
   Khang)...A4
6 Tsechokling Gompa...........................A2

◉ Activities, Courses & Tours
7 Himalayan Iyengar Yoga
   Centre...B1
Library of Tibetan Works &
   Archives...................................(see 4)
8 Regional Mountaineering
   Centre...B1
9 Tushita Meditation Centre.................B1
10 Vipassana Meditation Centre.............B1

◉ Sleeping
11 Greenwoods Inn..................................B1
12 Kashmir House....................................A4
13 New Blue Heaven Guesthouse..........B1

◉ Eating
14 Andey's Midtown Restaurant............A5

◉ Entertainment
15 Tibetan Institute of
   Performing Arts..............................B1

◉ Shopping
Namgyal Bookshop.....................(see 3)

◉ Information
16 Delek Hospital...................................A4
17 State Bank of India............................A5
18 State Bank of India ATM...................A5

◉ Transport
19 Dharamsala Bus Station....................A5
20 Rail Reservation Centre.....................A5

HIMACHAL PRADESH DHARAMSALA

**Andey's Midtown
Restaurant**   MULTICUISINE $$
(Map p319; mains ₹100-300; ⊙10am-10.30pm)
Lower Dharamsala's best restaurant. Come
for kebabs, creamy curries and thalis, or sit
on a saddle at the (otherwise crummy) bar.

ℹ Getting There & Away

BUS
There's a regular shuttle service from **Dharamsala bus station** (Map p319) to McLeod Ganj
(₹10, 35 minutes) about every half-hour till
about 8pm. For the 12-hour ride to Delhi there's
a deluxe Volvo bus at 8pm (₹1040), an AC deluxe
bus at 8.30pm (₹760) and a deluxe service at
7pm and 8pm (₹610).

TAXI
The taxi stand is up some steep steps from the
bus stand, though some taxis also wait at the
bus station exit. Cramped shared jeeps (₹10 per
person, 30 minutes) to McLeod Ganj leave when
full or hire a taxi for ₹200.

TRAIN

The nearest train station is Kangra Mandir, on the slow narrow-gauge line from Pathankot to Jogindarnagar. Reservations for other services from Pathankot can be made at the **Rail Reservation Centre** (Map p319; ☑ 226711; Hotel Dhauladhar; ⊗ 8am-2pm).

McLeod Ganj

☑ 01892 / ELEV 1770M

When travellers talk of heading up to Dharamsala (to see the Dalai Lama...), this is where they mean. Around 4km north of Dharamsala town – or 10km via the looping bus route – McLeod Ganj is the headquarters of the Tibetan government in exile and the residence of His Holiness the 14th Dalai Lama. Along with Manali, it's the big traveller hang-out in Himachal Pradesh, with many budget hotels, trekking companies, internet cafes, restaurants and shops selling Tibetan souvenirs crammed in just a couple of blocks, like a mini-Kathmandu. Naturally, there's a large Tibetan population here, many of whom are refugees, so you'll see plenty of maroon robes about, especially when the Dalai Lama is in residence.

McLeod (named after David McLeod, Lieutenant-Governor of Punjab) was established in the mid-1850s as a British garrison and it served as an administration centre for the colonial government until the earthquake of 1905. It was a backwater until 1960, when the Dalai Lama claimed asylum here following the Chinese invasion of Tibet.

Since then, McLeod has become a centre for the study of Buddhism and Tibetan culture. There are all sorts of holistic activities and courses on offer, and lots of travellers come here to volunteer on community projects that focus on the refugees. With an interesting mix of travellers, volunteers, monks and the dharma crowd, you are never far from an interesting conversation here.

A raincoat is handy for McLeod Ganj during the monsoon (June to August) and warm clothes are useful between November and March. Many shops and businesses are closed on Monday.

Taxis will drop you off at the Main Chowk. From here noisy Jogibara Rd runs south to Gangchen Kyishong and the main centre of the Tibetan government in exile. For Dharamkot, Tipa Rd climbs gently via the Tibetan Institute of Performing Arts, and Dharamkot Rd climbs very steeply but more directly.

◉ Sights

★**Tsuglagkhang Complex** BUDDHIST TEMPLE
(Map p322; Temple Rd, Central Chapel; ⊗ 5am-8pm) The main focus of visiting pilgrims, monks and many tourists is the Tsuglagkhang, comprising the *photrang* (official residence) of the Dalai Lama, the Namgyal Gompa, Tibet Museum and the Tsuglagkhang itself.

The revered Tsuglagkhang is the exiles' concrete equivalent of the Jokhang Temple in Lhasa. Sacred to Avalokitesvara (Chenrezig in Tibetan), the Tibetan deity of compassion, it enshrines a 3m-high gilded statue of the Sakyamuni Buddha, flanked by Avalokitesvara and Padmasambhava, the Indian scholar who introduced Buddhism to Tibet. The Avalokitesvara statue contains several relics rescued from the Jokhang Temple during the Cultural Revolution.

Before visiting the main chapel, pilgrims first visit the **Kalachakra Temple** (Map p322; Temple Rd), built in 1992, which contains mesmerising murals of the Kalachakra (Wheel of Time) mandala, specifically linked to Avalokitesvara, of whom the Dalai Lama is a manifestation. Sand mandalas are created here annually on the fifth day of the third Tibetan month. Photography is allowed in the Tsuglagkhang, but not in the Kalachakra Temple. Note that during teachings, cameras, mobile phones, cigarettes and lighters are not permitted in the temple.

The remaining buildings form the **Namgyal Gompa** (Namgyal Monastery; Map p319; Temple Rd), where you can watch monks debate most afternoons (not Sunday), driving their points home with a theatrical clap of the hands.

Just inside the main entry gate is the **Tibet Museum** (Map p322; admission ₹5; ⊗ 9am-5pm Tue-Sun, closed 2nd and 4th Sat), telling the story of the Chinese occupation and the subsequent Tibetan exodus, through photographs, interviews and video clips. A visit here is a must. Documentaries (₹10) are shown daily at 3pm.

Most Tibetan pilgrims make a clockwise *kora* (ritual circuit) of the outer Tsuglagkhang Complex. Take the downhill road to the left at the entrance to the temple and follow the winding path leading off to the right. The 20-minute walk passes through forest draped with prayer flags before climbing back onto Temple Rd.

Secretariat of the
Tibetan Government in Exile   MUSEUM

(Map p319) Inside the government compound at Gangchen Kyishong, the **Library of Tibetan Works & Archives** (p325) preserves Tibetan texts spared from the Cultural Revolution. Many have since been translated into English and other European languages. Regular visitors can become temporary members (₹50 per month; passport needed for ID) to access the foreign-language collection.

Upstairs is a fascinating **cultural museum** (Map p319; admission ₹10; ⊘ 9am-1pm & 2-5pm Mon-Sat, closed 2nd & 4th Sat each month) with statues, old Tibetan artefacts and books and some astonishing three-dimensional mandalas in wood and sand. Also worth a visit is the **Nechung Gompa** (Map p319) just below, home to the Tibetan state oracle.

It's a stiff walk back up to McLeod centre, or take a taxi for ₹100.

Tibetan Medical & Astrological
Institute (Men-Tsee-Khang) TIBETAN MEDICINE

(Map p319; ☑ 223113; www.men-tsee-khang.org; Gangchen Kyishong, Dharamsala) Established to preserve the ancient arts of traditional Tibetan medicine and astrology, the Men-Tsee-Khang is a five-minute walk from the Secretariat. If you know the exact time you were born, you can have a whole life horoscope prepared in English here.

The **Men-Tsee-Khang Museum** (Map p319; admission ₹5; ⊘ 9am-1pm & 2-5pm Mon-Sat) has fascinating displays on traditional Tibetan medicine, told via preserved specimens and illustrative *thangkas* (Tibetan cloth paintings). Learn useful facts such as cinnamon wards agains flatulence and that red-hot hammers were once the traditional Tibetan treatment for insanity (gulp).

Tsechokling Gompa   BUDDHIST MONASTERY

(Map p319) At the base of a long flight of steps off Nowrojee Rd, this peaceful gompa was built in 1987 to replace the original Dip Tse Chokling Gompa in Tibet, destroyed in the Cultural Revolution. The prayer hall enshrines a statue of Sakyamuni in a magnificent jewelled headdress.

Gu Chu Sum Movement Gallery   GALLERY

(Map p322; ☑ 220680; www.gu-chu-sum.org; Jogibara Rd; ⊘ 9am-5pm Mon-Sat, closed 2nd and 4th Sat) **FREE** Run by a local charity that works with former political prisoners, this houses a harrowing exhibition of photos telling the story of political oppression in Chinese-occupied Tibet and the brutally suppressed demonstrations of 1987, 1988 and 2008. The hall is open on request; ask at the Gu Chu Sum office above Lung Ta Restaurant.

Church of St John
in the Wilderness   CHURCH

(Map p319) Just off the main road into McLeod, this brooding church (dating from 1852) has handsome stained-glass windows and is one of the few remaining traces of McLeod's days as a British hill station. It's open on Sunday mornings for a weekly 10am service. The cemetery contains the graves of many victims of the 1905 earthquake, as well as the rocket-like tomb of the Earl of Elgin, 23rd Viceroy of India.

🏃 Activities

Alternative Therapies, Yoga & Massage

McLeod Ganj has dozens of practitioners of holistic and alternative therapies, some legitimate and some making a fast buck at the expense of gullible travellers. Adverts for courses and sessions are posted on noticeboards all over McLeod Ganj and in *Contact* magazine, but talking to other travellers is a better way to find the good practitioners. **Lha** (p324) offers reliable massage treatments for ₹800 and occasional two-week courses in Swedish or Tibetan massage (₹3000).

Holistic Ayurvedic
Massage Centre   MASSAGE

(Map p322; ☑ 9418493871; Jogibara Rd, Ladies Venture Hotel; 30/60min ₹300/600; ⊘ 9.30am-9pm) Resident masseur Shami gets rave reviews, so book ahead.

Universal Yoga Centre   YOGA

(Map p322; ☑ 9418291929; www.vijaypoweryoga.com; Jogibara Rd, Yongling School; ⊘ Apr-Nov) Gets good reports for drop-in yoga classes and longer courses.

Walks

Short walks around McLeod include the 1.5km stroll to Bhagsu and the 2km uphill walk northeast to Dharamkot for uplifting views south over the valley and north towards the Dhauladhar Ridge. Both walks follow the road but pass through lovely pine forest. You can do a loop to Bhagsu, visit the waterfall there, wind up and across to Dharamkot for lunch and then head back down to McLeod in a half-day walk.

About 4km northwest of McLeod Ganj on Mall Rd, the underwhelming Dal Lake

McLeod Ganj

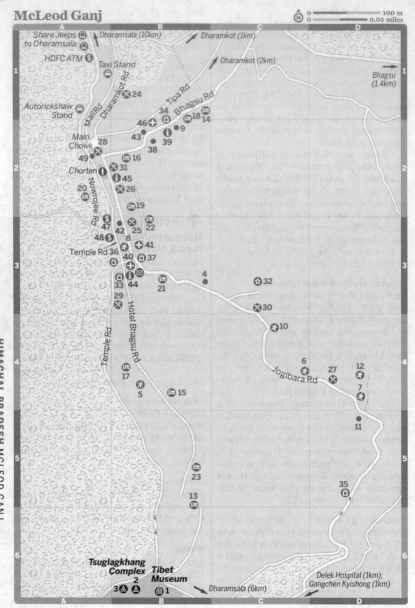

0 — 100 m
0 — 0.05 miles

is home to the **Tibetan Children's Village** (☎ 221348; www.tcv.org.in; ⊙ 9.30am-5pm Mon-Fri), which provides free education for some 2000 refugee children. Visitors are welcome and there may be opportunities for volunteers. One good 45-minute hike is to walk

above the school along forested hillside paths to the dirt road that runs from Galu Devi Temple back to Dharamkot.

A tough but popular longer walk is the long day or overnight return hike up the steep ridge east of Dharamkot to **Triund**

McLeod Ganj

(2900m), a 7km walk that gains 900m altitude in a strenuous three hours. The little meadow of Triund has a couple of simple rest houses and shops, which rent out sleeping bags and places to sleep or camp, and can provide simple meals. An overnight stop gives you the best chance of clear weather, and time to hike for one hour up to the teashop and viewpoint at **Laka Got** (3350m), sometimes called 'Snowline', before returning to McLeod Ganj.

Trekking

It's possible to trek from McLeod Ganj to the Kullu, Chamba, Lahaul and Spiti Valleys, and there are several agencies in town that can make the necessary camping arrangements. Apart from the demanding trek to Chamba over the Indrahar La (4300m), the most popular option is the easy six-day loop to Kareri Lake. All-inclusive treks costs around ₹1500 to ₹2000 per person, per day.

Regional Mountaineering Centre TREKKING (Map p319; ☑221787; ⊙10am-5pm Mon-Sat) Uphill from the bus stand on the direct road to Dharamkot, this government-run organisation can arrange treks and adventure activities and offers courses and expeditions on set dates. It can also provide a list of registered guides and porters.

High Point Adventure TREKKING (Map p322; ☑9816120145; www.trek.123himachal. com; Hotel Bhagsu Rd, Kareri Lodge) Offers some of the best prices in town, including the popular Indrahar La and Kareri Lake treks.

 ## Volunteering

McLeod Ganj has more volunteering opportunities than anywhere else in Himachal Pradesh. Travellers can generally find short-term opportunities such as English-language conversation classes right on the spot, though it's best to contact the following organisations a couple of weeks in advance. For longer-term placements always look for a position that matches your existing skills. Volunteers generally make their own arrangements for accommodation and meals, though Lha can arrange long-term homestays with Tibetan families (US$550 per month, including meals).

Many organisations seeking volunteers also advertise in the free magazine *Contact*. The magazine itself looks for volunteers to help with writing, proofreading or design.

➜ **Lha** (Map p322; ☎ 220992; www.lha socialwork.org; Temple Rd; ⊙10am-noon & 1-5pm Mon-Fri) is the best places to start. Lha arranges placements at a variety of local community projects, including those for English- and French-language teachers, grant writers, photographers or IT professionals. Volunteers with a month or more to spare are preferred. Come to the office at 4pm on weekdays to join an English conversation class with local refugees.

➜ **VolunteerTibet** (Map p322; ☎ 220894; www.volunteertibet.org.in; Jogibara Rd; ⊙10am-1.30pm & 2-5pm Mon-Fri) is a community organisation that arranges placements in areas of need – eg teaching, computer training and social services. Contact Yeshi Lhundup.

➜ **Tibet Hope Center** (Map p322; ☎ 9218947689; www.tibethopecenter.org), off Jogibara Rd, runs conversational English classes for Tibetan refugees from 4.30pm to 6pm Monday to Friday, often held informally over coffee at nearby Hope Cafe. Anyone is welcome to turn up.

➜ **Rogpa** (Map p322; www.tibetrogpa.org) is a good choice for volunteers interested in child care and who can baby sit for refugees, freeing parents to earn an income.

➜ **Learning & Ideas for Tibet** (LIT; Map p322; ☎ 9418794218; www. learningandideasfortibet.org; Jogibara Rd; ⊙9am-5pm) has a variety of positions, including teaching and editing the autobiographies of Tibetan political prisoners and exiles. Volunteers can drop in to the 2pm English conversation classes and can attend a free Tibetan language class daily at 10am.

MCLEOD GANJ TO BHARMOUR TREK

This popular five-day route crosses over the Indrahar La (4300m) to the ancient village of Bharmour in the Chamba Valley. The pass is open from June to early November, but the best months are September and October. You can start the trek in either McLeod Ganj or Bharmour.

From McLeod, the first day climbs three hours to Triund, where there are a couple of simple rest houses and camping spots. The next stage climbs to the glacier at Laka Got (3250m) and continues to the rocky shelter known as Lahesh Cave (3600m). With an early start the next day, you can cross the Indrahar La – and be rewarded with astounding views – before descending to the meadow campground at Chata Parao.

The stages on to Bharmour can be tricky without a local guide. From Chata Parao, the path moves back into the forest, descending to Kuarsi, Lamu or Dali, depending on the current state of road construction in the valley.

STAGE	ROUTE	DURATION (HR)	DISTANCE (KM)
1	McLeod Ganj to Triund	3	9
2	Triund to Lahesh Cave	3	8
3	Lahesh Cave to Chata Parao over Indrahar La	6	10
4	Chata Parao to Kuarsi	5-6	15
5	Kuarsi to Lamu	4	10

🎓 Courses

Yoga, Meditation & Philosophy

Several organisations offer long-term courses in Buddhist philosophy and meditation. They have strict rules on silence, alcohol and smoking. Lha offers courses in massage treatment, Tibetan art and cooking (₹300 for two hours).

Himalayan Iyengar Yoga Centre   YOGA
(Map p319; ☑ 221312; www.hiyogacentre.com; Tipa Rd; 5-day course ₹3000; ☺ Apr-Oct) Five-day courses start every Thursday.

Tushita Meditation Centre   MEDITATION
(Map p319; ☑ 221866; www.tushita.info; course ₹4800; ☺ registration 9.30-11.30am & 12.30-4pm Mon-Sat) At the junction of the two roads from McLeod to Dharamkot, Tushita offers 10-day residential retreats in Tibetan Buddhist philosophy, courses for advanced students and shorter programs, including drop-in meditation – see the website for course dates.

Vipassana Meditation Centre   MEDITATION
(Map p319; ☑ 221368; www.sikhara.dhamma.org; ☺ registration 4 5pm) Located in Dharamkot, this centre runs strict and physically rigorous 10-day silent retreats on *vipassana* (mindfulness meditation) starting on the first and 15th of the month, from April to November. Fees are by donation only.

Library of Tibetan Works & Archives   PHILOSOPHY
(Map p319; ☑ 222467; www.ltwa.net; Secretariat Complex; 9am-1pm & 2-5pm Mon-Sat, closed 2nd & 4th Sat of month) At the Gangchen Kyishong complex, there are two-month Buddhist philosophy courses for ₹300 per month, plus ₹50 registration.

Cooking

Cooking courses in McLeod Ganj cover everything from masalas to *momos*, with the advantage that you get to eat your homework afterwards. Book the following courses one day in advance.

Bhimsen's Cooking Class   COOKING
(Map p322; ☑ 9418909065; Jogibara Rd; classes ₹300; ☺ 11am-1pm & 4-6pm) The Punjabi Dhaba restaurant offers courses in North Indian cooking, starting at 3pm.

Lhamo's Kitchen   COOKING
(Map p322; ☑ 9816468719; Bhagsu Rd; classes ₹300, 3-day courses ₹550; ☺ 10.30am-12.30pm, 5-7pm) Recommended courses in vegetarian Tibetan cooking.

Sangye's Kitchen   COOKING
(Map p322; ☑ 9816164540; Jogibara Rd; classes ₹250; ☺ 10am-12.30pm & 4.30-6.30pm Thu-Tue) Tibetan treats, focusing on *momos* (including chocolate *momos!*) every Sunday and Thursday, and noodles on Tuesday and Saturday. It's next to Tashi Choeling Monastery.

Language

Inside the Gangchen Kyishong complex, the **Library of Tibetan Works & Archives** (☑ 222467; www.ltwa.net; ☺ classes Mon-Sat) runs three-month Tibetan-language courses for beginners and experienced students for ₹550 per month, plus a ₹50 registration fee. Courses start in mid-March, mid-June and at the end of September.

Lha offers Tibetan language classes and private tuition (₹150 per hour), as does VolunteerTibet.

There are several independent Tibetan teachers – check *Contact* magazine for details. Classes run by **Pema Youton** (☑ 9418603523) get good reports.

✨ Festivals & Events

Performances of traditional lhamo (Tibetan opera) and musical theatre are held on special occasions at the **Tibetan Institute of Performing Arts** (TIPA; Map p319; ☑ 221478; www.tibetanarts.org), east of Main Chowk. The annual **Opera Festival** is held in February or March, while the **TIPA Anniversary Festival** takes place in August.

In December or January, McLeod celebrates Losar with processions and masked dances at local monasteries. The Dalai Lama often gives public teachings at this time. The **Dalai Lama's birthday** (☺ 6 Jul) is also celebrated with aplomb.

In December, McLeod Ganj hosts the **International Himalayan Festival** (McLeod Ganj; ☺ 10-12 Dec) to commemorate the Dalai Lama's Nobel Peace Prize, featuring cultural troupes from all the Himalayan nations.

Several film festivals liven up McLeod in October and November. The **Free Spirit Film Festival** (www.freespiritfilmfestival.com) and **Tibet Film Festival** (www.filmingfortibet.org) in late October spotlight Tibetan and international documentaries, followed shortly afterwards by the **Dharamsala International Film Festival** (www.diff.co.in).

📖 Sleeping

Popular places fill up quickly; advance bookings are advised year-round, especially from April to June and October.

Om Hotel
HOTEL $

(Map p322; ☑ 221313; omhotel@hotmail.com; Nowrojee Rd; d with/without bathroom ₹450/250) Conveniently located down a lane below the main square, the friendly family-run Om has simple but pleasing rooms with good views and the good Namgyal Restaurant whose terrace catches the sunset over the valley. This might be the best deal in town; the main downside is that it's often full.

Tibetan Ashoka Guest House
GUESTHOUSE $

(Map p322; ☑ 221763; d with/without bathroom ₹550/220) Off Jogibara Rd, down an alley near the chorten (Tibetan for stupa), this big place looks out on the valley and catches plenty of sunlight on the communal upper terrace. Its clean, simple rooms are good value and so fill up in season, but advance reservations aren't accepted.

Greenwoods Inn
HOTEL $

(Map p319; ☑ 220622; www.greenwoodsinn.org; r ₹880-990; 🖧) Clean, bright, spacious rooms here come with flat-screen TV and balconies with fine views over the valley. It's a great deal and a quiet option, as long as you don't mind the heart-pounding 15-minute uphill walk from McLeod. It's 250m past TIPA on the way to Dharamkot. Rooms are half-price outside high season.

Loseling Guest House
GUESTHOUSE $

(Map p322; ☑ 9218923305; d ₹260-330) Down an alley of Jogibara Rd, Loseling is run by a Tibetan monastery based in Karnataka. It's a good cheapie and all rooms have a hot shower; cheaper ones have squat toilets. The three rooftop rooms are easily the best.

Kareri Lodge
HOTEL $

(Map p322; ☑ 221132; karerihl@hotmail.com; Hotel Bhagsu Rd; r ₹660-990, ste ₹1540; 🖧) Squeezed in among a string of more upmarket hotels, Kareri has five well-worn but clean rooms, some with huge windows and prime views. There's a good vibe here, helped by the friendly manager who offers a reliable trekking service.

Takhyil Guest House
HOTEL $

(Map p322; ☑ 221152; Jogibara Rd; r ₹880-990) A calm vibe and neat, tidy rooms with TVs and hot showers add up to a decent, if somewhat overpriced, package at this Tibetan-run hotel that's just downhill from the chorten.

Kunga Guesthouse
GUESTHOUSE $$

(Map p322; ☑ 221180; Bhagsu Rd; d ₹550-2935, without bathroom ₹220-330) 🍴 Above (and below) Nick's Italian Kitchen, Kunga offers a huge range of rooms dotted around several buildings, but all are clean and offer reasonable value. According to the Clean Upper Dharamsala Project, this hotel stands out for its responsible waste disposal and efforts towards recycling.

Green Hotel
HOTEL $$

(Map p322; ☑ 221200; www.greenhotel.biz; Bhagsu Rd; r ₹880-2936; @🖧) A favourite with mid-range travellers and groups, Green has a diverse range of sunny, stylish and super-clean rooms in two buildings, some with valley and mountain views. The pricier rooms have their own balconies. The busy lounge cafe feels like the hip place to be.

Hotel Tibet
HOTEL $$

(Map p322; ☑ 221587; hoteltibetdasa@yahoo.com; Bhagsu Rd; r ₹660-1100; ❄) Bang in the centre of town, this place has the feel of an upmarket hotel yet it has almost budget prices. All rooms have TV and hot water and there's a cosy restaurant; credit cards accepted. Proceeds go to Tibetan settlements in India.

Hotel Bhagsu
HOTEL $$

(Map p322; ☑ 221091; Hotel Bhagsu Rd; d ₹1380-2875; ❄) On the road above the bazaar and Tsuglagkhang, this popular but old-fashioned HPTDC hotel has a solid Raj-era feel and attractively decorated rooms, some with partial valley views.

★Chonor House
BOUTIQUE HOTEL $$$

(Map p322; ☑ 221006; www.norbulingka.org; s/d from ₹3240/4086; ❄@🖧) Hidden down a track off Hotel Bhagsu Rd, Chonor House is a real gem. It's run by the Norbulingka Institute, and rooms are decked out with its wonderful handicrafts and fabrics. Each of the bright and sunny 11 rooms has a Tibetan theme that runs from the bedspreads to the murals on the walls. Even the cheapest rooms are spacious. There's also a lovely garden, with a reasonably priced terrace restaurant.

Zambala House
HOTEL $$$

(Map p322; ☑ 9418833838; www.zambalahouse.com; Hotel Bhagsu Rd; d ₹2348-3405, ste ₹3992; 🖧) Still feeling fresh-out-of-the-box, this place down the same lane as Chonor House has spacious modern rooms with the best bathrooms in town. The views from the upper-floor suites are so good you might never turn on the flat-screen TV. Ask for breakfast on the rooftop terrace.

🍴 Eating

Restaurants

McLeod Ganj is crammed with backpacker restaurants serving identical traveller menus – pizzas, pasta, omelettes, Indian and Chinese staples – and commendable attempts at European and Mexican food. For a quick snack, local women sell veg *momos* around the chorten and at the entrance to the Tsuglagkhang.

★ Nick's Italian Kitchen ITALIAN $
(Map p322; Bhagsu Rd; mains ₹50-100; ⏰7am-9pm; 🛜) At Kunga Guesthouse, Nick's is a well-run and unpretentious place has been serving up tasty vegetarian pizzas, lasagne and gnocchi for years. Follow up a ground coffee with a heavenly slice of lemon cheesecake – apparently Richard Gere's favourite when he stayed here. Eat inside or out on the sunny terrace.

Khana Nirvana MULTICUISINE $
(Map p322; www.khananirvana.org; Temple Rd; meals ₹35-85; ⏰9.30am-9.30pm) 🌿 Up a steep stairway and easily missed, this community cafe is a relaxed hang-out serving healthy vegetarian breakfasts, soups and salad, pita sandwiches, burritos and smoothies (try the apple cardamom cooler). There's local entertainment most nights, including open-mic jams on Monday and Wednesday, documentary films about Tibet on Thursday, and occasional Tibetan speakers on Sunday. Staff can often put you in touch with volunteer opportunities.

Lung Ta JAPANESE $
(Map p322; Jogibara Rd; set meals ₹150; ⏰noon-8.30pm Mon-Sat) 🌿 The daily set menus are the best choice at this popular, nonprofit, vegetarian Japanese restaurant, especially on Tuesdays and Fridays when there's always a rush for the sushi rolls and miso soup. The food and ambience are authentic and many Japanese travellers come here for a taste of home.

Four Seasons Cafe MULTICUISINE $
(Map p322; Jogibara Rd; mains ₹60-180) This bustling hole-in-the-wall place serves up mainly Italian fare, but also waffles, baked potatoes and good breakfasts, with some of the best prices in town. There are only five tables so be prepared to share.

Taste of India INDIAN $
(Map p322; Jogibara Rd; mains ₹90-130) This tiny dive has just five tables and is often full of diners savouring North Indian veg and nonveg curries. The capsicum with cottage cheese is excellent but the chicken dishes can be skimpy so order a 'half chicken' portion if you're hungry.

Green Hotel Restaurant MULTICUISINE $
(Map p322; Bhagsu Rd; mains ₹60-150; ⏰6.30am-9.30pm; 🛜) This traveller-oriented hotel restaurant with comfy chairs and couches serves good vegetarian food and the earliest breakfasts in town.

Peace Cafe TIBETAN $
(Map p322; Jogibara Rd; dishes ₹50-140; ⏰7.30am-9.30pm) This cosy little cafe below Takhyil Guest House is always full of monks chatting and dining on tasty Tibetan *momos*, *chow chow* (stir-fried noodles with vegetables or meat) and *thukpa*.

★ Tibet Kitchen MULTICUISINE $$
(Map p322; Jogibara Rd; mains ₹90-150; ⏰noon-9.30pm) It's worth queueing here to get the opportunity to try spicy Bhutanese food including *kewa datse* (potatoes and cheese) and unusual Tibetan dishes like *shapta* (roasted lamb and onion) and *moktuk* (*momos* in soup). There are also Thai and Chinese flavours, from green curry to kung pao chicken. Even with three floors and a lounge on top, it's often full with a good mix of travellers, monks and locals.

Namgyal Cafe PIZZA $$
(Map p322; Nowrojee Rd, Om Hotel; mains ₹80-150; ⏰10am-10pm Tue-Sun) 🌿 The busy restaurant attached to Om Hotel serves some of the best pizza in town, as well as most other dishes, to a reassuring soundtrack of classic '80s music. Choose between the cosy interior restaurant or the sunny terrace, either way service can be patchy. It also provides vocational training for refugees.

Common Ground Cafe ASIAN $$
(Map p322; www.commongroundsproject.org; Dharamkot Rd; mains ₹65-170; ⏰11am-9pm; 🛜) 🌿 The mission of the NGO that runs this restaurant is to promote understanding between Tibetan and Chinese people, and food is used symbolically here. The menu is a sizzling variety of cross-cultural dishes, from Taiwanese pork rice to Sichuanese hot pot,

though some dishes can end up being bland. The atmosphere is pleasingly laid-back, with communal tables, floor cushions and a small library, and the coffee's good too.

Jimmy's Italian Kitchen
ITALIAN $$

(Map p322; Jogibara Rd; dishes ₹90-200; 🕾) Jimmy's is a well-established Italian place opposite the chorten with pleasant seating and a sunny rooftop. The baked potatoes and Greek or fattoush salads are a nice change, and there are a dozen types of pasta, though, as one expat warned us, 'It's good for everything except Italian'.

McLlo Restaurant
MULTICUISINE $$

(Map p322; Main Chowk; mains ₹150-250; ⊘ 10am-10pm) Crowded nightly and justifiably popular, this big place above the noisy main square serves a mind-boggling menu of Indian, Chinese and international fare, including pizzas and grilled trout (₹320). It's also one of the best places to enjoy an icy cold beer (₹150) on the top-floor terrace.

Cafes

McLeod has some of the best cafes in North India, with many places serving good espresso coffee, cappuccino and English-style tea.

Moonpeak Espresso
MULTICUISINE $

(Map p322; www.moonpeak.org; Temple Rd; coffees & meals ₹50-170; ⊘7.30am-8pm; 🕾) A little chunk of Seattle, transported over to India. Come for excellent coffee, cakes, imaginative sandwiches and dishes such as poached chicken with mango, lime and coriander sauce. Among the culinary highlights is the Himachali Thali (₹200), a sampler of regional dishes.

Tibetan Mandala Cafe
CAFE $

(Map p322; Temple Rd; snacks ₹25-90; ⊘7am-8pm; 🕾) Mandala has comfy sofas and an inviting terrace and serves tasty wraps, sandwiches and coffee.

🍷 Drinking & Entertainment

Two of the best places for a drink are McLlo Restaurant or the lawn of the Hotel Bhagsu. Takeaway beer and spirits are available from several small wine shops, including one right opposite the bus stand.

Tibetan Music Trust
LIVE MUSIC

(Map p322; ⬚ 9805661031; admission by donation) Performances of Tibetan folk music are held with varying regularity at Yongling School,

off Jogibara Rd. The live shows feature demonstrations of traditional regional Tibetan instruments and song. It's a great cultural and educational experience.

Shopping

Dozens of shops and stalls sell Tibetan artefacts, including *thangkas,* bronze statues, metal prayer wheels, bundles of prayer flags and gemstone rosary beads. Some are Tibetan-run, but many are run by Kashmiri traders who apply a fair amount of sales pressure. Several local cooperatives offer the same goods without the hassle.

Tibetan Handicrafts Centre
HANDICRAFTS

(Map p322; ⬚ 221415; Jogibara Rd; ⊘ 8.30am-5pm Mon-Sat) 🖉 Employs newly arrived refugees in the weaving of Tibetan carpets. You'll pay around ₹8000 for a 0.9m by 1.8m traditional wool carpet, and visitors are welcome to watch the weavers in action. For made-to-order clothing, including Tibetan dresses, blouses and waistcoats, head over the road to the tailoring section. A Tibetan dress takes three days to make and costs from ₹725 (cotton) to ₹2200 (silk). Shipping is available.

Stitches of Tibet
CLOTHING

(Map p322; ⬚ 221527; www.tibetanwomen.org; Jogibara Rd; ⊘10am-5pm Tue-Sun) 🖉 This organisation offers a similar tailoring service to that of the Tibetan Handicrafts Centre of Tibet, providing work for newly arrived women refugees.

TCV Handicraft Centre
SOUVENIRS

(Map p322; ⬚ 221592; www.tcvcraft.com; Temple Rd; ⊘10am-5pm Tue-Sun) 🖉 Has a huge range of Tibetan souvenirs at fixed prices, including good value T-shirts and traditional wall hangings. Sales benefit the Tibetan Children's Village.

Green Shop
PAPER PRODUCTS

(Map p322; Bhagsu Rd; ⊘10am-5pm Tue-Sun) 🖉 Sells handmade recycled paper products, with a sideline in tangy rhododendron jam.

Bookworm
BOOKS

(Map p322; ⬚ 221465; Hotel Bhagsu Rd; ⊘9am-6.30pm Tue-Sun) The best all-round bookshop.

Hills Bookshop
BOOKS

(Map p322; ⬚ 220008; Bhagsu Rd; ⊘10am-9.30pm) This place is well stocked with novels and guidebooks.

Namgyal Bookshop BOOKS
(Map p319; 221492; Tsuglagkhang Complex; 9.30am-noon & 1-6pm Tue-Sun) Specialises in Buddhist texts.

ℹ Information

MEDIA

Contact (www.contactmagazine.net) is an informative, free local magazine that contains some useful listings, as well as details regarding courses and volunteer work. It's also a useful website.

MEDICAL SERVICES

Traditional Tibetan medicine is a popular form of treatment in McLeod Ganj; see p316.

Delek Hospital (Map p319; 222053; Gangchen Kyishong; consultations ₹10; outpatient clinic 9am-1pm & 2-5pm)

MONEY

Several places around town offer Western Union money transfers.

HDFC ATM (Map p322; Lower Rd; 24hr) Located upstairs at the new bus depot.

State Bank of India (Map p322; Temple Rd; 10am-4pm Mon-Fri, to 1pm Sat) Has a busy international ATM.

Thomas Cook (Map p322; Temple Rd; 9.30am-6.30pm Mon-Fri, 9.30am-5pm Sat) Changes cash and travellers cheques for ₹60 commission and gives advance on credit cards for a 3% charge.

POST

Post Office (Map p322; Jogibara Rd; 9.30am-5pm Mon-Fri, to noon Sat, parcel post to 1pm Mon-Fri)

TOURIST INFORMATION

Clean Upper Dharamsala Project (Map p322; www.tsodhasa.org; Bhagsu Rd; 9am-5pm Mon-Sat, closed second and fourth Sat) This impressive centre provides education on environmental issues and offers an interesting free tour of McLeod's recycling system every Wednesday afternoon.

HPTDC Tourist Office (Map p322; 221205; Hotel Bhagsu Rd; 10am-5pm, closed Sun in Jul, Aug & Dec-Mar) Offers basic local informa-

tion and can make bookings for HPTDC hotels and buses around Himachal.

Information Office of Central Tibetan Administration (Map p322; 222457; www.tibet. net; Jogibara Rd; 9am-5.30pm Tue-Sun) For publications on Tibetan issues.

TRAVEL AGENCIES

Numerous travel agencies can book bus tickets, and can also arrange tours and treks.

Himalaya Tours & Travels (Map p322; 220714; www.himalayatravels.net; Bhagsu Rd)

Himachal Travels (Map p322; 221428; himachaltravels@sancharnet.in; Jogibara Rd)

ℹ Getting There & Around

Many travel agencies in McLeod Ganj will book train tickets for a commission of ₹100.

AIR

McLeod Ganj's nearest airport is at Gaggal, 15km southwest of Dharamsala. At the time of research no flights were operating but seasonal services to Delhi should resume eventually.

AUTORICKSHAW

Autorickshaws are useful for getting around the immediate area – the **autorickshaw stand** (Map p322) is just north of the Main Chowk. Sample fares include Bhagsu (₹40), Dal Lake (₹80) and Dharamkot (₹60).

BUS

Book long-distance government buses in advance at the **bus ticket office** (Map p322; 10am-1.30pm & 2-4.30pm) in McLeod's Main Chowk. More frequent departures leave from the lower Dharamsala bus station. Travel agencies can book seats on deluxe private buses to Delhi (₹700 to ₹1100, 12 hours, 6pm), Manali (₹550, 10 hours, 8pm) and other destinations.

TAXI

McLeod's **taxi stand** (Map p322; 221034) is on Mall Rd, north of the Main Chowk. To hire a taxi for the day, for a journey of less than 80km, expect to pay ₹2000.

One-way fares for short hops include Gangchen Kyishong (₹100), Dharamkot (₹100), Dharamsala bus station (₹200), Norbulingka

BUSES FROM MCLEOD GANJ

DESTINATION	FARE (₹)	DURATION (HR)	FREQUENCY
Dehra Dun	435	13	8pm
Delhi	450-1065	12	4am, 6pm & 7.30pm (ordinary); 5pm (semi-deluxe); 6.30pm & 7.45pm (deluxe); 7pm (Volvo)
Manali	300	11	4.30pm
Pathankot	115	4	5 daily

TIBETAN EXILES

In October of 1950, about a year after Mao Zedong declared the founding of the People's Republic of China, Chinese troops invaded Tibet. At the time, Tibet was a de facto independent state led by the Dalai Lama, with a hazy, complicated relationship with China. A year later, in October 1951, Lhasa, the Tibetan capital, fell. After resistance simmered for years in the countryside, protests against the Chinese occupation broke out on the streets of Lhasa in 1959. As the Chinese Army moved against the uprising, it fired upon the Norbulingka, the Dalai Lama's summer palace. Believing his life or his freedom was at risk, the Dalai Lama secretly fled across the Himalayas to India, where he received asylum.

China says its army was sent to Tibet as liberators, to free Tibetans from feudal serfdom and improve life on the vast high plateau. It hasn't worked out that way. While the commonly quoted figure of 1.2 million Tibetans killed since 1950 is seriously disputed – even by Western scholars – no independent observers question the reality of the suffering and human-rights abuses, as well as huge losses to Tibet's cultural legacy, that have occurred under Chinese occupation. Each year hundreds of Tibetans risk the dangerous, clandestine crossing over the mountains into India, and it's estimated that about 130,000 refugees are now living outside their homeland. Most come first to the Dharamsala area, where they find support from their community, their government in exile and a legion of NGOs. About 80,000 exiles live around Dharamsala today.

Institute (₹400) and the airport at Gaggal (₹700). Return fares are about a third more.

Around McLeod Ganj

Bhagsu & Dharamkot

☑ 01892

Through pine trees to the north and east of McLeod lie the villages of Dharamkot and Bhagsu, which can both be visited on a pleasant half-day stroll, or used as an alternative accommodation base. Both places are true Backpackerland heavy with Hebrew signage, where you can lounge in cafes, take drumming lessons and yoga classes and forget there's any crisis in Tibet.

Of the two Dharamkot is by far the more mellow and laid-back and still retains a charming village vibe. It's a particularly good base for day hikes around the valleys, to Triund, Dal Lake and the nearby Galu Devi Temple on the top of the ridge.

Bhagsu (Bhagsunag) is busier and much more built-up, and the lower village in particular is lined with concrete hotels, shops and discos aimed squarely at domestic visitors. The village has a small **Shiva temple** and cold spring-fed pool built by the raja of Kangra in the 16th century. Walking paths lead from here up for 1.5km to the Bhagsu **waterfall**, which is most impressive during the monsoon. Further up in the village is

the awesomely cheeesy **Mata Temple**, with stairways leading through the open mouths of a cement crocodile and lion.

🛏 Sleeping & Eating

🛏 Bhagsu

Bhagsu is lined with German bakeries and backpacker cafes serving falafel, hummus and Tibetan food.

Sky Pye Guesthouse   GUESTHOUSE $
(☑0941805966; d ₹250-800; @🛜) A five-minute walk up through the village, Sky Pye is a good-value traveller hang-out that's often full. There are views from the sunny terrace and from the balconies of the pricier rooms, and there's a great little restaurant with low tables and cushions on the floor. Music jams get things going on Tuesday evenings.

Oak View Guesthouse   GUESTHOUSE $
(☑221530; d ₹300-500) Clean guesthouse on the path to Upper Bhagsu with a modern backpacker vibe – right down to the Bob Marley flag in the common lounge. The clean, spacious rooms have hot water and TVs, and there's a good restaurant.

🛏 Dharamkot

Dharamkot is much more low-key than Bhagsu, and you'll have to seek out the many unmarked guesthouses and home-stays in the sleepy village lanes. There are several particularly good backpacker cafes in the main upper village, including Moon-light Cafe, Trek and Dine and Milky Way Restauarant.

New Blue Heaven Guesthouse   HOTEL **$**
(Map p319; ☑ 9736221095; www.hotelnewblue-heaven.com; d ₹880) This budget place is in the lower village, by the Himalayan Iyen-gar Yoga Centre. Spotless carpeted rooms with TVs, hot water and balconies over-looking the valley make it a decent choice, though you'll find plenty of cheaper and better value places in the village if you dig around.

Sidhibari

About 6km southeast of Dharamsala, the lit-tle village of Sidhibari is the adopted home of Ogyen Trinley Dorje, the 17th Karmapa of Tibetan Buddhism, who fled from Tibet to India in 2000. Although his official seat is Rumtek Monastery in Sikkim, the young leader of the Kagyu (Black Hat) sect has been banned from taking up his seat be-cause of rival claims and fear this would up-set the Chinese government.

The temporary seat of the Karmapa is the large **Gyuto Tantric Gompa** (☑ 01892-230637; www.kagyuoffice.org). Public audi-ences take place here on Wednesday and Saturday at 2.30pm; foreign visitors are welcome but security is tight, and bags, phones and cameras are not allowed inside the auditorium.

Frequent local buses run from Dharam-sala to Palampur, passing through Sidhibari (₹8, 15 minutes), or you can take a taxi for ₹250 return. Sidhibari is 3km from the Nor-bulingka Institute.

Norbulingka Institute

About 6km from Dharamsala, the wonder-ful **Norbulingka Institute** (☑ 01892-246405; www.norbulingka.org; ☺ 9am-5.30pm) FREE was established in 1988 to teach and preserve traditional Tibetan art forms, and you can watch woodcarving, statue-making, *thang-ka* painting and embroidery as you tour the various workshops. The **shop** (www.norbulingkashop.com) here sells the centre's expensive but stylish craftworks and home-decor items, including embroidered clothes, cushions and wall hangings, and sales ben-

efit refugee artists. Also here are delightful Japanese-influenced gardens and the cen-tral **Deden Tsuglakhang temple** with a 4m-high gilded statue of Sakyamuni. Next to the shop is the **Losel Doll Museum** (Indian/foreigner ₹5/20; ☺ 9am-5.30pm), which uses charming puppet dioramas to illustrate as-pects of traditional Tibetan culture. A short walk outside the complex is the large **Dolma Ling** Buddhist nunnery. On Sundays and the second Saturday of each month, the work-shops are closed but the rest of the grounds are open.

Set in the Norbulingka gardens, peaceful and stylish **Norling Guest House** (☑ 01892-246406; www.norbulingka.org; s/d ₹2220/2853, ste ₹3329-4280; ☎) offers comfortable rooms decked out with Buddhist murals and handicrafts from the institute, and arranged around a sunny atrium. Waffles, wraps and sandwiches are available at the institute's lovely **Norling Cafe** (mains ₹70-180; ☎).

To get here, catch a Palampur-bound bus from Dharamsala and ask to be let off at Sidhpur (₹8, 15 minutes), near the Sacred Heart School, from where it's a 15-minute gentle uphill walk. A taxi from McLeod Ganj or Dharamsala costs ₹400/600 one-way/return.

Southwest of Dharamsala

Kangra

☑ 01892 / ELEV 734M
The former capital of the princely state of Kangra, this bustling pilgrim town is a good day trip from McLeod Ganj. Hindus visit to pay homage at the **Brajeshwari Devi Tem-ple**, one of the 51 Shakti *peeths*, the famous temples marking the sites where body parts from Shiva's first wife, Sati, fell after the goddess was consumed by flames (the tem-ple marks the final resting place of Sati's left breast). It's reached through an atmospheric bazaar winding uphill, 10 minutes from the main road, lined with shops selling *prasad* and religious trinkets.

On the far side of town, a ₹100 autorick-shaw ride from the bus stand, impregnable-looking **Kangra Fort** (www.royalkangra.com; Nagar Kot; Indian/foreigner ₹5/100, audio guide ₹95/150; ☺ 9am-5pm) soars above the con-fluence of the Manjhi and Banganga Riv-ers. The fort was occupied by Hindu rajas, Mughal warlords and even the British (in

KANGRA VALLEY TOY TRAIN

A lumbering narrow-gauge train runs east from Pathankot, providing a scenic, if slow, back route to Kangra (2½ hours), Palampur (four hours), Baijnath (6½ hours) and Jogindarnagar (nine hours). There are seven trains a day – two as far as Jogindarnagar and five as far as Baijnath. Ordinary trains cost ₹42 or less to any destination on the route, but carriages are generally packed and seats cannot be booked in advance. Board early to grab a window seat and enjoy the views en route.

1846), before it was finally toppled by the earthquake of 1905. Head up to the battlements for views north to the mountains and south to the plains. A small museum back at the entrance has stone carvings from temples inside the compound and miniature paintings from the Kangra School.

Just above the fort entrance is the **Maharaja Sansar Chand Museum** (☑ 265866; Indian/foreigner ₹5/100, audio guide ₹95/150; ☺ 9am-5pm), whose uniforms, ornate palanquins and sets of armour give a fine insight into the twilight years of the local Katoch royal family.

Royal Hotel & Restaurant (☑ 265013; royalhotel@rediffmail.com; s/d ₹650/750, r with AC ₹1400; ✳) on the main road between the temple bazaar and the bus stand has acceptable, tiled rooms with hot showers, plus a decent restaurant, though rooms are a bit overpriced.

❶ Getting There & Away

Kangra's bus stand is 1.5km north of the temple bazaar, a ₹25 autorickshaw ride from the centre. There are frequent buses to Dharamsala (₹20, one hour), Palampur (₹40, 1½ hours), Pathankot (₹100, three hours) and Jawalamukhi (₹40, 1½ hours).

Seven trains a day pull into Kangra Mandir station, 3km east of town, and Kangra station, 5km south. Travellers have reported problems getting a taxi from the stations into town (₹150).

A return taxi from McLeod Ganj to Kangra Fort costs ₹1200, including waiting time. Taxis in Kangra charge ₹400/600 to Dharamsala/McLeod Ganj, ₹700 to Jawalamukhi and ₹1000 to Masrur.

Masrur

A winding road runs southwest from Gaggal through pleasant green hills to the 10th-century **temples** (Indian/foreigner ₹5/100; ☺ dawn-dusk) at Masrur. Although badly damaged by the 1905 earthquake, the elaborately carved monolithic sandstone *sikharas* owe more than a passing resemblance to the Hindu temples at Angkor Wat in Cambodia or to Ellora in Maharshtra. You can climb to the upper level for mountain views.

The easiest way to get here is a day trip by taxi from Dharamsala together with a visit to Kangra Fort (₹2200 return). Alternatively you can get as far as Lunj (₹50, 1½ hours) from Dharamsala by public bus, then take a Nagrota Surian–bound bus for 4km south to the junction at Pir Bindli and then either walk the last 2.5km or wait for one of the hourly buses to the temples.

Jawalamukhi
☑ 01970

About 34km south of Kangra is the town and temple of Jawalamukhi, the goddess of light, worshipped in the form of a natural-gas eternal flame issuing from the rocks. The temple is one of the 51 *Shakti peeths,* marking the spot where the tongue of Shiva's first wife, Sati, fell after her body was consumed by flames. The gold dome and spire were installed by Maharaja Ranjit Singh, the 'Lion of Punjab', who purportedly never went into battle without seeking a blessing from the temple.

Hotel Jawalaji (☑ 222280; d ₹1495, with AC ₹2415, ste ₹3680; ✳) is a superior HPTDC property, with well-loved rooms, conveniently located for walks to the temple and outlying countryside.

Buses to Dharamsala (₹60, 1½ hours) and Kangra (₹30, 1½ hours) leave all day from the stand below the road leading up to the temple. Taxis charge ₹1500 return from McLeod Ganj.

Dharamsala to Mandi

Palampur
☑ 01894 / ELEV 1249M

About 30km southeast of Dharamsala, Palampur is a small junction town surrounded by tea plantations and rice fields. A short walk from town takes you to the pretty waterfall in **Bundla Gorge**, or you can pass a few hours observing the tea-making process at the **Palampur Tea Cooperative** (☎230220; ☉10.30am-12.30pm & 1.30-4.30pm Tue-Fri), about 2km south of town on the main road between Kangra and Mandi.

The HPTDC-run **Hotel T-Bud** (☎231298; palampur@hptdc.in; d ₹1725-2530), 1km north of Main Bazar on the edge of town, has large grounds and a good restaurant; rooms are spacious and well kept. The more expensive rooms are in a newer block, but the old ones aren't bad.

The bus station is 1km south of Main Bazar; an autorickshaw from the centre costs ₹30. Buses leave all day for Dharamsala (₹40, two hours). A taxi from Dharamsala costs ₹800. Palampur is a stop on the Pathankot–Jogindarnagar rail line.

Tashijong & Taragarh

About 5km west of Baijnath, and 2km north from the Palampur road, the village of Tashijong is home to a small community of Drukpa Kagyud monks and refugees. The focus of life here is the impressive **Tashijong Gompa**, with several mural-filled prayer halls and a carpet-making, *thangka*-painting and wood-carving cooperative.

About 2km south of Tashijong, at Taragarh, is the extraordinary **Taragarh Palace** (☎242034, in Delhi 24692317; www.taragarh.com; r ₹5870-8220), the summer palace of the last maharaja of Jammu and Kashmir. Now a luxury hotel, this elegant country seat is full of portraits of the Dogra royal family, Italian marble, crystal chandeliers, tiger skins and other ostentatious furnishings. It's set in beautiful grounds with a pool and tennis courts. The restaurant serves lavish buffet meals.

Both villages can be reached on the buses that run along the Mandi–Palampur Hwy.

Baijnath

☎ 01894 / ELEV 1010M

The small town of Baijnath, set on a mountain-facing ridge 46km southeast of Dharamsala, is an important pilgrimage destination. In the middle of the village, next to the bus station, is the exquisitely carved **Vaidyanath Temple**, sacred to Shiva in his incarnation as Vaidyanath, Lord of the Physicians, dating from the 8th century. Thousands of pilgrims make their way here for the **Shivaratri Festival** (☉late Feb-early Mar).

Most people visit on a day trip, or a stop on the journey from Mandi to Dharamsala. The Pathankot–Jogindarnagar rail line passes through Paprola, about 1km west of the main bus stand.

Bir & Billing

About 9km east of Baijnath, a road winds uphill to the village of Bir (1300m), a small Tibetan colony with three peaceful **gompas** that welcome passing visitors, and Billing (2600m), a famous launch pad for paragliding and hang-gliding. In 1992 the world record of 132.5km for an out-and-return flight was set here. International teams come to challenge the record every May for the **Himalayan Hang-Gliding Rally**, while paragliders compete in the **Himalayan Open** in autumn.

A taxi from McLeod Ganj to Billing will cost ₹2200. Alternatively, travel by bus or train to Jogindarnagar (on the route to Mandi) and take a taxi there for ₹400 return.

Chamba Valley

The Chamba Valley is a splendidly isolated valley system, cut off from the Kangra Valley by the Dhauladhar Range and from Kashmir by the Pir Panjal. This area was ruled for centuries as the princely state of Chamba, the most ancient state in North India. Even though good roads connect Chamba with Pathankot and Kangra, surprisingly few travellers make it out here, with even fewer continuing up the valley beyond the old hill station of Dalhousie.

Dalhousie

☎ 01899 / POP 10,500 / ELEV 2036M

With its plunging pine-clad valleys and distant mountain views, Dalhousie is another of those cool hill retreats left behind by the British. Since independence, the old colonial mansions have been joined by an army cantonment, the posh Dalhousie Public School and numerous modern hotels catering to honeymooners from the plains. There's not a lot to do here other than stroll around appreciating the crisp air and mountain views.

Quite a few Tibetan refugees have made a home in Dalhousie and there are **painted rock carvings** of Buddhist deities along the south side of the ridge. You can also visit the

Dalhousie

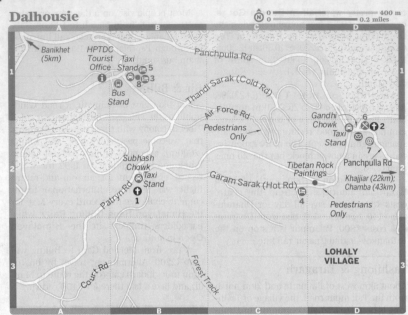

British-era churches of **St John** (1863) and **St Francis** (1894), set among the pines at opposite ends of the ridge.

Unusually for a hill station there are few truly steep roads, but Dalhousie is spread out far enough to be tiring. The market areas at Subhash Chowk and Gandhi Chowk are linked by lanes – Thandi Sarak (Cold Rd), and Garam Sarak (Hot Rd). The latter lane receives more sunshine.

🛏 Sleeping

Dalhousie has more than 100 hotels spread across various ridges and lanes. Most are either old or just look old. High season runs from April to July, and Christmas to New Year; expect up to 50% off at other times.

Hotel Crags
GUESTHOUSE $

(📞 242124; hotelcrags@hotmail.com; Garam Sarak; r ₹600-900, cottage ₹1200) For creaky colonial character and valley views, Crags is the pick of the budget places. The rickety old house has huge rooms and a large front terrace offering spectacular sunny views of the valley, but the wooden walls mean that you'll hear your neighbours sneezing. The upper-floor suite comes with a front sitting room, but the choicest option is the self-contained cottage above the main house. Rates are discounted by 30% much of the year.

Grand View Hotel
HERITAGE HOTEL $$$

(📞 240760; www.grandviewdalhousie.in; d incl breakfast ₹3335-4485, ste ₹5520; 🛜) The Grand has a range of rooms, some in the new modern deluxe block and others with more colonial-era character, including some with four-poster beds. The stately 1920s hotel is surrounded by terraces gazing across to views of the Pir Panjal peaks. There's a spa and exercise room.

Hotel Mount View
HOTEL $$$

(📞 242120; www.hotelmountview.com; Club Rd; r ₹3042-3627, ste ₹3978-4446) There's a faint Raj-era charm here in the dark-wood finishes and wicker furnishings, and there are good valley views from the well-tended garden terrace. The less expensive rooms are small, with slightly dingy bathrooms but there are good discounts in the off season.

🍴 Eating

The restaurants at Hotel Grand View and Mount View offer a charming setting and multicuisine menus (mains ₹200 to ₹300).

Dalhousie

⊙ **Sights**
1 St Francis Church B2
2 St John Church D2

🛏 **Sleeping**
3 Grand View Hotel B1
4 Hotel Crags C2
5 Hotel Mount View B1

✕ **Eating**
6 Kwality Restaurant D2

ℹ **Information**
7 Manimahesh Cyber Cafe D2
8 Trek-n-Travels B1

For cheap eats, there are several Punjabi *dhabas* on the south side of Subhash Chowk.

★ **Kwality Restaurant**   MULTICUISINE **$$**
(Gandhi Chowk; dishes ₹135-220) Regarded as Dalhousie's best independent restaurant, the extensive menu at this modern and stylish place spreads to Chinese dishes and burgers, though the Indian dishes are easily the best choice.

ℹ Information

HPTDC Tourist Office (☎ 242225; ⊙ 10am-5pm, closed 2nd and 4th Sat Apr-Jul, closed Sun & 2nd Sat Aug-Mar) Opposite the bus stand.
Manimahesh Cyber Cafe (Gandhi Chowk; per hr ₹40; ⊙ 8.30am-9pm)
Trek-n-Travels (☎ 242160; Tibetan Market) Near the bus stand; can arrange treks around Chamba Valley from ₹2000 to ₹3000 per day.

ℹ Getting There & Away

BUS
The booking office at the **bus stand** is invariably closed, but Prince Travels next door can help with bus information. For long-distance services, there are more options from Banikhet, a major transport junction about 10 minutes' ride from Dalhousie (bus/taxi ₹7/200), though you aren't guaranteed a seat here. Four buses run from Dalhousie to Chamba (₹60 to ₹70, two hours); two through Khajjiar (₹25, one hour, 9am and 4.30pm). For more frequent Chamba buses, head to Banikhet first.

TAXI
There are taxi stands with fixed fares at Subhash Chowk, Gandhi Chowk and the bus stand. From the bus stand, you'll pay ₹100 to Subhash Chowk or Gandhi Chowk. A day tour to Kalatop, Dhainkot and Khajiar costs ₹1230.
Other fares:
Bharmour ₹3500
Chamba ₹1130 (₹1450 return)
Dharamsala ₹2500
Kalatop ₹520 (₹620 return)
Khajjiar ₹720 (₹870 return)
Pathankot ₹1700

Around Dalhousie
KALATOP WILDLIFE SANCTUARY
Midway between Dalhousie and Chamba, accessible by taxi or public bus, the forested hills around Khajjiar are preserved as the **Kalatop Wildlife Sanctuary** (vehicle entry ₹200). The flat 3km unpaved road and shortcut walking paths to Kalatop provide excellent forest walks and you have a chance of spotting langur monkeys and musk deer. Buses between Dalhousie and Khajjiar pass the park entrance at Lakkar Mandi. It's possible to hike the 10km from Kalatop down to Khajjiar but you would need a guide from the park entrance to navigate the forest trails. Buses head back to Dalhousie between 1.30pm and 4pm.

On the other side of the road from the park entrance a looping paved road (and more direct shortcut hiking trails) leads 5km uphill to **Dhainkund** (2745m) to

HIMACHAL PRADESH CHAMBA VALLEY

BUSES FROM DALHOUSIE

DESTINATION	FARE (₹)	DURATION (HR)	FREQUENCY
Amritsar	170	7	9.40am
Delhi	370/590/870	12	3pm/6.30pm/7.30pm (ordinary/semideluxe/deluxe)
Dharamsala	160	6	7.15am, 11.50am & 1.45pm
Pathankot	70	3	10 daily
Shimla	350	12	12.45pm

reveal the region's best views of the expansive Pir Pinjal range. Taxis have to park at a military checkpost, from where it's a 1.5km ridgeline walk to the **Jai Pohlani Mata Temple** and several teahouses. A taxi from Dalhousie costs ₹720 return.

KHAJJIAR

India's so-called 'Mini Switzerland', this grassy bowl-shaped *marg* (meadow), 22km east from Dalhousie, is ringed by pines and thronged by Indian holidaymakers. In among the *dhabas* on one side is the **Khajjinag Temple**, with fine woodcarvings and crude effigies of the five Pandavas, installed here in the 16th century.

In season, pony rides around the meadow and its small central lake cost ₹300, and zorbing in giant inflatable balls costs from ₹300 for a quick roll. Since there are no big slopes as such, you get pushed along – not exactly high adrenaline!

There are a handful of hotels popular with Indian holidaymakers, but most travellers make a day trip here by bus from Chamba (₹25, 1½ hours) or Dalhousie (₹25, one hour). Buses run from Dalhousie between 9am and 9.30am, returning between 2.30pm and 3.30pm.

If you do decide to stay, the option with the best location is the **HPTDC Hotel Davdar** (☏236803; ₹2185-3220), with its deliciously isolated Khajjiar Cottage.

Chamba

☏ 01899 / POP 19,900 / ELEV 996M

Ensconced in the valley of the fast-flowing Ravi River, the bustling capital of Chamba district is dominated by the former palaces of the local maharajas. The princely state of Chamba was founded in AD 920 by Raja Sahil Varman and it survived for 1000 years until it finally fell to the British in 1845. Every year since 935, Chamba has celebrated the annual harvest with the **Minjar Festival** (☉ Jul/Aug), in honour of Raghuvira (an incarnation of Rama).

Although en route to Bharmour and fine trekking country, Chamba is well off the tourist radar. The de facto centre is the open grassy sports field known as the Chowgan, the focus for festivals, impromptu cricket matches, picnics and promenades. Most places of interest are tucked away in the alleyways of Dogra Bazar, which spread uphill from the Chowgan.

Sights & Activities

★ Lakshmi

Narayan Temple Complex   HINDU TEMPLE

(☉ dusk-dawn) Opposite the Akhand Chandi Palace are six corn-cob-style stone *sikharas* dating from the 10th to the 19th centuries and covered in carvings. The largest (and oldest) is dedicated to Lakshmi Narayan (Vishnu). Just outside the complex is a distinctive Nepali-style pillar topped by a statue of Vishnu's faithful servant, the man-bird Garuda. The remaining temples are sacred to Radha Krishna, Shiva, Gauri Shankar, Triambkeshwar Mahdev and Lakshmi Damodar. The compound has a small **museum** (admission free; ☉ 11am-5pm Mon-Sat) displaying religious artefacts.

Hindu Temples   TEMPLES

On the hilltop above the Rang Mahal (Old Palace), reached via a set of steps near the bus stand, or by taxi along the road to Jhumar, the stone **Chamunda Devi Temple** features impressive carvings of Chamunda Devi (Durga in her wrathful aspect) and superior views of Chamba and the Ravi Valley. About 500m north along the road to Saho, accessed by a red and white roadside gate, the **Bajreshwari Devi Temple** is a handsome hut-style mandir with exquisite effigies of Bajreshwari (an incarnation of Durga) set into plinths around the walls.

Between the two is a small shrine to **Sui Mata**, a local princess who gave her life to appease a water spirit that was causing a terrible drought in Chamba. The goddess is highly venerated by local women, and the four-day Sui Mata Mela is celebrated each April on the Chowgan in her honour.

By the Chowgan is the 11th-century **Harirai Mandir**, sacred to Vishnu. Dotted near the Akhand Chandi Palace are similar stone temples to Radha Krishna, Sitaram (Rama) and **Champavati**, daughter of Raja Sahil Varman, worshipped locally as an incarnation of Durga.

Former Palaces   HISTORIC BUILDINGS

Uphill from the Chowgan and lording over the town is the unmissable stately white **Akhand Chandi Palace**, the former home of the Chamba raja. Built in 1764, the central Darbar Hall is reminiscent of many civic buildings in Kathmandu. It now houses a postgraduate college; you can peek inside during school hours.

A few blocks southeast is the fortress-like, rusty-coloured **Rang Mahal** (Old Palace),

Chamba

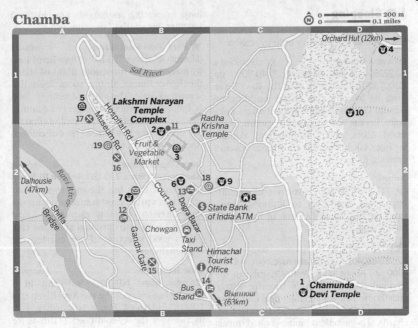

Orchard Hut (12km)→

Sal River

Lakshmi Narayan
Temple
Complex

Radha
Krishna
Temple

Fruit &
Vegetable
Market

Dalhousie
(47km)

Ravi River

Shitla
Bridge

Chowgan

Taxi
Stand

Himachal
Tourist
Office

State Bank
of India ATM

Bus
Stand

Bharmour
(63km)

Chamunda
Devi Temple

---

which once housed the royal granary and treasury.

Bhuri Singh Museum MUSEUM

(☎222590; Museum Rd; Indian/foreigner ₹20/100, camera ₹50/100; ◷10am-5pm Tue-Sun) Founded in 1908 and named after the Chamba ruler of that time, this museum has a wonderful collection of miniature paintings from the Chamba, Kangra and Basohli schools, plus wood carvings, weapons, *rumal* (embroideries), intriguing copper-plate inscriptions and ornately carved centuries-old fountain slabs from around the Chamba Valley. There's detailed labelling in English.

Tours

Mani Mahesh Travels TREKKING

(☎9816620401; www.himalayanlap.com) Near the Lakshmi Narayan complex, Mani Mahesh Travels can arrange treks with guides and porters in the surrounding Pir Panjal and Dhauladhar ranges, as well as informative tours of Chamba's temples (from ₹550). If you don't have time for a long trek, ask about overnight stays in the deliciously isolated Ridgemoor Cottage, three hours' walk and 1000m climb above the Orchard Hut at Rulpalli meadow. Contact Prakash.

HIMACHAL PRADESH CHAMBA VALLEY

🛏 Sleeping

Unlike Dalhousie, Chamba is not a tourist town, so hotel prices vary little by season.

Chamba House   GUESTHOUSE $
(📞 222564; Gopal Nivas; d ₹440-800, ste ₹1100) With fine views over the Ravi River from its balcony, this creaky building by Gandhi Gate is Chamba's best budget bolt-hole. Rooms are small but quaint, with wood floors, giving it a homey cottage feeling. Ask about the charming upstairs drawing room.

Jimmy's Inn   HOTEL $
(📞 224748; r ₹300-500) If you're really count-ing rupees, head over to Jimmy's, across from the bus stand. Get one of the upper-floor rooms.

★ Orchard Hut   GUESTHOUSE $$
(📞 9816620401; www.himalayanlap.com; r ₹350-2000; 🚗) About 12km from Chamba in the tranquil Saal Valley, this friendly village guesthouse is a wonderfully peaceful place to unwind amid the plum and apricot or-chards. The excellent home-cooked meals are recommended (₹500 half-board per person) and there are even cooking courses, and stafff can lead you on some fine walks in the area, including around the surround-ing organic farm. Staff at sister company Mani Manesh Travels in Chamba will ar-range transfers, either by taxi (₹300) or public bus (₹15) to Chaminoo village, from where it's a steep 20-minute walk to the resort. Do yourself a favour and budget an extra day here.

Hotel Aroma Palace   HOTEL $$
(📞 225177; www.hotelaromapalacechamba.com; r ₹690-1380, ste with AC ₹1725-4025; @🖥🖂) Up-hill from the taxi stand and past the court-house, this modern place has a range of tidy rooms, an internet cafe, a restaurant and a sunny terrace with views over Chowgan. The cheaper rooms are disappointing – some are dark and have their own bathroom outside off the hall – but if you pay a bit more you get the real deal.

🍴 Eating & Drinking

Chamba is known for its *chukh* – a chilli sauce that consists of red and green pep-pers, lemon juice and mustard oil, served as a condiment in most restaurants. Chamba's most interesting restaurants are clustered together just south of the museum.

★ Park View Restaurant   INDIAN $
(Museum Rd; dishes ₹50-150; ⊕ 8am-11pm) Eas-ily missed up an innocuous flight of stairs, the low-ceilinged dining room feels like someone's attic. The veg and nonveg food is fantastic – order some *jheera* (cumin) rice and curd and a copper pail of dhal on the side, or one of a dozen types of chicken (including lemon chicken).

Jagan Restaurant   INDIAN $
(Museum Rd; dishes ₹30-180; ⊕ 11am-10.30pm) It's nothing flash but the uniformed wait-ers at this upstairs restaurant serve up the tasty Chamba speciality *chamba madhra* (kidney beans with curd and ghee) for ₹90, plus a good selection of veg curries and chicken dishes.

Cafe Ravi View   INDIAN $$
(Chowgan; mains ₹40-160; ⊕ 9am-9pm) In a circular hut overlooking the Ravi River, this HPTDC-run snack house is worth a visit as much for the icy-cold beers (₹110) as for the Indian and Chinese veg food, including *dosas* and bargain veg thalis (₹80).

ℹ Information

There's an international ATM (but no currency exchange) at the State Bank of India, near the courthouse.

Cyberia (per hr ₹30; ⊕ 9am-8pm Mon-Sat) Near Hotel Aroma Palace; has broadband con-nection and helpful staff.

Dhiman Cyber Cafe (Museum Rd; per hr ₹30; ⊕ 9.30am-8.30pm Mon-Sat)

Himachal Tourist Office (📞 224002; Court Rd; ⊕ 10am-5pm Mon-Sat) In the courtyard of Hotel Iravati.

Post Office (Museum Rd; ⊕ 9.30am-5.30pm Mon-Sat)

ℹ Getting There & Away

Six daily buses make the hair-raising ride to Bharmour (₹70, three hours); sit on the left for the best views. Buses for Dalhousie run every two hours (₹60, 2½ hours), with four going via Khajjiar (₹30, 1½ hours). There are also one or two buses a day to Dharamsala (₹175, eight hours).

Official taxi fares include Khajjiar (₹600/1000 one way/return), Bharmour (₹1200/1500 one way/return), Dalhousie (₹1200) and Dharamsala (₹2500).

Bharmour

☎ 01895 / ELEV 2195M

Hovering on the edge of a seemingly bottom-less valley, the charming mountain village of Bharmour is reached by a mountain road as scenic as it is perilous, winding 65km east of Chamba. This ancient slate-roofed settlement was the capital of the princely state of Chamba until AD 920, and there are some beautiful temples, though the main reason to come here is for treks to the surrounding valleys and passes. The villages around Bharmour are home to the seminomadic Gaddis, pastoralists who move their flocks up to alpine pastures during the summer, and descend to Kangra, Mandi and Bilaspur in winter.

◉ Sights & Activities

Chaurasi Temples   HINDU TEMPLE
Reached through the bazaar leading uphill from the jeep stand, the Chaurasi temples ('chaurasi' means 84) are some of Himachal's finest. Built in the classic stone-*sikhara* style, with wide slate canopies, the three main Shaivite temples occupy a flagstone courtyard that doubles as an outdoor classroom and cricket ground. Highlights of the compound are the **Manimahesh Temple**, built in the 6th century AD and dwarfed by a huge cedar, and the squat **Lakshna Devi Temple**, featuring an eroded but wildly carved wooden doorway.

For the best valley views, hike 3km up to the Brahmani Mata Temple above town.

Trekking   TREKKING
Treks from Bharmour can be arranged through **Anna Adventures & Tours** (☎981 7710758; www.bharmourtreks.com), opposite the Chaurasi Hotel; contact Gopal Chauhan. Expect to pay around ₹2500 a day for a full camping trek. The trekking season lasts from May to late October, though July and August see some monsoon rain.

Treks include from Kugti to Jelma in Lahaul over the 5040m Kugti Pass (five days); to McLeod Ganj over the Indrahar Pass (five days); and longer treks via Bara Bhangal to Manali or Bir in the Kangra Valley.

One popular shorter trek is to the sacred lake at Manimahesh, a three-day, 35km return hike that starts from Hadsar, 13km from Bharmour. In August/September, thousands of pilgrims take a freezing dip in Manimahesh Lake as part of the **Manimahesh Yatra** in honour of Lord Shiva.

🛏 Sleeping & Eating

Chaurasi Hotel & Restaurant   HOTEL $
(☎9418025004; r ₹350-1000) You can't miss this blazing red multistorey building on the temple road. Though carpets are a little ratty, this is a good-value hotel with generous-sized rooms offering soaring views over the valley, especially from the top-floor room with balcony. The ground-floor restaurant (mains ₹80 to ₹140) is Bharmour's best, which isn't saying much.

ℹ Getting There & Away

Buses leave hourly until 5pm for the rugged trip to Chamba (₹65, four hours), but expect delays during monsoon landslides. If you want to get a seat, board early! For the ride to Chamba, the best views are from the right side of the bus. Taxis charge ₹1500 but you can bargain at the jeep stand.

LAHAUL & SPITI

This vast, desolate corner of Himachal Pradesh is one of the most spectacular and sparsely populated regions on Earth. Lahaul is a relatively green valley north of the Rohtang La, but as you travel east into Spiti the landscape transforms into a rugged network of interlocking river valleys hidden in the rain shadow of the Himalaya. It's 12,000 sq km of snow-topped mountains and high-altitude desert, punctuated by tiny patches of greenery and villages of whitewashed mud-brick houses clinging to the sides of rivers and melt-water streams.

As in Zanskar and Ladakh, Buddhism is the dominant religion, though there are small pockets of Hinduism in Lahaul, where many temples are sacred to both Buddhist and Hindu deities. According to legend, some monasteries in Lahaul were founded personally by Padmasambhava (Guru Rinpoche in Tibetan), the Indian monk-magician who converted Tibet to Buddhism in the 8th century AD.

Manali is the main gateway to Lahaul and Spiti. A seasonal highway runs north over the Rohtang La (3978m) to Keylong, the capital of Lahaul, continuing to Ladakh over the mighty Baralacha La (4950m) and Taglang La (5328m). Side roads branch west to the little-visited Pattan Valley and east to Spiti over Kunzum La (4551m).

HIMACHAL PRADESH LAHAUL & SPITI

Growing numbers of travellers are visiting Lahaul and Spiti as part of the Great Himalayan Circuit from Kashmir to Kinnaur. The Rohtang La, Baralacha La and Taglang La are normally open from June to late October, while the Kunzum La to Spiti is accessible from July to October, with exact dates depending on snow conditions. At other times, Lahaul is virtually cut off from the outside world, with Spiti connected only by the rugged Hindustan–Tibet Hwy from Kinnaur. A new tunnel currently under construction between Solang, just north of Manali, and Gramphu in Lahaul, will eventually cut driving time by several hours and open the valley to year-round traffic. The (very) tentative completion date is 2015.

For more information on Lahaul and Spiti, visit the local government website at http://hplahaulspiti.gov.in.

Losar, the Tibetan New Year, is celebrated in villages throughout Lahaul and Spiti in January or February, depending on the lunar calendar.

History

Buddhism arrived in Spiti and Lahaul during the 8th century AD with the Indian missionary Padmasambhava (Lahaul comes from *lha-hi-yul* meaning 'Land of the Gods' or *lho-yul* meaning 'Land in the South') . By the 10th century, upper Lahaul, Spiti and Zanskar had been incorporated into the vast Guge kingdom of western Tibet. The Great Translator, Ringchen Zangpo, founded a series of centres of Buddhist learning along the Spiti Valley, including Tabo, one of the most remarkable Buddhist monasteries in the Indian Himalaya.

After the kings of Ladakh were defeated by Mongol-Tibetan armies in the 18th century, the region was divided and ruled by various rajas, then fell under the British administration. Yet it maintained strong links with Tibet right up until the Chinese occupation in 1949.

Since then, there has been a major resurgence in the cultural and religious life of Spiti, aided by the work of the Tibetan government in exile in Dharamsala. The gompas of Lahaul and Spiti are being restored, and money from tourism and hydroelectricity is improving living conditions for the farming communities who get snowed in here each winter.

Climate

Lahaul and Spiti have a markedly different climate from the rest of Himachal Pradesh. The limited rainfall and high altitude – mostly above 3000m – ensures desperately cold conditions in winter. Even in summer, temperatures rarely rise above 15°C, and winter temperatures can plummet below -30°C! On the plus side, when monsoons are drenching the rest of the state, it's usually sunny here.

Realistically, the region is only open to travellers when the mountain passes are open, from early June/July to late October. Whenever you travel, bring plenty of clothing for cold weather.

Lahaul

Separated from the Kullu Valley by the 3978m Rohtang La and from Spiti by the 4551m Kunzum La, Lahaul is greener and more developed than Ladakh and Spiti, but most travellers whistle straight through on the road between Manali and Leh, missing most of what Lahaul has to offer. The capital, Keylong, is an easy stop on the popular Leh to Manali bus trip and you can detour to a number of mountain villages and medieval monasteries that remain blissfully untouched by mass tourism.

Normally, government buses between Manali and Leh run from mid-July to mid-September, with private buses and shared minivans operating from late June to mid-October. Services as far as Keylong continue until the Rohtang La closes in November, and buses east to Kaza stop when the Kunzum La closes in October. Check the status of the passes before visiting late in the season – once the snows arrive, you might be stuck for the winter.

Manali to Keylong

From Manali the road to Leh strikes north along the Beas River valley and climbs slowly through pine forests and switchbacks to the bare rocky slopes below Rohtang La. The name literally translates as 'pile of dead bodies' – a reference to the hundreds of travellers who have frozen to death here over the centuries. In the height of summer, the pass is chock-a-block with Indian tourists riding horses and enjoying the novelty of a summertime snowball fight. At the pass, look out for the small, dome-shaped temple that marks the source of the Beas River.

On the far side of the pass, the road plunges spectacularly down into the awesome Lahaul Valley, a rugged landscape of soaring crags, alpine meadows and mesmerising waterfalls plunging from glacial heights. About 66km northwest of Manali, the tiny hamlet of **Gramphu** marks the turn-off to Spiti. There is only one building in Gramphu – a rustic stone *dhaba* beside a stream where you'll have to wait for the bus if you're heading to Kaza from Keylong.

Khoksar, 5km northwest of Gramphu, has several *dhabas* and a police checkpoint where foreigners must show their passports. The road passes through a sheer-sided valley, hemmed in by skyscraping rocky peaks. The planned tunnel underneath the Rohtang La will eventually join the main road 4km west of here.

About 18km before Keylong, **Gondla** is famous for its eight-storey tower fort, built from alternating layers of stone and timber. Once the home of the local *thakur*, the fort is no longer occupied, but it's still an impressive sight. Try to visit during the lively Gondla Fair in July. An epic day- or overnight-hike leads from Keylong to Gondla up over the high Drilbu La (Bell Pass); Brokpa Adventure Tours can supply a guide for ₹1000 per day.

From the nearby road and river junction of Tandi, 7km from Keylong, you can hike 15 minutes to the village of **Tupchiling** and then continue for a further hour to historic **Guru Ghantal Gompa**, the oldest monastery in Lahaul and allegedly founded by Padmasambhava. Although crumbling, the gompa contains ancient murals and wooden statues of bodhisattvas (Buddhist enlightened beings). Ask monks in Tupchiling for the key.

Keylong

☎ 01900 / ELEV 3350M

The capital of Lahaul stretches along one side of the green Bhaga Valley just below the Manali–Leh Hwy, and it's a popular overnight stop for many buses plying that route. Many travellers only see Keylong briefly and in the dark, but a longer stay reveals grand mountain views, a laid-back village lifestyle and plenty of scenic walks. For tips on day hikes or to arrange longer treks to Zanskar, talk to Amar at **Brokpa Adventure Tours**

PATTAN VALLEY

About 8km south of Keylong at Tandi, a side road branches northwest along the Pattan Valley towards **Udaipur**. Overlooking the Chenab River, it's a peaceful spot with a few basic hotels and the plain-looking **Markula Devi Temple**, which hides fabulous wooden panels depicting scenes from the Mahabharata and Ramayana, carved in the 12th century.

From Udaipur, you can backtrack 9km along the valley to the squat stone temple at **Triloknath**, where Hindus worship the idol inside as Shiva while Buddhists venerate it as Avalokitesvara. It's a major pilgrimage site for both religions during the **Pauri Festival** (☉Aug).

(☎9418165176; www.brokpatreks.webs.com) in the bazaar (it's under the Hotel Dupchen).

The bus stand is off the highway, just above the main bazaar. At the west end of town is the sort-of-interesting **Lahaul & Spiti Tribal Museum** (admission free; ☉10am-1.30pm & 2-5pm Tue-Sun), with examples of the distinctive brown Lahauli dress known as a *dukpo*, plus old dance masks and photos of the local monasteries.

There is a State Bank of India ATM at the north end of the bazaar and an internet cafe opposite the Hotel Tashi Deleg, with wi-fi and patchy connections.

Keylong celebrates the annual **Lahaul Festival** (☉Jul) with a big, bustling market and various cultural activities.

🛏 Sleeping & Eating

Prices listed here are for July and August but expect discounts of 50% in June and September. All hotels are closed November to April.

Hotel Nordaling GUESTHOUSE $
(☎222294; www.nordaling.com; r ₹800, ste ₹1500) Just two minutes above the bus stand is this pleasant place, set in an apple orchard with a relaxing garden restaurant. Rates drop to ₹400 when things are quiet, making it great value.

Hotel New Gyespa HOTEL $
(☎9418136055; www.gyespahotels.webs.com; r ₹800-1000) Another option, just above the

bus stand, though rooms are a bit over-priced. Clean, carpeted rooms have balconies and half of them have views of the valley. Cheaper rooms are available at the affiliated **Hotel Gyespa** (r ₹300-800) lower down in the bazaar, which also has a good restaurant.

Hotel Tashi Deleg
HOTEL **$$**

(☑ 222450; r ₹850-1750, ste ₹2000) At the eastern end of the main bazaar, this big white place is Keylong's nicest hotel. Rooms on upper floors cost more, but all open out onto a balcony with mountain and valley views. The restaurant is also Keylong's best, serving excellent Indian, Chinese and Tibetan food (mains ₹60 to ₹130), as well as cold beers.

ℹ Getting There & Away

Keylong is the official overnight stop for government buses travelling between Manali and Leh, between mid-June and mid-September. Through bookings are only taken in Manali, so arrange a seat the day before, if you break the journey. Buses to Leh (₹525, 15 hours) leave at 5am, arriving at about 8pm the same evening. Private minibuses and shared jeeps (₹1000 to ₹1500, 50% less at the end of the season) run until October, depending on snow conditions.

There are six daily buses to Manali (₹130, six hours), as well as early morning shared taxis (₹300 to ₹400). For Kaza in Spiti take the 5.30am bus and change at Gramphu (₹60, two hours); the bus from Manali to Kaza pulls in around 8.30am.

For the Pattan Valley, there are seven daily buses to Udaipur (₹65, 3½ hours).

Around Keylong

About 3km (one hour) above Keylong is **Shashur Gompa**, dedicated to the Zanskari lama Deva Gyatsho. The original 16th-century gompa is now enshrined inside a modern concrete gompa, with fine views over the valley. Frenetic masked *chaams* (ritual masked dances performed by Buddhist monks in gompas to celebrate the victory of good over evil and of Buddhism over pre-existing religions) are held here every June or July, depending on the Tibetan calendar. The path to the gompa cuts uphill near the old bus stand – follow the dirt path opposite the Yarkid Guesthouse until you see the white chortens visible on the ridge.

Propped up on stilts on the far side of the valley, **Khardong Gompa** is a steep two-hour walk from Keylong. A monastery has existed

here for 900 years, but the current building is a modern one. Maintained by an order of Drukpa Kagyud monks and nuns, the monastery enshrines a mighty prayer wheel said to contain a million strips of paper bearing the mantra '*om mani padme hum*' (hail to the jewel in the lotus). The surrounding scenery is magnificent and there are excellent frescoes, but you'll have to track down a monk or nun to open the doors. To get to the monastery, head through the bazaar, follow the stepped path down to the hospital and take the bridge over the Bhaga River, from where it's a 4km slog uphill.

Perched on the side of the valley above the village of Satingri, 6km from Keylong, ancient **Tayul Gompa** has elegant mural work and a 4m-high statue of Padmasabhava. High above Tayul is the cave where British nun Diane Perry meditated for 12 years, as told in the book *Cave in the Snows*. Take a taxi to Satingri (₹200 to ₹300), from where it's a 45-minute hike.

About 20km northeast of Keylong, the pretty village of **Jispa** is a popular overnight stop for mountain bikers and motorcyclists. There's a small and interesting **folk museum** (admission ₹25; ⊙ 9am-6pm) on the main road, and a 2km walk south is the 16th-century **Ghemur Gompa**.

For accommodation, there's the inviting **Hotel Ibex Jispa** (☑ 01900-233203; www.hotelibexjispa.com; d ₹1800) on the main road.

Spiti

Separated from the fertile Lahaul Valley by the soaring 4551m Kunzum La, Spiti is another chunk of Tibet marooned in India. Villages are few and far between in this serrated moonscape and they arrive like mirages, with clusters of whitewashed homes huddled by green barley fields below monasteries perched on crags a thousand feet above.

In many ways Spiti is even more rugged and remote than Ladakh, but buses run over the Kunzum La from Manali from July to mid-October, and the Hindustan–Tibet Hwy to Kaza is theoretically open all year. A steady stream of motorcyclists and mountain bikers pit their machines against some of the most challenging roads in India. Sections of the road are occasionally washed away by monsoon floods and landslides, especially between Nako and Rekong Peo, so build some extra time into your itinerary in case of delays.

In either direction, an inner line permit is required for the stretch from Tabo to Rekong Peo.

Gramphu to Kaza

From the *dhaba* at Gramphu, the road to Spiti follows the dramatic glacier-carved Chandra River gorge.

At **Battal**, a rough track runs 14km north to lovely **Chandratal** (Moon Lake), a tranquil glacial pool set among snow peaks at 4270m. From June to September you can stay in comfortable tents (per person including meals ₹900) on the lakeshore. Battal is also the starting point for treks to nearby **Bara Shigri** (Big Glacier), one of the longest glaciers in the Himalaya, but the route is treacherous and it's essential to travel with an experienced guide.

From Battal, the road leaves the river and switchbacks precipitously up to the Kunzum La, the watershed between the Spiti and Lahaul Valleys. Buses perform a respectful circuit of the stupas strewn with fluttering prayer flags at the top before continuing down into the Spiti Valley. An alternative 10.5km footpath to Chandratal starts at the pass, continuing to Baralacha La on the Manali–Leh road in three strenuous but heavenly days.

The first village of any size is **Losar**, a cluster of concrete and mud-brick houses, where there's a passport check. If you want to break the journey here, the friendly **Samsong Cafe & Guesthouse** (r with/without bathroom ₹400/300) has simple but clean rooms and hot meals, while the less atmospheric **Tashi Gatsel Hotel** (r ₹500) offers fancier rooms with great views.

The final stretch to Kaza follows the edge of the Spiti River, passing the large Yangchen Choling nunnery at Pangmo, and the Sherab Choling monastery school at Morang. Experienced teachers may be able to arrange volunteer teaching placements at these schools through the US-based **Jamyang Foundation** (www.jamyang.org).

Kaza

01906 / ELEV 3640M

The capital of Spiti, Kaza sits on the eroded flood plain of the Spiti River and is the biggest settlement you'll encounter in this empty corner of the state. Still, it's relatively small, feeling like a frontier town with an easygoing pace. The setting is wonderfully rugged – jagged mountains rise on either side and the river coils across the valley

HIMACHAL PRADESH SPITI

SUSTAINABLE SPITI

While tourism brings money and development to remote rural areas like Spiti, it can also do unintentional damage to fragile cultures and ecosystems. Recognising this, a number of villages here are partnering with **Ecosphere** (222724; www.spitiecosphere.com; 9.30am-6.30pm Mon-Sat, closed Jan), a Kaza-based NGO, to create a home-grown sustainable tourism industry.

Homestays (per night ₹600, including meals) have been set up in six villages, five of which (Langza, Komic, Demul, Lhalung and Dhankar) can be linked into a five-day trekking route called the Homestay Trail. Visitors get a taste of authentic Spitian life, sleeping in traditional whitewashed houses and eating home-cooked food in the family kitchen. From the villages, wildlife-watching hikes offer a chance of spotting the shanku, or Spitian wolf – the world's oldest wolf species. Trained guides (per day ₹1000), which are recommended but not required, translate and explain about the culture and the land.

Part of the homestay fee supports the host family; part of it is deposited into a village fund and used for something that benefits the community as whole – such as restoring the local Buddhist monastery, which is the heart of their cultural life. Volunteers who can spare two or more weeks can work on ecofriendly projects, such as building greenhouses used as solar home-heating systems, which reduce fuelwood consumption and cut soot emissions that settle on nearby glaciers and speed their melting.

For more information on Spitian homestays, treks, volunteer opportunities and grassroots environmental initiatives, visit Ecosphere's website (www.spitiecosphere.com) or drop by their office in Old Kaza's bazaar. Refill your bottle with filtered water while you're there.

INNER LINE PERMITS IN KAZA

To travel between Tabo in Spiti and Re-kong Peo in Kinnaur, travellers need an inner line permit. This is easily arranged in Kaza – free permits are issued in around 20 minutes by the **Additional District Commissioner's Office** (✆222202; ⊙10am-1pm & 1.30-5pm Mon-Sat, closed 2nd Sat each month) in New Kaza – look for the big green-roofed building behind and to the left of the hospital. You'll need two passport photos and a photocopy of the identity and visa pages from your passport and you'll need to bring your own applica-tion form (available at internet cafes). Solo travellers have no problems get-ting permits here, unlike in Rekong Peo or Shimla.

floor like twisted locks of Medusa's hair. The colourful new **Sakya Gompa** dominates the high road in New Kaza – where the town's administrative centre is located – while the ramshackle bazaar and whitewashed build-ings of Old Kaza spread out on the other side of the stream that divides the town.

Most people stay at least one night to arrange the inner line permit for travel be-yond Tabo. Kaza is also the starting point for trips to Ki Gompa and Kibber and treks into the mountains. **Spiti Holiday Adventure** (✆222711; www.spitiholidayadventure.com; Main Bazar) organises all-inclusive treks from two to nine days, as well as jeep safaris and mon-astery tours, and is a good place for travel information.

The bus and jeep stand is below the ba-zaar in the old village. The bazaar pretty much closes down on Sundays.

In August, villagers from across Spiti descend on Kaza for the Ladarcha Fair. All sorts of goods are bought and sold and trad-ers wear their finest clothes.

🛏 Sleeping & Eating

There are a surprising number of guest-houses squirrelled away close to the bus and taxi stands in Old Kaza, as well as a few places along the highway and across the stream in New Kaza. Most places close down by November.

Of the several traveller-friendly restau-rants in the old town, the best are **Dragon Restaurant** (Old Kaza; mains ₹60-200) and **Sachin Kunga Restaurant** (Old Kaza; mains ₹60-150), the former with a sunny terrace. Both close in early September.

Sakya Abode   HOTEL $
(✆9418855963; r ₹660-990; @) On the main road in New Kaza, near the gompa, this is one of the best value places in town. Bright, comfy rooms open onto shared terraces that overlook a grassy-lawned courtyard, and the restaurant is excellent – try the bizarrely-named but addictively delicious 'copper Eliza' (a pancake with dried fruit, banana, nuts and chocolate sauce).

Mahabaudha Homestay   GUESTHOUSE $
(✆9418686272; drnorgyal@yahoo.com; d without bathroom ₹350) Trained *amchi* (Tibetan doc-tor) Norbu Gyalten runs this homestay-style guesthouse beside his traditional medicine clinic in the upper old town, just below the main road. The six rooms are well main-tained and there's a shared hot-water bath-room down the hall. Meals can be booked in advance.

Zanchuk Guest House   HOTEL $
(✆9418903516; r ₹250-500, without bathroom ₹150) Near the footbridge between Old and New Kaza, this popular backpacker place has good views from a sunny terrace. Rooms are a bit grungy, but prices for those with bathrooms are negotiable.

Grand Dewachen   HOTEL $$$
(✆9459566689; www.dewachenretreats.com; Rangrik village; d ₹4000) This somewhat isolat-ed roadside place, 8km outside Kaza, is the best hotel in Spiti. Rammed earth walls give it the look of a Tibetan *dzong* (fort), while inside rooms are well decorated with Tibet-an carpets and polished wood floors.

Sol Cafe   CAFE $
(coffee ₹30-65, snacks ₹40-100; ⊙9am-5pm) 🌿 Ecosphere operate this cool cafe, offering coffee and baked goods from their solar-powered oven, plus snacks that showcase local ingredients, such as barley nachos or waffles with seabuckthorn jam. There are sometimes documentary showings in the evening.

ℹ Information

There is nowhere to change money, but there is a State Bank of India ATM in the bazaar. The inter-net cafe opposite Shambhala Homestay in the bazaar charges ₹80 per hour and has inner line permit forms (₹10). The post office is just below the gompa in New Kaza.

ℹ Getting There & Away

The bus station is at the bottom of the old town, just off the main road or reached on foot through the bazaar. There is one bus to Manali (₹230, 10 hours) at 5am; buy tickets at 5pm the day before. For Keylong, change at Gramphu (₹155, eight hours). A bus leaves for Shimla via Rekong Peo (₹260, 12 hours) at 7am, passing through Sichling (for Dhankar; ₹30, one hour) and Tabo (₹55, two hours). There's a second Tabo bus at 2pm.

There's a single daily bus to Kibber (₹25, 50 minutes) via Ki (₹20, 30 minutes) at 4.20pm, but it doesn't return until 8.30am, so you'll have to hire a taxi if you don't want to spend the night. Jeep drivers hang around the bazaar, or you can make arrangements at your hotel. Fixed rates include Tabo (₹1200, 1½ hours), Dhankar (₹1500), Keylong (₹6000, seven hours), Manali (₹6000, nine hours) and Rekong Peo (₹5000, 10 hours). Day trips include Ki and Kibber (₹900 return) and Dhankar and the Pin Valley (₹2000 return). A seat in a shared jeep to Manali (₹600) is usually easy to arrange in high season.

Ki

On the road up to the village of Kibber, about 12km from Kaza, the tiny village of Ki is dominated by the whitewashed buildings of **Ki Gompa** (☉6am-7pm). Set atop a 4116m-high conical hillock, this is the largest gompa in Spiti and the views from the surrounding hillsides are wonderfully photogenic. Around 300 monks, including many students from surrounding villages, live here. An atmospheric *puja* is held in the new prayer hall every morning at around 7am (8am in winter). On request, the monks will open up the medieval prayer rooms, including the Zimshung Lhakhang, which houses the bed slept in by the Dalai Lama during his visits in 1960 and 2000. Dance masks are brought out for the annual **Ki Chaam Festival** (☉Jun/Jul) and again for Losar.

The **Noryang Guest House** (Ki Gompa; r ₹400-500; ☉May-Sep) at the monastery entrance offers rooms; if it's closed monks can help arrange a **room** (☎01906 262201; Ki Gompa; dm without bathroom ₹150) in the monastery.

Kibber
☎ 01906

A further 8km above Ki, this charming village of traditional whitewashed homes was once a stop on the overland salt trade. Catch your breath because at 4205m, beautiful but desolate Kibber for a time laid claim to being the highest village in the world with a drivable road and electricity.

Kibber is a great place to hang out for a couple of days. The village gompa has a lovely *lhakhang* (chapel), and you can hike out to the nearby village of Chicham across the gorge, returning down the gorge and steeply back up the other side to Kibber. Chicham has a guesthouse, though it's often closed.

One daily bus leaves for Kaza at 8.30am, travelling via Ki Gompa.

🛏 Sleeping & Eating

There are several village guesthouses offering rooms and meals. Most have bucket hot water (for ₹10 to ₹15) and close down for the winter from early October to April.

★ Norling Home Stay   GUESTHOUSE $
(r without/with bathroom ₹250/400) 🍃 At the far end of the village, rooms in this traditional whitewashed home at the top of the village are easily the best in town, and the organic food is excellent. Those with private bathrooms have geysers.

Serkong Homestay   GUESTHOUSE $
(☎9418538140; cdorjeserkong@yahoo.in; s/d without bathroom ₹150/200) Rooms at this ramshackle place are fairly neat and clean, especially on the brighter upper floor, and the bohemian front terrace has couches and old photos of Spiti.

Dhankar

Southeast of Kaza, the snaking Spiti River merges with the Pin River, creating a single ribbon of grey in the midst of dust-coloured badlands. Perched high above the confluence in a hidden bowl is the tiny village of Dhankar, the former capital of the Nono kings who ruled Spiti.

The spectacular 1200-year-old **Dhankar Gompa** (admission ₹25; ☉8am-7pm) perches precariously between eroded rocky pinnacles on the edge of a cliff. The monastery's name means palace *(khar)* on a cliff *(dhak)*. One glance at the crumbling cliffs and it's clear why it was listed in 2006 as one of the world's 100 most endangered monuments. There are four chapels in the upper building and a second prayer hall on the hilltop above, accessed by a separate set of concrete steps.

HIMACHAL PRADESH SPITI

Just downhill is a small **museum** (admission ₹25; ⊙ 8am-6pm) with costumes, instruments, old saddles and Buddhist devotional objects. In November, Dhankar monks celebrate the **Guktor Festival** (⊙ Nov) with energetic masked dances.

High above the gompa are the ruins of the mud-brick **fort** that sheltered the entire population of the valley during times of war. An hour's climb above the village is the small lake of **Dhankar Tso**, offering views over the valley and towards the twin peaks of Mane Rang (6593m).

Dhankar is a steep 10km walk or drive from Sichling on the Kaza–Tabo Hwy. There are several signed homestays in the village. One good place to stay is **Tashi Cafe Homestay** (s/d ₹500/600), 100m before the old monastery, which offers comfortable en-suite rooms above a small restaurant. You can also stay at a privately run **guesthouse** (☑ 9418817761; dm ₹150, r ₹350-800; ⊙ Apr-Sep) at the new monastery, where most of the red-carpeted rooms have windows with picture-postcard views.

Buses from Kaza to Tabo pass through Sichling (₹25, one hour) or you can do a day trip by taxi from Kaza for ₹1000. You might find a taxi from Sichiling to Dhankar for around ₹300. One shared jeep normally leaves Dhankar around 9am to Kaza (₹100 per seat), returning around 2pm.

Lhalung

Hidden up the Lingti valley beneath Chogula peak, 11km north of Dhankar, the charming traditional village of Lhalung is worth a detour for its fantastic, medieval **monastery** (admission ₹50). The atmospheric main chapel is the highlight, with superb murals dating from the same era as Tabo and featuring an incredibly ornate carved wooden back frieze. The separate Langkharpo chapel holds a unique four-sided statue of the white deity atop a plinth of snow lions. Don't miss the skin prayer wheel in a side chapel.

The village is easily visited from Dhankar or Lingti with your own transport or you could walk the dirt roads from Dhankar. The village below the monastery offers several homestays, which you can arrange privately or through Ecosphere (p343).

Pin Valley National Park

Running south from the Spiti Valley, the wind-scoured Pin Valley National Park (1875 sq km) is famous as the 'land of ibex and snow leopards', though in reality, sightings of either species are rare. From July to October, a spectacular but logistically complicated six- to eight-day trek runs from here over the 5319m Pin-Parvati Pass to the Parvati Valley near Kullu. Easier to arrange is the four-day trek over the 4850m Bhaba Pass to Kaphnu in Kinnaur.

The road to the Pin Valley branches off the Kaza–Tabo Hwy about 10km before Sichling, climbing through winter meadows to the cluster of whitewashed farmhouses at **Gulling**, which has a couple of simple guesthouses. About 2km above Gulling at Kungri, the 600-year-old **Ugyen Sangnak Choling Gompa** has a huge new monastery building and two much more interesting medieval side chapels, featuring blackened murals, festival masks and carved wooden snowlions. The **monastery guesthouse** (r without bathroom ₹450) has four plain but clean rooms.

Southwest of Gulling, the charming traditional village of **Sagnam** marks the turn-off to the village of **Mudh** (3770m), trailhead for the trek over the Pin-Parvati Pass and an increasingly popular hang-out for the Israeli backpacker crowd. The excellent **Tara Guesthouse** (☑ 9418441453; sonamtara@gmail.com; r without bathroom ₹300-500) is a fine place to soak up the views, and the owner Sonam can arrange porters and full treks.

Buses run daily from Kaza to Mudh (₹70, two hours) at 3pm, returning to Kaza the next day at 8am. Taxis in Kaza charge ₹1500 to Mudh.

Tabo

☑ 01906

About 47km east of Kaza, tiny Tabo is the only other town in the Spiti Valley. The setting, hemmed in by scree slopes, is wind-blown and dramatic, and the ridge north of town is riddled with caves once used as meditation cells by local hermits. It's a fine place to kick back for a couple of days.

The village is completely dominated by **Tabo Gompa** (www.tabomonastery.org; admission by donation; ⊙ 6am-10pm, chapels 9am-5pm), a World Heritage Site whose dull mud-brick walls hide some of the finest Indo-Tibetan art in the world. Founded in AD 996, the gompa's fantastically adorned chapels were painted by some of the best Buddhist muralists of the era, blending western Tibetan, Indian and Kashmiri styles. Bring a torch. Beyond the intricate mandalas and portraits of gods and demons, the moody chambers are graced with life-size stucco statues of bodhisattvas and detailed wood carvings. The modern gompa outside the ancient compound has a well-attended morning *puja* at 6.30am, and the monastery guesthouse contains a **Buddhist library** (admission free; ☉9.45-11.45am & 2-4pm Jun–mid-Sep) and a small **religious museum** (admission ₹20, camera/video ₹25/50; ☉8.30am-5pm Mon-Sat).

🛏 Sleeping & Eating

Most of Tabo's guesthouses are clustered around the gompa. Stock up on cinnamon rolls and yak cheese at the German Bakery in front of the monastery entrance.

Tashi Khangsar Hotel HOTEL $
(☎9418817761; vaneetrana23@gmail.com; s/d ₹400/600; ☉Apr–mid-Oct) The bright and inviting rooms here surround a lawn where tables sit shaded beneath a large parachute canopy. There's a small lending library, a good restaurant, a flat grassy area for tent camping (₹200), and a relaxed vibe, all adding up to solid value. It's on the southwest side of the monastery.

Kesang Homestay
Guest House GUESTHOUSE $
(☎223451; sherabtabo@gmail.com; r without/with bathroom ₹400/700; @) Just in front of monastery gates, this place is run by a super-friendly family and has clean, spacious rooms, plus internet access (₹80 per hour). Discounts of up to 50% are possible in September.

Millennium Monastery Guesthouse HOTEL $
(☎223315; dm ₹50, r with/without bathroom from ₹350/200, ste ₹800) Run by the monastery, this ageing but popular place has fairly average rooms but bags of atmosphere. Rooms have piped hot water for washing, but guests are asked to refrain from smoking, drinking alcohol and other activities that might offend monastic sensibilities. The attached monastery restaurant serves *momos* and has outdoor seating.

Cafe Kunzum Top TIBETAN $
(mains ₹60-100) This is our favourite restaurant in town, both for its cosy interior and sunny garden and its tasty Tibetan and local Spiti dishes, plus it's got decent coffee. The rooms of the attached **Sonam Homestay** (☎9418503966; r ₹400-700, r without bathroom ₹300) are also some of the best value in town.

ℹ Getting There & Away

Buses to Kaza (₹55, two hours) pass through town at around 9am and 3pm, give or take an hour. There's a daily bus to Rekong Peo (₹270, nine hours) at 9am, going through Nako (₹80, four hours), but since this originates in Kaza it can be packed.

Taxis charge ₹1500 to ₹1800 to Kaza (1½ hours), ₹1200 to Dhankar (40 minutes), ₹2500 to Nako (three hours) and ₹4500 to Rekong Peo (nine hours).

Tabo to Rekong Peo

One of India's most dramatic mountain roads, the Tabo–Rekong Peo Hwy in Kinnaur offers some great adventure. In theory, this highway is open year-round, providing the only winter access to the Spiti Valley; however, the Sutlej River frequently floods, washing away parts of the precarious road, and snowfalls can occasionally cut off this route in winter, so it's worth checking if the road is intact before heading east of Tabo. You will need to show your passport and inner line permit at Sumdo and Jangi. Some of the following places are technically in Kinnaur, but they are covered here because they form part of the Spiti circuit.

From Tabo, the road follows the narrowing Spiti Valley, passing villages full of apple orchards, before climbing high over the valley. If you're on a bus, you may have some tense moments as the bus skids around hairpin bends with millimetres to spare. The views of the Spiti River flashing hundreds of metres below, and the road ahead zigzagging across the mountainside are mesmerising. Views are best – and scariest – from the right-side window seats.

The first permit checkpost is at **Sumdo**. Just before that, if you've got your own transport, look for the turn-off to **Giu**, a village 8km up the side valley where you can see the mummified remains of a Buddhist monk who died over 500 years ago. The mummy still has hair and fingernails and, according to local lore, spurted blood when unearthed by the shovels of an ITBP construction crew in 2004.

Beyond Sumdo, the main highway starts its ascent into the hills at **Chango**, which has several Buddhist temples in the village above the road.

The first settlement with accommodation is **Nako**, a charming medieval village of stone and mud-brick houses and a popular stop for motorcyclists. Even if you're on the bus, this is a great place to break the journey for a day or two. The village is centred on a small sacred lake, behind which rise towering rock-strewn mountains dotted by stupas. A remote hiking trail leads up over a pass to Tashigang village and monastery (3½ hours), from where hard-core hikers can continue 90 minutes to caves and a shrine at **Tsomang**; take a guide at the Youth Camp in Nako centre and check with them whether you need to register with the local police. Just below Nako town you'll find the four 11th-century chapels of **Nako Gompa**, containing some fine Tabo-style murals and sculptures, alongside a shrine to local mountain deity Purgyal.

There are several simple guesthouses offering rooms for around ₹200 to ₹500, or there's the posher **Reo Purgil Hotel** (✆236339; d ₹1500-2000). Better still is the bright **Lake View Guest House** (r ₹500-700), a short walk through the old village and

overlooking the lake. One bus passes through Nako each morning en route to Rekong Peo.

The final stage of the journey passes through greener country in the narrow gorge of the Sutlej River. At Khab, near where the Sutlej River joins the Spiti, a side road branches off to the Chinese border at the Shipki La (off-limits to foreigners). The village of **Puh** marks the official crossing into Kinnaur.

There are more monasteries and temples at **Khanum**, high above the road near Spillo, founded by Ringchen Zangpo in the 10th century. **Jangi** marks the turn off to Lambar and the start of the three-day *parikrama* (ritual circumnavigation) trek around 6050m Kinner Kailash via the Charang La (inner line permits required). As you pass Jangi look for the fort-like Kinnauri-style temples across the river at Moorang. The police check post at **Akpa** a few kilometres further marks the end of the inner line permit zone.

Uttar Pradesh & the Taj Mahal

Best Places to Eat

➡ Pinch of Spice (p365)
➡ El Chico (p386)
➡ Sakhawat (p378)
➡ Esphahan (p364)

Best Places to Stay

➡ Hotel Ganges View (p397)
➡ N Homestay (p363)
➡ Kanchan Villa (p385)
➡ Ganpati Guesthouse (p396)

Why Go?

Agra's Taj Mahal rises from the beaten earth of Uttar Pradesh (UP) as it does in dreams, but even the wildest imaginations leave travellers underprepared for that breath-stealing moment its gates are traversed and this magnificent world wonder comes into focus – skipping it would be a bit like drinking chai without spoonfuls of sugar: absurd.

But it's the unmistakable spirituality and religious fervour in this enormous state that leaves the longest-lasting impressions: being slapped by a divine punch of wow along atmospheric riverside ghats such as Manikarnika and Dashashwamedh in India's holiest city, Varanasi; the contemplative aura that emanates from ancient Buddhist stupas in Kushinagar; and the serenity of waking up before dawn to watch locals perform *puja* (offerings or prayers) in sacred Chitrakut. Along the way, a groundswell of Mughal and Nawab architectural and gastronomic highpoints – especially in Lucknow – ensure all-sensory satisfaction in India's imperial heartland.

When to Go

Agra

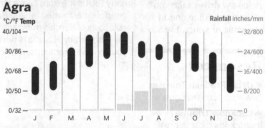

Sep–Oct Monsoon rains are mostly over and temperatures have cooled ...just enough.

Nov–Feb Comfortable winter days and nippy nights mean it's cool but overcrowded.

Mar–Apr With evening chills subsided and raging midsummer heat still at bay, some say it's perfect.

MAIN POINTS OF ENTRY

International connections include Varanasi–Kathmandu and Lucknow–Dubai. Many travellers come overland from Nepal, usually at Sunauli. Best-connected train stations are Agra, Lucknow, Allahabad and Varanasi.

Fast Facts

➜ **Population**: 200 million

➜ **Area**: 231,254 sq km

➜ **Capital**: Lucknow

➜ **Language**: Hindi

➜ **Sleeping prices**: $ below ₹1000, $$ ₹1000 to ₹3000, $$$ above ₹3000

Top Tip

When arriving by train or bus in Agra or Varanasi, ignore anyone who approaches you in the station; head straight for the prepaid autorickshaw booth (opposite the main entrance). Do not let any guide or autorickshaw driver take you to a shop, whether one of his choosing or yours. Ever.

Resources

➜ **Uttar Pradesh Tourism** (www.up-tourism.com)

➜ **Lucknow Tribune** (www.thelucknowtribune.org)

➜ **Lonely Planet** (www.lonelyplanet.com/india/agra)

Food

Mughlai cuisine – rich, meaty and impossibly tasty – is the order of the day across much of Uttar Pradesh, with the best restaurants often attached to the top hotels in the big cities. Lucknow is the undisputed king of UP cuisine. You'll find some excellent Mughlai kitchens here as well as great *chaat* (snacks) and some simply sumptuous kebabs.

DON'T MISS

There are two things you shouldn't leave Uttar Pradesh without doing: seeing the **Taj Mahal** at sunset and taking a dawn boat ride along the Ganges in the holy city of **Varanasi**.

Top State Festivals

➜ **Magh Mela** (⊙ Jan/Feb, Allahabad, p382) A huge annual religious fair that transforms into the world's largest human gathering, the Purna Kumbh Mela, every 12th year (next in 2025).

➜ **Holi** (⊙ Feb/Mar, Mathura, p372, and Vrindavan, p374) This national festival is celebrated with particular fervour around Mathura and Vrindavan, spiritual home of Krishna.

➜ **Purnima** (⊙ Apr/May, Sarnath, p402) Also known as Vesak, Buddha Jayanti or, informally, Buddha's birthday, Purnima actually celebrates the birth, enlightenment and death of Buddha. Sarnath, just outside Varanasi, takes on a particularly festive air on this day, when Buddhists from many countries take part in a procession and a fair is held.

➜ **Janmastami** (⊙ Aug/Sep, Mathura, p372) You can barely move here during Krishna's birthday, when temples are swathed in decorations and musical dramas about Krishna are performed.

➜ **Ram Lila** (⊙ Sep/Oct, Varanasi, p388) Every year since the early 1800s the Ram Lila, a lengthy version of the Ramayana, has been performed beside Ramnagar Fort in Varanasi. The epic saga of Rama's marriage to Sita and his battle against the demon king Ravana is performed mainly by Brahmin youths aided by masks, music, dancing and giant papier-mâché figures.

History

Over 2000 years ago this region was part of Ashoka's great Buddhist empire, remnants of which can be found in the ruins at the pilgrimage centre of Sarnath near Varanasi. Muslim raids from the northwest began in the 11th century, and by the 16th century the region was part of the Mughal empire, with its capital in Agra, then Delhi and, for a brief time, Fatehpur Sikri.

Following the decline of the Mughal empire, Persians stepped in briefly before the nawabs of Avadh rose to prominence in the central part of the region. The nawabs were responsible for turning Lucknow into a flourishing centre for the arts, but their empire came to a dramatic end when the British East India Company deposed the last nawab, triggering the First War of Independence (Indian Uprising) of 1857. Agra was later merged with Avadh and the state became known as United Province. It was renamed Uttar Pradesh after Independence and has since been the most dominant state in Indian politics, producing half of the country's prime ministers, most of them from Allahabad. The local population doesn't seem to have benefited much from this, though, as poor governance, a high birth rate, a low literacy rate and an erratic electricity supply have held back economic progress in UP in the past 60 years.

In 2000 the mountainous northwestern part of the state was carved off to create the new state of Uttaranchal.

Agra

📞 0562 / POP 1.7 MILLION

The magical allure of the Taj Mahal draws tourists to Agra like moths to a wondrous flame. And despite the hype, it's every bit as good as you've heard. But the Taj is not a stand-alone attraction. The legacy of the Mughal empire has left a magnificent fort and a liberal sprinkling of fascinating tombs and mausoleums; and there's also fun to be had in the bustling *chowks* (marketplaces).

The downside comes in the form of hordes of rickshaw-wallahs, touts, unofficial guides and souvenir vendors, whose persistence can be infuriating at times.

Many tourists choose to visit Agra on a whistle-stop day trip from Delhi. This is a shame. There is much more of interest here than can be seen in that time. In fact, you can enjoy several days' sightseeing with side trips to the superb ruined city of Fatehpur Sikri and the Hindu pilgrimage centre of Mathura.

Agra sits on a large bend in the holy Yamuna River. The fort and the Taj, 2km apart, both overlook the river on different parts of the bend. The main train and bus stations are a few kilometres southwest.

The labourers and artisans who toiled on the Taj set up home immediately south of the mausoleum, creating the congested network of alleys known as Taj Ganj, now a popular area for budget travellers.

History

In 1501 Sultan Sikander Lodi established his capital here, but the city fell into Mughal hands in 1526, when Emperor Babur defeated the last Lodi sultan at Panipat. Agra reached the peak of its magnificence between the mid-16th and mid-17th centuries during the reigns of Akbar, Jehangir and Shah Jahan. During this period the fort, the Taj Mahal and other major mausoleums were built. In 1638 Shah Jahan built a new city in Delhi, and his son Aurangzeb moved the capital there 10 years later.

In 1761 Agra fell to the Jats, a warrior class who looted its monuments, including the Taj Mahal. The Marathas took over in 1770, but were replaced by the British in 1803. Following the First War of Independence of 1857, the British shifted the administration of the province to Allahabad. Deprived of its administrative role, Agra developed as a centre for heavy industry, quickly becoming famous for its chemicals industry and air pollution, before the Taj and tourism became a major source of income.

👁 Sights & Activities

The entrance fee for Agra's five main sights (the Taj, Agra Fort, Fatehpur Sikri, Akbar's Tomb and Itimad-ud-Daulah) is made up of charges from two different bodies, the Archaeological Survey of India (ASI) and the Agra Development Association (ADA). Of the ₹750 ticket for the Taj Mahal, ₹500 is a special ADA ticket, which gives you small savings on the other four sights if visited in the same day. You'll save ₹50 at Agra Fort and ₹10 each at Fatehpur Sikri, Akbar's Tomb and Itimad-ud-Daulah. You can buy this ₹500 ADA ticket at any of the five sights. Just say you intend to visit the Taj later that day.

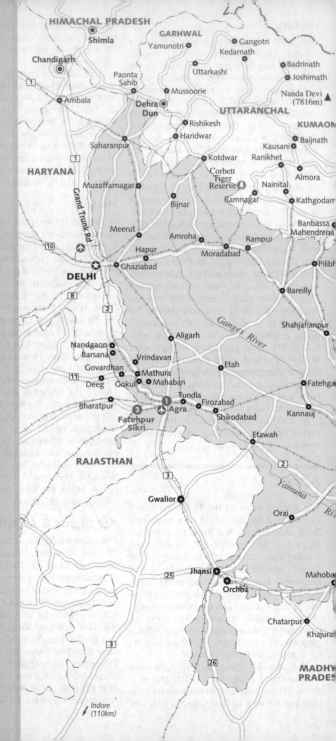

Uttar Pradesh & the Taj Mahal Highlights

1 Watch in awe as the colours of the majestic **Taj Mahal** (p354) in Agra dance by day and night

2 Take in a dramatic sunrise amid a hubbub of holiness on a pre-dawn boat ride along the Ganges River in **Varanasi** (p388)

3 Be wowed while wandering immense Mughal monuments in **Fatehpur Sikri** (p368)

4 Explore fascinating back lanes and ornamented Mughal architecture on a Heritage Walking Tour in **Lucknow** (p377)

5 Escape chaotic cities at the pilgrimage centre of **Kushinagar** (p404), Buddha's final resting place

6 Experience the spirituality of Varanasi without the hassle at the more chilled-out riverside ghats of **Chitrakut** (p387)

7 Imagine 100 million Kumbh Mela devotees on your tail as you're rowed out to the confluence of two holy rivers in **Allahabad** (p382)

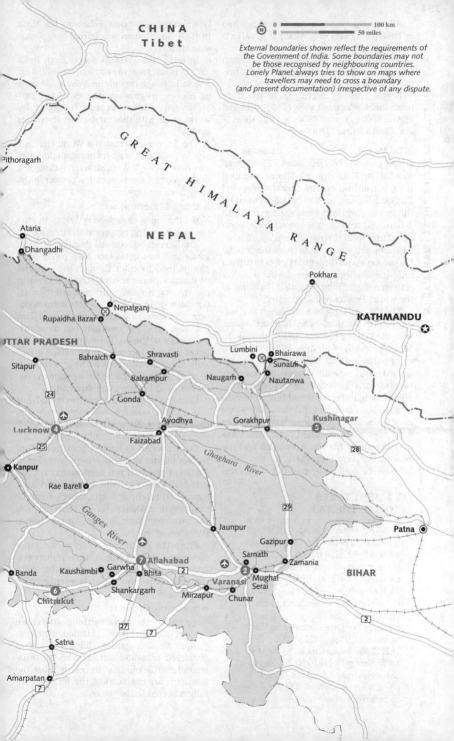

External boundaries shown reflect the requirements of
the Government of India. Some boundaries may not
be those recognised by neighbouring countries.
Lonely Planet always tries to show on maps where
travellers may need to cross a boundary
(and present documentation) irrespective of any dispute.

Pithoragarh

GREAT HIMALAYA RANGE

NEPAL

Pokhara

KATHMANDU

Ataria
Dhangadhi

Nepalganj
Rupaidha Bazar

UTTAR PRADESH

Sitapur

Bahraich
Shravasti
Balrampur
Gonda

Lumbini
Bhairawa
Sunauli
Nautanwa

Naugarh

Lucknow ④

Ayodhya
Faizabad

Gorakhpur
Kushinagar ⑤

Ghaghara River

Kanpur

Rae Bareli

Ganges River

Jaunpur

Gazipur
Sarnath
Zamania

Patna

BIHAR

Banda
Kaushambi
Garwha
Allahabad ⑦
Bhita
Shankargarh

Chitrakut ⑥

Mirzapur

Varanasi ②
Mughal
Serai
Chunar

Satna

Amarpatan

All the other sights in Agra are either free or have ASI tickets only which aren't affected by the ADA one-day offer.

Admission to all sights is free for children under 15. On Fridays, many sites offer a tax-free discount of ₹10.

Hotels allowing nonguests to use their pools include Yamuna View (₹400), Howard Plaza (₹562), Amar (₹500) – with slide! – and Clarks Shiraz (₹1000).

★ Taj Mahal   HISTORIC BUILDING

(Indian/foreigner ₹20/750, video ₹25; ☺ dawn-dusk Sat-Thu) Rabindranath Tagore described it as 'a teardrop on the cheek of eternity', Rudyard Kipling as 'the embodiment of all things pure', while its creator, Emperor Shah Jahan, said it made 'the sun and the moon shed tears from their eyes'. Every year, tourists numbering more than twice the population of Agra pass through its gates to catch a once-in-a-lifetime glimpse of what is widely considered the most beautiful building in the world. Few leave disappointed.

The Taj was built by Shah Jahan as a memorial for his third wife, Mumtaz Mahal, who died giving birth to their 14th child in 1631. The death of Mumtaz left the emperor so heartbroken that his hair is said to have turned grey virtually overnight. Construction of the Taj began the following year and, although the main building is thought to have been built in eight years, the whole complex was not completed until 1653. Not long after it was finished Shah Jahan was overthrown by his son Aurangzeb and imprisoned in Agra Fort where, for the rest of his days, he could only gaze out at his crea-tion through a window. Following his death in 1666, Shah Jahan was buried here along-side Mumtaz.

In total, some 20,000 people from India and Central Asia worked on the building. Specialists were brought in from as far away as Europe to produce the exquisite marble screens and pietra dura (marble inlay work) made with thousands of semiprecious stones.

The Taj was designated a World Heritage Site in 1983 and looks as immaculate today as when it was first constructed – though it underwent a huge restoration project in the early 20th century.

➤ Entry & Information

Note: the Taj is closed every Friday to any-one not attending prayers at the mosque.

The Taj can be accessed through the west, south and east gates (see Map p362). Tour groups tend to enter through the east and west gates. Independent travellers tend to use the south gate, which is nearest to Taj Ganj, the main area for budget accommodation, and generally has shorter queues than the west gate. The east gate has the shortest queues of the lot, but this is because the ticket office is inconveniently located a 1km walk away at Shilpgram, a dire government-run tourist centre. There are separate queues for men and women at all three gates.

Cameras and videos are permitted but you cannot take photographs inside the mausoleum itself, and the areas in which you can take videos are quite limited.

Do not forget to retrieve your free 500ml bottle of water and shoe covers (included in Taj ticket price). If you keep your ticket you get small entry-fee reductions when visiting Agra Fort, Fatehpur Sikri, Akbar's Tomb or the Itimad-ud-Daulah on the same day. You can also store your luggage for free beside the ticket offices.

From the south gate, entry to the inner compound is through a very impressive, 30m red sandstone **gateway** on the south side of the forecourt, which is inscribed with verses from the Quran.

➤ Inside the Grounds

Once inside, the **ornamental gardens** are set out along classical Mughal *charbagh* (formal Persian garden) lines – a square quartered by watercourses, with an ornamental marble plinth at its centre. When the fountains are not flowing, the Taj is beautifully reflected in the water.

ℹ BEST TIMES TO SEE THE TAJ

The Taj is arguably at its most atmospheric at **sunrise**. This is certainly the most comfortable time to visit, with far fewer crowds. **Sunset** is another magical viewing time. You can also view the Taj for five nights around **full moon**. Entry numbers are limited, though, and tickets must be bought a day in advance from the **Archaeological Survey of India office** (Map p355; ☎ 2227263; www.asi.nic.in; 22 The Mall; Indian/foreigner ₹510/750; ☺10am-6pm). See its website for details. Note, this office is known as the Taj Mahal Office by some rickshaw riders.

Agra

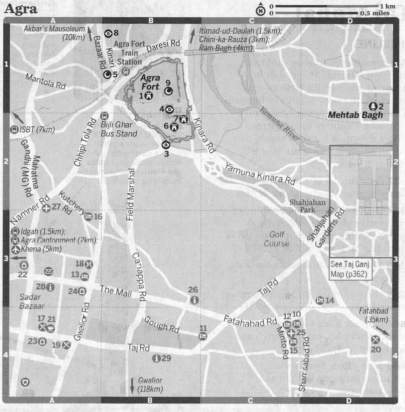

Agra

◉ Top Sights

1 Agra Fort	B1
2 Mehtab Bagh	D1

◉ Sights

3 Amar Singh Gate	B2
4 Diwan-i-Am	B1
5 Jama Masjid	B1
6 Jehangir's Palace	B2
7 Khas Mahal	B2
8 Kinari Bazaar	B1
9 Moti Masjid	B1

◉ Sleeping

10 Amar Yatri Niwas	C4
11 Clarks Shiraz Hotel	C4
12 Hotel Amar	C4
13 Hotel Yamuna View	A3
14 Howard Plaza	D3
15 N Homestay	C4
16 Tourists Rest House	A3

◉ Eating

17 Brijwasi	A4
18 Dasaprakash	A3
19 Lakshmi Vilas	A4
20 Pinch of Spice	D4

◉ Drinking & Nightlife

21 Café Coffee Day	A4

◉ Shopping

22 Khadi Gramodyog	A3
23 Modern Book Depot	A4
24 Subhash Emporium	A3

◉ Information

25 Amit Jaggi Memorial Hospital	C4
26 Archaeological Survey of India Office	B3
27 District Hospital	A2
28 India Tourism	A3
29 UP Tourism	B4

Taj Mahal

TIMELINE

1631 Emperor Shah Jahan's beloved third wife, Mumtaz Mahal, dies in Buhanpur while giving birth to their 14th child. Her body is initially interred in Buhanpur itself, where Shah Jahan is fighting a military campaign, but is later moved, in a golden casket, to a small building on the banks of the Yamuna River in Agra.

1632 Construction of a permanent mausoleum for Mumtaz Mahal begins.

1633 Mumtaz Mahal is interred in her final resting place, an underground tomb beneath a marble plinth, on top of which the Taj Mahal will be built.

1640 The white-marble mausoleum is completed.

1653 The rest of the Taj Mahal complex is completed.

1658 Emperor Shah Jahan is overthrown by his son Aurangzeb and imprisoned in Agra Fort.

1666 Shah Jahan dies. His body is transported along the Yamuna River and buried underneath the Taj, alongside the tomb of his wife.

1908 Repeatedly damaged and looted after the fall of the Mughal empire, the Taj receives some long-overdue attention as part of a major restoration project ordered by British viceroy Lord Curzon.

1983 The Taj is awarded Unesco World Heritage Site status.

2002 Having been discoloured by pollution in more recent years, the Taj is spruced up with an ancient recipe known as *multani mitti* – a blend of soil, cereal, milk and lime once used by Indian women to beautify their skin.

Today More than three million tourists visit the Taj Mahal each year. That's more than twice the current population of Agra.

Go Barefoot
Help the environment by entering the mausoleum barefoot instead of using the free disposable shoe covers.

Pishtaqs
These huge arched recesses are set into each side of the Taj. They provide depth to the building while their central, latticed marble screens allow patterned light to illuminate the inside of the mausoleum.

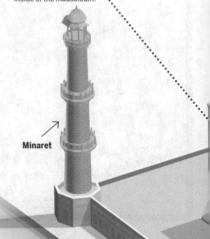

Minaret

Plinth

Entranc

Marble Relief Work
Flowering plants, thought to be representations of paradise, are a common theme among the beautifully decorative panels carved onto the white marble.

Be Enlightened
Bring a small torch into the mausoleum to fully appreciate the translucency of the white marble and semiprecious stones.

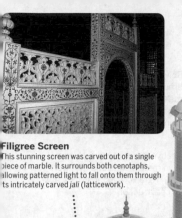

Filigree Screen
This stunning screen was carved out of a single piece of marble. It surrounds both cenotaphs, allowing patterned light to fall onto them through its intricately carved *jali* (latticework).

Central Dome
The Taj's famous central dome, topped by a brass finial, represents the vault of heaven, a stark contrast to the material world, which is represented by the square shape of the main structure.

Yamuna River

NORTH →

Pietra Dura
It's believed that 35 different precious and semi-precious stones were used to create the exquisite pietra dura (marble inlay work) found on the inside and outside of the mausoleum walls. Again, floral designs are common.

Calligraphy
The strips of calligraphy surrounding each of the four pishtaqs get larger as they get higher, giving the impression of uniform size when viewed from the ground. There's also calligraphy inside the mausoleum, including on Mumtaz Mahal's cenotaph.

Cenotaphs
The cenotaphs of Mumtaz Mahal and Shah Jahan, decorated with pietra dura inlay work, are actually fake tombs. The real ones are located in an underground vault closed to the public.

TAJ MAHAL MYTHS

The Taj is a Hindu Temple

The well-publicised theory that the Taj was in fact a Shiva temple built in the 12th century and only later converted into Mumtaz Mahal's famous mausoleum was developed by Purushottam Nagesh Oak. In 2000 India's Supreme Court dismissed his petition to have the sealed basement rooms of the Taj opened to prove his theory. Oak also claims that the Kaaba, Stonehenge and the Papacy all have Hindu origins.

The Black Taj Mahal

The story goes that Shah Jahan planned to build a negative image of the Taj Mahal in black marble on the opposite side of the river as his own mausoleum, and that work began before he was imprisoned by his son Aurangzeb in Agra Fort. Extensive excavations at Mehtab Bagh have found no trace of any such construction.

Craftsmen Mutilations

Legend has it that on completion of the Taj, Shah Jahan ordered that the hands of the project's craftsmen be chopped off, to prevent them from ever building anything as beautiful again. Some even say he went so far as to have their eyes gouged out. Thankfully, no historical evidence supports either story.

Sinking Taj

Some experts believe there is evidence to show that the Taj is slowly tilting towards and sinking into the riverbed due to the changing nature of the soil beside an increasingly dry Yamuna River. The Archaeological Survey of India has dismissed any marginal change in the elevation of the building as statistically insignificant, adding that it has not detected any structural damage at its base in the seven decades since its first scientific study of the Taj was carried out, in 1941.

The Taj Mahal itself stands on a raised marble platform at the northern end of the ornamental gardens, with its back to the Yamuna River. (See also the colour illustration, p356.) Its raised position means that the backdrop is only sky – a masterstroke of design. Purely decorative 40m-high white minarets grace each corner of the platform. After more than three centuries they are not quite perpendicular, but they may have been designed to lean slightly outwards so that in the event of an earthquake they would fall away from the precious Taj. The red sandstone mosque (Map p362) to the west is an important gathering place for Agra's Muslims. The identical building to the east, the jawab (Map p362), was built for symmetry.

The central Taj structure is made of semitranslucent white marble, carved with flowers and inlaid with thousands of semiprecious stones in beautiful patterns. A perfect exercise in symmetry, the four identical faces of the Taj feature impressive vaulted arches embellished with pietra dura scrollwork and quotations from the Quran in a style of calligraphy using inlaid jasper. The whole structure is topped off by four small domes surrounding the famous bulbous central dome.

Directly below the main dome is the **Cenotaph of Mumtaz Mahal**, an elaborate false tomb surrounded by an exquisite perforated marble screen inlaid with dozens of different types of semiprecious stones. Beside it, offsetting the symmetry of the Taj, is the **Cenotaph of Shah Jahan**, who was interred here with little ceremony by his usurping son Aurangzeb in 1666. Light is admitted into the central chamber by finely cut marble screens. The real tombs of Mumtaz Mahal and Shah Jahan are in a locked basement room below the main chamber and cannot be viewed.

★ Agra Fort
FORT

(Map p355; Indian/foreigner ₹20/300, video ₹25; ☉dawn-dusk) With the Taj Mahal overshadowing it, one can easily forget that Agra has one of the finest Mughal forts in India. Construction of the massive red-sandstone fort, on the bank of the Yamuna River, was begun by Emperor Akbar in 1565. Further additions were made, particularly by his grandson Shah Jahan, using his favourite building material – white marble. The fort was built primarily as a military structure, but Shah Jahan transformed it into a palace, and later it became his gilded prison for eight years after his son Aurangzeb seized power in 1658.

The ear-shaped fort's colossal double walls rise over 20m in height and measure 2.5km in circumference. The Yamuna River originally flowed along the straight eastern edge of the fort, and the emperors had their own bathing ghats here. It contains a maze of buildings, forming a city within a city, including vast underground sections, though many of the structures were destroyed over the years by Nadir Shah, the Marathas, the Jats and finally the British, who used the fort as a garrison. Even today, much of the fort is used by the military and so is off-limits to the general public.

The **Amar Singh Gate** (Map p355) to the south is the sole entry point to the fort these days and where you buy your entrance ticket. Its dogleg design was meant to confuse attackers who made it past the first line of defence – the crocodile-infested moat.

A path leads straight from here up to the large **Moti Masjid** (Pearl Mosque; Map p355), which is always closed. To your right, just before you reach Moti Masjid, is the large open **Diwan-i-Am** (Hall of Public Audiences; Map p355), which was used by Shah Jahan for domestic government business, and features a throne room where the emperor listened to petitioners. In front of it is the small and rather incongruous **grave of John Colvin**, a lieutenant-governor of the northwest provinces who died of an illness in the fort during the 1857 First War of Independence.

A tiny staircase just to the left of the Diwan-i-Am throne leads up to a large courtyard. To your left, is the tiny but exquisite **Nagina Masjid** (Gem Mosque), built in 1635 by Shah Jahan for the ladies of the court. Down below was the **Ladies' bazaar**, where the court ladies bought goods.

On the far side of the large courtyard, along the eastern wall of the fort, is **Diwan-i-Khas** (Hall of Private Audiences), which was reserved for important dignitaries or foreign representatives. The hall once housed Shah Jahan's legendary Peacock Throne, which was inset with precious stones including the famous Koh-i-noor diamond. The throne was taken to Delhi by Aurangzeb, then to Iran in 1739 by Nadir Shah and dismantled after his assassination in 1747. Overlooking

the river and the distant Taj Mahal is **Takhti-i-Jehangir**, a huge slab of black rock with an inscription around the edge. The throne that stood here was made for Jehangir when he was Prince Salim.

Off to your right from here (as you face the river) is **Shish Mahal** (Mirror Palace), with walls inlaid with tiny mirrors. At the time of research it had been closed for some time due to restoration, although you could peek through cracks in the doors at the sparkling mirrors inside.

Further along the eastern edge of the fort you'll find **Musamman Burj** and **Khas Mahal** (Map p355), the wonderful white-marble octagonal tower and palace where Shah Jahan was imprisoned for eight years until his death in 1666, and from where he could gaze out at the Taj Mahal, the tomb of his wife. When he died, Shah Jahan's body was taken from here by boat to the Taj. The now closed **Mina Masjid**, set back slightly from the eastern edge, was his private mosque.

The large courtyard here is **Anguri Bagh**, a garden that has been brought back to life in recent years. In the courtyard is an innocuous-looking entrance – now locked – that leads down a flight of stairs into a two-storey labyrinth of underground rooms and passageways where Akbar used to keep his 500-strong harem.

Continuing south, the huge red-sandstone **Jehangir's Palace** (Map p355) was probably built by Akbar for his son Jehangir. It blends Indian and Central Asian architectural styles, a reminder of the Mughals' Afghani cultural roots. In front of the palace is **Hauz-i-Jehangir**, a huge bowl carved out

TAJ MUSEUM

Within the Taj complex, on the western side of the gardens, is the small but excellent **Taj Museum** (Map p362; admission ₹5; ⊙10am-5pm Sat-Thu), housing a number of original Mughal miniature paintings, including a pair of 17th-century ivory portraits of Emperor Shah Jahan and his beloved wife Mumtaz Mahal. You'll also find here some very well preserved gold and silver coins dating from the same period, plus architectural drawings of the Taj and some nifty celadon plates, said to split into pieces or change colour if the food served on them contains poison.

of a single block of stone, which was used for bathing. Walking past this brings you back to the main path to Amar Singh Gate.

You can walk here from Taj Ganj, or it's ₹25 in a cycle-rickshaw.

Akbar's Mausoleum HISTORIC BUILDING

(Indian/foreigner ₹10/110, video ₹25; ☉ dawn-dusk) This outstanding sandstone and marble tomb commemorates the greatest of the Mughal emperors. The huge courtyard is entered through a stunning gateway. It has three-storey minarets at each corner and is built of red sandstone strikingly inlaid with white-marble geometric patterns.

The mausoleum is at Sikandra, 10km northwest of Agra Fort. Buses (₹22, 45 minutes) heading to Mathura from Bijli Ghar bus stand go past the mausoleum.

Itimad-ud-Daulah HISTORIC BUILDING

(Indian/foreigner ₹10/110, video ₹25; ☉ dawn-dusk) Nicknamed the Baby Taj, the exquisite tomb of Mizra Ghiyas Beg should not be missed. This Persian nobleman was Mumtaz Mahal's grandfather and Emperor Jehangir's *wazir* (chief minister). His daughter Nur Jahan, who married Jehangir, built the tomb between 1622 and 1628 in a style similar to the tomb she built for Jehangir near Lahore in Pakistan.

It doesn't have the same awesome beauty as the Taj, but it's arguably more delicate in appearance thanks to its particularly finely carved *jali* (marble lattice screens). This was the first Mughal structure built completely from marble, the first to make extensive use of pietra dura and the first tomb to be built on the banks of the Yamuna, which until then had been a sequence of beautiful pleasure gardens.

You can combine a trip here with Chini-ka-Rauza, Mehtab Bagh and Ram Bagh, all on the east bank. A cycle-rickshaw covering all four should cost about ₹250 return from the Taj, including waiting time. An autorickshaw should be ₹350.

Chini-ka-Rauza HISTORIC BUILDING

(☉ dawn-dusk) This Persian-style riverside tomb of Afzal Khan, a poet who served as Shah Jahan's chief minister, was built between 1628 and 1639. Rarely visited, it is hidden away down a shady avenue of trees on the east bank of the Yamuna. Bright blue tiles, which once covered the whole mausoleum, can still be seen on part of the exterior, while the interior is painted in floral designs.

★ Mehtab Bagh PARK

(Map p355; Indian/foreigner ₹5/100, video ₹25; ☉ dawn-dusk) This park, originally built by Emperor Babur as the last in a series of 11 parks on the Yamuna's east bank, long before the Taj was conceived, fell into disrepair until it was little more than a huge mound of sand. To protect the Taj from the erosive effects of the sand blown across the river, the park was reconstructed and is now one the best places from which to view the great mausoleum. The gardens in the Taj are perfectly aligned with the ones here, and the view of the Taj from the fountain directly in front of the entrance gate is a special one.

Jama Masjid MOSQUE

(Map p355; Jama Masjid Rd) This fine mosque, built in the Kinari Bazaar by Shah Jahan's daughter in 1648, and once connected to Agra Fort, features striking marble patterning on its domes.

☞ Tours

Amin Tours CULTURAL TOURS

(☑ 9837411144; www.daytourtajmahal.com) If you can't be bothered handling the logistics, look no further than this recommended agency for all-inclusive private Agra day trips from Delhi by car (₹6250) or train (₹6000).

UP Tourism COACH TOURS

(www.up-tourism.com; incl entry fees Indian/foreigner ₹400/1700) **Agra Cantonment train station** (☑ 2421204; Agra Cantonment Train Station; ☉ 7am-10pm) **Taj Rd** (☑ 2226431; www.up-tourism.com; 64 Taj Rd; ☉ 10am-5pm Mon-Sat) UP Tourism runs daily coach tours that leave Agra Cantonment train station at 10.30am, after picking up passengers arriving from Delhi on the Taj Express. The tour includes the Taj Mahal, Agra Fort and Fatehpur Sikri with a 1¼-hour stop in each place. Tours return to the station so that day trippers can catch the Taj Express back to Delhi at 6.55pm. Contact either of the UP Tourism offices to book a seat, or just turn up at the train station tourist office at 9.45am to sign up for that day.

🛏 Sleeping

The main place for budget accommodation is the bustling area of Taj Ganj, immediately south of the Taj, while there's a high concentration of midrange hotels further south, along Fatehabad Rd. Sadar Bazaar, an area boasting good quality restaurants, offers another option.

TOP TAJ VIEWS

Inside the Taj Grounds

You may have to pay ₹750 for the privilege, but it's only when you're inside the grounds themselves that you can really get up close and personal with the world's most beautiful building. Don't miss inspecting the marble inlay work (pietra dura) inside the *pishtaqs* (large arched recesses) on the four outer walls. And don't forget to bring a small torch with you so that you can shine it on similar pietra dura work inside the dark central chamber of the mausoleum. Note the translucency of both the white marble and the semi-precious stones inlaid into it.

From Mehtab Bagh

Tourists are no longer allowed to wander freely along the riverbank on the opposite side of the Yamuna River, but you can still enjoy a view of the back of the Taj from the 16th-century Mughal park Mehtab Bagh, with the river flowing between you and the mausoleum. A path leading down to the river beside the park offers the same view for free, albeit from a more restricted angle.

Looking Up from the South Sank of the River

This is a great place to be for sunset. Take the path that hugs the outside of the Taj's eastern wall and walk all the way down to the small temple beside the river. You should be able to find boat hands down here willing to row you out onto the water for an even more romantic view. Expect to pay around ₹100 per boat. For safety reasons, it's best not to wander down here on your own for sunset.

On a Rooftop Cafe in Taj Ganj

Perfect for sunrise shots, there are some wonderful photos to be had from the numerous rooftop cafes in Taj Ganj. We think the cafe on Saniya Palace Hotel is the pick of the bunch, with its plant-filled design and great position, but many of them are good. And all offer the bonus of being able to view the Taj with the added comfort of an early-morning cup of coffee.

From Agra Fort

With a decent zoom lens you can capture some fabulous images of the Taj from Agra Fort, especially if you're willing to get up at the crack of dawn to see the sun rising up from behind it. The best places to picture it from are probably Musamman Burj and Khas Mahal, the octagonal tower and palace where Shah Jahan was imprisoned for eight years until his death.

🛏 Taj Ganj Area

Hotel Sheela   HOTEL $

(Map p362; ☎ 2333074; www.hotelsheelaagra.com; Taj East Gate Rd; d with fan ₹600-800, with AC ₹1000; ※) If you're not fussed about looking at the Taj Mahal 24 hours a day, and don't mind doing a little legwork for an autorickshaw, Sheela is a superb budget option. Rooms are simple (no TVs here, and – perhaps absurdly – no internet) but are set around a beautifully landscaped garden with singing birds, plenty of shade and an inviting restaurant area (better for atmosphere than food). Book ahead.

Saniya Palace Hotel   HOTEL $

(Map p362; ☎ 3270199; www.saniyapalace.com; Chowk Kagziyan, Taj South Gate; d without bathroom ₹200, with bathroom ₹400-600, with AC ₹800-1000; ※@🛜) Set back from the main strip down a tiny alleyway, this place has more character than its rivals, with marble floors and Mughal-style framed carpets hung on the walls. The rooms (apart from the cramped bathroomless cheapies) are clean and big enough, although the bathrooms in the non-air-con rooms are miniscule. The very pleasant, plant-filled rooftop restaurant has fabulous Taj views.

Taj Ganj

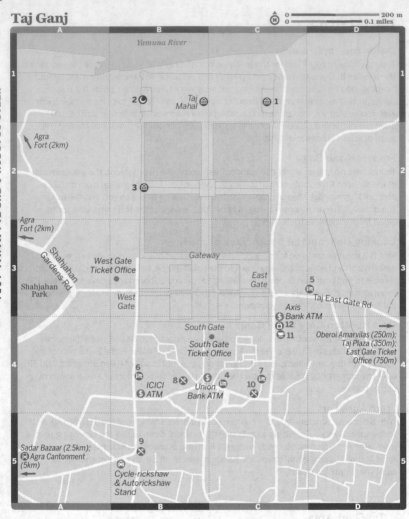

Hotel Sidhartha

HOTEL $

(Map p362; ☑ 2230901; www.hotelsidhartha.com; Taj West Gate; s/d/tr ₹500/600/700, s/d with AC ₹850/950; ❉@🛜) The 18 very smart double rooms are bright and clean and are set around a small, leafy courtyard. Hot water is available for all the rooms but only the air-con ones have hot-water showers. It was weaving through the bureaucracy of opening a rooftop restaurant when we came though, but most of the Taj is obscured by neighboring buildings.

Hotel Kamal

HOTEL $

(Map p362; ☑ 2330126; hotelkamal@hotmail.com; Taj South Gate; d ₹600-850, with AC ₹1500-1750; ❉🛜) The smartest hotel in Taj Ganj proper, Kamal has very clean, comfortable rooms with nice touches such as framed photos of the Taj on the walls and rugs on the tiled floors (five are newly renovated with welcoming woodwork and extra space). There's a cozy, bamboo-enclosed ground-floor restaurant and a perhaps slightly underutilised rooftop restaurant with a slightly obscured Taj view.

Taj Ganj

Taj Plaza
HOTEL $$

(☑2232515; www.hoteltajplaza.com; Taj East Gate Rd; d ₹1500, with AC ₹2200, Taj-facing ₹2800; ❄@❂) This former good-quality budget hotel has been stretched into a midrange price bracket in recent years. You won't be disappointed if you stay here – rooms are clean and have TV, and six eye the Taj – and there's a pleasant rooftop with decent Taj and sunset views. And it's a whole lot closer to the Taj than most hotels in the same price range.

Oberoi Amarvilas
HOTEL $$$

(☑2231515; www.oberoihotels.com; Taj East Gate Rd; d with/without balcony ₹56,210/48,901; ❄@❂❋) Following Oberoi's iron-clad MO of Maharaja-level service, exquisite dining and properties that pack some serious wow, Agra's best hotel by far oozes style and luxury. Elegant interior design is suffused with Mughal themes, a composition carried over into the exterior fountain courtyard and swimming pool, both of which are set in a delightful water garden. All rooms (and even some bathtubs) have wonderful Taj views.

⊨ Fatahabad Road Area

★ N Homestay
B&B $$

(Map p355; ☑9690107860; www.nhomestay.com; 15 Ajanta Colony, Vibhav Nagar; s/d incl breakfast ₹1200/1500; ❄@❂) Naghma, the family matriarch at this wonderful homestay, and her son, Shiron, are both a riot and their beautiful home, tucked away in a residen-tial neighborhood 15 minutes' walk from the Taj's Western Gate, is nothing short of a fabulous place to stay. The three-storey house features marble floors throughout; and some of the six large and authentically appointed rooms have pleasant balconies (first-come, first-served). Naghma will even cook you dinner. You'll rarely break through the cultural surface with such ease.

Amar Yatri Niwas
HOTEL $$

(Map p355; ☑2233030; www.amaryatriniwas.com; Fatahabad Rd; s/d from ₹1800/2137; ❄@❂) Sandwiched between a Costa Coffee and a Pizza Hut (but don't let that put you off), this place has had a recent makeover. The standard rooms are now smart, clean and come with modern furnishings and bright bathrooms and the renovated 4th floor is now borderline boutique. Be warned, wi-fi is chargeable at the ludicrous rate of ₹100 per hour!

Howard Plaza
HOTEL $$$

(Map p355; ☑4048600; www.howardplaza agra.com; Fatahabad Rd; s/d incl breakfast from ₹6745/7869; ❄@❂❋) Standard (formerly deluxe) rooms in this very welcoming hotel are decked out in elegant dark-wood furniture and stylish decorative tiling. New deluxe rooms boast soothing aqua color schemes – the results of ongoing renova-tions (there's a new coffee shop coming down the pike as well). There's an unusual splash-shaped pool out the back, a small but well-equipped gym, and a very pleasant spa offering a whole range of ayurvedic treat-ments. The breezy open-air rooftop restau-rant doubles as an atmospheric bar at night, one of the few. Wi-fi-enabled throughout.

Hotel Amar
HOTEL $$$

(Map p355; ☑2331884; www.hotelamar.com; Fa-tahabad Rd; s/d incl breakfast from ₹3859/4313; ❄@❂❋) A little worn, wi-fi–enabled rooms come with big TVs and clean bath-rooms as well as marble inlay entrance halls to drive home a paltable sense of place. The great pool area, complete with a lush green lawn and a 3.5m-tall water slide, is gravy.

⊨ Sadar Bazaar Area

Tourists Rest House
HOTEL $

(Map p355; ☑2463961; www.dontworrychicken curry.com; Kutchery Rd; s/d ₹350/450, with AC from ₹650/850; ❄@❂) Folks seem to either love it or hate it, but if you aren't dead set on sleeping under the nose of the Taj, this far more centrally located travellers' hub offers better bang for the buck than most Agra spots. Rooms of varying sizes and conditions (you'll be happier if you take a look before committing) all come with free wi-fi, TV, hot water and large windows and are set around a peaceful plant-filled, palm-shaded courtyard restaurant (the real coup here). Brand-new 3rd-floor rooms step it up with four-poster beds and expansion plans include a rooftop restaurant. The bend-over-backwards owners speak English and French and couldn't be more helpful, right down to occasionally carting you off somewhere in their hotel rickshaw. Phone ahead for a free pick-up; otherwise, it's ₹30 in a cycle-rickshaw from the train station. Damn fine masala chai, too.

Clarks Shiraz Hotel HOTEL $$$

(Map p355; ☑2226121; www.hotelclarksshiraz. com; 54 Taj Rd; s/d from ₹7307/7869; ❈@🛜≋) One of Agra's original five-star hotels has seen some recent renovation. The standard doubles are still nothing special, but marble-floored deluxe versions are excellent and all bathrooms are retiled and spotless. There are two very good restaurants, two bars (three in season), a gym, a shaded garden pool area and ayurvedic massages. Some rooms have distant Taj views.

Hotel Yamuna View HOTEL $$$

(Map p355; ☑2462990; www.hotelyamunaview agra.com; 6B The Mall; s/d from ₹5500/6000; ❈@🛜≋) A veteren Marriott manager has swooped in and taken over this good-value spot, where a newly renovated pool in the garden, a sleek new cocktail bar, a plush Chinese restaurant and spacious rooms with gleaming bathrooms make this friendly hotel in a quiet part of Sadar Bazaar worth the splurge. It also has a 24-hour cafe. Free wi-fi is in the lobby only.

🍴 Eating

Dalmoth is Agra's famous version of *namkin* (spicy nibbles). *Peitha* is a square sweet made from pumpkin and glucose that is flavoured with rosewater, coconut or saffron. You can buy it all over Agra. From October to March look out for *gajak,* a slightly spicy sesame-seed biscuit strip.

🍴 Taj Ganj Area

This lively area directly south of the Taj has plenty of budget rooftop restaurants, where menus appear to be carbon copies of one another. None are licensed but most will find you a beer if you are discreet.

Shankar Ji Restaurant INDIAN $

(Map p362; mains ₹35-100; ⊙9am-10pm) Those who are bored of the multicuisine Western-friendly tourist restaurants in Taj Ganj, and are after something a bit more down to earth and authentic, should head round the corner to the *dhabas* (snack bars) near the autorickshaw stand. Shankar Ji is as basic as any, but it's all smiles, has an English menu and dishes out the *dhabi* experience without taking a toll on your gut.

Joney's Place MULTICUISINE $

(Map p362; Kutta Park, Taj Ganj; mains ₹20-80; ⊙5am-10.30pm) This pocket-sized institution whipped up its first creamy lassi in 1978 and continues to please despite cooking its meals in what must be Agra's smallest kitchen. The cheese and tomato 'jayfelles' (toasted sandwich), the banana lassi (money-back guarantee!) and the *malai* kofta all come recomended, but it's more about crack-of-dawn sustenance than gastronomic super-feats.

Yash Cafe MULTICUISINE $

(Map p362; 3/137 Chowk Kagziyan; mains ₹30-130; ⊙7am-10.30pm; 🛜) This chilled-out 1st-floor cafe has wicker chairs, sports channels on TV, DVDs shown in the evening and a good range of meals, from good-value set breakfasts to thali (₹70), pizza (₹80 to ₹275) and Indian-style French toast (with coconut; we think they made that up). It also offers a shower and storage space (₹50 for both) to day visitors.

Saniya Palace Hotel MULTICUISINE $$

(Map p362; mains ₹30-180; ⊙6am-11pm) With cute tablecloths, dozens of potted plants and a bamboo pergola for shade, this is the most pleasant rooftop restaurant in Taj Ganj. It also has the best rooftop view of the Taj bar none. The kitchen isn't the cleanest in town, but its usual mix of Western dishes and Western-friendly Indian dishes usually go down without complaints.

Esphahan NORTH INDIAN $$$

(☑2231515; Taj East Gate Rd, Oberoi Amarvilas Hotel; mains ₹775-1250; ⊙dinner 6.30pm & 9pm) There are only two sittings each evening at Agra's finest restaurant (6.30pm and 9.30pm) so booking a table is essential. Highlights of the small but exquisite menu include succulent North Indian tandoor preparations (anything is good), a lamb *raan* steeped in chocolate and coffee undertones that packs a wallop of velvety spice, and some memorable unpolished rice topped with decadent Kerala shrimp curry. It's all set to a romantic background soundtrack of a live *santoor* player. Skip the espresso.

Sadar Bazaar

This area offers better-quality restaurants and makes a nice change from the please-all, multicuisine offerings in Taj Ganj.

Lakshmi Vilas
SOUTH INDIAN $
(Map p355; 50A Taj Rd; meals ₹38-120) This no-nonsense, plainly decorated, nonsmoking restaurant is *the* place in Agra to come for affordable South Indian fare. The thali meal (₹120), served noon to 3.30pm and 7pm to 10.30pm, is good though comes across as relatively expensive.

Brijwasi
SWEETS $
(Map p355; www.brijwasisweethouse.com; Sadar Bazaar; sweets per kg from ₹280, meals ₹70-150; ⊙6.30am-11pm) Mouth-watering selection of traditional Indian sweets, nuts and biscuits on the ground floor, with a decent-value Indian restaurant upstairs. It's most famous for its *peda* milk sweets.

★ Dasaprakash
SOUTH INDIAN $$
(Map p355; www.dasaprakashgroup.com; 1 Gwalior Rd; meals ₹110-150; ⊙noon-11pm) Fabulously tasty and religiously clean, Dasaprakash whips up consistently great South Indian vegetarian food, including spectacular thalis (₹125 to ₹300), dosa and a few token Continental dishes. The ice-cream desserts (₹70 to ₹145) are another speciality. Comfortable booth seating and wood-lattice screens make for intimate dining.

★ Pinch of Spice
NORTH INDIAN $$$
(Map p355; www.pinchofspice.in; 1076/2 Fatahabad Rd; mains ₹190-350; ⊙noon-11pm) This modern North Indian superstar at the beginning of Fatahabad Rd is the best spot outside a five-star hotel to indulge yourself in rich curries and succulent tandoori kebabs. The *murg boti masala* (chicken tikka swimming in a rich and spicy country gravy) and the *paneer lababdar* (fresh cheese cubes in a spicy red gravy with sauteed onions) are outstanding.

Drinking & Nightlife

A night out in Agra tends to revolve around sitting at a rooftop restaurant with a couple of bottles of beer. None of the restaurants in Taj Ganj are licensed, but they can find alcohol for you if you ask nicely, and don't mind if you bring your own drinks, as long as you're discreet. You can catch live Indian classical music and *ghazals* (Urdu love songs) at restaurants in several of Agra's top-end hotels, most of which also have bars, albeit of the rather soulless variety.

Café Coffee Day
CAFE
(Map p362; www.cafecoffeeday.com; 21/101 Taj East Gate; items ₹49-114; ⊙6am-8pm) This AC-cooled branch of the popular cafe chain is the closest place to the Taj selling proper coffee. Another branch is located at Sadar Bazaar (Map p355; www.cafecoffeeday.com; Sadar Bazaar; items ₹49-114; ⊙7am-11pm).

Amarvilas Bar
BAR
(Taj East Gate Rd, Oberoi Amar Vilas Hotel; ⊙noon-midnight) For a beer (₹375) or cocktail (₹525) in sheer opulence, look no further than the bar at Agra's best hotel. A terrace opens out to views of the Taj, which nonguests can wander onto, but staff can be funny about it.

Shopping

Agra is well known for its marble items inlaid with coloured stones, similar to the pietra dura work on the Taj. Sadar Bazaar, the old town and the area around the Taj are full of emporiums. Taj Mahal models are all made of alabaster rather than marble. Very cheap ones are made of soapstone, which scratches easily.

Other popular buys include rugs, leather and gemstones, though the latter are imported from Rajasthan and are cheaper in Jaipur.

Be sure to wander narrow streets behind Jama Masjid where the crazy maze of overcrowded lanes bursting with colourful markets is known collectively as **Kinari Bazaar** (Map p355; ⊙dawn-late).

Fabindia
CLOTHING
(Map p362; www.fabindia.com; 21/101 Eastern Gate; ⊙7.30am-7.30pm) India's best high-quality clothing outfitter for stylish Indian wear that's cool enough to ward off self-consciousness at home snatched up a real coup location here at the Taj's East Gate.

ℹ STAYING AHEAD OF THE SCAMS

As well as the usual commission rackets and ever-present gem import scam, some specific methods to relieve Agra tourists of their hard-earned include the following.

Rickshaws

When taking an auto or cycle-rickshaw to the Taj, make sure you are clear which gate you want to go to when negotiating the price. Otherwise, almost without fail, riders will take you to the roundabout at the south end of Shahjahan Gardens Rd – where expensive tongas (horse-drawn carriage) or camels wait to take tour groups to the west gate – and claim that's where they thought you meant. Only nonpolluting autos can go within a 500m radius of the Taj because of pollution rules, but they can get a lot closer than this.

Fake Marble

Lots of 'marble' souvenirs are actually alabaster, or even just soapstone. The mini Taj Mahals are always alabaster because they are too intricate to carve quickly in marble.

Subhash Emporium HANDICRAFTS
(Map p355; www.subhashemporium.com; 18/1 Gwalior Rd; ⊙9am-6pm) This expensive but honest marble-carving shop has been knocking up quality pieces for more than 35 years and offers a fairer price vs experience than others in town.

Subhash Bazaar MARKET
Skirts the northern edge of Agra's Jama Masjid and is particularly good for silks and saris.

Khadi Gramodyog CLOTHING
(Map p355; MG Rd; ⊙11am-7pm, closed Tue) Stocks simple, good-quality men's Indian clothing made from the homespun *khadi* fabric famously recommended by Mahatma Gandhi. No English sign: on Mahatma Gandhi (MG) Rd, look for the *khadi* logo of hands clasped around a mud hut.

Modern Book Depot BOOKS
(Map p355; Sadar Bazaar; ⊙10.30am-9.30pm, closed Tue) Great selection of novels, plus Lonely Planet guides, at this 60-year-old establishment.

ℹ Information

Agra is more wired than most, even in restaurants. Taj Ganj is riddled with internet cafes, most charging between ₹30 and ₹40 per hour.

EMERGENCY

Tourist Police (Agra Cantonment Train Station; ⊙24hr) The guys in sky-blue uniforms are based on Fatahabad Rd, but have an office here just outside the train station, as well as officers that hang around the East Gate ticket office and the UP Tourism office on Taj Rd as well as major sites.

MEDICAL SERVICES

Amit Jaggi Memorial Hospital (Map p355; www.ajmh.in; Vibhav Nagar, off Minto Rd) If you're sick, Dr Jaggi, who runs this private clinic, is the man to see. He accepts most health insurance plans from abroad; otherwise a visit runs ₹1000 (day) or ₹2000 (night). He'll even do house calls.

District Hospital (Map p355; MG Rd) Government-run local hospital.

MONEY

ATMs are all over the city. There are three close to the Taj, one near each gate. If you need to change money and are worried about being swindled in Taj Ganj, there is a Thomas Cook in the East Gate ticket office complex.

POST

India Post (Map p355; www.indiapost.gov. in; The Mall; ⊙10am-5pm Mon-Fri, to 4pm Sat) Includes a handy 'facilitation office' for foreigners.

TOURIST INFORMATION

India Tourism (Map p355; www.incredibleindia.org; 191 The Mall; ⊙9am-5.30pm Mon-Fri, to 2pm Sat) Very helpful branch; has brochures on local and India-wide attractions and can arrange guides (half-/full day ₹750/950).

Tourist Facilitation Centre (Taj East Gate; ⊙9am-5pm Sat-Thu) This helpful tourist office is part of the East Gate ticket office complex at Shilpgrram.

UP Tourism (www.up-tourism.com; ⊙6am-10pm summer, to 9pm winter) The friendly train station branch has round-the-clock help and advice. Both this branch and the one on **Taj Rd** (Map p355; www.up-tourism.com; 64 Taj Rd; ⊙10.30am-5pm Mon-Sat) can arrange guides (half-/full day ₹750/950).

ℹ Getting There & Away

AIR

Commercial flights to Agra's Kheria Airport began again in late 2012 after a long absence. **Air India** (www.airindia.com) now flies Mondays, Wednesdays and Saturdays to Varanasi (1.50pm) via Khajuraho. A new international airport, something Delhi lobbyists have fought against for years, was also greenlighted at time of research, but don't expect to see it in this edition's lifespan.

To access the airport, part of Indian Air Force territory, your name must be on the list of those with booked flights that day. Tickets must be purchased online or by phone.

BUS

The opening of the 165km Yamuna Expressway toll highway in 2012 cut drive time from Delhi to Noida, a southeastern suburb, by 30%. Some luxury coaches now use this route and reach central Delhi faster.

Some services from **Idgah bus stand** (off National Hwy 2, near Sikandra):

Bharatpur ₹56, 1½ hours, every 30 minutes, 4.30am to 11pm

Delhi Non-AC (₹171 4½ hours, every 30 minutes 5am to 11.30pm); AC (₹443, 4½ hours, 7am, 1pm, 3pm and 6.30pm)

Fatehpur Sikri ₹34, one hour, every 30 minutes, 6am to 7pm

Gwalior ₹105, three hours, hourly, 5am to 1.30pm

Jaipur ₹199, six hours, every 30 minutes, 5am to 1.30pm

Jhansi ₹180, six hours, 5am, 12.30pm, 2pm, 8.30pm, 9.30pm and 10.30pm

Khajuraho ₹250, nine hours, 5.30am

A block east of Idgah, in front of Hotel Sakura, the **Rajasthan State Road Transport Corp** (RTDC; www.rsrtc.rajasthan.gov.in) runs more-comfortable coaches to Jaipur throughout the day. Services include non-AC (₹218, 5½ hours, 7.30am, 1pm and 4.30pm), AC (₹392, five hours, 6.30am, 8.30am and 11.30am) and luxury Volvo (₹453, 4½ hours, 2.30pm).

From ISBT bus stand, luxury Volvo coaches leave for Delhi (₹490, four hours, 7am, 11.30am, 1pm and 6pm) and Lucknow (₹772, eight hours, 10am and 10pm); as well as standard non-AC services to Allahabad (₹314, 12 hours, 6.30pm), Varanasi (₹389, 16 hours,

---

TRANSPORT TO/FROM AGRA

Delhi–Agra Trains – Day Trippers

TRIP	TRAIN NO & NAME	FARE (₹)	DURATION (HR)	DEPARTURES
New Delhi–Agra	12002 Shatabdi Exp	384/805 (A)	2	6am (except Fri)
Agra–New Delhi	12001 Shatabdi Exp	415/850 (A)	2	8.35pm (except Fri)
Hazrat Nizamuddin–Agra	12280 Taj Exp	75/273 (B)	3	7.10am
Agra–Hazrat Nizamuddin	12279 Taj Exp	75/273 (B)	3	6.55pm

Fares: (A) AC chair/1AC, (B) 2nd-class/AC chair

More Handy Trains from Agra (AGC/AF)

DESTINATION	TRAIN NO & NAME	FARE (₹)	DURATION (HR)	DEPARTURES
Gorakhpur*	19037/19039 Avadh Exp	249/697/1050 (A)	15½	10pm
Jaipur*	12036 Shatabdi Exp	415/890 (C)	3½	4.20pm (except Thu)
Khajuraho	12448 UP SMPRK KRNTI	207/546/805 (A)	8	11.20pm (except Wed)
Kolkata (Howrah)	13008 UA Toofan Exp	394/1119 (B)	31	12.40pm
Lucknow	93238/93237 Kota PNBE Exp	164/446/655 (A)	6½	11.30pm
Mumbai (CST)	12138/12137 Punjab Mail	410/1139/1770 (A)	23	8.55am
Varanasi	93238/13237 Kota PNBE Exp	262/733/1110 (A)	12	11.30pm

Fares: (A) sleeper/3AC/2AC, *leaves from Agra Fort station; (B) sleeper/3AC only; (C) AC chair/1AC only

4.30pm) and Gorakhpur (₹517, 16 hours, 1.30pm, 3pm, 5pm, 9pm and 10pm). Dehra Dun buses also depart from here (AC/non-AC ₹523/320, 11 hours, 6pm, 8pm and 9.30pm, latter two non-AC) as well as three overnight buses to Rishikesh (seat/sleeper ₹348/464, 10 hours, 6.30pm, 7.30pm and 10pm) if you're shut out of the capital.

Bijli Ghar bus stand (Map p355) serves Mathura (₹49, 90 minutes, every 30 minutes, 6am to 7pm) as well as Tundla (₹25, one hour, every 30 minutes, 6am to 8.30pm), from where you can catch 12382 Poorva Express at 8.35pm to Varanasi if the trains from Agra are sold out.

Shared autos (₹10) run between Idgah and Bijli Ghar bus stands. To get to ISBT, take the AC public bus from Agra Cantt train station to Dayalbagh (₹22) but get off at Baghwan Talkies (₹16), from where shared autos (₹8) can take you to ISBT; or catch a autorickshaw from Taj Ganz (₹120).

TRAIN

Most trains leave from **Agra Cantonment (Cantt) train station**, although some go from Agra Fort station. A few trains, such as Marudhar Express, run as slightly different numbers on different days than those listed, but timings remain the same.

Express trains are well set up for day trippers to/from Delhi but trains run to Delhi all day. If you can't reserve a seat, just buy a 'general ticket' for the next train (about ₹62), find a seat in Sleeper class then upgrade when the ticket collector comes along. Most of the time, he won't even make you pay any more.

For Orchha, catch one of the many daily trains to Jhansi (sleeper from ₹127, three hours), then take a shared auto to the bus stand (₹10) from where shared autos run all day to Orchha (₹15). An autorickshaw runs ₹45 and ₹225, respectively, for same route.

🛈 Getting Around

AUTORICKSHAW

Agra's green-and-yellow autorickshaws run on CNG (compressed natural gas) and are less environmentally destructive. Just outside Agra Cantt station is the prepaid autorickshaw booth, which gives you a good guide for haggling elsewhere. Note, autos aren't allowed to go to Fatehpur Sikri.

Sample prices from Agra Cantt station: Fatahabad Rd ₹100; ISBT bus stand ₹150; Sadar Bazaar ₹60; Sikandra ₹150; Taj Mahal ₹100; Shilpgrarm (Taj East Gate) ₹120; half-day (four-hour) tour ₹400; full-day (10-hour) tour ₹500. Prices do not include a ₹5 booking fee.

CYCLE-RICKSHAW

Prices from the Taj Mahal include: Agra Cantt train station ₹40; Agra Fort ₹30; Biili Ghar bus stand ₹30; Fatahabad Rd ₹20; Kinari Bazaar ₹30; Sadar Bazaar ₹30; half-day tour ₹200.

TAXI

Outside Agra Cantt the prepaid taxi booth gives a good idea of what taxis should cost. Non-AC prices include: Delhi ₹3000; Fatahabad Rd ₹150; Sadar Bazaar ₹100; Taj Mahal ₹150; half-day (four-hour) tour ₹650; full-day (eight-hour) tour ₹850. Prices do not include a ₹10 booking fee.

Around Agra

Fatehpur Sikri

🕿 05613 / POP 29,000

This magnificent fortified ancient city, 40km west of Agra, was the short-lived capital of the Mughal empire between 1571 and 1585, during the reign of Emperor Akbar. Akbar visited the village of Sikri to consult the Sufi saint Shaikh Salim Chishti, who predicted the birth of an heir to the Mughal throne. When the prophecy came true, Akbar built his new capital here, including a stunning mosque – still in use today – and three palaces for each of his favourite wives, one a Hindu, one a Muslim and one a Christian (though Hindu villagers in Sikri dispute a few of these claims). The city was an Indo-Islamic masterpiece, but erected in an area that supposedly suffered from water shortages and so was abandoned shortly after Akbar's death.

It's easy to visit this World Heritage Site as a day trip from Agra, but there are a couple of decent places to stay, and the colourful bazaar in the village of **Fatehpur**, just below the ruins, as well as the small village of **Sikri**, a few kilometres north, are worth exploring. Also, the red-sandstone palace walls are at their most atmospheric, and photogenic, at sunset.

The bus stand is at the eastern end of the bazaar. Walking another 1km northeast will bring you to Agra Gate and the junction with the main Agra–Jaipur road, from where you can catch buses.

👁 Sights

The palace buildings lie beside the Jama Masjid mosque. Both sit on top of a ridge that runs between the small villages of Fatehpur and Sikri. See also the colour illustration, p370.

Jama Masjid MOSQUE

This beautiful, immense mosque was completed in 1571 and contains elements of Persian and Indian design. The main entrance, at the top of a flight of stone steps, is through the spectacular 54m-high **Buland Darwaza** (Victory Gate), built to commemorate Akbar's military victory in Gujarat.

Inside the courtyard of the mosque is the stunning white-marble **tomb of Shaikh Salim Chishti**, which was completed in 1581 and is entered through an original door made of ebony. Inside it are brightly coloured flower murals while the sandlewood canopy is decorated with mother-of-pearl shell. Just as Akbar came to the saint four centuries ago hoping for a son, childless women visit his tomb today and tie a thread to the *jali*, which are among the finest in India. To the right of the tomb lie the gravestones of family members of Shaikh Salim Chishti and nearby is the entrance to an underground tunnel (barred by a locked gate) that reputedly goes all the way to Agra Fort! Behind the entrance to the tunnel, on the far wall, are three holes, part of the ancient ventilation system. You can still feel the rush of cool air forcing its way through them. Just east of Shaikh Salim Chishti's tomb is the red-sandstone **tomb of Islam Khan**, the final resting place of Shaikh Salim Chishti's grandson and one-time governor of Bengal.

On the east wall of the courtyard is a smaller entrance to the mosque – the **Shahi Darwaza** (King's Gate), which leads to the palace complex.

Palaces & Pavilions PALACES

(Indian/foreigner ₹20/260, video ₹25; ☺dawn-dusk) A large courtyard dominates the northeast entrance at **Diwan-i-Am** (Hall of Public Audiences). Now a pristinely manicured garden, this is where Akbar presided over the courts from the middle seat of the five equal seatings along the western wall, flanked by his advisors. It was built to utilise an echo soundsystem, so Akbar could hear anything at any time from anywhere in the open space. Justice was dealt with swiftly if legends are to be believed, with public executions said to have been carried out here by elephants trampling to death convicted criminals.

The **Diwan-i-Khas** (Hall of Private Audiences), found at the northern end of the Pachisi Courtyard, looks nothing special from the outside, but the interior is dominated by a magnificently carved stone central column. This pillar flares to create a flat-topped plinth linked to the four corners of the room by narrow stone bridges. From this plinth Akbar is believed to have debated with scholars and ministers who stood at the ends of the four bridges.

Next to Diwan-i-Khas is the **Treasury**, which houses secret stone safes in some corners (one has been left with its stone lid open for visitors to see). Sea monsters carved on the ceiling struts were there to protect the fabulous wealth once stored here. The so-called **Astrologer's Kiosk** in front has roof supports carved in a serpentine Jain style.

Just south of the Astrologer's Kiosk is **Pachisi Courtyard**, named after the ancient game known in India today as ludo. The large, plus-shaped gameboard is visible surrounding the block in the middle of the courtyard. In the southeast corner is the most intricately carved structure in the whole complex, the tiny but elegant **Rumi Sultana**, which was said to be the palace built for Akbar's Turkish Muslim wife, but other theories say it was used by Akbar himself as a palace R&R/powder room during court sessions. On one corner of the **Ladies Garden** just west of Pachisi is the impressive **Panch Mahal**, a pavilion whose five storeys decrease in size until the top one consists of only a tiny kiosk. The lower floor has 84 columns, all different, and total colums clock in at 176.

Continuing anticlockwise will bring you to the **Ornamental Pool**. Here, singers and musicians would perform on the platform above the water while Akbar watched from the pavilion in his private quarters, known as **Daulat Khana** (Abode of Fortune). Behind the pavilion is the **Khwabgah** (Dream House), a sleeping area with a huge stone bunk bed. Nowadays the only sleeping done here is by bats, hanging from the ceiling. The small room in the far corner is full of them!

Heading west from the Ornamental Pool beholds the **Palace of Jodh Bai**, and the one-time home of Akbar's Hindu wife, said to be his favourite. Set around an enormous courtyard, it blends traditional Indian columns, Islamic cupolas and turquoise-blue Persian roof tiles. Just outside, to the left of Jodh Bai's former kitchen, is the **Palace of the Christian Wife**. This was used by Akbar's Goan wife Mariam, who gave birth

(Continued on page 372)

Fatehpur Sikri

A WALKING TOUR OF FATEHPUR SIKRI

You can enter this fortified ancient city from two entrances, but the northeast entrance at Diwan-i-Am (Hall of Public Audiences) offers the most logical approach to this remarkable Unesco World Heritage site. This large courtyard (now a garden) is where Emperor Akbar presided over the trials of accused criminals. Once through the ticket gate, you are in the northern end of the **Pachisi Courtyard 1**. The first building you see is **Diwan-i-Khas 2** (Hall of Private Audiences), the interior of which is dominated by a magnificently carved central stone column. Pitch south and enter **Rumi Sultana 3**, a small but elegant palace built for Akbar's Turkish Muslim wife. It's hard to miss the **Ornamental Pool 4** nearby – its southwest corner provides Fatehpur Sikri's most photogenic angle, perfectly framing its most striking building, the five-storey Panch Mahal, one of the gateways to the Imperial Harem Complex, where the **Lower Haramsara 5** once housed more than 200 female servants. Wander around the Palace of Jodh Bai and take notice of the towering ode to an elephant, the 21m-high **Hiran Minar 6**, in the distance to the northwest. Leave the palaces and pavilions area via Shahi Darwaza (King's Gate), which spills into India's second-largest mosque courtyard at **Jama Masjid 7**. Inside this immense and gorgeous mosque is the sacred **Tomb of Shaikh Salim Chishti 8**. Exit through the spectacular **Buland Darwaza 9** (Victory Gate), one of the world's most magnificent gateways.

Buland Darwaza
Most tours end with an exit through Jama Masjid's Victory Gate. Walk out and take a look behind you: Behold! The magnificent 15-storey sandstone gate, 54m high, is a menacing monolith to Akbar's reign.

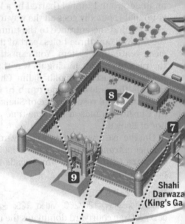

Shahi Darwaza (King's Ga

Tomb of Shaikh Salim Chishti
Each knot in the strings tied to the 56 carved white marble designs of the interior walls of Shaikh Salim Chishti's tomb represents one wish of a maximum three.

Jama Masjid
The elaborate marble inlay work at the Badshahi Gate and throughout the Jama Masjid complex is said to have inspired similar work 82 years later at the Taj Mahal in Agra.

Hiran Minar

This bizarre, seldom-visited tower off the north-west corner of Fatehpur Sikri is decorated with hundreds of stone representations of elephant tusks. It is said to be the place where Minar, Akbar's favourite execution elephant, died.

6

Pachisi Courtyard

Under your feet just past Rumi Sultana is the Pachisi Courtyard where Akbar is said to have played the game *pachisi* (an ancient version of ludo) using slave girls in colourful dress as pieces.

Diwan-i-Khas

Emperor Akbar modified the central stone column inside Diwan-i-Khas to call attention to a new religion he called Din-i-Ilahi (God is One). The intricately carved column features a fusion of Hindu, Muslim, Christian and Buddhist imagery.

Panch Mahal

1　**2**

Diwan-i-Am
(Hall of Public Audiences)

5

4　**3**

Rumi Sultana

Don't miss the headless creatures carved into Rumi Sultana's palace interiors: a lion, deer, an eagle and a few peacocks were beheaded by jewel thieves who swiped the precious jewels that originally formed their heads.

Lower Haramsara

Akbar reportedly kept more than 5000 concubines, but the 200 or so female servants housed in the Lower Haramsara were strictly business. Knots were tied to these sandstone rings to support partitions between their individual quarters.

Ornamental Pool

Tansen, said to be the most gifted Indian vocalist of all time and one of Akbar's treasured nine *Navaratnas* (Gems), would be showered with coins during performances from the central platform of the Ornamental Pool.

(Continued from page 369)

to Jehangir here in 1569, though some believe Akbar never had a Christian wife at all, and that Mariam was short for Mariam-Ut-Zamani, a title he gave to Jodh Bai meaning 'Beautiful like a Rose', or 'Most Beautiful Woman on Earth'. Like many of the buildings in the palace complex, it contains elements of different religions, as befitted Akbar's tolerant religious beliefs. The domed ceiling is Islamic in style, while remnants of a wall painting of the Hindu god Shiva can also be found.

Walking past the Palace of the Christian Wife once more will take you west to **Birbal Bhavan**, ornately carved inside and out, and thought to have been the living quarters of one of Akbar's most senior ministers. The **Lower Haramsara**, just to the south, housed Akbar's large inventory of live-in female servants.

Plenty of ruins are scattered behind the whole complex, including the **Caravanserai**, a vast courtyard surrounded by rooms where visiting merchants stayed. Badly defaced carvings of elephants still guard **Hathi Pol** (Elephant Gate), while the remains of the small **Stonecutters' Mosque** and a **hammam** (bath) are also a short stroll away. Other unnamed ruins can be explored north of what is known as the **Mint** but is thought to have in fact been stables, including some in the interesting village of Sikri to the north.

Tours

Official Archaeological Society of India guides can be hired from the ticket office for ₹300 (English), but they aren't always the most knowledgeable (some have been birthrighted in). Official Uttar Pradesh Tourism guides have gone through more rigorous training and can be hired for ₹750. Our favorite is **Pankaj Bhatnagar** (8126995552; www.tajinvitation.com).

Sleeping & Eating

Fatehpur Sikri's culinary speciality is *khataie*, the biscuits you can see piled high in the bazaar.

Goverdhan Tourist Complex HOTEL **$**
(9412526585; www.hotelfatehpursikriviews.com; Agra Rd; d ₹400-650, with AC ₹950-1250; ❈ @ ❖) Brightly painted, spotless rooms set around a very well-kept garden. There's communal balcony and terrace seating, free internet and wi-fi. The restaurant is decent (meals ₹80 to ₹180) but our four pieces of *paneer* means portions leave something to be desired. The friendly owner chucks off 20% for singles.

Hotel Ajay Palace GUEST HOUSE **$**
(282950; Agra Rd; d ₹300) This very friendly family guesthouse has three simple double rooms with marble floors and sit-down flush toilets. It's also a very popular lunch stop (mains ₹40 to ₹120). Sit on the rooftop at the large, elongated marble table and enjoy a view of the village streets with the Jama Masjid towering above. Note it is not 'Ajay Restaurant By Near Palace' at the bus stand – it's 50m more along the road.

❶ Information

DANGERS & ANNOYANCES

Take no notice of anyone who gets on the Fatehpur Sikri–Agra bus before the final stop at Idgah Bus Stand, telling you that you have arrived at the city centre or the Taj Mahal. You haven't. You're still a long autorickshaw ride away, and the man trying to tease you off the bus is, surprise surprise, an autorickshaw driver.

❶ Getting There & Away

Tours and taxis all arrive at the Gulistan Tourist Complex parking lot, from which shuttle buses (₹5) depart for Fatehpur Sikri's Diwan-i-Am entrance (right side of the street) and Jodh Bai entrance (left side of the street). Note that if you have hired an unauthorised guide, you will not be allowed to enter at Diwan-i-Am.

Buses run to Agra's Idgah Bus Stand from the bazaar every half-hour (₹34), from 6am to 7pm. If you miss those, walk to Agra Gate and wave down a Jaipur–Agra bus on the main road. They run regularly, day and night.

For Bharatpur (₹20, 40 minutes) or Jaipur (₹170, 4½ hours), wave down a westbound bus from Agra Gate.

Regular trains for Agra Fort Station leave Fatehpur Sikri at 4.51am (59811 Haldighati Pass) and 8.12pm (19037 Avadh Express), but there are simpler passenger trains at 10.30am and 3.55pm as well as four other trains that fly through at various times. Just buy a 'general' ticket at the station and pile in (₹6, one to two hours).

Mathura

0565 / POP 395,000

Famed for being the birthplace of the much-loved Hindu god Krishna, Mathura is one of Hinduism's seven sacred cities and attracts floods of pilgrims, particularly during **Janmastami** (Krishna's birthday; ⊘ Aug/Sep) in August/September; and Holi in February/March. The town is dotted with temples from various ages and the stretch of the sacred Yamuna River which flows past here is lined with 25 ghats, best seen at dawn, when many people take their holy dip, and just after sunset, when hundreds of candles are sent floating out onto the river during the evening *aarti* ceremony.

Mathura was once a Buddhist centre with 20 monasteries that housed 3000 monks but, after the rise of Hinduism, and later sackings by Afghan and Mughal invaders, today all that's left of the oldest sights are the beautiful sculptures recovered from ruins, now on display in the archaeological museum.

◉ Sights

Kesava Deo Temple
HINDU TEMPLE

(Shri Kirshna Janmbhoomi; ⊘ summer 5am-9.30pm, winter 5.30am-8.30pm) Among the foundations of the mural-filled Kesava Deo temple complex is a small, bare room with a slab of rock on which Krishna is said to have been born, some 3500 years ago. Next door is **Katra Masjid**, a mosque built by Aurangzeb in 1661 on the site of a temple he ordered to be destroyed. The mosque is now guarded round the clock by soldiers to prevent a repeat of the tragic events at Ayodhya in 1992 (p381). Cameras and mobiles must be checked here for ₹2 per piece.

Archaeological Museum
MUSEUM

(Museum Rd; Indian/foreigner ₹5/25; ⊘ 10.30am-4.30pm Tue-Sun) This large museum house superb collections of religious sculptures by the Mathura school, which flourished from the 3rd century BC to the 12th century AD.

Vishram Ghat & Around
AREA

A string of ghats and temples lines the Yamuna River north of the main road bridge. The most central and most popular is Vishram Ghat, where Krishna is said to have rested after killing the tyrannical King Kansa. Boats gather along the banks here to take tourists along the Yamuna (₹100 per half hour). Beside the ghat is the 17m **Sati Burj**, a four-storey tower built by the son of Behari Mal of Jaipur in 1570 to commemorate his mother's *sati* (self-immolation on her husband's funeral pyre).

Mathura

◉ Sights
1 Archaeological Museum B2
2 Katra Masjid A1
3 Kesava Deo Temple A1
4 Sati Burj B1

⊜ Sleeping
5 Agra Hotel B1
6 Hotel Brijwasi Royal B2

ⓘ Information
7 Internet Paradise A2
8 State Bank of India B2

Gita Temple
HINDU TEMPLE

(⊘ dawn-dusk) This serene marble temple, on the road to Vrindavan, has the entire Bhagavad Gita written on a red pillar in the garden.

🛏 Sleeping & Eating

Agra Hotel
GUESTHOUSE $

(☑ 2403318; Bengali Ghat; s ₹350-350, d ₹500-550, tr ₹650, d/tr with AC ₹800/900; ❈) This area, with narrow lanes winding their way down to the ghats and temples that line the Yamuna River, is easily the most interesting place to stay. Rooms here are basic but have character and some overlook the river, while staff members are very welcoming.

Hotel Brijwasi Royal   HOTEL $$
(☎ 2401224; www.brijwasiroyal.com; Station Rd; s/d incl breakfast from ₹2467/2867; ❉ ☎) A clean and contemporary hotel with businesslike rooms that come with either marble floors or carpets, some overlooking a buffalo pond behind. The restaurant (meals ₹105 to ₹175) does good quality Indian veg dishes, South Indian breakfasts and Chinese meals, and is deservedly popular. There's also a smoky, male-dominated bar (beer from ₹130).

ℹ Information

Near New bus stand is a **State Bank of India** (Station Rd; ⊙ 10.30am-4pm Mon-Fri, to 1pm Sat), which has a 1st-floor money-exchange desk and an ATM outside. The small **Internet Paradise** (Vrindavan Rd; per hr ₹30; ⊙ 6am-10pm) just across the roundabout from the bank on the way towards the New bus stand offers internet access.

ℹ Getting There & Around

BUS

The so-called **New bus stand** has regular buses to Delhi (₹109, four hours) and Agra (₹49, 90 minutes) that run every 15 to 30 minutes throughout the day and night. Tempos (large autorickshaws) charge ₹15 for the 10km Mathura–Vrindavan run.

TRAIN

Regular trains go to Delhi (sleeper/AC chair ₹140/206, three hours), Agra (sleeper/AC chair ₹140/202, one hour), and Bharatpur (sleeper/AC chair ₹80/218, 45 minutes). The Bharatpur trains continue to Sawai Madhopur (for Ranthambhore National Park, two hours) and Kota (5½ hours).

Vrindavan

☎ 0565 / POP 65,000

The village of Vrindavan is where the young Krishna is said to have grown up. Pilgrims flock here from all over India and, in the case of the Hare Krishna community, from all over the world. Dozens of temples, old and modern, dot the area. They come in all shapes and sizes and many have their own unique peculiarities, making a visit here more than just your average temple hop.

◉ Sights

The **International Society for Krishna Consciousness** (Iskcon; ☎ 2540343; www.iskcon.com), also known as the Hare Krishnas, is based at the **Krishna Balaram temple complex** (Ishkon Temple), accessed through a beautiful white-marble gate, which houses the tomb of Swami Prabhupada (1896–1977), the founder of the Hare Krishna organisation. Several hundred foreigners attend courses and seminars here annually. The temple is closed to the public at various times of the day, most significantly from noon to 4pm.

The cavernous, red sandstone **Govind Dev Temple**, built in 1590 by Raja Man Singh of Amber, has cute bells carved on its pillars. Resident monkeys here are as cheeky as any in India. We caught one running off with a lady's purse and saw another sitting in the rafters wearing a pair of sunglasses!

The 10-storey **Pagal Baba Temple** (admission ₹3), a fairytale-castle lookalike, has an amusing succession of animated puppets and dioramas in glass cases on the ground floor, which depict scenes from the lives of Rama and Krishna.

Rangaji Temple, dating from 1851, **Radha Ballabh Temple**, built in 1626, **Madan Mohan Temple** and **Nidhivan Temple** are also worth a visit.

🛏 Sleeping & Eating

It's possible to stay at the **guesthouse** (☎ 9634073197; www.iskconvrindavan.com; d without AC ₹700, d/tr with AC ₹950/1470) at the back of the temple complex (though devotees are prioritised). Here you'll also find the clean, cool and healthy **Sri Govinda Restaurant** (mains ₹90-200; ⊙ 8am-2:30pm & 6-9.30pm), which does Indian veg dishes, pasta, cakes, shakes, salads and soups. There's a small bakery beside it.

ℹ Information

There is an **information office** (⊙ 10am-1pm & 5-8.30pm) in the Krishna Balaram temple complex which has lists of places to stay in Vrindavan and can help with booking Gita (studies in the Bhagavad Gita, an ancient Hindu scripture) classes.

There's an ATM beside the temple and you can check internet (with wi-fi!) at **Priya Travels** (priyatravels59@yahoo.in; Shop 20, opp Ishkon Temple, Main Gate; per hr ₹30; ⊙ 6am-10pm) opposite.

ℹ Getting There & Around

Most temples are open from dawn to dusk and admission is free, but they are well spread out so a cycle-rickshaw tour is a good way to see them. Expect to pay ₹150 to ₹200 for a half-day tour.

Tempos, shared autos and buses all charge ₹15 from Vrindavan to Mathura.

Vrindavan

0 — 1 km
0 — 0.5 miles

Lucknow

📋 0522 / POP 2.9 MILLION

Liberally sprinkled with British Raj–era buildings – including the famous Residency – and boasting two superb mausoleums, the capital of Uttar Pradesh plays a somewhat unwarranted third fiddle to Agra and Varanasi, but caters well to history buffs without attracting the hordes of tourists that sometimes make sightseeing tiresome. By contrast, Lucknow's modern side boasts a unique Iron Curtain-esque feel, with grandiose monuments and overstated parks and gardens, many boasting marble sidewalks and pink sandstone a plenty (we imagine they were going for a Washington, DC aesthetic but ended up more Pyongyang). It's nothing if not interesting.

The city rose to prominence as the home of the Nawabs of Avadh (Oudh) who were great patrons of the culinary and other arts, particularly dance and music. Lucknow's reputation as a city of culture, gracious living and rich cuisine has continued to this day (it conveniently rhymes in Hindi: '*Nawab, Aadaab [Respect], Kebab* and *Shabab [Beauty]*'). And eating out is still a major highlight of a visit to the city.

In 1856 the British annexed Avadh, exiling Nawab Wajid Ali Shah to a palace in Kolkata (Calcutta). The disruption this caused was a factor behind the First War of Independence of 1857, culminating in the dramatic Siege of Lucknow at the Residency.

⊙ Sights

★ **Residency**   HISTORIC SITE
(Indian/foreigner ₹5/100, video ₹25; ☉ dawn-dusk) The large collection of gardens and ruins that makes up the Residency offers a fascinating historical glimpse of the beginning of the end for the British Raj. Built in 1800, the Residency became the stage for the most dramatic events of the 1857 First War of Independence, the Siege of Lucknow, a 147-day siege that claimed the lives of thousands. The compound has been left as it was at the time of the final relief and the walls are still pockmarked from bullets and cannon balls.

The focus is the well-designed **museum** (☉ 9am-4.30pm Sat-Thu) in the main Residency building, which includes a scale model of the original buildings. Downstairs are the huge basement rooms where many of the British women and children lived throughout the siege.

The **cemetery** around the ruined St Mary's church is where 2000 of the defenders were buried, including their leader, Sir Henry Lawrence, 'who tried to do his duty' according to the famous inscription on his weathered gravestone.

★ **Bara Imambara**   HISTORIC BUILDING
(Hussainabad Trust Rd; Indian/foreigner ₹35/350; ☉ dawn-dusk) This colossal tomb is worth seeing in its own right, but the highly unusual labyrinth of corridors inside its upper floors make a visit to this *imambara* (tomb dedicated to a Shiite holy man) particularly special. The ticket price includes entrance to Chota Imambara, the clock tower and the

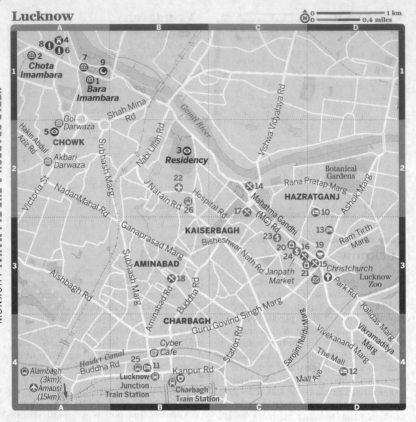

baradari (summer palace), all walking distance from here.

The complex is accessed through two enormous gateways which lead into a huge courtyard. On one side is an attractive **mosque**, on the other a large **baori** (stepwell) which can be explored. Bring a torch (flashlight). At the far end of the courtyard is the huge central hall, one of the world's largest vaulted galleries. *Tazias* (small replicas of Imam Hussain's tomb in Karbala, Iraq) are stored inside and are paraded around during the Shiite mourning ceremony of Muharram.

But it's what's beyond the small entrance (intriguingly marked 'labyrinth') to the left of the central hall, that steals the show. It leads to the **Bhulbhulaiya**, an enticing network of narrow passageways that winds its way inside the upper floors of the tomb's structure, eventually leading out to rooftop balconies. As with the step-well, it's handy to have a torch.

Just beyond the Bara Imambara is the unusual but imposing gateway **Rumi Darwaza** (Hussainabad Trust Rd), said to be a copy of an entrance gate in Istanbul. 'Rumi' (relating to Rome) is the term Muslims applied to Istanbul when it was still Byzantium, the capital of the Eastern Roman empire. Over the road is the beautiful white mosque **Tila Wali Masjid**, a deceptively shallow building built in 1680. The interior is repainted periodically over the original designs.

⭐ **Chota Imambara** HISTORIC BUILDING
(Hussainabad Imambara; Hussainabad Trust Rd; admission with Bara Imambara ticket) About 500m beyond the Bara Imambara, through a second beautiful gateway, is another tomb that was constructed by Mohammed Ali Shah in 1832, who is buried here, alongside his mother. Smaller than the Bara Imambara

Lucknow

Top Sights
1 Bara Imambara A1
2 Chota Imambara A1
3 Residency B2

Sights
4 Baradari A1
5 Chowk A2
6 Clock Tower A1
7 Rumi Darwaza A1
8 Satkhanda A1
9 Tila Wali Masjid A1

Activities, Courses & Tours
UP Tourism Heritage Walking Tour .... (see 10)

Sleeping
10 Hotel Gomti D2
11 Hotel Mayur B1
12 Lucknow Homestay D4
13 Tokaroos Inn D3

Eating
14 Falaknuma C2
15 Moti Mahal Restaurant D3
16 Royal Cafe C3
17 Sakhawat C2
18 Tunday Kababi B3

Drinking & Nightlife
19 Cafe Coffee Day D3
Strokes Sports Bar .... (see 16)
Tashna Bar .... (see 10)

Shopping
20 Ram Advani Bookshop C3
21 Sugandhco C3

Information
22 Balrampur District Hospital B2
23 HDFC ATM C3
24 ICICI Bank C3
UP Tourism .... (see 10)
UP Tourism Kiosk .... (see 19)

Transport
25 Charbagh Bus Stand B4
26 Kaiserbagh Bus Stand B2

but adorned with calligraphy, it has a more serene and intimate atmosphere.

Mohammed's silver throne and red crown can be seen here as well as countless chandeliers and some brightly decorated *tazias*. In the garden is a water tank and two replicas of the Taj Mahal that are the **tombs** of Mohammed Ali Shah's daughter and her husband. A traditional **hammam** is off to one side.

Outside the complex, the decaying watchtower on the other side of the road is known as **Satkhanda** (Seven Storey Tower; Hussainabad Trust Rd), although it has only four storeys because construction was abandoned in 1840 when Mohammed Ali Shah died.

The 67m red-brick **clock tower** (admission with Bara Imambara ticket; ⌚ dawn-dusk), the tallest in India, was built in the 1880s. Nearby is a **baradari** (summer palace; admission with Bara Imambara ticket; ⌚ 7am-6.30pm), a striking red-brick building, built in 1842, which overlooks an artificial lake and houses portraits of the nawabs.

Tours

★ UP Tourism Heritage Walking Tour WALK
UP(☎ 9415013047; 6 Sapru Marg, Hotel Gomti; 3hr tour Indian/foreigner ₹75/150; ⌚ tours 8am) This fabulous three-hour Heritage Walking Tour run by UP Tourism could well turn out to be the best ₹150 you ever spend. Meet your English-speaking guide outside Tila Wali Masjid then follow him first around the mosque, then the Bara Imambara, before delving in to the architectural delights of the crazy maze of alleyways in the incredibly fascinating **Chowk** district, sampling interesting nibbles along the way like *Namash* (a surprisingly light and tasty concoction made from milk, cream and morning dew!). This is an eye-popping way to get your bearings amongst Lucknow's oldest neighborhoods before returning on your own in the evening when things really get started.

Sleeping

Lucknow Homestay HOMESTAY $
(☎ 6460592; www.lucknowhomestay.wordpress.com; 110D Mall Ave; s/d ₹600/700, without bathroom ₹500/600, with AC ₹900/1000, all incl breakfast; ❄ wi-fi) It's not without issues (mosquitoes, negligable hot water, poor attention to email), but this remains Lucknow's most accomodating budget option. In the leafy neighbourhood home, Naheed and family keep their distance but offer 11 simple rooms – two with private bathrooms. The house number isn't marked, but a sign

reading 'Munni's Dream' is above the front door. Rickshaw drivers know Mall Ave, which is actually a neighborhood (not merely a street), but you'll need to orient yourself upon arrival if you want to find your way back home, as the address is amid the maze if you enter the neighborhood from anywhere other than the Mahatma Gandhi (MG) Rd side. Better yet, get to know Naheed's favorite rickshaw driver, the honest, reliable and English-speaking Guatam, and keep him close.

Hotel Mayur
HOTEL $

(☎2451824; Subhash Marg; s/d ₹400/500, without bathroom ₹300/350, with AC ₹850/950; ❄) Good-value rooms in this well-run establishment with limited English are basic but come with cable TV and some have huge bathrooms. Definitely one of the better cheapies near the train station. It's hard to spot – look up for a small sign on Subhash Marg just around the corner from Kanpor Rd/Charbagh bus stand.

Hotel Gomti
HOTEL $$

(☎2611463; hotelgomti@up-tourism.com; 6 Tej Bahadur, Sapru Marg; s/d ₹800/900, with AC from ₹1463/1575; ❄) A better government-run hotel than most, though bottom of the barrel rooms with air coolers are a bit musty. From there, the four catagories of AC rooms won't knock you out, but all come reasonably well equipped, with TV, sofa, table and chairs. A restaurant, a bar with a garden and a UP Tourism office are all here, too.

Vivanta by Taj
HOTEL $$$

(☎6771000; www.vivantabytaj.com; Vipan Khand, Gomti Nagar; s/d incl breakfast from ₹11,242/12,366; ❄@🅰❄) Lucknow's top hotel resides in an enormous stately building built as a domed homage to Taj's famous Taj Mahal Hotel in Mumbai and instills a sense of head-of-state in those alighting here. Rooms are modest but well-honed at the 110-room property, with newer rooms offering whimsical refinement without stuffiness, with fun cubicle showers and hardwood headboards. There's a scrumptious bakery, the excellent Nawab restaurant Oudhyana, a small spa and gym, a legitimate bar with a fiercely creative cocktail list (drinks ₹499 to ₹699) and a wonderful marble-flanked pool.

Tekarees Inn
HOTEL $$$

(☎2288928; www.tekareesinn.com; 17/3 Ashok Marg; s/d from ₹2248/3147; ❄@🅰) Neat and tidy 20-room businesslike hotel with marble floors in decent-sized twin rooms. Bathrooms are spartan but clean and the owner is extremly friendly.

✖ Eating

The refined palates of the Nawabs left Lucknow with a reputation for rich Mughlai cuisine, and the city's dinner tables are heavily influenced by the Arab world. Lucknow is famous for its biryani dishes as well as its wide range of kebabs. It's also known for *dum pukht* – the 'art' of steam-pressure cooking, in which meat and vegetables are cooked in a sealed clay pot.

★ Sakhawat
NORTH INDIAN $

(www.sakhawatrestaurant.com; 2 Kaiserbagh Ave, behind Awadh Gymkhana Club; kebabs ₹80; ⊙5-10pm) This highly recommended hole-in-the-wall place doesn't look like much, but the mutton *galawat* kebabs at this locals' haunt are actually the best we had in Lucknow – the smoky, perfectly crispy char makes the difference – and, despite appearances, it has won international accolades and doubles as an Awadh cooking institute (it can whip out some 72 different dishes per week). The present owner's great-grandfather was a brigadier in the British Army and a Nawab chef.

Tunday Kababi
NORTH INDIAN $

(Naaz Cinema Rd, just off Aminabad Rd; dishes ₹55-95; ⊙11am-12.30am) Tucked away down a small street in the bustling Aminabad district, this renowned, 100-year-old kebab shop serves up delicious plates of mutton biryani, kebabs and tandoori chicken. The mutton kebab here is impossibly delicious. Consider coming along early to give yourself time for a wander around the bazaar here, a prime location for picking up *chikan* (delicately embroidered muslin cloth). Rickshaw riders know how to find this place. You'll find other Tunday kebab restaurants around the city, some of which are franchises, most of which are copies.

Moti Mahal Restaurant
INDIAN $$

(75 MG Rd; mains ₹50-150; ⊙11am-11pm) If Mughlai meat country has got you down, seek refuge in popular veg hideway on MG Rd. It's perfect for a late breakfast (best *poori sabji* we had in UP!) or lunch. Come evening, head upstairs for more-refined dining in the good-quality, low-lit air-con restaurant. You could do worse than try

LUCKNOW'S KEBABS DECONSTRUCTED

Kakori Kebab

Originates from Kakori, a small town outside Lucknow. Legend has it that the old and toothless Nawab of Kakori asked his royal *bawarchi* (chef) to make kebabs that would simply melt in the mouth. So these kebabs are made adding papaya as a tenderiser to raw mincemeat and a mix of spices. They are then applied to skewers and barbecued over charcoals.

Galawat Kebab

This is the mouth-watering creation that is served up in Lucknow's most famous kebab restaurant, Tunday Kababi. There it is simply referred to as a mutton kebab, and in other restaurants it is often called Tunday. *Galawat* is the name of the tenderiser that's used for these kebabs. Essentially, they are the same as Kakori kebabs except that rather than being barbecued they are made into patties and shallow fried in oil or ghee. It also comes in a beef version, a rarity in India.

Shami Kebab

Raw mincemeat is boiled with spices and black gram lentil. It is then ground on stone before being mixed with finely chopped onions, coriander leaves and green chillies and shaped into patties and then shallow fried.

the Lucknow *dum aloo* (potatoes stuffed with nuts and paneer in a tomato-based sauce) but it's all excellent.

Royal Cafe
MUGHLAI $$

(51 MG Rd; chaat from ₹35, mains ₹135-285; ⊙11am-11pm) Even if you don't step inside this excellent restaurant, don't miss its exceedingly popular *chaat* (spicy snack) stand at the front where mixed *chaat* are served in an *aloo* (potato) basket or in mini *puris*. Inside you can dine on an extensive menu of fine Mughlai cuisine, mouth-watering kebabs, Chinese and even pizza. Our *murg mirch masala* (chicken in a spicy coconut and poppyseed tomato gravy) was perfect.

Oudhyana
MUGHLAI, NORTH INDIAN $$$

(www.vivantabytaj.com; Vivanta by Taj Hotel, Vipin Khand, Gomti Nagar; mains ₹550-900) If you want to savor the flavors of the Nawabs performing at their culinary best, look no further than Oudhyana, where chef Nagendra Singh gives Lucknow's famous Awadh cuisine its royal due at the signature restaurant inside the city's top hotel. The flavors of everything Singh does, from the famous *galawat* and *kakori* kebabs to an entire menu of long-lost heritage dishes, unravel like an intricate gastronomic spy novel in your mouth. The intimate room is impossibly striking as well, dressed up in soothing baby blues with chandelier accoutrements. A special night out.

Falaknuma
MUGHLAI, NORTH INDIAN $$$

(Hotel Clarks Avadh, 8 MG Rd; mains ₹230-460; ⊙12.30-3pm & 8-11.30pm) The stylish rooftop dining room of the upmarket Clarks Avadh Hotel has fabulous bird's-eye views and serves up sumptuous Nawab cuisine, including the famous kebabs and an outstanding list of rich, vibrant curries. There's a small bar area (beer from ₹250) if you just want to enjoy the views; or even use the ultra-clean bathroom, which offers death-by-lemon-verbena, a welcomed demise.

🍷 Drinking & Nightlife

Cafe Coffee Day
CAFE

(www.cafecoffeeday.com; 31/82 MG Marg; coffee from ₹53; ⊙9am-11pm) Our favourite Indian coffee chain – known as CCD by locals – sits in prime position at the beginning of MG Rd's upscale shopping district.

Strokes Sports Bar
BAR

(Capoor's Hotel, MG Rd; ⊙11am-11pm Sun-Fri, to midnight Sat) With metallic decor, zebra-print chairs, ultraviolet lights and a backlit bar, this must be one of the strangest places in India to come to watch the latest cricket match on TV. Set it all to an international, pop-heavy soundtrack and the results are surreal. Even the middle-modern Indian ladies go, albeit in smaller numbers. Good times.

Tashna Bar
BAR

(Sapru Marg, Hotel Gomti; ⊙noon-11pm Mon-Fri, to midnight Sat & Sun) Has the usual AC bar with little atmosphere found in many hotels, but with the added attraction of a beer garden on a well-tended lawn.

 ## Shopping

Lucknow is famous for *chikan*, an embroidered cloth worn by men and women. It is sold in a number of shops in the bazaars near Tunday Kebab, in the maze of streets in Chowk and in the small, traffic-free Janpath Market, just south of MG Rd in Hazratganj.

Sugandhco   PERFUME
(www.sugandhco.com; D-4 Janpath Market; ⊙ noon-7.30pm Mon-Sat) A family business since 1850, the sweet-scented Sugandhco sells attar (pure essence oil extracted from flowers by a traditional method) in the form of women's perfume and men's cologne as well as incense sticks.

Ram Advani Bookshop   BOOKS
(Mayfair Bldg, MG Rd; ⊙ 10am-7.30pm Mon-Sat) This Lucknow institution is worth visiting just to meet the fantastically friendly and exceedingly knowledgeable owner, Mr Advani (in his 90s!). Be aware, though, that he takes his siestas very seriously and is rarely seen between noon and 4pm. There's a strong collection of books on Lucknow history here as well as some popular India-based contemporary literature.

ⓘ Information

INTERNET ACCESS
Cyber Cafe (Buddha Rd; per hr ₹20; ⊙ 8am-10pm) If you need to check in while waiting on a train, this small cyber cafe is nearby.

EMERGENCY
Tourist Police (⊙ 6am-10pm) This helpful branch of the tourist police doubles as a tourist information centre. It's just inside the lobby at Charbagh Station.

MEDICAL SERVICES
Balrampur District Hospital (Hospital Rd)

MONEY
Foreign-friendly ATMs are dotted around Hazratganj. There's also one at the train station and the airport.
ICICI Bank (Shalimar Tower, 31/54 MG Rd, Hazratganj; ⊙ 8am-8pm Mon-Fri, 9am-2pm Sat) Changes travellers cheques (Monday to Friday only, 10am to 5pm) and cash, and has an ATM.

POST
Main Post Office (www.indiapost.gov.in; MG Rd; ⊙ 10am-4pm Mon-Sat) Grand Raj-era architecture.

TOURIST INFORMATION
UP Tourism (www.up-tourism.com; 6 Tej Bahadur, Sapru Marg; ⊙ 10am-5.30pm Mon-Sat) Helpful government tourist office, which also runs Lucknow's excellent Heritage Walking Tour. It operates a smaller **kiosk** (MG Rd; ⊙ 11am-9pm) on MG Rd's main drag.

ⓘ Getting There & Away

AIR
The new and modern Chaudhary Charan Singh International Airport is 15km southwest of Lucknow. **Jet Airways** (www.jetairways.com; Chaudhary Charan Sungh Airport) is one of a number of airlines that has offices at the airport. Daily flights serving Lucknow include Delhi (from ₹3225), Kolkata (Calcutta; ₹3854), Mumbai (Bombay; ₹5048) and Dubai (from ₹9845).

HANDY TRAINS FROM LUCKNOW (LKO/LJN)

DESTINATION	TRAIN NO & NAME	FARE (₹)	DURATION (HR)	DEPARTURES
Agra	13239 PNBE-Kota Exp	164/446/665 (A)	6	11.55pm
Allahabad	14210 Intercity Exp	253 (B)	4	7.30am
Faizabad	13010 Doon Exp	120/247/610 (A)	2½	8.35am
Gorakhpur	15708 ASR-KIR Exp	146/394/610 (A)	5	12.50am
Jhansi	11016 Kushinagar Exp	150/408/610 (A)	6½	12.40am
Kolkata (Howrah)	13006 ASR-HWH Mail	347/982/1520 (A)	20½	10.50am
Mumbai (CST)**	12533 Pushpak Exp	426/1185/1845 (A)	24	7.45pm
New Delhi	12553 Vaishali Exp	247/662/975 (A)	8	10.25pm
Varanasi	14236 BE-BSB Exp	161/438 (C)	7½	11.15pm

Fares: (A) sleeper/3AC/2AC, (B) AC chair class only, (C) sleeper/3AC, **leaves from Lucknow Junction

BUS

Long-distance buses leave from **Alambagh bus station**, 4km southwest of the town centre. Services include the following:

Agra Non-AC (₹237, seven hours, 5am, 7am and 11pm); Volvo AC (₹772, six hours, 10am and 10pm)

Allahabad Non-AC (₹152, six hours, every 30 minutes); AC (₹412, 4½ hours, 7.45am, 10am, 11.30am, 1pm, 3.15pm, 4.45pm, 6.15pm and 8.30pm)

Faizabad ₹112, three to four hours, every 30 minutes

Gorakhpur Non-AC (₹230, seven hours, hourly); AC (₹630, seven hours, 10am, 9pm, 10pm and 11pm)

Jhansi ₹242, eight hours, 6am, 7.30am, 6.15pm, 7.15pm, 8.30pm and 10.30pm

Varanasi Non-AC (₹250, seven hours, hourly); Volvo AC (₹623, seven hours, 8am, 3pm and 10pm)

Regular local buses (₹5) run to Alambagh bus station from the road in front of **Charbagh bus stand** (Kanpor Rd at Subhash Marg), near the train station.

Kaiserbagh bus stand (J Narain Rd) also has hourly services to Faizabad (₹102) and Gorakhphur (₹210) as well as buses to Rupaidha (₹136, seven hours, 9.30am, 11am, 7.30pm, 8.30pm, 9.30pm and 10.30pm), a rickshaw ride away from the rarely used Nepal border crossing of Jamunaha.

TRAIN

The two main stations, Charbagh and Lucknow Junction, are side by side. Services for most major destinations leave from Charbagh, including several daily to Agra, Varanasi, Faizabad, Gorakhpur and New Delhi. Lucknow Junction handles the one daily train to Mumbai. Foreign traveller help is at window 601 inside the Computerized Reservation complex just off to your right as you exit Charbagh.

❶ Getting Around

TO/FROM THE AIRPORT

An autorickshaw to the airport in Amausi from the prepaid taxi stand outside the train station costs ₹120 and takes about 30 minutes.

LOCAL TRANSPORT

A short cycle-rickshaw ride is ₹20. From the prepaid autorickshaw stand outside the train station (no English sign – look for the small blue booth with a sign reading 'G.R.P.' on top), a trip to the Residency costs about ₹100, as does Bara Imambara. Hazratganj and Mall Ave are ₹65. A half-day (four-hour) autorickshaw tour covering all the main sights costs ₹250. Prices do not include a ₹5 booking fee.

Ayodhya

☑ 05278 / POP 58,000

With monkeys galore, the usual smattering of cows and even the odd working elephant, the relatively traffic-free streets of Ayodhya would be an intriguing place to spend some time even if it wasn't for the religious significance of the place. This is not only the birthplace of Rama, and as such one of Hinduism's seven holy cities, nor just the birthplace of four of Jainism's 24 *tirthankars* (religious teachers), this is also the site of one of modern India's most controversial religious disputes.

Ayodhya became tragically synonymous with Hindu extremism in 1992, when rioting Hindus tore down the Babri Masjid, a mosque built by the Mughals in the 15th century, which Hindus claimed stood on the site of an earlier Rama temple, marking Lord Rama's birthplace. Hindus built Ram Janam Bhumi in its place. Tit-for-tat reprisals soon followed, including reactionary riots across the country that led to more than 2000 deaths, and the problem eventually reached the High Court. Archaeological investigations were carried out at the site and, in September 2010, the Allahabad High Court ruled that the site should be split equally between three religious groups; two Hindu, one Muslim. The Muslim group, Sunni Waqf Board, appealed parts of the ruling but the Supreme Court of India ruled in favor of the Allahabad ruling in 2011. Since the verdict, things have remained relatively calm. Meanwhile, security around the Ram Janam Bhumi remains incredibly tight.

The slightly larger town of Faizabad, 7km away, is the jumping-off point for Ayodhya and where you'll find more accommodation. From the Faizabad bus stand, turn left onto the main road where you'll find tempos (₹12, 20 minutes) to Ayodhya, where you can make a walking tour of the temples.

◉ Sights

Hanumangarhi TEMPLE
(☉dawn-dusk) This is one of the town's most popular temples, and is the closest of the major temples here to the main road. Walk up the 76 steps to the ornate carved gateway and the fortresslike outer walls, and join the throng inside offering *prasad* (temple-blessed food).

Dashrath Bhavan TEMPLE

(⊙dawn-dusk) A further 200m up the side road from Hanumangarhi, this temple is approached through a colourful entrance-way. The atmosphere inside is peaceful, with musicians playing and orange-clad sadhus reading scriptures.

Kanak Bhavan TEMPLE

(Palace of Gold; ⊙8.30-noon & 4.30-8pm) A few minutes' walk straight on from Dashrath Bhavan is this impressive, ancient but often rebuilt palace-cum-temple.

Ram Janam Bhumi TEMPLE

(⊙7-11am & 3-6pm) If you turn left at Dashrath Bhavan, when coming from Hanumangarhi, you soon reach the highly contentious temple that marks the birthplace of Rama. Security here is staggering (think crossing from West Bank into Israel!). You must first show your passport then leave all belongings apart from your passport and money (even your belt!) in nearby lockers. You are then searched several times before being accompanied through a caged corridor that leads to a spot 20m away from a makeshift tent of a shrine, which marks Rama's birthplace.

Ramkatha Museum MUSEUM

(☎9452172060; ⊙10.30am-4.30pm Tue-Sun, performances 6-9pm) FREE A 10-minute walk on the other side of the main road from the temples in this area brings you to Ramkatha Museum, a large, unsigned in English yellow-and-red building with paintings and ancient sculptures. Every evening except Monday the museum hosts free performances of the Ram Lila (a dramatic re-enactment of the battle between Lord Ram and Ravan, as described in the Hindu epic, the Ramayana). Walk about 500m or so along the main road deeper into Ayodhya, turn right at the police station across from Akash Cycle Company, and it's another 500m or so on your right.

🍴 Sleeping & Eating

Hotel Shane Avadh HOTEL $

(☎223586; shane_avadh@yahoo.com; Civil Lines, Faizabad; s/d from ₹600/700, without bathroom from ₹350/400, with AC from ₹990/1300; ❋) There's a huge range of rooms at this well-run establishment in Faizabad, and even the cheapest ones are neat and spacious, if a little basic. There's also a good restaurant (mains ₹70 to ₹170). This place is popular so try to book ahead.

Hotel Krishna Palace HOTEL $

(☎221367; hotelkrishnapalace@gmail.com; Faizabad; s/d from ₹500/700, with AC from ₹990/1250, restaurant mains ₹70-200, bar beer ₹90; ❋) If Shane Avadh is full, this lowlit white monolith of a hotel is a decent alternative in Faizabad. Also has a moody restaurant and a small basement bar.

★ Awantika MULTICUISINE $

(Civil Lines, Faizabad; mains ₹75-170; ⊙11am-10.30pm) Clean and hip, this out-of-place restaurant does a seriously good all-veg menu that runs the gamut from Chinese to Italian to Indian. The special thali (₹165) was a real treat and it's all set to trendy tunes in a funky lounge atmosphere.

❶ Information

There's an HDFC Bank ATM 100m from Hotel Krishna Palace. **Cyber Zone** (Civil Lines, Faizabad; per hr ₹20; ⊙10am-8.30pm) is an internet cafe just past Hotel Shane Avadh.

❶ Getting There & Away

From Faizabad bus stand, buses run to Lucknow (₹112, three hours), Gorakhpur (₹124, five hours) and Allahabad (₹127, five hours) every 15 to 20 minutes.

Daily trains include Lucknow (13307 Gangas-utlej Express, sleeper/3AC/2AC ₹120/247/610, four hours, 10.55am), Varanasi (13010 Doon Express, sleeper/3AC/2AC ₹120/317/610, five hours, 11.10am) and Delhi (14205 Faizabad-Delhi Express, ₹252/703/1065, 12 hours, 9.30pm).

A cycle-rickshaw from the bus stand to the train station is ₹20.

Allahabad

📞0532 / POP 1.2 MILLION

For all its importance in Hindu mythology, Indian history and modern politics, Allahabad is a surprisingly relaxed city that offers plenty in terms of sights, but little in the way of in-yer-face hassle.

Brahma, the Hindu god of creation, is believed to have landed on earth in Allahabad, or Prayag as it was originally known, and to have called it the king of all pilgrimage centres. Indeed, Sangam, a river confluence on the outskirts of the city, is the most celebrated of India's four Kumbh Mela locations. The vast riverbanks here attract tens of millions of pilgrims every six years for either the Kumbh Mela or the Ardh (Half) Mela, but every year there is a smaller Magh Mela.

Of more immediate interest to casual visitors are Allahabad's grand Raj-era buildings, its Mughal fort and tombs, and the historic legacy of the Nehru family.

Allahabad's Civil Lines is a district of broad avenues, Raj-era bungalows, hotels, restaurants and coffee shops. The Civil Lines bus stand – the main bus terminal – is also here. This area is divided from Chowk, the crowded, older part of town, by the railway line. Sangam is 4km southeast of the city centre.

⊙ Sights & Activities

★ Sangam
SACRED SITE

This is the particularly auspicious point where two of India's holiest rivers, the Ganges and the Yamuna, meet one of Hinduism's mythical rivers, the Saraswati. All year round, pilgrims row boats out to this holy spot, but their numbers increase dramatically during the annual **Magh Mela** (Allahabad; ⊙ Jan-Mar), a six-week festival held between January and March, which culminates in six communal 'holy dips'. Every 12 years the massive **Kumbh Mela** takes place here, attracting millions of people, while the **Ardh Mela** (Half Mela) is held here every six years.

In the early 1950s, 350 pilgrims were killed in a stampede to the soul-cleansing water (an incident re-created vividly in Vikram Seth's immense novel *A Suitable Boy*). The last Ardh Mela, in 2007, attracted more than 70 million people – considered to be the largest-ever human gathering until the 2013 Kumbh Mela, which attracted a guestimated 32 million on Mauni Amavasya, the main bathing day, and 100 million across the 55-day festival; expect equally astonishing numbers at the next Allahabad Kumbh Mela in 2025.

Old boat hands will row you out to the sacred confluence for around ₹15 per person (hard-bargaining Indian) or ₹50 (hard-bargaining foreigner), or ₹400 to ₹500 per boat.

Around the corner from Sangam (skirt the riverbank around the front of Akbar's Fort) are the **Saraswati** and **Nehru Ghats**, home to a nightly *aarti* (an auspicious lighting of lamps/candles).

★ Akbar's Fort & Patalpuri Temple
FORT

(Patalpuri temple admission by donation; ⊙ Patalpuri temple 7am-5pm) Built by the Mughal Emperor Akbar, this 16th-century fort on the northern bank of the Yamuna has massive walls with three gateways flanked by towers. Most of it is occupied by the Indian army

and cannot be visited, but a small door in the eastern wall by Sangam leads to one part you can enter, the underground Patalpuri Temple. This unique temple is crowded with all sorts of idols – pick up some coins from the change dealers outside so you can leave small offerings as you go. You may be pressured into giving ₹10 to ₹100 at some shrines. A few coins are perfectly acceptable.

Outside the temple – though its roots can be seen beneath ground – is the **Undying Banyan Tree** from which pilgrims used to leap to their deaths, believing it would liberate them from the cycle of rebirth.

★ Khusru Bagh
PARK

(Mughal tombs admission free; ⊙ Mughal tombs dawn-dusk) This intriguing park, surrounded by huge walls, contains four highly impressive **Mughal tombs**. One is that of **Prince Khusru**, the eldest son of Emperor Jehangir, who tried to assassinate his father but was blinded and imprisoned, finally dying in 1622. If Khusru's coup had succeeded, his brother, Shah Jahan, would not have become emperor and the Taj Mahal would not exist.

A second tomb belongs to **Shah Begum**, Khusru's mother (Jehangir's first wife), who committed suicide in 1603 with an opium overdose because of the ongoing feud between her son and his father. Between these two, a third, particularly attractive tomb was constructed by **Nesa Begum**, Khusru's sister, although was never actually used as a tomb. A smaller structure, called **Tamolon's Tomb**, stands to the west of the others, but its origin is unknown.

★ Anand Bhavan
MUSEUM

(Indian/foreigner ₹10/50; ⊙ 9.30am-5pm Tue-Sun) This picturesque two-storey building is a shrine to the Nehru family, which has

DIP DATES

The following are the auspicious bathing dates for upcoming mela to be held at Sangam in Allahabad.

2014	2015	2016	2017
14 Jan	5 Jan	15 Jan	12 Jan
16 Jan	14 Jan	24 Jan	14 Jan
30 Jan	20 Jan	8 Feb	27 Jan
4 Feb	24 Jan	12 Feb	1 Feb
14 Feb	3 Feb	22 Feb	10 Feb
28 Feb	17 Feb	7 Mar	24 Feb

Allahabad

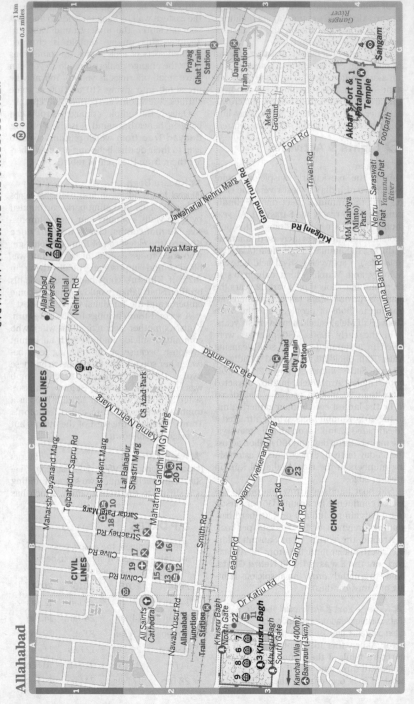

0 1 km
0 0.5 miles

POLICE LINES

CIVIL LINES

CHOWK

Ganges River

Sangam 4

Akbar's Fort & 1 Patalpuri Temple

Footpath

Nehru Saraswati Ghat
Ghat Yamuna Ghat
Yamuna Bank Rd River

MM Malviya (Minto) Park

Triveni Rd

Fort Rd

Mela Ground

Daraganj Train Station

Prayag Ghat Train Station

Kidganj Rd

Grand Trunk Rd

Jawaharlal Nehru Marg

Malviya Marg

2 Anand Bhavan

Allahabad University

Motilal Nehru Rd

Lala Stranm Rd

Allahabad City Train Station

CS Azad Park

Kamla Nehru Marg

5

Maharshi Dayanand Marg

Tejbahadur Sapru Rd

Tashkent Marg

Lal Bahadur Shastri Marg

Sardar Patel Marg

18 10

Strachey Rd 14

16

17

15

19

13 12

Clive Rd

Colvin Rd

Mahatma Gandhi (MG) Marg

20 21

Swami Vivekenand Marg

Smith Rd

Leader Rd

Zero Rd

23

Grand Trunk Rd

All Saints Cathedral

Nawab Yusuf Rd

Allahabad Junction Train Station

Dr Katju Rd

Khusru Bagh North Gate

22 11

3 Khusru Bagh

Khusru Bagh South Gate

9 8 6 7

Kanchan Villa (400m);
Bamrauli (13km)

Allahabad

produced five generations of leading politicians from Motilal Nehru to the latest political figure, Rahul Gandhi. This stately home is where Mahatma Gandhi, Jawaharlal Nehru and others successfully planned the overthrow of the British Raj. It is full of books, personal effects and photos from those stirring times. Indira Gandhi was married here in 1942. The run-down Swaraj Bhaven next door is where former Prime Minister Indira Gandhi was born.

Allahabad Museum   MUSEUM
(Kamla Nehru Marg; Indian/foreigner ₹5/100; ⊙10.30am-4.45pm Tue-Sun) This extensive museum in the grounds of a pleasant park has archaeological and Nehru family items, modern paintings, miniatures and ancient sculptures.

⌂ Sleeping

Many of Allahabad's hotels got a major makeover for the 2013 Kumbh Mela, so expect better-than-average conditions across the board.

Royal Hotel   HOTEL $
(☑2427201; royalhotel.666@rediffmail.com; Nawab Yusef Rd; dm ₹200, s/d from ₹450/650; @ ☎) This wonderful old building above a small bustling market near the train station used to be royal stables but was converted into a hotel by the king of Kalakankar, a former princely state, after he was refused entry into a British-run hotel nearby. It's basic and very run down, but has bags of character and is foreign-traveller at the ready. The rooms (with 6m-high ceilings) and their bathrooms are absolutely enormous.

Hotel Prayag   HOTEL $
(☑2656416; Noorullah Rd; s/d from ₹300/450, without bathroom ₹225/275, with AC ₹900/990; ❄@☎) A stone's throw south of the train station, this sprawling, well-run place is helpful and boasts an internet cafe (per hour ₹20), an ATM and a funky restaurant on the premises. There's a wide variety of old-fashioned, basic rooms but staff are friendly and will even help negotiate autorickshaws. The downside of the wi-fi is it works in the lobby cafe only, the upside is they don't seem overly concerned about charging for it.

★ **Kanchan Villa**   HOMESTAY $$
(☑983863111; www.allahabadbnb.com; 64, Lukerganj; s/d ₹2250/2750, apt ₹4250, all incl breakfast; ❄@☎) Ivan, a single malt connoisseur, and his wife, Purnima, are your South Indian Christian hosts at this fabulous homestay that offers a window into a rarely seen side of Indian culture. In a historic home pushing 90 years old, the five rooms are decked out with period furnishings (Bengali is the best) and breakfast is on a lush, 2nd-floor patio. They'll cook for you as well, serving up fresh kebabs from the outdoor tandoor, for example, and you'll feel right at home in the living room/bar. Pickup and drops-offs included; otherwise it's a short ₹20 cycle-rickshaw ride from the train station.

Hotel Valentines
HOTEL $$

(2560030; www.hotelvalentines.com; 7/3/2A Clive Rd; r incl breakfast from ₹2500; ❄️ 🛜) Not as romantic as the name suggests, but smart, comfortable rooms have TV, AC, carpeted floors and big bathrooms with towels and toiletries provided.

Grand Continental
HOTEL $$$

(2260631; www.birhotel.com; Sardar Patel Marg; s/d from ₹3935/5058, ste ₹7306, all incl breakfast; ❄️@🛜🏊) Go for the 17 newer standard rooms on the pool side, with rust-sunset curtains and wildly contrasting, brightly colored bathrooms, and you're getting a bangup room as nice as some five-stars for a fraction of the price. Staying here means you can also use the delightful swimming pool, housed in a beautiful open-air marble courtyard. There's also a good-quality restaurant and a bar where evening *ghazal* performances are held. Wi-fi is free. It's across the street from the modern Vinayak City Centre shopping mall.

✗ Eating

Shahenshah
INDIAN $

(18/A MG Marg; mains ₹40-115; ⊙11am-10pm) Watch young chefs frying up their creations from a couple of stalls set around a half open-air seating area with plastic tables and chairs and a high corrugated iron roof. This is no-nonsense, cheap eating, but it's popular with the locals so there's a nice atmosphere. The menu includes *uttapam, paratha* (flaky bread made with ghee and cooked on a hot-plate), a few Chinese dishes, pizza and some absolutely cracking dosa. The fruit beer isn't alcoholic. Don't miss it!

Indian Coffee House
CAFE $

(15 MG Marg; coffee from ₹18, mains ₹20-45; ⊙8am-9pm) Rickshaw drivers call this large, airy 50-year-old coffee hall simply 'Coffee House' (like the French call them fries). It's a top choice for a budget breakfast, with waiters in fan-tailed headgear serving up delicious South Indian fare – dosa, *idli, uttapam* – as well as eggs, omelettes and toast. The annex closest to the road is often closed, but the main building set back from the street should be open.

Kamdhenu Sweets
SWEETS $

(MG Marg; snacks ₹10-70; ⊙9.30am-10pm) Very popular snack shop selling delicious home-baked sweets (from ₹320 per box) as well as cakes, samosas, sandwiches and ice cream.

★ El Chico
MULTICUISINE $$

(24 MG Marg; mains ₹165-375; ⊙9am-11pm) The refined original restaurant serves up absolutely wonderful Indian (the chicken chilli garlic kebab is every bit as delicious as it sounds), tasty-looking Chinese and Continental fare along with coffee in pewter carafes. Next door, **El Chico Cafe** (24/28 MG Marg; items ₹12-425; ⊙10am-11pm; 🛜) tempts diners downstairs with takeaway ice creams, cakes, cookies and savoury snacks; and upstairs, a shockingly chic fusion cafe that's wildly but thankfully out of place. Here, you'll cure your homesick in a heartbeat among a forward-thinking Indian crowd. Think big breakfasts (cinnamon pancakes, waffles, bacon and egg pizza and espresso); and paninis, wood-fired pizzas and more sophisticated fusion fare throughout the day.

🍷 Drinking & Nightlife

Patiyala Peg Bar
BAR

(Grand Continental Hotel, Sardar Patel Marg; ⊙11am-11pm) The most interesting bar for tourists has live *ghazal* music nightly from 7pm to 10.30pm

HANDY TRAINS FROM ALLAHABAD (ALD)

DESTINATION	TRAIN NO & NAME	FARE (₹)	DURATION (HR)	DEPARTURES
Agra	12403 ALD MTJ Exp	220/582/855 (A)	7½	11.30pm
Kolkata (Howrah)	12312 Kalka Mail	318/872/1315 (A)	14	5.30pm
Lucknow	14209 ALD-LKO Intercity	253 (B)	4½	3.20pm
New Delhi	12559 Shiv Ganga Exp	277/750/1115 (A)	9	10.30pm
Satna	13201 RJPB LTT EXP	120/298/610 (A)	4½	8.25am
Varanasi	15017 Gorakhpur Exp	120/252/610 (A)	4	8.35am

Fares: (A) sleeper/3AC/2AC, (B) AC chair only

ⓘ Information

ATMs dot the Civil Lines area.

A23 Sewa Cyber Cafe (18/A MG Marg; per hr ₹20; ⊘10am-9pm) Inside the Shahenshah restaurant complex.

Apollo Clinic (28B MG Marg; ⊘24hr) A modern private medical facility/24-hour pharmacy.

Post Office (www.indiapost.gov.in; Sarojini Naidu Marg; ⊘9am-1.30pm & 2-4pm Mon-Sat)

UP Tourism (www.up-tourism.com; 35 MG Marg; ⊘10am-5pm Mon-Sat) At the Rahi Ilawart Tourist Bungalow. Very helpful.

ⓘ Getting There & Away

AIR

Allahabad Airport is 15km west of Allahabad. **Air India** (www.airindia.com) has daily flights to Delhi from ₹3239, except on Sunday some months of the year. An autorickshaw to the airport costs ₹350 to ₹400 and taxis ₹600.

BUS

From the **Civil Lines bus stand** (MG Marg) regular non-AC buses run to Varanasi (₹109, 3½ hours, every 15 minutes), Faizabad (₹130, five hours, every 30 minutes) and Gorakhpur (₹216, eight hours, every 30 minutes). There are 19 comfortable AC buses running to Lucknow (₹412, five hours, 5.30am to 8.30pm) daily. To get to Delhi or Agra, change in Lucknow, or take a train.

For buses to Chitrakut every two hours (₹101, four hours, 6am to 10pm), head to **Zero Road bus stand** (Zero Rd).

TRAIN

Allahabad Junction is the main station. A few daily trains run to Lucknow, Varanasi, Delhi, Agra and Kolkata. Frequent trains also run to Satna, from where you can catch buses to Khajuraho.

ⓘ Getting Around

Cycle-rickshaws (₹10 for a short trip of 1km to 2km but be prepared to go to war for it) are plentiful. The train station is your best bet for autorickshaws. A return autorickshaw to Sangam should cost around ₹200. Consider hiring one for half a day (₹400, four hours) to take in more of the sights. *Vikrams* (large shared autorickshaws) hang about on the south side of the train station. Destinations include Zero Road Bus Stand (₹8) and Sangam (₹16).

Chitrakut

🕿 05198 / POP 49,000

Known as a mini Varanasi because of its many temples and ghats, this small, peaceful town on the banks of the River Mandakini is the stuff of Hindu legends. It is here that Hinduism's principal trinity – Brahma, Vishnu and Shiva – took on their incarnations. It is also the place where Lord Rama is believed to have spent 11½ years of his 14-year exile after being banished from his birthplace in Ayodhya at the behest of a jealous stepmother.

Today Chitrakut attracts throngs of pilgrims, giving the area a strong religious quality, particularly by Ram Ghat, the town's centre of activity, and at the holy hill of Kamadgiri, 2km away.

Dozens, sometimes hundreds, of devotees descend onto **Ram Ghat** to take holy dips at dawn before returning at the end of the day for the evening *aarti*. Colourful **rowboats** (with rabbits!) wait here to take you across to the opposite bank (₹20), which is actually in Madhya Pradesh, or to scenic spots along the river. The 2km-trip to the **Glass Temple** (₹100 return per person, ₹300 minimum), a building covered in religious mosaics made with thousands of pieces of coloured glass, is popular. During the day, many people make their way to **Kamadgiri** (₹5 by tempo), a hill revered as the holy embodiment of Lord Rama. A 5km-circuit (90 minutes) around the base of the hill takes you past prostrating pilgrims, innumerable monkeys and temples galore.

The most enjoyable place to stay in Chitrakut is **Pitra Smiviti Vishramgrah** (🕿9450223214; varun.ckt@gmail.com; Ram Ghat; r ₹300-500, without bathroom ₹200). Rooms built just in front of Bada Math, a 300-year-old red-stone palace, are very basic, but lead out onto a huge shared balcony overlooking Ram Ghat. Look for the word 'Lodge' painted on the balcony. There are more comfortable rooms at **UP Tourist Bungalow** (rahitbchitrakoot@up-tourism.com; dm ₹150, s/d with AC from ₹900/950; ▣), which also has a distinctly average **restaurant** (mains ₹35-130; ⊘6am-midnight), but Chitrakot isn't exactly a culinary hotspot.

Shared minivans and tempos ply the 10km route from the train station to Ram Ghat (₹10), passing the bus stand (2km from the train station) and the UP Tourist Bungalow (1km before Ram Ghat).

With the exception of buses to Allahabad (₹95, four hours, every 30 minutes 5am to 9.30pm), buses in Chitrakut are notoriously unreliable. There *should* be three per day to Varanasi (₹190, eight hours, noon, 12.30pm and 1pm) but they don't always materialise –

you're better off changing in Allahabad. There are no bus services to Khajuraho.

Trains tend to pass through Chitrakut at stupid o'clock. Ones you may consider anyway: Agra (12189 Mahakaushal Express, sleeper/3AC/2AC ₹226/598/885, nine hours, 11pm), Varanasi (11107 Bundelkhand Express, ₹143/385/610, seven hours, 3.35am) and Khajuraho (21108 BSB-KURJ Link E, sleeper/3AC ₹120/308, four hours, 1.01am Tuesday, Thursday and Sunday).

Jhansi

This nondescript town is in fact in Uttar Pradesh. The town is famous for its link to the Rani of Jhansi, a key player in the 1857 War of Independence, and it is commonly used as a gateway to Orchha, Khajuraho and Gwalior. If you're here, check out **Jhansi Fort** (Indian/foreigner ₹5/100, video ₹25; ☉ dawn-dusk), built in 1613 by Maharaja Bir Singh Deo of Orchha.

Madhya Pradesh Tourism (www.mptourism.com; ☉ 10am-5pm) has an information centre on Platform 1 at the train station, which can make real-time hotel reservations in Khajuraho and Orchha.

🍴 Sleeping & Eating

There are a number of cheap places around the bus station where you can grab a snack on the run and a great multicuisine restaurant at Hotel Samrat.

Hotel Samrat   HOTEL **$**
(☎ 05102444943; Elite Rd; s/d from ₹600/675, with AC from ₹1250/1400; ❄) Worsening for wear but friendly and well-run, this hotel, walking distance from the train station, will do for a night. All rooms have TV and bathroom although the cheaper ones have squat toilets. There's no beer in Red Tomato, the hotel's excellent restaurant, but they will serve you in your room.

ℹ Getting There & Away

BUS
Buses leave from the bus stand for Khajuraho (₹119, five to six hours, 11.30am, 3pm and 7.30pm); Chitrakut (₹195, three hours, 8am); and Gwalior (₹105, three hours, 6.30am, 7.15am, 12.30pm, 2pm, 3.30pm, 5.30pm, 6.30pm and 8.30pm).

TRAIN
Several daily trains run to Gwalior, Agra and Delhi and there's a thrice-weekly fast train to Khajuraho.

Varanasi

☑ 0542 / POP 1.4 MILLION

Brace yourself. You're about to enter one of the most blindingly colourful, unrelentingly chaotic and unapologetically indiscreet places on earth. Varanasi takes no prisoners. But if you're ready for it, this may just turn out to be your favourite stop of all.

Also known at various times in history as Kashi (City of Life) and Benares, this is one of the world's oldest continually inhabited cities and is regarded as one of Hinduism's seven holy cities. Pilgrims come to the ghats lining the River Ganges here to wash away a lifetime of sins in the sacred waters or to cremate their loved ones. It's a particularly auspicious place to die, since expiring here offers moksha (liberation from the cycle of birth and death), making Varanasi the beating heart of the Hindu universe. Most visitors agree it's a magical place, but it's not for the faint-hearted. Here the most intimate rituals of life and death take place in public and the sights, sounds and smells in and around the ghats – not to mention the almost constant attention from touts.– can be overwhelming. Persevere. Varanasi is unique, and a walk along the ghats or a boat ride on the river will live long in the memory.

HANDY TRAINS FROM JHANSI (JHS)

DESTINATION	TRAIN NO & NAME	FARE (₹) (SLEEPER/3AC/2AC)	DURATION (HR)	DEPARTURE
Agra	12137 Punjab Mail	147/368/640	3½	2.30pm
Delhi	12615 Grand Trunk Exp	204/538/790	6½	11.42pm
Gwalior	12137 Punjab Mail	140/249/640	1½	2.30pm
Mumbai	12138 Punjab Mail	379/1047/1610	19	12.35pm
Varanasi	11107 Bundelkhand Exp	229/638/1215	12½	10.30pm

The old city of Varanasi is situated along the western bank of the Ganges and extends back from the riverbank ghats in a labyrinth of alleys called *galis* that are too narrow for traffic. They can be disorienting, but the popular hotels and restaurants are usually signposted and, however lost you become, you will eventually end up at a ghat and get your bearings. You can walk all the way along the ghats, apart from during and immediately after the monsoon, when the river level is too high.

Most places of interest, and much of the accommodation, are in the old city. Behind the station is the peaceful Cantonment area, home to most of the top-end hotels.

History

Thought to date back to around 1200 BC, Varanasi really rose to prominence in the 8th century AD, when Shankaracharya, a reformer of Hinduism, established Shiva worship as the principal sect. The Afghans destroyed Varanasi around AD 1300, after laying waste to nearby Sarnath, but the fanatical Mughal emperor Aurangzeb was the most destructive, looting and destroying almost all of the temples. The old city of Varanasi may look antique, but few buildings are more than a couple of hundred years old.

◉ Sights

★ Ghats   GHATS

Spiritually enlightening and fantastically photogenic, Varanasi is at its brilliant best by the ghats, the long stretch of steps leading down to the water on the western bank of the Ganges. Most are used for bathing but there are also several 'burning ghats' where bodies are cremated in public. The main one is Manikarnika: you'll often see funeral processions threading their way through the backstreets to this ghat. The best time to visit the ghats is at dawn when the river is bathed in a mellow light as pilgrims come to perform *puja* to the rising sun, and at sunset when the main *ganga aarti* (river worship ceremony) takes place at Dashashwamedh Ghat.

About 80 ghats border the river, but the main group extends from Assi Ghat, near the university, northwards to Raj Ghat, near the road and rail bridge.

A boat trip along the river provides the perfect introduction, although for most of the year the water level is low enough for you to walk freely along the whole length of the ghats. It's a world-class 'people-watching' stroll as you mingle with the fascinating mixture of people who come to the Ganges not only for a ritual bath but also to wash clothes, do yoga, offer blessings, sell flowers, get a massage, play cricket, wash their buffaloes, improve their karma by giving to beggars or simply hang around.

➡ *Southern Stretch*

★ **Assi Ghat** (Map p394), the furthest south of the main ghats, and one of the biggest, is particularly important as the River Assi meets the Ganges near here and pilgrims come to worship a Shiva lingam (phallic image of Shiva) beneath a peepul tree. Evenings are particularly lively, as the ghat's vast concreted area fills up with hawkers and entertainers. It's a popular starting point for boat trips and there are some excellent hotels here.

Nearby **Tulsi Ghat**, named after a 16th-century Hindu poet, has fallen down towards the river but in the month of Kartika (October/November) a festival devoted to Krishna is celebrated here. Next along, **Bachraj Ghat** has three Jain temples. A small Shiva temple and a 19th-century mansion built by Nepali royalty sit back from **Shivala Ghat**, built by the local maharaja of Benares. The **Dandi Ghat** is used by ascetics known as Dandi Panths, and nearby is the very popular **Hanuman Ghat**.

Harishchandra Ghat is a cremation ghat, smaller and secondary in importance to Manikarnika but one of the oldest ghats in Varanasi. Above it, **Kedar Ghat** has a shrine popular with Bengalis and South Indians.

➡ *Old City Stretch*

Varanasi's liveliest and most colourful ghat is **Dashashwamedh Ghat** (Map p394), easily reached at the end of the main road from **Godaulia Crossing**. The name indicates that Brahma sacrificed (*medh*) 10 (*das*) horses (*aswa*) here. In spite of the oppressive boat owners, flower sellers and touts trying to drag you off to a silk shop, it's a wonderful place to linger and people-watch while soaking up the atmosphere. Every evening at 7pm an elaborate *ganga aarti* ceremony with *puja*, fire and dance is staged here.

Just south of here, **Someswar Ghat** (Lord of the Moon Ghat) is said to be able to heal diseases. **Munshi Ghat** is very photogenic,

Varanasi

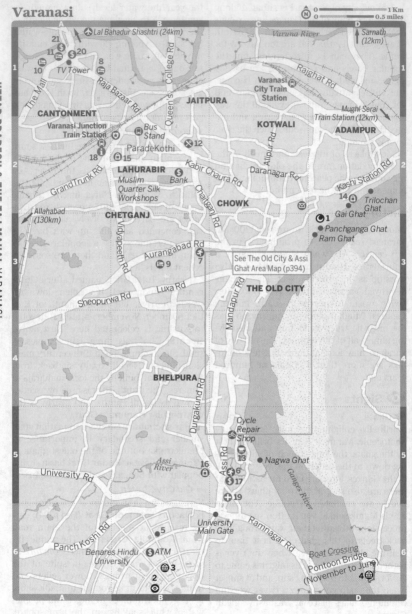

while **Ahalya Bai's Ghat** is named after the female Maratha ruler of Indore.

Just north of Dashashwamedh Ghat, Raja Man Singh's **Man Mandir Ghat** was built in 1600, but was poorly restored in the 19th century. The northern corner of the ghat has a fine stone balcony.

★**Manikarnika Ghat** (Map p394), the main burning ghat, is the most auspicious place for a Hindu to be cremated. Dead bodies are handled by outcasts known as

Varanasi

⊙ Sights

1	Alamgir Mosque	D3
2	Benares Hindu University	B6
3	Bharat Kala Bhavan	B6
4	Ramnagar Fort & Museum	D6

⊙ Activities, Courses & Tours

	Aarna Spa	(see 11)
5	International Centre	B6
6	Kiran	C5
7	Learn for Life Society	B3
	UP Tourism Office	(see 18)

⊙ Sleeping

8	Gateway Hotel Ganges	A1
9	Homestay	B3
10	Hotel Clarks Varanasi	A1
11	Hotel Surya	A1

⊗ Eating

	Canton Royale	(see 11)
12	Eden Restaurant	B2
	Varuna Restaurant	(see 8)

⊙ Drinking & Nightlife

	Mango Verra	(see 11)
13	Open Hand	C5
	Prinsep Bar	(see 8)

⊙ Shopping

14	Mehrotra Silk Factory	D2
15	Mehrotra Silk Factory	B2
16	Shri Gandhi Ashram Khadi	B5

⊙ Information

17	Axis Bank ATM	C5
18	Foreign Tourist Centre	A2
19	Heritage Hospital	C5
20	ICICI Bank ATM	A1
21	State Bank of India	A1
	UP Tourism	(see 18)

doms, and are carried through the alleyways of the old city to the holy Ganges on a bamboo stretcher swathed in cloth. The corpse is doused in the Ganges prior to cremation. Huge piles of firewood are stacked along the top of the ghat; every log is carefully weighed on giant scales so that the price of cremation can be calculated. Each type of wood has its own price, sandalwood being the most expensive. There is an art to using just enough wood to completely incinerate a corpse. You can watch cremations but always show reverence by behaving respectfully. Photography is strictly prohibited.

You're almost guaranteed to be led by a priest, or more likely a guide, to the upper floor of a nearby building from where you can watch cremations taking place, and then asked for a donation (in dollars) towards the cost of wood. If you don't want to make a donation, don't follow them.

Above the steps here is a tank known as the **Manikarnika Well**. Parvati is said to have dropped her earring here and Shiva dug the tank to recover it, filling the depression with his sweat. The **Charanpaduka**, a slab of stone between the well and the ghat, bears footprints made by Vishnu. Privileged VIPs are cremated at the Charanpaduka, which also has a temple dedicated to Ganesh.

Dattatreya Ghat bears the footprint of the Brahmin saint of that name in a small temple nearby. **Scindhia Ghat** was original-ly built in 1830, but was so huge and magnificent that it collapsed into the river and had to be rebuilt.

➡ *Northern Stretch*

Continuing north from Scindhia Ghat, you soon reach **Ram Ghat**, which was built by a maharaja of Jaipur. Just beyond it **Panchganga Ghat**, as its name indicates, is where five rivers are supposed to meet. Dominating the ghat is Aurangzeb's smaller mosque, also known as the **Alamgir Mosque** (Map p390), which he built on the site of a large Vishnu temple. **Gai Ghat** has a figure of a cow made of stone. **Trilochan Ghat** has two turrets emerging from the river, and the water between them is especially holy.

★ **Vishwanath Temple**   HINDU TEMPLE
(Golden Temple; Map p394) There are temples at almost every turn in Varanasi, but this is the most famous of the lot. It is dedicated to Vishveswara – Shiva as lord of the universe. The current temple was built in 1776 by Ahalya Bai of Indore; the 800kg of gold plating on the tower and dome was supplied by Maharaja Ranjit Singh of Lahore 50 years later.

The area is full of soldiers because of security issues and communal tensions. Bags, cameras, mobile phones, pens or any other electronic device must be deposited in lockers (₹20) before you enter the alleyway it's in. Non-Hindus are not allowed inside the temple itself, although this is not always strictly enforced – bring your original passport (not a copy) if you want to enter.

On the northern side of Vishwanath Temple is the **Gyan Kupor Well** (Well of Knowledge). The faithful believe drinking its water leads to a higher spiritual plane, though they are prevented from doing so by a strong security screen. Non-Hindus are also not allowed to enter here, and here the rule is enforced more strictly.

Benares Hindu University   HISTORIC SITE
(BHU; Map p390; www.bhu.ac.in) Long regarded as a centre of learning, Varanasi's tradition of top-quality education continues today at Benares Hindu University, established in 1916. The wide tree-lined streets and parkland of the 5-sq-km campus offer a peaceful atmosphere a world away from the city outside. On campus is **Bharat Kala Bhavan** (Map p390; ☏ 2369227; Indian/foreigner ₹10/100, camera ₹50; ☉10.30am-4.30pm Jul-Apr, 7.30am-1pm May-Jun, closed Sun), a roomy museum with a wonderful collection of miniature paintings, as well as 12th-century palm-leaf manuscripts, sculptures and local history displays.

Ramnagar Fort & Museum   MUSEUM
(Map p390; museum Indian/foreigner ₹20/150; ☉10-5pm) This crumbling 17th-century fort and palace, on the eastern bank of the Ganges, isn't worth coming out to if you only have a few days in Varanasi, but it is a beautiful place to watch the sun set over the river. It also houses an eccentric museum. There are vintage American cars, jewel-encrusted sedan chairs, a superb weaponry section and an extremely unusual astrological clock. The current maharaja, Anant Narayan Singh – still known in these parts as the Maharaja of Benares despite such royal titles being officially abolished in 1971 – continues his family tradition of attending the annual month-long **Ram Lila drama festival** (Varanasi; ☉ Sep/Oct) held in the streets behind the fort.

Boats operate a shuttle service across the river (₹20 return, 10 minutes) between 5am and 8pm, but from November to June, you can also cross on a somewhat steady pontoon bridge. A new bridge, under contruction at time of writing, means most folks will just drive across. A boat all the way back to Dashashwamedh Ghat is ₹200 to ₹300.

 Activities

It's worth an early rise two of your mornings in Varanasi, one to take in the action on a river boat trip and another to experience the

---

THE VARANASI SHAKEDOWN

If you thought the touts and rickshaw-wallahs were annoying in Agra, wait till you get to Varanasi. The attention here, particularly around the ghats and the Old City, is incredible: you will have to put up with persistent offers from touts and drivers of 'cheapest and best' boat trips, guides, tour operators, travel agents, silk shops and money changers (to name a few). Take it in good humour but politely refuse.

Words to live by in Varanasi:

➡ Don't take photos at the 'burning' ghats and resist offers to 'follow me for a better view', where you'll be pressured for money and possibly be placed in an uncomfortable situation.

➡ Do not go to any shop with a guide or autorickshaw driver. Be firm and don't do it. *Ever.* You will pay 40% to 60% more for your item due to insane commissions and you will be passively encouraging this practice. Do yourself a favor and walk there; or have your ride drop you a block away.

➡ Imposter stores are rampant in Varanasi, usually spelled one letter off or sometimes exactly the same. The shops we have recomended are the real deal. Ask for a visting card (ie business card) – if the info doesn't match, you have been had.

➡ When negotiating with boatsmen, confirm the price *and* currency before setting out. They just love to say '100!' and then at the end claim they meant dollars or euros.

➡ Do not book unoffical guides, which are hired by most guesthouses. If you want a guide, go through UP Tourism (p395) to avoid most of the hassles listed here. If not, have fun shopping!

hubbub of activity on the ghats themselves. Nonguests can use the outdoor **swimming pools** at Hotel Surya (₹200) and Hotel Clarks Varanasi (₹500).

★ **River Trips**   BOATING

A dawn rowing boat ride along the Ganges is a quintessential Varanasi experience. The early-morning light is particularly inspiring, and all the colour and clamour of pilgrims bathing and performing *puja* unfolds before you. An hour-long trip south from Dashashwamedh Ghat to Harishchandra Ghat and back is popular, but be prepared to see a burning corpse at Harishchandra. Early evening is also a good time to be on the river, when you can light a lotus flower candle (₹10) and set it adrift on the water before watching the nightly *ganga aarti* ceremony (7pm) at Dashashwamedh Ghat directly from the boat.

The official government price of boats is ₹50 per person per hour, but it is not enforced. Count yourself lucky if you manage ₹100 per person per hour and be prepared for some hard bargaining. And be warned: it's best to arrange a boat the day before. If you show up as the sun is about to rise, you'll find yourself in a Varanasi Standoff: a battle of wills between yourself, a boatsman and the unforgiving rising sun – to the tune of ₹1000 per person.

Many guesthouses offer boat trips, although they're more expensive than dealing with the boatmen directly. Brown Bread Bakery can arrange a hassle-free boat for less than riverside (₹100 for one to two people, ₹50 for each additonal person) with some à la carte coffee and cakes to boot.

Aarna Spa   MASSAGE

(Map p390; ☑2508465; www.hotelsuryavns. com; Hotel Surya, 20/51A The Mall; massage from ₹1400; ☺8am-8pm) Hotel Surya's spa is a nice choice for soothing Ayurvedic massages such as Abhyanga and Potli as well as standard aromatherpy and pressure point treatments.

Swasthya Vardhak   AYURVEDA

(Map p394; ☑2312504; www.swasthyavardhak. com; Assi Crossing; ☺8am-8pm) 🖉 Varanasi is full of ayurvedic imposters. Serious seekers should come here, the city's real deal ayurvedic pharmacy. Consultations with a doctor are free; prescriptions from the 500 stocked medicines run from ₹15 to ₹1500. Addtionally, they work with a government

initiative that encourages struggling local farmers to turn over a new leaf planting ayurvedic herbs.

🏃 **Volunteering**

Learn for Life Society   VOLUNTEERING

(Map p390; ☑2390040; www.learn-for-life.net; D55/147 Aurangabad) This small charity, run by two foreigners and contacted through Brown Bread Bakery, has established a small school for disadvantaged children and a women's empowerment group, offering fairly paid work to local women, some of whom are mothers of the school's students. The women make produce such as jams and muesli, which are available at the bakery. Pop into Brown Bread's Infocentre nightly at 7pm when representatives meet interested travellers. No cash donations.

Kiran   VOLUNTEERING

(Map p390; ☑5122670; www.kiranvillage.org; Madhopur, Post Office: Kuruhuan) This Swiss-run organisation works with underprivileged children in its village in Madhopur, 12km south of Benares Hindu University. It requires a five-month commitment (as well as enrollment in Hindi classes), but the program is as recommended as they come. Time is spent helping to produce handicrafts, assisting an Indian sports teacher or helping with evening and weekend entertainment at the boys and girls hostels, but roles are catered to meet individual volunteer needs and interests. You must be 25 or older. Stop by the Varanasi office for info.

🖉 **Courses**

Yoga Training Centre   YOGA

(Map p394; ☑9919587895; www.yogatrainingcentre .com; 5/15 Sakarkand Gali; 2hr class ₹400, reiki from ₹1800; ☺8am, 10am & 4pm) Yoga master Sunil Kumar and his wife, Bharti, run classes three times a day on the 3rd floor of a small backstreet building near Meer Ghat. He teaches an integrated blend of hatha, Iyengar, pranayama, satyananda and shivananda, and serious students can continue on certificate and diploma courses in both yoga and reiki. This place is highly recommended by travellers.

Pragati Hindi   LANGUAGE

(Map p394; ☑9335376488; www.pragatihindi.com; B-7/176 Harar Bagh) Readers recommend the flexibility of the one-to-one classes taught

The Old City & Assi Ghat Area

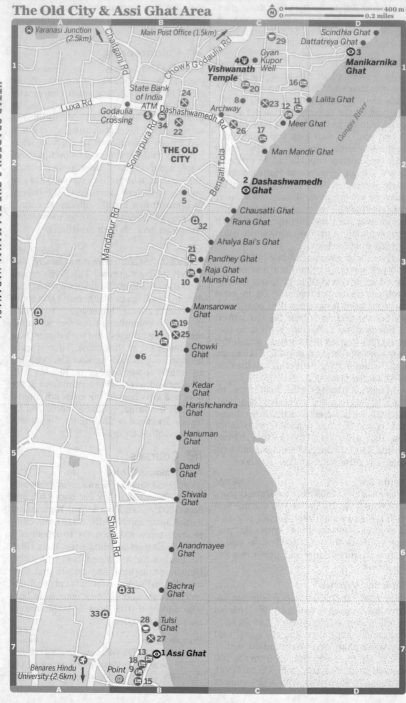

0   400 m
0   0.2 miles

Varanasi Junction (2.5km)

Main Post Office (1.5km)

Chaitganj Rd

Scindhia Ghat
Dattatreya Ghat
29
3 **Manikarnika Ghat**

Chowk Godaulia Rd

Gyan Kupor Well
4
16
11 Lalita Ghat
12 Meer Ghat
20
8
23
26
17
Man Mandir Ghat

Luxa Rd
State Bank of India ATM
Godaulia Crossing
24
Dashashwamedh Rd
Archway
34
5
22

Vishwanath Temple

THE OLD CITY

Sonarpura Rd

Mandapur Rd

Bengali Tola

2 **Dashashwamedh Ghat**

Ganges River

5
Chausatti Ghat
32
Rana Ghat
Ahalya Bai's Ghat
21
Pandhey Ghat
10 Raja Ghat
Munshi Ghat

30

Mansarowar Ghat

14
19
25
Chowki Ghat

6

Kedar Ghat

Harishchandra Ghat

Hanuman Ghat

Dandi Ghat

Shivala Ghat

Shivala Rd

Anandmayee Ghat

31
Bachraj Ghat

33

28 Tulsi Ghat
27

13
18
9
15
1 **Assi Ghat**

7
Benares Hindu University (2.6km)
Point @

The Old City & Assi Ghat Area

⊙ Top Sights

⊕ Activities, Courses & Tours

⊜ Sleeping

⊗ Eating

⊙ Drinking & Nightlife

⊜ Shopping

ⓘ Transport

here by the amiable Rajeswar Mukherjee (Raju). Private classes start from ₹250 per hour. Call ahead, or just drop in, to meet Raju and arrange a schedule. Walk up the lane opposite Chowki Ghat and take the first left.

International Music Centre Ashram   INDIAN MUSIC

(Map p394; ☏ 2452302; keshavaraonayak@hot mail.com; 33/81 Khalishpura; per hr ₹200) This family-run centre is hidden in the tangle of backstreets off Bengali Tola. It offers sitar, tabla, flute and classical-dance tuition, and performances are held every Saturday and Wednesday evening at 8pm (₹100). There's a small, easy-to-miss sign on Bengali Tola directing you here. If you can't find it, there are loads of **musical-instrument shops** (Map p394) on Bengali Tola, many of which offer tuition.

International Centre   VARIOUS

(Map p390; ☏ 2368130; www.bhu.ac.in; C/3/3 Tagore House; ⊙10am-5pm Mon-Sat) If you're interested in studying at Benares Hindu University, contact this centre. Courses on offer include Hindi, Sanskrit, yoga, ayurveda studies, and weaving and handicraft.

⌒ Tours

Varanasi Walks   WALKING TOUR

(☏8795576225; www.varanasiwalks.com; tour ₹1500-1800) ✎ Travellers have raved about cultural walks on offer from this foreigner run agency specialising in themed walks that explore beyond the most popular ghats and temples. Walks are usually available between 6am and 9am and 3pm and 7pm and can be reserved online. Three of the five guides were born and raised in Varanasi.

UP Tourism Office   CITY TOUR

(Map p390; Varanasi Junction Train Station; half-/full-day tour ₹1500/3000; ⊙7am-7pm) If time is short, UP Tourism can arrange guided tours by taxi of the major sites, including a 5.30am boat ride and an afternoon trip to Sarnath.

⌷ Sleeping

The majority of Varanasi's budget hotels – and some midrange gems – are concentrated in the tangle of narrow streets back from the ghats along the River Ganges. There's a concentration around Assi Ghat, while others are in the crazy, bustling northern stretch of alleys between Scindhia and Meer Ghat, part of an area we refer to as the Old City.

Varanasi has an active paying-guesthouse scheme with more than 100 family homes available for accommodation from ₹200 to ₹1500 a night (most are under ₹400). UP Tourism has a full list.

Old City Area

Ganpati Guesthouse   GUESTHOUSE $

(Map p394; ☎ 2390059; www.ganpatiguesthouse. com; 3/24 Meer Ghat; r ₹1000-1800, without bathroom ₹700, with AC ₹1200-3500; ❄ @ ☏) Ganpati infuriates us. On one hand, this old red-brick building has a pleasant, shaded courtyard as well as plenty of balcony space dotted around offering fine river views. Nicely painted rooms are colourful and clean and the ones facing out onto the Ganges (from ₹700) are cutesy and spacious. Free wi-fi works everywhere (except the lovely rooftop restaurant, unfortunately). On the other, there have been complaints about its hiring of pushy guides, the front desk can be hard-headed, it irritatingly locks the doors at 10pm and we met two Irish girls fleeing the hotel at midnight after a rat was crawling in their room! Though it stands out in the crowded riverside pack, don't expect it to not agitate you at some point or another.

Hotel Alka   GUESTHOUSE $

(Map p394; ☎ 2401681; www.hotelalkavns.com; Meer Ghat; r ₹600-800, without bathroom ₹500, with AC ₹1124-3597; ❄ @ ☏) An excellent ghatside option, Alka has pretty much spotless rooms that open onto, or overlook, a large, plant-filled courtyard. In the far corner, a terrace juts out over Meer Ghat for one of the best views in all of Varanasi, a view shared from the balconies of eight of the pricier rooms.

Teerth Guesthouse   GUESTHOUSE $

(Map p394; www.teerthguesthouse.com; 8/9 Kalika Gali; r without bathroom ₹350, r ₹600-800; ☏) This newish guesthouse is a pleasant surprise as you leave the undesirable alleyways that lead to it and enter into a spic-and-span, marble lobby laced with the scent of jasmine. Rooms are on the smaller size, but are new and spotless and the whole place hogs a load of sunlight through the open atrium. A pleasant rooftop offers Old City views. Best of all, though, it's relatively quiet. Wi-fi is ₹100 per stay.

Vishnu Rest House   GUESTHOUSE $

(Map p394; ☎ 2500206; 24/17 Pandhey Ghat; dm ₹90, s/d from ₹200/300; @ ☏) Accessed through a small courtyard with family homes coming off it, or directly from Pandhey Ghat itself, this simple guesthouse offers poky rooms that aren't the cleanest, but the atmosphere is friendly and the stone terrace overlooking the ghat is a winner. Free wi-fi.

Puja Guest House   GUESTHOUSE $

(Map p394; ☎ 2405027; www.pujaguesthouse.com; 1/45 Lalita Ghat; r ₹400-800, without bathroom ₹200-250, with AC ₹1000-1500; ❄ @) Hidden away up an alley overlooking Lalita Ghat, this towering building offers extremely basic, but clean enough, cheap rooms. The rooftop restaurant is one of Varanasi's tallest, with superb 180-degree views of the river and free sitar-and-tabla performances every evening from 8pm. Rooms ₹800 and up have river views and ₹1500 rooms include breakfast. Internet is ₹50 per hour.

Eden Halt   GUESTHOUSE $

(Map p394; ☎ 2454612; dtripathi23@yahoo.co.in; Ganga Mahal, Raja Ghat; s/d ₹300/600; @ ☏) We are not as bowled over by this deadsimple, pocket-sized guesthouse as many travellers, but the four rooms (two have private bathrooms, two have river views) here are clean and spacious and come with interesting alcoves and built-in shelving. A simple roof terrace overlooks peaceful Raja Ghat, but be prepared to fight monkeys for space on it.

Kedareswar   HOTEL $$

(Map p394; ☎ 2455568; www.kedareswarguesthouse.com; 14/1 Chowki Ghat; r ₹1400, with AC ₹2400, all incl breakfast; ❄ ☏) Housed in a brightly painted, aquamarine green building, this friendly six-room place has cramped but immaculate rooms with sparkling bathrooms. There are only two cheaper non-AC rooms, so it might be worth phoning ahead. Chowki Ghat is right beside Kedar Ghat.

Shiva Ganges View
Paying Guest House   GUESTHOUSE $$$

(Map p394; ☎ 2450063; www.varanasiguesthouse. com; 14/24 Mansarowar Ghat; r ₹3500, with AC ₹4500-5000, ste ₹6000; ❄ @ ☏) The best Old City top-end option is a delightful, brightred brick building and part of the city's paying-guesthouse scheme. Huge rooms here ooze character, with central double beds (all with mosquito nets), high ceilings and chunky door and window shutters. All have river views and spotlessly clean bathrooms. Home-cooked food is also available. The one downside – the manager can be a bit pushy.

Rashmi Guest House   HOTEL $$$
(Map p394; ☏2402778; www.rashmiguesthouse. com; 16/28A Man Mandir Ghat; r incl breakfast ₹2780-6670; ❄@🖥) Sparkling white-tiled corridors and marble staircases lead to clean and modern rooms, which are tiny but smart. Many have views of Man Mandir Ghat (in fact, the only difference between a deluxe and super deluxe is the view and a courtesy minibar), although the excellent rooftop Dolphin Restaurant offers the best views of all. Ayurvedic massage (₹1200) is also available.

🛏 Assi Ghat Area

Sahi River View Guesthouse   GUESTHOUSE $
(Map p394; ☏2366730; sahi_rvgh@sify.com; 1/158 Assi Ghat; s/d from ₹300/350, with AC from ₹950/1250, all incl breakfast; ❄@) There's a huge variety of rooms at this friendly place. Most are good quality and clean, and some have interesting private balconies. Each floor has a pleasant communal seating area with river view, creating a great feeling of space throughout.

Chaitanya Guest House   GUESTHOUSE $
(Map p394; ☏2313686; knpsahi@yahoo.com; 1/158A Assi Ghat; r ₹500, with AC ₹1000; ❄) Chaitanya has just four rooms: a single, two doubles and a double with AC. All are comfortable, with high ceilings and clean bathrooms (though some mattresses are warped), and are well looked after by friendly staff.

Homestay   HOMESTAY $$
(Map p390; ☏9415449348; www.homestayvarana si.in; 61/16 Sidhgiri Bagh; s ₹2300-2800, d ₹2500-3000; ❄@🖥) Travellers rave about this friendly homestay in a 1936 colonial home in a residential neighborhood 1.5km from the Old City. Host Harish, a 30-year veteran of the textile industry (shop on premises) has seven rooms: a few deluxe emptying out into a small garden and enormous super deluxes with minibars and enough space for a small army. His wife, Malika, whips up home-cooked meals and has been known to give impromptu cooking classes. If you don't mind being a bit away from the heart of the action, it's a great choice.

★ **Hotel Ganges View**   HOTEL $$$
(Map p394; ☏2313218; www.hotelgangesview. com; Assi Ghat; r with AC ₹4500-5500; ❄🖥) Simply gorgeous, this beautifully restored and maintained colonial-style house overlooking Assi Ghat is crammed with books, artwork and antiques. Rooms are spacious and immaculate and there are some charming communal areas in which to sit and relax, including a lovely 1st-floor garden terrace. Book ahead.

Palace on Ganges   HOTEL $$$
(Map p394; ☏2315050; www.palaceonganges.com; 1/158 Assi Ghat; r ₹6184; ❄@🖥) Each of the 24 rooms (the four river views are first-come, first-served) in this immaculate heritage accommodation is individually themed on a regional Indian style, using antique furnishings and colourful design themes. The colonial, Rajasthan and Jodhpur rooms are among the best.

🛏 Cantonment Area

Hotel Surya   HOTEL $$
(Map p390; ☏2508485; www.hotelsuryavns. com; 20/51A The Mall; s/d incl breakfast from ₹2280/2700; ❄@🖥) Varanasi's cheapest hotel with a swimming pool, Surya has standard 3-star Indian rooms, but a modern makeover in the superior and premium rooms means everything has been tightened up a bit, with new furnishings, upholsteries and the like. Value here is palpable, as all is built around a huge lawn area that includes a laid-back Middle Eastern–style cafe (Mango Verra) flanked by a gorgeous, nearly 200-year-old heritage building (the former stomping grounds of a Nepali king), where the excellent-value Canton Royale is housed. There's also the good (but smoky) Sol Bar and the recomended Aarna Spa.

Gateway Hotel Ganges   HOTEL $$$
(Map p390; ☏6660001; www.thegatewayhotels. com; Raja Bazaar Rd; r/ste from ₹12,366/15,738; ❄@🖥) Varanasi's best hotel is on nearly 2 hectares of beautiful gardens with fruit trees, a tennis court, a pool, an outdoor yoga centre and the old maharaja's guesthouse. All the rooms were madeover between 2010 and 2012. There's little size difference between standard and deluxe catagories, but the latter are far classier with refined art on the walls and new whimsically coloured carpeting throughout the hallways that lead to them. Service is expectedly top class and

there are two fine restaurants, two bars and two spa treatment rooms (massages from ₹3000).

Hotel Clarks Varanasi

HOTEL **$$$**

(Map p390; ☐ 2501011; www.clarkshotels.com; The Mall; s/d from ₹7782/8338; ❇@🛜🏊) While executive rooms are enormous, a smart overhaul to all rooms means standards now come with hardwood floors and soothing blue or red colour schemes with small alcoves for a sofa and table. The garden out the back has a delightful teardrop-shaped swimming pool shaded by bamboo and palm trees. There's also a 24-hour cafe and fitness center but sadly no spa. Wi-fi is ₹600 per day.

Eating

Look out for locally grown *langda aam* (mangoes) in summer or *sitafal* (custard apples) in autumn. *Singhara* is a blackish root that tastes like water chestnut.

Old City Area

Keshari Restaurant

INDIAN **$**

(Map p394; 14/8 Godaulia; mains ₹65-130; ⏰9.30am-11pm) Known as much for excellent cusine as surly service, this atmospheric spot (carved wood panelling dons the walls and ceilings) has been famously at it for nearly a half-century. Indians pack in here for high-quality veg from all over India – a dizzying array of dishes are on offer (41 paneer curries alone). Those who like to dance with the devil should spring for the paneer Kadahi (spicy tomato-based gravy), sure to make your nose run. Do not confuse it with the less-desirable Keshari Ruchiker Byanjan around the corner on Dashashwamedh Rd.

Ayyar's Cafe

SOUTH INDIAN **$**

(Map p394; Dashashwamedh Rd; mains ₹30-75; ⏰8am-10pm) Excellent, no-nonsense choice off the tourist beaten path for South Indian masala dosa (₹30), and its spicier cousin, the Mysore dosa (₹70); and one of the few cheapies to serve filtered coffee. It's tucked away at the end of a very short alley signed 'New Keshari Readymade' off Dashashwamedh Rd.

Madhur Milan Cafe

INDIAN **$**

(Map p394; 15/81 Dashashwamedh Rd; mains ₹32-85; ⏰6am-11pm) Popular with locals, this simple but friendly restaurant serves up a range of good-value, mostly South Indian dishes. Thalis start from ₹60. The early opening time means it's packed for breakfast, with most folks going for the extremely popular *poori sabji* set breakfast (₹40; fried wheat flour patties used to scoop up spiced potato curry), which comes with *jalebi* (fried batter soaked in sugar syrup).

★ Brown Bread Bakery

MULITCUISINE **$$**

(Map p394; ☐ 9838888823; www.brownbreadbak ery.com; 5/127 Tripura Bhairavi; mains ₹120-350; ⏰7am-10pm; 🛜) 🌱 This restaurant and organic shop's fabulous menu includes more than 40 varieties of European-quality cheese and more than 30 types of bread, cookies and cakes. The partly-AC ambiance – with seating on cushions around low tables on the nonsmoking bottom floor, astounding views from the rooftop patio and live classical-music performances in the evenings – is spot on. Part of the profits go to the charity Learn for Life (p393). Warning: not to be confused with the location across the street, abandoned by Micha, the 5th-generation German baker, but carried on by his local ex-partners. If there are not four floors and a rooftop, you're at a different place. Call to confirm if you're unsure.

Lotus Lounge

MULTICUISINE **$$**

(Map p394; 14/27 Mansarowar Ghat; mains ₹70-240; ⏰8am-10pm; 🛜) The food doesn't move mountains, but Lotus is a supremely great place to chill. The laid-back, half-open-air restaurant, with broken-tile mosaic flooring, wicker chairs and a terrace that juts out over Mansarowar Ghat with lounge cushions and tatami mats, dishes out a world fusion potpourri from its kitchen and there's wi-fi and French Press coffee.

Dolphin Restaurant

INDIAN **$$$**

(Rashmi Guest House; Map p394; 16/28A Man Mandir Ghat; mains ₹110-300; ⏰7am-10pm) The atmosphere trumps the food at Dolphin – the rooftop restaurant at Rashmi Guest House – which is perched high above Man Mandir Ghat, but it's still a fine place to enjoy an evening meal. The breezy balcony is the most refined table in the Old City and one of the few that serves non-vegetarian as well.

Assi Ghat Area

★ Open Hand

CAFE

(Map p390; www.openhandonline.com; 1/128-3 Dumraub Bagh; ₹70-210; ⏰8am-8pm ; 🛜) 🌱 This shoes-off cafe-cum–gift shop serves the best espresso we had in India (from

₹45) and a range of excellent muffins, pancakes, muesli and juices that will delight you no end. Take breakfast (₹70 to ₹210) on the narrow balcony or lounge around the former home all day on the free wi-fi. There's also a large selection of gorgeous handicrafts (jewellery, toys, clothing) made in the local community. Couldn't be more pleasant.

Aum Cafe CAFE $$
(Map p394; www.touchoflight.us; 1/201 Assi Ghat; mains ₹60-155; ☺7am-4.30pm Tue-Sun; 🛜) ⬭
Run by a hippie dippie American woman who has been coming to India for more than 20 years, this colourful cafe has breakfast all day (₹65 to ₹120; good lemon pancakes!), astounding lemon and organic green tea lassis and a handful of light sandwiches and mains. There's also massage therapies and body piercing available.

Pizzeria Vaatika Cafe MULTICUISINE $$
(Map p394; www.pizzeriavaatika.in; Assi Ghat; pizza ₹150-220; ☺7.30am-10pm) Italians stop reading now. As for the rest of you, decent (for India) thin-crust pizza is churned out of a wood-fired oven and served on a shady garden terrace overlooking Assi Ghat. An Italian friend of the Indian owner originally showed him the ropes, so his heart is in the right place. Don't forget to leave some room for the delicious apple pie – it's legitimately tasty.

✗ Cantonment Area

Varuna Restaurant INDIAN $$$
(Map p390; www.thegatewayhotels.com; Gateway Hotel Ganges, Raja Bazaar Rd; mains ₹425-1700; ☺12.30-2.45pm & 7.30-11pm) Taj Hotels takes its restaurants very seriously and you'll indeed find one of UP's most innovative and interesting menus at the elegant but not stuffy main restaurant at the best hotel in town. New Zealand lamb chops doused with masala, spiritual veg thalis (₹800) and stone-ground mustard-marinated prawns are just a few of the intriguing choices. Service is appropriately on point and there's live sitar and tabla music every evening.

Canton Royale INDIAN $$$
(Map p390; www.hotelsuryavns.com; Hotel Surya, 20/51A The Mall; mains ₹150-280; ☺11am-11pm) Housed in a nearly 200-year-old heritage building, Hotel Surya's excellent main restaurant has a colonial elegance, and on

VARANASI'S TOP FIVE RIVERSIDE RETREATS

Pizzeria Vaatika Cafe Tree-shaded verandah overlooking Assi Ghat.

Lotus Lounge Laid-back yet chic.

Hotel Ganges View (p397) Sip tea in style from the gorgeous 1st-floor garden terrace.

Puja Guest House (p396) Offers 180-degree rooftop views with live classical music every evening.

Vishnu Rest House (p396) Simple stone terrace sandwiched between Pandhey Ghat and a colourful temple.

warm evenings you can eat out on the large lawn. Value for money, it's one of the best of Varanasi's top-end choices, offering a global hodgepodge that extends from Mexican and Thai to Chinese and Continental. But really, it's the Indian that's excellent, including a wonderful thali (₹280).

Eden Restaurant INDIAN $$$
(Map p390; www.hotelpradeep.com; Hotel Pradeep, Jagatganj; 125-300; ☺7am-11pm) Hotel Pradeep's rooftop restaurant, complete with garden, manicured lawns and wrought-iron furniture, is a very pleasant place for a candle-lit evening meal. The good-quality Indian menu comes from the lobby-level Poonam restaurant – and as we all know, heat rises! If you ask for Indian-spicy here, you'll get it.

🍷 Drinking & Nightlife

Wine and beer shops are dotted discreetly around the city, usually away from the river. Note that it is frowned upon to drink alcohol on or near the holy Ganges, and liquor laws regarding proximity of temples insure nobody is licensed, but rooftops here can usually discreetly fashion up a beer. For bars, head to midrange and top-end hotels away from the ghats.

There's nightly live **classical music** at Brown Bread Bakery, Puja Hotel and Varuna Restaurant at Gateway Hotel Ganges, to name but a few.

The International Music Centre Ashram has small **performances** (₹100) on Wednesday and Saturday evenings.

NO 1 LASSI IN ALL VARANASI

Your long, thirsty search for the best lassi in India is over. Look no further than **Blue Lassi** (Map p394; lassis ₹20-80; ☺ 7.30am-10.30pm; 🔊), a tiny, hole-in-the-wall yoghurt shop that has been churning out the freshest, creamiest, fruit-filled lassis since 1925. The grandson of the original owner still works here, sitting by his lassi-mixing cauldron in front of a small room with wooden benches for customers and walls plastered with messages from happy drinkers. There are 70 delicious flavour combos, but of the main ones – plain, banana, apple and pomegranate – we think banana and apple, the latter flecked with fresh apple shreds, just about top of the bunch (yes, we went twice!). The whole scene here is surreal: the lassi takes ages to arrive and when it does, it's handed off to you with the care of a priceless work of art as the deceased are carried by the front of the shop on the way to Burning Ghat. *Namaste!*

Prinsep Bar BAR
(Map p390; www.tajhotels.com; Gateway Hotel Ganges, Raja Bazaar Rd; ☺ noon-11pm Mon-Fri, to midnight Sat & Sun) For a quiet drink with a dash of history try this tiny bar, named after James Prinsep, who drew wonderful illustrations of Varanasi's ghats and temples, but stick to beer (from ₹195) as our cocktail (from ₹450) was weak.

Mango Verra CAFE
(Map p390; www.hotelsuryavns.com; 20/51A The Mall; ☺ 11am-11pm) This laid-back cafe in the garden at Hotel Surya is a relaxing place where you can smoke hookah pipes (₹300) while sipping a beer.

🔒 Shopping

Varanasi is justifiably famous for silk brocades and beautiful Benares saris, but don't believe much of what the silk salesmen tell you about the relative quality of products, even in government emporiums. Instead, shop around and judge for yourself.

Varanasi is also a good place to shop for sitars (starting from ₹3000) and tablas (from ₹2500). The cost depends primarily on the type of wood used. Mango is cheapest (and cracks or warps correspondingly), while black shisham or mahogany are of the highest quality. Serious buyers should be sure to double-check their chosen wood isn't banned for export.

⭐ **Baba Blacksheep** SILK
(Map p394; www.bababalcksheep.co; B 12/120 A-9, Bhelpura; ☺ 9.30am-8pm) If the deluge of traveller enthusiasm is anything to go by, this is the most trustworthy, non-pushy shop in India. Indeed it is one of the best places you'll find for silks (scarves/saris from ₹300/2500) and pashminas (shawls from ₹1500). Prices are fixed and the friendly owner refuses to play the commssion game, so autorickshaws and taxis don't like to come here (ignore anyone who says you cannot drive here). It's located at Bhelpura crossing under the mosque.

Benares Art & Culture HANDICRAFTS
(Map p394; Shivala Rd; ☺ 10am-8pm Mon-Sat) This centuries-old *haveli* (traditional, ornately decorated residence) stocks fixed-price quality carvings, sculptures, paintings and wooden toys all made by local artists.

Organic by Brown Bread Bakery COSMETICS
(Map p394; www.brownbreakbakery.com; 2/225 Shivali; 🔊) ⌀ This small shop and garden cafe sells natural and organic cosmetics from the government-sponsored Khadi program. Honey, muesli and other small foodstuffs, baked goods and fresh juices and coffee are on offer.

Shri Gandhi Ashram Khadi CLOTHING
(Map p390; Khabir Chaura Rd; ☺ 10am-7.30pm) Stocks shirts, kurta pyjamas, saris and head scarves, all made from the famous homespun *khadi* fabric. Next day tailoring can be arranged.

Mehrotra Silk Factory SILK
(Map p390; www.mehrotrasilk.in; 21/72 Englishia Line; ☺ 10am-8pm) Tucked away down a tiny alleyway near the main train station, this pocket-sized, fixed-priced shop is a fun place to buy silk scarves (from ₹250), saris (from ₹1600) and bedspread sets (from ₹5000). The **Lal Ghat location** (Map p390; 4/8A, Lal Ghat; ☺ 10am-8pm) is more convenient for Old City shoppers.

ℹ️ Information

Varanasi is pretty wired – even Blue Lassi has wi-fi! Some charge. Many don't. Internet cafes are everywhere, charging between ₹25 and ₹50 per hour. There are several ATMs scattered around town, including State Bank of India in the lobby as you exit the train station.

Heritage Hospital (Map p390; www.heritage hospitals.com; Lanka) English-speaking staff and doctors; 24-hour pharmacy.

Main Post Office (Map p390; GPO; Kabir Chaura Rd; ⊙9am-6pm Mon-Sat) Best PO for sending parcels abroad.

Point (Map p394; 1/156 Assi Ghat Rd; per hr ₹25; ⊙8am-10.30pm) Friendly internet near Assi Ghat.

State Bank of India (Map p390; The Mall; ⊙10am-2pm & 2.30-4pm Mon-Fri, 10am-1pm Sat) Changes travellers cheques and cash.

State Bank of India ATM (Map p394; cnr Dashashwamedh Rd & Mandapur Rd)

Tourist Police (Map p390; UP Tourism office, Varanasi Junction train station; ⊙7am-7pm) Tourist police wear sky-blue uniforms.

UP Tourism (Map p390; www.up-tourism.com; Varanasi Junction Train Station; ⊙7am-7pm) The patient Mr Umashankar at the office inside the train station has been dishing out reasonably impartial information to arriving travellers for years; he's a mine of knowledge, so this is a requisite first stop if you arrive here by train. Get the heads up on autorickshaw prices, the best trains for your travels, the lay of the land, details on Varanasi's paying-guesthouse scheme or arrange a guided tour.

ℹ️ Getting There & Away

AIR

Lal Bahadur Shashtri Airport, 24km north of town, is served by **Jet Airways** (www.jetairways. com; Lal Bahadur Shastri Airport), with direct flights to Delhi (from ₹7400, daily), Mumbai (from ₹7600, daily) and Kolkata (from ₹2900, daily); and **Air India** (www.airindia.com; Airlines Bhavan 52, Yadunath Marg) to Delhi (₹1799, daily), Mumbai (₹3699, daily), Agra (₹3028; Monday, Wednesday and Saturday), Khajuraho (₹3532, Monday, Wednesday and Saturday) and Kathmandu (₹12,159, Tuesday, Thursday, Saturday and Sunday). Some other airlines are based at the airport.

BUS

The main **bus stand** (Map p390) is opposite Varanasi Junction train station.

Allahabad Non-AC (₹110, three hours, every 30 minutes); AC (₹169, three hours, 7am, 10am and 4pm)

Faizabad ₹160, six hours, daily at 1.30pm, 2pm and 6pm

Gorakhpur ₹168, seven hours, every two hours or so from 4am to 5.30pm

Lucknow Non-AC (₹232, seven to eight hours, 7am and 3pm); Pawan Gold (nonstop, ₹623, six hours, 8am, 9am, 4pm and 4.30pm); AC (₹623, six hours, 7am, 8am, 3pm and 10.30pm)

TRAIN

Luggage theft has been reported on trains to and from Varanasi so you should take extra care. Reports of drugged food and drink aren't uncommon, so it's probably still best to politely decline any offers from strangers.

Varanasi Junction train station, also known as Varanasi Cantonment (Cantt), is the main station. Foreign tourist quota tickets must be purchased at the helpful **Foreign Tourist Centre** (Map p390; ⊙8am-12.50pm & 2-8pm Mon-Sat, 8am-2pm Sun), a ticket office just past the UP Tourism office, on your right as you exit the station.

There are several daily trains to Allahabad, Gorakhpur and Lucknow. A few daily trains leave for New Delhi and Kolkata, but only two daily trains go to Agra. The direct train to Khajuraho only runs on Monday, Wednesday and Saturday.

HANDY TRAINS FROM VARANASI (BSB)

DESTINATION	TRAIN NO & NAME	FARE (₹)	DURA-TION (HR)	DEPARTURES
Agra	13237/13239 PNBE-Kota Exp	262/733/1110 (A)	13	4.40pm
Allahabad	11094 Mahangari Exp	120/287/610 (A)	3	11.25am
Gorakhpur	15003 Chaurichaura Exp	132/353/610 (A)	6½	12.40am
Jabalpur	11062/11066 MFP/DBG-LTT Exp	212/585/880 (A)	10½	11.20pm
Khajuraho	21108 BSB-Kurj Link E	200/551 (B)	12	6.05pm*
Kolkata (Howrah)	12334 Vibhuti Exp	306/836/1255 (A)	14	6.10pm
Lucknow	14235 BSB-BE Exp	161/438 (B)	7¼	11.45pm
New Delhi	12559 Shiv Ganga Exp	306/836/1255 (A)	12½	7.15pm

Fares: (A) sleeper/3AC/2AC, (B) sleeper/3AC; *Mon, Wed, Sat only

BORDER CROSSING – TO/FROM NEPAL

From Varanasi's bus stand there are regular services to Sunauli (₹239, 10 hours, 7am to 7.30pm).

By train, go to Gorakhpur then transfer to a Sunauli bus.

Air India has four weekly flights to Kathmandu (from ₹12,159). Nepali visas are available on arrival.

On other days, go via Satna from where you can catch buses to Khajuraho.

Getting Around

TO/FROM THE AIRPORT

An autorickshaw to the airport in Babatpur, 22km northwest of the city, costs ₹200. A taxi is about ₹400.

BICYCLE

You can hire bikes (per day ₹20) from a small **cycle repair shop** (Map p390) near Assi Ghat.

CYCLE-RICKSHAW

A small ride – up to 2km – costs ₹10 to ₹15. Rough prices from Dashashwamedh Rd include: Assi Ghat ₹40, Benares Hindu University ₹60 and Varanasi Junction train station ₹45. Be prepared for hard bargaining.

TAXI & AUTORICKSHAW

Prepaid booths for autorickshaws and taxis are directly outside Varanasi Junction train station and give you a good benchmark for prices around town. First pay a ₹5 administration charge at the booth then take a ticket which you give to your driver, along with the fare, once you've reached your destination. Note that taxis and autorickshaws cannot access the Dashashwamedh Ghat area between the hours of 8am and 8pm due to high pedestrian traffic. You'll be dropped at Godaulia Crossing and will need to walk the remaining 400m or so to the entrance to the Old City; or 700m or so all the way to Dashashwamedh Ghat. Sample fares:

Airport auto/taxi ₹200/400

Assi Ghat auto/taxi ₹70/200

Dashashwamedh Ghat auto/taxi ₹60/150

Godaulia (by St Thomas' Church) auto/taxi ₹50/₹150

Ramnagar Fort auto/taxi ₹155/₹350

Sarnath auto/taxi ₹80/250

Half-day tour (four hours) auto/taxi ₹455/₹600

Full-day tour (eight hours) auto/taxi ₹905/₹1200

Tempos to Assi Ghat (₹10) and Benares University (₹15) leave from southeast corner of Dashashwamedh Rd.

Sarnath

📞 0542

Buddha came to Sarnath to preach his message of the middle way to nirvana after he achieved enlightenment at Bodhgaya and gave his famous first sermon here. In the 3rd century BC emperor Ashoka had magnificent stupas and monasteries erected here as well as an engraved pillar. When Chinese traveller Xuan Zang dropped by in AD 640, Sarnath boasted a 100m-high stupa and 1500 monks living in large monasteries. However, soon after, Buddhism went into decline and, when Muslim invaders sacked the city in the late 12th century, Sarnath disappeared altogether. It was 'rediscovered' by British archaeologists in 1835.

Today it's one of the four important sites on the Buddhist circuit (along with Bodhgaya, Kushinagar and Lumbini in Nepal) and attracts followers from around the world, especially on Purnima (or, informally, Buddha's birthday), when Buddha's life, death and enlightenment are celebrated, usually in April or May.

⊙ Sights

Dhamekh Stupa & Monastery Ruins
HISTORIC SITE

(Indian/foreigner ₹5/100, video ₹25; ⊙ dawn-dusk) Set in a peaceful park of monastery ruins is the impressive 34m Dhamekh Stupa, which marks the spot where the Buddha preached his first sermon. The floral and geometric carvings are 5th century AD, but some of the brickwork dates back as far as 200 BC.

Nearby is a 3rd-century BC **Ashoka Pillar** with an edict engraved on it. It once stood 15m tall and had the famous four-lion capital (now in the museum) perched on top of it, but all that remains are five fragments of its base.

Chaukhandi Stupa
BUDDHIST SACRED SITE

(⊙ dawn-dusk) This large ruined stupa dates back to the 5th century AD, and marks the spot where Buddha met his first disciples. The incongruous tower on top of the stupa is Mughal and was constructed here in the 16th century to commemorate the visit of Emperor Humayun.

Mulgandha Kuti Vihar

BUDDHIST TEMPLE

(camera/video ₹20/100; ⊙4-11.30am & 1.30-8pm) This modern temple was completed in 1931 by the Mahabodhi Society. Buddha's first sermon is chanted daily, starting between 6pm and 7pm depending on the season. A **bodhi tree** growing outside was transplanted in 1931 from the tree in Anuradhapura, Sri Lanka, which in turn is said to be the offspring of the original tree in Bodhgaya under which Buddha attained enlightenment.

Archaeological Museum

MUSEUM

(admission ₹5; ⊙9am-4.45pm) This fully modernised, 100-year-old sandstone museum houses wonderfully displayed ancient treasures such as the very well preserved 3rd-century BC lion capital from the Ashoka pillar, which has been adopted as India's national emblem, and a huge 2000-year-old stone umbrella, ornately carved with Buddhist symbols.

🛏 Sleeping

Jain Paying Guest House

GUESTHOUSE $

(☎2595621; jainpgh@gmail.com; d ₹500, without bathroom ₹450) This simple, good-value guesthouse is run by a friendly doctor of geography, whose wife whips up home-cooked thalis (₹120). The five rooms are spacious and prices drop to ₹250 between April and September.

Tibetan Temple & Monastery

MONASTERY $

(☎2595990; chotrulmonlam@gmail.com; d ₹500, tr without bath ₹300) The modest, well-kept Tibetan monastery offers simple rooms and a small restaurant serving Tibetan and Chinese specialties (₹60 to ₹150).

Agrawal Paying Guest House

GUESTHOUSE $$

(☎2595316; agrawalpg@gmail.com; r ₹700-800, with AC ₹1400; ❄) Peaceful place with a refined owner and spotless marble-floored rooms overlooking a large garden.

🍴 Eating

Vaishali Restaurant

INDIAN, CHINESE $

(mains ₹30-160; ⊙8am-7.30pm) Large and modern 1st-floor restaurant serving mostly Indian dishes, but some Chinese too. It's the best in town.

Green Hut

INDIAN, CHINESE $

(meals ₹35-165; ⊙9am-9pm) A breezy open-sided cafe-restaurant offering snacks, thalis (₹60 to ₹160) and Chinese dishes.

Sarnath

Sarnath

◎ Sights

🛏 Sleeping

🍴 Eating

ℹ Information

ℹ Information

Power cuts mean internet cafes are unreliable, but there are a few in town.

ℹ Getting There & Away

Local buses to Sarnath (₹15, 40 minutes) pass in front of Varanasi Junction train station, but you may wait a long time for one. An autorickshaw costs about ₹110 from Varanasi's Old City. On the way back you can snag a lift in a shared auto or *vikram* (₹30) but you may have to change on the outskirts of the city. Some trains running between Varanasi and Gorakhpur also stop here. Trains for Sarnath leave Varanasi Junction at 7am, 11.30am and 1.20pm. Returning to Varanasi, trains leave Sarnath at 9am, 7.30pm and 9.50pm. The journey takes around 20 minutes and a 'general' ticket for an unreserved 2nd-class seat will cost you just a few rupees.

Gorakhpur

☑ 0551 / POP 623,000

There's little to see in Gorakhpur itself, but this well-connected transport hub is a short hop from the pilgrimage centre of Kushinagar – the place where Buddha died – making it a possible stopover on the road between Varanasi and Nepal.

🛏 Sleeping & Eating

There are loads of standard-issue hotels across from the railway station that will do for a get-in, get-out overnight. Try **Hotel Adarsh Palace** (☑ 2201912; hotel.adarshpalace @rediffmail.com; Railway Station Rd; dm ₹150, s/d from ₹400/600, d with AC ₹660-990; ❄). Same goes for food – *dhabas* line the same street. We like **Mirch Masala** (mains ₹40-120; ☺ 9am-2.30am).

Hotel Vivek   HERITAGE HOTEL $
(☑ 2342800; hotelvivek@yahoo.co.in; Bank Rd; s/d ₹600/700, with AC from ₹990/1050; ❄ 🛜) This 1939 colonial mansion 1.5km from the railway station, is a great budget option if you don't mind venturing into town a bit. In the former home of India's first Indian Police Inspector General, budget rooms are simple but spacious and things only improve into a smattering of air-con options, all facing a U-shaped courtyard. The appeal here is the crumbling history and a hands-on owner, the Inspector General's grandson. There's a good restaurant and great chai as well. It's a ₹20 cycle-rickshaw ride from the railway station and walking distance from many good restaurants.

Chowdhry Sweet House   MULTICUISINE, DESSERTS $
(Cinema Rd; mains ₹55-170; ☺ 8am-10.45pm) This bi-level madhouse is packed with locals taking in an extensive array of Indian and Chinese veg dishes in a diner atmosphere, including ginormous *dosas* and excellent thalis (₹125 to ₹165). It specialises in sundaes,

too, and there is an absolute boatload from which to choose. It's a ₹20 cycle-rickshaw ride from the railway station.

❶ Information

UP Tourism (☺ 10am-6pm Mon-Sat) is inside the train station. There are State Bank of India ATMs in the train station parking lot and across from Adarsh Palace. **Varden Cyber Hut** (per hour ₹20; ☺ 7am-midnight) is opposite the train station, below Hotel Varden.

For the main bus stand, come out of the train station and keep walking straight for about 300m. For Varanasi buses you need the Katchari bus stand, about 3km further south.

❶ Getting There & Away

Frequent bus services run from the main bus stand to Faizabad (₹124, five hours, every 30 minutes), Kushinagar (₹42, two hours, every 30 minutes until 8pm) and Sunauli (₹68, three hours, hourly), along with Volvo AC buses to Lucknow (₹613, six hours, 9am, 11am and 10pm). Faster collective jeeps leave for Sunauli when full from 5am to 6pm directly across from the train station (per person ₹150 to ₹200, two hours).

Buses to Varanasi (₹165, seven hours, hourly from 7am to 9.30pm) leave from the Katchari bus stand, including two express buses (₹173, five hours, 7am and 4pm), as do buses to Allahabad (₹215, eight hours, hourly from 7am to 10pm).

There are five daily trains (six on Monday, Wednesday and Friday) from big and bustling Gorakhpur Junction to Varanasi (sleeper/3AC/2AC ₹132/353/610, 5½ hours), including one slower, cheaper night train (55149 Gkp Muv Pass, seven hours, 11.05pm). A number of daily trains also leave for Lucknow (sleeper/3AC/2AC ₹144/390/610, six hours) and Delhi (₹314/860/1295, 13 hours) and one for Agra Fort (19038/19040 Avadh Express, ₹249/697/1050, 1.20pm, 15½ hours).

The train ticket reservation office is 500m from the train station; to the right of the station as you exit.

JetKonnect (www.jetkonnect.com; Civil Air Terminal) operates one daily flight from Delhi Monday to Friday but it is comparatively expensive.

Kushinagar

☑ 05564 / POP 18,000

One of the four main pilgrimage sites marking Buddha's life – the others being Lumbini (Nepal), Bodhgaya and Sarnath – Kushinagar is where Buddha died. There are several peaceful, modern temples where you can stay, chat with monks or simply contemplate your place in the world, and there are three

Kushinagar

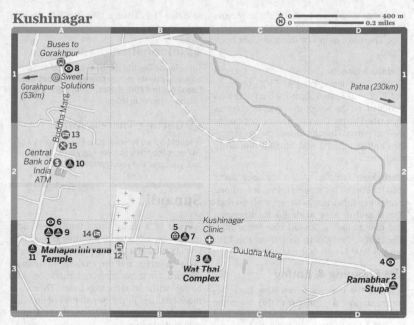

main historical sights, including the simple but wonderfully serene stupa where Buddha is said to have been cremated.

◉ Sights

★**Mahaparinirvana Temple** BUDDHIST TEMPLE
(Buddha Marg) The highlight of this modest temple, rebuilt in 1927 and set among extensive lawns and ancient ruins with a circumambulatory path, is its serene 5th-century reclining Buddha, unearthed in 1876. Six metres long, it depicts Buddha on his ancient death-bed and is one of the world's most moving Buddhist icons. Behind the temple is an ancient 19m-tall **stupa**, and in the surrounding park is a large **bell** erected by the Dalai Lama.

★**Ramabhar Stupa** BUDDHIST SITE
Architecturally, this half-ruined, 15m-high stupa is little more than a large, dome-shaped clump of red bricks, but there is an unmistakable aura about this place which is hard to ignore. This is where Buddha's body is said to have been cremated and monks and pilgrims can often be seen meditating by the palm-lined path that leads around the stupa.

★**Wat Thai Complex** BUDDHIST TEMPLE
(☎9005007064; www.tkr980.org; Buddha Marg; ◷6am-9pm) Features an elaborate temple,

beautifully maintained gardens with bonsai-style trees, a monastery and a temple containing a gilded Buddha. There's also a Sunday school and health clinic (across the street), each of which welcomes visitors. There are rooms by donation, but book ahead!

Buddha Museum MUSEUM
(Buddha Marg; Indian/foreigner ₹3/10, photography ₹20; ⊙10.30am-4.30pm Tue-Sun) Exhibits Buddhist relics, sculptures and terracottas unearthed from the Kushinagar region, as well as some Tibetan *thangkas* (rectangular cloth paintings) and Mughal miniature paintings.

Mathakuar Temple BUDDHIST TEMPLE
(Buddha Marg) This small shrine, set among monastery ruins, marks the spot where Buddha is said to have made his final sermon and now houses a 3m-tall blue-stone Buddha statue, thought to date from the 10th century AD.

🛏 Sleeping & Eating

Some of the temples which have basic accommodation for pilgrims also welcome tourists. Wat Thai is the most serene and beautiful, but books up well in advance, usually with Thai folks.

Tibetan Temple PILGRIMS' REST HOUSE $
(☑9931276680; Buddha Marg; d/tr ₹600/700) Some 25 brand-new rooms make this a great temple choice – some are nicer than neighbouring hotels. There is also a dormitory offering rooms by donation. Call the manager, Thinlay, who speaks decent English.

Linh Son Vietnam Chinese Temple PILGRIMS' REST HOUSE $
(☑273093; www.linhsonnepalindiatemple.org; Buddha Marg; tr ₹700, ste tr ₹1700) Simple, clean triples with private bathroom and hot water.

Japan-Sri Lanka Buddhist Centre PILGRIMS' REST HOUSE $
(☑273042; assajikushinagar@hotmail.com; Buddha Marg; tr/q ₹300/600) Set up for large groups, so call ahead, but has decent-quality, clean rooms.

★ Yama Cafe MULTICUISINE $
(Buddha Marg; mains ₹30-80; ⊙8am-8pm) Run by the welcoming Mr and Mrs Roy, this Kushinagar institution has a traveller-friendly menu which includes toast, omelettes, fried rice and *thukpa* (Tibetan noodle soup) and is the best place to come for information about the area. Ask about the so-called Holy Hike, a 13km-walk in the surrounding farmland.

ℹ Information

There is one Central Bank of India ATM and a couple of private money changers. **Sweet Solutions** (per hr ₹400; ⊙8am-6pm) is the most reliable internet in town.

ℹ Getting There & Away

Frequent buses to Gorakhpur (₹42, two hours, 24 hours though less frequently after dark) will pick you up at the yellow archway.

Sunauli

✐05522

Sunauli is a dusty town that offers little more than a bus stop, a couple of hotels, a few shops and a border post. The border is open 24 hours and the crossing is straightforward so most travellers carry on into Nepal without stopping here. There are more facilities in the Nepali part of Sunauli; Bhairawa, a further 4km north, is a more substantial town.

Buses drop you just a few hundred metres from the Indian immigration office, so you can ignore the cycle-rickshaws.

If you need to bed down here for a night, **Hotel Indo-Nepal** (☑238142; r ₹400-650), by the bus stand, has underwhelming rooms set around a cool courtyard. Its simple **restaurant** (mains ₹40-150, thali ₹75-120; ⊙6.30am-10pm) doesn't instill confidence but actually makes a nice lunch stop even if you don't stay.

If you're leaving India, the very helpful **Nepal Tourism Board information centre** (www.welcomenepal.com; ⊙10am-5pm Sun-Fri) is on your right, in no-man's land.

The Nepali side of Sunauli has a few cheap hotels, outdoor restaurants and a more upbeat atmosphere, but most travellers prefer to stay in Bhairawa, or get straight on a bus to Kathmandu or Pokhara.

Regular buses run from Sunauli to Gorakhpur (₹81, three hours, 5am to 7pm) from where you can catch trains to Varanasi. A few morning (4.30am to 10.30am) and afternoon (4.30pm to 7pm) buses run direct to Varanasi (₹242, 11 hours), but it's a long, bumpy ride. For faster collective jeeps to Gorakhpur, take your second left after Indian immigration down a small side street and walk about 75m past the water tower into a

BORDER CROSSING – INTO NEPAL FROM SUNAULI

Border Hours

The border is open 24 hours but closes to vehicles from 10pm to 6am, and if you arrive in the middle of the night you may have to wake someone to get stamped out of India. For further information, head to shop.lonelyplanet.com to purchase a downloadable PDF of the Kathmandu chapter from Lonely Planet's *Nepal* guide.

Foreign Exchange

There's nowhere to change money in Sunauli, but there are foreign-exchange places just across the border on the Nepal side. Small denominations of Indian currency are accepted for bus fares on the Nepal side.

Onward Transport

Buses and shared jeeps leave all day until around 8pm from the Nepal side of the border for Kathmandu (NRs600, six hours) and Pokhara (NRs500, eight hours). The most comfortable option is the **Golden Travels** (☏0977 71520194) AC bus to Kathmandu (NRs1000, six to seven hours); it leaves Sunauli at 7am. Shared autorickshaws or jeeps (NRs10) can take you from the border to Bhairawa, 4km away, where you can also catch buses to Kathmandu (NRs 467, eight hours) via Narayangarh (NRs 230, three hours); Pokhara (NRs 367, nine hours) via Tansen (NRs 120, five hours) along the Siddhartha Hwy or via the Mugling Hwy (NRs 450, eight hours). Local buses for Buddha's birthplace at Lumbini (NRs 70, one hour) leave from the junction of the Siddhartha Hwy and the road to Lumbini, about 1km north of Bank Rd.

  Buddha Air (www.buddhahair.com) and **Yeti Airlines** (www.yetiairlines.com) offer flights to Kathmandu from Bhairawa (from US$121).

Visas

Multiple-entry visas (15/30/90 days US$25/40/100 – cash, not rupees) are available at the Nepal immigration post. You will need two recent passport photos. Always check with **Nepal Department of Immigration** (☏0977 1 4433934; www.immi.gov.np; Kalikasthan, Kathmandu) for the latest information.

parking lot where they congregate and leave when full (₹150 to ₹200, two hours).

  Be wary of buying 'through' tickets from Kathmandu or Pokhara to Varanasi. Some travellers report being intimidated into buying another ticket once over the border. Travelling in either direction, it's better to take a local bus to the border, walk across and take another onward bus (pay the conductor on board). Travellers have also complained about being pressured into paying extra luggage charges for buses out of Sunauli. You shouldn't have to, so politely decline.

Uttarakhand

Why Go?

Soaring Himalayan peaks and steamy lowland jungles. Revered temples and renowned ashrams. Peaceful hill stations and busy cities. Uttarakhand is truly a thali of a state, with some of India's best trekking, yoga schools, holiday towns and wildlife-watching all tucked into one little corner of the country.

Hindus think of Uttarakhand as *Dev Bhoomi* – the Land of Gods – and the dramatic terrain is covered with holy mountains, lakes and rivers. Twisting roads and high-altitude hiking trails lead to spectacular pilgrimage sites where tales from the Hindu epics are set. And something of these ancient stories seems to have been absorbed by the land, which exudes a subtle sense of actually being sacred – even to ultra-orthodox agnostics. Many travellers flock here for this vibe, finding it a powerful place to pursue a spiritual practice.

Others come here for the tigers!

Best Off the Beaten Path

➡ Munsyari (p448)

➡ Tungnath & Chandrasila (p437)

➡ Binsar Wildlife Sanctuary (p446)

➡ Har-ki-Dun (p434)

Best for Culture

➡ Kedarnath (p432)

➡ Hem Kund (p437)

➡ Haridwar (p419)

➡ Nanda Devi Fair (p445)

When to Go
Rishikesh

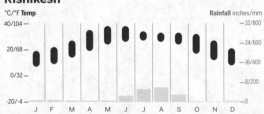

Apr–mid-Jun
The best season for tiger spotting at Corbett Tiger Reserve.

Jul–mid-Sep Monsoons may make travel difficult; Valley of Flowers bloom is best July and August.

Mid-Sep–Oct
The perfect time to trek the Himalaya.

Food

Uttarakhand is not famous for its food, and cuisine is typically North Indian. The most variety is found in Mussoorie, Rishikesh, Nainital and Dehra Dun. A warning to meat-eaters: towns with top-tier religious significance are all-vegetarian, all the time.

DON'T MISS

Every evening around sunset, hundreds of Hindu worshippers converge at Haridwar's **Har-ki-Pairi Ghat** to perform *puja* (prayer offering) on the Ganges canal. Leaf baskets filled with a fragrant rainbow of flower petals, each softly lit by a candle nestled in the centre, are launched onto the water. Beautiful and intense, this might be the most potent scene of archetypal 'India' in all of Uttarakhand. Just north of Haridwar, follow the footsteps of The Beatles to **Rishikesh** (p424), the world-renowned spiritual-seekers' city, where you'll surely find a yoga or meditation course to suit your needs – whether you're a serious practitioner or an undisciplined dabbler. Spanning the northern half of the state are the mighty **Himalaya** (p434). A vast land of soaring, snowy summits and alpine meadows, Uttarakhand is a trekking paradise. Choose between busy pilgrims' trails on the **Char Dham route** (p431) or remote wilderness where you'll hardly see another soul.

Top State Festivals

➡ **Magh Mela** (Jan & Feb, Haridwar, p419) Hundreds of thousands of pilgrims come to bathe in the soul-cleansing Ganges during this huge annual religious fair. The Ardh Kumbh Mela is held every six years; and millions of pilgrims attend the mega Kumbh Mela every 12 years.

➡ **International Yoga Festival** (Mar, Rishikesh, p427) Rishikesh hosts the International Yoga Festival, attracting swamis and yoga masters from around the world for discourses and lectures. Most of the action is centred on the Parmarth Niketan Ashram in Swarg Ashram. Check the festival website for dates.

➡ **Shivaratri** (usually Mar, Dehra Dun, p413) A festival celebrated in style with carnival rides and stalls at a picturesque riverside cave temple on the outskirts of Dehra Dun.

➡ **Nanda Devi Fair** (Sep, Almora, p445) During this five-day fair, thousands of devotees parade the image of the goddess around and watch dancing and other cultural shows.

MAIN POINTS OF ENTRY

Haridwar, Dehra Dun and Haldwani are easily reached by train or bus. Jolly Grant Airport is convenient to Rishikesh and Dehra Dun. Enter or exit Nepal at Banbassa.

Fast Facts

➡ **Population**: 10.1 million

➡ **Area**: 51,125sq km

➡ **Capital**: Dehra Dun

➡ **Main languages:** Hindi, Garhwali, Kumaoni

➡ **Sleeping prices**: **$** below ₹800, **$$** ₹800 to 1800, **$$$** above ₹1800

Top Tip

If travelling through the hills or mountains, get to buses early to claim a window seat. The landscape, much of which you'll never stop to explore, is gorgeous.

Resources

➡ **US Military maps** (www.lib.utexas.edu/maps/ams/india), useful for trekking.

➡ Background on the **Chipko movement** (http://spot.colorado.edu/~wehr/491R10.TXT), the original 'tree-huggers'.

➡ Read up on **Transcendental Meditation** (www.tm.org), founded by Maharishi Mahesh Yogi.

Uttarakhand Highlights

1 Visit the temple at **Gangotri** (p431) and trek beyond it to **Gaumukh** (p431), the source of the holy Ganges River

2 Float a candle down the Ganges at the gorgeous nightly ceremony at Haridwar's **Har-ki-Pairi Ghat** (p419)

3 Scout for rare Bengal tigers and ride an elephant in **Corbett Tiger Reserve** (p438)

4 Get your asanas and chakras sorted at **Rishikesh** (p424), the yoga and ashram capital of the universe

5 Cool off in a scenic Raj-era hill station in **Mussoorie** (p415) or **Nainital** (p440)

6 Trek to the sublime **Valley of Flowers National Park** (p436) and nearby **Hem Kund** (p437) for an unforgettable combo of the scenic and sacred

7 Immerse yourself in a mind-blowing Himalayan landscape while trekking the **Kuari Pass** (p434) through Nanda Devi Sanctuary

History

Uttarakhand consists of the culturally distinct Garhwal (in the west) and Kumaon (east) districts. Over the centuries various dynasties have dominated the region, including the Guptas, Kuturyi and Chand rajas. In the 18th century the Nepalese Gurkhas attacked first the kingdom of Kumaon, then Garhwal, prompting the British to step in and take most of the region as part of the Treaty of Sigauli in 1817.

After Independence, the region was merged with Uttar Pradesh, but a vocal separatist movement follwed, and the present-day state of Uttaranchal was formed in 2000. In 2007 it was officially renamed Uttarakhand, a traditional name meaning 'northern country'.

Climate

Temperatures are determined by altitude in this state of elevation extremes. Trekking the Himalaya is possible from May to October, but can be dangerous between July and mid-September, during the monsoon, when violent cloudbursts cause landslides. Hill stations offer a welcome escape from summertime heat, while low-lying Rishikesh is most comfortable from October to March.

ℹ Information

Most towns in the region have an Uttarakhand Tourism office, however the main responsibility for the region's tourism rests with the **Garhwal Mandal Vikas Nigam** (GMVN; www.gmvnl.com), in the Garhwal district, and **Kumaon Mandal Vikas Nigam** (KMVN; www.kmvn.org), in the Kumaon district.

ℹ Getting Around

Tough old government buses are the main means of travelling around Uttarakhand. In addition, crowded share jeeps (often called 'sumos') criss-cross the state, linking remote towns and villages to important road junctions. Pay 10 times the share-taxi rate to hire the whole vehicle and travel in comfort. Roads that snake through the hills can be nerve-racking and stomach-churning, and are sometimes blocked by monsoon-season landslides.

DEHRA DUN

☑ 0135 / POP 578,420 / ELEV 700M

Perhaps best known for the institutions the British left behind – the huge Forest Research Institute Museum, the Indian Military Academy, the Wildlife Institute of India and the Survey of India – the capital of Uttarakhand is a hectic, congested city sprawling in the Doon Valley between the Himalayan foothills and the Siwalik Range. Most travellers merely pass through on their way to nearby Rishikesh, Haridwar, Mussoorie or Himachal Pradesh, but if you have time, there's enough to do here to make Dehra Dun worth a stop.

◉ Sights & Activities

Mindrolling Monastery   MONASTERY
(☑ 2640556; www.mindrolling.org) The region around Dehra Dun is home to a thriving Tibetan Buddhist community, mainly focused on the Mindrolling Monastery, about 10km south of the centre in Clement Town. Everything about the monastery is on a grand scale: it boasts a large college, manicured gardens and the five-storey **Great Stupa** (admission free; ⊙ 5am-9pm). At over 60m tall, it's believed to be the world's tallest stupa and contains a series of shrine rooms displaying relics, murals and Tibetan art. Presiding over the monastery is the impressive 35m-high gold **Buddha Statue**, dedicated to the Dalai Lama.

The streets around the monastery have several Tibetan-run cafes. Unfortunately, due to a change in government regulations, foreigners are no longer allowed to stay overnight in Clement Town. Take *vikram* (large tempo) 5 from the city centre (₹10). An autorickshaw costs about ₹150.

**Forest Research
Institute Museum**   NOTABLE BUILDING
(☑ 2759382; www.icfre.org; admission ₹10, guide ₹50; ⊙ 9.30am-4.30pm Mon-Fri) The prime attraction of this museum is the building itself. Set in a 5-sq-km park, the institute – where most of India's forest officers are trained – is larger than Buckingham Palace and is a grand remnant of the Raj era. Built between 1924 and 1929, this red-brick colossus has Mughal towers, perfectly formed arches and Roman columns in a series of quadrangles edged by elegant cloisters. Six huge halls have displays on Indian forestry that look like leftovers from a middle-school science fair. Highlights include beautiful animal, bird and plant paintings by Afshan Zaidi, exhibits on the medicinal uses of trees, and a cross-section of a 700-year-old deodar tree. A return autorickshaw from the city centre, including waiting time, costs around ₹250.

Dehra Dun

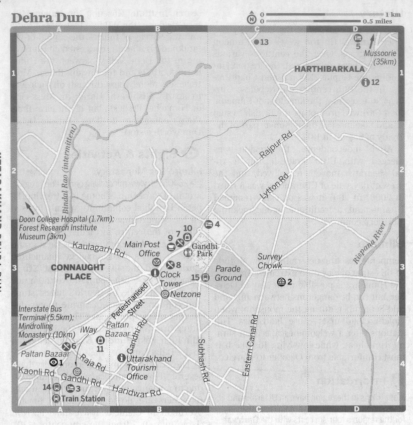

Or take *vikram* 6 from Connaught Place and get out at the institute's entry gate.

Ram Rai Darbar
MAUSOLEUM

(Paltan Bazaar; ⊙ dawn-dusk) FREE The unique mausoleum of Ram Rai, the errant son of the seventh Sikh guru, Har Rai, is made of white marble, with paintings covering the walls, archways, and ceilings. Four smaller tombs in the garden courtyard are those of Ram Rai's four wives. A free communal lunch of dhal, rice and chapatis is offered to anyone who wants it, for a donation.

Survey of India Museum
MUSEUM

(Survey Chowk; ⊙ 10.30am-5pm Mon-Fri) FREE Instruments used to accomplish the monumental task of mapping India in the 19th century are on display here, including some designed especially for the mission by its leader, George Everest. Among them are beautiful transits and scopes of gleaming brass, and a bar made partly of iron, partly of brass, which allowed surveyors to compensate for inaccuracies in their measurements caused by the expansion and contraction of their instruments due to heat and cold. Small placards tell snippets of the story of one of the most impressive geographical feats ever achieved.

The museum, however, is not officially opened to the public. To get permission to see it, go to the Surveyor General's office at the **Survey of India Compound** in Harthibarkala. There, you'll have to write a brief letter explaining why you want to view the collection. Permits are given only to those with an academic or professional interest in the subject – like a geography student or a historian – but proof of your vocation or college major isn't demanded.

Tapkeshwar Temple
HINDU TEMPLE

(⊙ dawn-dusk) In a scenic setting on the banks of the Tons Nadi River, you'll find

Dehra Dun

an unusual and popular Shiva shrine inside a small, dripping cave, which is the site of the annual **Shivaratri** (Tapkeshwar Temple; ☺usually Mar) festival. Turn left at the bottom of the steps for the main shrine. Cross the bridge over the river to visit another one, where you have to squeeze through a narrow cave to see an image of Mata Vaishno Devi. The temple is about 5km north of the centre. Take a rickshaw for ₹300 round trip.

🛏 Sleeping

There are plenty of grungy cheapies along the Haridwar road outside the train station, some charging as little as ₹300 a double, but the better places can be found along Gandhi Rd and Rajpur Rd.

Hotel GP Grand   HOTEL $$
(☎2625555; www.hotelgpgrand.com; 68 Gandhi Rd; s/d from ₹750/900, with AC from ₹1325/1450; ❊) If you want to be near the train station,

you can't get much closer or cleaner than the GP Grand. Good rooms, surprisingly quiet, with a restaurant in the lobby.

Samar Niwas Guest House   GUESTHOUSE $$
(☎2740299; www.samarniwas.com; M-16 Chanderlok Colony; d ₹1000-1800; ❊ @) This charming four-room guesthouse, in a peaceful residential area just off Rajpur Rd, is as welcoming as it gets. The owners are descendants of the Tehri royal family, but the rulers of the house seem to be the friendly pugs that roam the comfortable lounge-cum-lobby. Rooms are well appointed, but cleanliness is less than meticulous.

Hotel President   HOTEL $$$
(☎2657082; www.hotelpresidentdehradun.com; 6 Astley Hall, Rajpur Rd; s ₹3320-3690, d ₹3690-4060; ❊) This Dehra Dun institution is one of the classiest hotels in town, despite being sandwiched within the complex of shops, restaurants and fast-food spots called Astley Hall. Rooms are thoroughly modern and even the least expensive have fridges, safes and complimentary slippers. There's a good restaurant, a coffee shop and the Polo Bar.

✖ Eating & Drinking

Dehra Dun has an eclectic range of restaurants, but by far the best hunting ground is along Rajpur Rd, northeast of the clock tower. The Astley Hall precinct is popular for fast food and has a couple of upmarket bars.

★ Chetan Puriwallah   INDIAN $
(near Hanuman Chowk, Paltan Bazaar; ₹12 per puri; ☺9am-4pm) If you're looking for that authentic (and delicious) local dining experience, you've found it. Unlimited thalis are served on plates made of leaves in this no-frills joint, and you just pay for the *puri* (deep-fried dough). The sweet *gulab jamun* (deep-fried dough in rose-flavoured syrup) is said to be some of the best in town.

Kumar Vegetarian & South Indian Restaurant   INDIAN $$
(15B Rajpur Rd; mains ₹90-180; ☺8.30am-4pm, & 7-10.30pm) This popular, sparkling clean restaurant serves what surely comes close to the Platonic Form of a masala dosa, which is the main reason locals flock here. Other Indian dishes are also cooked to near perfection and even the Chinese food is quite good. The waitstaff are very attentive.

Motimahal
SOUTH INDIAN $$

(7 Rajpur Rd; mains ₹160-325; ⊘11am-11pm) Locals consistently rate Motimahal as one of the best midrange diners along Rajpur Rd. An interesting range of vegetarian and non-vegetarian includes Goan fish curry and Afghani *murg* (chicken), along with traditional South Indian fare and Chinese food.

Polo Bar
BAR

(6 Astley Hall, Rajpur Rd; ⊘11am-3pm & 7-11pm) One of the more salubrious of Dehra Dun's many hotel bars, this one is at Hotel President.

Barista
CAFE

(15a Rajpur Rd; drinks & snacks ₹50-150; ⊘9am-11pm; 🛜) A popular modern cafe with board games, wi-fi and an excellent bookshop out back.

🛍 Shopping

Among the best bookshops in town are **Natraj Booksellers** (17 Rajpur Rd; ⊘10.30am-1.30pm & 3-8pm Mon-Sat), which gives plenty of shelf to local author Ruskin Bond, and **English Book Depot** (✉2655192; www.englishbookdepot.com; 15 Rajpur Rd; ⊘10am-1.30pm & 2.30-8pm), attached to the Barista coffee shop.

Paltan Bazaar
MARKET

The congested but virtually traffic-free street through Paltan Bazaar, running south from the clock tower, is a popular spot for an evening stroll. Here you can pick up everything from cheap clothing and souvenirs to camping and trekking gear.

Survey of India Map Counter
MAPS

(maps ₹20-70; ⊘9am-5.30pm Mon-Fri) Though the Survey of India Map Counter in Harthibarkala is mostly good for being told which topographical maps you're not allowed to buy, you can pick up trekking maps that aren't bad for getting from village to village, but are worthless for backcountry navigation.

ℹ Information

The banks located on Rajpur Rd exchange travellers cheques and currency, and there are numerous ATMs that accept foreign credit cards.

Ambulance (✉2650102)

Doon College Hospital (✉2760330; General Mahadev Singh Rd)

GMVN Office (74/1 Rajpur Rd; ⊘10am-5pm Mon-Sat) For some of the most helpful information on trekking in Garwhal, whether booking a GMVN trip or going independently, talk to Satish Khanduri (⊘9568006696) in the Adventure Tourism office, two flights up.

iWay (Hotel Grand, Shri Laxmi Plaza, 64 Gandhi Rd; per hr ₹30; ⊘10am-8pm)

Main Post Office (Rajpur Rd; ⊘10am-6pm Mon-Fri, 10am-1pm Sat)

Netzone (per hr ₹30; ⊘9.30am-9.30pm) Located one block southeast of the clock tower.

Police (✉2653333)

Uttarakhand Tourism Office (✉2653217; 45 Gandhi Rd; ⊘10am-5pm Mon-Sat, closed 2nd Sat of month) The local tourist office, attached to the Hotel Drona. There's also a tourist information counter at the train station.

BUSES FROM DEHRA DUN

The following buses depart from the Interstate Bus Terminal (ISBT).

DESTINATION	FARE (₹)	DURATION (HR)	FREQUENCY
Chandigarh	175	6	hourly 4am-10pm
Delhi (standard)	200	7	hourly 4am-10.30pm
Delhi (AC Volvo)	480	7	7 daily
Delhi (deluxe)	290/350AC	7	hourly 4am-11pm
Dharamsala	658	14	1.45pm & 5pm
Haldwani (for Nainital)	275	10	hourly
Haridwar	50	2	half-hourly
Joshimath	380	12	5.30am
Manali	300	14	3pm
Ramnagar	210	7	7 per day
Rishikesh	41	1½	half-hourly
Shimla	260/460AC	10	6 per day
Uttarkashi	225	8	5.30am & 7am

🛈 Getting There & Away

AIR

A few airlines fly daily between Delhi and Dehra Dun's Jolly Grant Airport – about 20km east of the city on the Haridwar road – with fares starting at around ₹3500 each way. A taxi to/from the airport costs ₹550, or take the AC coach for ₹100 (call the Uttarakhand Tourism office for details).

BUS

Nearly all long-distance buses arrive and depart from the huge Interstate Bus Terminal (ISBT), 5km south of the city centre. To get there take a local bus (₹5), vikram 5 (₹10) or an autorickshaw (₹100). A few buses to Mussoorie leave from here but most depart from the **Mussoorie bus stand** (₹41, 1½ hours, half-hourly between 6am and 8pm) next to the train station. Some head to Mussoorie's Picture Palace bus stand while others go to the Library bus stand across town. There are also buses from the Mussoorie bus stand to Barkot – for Yamnotri – (₹190, five hours, 5.30am, 7.30am and 11.30am) and Sankri – for Har-Ki-Dun – (₹200, seven hours, 6.30am, 9.30am and 1.30pm).

Private buses to Joshimath (₹300, 12 hours, 7am) and Uttarkashi (via Mussoorie ₹180, seven hours, 7.30am and 1.30pm; or via Rishikesh ₹230, eight hours, 7am and 1pm) leave from the **Parade Ground bus stand**.

TAXI

A taxi to Mussoorie costs ₹610, while a share taxi should cost ₹120 per person; both can be found in front of the train station. Taxis charge ₹910 to Rishikesh and ₹1010 to Haridwar.

TRAIN

Dehra Dun is well connected by train to Delhi, and there are a handful of services to Lucknow, Varanasi, Chennai (Madras) and Kolkata (Calcutta). Of the multiple daily trains between Dehra Dun and Delhi, the best are the expresses: Shatabdi (chair/executive ₹510/1055, six hours; train 12017 from New Delhi station to Dehra Dun at 6.50am; train 12018 from Dehra Dun to New Delhi station at 5pm) and Janshatabdi (2nd class/chair ₹137/410, six hours; train no. 12055 from New Delhi station to Dehra Dun at 3:25pm; train 12056 from Dehra Dun to New Delhi station at 5.10am).

The overnight Dehradun–Amritsar Express (sleeper/3A ₹203/539, 12 hours) to Amritsar departs nightly at 7.40pm.

🛈 Getting Around

Hundreds of eight-seater vikrams (₹3 to ₹10 per trip) race along five fixed routes (look at the front for the number). Most useful is vikram 5, which runs between the ISBT stand, the train station and Rajpur Rd, and as far south as the Tibetan colony at Clement Town. Vikram 1 runs up and down Rajpur Rd above Gandhi Park, and also to Harthibarkala (check with the driver to see which route he's on). Autorickshaws cost ₹30 for a short distance, ₹150 from ISBT to the city centre or ₹160 per hour for touring around the city.

MUSSOORIE

☑ 0135 / POP 29,500 / ELEV 2000M

Perched on a ridge 2km high, the 'Queen of Hill Stations' vies with Nainital as Uttarakhand's favourite holiday destination. When the mist clears, views of the green Doon Valley and the distant white-capped Himalayan peaks are superb, and in the hot months the cooler temperatures and fresh mountain air make a welcome break from the plains below.

Established by the British in 1823, Mussoorie became hugely popular with the Raj set. The ghosts of that era linger on in the architecture of the churches, libraries, hotels and summer palaces. The town is swamped with visitors between May and July, when it can seem like a tacky holiday camp for families and honeymooners, but at other times many of the 300 hotels have vacancies and their prices drop dramatically. During monsoon, the town is often shrouded in clouds.

Central Mussoorie consists of two developed areas: Gandhi Chowk (also called Library Bazaar) at the western end, and the livelier Kulri Bazaar and Picture Palace at the eastern end, linked by the (almost) traffic-free 2km Mall. Beyond Kulri Bazaar a narrow road leads 1.5km to Landour Bazaar.

◉ Sights & Activities

Gun Hill   VIEWPOINT

From midway along the Mall, a **cable car** (return ₹75; ⊙ 8am-10pm May-Jul & Oct, 10am-7pm Aug-Sep & late Nov-Apr) runs up to Gun Hill (2530m), which, on a clear day, has views of several big peaks. A steep path also winds up to the viewpoint. The most popular time to go up is an hour or so before sunset and there's a minicarnival atmosphere in high season, with kids' rides, food stalls, magic shops and honeymooners having their photos taken in Garhwali costumes.

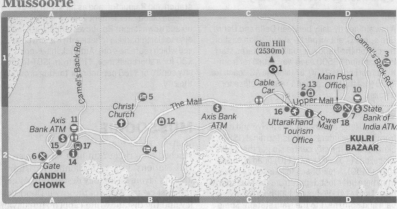

Mussoorie

Sights
1 Gun Hill.......................................C1

Activities, Courses & Tours
GMVN Booth...............................(see 17)
2 Trek Himalaya............................D1

Sleeping
3 Hotel Broadway..........................D1
4 Hotel Padmini Nivas...................B2
5 Kasmanda Palace Hotel..............B1

Eating
6 Imperial Square..........................A2
7 Kalsang Friends Corner...............D2
Kasmanda Palace Restaurant......(see 5)
8 Lovely Omelette Centre...............E1
9 Tavern..E1

Drinking & Nightlife
10 Café Coffee Day........................D1
11 Café Coffee Day........................A2

Shopping
12 Tibetan Market.........................B2
13 Wildcraft..................................D1

Information
Connexions..................................(see 9)
14 GMVN Booth.............................A2
Trek Himalaya.............................(see 2)

Transport
15 Cycle-rickshaw Stand...............A2
16 Cycle-rickshaw Stand...............C2
17 Library Bus Stand.....................A2
18 Northern Railway Booking Agency.......D2
19 Picture Palace Bus Stand..........F2
Taxi Stand..................................(see 19)
Taxi Stand..................................(see 17)

Walks

WALKING

When the clouds don't get in the way, the walks around Mussoorie offer great views. **Camel's Back Rd** is a popular 3km promenade from Kulri Bazaar to Gandhi Chowk, and passes a rock formation that looks like a camel. There are a couple of good mountain viewpoints along the way, and you can ride a horse (one way/return ₹200/250) along the trail if you start from the Gandhi Chowk end. An enjoyable, longer walk (5km one way) starts at the **Picture Palace Cinema**, goes past **Union Church** and the clock tower to Landour and the Sisters' Bazaar area.

West of Gandhi Chowk, a more demanding walk is to the **Jwalaji Temple** on Benog Hill (about 20km return) via Cloud's End Hotel. The route passes through thick forest and offers fine views. Taking a taxi to Cloud's End (₹500) cuts the walk by more than half. A slightly shorter walk is to the abandoned **Everest House** (16km return), former residence of Sir George Everest, first surveyor-general of India and namesake of the world's highest mountain. You can also take a cycle rickshaw (₹100) to Park Toll, cutting 5km off

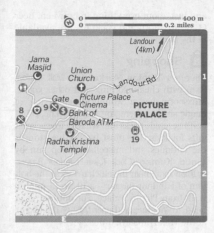

the distance. Trek Himalaya (p417) can organise guides for around ₹700 a day.

🐾 Courses

Mussoorie is home to many schools and colleges, including the **Landour Language School** (☑2631487; www.landourlanguageschool. com; Landour; group ₹175 per hr, private ₹275 per hr; ☺Feb-Dec), one of India's leading schools for teaching conversational Hindi at beginner, intermediate and advanced levels. There's an enrollment fee of ₹250, and course books are an extra ₹2000.

🧭 Tours

A full day of sightseeing around Mussoorie by taxi costs around ₹2700, including visits to the popular and overdeveloped Kempty Falls, 15km west, and to Dhanolti – a serene spot 25km east, set in deodar forests with Himalayan views

GMVN Booth   SIGHTSEEING
(☑2631281; Library bus stand; ☺8am-6pm Mon-Sat) GMVN organises a number of local bus tours, including to Kempty Falls (three-hour tour ₹100), and Dhanolti, Surkhanda Devi Temple and Mussoorie Lake (full-day tour ₹225). Tours can also be booked at the Utterakhand Tourism Office on the Lower Mall.

Trek Himalaya   TREKKING
(☑2630491; www.trekhimalaya.com; Upper Mall; ☺11am-9pm) For around ₹2500 per day, long-time local trekker Neelambar Badoni organises three-day treks to unspoilt Nagtibba, as well as customised treks to Dodital, Har-ki-Dun and Gaumukh Glacier, and safaris as far as Ladakh.

🛏 Sleeping

Peak season is summer (May to July) when hotel prices shoot to ridiculous heights. There's a midseason during the honeymoon period around October and November, and over Christmas and New Year. At other times you should be able to get a bargain. The following prices are for midseason, unless otherwise specified.

Budget places are few – you'll find some dives near Picture Palace. But there are scores of hotels that drop their rates into budget territory out of season. We list just a few here, which are outstanding for one reason or another.

Hotel Broadway   HOTEL $
(☑2632243; Camel's Back Rd, Kulri Bazaar; d ₹600-1500) The best of the budget places by a country mile, this historic 1880s wooden hotel with colourful flowerboxes in the windows oozes character. It's in a quiet location but close to the Mall. Cheaper downstairs rooms could use a refresh, but upstairs rooms are nice; the best has lovely sunlit bay windows.

⭐**Kasmanda Palace Hotel**   HERITAGE HOTEL $$$
(☑2632424; www.kasmandapalace.com; d ₹5000-7200) Located off the Mall, this is Mussoorie's most romantic hotel. The white Romanesque castle was built in 1836 for a British officer and was bought by the Maharaja of Kasmanda in 1915. The red-carpeted hall has a superb staircase flanked by moth-eaten hunting trophies (the tiger and leopard skins are a sad anachronism). All of the rooms have charm but the wood-panelled and antique-filled Maharaja Room is the royal best. There's also a separate cottage with six renovated contemporary-style rooms. Excellent restaurant and pretty garden area complete the picture.

Hotel Padmini Nivas   HERITAGE HOTEL $$$
(☑2631093; www.hotelpadmininivas.com; The Mall; d ₹2250-2850, ste ₹3450-4050; @) Built in 1840 by a British colonel, this heritage hotel has real old-fashioned charm. Large rooms with quaint sun rooms are beautifully furnished; those in the main house are significantly nicer than those in the side building. The dining room, with its antique furniture, is an outstanding feature.

The whole place is set on 2 hectares of landscaped gardens.

Eating & Drinking

Most of Mussoorie's best eating places are at the Kulri Bazaar and Picture Palace end of town. True to the holiday feel there are lots of fast-food places, and most hotels have their own restaurants. There is a **Café Coffee Day** in Kulri Bazaar and another **branch** near Gandhi Chowk.

★ Lovely Omelette Centre   FAST FOOD $
(The Mall, Kulri Bazaar; mains ₹30-80; ⊙9am-9.30pm Wed-Mon) Mussorie's most famous eatery is also its smallest – a cubbyhole along the Mall that serves what many say are the best omelettes in India. The specialty is the cheese omelette, with chillies, onions and spices, served over toast, but the maestro at the frying pan will whip up a chocolate omelette on request.

★ Imperial Square   CONTINENTAL $$
(☑2632632; Gandhi Chowk; mains ₹190-350; ⊙7am-11pm; 🛜) With huge windows overlooking Gandhi Chowk, Imperial Square scores high on everything – decor, service and food. The menu is strong on Continental dishes, with long lists of platters and sizzlers, plus big toasted sandwiches. For breakfast you can even have waffles. Upstairs features a tea room–cum–hookah lounge, and the attached hotel (doubles ₹5000) has excellent rooms with valley views.

Kasmanda Palace Restaurant   MULTICUISINE $$
(☑2632424; Kasmanda Palace Hotel; mains ₹110-350) The regal restaurant at this Raj-era hotel (found north of the Mall) is the perfect escape from Mussoorie's holiday bustle. The dining room is intimate but not stuffy, and the garden restaurant is fine for a lazy lunch or summer evening. The food lives up to the setting with North and South Indian dishes, as well as Continental (moussaka and pastas) and Chinese offerings.

Kalsang Friends Corner   TIBETAN $$
(Kulri Bazaar, The Mall; mains ₹90-220; ⊙11am-11pm) Tibetan-run, Kalsang has a longer list of *momos* (dumplings) than you might think possible.

Tavern   MULTICUISINE $$$
(Picture Palace, The Mall; mains ₹190-400; ⊙11am-11pm) A global range of food, from tons of tandoori to roast lamb, fish curry and just about everything in between. Beer (₹200 to ₹300) and cocktails are available at the bar.

Shopping

There's a **Tibetan Market** (The Mall; ⊙from 9am) with cheap clothing and other goods. Mussoorie has a wonderful collection of magic shops, where you can buy cheap but baffling magic tricks and whacky toys – great gifts for kids. The most interesting store is the antiques and miscellany shop run by **Vinod Kumar** (Clock Tower, Landour Bazaar; ⊙10am-7pm), near the clock tower at the bottom of Landour Bazaar – a 10- to 15-minute walk from Picture Palace. For outdoor gear, head to **Wildcraft** (Upper Mall; ⊙11am-9pm), at the Trek Himalaya office.

Information

Connexions (Kulri Bazaar, The Mall; per hr ₹60; ⊙10.30am-10.30pm) Above the Tavern.

GMVN Booth (☑2631281; Library bus stand; ⊙8am-6pm) Can book local tours, treks and far-flung rest houses.

Main Post Office (☑2632206; Kulri Bazaar, Upper Mall; ⊙9am-5pm Mon-Sat)

Trek Himalaya (☑2630491; Upper Mall; ⊙11am-9pm) Exchanges major currencies at a fair rate.

Uttarakhand Tourism Office (☑2632863; Lower Mall; ⊙10am-5pm Mon-Sat) Near the cable-car station.

Getting There & Away

BUS
Frequent buses head to Mussoorie (₹47, 1½ hours) from Dehra Dun's Mussoorie bus stand. Some go to the **Picture Palace bus stand** (☑2632259) while others go to the **Library bus stand** (☑2632258) at the other end of town – if you know where you're staying, it helps to be on the right bus. There's no direct transport from Mussoorie to Rishikesh or Haridwar – change at Dehra Dun.

To reach the mountain villages of western Garhwal, buses and jeeps leave from around the Library bus stand. For Yamunotri, hop on a bus to Barkot (₹160, 3½ hours, departs around 7am, 9am and 1pm), then another to Hanuman Chatti (₹60, 2½ hours). A few direct buses go to Sankri (₹200, five hours, departs around 8am, 10.30am and 3pm). For Uttarkashi, leave from the Tehri bus stand at Landour and change at Chamba.

TAXI
From taxi stands at both bus stands you can hire taxis to Dehra Dun (₹610) and Rishikesh

(₹1610), or jeeps to Uttarkashi (₹3500). A shared taxi to Dehra Dun should cost ₹100 per person.

TRAIN

The **Northern Railway booking agency** (☑2632846; Kulri Bazaar, Lower Mall; ⊘8am-2pm Mon-Sat) books tickets for trains from Dehra Dun and Haridwar.

ⓘ Getting Around

Central Mussoorie is very walkable – for a hill station, the Mall and Camel's Back Rd are surprisingly flat. Cycle-rickshaws along the Mall cost ₹30, but can only go between Gandhi Chowk and the cable-car station.

HARIDWAR

☑ 01334 / POP 225,235 / ELEV 249M

Propitiously located at the point where the Ganges emerges from the Himalaya, Haridwar (also called Hardwar) is Uttarakhand's holiest Hindu city, and pilgrims arrive here in droves to bathe in the fast-flowing Ganges. The sheer numbers of people gathering around Har-ki-Pairi Ghat give Haridwar a chaotic but reverent feel. Within the religious heirarchy of India, Haridwar is much more significant than Rishikesh, an hour further north, and every evening the river comes alive with flickering flames as floating offerings are released onto the Ganges. It's especially busy during the *yatra* (pilgrimage) season from May to October, and is the site of the annual Magh Mela religious festival.

Haridwar's main street is Railway Rd, becoming Upper Rd, which runs parallel to the Ganges canal (the river proper runs further to the east). Generally only cycle-rickshaws are allowed between Laltarao Bridge and Bhimgoda Jhula (Bhimgoda Bridge), so vehicles travel around the opposite bank of the river. The alleyways of Bara Bazaar run south of Har-ki-Pairi Ghat.

⊙ Sights & Activities

★Har-ki-Pairi Ghat   GHAT

Har-ki-Pairi (The Footstep of God) is where is said to have dropped some divine nectar and left behind a footprint. Hindu pilgrims flock here to immerse in the Ganga's spiritually purifying currents.

The ghat sits on the western bank of the Ganges canal, and every evening hundreds of worshippers gather for the *ganga aarti*

(river worship ceremony). Officials in blue uniforms collect donations (and give out receipts) and, as the sun sets, bells ring out a rhythm, torches are lit, and leaf baskets with flower petals inside and a candle on top (₹10) are lit and put on the river to drift away downstream.

Tourists and travellers can mingle with the crowd to experience the rituals of an ancient religion that still retains its power in the modern age. Someone may claim to be a priest and help you with your *puja* before asking for ₹200 or more. If you want to make a donation, it's best to give it to a uniformed collector.

The best times to visit the ghat are early morning or just before dusk.

Mansa Devi & Chandi Devi Temples   HINDU TEMPLE

Take the **cable car** (return ₹58; ⊘7am-7pm Apr-Oct, 8am-6.30pm Nov-Mar) to the crowded hilltop temple of **Mansa Devi** (return ₹48; ⊘7.30am-7pm Apr-Oct, 8.30am-6pm Nov-Mar), a wish-fulfilling goddess. The path to the cable car is lined with stalls selling packages of *prasad* (food offering used in religious ceremonies) to take up to the goddess on the hill. You can walk up (1.5km) but beware of *prasad*-stealing monkeys. Photography is forbidden in the temple.

Many visitors and pilgrims combine this with another **cable car** (return ₹102; ⊘8am-6pm) up Neel Hill, 4km southeast of Haridwar, to **Chandi Devi Temple** (cable car return ₹70; ⊘8am-6pm). The temple was built by Raja Suchet Singh of Kashmir in 1929. Pay ₹210 at Mansa Devi and you can ride both cable cars and take an AC coach between the two temples.

⌖ Tours

Mohan's Adventure Tours   ADVENTURE TOUR

(☑9412022966, 9837100215; www.mohansadventure.in; Railway Rd; ⊘8am-10.30pm) Sanjeev Mehta of Mohan's Adventure Tours can organise any kind of tour, including trekking, fishing, birdwatching, cycling, motorcycling and rafting. An accomplished wildlife photographer, he specialises in five-hour safaris (₹1950 per person with two or more, singles pay ₹2750) within Rajaji National Park. Sanjeev also runs three-day trips to Corbett Tiger Reserve (from ₹7000). Tours operate year-round.

Haridwar

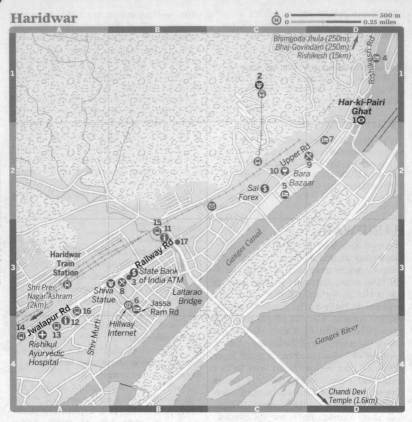

Haridwar

🛏 Sleeping

Haridwar has loads of hotels catering to Hindu pilgrims. The busiest time of year is the *yatra* season from April to November – outside this time you should have no problem finding a room at discounts of 20% to 50%.

Jassa Ram Rd and the other alleys running off Railway Rd have plenty of budget hotels and although some of the fancy foyers and neon signs may raise your hopes, none are great. Rishikesh has far superior budget accommodation.

Down by the ghats are a number of highrise hotels that have good views but very average rooms.

Hotel Arjun HOTEL $
(☎ 220409; www.hotelarjun.com; Jassa Ram Rd; r with/without AC from 700/350; ❄) Currently the best of the budget choices, the Arjun beats its neighbours for cleanliness and comfort. Some rooms have balconies. Most have their quirks, though – one a broken tv, another a dead overhead light – so take a look at a few if you can. It's walking distance from the train and bus stations.

Yatri Niwas HOTEL $$
(☎ 226004, 9675947484; www.yatriniwas.com; Upper Rd; r ₹1000; ❄) Just a few minutes' walk from Har ki Pairi Ghat and the Mansa Devi cable car, this place is set back from the road around a surprisingly quiet courtyard. Rooms are good value, with nice wooden furnishings, glass and steel light fixtures, flat-screen TVs and modern bathrooms.

Bhaj-Govindam HOTEL $$
(☎ 261682; www.bhajgovindam.com; Upper Rd; r from ₹1500; ❄) On Upper Rd about 100m north of Bhimgoda Jhula, Bhaj-Govindam is the most peaceful hotel in town, set around a grassy garden, with river frontage on the banks of the Ganges. Rooms are comfortable and suites are huge, but cleanliness is spotty. Fortunately, prices are very negotiable.

★ Haveli Hari Ganga HERITAGE HOTEL $$$
(☎ 226443; www.havelihariganga.com; 21 Ram Ghat; r ₹5500-7000; ❄ ☎) Hidden away in Bara Bazaar, but right on the Ganges, this superb 1918 *haveli* (traditional, ornately decorated residence) is Haridwar's finest hotel. Airy courtyards, marble floors, hanging flower baskets and balconies overlooking the river give it a regal charm. Room rates include breakfast, steam bath, yoga and the hotel's own *ganga aarti* on its private ghat. The Ganges laps one terrace, and downstairs an ayurvedic health spa offers treatments as well as yoga classes. It's hard to find, so call ahead for a pick-up.

🍴 Eating & Drinking

Being a holy city, only vegetarian food and nonalcoholic drinks are available.

★ Prakash Lok LASSI $
(Bara Bazaar; lassis ₹40) Don't miss a creamy lassi at this Haridwar institution, famed for its ice-cold, best-you'll-ever-have lassis served in tin cups. Just about anyone in the Bara Bazaar can point you to it.

Hoshiyar Puri INDIAN $
(Upper Rd; mains ₹60-120; ◷ 11am-4pm & 7pm-4am) Established in 1937, this place still has a loyal (and well-deserved) local following. The *dal makhani* (beans and lentils), *lacha paratha* (layered fried bread), *aloo gobi* (potato-and-cauliflower curry) and *kheer* (rice pudding) are lip-smackingly good.

Big Ben Restaurant MULTICUISINE $$
(Hotel Ganga Azure, Railway Rd; mains ₹80-190; ◷ 8am-11pm; ☎) Watch the passing parade through the big windows and enjoy some of Haridwar's best food in this restaurant of mirrors, soft music and polite staff. It's a solid choice for breakfast, with good coffee. There's wi-fi in the adjoining lobby.

Haveli Hari Ganga Restaurant INDIAN $$$
(☎ 226443; www.havelihariganga.com; 21 Ram Ghat; lunch thali ₹350, dinner buffet ₹450; ◷ 1-3pm & 7.30-10pm) The Indian vegetarian buffet at this lovely heritage hotel is the classiest in Haridwar.

ℹ Information

There are a number of internet places on Railway Rd near the train station and down the side lanes, but most have only one or two terminals.

GMVN Tourist Office (☎ 224240; Railway Rd; ◷ 10am-5pm Mon-Sat)

Hillway Internet (Jassa Ram Rd; per hr ₹30; ◷ 9am-10pm)

Main Post Office (Upper Rd; ◷ 10am-6pm Mon-Sat) Main post office.

Rishikul Ayurvedic Hospital (☎ 221003; Railway Rd) A long-established medical college and hospital with a good reputation.

Sai Forex (Upper Rd; ◷ 10am-2pm & 4-9pm) Changes cash and travellers cheques for a commission of 1%. Also has internet for ₹40 per hour.

Uttarakhand Tourism Office (☑265304; Rahi Motel, Railway Rd; ☉10am-5pm Mon-Sat)

❶ Getting There & Away

Haridwar is well connected by bus and train, but book ahead for trains during the pilgrimage season (May to October).

BUS

Private deluxe buses and sleeper buses run to Delhi (deluxe/Volvo ₹250/350), Agra (seat/sleeper ₹400/450), Jaipur (₹400/500) and Pushkar (₹450/500). The buses leave from a **stand** around the corner from the GMVN tourist office and by the gurdwara (Sikh temple). Otherwise, any travel agent in town can make a booking.

TAXI & VIKRAM

The main **taxi stand** (Railway Rd) is located just outside the train station. Destinations include Chilla (for Rajaji National Park, ₹570), Rishikesh (₹770, one hour) and Dehra Dun (₹1250), but it is usually possible to arrange a taxi for less than these official rates.

You can hire private jeep Sumos to go to one or all of the pilgrimage sites on the Char Dham between April and October. One-way rates for Gangotri and Badrinath are ₹7500 each; Kedarnath and Yamnotri cost ₹7000; a nine-day tour of all four is ₹22,600. Taxis to Jolly Grant Airport cost ₹1020.

Shared *vikrams* run up and down Railway Rd (₹10) and to Rishikesh (₹40, one hour) from Upper Rd at Laltarao Bridge, but for that trip buses are more comfortable. You can hire the whole thing to Rishikesh's Lakshman Jhula for ₹400.

GETTING AROUND

Cycle-rickshaws cost ₹10 for a short distance and ₹30 for longer hauls, such as from the Haridwar train station to Har-ki-Pairi. Hiring a taxi for three hours to tour the local temples and ashrams costs around ₹800; an autorickshaw costs ₹350.

BUSES FROM HARIDWAR

The following buses depart from the **UK Roadways bus stand** (Railway Rd). Information about buses to Dharamsala and Shimla is available at the Himachal Pradesh transport company office (shack, really) about 1km south on Railway Rd, but the buses leave from the main bus stand.

DESTINATION	FARE (₹)	DURATION (HR)	FREQUENCY
Agra	300	12	early morning
Almora	370	10	early morning & evening
Chandigarh	164	10	hourly
Dehra Dun	55	2	half-hourly
Delhi	147	6	half-hourly
Dharamsala	400	15	2.30pm & 4.30pm
Jaipur	345	12	early morning
Nainital	300	8	early morning & evening
Ranikhet	240	10	6am & 4.30pm
Rishikesh	30	1	half-hourly
Shimla	255	14	1.30am, 12.30pm & 5.30pm
Uttarkashi	257	10	5.30am, 7.30am & 9.30am

In the *yatra* (pilgrimage) season from May to October, the following buses run from the **GMOU bus stand** (Railway Rd). During monsoon season (July to mid-September), service is occasionally suspended. For current info, call ☑9897924247 for the Gangotri route and ☑9634936474 for Kedarnath and Badrinath buses. For Yamunotri, go to Dehra Dun, then take a bus to Barkot.

DESTINATION	FARE (₹)	DURATION (HR)	FREQUENCY
Badrinath (via Joshimath)	350	15	6 buses, early morning
Gangotri	350	10	5am
Kedarnath	255	10	5.30am & 7am

TRAINS FROM HARIDWAR

DESTINATION	TRAIN NUMBER & NAME	FARE (₹)	DURATION (HR)	DEPARTURE/ARRIVAL
Amritsar	12053 Jan Shatabdi	137/467 2nd class/chair car	7½	2.35pm/10pm
Amritsar	14631 Dehra Dun–Amritsar Express	187/496/615 sleeper/3AC/1st class	9¾	9.45pm/7.30am
Delhi (Old Delhi Station)	14042 Mussoorie Express	147/384/585 sleeper/3AC/2AC	8¾	11.15pm/7.55am
Delhi (New Delhi Station)	12018 Shatabdi Express	524/1075 chair car/executive	4½	6.13pm/10.45pm
Delhi (New Delhi Station)	12056 Jan Shatabdi Express	107/345 2nd class/chair car	4½	6.22am/11.10am
Haldwani(for Nanital and Almora)	14120 Dehra Dun–Kathgodam Express	146/585/990 sleeper/2AC/1AC	6½	12.20am/6.50am
Kolkata/Howrah	13010 Doon Express	418/1145/1810 sleeper/3AC/2AC	32	10.20pm/7am (two nights later)
Lucknow	13010 Doon Express	212/564/850 sleeper/3AC/2AC	10	10.20pm/8.20am
Varanasi	13010 Doon Express	298/811/1235 sleeper/3AC/2AC	18	10.20pm/4.00pm

RAJAJI NATIONAL PARK

ELEV 300-1000M

This unspoilt **park** (www.rajajinationalpark.in; Indian/foreigner per day ₹150/600; ⊙15 Nov-15 Jun), covering 820 sq km in the forested foothills near Haridwar, is best known for its wild elephants, numbering around 600 at last count.

As well as elephants, the park contains some 32 tigers and 250 leopards. Although they're not easily seen, there are thousands of chital (spotted deer) and hundreds of sambars (India's largest species of deer) to feed on. A handful of rarely seen sloth bears are hidden away. Some 300 species of birds also add interest.

Rajaji's forests include the traditional winter territory of over 1000 families of nomadic Van Gujjar buffalo herders – most of whom have been evicted from the park against their will. For more on this and other issues affecting the unique Van Gujjar tribe, visit www.sophiaindia.org.

The village of **Chilla**, 13km northeast of Haridwar, is the base for visiting the park. At the Forest Ranger's office, close to the tourist guesthouse at Chilla, you can pick up a brochure, pay entry fees and organise a jeep. These take up to eight people and cost ₹1000 for the standard safari (plus a ₹500 entry fee for the vehicle). Elephant rides are no longer offered at Rajaji.

Before visiting, contact the GMVN tourist office (p421) in Haridwar and **Mohan's Adventure Tours** (☑220910; www.mohansadventure.in; Railway Rd, Haridwar; ⊙8am-10.30pm), which offers abridged safaris even when the park is officially closed. These are five-hour trips (₹1950 per person) that include being taken on a short safari, hopefully seeing a parade of wild elephants, and maybe visiting a Van Gujjar forest camp.

Sleeping & Eating

The **Chilla Guesthouse** (☑0138-226678; r from ₹1500; ❄) is the GMVN rest house and the most comfortable place to stay in Chilla. There's a good restaurant here and a pleasant garden.

You can stay inside the park at one of the rest houses run by the Forest Department. For information and reservations, contact the director at the **Rajaji National Park Office** (☑0135-2621669; Dehra Dun). Mohan's Adventure Tours can also make bookings.

Also within the park, the **Camp King Elephant** (☑9871604712; cottage incl full board Indian/foreigner from ₹8500/US$240) resort has solar electricity, private bathrooms, full meal service and optional jeep tours.

ℹ Getting There & Away

Buses to Chilla (₹25, one hour) leave the GMOU bus stand in Haridwar every hour from 7am to 2pm. The last return trip leaves Chilla at 5.30pm. Taxis charge ₹570 one way for the 13km journey.

RISHIKESH

📞 0135 / POP 102,130 / ELEV 356M

Ever since the Beatles rocked up at the ashram of the Maharishi Mahesh Yogi in the late '60s, Rishikesh has been a magnet for spiritual seekers. Today it styles itself as the 'Yoga Capital of the World', with masses of ashrams and all kinds of yoga and meditation classes. Most of this action is north of the main town, where the exquisite setting on the fast-flowing Ganges, surrounded by forested hills, is conducive to meditation and mind expansion. In the evening, the breeze blows down the valley, setting temple bells ringing as sadhus (holy people), pilgrims and tourists prepare for the nightly *ganga aarti*. You can learn to play the sitar or tabla; try Hasya yoga (laughter therapy); practise humming or gong meditation; and experience crystal healing.

But Rishikesh is not all spirituality and contorted limbs; it's now also a popular white-water rafting centre, a backpacker hang-out, and the gateway to treks in the Himalaya.

Rishikesh is divided into two main areas: the crowded, unattractive downtown area (Rishikesh town), where you'll find the bus and train stations as well as the Triveni Ghat; and the riverside communities 2km upstream around Ram Jhula and Lakshman Jhula, where most of the accommodation, ashrams, restaurants and travellers are ensconced. The two *jhula* (suspension bridges) that cross the river are pedestrian-only – though scooters and motorcycles freely use them. Swarg Ashram, located on the eastern bank, is the traffic-free 'spiritual centre' of Rishikesh, while High Bank, west of Lakshman Jhula, is a small enclave popular with backpackers.

◉ Sights

Lakshman Jhula & Around   AREA

The defining image of Rishikesh is the view across the Lakshman Jhula hanging bridge to the huge, 13-storey wedding-cake temples of **Swarg Niwas** and **Shri Trayan-**bakshwar. Built by the organisation of the guru Kailashanand, they resemble fairyland castles and have dozens of shrines to Hindu deities on each level, interspersed with jewellery and textile shops. Sunset is an especially good time to photograph the temples from the bridge itself, and you'll hear the bell-clanging and chanting of devotees in the morning and evening. Shops selling devotional CDs add to the cacophony of noise on this side of the river. Markets, restaurants, ashrams and guesthouses sprawl on both sides of the river; in recent years the area has grown into the busiest and liveliest part of upper Rishikesh.

Swarg Ashram   AREA

A pleasant 2km walk south of Lakshman Jhula along the path skirting the east bank of the Ganges leads to the spiritual community of Swarg Ashram, made up of temples, ashrams, a crowded bazaar, sadhus and the bathing ghats where religious ceremonies are performed at sunrise and sunset. The colourful, though rather touristy, *ganga aarti* is held at the riverside temple of the Parmarth Niketan Ashram (p425) every evening at 6.30pm, with singing, chanting, musicians and the lighting of candles.

Maharishi Mahesh Yogi Ashram   HISTORIC BUILDING

(entry ₹50; ⏱ 8am-6pm) Just south of Swarg Ashram, slowly being consumed by the forest undergrowth, is what's left of the original Maharishi Mahesh Yogi Ashram. It was abandoned in 1997 and is now back under the control of the forest department. However, the shells of many buildings, meditation cells and lecture halls can still be seen, including Maharishi's own house and the guesthouse where the Beatles stayed and apparently wrote much of the *White Album*. Be sure to see the weirdly effective art installation called The Beatles Cathedral Gallery.

🏃 Activities

Yoga & Meditation

Rishikesh styles itself as the yoga capital of the world, and yoga and meditation are ubiquitous. Teaching and yoga styles vary tremendously, so check out a few classes and ask others about their experiences before committing yourself to a course.

THE MAHARISHI & THE BEATLES

In February 1968 Rishikesh hit world headlines when the Beatles and their partners stayed at Maharishi Mahesh Yogi's ashram in Swarg Ashram, following an earlier visit by George Harrison. Ringo Starr and his wife didn't like the vegetarian food, missed their children and left after a couple of weeks, but the others stayed for a month or two. They relaxed and wrote tons of songs, many of which ended up on their double album *White Album*. But rumours of the Maharishi's demands for money and his behaviour towards some female disciples eventually disillusioned all of them. 'You made a fool of everyone', John Lennon sang about the Maharishi. In later years, Harrison and Paul McCartney said, on record, that the rumours were unfounded. The original ashram is now abandoned, but nearly 40 years on, idealistic foreigners still swarm into Rishikesh seeking spiritual enlightenment from teachers and healers in their tranquil ashrams scattered along the Ganges River.

Many places also offer ayurvedic massage. Among the many yoga-instructor training courses in town, **Rishikesh Yog Peeth** (☎ 2440193; www.rishikeshyogpeeth.com; Swarg Ashram; 40-day course US$1350) has a good reputation.

Sri Sant Seva Ashram   MIXED YOGA
(☎ 2430465; santsewa@hotmail.com; Lakshman Jhula; d ₹200-500, with AC ₹1000; ☎) The yoga classes are mixed styles and open to all. Beginner (₹100) and intermediate and advanced (₹200) sessions run daily. There are also courses in reiki, ayurvedic massage and cooking. Overlooking the Ganges in Lakshman Jhula, the large rooms here are popular, so book ahead. The more expensive rooms have balconies with superb river views.

Omkarananda Ganga Sadan   IYENGAR YOGA
(☎ 2430763; www.iyengaryoga.in; Lakshman Jhula Rd; r with/without AC ₹1500/350, minimum 3-day stay) On the river at Ram Jhula, this ashram has comfortable rooms and specialises in highly recommended Iyengar yoga classes at the Patanjala Yoga Kendra centre. There are intensive seven- to 10-day courses (₹1200) on offer from October to May, advance reservations recommended; in the gaps between the intensives, day classes are offered (6pm to 7.30pm Monday to Saturday, ₹250). The ashram has its own ghat and evening *ganga aarti*.

Parmarth Niketan Ashram   HATHA YOGA
(☎ 2434301; www.parmarth.com; Swarg Ashram; s/d ₹500/600) Dominating the centre of Swarg Ashram and drawing visitors to its evening *ganga aarti* on the riverbank, Parmarth has a wonderfully ornate and serene garden courtyard. The price includes a room with a private bathroom, all meals and hatha yoga lessons.

Anand Prakash Yoga Ashram   AKHANDA YOGA
(☎ 2442344; www.anandprakashashram.com; Badrinath Rd, Tapovan; r incl full board ₹900, without bathroom ₹400) About 1km north of Lakshman Jhula, you can stay here as long or short as you like, taking part in morning and afternoon yoga classes (included in the price). Food is excellent and rooms are simple but comfortable and clean. Silence is the rule from 9pm to 9am. If you're not staying, drop in for classes for ₹150.

Rafting, Kayaking & Trekking

Over 100 storefronts offer full- and half-day rafting trips, launching upstream and paddling down to Rishikesh. Some also offer multiday rafting trips, with camping along the river. The official rafting season runs from 15 September to 30 June. A half-day trip starts at about ₹600 per person, while a full day costs from ₹1600. Most companies also offer all-inclusive Himalayan treks to places such as Kuari Pass, Harki Dun and Gangotri from around ₹2500 per day.

Red Chilli Adventure   TREKKING, RAFTING
(☎ 2434021; www.redchilliadventure.com; Lakshman Jhula Rd; ⊙ 9am-9pm) Reliable outfit offering Himalayan trekking and rafting trips throughout Uttarakhand and to Himachal Pradesh and Ladakh.

De-N-Ascent Expeditions   KAYAKING, TREKKING
(☎ 2442354; www.kayakhimalaya.com; Lakshman Jhula, Tapovan Sarai) Specialist in kayaking lessons and expeditions. Learn to paddle and

Rishikesh

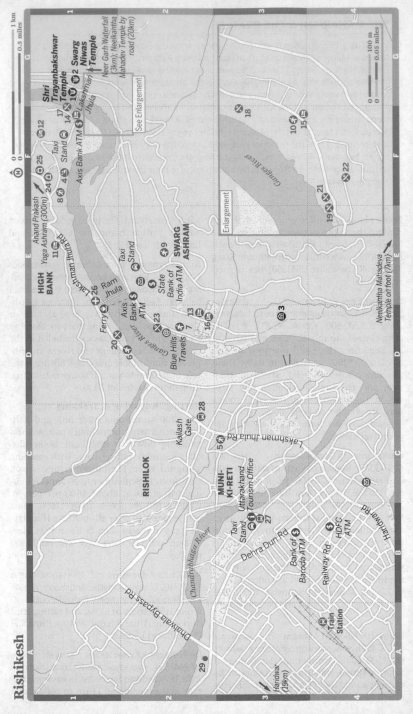

Neer Garh Waterfall (3km); Neelkantha Mahadev Temple by road (20km)

Shri Trayanbakshwar Temple

Swarg Niwas Temple

Lakshman Jhula

Shri Trayanbakshwar Temple

See Enlargement

Axis Bank ATM

Taxi Stand

Anand Prakash Yoga Ashram (300m)

HIGH BANK

Lakshman Jhula

Ram Jhula

SWARG ASHRAM

Taxi Stand

State Bank of India ATM

Ferry

Axis Bank ATM

Blue Hills Travels

Ganges River

Neelkantha Mahadeva Temple on foot (7km)

Kailash Gate

Lakshman Jhula Rd

RISHILOK

MUNI-KI-RETI

Uttarakhand Tourism Office

Taxi Stand

Chandrabhaga River

Dehra Dun Rd

Bank of Baroda ATM

Railway Rd

HDFC ATM

Haridwar Rd

Dhalwala Bypass Rd

Train Station

Haridwar (19km)

Enlargement

Ganges River

1 km
0.5 miles

100 m
0.05 miles

Rishikesh

eskimo roll with an experienced instructor, or go on multiday kayaking or rafting adventures. Also organises trekking trips.

GMVN Trekking & Mountaineering Division TREKKING
(2430799; www.gmvnl.com; Lakshman Jhula Rd, Muni-ki-Reti; 10am-5pm) Can arrange high-altitude treks in the Garhwal Himalaya and hires out trekking equipment, guides and porters.

Walks & Beaches
An easy, 15-minute walk to two small **waterfalls** starts 3km north of Lakshman Jhula bridge on the south side of the river. The start is marked by drink stalls and a roadside shrine, and the path is easy to find. Four-wheel-drive taxis cost ₹100 from Lakshman Jhula.

On the other side of the river, it's about 2km north to the signposted walk to lovely **Neer Garh Waterfall** (admission ₹30), from where it's a 20-minute uphill walk.

For a longer hike, follow the dedicated pilgrims who take water from the Ganges to offer at **Neelkantha Mahadev Temple**, a 7km, approximately three-hour walk, along a forest path from Swarg Ashram. You can also reach the temple by road (20km) from Lakshman Jhula.

✦ Festivals & Events

In the first week of March, Rishikesh hosts the **International Yoga Festival** (www.internationalyogafestival.com; Mar), attracting swamis and yoga masters from around the world for discourses and lectures. Most of the action is centred on the Parmarth Niketan Ashram (p425) in Swarg Ashram. Check the festival website for dates.

◎ Sleeping

Most of the accommodation is spread on both sides of the river around Lakshman Jhula; there are a handful of hotels among the ashrams at Swarg Ashram and directly across the river around Ram Jhula, and some good budget places at High Bank.

Midrange and top-end hotels are in relatively short supply in budget-minded Rishikesh.

◎ High Bank

This small, leafy travellers' enclave is a 20-minute walk up the hill from Lakshman Jhula and has some of the best backpacker accommodation in Rishikesh.

Bhandari Swiss Cottage HOTEL $
(☎2432939; www.bhandariswisscottagerishikesh.com; r from ₹200, with AC from ₹1000; ❀@☎) The first place you come to, this is a well-run backpacker favourite with rooms in several budgets – the higher up you stay, the higher the price. Rooms with big balconies have expansive views of the river backed by green mountains. Excellent little restaurant, internet cafe and yoga classes.

New Bhandari Swiss Cottage HOTEL $
(☎2435322; www.newbhandariswisscottag.com; r ₹300-800, with AC ₹1000-1200; ❀@☎) One of the last places on the High Bank lane, this is a large, popular place with rooms ranging from clean and simple to simply impressive. There's a massage centre, a good restaurant, and a helpful travel desk in the internet cafe. It also runs the White House, in the back, with huge, excellent rooms (₹1200 to ₹1500) that feel like part of a mansion.

Lakshman Jhula

There are several good budget options on both sides of the river here, which is the liveliest part of Rishikesh.

Divine Ganga Cottage HOTEL $
(☎2442175; www.divinegangacottage.com; r ₹800, with AC ₹2000; ❀@) Tucked away from the hubbub and surrounded by small rice paddies and local homes with gardens, the huge upstairs terrace has supreme river views. Downstairs non-AC rooms are small and overpriced, but the larger stylish upstairs AC rooms are some of the best in town, with writing tables and modern bathrooms. There's an ayurvedic spa and yoga instruction on some days.

Hotel Ishan HOTEL $
(☎2431534; r ₹250-1000; ❀@☎) This long-running riverfront place near Lakshman Jhula has a wide range of rooms at a wide range of prices. Here, you get what you pay for: the best are large and clean with terraces overlooking the river, the cheapest are unpleasantly musty. The top-floor room with TV and balcony has great views.

Hotel Surya HOTEL $
(☎2440211; www.hotelsuryalaxmanjhula.com; r ₹300-500, with AC ₹1200; ❀) Above Café Coffee Day, the newly renovated Surya is good value in a good location. Even some of the

cheapest rooms have balconies with river views, and all are very spacious.

Swarg Ashram

If you're serious about yoga and introspection, stay at one of Swarg's numerous ashrams. Otherwise, there's a knot of guesthouses a block back from the river towards the southern end of Swarg.

Vashishth Guest House BOUTIQUE HOTEL $
(☎2440029; www.vashishthgroup.com; r ₹500, with AC ₹850, with AC & kitchen ₹1000) This sweet little boutique hotel has colorfully painted walls, comfortable mattresses, and a small lending library. A couple of the rooms boast good-sized kitchens with cooking utensils and table and chairs. For what you get, this is one of the best deals in Rishikesh.

Green Hotel HOTEL $$
(☎2434948; www.hotelgreen.com; Swarg Ashram; d ₹750, with AC ₹950-2000; ❀@) In a small enclave of hotels down an alleyway, the Green has bright rooms with tasteful furnishings, hot showers and flat-screen TVs. Oddly, the cheapest rooms are the best, since they open onto a rooftop terrace with fantastic views of the hills. Cleanliness is hit and miss. Hallways on some floors are connected by wooden bridges over the atrium. The sibling **Green View Hotel** (d ₹500-900) around the corner is a bit cheaper, but not as nice.

Eating

Virtually every restaurant in Rishikesh serves only vegetarian food, but there are lots of travellers' restaurants whipping up various interpretations of Continental and Israeli food, as well as Indian and Chinese.

Lakshman Jhula

★**Devraj Coffee Corner** CAFE $
(snacks & mains ₹30-150; ☺8am-9pm) Perched above the bridge and looking across the river to Shri Trayanbakshwar temple, this German bakery is a sublime spot for a break at any time of the day. The coffee is the best in town and the menu ranges from specialties like brown bread with yak cheese to soups and sizzlers, along with the usual croissants and apple strudel. There's a good new and used bookshop next door.

Prem's Namaste Cafe
MULTICUISINE $

(mains ₹55-150; ⊙8am-midnight) With a menu and atmosphere similar to most of the other restaurants on this strip, what sets Prem's apart are the super-friendly staff and the nightly jam sessions in the cushioned top-floor eating lounge.

Pyramid Cafe
MULTICUISINE $

(mains ₹60-95; ⊙8.30am-10pm; 🛜) Sit on cushions inside pyramid-shaped tents and choose from a menu of home-cooked Indian food, plus a few Tibetan and Western dishes including pancakes. The family that runs it is super-friendly and they also rent out a couple of peaceful, well-kept pyramid tents with double bed and attached bath (₹250 and ₹500).

★ Little Buddha Cafe
MULTICUISINE $$

(mains ₹60-140; ⊙8am-11pm) This funky tree-house-style restaurant has an ultraloungey top floor, tables overlooking the Ganga, and really good international food. Pizzas are big and the mixed vegetable platter is a serious feast. It's one of the busiest places in Lakshman Jhula, for good reasons.

Ganga Beach Restaurant
MULTICUISINE $$

(mains ₹80-140; ⊙6.30am-11pm) Great riverside location with a spacious terrace and big menu including crepes and ice-cold lassis.

🍴 Swarg Ashram & Ram Jhula

Madras Cafe
INDIAN $

(Ram Jhula; mains ₹80-120; ⊙8am-10pm) This local institution dishes up tasty South and North Indian vegetarian food, thalis, a mean mushroom curry, whole-wheat pancakes and the intriguing Himalayan 'health *pilau*', as well as super-thick lassis.

Tip Top Restaurant
MULTICUISINE $

(Swarg Ashram; mains ₹60-170; ⊙8am-10pm) This friendly little joint is perched up high, catching river views and breezes. Customise your own sandwich, or dig into the three 'I's – Indian, Italian or Israeli dishes.

🍴 High Bank

Backpackers gather at the popular restaurants on High Bank. This is the only area in town where you'll find meat on the menu.

Oasis Restaurant
MULTICUISINE $$

(mains ₹90-170; ⊙8am-10pm) At New Bhandari Swiss Cottage, this place has some character, with candlelit tables in the garden and hanging lanterns inside. The menu covers oodles of world cuisines, from Mexican and Thai to Israeli and Tibetan, and features a number of chicken dishes including a delicious chilli chicken. Great desserts include apple crumble.

🛍 Shopping

Swarg Ashram is the place to go for bookshops, ayurvedic herbal medicines, clothing, handicrafts and tourist trinkets such as jewellery and Tibetan singing bowls, though there are also plenty of stalls around Lakshman Jhula. Many stalls sell *rudraksh mala* (the strings of beads used in *puja*), made from the nuts of the rudraksh tree, which originally grew where Shiva's tears fell. Beads with *mukhi* (different faces) confer various blessings on the wearer.

If you need outdoor gear, your best bet is either **Adventure Compass** (☑9899297904; www.adventurecompass.com; Badrinath Rd, Lakshman Jhula; ⊙9am-9pm) or **Adventure Axis** (Badrinath Rd, Lakshman Jhula; ⊙10am-8pm), which stock everything from sleeping bags and carabiners to climbing harnesses and trekking boots.

ⓘ Information

DANGERS & ANNOYANCES

Be cautious of befriending sadhus – while some are on genuine spiritual journeys, the orange robes have been used as a disguise by fugitives from the law since medieval times.

The current in some parts of the Ganges is very strong, and as inviting as a dip from one of the beaches may seem, people drown here every year. Don't swim out of your depth.

INTERNET ACCESS

Internet access is available all over town, usually for ₹20 or ₹30 per hour.

Blue Hills Travels (Swarg Ashram; per hr ₹20; ⊙8am-10pm) Skype is ₹30 per hour.

Lucky Internet (Lakshman Jhula; per hr ₹30; ⊙8.30am-10pm) Wi-fi access.

Red Chilli Adventure (Lakshman Jhula Rd; per hr ₹30; ⊙9am-9pm) Surf with a view.

MEDICAL SERVICES

Himalayan Institute Hospital (☑2471133; ⊙24hr) The nearest large hospital, 17km along the road to Dehra Dun and 1km beyond Jolly Grant airport.

Shivananda Ashram (☑2430040; www.
sivanandaonline.org; Lakshman Jhula Rd)
Provides free medical services and has a
pharmacy.

MONEY

Several travel agents around Lakshman Jhula
and Swarg Ashram will exchange travellers
cheques and cash.

POST

Main Post Office (Ghat Rd; ⊙10am-4pm Mon-
Fri, 10am-1pm Sat) Near Triveni Ghat.
Post Office (Swarg Ashram; ⊙10am-4pm
Mon-Fri, 10am-1pm Sat)

TOURIST INFORMATION

Uttarakhand Tourism Office (☑2430209;
main bus stand; ⊙10am-5pm Mon-Sat) A
brand new building behind the bus stand, with
eager staff.

❶ Getting There & Away

BUS

There are regular buses to Haridwar and Dehra
Dun; for Mussoorie change at Dehra Dun. Buses
run north to pilgrimage centres during the *yatra*
season (April to November), and to Joshimath
and Uttarkashi year-round.

Private deluxe buses to Delhi (₹475, seven
hours) leave from Kailash Gate, just south of
Ram Jhula, at 1.30pm and 9.30pm. There's also
one direct overnight bus daily from Rishikesh to
Dharamsala (₹925) at 4pm.

Private night buses to Jaipur (seat/sleeper/
Volvo ₹550/625/1350, 13 hours), Agra (seat/
sleeper ₹475/550, 12 hours) and Pushkar
(₹550/625, 16 hours) can be booked at travel
agents in Lakshman Jhula, Swarg Ashram and
High Bank, but they leave from Haridwar.

SHARE JEEPS & TAXI

Share jeeps leave, when overfull, from the corner of Dehra Dun Rd and Dhalwala Bypass Rd,
to Uttarkashi (₹250, five hours) and Joshimath
(₹300, eight hours), mostly early in the morning,
starting from 4am.

Private taxis can be hired from Lakshman
Jhula, Ram Jhula, and in between the main and
yatra bus stands. Rates to various destinations
include: Haridwar (₹660, one hour), Dehra Dun
(₹970, 1½ hours), Jolly Grant Airport (₹610, one
hour), Uttarkashi (for Gangotri; ₹3050, seven
hours), Joshimath (₹4500, nine hours) and Almora (₹4600, 10 hours). For long-distance trips
you may find a cheaper rate by asking around at
travel agents and guesthouses.

Vikrams charge ₹400 to make the trip to
Haridwar.

TRAIN

Bookings can be made at the reservation office
at the train station, or at travel agents around
Lakshman Jhula and Swarg Ashram (for a fee).
Only a handful of slow trains run from Rishikesh
to Haridwar, so it's usually better to go by bus
or taxi.

❶ Getting Around

Shared *vikrams* run from the downtown Ghat Rd
junction up past Ram Jhula (₹10 per person)
and the High Bank turn-off to Lakshman Jhula.
To hire the entire *vikram* from downtown to Lakshman Jhula should cost ₹80 to 'upside' – the
top of the hill on which the Lakshman Jhula area
sits – and ₹100 to 'downside' – closer to the
bridge. From Ram Jhula to High Bank or Lakshman Jhula is ₹40.

To get to the eastern bank of the Ganges you
either need to walk across one of the suspension bridges or take the **ferry** (one way/return
₹10/15; ⊙7.30am-6.15pm) from Ram Jhula.

BUSES FROM RISHIKESH

The following buses depart from the **main bus stand** (A) or the **yatra bus stand** (B). The latter
leave when full.

DESTINATION	FARE (₹)	DURATION (HR)	FREQUENCY
Badrinath (B)	330	12	4am, 5am & 6am
Dehra Dun (A)	41	1½	half-hourly
Delhi (A)	ordinary/deluxe 177/265	7	half-hourly
Gangotri (B)	300	12	5.30am & 6.15am
Haridwar (A)	30	1	half-hourly
Joshimath (B)	280	10	4am, 5am & 6am
Kedarnath (B)	230	12	3.45am & 5am
Uttarkashi (B)	180	7	4.15am, 5.30am, 8am & 12.30pm
Yamnotri (B)	260	12	5.30am & 6.15am

On the eastern bank of the Ganges, taxis and share jeeps hang around to take passengers to waterfalls and Neelkantha temple (shared/private ₹100/700), but it's a 16km trip by road to get from one side of the river to the other. From Lakshman Jhula to Swarg Ashram costs ₹5 in a shared jeep, or ₹50 for the whole thing.

Bicycles (per day ₹100), scooters (per day ₹300) and motorcycles (per day ₹400 to ₹600) can be hired around the Lakshman Jhula area. There are no actual shops – rent from guys on the street or ask around at guesthouses.

THE CHAR DHAM

High in the Garhwali Himalayas sit some of the holiest sites in the Hindu religion – Yamunotri, Gangotri, Kedarnath, and Badrinath – where temples mark the spiritual sources of four sacred rivers: the Yamuna, the Ganges, the Mandakini and the Alaknanda. Together, they make up one of the most important pilgrimage circuits in all of India, known as the *char dham* (four seats). Every year between April and November, hundreds of thousands of worshipers brave hair-raising mountain roads and high-altitude trails to reach them.

Travelling to one or more of these temples is a great way to get a feel for the religious pulse of the subcontinent, amid incredible alpine scenery. Since the *yatra* is big business, numerous buses, share jeeps, porters, ponies and palanquins are on hand for transport, along with a well-established network of guesthouses, ashrams and government rest houses. As a result, getting to these temples is easy enough without hiring a guide or carrying supplies. Only Gangotri and Badrinath temples can be visited without having to hike.

Yamunotri

ELEV 3185M

Yamunotri Temple is tucked in a tight gorge close to the source of the Yamuna, Hinduism's second-most sacred river after the Ganges. Yamunotri is the least visited hence least developed of the *char dham* sites, but once you get to the trailhead it's an easy trek in.

The 5km, two-hour hike begins where the road ends at Janki Chatti, 6km beyond the village of **Hanuman Chatti** (2400m).

At Yamunotri Temple there are several hot springs where you can take a dip, and others where pilgrims cook potatoes and rice as *prasad*. One kilometre beyond the temple, the Yamuna River spills from a frozen lake of ice and glaciers on the **Kalinda Parvat** mountain at an altitude of 4421m, but this is a very tough climb that requires mountaineering skills.

Across the river from Janki Chatti is the pretty village of **Kharsali**, which is worth a stroll if you've got the time.

Accommodation is available at basic guesthouses or the GMVN tourist lodges in Janki Chatti and Hanuman Chatti.

Buses only go as far as Hanuman Chatti, where you need to catch a share jeep to Janki Chatti (₹35). During peak *yatra* season buses run from Dehra Dun, Mussoorie and Rishikesh to Hanuman Chatti, but the most frequent transport services originate in Barkot. From Janki Chatti, share jeeps go to Barkot (₹70, two hours); from Hanuman Chatti, buses go to Barkot (₹60, 2½ hours) and Uttarkashi (₹125, seven hours) for those heading to Gangotri.

Gangotri & Gaumukh Glacier Trek

⟋ 01377 / ELEV 3042M

In a remote setting at an altitude of 3042m, **Gangotri Temple** is one of the holiest places in India. Near the source of the Ganges (known as the Bhagirathi until it reaches Deoprayag), the shrine is dedicated to the origin of Hinduism's most sacred river – nearby is the rock on which Shiva is said to have received the flowing waters in his matted locks.

Erected by Gorkha commander Amar Singh Thapa in the 18th century, the temple is surprisingly underwhelming for a site of such significance. Unless you're a devout Hindu, to get a real sense of awe you'll probably have to trek from **Gangotri** to the true source of the river, at **Gaumukh**, 18km upstream. There, the water flows out of **Gangotri Glacier** beneath the soaring west face of **Baghirathi Parvat** (6856m), with the peak of **Shivling** (the 6543m 'Indian Matterhorn') towering to the south.

Don't be daunted by the trek – the trail rises gradually and is totally solid. Fourteen kilometres (four to six hours) up the trail, at Bhojbasa (3790m), there's a **GMVN Tourist Bungalow** (Bhojbasa; dm ₹300) and other basic lodging; Gaumukh is 4km (1½ hours) past that. On clear days, the best time to visit the source is early-to-mid-afternoon, when it's out of the shadows. Porters (₹500 each way) and horses (one way/return ₹850/1250) can be hired in Gangotri. More ambitious hikers with their own gear often continue to the gorgeous meadow at **Tapovan**, 6km beyond Gaumukh.

Before trekking to Gaumukh, you must first get a permit, since access is limited to 150 people per day. These can be obtained from the **District Forest Office** (☑225693; ⊙10am-5pm Mon-Sat, closed 2nd Sat of month), 3km north of the Uttarkashi bus stand, or from the satellite office above the bus stand at Gangotri, which is open every day from 7am to 7pm. At both places, you'll need to bring a copy of your passport ID page and visa. The permit is valid for two days and costs ₹150/600 per Indian/foreigner (then ₹50/250 for each extra day).

Gangotri village has plenty of guesthouses, ashrams and *dharamsalas* charging ₹300 or less per room. There's also a **GMVN Tourist Bungalow** (☑222221; dm ₹300). When hungry, follow the Indian families to the **Hotel Gangaputra Restaurant** (mains ₹45-100; ⊙7am-11pm), which is busy for a good reason.

Buses run from Gangotri to Uttarkashi (₹110, six hours) and, during peak season, to Rishikesh (₹300, 12 hours). Share jeeps (₹150) and private taxis (one-way/return ₹2500/3000) also run to Gangotri. To Rishkesh, shared jeeps/private taxis cost ₹300/4000.

Kedarnath

☑ 01364 / ELEV 3584M

Kedarnath is revered as the source of the Mandakini River, but this magnificent temple – built in the 8th century by Guru Shankara – is primarily dedicated to the hump that Shiva (who had taken the form of a bull) left behind when he dove into the ground to escape the Pandavas. The actual source of the river is 12km past Kedarnath.

Tucked at the base of 6970m peaks, 14-km from the nearest road, Kedarnath is in the most dramatic location of any of the *char dham* temples. The *puja* offered inside, especially around the stone 'hump', is fervent and can be quite intense. The site is so auspicious that pilgrims used to throw themselves from one of the cliffs behind the temple in the hope of instantly attaining *moksha* (liberation).

The 14km uphill hike to the temple (3584m) takes six hours on foot (five hours on a pony) and begins at Gaurikund, which has basic accommodation. When you arrive, expect to be pounced on by a pack of hotel touts. If in doubt, head for the reliable **Sunil Lodge** (☑01364 269205; r from 200) or the **GMVN Tourist Bungalow** (Gaurikund; dm/d ₹150/450), one of the few places with geysers in the bathrooms. Stalls store luggage, and porters and ponies can be hired; make arrangements through your hotel or go to the booking office at the start of the trail, which has an official price list. The wide, paved trail to the temple is lined with *dhabas* and chai stalls.

Kedarnath also has plenty of pilgrim accommodation: **Maharashta Mandal** (☑8979 746197; r from ₹200) is good, and there's always the **GMVN Tourist Bungalow** (☑263218; dm ₹200, d ₹640-800). If you want to take photos of the sadhus at the temple, bring a pocketful of ₹10 notes.

Buses run from Gaurikund to Rishikesh (₹230, 12 hours) and Joshimath/Badrinath (₹180/200) in the morning, or you can use share jeeps to make the same journey, heading first to Guptakashi then changing there.

Other portions of Shiva's bull-form-body are worshipped at the other four Panch Kedar shrines, which take some effort to reach but can be visited: the arms at **Tungnath**; the face at **Rudranath**; the navel at **Madmaheshwar**; and the hair at **Kalpeshwar**.

Badrinath & Mana Village

☑ 01381 / ELEV 3133M

Basking in a superb setting in the shadow of snow-topped Nilkantha, **Badrinath Temple** appears almost lost in the tatty village that surrounds it. Sacred to Lord Vishnu, this vividly painted temple is the most easily accessible and popular of the *char dham* temples. It was founded by Guru Shankara in the 8th century, but the current structure is much more recent. Below the temple are hot springs that reach a scalding 40°C and serve as a laundry for locals.

A scenic 3km walk beyond Badrinath along the Alaknanda River (cross over to the temple side to pick up the path), past fields divided by dry-stone walls, leads to tiny but charismatic **Mana Village**. (You can also take a taxi there for ₹200.) The village is crammed with narrow stone laneways and traditional houses of varying designs – some have slate walls and roofs while others are wooden with cute balconies. You can wander around and watch the village ladies knitting colourful jerseys or hauling loads of fodder while the men tend goats or play cards or carom billiards. Carpets, blankets, jerseys, hats and gloves are all on sale.

Just outside the village in a small cave is the tiny, 5000-year-old **Vyas Temple**. Nearby is **Bhima's Rock**, a natural rock arch over a river that is said to have been made by Bhima, strongest of the Pandava brothers, whose tale is told in the Mahabharata. The 5km hike along the Alaknanda to the 145m **Vasudhara Waterfall** has a great reward-to-effort ratio, with views up the valley of the Badrinath massif jutting skyward like a giant fang. The villagers migrate to somewhere warmer and less remote – usually Joshimath – between November and April.

Badrinath can easily be visited in a day from Joshimath if you get an early start, but it's worth staying if you also want to see Mana Village and do any hiking. There is a slew of mediocre budget guesthouses lining the main road into town, charging ₹400 to ₹600 per room, which can be loud with pilgrims. Among the best values in town are **Himgiri Guest House** (7579257765; r ₹500), **Narayan Palace Hotel** (9420358998; www.narayanpalace.com; r ₹3600-4500), and **Hotel Snow Crest** (9412082465; www.snowcrest.co.in; r ₹4500-6000), which is Badrinath's most expensive, but has heaters in the rooms. Even in summer, it can be quite cold here.

From the large bus station at the entrance to Badrinath, GMOU buses run to Haridwar (₹350) via Rishikesh (₹320) at 5.30am and Gaurikund (for Kedarnath, ₹255) at 7am, but check scheduled departure times or you may end up stranded. Private buses to Joshimath and beyond leave sporadically throughout the morning. For Joshimath or Govindghat (for Valley of Flowers) try to take a shared jeep around 7am.

UTTARKASHI

01374 / POP 17,120 / ELEV 1158M

Uttarkashi, 155km from Rishikesh and the largest town in northern Garhwal, is a major stop on the road to Gangotri Temple and the Gaumukh Glacier trek. The main bazaar is worth a wander and has all the supplies you might need. Guides and porters can be arranged here for treks in the region.

There's a State Bank of India ATM in the market.

The town is probably best known for the **Nehru Institute of Mountaineering** (222123; www.nimindia.net; 10am-5pm), which trains many of the guides running trekking and mountaineering outfits in India. The centre has a museum and outdoor climbing wall. Basic and advanced mountaineering and adventure courses are open to all – check the website for details and admission information. Across the river from the main market.

Uttarkashi also hosts the annual **Makar Sakranti** festival in January.

There are plenty of hotels and *dhabas* (snack bars) around the bus stand and in the nearby market.

Buses depart at 7am for Gangotri (₹110, six hours). Five head to Haridwar (₹220, eight hours) at 7am, and Dehradun (₹230, nine hours) via Rishikesh (₹2000, seven hours) between 5.30am and 2pm. There are buses to Hanuman Chatti, for Yamunotri Temple, at 7.45am and 10.45am (₹140, seven hours), and multiple services to Barkot (₹90, five hours) until 3pm.

Monal Guest House HOTEL $

(222270; www.monaluttarkashi.com; Kot Bungalow Rd; r ₹500-1700;) Off the Gangotri road 3km north of town, about 100m from the office that issues permits to Gamukh, this hillside hotel feels like a large comfortable house with lean, airy rooms, a big-windowed restaurant and peaceful garden setting. Wing A has a more homely feel than Wing B.

Hotel Govind Palace HOTEL $

(9411522058, 223815; near bus stand; r from ₹500) One of the best value choices if you've got to catch an early morning bus. It's got good beds, hot showers, TVs and manager GS Bhandari, who is super-helpful.

Shangri-La Restaurant MULTICUISINE $

(mains ₹40-130; 10am-9pm) In the main bazaar, this restaurant has the most diverse menu in Uttarkashi: pizza, vegie burgers and banana pancakes as well as Indian and Tibetan food.

TREKKING THE HIMALAYA

There are many sublime trekking routes in Uttarakhand. Here are details on a few, listed from west to east. For more information or more options, pick up Lonely Planet's *Trekking the Indian Himalayas* or contact GMVN in Dehra Dun or the local trekking outfitters mentioned in this chapter.

Har-ki-Dun Valley Trek

The wonderfully remote Har-ki-Dun (3510m) is a botanical paradise criss-crossed by glacial streams and surrounded by pristine forests and snowy peaks, within **Govind Wildlife Sanctuary & National Park** (Indian/foreigner up to 3 days ₹50/350, subsequent days ₹20/175). You might be lucky enough to glimpse the elusive snow leopard above 3500m.

The trail begins at Sankri (also called Saur), and there are very basic GMVN Tourist Bungalows at Sankri, Taluka and Osla, but at the valley itself you have to stay in the Forest Department rest house or have a tent. It's a 38km hike to Har-ki-Dun, which takes three days – or two days if you take a share jeep to Taluka. A side trip to Jamdar Glacier takes another day. The trek can be busy during June and October.

A couple of reputable guides work out of Sankri – Chain Singh and Bhagat Singh – who run the **Har Ki Dun Protection & Mountaineering Association** (☑ 9410134589, 9412918140; www.harkidun.org). In addition to outfitting trips to Har-ki-dun, they can take you to the unique villages of the Rupin and Supin Valleys. They also lead treks from Sankri to the Baspa Valley in Himachal Pradesh and along other beautiful routes.

To get to Sankri, take a direct bus from Gandhi Chowk in Mussoorie or from Dehra Dun's Mussoorie Bus Stand – or hop on a series of buses and share jeeps until you get there.

Kuari Pass Trek

Also known as the Curzon Trail (though Lord Curzon's party abandoned its attempt on the pass following an attack of wild bees), the trek over the Kuari Pass (3640m) was popular in the Raj era. It's still one of Uttarakhand's finest and most accessible treks, affording breathtaking views of the snow-clad peaks around Nanda Devi – India's highest mountain – while passing through the outer sanctuary of Nanda Devi Sanctuary. The trailhead is at Auli and the 75km trek to Ghat past lakes, waterfalls, forests, meadows and small villages takes five days, though it's possible to do a shorter version that finishes in Tapovan in three days. A

JOSHIMATH

☑ 01389 / POP 13,860 / ELEV 1845M

As the gateway to Badrinath Temple and Hem Kund, Joshimath sees a steady stream of Hindu and Sikh pilgrims from May to October. And as the base for the Valley of Flowers and Kuari Pass treks, and Auli ski resort, it attracts adventure travellers year-round.

Reached from Rishikesh by a serpentine mountain road, Joshimath is a ramshackle two-street town with erratic power supply and limited places to eat. Although the mountain views are lost from the town itself, it's only a short cable-car ride from here to magnificent vistas of Nanda Devi.

🏃 Activities

To trek the Kuari Pass and other routes in Nanda Devi Sanctuary, you need a permit and a registered guide. There are three excellent operators in town who can organise everything.

Adventure Trekking   OUTDOOR ADVENTURE
(☑ 9837937948; www.thehimalayanadventures.com; Main Bazaar) Treks of anything from two to 10 days can be arranged here for around US$45 per person per day (with more than one person), as well as white-water rafting, skiing and mountain climbing. The owner, Santosh, is helpful and runs a guesthouse on the way up to Auli (rooms ₹1000 to ₹2000).

Eskimo Adventures   OUTDOOR ADVENTURE
(☑ 9411508060; adventure22@rediffmail.com) Offers treks and rock-climbing expeditions from about ₹2300 per day, and equipment rental (for trekking and skiing), as well as white-water rafting trips on the Ganges.

tent, guide, permit and your own food supplies are necessary, all of which can be organised easily in Joshimath.

Pindari Glacier Trek

This six-day, 94km trek passes through truly virgin country that's inhabited by only a few shepherds, and it offers wonderful views of Nanda Kot (6860m), and Nanda Khat (6611m) on the southern rim of Nanda Devi Sanctuary. The 3km-long, 365m-wide Pindari Glacier is at 3353m, so take it easy to avoid altitude sickness. Permits aren't needed but bring your passport.

The trek begins and finishes at Loharket (1700m), a village 36km north of Bageshwar. Guides and porters can be organised easily there, or in the preceding village of Song (1400m), or you can organise package treks through companies in Almora. KMVN operates all-inclusive eight-day treks out of Loharket for ₹5100 per person, staying at government rest houses. KMVN dorms (mattresses on the floor for ₹200), basic guesthouses or *dhaba* huts (₹100 to ₹300) are dotted along the route, and food is available.

Buses (₹50, two hours) or share jeeps (₹60, 1½ hours) run between Song and Bageshwar. Private taxis between Bageshwar and Song/Loharket cost ₹1500/2000.

Milam Glacier Trek

A challenging eight-day, 118km trek to this massive glacier at 3450m is reached along an ancient trade route to Tibet that was closed in 1962 following the war between India and China. It passes through magnificent rugged country to the east of Nanda Devi (7816m) and along the sometimes spectacular gorges of the Gori Ganga River. A popular but tough side trip to Nanda Devi East base camp adds another 32km or three days.

Free permits (passport required) are available from the District Magistrate in Munsyari. You will also need a tent and your own food supplies, as villages on the route may be deserted. KMVN organises all-inclusive eight-day treks (from ₹6325).

The base for this excursion is the spectacularly located village of **Munsyari** (p448), where a guide, cook and porters can be hired and package treks can be arranged through **Nanda Devi Tour N Trek** (☎05961-222324; trek_beeru@rediffmail.com) or **Johar Tour & Treks** (☎05961-222752).

Himalayan Snow Runner OUTDOOR ADVENTURE (☎9412082247; www.himalayansnowrunner.com) Recommended outfit for trekking (from around ₹2250 per day), skiing and adventure activities. The owner, Ajay, also takes cultural tours to Bhotia and Garhwali villages, and runs a guesthouse in his home in Mawari village, 5km from Joshimath (doubles ₹1060).

🍴 Sleeping & Eating

There are lots of cheap lodgings and a few pricier hotels scattered around town. Joshimath's trekking outfits also operate upmarket homestay-style guesthouses that are worth considering.

Several *dhabas* in the main bazaar serve similar vegetarian thalis and dosas from ₹20 to ₹90.

Hotel New Kamal HOTEL $
(☎221891; r ₹300) Small and clean with bucket hot water and TV; one of the better cheapies in the town centre.

Hotel Kamet HOTEL $
(☎222155; d ₹400-600, annexe r ₹700-1600) Decent enough central budget option, but check a few rooms to find the least worn. There's a new, more modern annexe in the back.

Malari Inn HOTEL $$
(☎222257; malari.inn@gmail.com; r ₹1200-3200) The newest and best place in Joshimath. Standard rooms are basic but spacious and clean; pay more for more amenities, a fatter mattress and a balcony with valley views. All have geysers. Discounts are offered outside of peak season.

Auli D's Food Plaza MULTICUISINE $$
(Main Market; mains ₹70-200; ⏱7am-10pm) Featuring a full menu of Indian, Chinese and Continental food, including veg and nonveg choices, this 1st-floor restaurant has plastic tablecloths and covered seats, and feels like a banquet hall.

ℹ Information

There's a **GMVN Tourist Office** (☑222181; ⏱10am-5pm Mon-Sat) located just north of the town (follow the Tourist Rest House sign off Upper Bazaar Rd), and there's a State Bank of India ATM. Tour companies have internet services.

ℹ Getting There & Away

Although the main road up to Joshimath is maintained by the Indian army, and a hydroelectric plant on the way to Badrinath has improved that road, the area around Joshimath is inevitably prone to landslides, particularly in the rainy season from mid-June to mid-September.

The best way to get to Badrinath or Govindghat (for Valley of Flowers and Hem Kund) is by shared jeep (₹70), leaving from the Badrinath taxi stand at the far end of Upper Bazar Rd. Hiring the whole jeep costs ₹1000. A few buses (₹60) leave throughout the day from the same place.

Buses run from Joshimath to Rishikesh (₹270, 10 hours) and Haridwar (₹300, 11½ hours) at 4am, 4.30am and 6am, departing from the tiny **GMOU booth** (Upper Bazaar Rd; ⏱4am-8pm), where you can also book tickets. From the main jeep stand, private buses leave occasionally for Karanprayag (₹90, four hours), with some continuing to Rishikesh.

To get to the eastern Kumaon region take any bus to Karanprayag, from where local buses and share jeeps can take you along the beautiful road towards Kausani, Bageshwar and Almora. You may have to change buses at Gwaldam (₹80, 3½ hours), to get to where you're going.

AROUND JOSHIMATH

Auli

☑ 01389 / ELEV 3019M

Rising above Joshimath, 14km by road – and only 4km by the gondola-style cable car – Auli is India's premier ski resort. But you don't have to visit in winter to enjoy the awesome views of Nanda Devi (India's highest peak) from the top of the cable-car station.

As a ski resort, Auli is hardly spectacular, with gentle 5km-long slopes, one 500m rope tow (₹100 per trip) that runs beside the main slope, and an 800m chairlift (₹200) that connects the upper and lower slopes. The snow is consistently good, though, and the setting is superb. The season runs from January to March, and equipment hire and instruction can be arranged here or in Joshimath.

The state-of-the-art **cable car** (return ₹500; ⏱every 20min 8am-6.50pm), India's longest, links Joshimath to the upper slopes above Auli. There's a cafe, of sorts, at the top, serving hot chai and tomato soup.

The **Cliff Top Club Resort** (☑223217, in Delhi 011-25616679; www.nivalink.com/clifftop; studio ₹4500, ste ₹7500, f ₹9500) wouldn't look out of place in the Swiss Alps, with its solid timber interior finish, cosy atmosphere and spacious rooms, some with views of Nanda Devi. Meals and all-inclusive ski packages, including equipment, are available.

If on a tighter budget, stay at the surprisingly good **GMVN Tourist Rest House** (☑223208; www.gmvnl.com; dm ₹250, r ₹1500-4000) at the start of the chairlift. There's also the new **Devi Darshan** (☑9719316777; www.mountainshepherds.com; r ₹3200), which has a restaurant and common room with full-on Nanda Devi views, though bedrooms are dark.

VALLEY OF FLOWERS & HEM KUND

British mountaineer Frank Smythe stumbled upon the Valley of Flowers in 1931. 'In all my mountain wandering,' he wrote, 'I have not seen a more beautiful valley where the human spirit may find repose'. The *bugyals* (high-altitude meadows) of tall wildflowers are a glorious sight on a sunny day, rippling in the breeze, and framed by mighty 6000m mountains that have glaciers and snow decorating their peaks all year.

The 300 species of flowers make the valley a unique and valuable pharmaceutical resource that may soon be a World Heritage Site. Unfortunately, most flowers bloom during the monsoon season in July and August, when the rains make access difficult and hazardous. There's a widespread misconception that the valley isn't worth visiting outside of peak flower season, but even without its technicolour carpet it's still ridiculously beautiful. And it's more likely to be sunny.

To reach the 87-sq-km **Valley of Flowers National Park** (Indian/foreigner up to 3 days ₹40/600, subsequent days ₹20/175; ⏱7am-5pm

TUNGNATH & CHANDRISILLA

One the best day hikes in Uttarakhand, the trail to **Tungnath Mandir** (3680m) and **Chandrisilla Peak** (4000m) features a sacred Panch Kedar temple and a stunning Himalayan panorama.

The trail starts at **Chopta**, a small village with no electricity, which is found on the winding road between Chamoli (south of Joshimath) and Kund (south of Gaurikund). A well-paved path switchbacks 3.5km uphill, gaining 750m in elevation, to **Tungnath**, the highest Shiva temple in the world, then a dirt trail continues 1.5km further to the top of Chandrisilla. From the summit, the Garhwali and Kumaoni Himalayas stretch out before you, with awesome vistas of major mountains including Nanda Devi, Trishul and the Kedarnath group. Start early before the clouds move in, or head up in the afternoon, stay at one of the spartan guesthouses around Tungnath, and hit Chandrisilla for sunrise. There's basic accommodation in Chopta: Hotel Neelkanth has the best rooms, but Hotel Rajkumar is the friendliest.

The drive from Chamoli to Chopta is a worthwhile diversion in itself, as it traverses steeply terraced hillsides dotted with rural villages before entering a lushly forested musk-deer sanctuary pierced by dramatic cliffs.

Jun-Oct, last entry 2pm) requires a full-day hike from Govindghat to the village of Ghangaria, less than 1km from the park. The fabled valley begins 2km uphill from the ticket office, and continues for another 5km. Tracks are easy to follow. No overnight stay is permitted here (or at Hem Kund) so you must stay in Ghangaria.

A tougher trek from Ghangaria involves joining the hundreds of Sikh pilgrims toiling up to the 4300m **Hem Kund**, the sacred lake surrounded by seven peaks where Sikh guru Gobind Singh is believed to have meditated in a previous life. The pilgrim season runs from around 1 June to 1 October. Ponies (₹350) are available if you prefer to ride up the 6km zigzag track.

Also called Govinddham, **Ghangaria** is a one-street village in a wonderful deodar forest with a busy market, a handful of budget hotels and mediocre restaurants, hundreds of ponies, a pharmacy and a doctor. Water and electricity supplies are erratic. It can get *cold*, so bring warm layers.

Hotel Pritam (☑0199-1322031; Ghangaria; s/d ₹300/400) is one of the better budget places to stay. **Hotel Priya** (Ghangaria; r from ₹200) is good, too. No hotels have heat, but they do have heaps of blankets.

Ghangaria is a scenic but strenuous 14km uphill trek from Govindghat, which takes five to seven hours. You can quicken the trip and help the local economy by hiring a pony (₹437) through the Eco Development Committee office at the bridge over the Alaknanda River. The return trip takes

four to five hours. You don't need to carry food because there are *dhabas* and drink stalls along the way serving the army of pilgrims heading to Hem Kund. Top tip: if you have the time, sleep at Badrinath the night before you trek to Ghangaria to acclimatise your body to the altitude; it'll make the hike easier.

Despite the distances and grades of the trails, treks to Ghangaria, the Valley of Flowers and Hem Kund are often undertaken by small children and people with weak legs or lungs – they ride up in a wicker chair hauled on the back of a *kandi* man (from ₹400) or reclining in a *dandi* litter (from ₹5000), carried on the shoulders of four men like the royalty of old. It's also possible to fly by **Deccan Air** (☑9412051036; www.deccanair.com) helicopter from Govindghat to Gangharia (one way/return ₹3500/7000); the booking office is at the top of the road leading down to the village.

At **Govindghat**, there are lots of lodging options for around ₹200, as well as the huge **gurdwara** (payment by donation), where VIP rooms are basic. The **Hotel Bhagat** (☑9412936360; www.hotelbhagat.com; r ₹1500-2400), up on the main road between Joshimath and Badrinath, has very clean rooms with river views, geysers and meals available.

All buses and share jeeps between Joshimath and Badrinath stop in Govindghat, so you can easily find transport travelling in either direction, though this trickles off later in the day and stops dead at night.

CORBETT TIGER RESERVE

☑ 05947 / ELEV 400-1210M

This famous **reserve** (☉ mid-Nov–mid-Jun, Jhrna zone open year-round) was established in 1936 as India's first national park. It's named for legendary tiger hunter Jim Corbett (1875–1955), who put Kumaon on the map with his book *The Man-Eaters of Kumaon*. The British hunter was greatly revered by local people for shooting tigers that had developed a taste for human flesh, but he eventually shot more wildlife with his camera than with his gun.

Tiger sightings take some luck, as the 200 or so tigers in the reserve are neither baited nor tracked. Your best chance of spotting one is late in the season (April to mid-June), when the forest cover is low and animals come out in search of water.

Notwithstanding tiger sightings, few serious wildlife enthusiasts will leave disappointed, as the 1318-sq-km park has a variety of wildlife and birdlife in grassland, sal forest and river habitats, and a beautiful location in the foothills of the Himalaya on the Ramganga River. Commonly seen wildlife include wild elephants (200 to 300 live in the reserve), sloth bears, langur monkeys, rhesus macaques, peacocks, romps of otters and several types of deer including chital (spotted deer), sambars, hog deer and barking deer. You might also see leopards, mugger crocodiles, gharials, monitor lizards, wild boars and jackals. The Ramganga Reservoir attracts large numbers of migrating birds, especially from mid-December to the end of March, and over 600 species have been spotted here.

Of Corbett's five zones – Bijrani, Dhikala, Domunda, Jhirna and Sonanadi – Dhikala is the highlight of the park. Forty-nine kilometres northwest of Ramnagar and deep inside the reserve, this is the designated core area, where the highest concentration of the animals you probably hope to see are found. It's only open from 15 November to 15 June and only to overnight guests, or as part of a one-day tour available only through the park's **reception centre** (☑ 251489; www.corbett nationalpark.in; Ranikhet Rd; ☉ 6am-4pm), opposite Ramnagar's bus stand.

Jhirna, in the southern part of the reserve, is the only zone that remains open all year. Short jeep safaris can be organised in Ramnagar, but your chances of seeing serious megafauna there are iffy. In certain years, depending on conditions, some of the other zones open in October, but the only way to find out is to contact the reception centre.

Be sure to bring binoculars (you can hire them at park gates) and plenty of mosquito repellent and mineral water. If you're inter-

PERMITS

The park controls tourist impact by limiting the number of vehicles into each zone each day. It's highly recommended to make advance reservations. You can book via the park's website or by signing up for a trip with a safari outfit. If you book online, give your reservation confirmation to your driver, whether you hire one from the reservation centre or use a tour operator. Day trips can be booked three months in advance; if you can't plan ahead, go to the reception centre and try to pick up a leftover vehicle permit. If they are all gone, you still might be able to visit the park; safari operators will ask each other if anyone is running a jeep with open seats that you can fill. Overnight trips to Dhikala are best booked by calling the reception centre or a safari company.

For a day trip, the vehicle fee (not including passengers) costs ₹250/500 for Indians/foreigners; for an overnight jaunt, it's ₹500/1500. Then there's the visitor entry fee, which is about the craziest system we've seen in a while. Officially, the single-day fee (valid for four hours, available for every zone except Dikhala) is ₹100/450 per Indian/foreigner; three-day permits cost ₹200/1000. But the park makes you pay visitor fees for every seat in the jeep, *even if they are empty*. Kindly, they imagine that unoccupied seats are filled by Indians, so if two foreigners are the only passengers in a jeep, they pay their entry fees, plus an extra ₹400 for their invisible Indian companions.

How much does this all cost? Add up your jeep hire fee, vehicle entry fee, visitor entry fees, and empty seat fees, and that's your total. Arranging everything yourself is marginally cheaper than taking a safari or hotel tour, but they provide expert guides fluent in English, which can be well worth the few extra rups.

ested in the life of Jim Corbett, his former house at Kaladhungi, 26km southeast of Ramnagar, is now a **museum** (Kaladhungi; admission ₹50; ☺ 8am-5pm).

☞ Tours

The reception centre in Ramnagar runs daily **bus tours** (Indian/foreigner ₹1000/2000) to Dhikala at 5.30am and noon.

Jeeps can be hired at the reception centre in Ramnagar, or through your accommodation or a tour agency. Jeep owners have formed a union, so in theory rates are fixed (on a per jeep basis, carrying up to six people). Half-day safaris (leaving in the morning and afternoon) should cost ₹1500 to Bijrani, ₹1800 to Jhirna, or ₹2100 to Domunda – not including the entry fees for you and your guide. Full-day safaris cost double. Overnight excursions to Dhikala cost ₹3300. Check the current prices at the reception centre and at your hotel before hiring a jeep. Safaris offered by Karan Singh, who runs Corbett Motel, are highly recommended.

Two-hour **elephant rides** (Indian/foreigner ₹300/1000) are available only at Dhikala and Bijrani, at 6am and 4pm on a first-come, first-served basis.

⌸ Sleeping & Eating

For serious wildlife viewing, Dhikala – deep inside the reserve – is the prime place to stay, though prices for foreigners are exorbitant. Book through the reception centre in Ramnagar at least one month in advance. The town of Ramnagar has budget accommodation, while upmarket resorts are strung out along the road skirting the eastern side of the park between Dhikuli and Dhangarhi Gate.

⌸ Dhikala

Easily the cheapest beds in the park are at **Log Huts** (dm Indian/foreigner ₹200/400), resembling 3AC train sleepers, with 24 basic beds (no bedding supplied). **Tourist Hutments** (Indian/foreigner ₹1250/2500) offer the best value accommodation in Dhikala and sleep up to six people. Dhikala has a couple of restaurants serving vegetarian food. No alcohol is allowed in the park.

The **New Forest Rest House** (r Indian/foreigner ₹1250/2500), three cabins (Indian/foreigner ₹1250/2500) and the VIP **Old Forest Rest House** (r ₹1500-5000) accommodation can all be booked at the reception centre in Ramnagar. Annexe (rooms Indian/foreigner ₹1000/2000) can be booked through the **Uttarakhand Tourism Development Board** (UTDB; ☏011-23319835) in Delhi.

⌸ Elsewhere In the Reserve

Bijrani Rest House HOTEL $$$
(s/d Indian ₹500/1000, foreigner ₹1000/2500) The first place in from Amdanda Gate; meals and elephant rides available.

Khinnanauli Rest House HOTEL $$$
(r Indian/foreigner ₹5000/12,000) VIP lodging near Dhikala, deep in the reserve.

Sarapduli Rest House HOTEL $$$
(r Indian/foreigner ₹2000/4000) Has a good location in the reserve's core area.

Gairal Rest House HOTEL $$$
(r Indian/foreigner from ₹1250/2500) On the Ramnagar River, accessed from Dhangarhi Gate; meals available.

⌸ Ramnagar

A busy, unappealing town, Ramnagar has plenty of facilities, including internet cafes (₹30 per hour), ATMs (State Bank of India ATM at the train station, and a Bank of Baroda ATM on Ranikhet Rd) and transport connections – mostly along Ranikhet Rd.

★ **Corbett Motel** HOTEL $
(☏9837468933; www.corbetmotel.com; tent ₹400, d/tr ₹500/600) Set in a beautiful mango orchard only a few hundred metres from the train station, Ramnagar's best budget accommodation is a world away from the traffic-clogged centre and offers exceptional service and hospitality. You can stay in sturdy tents or basic but spotless rooms, and the restaurant serves fine food. The owner, Karan, is a well-known local naturalist and can organise jeep safaris into the park. Call ahead for a pick-up.

Hotel Anand HOTEL $
(☏255297; Ranikhet Rd; s/d ₹300/500) A noisy budget option located about 100m from the bus stand, many rooms only have windows onto a corridor. Its **Delhi Darbar Restaurant** (mains ₹50-100; ☺7am-11pm) is one of the

cleanest, quietest places to eat in town, with a typical Indian menu plus pizzas.

Krishna Nidhi Corbett Inn HOTEL $$
(253028; Ranikhet Rd; d with/without AC ₹1300/1100; ※) Large and clean but simple rooms with balconies or verandahs make this an alright option at the northern end of Ramnagar's main street, if you want to be right in town. The manager can help organise safaris.

🛏 North of Ramnagar

Half a dozen upmarket African-style safari resorts are strung along the Ramnagar–Ranikhet road that runs along the reserve's eastern boundary. Most are around a settlement called Dhikuli – not to be confused with Dhikala! When most of the reserve is closed (15 June to 15 November), discounts of up to 50% are offered. Rates given here are for a room only, but most have packages that include meals and safaris. All places have resident naturalists, recreational facilities, restaurants and bars.

Infinity Resorts HOTEL $$$
(251279; www.infinityresorts.com; Dhikuli; s/d incl breakfast from ₹8000/10,000; ※※) The most impressive of the resorts in this area, Infinity has luxurious rooms, a roundhouse with restaurant and bar, and a swimming pool in a lovely garden backing onto the Kosi River (where you can see hordes of golden mahseer fish). The rooms in the 'old block' are better located and have more character than those in the 'new block'. Big discounts are offered if booking online.

Corbett Hideaway HOTEL $$$
(284132; www.corbetthideaway.com; Dhikuli; cottages ₹14,000-18,000; ※※) The luxurious ochre cottages offer privacy, the riverside garden is relaxing, and there's a poolside bar and thatched restaurant at this quality resort, 12km north of Ramnagar. Rooms are unique, so look at few if possible; the 'Kumaon Maneater' suite is impressive.

Tiger Camp RESORT $$$
(9891852004; www.tiger-camp.com; cottages ₹3450-4450; ※) This intimate, excellent-value resort is nestled in a shady jungle-style garden by the Kosi River, 8km from Ramnagar. Cosy cottages and bungalows have modern facilities, and nature walks and village tours are offered.

ℹ Getting There & Away

Buses run almost hourly from Ramnagar to Delhi (₹178, seven hours), Haridwar (₹155, six hours) and Dehra Dun (₹171, seven hours). For Nainital (₹51, 3½ hours) there are four direct buses, or take one to Haldwani and change there. A bus to Ranikhet (₹77, 4½ hours) leaves around 11am. Frequent buses run to Haldwani (₹51, two hours).

Ramnagar train station is 1.5km south of the main reception centre. The nightly 15013-Slip Ranikhet Express Slip (sleeper/3AC/2AC ₹133/345/585) leaves Delhi at 10.40pm, arriving in Ramnagar at 4.55am. The return trip on train 25014 leaves Ramnagar at 9.55pm, arriving in Old Delhi at 3.55am. A daytime run from Old Delhi on train 15035-Slip (2nd class/chair ₹77/271) departs at 4pm, reaching Ramnagar at 8:35pm; the return on train 25036 departs Ramnagar at 9.50am, hitting Delhi at 3.20pm.

NAINITAL

🕿 05942 / POP 40,000 / ELEV 1938M

Crowded around a deep, green volcanic lake, Nainital is Kumaon's largest town and favourite hill resort. It occupies a steep forested valley around the namesake lake Naini and was founded by homesick Brits reminded of the Cumbrian Lake District.

Plenty of hotels are set in the forested hills around the lake, there's a busy bazaar, and a spider's web of walking tracks covers the forested hillsides to viewpoints overlooking the distant Himalayan peaks. For travellers, it's an easy place to kick back and relax, eat well, go horse riding or paddling on the lake. In peak seasons – roughly May to mid-July and October – Nainital is packed to the gills with holidaying families and honeymooners, and hotel prices skyrocket.

Tallital (Lake's Foot) is at the southeastern end of the lake where you'll find the bus stand and the main road heading east towards Bhowali. The 1.5km promenade known as the Mall leads to Mallital (Lake's Head) at the northwestern end of the lake. Most hotels, guest houses and restaurants are strung out along the Mall between Mallital and Tallital. You'll most find shops, including pharmacies, in Bara Bazaar; check out the **Panchachuli** (Bara Bazaar; ⊙10am-8pm Mon-Sat) outlet, where you can buy shawls and other textiles handwoven by women from the Kumaon hills.

⊙ Sights & Activities

★ **Naini Lake** LAKE

This pretty lake is Nainital's centrepiece and is said to be one of the emerald green eyes of Shiva's wife, Sati (*naina* is Sanskrit for eye). **Naina Devi Temple**, rebuilt after the 1880 landslide, is on the precise spot where the eye is believed to have fallen. Nearby is the **Jama Masjid** and a **gurdwara**. You can walk around the lake in about an hour – the southern side is more peaceful and has good views of the town.

Boatmen will row you around the lake for ₹160 in the brightly painted gondola-like boats, or the **Nainital Boat Club** (Mallital; ☺10am-4pm) will sail you round for ₹270. Pedal boats can also be hired for ₹100 per hour.

Snow View & Cable Car VIEWPOINT

A cable car (adult/child return ₹150/100; ☺8am-8pm May & Jun, 10.30am-4pm Jul-Apr) runs up to the popular **Snow View** at 2270m, which (on clear days) has panoramic Himalayan views, including of Nanda Devi. The ticket office is at the bottom. At the top you'll find the usual food, souvenir and carnival stalls, as well as **Mountain Magic** (rides ₹30-100), an amusement park with kids' entertainment including bumper cars, trampolines and a flying fox.

A highlight of the trip to Snow View is hiking to viewpoints such as Cheena/Naina Peak, 4km away. Local guides may offer to lead you on walks.

If you want to get up to Snow View for sunrise, taxis charge ₹200.

Tiffin Top & Land's End HORSE RIDING, WALKING

A 4km walk west of the lake brings you to Tiffin Top (2292m), also called Dorothy's Seat. From there, it's a lovely 30-minute walk to Land's End (2118m) through forest of oak, deodar and pine. Mangy horses gather 3km west of town on the road to Ramnagar to take you on rides to these spots. A two-hour ride costs about ₹775, but you can take shorter rides (eg Tiffin Top for ₹350), and you can always negotiate. Touts for these rides will accost you in Mallital near the ropeway.

Rock Climbing & Trekking OUTDOOR ADVENTURE

(all inclusive per day from ₹3000) The enthusiasts at **Nainital Mountaineering Club** (☎9412905949; http://ntmcindia.pirengo.org; Mallital; per day ₹600) offer rock-climbing courses on an artificial tower and at the rock-climb-ing area, a 15m-high rock outcrop to the west of the town.

Snout Adventures (☎9411374560; www.snoutadventure.com; Ashok Cinema Bldg, Mallital) is a recommended outfit offering treks in the Kumaon and Garhwal mountains, rock-climbing courses (₹600 per day) and adventure camps.

For details on KMVN's rest houses and trekking packages, visit **KMVN Parvat Tours** (☎235656; www.kmvn.org; Tallital; ☺8am-7pm).

Nature Walks WALKING

Experienced guide **Sunil Kumar** (☎9411196837) leads hikes and focuses on bird and wildlife-watching. He can take you on day walks (₹1500), overnight hikes where you stay in local villages (₹2000), and two-week all-inclusive nature trips (from ₹75,000).

⌷ Tours

Travel agencies along the Mall such as **Hina Tours & Travel** (☎237126, 235860; www.nainitalhinatours.com) and **Anamika Travels** (☎235186) offer bus tours of the local lakes and trips to Corbett Tiger Reserve.

🛏 Sleeping

Nainital is packed with hotels but they fill up fast in peak seasons, making it hard to find a bargain at those times. The prices given below are for the main peak season; virtually all hotels offer around 50% discounts in the low season. The main peak season is generally 1 May to 30 June, and some hotels have a semipeak in October, at Diwali (October/November) and at Christmas.

Traveller's Paradise HOTEL $$

(☎9411107877; www.travellersinparadise.com; Mallital; r ₹1500-4500) A bit north of the Mall, this exceptionally friendly hotel is excellent value. Standard rooms are basic, but have comfy beds, along with chairs, coffee tables, TVs and colourfully tiled bathrooms with geysers. Deluxe rooms are more stylish, and have sofas. It's run by the amiable Anu Consul, who spent 10 years living in Mexico and knows what it's like to be on the road. Off-season prices start at ₹600.

★ **Palace Belvedere** HERITAGE HOTEL $$$

(☎237434; www.palacebelvedere.com; Mallital; s/d/ste from ₹5500/6300/7500; ☎) Built in 1897, this was the summer palace of the rajas of Awagarh. Animal skins and old prints adorn

Nainital

UTTARAKHAND NAINITAL

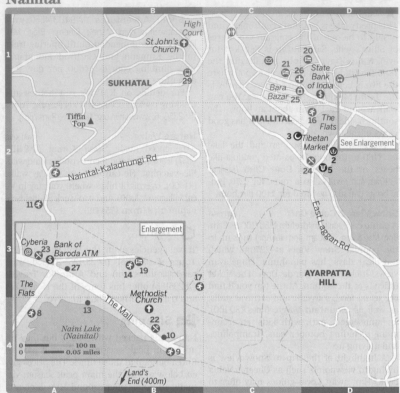

the walls and lend a faded Raj-era charm. Rooms are spacious, high-ceilinged, and have a finely aged, if slightly worn, kind of soul. Downstairs is an elegant dining room/lounge/verandah. It can be cold in winter. Good discounts off-season.

Hotel City Heart HOTEL $$$
(☎235228; www.cityhearthotelnainital.com; Mallital; d ₹2250-4500) Located off the Mall, the rooftop terrace restaurant has fine lake views. Rooms range from small but cute to fabulous deluxe rooms with a view. This place discounts more than most and is one of Nainital's best off-season bargains, with rooms from ₹800. The effusive owner will gladly play the CD of his band covering tunes by Pink Floyd and Dire Straits.

Evelyn Hotel HOTEL $$$
(☎235457; www.hotelevelynnainital.com; The Mall, Tallital; d ₹1700-3000, ste ₹3800-5500) This large Victorian-looking hotel overlooking the lake is quintessential Nainital – charming and slightly eccentric. It's big, with stairways and terraces cascading down the hillside. It's a bit old-fashioned, but the well-tended rooms with retro furniture have a nice, cosy feel.

✕ Eating & Drinking

Nainital has a host of restaurants, mostly along the Mall on the north side of the lake. For cheap eats, head to the food stalls around the Tibetan Market or to the *dhabas* in Bara Bazar.

Sonam Chowmein Corner FAST FOOD $
(The Flats, Mallital; mains ₹20-60; ⊙11am-7.30pm) In the covered alley part of the Tibetan Market, this authentic Tibetan *dhaba* whips up fabulous chow mein and *momos* for the best cheap eats in town.

Embassy   INDIAN **$$**

(The Mall, Mallital; meals ₹80-320; ⊙10.30am-
11pm) With a wood-lined chalet interior and
snappily dressed staff, Embassy has been
serving up five pages of menu items for over
40 years. For drinks try 'dancing coffee' or
a rosewater lassi. There's a good terrace for
people-watching.

Sakley's Restaurant   MULTICUISINE **$$**

(Mallital; mains ₹100-425; ⊙9am-10pm) A spotless restaurant found off the Mall, serving
up a range of unusual global items such as Thai
curries, honey chicken, roast lamb, pepper
steaks, and plenty of Chinese dishes, pizzas
and sizzlers. The cakes and pastries are great;
even if you don't dine here, swing by and pick
up some dessert to take back to your room.

Nainital Boat Club   BAR

(The Mall, Mallital; temp membership men/women/
couples ₹850/425/850; ⊙10am-10pm) This club
is a classic remnant of the Raj-era. Temporary membership is ridiculously steep, but
the atmospheric bar – with timber beams,
buttoned-up barmen with handlebar moustaches, and an outdoor deck overlooking the
lake, is perfect for an afternoon drink. The
dress code specifies no shorts or slippers,
and signs warn that 'decorum should be
maintained'.

ⓘ Information

BD Pandey Government Hospital (☎235012; Mallital) Located off the Mall.

Cyberia (Mallital; per hr ₹25; ☺10am-7.30pm) Nainital's best internet cafe offers CD burning, printing and wi-fi access. Found off the Mall.

HDFC Bank (The Mall; ☺10am-4pm Mon-Fri, to 1pm Sat) Twenty-four-hour ATM.

Main Post Office (Mallital; ☺10am-5pm Mon-Sat)

State Bank of India (The Mall, Mallital; ☺10am-4pm Mon-Fri, to 1pm Sat) Exchanges major foreign currencies and travellers cheques.

Uttarakhand Tourism Office (☎235337; The Mall; ☺10am-5pm Mon-Sat) Doesn't always follow official hours.

ⓘ Getting There & Away

BUS

Most buses leave from the **Tallital bus stand**.

Although there are direct buses from Nainital, many more services leave from the transport hubs of Haldwani and Bhowali. From Haldwani, regular buses head to Ramnagar, Delhi, Haridwar and the Nepal border at Banbassa. Haldwani is also a major train terminus. For points north, take a bus or share jeep from Nainital to Bhowali (₹10, 20 minutes) and catch one of the regular onward buses to Almora, Kausani and Ranikhet.

Five private buses direct to Ramnagar (₹70, 3½ hours) leave from the **Sukhatal bus stand**, northwest of Mallital, between 9am and 3.30pm.

Travel agencies sell tickets for private overnight deluxe coaches (with reclining seats) to Delhi (₹350 to ₹800, nine hours), which leave from Tallital around 11am and 10pm.

TAXI & SHARE JEEP

From the Kumaon Taxi Union stand in Tallital, taxis cost ₹100/500 (shared/private) to Kathgodam or Haldwani (1½ hours), ₹1200 to Ramnagar (three hours) and ₹1500 to Almora (three hours) or Ranikhet (three hours).

Share jeeps leave when full, and go to Bhowali (₹15, 20 minutes) and Kathgodam/Haldwani (₹60, 1½ hours).

TRAIN

Kathgodam (35km south of Nainital) is the nearest train station, but Haldwani, one stop further south, is the regional transport hub. The **train booking agency** (☺9am-noon & 2-5pm Mon-Fri, 9am-2pm Sat), next to the Tallital bus stand, has a quota for trains to Dehra Dun, Delhi, Moradabad, Lucknow, Gorakhpur and Kolkata. The daily 15014 Ranikhet Express (sleeper/3AC/2AC ₹146/380/585) departs Kathgodam at 8.40pm, stops at Haldwani at 8.56pm, and arrives at Old Delhi station at 4.15am. In the other direction, it departs Delhi at 10.40pm, arriving at Kathgodam at 5.05am.

ⓘ Getting Around

Cycle-rickshaws charge a fixed ₹10 along the Mall, but can only pick up and drop off at the ticket booths at either end. Taxi rides within town cost ₹50 to ₹200.

ALMORA

☎ 05962 / POP 33,000 / ELEV 1650M

Clinging to a steep-sided valley, Almora is the regional capital of Kumaon, first established as a summer capital by the Chand rajas of Kumaon in 1560. These days you'll find some colonial-era buildings, reliable trekking outfits and a couple of community-based weaving enterprises. Don't be put off by the ugly, shambolic main street when you're first deposited at the bus stand – just head one block south to the pedestrian-

BUSES FROM NAINITAL

The following buses leave from the Tallital bus stand. For Kathgodam, take the Haldwani bus.

DESTINATION	FARE (₹)	DURATION (HR)	FREQUENCY
Almora	100	3	7am
Dehra Dun	308-505	10	3 early morning, 4 evening
Delhi	250-385	9	9am, 9.30am, 7pm, 8.30pm
Haldwani	50	2	half-hourly
Haridwar	250-450	8	same as Dehra Dun
Kathgodam (A)	46	1½	half-hourly
Rishikesh	280	9	5am

only cobbled Lalal Bazaar, which is lined with intricately carved and painted traditional wooden shop facades. It's a fascinating place to stroll, people-watch and go shopping.

◉ Sights & Activities

Nanda Devi Temple HINDU TEMPLE
The stone Nanda Devi Temple in Lalal Bazaar dates back to the Chand raja era, and is covered in folk-art carvings, some erotic. Every September, the temple hosts the **Nanda Devi Fair**.

Panchachuli Weavers Factory HANDICRAFTS
(☑ 232310; www.panchachuli.com; ◷ 10am-5pm Mon-Sat) FREE The Panchachuli Weavers Factory, off Bageshwar Rd, employs some 700 women to weave, market and sell woollen shawls. The shop here has a wider range of products than at the small shop in the Mall. Taxis charge ₹150 return to the factory, or you can walk the 3km – follow the continuation of Mall Rd to the northeast and ask for directions.

High Adventure TREKKING
(☑ 9012354501; www.trekkinghimalayas.in; The Mall) Organises eight-day treks to Pindari Glacier and 10-day treks to Milam Glacier for around ₹2000 per person, per day.

Discover Himalaya TREKKING
(☑ 9411346550; bobbyalmora@hotmail.com; The Mall) Also runs trips to Pindari and Milam Glaciers.

🛏 Sleeping

Unlike most hill stations, prices here are not seasonal.

Savoy Hotel HOTEL $
(☑ 262601; www.ashoknainital.com; Mall Rd; r ₹500-1000) At the southern end of the Mall, just past the tourist office, the Savoy is in a quiet location. Cheaper downstairs rooms are simple, musty affairs, but the pricier upstairs rooms strive for comfort and style; best of all, they have tables and chairs on a shared terrace that overlooks the valley below Almora.

Bansal Hotel HOTEL $
(☑ 230864; Lalal Bazaar; d ₹300-400) Above Bansal Cafe in the bustling bazaar, but easily reached from the Mall, this is a fine budget choice with small, tidy rooms (some with TV) and a rooftop terrace.

Hotel Shikhar HOTEL $$
(☑ 230253; www.hotelshikhar.com; The Mall; r ₹700-1800, ste ₹2500-3500; ❇) Dominating the centre of town and built to take in the views, this large, boxlike hotel is perched on a hillside and offers a maze of rooms covering all budgets. In the original building, higher-end rooms aren't much better than cheaper ones; all are a bit worn, but not too foul. The top-tier rooms in the new building are Almora's nicest. The hotel also has the reasonable Mount View Restaurant.

🍴 Eating

Almora's speciality sweet is *ball mithai* (fudge coated in sugar balls), available for ₹5 in sweet shops all along the Mall and bazaar.

Glory Restaurant INDIAN $
(I R Sah Rd; mains ₹60-170; ◷ 8.30am-9.30pm) This long-running family eatery features popular South and North Indian veg and nonveg dishes, including biryanis and lemon chicken. Pizzas are extra cheesy.

Saraswati Sweet & Restaurant TIBETAN $
(Pithoragarh Rd; dishes ₹30-60; ◷ 7am-8pm) This busy place with upstairs tables quickly dishes up veg and nonveg *momos* and other Tibetan food, along with Chinese. The *thupka* is spicy enough to clear your sinuses. It has also got mutton burgers and a substantial list of cold drinks.

ℹ Information

Internet access is available at several places in Lalal Bazaar and the Mall, usually from ₹25 per hour.
HDFC (The Mall; ◷ 9.30am-3.30pm Mon-Fri, to 12.30pm Sat)
Sify iWay (The Mall; per hr ₹25; ◷ 9am-8.30pm) One of several places with internet.
State Bank of India (The Mall; ◷ 10am-4pm Mon-Fri, to 1pm Sat)
Uttarakhand Tourism Office (☑ 230180; Upper Mall; ◷ 10am-5pm Mon-Sat)

ℹ Getting There & Away

The vomit-splattered sides of the buses and jeeps pulling into Almora tell you all you need to know about what the roads are like around here.

KMOU buses operate from the Mall – starting early morning until 2.30pm or 3pm – to Ranikhet (₹55, two hours), Kausani (₹75, 2½ hours), Bageshwar (₹105, two hours) and Haldwani (₹115, three hours) via Bhowali (₹65, two hours) near Nainital. Buses to those places – except Ranikhet – also leave from the adjacent Roadways stand, where you'll find buses to

Delhi (₹325, 12 hours) at 7am, 4pm, 5pm and 6pm. For Pithoragarh, head to the Dharanaula bus stand east of the bazaar on Bypass Rd, where several buses (₹155, five hours) depart between about 7.30am and 11.30am. For Banbassa on the Nepal border, take a bus to Haldwani and change there.

Taxis or jeeps can be picked up to Ranikhet (shared/private ₹80/1000, two hours), Kausani (₹100/1000, 2½ hours), Bageshwar (₹250/2000, two hours), Bhowali (₹100/1000, three hours), Kasar Devi (₹30/250), Pithoragarh (₹250/2000, five hours) and Munsyari (private only ₹4000, 10 hours). All leave from the Mall, except the shared taxis to Pithoragarh, which leave from Dharanaula bus stand.

There's a **Railway Reservation Centre** (◷ 9am-noon & 2-5pm Mon-Sat) at the KMVN Tourist Holiday Home.

AROUND ALMORA

Kasar Devi

This peaceful spot about 8km north of Almora has been luring alternative types for close to 100 years – as a result, it's also known as Crank's Ridge. The list of luminaries who've visited, some for extended stays, includes Bob Dylan, Cat Stevens, Timothy Leary, Allen Ginsburg, and Swami Vivekananda, who meditated at the hilltop **Kasar Devi Temple**. Today, the village is a low-key backpacker destination, with a mellow vibe and clear-day Himalayan views. There's not a lot to do here, but it's a great place to chill. Get there from Almora by share jeep (₹20) or private taxi (₹300).

🛏 Sleeping & Eating

There are some great budget to midrange guesthouses here, along with a few restaurants and shops.

Manu Guest House GUESTHOUSE **$**
(☏ 9410920696; r ₹400-600) Set amid an orchard with a resident water buffalo, this place feels like a rural homestay. The largest stone or brick cottages include kitchenettes, making it a great choice for long stays.

Freedom Guest House GUESTHOUSE **$**
(☏ 9411542477; r with/without kitchen ₹800/600) Big, nice rooms open onto shared terraces with west-facing valley views, catching the

afternoon and sunset light. Pay a little more and you'll get a room with a kitchen.

★ **Mohan's** GUESTHOUSE **$$**
(☏ 9412162816; www.mohansbinsarretreat.com; r ₹1200-2400; @ 🖃) Arguably the nicest place in Kasar Devi, Mohan's has huge rooms with super comfy beds – and the pricier rooms are beautiful, with wooden ceilings and floors, and wood stoves for warmth. The real draw may be the indoor-outdoor terrace restaurant, with great views of the valley below and a shot of distant Himalayan peaks. Staff are incredibly helpful, and there's an internet cafe and a library.

Binsar Wildlife Sanctuary

Beyond Kasar Devi, picturesque Binsar, 26km from Almora, was once the hilltop summer capital of the Chand rajas. Now it's a sanctuary protecting 45 sq km, and you may spot a leopard or some barking deer, but many people come here for the 200-plus species of birds. On clear days, the Himalayan panorama is breathtaking – from the tower at 'Zero Point,' Binsar's summit (2420m), you can see Kedarnath, Nanda Devi, Panchachuli and more. Hiking trails wend throughout the lush forest; their main nexus is the KMVN Rest House. There is one good map of Binsar put out by the Forest Department, with trails and topo lines, but this is very hard to find; it's not offered at the entry gate.

It's possible to trek between the villages that are in the sanctuary, sleeping in rural homestays (which vary in quality and price). For something uniquely special, stay at the **Nandadevi Estate** (☏ 8006658964; www.nandadevi.in; cottages incl full-board from ₹7000), set amid an organic farm on Binsar's summit ridge, with beautifully restored 155-year old bungalows that exude a soulful kind of luxury. The larger ones come with kitchens and your own personal cookstaff, and the views from the property are mesmerising.

The fee to enter the sanctuary is ₹150/600 per Indian/Foreigner, plus a ₹250 to ₹500 vehicle fee depending on what you're driving. Guides, who can be hired at the sanctuary gate or the Rest House, charge ₹250 for a 1½-hour hike. A return taxi from Almora costs about ₹1100.

Jageshwar

An impressive and active **temple complex** is set along a creek in a forest of deodars at the village of Jageshwar, 38km northeast of Almora. The 124 temples and shrines date to the 7th century AD and vary from linga shrines to large *sikhara* (Hindu temples) dedicated to different gods and goddesses. Down the street is the **Jageshwar Archaeological Museum**, which houses a small collection of exquisite religious carvings taken from the temples for preservation purposes, and is well worth a look; among the highlights are the 'Dancing Ganesha' and the highly detailed version of 'Uma/Maheshwar Sitting on Nandi' with the intense snake action.

A 3km trail that starts below the centre of the village leads to the top of the ridge behind it, which has dizzying views of the sculpted valley on the other side and the big peaks in the distance.

There are a number of *dhabas* in Jageshwar, plus a handful of hotels. The best of the bunch is **Tara Guest House** (258330; 9411544736; www.jageshwar.co.uk; r ₹200), surrounded by gardens with views of the forest and the temple, with basic but decent rooms. The easiest way to get from Almora to Jageshwar is by taxi (₹900 return) or shared taxi (₹60). There's one direct bus daily around noon, which returns to Almora at 8am the following day. You can also take any bus going through Artola, get off there, and either walk 4km to Jageshwar or take a taxi for ₹80.

KAUSANI

05962 / POP 4100 / ELEV 1890M

Perched high on a forest-covered ridge, the tiny village of Kausani has lovely panoramic views of distant snowcapped peaks, fresh air and a relaxed atmosphere. Mahatma Gandhi found the village an inspirational place to retreat and write his Bhagavad Gita treatise *Anasakti Yoga* in 1929, and there is still an ashram devoted to him here. Nineteen kilometres north, Baijnath village has an intriguing complex of 12th-century *sikhara*-style temples in a lovely location shaded by trees, with other shrines in the nearby old village.

⊙ Sights & Activities

Kausani Tea Estate TEA ESTATE
(258330; www.uttaranchaltea.com; ⊙9am-6pm mid-Mar–mid-Nov) FREE At Kausani Tea Estate – a tea plantation that involves private enterprise, the government and local farmers – you can look around and sample and buy products that are exported around the world. It's 3.5km north of the village on the road to Baijnath, an easy and scenic walk.

Anasakti Ashram HISTORIC SITE
(258028; Anasakti Ashram Rd) About 1km uphill from the bus stand, Anasakti Ashram is where Mahatma Gandhi spent two weeks pondering and writing *Anasakti Yoga*. It has a small **museum** (admission free; ⊙6am-noon & 4-7pm) that tells the story of Gandhi's life through photographs and words. Visit at 6pm to attend nightly prayers in his memory. You can stay at the ashram for ₹300 but you must respect the rules, including attending evening prayers. Meals cost ₹50.

⊨ Sleeping & Eating

Outside the two short peak seasons (May to June and October to November) the accommodation listed below is discounted by 50%.

There are lots of cheap *dhabas* around the main bazaar and the road leading uphill from the bus stand.

Hotel Uttarakhand HOTEL $$
(258012; www.uttarakhandkausani.com; d ₹1050-2550; @) Up some steps from the bus stand but in a quiet location with a panoramic view of the Himalaya from your verandah, this is Kausani's best-value accommodation. The cheaper rooms are small, with bucket hot water, but upper-floor rooms are spacious and have hot showers and TVs. The manager is helpful and friendly, and credit cards are accepted.

Krishna Mountview HOTEL $$$
(258008; www.krishnamountview.com; Anasakti Ashram Rd; d ₹3200-5500, ste ₹7500-9000; ☎) Just past Anasakti Ashram, this is one of Kausani's smartest hotels, with clipped formal gardens (perfect for mountain views), the good Vaibhav restaurant, a gym and a pool table. All rooms are well kept and comfy, but the spacious upstairs rooms with balcony, bay windows and even rocking chairs are the pick.

Garden Restaurant MULTICUISINE $$
(Hotel Uttarakhand; mains ₹70-250; ⊙7am-10pm)
In front of Hotel Uttarkhand and enjoy-
ing fine Himalayan views, this bamboo
and thatch-roofed restaurant is Kausani's
coolest. The food comprises first-class dish-
es from Swiss rösti to chicken tikka and im-
ported pasta, as well as some Kumaon speci-
alities, using fresh ingredients.

Information

Kausani has a State Bank of India ATM in the
main bazaar, but no foreign currency exchange.
Sanchar Dhaba Cyber Cafe (Anasakti Ashram
Rd; per hr ₹40; ⊙6am-8pm) At Hill Queen
Restaurant.
Uttarakhand Tourism Office (☑258067; The
Mall; ⊙10am-5pm Mon-Sat)

Getting There & Away

Buses and share jeeps stop in the village centre.
Several buses go to Almora (₹105, 2½ hours),
but in the afternoon they generally stop at Kar-
bala on the bypass road, from where you need
to take a share jeep (₹10). Heading north, buses
run every hour or so to Bageshwar via Baijnath
(₹45, 1½ hours). Share jeeps (₹20, 30 minutes)
run to Garur, 16km north of Kausani, which is
a much more active transport hub, and where
you can find share jeeps to Gwaldam for onward
buses and jeeps to Garhwal (via Karanprayag).
A taxi to Almora costs around ₹1000; to Nainital
or Karanprayag it costs ₹2000.

BAGESHWAR

☑ 05963 / POP 8000 / ELEV 975M

Hindu pilgrims visit Bageshwar, at the con-
fluence of the Gomti and Sarju Rivers, for its
ancient stone **Bagnath Temple**. For travel-
lers, it's more important as a transit town to
or from the Milam or Pindari Glacier trail-
heads. There are a couple of internet cafes
around, and there's a State Bank of India
ATM in the main bazaar.

The OK **Hotel Annapurna** (☑220109;
r ₹200-400, s/d without bathroom ₹70/150) is
conveniently located next to the bus stand,
but for something much better, head for **Ho-
tel Narendra Palace** (☑9319083181; Pindari
Rd; ₹700-1500), about 1km from the bus stand
on Pindari Rd.

Several daily buses go to Almora (₹115,
three hours), and Ranikhet (₹115, three
hours) via Kausani (₹45, 1½ hours). Fre-
quent buses run to Bhowali (₹150, six hours)
and Haldwani (₹200, 7½ hours). For con-
nections to Garhwal, take a bus to Gwaldam
(₹60, two hours) and change there. For the
Pindari Glacier trek, there are two daily
buses to Song (₹50, two hours). For Milam
Glacier, there's a 9am bus to Munsyari (₹150,
six hours). There are also 6.30am and 8am
buses to Pithoragarh (₹180, seven hours).
There's a jeep stand near the bus stand,
along with a few other spots around town.
Share jeeps go to Garur (₹30, 45 minutes),

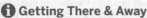

MUNSYARI

Perched on a mountainside surrounded by plunging terraced fields, where the 6000m
Panchachuli peaks scrape the sky across the Johar Valley, Munsyari (2290m) is one of
the most scenic villages in Uttarakhand. Visited mostly by trekkers heading to the Milam
Glacier – and on the way to nowhere else – the surrounding landscape makes this a
worthwhile destination even if you don't plan on lacing up your boots and hitting the trail.

There are some nice day hikes in the area and, 2km downhill from the bazaar, the
small **Tribal Heritage Museum**, run by the charming scholar SS Pangtey, with arte-
facts from the days when Munsyari was an important nexus of trade with Tibet. This is
also a unique place to experience the Nanda Devi Festival in September.

The **Hotel Pandey Lodge** (☑9411130316; www.munsyarihotel.com; r ₹200-1850) by
the bus stand has a wide range of good-value rooms, some with amazing views, and an
extremely helpful owner. Munsyari's dining situation is sparse. For motherly urging to
eat until you're stuffed (plates refilled free), try the hole-in-the-wall *dhaba* (₹40) just to
the left of the shuttered Bugyal Restaurant, at the main chowk.

Buses run to and from Pithoragarh (₹180, eight hours), Bageshwar (₹150, six hours)
and Almora (₹200, 11 hours). Share jeeps run to Pithoragarh (₹180, eight hours) and Thal
(₹120, three hours), where you can change for onward transport. If travelling to Munsyari
via Thal, get a right-side window seat for the best views along the road. If you came from
Thal and are heading to Pithoragarh, consider taking the longer route via Jauljibi for a
change of scenery, including some amazing vistas of the Kumaon and Nepali Himalayas.

BORDER CROSSING – INTO NEPAL FROM BANBASSA

Banbassa is the closest Indian village to the Nepal border post of Mahendranagar, 5km away. Check the current situation in western Nepal before crossing here, as roads during monsoon or immediate postmonsoon season may be impassable due to landslides and washed-out bridges. Buses run between Banbassa and Delhi, Haldwani, Haridwar and Pithoragarh.

Border Hours

The border is open 24 hours, but before 6am and after 6pm you're unlikely to find anyone to stamp you in and out of the respective countries. While officially open to vehicles only from 6am to 7am, noon to 2pm and 5pm to 6pm, rickshaws and motorcycles are usually allowed to make the 1km trip across the bridge between the border posts at any time. Otherwise, you have to walk it.

Foreign Exchange

Hotels in Banbassa exchange Indian and Nepali rupees, as will a small office near the Nepal border post. Nabil Bank in Mahendranagar has an ATM and foreign currency exchange.

Onward Transport

From the border, take a rickshaw or shared taxi to Mahendranagar. The bus station is about 1km from the centre on the Mahendra Hwy, from where buses leave for Kathmandu (₹1100, 16 hours) three times a day. There's also a single Pokhara service at 10.30am (₹1000, 16 hours).

Visas

Visas are available for US$30 (cash only) at the Nepali side of the border between 9am and 5pm.

Kausani (₹50, 1½ hours) and Gwaldam (₹80, two hours). A taxi to Song costs ₹1500 (two hours); to Loharket costs ₹2000 (2½ hours).

PITHORAGARH

☑ 05964 / POP 42,000 / ELEV 1815M

Spread across the hillsides above a scenic valley that's been dubbed 'Little Kashmir', Pithoragarh is the main town of a little-visited region that borders Tibet and Nepal. Its sights include several Chand-era temples and an old fort, but the real reason to come here is to get off the tourist trail. The busy main bazaar is good for a stroll, and townspeople are exceptionally friendly. Picturesque hikes in the area include the rewarding climb up to **Chandak** (7km) for views of the Panchachuli (Five Chimneys) massif.

The **tourist office** (☑ 225527), 50m uphill from the jeep stand, can help with trek-king guides and information; a State Bank of India ATM and a few internet cafes (₹30 per hour) are in the bazaar. Cheap hotels can be found around the bus stand (rooms from ₹250), but for something much better head 200m uphill to **Hotel Yash Yatharth** (☑ 225005; www.punethahotels.com; Naya Bazaar; dm ₹100, r ₹1000-3400); rates can be halved if business is slow. For a good meal at a good price, locals swear by **Jyonar Restaurant** (Gandhi Chowk; mains ₹60-200; ☺ 7.30am-10pm) in the bazaar.

Several buses leave in the morning for Almora (₹150, five hours). Frequent buses go to the transport hub of Haldwani and on to Delhi. There are hourly services from 5am to 2pm to Banbassa (₹210, six hours), the border crossing into Nepal. A bus runs north to Munsyari (₹180, eight hours) at 5.30am, as do the ubiquitous share jeeps (₹200, seven hours).

Kolkata (Calcutta)

Best Places to Eat

➡ Bhojohari Manna (p475)
➡ Oh! Calcutta (p474)
➡ Fire and Ice (p474)
➡ Amigos (p474)

Best Places to Stay

➡ Oberoi Grand (p468)
➡ Chrome (p468)
➡ Hotel Kempton (p467)

Why Go?

India's second-biggest city is a daily festival of human existence, simultaneously noble and squalid, cultured and desperate. By its old spelling, Calcutta conjures up images of human suffering to most Westerners. But locally, Kolkata is regarded as India's intellectual and cultural capital. While poverty is certainly in your face, the dapper Bengali gentry continues to frequent grand old gentlemen's clubs, back horses at the Calcutta Racetrack and tee off at some of India's finest golf courses.

As the former capital of British India, Kolkata retains a feast of colonial-era architecture, albeit much in a photogenic state of disrepair. Meanwhile urban slums contrast with dynamic new-town suburbs and a rash of air-conditioned shopping malls. Kolkata's also the ideal place to experience the mild, fruity tang of Bengali cuisine. Friendlier than India's other metropolises, this is a city you 'feel' more than simply visit.

When to Go
Kolkata (Calcutta)

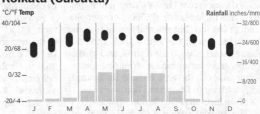

Sep/Oct The city dresses up magnificently for the colourful mayhem of Durga Puja.

Nov–Jan Cool and dry; there's a November film festival and a big book fair in January.

May–Sep Best avoided unless you're prepared for a very serious drenching.

Food

Fruity and mildly spiced, Bengali food favours the sweet, rich notes of jaggery (palm sugar), *daab* (young coconut), *malaikari* (coconut milk) and *posto* (poppy seed). Typical Bengali curry types include the light, coriander-scented *jhol,* drier spicier *jhal* and richer, ginger-based *kalia.* Strong mustard notes feature in *shorshe* curries and *paturi* dishes that come steamed in a banana leaf. *Gobindobhog bhaat* (steamed rice) or *luchi* (small puris – dough that puffs up when fried) are the usual accompaniment. More characteristic than meat or *murgir* (chicken) are *chingri* (river prawns) and excellent fish, particularly *rohu* (white rui), fatty chital and cod-like bhekti. If you can handle the bones, *ilish* (hilsa) is considered the tastiest fish, kachki are very small and *lau ghonto* – an acquired taste – is fish head pounded with pumpkin. Excellent vegetarian choices include *mochar ghonto* (mashed banana-flower, sometimes with potato and coconut), *doi begun* (eggplant in curd) and *shukto,* a favourite lunchtime starter combining at least five different vegetables in a milk-based sauce. Bengali desserts and sweets are legendary. Most characteristic are *mishti dhoi* (curd deliciously sweetened with jaggery), *rasgulla* (rosewater-scented cream-cheese balls) and *cham-cham* (double-textured curd-based fingers).

For a colourful and very affectionate portrait of Kolkata's ever-vibrant street food scene, see http://streetfoodkolkata.com which includes recipes, films and sells a brilliantly evocative book.

DON'T MISS

Sampling distinctive Bengali food, walking the chaotic back alleys, riding the Hooghly ferries, taking a motorbike tour to see more of the city and – if you've got more time – an excursion to the Sunderbans.

Top Festivals

→ **Dover Lane Music Conference** (late Jan) Indian classical music and dance at Rabindra Sarovar.

→ **Kolkata Boi Mela** (late Jan/early Feb) Kolkata Boi Mela Asia's biggest book fair.

→ **Sarawati Puja** (early Feb) Prayers for educational success – all dress in yellow.

→ **Rath Yatra** (Jun/Jul) Major Krishna chariot festival similar to the Puri equivalent.

→ **Durga Puja** (Sep or Oct) Kolkata's biggest festival.

→ **Kolkata Film Festival** (mid-Nov) Week-long festival of Bengali and international movies.

MAIN POINTS OF ENTRY

The city has three major train stations: Howrah, Sealdah and Kolkata (Chitpore).

The newly rebuilt airport area has a growing range of international flights.

Buses arrive frequently from Bangladesh and regional destinations.

Top Tip

Come for the head-spinning contrasts and disarmingly human quality of the city rather than for specific sights.

Fast Facts

→ **Population**: 14.7 million
→ **Area**: 185 sq km
→ **Telephone code**: 033
→ **Main language**: Bengali
→ **Sleeping prices**: $ below ₹1200, $$ ₹1200 to ₹10,000, $$$ above ₹10,000

Resources

→ **Bengali Recipes** (http://sutapa.com)

→ **Tourist office** (http://westbengaltourism.gov.in/web/guest/kolkata)

→ **News & Listings** (www.calcuttaweb.com)

→ **Curiosities** (http://rangandatta.wordpress.com/blog-index/calcutta-kolkata)

→ **Classified ads** (http://kolkata.clickindia.com)

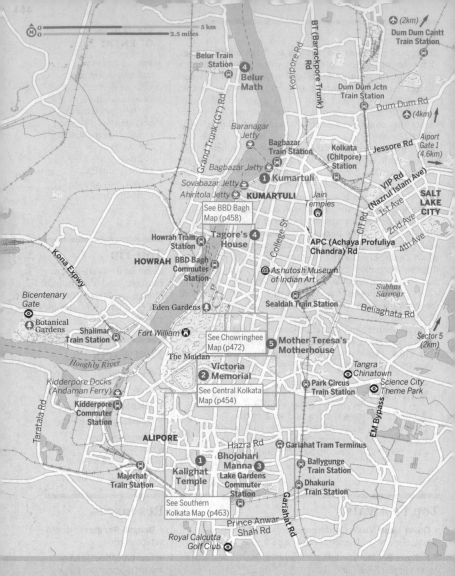

Kolkata Highlights

1 Watch goddesses coming to life in the curious lanes of **Kumartuli** (p461) or on Kalighat Rd near the famous **Kalighat Temple** (p462)

2 Ponder the contradictions of the magnificent **Victoria Memorial** (p453) which remains Kolkata's most splendid building, over 65

years after the end of the colonial era

3 Sample lip-smackingly authentic Bengali cuisine at **Bhojohari Manna** (p475)

4 Discover the enlightened universalist idealism of Ramakrishna in **Belur Math** (p462) and Rabindranath

Tagore at **Tagore's House** (p460)

5 Volunteer to help the destitute with the organisation founded by **Mother Teresa** (p460)

History

Although Kalikata (now Kalighat) had been a much-revered temple for centuries, the Kolkata area was very much a rural backwater when British merchant Job Charnock showed up in 1686. He considered the site appropriate for a new, defendable colonial settlement and within a few decades a miniature version of London was sprouting stately buildings and English churches amid wide boulevards and grand formal gardens. But the grand illusion vanished abruptly at Calcutta's frayed edges where Indians servicing the British Raj mostly lived in cramped, overcrowded slums.

The most notable hiccup in the city's meteoric rise came in 1756, when Siraj-ud-daula, the nawab (Muselim ruling prince) of nearby Murshidabad, recaptured the city. Dozens of members of the colonial aristocracy were imprisoned in a cramped room beneath Fort William. By morning, around 40 of them were dead from suffocation. The British press exaggerated numbers, drumming up moral outrage back home: the legend of the 'Black Hole of Calcutta' was born.

The following year, Clive of India retook Calcutta for Britain. The nawab sought aid from the French but was soundly defeated at the Battle of Plassey (now Palashi), thanks mainly to the treachery of former allies. A stronger fort was built and the town became British India's official capital, though well into the late 18th century one could still hunt tigers in the bamboo forests around where Sudder St lies today.

The late-19th-century Bengali Renaissance movement saw a great cultural reawakening among middle-class Calcuttans. This was further galvanised by the massively unpopular 1905 division of Bengal, sowing the seeds of the Indian Independence movement. Bengal was reunited in 1911, but the British promptly transferred their colonial capital to less troublesome Delhi.

Initially, loss of political power had little effect on Calcutta's economic status. However, the impact of 1947's partition was devastating. While West Pakistan and Punjab saw a fairly equal (if bloody) exchange of populations, migration in Bengal was almost entirely one way. Around four million Hindu refugees from East Bengal arrived, choking Calcutta's already overpopulated *bastis* (slums). For a period, people really were dying of hunger in the streets, creating Calcutta's abiding image of abject poverty. No sooner had these refugees been absorbed than a second wave arrived during the 1971 India–Pakistan War.

After India's partition, the port of Calcutta was hit very hard by the loss of its main natural hinterland, now behind the closed Pakistan (later Bangladesh) border. Labour unrest spiralled out of control while the city's dominant party (Communist Party of India) spent most of its efforts attacking the feudal system of land ownership. Well-intentioned attempts to set strict rent controls backfired: where tenants pay only a few rupees in monthly rent, landlords have no interest in maintaining or upgrading properties, so many fine old buildings spent years crumbling.

In 2001 Calcutta officially adopted the more phonetic spelling Kolkata. Around the same time the city administration implemented a new, relatively business friendly attitude that has encouraged a noticeable economic resurgence. The most visible results are numerous suburban shopping malls and apartment towers plus the rapid emergence of Salt Lake City's Sector 5 as Kolkata's alternative corporate and entertainment centre, albeit well off most tourists' radar.

⊙ Sights

⊙ Central Kolkata

★**Victoria Memorial**   HISTORIC BUILDING
(VM; Map p454; ☑22235142; www.victoriamemorial-cal.org; Indian/foreigner ₹10/150; ⊙10am-5pm Tue-Sun, last tickets 4.30pm) The incredible Victoria Memorial is a vast, beautifully proportioned festival of white marble: think US Capitol meets Taj Mahal. Had it been built for a beautiful Indian princess rather than a dead colonial queen, this would surely be considered one of India's greatest buildings. It was designed to commemorate Queen Victoria's 1901 diamond jubilee, but construction wasn't completed until nearly 20 years after her death.

Don't miss the statues as you enter the first hallway: King George V faces his wife, Mary, but looks more a queen himself in his camp breeches. To the left, prints and paintings are displayed on hardboard hoardings that jar with the gallery's original splendour. The soaring central chamber remains

Central Kolkata

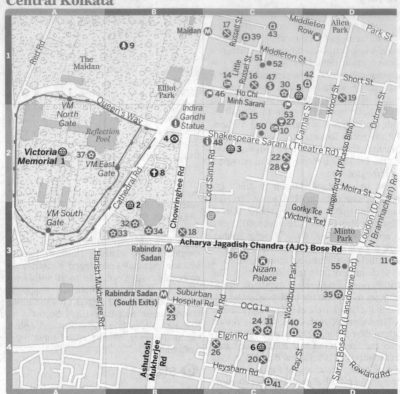

very impressive and leads through to the **Calcutta Gallery**, an excellent, even-handed exhibition tracing the city's colonial-era history.

Even if you don't want to go in, the building is still worth admiring from afar: there's a magnificently photogenic view across reflecting ponds from the northeast. Or you can get closer by paying your way into the large, well-tended **park** (⏱5.30am-6.45pm). By day, entrance is from the north or south gates (with ticket booths at both). To exit you can also use the east gate.

In the evenings the VM makes a spectacular canvas for a 45-minute English-language **sound & light show** (Map p454; Indian/foreigner ₹10/20; ⏱ 7.15pm Tue-Sun mid-Oct–Feb, 7.45pm Tue-Sun Mar-Jun) that's better than you might initially fear from the very dated opening slide sequence. The ticket booth (from 5pm) and entry are at the east gate. Seating is outside and uncovered. No shows in summer.

St Paul's Cathedral
CHURCH

(Map p454; ☎22230127; Cathedral Rd; ⏱9am-noon & 3-6pm) With its central crenellated tower, St Paul's would look quite at home in Cambridgeshire. Built 1839–47, it has a remarkably wide nave and features a stained-glass west window by Pre-Raphaelite maestro Sir Edward Burne-Jones.

Academy of Fine Arts
ART GALLERY

(Map p454; ☎22234302; 2 Cathedral Rd; ⏱3-8pm) **FREE** Several bright, ground-floor gallery rooms feature changing exhibitions by local living artists. A small museum section upstairs (closes 6pm) has some original works by Tagore.

Harrington Street Arts Centre
ART GALLERY

(Map p454; www.hstreetartscentre.com; 2nd fl, 8 Ho Chi Minh Sarani; ⏱2-8pm Mon-Sat) Imaginative exhibitions, normally photographic, are spread through four spacious rooms of a classic Kolkata colonial building.

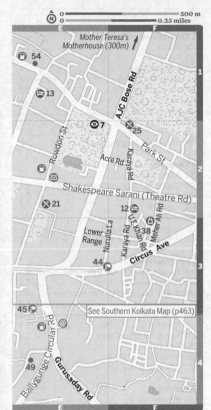

See Southern Kolkata Map (p463)

Birla Planetarium
PLANETARIUM

(Map p454; 22231516; Chowringhee Rd; admission ₹30; in English 1.30pm & 6.30pm) Loosely styled on Sarnath's classic Buddhist stupa, this 1962 dome presents slow-moving, half-hour star shows.

Aurobindo Bhawan
HISTORIC BUILDING

(Map p454; 8 Shakespeare Sarani; 8am-8pm) Revolutionary turned guru Sri Aurobindo was born in Calcutta in 1872 and his grand childhood mansion-home has been preserved as an oasis of peace in the city centre.

The Maidan
PARK

(Map p454) After the 'Black Hole' fiasco, a moated 'second' Fort William was constructed in 1758 in octagonal, Vaubanesque form. The whole village of Gobindapur was flattened to give the new fort's cannons a clear line of fire. Though sad for then-residents, this created the Maidan (moi-dan), a 3km-long park that is today as fundamental to Kolkata as Central Park is to New York City. Fort William itself remains hidden within a walled military zone.

New Market
MARKET COMPLEX

(Map p472; Hogg Bazaar, Lindsay St) Marked by a distinctive red-brick **clocktower** (Map p472), this enormous warren of a place was originally opened in 1874. It was substantially rebuilt after a 1980s fire. By day it is plagued by handicraft touts, but early morning it is fascinating to see the arrival of vegetables and animals in the old pillared food section.

Indian Museum
MUSEUM

(Map p472; 22499979; www.indianmuseumkolkata.org; Chowringhee Rd; Indian/foreigner ₹10/150, camera ₹50; 10am-4.30pm Tue-Sun, last entry 4pm) Kolkata's old-fashioned main museum fills a colonnaded palace ranged around a central lawn. Extensive exhibits include fabulous 1000-year-old Hindu sculptures, lumpy minerals, a dangling whale skeleton and an ancient Egyptian mummy. Gag at the pickled human embryos (gallery 19), spot the surreal Glyptodon dinosaur-armadillo (gallery 11) and don't miss the reassembled 2nd-century-BC **Barhut Gateway** (gallery 2). Gallery 15 displays rings and bangles found in the tummy of a gigantic man-eating crocodile.

Note that no bags are allowed inside: handbags can be stored at the entrance but don't arrive with a backpack.

Mother Teresa's Motherhouse
HISTORIC BUILDING

(Map p452; 22172277; www.motherteresa.org; 54A AJC Bose Rd; 8am-noon & 3-6pm Fri-Wed) A regular flow of mostly Christian pilgrims visit the Missionaries of Charity's 'Motherhouse' to pay homage at Mother Teresa's large, sober tomb. A small adjacent museum room displays Teresa's worn sandals and battered enamel dinner bowl. Located upstairs is the room where she worked and slept from 1953 to 1997, preserved in its simplicity with her modest camp bed and an unexplained framed airline route map. The site is around 15 minutes' walk from Sudder St; walk along Alimuddin St, then two minutes' south. It's in the second alley to the right (after Hotel Heaven).

South Park Street Cemetery
CEMETERY

(Map p454; donation ₹20, guide booklet ₹100; 8am-4.45pm) In use from 1757 to 1840, this historic cemetery remains a wonderful oasis of calm, featuring mossy Raj-era graves from rotundas to soaring pyramids, all jostling for space in a lightly manicured jungle.

Central Kolkata

Netaji Bhawan　　　　MUSEUM
(Map p454; ☎ 24756139; www.netaji.org; 38/2 Elgin Rd; adult/child ₹5/2; ⊙11am-4pm Tue-Sun) Celebrating the life and vision of controversial independence radical Subhas Chandra Bose, this house museum from Bose's brother's residence from which Subhas made his famous 'Great Escape' from British-imposed house arrest in January 1941. Some rooms retain a 1940s feel and the original getaway car is parked in the drive.

◉ BBD Bagh Area

Esplanade　　　　AREA
Rising above chaotic Esplanade bus station, the 1828 **Sahid Minar** (Map p458) is a 48m-tall round-topped obelisk originally celebrating an 1814 British military victory over Nepal.

Across one of Kolkata's busiest junctions, the striking **Metropolitan Building** (Map p458) was originally a colonial-era department store. Left derelict for years, a long overdue 2009 restoration saw its corner domes regilded. A block north, the fanciful **Tippu Sultan's Mosque** (Map p458) hides almost invisibly behind street stalls.

BBD Bagh　　　　AREA
(Dalhousie Sq) Once one of Raj-era Calcutta's foremost squares, BBD Bagh is centred on a palm-lined central reservoir-lake ('tank') that once supplied the young city's water. Although concrete intrusions detract from the overall spectacle, many splendid colonial-era edifices remain, including the grand cupola-topped 1860s **GPO** (Map p458) and the 1780 **Writers' Building** (Map p458), whose glori-

KOLKATA IN...

Three Days

On the first day admire the Victoria Memorial (p453) and surrounding attractions, then visit India Tourism to grab a Marble Palace permit (to be used two days hence), before dining and dancing on Park St. On day two wander through the colonial-era wonderland of BBD Bagh (p456), experience the fascinating/disturbing alley-life of Old Chinatown (p460) and Barabazar (p459) and observe Howrah Bridge from colourful Mullik Ghat flower market (p459). Refresh yourself with a beer at the Fairlawn (p475). Day three visit Marble Palace (p460) and surrounding attractions, continuing to Kumartuli (p461) directly or by a vastly longer loop via Dakshineswar (p462) and Belur Math (p462).

One Week

In addition to the three-day itinerary, experience the contrasts of Southern Kolkata (p462), its art galleries, golf clubs, dawn laughing clubs, the great Bengali food and the goat sacrifices at Kalighat (p462). Ponder the moral dilemmas of taking/not taking a hand-drawn rickshaw. Then take a multiday tour to the Sunderbans Tiger Reserve (p485) in West Bengal or consider volunteering for a few days having visited Mother Teresa's Motherhouse (p455).

ous south facade looks something like a French provincial city hall originally built for clerks ('writers') of the East India Company. **St Andrews Church** (Map p458; www.standrewschurch-kolkata.org; 14 BBD Bagh) has a fine Wren-style spire and the former **Standard Chartered Building** (Map p458; Netaji Subhash Rd) has a vaguely Moorish feel.

High Court   HISTORIC BUILDING
(Map p458; http://calcuttahighcourt.nic.in; Esplanade Row West; ⊙ 10.30am-1.15pm & 2-4.30pm Mon-Fri) Another of Kolkata's greatest architectural triumphs, the High Court building was built between 1864 and 1872, loosely modelled on the medieval Cloth Hall in Ypres (Flanders). The grand Gothic exterior is best viewed from the south. To look around its Kafkaesque interior replete with ribbon-tied paper bundles, ask for a gate pass at the eastern entrance security desk.

Kolkata Panorama   MUSEUM
(Map p458; ☑ 22131098; http://tinyurl.com/Kolkpan; 4 Esplanade West; Mon-Fri ₹10, Sat ₹15; ⊙ 11am-6pm Mon-Sat, last entry 5pm) Within the former 1814 Town Hall building, this interactive museum introduces the city's heritage through a lively collection of working models. It's well designed, though historically selective; some may struggle to appreciate fully the detailed sections on Bengali popular culture. You'll be accompanied by a guide. Directly east, the vast building vaguely resembling the US White House is the 1799 **Raj Bhavan** (Map p458; http://rajbhavankolkata.nic.in; ⊙ closed to public), now the official residence of the West Bengal governor.

St John's Church   CHURCH
(Map p458; ☑ 22436098; KS Roy Rd; admission ₹20; ⊙ 8am-5pm) This stone-spired 1787 church is ringed by columns and contains a small, portrait-draped room once used as an office by Warren Hastings, India's first British governor-general (on the right as you enter). The graveyard is now partly a car park but retains two curious octagonal monuments. The **mausoleum of Job Charnock** (Map p458) celebrates Kolkata's disputed 'founder'. The 1902 **Black Hole Memorial** (Map p458) was moved here in 1940.

Banking Museum   MUSEUM
(Map p458; ☑ 22318164; 11th fl, SBI Bldg, Strand Rd; ⊙ 2.30-5pm Tue-Fri) This small, professionally presented new museum brings alive the history of Indian banking using archive materials such as the original account ledgers of Tagore and of Nehru's father.

○ North-Central Kolkata

Howrah Bridge   LANDMARK
(Rabindra Setu; Map p458) Howrah Bridge is a 705m-long abstraction of steel cantilevers and traffic fumes. Built during WWII, it's one of the world's busiest bridges and one of Kokata's greatest architectural icons. Photography of the bridge is technically prohibited but you might sneak a discreet shot from one of the various ferries that ply the Hooghly River to the vast 1906 Howrah train station.

BBD Bagh

SALKIYA

0 — 400 m
0 — 0.2 miles

Howrah Bridge
11

Howrah Station
43

Hooghly River

Mullik Ghat

16
45

Tagore St

Strand Rd North

Netaji Subhash Rd

H Goenka St

Tagore's House
1

Marble Palace (120m)

Cotton St

Mahatma Gandhi (MG) Rd (Harrison Rd)

J Mullick La

Burtala St

Armenian Ghat

Bonfield La

Armenian St

2

Clive Row

Canning St (BRB Basul Rd)

Jackson La

Portuguese Church St

10

Fruit Market

Tarachand Dutta St

BBD Bagh Commuter Station

NC Dutta Sarani

Old China Bazaar Rd

15
20

Brabourne Rd

Zakaria St

17

Bolai Dutta St

Coolotola Rd

Fairlie Ghat (Private Ferry)

Fairlie Ghat

Strand Rd South

Fairlie Pl
37

ATM

India Exchange Pl
26

Mahakaran (Planned)
4

Ezra St

Tiretta Bazaar St

Rabindra Sarani

Marinbari La

18 **6**
Ashutosh Museum of Indian Art (400m)

OLD CHINATOWN

Peter La

New CIT Rd (Lushun Sarani)

19

Sun Yat Sen St

8
35

Hide La

Phears La

28

Bishe June Ghat
44

Koilaghat St
36

7

24

Bipin Behari Ganguly St

CR (Central Ave)

Central (South Exits)

Babughat (220m)

Dharbanga Statue

Hare St

13

5 **25**

Hastings St

3

9

Esplanade Row West

12

Government Pl

Netaji Subhash (NS) Rd

Gate

42

Mission Row

Mission Church

38

Bentinck St

Buddhist Temple St

RN Mukherjee Rd

Weston St

Bow St

29

ATM
30

40

Chandni Chowk (North Exits)

Mangoe La

Sooterkin St

British Indian St

Waterloo St

34

Princep St

Prafulla Sakar St

32

31

Madan St

Chandni Chowk (South Exits)

Biplabi Ankul Chamba St

Ganesh Chandra (GC) Ave

21

Crooked La

Chandni Chowk (South Exits)

Chowringhee Sq
27

Chandni Chowk Temple St

Chandni Chowk Market

22

Tram 22 (Northbound)

33

Lenin Statue

Esplanade (North Exits)

Chowringhee Rd

Moti Sil La

14

Grant St

Rani Rashmmoni Sarani

Lenin Sarani

The Maidan

WWI Cenotaph

23 **41** **39**

BBD Bagh

Mullik Ghat Flower Market FLOWER MARKET
(Map p458) Near the southeast end of Howrah Bridge, the flower market is fascinatingly colourful virtually 24 hours a day. Many workers live in makeshift shacks, bathing in the river behind, while at around 7am local wrestlers practise their art on a small caged area of sand set just back from the river.

Barabazar AREA
Finding the following minor religious sights walks you through some of Kolkata's most vibrantly chaotic alleys teeming with traders, rickshaw couriers and baggage wallahs with impossibly huge packages balanced on their heads. Hidden away amid the paper-merchants of Old China Bazaar St, the **Armenian Church of Nazareth** (Map p458; Armenian St; ⊙6am-6pm) was founded in 1707 and is claimed to be Kolkata's oldest place of Christian worship. The larger 1797 Portuguese-Catholic **Holy Rosary Cathedral** (Map p458; Brabourne Rd; ⊙6am-11am) has eye-catching crown-topped side towers and an interior whose font is festively kitsch.

Kolkata's Jewish community once numbered around 30,000 but these days barely 40 ageing co-religionists turn up at **Moghan David Synagogue** (Map p458; Canning St; ⊙by discussion with doorkeeper). Around the corner, the derelict **Neveh Shalome Synagogue** (Map p458; Brabourne Rd) is almost invisible behind shop stalls, and opposite decrepit Pollock St Post Office (once a grand Jewish school building) is **BethEl Synagogue** (Map p458; Pollock St) whose colonnaded interior can only be visited with written permission from **Nahoum Bakery** (Map p472; Stall F-20, New Market; ⊙9.30am-8pm Mon-Sat, to 1pm Sun). Allow two days!

Rising above the colourful shopfronts of ever-fascinating Rabindra Sarani, the 1926 **Nakhoda Mosque** (Map p458; 1 Zakaria St) was loosely modelled on Akbar's Mausoleum at Sikandra.

MOTHER TERESA

For many people, Mother Teresa (1910–97) was the living image of human sacrifice. Born Agnes Gonxha Bojaxhiu to Albanian parents in then-Ottoman Üsküp (now Skopje in Macedonia), she joined the Irish Order of Loreto nuns and worked for over a decade teaching in Calcutta's **St Mary's High School** (Map p472; ☎ 033 22298451; 92 Ripon St). Horrified by the city's spiralling poverty, she established a new order, the Missionaries of Charity (p465) and founded refuges for the destitute and dying. The first of these, Nirmal Hriday (p464), opened in 1952 in a former Kalighat pilgrims' hostel. Although the order expanded into an international charity, Mother Teresa herself continued to live in absolute simplicity. She was awarded the Nobel Peace Prize in 1979 and beatified by the Vatican in October 2003, the first official step towards being made a saint.

But this 'Saint of the Gutters' is not universally beloved. For some Kolkatans it's slightly galling to find their cultured, predominantly Hindu city popularly linked in the world's mind with a Catholic heroine whose work underlined the city's least appealing facet. Germaine Greer has accused Mother Teresa of religious imperialism, while Christopher Hitchens' book, *The Missionary Position,* decried the donations from dictators and corrupt tycoons. Many have questioned the Missionaries of Charity's minimal medical background and Teresa's staunchly Catholic position against contraception, which seems particularly untenable given Kolkata's AIDS and hepatitis problems. However, the organisation was never primarily focused on saving lives, simply offering a little love and dignity to the dying. Before Mother Teresa, even that was an unknown luxury for the truly destitute.

Old Chinatown
AREA

For nearly two centuries the area around Phears Lane was home to a predominantly Christian Chinese community, many of whom fled or were interned during a fit of anti-Chinese fervour during the 1962 Sino-Indian war. These days 'old' Chinatown is pretty run down and predominantly Muslim – a fascinating place to glimpse Kolkata's contrasts. On the turn of ragged little Damzen Lane you'll find the shrine-like Chinese church, **Nam Soon** (Map p458). A little further along is an oversized turquoise **gateway** (Map p458; 10 Damzen Lane), built to allow passage for domestic elephants. The once-grand 1924 **Nangking Restaurant** (Map p458; Lushun Sarani) is now a wreck beside which a rubbish heap supports a community of destitute scavengers who scrape together a miserable existence living in tent-and-box shacks on neighbouring pavements. Very humbling.

Just after dawn, there's a lively market scene on Tiretta's Bazaar. It's all closed by 10am, as is the archetypal old shop, **Hap Hing** (Map p458; 10 Sun Yat Sen St; ⊙ 6am-10am Mon-Sat, to 8.30am Sun) where owner Stella Chen can tell you lots more about the Chinese community.

Marble Palace
MUSEUM

(☎ 22393310; 46 Muktaram Babu St; ⊙ 10am-4pm, last entry 3.30pm, closed Mon & Thu) Re-splendent yet slightly run down, this grand 1835 raja's mansion is astonishingly overstuffed with statues, Victoriana, Belgian glassware and fine if bedraggled paintings including supposedly original works by Murillo, Joshua Reynolds and three by Rubens. Napoleons beat Wellingtons two to one in the music room, which is lavishly floored with marble inlay. The ballroom retains its vast array of candle chandeliers with globes of silvered glass to spread illumination: original 19th-century disco balls! Before arriving you need to get a permission note from one of the tourist offices. With this note, admission is technically free. However, the (obligatory) guide very pointedly solicits tips (expecting around ₹100 per group) and the spear-wielding guard would love some too.

To find Marble Palace from MG Rd metro, walk north and turn left at the first traffic light (Chittaranjan Ave).

★ Tagore's House
MUSEUM

(Jorasankho Thaurbari; ☎ 22695242; www.rabindrabharatimuseum.org; 246D Rabindra Sarani; Indian/foreigner ₹10/50, student ₹5/25; ⊙ 10.30am-5pm Tue-Sun, last entry 4.30pm) Within Rabindra Bharati University, the comfortable 1784 family mansion of Rabindranath Tagore has become a shrine-like museum to India's greatest modern poet. Even if his personal effects don't inspire you, some of the well-chosen quotations might spark an interest in Tagore's deeply universalist philosophy. There's also a decent gallery of paintings by his family and contemporaries, and an exhibition on his links with Japan. The 1930 photo of Tagore taken with Einstein could win a 'World's Wildest Hair' competition. You'd need an hour to see everything but for many casual visitors a brief glimpse is enough.

Kumartuli   AREA

Many of the giant god effigies that are immersed in the holy Hooghly during Kolkata's colourful *pujas* (offerings) have been made by the *kumar* (sculptors) of this enthralling district. Different workshops specialise in creating the straw frames, adding clay coatings or painting the divine features. Craftsmen are busiest from August to November for the Durga and Kali festivals.

There's a great selection of workshops on the narrow lane running two blocks west from 499 Rabindra Sarani. Where that makes a T-junction turn right for more (Banamali Sakar St). That road ends 300m north at Durgacharan Banerjee St. Turning left here brings you quickly to a ghat where the sculptors' mud clay is brought in by boat. A tree-shaded riverside stroll north of here passes several small shrines en route to Bagbazar Jetty, from where passenger ferries cross to Howrah (₹5, 20 minutes with two stops, four hourly) and Baranagar (twice hourly).

Ashutosh Museum of Indian Art   MUSEUM

(Map p452; ☎22410071; www.caluniv.ac.in/museum/museum.html; Centenary Bldg, 87/1 College St; admission ₹10; ◷10am-4pm Mon-Fri) Priceless antique Indian sculptures, brasswork and Bengali terracotta are displayed with very little fanfare in this dry, but brilliantly endowed museum tucked behind Kolkata University's Central Library. Permission is required for photography and even for sketching museum items. Entrance is off College St down the first lane to the left as you walk north from Coolootola Rd. Trams 5 and 6 link Esplanade and College St.

Indian Coffee House   HISTORIC CAFE

(1st fl, 15 Bankim Chatterjee St; coffee ₹12; ◷9am-9pm Mon-Sat, 9am-12.30pm & 5-9pm Sun) If you're walking down College St to the Ashutosh Museum from intriguing MG Rd, after one block turn left, take the fourth doorway on the left and climb the stairs to this mythic cafe. The cheap coffee can hardly be recommended, but it's perversely fascinating to look inside this unpretentious high-ceilinged place that was once a meeting place of freedom fighters, bohemians and revolutionaries.

◉ Northern Kolkata

This area's long distances and tedious traffic are mitigated if you use the public riverboat from Dakshineswar to Belur Math. It's better still if you can charter a boat on from Belur Math to Bagbazar (around ₹400) for Kumartuli, but finding an available boatman is very much hit and miss.

Sheetalnathji Mandir   JAIN TEMPLE

(www.jaindharmonline.com/pilgri/shitala.htm; Badridas Temple St; donation appropriate;

KOLKATA (CALCUTTA) SIGHTS

DURGA PUJA

Much as Carnival transforms Rio or New Orleans, **Durga Puja** brings Kolkata even more colourfully to life. For five days around September/October people venerate gaudily painted idols of the 10-armed goddess Durga and her entourage displayed in *pandals* (temporary shrines) that dominate yards, block roads and fill little parks. In the last 30 years, design competitions and increasing corporate sponsorship have seen *pandals* growing ever more ornate and complex, some with topical or political messages. West Bengal Tourism tours try to take tourists around a selection of the best *pandals* but getting anywhere within the city can take hours given the general festive pandemonium. At the festival's climax, myriad Durga idols are thrown into the sacred Hooghly River amid singing, water throwing, fireworks and indescribable traffic congestion. If you just want *pandal* photos and not the festival aspect, consider visiting just after Durga Puja when the idols have gone but *pandals* have yet to be deconstructed. Or come back for Kali Puja three weeks later when the city does the whole thing all over again, this time with statues of blue-faced, red-tongued Kali.

⊘ 6am-noon & 3-7pm) The best known of a closely grouped trio of Jain temples, this 1867 complex is a dazzling if unrefined pastiche of colourful mosaics, spires, columns and slivered figurines that looks like a work by Gaudi. It's 1.6km from Shyambazar metro.

Dakshineswar HINDU TEMPLE
(www.dakshineswarkalitemple.org; ⊘ 6.30am-noon & 3-8.30pm) The heart of this vibrant riverside complex is a cream-and-red 1847 Kali Temple shaped like an Indian Sacré-Coeur. The site is where Ramakrishna (see below) started his remarkable spiritual journey, and his small room in the outer northwest corner of the temple precinct is now a place of special meditative reverence.

A metro extension is under construction. Meanwhile Dakshineswar train station, 400m south of the temple, has roughly hourly suburban train services from Sealdah (20 minutes) and is the terminus of bus DN9/1 from Dum Dum metro (₹5). Uncovered boats to Belur Math (per passenger/boat ₹8/240, 20 minutes) leave when full from the temple's tree-shaded riverbank. Bring a hat or umbrella.

★**Belur Math** SACRED SITE
(Map p452; ☎ 26545892; www.sriramakrishna.org/belur.htm; Grand Trunk Rd; ⊘ 6.30am-noon & 3.30-8.30pm) Set very attractively amid palms and manicured lawns, this large religious centre is the headquarters of the Ramakrishna Mission, inspired by 19th-century Indian sage Ramakrishna Paramahamsa, who preached the unity of all religions. Its centrepiece is the 1938 **Ramakrishna Mandir** (⊘ closes 8pm) which somehow manages to look like a cathedral, Indian palace and Istanbul's Aya Sofya all at the same time. Several smaller shrines near the Hooghly riverbank include the **Sri Sarada Devi Temple** (⊘ 6.30-11.30am & 3.30-5.15pm), entombing the guru's wife.

Accessed from the car park, the beautifully presented dual-level **museum** (admission ₹5; ⊘ 8.30-11.30am & 3.30-5.30pm Tue-Sun) charts Ramakrishna's life and the travels of his great disciple Swami Vivekananda, with mock-ups of buildings in which the latter stayed from Rajasthan to New York.

From the main road outside Belur Math, minibus 11 and bus 54 run to Esplanade, bus 56 to Howrah. The stop-start traffic is miserable. Six daily suburban trains run from Belur Math to Howrah (₹4, 25 minutes)

⊙ West Kolkata

Botanical Gardens PARK
(Map p452; ☎ 26685357; http://164.100.52.111/indianBotanicgarden.shtm; Indian/foreigner ₹10/100; ⊘ 5.30am-5pm Tue-Sun) If it weren't such an awkward trek by public transport, Kolkata's lovely 109-hectare Botanical Gardens would make a great place to escape from the city's sounds and smells. Founded in 1786, the gardens played an important role in cultivating tea long before the drink became a household commodity. Today there's a cactus house, palm collection, river overlook and a boating lake with splendid giant Amazon lily pads. The most touted attraction is the 250-year-old 'world's largest banyan tree'. That's a little misleading: the central trunk rotted away in the 1920s, leaving an array of cross-branches and linked aerial roots so it looks more like a copse than a single tree.

The banyan is five minutes' walk from the park's **Bicentenary Gate** (Map p452; Andul Rd) on bus route 55A, or 25 minutes' walk from the gardens' main gate where bus 55 and minibus 6 terminate after a painfully slow drive from Esplanade (₹7) via Howrah. Taxis from Shakespeare Sarani charge around ₹150 via the elegant Vidyasagar Setu (Hooghly Suspension Bridge).

⊙ Southern Kolkata

★**Kalighat Temple** HINDU TEMPLE
(Map p463; ☎ 22231516; ⊘ 5am-10pm, central shrine closed 2-4pm) This ancient Kali temple is Kolkata's holiest spot for Hindus and possibly the source of the city's name. Today's version, an 1809 rebuild, has floral- and peacock-motif tiles that look more Victorian than Indian. More interesting than the architecture are the jostling pilgrim queues that snake into the main hall to fling hibiscus flowers at a crowned, three-eyed Kali image. There's no need to join them to feel the atmosphere. Behind the bell pavilion but still within the mandir complex, goats are ritually beheaded (generally mornings) to honour the ever-demanding goddess, or, as a local guide described it, to buy 'God power'. To the direct east is a pea-green 'holy pond' and just by the north perimeter a 'tree of fertility'.

Unless using their services to queue-jump into the central shrine hall, there's no need to make more than a token donation to the impromptu temple guides: ₹10 or ₹20

Southern Kolkata

KOLKATA (CALCUTTA) SIGHTS

Southern Kolkata

◎ Top Sights
1 Kalight Temple.......................................B3

◎ Sights
2 Alipore Zoo...A1
3 Birla Academy of Art & Culture...........C3
4 Birla Mandir..D2
5 CIMA..D1
6 Curzon Mansion.....................................A1
7 Experimenter..D3
8 Horticultural Gardens...........................A2
9 National Library.....................................A1
Nirmal Hriday.................................(see 1)
10 Rabindra Sarovar....................................C3
11 Shanagar Burning Ghat.........................B3

◎ Activities, Courses & Tours
12 Help Tourism..B3

◎ Sleeping
13 Bodhi Tree...B4
Hotel Aston....................................(see 16)

◎ Eating
14 Bhojohari Manna....................................D3

◎ Drinking & Nightlife
15 Dolly's Tea Shop.....................................D4
16 Tea Bush Table.......................................C1

◎ Entertainment
17 Basement...C1
18 Calcutta School of Music......................D1
19 Ginger..B2

◎ Shopping
20 Dakshinapan Shopping Centre............D4

◎ Information
21 German Consulate..................................A2
22 Mizoram State Office.............................D2
23 Myanmar Consulate...............................D2

should be fine, while ₹11 or ₹21 is even better, as giving a sum ending in one is considered lucky and implies that you are familiar with local customs. It also prevents unscrupulous scribes adding extra zeros into the donation book after you have left, exaggerating your gift to naive future visitors.

The temple is hidden in a maze of alleys jammed with market stalls selling votive flowers, brassware, religious artefacts and pictures of Kali. From Kalighat metro station (with its four-storey Mother Teresa mosaic) walk towards the putrid Tolisnala Stream where **Shanagar Burning Ghat** (Map p463; Tolisnala Stream) hosts an impressive gaggle of monuments celebrating those cremated here. Turn north up Tollygunge Rd, which becomes Kalighat Rd after one block. The temple is to the right down the

footpath beside **Nirmal Hriday** (Map p463; 251 Kalighat Rd). That's Mother Teresa's world-famous, if surprisingly small, home for the dying, its roof corners pimpled with neo-Mughal mini-domes.

Further north up lively Kalighat Rd, after it curves across Hazra Rd, you'll find numerous image makers – less famous but almost as intriguing as those in Kumartuli.

Alipore   AREA

First opened in 1875, Kolkata's 16-hectare **zoo** (Map p463; Alipore Rd; admission ₹10; ☺9am-5pm Fri-Wed) includes lawns and lakeside promenades that are very popular with weekend picnickers, hence all the rubbish. Bus 230 from Rabindra Sadan passes outside. Directly south of the zoo entrance, the (private) access road to India's **National Library** (Map p463; www.nlindia.org) loops

STREET NAMES

Since Independence, street names with Raj-era connotations have been officially changed, but while street signs and business cards use the new variant, citizens and taxis often still refer to the British-era names. This chapter uses what we found, quite unscientifically, to be the most commonly employed variant, *italicised* in the list below:

OLD NAME	NEW NAME
Allenby Rd	Dr Sisir Kumar Bose Sarani
Ballygunge Rd	Ashutosh Chowdhury Ave *(AC Rd)*
Brabourne Rd	Biplabi Trailokya Maharaja Rd
Camac St	Abinindranath Tagore St
Central Ave	*Chittaranjan (CR) Ave*
Chitpore Rd	*Rabindra Sarani*
Chowringhee Rd	Jawaharlal Nehru Rd
Dalhousie Sq	*BBD Bagh*
Free School St	*Mirza Ghalib St*
Harrington St	*Ho Chi Minh Sarani*
Harrison Rd	Mahatma Gandhi *(MG)* Rd
Hungerford St	Picasso Bithi
Kyd St	Dr M Ishaque Rd
Lansdowne Rd	*Sarat Bose Rd*
Loudon St	Dr UM Bramhchari St
Lower Circular Rd	*AJC Bose Rd*
Old Courthouse St	Hemant Basu Sarani
Park St	Mother Teresa Sarani
Rawdon St	Sarojini Naidu Sarani
Theatre Rd	*Shakespeare Sarani*
Victoria Terrace	*Gorky Terrace*
Waterloo St	Nawab Siraj-ud-Daula Sarani
Wellesley St	*RAK* (Rafi Ahmed Kidwai) *Rd*
Wood St	Dr Martin Luther King Sarani

around the very regal **Curzon Mansion** (Map p463), which was once the colonial Viceroy's residence. Around 1km southeast, the delightful **Horticultural Gardens** (Map p463; Belvedere Rd; admission ₹10; ⊘ 6-10am & 2-7pm) offer some respite from the traffic rumble.

Rabindra Sarovar   PARK
(Map p463) The parkland here is less beautiful than Kolkata's Botanical Gardens but the lake prettily reflects hazy sunrises while middle-class Kolkatans jog, row and meditate. Some form circles to do group-yoga routines culminating in ho-ho ha-ha-ha laugh-ins, engagingly described by Tony Hawks as Laughing Clubs in *The Weekenders: Adventures in Calcutta*. Even if forced, a good giggle can be refreshingly therapeutic.

Birla Academy of Art & Culture   GALLERY
(Map p463; ☑ 24666802; www.birlaart.com; 109 Southern Ave; exhibition/museum free/₹5; ⊘ 3-8pm Tue-Sun) This multi-storey gallery displays frequently changing exhibitions, both from contemporary artists and from its vast collection encompassing all Indian styles back to some classic medieval work.

Gariahat   AREA
This wealthy area isn't really a tourist draw but has a good scattering of restaurants, shops and galleries. In an apartment block near the large, distinctive 20th-century **Birla Mandir** (Map p463; Gariahat Rd; ⊘ 6-11am & 4.30 9pm), **CIMA** (Map p463; ☑ 24858509; www.cimaartindia.com; Sunny Towers, 2nd fl, 43 Ashutosh Chowdhury Rd; ⊘ 11am-7pm Tue-Sat, 3-7pm Mon) is an appealing private gallery of modern Bengali art, while relatively small **Experimenter** (Map p463; www.experimenter.in; 2/1 Hindustan Rd; ⊘ 11am-7pm Mon-Sat) behind Kanishka's, is about as cutting edge as any Kolkata gallery gets.

🏃 Activities

Cooking
Kali Travel Home (☑ 25550581; www.traveleastindia.com; ₹600-800) arranges personal three-hour Bengali cooking courses led by local women in their homes. Costs include food. Several days' notice required.

Golf
The 1829 **Royal Calcutta Golf Club** (Map p452; ☑ 24731288, 24731352; www.rcgc.in; 18 Golf Club Rd), the world's oldest outside Britain, allows foreign nonmembers to play a round for US$50.

Yoga
Type 'Kolkata' into the **Art of Living** (☑ 24631018; www.artofliving.org/in-en/search/course) website to find courses at various venues.

🏃 Volunteering

Several organisations welcome foreign volunteers. A good place to meet other volunteers informally is at Raj's Spanish Cafe (p471).

Mother Teresa's **Missionaries of Charity** (www.motherteresa.org) welcomes all comers. There's no minimum service period and no specific skills required other than a warm heart and patience to listen to and empathise with those whose language you might not understand. Start by attending a briefing at **Sishu Bhavan** (78 AJC Bose Rd; ⊘ 3pm Mon, Wed & Fri), two blocks north of Mother Teresa's Motherhouse.

Calcutta Rescue (Map p472; ☑ 22175675; www.calcuttarescue.org; 4th fl, 85 Collins St) provides medical care and health education for the disadvantaged of Kolkata and other parts of West Bengal. There are six- to nine-month openings for experienced professionals.

👉 Tours

See p486 for excursions to the Sunderbans.

Walking Tours
Small group, accompanied city walks are available through several outfits, some aimed specifically at photographers. Most start after dawn and last till midmorning, but tailor-made options are possible.

Kali Travel Home   WALKING
(☑ 25550581, 9007778504; www.traveleastindia.com; ₹400-700)

CalWalks   WALKING
(☑ 9830184030; www.calcuttawalks.com; from ₹1500)

Footsteps   WALKING
(☑ 9830008033, 9830052688; www.braindropsindia.com/footsteps; from ₹800) Relatively few fixed dates.

Calcutta Photo Tours   WALKING, PHOTOGRAPHY
(☑ 9831163482; calcuttaphototours.com; from ₹1500)

Tour-hosting Service
Tailor-made tours by car and foot for up to four people are part of the bespoke non-residential hosting service offered

KOLKATA (CALCUTTA) ACTIVITIES

by dapper art-dealer **Bomti** (Surajit Iyengar; ✎9831314990; bomtiyengar@yahoo.com; per group per day ₹5000-8000). Tours end up with a traditional Bengali lunch in Bomti's remarkable art-filled apartment (₹1500 per person extra including drinks) which once featured in *Elle Decor* (www.elledecor.com/design-decorate/artful-patina).

Motorbike/Car Tours

Best known for their mangrove boat trips, Backpackers (p486) also offers innovative two-part city tours on the back of a motorbike (₹1500). Tours drive past several well-known sites and add curiosities such as Kolkata's giant trash mountain, Tangra Chinatown, a burning ghat, a Shiva temple (join the prayers) and a brief drive through the red-light district. A similar, if adapted, tour by car costs ₹3000 for up to three people, ₹3500 with air-con. Longer car tours to Belur Math, Dakshineswar and the Hooghly river-town sites as far as Bansberia's Kremlin-styled palace **temple** (p487) costs ₹3500/4000.

Bus Tours

Full-day sightseeing bus tours are operated by **West Bengal Tourism** (tour ₹450; ⊙8.30am Tue-Sun) on BBD Bagh. Though a relative bargain, they give only sweaty, drive-by glimpses of most sights, and rush you round Belur Math and Dakshineswar in barely half an hour apiece. Tours are cancelled if there are fewer than 10 customers, least likely on Sundays.

🛏 Sleeping

Looks can be deceptive. Some eye-catchingly smart facades mask lacklustre, mustily disappointing rooms. Other very survivable places are hidden within buildings that look like crumbling wrecks. Decent hotel accommodation in Kolkata often costs about the same as in Western Europe, so if you want to pay less than ₹700 for a room, don't expect to enjoy the experience. Even in many midrange hotels, peeling paint, loose wires, battered furniture and damp patches come as standard. Many cheaper hotels lock their gates by midnight so if you're planning a night on the tiles, check if there's a late-entry procedure.

Many of Kolkata's better hotels are in Salt Lake, Southern Kolkata and other peripheral areas. Until the metro extension makes these areas less painful to reach from most

points of touristic interest, we have chosen not to review most such options.

Hotels typically add at least 5% tax on rooms over ₹1000 and 17.42% on those over ₹3000, but some quote inclusive rates. When bargaining, double-check whether the offer is 'plus tax'. This chapter gives total quoted prices. Top-end hotels are often very significantly discounted on websites such as www.yatra.com and www.booking.com. Most places charging under ₹1200 won't take bookings.

Don't get overexcited by places that call themselves 'boutique hotels', a term that seems to imply little more than a new building and a splash of colour while often excusing a comparative lack of staff in comparison to older, full-service business hotels.

Accommodation fills to bursting before and during Durga Puja. Occupancy drops noticeably afterwards (October), but from November to February occupancy is heavy again.

🗺 Sudder Street Area

The nearest Kolkata gets to a traveller ghetto is the area around helpfully located Sudder St. There's a range of backpacker-oriented services, and if you don't have any booking a big advantage of arriving here is that virtually every second building is a guesthouse or hotel. The area has a very wide range of qualities including arguably Kolkata's very best hotel, but it's also virtually the only area in Kolkata where ultra-cheap dives accept foreigners. Be aware that many such dives scrape the barrel of acceptability. As one backpacker quipped, 'Kolkata's budget accommodation represents a whole new league of nastiness'. Nonetheless, many travellers do insist on subjecting themselves to coffin-sized rooms where the main decor is the graffiti of previous inmates. Consider putting a mat on the bed to reduce bed-bug bites. When we list Sudder St area accommodation much under ₹1000, we're usually identifying the least objectionable options rather than making a recommendation. And as few cheapies take reservations, finding a cheap room is generally a case of simply visiting a whole series of options.

Long-serving cheapies include bearable if unfriendly **Maria** (Map p472; from ₹250), worn-if-quirky **Modern Lodge** (Map p472; ✎22524960; Stuart Lane; from ₹300) and deeply depressing cheapy **Paragon** (Map p472; Stuart Lane; from ₹230).

Hotel Aafreen
HOTEL $

(Map p472; ☑ 22654146; www.goldenapplehotel. in/aafreen.aspx; Nawab Abdur Rahman St; d with fan/AC ₹700/950, ste ₹2000; ✴) Offering midrange quality at budget prices, the Aafreen has been recently repainted, and en-suite bathrooms have decent geysers. Bed quality varies considerably between rooms and the lift can be temperamental.

Hotel Pioneer International
GUESTHOUSE $

(Map p472; ☑ 22520557; 1st fl, 1 Marquis St; d without/with AC ₹650/900; ✴) From outside the house looks semi-derelict and the wobbly wooden stairs don't improve expectations, yet the guesthouse's six rooms in two-tones of yellow are unexpectedly neat with clean tiled floors and multilingual TV. Staff are friendly and helpful.

Aafreen Tower
HOTEL $

(Map p472; ☑ 22293280; 9A Kyd St; d with fan/AC ₹800/1200; ✴) A creaky glass elevator plays pinball music and rises to bright orange corridors and good-sized rooms with paintwork designed in a Disneyesque caricature of oldworld style. Walls have suffered the usual battering and cleaning seems a little cursory, but furniture damage is relatively limited. Good value in this price range.

Hotel Galaxy
BACKPACKER GUESTHOUSE $

(Map p472; ☑ 22524565; hotelgalaxy.kol@gmail. com; 3 Stuart Lane; r with fan/AC ₹750/900; ✴) This ageing mansion block has highceilinged rooms that have been reasonably well upgraded for a cheaper guesthouse, albeit with a typical share of peeling paint. Hot water in en-suite bathrooms.

Shams Hotel
BACKPACKER GUESTHOUSE $

(Map p472; ☑ 30222722; 3 Tottie Lane; r from ₹300; ✴🛜) The nine rooms vary from bare and simple to windowless boxes for which you'll need to bend double, but it's relatively clean and rare among basic backpacker places in offering free wi-fi.

★ Hotel Kempton
HOTEL $$

(Map p472; ☑ 40177888; www.hotelkempton.in; 3 Marquis St; s/d from ₹3757/4110; ✴🛜) The Kempton's feast of white marble and artificial orchids hint at standards far above the prices actually charged in this new, relatively suave tower that brings a new level of class to the Sudder St zone. Prices include buffet breakfast.

Fairlawn Hotel
HOTEL $$

(Map p472; ☑ 22521510; www.fairlawnhotel.com; 13A Sudder St; s/d incl breakfast ₹3167/3871; ✴🛜) Taking guests since 1936, the Fairlawn is a characterful 1783 Raj-era home fronted by tropical greenery. The stairs and sitting room are smothered with photos, family mementos and articles celebrating the hotel's nonagenarian owner. While not luxurious, most rooms are spacious and well equipped though some bathrooms retain very old tubs. At least one of the downstairs rooms has limited natural light. Wi-fi (₹250) is turned off at midnight.

Golden Apple Hotel
GUESTHOUSE $$

(Map p472; ☑ 66077500; www.goldenapplehotel. in; 9 Sudder St; cubicle ₹500, r ₹1300-2000) The Golden Apple is probably the best-value hotel on Sudder St. Rooms are mostly very fresh and stylishly appointed, but do try to look before booking as a few are darker, damp-afflicted boxes with feeble AC. A very cool backpacker feature is the set of 15 topfloor budget 'cubicles': like a dorm deluxe, each is a lockable bedspace partitioned off by smoked-glass walls and with storage area beneath the mattress.

Housez 43
HOTEL $$

(Map p472; ☑ 22276020; www.housez43.com; 43 Mirza Ghalib St; s/d ₹2811/3373; ✴🛜) Housez 43 calls itself a 'value boutique hotel', based perhaps on the beanbags on landings and jauntily shaped mirrors in brightly pastelcoloured rooms. It's certainly neat, clean and fair value though road noise can be disturbing by day.

DK International
HOTEL $$

(Map p472; ☑ 22522540; www.dkinthotel.com; 11/1A Marquis St; r from ₹2000; ✴) Being very slightly removed from the main Sudder St traveller area, this good-value, relatively new five-storey glass tower is little known to foreigners. Corridors have an effective neo-art-deco feel and rooms are unusually lacking in scuffed furniture.

Hotel Neelam
GUESTHOUSE $$

(Map p472; ☑ 22269198; hotelneelam@gmail.com; 11 Kyd St; s/d with fan ₹800/900 old/new AC r from ₹1100/2000; ✴) This odd guesthouse was once a grand colonial villa, became a basic backpacker guesthouse and is now partly transformed into a 'boutique' wannabe. Reception hides in a cubicle booth on the 1st floor where unreconstructed rooms are mostly large but forgettable. A floor above, however, suite-sized rooms were stylishly rebuilt in 2012. At first glimpse they seem a great deal at ₹2000 but the flashy showers don't work (yet?), hot water is by bucket and the management seems haphazard, if friendly.

★ **Oberoi Grand** HERITAGE HOTEL $$$
(Map p472; ☎22492323; www.oberoikolkata.com; 15 Chowringhee Rd; s/d/ste from ₹22,310/24,071/52,840; ❋@✿❋) Passing through the almost hidden courtyard gateway, you're transported from the chaos of Chowringhee Rd into a regal oasis of genteel calm that deserves every point on its five stars. Immaculate accommodation oozes atmosphere, the swimming pool is ringed with palms, and proactive staff anticipate your every need.

Park Street Area

Sunflower Guest House GUESTHOUSE $
(Map p472; ☎22299401; www.sunflowerguesthouse.com; 5th fl, 7 Royd St; d/tr ₹1000/1290, with AC ₹1380/1688; ❋) The Sunflower occupies much of a once-grand 1865 building with a memorably antiquated layered atrium and an original 1940s lift. Take it to the top: check-in is a short walk across the little roof garden. Rooms can be slightly spartan but they're assiduously cleaned, with high ceilings and several communal spaces.

YWCA HOSTEL $
(Map p472; ☎22297033; 1 Middleton Row; s/d ₹555/760, with AC ₹800/1000, without bathroom ₹305/610; ❋) No you don't have to be female to get a room in the illustrious YWCA, founded 1872. Spartan old high-ceilinged rooms have slatted green doors opening onto a wide corridor whose other open side faces a central tennis court. Large, sparse sitting rooms have a sense of bygone times without any hint of luxury.

The Corporate HOTEL $$
(Map p472; ☎22267551; www.thecorporatekolkata.com; 4 Royd St; s/d/tw/superior ₹4140/4560/5210/5860; ❋✿) In the suave little designer lobby, the receptionist seems to float in luminous marble. Rooms are competent, 21st-century business affairs though not especially spacious and staff seem a little overstretched at times.

Park Hotel HOTEL $$$
(Map p472; ☎22499000; www.theparkhotels.com; 17 Park St; rack rate r from ₹14,090; ❋@✿❋) Popular with airline crews and hosting much of the city's nightlife, the Park is a top central choice for hip, upmarket accommodation. Some floors have 'a dark side', where corridors use a very stylish black-on-black decor. In contrast the slightly less expensive 'light side' whispers pseudo 1920s-style elegance. Hidden on the 1st floor is an arty sitting space, a trio of restaurants and the passage to the lounger-lined swimming pool. Reverberating music might disturb light sleepers on the lower floors. The small reception area is accessed bizarrely from Park St by walking through The Street, a cafe-deli.

City Centre

★ **Chrome** ART HOTEL $$
(Map p454; ☎30963096; www.chromehotel.in; 226 AJC Bose Rd; s/d from ₹9400/9980; ❋@✿❋) Sleep in a brilliantly executed artistic statement that looks like a seven-storey Swiss cheese by day and a colour-pulsing alien communicator by night. Rooms have optical-illusion decor, and the 5th-floor landing hides a mini-library. Droning air-conditioner motors undermine relaxation at the rooftop swimming pool (open 7am to 7pm).

Fortune Select Louden BUSINESS HOTEL $$
(Map p454; ☎39884422; www.fortunehotels.in; 21B Loudon St; s/d from ₹8219/9393; ❋✿❋) This sizeable new business hotel ticks most of the right boxes in terms of convenience, comfort and gently stylish decor without any funky pretence. The outdoor rooftop pool is pleasant. Wi-fi is payable after two free hours. Online discounts are available.

Golden Park HOTEL $$
(Map p454; ☎22883939; www.goldenparkk.com; 13 Ho Chi Minh Sarani; s/d ₹9394/10,568, discount rate ₹5870/7045; ❋) Fair value by central Kolkata standards, rooms are kitted out with a slightly exaggerated attempt at class that ends up feeling a little dated yet undoubtedly pleasant. The eccentric lobby atrium features oddly mismatched nymphs, wood panelling, glass elevators and a Shakespeare-versus-Zoroaster relief over four stories. Shakespeare wins 3–1.

Hotel Aston HOTEL $$
(Map p463; ☑24863145; hotelaston@gmail.com; 3 Aston Rd; s/d ₹1574/1687; ❋@) Compact but gently attractive all-AC rooms have various sizes and shapes, but are generally far better than most central Kolkata options at this price point. It's just off Sarat Bose (Lansdowne) Rd on the road heading southwest directly south of the Samilton Hotel (nearly opposite the Laxmi Narayan Mandir).

Astor HOTEL $$
(Map p454; ☑22829950; www.astorkolkata.com; 15 Shakespeare Sarani) Artful evening floodlighting brings out the best of the Astor's solid 1905 architecture, and rooms should offer standards to match once the wholesale interior reconstruction is complete, which should be any day now.

Diamond Suites GUESTHOUSE $$
(Map p454; ☑64582564; http://diamondsuites. webs.com; 17A Karaya Rd; s/d ₹1500/1800) This friendly 12-room family hotel is perched above an internet cafe in a residential area that's calm yet relatively handy for the city centre and Motherhouse. Some rooms are small and oddly shaped, but they're tastefully designed with age-effect woodwork, many with hotplates and tiny kitchen sink units.

Kenilworth HOTEL $$$
(Map p454; ☑22823939; www.kenilworthhotels. com/kolkata; 1 Little Russell St; s/d ₹11,750/13,000; ❋☎) The deep lobby of marble, dark wood and chandeliers contrasts successfully with a more contemporary cafe that spills out onto an attractive lawn. Pleasingly bright, fully equipped rooms have some of Kolkata's most comfortable beds. Discount rates from around ₹7000 are often available. Wi-fi costs ₹335/670 per hour/day.

🛏 BBD Bagh Area

There's no traveller scene here but there are a trio of options that are handy for Chandni Chowk metro and very fair value by Kolkata standards. Also, by 2014, the classic 1840 Great Eastern Hotel should finally be luxuriously restored/rebuilt as the Kolkata Lalit.

Esplanade Chambers GUESTHOUSE $$
(Map p458; ☑22127101; www.esplanadechambers. com; 2 Chandni Chowk St; r ₹800-2100; ❋☎) These two floors of former apartments are more homestay than hotel. Rooms vary wildly from unadorned claustrophobic basic fan singles to comfortable 'executive' mini-suites complete with ornaments, wooden bed frames and attractive bold art in some. Prices include wi-fi (best downstairs), breakfast, hot water and toiletries. Access is via a narrow alley beside Gypsy Restaurant.

Broadway Hotel HOTEL $
(Map p458; ☑22363930; www.broadwayhotel.in; 27A Ganesh Chandra Ave; s/d/tr/ste ₹675/775/ 1125/1425, without bathroom s/d ₹630/715) This simple but well-maintained old hotel has an antiquated lift, 1950s furniture and a classic bar downstairs. Most rooms are generously large with high ceilings, and corner rooms offer plenty of light. The free newspaper under the door is a nice touch. It's clean and great value, but also noisy, and showers are cold.

Bengal Buddhist Association GUESTHOUSE $
(Bauddha Dharmankur Sabha; Map p458; ☑22117138; http://bengalbuddhist.com/guesthouse.html; Buddhist Temple Rd; tw ₹400-600; ❋) Although intended for Buddhist students, anyone can rent these simple rooms, which are unadorned except for the window bars shaped into lama form. Shared bathrooms are basic but have geysers. A couple of rooms have AC and private bathrooms. The courtyard location is quiet. And to keep it that way gates are locked from 10.30pm to 5am with no way in, so forget nightlife.

🛏 Outer Kolkata

Due to distant locations and lack of convenient transport links, we don't review several of the city's top business hotels, including the impressive **Hyatt Regency** (☑23351235; http://kolkata.regency.hyatt.com), ecofriendly **Sonar** (www.itcwelcomgroup.in/hotels/itcsonar. aspx) and the antique-softened 1990s **Taj Bengal** (Map p463; ☑22233939; www.tajhotels. com). Hotels in distant Salt Lake will eventually become more useful to tourists once metro Line 2 is built.

Bodhi Tree GUESTHOUSE $$
(Map p463; ☑24243871, 24246534; www.bodhi treekolkata.com; 48/44 Swiss Park; r incl breakfast ₹2200-4500; ❋☎) The well-travelled owners dub Bodhi Tree's intriguing little **gallery-cafe** (⊙2-7pm during exhibitions) a 'monastery of art'. Above, five uniquely characterful Buddha-themed rooms come with stone walls and decent facilities. Bathrooms aren't as memorable and the cheapest room is pretty cramped, but the two best rooms

share a super sitting room-cum-kitchen. The unlikely suburban location is under 10 minutes' stroll from Rabrindra Sarovar metro (walk east from behind the southeast exit and keep going).

Airport Area

As part of the airport's massive reconstruction there is likely to be a lot more accommodation choice in coming years for those stuck overnight in transit. Most notably, a Westin is due to open near the airport's southeastern perimeter. As yet, there is no real 'airport hotel' and the mostly uninspired options within 10 minutes' drive fall into two categories:

➡ Within 15 minutes' walking (or cycle-rickshaw) distance of the terminals, on and around Jessore Rd, are several simple hotels (from ₹1200) and ultra-basic dives (from ₹500).

➡ Bigger, flashier but still not necessarily luxurious hotels are dotted along VIP road between 1.5km and 3km from the terminals.

O2 HOTEL **$$**
(☑ 25250113; VIP Rd, Ramkrishna Pally; r ₹3500-9400; ✺) Of the larger VIP Road options, the two closely located O2 (oh-two) hotels are about the closest to the terminals. Finding a taxi isn't always a breeze, but an advantage here is that you're on the west side of the thunderingly busy dual carriageway so your vehicle to the airport doesn't have to make a traffic-plagued detour just to start heading in the right direction. Choose the O2's newer, smarter VIP building over the older scrappier 'Oxygen' but be aware that neither is really great value for money unless you get a very hefty online discount.

KATI ROLLS

Bengal's trademark fast food is the *kati* roll: take a *paratha* roti, fry it with a coating of egg then fill with sliced onions, chilli and your choice of stuffing (curried chicken, grilled meat or paneer). Roll it up in a twist of paper and it's ready to eat, generally on the street from hole-in-the-wall serveries. Standards vary considerably but a classic is **Hot Kati Rolls** (Map p472; 1/1 Park St; rolls ₹15-65; ⊙ 11am-10.30pm).

Swagatam Inn HOTEL **$$**
(☑ 9883031486; 10/1 Jessore Rd; s ₹1000, d ₹1500-2300; ✺) Being brand new in October 2012, this no-frills hotel is the freshest of several lower-midrange options near airport gate 2 within 10 minutes' walk from the (old) main terminals. It's between better-known but more claustrophobic hotels: Airways (from ₹500) and Sheela's. Though its restaurant is well signed, the tiny reception booth is hidden down a small alley.

Eating

Don't miss sampling Bengali cuisine, a wonderful discovery once you've mastered a whole new culinary vocabulary (see p451). Cheaper Bengali places often serve tapas-sized portions so order two or three dishes per person along with either rice or *luchi* plus some sweet *khejur* (chutney).

Most restaurants add 13% tax to bills. Posher places add 18.3%. Tips are welcome at cheaper places and expected at most expensive restaurants. **Times Food Guide** (www.timescity.com/kolkata; book ₹100) and **Zomato** (www.zomato.com/kolkata) offer hundreds of restaurant reviews.

Upper Chowringhee Area

A few relatively basic traveller cafes around Sudder St serve backpacker favourites, including banana pancakes, muesli and toasted sandwiches, complemented by fresh fruit juices and a range of good-value Indian dishes. Eateries across Mirza Ghalib St cater predominantly to Bangladeshi tastes. Cheap places for regional Indian food lie around New Market (notably Hogg St) with many more food stalls lining Madge Lane, Bertram St and Humayan Pl, where fast-food chains join vendors of dosas, chow mein and fresh juices. For something more upmarket, walk 10 minutes south towards Park St where you'll find many of Kolkata's age-old family favourites facing off with KFC and a beef-free McDonald's.

Around Sudder Street & New Market

Bhoj Company BENGALI, MULTICUISINE **$**
(Map p472; Sudder St; Bengali dishes ₹40-120, other mains ₹65-180; ⊙ 8.30am-11.30pm) Excellent, inexpensive Bengali food served in a bijou

little restaurant, where colourful naive art sets off white walls inset with little terracotta statuette niches. You'll need some basic knowledge to decode the menu, but it's hard to find a better ₹160 dinner than their *ruhi kalia* with *doi begun* and rice. A second menu offers a full range of pancakes, breakfasts, Chinese, Indian and tandoori dishes.

Raj's Spanish Cafe
CAFE $

(Map p472; off Sudder St; mains ₹80-150; ⊙8am-10pm; 🖰) Excellent coffee, juices, pancakes and relatively reliable wi-fi (₹25 per hour, from around 11am) makes this a popular hang-out for medium-term charity volunteers. The menu includes a well-made selection of Spanish dishes (tortilla, *pisto manchego* – pureed ratatouille) and various traveller favourites. Decor is simple but welcoming and the small outdoor area has some cursory foliage. It's hidden behind Roop Shrinagar fabric shop.

Sidheshwari Ashram
BENGALI $

(Map p472; 19 Rani Rashmoni Rd; mains ₹8-100; ⊙noon-4pm & 7-11pm) For a really local experience, venture into this archetypal old-fashioned eating house serving excellent Bengali food eaten with the (right) hand at old stone-topped tables. Women are rare, some waiters shoeless and the blackboard menu offers no explanations so ideally bring a local friend. The entrance is easily missed as it's between shops, then up an unlikely stairway.

Fresh & Juicy
MULTICUISINE $

(Map p472; Chowringhee Lane; mains ₹30-90, rice ₹25; ⊙7.30am-10.30pm) Tiny, two-floored box-cafe recently smartened up a tad but still serving excellent-value curries, snacks and traveller favourites.

Aminia
TANDOORI, MUGHLAI $

(Map p472; Hogg St; mains ₹70-135; ⊙10.30am-10.30pm) Aminia's age-old interior has been mildly spruced up to give a vaguely retro-1940s cool feel, the ceiling fans whirring high above a single big white cacophonous hall. Henna-bearded wait-staff in monogrammed magenta tunics slap down dishes including good chicken tikka and overly oily biryanis.

Kathleen Confectioners
BAKERY $

(Map p472; 12 Mirza Ghalib St; snacks ₹8-35; ⊙8.30am-10pm) Their sickly sweet cakes aren't exactly the promised 'Taste of Hapinezz', but flaky pastry savouries such as the ₹22 paneer patties are scrumptious. Numerous alternative branches.

DINING CLASSICS

A few classic multicuisine dining experiences huddle within a block of the attractive (if overrated) art-deco teashop-restaurant **Flurrys** (Map p472; Park St; coffees Rs60-145, sandwiches Rs40; ⊙7.30am-9.45pm). Contrasting conspicuously with the 21st-century decor trends so beloved of most cutting-edge Kolkata restaurants, **Mocambo** (Map p472; ☑033 22290095; Mirza Ghalib St; mains ₹150-320; ⊙11am-11.15pm) and **Peter Cat** (Map p472; ☑033 22298841; Middleton Row; mains ₹150-310; ⊙11am-11.15pm) seem almost self-conscious parodies of 1970s British steak-house design. The latter serves beers in pewter tankards and dresses its waiters in Khan-Afghani costumes. The draw at all is both a reputation among middle-class Kolkatans for ever-reliable food, and snappy service that can prove quietly witty. None usually takes reservations. Indeed, meeting fellow diners in the queue for a late dinner spot is an integral part of the experience.

JoJo's Cafe
TRAVELLER CAFE $

(Map p472; snacks ₹30-70, mains ₹50-110, rice ₹20; ⊙8am-11pm; 🖰) Traveller cafe with free wi-fi.

UP Bihar
BIHARI $

(Map p472; H12 Hogg St; mains ₹45-80, kati rolls ₹15-38, dhal/rice ₹4/5; ⊙6am-11pm) Very basic, if not quite as grimy as it appears from outside, this inexpensive restaurant looks little changed since 1937 while the beef-chunk curries are far better than at other gristle-merchants nearby. Curtained 'family' booths available.

Blue & Beyond
MULTICUISINE $$

(Map p472; ☑22521039; 9th fl, Lindsay Hotel, Lindsay St; mains ₹200-300, beer/cocktails from ₹165/200; ⊙12.30-10.30pm) The drawcard here is an open-air rooftop terrace with wide views over New Market and prices that are relatively reasonable for a restaurant that's licensed to serve alcohol. Menu wild-cards include Greek chicken, vegetable platters and Tom Yam soup.

Blue Sky Cafe
TRAVELLER CAFE $$

(Map p472; Chowringhee Lane; snacks ₹20-65, mains ₹50-230, rice ₹35; ⊙6.30am-10.30pm)

Chowringhee

Wise-cracking staff serve up a vast selection of reliable traveller standbys in a trying-to-be-stylish air-conditioned room with high-backed zinc chairs at long glass tables. The garlic-ginger chicken is delicious if totally mis-described as 'chicken pepper-steak' (₹140). Prices include tax.

Jong's/Zaranj
ASIAN, INDIAN $$$

(Map p472; ☑ 22490369; www.facebook.com/ZaranjJongs; Sudder St; mains ₹400-840; ⊙12.30-3pm & 7.30-11pm Wed-Mon) Two suave if pricey restaurants in one. Jong's serves Chinese, under-spiced Thai and other Asian cuisines in a magnificently wood-panelled room that feels like a Raj-oriental gentleman's club. Less visually successful, the interconnected Indian section, Zaranj, has magenta table cloths and a little 'stream' running down the middle. Some meals include rice but with most it's ₹175 extra.

✕ Park Street Area

Arsalan
MUGHLAI $$

(Map p472; 119A Ripon St; mains ₹95-205; ⊙noon-11.30pm) High ceilinged and modern without being fashion-conscious. The main attractions are melt-in-mouth chicken tikka and celebrated biryanis that come with a free palette of extras (lemon, chilli, onion, mint chutney).

Bistro by the Park
MULTICUISINE $$

(Map p472; ☑ 22296494; www.bistrobythepark.com; 2A Middleton Row; mains ₹390-550; ⊙11am-11pm) This enticing if pricey new cafe manages to combine hip 21st-century design with 1970s retro, yet keeps the colours muted and the ambience cosily approachable. Menus are iPads: click the price for a photo of the dish.

Teej
RAJASTHANI $$$

(Map p472; ☑ 40062787; www.teej.in; 1st fl, 2 Russell St; mains ₹205-250, rice ₹175, thalis ₹360, beer

Chowringhee

₹170; ⊘noon-3.30pm & 7-10.30pm) Superbly painted with Mughal-style murals, the interior feels like an ornate Rajasthani *haveli* (traditional residence) and the excellent, 100% vegetarian food is predominantly Rajasthani, too. A la carte portions are often big enough for two people; not so the thalis.

Marco Polo   MULTICUISINE **$$$**
(Map p472; ☑22273939; 24 Park St; mains ₹395-600, rice ₹225; ⊘noon-10.30pm) Stylish deep-brown panels incised with flower patterns are back-lit to create a moody yet contemporary atmosphere in this split-level restaurant where lamps are kept so low that you almost need a torch. Curiosities such as Lebanese chops and Hungarian-sauce veg gratin add to a wide menu of high-class Bengali, Indian, Chinese and continental dishes,

but don't expect much change from ₹1000 per head.

✕ City Centre

As well as the places reviewed there are dining options scattered around Camac St, Shakespeare Sarani and in the Forum Mall (Elgin St), plus three cheap Tibetan eateries at **Momo corner** (Map p454; cnr Suburban Hospital Rd & Chowringhee Rd).

Drive Inn   MULTICUISINE **$**
(Map p454; ☑32000025; 10 Middleton St; mains ₹70-125; ⊘11am-9.30pm) Great-value vegetarian fare served in a modest little part-covered garden area or available for delivery.

Kookie Jar BAKERY $
(Map p454; www.kookiejar.in; Rawdon St; pastries ₹30-80; ⊙8am-10pm) Takeaway cakes, multi-grain bread, wraps, fluffy pastries and Kolkata's most heavenly fudge brownies.

Haldiram FAST FOOD $
(Map p454; 58 Chowringhee Rd; ⊙7.30am-10pm) Chain cafeteria with great value pay-then-queue vegetarian thalis (₹90), dosas (from ₹52), vegi-burgers (₹50) and Bengali sweets.

Kewpies BENGALI $$
(Map p454; ☑24861600; 2 Elgin Lane; dishes ₹115-225, thalis ₹335-775; ⊙12.30-3pm & 7.30-10.30pm Tue-Sun) Dining at Kewpies feels like being invited to a dinner party in the chef's eclectic, gently old-fashioned home (so long as you avoid the far less charming smaller room entered via the north door). The thalis are a good introduction to Bengali food, though cuisine at Oh Calcutta! and Bhojohari Manna is arguably better. Minimum spend is ₹355 per person.

Vanilla Creperie CAFE $$
(Map p454; 32 Elgin Rd; pancakes ₹180-250, coffee from ₹50; ⊙9am-11pm) Handy as an Elgin St meeting place, this all-white cafe sports faux shutters and serves baguette sandwiches along with its range of savoury filled pancakes.

Shiraz AWADHI $$
(Map p454; 135 Park St; mains ₹110-210; ⊙5am-11.30pm) Synonymous with Kolkata biryani, the Shiraz also offers a range of curries, and a succulent mutton *chaap special* (rib-meat dish, ₹200). The location, handy for South Park St Cemetery, has two almost next-door branches. The smarter section only opens from lunchtime but the functional older branch serves a superb ₹60 mutton *keema* (spiced mince meat) breakfast until noon.

Jalapenos MULTICUISINE $$
(Map p454; ☑22820204; 10 Wood St; mains ₹110-295; ⊙11.30am-10pm) The menu promises a range of world cuisines. None taste quite like the originals, but that's forgivable given the relatively reasonable prices and the attractive low-key decor with wrought-iron chairs, mock beamed ceilings and little spice-bottle alcoves. It's behind Aqua Java coffee shop.

★**Oh! Calcutta** BENGALI $$$
(Map p454; ☑22837161; 4th fl, Forum Mall, Elgin Rd; mains ₹240-650, rice ₹180; ⊙12.30-3.15pm & 7.30-10.45pm) Shutter-edged mirror 'windows',

bookshelves and B&W photography create a casually upmarket atmosphere in this Bengali-fusion restaurant that is far more suave than you might expect from its shopping-mall location, and portions are unusually large. *Luchi* (₹140 for six) are feather-light, and fresh lime brings out the subtleties of *koraishatir dhokar dalna* (pea-cakes in ginger, ₹430).

★**Amigos** MEXICAN $$$
(Map p454; ☑40602507; www.facebook.com/Amigos.calcutta; 11/1A Ho Chi Minh Sarani; mains ₹300-450; ⊙noon-3pm & 7.30-10.30pm) Excellent Tex-Mex food supplemented with pizzas, served to a relaxed crowd of upwardly mobile 30-somethings whose reverberant chatter combines with two different salsa music tracks to create quite a din in the tidy stone-effect dining rooms. Delicious guacamole (extra) comes in spoon-sized portions; the bill arrives in a sombrero.

★**Fire and Ice** ITALIAN $$$
(Map p454; ☑22884073; www.fireandicepizzeria.com; Kanak Bldg, Middleton St; mains ₹350-670, beer/wine/cocktails from ₹210/280/350; ⊙noon-11.15pm) Self-consciously handsome waiters sporting black shirts, red aprons and bandanas bring forth real Italian pastas and pizzas with fresh-baked thin crusts that are Kolkata's best.

Little Italy ITALIAN $$$
(Map p454; ☑22825152; 8th fl, Fort Knox Bldg, 6 Camac St; mains ₹340-520; ⊙noon-2.45pm & 7-10.45pm) While the pastas and pizzas at Fire and Ice have more pizazz, those wanting a pure veg kitchen and an artily upmarket environment might prefer Little Italy. What appear to be rhino horns protrude from the walls, there are seven waving ceramic monoliths, a wall-of-water fountain and some city views. Lounge bar attached.

🍴 BBD Bagh Area

Anand SOUTH INDIAN $
(Map p458; ☑22128344; 19 CR Ave; dosas ₹40-120; ⊙9am-9.30pm, closed Wed) Prize-winning pure-veg dosas served in a well-kept if old-fashioned family restaurant with bamboo and mirror-tiled ceilings.

KC Das SWEETS $
(Map p458; Lenin Sarani; mishit doi ₹28; ⊙7.30am-9.30pm) Bustling Bengali sweet shop that

claims to have invented *rasgulla* in 1868. Seating available.

Manthan CHINESE **$$**
(Map p458; ☑ 22105065; 3 Waterloo St; mains ₹85-125, ₹beer 130; ☺ 11am-10.30pm) Hidden away on the 1st floor of a partly timbered house-hotel, this calm, 'secret' restaurant-bar would feel pretty special if they bothered to add a few artworks to the blank, chandelier-lit white walls. The tasty Chinese food is good value without being gourmet.

✕ Gariahat Area

★**Bhojohari Manna** BENGALI **$$**
(Map p463; ☑ 24663941; www.bhojohorimanna.com; 18/1 Hindustan Rd, Branch 6; dishes ₹50-270, rice ₹45; ☺ 12.30-10.30pm) Although it's a small chain, each Bhojohari Manna branch feels very different and has a somewhat different menu, though all feature top-quality Bengali food at sensible prices. Our favourite, Branch 6, is comparatively spacious, decorated with tribal implements and has live traditional music some Saturdays. The menu allows diners to pair a wide selection of fish types with the sauce of their choice. Some dishes are rather small so order a spread not missing the *echorer dalna* (green jackfruit curry).

🍷 Drinking & Nightlife

Most better bars are in hotels or restaurants. Cheaper places are usually dingy and overwhelmingly male-dominated with a penchant for over-loud music, often sung by scantily clad females. Plentiful branches of Starbuck-style chains Barista, Aqua Java and Café Coffee Day make air-conditioned oases in which to sip a decent Americano, though coffee prices can vary substantially by location. A Kolkata delight is making streetside tea stops for mini-cuppas served in disposable *bhaar* (environmentally friendly earthenware thimbles, around ₹5).

On Kolkata's party nights (Wednesday, Friday and Saturday) clubs open till 2am. On other nights most are half empty and close at midnight. Note the difference between entry charge and cover charge: the latter can be recouped in drinks or food to the same value. Either is charged per couple. Women can sometimes enter free but single men (known as 'stags') are generally excluded and aren't expected to dance without a female partner. Ginger is an exception.

🍷 Chowringhee Area

There's a pub on Sudder St and several more in and around the Park Hotel.

Fairlawn Hotel BAR
(Map p472; 13A Sudder St; beers ₹110; ☺ 10am-10pm) The small tropical garden of the historic Fairlawn Hotel is great for a cold brew.

Urban Desi BAR-RESTAURANT
(Map p454; 9th fl, 6 Camac St; small beers ₹150; ☺ noon-11.30pm) Low-key rooftop party lounge with shisha pipes (₹390) to smoke, pool and table football to play, and sofa seating amid luminous cube lamps and trancy music. From the balcony of the restaurant section (mains ₹200 to ₹435) there's a great city panorama, including an original view of Victoria Memorial.

OlyPub BAR
(Map p472; 21 Park St, 1st fl; beers ₹134, steak ₹165) With ragged chairs and jute carpets, this grungy yet oddly convivial central watering hole is a low-key Kolkata classic.

Tantra NIGHTCLUB
(Map p472; Park Hotel, 17 Park St; entry ₹500-1000) Often considered Kolkata's top club, contemporary sounds throb through the single dance floor and not-so-chilled chill-out zone around a central island bar with an overhead observation bridge.

🍷 Central Kolkata

Big Ben PUB
(Map p454; Kenilworth Hotel, 1 Little Russell St; small beers ₹300; ☺ 10am-midnight) British-style pub with DJ after 8pm and small dance space between the green-leather padded seats.

Plush LOUNGE BAR
(Map p454; Astor Hotel, 15 Shakespeare Sarani; small beer/cocktail/wine from ₹250/390/670; ☺ 3pm-close) This stylish yet unthreateningly casual, low-lit bar is most appealing on Thursday evenings when young local musicians perform at the open mic (from 7pm). Wednesdays (₹1000) and Fridays (₹1500) are set-price all-you-can-drink nights, open till 2am.

Soho NIGHTCLUB, RESTAURANT
(Map p454; ☑ 40036605; Ideal Plaza, 11/1 Sarat Bose Rd; beer ₹500; ☺ 6pm-close Mon-Sat) Central Kolkata's latest upper-market party address has a sweep of bar and reverse conical

columns. Entrance is free except on Saturdays when there's a ₹1000 cover. Call ahead especially on Fridays to check if the venue is closed for a private function.

Underground
NIGHTCLUB
(Map p454; HHI Hotel, AJC Bose Rd) Small dance floor in a pub-bar with Hard Rock Café–style elements.

BBD Bagh Area

If you want ear-shattering 'live' (if karaoke quality) music, there are several choices along eastern Waterloo St.

Broadway Bar
BAR
(Map p458; Broadway Hotel, 27A Ganesh Chandra Ave; small/standard beer ₹60/120, shots ₹30-105; ⊙11am-10.30pm) Backstreet Paris? Chicago 1930s? Prague 1980s? This cavernous, unpretentious old-men's pub defies easy parallels but has a compulsive Left Bank fascination with cheap booze, 20 ceiling fans, bare walls, marble floors and, thankfully, no music.

Southern Kolkata

Tea Bush Table
TEA ROOM
(Map p463; www.ttbt.in; 5b Aston Rd; tea ₹60-200; ⊙11am-11pm Mon-Fri, 9am-11pm Sat-Sun) Connoisseurs will swoon at a choice of over 130 local and imported teas, only a few of which (oolong, pu-erh, kukicha, Moroccan mint) are even mentioned on the menu. The small cafe has just five stone-topped tables with white wicker chairs, staff are super knowledgeable and the company has its own Assam plantation.

Basement
NIGHTCLUB
(Map p463; Samilton Hotel, 25 Lansdowne Rd; ⊙live music Wed-Fri) Relaxed and inexpensive mini-club, under renovation at the time of research.

Ginger
NIGHTCLUB, RESTAURANT
(Map p463; 104 SP Mukherjee Rd; ⊙8pm-2am Fri-Sun; M Jatin Das Park) A majority male clientele whoop to 1990s dance hits, 'stags' are admitted and it's modestly gay-friendly.

Entertainment

Events and cultural happenings are announced in the *Telegraph* newspaper's Metro section and the various listings brochures.

Cultural Programs
Nandan Complex
CULTURAL CENTRE
(Map p454; 22239936, 22235317; 1/1A AJC Bose Rd) Comprises theatre halls **Rabindra Sadan** (22239936) and **Sisir Mancha** (22235317), plus the art-house **Nandan Cinema** (22231210).

ICCR
CULTURAL CENTRE
(Rabindranath Tagore Centre; Map p454; 22872680; www.iccrindia.org; 9A Ho Chi Minh Sarani) Large, multilevel cultural centre sporadically hosting exhibitions, dance shows and recitals. Often free.

Calcutta School of Music
MUSIC
(Map p463; www.calmusic.org; 6B Sunny Park) See the website for a timetable of musical events in a variety of styles.

Char So Bees
EVENTS
(www.facebook.com/420rooftop) Led by social media, this is a 'free-flowing event cycle' held once or twice monthly, with musicians, artists and a flea market on a city rooftop.

Akhra
CULTURAL EVENINGS
(Map p454; 24178561; www.banglanatak.com; 4 Elgin Rd; ⊙6.30pm-8pm most Sat & Sun) Showcasing an ever-changing melange of art, theatre and folk or fusion music both rural and urban. Operates most but not all weekends.

Cinema
Inox Elgin Rd
CINEMA
(Map p454; 23584499; www.inoxmovies.com; Forum Shopping Mall, 10/3 Elgin Rd; tickets ₹90-280) One of several modern multiplex cinemas, bookable online. Cheapest midweek at 9am.

Live Music
Someplace Else
LIVE MUSIC
(Map p472; Park Hotel, 17 Park St) Showcases local bands, predominantly rock-oriented, without a cover charge.

Spectator Sports
Even if you don't know Ganguly from a googly, the electric atmosphere of a cricket match at **Ranji Stadium** (Map p458; Eden Gardens) is an unforgettable experience. For Kolkata Knight Riders' IPL fixtures see www.kkr.in.

At **Maidan racecourse** (22291104; www.rctconline.com; Acharya Jagdish Rd; admission from ₹15; 36), you can watch some of India's best horse racing from 19th-century grandstands, with the Victoria Memorial providing a beautiful backdrop. Over 40 annual meets.

🔒 Shopping

Books

Several small traveller-oriented bookstalls huddle around the junction of Sudder St and Mirza Ghalib St. For more choice visit the following.

Classic Books/Earthcare Books
(Map p454; ✑ 22296551; www.earthcarebooks.com; 10 Middleton St; ⊙ 11am-7pm Mon-Sat) Family publisher-bookshop.

Crossword
(Map p454; ✑ 22836502; www.crosswordbookstores.com; 8 Elgin Rd; ⊙ 10.30am-8.30pm) Three-storey chain bookshop with cafe.

Oxford Bookstore
(Map p472; ✑ 22297662; www.oxfordbookstore.com; 17 Park St; ⊙ 10am-10pm) Excellent full-range bookshop with seating and cafe. Stocks many Lonely Planet guides.

Clothing

Kolkata is great value for clothing, with pre-cut shirts costing under ₹100 from the Chowringhee Rd **Hawkers' Market** (Map p472). **Local tailors** (Map p472) on Elliot Rd are less tourist-oriented than those around New Market. Fashion-conscious locals head to Hazra Rd and Gariahat.

Crafts & Souvenirs

State-government emporia sell good-quality souvenirs at decent fixed prices, while several charity cooperatives allow you to feel good about your purchases.

➡ *Government Emporia*

Dakshinapan
Shopping Centre   SHOPPING CENTRE
(Map p463; Gariahat Rd; ⊙ 10.30am-7.30pm Mon-Sat) It's worth facing the soul-crushing 1970s architecture for Dakshinapan's wide range of government emporia. There's plenty of tack but many shops offer excellent-value souvenirs, crafts and fabrics. **Kashmir Emporium** (Shop F38) has colourful papier-mâché boxes from ₹55, **Tribes India** (Shop F48) has brass figures and appealing greetings cards, **Sonali** (Shop F1) specialises in jute-ware, and **Purbasha Tripura** (Shop F4) has bargain caneware, from intricate lamp-shades to Marx and Lenin portraits (₹60). On the lower level don't miss **Dolly's Tea Shop** (Map p463; ✆ 9830115787, 24237838; G62; teas ₹25-50, snacks ₹30-120) where teak panels, rattan chairs and tea-crate tables create a charming little oasis that attracts a wonderfully eclectic clientele, especially society ladies.

Pragjyotika   HANDICRAFTS
(Map p454; Assam House, 8 Russell St; ⊙ 10.30am-6pm Mon-Fri, 11am-1pm Sat) Cane vases, jute handbags, pearls, fabrics and Assam tea.

Nagaland Emporium   SOUVENIRS
(Map p454; 11 Shakespeare Sarani; ⊙ 10am-5.30pm Mon-Fri, 10am-2pm Sat) Naga crafts including shawls and face necklaces for wannabe head-hunters.

Manjusha   HANDICRAFTS
(Map p454; 4 Camac St; ⊙ 10.30am-7pm Mon-Sat) West Bengal fabrics, handicrafts and costumed dolls.

Karnataka State Arts & Crafts   EMPORIUM
(Map p458; www.cauverycrafts.com; Metropolitan Bldg, 7 Chowringhee Rd; ⊙ 10am-7pm Mon-Sat) Sandalwood, silk and other crafts.

➡ *Boutiques*

Doel's Choice   HANDICRAFTS
(Map p472; 1 Kyd St; ⊙ 11am-7pm Mon-Sat) Quality hand-carved wooden products at OK prices though you'd pay less for some of the same items at Dakshinapan.

FabIndia   HANDICRAFTS
(Map p454; www.fabindia.com; 11a Allenby Rd; ⊙ 11am-8.30pm Mon-Sat) Quality Indian textiles and handicrafts that are colourful without that full-on hippie vibe. The shop is a modern, Western-style boutique and prices are clearly labelled.

Karmyog   HANDICRAFTS
(Map p472; 12B Russell St; ⊙ 10am-6pm Mon-Sat) Elegant gallery of paper products.

➡ *Charity Cooperatives*

Ankur Kala   SOUVENIRS
(Map p454; ✑ 22878476; www.ankurkala.org; 3 Meher Ali Rd; ⊙ 10am-1pm & 2-5pm Mon-Sat) This cooperative training centre empowers women from the slums. Their small, hidden shop sells batik, embroidered goods, greeting cards and leather goods.

Ashalayam   HANDICRAFTS
(Map p472; www.ashalayamfrance.org; 1st fl, 44 Mirza Ghalib St; ⊙ 10.30am-7pm Mon-Fri, to 4pm Sat) Buying cards, handmade paper and fabrics funds the (ex)street kids who made them. There's also a simple cafe (coffee ₹10) and a one-case library including guidebooks.

Incense

Good selection from two street stalls outside 203 Bidhan Sarani (the northern extension of College Street) at the Vivekananda St junction.

Musical Instruments

Shops and workshops along Rabindra Sarani sell a great range of musical instruments. For tablas (from ₹1200), rayas (from ₹500) and other percussion instruments, try numbers 248, 264 and 268B near Tagore's House. For sitars (from ₹4000) or violins (from ₹2000) visit **Mondal & Sons** (Map p458; ☑ 22349658; 8 Rabindra Sarani; ⊙10am-6pm Mon-Fri, to 2.30pm Sat). Family-run since the 1850s, Mondal & Sons has counted Yehudi Menuhin among its satisfied customers.

 Information

DANGERS & ANNOYANCES

Kolkata feels unthreatening. Predictable beggar-hassle around the Sudder St traveller ghetto is a minor irritant and *bandhs* (strikes) can prove annoying, closing shops and stopping all land transport (including taxis to the airport). Monsoon-season flooding can be highly inconvenient.

INTERNET ACCESS

Cyber Zoom (Map p472; 27B Park St; per hr ₹15; ⊙10am-9pm)

Gorukh (Map p472; 7 Sudder St; per hr ₹20; ⊙9am-9.30pm) Traveller-friendly; at the back of a fabric shop beside Raj's Spanish Cafe. Cheap international phone calls.

MAJOR TRAINS FROM KOLKATA

Departures daily unless otherwise stated.

USEFUL FOR	TRAIN	DURATION (HR)	DEPARTURES	FARES (₹; SLEEPER/3AC/2AC UNLESS OTHERWISE STATED)
Bhubaneswar	12839 Chennai Mail	6½	11.45pm (HWH)	214/564/830
Chennai	12841 Coromandal	26½	2.50pm (HWH)	461/1288/2025
	12839 Chennai Mail	28	11.45pm (HWH)	461/1288/2025
Delhi	12303/12381 Poorva	23	8.10am/8.15am (HWH)	442/1187/1860
	12313 SDAH Rajdhani	17½	4.50pm (SDAH)	3AC/1AC 1592/3395
Gorakhpur	15047/15049/15051 Poorvanchal	17½-19	2.30pm (KOAA)	311/845/1295
Guwahati	12345 Saraighat	17¾	3.50pm (HWH)	359/954/1460
	15657 Kanchenjunga	22	6.35am (SDAH)	332/935/1440
Hooghly	Bandel Local	51 mins	several hourly (HWH)	Unreserved 9
Lucknow	13151 Jammu Tawi	22¾	11.45am (KOAA)	339/958/1480
	12327/12369 Upasana/Kumbha	18	1.10pm (HWH)	363/1002/1530
Mumbai CST	12810 Mumbai Mail	33¼	8.15pm (HWH)	508/1425/2265
New Jalpaiguri	12377 Padatik	10¼	10.55pm (SDAH)	259/673/1000
Patna	12351 Danapur	9½	8.35pm (HWH)	252/653/965
	13039 Janta	12	8.20pm (HWH)	161
Puri	12837 Howrah-Puri	9	10.35pm (HWH)	244/654/965
	18409 Sri Jagannath	10	7pm (HWH)	244/654/965
Siliguri Jctn	12343 Darjeeling Mail	10	10.05pm (SDAH)	259/698/1035
Varanasi	13005 Amritsar Mail	14	7.10pm (HWH)	286/805/1225

HWH=ex-Howrah, SDAH=ex-Sealdah, KOAA=ex-Chitpur

MEDICAL

Handy for Sudder St, **Eastern Diagnostics** (Map p472; ☑ 22178080; www.easterndiagnostics. com; Mirza Ghalib St; ☺10am-2pm or by appointment) offers doctors' consultations from ₹200.

Medical services are listed on www.calcutta web.com/doctor.php.

MONEY

ATMs are widespread. Many private money-changers around Sudder St offer commission-free exchange rates several per cent better than banks, and some will exchange travellers cheques. Shop around and double-check the maths. Airport moneychangers charge up to 5% tax/commission. In the city centre, **Globe Forex** (Map p454; ☑ 033 22828780; 11 Ho Chi Minh Sarani; ☺10am-6pm Mon-Fri, to 2.30pm Sat) gives reasonable rates but charges commission.

TELEPHONE

Getting a SIM card requires ID (and copies), a passport photo and proof of residential address; a copy of your hotel bill will suffice for some Sudder St agency-shops. A day or two later you'll be called or messaged to confirm your identity.

TOURIST INFORMATION

ExploCity (http://kolkata.explocity.com) Advertisement-led listings pamphlet marked ₹50 but available free from better hotels. Reviews can be somewhat misleading.

India Tourism (Map p454; ☑ 22825813; www. incredibleindia.org; 4 Shakespeare Sarani; ☺9am-6pm Mon-Fri, to 1pm Sat) Free maps of greater Kolkata.

West Bengal Tourism (Map p458; ☑ 22437260; westbengaltourism.gov.in; 3/2 BBD Bagh; ☺10.30am-1.30pm & 2-5.30pm Mon-Fri, 10.30am-1pm Sat) Useful website. Office primarily sells their own tours; last sales 4.30pm.

VISAS & PERMITS

Bangladeshi Consulate (Map p454; ☑ 40127500; www.bdhckolkata.org/indexEng. htm; 9 Circus Ave; ☺applications 9-11am Mon-Fri) For a Bangladeshi tourist visa, download the application form, and take it with two photos (3.7cm square) and photocopies of your passport and Indian visa to counter 3 (in the building's curved outer southwest corner). Fees vary by nationality. Then return as advised (usually around 11.30am) to the second door up Nurulla Lane (speakerphone) for a cursory interview. The visa is usually ready next afternoon at 4.30pm.

For Indian citizens, take the same documents but join the horrendous melee at the main Circus Ave window to apply.

Sikkim House (Map p454; ☑ 22817905; 4/1 Middleton St; ☺10.30am-4pm Mon-Fri, to 2pm Sat) Sikkim arranges permits free and they are usually issued within 24 hours.

ⓘ Getting There & Away

The tourist quota on train tickets can be a saviour around Durga Puja (September/October) when local travel is at a peak.

AIR

The total reconstruction of **Netaji Subhash Bose International Airport** (NSBIA; ☑ 25118787; http://www.aai.aero/kolkata /index.jsp) is likely to vastly increase international traffic to Kolkata from 2013. Already there are direct connections to around 30 Indian cities as well as the following international destinations:

Bangkok Air Asia, Thai, IndiGo, Jet
Dhaka Biman, Jet, United Airways Bangladesh
Doha Qatar Airways
Dubai Emirates
Hong Kong Dragonair
Kathmandu Air India
Kuala Lumpur Air Asia
Kunming China Eastern
Paro, Bhutan Druk
Singapore SilkAir/Singapore Air, Druk
Yangon Air India

Useful local airline contacts:

Air India (Map p458; ☑ 22114433; 39 Chittaranjan Ave; ☺10am-6pm Mon-Fri, to 5pm Sat)

Biman (Map p454; ☑ 22266672; www.biman-airlines.com; 6th fl, 99A Park St)

China Eastern Airlines (Map p454; ☑ 40448887; InterGlobe, 1st fl, Landmark Bldg, 228A AJC Bose Rd) Flies to Kunming (Yunnan).

Druk Air (Map p454; ☑ 22902429; 3rd fl, 51 Tivoli Court, 1A Ballygunge Circular Rd) Most foreigners need to make tour arrangements before flying into Bhutan.

United Airways Bangladesh (Map p472; ☑ 9007095363; www.uabdl.com; Saberwal House, 55b Mirza Galib St) Single/return to Dhaka from ₹3052/5400.

BOAT

Sporadic ferries to Port Blair (Andaman Islands) depart from **Kidderpore Docks** (Map p452; Karl Marx Sarani), entered from Gate 3 opposite Kidderpore commuter train station. Tickets (bunk/cabin/deluxe ₹2160/4280/8420) go on sale at the **Shipping Corporation of India** (Map p458; ☑ 22484921; calcps.dept@sci.co.in; Hare St; ☺10am-1pm & 2.30-5pm Mon-Fri) around 10 days before departure.

CAR & MOTORBIKE HIRE

Car-rental companies including **Wenz** (☑ 9330018001; http://wenzcars.com) can organise long-distance chauffeured rides. Sudder St agencies might be able to find you better deals: Backpackers (p486) can find cars at ₹2200 for up to eight hours (add ₹22 per km if driving more than 80km).

BUS

International

Bangladesh Shohagh Paribahan (Map p472; ☑ 22520757; 21A Marquis St; ⊙5am-10.30pm) and **GreenLine** (Map p472; ☑ 22520571; 12B Marquis St; ⊙4am-10.30pm) each have three early morning buses to Dhaka (₹1050 to ₹1150, 13 hours) involving a change of vehicle at the Benapol border.

Bhutan A Bhutan Government postbus to Phuentsholing (₹400, 17 hours) leaves 7pm except Sunday from the northeast yard of Esplanade bus station where there are special **ticket booths** (⊙9.30am-1pm & 2-6pm Mon-Sat).

Domestic

For shorter-distance services from Esplanade (eg to Diamond Harbour) use the central CSTC ticket office.

For Darjeeling or Sikkim, start by taking a bus to Siliguri (around 12 hours). Numerous private Siliguri buses drive overnight departing between 6pm and 8pm (from ₹355). SBSTC (₹300) and NBSTC (₹360), with ticket desks in the walled area in the bus station's northeastern corner, also have a few morning services to Siliguri.

Lined up along the roadside south of Eden Gardens commuter train station are buses for Odisha (Orissa) and Bihar, most running overnight, so departing between 5pm and 8.30pm. Arrive very early if you have baggage. Destinations include the following:

Bhubaneswar (seat/sleeper ₹350/400, 9½ hours)

Bodhgaya (seat/sleeper ₹240/300, 13 hours) Leaves at 5pm with Maharani Express.

Puri (seat/sleeper ₹400/450, 12 hours) On Dolphin (www.odishabusservice.com).

Ranchi (seat/sleeper from ₹220/270, 10 hours)

TRAIN

Stations

Long-distance trains depart from three major stations. Gigantic Howrah (Haora; HWH) is across the river, often best reached by ferry, Sealdah (SDAH) is at the eastern end of MG Road, and Kolkata (Chitpore; KOAA) Station is around 5km further north (nearest metro Belgachia).

Tickets

To buy long-distance train tickets, foreigners should use the **Eastern Railways' Foreign Tourist Bureau** (Map p458; ☑ 22224206; 6 Fairlie Pl; ⊙10am-5pm Mon-Sat, to 2pm Sun). Bring a book to read as waits can be very long but there are sofa-seats. Some folks arrive before opening time and sign a waiting list. Indian citizens can buy from computerised booking centres next door or on Koilaghat St.

For Dhaka, Bangladesh, the Maitree Express (2nd class/AC chair/1AC ₹425/659/1095, 12½ hours) departs Kolkata (Chitpore) Station at 7.10am Saturday and Tuesday, returning from Dhaka Cantt at 8.30am Wednesday and Sunday. You must have 'Darsana' marked on your Bangladeshi visa. Buy tickets up to 10 days ahead.

For a certain commission, Sudder St travel agencies can save you the trek to the ticket office and can sometimes manage to find tickets on 'full' trains.

ⓘ Getting Around

Tickets on most city transport routes cost from ₹4 to ₹8. Men shouldn't sit in assigned 'Ladies' seats'.

TO/FROM THE AIRPORT

NSBIA Airport is around 16km northeast of central Kolkata. By the time you read this, the brand new integrated terminal should have opened 300m/600m south of the ageing former domestic/international terminals. A big new feeder loop road accesses the new terminal from VIP Rd in the south at Airport Gate 1. Busy Jessore Rd approximately parallels the runway and the western airport access road, offering a second, smaller access through Airport Gate 2, around 400m west of the old terminals.

Air-Con Bus

Air-conditioned airport buses (₹40, around one hour) run every half-hour (9am to 9pm) to Esplanade and/or Howrah.

City Bus

Minibus 151 to BBD Bagh and relatively infrequent bus 46 to Esplanade (₹8, one hour) via VIP Rd start from the VIP Rd/Jessore Rd junction. Bus 30B from Jessore Rd is bound eventually for Babughat.

Metro

An airport metro extension is mooted but for now the closest station is Dum Dum, 5km southwest. By suburban train, change at Dum Dum Junction not Dum Dum Cantt. By bus from Jessore Rd you could jump aboard 30B or DN9/1, which reach Dum Dum in around 20 minutes.

Suburban Train

Biman Bandar train station, on concrete piles around 300m west of the old terminals, is a dead-end spur line with just a handful of daily services.

Taxi

Prepaid, fixed-price taxis cost ₹290 to Sudder St, taking around 50 minutes. Long waits are possible after 10pm.

BUS & TRAM

Most buses' route numbers are written in Western script even when destination signboards aren't. Photogenically battered old trams are slower but follow somewhat more predictable routes. Pay on board.

FERRY

Generally faster and more agreeable than road travel, especially between central Kolkata and Howrah train station, **river ferries** (ticket ₹4; ☺8am-8pm) depart every 15 minutes from various jetties including Bagbazar (Map p452), Armenian (not Sundays, Map p458), Fairlie (Map p458), Bishe June (Map p458) and Babu Ghat. Reduced service on Sundays.

METRO

Kolkata's busy **metro** (www.mtp.indianrailways.gov.in; ticket ₹4-12; ☺7am-9.45pm Mon-Sat, 2-9.45pm Sun) has trains every five to 15 minutes. For Sudder St use Esplanade or Park St.

There's one operational line but several extensions are planned. Due for completion by 2015, Line 2 (http://kmrc.in) between Howrah, Sealdah and Salt Lake, will massively improve the city's navigability.

Theoretically you may not carry bags over 10kg.

RICKSHAW

Human-powered 'tana rickshaws' work within limited areas, notably around New Market. Although rickshaw pullers sometimes charge foreigners disproportionate fares, many are virtually destitute, sleeping on the pavements beneath their rented chariots at night, so tips are heartily appreciated.

Autorickshaws operate as share-taxis along fixed routes. Usefully for Sudder St travellers, one such route shuttles the length of Mirza Ghalib and Royd streets (₹5, northbound mornings, southbound afternoons).

SUBURBAN TRAINS

Sealdah–Dum Dum–Dakshineswar trains run roughly hourly. The Kidderpore–BBD Bagh–Bagbazar–Chitpore–Dum Dum route is rush hour only. For timetables see http://erail.in/kolkatasuburbantrains.htm.

TAXI

Kolkata's yellow Ambassador cabs are ubiquitous by day but can become hard to find after 10pm.

They charge a minimum fare of ₹25 for up to 1.9km. Be aware that taxi meters do NOT show what you'll pay: the real fare is around 250% of the meter reading. Drivers have a conversion chart. Some cabs, typically stationary ones, won't use the meter especially after 9pm when drivers might ask double if they can't expect to find a return fare.

Beware: around 1pm much of the city's one-way road system reverses direction! Taxis can prove reluctant to make journeys around this time.

There are prepaid taxi booths at Howrah Station, Sealdah Station and the airport.

West Bengal & Darjeeling

Best Places for a Cuppa

➡ Windamere Hotel (p502)

➡ Sunset Lounge (p503)

➡ Makaibari (p494)

Best Places to Stay

➡ Dekeling Hotel (p500)

➡ Holumba Haven (p510)

➡ Backpackers (p486)

Why Go?

A sliver of fertile land running from the tea-draped Himalayan foothills to the sultry mangroves of the Bay of Bengal, West Bengal offers a range of destinations and experiences that few other states can match. In the tropical southern areas, the sea-washed hamlet of Mandarmani vies for attention with Bishnupur's ornate terracotta-tiled Hindu temples and palaces. The striped Bengal tiger sizes you up as you float down muddy rivulets in the Sunderbans, while a bunch of European ghost towns line the banks of the Hooghly (Ganges) further upstream as vestigeal reminders of the state's maritime heydays. And in the cool northern hills, the 'toy train' chugs its way up the charming British-era hill station of Darjeeling, revered for its ringside views of massive Khangchendzonga. Combine all these with a vibrant art scene, a delectable cuisine and a genuinely friendly population, and you've got a cracker of an itinerary.

When to Go
Darjeeling

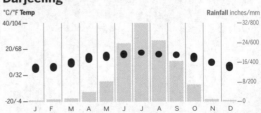

Oct–Dec & Mar–May Best for West Bengal hill views, trekking and spring bloom.

Oct–Mar Best for avoiding the heat on the lower plains.

Jan The best time to navigate the dense mangrove forests of the Sunderbans Tiger Reserve.

Food & Drink

Darjeeling is *the* place to taste a range of teas from local tea estates. Noted for its delicate taste, the teas range from black to green to white and are best taken alone or with a slice of lemon (and/or a pinch of sugar), but never with milk. Not to be outdone, Bengali food – with its varied fish preparations and sweetmeats – is considered iconic by locals and visitors alike.

DON'T MISS

The views of 8598m Khangchendzonga, the world's third-highest mountain, are easily one of the West Bengal hills' highlights. The classic viewpoints are from **Tiger Hill** or from the **Singalila Trek**, where the Himalayan skyline stretches from Nepal to Bhutan. **Darjeeling** town also has great views, as does Deolo Hill in **Kalimpong**. The major potential spoiler is the weather. The most reliable clear skies are at dawn during the post-monsoon months of October to December.

Top State Festivals

➡ **Ganga Sagar Mela** (⊙mid-Jan, Sagar Island, p486) Hundreds of thousands of Hindu pilgrims converge where the Ganges meets the sea, to bathe en masse in a riotous festival.

➡ **Bengali New Year** (⊙mid-Apr, statewide) A statewide holiday celebrating the first day of the Bengali calendar, also called Nabo Barsho.

➡ **Rath Yatra** (⊙Jul/Aug, statewide) Celebrated by pulling the juggernaut of Lord Jagannath's chariot.

➡ **Dussehra** (Durga Puja; ⊙Sep/Oct, statewide) Across the state, especially in Kolkata (Calcutta), temporary *pandals* (temple shrines) are raised and intense celebrations take place to worship the goddess Durga. After four colourful days, beautiful clay idols of the 10-armed deity are immersed in the rivers.

➡ **Jagaddhatri Puja** (⊙Nov, Chandarnagar, p486) Honours the goddess Jagaddhatri, an incarnation of Durga.

➡ **Poush Mela** (⊙23-26 Dec, Shantiniketan, p488) Folk music, dance, theatre and Baul (a sect of mystical minstrels) songs radiate across the university town.

MAIN POINTS OF ENTRY

Kolkata Airport; Howrah, Sealdah and Kolkata (Chitpore) train station; Bagdogra Airport; New Jalpaiguri train station.

Fast Facts

➡ **Population**: 91.3 million

➡ **Area**: 87,853 sq km

➡ **Capital**: Kolkata

➡ **Main language**: Bengali

➡ **Sleeping prices**: $ below ₹1000, $$ ₹1000 to ₹2500, $$$ above ₹2500

Top Tip

During the month-long *puja* (prayers) season', from Durga Puja to Diwali, hotels, jeeps and trekking huts are often booked out by travelling Bengali tourists. Pack a jumper and visit in November to avoid the crowds.

Resources

➡ **West Bengal Tourism** (www.westbengaltourism. gov.in) Information and online booking for West Bengal Tourism Development Corporation (WBTDC) lodges, such as Jaldhapara and boat cruises.

➡ **Kalimpong** (www. kalimpong.org) Travel information with an emphasis on accommodation.

West Bengal Highlights

1 Enjoy 360-degree mountain views over breakfast at hilltop lodges on the **Singalila Ridge Trek** (p506)

2 Ride the steam-driven **toy train** (p501) as it puffs and pants its way between the tea towns of Kurseong and Darjeeling

3 Explore rural wonders and get arty on a visit to the university town of **Shantiniketan** (p488)

4 Visit a tea estate, sip a delicate local brew and enjoy the fantastic views from the historic hill station of **Darjeeling** (p494)

5 Watch dawn break over the world's third-highest peak from **Tiger Hill** (p495)

6 Admire intricate scenes from the Hindu epics carved on the medieval terracotta temples of **Bishnupur** (p487)

7 Cruise the river channels of the **Sunderbans** (p485) through the world's most extensive mangrove forest, to spot darting kingfishers, spotted deer and the elusive Royal Bengal tiger

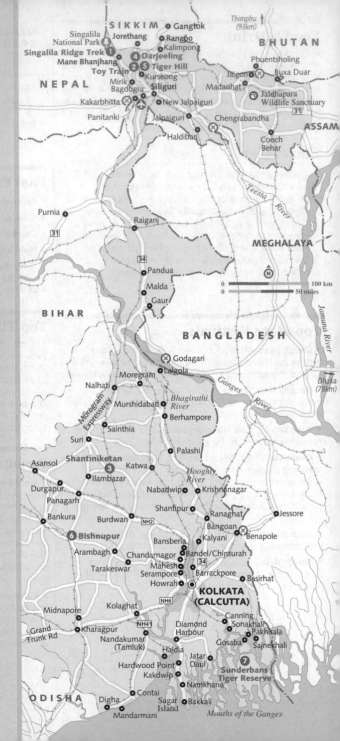

History

Referred to as Bongo in the Mahabharata, this region has a long history predating the Aryan invasions of India. It was part of the Mauryan empire in the 3rd century BC before being overrun by the Guptas. For three centuries from around the 9th century AD, the Buddhist Pala dynasty controlled a large area based in Bengal and including parts of Odisha (Orissa), Bihar and modern Bangladesh.

Bengal was brought under Muslim control by Qutb-ud-din, first of the sultans of Delhi, at the end of the 12th century. Following the death of Aurangzeb in 1707, Bengal became an independent Islamic state.

The British East India Company established a trading post in Kolkata (Calcutta) in 1698, which quickly prospered. Annoyed by the rapid British expansion, Siraj-ud-daula, the nawab of Bengal, came down from his capital at Murshidabad and easily took Kolkata in 1756. Robert Clive defeated him the following year at the Battle of Plassey, helped by the treachery of Siraj ud-daula's uncle, Mir Jafar, who commanded the greater part of the nawab's army. Jafar succeeded his nephew as nawab but his reward was short-lived; after the Battle of Buxar in 1764 the British took full control of Bengal.

West Bengal was the cradle of the Indian Renaissance in the late 19th century and early 20th century and the national freedom movement (1857-1947), and has long been considered the country's cultural heartland. In 1947, Indian independence from Britain and the subsequent partition of the country saw the state of Bengal (already divided for administrative purposes in 1905) divided into Hindu-predominant West Bengal and Muslim-oriented Bangladesh, causing the upheaval and migration of millions of Bengalis.

Activities

Trekking

While pleasant walks along pine-scented trails are possible in all of West Bengal's hill stations, the most popular place for a multiday trek is Singalila Ridge, near Darjeeling, where teahouse-style trekking is possible. Camping treks are possible elsewhere, including around Kalimpong.

Rafting

White-water rafting trips on the Teesta and Rangeet Rivers can be easily arranged and accessed from Darjeeling and Kalimpong.

ⓘ Getting There & Around

The vast majority who enter West Bengal arrive in Kolkata, which is connected by air to Delhi, Mumbai, Bangkok, Kathmandu and Dubai. Siliguri's Bagdogra airport has services to Kolkata, Delhi and Guwahati, as well as daily helicopter flights to Gangtok.

Most land arrivals are by train: main lines run south to Bhubaneswar and Chennai (Madras), and west to Gaya, Varanasi and Delhi. Other lines connect the state to Assam in the northeast and Jharkhand in the west. Numerous long-distance buses also connect surrounding states.

Overcrowded 'share jeeps' ply the winding roads of the West Bengal hills. Try to avoid the cramped back seats.

SOUTH OF KOLKATA

Sunderbans Tiger Reserve

Home to one of the largest concentrations of Royal Bengal tigers on the planet, this 2585 sq km **reserve** (⌨ 03218255280; per person per day/video ₹40/200; ☉ dawn-dusk) is a network of channels and semi-submerged mangroves that forms the world's largest river delta. Tigers (officially estimated to number close to 300) lurk in the impenetrable depths of the mangrove forests, and also swim the delta's innumerable channels. Although they do sometimes kill villagers and their livestock, tigers are typically shy and sightings are rare. Nevertheless, cruising the broad waterways through the world's biggest mangrove sanctuary (now a Unesco World Heritage Site) and watching wildlife, whether it be a spotted deer, 2m-long water monitor or luminescent kingfisher, is a world away from Kolkata's chaos.

The best time to visit the reserve is between November and March – entry is restricted through the monsoon months. Organised tours are the best way to navigate this tricky and harsh landscape, not least because all your permits, paperwork, guiding duties and logistical problems are taken care of. In fact, travelling alone is not recommended.

At Sajnekhali, the official gateway into the reserve, you'll find the **Mangrove Interpretation Centre** (☉ 8.30am-5pm) with a small turtle and crocodile hatchery, a collection of pickled wildlife and a blackboard with the date of the last tiger-spotting chalked up. Rowboats (₹400), motorboats (₹500) and guides (₹600) are available for hire near the site.

☞ Tours

Tour prices vary widely. They typically include return transport from Kolkata, accommodation, food, park entry fees as well as guide- and boat-hire charges, but do check what is and isn't included.

Backpackers   WILDLIFE-WATCHING
(☏9836177140; www.tourdesundarbans.com; 11 Tottee Lane, Kolkata; 1/2 nights per person all-inclusive ₹4000/4500; ☺10am-7pm) An extremely professional and knowledgeable outfit that conducts highly recommended tours of the jungles, including birdwatching and local music sessions. Accommodation is in a cruise boat converted from a fishing trawler, or a traditional village-style guesthouse, with folk music in the evenings.

West Bengal Tourism   CRUISE
(☏03344012660; www.westbengaltourism.gov.in) West Bengal Tourism organises weekly boat cruises from September to April, costing from ₹2800 per person for one night and two half-days, including food and on-board accommodation. Trips that include a worthwhile extra day start from ₹3700.

Sunderban Tiger Camp   WILDLIFE-WATCHING
(☏03332935749; www.waxpolhotels.com; 71 Ganesh Chandra Ave, Kolkata; 1/2 nights per person all-inclusive from ₹3700/6200) Provides expert guides and quality accommodation (on dry land) in lovely red-brick cottages with forest-themed wall murals.

SAGAR FESTIVAL

According to Hindu legend, Sagar Island – at the confluence of the Ganges – was where King Sagar's 60,000 sons were brought back to life by the flowing river after they had been reduced to ashes by a sage named Kapil Muni. Each year in January, the **Ganga Sagar Mela** (Sagar Island; ☺mid-Jan) is held here, near the Kapil Muni Temple, honouring the legend. The best way to see the festival is the two-day, one-night boat tour operated from Kolkata by **West Bengal Tourism** (www.westbengaltourism.gov. in), with accommodation on board (per person all-inclusive deck/berth ₹5500/10000). The island hibernates for the rest of the year.

Help Tourism   WILDLIFE-WATCHING
(Map p463; ☏033-24550917; www.helptourism. com; 67A Kali Temple Rd, Kalighat, Kolkata; 2 nights per person all-inclusive ₹15,950) Actively associated with local communities, this tour takes you in close proximity to rural life in the delta, in addition to providing wonderful access into the forest. Accommodation is in a luxury eco-themed camp.

Mandarmani
☏03220

About 180km south of Kolkata, Mandarmani is a sleepy fishing village that sports a heavenly beach stretching nearly 15km. It remains one of the more unpolluted beaches in the country, and supports countless colonies of sand bubbler crabs. The beaches see some additional action at dawn, when fishing boats drop anchor and disgorge their catches of marine goodies.

Adventure Zone (☏9830033896; www.about adventure.org) conducts parasailing (₹500) on the beaches, and offers an adventure sports package (₹1000) that includes kayaking, ziplining, rock climbing and rappelling.

Sana Beach (☏9330633111; www.thesana-beach.com; d incl breakfast from ₹2800; ❋☒), at the far end of the beach, is by far the best among all the resorts lining Mandarmani beach. It has a mix of comfy rooms done up in cheerful hues, ethno-chic cottages and tents, a lovely swimming pool and a good bar-cum-restaurant.

To get there, take the 6.40am 12857 Tamralipta Express (2nd class/chair ₹75/273, 3½ hours) from Kolkata's Howrah Station to Digha. A taxi drop from there costs about ₹500.

NORTH OF KOLKATA

Up the Hooghly

On the Hooghly River, about 25km north of Kolkata, Serampore was a Danish trading centre until Denmark's holdings in India were transferred to the British East India Company in 1845. **Serampore College** was founded in 1818 by the first Baptist missionary to India, William Carey, and houses a library that was once one of the largest in India.

Further upstream is the former French outpost of **Chandarnagar**, where you can

SPA TREATS

Looking to experience the best of rural Bengal while treating yourself to a spot of wellness and luxury? Then head out to one of these two recommended spa resorts, which are set amid scenic landscapes and pack in some of the best comforts and therapies for you to indulge in, even while allowing you to soak up the bucolic charms of the region.

Hemmed by blooming vegetable gardens and centred around a tree-lined lake only an hour's drive north of Kolkata is **Vedic Village** (☏ 03366229900; www.thevedicvillage. com; Shikharpur village; r from ₹8500; ❄ @ ☀), a luxury resort that's known as much for its fine hospitality as its showcase facility – a speciality spa-cum-naturopathy clinic that's touted to be the first (and best) medical spa in the country. Long-stay treatment packages, built around several sessions of consultation with in-house doctors, can be customised upon prior notice, while casual holidaymakers have the option of simply kicking back in one of its luxury villas, de-stressing to the chirping of myriad bird species and tucking into mouth-watering cuisine in between floating sessions in the ultramarine waters of its swimming pool.

En route to Diamond Harbour, about two hours south of Kolkata, stands **Ganga Kutir** (☏ 03340404040; www.gangakutir.com; Sarisa village, Raichak; rooms from ₹14,500; ❄ @ ☀), yet another popular destination for those wanting to catch up with solitude. Located on the banks of the Hooghly, this swish resort brings together a range of wellness packages which – paired with yoga and meditation – are a great nourisher for tired sinews. Accommodation is in chic suites appointed with snazzy muralled walls and great river views.

visit the **Eglise du Sacre Coeur** (Sacred Heart Church) and the nearby 18th-century mansion now housing the **Cultural Institut de Chandernagar** (admission free; ⏱ 11am-5.30pm, closed Thu & Sat), with collections documenting this colonial outpost. November sees Chandarnagar deck up in gorgeous public lighting for the **Jagaddhatri Puja**. This festival is devoted to the worship of an incarnation of the Hindu mother goddess, even as enthusiastic locals throng festive arenas to pay their respects to gigantic clay idols of the four-armed deity, housed in temporary pavilions called *pandals*.

In 1571 the Portuguese set up a factory in **Bandel**, 41km north of Kolkata and close to Saptagram, which was an important trading port long before Kolkata rose to prominence. Here, you can climb the lofty clock tower of the romantically crumbling **Imambara** (admission ₹5; ⏱ 8am-6pm Apr-Jul, to 5.30pm Aug-Nov, to 5pm Dec-Mar), which has breathtaking (in more ways than one!) views of the river. The building was constructed in 1861 as a centre for learning and worship. Only 1km south of Bandel, **Chinsurah** was exchanged by the Dutch for the British possessions on the (Indonesian) island of Sumatra in 1825. There are dilapidated ruins of a fort and a cemetery, about 1km to the west.

About 6km north of Hooghly, **Bansberia** has two interesting temples. The 13 *sikhar-as* (spires) of the **Hanseswari Temple** look like something you'd expect to see in St Petersburg, while the ornate terracotta tiles covering the **Vasudev Temple** resemble those seen in Bishnupur.

To visit these settlements on a day tour from Kolkata, take any Bandel-bound local train (₹10, one hour, hourly) from Howrah Station, or hire a taxi (₹1500). For river cruises, see p488.

Bishnupur

☏ 03244 / POP 61,900

Known for its beautiful terracotta temples, Bishnupur flourished as the capital of the Malla kings from the 16th to the early 19th centuries. The architecture of these intriguing **temples** (Indian/foreigner ₹10/250; ⏱ dawn-dusk) is a bold mix of Bengali, Islamic and Oriya (Odishan) styles. Intricately detailed facades of numerous temples play out scenes of the Hindu epics, the Ramayana and the Mahabharata. The most striking structures include the **Jor Bangla**, **Madan Mohan Temple**, the multiarched **Ras Mancha** and the elaborate **Shyam Rai Temple**. You need to pay for your ticket at Ras Mancha and show it at the other temples. Cycle-rickshaw wallahs offer tours (the best way to negotiate the labyrinth of lanes) for ₹250.

RIVER CRUISES

For those with a piscean bent of mind (and deep pockets), there's news. The Hooghly River now doubles as a corridor for luxury cruises that slosh their guests with a host of the finest onboard comforts, while allowing them to visit the riverine areas of Bengal in a most memorable manner. Cruises usually range from a week to 10 days, and stop in places such as Chandarnagar, Bandel, Mayapur, Murshidabad and Farakka (for Gaur and Pandua). **Bengal Ganga** (☑ 011-26122290; www.bengalganga.com; d all-inclusive ₹390,000) and **Assam Bengal Navigation** (☑ 9207042330; www.assam-bengalnavigation.com; per person per day all-inclusive from US$195) come highly recommended.

There's a small **museum** (admission ₹10; ☺ 11am-7pm Tue-Sun) that's worth a look for its painted manuscript covers, stone friezes, musical instruments and folk art gallery.

Bishnupur is in Bankura district, famous for its Baluchari silk saris and its pottery, particularly the stylised terracotta Bankura horse. Reproductions of detailed terracotta tiles from the temples are sold everywhere.

Bishnupur Tourist Lodge (☑ 252013; www.westbengaltourism.gov.in; College Rd; d from ₹900; ✵), flaunting a red-and-white exterior, is perhaps the best place to sleep in town, with clean, pastel-shaded rooms and a good bar-cum-restaurant. It's close to the museum and a ₹50 rickshaw ride from the train station. It's often full, so book ahead.

Regular buses run from Bishnupur to Kolkata (₹130, five hours). For Shantiniketan (₹90, four hours) you have to change in Durgapur. Two fast trains run daily to Howrah (2nd class/chair ₹80/281, 3½ hours): the 6am 12883 Rupashi Bangla Express and the 4.50pm 12827 Howrah Purulia Express.

Shantiniketan

☑ 03463

In addition to epitomising its Bengali name (meaning 'abode of peace'), Shantiniketan is a veritable nerve centre of Bengal's art and culture. Nobel laureate, poet and artist Rabindranath Tagore (1861–1941) founded a school here amid pastoral settings in 1901, which later developed into the **Visva Bharati University**, with an emphasis on the study of liberal arts as well as humanity's relationship with nature. A relaxed place, it attracts students from all over India and abroad.

Spread throughout the leafy university grounds are eclectic **statues**, the celebrated **Shantiniketan murals** and the Belgian glass-panelled **university prayer hall**. The **museum and art gallery** (adult/student ₹5/3; ☺ 10.30am-1pm & 2-4.30pm Thu-Mon, to 1pm Tue) within the **Uttarayan complex** (Tagore's former home) are worth a peek if you are a Tagore aficionado. Reproductions of his sketches and paintings are sold here.

Subarnarekha bookshop near the post office has plenty of Tagore's titles (₹80 to ₹250) in English. Around Shantiniketan, several practitioners of classical dance, music, pottery and painting offer casual short-term courses to visiting students. Ask the helpful staff at Subarnarekha.

✹ Festivals & Events

Poush Mela CULTURE, MUSIC
(☺ 23-26 Dec) The highpoint of Shantiniketan's festive calendar, this four-day gala brings together artists, musicians, artisans and poets from places as diverse as nearby villages to far-flung continents. There's food, fun, frolic, song, dance and poetry round the clock, with sessions of vigorous souvenir shopping in between.

🛏 Sleeping & Eating

Park Guest House GUESTHOUSE $$
(☑ 9434012420; www.parkguesthouse.co.in; Deer Park; d from ₹1200; ✵) Bordering a quaint tribal village, this peaceful and pretty place is clearly the best deal in town. The rooms are beautifully embellished with tribal decor, and the elaborate *thali* meals (prepared upon advance notice) are simply awesome. There's a lovely lawn where you can nurse a quiet beer in the evening.

Shantiniketan Tourist Lodge HOTEL $$
(☑ 252699; www.westbengaltourism.gov.in; Bhubandanga; d from ₹900; ✵) Industrial but friendly, this large-scale government operation is really worth considering if you go for one of its deluxe air-conditioned rooms (₹2400), located in cottages standing around a pretty lawn. There's a decent restaurant

(mains ₹100) which works up a limited range of Indian standards.

⭐ **Alcha**   CAFE **$**
(☑329619; Ratanpalli; mains ₹40-80; ◎8am-10.30am, noon-2pm & 4-8pm) This lovely cafe on one edge of the university campus is a melting pot for free-thinking students. It's got a cool shack-style seating space that often doubles as an art gallery, and there's a boutique which sells a fantastic selection of jewellery, textiles and handicrafts made by local artisans. Try the delectable set-menu vegetarian lunch (₹100), prepared upon advance order.

ℹ Information

Post office (Santiniketan Rd; ◎10am-4pm Mon-Sat) On the main road, opposite the turn-off to the university entrance.

State Bank of India (Santiniketan Rd; ◎10am-2pm Mon-Fri, to noon Sat) Has an ATM and changes foreign currency.

Train booking office (Santiniketan Rd; ◎8am-noon & 12.30-2pm Thu-Tue) Near the post office, with information on trains to and from Kolkata or Darjeeling, as well as reservation facilities.

ℹ Getting There & Away

Several trains ply the route between Bolpur station, 2km south of the university, and Kolkata

daily. The best is 12337 Shantiniketan Express (2nd class/chair ₹68/232, 2½ hours) departing at 10.10am from Howrah. For New Jalpaiguri, take the 9.25am 15657 Kanchenjunga Express (sleeper/3AC ₹187/496, nine hours).

Bolpur's Jambuni bus stand has connections to Berhampore/Murshidabad (₹95, four hours) and Bishnupur (₹90, four hours). Change in Suri and Durgapur respectively.

Nabadwip & Mayapur
☑03472 / POP 125,300

Nabadwip, 114km north of Kolkata, is an important Krishna pilgrimage centre, attracting throngs of devotees, and is also an ancient centre of Sanskrit culture. The last Hindu king of Bengal, Lakshman Sen, moved his capital here from Gaur.

Across the river from Nabadwip, Mayapur is the home of the Iskcon (Hare Krishna) movement. There's a large, colourful temple and the basic but clean **Iskcon Guest Houses** (☑245620; mghb@pamho.net; d/tr/q from ₹500/600/800; ❄). Iskcon runs a package tour in a private bus from Kolkata, leaving early on Friday, Saturday and Sunday mornings, returning the subsequent evening. For details or to make a booking call **Iskcon Kolkata** (☑9830955124).

GAUR & PANDUA

Rising from the flooded paddy fields of Gaur (355km from Kolkata) are mosques and other crumbling ruins of the 13th- to 16th-century capital of the Muslim nawabs of Bengal. Little remains from the 7th- to 12th-century pre-Muslim period, when Gaur was the capital of the successive Buddhist Pala and Hindu Sena dynasties.

Hiding behind lush mango orchards, the most graceful monuments in this area are the impressive **Baradwari Mosque** (1526) – the arcaded aisle of its corridor still intact – and the fortress-like gateway of **Dakhil Darwaza** (1425). The **Qadam Rasul Mosque** enshrines the flat footprint of the Prophet Mohammed, while the adjacent **tomb of Fateh Khan** (1707) startlingly informs you that its occupant 'vomited blood and died on this spot'. Remnants of colourful enamel cling to the **Chamkan Mosque** and the **Gumti Gate** nearby.

In Pandua (about 25km from Gaur) are the vast ruins of the 14th-century **Adina Masjid**, once India's largest mosque. About 2km away is the **Eklakhi Mausoleum**, so called because it cost ₹1 lakh (₹100,000) to build back in 1431.

To visit these forgotten relics, board the 13011 Howrah-Malda Intercity Express (2nd class/chair ₹95/337, 7½ hours) from Kolkata. Accommodation is available in Malda (15km from Gaur and 30km from Pandua) at **Hotel Kalinga** (☑03512-283567; hotel-kalinga@gmail.com; NH34, Ram Krishna Pally; d with/without AC ₹1050/680; ❄), which has basic rooms, friendly service and palatable in-house food. For touring the monuments, it's best to hire a taxi from Malda for the day (₹2000).

Murshidabad & Berhampore

📞 03482 / POP 170,300

In Murshidabad, rural Bengali life and 18th-century architecture meld on the verdant shores of the Bhagirathi River. When Siraj-ud-daula was nawab of Bengal, Murshidabad was his capital, and he was assassinated here after the defeat at Plassey (now Palashi).

The main draw here is the **Hazarduari** (Indian/foreigner ₹5/100; ⊘10am-4.30pm Sat-Thu), a palace famous for its 1000 doors (real and false), built here for the nawabs in 1837. It houses an astonishing collection of antiquities from the 18th and 19th centuries. Other beautiful structures in the complex include the **Nizamat Imambara**, the clock tower, the **Wasef Manzil**, a former regal residence, and the elegant **Madina Mosque**.

Murshid Quli Khan, who moved the capital here in 1700, is buried beneath the stairs at the impressive ruins of the **Katra Mosque**. Siraj-ud-daula was assassinated at the **Nimak Haram Deori** (Traitor's Gate). Within the **Kathgola Gardens** (admission ₹7; ⊘6.30am-5.30pm) is an interesting family mansion of a Jain trading family, dating back to 1873.

Berhampore is 15km south of Murshidabad and acts as its bus and railway hub.

🛏 Sleeping & Eating

Hotel Sagnik   HOTEL $

(📞270051; Omrahaganj; s/d from ₹750/850; ❄) Conveniently located between Murshidabad and Berhampore, this friendly place has good-value rooms and a decent restaurant, but scores mostly on service, which is prompt and personalised. It's a 10-minute cycle-rickshaw ride from Murshidabad train station.

Hotel Samrat   HOTEL $

(📞251147; NH34 Panchanantala; s/d from ₹650/850; ❄) This is one of Berhampore's longest-running operations, and offers spacious and clean rooms opening along corridors painted in orange and cream. The Mahal restaurant (mains ₹140) downstairs is a good place for meals. It's located on the main highway, though, so expect some vehicular noise through the night.

ℹ Getting There & Around

The 13103 Bhagirathi Express (2nd class/chair ₹68/241, four hours) departs Kolkata's Sealdah station at 6.20pm. Regular buses leave for Kolkata (₹130, six hours) and Malda (₹90, four hours). To Shantiniketan/Bolpur (₹95, four hours) there are occasional direct buses but you may need to change in Suri.

Shared autorickshaws (₹30) whiz between Murshidabad and Berhampore. Cycle-rickshaws/taxis offer guided half-day tours to see the spread-out sites for ₹300/800.

WEST BENGAL HILLS

Siliguri & New Jalpaiguri

📞 0353 / POP 701,000 / ELEV 120M

The crowded and noisy transport hub encompassing the twin towns of Siliguri and New Jalpaiguri (NJP) is the jumping-off point for Darjeeling, Kalimpong, Sikkim, the northeast states, eastern Nepal and Bhutan. Despite being one of the largest cities in the state, there's little to see here: for most travellers, Siliguri is an overnight transit point to cooler climes.

Most of Siliguri's hotels, restaurants and services are spread along Tenzing Norgay Rd, better known as Hill Cart Rd. NJP Station Rd leads southward 6km to NJP station, while branching northeastward off Hill Cart Rd are Siliguri's other main streets, Sevoke and Bidhan Rds, the latter hiding the city's most interesting bazaars.

🛏 Sleeping

Conclave Lodge   HOTEL $

(📞2514102; Hill Cart Rd; s/d/tr ₹332/500/650, r without bathroom ₹200-250) Tucked away behind the more visible Hotel Conclave this central lodge is the best budget option, with cleanish, quietish and high-ceilinged rooms with TV and hot-water bathrooms.

Hotel Rajdarbar   HOTEL $$

(📞2511189; www.hotelrajdarbarsiliguri.com; Hill Cart Rd; s/d incl breakfast ₹1889/2099; ❄ 🛜) The stylish and modern Rajdarbar was completely refurbished in 2012, making it fresher and better run than its popular neighbour, the Hotel Conclave. There's a good restaurant and lobby wi-fi.

Hotel Conclave   HOTEL $$

(📞2518536; www.hotelconclave.in; Hill Cart Rd; s/d from ₹770/880, with AC from ₹1334/1524; ❄) Grumpy staff can't detract from this solid contemporary hotel, conveniently close to all the transport options. Quality mattresses and a glass elevator add a touch of class, though rooms could use some freshening. The cheaper rooms are quieter, since the luxury rooms face the road. Pricier rooms come with breakfast at the excellent **Eminent Restaurant** (mains ₹85-150).

Evergreen Inn　　　　HOTEL $$
(✆2510426; innevergreen@yahoo.in; Pradhan Nagar, Ashana Purna Sarani; d ₹1035, with AC ₹1438-1725; ❄) This modern new place is just 100m from the bus terminal but the location down a side street means it's surprisingly peaceful. There are three different grades of room but all are clean and fresh with flat screens and stylish bathrooms. The side street is one block south of the Delhi Hotel, on the opposite side of Hill Cart Rd from the bus terminal. Not much English is spoken.

Hotel Sinclairs　　　　HOTEL $$$
(✆2517674; www.sinclairshotels.com; off NH31; s/d incl breakfast from ₹5284/5577, ste from ₹7632; ❄🖥❄) This comfortable three-star hotel, 1km north of the bus terminal, offers an escape from the noise of Hill Cart Rd. The carpeted rooms are spacious and there's an excellent patio restaurant-cum-bar and the chance to dive into a cool, clean pool.

Cindrella Hotel　　　　HOTEL $$$
(✆2544130; www.cindrellahotels.com; Sevoke Rd; s/d incl breakfast from ₹5284/5870; ❄🖥❄) The top place in town offers comfortable rather than luxurious rooms, with a terrace bar, small gym and pool (closed November to February) and free wi-fi. It's 3km northeast of the centre on the road to Kalimpong.

✖ Eating

★ Khana Khazana　　　　MULTICUISINE $
(Hill Cart Rd; mains ₹70-140) On a side alley off the busy main highway, the secluded outdoor garden here offers merciful relief from the chaos outside. The extensive menu ranges from Chinese and South Indian specialities to Mumbai street snacks, and includes plenty of vegetarian options.

Sartaj　　　　INDIAN $$
(Hill Cart Rd; mains ₹95-240) A sophisticated and cool (literally – the air-con is heaven) bar-restaurant with a huge range: first-rate North Indian tandooris and curries, good Continental options and top-notch service, including a fantastically uniformed doorman. It's also a good place just for a cold beer.

❶ Information

INTERNET ACCESS
Krishna Travels (Hill Cart Rd; per hr ₹40; ◷9am-8pm) Internet access down a side street across from Hotel Conclave.

MEDICAL SERVICES
Sadar Hospital (✆2436526; Hospital Rd)

MONEY
Bagdogra Airport has a moneychanger with decent rates.

Delhi Hotel (Hill Cart Rd; ◷8am-8pm) Currency and travellers cheques exchanged, opposite the bus station; ₹30 tax per transaction.

TOURIST INFORMATION
Sikkim Tourist Office (Hill Cart Rd, SNT Terminal; ◷10am-4pm Mon-Sat) Issues permits for Sikkim on the spot. Bring copies of your passport and visa and one passport-sized photo.

West Bengal Tourist Office (✆bookings 2517561, information 2511974; www.westbengaltourism.gov.in; Hill Cart Rd; ◷10.30am-5.30pm Mon-Fri, to 1.30pm Sat) Can book accommodation and tours for Jaldhapara Wildlife Sanctuary, including forestry lodges.

TRAVEL AGENCIES
Private transport booking agencies line Hill Cart Rd.

Help Tourism (✆2535896; www.helptourism.com; 143 Hill Cart Rd) A recommended agency with a strong environmental and community-development focus, including voluntourism. It has links to dozens of homestays and lodges around the hills, including a historic tea estate at Damdin and the stylish Neora Valley Jungle Camp outside Lava.

❶ Getting There & Away

AIR
Bagdogra Airport is 12km west of Siliguri. There are daily flights to Delhi, Kolkata and Guwahati but not all are direct. Check websites for fares, which vary widely.

Five-seater helicopters (₹2200, 30 minutes, 10kg luggage limit) travel daily from Bagdogra to Gangtok at 2.30pm in good weather. You need to book in advance through Sikkim Tourism Development Corporation (p539) in Gangtok.

BUS
Most North Bengal State Transport Corporation (NBSTC) buses leave from **Tenzing Norgay Central Bus Terminal** (Hill Cart Rd), as do many private buses plying the same routes. Private long-distance bus companies line the entrance.

NBSTC buses include frequent buses to Malda (₹140, 6½ hours) and Madarihat, plus six daily services to Kolkata (₹360 to ₹390, AC ₹710). Assam State Transportation Corporation runs a daily 4pm bus to Guwahati (₹450, 15 hours).

For Patna (₹225, 12 hours, departs 6pm) try **Gupta Travels** (🖉 2513451), just outside the bus station. Deluxe Volvo buses for Kolkata (₹1200, 11 hours) leave around 7pm from this and many other agencies.

Sikkim Nationalised Transport (SNT) buses to Gangtok (₹135 to ₹210, 4½ hours) leave at 7.30am, 11.30am, 12.30pm and 1.30pm from the **SNT terminal** (Hill Cart Rd), 250m southeast of the bus terminal. At least one of the departures is air-con (₹220). Arrange your permit in advance at the Sikkim Tourist Office next door.

JEEP

A faster and marginally more comfortable way of getting around the hills is by share jeep. There are a number of jeep stands lining Hill Cart Rd: for Darjeeling (₹120, three hours) and Kurseong (₹60, 1½ hours) look around opposite the bus terminal or outside the Conclave Hotel until late afternoon; for Kalimpong (₹100, 2½ hours) head to the Panitanki Mall stand on Sevoke Rd (take an autorickaw); and for Gangtok (₹200, four hours) jeeps leave from next to the SNT terminal until around 4pm. Share and charter jeeps for all these destinations also leave from NJP train station. Mirik-bound jeeps (₹80, 2½ hours) leave most frequently from Siliguri Junction train station, 200m from the central bus terminal.

Chartering a jeep privately costs roughly 10 times that of a shared ticket. An option for XL-sized Westerners is to pay for and occupy the front two or three seats next to the driver.

A prepaid taxi stand at Bagdogra Airport offers fixed fares to Darjeeling (₹1800), Gangtok (₹1850), Kakarbhitta (₹450) and even Bhadrapur in Nepal (₹1000), allowing you to bypass Siliguri completely. It's not difficult to hook up with other airline passengers to share the cost.

TRAIN

Buy tickets at Siliguri Junction station or at the **train booking office** (🖉 2537333; cnr Hospital & Bidhan Rds; ⊙ 8-11am, 11.30am-2pm & 2.15-8pm Mon-Sat, to 2pm Sun), 1.5km southeast of the Hotel Conclave.

The 12344 Darjeeling Mail is the fastest of the four daily services to **Kolkata** (sleeper/3AC ₹264/695, 10 hours, departs 5.25pm), via Malda.

BORDER CROSSING – BANGLADESH, BHUTAN & NEPAL

To/From Bangladesh

A number of private agencies in Siliguri, including **Shyamoli** (🖉 9932628243; Hotel Central Plaza complex, Hill Cart Rd, 1km northwest of the central bus station, Mallagauri More), run a daily AC bus direct to Dhaka (₹950, 18 hours), departing at 1.30pm. You'll need to complete border formalities at Chengrabandha. Book a day or two in advance.

Buses also run every 45 minutes from the Tenzing Norgay Central Bus Terminal to Chengrabandha (₹55, 2½ hours) between 7am and 6pm. The border post is open from 8am to 6pm daily. From near the border post you can catch buses on to Rangpur, Bogra and Dhaka. Visas for Bangladesh can be obtained in Kolkata and New Delhi.

For further information, head to http://shop.lonelyplanet.com to purchase a downloadable PDF of the Dhaka chapter from Lonely Planet's *Bangladesh* guide.

To/From Bhutan

Bhutan Transport Services runs two daily buses from Sevoke Rd to Phuentsholing (₹75, departs 7.15am and noon), and there are many more local buses to Jaigon on the Indian side of the border, where you clear Indian immigration. Non-Indian nationals need visa clearance from a Bhutanese tour operator to enter Bhutan. See www.tourism.gov.bt and Lonely Planet's *Bhutan* guide for details.

To/From Nepal

For Nepal, local buses pass the Tenzing Norgay Central Bus Terminal on Hill Cart Rd every 15 minutes for the border town of Panitanki (₹20, one hour). Nearby shared jeeps to Kakarbhitta (₹80 to ₹100) are faster but only leave when full. The Indian border post in Panitanki is officially open 24 hours but the Nepali post in Kakarbhitta is open from 7am to 7pm. Onward from Kakarbhitta there are numerous buses to Kathmandu (17 hours) and other destinations. Bhadrapur Airport, 23km southwest of Kakarbhitta, has regular flights to Kathmandu (US$164) on **Yeti Airlines** (www.yetiairlines.com), **Buddha Air** (www.buddhaair.com) or **Agni Air** (www.agniair.com). Visas for Nepal can be obtained at the border (bring two passport photos).

The 12364 Haldibari Koaa SF Express is a better option for **Malda** (2nd class/chair ₹108/343, 3½ hours, departing 9.40am Wednesday, Friday and Sunday).

The 12505 North East Express is a fast service to **Delhi** (sleeper/3AC ₹458/1214, 27 hours, departs 5pm), via **Patna** (₹229/587, 10 hours); the 12435 Rajdhani Express is the fastest service to Delhi (2AC/3AC ₹2194/1735, 26 hours, departs 12.05pm).

Take the 12506 North East Express for **Guwahati** (sleeper/3AC ₹228/569, eight hours, departs 8.20am).

The toy train is currently not running from Siliguri, due to destroyed track near Dindaria. For the next few years the only option will be to drive to Kurseong and then catch the toy train on to Darjeeling.

❶ Getting Around

From the bus terminal to NJP train station a taxi/autorickshaw costs ₹200/100. Taxis/autorickshaws between Bagdogra Airport and Siliguri cost ₹350/200.

Jaldhapara Wildlife Sanctuary

◢ 03563 / ELEV 60M

This little-visited **sanctuary** (◢ 262239; www.jaldapara.com; Indian/foreigner ₹50/50, camera/video ₹50/500; ⊙ mid-Sep–mid-Jun) protects 114 sq km of lush forests and grasslands along the Torsa River and is a refuge for 150 Indian one-horned rhinoceros (*Rhinoceros unicornis*).

The best time to visit is mid-October to May, particularly March and April when wild elephants, deer and tigers (rarely seen) are attracted by new grass growth. Your best chance of spotting a rhino is on an **elephant ride** (Indian/foreigner per hr ₹200/600; ⊙ 5-8am), though these lumbering safaris are often booked out by the tourist lodges. Even if you are staying at Jaldaphara Tourist Lodge for a night you are not guaranteed a ride, as full occupancy is double that of their daily elephant quota. Weekdays offer the best chance.

Jeep safaris (4/8 passengers ₹1860/2260, 40% less for Indians) operate in the early morning and afternoon and stop at viewing platforms, but again these can be hard to arrange unless you are on a tour.

The West Bengal tourist offices in Kolkata and Siliguri organise weekend **tours** (per person Indian/foreigner ₹4300/5225; ⊙ departs 10am Sat, returns 5pm Sun) from Siliguri to Jaldhapara, which include an elephant ride, transport, accommodation at the Hollong Tourist Lodge and all meals.

Mithun of **Wild Planet Travel Desk** (◢ 9735028733; easthimalayan3@yahoo.com) and Hotel Relax can often book accommodation and elephant rides when no-one else can and is probably your best option for a DIY trip. Budget travellers should bear in mind that an hour-long elephant ride is probably going to end up costing a minimum US$40 per person, after all costs are added in.

Bring mosquito repellent.

🛏 Sleeping & Eating

The two lodges should be booked well in advance through the West Bengal Tourist Office in Siliguri, Darjeeling or Kolkata, or online at www.westbengaltourism.gov.in. The lodges don't take direct bookings.

Hotel Relax HOTEL $
(◢ 262304; Madarihat; d ₹500-900) The Relax is the best private budget option, opposite the Jaldhapara Tourist Lodge, with simple standard rooms and larger deluxe rooms with hot-water bathrooms. Meals are available.

Hollong Tourist Lodge JUNGLE LODGE $$
(◢ 262228; d ₹2000) This wooden forestry lodge right in the heart of the park is easily the best place to stay, though booking one of the six rooms can be a real challenge. You can spot animals right from the verandah and you are guaranteed a morning elephant ride. Book up to three months in advance.

Jaldhapara Tourist Lodge HOTEL $$
(◢ 262230; Madarihat; d ₹1800, with AC ₹2300-3500; ❄) This functional WBTDC hotel is just outside the park in Madarihat town and has rooms in wooden and concrete blocks or in new cottages. All meals are included in the room rates, so singles get a 25% discount.

❶ Getting There & Away

Jaldhapara is 124km east of Siliguri. Local buses run frequently from Siliguri to Madarihat (₹66, four hours) between 11.40am and 4.30pm. There are also slow but scenic mail trains (unreserved seat ₹19 to ₹38, three to four hours), leaving Siliguri Junction at 8.20am, 5.10pm and 6pm, returning from Madarihat at 6.05am, 7.50am and 1.30pm.

From Madarihat to the park headquarters at Hollong is 7km. A return taxi costs ₹500, including waiting time, plus you'll also have to pay the ₹200 vehicle entry fees.

Kurseong

☎ 0354 / POP 40,100 / ELEV 1460M

Kurseong, 32km south of Darjeeling, is the shy, often-overlooked little sister of the more glamourous Queen of the Hills further up the track. Its name derives from the Lepcha word *kurson-rip*, a reference to the small white orchid prolific in this area. Surrounded by manicured tea estates, it is also currently the southern terminus for the charming toy trains of the Darjeeling Himalayan Railway.

Hill Cart Rd (Tenzing Norgay Rd) – the noisy, traffic-choked main thoroughfare from Siliguri to Darjeeling – and its remarkably close shadow, the railway line, wind through town.

There are numerous good walks in the area, including one to Eagle's Crag (2km return) that affords splendid views down the Teesta Valley and the steamy plains to the south.

👁 Sights & Activities

Makaibari   TEA ESTATE,
(☎ 2330181; www.makaibari.com; Pankhabari Rd; ☉ Tue-Sat) Anyone interested in tea should visit this organic and biodynamic tea estate. The factory is open to visitors and in between the huge sorting and drying machines and the fields of green bushes you may just run into the owner, tea guru and local character Rajah Banerjee. Mornings are the best time to see the production process. Visits are free, or you can opt for a program of tea plucking, tasting and lunch in a local home-stay for ₹200.

The estate is 3km below Kurseong along Pankhabari Rd, and 1km below Cochrane Place. A taxi here costs ₹150, or it's a pleasant downhill walk (it's much steeper coming back so take a ₹10 shared taxi from Cochrane Place. En route, the lushly overgrown old graveyard at St Andrew's has poignant reminders of the tea-planter era.

Makaibari also runs a pioneering homestay and volunteer program (www.volmakaibari.org) from a separate office 50m below the main entrance. Volunteers can find placements in teaching, health and community projects.

🛏 Sleeping & Eating

Makaibari Homestays   HOMESTAY $
(☎ 9832447774; Makaibari Tea Estate; incl full board per person ₹700) This pioneering program aims to harness tourism to empower local women tea pickers. There are 21 family houses and more are planned in a new environmentally sustainable village below. Houses are simple but comfortable and families speak English. Activities on offer include tea picking and birdwatching trips. Contact Nayan Lama.

Kurseong Tourist Lodge   HOTEL $$
(☎ 2345608; Hill Cart Rd; d ₹1350-1686, restaurant mains ₹60-100) This old-fashioned, government-run lodge has inviting wood-lined rooms that feature valley views. The toy train whistles past the popular cafe, where you can snack on *momos* (Tibetan dumplings), or you can enjoy a meal at its scenic restaurant. Look for the much-photographed 'Hurry burry spoils the curry' traffic sign across the road.

★ **Cochrane Place**   BOUTIQUE HOTEL $$$
(☎ 2330703; www.imperialchai.com; 132 Pankhabari Rd; s/d from ₹2954/3545, ste ₹5370; @) With 360-degree views over tea plantations and the twinkling lights of Siliguri, this quirky, charming boutique hotel is a destination in its own right. The 31 rooms are individually decorated with divans and antiques come with either a view or a balcony. Delicious meals feature unique Anglo-Indian cuisine (think ginger pudding with tea sauce), making it a good lunch stop if you have your own transport. The hotel is wheelchair-friendly and can provide Bagdogra Airport and NJP train station pick-ups. It's worth budgeting an extra day to take in one of the excellent guided village and tea estate walks, topped off by a local-style stick massage or an expert tea tasting.

ⓘ Getting There & Away

Numerous share jeeps run to Darjeeling (₹60, 1½ hours) and Siliguri (₹60, 1½ hours), with 8am departures for Kalimpong (₹130, 3½ to four hours) and Mirik (₹70, 2½ hours).

The Darjeeling Himalayan Railway's toy train to Darjeeling (1st/2nd class ₹160/27, three hours) leaves at 7am and 3pm and takes twice as long as a shared jeep.

Darjeeling

☎ 0354 / POP 120,400 / ELEV 2135M

Spread in ribbons over a steep mountain ridge, surrounded by emerald-green tea plantations and with a backdrop of jagged white Himalayan peaks floating over distant clouds, the archetypal hill station of Darjeeling is rightly West Bengal's premier attraction. When you aren't gazing open-mouthed at Khangchendzonga (8598m), you can explore colonial-era architecture, visit Buddhist monasteries and spot snow leopards and red pandas at the nearby zoo. The steep narrow streets bustle with an array of Himalayan faces from Sikkim, Bhutan, Nepal and Tibet and when energies start to flag a good, steaming Darjeeling brew is never far away.

Most tourists visit after the monsoon (October and November) and during spring (mid-March to the end of May) when skies are dry, panoramas are clear and temperatures are pleasant. This is considered high season. Winters can be cold here, so bring an extra jumper if visiting from December to February.

Darjeeling sprawls over a west-facing slope in a confusing web of interconnecting roads and steep flights of steps. Expect an uphill hike to your hotel if arriving at the train station or jeep stand. The two main squares are Chowrasta, near the top of town, and Clubside Junction, which are linked by pedestrianised Nehru Rd (aka The Mall), the main shopping street. Hill Cart Rd (aka Tenzing Norgay Rd) runs the length of the bustling lower bazaar and is Darjeeling's major vehicle thoroughfare.

History

This area belonged to the Buddhist chogyals (kings) of Sikkim until 1780, when it was annexed by the invading Gurkhas from Nepal. The East India Company gained control of the region in 1816 then returned most of the lands back to Sikkim in exchange for British control over any future border disputes.

During one such dispute in 1828, two British officers stumbled across the Dorje Ling monastery, on a tranquil forested ridge, and passed word to Kolkata (Calcutta) that it would be a perfect site for a sanatorium; they were sure to have also mentioned its strategic military importance in the region. The chogyal of Sikkim (still grateful for the return of his kingdom) agreed to lease the uninhabited land to the East India Company for the annual fee of £3000. In 1835 the hill station of Darjeeling (Dorje Ling) was born and the first tea bushes were planted that same year. By 1857 the population of Darjeeling had reached 10,000, mainly because of a massive influx of Gurkha tea labourers from Nepal.

Since Independence, the Gurkhas have become the main political force in Darjeeling and friction with the state government led to calls for a separate state of Gorkhaland in the 1980s. In 1986 violence and riots orchestrated by the Gurkha National Liberation Front (GNLF) brought Darjeeling to a standstill, leading to the Darjeeling Gorkha Hill Council (DGHC) being given a large measure of autonomy from the state government. Calls for full secession have resurfaced in recent years, leading to the replacement in 2012 of the DGHC by the Gorkhaland Territorial Administration (GTA). The political situation remains calm at the time of research but tensions (and strikes) could resurface so keep an eye on the news.

⊙ Sights

Tiger Hill   VIEWPOINT

To watch the dawn light break over a spectacular 250km stretch of Himalayan horizon, including Everest (8848m), Lhotse (8501m) and Makalu (8475m) to the far west, rise early and jeep out to Tiger Hill (2590m), 11km south of Darjeeling, above Ghum. The skyline is dominated by Khangchendzonga ('great five-peaked snow fortress'; 8598m), India's highest peak and the world's third-highest mountain (until 1852 it was thought to be the world's highest). On either side of the main massif are Kabru (7338m), Jannu (7710m) and Pandim (6691m), all serious peaks in their own right.

Seeing the sunrise over the Himalaya from here has become a major tourist attraction, with hundreds of jeeps leaving Darjeeling for Tiger Hill every morning at 4am. At the summit you can either pay ₹10 to stand in the pavilion grounds or warm up in one of the heated lounges in the pavilion (₹20 to ₹40). It can be a real bunfight, even outside of the high season, with dawn traffic jams snaking down the hillside and crowds of hundreds jostling for the best viewing spots.

Organised sunrise trips (usually with a detour to Batastia Loop on the way back) can be booked through a travel agency or directly with jeep drivers at the Clubside taxi stand. Return trips cost ₹800 to ₹1000 per vehicle.

Observatory Hill   SACRED SITE

Sacred to both Buddhists and Hindus, this hill was the site of the original Dorje Ling monastery that gave the town its name.

Darjeeling

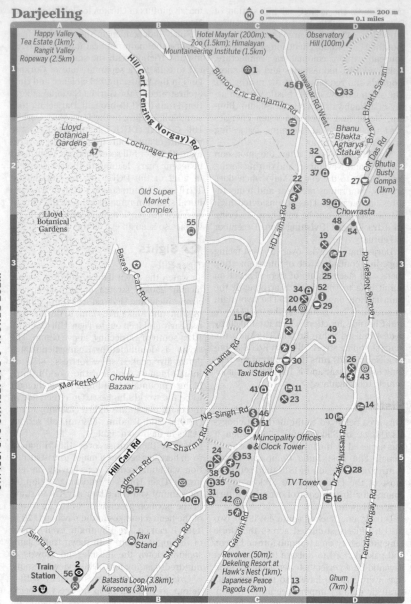

0 — 200 m
0 — 0.1 miles

Today, devotees come to a temple in a small cave to honour Mahakala, a Buddhist deity and wrathful form of the Hindu god Shiva. The summit is marked by several shrines, a flurry of colourful prayer flags and the ringing notes from numerous devotional bells. A path leading up to the hill through giant Japanese cedars starts about 300m along Bhanu Bhakta Sarani from Chowrasta; watch out for marauding monkeys. Disappointingly, there are no mountain views.

Darjeeling

◎ Sights
1 Bengal Natural History Museum	C1
2 Darjeeling Himalayan Railway	A6
3 Dhirdham Mandir	A6
Himalayan Tibet Museum	(see 18)

◎ Activities, Courses & Tours
4 Adventures Unlimited	D4
5 Himalayan Travels	C6
6 Manjushree Centre of Tibetan Culture	C5
7 Samsara Tours, Travels & Treks	C5
8 Somewhere Over the Rainbow Treks & Tours	C2
9 Trek Mate	C4

◎ Sleeping
10 Andy's Guesthouse	D5
11 Dekeling Hotel	C4
12 Elgin	C2
13 Hotel Aliment	C6
14 Hotel New Galaxy	D4
15 Hotel Seven Seventeen	C4
16 Hotel Tranquillity	D5
17 Olde (Main) Bellevue Hotel	D3
18 Tibet Home	C5
Windamere Hotel	(see 33)

◎ Eating
Dekeva's	(see 23)
19 Footsteps	D3
20 Glenary's	C3
21 Hasty Tasty	C4
22 Hot Pizza Place	C2
23 Kunga	C4
Lunar Restaurant	(see 11)
24 Park Restaurant	C5
25 Shangri-La	D3
26 Sonam's Kitchen	D4

◎ Drinking & Nightlife
27 Café Coffee Day	D2
Café Coffee Day	(see 40)
28 Gaddi's Cafe	D5
29 Glenary's	D3
30 House of Tea	C4
31 Joey's Pub	C5
32 Sunset Lounge	D2
33 Windamere Hotel	D1

◎ Shopping
34 Das Studios	D3
35 Dorjee Himalayan Artefacts	C5
36 Hayden Hall	C5
37 Life & Leaf Fair Trade Shop	D2
38 Nathmull's Tea Room	C5
39 Oxford Book & Stationery Company	D2
40 Rink Mall	B5
41 Rope	C4

◎ Information
42 Compuset Centre	C5
43 Cyber Planet	D4
44 Glenary's	C3
45 Gorkhland Terriorial Administration (GTA) Tourist Reception Centre	C1
46 ICICI Bank ATM	C5
47 Lloyd Botanical Gardens Entrance	A2
48 Pineridge Travels	D3
49 Planter's Hospital	D4
50 Poddar's	C5
51 Ridhi Siddhi	C5
52 Sikkim Tourist Office Darjeeling	D3
53 State Bank of India	C5
State Bank of India ATM	(see 37)

◎ Transport
54 Air India	D3
55 Chowk Bazaar Bus & Jeep Station	B3
56 Darjeeling Himalayan Railway (Toy Train)	A6
57 Darjeeling Transport Corporation	B5

Bhutia Busty Gompa
MONASTERY

This temple originally stood on Observatory Hill, but was rebuilt in its present location by the chogyals of Sikkim in the 19th century. It houses fine murals depicting the life of Buddha, and Khangchendzonga provides a spectacular backdrop. To get here, follow CR Das Rd steeply downhill for five minutes from Chowrasta, past a trinity of colourful Buddhist rock carvings. Climbing back up is a 10-minute slog.

Himalayan Tibet Museum
MUSEUM

(www.himalayantibetmuseum.org; Gandhi Rd) This new museum on the ground floor of the Manjushree Centre of Tibetan Culture is an introduction to Tibetan culture, from its 3D geographical map of the plateau to the sand mandala (visual meditation aid) signifying the nature of impermanence. It's scheduled for completion in 2013, funds allowing.

Japanese Peace Pagoda
BUDDHIST TEMPLE

(☺ puja 4.30-7am & 4.30-6.30pm) Perched on a hillside at the end of AJC Bose Rd, this gleaming white pagoda is one of more than

70 pagodas built around the world by the Japanese Buddhist Nipponzan Myohoji organisation. During the drumming *puja* (prayers) visitors are offered a hand drum and encouraged to join in the fun. It's a pleasant, gentle 30-minute walk from Clubside along Gandhi and AJC Bose Rds, past the implausible-sounding Institute of Astroparticle Physics and Space Science.

Padmaja Naidu
Himalayan Zoological Park ZOO
(☑ 2253709; www.pnhzp.gov.in; admission incl Himalayan Mountaineering Institute Indian/foreigner ₹40/100; ☉ 8.30am-5pm Fri-Wed, ticket counter closes 4pm) This zoo, one of India's best, was established in 1958 to study, conserve and preserve Himalayan fauna. Housed within the rocky and forested environment are Himalayan megafauna such as Himalayan bears, clouded leopards, red pandas and Tibetan wolves. The zoo, and its attached snow-leopard breeding centre (closed to the public), are home to the world's largest single captive population of snow leopards.

The zoo is a pleasant 20-minute downhill walk down from Chowrasta along Jawahar Rd West; alternatively, take a share jeep (₹10, about 10 minutes) from the Chowk Bazaar bus/jeep station, or hire a taxi (₹200).

Himalayan
Mountaineering Institute MUSEUM
(HMI; ☑ 2254087; www.himalayanmountaineeringinstitute.com; admission incl zoo Indian/foreigner ₹40/100; ☉ 8.30am-4.30pm Fri-Wed) Tucked away within the grounds of the zoo, this prestigious mountaineering institute was founded in 1954 and has provided training for some of India's leading mountaineers. Within the complex is the **Mountaineering Museum**, with fascinating details of the 1922 and 1924 Everest expeditions, both of which set off from Darjeeling. Look for the Carl Zeiss telescope presented by Adolf Hitler to the head of the Nepali army.

Just beside the museum, near the spot where Tenzing Norgay was cremated, stands the **Tenzing statue**. The intrepid Everest summiteer lived in Darjeeling for most of his life and was the director of the institute for many years.

Rangit Valley Ropeway CABLE CAR
(return ticket child/adult ₹75/150; ☉ 10am-2pm, closed 19th of every month) This scenic ropeway reopened in 2012, after a fatal accident halted operations in 2003. The 40-minute ride takes you from North Point down to the Takvar Valley tea estate, gliding over manicured tea bushes that from this perspective look like giant broccoli. Get here early if you want to explore the village and tea plantation.

Tibetan Refugee
Self-Help Centre HANDICRAFTS WORKSHOP
(Lebong Cart Rd; ☉ 9am-4.30pm Mon-Sat) 🖉 Established in 1959, this refugee centre comprises a home for the aged, a school, an orphanage, a clinic, a gompa and craft workshops that produce carpets, woodcarvings, leather work and woollen items. There's also an interesting, politically charged pho-

---

ⓘ SEEING THE SIGHTS IN DARJEELING

Darjeeling's sights are quite spread out and road transport is a bit of a hassle so you'll make your life easier by visiting certain sights together.

One excellent idea is to take the toy train to Ghum and then spend the morning/day visiting the monasteries there before wandering back to Darjeeling along quiet hill Cart Rd, via the monastery of Alu Bari (1½ hours). Despite the lack of mountain views this also makes a nice cycling route.

If you can't face a dawn trip to Tiger Hill, an early-morning stroll around Bhanu Bhakta Sarani, which runs from Chowrasta Sq around the north side of Observatory Hill, offers several stunning viewpoints. Combine the stroll with a visit to down to Bhutia Busty Monastery or up to Observatory Hill.

One good half-day itinerary is to walk out to the zoo and mountaineering institute, then continue around the hill on the road above busy Hill Cart Rd to the Rangit Valley Ropeway. From here take a shared minivan from North Point back to Darjeeling, getting off at Happy Valley Tea Estate, and then walk the shortcut footpath to the Chowk Bazaar jeep stand via Lloyd's Botanical Garden. Alternatively, walk 30 minutes from the ropeway along Lebong Cart Rd to the Tibetan Refugee Self-Help Centre and hike back steeply uphill to Chowrasta via Bhutia Busty Monastery.

tographic exhibition portraying the early years of the Tibetan refugees in Darjeeling.

Visitors are welcome to wander through the workshops. The handicrafts are for sale in the showroom (p504), where proceeds go straight back into the Tibetan community.

The quickest way to reach the centre is to walk steeply downhill from the north side of Bhanu Bhakta Sarani; take the alley down beside the Hotel Dolphin. To return to Chowrasta take a side path 10 minutes to the Bhutia Busty Gompa and climb back uphill from there. A chartered taxi via North Point costs around ₹400/600 one way/return.

Happy Valley Tea Estate   TEA ESTATE
(Pamphawati Gurungni Rd; ⊙8am-4pm Tue-Sun) This 1854 tea estate below Hill Cart Rd is worth visiting, especially when the plucking and processing are in progress (March to November). An employee will guide you through the aromatic factory and its withering, rolling, fermenting and drying processes, explaining how green, black and white teas all come from the same leaf. Take the marked turn-off about 1km northwest of town on Hill Cart Rd.

Lloyd Botanical Gardens   BOTANICAL GARDENS
(⌨2252358; admission free; ⊙8am-4.30pm) These pleasant gardens contain an impressive collection of Himalayan plants, most famously orchids and rhododendrons. Follow the signs along Lochnagar Rd from the Chowk Bazaar bus/jeep station, until the hum of cicadas replaces the honking of jeeps at the main entrance. A map is posted at the office at the top of the park.

Batastia Loop   MONUMENT
If you're travelling on the toy train, or walking back from Tiger Hill, look out for this famous railway loop and the **Gorkha war memorial** (admission ₹50; ⊙dawn-dusk). Some tours stop here after the sunrise trip at Tiger Hill; the views are almost as good, and the atmosphere much more serene.

Ghum   MONASTERIES
The junction of Ghum, 7km from Darjeeling, is home to a number of colourful Buddhist monasteries. You can get here by toy train (₹21), shared taxi (₹15) or chartered taxi (₹300 one way).

Yiga Choling Gompa (Ghum; camera per photo ₹10), the region's most famous monastery, has wonderful old murals and is home to 30 monks of the Gelugpa school. Built

in 1850, it enshrines a 5m-high statue of Jampa (Maitreya, or 'Future Buddha') and 300 beautifully bound Tibetan texts. It's just west of Ghum, about a 10-minute walk off Hill Cart Rd.

Other gompas of interest nearby include the fortress-style **Sakya Guru Gompa**, which has *puja* between 5.30am and 7.30am (useful if returning from a dawn visit to Tiger Hill). The active **Samten Choling Gompa**, just downhill, has the largest Buddha statue in West Bengal, a memorial chorten (stupa) dedicated to German mystic Lama Govinda and even a small cafe. All three gompas are within 10 minutes' walk of each other on Hill Cart Rd.

About halfway between Ghum and Darjeeling is the huge **Druk Sangak Choling Gompa**, also known as Dali Gompa, inaugurated by the Dalai Lama in 1993. Known for its vibrant frescoes, it is home to 300 Himalayan monks who study philosophy, literature, astronomy, meditation, dance and music. Come for prayers between 4pm and 6pm.

Bengal Natural History Museum   MUSEUM
(Bishop Eric Benjamin Rd; adult ₹10; ⊙9am-4.30pm) Established in 1903, this minor sight houses a moth-eaten collection of Himalayan and Bengali species, hidden away in a compound just off Bishop Eric Benjamin Rd. The giant leeches and horrific baby animals pickled in jars are guaranteed to provoke a shudder.

Dhirdham Mandir   HINDU TEMPLE
Darjeeling's most conspicuous Hindu temple is a replica of the famous Pashupatinath Temple in Kathmandu. It's easy to find – just below the Darjeeling train station. There's a good view over Darjeeling from its grounds.

🏃 Activities

White-Water Rafting   RAFTING
The GTA Tourist Reception Centre can book scenic family-orientated rafting trips on the Teesta. Trips cost around ₹450 per person, with a minimum of four people. Transport will cost another ₹2000 per jeep, or take a shared jeep for Gangtok and get off at the **Chitrey Wayside Inn** (⌨9434862561), 1.5km above Teesta bazaar. The rapids are mostly Grade II to III and dam construction has limited runs in recent years. The best times for rafting are September to November and March to June.

Pony Rides
HORSE RIDING

From Chowrasta, children can take a ride around Observatory Hill for ₹200, or through tea estates to visit a monastery for ₹400 per hour.

Courses

Manjushree Centre
of Tibetan Culture
LANGUAGE

(☎2252977; www.manjushreetibcentre.org; 12 Ghandi Rd; 2-/3-/6-month courses US$180/260/380, plus registration US$30; ☺mid-Mar–mid-Dec) Beginner and advanced lessons in written and spoken Tibetan are offered at this Tibetan cultural centre, with beginner courses starting every two months. Students can lodge with local Tibetan families.

Himalayan
Mountaineering Institute
MOUNTAINEERING

(HMI; ☎2254087; www.himalayanmountaineering institute.com) The HMI runs 15-day adventure courses (Indian/foreigner ₹2000/US$325) in January and February, which include climbing, jungle survival and canoeing, for those aged between 18 and 30. There are also 28-day basic and advanced mountaineering courses (Indian/foreigner ₹4000/US$650), from March to May and September to December. Some courses are for women only. Foreigners should apply directly to the centre at least three months in advance.

Tours

The GTA Tourist Reception Centre, taxi stands and travel agencies offer a variety of tours around Darjeeling, usually including the zoo, Himalayan Mountaineering Institute, Tibetan Refugee Self-Help Centre and several viewpoints. Taxis can be hired for custom tours for ₹800 per half-day.

Sleeping

Only a small selection of Darjeeling's many hotels is mentioned here. The main backpacker enclave is Dr Zakir Hussain Rd, which follows the highest ridge in Darjeeling, so be prepared for a hike to the best budget accommodation.

Prices given are for the high season (October to early December and mid-March to June), when it's wise to book ahead. In the low season prices can drop by 50%. A recently introduced rule requires foreigners to present a passport photo when checking in to a hotel, so carry some with you until this bemusing rule is withdrawn.

★ Andy's Guesthouse
GUESTHOUSE $

(☎2253125; 102 Dr Zakir Hussain Rd; d ₹500-600) This simple, spotless, stone-walled place has airy, carpeted rooms, a comfy common area and a rooftop terrace with a great view. Mrs Gurung provides a friendly boarding-house atmosphere but runs a tight ship, with dozens of post-it notes admonishing the guests to follow the many house rules, including no smoking and 'complete silence after 9.30pm'. There's a good laundry service.

Hotel Aliment
HOTEL $

(☎2255068; alimentwe@sify.com; 40 Dr Zakir Hussain Rd; s ₹330, d ₹660-880; @) A budget travellers' favourite, with a good top-floor restaurant (and cold beer), lending library, helpful owners and wood-lined rooms. The upstairs rooms (₹600) have a TV and valley views. All the double rooms have geysers, but they only operate between 6pm and 8pm. The singles are a big step down in quality.

Hotel Tranquillity
HOTEL $

(☎2257678; hoteltranquillity@yahoo.co.in; Dr Zakir Hussain Rd; d ₹550-660; ☎) This good-value place is sparkling clean, with 24-hour hot water, nice lobby seating and small but neat baby-blue rooms. The helpful owner is a local schoolteacher, and can provide all kinds of info about the area. Wi-fi costs ₹100 per day.

Hotel New Galaxy
HOTEL $

(☎2252077; Dr Zakir Hussain Rd; s ₹300-450, d ₹500) A clean, simple budget option almost opposite Andy's, with wood-panelled walls, smallish rooms and hot-water buckets in the cheaper rooms. Try for room 104 – it has the best views across to the mountains. If it's full, try across the road.

★ Dekeling Hotel
GUESTHOUSE $$

(☎2254159; www.dekeling.com; 51 Gandhi Rd; d ₹1644-2935, without bathroom ₹935; @☎) Spotless Dekeling is full of charming touches such as coloured diamond-pane windows, a traditional *bukhari* (wood-burning heater) in the cosy and sociable lounge-library, wood panelling and sloping-attic ceilings, plus some of the best views in town. Tibetan owners Sangay and Norbu are the perfect hosts. The whole place is a perfect combination of clean and homey, right down to the adorable dog, Drolma.

Revolver
BOUTIQUE HOTEL $$

(☎2253711; www.revolver.in; 110 Gandhi Rd; r ₹1174-1409; ☎) This Beatles-themed hotel is a must for fans. The five small but stylish rooms are each named after one of the Fab Four (plus Brian Epstein), so you can choose your favourite moptop (John fills up first; no-one likes Ringo). The hotel is chock-a-block with Beatles memorabilia, including 'Beatles Rock Band' on the resident PlayStation 3. The downstairs restaurant serves good coffee and interesting Naga set meals (₹80 to ₹110). It's certainly well thought out but it could perhaps do with a bit more old-fashioned family warmth. The entrance is easily missed behind the Union Church.

Hotel Seven Seventeen HOTEL $$

(2255099; www.hotel717.com; 26 HD Lama Rd; main block s/d ₹1878/2348, deluxe r ₹2935-3522;) A friendly Tibetan-themed place on the edge of the bazaar with a good restaurant and clean, fresh rooms. The older annexe (single/double ₹1400/1700) is cheaper but darker and less cheery.

Olde (Main) Bellevue Hotel HOTEL $$

(2254178; www.darjeelinghotel.co.uk; Chowrasta; budget/deluxe d ₹1250/1950) Rooms at this 19th-century hotel are spacious and fairly well maintained and have a great location, though the service is sleepy at best. Opt for a room in the creaky chalet-style upper building, as these have a lot more colonial-era charm. Don't confuse this with the next-door Bellevue Hotel, run by a feuding brother.

Tibet Home HOTEL $$

(2252977; 12 Gandhi Rd; r ₹1870) Clean, bright and modern rooms make this a solid, central option, with profits going to the attached Manjushree Centre of Tibetan Culture. There are great views from the rooftop.

★Windamere Hotel HERITAGE HOTEL $$$

(2254041; www.windamerehotel.com; Jawahar Rd West; incl full board s/d from ₹9133/11,807; @) This quaint, rambling relic of the British Raj on Observatory Hill offers Darjeeling's most atmospheric digs. The charming colonial-era Ada Villa was once a boarding house for British tea planters, and the well-tended grounds are spacious with lots of pleasant seating areas. The comfortable rooms, fireplaces and hot-water bottles offer just the right measures of comfort and fustiness; a bit like staying at a rich aunt's house. It's a particularly great place to spend Christmas. Keep your eyes peeled for the Jan Morris poem in the tearoom.

Elgin HERITAGE HOTEL $$$

(2257226; www.elginhotels.com; HD Lama Rd; s/d/ste incl half board ₹8806/9159/10,450; @)

THE TOY TRAIN

The **Darjeeling Himalayan Railway**, known affectionately as the toy train, is one of the few hill railways still operating in India. The panting train made its first journey along its precipice-topping, 2ft-wide tracks in September 1881 and these days passes within feet of local storefronts as it weaves in and out of the main road, bringing traffic to a standstill and tooting its whistle incessantly for almost the entire trip. The train has been a Unesco World Heritage Site since 1999.

Services on the line have been in flux since 2009, when landslides destroyed a section of track. Services to and from NJP station are not expected to resume for the next couple of years, which leaves only the two daily diesel services to Kurseong via Ghum:

TRAIN NO	DARJEELING	GHUM	KURSEONG
52544	10.15am	10.45am	1.10pm
52588	4pm	4.30pm	6.40pm
TRAIN NO	**KURSEONG**	**GHUM**	**DARJEELING**
52587	7am	9.15am	9.45am
52545	3pm	5.20pm	5.50pm

During the high season there are also joy rides (₹270) that leave Darjeeling at 8am, 10.40am, 1.20pm and 4pm for a two-hour steam-powered return trip. The service pauses for 10 minutes at the scenic Batasia Loop and then stops for 20 minutes in Ghum, India's highest railway station, to visit the small **railway museum** (admission ₹20; ⊙10am-1pm & 2-4pm). Enthusiasts can see the locomotives up close in the shed across the road from Darjeeling station. For a budget ride take the 10.15am diesel passenger service to Ghum (₹21).

Book at least a day or two ahead at the train station (p506) or online at www.irctc.co.in. For more on the service and efforts to maintain it, see www.dhrs.org.

TEA TOURISM

After days of sipping teas, nibbling cucumber sandwiches and hiking tea estates in the name of thorough research, the following are our best tips on where to indulge in Darjeeling's most famous export.

Visit The easiest places to learn about tea production are Makaibari Estate (p494) in Kurseong and Happy Valley (p499) outside Darjeeling. March to May is the busiest time, but occasional plucking also occurs from June to November. Outside of high season there's no plucking on Sunday, which means most of the machinery isn't working on Monday.

Stay Overnight with a tea pickers' family at a **homestay** (☑9832447774; www.volmakaibari.org; per person incl food ₹600) at Makaibari Estate and you'll get to join your hosts for a morning's work in the tea bushes. Pick your own leaves, watch them being processed and then return home with a batch of your very own hand-plucked Darjeeling tea. How's that for a personalised gift! If you're in the mood for splurging, accommodation doesn't get any more exclusive than top-end **Glenburn** (www.glenburnteaestate.com; s/d ₹14,500/23,000), between Darjeeling and Kurseong, a working tea estate/resort that boasts five staff for every guest. A stay at Glenburn is rumoured to have given director Wes Anderson inspiration for his film *The Darjeeling Limited*.

Drink Where better to sip a cup of Darjeeling tea? You can sample different grades of black, white and green teas by the cup at Sunset Lounge and House of Tea. The pukka afternoon tea at the **Windamere Hotel** (₹450; ⊙4-6pm) is a joy for aficionados of all things colonial, with shortcake, scones, cheese and pickle sandwiches and brews from the Castleton Tea Estate.

A grand yet friendly hotel full of classy ambience, the Elgin is more modern and formal than the Windamere but has less of a sense of history. The restaurant is elegant, as is the great bar and small library, and the small-but-lovely garden terrace is the perfect place to relax over a beer (₹185) or high tea (₹370, 4pm to 6pm). The cosy 'attic room' underneath the dripping eaves is especially charming.

**Dekeling Resort
at Hawk's Nest** HERITAGE HOTEL $$$
(☑2253298; www.dekeling.com; 2 AJC Bose Rd; d ₹3899-4462; ﹫) Run by the good people at Dekeling, this is a quieter, more exclusive place, 1km outside of Darjeeling en route to the Japanese Pagoda. The four 130-year-old, colonial-style two-room suites come with antique touches and fireplaces and there's a nice sunny terrace. It's a great escape from Darjeeling's increasingly noisy centre. Five new mountain-facing super-deluxe rooms were added in 2013.

Mayfair Darjeeling HOTEL $$$
(☑2256376; www.mayfairhotels.com; Jawahar Rd West; d incl breakfast & dinner from ₹11,742; ﹫) Originally a maharaja's summer palace but renovated to within an inch of its life, this plush choice sits among manicured gardens and a bizarre collection of kitschy

sculptures. The outside and common areas don't have quite the charm of the Elgin, but the plush rooms are well decorated and many have balconies. Soft carpets and coal fires add to the warm welcome, the bar has fine sunset views and the cosy library has a choice of DVDs for a rainy day. The children's playroom makes it good for families.

 Eating

Most restaurants close by 8pm or 9pm. Tax will add on 13.5% to most bills.

Sonam's Kitchen CONTINENTAL $
(142 Dr Zakir Hussain Rd; mains ₹80-120; ⊙8am-2.30pm & 5.30-8pm Mon-Sat, to 2pm Sun) Providing an island of real brewed coffee in an ocean of tea, Sonam serves up lovely breakfasts, French toast, pancakes, fresh soups (nettle in season) and pasta; the deliciously chunky wholemeal sandwiches can be packed to go for picnics. It's a tiny place so try not to linger during mealtimes.

Kunga TIBETAN $
(51 Gandhi Rd; mains ₹90-120) Kunga is a cosy wood-panelled place run by a friendly Tibetan family, strong on noodles and *momos*, with excellent juice, fruit museli curd and *shabhaley* (Tibetan pies).

Dekeva's
TIBETAN $

(51 Gandhi Rd; mains ₹80-120) Next door to Kunga, this is a similarly good place, offering Tibetan butter tea, *tsampa* (roast barley flour), good Chinese dishes and a range of noodles for connoisseurs who can tell their *thenthug* (Tibetan noodles) from their *sogthug* (different Tibetan noodles).

Hasty Tasty
INDIAN $

(Nehru Rd; mains ₹40-80, thali ₹95-130) There's nothing fancy at this vegetarian self-service canteen, but the open kitchen churns out great paneer *masala dosas* (lentil-flour pancake filled with vegetables) and several types of veg *thali* (set meals). It's tasty but not hasty, so don't be in a hurry.

Lunar Restaurant
INDIAN $$

(51 Gandhi Rd; mains ₹90-150) This bright and clean space just below Dekeling Hotel is perhaps the best vegetarian Indian restaurant in town, with good service and great views from the large windows. The *masala dosas* come with yummy dried fruit and nuts.

Hot Pizza Place
ITALIAN $$

(HD Lama Rd; pizza ₹120-215) A cramped but sociable one-table pizza joint with excellent French-accented pizza, pasta, panini and salads. Come at breakfast for such rarities as bacon, merguez (spicy beef sausage) and Nepali cheese. Expect to wait 15 minutes for a pizza.

Footsteps
MULTICUISINE $$

(19 Nehru Rd; mains ₹160-240; ⊘7.30am-9.30pm) There's a refreshing focus on healthy options at this new place, with gluten-free baked goods and brown breads on the menu. The best options are the all-day breakfasts, particularly the waffles and pancakes, but there are also good grilled sandwiches and dinner *thalis*. The baked cookies and muffins are served with a Darjeeling brew as a range of afternoon set teas.

Park Restaurant
INDIAN, THAI $$

(☑2255270; 41 Laden La Rd; mains ₹85-180) The intimate Park is deservedly very popular for its tasty North Indian curries (great chicken tikka masala!) and surprisingly authentic Thai dishes, including small but tasty *tom kha gai* (coconut chicken soup) and spicy green papaya salad. Grab a seat early or make a reservation. The tables are a little too closely packed for our liking.

Shangri-La
INDIAN $$

(Nehru Rd; mains ₹120-180) This classy modern bar-restaurant near the top of the Mall offers an upmarket version of the usual Indian/Chinese/Continental food mix in stylish surrounds, with sleek wooden floors, clean tablecloths and roaring fires in winter. There are also a couple of stylish hotel rooms upstairs (double ₹3000).

Glenary's
MULTICUISINE $$

(Nehru Rd; mains ₹100-225; ⊘noon-9pm, later in high season) This elegant restaurant atop the famous bakery and cafe receives mainly rave reviews: of note are the Continental sizzlers, Chinese dishes, tandoori specials and veg gratin (good if you're off spicy food). The wooden floors, linen tablecloths and fabulous tin roof just add to the classy atmosphere.

🍷 Drinking

Glenary's
TEAHOUSE

(Nehru Rd; small pot ₹45-75, pastries ₹15-35; ⊘8am-8pm; 🛜) Below the restaurant, this teahouse and bakery has massive windows and good views – order your tea, select a cake, grab your book and sink into some wicker. It's a good place to grab breakfast.

Café Coffee Day
CAFE

(coffee from ₹60, ⊘8am-8pm) It's almost heresy to drink espresso in Darjeeling but if the caffeine calls you, this reliable chain has locations at the Rink Mall and at Chowrasta (coffee from ₹60; ⊘8am-8pm), the latter with a fine sunny terrace.

House of Tea
TEAHOUSE

(Nehru Rd; tea ₹30-50; ⊘9.30am-8pm) Sit and sip a range of brewed teas from several local Goodricke estates before purchasing a package of your favourite leaves.

Sunset Lounge
TEAHOUSE

(20 Chowrasta; cup of tea ₹25-130; ⊘9am-8pm; 🛜) This tearoom run by Nathmull's Tea offers aficionados a range of white, green and black teas by the cup, with baked treats, fine valley views and wi-fi.

Bars

The top-end hotels all have classy bars; the Windamere is the most atmospheric place to kick back with an early-evening G&T (₹225).

Joey's Pub
PUB

(SM Das Rd; beer ₹150; ⊘11am-10pm) If your preferred beverage comes in a pint not a pot, this long-standing pub near the post office is a great place to strike up conversations with other travellers. It has sports on TV, cold beer, and hot toddys in the winter.

Gaddi's Cafe
BAR

(Dr Zakir Hussain Rd; 📞) Backpacker-friendly Gaddi's is the only place in town that has a pulse after 9pm, with live music on the weekend and open mike and movie nights during the week. The food runs to house-made ravioli and decent breakfasts (mains ₹150 to ₹200) with Lavazza coffee.

🔒 Shopping

Nathmull's Tea Room
TEA

(www.nathmulltea.com; Laden La Rd; ⏰ 10am-8pm Mon-Sat, daily high season) Darjeeling tea is some of the finest tea in the world and Nathmull's is the best place to pick up some, with over 50 varieties. Expect to pay ₹80 to ₹150 per 100g for a decent tea and up to ₹2000 per 100g for the finest flushes. You can ask for a tasting, which will be expertly brewed, and you can also buy attractive teapots, strainers and cosies. The Sarda family has run the business for 80 years and are very knowledgeable.

Tibetan Refugee Self-Help Centre
CARPETS

(📇 2252552; www.tibetandarj.yolasite.com; carpet incl shipping US$216) 🍃 This centre makes gorgeous Tibetan carpets to order, if you don't mind waiting around six months for one to be made. Choose from the catalogue and they will ship the finished carpet to your home address.

Hayden Hall
HANDICRAFTS

(www.haydenhall.org; Laden La Rd; ⏰ 9am-6pm) 🍃 Sells Tibetan-style yak wool carpets as part of its charitable work (₹6000 for a 1m by 1.8m carpet) and offers shipping. There are also good knitwear items and bags made by local women.

Dorjee Himalayan Artefacts
HANDICRAFTS

(Laden La Rd) This tiny Aladdin's cave is crammed full of Himalayan knick-knacks, from Tibetan *gau* (amulets) to cast Buddhas and silver prayer wheels. Walking in through the door is like entering a scene from Kipling's novel *Kim*.

Life & Leaf Fair Trade Shop
HANDICRAFTS

(www.lifeandleaf.org; Chowrasta) 🍃 Supports local artisans and environmental projects through the sale of organic honey and tea

sourced from local small farmers, plus jute bags and Assamese silk stoles.

Oxford Book & Stationery Company
BOOKS

(Chowrasta; ⏰ 9.30am-7.30pm Mon-Sat, daily high season) The best bookshop in Darjeeling, selling a good selection of novels and Himalayan-related titles.

Das Studios
PHOTOGRAPHY

(Nehru Rd; ⏰ 9.30am-7.30pm Mon-Fri, to 2.30pm Sat, daily in high season) Digital photo accessories, printing and passport pics (six for ₹60). The reprinted 19th-century photographs make for a great souvenir (₹450); ask to look at the catalogue.

Rope
OUTDOOR GEAR

(NB Singh Rd) An unexpected find in the bazaar just below Clubside, this shop stocks quality imported gear alongside the Chinese knock-offs, including backpacks, stoves and trek boots.

ℹ️ Information

EMERGENCY

Police assistance booth (Chowrasta)
Sadar Police Station (📇 2254422; Market Rd)

INTERNET ACCESS

There are dozens of internet cafes around town; all generally charge ₹30 per hour.
Compuset Centre (Gandhi Rd; ⏰ 8am-8pm; 📞) Does printing and will burn photos to a CD/DVD, but doesn't offer Skype.
Cyber Planet (Dr Zakir Hussain Rd; ⏰ 8am-10pm) Opposite Sonam's Kitchen.
Glenary's (The Mall; 📞) Most convenient to the Mall and has wi-fi.

MEDICAL SERVICES

Planter's Hospital (D&DMA Nursing Home; 📇 2254327; Nehru Rd) The best private hospital.

MONEY

ICICI Bank ATM (Laden La Rd) Accepts most international bank and credit cards.
Poddar's (📇 2252841; Laden La Rd; ⏰ 9.30am-8pm) Better rates, longer hours and shorter queues than the State Bank next door; changes most currencies and travellers cheques at no commission. It accepts credit cards and is a Western Union agent. It's inside a clothing store.
Ridhi Siddhi (Laden La Rd; ⏰ 9.30am-8.30pm) Changes cash at good rates with no commission.
State Bank of India (Laden La Rd; ⏰ 10am-2pm & 3-4pm Mon-Fri, to 1pm Sat) Changes cash US dollars, euros and pounds sterling, plus US-dollar Amex travellers cheques, with a

commission of ₹100 per transaction. It has an adjacent ATM, another in Chowrasta.

POST
Main post office (Laden La Rd; ⊙9am-5pm Mon-Fri, 9am-1pm Sat)

SIKKIM TRAVEL PERMIT
Sikkim Tourist Office Darjeeling
(⌨9832438118; Nehru Rd; ⊙10am-4pm Mon-Sat) For an on-the-spot Sikkim permit bring a photocopy of your passport and Indian visa, plus one photo. It's opposite Glenary's in the Olde (Main) Bellevue Hotel annexe.

TOURIST INFORMATION
Gorkhland Terriorial Administration (GTA) Tourist Reception Centre (⌨2255351; Jawahar Rd West, Silver Fir Bldg; ⊙10am-5pm Mon-Sat, except 9am-1pm every 2nd and 4th Sat, 9am-1pm Sun high season) The staff are friendly, well organised and the best source of information in Darjeeling.

TRAVEL & TREKKING AGENCIES
Most travel agencies in town can arrange local tours. Other reliable agencies and their specialities include the following:

Adventures Unlimited (⌨9933070013; www.adventuresunlimited.in; Dr Zakir Hussain Rd) Offers treks (US$40 to US$45 per day), kayaking, motor paragliding, Enfield motorbike hire and mountain-bike trips (ask about the overnight trip to Kurseong and back via Senchul Reservoir). It also offers internet access, a laundromat and gear rental, including trek boots and sleeping bags (₹100 to ₹750). Contact Gautam.

Himalayan Travels (⌨2252254; kkgurung@cal.vsnl.net.in; 18 Gandhi Rd; ⊙8.30am-7pm) Experienced company arranging treks (US$55 to US$65 per person per day) and mountaineering expeditions in Darjeeling and Sikkim.

Samsara Tours, Travels & Treks (⌨2252874; www.samsaratourstravelsandtreks.com; 7 Laden La Rd) Helpful and knowledgeable agency offering trekking trips and domestic Nepali bus and air tickets to Kathmandu.

Somewhere Over the Rainbow Treks & Tours (⌨9832025739; kanadhi@yahoo.com; HD Lama Rd; ⊙8am-6pm, later in high season) Organises off-the-beaten track walks around Darjeeling, as well as rafting, rock climbing, cycling and trekking in Sikkim (including interesting routes from Uttarey). Treks start from US$40 per day.

Trek Mate (⌨2256611, 9832083241; trekmatedarj@gmail.com; Nehru Rd) All-inclusive guided treks cost from US$45 per person per day, or US$50 for Goecha La in Sikkim, depending on group size. Clothing or gear can be hired (sleeping bag ₹50 to ₹80 per day, plus ₹1500 to ₹2500 deposit), but the quality is pretty low.

Getting There & Away

AIR
The nearest airport is 90km away at Bagdogra, about 12km from Siliguri. Budget four hours for the drive, to be safe.

Air India (⌨2254230; www.airindia.com; Chowrasta; ⊙9.30am-1pm & 1.45-5.30pm Mon-Fri)

Pineridge Travels (⌨2253912; pineridge@mail.com; Nehru Rd; ⊙10am-5pm Mon-Sat) For domestic and international flight tickets.

BUS
Samsara Tours, Travels & Treks can book 'luxury' air-con buses from Siliguri to Kolkata (₹1000 to ₹1500, 12 hours) and ordinary night buses to Guwahati (₹550, 6pm) and Patna (₹450, 6pm). These tickets don't include transfers to Siliguri.

JEEP & TAXI
Numerous share jeeps leave the crowded Chowk Bazaar bus/jeep stand for Siliguri (₹120, three hours) and Kurseong (₹60, 1½ hours). Jeeps for Mirik (₹80, 2½ hours) leave from the northern end about every 1½ hours. A ticket office inside the ground floor of the Old Super Market Complex sells advance tickets for the frequent jeeps to Kalimpong (₹100, 2½ hours), while two roadside stands sell advance tickets for Gangtok (₹180, four hours). All jeeps depart between 7am and 3.30pm.

At the northern end of the station, three to four jeeps a day leave before noon for Jorethang

BORDER CROSSING – INTO NEPAL FROM DARJEELING

Foreigners can only cross the border into Nepal at Kakarbhitta/Panitanki (not at Pasupati, en route to Mirik).

Samsara Tours, Travels & Treks can book day and night buses from Kakarbhitta to Kathmandu (₹950 to ₹1200, departure 4am and 4pm), leaving you to hire a jeep to Kakarbhitta (₹1600), or catch a shared jeep to Siliguri and then Karkabhittha. Samsara can also book Nepali domestic flights from Bhadrapur to Kathmandu (US$164), which will save you the overnight bus trip.

Any tickets you see advertised from Darjeeling to Kathmandu are not direct buses and involve transfers in Siliguri and at the border – leaving plenty of room for problems – it's just as easy to do it yourself.

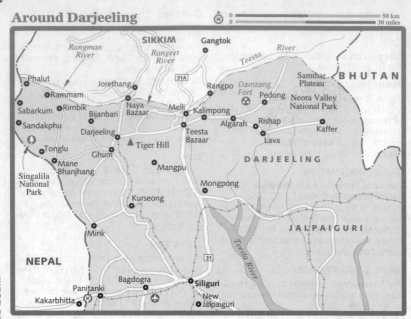

(₹120, two hours) in Sikkim. You must already have a permit to enter Sikkim via this route.

To New Jalpaiguri or Bagdogra, get a connection in Siliguri, or charter a jeep or taxi from Darjeeling.

Darjeeling Transport Corporation (☎9933071338; 30 Laden La Rd) offers charter jeeps to Gangtok (₹2000), Kalimpong (₹1700), Kurseong (₹1200), Kakarbhitta (₹2000) and Siliguri/Bagdogra Airport (₹1500/1700).

TRAIN
The nearest major train station is at New Jalpaiguri (NJP), near Siliguri. Tickets can be bought for major services out of NJP at the **Darjeeling train station** (☎2252555; ◷8am-5pm Mon-Sat, to 2pm Sun). Fares from Darjeeling include Ghum (1st/2nd class ₹115/21, 30 minutes) and Kurseong (₹160/27, three hours).

❶ Getting Around

There are several taxi stands around town, but rates are absurdly high for short hops. Darjeeling's streets can be steep and hard to navigate. You can hire a porter to carry your bags up to Chowrasta from Chowk Bazaar for around ₹60.

Share minivans to anywhere north of the town centre (eg to North Point) leave from the northern end of the **Chowk Bazaar bus/jeep station**. To Ghum, get a share jeep (₹15) from along Hill Cart Rd.

Singalila Ridge Trek

The most popular multiday walk from Darjeeling is the five-day Singalila Ridge Trek from Mane Bhanjhang to Phalut, through the scenic **Singalila National Park** (Indian/foreigner ₹100/200, camera/video ₹100/400). The highlights are the great views of the Himalayan chain stretching from Nepal to Sikkim and Bhutan, with Sandakphu in particular offering a superb panorama that includes Lhotse, Everest and Khangchengdzonga peaks. October and November's clear skies and warm daytime temperatures make it an ideal time to trek, as do the long days and incredible rhododendron blooms of May and early June.

Local guides (₹700 per day) are mandatory within the park and must be arranged at the office of the **Highlander Trekking Guides Association** (☎9734056944; www.highlanderguidesandporters.com) at Mane Bhanjhang, along with porters (₹350) if required.

Mane Bhanjhang is 26km from Darjeeling and is served by frequent shared jeeps (₹70, 1½ hours) as well as a 7am bus from Darjeeling's Chowk Bazaar bus/jeep station. A chartered jeep costs ₹1000. From Rimbik, there are shared jeeps back to Darjeeling

(₹120, five hours) at 7am and noon and a bus at 6.30am (₹72). Book seats in advance.

If you have to overnight in Rimbik the best lodges are **Hotel Sherpa** (☎9434212810; d ₹400-1000), with pleasant lawns and Alpine-style huts, and **Green Hill** (dm ₹100, r ₹450-750), with quieter wooden rooms out back.

The usual trekking itinerary is 83km over five days (see below). A shorter four-day option is possible by descending from Sandakphu to Sri Khola on day three. A very rough jeep road follows the trek from Mane Bhanjhang to Phalut but traffic is very light and the walking trail partly avoids the road.

Private lodges, some with attached bathrooms, are available along the route for around ₹150 for a dorm bed or ₹400 to ₹700 per room. All offer food, normally a filling combo of rice, dhal and vegetables (₹100). Rooms have clean bedding and blankets so sleeping bags are not strictly necessary, though they are nice to have. At a minimum bring a sleeping bag liner and warm clothes for dawn peak viewing. Bottled and boiling water is available along the route. Trekkers' huts can be booked at the GTA Information Centre but even they will tell you that you are better off at one of the private lodges. The main lodges are listed below in ascending order of price and quality:

Tumling Trekkers' Hut, Mountain Lodge, Siddharta Lodge, Shikhar Lodge

Tonglu Trekkers' Hut

Kalipokhari Chewang Lodge, five others

Sandakphu Trekkers' Hut, Namobuddha, Sunrise, Sherpa Chalet Lodge

Phalut Trekkers' Hut, Forest Rest House

Gurdum Himalayan Sherpa Lodge

Sri Khola Trekkers' Hut, Goparma Lodge

Gorkhey Trekkers' Hut, Shanti Lodge, Eden Lodge

Ramman Trekkers' Hut, Namobuddha Lodge, Sherpa Lodge

Molley Trekkers' Hut

All-inclusive guided treks on this route are offered by Darjeeling agencies for ₹1600 to ₹1800 per day, though it's easy enough to arrange a DIY trek for much less. See p505 for some reliable trekking agencies. Lodges can get booked out in the busy month of October, so consider a November trek.

Remember to bring your passport, as you'll have to register at half a dozen army checkpoints. The ridge forms the India–Nepal border and the trail actually enters Nepal in several places.

For a relaxing end to a trek, consider a stay at **Karmi Farm** (www.karmifarm.com; per person incl full board ₹1800), a one- to two-hour drive from Rimbik near Bijanbari. It's managed by Andrew Pulger-Frame, whose Sikkimese grandparents once ran an estate from the main house here. The simple but comfortable rooms are attractively decorated with colourful local fabrics, and bathrooms have 24-hour hot water. A small clinic for villagers is run from the farm, providing a volunteer opportunity for medical students and doctors. Singalila treks and other activities can be organised, but it would be just as easy to sit here for a week with a book and a pot of tea, overlooking the bird- and flower-filled gardens in the foreground and towering peaks in the distance. The adventurous could walk here in a day from Darjeeling, via North Point, Singtom Tea Estate and Pul Bazaar.

Kalimpong

☎03552 / POP 43,000 / ELEV 1250M

This bustling bazaar town sprawls along a ridge overlooking the roaring Teesta River and within sight of Khangchendzonga. It's not a must-see but it does boast Himalayan views, Buddhist monasteries, colonial architecture and a fascinating nursery industry, all linked by some fine hikes.

Kalimpong's early development as a major Himalayan trading centre focused on the wool trade with Tibet, across the Jelepla pass. Like Darjeeling, Kalimpong once

WEST BENGAL & DARJEELING KALIMPONG

SINGALILA RIDGE TREK

DAY	ROUTE	DISTANCE
1	Mane Bhanjhang (2130m) to Tonglu (3070m)/Tumling (2980m) via Meghma Gompa	14km
2	Tonglu to Sandakphu (3636m) via Kalipokhri & Garibas	17km
3	Sandakphu to Phalut (3600m) via Sabarkum	17km
4	Phalut to Rammam (2530m) via Gorkhey	16km
5	Rammam to Rimbik (2290m) via Sri Khola	19km

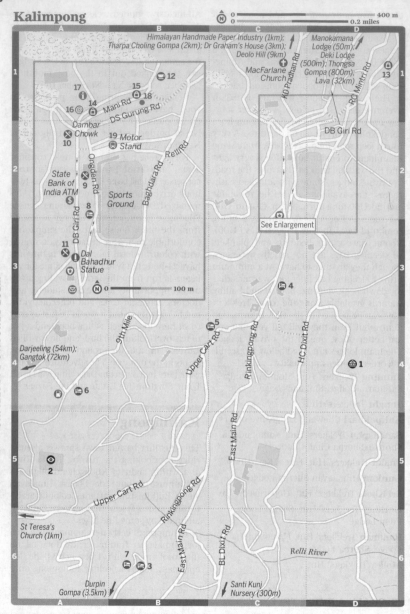

Himalayan Handmade Paper Industry (1km);
Tharpa Choling Gompa (2km); Dr Graham's House (3km);
Deolo Hill (9km)

Manokamana
Lodge (50m);
Deki Lodge
(500m); Thongsa
Gompa (800m);
Lava (32km)

MacFarlane
Church

DB Giri Rd

See Enlargement

KD Pradhan Rd

RC Mintri Rd

17
15
12
14
16
Mani Rd
18
DS Gurung Rd
Dambar
Chowk
10
19 Motor
Stand
Relli Rd

State
Bank of
India ATM
9
Onden Rd
Baghdara Rd
Sports
Ground
8

11
Dal
Bahadhur
Statue
DB Giri Rd

100 m

4

9th Mile
5
Upper Cart Rd
Rinkingpong Rd
HC Dixit Rd

Darjeeling (54km);
Gangtok (72km)

6

East Main Rd

1

2

Upper Cart Rd
Rinkingpong Rd

St Teresa's
Church (1km)

7
3
Bt Dixit Rd
East Main Rd

Relli River

Durpin
Gompa (3.5km)

Santi Kunj
Nursery (300m)

13

WEST BENGAL & DARJEELING KALIMPONG

belonged to the chogyals of Sikkim, but it
fell into the hands of the Bhutanese in the
18th century and later passed to the British,
before becoming part of India at Independence. Scottish missionaries, particularly the
Jesuits, made great efforts to win over the

local Buddhists in the late 19th century and
the town remains an important educational
centre for the entire eastern Himalaya.

Kalimpong is centred on its chaotic Motor Stand. Most sights and quality accom-

Kalimpong

⦿ Sights
1 Lepcha Heritage Museum D4
  Nurseryman's Haven.......................(see 6)
2 Pineview Nursery A5

⊜ Sleeping
3 Cloud 9... B6
4 Elgin Silver Oaks C3
5 Himalayan Hotel C4
6 Holumba Haven A4
7 Kalimpong Park Hotel B6
8 Sherpa Lodge.. A2

⊗ Eating
9 3C's.. A2
10 Gompu's Bar & Restaurant A2
11 King Thai.. A3
  Lee's ....(see 12)

⊙ Drinking & Nightlife
12 One Shot... B1

⊜ Shopping
13 Haat Bazaar D1
14 Kashi Nath & Sons A1
15 Lark's Provisions B1

ⓘ Information
16 Bits N Bytes... A1
  Helpdesk ....(see 8)
17 Tourist Reception Centre...................... A1

ⓘ Transport
18 Kalimpong Railway Out Agency B1
19 Motor Stand..B2

modation are a kilometre or two from town, along DB Giri and Rinkingpong Rds.

⊙ Sights

Durpin Gompa   MONASTERY
Kalimpong's largest monastery, formally known as Zangtok Pelri Phodang, sits atop panoramic Durpin Hill (1372m) and was consecrated by the Dalai Lama in 1976. There are impressive wall and ceiling paintings in the main prayer room downstairs (photography is permitted), and interesting 3D mandalas on the 2nd floor. Prayers are held at 4pm. The monastery is located about 5km south of the town centre, and most easily reached by taxi (₹200 drop). It's a pleasant walk back down to town, passing the army golf course and stopping for a drink at charming Morgan House, now a WBTDC hotel. A viewpoint about 300m below the gompa looks north towards the Jelepla and south over the Relli and Teesta Rivers.

Tharpa Choling Gompa   MONASTERY
(www.tharpacholing.org) Built in 1922, this Gelugpa-school Tibetan monastery, off KD Pradhan Rd, contains statues of the past, present and future Buddhas. A Garuda (man-bird Vehicle of Vishnu) protects each Buddha from above, his mouth devouring hatred and anger (in the form of a snake). It's a 30-minute walk (uphill) from town, 50m past Tripai Rd.

Thongsa Gompa   MONASTERY
Near the junction of RC Mintri and KD Pradhan Rds is this charming Nyingmapa-school monastery, also known as the Bhuta-nese Monastery. The gompa was founded in 1692, but the present building, surrounded by 219 small prayer wheels, was built in the 19th century after the Gurkhas rampaged across Sikkim.

Dr Graham's Home   HISTORIC BUILDING
(museum admission free; ⊙ museum 9am-noon, 1.15-3.30pm Mon-Fri) This working orphanage and school was built in 1900 by Dr JA Graham, a Scottish missionary, to educate the children of tea estate workers, and now has more than 1300 students. There's a small **museum** that commemorates the founder and his wife, Katherine. The 1925 chapel above the school seems lifted straight out of a Scottish parish, with its grey slate, spire and fine stained-glass windows. The gate is 4km up the steep KD Pradhan Rd. Many people charter a taxi to get here (₹100) and then walk back to town via Tharpa Choling Gompa and the Himalayan paper workshop.

Deolo Hill   VIEWPOINT
(9km from Kalimpong; admission ₹50, Tourist Lodge breakfast ₹80-150; ⊙ Tourist Lodge from 8am) On a clear day the sunrise views of Khangchendzonga from this hilltop park are superb. After savouring the views you can have breakfast at the attached **Tourist Lodge** and then walk down to Kalimpong via Dr Graham's. A taxi here costs around ₹300. If it's cloudy, stay in bed.

Himalayan Handmade
Paper Industry   HANDICRAFTS WORKSHOP
(🖉 255418; www.rupeshpradhan.com; KD Pradhan Rd; ⊙ 9am-noon & 1-4pm Mon-Sat) Visitors are

welcome to drop into this small workshop to see the traditional papermaking process, from boiling and pulping of the local *argayli* (daphne) bush to sifting, pressing and drying. The resulting insect-resistant paper is used to block print monastic scriptures. Morning is the best time to see production. It's a 10-minute walk from the centre, on the right side of the road.

Nurseries
NURSERIES

Kalimpong is a major flower exporter and produces about 80% of India's gladioli as well as many orchid varieties. Visit **Nurseryman's Haven** (☎256936; 9th Mile) at Holumba Haven to have a look at its 200-odd species of orchids; **Santi Kunj** (BL Dixit Rd; ⊗8.30am-noon & 1.30-4pm Sun-Fri) to see anthuriums and the bird of paradise flower; and **Pineview Nursery** (☎255843; www.pineviewcactus.in; Atisha Rd; admission ₹10; ⊗9am-5pm Mon-Sat) to gaze at its eminently photographable cactus collection.

Lepcha Heritage Museum
MUSEUM

(☎9933780295; ⊗10.30am-4.30pm Mon-Fri, 10am-noon Sat) FREE A visit to this offbeat collection of Lepcha treasures is best likened to rummaging through the attic of your grandfather's house (if he were a Lepcha tribal elder). A guide will explain Lepcha creation myths, while pointing out the religious texts, sacred porcupine quill hat and several old pangolin skins. It's a 10-minute walk downhill below the sports ground, just past the Kamudini Homes School. Calling ahead is advised.

St Teresa's Church
CHURCH

A fascinating missionary church built in 1929 by Swiss Jesuits, St Teresa was constructed to incorporate designs from a Bhutanese gompa. The wooden apostles look suspiciously like Buddhist monks, and the carvings on the doors resemble the *tashi tagye,* eight auspicious symbols of Himalayan Buddhism. The church is found off 9th Mile, about 2km from town. If it's locked ask at the next-door residence.

🏃 Activities

Gurudongma Tours & Travels
TOUR COMPANY

(☎255204; www.gurudongma.com; Rinkingpong Rd, Hilltop) This local operator organises interesting trekking, mountain-biking and birdwatching tours, based around its luxury Farm House on the Samthar Plateau. Pricey

homestays (single/double US$45/65) are also possible here.

Himalayan Eagle
PARAGLIDING

(☎9635156911; www.paraglidingkalimpong.com) Kalimpong-based Swede Roger Lenngren offers paragliding flights from Deolo Hill. Tandem flights cost ₹3000/4500 for a 15-/30-minute flight, which includes transport. Weather conditions have to be perfect.

🛏 Sleeping

High-season rates (October to early December and mid-March to early June) are given here.

Manokamana Lodge
GUESTHOUSE $

(☎257047; DB Giri Rd; ₹350-600; @🛜) This family-run budget place is well set up for backpackers, with a central location, an internet cafe and an excellent-value restaurant. Mattresses may be thin but the bathrooms are clean (hot water by the bucket). Of the five rooms, the two at the back are quietest.

Sherpa Lodge
HOTEL $

(☎8972029913; Ongden Rd; s ₹200-400, d ₹400-600) This simple but decent cheapie is slap bang in the centre of town, offering bright, clean rooms and buckets of hot water for the attached bathrooms. The rooftop terrace has great potential. Ask for Raju.

Deki Lodge
GUESTHOUSE $

(☎255095; Tripai Rd; s ₹350-1100, d ₹650-1611, ste ₹2348) This pleasant upper-budget lodge is close to the Thongsa and Tharpa Choling gompas and still handy to town. It's a friendly, peaceful place set in a garden with lots of terrace seating and a cafe. Rooms are overpriced without discounts but all except the cheapest are appealing, particularly the pricier upper-floor rooms.

★ Holumba Haven
BOUTIQUE HOTEL $$

(☎256936; www.holumba.com; 9th Mile; r ₹1200-2000; 🛜) Described by its welcoming owners as 'more of a homestay than a hotel', this family-run place is situated in a splendid orchid nursery just 1km below town. The spotless, comfy rooms are arranged in cosy cottages around the lush gardens and good homestyle meals (₹350, preorder) are available in the sociable dining room. Owner Norden is a fantastic source of local information.

Kalimpong Park Hotel
HERITAGE HOTEL $$

(☎255304; www.kalimponghotel.com; s/d/ste ₹2223/2818/3757; @🛜) This former maha-

KALIMPONG WALKS

There's plenty of scope for some great walking around Kalimpong, so budget an extra day or two to stretch the legs. Helpdesk (p513) and Holumba Haven offer information on all these walks and can arrange guides and transport if needed.

In Kalimpong itself, Helpdesk can arrange a guided crafts walk, taking in a traditional incense workshop, working silversmiths, noodle makers and a *thangka* (Tibetan cloth painting) studio, all hidden in the backstreet bazaars.

One good half-day walk close to town leads from near Holumba Haven to the villages of **Challisey** and **Chibo Busty** to a grand viewpoint over the Teesta River. With a guide you can visit en route the LK Pradhan Cactus Nursery and a small curd production centre at Tharker Farm, with the option of descending to see two fascinating traditional Lepcha houses at Ngassey village.

Heading further afield, one potential DIY hike starts at a wide track 2km past Algarah on the road to Pelling. The track climbs gently along a forested ridge to the faint 17th-century ruins of **Damsang Dzong**, site of the last stand of the Lepcha kings against the Bhutanese. Continue along the ridge and then descend to views of Khangchendzonga at Tinchuli Hill, before following the dirt road back to the main Algarah–Pedong road. From here you can walk back 4km to Algarah to catch a shared jeep to Kalimpong, or continue 3km to Pedong via the Shangchen Dorje Gompa in Sakyong Busty. Shared jeeps run between Kalimpong and both Pedong (₹40) and Algarah (₹30). To make an overnight of it, try the **Silk Route Retreat** (☑9932828753; www.thesilkrouteretreat.com; 21st Mile, Pedong; r/cottage ₹880/1650) in Pedong.

For the ultimate dawn and dusk views of Khangchendzonga, head to the **Tiffin Dara viewpoint**, just above the village of Rishap, about 30km from Kalimpong. A rough road climbs from the main Kalimpong–Lava road for 3km to a signed footpath 1km before Rishap. The path detours left after 20 minutes to the viewpoint then continues through forest for 45 minutes to rejoin the main Lava–Kalimpong road. Just before this junction, by some prayer flags, a shortcut footpath drops down to Lava village via the Forest Lodge. For transport take the 7am shared jeep to Lava or the slower 8am bus. A chartered one-way jeep costs ₹1400 to Rishap, ₹1000 to Lava, or ₹2000 for a day's return hire.

Lava (2353m) is a worthy destination in itself, especially if you time your walk with the bustling Tuesday market or the 10am debating or 3.30pm prayers at the modern Kagyupa Thekchenling Gompa. Adjoining Lava is **Neora Valley National Park** (Indian/foreigner ₹100/200, vehicle entry ₹80, guide ₹600; ☺15 Sep-15 Jun), featuring lush forests that are home to red pandas and clouded leopards. There are some fine day hikes here but you have to hire a jeep (₹1200) to take you the 8km to the park entrance. Travel agents can arrange a four-day camping trek to Roche La (3155m), at the high junction of West Bengal, Sikkim and Bhutan. The cottages of the **Lava Forest Lodge** (www.wbfdc.com; d ₹600-1200) just above town offer the nicest accommodation but can be hard to book; try through WBTDC in Siliguri or Holumba Haven in Kalimpong. The private **Hotel Orchid** (☑03552-282213; www.hotelorchidlava.com; d ₹750-1200) is another decent choice. Avoid October when Bengali tourists flood the town. Shared jeeps run when full back to Kalimpong until around 3.30pm.

raja's summer residence has oodles of Raj-era charm. Wicker chairs and flowerpots line the verandah and there's a charming lounge bar, along with a restaurant offering such British boarding-school staples as jelly custard. Rooms in the new wing lack the period charm of the old house's Tibetan rungs and antique dressers but are still appealing. Request a front-facing room, preferably on the upper floors.

Cloud 9 HOTEL **$$**
(☑9832039634; cloud9.kpg@gmail.com; Rinkingpong Rd; d ₹1200-1500) There's no chance of a tour-group invasion in this friendly place, since there are just five wood-panelled rooms, plus a cosy TV lounge and a good restaurant serving interesting Bhutanese and Sikkimese dishes (try the *kewa tachi* – potato and cheese). Guitars in the lounge attest to the owner's love of late-night Beatles covers.

Himalayan Hotel
HERITAGE HOTEL $$$

(☎255248; www.himalayanhotel.com; Upper Cart Rd; s/d ₹2349/3552; @) This classic hotel was opened by David MacDonald, an interpreter from Francis Younghusband's mission to Lhasa in 1904 and one of those who helped the 13th Dalai Lama escape Tibet in 1910. The original rooms have loads of Raj-era appeal with fireplaces and sloping Himalayan oak ceilings, while the new suites mesh old-world charm with modern comfort and private balconies. You're in fine company here; the former guest list reads like a 'who's who' of great 19th-century Himalayan travellers, from Alexandra David-Néel and Heinrich Harrer to Charles Bell. Head to the lawn to savour the Himalayan views over an al fresco breakfast or afternoon beer (₹120).

Elgin Silver Oaks
HERITAGE HOTEL $$$

(☎255296; www.elginhotels.com; Rinkingpong Rd; s/d incl half board ₹7750/8102; @🖥) This centrally located Raj-era homestead has been renovated into a modern and very comfortable Elgin hotel. The rooms are plushly furnished and offer grand views down the valley (ask for a garden-view room). The tariff includes all meals in the classy restaurant and the sociable bar packs bags of atmosphere.

✖ Eating & Drinking

Gompu's Bar & Restaurant
TIBETAN $

(☎257456; Gompu's Hotel, off DB Giri Rd; mains ₹60-120, beer ₹150; ⊙7am-9pm) Gompu's is famous for its oversized pork *momos* (and smaller chicken varieties), which have been drawing locals and travellers alike for as long as anyone can remember. It's also a good place for a cold beer chased by a plate of garlic chilli potatoes.

BORDER CROSSING – TO/FROM BHUTAN & NEPAL

A West Bengal government bus travels to the Bhutan border, Jaigon (₹140, 5½ hours) at 8.15am, and there are also early-morning jeeps (₹130, five hours). There is one early-morning bus (₹90, 5.45am) and jeep (₹110, 6.30am) to the Nepal border at Kakarbhitta (₹110, three hours).

Lee's
CHINESE $

(☎9593305812; DB Giri Rd; mains ₹80-120; ⊙11am-7.30pm Mon-Sat) Mr Lee and his daughter serve up fantastic home-made southern Chinese dishes, many of which you won't find anywhere else. Stand-out dishes include the *mun* wontons (dumplings fried in egg), *sao moi* (open dumplings), red pork and the golden chicken in garlic gravy. It's just above One Shot cafe. Ring ahead to check it is open.

3C's
BAKERY $

(DB Giri Rd; cakes & snacks ₹10-30; ⊙8.30am-7.15pm) If you need a quick break, this popular bakery and fast-food restaurant offers a variety of pastries and cakes, both sweet and savoury, with seating in the back.

King Thai
CHINESE $$

(DB Giri Rd, 3rd fl supermarket; mains ₹50-110; ⊙11am-9.30pm) A multicultural hang-out with a Thai name, Chinese food and Bob Marley posters on the walls. The regulars here include monks, businesspeople and Tibetan cool kids drawn to the noisy live music in the evenings. The generously portioned food is mainly Chinese with some Thai and Indian accents and there's a bar with comfy chairs and even a mirror ball.

One Shot
CAFE

(DB Giri Rd; coffee ₹50; ⊙11am-6.30pm Mon-Sun) Kalimpong's first coffeehouse serves a decent espresso hit, alongside some quality cakes and ice-cream specials.

🔒 Shopping

Lark's Provisions
FOOD & DRINK

(DB Giri Rd) The best place to pick up local cheese (₹320 per kg), produced in Kalimpong since the Jesuits established a dairy here in the 19th century. Also sells locally made sweet, milky lollipops (₹5) and yummy home-made pickles.

Haat Bazaar
MARKET

(btwn Relli & RC Mintri Rds) On Wednesday and Saturday this normally quiet bazaar roars to life.

Kashi Nath & Sons
BOOKS

(DB Giri Rd; ⊙10am-6.30pm) This place, and the shop next door, has a small collection of books on Buddhism, Nepal and Tibet, plus some novels.

ℹ Information

Bits N Bytes (per hr ₹30; ⊙8.30am-7pm; 🖭)
Reliable internet connections and wi-fi.

Helpdesk (📋8972029913; helpdesk_kpg@
hotmail.com; ⊙9am-5pm) This private information centre on the ground floor of the
Sherpa Lodge offers guides, a useful map and
information on trips around Kalimpong.

Post office (Rinkingpong Rd; ⊙9am-5pm
Mon-Fri, to 4pm Sat)

Sikkim permit There is nowhere in Kalimpong
to obtain permits for Sikkim, but free 30-day
permits are available at the border at Rangpo,
en route to Gangtok. You need to present three
passport photos.

State Bank of India ATM (DB Giri Rd) One of
several ATMs located together on DB Giri Rd.

Tourist reception centre (DGHC; 📋257992;
DB Giri Rd; ⊙10am-4.30pm Mon-Sat, closed
2nd & 4th Saturday) Sleepy staff can organise
local tours and rafting in Teesta Bazaar.

ℹ Getting There & Away

All the bus and jeep options and their offices are
found next to each other at the chaotic **Motor
Stand**.

BUS & JEEP

Bengal government buses run hourly to Siliguri
(₹70, 2½ hours). A single **Sikkim Nationalised
Transport** (SNT; Ongden Rd) bus to Gangtok
(₹80, three hours) leaves at 1pm from across
the road.

Himalayan Travellers (📋9434166498; Motor
Stand) Helpful transport company runs share
jeeps to Gangtok (₹120, three hours, four daily)
and Lava (₹70, 1½ hours, five per day) and a
bus to Kaffer (₹60, 2½ hours, 8am).

**Kalimpong Mainline Taxi Driver's Welfare
Association** (KMTDWA; Motor Stand) Frequent
share jeeps to Siliguri (₹100, 2½ hours) and
Gangtok (₹120, 2½ hours) and one daily to
Jorethang (₹80, two hours, departs 7.15am).

KS & AH Taxi Driver's Welfare Association
(Motor Stand) Share jeeps to Gangtok (₹120,
hourly), Ravangla (₹130, 3½ hours, 2pm) and
Namchi (₹100, four daily) in Sikkim.

Kalimpong Motor Transport (Motor Stand)
Frequent share jeeps (₹100, 2½ hours) to
Darjeeling until mid-afternoon, plus charters
(₹1400).

TRAIN

Kalimpong Railway Out Agency (Mani Rd;
⊙10am-6pm Mon-Sat, to 1pm Sun) Sells train
tickets out of New Jalpaiguri (NJP) train station
and runs a daily shared jeep to NJP station at
1pm (₹110).

ℹ Getting Around

Taxis (mostly unmarked minivans) can be chartered for local trips from along DB Giri Rd. A
half-day rental to see most of the sights should
cost ₹700.

Bihar & Jharkhand

Best Places to Eat

➜ Bellpepper Restaurant (p520)

➜ Tandoor Hut (p520)

➜ To Kiy Restaurant (p528)

➜ Siam Thai (p528)

Best Places to Stay

➜ Indo Hokke Hotel (p530)

➜ Chanakya BNR Hotel (p532)

➜ Taj Darbar (p527)

➜ Hotel Windsor (p520)

➜ Bodhgaya Regency (p527)

Why Go?

The landlocked states of Bihar and Jharkhand promise an eclectic mix of attractions cherry-picked from India's vast artistic and natural heritage. Spirituality is a huge draw here: Bihar is the birthplace of Buddhism and plays host to countless pilgrims who flock to its many places of religious significance. Parasnath Hill, Jharkhand's highest point, is the most significant Jain pilgrimage site in north-central India. The city of Patna commands academic respect as one of ancient India's greatest power centres, in addition to housing some curious monuments from the British Raj era. On the other hand, wallowing far off the beaten track, the remote hills and forests of Jharkhand are a nature lover's paradise, where one can spy on myriad animal and bird species, including the elephants and tigers. All in all, this is a very different kind of experience compared to holidays in more touristy states, so come with an open mind and a sense of adventure.

When to Go
Patna

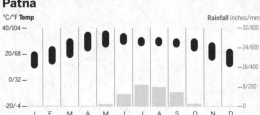

Jan & Feb Temperatures hover between a chilly-to-pleasant 12°C and 25°C.

Oct & Nov The region's forests assume a moody autumn look as winter sets in.

Nov & Dec Bihar's Sonepur Mela puts Pushkar's Camel Fair to shame.

Food

Bihar and Jharkhand are lands of robust, rustic culinary flavours. In Bihar, look out for the ubiquitous *litti*, balls of spiced chickpea flour covered in dough and baked on coals, which are served with *chokha*, a spicy mashed potato gravy seasoned with local five-spice. Jharkhand's answer to *litti* is *dhuska*, rice-flour pancakes deep fried in oil and served with a potato and gram curry. A string of upmarket restaurants in Patna and Ranchi specialise in the best of traditional Mughlai and Afghani cuisine, mostly of the meaty kebab kind. Eateries in Bodhgaya bring together a smattering of flavours from around the world, including Japanese, Thai and Continental. Sweet tooths in Bihar and Jharkhand are satiated with dry sweets, like the strange but satisfying *tilkut*, pounded sesame-seed cookies made with jaggery batter or melted sugar.

DON'T MISS

The **Mahabodhi Temple** in Bodhgaya was where Prince Siddhartha attained enlightenment beneath a bodhi tree and became Buddha. The temple complex was declared a Unesco World Heritage Site in 2002, and is visited daily by thousands of pilgrims, predominantly from India, Sri Lanka, Southeast Asia, China and Japan. It's a supernova of ritualistic splendour and is not to be missed. Other treats in the region include the Jain Holy Ground at **Parasnath Hill**, the elephant-rich **Betla National Park** and the ancient ruins in and around **Rajgir**.

Top State Festivals

→ **Pataliputra Mahotsava** (Mar; Patna, p519) Patna's historic past is celebrated with parades, sports, dancing and music.

→ **Rajgir Mahotsava** (Oct; Rajgir, p529) A performing arts gala with dances, devotional songs and instrumental music.

→ **Chhath Festival** (Oct/Nov; Bihar & Jharkhand, p531) People perform spectacular rituals on the banks of rivers and water bodies to honour Surya, the sun god.

→ **Sonepur Mela** (Nov/Dec; Sonepur, p522) With 700,000 attendees and countless thousands of animals taking part, this three-week festival is four times the size of Pushkar's Camel Fair.

MAIN POINTS OF ENTRY

Most travellers arrive at Patna's Jaiprakash Narayan International Airport, Ranchi's Birsa Munda Airport or by train into Patna (PNBE) or Ranchi junctions (RNC).

Fast Facts

→ **Population**: 103.8 million (Bihar), 32.9 million (Jharkhand)

→ **Area**: 99,200 sq km (Bihar), 74,677 sq km (Jharkhand)

→ **Capital**: Patna (Bihar), Ranchi (Jharkhand)

→ **Language**: Hindi, English

→ **Sleeping prices**: $ below ₹1000, $$ ₹1000 to ₹2500, $$$ above ₹2500

Top Tip

Steer clear of this region during monsoon season (June to September) – Bihar is the country's most flood-prone state.

Resources

→ **Bihar Tourism** (www.bihartourism.gov.in) The official department of tourism site of Bihar.

→ **Jharkhand Tourism** (www.jharkhandtourism.in) The official department of tourism site of Jharkhand.

BIHAR & JHARKHAND

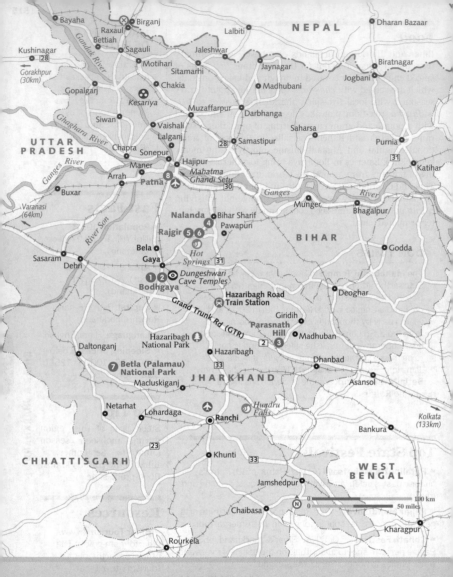

Bihar & Jharkhand Highlights

❶ Witness the spiritual dawn spectacle at the **Mahabodhi Temple** (p524) in Bodhgaya

❷ Take a walking tour through the Buddhist world at **Bodhgaya**'s numerous **temples and monasteries** (p524)

❸ Join the Jain pilgrimage to the 1366m-high **Parasnath Hill** (p533)

❹ Visit the ancient university at **Nalanda** (p530) and imagine what life was like for its 10,000 pupils from all over Asia

❺ Explore the lost capital of Magadha, spread over the timeless hilly landscape of **Rajgir** (p529)

❻ Trade noise pollution for silent lucidity at the stunning **Vishwashanti Stupa** (p529) in Rajgir

❼ Prowl the forested **Betla (Palamau) National Park** (p532) on the back of an elephant in search of elusive tigers

❽ Gorge on the memorable frontier cuisine in the excellent restaurants of **Patna** (p517)

History

Bihar's ancient history kicks off with the arrival of Prince Siddhartha during the 6th century BC, who spent many years here before leaving enlightened as Buddha. Mahavira, a contemporary of Buddha and the founder of Jainism, was born in Bihar and attained nirvana near Nalanda at the age of 72. In the 4th century BC, after Chandragupta Maurya conquered the Magadha kingdom and its capital Pataliputra (now Patna), he expanded into the Indus Valley and created the first great Indian empire. His grandson and successor, Ashoka, ruled the Mauryan empire from Pataliputra, which was one of the largest cities in the world at that time. Emperor Ashoka embraced Buddhism, erecting stupas, monuments and his famous Ashokan pillars throughout northern India, notably at Sarnath (Uttar Pradesh) and Sanchi (Madhya Pradesh). In Bihar, Ashoka built the original shrine on the site of today's Mahabodhi Temple in Bodhgaya and the lion-topped pillar at Vaishali.

Bihar continued to be coveted by a succession of major empires until the Magadha dynasty rose to glory again during the reign of the Guptas (7th and 8th centuries AD). With the decline of the Mughal empire in the 17th century AD, Bihar came under the control of Bengal until 1912, when a separate state was formed. Part of this state later became Orissa (now Odisha) and, more recently in 2000, Jharkhand.

ⓘ Dangers & Annoyances

Bihar and Jharkhand have a deserved reputation for lawlessness throughout India. Conditions have improved in recent times, but bandit activity – such as holding up cars, buses and trains – is still a possibility, and Maoist and Naxalite bombings are not uncommon. Although foreign and domestic tourists are not specific targets, it's a good idea to split up your valuables on long journeys and avoid night travel where possible, especially by road. Women should take extra precautions throughout the state – never travel alone, avoid befriending strangers and don't stay out after dark, especially in secluded places. In Patna, security has improved, but do take care at night, especially if alone. For more info, check the newspapers *Bihar Times* (www.bihartimes.in) or *Patna Daily* (www.patnadaily.com), or the English portal of Ranchi Express (www.ranchiexpress.com) before arrival.

ⓘ Information

State tourism offices exist in every major town but do little besides handing out leaflets – if that.

BIHAR

Most people travel to Bihar to visit the hallowed Buddhist circuit of Bodhgaya, Rajgir, Nalanda and Vaishali, with Patna as a transport hub. There's little else to see in the state, so don't plan on staying for too long.

Patna

⤴ 0612 / POP 1,697,900

Bihar's busy capital sprawls out over the south bank of the polluted Ganges, just east of the river's confluence with three major tributaries. There's nothing for the traveller along the river itself, and Patna only has a handful of worthwhile sights. Otherwise, it's a chaotic eyesore that would be an odd place to voluntarily spend any considerable length of time. For what it's worth, though, Patna is home to the region's best eats, so tuck in generously before moving on to more interesting destinations such as Bodhgaya or Rajgir.

Patna was once a powerful city. Early in the 5th century BC, Ajatasatru shifted the capital of his Magadha kingdom from Rajgir to Pataliputra, fulfilling Buddha's prophecy that a great city would arise here. Emperors Chandragupta Maurya and Ashoka also called Pataliputra home, and it remained one of India's most important cities for almost 1000 years.

The old and newer parts of Patna stretch along the southern bank of the Ganges for about 15km. The main train station, airport and hotels are in the western half, known as Bankipur, while most of the historic sites are in the teeming older Chowk area to the east. The 5.7km-long Mahatma Gandhi Setu, the longest single river bridge in the world, connects Patna with Hajipur.

⊙ Sights & Activities

★**Patna Museum**   MUSEUM

(Buddha Marg; Indian/foreigner ₹15/250; ☺10.30am-4.30pm Tue-Sun) Behind its impressive and freshly renovated exterior, this museum houses a splendid collection of Mauryan and Gupta stone sculptures. There's the usual scattering of period weapons, including Humayun's dagger, and a gallery of

Patna

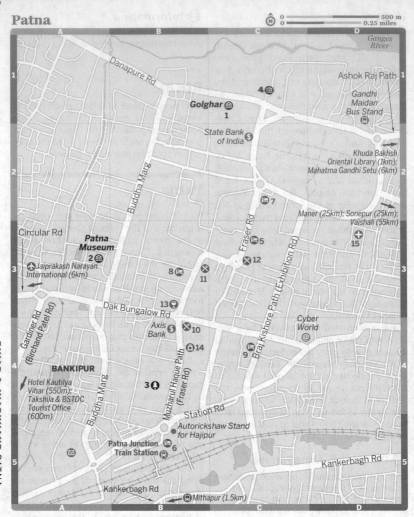

wonderful Rajasthani miniatures. Don't miss the fabulous collection of Tibetan antiques and *thangkas* (cloth paintings) brought to India by the scholar and traveller Rahul Sankrityayan in the early 20th century.

Upstairs in a locked gallery (an extra ₹500) you can glimpse a tiny casket believed to contain some of Buddha's ashes that were retrieved from Vaishali. In another gallery is a motley collection of stuffed animals, including tigers, a large gharial (a type of crocodile), a bizarre three-eared and eight-legged goat kid, and a wombat.

★Golghar   HISTORIC BUILDING
(Danapure Rd; admission ₹2; ☉6am-6pm) For a dome with a view, climb this massive, bulbous granary, built by the British army in 1786. The idea behind its construction was to avoid a repeat of the 1770 famine; fortunately it was never required. Its dual spiralling staircases (250 steps each) were designed so that workers could climb up one side and down the other.

The viewing gallery on top of the monument affords unparalleled vistas of the city and the Ganges. Golghar is a short walk west of Gandhi Maidan, a large, messy park

Patna

with a couple of sights located south of the river.

Buddha Smriti Park   PARK
(◎ dawn-dusk Tue-Sun) This 9-hectare park on Fraser Rd, inaugurated by the Dalai Lama in 2010, is notable for its massive sandblasted charcoal stupa, which houses a unique bulletproof chamber inside, and sapling plantings from both the Bodhi Tree in Bodhgaya and Anuradhapura in Sri Lanka. There is also a colour-coordinated museum and meditation centre, which makes for a striking architectural panorama.

Khuda Bakhsh Oriental Library   MUSEUM
(Ashok Raj Path; ◎ 9.30am-5pm Sat-Thu) FREE This fascinating library, founded in 1900, contains a renowned collection of Arabic and Persian manuscripts, Mughal and Rajput paintings, and even the Quran, inscribed in a book just 25mm wide. A significant exhibit is Nadir Shah's sword – perhaps the very weapon he raised at Delhi's Sunehri Mosque in 1739 to order the massacre of the city's residents.

Har Mandir Takht   SIKH TEMPLE
Behind a grand gate and sheltered from the mayhem of Patna's Chowk area lies this important Sikh shrine. Its miniature marble domes, sweeping staircases and fine latticework mark the spot where Guru Gobind Singh, last of the 10 Sikh gurus, was born in 1666. It's 11km east of Gandhi Maidan.

Gandhi Museum   MUSEUM
(Danapure Rd; ◎ 10am-6pm Sun-Fri) This museum contains a pictorial history of Mahatma Gandhi's life, plus some of his meagre belongings. On your way in, don't miss the glass-boxed statues of Gandhi and Nobel laureate Rabindranath Tagore in conversation.

✦ Festivals & Events
Patna honours its historic past every March with **Pataliputra Mahotsava** (Patna; ◎ Mar), a celebration featuring parades, sports, dancing and music.

🛏 Sleeping
Most accommodation choices are around Fraser, Exhibition and Station Rds.

Garden Court Club   HOTEL $
(☎ 3202279; www.gardencourtclub.com; Fraser Rd; s/d ₹550/770, with AC from ₹1100/1350; ❄) Take the lift within a small shopping complex up to the intimate 13-room Garden Court Club. With a vague homestay feel, it has rooms of varying standards: some have views, some have squat toilets. The faux-forest open-air rooftop restaurant is a pleasant retreat from street level, except when a wedding party is on.

Hotel President   HOTEL $
(☎ 2209203; www.hotelpresidentpatna.com; off Fraser Rd; s/d ₹880/990, with AC ₹1350/1700; ❄ @) This family-run hotel is in a relatively quiet location off Fraser Rd and close to Patna Museum. Rooms are simple, clean and good value with TV, seating areas and hot water. It takes block bookings from corporate groups, so check in advance to see if rooms are available.

Hotel Kautilya Vihar   HOTEL $$
(☎ 2225411; bstdc@rediffmail.com; Gardiner Rd; d with/without AC from ₹1400/1200; ❄) This

BIHAR & JHARKHAND PATNA

government-run hotel on Gardiner Rd (Birchand Patel Rd) has typically well-worn rooms which lack atmosphere. However, there's a restaurant and eager staff. Those on a shoestring budget will love the idea of scoring a dorm bed here for a mere ₹200.

★ Hotel Windsor
HOTEL $$

(☏2203250; www.hotelwindsorpatna.com; Exhibition Rd; s/d ₹1400/1700; ❄@) If there's one hotel in Patna which offers business-class luxuries within a budget, it's the Windsor. With well-designed rooms, spotless bathrooms, cheery and prompt service, plenty of complimentary offerings (from medical pouches to sewing kits), a superb restaurant and internet centre, it's the coolest place to spend a few nights. With a bar, it'd be just awesome.

Hotel City Centre
HOTEL $$

(☏2208687; hotelcitycentrepatna@rediffmail.com; Station Rd; d incl breakfast with/without AC ₹1700/1000; ❄) This modern glass tower to your right just as you exit the train station is perfect for a comfy transit overnighter. The rooms are great value for the price (the non-air-con rooms have squat toilets), and there's a buzzing bar and restaurant within the premises.

Hotel Maurya Patna
HOTEL $$$

(☏2203040; www.maurya.com; South Gandhi Maidan; s/d incl breakfast ₹12,000/14,000; ❄@☏) Fine appointments and luxurious surroundings distinguish Patna's top business hotel. The large gardens host a tempting pool with dolphin murals on the floor, and there are a few nice restaurants and a bar. Rooms are tastefully furnished, centrally air-conditioned and feature fresh floral arrangements.

✗ Eating & Drinking

Animated Fraser Rd is the main shopping street, with a buzz of restaurants and bars.

★ Bellpepper Restaurant
INDIAN $$

(Exhibition Rd, Hotel Windsor; mains ₹120-250; ☺noon-3pm & 7pm-10.30pm) Intimate and contemporary, this restaurant is hugely popular for its tandoori dishes. The *murg tikka lababdar* (boneless tandoori chicken basted with garlic, ginger, green chillies, and a pistachio- and cashew-nut paste) is melt-in-your-mouth sinful, as is the subtly spiced Hyderabadi biryani. No booze to wash it down, though, but that's hardly any reason to complain.

★ Tandoor Hut
INDIAN $$

(☏delivery 9304871717; Fraser Rd; mains ₹70-130; ☺noon-3pm & 7pm-11pm) The moment you walk past the delicious dangling kebabs in the display of this takeaway-only stand, you'll want to throw your money across the counter. The chicken tikka and chicken *reshmi* kebabs (cooked in the tandoor; feeds two) are both extraordinary. For a royal treat, try the executive meal box, with generous portions of naan, pulao, paneer, chicken and dhal.

Anarkali
INDIAN $$

(cnr Fraser & Dak Bungalow Rds, Mamta Hotel; mains ₹90-180; ☺noon-10pm) One of the friendliest restaurants in Patna, this oldie is a wonderful place to get sloshed in style. What's more, it tosses up some great eats to accompany your poison for the evening. The best pairing? Chicken leg kebab with a chilled bottle of Kingfisher. Hurts so good.

Nirula's
FAST FOOD $$

(Fraser Rd; dishes ₹80-140; ☺11am-10pm) A brand new eatery brought to town by a popular Delhi fast-food chain, this swish restaurant does a good job belting out snacky treats such as pizzas, sandwiches, burgers, sundaes and shakes. There are a few items on the menu that come with a twist of taste, like the chilli chicken pizza (which is actually quite good!).

Bollywood Treats
INDIAN $$

(Maurya Patna Hotel Arcade; mains ₹80-150; ☺noon-9pm) This spotless, modern self-service cafe dishes out dosas (thin lentil-flour pancakes), Chinese stir-fries, shwarma, chicken hot dogs, decent pizza and tempting brownies to Patna's blossoming middle class in self-proclaimed 'American style'. There is a Baskin Robbins ice-cream stand just outside its doors, if you want to top your meal off with a snowy dessert.

Elevens
LOUNGE

(Fraser Rd, Dumraow Kothi; mains ₹150-200, beers ₹140; ☺noon-10pm) Owned by former Indian cricketer Kapil Dev, this place works up some decent cocktails and shooters for tipplers. The interiors are sufficiently plushed up with lounge chairs and accent lighting. The adjacent restaurant (family seating only) features an atypical menu of recipes collected from the owner's sporting travels throughout Asia.

🛍 Shopping

Ajanta   HANDICRAFTS
(Fraser Rd; ☺10.30am-8.30pm Mon-Sat) Come
here for Patna's best selection of Mithila
(Madhubani) paintings. Although most of
the stock on display is bronzes, the owner
can show you a wide range of unmounted
paintings starting from ₹400 (handmade
paper) to ₹1500 (silk). Bargain hard.

ℹ Information

INTERNET ACCESS
Cyber World (Rajendra Path; per hr ₹25;
☺9.30am-9pm) Internet cafe.
Rendezvous Cyber Cafe (Exhibition Rd, Hotel
Windsor; per hr ₹25; ☺10am-8pm) Internet
cafe.

MEDICAL SERVICES
Dr Ruban Memorial Hospital (📞2320404/446;
Gandhi Maidan; ☺24hr) Emergency room,
clinic and pharmacy.

MONEY
Axis Bank (Fraser Rd; ☺10am-4pm Mon-Sat)
Exchanges currency and has ATMs.
State Bank of India (Gandhi Maidan; ☺10am-
2pm Mon-Fri, to noon Sat) Currency and travel-
lers cheques exchanged. Has ATMs.

POST
Post office (Buddha Marg; ☺10am-4pm
Mon-Fri, to 2pm Sat) Ordinary and speed post
facilities.

TOURIST INFORMATION
BSTDC Tourist Office (📞2225411; Gardiner
Rd, Hotel Kautilya Vihar; ☺10am-5pm Mon-
Sat) Limited information.

TRAVEL AGENCIES
Thomas Cook (📞2221699; www.thomascook.
in; Hotel Maurya Patna Arcade; ☺10.30am-
6pm Mon-Sat) Helpful for booking airline
tickets and car rental. Also exchanges currency.

ℹ Getting There & Away

Patna's Jaiprakash Narayan International
Airport is 8km from the city centre. **Air India**
(📞2223199), **IndiGo** (📞1800 1803838) and
JetKonnect (📞2223045) fly daily to Delhi and
Kolkata, and all have offices at Patna airport. The
Air India flight calls at Ranchi en route. IndiGo
also flies to Mumbai via Lucknow.

BUS
The Mithapur bus station occupies a large, dusty
space about 1.5km from the train station. Services include buses to Gaya (₹70, three hours,
hourly), Ranchi (₹260, eight hours, several

MITHILA (MADHUBANI) PAINTINGS

Bihar's unique and most famous folk
art is its Mithila (Madhubani) paintings.
Traditionally, women from Madhubani
and surrounding villages started creating strong line drawings on the walls of
their homes from the first day of their
marriage. Using pigments from spices,
minerals, charcoal and vegetable
matter, they painted local deities and
scenes from mythology, often intermin-
gled with special events and aspects of
everyday life.

These paintings, in both black-and-
white and strong primary colours, are
now professionally produced on paper,
canvas and silk and marketed for sale.
Original wall paintings can still be seen
in homes around Madhubani, 160km
northeast of Patna.

---

between 5pm and 9pm) and Raxaul (₹140, eight
hours, five daily from 6am).

From the **Gandhi Maidan bus stand**, government bus services travel to Ranchi (₹240, 10
hours, 8pm, 9.30pm and 10pm) and Raxaul
(₹140, eight hours, 7.15am and 10pm).

CAR
Hiring a car and driver is the best way for day
trips from Patna. Most hotels and Thomas Cook
can arrange this service, starting from ₹8 per
kilometre (minimum 200km) plus a driver allowance of ₹200. Arrange an early start, as few
drivers operate after dark.

TRAIN
Patna Junction is a chaotic station, but there's a
foreign-tourist ticket counter (window 7, Patna
Junction; ☺8am-8pm Mon-Sat, to 2pm Sun) at
the 1st-floor reservation office, in the right-hand
wing of the station. Destinations with regular
daily services include the following:
Kolkata (Howrah station) (2nd class/chair/
sleeper/3AC/2AC ₹180/630/270/710/1035,
eight to 12 hours)
Delhi (sleeper/3AC/2AC ₹415/1085/1555, 12
to 16 hours)
**Siliguri/New Jalpaiguri (for Darjeeling and
Sikkim)** (sleeper/3AC/2AC ₹255/650/915, 10
to 14 hours)
Varanasi (sleeper/3AC ₹145/445, five hours)
Gaya (2nd class/sleeper ₹15/135, 2½ hours)
Ranchi (2nd class/chair/sleeper/3AC/2AC
₹160/515/265/705/1005, eight to 10 hours)

There is no direct train to Raxaul. It's possible to cross the Mahatma Gandhi Setu to Hajipur, then take a train to Muzaffarpur, and then again change for Raxaul, but this would only make sense if you were vehemently opposed to the bus.

❶ Getting Around

The airport is located 7km west of the city centre. Autorickshaws to/from the city cost ₹140, while prepaid taxis start at ₹360.

Shared autorickshaws shuttle between the train station and Gandhi Maidan bus stand (₹5), departing from the rear of the train station. For short trips, cycle-rickshaws are best.

Around Patna

The sights of Vaishali and Kesariya are scattered and transport is sporadic. It's wise to organise a car and driver for a longish day.

Vaishali

☑ 06225

Most sites in Vaishali, 55km northwest of Patna, surround a large ancient coronation water tank. Dominating the skyline is a gleaming, modern **Japanese Peace Pagoda** (Indian/foreigner ₹5/100; ☺ dawn-dusk), while opposite is a small **museum** (☑ 229404; admission ₹5; ☺ 10am-5pm Tue-Sun) presenting clay and terracotta figures plus an intriguing 1st- to 2nd-century AD toilet pan with appropriately sized exit holes. Nearby are the ground-floor remains of a **stupa** that once contained Buddha's ashes, which now reside in Patna Museum.

Three kilometres from the Japanese Peace Pagoda, **Basokund** is – among three debated locations – the most widely accepted birthplace of Lord Mahavira, the 24th and final Jain *tirthankar* (teacher) and founder of Jainism. An engraved stone marks the place in a flower-decorated plot.

At a similar distance are the ruins of the **Kolhua Complex** (Indian/foreigner ₹5/100; ☺ 7am-5pm), comprising a hemispherical brick stupa guarded by a lion squatting atop a 2300-year-old Ashoka pillar. The pillar is plain and contains none of the Ashokan edicts usually carved onto these pillars. Nearby are the ruins of smaller stupas and monastic buildings. According to legend, Buddha was given a bowl of honey here by monkeys, who also dug out a rainwater tank for his water supply.

Kesariya

Rising high out of the earth from where the dying Buddha donated his begging bowl, this stupa is an enthralling example of how nature reclaimed a deserted monument. Excavated from under a grassy and wooded veil is what's likely to be the world's second-tallest (38m) Buddhist stupa dating from the Pala period. Above the 425m-circumference pedestal are five uniquely shaped terraces that form a gargantuan Buddhist tantric mandala. Each terrace has a number of niches containing disfigured Buddha statues, which were destroyed during attacks by foreign invaders in the Middle Ages.

Maner

Worth visiting 30km west of Patna is **Chhoti Dargah**, an architecturally elegant three-storey mausoleum fronted by a large tank. The venerable Muslim saint Makhdum Shah Daulat was buried here in 1619 under a canopied tomb. As it is auspicious to be buried close to a saint, several cloth-covered graves in front of the mausoleum keep him company. The large body of water is a favourite swimming spot for local children.

WORTH A TRIP

SONEPUR MELA

According to Hindu legend, Sonepur, 25km north of Patna, is where Vishnu ended the prehistoric battle between the lords of the forest (elephants) and the lords of the water (crocodiles). Each November/December, during the full moon of Kartik Purnima, the three-week **Sonepur Mela** (Sonepur; ☺ Nov/Dec) celebrates this famous tale. Devotees bathe where the Ganges joins with the Gandak and Mehi Rivers, while Asia's largest cattle fair takes place nearby at Hathi Bazaar. More than mere bovines are on sale – Marwari horses, brindled goats, camels, birds and elephants change hands, although trade in the latter is illegal.

Raxaul

☎ 06255 / POP 41,600

Raxaul is a grim, dirty and horribly congested border town that provides passage into Nepal. It's no place to linger, but if you must spend the night **Hotel Kaveri** (☎ 221148; Main Rd; d from ₹800; ❄) is tolerable, with clean rooms and loos and a vague semblance of tourist-friendliness. Restaurants are scarce. You can check your email at **Soni Cyber Cafe** (Main Rd; per hr ₹30)

The Karai Tala bus stand is 200m down a western side road about 2km south of the border. There are supposedly five daily buses to Patna, but times are extremely variable (₹160, six hours). The 13022 Mithila Express train runs daily to Kolkata (sleeper/3AC/2AC ₹315/835/1200, 18 hours, 10am).

Gaya

☎ 0631 / POP 395,000

Brash and loud Gaya, 100km south of Patna, is a religious centre for Hindu pilgrims who believe temple offerings here relieve the recently departed from the cycle of birth and rebirth. For foreign tourists, it merely serves as a transit point for Bodhgaya.

◉ Sights & Activities

Vishnupad Temple　　HINDU TEMPLE

Close to the banks of the Falgu River south of town, this stone-spired temple was constructed in 1787 by Queen Ahilyabai of Madhya Pradesh and houses a 40cm 'footprint' of Vishnu imprinted into solid rock. Non-Hindus are not allowed entry. Along the ghats on the river's edge, Hindus bathe and light funeral pyres; be discreet if you visit.

🛏 Sleeping & Eating

Overnighting in Gaya is not a pleasant affair. Consider it only if you arrive late or have an early departure en route to Bodhgaya.

Hotel Vishnu International　　HOTEL $

(☎ 2224422; Swarajpuri Rd; s/d from ₹600/800; ❄) Apart from a caricature-like French castle exterior, this nondescript hotel has nothing to write home about. It's good value though; rooms are clean with high-powered fans, and a couple of costlier rooms have AC.

Ajatsatru Hotel　　HOTEL $

(☎ 2222961; Station Rd; s/d from ₹600/800; ❄) This hotel across from the train station has

clean rooms plagued by street noise. It's home to an excellent and friendly multicuisine restaurant called Sujata (mains ₹40 to ₹80) that can't be beat while waiting for a train.

Khushi　　INDIAN, CHINESE $$

(Swarajpuri Rd; mains ₹80-160; ⊙11am-10pm) A superb selection of Indian and Chinese dishes are available at this smart air-conditioned eatery on the main drag near Hotel Vishnu International. The paneer and chicken dishes score well with local diners.

ℹ Information

There's a **Bihar state tourist office** (☎ 2223635; ⊙10am-5pm Mon-Sat) and a State Bank of India ATM at the train station. Several **internet cafes** (Swarajayapur Rd; per hr ₹30) line Swarajpuri Rd near Hotel Vishnu International.

ℹ Getting There & Away

BUS

Patna (₹80, three hours, hourly) Buses leave from the Gandhi Maidan bus stand and from a stand next to the train station.

BORDER CROSSING – INTO NEPAL FROM RAXAUL

Border Hours

The border at Raxaul is open from 6am to 10pm.

Foreign Exchange

No banks change money in Raxaul but there are many private money changers on both sides of the border. The State Bank of India in Raxaul has an ATM.

Onward Transport

Catch a cycle-rickshaw (₹100), autorickshaw or tonga (two-wheeled horse or pony carriage) from Raxaul's bus or train station to Birganj, 5km away on the Nepali side. From Birganj, you can find jeeps to Kathmandu and Pokhara every morning between 7am and 10am. There are also regular day and night bus departures to Kathmandu.

Visas

Nepali 15-, 30- and 90-day visas (US$25/40/100 and one passport photo) are only available from 6am to 6pm on the Nepal side of the border.

SASSARAM

If you're motoring from Gaya to Varanasi, a short detour to the **Mausoleum of Sher Shah** (Indian/foreigner ₹5/100; ⊙ dawn-dusk) at Sassaram is worthwhile. Seemingly floating within a large tank, the mausoleum of the historically significant emperor is an exercise in architectural restraint, and still bears vestiges of deep-blue Persian tiling. Note the aesthetic use of proportion, from its rounded dome down through a ring of *chhatris* (cenotaphs) to its solid pedestal. Within is the tomb of Sher Shah and his family. Hasan Shah, father of Sher Shah, has his own less spectacular tomb 200m away.

Rajgir (₹70, 2½ hours, every 30 minutes) Use the bus stand across the river in Manpur.
Ranchi (₹150, seven hours, two-hourly) Buses leave from the Gandhi Maidan bus stand.

TRAIN

Gaya is on the Delhi–Kolkata railway line.
Delhi (3AC/2AC/1AC ₹1244/1749/2987, 11½ hours, 22.39pm) The fastest train to Delhi is the 12301 Rajdhani Express.
Kolkata (3AC/2AC/1AC ₹756/1014/1747, six hours, 4.04am) Catch the 12302 Rajdhani Express for the most convenient connection to Kolkata.
Patna (2nd class/chair ₹67/210, two hours, 8.20pm) The 12366 Ranchi-Patna Janshatabdi Express is the fastest and most comfy.
Varanasi (sleeper/3AC/2AC ₹145/445/625, 5½ hours, 5am) Your best bet is the 13009 Doon Express.

Autorickshaw drivers will make the trip to Bodhgaya for ₹200 but can usually be bargained down to about ₹150.

Bodhgaya

📞 0631 / POP 30,900

The undisputed melting pot of Buddhism, Bodhgaya was where Prince Siddhartha attained enlightenment beneath a bodhi tree and became Buddha 2600 years ago. In terms of blessedness, this tiny temple town is to Buddhists what Mecca is to Muslims. Unsurprisingly, it attracts thousands of pilgrims from around the world every year, who come for prayer, study and meditation.

The most hallowed spot in town is a bodhi tree which flourishes amid a beautiful

garden setting, its roots embedded in the same soil as its celebrated ancestor. Additionally, many monasteries and temples dot the bucolic landscape, built in their national style by foreign Buddhist communities. The ambience is a mix of monastic tranquility and small-town commotion (a booming non-religious tourism industry has brought along with it the usual invasion of tourist paraphernalia, souvenir stalls and a serious rubbish problem). Incidentally, Bodhgaya has the best range of accommodation in Bihar and offers the most traveller camaraderie anywhere in Bihar and Jharkhand.

The best time to visit is November to March, when Tibetan pilgrims come down from McLeod Ganj in Dharamsala. The high season is from December to January, which is also when the Dalai Lama often visits.

⊙ Sights & Activities

★ **Mahabodhi Temple**   BUDDHIST TEMPLE
(camera/video ₹20/300; ⊙ 4am-9pm) The magnificent Unesco World Heritage–listed Mahabodhi Temple, marking the hallowed ground where Buddha attained enlightenment and formulated his philosophy of life, forms the spiritual heart of Bodhgaya. Built in the 6th century AD atop the site of a temple erected by Emperor Ashoka almost 800 years earlier, it was razed by foreign invaders in the 11th century and subsequently underwent several major restorations.

Topped by a 50m pyramidal spire, the inner sanctum of the ornate structure houses a 10th-century, 2m-high gilded image of a seated Buddha. Amazingly, four of the original sculpted stone railings surrounding the temple, dating from the Sunga period (184–70 BC), have survived amid the replicas.

Pilgrims and visitors from all walks of life and religions come to worship or just soak up the atmosphere of this sacred place. There's a well-manicured **Meditation Park** (Mahabodhi Temple; visitors/meditators ₹20/25; ⊙ visitors 10am-5pm, meditators 5-10am & 5-9pm) for those seeking extra solitude within the temple grounds. An enthralling way to start or finish the day is to stroll around the perimeter of the temple compound (in an auspicious clockwise pattern) and watch a sea of maroon and yellow dip and rise as monks perform endless prostrations on their prayer boards.

Monasteries & Temples   MONASTERIES, TEMPLES
One of Bodhgaya's great joys is its collection of monasteries and temples, each offering visitors a unique opportunity to peek into

Bodhgaya

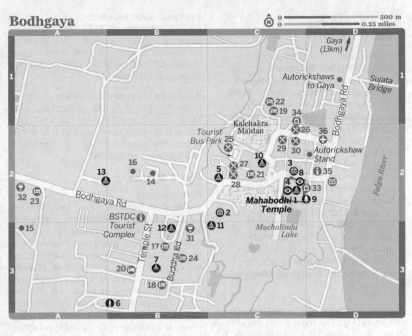

Bodhgaya

◉ Top Sights
1 Mahabodhi Temple.................................C2

◎ Sights
2 Archaeological Museum........................C2
3 Bodhgaya Multimedia Museum............C2
4 Bodhi Tree...C2
5 Chinese Monastery................................C2
6 Great Buddha Statue.............................B3
7 Indosan Nipponji Temple......................B3
8 Mahabodhi Temple Entrance................C2
9 Meditation Park.....................................D2
10 Namgyal Monastery...............................C2
11 Nepali Monastery...................................C3
12 Thai Monastery......................................B3
13 Vietnamese Monastery..........................A2

⊕ Activities, Courses & Tours
14 International Meditation Centre...........B2
15 Root Institute for Wisdom
    Culture...A3
16 Tergar Monastery..................................B2

🛏 Sleeping
17 Bhutanese Monastery............................B3
18 Bodhgaya Regency.................................B3
19 Gupta House...C1

20 Karma Temple..B3
21 Kirti Guest House...................................C2
22 Rahul Guest House.................................C1
23 Taj Darbar...A2
24 Tokyo Vihar..B3

✕ Eating
25 Fujiya Green...C2
26 Mohammad Restaurant.........................C2
27 Ram Sewak Tea Corner.........................C2
28 Siam Thai...C2
29 Tibet Om Cafe..C2
30 To Kiy Restaurant..................................C2

🍷 Drinking & Nightlife
31 Hotel Sujata...B3
32 Royal Residency.....................................A2

🛍 Shopping
33 Mahabodhi Bookshop.............................D2
34 Tibetan Refugee Market.........................C1

❶ Information
35 Middle Way Travels................................D2
    State Bank of India......................(see 28)
36 Verma Health Care
    Centre..D2

CHOOSING THE RIGHT CHARITY

Central Bihar is one of the poorest parts of India and, with its influx of visitors and Buddhist pilgrims, Bodhgaya has become home to numerous charity organisations and schools that rely on donations and volunteers. Some are set up by dodgy characters jumping on the charity bandwagon to fleece tourists. Be wary of those who approach you in the street for donations, especially children who besiege tourists asking for money for everything from school books and educational sponsorship to new cricket bats – they may speak several languages but are most likely illiterate. Genuine charities advise that you never give money directly to children. It's far better to help by donating to legitimate institutions or volunteering.

different Buddhist cultures and compare architectural styles. A tour of this global Buddhism microcosm takes an entire day, but you can always linger for longer.

Start your explorations at the **Indosan Nipponji Temple** (⊙5am-noon & 2-6pm), an exercise in quiet Japanese understatement compared to the richly presented Bhutanese Monastery nearby. The most impressive is the newer **Tergar Monastery** of the Karmapa, a glory of Tibetan decorative arts that will leave you slack-jawed as you enter. A none-too-distant runner-up is the impressive **Thai Monastery**, a brightly coloured *wat* with gold leaf shimmering from its arched rooftop and manicured gardens. Meditation sessions are held here mornings and evenings. The Tibetan **Karma Temple** and **Namgyal Monastery** each contain large prayer wheels. Other noteworthy monasteries include the **Chinese Monastery**, **Vietnamese Monastery** and **Nepali Monastery**. Monasteries are open sunrise to sunset.

Great Buddha Statue　　　MONUMENT
(off Temple St; ⊙7am-noon & 2-5pm) This 25m-high statue towers above a pleasant garden at the end of Temple St. The impressive monument was unveiled by the Dalai Lama in 1989, and is surrounded by 10 smaller sculptures of Buddha's disciples. The statue is partially hollow and is said to contain some 20,000 bronze Buddhas.

Archaeological Museum　　　MUSEUM
(⊉2200739; admission ₹10; ⊙8am-5pm) This museum contains a small collection of local Buddha figures and parts of the original granite railings and pillars rescued from the Mahabodhi Temple.

Bodhgaya Multimedia Museum　　　MUSEUM
(Indian/foreigner ₹30/100; ⊙8am-8pm) The Dalai Lama himself blessed the 2010 opening of this visual museum, which is low on production value but big on information and historical perspective.

🎓 Courses

Root Institute for Wisdom Culture　　　MEDITATION, YOGA
(⊉2200714; www.rootinstitute.com; ⊙office 8.30-11.30am & 1.30-4.30pm) This foreign-run institute holds various meditation courses (from two to 21 days) between late October and March. A requested donation of ₹750 per day covers your expenses. The 6.45am meditation session is open to all; you can also catch drop-in yoga classes at 11.45am Tuesday to Saturday. There's a charitable health program running six days a week; volunteering is welcome.

Bodhgaya Vipassana Meditation Centre　　　MEDITATION
(Dhamma Bodhi; ⊉2200437; www.bodhi.dhamma.org) Runs intensive 10-day *vipassana* courses twice each month on a donation basis. The small compound is 4km west of town on Boghgaya Rd.

International Meditation Centre　　　MEDITATION
(⊉2200707; per day from ₹200) The courses here are more informal compared to other meditation centres, and run through the year. However, anything less than a three-day commitment is frowned upon.

Tergar Monastery　　　MEDITATION
(⊉2201256; www.tergar.org) Offers courses on Tibetan Buddhism and welcomes long-term qualified volunteer English teachers.

🛏 Sleeping

Rates listed are for the high season (from December to January) but can fall by as much as 50% in the low season, so it pays to negotiate. If you don't mind the simple rules, it's also possible to stay at some of the monasteries and dharma centres, which give out simple beds for a nominal fee. Enquire at **Bhutanese Monastery** (⊉2200710; Buddha Rd; d with/without bathroom ₹300/250),

Karma Temple (☎2200795; Temple St; d with shared bathroom ₹250) and Root Institute for Wisdom Culture.

Gupta House GUESTHOUSE $
(☎2200933; jyoti_gupta2000in@yahoo.com; d ₹500) This homestay-style guesthouse has small but clean rooms, and is run by an affable local family. Its main selling point, however, is the al fresco Hari Om International Cafe located out front, which serves real coffee and some tasty North Indian, Italian, Tibetan, Korean and Japanese grub (mains ₹60 to ₹120), made from organic produce.

Rahul Guest House GUESTHOUSE $
(☎2200709; rahul_bodhgaya@yahoo.co.in; d ₹500) Clean, serene and seemingly popular with Russian travellers, this family home makes for an excellent stay away from the din – you'll find it down a lane at the far end of Kalachakra Maidan. The rooms upstairs, with whitewashed walls, nice breezes and simple furnishings, are better than those on the ground floor.

Kirti Guest House GUESTHOUSE $$
(☎2200744; kirtihouse744@yahoo.com; Off Bodhgaya Rd; d incl breakfast ₹2400; ✲@) Run by the Tibetan Monastery and one of the best of the midrange places, Kirti is known for its clean, bright rooms which are often occupied by pilgrim groups from Himachal Pradesh, Bhutan, Sikkim and Nepal. Its monastery-like facade is particularly pretty, and the staff never tire of meeting your requests with a smile. It's down a narrow bylane branching off the main road.

★**Taj Darbar** HOTEL $$$
(☎2200053; www.hoteltajdarbar.com; Bodhgaya Rd; s/d from ₹5000/5600; ✲☎) An excellent-value top-end choice in town, this hotel comes with polished marble hallways and spacious rooms with ivory-white bed sheets, small seating areas, working desks and sporadic bathtubs. The restaurant is also very popular with expats, and throws up a good range of frontier cuisine as well as Thai and Sri Lankan fare.

Bodhgaya Regency HOTEL $$$
(☎2200415; www.bodhgayaregency.com; s/d incl breakfast from ₹5200/5800; ✲☎) A smart and spanking new property off a quiet back road, this luxury address had just started operations when we visited. The rooms are of excellent value, boasting comfy twin beds, fresh pastel-print upholstery, squeaky clean bathrooms with bathtubs and views of temples in its vicinity.

Tokyo Vihar HOTEL $$$
(☎2201141; www.hoteltokyovihar.com; opposite Indosan Nipponji Temple; s/d ₹3000/4000; ✲☎) The name's a giveaway – this spiffy hotel is patronised by large Japanese groups. The decor, however, is unmistakeably midrange Indian, with the airy rooms sporting heavy upholstery, some generic woodwork, and standard creature comforts such as satellite TV and high-speed wi-fi. Go for a room with a balcony.

 Eating & Drinking

During high season between October and March, when pilgrims pour into Bodhgaya

---

TREE OF WISDOM

Undoubtedly, the most sacred fig tree ever to grace the earth was the **Bodhi Tree** at Bodhgaya, under which Prince Siddhartha, the founder of Buddhism, achieved enlightenment. Known as Sri Maha Bodhi, the original tree was paid special attention by Ashoka, a mighty Indian emperor who ruled most of the subcontinent from 269 to 232 BC, a century or so after Buddha's believed death. His wife, Tissarakkhā, wasn't such a fan of the tree and in a fit of jealousy and rage, caused the original Bodhi Tree's death by poisonous thorns shortly after becoming queen.

Thankfully, before its death, one of the tree's saplings was carried off to Anuradhapura in Sri Lanka by Sanghamitta (Ashoka's daughter), where it continues to flourish. A cutting was later carried back to Bodhgaya and planted where the original once stood. The red sandstone slab between the tree and the adjacent Mahabodhi Temple was placed by Ashoka to mark the spot of Buddha's enlightenment – it's referred to as the Vajrasan (Diamond Throne). Buddha was said to have stared unblinkingly at the tree in an awed gesture of gratitude and wonder after his enlightenment. Today, pilgrims and tourists alike flock here and attempt to do exactly the same thing, and the tree is considered the most important of Buddhism's four holiest sites.

by the thousands, temporary tent restaurants are set up around the Tibetan Refugee Market, serving a range of Tibetan, Continental and Indian dishes and sweets. **Royal Residency** (Bodhgaya Rd; mains ₹85-200, beers ₹250) and **Hotel Sujata** (Buddha Rd; mains ₹120-250, beers ₹250), two of Bodhgaya's upmarket hotels, are possibly the only places in town which officially serve alcohol.

★ To Kiy Restaurant   TIBETAN $
(dishes ₹40-80; ⊘8am-8pm Oct-Mar) You don't need to look beyond the hordes of maroon-robed monks with their heads immersed in steaming bowls of *thanthuk* (noodle soup) to tell that this ambient restaurant makes the best Tibetan food in town. Don't forget to sample the juicy, cricket-ball-sized *momos* and some yummy *phing* (rice noodles) while you're here.

Mohammad Restaurant   CAFE $
(mains ₹30-110; ⊘8am-8pm Nov-Mar) Hands-on Mohammed has been cooking professionally since he was 13 and it shows: his traveller tent serves up fresh, cheap food that you miss no matter where you are from. Gorge on Tibetan *momos*, Israeli *saksuka* (eggs poached in tomato sauce), quesadillas, Japanese food, Chinese fare, Greek salads and homemade soups, before topping it off with a tasty chocolate ball.

Tibet Om Cafe   TIBETAN, CAFE $
(dishes ₹30-100; ⊘8am-8pm Nov-Mar) A sweet Tibetan family has been coming down from Dharamsala every winter since 1986 to feed travellers hungry for *momos*, pancakes, brown bread, pies and cakes. The food is cheap and tasty and you can loiter endlessly. It lies within the Mayayana Guesthouse of the Namgyal Monastery.

Fujiya Green   CAFE $
(off Kalachakra Maidan; mains ₹30-85; ⊘8am-8pm) Another makeshift restaurant that's hugely popular with travellers, with the exception (and advantage) of running outside the high season. It has brightly coloured walls, tiled flooring and shiny chrome chairs, and the menu – running the gamut of Asian travel staples – excels across the board.

Ram Sewak Tea Corner   SWEETS $
(items ₹10-40; ⊘7am-7pm) If you seek sustenance at rock-bottom prices, look no further than this eatery, little more than a glorified roadside stand, for excellent snacks, sweets, lassis and basic thalis (set meals). Outdoor seating is a great spot to lounge with a cup of masala chai and watch Bodhgaya go by.

Siam Thai   THAI $$
(Bodhgaya Rd; mains ₹100-180; ⊘9am-10pm) If you're not particularly looking for culinary authenticity, you'll love the flavourful Thai dishes belted out by this restaurant near the Chinese Monastery. Staples like the green/red curries, raw papaya salad and tom yum soup are a pleasant departure from Indian spices, and you might have to queue for a table when the Thai direct flight operates during high season.

🛍 Shopping

Mahabodhi Bookshop   BOOKS
(Mahabodhi Temple; ⊘5am-9pm) A range of Buddhist literature within the temple complex.

Tibetan Refugee Market   CLOTHING
(⊘8am-8pm Oct-Jan) There are slim pickings here for winter woollens and textiles – most items are carted in from wholesale markets in Darjeeling and Delhi. There are scores of souvenir stalls around, peddling the usual religious trinkets such as rosaries and prayer wheels, as well Tibetan-style jewellery.

ℹ Information

Internet cafes (per hour ₹30) cluster around Hotel Tathagat International and across from the Mahabodi Temple entrance.
Middle Way Travels (☎2200648; Bodhgaya Rd; ⊘9am-10pm) Located opposite the temple entrance, this agency exchanges currency and travellers cheques, sells or swaps books, and deals with ticketing and car hire.
Main post office (cnr Bodhgaya & Godam Rds; ⊘10am-4pm Mon-Fri, to 2pm Sat) Main post office.
State Bank of India (Bodhgaya Rd; ⊘10am-2pm Mon-Fri, to noon Sat) Best rates for cash and travellers cheques; has an ATM.
Verma Health Care Centre (☎2201101; ⊘24hr) Emergency room and clinic.

ℹ Getting There & Away

Gaya airport is 8km west of town. **Air India** (☎2201155; www.airindia.com) flies twice a week to Kolkata; during the high season there are direct international flights from Bangkok (Thailand), Colombo (Sri Lanka), Thimphu (Bhutan) and Yangon (Myanmar).

Overcrowded shared autorickshaws (₹30) leave from the T-junction of Bodhgaya Rd and Sujata Bridge for the 13km trip to Gaya. A private autorickshaw to Gaya should cost ₹150 in high season.

Rajgir

🗹 06112 / POP 33,700

The fascinating surrounds of Rajgir are bounded by five semi-arid rocky hills, each lined with ancient stone walls – vestiges of the ancient capital of Magadha. Thanks to both Buddha and Mahavira spending some serious time here, Rajgir is an important pilgrimage site for Buddhists and Jains. A mention in the Mahabharata also ensures that Rajgir has a good supply of Hindu pilgrims who come to bathe in the hot springs at the Lakshmi Narayan Temple. However, foreign travellers are relatively rare.

If you're visiting, it's best to schedule a couple of days for exploring the many historic Buddhist and Jain sites around town and the ancient university site of Nalanda (12km south) which provides the perfect complement to Bodhgaya, 80km away. The centre of town is 500m east of the main road, on which you'll find the train station, bus stand and a number of hotels.

Rajgir Mahotsava (Rajgir; ☉ Oct), in October, is the town's three-day cultural festival, featuring classical Indian music, folk music and dance.

◉ Sights & Activities

The easiest way to see Rajgir's scattered sites is to rent a tonga. A four-hour tour including the hot springs, Vishwashanti Stupa, the Son Bhandar caves, Naulakha Mandir, Jain Temple, Japanese Temple, Veerayatan, Venuvana Vihar and the shrine of Maniyar Math is ₹600.

★ Vishwashanti Stupa   BUDDHIST TEMPLE

(chairlift return ticket ₹60; ☉ ropeway 8.15am-1pm & 2pm-5pm) This blazing-white, 40m stupa stands atop the Ratnagiri Hill about 5km south of town (take a tonga). Recesses in the stupa feature golden statues of Buddha in four stages of his life – birth, enlightenment, preaching and death. A wobbly, single-person ropeway runs to the summit, which affords expansive views of hills and a few Jain shrines dotting the landscape.

If you walk back down, you can detour to the remains of a stupa and **Griddhakuta** (Vulture's Peak), where Buddha preached to his disciples.

Veerayatan   MUSEUM

(www.veerayatanbihar.org; admission ₹20; ☉ 7am-6pm) This fascinating Jain museum tells the history of each of the 24 Jain *tirthankars* through ornate dollhouse-like 3D panel depictions made from wood and metal. The level of detail is astonishing. Don't miss the display by artist-in-residence Arharya Shri Chandanaiji Maharaj, made by hand out of flour.

Lakshmi Narayan Temple   TEMPLE

(admission free; ☉ dawn-dusk) Spread around Rajgir are numerous relics and sites associated with kings Ajatasatru and Bimbisara. Hindu pilgrims are drawn to the noisy Lakshmi Narayan Temple, about 2km south of town, to enjoy the health benefits of the hot springs. The murky grey Brahmakund, the hottest spring, is a scalding 45°C.

Temple priests will show you around, pour hot water on your head (in the manner of bathing a pilgrim) and ask for generous donations (don't feel pressured to give more than a small donation). It's a fascinating but confusing place with no English signs; tread carefully so you don't unintentionally offend.

Buddha Jal Vihar   SWIMMING

(Indian/foreigner ₹25/50; ☉ men 5-10am & noon-9pm, women 10am-noon) The Jaipur-pink Buddha Jal Vihar is an inviting, crystal-clear swimming pool set in well-manicured gardens and perfect to beat the heat.

🛏 Sleeping & Eating

Siddharth Hotel   HOTEL $

(🗹 255216; siddharthrajgir@gmail.com; s/d from ₹1050/1200; 🏨 @) Near the hot springs, Siddharth features fresh, clean rooms with a fair sprinkling of creature comforts. Prices swing wildly through the year: they increase con-

PILGRIMAGE ON RAILS

A unique way to explore the Buddhist circuit in North India is by hopping onto the **Mahaparinirvan Express** (www.railtourismindia.com/buddha), operated by Indian Railways on set dates between September and March. The eight-day package tour starts in Delhi, and guides you through Bodhgaya, Rajgir, Nalanda, Varanasi, Sarnath, Kushinagar, Lumbini (in Nepal) and Sravasti before returning to Delhi via Agra. Per person all-inclusive rates for the tour (on-board amenities are similar to the Rajdhani Expresses) start from US$110 per day. Note that the tariff doesn't include your visa fees for Nepal.

siderable between November and January (when rates also include breakfast, mineral water and tea) but come with a 30% discount between April and August. Most rooms are non-air-con; pay double for a chilled room.

Tathagat Tourist Bungalow　　HOTEL $$
(☎ 255176; tathagatrajgir@rediffmail.com; d with/ without AC ₹1600/1000; ❄) A standard-issue government hotel, this place has well-appointed rooms thrown around a hulking white building with dark-tinted windows close to the Veerayatan museum. It is chronically packed with domestic tourists during high season, who partly flock to it for the tasty Indian food served up in the in-house restaurant.

★**Indo Hokke Hotel**　　BOUTIQUE HOTEL $$$
(☎ 255245; centaur@bsnl.in; s/d ₹4600/5000; ❄@令❄) Surrounded by lovely gardens, this red-brick building has some of Bihar's comfiest beds. It's a unique sleeping experience here, in Japanese-style rooms furnished with tatami mats, teak furniture and Eastern decor. Other signature amenities include a Japanese bathhouse (different time slots for men and women), and meditation facilities for guests in the towering cylindrical Buddhist prayer hall.

Rajgir Residency　　HOTEL $$$
(☎ 255404; www.residencygrouphotels.com; s/d ₹5500/6600; ❄令) Overpriced, self-pampering and lacking in personality, this Vegas-sized hotel somehow manages to attract large international pilgrim and tourist groups. Comfort is top-end, with cosy beds and bathtubs in rooms and three air-con restaurants that can whip up Thai, Japanese, Chinese or Korean if you ask. You'll find it right next to Indo Hokke Hotel.

Green Restaurant　　INDIAN $
(mains ₹60-100, thali ₹100) Opposite the Lakshmi Narayan temple complex and hot springs, this simple restaurant offers great Indian meals, including an elaborate vegetarian thali. It can be crowded though, especially during lunch.

Lotus Restaurant　　INDIAN, JAPANESE $$$
(meals ₹450-500) It's expensive all right, but a meal at this upscale restaurant in the Indo Hokke Hotel is an experience you won't mind paying for. Part Japanese in decor with high-backed chairs, it has superb Indian food and a pricier Japanese menu featuring soba noodles, teriyaki and tempura, with authentic flavours and fresh ingredients (including pepper, pickles and tea).

❶ Information

There's a BSTDC tourist office at the Hotel Gautam Vihar, about 1km south of the train station on Nalanda Rd. SBI has an ATM on Bank Rd, about 200m west of the bus stand, and another across from the temple complex.

❶ Getting There & Around

Frequent buses run to Gaya (₹50, 2½ hours) and Nalanda (₹10, 30 minutes) from the bus stand on the road to Nalanda. Ridiculously crowded shared jeeps also shuttle between Rajgir and Nalanda (₹10). There is only one direct bus to Patna (₹70, three hours, 4.30pm). Of the five trains connecting Rajgir to Patna, the 13233 Rajgriha Express (2nd class/chair ₹33/225, 2.40pm, three hours) is the best.

Around Rajgir

Nalanda
☑ 061194

Founded in the 5th century AD, Nalanda was one of the ancient world's great universities and an important Buddhist centre of academic excellence. When Chinese scholar and traveller Xuan Zang visited sometime between 685 and 762 AD, about 10,000 monks and students lived here, studying theology, astronomy, metaphysics, medicine and philosophy. It's said that Nalanda's three libraries were so extensive they burnt for six months when foreign invaders sacked the university in the 12th century.

Allow an hour or two for wandering the extensive **ruins** (Indian/foreigner ₹5/100, video camera ₹25; ☺ 9am-5.30pm). They're peaceful and well maintained with a park-like atmosphere of clipped lawns, shrubs and roses. A guide (₹100 plus tip) is a worthwhile investment in unravelling the labyrinthine buildings and their history. The red-brick ruins consist of nine monasteries and four main temples. Most impressive is the **Great Stupa**, with steps, terraces, a few intact votive stupas, and monks' cells (climbing the structure is not allowed).

Across from the interesting Multimedia Museum is the **archaeological museum** (admission ₹5; ☺ 9am-5pm), a small but fascinating museum housing the Nalanda University seal and a host of sculptures and bronzes unearthed from Nalanda and Rajgir. Among the many Buddha figures and a 9th-century Kirtimukha (gargoyle) is a bizarre multiple-spouted pot.

About 2km further on from the museum is the huge **Xuan Zang Memorial Hall** (Indian/foreigner ₹5/50; ☉8am-5pm), built by the Chinese as a peace pagoda in honour of the famous Chinese traveller who studied and taught for some years at Nalanda. Modern-day backpackers will appreciate the statue of Xuan Zang at the front!

Regular shared jeeps run between Rajgir and Nalanda village (₹10), and from there you can take a shared tonga (per person ₹10 when full) for the final 3km to the site of Nalanda.

Kundalpur

Just outside Nalanda you'll find the striking **Nandyavarta Mahal** (☉5am-9pm) at Kundalpur, believed by the Digambar Jain sect to be the birthplace of Lord Mahavira, the final *tirthankar* and founder of Jainism. The small temple complex houses three white temples, the main featuring a to-scale postured idol of Mahavira. Inside the serene **Trikal Chaubeesi Jinmandir** within the same complex you'll find 72 *tirthankar* idols representing 24 *tirthankars* each of the past age, the present age and the future age.

JHARKHAND

Hewn out of neighbouring Bihar in 2000 to meet the autonomy demands of the Adivasi (tribal) population, Jharkhand is a land of immense natural and anthropological wealth. However, despite boasting an incredible 40% of the country's mineral wealth (mostly coal, copper and iron ore), rich forests and cash-rich industrial hubs, it is plagued by poverty, social injustice, corruption and outbursts of Maoist and Naxalite violence. For travellers, Jharkhand's prime attractions are the Jain pilgrimage centre at Parasnath Hill, its national parks and the chance to explore a relatively tourist-free and unspoilt part of India.

Ranchi

☏0651 / POP 863,500

Set on a plateau at 700m and marginally cooler than the plains, Jharkhand's capital, Ranchi, was the summer capital of Bihar

under the British. There's little of interest here for travellers, and it's not really on the way to anywhere except Betla (Palamau) National Park.

◉ Sights & Activities

Jagannath Temple   HINDU TEMPLE

This temple, about 12km southwest of town (₹250 return by autorickshaw), is a smaller version of the great Jagannath Mandir at Puri, and is open to non-Hindus. Every year during the Rath Yatra (Cart Festival), in the same manner as in Puri, Jagannath and his brother and sister gods are charioted to their holiday home, a smaller temple some 500m away.

✯ Festivals & Events

Chhath Festival   HINDU FESTIVAL

People line the banks of rivers and water bodies to honour Surya, the Sun God. For four days every October/November, it sees pious locals perform a series of rites that culminate in a social jamboree on the third day, marked by water rituals, traditional music and social mingling. At sunset on the sixth day after Diwali, married women, having fasted for 36 hours, immerse themselves in the water and offer fruits and flowers to the deity.

⌂ Sleeping

Station Rd, running between the train and bus stations, is lined with hotels of varying quality. Other hotels and restaurants can be found on the seemingly endless Main Rd, which runs at right angles to Station Rd. Hotel prices are steep since they cater more to business travellers than tourists. Many budget hotels may not have permits for hosting foreigners.

Hotel Embassy   HOTEL **$**

(☏2460813; embassyhotel@rediffmail.com; Station Rd; s/d from ₹880/990; ❄) A budget hotel that offers surprisingly good value by Ranchi's standards, this place is worth considering if you want a cheap bed for the night. The rooms are contemporary and decently clean – the costlier rooms have air-conditioning, and those out front have views of the train station.

Hotel Birsa Vihar   HOTEL **$$**

(Hans Regency; ☏2332816; Main Rd; d ₹2475; ❄) This government-owned property has received a much-needed renovation and now boasts spacious rooms with good toilets, clean linen, flat-screen TVs and tasty in-house food. The management is exceptionally efficient and friendly for a state-run property.

★**Chanakya BNR Hotel** HERITAGE HOTEL $$$
(☑2461211; www.chanakyabnrranchi.com; Station Rd; s/d incl breakfast from ₹3300/4000; ✳@☎) Spending a night at this charming hotel alone could be your reason for visiting Ranchi. A part-historic railways property located outside the train station, it's a superbly renovated terracotta-roofed Raj relic that oozes a flattering combination of vintage and boutique appeal. The trees on the property are home to parrots, and a swimming pool was under construction during research.

While the deluxe rooms are luxurious enough, try and grab a 110-year-old heritage room, with antique furniture, plush beds, high ceilings and glass-panelled views of manicured lawns outside. The hotel also prides itself on a superb in-house kitchen, which works up a formidable range of flavourful Indian and Continental dishes.

✗ Eating & Drinking

Planet Masala CAFE $
(56C Main Rd; mains ₹70-100; ⊙11am-9pm) A lively modern cafe thronged by college kids and young lovebirds, this smart and modern place offers two-dozen-odd dosas, along with a few other usual fast-food suspects such as pizzas and sundaes. There's a decent espresso on offer as well.

Hooch BAR
(Main Rd; beers ₹120; ⊙11am-11pm) Loud, flash and irreverently stylish, this bar is where Ranchi's yuppies meet in the evenings over booze and platters of tasty finger food. The comfy interiors sport funky neon trimmings, and there's live music on select evenings. Oh, we almost forgot the stadium-sized TV screen which plays live cricket matches if and when they're on.

❶ Information

The **State Bank of India** (Main Rd; ⊙10am-2pm Mon-Fri, to noon Sat) changes cash and travellers cheques, and has an ATM. **Chawla Travels & Cafe** (Station Rd, Gurunanak Market; internet per hr ₹30; ⊙8am-10pm), within a small shopping centre next to Hotel Embassy, has fast internet access. In the same shopping centre is **Suhana Tour and Travels** (☑9431171394; suhana_jharkhandtour@yahoo.co.in; ⊙8am-8pm

Mon-Sat, to 2pm Sun), which (due to the lack of better information centres) serves as Ranchi's de facto tourism office. The friendly Amardeep Sahay dispenses valuable tourist information, in addition to organising day trips to local waterfalls (from ₹400), two- and three-day trips to Betla (Palamau) National Park (from ₹3500 per person), and other transport ticketing.

❶ Getting There & Away

Ranchi's Birsa Munda Airport is 6km from the city centre. **Air India** (☑2503255; www.airindia.com) flies daily to Kolkata, Delhi and Patna, while **GoAir** (☑1800-222111; www.goair.in) has flights to Mumbai. A pre-paid taxi to Station Rd from the airport is ₹250.

From the government bus stand on Station Rd, there are five hourly departures to Gaya (₹160, six hours) from 6.30am to 10.30am; and one to Patna (₹225, nine hours, 9.30pm). There's also an overnight AC Volvo service to Patna (₹500, seven hours, 9pm) – tickets can be booked from the Volvo Service counter outside Birsa Vihar.

The 12366 Ranchi-Patna Janshatabdi connects to Patna (2nd class/chair ₹137/450, eight hours, 2.25pm), calling at Gaya (2nd class/chair ₹117/380, 5½ hours). For Kolkata, you can take the 12020 Ranchi-Howrah Shatabdi Express (chair/executive ₹645/1350, 7½ hours, 1.45pm).

Betla (Palamau) National Park

☑06562

Wild elephants freely roam the virgin forests of this lovely **national park** (☑222650, 9939341211; admission per vehicle ₹100, camera/video ₹100/500; ⊙6-10am & 2-5pm), spread over the hilly landscape of picturesque Palamau district 140km west of Ranchi. Tiger sightings are relatively rare, but a trip to this primeval region of Jharkhand is nonetheless worth considering because it guarantees a glimpse into the rich tribal heritage of the state. The park covers around 1026 sq km, about 232 sq km of which was declared as Betla National Park in 1989. Hiding behind stands of sal forest, rich evergreens, teak trees and bamboo thickets here are some 17 tigers, 52 leopards, 216 elephants and four lonely nilgai (antelope) according to a 2007 census (newer figures are yet to be derived).

The park is open year-round, but the best time to visit is November to April. If you can stand the heat, May is prime time for tiger spotting as forest cover is reduced and animals venture out in search of waterholes.

THE HOLY PARASNATH

Dusty Parasnath sits in a secluded spot of eastern Jharkhand, attracting a steady stream of devotees who come to pay obeisance at **Parasnath Hill**, a major Jain pilgrimage centre. The mountain (the highest landform in Jharkhand), is studded with 31 temples of religious importance. At the summit (1366m), where the **Parasnath Temple** now stands, 20 of the 24 Jain *tirthankars* are believed to have reached salvation, including Parasnath (the 23rd *tirthankar*) at the age of 100.

The best approach is from the auspicious town of Madhuban, 13km northeast of Parasnath, and itself home to some magnificent temples. The daily pilgrimage begins at 3am from the village: it's a 9km jaunt to the top, followed by a 9km loop visiting each of the temples. The entire 27km circuit takes about 12 hours. If you don't want to walk you can hire a *dandy* (a palanquin carried by two men) for ₹2500 return. Water and snacks are available along the way. During holidays and major festivals, you could have up to 15,000 people walking along with you.

You're likely to spend a night here, if only to rest your tired calves after the trek! There are several *dharamsalas* (pilgrim's rest houses) in Madhuban, which are more or less free save for a nominal upkeep fee, but nearly always jam-packed. For a proper hotel, the government-run and efficient **Yatri Nivas** (☑ 0658-232265; d from ₹300) has refreshingly comfortable rooms (with TV, lockers and hot water). Don't miss the small but well-kept **Jain Museum** (admission ₹5; ☺ 8am-6.30pm Mar-Oct, 8.30am-6pm Nov-Feb).

Parasnath is on the Kolkata–Gaya–Delhi train line. The best options are the 12801 Purushottam Express to Gaya (sleeper/3AC/2AC ₹140/303/640, three hours, 11.15am) and Mughalsarai for Varanasi (sleeper/3AC/2AC ₹190/495/720, seven hours), and the 12308 Jodhpur Howrah Superfast Express to Kolkata (sleeper/3AC/2AC ₹175/450/655, 5½ hours, 10.26pm). Regular minibuses run from Parasnath's bus stand to Madhuban every half-hour (₹40, 40 minutes). From Ranchi, you'll need to hire a car for about ₹3000 return.

Jeep safaris (per hr ₹350) can be arranged privately at the park gate – you must additionally hire a local guide (per hour ₹50) to accompany you. The park has two pachyderms for **elephant safaris** (per hr ₹200, up to 4 people), which offer a better chance at wildlife spotting, that too from a photo friendly perspective.

If you have time on your hands, consider an excursion to the ruined **Palamau Fort**, a 16th-century citadel of the local tribal Chero dynasty sited spectacularly within the forest. Alternatively, plan a picnic on the sandy banks of the scenic **Kechki River**. Jeep tours to each of these places from the park gate cost ₹350 per vehicle.

The best accommodation within the park is the superbly renovated **Forest Lodge** (d from ₹920; ✳), which boasts clean rooms with viewing balconies, LCD TV and spacious bathrooms. The canteen arranges a hearty vegetarian thali (₹100) for lunch and dinner upon advance notice. About 50 paces from the lodge is the **Tree House** (r ₹318), with two elevated sets of rooms built

out of teak and containing two bedrooms, a bathroom and an observation deck. Both can be booked through the park office. If they are booked out, spend the night at the gloomy government-run **Van Vihar** (☑ 9430725647; d with/without AC ₹900/550; ✳), a hulking property with spacious but musty rooms, scruffy paint-peeled walls and patchy service.

The nearest town to the park entrance is Daltonganj (Medininagar), 25km away, which has connections to Ranchi. It makes much more sense, however, to organise a tour through a Ranchi travel agency that will take you directly to the park. Suhana Tour and Travels has two- and three-day trips from ₹3500 per person, including transport, accommodation, park fees and safari. Travelling through an agency is highly recommended owing to inadequate local transport and safety issues in this isolated and sometimes lawless part of the state. In any case, call the park office or ask your travel agent for security advice before coming.

BIHAR & JHARKHAND EETLA (PALAMAU) NATIONAL PARK

Sikkim

Why Go?

Legend has it that the great Buddhist guru Padmasambhava regarded Sikkim as one of the last utopias on earth. Arguably one of the prettiest destinations in India, this tiny former Himalayan kingdom is a haven for travellers. From North Sikkim's plunging mountain valleys and emerald alpine forests to West Sikkim's picturesque patchwork of terraced paddy fields and flowering rhododendrons, there's plenty to feast your eyes on here – not least of which are stunning views of Khangchendzonga, the world's third-highest mountain (8598m), visible from almost anywhere in the state.

A strong preserve of Mahayana Buddhism, Sikkim's superb public buildings are lined with ritualistic vermilion, gold, blue and green. To top it all off, the resident population here is gracious, happy and hospitable, and your trip through the state is bound to leave you richer by a few friends.

Best Places to Stay

➡ Elgin Mount Pandim (p552)

➡ Mt Narsing Resort (p549)

➡ Mintokling Guest House (p541)

Best Monasteries

➡ Tashiding Gompa (p556)

➡ Pemayangtse Gompa (p552)

➡ Rumtek Gompa (p544)

When to Go
Gangtok

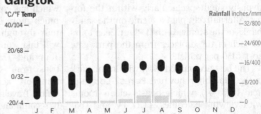

Oct–mid-Nov Clearest weather for views, but high-season crowds and prices.

Apr–May Spring blooms and warmth make up for cloudier skies.

Mid-Jun–Sep Good for rain-shadow areas of northern Sikkim but the monsoon plays spoilsport elsewhere.

Food & Drink

Sikkim's cuisine is a melange of robust Tibetan flavours and local tribal recipes, garnished with hints of Nepali and Bengali cuisine. The one 'don't-miss' beverage here is tongba, an alcoholic millet beer enjoyed across the entire eastern Himalaya. The beer (also known as chhang) is sipped through a bamboo straw and the wooden container (the tongba) is topped up periodically with boiling water to let the brew gain strength. Traditional Sikkimese dishes include *sisnoo/sochhya* (nettle soup), *ningro* (fried fiddlehead ferns), Tibetan-style *churpi* (dried yak cheese) and the Nepali speciality *gundruk ko jhol* (fermented mustard-leaf soup).

DON'T MISS

Sikkim's monastic **chaam masked dances** are when the hills come alive with unmatched ritualistic splendour. Part morality play, part country fair and part exorcism, the dances feature masked monks acting out Buddhist parables, stories from the life of Guru Padmasambhava and the victory of good over evil. Performances are supported by a crew of clowns, demons and dancing snowlions, all entertaining a crowd of spellbound locals dressed in their festive best.

Top State Festivals

➡ **Losar** (⊙ Feb/Mar; Pemayangtse, Rumtek, Enchey) Sikkim's biggest *chaam* dance takes place just before Tibetan New Year.

➡ **Bumchu** (⊙ Feb/Mar; Tashiding Gompa, p557) Lamas (Tibetan Buddhist priests or monks) open a pot (*bum*) containing holy water (*chu*) to foretell the year's fortunes.

➡ **Saga Dawa** (⊙ May/Jun; all monastery towns) Religious ceremonies and parades commemorate Buddha's birth, enlightenment and death.

➡ **Pang Lhabsol** (⊙ Aug; Ravangla, p549) Prayers and religious dances are performed in honour of Sikkim's guardian deity Khangchendzonga.

➡ **Losoong** (⊙ Dec/Jan; Old Rumtek, p544) Sikkimese New Year, preceded by *chaam* dances in many locations including Lingdum, Phodong, Phensang and Ralang.

MAIN POINTS OF ENTRY

Rangpo, on NH31A (connecting Siliguri to Gangtok) is the main entry point. Permits are available at the Rangpo border checkpost. For entry via Jorethang, permits must be arranged in advance.

Fast Facts

➡ **Population**: 607,700
➡ **Area**: 7096 sq km
➡ **Capital**: Gangtok
➡ **Main language**: Nepali
➡ **Sleeping prices**:
$ below ₹1000, $$ ₹1000 to ₹3000, $$$ above ₹3000

Top Tip

Shared jeeps are the best way to get around the hills. Jeeps between smaller towns depart early in the morning, and no connections may be available for the rest of the day. Book a front seat in advance, to save yourself from the physical torture of the journey that's typically felt in the side-facing rear seats.

Resources

➡ **Cultural Affairs & Heritage Department** (www.sikkim-culture.gov.in) Offers cultural background.

➡ **Sikkim Tourism** (www.sikkimtourism.travel) Lists sights, homestays and entry formalities.

➡ **Sikkim Government portal** (www.sikkim.nic.in) Provides a comprehensive overview.

Sikkim Highlights

1 Enjoy a roller-coaster journey over mountain tops and through abyss-like valleys on a road trip to the **Yumthang Valley** (p547)

2 Be enthralled by a colourful *chaam* (masked monk dance) at **Rumtek Gompa** (p544)

3 Wake up to dazzling Khangchendzonga views in **Pelling** (p551), visit Pemayangtse Gompa, and then help out the local schoolkids by eating banana cake

4 Wander among prayer flags, flower hedges and ancient chortens (stupas) at **Tashiding Gompa** (p556)

5 Get closer to sublime Himalayan peaks and flex your calves on the **Goecha La** (p556) trek

6 Sip garden fresh tea while taking in sweeping mountain vistas in **Temi** (p550)

7 Overnight at peaceful **Khecheopalri Lake** (p553) before hiking up to a nearby meditation cave

History

According to popular belief, Sikkim was supposedly uninhabited before the Lepchas migrated here from Assam or Myanmar (Burma) in the 13th century, followed by Bhutias who moved out of Tibet during the 15th century. The Nyingmapa form of Vajrayana (Tibetan) Buddhism arrived with three refugee Tibetan lamas who encountered each other at the site of modern-day Yuksom. Here in 1641 they crowned Phuntsog Namgyal as first chogyal (king) of Sikkim. The capital later moved to Rabdentse (near Pelling), then to Tumlong (now Phodong) before finally settling in Gangtok following a Nepali invasion.

In their heydays, the chogyals' rule encompassed eastern Nepal, upper Bengal and Darjeeling. However, much territory was later lost during wars with Bhutan and Nepal, and throughout the 19th century large numbers of Hindu Nepali migrants arrived, eventually coming to form a majority of Sikkim's population.

In 1835 the British bribed Sikkim's chogyal to cede Darjeeling to the East India Company. Tibet, which regarded Sikkim as a vassal state, raised strong objections. In 1849, amid rising tensions, the British annexed the entire area between the present Sikkim border and the Ganges plains, repulsing a counter-invasion by Tibet in 1886. In 1903–04, Britain's ultimate imperial adventurer Francis Younghusband twice trekked up to the Sikkim–Tibet border. There, with a small contingent of soldiers, he set about inciting a fracas that would 'justify' an invasion of Tibet.

Sikkim's last chogyal ruled from 1963 to 1975, after which the kingdom merged with the Indian dominion and was given statehood.

Activities

Going on a trek is the high point of any Sikkim sojourn. From day hikes between villages along centuries-old foot trails to multiday slogs across high mountain passes, there are plenty of trekking options available in the state. The most popular short hikes are the routes between Yuksom and Tashiding and Yuksom and Khecheopalri Lake. Longer options that score well with experienced adventurers are the trek to Goecha La at the base of Khangchendzonga, and the Singalila Ridge trek that connects Yuksom to West Sikkim along the eponymous mountain ridge. Treks to remote areas such as Zemu Glacier and Green Lake are yet to be opened up, though it's possible to visit these areas with lots of money and permit-processing time to spare.

Apart from trekking, adventure activities such as mountain biking and paragliding are slowly becoming popular in Sikkim. The **Sikkim Paragliding Festival** (http://www.paraglidingassociationofindia.org), held in Gangtok in winter, is one of the latest events to seize the imagination of travellers and sports buffs alike.

Permits

STANDARD PERMITS

Foreigners require an Inner Line Permit to enter Sikkim (Indians don't). These are free and a mere formality, although to apply you'll need photos and passport photocopies. Permits are most easily obtainable at the Melli police checkpost and Rangpo border post on arrival, but can also be obtained at Indian embassies abroad when getting your visa and at the following places:

Foreigners' Regional Registration Offices (FRRO: ☎ 011-26711384, 033-22837084; www.immigrationindia.nic.in; ⊗ 10am-5pm Mon-Fri) Delhi or Kolkata offices.

Sikkim House (☎ 011-26883026, 033-22817905; www.sikkim.nic.in/sikkimhouse; ⊗ 10.30am-4pm Mon-Fri, until 2pm Sat) Delhi or Kolkata offices.

Sikkim Tourist Office (www.sikkimtourism.travel; ⊗ 10am-5pm Mon-Sat) Darjeeling, Siliguri and Rangpo offices. For an on the spot Sikkim permit, bring a photocopy of your passport and Indian visa, plus one photo.

EXTENSIONS

Permits are generally valid for 30 days (sometimes 15 days from embassies abroad). These can be extended at government offices in Gangtok and Tikjuk (5km below Pelling) for a further 30 days, giving a maximum of 60 days. Once you leave Sikkim, you must wait three months before applying for another permit.

PERMIT VALIDITY

The standard permit is valid for visits to the following areas:
➡ Gangtok, Rumtek and Lingdum
➡ South Sikkim
➡ Anywhere on the Gangtok–Singhik road
➡ Most of West Sikkim where paved roads extend.

SPECIAL PERMITS

High-altitude treks, including the main Goecha La and Singalila Ridge routes, require **trekking permits** valid for up to 15 days and organised by trekking agents.

For travel beyond Singhik up the Lachung and Lachen Valleys, foreigners need additional **restricted area permits** from the tourism department and police and, even with these, cannot go further than the Tsopta Valley or Yume Samdong (Zero Point). Indian citizens need a **police permit** to travel north of Singhik, but can travel further up the Thangu Valley to Gurudongmar Lake.

Foreigners also need a restricted area permit to visit Tsomgo (Changu) Lake. Only Indians are permitted to travel past Tsomgo Lake to the Tibetan border at Nathu La.

Trekking permits as well as restricted area permits are issued locally through approved tour agencies and you will have to join a tour to get one. You'll need a minimum group of two, a passport photo, and copies of your existing permit, visa and passport details page. Permits take 24 hours to arrange.

EAST SIKKIM

Thanks to a national highway that connects it with the rest of the country, East Sikkim sees a higher tourist footfall compared to other parts of the state. Focused around the urban hub of Gangtok, it's also the most populous area in the region. Regardless of your destination, you are likely to spend a few days here, even if only in transit.

Gangtok

✔ 03592 / POP 29,300 / ELEV 1750M

Irreverent, laid-back and happy-go-lucky, Sikkim's capital is mostly a functional sprawl of urban concrete interspersed with patches of forestry. True to its name (meaning 'hilltop'), the city perches along a precipitous mountain ridge, descending down the hillside in steep tiers. Apart from a few sights of religious importance and an inspiring view of Khangchendzonga soaring above the western horizon, there isn't much to see in town. That said, travellers love its relaxed atmosphere and often linger here for a few days, soaking up the local culture while arranging their travels (eg treks and tours) around the state.

Gangtok's crooked spine is the Rangpo–Mangan road, marked NH31A. The tourist office, banks and many shops line the central pedestrianised Mahatma Gandhi (MG) Marg, a pretty district patronised by shoppers, lovers, diners and local fashionistas.

◉ Sights

★ **Namgyal Institute of Tibetology**   MUSEUM

(www.tibetology.net; Deorali; admission ₹10; ⊙10am-4pm) This fantastic museum housed in a traditional Tibetan-style mansion boasts a jaw-dropping collection of artefacts related to Vajrayana Buddhism and Tibetan culture. Established in 1958 to promote scholastic and cultural research, its ground-floor hall displays Buddhist manuscripts, icons, *thangkas* (Tibetan cloth paintings) and Tantric ritual objects, such as a *thöpa* (bowl made from a human skull) and *kangling* (human thighbone trumpet).

The library on the 1st floor houses precious Buddhist tomes, some dating back several hundred years. The **publication sales counter** within the building sells a collection of documentaries on Sikkimese rituals and culture, but timings are flexible.

Further up along the same road is the **Do-Drul Chorten**, a large white Tibetan pagoda surrounded by dormitories for novice monks and glass-walled galleries with countless flaming butter lamps burning within.

The institute sits in a park and is conveniently close to the lower station of Damodar Ropeway, a cable car running to the Secretariat ridge with great views of town.

Ridge   AREA

With gorgeous views both to the east and west, the ridge is a shaded promenade cresting Gangtok's upper reaches. It's a pleasant place to stroll away your time in manicured parks and gardens. The imposing structure of **Chogyal Palace** (former royal residence) is closed to visitors, but is a fine sight from a distance nonetheless.

The impressive **Tsuglhakhang** temple near the palace is often open early in the morning (and during major festivals) to pilgrims and curious tourists. During the spring bloom (March and April) it's worth peeping inside the **Flower Exhibition Centre** (admission ₹10; ⊙9am-5pm), a modestly sized greenhouse full of exotic orchids, anthuriums and Easter lilies.

Enchey Gompa   MONASTERY

(⊙4am-4pm Mon-Sat, to 1pm Sun) On the northern outskirts of Gangtok, approached through gently rustling conifers, stands this ambient monastery. It's easily Gangtok's most attractive, with some decent murals and statues of Tantric deities. The monastery founder was apparently famous for his levitational skills. It comes alive for the colourful **Detor Chaam** masked dances in December/January (28th and 29th day of the 11th Tibetan lunar month).

Ganesh Tok & Around · VIEWPOINTS
From Enchey Gompa, the main road swings northeast around the telecom tower to a collection of prayer flags, where a footpath scrambles up in around 15 minutes to **Ganesh Tok viewpoint**. Festooned in colourful prayer flags, Ganesh Tok offers superb city views and its minicafe serves hot tea and Indian snacks.

Hanuman Tok, another impressive viewpoint, sits on a hilltop around 4km drive beyond Ganesh Tok, though there are shortcuts for walkers.

Gangtok's best view of Khangchendzonga can be found from the **Tashi viewpoint**, 4km northwest of town, beside the main route to Phodong.

Himalayan Zoological Park · ZOO
(Indian/foreigner ₹25/50, vehicle ₹40, video ₹500; ⊙9am-4pm Fri-Wed) Among the better-maintained zoos in the country, the Gangtok zoo occupies an entire hill opposite Ganesh Tok viewpoint. Red pandas, civet cats, Himalayan bears, clouded leopards and snow leopards roam around in extensive forested enclosures so large that you'll value a car to shuttle between them. There's a cafe within for refreshments (snacks ₹30).

🕯 Activities

Classic early-morning 'three-point tours' show you Ganesh Tok, Hanuman Tok and Tashi viewpoints (₹600). Almost any travel agent, hotel or taxi driver offers variants, including a 'five-point tour' adding Enchey Gompa and Namgyal Institute (₹800), or 'seven-point tours' tacking on old-and-new Rumtek (₹1200) or Rumtek plus Lingdum (₹1500). Prices are per vehicle holding three or four passengers.

For high-altitude treks, visits to Tsomgo Lake or tours to northern Sikkim, you'll need a tour agency. Not all agents, however, work with foreigners, so look for a company that's registered with the **Travel Agents Association of Sikkim** (TAAS; www.taas.org.in). Inclusive trekking charges for foreigners range from US$55 to US$80 per person per day.

Damodar Ropeway · SIGHTSEEING
(per person adult/child return ₹60/40, video ₹70; ⊙9.30am-4.30pm) The Damodar Ropeway is a cable car that shuttles from just below the Namgyal Institute of Tibetology to the Secretariat ridge. It provides a bird's-eye view of Gangtok, along with stupendous vistas of the surrounding mountain ranges and valleys. Avoid if you have vertigo.

Sikkim Tourism Development Corporation · OUTDOOR ADVENTURE
(STDC; ☎203960; www.sikkimtourism.travel; MG Marg) Memorable eagle-eye views of Sikkim can be enjoyed from scenic **helicopter flights** operated by STDC. Choose between a buzz over Gangtok (₹7590, 15 minutes), a circuit of West Sikkim (₹66,000, 55 minutes), a circuit of North Sikkim (₹78,500, 65 minutes) and the Khangchendzonga ridge (₹90,000, 75 minutes). Prices are for five people (four for Khangchendzonga). Book in advance.

STDC also has information regarding **white-water rafting** on the Teesta River, **paragliding** and **mountain biking**.

Potala Tours & Treks · TREKKING
(☎9434257036; www.potalatreks.in; PS Rd) A pricey but professional outfit with operations in Sikkim, Darjeeling and Bhutan.

Yak and Yeti Travels & Expeditions · TREKKING
(☎9434117418; www.yaknyeti.com; Zero Point) Highly recommended for trekking and mountaineering.

Blue Sky Treks & Travels · TREKKING
(☎205113; blueskytourism@yahoo.com; Tourism Bldg, MG Marg) For trekking and customised tours.

Galaxy Tours & Treks · TREKKING
(☎201290; galaxytvls@gmail.com; Metro Point) Arranges tours to North Sikkim and runs several hotels in the Lachung Valley.

🛏 Sleeping

Ecotourism & Conservation Society of Sikkim · HOMESTAY $
(ECOSS; ☎232798; www.sikkimhomestay.com; Daragaon/Tadong) For a rustic experience, ECOSS can arrange homestays (₹600 to ₹1500 per person) in the villages of Dzongu (permits required), Pastanga and Yuksom.

Hotel Pandim · HOTEL $$
(☎9832080172; www.hotelpandim.com; Bhanu Path; s/d from ₹850/1550; 🖥) In a quiet roadside location along the ridge, this hotel offers superb value, commendable service and the best beds in town within a budget.

Gangtok

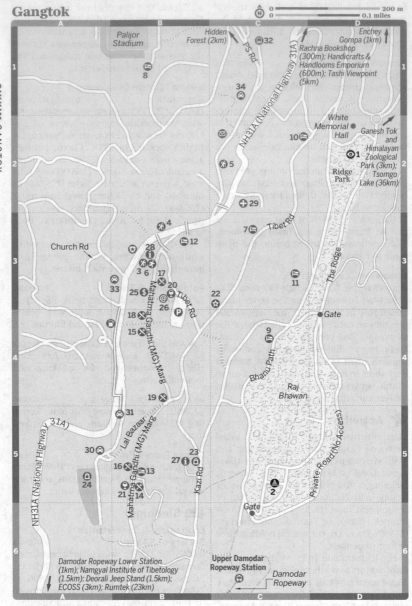

Top-floor deluxe rooms have the coolest mountain views, but the cheaper basement rooms are eminently liveable too. There's good food (advance order) served at the cosy terrace sit-out. The reception is on the top floor.

Modern Central Lodge GUESTHOUSE $
(☎204670; moderntreks@hotmail.com; NH31A; d/tr ₹880/900) This is one of several budget hotels lining the main drag in Gangtok, with the added advantage of an in-house travel agency that can organise treks and tours

Gangtok

for residents. Combining a stay in the guesthouse's spartan rooms (with hand-painted furniture, clean sheets and town views) with a tour often works out in your favour money-wise.

★ **Mintokling Guest House**　　GUESTHOUSE **$$**
(☑208553; www.mintokling.com; Bhanu Path; s/d from ₹1650/1850; @ 🕾) Draped by exotic foliage and secluded from urban din, this lodge-like family home is an oasis of peace and quiet. The rooms are non-fussy, but come with pinewood wall panels and sport fresh upholstery made from traditional fabric. The pretty lawns are dotted with prayer flags and cane garden chairs. The traditional menu at the restaurant is a must-try.

Hotel Sonam Delek　　HOTEL **$$**
(☑202566; www.hotelsonamdelek.com; Tibet Rd; d incl breakfast from ₹1540; 🕾) Part art deco, part Tibetan, this long-standing favourite continues to offer matchless service, hearty food and great value for money. The standard rooms in the basement have direct access to a superb rear terrace (studded with colourful flags) with sweeping views of Khangchendzonga across the valley. The pricier rooms (₹3000) above have private balcony views, king-size beds and prim furnishings.

Oriental　　BOUTIQUE HOTEL **$$**
(☑221181; www.orientalsikkim.com; MG Marg; s/d incl breakfast ₹2450/3200; @) Stylish though understated, this appealing hotel behind a flora-lined glass-and-teak facade sees a lot of guests who desire comfort and privacy without having to venture far from the town centre. Rooms are smallish, but appointed with inviting beds (some with canopies), pinewood panelling and good views of the pedestrianised district below.

Hidden Forest　　HOMESTAY **$$**
(☑205197; www.hiddenforestretreat.org; Middle Sichey Village; s/d from ₹1700/2000) 🖉 If you don't mind traipsing 2km from town, this family-run homestay – secluded amid fruit trees, orchids and flower nurseries – could be your ideal hideaway. The Tibetan-themed rooms have private balconies and the terrace is great for evening chhangs. The lip-smacking food comes from the solar-powered kitchen, a resident cow provides dairy produce and all vegetable matter is composted.

A taxi from the centre costs ₹150.

Hotel Nor-Khill　　HERITAGE HOTEL **$$$**
(☑205637; www.elginhotels.com; PS Rd; s/d incl full board ₹8400/8700; 🕾) Checking into the

Nor-Khill is like time travelling back to the pre-Independence era, when this stately property served as the chogyal's royal guesthouse. Bearing testimony to its heydays are countless historical photos, period furniture and exquisite Tibetan carpets that lend vintage appeal to the hallways and the lobby. The spaciously luxurious rooms are an absolute splurge, and attract diplomats and the Dalai Lama.

Chumbi Residency BOUTIQUE HOTEL $$$
(206618; www.thechumbiresidency.com; Tibet Rd; s/d incl breakfast from ₹2600/3400;) A spot of luxury only five minutes from the town centre, this place is extremely popular with top-end tour groups. Boasting interiors and comforts that remind you of the 1980s, its smallish rooms sport fresh white walls and tasteful furniture. Ask for a room with a view. The cool Tangerine bar-restaurant in the basement is great for dinner.

✗ Eating

★ Taste of Tibet TIBETAN $
(MG Marg; mains ₹70-100; ⊙10am-9pm) This bustling upstairs place, incredibly popular with Gangtok's youth brigade, serves the best Tibetan morsels in Gangtok. Jostle with college students and maroon-robed monks aorund tiny tables and wolf down generous servings of *momos*, noodle soup, *shyabhale* (fried meat pasty) and cold beef salad – best paired with a bottle of local Dansberg beer.

Parivar Restaurant SOUTH INDIAN $
(MG Marg; dishes ₹60-100; ⊙8am-8pm) Eat here for good-value South Indian vegetarian food. Go for the various *masala dosas* (savoury crepes stuffed with spiced potatoes) and *choley paneer* (chickpeas with cottage cheese) for breakfast. For lunch, try the all-inclusive mini/full thali (set meal; ₹100/160).

Bakers Cafe BAKERY $
(MG Marg; pastries from ₹20, mains ₹40-90; ⊙9am-8pm) The coolest breakfast escape on MG Marg, this cosy Western-style cafe has strong espresso (₹40), refreshing lemon iced tea, croissants, baguettes, panini, pizzas and pastries. You might have to wait for a table in the evening.

★ 9'INE SIKKIMESE $$
(MG Marg; set meals ₹180-200; ⊙11am-9pm) This glass-fronted restaurant up a flight of stairs serves an awesome spread of local delicacies such as *sisnoo*, *gundruk ko jhol*, fermented soybean chutney and fiery pork

curry. The lounge-style seating complements lazy lunch sessions, and the proprietors have thankfully done away with karaoke (an earlier accompaniment), making it a better place to dine in.

Gangtalk MULTICUISINE $$
(MG Marg; mains ₹140-270; ⊙11am-9pm) Grab a cane table on the lovely sit-out overlooking MG Marg, and make short work of a wide range of tasty eats that emerge from this restaurant's busy kitchen. Call in a serving of creamy chicken and mushroom sandwich followed by fish *momos*, or simply go for the elaborate Gangtalk sampler (₹495), which has a little bit of everything.

Chopsticks MULTICUISINE $$
(MG Marg; mains ₹140-180; ⊙11am-9pm) Craving some spare pork ribs glazed in honey, or a giant serving of grilled sausages with mashed potato and barbecue sauce? Then walk into this fancy place and hog away to glory, all the while catching up on cricketing action on the wall-mounted giant TV screen.

🍷 Drinking & Entertainment

Two of the nicest locations for a quiet drink are the large terrace of the **Tashi Delek Hotel** (MG Marg) or the bar and garden of the Hotel Nor-Khill.

Indulge BAR
(www.thriceasmuch.com; Tibet Rd; beers from ₹110; ⊙11am-10pm) Funky neon streaks on the walls and ceiling add a touch of space-age cool to this modern bar-restaurant. The bar menu stretches to pizzas and steaks (mains ₹90 to ₹220), and the company is pleasant. Now only if the karaoke could be toned down a wee bit.

Cafe Live & Loud LIVE MUSIC
(www.thriceasmuch.com; Tibet Rd; beers from ₹120; ⊙10am-11pm;) A happening venue for live music, this flashy lounge-bar hosts gigs by live rock, blues and alternative bands every Thursday, Friday and Saturday evenings. There's a full bar and food menu, with some unusual Southeast Asian offerings (mains ₹130 to ₹180), and a pleasant cafe terrace if you wish to distance yourself from the sound blast within.

🔒 Shopping

Several souvenir shops on MG Marg and PS Rd sell Tibetan and Sikkimese handicrafts such as wooden tongba pots, prayer flags, Tibetan curios and Nepali-style *khukri* knives.

Owing to its tax-free status, Sikkim sells booze at rock-bottom prices. Apart from generic Indian and foreign labels being sold almost at half price, a few local brands are are available in novelty souvenir containers. Fireball brandy comes in a bowling-ball-style red sphere, while Old Gold whiskey is bottled in a *khukri*-shaped glass dagger.

★ Golden Tips FOOD & DRINK

(www.goldentipstea.com; Kazi Rd; tea per pack from ₹300; ☺9am-9pm) This boutique tea store stocks a mind-blowing repertoire of premium Darjeeling teas, including selections of Sikkimese tea from Temi. The produce is sold in souvenir-sized packages (175g to 250g), and the store reps are happy to brew you a cup of your chosen tea for free.

Rachna Books BOOKS

(www.rachnabooks.com; Development Area; ☺10am-7pm) Gangtok's best-stocked and most convivial bookshop also has occasional film and music events on the upstairs terrace. Its catalogue of titles on Sikkimese and Tibetan history as well as Vajrayana Buddhism is well worth browsing.

Handicrafts & Handloom Emporium HANDICRAFTS

(Zero Point; ☺10am-4pm, closed Sun Apr-Jun) This government initiative teaches traditional crafts to local students and markets their products – including toy red pandas, 1m by 2m handwoven carpets (₹6000), Tibetan furniture, handmade paper and traditional Sikkimese-style ensembles (₹1500 to ₹2000).

Khangchendzonga Market FOOD & DRINK

(☺8am-8pm) This covered multi-storey market is interesting for its range of traditional Himalayan produce, including *churpi*, Tibetan *tsampa* (ground roasted barley), dried *phing* noodles and circular yeast patties used for brewing chhang.

ℹ Information

Many ATMS and internet cafes line MG Marg.

Axis Bank (MG Marg; ☺10am-5pm Mon-Sat) Changes cash and travellers cheques and has an ATM. Stock up with rupees in Gangtok: exchange is virtually impossible elsewhere in Sikkim.

Cyber Cafe (MG Marg; per hr ₹30; ☺9am-9pm) Internet access in a bylane.

Foreigners' Registration Office (Kazi Rd; ☺10am-4pm Mon-Sat) In the lane beside Indian Overseas Bank, for permit extensions.

Main post office (PS Rd; ☺10am-4pm Mon-Sat, to 2pm Sun for stamps) Normal and speed post services.

Police station (☑202033; NH31A) A helpful lot.

Sikkim Tourist Information Centre (☑toll free 204408; www.sikkimtourism.travel; MG Marg; ☺10am-7pm) Offers general advice. Open 10am to 4pm outside peak seasons.

STNM Hospital (☑222059; NH31A) Emergency and outpatient facilities.

ℹ Getting There & Away

AIR

The nearest airport to Sikkim is Bagdogra, 124km from Gangtok, near Siliguri in West Bengal, which has flights to Kolkata, Delhi and Guwahati.

Helicopters shuttle from Gangtok to Bagdogra (₹2200, 35 minutes), departing at 11am and returning at 2.30pm, but services are cancelled in adverse weather. There's a strict maximum 10kg baggage allowance. Sikkim Tourism Development Corporation (p539) sells the tickets for this and scenic flights.

Fixed-price taxis and Sumos (jeeps) go directly to Bagdogra (₹2500, five hours).

Sikkim's first airport is planned at Pakyong, 35km from Gangtok, with a tentative completion date of 2014.

BUS

Buses run from the government **SNT bus station** (☑03592-202016; PS Rd) at 7am to Jorethang (₹90), Kalimpong (₹90) and Namchi (₹100), at 1.15pm to Pelling (₹145) and hourly to Siliguri (₹180, 6am to 1pm). Shared jeeps, however, are quicker and more frequent.

SHARED JEEPS

Some jeep departures are fixed, others leave when all the seats are filled. Departures usually start at 6.30am for the more distant destinations and continue up to about 2pm.

From the hectic but well-organised **Private Jeep Stand** (NH31A), 1.5km below Gangtok, shared jeeps depart every 30 minutes or so to Darjeeling (₹160, five hours), Kalimpong (₹90, three hours) and Siliguri (₹170, five hours), some continuing to New Jalpaiguri train station. Buses to Siliguri (₹120) also run from here.

West Sikkim vehicles depart from **Southwest Jeep Stand** (Church Rd) for Geyzing (₹180, 4½ hours, four daily), Ravangla (₹100, three hours, four daily), Namchi (₹120, three hours, every half-hour) and Jorethang (₹120, three hours, hourly). Jeeps for Yuksom, Tashiding and Pelling (₹180 to ₹200, five hours) depart around 7am and possibly again around 12.30pm. For independent travel, small groups can charter a vehicle (per day ₹3000).

BORDER CROSSING – NEPAL, BHUTAN & TIBET

There are daily jeeps from the Private Jeep Stand to Kakarbhitta (₹200, six hours, 6.30am) on the Nepalese border and Jaigon (₹280, five hours, 7am) on the Bhutanese border.

The border crossing at Nathu La is currently open to Indian traders. This means that merchants with special permits can cross over to Tibet with merchandise for sale on designated days of the week. Staying overnight on the Chinese side is not allowed and traders must return to India before dusk. Chinese traders with similar permits are also allowed to enter India for business during the day. For travellers, however, the checkpost continues to remain sealed. While Indian tourists are allowed to visit the international border for sightseeing and photo-ops, the area is strictly out of bounds for foreigners.

TRAIN

The nearest major train station is over 125km away at New Jalpaiguri (NJP). There's a computerised **railway booking counter** (⊙8am-2pm Mon-Sat,to 11am Sun & public holidays) at the SNT bus station.

❶ Getting Around

There's a **taxi stand** in Lal Bazaar opposite the Denzong Cinema, and another in **PS Rd** just north of the post office. **Shared taxis** to Tadong (₹20, every 10 minutes) depart from just under the pedestrian bridge on NH31A.

Around Gangtok

Rumtek

Facing Gangtok distantly across a plunging green valley, Rumtek village is dominated by its extensive and eponymous gompa complex, considered one of Tibetan Buddhism's most venerable institutions and currently the home-in-exile of Buddhism's Kagyu (Black Hat) sect. Time permitting, you can make a quick sortie to Lingdum Gompa as well, linked to Rumtek by beautiful country lanes that wind through mossy forests high above river valleys and artistically terraced rice slopes.

◉ Sights

Rumtek Gompa　　　　　　　　MONASTERY

(📞252329; www.rumtek.org; monastery building admission ₹10; ⊙monastery building 6am-6pm) The rambling and walled complex of this monastery contains religious buildings, schools and several small lodge-hotels. Unusually for a monastery, the place is guarded by armed forces, following heated altercations and even an invasion by partisan monks in the wake of the Karmapa controversy. To enter, foreigners must show their passport and Sikkim permit at the checkpost.

Meant to replace the Tsurphu Monastery in Tibet, which had been partially destroyed during China's Cultural Revolution, Rumtek's main monastery building was constructed between 1961 and 1966. There's a mural of the original monastery beside the metal detector. The giant throne within awaits the crowning of Kagyu's current spiritual leader, the (disputed) 17th Karmapa, who currently resides in Dharamsala. An ornate scroll, hand-painted by the young leader, hangs within the monastery in his absence.

Behind the monastery building, up a flight of stairs running past a snack shop (good tea and *momos*!) stands the **Golden Stupa** (⊙6-11.45am & noon-5pm) 〈FREE〉. Stuffed with religious paraphernalia, the smallish room holds the ashes of the 16th Karmapa in an amber, coral and turquoise-studded reliquary to which pilgrims pay their deepest respects. The keys to the shrine are usually with obliging lamas enrolled at the Karma Shri Nalanda Institute of Buddhist Studies opposite. Leave a donation, and you'll be blessed with a holy metal dorje (Tibetan-Buddhist talisman symbolising lightning).

The knowledgeable, witty and dapper Monay Rai gives a wonderful tour of the monastery (₹150).

Old Rumtek Gompa　　　　　　MONASTERY

(⊙dawn-dusk) About 1.5km beyond the Rumtek Gompa towards Sang, a long avenue of white prayer flags and junipers leads photogenically down to the forlorn and atmospheric Old Rumtek Gompa, looking out to some fabulous west-facing views. The monastery is still in use, and the main prayer hall has been thoroughly renovated. Two days before **Losoong** (Old Rumtek; ⊙Dec/Jan) (Sikkimese New Year), the monastery holds the celebrated **Kagyed Chaam** dance.

Lingdum Gompa — MONASTERY

(www.zurmangkagyud.org) Completed as recently as 1998, peaceful Lingdum Gompa grows out of pine forests in impressive layers, with pleasant side gardens and a photogenic chorten. The extensively muralled main prayer hall enshrines huge statues of Sakyamuni (historic) Buddha, Guru Rinpoche and the 16th Karmapa.

✴️ Festivals & Events

Rumtek holds impressive masked *chaam* dances during the annual **Drupchen** (group meditation) in May/June, and two days before Losar (Tibetan New Year; p535). The much-fancied **Mahakala Dance** (Ralang; ⊙Nov) takes place in February, when giant figurines of the protector deity come to life in the central courtyard.

🛏️ Sleeping & Eating

Sangay Guesthouse — GUESTHOUSE $

(☎9933805553; s/d ₹300/500) A budget inn that strives to offer the best bang for your buck, this Tibetan establishment within the monastery complex is a good place to overnight if you want to explore the region at leisure. Rooms are comfortable; all have hot-water bathrooms and some have balconies. It's just inside Rumtek's main entrance gate.

Rumtek Dzong — HOTEL $$

(☎9233504474; www.hotelrumtekdong.com; d incl breakfast from ₹2200) Midway up the Rumtek road, overlooking the Santi viewpoint, is this smart hotel commanding fabulous views of Gangtok across the valley. Rooms are prim and well appointed, and there's a cute lawn in front where you could laze away a sunny afternoon with a paperback in hand.

Bamboo Retreat — RESORT $$$

(☎9434382036; www.bambooretreat.in; Sajong; per person incl breakfast from ₹3375; 🛜) This fantabulous resort just below Rumtek is lounged amid conifers and blooming gardens, and seamlessly blends its innate tranquillity with a horde of activities, such as mountain biking, guided hikes, Lepcha cultural programs, herbal baths and refreshing massages. The colourful rooms are all ethnically decorated, and much of the yummy food comes from the property's organic gardens.

ℹ️ Getting There & Away

Rumtek is 26km (1½ hours) from Gangtok by a winding but scenic road. Lingdum Gompa is a 2km walk from Ranga (Ranka) village, reached by rough backlanes from Gangtok. Shared jeeps run to Rumtek (₹40) every hour or so, with the last jeep returning to Gangtok between 2pm and 3pm. A return taxi costs around ₹900. Going to both sites requires private transport (₹1500).

Towards Tibet

Tsomgo (Changu, Tsangu) Lake

Pronounced 'changu', this scenic high-altitude lake (3780m) 38km from Gangtok is madly popular with Indian travellers, though foreigners require a permit to visit. To get one, sign up for a tour by 2pm, and most Gangtok agents can get the permit for next-day departure (two photos required). A budget day tour will cost around ₹3500 per vehicle or ₹600 per person if you can get a group together.

THE KARMAPA CONTROVERSY

The 'Black Hat' sect takes its name from priceless ruby-topped black headgear traditionally worn by the Karmapas. Supposedly woven from the hair of *dakinis* (angels), the hat must be kept locked in a box to prevent it from flying back to the heavens.

Nobody, however, has actually seen the hat since 1993, when a bitter controversy flared within the Kagyu sect over the legitimacy of two candidates, both of whom claimed their right to the throne following the death of the 16th Karmapa. The main candidate, Ogyen Trinley Dorje, fled Tibet in 2000 and remains based at Dharamsala: Indian authorities are believed to have prevented him from officially taking up his Rumtek seat for fear of upsetting Chinese government sensibilities. The rival candidate, Thaye Dorje, lives in nearby Kalimpong in West Bengal. Supporters of the two are locked in a legal dispute over who can control Rumtek. To learn more about the controversy, read *The Dance of 17 Lives* by Mick Brown.

Only when the dispute is resolved and the 17th Karmapa is finally crowned will anyone dare to unlock the box and reveal the sacred black hat.

At the lakeside, food stalls sell hot chai, chow mein and *momos*, while yaks taking people for short rides potter along the shore.

Nathu La

Indian citizens are permitted to continue 18km along the spectacular road from Tsomgo Lake to the 4130m Nathu La (Listening Ears Pass), whose border opened with much fanfare in 2006 but to local border trade only.

A few kilometres southeast of Nathu La, **Jelepla** was the pass used by Francis Younghusband in the British Great Game–era attack on Tibet (1903–04). Until 1962, Jelepla was the main trade route between Kalimpong and Lhasa, but it shows no signs of reopening.

NORTH SIKKIM

🎵 03592

Blessed with nature's unspoilt bounties, the pristine mountains of North Sikkim boast two big draws for landscape lovers: the idyllic valleys of Yumthang and Tsopta. Travelling here requires a special permit, which is easy to obtain if you sign up for a tour. The upper reaches of the region are very cold by October, and become fingertip numbing between December and February.

ℹ NORTH SIKKIM TOUR TIPS

A group size of four people is ideal for sharing costs while not overfilling the jeep. To find jeep-share partners, try asking around at the cafe at New Modern Central Lodge in Gangtok, a few days before you plan to travel.

Slot in at least five days to comfortably visit Yumthang, Lachung and Lachen. Three days is enough to see just Yumthang. Three-night, four-day tours start from around ₹8000 per person for groups of four.

Leave Gangtok early on the first day: it's a shame to arrive in the dark.

Your (obligatory) 'guide' is actually more of a translator. Don't assume he'll stop at all potential points of interest without prodding.

Bring a torch (flashlight) and plenty of warm clothes.

Gangtok to Singhik

Going north past Gangtok, the narrow NH31A clings dangerously to steep wooded slopes above the Teesta River, occasionally descending in long coils of hairpin bends to a bridge photogenically draped in prayer flags, only to climb the switchback up again on the other side. Consider several photo stops along the way.

Kabi Lunchok, an atmospheric glade decorated with memorial stones 17km north of Gangtok, is the site of a 13th-century peace treaty between the chiefs of the Lepcha and Bhutia peoples. The small 290-year-old Nyingmapa-school **Phensang Gompa** is further north, 1km off the main road. Rebuilt after a 1957 fire, it has beautifully decorated lower- and upper-floor prayer halls.

Just over 30km north of Gangtok, **Seven Sisters Waterfall**, a multistage cascade, cuts a chasm above a roadside cardamom grove and plummets into a rocky pool. Further down the road is **Phodong** (1815m), a popular lunch stop with a strip of roadside restaurants. About 1km southeast, near the Km39 post, a 15-minute walk along a side road leads to the **Phodong Gompa** (established in 1740). Belonging to the Kagyu sect, it houses extensive murals and a large statue of the 9th Karmapa, while a rear room contains a hidden statue of Mahakala, a protective deity.

Drive or walk another 1.5km uphill to the much more atmospheric **Labrang Gompa** (established in 1884), home to 100 monks. The inner walls of the eight-sided main building are lined with over 1000 icons of Padmasambhava, while upstairs a fearsome statue of the guru sports a necklace of severed heads.

Between the two monasteries, just below the road, lie the 19th-century foundations of **Tumlong**, Sikkim's third capital. The enigmatic palace ruins are worth a scramble.

North Sikkim's district headquarters are located in **Mangan**, 28km from Phodong. Some 1.5km beyond, concrete stupas on a sharp bend mark a small footpath; a three-minute descent leads to a panoramic **viewpoint** and an excellent tea stop.

Beyond Singhik

With relevant permits and an organised tour you can continue north beyond Singhik. At Chungthang, the next settlement, the road branches up the Lachung Chu and Lachen

Chu Valleys. If you only have time to visit one valley, the Lachung Chu has the most impressive scenery.

Accommodation is available in Lachung and Lachen, with some basic options in Thanggu. In most cases, your tour operator will have preselected a hotel for you.

Lachung

3592 / ELEV 2910M

Soaring rock-pinnacled valley walls embroidered with long ribbons of waterfall surround the scattered village of Lachung. To appreciate the full drama of its setting, take the metal cantilever bridge across the wild Yumthang River to the Sanchok side then climb 1.5km along the Katao road for great views from the **Lachung (Sarchok) Gompa** (established 1880).

Over a dozen hotels are dotted around Lachung. Many outwardly modern places maintain traditional Tibetan-style wood-fire kitchens that are a cosy place to linger over a butter tea or a tongba of chhang.

The gompa-style **Modern Residency** (214888; www.modernresidency.com; Singring village; d ₹3000) hotel 3km south of Lachung has comfortable, well-decorated rooms, a mini-museum, library and bar. Walk-in prices can be steep.

The fancy resort **Mayfair Yarlam** (9434330033; www.yarlamresort.com; d incl full board ₹8000), possibly the top place in town, is preferred by many tour operators for their groups.

Yumthang Valley

The main reason to come to Lachung is to continue 23km further north to admire the majestic Yumthang Valley, which starts some 10km after leaving Lachung. This point is also the entry to the **Singba Rhododendron Sanctuary**, whose network of hiking trails offers a welcome chance to get out of the jeep. From March to early May a host of primulas, 24 species of rhododendrons and other alpine flora burst forth in riotous blossom, carpeting the valley floor.

At the Km23 point, a number of snack shacks operate in the high season. As the valley widens and flattens, the scenery slowly transforms into a montage of jagged peaks, lush pastures and bridges draped with colourful prayer flags.

From Yumthang you can continue up switchbacks for 14km onto the snowy plateau

---

NATURE'S FURY

Jaw-dropping sceneries apart, North Sikkim is severely prone to natural calamities. In September 2011 a 6.9-magnitude earthquake rocked the region, claiming more than 100 lives and leaving indelible marks of destruction on the landscape, architecture and the minds of citizens. Further damages were inflicted by another earthquake and a flash flood in September 2012, which washed away large sections of NH31A and cut the region off from the rest of India for several weeks. The region was limping back to normalcy at the time of research, and it may be a while before the tourist infrastructure in these hills sees a complete revival.

---

of **Yume Samdong (Zero Point)** at a head-pounding 4640m, where a candelabra of saw-edged peaks rises towards Tibet. This is as far as you can go as a tourist. The road starts to get blocked by snow from mid-October.

Lachen

POP 2000 / ELEV 2700M

Despite burgeoning development, the traditional mountain village of Lachen retains its quaintness in the form of old wooden homes on sturdy stone bases, decorated with colourful Tibetan-style window frames. Logs are stacked everywhere for winter fuel.

Lachen (Nyudrup Choeling) Gompa is a 15-minute walk above the town and is most likely to be open early morning or late afternoon. At the beginning of town, beside a giant cypress tree, is a huge mounted prayer wheel and a spooky collection of geometric threads designed to trap evil spirits.

Lachen is the trailhead for eight-day expeditionary treks to **Green Lake** (5050m) along the yeti-infested **Zemu Glacier** towards Khangchendzonga's northeast face. These require long advance planning and very expensive permits.

Of the few accommodation options available, most groups prefer either the **Lachen View Point** (9434867312; d incl full board from ₹2400), which has decent rooms, or the luxurious **Apple Orchard Resort** (9474837640; www.theappleorchardresort.com; d incl full board ₹7000), above the village next to the *ani gompa* (nunnery).

OFF THE BEATEN TRACK

THANGGU & TSOPTA

Beyond a sprawling army camp 32km north of Lachen, Thanggu (3850m) has an end-of-the-world feel. There are no phones (mobile or otherwise), the electricity is solar generated and the Chinese are only 15km away.

Thanggu Resort (snacks ₹50; ⊙ May-Nov) is a simple wooden house incorporating a traditional-style kitchen and tongba-drinking den (tongba ₹20) that offers a popular breakfast stop. There are a couple of grubby rooms upstairs (₹500), if you're feeling particularly sleepy.

A boulder-strewn stream leads on 2km to the Tsopta Valley. Just above the tree line, the scenery takes on the added drama of a glacier-toothed mountain wall framing the western horizon. A two-hour hike leads up to a pair of meditation caves, one of which was used for two years by the famous French traveller and mystic Alexandra David-Néel.

Indian visitors can continue 30km north to spectacular **Gurudongmar Lake** (5150m), right on the border with Tibet, but the glacial lake is off-limits to foreigners.

SOUTH SIKKIM

Tourists flock to the lofty hills of South Sikkim mainly to gaze at the sky-piercing statues of Namchi, or to find religion in the atmospheric monasteries of Ravangla. This is also the state's only tea-growing region, and the gardens of Temi are a wonderful stopover for anyone travelling the road between Gangtok and West Sikkim.

Namchi

☎ 03595 / ELEV 1525M

The hulking religious superstructures that dot the jagged horizon of Namchi are perhaps the only reason why travellers swing by this tiny settlement. There are several internet cafes in the central pedestrianised plaza, along with an Axis Bank ATM, two ancient bodhi and pipal trees and, oddly, an aquarium with angel fish, parrot fish and piranhas.

 Sights

Samdruptse MONUMENT
(Padmasambhava statue; Indian/foreigner ₹10/20; ⊙ dawn-dusk) Painted in shimmering copper, pink and bronze, the 45m-high **statue of Guru Padmasambhava** lords over the forested Samdruptse ridge and is visible for miles around. Completed in 2004 on a foundation stone laid by the Dalai Lama, the statue of the hallowed Buddhist leader sits atop a giant lotus plinth and makes for an interesting photo-op.

Within the complex, there's a permanent photo exhibition of archival images from India's history, including a rare photo of Mahatma Gandhi breaking into a jig.

The site is 7km from Namchi, 2km off the Damthang–Ravangla road. Taxis from town charge around ₹600 return. Alternatively, pay ₹400 for a one-way drop and walk back to Namchi, following the road down to the atmospheric **Ngadak Gompa**, via the ruined **Ngadak Dzong** (fort), which dates back to 1717 and still exudes a sense of old Sikkim.

Char Dham MONUMENT
(Siddesvara Dham; ₹100 per vehicle; ⊙ 8am-noon & 1pm-7pm) Even grander than Samdruptse's Padmasambhava is the massive 33m **Shiva statue** which sits within the complex of Char Dham. Spread over the Solophuk hilltop 5km south of Namchi, the site intends to bring together all revered Hindu pilgrimages from across India (albeit in the form of replicas), and is strewn with temples and pagodas built on an epic scale.

Apart from visiting these concrete behemoths (each of which enshrines sundry deities of the Hindu pantheon), there's a **4D simulator show** (₹50) within the complex that recreates popular pilgrimages, airplane flights and car races for kids. Nearby, the **Yatri Nivas** dishes out a superb thali (₹160) for lunch.

A taxi here costs ₹600/400 for a return/one-way drop.

Sleeping

Dungmali Heritage Resort GUESTHOUSE $$
(☎ 9434126992; Solophuk Rd; s ₹500, d from ₹2500) Overlooking the road to Solophuk about 4km from Namchi, this friendly family-run guesthouse is an island of quiet tranquility. It prides itself on the mantra of simple living; the rooms are spotless and fresh, and many come with balconies

and great valley views. The family grows its own organic vegetables and offers bird-watching walks in 2.4 hectares of private jungle.

★ Seven Hills Resort   RESORT $$$
(☏ 8348171672; www.sevenhillsresort.com; Phali-dara; d from ₹3200) For peace and luxury in equal measures, there's no better place in Namchi than this relaxing resort on a re-mote ridge 7km northeast of town. Boasting a collection of rural-themed cottages done up in tasteful ethnic decor, the property has a carefully manicured garden dotted with passionfruit, bamboo and orchids, and the views from the balconies are superb.

Warm up on cold evenings with a glass of house-made rhododendron brandy.

❶ Getting There & Around

Shared jeeps leave frequently when full to Ravangla (₹50, one hour), Gangtok (₹120, three hours) and Siliguri (₹130, three hours) from stands around the pedestrian mall. Services dry up around 2pm.

Buses leave early in the morning from the SNT bus stand on the east of town, heading to Ravangla (₹35, one hour) and Gangtok (₹90, four hours).

Ravangla (Rabongla)

☏ 03595 / ELEV 2010M

Lined by conifer forests and spectacularly perched on a ridge overlooking a wide sweep of western Sikkim, Ravangla promises some of the best mountain views in the region. The gompas of Ralang, Tashiding, Pemay-angtse and Sangacheoling are all distantly visible against a horizon that's sawtoothed with snow-capped peaks.

A cheerful but characterless town, Ra-vangla is useful as a hub to visit surround-ing sights. Joining the main highway is Main Bazaar, a concentration of shops, cheap ho-tels, the jeep stand and the Cyber Cafe (per hr ₹30; ⊙ 9am-7pm).

◉ Sights

Mane Choekhorling Gompa   MONASTERY
(⊙ dawn-dusk) Steps lead up from the end of Main Bazaar to this handsome new stone-and-wood gompa. The festival ground here is the site of the annual Pang Lhabsol festival (www.panglhabsol.blogspot.com; Ra-vangla; ⊙ Aug), held each August in honour of

Kanchendzonga. *Chaam* dances take place on the 15th day of the seventh lunar month.

Sakyamuni Complex   MONUMENT
(www.sakyamuniproject.com) On the edge of town is the sprawling new Sakyamuni Com-plex, the centrepiece of which is a giant 41m-tall Buddha statue. Still receiving finishing touches during research, the statue holds Buddhist relics from 13 countries and will eventually include a meditation and hotel complex when completed in 2013. The Dalai Lama blessed the site in 2010.

Until admission rules are finalised, it's free to visit.

🛏 Sleeping & Eating

Hotel 10zing   GUESTHOUSE $
(☏ 9733122491; s/d from ₹250/300) This de-lightful cheapie remains a favourite with budget travellers for its genuine hospitality and friendliness. Rooms are basic but clean, and only the doubles have running hot wa-ter. The restaurant has nice outdoor seating, ideal for an evening beer.

Mt Narsing Resort   RESORT $$
(☏ 9434026822; www.rabong-borong.com; d lower resort from ₹1300, upper annexe from ₹2500) This rustic bungalow occupies a glade-like road-side plot 5km southwest of Ravangla. The lower main building is cheaper but the am-bience and views are far better at the upper annexe, featuring cottage-style rooms with wooden interiors. There's good food and fine views over the lawn towards the summits of Narsing and Pandim. A taxi to the lower/upper resort costs ₹100/250.

Kookay Restaurant   TIBETAN $
(mains ₹70-90; ⊙ 7am-8pm) A cheerful eatery perpetually packed with happy diners, this clean restaurant is easily the best in town. The menu includes a wide range of Tibetan delicacies, along with rice and curry sets and Chinese staples. Slurp down a steam-ing bowl of noodle soup or beef *momos*, and leave a note of appreciation on the 'We Were Here' noticeboard.

❶ Getting There & Away

Travel agents on the main highway book shared jeeps to Gangtok (₹100, 8am to noon), Pelling (₹100, 1pm) and Siliguri (₹170, 7am to 8am). For Yuksom, change at Geyzing (₹90, 9am). Jeeps to Namchi (₹50) and Legship (₹50) leave peri-odically from near Hotel 10zing.

The SNT bus booking office is part of Hotel 10zing. Morning buses run to Namchi (₹35, one hour, 9am) and Siliguri (₹170, five hours, 6.30am).

Around Ravangla

Beside the main Legship road, 5.5km from central Ravangla, the small but fascinating **Yungdrung Kundrakling** is the only Bon monastery in Sikkim. Animistic in nature, Bon preceded Buddhism in Tibet but has since been largely subsumed by it. The deities look slightly different and prayer wheels are turned anticlockwise. Flash photography is prohibited within. You can get here from Ravangla on a Kewzing-bound shared jeep (₹20).

Back in town, a steep four-hour hiking trail leads from above the Sakyamuni statue to the top of **Maenam Hill** (3150m). En route, you'll pass the springtime rhododendrons and magnolia blooms of the **Maenam Wildlife Sanctuary**. From the summit, continue 2km to **Bhaledunga rock**, where you can enjoy sweeping views and a chance encounter with red pandas and monal pheasants (Sikkim's state bird). Hire a guide (₹500) at the forestry checkpost to avoid getting lost.

Ralang

At Ralang, 13km below Ravangla, the splendid 1995 Palchen Choeling Monastic Institute (New Ralang Gompa) is home to about 200 Kagyu-order monks. Arrive early morning or around 3pm to hear them chanting in mesmerising unison. There's a 9m-high golden statue of the historical Buddha in the main hall, and the gompa is famous for elaborate butter sculptures. Peek into the side room to see the amazing effigies used in November's impressive Mahakala dance.

SO NEAR, YET SO FAR

Sikkim is tiny, only approximately 80km from east to west and 100km north to south, but due to the seriously vertical terrain it is slow to traverse. Your next destination, just across the valley, could be reached in 15 minutes flat if someone were to string a cable car between the mountains. Driving down, however, would take anything between three or four hours!

About 1.5km downhill on the same road is peaceful (and still active) Old Ralang Gompa, established in 1768 and worth a visit. A chartered taxi to Ralang costs around ₹600 from Ravangla (return with two hours' wait).

Temi

Located 16km south of Ravangla, the jade-green estate of Temi is as famous for its fine quality tea as the gorgeous mountain scenery it offers to travellers. The only tea garden in Sikkim, it drapes some 450 acres of hill slopes that are fronted by a stupendous hill-lined horizon, lorded over by the Khangchendzonga massif.

Accommodation is available at the **Cherry Resort** (☑ 9733098737; www.cherry resort.com; Temi Tea Estate; s/d incl breakfast from ₹2500/3200), a stylish property slap-bang in the middle of the plantations overlooking the Teesta Valley far below. The spacious rooms here have fantastic sit-outs and a terrace which affords magnificent views of summits and the plantations.

Shared jeeps (₹40, 30 minutes) bound for Siliguri via Damthang and Rangpo can drop you at the resort.

WEST SIKKIM

Towered over by the sublime Khangchendzonga, West Sikkim's breathtaking landscape is strung out along spectacular mountain ridges draped in evergreen alpine forests. A handful of intriguing monasteries, villages and waterfalls add to its overall appeal, and make it ideal for a spot of walking. The fabulous Goecha La trek, which takes hikers to the icy base of Khangchendzonga, begins in the village of Yuksom (which is also the trailhead for a few pleasant day hikes). Comfort seekers, on the other hand, can simply settle for stupendous mountain views from Pelling.

Geyzing & Tikjuk

☑ 03595

More practical stops than anything else, these two contiguous towns have little to offer a visitor apart from transport changes at Geyzing and permit extension facilities at Tikjuk, half way to Pelling.

Tikjuk is the district administrative centre for West Sikkim. Permits can be extended at the **Superintendent of Police office** (side wing, 3rd fl; ⊙ 10am-4pm Mon-Sat, closed 2nd Sat of month).

Geyzing is most useful as West Sikkim's transport hub. Frequent shared jeeps go to Jorethang (₹80, 1½ hours), Pelling (₹40, 20 minutes), Tashiding (₹70, 1½ hours) and Yuksom (₹90, 2½ hours). Several serve Gangtok (₹180, seven to nine hours, 7am to 12.30pm), Ravangla (₹80, one hour, 9am and 11.45am) and Siliguri (₹190, four hours, 7am and 12.30pm).

Pelling

☑ 03595 / ELEV 2085M

Pelling's raison d'être is its stride-stopping view of Khangchendzonga at dawn (weather permitting, that is!). A 2km stretch of boxed-out tourist hotels that line its main thoroughfare, it's otherwise a characterless town frequented by hordes of local tourists through the year. Unsurprisingly, there's more noise and vehicle exhaust here than you bargained for, so once you've taken in the good views, consider moving on.

Pelling is nominally divided into upper, middle and lower areas. A focal point of Upper Pelling is a small roundabout where the main road from Geyzing turns 180 degrees in front of Hotel Garuda. At the same point, minor roads branch south to Dentam and southwest to the tourist office and the helipad – which affords magnificent panoramic views at dawn.

☞ Tours

Popular day tours (offered by most hotels and travel agencies) include Yuksom via Khecheopalri Lake and three waterfalls (₹2800 per jeep) or Khecheopalri Lake, Pemayangtse Gompa and Rabdentse (₹2200).

Hotel Garuda SIGHTSEEING TOURS
(☑ 258319; Upper Pelling; tours per day per jeep ₹2200) Half-day tours to Khecheopalri Lake cost ₹1400; to Pemayangtse and Rabdentse costs an extra ₹800.

Simvo Tours & Travels SIGHTSEEING TOURS
(☑ 9733021577; Upper Pelling; day tour per person/jeep ₹300/2200) This outfit offers guided and independent tours of local sights.

🛏 Sleeping

Most of Pelling's hotels are drab and cater to midrange domestic tourists. Rates typically drop 30% in low season (June to September)

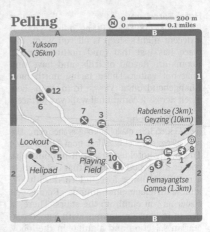

Pelling

🏃 Activities, Courses & Tours
    Hotel Garuda .... (see 2)
1 Simvo Tours & Travels B2

🛏 Sleeping
2 Hotel Garuda B2
3 Hotel Paradzong A1
    Hotel Phamrong .... (see 2)
4 Hotel Sonamchen A2
5 Norbu Ghang Resort A2

🍴 Eating
6 Anjali Restaurant A1
7 Melting Point A1

ⓘ Information
8 Paylink Cyher Zone B2
9 SBI ATM B2
10 Tourist Office B2

ⓘ Transport
11 Father Tours B2
12 SNT Counter A1

and are highly negotiable during low occupancy.

Hotel Garuda HOTEL $
(☑ 9733076484; garuda_pelling@rediffmail.com; Upper Pelling; d from ₹700; @) This old-school backpacker ghetto has clean, spacious rooms (all with hot showers and TV), a library with book-swap facilties, good Khangchendzonga views and a superb restaurant ideal for hooking up with other travellers. The 'suites' upstairs have Tibetan names such as Nima and Pema. Krishna, the friendly receptionist, is always ready to help with trip planning.

Hotel Paradzong
HOTEL $

(📞9733084348; Middle Pelling; d from ₹700) If a decent night's sleep is all you want, this place has just that (and nothing more!). Rooms are devoid of frills, and have running hot water. Those facing north have Khangchendzonga views from your bed, albeit across a communal walkway terrace.

Hotel Phamrong
HOTEL $$

(📞9733085318; mailphamrong@yahoo.com; Upper Pelling; s/d incl breakfast from ₹1850/2350) This pretty hotel features stylish rooms with wicker and wood interiors that open out to a multilevel inner foyer adorned with Sikkimese artefacts and murals. Rooms get cosier as you climb up the stairs. There's a decent in-house restaurant with a good vegetarian selection and a guitar in the lobby, if you wish to improve your fretting skills.

Hotel Sonamchen
HOTEL $$

(📞258346; sonamchen07@yahoo.com; Upper Pelling; s/d from ₹1500/2000) A largish place patronised by domestic tourists, this hotel scores with good mountain views from most rooms. Service and housekeeping are commendable, and the ornate lobby has an adjoining restaurant for snacks and meals.

Norbu Ghang Resort
HERITAGE HOTEL $$$

(📞258272; www.norbughangresort.com; Upper Pelling; s/d incl breakfast from ₹3500/4000; 📶) A charming property comprising pretty cottages dotting a hillside, this place has rooms caringly done up with traditional upholstery and polished wood flooring. The biggest draw are the giant windows which offer gorgeous mountain views that you can savour at dawn from the toasty-warm comfort of your own bed. An afternoon drink on the lawn is another highlight.

Elgin Mount Pandim
HERITAGE HOTEL $$$

(📞250756; www.elginhotels.com; Pemayangtse; s/d incl full board ₹7700/8000; @📶) Classy, self-indulgent and luxurious, this erstwhile royal residence is a five-minute stroll from Pemayangtse Gompa. A stately lounge – stacked with fresh flowers, wicker and antiques – leads to indulgent rooms that are islands of tranquillity, and come lined with the best creature comforts. Some rooms have gorgeous Khangchendzonga views; others have vistas of the Singalila Ridge to match.

✖ Eating

Pelling's best dining is in the hotels, and standalone places are numbered.

Melting Point
MULTICUISINE $

(Middle Pelling; mains ₹80-120; ⊙8am-9pm) Pelling's equivalent to a fine-dining resturant, this eatery has a cosy lounge and an adjoining alfresco terrace with superb mountain views. The excellent menu features wholesome Sikkimese fixed meals (₹380, ordered in advance) and some Western favourites (try the penne in mushroom sauce). There's 20% discount between 5pm and 7pm.

Anjali Restaurant
MULTICUISINE $

(Middle Pelling; mains ₹80-110; ⊙8am-9pm) Don't mind the grubby interiors – the food at this slapdash restaurant is finger-licking good. Choose from Sikkimese specials (advance orders only) such as *sisnoo* and *ningro*, and pair it with a glass of chhang. Or go for the fiery chilli chicken with noodles.

ℹ Information

Paylink Cyber Zone (per hr ₹50; ⊙8am-7pm) Internet access on the main road.

SBI ATM Opposite the Hotel Garuda.

Tourist office (📞7797887401; ⊙10am-5pm Mon-Sat) The helpful tourist office sits en route to the helipad.

ℹ Getting There & Away

SNT buses run to Siliguri (₹175, five hours, 7am) via Jorethang (₹60, 2½ hours); book at the **SNT counter** (Hotel Pelling) in Lower Pelling from where the buses depart.

Father Tours (📞9733286872; Upper Pelling) runs shared jeeps at 7am for Gangtok (₹200, five hours) and Siliguri (₹200, 4½ hours).

Shared jeeps to Geyzing (₹40, 20 minutes) leave frequently from near the Hotel Garuda, passing close to Pemayangtse, Rabdentse and Tikjuk district administrative centre. For Khecheopalri Lake (₹60) or Yuksom (₹80), jeeps start from Geyzing, passing through Pelling between noon and 1pm.

Around Pelling

Pemayangtse Gompa

Literally translated as 'Perfect Sublime Lotus', the 1705 **Pemayangtse Gompa** (admission ₹20; ⊙7am-5pm) is one of Sikkim's oldest and most significant Nyingmapa gompas. Magnificently set on a hilltop (2100m) overlooking the Rabdentse ruins, the atmospheric compound is ringed by gardens and traditional cottages used by the resident monks. The ground floor features a central Buddha, while upstairs fierce-looking statues depict all eight reincarnations of Padmasambhava. On the top floor is an astounding seven-tiered model representing Padmasambhava's heavenly abode of Zangtok Palri, hand-made over five laborious years by a single dedicated lama.

During February/March, impressive *chaam* dances celebrating Losar (p535) culminate with the unfurling of a huge *gyoku* (giant embroidered *thangka*) and the zapping of evil demons with a great fireball.

Pemayangtse is 1.5km from Upper Pelling, along the road to Geyzing, and is easily combined with a visit to Rabdentse. The signposted turn-off is near an obvious stupa.

If you are walking to or from Pemayangtse, pop into the self-service **Lotus Bakery** (cakes ₹10-20; ⊙8am-5pm), about 15 minutes from town, for a restorative slice of carrot or banana cake. All money raised goes to the nearby Denjog Pema Choling Academy, which works with underprivileged children.

Rabdentse

The royal capital of Sikkim from 1670 to 1814, the now-ruined **Rabdentse** (⊙dawn-dusk) consists of chunky wall stubs with a few inset inscription stones. The selling point of the site, however, is the utterly fabulous viewpoint on which the ruins are located. The entrance to the site is around 3km from Upper Pelling, along the road to Geyzing. The ruins are a 10-minute walk from the site's yellow gateway – beware of leeches in the undergrowth.

The Monastery Loop

The picturesque western frontiers of Sikkim can technically be rounded off on a day-long or overnight jeep tour from Pelling. Time permitting, however, you can do an adventurous three-day trip from Pelling to Tashiding via Khecheopalri Lake, using a combination of jeeps and hiking. Alternatively, consider an outing to wonderful Yuksom via Khecheopalri Lake, and a subsequent multi-day high-altitude trek that takes you up close and personal with Khangchendzonga.

Pelling to Yuksom

Apart from dipping your toes in the cascading waters of the **Rimbi, Khangchendzonga** and **Phamrong Falls**, the only major sight on this stretch is the hallowed

THE RHODODENDRON TRAIL

In the far southwest corner of Sikkim, close to the India–Nepal border, lies the **Varsey Rhododendron Sanctuary**, known to be the native habitat of more than 500 species of rhododendrons. Well off the tourist route, this exotic forest (at an altitude of about 3048m) can be accessed by a two-hour trek through enchanted pine forests from the village of Hilley, which lies about 28km from Pelling. Hemmed by the Singalila Ridge, the forest bursts into a riot of colours in April and May. A few basic lodges provide overnight accommodation in the sanctuary – contact Sikkim Tourism Development Corporation (p539) for details.

Khecheopalri Lake (admission ₹10). Located at 1950m, this placid natural reservoir – pronounced 'ketchup-perry' - is highly revered by both Sikkimese Buddhists and Lepcha animists who believe its shape to be akin to the footprint of the goddess Tara. Legend also has it that birds assiduously remove any leaves from its surface, keeping it clean through the year.

During **Khecheopalri Mela** (Khecheopalri Lake; ⊙Mar/Apr), butter lamps are floated out across the lake. Prayer wheels line the lake's jetty, backed by fluttering prayer flags and Tibetan inscriptions, but the setting, ringed with forested hills, is serene rather than dramatic.

Day jeep tours typically drop you at a car park five minutes from the lake, allowing you 30 minutes' sightseeing time. The best way to appreciate the site, however, is to stay overnight and visit once the tourists have left.

Around the car park are a Buddhist nunnery, a couple of shops and the simple **Jigme Restaurant** serving tea and chow mein. From the car park, a path to the left leads uphill for 20 minutes to **Khecheopalri Gompa** and stupa, from where you can hike up to several viewpoints.

Just beside the gompa and run by a local lama is **Pala's Guest House** (☑9832471253; per person incl 3 meals ₹450), with more rooms available at next-door Sonam's nicer annexe.

On the main approach to the car park, Teng Hang Limboo operates a basic homestay at the **Family Guest House** (☑9609874677; per person ₹300).

Shared jeeps to Pelling (₹50, two hours) leave the car park at 6am.

A hiking trail to Yuksom (9km, three to five hours) leaves the road just opposite Family Guest House, descending steeply to the main road (take the right branch after crossing the Runom Khola river) and emerging near Khangchendzonga Falls. After the road suspension bridge, follow the concrete steps uphill to meet the Yuksom road, about 2km below Yuksom village.

Yuksom

☑ 03595 / ELEV 1780M

Loveable little Yuksom is historic, charming and unspoilt, although concretisation is fast taking over. The town is the main trailhead for the treks towards Mt Khangchendzonga, and remains a good place to kick back for a few quiet nights.

⊙ Sights

Norbugang Park   HISTORIC SITE

Yuksom means 'meeting place of the three lamas', referring to the trio of Tibetan holy men who crowned the first chogyal of Sikkim at this historic site in 1641. The charming complex contains a small temple, a huge prayer wheel, a chorten and the supposedly original **Coronation Throne** (Norbugang), from which it takes its current name.

Standing beneath a vast cryptomeria pine, the site looks something like an ancient Olympic podium hewn out of stone. Just in front is a spooky footprint fused into stone, believed to be that of one of the crowning lamas!

Walking up to Norbugang Park past Hotel Tashi Gang, you'll pass the murky prayer-flag-lined **Kathok Lake**, from which anointing waters were taken for the original coronation.

ⓘ BLOODY LEECHES

Walks in West Sikkim are generally a safe activity, with the exception of nasty leeches that infest the undergrowth, especially during the wet months (June to September). Stick to dry, wide paths and slap on a generous amount of mosquito repellent (try the local brand Odomos), which does well to keep these pesky bloodsuckers away.

Tashi Tenka   RUINS

When Yuksom was Sikkim's capital, a royal palace complex known as Tashi Tenka sat on a ridge to the south with superb (almost 360-degree) views. Today, barely a stone remains but the views are still superb. To get here, head south out of town and take the small uphill path marked by two weathered stupas near the school football pitch.

Dubdi Gompa   MONASTERY

High on the ridge above Yuksom, this atmospheric gompa (its name means 'hermit's cell') is set in beautifully tended gardens behind three coarsely hewn stupas. Established in 1701, it is said to be Sikkim's oldest monastery, though the current chapel looks much newer.

Start the steep 40-minute climb from upper Yuksom's primary health centre; the clear path rises through thickets of trumpet lilies and some lovely mature forest.

Kathok Wodsallin Gompa   MONASTERY

This newly contructed gompa near Hotel Tashi Gang has an impressively stern statue of Guru Padmasambhava surrounded by a collection of yogis, gurus and lamas in glass-fronted compartments.

Ngadhak Changchub Choling Gompa   MONASTERY

This other new and colourful gompa is accessed through an ornate gateway opposite Hotel Yangri Gang. The main statue is of an 11-headed Chenresig, the Bodhissatva of Compassion.

🏃 Activities

Several trekking agencies in Yuksom can organise a **Khangchendzonga trek** given a couple of days. Prices start around US$55 per person per day assuming a group of four. Try the following outfits.

Red Panda Tour & Travel   TREKKING

(☑9733196470; sikkimtraveler@gmail.com) Run by a former porter–turned-guide (nicknamed 'panda') with great expertise and experience.

Alpine Exodus Tours & Travel   TREKKING

(☑9735087508; nawang.bhutia@gmail.com) The in-house agency at Hotel Yangri Gang.

Mountain Tours and Treks   TREKKING

(☑9641352656; www.sherpatreks.in) A reputed outfit with a good repertoire of high-altitude gear.

WORTH A TRIP

YUKSOM TO TASHIDING HIKE

This wonderful one-day hike requires no permits, and can be done quite easily if you start in Yuksom. Figure on six hours of walking (19km), plus another two hours visiting the monasteries. Porter-guides are available in Yuksom for around ₹500.

Start by ascending to **Dubdi Gompa**, from where a path dips into a side valley for 40 minutes to **Tsong**. The trail splits here, with the lower route returning to Yuksom, while the upper route leads uphill past cardamom fields to lonely **Hongri Gompa**, a small, unusually unpainted ancient monastery with a superlative ridge-top location. Local folklore claims the gompa was moved here from a higher spot where monks kept being ravaged by yeti.

A signpost points the way downhill for 20 minutes to **Nessa** hamlet, 10 minutes below which is the village of **Pokhari Dara** (four hours from Yuksom). Follow the road until a footpath branches towards **Sinon Gompa** (built 1716), high above Tashiding. The path then drops steeply down steps behind the yellow monastic school, following village trails down to Tashiding.

🛏 Sleeping & Eating

Tourist traffic is heavy during peak trekking seasons, so book early. Khangchendzonga Conservation Committee arranges homestays (per person full board ₹500-700), offering travellers the chance to connect with locals. It also has information on trekking, sustainable tourism and responsible ecotourism.

Hotel Yangri Gang HOTEL $
(📱9434164408; s/d from ₹600/800; @) The better rooms at this functional hotel at the head of Yuksom's main street are on the upper floors. Beds are comfy, the wooden half-panelling is pleasant to the eye and there are hot showers through the day. Thanks to its in-house trekking agency, it's a good upper budget option favoured by trekkers.

Hotel Demazong HOTEL $
(📱9775473687; dm ₹100, d from ₹500) Used by domestic trekking groups, this place has simple but clean rooms behind its boxy facade. The more expensive rooms have balconies.

Yuksom Residency HOTEL $$
(📱9933133330; www.travel-sikkim.com/Yuksom_Residency; s/d from ₹2500/2900; ☎) Very plush, very stylish and very comfortable by Yuksom's standards, this upscale hotel has large rooms with giant windows overlooking soothing greenery. It has a pleasant terrace which doubles as a dining area in the evenings. All in all, the perfect place for returning trekkers in need of a hot shower and creature comforts.

Hotel Tashi Gang HOTEL $$
(📱9733077249; hoteltashigang@gmail.com; d from ₹1800) Done up in rich Sikkimese motifs and colourful *thangkas*, the rooms at this popular hotel are comfortable and, as a result, mostly booked out. There's good food at the in-house restaurant, and the rooms out front have balconies opening in the direction of Khangchendzonga. There's a patch of a front lawn hemmed by flowering plants.

Gupta Restaurant MULTICUISINE $
(mains ₹40-80; ☺5am-9pm) Arguably the only 'piazza' in Yuksom for tourists, this alfresco restaurant belts out curries, pizza, instant noodles, breakfast platters and dinner thalis for a steady stream of diners who filter in through the day. The sociable thatched cabana outside is good for a beer in the afternooon (or a stiff drink in the evening) with fellow travellers.

ℹ Information

Khangchendzonga Conservation Committee (📱9733158268; ☺10am-4pm Mon-Sat) Khangchendzonga Conservation Committee arranges homestays, offering travellers the chance to connect with locals. It also has information on trekking, sustainable tourism and responsible ecotourism.

ℹ Getting There & Away

Around 6.30am, several shared jeeps leave for Jorethang (₹140, four hours) via Tashiding (₹60, 1½ hours), Geyzing via Pelling (₹80, 2½ hours) and Gangtok (₹200, six hours). Book the day before, either at the shop next to Gupta Restaurant or at the hut opposite.

Dzongri & Goecha La – The Khangchendzonga Trek

For guided groups with permits, Yuksom is the starting point for Sikkim's classic seven- to 10-day trek to Goecha La, a 4940m pass with jaw-dropping views of Khangchendzonga.

Trek costs start at around US$55 per person per day (assuming a group of four), including food, guides, porters and yaks. You have to arrange your trek through a trekking agency. The paperwork is done in Gangtok, but given two or three days your agent can organise things by sending a fixer to the capital.

Don't underestimate the rigours of the trek – it's considered one of the most challenging hikes in the Indian Himalaya. Don't climb too high too quickly: altitude sickness often strikes those who are fittest and fastest. Starting early makes sense, as rain is common in the afternoons, spoiling views and making trails annoyingly muddy. Check all your equipment before setting off – bring good-quality sleeping bags, torches (flashlights), some heavy woollens and rain gear.

March to May is an ideal time to trek. Monsoon clouds move in by the end of May, rendering the mountains unwalkable. The clearest skies are from October to December, but remember that snow starts to block the trails with the advent of winter.

The route initially follows the Rathong Valley through unspoilt forests before steeply ascending to **Baktim** (Bakhim; 2750m) and the rustic Tibetan village of **Tsokha** (3050m), established in 1969 by Tibetan refugees. This is the last village on the trail, where spending two nights helps with acclimatisation.

The next stage climbs to pleasant meadows around **Dzongri** (4020m). Consider another acclimatisation day here, best spent by strolling up to **Dzongri La** (4550m, four-hour round trip) for fabulous views of Mt Pandim (6691m).

From Dzongri, the trail drops steeply to **Kokchurong** and follows the river to **Thangsing** (3930m). Trekkers have recommended spending an extra day here to visit the beautiful lake at Lampokhari, three hours' walk away. Next day takes you to camping at **Lamuni**, 15 minutes before **Samiti Lake** (4200m). From here, a dawn assault the following morning takes you to the head-spinning **Goecha La** (4940m) for those incredible views of Khangchendzonga. A further viewpoint, another hour's walk ahead, offers even closer views.

The return is essentially by the same route. Alternatively, you could cut south at Dzongri for an extra week, following the **Singalila Ridge** along the India–Nepal border to emerge at **Uttarey**, from where public transport runs to Pelling and Jorethang (for Siliguri).

There are government-run **trekkers' huts** at Baktim, Tsokha, Dzongri, Kokchurong and Thangsing, but most have neither furniture nor mattresses. Besides, they can get booked out with noisy student groups during peak trekking seasons. It's far better to bring all camping equipment and food.

Dzongri & Goecha La

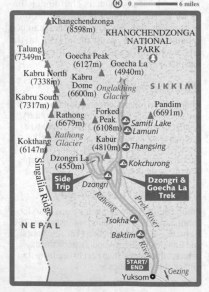

Tashiding

ELEV 1490M

Little Tashiding is a single, sloping market street forking north off the Yuksom–Legship road. Walking 400m south from the main junction takes you past a series of **mani walls** with painted mantras to a colourful **gateway**. A 2.5km uphill track leads to a car park from where a footpath leads up between an avenue of prayer flags to the atmospheric Nyingmapa-school **Tashiding Gompa**, about 30 minutes' away.

KHANGCHENDZONGA TREK SCHEDULE

STAGE	ROUTE	DURATION
1	Yuksom to Tsokha, via Baktim	6-7 hr
2	Optional acclimatisation day at Tsokha	1 day
3	Tsokha to Dzongri	4-5 hr
4	Acclimatisation day at Dzongri, or continue to Kokchurong	1 day
5	Dzongri (or Kokchurong) to Lamuni, via Thangsing	6-7 hr
6	Lamuni to Goecha La, then down to Thangsing	8-9 hr
7	Thangsing to Tsokha	6-7 hr
8	Tsokha to Yuksom	5-6 hr

Founded in 1641 by one of the three Yuksom lamas, the monastery's five colourful religious buildings are strung out between more functional monks' quarters. Beautifully proportioned, the four-storey **main prayer hall** has a delicate filigree topknot, with wonderful views across the semi-wild flower garden towards Ravangla. The Dalai Lama chose this magical spot for a two-day meditation retreat in 2010. Notice the cracks left in the marble flooring by the 2011 earthquake.

Beyond the last monastic building, an unusual compound contains dozens of white chortens, including the **Thongwa Rangdol**, said to absolve the sins of anyone who gazes upon it. More visually exciting is the golden **Kench Chorgi Lorde** stupa. Propped up all around are engraved stones bearing the Buddhist mantra *om mani padme hum*; at the back of the compound is the engraver's lean-to.

In February the monastery celebrates the **Bumchu Festival**, when lamas gingerly open a sacred pot containing holy water and make important predictions by studying the level of water within.

There are a few scruffy lodges within Tashiding. The best beds, however, are at the government-run **Yatri Niwas** (☑9832623654; s/d ₹1500/2000). This is an excellent midrange place, by the turn-off to the monastery, and it offers spacious rooms, lovely gardens and a good restaurant.

Shared jeeps to Gangtok (₹170, four hours) and Geyzing (₹80, 1½ hours) leave from the main junction between 6.30am and 8am. For Siliguri, take a jeep to Jorethang (₹90, two hours) and change. A few jeeps to Yuksom (₹60, one hour) pass through during the early afternoon.

Northeast States

Includes ➡

Best Places to Stay

➡ Diphlu River Lodge (p568)

➡ Ri Kynjai (p589)

➡ Razhu Pru (p579)

➡ Baruah Bhavan (p563)

➡ Classic Hotel (p582)

Best Adventures

➡ Kaziranga elephant safari (p567)

➡ Rafting the Siang (p576)

➡ Exploring Naga villages in Mon (p581)

➡ Trekking in Cherrapunjee (p590)

Why Go?

Teetering on the farthest brink of India's map, popular perception and prime-time TV, the Northeast States are one of Asia's last great unknowns. Sharing borders with Bhutan, Tibet, Myanmar and Bangladesh, these remote frontiers are a collision zone of tribal cultures, climates, landscapes and peoples. A region of rugged beauty, it's a wonderland where glacial rivers flow through plunging Himalayan gorges, faith moves mountains on perilous pilgrimages to Tawang and Pemako, rhinoceros graze in Kaziranga's swampy grasslands and former head-hunters slowly awake from opium-induced dreams to embrace modernity in their primordial longhouses in Nagaland.

Of course, it's not all smooth sailing in these faraway states, and you have a horde of everyday obstacles (bad roads, poor infrastructure and social unrest, to name a few) to battle along the way. Needless to say, only those with a taste for raw adventure would return from here feeling truly rewarded.

When to Go
Assam (Guwahati)

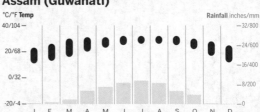

Mar The best season for rhino spotting in Kaziranga.

Oct Best for dazzling Himalayan vistas and trips to remote outposts such as Tawang and Mechuka.

Dec Fierce Naga warriors in ethnic regalia assemble for Kohima's Hornbill festival.

Food

Good news for gastronomes: the food in the Northeast is as varied and exotic as its cultures and terrains. Start your culinary journey in Guwahati with a helping of fish *tenga* (sour curry), a subtly flavoured Assamese speciality, before hitting Tawang's highlands, where Tibetan staples such as *momos*, fermented cheese chutney and salted yak butter tea are all the rage. For a change of palate, head to eastern Arunachal Pradesh, where barbecued rats and sun-dried fish feature boldly on menus. Dollops of fermented (and super pungent!) bamboo shoot liven up fiery servings of stewed pork in Nagaland, while complementing a range of exotic delicacies including maggots, silkworms and – wait for it – dog meat. If you fancy fish and soyabean in their fermented, piquant avatars, Manipur is the place for you. And finally, for those with less-adventurous taste buds, there's always some generic pan-Indian fare to be found along the way.

DON'T MISS

Being one of the last few sanctuaries in the world where maps still have blank spaces on them, Northeast India offers travellers a priceless opportunity to explore virgin forests filled with unnamed creatures or hike through rolling mountainscapes dotted with unmolested tribal villages. Areas that are safe yet largely unexplored include most of rural **Mizoram**, far eastern **Nagaland** and, best of all, ageless forests, gushing rivers and alpine meadows in **Arunachal Pradesh**.

Top Festivals

➡ **Losar** (Jan/Feb; Tawang, p577) Masked Tibetan Buddhist dances.

➡ **Rongali Bihu** (mid-Apr, statewide) Assamese New Year festivities featuring good food, dance and merriment.

➡ **Ambubachi Mela** (Jun; Kamakhya Mandir, Guwahati, (p561) A melange of tantric fertility rituals.

➡ **Wangala** (Oct/Nov; Tura, p587) Garo harvest festival with dance and drum rolls.

➡ **Ras Mahotsav** (Nov; Majuli Island, p569) Hindu festival marked by traditional dance performances.

➡ **Hornbill Festival** (1-7 Dec; Kohima, p580) Naga tribes take the stage in full warrior gear.

MAIN POINTS OF ENTRY

Guwahati airport has flights to most Indian cities. It's the only big city in the northeast with a major train line connecting it to the rest of India.

Fast Facts

➡ **Population**: 44.98 million
➡ **Area**: 255,083 sq km
➡ **Main languages:** Assamese, Hindi, Nagamese, English, Manipuri, Mizo, Khasi, Garo, Bengali
➡ **Sleeping prices:** $ below ₹1000, $$ ₹1000 to ₹2500, $$$ above ₹2500

Top Tip

Check weather forecasts, road conditions, security issues and availability of transport and accommodation in advance, especially for remote places. Things can change at short notice; stay clued in to the latest situation on the ground.

Resources

➡ **Assam Tourism** (www.assamtourism.org)
➡ **Arunachal Tourism** (www.arunachaltourism.com)
➡ **Nagaland Tourism** (www.tourismnagaland.com)
➡ **Tourism in Manipur** (www.manipur.nic.in/tourism.htm)
➡ **Dept of Tourism** (www.tourism.mizoram.gov.in)
➡ **Tripura Tourism** (www.tripuratourism.nic.in)
➡ **Dept of Tourism, Government of Meghalaya** (www.megtourism.gov.in)

NORTHEAST STATES

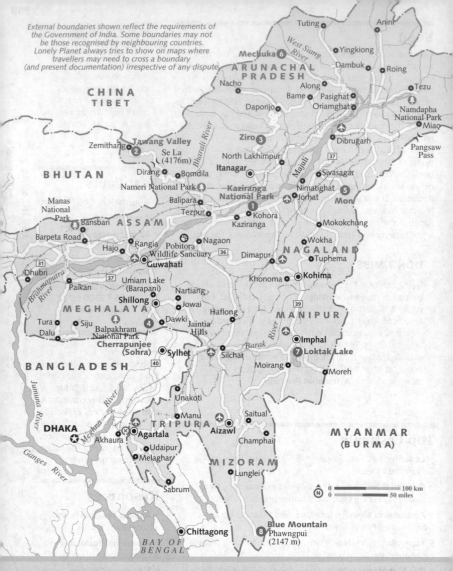

External boundaries shown reflect the requirements of the Government of India. Some boundaries may not be those recognised by neighbouring countries. Lonely Planet always tries to show on maps where travellers may need to cross a boundary (and present documentation) irrespective of any dispute

Northeast States Highlights

① Ride atop an elephant in search of rhinos in **Kaziranga National Park** (p567)

② Touch the clouds at the 4176m pass of Se La before descending to **Tawang Valley** (p577), Arunachal Pradesh's 'little Tibet'

③ Visit intriguing tribal villages around **Ziro** (p573) and meet the last of the bizarrely adorned Apatani women

④ Gaze down on the plains of Bangladesh from the lofty escarpment around **Cherrapunjee** (Sohra; p590)

⑤ Feel as if you've stepped out of India into a different culture and country in Nagaland's **Mon** (p581)

⑥ Search for the last Shangri La in **Mechuka** (p575)

⑦ Explore the unique ecosystem and floating islands of **Loktak Lake** (p583) in Manipur

⑧ Avoid the ghosts and hang with the Gods on the **Blue Mountain** (p584) of Mizoram

ASSAM

Fascinating, expansive Assam – also known as Axom (or simply Ahom) – sprawls lazily along the length of the Brahmaputra valley, and happens to be the most accessible of India's Northeast States. The archetypal Assamese landscape is a picturesque golden-green vista of seemingly endless rice fields and manicured tea estates, framed in the distance by the hazy-blue mountains of Arunachal in the north and the highlands of Meghalaya and Nagaland to the south. A hospitable population, a cuisine redolent with a volley of aromas, and a vibrant artistic heritage marked by exotic dance forms and a string of elegant Hindu temples only add to the list of local attractions, making Assam a delight to travel in.

Despite many similarities to people in neighbouring West Bengal and Orissa, Assamese culture is proudly sovereign. While the *gamosa* (a red-and-white scarf worn around the neck by most men) and the *mekhela sador* (the traditional ensemble for women) are visible proclamations of regional costume and identity, there are several subtle nuances in the local culture that are quintessentially Assamese. Hang around for long enough, and you can spot the difference.

Guwahati

☎ 0361 / POP 818,800

The gateway to the northeast and the largest and most cosmopolitan city in the region, Guwahati serves as the starting block for most northeastern itineraries. A prosaic heap of glass and concrete for the most part, Guwahati resembles any other Indian city at first glance. But walk its back alleys and old quarters, and you will still be able to salvage a generous amount of local flavour that lingers amid its suburban sprawl of ponds, palm trees, small single-storey traditional houses and old colonial-era mansions.

History

Guwahati is considered the site of Pragjyotishpura, a semimythical town founded by Asura King Naraka who was later killed by Lord Krishna for a pair of magical earrings. The city was a vibrant cultural centre well before the Ahoms arrived from Southeast Asia around the 13th century, and it was subsequently the theatre of intense Ahom-Mughal strife, changing hands eight times in 50 years before 1681. In 1897 a huge earthquake, followed by a series of devastating floods, wiped out most of the old city.

Dormant through much of India's colonial history, Guwahati gained metropolitan prominence after the formation of Assam state in the post-Independence era. Though technically not the state capital (the title goes to neighbouring Dispur), Guwahati is, for all purpose and intent, Assam's numero uno city.

◉ Sights

Kamakhya Mandir HINDU TEMPLE
(admission for no queue/short queue/queue ₹500/100/free; ⊙ 8am-1pm & 3pm-dusk) While Sati's disintegrated body parts rained toes on Kolkata, her yoni fell on Kamakhya Hill. This makes Kamakhya Mandir important for *shakti* (tantric worship of female spiritual power). Goats, pigeons and the occasional buffalo are ritually beheaded in a gory pavilion and the hot, dark inner womblike sanctum is painted red to signify sacrificial blood.

The huge June/July **Ambubachi Mela** (Kamakhya Mandir, Guwahati; ⊙ Jun/Jul) celebrates the end of the mother goddess' menstrual cycle with even more blood.

Kamakhya is 7km west of central Guwahati and 3km up a spiralling side road. Occasional buses from Guwahati's Kachari bus stand run all the way up (₹20, 20 minutes).

Assam State Museum MUSEUM
(Gopi Nath Bordoloi (GNB) Rd; admission/camera/video ₹5/10/100; ⊙ 10am-5pm Tue-Sun, to 4pm winter) Housed in an imposing colonial building, this museum has a large sculpture collection, while the upper floors are devoted to informative tribal culture displays. You get to walk through reconstructed tribal homes. Time permitting, it's worth a visit.

Old Guwahati AREA
This quainter area of Guwahati, bordering the Brahmaputra River, is best explored on foot. Walk past the distinctive beehive dome of the **Courthouse** (MG Rd) which rises above attractive **Dighulipukhuri Park** (HB Rd; admission ₹5, boats per person ₹15; ⊙ 9.30am-8pm), with its large tank full of row boats. The nearby **Guwahati Planetarium** (MG Rd; shows ₹15; ⊙ noon & 4pm, closed 1st & 15th of the month) looks somewhere between a mosque

Guwahati

Guwahati

and a landed UFO. A short walk due northwest takes you to the **riverbanks**, where you can take in sweeping views of the Brahmaputra River while walking along a well-maintained promenade.

🛏 Sleeping

Most midrange and top-end hotels add a 15% tax and 10% service charge to their nightly rates. These have been included in the prices listed here.

Sundarban Guest House HOTEL $
(☎ 2730722; Paltan Bazaar; s/d from ₹500/700; ❄) Reminiscent of a classic backpacker hangout, this cheery and colourful hotel sits in Guwahati's central market area and offers great value for those travelling on a budget. Rooms are atypically clean and tidy with fresh sheets, and the management is helpful. It's off Manipuribasti East (ME) Rd, in the first side lane and away from road noise.

Prashaanti Tourist Lodge HOTEL $
(☎ 9207017841; Station Rd; s/d from ₹680/800; ❄) A standard-issue government outfit, this centrally located hotel is convenient for the train station. The staff go about dispensing cold hospitality, and there's some train noise to put up with, but the rooms are clean and, most importantly, a genuine bargain for the price. There's no room service after 9pm.

★ Baruah Bhavan GUESTHOUSE $$
(☎ 9954024165; www.heritagehomeassam.com; Manik Chandra (MC) Rd, Uzanbazar; d incl breakfast from ₹2000; ❄ @) Owned and managed by the affable Baruah family, this charming bungalow dating back to the 1970s oozes nostalgia in the form of innumerable antiques and memorabilia strewn across its living areas. The six plush rooms are appointed with elegant period furniture and brocaded upholstery, adding to their quaintness. The manicured front lawns go excellently with chilled beer.

Rains Inn HOTEL $$
(☎ 2730025; www.rainsinn.com; Solapara Rd; s/d from ₹1800/2000; ❄ ☎) A fresh new entrant in Guwahati's hospitality scene, this stylish hotel makes great use of ethno-chic decor (read cane furniture and reed blinds) in its well-appointed rooms stuffed with modern creature comforts. Some of the furniture is made from recycled wood, while water conservation is given top priority by the management. Wi-fi, tea and coffee come complimentary.

WORTH A TRIP

RIVER RIDES

To experience the innate beauty of Assam in a delightfully alternative way, consider signing up for a river cruise. Departing Guwahati on set dates, these multiday luxury rides take you upstream along the Brahmaputra all the way to Dibrugarh, dropping anchor at essential hotspots such as Kaziranga. Attractions en route include wildlife tours, cultural excursions, or simply lazing on the sun-deck with a chiller in hand. Guwahati-based **Assam Bengal Navigation** (☎ 9207042330; www.assambengalnavigation.com; Gopi Nath Bordoloi (GNB) Rd; per person per day all-inclusive from US$195) has all the information, and is recommended.

Hotel Siroy Lily HOTEL $$
(☎ 2608492; www.hotelsiroylilygroup.com; Solapara Rd; s/d incl breakfast from ₹1275/1485; ❄) This trusted oldie has finally started showing signs of old age, but it's still professionally run and thereby a favourite with midrange travellers transiting through Guwahati. Rooms are well serviced, and the air-conditioned rooms offer a significantly better deal for a few hundred extra rupees.

Kiranshree Portico HOTEL $$$
(☎ 2735300; www.kiranshreeportico.com; Guwahati Shillong (GS) Rd; s/d from ₹4600/5300; ❄ ☎) This luxurious and modern hotel on Guwahati Shillong (GS) Rd is arguably the most upscale address in town. The prim and elegantly appointed rooms boast soft beds, moody lighting, giant LCD TVs and well-stocked minibars, and guests have complimentary access to the fitness centre. The coffee shop has a delectable range of bakes and brews to keep you occupied through the lean hours.

🍴 Eating

Beatrix MULTICUISINE $
(Manik Chandra (MC) Rd; dishes ₹60-100; ⊙ noon-10pm) Upbeat and cartoon-walled, Beatrix is just a peg above a student hangout, and serves food with canteen-like irreverence. Its eclectic menu offers fish and chips, *momos* and Hakka Chow, all of which can be wolfed down while admiring the beautiful old villa it sits next door to.

NORTHEAST TOURS

Most foreign tourists visiting the Northeast States travel – perhaps wisely so – as part of an organised tour. Indeed, in Arunachal Pradesh, Nagaland, Manipur and Mizoram, independent travel is almost impossible – you will be left to grapple with crippling issues like language barriers, poor connectivity, strikes, curfews and roadblocks all by yourself. Going with a reputed agent would greatly help with troubleshooting, thus allowing you to travel peacefully and actually enjoy your trip (albeit for a marginally higher fee). Travelling with a local go-between also goes a long way in earning the trust of xenophobic villagers in remote areas, thereby giving you greater cultural and artistic access into their lives.

The following companies organise permits and tours throughout the northeast.

Aborcountry Travels & Expeditions (☑9436053870, 0360-2292969; www.abor countrytravels.com; B Sector, Itanagar) Based in Itanagar, with an exhaustive footprint across the region. Specialises in customised adventure tours and treks in remote areas.

Alder Tours & Travels (☑9402905046; www.altertoursntravels.com; Imphal Rd, opp War Cemetery, Kohima; ☺9am-5pm) Can provide matchless service (thanks to being located in Kohima) during the rushed Hornbill Festival.

Network Travels (☑0361-2605335; www.networktravelsindia.net; Guwahati Shillong (GS) Rd, Guwahati; ☺6am-9pm) A reputed Guwahati agency with tailor-made, fixed-itinerary tours and a fantastic regional network.

Purvi Discovery (☑0373-2301120; www.purviweb.com; Medical College Rd, Jalan Nagar, Dibru-garh) This Dibrugarh-based agency offers culinary, wildlife and cultural tours in Upper Assam.

Rhino Travels (☑0361-2540666; www.rhinotravels.com; M Nehru Rd, Guwahati; ☺10am-5pm Mon-Sat) Located in Guwahati, this outfit has set-date tours and cruises in Assam and Arunachal Pradesh.

Maihang NORTHEAST INDIAN $$
(☑9854373978; Guwahati Shillong (GS) Rd; mains ₹150-170; ☺noon-3pm & 7-10pm) Want a delectable sampling of local cuisines from across the Northeast, all in one place? Choose from an assortment of regional dishes at this smart restaurant, and feel like you've stepped into a parallel culinary universe. The pork with bamboo shoot, charcoal grilled fish *khorika,* chicken in fermented soyabean and duck in sesame gravy find lots of takers.

Paradise ASSAMESE $$
(GNB Rd; mains ₹100-200; ☺noon-3pm & 7-10pm) The lunch thali at Paradise is considered by many to be the archetypal Assamese spread, bringing together a wide range of local culinary flavours in one platter. Try the subtly flavoured fish *tenga* (sour curry), and you're bound to become a fan for life.

Tandoori NORTH INDIAN $$
(☑2516021; Sir Shahdullah (SS) Rd; mains ₹200-300; ☺noon-3pm & 7-11pm) Inside the stately Dynasty Hotel, Tandoori concocts majestic North Indian dishes which are served at stylish low tables by waiters in Mughal uniforms accompanied by gentle live tabla music.

Drinking & Nightlife

Café Coffee Day CAFE
(Taybullah Rd; coffees ₹45-80; ☺10am-10pm) Guwahati's central coffee shop, pumping out contemporary music, attracts the city's students and nouveau-riche youth with perfect (if very slow) macchiato. There are some tasty snacks on offer to go with your cuppa.

Trafik BAR
(GNB Rd; beers ₹120; ☺10am-10pm; ☎) Underlit and buzzy, this popular bar is a hit with the city's working class and, true to its name, attracts heavy traffic after sundown. There's a vast screen for cricket matches or Bollywood music, and the vibe is generally pleasant.

Information

EMERGENCY
Police Station (☑2540126; Hem Barua (HB) Rd) Calls are promptly answered.

INTERNET ACCESS
iWay (Lamb Rd; per hr ₹20; ☺9am-8pm) Internet access.

MEDICAL SERVICES
Downtown Hospital (☑2331003; Guwahati Shillong (GS) Rd, Dispur) The area's best.

MONEY

ATMs and banks abound. It's a good idea to stock up on local currency here as ATMs in smaller centres can be unreliable.

Axis Bank (M Nehru Rd; ⊙10am-4pm Mon-Sat) Has an ATM and handles foreign exchange.

State Bank of India (SBI; MG Rd, 3rd fl; ⊙10am-2pm Mon-Fri, to noon Sat) Has an ATM, changes major currencies and cashes travellers cheques.

POST

Main Post Office (Ananda Ram Barua (ARB) Rd; ⊙10am-4pm Mon-Sat)

TOURIST INFORMATION

Assam Tourism (☑2542748; www.assamtourism.org; Station Rd; ⊙10am-5pm Mon-Sat) Informal help desk within the Prashaanti Tourist Lodge, with a tour booth just outside.

ⓘ Getting There & Away

AIR

Air India (☑2264420; Ganeshguri), IndiGo, Jet Airways and SpiceJet fly to Guwahati from most major Indian cities (often with a stopover in Kolkata). Getting into town from Guwahati's orderly Lokpriya Gopinath Bordoloi International Airport costs ₹500/150/100 for taxi/shared taxi/airport bus.

Arunachal Helicopter Service (☑2229501; Guwahati airport; ⊙10am-2pm) has flights to Itanagar (₹3000, 1½ hours, 1.30pm Monday, Tuesday, Thursday and Saturday).

Meghalaya Helicopter Service (☑9859 021473; Guwahati Airport; ⊙8.30am-2pm) shuttles to Shillong (₹1500, 40 minutes, 9am and 12.30pm Monday to Saturday) and Tura (₹1900, 50 minutes, 10.30am Monday, Wednesday, Friday and Saturday). Note that helicopter travel in India has a poor safety record.

BUS & SUMO

Distance buses leave from the Interstate Bus Terminal (ISBT) 8km east of Guwahati. Private bus operators run shuttle services from their offices to the ISBT. With extensive networks are **Blue Hill** (☑2601490; HPB Rd; ⊙6am-8pm), **Deep** (☑2152937; Heramba Prasad Borua (HPB) Rd; ⊙6am-9pm) and **Network Travels** (☑2522007; Guwahati Shillong (GS) Rd; ⊙5am-9pm). All companies hire out Sumos and other sturdy 4WD vehicles for travel in the region, and charge the same regulated fares.

TRAIN

Of the four daily trains connecting Guwahati to Delhi, the 12423 Dibrugarh Rajdhani Express (3AC/2AC ₹1950/2875, 27 hours, 7.05am) is the fastest and most comfortable. For travelling to Darjeeling and Sikkim, simply get off at New Jalpaiguri (3AC/2AC ₹690/965, six hours). The best daily train to Kolkata (Howrah Junction) is the 12346 Saraighat Express (sleeper/3AC/2AC ₹425/989/1510, 16½ hours, 12.45pm).

ⓘ PERMIT CHECK

Permits All states in the Northeast except Arunachal Pradesh have done away with Restricted Area Permits (RAP) for travellers, allowing free movement in areas which are officially open for tourism. However, foreigners are still technically required to register at the nearest police station upon their arrival in any state capital.

The following information pertains to visitors interested in travelling to Arunachal Pradesh only.

Minimum Group Size Permit applications need a two-person minimum group. In reality, though, it's possible for single travellers to get a permit, but only if you use a tour company.

Permit Requirements An application for a permit must be accompanied by a covering letter, photocopies of passport and valid visa, two passport-size photographs and a US$50 processing fee.

Validity Permits are valid for 30 days from a specified starting date. If you wish to overstay, you have to apply for a fresh permit. Permits only allow you to visit specified districts between specified dates, so plan your itinerary carefully. Make multiple photocopies of your permit to hand in at each checkpoint, police station and hotel.

Where to Apply Permits are issued at the state secretariat in Itanagar, which accepts applications only from reputed and registered travel agencies. Ergo, you must go through a tour operator even if you plan to travel independently in the region afterward. Some agents nowadays offer to secure permits for independent travellers for an extra fee.

Several trains serve Dimapur (sleeper/3AC/2AC from ₹150/380/575, four to six hours), Jorhat (sleeper/3AC ₹192/505, seven to 11 hours) and Dibrugarh (3AC/2AC ₹900/1250, 11 hours).

ⓘ Getting Around

Shared taxis to the airport (per person/car ₹150/500, 23km) leave from outside the Hotel Mahalaxmi on Guwahati Shillong (GS) Rd. From the Adabari bus stand, city buses travel to Hajo (bus 25, ₹60, one hour) and Sualkuchi (bus 22, ₹60, one hour). Autorickshaws charge ₹25 to ₹70 for shorter hops.

Around Guwahati

Hajo

Some 30km northwest of Guwahati, the pleasant little town of Hajo attracts Hindu and Buddhist pilgrims to its five ancient temples topping assorted hillocks. **Haigriv Madhav Temple** is the main shrine, which is accessed by a long flight of steps through an ornate quasi-Mughal gateway. The images inside of Madhav, an avatar of Krishna, are believed to be 6000 years old.

Pobitora Wildlife Sanctuary

Only 40km from Guwahati, this small wildlife sanctuary has a generous sprinkling of one-horned rhinoceros. Entrance fees are Indian/foreigner ₹50/500. Getting into the park involves a boat ride over the river boundary to the elephant-mounting station. From there it's a one-hour trip atop an elephant lumbering through boggy grassland and stirring up petulant rhinos.

Tezpur

☏ 03712 / POP 105.300

An essential stopover for travellers journeying into Arunachal Pradesh or Upper Assam, Tezpur is a charming city that boasts a handful of beautifully kept parks, attractive lakes and enchanting views of the mighty Brahmaputra River as it laps the town's edge.

◉ Sights

Chitralekha Udyan (Cole Park; Jenkins Rd; adult/camera/video ₹20/20/100; ☺9am-7pm) has a U-shaped pond (paddleboat hire ₹10 per person) wrapped around pretty manicured lawns, dotted with fine **ancient sculptures**. The park also contains bumper cars and waterslides (April to September)! A block east, then south, stands **Ganeshgarh Temple**, which backs onto a ghat overlooking the surging river, a good place for Brahmaputra sunsets. Nearly 1km east along the narrow, winding riverside lane is **Agnigarh Hill** (Padma Park; adult/camera/video ₹20/20/100; ☺8.30am-7.30pm), which might have been Banasura's fire fortress site.

⌕ Sleeping

Prashaanti Tourist Lodge   HOTEL **$**
(☏9207044435; Jenkins Rd; s/d from ₹648/762) Facing Chitralekha Udyan, two blocks south of the bus station, this government-run hotel is manned by efficient staff who (unlike most state-run ops) actually care about the well-being of their guests and the cleanliness of their hotel. The place offers good-value spacious rooms with bathrooms (cheaper rooms come with squat toilets) and mosquito nets.

BUSES FROM GUWAHATI

DESTINATION	FARE (₹)	DURATION (HR)
Agartala (Tripura)	750	24-26
Aizawl (Mizoram)	720	28
Dibrugarh	470	10
Imphal (Manipur) via Mao	870	20
Jorhat	290	8
Kaziranga	260-300	6
Kohima (Nagaland)	390	13
Shillong (Meghalaya)	90-110	3½
Sivasagar	390	8
Tezpur	180	5

KF HOTEL $$

(☑237825; skfood@gmail.com; Mission Charali; s/d from ₹1800/2100; ❈ 🔊) With slick, contemporary rooms, good customer service and plenty of attention to detail, this hotel – located about 3km north of the town centre – has lots going for it. There's an in-house restaurant, a coffee shop and, most importantly, a departmental store downstairs where you can stock up on essential commodities before venturing into remote areas.

Hotel Centre Point HOTEL $$

(☑232359; hotelcentrepoint.tezpur@gmail.com; Main Rd; d incl breakfast from ₹1300; ❈) The smart, freshly painted rooms at this well-run and centrally located hotel feature flat-screen TVs, hot showers and polished wooden floors, which gives them a swanky business-class feel. The in-house travel desk can organise local sightseeing trips as well as longer tours.

🍴 Eating & Drinking

The modern glass tower **Baliram Building**, on the corner of Naren Bose (NB) and NC/SC Roads, contains several floors of good dining. The ground-floor stand-up-and-eat **Dosa House** (dishes ₹30-60; ⊙6am-9pm) has South Indian fare and cheap breakfasts. Semi-smart **China Villa** (meals from ₹120; ⊙10am-10.30pm) offers Indian and Chinese food in air-con comfort, while the rooftop **Chat House** (snacks from ₹30; ⊙8am 9.30pm) has good views, noodles, pizzas and *momos*.

Oasis BAR

(Jonaki Cinema Rd; beers from ₹110; ⊙11am-10pm) Chilled bottles of Kingfisher are served with a wide array of kebabs at this popular and friendly bar a short walk from Hotel Centre Point. It's adjacent to Jonaki Cinema.

ℹ Information

Cinex Computers (Santa Plaza; per hr ₹30; ⊙10am-9pm) Cinex Computers on Shyama Charan (SC) Rd, 250m north of the Baliram Building restaurants, has internet.

HDFC Bank (Mission Chariali; ⊙10am-4pm Mon-Sat) Has an ATM.

ℹ Getting There & Away

Sumos have their booking counters in Jenkins Rd and run to Bomdila in Arunachal Pradesh (₹300, eight hours) and Tawang (₹650, 15hrs). Bargain for a private taxi in the same street for the Eco-Camp at Nameri (₹2000) and Kaziranga (₹2000). A little further on is the **bus station** (Jenkins Rd) with frequent services to Guwahati (₹150, five hours), Jorhat (₹150, four hours) and Kohora for Kaziranga (₹80, two hours).

Around Tezpur

Scenic **Nameri National Park** (Indian/camera/video ₹20/50/500, foreigner/camera/video ₹250/500/1000; ⊙Nov-Apr) specialises in low-key, walk-in birdwatching treks. Around 374 bird species have been recorded in the park, including such rarities as the greater spotted eagle and the white-winged duck. Mammals include wild elephants, a few rarely seen tigers and the critically endangered dwarf hog. Park fees include the compulsory armed guard. Access is from **Potasali**, 2km off the Tezpur–Bhalukpong road.

Eco-Camp (☑9854019932, 9435220697; assamangling@yahoo.com; dm/d incl membership per person ₹250/1720) organises all Nameri visits, including two-hour birdwatching rafting trips (two people Indian/foreigner ₹1500/2000). Accommodation is in 'tents', but colourful fabrics, private bathrooms, sturdy beds and thatched-roof shelters make the experience relatively luxurious. The camp is set within lush gardens full of tweeting birds and butterflies drunk on tropical nectar.

Wild Mahseer (☑9435197650; www.wild mahseer.com; d incl full board from ₹8500; ❈), located amid rolling tea gardens about 30km northeast of Tezpur, offers a luxurious stay in its four superbly renovated planter's bungalows thrown about a picturesque 22-acre campus canopied with evergreen trees. For a particularly memorable experience, consider spending a night in the Heritage Bungalow, a stately 100-year-old building that carefully preserves a slice of high life from its bygone era. To get to the estate, turn right from Balipara crossing and take the village road going left after the bridge on the Bhorelli River.

Kaziranga National Park

☑03776

One of India's best-known tourism mascots, the famed one-horned rhinoceros calls the expansive grasslands of this **national park** (Indian/foreigner ₹50/500; ⊙1 Nov-30 Apr, elephant rides 5.30-8.30am, jeep access 7.30am-noon & 2.30pm-dusk) its native place. The park's population of 1800-odd rhinos (just 200 in

1904) represents more than two-thirds of the world's total.

The park consists of a western, central and an eastern range, the central range doubling as the venue for the thoroughly enjoyable elephant safari, a must-do for anyone visiting Kaziranga. Lasting an hour each, these rides are especially satisfying when a 'team' of elephants makes pincer movements, surrounding rhinos without frightening them off.

🛏 Sleeping & Eating

In season, booking ahead against advance payment is recommended. All the better hotels listed here sell 'Jungle Plan' packages, including full-board accommodation, park fees, a morning elephant safari and an afternoon jeep safari. Unless stated otherwise, the prices we list are for rooms only.

🛏 Tourist Complex

There are a number of budget and mid-range options (mostly run by Assam Tourism) across the well-maintained complex, all within a short walk of the range office. The following are the best options.

Aranya Tourist Lodge   HOTEL $$
(📷 262429; d from ₹1572; 🕸) A somewhat characterless operation masquerading as a forest getaway, this garden-fronted hotel otherwise features clean rooms, prompt service, decent food and a well-stocked bar. It's popular with large groups, so expect some noisy company.

Jupuri Ghar   RESORT $$
(📷 9435196377, 0361 2605335; d incl breakfast ₹2886; 🕸) A general holidaying atmosphere lends itself to the appeal of this pretty property, comprising traditional-style cabins set around pleasant, mature gardens in a tranquil setting. It's well managed and has an open-air restaurant where you can compare your elephant safari notes with other guests over complimentary breakfast.

🛏 Beyond the Complex

Wild Grass Resort   RESORT $$
(📷 9954416945, 262085; www.oldassam.com; d incl breakfast ₹2400) This delightful and slightly ramshackle ecofriendly resort is so justifiably popular that it doesn't bother with a sign – it carefully labels all the trees instead! Colonial-era decor makes you feel the clock has slowed. The dining

room serves tasty Indian food. The affable, bearded proprietor is a fount of local information. In season, bookings are absolutely essential.

Bonhabi Resort   RESORT $$
(📷 262675; www.bonhabiresort.com; d from ₹1610; 🕸) A short way east of the tourist complex, this place consists of an old villa with a colonial-era look and feel, and a series of comfortable cottages set around gorgeous gardens. It's on the way to the eastern range, and is well signposted.

⭐ Diphlu River Lodge   RESORT $$$
(📷 9954205360, 0361-2667871; www.diphlu riverlodge.com; jungle plan per person Indian/foreigner ₹7000/12,500; 🕸 🕿) Easily the classiest place to stay in the Kaziranga region, this lovely resort combines fine luxuries with a rustic look and an ethno-chic theme. The bamboo cottages lining the Diphlu River boast soft beds, rain showers in stylish bathrooms and pleasant sit-outs from where lucky guests might spot rhinos grazing in the grasslands. And oh, the food is delicious.

There's no marker: if you're travelling from Guwahati, look for the dirt track on the left after the Bagori police outpost, leading to a gate with a signage saying 'private property'.

Iora   RESORT $$$
(The Retreat; 📷 9957193350; www.kazirangasafari. com; s/d incl breakfast from ₹3350/3750; 🕸 @🕿🏊) Flashier than most other resorts in Kaziranga, this sprawling property has excellently maintained rooms (42 in all) featuring tasteful decor, modern amenities and efficient service. The swimming pool is a big draw for kids, while adults can spend a lazy afternoon indulging in a range of therapies at the in-house spa.

ℹ Information

The forest administration offices are clubbed together in the Kaziranga Tourist Complex (marked by an obvious Rhino Gate) about 800m south of Kohora village. Here you'll find the **rangers office** (📷 262428; ⏱ 24hr), **elephant-ride booking office** (Kaziranga Tourist complex; rides incl park fee Indian/foreigner ₹525/1525; ⏱ 5-7pm, book the previous night) and **jeep rental stand** (Kaziranga Tourist complex; rental per vehicle incl toll fee ₹1500). Pay your fees at the rangers office before entering the park, 2km north.

Fees for Indians/foreigners are: entry ₹50/500, cameras ₹50/500 and videos

₹500/1000. An armed guard accompanies all vehicles (and some elephants) entering the park. A ₹50 tip for mahouts, drivers and guards is customary.

ⓘ Getting There & Away

Buses travel from Kohora village to Guwahati (₹330, five hours, hourly 7.30am to 4.30pm), Dibrugarh (₹310, four hours) and Tezpur (₹80, two hours).

Jorhat

📞 0376 / POP 137,800

Apart from being the access point for Majuli Island, bustling Jorhat has little on offer for travellers. Gar Ali, the town's commercial street, meets the main east–west thoroughfare – Assam Trunk (AT) Rd (NH37) – in front of a lively central market area. AT Road is also home to an **SBI ATM** and the **Netizen Cyberspace** (₹20 per hr; ⊙ 9am 8pm) Internet cafe.

Tucked conveniently behind the Assam State Transport Corporation (ASTC) Bus Station (AT Rd), Solicitor Rd has half a dozen reasonable hotels. The best of the lot is **Hotel Paradise** (📞 2321521; Solicitor Rd; s/d incl breakfast from ₹600/850; ❀ 🖥), a trusted address with well-kept, wallpapered interiors, friendly service, deep-fried snacks and free wi-fi. **Hotel Heritage** (📞 2301839; heritagejorhat2009@yahoo.in; Solicitor Rd; s/d from ₹550/650; ❀) has well-maintained rooms, obliging staff and an old-fashioned character. At the end of the lane is **New Park** (📞 2300/45; hotelnewparkjorhat@gmail.com; Solicitor Rd; s/d from ₹625/800; ❀), a smart establishment with tidy, breezy rooms, hot showers and lots of daylight.

The **ASTC bus station** (AT Rd) has frequent services to Sivasagar (₹60, 1½ hours), Tezpur (₹155, four hours) and Guwahati (₹290, eight hours, eight buses 6am to noon; buses pass Kaziranga en route).

The 12068 Jan Shatabdi Express (AC Chair ₹436, 6¾ hours, 2.10pm Monday to Saturday) is the most convenient of the two trains to Guwahati.

Majuli Island

📞 03775 / POP 168,000

Beached amid the mighty Brahmaputra River's ever-shifting puzzle of ochre sandbanks is Majuli, which at around 452 sq km is India's largest river island. For a place continually ravaged by the primal forces of nature (much of the island disappears under water every monsoon), Majuli flaunts unparalleled scenic beauty. The island is a relaxed, shimmering mat of glowing rice fields and water meadows bursting with flowers. Aside from relishing the laid-back vibe that permeates island life, highlights of a visit include birdwatching and learning about neo-Vaishnavite philosophy at one of Majuli's 22 ancient *satras* (Hindu Vaishnavite monasteries and centres for art). If all this makes Majuli sounds like your kind of place then don't waste time getting there – surveys indicate that at current levels of erosion the island will cease to exist within 20 years.

The two main villages are **Kamalabari**, 3km from the ferry port, and **Garamur**, 5km further north. The most interesting, accessible *satras* are the large, beautifully peaceful **Uttar Kamalabari** (1km north, then 600m east of Kamalabari) and **Auni Ati** (5km west of Kamalabari), where monks are keen to show you their little **museum** (Indian/foreigner/camera/video ₹10/50/50/200; ⊙ 9.30-11am & 12-4pm) of Ahom royal artefacts. The best chances of observing chanting, dances or drama recitations are around dawn and dusk or during the big **Ras Mahotsav Festival** (Majuli Island; ⊙ 3rd week of Nov).

To add to list of Majuli's attractions, birdwatchers would love the fact that the island is home to nearly 100 species of birds. **Majuli Tourism Information Centre** (📞 9435657282; jyoti24365@gmail.com; per day ₹500), manned by the friendly and knowledgeable Jyoti Narayan Sarma, conducts birdwatching tours.

🛏 Sleeping & Eating

As well as the options listed here, many of the *satras* have very basic **guesthouses** (₹150). Remember to dress conservatively within the premises.

La Maison de Ananda　　　　GUESTHOUSE $
(📞 9957186356; monjitrisong@yahoo.in; r ₹300-600) On a Garamur back lane, this traditionally styled thatched house on bamboo stilts has rooms decked out in locally made fabrics, giving it a hippie-chic atmosphere. The best value-for-money lodging on the island, it is run by a friendly tribal family, and the kitchen tosses up a delicious range of local dishes.

SATRAS

A *satra* is a monastery for Vishnu worship, Assam's distinctive form of everyman Hinduism. Formulated by 15th-century Assamese philosopher Sankardev, the faith eschews the caste system and idol worship, focusing on Vishnu as God, especially in his Krishna incarnation. Much of the worship is based around dance and melodramatic play-acting of scenes from the holy Bhagavad Gita. The heart of any *satra* is its *namghar,* a large, simple, prayer hall housing an eternal flame, the Gita and possibly a horde of instructive (but not divine) images. Traditionally, *satras* have also patronised the elegantly choreographed Satriya dance form, as well as the folk-performing-arts tradition of Ankiya Bhawna, in which masked dancers play out tales from Hindu mythology. To purchase traditional dance masks (₹300 to ₹1500) as souvenirs, visit **Samaguri Satra**, a 15-minute drive from Garamur.

Ygdrasill Bamboo Cottage   GUESTHOUSE **$**
(📞8876707326; bedamajuli@gmail.com; d/q ₹600/1200) En route from Kamalabari to Garamur, this stilted guesthouse perches on a marshy, avian-filled lake. Watch fish plopping about in the water, and listen to the chorus of a thousand cicadas before to sleep in a comfy bamboo bed in one of the spartan, traditionally furnished cottages. Dinner (₹350) can be organised upon prior request.

❶ Getting There & Away

The windswept sandbank of Nimatighat in Jorhat, pockmarked with chai shacks, is the departure point for photogenically overcrowded ferries to Majuli Island. It's a 12km-ride from Jorhat by bus (₹30, 40 minutes).

Ferries (adult/jeep ₹50/600, 1½ hours) leave Nimatighat at 8.30am, 10.30am, 1.30pm and 3pm; return trips are at 7.30am, 8.30am, 1.30pm and 3pm. Departures depend on tidal conditions and season.

❶ Getting Around

Jam-packed buses/vans (₹20/30) meet arriving ferries then drive to Garamur via Kamalabari where three-wheelers are easier to rent. For a few days consider arranging a bicycle (₹100) through Majuli Tourism Information Centre.

Sivasagar

📞03772 / POP 53,800

Once the capital of the Ahom dynasty, sleepy Sivasagar takes its name (literally 'waters of Shiva') from the graceful central reservoir in the heart of town, commissioned by the Ahom Queen Ambika in 1734. Three typical Ahom **temple towers** rise proudly above the tank's partly wooded southern banks – to the west **Devidol**, to the east **Vishnudol** and in the centre, the 33m-high **Shivadol Mandir**.

Around 500m from Shivadol, a gaggle of hotels line AT Rd, the most appealing of which is the surprisingly swish **Hotel Shiva Palace** (📞222629; hotelshivapalace.1811@rediff mail.com; s/d from ₹900/1000; ❄), incorporating a decent restaurant, the **Sky Chef Restaurant** (mains ₹140).

About 1.5km along Bhuban Gogoi (BG) Rd stands **Hotel Siddhartha** (📞222276; e7safari@rediffmail.com; s/d from ₹550/880; ❄), a sparkly place with a combination of basic and swanky rooms.

The **ASTC bus station** (cnr AT & Temple Rds) has frequent services to Jorhat (₹60, one hour), Dibrugarh (₹75, two hours), Tezpur (₹220, five hours) and Guwahati (₹390, eight hours, frequent from 7am).

For sightseeing to Talatalghar and Kareng Ghar, use a tempo (large autorickshaw; ₹200 per tour). You'll find them at an unmarked stop about 300m up BG Rd from AT Rd.

Around Sivasagar

A sprinkling of graceful temples and red-brick pavilions, built by the Ahom monarchs during their 17th- and 18th-century heydays, make for a wonderful half-day excursion out of Sivasagar.

Talatalghar

This famous Ahom ruin is 4km down AT Rd from central Sivasagar, and is marked by the elegant **Rang Ghar** (Indian/foreigner ₹5/100; ☉dawn-dusk), a two-storey oval-shaped pavilion from where Ahom monarchs once watched buffalo and elephant fights in an arena that's now been converted into a manicured garden.

Past Talatalghar along AT Rd, a left turning passes the barrack-shaped **Golaghar** (Ahom ammunition store). Beyond are the ruins of **Talatalghar** (Indian/foreigner ₹5/100; ☉dawn-dusk), an expansive, two-storey

Ahom palace built by Ahom King Rajeswar Singha in the mid-18th century.

Karenghar

Dramatic if largely unadorned, this 1752 brick palace is the last remnant of the Ahom's pre-Sivasagar capital. The unique four-storey structure rises like a sharpened, stepped pyramid above an attractive forest-and-paddy setting. It's about 15km along the Sivasagar–Sonari highway down a village road: turn left just before Gargaon.

Dibrugarh

🕿 0373 / POP 137,600

Cheerful, clement Dibrugarh – Assam's original tea city – usefully closes a loop between Kaziranga and the Ziro–Along–Pasighat route in Arunachal Pradesh, and is also the terminus (or starting point) for the fascinating ferry ride along the Brahmaputra to Pasighat. Despite being a rapidly growing urban agglomeration, Dibrugarh has managed to retain some charm from its glory days – it's probably the only town in India with pretty tea gardens smack in the heart of the business district!

Dibrugarh is a reliable place to change money; **State Bank of India** (Thana Chariali; ⌚10am-2pm Mon-Fri, to noon Sat) cashes travellers cheques and foreign currency; there's also an **SBI ATM** in the main bus station complex. **Cyber@Generation Next** (HS Rd; per hr ₹30; ⌚9am-10pm) is one of several internet cafes.

Hotel Mona Lisa (☎2320416; monalisahotel@gmail.com; Mancotta Rd; d from ₹1000; ❋), a multistoreyed establishment accessed through an alfresco coffee shop sporting ethno-tribal decor, is a superb budget hotel

with character. The rooms are airy, spacious and well maintained, service (overseen by the lovely old proprietor) is good and there's a mess-like bar on the 1st floor (beers ₹120) where you can quaff booze in peace.

Hotel Little Palace (☎2328700; www.hotellp.com; AT Rd; d from ₹1000; ❋), on the edge of town, is anything but little. Its 48 rooms are well appointed with clean linen, and the views of the Brahmaputra River from the verandah at the end of the corridor comes free. The flashy lobby downstairs has a well-stocked bar and a decent restaurant (mains ₹160).

ℹ️ Getting There & Away

From Mohanbari airport, 16km northeast of Dibrugarh and 4km off the Tinsukia road, Air India and Jet Airways fly to Guwahati, Kolkata and Delhi, while IndiGo flies to Guwahati.

From the main **bus station** (Mancotta Rd), both ASTC and private buses depart for Sivasagar (₹85, two hours, frequent 6am to 9am), Jorhat (₹150, three hours, frequent 6am to 9am), Tezpur (₹330, six hours) and Guwahati (₹470, 10 hours). There's also an air-conditioned Volvo service to Guwahati (₹660, eight hours, 9.45pm).

The 12423 Dibrugarh Rajdhani Express is the overnight train for Guwahati (3AC/2AC ₹939/1270, 10 hours, 8.35pm).

Rough-and-ready **ferries** (Indian/foreigner ₹70/200, vehicle ₹800, hourly 9am to 3pm) cruise daily to Bogibil Ghat on the Arunachal side of the Brahmaputra River, where the boat is met by a bus to Pasighat in Arunachal Pradesh. Cheekily challenging the basic laws of floatation, the rickety steamboats carry two jeeps, a few dozen motorcycles and an army of humans. There's little shelter and the journey takes around 1½ hours, so bring shades, water and sunscreen. It's quite an adventure, with boats

---

WORTH A TRIP

IT'S TEA TIME, FOLKS!

To get a hang of Dibrugarh's centuries-old tryst with tea, try scheduling a night at one of the vintage planters bungalows in and around town. Superbly renovated and stacked with layers of carefully preserved memorabilia from their heydays in the late 18th and early 19th centuries, these bungalows allow you to relive the high life that was once the sole preserve of the topmost echelons of society. The best places to indulge in this mothballed luxury are the **Mancotta Heritage Chang Bungalow** (☎2301120; purvi@sancharnet.in; Mancotta Rd; d incl full board ₹7650-8100; ❋ 🛜), 4km from town, and the **Chowkidinghee Chang Bungalow** (Convoy Rd; r incl full board ₹3600-6750; ❋ 🛜), about 700m from the bus station. Apart from guaranteeing you a lavish stay, both properties can arrange tea estate tours and boat rides upon prior request. To book, contact Purvi Discovery (p564).

sometimes running into sandbanks and then being pushed back into deeper waters by the boat's crew! Exact departure times depend on the Brahmaputra's water level. During the dry season, ferries cruise further upstream to Majer Ghat or Oiram Ghat, which can take up to five hours.

ARUNACHAL PRADESH

The final frontier of Indian tourism, virginal Arunachal Pradesh shows up as a giant patch of green on the country's map. India's wildest and least explored state, Arunachal – literally the 'Land of Dawn-lit Mountains' – rises abruptly from the Assam plains as a mass of densely forested, and impossibly steep, hills, which eventually top off as snow-capped peaks along the Tibetan border. Home to 26 indigenous tribes, from the robust Monpas of Tawang to the artistic Apatanis of Ziro, Arunachal is perhaps the last sanctuary for India's natural and anthropological heritage. Much of the state still remains beyond tourism's reach, but new areas (comprising lush river gorges and craggy mountainscapes) are slowly being opened to visitors.

China has never formally recognised Indian sovereignty here, and it took the surprise Chinese invasion of 1962 for Delhi to really start funding significant infrastructure (the Chinese voluntarily withdrew). These days, border passes are heavily guarded by the Indian military and the atmosphere is extremely calm. In a stark contrast to its neighbours, Arunachal has virtually no history of communal insurgency.

Arunachal Tourism (www.arunachaltourism.com) has additional information.

Itanagar

📞 0360 / POP 35,000

Arunachal's capital takes its name from the mysterious Ita Fort, the residual brick ruins of which crown a hilltop above the rapidly booming town. A concrete-fest of sorts, this somewhat characterless urban hub merely serves as the state's power centre (your travel permits for Arunachal are issued here). There's a stack of ATMs and internet cafes along Mahatma Gandhi (MG) Marg.

The few sights in town include the decent but shoddily curated **Jawaharlal Nehru State Museum** (Indian/foreigner/camera/video ₹10/75/20/100; ⊙ 9.30am-4pm Sun-Thu), and the brightly coloured gompa of the **Centre for Buddhist Culture** set in the gardens nearby.

The good-value **Hotel Blue Pine** (📞 2211118; Ganga Market; s/d from ₹800/1000; ❄) stands near the APST bus station, with simple but prim rooms, and positions itself 'between you and your sweet home'. Oversized **Hotel Arun Subansiri** (📞 2212806; Zero Point Tinali; s/d ₹1200/1400; ❄), en route to the

NAMDAPHA NATIONAL PARK

Nearly half of India's biodiversity is indigenous to Arunachal Pradesh. If that's saying a lot, wait until you hear that most of this wilderness is gathered in the far eastern corner of the state, in and around the staggering **Namdapha National Park** (📞 0360-2244328; www.changlang.nic.in/namdapha.html; Indian/foreigner/camera/camera with zoom lens/video ₹10/50/75/400/750). Spread over 1985 sq km of dense forest land, this ecological hotspot contains a mind-boggling array of animal and plant species, with habitats ranging from warm tropical plains to icy Himalayan highlands. Namdapha is famous for being the only park in India to have four big cat species (leopard, tiger, clouded leopard and snow leopard). It's also a birdwatcher's delight, with around 500 species recorded.

The park is a long haul from anywhere, and visiting the park can be a pain unless you're travelling with a tour operator. Aborcountry Travels & Expeditions (p564) has a good grasp of these jungles.

The access point to the park is the small town of **Miao**, from where you will have to drive 26km to **Deban** where the park headquarters are located. Simple accommodation is available in Miao at the **Eco-Tourist Guest House** (📞 03807-222296; per person Indian/foreigner ₹400/600), or in Deban at the **Forest Rest House** (📞 03807-222249; d ₹350). To really get into the middle of nowhere, you'll have to stay at one of the **campsites** inside the park (virtually a non-option unless you're on a guided tour).

ARUNACHAL'S TRIBAL GROUPS

An astonishing patchwork quilt of ethnic populations, Arunachal is home to as many as 26 different tribes. Some of the more prominent tribes include the Adi (Abor), Nishi, Tajin, Hill Miri, Galo, Apatani and Monpa people. Many tribes are related to each other, while some consider themselves unique. While modernity is slowly making inroads into the local society, most tribes have brought about a seamless blending of the old and the new – it's not uncommon in many areas to see a modern concrete building outfitted with a traditional open-hearth kitchen over stilted bamboo flooring. The traditional animistic religion of Donyi-Polo (sun-and-moon worship) is still prevalent in the region, although Christian missionaries have contributed to bringing about a change in the region's traditional cultures, religious beliefs and ways of life. For ceremonial occasions, village chiefs typically wear scarlet shawls and a bamboo wicker hat spiked with porcupine quills or hornbill beaks. Women favour hand-woven wraparounds like Southeast Asian sarongs, while some of the older men still wear their hair long, with a topknot above their foreheads. The artistic traditions of weaving and wicker-work are very much alive in these hills. Architecture varies from tribe to tribe – traditional Adi villages are generally the most photogenic, with luxuriant palmyra-leaf thatching and wobbly bamboo suspension bridges precariously strung across river gorges.

Jawaharlal Nehru State Museum, has large rooms, soft beds and an overall officious feel. For business-class luxury, try the spanking new **Hotel SC Continental** (☑9436075875; www.hotelsccontinental.com; Vivek Vihar; s/d from ₹2000/2400; ❄ @), a 15-minute walk southwest of the bustling Ganga Market area.

The **APST bus station** (Ganga Market) has services to Guwahati (₹480, 11 hours, 6am), Bomdila (₹300, eight hours, 6am), Pashighat (₹250, 10 hours, 5.30am and 6am) and Shillong (₹380, 12 hours, 5pm).

Across the road, the **Royal Sumo Counter** has daily services to Ziro (₹300, five hours, 5.30am and 2.50pm), Along (₹600, about a million hours, 5.30am) and Pasighat (₹350, eight hours, 5.30am).

Central Arunachal Pradesh

Most travellers visit Central Arunachal Pradesh with the intention of spending a few quiet days in the bucolic and picturesque setting of Ziro Valley. For a few intrepid types, on the other hand, the region promises some great adventure options, from rafting on the Siang River to trekking to remote settlements, such as Mechuka.

Ziro Valley

☑ 03788

By far one of the prettiest landscapes in all of India, the fertile Ziro Valley nestles within Arunachal's formidable mountainscape like a mythical kingdom. A layered landscape of wind-kissed rice fields, gurgling rivulets and picture-postcard villages of the Apatani tribe, it is an undisputed high point of any trip into Arunachal's interiors.

Scenery and village architecture apart, the main attraction here is meeting the friendly older Apatani folk who sport facial tattoos and nose plugs that would be the envy of any self-respecting tattoo artist back home. The most authentic Apatani villages are **Hong** (the biggest and best known), **Hija** (more atmospheric), **Hari**, **Bamin** and **Dutta**; none of which are more than 10km apart. It's vital to have a local guide to take you to any of these villages, or you won't see much and might even be made to feel quite unwelcome.

Ngunu Ziro (☑9436224834; hibuatotatu@gmail.com; homestay Indian/foreigner per person ₹800/1000), a local self-help group that works towards sustainable community development in Apatani villages, provides superb access into the lives of local villagers. It runs a string of comfortable and thoroughly atmospheric homestays with friendly and hospitable hosts – an evening treat of local rice beer and smoked beef often comes free! Ngunu Ziro also provides guides (₹1000) and bicycles (₹500) for village tours.

Sprawling **Hapoli** (New Ziro), starting 7km further south than Ziro, has hotels and road transport. Just below the Commissioner's office, on a bend in MG Rd, is an **SBI ATM**.

MEET THE APATANIS

Numbering around 25,000 and native to the Ziro Valley, the Apatanis are one of Northeast India's most intriguing tribes. Believed to have migrated to the valley from the less hospitable northern highlands, the Apatanis are strongly rooted to their ancient culture. Most people are adherents of the animistic Donyi-Polo religion, and continue to live in pretty traditional houses fabricated out of bamboo and wood (the interiors are considerably modern though). Apatani villages are immensely photogenic, with T-shaped totem poles called *babos* towering over rows of huts that line every thoroughfare. Farmers by occupation, the tribe practises a unique system of agriculture, where terraced rice fields are flooded with water to double as shallow fish farms. Apatanis also have refined aesthetic sensibilities, and excel in arts such as weaving and wicker work.

Historically famous for their beauty, Apatani women were all too often kidnapped by warriors of the neighbouring Nishi tribes. As a 'defence', Apatani girls were deliberately defaced with facial tattoos, like graffitied beards scribbled onto living Mona Lisa paintings, and extraordinary nose plugs known as *dat* fitted into holes cut in their upper nostrils. Peace with the Nishis in the 1960s meant an end to the brutal practice, and only a few surviving locals from the older generations can now be seen wearing *dat*. Photography is an understandably sensitive issue, so ask first (and have a few smaller banknotes to hand out as posing fees).

Hotel Blue Pine (☏ 224812; Pai Gate; s/d from ₹1000/1200) is the best-value lodgings in the town itself (though it's still a bit of a walk from the centre). It has wood-panelled rooms with plenty of character.

Out of town, and by far the best place to stay, is the new log-cabin style **Siiro Resort** (☏ 9402464985; siiroresort@hotmail.com; Siiro Village; d from ₹1600), which has pastel-shaded rooms, lounge-sized bathrooms and prompt service.

Sumos depart from MG Rd, Hapoli (near SBI ATM), for Itanagar (₹300, five hours, 5am and 11am), Lakhimpur (₹300, four hours) and Daporijo (₹400, six hours, around 9.30am).

Ziro to Pasighat

Passing through a most pristine landscape marked by forested hills and tribal settlements, the highway linking Ziro to Pasighat via Along offers great photo-ops of dizzying suspension footbridges and thatched Adi villages. Attractions along this rough and remote route are low-key in the touristy sense of the term, and villagers around Along are much less welcoming unless you go with a friendly local tour guide. Unless you're an intrepid traveller who's willing to stray off the beaten track and head to isolated destinations such as Mechuka or Tuting, this route is probably not your oyster.

DAPORIJO
☏ 03792 / POP 15,700 / ELEV 700M

A necessary stopover midway along the long drive from Ziro to Along, Daporijo is probably the dirtiest and most unsophisticated town in Arunachal Pradesh. If you start at the crack of dawn from Ziro, you might just be able to course the 250km distance to Along in about 10 hours, thereby giving Daporijo a miss. If you can't, the only half-decent beds in town are at **Hotel Kanga Karo Palace** (☏ 223531; r ₹900), which has shabby and uninspiring interiors. With your own transport, however, you could possibly spend the night in the traditional thatched village of **Ligu** (coming from Ziro take the left turning just before the bridge at the entrance to Daporijo), where you'll find the basic but delightful **Ligu Tourist Resort** (☏ 223114; r ₹900). The proprietor's family cooks up fantastic meals, and you can spend the evening wandering under the shadow of trees, exploring the village and its friendly population.

Sumos leave New Market at 6am for Itanagar (₹550, 12 hours) and Ziro (₹300, six hours).

ALONG
☏ 03783 / POP 17,000 / ELEV 300M

This nondescript market town offers internet at **Eastern Infotech Cyber Cafe** (Nehru Chowk; per hr ₹40; ☺8am-6pm Mon-Sat) opposite the APST bus station and an **SBI ATM** (Main Rd). Next to the Circuit House, also on

Main Rd, is an informative little **district museum** (◷10am-4pm Mon-Fri) FREE.

The saving grace of Along is the new and surprisingly upmarket **Hotel West** (☏222411; booking@hotelwestaalo.com; Medical Rd; d from ₹1000; ❄), which has lavish rooms (for this part of the world), good service and a central location – making it the perfect place to retire in after your tiresome traverse through Arunachal. **Hotel Toshi Palace** (☏9436638196; toshipalaceaalo@gmail.com; Rime Market; d from ₹600; ❄), opposite the APST bus station, has clean rooms and a pleasant terrace restaurant where beers flow freely after sundown.

There are Sumos to Itanagar (₹600, about a million hours, 5.30am) and Pasighat (₹250, five hours, 5.30am and 11.30am).

Of the many Adi villages around Along, **Kabu** and **Pobdi** (2km and 7km north of town respectively) are best known and most easily accessible. Once again, it's easier to secure entry in the company of a local guide, and you can study the Adis slowly warming to modernity (heralded by zippy cars and the ubiquitous satellite TV dish outside most huts) from a much closer range.

There are many more interesting and less-visited Adi villages along the onward journey to Pasighat. The top sight, however, is a wobbly, cable-trussed bamboo-decked **suspension bridge** that runs nearly 200m across the valley of the Siang River.

Pasighat

☏0368 / POP 21,900

Laid out along forested plains by the banks of the Siang River, Pasighat feels more like Assam than Arunachal Pradesh. The town hosts the interesting Adi festival of **Solung** (1–5 September). Through the rest of the year, the most interesting sight around here is the sunrise over the Siang. The **internet cafe** (per hr ₹60; ◷7.30am-8pm) is 50m from Hotel Aane and there's an **SBI ATM** near the Sumo stand in the central market area.

Most tourists passing through Pasighat sleep at **Hotel Aane** (☏2222777; MG Rd; d from ₹1400; ❄), which has floral shades adorning its walls, clean sheets, and a good in-house restaurant. The friendly and centrally located **Hotel Oman** (☏2900430; Main Market; s/d from ₹550/800) is a tad cheaper, but there's no hot water and you'll have to traipse to the market for meals.

For a more rewarding stay, head 25km south of Pasighat along NH52 to Oyan village, where you can spend a few days lounging amid lush tea gardens at the **Siang Tea Garden Lodge** (☏0436675824; Oyan village; per person incl full board ₹2500), which has simple but comfy rooms, garden-fresh tea and awesome food prepared by Babul, the in-house chef. Contact Aborcountry Travels & Expeditions (p564) for bookings.

❶ Getting There & Away

Sumos run to Along (₹250, five hours, 6am and noon) and Itanagar (₹350, eight hours, 6am). The road to Along is in a dreadful state – be prepared for a very long and rough day. Sumos also run to Tuting (₹950) but only when demand warrants it. **Ferries** (Indian/foreigner ₹70/200, vehicle ₹800) drift lazily down the Brahmaputra to Dibrugarh in Assam from Bogibil Ghat, and from Oiram Ghat and Majerbari Ghat during the dry season (Sumos take one hour from Pasighat, depart at 6am and cost ₹120). Ferry tickets are sold by agents at the Sumo stand in town.

OFF THE BEATEN TRACK

MECHUKA

For many travellers, the drive from Along to Mechuka – a remote outpost very close to the Tibetan border – qualifies as one of the most enthralling road trips in Arunachal Pradesh. Recently opened for tourism by the government, Mechuka often goes by the moniker of 'forbidden valley' or the 'last Shangri La' – possibly owing to the fact that there was no real road connecting it to the rest of Arunachal until a few years ago. Populated by the Buddhist Memba tribe, the tiny village sitting on the banks of the Siang River is notable for both the 400-year-old **Samten Yongcha Monastery** and the stunning landscapes surrounding the town, which culminate in a massive hulk of snow-draped mountains running along the border.

Sumos ply the 180km from Along (₹450, seven hours, 5.30am). Unless you are able to find accommodations with a local family, the only accommodation is the government **Circuit House**, which rents out rooms on an ad hoc basis. Remember that bookings can be overriden by visiting government officials.

TUTING & PEMAKO

In the far northern extent of Arunachal lies the isolated region of Tuting, visited yearly by none other than a handful of hardcore adventure seekers. Accessible from Pasighat by a long rough road, this less-travelled route is all about two things: rafting on the Siang River and trekking to the mysterious Buddhist land of Pemako.

Tuting, which sits near the Tibetan border, is the point at which the Tsang Po River – having left the Tibetan Plateau and burrowed through the Himalayas via a series of spectacular gorges – enters the Indian subcontinent and becomes the Siang (which in turn becomes the Brahmaputra in Assam). Steadily gaining a reputation as one of the the world's most thrilling white-water rafting destinations, the perilous 180km route is littered with grade 4–5 rapids, strong eddies and inaccessible gorges. Needless to say, this is the stuff of pros.

Tuting also serves as the launchpad for searching out the fabulous land of Pemako, known in Buddhist legend as a hidden earthly paradise and the earthly representation of Dorje Pagmo, a Tibetan goddess. A revered place of worship and pilgrimage for Buddhists, it lies in a region where the Tsang Po tumbles into India over a giant waterfall and passes through a rich and fertile valley populated by Memba Buddhists, completely isolated from the rest of the world. Pemako is accessible to those willing to endure days of incredibly tough hiking (and permit hassles).

Finally, if you do manage to get here and back again, consider kicking back for a few nights at **Yamne Abor** (Damro village; per person full board ₹2500), a solitary resort comprising a mix of luxury tents and eco-cottages that stands in the remote Yamne valley amid pretty Adi villages, rice fields and verdant forests. To get here, turn off the Pasighat–Tuting road at Yinkyiong. Book through Aborcountry Travels & Expeditions (p564).

Western Arunachal Pradesh

An impelling sense of journey is the core essence of any trip into the culturally magical and scenically spectacular land of Western Arunachal. Two full days of hobbling along what could easily be called the worst road in the world takes you through layer after layer of magnificent blue mountains until you reach Tawang, the archetypal Shangri La guarded by ageless hills and inhabited by the Monpa (a people of Buddhist-Tibetan origin) people. Ideally budget at least one week for a return trip from Guwahati (or Tezpur), breaking the journey each way at Dirang (allow one full day here) or Bomdila. Be prepared for intense cold in winter, and vehicular breakdowns during monsoons.

Bomdila

☎ 03782 / ELEV 2680M

An alternative sleeping place to Dirang, this district town accommodates visitors in the traditionally decorated **Doe-Gu-Khill Guest House** (☎ 223232; yipe_bg@yahoo.com; r from ₹800) just below the large monastery, providing fabulous views. **Hotel Tsepal**

Yangjom (☎ 223473; www.hoteltsepalyangjom .in; d from ₹2200), with wood-panelled rooms and a busy restaurant playing cricket matches on a cricket-field-sized TV, is the town's most popular inn. It's also centrally located.

Dirang

☎ 03780 / ELEV 1620M

Tiny **Old Dirang**, 5km south of Dirang, is a picture-perfect Monpa stone village. The main road separates its rocky **mini citadel** from a huddle of picturesque streamside houses above which rises a steep ridge topped with a timeless **gompa**. Heading the other way, just north of New Dirang, the valley opens out and its floor becomes a patchwork of rice and crop fields through which gushes the icy blue river. A fun day could be spent walking along the footpaths between fields and little hamlets.

All Dirang's commercial services are in **New Dirang**, with a strip of cheap eateries and Sumo counters around the central crossroads. **Hotel Pemaling** (☎ 242615; pema lingdirang@yahoo.co.in; d from ₹2200), a kilometre south and overlooking New Dirang, is a wonderful family-run hotel with smart rooms, great service and a very pleasant garden where you can enjoy views of the river below and the high mountains above. The new and flashy **Awoo Resort** (✆242036; www.awooresort.com; d from ₹1000), located a short hike away, has good-value rooms with cozy wood panelling, a decent restaurant and a children's park with swings and slides.

Dirang to Tawang Valley

Climbing from Dirang, the road is a seemingly endless series of zigzags which crosses several army camps and landslide zones to finally top off at **Se La**, an icy 4176m pass that breaches the mountains and provides access to Tawang. From here, the road plummets down the mountainside into the belly of Tawang Valley.

Tawang Valley

✆03/94 / ELEV 3050M

A mighty gash in the earth ringed by hulking mountains, Tawang Valley begins to work its magic on the minds of travellers the moment they start descending along patchworked sloping ridges to its lower floor, swept by vast fields and dotted with Buddhist monasteries and Monpa villages. Autumn is a particularly beautiful season for travelling this route, when waterfalls are in spate and cosmos shrubs lining the tarmac come alive with a riotous blossom of red and pink.

Tawang town is a transport hub and service centre for the valley's villages; its setting is more beautiful than the town itself. Nonetheless, colourful prayer wheels and murals of auspicious Buddhist emblems add interest to the central old market area. These are turned by apple-cheeked Monpa pilgrims, many of whom sport traditional black yak-wool gurdam (skullcaps that look like giant Rastafarian spiders).

👁 Sights & Activities

The biggest attraction is magical **Tawang Gompa** (camera/video ₹20/100; ⏰dawn-dusk) FREE, backdropped by snow-speckled peaks. Founded in 1681, this medieval citadel is reputedly the world's second-largest Buddhist monastery complex and famed in Buddhist circles for its library. Within its fortified walls, narrow alleys lead up to the majestic and magnificently decorated prayer hall containing an 8m-high statue of Buddha Shakyamuni. Come here at dawn (4am to 5am) to see row after row of monks performing their early-morning prayers. Across the central square is a small but interesting **museum** (admission ₹20; ⏰8am-5pm) containing images, robes, telescopic trumpets and some personal items of the sixth Dalai Lama. Spectacular chaam (ritual masked dances performed by some Buddhist monks in gompas to celebrate the victory of good over evil) are held in the monastery courtyard during the Torgya, Losar and Buddha Mahotsava festivals.

Other enchanting gompas and anigompas (nunneries) offer great day hikes from Tawang, including the ancient if modest Urgelling Gompa where the sixth Dalai Lama was born. By road, it's 6km from Tawang town but closer on foot downhill from Tawang Gompa. Note that the monastery remains closed on random days, so consider yourself lucky if you find the caretaker (the guy with the only set of keys) around.

🛏 Sleeping

Tawang has a number of small hotels. On the cheap end is **Hotel Nefa** (✆222419; Nehru Market; d from ₹1000), with tidy, wood-panelled rooms and hot showers but lackadaisical service. **Monyul Lodge** (✆222196; Old Market; d ₹900), in the heart of the market area, has fresh linen and plenty of air and sunlight.

THE BATTLE THAT WAS

The rolling hills of Tawang were the scene of bloody strife between Indian and Chinese forces during China's invasion of Arunachal in 1962. The month-long war – which ended with the voluntary withdrawal of Chinese personnel – left indelible marks on the collective memory of the local populace. To know more about the event, break your journey from Dirang at the **Jaswantgarh War Memorial**, about 20km down the road from Se La. Named after an Indian soldier who single-handedly fended off advancing Chinese forces while staring death in the eye, the camp has a statue of the deceased soldier, some of his personal memorabilia, a few plaques recording the events of the day as well as a mass graveyard of soldiers within walking distance.

ℹ MEAT MATTERS

Slaughtering of animals is banned in Tawang, and all edible meat served in local restaurants comes by road from Tezpur. From the abbatoir to the kitchen, the journey sometimes takes a couple of days. If you're ordering nonveg, always enquire if the supplies are fresh.

Hotel Gakyi Khang Zhang (☑ 9402605115; www.gkztawang.com; d from ₹1300), a couple of kilometres out of town on the road to the monastery, offers by far the best rooms in town – colourful sky-blue affairs with polished wooden floors. The distant views of the monastery (from most rooms) are a dealmaker. There's power back-up and, most bizarrely, a lounge bar/nightclub complete with strobe lights that comes alive over weekends.

✕ Eating & Drinking

While each of these hotels have good restaurants, the cosy **Dragon Restaurant** (Old Market; mains ₹60-170) is the town's best eatery with freshly made local dishes such as churpa (₹150), a delicious fermented cheese broth with fungi and vegetables, *momos* and a fiery chilli chicken. Also don't miss the salted Tibetan yak-butter tea, an acquired taste if ever there were one.

Located along the main drag, the convivial **Orange Restaurant & Lounge Bar** (Old Market; beers ₹90; ⊙10am-9pm) comes alive in the evenings with chilled beers (₹90), pleasant company, fairy lights on the walls, loud music and TV.

ℹ Information

In the market area is **D-Zone** (per hour ₹40; ⊙9am-4pm), which has pool and video games when it doesn't have internet. There's a **State Bank of India** branch with an ATM just past the market on the road to the monastery.

ℹ Getting There & Away

Sumos manned by kamikaze drivers ply daily from Tawang to Tezpur (₹900, 5.30am, 14 hours), calling at Dirang (₹500, six hours), Bomdila (₹600, eight hours) and Bhalukpong (₹750, 11 hours).

NAGALAND

The uncontested 'wild east' of India, Nagaland is probably one of the reasons you came to the Northeast in the first place. A place of unparalleled primeval beauty, Nagaland's dazzling hills and valleys – right on the edge of the India–Myanmar border – are an otherworldly place where until very recently some 16-odd headhunting Naga tribes valiantly fought off any intruders. Of course, the place is a shadow of its once savage self today, and much of the south of the state is fairly developed. In the north, however, you still stand a good chance of meeting tribesmen in exotic attire who continue to live a lifestyle that is normally only seen within the pages of *National Geographic* magazine.

Dimapur

☑ 03862 / POP 98,100 / ELEV 260M

Unless you're transiting via its airport (70km northwest from Kohima), there is little reason to linger in this flat, uninspiring commercial centre of Nagaland. Of the central hotels, **De Oriental Dream** (☑231211; Kohima Rd; d from ₹900; ❄@) is the smartest option.

Air India (☑229366, 242441) flies to Kolkata, Guwahati and Imphal. The **NST bus station** (Kohima Rd) runs services to Kohima (₹85, three hours, hourly) and Imphal (₹220, seven hours, 6am).

Kohima

☑ 0370 / POP 77,100 / ELEV 1450M

If not for its crazy traffic and rampant urbanisation, Nagaland's agreeable capital – scattered across a series of forested ridges and hilltops – could easily rub shoulders with the best hill stations of India. Avoid Kohima on Sundays as apart from hotels, everything is closed.

ℹ BRING YOUR OWN BOTTLE

Nagaland is officially a dry state (as are Manipur and Mizoram) – sale and purchase of alcohol is prohibited by law, at least on paper. However, authorities don't seem to mind minor amounts of booze being brought in for personal consumption. In any case, it's safer than going about town shopping for contraband.

OFF WITH THE HEADS

Long feared for their ferocity in war and their sense of independence, Naga tribes considered headhunting a sign of strength and machismo. Every intervillage war saw the victors lopping off the heads of the vanquished and instantly rising in social stature (as well as in the eyes of women). Among certain tribes such as the Konyaks of Mon, men who had claimed heads were adorned with face tattoos and V-shaped marks on their torsos, in addition to being allowed to wear brass pendants called *yanra* denoting the number of heads the wearer had taken.

Headhunting was outlawed in 1953 (the last recorded occurrence was in 1963). However, it wasn't so much for the government ban that the Nagas gave up the practice, but for Christian missionaries in the region waxing eloquent about nonviolence and peaceful coexistence over decades. Almost 90% of the Nagas now consider themselves Christian, their unshakeable faith marked by behemoth-like churches that are a prominent landmark in any settlement. Now seen as immoral possessions, most hamlets have gotten rid of their trophies, although in some villages such as Singha Chingnyu and Shangnyu in Mon district, it's still possible to see a few skulls retained in 'hidden' collections.

◎ Sights

★ War Cemetery   HISTORIC SITE
(◎9am-5pm, to 4pm winter) A fascinating example of modern architecture, this immaculate cemetery contains the graves of 1400 British, Commonwealth and Indian soldiers laid out across stepped and manicured lawns. It stands at the strategic junction of the Dimapur and Imphal roads, the site of intense fighting against the Japanese during a 64-day WWII battle.

Central Market   MARKET
(Stadium Approach; ◎6am-4pm) At this fascinating if tiny market, tribal people sell such 'edible' delicacies as *borol* (wriggling hornet grubs).

State Museum   MUSEUM
(admission/camera/video ₹5/20/100; ◎9.30am-3.30pm Mon-Sat) This superbly presented museum, 3km north, includes tribal artefacts, jewellery, tableaux with mannequins in action and a display of 'hunted' human skulls.

🛏 Sleeping & Eating

Accommodation becomes pricier and extremely scarce during the Hornbill Festival, so book well in advance. For cheap beds in town, try any of the paying guest options approved by **Nagaland Tourism** (☑2243124; www.tourismnagaland.com; Secretariat Bldg; ◎10am-4pm Mon-Sat).

★ Razhu Pru   HERITAGE HOTEL $$
(☑2290291; razhupru@yahoo.co.in; Mission Compound, Kohima Village; d incl breakfast from ₹2000; ✳🕸) A family home thoughtfully converted into a heritage hotel, this lovely guesthouse packs in a diverse array of heirlooms and artefacts in its moodily lit, wood-panelled living areas. Elegant cane furniture and potted ferns only add to its appeal. Rooms are spacious with comfy beds, ethnic upholstery and fireplaces for cold winter nights. The proprietors make for delightful company.

Hotel Japfü   HOTEL $$
(☑2240211; hoteljapfu@yahoo.co.in; PR Hill; s/d from ₹2000/2500; ✳@) Sporting that classy '70s high-service look, this hotel sits on a small hill directly above Police Station Junction. Rooms are smallish but well appointed, with glassed-in balconies, hot showers and snug beds. Food at the in-house Shilloi Restaurant is superb, but service is a little patchy.

Hotel Vivor   HOTEL $$$
(☑2806243; www.niathugroup.com; NH 61; s/d incl breakfast from ₹3500/4000; ✳🕸) The newest and swankiest hotel in Kohima, this upscale affair is located about 3km out of town. Rooms are lavishly outfitted with spongy beds, snow-white linen, ultra-clean loos and large windows. Service is prompt, and the lobby overlooks the terrace of a girls' hostel next door, where young women strum their guitars on sunny mornings!

Dream Café   CAFE $
(Cnr Dimapur & Imphal Rds, opp War Cemetery; mains ₹80-120; ◎10am-6pm Mon-Sat) The melting pot for most of Kohima's youth, this busy and cheerful place works up daily lunch specials such as fried noodles or pizzas as well as coffee and snacks. Great hill views

HORNBILL FESTIVAL

Nagaland's biggest annual jamboree, the **Hornbill Festival** (www.hornbillfestival .com; Kohima; ☉ 1-7 Dec) is celebrated at Kisama Heritage Village with various Naga tribes converging for a weeklong cultural, dance and sporting bash, much of it in full warrior costume. Of all the festivals in the Northeast this is the most spectacular and photogenic. Capering in step with former headhunters are headbangers who play out acid riffs at the **rock & metal festival** (www .hornbillmusic.org), held simultaneously in Kohima. City-based Alder Tours & Travels (p564) organises customised festival tours.

from bay windows, displays by local artists and lots of friendly diners make this a good place to linger.

ℹ Information

NIIT Internet Cafe (Opp NST bus station; per hr ₹30; ☉ 8am-7pm Mon-Sat) The internet cafe with the longest opening hours.

SBI (Police Bazar) One of several ATMs in town.

Tribal Discovery (☎ 9436000759; yiese_nei-tho@rediffmail.com; Science College Rd; guides per day ₹1000; ☉ 10am-4pm) Provides guiding services to local sites and general tourist information.

ℹ Getting There & Away

The **NST bus station** (Main Rd) has services to Dimapur (₹85, three hours, hourly Monday to Saturday), Mokokchung (₹190, seven hours, 6.30am Monday to Saturday) and Imphal (₹170, six hours, 7.30am Monday to Saturday). The taxi stand opposite has share taxis to Dimapur (₹170, 2½ hours). A car for a day out to Kisama and Khonoma costs about ₹1200.

Around Kohima

Kisama Heritage Village

This open-air museum hosts the annual Hornbill Festival, and has a representative selection of traditional Naga houses and *morungs* (bachelor dormitories) with full-size log drums. Within the complex is the World War II Museum, which has a collection of war memorabilia and flexi-timings. Kisama

is 10km from central Kohima along the well-surfaced Imphal road.

Khonoma

This historic Angami-Naga village was the site of two major British-Angami siege battles in 1847 and 1879. Built on an easily defended ridge, Khonoma looks beautifully traditional. There are several simple homestay guesthouses in the village.

Tuophema

Forty-five kilometres north of Kohima is the village of Tuophema, a possible overnight stop en route to Mon. The highlight here is the **Tuophema Tourist Village** (☎ 9436005002; d ₹1500), where you sleep in comfortable traditionally styled Naga thatched huts, and eat traditional food in a glass-paned cafeteria (meals ₹180 to ₹260). Notify them of your arrival in advance or it will probably be closed.

Kohima to Mon

A thoroughly enjoyable – and bumpy! – ride takes you through beautiful forested hillsides from Kohima to Mon. A section of this road passes through Assam. A convenient stopover en route, **Mokokchung** is a laid-back town with a spectacular hillside setting. The spiffy **Hotel Metsuben** (☎ 9206198221; www.metsuben.com; d from ₹750; ❈ @ ⊗) is the best place to look for a bed, and a range of delectable and fiery Naga dishes.

Northern Nagaland

The most unspoiled part of the state, Northern Nagaland is a rugged and divinely beautiful country where antiquity still thrives in tribal villages composed of thatched longhouses, many of whose inhabitants continue to live a fairly traditional hunting and farming lifestyle. The most accessible villages are the Konyak settlements around Mon (where traditional houses abound), and some villages still have *morungs* and religious relics from pre-Christian times. Village elders may wear traditional costumes and Konyaks of all ages carry the fearsome-looking *dao* – a crude machete (originally used for headhunting) as a standard accessory.

Visiting a Naga village without a local guide is hopelessly unproductive. You'd also do well to have your own sturdy vehicle, as there's virtually no public transport and roads are bad.

Mon & Around

The haggard hill town of Mon merely serves as an access point for the many Konyak villages in the area. There's an SBI ATM in town which rarely works.

Of the numerous tribal villages in the area, the most popular is Longwa about 35km from Mon, where the headman's longhouse spectacularly straddles the India–Myanmar border and contains a fascinating range of weapons, dinosaur-like totems and a WWII metal aircraft seat salvaged from debris scattered in nearby jungles! You can spend some time at a local house here, and see the men waste their days smoking opium while the women toil away in the fields. Several tattooed former headhunters can be photographed for a fairly standard ₹100 fee. Tribal jewellery, carved masks and other collectibles (₹200 to ₹1000) can also be bought from many households.

Other villages that can be visited from Mon include Old Mon (5km), with countless animal skulls adorning the walls of the headman's house; Singha Chingnyu (20km), which has a huge longhouse decorated with animal skulls, three stuffed tigers, and a store of old human trophies; and Shangnyu (25km), with a friendly headman, a wooden shrine full of fertility references such as tumescent warriors, fornicating couples and a crowing cock, and a pile of old skulls in the hollow of a tree.

The only hotel in town is the scrappy but friendly Helsa Cottage (☑9862345965; d ₹1500) run by the influential, affable Aunty. Running water and electricity are seldom your companions here. Aunty's daughter Suzanne runs the Helsa Resort (☑9436000028; d ₹1500), slightly out of town en route to Longwa, which has six traditional thatched Konyak huts with springy bamboo floors, sparse furnishings and hot water by the bucket. Both places arrange for meals on request.

Share jeeps bounce painfully to Dimapur (₹350, 12 hours, 3pm) and Sonari in Assam (₹80), where you can change for Jorhat. Note there's no public transport leaving Mon over weekends.

MANIPUR

A breeding ground for graceful classical dance traditions, intricate art forms, spicy sumptuous cuisine and (supposedly) the sport of polo, Manipur sits pretty amid rolling hills along India's border with Myanmar. This 'Jewelled Land' is home to Thadou, Tangkhul, Paite, Kuki, Mao Naga and many other tribal peoples, but the predominant community is the Hindu Meitei tribe, who adhere to a neo-Vaishnavite order. Much of the state is carpeted with dense forests which provide cover for rare birds, drug traffickers and guerrilla armies, making it by far the Northeast's most dangerous state.

Foreign travellers are currently restricted to Imphal and its outskirts, an area which is deemed 'safe'. Most foreigners fly into Imphal; it is also possible to drive in from Kohima (Nagaland) or Silchar (Assam) if you have a guide. Travelling east of Kakching towards the Myanmar border is not permitted.

Imphal

☑ 0385 / POP 250,200

A raucous melange of ethnicities and its positioning near the border of India and Southeast Asia makes Imphal a vibrant melting pot of local cultures. A few days in this noisy, polluted city is (for some) an undeniably fascinating experience. The airport is 9km to the southwest.

◉ Sights

Kangla PARK

(admission ₹5; ⊙9am-4pm Nov-Feb, to 5pm Mar-Oct) This expansive, low-walled fort was the off-and-on-again regal capital of Manipur until the Anglo-Manipuri War of 1891 saw the defeat of the Manipuri maharaja and a British takeover. Entrance is by way of an

---

ⓘ REGISTERING ON ARRIVAL IN MANIPUR

On arrival at Imphal airport, all foreigners must register with the police stationed next to the luggage collection point. You must then register again with the CID at the main police station. In both cases it's a fairly painless affair (assuming your papers are in order). If you're travelling by road, you must register at the security checkpoint on the state border.

exceedingly tall gate on Kanglapat. The interesting older buildings are at the rear of the citadel, guarded by three restored large white *kangla sha* (dragons).

Manipur State Museum   MUSEUM
(Off Kangla Rd; Indian/foreigner ₹3/20; ⊙10am-4pm Tue-Sun) This government-run museum has a curious collection of historical, cultural and natural-history ephemera. Tribal costumes, royal clothing, historical polo equipment and stuffed carnivores in action compete with pickled snakes for the attention of visitors. Fronting the museum is the **Polo Ground**, where polo is said to have been invented.

Shri Govindajee Mandir   HINDU TEMPLE
The 1776-built Shri Govindajee Mandir, with two rather pronounced domes, is a neo-Vaishnavite temple with Radha and Govinda as the presiding deities. Adjacent to the temple is the **Royal Palace** (closed to visitors).

Khwairamband Bazaar   MARKET
(Ima Market; ⊙7am-5pm) A spectacular photo-op for shutterbugs, this vast all-women's market is run by some 3000 *ima* (mothers). Divided by a road, one side sells vegetables, fruit, fish and groceries while the other deals in household items, fabrics and pottery. It's easily one of the largest markets in the Northeast.

Imphal War Cemetery   HISTORIC PARK
(Imphal Rd; ⊙8am-5pm, Indian War Cemetery 8am-5pm) This peaceful and well-kept memorial contains the graves of more than 1600 British and Commonwealth soldiers killed in the battles that raged around Imphal in 1944. Off Hapta Minuthong Rd is a separate **Indian War Cemetery**.

🛏 Sleeping & Eating

A state tax adds 30% to your bill. This is included in the prices listed.

Hotel Nirmala   HOTEL $
(☑2459014; MG Ave; s/d incl breakfast from ₹750/900; ❄) Don't expect any frills at this middle-of-the-market establishment. But there's a genuine sense of belonging when you stay here, and the staff go about their chores with dedication. Rooms are unfussy and prim, and the air-conditioned in-house **Chamu Restaurant** serves up decent food.

★ Classic Hotel   HOTEL $$
(☑2443967; www.theclassichotel.in; North AOC Rd; s/d from ₹1400/1800; ❄@☎) Luxury couldn't come at a more affordable price. Featuring large, spotless rooms stuffed with requisite business-class comforts, this unexpectedly classy hotel is one of the best-value hotels in the northeast. The cheerful lobby downstairs has souvenir shops, accent lighting and an overall hospitable vibe. The staff love to please, and the restaurant serves the best dishes in town.

Anand Continental   HOTEL $$
(☑2449422; hotel_anand@rediffmail.com; Khoyathong Rd; s/d from ₹1000/1400; ❄) A recent facelift shows in the form of freshly daubed paint on this trusted oldie. The tidy rooms are smallish with more furniture than may be necessary, but the management is friendly and you have the advantage of power backup, which is vital considering the power situation in town.

ⓘ TRAVELLING SAFELY IN THE NORTHEAST STATES

In recent decades, many ethno-linguistic groups in the Northeast have jostled – often violently – to assert themselves in the face of illegal immigration from neighbouring countries, governmental apathy and a heavy-handed defence policy. Some want independence from India, others autonomy, but most are fighting what are effectively clan or turf wars. At the time of writing, Arunachal Pradesh, Meghalaya, Mizoram, Nagaland and the tourist areas of Tripura were fairly peaceful.

However, trouble can flare up suddenly and unpredictably. In 2010 bombings hit parts of Assam and the Garo hills area of Meghalaya. Ethnic violence erupted in Assam, while a bomb blast and curfews shattered the veneer of peace in Manipur during on-road research for this book in late 2012. To make things worse, Assam and Manipur are often paralysed by strikes and shutdowns, which can set back travel itineraries by several days. Clearly, it helps to keep abreast of the latest headlines on TV even as you move (satellite television has penetrated the remotest villages in the region). If you're with a tour group, ensure your guide is up to date with the latest situation.

ℹ Information

Internet Cafe (MG Ave; per hr ₹30; ⊘8am-7pm Mon-Sat)

SBI ATM (MG Ave) About 100m from Hotel Nirmala. Note that ATMs in Imphal have enormous queues of people and run out of cash quickly. It's better to bring enough money with you.

Tourist Office (http://manipur.nic.in/tourism.htm; Jail Rd; ⊘10am-4pm Mon-Sat) Generally useless. It didn't have a working phone connection at the time of research.

ℹ Getting There & Away

Private buses to head to Guwahati (₹700, 20 hours, hourly 6am to 10am) and Dimapur (₹400, 10 hours, 10am) via Kohima (₹300, five hours). If you're heading to Aizawl you must change in Dimapur first. All the bus company offices are found on North AC Rd.

Air India, IndiGo and Jet Airways all fly to Guwahati and Kolkata. Air India also flies to Aizawl and Dimapur.

MIZORAM

Seated precariously along rows of north–south-running mountain ridges, gorgeous Mizoram is perhaps the most picturesque of all the states in the Northeast. Feature-wise, there's very little to identify this place as India: the population (ethnically more Southeast Asian than Indian) is almost wholly local, and the predominant religion is Christianity. Mizo culture – in a significant departure from the rest of the country – has no caste distinctions and women are more liberated than their counterparts in many other Indian states. In Aizawl girls smoke openly, wear modern clothes and hang out in unchaperoned posses meeting up with their beaus at rock concerts.

Mizoram runs to its own rhythm. Most businesses open early and shut by 6pm; virtually everything closes tight on Sunday. Upon arrival, you must register at the Office of the Superintendent of Police in Aizawl. Domestic tourists require a temporary Inner Line Permit, issued for ₹120 on arrival at the airport.

✯ Festivals & Events

Two main Mizo festivals, **Chapchar Kut** (Kut is Mizo for festival) and **Pawl Kut** celebrate elements in the agricultural cycle. Chapchar Kut takes place towards the end of

LOKTAK LAKE

A most intriguing and picturesque ecosystem if there ever was one, the fascinating Loktak Lake is one of the few places a foreigner is allowed to visit outside Imphal. A shimmering blue lake broken up into small lakelets by clumps of thick matted weeds (called *phumdis*), the lake is inhabited by local villagers who build thatched huts on these floating 'islands' and make their way about the lake in dugout canoes. More peculiar than floating villages are the large, perfectly circular fishing ponds created out of floating rings of weeds. The best view is atop **Sendra Island**. You can hire a boat (per person ₹150) in order to get a closer look at lake life. The lake is 45km by road south from Imphal; a return taxi costs about ₹1800.

February and signals the start of the spring sowing season, while Pawl Kut, held at the end of November celebrates the harvest. In both festivals, participants don traditional costumes and celebrate with music and dance.

Aizawl

📞 0389 / POP 228,200

Clinging to a near-vertical ridge by its fingernails, Aizawl (pronounced eye-zole) is easily the most languid and unhurried among all Indian state capitals. There's little to do here, apart from soaking up its relaxed grain and peaceful way of life. The area around Chanmari is the most interesting, and most tourist establishments are located in and around it.

◉ Sights

Mizoram State Museum　　　　MUSEUM
(Macdonald Hill, Zarkawt; admission ₹5; ⊘10am-5pm Mon-Fri) This museum has interesting exhibits on Mizo culture. It's up a steep lane from Sumkuma Point past Aizawl's most distinctive **church**, whose modernist bell-tower spire is pierced by arched 'windows'.

KV Paradise　　　　MONUMENT
(Durtlang; admission ₹10; ⊘10am-4pm Mon-Sat) When Varte (V) died in a 2001 motor accident, her husband Khawlhring (K) lavished

his entire savings and energy to create this three-storey mausoleum to her memory. A grand but spartan affair, it's located 8km from the town centre, 1km off Durtlang via an improbably narrow dirt lane. The marble fountain-patio has wonderful views of Aizawl on a facing ridge.

Sleeping

Hotel Chief HOTEL $
(2341097; Zarkawt; s/d from ₹770/1520) A pleasant budget option in the heart of town, this hotel has decent beds and good in-house food. The costlier rooms come with cane furniture. It's near the KTM motorcycle showroom.

Hotel Clover HOTEL $$
(9508653520; www.davids-hotel-clover.com; G-16 Chanmari; s/d incl breakfast from ₹950/1500; @ 🛜) It may not be the plushest address in town, but it's definitely the friendliest. The well-kept rooms receive fancy touches by way of colourful accent lighting and fancy bathroom fittings. And Dolly, the excellent host, makes you feel instantly at home with her courtesy and helpfulness.

Hotel Regency HOTEL $$
(2349334; www.regencyaizawl.com; B49 Zarkawt Main St; s/d from ₹1300/2850; ❄ 🛜) Posh by Aizawl's standards, this stylish hotel has inviting rooms opening along marbled corridors, each with cosy beds, clean baths and LCD TVs. The staff are smart and cooperative, and there's a great in-house restaurant overlooking the main street.

OFF THE BEATEN TRACK

RURAL MIZORAM

Mizoram's pretty, green hills get higher as you head east towards the Myanmar border. **Champhai** is widely considered the most attractive district, where you'll find the **Murlen National Park**, known for its hoolock gibbons. The small town of **Saitual** is a good stopover on the road to Champhai. Very close to Champhai is pretty **Tamdil Lake**, ringed by lush mountains. Further afield is the stunning **Blue Mountain** (Phawngpui), Mizoram's highest peak at 2147m. It's considered by Mizos to be the abode of Gods, but its slopes are haunted by ghosts.

Eating

Aizawl Masala CHINESE $
(Zarkawt; mains ₹70-100; ⏱noon-8pm) One flight of stairs below road level, this trendy place serves a host of usual quasi-Chinese suspects (noodles, fried rice, meat in chilli/garlic/pepper sauce etc). There's good music to go with your food.

David's Kitchen MULTICUISINE $$
(Zarkawt; mains ₹100-140; ⏱10am-8pm Mon-Sat, noon-9pm Sun) The super-popular David's churns out yummy Mizo, Thai, Indian, Chinese and Continental food, not to mention a decent range of mocktails. Try the smoked pork with mustard leaves (₹150), served with rice and Mizo chutney.

ℹ Information

Directorate of Tourism (2333475; www.mizotourism.nic.in; PA-AW Bldg, Bungkawn)
ICICI Bank (Zarkawt; ⏱10am-4pm Mon-Sat) Has an ATM.
Mizo Holidays (2306314; Hauva Bldg, Chanmari; ⏱10am-5pm Mon-Sat) Arranges a variety of state-wide tours including village visits. Also doubles as representatives for Thomas Cook.
Sify e-port (Chanmari; per hour ₹30; ⏱9am-5pm Mon-Sat) High-speed internet.

ℹ Getting There & Away

Taxis charge ₹800 and shared Sumos charge ₹80 to Lengpui airport, 35km west of Aizawl. **Air India** (2322283) flies to Guwahati, Kolkata and Imphal, while Jet Konnect goes to Kolkata.

Counters for long-distance Sumos are conveniently clustered around Zarkawt's Sumkuma Point.

Guwahati (₹950, 28 hours, 6pm Monday to Saturday)
Shillong (₹800, 16 hours, 6pm Monday to Saturday)
Silchar (₹360, six hours, four daily)

TRIPURA

Far from India's popular tourist circuits, Tripura is a culturally charming place which thrives on the hope that its handful of royal palaces and temples will draw the world's attention some day. For the moment, though, foreign travellers remain very rare.

Foreigners must register with the police on arrival at the airport.

Agartala

☏ 0381 / POP 189,900

Tripura's only 'city', this low-key settlement with its semirural atmosphere feels like an India of yore. It's a congested but relaxed place, and in many ways feels more like a small town than a state capital. The pace of life is slow, and in the absence of rampant commercial tourism, people are much more likely to welcome you as a guest than a gullible traveller. Apart from the town's main sights, there are several royal mausoleums decaying quietly on the riverbank behind Battala market. To get to them, walk west down HGB Rd, turn left at Ronaldsay Rd and right along the riverbank. Be discrete as the burning ghats are located nearby.

◉ Sights

Ujjayanta Palace PALACE

Agartala's indisputable centrepiece is this striking, dome-capped palace. Flanked by two large reflecting ponds, the whitewashed 1901 edifice was built by Tripura's 182nd maharaja. It was closed for maintenance and restoration work during research, but still looked impressive in its floodlit night avatar.

Jagannath Mandir HINDU TEMPLE

(◷ 4am–2pm & 4-9pm) Of the four Hindu temples around the palace compound, the most fanciful is Jagannath Mandir. Its massive sculptured portico leads into a complex with wedding-cake architecture painted in ice-cream sundae colours.

Tripura Government Museum MUSEUM

(http://tripura.nic.in/museum/welcome.html; Post Office Circle; admission ₹5; ◷ 10am-1pm & 2-5pm Mon-Sat) This small state-operated museum has a variety of tribal displays plus some interesting musical instruments made from bamboo.

🛏 Sleeping

Ginger HOTEL $$

(☏ 2411333; www.gingerhotels.com; Airport Rd; s/d ₹2350/2750; ✸ @ 🛜) Part of the Tata-owned Ginger chain of hotels, this well-run low-cost business hotel has delightful rooms done up in orange and blue pastel shades. There's wi-fi, real coffee, a small gym and an in-house SBI ATM. Coming from the airport, you'll find the hotel on your right about 2km short of town.

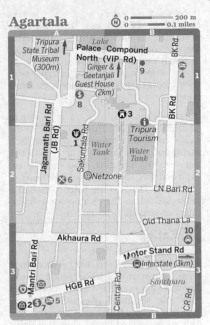

Agartala

◉ Sights
1 Jagannath Mandir...................................A2
2 Tripura Government Museum...........A3
3 Ujjayanta Palace.....................................B1

🛏 Sleeping
4 Hotel Rajdhani...B1
5 Hotel Welcome Palace.........................A3

🍴 Eating
6 Abhishek Restaurant............................A2
   Restaurant Kurry Klub................(see 5)

ℹ Information
7 Axis Bank ATM...A3
8 SBI ATM...A1

ℹ Transport
9 Air India..B1
10 Motor Stand...B3

Geetanjali Guest House HOTEL $$

(☏ 2410009; Airport Rd; d ₹1650; ✸ @) The only match for Ginger in terms of luxe quotient, this government-run guesthouse just across the road has large, perfect rooms done up in clean upholstery and washed with disinfectants and sunlight. Note that half the guesthouse is reserved only for officials.

Hotel Welcome Palace HOTEL $$

([2384940; HGB Rd; d from ₹1100; [*]) Bang in the heart of Agartala's main market, this friendly hotel has helpful English-speaking staff and superb food. Rooms are neat, although some may not have external windows (those that do may suffer from street noise).

Hotel Rajdhani HOTEL $$

([2323387; BK Rd; [*]) This hotel close to the palace compound proudly proclaims itself as Tripura's 'only three star hotel with five star comfort'. Bragging apart, rooms are clean and tidy, and some have nice views of the palace. The staff are helpful, though a tad lackadaisical. There's a decent in-house eatery serving multicuisine fare.

✕ Eating

Abhishek Restaurant INDIAN $

(LN Bari Rd; mains ₹60-100; ⊙noon-10pm) Choose between a marine-themed air-con dining room, or an outdoor seating area with tables set amid bushes and sculptures, and then proceed to put away a hearty meal comprising some eminently enjoyable North Indian and local savouries.

Restaurant Kurry Klub INDIAN, CHINESE $$

(HGB Rd, Hotel Welcome Palace; mains ₹80-140; ⊙10am-10pm) The in-house restaurant at Hotel Welcome Palace serves generous helpings of tasty Indian food, including some fantastic fish prepartations. It is particularly busy during dinner.

BORDER CROSSING INTO BANGLADESH FROM AGARTALA

Border Hours

The border at Agartala is open from 8am to 6pm.

Foreign Exchange

There's no exchange booth. Ask local traders or border officials.

Onward Transport

From central Agartala, the border is just 3km along Akhaura Rd (₹50 by rickshaw). On the Bangladesh side the nearest town is Akhaura, 5km beyond, reached by 'baby taxi' (autorickshaw). From Akhaura trains head to Dhaka, Comilla and Sylhet.

ℹ Information

Axis Bank ATM (HGB Rd, Hotel Welcome Palace)

Netzone (6 Sakuntala Rd; per hr ₹30; ⊙10am-8pm) Best of several closely grouped options.

State Bank of India ([2311364; HGB Rd, top fl, SBI Bldg) Changes cash and travellers cheques and has an ATM; west of Mantri Bari Rd. There's also an ATM on Palace Compound West.

Tripura Tourism ([2225930; www.tripura tourism.nic.in; Swet Mahal, Palace Complex; ⊙10am-5pm Mon-Sat) A helpful and enthusiastic lot.

ℹ Getting There & Around

Air India ([2325470; VIP Rd), Spicejet and Jet Konnect fly to Kolkata and Guwahati; IndiGo flies only to Kolkata. Agartala's airport is 12km north and a taxi costs ₹250.

Private bus operators are clustered on LN Bari Rd; others leave from the new **Interstate Bus Terminal** 3km east of the centre (autorickshaw ₹50). Sumos use the **Motor Stand** (Motor Stand Rd) and **South Bus Station** (SBS; off Ronaldsay Rd). Destinations and their respective departure stations for bus and Sumo trips:

Guwahati (bus ₹800, 24 hours, 6am and noon) Interstate Bus Terminal.

Shillong (bus ₹750, 20 hours, 6am and noon) Interstate Bus Terminal.

Silchar (bus ₹210, 12 hours, 6am) Interstate Bus Terminal.

Udaipur (bus ₹45, 1¾ hours; Sumo ₹50) South Bus Station.

Around Agartala

Southern Tripura's best-known sights can be combined into a long day trip from Agartala, though sleeping at Neermahal is worthwhile. Any of Agartala's hotels can arrange a taxi; try **Hindustan Tours & Travels** ([9206348911; Airport Rd) in Ginger. An aircon car hired for the day will cost you ₹800 plus ₹8 per km.

Udaipur

[03821

Udaipur was Tripura's historic capital and remains dotted with ancient temples and a patchwork of tanks.

MATABARI

When Sati's toes fell on Kolkata, her divine right leg dropped on Matabari. This gruesome legend is piously celebrated at the

GARO HILLS

Well off the beaten path, the lush, green Garo Hills in the far west of Meghalaya are worth exploring if you have a few days to spare. Easier to reach from Guwahati than Shillong, its main urban hub is the tiny settlement of Tura, where the friendly **tourist office** (☏03651-242394; ◷10am-4pm Mon-Fri) can arrange for local guides. Accommodation is available at the **Rikman Continental** (☏03651-220744; hotelrikman@gmail.com; Circular Rd; s/d incl breakfast from ₹950/1100; ✲), which has a mix of basic and semiluxury rooms.

For most people, a visit to the Garo Hills involves an encounter with the endangered Hoolock gibbon, a cuddly and friendly primate that lives in the forests of the **Nokrek Biosphere Reserve**. The other highlight of the region is an excursion to **tribal villages** deep in the mountains, where you can see villagers practise the 'slash-and-burn' method of *jhum* cultivation. Intriguing *borangs* (traditional tree houses) dot the lush landscape in these hills. If you're with a reliable local guide, it's also possible to visit a traditional Garo village, where you can sit around a traditional kitchen with villagers and quaff rancid *chu bitchi* (rice wine) from calabash vessels called *phong*. **Sadolpara**, with a friendly headman, is the most accessible. Remember to leave a tip in return for their hospitality.

Tripura Sundari Mandir (◷4.30am-1.30pm & 3.30-9.30pm), a 1501 Kali temple where a steady stream of pilgrims make almost endless animal sacrifices that leave the grounds as bloody as the temple's vivid-red *shikhara* (spire). Even more people come here during the Diwali festival (October/November) to bathe in the fish-filled tank by the temple. The temple is 100m east of the NH44, 4km south of Udaipur. A rickshaw from Udaipur costs ₹50.

ℹ️ Getting There & Around

Udaipur's bus stand has quarter-hourly departures to Agartala (₹45, 1¾ hours) and Melagarh (₹25, 45 minutes).

Neermahal & Melaghar

☏0381

Tripura's most iconic building, the 1930 **Neermahal** (admission/camera/video ₹5/10/25; ◷8.30am-4pm, to 4.30pm Apr-Sep), is a long, red-and-white water palace which is empty but shimmering on its own boggy island in the lake of Rudra Sagar. Like its counterpart in Rajasthan's Udaipur, this was a princely exercise in aesthetics. The finest craftsmen built a summer palace of luxury in a blend of Hindu and Islamic architectural styles, and the pavilion was christened by the Bengali Nobel laureate Rabindranath Tagore.

The delightful waterborne approach by motorboat (passenger/boat ₹20/400) or fancy rowboat (boat ₹100) is the most enjoyable part of visiting. Boats leave from beside the remarkably decent **Sagarmahal Tourist Lodge** (☏9436185313; d from ₹825; ✲), where most rooms have lake-facing balconies and a good restaurant presides downstairs.

MEGHALAYA

Separating the Assam valley from the plains of Bangladesh, hilly Meghalaya – the 'abode of clouds' – is a cool, wet and pine-fresh mountain state set on dramatic horseshoes of rocky cliffs. Cherrapunjee and Mawsynram are statistically the wettest places on earth. Most of the rain falls between June and September, creating very impressive waterfalls and carving out some of Asia's longest caves.

The state's population predominantly comprises the Jaintia, Khasi and Garo tribes, who live in the eastern, central and western parts respectively. A good time to be in Meghalaya is when the four day **Wangala festival** (Garo Hills in Meghalaya; ◷Oct/Nov) takes place in autumn. Renowned for its impressive tribal dancing, this harvest festival is also noted for its traditional drum recitals.

Shillong

☏0364 / 267,600

Until 1972, irreverent Shillong was the capital of British-created Assam. Since becoming the state capital of Meghalaya, it has rapidly developed into a typical modern Indian town, but still retains some its colonial-era

Shillong

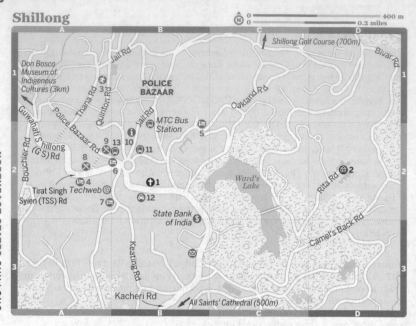

Shillong

◉ Sights
- 1 Anglican Church................................B2
- 2 Pinewood Hotel................................D2

✪ Activities, Courses & Tours
- 3 Cultural Pursuits Adventures..............A1

⊜ Sleeping
- 4 Baba Tourist Lodge...........................A2
- 5 Earle Holiday Home...........................B2
- 6 Hotel Centre Point............................B2
- 7 Silk Route.......................................A2

✕ Eating
- 8 Broadway.......................................A2
- 9 Trattoria's......................................A2

⊙ Information
- 10 Meghalaya Tourism..........................B2

⊙ Transport
- 11 Deep..B2
- 12 Khasi Hills Tourist Taxi
     Cooperative..................................B2
- 13 Network Travels..............................B2

charm in certain pockets. Overhauled cars are all the rage here – take a ride in one of Shillong's many taxis, and you'll know.

◉ Sights & Activities

Colonial-Era Shillong   NOTABLE BUILDINGS
The city's half-timbered architecture has been rather swamped by lots of drab modern concrete, but areas such as Oakland and Lumsohphoh retain many older houses. More centrally located is the **Pinewood Hotel** (Rita Rd), a 1920s tea-growers retreat, which is particularly representative and looks great at night. The 1902 **All Saints' Cathedral** (Kacheri Rd) would look perfect pictured on a biscuit tin. The **Anglican Church** (Police Bazaar), perched above Police Bazaar, is a graceful structure fronted by pretty lawns.

Ward's Lake   LAKE
(admission/camera/video ₹5/10/20; ⊙8.30am-5.30pm Nov-Feb, 8.30am-7pm Mar-Oct) This attractive lake has a pretty ornamental bridge, flower beds, coy courting couples and gaggles of geese. Walk 15 minutes northeast of the lake to visit the rolling meadows of **Shillong Golf Course** (Golf Links), which is bordered by pine trees and fronted by a pretty **clubhouse**.

★**Don Bosco Museum of Indigenous Cultures**   MUSEUM
(☑2550260; Mawlai; Indian/foreigner ₹60/150; ⊙9.30am-4.30pm Mon-Sat, 1.30-4.30pm Sun, to

5.30 Apr-Sep) This well-maintained museum is a fabulous repository of innumerable tribal artefacts interspersed occasionally with gratuitous galleries on Christian missionary work. Tours (which are compulsory) last over an hour, departing on the half-hour. Sights in the seven-storey museum include tribal basketry, musical instruments, weapons, objects of daily life, costumes and jewellery, along with plenty of photographic documentation.

Cultural Pursuits Adventures
OUTDOOR ADVENTURE
(📞 9856041205; www.culturalpursuits.com; Thana Rd, Hotel Alpine Continental; ⊙ 10am-4pm) Experienced agency for caving, trekking, village stays and off-the-beaten-track stuff.

🛏 Sleeping

Taxes add a discouraging 27% to your bill (included in the prices listed here), but off-season discounts are available.

Earle Holiday Home
HOTEL $
(📞 2228614; Oakland Rd; s/d from ₹750/1000; ❄) This hotel has character and is amusingly disorganised. The cheaper rooms are the original half-timbered affairs within a classic 1920 Shillong hill house adorned with sweet little turrets. Pricier rooms in the concrete annexe are less atmospheric but more comfortable.

Baba Tourist Lodge
HOTEL $
(📞 2211285; Guwahati Shillong (GS) Rd; d ₹850) Popular with backpackers, Baba hides many floors below the road level, and offers clean and spartan accommodation in rooms that open past a prim wood-panelled reception area lined with fish-filled aquariums. The pricier rooms have running hot water.

Hotel Centre Point
HOTEL $$
(📞 2220100; www.shillongcentrepoint.com; d incl breakfast from ₹2800/3300; ❄🖥) Located bang on Police Bazaar, this is clearly the best business hotel in Shillong. Run by professional and helpful staff, it has smart rooms with wood flooring and large windows overlooking the town centre. All requisite creature comforts are at your disposal, and the Cloud-9 rooftop lounge bar is a good place for evening beers and (occasionally) live music.

Silk Route
HOTEL $$
(📞 2503301; hotelsilkroute@yahoo.in; Keating Rd; s/d from ₹2100/2500; ❄@🖥) Simple, stylish, well managed and clean, this modern establishment boasts memorably colourful rooms with rain-shower fitted loos. It's popular, so book ahead.

★ Ri Kynjai
RESORT $$$
(📞 9862420300; www.rikynjai.com; Umiam Lake; d incl breakfast from ₹6500; ❄) This divine resort on the banks of pristine Umiam Lake, 22km from Shillong, is a gem of a getaway. Spacious wood-pillared cottages with fabulous lake views lie scattered about its lush, green gardens and each is impeccably presented with elegant furnishings and lavish bathrooms. There's a spa done up in traditional decor, a restaurant and a bar with lake views.

Royal Heritage Tripura Castle
HERITAGE HOTEL $$$
(📞 2501111; www.tripuracastle.com; Cleve Colony; d from ₹4500; ❄@🖥) The distinctively turreted summer villa of the former Tripura maharajas, this private 'castle' offers luxurious rooms in a new (pseudo-heritage) building behind. Pine-framed rooms have a gently stylish vibe with period furniture and excellent service. For the full royal experience opt for a suite. The hotel is 2.5km southeast of the centre.

🍴 Eating & Drinking

Trattoria's
KHASI $
(mains ₹60-80; ⊙ 11am-4pm) No visit to Shillong is complete without a midday meal at this busy proletarian eatery patronised by locals. Some of the best local Khasi dishes such as *ja doh* (rice stewed in pig blood) and curried pig innards are (literally) hot favourites here.

SIAT KHNAM

A unique local 'sport' that doubles as a system of local lottery, Siat Khnam involves a group of Khasi marksmen shooting dozens of arrows into a barrel-shaped straw target. At the end of the shooting session, the number of on-target arrows are counted, and the last two digits of the total are taken as the lucky number. If you've bet on this particular number (before the shootout, of course), the evening's beers are on you. A gently fascinating spectacle, Siat Khnam is usually scheduled around 4pm, though timings can vary somewhat by season.

Broadway INDIAN, CHINESE $$

(Guwahati Shillong (GS) Rd; mains ₹80-150; ☉11am-8pm) With a relaxed and pleasant atmosphere and an impressive array of aquariums full of goldfish, this no-nonsense restaurant serves a tasty mix of Indian and Chinese meals.

Café Shillong CAFE

(☑2505759; Laitumkhrah; coffee ₹45-60, mains ₹120-200; ☉11am-9pm) Its fashionable decor featuring a Les Paul guitar signed by performing musicians, this cool hangout in bustling Laitumkhrah (pronounced Lai-muk-rah) has the best coffee in town, yummy steaks and rock, jazz and blues on tap. Weekends are the busiest with live acts.

ℹ Information

INTERNET ACCESS

Techweb (Keating Rd, basement Zara's Arcade; per hr ₹20; ☉9am-7pm) Bright and relatively comfy. Internet available.

MONEY

There are many ATMs.

State Bank of India (Kacheri Rd; ☉10am-4pm Mon-Fri, to noon Sat) Exchanges foreign currency and travellers cheques; ATM outside.

TOURIST INFORMATION

Meghalaya Tourism (☑2226220; www.meg tourism.gov.in; Jail Rd) Lots of brochures and useful information.

ℹ Getting There & Away

The **MTC bus station** (Jail Rd) also has a computerised railway-reservation counter (nearest train station is Guwahati). Private buses depart from Dhanketi Point; book tickets from counters

---

BORDER CROSSING – INTO BANGLADESH FROM DAWKI

Border Hours

The border is open from 9am to 6pm.

Foreign Exchange

There's no exchange booth, though you might find helpful personnel on the Bangladesh side.

Onward Transport

The border post is at Tamabil, 1.5km from Dawki market (taxis are ₹50). There are frequent Tamabil–Sylhet minibuses.

---

around Police Bazaar, including **Deep** (Ward's Lake Rd) and **Network Travels** (☑2210981; Shop 44, MUDA Complex, Police Bazaar).

Frequent buses and Sumos run to the following towns:

Aizawl (₹600, 15 hours)

Cherrapunjee (bus/Sumo ₹270/250, three hours)

Dimapur (₹430, 14 hours)

Guwahati (government bus/private bus ₹110/150, 3½ hours)

Silchar (₹350, 10 hours)

Siliguri (₹450, 16 hours)

Tura (bus/Sumo ₹320/450, 12 hours via Guwahati)

Khasi Hills Tourist Taxi Cooperative (☑2223895; Kacheri Rd) charges ₹2000 to ₹2500 for a day trip to Cherrapunjee; for a ride to the Bangladesh border near Dawki it's ₹1800. For Guwahati airport, a full taxi costs ₹2000, or you can share with other passengers for ₹300.

Cherrapunjee (Sohra)

☑03637 / POP 10,100

Laid out along razor-like ridges of a high mountain wall, Cherrapunjee sits on the edge of the Himalayas, overlooking the pancake-flat plains of Bangladesh. The road from Shillong to this tiny village passes through pretty scenery that becomes dramatic at **Dympep viewpoint**, where a photogenic V-shape valley slits deeply into the plateau.

Although straggling for several kilometres, Cherrapunjee (known locally as Sohra) has a compact centre. Huddling beside the marketplace is the Sumo stand.

◉ Sights & Activities

★ Root Bridges NATURE RESERVE

The most fascinating sight around Cherrapunjee are the incredible **root bridges** – living rubber fig-tree roots which ingenious Khasi villagers have trained across streams to form natural pathways. Three of these root bridges (including an amazing 'double-decker') are near **Nongriat**. Access is via the pretty village of **Tyrna**, 2km from Mawshamok. The round trip from Cherrapunjee Holiday Resort is an eight-hour slog, involving a 2000-step ascent and descent through very steep terrain.

Moors & Waterfalls VIEWPOINT

(Viewpoint admission/camera/video ₹10/20/50; ☉ Viewpoint 8am-5pm) The grassy moors surrounding Cherrapunjee justify Meghalaya's over-played 'Scotland of the East' tourist-office soubriquet, although they're dotted with monoliths and scarred by quarrying. Much more impressive is the series of 'grand canyon' valleys that plunge into deep lush chasms of tropical forest sprayed by a succession of seasonally inspiring waterfalls. The **Nohkalikai Falls** are particularly dramatic, especially in the monsoon when their capacity increases 20-fold. You can see them easily enough without quite entering the official **viewpoint**, 4.4km southwest of Sohra market.

Mawsmai Cave
CAVE

(admission/camera/video ₹10/15/50; ⊘ 9.30am-5.30pm) The popularity of this cave with domestic tourists translates to the incongruous sight of sari-clad women stooping through the low passages of the 150m-long natural limestone formation. Mawsmai's tall row of roadside **monoliths** is as impressive as the cave but don't receive the same attention.

🛏 Sleeping & Eating

Cherrapunjee Holiday Resort   RESORT **$$**
(☑ 09436115925; www.cherrapunjee.com; Laitkynsew village; d from ₹2100; @) The new multistoreyed block (which has newer deluxe rooms) may have undercut the beauty of this old-time favourite, but the hosts remain just as warm and affable, and the older building (with cheaper rooms thrown around a spacious refectory) is still a delightful place to stay. The resort provides guides for local hikes, and tented accommodation in the dry season.

A daily bus leaves nearby Laitkynsew village for Shillong (₹65, 6am). Going the other way it leaves Shillong at 1pm. Otherwise a taxi from Cherrapunjee costs ₹300.

Polo Orchid   RESORT **$$$**
(☑ 8794701636; www.hotelpolotowers.com; Seven Sisters Falls; d incl breakfast from ₹4800; ✳) A stylish place with a spectacular setting, this mint-fresh resort has clusters of rooms located along a ridge which overlooks the vast sweep of the Bangladesh plains. Rooms are a lavish affair, with eco-chic furnishings and vermilion-and-purple upholstery. A string of uber-swish suites are currently under contruction. Nonresidents can access its fabulous viewpoint for a ₹30 fee.

Odisha

Best Far-Flung Sleeps

➡ Gajlaxmi Palace (p600)

➡ Chandoori Sai (p617)

➡ Nature Camp Bhitarkanika (p618)

➡ Roopark Village (p618)

➡ Nature Camp Chhotkei (p604)

Best Places to Eat

➡ Kanika (p601)

➡ Odisha Hotel (p600)

➡ Tangerine 9 (p601)

➡ Chung Wah (p609)

➡ Nature Camp Bhitarkanika (p618)

Why Go?

Though travellers are waking up to Odisha's (Orissa) intricate patchwork of culture, tradition, sun and sand, it continues content as relatively undiscovered. For those that go, Odisha affords an escape from the frenzy of other Indian traveller epicentres and boasts the World Heritage–listed Sun Temple in Konark, bursting with brilliantly worked scenes of Odisha life. Medieval temples pepper the streets of the capital, Bhubaneswar. Wonderful national parks and wildlife sanctuaries are crammed with tigers, elephants, Irrawaddy dolphins, monster crocodiles and millions of migratory birds. Chilika Lake, Asia's largest brackish lagoon, is flanked by inexpensive seaside retreats along one of India's prettiest coasts. Inland, the Adivasis (tribal people) live precariously on the edge of mainstream society, yet retain their colourful, fascinating traditions – a metaphor for Odisha itself.

When to Go
Bhubneswar

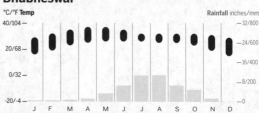

Nov–Mar Warm and dry, just like fresh laundry from the dhobi-wallah.

June/July It's baking, but Puri's Rath Yatra Festival is Odisha's biggest party.

Dec The Unesco-betrothed Sun Temple is the backdrop for the seductive Konark Festival.

Food

Mustard is the staple in Odishan kitchens, used ubiquitously in seed, paste and oil forms, giving many Odisha dishes a distinct pungent flavour. A typical meal consists of *bhata* (rice) served alongside a variety of tasty side dishes such as *kaharu phula bhaja* (fried pumpkin flower); *dalma* (dahl cooked with pumpkin, potato, plantains and eggplant, then fried in a five-spice oil of fenugreek, cumin, black cumin, anise and mustard, topped with grated coconut); and *besara* (vegetables or river fish with mustard-paste gravy). *Saga bhaja*, leafy greens lightly fried with garlic paste and a five-seed mixture called *pancha phutan* (cumin, mustard, anis, black cumin and chilli), is also a treat here. On the coast, fish and prawns are omnipresent: *sarison macha* is a superb favourite fish dish cooked in a mustard-based curry.

DON'T MISS

Odisha's masterstroke is undeniably its 13th-century **Sun Temple** at Konark; one of the state's most unforgettable journeys is a tour through the **Southwestern tribal regions**, where colour and culture collide in the fascinating villages and markets of some 62 tribal (Adivasi) societies.

Top State Festivals

→ **Adivasi Mela** (⊙ Jan, Bhubaneswar, p595) Features art, dance and handicrafts of Odisha's tribal groups.

→ **Rath Yatra** (⊙ Jun/Jul, Puri, p605) Immense chariots containing Lord Jagannath, brother Balbhadra and sister Subhadra are hauled from Jagannath Temple to Gundicha Mandir.

→ **Puri Beach Festival** (⊙ late Nov, Puri, p605) Song, dance, food and cultural activities on the beach.

→ **Konark Festival** (⊙ Dec, Konark, p610) Features traditional music and dance and a seductive temple ritual.

MAIN POINTS OF ENTRY

Most travellers usually arrive at Bhubaneswar's Biju Patnaik Airport or by the rails into Bhubaneswar or Puri junctions.

Fast Facts

→ **Population:** 42 million
→ **Area:** 155,707 sq km
→ **Capital:** Bhubaneswar
→ **Main language:** Odia
→ **Sleeping prices:** $ below ₹1200, $$ ₹1200 to ₹3500, $$$ above ₹3500

Top Tip

Permission from the District Collector is needed to visit sensitive tribal areas. Give yourself at least 10 days for this process to play itself out.

Resources

→ **Visit Odisha** (www.orissatourism.gov.in) Official Department of Tourism site.

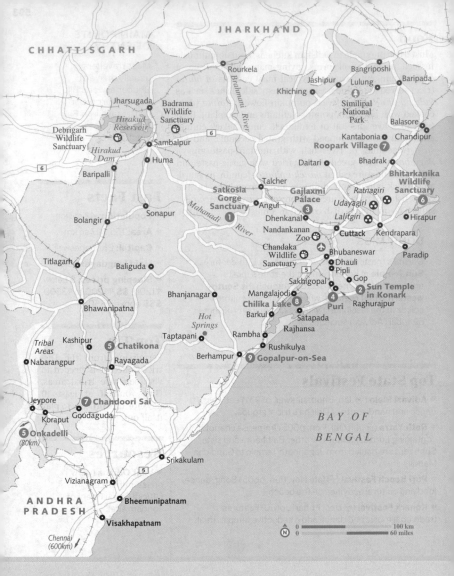

Odisha Highlights

1 Breathe a sigh of serenity along the sands of the Mahanadi River in breathtaking **Satkosia Gorge Sanctuary** (p604)

2 Relish the colour of the Konark Festival with the **Sun Temple** (p611) as a backdrop

3 Lose a few days among royalty and wild elephants at **Gajlaxmi Palace** (p600)

4 Bliss-out beachside in traveller favourite **Puri** (p605)

5 Respectfully immerse yourself in the colourful tribal marketplaces in **Onkadelli** (p616) and **Chatikona** (p615)

6 Ply wildlife-rich mangroves on the prowl for crocodiles in **Bhitarkanika Wildlife Sanctuary** (p618)

7 Go deeper into rural Odishan village life at **Chandoori Sai** (p617) and **Roopark Village** (p618)

8 Enjoy an overnight trip to **Chilika Lake** (p612), Asia's largest brackish lagoon

9 Sip masala chai on the bygone boardwalk at **Gopalpur-on-Sea** (p613)

History

Formerly known as Kalinga, then Orissa, Odisha (per a longstanding name-change campaign that finally received Lok Sabha approval in 2010) was once a formidable maritime empire that had trading routes leading down into Indonesia, but its history is somewhat hazy until the demise of the Kalinga dynasty in 260 BC at the hands of the great emperor Ashoka. Appalled at the carnage he had caused, Ashoka forswore violence and converted to Buddhism.

Around the 1st century BC Buddhism declined and Jainism was restored as the faith of the people. During this period the monastery caves of Udayagiri and Khandagiri (in Bhubaneswar) were excavated as important Jain centres.

By the 7th century AD Hinduism had supplanted Jainism. Under the Kesari and Ganga kings, trade and commerce increased and Odishan culture flourished – countless temples from that classical period still stand. The Odishans defied the Muslim rulers in Delhi until finally falling to the Mughals during the 16th century, when many of Bhubaneswar's temples were destroyed.

Until Independence, Odisha was ruled by Afghans, Marathas and the British.

Since the 1990s a Hindu fundamentalist group, Bajrang Dal, has undertaken a violent campaign against Christians in Odisha in response to missionary activity. The often illiterate and dispossessed tribal people have suffered the most from the resulting communal violence, which has been as much about power, politics and land as religious belief.

Violence flared up again in 2008 after the killing of a Hindu leader in Kandhamal district, and thousands of Christians were moved to government relief camps outside the district after their homes were torched.

The creation of the neighbouring states of Jharkhand and Chhattisgarh has prompted calls for the formation of a separate, tribal-oriented state, Koshal, in the northwest of Odisha, with Sambalpur as the capital. A separatist political party, the Kosal Kranti Dal (KKD), fielded candidates in the 2009 state election and took to disruptive transport protests in 2010.

The last few years have seen something of an industrial boom in Odisha, with an influx of big steel plants and controversial mining.

Climate

Monsoonal rains and cyclones in July to October can seriously affect transport. Particularly devastating monsoonal disasters struck Odisha in 1999 and 2008, causing significant damage, loss of life massive flooding.

National Parks

The admission fee for foreigners to visit most of Odisha's national parks and wildlife sanctuaries is ₹1000 per day – including the day you depart.

ⓘ Dangers & Annoyances

Mosquitoes here have a record of being dengue and malaria carriers. Consider bringing a mosquito net and arming yourself with repellent.

ⓘ Information

Odisha Tourism (www.orissatourism.gov.in) has a presence in most towns, with offices for information and tour/hotel booking. It also maintains a list of approved guides for tribal-area visits. **Odisha Tourism Development Corporation** (www.otdc.in), the commercial arm of Odisha Tourism, runs tours and hotels throughout the state.

ⓘ Getting There & Away

Air routes connect Bhubaneswar with Bengaluru (Bangalore), Delhi, Hyderabad, Mumbai (Bombay), Kolkata (Calcutta) and Chennai (Madras). Major road and rail routes between Kolkata and Chennai pass through coastal Odisha and Bhubaneswar with spur connections to Puri. Road and rail connect Sambalpur with Kolkata, Chhattisgarh and Madhya Pradesh.

ⓘ Getting Around

Public transport in the coastal region is good with ample long-distance buses and trains. For touring around the interior hiring a car is the best option, although buses and trains are available if you're not in a hurry.

BHUBANESWAR

☏ 0674 / POP 658,000

At first glance, Bhubaneswar's wide avenues, green belts and public-highway murals that reflect its temple-town heritage – all on the outskirts – seem quite pleasant. Its inner sanctum, where the many gorgeous and well-preserved Hindu temples inspired the nickname of India's Temple City, is also a serene spiritual epicentre and a living museum of medieval temple

Bhubaneswar

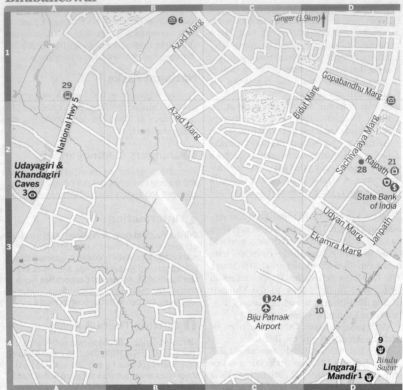

architecture. Though typically noisy and congested around the rest of it, the Temple City is an enthralling pit stop for a day or two to take in the old city's holy centre around Bindu Sagar where, from the thousands that once stood here, 50-odd stone temples remain; and the city is a fantastic spot to take in Odisha's distinct regional cuisine.

⊙ Sights

According to legend, Bhubaneswar once boasted over 7000 temples and is a long-harnessed religious centre dating back 2000 years. Today, it's most famous for its surviving medieval temples, a mix of 'live' (still in use as places of worship) and 'dead' (archaeological sites).

★ Lingaraj Mandir HINDU TEMPLE
The 54m-high Lingaraj Mandir, dedicated to Tribhuvaneswar (Lord of Three Worlds),

dates from 1090 to 1104 (although parts are over 1400 years old) and is surrounded by more than 50 smaller temples and shrines. The granite block, representing Tribhuvaneswar, is bathed daily with water, milk and bhang (marijuana). The main gate, guarded by two moustachioed yellow lions, is a spectacle in itself as lines of pilgrims approach, *prasad* (temple-blessed food offering) in hand.

Because the temple is surrounded by a wall, and closed to non-Hindus, foreigners can see it only from a viewing platform (by the way, this can also include foreign Hindus). Face the main entrance, walk around to the right and find the viewing platform down a short laneway to the left. There have been reports of aggressive hassling for 'donations' at the viewing platform. The money will not go to the temple; stand your ground and do not pay.

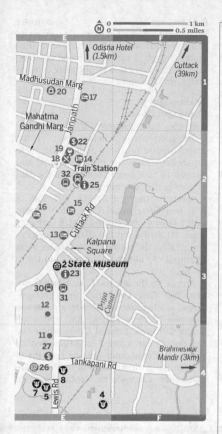

ODISHA BHUBANESWAR

Bhubaneswar

Mukteswar, Siddheswar & Kedargauri Mandirs
HINDU TEMPLES

Not far from Parsurameswar is the small but beautiful 10th-century **Mukteswar Mandir**, one of the most ornate temples in Bhubaneswar; you'll see representations of it on posters and brochures across Odisha. Intricate carvings show a mixture of Buddhist, Jain and Hindu styles – look for the Nagarani (Snake Queen), easily mistaken by Westerners for a mermaid, who you'll also see at the Raja Rani Mandir. The ceiling carvings and stone arch are particularly striking, as is the arched *torana* (architrave) at the front, clearly showing Buddhist influence.

Siddheswar Mandir, in the same compound, is a later but plainer temple with a fine red-painted Ganesh. Over the road is **Kedargauri Mandir**, one of the oldest temples in Bhubaneswar, although it has been substantially rebuilt.

Vaital Mandir
HINDU TEMPLE

This 8th-century temple, with a double-storey 'wagon roof' influenced by Buddhist cave architecture, was a centre of Tantric worship, eroticism and bloody sacrifice. Look closely and you'll see some very early erotic carvings on the walls. Chamunda (a fearsome incarnation of Devi), representing old age and death, can be seen in the dingy interior, although her necklace of skulls and her bed of corpses are usually hidden beneath her temple robes.

Parsurameswar Mandir
HINDU TEMPLE

Just west of Lewis Rd lies a cluster of about 20 smaller but important temples. Best preserved is Parsurameswar Mandir, an ornate Shiva temple built around AD 650. It has lively bas-reliefs of elephant and horse processions, and Shiva images.

Raja Rani Mandir
HINDU TEMPLE

(Indian/foreigner ₹5/100, video ₹25; ⊙dawn-dusk) This temple, built around 1100 and surrounded by manicured gardens, is famous for its ornate *deul* (temple sanctuary) and tower. Around the compass points are pairs of statues representing eight *dikpalas* (guardians) who protect the temple. Between them, nymphs, embracing couples, elephants and lions peer from niches and decorate the pillars.

Brahmeswar Mandir
HINDU TEMPLE

Standing in well-kept gardens, flanked on its plinth by four smaller structures, this 9th-century temple is a smaller version of Lingaraj Mandir. It's notable for its finely detailed sculptures with erotic elements.

★ Udayagiri & Khandagiri Caves
HISTORICAL SITE

(both sites Indian/foreigner ₹5/100, video ₹25; ⊙dawn-dusk) Six kilometres west of the city centre are two hills riddled with rock-cut shelters. Many are ornately carved and thought to have been chiselled out for Jain ascetics in the 1st century BC.

Ascending the ramp at Udayagiri (Sunrise Hill), note **Swargapuri** (Cave 9) to the right with its devotional figures. **Hathi Gumpha** (Cave 14) at the top has a 117-line inscription relating the exploits of its builder, King Kharavela of Kalinga, who ruled from 168 to 153 BC.

Around to the left you'll see **Bagh Gumpha** (Tiger Cave; Cave 12), with its entrance carved as a tiger mouth. Nearby are **Pavana Gumpha** (Cave of Purification) and small **Sarpa Gumpha** (Serpent Cave), where the tiny door is surmounted by a three-headed cobra. On the summit are the remains of a defensive position. Around to the southeast is the single-storey elephant-guarded

---

ODISHA'S INDIGENOUS TRIBES

Sixty-two tribal (Adivasi) groups live in an area that encompasses Odisha, Chhattisgarh and Andhra Pradesh. In Odisha they account for one-quarter of the state's population and mostly inhabit the jungles and hilly regions of the centre and southwest. Their distinctive cultures are expressed in music, dance and arts.

Of the more populous tribes, the **Kondh** number about one million and are based around Koraput in the southwest, Rayagada and the Kandhamel District in the central west. The 500,000-plus **Santal** live around Baripada and Khiching in the far north. The 300,000 **Saura** live near Gunupur near the border with Andhra Pradesh. The **Bonda**, known as the 'Naked People' for wearing minimal clothing but incredibly colourful and intricate accessories, have a population of about 5000 and live in the hills near Koraput.

Private tour operators in Bhubaneswar and Puri organise customised tours into Odisha's tribal areas. Prices will depend on number of people, transport and hotel standards, but expect to pay around US$60 to US$100 per person per day for tours that include transport, accommodation and a professional guide. Tribal tours usually start on a Sunday or Monday to synchronise with village markets.

As of 2012, permission from the District Collector is required to visit areas designated as home to Particularly Vulnerable Tribal Groups (PVTGs) and bans on overnight lodging, private home visits, photographs and video or even getting within close proximity to them were all put in place. Until this new legislation shakes itself out, tribal tours are touch and go, but you will definitely need an agency in Bhubaneswar or Puri to facilitate the red tape. Once the bureaucracy is navigated, the rewards easily outweigh the pain, and a tribal tour is one of Eastern India's most memorable experiences.

Ganesh Gumpha (Cave 10), almost directly above the two-storey **Rani ka Naur** (Queen's Palace Cave; Cave 1), carved with Jain symbols and battle scenes.

Continue back to the entrance via **Chota Hathi Gumpha** (Cave 3), with its carvings of elephants, and the double-storey **Jaya Vijaya Cave** (Cave 5), with a bodhi tree carved in the central area.

Across the road, Khandagiri offers fine views over Bhubaneswar from its summit. The steep path splits about one-third of the way up the hill. The right path goes to **Ananta Cave** (Cave 3), with its carved figures of athletes, women, elephants and geese carrying flowers. Further along is a series of **Jain temples**; at the top is another (18th-century) Jain temple.

Buses don't go to the caves, but plenty pass nearby on NH5, or take an autorickshaw (₹200 to ₹300 return).

⭐ **State Museum**   MUSEUM
(www.odishamuseum.nic.in; Lewis Rd; Indian/foreigner ₹5/50, camera ₹10/100; ◷10am-4.30pm Tue Sun) Odisha's best collection of rare palm-leaf manuscripts, traditional and folk musical instruments, Bronze Age tools, an armoury, and an impressive collection of Buddhist, Jaina and Brahmanical sculptures.

Museum of Tribal Arts & Artefacts MUSEUM
(◷10am-5pm Tue-Sun) **FREE** For anyone considering a visit to the tribal areas, this museum, off National Hwy 5 (NH5), is recommended. Dress, ornaments, weapons, household implements and musical instruments are displayed.

☞ **Tours**

The OTDC runs a **city tour** (AC ₹285, 9am daily), covering the Nandankanan Zoo, Dhauli, the Lingaraj and Mukteswar temples, the State Museum, and Udayagiri and Khandagiri Caves. Another tour goes to Pipli, Konark and Puri (AC ₹350, 9am daily). Both tours leave from the Panthanivas Bhubaneswar hotel. These prices do not include entry fees.

Alternative Tours   TRIBAL, CULTURAL
(☏2590830; www.travelclubindia.com; Room 5, BDA Market Complex) 🏳 A veteran for tribal tours in Odisha, Nagaland and Arunchal Pradesh.

Discover Tours   TRIBAL, WILDLIFE
(☏2430477; www.orissadiscover.com; 463 Lewis Rd; ◷9.30-7pm Mon-Sat) Specialises in tribal and textile village tours as well as Bhitarkanika and Similipal.

Odisha Tourism Development Corporation   CITY TOUR
(OTDC; www.otdc.in; Lewis Rd, behind Panthanivas Bhubaneswar; ◷10am-5pm Mon-Sat) Commercial arm of Odisha Tourism. Books sightseeing tours and hotels.

🎎 **Festivals & Events**

Adivasi Mela   CULTURE
(◷26-31 Jan) Bhubaneswar goes tribal for the annual Adivasi Mela festival, celebrating the art, dance and handicrafts of Odisha's tribal groups.

🛏 **Sleeping**

Bhubaneswar has plenty of accommodation, but a real dearth of anything in the way of clean or appealing family run places or traveller dens in the budget and lower-midranges. Conversely, it has a great selection of top-end hotels.

Kasturi Guest House   GUESTHOUSE $
(☏2537054; Ashok Nagar; r ₹750-1200, with AC ₹1000-1500; ❄) Located in the heart of Bhubaneswar's commercial district (read: noisy), the intimate Kasturi guesthouse offers numerous categories for all budgets and is a little more welcoming than others in its price range. Rooms vary in size so there is something for everyone – except hot water.

Hotel Upasana   HOTEL $
(☏2310044; upasana_bbsr@rediffmail.com; 2282 Laxmisagar, off Cuttack Rd; s/d ₹850/950, with AC from ₹870/1147; ❄@) One of the friendlier and more welcoming budgets in town, located behind Bhubaneswar Hotel.

Hotel Richi   HOTEL $
(☏2534619; www.hotelrichi.com; 122A Station Sq; s ₹500-550, d ₹750-950, d with AC from ₹1150, all incl breakfast; ❄) The management here is definitely not familiar with the red carpet concept, but its proximity to the train station makes this half-hearted choice (very) popular.

Hotel Pushpak   HOTEL $$
(☏2310185; www.hotelpushpak.com; 68 Budha Nagar, Kalpana Sq; s/d/tr from ₹1289/1504/1719, with AC ₹2148/2363/2578; ❄🛜) Some of the colourful AC rooms at this vaguely institutional choice are a bit cramped, but across the board the rooms here are in pretty good

SLEEP LIKE A KING

Located a mere 3km from the Dhenkanal railway station (an easy train ride from Bhubaneswar), the wonderful **Gajlaxmi Palace** (☑9861011221; www.gajlaxmipalace.com; s/d incl meals ₹2500/5000), tucked away amid stunning scenery in the untapped forests of the Dhenkanal district, dates back to 1935. The palace belonged to Rajkumar Shri Shesh Pratap Singh Deo, a member of the Dhenkanal royal family. Today, his grandson, JP Singh Deo, and Navneeta, his lovely wife, have opened up at least two rooms inside their tranquil slice of royal history to guests. Sleeping here is like overnighting in a museum – the whole place is chock full of Singh Deo's antiques collected around the world and the whole place lives and breathes of decadent days gone by. The surrounding forest hides at least 22 wild elephants, a common sight on JP's morning and evening nature walks. Wild boar, jungle fowl and barking deer also roam freely outside the palace doors. JP grew up here and is ever-too-pleased to take you to rarely visited Sabara tribal villages or nearby Joranda Temples; or spit tales of elephant and tiger kills in crazier days over wonderful meals sourced from their own organic gardens. Paradise found.

shape, and the service and amenities evoke that of a pricier hotel. A new executive floor (from ₹3008) offers near-boutique-hotel qualities. There are three restaurants and a bar in-house.

★**Ginger** BOUTIQUE HOTEL **$$$**
(☑6663333; www.gingerhotels.com; Jayadev Vihar; s/d ₹3759/4296; ❄@☎) Ginger is a modern boutique business hotel chain (owned by Tata) with an IKEA-like self-service philosophy that means you're not constantly surrounded by tip-demanding bag-carriers, laundry peons etc. Staff are more young and hip than efficient or helpful – truth be told, they're not helpful at all – but with fresh, spotless rooms with LCD TVs, mini-fridge and silent AC, it's a tradeoff. Meals are served buffet style in the popular restaurant and there's a 24-hour branch of Café Coffee Day (the true coup here, let's be honest!). Advanced internet booking can cut rates up to 40% – Bhubaneswar's best bang for the buck.

Mayfair Lagoon HOTEL **$$$**
(☑6610181; www.mayfairhotels.com; Jaydev Vihar; d cottages from ₹10,852, d villas ₹43,408, all incl breakfast; ❄@☎) Quirky, colourful, even kitschy, but luxuriously Indian at the same time. In the jungle-like grounds you'll find static tigers, an elephant, even a twin-prop 1942 aircraft. The cottages are scattered around a serene lagoon and facilities run to a complimentary breakfast, six excellent restaurants, and Bhubaneswar's pub, nightclub and mini-bowling alley, the Cellar.

New Marrion HOTEL **$$$**
(☑2380850; www.hotelnewmarrion.com; 6 Janpath; s/d from ₹6552/6982; ❄@☎) A centrally located hotel where rooms have contemporary, classy design – LCD TVs, dark-wood panelling and a small sofa space. Restaurants here include South Indian, Italian-Mexican combo and Chinese, a great kebab house, a Café Coffee Day adjacent and a contemporary Scottish bar. The new Thai spa (massages from ₹2000) rounds out the allure.

✗ Eating

Bhubaneswar is a wonderful spot to twist up your tastebuds with a whole new set of regional flavors.

★**Odisha Hotel** ODISHAN, REGIONAL **$**
(☑9437419279; Sahid Nagar, Market Bldg; thalis ₹140-220; ☺12.30-4pm) This dead-simple restaurant (not a hotel!) is the best budget spot to try authentic Odishan cuisine, served in huge proportions thali-style on plantain leaves resting in traditional Bell Metal dishware. The menu board is entirely in Odia, so just order veg or non-veg (not always available, depending on the religious calendar) and sit back and await this Hindu Last Supper! If you're lost, call the owner, who speaks some English.

Khana Khazana INDIAN **$**
(Kalpana Sq, outside Hotel Padma; mains ₹40-140; ☺5.30-10.30pm) This longstanding fast-food street stall does a bang-up job with tandoori chicken, delicious chow mein and tasty chicken biryani at laughable prices.

Hare Krishna Restaurant   INDIAN $$

(Station Sq, Lalchand Market Complex; mains ₹120-205; ⏱noon-11.30pm) The beautifully laquered Gujarati *sankheda* furniture stands out in this dimly lit veg restaurant where you can enjoy mainly Indian dishes, including a wide range of tasty biryanis and pilaus in a truly gorgeous setting.

Tangerine 9   INDIAN, MULTICUISINE $$

(Station Sq, 108A Lotus House; mains ₹99-409; ⏱noon-3.30pm & 7-10.30pm) Everything on the panic-inducing menu here (What to order? I want it all!) – North Indian (especially tandoori), Chinese and a few Thai thrown in – bursts with the flavour of fresh herbs and spices. It's five-star dining for half the price and a cool crowd to boot.

Maurya Gardens   INDIAN, CHINESE $$

(Hotel Richi, Station Sq; mains ₹95-250; ⏱noon-11pm) This darkened restaurant is a welcome respite from the train-station chaos outside, as well as a dramatic contrast from the hotel in which it's located. The curries are nice and hot, but if you want a beer to cool it down you'll have to eat (same menu) in the bar next door.

★Kanika   ODISHAN, REGIONAL $$$

(www.mayfairhotels.com; Jaydev Vihar, Mayfair Lagoon ; mains ₹110-595; ⏱noon-3pm & 7-11pm) Just when you thought all Indian food was starting to taste the same, you went and arrived in Odisha. Tiny Kanika does a don't-miss job with regional Odishan recipes, excelling most memorably with local seafood. Specialities include *kankada yurkari* (crab curry; ₹595); anything made with mustard (the off-menu mustard paste river fish *besara* is freak-out good); and Odisha's most traditional dessert, the seriously addictive *chhena poda* (literally 'burnt cheese', cooked with sugar, cashew nuts and raisins), served here uncharacteristically warm.

🍷 Drinking & Nightlife

Cha Bar   CAFE

(www.oxfordbookstore.com; 2nd fl, PAL Heights, Jaydev Nagar; tea ₹30-90; ⏱10am-10pm) This Mumbai import serves a wide range of exotic teas, including organic, ayurvedic and single estate; as well as organic South Indian and Brazilian espresso. It's inside the megachain Oxford Bookstore in modern Pal Heights shopping mall and draws a modern, forward-thinking crowd.

★Cellar   BAR/NIGHTCLUB

(www.mayfairhotels.com; Jaydev Vihar, Mayfair Lagoon; ⏱noon-midnight) The Cellar is Bhubaneswar's best watering hole, boasting a colonial British–style megapub (beers from ₹150) with a few nice pool tables, cricket and footy on the TV, and a small dance floor, too, with DJ's spinning house, R&B and Bollywood from 7.30pm nightly (couples only, though, so make a quick friend). Oh. *Wait.* There's also a mini-bowling alley!

Oceana   COCKTAIL BAR

(www.swostihotel.com; 103 Janpath; ⏱noon-11.30pm) A trendy new cocktail bar, part of the swanky makeover of the Swosti Hotel in which its located. There's a maritime-on-acid theme, with fuchsias and blues bouncing off the beautiful black Thai marble bar. Cocktails (from ₹275) and interesting bar snacks – tasty chickpeas laced with onion cucumbers, lime and salt – are served.

🛍 Shopping

Ekamra Haat   MARKET

(www.ekamrahaat.in; Madhusudan Marg; ⏱10am-10pm) A wide-ranging exposition of Odishan handicrafts (and snack stalls) can be found at this permanent market.

Utkalika   HANDICRAFTS

(Odisha State Handloom Cooperative; Eastern Tower, Market Bldg; ⏱10am-8.30pm) Features Odishan textiles, including appliqué and *ikat* (a technique involving tie-dyeing the thread before it's woven).

Modern Book Depot   BOOKS

(Station Sq; ⏱9.30am-2pm & 4.30-9pm) Maps, English-language novels, coffee-table books, postcards and books on Odisha. If you're interested in learning some Odia, ask the owner about the well-regarded *Oriya in Small Bites*.

ℹ Information

ATMs are plentiful along Janpath and elsewhere in the city. Cyber cafes are decliningly scarce.

Apollo Hospital (www.apollohospitals.com; ⏱24hr) This new modern private medical facility with a round-the-clock trauma center and pharmacy is where you want to be if you're ill.

India Tourism (www.incredibleindia.org; Paryatan Bhavan, 2nd fl, Lewis Rd, behind State Museum; ⏱9am-6pm Mon-Fri, to 1pm Sat) Dishes out national information, and is the friendliest and most accommodating spot for local info as well. It's is the same building as Odisha Tourism.

ODISHA BHUBANESWAR

SIMILIPAL NATIONAL PARK

Located some 250km north of Bhubaneswar, the 2750-sq-km **Similipal National Park** (www.similipal.org; Indian/foreigner per day ₹40/1000, camera per 3 days ₹50/100; ☺ closed 16 Jun-Oct) has long been Odisha's prime wildlife sanctuary. However, due to several issues, including ongoing Maoist activity in the region, animal and timber poaching, a kidnapping or two, sensitive tribal villages within the park, staff shortages and lack of resources to properly track animal movements or protect tourists, accessing the park has become more and more difficult for foreigners in recent years (though it seems Indians don't have issues with access).

For those out of the bureaucracy unscathed, a massif of prominent hills creased by valleys and gorges, made dramatic by plunging waterfalls, including the spectacular 400m-high **Barheipani Waterfall** and the 150m-high **Joranda Waterfall**, awaits. The jungle is an atmospheric mix of dense sal forest and rolling open savannah and there's a huge range of reptile, bird and mammal species. The tigers aren't tracked and sightings are extremely rare – the best chance to spot them will be at the **Joranda salt lick**. More realistic sighting possibilities include wild elephants (there are over 400 in the park), most probably at the **Chahala salt lick**. Mankida and Khadia PVTGs (Particulary Vunerable Tribal Groups) live inside the park – bear in mind, it is now prohibited in Odisha to photograph them.

There are two entrances, **Tulsibani**, 15km from Jashipur, on the northwestern side; and **Pithabata**, near Lulung, 25km west of Baripada – the most convenient for travellers coming from Bhubaneswar or Puri. At time of writing, the park was open for day trips only, though very few agencies in Bhubaneswar or Puri are willing to go through the rigamarole to take foreigners to the park. The uneventful **Forest Department bungalows** (d Indian ₹600, foreigner ₹800-1200) inside the park were off limits during research.

If you go, the dusty transit hub of **Baripada** is the best and most convenient place to organise a visit; if you're planning an independent trip, recommended agency **Mayur Tours & Travels** (☏9437218602, 253567; mayurtour@rediffmail.com; Lal Bazaar) can organise tours with capable guides and is the best place to initiate the permission process, which supposedly takes three to five working days, subject to the availability of the District Collector. **Odisha Tourism** (www.orissatourism.gov.in; Baghra Rd; ☺10am-5pm Mon-Sat) is also an option. The clean-but-fading **Hotel Ambika** (☏252557; hotel_ambika@yahoo.com; Roxy Rd; s/d from ₹375/425, d with AC ₹990; ✱) is friendly, has a great restaurant, local workers' bar and large rooms, but is a little dark. The most comfortable spot near the park is unfortunately on the Jashipur side (which is a long drive out of the way from the main entrance and park infrastructure): **Toshali Jungle Lodge** (☏9937298099; www.toshalivalyou.com; d incl meals ₹2670), run by concession in cottages built by the Forest Department, offers basic but well-maintained rooms with mosquito nets, nice bathrooms and a professional manager. It's 15km from the Tulsibani entrance.

From the Baripada bus stand on Kacheri Rd, buses go to Kolkata (non-AC/AC ₹190/220, five hours, 4.45am, 9.20am, 10.30pm, 10.40pm and 11pm), Bhubaneswar (non-AC/AC ₹200/250, five hours, 20 per day), Balasore (₹36 to ₹56, 1½ hours, every 30 minutes from 5.15am to 8.40pm), Jashipur (₹70, 2½ hours, every 30 minutes from 5am to 10pm) and one night bus to Puri (₹310, seven hours, 11pm). The 12892 Bhubaneswar-Baripada Express train (2nd class/AC chair ₹92/336, five hours, 5.10pm) runs from Bhubaneswar every day except Saturday, and returns as the 12891 at 5.09am every day except Sunday.

Odisha Tourism (www.orissatourism.gov.in, www.visitodisha.com) main branch (2nd fl, Paryatan Bhavan, Lewis Rd, behind State Museum; ☺10am-5pm Mon-Sat); airport (☺by flight schedule); train station (☏2431299; ☺6am-10pm) Tourist information, maps and lists of recommended guides.

Om Sai Communication (Ravi Talkies; internet per hr ₹15; ☺9am-9pm) Internet access conveniently located near temples.

Police (Rajpath, Capitol Police Station)

Post Office (www.indiapost.gov.in; cnr Mahatma Gandhi & Sachivajaya Margs; ☺9am-7pm Mon-Sat, 3-7pm Sun)

State Bank of India (Rajpath; ☉10am-5pm Mon-Sat) Travellers cheques and foreign currency exchange.

❶ Getting There & Away

AIR

Bhubaneswar's Biju Patnaik Airport is a 7km drive from town and was undergoing a major upgrade at time of research. Among others, **Jet Airways** (www.jetairways.com; Biju Patnaik Airport) flies direct to Mumbai, Chennai, Kolkata and Bengaluru; and **Air India** (www.airindia.com; Rajpath; ☉10am-4.45pm Mon-Sat) flies daily to Delhi and Mumbai.

BUS

Baramunda bus station (NH5) has frequent government buses to Cuttack (₹20, one hour) and Puri (₹35, 1¼ hours) and Konark (₹40, two hours); and less-frequent services to Berhampur (₹140, four hours, every two hours), Rayagada (₹320, 12 hours, 1pm, 3pm and 7pm) and Jeypore (AC ₹620, 13 hours, 5.30pm, 6.30pm and 7.30pm). Private buses head to Baripada (₹250, six hours, every 45 minutes 5.30am to 11.30am) and Gopalpur-on-Sea (₹140, four hours, every 30 minutes 7pm to 10.30am).

For Kolkata (non-AC/AC ₹280/400, 12 hours), buses depart hourly from 6.30pm to 9.30pm, with AC's going at 8.30pm and 9pm.

To reach the bus stand, catch bus 801 from the city bus stand (₹7, 45 minutes).

TRAIN

Foreigners queue up at window 3 at the Computerised Reservation Office at Bhubaneswar Station. There are regular trains to Chennai, Kolkata, Delhi and Mumbai.

❶ Getting Around

Bhubaneswar's city bus system runs from 7am to 9pm. From the **city bus stand** (known as Master Canteen), bus 207 goes to the airport (₹7, 15 minutes) and Nandankanan (₹18, one hour). Bus 171 goes to Dhauli (₹15, 30 minutes), Pipli (₹20, 50 minutes) and Puri (₹35, two hours). An autorickshaw to the airport costs about ₹200. Prepaid **Cool Cab** (☑3255552) AC taxis from the airport to central Bhubaneswar cost ₹250, and to Puri or Konark ₹1200 to ₹1500. Autorickshaws cannot access the terminal, but if you exit to the right and walk 100m or so, they should be waiting. They charge about half that of taxis.

To visit the attractions around Bhubaneswar in comfort by taxi, the haggle free and fairest option is to hire a car and driver from OTDC (p599). For destinations within 200km (Nandankanan, Pipli, Dhauli and Hirapur included), charges are ₹110 per hour and ₹10 per kilometre minus a 10km free allotment per hour for an AC Indigo. Book in person at least a day in advance.

AROUND BHUBANESWAR

Nandankanan Zoological Park

Famous for its handful of blue-eyed white tigers, the zoo (www.nandankanan.org; Indian/foreigner ₹20/100, digital camera/video ₹10/500; ☉7.30am-5.30pm Tue-Sun Apr-Sep, 8am-5pm Tue-Sun Oct-Mar), one of India's best, also boasts

ODISHA NANDANKANAN ZOOLOGICAL PARK

HANDY TRAINS FROM BHUBANESWAR

DESTINATION	TRAIN NO & NAME	FARE (₹)	DURATION (HR)	DEPARTURES
Chennai	12841 Coromandal Express	₹391/1082/1670 (A)	20	9.25pm
Delhi	12801 Purushotlam Express	₹481/1344/2125 (A)	31	11.20pm
Kolkata (Howrah)	12074 Jan Shatabdi	₹142/477 (B)	7	6am Mon-Sat
Koraput	18447 Hirakhand Express	₹267/623/935 (A)	15	7.35pm
Mumbai	11020 Konark Express	₹484/1382/2210 (A)	37	3.20pm
Puri	18426 Durg Puri Exp	₹120/218/610 (A)	2	7.35am
Rayagada	18447 Hirakhand Express	₹224/748/1130 (A)	10	7.35pm
Sambalpur	12893 Bhubaneswar-Balangir Express	₹93/339 (B)	5	6.45am

Fares: (A) sleeper/3AC/2AC, (B) 2nd Class/AC Chair

SATKOSIA GORGE SANCTUARY

This 525-sq-km sanctuary (☑8763102681; www.satkosia.org; per day Indian/foreigner ₹20/1000; ☺6am-6pm), 190km west of Bhubaneswar, is one of India's eco-tourism triumphs. Part of the larger **Satkosia Tiger Reserve**, inaugurated in 2007 by combining adjoining Satkosia Gorge and Baisipalli wildlife sanctuaries, the park is one of the best and most organised parks in Odisha as well as the most accessible both geographically (from Bhubaneswar or Puri) as well as bureaucratically.

The reserve is straddled by the breathtaking gorge, cut by the mighty Mahanadi River, one of the most beautiful natural spots in all of Odisha, if not India. In addition to significant populations of Gharial crocodiles, 38 species of mammals have been recorded, with elephants the most often spotted, but leopards, sambar, wild dogs, jackals and giant squirrels all call the reserve home – and a handful of tigers that visitors will likely never see. The sanctuary is managed through a groundbreaking community-based eco-tourism initiative that chose 17 of the 116 villages within the park's bounderies to work together to convert their income-dependance on the forest (often from timber poaching and other illegal activities) to running nature camps and becoming forest rangers. These communties now live off an alternative source of income that doesn't harm the forest, and improvements in their livelihoods (solar panel fencing, irrigation support and general health and sanitation improvements) are being provided by a portion of the park's profits.

The main entry gate of the tiger reserve is at Pampasar, 30km southwest of Angul. **Satkosia Wildlife Division** (☑8763102681; www.satkosia.org; Hakimpada, Angul) manages three sets of accomodations run by local communities. The nicest is the new **Nature Camp Chhotkei** (www.satkosia.org; d incl meals, guide & nature hike ₹2300) ✎, where you'll find five spacious eco-cottages made from compressed earth bricks and bamboo (and very un-eco asbestos roofing), running on solar energy. Meals here are simple, but tasty and served proudly and substantially by villagers. Simpler cottages and tents are available at **Nature Camp Purunakote** (www.satkosia.org; per person ₹1000). And, although its been moved back from the spectacular riverbank setting it once occupied, the seasonal **Nature Camp Tikarpada** (www.satkosia.org; d incl meals ₹1600; ☺1 Dec-31 Mar), perched near the golden sand beaches of the Mahanadi River with the gorge as the scenic backdrop, remains Odisha's most storybook setting. Here you'll find eight deteriorating double-bedded tents and four VIP tents with toilets and water supply.

Most folks visit Satkosia on a tour, but it's possible to do so independently. There are 10 daily buses from Bhubaneswar to Angul (₹85, four hours), the nearest city to the reserve, and another three from Kolkata (non-AC/AC ₹330/400, eight hours). Alternatively, catch the 12893 Bhubaneswar-Balangir Express from Bhubaneswar (2nd class/AC chair ₹63/222, 2½ hours, 6.45am). You'll need to stop by Satkosia Wildlife Division for permissions and reservations – a mere formality but bring a copy of your passport and visa.

From Angul, a car and driver is the only feasible way to get you the last 50km to 60km to most of the lodgings within the park, which can also be arranged at the wildlife division (from ₹450 plus fuel and overnight charges).

rare Asiatic lions, rhinoceroses, copious reptiles and long-snouted crocodiles, monkeys, deer, a vulture that is believed to have worked for the Pakistan Inter-Services Intelligence agency and India's only orangutan.

The highlight is the hour-long **lion and tiger safari** (₹30), which leaves every 30 minutes from 9am to 5pm; other attractions include a toy train, boat rides, a cable car and the State Botanical Garden. Early or late in the day you might catch the elephants having a bath in the lake.

OTDC tours stop here for an (insufficient) hour or so. From Bhubaneswar, frequent public buses (₹15, one hour) leave from Kalpana Sq (near Hotel Padma) and from outside the former Capital bus stand for Nandankanan village, about 400m from the entrance to the zoo. By taxi, a return trip (including waiting) costs about ₹800.

Dhauli

In about 260 BC one of Ashoka's famous edicts was carved onto a large rock at Dhauli, 8km south of Bhubaneswar. The rock is now protected by a grill-fronted building and above, on top of a hillock, is a carved elephant.

On a nearby hill is the huge, white **Shanti Stupa** (Peace Pagoda), built by Japanese monks in 1972. Older Buddhist reliefs are set into the modern structure. You have to climb the stairs barefoot (hot! hot! hot!) but it's worth it for the four lovely images of Buddha and great views of the surrounding countryside.

Bus 171 goes to Dhauli (₹15, 30 minutes) from Bhubaneswar or Puri. From the turnoff, it's a flat 3km walk to the rock, and then a short, steep walk to the stupa. A return trip costs about ₹400 to ₹500 by autorickshaw, and about ₹800 by taxi.

Hirapur

Among iridescent-green paddies 15km from Bhubaneswar is a small village with an important **Yogini Temple**, one of only four in India. The low, circular structure, open to the sky, has 64 niches within, each with a black chlorite goddess. Getting here requires hired transport or coming on a customised tour from Bhubaneswar.

Pipli

This colourful town, 16km southeast of Bhubaneswar, is notable for its brilliant appliqué craft, which incorporates small mirrors and is used for door and wall hangings and the more traditional canopies hung over Lord Jagannath and family during festival time. Lampshades and parasols hanging outside the shops turn the main road into an avenue of rainbow colours. The work is still done by local families in workshops behind the shops; you may be able to go back and have a look. During Diwali, it's particularly vibrant. Pipli is easily accessible by any bus between Bhubaneswar and Puri or Konark.

SOUTHEASTERN ODISHA

Southeastern Odisha hugs the coast of the Bay of Bengal and is home to the state's most visited areas: the backpacker outpost of Puri, the Unesco World Heritage Sun Temple at Konark and the ecotourism hotbeds of Chilika Lake and Mangalajodi.

Puri

☑ 06752 / POP 158,000

Hindu pilgrims, Indian holidaymakers and foreign travellers all make their way to Puri, setting up camp in different parts of town. For Hindus, Puri is one of the holiest pilgrimage places in India, with religious life revolving around the great Jagannath Mandir and its famous Rath Yatra (Car Festival).

Puri's other attraction is its long, sandy beach and esplanade. Backing this, on New Marine Rd, is a long ribbon of hotels, resorts and company holiday homes that become instantly full when Kolkata rejoices in a holiday – great for an evening stroll.

In the 1970s travellers on the hippie trail through Southeast Asia were attracted here by the sea and bhang, legal in Shiva's Puri. There's little trace of that scene today (though the bhang hasn't departed); travellers come just to hang out and recharge their backpacking spirit.

The action is along a few kilometres of coast. The backpacker village is clustered around Chakra Tirtha (CT) Rd to the east while Bengali holidaymakers flock to busy New Marine Rd (the 'Indian side' or 'Puri I'), where there is lots of hangout action on the long esplanade.

ⓘ Dangers & Annoyances

Muggings and attacks on women have been reported along isolated stretches of beach, even during the day, so take care. Ocean currents can become treacherous in Puri, and drownings are not uncommon, so don't venture out beyond your depth. Ask one of the *nolias* (fishermen/lifeguards), with their white-painted, cone-shaped wicker hats, for the best spots and keep a look out for **Sea Riders**, a group of traditional fishermen turned lifeguards through an initiative of a local NGO.

◉ Sights

Jagannath Mandir   HINDU TEMPLE

This mighty temple belongs to Jagannath, Lord of the Universe and incarnation of Vishnu. The jet-black deity with large,

round, white eyes is hugely popular across Odisha; figures of Jagannath are tended and regularly dressed in new clothes at shrines across the state. Built in its present form in 1198, the temple (closed to non-Hindus) is surrounded by two walls; its 58m-high *sikhara* (spire) is topped by the flag and wheel of Vishnu.

Guarded by two stone lions and a pillar crowned by the Garuda that once stood at the Sun Temple at Konark, the eastern entrance (Lion Gate) is the passageway for the chariot procession of Rath Yatra.

Jagannath, brother Balbhadra and sister Subhadra reside supreme in the central *jag-amohan* (assembly hall). Priests continually garland and dress the three throughout the day for different ceremonies. Incredibly, the temple employs about 6000 men to perform the complicated rituals involved in caring for the gods. An estimated 20,000 people –

divided into 36 orders and 97 classes – are dependent on Jagannath for their livelihood.

Non-Hindus can spy from the roof of **Raghunandan Library** (cnr Temple Rd & Swargadwar Rd; ☺ 9am-1.30pm & 4-6pm Mon-Sat) opposite; a 'donation', while not officially compulsory, is expected (₹10 is fine though they will whine about it). The library is closed on Sunday, so touts who will help you to a nearby rooftop prey on tourists and demand ₹100 – easily negotiated down to ₹50. Enter around the back of the building to the right-hand side and follow the arrows and signs through a fascinating ruined monastery.

Model Beach
BEACH

(www.puribeach.net) 🖉 Puri is no palm-fringed paradise – the beach is wide, shelves quickly with a nasty shore break and is shadeless, but the newly crowned Model Beach, art of a sustainable, community-run beach tourism initiative by Barefoot (see opposite), offers a 700m stretch of sand that's easily Puri's

Puri

👁 Sights
1 Model Beach...................................... A4

🏃 Activities, Courses & Tours
2 Ayurshree Spa.................................. A4
Heritage Tours .... (see 8)
3 OTDC Booking Office...................... A4

🛏 Sleeping
4 Chanakya BNR Hotel C3
5 Hotel Gandhara................................ C3
6 Hotel Lee Garden A4
7 Hotel Lotus...................................... D3
8 Mayfair Beach Resort A4
9 Z Hotel D3

🍴 Eating
Chung Wah.................................. (see 6)
10 Honey Bee Bakery & Pizzeria C3
11 Peace Restaurant............................. D3
12 Wildgrass Restaurant A4

ℹ Information
13 District Headquarters Hospital...........A1
14 Gandhara International...................... C3
15 Odisha Tourism................................ A4
16 Odisha Tourism................................ B2
17 Swapu... A4

🚍 Transport
Bike & Motorcycle Rental .... (see 7)
18 Konark Bus Stand B1
19 Medical Square A1

finest and cleanest. Palm umbrellas provide shade and cabana boys/lifeguards, known as **Sea Riders**, hawk fixed-price beach chairs (₹20) and massages (₹50 to ₹200) and are responsible for keeping the beach clean.

Swargdwar   SACRED SITE
(off New Marine Rd; ⏰ 24hr) These hallowed cremation grounds are the end stop of choice for Eastern India's Hindu population and beyond – some 40 bodies are cremated here daily. Anyone can watch or walk among the open-air ceremonies providing you are behaving in a respectful manner and not taking photos. It's an obviously solemn affair, but a fascinating glimpse into Puri's role as one of India's holiest cities.

🏃 Activities & Tours

OTDC   TOURS
(☎ 223524; www.otdc.in; CT Rd; ⏰ 6am-10pm) Runs a series of day trips. Tour 1 (₹400, departs 6.30am Tuesday to Sunday) skips through Konark, Dhauli, Bhubaneswar's temples, Udayagiri and Khandagiri Caves plus Nandankanan zoo. Tour 2 (₹290, departs 7am daily) goes for a boat jaunt on Chilika Lake. Admission fees are not included. Tours begin and end at various points including the Odisha Tourism office (which is likely to move a few hundred metres to the northwest corner of VIP Rd and CT Rd during the lifespan of this book) and the Chanakya BNR Hotel.

Heritage Tours   CULTURAL, WILDLIFE
(☎ 223656; www.heritagetoursodisha.com; Mayfair Beach Resort; ⏰ 8am-8pm) 🌿 A sustainable tribal and cultural tourism veteran focusing on rural and special-interest ethnic tourism, but also interesting for its **Green Riders** program in which 75 cycle-rickshaw drivers are trained weekly in fixed pricing, self-respect and why spiking prices for foreign tourists is uncool. In addition to transport, the program offers a wealth of local cycle-rickshaw tours to fascinating parts of old Puri.

Ayurshree Spa   SPA
(☎ 8895353960; www.ayurshree.com; Ramaballav Rd; ⏰ 9am-2pm & 4-7.30pm) This Ayurvedic spa housed in a simple but atmospheric heritage home is run by the welcoming Dr Sidhu. Massages start at ₹600.

Volunteering

Barefoot   VOLUNTEERING
(www.teambarefoot.org) The small local NGO works to improve community lifestyles through sustainable tourism development. Volunteers must commit to a two-week minimum, which can involve teaching English, beach maintance supervision and training in tourism. From ₹1400 per week including lodging and meals.

🎆 Festivals & Events

Highlights of the festival-packed year include the celebrated festival of **Rath Yatra** (⏰ Jun/Jul) and the **Puri Beach Festival** (www.puribeachfestival.com; ⏰ late Nov) featuring magnificent sand art, food stalls, traditional dance and other cultural programs.

🛏 Sleeping

For Rath Yatra, Durga Puja (Dussehra), Diwali or the end of December and New Year, book well in advance.

Prices given are for October to February. Significant discounts can be negotiated during the monsoon, while prices can triple during a festival. Many hotels have early

ODISHA PURI

PURIFECTLY SWEET

The narrow lanes of Puri's holy quarter are full of makeshift sweet shops, perhaps none more famous than **Puri Cheesecake** (Temple Rd, Dolamandap Sahi; per piece ₹16; ⊙7am-11pm). Bikram Sahoo and his six brothers have been churning out this unique Odishan delight, known as *chhena poda* ('burnt cheese'), for 45 years. It's cottage cheese, sugar and cardamom cooked in an iron pan over an open flame. Though it's more like a flan than traditional cheesecake, it's off the mark by name only. A real treat for just ₹16 per piece. To find it, walk down Temple Rd from Jagganath Mandir, pass a small public square about 300m on the right, and it's another 100m on your right next door to Jagganath Pump House.

checkout times – as early as 7am. A 10% service charge is frequently levied.

Z Hotel HERITAGE HOTEL **$**
(☑222554; www.zhotelindia.com; CT Rd; dm women only ₹100, s/d without bathroom ₹500/1000, d ₹3000, with AC ₹3500; ❄☎) Inside this former maharaja's home, the Z has a lock on traveller vibe pretty much across the board in Odisha; and offers huge, clean, airy rooms, many of them facing the sea. The entire 2nd floor has been gutted and redone; and upgraded digs begat upgraded prices. The heritage vibe and traveller scene here trumps the hospitality, which is nonexistent, but it remains Puri's most atmospheric choice.

Hotel Lee Garden HOTEL **$**
(☑229986; lee_garden@rediffmail.com; VIP Rd; d from ₹1000, d/tr with AC from ₹1700/2100; ❄@☎) A sleek renovation has upped the ante on this spotless Chinese-run establishment, which has a painful but negotiable 7am checkout time. Rooms are spacious and contemporary, with new tasteful doors and headboards (the bathrooms get the treatment next), but it is its proximity all too dangerously close to the excellent Chinese restaurant, Chung Wah, that is perhaps it's most valuable asset.

Hotel Lotus HOTEL **$**
(☑227033; www.hotellotuspuri.com; CT Rd; d/q from ₹550/1200, d with AC ₹1200; ❄☎) Friendly and humbly run, the Lotus is a great budget option offering a range of inexpensive rooms that are clean and comfortable. The non-AC rooms are some of the best value for money in Puri, though the front rooms may suffer a bit of street noise. Travellers fight over the one rooftop room (₹600).

★**Hotel Gandhara** HOTEL **$$**
(☑224117; www.hotelgandhara.com; CT Rd; s/d ₹1435/1565, with AC & breakfast ₹2217/2347; ❄@☎❅) Though prices on non-AC rooms have considerably outrisen inflation, the new pool eases the blow, and the Gandhara continues to steamroll the competition for friendliness, services and value. There's a range of bright rooms for different budgets in the whitewashed, once-regal building. The rear five-storey block has rooftop AC rooms catching breezes and views; others are arrayed around a tree-shaded garden with balconies, with one cheapie set aside for shoestringers (₹750). Amenities include a friendly dog named after an Indian soda, international cable channels, free wi-fi (the only in our entire India travels that worked seamlessly), newspapers slipped under doors and self-service beer. Japanese spoken.

Chanakya BNR Hotel HERITAGE HOTEL **$$**
(☑223006; www.therailhotel.com.com; CT Rd; r incl breakfast ₹3342; ❄) Looming archways and wide hallways leading to spacious, hardwood-floored rooms with 2.7m doors and modern furnishings highlight this renovated sprawling historic railway hotel. There are beautiful bygone touches throughout, most notably the dark, 90-year-old Lac mural art in the lobby stairwell and restaurant.

Mayfair Beach Resort HOTEL **$$$**
(☑227800; www.mayfairhotels.com; CT Rd; d incl breakfast & dinner from ₹11,017; ❄☎❅) The benchmark for Puri luxury features spacious units nestled in idyllic gardens dotted with carved statues. Its stretch of beach is cleaned and maintained by the resort and a good spot to kick away a day, guest or not, and the white-wicker charm of the Verandah deck restaurant (serving Continental, Chinese and even Thai; mains ₹200 to ₹400) makes for a great refuelling stop.

✖ Eating

There's excellent fresh seafood to be enjoyed almost anywhere in Puri, and in CT Rd homesick travellers can find muesli and pancakes. A few restaurants here can 'find' a beer for you.

Peace Restaurant INDIAN $

(CT Rd; mains ₹45-200) The most pleasant budget option, doing nice work with curries, macaroni, the best muesli in town (₹70) and tasty fish dishes, including a nice chilli fish. Save room for the house dessert, a fried empanada-like banana or apple turnover laced with sugar, cinnamon and honey.

★Chung Wah INDO-CHINESE $$

(VIP Rd; mains ₹120-230; ⊙11.30am-3pm & 6.30-11.30pm) The real thing courtesy of a Chinese family transplanted from Kolkata 40 years ago. Chung Wah's menu is loaded down with spicy Szechuan dishes that bite back. Try the excellent hot garlic chicken, Szechuan prawns or go fusion: Kung Pao *paneer,* which has a much catchier ring to it than Kung Pao chicken.

Wildgrass Restaurant REGIONAL, INDIAN $$

(VIP Rd; mains ₹50-200; ⊙noon-11pm) With mismatched sculptures and precarious tree huts scattered throughout its grounds, Wildgrass is an atmospheric secret garden gone wild. The Indian side of the menu is enlivened with excellent regional specials, categorised by their origins (Odishan, Chilikan and Puriwala), many of which you no longer see on menus.

Grand NORTH INDIAN $$

(✉222829; Grand Centre, Grand Rd; mains ₹80-130; ⊙11.30am-3.30pm & 7.30-10.30pm) This locals' pure-veg monstrosity offers two menus, so even if you don't see scrumptious dishes like the *bhindi chatpati* (okra), *gobi Hyderabadi* (cauliflower), or *kadai* veg (creamy curried veggies), ask for them anyway, along with a healthy list of *dosas* (₹30 to ₹75). A bonus to the fab food is the open-air terrace, from which there are striking views of Jagannath Mandir and the hubbub of Grand Rd below. From the temple, it's 100m down Grand Rd.

Honey Bee Bakery & Pizzeria CAFE $$

(CT Rd; pizza ₹165-425, mains ₹85-260; ⊙8.30am-2pm & 6-10pm) Decent pizzas and pancakes, filtered coffee and espresso, toasted sandwiches and fry-up brekkies (including bacon!) – all the comforts of home are here in newly upgraded digs complete with a small rooftop setting.

ⓘ Information

The main traveller-hotel stretch of CT Rd is a zoo of travel agents, cheap shops, moneychangers and internet cafes (₹30 to ₹40 per hour.)

District Headquarters Hospital (Grand Rd)

Gandhara International (www.hotelgandhara. com; CT Rd, Hotel Gandhara; internet per hr ₹40; ⊙8am-7pm Mon-Sat, to 1pm Sun) Friendly travel agency, moneychanger and internet.

Odisha Tourism (www.orissatourism.gov.in; CT Rd; ⊙10am-5pm Mon-Sat) Tourist info, hotel,

ODISHA PURI

HANDY TRAINS FROM PURI

DESTINATION	TRAIN NO & NAME	FARE (₹)	DURATION (HR)	DEPARTURES
Balisore	18410 Sri Jagannath Express	₹218/385/610 (A)	4½	10.30pm
Bhubaneswar	18419 Puri Durg Express	₹120/218/610 (A)	1½	1.45pm
Delhi	12801 Purushottam Express	₹493/1379/2185 (A)	32	9.50pm
Gopalpur-on-Sea	17479 Puri-Tirupati Express	₹120/520 (C)	5	12.25pm except Tue & Sat
Kolkata	12838 Puri-Howrah Express	₹244/654/965 (A)	9	8pm
Sambalpur	18304 Puri-Sambalpur Express	₹95/349 (B)	6	3.25pm
Varanasi	12875 Neelachal Express	₹371/1025/1570 (A)	21	10.55am Tue, Fri & Sun

Fares: (A) sleeper/3AC/2AC, (B) 2nd Class/AC Chair, (C) sleeper/3AC

vehicle and tour booking, and a convenient start/finish point for day tours, though not particularly friendly. Also a branch at the **train station** (⏲ 7am-10pm).

Post Office (www.indiapost.gov.in; cnr Kutchery & Temple Rd; ⏲ 10am-6pm Mon-Sat)

Swapu (VIP Rd; ⏲ 8am-11pm) Probably Odisha's nicest pharmacy.

Tourist Police Aid Post (CT Rd, Seabeach)

ⓘ Getting There & Away

BUS

The easiest way to Bhubaneswar is bus 171 (₹35, two hours), which leaves from **Medical Square** on Grand Rd every 30 to 45 minutes between 7.45am and 5.30pm and will drop you at the city bus stand (Master Canteen) next to Bhubaneswar's train station. Bus 441 goes to Konark (₹40, one hour) – flag it down heading east on CT Rd. Alternatively, flag down Bus 450 heading west on CT Rd, which heads to the railway station (₹6, 15 minutes) and on to the Konark bus station where you can catch a local bus to Konark (₹22, 45 minutes, every 30 minutes from 5am to 6pm).

Next to the **Konark bus stand** is the sprawling main **bus stand** (📞 224461) near Gundicha Mandir, where frequent buses head to Bhubaneswar (₹35, two hours), Cuttack (₹50, 2½ hours) and Satapada (₹335, two hours) as well as private AC (₹430, 12 hours, 6pm) and non-AC (₹300, 15 hours, 2.30pm) buses to Kolkata. Keep in mind that Cuttack buses stop in Bhubaneswar but not at Baramunda bus stand.

For Pipli and Raghurajpur, take the Bhubaneswar bus. For other destinations change at Bhubaneswar.

TRAIN

Book well ahead if traveling during holiday and festival times.

ⓘ Getting Around

A few places along CT Rd (around the Hotel Lotus) rent bicycles from ₹40 per day, and mopeds and motorcycles for ₹250 to ₹500. From CT Rd, cycle-rickshaws charge about ₹30 to the train station and ₹40 to the bus station or Jagannath Mandir. Look for the appropriately attired Green Riders for no-hassle pricing.

Raghurajpur

The fascinating artists' village of Raghurajpur, 14km north of Puri, is two streets and 120 thatched brick houses adorned with murals of geometric patterns and mythological scenes – a traditional art form that has almost died out in Odisha.

The village is most famous for its *patachitra* – work made using cloth coated with a mixture of gum and chalk made from tamarind seeds and then polished. With eye-aching attention and a very fine brush, artists mark out animals, flowers, deities and demons, which are then illuminated with bright colours. It makes for very beautiful and unique souvenirs.

Take the Bhubaneswar bus and look for the 'Raghurajpur The Craft Village' signpost 11km north of Puri, then walk the last 1km (don't get cornered by the few shops that have set up first but which are technically outside the village itself).

Konark

📞 06758 / POP 15,000

The iconic Sun Temple at Konark – a Unesco World Heritage Site – is one of India's signature buildings and Odisha's raison d'être. Most visitors are day-trippers from Bhubaneswar or Puri, but fine accomodation options along the beaches of the Ramchandi River should tempt more travellers to sleep over. After all, the temple is most majestic at dawn.

Originally nearer the coast (the sea has receded 3km), Konark was visible from far out at sea and known as the 'Black Pagoda' by sailors, in contrast to Puri's whitewashed Jagannath. The inland lighthouse near Chandrabhaga Beach is odd testament to that fact.

◉ Sights

Archaeological Museum   MUSEUM
(admission ₹10; ⏲ 8am-5pm, closed Fri) This interesting (and refreshingly cool and quiet) museum, just west of Yatrinivas, contains many impressive sculptures and carvings found during excavations of the Sun Temple.

✵ Festivals & Events

Konark Festival   DANCE
(⏲ 1-5 Dec) Steeped in traditional music and dance, the Konark Festival takes place in the open-air auditorium with the gorgeous Sun Temple as a backdrop.

🛏 Sleeping & Eating

Labanya Lodge   HOTEL $
(📞 9937073559; labanyalodge1@rediffmail.com; Sea Beach Rd; s ₹150-250, d ₹250-750, r with AC ₹1050; ❄ @) The best shoestringer choice, offering bright-coloured rooms in varying

SUN TEMPLE

The massive **Sun Temple** (Indian/foreigner ₹10/250, video ₹25, guide per hr ₹100; ⊙ dawn-8pm) was constructed in the mid-13th century, probably by Odishan king Narashimhadev I to celebrate his military victory over the Muslims, and was in use for maybe only three centuries. In the late 16th century the 40m-high *sikhara* (spire) partially collapsed: speculation about causes range from marauding Mughals removing the copper over the cupola to a ransacking Kalapahad displacing the Dadhinauti (arch stone), to simple wear and tear from recurring cyclones – the truth was apparently lost with Konark's receding shoreline. The entire temple was conceived as the cosmic chariot of the sun god Surya. Seven mighty prancing horses (representing the days of the week) rear at the strain of moving this stone leviathan on 24 stone cartwheels (representing the hours of the day) that stand around the base. The temple was positioned so that dawn light would illuminate the *deul* (temple sanctuary) interior and the presiding deity, which may have been moved to Jagannath Mandir in Puri in the 17th century.

The **gajasimha** (main entrance) is guarded by two stone lions crushing elephants and leads to the intricately carved **nritya mandapa** (dancing hall). Steps, flanked by straining horses, rise to the still-standing **jagamohan**. Behind is the spireless **deul**, with its three impressive chlorite images of Surya aligned to catch the sun at dawn, noon and sunset.

The base and walls present a chronicle in stone of Kalinga life; you'll see women cooking and men hunting. Many are in the erotic style for which Konark is famous and include entwined couples as well as solitary exhibitionists.

If there's anywhere worth hiring a guide, it's here. The temple's history is a complicated amalgam of fact and legend, and religious and secular imagery, and the guides' explanations are thought-provoking. They'll also show you features you might otherwise overlook – the woman with Japanese sandals, a giraffe (proving this area once traded with Africa) and even a man treating himself for venereal disease! Be sure your guide is registered. There are only 29 registered guides listed on the ancient board at the entrance to Konark, but there are actually a good 90 or so certified by various entities recognised by the Odisha goverment. Ask to see credentials.

sizes (bucket hot water only under ₹750), and a rooftop terrace.

⭐ **Nature Camp,**
Konark Retreat CAMPGROUND $$
(☑ 9437029989; www.naturecampindia.com; s/d/tr/q incl breakfast ₹2000/3000/4000/5000) Plopped down on the banks of the Ramchandi River 10km south of Konark in 2013, this new luxury tented camp is fashioned from stylish Swiss cottages fully equipped with electricity, fans, sit-down flush toilets, pleasant terraces and hot-water showers. It's right across the river from a sandy Bay of Bengal beach.

Yatrinivas HOTEL $$
(☑ 236820; yatrinivaskonark.das@gmail.com; r with AC ₹1182-2363, ste ₹3867, all incl breakfast & bed tea; ❄ @) One of the more pleasant OTDC hotels, set in a large, well-manicured garden next to the museum. It's especially atmospheric during the Konark Festival.

Lotus Eco Village HOTEL $$$
(☑ 236161; www.lotusresorthotels.com; Puri-Konark Marine Dr; villas/cottages incl breakfast from ₹6445/8594; ❄) About 7km from the Sun Temple on pretty Ramchandi Beach, this collection of rustic and weathered Canadian pine cottages are a beautiful getaway across a calm and swimmable islet catering to a few local fisherman and not much else; villas are surprisingly stylish inside and amenities include a small ayurvedic spa and a nice sandside restaurant (mains ₹120 to ₹350).

Suntemple Hotel INDIAN $$
(☑ 236890; Bus Stand Rd; mains ₹60-350; ⊙ 8am-3.30pm & 6-10pm) A busy, friendly place with a big range of Indian veg and non-veg dishes, recommended seafood dishes and traveller favourites such as chips and banana pancakes. There are two locations, a small one on the main road to the temple; and a bigger, better and cleaner version around the corner on Bus Stand Rd.

ℹ️ Information

The road from Bhubaneswar swings around the temple and past a couple of hotels and eateries before continuing to meet the coastal road to Puri. To the north and east of the temple is the **post office** (www.indiapost.gov.in; ⏲10am-5pm Mon-Sat), which sits next door to **Mahaveer Communication** (per hr ₹50; ⏲9am-10pm), where you can check internet; a State Bank of India ATM, the bus station and numerous souvenir shops. The **tourist office** (Yatrinivas hotel; ⏲10am-5pm Mon-Sat) can line up a registered guide to meet you at the temple.

ℹ️ Getting There & Away

Bus 441 is the most comfortable to Puri (₹40, one hour), though crowded minibuses regularly run along the coastal road as well (₹25, one hour). There are also regular departures to Bhubaneswar (₹40, two hours). An autorickshaw will take you to Puri, with a beach stop along the way, with negotiations usually beginning around ₹300 depending on the season.

Chilika Lake

Chilika Lake is Asia's largest brackish lagoon. Swelling from 600 sq km in April/May to 1100 sq km in the monsoon, the shallow lake is separated from the Bay of Bengal by a 60km-long sand bar called Rajhansa.

The lake is noted for the million-plus migratory birds – including grey-legged geese, herons, cranes and pink flamingos –

OFF THE BEATEN TRACK

MANGALAJODI

On Chilika's north shore, 60km northwest of Bhubaneswar, is this haven for resident and migratory birds, an ecotourism success story virtually unknown to the outside world until 2006. Six years prior, NK Bhujabal started **Wild Orissa** (www.wildorissa.org), a waterfowl safeguard committee that began the arduous process of converting bird poachers into protectors...and now ecotourism guides. In just a decade, the waterfowl population has climbed from 5000 to an estimated 40,000, spread among some 160 species. It's all best viewed on a sunrise canoe ride in winter, when tepid sunlight illuminates the waters and the cackle of various species of ducks provides the only soundtrack.

---

that flock here in winter (from November to mid-January) from as far away as Siberia and Iran and concentrate in a 3-sq-km area within the bird sanctuary on Nalabana Island.

Other attractions are rare Irrawaddy dolphins near Satapada, the pristine beach along Rajhansa, and Kalijai Island temple where Hindu pilgrims flock for the Makar Mela festival in January.

Satapada

☎ 06752

This small village, on a headland jutting southwestwards into the lake, is the starting point for most boat trips.

Boat trips from Satapada usually cruise towards the new sea mouth for a paddle in the sea and some dolphin- and bird-spotting en route. Travellers have reported dolphins being (illegally) herded and otherwise harassed; make it clear you don't want this.

OTDC (☎262077; Yatri Nivas hotel) has boats for hire (from ₹600) or a three-hour tour (per person ₹130) at 10am.

Dolphin Motor Boat Association (☎9040993732; Satapada jetty; 1½-8hr trips per boat ₹800-2500), a cooperative of local boat owners, has set-price trips mixing in dolphin sightseeing, Nalabana Bird Sanctuary and Kalijai Island temple.

Chilika Visitor Centre (admission ₹10; ⏲10am-5pm) is an exhibition on the lake, its wildlife and its human inhabitants. The centre has an upstairs observatory with a telescope and bird identification charts.

Considering the potential storybook lakeside setting, **Yatrinivas** (☎262077; d ₹550, with AC ₹1400; ❄) is surprisingly uninspired but perhaps the most architecturally interesting of the government-run hotels, with its crumbling elevated walkways. The AC complex is in better condition and offers lakeview rooms with balconies. A better-late-than-never renovation with 18 new rooms was started in late 2012. The restaurant (mains ₹35 to ₹140) has a good selection of Odishan fare, seafood dishes fresh from the lake and thalis (₹70 to ₹115).

It's no longer possible to cross the lake by ferry. Instead, daily ferries (vehicles ₹300, pedestrians ₹4, 30 minutes) ply between Satapada and the Janhikuda jetty just to the west, where vehicles can then head west and around to the north side of the lake. Daily departures are 7am, 10am, 1pm and 4pm, returning at 8am, 10.30am, 1.30pm and 4.30pm.

Travel agents in Puri can organise return trips on crowded buses for around ₹200 or far-more comfortable taxis for four or more (non-AC/AC ₹900/1200), including four hours in Satapada where you can organise your own boat. You can also catch the OTDC (p599) 7am AC bus from Puri, which returns at 5.30pm. Heritage Tours (p607) in Puri arranges a day on the lake, including transport, boat and lunch on fresh catch with a local fisherman (per person ₹900).

Several shops and *dhabas* (food stalls) line the road to the jetty. Hotel Avinandan is the cleanest. Don't forget to take water on your boat trip.

Barkul
☑06756

On the northern shore of Chilika, Barkul is just a scatter of houses, basic 'lodges' and food stalls on a lane off NH5. From here boats go to Nalabana and Kalijai Island. Nalabana is best visited in theearly morning and late afternoon, November to late February.

With a minimum of seven people, the OTDC (Panthanivas Barkul) runs tours to Kalijia and Nalabana for ₹730 per hour for a boat that holds up to seven. Taking in both sights takes about three hours. It's faster and costlier by speedboat (₹4000). You can also get out on the lake in a paddleboat (from ₹40).

Panthanivas Barkul (☑227488; pns. barkul@gmail.com; d ₹900, with AC ₹2256, d houseboat ₹3277, all incl breakfast; ☀@) has a great setting, and is one of the best government-run hotels in Odisha, with comfortable rooms overlooking the garden to the lake. Newer cottages are clean and inviting with lake views. The chilly air-con restaurant here does local seafood (at questionable value) and Chinese (mains ₹45 to ₹170).

Frequent buses dash along NH5 between Bhubaneswar (₹80, two hours) and Berhampur (₹76, 2½ hours). You can get off anywhere en route. Autorickshaws make long-hauls from Barkul village, stopping at Gopalpur-on-Sea (₹820, 1¾ hours), Berhampur railway station (₹820, two hours) as well as the nature reserve at Mangalajodi (₹850, 45 minutes).

A ferry (vehicles ₹300, pedestrians ₹4, 30 minutes) leaves from the Janhikuda jetty 62km west of Rambha for Satapada at 8am, 10.30am, 1.30pm and 4.30pm.

Rambha
☑06810

The small town of Rambha is the nearest place to stay for turtle-watching on Rushikulya beach.

Panthanivas Rambha (☑278346; rabi. dash09@gmail.com; dm ₹180, d ₹800, s/d cottage with AC ₹1450/2900, all incl breakfast & bed tea; ☀), about 200m off the main road, and 1km west of Rambha centre, looks a tad battered outside but has fine rooms (the AC rooms are better) with big clean bathrooms and balconies overlooking the lake. Newer cottages hog the charm (but views are partially obscured), and all beds have mozzie nets. The restaurant (mains ₹35 to ₹155) is very good, especially the seafood. One-hour speedboat (₹2000) or motorboat (₹600) tours of the lake are available by the hour.

There are regular bus services to/from Barkul (₹10, 30 minutes), Berhampur (₹25, one hour) and Bhubaneswar (₹100, 2½ hours).

Gopalpur-on-Sea
☑0680 / POP 6660

If you dig nosing about decaying seaside resorts, Gopalpur-on-Sea, a seaside town the British left to slide into history until Bengali holidaymakers rediscovered its attractions in the 1980s, is your bygone living museum on the ocean. Prior to this, it had a noble history as a seaport with connections to Southeast Asia, the evidence of which is still scattered through the town in the form of romantically deteriorating old buildings.

It's no paradise, but the peaceful and relatively clean beach is great for a stroll and it's oddly charismatic in its own strange, antiquated way.

For cash, there's an Axis Bank ATM on the main drag.

◎ Sights

Lighthouse   LANDMARK
(Indian/foreigner/child ₹10/25/3, camera ₹20; ◷3.30-5.30pm) Peering over the town is the lighthouse, with its immaculate gardens and petite staff cottages. It's a late-afternoon draw card and after puffing up the spiral staircase you're rewarded with expansive views and welcome cooling breezes.

🛏 Sleeping & Eating

Gopalpur-on-Sea can be booked out during holiday and festival time. Prices here are for the high season (November to January); discounts are available at other times. There is no power from 6pm to 7pm nightly.

Seaside Breeze HOTEL $
(☑ 2343075; s/d ₹600/750, with AC ₹1000/1250; ❄) Don't judge a hotel by its facade – you'll be pleasantly surprised how much character is packed into this great-value budget option shining sea-evoking blue right on the sand. While bathrooms are standard-issue, the well-kept rooms come in vibrant colors with cute bedspreads and tasteful artwork. The kitchen, run by the amicable Krishna, churns out home-cooked meals for guests (₹250 for three meals).

Hotel Sea Pearl HOTEL $
(☑ 2343557; www.hotelseapearlgopalpur.com; d ₹700-900, with AC ₹1380-1751; ❄ @) Any nearer the sea and it'd be in it; the big and popular Sea Pearl has some great rooms, especially the upper-storey, beach-facing, non-AC rooms, and a little private entrance to the beach.

Hotel Green Park HOTEL $
(☑ 2243716; greenpark016@yahoo.com; s ₹350, d ₹650, d with AC ₹850; ❄) One street back from the beach, Green Park is a friendly and good-value option. Some rooms have front-facing balconies and marble flooring throughout means it's easy to keep clean.

Mayfair Palm Beach HOTEL $$$
(☑ 6660101; www.mayfairhotels.com; d/ste incl breakfast & dinner from ₹11,018/16,527; ❄ @ 🛜 🏊) This brand new Mayfair is aiming to single-handedly put Gopalpur back on the tourist map. This historic property, originally built as Odisha's first luxury beach resort in 1914, boasts no shortfall of highlights: a long, winding walkway and manicured lawn down to a three-layer beach; a huge indoor lounge with a striking

---

ODISHA'S OLIVE RIDLEY TURTLES

One of the smallest sea turtles and a threatened species, the olive ridley marine turtle swims up from deeper waters beyond Sri Lanka to mate and lay eggs on Odisha's beaches. The main nesting sites are Gahirmatha (Bhitarkanika National Park), Devi river mouth near Konark and Rushikulya River mouth in Southern Odisha.

Turtle deaths due to fishing practices are unfortunately common. Although there are regulations, such as requiring the use of turtle exclusion devices (TEDs) on trawl nets and banning fishing from certain prohibited congregation and breeding areas, these laws are routinely flouted in Odisha.

Casuarina trees have been planted to help preserve Devi beach but they occupy areas of soft sand that are necessary for a turtle hatchery. Other potential threats include the upcoming Astaranga Seaport and Thermal Power Plant and the proposed Palur port, which is planned right next to the Rushikulya River mouth nesting site (which it would destroy if allowed to continue as planned).

In January and February the turtles congregate near nesting beaches and, if conditions are right, come ashore. If conditions aren't right, they reabsorb their eggs and leave without nesting.

Hatchlings emerge 50 to 55 days later and are guided to the sea by the luminescence of the ocean and stars. They can be easily distracted by bright lights; unfortunately NH5 runs within 2km of Rushikulya beach. Members of local turtle clubs in Gokharkuda, Podampeta and Purunabandha village gather up disoriented turtles and take them to the sea. It is best to visit the nesting beach at dawn when lights are not necessary.

The best place to see nesting and hatching is on the northern side of Rushikulya River, near the villages of Purunabandh and Gokharkuda, 20km from the nearest accommodation in Rambha. During nesting and hatching, activity takes place throughout the night: don't use lights.

Ask staff at OTDC Panthanivas Rambha what conditions are like, or contact the **Wildlife Society of Odisha** (☑ 6712311513; kachhapa@gmail.com; Shantikunj, Link Rd, Cuttack). Rickshaws between Rambha and Rushikulya cost ₹400 return for a half day and ₹800 for the full day.

teakwood bar; private in-water cabanas at the gorgeous pool; and classy, understated rooms with sink-in bathtubs, some of which boast massive private plunge pools and extensive terraces with large baybeds. The restaurant does outstanding seafood (mains ₹250 to ₹750), including culture-clash cusine like Thai crab tandoori. Class act.

Krishna's INDIAN, CHINESE $
(mains ₹30-70; ⊙ 8am-10pm) Mainly Indian and Chinese standards (nicely executed) and excellent *kati rolls*. Ask nicely in quiet season and the kitchen can produce good pancakes, pasta, fish and chips or a bang-up garlic calamari. Expect to pay ₹100 and up for some of the seafood. Eat outside or grab a provided laptop and eat inside a small AC internet room the super-friendly owner has installed.

ⓘ Getting There & Away

Frequent, crowded minibuses travel to Berhampur (₹10, one hour), where you can catch onward transport by rail or bus. Alternatively, an autorickshaw will cost you about ₹180 and a taxi ₹300.

SOUTHWESTERN ODISHA

As of 2012, permits are once again required for foreigners venturing into the tribal areas. The process will likely be taken care of by a government-approved tour agency, but play it safe and give yourself a good 10 days for the paperwork to play itself out. Photography and overnight stays are now strictly prohibited by law. If you are going independently, you will need to visit the district tourist officer to initiate permissions.

Rayagada

☑ 06856 / POP 58,000
Rayagada is the base for visiting the weekly Wednesday **Chatikona market** at Bissamcuttack (about 40km north). Here, highly ornamented Dongria Kondh and Desia Kondh villagers from the surrounding Niayamgiri Hills bring their produce and wares to sell. Alongside piles of chillies and dried fish are bronze animal sculptures made locally using the lost wax method. The market is considered tourist-friendly, but it's a process.

Tejasvi International (☑ 224925; www.hoteltejasvi.com; Collector Residence Rd; s/d/ste incl breakfast ₹1173/1386/2665; ❉ ☜), a smart business hotel done up according to the ancient Indian architectural science of Vastu Shatra (Hindu Feng Shui!), is the best-equipped hotel in Southern Odisha as well as being the same price as far more drab places in town. At the friendly **Hotel Rajbhavan** (☑ 223777; Main Rd; d/tr ₹700/900, r with AC from ₹1100-1400; ❉), stick to higher category rooms. There's a good multicuisine restaurant (mains ₹50 to ₹170). The latter is just across the main road from the train station while Tejasvi is also walkable – take a right out of the station and then your first left and it's about 500m down the road on your left.

To visit Chatikona independently, you'll need to get in touch with Rayagada's tourist officer, **Ramal Loechan Gamango** (☑ 9439838936), and provide a copy of your passport and visa. He will then facilitate your paperwork through the appropriate channels. Note that although you are not required to visit Chatikona with a tour group, the local district will provide you with an escort.

From the Rayagada bus stand, there are three early-morning local buses to Chatikona (₹25, two hours, 4.45am, 6.30am and 9.30am). Buses to Jeypore (₹80, five hours, 7am, 10.30am, noon, 2pm, 3pm and 4.50pm) and Bhubaneswar (₹320, 12 hours, 4pm, 5pm, 6pm, 6.30pm and 7.30pm) also depart from here. The 18447 Hirakhand Express departs Bhubaneswar daily at 7.35pm reaching Rayagada at 4.50am and Koraput at 9.50am.

Jeypore

☑ 06854 / POP 77,000
Jeypore is the least interesting base for visiting the amazingly colourful Onkadelli market. There is little reason to choose here over Koraput other than the 22km head start to Onkadelli. If you plan to visit the market, you'll need to obtain permission at Odisha Tourism (p616) in Koraput.

Modern, two-star side-by-side sister hotels **Hotel Mani Krishna** (☑ 231139; www.hotelmanikrishna.com; MG Rd; s/d ₹695/795, with AC from ₹995/1095; ❉) and **Hotel Sai Krishna** (☑ 230253; www.hotelsaikrishna.com; MG Rd; s/d ₹695/795, with AC from ₹1095/1195, all incl breakfast; ❉ ☜) both offer spotless rooms, international cable and room service (at Mani)

ODISHA RAYAGADA

WORTH A TRIP

ONKADELLI

This small village, 65km from Jeypore, has a most remarkable and vibrant Thursday **market** (best time 10am to 1pm) that throngs with Bonda, Gadaba, Mali and Didai villagers. In the morning it's all business on the vegetable side; in the afternoon, the alcohol market revs up, and entire families get sloshed – *including* infants.

The market has been traditionally popular with tour groups; however, due to Maoist activity in the region, outcries of 'Human Safari!' by some and an Odishan goverment that cannot (or will not) ensure security of tourists, visits to Onkadelli were declining during research for this edition and some conservative local tour operators have dropped it from their regularly scheduled tours. Check ahead with the recomended tour operators on the ground in Bhubaneswar or Puri as the situation was very fluid at time of research.

Onkadelli is best accessed by hire car and can only be visited with a professional guide, who will palpably enrich your experience, keep the peace if things get ugly among the alcohol and the bows and arrows and enforce the new rules. It's feasible to come to Jeypore or Koraput independently and organise a guide (₹1000 to ₹1500). If you opt to go on your own, photographs are now strictly prohibited by law, and you'll need to stop by the tourist office in Koraput to handle the paperwork. Plan ahead – at least 10 days to be safe – and bring copies of your passport and visa.

For those willing to put in the effort, Onkadelli is a sight for the senses and a true Odisha highlight.

and a great Indian restaurant (at Sai). The all-AC **Hello Jeypore** (✆ 231127; www.hoteljeypore.com; NH43 ; s/d incl breakfast from ₹795/995; ✳@🛜❄) is the most comfortable.

From the old bus stand there are frequent buses to Koraput (₹15, one hour, every 30 minutes); others go to Berhampur (₹350, 12 hours, 7.30pm, 8.30pm, 9pm and 9.30pm), Bhubaneswar (non-AC/AC ₹450/550, 12 to 16 hours, 5.30pm, 6pm, 6.30pm, 6.45pm, 7pm and 7.15pm) and Rayagada (₹90, five hours, 4.35am, 5.45am, 7.15am, 8.15am, noon, 5.30pm and 7pm).

To reach Onkadelli (₹40, three hours) there are three morning buses of interest to marketgoers, at 7.30am and 9am from the Ghoroi Bus Union's office on Byepass Rd; and at 8.30am from the new private bus stand on NH43. A private taxi including waiting time runs ₹2500 for up to four passengers.

Koraput

✆ 06852 / POP 40,000

Koraput is just a few kilometres from Jeypore and is a far more interesting base for visits to Onkadelli. The temple is fascinating, especially for non-Hindus who couldn't enter the Jagannath temple in Puri.

Odisha Tourism (www.orissatourism.gov.in; Tourist Complex, near Station Circuit House; ⊙10am-5pm Mon-Sat) has information and can arrange car hire as well as initiate the permission process for Onkadelli market.

The **Jagannath temple** has an exhibition of deities of the different states of India. There's also a selection of local forms of *ossa* (also known as *rangoli*), traditional patterns made with white and coloured powders on doorsteps. At the back of the temple is a series of apses containing statuettes of Jagannath in his various guises and costumes. Nearby, there is a **Tribal Museum** full of English information on the tribes from the highland areas, but it never seems to be open when we visit.

The **Raj Residency** (✆ 251591; www.hotelrajresidency.com; Post Office Rd; s/d ₹550/750, with AC from ₹900/1100; ✳🛜) is the best digs in town, offering modern rooms with plasma TVs, friendly service and free wi-fi (lobby only). Chicken tikka butter masala at the dimly lit Indian/Chinese restaurant (mains ₹40 to ₹150) was the best hotel meal we had in Southwestern Odisha four years running!

The temple manages three budget hotels just outside its grounds. **Atithi Bhaban** (✆ 250610; atithibhaban@gmail.com; d ₹250, with AC ₹500; ✳) has a pure veg restaurant (thalis ₹50) and simple but great-value AC doubles. **Atithi Nivas** (✆ 250610; atithibhaban@gmail.com; s ₹150) is singles only, but solo travellers are better off springing for a much nicer double at Atithi Bhaban. **Yatri Nivas**

(☎9337622637; d ₹175) has distinctly basic crashpads.

The 18447/8 Hirakhand Express plies daily between Bhubaneswar and Koraput. There are buses every 30 minutes to Jeypore (₹20, 40 minutes) and services to Rayagada (₹70 to ₹100, three hours, 11 per day), Sambalpur (₹260, eight hours, 3pm) and Bhubaneswar (₹470, 12 hours, 5pm, 5.45pm, 6.15pm and 7.15pm). Fares to Bhubaneswar increase ₹100 for AC.

There is a handy State Bank of India ATM and internet at the bus stand.

NORTHEASTERN ODISHA

Northeastern Odisha is best known for its nature sanctuaries, notably Bhitarkanika and Similipil National Park (though foreigners were being denied entry to the latter at time of research due to an array of safety issues within the park) and the excellent triple Buddhist ruins at Ratnagiri, Udayagiri and Lalitgiri.

Balasore

☑ 06782 / POP 156,500

Balasore, the first major town in northern Odisha geographically, was once an important trading centre. Now it's a noisy, ramshackle staging post for Chandipur, Similipal National Park and the main rail line.

Odisha Tourism (www.orissatourism.gov.in; ☺10am-5pm Mon-Sat) is located in Panthanivas Balasore but skip the hotel. Hotel Chandrabhaga (☎261808; s/d from ₹400/500, with AC from ₹800/900; ❄), 1km from the bus station, has spotless, good-value rooms with large balconies, though it's amazing what just a few years of wear and tear can do to a new Indian hotel. Tolerable for a quick overnight is Hotel Swarnachuda (☎262657; swarnachuda@yahoo.com; s/d/tr from ₹150/200/250, s/d with AC from ₹600/700; ❄), just 100m from the bus stand; go AC here, trust us!

From the bus stand at Remuna Golai, there are private buses for Kolkata (₹230, 4½ hours, 6am), Bhubaneswar (₹199, 4½ hours, 7.30am, 9.25am and 4pm) and Baripada (₹50, two hours, several between 9am and 10am). The sporadic service to Chandipur makes an autorickshaw (₹230) a better option.

Balasore is on the main rail line. Options include the 12837 Howrah-Puri Express departing for Puri daily at 1.55am (sleeper/3AC/2AC ₹163/416/640, five hours). For Chennai, the 12841 Howrah-Chennai Coromandel Express calls at 6.02pm (sleeper/3AC/2AC ₹426/1185/1845, 11½ hours).

Chandipur

☑ 06782

The laid-back seaside village of Chandipur, which ambles down to the ocean through a short avenue of casuarina and palm trees,

ODISHA BALASORE

OFF THE BEATEN TRACK

CHANDOORI SAI

Some 50km northeast of Koraput in the tiny Adivasis village of Goudaguda, you'll find this Australian-run retreat (☎9443342241; www.chandoorisai.com; Goudaguda; s/d incl meals 3500/5000; @), Odisha's most stylish rural accommodation bar none. Built from the ground up by the hands of some 60 Poraja tribal men and women, it's a sustainable earthen-walled refuge with beautiful terracotta flooring and bamboo-sheeted ceilings. The main lobby is dressed up with colourful hanging saris and the local village pottery present throughout. House specialities include supreme tranquility and curing of culinary homesickness. But the real coup is the guest interaction with tribal women, who act as cultural ambassadors on the property and guides through the village. This brief assimilation into the vibrant Adivasis way of life is priceless. The owner is a hard-driving ex–oil man, who holds the hospitality on a tight leash.

To reach Chandoori Sai, catch the 18447 Hirakhand Express towards Koraput and get off at Kakirigumma, an 8.09am arrival; or, most scenically, on the 18512 Visakhapatnam-Koraput Intercity Express on Mondays or Fridays, leaving Visakhapatnam in Andhra Pradesh at 2.25pm, getting off at Laxmipur Rd at 8pm. The guesthouse will pick you up.

seems content as a declining underachiever. The draw here is a huge 'vanishing sea': the bay recedes an astonishing 4km at low tide – a sight to see. It's safe to swim here when there's enough water.

The new and contemporary **Arpita Beach Resort** (☑270041; www.arpitabeachresort.com; d from ₹2147; ☒@☎), 300m from the beach, is the nicest place to stay, with rain-style showers, LCD televisions and wi-fi. The colourful restaurant (mains ₹55 to ₹170) far outclasses the town. **Hotel Shubham** (☑270025; www.hotelshubham.com; d ₹800-1050, with AC from ₹1275; ☒@) offers a dizzying range of spotless and comfortable rooms (stick to the new wing), a pleasant garden and an average restaurant. **Panthanivas Chandipur** (☑270051; dm ₹280, d from ₹900, with AC from ₹1503; ☒@) is set on a sprawling campus in a great location overlooking the beach, but seems overpriced.

Regular buses ply the NH5 between Bhubaneswar and Balasore. From Balasore, taxis and autorickshaws (₹170 to ₹230) can take you the 15km to Chandipur.

Bhitarkanika Wildlife Sanctuary

Three rivers flow out to sea at Bhitarkanika forming a tidal maze of muddy creeks and mangroves. Most of this 672-sq-km delta forms this wonderful **sanctuary** (www.bhitarkanika.org; Indian/foreigner per day ₹20/1000, camera/video ₹50/1000; ☼closed 1 May-30 Sep), a significant biodiversity hotspot. The only way to get around the sanctuary is by boat. Many boats are a little battered, with old tyres on ropes acting as life preservers: this definitely adds piquancy to the thrill of boating on waters where enormous crocodiles – 1646 at last count – can suddenly surface rather close by.

The best time to visit is from December to February. Hundreds of massive estuarine crocodiles bask on mud flats waiting for the next meal to swim by. Birdwatchers will find eight species of brilliantly coloured kingfishers, plus 207 other species.

First stop is a permit check at Khola jetty before chugging on to **Dangmal Island**, where you'll find a successful crocodile breeding and conservation program (and accommodation). Pythons, water monitors, baboons, wild boar and numerous spotted deer can also be seen. Herons arrive at **Bagagahan Island** in early June and nest until early December, when they move on to Chilika Lake. Raucous open-billed storks have set up a permanent rookery here.

🛏 Sleeping & Eating

★**Nature Camp Bhitarkanika**   CAMPGROUND $$$
(☑9437016054; www.bhitarkanikatour.com; dm/s/d/tr/q incl meals & excursions ₹2000/3000/4000/5000/6000) ❧ A special experience awaits at this small tented camp in the heart of Dangmal Village, built with the help of villagers and with a sustainable foot on the ground just steps from the sanctuary. The stylish Swiss cottage tents are fully equipped with electricity, fans, sit-down

---

OFF THE BEATEN TRACK

ROOPARK VILLAGE

Tucked way, way off the grid 37km from Balasore in the rural village of Katabonia, this Santali village-themed **guesthouse** (☑9830304049, 033 32419633; www.roopark.co.in; Kantabonia; tent ₹1275, cottage ₹1675, with AC ₹2275; ☒) ❧ is chock-full of tribal kitsch and is a great getaway for those wanting to immerse yourself in local culture without a foreigner in sight (apparently, we were the first to visit!). Built with sustainable materials, the homey thatched cottages, nearly indistinguishable from the actual surrounding villages, are bedazzled with tribal designs and are surprisingly comfortable and sit under the massive Nilgiri mountains that serve as the postcard-perfect backdrop. You can laze about the hammocks strewn amongst the lush and colourful gardens watching local villagers slap *Chita* designs on the ground; or get out and about on local treks to visit village temples, or go mountain biking in the hills or rock climbing in the towering surrounding mountains.

As of our visit, there was virtually no English spoken, so you'll need to get by on flagrant gestures, cutesy winks and convoluted facial expressions, but you won't find anything else quite like this in Northeastern Odisha.

flush toilets and pleasant terraces, and, even if you didn't see a crocodile, wonderful rustic Odisha cuisine is worth the trip alone. Tour options include three-day/two-night packages (₹5125 per person based on double occupancy); these begin and end in Bhubaneswar and include full board, entrance fees, a boat trip, a nature trek and transport.

ℹ️ Information

Permits, accommodation and boat transport can all be organised in Dangmal. Organise boats (per day week/weekend from ₹3300/4000, negotiable) with one of the private operators whose mobile numbers are posted at the jetty and park entrance.

ℹ️ Getting There & Away

You'll save yourself some sanity by visiting Bhitarkanika on an organised tour arranged in Bhubaneswar, but die-hards have a few options. A newly paved road all the way to Dangmal means you can bypass the old route via Chandbali and arrive at Nature Camp, Khola Jetty and the main Dangmal gate by road. Catch the once-daily OSRTC bus from Bhubaneswar's bus stand to Ishwarpur (₹80, 5½ hours, noon) and then an autorickshaw the final 15km to Dangmal village (₹250 to ₹300, 45 minutes) as you will likely miss the one Sujata bus to Dangmal (₹15, 30 minutes, 5.30pm).

Ratnagiri, Udayagiri & Lalitgiri

These Buddhist ruins are about 60km northeast of Cuttack. You can now sleep here, which is quite a peaceful proposition for those looking for a countryside experience. Visiting is still easiest by car hire organised in Bhubaneswar or Puri but public transport is available.

Ratnagiri

Ratnagiri has the most interesting and extensive **ruins** (Indian/foreigner ₹5/100, video

₹25; ☉ dawn-dusk). Two large monasteries flourished here from the 6th to 12th centuries. Noteworthy are an exquisitely carved doorway and the remains of a 10m-high stupa. The excellent **museum** (☉8am-5pm) contains beautiful sculptures from the three sites. The new **Toshali Ratnagiri Resort** (📞9937023791; www.toshaliratnagiri.com; s/d incl breakfast ₹2000/3500; ❄️ @ 🏊), just across the street, is tranquilly located surrounded by rice fields and a peaceful village pond. Nice rooms flank an interior enclosed courtyard and a renovation underway on our visit was bringing in a pool, a bar, an ayurvedic spa and a coffee shop. Toshali is also planning additional hotels at Udayagiri and Lalitgiri.

Udayagiri

Another **monastery complex** is being excavated here in lush surrounds. There's a large pyramidal brick stupa with a seated Buddha and some beautiful doorjamb carvings. There's no entry fee, but unhelpful guides may attach themselves to you then ask for a donation (not compulsory).

Lalitgiri

Several **monastery ruins** (Indian/foreigner ₹5/100, video ₹25; ☉ dawn-dusk) are scattered up a hillside leading to a small museum and a hillock crowned with a shallow stupa. During excavations of the stupa in the 1970s, a casket containing gold and silver relics was found. It's also notable for its surrounding village atmosphere.

ℹ️ Getting There & Away

From Bhubaneswar's bus stand, you can catch a bus to Chandikhol (₹55, two hours), where options to Ratnagiri – the best spot to sleep at time of research – include public buses (₹20, one hour) or a taxi (₹400, 45 minutes).

Madhya Pradesh & Chhattisgarh

Includes ➡

Best Places to Eat

- ➡ Raja's Café (p642)
- ➡ Bapu Ki Kutia (p648)
- ➡ Silver Saloon (p627)
- ➡ Under the Mango Tree (p648)

Best Places to Stay

- ➡ Kipling Camp (p676)
- ➡ Usha Kiran Palace (p627)
- ➡ Orchha Homestay (p632)
- ➡ Labboo's Cafe (p667)

Why Go?

The vast state of Madhya Pradesh (MP) doesn't enjoy the same prominence as its more celebrated neighbouring states, which is why it can reward travellers with unparalled opportunities to take a detour off the tourist trail and delve into India's heartland.

At the top of your list should be Khajuraho's temples displaying some of the finest stone carvings in India. The famous erotic sculptures are just a portion of this architectural highlight in a region blessed with palaces, forts and stupas. Tigers are the other big attraction here, and your chances of spotting a tiger in MP's national parks are as good as anywhere in India. Laid-back traveller havens such as Orchha and Omkareshwar display the spiritual, scenic, and chill-out flavours for which India is renowned, while the adventurous can foray into tribal Chhattisgarh, which split from Madhya Pradesh in 2000 and remains far removed from mainstream Indian culture.

When to Go
Bhopal

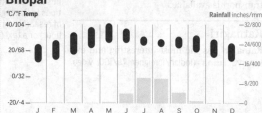

Nov–Feb Most pleasant time to visit central India, although mornings will be chilly.

Apr–Jun Best chance of spotting tigers; vegetation is thin and water sources are few.

Jul–Sep Monsoon time, but places such as Chhattisgarh are at their most beautiful.

Food & Drink

The combined region of Madhya Pradesh and Chhattisgarh is enormous, so naturally food varies across the land. Bhopal produces some exquisite meat and fish dishes as well as some great biryanis and kebabs. In the drier regions of the north and west, you'll find more wheat-based foods and less rice. There's wonderful fruit to be had, especially in the lush south and southeast regions – mangoes and custard apples are the highlights – and those brave enough to venture to the tribal markets of Chhattisgarh will see locals eating live ants. The favourite tipple, meanwhile, is a liquor made from the flowers of the *mahuwa* tree, which you'd be advised to drink with caution – it's potent.

DON'T MISS

Madhya Pradesh is bursting at the seams with fabulous places to visit, but two things you really shouldn't leave without seeing are the exquisite temples of **Khajuraho** and the national parks that are home to India's most magnificent creature – the tiger.

Top State Festivals

➡ **Festival of Dance** (🕙 Feb/Mar, Khajuraho, p633) Weeklong event with the cream of Indian classical dancers performing amid floodlit temples.

➡ **Shivaratri Mela** (🕙 Feb/Mar, Pachmarhi, p655) Up to 100,000 Shaivite pilgrims, sadhus (holy people) and Adivasis (tribal people) attend celebrations at Mahadeo Temple. Participants bring symbolic tridents and hike up Chauragarh Hill to plant them by the Shiva shrine.

➡ **Magh Mela** (🕙 Apr/May, Ujjain, p659) Huge annual religious fair held on the banks of the Shipra River at Ujjain; pilgrim numbers increase dramatically every 12th year for the masmsive Kumbh Mela (next held in Ujjain in 2016).

➡ **Ahilyabai Holkar's Birthday** (🕙 Apr/May, Maheshwar, p666) The Holkar queen's birthday is celebrated with palanquin (enclosed seats carried on poles on four men's shoulders) processions through the town.

➡ **Navratri** (🕙 Sep/Oct, Ujjain, p659) The Festival of Nine Nights, leading up to Dussehra, is celebrated with fervour in Ujjain. Lamps on the large pillars in Harsiddhi Mandir are lit.

➡ **Dussehra** (🕙 Oct, Jagdalpur, p680) Dedicated to local goddess Danteshwari, this 75-day festival culminates in eight days of (immense) chariot pulling around the streets.

➡ **Tansen Music Festival** (🕙 Nov/Dec, Gwalior, p623) Four-day music festival attracting classical musicians and singers from all over India; free performances are usually staged at the tomb of Tansen, one of the most revered composer-musicians of Hindustani classical music.

MAIN POINTS OF ENTRY

No international airports, but the main cities – Bhopal, Indore, Jabalpur and Raipur – plus big tourist spots such as Khajuraho are connected by rail and air to one or more of Delhi, Mumbai (Bombay) and Kolkata (Calcutta).

Fast Facts

➡ **Population:** 72.6 million (Madhya Pradesh), 25.5 million (Chhattisgarh)

➡ **Area:** 308,000 sq km (Madhya Pradesh), 135,000 sq km (Chhattisgarh)

➡ **Capital:** Bhopal (Madhya Pradesh), Raipur (Chhattisgarh)

➡ **Main languages:** Hindi, regional tribal languages

➡ **Sleeping prices:** $ below ₹1000, $$ ₹1000 to ₹5000, $$$ above ₹5000

➡ **Eating prices:** $ mains below ₹150, $$ ₹150 to ₹300, $$$ above ₹300

Top Tip

If you're serious about seeing a tiger, plan and budget for at least three days of jeep safaris, with two safaris each day.

Resources

➡ **Chhattisgarh Tourist Board** (www.chhattisgarhtourism.net)

➡ **Madhya Pradesh Tourist Board** (www.mptourism.com)

➡ **Save Our Tigers** (www.saveourtigers.com) Tiger protection.

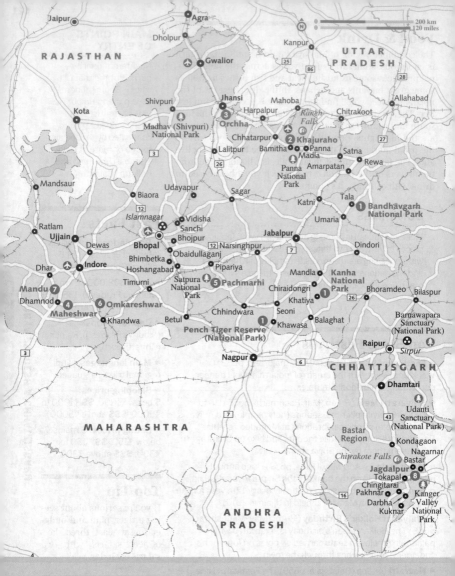

Madhya Pradesh & Chhattisgarh Highlights

1 Venture deep into tiger territory at one of Mahdya Pradesh's three big tiger parks: **Pench Tiger Reserve** (p678), **Kanha National Park** (p674) and **Bandhavgarh National Park** (p676)

2 Blush at the erotic carvings on the exquisite temples in **Khajuraho** (p633)

3 Bed down in a former palace or a mud-hut homestay in laidback **Orchha** (p632)

4 Soak up the spiritual vibe at the bathing ghats in magical **Maheshwar** (p666)

5 Cool off under a waterfall in **Pachmarhi** (p655), Madhya Pradesh's only hill station

6 Chill out on the Om-shaped holy island of **Omkareshwar** (p665)

7 Cycle around India's finest Afghan ruins at the hilltop getaway of **Mandu** (p668)

8 Watch locals eat live red ants at a tribal market near **Jagdalpur** (p680)

History

Virtually all phases of Indian history made their mark on the region historically known as Malwa, starting with the rock paintings at Bhimbetka and Pachmarhi, which date back more than 10,000 years. They tell of a cultural succession through the late Stone Age to the start of recorded history in the 3rd century BC, when the Buddhist emperor Ashoka controlled the Mauryan empire from Malwa and built Sanchi's Great Stupa.

The Mauryas were followed by the Sungas and the Guptas – Chandragupta II (r AD 382–401) ruled from Ujjain and had the caves cut at Udaigiri – before the Huns rampaged across the state. Around 1000 years ago the Parmaras reigned in southwest Madhya Pradesh – notably Raja Bhoj, who ruled for over half a century across this region and who founded the now-ruined town of Bhojpur, the magnificent fort of Mandu and, according to some scholars, the city of Bhopal.

The Chandelas ruled over much of central India from the 9th to the 13th centuries. It was their nimble-fingered sculptors who enlivened the facades of some 85 temples in Khajuraho with erotic scenes before the dynasty eventually moved its capital from Khajuraho to Mahoba. Between the 12th and 16th centuries, the region experienced continuing struggles between Hindu and Muslim rulers, and Mandu was the scene of some decisive clashes. The Mughals were eventually superseded by the Marathas after a 27-year war (1681–1707) – the longest in India's history. The Marathas went on to rule the region for more than a century before they fell to the British (1818) for whom the Scindia maharajas of Gwalior were powerful allies.

With the States Reorganisation Act of 1956, several former states were combined to form Madhya Pradesh. In 2000, Chhattisgarh became an independent state.

NORTHERN MADHYA PRADESH

Gwalior

📳 0751 / POP 1.05 MILLION

Famous for its medieval hilltop fort, and described by Mughal emperor Babur as 'the pearl amongst fortresses in India', Gwalior makes an interesting stop en route to some of the better-known destinations in this part of India. The city also houses the elaborate Jai Vilas Palace, the historic seat of the Scindias, one of the country's most revered families.

History

Gwalior's legendary beginning stems from the 8th century when a hermit known as Gwalipa is said to have cured the Rajput chieftain Suraj Sen of leprosy using water from Suraj Kund tank (which remains in Gwalior Fort). Renaming the chieftain Suhan Pal, Gwalipa foretold that Suhan's descendants would remain in power as long as they retained the name Pal. Suhan's next 83 descendants did just that, but number 84 changed his name to Tej Karan and, naturally, lost his kingdom.

In 1398 the Tomar dynasty came to power. Gwalior Fort became the focus of continual clashes with neighbouring powers and reached its ascendancy under Raja Man Singh (r 1486–1516). Two centuries of Mughal rule followed, ending with the fort's capture by the Marathas in 1754.

Over the next 50 years the fort changed hands several times, including twice to the British before finally passing to the Scindias.

During the First War of Independence (Indian Uprising) in 1857, Maharaja Jayajirao remained loyal to the British but his troops rebelled, and in mid-1858 the fort was the scene of some of the uprising's final events. Near here the British defeated rebel leader Tantia Topi and it was in the final assault on the fort that the rani (wife) of Jhansi was killed.

⊙ Sights

★ **Gwalior Fort**   FORT

(⏱ dawn–dusk) Perched majestically on top of a 3km-long plateau overlooking Gwalior, this hilltop fort is an imposing, eye-catching sight, with the circular towers of the dominating Man Singh Palace ringed with turquoise tiles.

There are two approaches to the fort, both steep treks. Rickshaws can drive you up to Urvai, the western gate, so it's tempting to go that way because vehicles cannot drive up from the eastern entrance. But the western entrance is an anticlimax compared with the formidable view of the fort from the eastern approach, which makes entering from the east well worth the climb. Don't, however,

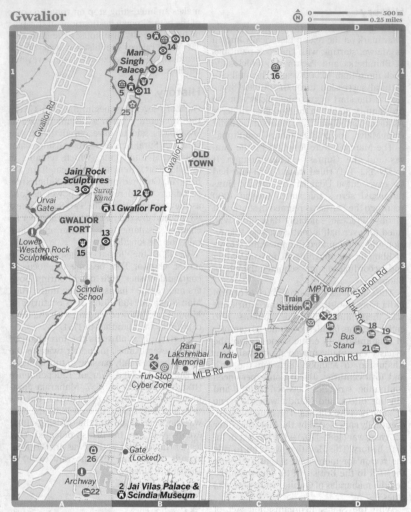

miss the rock sculptures, which are part of the way down the western side.

A **sound-and-light show** (Indian/foreigner ₹75/250; ⏰ English 8.30pm Mar-Oct, 7.30pm Nov-Feb, Hindi 7.30pm Mar-Oct, 6.30pm Nov-Feb) is held nightly in the amphitheatre.

Much of the fort is now occupied by the prestigious private Scindia School, established by Maharaja Madhavrao Scindia in 1897 for the education of Indian nobility.

➡ **Eastern Entrances**

From the east a series of gates punctuates the worn steps of the path leading up to the fort. At the bottom, the first gate you pass

through is **Gwalior Gate** (Alamgiri Gate), dating from 1660, and leading to the State Archeological Museum. The second, Bansur (Archer's Gate), has disappeared, so the next is **Badalgarh**, named after Badal Singh, Man Singh's uncle.

Further up is **Ganesh Gate**, built in the 15th century. Nearby is **Kabutar Khana**, a small pigeon house, and a small four-pillared **Hindu temple** to the hermit Gwalipa, after whom both fort and town are named.

You'll pass a 9th-century Vishnu shrine known as **Chatarbhuj Mandir** (Temple of the Four-Armed) before reaching the fifth gate,

Gwalior

Hathiya Paur (Elephant Gate), now the entrance to the palace grounds (as the sixth gate, Hawa Gate, no longer exists).

➡ **State Archaeological Museum**

(Indian/foreigner ₹10/100, camera/video ₹50/200; ⏱10am-5pm Tue-Sun) This museum is within **Gujari Mahal**, just through Gwalior Gate at the base of the fort. Built in the 15th cen-tury by Man Singh for his favourite rani, the palace is now rather deteriorated. There's a large collection of Hindu and Jain sculp-tures, including the famed Salabhanjika (an exceptionally carved female figure) plus cop-ies of Bagh Caves frescoes.

➡ ★**Man Singh Palace**

(Indian/foreigner ₹5/100, video ₹25; ⏱ dawn-dusk) This imperial-style palace is one of the more unusually decorated monuments you'll see in India: the outer walls include a frieze of yellow ducks! These – and mosaic tiling of elephants, tigers and crocodiles in blue, yel-low and green – give it its alternative iden-tity of Chit Mandir (Painted Palace).

Built by Tomar ruler Man Singh between 1486 and 1516, this fine example of early Hindu architecture consists of two open courts surrounded by apartments on two levels. Below ground lie another two sto-reys constructed for hot weather, connected by 'speaking tubes' built into the walls, and used by the Mughals as prison cells.

The ticket counter is opposite the palace, while another ticket counter nearby sells tickets for the ruins of Shah Jahan Palace, Karan Palace and several other dilapidated palaces in the northwest of the fort. Also opposite the palace is the small **Archeo-logical Survey of India (ASI) museum** (admission ₹5; ⏱9am-5pm Sat-Thu) that was a hospital under British rule.

➡ **Sasbahu Temples**

The Mayan-like Sasbahu, or Mother-in-Law and Daughter-in-Law Temples, date from the 9th to 11th centuries. Mother-in-Law, dedicated to Vishnu, has four gigantic pil-lars supporting its heavy roof, layered with carvings. The smaller Daughter-in-Law, dedicated to Shiva, is also stacked with sculptures.

➡ **Teli ka Mandir**

Used as a drinks factory and coffee shop by the British after the First War of Independ-ence (Indian Uprising) of 1857, this 30m-high, 8th-century temple is the oldest monu-ment in the compound.

The modern, gold-topped **gurdwara** (Sikh Temple) nearby is dedicated to Sikh hero Guru Har Gobind, who was imprisoned in Man Singh Palace from 1617 to 1619.

➡ ★**Jain Rock Sculptures**

While there are sculptures carved into the rock at a few points on the plateau, includ-ing on the way up from Gwalior Gate, the most impressive is the upper set on the western approach, between Urvai Gate and the inner fort walls. Mostly cut into the cliff face in the mid-15th century, they represent nude figures of *tirthankars* (the 24 great Jain teachers). They were defaced by Babur's Muslim army in 1527 but have been more recently repaired.

There are more than 30 images, including a splendid 17m-high standing sculpture of the first *tirthankar,* Adinath.

★ Jai Vilas Palace & Scindia Museum PALACE

(Indian/foreigner ₹60/350, camera/video ₹70/120; ⊙10am-5.30pm Thu-Tue) The museum occupies some 35 rooms of the Scindias' opulent Jai Vilas Palace, built by Maharaja Jayajirao in 1874 using prisoners from the fort. The convicts were rewarded with the 12-year job of weaving the hall carpet, one of the largest in Asia.

Supposedly, eight elephants were suspended from the durbar (royal court) hall ceiling to check it could cope with two 12.5m-high, 3.5-tonne chandeliers with 250 lightbulbs, said to be the largest pair in the world.

Bizarre items fill the rooms: cut-glass furniture, stuffed tigers and a ladies-only swimming pool with its own boat. The cavernous dining room displays the pièce de résistance, a model railway with a silver train that carried after-dinner brandy and cigars around the table.

Note: the gates to the north and south are locked so you have to enter the palace from the west.

Tomb of Tansen HISTORIC BUILDING

Tucked away in the winding lanes of the Old Town, and in the same compound as the resplendent tomb of Mohammed Gaus, is the smaller, simpler tomb of Tansen, a singer much admired by Akbar and held to be the father of Hindustani classical music. Chewing the leaves from the tamarind tree here supposedly enriches your voice. Free performances are staged during the four-day Tansen Music Festival in November/December.

Tours

MP Tourism's little yellow bus, Gwalior Darshan, takes passengers on a full-day **city tour** (per person ₹105; ⊙10.30am-6pm), taking in all the main sights, including Gwalior Fort and Jai Vilas Palace. Enquire at the tourist office at Tansen Residency (p627).

🛏 Sleeping

Hotel Mayur HOTEL $

(☑2375559; www.hotelmayurgwalior.com; Station Rd, Padav; dm ₹110, s/d from ₹341/451, with AC from ₹611/721; ※) Acceptable for the price, but slightly grubby rooms set around a lightwell extend up three floors. Twenty-four-hour checkout.

Hotel DM HOTEL $

(☑2342083; Link Rd; s/d from ₹550/660, with AC from ₹1320; ※) It's a bit like a cell block and rooms are small, but they are slightly better than the other budget options around town. All have clean bathrooms and an old TV

TOP TIGER PARKS

Madhya Pradesh is blessed with five tiger parks, but most tourists don't have the time or money to visit more than one. To help you decide where best to prowl, here's a quick guide to tiger territory in MP:

➡ **Kanha** (p674) The biggest and possibly the best of the lot, where you can venture deep into the forests. Chances of a tiger: very good.

➡ **Bandhavgarh** (p676) Budget-travellers' favourite with highest density of tigers, but sightings can feel a bit 'rush and grab'. Chances: very good.

➡ **Pench** (p678) Quiet and more exclusive. Most people book ahead here. Chances: good.

➡ **Panna** (p644) The tiger population is slowly rebuilding thanks to relocation. Boat safaris here can be fun. Chances: slim.

➡ **Satpura** (p655) Beautiful hilltop landscape, but come here for the waterfalls and the hiking rather than the tigers. Chances: slim.

SHIVPURI'S MARBLE CENOTAPHS

A possible day trip from Gwalior is to the old Scindia summer capital of Shivpuri. This rarely visited town is the site of the Scindia family's *chhatris* (cenotaphs), appropriately grand memorials to maharajas and maharanis gone by.

Two kilometres' walk from the bus stand (autorickshaw ₹30), and set in formal gardens, the **chhatris** (admission ₹40, camera/video ₹10/40; ⊙ 8am-noon & 3-8pm) are magnificent walk-in marble structures with Mughal-style pavilions and *sikharas* (Hindu temple-spires) facing each other across a pool with a criss-cross of walkways. The *chhatri* to Madhorao Scindia, built between 1926 and 1932, is exquisitely inlaid with intricate pietra dura (marble inlay work).

Buses leave regularly from the Shivpuri bus stand for Gwalior (₹90, 2½ hours) and Jhansi (₹85, three hours), meaning you don't have to backtrack.

locked securely inside a cabinet (when was the last time you stole a hotel TV?).

Hotel Chandralok   HOTEL $
(☏ 4084096; Station Rd; s/d from ₹450/750, with AC ₹1320; ❄) The only hotel on Station Rd that accepts foreigners. Rooms are grungy, but some have sit-down flush toilets, and there's a veg restaurant with South Indian dishes.

Tansen Residency   HOTEL $$
(☏ 4056789; www.mptourism.com; 6A Gandhi Rd; r from ₹2689; ❄) MP Tourism hotel with tidy but musty rooms. Has a bar and a restaurant but little character.

Hotel Gwalior Regency   HOTEL $$
(☏ 2340670; www.hotelregencygroup.com; Link Rd; s/d incl breakfast from ₹2818/3992; ❄@☏) Very friendly staff, but the building needs some work. Standard rooms in this business hotel are fine, albeit a little musty, with the central air-con struggling to make much of an impact. You can pay an extra ₹900 for 'grande deluxe' rooms with modern furnishings (wall-mounted wide-screen TV, glass-walled shower room, free wi-fi).

★ Usha Kiran Palace   HERITAGE HOTEL $$$
(☏ 2444000; www.tajhotels.com; Jayendraganj; r from ₹8800; ❄@☏) Live like royalty in this grand, 125-year-old building that was built as a guesthouse for the Prince of Wales (later King George V). Every room has its own unique touches, but all feature understated heritage luxury – while the villas even come with their own private pool! There's a gorgeous main pool with separate kids' pool, the soothing Jiva Spa (p41), the excellent Silver Saloon (p627) restaurant and the spiffing Bada Bar (p627).

✖ Eating & Drinking

Indian Coffee House   SOUTH INDIAN $
(Station Rd; mains ₹50-130; ⊙ 7.30am-11pm) Hugely popular branch that does all the breakfast favourites – real coffee, dosas, scrambled eggs – but also has a main-course menu, including an excellent thali, in a separate 1st-floor family section.

Zayka   MULITCUISINE $
(MLB Rd; mains ₹80-180; ⊙ 11am-11pm) This cafe-style restaurant with glass tabletops and brightly painted walls pulls in young professionals with its foreign menu – noodles, burgers, pizza – but the Indian veg dishes are still very good.

★ Silver Saloon   INDIAN $$$
(☏ 2444000; Usha Kiran Palace, Jayendraganj; mains ₹360-800; ⊙ 7-10.30am, 12.30-3pm & 7.30-10.30pm) Mouth-watering India and Continental dishes, as well as some Nepali and Marathi specialities, are served in the air-con restaurant or the palm-shaded verandah of this exquisite heritage hotel.

Bada Bar   BAR
(☏ 2444000; Usha Kiran Palace, Jayendraganj; beer ₹415; ⊙ 6-11pm) Take a peek inside Gwalior's most luxurious hotel, order a beer or a glass of French wine, then rack up for a frame or two on the century-old, four-ton, Italian-slate snooker table.

🔒 Shopping

Arihant Emporium   HANDICRAFTS
(www.jewelncrafts.com; Moti Mahal Rd; ⊙ 10.30am-6pm Mon-Sat) Near Jai Vilas Palace, this place has all sorts of handicrafts including a Gwalior favourite – silver boxes (₹500) decorated with enamel images imitating the tilework on Man Singh Palace.

MADHYA PRADESH & CHHATTISGARH GWALIOR

ℹ Information

Fun Stop Cyber Zone (MLB Rd; per hr ₹30;
⊙9.30am-10pm) Internet access and webcams
for Skype use.

MP Tourism (☐2340370; Tansen Residency,
6A Gandhi Rd; ⊙10am-5pm Mon-Sat) Organises daily Gwalior bus tour. Very helpful.

MP Tourism (☐4040777; Train Station;
⊙9am-7.30pm) Tourist office branch at the
train station.

Post Office (Station Rd; ⊙10am-4pm Mon-Fri,
10am-3pm Sat) A convenient branch near the
train station. The GPO is at Jayaji Chowk.

ℹ Getting There & Away

AIR

Air India (☐2376872; MLB Rd; ⊙10am-5pm
Mon-Sat) Daily flights to Delhi (from ₹4500)
and Mumbai (from ₹5500).

BUS

Services from the bus stand on Link Rd include:
Agra ₹104, 3½ hours, frequent from 4.30am
to 9pm
Jaipur seat/sleeper ₹220/350, 10 hours, four
daily at 6.30am, 7.15am, 6.30pm & 7.30pm
Jhansi ₹80, three hours, frequent
Khajuraho ₹200, seven hours, one daily at
8.30am
Shivpuri ₹100, 2½ hours, frequent from 5am
to 10pm

TRAIN

More than 20 daily trains go to Agra's Can-
tonment station and to Jhansi for Orchha or
Khajuraho, while more than 10 go to Delhi and
Bhopal.

ℹ Getting Around

Cycle-rickshaws, autorickshaws and taxis are
plentiful. An auto to the airport will cost at least
₹200.

Jhansi

This nondescript town is in fact in Uttar
Pradesh (p388). The town is famous for
its link to the Rani of Jhansi, a key player
in the 1857 War of Independence, and it is
commonly used as a gateway to Orchha,
Khajuraho and Gwalior. If you're here, check
out **Jhansi Fort** (Indian/foreigner ₹5/100, video
₹25; ⊙dawn-dusk), built in 1613 by Maharaja
Bir Singh Deo of Orchha.

Madhya Pradesh Tourism (www.mptour
ism.com; ⊙10am-5pm) has an information
centre on Platform 1 at the train station,
which can make real-time hotel reservations
in Khajuraho and Orchha.

Orchha

☐ 07680 / POP 10,200

This historic village on the banks of the
boulder-strewn Betwa River showcases
some fabulous architecture similar to that
of nearby Khajuraho, albeit without such
high-quality artistry. The atmosphere in
Orchha, though, is far more laid-back and
hassle-free, which makes for a relaxing stay.
There are great homestay options as well
as opportunities to enjoy the surrounding
countryside, with walking, cycling and rafting all on the agenda.

History

Orchha was the capital of the Bundela rajas
from the 16th century to 1783, when they
decamped to nearby Tikamgarh. Bir Singh
Deo ruled from Orchha from 1605 to 1627
and built Jhansi Fort. A favourite of Mughal
prince Salim, Bir Singh feuded with Salim's
father, Emperor Akbar, who all but ruined
his kingdom.

HANDY TRAINS FROM GWALIOR

DESTINATION	TRAIN NO. & NAME	FARE (₹)	DURATION (HR)	DEPARTURE
Agra	12617 Mangala Ldweep	245/482/845 (A)	2	8.15am
Bhopal	12920 Malwa Express	273/728/970 (A)	7	12.35am
Delhi	12625 Kerala Express	364/667/875 (A)	5	8.30am
Indore	12920 Malwa Express	357/972/1440 (A)	12	12.35am
Jhansi	12002 Delhi-Bhopal-SHATABDI	327/745 (B)	1	9.35am

Fares: (A) sleeper/3AC/2AC, (B) chair/1AC only

In 1605 Prince Salim became Emperor Jehangir, making Bir Singh a powerful figure. The Jehangir Mahal was built for the emperor's state visit the following year.

◉ Sights

The **ticket** (Indian/foreigner ₹10/250, camera/video ₹25/200) for Orchha's sites covers seven monuments – Jehangir Mahal, Raj Mahal, Raj Praveen Mahal, the camel stables, the *chhatris,* Chaturbhuj Temple and Lakshmi Narayan Temple – and is only for sale at the **ticket office** (◷8am-6pm). You can walk around the palace grounds for free.

Palaces   HISTORIC SITE
Crossing the granite bridge from the village centre over the often dry water channel brings you to a fortified complex dominated by two wonderfully imposing 17th-century palaces – Jehangir Mahal and Raj Mahal. If you look closely at the top of some buildings, you can still see some of the few remaining turquoise-coloured tiles that once decorated the palaces here.

★**Jehangir Mahal**, an assault course of steep staircases and precipitous walkways, represents a zenith of medieval Islamic architecture. Behind the palace sturdy **camel stables** overlook a green landscape dotted with monuments.

In the nearby **Raj Mahal**, the caretaker will open the painted rooms where Rama, Krishna and Orchha royalty wrestle, hunt, fight and dance across the walls and ceilings.

Downhill from the palace compound are the smaller **Raj Praveen Mahal**, a pavilion and formal Mughal garden, and **Khana Hammam**, with some fine vaulted ceilings.

On the other side of the village, **Palki Mahal** was the palace of Dinman Hardol (the son of Bir Singh Deo), who committed suicide to 'prove his innocence' over an affair with his brother's wife. His memorial is in the adjacent **Phool Bagh**, a traditional *charbagh* (formal Persian garden, divided into quarters). Prince Hardol is venerated as a hero in Bundelkhand culture. Women sing songs about him, tie threads onto the *jali* (carved marble lattice screen) of his memorial and walk around it five times, clockwise, to make wishes they hope he'll grant.

Temples   HINDU TEMPLE
Orchha's impressive 16th-century temples still receive thousands of Hindu pilgrims. At the centre of a lively square is the pink- and gold-domed **Ram Raja Temple** (◷8am-noon & 8-10pm), the only temple where Rama is worshipped as a king. Built as a palace for Madhukar Shah's wife, it became a temple when an image of Rama, temporarily installed by the rani, proved impossible to move.

Ram Raja is overlooked by the spectacular towers of **Chaturbhuj Temple**, an immensely solid building on a cruciform plan. Buy a cheap torch from the bazaar and climb the internal stairs to the roof where, from among the mossy spires and domes, you get the best view in town.

Lakshmi Narayan Temple, on the road out to Ganj village, has fine rooftop views and well-preserved murals on the ceilings of its domed towers.

Chhatris   HISTORIC SITE
Cenotaphs to Orchha's rulers, including Bir Singh Deo, the immense and serene *chhatris* rise beside the river about a kilometre south of the village. They're best seen at dusk, when the birds reel above the children splashing at the river ghats.

🏃 Activities

Nature Trails   WALKING
Some paths in the vast palace grounds lead down to the river through gates in the wall. Another option is the 8km-long nature trail in Orchha Nature Reserve, a 44-sq-km island surrounded by the Betwa and Jamni Rivers. You need to buy a ticket (Indian/foreigner ₹15/150) from the ticket office (open 8am to 6pm) to enter the reserve, then you are free to explore. The nature trail is well marked and the roads are signposted, making this a nice place to cycle. Wildlife you're likely to see on the trail includes monkeys, deer, monitor lizards and peacocks.

Massage & Yoga   AYURVEDA
Amar Mahal and **Orchha Resort** (☎252222; www.orchharesort.com; ◷8.30am-8.30pm) offer good-quality ayurvedic massage treatments (from ₹800) and hold yoga classes (₹500) on demand.

Rafting   RAFTING
(per raft per 1½/3hr ₹1200/2000) River-rafting trips start from the boat club, but tickets must be bought through MP Tourism at Hotel Sheesh Mahal or Betwa Retreat. Rafts take one to six people.

Orchha

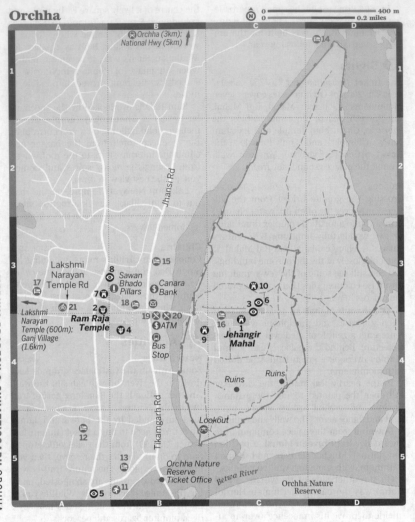

MADHYA PRADESH & CHHATTISGARH ORCHHA

Swimming

SWIMMING

Locals swim in the Betwa River every day, although the river rocks appear to be used as toilets and the river flows swiftly. A popular spot is in front of the boat club by the bridge that leads into the Orchha Nature Reserve. Another option is the boulder-strewn section beside Bundelkhand Riverside hotel.

Nonguests can use the swimming pools at the following hotels: Betwa Retreat (₹200), Amar Mahal (₹300) and Orchha Resort (₹300).

🛏 Sleeping

Shri Mahant Guest House   HOTEL **$**

(☑ 252715; r from ₹250, with AC from ₹600; ❄) Overlooking the souvenir market at the entrance to Ram Raja Temple and overlooked itself by the wonderful Chaturbhuj Temple, this tiny budget option has a superb location and clean though pokey rooms, some with TV, others with balconies. If full, you'll be directed to its larger sister property, Hotel Shri Mahant, a few hundred metres west of town.

Orchha

Hotel Shri Mahant HOTEL $
(☎9893447392, 252341; shri.mahant.hotel@gmail.com; off Lakshmi Narayan Temple Rd; r from ₹450-650, with AC ₹800-1200; ❄☎) Sri Mahant Guest House's laid-back sister property has a quiet location with huge rooms and good views from the rooftop. It is convenient to town, Laxmi Narayan Temple and Ganj village.

Fort View Guest House HOTEL $
(☎252701; fortvieworchha@rediffmail.com; Jhansi Rd; r incl breakfast ₹300-700, with AC from ₹1500; ❄) Simple rooms off a cute courtyard come with marble floors and clean bathrooms. The air-con rooms have huge windows with palace views, while one has a marble bed! Also signposted as Fort View Hotel.

Betwa Retreat HOTEL $$
(☎252618; www.mptourism.com; tents & cottages ₹2689, ste ₹5859; ❄☎☎) Set in shady gardens with a small swimming pool this MP Tourism property, overlooking the river and with views of the *chhatris,* makes an excellent family choice. Rooms come in Mughal-style cottages or Swiss tents and have nice touches such as iron bed frames. There's a restaurant, a bar and an outdoor terrace, and it's only a five-minute walk from the main drag.

Hotel Sheesh Mahal HERITAGE HOTEL $$
(☎252624; www.mptourism.com; Jehangir Mahal; r ₹2690, ste ₹4685-5859; ❄) Literally palatial, this hotel is located in a wing of Jehangir Mahal. As you'd expect, the surrounding architecture is stunning – arches, columns, lattice windows – but the rooms themselves are gorgeous too, and each is unique, some with regal touches such as throne-like toilets.

★**Bundelkhand Riverside** HOTEL $$$
(☎252612; www.bundelkhandriverside.com; s/d incl breakfast from ₹3000/3600; ❄☎) Owned by the grandson of Orchha's last king, Vir Singh, this hotel feels authentically heritage, although the main building is only 13 years old. Antique-style furniture abounds and some of the maharaja's personal art collection is displayed in the corridors. Exquisite rooms overlook either the river or the graceful gardens, which contain some 16th-century monuments as well as a small swimming pool. Budget-priced cabins were under construction beside the river when we visited.

Amar Mahal HOTEL $$$
(☎252102; www.amarmahal.com; s/d from ₹3757/4697, ste ₹8454; ❄@☎☎) Grand rooms containing lovely wood-carved four-poster beds are set around a courtyard with white pillar verandahs. There's an ayurvedic massage and yoga centre beside the large pool. This is probably Orchha's most luxurious stay.

✗ Eating & Drinking

Ram Raja INDIAN $
(Jehangir Mahal Rd; mains ₹45-150; ⊙7.30am-11pm) A friendly, family-run streetside

MUD-HUT HOMESTAYS IN THE VILLAGE OF GANJ

Thanks to **Friends of Orchha** (☑ 9993385405; www.orchha.org; s/d ₹500/600, meals ₹80-130), a nonprofit organisation run by Dutchman Louk Vreeswijk and his Indian wife, Asha D'Souza, travellers have the opportunity to stay with local villagers.

This is a wonderful chance to experience Indian village life, so don't expect anything but the most basic of facilities. Friends of Orchha helped provide loans for some renovations, including installing ecofriendly dry toilets in the yards of each homestay house, but you will still be staying in mud huts and eating the simple veg dishes that your host family eats every day.

Staying for a single night is discouraged for logistical reasons. If you really want to stay one night only, you can, but room rates will be slightly higher. In any case, the slow pace of life in Ganj is something that should be savoured.

Friends of Orchha also runs an after-school youth club for village children. Options to volunteer and donate are available. The Friends of Orchha office is in Ganj Village itself, on the left-hand side of the main road as you are coming from Orchha.

restaurant offering eggy breakfasts and tasty vegetarian fare under the shade of a large tree. Next door, Milan Restaurant has a carbon-copy menu.

Bhola Restaurant INDIAN $
(cnr Jehangir Mahal & Tikamgarh Rds; mains ₹40-150; ☺ 7am-10pm) A great spot for people-watching and fresh juices, this streetside veg restaurant does mostly Indian fare, but also some Korean and Dutch dishes as well as pizza and veg burgers.

Betwa Tarang INDIAN $
(Jehangir Mahal Rd; mains ₹90-200; ☺ 7.30am-10pm) This place does the best pure veg food out of any of Orchha's budget restaurants – the thalis (₹130 to ₹200) are particularly good. It also has the attraction of a rooftop terrace where you can sit and overlook the market.

Jharokha Restaurant INDIAN $$
(mains ₹75-310) Good food, cold beer and friendly waiters belie the fact that this is in a government-run hotel. Indian, Chinese and Continental dishes are on offer, but as usual the Indian (especially tandoori items) are recommended, especially in this grand dining room with live Indian music.

Turquoise Diner INDIAN $$
(☑ 252612; Bundelkhand Riverside; mains ₹180-350; ☺ 7-10am, 12.30-3.30pm & 7-10.30pm) Fabulous green- and blue-tiled air-conditioned restaurant inside the sumptuous Bundelkhand Riverside knocks out arguably the best Indian food in Orchha, including the speciality Bundelkhand chicken. There's a smattering of Continental options too, and if a tour group is in, the buffet will have toned-

down Indian food, but stick to the local dishes and you shouldn't leave disappointed.

ℹ️ Information

Canara Bank (☑ 252689; Jhansi Rd; ☺ 10.30am-2.30pm & 3-4pm Mon-Fri, 10.30am-1pm Sat) Changes travellers cheques and cash. There's an ATM by the bus stand.

MP Tourism (☑ 252624; Betwa Retreat; ☺ 7am-10pm)

MP Tourism (Hotel Sheesh Mahal; ☺ 7am-10pm)

Post Office (cnr Jhansi & Jehangir Rds; ☺ 10am-4pm Mon-Fri, 10am-3pm Sat)

ℹ️ Getting There & Around

Tempos (₹20) go between Jhansi bus stand and Orchha all day. Private autorickshaws charge ₹200. Coming from Khajuraho, you can ask the bus driver to drop you off at the Orchha turn-off on the National Hwy, where you should be able to wave down a vehicle to take you to Orchha.

There are no buses between Orchha and Khajuraho. You need to go to Jhansi first then catch a bus (₹150, six hours, 6am to 2pm) from there as Jhansi–Khajuraho buses tend not to stop for you if you wait on the side of the highway. Taxis to Khajuraho cost at least ₹2300.

You can take a slow passenger train (no. 51821) to Khajuraho from Orchha's tiny train station, which is on the Jhansi Rd, about 3km from the village centre. The train leaves daily at 7.25am and takes five hours (if it's on time). It has 2nd-class seats only so you can't reserve tickets. Just turn up at the station and buy a 'general' ticket (₹36). The return train leaves Khajuraho at 12.30pm.

Raju Bikes (Lakshmi Narayan Temple Rd; per hr/day ₹10/50; ☺ 7am-6pm) hires out rickety bicycles at great rates.

Khajuraho

📌 07686 / POP 23,200

The erotic carvings that swathe Khajuraho's three groups of World Heritage–listed temples are among the finest temple art in the world. The Western Group of temples, in particular, contains some stunning sculptures. See our special colour illustration for details.

Many travellers complain about the tiring persistence of touts here. Their complaints are well founded, but its not so bad that you should contemplate missing out on these beautiful temples.

Come February/March, the Western Group of temples becomes the stage for the weeklong Festival of Dance.

History

Legend has it that Khajuraho was founded by Chardravarman, the son of the moon god Chandra, who descended and saw a beautiful maiden as she bathed in a stream. Historians tell us that most of the 85 original temples (of which 25 remain) were built from AD 950 to 1050 during the Chandela dynasty, and they remained active long after the Chandelas moved their capital to Mahoba.

Khajuraho's isolation may well have helped preserve it from the desecration Muslim invaders inflicted on 'idolatrous' temples elsewhere, but perhaps for the same reason the area was slowly abandoned and eventually fell into ruin, letting the jungle take over. The wider world remained largely ignorant until British officer TS Burt was apparently guided to the ruins by his palanquin bearers in 1838.

⊙ Sights

Temples

The temples are superb examples of Indo-Aryan architecture, but it's their liberally embellished carvings that have made Khajuraho famous throughout India and the world. Around the outsides of the temples are bands of exceedingly artistic stonework showing a storyboard of life a millennium ago – gods, goddesses, warriors, musicians, and real and mythological animals.

Two elements appear repeatedly – women and sex. Sensuous, posturing *surasundaris* (heavenly nymphs), *apsaras* (dancing *surasundaris*) and *nayikas* (mortal *surasundaris*) have been carved with a half-twist and slight sideways lean that make the playful figures dance and swirl out from the temple. The *mithuna* (pairs, threesomes etc of men and women depicted in erotic poses) display the great skill of the sculptors and the dexterity of the Chandelas.

➡ Western Group –
inside the fenced enclosure

Khajuraho's most striking and best-preserved temples are those within the fenced-off section of the **Western Group** (Indian/foreigner ₹20/250, video ₹25; ⊙dawn-dusk) and are the only temples here you have to pay to see. An Archaeological Survey of India (ASI) guidebook to Khajuraho (₹99) and a 90-minute audio guide (₹113) are available at the ticket office.

Varaha, dedicated to Vishnu's boar incarnation, and the locked **Lakshmi** are two small shrines facing the large Lakshmana Temple. Inside Varaha is a wonderful, 1.5m-high sandstone boar, dating from AD 900 and meticulously carved with a pantheon of gods.

The large **Lakshmana Temple** took 20 years to build and was completed in about AD 954 during the reign of Dhanga, according to an inscribed slab in the *mandapa* (pillared pavilion in front of a temple). It's arguably the best preserved of all the Khajuraho temples. You'll see carvings of battalions of soldiers here – the Chandelas were generally at war when they weren't inventing new sexual positions. On the south side is a highly gymnastic orgy, including one gentleman proving that a horse can be a man's best friend, while a shocked figure peeks out from behind her hands. More sensuous figures intertwine between the elephants in the frieze ringing the basement, while some superb carvings can be found around the *garbhagriha* (inner sanctum). Lakshmana is dedicated to Vishnu, although it is similar in design to the Shiva temples Vishvanath and Kandariya-Mahadev.

The 30.5m-long **Kandariya-Mahadev**, built between 1025 and 1050, is the largest temple and represents the highpoint of Chandelan architecture. It also has the most representations of female beauty and sexual acrobatics. There are 872 statues, most nearly 1m high – taller than those at the other temples. One frequently photographed sculpture illustrates the feasibility

Khajuraho

of the handstand position. The 31m-high *sikhara* here is, like linga, a phallic Shiva symbol, worshipped by Hindus hoping to seek deliverance from the cycle of reincarnation. It's decorated with 84 subsidiary spires, which make up a mountain-like rooftop scene reminiscent of the Himalayan abode of the gods.

Mahadeva, a small ruined temple on the same platform as Kandariya-Mahadev and Devi Jagadamba, is dedicated to Shiva, who is carved on the lintel of its doorway. It houses one of Khajuraho's finest sculptures – a *sardula* (mythical beast – part lion, part other animal – possibly human) caressing a 1m-high lion.

Devi Jagadamba was originally dedicated to Vishnu, but later to Parvati and then Kali. The carvings include *sardulas* accompanied by Vishnu, *surasundaris,* and *mithunas* frolicking in the third uppermost band. Its three-part design is simpler than

Kandariya-Mahadev and Chitragupta. It has more in common with Chitragupta, but is less embellished with carvings so is thought to be a little older.

North of Devi Jagadamba, **Chitragupta** (1000–25) is unique in Khajuraho – and rare among North Indian temples – in being dedicated to the sun god Surya. While its condition is not as good as the other temples, it has some fine carvings of *apsaras* and *surasundaris,* elephant fights and hunting scenes, *mithuna* and a procession of stone-carriers. In the inner sanctum, Surya drives his seven-horse chariot, while in the central niche on the south facade is an 11-headed statue of Vishnu, representing the god and 10 of his 22 incarnations.

Continuing around the enclosure, the closed-up **Parvati Temple** is on your right, a small temple originally dedicated to Vishnu and now with an image of Gauri riding a *godha* (iguana).

Khajuraho

Believed to have been built in 1002, the **Vishvanath Temple** and **Nandi Shrine** are reached by steps on the northern and southern sides. Elephants flank the southern steps. Vishvanath anticipates Kandariya-Mahadev, with which it shares *saptamat-trikas* (seven mothers) flanked by Ganesh and Virabhandra, and is another superlative example of Chandelan architecture. Its sculptures include sensuous *surasundari* writing letters, cuddling babies and playing music while languishing more provocatively than at other temples. At the other end of the platform, a 2.2m-long statue of Nandi, Shiva's bull vehicle, faces the temple. The basement of the 12-pillared shrine is decorated with an elephant frieze that recalls similar work on Lakshmana's facade.

The nearby white temple, **Pratapeswar**, is a much more recent bricks-and-mortar structure built around 200 years ago.

➜ **Western Group –**
outside the fenced enclosure

Skirting the southern boundary of the fenced enclosure, **Matangesvara** is the only temple in the Western Group still in everyday use. It may be the plainest temple here (suggesting an early construction), but inside it sports a polished 2.5m-high lingam (phallic image of Shiva). From its platform you can peer into an open-air storage facility scattered with temple finds, but it's not open to the public.

The ruins of **Chausath Yogini**, beyond Shiv Sagar, date to the late 9th century and are probably the oldest at Khajuraho.

(Continues on page 640)

Khajuraho Temples

WESTERN GROUP

The sheer volume of artwork at Khajuraho's best-preserved temples can be overwhelming. Initiate yourself with this introductory tour, which highlights some of those easy-to-miss details.

First, admire the **sandstone boar 1** in the Varaha shrine before heading towards **Lakshmana Temple 2** to study the south side of the temple's base, which has some of the raunchiest artwork in Khajuraho: first up, a nine-person orgy; further along, a guy getting very friendly with a horse. Up on the temple platform see a superb dancing Ganesh carved into a niche (south side), before walking to the west side for graceful *surasundaris* (nymphs): one removing a thorn from her foot; another draped in a wet sari; a third admiring herself in a mirror.

Next is Khajuraho's largest temple, **Kandariya-Mahadev 3**. Carvings to look for here include the famous handstand position (south side), but the most impressive thing about this temple is the scale of it, particularly its soaring rooftops. **Mahadeva 4** and **Devi Jagadamba 5** share the same stone plinth as Kandariya-Mahadev, as do four beautifully carved *sardula* (part-lion, part-human mythical beasts), each caressing a stone lion – one is at the entrance to Mahadeva; the other three stand alone on the plinth.

Walk north from here to **Chitragupta 6**, with beautiful carvings hidden on the west side, as well as elephant friezes around the temple's base (north side). The interior here is particularly impressive.

Continue east to **Vishvanath Temple 7** for more fabulous carvings before admiring the impressive statue of Vishnu's bull in the **Nandi shrine 8** opposite.

Handstand Position
Perhaps Khajuraho's most famous carving, this flexible flirtation is above you as you stand on the south side of the awesome Kandariya-Mahadev.

Sikharas
Despite its many fine statues, perhaps the most impressive thing about Kandariya-Mahadev is its soaring *sikharas* (temple rooftops), said to represent the Himalayan abode of the gods.

Devi Jagadamba Temple 5

3

Kandariya-Mahadev Temple

Mahadeva Temple 4

NORTH →

Toilets

Sardula Statue
There are four lion-stroking *sardula* (part-lion, part-human mythical beasts) on this huge stone plinth, but this one, guarding the entrance to Mahadeva, is our favourite.

Kama Sutra Carvings
Although commonly referred to as Kama Sutra carvings, Khajuraho's erotic artwork does not properly illustrate Vatsyayana's famous sutra. Debate continues as to its significance: to appease evil spirits or imply rulers here were virile, thus powerful? Interestingly, the erotic carvings are never located close to the temple deity.

Listen Up

The audio guide provides a detailed insight into the stories behind the temples and their carvings.

6 Chitragupta Temple

Toilets

Just the Ticket

For an extra-close look at Khajuraho artwork, use your ticket for same-day entrance to the small Archaeological Museum nearby.

7 Vishvanath Temple

Parvati Temple

8 Nandi Shrine

Lakshmana Temple
2

Pratapeswar Temple

Lakshmi Shrine

Varaha Shrine **1**

Entrance

Matangesvara Temple

Nandi Statue

This massive 2.2m-long statue of Nandi, the bull-vehicle of Shiva, is enshrined in a pavilion facing Vishvanath Temple.

Surasundaris

Beautifully graceful depictions of nymphs are found on a number of Khajuraho temples. And despite all the depictions of gymnastic orgies, the wonderfully seductive *surasundari* draped in a wet sari is arguably the most erotic of all.

Vishnu's Boar

This 9th-century statue of Varaha, the boar incarnation of Vishnu, is carved all over with figures of Bramanical gods and goddesses. Under Varaha's foot notice the serpent Seshanaga in a devotional posture, and the feet of a goddess, now missing.

The Sacred Centre

With its melting pot of religious denominations, India is blessed with a formidable array of sacred sites, from ancient cave temples and solemn contemporary shrines to more frisky architectural creations, such as the sensuous temples of Khajuraho (p633). In this section, we focus on some of central India's most renowned places of worship.

1. Mahabodhi Temple (p524), Bodhgaya
The temple marks the hallowed ground where Buddha attained enlightenment.

2. Ellora (p785), Maharashtra
These rock-cut cave temples were worked on by generations of Buddhist, Hindu and Jain monks.

3. Jain temple carvings
Jain temple covered in detailed, wrought carvings.

4. Ranakpur (p169), Rajasthan
This milk-white marble Jain temple has 1444 individually engraved pillars.

(Continued from page 635)

Constructed entirely of granite, it's the only temple not aligned east to west. The temple's name means 64 – it once had 64 cells for the *yoginis* (female attendants) of Kali, while the 65th sheltered the goddess herself. It is reputedly India's oldest *yogini* temple.

A further 600m west, down a track and across a couple of fields (just ask the locals), is the sandstone-and-granite **Lalguan Mahadev Temple** (AD 900), a small ruined shrine to Shiva.

➡ **Eastern Group – Old Village Temples**

The eastern group includes three Hindu temples scattered around the old village and four Jain temples further south, three of which are in a walled enclosure.

The **Hanuman Temple** (Basti Rd) contains a 2.5m-tall statue of the Hindu monkey god. It's little more than a bright orange shrine, but the interest is in the pedestal inscription dating to AD 922, the oldest dateable inscription in Khajuraho.

The granite **Brahma Temple**, with its sandstone *sikhara* overlooking Narora Sagar, is one of the oldest in Khajuraho (about AD 900). The four-faced lingam in the sanctum led to it being incorrectly named, but the image of Vishnu above the sanctum doorway reveals its original dedication to Vishnu.

Resembling Chaturbhuja Temple in the southern group, **Javari Temple** (1075–1100) stands just north of the old village. It's dedicated to Vishnu and is a good example of small-scale Khajuraho architecture for its crocodile-covered entrance and slender *sikhara*.

Vamana Temple (1050–75), 200m further north, is dedicated to the dwarf incarnation of Vishnu. It has quirky touches such as elephants protruding from the walls, but its *sikhara* is devoid of subsidiary spires and there are few erotic scenes. Its roofed *mahamandapa* (main hall) is an anomaly in Khajuraho but typical among medieval west Indian temples.

Located between the old village and the Jain Enclosure, the small **Ghantai Temple**, also Jain, is named after the *ghanta* (chain and bell) decorations on its pillars. It was once similar to nearby Parsvanath, but only its pillared shell remains, and it's normally locked.

➡ **Eastern Group – Jain Enclosure**

While not competing in size and erotica with the western-enclosure temples, **Parsvanath Temple**, the largest of the Jain temples in the walled enclosure, is notable for the exceptional precision of its construction, and for its sculptural beauty. Some of the best preserved of Khajuraho's most famous images can be seen here, including the woman removing a thorn from her foot and another applying eye makeup, both on the south side. Although the temple was originally dedicated to Adinath, a jet-black image of Parsvanath was substituted about a century ago. Both an inscription on the *mahamandapa* doorway and its similarities with the slightly simpler Lakshmana Temple date it to AD 950–70.

The adjacent, smaller **Adinath** has been partially restored over the centuries. With fine carvings on its three bands of sculptures, it's similar to Khajuraho's Hindu temples, particularly Vamana. Only the striking black image in the inner sanctum triggers a Jain reminder.

Shanti Nath, built about a century ago, houses components from older temples, including a 4.5m-high Adinath statue with a plastered-over inscription on the pedestal dating to about 1027.

➡ **Southern Group**

A dirt track runs to the isolated **Duladeo Temple**, about 1km south of the Jain enclosure. This is the youngest temple, dating to 1100–1150. Its relatively wooden, repetitious sculptures, such as those of Shiva, suggest that Khajuraho's temple builders had passed their artistic peak by this point, although they had certainly lost none of their zeal for eroticism.

Anticipating Duladeo and its flaws, the ruined **Chaturbhuja Temple** (c 1100) has a fine 2.7m-high, four-armed statue of Vishnu in the sanctum. It is Khajuraho's only developed temple without erotic sculptures.

Just before Chaturbhuja there's a signed track leading to **Bijamandala Temple**. This is the excavated mound of an 11th-century temple, dedicated to Shiva (judging by the white marble lingam at the apex of the mound). Although there are some exquisitely carved figures, unfinished carvings were also excavated, suggesting that what would have been Khajuraho's largest temple was abandoned as resources flagged.

Other Sights

Archaeological Museum MUSEUM
(Main Rd; with same-day Western Group ticket ₹10; ⊘ Sat-Thu 9am-5pm) The Archaeological Museum, announced by a wonderful 11th-century statue of Ganesh dancing sensuously for an elephant-headed deity, has a small but well-presented collection of sculptures from around Khajuraho. At the time of research, there were plans to move this museum to a larger site north of the Western Group, but don't hold your breath; they've been telling us that since 2006.

Adivart Tribal & Folk Art Museum MUSEUM
(Chandela Cultural Centre, Link Rd No 1; guide ₹20; ⊘10am-5pm) FREE The museum-cum-art gallery makes a colourful change from the temples. It gives a taste of Madhya Pradesh's vibrant tribal culture of both Madhya Pradesh and Chhattisgarh through paintings, terracotta sculptures, masks and statues. Original signed paintings are for sale from around ₹10,000. Prints can be bought from around ₹200.

Old Village AREA
If you can put up with the persistent requests from local children for pens and money, then a stroll or cycle around the dusty narrow streets of the old village can be very rewarding. Homes here are whitewashed or painted in colourful pastels and the lanes are dotted with small shrines, old wells and water pumps.

Activities

Massage AYURVEDA
Many budget hotels offer cheap ayurvedic massage treatments of varying levels of authenticity. Top-end hotels offer more luxurious versions. For the real deal, though, head to **Ayur Arogyam** (⌨272572; treatment ₹1500-2300). The lovely Keralan couple who run this small place from their home also have two simple double rooms to rent.

Yoga YOGA
Apart from the hotels offering yoga, the inspiring **Yogi Sudarshan Dwiveda** (⌨9993284940; Vidhya Colony; by donation; ⊘6am) runs sessions at his home in Vidhya Colony 1.5km north of the town centre. Accommodation can be arranged here as well. There is no English sign. If you have trouble contacting him, go through the **Rajesh Medical Store** (⊘9am-9pm) located in Gole Market.

Sleeping

Hefty discounts (20% to 50%) are available out of season (April to September), although it's worth bargaining at any time of year.

★ Hotel Harmony HOTEL $
(⌨274135; www.hotelharmonyonline.com; Jain Temples Rd; s/d ₹600/800, with AC s ₹1100, d ₹1200-1600; ✳@ ⊛) Cosy, well-equipped rooms off marble corridors are tastefully decorated and come with effective mosquito screens and cable TV. Great food is available at the Zorba the Buddha restaurant and you can eat under the stars on the rooftop. Yoga, massage, face- and palm-reading and numerology are all available.

Hotel Surya HOTEL $
(⌨274144; www.hotelsuryakhajuraho.com; Jain Temples Rd; r ₹500-800, with AC ₹1000-1600; ✳@ ⊛) There's quite a range of rooms in this sprawling, well-run hotel with whitewashed corridors, marble staircases and a lovely courtyard garden out the back. Some rooms have TV. Some have balconies. There's yoga, massage, cycling tours and cooking classes available. Wi-fi costs ₹100 per day.

Hotel Zen HOTEL $
(⌨274228; www.hotlzenkhajuraho.co.in; Jain Temples Rd; r ₹400-600, with AC ₹1200; ✳@ ⊛) A popular backpacker hang-out. Rooms have cable TV. Upstairs rooms are brighter and overlook a series of courtyards with lotus ponds, winter bonfires, candles flickering at night and a decent restaurant. The attentive staff are more than happy to organise tours and travel.

Osaka Guesthouse GUESTHOUSE $
(⌨272839; imrankhankhj@yahoo.co.in; off Basti Rd; r ₹400, with AC ₹700; ✳⊛) Spacious rooms here are pretty basic, but have a homey feel to them and the owner is very welcoming. Osaka is set back off the main drag, down a dirt track, so is quieter than elsewhere, and has some nice temple views from its rooftop (which may be reincarnated as a restaurant by the time you visit).

Yogi Lodge GUESTHOUSE $
(⌨274158; yogi_sharm@yahoo.com; s ₹150, d ₹250-400, r with AC ₹600; ✳) Rooms are basic – some share showers though they have a private toilet. The small courtyards, narrow corridors and the cute stone tables in the rooftop restaurant give this place character. There's a lone air-con room but it's not worth the extra cost.

Ayur Arogram GUESTHOUSE $
(☏272572; r ₹200) There are just two simple rooms with private bathrooms at this small, family-run ayurvedic massage lodge.

Hotel Payal HOTEL $$
(☏274076; payal@mptourism.com; Link Rd No 1; r ₹1515, with AC ₹2337; ❋⛾) This MP Tourism hotel has smart rooms with dark-wood furniture set around very nice gardens with an inviting swimming pool out the back. It also rents bikes (₹50 per day).

Radisson Jass Hotel HOTEL $$$
(☏272777; www.radisson.com; Bypass Rd; r from ₹6600; ❋@⛾⛾) A marble spiral staircase winds its way up from the fountain in the lobby to stylish 1st-floor rooms that are very smart and fully appointed, albeit with small bathrooms. There's a comfortable bar (with pool table), a restaurant, tennis and badminton courts, and a fine swimming pool and spa. Check the website for latest room deals.

Lalit Temple View HOTEL $$$
(☏272111; www.thelalit.com; Main Rd; r from ₹11,700; ❋@⛾⛾) Sweeps aside all other five-star pretenders with supreme luxury, impeccable service and high prices. Rooms are immaculate with large-screen TVs, wood-carved furniture and tasteful artwork. Guests who don't have temple-view rooms can see the Western Group from the delightful lotus-shaped pool.

✗ Eating

Madras Coffee House SOUTH INDIAN $
(cnr Main & Jain Temples Rds; mains ₹40-150; ☺8.30am-9.30pm) Good, honest South Indian fare – dosa, *idli* (spongy round fermented rice cakes), *uttapam* (thick savoury rice pancakes), thali – as well as coffee and chai, served in a narrow cafe. Ideal for breakfast. House speciality is the egg, cheese and veg dosa (₹150).

Blue Sky Restaurant MULTICUISINE $
(Main Rd; mains ₹40-250; ☺7.30am-10pm) A rickety wooden platform, three storeys up, leads out to the most unusual place to eat in Khajuraho – a one-table treehouse with an unrivalled view of the western temples. The view from the ordinary, terraced balcony is good too, while the menu is the usual Indian and Chinese, plus Western breakfasts. The grumpy service is perhaps understandable. Would you like to serve food to customers in a tree?

Paradise Restaurant MULTICUISINE $
(Main Rd; mains ₹55-250; ☺8am-11pm; 🕸) This casual restaurant has an open terrace overlooking the lake. The menu includes Chinese, Continental and pizza as well as the recommended Indian food.

Lassi Corner INDIAN $
(Jain Temples Rd; mains ₹35-45, lassis ₹10-35; ☺9.30am-9.30pm) This tarpaulin-covered bamboo shack is a great place for a quick chai break or a lazy lassi. Also does pancakes as well as simple Indian fare such as *pakora* (deep-fried vegetables), *paratha* (bread stuffed with grated vegetables), pulao and kofta.

★ Raja's Café MULTICUISINE $$
(Main Rd; mains ₹80-280; ☺8am-10pm; 🕸) Raja's has been on top of its game for more than 30 years, with espresso coffee, English breakfasts, wood-fired pizzas, and superb Indian, Italian and Chinese dishes. Try the *palak paneer* (unfermented cheese and spinach) and tandoori chicken, in particular. The location, with a temple-view terrace, is great, as is the restaurant design, with a delightful courtyard shaded by a 170-year-old neem tree. But it's the food that steals the show.

Agrasen MULTICUISINE $$
(Jain Temples Rd; mains ₹65-280; ☺7.30am-10pm) This smart place with gingham tablecloths and a 1st-floor terrace serves up salads, pasta and pizza as well as a variety of Indian vegetable and meat dishes.

Mediterraneo ITALIAN $$
(Jain Temples Rd; mains ₹200-350, pizza ₹290-430; ☺7.30am-10pm) Far removed from its Italian roots, Mediterraneo manages acceptable Italian fare served on a lovely terrace overlooking the street. Dishes includes chicken, salads, organic wholewheat pasta and wood-fired pizzas, and beer and wine are also available.

☆ Entertainment

Admittedly, the temples do look magical illuminated with technicolour floodlights, but the one-hour **sound-and-light show** (Indian/foreigner ₹120/350, child ₹60/200; ☺English 6.30pm Nov-Feb, 7.30pm Mar-Oct, Hindi 7.45pm Nov-Feb, 8.45pm Mar-Oct) chronicling the history of Khajuraho is still about 45 minutes too long.

Folk dancing can be seen at the comfortable indoor theatre at **Kandariya Art &**

Culture (☎274031; Jhansi Rd; admission ₹350; ⊗7-8pm & 8.45-9.45pm).

 Shopping

Kandariya Art & Culture HANDICRAFTS
(Jhansi Rd; ⊗9am-9pm) Huge emporium where full-size replicas of some of Khajuraho's temple carvings can be bought – if you have a spare ₹150,000. Smaller, more affordable versions, along with textiles, wood carvings and marble inlay, can be found indoors.

❶ Information

Community Health Centre (☎272498; Link Rd No 2; ⊗9am-1pm & 2-4pm) Limited English, but helpful staff.

Post Office (☎274022; ⊗10am-4pm Mon-Sat)

State Bank of India (☎272373; Main Rd; ⊗10.30am-4.30pm Mon-Fri, 10.30am-1.30pm Sat) Changes cash and travellers cheques. There are ATMs beside Raja's Cafe and Paradise Restaurant.

Tourist Interpretation & Facilitation Centre (☎274051; khajuraho@mptourism.com; Main Rd; ⊗10am-5pm Mon-Sat, closed 2nd & 3rd Sat of month) Leaflets on statewide tourist destinations. Also has a stand at the airport and train station.

Tourist Police Booth (☎272690; Main Rd; ⊗6am-10pm)

❶ Getting There & Away

AIR

Jet Airways (☎274406; ⊗10am 3.30pm), at the airport, has a daily 1.45pm flight to Delhi (from ₹5900, 3½ hours) via Varanasi (from ₹4800, 40 minutes). **Air India** (☎274035; Jhansi Rd; ⊗10am-4.50pm Mon-Sat) has 5.20pm flights to the same two cities, but only on Monday, Wednesday and Friday.

BUS

If the **bus tickets office** (⊗7-10am & 2-3pm) is closed, the owner of the Madhur coffee stand, just opposite, is very helpful and trustworthy.

There are three daily buses to Jhansi (₹130, five hours, 5.30am, 7am and 9am), which will all drop you at the junction to Orchha from where you can wave down a shared autorickshaw (₹10) to Orchha. One of these buses (time varies) continues on from Jhansi to Gwalior (₹170, seven hours) and Agra (₹320, 10 hours). Regular buses run to Madla (for Panna National Park; ₹30, one hour, 8am to 7pm), where you can change for Satna (₹75, three hours). There are three direct buses to Satna (₹130, four hours, 8am, 10am and 3pm) from where you can catch trains to various destinations.

Much more frequent buses can be caught at the Bamitha crossroads, 11km away on Hwy 75, where buses between Gwalior, Jhansi and Satna shuttle through all day. Catch a shared jeep (₹10, 7am to 7pm) to Bamitha from the bus stand or as they drive down Jhansi Rd.

TAXI

Yashowaran Taxi Driver Union is opposite Gole Market under a neem tree. Fares including all taxes and tolls: airport (₹200), train station (₹300), Raneh Falls (₹600), Panna National Park (in 4WD, ₹1500), Satna (₹1500), Orchha (₹2300), Chitrakut (₹2800), Bandhavgarh (₹4500), Varanasi (₹6000) and Agra (₹6000).

TRAIN

Three useful trains leave from Khajuraho train station:

A daily passenger train (no. 51822) leaves at 12.30pm for Jhansi, stopping at the tiny train station of Orchha (₹30, four hours). There are 2nd-class seats only, so you can't buy tickets in advance. Just turn up at the train station, buy a 'general' ticket and squeeze in.

The daily 22447 Khajuraho–Nizamuddin Express leaves for Delhi (sleeper/3AC/2AC ₹344/935/1365, 6.20pm, 11½ hours) via Agra (sleeper/3AC/2AC ₹282/753/1015, 8½ hours).

On Tuesdays, Fridays and Sundays the 21107 Khajuraho–Varanasi Express leaves for Varanasi (sleeper/3AC ₹275/758, 11.40pm, 11 hours).

Train tickets can be bought from the **train reservation office** (☎274416; ⊗8am-noon & 1-4pm Mon-Sat, 8am-2pm Sun) at the bus stand. You must book tickets at least four hours before departure.

Coming to Khajuraho, the 21108 Varanasi–Khajuraho Express leaves Varanasi on Mondays, Wednesdays and Saturdays at 6.05pm and arrives in Khajuraho at 5.15am. The 22448 Nizamuddin–Khajuraho Express leaves Delhi's Hazrat Nizamuddin station daily at 8.15pm and passes Agra (11.20pm) before arriving in Khajuraho (6.35am). The daily passenger train leaves Jhansi at 7.10am, passing Orchha (7.25am) before arriving in Khajuraho at around noon.

❶ Getting Around

Bicycle is a great way to get around. Several places along Jain Temples Rd rent them (per day ₹50). Cycle-rickshaws cost around ₹20 wherever you go in Khajuraho.

Taxis to and from the airport/train station charge ₹200/250, autorickshaws ₹150/200, but if you don't have too much luggage it's easy enough to wave down a bus or a shared jeep (₹10) as they head along Jhansi Rd either into or out of town.

Around Khajuraho

Raneh Falls

These 30m-high **waterfalls** (Indian/foreigner ₹15/150, motorbike ₹40/200, autorickshaw ₹80/400, car ₹200/1000, compulsory guide ₹40; ⏰ 6am-6pm), 18km from Khajuraho, at times tumble as a churning mass over rocks but are only really worth the trip just after rain. The ticket office is 3km before the falls so if you don't want to pay the fees for vehicle entry be prepared for a walk. It's possible to view gharials – an endangered species of crocodile – at **Ken Gharial Sanctuary** (⏰ 9am-5pm, closed during monsoon), 8km from the ticket office, beyond the falls. The road to Raneh Falls is signposted if you fancy cycling through the countryside from Khajuraho, or else its ₹350/600 return in an autorickshaw/taxi.

Panna National Park

Tigers are now making a comeback after being reintroduced to this **reserve** (☎ 07732252135; vehicle with up to 8 passengers Indian/foreigner ₹1000/2000, 6-person jeep hire ₹1500; ⏰ 6.30-11am & 2.30-5.30pm Oct 16-Jun 30, closed Wed) from Bandhavgarh, Pench and Kanha, and after some cubs have been born to these new settlers. This is a good place to see crocodiles and, with the Ken River flowing through it, Panna is a peaceful, picturesque place to spend a day on your way to or from Khajuraho. In fact, it's easy enough to do an afternoon safari here as a day trip from Khajuraho, using public transport to get to and from Madla.

Even if you don't stay the night here, it's worth making **Jungle Camp** (☎ 07732275275; jcmadla@mptourism.com; r ₹2336) your base. It is on the edge of Madla village, 200m past the large Ken River bridge (if you're coming from Khajuraho), and right by Madla Gate, the main entrance to the park. There's a restaurant (mains ₹80 to ₹200), you can arrange jeep safaris and there's a nicely kept garden dotted with children's play areas in which the comfortable air-conditioned tents for guests are located. Upmarket packages including full board and jungle safaris are available through **Ken River Lodge** (www.kenriverlodge.com; safari packages from ₹15,000) and Taj Hotel's **Pashan Garh** (www.tajhotels.com; packages from ₹17,000).

Regular buses run between Madla and Khajuraho (₹30, one hour) and between Madla and Satna (₹75, three hours), although for Satna you sometimes have to change at the nearby town of Panna (₹10, 30 minutes).

Satna

☎ 07672 / POP 280.248

Satna is of no interest to tourists but is a transport link between Khajuraho and Madhya Pradesh's three big tiger parks – Bandhavgarh, Kanha and Pench.

The bus and train stations are 3km apart (cycle-rickshaw/autorickshaw ₹20/50). There is an ATM opposite the bus stand and one at the train station, where you'll also find **MP Tourism** (☎ 225471; ⏰ 9am-5pm Mon-Sat), which is occasionally open.

If you get stuck here, **Hotel Chandra View** (☎ 410600; Rewa Rd; s/d from ₹900/1275; ❄) is 50m right of the bus stand and has decent rooms and a restaurant.

Three buses go to Khajuraho (₹130, four hours, 6.30am, 9.15am and 2.30pm). At other times you can go via Panna (last bus 6pm). There are also regular buses towards Chitrakut (₹80, three hours, 6am to 8pm), although you often have to change.

Six daily trains go to Varanasi (sleeper/3AC/2AC, ₹233/636/845, seven hours), frequent daily trains go to Jabalpur (₹215/547/845, three hours), and two to Umaria (₹195/484/815, three hours and four hours, 7pm and 10.05pm) for Bandhavgarh National Park.

CENTRAL MADHYA PRADESH

Bhopal

☎ 0755 / POP 1.80 MILLION

Split by a pair of lakes, Bhopal offers two starkly contrasting cityscapes. In the north is the Muslim-dominated old city, a fascinating area of mosques and crowded bazaars. Bhopal's population is 40% Muslim – one of India's highest concentration of Muslims – and the women in black *niqabs* (veils) are reminders of the female Islamic rulers who built up Bhopal in the 19th century. North of here is a reminder of a more recent, tragic history – the Union Carbide plant, site of the world's worst industrial disaster.

South of the two lakes, Bhopal is more modern, with wide roads, shopping complexes and upmarket hotels and restaurants nestled comfortably in the Arera and Shamla Hills, which overlook the lakes and the old city beyond. The central district here is known as New Market.

The main train and bus stations are just off Hamidia Rd – the main budget hotel area – with the bustling *chowk* (marketplace) slightly further southeast. Hamidia Rd is accessed via the Platform 5 end of the train station. The Platform 1 end is where you'll find left luggage (you need your own padlock), MP Tourism, the post office and an ATM.

◉ Sights & Activities

★ State Museum
MUSEUM

(✆2661856; Shamla Hills; Indian/foreigner ₹10/100, camera/video ₹50/200; ⊙noon-7pm Tue-Sun) This first-class archaeological museum includes some wonderful temple sculptures as well as 87 Jain bronzes unearthed by a surprised farmer in western Madhya Pradesh. Keep an eye out for the tiny, but remarkably animated, metal carpet seller in the Royal Collections Gallery.

Mosques
MOSQUE

Bhopal's third female ruler, Shah Jahan Begum, wanted to create the largest mosque in the world, so in 1877 she set about building **Taj-ul-Masjid** (⊙closed to non-Muslims Fri). It was still incomplete at her death in 1901, after funds had been diverted to other projects, and construction did not resume until 1971. It is now one of the largest mosques in India, thanks to its huge courtyard. The main structure is enormous too; fortresslike terracotta walls surround three gleaming white onion domes and a pair of towering pink minarets with white domes. If you can make the dawn azan (Muslim call to prayer), you won't regret it. And while you're in the area, don't forget to pop over the road to see **Dhai Seedi Ki Masjid**, the city's oldest and teeniest mosque inside the grounds of Hamidia Hospital.

The gold spikes crowning the squat minarets of the **Jama Masjid**, built in 1837 by Bhopal's first female ruler, Qudsia Begum, glint serenely above the skull caps and veils swirling through the fascinating bazaar below.

THE BHOPAL DISASTER – A CONTINUING TRAGEDY

At five minutes past midnight on 3 December 1984, 40 tonnes of deadly methyl isocyanate (MIC) gas leaked out over Bhopal from the US owned Union Carbide chemical plant. Blown by the wind, rivers of the heavy gas coursed through the city. In the ensuing panic, people were trampled trying to escape while others were so disorientated that they ran into the gas.

There were 3828 initial fatalities according to official figures, but the continuing death toll stands at over 20,000. More than 120,000 people suffer from a catalogue of illnesses from hypertension and diabetes to premature menopause and skin disorders, while their children experience growth disorders, such as shrunken rib cages.

The leak at the plant resulted from a saga of untested technology, negligent maintenance and cost-cutting measures. Damages of US$3 billion were demanded, and in 1989 Union Carbide paid the Indian government US$470 million, but winning compensation for the victims has been a tortuous process slowed by the Indian government's wrangling over who was a victim and Dow Chemical's acquisition of Union Carbide in 2001. Both buyer and seller deny ongoing liability.

Union Carbide also financed the building of a multimillion dollar hospital, while charity **Sambhavna Trust Clinic** (✆2730914; www.bhopal.org; Berasia Rd, Bafna Colony; ⊙8.30am-3pm) treats more than 200 people a day using yoga, ayurvedic treatments, conventional medicine and herbal remedies. Volunteers can work in a range of areas from water testing and medical research to gardening and internet communications; they are hugely appreciated and offered board and lodgings in the medical centre. Visitors are welcome and donations can be made.

Bafna Colony is off Berasia Rd. If walking from Hamidia Rd, turn right after about 500m and keep asking for Sambhavna.

Bhopal

The **Moti Masjid** near Sadar Manzil was built by Qudsia Begum's daughter and Bhopal's second female ruler, Sikander Jahan Begum, in 1860. Similar in style to the Jama Masjid in Delhi, this smaller marble-faced mosque has two dark-red minarets and gold-spiked cupolas. Inside, the kiblah has 11 white arches. The five most central are marble.

Bharat Bhavan   ART GALLERY
(☑ 2660239; galleries/performances ₹10/20, galleries Fri free; ⊙ 2-8pm Tue-Sun Feb-Oct, 1-7pm Nov-Jan) This cultural centre is a serene place to take in modern Indian art, tribal carvings and paintings. There is a library, contemporary art galleries, a cafe, and regular evening performances (7pm) of poetry, music and theatre.

Rashtriya Manav Sangrahalaya   PARK
(Museum of Man; ☑ 2661319; Shamla Hills; admission ₹10, vehicle ₹10, video ₹50; ⊙ 10am-5pm Tue-Sun Sep-Feb, 11am-6.30pm Mar-Aug) A kind of tribal safari park, only without the tribes, this open-air hillside complex is possibly your best chance to get a taste of India's 450-plus tribes without actually visiting an Adivasi village. Authentic-looking dwellings – built and maintained by Adivasis (tribespeople) using traditional tools and materials – dot the hillside. There's a mythological trail and a more conventional museum found on the hilltop.

Upper Lake   LAKE
The MP Tourism Boat Club offers motorboat rides (per person ₹60, five minutes, minimum three people), pedal boats (per boat ₹60, 30 minutes) and even jet skiing (per person ₹350). Children might enjoy feeding the gaggle of geese that make their home by the boat club.

Bhopal

☞ Tours

Bhopal-On-Wheels (☎ 3295040; 3½hr tour adult/child ₹60/30; ⊙ 11am-3.30pm Tue-Sun) is a guided tour on a toy-train lookalike open bus, departing from Palash Residency and winding through the hills and the old city. Stops include Taj-ul-Masjid, MP Tourism Boat Club and Rashtriya Manav Sangrahalaya. Minimum five passengers.

🛏 Sleeping

Hotel Ranjeet   HOTEL $
(☎ 2740500; ranjeethotels@sancharnet.in; 3 Hamidia Rd; s/d from ₹518/805, with AC from ₹863/1150; ✸ @) They look after you in Ranjeet. Even in the cheapest rooms you get your own soap, towel, bottle of mineral water and a complimentary breakfast, plus there's one computer terminal in the lobby for brief (free) internet use. The restaurant here is good, there's a bar, and it's convenient to the bus and train stations.

Hotel Sonali   HOTEL $
(☎ 2740880; sonalinn@sancharnet.in; Radha Talkies Rd; s/d from ₹575/748, with AC incl breakfast from ₹1250/1450; ✸ @ 🛜) Excellent service and shiny tiled floors in big rooms make this a quality option near Hamidia Rd. Some non-AC rooms come with slightly shabby carpets, but all have TV and there's 24-hour internet and free wi-fi in the lobby. Also has a restaurant. From Hamidia Rd, turn left down the lane alongside Hotel Ranjit and follow it around to the right.

Park Hotel   HOTEL $
(☎ 4057711; parkhotelbhopal@yahoo.com; Rang Mahal Rd; s/d from ₹690/920, with AC from ₹920/1150; ✸) This neat place is a good-value option for New Market, with a great location close to restaurants, shops and market stalls. The rooms are decent, with marble floors, TV and hot-water showers and 24-hour checkout.

★ **Jehan Numa Palace Hotel**   HERITAGE HOTEL $$$
(☎ 2661100; www.hoteljehanumapalace.com; 157 Shamla Hill; patio s/d ₹4872/6090, s ₹7916-10,352, d ₹9134-1157, ste from ₹19,486, incl breakfast; ✸ @ 🛜 ⌇) This former 19th-century palace lost none of its colonial-era charm through conversion into a top-class hotel. Arched walkways and immaculate lawns lead you to beautifully decorated rooms. There's a palm-lined pool, an excellent health spa and three restaurants and a coffee shop.

Palash Residency   HOTEL $$$
(☎ 2553066; palash@mptourism.com; TT Nagar; s/d from ₹3395/3865; ✸ @ 🛜) Walking distance from New Market, this MP Tourism hotel has smart rooms with heavy wood furniture, wall-mounted flat-screen TVs, kettles, complimentary toiletries and free wi-fi in the lobby. Has a bar and restaurant.

✖ Eating & Drinking

★ Bapu Ki Kutia   INDIAN $

(Sultania Rd; mains ₹50-120, special thali ₹110; ☺10am-11pm) Papa's Shack has been serving up delicious Indian veg dishes since 1964 and is so popular you often have to share a table. Does handy half portions if you just fancy a snack. There's an English menu, but no English sign. Look for the picture of a beach hut and palm tree above the door.

New Inn   INDIAN $

(Bhadbhada Rd, New Market; mains ₹35-135; ☺8am-10pm) Clean and colourful split-level restaurant with a well-priced veg and meat menu delivered by staff in waistcoats and bow ties. There are good breakfast choices, including filter coffee (₹15), but it's the delicious main courses that hit the spot. If you like a bit of spice, don't leave this place without trying the *mattar paneer* (unfermented cheese and pea curry). Has good tandoori too.

Indian Coffee House   SOUTH INDIAN $

(New Market Rd, New Market; mains ₹50-140; ☺7am-11pm) As always, Indian Coffee House is a top spot for breakfast, with waiters in fan-tailed hats serving good-value coffee plus South Indian favourites such as dosa, *idli* and *vada* (doughnut-shaped deep-fried lentil savoury). The upstairs 'family' restaurant is the more relaxed and welcoming of the two dining options.

Manohar   INDIAN $

(6 Hamidia Rd; mains ₹40-100, thali ₹110; ☺8am-11pm) This bright, clean, canteen-style restaurant is a decent place to come for South Indian breakfasts. After midday it also does thalis and 'mini-meals' as well as some Chinese dishes and pizza. Has an impressive range of cakes, cookies and sweets at a side counter.

★ Under the Mango Tree   INDIAN $$$

(Jehan Numa Palace Hotel, 157 Shamla Hill; mains ₹350-700; ☺noon-3pm & 7-11pm) One of spiffy Jehan Numa Palace's three restaurants (four if you include the coffee shop). This one specialises in barbecue kebabs and tandoor. The succulent pieces of meat are cooked and smoked before your eyes and brought to the table in mini copper tandoors. Good food, wine, draught beer, cocktails and live music all combine under a romantic white pavilion and the heavy boughs of a venerable centenarian mango tree.

Café Coffee Day   CAFE

(Lake Drive Rd; coffee ₹35-110; ☺8.30am-10.30pm) Quality fresh coffee and the best views in town.

Wine Shop   BAR

(Hamidia Rd; ☺10am-10pm) There are a number of bottle shops on this grotty stretch of Hamidia Rd, but this one has the added attraction of beer on tap.

🛍 Shopping

Bhopal's two main shopping areas are the small shops and stalls around New Market, which really come to life in the evenings, and the labyrinthine old-city alleys that weave their way towards the Jama Masjid. Both areas stock delicate gold and silver jewellery, fancifully woven saris, hand-embroidered appliqué skirts and *jari* (glittering embroidery, often including shards of mirror or glass) shoulder bags, a speciality of Bhopal.

Mrignayani   HANDICRAFTS

(23 New Market Shopping Centre; ☺11am-2.30pm & 3.30-8pm Tue-Sun) This state-owned place offers stress-free handicraft shopping, though the fixed prices are higher than in the market behind it.

Khadi Gramodyog Bhavan   CLOTHING

(Bhadbhada Rd; ☺11am-8pm Tue-Sun) Kurta, pyjamas, head scarves and shirts made from the famous *khadi* cotton, plus some quality *khadi* silk garments. Next-day tailoring service available.

Variety Book House   BOOKS

(Bhadbhada Rd, 14-15 GTB Complex; ☺10am-10pm) Stationery, maps and a fabulous selection of contemporary novels and Indian history books.

ℹ Information

Hamidia Hospital (☏2540222; Royal Market Rd) Housed within the grounds of the now ruined Fatehgarh Fort.

Main Post Office (Sultania Rd; ☺10am-7pm Mon-Sat) Also a counter at the train station.

MP Tourism (☏2550588; regional office, Palash Residency, TT Nagar; ☺10am-8pm Mon-Fri, 10am-5pm Sat & Sun) Also has desks at the airport and train station.

Raj Medical Store (Hamidia Rd; ☺9am-9.30pm) Medicines.

State Bank of India (Rang Mahal Rd; ☺11am-5pm Mon-Fri, 11am-2pm Sat) 'International Division' on 1st floor changes travellers cheques and cash. Has ATM. There's also an ATM at the train station.

ⓘ Getting There & Away

AIR

Air India (☎2770480; Bhadbhada Rd; ◷10am-5pm Mon-Sat) flies daily to Delhi (from ₹4200, one hour, 5.50pm) and Mumbai (from ₹3800, two hours, 7.45pm).

BUS

For Jabalpur (₹230, eight hours, 10am) go to the ISBT bus stand in Habidganj, east of the city. Services from the **central bus stand** (☎0755 4257602; Hamidia Rd) off Hamidia Rd:

Bhimbetka ₹40, one hour, many departures to Hoshongabad, 6am to 6pm, alight at Highway Treat

Indore ₹150, five hours, many departures throughout day

Pachmarhi ₹150, six hours, six daily at 5.15am, 6.15am, 8.15am, 3pm, sleeper 1am and 2.30am

Sanchi ₹35, 1½ hours, every 15 minutes from 5am to 9.30pm

TRAIN

There are more than 20 daily trains to Gwalior and Agra and more than 10 to Ujjain and Delhi.

ⓘ Getting Around

Minibuses and buses (both ₹10) shuttle between New Market and Hamidia Rd all day and all evening. Catch ones to New Market at the eastern end of Hamidia Rd. Returning from New Market, you can catch them from the Nehru Statue. Autorickshaws cost about ₹50 for the same journey. The autorickshaw fare from New Market to MP Tourism Boat Club is ₹60, and from Hamidia Rd to Taj-ul-Masjid it's ₹40.

The airport is 16km northwest of central Bhopal. Expect to pay at least ₹200/400 for an autorickshaw/taxi.

Around Bhopal

Islamnagar

This now-ruined fortified city 11km north of Bhopal was the first capital of Bhopal state, founded as Jagdishpur by the Rajputs before Dost Mohammed Khan occupied and renamed it in the early 18th century. The still-standing walls enclose two villages as well as the remains of two palaces: Chaman Mahal and Rani Mahal.

The 18th-century **Chaman Mahal** (Indian/foreigner ₹5/100; ◷dawn-dusk) is a synthesis of traditional Indian and Islamic architecture with Bengali-influenced drooping eaves. The main attraction is the Mughal water garden. There's also a *hammam* (Turkish bath) with changing rooms and water troughs in the dark, cool interior.

Adjacent is the dusty 19th-century **Rani Mahal** (Indian/foreigner ₹5/100; ◷dawn-dusk) with a colonnaded Diwan-i-Am (Hall of Public Audience). Outside stand eight massive iron treasure chests, presumably delivered by outsized porters from the nearby *hathi khana* (elephant stables).

Catch a tempo, bus or shared jeep (all ₹20) up Berasia Rd, though you may have to change, or take an autorickshaw (₹200).

Bhojpur

Built by the founder of Bhopal, Raja Bhoj (1010–53), Bhojpur used to be home to a 400-sq-km manmade lake, which was destroyed in the 15th century by the dam-busting Mandu ruler Hoshang Shah. Thankfully, the magnificent **Bhojeshwar Temple** survived the attack.

HANDY TRAINS FROM BHOPAL

DESTINATION	TRAIN NO & NAME	FARE (₹)*	DURATION (HR)	DEPARTURE
Agra	12627 Karnataka Express	319/862/1215	7	11.35pm
Delhi	12621 Tamil Nadu Express	370/1008/1510	10½	8.30pm
Gwalior	11077 Jhelum Express	253/697/940	6	9.15am
Indore	12920 Malwa Express	236/619/845	5	7.50am
Jabalpur	18233 Narmada Express	239/653/870	7	11.35pm
Mumbai (CST)	12138 Punjab Mail	405/1120/1655	14½	4.55pm
Raipur	18238 Chhattisgarh Express	344/962/1455	14½	6.50pm
Ujjain	12920 Malwa Express	215/541/845	3½	7.50am

*Fares: sleeper/3AC/2AC

Around Bhopal

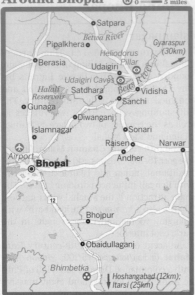

A gamut of figures and scenes dance across the rocks: gaurs (Indian bison), rhinoceroses, bears and tigers share space with scenes of hunting, initiation ceremonies, childbirth, communal dancing, drinking, religious rites and burials.

The oldest paintings (Upper Palaeolithic) in red, often of huge animals, are thought to be 12,000 years old. Successive periods depict hunting tools, trade with the agricultural communities on the Malwa plains, and religious scenes involving tree gods. The latest are crude geometric figures probably dating from the medieval period, when much of the artistry was lost.

The rock shelters are easy to find. The 15 most accessible are numbered, signposted and linked by a concrete path. Zoo Rock Shelter (Shelter 4), famous for its variety of animal paintings, is one of the first you come to; Shelter 15 features a magnificent red bison attacking a helpless stick figure. There are no facilities here, so bring water.

Highway Treat Bhimbetka (☎ 07480 281558; r ₹1777; ❄), with a pleasant restaurant-cafe (mains ₹60 to ₹170; open 8am to 10pm), a children's playground and three comfortable AC rooms, is by the Bhimbetka turn-off, 3km from the rock shelters. The ticket office is halfway up the road to the rocks from here.

Ask your bus driver to drop you at the turn-off for Bhimbetka, about 6.5km beyond Obaidullaganj. It's a 45-minute, 3km walk from here. Alternatively, take an autorickshaw from Obaidullaganj.

On the return journey, flag down anything that moves (buses often won't stop for you) and go as far as Obaidullaganj (₹5), where you'll find buses to Bhopal (₹34) via the Bhojpur turn-off (₹20).

Square in shape and simple in design, this 1000-year-old Hindu temple doesn't look much from the outside, but the interior of the sanctum, supported by four gargantuan pillars and housing a large Shiva lingam, is very powerful indeed.

Around the back, a stony ramp illustrates how huge pieces of rock would have been moved into position onto the temple's 5m-tall platform. To the side, fenced-off areas of rocky slopes show etchings of grander plans for a temple complex that was never finished.

Take the Bhimbetka bus to the turn-off for Bhojpur (₹17, 30 minutes), where tempos (₹20) ply the 11km road to the temple.

Bhimbetka

Secreted in a forest of teak and sal in craggy cliffs 46km south of Bhopal are more than 700 **rock shelters** (Indian/foreigner ₹10/100, motorbike or car ₹50/200, autorickshaw ₹80/400; ☉ dawn-dusk). Around 500 of them contain some of the world's oldest prehistoric paintings.

Thanks to their natural red and white pigments, the colours are remarkably well preserved and, in certain caves, paintings of different eras adorn the same rock surface.

Sanchi

☎ 07482 / POP 7305

Rising from the plains, 46km northeast of Bhopal, is a rounded hill topped with some of India's oldest Buddhist structures.

In 262 BC, repentant of the horrors he had inflicted on Kalinga in present-day Odisha, the Mauryan emperor Ashoka embraced Buddhism. As a penance he built the Great Stupa at Sanchi, near the birthplace of his wife. A domed edifice used to house religious relics, it was the first Buddhist monument in the region, although many other religious structures followed.

As Hinduism gradually reabsorbed Buddhism, the site decayed and was forgotten, until being 'rediscovered' in 1818 by a British army officer.

Although Sanchi can be visited as a day trip from Bhopal, this crossroads village is a relaxing spot to spend the night, and a number of side trips can be taken from here.

◉ Sights

The hilltop **stupas** (Indian/foreigner ₹10/250, audio guide Indian languages/foreign languages ₹68/113; ☻ dawn-dusk) are reached via a path and stone steps at the end of Monuments Rd (which is a continuation of the road that leaves the train station), where the **ticket office** is located.

If you're going up to the stupas for sunrise, buy a ticket the day before. Remember, it is auspicious to walk clockwise around Buddhist monuments.

Stupa 1   BUDDHIST SITE
(Great Stupa) Beautifully proportioned, the Great Stupa is the main structure on the hill, directly in front of you as you enter the complex from the north. Originally constructed by Ashoka, it was later enlarged and the original brick stupa enclosed within a stone one. Presently it stands 16m high and 37m in diameter. Encircling the stupa is a wall with four entrances through magnificently carved *toranas* (gateways) that are the finest Buddhist works of art in Sanchi, if not India.

Toranas   SACRED SITE
The Great Stupa's four gateways were erected around 35 BC, but had all fallen down by the time the site was rediscovered. They have since been repositioned. Scenes carved onto the pillars and their triple architraves are mainly tales from the Jatakas, episodes from Buddha's various lives. At this stage in Buddhist art he was never represented directly – his presence was alluded to through symbols. The lotus stands for his birth, the bodhi tree for his enlightenment, the wheel for his teachings, and the footprint and throne for his presence. The stupa itself also symbolises Buddha.

The **Northern Gateway**, topped by a broken wheel of law, is the best preserved of the *toranas*. Scenes include a monkey offering a bowl of honey to Buddha, who is represented by a bodhi tree. Another panel depicts the Miracle of Sravasti – one of several miracles

represented here – in which Buddha, again in the form of a bodhi tree, ascends a road into the air. Elephants support the architraves above the columns, while delicately carved *yakshis* (maidens) hang nonchalantly on each side.

The breathtakingly carved figure of a *yakshi,* hanging from an architrave on the **Eastern Gateway**, is one of Sanchi's best-known images. One of the pillars, supported by elephants, features scenes from Buddha's entry to nirvana. Another shows Buddha's mother Maya's dream of an elephant standing on the moon, which she had when he was conceived. Across the front of the middle architrave is the Great Departure, when Buddha (a riderless horse) renounced the sensual life and set out to find enlightenment.

The back-to-back lions supporting the **Southern Gateway**, the oldest gateway, form the state emblem of India, which can be seen on every banknote. The gateway narrates Ashoka's life as a Buddhist, with scenes of Buddha's birth and another representation of the Great Departure. Also featured is the Chhaddanta Jataka, a story in which Bodhisattva (Buddha before he had reached enlightenment) took on the form of an elephant king who had six tusks. The less favoured of the elephant king's two wives was so jealous of the other that she decided to starve herself to death, vowing to come back to life as the queen of Benares in order to have the power to avenge her husband's favouritism. Her wish came true, and as queen she ordered hunters to track down and kill the elephant king. A hunter found the great elephant but before he could kill it, the elephant handed over his tusks, an act so noble it led to the queen dying of remorse.

Pot-bellied dwarves support the architraves of the **Western Gateway**, which has some of the site's most interesting scenes. The top architrave shows Buddha in seven different incarnations, manifested three times as a stupa and four times as a tree. The rear of one pillar shows Buddha resisting the Temptation of Mara (the Buddhist personification of evil, often called the Buddhist devil), while demons flee and angels cheer.

Other Stupas   BUDDHIST SITE
Stupa 2 is halfway down the hill to the west (turn right at Stupa 1). If you come up

Sanchi

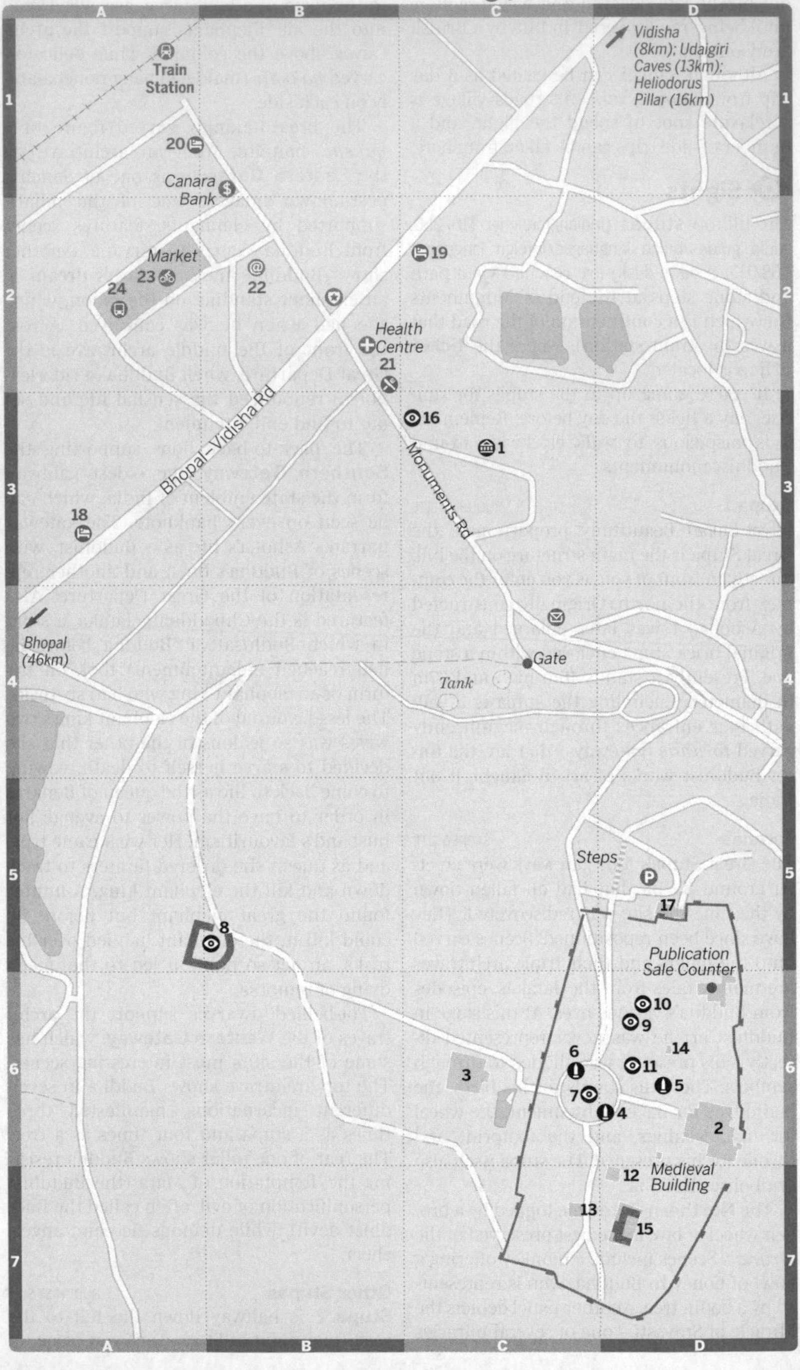

N ⌃ 0 ————————— 200 m
0 ————————— 0.1 miles

Train Station

Vidisha (8km); Udaigiri Caves (13km); Heliodorus Pillar (16km)

20

Canara Bank

Market
24 23
22

19

Health Centre
21

16

1

Bhopal–Vidisha Rd

18

Monuments Rd

Bhopal (46km)

Tank

Gate

Steps
P

17

Publication Sale Counter

10
9
14

6
3
11
7
5
4

2

Medieval Building

12

13

15

8

Sanchi

from the village by the main route you can walk back down via Stupa 2, although be prepared for some fence-hopping at the bottom. Instead of gateways, 'medallions' decorate the surrounding wall – naive in design, but full of energy and imagination. Flowers, animals and people – some mythological – ring the stupa.

Stupa 3 is northeast of the Great Stupa (you pass it on your left as you approach the Great Stupa from the main entrance) and similar in design, though smaller, with a single, rather fine gateway. It once contained relics of two important disciples of Buddha: Sari Puttha and Maha Moggallana. They were moved to London in 1853 but returned in 1953 and are now kept in the modern *vihara* (resting place).

Only the base is left of the 2nd-century-BC **Stupa 4**, which stands behind Stupa 3. Between Stupas 1 and 3 is the small **Stupa 5**, unusual in that it once contained a statue of Buddha, now displayed in the museum.

Pillars
MONUMENT

Of the scattered remains of pillars, the most important is **Pillar 10**, erected by Ashoka but later broken. Two upper sections of this beautifully proportioned and executed shaft lie side by side behind Stupa 1; the capital (head of the pillar, usually sculpted) is in the museum. **Pillar 25** (to the east of Stupa 1) dating from the Sunga period (2nd century BC), and the 5th-century-AD **Pillar 35** (to the west of Stupa 1) are less impressive.

Temples
TEMPLES

Temple 18 (behind Stupa 1) is a *chaitya* (prayer room or assembly hall) remarkably similar in style to classical Greek columned buildings. It dates from around the 7th century AD, but traces of earlier wooden buildings have been discovered beneath it. To its left is the small, also Greek-like **Temple 17**. Beyond both of them, the large **Temple 40** dates back to the Ashokan period, in part.

The rectangular **Temple 31** (beside Stupa 5) was built in the 6th or 7th century but reconstructed during the 10th or 11th century. It contains a well-executed image of Buddha.

Monasteries
MONASTERY

The earliest monasteries were made of wood and are long gone. The usual plan was of a central courtyard surrounded by monastic cells. These days only the courtyards and stone foundations remain. **Monasteries 45 and 47**, standing on the eastern ridge to the left of Stupa 1, date from the transition from Buddhism to Hinduism, with strong Hindu elements in their design. The former has two sitting Buddhas. The one housed inside is exceptional.

Behind **Monastery 51**, partway down the hill towards Stupa 2, is the **Great Bowl**, carved from a boulder, into which food and offerings were placed for distribution to the monks.

Vihara
MUSEUM

(⊙9am-5pm) The *vihara*, literally 'resting place', was built to house the returned relics from Stupa 3. They can be viewed on the last Sunday of the month. It's immediately on your left as you enter the complex.

MADHYA PRADESH & CHHATTISGARH SANCHI

Archaeological Museum
MUSEUM

(incl with Stupa ticket; ⊙ 8am-5pm Sat-Thu) This fine museum has a small collection of sculptures from the site. The centre piece is the 3rd-century-BC lion capital from the Ashoka Pillar 10. Other highlights include a *yakshi* hanging from a mango tree, and beautifully serene Buddha figures in red sandstone. There are also some interesting photos showing the site, pre-restoration.

🛏 Sleeping & Eating

New Jaiswal Lodge
GUESTHOUSE $

(⌨ 266508; Monuments Rd; r ₹350-550) This friendly place has basic but colourful rooms and small private bathrooms with sit-down flush toilets. It is on your right as you exit the train station. Does basic meals and air-coolers can be provided.

Krishna Hotel
GUESTHOUSE $

(⌨ 266610; Bhopal–Vidisha Rd; r from ₹150, s/d ₹300/400) Simple rooftop rooms, some with sit-down flush toilets, are slightly more expensive than the darker, noisier rooms at the front. It's above Jaiswal Medical Store. Pancakes and a few traveller favourites are available from the kitchen. Come out of the train station along Monuments Rd, turn left at the crossroads and it's on your right.

Gateway Retreat
HOTEL $$

(⌨ 266723; www.mptourism.com; Bhopal–Vidisha Rd; s/d incl breakfast ₹1162/1280, with AC from ₹2102/2340; ❄☲) This family-friendly MP Tourism hotel is the most comfortable place to stay in Sanchi. AC bungalows are set among well-kept gardens, with a small children's play area and a swimming pool with slide. There's a restaurant (mains ₹60 to ₹145; open 7am to 11pm) and bar. Come out of the train station, turn right at the crossroads and it's on your right.

Gateway Cafeteria
INDIAN $

(⌨ 266743; Monuments Rd; mains ₹50-120; ⊙ 7am-10.30pm) This clean MP Tourism place has a simple Indian menu plus coffee. Come out of the train station and keep going. It's on your left, just before the ticket office for the stupas.

❶ Information

There's a State Bank ATM outside the Gateway Hotel. A couple of places in the market by the bus stand have **internet access** (per hr ₹30; ⊙ 8am-10.30pm).

❶ Getting There & Around

BIKE
You can rent **bicycles** (per hour/day ₹5/30) at the market by the bus stand.

BUS
Every half-hour, buses connect Sanchi with Bhopal (₹35, 1½ hours, 6am to 10pm) and Vidisha (₹10, 20 minutes, 6am to 11pm). It's better to wait at the village crossroads for buses rather than going into the **bus stand**, which is on your right as you exit the train station.

TRAIN
Train is a decent option for getting to Sanchi from Bhopal. It takes less than an hour so there's no need to book a seat: just turn up with enough time to queue for a 'general' ticket (₹26), and squeeze on. Six daily trains leave from Bhopal (8am, 10.20am, 3.15pm, 4.10pm, 6pm and 8.55pm). Only four run in the other direction (8am, 8.50am, 4.30pm and 7.10pm).

Around Sanchi

Vidisha

⌨ 07592 / POP 155,959

This small but thriving market town, 8km northeast of Sanchi, was a commercial centre in the 5th and 6th centuries BC. These days it's an interesting place for a wander or a chai break en route to the Udaigiri Caves.

Many of the attractive whitewashed or painted buildings still have old wooden balconies that overlook the market streets where horse-drawn carts share space with scooters and rickshaws. There are also a number of brightly coloured temples dotted around the old town, which is located to the left of the main road from Sanchi.

Past the town, and over the railway line, is the dusty **District Museum** (Sagar–Vidisha Rd; Indian/foreigner ₹5/50, camera ₹50; ⊙ 10am-5pm Tue-Sun), which houses some beautiful sculptures recovered from local sites, the most impressive of which is a 3m-high, 2nd-century-BC stone statue of Kuber Yaksha, treasurer of the gods, on display as you enter.

It's a straightforward 30-minute cycle from Sanchi or else there are frequent buses (₹10, 20 minutes).

Udaigiri Caves

Cut into a sandstone hill, about 5km northwest of Vidisha, are some 20 Gupta **cave shrines** (⊙ dawn-dusk) dating from the reign of Chandragupta II (AD 382–401). Most are Hindu but two, near the top of the hill, are Jain (Caves 1 and 20) – unfortunately both are closed due to unsafe roofs.

In Cave 4 is a lingam bearing Shiva's face complete with a third eye. Cave 5 contains the finest carving – a superb image of Vishnu in his boar incarnation topped with a frieze of gods, who also flank the entrance to Cave 6. Lotus-ceilinged Cave 7 was cut out for the personal use of Chandragupta II. On the top of the hill are ruins of a 6th-century Gupta temple dedicated to the sun god.

To get here by bike from Sanchi, head towards Vidisha, but turn left about 1km before the town, following a sign for Udaigiri. Follow the road to the Betwa River, cross the river then take the first left and keep going until you reach the caves. Alternatively, take a bus to Vidisha then a rickshaw (₹150 return). A return rickshaw from Sanchi is about ₹400.

If you want to cycle back via Vidisha, cross back over the river and keep going straight instead of bearing round to the right on the road you took from Sanchi.

Heliodorus Pillar

The Heliodorus Pillar (Khamb Baba), just beyond the Udaigiri Caves turn-off, was erected by a Greek ambassador, Heliodorus from Taxila (now in Pakistan), in about 140 BC, and dedicated to Vasudeva. The pillar is worshipped by local fishermen who chain themselves to it on full-moon nights. It is said they then become possessed and are able to drive evil spirits from other locals. When someone has been exorcised, they drive a nail into the tamarind tree nearby, fixing to it a lime, a piece of coconut, a red thread and supposedly the spirit. The large tree is bristling with old nails.

The pillar is close to the Udaigiri Caves. Once you cross the Betwa River, carry straight on, rather than turning left for the caves, and you'll soon see a sign directing you up a small lane on your right, which leads to the pillar.

Pachmarhi

📞 07578 / POP 13,700 / ELEV 1067M

Madhya Pradesh's only hill station is surrounded by waterfalls, cave temples and the forested ranges of the Satpura Tiger Reserve and offers a refreshing escape from steamy central India.

Even if you don't go on an organised trek or jeep safari, you can easily spend a couple of days here cycling or hiking to the numerous sights before taking a dip in one of the natural pools that dot the area.

Explorer Captain J Forsyth 'discovered' Pachmarhi as late as 1857 and set up India's first Forestry Department at Bison Lodge in 1862. Soon after, the British army set up regional headquarters here, starting an association with the military that remains today.

A number of colonial buildings from that era have been converted into delightful guesthouses, which can be found in the Jaistambha area, 2km southwest of the small town.

⊙ Sights

Satpura National Park   NATURE RESERVE
(Indian/foreigner per day ₹20/200, per jeep ₹500/1700; ⊙ dawn-dusk) A ticket for Satpura National Park must be bought at the **ticket office** (⊙ 8.30am-1pm & 2-5pm) outside Bison Lodge. It includes entry to Bison Lodge, Bee Falls, Duchess Falls, Reechgarh, Astachal, Ramykund and Rajat Prapat (including Panchuli Kund and Apsara Vihar). Other sights are free.

Bison Lodge   MUSEUM
(⊙ 8.30am-1pm & 2-5pm) Captain Forsyth named Bison Lodge after a herd of 'bison' (gaur) he spotted here. It's now an old-fashioned, dilapidated museum focusing on the history, flora and fauna of the Satpura region.

Caves   CAVES
The nearest sight to Pachmarhi village is **Jata Shankar**, a cave temple in a beautiful gorge about 2.5km along a good track that's signed just north of the town limits. The small Shiva shrine is hidden under a huge overhanging rock.

Just southeast of Jaistambha, you'll find **Pandav Caves**, which are believed to have been carved by Buddhists as early as the 4th century. The foundations of a brick Buddhist stupa have been excavated on top of them.

Pools & Waterfalls   WATERFALL
Just south of town, past Christchurch, the trailhead for **Bee Falls** is easily accessed by bike. There are chai and snack stalls along the way to the bottom of the trail.

Further along the main road, past the trailhead, you'll find the access roads for **Duchess Falls**, the two beauty points

Pachmarhi

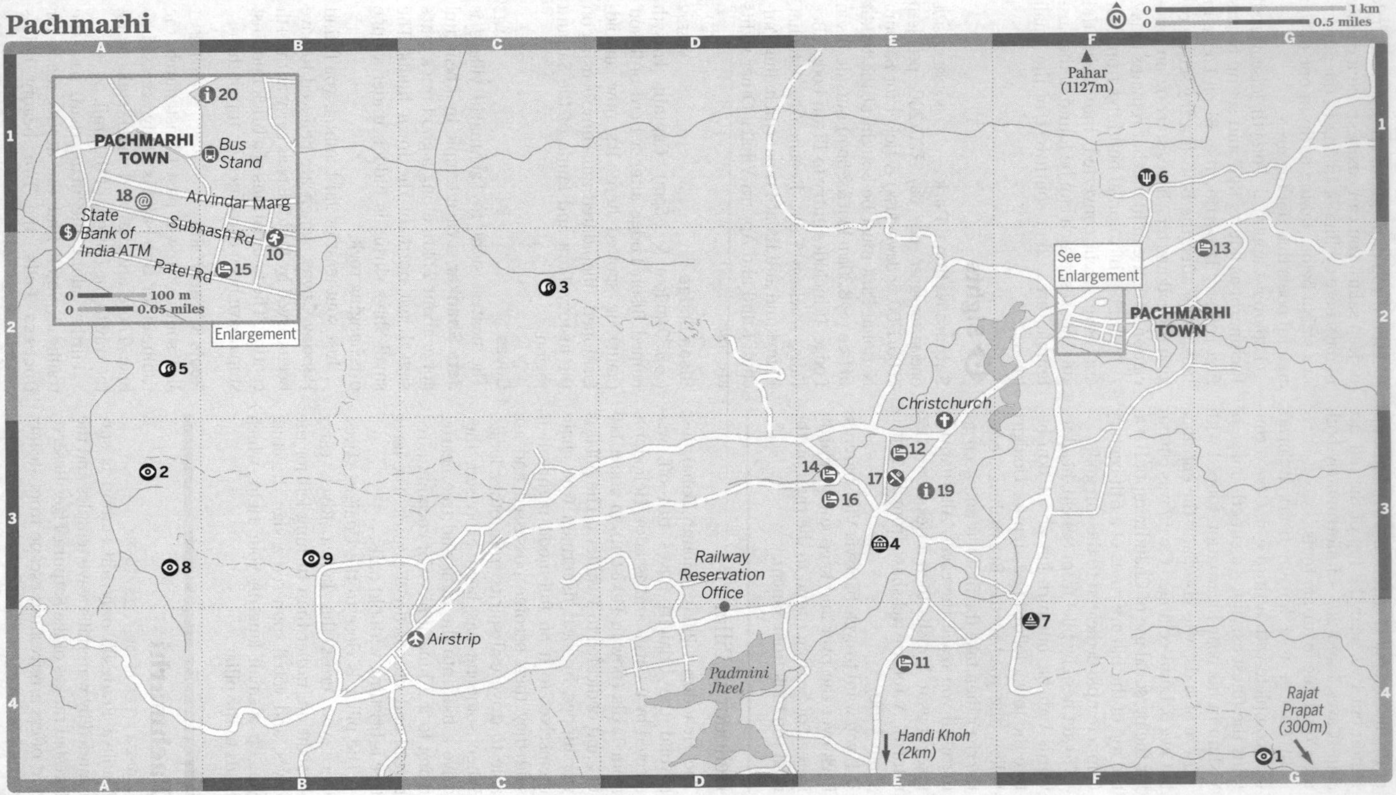

1 km
0.5 miles

Rajat Prapat (300m) ◉ 1

PACHMARHI TOWN

⚐ 13

♨ 6

Pahar (1127m) ▲

See Enlargement

▲ 7

Handi Khoh (2km) →

Christchurch

ⓘ 19
✉ 12
17 ✕
⚔ 4
🏛 11

14 🏛
🏛 16

Railway Reservation Office

Padmini Jheel

Airstrip ✈

◉ 9

◉ 3

Enlargement

PACHMARHI TOWN

ⓘ 20
Bus Stand
Arvindar Marg
Subhash Rd
10 ★
18 @
State Bank of India ATM $
Patel Rd
15 ⊙

100 m
0.05 miles

◉ 5

⊙ 2

◉ 8

Pachmarhi

◎ Sights

known as **Reechgarh** and **Astachal,** and a small, crystal-clear pool called **Ramykund.**

On the other side of Jaistambha, 1km past Pandav Caves, is the trailhead for **Apsara Vihar** (Fairy Pool), a pool underneath a small waterfall, which is the best of Pachmarhi's natural pools for swimming. Upstream from here is **Panchuli Kund,** five descending rock pools that are great for a paddle. Steps up from the snack stall by Apsara Vihar lead to a point with magnificent views of the gorge and of **Rajat Prapat** (Big Fall), the tallest of Pachmarhi's waterfalls, which tumbles down a gully in a sheer cliff.

Chauragarh   VIEWPOINT

South of Jaistambha is the road that leads towards Chauragarh (1308m), Madhya Pradesh's third-highest peak. The Shiva shrine at the top attracts tens of thousands of pilgrims during Shivaratri Mela. On the way, stop at **Handi Khoh,** also known as Suicide Point, to gawk down the 100m canyon into the dense forest. You'll spy Chauragarh in the distance from here as well as Priyadarshini (Forsyth Point), further along the road.

About 3km beyond Priyadarshini the road ends at **Mahadeo Cave,** where a path 30m into the damp gloom reveals a lingam with attendant priest. This is the beginning of the 1365-step pilgrim trail to Chauragarh (five hours' return hike). A kilometre further on, another **Shiva shrine** is at the back of a terrifyingly narrow passage created by sticks (apparently) holding open a fissure in the cliff.

Satpura Tiger Reserve   NATURE RESERVE

(per jeep Indian/foreign ₹2200/3200; ☉ 16 Oct-30 Jun) Has tigers and leopards, although you're unlikely to see either. What you will get, though, are scenic forest tracks without another tourist in sight, plus plenty of monkeys, deer and birds of all types. Safaris are best arranged at Bison Lodge. On top of your group and jeep entrance fee, you will need to pay for a guide (₹350). Fees are per jeep, not per person. Unlike in other tiger parks, where safaris are split into morning and afternoon outings, here you get a full day in the reserve. Enquire at Bison Lodge about two-day packages with the opportunity to stay overnight in the reserve at a Forest Rest House.

☊ Activities

All the places mentioned here can be reached by bike, although bikes have to be left at the trailheads from where the hiking begins.

Baba Cycles   BIKE HIRE

(Subhash Rd; per hr/day ₹5/50; ☉ 9.15am-9pm) Baba Cycles rents bikes.

Bison Lodge   SAFARIS, TREKKING

Forestry commission guides (trekking per day ₹350 to ₹510) can be arranged at Bison Lodge ticket office; some speak English. This is also the best place to arrange jeep safaris to Satpura Tiger Reserve.

Satpura Adventure Club   ADVENTURE SPORTS

(☏ 252256, 09425367365; ☉ 9am-5pm) Based at Hotel Saketh; can arrange parasailing (per person ₹600) at the airstrip near Reechgarh, and guides (per day ₹300; Hindi-speaking only) to take you on treks around the area.

Swimming   SWIMMING

Locals paddle at the bottom of Bee Falls and Duchess Falls, and Ramykund is good for an invigorating plunge, but for a proper swim, try Apsara Vihar.

🛏 Sleeping & Eating

High seasons are from April to July and December to January, when places fill up and room rates rocket. The same applies during national holidays and major festivals.

🛏 Pachmarhi Town

Hotel Saket   HOTEL $
(☎ 252165; www.pachmarhihotel.com; r ₹300-800, with AC ₹1100; ❄) There is a wide range of rooms in this welcoming hotel on a quiet side street off Patel Rd, from budget classics to midrange options. The attached restaurant **Raj Bhoj** (mains ₹40-100) does Gujarati, Bengali, Chinese and South Indian dishes, including delicious breakfast dosa and thali.

Hotel Highlands   HOTEL $$
(☎ 252099; highland@mptourism.com; Pipariya Rd; r ₹1945, with AC ₹2635; ❄) This family-friendly MP Tourism property on the approach road into Pachmari has rooms with high ceilings, dressing rooms, modern bathrooms and verandahs, which are dotted around well-tended gardens. There's a children's play area and a restaurant.

🛏 Jaistambha Area

Evelyn's Own   GUESTHOUSE $$
(☎ 252056; evelynsown@gmail.com; r incl breakfast ₹1000-4000; ❄ ≋) A rustic colonial-era cottage built by a reverend then bought and converted into a charming guesthouse by the welcoming Colonel Balwant Rao and his wife Pramilla. The main cottage, where you can share meals with the colonel and his wife, is full of family portraits and period furniture. Guest rooms are in buildings dotted around the gardens, which also contain a small swimming pool. Follow the signs to Satpura Retreat, which is down the same dirt track.

Glen View   HERITAGE HOTEL $$
(☎ 252533; gview@mptourism.com; s/d incl breakfast ₹3290/3990, heritage rooms ₹4190/4690; ❄) Large, comfortable AC tents and cottages are dotted around the shaded gardens of a huge colonial-era cottage, which has also been converted to house the luxury 'heritage' rooms. Has restaurant and bar.

Hotel Panchvati   HOTEL $$
(☎ 252096; panchvati@mptourism.com; r ₹1945, with AC ₹2290) A cute colonial bungalow houses the hotel's reception while its restaurant, **China Bowl** (mains ₹70-160), occupies much of the wide verandah. The rooms are out in the back garden, in simple cement cottages, which frankly are in need of an overhaul, but will do if the other eight MP Tourism hotels in town are full.

Rock-End Manor   HERITAGE HOTEL $$
(☎ 252079; mptremph@sancharnet.in; r incl breakfast ₹4490; ❄) Another gorgeous colonial-era building, whitewashed Rock-End is perched above the parched fairways of the army golf course. Spacious rooms (there are only six) have wonderfully high ceilings, and furnishings are luxurious with quality upholstery and framed paintings. There are also great views to be had from seating areas around the covered walkway.

Nandavan Restaurant   INDIAN $
(mains ₹40-130; ⊙ 9.30am-11pm) An outdoor restaurant and a sort of reverse zoo, as monkeys sit outside watching humans eating in a cage. South Indian, Gujarati and thalis.

ℹ Information

Internet Cafe (Subhash Rd; per hr ₹30; ⊙7am-11pm)

MP Tourism Near Jaistamba.

MP Tourism Kiosk (☎252100; ⊙10am-5pm Mon-Fri) By the bus station.

State Bank of India ATM (cnr main road & Patel Rd)

ℹ Getting There & Away

Eight daily buses go to Bhopal (₹150, six hours). The two evening ones (7pm and 8pm) are sleepers and continue on to Indore (seat/bed ₹345/405, 12 hours). There are three buses – all nonsleeper – to Nagpur (₹218, eight hours, 8am, 10am and 9pm). The friendly guys at the bus-ticket counter are around from 7am to 9pm.

All Bhopal buses, plus some extra local ones, go via Pipariya (₹56, two hours), from where you can catch trains to onward destinations such as Jabalpur and Varanasi without having to go all the way to Bhopal. Train tickets can be bought at the **Railway Reservation Office** (⊙ 8am-2pm) inside the forlorn Woodlands Adventure Camp in Pachmarhi. The bus station and train station in Pipariya are next to each other.

If you're coming from Pipariya, shared jeeps to Pachmarhi leave far more frequently than buses and cost the same.

ℹ Getting Around

A place in a shared jeep costs about ₹200 for a day. Cycling or hiking will give you more freedom.

WESTERN MADHYA PRADESH

Ujjain

☏ 0734 / POP 515,215

First impressions do not always impress. And that's the case with Ujjain. The area around the train and bus stations is chaotic and nothing special, but wander towards the river ghats, via Ujjain's maze of alleyways, and you'll discover an older, more spiritual side to this city that has been attracting traders and pilgrims for hundreds of years. An undeniable energy pulses through the temples here – perhaps because this is one of Hinduism's seven sacred cities.

The town is also one of four sites in India that hosts the incredible Kumbh Mela, during which millions bathe in the Shipra River. It takes place here every 12 years, normally during April and May. The next one is in 2016 (22 April to 21 May). Six years before and after each Kumbh Mela there is a slightly smaller Ardh (Half) Mela. On all other years a smaller festival called Magh Mela is held.

History

The Guptas, the Mandu sultans, Maharaja Jai Singh (of Jaipur fame), the Marathas and the Scindias have all had a controlling hand in Ujjain's long and chequered past, which stretches back to when the city, originally called Avantika, was an important trade stop. When the Scindias moved their capital to Gwalior in 1810, Ujjain's prominence declined rapidly.

◎ Sights

Temples

Mahakaleshwar Mandir   HINDU TEMPLE

While this is not the most stunning temple on offer, tagging along behind a conga-line through the underground chambers can be magical. At nonfestival times, the marble walkways are a peaceful preamble to the subterranean chamber containing one of India's 12 sacred Shiva shrines known as *jyoti linga* – naturally occurring linga believed to derive currents of *shakti* (creative energies) from within themselves rather than being ritually invested with *mantra-shakti* by priests.

The temple was destroyed by Altamish in 1235 and restored by the Scindias in the 19th century. You may be asked to give a donation, but it's not compulsory.

Gopal Mandir   HINDU TEMPLE

The Scindias built this marble-spired temple, a magnificent example of Maratha architecture, during the 19th century. Muslim pillagers originally stole the sanctum's silver-plated doors from Somnath Temple in Gujarat and installed them in Ghazni, Afghanistan. Mohammed Shah Abdati later took them to Lahore (in present-day Pakistan), before Mahadji Scindia brought them back here. The winding alleyways north, east and west of here are wonderful places to explore.

Harsiddhi Mandir   HINDU TEMPLE

Built during the Maratha period, this temple enshrines a famous image of goddess Annapurna. At the entrance, two tall blackened stone towers bristling with lamps are a special feature of Maratha art. They add to the spectacle of Navratri (Festival of Nine Nights; Hindu festival leading up to Dussehra) in September/October when filled with oil and ignited.

Chintaman Ganesh Mandir   HINDU TEMPLE

This temple is believed to be of considerable antiquity   the assembly hall's artistically carved pillars date to the Parmara period (c 800–1305). Worshippers flock here to pray to the deity, whose name means 'assurer of freedom from worldly anxieties'. It's an easy cycle from the centre, mostly through farmland. Pass the observatory and keep to the left.

Other Sights

Ram Ghat   GHAT

The most central and most popular of Ujjain's river ghats is best visited at dawn or dusk when the devout chime cymbals and light candles at the water's edge. People bathe here at all times of the day, though. You can also rent pedal boats (₹10).

Vedh Shala   HISTORIC BUILDING

(Observatory; Jantar Mantar; admission ₹10; ⊙ dawn-dusk) Ujjain has been the country's Greenwich since the 4th century BC, and this simple but interesting observatory was built by Maharaja Jai Singh in about 1730. He also built observatories in Jaipur, Delhi, Varanasi and Mathura, but Ujjain's is the

MADHYA PRADESH & CHHATTISGARH UJJAIN

Ujjain

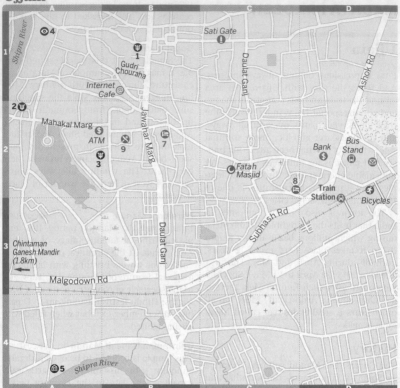

only one still in use. Among the instruments in the small garden are two marble-topped sundials – one a conventional sundial, the other made up of two large quadrants split by a tall staircase whose shadow tells the time.

🛏 Sleeping

Hotel Rama Krishna
HOTEL $

(☎2553017; www.hotelramakrishna.co.in; Subhash Rd; s/d ₹400/500, with AC ₹800/1000; ❄) This cleaner-than-average Subhash Rd hotel has rooms with white-tiled floors, TV and sit-down flush toilets in the air-con rooms.

Hotel Pleasure Landmark
HOTEL $$

(☎2557867; 98 Mahakal Marg; r ₹800, with AC ₹1200; ❄) Rooms here are small, cluttered with chunky wooden furniture and cop a bit of noise, but are clean and it's a great location from which to launch yourself into the old town. Some of the air-con rooms have sit-down flush toilets.

Hotel Grand Tower
HOTEL $$

(☎2553699; 1 Vikram Marg; s/d from ₹1420/1640; ❄) In a very busy part of town convenient to both the bus stand and train station, the GT has large, clean, well-kept air-con rooms, plus efficient service and a very good restaurant.

🍴 Eating

Thali restaurants line Subhash Rd and are good value (from ₹30) but have no English menus and don't open before around 9.30am.

★ Shivam Restaurant
INDIAN $

(Hotel Satyam; mains ₹90-140, thalis from ₹60; ⊙7am-11pm) This friendly and very popular veg restaurant in the basement below Hotel Satyam has a fabulous menu with detailed descriptions of every dish. Choose from tan-

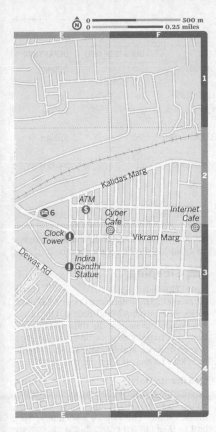

Cyber Cafe (per hr ₹10; ⊙10am-10pm) Walk up Vikram Marg, turn left at the roundabout and it's on your right in a basement. You can you hook up your laptop.

ⓘ Getting There & Away

BUS

Services from the **bus stand** include the following. For Mandu or Maheshwar, change at Dhar.

Bhopal ₹150, five hours, two daily at 6am and 7.30am

Dhar ₹84, four hours, four daily at 5.30am, 8.30am, 9am and 9.45am

Indore ₹35, two hours, every 15 minutes, 5.30am to 11pm

Omkareshwar ₹110, four hours, four daily at 6am, 8am, 11am and 4pm

TRAIN

The two direct trains to Gwalior and Agra arrive at stupid o'clock so you're better off going via Bhopal which, like Indore, is served by more than 10 daily trains.

ⓘ Getting Around

A cycle rickshaw from the train station to Ram Ghat costs ₹30. You can also rent dirt-cheap **bicycles** (per day ₹20; ⊙7am-11pm) from a place behind the bus stand.

Bus 9 (₹4) runs between Jawahar Marg in the old town and Chintaman Ganesh Mandir, via the train station and the clock tower.

Prices from the prepaid autorickshaw booth outside the train station:

Chintaman Ganesh Mandir ₹150 return

Four-hour tour around Ujjain ₹500

Ram Ghat ₹50

doori kebabs, a selection of paneer dishes, koftas and a variety of stuffed vegetables, or just come for the South Indian breakfasts or a thali.

New Sudama   INDIAN $
(Hotel Rama Krishna; mains ₹50-100; ⊙8.30am-11pm) One of the better Subhash Rd offerings, this clean restaurant attached to Hotel Rama Krishna has inexpensive North Indian food.

Zharokha Restaurant   INDIAN $$
(mains ₹50-130; ⊙7am-3.30pm & 7-11pm) The vegetarian restaurant at Hotel Grand Tower serves excellent Kashmiri, Punjabi and Chinese food and has 1st-floor balcony seating.

ⓘ Information

There are ATMs all over Ujjain, including two next to the Hotel Grand Tower.

HANDY TRAINS FROM UJJAIN

DESTINATION	TRAIN NO & NAME	FARE (₹)*	DURATION (HR)	DEPARTURE
Bhopal	19313 Indore RJN Express	195/510/815	3½	3.20pm
Delhi	12919 Malwa Express	415/1152/1695	15	2pm
Indore	18234 Narmada Pas Express	155/425/815	2	8.40am
Jaipur	12465 Ranthambhore Express	146/322/648/869**	8½	8.05am
Mumbai (Central)	12962 Avantika Express	380/1044/1560	13	5.40pm

*Fares: sleeper/3AC/2AC **2nd class/sleeper/chair car/3AC

Indore

☎ 0731 / POP 1.96 MILLION

The Holkar dynasty left behind some fine buildings here, and you'll find some cool cafes thanks to the city's ever-burgeoning coffee culture, but Indore – Madhya Pradesh's business powerhouse – is primarily used by tourists as the gateway to Omkareshwar, Maheshwar or Mandu.

⊙ Sights

Lal Bagh Palace   MUSEUM

(Indian/foreigner ₹5/100; ⊙ 10am-5pm Tue-Sun) Built between 1886 and 1921, Lal Bagh Palace is the finest building left by the Holkar dynasty. Replicas of the Buckingham Palace gates creak at the entrance to the 28-hectare garden, where, close to the palace, there is a statue of Queen Victoria. The palace is dominated by European styles, with baroque and rococo dining rooms, an English library with leather armchairs, a Renaissance sitting room with ripped sofas and a Palladian queen's bedroom. An autorickshaw from the town centre to here is about ₹50.

Central Museum   MUSEUM

(AB Rd; Indian/foreigner ₹10/100, camera/video ₹50/200; ⊙ 10am-5pm Tue-Sun) Housed in another fine Holkar building, this museum has one of Madhya Pradesh's best collections of medieval and premedieval Hindu sculptures, along with tools, weaponry and copper-engraved land titles. Skirmishes took place here during the First War of Independence (Indian Uprising) – the well in the garden was poisoned during the struggle.

Gandhi Hall   HISTORIC BUILDING

This Gothic town hall, built in 1904 and once called King Edward's Hall, stands incongruously on MG Rd like a ghost of the Raj.

🛏 Sleeping

Hotel Neelam   HOTEL $

(☎ 2466001; 33/2 Patel Bridge Corner; s ₹375-425, d ₹550-650, s/d with AC ₹650/850; ▒) One of the few budget places near the train and bus stations that happily accepts foreigners, Neelam is very well run and friendly, and has simple but clean rooms off a central courtyard.

Maasharda Hotel   HOTEL $

(☎ 4006562; 4 Nasia Rd, Sarvate bus stand; r ₹300, with AC ₹600; ▒) Good-value, clean choice near the bus stand. This hotel is sometimes reluctant to take foreign guests, but smile sweetly when you arrive and you should be OK.

Hotel Chanakya   HOTEL $

(☎ 2704497; RNT Marg, Chhawni Chowk; s/d from ₹600/700, with AC from ₹990/1100; ▒) Rooms here are functional rather than flash. The cheapest have no windows and it's worth paying ₹100 more for the air-cooled 'semideluxe' rooms or the air-con rooms. On the plus side, staff are friendly and it's right in the heart of an interesting section of the old town. There's a restaurant upstairs and a popular sweet shop on the ground floor.

★ Hotel Shreemaya   HOTEL $$

(☎ 2515555; shree@shreemaya.com; 12 RNT Marg; s/d from ₹2525/3290; ▒ @ 🛜) This professionally run place is quality throughout. Modern rooms with flat-screen TVs and coffee makers are in immaculate condition and there's free wi-fi in all of them. Rates include breakfast and airport drop-off, while the multicuisine veg restaurant is all class.

Indore

Hotel Surya
HOTEL $$

(☑ 407911; www.suryaindore.com; s/d from 1720/2150; ❋) The rooms, restaurant and bar are all rather dim for a place with a sunny name. Nevertheless, it is a clean and welcoming hotel with comfortable and functional rooms and a recommended restaurant.

🍴 Eating & Drinking

Indian Coffee House
SOUTH INDIAN $

(MG Rd; mains ₹40-80, coffee ₹10; ⊘ 7.30am-10pm) Drink coffee with Indore's judiciary at this branch of the excellent Indian Coffee House set inside the grounds of the commissioner's office and near the district court. A top spot for breakfast, with dosa and particularly good *idli* sharing the menu with eggs and toast.

Shree Chotiwala
INDIAN $

(Nath Mandir Rd; mains ₹50-115; ⊘ 11am-11pm) This very popular restaurant has comfy booth seating and a family-friendly veg menu that includes Jain and Chinese dishes and a children's thali (₹70). An excellent choice for an evening meal.

Shreemaya Celebration
BAKERY $

(Tuko Ganj; mains ₹85-145; ⊘ 7.30am-10.30pm) This modern bakery next to Hotel Shreemaya sells pastries, sandwiches, cookies and cakes, as well as a handful of mains, including South Indian, Chinese and pizza. Also has juices, shakes and coffee, making this a good pick for breakfast.

Apna
INDIAN $

(Sarvate bus stand; mains ₹60-160; ⊘ 10am-11.30pm) This 50-year-old bar and restaurant right opposite the bus stand serves up delicious veg and meat dishes from an all-Indian menu, as well as the usual selection of beers and cheap whiskeys.

Mr Beans
CAFE

(MG Rd; cappuccino ₹65; ⊘ 9am-11pm) Slick cafe housed in a charming 100-year-old colonial-era building serving decent coffee and snacks.

Monkey Cafe
CAFE

(MG Rd; coffee from ₹40; ⊘ 11am-midnight; 🖥) Good-quality coffee, wi-fi and DVDs shown on a giant screen. Music, though, is often deafeningly loud and sometimes of the karaoke variety.

🛍 Shopping

Mrignayani
HANDICRAFTS

(165 MG Rd; ⊘ 11am-1.30pm & 2.30-8pm Mon-Sat) Fixed-price government emporium with two floors crammed with handicrafts from across the state, including leather toy animals – an Indore speciality.

ℹ Information

ATMs are all over town.

007 Cyber Gallery (Silver Mall; per hr ₹10; ⊘ 9am-11pm) Internet cafe serving drinks and snacks.

Bombay Hospital (☑ 4077000; www.bombayhospitalindore.com; Indore Ring Rd) Indore's best general hospital.

Main Post Office (AB Rd; ⊘ 8am-8pm Mon-Sat, 10am-4pm Sun)

Royal Chemist (MY Hospital Rd; ⊘ 9.15am-10pm)

State Bank of India (AB Rd; ⊘ 10.30am-4.30pm Mon-Fri, 10.30am-2.30pm Sat) Changes travellers cheques and cash, and has an ATM.

Wintech Cyber (1st fl; per hr ₹10; ⊘ 11am-10pm) Internet cafe set back from Ushaganj Main Rd.

ℹ Getting There & Away

AIR

Air India (☑ 2431595, 2431596; Racecourse Rd; ⊘ 10am-1pm & 2-5pm Mon-Sat) flies daily to Mumbai and Delhi (both from around ₹4000).

Jet Airways (☑ 2544590; Racecourse Rd; ⊘ 9.30am-6pm Mon-Sat) has daily flights to Mumbai, Delhi, Hyderabad, Ahmedabad and Raipur.

MADHYA PRADESH & CHHATTISGARH INDORE

HANDY TRAINS FROM INDORE

DESTINATION	TRAIN NO & NAME	FARE (₹; SLEEPER/3AC/2AC)	DURATION (HR)	DEPARTURE
Bhopal	12919 Malwa Express	236/619/845	5	12.25pm
Delhi	12919 Malwa Express	437/1214/1775	16½	12.25pm
Mumbai	12962 Avantika Express	398/1107/1635	15	4.05pm
Ujjain	12919 Malwa Express	215/456/845	2	12.25pm

BUS

For Mandu, catch a bus from **Gangwal bus stand** (📞 0731 2380688; Jawahar Rd) to Dhar (₹55, three hours, 6am to 10.30pm) from where you can change for Mandu (₹25, one hour, last bus 7pm). Shared minivans (₹10) go between Gangwal bus stand and the centre. Private autorickshaws charge around ₹80.

Bus services from **Sarwate bus stand** (📞 2465688) include those listed below. For Maheshwar, change at Dhamnod.

Bhopal ₹150, five hours, every 30 minutes from 5am to midnight

Dhamnod ₹60, three hours, every 30 minutes from 7am to 5pm

Gwalior seat/sleeper ₹210/265, 12 hours, three daily at 7pm, 8pm and 9pm

Omkareshwar ₹150, three hours, frequent from 7am to 4.30pm

Pachmarhi seat/sleeper ₹215/270, 12 hours, four daily at 5pm, 6pm, 7pm and 8pm

Ujjain ₹35, two hours, frequent from 6am to 10pm

TAXI

Private taxi firms on the service road parallel to Valiash Nagar charge around ₹2000 return to Mandu and the same price for a trip incorporating Omkareshwar and Maheshwar.

TRAIN

There are six daily trains to Bhopal and more than 10 to Ujjain. The **train reservation office** (🕑 8am-8pm Mon-Sat, 8am-2pm Sun) is 200m east of the train station.

🛈 Getting Around

The airport is 9km from the city. Allow 45 minutes. Autorickshaws charge around ₹200, taxis ₹150 to ₹300. Autorickshaw journeys around Indore cost ₹30 to ₹50.

Omkareshwar

📞 07280 / POP 10,062

One of a number of holy places with ghats referred to as a 'mini Varanasi', the Om-shaped island of Omkareshwar attracts pilgrims in large numbers and has become a popular chill-out destination on the backpacker trail.

The controversial dam has changed the look of Omkareshwar considerably, but the island has retained its spiritual vibe and remains a pleasant place to stay.

Much activity takes place off the island, at a market square known as Getti Chowk (from where the old bridge crosses to the island), and on Mamaleshwar Rd,

which links Getti Chowk to the bus stand. If you continue straight along Mamaleshwar Rd from the bus stand, without turning left to Getti Chowk, you'll find steps leading down to the ghats (where you can cross the river on boats for ₹5). Beyond is the new bridge and the dam.

The path leading from the old bridge to Shri Omkar Mandhata temple is the hub of the island.

👁 Sights & Activities

Shri Omkar Mandhata   HINDU TEMPLE

Tourists can rub shoulders with sadhus in the island's narrow lanes, browse the colourful stalls selling chillums and souvenir linga, or join pilgrims attending the thrice daily *puja* (prayer) at Shri Omkar Mandhata. This cave-like temple, which houses the only shapeless *jyothi lingam* (12 important shrines dedicated to Shiva), is one of many Hindu and Jain monuments on the island.

Other Temples   HINDU TEMPLES

From the old bridge, instead of turning right to Shri Omkar Mandhata, you can also head left and walk up the 287 steps to the 11th-century **Gaudi Somnath Temple**, from where you can descend the hill to the northern tip of the island, where sadhus bathe in the confluence of the holy Narmada and Keveri Rivers. You can climb the narrow, inner staircase of the temple or just sit and watch the langur monkeys play. Nearby, is a 30m-tall Shiva statue. The path passing in front of the statue can be followed back to the ghats (45 minutes), up and down hills and past a number of temple ruins. Don't miss the beautifully sculpted **Siddhanatha Temple** (left at the T-junction in the pathway) with marvellous elephant carvings around its base.

🛏 Sleeping & Eating

★ Manu Guest House   GUESTHOUSE $

(📞 9826749004; r ₹200) Give it a couple of days and you'll feel like part of the family at this welcoming guesthouse. Rooms are simple yet well looked after and bathrooms are shared only, but kept clean. There's no restaurant, though your hosts can whip up a delicious thali (₹100) if you ask in advance. This is pretty much the only place to stay on the island itself that isn't a *dharamsala* (pilgrim's rest house) and it's perched high above the old bridge meaning that it's lovely and quiet, but has great views. It's hard to find, though. Cross the bridge from Getti Chowk and turn right. After 100m, you may spot a tiny sign for the guesthouse that leads you vaguely in the right direction, up a lot of steep steps. Keep asking the way as you climb and be prepared for the odd territorial dog.

Ganesh Guest House
GUESTHOUSE $

(☑ 271370; r with bathroom ₹150-300, r without bathroom ₹100) Follow the signs as you zig-zag off the path leading down to the ghats from Mamaleshwar Rd to reach Ganesh, with its decidely budget rooms with thin mattresses. Upstairs rooms are brighter and have air-coolers, while its shaded garden restaurant (mains ₹60 to ₹130), overlooking the ghats, has a multicuisine menu including Western breakfasts and a peaceful ambience.

Maharaja Guesthouse
GUESTHOUSE $

(☑ 271237; r ₹250-750) This 600-year-old stone building, accessed off Getti Chowk, is slowly being swallowed up by the jungle growing on the river banks. Its nine extremely basic rooms are all in various states of disrepair, and come with tap-and-bucket showers and squat toilets only. Bring your own mosquito net! Room 1, with family portraits on the walls and two doorways that lead out to private clifftop river views, is certainly atmospheric.

Narmada Resort
HOTEL $$

(☑ 271455; omkareshwar@mptourism.com; r incl breakfast ₹1280, with AC from ₹2012; ✳) Overlooking the island and ghats, about 300m from the old bridge and 500m from the bus stand, MP Tourism's midrange option provides the most spacious and comfortable accommodation in Omkareshwar. The pure veg restaurant can do (non-egg) Western breakfasts and decent curries, and enjoys a great view of the island.

Brahmin Bhojanalaya
INDIAN $

(Mamaleshwar Rd; mains ₹35-70; ⊙ 8am-10pm) There are a number of no-nonsense, pure-veg *dhabas* (snack bars) in Omkareshwar, both on the island and on the mainland, especially in Getti Chowk. None has an English sign, although this one does at least have an English menu. It's on your left as you walk up from the bus stand, 50m before the road bears left towards Getti Chowk.

Lassi & Juice Centre
CAFE $

(Getti Chowk; drinks ₹12-30; ⊙ 7am-10pm) A great place to sit and while away time with some people-watching, this pocket-sized cafe on Getti Chowk does magnificent lassis and delicious fruit salads as well as breakfasts and snacks.

❶ Information

Some telephone stalls on Mamaleshwar Rd and on the island have a computer and a stuttering **internet connection** (per hr ₹40). A **State Bank of India ATM** (Mamaleshwar Rd) is near the bus stand. There's a **pharmacy** (⊙ 9am-9pm) diagonally opposite.

❶ Getting There & Away

Services from the bus stand:

Dhamnod (for Mandu, via Oonera) ₹70, 3½ hours, frequent from 6am to 5pm

Indore ₹65, two hours, hourly from 6am to 6pm

Maheshwar ₹55, three hours, hourly from 6am to 4.30pm

Ujjain ₹110, four hours, four daily at 6am, 11.30am, 2.30pm and 5.30pm

Maheshwar

☑ 07283 / POP 23,600

The peaceful, riverside town of Maheshwar has long held spiritual significance – it's mentioned in the Mahabharata and Ramayana under its old name, Mahishmati, and still draws sadhus and *yatris* (pilgrims) to its ancient ghats and temples on the holy Narmada River. The town enjoyed a golden age in the late 18th century under Holkar queen Ahilyabai, who built the palace in the towering fort and many other monuments. Away from the ghats and historic buildings, Maheshwar's colourful streets display brightly painted wooden houses with overhanging balconies.

The river, and the fort which overlooks it, is about 1.5km south of the bus stand. Leaving the bus stand, walk straight over the crossroads and continue past the internet cafe and ATM until you reach a floodlit roundabout. Take the left fork to get to the ghats via Hansa Heritage hotel, Labboo's Café and the fort. Take the right fork to head directly to the ghats.

◉ Sights & Activities

Fort & Palace
HISTORIC SITE

Dominating the town is this 16th-century fort. The huge, imposing ramparts were built by Emperor Akbar, while the **Maheshwar Palace** and several temples within its grounds were added during the reign of Holkar queen Ahilyabai (r 1767–95). The palace is part public courtyard, part posh hotel. Housed within the courtyard, among a collection of rusty matchlocks and dusty palanquins, is a glass-cased statue of Ahilyabai, treated with the reverence of a shrine. Nearby is a Shiva temple with a golden lingam – the starting point for palanquin processions on Ahilyabai's birthday and Dussehra.

Temples
HINDU TEMPLES

From the ramparts of the fort you can see boats (return trip per person/boat ₹10/100) and incense smoke drifting across the water to **Baneshwar Temple**, located on a tiny island in the middle of the river. Descending to the dhobi-wallahs (clothes washers) at the ghats, you pass two impressive **stone temples**. The one on the right, guarded by stone Holkar sentries and a frieze of elephants, houses more images of Ahilyabai and two candle towers, lit during festivals.

Rehwa Society
HANDICRAFTS WORKSHOP

(☑ 273203; www.rehwasociety.org; ⊙ 10am-6pm Wed Mon, shop open daily) Between the palace and the two stone temples a small doorway announces the NGO Rehwa Society, a craft cooperative where profits are ploughed back into the education, housing and welfare of the weavers. A local school, run entirely by Rehwa, is behind the workshop. Maheshwar saris are famous for their unique weave and simple, geometric patterns. You can watch the weavers at work and buy shawls (₹1800), saris (from ₹2500), scarves (₹550) and fabrics made from silk, cotton and wool. Volunteers with some design background are always welcome, as are those interested in volunteering to teach at the school.

🛏 Sleeping & Eating

Akash Deep
GUESTHOUSE $

(☑ 9425334138; Kila Rd; r ₹300-600) The best budget option in town, friendly Akash has clean, spacious rooms, some with TV. Checkout time is 10am. Next door to Hansa Heritage.

Hansa Heritage
HOTEL $

(☑ 273296; r ₹700, with AC ₹1050; ❄) This place has been built with style and quality throughout. Smart, modern rooms have a rustic feel with mud-and-grass daubed interior walls, antique-looking wooden furniture and attractive coloured-glass window panes. Bathrooms are also very modern and spotlessly clean. Indian breakfasts and thali are available.

★ Labboo's Café
GUESTHOUSE $$

(☑ 09229125267; r incl breakfast ₹1210, with AC ₹1650-2090; ⊙ 6.30am-8pm; ❄) Not only a delightful cafe (snacks ₹10 to ₹45, thali ₹250) in a glorious tree-shaded courtyard, but also a place with six wonderful rooms to stay in. Each is different, being part of the fort gate and walls, but is decorated with care and attention. The upper room features its own fort-wall verandah. The cafe menu is snacks only, but staff will whip up a delicious, unlimited thali. It can also organise river trips (per hour per boat ₹200).

Ahilya Fort
HERITAGE HOTEL $$$

(☑ 273329, Delhi 01141551575; www.ahilyafort.com; Indian/foreigner r from ₹10,500/15,500; ❄ @ ≋) This heritage hotel is owned by Prince Shivaji Rao Holka, a direct descendent of Ahilyabai, and forms part of Maheshwar Palace. The best rooms are indeed palatial and some come with fabulous river views, while lush gardens house exotic fruit trees, vegetable patches and a lovely swimming pool. Rates include all meals as well as boat trips on the river. Booking ahead is pretty much essential. Nonguests who fancy a splurge can eat lunch or dinner here. The sumptuous menu is set, as is the ₹1650 per person price. You'll need to book your place at a table in advance and pay a deposit.

❶ Getting There & Away

There are frequent buses to Omkareshwar (₹55, three hours, 9am to 5.30pm) and Dhamnod (₹15, 30 minutes, 7am to 11pm) where you can change for Indore (₹65, two hours, last bus 9pm). For Mandu, first head to Dhamnod then take a Dhar-bound bus as far as a forked junction in the main road, known as Oonera (₹30, two hours). From there flag down a bus (₹10, 30 minutes) or hitch the final 14km to Mandu.

Mandu
☑ 07292 / POP 10,300 / ELEV 634M

Perched on top of a pleasantly green, thinly forested 20-sq-km plateau, picturesque Mandu is home to some of India's finest examples of Afghan architecture as well as impressive baobab trees, originally from Africa. The area is littered with palaces, tombs, monuments and mosques, all within easy cycling distance of each other. Some cling to the edge of ravines, others are beside lakes, while Rupmati's Pavilion, the most romantic of them all, sits majestically at the far end of the plateau, overlooking the vast plains below.

History

Raja Bhoj, of Bhopal fame, founded Mandu as a fortress retreat in the 10th century before it was conquered by the Muslim rulers of Delhi in 1304. When the Mughals captured Delhi in 1401, the Afghan Dilawar Khan, governor of Malwa, set up his own little kingdom and Mandu's golden age began.

Although Dilawar Khan established Mandu as an independent kingdom, it was his son, Hoshang Shah, who shifted the capital from Dhar to Mandu and raised it to its greatest splendour.

In 1526, Bahadur Shah of Gujarat conquered Mandu, only to be ousted in 1534 by the Mughal Humayun, who in turn lost the kingdom to Mallu Khan, an officer of the Khalji dynasty. Ten more years of feuds and invasions saw Baz Bahadur eventually emerge in the top spot, but in 1561 he fled Mandu to avoid facing Akbar's advancing troops.

After Akbar added Mandu to the Mughal empire, it kept a considerable degree of independence, until taken by the Marathas in 1732. The capital of Malwa was then shifted back to Dhar, and the slide in Mandu's fortunes that had begun with the absconding of Baz Bahadur became a plummet.

⊙ Sights & Activities

There are three main groups of ruins: the Royal Enclave, the Village Group and the Rewa Kund Group. Each requires its own separate ticket. All other sights are free.

Royal Enclave　　　　　HISTORIC SITE
(Indian/foreigner ₹5/100, video ₹25; ⊙ dawn-dusk Sat-Thu) These ruins are the only ones fenced off into one single complex. There's a **Publication Centre** (⊙ 10am-6pm) selling guidebooks by the entrance and a shaded garden canteen selling tea, coffee and snacks by Hindola Mahal.

➡ Jahaz Mahal

(Ship Palace) This is the most famous building in Mandu. Built on a narrow strip of land between Munja and Kapur Tanks, with a small upper storey like a ship's bridge (use your imagination), it's far longer (120m) than it is wide (15m). Ghiyas-ud-din, who is said to have had a harem of 15,000 maidens, constructed its lookouts, scalloped arches, airy rooms and beautiful pleasure pools.

➡ Taveli Mahal

(⊙ 9am-5pm Sat-Thu) These former stables now house small **Archaeological Museum** (⊙ 8am-6pm), which features a handful of artefacts found here including 11th- and 12th-century sculptures as well as stone slabs with Quranic text dating back to the 15th century.

➡ Hindola Mahal

(Swing Palace) Just north of Ghiyas' stately pleasure dome is Hindola Mahal (Swing Palace), so-called because the slope of the walls is supposed to create the impression that they are swaying. While it doesn't give that impression, it is an eye-catching design nonetheless.

➡ House & Shop of Gada Shah

The house is within the enclave, but the shop is outside on the road to Delhi Gate. As the buildings' size and internal workmanship suggest, their owner was more than a shopkeeper. His name, which means 'beggar master', is thought to identify him as Rajput chief Medini Ray, a powerful minion of the sultans. The 'shop' was a warehouse for saffron and musk, imported and sold at a handsome profit when there were enough wealthy people to shop here.

➡ Mosque of Dilawar Khan

Built by Dilawar Khan in 1405, this mosque is Mandu's earliest Islamic building. There are many Hindu elements to the architecture, notably the pillars and ceilings inside, which was typical for this era.

➡ Champa Baodi

So-called because its water supposedly smelled as sweet as the champak flower, Champa Baodi is a step-well surrounded by subterranean vaulted chambers, some of which you can explore.

➡ Turkish Bath

Stars and octagons perforate the domed roofs of this tiny *hammam*, which had hot and cold water and a hypocaust (underfloor heated) sauna.

Village Group
HISTORIC SITE
(Indian/foreigner ₹5/100, video ₹25; ☉ dawn-dusk) This group, located by the bus stand in the centre of the village, contains three monuments. One ticket, which you buy at the entrance to Jama Masjid, covers all three.

➡ **Jama Masjid**

Entered by a flight of steps leading to a 17m-high domed porch, this disused redstone mosque dominates the village of Mandu. Hoshang Shah begun its construction around 1406, basing it on the great Omayyad Mosque in Damascus in Syria, and Mohammed Khalji completed it in 1454. Despite its plain design, it's reckoned to be the finest and largest example of Afghan architecture in India.

➡ **Hoshang's Tomb**

Reputed to be India's oldest marble building, this imposing tomb is crowned with a crescent thought to have been imported from Persia or Mesopotamia. Inside, light filters into the echoing dome through stone *jalis* (carved lattice screens), intended to cast an appropriately subdued light on the tombs. An inscription records Shah Jahan sending his architects – including Ustad Hamid, who worked on the Taj Mahal – here in 1659 to pay their respects to the tomb's builders.

➡ **Ashrafi Mahal**

Mohammed Shah originally built his tomb as a madrasa (Islamic college), before converting and extending it. The overambitious design later collapsed – notably the sevenstorey circular tower of victory. The building is an empty shell, but intricate Islamic pillarwork can be seen at the top of its great stairway.

Rewa Kund Group Ruins
HISTORIC SITE
(Indian/foreigner ₹5/100, video ₹25; ☉ dawn-dusk) A pleasant 4km-cycle south of Mandu village, past Sagar Talao, brings you to two more ruins. Tickets for both should be bought from outside Baz Bahadur's Palace.

➡ **Baz Bahadur's Palace**

Baz Bahadur was the last independent ruler of Mandu. His palace, constructed around 1509, is beside the Rewa Kund Tank where a water lift at the northern end supplied water to the palace. A curious mix of Rajasthani and Mughal styles, it was actually built decades before Baz Bahadur came to power.

➡ **Rupmati's Pavilion**

Standing at the top of a cliff plunging 366m to the plains, Rupmati's Pavilion has a subtle beauty unmatched by the other monuments – and some of the dinkiest stone staircases you'll ever climb.

According to Malwa legends, the musicloving Baz Bahadur built it to persuade a beautiful Hindu singer, Rupmati, to move here from her home on the plains. From its terrace and domed pavilions Rupmati could gaze down at the distant glint of the sacred Narmada River.

In fact, the pavilion was built in two or three phases and the style of its arches and pillars suggest it was completed 100 years before Rupmati's time. Nonetheless, the love story is a subject of Malwa folk songs – not least because of its tragic ending. Lured by tales of Rupmati's beauty, Akbar marched on the fort and Baz Bahadur fled, leaving his lover to poison herself.

This place is simply gorgeous at sunset.

Nil Kanth Palace
HISTORIC SITE
If you're looking for a great reason to cycle out into the countryside, consider visiting this unusual former palace turned temple. It stands at the head of a ravine, on the site of an earlier Shiva shrine – its name means God with Blue Throat – and is now once again used as a place of worship. A stream built by one of Akbar's governors trickles through a delightful spiral channel and is usually filled with scented water, giving the palace a sweet aroma. To get here cycle south along Main Rd for less than 1km until you see a large white water tower. Turn right here and follow the road as it twists and turns past villages all the way to Nil Kanth (about 2km). You can continue from here, past more remote villages, for about another kilometre to reach the still-standing gateway of the now ruined Songarh Fort, from where there are more great views.

Lohani Caves
CAVE
Local guides seem unsure as to just how old these sculpted caves are, but some insist that a now-blocked tunnel leads from the caves to Dhar, 35km away. One thing is certain, they command a fabulous view of the ravine below, which you can hike down to from here.

Jain Temple
JAIN TEMPLE
Entered by a turquoise doorway, this complex is a splash of kitsch among the Islamic monuments. The richly decorated temples

Mandu

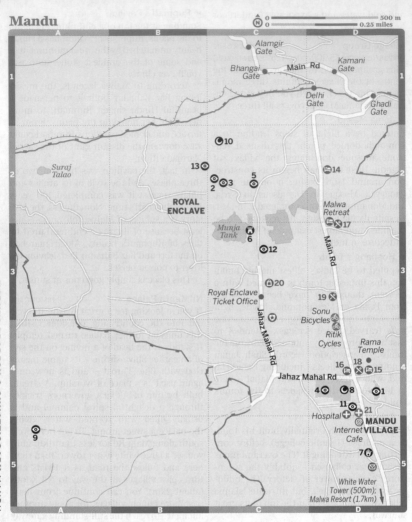

feature marble, silver and gold *tirthankars* with jade eyes, and behind them is a theme park–like museum with a walk-on replica of Shatrunjaya, the hilltop temple complex at Palitana in Gujarat. In the colourful murals, bears devour sinners' arms, crocodiles chew their heads, and demons saw one evil character in half, lengthways.

Saturday Haat
MARKET

(☉10am-dusk) This colourful weekly market, behind Jama Masjid, is similar to ones held all over the Bastar region, a tribal stronghold of Chhattisgarh. Adivasis (tribespeople)

walk kilometres to come here to buy and sell goods ranging from mountains of red chillies to dried *mahuwa,* a flower used to make a potent liquor of the same name.

🛏 Sleeping & Eating

Rama Guesthouse
GUESTHOUSE **$**

(☑ 263251; bus stand; r ₹300) Made up of a row of simple rooms off a courtyard that leads to the small Rama Temple, accommodation here is slightly better than at nearby Tourist Resthouse. Some bathrooms have showers and sit-down flush toilets, but this is still very basic digs. Walk through an archway

Mandu

between two shops by the bus stand. Reception is beyond the rooms, inside the temple grounds.

Tourist Resthouse   GUESTHOUSE $
(☑ 263264; Jahaz Mahal Rd; r ₹150) This row of seven identical and extremely basic rooms with squat toilets and tap-and-bucket showers is the cheapest place in town. Rooms come with small, private verandahs, but they're right on the roadside (albeit it's not a very busy road).

Malwa Resort   HOTEL $$
(☑ 263235; mresortm@mptourism.com; Main Rd; r ₹2337, with AC ₹3041; ❋ ❦) This family-friendly MP Tourism property, 2km south of the village, has large gardens containing comfortable cottages, children's play areas, tree swings and a pool (which isn't always open). There is a restaurant and bar plus pleasant views of the neighbouring lake Sagar Talao.

Malwa Retreat   HOTEL $$
(☑ 263221; mretreatm@mptourism.com; Main Rd; r ₹1515, with AC from ₹2337; ❋) This is MP Tour-

ism's cheaper option, with air-cooled and air-con rooms and tents, that is handy to the village. It can hire out bikes, and the new spick-and-span Malwa Retreat Cafeteria is a step up for Mandu's dining scene.

Hotel Rupmati   HOTEL $$
(☑ 263270; Main Rd; r from ₹1010, with AC ₹1430; ❋) Clean, colourful row of rooms, with large bathrooms, are perched on the edge of a cliff with great views of the valley below. Air-con rooms can be had for a discount if you don't use the air-con. Has a restaurant and a delightful outdoor eating area with views.

Malwar Retreat Cafeteria   INDIAN $$
(Main Rd; mains ₹80-90; ⊙ 8-10am, noon-3pm & 7-10pm) A delightful restaurant that dishes out veg and non-veg Indian meals in very flash (for Mandu) contemporary premises. It was still ironing out a few wrinkles when we visited but this place is definitely worth a try. Unfortunately if you want a cold beer you will need to head to the sister property, the Malwar Resort.

Shivani Restaurant   INDIAN $
(Main Rd; mains ₹35-90; ⊙ 8.30am-10pm) This large, no-nonsense diner with plastic tables and chairs has a big menu that includes thalis (₹60) plus local specialities such as *Mandu kofta* (dumplings in a mild sauce). South Indian breakfasts are also available, as are lassis and coffee.

Relax Point   INDIAN $
(Main Rd; snacks ₹10-40, thali ₹80; ⊙ 8am-9pm) A village shop, gathering point and restaurant-cafe rolled into one. The menu is often limited to snacks such as samosas and *aloo parathas*, but these can make a great light lunch. The rest of the shop is literally packed to the ceiling with every imaginable consumer item.

🛍 Shopping

Roopayan   HANDICRAFTS
(Main Rd; ⊙ 9am-7pm) Next to Malwa Resort, this small shop sells good-quality scarves, shawls, bed spreads, and clothing made from material that has been block printed in the nearby village of Bagh.

❶ Information

The only **internet cafe** (Main Rd; per hr ₹50; ⊙ 7am-10pm) has just one terminal. There's a small **pharmacy** (⊙ 8am-9.30pm) next door, while the **post office** (☑ 263222; Main Rd; ⊙ 9am-5pm) is further south. There's nowhere to change money. Malwa Retreat can help arrange local guides (₹500).

ⓘ Getting There & Away

There are two direct buses to Indore (₹80, 3½ hours, 9am and 3.30pm), one to Ujjain (₹96, six hours, 6am) and regular services to Dhar (₹25, one hour, 6am to 6pm), where you can change for buses to Dhamnod (₹40, two hours), then, in turn, for Maheshwar (₹10, 30 minutes, last bus 11pm) or Omkareshwar (₹65, 3½ hours, last bus 7pm). If doing this, it's quicker to get off 14km before Dhar at a junction called Oonera (₹10, 30 minutes) from where you can flag down Dhamnod-bound buses.

ⓘ Getting Around

Cycling is best, as the terrain is flat, the air clear and the countryside beautiful. Overly confident little Ritik (a transport baron in the making) operates **Ritik Cycles** (per day ₹50), and right next door is **Sonu Bicycles** (Main Rd; per hr/day ₹10/50; ☉6am-6pm).

You can tour the monuments in half a day in an autorickshaw (about ₹300).

EASTERN MADHYA PRADESH

Jabalpur

☑ 0761 / POP 1.27 MILLION

Domestic tourists mostly come here to visit Marble Rocks, an attractive river gorge nearby, but for foreigners this industrial city of *chowks* and working men's taverns is used mainly as a launchpad for the famous tiger parks – Kanha, Bandhavgarh and Pench.

Most of the action takes place north of the railway line, in the dusty lanes of the Old Bazaar, along Vined Talkies Rd and as far south as Russell Chowk, which is where most of the hotels are located. The Civil Lines district, south of the train station, is less interesting, but more peaceful.

⊙ Sights

Rani Durgavati Museum   MUSEUM
(Indian/foreigner ₹10/100, camera/video ₹40/200; ☉10am-5pm Tue-Sun) Displays a collection of 10th-century sculptures from local sites, while upstairs are letters and photographs relating to Mahatma Gandhi and an old-fashioned gallery exploring tribal culture.

🛏 Sleeping & Eating

Lodge Shivalaya   HOTEL $
(☑2625188; Napier Town; s/d from ₹530/550, r with AC from ₹900; ✱) There are loads of hotels around Russell Chowk but this is the best value of the lot. Rooms are basic, but are clean enough for one night and come with TVs and small bathrooms. They also open onto shared balconies that overlook the bustling street below. Twenty-four-hour checkout.

Hotel Sidharth   HOTEL $
(☑4007779; hotel_sidharth@hotmail.com; Russell Chowk; s/d ₹570/633, with AC ₹780-1145; ✱) An old-fashioned lift leads to comfortable, compact rooms in this modest, well-run business hotel. AC rooms are no smarter than non-AC. Has a restaurant and 24-hour checkout.

Kalchuri Residency   HOTEL $$
(☑2678491; kalchuri@mptourism.com; r incl breakfast from ₹3510; ✱) This MP Tourism property, located in the quieter Civil Lines area just south of the train station, has large, neat and tidy rooms with TVs, kettles and clean, spacious bathrooms. Some rooms have private balconies. There's a restaurant and a bar.

Indian Coffee House   SOUTH INDIAN $
(Hotel India; coffee from ₹10, mains ₹30-130; ☉7am-10.30pm) As well as serving good-value filter coffee, the guys in fan-tailed hats serve up delicious breakfasts, from dosa and *uttapam* to French toast and omelettes, and hearty Indian and Chinese mains.

Options   INDIAN $$
(Vined Talkies Rd; mains ₹50-120; ☉10am-10pm) Popular with families, courting couples and students, this child-friendly veg restaurant with funky decor serves up good-quality Indian and Chinese cuisine to a backdrop of Bollywood soundtracks.

Satyam Shivam Sundram   INDIAN $$
(Napier Town; mains ₹40-100, thalis from ₹70; ☉9am-11pm) The veg menu is spot on and includes some generous thalis.

ⓘ Information

City Hospital (☑2628154; North Civil Lines; ☉24hr) Modern, private healthcare facility.
Cyber Cafe (Russell Chowk; per hr ₹10; ☉10.30am-10.30pm) Has wi-fi.
MP Tourism (☑2677690; ☉7am-8pm) At train station (south entrance).
Post Office (Residency Rd; ☉10am-5pm Mon-Fri, 10am-2pm Sat) An unusual 1860s,

Jabalpur

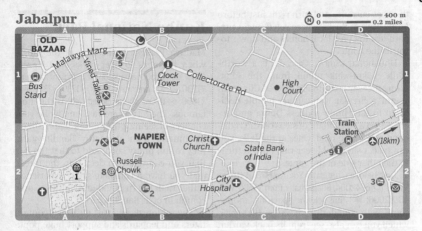

English-made, red postbox stands outside the entrance.

State Bank of India (☎ 2677777; South Civil Lines; ◷ 10.30am-4.30pm Mon-Fri, to 1pm Sat) Changes American Express travellers cheques and cash, and has ATM; there's also an ATM at the train station and others around the city.

❶ Getting There & Away

AIR

Air India (☎ 6459333) flies to Delhi (₹5000, 6pm) on Tuesdays, Thursdays, Saturdays and Sundays.

BUS

Two daily buses go to Kanha National Park (₹140, six hours, 7am and 11am). For Pench Tiger Reserve, take any Nagpur-bound bus as far as Khawasa (₹150, five hours, 7am to 11pm), then take a shared jeep (₹10) for the final 12km. For Bandhavgarh National Park, it's best to take a direct train to Umaria, but you can also take a bus to Katni (₹75, three hours, every 30 minutes, 4am to 11pm), from where there are trains and buses to Umaria.

TRAIN

More than 10 daily trains leave for Satna, from where you can take a bus to Khajuraho. You may have to catch a bus from Satna to Panna and change again for Khajuraho. For Bandhavgarh National Park, take a train to Umaria. There are several trains to Varanasi but they may not be daily and they may leave or arrive at an unearthly hour, so check when you book your ticket.

❶ Getting Around

A cycle rickshaw from the train station to Russell Chowk is about ₹30. Autorickshaws are usually double the price.

Around Jabalpur

Marble Rocks

Known locally as Bhedaghat, the marblelike magnesium-limestone cliffs at this gorge on the holy Narmada River, 22km west of Jabalpur, change colours in different lights, from pink to black. They're particularly impressive by moonlight, and parts are floodlit at night.

The trip up the 2km-long gorge is made in a shared **motorboat** (per person 30/50min ₹21/31; ◷ 7am-7pm, full moon 8pm-midnight, closed 15 Jun-15 Oct due to monsoon) from the jetty at Panchvati Ghat. Alternatively hire a boat (standard/large ₹200/320) to yourself. For a nice postboating stroll, and a closer look at village life, carry on up the hill past the ghat entrance and turn right just before Motel Marble Rocks, where you'll find a tiny path leading past local homes and down towards the gorge.

Dhuandhar (Smoke Cascade) is a worthwhile 1.5km-walk uphill from the ghat. Along the way is the much-revered Chausath Yogini, a circular 10th-century temple dedicated to the Hindu goddess Durga and accessed via a steep flight of steps on the right-hand side of the road. Once at the falls, you can take a short cable-car ride (₹60 return) to the other side of the gorge.

Just before Chausath Yogini, **Hotel River View** (⏹ 6942004; Bhedaghat; r from ₹1500, with AC ₹2000; ❄) has clean, spacious rooms, some with wonderful views of the river, which you can also see from its back-garden restaurant (mains ₹50 to ₹120).

Local buses leave regularly for Bhedaghat (₹20, 40 minutes, 6am to 8pm) from Jabalpur bus stand. They drop you at a crossroads from where shared autorickshaws wait to take you the final 5km to Panchvati Ghat (₹5) or 6.5km to Dhuandhar (₹10). Getting back is just a case of waiting at the crossroads for a passing bus. The impatient might like to try squeezing into a jam-packed, Jabalpur-bound shared autorickshaw (₹15).

Kanha National Park

⏹ 07649

Madhya Pradesh is the king of the jungle when it comes to tiger parks, and **Kanha** (www.kanhanationalpark.com; Indian/foreigner ₹1230/2230, premium zones ₹1730/3230, jeep ₹1800; ⏰ 16 Oct-30 Jun, closed Wed) is the most famous. The forests are vast, and while your chances of seeing a tiger are probably slightly slimmer than at nearby Bandhavgarh, they're still pretty good. Add to that the fact that you can really go deep into the forest, and you have a complete safari experience, rather than the rush-and-grab outings some complain of at Bandhavgarh.

The sal forests and vast meadows contain tigers and leopards and support huge populations of deer and antelope, including the extremely rare *barasingha*. You'll see plenty of langur monkeys, the odd gaur (Indian bison) and maybe even a family or two of wild boar. The park is also home to more than 300 bird species.

There are a few gates into the park, but we focus here on Khatiya Gate, easily the most popular.

◉ Sights & Activities

Jeep Safaris   JEEP SAFARIS
(www.mponline.gov.in) This is why everyone comes to Kanha and pretty much everyone

HANDY TRAINS FROM JABALPUR

DESTINATION	TRAIN NO & NAME	FARE (₹)	DURATION (HR)	DEPARTURE
Agra	12189 Mahakaushal Express	385/1066/1590	14	6.10pm
Bhopal	11472 Jbp–Bhopal Express	239/653/870	7	11pm
Delhi	12192 Jbp–NDLS Express	454/1267/1840	18	5.45pm
Kolkata (Howrah)	12322 Kolkata Mail	486/1357/1960	22	1.35pm
Mumbai (CST)	12321 Howrah–Mumbai Mail	444/1237/1800	17½	6.05pm
Raipur	12854 Amarkantak Express	322/869/1230	9½	9.30pm
Satna	22131 Pune–Darbhanga Exp	215/547/845	3	9.05am
Umaria	18233 Narmada Express	155/479/815	4	6.40am
Varanasi*	12165 Lokmanya Tilak Express	319/862/1215	10	1.15am

Fares: sleeper/3AC/2AC; *departs Tuesday, Friday, Saturday.

who lives here can hook you up with a jeep (Gypsy 4WD) for a safari. Safari bookings are made online but you will save a lot of hassle by allowing your hotel to do this. Ten percent of safari tickets are reserved for gate sales and are sold 30 minutes before the gate opens. Vehicle fees may be higher than stated here if you need to drive further to enter from a more distant gate (depending on the zone you are visiting). The key, if you haven't booked safaris through your hotel, is to find other independent travellers with whom you can share costs because vehicle fees are per jeep load (maximum six adults), not per person. Budget guesthouses are the best place to enquire; try at Motel Chandan. Otherwise, just ask around. Note, a jeep containing Indian nationals *and* foreigners costs the foreign-tourist price. There are two safari slots each day: morning (roughly 6am to 11am) and afternoon (roughly 3pm to 6pm). The morning safaris are longer and tend to produce more tiger sightings.

Nature Trails
WALKING

(guide ₹300) A well-marked 7km trail leads from just inside Khatiya Gate and skirts along the edge of the park before looping back to the village. Mostly you'll see a lot of monkeys and birds, but tigers do venture into this area on occasions and an accompanying guide is essential. Rahul, the manager at Pugmark Resort, is well informed.

🛏 Sleeping & Eating

All hotels listed here have restaurants. There's a row of small *dhabas* just before Khatiya Gate serving cheap food and chai. If you're on a morning safari, you can grab breakfast (₹20), tea and coffee when you stop at the visitor centre inside the park.

Note, while lodgings in the buffer zone enjoy a wonderfully natural forest location, there are none of the facilities that are available in the village outside Khatiya Gate.

🛏 Inside the Buffer Zone

Tourist Hostel
HOSTEL **$$**

(✆277310; Kisli Gate; American Plan dm ₹1280) This MP Tourism property, made up of a few huge, well-kept multibed dorms with clean shared bathrooms, is inside the buffer zone, right by Kisli Gate, which leads into the park's core zone. There are no facilities here apart from the dorms, the nearby

> ### MORNING CHILL
>
> No matter how hot a time of year it is, make sure you bring warm clothing with you for morning jeep safaris. It's fr-fr-freezing in the forests before the sun comes up properly.

canteen and the adjacent Baghira Log Huts (another MP Tourism property), but the attraction is that you're staying right in among the monkey-filled forest, and a stone's throw from meadows that attract deer and *gaur* throughout the day. You'll need to have a room booked in advance in order to get past security at Khatiya Gate, then you can hitch a ride to Kisli Gate on any passing vehicle, or on one of the buses that swing by both gates.

Baghira Log Huts
GUESTHOUSE **$$$**

(✆277227; Kisli Gate; American Plan s/d from ₹5977/6682; ❄) Apart from the nearby Tourist Hostel, this is the only place inside the buffer zone. Comfortable rather than luxurious log-cabin-lookalike rooms are set among the trees and overlook a beautiful meadow. There's a restaurant and a bar. As with Tourist Hostel, you'll need to have a room booked here in advance in order to get past security at Khatiya Gate.

🛏 In the Village by Khatiya Gate

Machan Complex
GUESTHOUSE **$**

(✆252457, 9993672827; dm ₹200, r ₹500) Like staying in a tiny village, Machan has rooms in different buildings, all a bit shabby, set around a huge banyan tree. There are dorms, basic mud-hut doubles, and larger rooms with sit-down flush toilets. The owner, Anil, is a naturalist and extremely welcoming. About 1km before Khatiya Gate, on the right.

Van Vihar
HOTEL **$**

(✆277241; vanvihar99@yahoo.com; r ₹550-1100, with AC ₹2200; ❄) Uninspiring rooms are pretty basic, but this is one of the cheapest options available. It's 300m left of Khatiya Gate.

Motel Chandan
HOTEL **$$**

(✆277220, 9425855220; www.motelchandan.com; r ₹750-1250, with AC ₹1850; ❄ @) Spotless modern rooms can be nabbed for great rates if

> ### AMERICAN/JUNGLE PLAN
>
> Many of the resorts at the tiger re-
> serves have part- and all-inclusive
> packages rather than straight accom-
> modation prices. The so-called Ameri-
> can Plan includes accommodation and
> all meals, while the Jungle Plan includes
> accommodation and meals plus a
> morning and an afternoon jeep safari.

you bargain hard. Staff members are friendly and are happy to help you find other travellers to share safari costs, and can organise
village walks. They will also do American
Plan (meals included) for ₹500 extra per
person. On the left-hand side of the main
road, 200m before Khatiya Gate.

Pugmark Resort   HOTEL $$
(☎277291; www.pugmarkresort.com; s/d American
Plan ₹1800/2400, r with AC ₹3400; ❈ ☎) Large,
clean cottages are bright and airy and set
around a lovely, if slightly overgrown, gar-
den. There's a gazebo-covered campfire and
restaurant, and Rahul, the manager, is very
knowledgeable. It's 700m down a track to
the right of Khatiya Gate.

★Kipling Camp   HOTEL $$$
(☎277218; www.kiplingcamp.com; Mocha Vil-
lage; American Plan s/d ₹18,700/26,600; ☎) ◢
Kipling Camp is a laid-back wildlife lodge
hosted by one of India's most formidable
tiger proponents, Belinda Wright. It's as informative as it is relaxing to stay in this jungle setting where wildlife discussions follow
meals. There's no TV or air-con, but nature
abounds in the fenceless grounds and you
can swim in the river with Tara, the camp's
50-year-old elephant, who has her own interesting story to tell.

Tuli Tiger Resort   HOTEL $$$
(☎277221; www.tulihotels.com; American Plan
s/d cottages US$115/135, luxury tents d US$325;
❈ @ ☎) Really two resorts in one, with the
new tented camp of Tuli Corridor outshin-
ing its older sibling and neighbour Tuli Tiger
Resort. Each section has its own reception,
excellent restaurant and pool. Both are fabu-
lously comfortable and set in peaceful bam-
boo grounds located 4km before Khatiya
gate, just outside the village of Mocha. The
luxury tents in Tuli Corridor are absolute
five-star luxury.

🛍 Shopping

There's a *haat* (village market) held in the
nearby village of Mocha (5km from Khatiya
Gate) every Wednesday.

Aranyak Art Emporium   HANDICRAFTS
(◷9am-9pm) This is a local enterprise, op-
posite Motel Chandan, where you can pur-
chase some tribal-inspired handicrafts as
well as general central Indian souvenirs.

🛈 Information

There's nowhere to change money and only a
couple of hotels have internet (when it is work-
ing). A Central Bank of India ATM next to Motel
Chandan accepts foreign cards.

🛈 Getting There & Away

There are five daily buses from Khatiya Gate to
Mandla (₹50, 2½ hours, 6am, 8.30am, 9am,
12.30pm and 6pm). The 6am, 12.30pm and 6pm
continue to Jabalpur (₹140, 5½ hours). All ex-
cept the 6pm swing by Kisli Gate too.

Services from Mandla Bus Stand:

Jabalpur ₹80, three hours, frequent from 4am
to 9pm

Kanha ₹50, 2½ hours, five daily at 10am,
10.15am, 11.15am, 2.30pm and 4.15pm

Nagpur buses go via Pench National Park
turn-off; ₹200, eight hours, frequent from 8am
to 11pm

Raipur ₹220, eight hours, four daily at 9am,
noon, 4.20pm and 9pm

Bandhavgarh National Park

☎07653

If your sole reason for visiting a national
park in India is to see a tiger, look no fur-
ther. A couple of days at **Bandhavgarh**
(www.bandhavgarhnationalpark.com; Indian/for-
eigner ₹1230/2230, premium zones ₹1730/3230,
jeep ₹1800; ◷16 Oct-30 Jun, closed Wed) almost
guarantees you a tiger sighting in this rela-
tively small park that boasts the highest
density of tigers in India. As well as the
star attraction, there are also more than 40
leopards (although they are rarely seen) and
more commonly sighted animals such as
deer, wild boar and langur.

Like Kanha, Bandhavgarh also has a lot
of budget accommodation, making this a
good place for independent travellers to find
other people to share safari costs.

The park takes its name from an ancient
fort perched on top of 800m-high cliffs. Its

ramparts provide a home for vultures, blue rock thrushes and crag martins. You can visit it on special jeep trips during the day, but you'll have to pay all the usual park entry fees.

The park is entered at the small, laid-back village of Tala, 32km from Umaria, the nearest train station.

Sights & Activities

Interpretation Centre MUSEUM
(admission ₹5; 11am-2pm & 5.30-8pm) Interesting exhibits detailing the history and legends of Bandhavgarh, plus some superb tiger photos on the 1st floor. On your right just before the village.

Jeep Safaris JEEP SAFARIS
(www.mponline.gov.in) Safari bookings are made online but you will save a lot of hassle by allowing your hotel to do this. Ten percent of safari tickets are reserved for gate sales and are sold 30 minutes before the gate opens. Try Hotel Pawan or Kum Kum Home if you want to find others with whom to share safari costs. Note, that Tala Gate (a short walk from the village) may have cheaper jeep charges. Otherwise, you'll have to settle for Maghdi Gate (7km from the village). With safari numbers drastically reduced in the 2012 review, early booking is essential.

Sleeping & Eating

All accommodation listed here is on the main strip (or within walking distance) and has a restaurant.

Hotel Pawan HOTEL $
(265336, 9425343812; bhainarayan603@gmail.com; s ₹300, d ₹350-400) The best of the budget choices with clean rooms, 24-hour hot water, and TVs. The boys here also run a cyber cafe and travel agency downstairs, plus there is a multicuisine vegetarian restaurant.

Kum Kum Home HOTEL $
(265324; r ₹350-400) Decent budget option – rooms are very basic but comfortable – come with large bathrooms (bucket hot water) and a verandah.

Nature Heritage Resort HOTEL $$
(265351, 265327; shalinidev@eth.net; s/d ₹2000/2500, with AC ₹2500/3000, American Plan ₹3500/4000;) A very good midrange choice with a slick safari operation. It's all about bamboo here, with comfortable, bamboo-trim cottages containing bamboo furniture, set around lush gardens shaded by...yep, bamboo. Has a very pleasant open-air restaurant and bar. It's 1km down a track opposite Kum Kum.

Tiger's Den HOTEL $$$
(265353; www.tigerdenbandhavgarh.com; American Plan s/d ₹4500/5500, ste ₹6500/7500;) Very smart bungalows with quality furnishings set around a lush, palm-lined garden with a gorgeous pool. The suites are sumptuous and some rooms feature rain showers and tubs. There is a spa, library and wildlife presentation hall.

Malaya Cafe CAFE $$
(breakfast ₹275; 9.30am-8pm) Real filter coffee, cakes and breakfasts of fruit, oats and

---

THE TIGER SHOW IS OVER

In 2012 dramatic changes were made to the management of tiger reserves (under Project Tiger), including Kanha, Bandhavgarh and Pench National Parks. Daily safari numbers were cut by almost 50%, core areas were further protected from tourism with only 20% allowed to be visited, and reserves were closed to tourism for one day of the week (Wednesday in Madhya Pradesh). And very significantly, the practice of using elephants to take tourists close to a previously located resting tiger, the so-called Tiger Show, was banned. Elephant rides may well be reinstated, but the practice of approaching resting tigers (responsible for most of those great tiger photos in the lodges) has been abolished. The upshot is that the chances of getting that elusive glimpse or magnificent photo are reduced to the probability of crossing a tiger's path on a jeep safari, which is marginally enhanced by chasing the warning calls from deers and monkeys. The intention is of course to reduce the impact of the ever-expanding tourist numbers on the ever-diminishing wildlife populations. For more on the establishment of Project Tiger, see the boxed text on p1166,.

pancakes. Breakfasts must be arranged the day before and are an ideal way to finish off a safari. This is also an excellent souvenir shop with crafts from all over India.

Kolkata Restaurant INDIAN $$
(mains ₹70-300, thali ₹100; ☺7.30-10pm) Kolkata Restaurant, at the end of the village before the petrol pump, does decent Indian veg and meat dishes plus some Chinese and breakfasts. The omelettes are popular.

ⓘ Information

There's internet access at **Angili Cyber Cafe** (per hr ₹30) and **Yadav Cyber Café** (per hr ₹40; ☺8am-11pm), but the nearest place to withdraw money is in Umaria. From the train station, walk to the end of the road, turn right and you'll find an ATM on your left after a few hundred metres.

ⓘ Getting There & Around

There's one early-morning bus from Umaria train station to Tala Village (₹30, one hour, 6.30am). After that you'll have to take a taxi (₹600). Alternatively, take a cycle rickshaw to Umaria bus stand (₹10, 10 minutes), from where there are one or two buses an hour to Tala (₹35).

The last bus from Tala Village back to Umaria bus stand is 7pm.

TRAIN

Trains from Umaria include the 18477 Utkal Express to Delhi (Nizamuddin; sleeper/3AC/2AC ₹393/1113/1655, 17 hours, 8.50pm) via Gwalior (₹314/874/1275, 11 hours), Agra (₹344/962/1455, 14 hours) and Mathura (₹360/1013/1525, 15 hours), and the 18234 Narmada Express, which goes to Jabalpur (₹8155/479/815, 4½ hours, 4.20pm) before continuing to Bhopal (₹284/783/1105, 12 hours), Ujjain (16½ hours) and Indore (18½ hours).

There's one daily train to Varanasi, but it's at 4.30am (15160 Sarnath Express; ₹281/775/1090, 12 hours). Trains to Satna (from where you can also catch buses to Khajuraho, are equally inconvenient, the least sleep-depriving being the 51754 Chirmiri-Rewa Passenger (sleeper ₹155, 3½ hours) leaving at 1am.

For Chhattisgarh, there are two daily trains to Raipur, the best being the 15159 Sarnath Express (₹248/679/910, eight hours, 10.18pm)

An alternative to Umaria is Katni, a busier railway junction from where there are direct trains to places like Jabalpur, Satna and Varanasi. You can catch a direct bus to Katni (₹60, three hours, three daily at 6.30am, 8am and 2pm) from Tala Mall, 3km beyond Tala Village.

Pench Tiger Reserve
☑07695

The third of Madhya Pradesh's trio of well-known tiger parks, **Pench** (www.penchnationalpark.com; Indian/foreigner ₹1230/2230, premium zones ₹1730/3230, jeep ₹1800; ☺16 Oct-30 Jun, closed Wed) is made up mostly of teak-tree forest rather than sal and has a different flavour from nearby Kanha or Bandhavgarh. It also sees fewer tourists so, as you're driving around the park, you'll often feel like you have the whole forest to yourself. Tigers are fewer too, but are occasionally spotted.

⊙ Sights & Activities

Jeep Safaris JEEP SAFARIS
(www.mponline.gov.in) As with the other tiger parks, safari bookings are made online, but you will save a lot of hassle by allowing your hotel to do this. Ten percent of safari tickets are reserved for gate sales and are sold 30 minutes before the gate opens. A lack of budget accommodation means it's tough to find other independent travellers to share jeep costs. Kipling's Court is your best bet. Otherwise, try hanging around the park gate and keep your fingers crossed that a jeep comes along with passengers who aren't on an all-inclusive package. As at the other tiger parks, there are morning (sunrise to 10am) and afternoon (3pm to sunset) safaris.

🛏 Sleeping & Eating

All of these hotels have restaurants.

Mowgli's Den HOTEL $$
(☑232832; junglecamps@gmail.com; s/d ₹1600/2800, American Plan ₹2200/4000) A nice choice for families; the reception and restaurant are set around a lush lawn with children's playground. Log-cabin-style concrete huts come with wrought-iron furniture and huge circular bathrooms with Jacuzzi-sized sunken baths. There's no TV to spoil the sounds of the jungle, and when you turn off the lights to sleep, a fluorescent night sky magically appears on your bedroom ceiling. It's 1km past the village of Turia.

Kipling's Court HOTEL $$
(☑232830; kcpench@mptourism.com; dm/s/d American Plan ₹1090/3090/3690, s/d with AC from ₹4090/4690; ❄) Considering prices

include all meals, the large dorms here are good value. There are two, with five beds each. They're both in tip-top condition and share a clean shower area. The private cottages aren't bad either and are dotted around well-kept gardens. Also has a bar. It's 2km past Turia, about 1km before the park gate.

Tuli Tiger Corridor　　　　HOTEL $$$
(🖉 232859, 09981994116, Nagpur office 07122534784; www.tulihotels.com; American Plan s/d cottages US$173/192, luxury tents s/d US$325/365; ❈@❈) Extravagance by the bucketload in exquisite cottages with verandahs and outdoor showers, plus luxury tents with private lawns. There's also a gorgeous pool, a spa and massage centre, a bar, library and full-size snooker table. It's 500m past Mowgli's Den.

ℹ Information

There's nowhere to change money and no reliable internet access.

ℹ Getting There & Away

Regular buses, day and night, link Khawasa with Nagpur (₹70, two hours) and Jabalpur (₹150, five hours, 7am to 11pm). Shared jeeps (₹10) run between Khawasa and Turia when full. The main gate to the park is about 3km beyond Turia. The nearest airport and major train station is in Nagpur.

You can go to Kanha National Park from Khawasa without going all the way to Jabalpur or Mandla. Flag down any north-bound bus to Seoni (₹40, one hour) then take a Mandla-bound bus to Chiraidongri (₹80, 2½ hours) where you can catch buses to Khatiya Gate (₹30, one hour, last bus 9pm).

CHHATTISGARH

Chhattisgarh is remote, its public transport system is poor and its tourist infrastructure outside the main cities is almost nonexistent, but for the intrepid traveller, time spent here may well prove to be the highlight of your trip to this part of India. The country's most densely forested state is blessed with natural beauty – waterfalls and unspoilt nature reserves abound. More interestingly, though, it is home to 42 different tribes whose pointillist paintings and spindly sculptures are as vivid as the colourful *haats* (markets) that take place across the region, particularly around Jagdalpur in Bastar.

Chhattisgarh is one of the eastern states associated with the Naxalite guerrillas (an ultra-leftist political movement that began in Naxal Village, West Bengal), but they rarely stray from their remote hideouts on Chhattisgarh's northern and southern borders.

Raipur

📞 0771 / POP 1.01 MILLION

Chhattisgarh's ugly capital is a centre for the state's steel industry and, apart from being a day trip away from Sirpur, has little in the way of tourist attractions. The Chhattisgarh Tourism Board head office here is worth visiting, though.

🛏 Sleeping & Eating

Hotel Jyoti　　　　HOTEL $
(🖉 24286721; Pandri; s/d from ₹400/500, with AC from ₹750/900; ❈) A welcome retreat after a long bus journey. Basic rooms are well

---

WORTH A TRIP

THE VENERABLE LAXMAN TEMPLE

A possible day trip from Raipur, Sirpur is home to dozens of ruined Hindu temples and Buddhist monasteries, all dotted around the village and surrounding countryside. Many of the excavations are works in progress. All are free to see apart from the star of the show, the 7th-century **Laxman Temple** (Indian/foreigner ₹5/100; ☉ dawn-dusk), one of the oldest brick temples in India.

Buses from Raipur bus stand drop you at Sirpur Mudh (₹40, two hours), a junction 17km from Sirpur where you'll have to wait for a bus or shared jeep (₹10, 25 minutes) to the village. For Laxman Temple, turn right past the snack stalls and keep walking for 1km. It's on the left, past the petrol pump.

looked after and the manager is helpful. Right opposite the Naya bus stand.

Hotel Radhika
HOTEL $$

(☎2233806; Jaistambh Chowk; r from ₹550, with AC from ₹1600; 🖃) A centrally located one-stop point for all your needs – a bank opposite, an ice-cream parlour below, a thali restaurant above and two bars next door. What more could you want? Rooms vary from basic budget to decent AC midrangers. Book ahead – it's popular.

Supreet Restaurant
INDIAN $

(Pandri; mains ₹50-90; ⊙9am-10pm) South Indian breakfasts and tasty veg mains at this cheap and cheerful place near the bus stand. Turn left out of the bus stand and it's 500m along on your left.

Girnar Restaurant
INDIAN $$

(Hotel Radhika, Jaistambh Chowk; mains ₹50-180; ⊙11am-10pm) This institution of a restaurant serves good-quality Indian food. It's right opposite Hotel Radhika reception. Upstairs, the separate **thali restaurant** (unlimited thali ₹100; ⊙11.30am-3.30pm & 7.30-10.30pm) is wonderful.

ℹ Information

There are ATMs outside the bus and train stands, and one opposite Hotel Radhika.

Chhattisgarh Tourism Board Head Office (☎6456336; train station; ⊙10am-5pm) Gives statewide advice and can help organise tribal visits, transport, accommodation and guides.

ANT-EDOTE

Red ants are more than just a painful nuisance to the Bastar tribes. Known as *chapura*, the ants also play an important role in food and medicine. They are often eaten live, served on a leaf with white ant eggs. Alternatively, villagers grind them into a paste and mix them with chilli to make chutney. The bodies of *chapura* contain formic acid believed to have useful medicinal qualities. If suffering from a fever, locals will sometimes put their hand into an ants nest, allowing it to be bitten hundreds of times so that the acid is administered into their bloodstream. Patients presumably soon forget their fever.

ℹ Getting There & Around

AIR

Air India (☎4060942; Pandri; ⊙10am-5.30pm Mon-Sat) flies direct daily to Mumbai (₹6000, 3½ hours) and to Delhi (₹7000, 1½ hours). Turn left out of the bus stand and the office is 1km along on your left, just past the level crossing.

An autorickshaw to the airport, 15km out of town, costs ₹100 to ₹150.

BUS

The government bus ticket office is invariably unstaffed so it is far easier to use private bus companies, which all operate out of the bus stand area, too.

Mahendra Travels, with a ticket desk directly opposite the bus stand, where the Jagdalpur buses leave from, is reliable.

Between government- and private-run buses you'll find frequent departures to Jagdalpur (seat/sleeper ₹245/310, seven hours, 10.45am to midnight), and early morning and late evening buses to both Jabalpur (₹320, 11 hours) and Nagpur (₹250, eight hours).

RICKSHAWS

Cycle-rickshaws (₹40) or autorickshaws (₹80) run between the bus stand and train station. Shared autos (₹10) ply the same route as well as the main GE Rd between Jaistambh Chowk and Chhattisgarh Tourism's head office.

TRAIN

Useful trains include the 18237 Chhattisgarh Express to Delhi's Nizamuddin station (sleeper/3AC/2AC ₹506/1442/2040, 27½ hours, 4.20pm) via Nagpur (5½ hours), Bhopal (14½ hours), Jhansi (19½ hours), Gwalior (21½ hours) and Agra (24 hours), and the 12859 Gitanjali Express to Kolkata's Howrah station (₹398/1107/1635, 13 hours, 11.35pm).

Jagdalpur

☎07782 / POP 125,345

The capital of the Bastar region is an ideal base for exploring tribal Chhattisgarh. The town itself hosts a *haat* every Sunday where you'll see Adivasis (tribespeople) buying, selling and bartering alongside town traders, but it's in the surrounding villages where Adivasi life can be fully appreciated. Some villages are extremely remote, and only really accessible with a guide. Others, though, are just a bus ride away and, particularly on market days, can be explored independently. For eight particularly lively days in October, Jagdalpur's streets transform into race tracks as immense, home-

THE EIGHT TRIBES OF BASTAR

Bhatra Women are distinguished by their particularly colourful saris and an abundance of jewellery, including their distinctive gold, conical nose studs.

Bhurwa Men wear simple headscarves wrapped around their foreheads, often coloured red and white.

Bison-Horn Maria Famed for their distinctive double-horned headdress worn during festivals.

Dorla The only tribe to make their homes from the branches and leaves of trees (instead of mud thatch) in the remote forests of the far south of Chhattisgarh.

Ghadwa The bell-metal specialists of Bastar.

Halba Excellent farmers, taller in stature than other Adivasis. Men often only wear a loincloth.

Hill Maria or Abhuj Maria Extremely remote tribe whose people very rarely venture out from their villages in the dense forests of the Bastar Hills.

Muria Known for the huge amount of jewellery worn by both men and women.

made chariots are pitted against each other in an unusual climax to the 75-day festival of Dussehra.

Sanjay Market, which hosts the Sunday *haat,* is the heartbeat of Jagdalpur. Hotel Rainbow is opposite, while Main Rd, a lively shopping street, is 200m away (turn left out of the market, then first right). The bus stand and train station are 3km and 4km south respectively (₹20 and ₹25 in a cycle-rickshaw).

◉ Sights

Anthropological Museum   MUSEUM
(Chitrakote Rd; ⊙10am-1pm & 2-5.30pm Mon-Fri) **FREE** This old-fashioned museum hoards a fascinating collection of artefacts collected from tribal villages in the 1970s and 1980s. Cycle-rickshaws from the centre of town cost ₹50. Shared autorickshaws from the Chitrakote Rd junction near Sanjay Market cost ₹10.

🛏 Sleeping & Eating

If the following are full, there are a couple of OK hotels opposite Shabari emporium.

Hotel Chetak   HOTEL **$**
(☏223503; r ₹425, with AC ₹800; ❄) Chetak is handy to the bus stand, and though its tidy rooms are smaller than Rainbow's they're clean enough. It has a dimly lit bar-restaurant (mains ₹50 to ₹150) where cold beer is available. Turn right out of the bus stand and walk 100m.

Hotel Rainbow   HOTEL **$$**
(☏221684; hotelrainbow@indiatimes.com; s/d from ₹500/630, with AC from ₹890/1050 ; ❄) Even the cheap, non-AC rooms are huge and well furnished in this good-value hotel, while the in-house, pure-veg restaurant (mains ₹60 to ₹190; no alcohol) is one of the best in town. Opposite Sanjay Market. Twenty-four-hour checkout.

🛍 Shopping

Shabari   HANDICRAFTS
(Chandi Chowk; ⊙11am-8pm Mon-Sat) Shabari is a fixed-price government emporium selling Adivasi handicrafts, from small, spindly iron figures to more expensive, heavy bell-metal statues. From the Sanjay Market end of Main Rd, take the third right and continue for 500m. Opposite the Bank of Baroda ATM.

ⓘ Information

Internet Garden (Main Rd; per hr ₹20; ⊙8.30am-10.30pm) lets you hook up your laptop and is walking distance from Sanjay Market. Turn left, take the first right (Main Rd) and it's 500m on your left. There's nowhere to change money, but there's an ATM opposite Shabari emporium, and others around town.

Contact the Chhattisgarh Tourism Board (p680) in Raipur to arrange a guide to help with trips to tribal areas of the Bastar region, or arrange your own.

ℹ Getting There & Away

BUS

There are frequent services to Raipur (seat/sleeper from ₹245/310, seven hours, 4.30am to midnight), via Kondagaon (₹60, 1½ hours).

Buses to Chitrakote Falls (₹40, 1½ hours) leave from Anumapa Takij, a local cinema about 2km (cycle-rickshaw ₹20) from the bus stand. From Hotel Rainbow, turn left then take the first right and buses, plus shared jeeps, will be on your left.

TRAIN

The 18448 Jagdalpur–Bhubaneswar Express heads over the Eastern Ghats on India's highest broad-gauge line to Bhubaneswar (sleeper/3AC/2AC ₹368/1043/1565, 18 hours) on the Odisha coast, via Koraput (₹195/451/815, three hours). It leaves Jagdalpur daily at 2.30pm. In the opposite direction, the 18447 arrives in Jagdalpur at 1.30pm. **Train reservations** (⊙8am-noon & 2-4pm Mon-Sat, 8am-noon Sun) can be made at the train station, a ₹10 cycle-rickshaw ride from the bus stand.

Around Jagdalpur

You can get to many local Adivasi villages by bus – this is certainly an option on market days – but some are pretty inaccessible, and if you want to actually meet tribespeople, rather than just look at them, a guide is essential as a translator if nothing else. They can also help you arrange homestays.

Awesh Ali (☑9425244925; aweshali@gmail.com; per day ₹1000) comes highly recommended. Contact him directly, or go through the Chhattisgarh Tourism Board. A car and driver will cost ₹1000 per day plus diesel (about ₹50 per 10km).

Haats

These colourful markets are the lifeblood of tribal Chhattisgarh, and visiting them is an excellent way to get a taste of Bastar's vibrant Adivasi culture. Tribes walk up to 20km to trade everything from their distinctive, almost fluorescent, saris to live red ants (see p680).

The large piles of what look like squashed dates are in fact dried *mahuwa*, a type of flower, either eaten fresh, or dried then boiled to create steam which is fermented to produce a potent liquor, the favourite tipple of many Bastar Adivasis.

Adivasi Villages

There are more than 3500 villages in Bastar. Earrakote, 3.5km beyond Tokapal, is a mixed-tribe village, made up largely of Ghadwa, specialists in the art of bell-metal craftwork. The skill has been passed down through generations, in some instances for as long as 300 years. A number of family members are involved in the process, from the initial clay moulding and melting of scrap metal to the painstaking job of cover-

BASTAR HAATS – HOW TO FIND ADIVASI MARKETS

Most *haats* (markets) run from around noon to 5pm. There are many markets – these are just some of the more popular ones. Ask at the Chhattisgarh Tourism Board in Raipur for details. Shared jeeps normally hang around markets to take people back to Jagdalpur.

WHEN	WHERE	DISTANCE FROM JAGDALPUR	BUS FROM JAGDALPUR	FEATURES
Mon	Tokapal	23km	₹18, 30min	Bell-metal craftwork from Ghadwa Adivasis
Tue	Pakhnar	70km	No direct bus	Beautiful forest setting
Wed	Darbha	40km	₹40, 1hr	Attended by Bhurwa Adivasis
Thu	Bastar	18km	₹35, 30min	Easy to reach from Jagdalpur
Fri	Nangur	35km	No direct bus	Attended by distant forest Adivasis
	Nagarnar	18km	No direct bus	Colourful Bhatra Adivasis
Sat	Kuknar	65km	₹55, 2hr	Bison-Horn Maria stronghold
Sun	Jagdalpur	-	-	City location, open late into the evening
	Chingitarai	52km	No direct bus	Open, meadow setting
	Pamela	12km	₹15, 20min	Animated crowds bet on cockfighting

ing the moulds in wax thread, a part of the process that is unique to Bastar. Awesh Ali can put you in touch with families here who will put you up for the night in exchange for scrap metal or wax, which you can buy for them in Jagdalpur.

Chitrakote Falls

India's broadest waterfall (300m), two-thirds the size of Niagara, is at its roaring best just after the rains, but beautiful all year round, particularly at sunset. When the water is low, it's possible to paddle in pools at the top of the drop. You should take extreme care.

In the river below the falls you can swim or get a local fisherman to row you up to the spray (₹25). Take the steps that lead down from the garden of the government-only hotel.

Chitrakote Log Huts (☑07859200194, 9993854165; cabins ₹1800; ❄), with comfortable AC cabins (some with views of the falls) and an eyesore of a restaurant, is a peaceful place to stay.

The last bus back to Jagdalpur is at 4pm.

Gujarat

Best Places to Eat a Gujarati Thali

➡ Vishalla (p695)

➡ Shaam-e-Sarhad Village Resort (p728)

➡ Geeta Lodge (p717)

➡ Zorba the Buddha (p730)

Best Tribal Fairs

➡ Tarnetar Fair (p731)

➡ Vautha Fair (p697)

➡ Dangs Darbar (p702)

Why Go?

Barely glimpsed by many travellers scurrying between Mumbai (Bombay) and Rajasthan, Gujarat is an easy side-step off the well-beaten tourist trail. While the capital, Ahmedabad, retains some charm amid its chaos, the countryside holds most of this state's treasures. Traditional artisans in tribal villages weave, embroider, dye and print some of India's finest textiles. Pristine parks harbour unique wildlife, including migratory birds, wild asses and the last remaining prides of Asiatic lions. For the spiritually inclined, sacred Jain and Hindu pilgrimage sites sit atop mountains that rise dramatically from vast flatlands. And colourful festivals burst with a cornucopia of culture.

Gujarat also claims a special relationship to the life and work of Mahatma Gandhi: he was born here, he ignited the *satyagraha* (nonviolent protest) movement from here, he made his Salt March here – and his legacy remains a vibrant part of public discourse and private lives.

When to Go
Ahmedabad

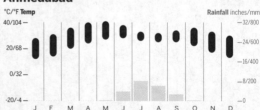

Sep/Oct Navratri festival brings music and dancing to every town and village.

Nov/Dec Mango milkshake time in Junagadh.

Nov–Mar The best months to visit Gujarat's national parks and wildlife sanctuaries.

Food

Gujarat is strong on vegetarian food, partly thanks to the Jain influence here, and the quintessential Gujarati meal is the all-veg Gujarati thali. It's sweeter, lighter and less spicy and oily than the Punjabi thali and locals have no doubts it's the best thali in the world. It begins with a large stainless-steel dish, onto which teams of waiters will serve most or all of the following: curries, chutneys, pickles, dhal, *kadhi* (a yoghurt and gram-flour preparation), raita, rotis, rice, *khichdi* (a blend of lightly spiced rice and lentils), *farsan* (savoury nibbles), salad and one or two sweet items – to be eaten concurrently with the rest. Buttermilk is the traditional accompanying drink. Normally the rice and/or *khichdi* don't come till you've finished with the rotis. In most thali restaurants the waiters will keep coming back until you can only say 'No more'.

DON'T MISS

Sasan Gir Wildlife Sanctuary offers the chance to see the only wild Asiatic lions in the world, the last of a species that once roamed from the Middle East to northern India. Lion numbers in this forest sanctuary have risen to over 400 and the chances of seeing some on a jeep safari are better than 50-50.

The complicated jigsaw of tribal groups and subcastes who inhabit the villages of **Kachchh** are some of India's finest artisans, practising a huge variety of crafts and especially textiles. Their embroidery, weaving, tie-dye and block printing are intensely colourful and infinitely varied, and visits to some of their workshops and sales outlets make a fascinating journey into a world of colour, pattern and endless hours of meticulous, amazingly skilled craftwork.

Sabarmati Ashram (p688), in Ahmedabad, where Mahatma Gandhi lived for 12 years, offers an informational and inspirational look at the great man's work.

Top State Festivals

➡ **Uttarayan** (⊙14-15 Jan; Ahmedabad, p691) Kite festival.

➡ **Modhera Dance Festival** (⊙around 20 Jan, Modhera, p698) Indian classical dance jamboree.

➡ **Bhavnath Mela** (⊙Jan/Feb; Girnar Hill, p715) Hindu festival at the foot of sacred Girnar Hill.

➡ **Mahakali Festival** (⊙Mar/Apr; Pavagadh, p703) Pilgrims pay tribute to Kali at Pavagadh hill.

➡ **Navratri** (⊙Sep/Oct; statewide) Nine nights of dancing all around Gujarat.

➡ **Kartik Purnima** (⊙Nov/Dec; Somnath, p712, & Shatrunjaya, p705) Large fair at Somnath; Jain pilgrims flock to Shatrunjaya hill.

MAIN POINT OF ENTRY

Ahmedabad (Amdavad) has direct flights from Singapore and several Persian Gulf cities, plus major Indian cities. It's also the main hub for trains and buses connecting Gujarat with the rest of India.

Fast Facts

➡ * **Population:** 60.4 million

➡ **Area:** 196,024 sq km

➡ **Capital:** Gandhinagar

➡ **Main language:** Gujarati

➡ **Sleeping prices:** $ below ₹1000, $$ ₹1000 to ₹5000, $$$ above ₹5000

Top Tip

Gujarat's most exhilarating destinations are away from its crowded, noisy cities. To enjoy it most, head out to its national parks and wildlife sanctuaries, to the tops of its sacred mountains, or to the handicraft hotbed of Kachchh.

GUJARAT

Resources

➡ **Gujarat Tourism** (www.gujarattourism.com)

➡ **Gujarat Forest Department** (www.gujaratforest.gov.in)

➡ **Diu Tourism Department** (www.diutourism.co.in)

➡ **Kala Raksha** (www.kala-raksha.org)

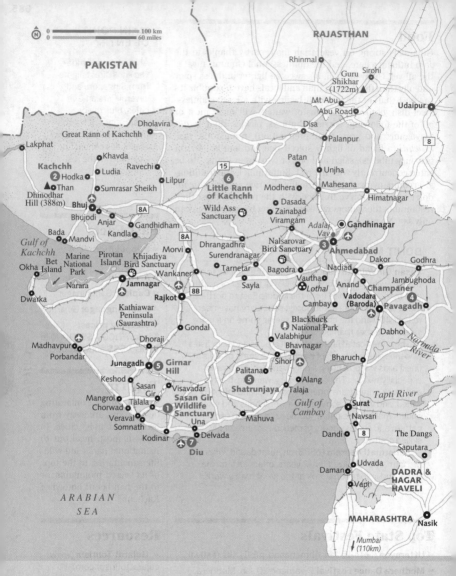

Gujarat Highlights

1 Take a forest safari in search of Asia's only wild lions at **Sasan Gir Wildlife Sanctuary** (p713)

2 Explore the villages of **Kachchh** (p724) to understand, admire and acquire some of India's best textiles

3 Tackle a thali, explore the old-city mosques, and pay homage to Mahatma Gandhi in bustling **Ahmedabad** (p687)

4 Explore an abandoned capital city and follow pilgrims up a mountain at the World Heritage Sites of **Champaner** and **Pavagadh** (p702)

5 Undertake a challenging dawn pilgrimage to the hill-top temples of **Shatrunjaya** (p705) near Palitana or **Girnar Hill** (p715) near Junagadh

6 Go looking for Indian wild asses on the flat salt plains of the **Little Rann of Kachchh** (p730)

7 Change down a gear and head for a sleepy island sojourn at the former Portuguese enclave of **Diu** (p706)

History

It's said that Gujarat's Temple of Somnath witnessed the creation of the universe; sometime later, the state became Krishna's stomping grounds. On a firmer historical footing, Lothal and Dholavira (Kachchh) were important sites of the Indus Valley civilisation more than 4000 years ago. Gujarat featured in the exploits of the mighty Buddhist emperor Ashoka, and Jainism first took root under a grandson of Ashoka who governed Saurashtra.

The rule of the Hindu Solanki dynasty from the 10th to the 13th centuries, with its capital at Patan, is considered Gujarat's cultural golden age. Solanki rule was ended when Ala-ud-din Khilji brought Gujarat into the Delhi sultanate after several campaigns around 1300. A century later the Muslim Gujarat sultanate broke free of Delhi rule and established a new capital at Ahmedabad. The Mughal empire conquered Gujarat in the 1570s and held it until the Hindu Marathas from central India occupied eastern and central Gujarat in the 18th century. The British set up their first Indian trading base at Surat on Gujarat's coast in about 1614, and replaced Maratha power in the early 19th century.

It's from Gujarat that Gandhi launched his program of non-violent resistance against British rule, beginning with protests and fasting, and culminating with the 390km Salt March, which drew the attention of the world and galvanised anti-British sentiment across India. After Independence, eastern Gujarat became part of Bombay state. Saurashtra and Kachchh, initially separate states, were incorporated into Bombay state in 1956. In 1960 Bombay state was divided on linguistic lines into Gujarati-speaking Gujarat and Marathi-speaking Maharashtra.

The Congress Party of India largely controlled Gujarat until 1991 when the Bharatiya Janata Party (BJP) came to power. In 2002, communal violence erupted after a Muslim mob was blamed for an arson attack on a train at Godhra that killed 59 Hindu activists. Hindu gangs set upon Muslims in revenge. In three days, an estimated 2000 people were killed (official figures are lower), most of them Muslims, and tens of thousands were left homeless. The BJP-led state government was widely accused of tacitly, and sometimes actively, supporting some of worst attacks on Muslim neighbourhoods for political gain; later that year Gujarat's chief minister, Nahendra Modi, won a landslide re-election victory. A decade hence, in 2012, a former BJP minister was convicted of criminal conspiracy and murder in the Naroda Patiya massacre during the Godhra riots, while Modi has thus far been cleared of all charges related to the violence. Since the 2002 riots, Gujarat has been peaceful, and continues to enjoy its reputation as one of India's most prosperous and businesslike states.

EASTERN GUJARAT

Ahmedabad (Amdavad)

☑ 0/9 / POP 5.57 MILLION

Ahmedabad (also called Amdavad, Ahmadabad or Ahemdavad) is Gujarat's major city and a startling metropolis with a long history, many remarkable buildings, a fascinating maze of an old quarter, excellent museums, fine restaurants and fabulous night markets. Yet the old-world charm is all but swamped by 21st-century traffic, crowding, pollution and the usual extremes of wealth and poverty. Many travellers stop off briefly en route to Rajasthan or Mumbai, sneaking in a visit to Sabarmati Ashram (Gandhi's former headquarters). You need a little stamina to get to know the city better, as it's quite spread out and moving around can be a bit of a task.

The old city lies on the east side of the Sabarmati River and used to be surrounded by a 10km-long wall, of which little now remains except 15 formidable gates standing as forlorn islands amid swirling, cacophonous traffic. The new city on the west side of the river, nearly all built in the last 50 years, has wider streets, several major universities, and many middle-class neighbourhoods.

History

Ahmedabad was founded in 1411 by Gujarati sultan Ahmed Shah at the spot where, legend tells, he saw a hare chasing a dog (he was impressed by its bravery). The city spread quickly beyond his citadel on the east bank of the Sabarmati, and by the 17th century it was considered one of the finest cities in India, a prospering trade nexus adorned with an array of fine Islamic architecture. Its influence waned, but from the second half of the 19th century Ahmedabad rose again as a huge textile centre (the 'Manchester of

GUJARAT AHMEDABAD (AMDAVAD)

Ahmedabad (Amdavad)

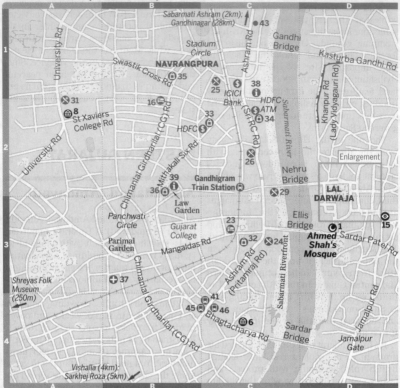

the East'). By the late 20th century many of the mills had closed and the subsequent economic hardship may have been a contributing factor in the communal violence that split the city in 2002, when up to 2000 people, mostly Muslims, were killed. Today Ahmedabad is booming again as a centre for IT, education and chemicals production on top of its traditional textiles and commerce, and has been officially dubbed a 'megacity'.

◉ Sights

★ Sabarmati Ashram   HISTORIC SITE
(www.sabarmati.org; Ashram Rd; ☺8.30am-6.30pm) **FREE** About 5km north of the centre, in peaceful, shady grounds on the river's west bank, this ashram was Gandhi's headquarters from 1917 to 1930 during the long struggle for Indian independence. It's said Gandhi chose this site because it lay between a jail and a cemetery, and any *satyagrahi* (nonviolent resister) was bound

to end up in one or the other. From here on 12 March 1930, Gandhi and 78 companions set out on the famous Salt March to Dandi on the Gulf of Cambay in a symbolic protest, with Gandhi vowing not to return to the ashram until India had gained independence. The ashram was disbanded in 1933, later becoming a centre for Dalit welfare activities and cottage industries. Gandhi's poignant, spartan living quarters are preserved, and there's a museum that presents an informative record of his life and teachings. After Gandhi's death some of his ashes were immersed in the river in front of the ashram.

Buses 84/1 and 83 (₹5) run here from Lal Darwaja bus stand. An autorickshaw from the city centre is about ₹40.

★ Calico Museum of Textiles   MUSEUM
(☎22868172; www.calicomuseum.com; Sarabhai Foundation; ☺tours 10.30am & 3pm Thu-Tue)

the Shahibag area, 3.5km north of the old centre, opposite the Shahibag Underbridge. You can get there by bus 101, 102, 105 or 21/1 (₹5) from Lal Darwaja local bus stand and through Delhi Gate. An autorickshaw should cost ₹50.

Bhadra Fort
FORT

(Lal Darwaja; ☺dawn-dusk) **FREE** Built immediately after the founding of Ahmedabad in 1411, Bhadra Fort now houses government offices and a Kali temple. Its gate formed the eastern entrance of the Ahmedabad citadel, which stretched west to the river. From the roof you can check out the formidable structure and views of the surrounding streets. Between the fort and the **Teen Darwaja** (Triple Gateway; Lal Darwaja) to its east was the Maidan Shahi (Royal Square), where royal processions and polo games took place. Today it's a seething market area.

Shreyas Folk Museum
MUSEUM

(Indian/foreigner ₹25/100; ☺3-5.30pm Tue-Sat, 10am-1.30pm & 3-5.30pm Sun) This museum, 3km west of the river in Bhudarpura, displays an impressive range of Gujarati folk arts, including woodcarvings, metalwork and some wonderful embroidered textiles and amazing tie-dyed quilts. Included in the ticket is the **Kalpana Mangaldas Museum**, with festival masks from around India and, just to round things off, an elephant skeleton. It's all set in the peaceful, peacock-dotted grounds of the Shreyas Foundation. Photos are not allowed. An autorickshaw from the centre costs around ₹40; say you want to go to Shreyas Foundation.

Lalbhai Dalpatbhai Museum
MUSEUM

(LD Museum; www.lldmuseum.in; University Rd; ☺10.30am-5pm Tue-Sun) **FREE** Part of the LD Institute of Indology, this museum houses a gorgeous collection of ancient and medieval Indian art treasures, including stone, marble, bronze and woodcarvings and 75,000 Jain manuscripts. A 6th-century-AD sandstone carving from Madhya Pradesh is the oldest-known carved image of the god Rama.

NC Mehta Gallery
ART GALLERY

(University Rd; ☺10.30am-5.30pm Tue-Sun Jul-Apr, 8.30am-12.30pm Tue-Sun May & Jun) **FREE** In the same building as the LD Museum, this gallery has an important collection of jewel-like illustrated manuscripts and miniature paintings. Best known is *Chaurapanchasika*

FREE This museum contains one of the world's finest collections of antique and modern Indian textiles, all handmade and up to 500 years old. There are some astoundingly beautiful pieces, displaying incredible virtuosity and extravagance. You'll see Kashmiri shawls that took three years to make, and double-ikat cloths whose 100,000 threads were each individually dyed before weaving.

The main textile galleries can only be visited in the morning session: the tour lasts two hours with a maximum 20 people. The afternoon tour (maximum 10 people) is devoted to the Sarabhai Foundation's collection of religious art, which explores depictions of Indian deities, including textile galleries. Advance booking is required, either by phone or by email. Kids under 10 are not welcome.

Photography is not permitted and bags are not allowed inside. The museum is in

Ahmedabad (Amdavad)

(Fifty Love Lyrics of a Thief), written by Vilhana, an 11th-century Kashmiri poet sentenced to be hanged for loving the king's daughter. Before his execution he was granted one final wish: he chose to recite these 50 poems, which so impressed the king that he gave Vilhana his daughter in marriage.

Sarkhej Roza HISTORIC BUILDING
(◎9am–dusk) FREE In the Sarkhej area, 8km southwest of the old centre, Sarkhej Roza is a mosque, tomb and palace complex dedicated to the memory of Ahmed Shah I's spiritual advisor, Ahmed Khattu Ganj Baksh. The elegant though dilapidated buildings cluster around a great (now often dry) tank, constructed by Sultan Mahmud Begada in the mid-15th century. It's an atmospheric place that was used as a retreat by several of Ahmedabad's rulers. The mausoleums of Mahmud Begada (by the entrance, with geometric *jalis* (carved lattice screens) casting patterns of light on the floor) and Ganj Baksh (the largest in Gujarat) are both here.

A return autorickshaw from the city centre will cost around ₹120; Sarkhej Roza could be combined with a visit to Vishalla restaurant and its utensil museum, about 1km back towards the city.

Hutheesingh Temple JAIN TEMPLE
(Balvantrai Mehta Rd) Outside Delhi Gate, north of the old city, the Jain Hatheesingh Temple is constructed of delicately carved white marble. Built in 1848, it's dedicated to Dharamanath, the 15th Jain *tirthankar* (great teacher).

Swaminarayan Temple
HINDU TEMPLE

(Kalupur; ⊙6am-7pm) The glorious, multicoloured, woodcarved Swaminarayan Temple, in the old city, was built in 1822 as the first temple of the Swaminarayan Hindu sect. Followers believe the sect's founder, Swaminarayan (1781–1830), was the supreme being. The start of the daily Heritage Walk here at 8am usually coincides with worship at the temple, with believers' passion on full display.

Sabarmati Riverfront
AREA

(www.sabarmatiriverfront.com) Replacing the slum camps that used to line the Sabarmati River, this newly built waterfront promenade will stretch for 10km through the heart of Ahmedabad. It's a pleasant place to stroll, popular with families and young lovers. Boat rides (motor and pedal) are available, and there are plans for water-zorbing. At the time of writing, the park had just opened and wasn't entirely complete. It can be accessed from numerous points on the western bank of the river.

★ Kankaria Lake
LAKE

(admission ₹10; ⊙9am-11pm) Built in 1451 and recently dandified as a recreation space for the city, this large lake is a nice respite from the hectic streets. Attractions include a tethered hot-air balloon (10-minute ride ₹100, 10am to 10pm), a mini-train and a zoo. One Tree Hill Garden on the west side (entered from outside) contains some quite grand colonial Dutch tombs.

City Museum
MUSEUM

(Bhagtacharya Rd, Sanskar Kendra; ⊙10am-6pm Tue-Sun) **FREE** The City Museum covers Ahmedabad's history with simple but diverse displays, and explanatory material in English and Gujarati. It includes sections on the city's religious communities, Gandhi and the Independence struggle. The ground floor houses the disappointing Kite Museum, where flattened tissue-paper contraptions resemble trapped butterflies.

Dada Hari Vav
NOTABLE BUILDING

(⊙dawn-dusk) **FREE** This step-well, built in 1499 by the supervisor of Sultan Begada's harem, has steps down through five levels of carved stone columns to two small wells, now often bone dry. The depths are cool, even on the hottest day, and it's a fascinating and eerie place. Overflow channels at the top are a reminder of times when water tables were much higher than today.

Behind the step-well, the 16th-century **Dai Halima Mosque** contains the mausoleum of a royal midwife named Halima, with nice *jali* screens.

Vechaar Utensil Museum
MUSEUM

(www.vishalla.com; Bye-Pass Rd; Indian/foreigner ₹10/20; ⊙2-4pm & 5-10.30pm Tue-Sun) At Vishalla restaurant, opposite Vasna Tol Naka, this museum displays the graceful practicality of pots and utensils, with more than 4500 items from all over India, some 1000 years old.

Festivals & Events

Uttarayan
KITE FESTIVAL

(Makar Sakranti, Ahmedabad; ⊙14-15 Jan) Each 14–15 January, Ahmedabad hosts Uttarayan, a traditional kite festival that attracts International participants and is well worth the stiff neck.

☞ Tours

The Municipal Corporation runs a fascinating daily **Heritage Walk** (☑9824032866; Indian/foreigner ₹30/50) through the old city. It starts at 8am at the Swaminarayan Temple in Kalupur and finishes at the Jama Masjid around 10.30am. It's advisable to book. The tours, through narrow, confusing streets and past dilapidated, carved wooden houses,

---

NAVRATRI & DUSSEHRA

Navratri (Festival of Nine Nights; ⊙Sep/Oct) is celebrated India-wide, but Gujarat has made it its own. The festival celebrates the feminine divinity in the forms of the goddesses Durga, Lakshmi and Saraswati – particularly Durga's slaying of the demon Mahishasura. Celebrations centre on special shrines at junctions, marketplaces and, increasingly today, large venues that can accommodate thousands. People dress up in sparkling finery to whirl the night away in entrancing *garba* or *dandiya rasa* circle dances till the early hours. Celebrated in every town and village in Gujarat, Navratri is a festival where you may well find yourself joining in.

The night after Navratri is Dussehra, which celebrates the victory of Lord Rama over the demon king Ravana, with more nocturnal dancing and fireworks, plus the burning of giant effigies of the defeated demon king.

MOSQUES & MAUSOLEUMS

Under the Gujarat sultanate in the 15th and 16th centuries, and especially under Ahmed Shah I (r 1411–42) and Mahmud Begada (r 1459–1511), Ahmedabad was endowed with a remarkable collection of stone mosques in a unique style incorporating elements of Hindu and Jain design. Note that women are not allowed into the actual prayer halls and at some mosques are restricted to the periphery.

Built by Ahmed Shah in 1423, the **Jama Masjid** (Friday Mosque; Mahatma Gandhi (MG) Rd) ranks as one of India's most beautiful mosques, enhanced by an enormous, peaceful courtyard. Demolished Hindu and Jain temples provided the building materials, and the mosque displays some architectural fusion with these religions, notably in the lotus-like carving of some domes, similar to that of many Jain temples. The prayer hall's 260 columns support 15 principal domes at different elevations. There were once two 'shaking' minarets, but they lost half their height in the great earthquake of 1819, though their lower portions still flank the prayer hall's central portico.

The **Mausoleum of Ahmed Shah** (Badshah-na-Hazira), outside the Jama Masjid's east gate, may have been constructed by Ahmed Shah himself before his death in 1442. His cenotaph is the central one under the main dome. An 11pm drumming session in the mausoleum's eastern gateway used to signal the closing of the city gates and still happens nightly. Through an arch a little further east is Ahmed Shah's queen's tomb, the **Rani-na-Hazira**, on a raised platform now engulfed by market stalls, and in poor shape, though the *jali* screens are nice.

★ **Siddi Sayid's Mosque** (Lal Darwaja) was built in the year the Mughals conquered Gujarat (1573), by an Abyssinian in the Gujarati army. One of Ahmedabad's most stunning buildings, it is famed for its exquisite *jali* windows, spiderweb fine, depicting the intricate intertwining branches of the 'tree of life'.

Southwest of Bhadra Fort, **Ahmed Shah's Mosque** was built in 1414 for the sultan and nobles within Ahmedabad's original citadel. The prayer hall is a forest of beautifully carved stone pillars and *jali* screens, and its elaborately carved ceiling has a circular symmetry reminiscent of Hindu and Jain temples.

The small **Rani Sipri's Mosque**, near the ST bus stand, is also known as the Masjid-e-Nagira (Jewel of a Mosque) because of its graceful construction, with delicate carved minarets and Rani Sipri's domed tomb with fine *jali* screens. Rani Sipri is said to have been a Hindu widow of Mahmud Begada; the buildings date from 1514.

Between Ahmedabad train station and Sarangpur Gate, the **Sidi Bashir Mosque** (outside Sarangpur Gate), built in 1452, is famed for its 21.3m-high shaking minarets (*jhulta minara*), built to shake to protect against earthquake damage. This certainly worked in 2001.

are an excellent way to get a feel for old Ahmedabad with its 600 *pols* – neighbourhoods of narrow streets with common courtyards, wells and *chabutaras* (bird-feeding towers). The tours are in English and there's a brief slide show beforehand. Wear slip-on footwear as you'll be visiting plenty of temples. Show up no later than 7.45am.

The House of MG offers an ingenious **audio guide walk** (₹200; ⊙7am-7pm). Beginning at the famed hotel (where you deposit your passport), the 80-minute walk takes an alternative route through the old city, ending at the **Mangaldas ni Haveli**, a finely carved old mansion that houses a crafts shop. It's recommended to do the walk between 7am and 10am or 5.30pm and

7.30pm, as midday traffic is loud enough to drown out the audio guide. We've had reports of the hotel refusing to let people take the tour in the afternoon. House of MG also hosts an hour-long **Heritage Night Walk** (House of MG; ₹200; ⊙9.30-11pm, Tue-Sun) through the old city.

The Municipal Corporation runs twice-daily four-hour **city tours** (₹200; ⊙Tue-Sun) by bus, with short stops at major sights. Buses depart from Bhadra Fort at 9am and 1.30pm.

🛏 Sleeping

Budget hotels are mostly clustered in the noisy, traffic-infested Lal Darwaja area, close to the old city, while the majority of midrange and top-end places are found on Khanpur Rd (paralleling the east bank of the Sabarmati) or west of the river, which is a more congenial environment but further from most of the interesting sights. Ahmedabad has most of the top-end hotels in Gujarat.

Hotel Volga
HOTEL $

(☑ 25509497; www.hotelvolga.in; off Relief Rd, Hanuman Lane, Lal Darwaja; s/d ₹750/850, s with AC ₹950-1200, d with AC ₹1150-1400; ✳ 🛜) This surprisingly good option tucked down a narrow street behind the House of MG is worth searching out. Rooms are smart and respectably clean, with a hint of 1970s design in the curved beige walls – some are more dashingly decorated. The front desk is friendly and efficient, checkout is 24 hours, and you can order decent multicuisine food (mains ₹95 to ₹175) to your room.

Hotel Good Night
HOTEL $

(☑ 25507181; www.hotelgoodnight.co.in; Lal Darwaja; s/d from ₹500/600, s with AC ₹950-1500, d with AC ₹1100-1700; ✳) This tidy hotel next door to the House of MG has a range of rooms that are better value than most in these parts. There are seven categories of room, all clean and well kept, so it shouldn't be too hard to find one that suits your budget and comfort needs, though the cheapest, ground-floor 'Ordinary' ones are dingy and can be odorous.

Hotel Cadillac
HOTEL $

(☑ 25507558; Advance Cinema Rd, Lal Darwaja; s/d ₹400/500, without bathroom ₹300/400) If you're counting every last rupee, you could do worse than this friendly option – an old-timer from 1934, which has kept its wooden balustrade. Mattresses are lumpy and smaller rooms are cell-like; larger rooms are OK, just grungy. Try to get a room on the balcony.

Hotel Royal Highness
HOTEL $$

(☑ 25507450; www.hotelroyalhighness.com; Lal Darwaja; s/d incl breakfast from ₹2750/3300; ✳ @ 🛜) The lobby is a bit tacky, with wood paneling and glass chandeliers, but the rooms are tasteful, spacious and clean. Deluxe rooms feature zebra-print furnishings and sparkling bathrooms with big, glassed-in showers. There is a 24-hour restaurant, free airport shuttle service, and helpful staff, all in a great location.

Hotel Ambassador
HOTEL $$

(☑ 25502490; www.ambassadorahmedabad.com; Khanpur Rd; s/d from ₹2100/2500; ✳ @ 🛜) With a bright white exterior and modern decor inside, the Ambassador greets you with a chilled lobby and friendly desk. It follows up with rooms that are quite stylish in browns and creams. With discounts often available, it's good value; ask to have breakfast included and it will be.

Ritz Inn
HOTEL $$

(☑ 22123842; www.hotelritzinn.com; Station Rd; s ₹2700-2900, d ₹3300-4800; ✳ @ 🛜) Near the railway station, this smart hotel has unusual class and is excellent value for money. The art-deco lobby, comfortable rooms with superb beds, and unusually slick and amiable service make it an outstanding option. There's a good veg restaurant, checkout is a civilised 24 hours, discounts are often available and it offers free airport and station transfers.

Comfort Inn President
HOTEL $$

(☑ 26467575; www.comfortinnpresident.com; off CG Rd, Navrangpura; s/d incl breakfast from ₹3125/3750; ✳ 🛜) This is a calm, well-run hotel on a quiet street close to the Chimanlal Girdharilal (CG) Rd shops in middle-class Navrangpura. Rooms aren't huge but are solidly comfortable and well equipped, and there's an in-house wine shop as well as a multicuisine restaurant. Good discounts are often available; airport transfers are free.

★ House of MG
HERITAGE HOTEL $$$

(☑ 25506946; www.houseofmg.com; Lal Darwaja; s/d from ₹4990/6490, ste from ₹9990/11,900, all incl breakfast; ✳ @ 🛜 ⊠) This 1920s building (with two excellent restaurants) opposite Siddi Sayid's Mosque was once the home of textile magnate Sheth Mangaldas Girdhardas; it was converted into a beautiful heritage hotel in the 1990s by his great-grandson. All the rooms are vast, verandah-edged and masterfully decorated, with a homey yet luxurious ambience. It's an icon of the upper classes, and hugely popular. Service is first-rate, and the indoor swimming pool and gym are divine. If you know your dates, book in advance online to receive a discount of up to 30% .

Royal Orchid Central
HOTEL $$$

(☑ 30912345; www.royalorchidhotels.com; Ellis Bridge; s ₹7000-8000, d ₹8000-9000, ste ₹12,000, all incl breakfast; ✳ @ 🛜 ⊠) Opposite Gujarat College, this luxury hotel has a waterfall in the lobby and aromatheraphy in the air. Rooms are tasteful and comfortable, with state-of-the-art gadgets, including universal electrical sockets and iPod docks. There's an excellent 24-hour restaurant and coffee shop. Free airport transfers too.

Le Meridien Ahmedabad   HOTEL $$$

(📞25505505; http://lemeridien.com/ahmedabad; Khanpur Rd; s/d from ₹6500/7500, ste ₹20,000, all incl breakfast; ❋@🛜❄) This luxurious option towers over the Sabarmati River's east bank. All rooms are super comfortable – making cheaper rooms the best deal – and the suites are palatial. Breakfast is excellent and as huge as you like, and there is a neat indoor swimming pool, spa and sauna. Ask for the best available rate, which can be about half the rack rate.

✖️ Eating

Ahmedabad has the best range of restaurants in Gujarat and is a great place to sample Gujarati thalis.

The Law Garden Night Market (p695) and Manek Chowk (p695) are good for street food after about 8pm. Halal grills are fired up nightly along Bhathiyar Gali, a small street parallel to MG Rd: you can get a good meaty feed for about ₹30 from the evening stalls.

New Lucky Restaurant   SOUTH INDIAN $

(Lal Darwaja; mains ₹40-80; ◷8am-11pm) For the best breakfast bang-for-your-buck in Ahmedabad, it's hard to beat the dosas at New Lucky (though they're good anytime!).

ALCOHOL PERMITS

Gujarat is a dry state, but alcohol permits for foreign visitors are easy to get at the 'wine shops' found in many large hotels; show your passport plus a certificate or letter from your hotel (your Gujarat 'residence form') to receive a one-month permit. Permits are only available within one month of your arrival in India. Although they are officially free, local authorities often demand ₹100 or so from the shops and the shops pass this cost on to the customer. The permit allows you two units over the month, equating to 20 bottles of standard beer or two 750ml bottles of liquor, which you must drink in private. Cheers.

There's booth-seating in a simple but clean dining hall, with friendly service and surprisingly drinkable black coffee.

Zen Cafe   CAFE $

(www.zencafe.co.in; University Rd; drinks ₹30-50, snacks ₹50-100; ◷4-8pm Tue-Sun) This peaceful spot in a tree-fringed garden is popular with students from Gujarat University and other colleges nearby. It's right next to the weird Amdavad ni Gufa (Amdavad Cave), an underground art gallery that looks like a heap of octopi with sawn-off tentacles. Offerings include panini, chocolate walnut brownies, organic coffee and capriosch mocktails – perfect icy coolers of mint, lime and soda.

Havmor   ICE CREAM $

(Navrangpura; scoops ₹20-40; ◷11am-11pm) Ahmedabad is famous for ice cream, and locals swear that the Havmor brand, found only in Gujarat, is best. Havmor has branches all over the city including at Lal Darwaja, Khanpur Rd and the Cinemasala building, Ashram Rd.

★ Green House   GUJARATI $$

(House of MG, Lal Darwaja; snacks ₹100-200, mains ₹340-470; ◷7am-10.45pm) We love the Green House, the casual front restaurant at the House of MG. Choose the fan-blasted outdoor courtyard or the AC room with a 15% surcharge. The selection of vegie Gujarati dishes is superb, as is the *chaat* (savoury snack); the house special *sharbat* (sherbet); and the divine *malpuva,* a sweet, deep-fried pancake in saffron syrup, topped with rose petals. And don't forget the hand-churned ice cream. Great anytime, there's nowhere in the city better for an afternoon break.

Hotel ZK   INDIAN, CHINESE $$

(Relief Rd, Lal Darwaja; mains ₹80-160; ◷9am-11pm) This popular AC, nonveg restaurant has tinted windows, low lighting and impeccable service. The boneless mutton kadai is fantastic, and (like a number of dishes here) comes served over a flame. The chicken Afghani curry is also recommended and locals love the chicken pesto Chinese. On weekends, there may be a wait.

Food Inn   INDIAN $$

(Lal Darwaja; ₹100-200; ◷11.45am-4pm & 7-11pm) A clean, bright and bustling curry house in the Hotel Good Night building (opposite Siddi Sayid's Mosque) where carnivores can tuck into numerous chicken, mutton and fish dishes, including spicy Punjabi curries, lip-smackin' tandoori, biryani and sizzlers.

Gopi Dining Hall
GUJARATI **$$**

(off Pritamraj Rd; thali ₹120-160; ⊙11am-10pm) Just off the west end of Ellis Bridge, this little restaurant is a much-loved thali institution, with a small garden and an AC dining room. You can choose from 'fix', 'full' and 'with one sweet' options depending how hungry you are.

Sankalp
SOUTH INDIAN **$$**

(CG Rd, Samir Bldg; mains ₹120-190; ⊙11am-11pm) A quality chain restaurant serving up excellent vegetarian South Indian food, Sankalp sits on a rooftop about five storeys high. Unusual fillings such as pineapple or spinach-cheese-garlic are available for its renowned dosas (paper-thin lentil-flour pancakes) and *uttapams* (thick, savoury rice pancakes) that come accompanied by seven different sauces. Order *masala papad* (thin, crisp wafer with a spicy topping) for a tasty starter.

★ Vishalla
INDIAN **$$$**

(☑26602422; www.vishalla.com; Bye-Pass Rd; lunch Mon-Sat ₹80, Sun ₹197, dinner ₹449; ⊙11am-11pm, 11am-3pm, from 7.30pm) On the southwest outskirts of town, just off the road to Sarkhej (opposite Vasna Tol Naka), Vishalla is a magical eating experience in an open-air setting that's something of a rural village fantasy. An endless thali of Gujarati dishes you won't find in other restaurants is served on plates of leaves, at low wooden tables under open-air awnings. Dinner includes excellent performances of folk music, and dance and puppet shows. The complex includes a fascinating utensil museum. An autorickshaw from the city centre costs about ₹100 return.

Agashiye
GUJARATI **$$$**

(☑25506946; House of MG, Lal Darwaja; meal regular/deluxe ₹490/650; ⊙noon-3.30pm & 7-10.30pm) On the rooftop terrace of the city's finest hotel, Agashiye features an all-veg menu, which changes daily, begins with a welcoming drink and is a cultural journey around the traditional thali, with a multitude of diverse dishes delivered to your plate. It finishes with hand-churned ice cream. For dinner, it is advisable to book ahead.

Neelkanth Patang
MULTICUISINE **$$$**

(☑26586200; Chinubhai Center, west end Nehru Bridge; lunch ₹400-450, dinner ₹450-500; ⊙11.30am-2.30pm & 7-10.30pm) For a meal with a view, the Neelkanth Patang has no rivals as it's 50m above the ground and revolves. The multicuisine buffet meals are bountiful. It's worth calling ahead to book.

🛍 Shopping

Law Garden
Night Market
HANDICRAFTS, CLOTHING

(Law Garden; ⊙dusk-11pm) An evening market packed with stalls selling glittering wares from Kachchh and Saurashtra. It's chock-a-block with fantastically decorated *cholis* (sari blouses) and *chaniyas* (long, wide traditional skirts), as well as embroidered wall hangings, costume jewellery and more.

Manek Chowk
HANDICRAFTS, FOOD

(Old City) This busy space and surrounding narrow streets are the commercial heart of the old city. Weave your way through the crowds to soak up the atmosphere and browse the vegetable and sweet stalls, and the silver and textile shops. **Gamthiwala** (⊙11am-7pm Mon-Sat), by the entrance to the Mausoleum of Ahmed Shah, sells quality block-printed textiles.

Garvi Gurjari
HANDICRAFTS, CLOTHING

(Ashram Rd; ⊙11am-7.30pm Mon-Sat) This state-government-run outlet has three floors of Gujarati crafts, including silk and hand-loomed-cotton saris, painted metal jewellery boxes and clothing in folksy designs. There are some good finds if you rummage around.

Hansiba
HANDICRAFTS

(CG Rd, 8 Chandan Complex; ⊙11am-9pm Mon-Sat, 11.30am-7.30pm Sun) The retail outlet of the Self-Employed Women's Association (SEWA), Hansiba sells colourfully woven and embroidered shawls, saris, other clothes and wall hangings.

Art Book Center
BOOKS

(www.artbookcenter.net; off Mangaldas Rd; ⊙10am-6pm) This specialist treasure trove is upstairs in a brightly painted building near Ellis Bridge. Indian architecture, miniature painting and textile design are the main topics stocked.

Crossword
BOOKS

(Mithakali Six Rd, Shree Krishna Centre; ⊙10.30am-9pm) A large, bustling book, music and DVD shop also boasting the Chocolate Room cafe (with chocolate drinks and snacks, plus coffee).

ℹ Information

INTERNET ACCESS

Cyberpoint (Mithakali Six Rd, Shree Krishna Centre; per hr ₹20; ☺10am-8pm Mon-Sat) Behind Crossword bookshop.

Relief Cyber Café (Relief Rd; per hr ₹20; ☺10am-midnight) It's air-conditioned, what a relief!

MEDICAL SERVICES

Apollo City Center (☎66305800; www.apolloahd.com; 1 Tulsibaug Society) Small but recommended private hospital opposite Doctor House, near Parimal Garden.

MONEY

For changing travellers cheques and currency, there's the **State Bank of India** (Lal Darwaja; ☺11am-4pm Mon-Fri, to 1pm Sat) opposite the local bus stand, and **ICICI Bank** (Ashram Rd, 2/1 Popular House; ☺9am-6pm Mon-Fri). There are numerous ATMs. **HDFC** (Relief Rd, Lal Darwaja) is off Mithakali Six Rd, Navrangpura.

POST

Main post office (Ramanlal Sheth Rd; ☺10am-7.30pm Mon-Sat, to 1pm Sun) The main post office branch.

TOURIST INFORMATION

Gujarat Tourism (☎26578044; www.gujarattourism.com; HK House, opposite Bata showroom, off Ashram Rd; ☺10.30am-6pm) The very helpful HK House office has all sorts of information at its fingertips and you can hire cars with drivers here. There is also an office at the Ahmedabad train station.

Tourism desk (☎32520878; Law Garden; ☺8am-8.30pm) Ahmedabad Municipal Corporation's office has city maps and puts effort into answering questions.

ℹ Getting There & Away

AIR

Ahmedabad's busy airport has direct flights to several Indian cities and, overseas, Doha (Qatar), Dubai (United Arab Emirates), Kuwait City (Kuwait), Muscat (Oman), Sharjah (United Arab Emirates) and Singapore. Many agencies sell air tickets, including **Express Travels** (☎26588602; expresstravel@eth.net; Jivabhai chambers, off Ashram Rd). Domestic airlines serving Ahmedabad:

Indian Airlines/Air India (☎25505198; www.airindia.in; Lal Darwaja)

IndiGo (☎9910383838; www.goindigo.in)

Jet Airways (☎022-39893333; www.jetairways.com; Ashram Rd, Ratnanabh Complex) Also their low-cost carrier, JetKonnect.

MAJOR TRAINS FROM AHMEDABAD

DESTINATION	TRAIN NO & NAME	DEPARTURE	DURATION (HR)	FARE (₹)
Bhavnagar	12971 Bandra-Bhavnagar Express	5.45am	5½	172/443/640 (A)
Bhuj	19115 Sayaji Nagari Express	11.59pm	7½	170/464/690 (A)
Delhi	12957 Rajdhani	5.45pm	14	1250/1790/3035 (B)
	12915 Ashram Express	6.30pm	15¾	343/943/1430/2455 (C)
Jamnagar	19005 Saurashtra Mail	5.05am	7	164/446/665/1125 (C)
Junagadh	19221 Somnath Express	10pm	6½	167/455/675 (A)
Mumbai (Bombay)	12010 Shatabdi	2.30pm (Mon-Sat)	7	721/1535 (D)
	12902 Gujarat Mail	10pm	8½	232/616/910/1560 (C)
Udaipur	19944 Udaipur Express	11pm	10½	152/585 (E)
Vadodara (Baroda)	12010 Shatabdi	2.30pm (Mon-Sat)	1¾	296/605 (D)

Fares: (A) sleeper/3AC/2AC, (B) 3AC/2AC/1AC, (C) sleeper/3AC/2AC/1AC, (D) AC chair/1AC, (E) sleeper/2AC

SpiceJet (☎1800 1803333; www.spicejet.com)

BUS

Private buses from the north may drop you on Naroda Rd, about 7km northeast of the city centre – an autorickshaw will complete the journey for ₹50 to ₹60.

From the main **ST bus stand** (known as Geeta Mandir or Astodia), frequent Gujarat State Road Transport Corporation (GSRTC, ST) buses go to Vadodara (₹82, two hours), Bhavnagar (₹100, five hours), Junagadh (₹160, eight hours), Jamnagar (₹163, seven hours), Rajkot (₹131, 4½ hours) and Bhuj (₹170, nine hours). Volvo AC buses go to Vadodara (₹170) throughout the day. Eleven daily buses go to Udaipur (₹200, 5½ hours), five head to Jodhpur (₹348), and three to Jaipur (₹480). A Volvo AC bus departs at 7pm for Udaipur (₹440), Jaipur (₹1115) and Delhi (₹1843, 20 hours).

For long distances, private buses are mostly quicker; most offices are close to Paldi Char Rasta.

Patel Tours & Travels (www.pateltoursandtravels.com; 8 Shroff Chambers) Runs Volvo AC buses to Rajkot (₹330, four hours, 18 daily), Jamnagar (₹400, six hours, nine daily) and Mumbai (sleeper ₹1000, 11 hours, 7.30pm), plus non-AC buses to Mumbai (seat/sleeper ₹300/500, 6pm and 10pm) and six daily buses to Bhuj (seat/sleeper non-AC ₹250/350, AC sleeper ₹500, eight hours).

Raj Express (8 Kanth Complex) Runs Volvo AC buses to Udaipur (seat/sleeper ₹300/460, five hours, hourly 5pm to midnight) and non-AC buses to Jaipur (seat/sleeper ₹400/700, 12 hours, 7pm, 10pm and 11pm).

Gujarat Travels (www.gujarattravels.co.in; 1 Medicine Market) Has buses to Mt Abu (seat/sleeper ₹260/410, seven hours, 7am and 11pm).

Shree Swaminarayan (22 Anilkunj Complex) Heads to Diu in non-AC buses (seat/sleeper ₹220/320, 10 hours, 10.30pm).

TRAIN

There's a **computerised booking office** (⊙8am-8pm Mon-Sat, to 2pm Sun) just outside Ahmedabad train station. Window 6 handles the foreign-tourist quota. Computerised booking is also available at the *relatively* quiet Gandhigram station, although there is no window dedicated to foreigners.

❶ Getting Around

TO/FROM THE AIRPORT

The airport is 8km north of the centre; a prepaid taxi should cost around ₹400 depending on your destination. An autorickshaw costs about ₹150 to the old city.

AUTORICKSHAW

Autorickshaw drivers are supposed to turn their meter to zero at the start of a trip then calculate the fare using a conversion chart at the end. Some meters have been rigged, but most work properly. In some cases, you'll have to negotiate fares in advance.

Around Ahmedabad

Adalaj Vav

Adalaj Vav, 19km north of Ahmedabad, is among the finest of the Gujarati step-wells. Built by Queen Rudabai in 1499, it has three entrances leading to a huge platform that rests on 16 pillars, with corners marked by shrines. The octagonal well is five storeys deep and is decorated with exquisite stone carvings; subjects range from eroticism to buttermilk. The Gandhinagar bus will get you within walking distance (ask the conductor where to get off). An autorickshaw costs ₹400 return.

Gandhinagar

With broad avenues and greenery, Gandhinagar forms a striking contrast to Ahmedabad. This is where state politicians live in large, fortified houses. Although Ahmedabad became Gujarat's capital when the old state of Bombay was split, this new capital was planned 28km north on the west bank of the Sabarmati River. Named Gandhinagar after Mahatma Gandhi, it's India's second planned city after Chandigarh. The secretariat was moved here in 1970.

The best reason for visiting is the spectacular **Akshardham** (www.akshardham.com; J Rd, Sector 20; ⊙9.30am-6.30pm Tue-Sun) **FREE**, belonging to the wealthy Hindu Swaminarayan group. The elaborately carved main temple, built by nearly 1000 artisans and opened in 1992, is constructed of 6000 tonnes of pink sandstone and surrounded by manicured gardens. Three underground **exhibition areas** (admission ₹170; ⊙10am-5.30pm Tue-Sun) have high-tech multimedia presentations on the Swaminarayan movement, the Hindu epics and other religions. At sunset (every day except Monday) a 45-minute **Water Show** (adult/child ₹75/50) presents the story of the Upanishads through fountains, music, fire and lasers, and promises to reveal the secret of life after death.

WORTH A TRIP

VAUTHA FAIR

Each November, Gujarat's largest livestock fair is held at Vautha, at the confluence of the Sabarmati and Vatrak Rivers, 50km south of Ahmedabad. Thousands of donkeys, camels and cows change hands here, and some 25,000 people – including many *maldhari* (herder) pastoralists – set up tents and stay for five days of buying, selling, eating, dancing, and making sunset *puja* in the river. Check with Gujarat Tourism for exact dates.

Buses from Ahmedabad to Gandhinagar (₹20, 45 minutes, every 15 minutes) depart from the back northwest corner of Lal Darwaja, from ST bus stand, and from the numerous stops along Ashram Rd.

Nalsarovar Bird Sanctuary

This 121-sq-km **sanctuary** (Indian/foreigner ₹30/250, car ₹20, camera/video ₹50/2500), around 60km southwest of Ahmedabad, protects Nalsarovar Lake, a flood of island-dotted blue dissolving into the sky and iron-flat plains, and its surrounding wetlands. Between November and February, the sanctuary sees flocks of indigenous and migratory birds, with as many as 250 species passing through. Ducks, geese, eagles, spoonbills, cranes, pelicans and flamingos are best seen at daybreak and dusk.

The sanctuary is busiest at weekends and on holidays. To see the birds it's best to hire a boat (around ₹100, negotiable, per hour). Gujarat Tourism offers **luxury tent** (☑ 9427725090; d ₹1680; ❀) accommodation 1.5km from the lake.

A taxi from Ahmedabad costs around ₹1800 for a day trip, and gives you the option of combining Nalsarovar with Lothal (40km south).

Lothal

About 80km southwest of Ahmedabad, the city that stood here 4500 years ago was one of the most important of the Indus Valley civilisation. Lacking dramatic buildings, this **archaeological site** (admission free; ☺ dawn-dusk) is best appreciated by true archaeology buffs. Excavations have revealed the world's oldest known artificial dock, which was con-nected to an old course of the Sabarmati River. Seals discovered here suggest that trade may have been conducted with Mesopotamia, Egypt and Persia.

The site **museum** (Indian/foreigner ₹2/50; ☺ 9am-5pm Sat-Thu) displays intricate seals, weights and measures, games and jewellery, plus an artist's impression of how Lothal looked at its peak.

Palace Utelia (☑ 02714-262222; r from ₹3000), 7km from the site, by the Bhugavo River, is an imposing palace – complete with aged retainers – that dwarfs the village it oversees. The shabby rooms are overpriced, but it's an unusual place with some charm if not comfort.

Lothal is a long day trip from Ahmedabad, and a taxi (around ₹1800 return) is the easiest bet. Trains from Ahmedabad's Gandhigram station at 7.15am and 9am run to Lothal-Bhurkhi station (2nd-class ₹45, two hours), 6km from the site, from where you can catch a bus. Take water and food with you.

Modhera

The beautiful **Sun Temple** (Indian/foreigner ₹5/100; ☺ 9am-5pm) was built from 1026 to 1027 by King Bhimdev I and is one of the greatest monuments of the Solanki dynasty, whose rulers were believed to be descended from the sun. Like the better-known Sun Temple at Konark in Odisha (Orissa), which it predates by 200 years, the Modhera temple was designed so that the dawn sun shone on the image of Surya, the sun god, during the equinox. The temple exterior is intricately carved with demons and deities, and the main hall and shrine are reached through a pillared pavilion. Within, 52 sculpted pillars depict scenes from the Ramayana and the Mahabharata, and a hall with 12 niches represents Surya's different monthly manifestations. Erotic sculpture panels complete the sensual decoration.

The temple is fronted by the **Surya Kund**, an extraordinary rectangular step-well that contains over 100 shrines, resembling a sunken art gallery.

Around 20 January, the temple is the scene for a three-day classical dance festival with dancers from all over India.

Modhera is 100km northwest of Ahmedabad. You can take a bus (₹65, two hours, half-hourly) from Ahmedabad's ST bus stand to Mahesana (Mehsana), and then another bus 26km west to Modhera (₹30, one hour). There are also trains from Ahmedabad to Mahesana. Buses run from Modhera to Patan (₹35, 1¼ hours) every 30 minutes till around 4pm. There are also two daily buses to/from Zainabad (₹45, 1½ hours). A taxi from Ahmedabad will cost about ₹1500 round trip.

Patan

📞 02766 / POP 125,502

About 130km northwest of Ahmedabad, Patan was Gujarat's capital for six centuries before Ahmedabad was founded in 1411. It was ruined by the armies of Ala-ud-Din Khilji around 1300, and today is a dusty, little-visited town with narrow streets lined by elaborate wooden houses. The only real sign of its former glory is the **Rani-ki-Vav** (Indian/foreigner ₹5/100; ⊙ 9am-5pm), an astoundingly beautiful step-well, incongruously grand in this unassuming town. Built in 1063 by Rani Udayamati to commemorate her husband, Bhimdev I, the step-well is the oldest and finest in Gujarat and is remarkably well preserved. Steps lead down through multiple levels with lines of carved pillars and over 800 sculptures, mostly on Vishnu-avatar themes.

Patan also has more than 100 Jain temples, the largest of which is **Panchasara Parshvanath**, and is famed for its beautiful Patola silk textiles produced by the torturously laborious double-ikat method. Both the warp (lengthways) and weft (transverse) threads are painstakingly tie-dyed to create the pattern *before* the weaving process begins. It takes about six months to make one sari, which might cost ₹100,000. To see double-ikat being made visit the Salvi family at **Patan Patola Heritage** (📞 232274; www.patanpatola.com; Patolawala St, Salvivado).

Food Zone (near train tracks; mains ₹65-90; ⊙ 11am-3pm & 7-11pm), by the railway tracks, has modern booth seating, air-con and great set meals. There's nowhere really worth staying in town, but if you must, try **Hotel Shyam Palace** (📞 222555; 2nd Railway Nala; s/d ₹300/400, with A/C ₹700/800).

Patan is 40km northwest of Mahesana. Buses leave Ahmedabad's ST bus stand about every hour (₹78, 3½ hours). There are also buses to/from Zainabad (₹65, 2½ hours, two daily), via Modhera.

Vadodara (Baroda)

📞 0265 / POP 1.66 MILLION

Vadodara (or Baroda as it's often known) lies 106km southeast of Ahmedabad, little over an hour's drive along National Expressway 1. Vadodara has some interesting city sights, but the main reason for coming here is the stunning nearby Unesco World Heritage Site of Champaner and Pavagadh. The city is way less hectic than Ahmedabad, and parts of the Sayajigunj area near the university have a college-town feel.

After the Marathas expelled the Mughals from Gujarat in the 18th century, their local lieutenants, the Gaekwad clan, made Vadodara their capital. Vadodara retained a high degree of autonomy even under the British, right up to Independence in 1947. Maharaja Sayajirao III (1875–1939) was a great moderniser and laid the foundations of Vadodara's modern reputation as Gujarat's cultural capital.

👁 Sights

★ **Laxmi Vilas Palace**   PALACE
(Nehru Rd; adult ₹150; ⊙ 9.30am-5pm Tue-Sun) Still the residence of Vadodara's royal family, Laxmi Vilas was built in full-throttle 19th-century Indo-Saracenic flourish at a cost of ₹6 million. The most impressive British Raj-era palace in Gujarat, its elaborate interiors boast well-maintained mosaics, chandeliers and artworks. It's set in expansive parklike grounds, including a golf course. A one-hour audio tour is included with admission.

Sayaji Bagh   PARK, MUSEUM
Within this shady park is the **Baroda Museum & Picture Gallery** (Indian/foreigner ₹10/200; ⊙ 10.30am-5pm), which houses a diverse collection, much of it gathered by Sayajirao III, including statues and carvings from several Asian regions, an Egyptian room and some rather mangy zoology exhibits. The gallery has lovely Mughal miniatures and a motley crew of European masters.

Tambekar Wada   HISTORIC BUILDING
(Pratap Rd, Raopura; ⊙ 8am-6pm) **FREE** This wooden multi-storey townhouse is a typical Maratha mansion, once the residence of Bhau Tambekar, diwan of Baroda (1849–54). Inside are beautiful 19th-century murals featuring scenes from the Mahabharata, Krishna's life and the 19th-century Anglo-Maratha War. Many are worn and poorly lit by ambient light, but they're still impressive.

Vadodara (Baroda)

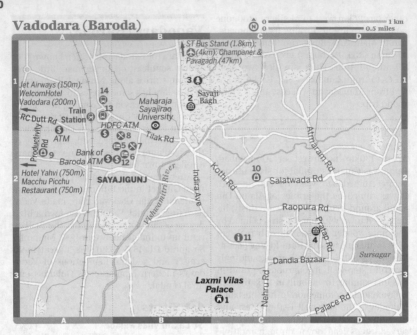

Vadodara (Baroda)

🛌 Sleeping

Most accomodation is in the conveniently central Sayajigunj area; there are a number of very cheap hotels (₹200 to ₹400) there, but they fill up early.

Hotel Valiant   HOTEL $
(☑2363480; www.hotelvaliant.com; 7th fl, BBC Tower, Sayajigunj; s/d ₹750/950, with AC from ₹995/1200; ❄@) The Valiant has surprisingly fresh rooms on the upper floors of a high-rise building. Take the lift up from the street entrance to find reception in a spacious lobby on the 7th floor. The clean, well-presented rooms are the best value in town.

Hotel Yahvi   HOTEL $$
(☑2350948; www.yahvihotels.com; Manisha Chowkri & OP Rd; s ₹2990-4590, d ₹3990-5590) Located in a quiet lane a five-minute rickshaw ride from the railway station, the new Yahvi is the closest thing Vadodara has to a boutique hotel. Each room is different, with some creatively designed beds, and a variety of artwork on the walls. Beds are

comforable, bathrooms are modern, and the staff is very attentive. Downstairs is the unique – if pricey – Macchu Picchu (p701) restaurant.

Hotel Ambassador HOTEL $$

(🖉2362727; www.hotelambassadorindia.com; Sayajigunj; s/d incl breakfast from ₹1250/1550; ❄ 🛜) With stylish rooms and comfortable beds, the Ambassador offers very good value. The cheapest ('deluxe') rooms have a vaguely Japanese air, while the 'executive' quarters have a slick contemporary feel, all pinks, oranges, squares and rectangles. There's civilised 24-hour checkout too.

Hotel Surya HOTEL $$

(🖉2361361; www.hotelsurya.com; Sayajigunj; s/d incl breakfast from ₹2500/3000; ❄ @ 🛜) Surya is a popular choice, with a cordial atmosphere and professional staff. Rooms are clean, though not particularly big or modern, and the mattresses are rather firm. Two excellent restaurants, Vega and Myra, flank the reception.

WelcomHotel Vadodara HOTEL $$$

(🖉2330033; www.itcwelcomgroup.in; RC Dutt Rd; s/d from ₹8000/9000; ❄ @ 🛜 ⛽) A swish five-star complex with predictable, well-appointed rooms, an unusual outdoor pool, plenty of cool lounge areas, an expensive 24-hour multicuisine restaurant and a wine shop.

✖ Eating

Kalyan SOUTH INDIAN $

(Sayajigunj; dishes ₹25-150; ⊙7am-11pm) Kalyan is a breezy student hang-out serving healthy portions of South Indian food and less healthy attempts at Western fast food (though all dishes are vegetarian).

Kansaar GUJARATI $$

(101 Unique Trade Centre, Sayajigunj; thali ₹150; ⊙11am-2.45pm & 7-10pm) A classy veg thali joint on the 1st floor with impeccable service and delicious food; the thali is bottomless and you can eat inside or out on the terrace for the street view.

Pizza Meo ITALIAN $$

(Sayajigunj; pizza & pasta ₹140-260; ⊙11am-11pm) This small Italian *ristorante e pizzeria* serves a reasonable veg pizza and so-so veg pasta. With a bizarrely frescoed ceiling in what's supposed to resemble Renaissance style, plus waiters with red, green and white aprons, they get an 'A' for effort.

Macchu Picchu MULTICUISINE $$$

(Hotel Yahvi; mains ₹175-700; ⊙12.30-3pm & 7-11pm) Brand new and ultra-modern, the restaurant at Hotel Yahvi is a blend of bubbles and squares, and blue lights and candles – but it works. The menu is largely Thai, Vietnamese and Indonesian – not quite authentic, but good. There's also wood-fired pizza and shwarma in the attached outdoor cafe.

🛍 Shopping

Baroda Prints HANDICRAFTS

(Productivity Rd, 3 Aires Complex; ⊙9am-9pm Mon-Sat, 8am-6pm Sun) A shop selling hand-printed dress materials in original, colourful and attractive designs. There's also a **branch** (Salatwada Rd; ⊙9am-9pm Mon-Sat, 8am-6pm Sun) on Salatwada Rd where you can see printers at work upstairs.

ℹ Information

There are ATMs at the train station, on RC Dutt Rd, and in Sayajigunj.

Gujarat Tourism (🖉2427489; Block C, Narmada Bhavan, Indira Ave; ⊙10.30am-6pm Mon-Sat, closed 2nd & 4th Sat of month) On the ground floor of a red and yellowy-white nine-storey building and not well signed. Unless you want to organise a tour or get brochures, this office is rather disappointing.

ICICI Bank (Sayajigunj) As well as the ATM, it changes travellers cheques and cash.

Speedy Cyber Cafe (Sayajigunj; per hr ₹20; ⊙8am-10pm) Cyber Cafe.

ℹ Getting There & Away

AIR

The airport is 4km northeast of the centre. **Jet Airways** (🖉022-39893333; www.jetairways. com; RC Dutt RD, 11 Panorama Bldg) and **IndiGo** (www.goindogo.com) fly to Mumbai and Delhi.

BUS

The **ST bus stand** (Nizampura) is about 3.6km north of the train station, with buses to many destinations in Gujarat and neighbourng states, including Ahmedabad (ordinary/deluxe ₹65/100, two hours, at least hourly), Bhavnagar (express ₹150, five hours, about hourly from 6am), Diu (deluxe ₹179, 12 hours, 6pm, 9pm and 10pm), Mumbai (deluxe ₹275, nine hours, 6pm, 7pm and 7.30pm) and Udaipur (₹195, eight hours, four daily). Volvo AC buses to Ahmedabad (₹170) leave throughout the day from the **local bus stand** (near train station). Many private bus companies have offices nearby, including **Sweta Travels** (🖉2786917; opposite train station), with Volvo AC buses to Mumbai (seat/sleeper ₹900/1100, eight hours, five daily), and buses to Udaipur (AC Volvo seat/sleeper ₹500/700, 9pm; non-AC ₹300/400 9pm, 10pm and 11pm).

Rickshaws from the ST bus stand to Sayajigunj cost about ₹50.

TRAIN

About 30 trains a day run to Ahmedabad, including the 12009 Shatabdi at 11.20am Monday to Saturday (AC chair/1AC ₹335/630, two hours). The 13 daily trains to Mumbai include the 12010 Shatabdi at 4.17pm Monday to Saturday (AC chair/1AC ₹627/1320, 5¼ hours).

Around Vadodara

Champaner & Pavagadh

This spectacular Unesco World Heritage Site, 47km northeast of Vadodara, combines a sacred, 762m volcanic hill (Pavagadh), looking like a chunk of the Himalaya dumped on the plain, and a ruined Gujarati capital with beautiful mosque architecture (Champaner). The whole area is referred to as Pavagadh.

Pavagadh hilltop may have been fortified as early as the 8th century. It became the capital of the Chauhan Rajputs around 1300, but in 1484 was taken by the Gujarat sultan Mahmud Begada, after a 20-month siege; the Rajputs committed *jauhar* – ritual mass suicide – in the face of defeat. Mahmud Begada turned Champaner, at the base of the hill, into a splendid new capital. But its glory was brief: when it was captured by Mughal emperor Humayun in 1535, the Gujarati capital reverted to Ahmedabad, and Champaner fell into ruin. Hindu and Jain pilgrims, however, continue to this day to climb to the temples atop Pavagadh.

The heart of **Champaner** (Indian/foreigner ₹10/250; ☺8am-6pm) is the Citadel, a rectangular area nearly 1km long, surrounded by high stone walls and now partly occupied by a village. A 6km-long outer wall enclosed the rest of the city. Champaner's most stunning features are its monumental mosques (which are no longer used for worship), with their beautiful blending of Islamic and Hindu decoration styles – above all the huge **Jami Masjid**, just outside the Citadel's east gate. Here a wonderful carved entrance porch leads into a lovely courtyard surrounded by a pillared corridor. The prayer hall has two tall central minarets, further superb stone carving, multiple domes, and seven mihrabs (prayer niches) along the back wall.

Other beautiful mosques include the **Saher ki Masjid**, behind the ticket office inside the Citadel, which was probably the private royal mosque, and the **Kevda Masjid**, 300m north of the Citadel and about 600m west of the Jami Masjid. Here you can climb narrow stairs to the roof, and higher up the minarets, to spot other mosques even further out into the countryside – **Nagina Masjid**, 500m north, with no minarets but exquisite geometric carving, and **Lila Gumbaj ki Masjid**, 800m east, on a high platform and with a fluted central dome. The twin minarets resembling factory chimneys, about 1km west, adorn the **Ek Minar ki Masjid**, a rare brick tomb.

To ascend **Pavagadh**, you can either walk up the pilgrim trail, which will take two to three hours, or you can take a shuttle (₹10) from opposite the Citadel's south gate. The shuttle deposits you about halfway up the

OFF THE BEATEN TRACK

SOUTH OF VADODARA

Gujarat stretches some 240km south from Vadodara to the border of Maharashtra, 150km short of Mumbai. **Surat**, 140km south of Vadodara, is where the British established their first Indian settlement in 1614. It's now Gujarat's hectic second-biggest city (population five million), and a busy commercial centre for textiles and diamonds. Around 40km south of Surat is **Dandi**, the destination of Gandhi's epic Salt March in 1930, with several Gandhi monuments by its strikingly empty beach. Just before the Maharashtra border is the ex-Portuguese enclave of **Daman**, an alcohol-infused resort town on a grey sea. Though it still retains a little of the piquancy of old Portugal, Daman is far less attractive than its counterpart, Diu, in Saurashtra. In the southeast, the hilly Dangs district is the northern extremity of the Western Ghats, with a large tribal population and little tourist infrastructure. The main town is the minor hill resort of Saputara. The **Dangs Darbar** (☺Feb/Mar), in the week before Holi, is a spectacular, largely tourist-free tribal festival.

hill, where you can either join the walking path (here lined by souvenir and drink stalls), or hop on the **Ropeway** (cable car; return ₹98; ⊙6am-6.45pm) which glides you up to within a 700m walk of the **Kalikamata Temple** on the hill's summit. The first version of this temple to Kali, an evil-destroying incarnation of the mother goddess, was built in the 10th or 11th century. The temple attracts a steady stream of pilgrims, especially during the nine days of Navratri (p691) and the month-long **Mahakali Festival** (Pavagadh; ⊙Mar/Apr). Near the top of the hill are also Pavagadh's oldest surviving monument, the 10th- to 11th-century Hindu **Lakulisha Temple**, and several Jain temples. The views are fantastic and so, if you're lucky, are the cooling breezes.

Hotel Champaner (☏02676-293041; s/d ₹400/600, with AC from ₹800/1200; ✳), near the foot of the Ropeway, has typically state-run rooms that are plain and unclean, but have balconies. There are plenty of eateries at the bottom of the Ropeway, and a few on top.

Buses to Pavagadh run about every half-hour from Vadodara (₹41, 1½ hours); a return taxi costs around ₹800. Some buses from Pavagadh travel via Vadodara to Ahmedabad (₹80, four hours).

SAURASHTRA

Before Independence, Saurashtra, also known as the Kathiawar Peninsula, was a jumble of over 200 princely states. Today it has a number of hectic industrial cities, but most of them retain a core of narrow old streets crowded with small-scale commerce. Outside the cities it's still villages, fields, forests and a timeless, almost feudal feel, with farmers and *maldhari* herders dressed head to toe in white, and rural women as colourful as their sisters in Rajasthan.

Saurashtra is mainly flat and its rare hills are often sacred – including the spectacular, temple-topped Shatrunjaya and Girnar Hill. The peninsula is liberally endowed with wildlife sanctuaries, notably Sasan Gir, where Asia's last wild lions roam. On the south coast lies the very quaint, laid-back ex-Portuguese island enclave of Diu. Saurashtra is also where Mahatma Gandhi was born and raised: you can visit several sites associated with his life.

Saurashtra has a reputation for being fond of its sleep, and siesta takes place from *at least* 1pm to 3pm.

Bhavnagar

☏0278 / POP 593,768

Bhavnagar is a hectic, sprawling industrial centre with a colourful old core that makes a base for journeys to nearby Shatrunjaya and Blackbuck National Park.

◉ Sights & Activities

Mahatma Gandhi attended university in Bhavnagar, and the dusty **Gandhi Smriti Museum** (admission free; ⊙9am-1pm & 3-6pm Mon-Sat, closed 2nd & 4th Sat of month), by the clock tower, has a multitude of Gandhi photographs and documents. Explanatory material is in Hindi only. Downstairs, the equally dusty **Barton Museum** (Indian/foreigner ₹2/50; ⊙9am-1pm & 3-6pm Mon-Sat, closed 2nd & 4th Sat of month), has religious carvings, betel-nut cutters, and a skeleton in a cupboard.

The old city, north of Ganga Jalia Tank, is well worth a wander, especially in early evening – it's busy with small shops and cluttered with dilapidated elaborate wooden buildings leaning over the colourful crowded bazaars. Don't miss the vegetable market!

★**Takhteshwar Temple** sits on a small hillock high enough to provide splendid views over the city and out onto the Gulf of Cambay.

🛏 Sleeping

The budget hotels, mostly in the old city and near the train station, are fairly grim, but midrange hotels are reasonable.

Hotel Sun 'n' Shine   HOTEL $$
(☏2516131; www.hotelsunnshine.com; ST Rd, Panwadi Chowk; s/d incl breakfast from ₹1800/2000; ✳@⊙) This well-run three-star hotel is excellent value. It has a Mediterranean-inspired and vertigo-inducing atrium, a very welcoming front desk, and the recommended RGB restaurant. The rooms are fresh and clean with comfortable beds and soft pillows: the more you pay, the more windows you get. The breakfast is substantial, and free airport transfers are offered.

Nilambag Palace Hotel   HERITAGE HOTEL $$
(☏2424241; http://nivalink.com/nilambagh; cottage room ₹1800/2500, palace room ₹3000/4000; ✳⊙≋) In large gardens beside the Ahmedabad road, about 600m southwest of the bus station, this former maharaja's palace was

Bhavnagar

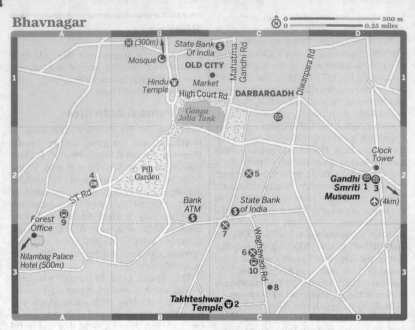

built in 1859. The lobby looks like an understated regal living room, with a beautiful mosaic floor. The 'cottage' rooms are good-sized but rather bare; the palace rooms are much nicer and bigger, in a stately early-20th-century style. Guests have use of a circular swimming pool (nonguests ₹100) in the Vijay Mahal in the extensive grounds, plus a gym and tennis facilities.

✗ Eating

Tulsi Restaurant　　　INDIAN, CHINESE $
(Kalanala Chowk; mains ₹75-110; ☺ lunch & dinner) Low-lit with plants and understated decor, this cosy and clean place with well-prepared Punjabi and Chinese veg dishes is rightly popular. Service is friendly and efficient, and it's excellent value.

Rasoi　　　INDIAN, CHINESE $
(thali ₹160; ☺ 11.30am-3.30pm & 7-11pm) This secluded bungalow and (in the evening) garden restaurant serves up great unlimited Gujarati thalis. It's behind the police post between two petrol stations, just north of the Galaxy Cinema.

Sankalp　　　SOUTH INDIAN $
(Waghawadi Rd; mains ₹50-120; ☺ 11am-3pm & 6-11pm) This place offers first-class South Indian vegetarian dishes in clean and contemporary surroundings.

ⓘ Information

State Bank Of India (Darbargadh; ☺ 10.30am-4.30pm Mon-Fri) Changes cash and travellers cheques and has a 24-hour ATM and a lovely, ornately carved, old-city portico. Other ATMs include locations at State Bank and HDFC near Tulsi Restaurant.

ⓘ Getting There & Around

AIR

Air **Jet Airways** (📞 2433371; www.jetairways.com; Waghawadi Rd, Surat House) has daily flights to and from Mumbai. A taxi to or from the airport costs around ₹150.

BUS

From the **ST bus stand** there are buses for Diu (₹125, seven hours, six daily), Rajkot (₹100, four hours, 12 daily) and Ahmedabad (₹110, five hours, 13 daily). Private bus companies include **Tanna Travels** (Waghawadi Rd), with AC buses to Ahmedabad (₹180, four hours, 15 daily), Vadodara (₹200, four hours, seven daily) and Mumbai (₹800, 13 hours, 4pm).

TRAIN

The 12972 Bhavnagar-Bandra Express departs at 8.30pm and arrives in Ahmedabad (sleeper/3AC/2AC ₹300/443/1225) at 1.52am on its way to Mumbai.

Blackbuck National Park

This beautiful, 34-sq-km **park** (Velavadar NP; Indian/foreigner car ₹250/1000, 4hr guide ₹100/500; ⊙ dawn-dusk 16 Oct-15 Jun), north of Bhavnagar, encompasses large areas of pale, custard-coloured grassland stretching between two seasonal rivers. Formerly called Velavadar National Park, it's famous for its blackbucks, beautiful, fast antelope that sport elegant spiralling horns – as long as 65cm in mature males. Some 1600 inhabit the park, which is also good for spotting birds such as wintering harriers from Siberia (about 2000 of them most years). The park has a good road network and is best explored by car. Pay your fees and pick up a guide (who is unlikely to speak English) at the reception centre about 65km from Bhavnagar, north of Valabhipur.

You can book accommodation in the four-room **Forest Department Guest House** (Indian/foreigner d ₹500/2600), by the reception centre, through the **Forest Office** (📞 0278-2426425; F-10, Annexe, MS Bldg; ⊙ 11am-5pm Mon-Fri) in Bhavnagar. The very comfortable stone-built villas of **Blackbuck Lodge** (📞 9824019877, 079-40020901; www.theblackbucklodge.com; s/d incl breakfast ₹7500/8000 Oct-Mar, ₹4500/5000 Apr-Sep) are just outside the park's western entrance.

A taxi day trip from Bhavnagar costs about ₹2000.

Palitana

📞 02848 / POP 55,000

The hustling, dusty town of Palitana, 51km southwest of Bhavnagar, has grown rapidly to serve the pilgrim trade around Shatrunjaya. Your best bet for general information is the helpful manager at Hotel Shravak.

⊙ Sights & Activities

Shatrunjaya   SACRED SITE

(Place of Victory; ⊙ temples 6.30am-6pm) One of Jainism's holiest pilgrimage sites, Shatrunjaya is an incredible hilltop sea of temples, built over a span of 900 years on a plateau dedicated to the gods. It is said that Adinath (also known as Rishabha), the founder of Jainism, meditated and gave his first sermon beneath the rayan tree at the summit. The temples are grouped into *tunks* (enclosures), each with a central temple and many minor ones. Some of the earliest were built in the 11th century, but were destroyed by foreign invaders in the 14th and 15th centuries; the current temples date from the 16th century onwards.

The 500m climb up 3300 steps to the temples adds to the extraordinary experience and takes most people about 1½ hours. The steps start on the southwest edge of Palitana, about 3.5km from the bus stand (₹20 by autorickshaw). Pilgrims make the climb in their hundreds most days, and in thousands around **Kartik Purnima** (Somnath & Shatrunjaya; ⊙ Nov/Dec).

As you near the top of the hill, the track forks. The main entrance, Ram Pole, is reached by taking the left-hand fork. To see the best views over the site first, take the right-hand fork. There are superb views in

---

ⓘ SHATRUNJAYA PRACTICALITIES

It's best to start the ascent around dawn, before it gets too hot. Dress respectfully (no shorts, etc). Leave behind leather items, including belts and bags, and don't eat or drink inside the temples. If you wish, you can be carried up and down the hill in a *dholi* (portable chair with two bearers), for about ₹1000 round trip.

Photo permits (₹100) must be obtained before you start the climb, from an office on the left just before the foot of the steps.

all directions; on a clear day you can see the Gulf of Cambay. Inside the Nav Tonk Gate, one path leads left to the Muslim shrine of **Angar Pir**, where women who want children make offerings of miniature cradles. The Muslim saint protected the temples from a Mughal attack. To the right, the second *tunk* you reach is the Chaumukhji Tunk, containing the **Chaumukh** (Four-Faced Shrine), built in 1618 by a wealthy Jain merchant. Images of Adinath, the first Jain *tirthankar* (believed to have attained enlightenment here), face the four cardinal directions.

You can easily spend a couple of hours wandering among the hundreds of temples up here. The biggest and one of the most splendid and important, with a fantastic wealth of detailed carving, is the **Adinath Temple**, on the highest point on the far (south) side.

Shri Vishal Jain Museum (admission ₹10; ☺8am-noon & 3.30-8.30pm), 500m down the street from the foot of the Shatrunjaya steps, exhibits assorted Jain artwork and artefacts up to 500 years old. In the basement is a surprising circular temple with mirror walls and centuries-old images of four *tirthankars*.

⊨ Sleeping & Eating

Hotel Shravak HOTEL $
(☑252428; s/d/tr/q ₹100/300/400/500; r with AC ₹850; ✻) The ultra-basic rooms at the friendly Shravak, opposite the bus stand, are the best bet in Palitana itself. They're shabby but clean, though bathrooms are hit or miss (mostly miss; doubles are much bigger than singles). Buckets of hot water are available from 5am to 10am.

★ **Vijay Vilas Adpur** HERITAGE HOTEL $$
(☑282371, 9427182809; www.vijayvilaspalitana. com; Adpur village; ✻) Vijay Vilas sits in deep, beautiful countryside beneath the western end of Shatrunjaya, 11km west of Palitana. It's a small 1906 palace with six large, plain but nicely decorated rooms, with original furniture. Three have terraces/balconies looking towards Shatrunjaya – which can be climbed from here by a slightly shorter, steeper path (2700 steps) than the one from Palitana. Vijay Vilas is family-run, with delicious home-cooked food (a mix of Gujarati and Rajasthani, veg and nonveg). You can also just pop in for lunch (₹300) – it's best to call first. This place was closed for renovations at the time of research, but was due to reopen soon.

Jagruti Restaurant INDIAN $
(thali ₹30-60; ☺24hr) Across the laneway from Hotel Shravak, Jagruti is a wildly busy thali house.

❶ Getting There & Away

Plenty of ST buses run to/from Bhavnagar (₹27, 1½ hours, hourly) and Ahmedabad (₹120, five hours, hourly). For Diu, take a bus to Talaja (₹21, one hour, hourly), where you can catch buses to Diu (₹90, 5½ hours, around six daily).

Three passenger trains run daily to/from Bhavnagar (2nd class ₹8).

Diu

☑02875 / POP 52,056

Diu is different. This tiny island linked by a bridge to Gujarat's southern coast is infused with Portuguese history. Its major architectural landmarks include three churches and a seafront fort. The streets of the main town are remarkably clean and quiet once you get off the tourist-packed waterfront strip; and alcohol is legal here. If you've been spending time immersed in the intensity of Gujarati cities, or just really need a beer, Diu offers a refreshing break.

Despite its draw as a seaside destination, Diu is not a great choice for a beach-centric vacation. Most of its sandy strips are littered with trash, and the throngs of families make them better for people-watching than sun-worshipping. Add in the random drunk-guy factor, and any fantasies you have of a tropical paradise will surely be dashed. Diu, however, is one of the safest places in India to ride a scooter, with minimum traffic and excellent roads, and zipping along the coast with the wind in your hair is a joy.

Like Daman and Goa, Diu was a Portuguese colony until taken over by India in 1961. With Daman, it is still governed from Delhi as part of the Union Territory of Daman & Diu and is not part of Gujarat. It includes Diu Island, about 11km by 3km, separated from the mainland by a narrow channel, and two tiny mainland enclaves. One of these, housing the village of Ghoghla, is the entry point to Diu from Una.

Diu town sits at the east end of the island. The northern side of the island, facing Gujarat, is tidal marsh and salt pans, while the southern coast alternates between limestone cliffs, rocky coves and sandy beaches.

Diu Town

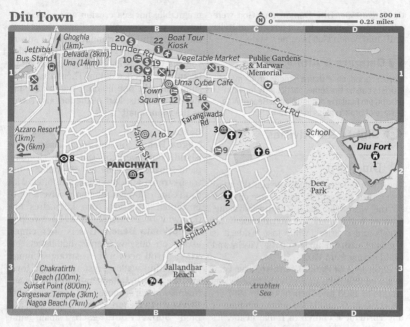

Diu Town

The island's main industries are fishing, tourism, alcohol and salt. Kalpana Distillery at Malala produces rum from sugar cane.

One custom of the Portuguese still very much respected by local businesses is that of the siesta.

History

Diu was the first landing point for the Parsis when they fled from Persia in the 7th centu-ry AD, and it became a major port between the 14th and 16th centuries, when it was the trading post and naval base from which the Ottomans controlled the northern Arabian Sea shipping routes.

The Portuguese secured control of Diu in 1535 and kept it until India launched Opera-tion Vijay in 1961. After the Indian Air Force unnecessarily bombed the airstrip and ter-minal near Nagoa, it remained derelict until the late 1980s. Diu, Daman and Goa were administered as one union territory of India until 1987, when Goa became a state.

ℹ Dangers & Annoyances

More an annoyance than a danger, drunk male tourists can be tiresome, particularly for women, and particularly around Nagoa Beach. Also, beware of broken glass in the sand.

◉ Sights & Activities

◉ Diu Town

The town is sandwiched between the massive fort at its east end and a huge city wall on the west. The main **Zampa Gateway**, painted bright red, has carvings of lions, angels and a priest, while just inside it is a chapel with an image of the Virgin and Child dating from 1702.

Cavernous **St Paul's Church** (⊘ 8am-6pm) is a wedding cake of a church, founded by Jesuits in 1600 and then rebuilt in 1807. Its neoclassical facade is the most elaborate of any Portuguese church in India. Inside, it's a great barn, with a small cloister next door, above which is a school. Daily mass is heard here. Nearby is white-walled **St Thomas' Church**, a lovely, simple building that is now the **Diu Museum** (admission free; ⊘ 9am-9pm), with a spooky, evocative collection of wooden Catholic saints going back to the 16th century. Once a year, on 1 November, this is used for a packed-out mass. The Portuguese-descended population mostly live in this area, still called Farangiwada (Foreigners' Quarter). The **Church of St Francis of Assisi**, founded in 1593, has been converted into a hospital, but is also sometimes used for services.

Many other Diu buildings show a lingering Portuguese influence. The western part of town is a maze of narrow, winding streets and many houses are brightly painted, with the most impressive being in the Panchwati area, notably **Nagar Sheth Haveli**, an old merchant's house laden with stucco scrolls and fulsome fruit.

◉ Around the Island

★ Diu Fort   FORT

(admission free; ⊘ 8am-6pm) Built in 1535, with additions made in 1541, the massive, well-preserved Portuguese fort with its double moat (one tidal) must once have been im-

pregnable, but sea erosion and neglect are leading to a slow collapse. Cannonballs litter the place, and the ramparts have a superb array of cannons. The lighthouse, which you can climb, is Diu's highest point, with a beam that reaches 32km. There are several small chapels, one holding engraved tombstone fragments. Part of the fort also serves as the island's jail.

Beaches   BEACHES

Nagoa Beach, on the south coast of the island, 7km west of Diu town, is long, palm-fringed and safe for swimming – but trash-strewn and very busy, and often with drunk men: foreign women receive a lot of unwanted attention. Two kilometres further west begins the sandy, 2.5km sweep of **Gomptimata Beach**. This is often empty, except on busy weekends, but it gets big waves – you need to be a strong swimmer here. Within walking distance of Diu town are the rocky **Jallandhar Beach**, on the town's southern shore; the longer, sandier **Chakratirth Beach**, west of Jallandhar; and pretty **Sunset Point Beach**, a small, gentle curve beyond Chakratirth that's popular for swimming and relatively hassle-free. Sunset Point itself is a small headland at the south end of the beach, topped by the **INS Khukhri Memorial**, commemorating an Indian Navy frigate sunk off Diu during the 1971 India-Pakistan War. Unfortunately, the region around Sunset Point is also a dumping ground, and any early-morning excursion will reveal that the tidal zone here is a popular toilet venue.

The best beach is **Ghoghla Beach**, north of Diu. A long stretch of sand, it's got less trash and fewer people than the others, along with gentle waves and some decent restaurants behind it.

Gangeswar Temple   HINDU TEMPLE

Gangeswar Temple, on the south coast 3km west of town, just past Fudam village, is a small coastal cave where five Shiva linga (phallic symbols) are washed by the waves.

Sea Shell Museum   MUSEUM

(adult/child ₹10/5; ⊘ 9am-6pm) This museum, 6km from town on the Nagoa road, is a labour of love. Captain Devjibhai Vira Fulbaria, a merchant navy captain, collected thousands of shells from literally all over the world in 50 years of sailing, and has displayed and labelled them in English with great care.

Parsi Bungali   HISTORIC SITE

A stone-paved path leads 200m inland from Gangeswar Temple to two Parsi 'towers of silence': squat, round stone towers where the Parsis laid their dead out to be consumed by vultures. Climb the ramp slowly and make some noise, so as not to startle the groups of dogs that hang out inside!

★ Vanakbara   FISHING VILLAGE

At the extreme west of the island, Vanakbara is a fascinating little fishing village and the highlight of the island. It's great to wander around the port, packed with colourful fishing boats and bustling activity – best around 7am to 8am when the fishing fleet returns and sells off its catch.

🖝 Tours

You can take 20-minute **boat trips** (per person ₹25, minimum charge ₹150; ⊗ 9.30am-1.30pm & 3-6.30pm) around the harbour. Get tickets at the kiosk in front of the tourist office. Other options include a one-hour **evening cruise** (per person ₹120, minimum charge ₹960) at 7.30pm, weather permitting.

🛏 Sleeping

Rates at most hotels are extremely flexible, with discounts of up to 60% available at the more expensive places when things are quiet. Some only charge the full rates at peak holiday times such as Diwali and Christmas/New Year. We've quoted the highest prices here.

🛏 Diu Town

★ Herança Goesa   GUESTHOUSE $

(☑ 253851; heranca_goesa@yahoo.com; Farangiwada; r ₹350-500) Behind Diu Museum, this friendly home of a Portuguese-descended family has eight absolutely spotless rooms that represent incredible value. Take one of the upstairs rooms that captures the sea breeze and just relax. Good breakfasts are served and delicious fish/seafood dinners (around ₹200) are available if you reserve in the morning.

Hotel São Tomé Retiro   GUESTHOUSE $

(☑ 253137; r ₹500, without bathroom ₹350) This atmospheric guesthouse, occupying rooms up on the side of old St Thomas' Church, is definitely the place to stay for a unique Diu experience. Your host, George D'Souza, is a gentle soul, and his barbecue parties are a treat. Rooms are getting run-down

these days, and range from small, hot and basic structures on the roof to breezy thick-walled abodes. The 360-degree views from the church roof are unrivalled on the island.

Hotel Super Silver   HOTEL $

(☑ 252020; hotel_supersilverdiu@yahoo.com; Super Silver Complex; r ₹400, with AC ₹900; ❄ @) Super Silver has a nice central location and is good value, with simple, very clean rooms, though the bathrooms could use some help. The affable manager raises and lowers prices according to demand on any given day, but likes foreign tourists and is willing to give them a break. The hotel has a handy cybercafe, and scooter and motorcycle rental.

Hotel Samrat   HOTEL $$

(☑ 252354; www.hotelsamratdiu.com; Old Collectorate Rd; r ₹1450, with AC from ₹2050; ❄ ☀) Hotel Samrat is the town's best midrange choice, with comfortable doubles, some with street-facing balconies. Credit cards are accepted and there's a decent Indian/Chinese restaurant (mains ₹70 to ₹160) with plenty of grog available.

Hotel Relax Inn   HOTEL $$

(☑ 9638741888; Bunder Rd; r ₹2850; ❄) With colourful exterior paintwork, Relax Inn offers bright rooms in blues and whites, all with balconies. If the weather's not too hot, you can score a good discount by having the AC turned off. Most rooms have huge windows with sea views. The substantial noise from the dance parties held at the streetfront club should end between 10pm and 11pm.

★ Azzaro Resort   HOTEL $$$

(☑ 255421; www.azzarodiu.com; Fudam Rd; d ₹4950-11,900; ❄ @ 🛜 ☀) Hands down Diu's most luxurious hotel, 1km outside the city gate, Azzarao features tastefully luxurious rooms with high-tech lighting controls and stylish glass walls between the bedroom and bath. All look out onto the garden surrounding the sapphire-blue pool, many with balconies. There's a spa, a gym, two restaurants and a 24-hour coffee shop. All in all, worth the money.

🛏 Nagoa Beach

Hoka Island Villa   HOTEL $$

(☑ 253036; www.resorthoka.com; r ₹1950-2250; ❄ 🛜 ☀) Hoka is a great place to stay, with colourful, clean and cool rooms in a small, palm-shaded complex with a small swimming pool. Some rooms have terraces over the palm trees. The management here is very helpful, you can hire mopeds, and the food is excellent. Stick to the main road, passing the turn into Nagoa Beach, and it's on the left about 300m along.

Radhika Beach Resort HOTEL **$$**
(☎252553; www.radhikaresort.com; d ₹2550-4050; ❉⚲❄) An immaculate, smart, modern place and Diu's best-located upmarket option, with comfortable, condo-like villas in grassy grounds. Rooms are spacious, clean and worth the money, and there's a very good multicuisine restaurant. The 'classic' and VIP rooms are set around a large pool.

✖ Eating

Fresh fish is excellent here, and drinks are blissfully cheap – around ₹50 for a Kingfisher or ₹150 for a bottle of port.

There is a **fish market** opposite Jethibai bus stand, and another one across the bridge in Ghoghla, which is active around 2.30pm and again at 6.30pm. The fresh fish and seafood are delicious; most guesthouses and hotels will cook anything you buy.

Ram Vijay ICE CREAM **$**
(scoops ₹20-25; ⊙8.30am-1.30pm & 3.30-9.30pm) For a rare treat head to this small, squeaky-clean, old-fashioned ice-cream parlour near the town square for delicious handmade ice cream and milkshakes. Going since 1933, this family enterprise started with soft drinks, and still makes its own brands (Dew and Leo) in Fudam village – try a mint or ginger lemon soda and then all the ice creams!

O'Coqueiro MULTICUISINE **$$**
(Farangiwada Rd; mains ₹65-260) Here, the dedicated Kailash Pandey has developed a soul-infused garden restaurant celebrating freshness and quality. The menu offers uncomplicated but very tasty pasta, chicken and seafood, plus a handful of Portuguese dishes learnt from a local Diu matriarch. There's also good coffee, cold beer, groovy music and friendly service.

Cat's Eye View MULTICUISINE **$$**
(Hoka Island Villa, Nagoa Beach; mains ₹100-275; ⊙8-10am, 12-2.30pm & 7-9.30pm) The open-air restaurant at Hoka Island Villa has excellent food, with inviting breakfasts and delicious choices such as penne with tuna and tomato, fish and chips, and prawn coconut curry. It's relaxed, pleasant and tree-shaded.

Hotel São Tomé Retiro SEAFOOD **$$**
(☎253137; buffet BBQ ₹200) From around October to April, hospitable George and family hold barbecue parties every other evening. The fresh fish and delicious salads are fantastic, beer is available and it's an atmospheric place to sit around a blazing campfire and meet other travellers.

Sea View Restaurant SEAFOOD **$$**
(Ghoghla Beach; ⊙7am-11pm) Just behind Ghoghla Beach, the open-air Sea View has a full menu of Indian and seafood, with the sand a stone's throw away. The prawn biryani (₹150) is big and spicy. Except at holiday time, the clientele is mostly men.

La Dolce Vita MULTICUISINE **$$**
(☎9824203925; Hospital Rd; mains ₹60-130; ⊙8am-10pm) This is a pretty garden restaurant on the beach side of town with excellent-value breakfasts (options include homemade muesli, fruit salad, pancakes and lassi), very good Moka coffee, and great service. Aside from the veg and nonveg standards, there's a good list of pasta and seafood, including tasty fish curry.

Apana Foodland MULTICUISINE **$$**
(Fort Rd, Apana Hotel; mains ₹60-225; ⊙7am-10.30pm) This outdoor restaurant facing the town waterfront does everything: breakfasts, South Indian, Gujarati, Punjabi and Chinese. The fish dishes, including shark tikka, or kingfish/prawns with rice, chips and salad, can be pre-ordered so you don't miss out. The Gujarati fruit salad is delicious.

☕ Drinking

Apart from the restaurants (most of which double as bars), there are a number of bars around town. Some are on the seedy side, but the almost publike **Casaluxo Bar** (⊙9am-1pm Mon-Sat, 4-9pm Tue-Sat), facing the town square, has a more salubrious air. It opened in 1963 and, except for some sexy swimsuit posters in the back room, might not have updated its decor since.

ℹ Information

Note that many shops around town change money.

A to Z (Vaniya St, Panchwati; per hr ₹30; ⊙9am-10pm) The best internet cafe is near Panchwati Rd.

Post office (⊙9am-5pm Mon-Sat) Upstairs, facing the town square.

State Bank of India (Main Bazaar; ⊙10am-4pm Mon-Fri) Changes cash and travellers cheques.

Tourist office (☑252653; www.diutourism.co.in; Bunder Rd; ⊙9.30am-1.30pm & 2.30-6pm Mon-Sat) Has maps, bus schedules and hotel prices.

Uma Cyber Café (per hr ₹30; ⊙9.30am-11pm)

ⓘ Getting There & Away

AIR

Jet Airways (☑255030; www.jetairways.com) flies to/from Mumbai via Porbandar. There are several ticketing agents in town. The airport is 6km west of town, just before Nagoa Beach.

BUS & CAR

Visitors arriving in Diu by road may be charged a border tax of ₹50 per person, though the practice seems to be erratic.

From **Jethibai bus stand** there are buses to Veraval (₹70, three hours, 12 daily), Junagadh (₹120, five hours, seven daily), Rajkot (₹140, six hours, six daily), Bhavnagar (₹150, seven hours, 10 daily) and Ahmedabad (₹200, 12 hours, 7am and 9pm). More frequent departures go from Una, 14km north of Diu. Buses run between Una bus stand and Diu (₹15, 40 minutes) every half-hour between 6.30am to 8pm. Outside these hours, shared autorickshaws go to Ghoghla or Diu from Tower Chowk in Una (1km from the bus stand), for about the same fare. An autorickshaw costs ₹250. Una rickshaw-wallahs are unable to proceed further than the bus station in Diu, so cannot take you all the way to Nagoa Beach (an additional ₹100).

At the bus stand, Ekta Travels runs private buses from Diu to Mumbai at 11am (sleeper ₹600, 20 hours) and to Ahmedabad at 7.30pm (seat/sleeper ₹200/300, 10 hours).

TRAIN

Delvada, 8km from Diu on the Una road, is the nearest railhead. Train 52951 at 2.25pm runs to Sasan Gir (2nd class ₹15, 3½ hours) and Junagadh (₹23, 6¼ hours). Train 52950 at 8.05am heads to Veraval (₹16, 3¼ hours). Half-hourly Diu–Una buses stop at Delvada (₹15, 20 minutes).

ⓘ Getting Around

Travelling by autorickshaw anywhere in Diu town should cost no more than ₹30. From the bus stand into town is ₹40. To Nagoa Beach and beyond pay ₹100 and to Sunset Point ₹50.

Scooters are a perfect option for exploring the island – the roads are deserted and in good condition. The going rate for 24-hour rental is ₹250 (not including fuel), and motorcycles can be had for ₹300. Most hotels can arrange rentals,

although quality varies. You will normally have to show your driving licence and leave a deposit of ₹500 to ₹1000.

Local buses from Diu town to Nagoa and Vanakbara (both ₹10) leave Jethibai bus stand at 7am, 11am and 4pm. From Nagoa, they depart for Diu town from near the police post at 1pm, 5.30pm and 7pm.

Veraval

☑02876 / POP 153,696

Cluttered and chaotic, Veraval is one of India's major fishing ports; its busy harbour is full of bustle and boat building. It was also the major seaport for Mecca pilgrims before the rise of Surat. The main reason to come here now is to visit the Temple of Somnath, 6km southeast, while the town of Somnath is a nicer place to stay, Veraval is more convenient to public transport.

⊙ Sights

One kilometre from Veraval towards Somnath, **Bhalka Tirth** is where Krishna was mistaken for a deer (he was sleeping in a deerskin) and fatally wounded by an arrow. The temple here is an architecturally mundane affair, but it contains an image of Krishna reclining, a tulsi tree planted in his memory growing out through the roof, a relief of his footprint and two Shiva linga. A sign outside tells us that this was where Krishna departed on his journey to Neejdham (final rest) at 2.27 and 30 seconds am on 18 February, 3102 BC.

The fishing harbour about 800m south of Bhalka Tirth towards Somnath is a striking sight with hundreds of wooden dhows flying colourful flags.

🛏 Sleeping & Eating

Hotel Kaveri HOTEL $
(☑220842; www.hotelkaveri.in; ST Rd, 2 Akar Complex; r ₹500, AC from ₹850, ste from ₹1500; ✳) Kaveri is the pick of the town's uninspiring accommodation, and the most convenient choice, with a range of well-kept rooms.

Toran Tourist Bungalow HOTEL $
(☑246588; College Rd; s/d ₹400/500, with AC ₹700/900; ✳) This state-government-run hotel, 1km west of the bus stand area, is not very conveniently situated. But it has sizeable, quiet, clean rooms with white-tile walls and floors, and terraces from which you can see the sea.

GUJARAT VERAVAL

Sagar INDIAN $

(ST Rd; mains ₹70-130; ⊙9am-3.30pm & 5-11pm)
With air-conditioning and fish tanks, this
all-veg restaurant is a cool, quiet oasis with
reliable food.

ℹ Information

There are HDFC and Axis Bank ATMs near the
municipal gardens.

JP Travels International (Satta Bazaar;
⊙10am-8.30pm Mon-Sat) Changes travellers
cheques and cash.

Magnet Cyber Café (ST Rd, 2nd fl, Chan-
dramauli Complex; per hr ₹20; ⊙9.30am-
10pm) Opposite the bus station.

ℹ Getting There & Away

BUS

ST buses go to Ahmedabad (₹210, nine hours,
five daily), Diu (₹85, three hours, 10 daily), Sasan
Gir (₹35, 1½ hours, hourly), Junagadh (₹83, 2½
hours, every 30 minutes) and Rajkot (₹140, four
hours, hourly). Krishna Travels, opposite the ST
bus stand, offers a nightly jaunt to Ahmedabad
(seat/sleeper ₹180/280) at 9.30pm.

TRAIN

The 11463 Jabalpur Express leaves at 9.55am for
Junagadh (sleeper/3AC/2AC ₹140/250/625, 1¾
hours), Rajkot (₹140/332/625, four hours) and
Ahmedabad (₹214/554/810, nine hours). Second-
class-only trains with unreserved seating head
to Sasan Gir (₹7, 1¼ to two hours) at 9.45am and
1.55pm, and to Delvada (for Diu) at 4.20pm (₹16,
3¼ hours). There's a **computerised reservation
office** (⊙8am-10pm Mon-Sat, to 2pm Sun) at the
station.

ℹ Getting Around

A shared/private autorickshaw to Somnath
should cost ₹10/50; buses are ₹8 and leave
from the ST bus stand.

Somnath

☑ 02876

Somnath's famous, phoenix-like temple
stands in neat gardens above the beach, 6km
southeast of Veraval. The sea below gives it a
wistful charm. The small town of Somnath
is an agglomeration of narrow, interesting
market streets with no car traffic, so it's easy
to walk around and enjoy. There's a State
Bank ATM on your right as you approach the
temple. Somnath celebrates Kartik Purnima
(p705), marking Shiva's killing of the demon
Tripurasura, with a large colourful fair.

◉ Sights

Temple of Somnath HINDU TEMPLE

(⊙6am-9pm) This temple has been razed
and rebuilt at least seven times. It's said
that Somraj, the moon god, constructed
a gold version, rebuilt by Ravana in silver,
by Krishna in wood and by King Bhimdev
I in stone. A description of the temple by
Al-Biruni, an Arab traveller, was so glowing
that it prompted a visit in 1024 by a most
unwelcome tourist – the legendary looter
Mahmud of Ghazni from Afghanistan. At
that time, the temple was so wealthy that it
had 300 musicians, 500 dancing girls and
even 300 barbers. Mahmud of Ghazni took
the town and temple after a two-day battle in which it's said 70,000 Hindu defenders died. Having stripped the temple of its
fabulous wealth, Mahmud destroyed it. So
began a pattern of destruction and rebuilding that continued for centuries. The temple
was again razed in 1297, 1394 and finally in
1706 by Aurangzeb, the notorious Mughal
fundamentalist.

After the 1706 demolition, the temple
wasn't rebuilt until 1950. The current serene, symmetrical structure was built to
traditional designs on the original coastal
site: it's painted a creamy colour and boasts
a little fine sculpture. The large black Shiva
lingam at its heart is one of the 12 most sacred Shiva shrines, known as *jyoti linga*.
Colourful dioramas of the Shiva story line
the north side of the temple garden, though
its hard to see them through the hazy glass.
A one-hour **sound-and-light show** (tickets
₹25) highlights the temple nightly at 7:45pm.

Cameras, mobile phones, and bags must
be left at the cloakroom before entering.

Prabhas Patan Museum MUSEUM

(Indian/foreigner ₹2/50; ⊙10.30am-5.30pm Thu-
Tue, closed 2nd & 4th Sat of month) This museum, 300m north of the Somnath temple,
is laid out in courtyard-centred rooms and
contains remains of the previous temples,
some intricately carved, though many are
very weathered.

🛏 Sleeping & Eating

Hotel Kailash HOTEL $

(☑9228205381; r ₹800, with AC ₹1000; ❄) This
brand-new hotel just north of Somnath
Temple is the best option close to the temple
and the markets. Rooms still shine, and have
modern AC units and flat-screen TVs.

New Bhabha Restaurant INDIAN, CHINESE **$**
(mains ₹50-80) The pick of a poor bunch of eateries, vegetarian New Bhabha sits 250m north of the ST bus stand. You can eat in a small AC room or outside, open to the street.

❶ Getting There & Away

Somnath has fewer departures than Veraval, but buses run to Diu (₹65, three hours, daily at 9.45am), Junagadh (₹90, two hours) and Rajkot (₹125, four hours) throughout the day. Shayam Travels, just north of the ST bus stand, has buses to Ahmedabad (seat/sleeper ₹250/350, nine hours) at 9.30pm and 10pm.

Sasan Gir Wildlife Sanctuary

☑ 02877

The last refuge of the Asiatic lion (*Panthera leo persica*) is this forested, hilly, 1412-sq-km sanctuary about halfway between Veraval and Junagadh. It feels beguilingly uncommercial, and simply driving through the thick, undisturbed forests would be a joy even if there wasn't the excitement of lions and other wildlife to spot.

The sanctuary was set up in 1965, and a 259-sq-km core area was declared a national park in 1975. Since the late 1960s, lion numbers have increased from under 200 to over 400. The sanctuary's 37 other mammal species, most of which have also increased in numbers, include the dainty chital (spotted deer), the sambar (a large deer), the nilgai or bluebull (a large antelope), the chousingha (four-horned antelope), the chinkara (a gazelle), crocodiles and rarely seen leopards. Sasan Gir is a great destination for birders too, with over 300 species, most of them resident. While the wildlife has been lucky, more than half the sanctuary's human community of distinctively dressed *maldhari* have been resettled elsewhere, ostensibly because their cattle and buffalo were competing for food resources with the antelopes, deer and gazelles, while also being preyed upon by the lions and leopards (*maldhari* livestock still provides a quarter of the lions' diet).

Sasan Gir is no longer big enough for the number of lions; some may be moved to Madhya Pradesh to protect genetic diversity, but the Gujarat government opposes this plan, vying to remain the sole home of India's lions.

The sanctuary access point is Sasan Gir village, on a minor road and railway between Veraval and Junagadh (about 40km from each). The best time to visit is from December to April; the sanctuary is closed from 16 June to 15 October and possibly longer if there has been a heavy monsoon.

◉ Sights & Activities

★ **Safaris** WILDLIFE-WATCHING
(permit vehicle with up to 6 passengers Indians/foreigners ₹400/US$40 Mon-Fri, ₹500/US$50 Sat & Sun, guide 4hr ₹50) As a general rule, about one in every two safaris has a lion sighting. So if you're determined to see lions, allow for a couple of trips. You'll certainly see a variety of other wildlife, and the guides are adept spotters.

Visits to the sanctuary are in jeeps which follow varied circuits of about three hours. The best time for seeing wildlife is early morning. Most hotels and guesthouses in and around Sasan Gir have jeeps and drivers or will arrange them for you, charging ₹1200 or more per safari for up to six passengers. Alternatively, you can hire an open jeep and driver for around ₹1000 outside the sanctuary **reception centre** (☑ 285541), next to Sinh Sadan Guest House in Sasan Gir village. Once you have a vehicle sorted, you must queue up at the reception centre to obtain a permit and a guide, and pay photography fees (camera up to seven megapixel free; over seven megapixel Indian/foreigner ₹100/500). Your driver will usually help with this; be at the reception centre with your passport when it opens to ensure you get a permit and an early start. Permit-issuing times are posted at the reception centre: at research time they were 6am, 9am and 3pm. Up to 90 permits can be issued each day and half of those can be booked in advance.

Gir Interpretation Zone WILDLIFE-WATCHING
(Indian/foreigner ₹75/1000 Mon-Fri, ₹100/1250 Sat & Sun; ◉ 8-11am & 3-5pm Thu-Tue) Twelve kilometres west of Sasan Gir village at Devalia, within the sanctuary precincts, is the Gir Interpretation Zone, better known as simply 'Devalia'. The 4.12-sq-km fenced-off compound is home to a cross-section of Gir wildlife. Chances of seeing lions here are good but stage-managed, and you're only likely to get 30 to 45 minutes looking for wildlife and only from a bus. An autorickshaw/taxi round trip to Devalia from Sasan Gir village costs around ₹80/120.

THE LAST WILD ASIATIC LIONS

The Asiatic lion (*Panthera leo persica*) once roared as far west as Syria and as far east as India's Bihar. Widespread hunting decimated the population, with the last sightings recorded near Delhi in 1834, in Bihar in 1840 and in Rajasthan in 1870. In Gujarat too they were almost hunted to extinction, with as few as 12 remaining in the 1870s. It was not until one of their erstwhile pursuers, the enlightened Nawab of Junagadh, decided to set up a protection zone at the beginning of the 20th century that the lions began slowly to recover. This zone now survives as the Sasan Gir Wildlife Sanctuary.

Separated from their African counterpart (*Panthera leo leo*) for centuries, Asiatic lions have developed unique characteristics. Their mane is less luxuriant and doesn't cover the top of the head or ears, while a prominent fold of skin runs the length of the abdomen. They are also purely predatory, unlike African lions, which sometimes feed off carrion.

Gir Orientation Centre EXHIBITION
(⊘8am-6pm) FREE Next to the reception centre, this has an informative exhibition on the sanctuary and a small shop. A creaking film about the park is screened behind the building at 7pm.

🛏 Sleeping & Eating

It's a good idea to make an advance booking. Sasan Gir has one main street and most accommodation is on it or nearby, with a few top-end options further away.

Nitin Ratanghayara
Family Rooms GUESTHOUSE $
(☑99790 24670; ratanghayaranitin@yahoo.com; r ₹400, with AC ₹700; ❋@) At his family's courtyard-style house in Sasan, friendly, golden-toothed Nitin Ratanghayara has a couple of good rooms reserved for travellers. They're well kept, and much better value than any of the budget joints on main street. Plus, you get to eat his sister-in-law's home cooking, and can help her in the kitchen if you like. Look for his sign over his shop along Sasan's main drag.

Hotel Umang HOTEL $
(☑285728; www.hotelumang.com; SBS Rd, Rameshwar Society; r without/with AC ₹750/1250; ❋) This is a quiet option with serviceable rooms, helpful management and decent meals. Discounts are available when business is slow, and it offers a two-night package with all meals for ₹3150. Head 150m west from Sinh Sadan then 200m south off the main road.

Gir Birding Lodge HOTEL $$
(☑9899810456; www.girbirdinglodge.com; cottage incl meals s/d standard ₹4500, deluxe ₹6000; ❋) Situated in a mango grove on the edge of the forest, this place is peaceful. Deluxe cottages are simple and almost sweet, with a few nice touches such as handmade wooden beds. Standard rooms and cottages seem plucked straight out of a low budget hotel. It's 2.5km from the village off the Junagadh road. Bird and river walks are available; naturalist guides cost ₹2000 per day.

★**Gateway Hotel** HOTEL $$$
(☑285551; www.thegatewayhotels.com; r from ₹7000, ste ₹9500-12,000; ❋@🛜🏊) 🅿 The remodelling of an old government property by the Taj Group is easily the finest – and greenest – choice in town. The rooms and huge suites are lush with comforts – they even come with yoga mats! All overlook a river where buffaloes wade and lions have been spotted. Booking online in advance gets serious discounts, and promotional packages that include meals and safaris are offered.

Amidhara Resort HOTEL $$$
(☑285950; www.amidhararesorts.com; r incl 3 meals ₹3900-7500, with AC ₹4900-8000; ❋🏊) Two kilometres south of the village on the Veraval road, the regular hotel rooms here are surprisingly basic and beginning to go downhill, but the cottages are modern, comfortable and great if you're travelling with kids. There's a pool, a playground, a gym and ping-pong tables.

Gir Rajwadi Hotel INDIAN $
(mains ₹60-70; ⊘lunch & dinner) This vegetarian joint is the best of several simple restaurants along the village's main street. Gujarati thali is ₹80.

ℹ️ Getting There & Away

Buses run from Sasan Gir village to both Veraval (₹34, 1½ hours) and Junagadh (₹40, two hours) about 10 times daily.

Second-class unreserved-seating trains run to Junagadh (₹12, 2¾ hours) at 5.57pm, to Delvada (for Diu, ₹15, 3½ hours) at 9.57am, and to Veraval (₹7, 1½ hours) at 12.07pm and 4.27pm.

Junagadh

📞 0285 / POP 320,250

Reached by few tourists, Junagadh is nestled against some of the most impressive topography in Gujarat. It's an ancient, fortified city with 2300 years of history (its name means 'old fort'), at the base of holy Girnar Hill. At the time of Partition, the Nawab of Junagadh opted to take his tiny state into Pakistan – a wildly unpopular decision as the inhabitants were predominantly Hindu, so the nawab departed on his own. Junagadh makes a good jumping-off point for seeing the lions at Sasan Gir.

◉ Sights & Activities

Parts of the centre are as traffic-infested, crowded and hot as any other city, but the area up towards Uparkot Fort and around Circle and Diwan Chowks is highly atmospheric, dotted with markets and half-abandoned palaces in Euro-Mughal style with grass growing out of their upper storeys.

Girnar Hill   SACRED SITE
The long climb up 10,000 stone steps to the summit of Girnar is best begun at dawn. Be prepared to spend a full day going up and down if you want to reach the furthest temples at the top. Starting out in the early morning light is a magical experience, as pilgrims and porters begin up the well-maintained steps. The start is 4km east of the city at Girnar Taleti. A road, which may or may not be open, goes up to about the 3000th step, which leaves you *only* 7000 to the top.

The refreshment stalls on the ascent sell chalk, so you can graffiti your name on the rocks. If you can't face the walk, *dholis* carried by porters cost ₹3850 (round trip) if you weigh between 50kg and 70kg, and ₹4250 for heavier passengers. If your weight range isn't obvious, you suffer the indignity of being weighed on a huge beam scale before setting off. Note that while photography is permitted on the trail, it's not allowed inside the temples.

Girnar is of great significance to the Jains, but several important Hindu temples mean that Hindus make the pilgrimage, too.

The Jain temples, a cluster of mosaic-decorated domes interspersed with elaborate stupas, are about two-thirds of the way up. The largest and oldest is the 12th-century **Temple of Neminath**, dedicated to the 22nd *tirthankar*: go through the first left-hand doorway after the first gate. Many temples are locked from around 11am to 3pm, but this one is open all day. The nearby triple **Temple of Mallinath**, dedicated to the ninth *tirthankar*, was erected in 1177 by two brothers. During festivals this temple is a sadhu (holy person) magnet.

Further up are various Hindu temples. The first peak is topped by the **Temple of Amba Mata**, where newlyweds worship to ensure a happy marriage. Beyond here there is quite a lot of down as well as up to reach the other four peaks and further temples. At 117m, the **Temple of Gorakhnath** is perched on Gujarat's highest peak. The steep peak Dattatraya is topped by a shrine to a three-faced incarnation of Vishnu. Atop the final outcrop, Kalika, is a shrine to the goddess Kali.

The **Bhavnath Mela** (Bhavnath Fair; ☺ Jan/Feb), over five days in the month of Magha, brings folk music and dancing and throngs of *nagas* (naked sadhus or spiritual men) to Bhavnath Mahadev Temple at Girnar Taleti. It marks the time when Shiva is believed to have danced his cosmic dance of destruction.

An autorickshaw from town to Girnar Taleti costs about ₹70.

★ Uparkot Fort   FORT
(☺ dawn-dusk) This ancient fort is believed to have been built in 319 BC by the Mauryan emperor Chandragupta, though it has been extended many times. In places the walls reach 20m high. It's been besieged 16 times, and legend has it that the fort once withstood a 12-year siege. It's also said that the fort was abandoned from the 7th to 10th centuries and, when rediscovered, was completely overgrown by jungle.

The views over the city and east to Girnar Hill are superb. The **Jumma Masjid**, the mosque inside the fort, was converted from a palace in the 15th century by Gujarat sultan Mahmud Begada and has a rare roofed courtyard with three octagonal openings which may once have been covered by domes.

Junagadh

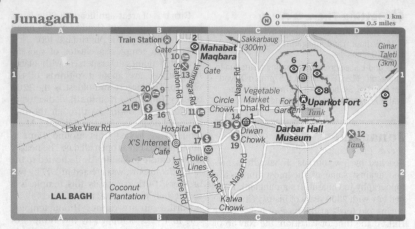

Close to the mosque is a set of **Buddhist caves** (Indian/foreigner ₹5/100; ⊙8am-6pm), not actually caves but monastic quarters carved out of the rock about 2000 years ago. The three-storey complex is quite eerie and the main hall contains pillars with weathered carvings.

The fort has two fine step-wells, both cut from solid rock. **Adi Kadi Vav** (named after two slave girls who used to fetch water from it) is 41m deep and was cut in the 15th century. **Navghan Kuvo**, 52m deep and designed to help withstand sieges, is almost 1000 years old and its magnificent staircase spirals around the well shaft.

★ **Mahabat Maqbara** MAUSOLEUM, MOSQUE
This stunning mausoleum of Nawab Mahabat Khan II of Junagadh (1851–82) seems to bubble up into the sky. One of Gujarat's most glorious examples of Euro-Indo-Islamic architecture, with French windows and Gothic columns, its lavish appeal is topped off by its silver inner doors. Boasting even more flourish is the neighbouring **Vazir's Mausoleum**, sporting four storybook minarets encircled by spiralling stairways.

Sakkarbaug Zoo ZOO, MUSEUM
(admission ₹20, camera/video ₹20/100; ⊙9am-6pm Thu-Tue) If you don't make it to Sasan Gir, Junagadh's zoo, 2km north of the centre, has Asiatic lions and a broad selection of other Indian wildlife. Most of the animal pens are rather depressing (though no more than what you see on the street every day); in the **'safari' park** (20min bus tour ₹25; ⊙bus tour 9am-1pm & 2.30-5.45pm) at the back, the big cats you view from a bus are in larger, more humane enclosures. Still, it's not a bad place to go, as it's shady, quiet, and the beauty of some of the animals is mesmeris-

ing despite the cages. The zoo also houses the **Junagadh Museum** (Indian/foreigner ₹2/50; ⊙9am-12.15pm & 2.45-6pm Thu-Tue, closed 2nd & 4th Sat of month), with paintings, manuscripts, archaeological finds and more. An autorickshaw from the centre costs around ₹25.

★ **Darbar Hall Museum**   MUSEUM
(Diwan Chowk; Indian/foreigner ₹5/50; ⊙10am-1.15pm & 2.45-6pm Thu-Tue, closed 2nd & 4th Sat of month) This museum displays weapons, armour, palanquins, chandeliers and howdahs from the days of the nawabs, as well as a huge carpet woven in Junagadh's jail. There's a royal portrait gallery, including photos of the last nawab with his numerous beloved dogs.

Ashokan Edicts   HISTORIC SITE
(Indian/foreigner ₹5/100; ⊙dawn-dusk) Just outside town on the road to Girnar Hill, a white building on the right encloses a large boulder on which the Buddhist emperor Ashoka had 14 edicts inscribed in Brahmi script in the Pali language about 250 BC. The spidery lettering instructs people to be kind to women and animals and give to beggars, among other things, and is one of several inscriptions that Ashoka placed all around his realm expounding his moral philosophy and achievements.

🛏 Sleeping

There are several cheap hotels around Kalwa Chowk which, because of the clientele they attract, are best avoided by women – even when travelling with a male companion.

Relief Hotel   HOTEL $
(☏2620280; www.reliefhotel.com; Chitta Khana Chowk; s/d ₹300/400, r with AC ₹700; ✳@) Mr Sorathia (Junagadh's unofficial tourist information officer) presides over the pick of the town's budget accommodation, which has simple, clean, colourfully painted rooms and the best set-up for travellers. There's also a fabulous restaurant and secure parking. Note: this hotel and its restaurant both close during the month of Ramadan.

Hotel Vishala   HOTEL $
(☏2631599; www.hotelvishala.com; 3rd fl, Dhara Complex; r from ₹600, with AC from ₹800; ✳☎) Almost opposite the bus station, this has good-sized rooms that are comfortable and clean. Staff are friendly and though there's some street noise during the day, it quietens

down at night. There's room service and a rooftop veg restaurant.

Lotus Hotel   HOTEL $$
(☏2658500; www.thelotushotel.com; Station Rd; s/d from ₹1200/1450; ✳☎) This luxurious and comfortable option occupies the totally renovated top floor of a former *dharamsala* (pilgrim's rest house). Pilgrims never had it so good, with split-system AC and LCD TVs. Rooms are beautifully bright, spacious and pristine, the beds are great, and everything works – incredible value for such quality. There isn't a restaurant, but there is room service and Geeta Lodge is in the same building.

🍴 Eating & Drinking

Junagadh is famous for its fruit, especially for *kesar* (mangoes) and *chiku* (sapodilla), which are popular in milkshakes in November and December.

★ **Geeta Lodge**   GUJARATI $
(Station Rd; thali ₹80; ⊙10am-3.30pm & 6-10.30pm) Geeta's army of waiters are constantly on the move serving up top-class, all-you-can-eat veg Gujarati thalis at a bargain price. Finish off with sweets, such as fruit salad or pureed mango, for ₹20.

Relief Restaurant   INDIAN $
(Relief Hotel, Chitta Khana Chowk; mains ₹60-100; ⊙11.30am-3.30pm & 6.30-11.30pm) This spotless, relaxed, AC restaurant serves up delicious Punjabi, tandoori and Chinese dishes. Meat-eaters can choose from chicken, mutton, fish or prawns, and there's a good choice of veg and paneer dishes.

Garden Cafe   INDIAN $
(mains ₹60-110; ⊙6.30-10.30pm Thu-Tue) Something different: this restaurant has a lovely garden setting next to Jyoti Nursery on the east side of town, and reasonable Jain, Punjabi and South Indian food. It's popular with families and young people, and worth the short rickshaw ride.

Jay Ambe Juice Centre   JUICE BAR
(Diwan Chowk; snacks & drinks ₹20-50; ⊙10am-11:30pm) Perfect retreat for a fresh juice, milkshake or ice cream – try a custard-apple shake.

ℹ Information

The very helpful management at Hotel Relief serves as an unofficial tourist information provider for the area.

Bank of Baroda (cnr MG Rd & Post Office Rd)

State Bank of India (Nagar Rd; ⊙11am-2pm Mon-Fri) Changes travellers cheques and cash; has an ATM.

X'S Internet Cafe (1st fl, Lake View Complex; per hr ₹20; ⊙9:30am-11pm)

ⓘ Getting There & Away

BUS

Buses leave the **ST bus stand** for Rajkot (₹80, two hours, hourly), Sasan Gir (₹55, two hours, hourly), Veraval (₹90, 2½ hours, eight daily), Diu (₹98, five hours, 2.30pm and 3.15pm), Una (for Diu, ₹112, 4½ hours, eight daily), Jamnagar (₹90, four hours, nine daily), Ahmedabad (₹167, eight hours, 6am and 7am) and Bhuj (₹170, seven hours, five daily).

Various private bus offices including **Mahasagar Travels** (☎0285-2629199) are on Dhal Rd, near the rail tracks. Services go to Mumbai (sleeper ₹600, 19 hours), Ahmedabad (with/without AC ₹350/250, eight hours), Rajkot (₹80, two hours), Jamnagar (₹100, four hours) and Udaipur (seat/sleeper ₹450/550, 14 hours).

TRAIN

There's a **computerised reservation office** (⊙8am-10pm Mon-Sat, to 2pm Sun) at the station.

The Jabalpur Express (11463 or 11465) departs at 11.35am for Rajkot (sleeper/3AC/2AC ₹140/229/585, 2½ hours) and Ahmedabad (₹177/469/685, seven hours).

Second-class train 52952 heads to Sasan Gir (₹12, 2¾ hours) and Delvada (for Diu, ₹23, six hours) at 7.15am.

Gondal

☎02825 / POP 112,064

Gondal is a small, leafy town, 38km south of Rajkot, that sports a string of palaces and a gentle river. It was once capital of a 1000-sq-km princely state ruled by Jadeja Rajputs.

⊙ Sights & Activities

Naulakha Museum   MUSEUM
(Naulakha Palace; admission ₹20; ⊙9am-noon & 3-6pm) This ecclectic museum in the old part of town is housed in a beautiful, 260-year-old riverside royal palace that was built in a mixture of styles, with striking gargoyles. It shows royal artefacts, including scales used to weigh Maharaja Bhagwat Singhji in 1934 (his weight in silver was distributed to the poor), a nine-volume Gujarati dictionary compiled by the same revered maharaja, and Dinky Toy collections. Two stables full of

mint-condition horse carriages can be seen for an extra ₹20.

**Bhuvaneshwari
Ayurvedic Pharmacy**   AYURVEDA
(www.bhuvaneshwaripith.com; Ghanshyam Bhuvan; ⊙9am-noon & 3-5pm Tue-Sat) Founded in 1910 by Gondal's royal physician, this pharmacy manufactures ayurvedic medicines, and it's possible to see all the weird machinery involved, as well as buy medicines for treating hair loss, vertigo, insomnia etc. The founding physician, Brahmaleen Acharyashree, is said to have coined the title 'Mahatma' (Great Soul) for Gandhi. Also here is a temple to the goddess Bhuvaneshwari.

**Udhyog Bharti
Khadi Gramodyog**   HANDICRAFTS WORKSHOP
(Udhyog Bharti Chowk; ⊙9am-noon & 3-5pm Mon-Sat) A large *khadi* (homespun cloth) workshop where women work spinning cotton upstairs, while downstairs embroidered *salwar kameez* (traditional dresslike tunic and trouser combination for women) and saris are on sale.

Vintage & Classic Car Collection   MUSEUM
(Orchard Palace; Indian/foreigner ₹60/210; ⊙9am-noon & 3-6pm) This is the royal collection of cars – 32 impressive vehicles, from a 1907 car made by the 'New Engine Company Acton' to racing cars raced by the present maharaja. All are still in working condition.

🛏 Sleeping & Eating

Orchard Palace   HERITAGE HOTEL **$$**
(☎220002; www.gondalpalaces.com; Palace Rd; r ₹3000; ✸) 🖋 This small palace, once the royal guesthouse, has seven well-kept, though hardly luxurious, high-ceilinged rooms of different sizes, filled with 1930s and '40s furniture. The parlors and patios, with more of the same, have an inviting, relaxed kind of charm. Guests get free admission to all of Gondal's attractions. Vegetables are from the on-site organic garden. Reservations recommended.

Riverside Palace   HERITAGE HOTEL **$$**
(☎220002; www.gondalpalaces.com; Ashapura Rd; r ₹3000; ✸) This is the erstwhile ruling family's other palace-hotel, built in the 1880s and formerly the crown prince's abode. Adorned with hunting trophies and four-poster beds, it's kind of like a royal time machine you can sleep in, and has river views. Reservations recommended.

ℹ Getting There & Around

Buses run frequently to/from Rajkot (₹25, one hour) and Junagadh (₹60, two hours). Slow passenger trains between Rajkot (₹7, one hour) and Junagadh (₹10, 1½ hours) also stop at Gondal.

Hiring a rickshaw to take you to all the sights and wait while you see them costs about ₹100 per hour.

Rajkot

♫ 0281 / POP 1.28 MILLION

Rajkot is a large, hectic commercial and industrial city that isn't easy to love with its heavy traffic, lack of open spaces and scant worthwhile sights. But the old city, east of the newer centre, still has plenty of character, with narrow streets, markets, and farmers still selling ghee on street corners.

Rajkot was founded in 1612 by Jadeja Rajputs, and in colonial times it became the headquarters of the Western India States Agency, Britain's administrative centre for some 400 princely states in Saurashtra, Kachchh and northern Gujarat. After Independence Rajkot was capital of the short-lived state of Saurashtra.

⊙ Sights & Activities

★ Watson Museum   MUSEUM

(Jubilee Gardens; Indian/foreigner ₹5/50; ⊙ 9am-12.45pm & 3-6pm Thu-Tue, closed 2nd & 4th Sat of month) The Watson Museum is named after Colonel John Watson, a political agent (administrator) in the 1880s who gathered many historical artefacts and documents from around Saurashtra. It's a jumbled attic of a collection, featuring 3rd-century inscriptions, delicate ivory work and taxidermy exhibits put together by someone with a bizarre sense of humor.

★ Kaba Gandhi No Delo   HISTORIC BUILDING

(Ghee Kanta Rd; ⊙ 9am-6pm) **FREE** This is the house where Gandhi lived from the age of six (while his father was diwan of Rajkot), and it contains lots of interesting information on his life. The Mahatma's passion for the hand loom is preserved in the form of a small weaving school.

Patola Sari Weaving   HANDICRAFTS WORKSHOPS

The Patola-weaving skill comes from Patan, and is a torturous process that involves dyeing each thread before it is woven. In Patan, both the warp and weft threads are dyed (double ikat), whereas in Rajkot only the

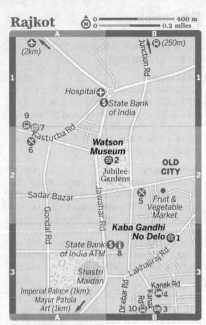

weft is dyed (single ikat), so the product is more affordable. You can visit workshops in people's houses in the Sarvoday Society area about 1km southwest of Shastri Maidan, including **Mayur Patola Art** (♫ 2464519; Street No 4; ⊙ 10am-6pm), behind Virani High School. Call for directions.

🛏 Sleeping

There are plenty of cheapies on Dhebar and Kanak Rds, either side of the ST bus stand, but many fill up early.

Hotel Bhakti
HOTEL $

(📞 2227744; Kanak Rd; s/d ₹700/950, s with AC ₹1000-1200, d with AC ₹1500-1800; ❊ 🛜) This reasonable semi-cheapie behind the bus station is a bit overpriced for what you get, but rooms are neat and in good shape, and mattresses are comfortable.

Hotel Kavery
HOTEL $$

(📞 2239331; www.hotelkavery.com; Kanak Rd; s ₹1000-2100, d ₹1850-2650, incl breakfast; ❊ 🛜) A popular midrange business hotel; the rooms here fill up quickly. Rooms are comfortable, a newspaper is delivered to your door in the morning, and desk staff are helpful. Part of the popularity is undoubtedly due to the excellent in-house Bukhara Restaurant.

Imperial Palace
HOTEL $$$

(📞 2480000; www.theimperialpalace.biz; Dr Yagnik Rd; s ₹4400-6900, d ₹4900-7700, ste from ₹9500; ❊ @ 🛜 🏊) The numero uno in town, with a masterful lobby and lavish, well-appointed rooms and a spa. There's a busy little wine shop and two excellent veg eateries. Breakfast is complimentary.

🍴 Eating

Shree Shakti Vijay Patel Soda Factory
ICE CREAM $

(Para Bazar; scoops & drinks ₹20-40; ⊙8.30am-11pm) Sit in a booth and treat yourself to a few scoops at this old-school ice cream and soda shop, with mirrored walls and pictures of previous generations of the owner's family. The cold coffee with ice cream hits the spot on a hot day!

Bukhara Restaurant
MULTICUISINE $$

(Kanak Rd, Hotel Kavery; mains ₹60-150, thali ₹140; ⊙11am-11pm) Bukhara is smart, cool and calm with good service and quality food, including a great Gujarati thali for lunch, and South Indian, among others, for dinner.

Senso
MULTICUISINE $$

(Dr Yagnik Rd, Imperial Palace; mains ₹150-220; ⊙24hr) The Imperial Palace's very good round-the-clock coffee shop, Senso, does everything from Lebanese to lasagne and sizzlers to South Indian – all without meat.

Temptations
MULTICUISINE $$

(Kasturba Rd; mains ₹120-200; ⊙noon-midnight) Popular Temptations has Mexican, Italian, falafel, baked potatoes, *parathas* (flaky flat bread with stuffings such as vegetables or paneer) and South Indian in a clean, brightly decorated, well-air-conditioned cafe.

ℹ Information

There are ATMs all over town, including SBI on Jawahar Rd.

Aaryans (Dr Yagnik Rd; internet per hr ₹20; ⊙8am-11pm) Go 100m south from the Imperial Palace hotel.

Buzz Cyber Café (Alaukik Bldg, Kasturba Rd; per hr ₹25; ⊙8.30am-9.00pm) Tucked away opposite Temptations restaurant.

State Bank of India (Kasturba Rd; ⊙10am-4pm) Changes cash and travellers cheques.

Tourist Office (📞 2234507; Bhavnagar House, Jawahar Rd; ⊙10.30am-6pm Mon-Sat) Behind a State Bank of India building.

ℹ Getting There & Around

AIR

There are daily flights to Mumbai with **Air India** (📞 2234122; www.airindia.in) and **Jet Airways** (📞 2450200; www.jetairways.com).

BUS

Regular **ST buses** connect Rajkot with Jamnagar (₹65, two hours, every half-hour), Junagadh (₹80, two hours, hourly), Ahmedabad (₹117, 4½ hours, every half-hour) and Bhuj (₹150, seven hours, about hourly). Private buses operate to Ahmedabad, Bhavnagar, Una (for Diu), Mt Abu, Udaipur and Mumbai. Several offices are on Limda Chowk. Head to **Jay Somnath Travels** (Umesh Complex, Kasturba Rd) for buses to Bhuj (₹180, seven hours, six daily).

TRAIN

The 19006 Saurashtra Mail leaves at 5.45pm and arrives in Ahmedabad (sleeper/3AC/2AC/1AC ₹137/354/585/990) at 10.25pm and Mumbai (₹282/764/1160/1980) at 7.10am. The 19005 departs at 10.30am and arrives at Jamnagar (₹140/250/625/1030) at 12.07pm. An autorickshaw to the station from the centre costs about ₹30.

Jamnagar
📞 0288 / POP 529,308

Jamnagar is another little-touristed but interesting city, brimming with ornate, decaying buildings and colourful bazaars displaying the town's famous, brilliant-coloured *bandhani* (tie-dye) – produced through a

Jamnagar

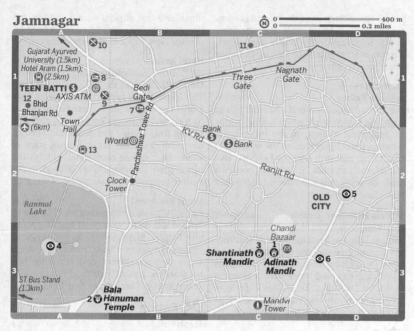

laborious 500-year-old process involving thousands of tiny knots in a piece of folded fabric. Perhaps best of all, people here are exceedingly friendly.

Before Independence, Jamnagar was capital of the Nawanagar princely state. Today, Jamnagar is quite a boom town, with the world's biggest oil refinery, belonging to Reliance Petroleum, not far west of the city. The whole central area is one big commercial zone, with more brightly lit shops and stalls at night than you'll find in many a larger city.

⊙ Sights

Old City   AREA

The heart of the old city is known as Chandi Bazaar (Silver Market – which it is, among other things) and it contains, besides a heaving commercial scene, three beautiful Jain temples. The larger two, **Shantinath Mandir** and **Adinath Mandir**, dedicated to the 16th and first *tirthankars,* explode with fine murals, mirrored domes and elaborate chandeliers. The Shantinath Mandir is particularly beautiful, with coloured columns and a gilt-edged dome of concentric circles.

Around the temples spreads the old city with its lovely buildings of wood and stone, peeling, pastel-coloured shutters and crum-

bling wooden balconies. **Willingdon Crescent**, a European-style arcaded crescent, was built by Maharaja Jam Ranjitsinhji to replace Jamnagar's worst slum. It now houses an assortment of shops, and is commonly known as Darbargadh after the now-empty royal residence across the street. **Subhas market**, the vegetable market, has lots of local colour.

Ranmal Lake & Lakhota Palace
LAKE, MUSEUM

The promenades around Ranmal Lake make for a nice stroll when temperatures are moderate. Flamingos and other birds can sometimes be spotted on the water. The diminutive mid-19th-century Lakhota Palace, a fort on an island in the lake, houses a small museum that was closed indefinitely at the time of research.

★ Bala Hanuman Temple
HINDU TEMPLE

This temple on the southeastern side of Ranmal Lake has been the scene of continuous chanting of the prayer *Shri Ram, Jai Ram, Jai Jai Ram* since 1 August 1964. This devotion has earned the temple a place in an Indian favourite, the *Guinness Book of Records*. Early evening is a good time to visit as the temple and lakeside area get busy.

🎓 Courses

Gujarat Ayurved University
AYURVEDA

(📞2664866; www.ayurveduniversity.edu.in; Hospital Rd, Chanakya Bhavan) The world's first ayurvedic university, founded in 1967, is 1.5km northwest of the centre. It has played a big part in the revival of ayurvedic medicine since Independence and also has a public hospital treating 800 to 1000 inpatients and outpatients daily, mostly free of charge. Its **International Center for Ayurvedic Studies** (📞2664866; icasjam@gmail.com; ⊘office 10.30am-1pm & 3-6.30pm Mon-Sat) runs a full-time, three-month introductory course (registration US$20, tuition per month US$375) teaching basic theory, treatment and medicine preparation, as well as longer certificate and degree courses in ayurveda, yoga and naturopathy. These courses are set up for foreign nationals with medical backgrounds; see the website for more information.

🛏 Sleeping

Hotel Ashiana
HOTEL $

(📞2559110; www.ashianahotel.com; New Super Market; s ₹450-1300, d ₹500-1500; ❄@🛜) Rambling, welcoming Ashiana has helpful management and a variety of well-kept rooms, from simple and plain to large and comfortable. There's a roof terrace to enjoy in the evenings, and free airport, station and bus station transfers. Enter by lift or stairs from inside the New Super Market shopping centre.

Hotel Aram
HERITAGE HOTEL $$

(📞2551701; www.hotelaram.com; Pandit Nehru Marg; r ₹1500-3000, ste ₹3600-6000; ❄@🛜) This former royal property has gotten an upgrade, creating either an interesting mix of historic and ultra-modern. Rooms also vary widely, from simple standards up to luxurious super-deluxe rooms and suites, some of which can't decide on a style. Still, it's the nicest place around. There's a good multicuisine veg restaurant with garden seating.

Hotel President
HOTEL $$

(📞2557491; www.hotelpresident.in; r ₹750, with AC ₹1600-2300; ❄🛜) This hotel has exceptionally helpful management and a range of reasonable rooms. The AC rooms have street views and are bigger and generally better than the non-AC, which are in the rear. Many rooms of both types have balconies.

🍴 Eating

Fresh Point
INDIAN, CHINESE $

(Town Hall Rd; mains ₹50-90; ⊘11am-3pm & 6pm-11pm) A simple, friendly, bustling restaurant with generous serves of Punjabi, South Indian and Chinese in clean surroundings.

Hotel Swati
MULTICUISINE $

(mains ₹50-125; ⊘10am-3pm & 5pm-11.30pm) This upstairs AC vegetarian restaurant has a faded ambience, but is well run and offers a big range of tasty South Indian, Chinese and Punjabi dishes, plus the odd pizza.

7 Seas Restaurant
MULTICUISINE $$

(Hotel President; mains ₹90-250; ⊘24hr) This cool, clean, efficient hotel restaurant has a nautical theme and a touch of class, offering a good range of veg and nonveg dishes, including seafood and tandoori options. The tandoori *bhindi* (okra) is a triumph.

ℹ Information

The **city's website** (www.jamnagar.org) is full of useful information for visitors.

The State Bank of India by the Town Hall roundabout, and Bank of Baroda and Bank of India on Ranjit Rd, change travellers cheques and cash between 10am and 4pm Monday to Friday. Hotel President will also change foreign currency.

Surf the internet at **IWorld** (Pancheshwar Tower Rd; 75 min ₹25; ⊘24hr) or **Cyber City** (ground fl, City Point Shopping Centre; per hr ₹20; ⊘9am-10pm).

WESTERN SAURASHTRA

Mahatma Gandhi was born in 1869 in the chaotic port town of Porbandar, 130km southwest of Jamnagar. You can visit **Gandhi's birthplace** – a 22-room, 220-year-old house – and a memorial next door, Kirti Mandir. **Dwarka**, 106km from Jamnagar at the western tip of the Kathiawar Peninsula, is one of the four holiest Hindu pilgrimage sites in India – Krishna is said to have set up his capital here after fleeing from Mathura. Its **Dwarkadhish Temple** is believed to have been founded over 2500 years ago, and has a fantastically carved, 78m-high spire. The town swells to breaking point for Janmastami in celebration of Krishna's birthday.

There are some good beaches on the ocean coast, including the beautiful, long, clean **Okhamadhi**, 22km south of Dwarka – waves can be strong here – and the calmer **Shivrajpur**, a long lagoon beach 12km north of Dwarka. En route to Porbandar, the **Barda Wildlife Sanctuary** is a hilly, forested area with stone-built villages, old temples and good hiking. A good contact for more information on visiting these and other off-the-beaten-track places in western Saurashtra is **Mustak Mepani** (☏9824227786) at Jamnagar's Hotel President.

ⓘ Getting There & Away

AIR

Indian Airlines (☏2554768; www.indian-airlines.nic.in; Bhid Bhanjan Rd) has daily flights to Mumbai.

BUS

ST buses run to Rajkot (₹53, two hours, half-hourly), Junagadh (₹80, four hours, about hourly) and Ahmedabad (₹166 to ₹186, seven hours, about hourly).

There are also numerous private companies, many based west of the clock tower, including **Patel Tours** with nine daily Volvo AC buses to Ahmedabad (₹380, seven hours) and three non-AC buses to Bhuj (seat/sleeper ₹210/280, six hours).

TRAIN

The 19006 Saurashtra Mail departs at 3.35pm for Rajkot (sleeper/3AC/2AC/1AC ₹140/250/625/1030, 1¾ hours), Ahmedabad (₹184/470/680/1125, seven hours) and Mumbai (₹320/857/1290/2170, 16 hours).

ⓘ Getting Around

An autorickshaw from the airport, 6km west, should be around ₹50, and a taxi ₹150. An autorickshaw from the bus stand to Bedi Gate costs ₹20.

Around Jamnagar

Permits for the following protected areas are available from the **Forest Office** (☏0288-2679357; ⊙10.15am-6.15pm Mon-Sat, closed 2nd & 4th Sat of month) in Jamnagar.

Khijadiya Bird Sanctuary   BIRDWATCHING
(up to 6 people ₹900) This small (6 sq km) sanctuary, about 12km northeast of Jamnagar, encompasses both salt- and freshwater marshlands and hosts over 200 bird species, including rarities such as the Dalmatian pelican and black-necked stork. The best months to visit are October to March and the best times of day are around sunrise or sunset. The evening arrival of cranes for roosting can be spectacular. A return taxi costs around ₹1500, or you can take a bus (₹10) to nearby Khijadiya, then walk 2km.

Marine National Park   NATURE RESERVE
(up to 6 people ₹900) This national park and the adjoining marine sanctuary encompass the intertidal zone and 42 small islands along some 120km of coast east and west of Jamnagar – an area rich in marine and bird life which faces growing challenges from industrialisation. Coral, octopus, anemones, puffer fish, sea horses, lobsters and crabs are among the marine life you may see in shallow water at low tide. The best time to visit is from December to March, when wintering birds are plentiful.

Access and obtaining permits can be a little complicated, so it's advisable to enlist local help such as that of Mustak Mepani (☏9824227786), manager at Hotel President. He can arrange tours to Narara island, 60km west of Jamnagar, for ₹4500 (₹5100 on weekends) including guide. Also check with him to see if Pirotan Island, which closed for conservation reasons, has reopened to visitors – a more expensive option which includes several hours riding a boat through the sanctuary's creeks and channels.

KACHCHH (KUTCH)

Kachchh, India's wild west, is a geographic phenomenon. The flat, tortoise-shaped land (*kachbo* means tortoise in Gujarati), edged by the Gulf of Kachchh and Great and Little Ranns, is a seasonal island. During the dry season, the Ranns are vast expanses of hard, dried mud. Come the monsoon, they're flooded first by seawater, then by fresh river water. The salt in the soil makes the low-lying marsh area almost completely barren. Only on scattered 'islands' above the salt level is there coarse grass which provides fodder for the region's wildlife.

The villages dotted across Kachchh's arid landscape are home to a jigsaw of tribal groups and sub-castes who produce some of India's finest handicrafts, above all their textiles which glitter with exquisite embroidery and mirrorwork. Each year, events for the glamorous **Rann Utsav** (⊗ Dec/Jan) cultural fair are held around Kachchh.

A branch of the Indus River once entered the Great Rann until a massive earthquake in 1819 altered its course. Another mammoth earthquake in January 2001 again altered the landscape, killing nearly 30,000 people and destroying many villages completely. Although the effects of the tragedy will resonate for generations, the residents have determinedly rebuilt their lives and are welcoming to visitors. Tax breaks to encourage economic recovery have brought in new industrial plants, but by and large Kachchh still remains a refreshingly pristine, rural environment.

Bhuj

📳 02832 / POP 147,123

The capital of Kachchh is an interesting city, mostly resurrected following the massive 2001 earthquake that destroyed most of the place. It sells amazing Kachchh handicrafts, and historic buildings such as the Aina Mahal and Prag Mahal possess an eerie beauty. Bhuj is an ideal springboard for visits to the surrounding villages, and textile tourism is attracting visitors from around the world.

The Jadeja Rajputs who took control of Kachchh in 1510 made Bhuj their capital 29 years later, and it has remained Kachchh's most important town ever since.

⊙ Sights

★ **Darbargadh**   PALACES

This walled complex from which Kachchh was once ruled is still in need of much repair after the 2001 earthquake. The 17th-century **Rani Mahal**, the former main royal residence, is completely closed up, though you can still admire the latticed windows of its *zenana* (women's quarters). Largest of the three palaces here is the 19th-century **Prag Mahal** (New Palace; admission ₹50; ⊗ 9-11.45am & 3-5.45pm). It's in a sad state and most sections are closed, but it's worth visiting for its ghostly Durbar Hall, a wonderful piece of decayed magnificence with broken chandeliers, rotting hunting trophies covered in bird droppings, and gold-skirted classical statues that wouldn't look out of place decorating a nightclub.

The beautiful **Aina Mahal** (Old Palace; admission ₹10, camera ₹30; ⊗ 9am-noon & 3-6pm Fri-Wed), built in the 1750s, was badly damaged in the earthquake, but the 1st and 2nd floors are open again and contain a fascinating museum with excellent explanatory information in English. The palace was built for Maharao Lakhpatji by Ramsingh Malam, a sailor from Dwarka who had learned European arts and crafts on his travels. The elaborately mirrored interior is a demonstration of the maharao's fascination with all things European – an inverted mirror of European Orientalism – with blue-and-white Delft-style tiling, a candelabra with Venetian-glass shades and the Hogarth lithograph series, *The Rake's Progress*. In the bedroom is a bed with solid gold legs (the king apparently auctioned his bed annually). In the Fuvara Mahal room, fountains played around the ruler while he sat watching dancers or composing poems. It's estimated that the Aina Mahal will cost ₹2.5 million to repair fully. Donations can be made – contact Pramod Jethi, the curator, at the museum for details (receipts are given).

★ **Kachchh Museum**   MUSEUM

(College Rd; Indian/foreigner ₹2/50; ⊗ 10am-1pm & 2-5pm Thu-Tue, closed 2nd & 4th Sat of month) Opposite Hamirsar Tank, Gujarat's oldest museum has eclectic and worthwhile displays spanning textiles, weapons, silverware, sculpture, wildlife, geography and dioramas of Kachchh tribal costumes and artefacts, with labelling in English and Gujarati.

Bhuj

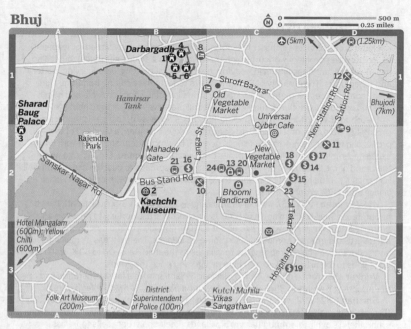

Bhuj

Folk Art Museum   MUSEUM
(Bhartiya Sanskriti Darshan; admission ₹50, camera ₹150; ☉10.30am-1pm & 2.30-5pm Tue-Sun) This museum has excellent displays on traditional Kachchh culture, including reconstructed Rabari *bhungas* (traditional mud-and-mirrorwork huts), musical instruments, many wood and stone carvings and much more. It's a further 700m south of the Kachchh Museum, off Mandvi Rd.

★ **Sharad Baug Palace**   PALACE
(admission ₹10, camera/video ₹20/100; ☉9am-noon & 3-6pm Sat-Thu) This graceful 1867 Italianate palace, on the west side of Hamirsar Tank in the middle of shady trees full of crows and bats, was the abode of the last Maharao of Kachchh, Madansingh, until his death in 1991. It lost most of its 3rd floor in the 2001 earthquake, and the remaining

KACHCHH CREATIVITY

Kachchh is one of India's richest areas for handicrafts, particularly famed for its beautiful, colourful embroidery work (of which there are at least 14 distinct styles), but it also has many artisans specialising in weaving, tie-dye, block printing, woodcarving, pottery and other crafts. The diversity of Kachchh crafts reflects the differing traditions of its many communities. Numerous local cooperatives invest in social projects and help artisans produce work that is marketable yet still preserves their artistic heritage.

Kutch Mahila Vikas Sangathan (☑256281) is a grass-roots organisation, comprising 12,000 rural women (1200 artisans), that pays members a dividend of the profits and invests money to meet social needs. The embroidery and patchwork are exquisite, employing the distinctive styles of several communities. Products go under the brand name Qasab and range from bags and bedspreads to cushion covers and wall hangings. Visit the head office in Bhuj, the Qasab outlet at Hotel Prince, or Khavda, a village about 80km north of Bhuj.

Kala Raksha (☑277237; www.kala-raksha.org; ☺10am-2pm & 3-6pm Mon-Sat), based at Sumrasar Sheikh, 25km north of Bhuj, is a nonprofit trust working to preserve and promote Kachchh arts. It works with about 1000 embroiderers and patchwork and appliqué artisans from six communities in some 25 villages. The trust has a small museum and shop, and can help arrange visits to villages to meet artisans. Up to 80% of the sale price goes to the artisans, who also help design and price the goods.

Vankar Vishram Valji (☑240723; Bhujodi; ☺8am-8pm) is a family operation and one of the leading weavers in Bhujodi; it sells beautiful blankets, shawls, stoles and rugs.

Shrujan (☑240272; www.shrujan.org; Bhujodi; ☺10am-7.30pm), just past the Bhujodi turn-off, behind the GEB Substation, is a nonprofit trust working with over 3000 women embroiderers of nine communities in 114 villages. Their showroom sells top-class shawls, saris, cushion covers and more.

Dr Ismail Mohammad Khatri (☑299786, 9427719313; dr.ismail2005@gmail.com; ☺9am-5pm) in Ajrakhpur, 6km east of Bhujodi along the Bhachau road, heads a 10-generation-old block-printing business of real quality, using all-natural dyes in bold geometric designs. Go in the morning if you want to see a demonstration of the fascinating, highly skilled process. You can buy tablecloths, shawls, skirts, saris and other attractive products.

Parmarth (☑273453; 106 Ramkrushn Nagar, New Dhaneti; ☺8.30am-9pm), run by a delightful family whose work has won national awards, specialises in Ahir embroidery. New Dhaneti is 17km east of Bhujodi on the Bhachau road.

Khamir (☑271272; www.khamir.org; Kukma Rd, Lakhond Crossroad, Kukma; ☺9am-5.30pm) is an umbrella organisation dedicated to preserving and encouraging Kachchh crafts in all their diversity. At the Kukma centre you can see demonstrations and buy some of the artisans' products. It's about 4km beyond Bhujodi in the Anjar direction.

The tourist office offers rickshaw tours that stop at most of these places (half/full day ₹600/1200) and can include visits to Ajir and Rabari villages; ask tourism director Pramod Jethi what's on the menu, and specify what you want to see and what you don't.

In Bhuj, textile dealers line Shroff Bazaar just east of the Darbargadh. However, plenty of so-called block-printed fabric is in fact screen-printed. **Bhoomi Handicrafts** (☑225808; Bus Stand Rd; ☺9am-9pm), across from the bus stand, is popular with locals.

If you're interested in antique embroidery, contact **Mr AA Wazir** (☑224187; awazir1@rediffmail.com; Plot 107B, Lotus Colony, Bhuj), opposite the General Hospital. He has a stunning collection of more than 3000 pieces, about half of which are for sale.

lower floors are closed. However, the adjacent former dining hall now houses the palace's eclectic museum collection. Standout exhibits are two huge stuffed tigers that the erstwhile maharao shot, and the maharao's coffin.

🛏 Sleeping

Hotel Gangaram   HOTEL **$**
(☑224231; off Shroff Bazaar; s/d ₹350/700, with AC ₹1000/1200; ✹🖹) In the old city, near the Darbargadh, this is a great place well away

from the din of the Bhuj's main thorough-fares – run by kindly Mr Jethi (not to be confused with the Aina Mahal curator) – where nothing is too much trouble. The rooms vary greatly so it might be worth inspecting a few. Meals here are delicious.

City Guest House
GUESTHOUSE **$**

(☎9913922669; Langa St; d ₹500, s/d without bathroom from ₹300/400) Just off Shroff Bazaar, this is unusually bright and cheery for a budget guesthouse, and has neat, basic rooms that are clean though they have peeling paint. Try for one with a window. Bathrooms have either squat toilets or the hybrid variety. Breakfast is available, there are two airy roof terraces, and you can rent motorbikes for ₹500 per day.

Hotel Ilark
HOTEL **$$**

(☎258999; www.hotelilark.com; Station Rd; s ₹1800-3200, d ₹2200-3800, ste from ₹4000; ❋@) One of Bhuj's top hotels, the stylish wood-panelled, wood-furnished rooms live up to the promise of the modern glass-and-red-paint exterior. Service is very professional. You can't go wrong here.

Hotel Mangalam
HOTEL **$$**

(☎220303; www.mangalamhotels.com; Mangalam Cross Roads; s/d ₹900/1200, s with AC ₹1200-2700, d with AC ₹1850-3600; ❋☎) Towards the south edge of town, the new Mangalam has big, bright, modern rooms with comfy furnishings and mostly good views. It's professionally run and on a nice human scale with just 17 rooms. The excellent Yellow Chilli restaurant is here, and free airport transfers are offered.

✗ Eating

Hotel Nilam
INDIAN, CHINESE **$**

(Station Rd; mains ₹60-115; ⏱11am-3pm & 7-11pm) Good service by bow-tied, waistcoated waiters complements tasty vegetarian North and South Indian and Chinese dishes at this long, white, AC and highly popular restaurant. There's Gujarati thali (₹120) at lunchtime.

Noorani Mahal
INDIAN **$**

(Station Rd; mains ₹55-200; ⏱11am-4pm & 6-11pm) This popular nonveg place gets packed out with mostly men eating chicken, but there's also mutton and veg cooked in the tandoor or a spicy North Indian curry.

★ Yellow Chilli
MUGHLAI **$$**

(Hotel Mangalam, Mangalam Cross Roads; mains around ₹150, buffet lunch ₹200; ⏱lunch & dinner) A branch of a franchise run by celebrity chef Sanjeev Kapoor, the Yellow Chilli serves up innovative, delicious, pure-veg Mughlai-based dishes. There's also a good kids' menu. Well worth a quick rickshaw ride from the city centre.

Green Rock
MULTICUISINE **$$**

(Bus Stand Rd; mains ₹90-150, thali ₹140-150; ⏱11am-3pm & 7-10.30pm) This 1st-floor, AC place serves up tasty lunchtime thalis as well as an extensive all-veg menu.

🔒 Shopping

Crossword
BOOKS

(Bus Stand Rd; ⏱8am-2pm & 4-9pm Mon-Sat, to 2pm Sun) A tiny branch of this franchise with some English-language books on Kachchh. Books are also sold at the Aina Mahal and Hotel Prince.

ℹ Information

You'll find Bank of Baroda and State Bank of India ATMs on Station Rd, and an HDFC ATM on Bus Stand Rd.

Ashapura Money Changer (Station Rd; ⏱9.30am-7pm Mon-Sat) Changes currency and travellers cheques.

State Bank of India (Hospital Rd; ⏱10am-4pm Mon-Fri, to 1pm Sat) Changes travellers cheques or currency.

Tourist information office (☎291702, 9374235379; Aina Mahal, Darbargadh; ⊗9am-noon & 3-6pm Sun-Fri) Pramod Jethi, the knowledgeable curator of the Aina Mahal, knows all there is to know about Bhuj and surrounding villages. He's also written a very useful guide to Kachchh (₹100), published in both English and French.

Universal Cyber Cafe (Anam Ring Rd; per hr ₹20; ⊗9am-10pm) Surf the internet in small cubicles here.

❶ Getting There & Away

AIR

Jet Airways (www.jetairways.com) has daily flights to Mumbai.

BUS

Numerous ST buses run to Ahmedabad (₹200 to ₹250, nine hours), Rajkot (₹145, seven hours) and Jamnagar (₹150, seven hours). Book private buses at **Hemal Travels** (Bus Stand Rd; ⊗8am-9pm), just outside the bus station, for Ahmedabad (seat/sleeper ₹250/350, without/with AC ₹300/400, nine hours, five daily) and Jamnagar (₹240/310, six hours, 3pm and 9pm), or at **Jay Somnath Travels** (Bus Stand Rd; ⊗8am-9pm) for Rajkot (without/with AC ₹180/210, seven hours, five daily).

TRAIN

Bhuj station is 1.5km north of the centre and has a **reservations office** (⊗8am-8pm Mon-Sat, to 2pm Sun). The 14312 Ala Hazrat Express leaves at 12.25pm (Tuesday, Thursday, Sunday) and arrives at Ahmedabad (sleeper/3AC/2AC ₹170/462/690) at 7.40pm, continuing to Abu Road, Jaipur and Delhi. The 19116 Sayaji Express leaves at 10.15pm daily and hits Ahmedabad (sleeper/3AC/2AC ₹170/462/665) at 5.05am.

❶ Getting Around

The airport is 5km north of town – a taxi will cost around ₹200, an autorickshaw ₹100. Autorickshaws to the train station cost ₹30.

Around Bhuj

The local Jat, Ahir, Harijan, nomadic Rabari and other communities have distinct, colourful craft traditions that make their villages fascinating to visit.

Bhujodi, about 7km southeast of Bhuj, is a village of weavers, mostly using pit looms, operated by both feet and hands. You can look into many workshops, which produce attractive shawls, blankets and other products. The village is 1km off Hwy 42. You can

take a bus towards Ahmedabad and ask the driver to drop you at the turn-off for Bhujodi (₹10). A return rickshaw from Bhuj costs ₹300.

In the hills about 60km northwest of Bhuj is the eerie monastery at **Than**. The holy man Dhoramnath, as penance for a curse he had made, stood on his head on top of Dhinodhar hill for 12 years. The gods pleaded with him to stop, and he agreed, provided the first place he looked at became barren – hence the Great Rann. He then established the Kanphata (Slit Ears) monastic order, whose monastery (dating back to at least the 12th century) stands at the foot of the hill. This is a laid-back place from which to explore the surrounding hills, and the architecture ranges from crumbling mud brick to Portuguese-style stucco, blue and whitewash bell towers, with a hint of basil and marigold in the air. There's one bus daily to Than from Bhuj (₹50, two hours) at 5pm, returning early next morning. The monastery and the temple atop Dhinodhar have very basic guest rooms with mattresses on the floor (pay by donation) but no drinking water.

You need a permit to visit some villages in the northern and western parts of Kachchh, but this is easy to obtain. Take a copy of your passport and visa (and the originals) to the office of the **District Superintendent of Police** (⊗11am-2pm & 3-6pm Mon-Sat), 800m south of Kachchh Museum in Bhuj, and complete a form listing the villages you want to visit – you should get the permit (free of charge; maximum 10 days) straight away. Drivers will need permits for themselves and their vehicles too.

Shaam-e-Sarhad Village Resort (☎02803-296222; www.hodka.in; tent s/d ₹2800/3200, bhunga s/d ₹3800/4800, incl meals; ⊗Oct-Mar) 🍴, just outside Hodka, in the beautiful Banni grasslands 70km north of Bhuj, is a fascinating and successful project in 'endogenous tourism'. Owned and operated by the Halepotra people, its accommodation consists of three *bhungas* with sloping roofs and neat interiors, and nine luxurious earth-floored tents, all with private bathroom. Local guides cost ₹200 per day for birdwatching or visits to villages in the area, such as Hodka, Khavda (known for its pottery and textiles) or Ludia (known for its mudwork), or Kalo Dungar (Black Hill, Kachchh's highest point at 462m above sea level), or the Great Rann itself, with its snow-glare of salt (you may need to provide your own transport). You can also just call in for a superb thali lunch (₹150).

Centre for Desert & Ocean (CEDO; ☑ 02835-221284, 9825248135; www.cedobirding.com) ✈, 53km northwest of Bhuj, is a wildlife conservation organisation run by passionate environmentalist Jugal Tiwari. It does birding and wildlife trips focusing on the wildlife-rich Banni grasslands (between Sumrasar Sheikh and Khavda). Accommodation is in plain but well-kept rooms with 24-hour solar-heated hot water; meals are Gujarati vegetarian. Staying costs ₹1750 per person per day, including meals. Safaris cost ₹3200 per day for a car and driver; an expert naturalist/birder guide costs an extra ₹1800 per day.

A long drive northeast from Bhuj is the fascinating and remote Harappan site of **Dholavira**, on a seasonal island in the Great Rann. Excavations have revealed a complex town of stone buildings 1 sq km in area, inhabited from around 2900 to 1500 BC. It's best to organise your own transport: the only bus to Dholavira leaves Bhuj at 2pm (₹80, seven hours) and starts back at 5am. The state-government-run **Toran Tourist Complex** (☑ 02837-277395; s/d ₹200/300, with AC ₹650/700; ✳) at Dholavira offers basic accommodation and meals.

Mandvi

☑ 02834 / POP 48,500

Mandvi is an hour down the road from Bhuj and is a busy little place with an amazing shipbuilding yard. Hundreds of men construct, by hand, these wooden beauties for faraway Arab merchants. The massive timbers apparently come from Malaysian rainforests. Mandvi suffered far less destruction than Bhuj in the 2001 earthquake, so the heart of town (around Mochi Bazar) is lined with beautiful old buildings in faded pastel hues and temples with wildly sculpted, cartoonlike facades. There are also some sweeping beaches, including the glorious, long, clean private beach (₹100) near Vijay Vilas Palace, and Kashivishvanath Beach, 2km from the centre just east of the Rukmavati River.

◉ Sights & Activities

Vijay Vilas Palace   PALACE
(admission Mon-Sat ₹25, Sun ₹35, vehicle ₹40, camera/video ₹50/200; ☺ 7am-7pm) Vijay Vilas Palace is a 1920s palace reminiscent of a large English country house, 7km west of town amid extensive orchards, and set by a magnificent private beach. Originally a summer abode for the Kachchh rulers, its 1st floor (out of bounds to visitors) is now the erstwhile royal family's main residence. The view from the roof is worth the climb, and the gardens make a nice stroll. Autorickshaws charge about ₹200/300 one way/return from town. You can walk back to town along the beach if you like.

Asher House   HISTORIC BUILDING
(☑ 9825311061; dilipchessasher@yahoo.com; Lakshmi Talkies; by donation) For a taste of Mandvi's past glory, call Dilip Asher, a chess instructor who is a loveable character and descendant of the town's once-richest merchant family. If he's around, he will give you an informal tour of his family's home, where he still lives with his blind sister. The house has definitely seen better days, but the Portuguese tiles, ceiling murals and other artworks – along with a dilapidated 1932 Chevrolet – still have a touch of magic. Donations help with the much-needed upkeep of the house.

Kutch Vipassana Centre   MEDITATION
(☑ 273303; www.sindhu.dhamma.org) At Bada village, 22km west of Mandvi, this centre runs 10-day *vipassana* meditation retreats for beginners. Courses, accommodation and food are free but donations are accepted.

🛏 Sleeping & Eating

Rukmavati Guest House   GUESTHOUSE $
(☑ 223558, 9429040484; www.rukmavatihotel.webs.com; Bridge Gate; dm ₹175, s/d from ₹300/400, r with AC ₹900; ✳) The best Indian hospital to spend the night in, this pleasant former medical centre, just by the bridge as you enter town, doesn't feel institutional. It's light, bright, clean and welcoming to travellers, with solar-water heaters and self-catering facilities. Some rooms have river-view balconies, and there's a nice terrace. Owner Vinod is a gentleman, and the town's unofficial tourist officer, with maps and heaps of helpful info.

Hotel Sea View   HOTEL $$
(☑ 224481; www.hotelseaviewmandvi.com; cnr ST & Jain Dharamsala Rds; r ₹700, with AC ₹1100-2000; ✳) A small hotel facing the river, this place has brightly decorated rooms with big windows that make the most of the views of the shipbuilding.

Beach at Mandvi Palace
HOTEL $$$

(📞277597, 9879013118; www.mandvibeach.com; 2-night package s/d ₹12,000/14,000) A small tent resort in a fantastic location on the private 2.5km beach stretching down from Vijay Vilas Palace. The luxurious air-cooled tents have big beds, white-tiled bathrooms and solid wood furniture. The resort's **Dolphin restaurant** (meal veg/nonveg ₹400/450; ⊙1-3pm & 7-9pm) is a beach pavilion that is open to nonguests if not full with guests. The beach is open to nonguest couples, families and foreigners for ₹100 per person unless you are having a meal at the Dolphin.

★ Zorba the Buddha
GUJARATI $

(1st fl, Osho Hotel, Bhid Gate; thali ₹70; ⊙11am-3pm & 7-10pm) In the heart of the town, Zorba's is a massively popular place for wonderfully flavourful, endless and cheap Kachchh-style thalis. It's also known as Rajneesh Hotel, and the sign outside says 'Osho'.

Gabha's Roti
STREET FOOD $

(roti ₹5; ⊙11am-1.30pm daily, plus 6-8.30pm Mon-Sat) Don't leave Mandvi without tracking down these famed bread rolls with their very spicy potato, garlic, chutney and masala filling. Mr Gabha frequently sells 1000 in an hour. At lunchtime his stall can be found at the vegetable market (Mochi Bazar) below the clock tower; in the evenings it's on Swaminarayan Rd.

❶ Getting There & Away

Regular buses to/from Bhuj (₹30) take 1½ to two hours. Or you can take faster shared jeep-taxis (₹35) which depart from the street south of Bhuj's main vegetable market. Several agencies, including **Patel Tours & Travels**, by the Sea View Hotel, sell tickets for private buses to Ahmedabad (seat/sleeper non-AC ₹270/370, with AC ₹350/450, 11 hours), leaving at 7pm and 7.30pm.

Wild Ass Sanctuary

The barren, blindingly white land of the Little Rann is nature at its harshest and most compelling. It's best known as the home of the last remaining population of the chestnut-coloured Indian wild ass (also called khur), as well as bluebulls, blackbuck and chinkara. There's also a huge bird population from October to March (this is one of the few areas in India where flamingos breed in the wild). The 4953-sq-km **Wild Ass Sanctuary** (jeep with up to 6 passengers Indians/foreigners ₹200/US$20 Mon-Fri, ₹250/US$25 Sat & Sun; guide per 4hr ₹50) covers a large part of the Little Rann. Easily accessible from Ahmedabad, it can be combined with trips to Nalsarovar Bird Sanctuary, Modhera and Patan.

The Little Rann is punctuated by desolate salt farms, where people eke out a living by pumping up groundwater and extracting the salt. Heat mirages disturb the vast horizon – bushes and trees seem to hover above the surface. Rain turns the desert into a sea of mud, and even during the dry season the solid-looking crust is often deceptive, so it's essential you take a local guide when exploring the area.

About 3000 wild asses live in the sanctuary, surviving off the flat, grass-covered expanses or islands, known as *bets*, which rise up to around 3m. These remarkable, notoriously untamable creatures are capable of running at an average speed of 50km/h for long distances.

Desert Coursers (📞9998305501, 9427 066070; www.desertcoursers.net), run by infectiously enthusiastic naturalist Dhanraj Malik, organises excellent Little Rann safaris and village tours from its **Camp Zainabad** (per person incl full board ₹2500; ⊙Oct-Mar; ✳), very close to the eastern edge of the Little Rann and just outside the small town of Zainabad, 105km northwest of Ahmedabad. The lodge has basic *koobas* (thatch-roofed huts) and excellent meals, in a peaceful, remote setting. The price includes a jeep safari. Advance booking is advised.

To get to Zainabad from Ahmedabad, you can take a bus from Ahmedabad's ST bus stand to Dasada, 10km away (₹75, 2½ hours, about hourly), where Desert Coursers does free pick-ups. There are direct buses between Zainabad and Patan (₹70, 2½ hours, two daily) via Modhera (₹45, 1½ hours). Desert Coursers can arrange taxis around the area for ₹7 per kilometre.

Rann Riders (📞9925236014; www.rannriders.com; s/d incl all meals & safari ₹5000/6000; ✳ 🛜 🏊), near Dasada, is also family-run and offers luxurious cottage accommodation in pretty gardens, plus highly recommended jeep and camel safaris and its own stable of indigenous horses for riding.

You may also approach from **Dhrangadhra**. The town itself is worth visiting, if only to break up the Bhuj–Ahmedabad hike.

The streets and alleys wind around each other, and almost every turn is a mosaic of whitewashed and coloured buildings of all periods, description and type. Temple bells ring out, and the locals aren't used to tourists, making for some refreshing dialogue. The personable **Devjibhai Dhamecha** (☑ 9825548090, 02754-280560; www.littlerann. com) is a wildlife photographer who makes a wonderful guide. You can stay at his appealing **house** (Dev Krupa, Jinplot, Dhrangadhra; per person incl meals ₹500) or his recently opened **Eco Tour Camp** (Jogad village; s/d incl full board ₹1500/2000; ⊙ Oct-Apr) which has colourful *koobas* near the edge of the sanctuary, 40km northwest of Dhrangadhra. Six-/eight-hour safaris to the sanctuary from either place cost ₹2000/3000 per jeep. If you can't get Devjibhai, try his son, **Ajaybhai** (☑ 9825548104).

Dhrangadhra is on the Bhuj–Ahmedabad rail route, 215km from Bhuj (3AC ₹350, five hours) and 120km from Ahmedabad (3AC ₹258, three hours). It's well served by buses, for example to and from Ahmedabad (₹50, three hours) and Bhuj (₹100, five hours).

The guides mentioned will arrange your permits for the reserve; the cost of these is normally additional to safari prices.

An hour south of Dhrangadhra on the Ahmedabad–Rajkot highway is **Sayla**, a peaceful, pastoral town that swells during the **Tarnetar Fair** (⊙ Aug/Sep). **Bell Guest House** (☑ 9724678145; www.ahbedabadcity/ sayla; r incl breakfast ₹3500; ❋), presided over by the former ruling family of Sayla (and their yellow labs), is an ageing heritage hotel retreat down a lane off the Sayla roundabout on Hwy 8A. Rooms have modern en-suite bathrooms. You can look for bluebulls and peacocks in the surrounding countryside or take trips further afield to see wild asses, blackbuck, the birds of Nalsarovar or a variety of artisans in area villages.

Mumbai (Bombay)

Best Places to Eat

➜ Koh (p759)

➜ Hotel Ram Ashraya (p760)

➜ Revival (p759)

➜ Pradeep Gomantak Bhojanalaya (p758)

➜ Culture Curry (p761)

Best Places to Stay

➜ Taj Mahal Palace, Mumbai (p752)

➜ Iskcon (p754)

➜ YWCA (p752)

➜ Anand Hotel (p754)

➜ ITC Maratha (p756)

Why Go?

Mumbai is big. It's full of dreamers and hard-labourers, starlets and gangsters, stray dogs and exotic birds, artists and servants and fisherfolk and *crorepatis* (millionaires) and lots and lots of other people. It has the most prolific film industry, some of Asia's biggest slums (and the world's most expensive home) and the largest tropical forest in an urban zone. It's India's financial powerhouse, fashion epicentre and a pulse point of religious tension. It's evolved its own language, Bambaiyya Hindi, which is a mix of...everything.

But Mumbai does not have to be overwhelming: it just has its own rhythm, which takes a little while to hear. Just give yourself some time to appreciate the city's lilting cadences, its harmonies of excess and restraint, and before you know it, Mumbai might just decide to take you in like you're one of her own.

When to Go
Mumbai (Bombay)

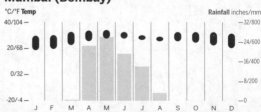

Dec–Jan The very best, least sticky weather.

Aug–Sep Mumbai goes Ganesh-crazy during its most exciting festival, Ganesh Chaturthi.

Oct–Apr Post-monsoon, best for festivals, and bird-watching in Sanjay Gandhi National Park.

Food

Mumbai is a city shaped by flavours from all over India and the world. Go on a cultural history tour by sampling Parsi *dhansak* (meat with curried lentils and rice), Gujarati or Keralan thalis ('all-you-can-eat' meals), Mughlai kebabs, Goan vindaloo and Mangalorean seafood. And don't forget, if you see Bombay duck on a menu, it's actually *bombil* fish dried in the sun and deep-fried. Streetwise, don't miss Mumbai's famous *bhelpuri* (puffed rice tossed with fried rounds of dough, lentils, onions, herbs and chutneys). Stalls offering *bhelpuri*, as well as samosas, *pav bhaji* (spiced vegetables and bread), *vada pav* (deep-fried spiced lentil-ball sandwich), bhurji pav (scrambled eggs and bread) and *dabeli* (a mixture of potatoes, spices, peanuts and pomegranate, also on bread), do a brisk trade around the city.

DON'T MISS

For many, a visit to cosmopolitan Mumbai is all about dining, nightlife and shopping, but the city offers far more than nocturnal amusement and retail therapy. Nowhere is that more evident than in the spectacular maze of Gothic, Victorian, Indo-Saracenic and art deco architecture, remnants of the British colonial era and countless years of European influence. **Chhatrapati Shivaji Terminus**, **High Court**, **University of Mumbai**, **Taj Mahal Palace** hotel and the **Gateway of India** are just the most prominent: the city is laced with architectural jewels, and stumbling upon them is one of Mumbai's great joys.

Top Festivals

⇒ **Mumbai Sanskruti** (⊙ Jan; Fort) This free, two-day celebration of Hindustani classical music is held on the steps of the gorgeous Asiatic Society Library.

⇒ **Kala Ghoda Festival** (⊙ Feb; citywide, p741) Getting bigger and more sophisticated each year, the two-week-long art fest sees tons of performances and exhibitions.

⇒ **Elephanta Festival** (⊙ Mar; Gateway of India, p736) Formerly on Elephanta Island, this classical music and dance festival now accommodates more people on waterfront Apollo Bunder.

⇒ **Nariyal Poornima** (⊙ Aug; Colaba) This Koli celebration marks the start of the fishing season and the retreat of monsoon winds.

⇒ **Ganesh Chaturthi** (⊙ Aug/Sep; citywide) Mumbai gets totally swept up by this 10- to 12-day celebration of the elephant-headed Hindu god Ganesh. On the festival's first, third, fifth, seventh and 11th days, families and communities take their Ganesh statues to the seashore and auspiciously submerge them.

⇒ **Mumbai Film Festival** (⊙ Oct; citywide) New films from the subcontinent and beyond are screened at the weeklong MFF.

MAIN POINTS OF ENTRY

Most arrive at Mumbai's Chhatrapati Shivaji International Airport, Mumbai Central train station (BCT) or Chhatrapati Shivaji Terminus (CST; Victoria Terminus).

Fast Facts

⇒ **Population:** 18.4 million

⇒ **Area:** 444 sq km

⇒ **Area code:** ☐ 022

⇒ **Languages:** Marathi, Hindi, Gujarati, English

⇒ **Sleeping prices:** $ below ₹1500, $$ ₹1500 to ₹5000, $$$ above ₹5000

Top Tips

Many international flights arrive after midnight. Beat the daytime traffic by heading straight to your hotel, and carry detailed landmark directions for your hotel: many airport taxi drivers don't speak English and may not use official street names.

Resources

⇒ **Mumbai Magic** (www.mumbai-magic.blogspot.com) Excellent blog on the city's hidden corners.

⇒ **Mumbai Boss** (www.mumbaiboss.com) The boss of what's on in Mumbai.

⇒ **Maharashtra Tourism Development Corporation** (www.maharashtratourism.gov.in) Official tourism site.

⇒ **Lonely Planet** (www.lonelyplanet.com/india/mumbai) Recommendations, planning advice, reviews, insider tips.

Mumbai Highlights

❶ Marvel at the magnificence of Mumbai's colonial-era architecture: **Chhatrapati Shivaji Terminus** (p737), **University of Mumbai** (p737) and **High Court** (p738)

❷ Get lost amid the millions of things for sale in Mumbai's ancient **bazaars** (p767)

❸ Dine like a maharaja at one of India's best **restaurants** (p756)

❹ Feel the city's sea breeze amongst playing kids, big balloons and a hot-pink sunset at **Girgaum Chowpatty** (p740)

❺ Ogle the Renaissance-revival interiors of the **Dr Bhau Daji Lad Mumbai City Museum** (p741)

❻ Learn to meditate at the awe-inspiring **Global Pagoda** (p744), then see how it was originally done at the **Kanheri Caves** (p749)

❼ Behold the commanding triple-headed Shiva at **Elephanta Island** (p745)

❽ Sleep in one of the world's iconic hotels, the **Taj Mahal Palace, Mumbai** (p752) or have a drink at its **bar** (p762), Mumbai's first

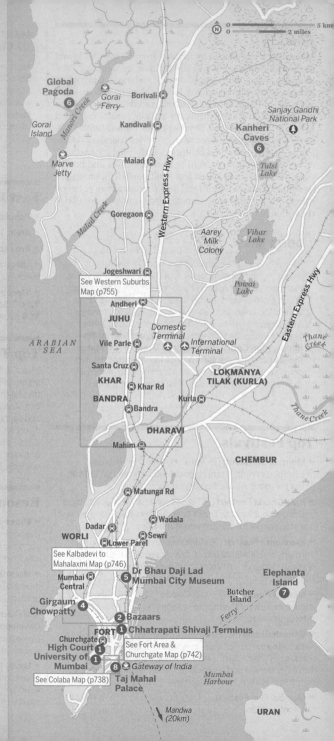

History

Koli fisherfolk have inhabited the seven islands that form Mumbai as far back as the 2nd century BC. Amazingly, remnants of this culture remain huddled along the city shoreline today. A succession of Hindu dynasties held sway over the islands from the 6th century AD until the Muslim Sultans of Gujarat annexed the area in the 14th century, eventually ceding it to Portugal in 1534. The only memorable contribution the Portuguese made to the area was christening it Bom Bahai, before throwing the islands in with the dowry of Catherine of Braganza when she married England's Charles II in 1661. The British government took possession of the islands in 1665 but leased them three years later to the East India Company.

Bombay flourished as a trading port, and within 20 years the East India Company presidency was transferred here. The city's fort was completed in the 1720s, and a century later ambitious land reclamation projects joined the islands into today's single landmass. The city continued to grow, and in the 19th century the fort walls were dismantled and massive building works transformed the city in grand colonial style. When Bombay became the principal supplier of cotton to Britain during the American Civil War, the population soared and trade boomed as money flooded into the city.

Bombay was a major player in the Independence movement, and the Quit India campaign was launched here in 1942 by frequent visitor Mahatma Gandhi. The city became capital of the Bombay presidency after Independence, but in 1960 Maharashtra and Gujarat were divided along linguistic lines – and Bombay became the capital of Maharashtra.

The rise of the pro-Marathi, pro-Hindu regionalist movement, spearheaded by the Shiv Sena (literally 'Shivaji's Army'), shattered the city's multicultural mould by actively discriminating against Muslims and non-Maharashtrians. Following Shiv Sena's rise to power in the city's municipal elections in 1985, communalist tensions increased, and the city's cosmopolitan self-image took a battering when 900 people, mostly Muslims, died in riots following the destruction of Ayodhya's Babri Masjid in December 1992 and January 1993. The riots were followed by a dozen retaliatory bombings in March 1993, which killed hundreds of people and damaged the Bombay Stock Exchange and Air India Building.

Shiv Sena's influence saw the names of many streets and public buildings – as well as the city itself – changed from their colonial names. In 1996 the city's name was officially changed to Mumbai, the Marathi name derived from the Hindu goddess Mumba, who was worshipped by the early Koli residents. The airport, Victoria Terminus and Prince of Wales Museum were all renamed after Chhatrapati Shivaji, the great Maratha leader.

Religious tensions continued to deepen and became intertwined with and supplanted by India's larger national religious tension and its struggles with Pakistan. Bombings in 2006 and 2011, and the 2008 attacks across the city, which lasted three days and killed 173 people, shifted the discussion to terrorism with origins outside Mumbai.

But in late 2012, when the Sena's charismatic founder Bal Thackeray died, the entire city shut down – due as much to fear of riots as to grief – and an estimated 500,000 people attended his funeral. Many predict the decline of the Shiv Sena mission – and a brighter future for harmony among Mumbaikars.

Sights

Mumbai, the capital of Maharashtra, is an island connected by bridges to the mainland. The city's commercial and cultural centre is at the southern, claw-shaped end of the island known as South Mumbai. The southernmost peninsula is Colaba, traditionally the travellers' nerve centre, with many of the major attractions, and directly north of Colaba is the busy commercial area known as Fort, where the British fort once stood. It's bordered on the west by a series of interconnected, fenced grassy areas known as maidans (pronounced may-*dahns*).

Though just as essential a part of the city as South Mumbai, the area north of here is collectively known as 'the suburbs'. The airport and many of Mumbai's best restaurants, shopping and nightspots are here, particularly in the upmarket suburbs of Bandra, Juhu and increasingly, Lower Parel.

◉ Colaba

Along the city's southernmost peninsula, Colaba is a bustling district packed with street stalls, markets, bars and budget-to-midrange lodgings. Colaba Causeway (Shahid Bhagat Singh Marg) dissects the promontory and Colaba's jumble of side streets and gently crumbling mansions.

If you're here in August, look out for the Koli festival, Nariyal Poornima, which is big in Colaba.

★ Taj Mahal Palace, Mumbai   LANDMARK

(Map p738) This stunning hotel is a fairy-tale blend of Islamic and Renaissance styles jostling for prime position among Mumbai's famous landmarks. Facing the harbour, it was built in 1903 by the Parsi industrialist JN Tata, supposedly after he was refused entry to one of the European hotels on account of being 'a native'. The image of smoke rising from the hotel became an iconic image of the 2008 terrorist attacks, when dozens were killed and much of the hotel was damaged. The hotel partly reopened less than a month later, dedicating the hotel to the victims; the fully restored hotel reopened on Independence Day 2010.

Gateway of India   MONUMENT

(Map p738) This bold basalt arch of colonial triumph faces out to Mumbai Harbour from the tip of Apollo Bunder. Incorporating Islamic styles of 16th-century Gujarat, it was built to commemorate the 1911 royal visit of King George V, but not completed until 1924. Ironically, the British builders of the gateway used it just 24 years later to parade the last British regiment as India marched towards Independence.

These days, the gateway is a favourite gathering spot for locals and a top spot for people-watching. Giant-balloon sellers, photographers, vendors making *bhelpuri* and touts rub shoulders with locals and tourists, creating all the hubbub of a bazaar. In March, they're joined by classical dancers and musicians who perform during the **Elephanta Festival** (www.maharashtratourism.gov.in).

Boats depart from the gateway's wharfs for Elephanta Island.

MUMBAI IN...

Two Days

Start at the grandaddy of Mumbai's colonial-era giants, the old Victoria Terminus, Chhatrapati Shivaji Terminus (CST; p737) and stroll up to Crawford Market (p767) and the maze of bazaars here. Lunch at Revival (p759), with a juice shake from Badshah Snacks & Drinks (p758).

Spend the afternoon admiring Mumbai's marvellous architecture at the High Court (p738) and the University of Mumbai (p737). Walk down to the Gateway of India (p736) and Taj Mahal Palace, Mumbai (p736). After sunset, eat streetside at Bademiya (p757). Swap tall tales with fellow travellers at Leopold's Café (p762).

The next day, visit the ornate Dr Bhau Daji Lad Mumbai City Museum (p741), then head to Kemp's Corner for lunch at Café Moshe (p758) and some shopping. Make your way down to Mani Bhavan (p743), the museum dedicated to Gandhi, and finish the day wandering the tiny lanes of **Khotachiwadi** followed by a beach sunset and a plate of *bhelpuri* at Girgaum Chowpatty (p740). A blow-out dinner at Khyber (p759) won't let you forget Mumbai soon.

Four Days

Head out to the Global Pagoda (p744) and learn to meditate, then return in the afternoon to visit the museums and galleries of **Kala Ghoda**. In the evening, head to Bandra for a candle-lit dinner at Caravan Serai, followed by some seriously hip bar action with a view at Aer (p763) in Worli.

Another day could be spent visiting the Dhobi Ghat (p743) and the nearby Mahalaxmi Temple (p743) and Haji Ali's Mosque (p741). Lunch at Olive Bar & Kitchen (p763) at Mahalaxmi Racecourse and then rest up for a night of avant-garde clubbing at Bluefrog (p764) in Worli.

Sassoon Dock
WATERFRONT

Sassoon Dock is a scene of intense and pungent activity at dawn (around 5am) when colourfully clad Koli fisher-folk sort the catch unloaded from fishing boats at the quay. The fish drying in the sun are *bombil*, the fish used in the dish Bombay duck. Photography at the dock is forbidden.

Fort Area & Churchgate

Lined up in a row and vying for your attention with aristocratic pomp, many of Mumbai's majestic Victorian buildings pose on the edge of **Oval Maidan**. This land, and the **Cross** and **Azad Maidans** immediately to the north, was on the oceanfront in those days, and this series of grandiose structures faced west directly out to the Arabian Sea.

Kala Ghoda, or 'Black Horse', is a sub-neighbourhood of Fort just north of Colaba and contains many of Mumbai's museums and galleries alongside a wealth of colonial-era buildings (best seen on a walking tour, p750).

★Chhatrapati Shivaji Terminus (Victoria Terminus)
HISTORIC BUILDING

(Map p742) Imposing, exuberant and overflowing with people, this is the city's most extravagant Gothic building, the beating heart of its railway network, and an aphorism for colonial India. As historian Christopher London put it, 'the Victoria Terminus is to the British Raj what the Taj Mahal is to the Mughal empire'. It's a meringue of Victorian, Hindu and Islamic styles whipped into an imposing Daliesque structure of buttresses, domes, turrets, spires and stained-glass windows.

Designed by Frederick Stevens, it was completed in 1887, 34 years after the first train in India left this site. Today it's Asia's busiest train station. Officially renamed Chhatrapati Shivaji Terminus (CST) in 1998, it's still better known locally as VT. It was added to the Unesco World Heritage list in 2004.

★Chhatrapati Shivaji Maharaj Vastu Sangrahalaya (Prince of Wales Museum)
MUSEUM

(Map p742; www.themuseummumbai.com; K Dubash Marg; Indian/foreigner ₹50/300, camera/video ₹200/1000; ⊙10.15am-6pm Tue-Sun) Mumbai's biggest and best museum displays a mix of exhibits from all over India. The domed behemoth, an intriguing hodge-podge of Islamic, Hindu and British architecture, was opened in 1923 to commemorate King George V's first visit to India (back in 1905, while he was still Prince of Wales). Its flamboyant Indo-Saracenic style was designed by George Wittet, who also designed the Gateway of India.

A recent renovation introduced a fascinating new miniature-painting gallery and a new gallery of contemporary art. Elsewhere, the vast collection includes impressive Hindu and Buddhist sculpture, terracotta figurines from the Indus Valley, porcelain and some particularly vicious-looking weaponry.

There's an outdoor cafeteria here, and the museum shop is excellent.

University of Mumbai (Bombay University)
HISTORIC BUILDING

(Map p742) Looking like a 15th-century French-Gothic masterpiece plopped incongruously amongst Mumbai's palm trees, this university on Bhaurao Patil Marg was designed by Gilbert Scott of London's St Pancras Station fame. There is an exquisite **University Library** and **Convocation Hall**, as

Colaba

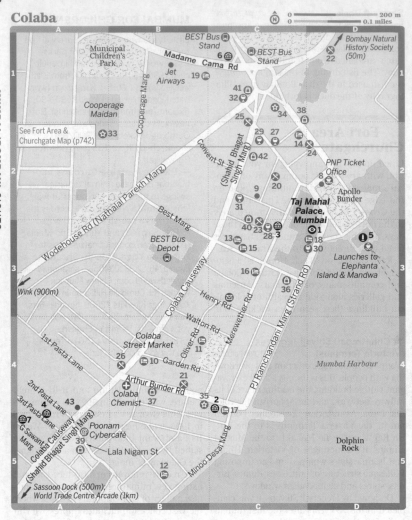

well as the 80m-high **Rajabai Clock Tower** (Map p742), decorated with detailed carvings, however, since the 2008 terror attacks, the public is not allowed inside the grounds. Admire the architecture on a stroll along Bhaurao Patil Marg (trees obscure much of the splendour when viewed from the Oval Maidan).

High Court   HISTORIC BUILDING
(Map p742; Eldon Rd) A hive of daily activity, packed with judges, barristers and other cogs in the Indian justice system, the High Court is an elegant 1848 neo-Gothic building. The

design was inspired by a German castle and was obviously intended to dispel any doubts about the authority of the justice dispensed inside, though local stone carvers presumably saw things differently: they carved a one-eyed monkey fiddling with the scales of justice on one pillar. You are permitted (and it is highly recommended) to walk around inside the building and check out the pandemonium and pageantry of public cases that are in progress – just walk right in! You'll have to surrender your camera to the guards, then make your way through the mazelike

Colaba

building to the original building's courtyard opposite Court 6.

Mumba Devi Temple   HINDU TEMPLE
(Map p746; Bhuleshwar) Pay a visit to the city's patron goddess at this 18th-century temple, about 1km north of CST. Among the deities in residence is Bahuchar Maa, goddess of the transgender *hijras*. Puja (prayer) is held several times a day.

Keneseth Eliyahoo Synagogue   SYNAGOGUE
(Map p742; www.jacobsassoon.org; Dr VB Gandhi Marg; admission free, camera/video ₹100/500; ⊙11am-6pm Mon-Sat, 1pm–6pm Sun) Built in 1884, this impossibly sky-blue synagogue still functions and is tenderly maintained by the city's dwindling Jewish community (and

protected to Baghdad Green Zone levels by Mumbai's finest).

National Gallery of Modern Art   MUSEUM
(NGMA; Map p738; www.ngmaindia.gov.in; MG Rd; Indian/foreigner ₹10/150; ⊙11am-6pm Tue-Sun) Increasingly well-curated shows of Indian and international artists in a bright and spacious exhibition space.

St Thomas' Cathedral   CHURCH
(Map p742; Veer Nariman Rd; ⊙7am-6pm) This charming cathedral, begun in 1672 and finished in 1718, is the oldest English building standing in Mumbai: it was once the eastern gateway of the East India Company's fort (the 'Churchgate'). The cathedral is a marriage of Byzantine and colonial-era architecture,

DHARAVI SLUM

Mumbaikars were ambivalent about the stereotypes in 2008's *Slumdog Millionaire*, but slums are very much a part of – some would say the foundation of – Mumbai city life. An astonishing 60% of Mumbai's population lives in slums, and one of the city's largest slums is Dharavi. Originally inhabited by fisher-folk when the area was still creeks, swamps and islands, it became attractive to migrant workers from South Mumbai and beyond when the swamp began to fill in due to natural and artificial causes. It now incorporates 1.75 sq km of land sandwiched between Mumbai's two major railway lines, and is home to more than one million people.

While it may look a bit shambolic from the outside, the maze of dusty alleys and sewer-lined streets of this city-within-a-city are actually a collection of abutting settlements. Some parts of Dharavi have mixed populations, but in other parts inhabitants from different parts of India, and with different trades, have set up homes and tiny factories. Potters from Saurashtra live in one area, Muslim tanners in another; embroidery workers from Uttar Pradesh work alongside metalsmiths; while other workers recycle plastics as women dry pappadams in the searing sun. Some of these thriving industries, around 10,000 in all, export their wares, and the annual turnover of business from Dharavi is thought to exceed US$650 million.

Up close, life in the slums is strikingly normal. Residents pay rent, most houses have kitchens and electricity, and building materials range from flimsy corrugated-iron shacks to permanent multistorey concrete structures. Many families have been here for many generations, and some of the younger Dharavi residents may work in white-collar jobs. They often choose to stay, though, in the neighbourhood they grew up in.

Slum tourism is a polarising subject, so you'll have to decide your feelings for yourself. If you opt to visit, Reality Tours & Travel (p751) does a fascinating tour, and puts a percentage of profits back into Dharavi. Some tourists opt to visit on their own, which is OK as well – just don't take photos. Take the train from Churchgate station to Mahim (₹6), exit on the west side and cross the bridge into Dharavi.

To learn more about Mumbai's slums, check out Katherine Boo's 2012 book *Behind the Beautiful Forevers*, about life in Annawadi, a slum near the airport, and *Rediscovering Dharavi*, Kalpana Sharma's sensitive and engrossing history of Dharavi's people, culture and industry.

and its airy interior is full of exhibitionist colonial memorials.

Jehangir Art Gallery ART GALLERY
(Map p742; 161B MG Rd; ⊙11am-7pm) **FREE**
Hosts shows by local artists and students, and the occasional big name. Rows of artists display their work on the pavement outside.

◉ Kalbadevi to Mahalaxmi

★ **Marine Drive &
Girgaum Chowpatty** BEACH
(Map p742; Netaji Subhashchandra Bose Rd)
Built on land reclaimed from Back Bay in 1920, Marine Drive arcs along the shore of the Arabian Sea from Nariman Point past Girgaum Chowpatty (where it's known as

Chowpatty Seaface) and continues to the foot of Malabar Hill. Lined with flaking art deco apartments, it's one of Mumbai's most popular promenades and sunset-watching spots. Its twinkling night-time lights earned it the nickname 'the Queen's Necklace'.

Girgaum Chowpatty (often referred to as just 'Chowpatty') remains a favourite evening spot for courting couples, families, political rallies and anyone out to enjoy what passes for fresh air. Evening *bhelpuri* at the throng of stalls at the beach's southern end is an essential part of the Mumbai experience. Forget about taking a dip: the water's toxic.

Chowpatty's also the place to be on the 10th day of the Ganesh Chaturthi festival (in August or September), when millions come to the shore to submerge the largest Ganesh statues: it's joyful mayhem.

Dr Bhau Daji
Lad Mumbai City Museum   MUSEUM
(Map p746; www.bdlmuseum.org; Dr Babasaheb
Ambedkar Rd; Indian/foreigner ₹10/100; ⊙ 10am-
5.30pm Thu-Tue) Jijamata Udyan – formerly
named Victoria Gardens – is a lush and
sprawling mid-19th-century garden and zoo.
It's home to this gorgeous museum, built in
Renaissance revival style in 1872 as the Victoria & Albert Museum. It reopened in 2007
after an impressive and sensitive four-year
renovation. In addition to extensive structural work, the building's Minton tile floors,
gilt ceiling mouldings, and ornate columns,
chandeliers and staircases were restored
to their former historically-accurate glory.
Even the sweet mint-green paint choice
was based on historical research. Also restored were the museum's 3500-plus objects
centering on Mumbai's history – clay models of village life, photography and maps,
textiles, books and manuscripts, Bidriware,
laquerware, weaponry and exquisite pottery,
all set against the museum's very distracting
stunning decor. The museum has also begun
hosting exhibitions of contemporary art and
other special shows. Skip the zoo.

Haji Ali Dargah   MOSQUE
(Map p746) Floating like a sacred mirage off
the coast, this exquisite Indo-Islamic shrine
is one of Mumbai's most striking symbols.
Built in the 19th century on the site of
a 15th-century structure, it contains the
tomb of the Muslim saint Pir Haji Ali Shah
Bukhari. Legend has it that Haji Ali died
while on a pilgrimage to Mecca and his casket miraculously floated back to this spot. A
long causeway reaches into the Arabian Sea,

THE ART DISTRICT

India's contemporary art scene has exploded in recent years, and Mumbai, along with
Delhi, is the centre of the action. A slew of galleries, mostly in Colaba, are showing incredible work in some gorgeous spaces. Kala Ghoda, meanwhile, Mumbai's traditional
art district, has a namesake two-week **festival** (www.kalaghodaassociation.com) each
February, with some great exhibitions.

Year-round, the second Thursday of each month is 'Art Night Thursday', when galleries stay open late and the vibe is social. Gallery crawls are sometimes organised; check
Mumbai Boss (www.mumbaiboss.com) for the latest. *Time Out Mumbai* is another
good gallery-hopping guide, as is the latest addition to the family, the free fold-up
Mumbai Art Map, available at galleries, bookstores and other art-friendly spots around
town. To go more in depth, check out the magazine *Art India*, available at most English-
language bookshops, which has news, background and criticism on work from across
the country.

Or, just read nothing and go see pretty things on your own: most of the following galleries are within walking distance of one another and make for a lovely afternoon art walk.

Chatterjee & Lal (Map p738; www.chatterjeeandlal.com; 1st fl, Kamal Mansion, Arthur Bunder Rd, Colaba; ⊙ 11am-7pm Tue-Sat)

Chemould Prescott Road (Map p742; www.gallerychemould.com; 3rd fl, Queens Mansion,
G Talwatkar Marg, Fort; ⊙ 11am-7pm Mon-Sat)

Galerie Mirchandani + Steinruecke (Map p738; www.galeriems.com; 1st fl, Sunny
House, 16/18 Mereweather Rd, Colaba; ⊙ 11am-7pm Tue-Sat)

Gallery Maskara (Map p738; www.gallerymaskara.com; 6/7 3rd Pasta Lane, Colaba; ⊙ 11am-
7pm Tue-Sat)

Guild (Map p738; www.guildindia.com; 2nd fl, Kamal Mansion, Arthur Bunder Rd ; ⊙ 10am-
6.30pm Mon-Sat)

Jhaveri Contemporary (www.jhavericontemporary.com; Krishna Niwas, 58A Walkeshwar
Rd, Walkeshwar, Malabar Hill ; ⊙ 11am-6pm Tue-Sat)

Project 88 (Map p738; www.project88.in; BMP Building, NA Sawant Marg, Colaba; ⊙ 11am-
7pm Tue-Sat)

Volte (Map p738; www.volte.in; 1st fl, Kamal Mansion, Arthur Bunder Rd, Colaba; ⊙ 11am-7pm
Mon-Sat)

Fort Area & Churchgate

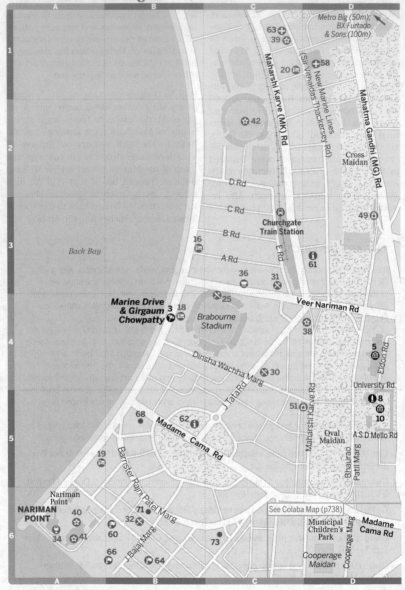

providing access to the dargah and mosque, but at high tide, water covers the causeway and the mosque becomes an island. Thousands of pilgrims, especially on Thursdays and Fridays (when there may also be *qawwali*, devotional singing), cross it to make their visit, many donating to beggars who line the way. Once inside, pilgrims fervently kiss the dressings of the tomb – or at least some do. In 2012, the dargah controversially adjusted its layout to bar women from entering the inner tomb. Discussions are ongoing.

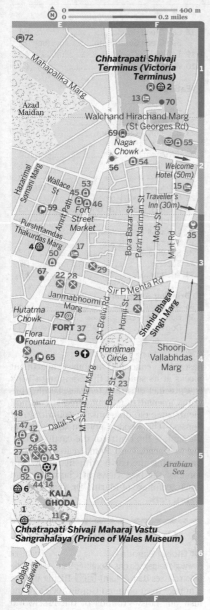

powered washing machine: every day hundreds of people beat the dirt out of thousands of kilograms of soiled Mumbai clothes and linen in 1026 open-air troughs. The best view, and photo opportunity, is from the bridge across the railway tracks near Mahalaxmi train station.

Mani Bhavan   MUSEUM
(Map p746; ☎23805864; www.gandhi-manibha van.org; 19 Laburnum Rd, Gamdevi; donation appreciated; ⊙9.30am-6pm) **FREE** As poignant as it is tiny, this museum is in the building where Mahatma Gandhi stayed during visits to Bombay from 1917 to 1934. The museum showcases the room where the leader formulated his philosophy of satyagraha (nonviolent protest) and launched the 1932 Civil Disobedience campaign that led to the end of British rule. Exhibitions include a photographic record of his life, along with dioramas and original documents, such as letters he wrote to Adolf Hitler and Franklin D Roosevelt. Nearby, August Kranti Maidan is where the campaign to persuade the British to 'Quit India' was launched in 1942.

Bombay Panjrapole   ANIMAL SHELTER
(Map p746; www.bombaypanjrapole.org.in; Panjrapole Marg, Bhuleshwar, near Madhav Baug Post Office; ⊙11am-6pm) In the middle of bustling Bhuleshwar market is, of all things, this shelter for 300 homeless cows. It was founded in the 18th century in response to the British approach to controlling the city's many stray dogs and pigs, which was, according to the Panjrapole, to shoot them. Cows were brought in to provide milk and eventually outnumbered the strays. Today, 1500 cows are cared for in seven centres across Gujarat and Maharashtra. You can wander around and pet the cows and calves and, for a small donation, feed them fresh greens.

Mahalaxmi Temple   HINDU TEMPLE
(Map p746) It's only fitting that in money-mad Mumbai one of the busiest and most colourful temples is dedicated to Mahalaxmi, the goddess of wealth. Perched on a headland, it is the focus for Mumbai's Navratri (Festival of Nine Nights) celebrations in September/October.

Babu Amichand Panalal Adishwarji Jain Temple   JAIN TEMPLE
(Walkeshwar, Malabar Hill; ⊙5am-9pm) This temple is renowned among Jains for its beauty;

Mahalaxmi Dhobi Ghat   GHAT
(Map p746) If you've had washing done in Mumbai, chances are your clothes have already visited this 140-year-old *dhobi ghat* (place where clothes are washed). The whole hamlet is Mumbai's oldest and biggest human-

Fort Area & Churchgate

given how beautiful Jain temples are, that's saying a lot. Check out the paintings and especially the ecstatically colourful zodiac dome ceiling – you've never seen anything like it. As this is a small temple, with usually a lot of prayer going on, tread lightly; you may wish to refer to the helpful 'Dear Tourist' sign at the entrance for guidelines (which include modest dress).

Nehru Centre CULTURAL COMPLEX
(☎24964676-80; www.nehru-centre.org; Dr Annie Besant Rd, Worli; Discovery of India admission free, planetarium adult/child ₹50/25; ⊙Tue-Sun, Discovery of India 11am-5pm, planetarium English show 3pm) This cultural complex includes a planetarium, theatre, gallery and an interesting history exhibition **Discovery of India**. The architecture is striking: the tower looks like a giant cylindrical pineapple, the planetarium a UFO.

Malabar Hill AREA
(around BG Kher Marg) Mumbai's most exclusive neighbourhood of sky-scratchers and private palaces, Malabar Hill is at the northern promontory of Back Bay. Surprisingly, one of Mumbai's most sacred and tranquil

oases lies concealed amongst apartment blocks at its southern tip: **Banganga Tank** is a precinct of serene temples, bathing pilgrims, meandering, traffic-free streets and picturesque old dharamsalas (pilgrims' rest houses). The wooden pole in the centre of the tank is the centre of the earth: according to legend, Lord Ram created the tank by piercing the earth with his arrow. For some of the best views of Chowpatty and the graceful arc of Marine Dr, visit **Kamala Nehru Park**.

◎ Gorai Island

★**Global Pagoda** LANDMARK
(www.globalpagoda.org; Gorai; ⊙9am-7pm, meditation classes 11am & 4pm) FREE Rising up like a mirage from polluted Gorai Creek and the lush but noisy grounds of the Esselworld and Water Kingdom amusement parks, is this breathtaking, golden 96m-high stupa modelled after Burma's Shwedagon Pagoda. The dome, which houses relics of Buddha, was built entirely without supports using an ancient technique of interlocking stones (it just snatched the record away from Bijapur's

Golgumbaz for being the world's largest unsupported dome), and the meditation hall beneath it seats 8000. A museum dedicated to the life of the Buddha and his teaching is also on site. The pagoda is affiliated with teacher SN Goenka, and two free 20-minute meditation classes are offered daily; an on-site meditation centre also offers 10-day meditation courses.

To get here, take a train from Churchgate to Borivali (exit the station the 'West' side), then an autorickshaw (₹40) to the ferry landing, where Esselworld ferries (return ₹35) come and go every 30 minutes. The last ferry to the Pagoda is 5.25pm.

◉ Elephanta Island

Nine kilometres northeast of the Gateway of India in Mumbai Harbour, the rock-cut temples on Gharapuri, better known as **Elephanta Island** (http://asi.nic.in/; Indian/foreigner ₹10/250; ☺ caves 9am-5pm Tue-Sun), are a Unesco World Heritage Site and worth crossing the waters for. The labyrinth of cave-temples, carved into the island's basalt rock, contain some of India's most impressive temple carving. The main Shiva-dedicated temple is an intriguing latticework of courtyards, halls, pillars and shrines; its magnum opus is a 6m-tall statue of Sadhashiva, depicting a three-faced Shiva as the destroyer, creator and preserver of the universe, his eyes closed in eternal contemplation.

The temples are thought to have been created between AD 450 and 750, when the island was known as Gharapuri (Place of Caves). The Portuguese called it Elephanta because of a large stone elephant near the shore, which collapsed in 1814 and was moved by the British to Mumbai's Jijamata Udyan. There's a small **museum** on-site, with informative pictorial panels on the origin of the caves.

Aggressive, expensive guides will meet you at the jetty and try to convince you to employ their services; you don't really need one. Opt instead for Pramod Chandra's *A Guide to the Elephanta Caves*, for sale at the stalls lining the stairway.

Launches (Map p738; economy/deluxe ₹120/150) head to Gharapuri from the Gateway of India every half-hour from 9am to 3.30pm.

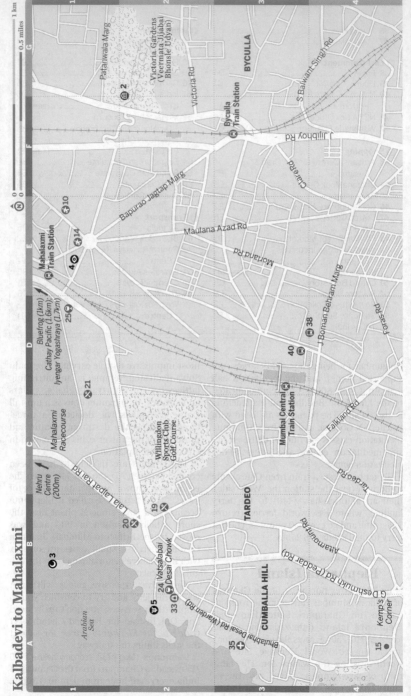

Kalbadevi to Mahalaxmi

1 km
0.5 miles

N

G
F
E
D
C
B
A

Patanwala Marg

Victoria Gardens (Veermata Jijabai Bhonsle Udyan)

Victoria Rd

BYCULLA

S Balwant Singh Rd

Byculla Train Station

Jijibhoy Rd

Clare Rd

Bapurao Jagtap Marg

Maulana Azad Rd

Morland Rd

J Boman Behram Marg

Foras Rd

Mahalaxmi Train Station

Bluefrog (1km); Cathay Pacific (1.6km); Iyengar Yogashraya (1.7km)

Mumbai Central Train Station

Falkland Rd

Tardeo Rd

Mahalaxmi Racecourse

Willingdon Sports Club Golf Course

TARDEO

Nehru Centre (200m)

Lala Lajpat Rai Rd

Altamount Rd

CUMBALLA HILL

Deshmukh Rd (Peddar Rd)

Arabian Sea

Vatsalabai Desai Chowk

Bhulabhai Desai Rd (Warden Rd)

Kemp's Corner

2
10
14
4
25
38
40
21
19
20
24
33
5
35
15
3

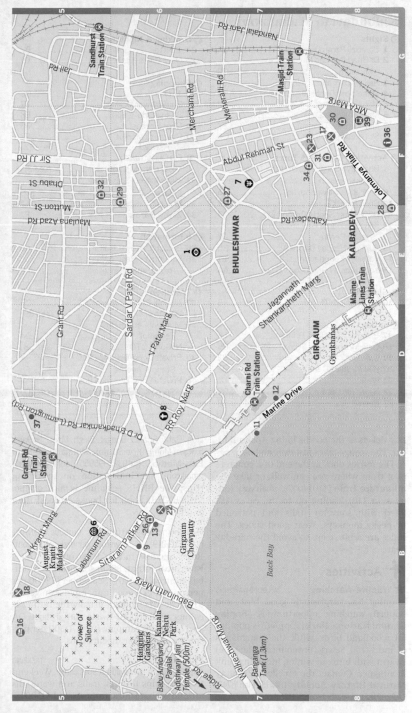

MUMBAI (BOMBAY) ACTIVITIES

Kalbadevi to Mahalaxmi

1 Bombay Panjrapole............................E6
2 Dr Bhau Daji Lad Mumbai City
   Museum......................................G2
3 Haji Ali Dargah................................B1
4 Mahalaxmi Dhobi Ghat....................E1
5 Mahalaxmi Temple...........................A2
6 Mani Bhavan...................................B5
7 Mumba Devi Temple.........................F7
8 St Teresa's Church..........................C6

⊕ Activities, Courses & Tours
Bharatiya Sangeet & Nartan
   Shikshapeeth..............................(see 9)
9 Bharatiya Vidya Bhavan....................B6
10 Child Rights & You...........................E1
11 H2O Water Sports Complex...............C7
12 Kaivalyadhama Ishwardas Yogic
   Health Centre..............................D7
13 Sumeet Nagdev Dance Arts...............B6
14 Vatsalya Foundation........................E1
15 Yoga Kids by Shraddha......................A4

🛏 Sleeping
16 Hotel Kemps Corner..........................A5

⊗ Eating
17 Badshah Snacks & Drinks...................F8
18 Café Moshe...................................B5
19 Cafe Noorani..................................B2
20 Haji Ali Juice Centre..........................B2
21 Neel...D1
22 New Kulfi Centre..............................B6
23 Revival...F8

⊜ Drinking & Nightlife
24 Ghetto..B2
25 Olive Bar & Kitchen...........................D1

⊜ Shopping
26 Anokhi..B6
27 Bhuleshwar Market............................F7
28 BX Furtado & Sons...........................E8
29 Chor Bazaar...................................F6
30 Crawford Market...............................F8
   Crossword..............................(see 18)
31 DD Dupattawala..............................F8
   Mangaldas Market.......................(see 31)
32 Mini Market/Bollywood
   Bazaar.....................................F5
33 Shrujan...A2
34 Zaveri Bazaar..................................F7

ⓘ Information
35 Breach Candy Hospital........................A3
36 Foreigners' Regional
   Registration Office.........................F8

ⓘ Transport
37 Allibhai Premji Tyrewalla.....................C5
   Citizen Travels...........................(see 39)
38 Mumbai Central Bus
   Terminal...................................D4
   National CTC.............................(see 38)
39 Private Long-Distance Bus
   Stand & Agents............................F8
40 Private Long-Distance Bus
   Stand & Ticket Agents......................D3

Buy tickets at the booths lining Apollo Bunder. The voyage takes just over an hour.

The ferries dock at the end of a concrete pier, from where you can walk or take the **miniature train** (₹10) to the **stairway** (admission ₹10) leading up to the caves. It's lined with souvenir stalls and patrolled by pesky monkeys. Wear good shoes. The stairs are a bit steep, so avoid the mid-day heat.

🏃 Activities

★ **Wildlife-Watching**　　WILDLIFE-WATCHING
Mumbai has surprisingly good bird- and butterfly-watching opportunities. **Sanjay Gandhi National Park** (Map p746) is popular for woodland birds, while the marshlands of industrial Sewri (pronounced shev-ree) swarm with birds in winter, including pink flamingoes. Contact the excellent **Bombay Natural History Society** (BNHS; Map p742; ☎22821811; www.bnhs.org; Hornbill House, opp Lion Gate, Shahid Bhagat Singh Marg; ⊘9am-5.30pm Mon-Fri) or Sunjoy Monga at **Yuhina Eco-Media** (☎9323995955; sunjoymonga@gmail.com) for information on upcoming trips; the BNHS schedule is also online. Visit BNHS's shop for books on local flora and fauna.

Outbound Adventure　　OUTDOOR ADVENTURE
(☎26315019; www.outboundadventure.com) Runs one-day rafting trips on the Ulhas River near Karjat, 88km southeast of Mumbai, from July to early September (₹2000 per person). After a good rain, rapids can get up to Grade III+, though usually the rafting is calmer with lots of twists and zigzags. OA also organises camping (from ₹1500 per person per day) and canoeing trips.

Wild Escapes　　TREKKING
(☎66635228; www.wild-escapes.com) Weekend trekking trips to forts, trails and waterfalls around Maharashtra, from around ₹1500.

OFF THE BEATEN TRACK

SANJAY GANDHI NATIONAL PARK

It's hard to believe that within 90 minutes of the teeming metropolis you can be surrounded by this 104-sq-km **protected tropical forest** (☑28866449; Borivali; adult/child ₹30/15, vehicle ₹100, safari admission ₹50; ⏰7.30am-6pm Tue-Sun, last entry 4pm). Here, bright flora, birds, butterflies and elusive wild leopards replace pollution and crowds, all surrounded by forested hills on the city's northern edge. Urban development tries to muscle in on the fringes of this wild region, but its national park status has allowed it to stay green and calm.

At research time, a trekking ban had been introduced to protect wildlife, but you can get inside the woods if you go with BNHS (p748). On your own, you can take the shuttle to the Shilonda waterfall, Vihar and Tulsi lakes (where there's boating), the zoolike lion and tiger safari and – the most intriguing option – the **Kanheri Caves** (admission/round-trip shuttle ₹5/30), a set of 109 dwellings and monastic structures for Buddhist monks 6km inside the park. The caves, not all of which are accessible, were developed over 1000 years, beginning in the 1st century BC, as part of a sprawling monastic university complex. They're no Ajanta, but worth a visit.

Inside the park's main northern entrance is an information centre with a small exhibition on the park's wildlife. The best time to see birds is October to April and butterflies August to November.

🏃 Volunteering

Child Rights & You
VOLUNTEERING

(CRY; Map p746; ☑23096845; www.cry.org; 189A Anand Estate, Sane Guruji Marg, Mahalaxmi) Child Rights & You works to raise funds for hundreds of projects India-wide that help marginalised children. Volunteers can assist with campaigns (online and on the ground), research, surveys and media, as well as occasional fieldwork. Note, a six-week commitment is required.

Vatsalya Foundation
VOLUNTEERING

(Map p746; ☑24962115; www.thevatsalyafoundation.org; Anand Niketan, King George V Memorial, Dr E Moses Rd, Mahalaxmi) The Vatsalya Foundation works with Mumbai's street children, focusing on rehabilitation into mainstream society. There are long- and short-term opportunities in teaching and sports activities.

Welfare of Stray Dogs
VOLUNTEERING

(Map p742; ☑64222838; www.wsdindia.org; Yeshwant Chambers, B Bharucha Rd, Kala Ghoda) This organisation works to help street dogs by eradicating diseases such as rabies, sterilising the animals, educating the public about strays and finding adoptive homes. Volunteers can walk dogs, mind kennels, treat street dogs, manage stores, educate kids in school programs or fundraise.

🎓 Courses

⭐ Yoga Institute
YOGA

(Map p755; ☑26122185; www.theyogainstitute.org; Shri Yogendra Marg, Prabhat Colony, Santa Cruz East; per 1st/2nd month ₹570/400) At its peaceful leafy campus near Santa Cruz, the almost-100-year-old Yoga Institute has daily classes as well as weekend and weeklong programs, and longer residential courses, including teacher training (with seven-day-course prerequisite).

⭐ Bharatiya Vidya Bhavan
LANGUAGE, MUSIC

(Map p746; ☑23871860; 2nd fl, cnr KM Munshi Marg & Ramabai Rd, Girgaum; per hr ₹500; ⏰4-8pm) Contact the Professor Shukla, a warm and worldly octogenarian, to arrange private Hindi, Marathi, Gujarati and Sanskrit classes here; prices for long-term study are negotiable. Also at the Bhavan is the **Bharatiya Sangeet & Nartan Shikshapeeth** (Indian Music & Dance Institute; Map p746; bhavansangeet@gmail.com; twice-weekly lessons per month ₹1000-5000; ⏰4-8pm). Connect with the friendly Professor Ghosh – a Grammy-winning composer and musician, and the principal – to join an ongoing group class or arrange private lessons in tabla, vocals (from classical Hindustani to playback), sitar, *sarangi* or Kathak or Orissi classical dance.

Yoga House
YOGA

(Map p755; ☑65545001; www.yogahouse.in; 53 Chimbai Rd, Bandra; classes ₹600; ⏰8am-10pm) A

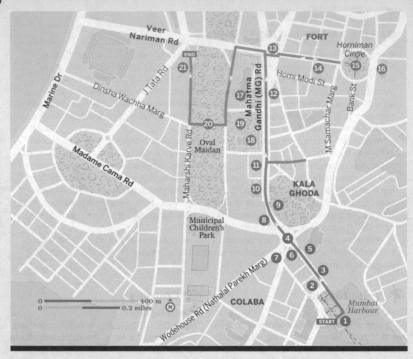

City Walk
Architectural Mumbai

START GATEWAY OF INDIA
END EROS CINEMA
DISTANCE 2.5KM
DURATION 1½ HOURS

Mumbai's defining feature is Its distinctive mix of colonial-era and art deco architecture .

Starting from the ❶ **Gateway of India** (p736), walk up Chhatrapati Shivaji Marg past the members-only colonial relic ❷ **Royal Bombay Yacht Club** and the art deco residential-commercial complex ❸ **Dhunraj Mahal**, towards ❹ **Regal Circle**. Walk the circle for views of the surrounding buildings – including the old ❺ **Sailors Home**, which dates from 1876 and is now the Maharashtra Police Headquarters, the art deco ❻ **Regal** (p765) cinema and the ❼ **Majestic Hotel**, now the Sahakari Bhandar cooperative store. Continue up MG Rd, past the beautifully restored facade of the ❽ **National Gallery of Modern Art** (p739). Opposite is the ❾ **Chhatrapati Shivaji Maharaj Vastu Sangrahalaya** (p737). Back across the road is the 'Romanesque Transitional' ❿ **Elphinstone College** and the ⓫ **David**

Sassoon Library & Reading Room, where members escape the afternoon heat lazing on planters' chairs on the upper balcony. Continue north to admire the vertical art deco stylings of the ⓬ **New India Assurance Company Building**. On an island ahead lies ⓭ **Flora Fountain**, depicting the Roman goddess of flowers. Turn east down Veer Nariman Rd, walking towards ⓮ **St Thomas' Cathedral** (p739). Ahead lies the stately ⓯ **Horniman Circle**, an arcaded ring of buildings laid out in the 1860s around a beautifully kept botanical garden. It's overlooked from the east by the neoclassical ⓰ **Town Hall**, home to the Asiatic Society library. Backtrack to Flora Fountain, continuing west and turning south onto Bhaurao Patil Marg to see the august ⓱ **High Court** (p738) and the ornate ⓲ **University of Mumbai** (p737). The university's 80m-high ⓳ **Rajabai Clock Tower** is best observed from within the ⓴ **Oval Maidan**. Turn around to compare the colonial edifices with the row of art deco beauties lining Maharshi Karve (MK) Rd, culminating in the wedding cake tower of ㉑ **Eros Cinema** (p765).

variety of yoga traditions are taught at this homey, Western-style yoga centre, housed in a Portuguese bungalow by the sea. Also has a charming cafe.

Kaivalyadhama Ishwardas Yogic Health Centre
YOGA

(Map p746; ☑ 22818417; www.kdhammumbai.org; 43 Marine Dr; ☺ 6am-7pm Mon-Sat) Several daily yoga classes, as well as workshops and special programs, are held here. Fees include a ₹600 monthly membership fee and a ₹500 admission fee. A medical consultation at the on-site health centre, as well as modest dress, are required.

Iyengar Yogashraya
YOGA

(☑ 24948416; www.bksiyengar.com; Elmac House, 126 Senapati Bapat Marg, Lower Parel; 1½hr classes ₹150) The Mumbai centre for the BKS Iyengar tradition of yoga has walk-in classes.

Sumeet Nagdev Dance Arts
DANCE

(☑ 24366777; www.sumeetnagdevdancearts.in; Silver Cascade Building, SB Marg, Dadar West; 1hr classes ₹400) SNDA offers tons of dance classes, from contemporary and ballet to Kalaripayattu (a Keralan martial art) and Bollywood. You can drop in on a class if it's early on in the session (or if you're a quick study); call to inquire. Classes are also held at a **Chowpatty location** (Map p746; Studio Balance, Krishna Kunj, 29/30 KM Munshi Marg).

☞ Tours

Fiona Fernandez's *Ten Heritage Walks of Mumbai* (₹395) contains walking tours in the city, with fascinating historical background. Jumping on a double-decker is an inexpensive and surprisingly good way to see South Mumbai.

The Government of India tourist office (p768) can provide a list of approved multilingual guides; most charge ₹750/950 per half-/full day.

Reality Tours & Travel
SLUM TOUR

(Map p738; ☑ 9820822253; www.realitytoursandtravel.com; 1st fl, Akbar House, Nawroji F Rd, Colaba; short/long Dharavi tours ₹650/1200) ✎ Photography is strictly forbidden on Reality's socially responsible tours of Dharavi, and 80% of post-tax profits go to the agency's own NGO, **Reality Gives** (www.realitygives.org), which runs a kindergarten and community centre in Dharavi. Reality also conducts village and Mumbai-by-bicycle tours. Enter the office through SSS Corner store.

Bombay Heritage Walks
WALKING

(☑ 23690992, 9821887321; www.bombayheritagewalks.com) Run by two enthusiastic architects, BHW has the best city tours in heritage neighbourhoods. Two-hour guided tours are ₹2000 for up to four people; longer tours are ₹3000 for three people; both include a 'handy keepsake'.

Mumbai Magic Tours
CITY TOUR

(☑ 9867707414; www.mumbaimagic.com; 2hr tours from ₹1500 per person) City tours, designed by the authors of the fabulous Mumbai Magic blog (www.mumbai-magic.blogspot.com), focus on food markets, traditional dance and music, and Jewish heritage, amongst others, and cover many places you would never find on your own.

Nilambari Bus Tours
BUS TOUR

(MTDC; 1hr tours ₹150; ☺ 7pm & 8.15pm Sat & Sun) Maharashtra Tourism open-deck bus tours of illuminated heritage buildings on weekends. They depart from and can be booked at both the MTDC booth (p768) and the MTDC office (p768).

Cruises
CRUISE

(☑ 22026364; ☺ 8am-8pm) A cruise on Mumbai Harbour is a good way to escape the city and see the Gateway of India as it was intended. Half-hour ferry rides (₹70) depart from the Gateway of India; tickets are sold on-site.

H2O Water Sports Complex
CRUISE

(Map p746; ☑ 23677584; www.drishtiadventures.com; Marine Dr, Mafatlal Beach; cruises per person day/night ₹400/500; ☺ 10am-10pm Sep-May) Arranges 45-minute day and night cruises (four-person minimum, so you may have to wait for them to fill), plus kayaking and parasailing.

🛏 Sleeping

You'll need to recalibrate your budget here: Mumbai has the most expensive accommodation in India, and you'll never quite feel like you're getting your money's worth. Welcome to Mumbai real estate!

Colaba is compact, has the liveliest tourist scene and many budget and midrange options. Fort is more spread out and convenient for the main train stations (CST and Churchgate). Most of the top-end places are dotted along Marine Drive and around the suburbs; Juhu and Bandra are good for nightlife, Juhu Beach and shopping. No matter where you stay, always book ahead.

Rates listed for five-star hotels are rack, but they go down, sometimes by 50%, depending on occupancy.

To stay with a local family, contact **India-tourism** (www.incredibleindia.com) for a list of homes across the city participating in Mumbai's **paying-guest and B&B program** (s/d from ₹400/800).

🛏 Colaba

Carlton Hotel
HOTEL $

(Map p738; ☎ 22020642; 1st fl, Florence House, Mereweather Rd; s/d/tr/q without bathroom from ₹900/1400/2150/2850, s/d with AC ₹2750/2950) Rooms here are quirky and tired, with about 100 different bathroom scenarios (most rooms have common showers, though they were recently renovated). But the hotel also has old tile floors, wood-beam ceilings and wooden railings, a balcony with plants and colonial-era Colaba views, and glittery old pictures of gods about – so it goes both ways.

Salvation Army
Red Shield Guest House
GUESTHOUSE $

(Map p738; ☎ 22841824; red_shield@vsnl.net; 30 Mereweather Rd; dm incl breakfast ₹250, d/tr/q incl breakfast & lunch ₹850/1150/1600; ✳ @) 'Salvies' is a Mumbai institution popular with rupee-pinching travellers. The large, ascetic dorms here are clean but cannot be reserved in advance: come just after the 9am kickout to ensure a spot. Curfew is midnight.

Sea Shore Hotel
GUESTHOUSE $

(Map p738; ☎ 22874237; 4th fl, Kamal Mansion, Arthur Bunder Rd; s/d without bathroom from ₹624/988) The Sea Shore's shoebox-size rooms are simple but nearly hotel-quality, with incongruously high-design communal bathrooms. Interior rooms have no window, but front-facing rooms have (through dingy, tiny screens) million-dollar views of Mumbai Harbour. The same owners run **India Guest House** (Map p738; ☎ 22833769; s/d without bathroom ₹416/520) downstairs, with similar bathrooms but not-as-nice rooms.

★ YWCA
GUESTHOUSE $$

(Map p738; ☎ 22025053; www.ywcaic.info; 18 Madame Cama Rd, Colaba; s/d/tr/q with AC incl breakfast & dinner ₹2126/3150/4462/6301; ✳ @ 🛜) The YWCA is immaculate – your room is scrubbed down every single day –

and ridiculously good-value: rates, which are a good ₹1000 cheaper than most in its class, include breakfast, dinner, early-morning tea, free wi-fi...*and a newspaper*. But there's a trade-off here with the long list of borderline-monastic rules, which some find off-putting.

Bentley's Hotel
HOTEL $$

(Map p738; ☎ 22841474; www.bentleyshotel.com; 17 Oliver Rd; r incl breakfast ₹1675-2295, with AC ₹1990-2610; ✳) People either love Bentley's or hate it, depending on which of the five buildings they end up in. Avoid Henry Rd and JA Allana Marg. The three buildings on Oliver Rd are good, but your first choice is the main building, where big rooms have old-school floor tiles, wooden furniture and colonial-era charm aplenty.

Regent Hotel
HOTEL $$

(Map p738; ☎ 22021518; www.regenthotelcolaba. com; 8 Best Marg; r with AC incl breakfast ₹4579-5284; ✳ @ 🛜) The friendly, Arabian-flavoured Regent has marble surfaces and soft beiges aplenty. More-expensive upper floors have tree views. The retro-chic breakfast area fills the 1st floor hallway, so avoid rooms 101–110 if you plan to sleep in.

Hotel Moti
GUESTHOUSE $$

(Map p738; ☎ 22025714; hotelmotiinternational @yahoo.co.in; 10 Best Marg; s/d/tr with AC ₹3000/3200/4500; ✳ @) Rooms here, in a gracefully crumbling, colonial-era building in prime Colaba, are simple and slightly overpriced. But all have fridges and some are huge and/or have whispers of charm, like ornate stucco ceilings. It's a family-run place, but the service gets complaints.

★ Taj Mahal Palace,
Mumbai
HERITAGE HOTEL $$$

(Map p738; ☎ 66653366; www.tajhotels.com; Apollo Bunder; s/d tower from ₹27,887/29,649, palace from ₹38,162/39,923; ✳ @ 🛜 🏊) With its sweeping arches, staircases and domes, the Taj really does feel like a palace. Following the 2008 terrorist attacks here, some 285 rooms were lavishly restored in fuchsia, saffron and willow-green colour schemes (and security is Fort Knox–level). Rooms in the tower wing lack the period details of the palace wing, but some have spectacular, full-on views of the Gateway. The hotel's Harbour Bar (p762), Mumbai's first licensed bar, is legendary.

Hotel Suba Palace
HOTEL $$$

(Map p738; ☏ 22020636–9; www.hotelsuba palace.com; Battery St; s/d with AC incl breakfast ₹5519/6341; ❈ ☎) Teetering precariously on the edge of boutique hotel, the Suba Palace oozes soothing neutral tones, from the tiny taupe shower tiles in the contemporary bathrooms to the creamy crown moulding and beige zebra-print quilted headboards in the tasteful rooms. Plus, wi-fi's free. Comfy, quiet and central.

Fariyas Hotel
HOTEL $$$

(Map p738; ☏ 61416141; www.fariyas.com; 25 D Vyas Marg; r with AC incl wi-fi from ₹11,742; @ ☎ ❈) This smart, friendly place has tasteful, traditional-style rooms (prices go up a couple notches for a harbour view) and a small pool, which nonguests can use (₹780 per day). With its peaceful spot on a residential street near the water, it's also a comfortable distance from the fray.

Ascot Hotel
HOTEL $$$

(Map p738; ☏ 66385566; www.ascothotel.com; 38 Garden Rd; r with AC incl breakfast from ₹7045; ❈ @ ☎) Marble-meets-modern at this well-designed hotel. Airy rooms have big headboards, bathtubs, desks and lots of natural light and, in front-facing rooms, tree views. Wi-fi's ₹300 per day.

🛏 Fort Area & Churchgate

Hotel Lawrence
GUESTHOUSE $

(Map p742; ☏ 22843618; 3rd fl, ITTS House, 33 Sai Baba Marg; s/d/tr without bathroom incl breakfast ₹700/850/1050) Tucked away in a little side lane, Lawrence has clean crashpads that are popular with shoestring meditators – and a management that tends to enforce moral judgements on guests.

Traveller's Inn
HOTEL $

(☏ 22644685; 26 Adi Marzban Path; dm/d ₹628/1579, d with AC incl breakfast ₹2260; ❈ @ ☎) On a quiet, tree-lined street, the tall and narrow Traveller's Inn has tiny rooms and rain-shower heads in even tinier bathrooms. But everything's squeaky clean, and the location's excellent. Free wi-fi in the lobby.

Hotel Oasis
HOTEL $$

(Map p742; ☏ 30227886–9; www.hoteloasisindia. in; 276 Shahid Bhagat Singh Rd; r from ₹1620; ❈) Rooms at this friendly place are incredibly small and need some paint, and some of the standard rooms are low on natural light. But they're spick and span and a stone's throw from CST. Plus, the kooky pastel design scheme makes you feel like you're inside an ice-cream cone. In a good way.

Sea Green Hotel
HOTEL $$

(Map p742; ☏ 66336525; www.seagreenhotel.com; 145 Marine Dr; s/d from ₹3974/5063) This excellent art deco hotel, and its twin, **Sea Green South** (Map p742; ☏ 22821613; www.seagreen south.com; 145A Marine Dr; s/d from ₹3974/5063), have spacious but spartan air-conditioned rooms, originally built in the 1940s to house British soldiers. Ask for one of the sea-view rooms: they're the same price.

CST Retiring Rooms
RAILWAY RETIRING ROOM $$

(Map p742; dm/d with AC ₹540/1600) Ticket-holders should try to snag one of VT's quaint and oddly quiet retiring rooms for a night; check in at the enquiry counter/station manager office.

Residency Hotel
HOTEL $$

(Map p742; ☏ 22625525; www.residencyhotel.com; 26 Rustom Sidhwa Marg; s/d with AC incl breakfast from ₹3640/3875; ❈ @ ☎) Recent renovations have transformed the friendly Residency into a contemporary design–style hotel, with mood lighting, rain showers and leather-walled elevators. Rooms also have fridges, flatscreens, slippers and wi-fi (free in the pricier rooms). But there are odd oversights (why only a single towel in double rooms?) that shouldn't happen in this price range.

Welcome Hotel
HOTEL $$

(☏ 6631488; welcomehotel@gmail.com; 257 Shahid Bhagat Singh Rd; s/d incl breakfast from ₹3082/3611, without bathroom from ₹1644/1820; ❈ ☎) Though the service needs some work, rooms here are simple and fresh, and shared bathrooms are nicer than most attached baths elsewhere. Top-floor executive rooms are more boutique than midrange, more LA than Bombay. Free wi-fi.

Trident
HOTEL $$$

(Oberoi Hotel; Map p742; ☏ 66324343; www. tridenthotels.com; Marine Dr; s/d from ₹22,016/23,480; ❈ @ ☎ ❈) The Trident is, along with the Oberoi, part of the Oberoi Hotel complex. But the Trident wins out both on price and on the spiffy, streamlined design of its restaurants, bars and pool area. The rooms, too, are as cool as the Oberoi's, but with earthy elements (and smaller bathrooms).

West End Hotel HOTEL $$$

(Map p742; ☑40839100; www.westendhotelmum bai.com; 45 New Marine Lines; s/d with AC from ₹5871/7045; ❄️🛜) The West End's spacious art-deco rooms have modish beds, balconies, and moments of mid-century modern and Hollywood regency. Bless their hearts, the look is totally accidental. The rest of the place is old-fashioned, down to the friendly service and the hotel's taglines: 'Honest Prices' and 'Good VFM' – Value For Money. If the rates were a wee bit lower, that would be TT – totally true.

InterContinental HOTEL $$$

(Map p742; ☑39879999; www.intercontinental. com; 135 Marine Dr; r incl breakfast from ₹22,897; ❄️@🛜🏊) Very sleek for an InterContinental. All earth tones and East Asian chic, deluxe sea-front rooms are sizeable, with a massive picture window, while halfmoon corner suites mirror the curve of Marine Drive. Lower-category rooms have poor views. Its lobby-level Koh (p759) turns Thai food on its head, while stunning Dome (p763) lounge stylishly graces the rooftop.

Western Suburbs

⭐ **Anand Hotel** HOTEL $$

(Map p755; ☑26203372; anandhote@yahoo.co.in; Gandhigram Rd, Juhu; s/d with AC from ₹2348/3875; ❄️) The rooms here are so clean, homey and old-fashioned – think embroidered artwork in the rooms, steel clothes-drying rods on the balconies and images of Ganesh everywhere – that they feel like they're in someone's Bombay apartment. It's around the corner from the ISKCON temple and upstairs from the excellent Dakshinayan restaurant, so the location couldn't be any better either.

⭐ **Iskcon** GUESTHOUSE $$

(Map p755; ☑26206860; guesthouse.mumbai @pamho.net; Hare Krishna Land, Juhu; s/d ₹3095/3495, with AC ₹3395/3995; ❄️@🛜) This efficiently managed guesthouse is part of Juhu's lively ISKCON complex. The lobby overlooks the temple, while rooms have Gujarati *sankheda* (lacquered country wood) furniture; some have balconies with pretty arches. Krishna's birthday (Janmastami; August) and the car festival (Rath Yatra; celebrated in January) are big here; the thrice-daily *aarti* (candle-lighting ritual) is also special.

Hotel Kemps Corner   HOTEL **$$**
(Map p746; ☎23634646; www.hotelkempscorner.
com; 131 August Kranti Marg; s/d with AC incl break-
fast from ₹2818/4697; ☀@☎) You can tell
this place is a family business from the TLC
given to rooms (spick-and-span bathrooms,
new TVs) and guests (free breakfast and

wi-fi, smiley service). The hotel is also in a
shady spot in the Kemp's Corner fashion bo-
nanza, which is much less frenzied than Co-
laba or Fort, and just 2km to Haji Ali Dargah
and Chowpatty.

Western Suburbs

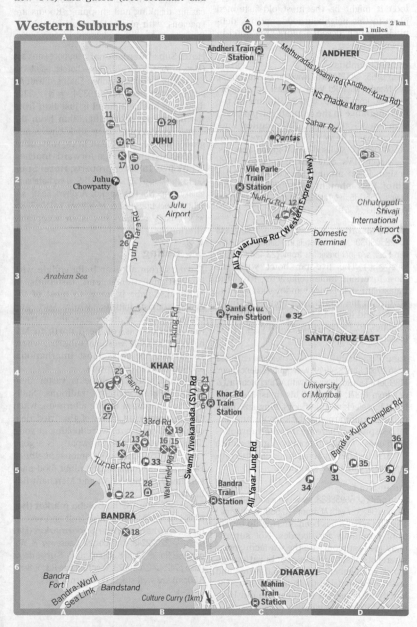

Hotel Neelkanth
HOTEL $$

(Map p755; ☑ 26495566-9; 354 Linking Rd, Khar West; s/d from ₹2231/2935; ❄) Rooms at the friendly Neelkanth are inadvertently retro, with lots of marble, chrome-trimmed wooden furniture and old-school plaid wool blankets. (Check out the sublimely mod logo too.) It might be the most old-fashioned place in this neighbourhood, and it's definitely the only decent Bandra-area hotel in this price range.

Hotel Columbus
HOTEL $$

(Map p755; ☑ 42144343; www.hotelcolumbus.in; 344 Nanda Patkar Rd, Vile Parle East, opposite BP; r with AC from ₹3523; ❄ @ ⓦ) Rooms at the best midrange in the domestic airport area aren't new – they are a little scuffed up – but are very homey. Super deluxe rooms (₹4697) have stylised wood-grain accents, flatscreen TVs and aspirations for high design. Right around the corner is **Adar Udipi Refreshment** (Map p755; Nehru Rd; mains ₹55-135; ⓢ 7am-10.30pm), with good veg thalis (₹75).

★ITC Maratha
HOTEL $$$

(☑ 28303030; www.itchotels.in; Sahar Rd, Andheri East; s/d incl breakfast from ₹23,484/25,832; ❄ @ ⓦ ❄) The five-star hotel with the most luxurious Indian character, from the Rajasthani-style lattice windows around the atrium, to the rooms with their silk throw pillows and lush raspberry and grey colour schemes, to Peshawri (p761), one of Mumbai's best restaurants.

Juhu Residency
BOUTIQUE HOTEL $$$

(Map p755; ☑ 67834949; www.juhuresidency.com; 148B Juhu Tara Rd, Juhu; s/d with AC incl breakfast & wi-fi from ₹5871; ❄ @ ⓦ) This quasi-boutique hotel has sleek marble floors, king-size beds in the premium rooms, dark woods and artful bedspreads. There are three restaurants – good ones – for just 18 rooms. A great choice if you're looking for something hip and intimate that won't cost a fortune.

Sun-n-Sand
HOTEL $$$

(Map p755; ☑ 66938888; www.sunnsandhotel.com; 39 Juhu Beach; r with AC from ₹10,568; ❄ @ ⓦ ❄) The Sun-n-Sand has been offering up beachfront hospitality for decades. Not surprisingly, the best rooms are the sea-facing ones, where lots of silk and pleasant burnt-orange motifs complement the pool, palm-tree and ocean views outside the huge window. The hotel's off Juhu Tara Rd, near the old Holiday Inn. Rates vary wildly.

Hotel Regal Enclave
HOTEL $$$

(Map p755; ☑ 67261111; www.regalenclave.com; 4th Rd, Khar West, near Khar market; r with AC incl breakfast from ₹6000) Regal Enclave has a stellar location: in an exceedingly leafy part of Khar, right near the station (some rooms have train views) and all of Bandra's best eating, drinking and shopping. Rooms are spacious, with pleasant if unoriginal decor. Rates include airport pick-up.

Hotel Suba International
BOUTIQUE HOTEL $$$

(Map p755; ☑ 67076707; www.hotelsubainterna tional.com; Sahar Rd, Andheri East; s/d with AC incl breakfast from ₹8102/9394; ❄ ⓦ) This 'boutique business' hotel is just 1km from the international terminal, 3km from the domestic. It's laid out in slick blacks and glossy marble, with clean lines, masculine hardwoods and design-forward touches. Wi-fi's free. Its sister property, **Hotel Suba Galaxy** (Map p755; ☑ 26821188; www.hotelsuba galaxy.com; NS Phadke Rd, Andheri East; s/d with AC incl breakfast & wi-fi from ₹4110/7985; ❄ ⓦ), isn't as shiny but is an acceptable alternative.

✗ Eating

Flavours from all over India collide with international trends and tastebuds in Mumbai. Colaba is home to most of the cheap tourist haunts, while Fort and Churchgate skew more upscale, a trend that continues as you head north to Mahalaxmi and the western suburbs, where you'll find Mumbai's most international and expensive restaurants.

Mumbai's street cuisine is vaster than many Western culinary traditions. Stalls tend to get started in late afternoon, when chai complements much of the fried deliciousness (*vada pav*, we're looking at you); items are ₹10 to ₹25. Chowpatty is a good place to try Mumbai's famous *bhelpuri*. During Ramadan, fantastic night food-markets line Mohammed Ali and Merchant Rds in Kalbadevi.

For self-caterers, the **Colaba market** (Map p738; Lala Nigam St) has fresh fruit and vegetables. **Saharkari Bhandar Supermarket** (Map p738; ☑ 22022248; cnr Colaba Causeway & Wodehouse Rd; ⓢ 10am-8.30pm) and **Suryodaya** (Map p742; ☑ 22040979; Veer Nariman Rd; ⓢ 8am-8.30pm) are well-stocked supermarkets.

✗ Colaba

Hotel OCH
INDIAN $

(Map p738; Shahid Bhagat Singh Rd; mains ₹65-110, thalis ₹65-105; ⊙ 7am-10.30pm) The best of the Colaba cheapies, with decent lunch thalis and evening *pav bhaji* in a cafeteria-like setting. Popular with families and cops working next door.

Bademiya
MUGHLAI, FAST FOOD $$

(Map p738; Tulloch Rd; light meals ₹60-150; ⊙ 8pm-1.30am) Formerly a tiny, outrageously popular late-night street stall, Bademiya recently added a dingy seating area across the street, a tiny eatery around the corner and a restaurant in Fort, which some say have been its downfall. It's true that prices have gone up while portions have shrunk, but the spicy, fresh-grilled kebabs and tikka rolls still hit the spot on a late night.

Theobroma
CAFE $$

(Map p738; Colaba Causeway; confections ₹40-95, light meals ₹180-200; ⊙ 7am-midnight) Perfectly executed cakes, tarts and brownies, as well as sandwiches and breads, go well with the coffee here. The pastries change regularly; if you're lucky, you'll find the Portuguese vanilla cinnamon custard tart (₹70). For brunch, have the *akoori* – Parsi-style scrambled eggs – with green mango. The **Bandra branch** (Map p755; 33rd Rd, near Linking Rd; ⊙ 8am-11.30pm) is big and airy, with the same menu.

Indigo
FUSION $$$

(Map p738; ☑ 66368980; www.foodindigo.com; 4 Mandlik Marg; mains ₹750-1100; ⊙ 12-3pm & 6.30pm-midnight) Colaba's finest eating option is a gourmet haven serving inventive European cuisine, a long wine list, sleek ambience and a gorgeous roof deck lit with fairy lights. Favourites include the kiwi margaritas (₹465), Cochin oysters (₹765) and zucchini-wrapped prawns with polenta and saffron butter (₹1100). Reserve on weekends.

Koyla
NORTH INDIAN $$$

(Map p738; www.koylaethniccuisine.com; 4th fl, Kamal Mansion, Arthur Bunder Rd; mains ₹280-550; ⊙ 7.30pm-1am Tue-Sun) This massive rooftop space has fairy lights, plants and sandy paths winding around the tented tables, while Mumbai Harbour and the Taj Palace

---

DABBA-WALLAHS

A small miracle of logistics, Mumbai's 5000 *dabba-wallahs* (literally 'food container person'; also called tiffin-wallahs) work tirelessly to deliver hot lunches to office workers throughout the city.

Lunch boxes are picked up each day from restaurants and homes and carried on heads, bicycles and trains to a centralised sorting station. A sophisticated system of numbers and colours (many wallahs don't read) identifies the destination of each lunch. More than 200,000 meals are delivered – always on time, come (monsoon) rain or (searing) shine.

This system has been used for over a century and there's only about one mistake per six million deliveries. (In a 2002 analysis, *Forbes Magazine* found that the *dabba-wallahs* had a six-sigma, or 99.99966%, reliability rating.)

Look for these master messengers mid-morning at Churchgate and CST stations.

---

twinkle in the distance. The menu is strong on tikkas and kebabs.

Basilico
MEDITERRANEAN $$$

(Map p738; ☑ 66345670; www.cafebasilico.com; Sentinel House, Arthur Bunder Rd; mains ₹360-690; ⊙ 9am-1am) Euro-style Basilico does creative steaks and fresh pastas, but the real draw is for vegies: exquisite salads (from ₹250) like grilled artichoke, Lebanese fattoush or the specials, which might include a spicy brown rice, baked tofu, and green salad in lemon-chilli-ginger dressing. The **Bandra branch** (Map p755; St John Rd, Pali Naka) has outdoor seating.

Indigo Delicatessen
CAFE $$$

(Map p738; Pheroze Bldg, Chhatrapati Shivaji Marg; mains ₹425-645; ⊙ 8.30am-midnight) Indigo's deli and bakery has cool tunes, warm decor and massive wooden tables. It has breakfast all day (₹155 to ₹385), inventive sandwiches and other casual meals, French-press coffee – including some from Andhra Pradesh's Araku region – and tons of teas, wine (₹350 to ₹790 per glass) and, alas, poor service.

✕ Fort Area & Churchgate

★ Pradeep

Gomantak Bhojanalaya
MAHARASHTRIAN $

(Map p742; Sheri House, Rustom Sidhwa Marg; mains ₹60-130; ⊙11am-4pm Mon-Sat) The *surmai* (seer) rice plate here looks plain – a fried piece of fish, some dhal, rice and chutneys on a stainless steel plate – but the meal will transport you. The food is home-style Malvani cuisine, from coastal Maharashtra, and so fresh you can taste the individual flavours dancing with one another. Savour the sublime, pink *sol kadhi*, a soothing, spicy drink of coconut milk and kokum.

A Taste of Kerala
KERALAN $

(Map p742; Prospect Chambers Annex, Pitha St, Fort; mains ₹50-140, thalis ₹80-120; ⊙6am-midnight) This humble little hotel is one of several little Keralan eateries on an alley in Fort and does a fine fish curry rice (if you can handle the bones) and lunch thali, served on a banana leaf. Lots of coconut and southern goodness.

Badshah Snacks & Drinks
INDIAN $

(Map p746; snacks & drinks ₹35-120; ⊙7am-12.30am) Opposite Crawford market, Badshah's been serving snacks, fruit juices and its famous *falooda* (rose-flavoured drink made with milk, cream, nuts and vermicelli) to hungry bargain-hunters for more than 100 years. Try the mango *falooda*.

K Rustom
SWEETS $

(Map p742; Stadium House, Veer Nariman Rd; desserts ₹25-70; ⊙9.30am-11pm Mon-Sat, 3-11pm Sun) Nothing but a few metal freezers, but the ice-cream sandwich (₹50) has been pleasing Mumbaikar palettes since 1953.

★ Suzette
FRENCH $$

(Map p742; www.suzette.in; Atlanta Bldg, Vinayak K Shah Marg, Nariman Point; light meals ₹200-330; ⊙9am-11pm Mon-Sat; 🖤) You'll feel like a cool Parisian when you eat here: there are newspapers, really good crepes, croques and coffee, water served in glass bottles, and loungy music that sways from old-timey French to Afropop. Also, a jaggery-and-butter crepe is a really good idea. Just one concern: it has no bathroom. The Bandra Suzette (Map p755; St John's St, Pali Naka) has outdoor seating and is open daily.

★ Samrat
GUJARATI $$

(Map p742; ☑42135401; www.prashantcaterers.com; Prem Ct, J Tata Rd; thalis lunch/dinner & Sundays ₹265/330, mains ₹170-250; ⊙noon-11pm) If this is your first thali, strap yourself in: the cavalcade of taste and texture (and sweetness – this is Gujarati food) will leave you wondering what just happened. Come hungry. Samrat is also the king of a pure-veg empire that includes 210°C (Map p742), an outdoor cafe and bakery, and Relish (Map p742), with Asian-Mexican-Lebanese fusion, at the same location.

Kala Ghoda Café
CAFE $$

(Map p742; www.kgcafe.in; 10 Ropewalk Lane, Kala Ghoda; light meals ₹100-275, dinners ₹375-525; ⊙8.30am-11.45pm; 🖤) 🍃 An artsy, modern and miniscule cafe that's a favourite among journalists and other creative types, who come for the organic coffee sourced from sustainable plantations, organic teas, excellent sandwiches and salads, and charming breakfasts – after fighting for one of the few tables.

Café Moshe
CAFE $$

(Map p738; www.moshes.in; Chhatrapati Shivaji Marg; light meals ₹175-375; ⊙9am-midnight) Teeny tiny Moshe's does excellent baked goods, coffees, smoothies, salads, fondue and sandwiches (the whole-wheat bagel sandwich with broccoli tapenade, rocket, basil, feta and mozzarella is to die for). The other outlets – the flagship restaurant (7 Minoo Manor, Cuffe Parade; ⊙9am-midnight), in a heritage building, and the bookstore cafe (Map p746; Crossword, NS Patkar Marg) at Kemp's Corner – all serve the same great food.

Bademiya Restaurant
MUGHLAI $$

(Map p742; ☑22655657; Botawala Bldg, Horniman Circle; mains ₹110-180; ⊙11am-1am) The grown-up, sit-down version of Bademiya's legendary Colaba streetside stand has the classic rolls and rotis, plus biryanis, tikka masalas and dhals. Delivers.

Brittania
PARSI $$

(Wakefield House, Ballard Estate; mains ₹100-350; ⊙12-4pm Mon-Sat) This Mumbai icon and its endearing owner have been going since 1923. The signature dishes are the *dhansak* and the berry *pulao* (from ₹250) – spiced and boneless mutton or chicken, or veg or egg, buried in basmati rice and tart barberries that are imported from Iran – in a shady spot in pretty Ballard Estate.

Samovar Café CAFE $$
(Map p742; Jehangir Art Gallery, MG Rd, Kala Ghoda; mains ₹90-160; ⏰ 11am-7pm Mon-Sat) This intimate place inside the art gallery, perfect for a snack and a tea, overlooks the gardens of the Prince of Wales Museum.

★ **Koh** THAI $$$
(Map p742; ☎ 39879999; InterContinental, Marine Dr; mains ₹495-1395; ⏰ 12.30-3pm & 7.30-midnight) India's first signature Thai restaurant is Mumbai's hottest and most beautifully designed dining destination. Celebrity chef Ian Kittichai works his native cuisine into an international frenzy of flavour with revelatory dishes like wok-tossed black-pepper tenderloin, and oven-roasted aubergine sprinkled with nori (paired with hot-stone garlic rice), throwing preconceived notions about Thai food to the curb.

★ **Revival** INDIAN $$$
(Map p746; 361 Sheikh Memon St, Kalbadevi, opp Mangaldas market; thalis ₹300; ⏰ 12-4pm & 7.30-10.30pm, lunch only Sun) It turns out that Tamil, Punjabi and Rajasthani food can work together in a jumbo thali if you know what you're doing – and Revival knows what it's doing. Servers in silken dhoti come one after another to fill your golden plates with dozens of dishes, sides and chutneys in a luscious onslaught. The thali changes daily and it's bigger on Sundays.

Khyber NORTH INDIAN $$$
(Map p742; ☎ 40396666; 145 MG Rd; mains ₹375-725; ⏰ 12.30-4pm & 7.30-11.30pm) The Afghan-inspired cave-like interior here sets off mouth-watering kebabs, biryanis and curries. Highlights of the meat-centric menu include the *reshmi kebab masala*, a transcendent dish of cream and yoghurt-marinated chicken drowning in the restaurant's intricate red masala; and its pièce de résistance, *raan* (a whole leg of slow-cooked lamb). Veggies, look elsewhere.

Trishna SEAFOOD $$$
(Map p742; ☎ 22703213/4; Ropewalk Lane, Kala Ghoda; mains ₹260-750; ⏰ noon-3.30pm & 6.30pm-midnight) An outstanding and intimate seafood restaurant focused on Mangalorean preparations. The crab with butter, black pepper and garlic, and Hyderabadi fish tikka are house specialities that warrant the hype, while service is underbearing, friendly and helpful. One of the best seafood places in town. Reservations unnecessary before 8pm.

Mahesh Lunch Home SEAFOOD $$$
(Map p742; ☎ 22023965; www.maheshlunchhome.com; Cowasji Patel St; mains ₹150-475; ⏰ 11.30am-4pm & 7pm-midnight) A great place to try Mangalorean seafood in Mumbai. It's renowned for its ladyfish, pomfret, lobster and crabs; the *rawas tikka* (marinated white salmon) and tandoori pomfret are outstanding. There's also a **Juhu branch** (Map p755; Juhu Tara Rd; mains ₹200-600; ⏰ 12-3.30pm & 7pm-12.30am).

5 Spice CHINESE $$$
(Map p742; 296A Perin Nariman St, Sangli Bank Bldg; mains ₹240-635; ⏰ noon-3pm & 7pm-midnight) A 30-minute wait is common at this Indo-Chinese godsend whose menu is packed with so many tantalising chicken, lamb, prawn/fish and veg dishes that choosing is an issue. In the end, the chicken in burnt-chilli sauce (₹290) works on a bed of burnt chilli-rice (₹265). Veggies should stick to the **veg branch** (Shalimar Bldg, G Rd) in Churchgate.

✖ **Kalbadevi to Mahalaxmi**

★ **New Kulfi Centre** SWEETS $
(Map p746; cnr Chowpatty Seaface & Sardar V Patel Rd; kulfi per 100gm ₹35-50; ⏰ 10am-1am) Serves the best *kulfi* (firm-textured ice cream) you'll have anywhere, which means it's pretty much the best thing in the world. Killer flavours include pistachio, *malai* (cream) and saffron.

Dakshinayan SOUTH INDIAN $
(183 Teen Batti, Walkeshwar Rd, Malabar Hill; light meals ₹75-110; ⏰ 11am-3pm & 6-11pm, from 8am Sun) This smaller, slightly faded Dakshinayan has the same excellent food as the Juhu branch (p760).

Haji Ali Juice Centre JUICE BAR $
(Map p746; Lala Lajpatrai Rd, Haji Ali Circle; juices & snacks ₹30-180; ⏰ 5am-1.30am) The Haji Ali Juice folks know all sweet, tasty things: fresh juices, milkshakes, *falooda*, and – don't miss this – fruit with fresh cream (the custard apple is so good you'll die). Strategically placed at the entrance to Haji Ali Mosque, it's a great place to cool off after the pilgrimage.

Cafe Noorani
NORTH INDIAN $$

(Map p746; Tardeo Rd, Haji Ali Circle; mains ₹75-275; ⊘8am-11.30pm) This almost-retro diner is a requisite stop before or after visiting Haji Ali Mosque. On the menu is the gamut of Mughlai and Punjabi staples, all done well and cheap. The chicken tikka biryani (₹190) is so good, you'll forgive a bite or two of gristle.

Neel
NORTH INDIAN $$$

(Map p746; ☑61577777; Gate No 5 & 6, Mahalaxmi Racecourse; mains ₹445-685; ⊘noon-3pm & 7pm-midnight) Funky, all-white tree-branch interiors and ridiculously beautiful crowds aside, this hip restaurant and lounge dishes out mostly Awadhi/Northwest Frontier cuisine with creative adjustments. The outdoor seating is canopied by grand old trees. Reserve on weekends.

Western Suburbs

North Mumbai is home to the city's trendiest dining, centered on Bandra West and Juhu. Look out for the Juhu branch of Mahesh Lunch Home (p759), and the Bandra outposts of Suzette (p758), Basilico (p757) and Theobroma (p757).

★ Hotel Ram Ashraya
SOUTH INDIAN $

(Bhandarkar Rd, King's Circle, Matunga East; light meals ₹30-50; ⊘5am-9.30pm) Tucked away in the Tamil enclave of King's Circle, 80-year-old Ram Ashraya is beloved by southern families for its spectacular dosas, *idli* (round steamed rice cakes), *upma* (semolina cooked with onions, spices and coconut) and filter coffee. The menu, written on a chalkboard, changes daily. To get here, take the Central Line from CST; it's just outside the Matunga station's east exit.

★ Dakshinayan
SOUTH INDIAN $

(Map p755; Hotel Anand, Gandhigram Rd, Juhu; light meals ₹75-110; ⊘11am-3pm & 6-11pm, from 8am Sun) With *rangoli* on the walls, servers in lungis and groups of women in saris lunching (*chappals* off under the table), Dakshinayan channels Tamil Nadu. The delicately textured dosas, *idli* and *uttapam*, fresh coconut chutney, sambar, tomato and onion chutneys all taste homemade. Finish them off with a South Indian filter coffee – served in a stainless-steel set, so you can pour it back and forth to cool just like your grandma in Madras used to do.

Candies
CAFE $$

(Map p755; Mac Ronells, St Andrews Rd, Pali Hill, Bandra West; meals ₹70-170; ⊘8.30am-11pm Tue-Sun) Reminiscent of an Escher etching, with outdoor patios, balconies, and interior spaces stacked on top of one another and connected by staircases, Candies is quirky. Each eating area has plants and trees, lanterns and fairy lights, mosaic artwork, and gorgeous students wearing fedoras. The food is self-service, cheap and fine-enough, with sandwiches, rolls, salads and curries well represented. Weekends are crowded.

Yoga House
CAFE $$

(Map p755; www.yogahouse.in; 53 Chimbai Rd, Bandra West; light meals ₹140-250; ⊘8am-10pm) On the balcony of Yoga House's bungalow by the sea is a little cafe with tasty and creative veg fare – much of it vegan, much of it raw and all of it wholesome. Designed to complement the yoga on offer, it's possibly the healthiest food in Mumbai.

Prithvi Cafe
CAFE $$

(Map p755; Juhu Church Rd; light meals ₹70-165; ⊘9am-11pm) This bohemian cafe attached to the Prithvi Theatre is a cultural hub of

---

OFF THE BEATEN TRACK

KHOTACHIWADI

This storied *wadi* (hamlet) is a bastion clinging onto Mumbai life as it was before high-rises. A Christian enclave of elegant two-storey wooden mansions, it's 500m northeast of Girgaum Chowpatty, lying amid Mumbai's predominantly Hindu and Muslim neighbourhoods. These winding lanes allow a wonderful glimpse into a quiet life free of rickshaws and taxis. It's not large, but you can spend a little while wandering the alleyways and admiring the old homes and, around Christmas, their decorations.

To find Khotachiwadi, aim for **St Teresa's Church** (Map p746) on the corner of Jagannath Shankar Sheth Marg (JSS Marg) and Rajarammohan Roy Marg (RR Rd/Charni Rd), then head directly opposite the church on JSS Marg and duck down the second and third lanes on your left.

intellectuals, artists and theatre types who tuck themselves away in the lush, bamboo-heavy spot for coffee, sandwiches, *chaat* and Punjabi standards. The food is OK, but the setting is fantastic.

★ Culture Curry   SOUTH INDIAN $$$

(Kataria Rd, Matunga West; mains ₹319-499; 12-3.45pm & 7pm-12.30am) There's a lot more to southern food than *idli* and dosas. Exquisite dishes from all over the south, ranging from Andhra and Coorg to Kerala, are the specialty here. Veggies are particularly well served: the *rajma* curry (kidney and green beans in coconut gravy; ₹259) is extraordinary. The same owners run **Goa Portuguesa**, specialising in fiery Goan dishes, and the Maharashtrian **Diva Maharashtracha**, on the same block. From Matunga station, they're about 750m west along Kataria Rd.

Peshawri   NORTH INDIAN $$$

(28303030; ITC Maratha, Sahar Rd, Andheri East; mains ₹1500-2850; 12.45-2.45pm & 7-11.45pm) Make this Northwest Frontier restaurant, outside the international airport, your first or last stop in Mumbai. It's pricy, but you won't regret forking out the ₹2850 (feeds two) for the exquisite Sikandari *raan* (leg of spring lamb braised in malt vinegar, cinnamon and black cumin). The buttery dhal Bukhara (a thick black dhal cooked for a day, ₹700) is renowned.

Salt Water Café   FUSION $$$

(Map p755; 87 Chapel Rd, Bandra West; mains ₹320-690; 9am-1am) This foodie find made a name for itself by marrying dramatically opposing flavours (green peppercorn chicken with grape jus, cardamom and carrot mash), but most of the menu is just mouthwatering global fusion. The cool, minimalist design is as nice a change as the recipes – a lovely spot to twist up your tastebuds.

Caravan Serai   NORTHWEST FRONTIER $$$

(Map p755; 42631000; 1st fl, 155 Waterfield Rd, Bandra West; mains ₹225-375; noon-4pm & 7pm-1am) With white, cave-like walls, gentle lighting and glass beads, Caravan Serai feels like a glamorous desert yurt. The mostly northern cuisine is accessorised with southern dishes and exciting creations like 'tandoori salad'. Also a great place for a drink. Reserve on weekends. Downstairs, **Bora Bora** (Map p755; mains ₹225-375; noon-1am) is super popular for all-evening-long drinks and starters.

Eat Around the Corner   CAFE $$$

(Map p755; cnr 24th & 30th Rd; light meals ₹150-200, mains ₹250-600; 7am-1am) The cool decor, cosy outdoor seating, modelesque clientele and novel salad and sandwich options make for a fun lunch, even if the food doesn't quite reach its potential.

Drinking & Nightlife

Mumbai has loads of places to drink – from hole-in-the-wall beer bars and chichi lounges to brash, multilevel superclubs – but the 25% liquor tax can bring bill shock. You're also technically supposed to have a licence to drink in Maharashtra; you won't have any problem without one, but some bars require you to buy a temporary one, for a nominal fee.

Wednesday and Thursday are big nights at some clubs, as well as the traditional Friday and Saturday; there's usually a cover charge. Dress codes apply, so don't rock up in shorts and sandals. The trend in Mumbai is towards resto-lounges as opposed to full-on nightclubs.

If it's the caffeine buzz you're after, Barista and Café Coffee Day cafes are ubiquitous in Mumbai.

Colaba

Cafe Mondegar   BAR

(Map p738; 22020591; Metro House, 5A Shahid Bhagat Singh Rd, Colaba; 7am-12.30am) 'Mondys' draws a healthy foreign crowd, but with a mix of locals, who all cosy up together in the small space, bonding over the excellent jukebox, one of Mumbai's few. Good music, good people.

5 All Day   LOUNGE

(Map p738; www.5allday.in; Lansdowne Rd; noon-12.30am;) The bartender here takes his work *really* seriously, and it works: the drinks, including several of his own invention, are fabulous, like the whisky crusta (whisky, fresh tomato, mint leaves and sour mix). The food (mains ₹295 to ₹555) is also great, all in a sleek, contemporary, all-white space lit with candles.

Woodside Inn   BAR

(Map p738; Wodehouse Rd, Regal Circle; 10am-1am) It's not a sleek lounge filled with Bollywood stars. It's just a cosy, friendly place with a traditional European look, not-too-loud classic rock (think Nirvana, Dire Straits), good wine and drinks (some served in jars), and excellent food (mains ₹295 to ₹425).

Harbour Bar
BAR

(Map p738; Taj Mahal Palace, Mumbai, Apollo Bunder; ⏱11am-11.45pm) The views here – of the Gateway of India and boats in the harbour – are spectacular, and the drinks are reasonably priced (for Mumbai; from ₹350/750 for a beer/wine). Snuggle up in a booth beside one of the big picture windows as the day's winding down on Apollo Bunder.

Busaba
BAR

(Map p738; ☎22043779; 4 Mandlik Marg; ⏱6.30pm-1am) Sunken couches and contemporary Buddha art give this restaurant-bar a loungey vibe. Cocktails are pricey but potent (₹425 to ₹550), and a DJ plays house on weekends. The upstairs restaurant serves pan-Asian (mains ₹425 to ₹575); its back room feels like a posh treehouse. Reserve ahead for dinner.

Leopold's Café
BAR

(Map p738; cnr Colaba Causeway & Nawroji F Rd, Colaba; ⏱7.30am-12.30am) Love it or hate it, most tourists end up at this Mumbai travellers' institution at one time or another. Around since 1871, Leopold's has wobbly ceiling fans, crap service and a rambunctious atmosphere conducive to swapping tales with strangers. There's food, but the lazy evening beers, especially the 3L yards, are the real draw.

Wink
NIGHTCLUB

(Vivanta by Taj - President, 90 Cuffe Pde; ⏱6pm-1am) Weekends, including Sunday, are thumping here, but it's a classy place even then, with its sophisticated decor (low beige sofas, intricately carved screens), long whiskey list and famous Winktinis. A DJ spins nightly, though, to a slightly more grown-up crowd, some of whom are guests at the hotel.

Fort Area & Churchgate

Mocha Bar
CAFE

(Map p742; 82 Veer Nariman Rd, Churchgate; coffees ₹60-150; ⏱10am-1.30am; 📶) This atmospheric Arabian-styled cafe is often filled to the brim with students deep in esoteric conversation or gossip. Cosy, low-cushioned seating (including some old cinema seats), exotic coffees, shakes and teas, and global comfort cuisine promote an intellectually chillaxed vibe. Sometimes the wi-fi works.

QUEER MUMBAI

Mumbai's LGBTQ scene is still not as big as you might expect, especially for women, but it's gaining momentum. Start with visiting **Gay Bombay** (www.gaybombay.org) and **Queer Azaadi Mumbai** (www.queerazaadi.wordpress.com) for listings of events and other queer-community info. Queer Azaadi organises Mumbai's **Pride Parade**, usually held in February.

Though published erratically, the pioneering magazine **Bombay Dost** (www.bombay-dost.co.in) is a great resource on happenings around town. *Bombay Dost* also founded the **Humsafar Trust** (Map p755; ☎26673800; www.humsafar.org; Old BMC Bldg, 1st fl, Nehru Rd, Vakola, Santa Cruz East), with tons of programs and workshops; one of its support groups organises the monthly gathering 'Sunday High'.

The excellent **Kashish Mumbai International Queer Film Festival** (www.mumbaiqueerfest.com), with a mix of Indian and foreign films, made its debut in 2010 and is held each May.

No dedicated LGBTQ bars/clubs have yet opened, but gay-friendly 'safe house' venues often host private gay parties (announced on Gay Bombay). The only regular club is **Voodoo Pub** (Map p738; ☎22841959; Kamal Mansion, Arthur Bunder Rd; cover ₹300), a dark and sweaty bar that has hosted Mumbai's only regular gay night on Saturdays since 1994. There's a DJ every night (usually free entry) and staff are screened for open-mindedness, so it's gay-friendly all week long too. The sign outside says 'Slip Disc Restaurant Bar & Permit Room'.

One of the best places to hook into the scene (and also buy stuff) is D'Kloset. Most of the merch is for men, but it also has films and books, including the story collection *Out!*, published by **Queer Ink** (www.queer-ink.com).

Starbucks CAFE

(Map p742; www.starbucks.in; Veer Nariman Rd; coffees ₹95-180; ☺8am-10pm) We were sceptical too, but when this first Starbucks cafe opened in 2012, Mumbai's young, fun and beautiful were so, so happy that it's worth a visit just to see their joy. The coffee is all fair-trade and sourced from India.

Amadeus LOUNGE

(Map p742; NCPA, Nariman Point; ☺7.30pm-1.30am Fri-Sun) The NCPA's elegant Spanish restaurant opens its lounge, with great DJs, on weekends for the SoBo crowd.

Café Universal BAR

(Map p742; 299 Shahid Bhagat Singh Rd, Fort; ☺9am-11pm Mon-Sat, 4-11pm Sun) A little bit of France near CST. The Universal has an art nouveau look to it, with butterscotch-colour walls, a wood-beam ceiling and marble chandeliers, and is a cosy place for happy hour and Kingfisher draughts (₹160).

Dome LOUNGE

(Map p742; Hotel InterContinental, 135 Marine Dr, Churchgate; ☺5.30pm-1.30am) This white-on-white rooftop lounge has awesome views of Mumbai's curving seafront while cocktails beckon the hip young things of Mumbai nightly.

Western Suburbs

⭐ **Aer** LOUNGE

(Four Seasons Hotel, 34th fl, 114 Dr E Moses Rd, Worli; cover ₹2000-2500 Wed-Sat after 8pm; ☺5.30pm-1.30pm) With astounding city views on one side and equally impressive sea and sunset views on the other, rooftop Aer is India's tallest and most stunning lounge. You'll need to remortgage your home for a cocktail (₹850), but the ₹350 Kingfishers are a steal at these views. A DJ spins low-key house and techno nightly from 9pm, but Aer is more about the eye candy, both near and far.

Mocha Mojo CAFE

(Map p755; Hill Rd, Bandra West, near Holy Family Hospital; ☺10am-12.30am; ☏) It's a little run-down, but the Mocha's Bandra branch is still good for coffee, all-day breakfasts or a beer in a funky, futuristic space.

Big Nasty BAR

(Map p755; 1st fl, 12 Union Park, Khar West, above Shatranj Napoli; ☺7pm-12.30am) The decor may be industrial, but the Nasty is fun and unpretentious. It's best known for its cheap drinks – beers (including, mysteriously, Miller High Life) from ₹160, glasses of wine from ₹350 – and its 'all-American classic beef burger' (₹240).

Trilogy NIGHTCLUB

(Map p755; Hotel Sea Princess, Juhu Tara Rd, Juhu; cover per couple after 11pm ₹2000; ☺closed Tue) Trilogy was closed at research time for 'renovations' (actually bureaucratic permit snafus), but Mumbaikars expect it to return to its throne as nightclub queen of Mumbai as soon as it's back. The trilevel space, like the clientele, is gorgeous, with a black granite dance floor lit up by LED cube lights that go off like an epileptic Lite-Brite. The imported sound system favours house and hip-hop.

Shiro LOUNGE

(☏66511201; www.shiro.co.in; Bombay Dyeing Mills Compound, Worli; ☺7.30pm-1.30am) At Shiro, water pours from the hands of towering Japanese faux-stone goddesses into lotus ponds, which reflect shimmering light on the walls. It's totally over the top, but the drinks (as well as the Asian-fusion dishes) are excellent and the DJs spin some mean house (Saturdays) and retro (Fridays).

Ghetto BAR

(Map p746; ☏23538418; 30 Bhulabhai Desai Marg, opposite Tirupathi Apts; ☺7pm-1am) Just a grungy, graffiti-covered hang-out blaring rock nightly to a dedicated set of regulars.

Olive Bar & Kitchen BAR

(Map p755; ☏26058228; www.olivebarandkitchen.com; 14 Union Park, Khar West; ☺7.30pm-1am daily, plus noon-3.30pm Sat & Sun) Hip, snooty and favoured by film stars, this gorgeous Mediterranean-style restaurant and bar has light and delicious food (mains ₹595 to ₹1095), soothing DJ sounds and pure Ibiza-meets-Mykonos decor. Thursday and weekends are packed. There's a second branch (Map p746; ☏40859595; Gate No 8, Mahalaxmi Racecourse; ☺noon-3.30pm & 7.30pm-1.30am) in Mahalaxmi.

Toto's Garage BAR

(Map p755; ☏26005494; 30th Rd, Bandra West; ☺6pm-1am) Forget the beautiful people. Toto's is a down-to-earth local dive done up in a mechanic's theme where you can go in your dirty clothes, drink pitchers of beer and listen to AC/DC. Get there early or you won't get a seat.

Elbo Room PUB
(Map p755; St Theresa Rd, Khar West, off 33rd Rd; ☺11am-1am) This reminiscent-of-home pub is a good bet for wines by the glass (₹350 to ₹500). The Italian-Indian menu is best enjoyed on the plant-filled terrace, where a screen is often set up for English Premier League and Bundesliga football matches.

Hungry Birds BAR
(Map p755; 3rd Khar Rd, Khar West; ☺7pm-1am) Conveniently around the corner from the train station in leafy Khar, the Hungry Birds has lots of bright colours, cheap drinks and chicken popcorn.

☆ Entertainment

The *Mumbai Mirror*, an insert of the *Times of India*, lists major events and other Mumbai happenings, as do **Time Out Mumbai** (www.timeoutmumbai.net; ₹50), **www.nh7.in**

(live-music listings) and **Mumbai Boss** (www.mumbaiboss.com).

It would be a crime not to see a movie in India's film capital. Unfortunately, Hindi films aren't shown with English subtitles. The cinemas we've listed all show English-language movies, along with some Bollywood numbers.

Mumbai has some great arts festivals: the **Mumbai Film Festival** (www.mumbaifilmfest. org; ☺Oct) in October is excellent, as is May's Kashish-Mumbai International Queer Film Festival (p762). Prithvi Theatre's November festival (p765) has a packed program of excellent drama, and **Mumbai Sanskruti** (☺Jan) sees two days of Hindustani classical music.

★**Bluefrog** LIVE MUSIC
(☎61586158; www.bluefrog.co.in; D/2 Mathuradas Mills Compound, Senapati Bapat Marg, Lower Parel;

BOLLYWOOD DREAMS

Mumbai is the glittering epicentre of India's gargantuan Hindi-language film industry. From silent beginnings with a cast of all-male actors (some in drag) in the 1913 epic *Raja Harishchandra* and the first talkie, *Lama Ara* (1931), it now churns out more than 1000 films a year – more than Hollywood. Not surprising considering it has a captive audience of one-sixth of the world's population, as well as a sizable Non-Resident Indian (NRI) following.

Every part of India has its regional film industry, but Bollywood continues to entrance the nation with its escapist formula in which all-singing, all-dancing lovers fight and conquer the forces keeping them apart. These days, Hollywood-inspired thrillers and action extravaganzas vie for moviegoers' attention alongside the more family-oriented saccharine formulas.

Bollywood stars can attain near godlike status in India and star-spotting is a favourite pastime in Mumbai's posher establishments. You can also see the stars' homes, as well as a film/TV studio with **Bollywood Tours** (www.bollywoodtours.in; 8hr tours per person ₹6000), but you're not guaranteed to see a dance number and you may spend much of it in traffic.

Extra, Extra!

Studios sometimes want Westerners as extras to add a whiff of international flair (or provocative dress, which locals often won't wear) to a film. It's become so common, in fact, that 100,000 junior actors nearly went on strike in 2008 to protest, among other things, losing jobs to foreigners, who work for less money and worse working conditions.

If you're still game, just hang around Colaba (especially the Salvation Army hostel) where studio scouts, recruiting for the following day's shooting, will find you. A day's work, which can be up to 16 hours, pays ₹500. You'll get lunch and snacks but usually no transport. The day can be long and hot with loads of standing around the set; not everyone has a positive experience. Complaints range from lack of food and water to dangerous situations and intimidation when extras don't comply with the director's orders. Others describe the behind-the-scenes peek as a fascinating experience. Before agreeing to anything, always ask for the scout's identification and go with your gut.

admission after 9pm Sun & Tue-Thu ₹350, Fri & Sat ₹600; ☉6.30pm-1.30am Tue-Sat, from 11.30am Sun) Bluefrog is a concert space, production studio, restaurant and one of Mumbai's most happening spaces. It hosts exceptional local and international acts, and has space-age booth seating in the intimate main room. Happy hour – also known as 'one on the Frog' – is buy one, get one free 6.30pm to 9pm.

National Centre for the Performing Arts THEATRE, LIVE MUSIC
(NCPA; Map p742; ☑66223737, box office 22824567; www.ncpamumbai.com; Marine Dr & Sri V Saha Rd, Nariman Point; tickets ₹200-800; ☉box office 9am-7pm) Spanning 800 sq metres, this cultural centre is the hub of Mumbai's music, theatre and dance scene. In any given week, it might host experimental plays, poetry readings, art exhibitions, Bihari dance troupes, ensembles from Europe or Indian classical music, as well as the occasional dance workshop open to the public. Many performances are free. The **box office** (Map p742) is at the end of NCPA Marg.

Prithvi Theatre THEATRE
(Map p755; ☑26149546; www.prithvitheatre.org; Juhu Church Rd, Juhu; tickets ₹80-300) A great place to see both Hindi and English-language theatre. Its excellent international theatre festival in November showcases what's going on in contemporary Indian theatre and includes performances by international troupes and artists. The theatre also has film screenings and a charming cafe.

Liberty Cinema CINEMA, LIVE MUSIC
(Map p742; ☑9820027841; 41/42 New Marine Lines, near Bombay Hospital) The stunning art-deco Liberty was once the queen of Hindi film – think red-carpet openings with Dev Anand – while Bombay's other cinemas were focused on Hollywood. It fell on hard times but has been making a valiant effort to be awesome again and now occasionally hosts film festivals and live music in terribly atmospheric surrounds.

Wankhede Stadium SPORTS
(Mumbai Cricket Association; Map p742; ☑22795500; www.mumbaicricket.com; D Rd, Churchgate; ☉ticket office 11.30am-7pm Mon-Sat) Test matches and One Day Internationals are played a few times a year in season (October to April). Contact the Cricket Association for ticket information; for a test match

you'll probably have to pay for the full five days.

Cooperage Football Ground SPORTS
(Map p738; ☑22024020; www.wifa.in; MK Rd, Colaba; tickets ₹50-250) The recently renovated Cooperage, home to FC Air India, Mumbai FC and ONGC FC, hosts national-league and local football (soccer) matches between September and April, as well as the Rose Cup in July/August. Tickets are available at the gate, though many local matches are free.

Regal Cinema CINEMA
(Map p738; ☑22021017; Shahid Bhagat Singh Rd, Regal Circle, Colaba) Check out the art deco architecture.

Eros CINEMA
(Map p742; ☑22822335; MK Rd, Churchgate; tickets ₹100-150) When in Mumbai it's hard to ignore the fact that you're at the epicentre of the world's biggest film industry. To experience Bollywood blockbusters in situ, the Eros is the place.

Metro Big CINEMA
(☑39894040; MG Rd, New Marine Lines, Fort; tickets ₹120-600) This grand dame of Bombay talkies was just renovated into a multiplex.

🛍 Shopping

Mumbai is India's great marketplace, with some of the best shopping in the country – in its stores, ancient bazaars and on sidewalks.

Be sure to spend a day at the markets around CST for the classic Mumbai shopping experience. In Fort, booksellers, with surprisingly good wares (not all pirated), set up shop daily on the sidewalks around Flora Fountain. Snap up a bargain backpacking wardrobe at **Fashion Street** (Map p742; MG Rd), the strip of stalls lining MG Rd between Cross and Azad Maidans, or on Bandra's Linking Rd, near Waterfield Rd. Hone your bargaining skills. Kemp's Corner has many good shops for designer threads.

🛍 Colaba

Bungalow 8 CLOTHING, ACCESSORIES
(Map p738; www.bungaloweight.com; 1st, 2nd & 3rd fls, Grants Bldg, Arthur Bunder Rd, Colaba; ☉10.30am-7.30pm) Bungalow 8 is so cool, you'll want to be it. Original, high-end, artisanal clothing, jewellery, home decor and

other objects of beauty, spread across three loftlike floors.

Phillips
ANTIQUES

(Map p738; www.phillipsantiques.com; Wodehouse Rd, Colaba; ⊙10am-7pm Mon-Sat) The 150-year-old Phillips has nizam-era royal silver, wooden ceremonial masks, Victorian glass and various other gorgeous things that you never knew you wanted. It also has high-quality reproductions of old photos, maps and paintings, and a warehouse shop of big antiques.

Search Word
BOOKS

(Map p738; ☑22852521; Metro House, Colaba Causeway, Colaba; ⊙11.30am-9pm) Small and tidy, with a choice selection of books and magazines.

Cottonworld Corp
CLOTHING

(Map p738; ☑22850060; Mandlik Marg; ⊙10.30am-8pm Mon-Sat, noon-8pm Sun) Small chain selling stylish Indian-Western-hybrid goods. Entrance is behind State Bank of India.

Bombay Electric
CLOTHING

(Map p738; www.bombayelectric.in; 1 Reay House, Best Marg, Colaba; ⊙11am-9pm) High fashion is the calling at this trendy, slightly overhyped unisex boutique, which it sells at top rupee alongside artisanal accessories and a handful of fashionable antiques.

Central Cottage Industries Emporium
HANDICRAFTS, SOUVENIRS

(Map p738; ☑22027537; www.cottageemporium. in; Chhatrapati Shivaji Marg; ⊙10am-6pm) Fairtrade souvenirs. Now has a second Colaba branch (Map p738; Kamal Mansion, Arthur Bunder Rd; ⊙11am-7pm Mon-Sat).

🔒 Fort Area & Churchgate

★Kitab Khana
BOOKS

(Map p742; www.kitabkhana.in; Somaiya Bhavan, 45/47 MG Rd, Fort; ⊙10.30am-7.30pm) This new bookstore has a brilliantly curated selection of books, all of which are 20% off all the time. Food for Thought (Map p742; www.cafe foodforthought.com; light meals ₹120-180), the little cafe in back, does a mean sabudana khichdi (sago fried with spices).

★Contemporary Arts & Crafts
HANDICRAFTS

(Map p742; www.cac.co.in; 210 DN Rd; ⊙10.30am-7.30pm) The CAC stocks contemporary, inventive takes on traditional crafts: these are not your usual handmade souvenirs. Home goods fill much of the store, but plenty of pieces will fit in a suitcase.

Artisans' Centre for Art, Craft & Design
CLOTHING, ACCESSORIES

(Map p742; ☑22673040; artisanscentre@gmail. com; 1st fl, 52-56 Dr VB Gandhi Marg, Kala Ghoda; ⊙11am-7pm) This heritage space hosts exhibitions of high-end handmade goods – from couture and jewellery to handicrafts and luxury khadi (homespun cloth) – by artisans from around the country.

Khadi & Village Industries Emporium
CLOTHING

(Map p742; Khadi Bhavan; 286 Dr Dadabhai Naoroji Rd, Fort; ⊙10.30am-6.30pm Mon-Sat) Khadi Bhavan is dusty, 1940s timewarp that's so old it's new again. Ready-made traditional Indian clothing, silk and khadi, shoes (including great handmade leather chappals for ladies and gents) and handicrafts are sublimely old-school.

Tribes India
HANDICRAFTS

(Map p742; Gate No 3, GPO; ⊙10.30am-6pm Mon-Sat) ✏ Right in the post office, this stall sells handmade goods from tribal communities across India.

Chimanlals
HANDICRAFTS

(Map p742; www.chimanlals.com; Wallace Rd, Fort; ⊙9.30am-6pm Mon-Fri, to 5pm Sat) The beautiful traditional printed papers here will make you start writing letters.

Royal Music Collection
MUSIC

(Map p742; 192 Kitab Mahal, Dr DN Rd, Fort; ⊙11am-9pm Mon-Sat) Brilliant street stall selling vintage records (from ₹250).

Fabindia
CLOTHING

(Map p742; www.fabindia.com; Jeroo Bldg, 137 MG Rd, Kala Ghoda; ⊙10am-8pm) Founded as a means to get traditional fabric artisans' wares to market, Fabindia has cotton and silk fashions and homewares in a modern-meets-traditional Indian shop.

Chetana Book Centre
BOOKS

(Map p742; www.chetana.com; K Dubash Marg, Kala Ghoda; ⊙10.30am-7.30pm Mon-Sat) This great spirituality bookstore has lots of books on Hinduism and a whole section on 'Afterlife/Death/Psychic'.

Cotton Cottage
CLOTHING

(Map p742; Agra Bldg, 121 MG Rd, Kala Ghoda; ⊙10am-9pm) Stock up on simple cotton kurtas and various pants – *salwars, churidars, patiala* – for the road.

Rhythm House
MUSIC STORE

(Map p742; ☑ 22842835; 40 K Dubash Marg, Fort; ⊙10am-8.30pm Mon-Sat, 11am-8.30pm Sun) Nonpirated CDs, plus tickets to concerts, plays and festivals.

Standard Supply Co
PHOTOGRAPHY

(Map p742; ☑ 22612468; Walchand Hirachand Marg, Fort; ⊙10.30am-7pm Mon-Sat) Everything you could possibly need for digital and film photography.

Oxford Bookstore
BOOKS

(Map p742; www.oxfordbookstore.com; Apeejay House, 3 Dinsha Wachha Marg, Churchgate; ⊙8am-10pm) Spacious, with a good selection of travel books and a tea bar.

🔒 Kalbadevi to Mahalaxmi

Markets
MARKET

You can buy just about anything in the dense bazaars north of CST, which tumble one into the next in a mass of people and stuff. **Crawford Market** (Mahatma Phule Market; Map p746; cnr DN & Lokmanya Tilak Rds), with fruit and vegetables, is the last outpost of British Bombay before the tumult of the central bazaars begins. Bas-reliefs by Rudyard Kipling's father, Lockwood Kipling, adorn the Norman Gothic exterior.

Mangaldas Market (Map p746), traditionally home to traders from Gujarat, is a mini-town, complete with lanes, of fabrics. Even if you're not the type to have your clothes tailored, drop by **DD Dupattawala** (Map p746; Shop No 217, 4th Lane, Mangaldas Market) for pretty scarves and dupattas at fixed prices. **Zaveri Bazaar** (Map p746) for jewellery and **Bhuleshwar Market** (Map p746; cnr Sheikh Menon St & M Devi Marg) for fruit and veg are just north of here.

Chor Bazaar (Map p746) is known for its antiques, though nowadays much of it is reproductions; the main area of activity is Mutton St, where shops specialise in 'antiques' and miscellaneous junk. Dhabu St, to the east, is lined with fine leather goods.

Mini Market/ Bollywood Bazaar
ANTIQUES, SOUVENIRS

(Map p746; ☑ 23472427; 33/31 Mutton St; ⊙11am-8pm Sat-Thu) Sells vintage Bollywood posters

and other movie ephemera as well as old little trinkets. Call if you get lost.

Anokhi
CLOTHING

(Map p746; www.anokhi.com; Dr AR Ragnekar Marg; ⊙10.30am-8pm Mon-Sat) Gets the East–West balance just right, with men's and women's clothes and bedding in block-printed silk and cotton.

Shrujan
HANDICRAFTS

(Map p746; www.shrujan.org; Sagar Villa, Bhulabhai Desai Marg, Breach Candy, opp Navroze Apts; ⊙10am-7.30pm Mon-Sat) 🖋 Selling the intricate embroidery work of 3500 women in 114 villages in Kutch, Gujarat, the nonprofit Shrujan helps women earn a livelihood while preserving the spectacular embroidery traditions of the area. The sophisticated clothing, wall hangings and purses make great gifts. There's also a (hard-to-find) **Juhu branch** (Map p755; Hatkesh Society, 6th North South Rd, JVPD Scheme; ⊙10am-7.30pm Mon-Sat).

Crossword
BOOKS

(Map p746; Mohammedbhai Mansion, NS Patkar Marg, Kemp's Corner; ⊙11am-8.30pm) Enormous, with a Café Moshe (p758) inside.

BX Furtado & Sons
MUSIC STORE

(Map p746; www.furtadosonline.com; Jer Mahal, Dhobi Talao; ⊙10.30am-7.30pm Mon-Sat) The best place in Mumbai for musical instruments – sitars, tablas, accordions and local and imported guitars. The branch around the corner on Kalbadevi Rd is pianos and sheet music only.

🔒 Western Suburbs

Indian Hippy
ART

(Map p755; ☑ 8080822022; www.hippy.in; 17/C Sherly Rajan Rd, off Carter Rd, Bandra West; portraits from ₹10,000; ⊙by appt) Because you need to have your portrait hand-painted in the style of a vintage Bollywood poster. Bring (or email) a photo. Also sells vintage LPs and film posters.

Play Clan
SOUVENIRS, CLOTHING

(Map p755; www.theplayclan.com; Libra Towers, Hill Rd, Bandra West; ⊙11am-8.30pm) Mumbai has a slew of stores selling fun, kitschy, design-y goods. Play Clan is the priciest, but also has the best stuff, like tote bags printed with futurist portraits of Vivekananda and pillows embroidered with sequined autorickshaws.

MUMBAI (BOMBAY) INFORMATION

Kishore Silk House CLOTHING, HANDICRAFTS
(Bhandarkar Rd, Matunga East; ⏰10am-8.30pm Tue-Sun) Handwoven saris and dhotis from Tamil Nadu and Kerala in all the best old-fashioned styles. But the real star here are the finely woven, surprisingly super-absorbant cotton towels – perfect for travelling.

ℹ️ Information

EMERGENCY

Call the police (📞100) for emergencies.

INTERNET ACCESS

Anita CyberCafé (Map p742; Cowasji Patel Rd, Fort; per hr ₹30; ⏰9.30am-10pm Mon-Sat, from 2pm Sun) Opposite one of Mumbai's best chai stalls (open evenings).

Poonam Cybercafé (Map p738; Lala Nigam St, Colaba Market; per hr ₹20; ⏰10am-10pm Mon-Sat, 8.30am-2pm Sun)

Portasia (Map p742; Kitab Mahal, Dr Dadabhai Naoroji Rd, Fort; per hr ₹30; ⏰9am-9pm Mon-Sat) Entrance is down a little alley; look for the sign hanging from the covered archway.

MEDIA

To find out what's going on in Mumbai, check out *Time Out Mumbai* and **Mumbai Boss** (www. mumbaiboss.com). The *Hindustan Times* is the best paper; its *Café* insert, as well as the *Mumbai Mirror* insert of the *Times of India*, are good what's-on guides.

Look for the free folding neighbourhood maps by **Locus City Cards** in high-end hotels and restaurants.

MEDICAL SERVICES

Bombay Hospital (Map p742; 📞22067676, ambulance 22067309; www.bombayhospital.com; 12 New Marine Lines)

Breach Candy Hospital (Map p746; 📞23672888, emergency 23667809; www. breachcandyhospital.org; 60 Bhulabhai Desai Marg, Breach Candy) Best in Mumbai, if not India.

Colaba Chemist (Map p738; 📞22832848; 27A Arthur Bunder Rd; ⏰8.30am-11pm) Delivers.

New Royal Chemists (Map p742; 📞22004051; 41/42 New Marine Lines; ⏰24hr) Free delivery 7am to 11pm.

MONEY

ATMs are everywhere, and foreign-exchange offices changing cash and travellers cheques – including Akbar Travels (p768) and Thomas Cook's Fort (p768) and **Colaba** (Map p738; 📞66092608; Colaba Causeway; ⏰9.30am-6pm) branches – are also plentiful.

POST

The **main post office** (Map p742; behind Chhatrapati Shivaji Terminus; ⏰10am-6pm) is an imposing building beside CST. **Poste restante** (⏰10am-3pm Mon-Sat) is at the 'Delivery Department'. Letters should be addressed c/o Poste Restante, Mumbai GPO, Mumbai 400 001. Bring your passport to collect mail. Opposite the post office, under the tree, are parcel-wallahs who will stitch up your parcel for ₹40.

Colaba Post Office (Map p738; Henry Rd) Convenient branch.

TELEPHONE

Call 📞197 for directory assistance.

TOURIST INFORMATION

Indiatourism (Government of India Tourist Office; Map p742; 📞22074333; www.incredibleindia.com; Western Railways Reservation Complex, 123 Maharshi Karve Rd; ⏰8.30am-6pm Mon-Fri, to 2pm Sat) Provides information for the entire country, as well as contacts for Mumbai guides and homestays.

Maharashtra Tourism Development Corporation Booth (MTDC; Map p738; 📞22841877; Apollo Bunder; ⏰8.30am-4pm Tue-Sun, 8.30am-9pm weekends) For city bus tours.

Maharashtra Tourism Development Corporation (MTDC; Map p742; 📞22044040; www. maharashtratourism.gov.in; Madame Cama Rd, opposite LIC Bldg, Nariman Point; ⏰10am-5pm Mon-Sat, closed 2nd & 4th Sat) Maharashtra Tourism Development Corporation has its head office in Mumbai. Most major towns throughout the state have offices, too, but they're generally only useful for booking MTDC accommodation and tours. Sunday is not a business day, and many government offices also remain closed on alternate Saturdays.

TRAVEL AGENCIES

Akbar Travels (www.akbartravelsonline.com; ⏰10am-7pm Mon-Fri, to 6pm Sat) Colaba (Map p738; 📞22823434; 30 Alipur Trust Bldg, Shahid Bhagat Singh Rd); Fort (Map p742; 📞22633434; 167/169 Dr Dadabhai Naoroji Rd) Extremely helpful, with good exchange rates.

Thomas Cook (Map p742; 📞61603333; 324 Dr Dadabhai Naoroji Rd, Fort; ⏰9.30am-6pm Mon-Sat)

VISA EXTENSIONS

Foreigners' Regional Registration Office (FRRO; Map p746; 📞22620446; www.immigrationindia.nic.in; Annexe Bldg No 2, CID, Badaruddin Tyabji Marg, near Special Branch; ⏰9.30am-1pm Mon-Fri) Technically, the FRRO can issue extensions on tourist visas with 'reasonable grounds of delay' for US$70, but applications are reviewed on a case-by-case basis; don't count on it.

ⓘ Getting There & Away

AIR
Airports

Mumbai is the main international gateway to South India and has the busiest network of domestic flights. **Chhatrapati Shivaji International Airport** (Map p755; BOM; ☑ 66851010; www.csia.in), about 30km from the city centre, has been undergoing a $2 billion modernisation since its privatisation in 2006. At press time, the shiny new terminal T2, serving both domestic and international flights, was expected to open in 2014 and the existing domestic terminals converted to cargo.

At time of writing, the airport comprises three domestic (1A, 1B and 1C; Map p746) and two international terminals (2B and 2C; Map p746). The domestic side is accessed via Vile Parle and is known locally as Santa Cruz airport, while the international, with its entrance 5km away in Andheri, goes locally by Sahar. Both terminals have ATMs, foreign-exchange counters and tourist-information booths. A free shuttle bus runs between the two every 30 minutes for ticket-holders.

Airlines

Travel agencies and websites are best for booking flights; airline offices are increasingly directing customers to their call centres. The following domestic and international airlines maintain offices in town and/or at the airport:

Major nonstop domestic flights from Mumbai include the following:

DESTINATION	SAMPLE LOWEST ONE-WAY FARE (₹)	DURATION (HR)
Bengaluru	5500	1½
Chennai	7200	2
Delhi	7600	2
Goa	4000	1
Hyderabad	4000	1½
Jaipur	5500	1¾
Kochi	7200	2
Kolkata	8200	2¾

Air India (Map p742; ☑ 27580777, airport 28318666; www.airindia.com; Air India Bldg, cnr Marine Dr & Madame Cama Rd, Nariman Point; ⊙ 9.15am-6.30pm Mon-Fri, to 5.15pm Sat & Sun)

Cathay Pacific (☑ 66572222, airport 66859002/3; www.cathaypacific.com; 2 Brady Gladys Plaza, Senapati Bapat Marg, Lower Parel; ⊙ 9.30am-5.30pm Mon-Sat)

Emirates Airlines (Map p742; ☑ 33773377, airport 26829917; www.emirates.com; 3 Mittal Chambers, 228 Nariman Point; ⊙ 9am-5.30pm Mon-Sat)

GoAir (☑ airport 26264789; www.goair.in)

IndiGo (Map p738; ☑ call centre 1800 1803838; www.goindigo.in)

Jet Airways (Map p738; ☑ call centre 39893333; www.jetairways.com; Amarchand Mansion, Madame Cama Rd, Colaba; ⊙ 9.30am-6pm Mon-Fri, to 4pm Sat) Also handles JetLite bookings.

Qantas (Map p755; ☑ 61111818, airport 66859110; www.qantas.com.au; 4th fl, Sunteck Centre, 37-40 Subhash Rd, Vile Parle; ⊙ 9am-1.15pm & 2.30-5.30pm Mon-Fri)

SpiceJet (☑ airport 9920172863; www.spicejet.com)

Swiss (☑ 67137200; www.swiss.com; 10th fl, Urmi Estate, Ganpatrao Kadam Marg, Lower Parel; ⊙ 9am-5.30pm Mon-Sat)

Thai Airways (Map p742; ☑ 1800 1021225, airport 26828950; www.thaiairways.com; 2A Mittal Towers A Wing, Nariman Point; ⊙ 9.30am-5.30pm Mon-Fri, to 4pm Sat)

BUS

Numerous private operators and state governments run long-distance buses to and from Mumbai.

Long-distance government-run buses depart from the well-organised **Mumbai Central bus terminal** (Map p746; ☑ inquiry 23024075) right by Mumbai Central train station. They're cheaper and more frequent than private services, but the quality and crowd levels vary; **MSRTC** (Maharashtra State Road Transport Corporation; ☑ 1800 221250; www.msrtc.gov.in) is not as well developed as some of its counterparts in other states.

Private buses are usually more comfortable and simpler to book but can cost significantly more than government buses. Most depart from Dr Anadrao Nair Rd near Mumbai Central train station, but many buses to southern destinations depart from Paltan Rd, near Crawford Market. To check on departure times and current prices, visit **Citizen Travels** (Map p746; ☑ 23459695; D Block, Sitaram Bldg, Paltan Rd) or **National CTC** (Map p746; ☑ 23015652; Dr Anadrao Nair Rd), though most private-bus operators are similar in price and quality. Fares to popular destinations (like Goa) are up to 75% higher during holiday periods.

More convenient for Goa and southern destinations are the private buses run by **Chandni Travels** (Map p742; ☑ 22713901, 22676840), which depart six times a day from in front of Azad Maidan.

POPULAR LONG-DISTANCE BUS ROUTES:

DESTINATION	PRIVATE NON-AC/AC SLEEPER (₹)	GOVERNMENT NON-AC (₹)	DURATION (HR)
Ahmedabad	500/800	N/A	13
Aurangabad	500/800	461 (four daily)	10
Hyderabad	800/1100	N/A	16
Mahabaleshwar	450/600	302 (three daily)	7
Panaji (Panjim)	600/900	N/A	15
Pune	300 (AC seater)	202 (half-hourly)	4
Udaipur	800/1400	508 (one daily)	16

TRAIN

Three train systems operate out of Mumbai, but the most important services for travellers are Central Railways and Western Railways. Tickets for either system can be bought from any station in South Mumbai or the suburbs that has computerised ticketing.

Central Railways (☑139), handling services to the east, south, plus a few trains to the north, operates from CST. The **reservation centre** (Map p742; ☺8am-8pm Mon-Sat, to 2pm Sun) is on the southern side of CST. Foreign tourist–quota tickets and Indrail passes can be bought at Counter 52. You can buy nonquota tickets with a credit card (₹90 fee) at counters 10 and 11.

Some Central Railways trains depart from Dadar (D), a few stations north of CST, or Lokmanya Tilak (LTT), 16km north of CST.

Western Railways (☑139) has services to the north from Mumbai Central train station, usually called Bombay Central (BCT). The **reservation centre** (Map p742; ☺8am-8pm Mon-Sat, to 2pm Sun), opposite Churchgate station, has foreign tourist–quota tickets at counter 14.

MAJOR TRAINS FROM MUMBAI

DESTINATION	TRAIN NO & NAME	SAMPLE FARE (₹)	DURATION (HR)	DEPARTURE
Agra	12137 Punjab Mail	410/1139/1770/3050 (A)	22	7.40pm CST
Ahmedabad	12901 Gujarat Mail	232/616/910/1560 (A)	9	10pm BCT
	12009 Shatabdi Exp	721/1535	7	6.25am BCT
Aurangabad	11401 Nandigram Exp	176/480/715 (B)	7	4.35pm CST
	17617 Tapovan Exp	102/376 (C)	7	6.10am CST
Bengaluru	16529 Udyan Exp	363/1028/1600/2750 (A)	25	8.05am CST
Bhopal	12534 Pushpak Exp	325/889/1345/2295 (A)	13	8.20am CST
Chennai	12163 Chennai Exp	403/1116/1730/2980 (A)	23½	8.30pm CST
Delhi	12951 Rajdhani Exp	1550/2270/3870 (D)	16	4.40pm BCT
	12137 Punjab Mail	442/1231/1925/3330 (A)	25½	7.40pm CST
Hyderabad	12701 Hussainsagar Exp	312/854/1285/2195 (A)	14½	9.50pm CST
Indore	12961 Avantika Exp	320/878/1325/2265 (A)	14	7.05pm BCT
Jaipur	12955 Jaipur Exp	383/1059/1630/2805 (A)	18	6.50pm BCT
Kochi	16345 Netravati Exp	430/1222/1935 (B)	26½	11.40am LTT
Margao	10103 Mandovi Exp	288/811/1235/2105 (A)	12	6.55am CST
	12133 Mangalore Exp	308/842/1265 (B)	9	11.05pm CST
Pune	12127 Intercity Exp	76/277 (C)	3	6.45am CST

Station abbreviations: CST (Chhatrapati Shivaji Terminus); BCT (Mumbai Central); LTT (Lokmanya Tilak); D (Dadar) Fares: (A) sleeper/3AC/2AC/1AC, (B) sleeper/3AC/2AC, (C) sleeper/CC, (D) 3AC/2AC/1AC

ℹ️ Getting Around

TO/FROM THE AIRPORTS
International

The international airport has a **prepaid-taxi booth**, with set fares for every neighbourhood, outside arrivals. Taxis are ₹650/750 (non-AC/AC) to Colaba, Fort and Marine Dr, and ₹380/450 to Bandra, plus a ₹10 service charge and ₹10 per bag. The journey to Colaba takes about 45 minutes at night and 1½ to two hours during the day. Tips are not required.

Meru Cabs (☑ 44224422; www.merucabs. com) has a counter in arrivals. The air-conditioned metered taxis charge ₹27 for the first kilometre and ₹20 per kilometre thereafter (25% more at night). Routes are tracked by GPS, so no rip-offs!

Autorickshaws queue up at a little distance from arrivals, but they only go as far south as Bandra. They also charge 25% more midnight to 5am, plus ₹3 per large bag.

If you arrive during the day (but not during 'rush hour' – 6am to 11am) and are not weighed down with luggage, consider the **train**: take an autorickshaw (around ₹55) to Andheri train station and then the Churchgate or CST train (₹8, 45 minutes). You can also take bus 308 to Andheri station, or 321 to Vile Parle station; the bus stand is a short walk from the arrivals area.

A taxi from South Mumbai to the international airport should be around ₹500; negotiate a fare beforehand. Add ₹10 per bag and 25% to the meter charge at night, and add an hour onto the journey time between 4pm and 8pm.

Domestic

There's a **prepaid taxi counter** in the arrivals hall. A non-AC/AC taxi costs ₹380/465 to Colaba or Fort and ₹220/265 to Bandra, plus ₹10/15 service charge, ₹10 per bag and 25% extra at night.

Alternatively, catch an autorickshaw (around ₹35) or bus 312 from the airport to Vile Parle station, where you can get a train to Churchgate (₹7, 45 minutes). Don't attempt this during rush hour (6am to 11am).

BOAT

Both **PNP** (Map p738; ☑ 22885220) and **Maldar Catamarans** (☑ 22829695) run regular ferries to Mandwa (oneway ₹110 to ₹135), useful for access to Murud-Janjira and other parts of the Konkan Coast, avoiding the long bus trip out of Mumbai. Buy tickets near the Gateway of India.

BUS

Mumbai's great and cheap local buses are run by BEST (www.bestundertaking.com), whose website has a useful search facility for city routes. Fares start at ₹5 (day passes are ₹40), which you pay on-board. It's handy to learn Devanagiri numerals so you can read the bus numbers on the front. Beware of 'LTD' buses, which make limited stops.

The following useful buses all stop along Colaba Causeway and outside the museum.

DESTINATION	BUS NO
Breach Candy	132, 133
Churchgate	70, 106, 123, 132
CST & Crawford Market	1, 3, 21, 103, 124
Girgaum Chowpatty	103, 106, 107, 123
Haji Ali	83, 124, 132, 133
Hanging Gardens	103, 106, 108
Mani Bhavan	123
Mohammed Ali Rd	1, 3, 21
Mumbai Central train station	70, 124, 125

CAR

Cars with driver are generally hired for an eight-hour day and an 80km maximum, with additional charges if you go over. For a nonair-conditioned car, the going rate is about ₹1200.

METRO

Construction of a new elevated **metro** (www. mumbaimetroone.com) is under way. Phase One, which links Versova (northwest of Andheri) to Ghatkopar, passing near the airports en route, should be completed in late 2013. The underground Colaba–Bandra–Airport line is several years away.

MOTORCYCLE

Allibhai Premji Tyrewalla (Map p746; ☑ 23099313/9417; www.premjis.com; 205 Dr D Bhadkamkar (Lamington) Rd; ⊙10am-7pm Mon-Sat), around since 1922, sells new and used motorcycles with a guaranteed buy-back option. For two- to three-week 'rental' periods you'll still have to pay the full cost of the bike upfront. The company prefers to deal with longer-term schemes (two months or more), which work out cheaper anyway. A used 150cc or 225cc Bajaj or Honda costs around ₹50,000, with a buy-back price of around 60% after three months. Smaller bikes (100cc to 180cc) start at ₹25,000. The company can also arrange shipment of bikes overseas (around ₹30,000 to the UK).

TAXI & AUTORICKSHAW

Mumbai's black-and-yellow taxis are the most convenient way to get around southern Mumbai, and drivers *almost* always use the meter without prompting. The minimum fare is ₹19; after the first 1.6km, it's ₹12 per additional kilometre.

Autorickshaws are the name of the game from Bandra going north. The minimum fare is ₹15, up to 1.6km, and ₹10 per additional kilometre.

Taxis and autorickshaws have a combination of mechanical and electronic meters, which are not calibrated to display current fares. Drivers by law should keep the most current conversion chart in their vehicle; don't hesitate to ask to see it, or print out copies from the **Mumbai Traffic Police** (www.trafficpolicemumbai.org/Tariff-card_Auto_taxi_form.htm).

Both taxis and autorickshaws tack 25% onto the fare from midnight to 5am.

Tip: Mumbaikars tend to navigate by land-marks, not street names (especially new names), so have some details before heading out.

TRAIN

Mumbai's suburban train network runs from 4am till 1am and has three main lines. The most useful is the **Western Line**, operating out of Churchgate north to Charni Rd (for Girgaum Chowpatty), Mumbai Central, Mahalaxmi (for the Dhobi Ghat), Vile Parle (for the domestic airport), Andheri (for the international airport) and Borivali (for Sanjay Gandhi National Park), among others.

The **Central Line** runs from CST to Byculla (for Veermata Jijabai Bhonsle Udyan, formerly Victoria Gardens), Dadar and as far as Neral (for Matheran).

From Churchgate, 2nd-/1st-class fares are ₹4/45 to Mumbai Central, ₹7/80 to Vile Parle, and ₹9/110 to Borivali.

To avoid the queues, buy a **coupon book** (₹50), good for use on either train line, then 'validate' the coupons at the machines before boarding.

'Tourist tickets' permit unlimited travel in 2nd/1st class for one (₹50/170), three (₹90/330) or five (₹105/390) days.

Avoid rush hours when trains are jam-packed; watch your valuables, and gals, stick to the ladies-only carriages except late at night, when it's more important to avoid empty cars.

Maharashtra

Best Places to Eat

→ Malaka Spice (p804)

→ New Sea Rock Restaurant (p795)

→ Khyber (p778)

→ Grapevine (p807)

→ Dario's (p804)

Best Places to Stay

→ Verandah in the Forest (p797)

→ Hotel Sunderban (p803)

→ Lemon Tree (p783)

→ Beyond (p779)

→ Hotel Plaza (p791)

Why Go?

India's third-largest and second-most populous state, Maharashtra is an expansive canvas showcasing many of India's iconic attractions. There are lazy, palm-fringed beaches; lofty, cool-green mountains; World Heritage historical sights; and bustling cosmopolitan cities.

A short excursion north of Mumbai brings you to Nasik, a curious blend of spirituality, meditation and India's premier wine region. Further inland are the extraordinary cave temples of Ellora and Ajanta, carved from 'living rock' that celebrate the rich cultural heritage of empires past. If you are looking for a cool change, head to Matheron, Maharashtra's only hill station, where a toy train chugs through verdant forests. Pilgrims and inquisitive souls should head south to cosmopolitan Pune, a city famous for its 'sex guru' and alternative spiritualism. Steer westward and you will be rewarded with a string of golden sands and crumbling forts along the romantic Konkan Coast of the Arabian Sea.

When to Go
Nasik

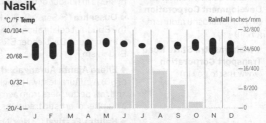

Jan It's party time in Nasik's wineries, marked by grape harvesting and crushing galas.

Sep The frenzied and energetic Ganesh Chaturthi celebrations reach fever pitch.

Dec Winter's a lovely time for the secluded beaches of Murud, Ganpatipule and Tarkarli.

MAIN POINTS OF ENTRY

Mumbai has an international and a domestic airport. Other domestic airports include Aurangabad, Pune and Nagpur. Jalgaon is an important rail hub between Delhi and Mumbai and is convenient to Ajanta and Ellora.

Fast Facts

➡ **Population:** 112.4 million

➡ **Area:** 307,690 sq km

➡ **Capital:** Mumbai

➡ **Main languages:** Marathi, Hindi, English

➡ **Sleeping prices: $** below ₹1000, **$$** ₹1000 to ₹4000, **$$$** above ₹4000

Money Matters

Maharashtra is among the most economically well-off states in India. Its per-capita income is 60% higher than the national average.

Resources

➡ **Maharashtra Tourism Development Corporation** (www.maharashtratourism. gov.in)

➡ **Maharashtra State Road Transport Corporation** (www.msrtc.gov.in)

Top Yoga & Meditation Centres

The Vipassana International Academy (p780) in Igatpuri has long been a destination for those wishing to put mind over matter through an austere form of Buddhist meditation. The boundaries of yoga, on the other hand, are constantly pushed at the Ramamani Iyengar Memorial Yoga Institute (p802) in Pune and the Kaivalyadhama Yoga Hospital (p798) in Lonavla. For a more lavish and indulgent form of spiritual engagement, there's the superluxurious Osho International Meditation Resort (p802) in Pune, where one can meditate in style, while flexing a few muscles in the unique game of 'zennis' (Zen tennis).

DON'T MISS

The ancient stone temples of **Ellora** and **Ajanta** are among India's top architectural and artistic wonders. Rock carving, sculpture and painting reach sublime levels of beauty and perfection at these World Heritage Sites.

In terms of medieval forts and citadels, Maharashtra comes second perhaps only to Rajasthan. The best of the lot is **Daulatabad**, a bastion that once played a cameo as India's capital. Equally intriguing is **Janjira**, a 12th-century island fortress that was once an outpost for the seafaring African traders. Others include the many forts associated with Chhatrapati Shivaji, including the **Raigad**, and **Shivneri**, where the Maratha leader was born.

Top State Festivals

➡ **Naag Panchami** (☉ Jul/Aug, Pune, p799; Kolhapur, p808) A traditional snake-worshipping festival.

➡ **Ganesh Chaturthi** (☉ Sep, Pune, p799) Celebrated with fervour all across Maharashtra; Pune goes particularly hysteric in honour of the elephant-headed deity.

➡ **Dussehra** (☉ Sep & Oct) A Hindu festival, but it also marks the Buddhist celebration of the anniversary of the famous humanist and Dalit leader BR Ambedkar's conversion to Buddhism.

➡ **Ellora Ajanta Aurangabad Festival** (☉ Nov, Aurangabad, p780) A cultural festival bringing together the best classical and folk performers from across the region, while promoting a number of artistic traditions and handicrafts on the side.

➡ **Kalidas Festival** (☉ Nov, Nagpur, p792) Commemorates the literary genius of legendary poet Kalidas through spirited music, dance and theatre.

➡ **Sawai Gandharva Sangeet Mahotsav** (☉ Dec, Pune, p799) An extravaganza where you can see unforgettable performances by some of the heftiest names in Indian classical music.

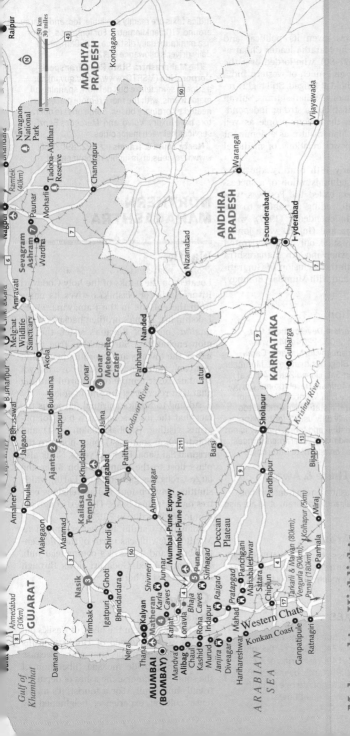

Maharashtra Highlights

❶ Be amazed by the intricate beauty of the **Kailasa Temple** (p786), the pièce de résistance in the monumental Ellora temple complex

❷ Wander through the ancient cave galleries of **Ajanta** (p788) to admire sublime ancient Buddhist art

❸ Sip on a glass of zinfanel, or lose yourself in a holy confluence of faith and ritual in **Nasik** (p776)

❹ Take a horse to spectacular viewpoints and breathe in the pollution-free air at the hill station of **Matheran** (p796)

❺ Delve into new-age spiritualism and modern Indian cuisine in diverse and bustling **Pune** (p799)

❻ Contemplate the power of nature while ambling around the primordial **Lonar Meteorite Crater** (p791)

❼ Rediscover the Gandhian way of life at the **Sevagram Ashram** (p793)

History

Maharashtra was given its political and ethnic identity by Maratha leader Chhatrapati Shivaji (1627–80), who lorded over the Deccan plateau and much of western India from his stronghold at Raigad. Still highly respected today among Maharashtrans, Shivaji is credited for instilling a strong, independent spirit among the region's people, as well as establishing Maharashtra as a dominant player in the power relations of medieval India.

From the early 18th century, the state was under the administration of a succession of ministers called the Peshwas who ruled until 1819, ceding thereafter to the British. After Independence (1947), western Maharashtra and Gujarat were joined to form Bombay state, only to be separated again in 1960, when modern Maharashtra was formed with the exclusion of Gujarati-speaking areas and with Mumbai (Bombay) as its capital.

ⓘ Information

Maharashtra Tourism Development Corporation (MTDC; ☑ 022-22044040; www.maharashtratourism.gov.in; Madame Cama Rd, opposite LIC Bldg, Nariman Point, Mumbai; ⊙ 10am-5pm Mon-Sat, closed 2nd & 4th S at) The Maharashtra Tourism Development Corporation's head office is in Mumbai. Most major towns throughout the state have offices, too, but they're generally only useful for booking MTDC accommodation and tours. Sunday is not a business day, and many government offices also remain closed on alternate Saturdays.

ⓘ Getting There & Away

Mumbai is Maharashtra's main transport hub, although Pune, Jalgaon and Aurangabad are also major players.

ⓘ Getting Around

Because the state is so large, internal flights (eg Pune to Nagpur) can help speed up your explorations. Airfares vary widely on a daily basis. AC

HOTEL TAXES

In Maharashtra, hotel rooms above ₹1000 attract a 7.42% Service Tax, plus a 'Luxury Tax' of 4% (for tariffs of ₹750 to ₹1200) or 10% (tariffs over ₹1200). Many hotels will negotiate one or both of the taxes away in quiet times.

Indica taxis are readily available, too, and charge around ₹10 per kilometre. For long trips, factor in a minimum daily distance of 250km, and a daily driver's allowance of ₹250.

The **Maharashtra State Road Transport Corporation** (MSRTC; www.msrtc.gov.in) has a superb semideluxe bus network spanning all major towns, with the more remote places connected by ordinary buses. Some private operators have luxury 'Volvo' and 'Mercedes Benz' services between major cities.

Neeta Tours & Travels (☑ 02228902666; www.neetabus.in) is highly recommended.

NORTHERN MAHARASHTRA

Nasik

☑ 0253 / POP 1.5 MILLION / ELEV 565M

Located on the banks of the holy Godavari River, Nasik (or Nashik) derives its name from the episode in the Ramayana where Lakshmana, Rama's brother, hacked off the *nasika* (nose) of Ravana's sister, the demon enchantress Surpanakha. True to its name, the town is an absorbing place, and you can't walk far without discovering yet another exotic temple or colourful bathing ghat that references the Hindu epic.

Adding to Nasik's spiritual flavour is the fact that the town serves as a base for pilgrims visiting Trimbak (33km west) and Shirdi (79km southeast), once home to the original Sai Baba. Every 12 years, Nasik also plays host to the grand Kumbh Mela, the largest religious gathering on Earth, which shuttles between four Indian religious centres on a triennial basis. The next congregation in Nasik is due in 2015.

Mahatma Gandhi Rd, better known as MG Rd, a few blocks north of the Old Central bus stand, is Nasik's commercial hub. The temple-lined Godavari flows through town just east of here.

⊙ Sights

★ **Ramkund**   GHAT

This bathing ghat in the heart of Nasik's old quarter sees hundreds of Hindu pilgrims arriving daily to bathe, pray and – because the waters provide moksha (liberation of the soul)– to immerse the ashes of departed friends and family. For a tourist, it's an intense cultural experience, heightened by

Nasik

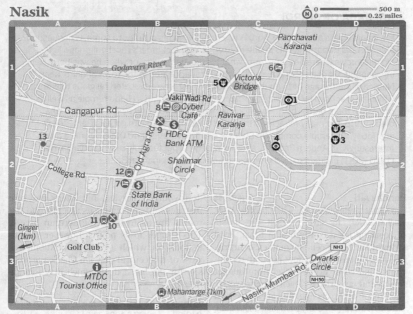

the presence of a colourful **market** downstream. It's OK to take photographs, but try not to be intrusive.

Temples HINDU TEMPLES

(⊙6am-9pm) A short walk uphill east of Ramkund is the **Kala Rama Temple**, the city's holiest shrine. Dating to 1794 and containing unusual black-stone representations of Rama, Sita and Lakshmana, the temple stands on the site where Lakshmana sliced off Surpanakha's nose. Nearby is the **Gumpha Panchavati**, where Sita supposedly hid while being assailed by the evil Ravana.

The ramshackle **Sundar Narayan Temple**, at the western end of Victoria Bridge, contains three black Vishnu deities. The modern **Muktidham Temple**, about 7km southeast of the city near the train station, has 18 muralled chapters of the Bhagavad Gita lining its interior walls.

🛏 Sleeping & Eating

Hotel Abhishek HOTEL $
(☏2514201; www.hotelabhishek.com; Panchavati Karanja; s/d ₹335/455, with AC ₹728/775; ❄) Found just off the Panchavati Karanja roundabout, this pleasant budget option packs hot showers, TV and appetising vegetarian food into its spotless, value-for-money

rooms. A few minutes' walk uphill from the Godavari River, it sits amid all the spiritual comings and goings, and is therefore a vantage point for familiarising oneself with the colour and ritual of sacred India.

SAI BABA OF SHIRDI

His iconic status as a national guru is legendary. And his divinity, to some, is unquestionable. But Sai Baba, for all his popularity, remains one of India's most enigmatic figures. No one knows where he came from, what his real name was, or when he was born. Having stepped out of an obscure childhood, he first appeared in the town of Shirdi near Nasik around the age of 16 (in the mid-1800s). There, he advocated religious tolerance, which he practised by sleeping alternately in a mosque and a Hindu temple as well as praying in them both. The masses took to him right away, and by the time Sai Baba died in 1918, the many miracles attributed to him had seen him gather a large following. Today, his temple complex in Shirdi draws an average of 40,000 pilgrims a day. Interestingly, in Andhra Pradesh, another widely respected holy man Sathya Sai Baba (1926–2011) claimed to be the reincarnation of the original Sai Baba.

Panchavati   HOTEL $$

(www.panchavatihotels.com; 430 Chandak Wadi, Vakil Wadi Rd) To save yourself the hassle of scouting for a comfy bed in town, head straight for this excellent complex, comprising four hotels (and a few popular restaurants) that cover every pocket from budget to top-end, and deliver each rupee's worth. Kicking off at the cheaper end is **Panchavati Guest House** (✆ 2578771; s/d from ₹550/650), which has slightly cramped rooms and prompt service. A more inviting option is **Panchavati Yatri** (✆ 2578782; s/d from ₹1530/1760; ❄), featuring top-notch rooms with hot showers, spot-on service, and an in-house health club. **Hotel Panchavati** (✆ 2575771; s/d from ₹2000/2410; ❄), fronting the complex, is pricier with classy rooms; it caters largely to business travellers. Last of all is the **Panchavati Millionaire** (✆ 2312318; s/d ₹2350/2950; ❄), a sumptuous affair where lavish rooms are complemented by cosy breakfast nooks that are perfect for a steaming morning cuppa.

Hotel Samrat   HOTEL $$

(✆ 2577211; www.hotelsamratnasik.com; Old Agra Rd; s/d ₹950/1290, with AC ₹1560/1775; ❄) You'll find little to complain about at the Samrat. Inviting rooms have large windows, are decorated in brown and beige, with pine furniture thrown in for good measure. Located right next to the bus stand, its spick-and-span vegetarian restaurant is open 24 hours, making it popular as a refuelling stop.

Ginger   HOTEL $$

(✆ 1860 2663333, 6616333; www.gingerhotels.com; Trimbak Rd, Plot P20, Satpur MIDC; s/d ₹2935/3520; ❄☎) Ginger hotels are formulaic, predictable and very, very comfortable. Primarily a business hotel, it features do-it-yourself service, but there are luxe features and conveniences aplenty, and the rooms are as fresh as the autumn breeze. This Ginger loses points, however, due to its location, which is a couple of kilometres west of the central district. Check the website for the latest deals which may include breakfast.

Annapoorna Lunch Home   FAST FOOD $

(MG Rd; mains ₹50-100) This joint has all the usual quick eats rolling endlessly off its culinary assembly line. No surprises on offer, but it would be hard to find fault with the pan-fresh food that's cheaper than peanuts. We recommend the dosas, but be warned, you might have trouble finding a seat at lunchtime.

★ Khyber   MULTICUISINE $$

(Panchavati Hotel Complex; mains ₹180-300) Taste one succulent morsel of any of Khyber's signature Afghani dishes and you might start wondering if you are actually in Kandahar. The Khyber is one of Nasik's top-notch fine-dining establishments, with a great ambience (soft lighting, sparkling glassware, teak furniture) to go with its wide range of delectable offerings. The *murgh shaan-e-khyber*, juicy pieces of chicken marinated with herbs and cooked in a creamy gravy, is not to be missed.

Talk of the Town   MULTICUISINE $$

(Old Agra Rd; mains ₹150-280) Next to the New Central bus stand, this multilevel dining experience attracts more tipplers than eaters, although that's no indication of the quality of its food. On offer is a good selection of coastal, North Indian and Chinese dishes, best washed down with a refreshing pint of lager.

ℹ Information

Cyber Café (Vakil Wadi Rd; per hr ₹20; ⊙10am-10pm) Near Panchavati Hotel Complex.

HDFC Bank ATM (MG Rd) Twenty-four-hour ATM.

MTDC Tourist Office (☏2570059; T/I, Golf Club, Old Agra Rd; ⊙10.30am-5.30pm Mon-Sat) About 1km south of the Old Central bus stand, behind the golf course.

State Bank of India (Old Agra Rd; ⊙11am-5pm Mon-Fri, 11am-1pm Sat) Opposite the Old Central bus stand. Changes cash and travellers cheques and has an ATM.

ℹ Getting There & Around

BUS

Nasik's **Old Central bus stand** (CBS; ☏02532309310) is useful for those going to Trimbak (₹30, 45 minutes). A block south, the **New Central bus stand** has services to Aurangabad (semideluxe ₹216, 4½ hours) and Pune (semideluxe/deluxe ₹230/389, 4½ hours). South of town, the **Mahamarg bus stand** has services to Mumbai (semideluxe ₹220, four hours) and Shirdi (₹90, 2½ hours).

Private bus agents based near the CBS run buses to Pune, Mumbai, Aurangabad and Ahmedabad. Fares are marginally lower than those charged on state buses. Note that buses depart from Old Agra Rd, and that most Mumbai-bound buses terminate at Dadar in Mumbai.

TRAIN

The Nasik Rd train station is 8km southeast of the town centre, but a useful **railway reservation office** (1st fl, Commissioner's Office, Canada Corner; ⊙8am-8pm Mon-Sat) is 500m west of the Old Central bus stand. The Panchavati Express is the fastest train to Mumbai (2nd class/chair ₹85/351, 3½ hours, 7.10am). Tapovan Express departs Mumbai CST at 6.10am, arrives at Nasik Rd at 9.45am, and is a convenient train to Aurangabad (2nd class/chair ₹76/319, 3½ hours, 9.50am). An autorickshaw to the station should cost about ₹80.

Around Nasik

Bhandardara

The picturesque village of Bhandardara is nestled deep in the folds of the Sahyadris, about 70km from Nasik. A little-visited place surrounded by craggy mountains, it is one of Maharashtra's best escapes from the bustle of urban India.

Most of Bhandardara's habitation is thrown around **Arthur Lake**, a horseshoe-shaped reservoir fed by the waters of the Pravara River. The lake is barraged on one side by the imposing **Wilson Dam**, a colonial-era structure dating back to 1910. If you like walking, consider a hike to the

---

GRAPES OF NASIK

From wimpy raisins to full-bodied wines, the grapes of Nasik have come a long way. The surrounding region had been producing table grapes since time immemorial. However, it was only in the early 1990s that a couple of entrepreneurs realised that Nasik, with its fertile soils and cool climate, boasted conditions similar to Bordeaux. In 1997 industry pioneer **Sula Vineyards** (☏09970090010; www.sulawines.com; Gangapur–Savargaon Rd, Govardhan; ⊙11am-10pm) fearlessly invested in a crop of sauvignon blanc and chenin blanc, and the first batch of domestic wines hit the shelves in 2000. It hasn't looked back.

These days, the wine list in most of Nasik's wineries stretch to include zinfandel, shiraz, merlot and cabernet as well as a few reserves and sparkling wines, and most of these drops can be sampled first-hand by visiting one of the estates. **York Winery** (☏02532230700; www.yorkwinery.com; Gangapur–Savargaon Rd, Gangavarhe; ⊙3-10pm) offers wine-tasting sessions (₹100) in a top-floor room that has scenic views of the lake and surrounding hills. Sula Vineyards, located 15km west of Nasik, rounds off a vineyard tour with a wine-tasting session (₹150) that features four of its best drops. It's also possible to stay among the vines. For an extremely indulging experience, head 3km inland to **Beyond** (☏09970090010; www.sulawines.com; d incl taxes & breakfast from ₹6100; ❋❋), Sula Vineyards' luxury resort set by a lake bordered by rolling hills, where you can roam the landscape on bicycles, go kayaking on the still waters or laze the hours away at the spa.

During harvest season (January to March), some wineries also organise grape-crushing festivals, marked by unbridled revelry. Events are usually advertised on the wineries' websites.

summit of **Mt Kalsubai**, which at 1646m was once used as an observation point by the Marathas. Alternately, you could hike to the ruins of the **Ratangad Fort**, another of Shivaji's erstwhile strongholds, which has wonderful views of the surrounding ranges.

The charming **Anandvan Resort** (☑ 9920311221; www.anandvanresorts.com; d from ₹7050; ❖), an ecoresort with a choice of comfy cottages and villas overlooking Arthur Lake, allows you to sleep in style. While the **MTDC Holiday Resort** (☑ 02424257032; d from ₹900; ❖), located further down the hill, is a reasonable budget option.

To get to Bhandardara, take a local bus from Nasik's Mahamarg bus stand to Ghoti (₹35, one hour), from where an autorickshaw ride costs ₹70. A taxi from Nasik can also drop you at your resort for about ₹1500.

Igatpuri

Heard of *vipassana,* haven't you? Well head to Igatpuri to see where (and how) it all happens. Located about 44km south of Nasik, this village is home to the headquarters of the world's largest *vipassana* meditation institution, the **Vipassana International Academy** (☑ 02553244076; www.dhamma.org), which institutionalises this strict form of meditation first taught by Gautama Buddha in the 6th century BC and reintroduced to India by teacher SN Goenka in the 1960s. Ten-day residential courses (advance bookings compulsory) are held throughout the year, though authorities warn that it requires rigorous discipline. Basic accommodation, food and meditation instruction are provided free of charge, but donations upon completion are accepted.

Trimbak

The moody **Trimbakeshwar Temple** stands in the centre of Trimbak, 33km west of Nasik. It's one of India's most sacred temples, containing a *jyoti linga,* one of the 12 most important shrines to Shiva. Only Hindus are allowed in, but non-Hindus can peek into the courtyard. Nearby, the waters of the Godavari River flow into the **Gangadwar bathing tank**, where all are welcome to wash away their sins. You also have the option of a four-hour return hike up the **Brahmagiri Hill**, where you can see the Godavari dribble forth from a spring.

Regular buses run from the CBS in Nasik to Trimbak (₹30, 45 minutes).

Aurangabad

☑ 0240 / POP 1,171,330 / ELEV 515M

Aurangabad lay low through most of the tumultuous history of medieval India and only hit the spotlight when the last Mughal emperor, Aurangzeb, made the city his capital from 1653 to 1707. With the emperor's death came the city's rapid decline, but the brief period of glory saw the building of some fascinating monuments, including a Taj Mahal replica (Bibi-qa-Maqbara), that continue to draw a steady trickle of visitors. These monuments, alongside other historic relics, such as a group of ancient Buddhist caves, make Aurangabad a good choice for a fairly decent weekend excursion. But the real reason for traipsing all the way here is because the town is an excellent base for exploring the World Heritage Sites of Ellora and Ajanta.

Silk fabrics were once Aurangabad's chief revenue generator, and the town is still known across the world for its hand-woven Himroo and Paithani saris.

The train station, cheap hotels and restaurants are clumped together in the south of the town along Station Rd East and Station Rd West. The MSRTC bus stand is 1.5km to the north of the train station. Northeast of the bus stand is the buzzing old town with its narrow streets and Muslim quarters. Interestingly, Aurangabad also has a sizeable Buddhist community who follow in the footsteps of eminent humanist and social leader BR Ambedkar, and celebrate his conversion to Buddhism during Dussehra.

◎ Sights

★ **Bibi-qa-Maqbara** MONUMENT (Indian/foreigner ₹5/100; ⊙ dawn-10pm) Built by Aurangzeb's son Azam Khan in 1679 as a mausoleum for his mother Rabia-ud-Daurani, Bibi-qa-Maqbara is widely known as the 'poor man's Taj'. With its four minarets flanking a central onion-domed mausoleum, the white structure bears a striking resemblance to Agra's Taj Mahal. It is much less grand, however, and apart from having a few marble adornments, namely the plinth and dome, much of the structure is finished in lime mortar. Apparently the prince conceived the entire mausoleum in white marble, but was thwarted by his frugal father who opposed his extravagant idea of draining state coffers for the purpose. However, despite the use of cheaper material and the obvious weathering, it's a sight far more impressive than the average gravestone.

Aurangabad Caves
CAVES

(Indian/foreigner ₹5/100; ☉ dawn-dusk) Architecturally speaking, the Aurangabad Caves aren't a patch on Ellora or Ajanta, but they do throw some light on early Buddhist architecture and, above all, make for a quiet and peaceful outing. Carved out of the hillside in the 6th or 7th century AD, the 10 caves, comprising two groups 1km apart (retain your ticket for entry into both sets), are all Buddhist. Cave 7, with its sculptures of scantily clad lovers in suggestive positions, is a perennial favourite. The caves are about 2km north of Bibi-qa-Maqbara. A return autorickshaw from the mausoleum shouldn't cost more than ₹180.

Panchakki
GARDEN

(Indian/foreigner ₹5/20; ☉ 6.15am-9.15pm) The garden complex of Panchakki, literally meaning 'water wheel', takes its name from the hydro-mill which, in its day, was considered a marvel of engineering. Driven by water carried through earthen pipes from a reservoir 6km away, it was once used to grind grain for pilgrims. You can still see the humble machine at work today.

Baba Shah Muzaffar, a Sufi saint and spiritual guide to Aurangzeb, is buried here. His memorial garden, flanked by a series of fish-filled tanks, is near a massive banyan tree on the southern side of the main cistern.

Shivaji Museum
MUSEUM

(Dr Ambedkar Rd; admission ₹5; ☉ 10.30am-6pm Fri-Wed) This simple museum is dedicated to the life of the Maratha hero, Shivaji. Its collection includes a 500-year-old chain-mail suit and a copy of the Quran handwritten by Aurangzeb.

☞ Tours

Classic Tours (p784) and the **Indian Tourism Development Corporation** (ITDC; ☑ 2331143) both run daily bus tours to the Ajanta and Ellora Caves. The trip to Ajanta Caves costs ₹450 and the tour to Ellora Caves, ₹300; prices include a guide but don't cover admission fees. The Ellora tour also includes all the other major Aurangabad sites along with Daulatabad Fort and Aurangzeb's tomb in Khuldabad, which is a lot

to swallow in a day. All tours start and end at the MTDC Holiday Resort. During quiet periods, these operators pool resources and pack their clients into a single bus.

For private tours, try Ashoka Tours & Travels (p784), which owns a decent fleet of taxis and can personalise your trip around Aurangabad and to Ajanta (₹1600 for up to four people) and Ellora (₹1100 for up to four people).

🛏 Sleeping

Hotel Panchavati
HOTEL $

(☑ 2328755; www.hotelpanchavati.com; Station Rd West; s/d ₹525/625, with AC ₹775/900; ※) Panchavati is popular with budget travellers, and for good reason. On offer are a range of compact, colour-themed and thoughtfully appointed rooms, with comfortable beds and balconies. Choose between front-facing, park-view rooms, or the much quieter, tree-view rooms at the rear. There are two restaurants and a bar. The managers are efficient and friendly and the hotel sits easily at the top of the value-for-money class.

Hotel Oberoi
HOTEL $

(☑ 2323841; www.hoteloberoi.in; Osmanpura Circle, Station Rd East; s/d ₹855/969, with AC ₹1082/1197; ※) Cheekily named, and nothing to do with the five-star chain, this recently renovated hotel is nevertheless a good budget option in a convenient location. Rooms are noticeably modern with flat-screen TVs and comfy beds, and the bathrooms are gleaming, with no loose plumbing! Also on offer is complimentary pick-up from rail or bus stations.

Hotel Nandanvan
HOTEL $

(☑ 2338916; Station Rd East; s/d ₹450/550, with AC ₹650/750; ※) Unusually large and clean rooms and bathrooms are on offer at this well-run hotel, set in a prime location close to Kailash Restaurant. The noise coming off the main road might get to you at times, though.

Tourist's Home
HOTEL $

(☑ 2337212; Station Rd West; dm ₹375, d ₹500, with AC ₹1000; ※) This one's as basic as it gets. Most rooms here are simply bare bones, but well-ventilated and clean. There are quite a few rules and regulations to be adhered to, going by the noticeboard at the entrance, but it's close to the train station.

Aurangabad

Hotel Amarpreet

HOTEL $$

(☎ 6621133; www.amarpreethotel.com; Jalna Rd; s/d from ₹3875/5166; ❄@☎) Old-fashioned though spacious rooms might trigger the occasional hunch that you'd have got more bang for your buck elsewhere, but the all-smiles management makes up for it with polite service, excellent housekeeping and a great selection of food and booze. Ask for a room in the western wing, with superb views of Bibi-qa-Maqbara. And look out for the new wing that will double the hotel's size and add a pool, gym and spa. It was all under construction when we visited.

MTDC Holiday Resort

HOTEL $$

(☎ 2331513; Station Rd East; d from ₹1260, with AC from ₹1560; ❄) Set around a verdant lawn and shaded by robust canopies, this curiously disorganised hotel is one of the better state-owned operations in Maharashtra. The rooms, though lacking in character, are spacious and tidy. Couples and solo travellers will be housed in the noisy rooms facing Station Rd; families get the quieter block. There's also a well-stocked bar, a decent restaurant and a couple of travel agencies (for Ellora and Ajanta tours) on-site. Come between March and July and you will pay 20% less.

Aurangabad

⭐ **Lemon Tree**   HOTEL **$$$**
(✐ 6603030; www.lemontreehotels.com; Airport Rd, R//2 Chikalthana; s/d incl breakfast from ₹7345/8815; 🕸@🛜❄) Fresh as lemonade, this swish hotel encircles what we thought was the best swimming pool in the Deccan. The standard rooms, although not large, are brightened by vivid tropical tones offset against snow-white walls. Adding a dash of class is the prim Citrus Café, and the Slounge bar, where you can down a drink while hustling a fellow traveller in a game of pool. It's one place you're sure to have a nice stay.

VITS   HOTEL **$$$**
(✐ 2350701; www.vitshotelaurangabad.com; Station Rd East; d incl breakfast ₹7632; 🕸@🛜❄) Handy to the train station, snazzy-lobbied VITS goes by the motto 'Guest. Rest. Best'. What that basically means is you have a delightfully luxurious room to flop about in, packed with all the usual luxe features you'd find in top-end hotels. Staff are eager to put you up, so it's worth asking for a discount here.

✖ Eating

Hotel Panchavati   MULTICUISINE **$**
(Station Rd West; mains ₹60-280) The 'family' restaurant at this budget hotel has a Chinese and Korean menu in addition to an extensive Indian menu. We can highly recommended its Korean food and tandoori chicken, as well as the cold beer. Ambience isn't a selling point here, but you can watch the soccer on the TV.

Swad Veg Restaurant   INDIAN **$**
(Station Rd East, Kanchan Chamber; mains ₹70-80) Swad offers a great range of Indian snacks and staples, such as dosas, plus a few pizzas, ice creams and shakes, in its clean basement premises. Try the Gujarati thali, an endless train of dishes that diners gobble up under the benevolent gaze of patron saint swami Yogiraj Hanstirth, whose portrait illuminates a far wall of the restaurant.

Kailash   INDIAN **$**
(Station Rd East; mains ₹85-110) Adjacent to Hotel Nandanvan, this busy pure-veg restaurant is a smart glass-and-chrome place where you can sit back after a long day out and wolf down a variety of local delicacies brought to your table by smartly dressed waiters.

China Town   CHINESE **$$**
(Hotel Amarpreet, Jalna Rd; mains ₹180-200) This is one of the two in-house restaurants that sit side by side in Hotel Amarpreet. The other one has the usual Indian and continental dishes, while China Town dishes up surprisingly fine quality Chinese food. A good range of noodles is on offer, which goes extremely well with the numerous chicken and lamb preparations all presented appetisingly in the restaurant's well-dressed interiors.

Tandoor   NORTH INDIAN **$$**
(Shyam Chambers, Station Rd East, ; mains ₹160-290) Offering fine tandoori dishes and flavoursome North Indian veg and non-veg options in a weirdly Pharaonic atmosphere, Tandoor is one of Aurangabad's top standalone restaurants. A few Chinese dishes are also on offer, but patrons clearly prefer the dishes coming out of, well, the tandoor.

🛍 Shopping

Hand-woven Himroo material is a traditional Aurangabad speciality. Made from cotton, silk and silver threads, it was developed as a cheaper alternative to Kam

Khab, the more ornate brocade of silk and gold thread woven for royalty in the 14th century. Most of today's Himroo shawls and saris are mass produced using power looms, but some showrooms in the city still run traditional workshops, thus preserving this dying art.

Himroo saris start at ₹1000 (cotton and silk blend). Paithani saris, which are of a superior quality, range from ₹5000 to ₹300,000 – before you baulk at the price, bear in mind that some of them take more than a year to make. If you're buying, ensure you're spending your money on authentic Himroo, and not 'Aurangabad silk'.

One of the best places to come and watch weavers at work is the **Paithani Weaving Centre** (Jalna Rd; ⊙11.30am-8pm), about 6km east of Kranti Chowk (behind the Indian Airlines office), so take a taxi.

ℹ Information

Bank of Baroda, ICICI, State Bank of India (SBI), State Bank of Hyderabad (SBH) and HDFC Bank have several ATMs along Station Rd East, Court Rd, Nirala Bazaar and Jalna Rd.

Ashoka Tours & Travels (☑2359102, 9890340816; atkadam88@gmail.com; Hotel Panchavati, Station Rd West) Personalised city and regional tours, car hire and hotel pick-ups. Run by former *Lonely Planet*–recommended autorickshaw driver Ashok T Kadam.

Classic Tours (☑2337788; www.classictours. info; MTDC Holiday Resort, Station Rd East) Books transport and tours, particularly to Ellora and Ajanta.

Cyber-dhaba (Station Rd West; per hr Rs20; ⊙8am-11pm) Also changes money.

MTDC Office (☑2331513; MTDC Holiday Resort, Station Rd East; ⊙10am-5.30pm Mon-Sat)

Post Office (Juna Bazaar; ⊙10am-6pm Mon-Sat)

Sai Internet Café (Station Rd East; per hr ₹15; ⊙8am-10pm)

State Bank of India (Kranti Chowk; ⊙11am-5pm Mon-Fri, 11am-1pm Sat) Handles foreign exchange.

ℹ Getting There & Away

AIR

The airport is 10km east of town. En route are the offices of **Indian Airlines** (☑2485241; Jalna Rd) and **Jet Airways** (☑2441392; www. jetairways.com; Jalna Rd). There are direct daily flights to Delhi (around ₹7000) and Mumbai (around ₹4000).

BUS

Buses leave roughly hourly from the **MSRTC bus stand** (Station Rd West) to Pune (semideluxe/deluxe/Volvo ₹250/270/530, five hours) and Nasik (semideluxe/deluxe ₹225/250, five hours). **Private bus agents** are located around the corner where Dr Rajendra Prasad Marg becomes Court Rd; a few sit closer to the bus stand. Deluxe overnight bus destinations include Mumbai (with/without AC ₹550/400, sleeper ₹750, eight hours), Ahmedabad (seat/sleeper ₹550/820, 15 hours) and Nagpur (₹450, 12 hours).

Ordinary buses head to Ellora from the MSRTC bus stand every half-hour (₹25, 45 minutes) and hourly to Jalgaon (₹140, four hours) via Fardapur (₹95, two hours). The T-junction near Fardapur is the drop-off point for Ajanta.

TRAIN

Aurangabad's **train station** (Station Rd East) is not on a main line, but two heavily booked trains run direct to/from Mumbai. The Tapovan Express (2nd class/chair ₹112/476, 7½ hours) departs Aurangabad at 2.35pm, and departs Mumbai at 6.10am. The Janshatabdi Express (2nd class/chair ₹142/555, 6½ hours) departs Aurangabad at 6am and Mumbai at 1.50pm. For Hyderabad (Secunderabad), take the Devagiri Express (sleeper/2AC ₹299/1180, 10 hours, 4.10am). To reach northern or eastern India, take a bus to Jalgaon (p791) and board a train there.

ℹ Getting Around

Autorickshaws are as common here as mosquitoes in a summer swamp. The **taxi stand** is next to the MSRTC bus stand; share jeeps also depart from here for destinations around Aurangabad, including Ellora and Daulatabad. Expect to pay ₹600 for a full-day tour in a rickshaw, or ₹1100 in a taxi.

Around Aurangabad

Daulatabad

This one's straight out of a Tolkien fantasy. A most beguiling structure, the 12th-century hilltop fortress of Daulatabad is located about 15km from Aurangabad, en route to Ellora. Now in ruins, the citadel was originally conceived as an impregnable fort by the Yadava kings. Its most infamous highpoint came in 1328, when it was named Daulatabad (City of Fortune) by eccentric Delhi sultan Mohammed Tughlaq and made the capital – he even marched the entire population of Delhi 1100km south to populate it.

Ironically, Daulatabad – despite being better positioned strategically than Delhi – soon proved untenable as a capital due to an acute water crisis, and Tughlaq forced the weary inhabitants all the way back to Delhi, which had by then been reduced to a ghost town.

Daulatabad's central bastion sits atop a 200m-high craggy outcrop known as Devagiri (Hill of the Gods), surrounded by a 5km **fort** (Indian/foreigner ₹5/100; ⊙ 6am-6pm). The climb to the summit takes about an hour, and leads past an ingenious series of defences, including multiple doorways designed with odd angles and spike-studded doors to prevent elephant charges. A tower of victory, known as the Chand Minar (Tower of the Moon), built in 1435, soars 60m above the ground to the right – it's closed to visitors. Higher up, you can walk into the Chini Mahal, where Abul Hasan Tana Shah, king of Golconda, was held captive for 12 years before his death in 1699. Nearby, there's a 6m cannon, cast from five different metals and engraved with Aurangzeb's name.

Part of the ascent goes through a pitch-black, bat-infested, water-seeping, spiralling tunnel. Guides (₹450) are available near the ticket counter to show you around, and their torch-bearing assistants will lead you through the dark passageway for a small tip. But on the way down you'll be left to your own devices, so carry a torch. The crumbling staircases and sheer drops can make things difficult for the elderly, children and those suffering from vertigo or claustrophobia.

Khuldabad

Time permitting, take a pit stop in the scruffy-walled settlement of Khuldabad (Heavenly Abode), a quaint and cheerful little Muslim pilgrimage village just 3km from Ellora. Buried deep in the pages of history, Khuldabad is where a number of historic figures lie interred, including emperor Aurangzeb, the last of the Mughal greats. Despite matching the legendary King Solomon in terms of state riches, Aurangzeb was an ascetic in his personal life, and insisted that he be buried in a simple tomb constructed only with the money he had made from sewing Muslim skullcaps. An unfussy affair of modest marble in a courtyard of the **Alamgir Dargah** (⊙ 7am-8pm) is exactly what he got.

Generally a calm place, Khuldabad is swamped with pilgrims every April when a robe said to have been worn by the Prophet Mohammed, and kept within the dargah (shrine), is shown to the public. Across the road from the Alamgir Dargah, another shrine contains strands of the Prophet's beard and lumps of silver from a tree of solid silver, which is said to have miraculously grown at this site after a saint's death.

Ellora

🗌 02437

Give a man a hammer and chisel, and he'll create art for posterity. Come to the World Heritage Site **Ellora cave temples** (Indian/foreigner ₹10/250; ⊙ dawn-dusk Wed-Mon), located 30km from Aurangabad, and you'll know exactly what we mean. The epitome of ancient Indian rock-cut architecture, these caves were chipped out laboriously over five centuries by generations of Buddhist, Hindu and Jain monks. Monasteries, chapels, temples – the caves served every purpose, and they were stylishly embellished with a profusion of remarkably detailed sculptures. Unlike the caves at Ajanta, which are carved into a sheer rock face, the Ellora caves line a 2km-long escarpment, the gentle slope of which allowed architects to build elaborate courtyards in front of the shrines, and render them with sculptures of a surreal quality.

Ellora has 34 caves in all: 12 Buddhist (AD 600–800), 17 Hindu (AD 600–900) and five Jain (AD 800–1000). The grandest, however, is the awesome Kailasa Temple (Cave 16), the world's largest monolithic sculpture, hewn top to bottom against a rocky slope by 7000 labourers over a 150-year period. Dedicated to Lord Shiva, it is clearly among the best that ancient Indian architecture has to offer.

Historically, the site represents the renaissance of Hinduism under the Chalukya and Rashtrakuta dynasties, the subsequent decline of Indian Buddhism and a brief resurgence of Jainism under official patronage. The increasing influence of Tantric elements in India's three great religions can also be seen in the way the sculptures are executed, and their coexistence at one site indicates a lengthy period of religious tolerance.

Official guides can be hired at the ticket office in front of the Kailasa Temple for ₹750. Most guides have an extensive knowledge of cave architecture, so try not to skimp. If your tight itinerary forces you to choose between Ellora or Ajanta, Ellora wins hands down.

◉ Sights

★ Kailasa Temple HINDU TEMPLE

This rock-cut temple, built by King Krishna I of the Rashtrakuta dynasty in AD 760, was built to represent Mt Kailasa (Kailash), Shiva's Himalayan abode. To say that the assignment was daring would be an understatement. Three huge trenches were bored into the sheer cliff face with hammers and chisels, following which the shape was 'released', a process that entailed removing 200,000 tonnes of rock, while taking care to leave behind those sections that would later be used for sculpting. Covering twice the area of the Parthenon in Athens and being half as high again, Kailasa is an engineering marvel that was executed straight from the head with zero margin for error. Modern draughtsmen might have a lesson or two to learn here.

Size aside, the temple is remarkable for its prodigious sculptural decoration. The temple houses several intricately carved panels, depicting scenes from the Ramayana, the Mahabharata and the adventures of Krishna. Also worth admiring are the immense monolithic pillars that stand in the courtyard, flanking the entrance on both sides, and the southeastern gallery that has 10 giant and fabulous panels depicting the different avatars of Lord Vishnu. Kailasa is a temple, still very much in use; you'll have to remove your shoes to enter the main shrine.

After you're done with the main enclosure, bypass the hordes of snack-munching day trippers to explore the temple's many dank, bat urine–soaked corners with their numerous forgotten carvings. Afterwards, hike up a foot trail to the south of the complex that takes you to the top perimeter of the 'cave', from where you can get a bird's-eye view of the entire temple complex.

Buddhist Caves CAVE

The southernmost 12 caves are Buddhist *viharas* (monasteries), except Cave 10, which is a *chaitya* (assembly hall). While the earliest caves are simple, Caves 11 and 12 are more ambitious, and on par with the more impressive Hindu temples.

Cave 1, the simplest *vihara*, may have been a granary. Cave 2 is notable for its ornate pillars and the imposing seated Buddha, which faces the setting sun. Cave 3 and Cave 4 are unfinished and not well preserved.

Cave 5 is the largest *vihara* in this group, at 18m wide and 36m long; the rows of stone benches hint that it may once have been an assembly hall.

Cave 6 is an ornate *vihara* with wonderful images of Tara, consort of the Bodhisattva Avalokitesvara, and of the Buddhist goddess of learning, Mahamayuri, looking remarkably similar to Saraswati, her Hindu equivalent. Cave 7 is an unadorned hall, but from here you can pass through a doorway to Cave 8, the first cave in which the sanctum is detached from the rear wall. Cave 9 is notable for its wonderfully carved fascia.

Cave 10 is the only *chaitya* in the Buddhist group and one of the finest in India. Its ceiling features ribs carved into the stonework; the grooves were once fitted with wooden panels. The balcony and upper gallery offer a closer view of the ceiling and a frieze depicting amorous couples. A decorative window gently illuminates an enormous figure of the teaching Buddha.

Cave 11, the Do Thal (Two Storey) Cave, is entered through its third basement level, not discovered until 1876. Like Cave 12, it possibly owes its size to competition with Hindu caves of the same period.

Cave 12, the huge Tin Thal (Three Storey) Cave, is entered through a courtyard. The locked shrine on the top floor contains a large Buddha figure flanked by his seven previous incarnations. The walls are carved with relief pictures.

Hindu Caves CAVE

Where calm and contemplation infuse the Buddhist caves, drama and excitement characterise the Hindu group (Caves 13 to 29). In terms of scale, creative vision and skill of execution, these caves are in a league of their own.

All these temples were cut from the top down, so it was never necessary to use scaffolding – the builders began with the roof and moved down to the floor.

Cave 13 is a simple cave, most likely a granary. Cave 14, the Ravana-ki-Khai, is a Buddhist *vihara* converted to a temple dedicated to Shiva sometime in the 7th century.

Cave 15, the Das Avatara (Ten Incarnations of Vishnu) Cave, is one of the finest at Ellora. The two-storey temple contains a mesmerising Shiva Nataraja, and Shiva emerging from a lingam (phallic image) while Vishnu and Brahma pay homage.

Caves 17 to 20 and caves 22 to 28 are simple monasteries.

Cave 21, known as the Ramesvara Cave, features interesting interpretations of familiar Shaivite scenes depicted in the earlier temples. The figure of the goddess Ganga, standing on her Makara (mythical sea creature), is particularly notable.

The large **Cave 29**, the Dumar Lena, is thought to be a transitional model between the simpler hollowed-out caves and the fully developed temples exemplified by the Kailasa. It has views over a nearby waterfall. When we visited the footpath to Cave 29 and the Jain temples was closed requiring a short rickshaw ride (₹100).

Jain Caves
CAVES

The five Jain caves may lack the artistic vigour and ambitious size of the best Hindu temples, but they are exceptionally detailed. The caves are 1km north of the last Hindu temple (Cave 29) at the end of the bitumen road.

Cave 30, the Chhota Kailasa (Little Kailasa), is a poor imitation of the great Kailasa Temple and stands by itself some distance from the other Jain temples.

In contrast, **Cave 32**, the Indra Sabha (Assembly Hall of Indra), is the finest of the Jain temples. Its ground-floor plan is similar to that of the Kailasa, but the upstairs area is as ornate and richly decorated as the downstairs is plain. There are images of the Jain *tirthankars* (great teachers) Parasnath and Gomateshvara, the latter surrounded by wildlife. Inside the shrine is a seated figure of Mahavira, the last *tirthankar* and founder of the Jain religion.

Cave 31 is really an extension of Cave 32. **Cave 33**, the Jagannath Sabha, is similar in plan to Cave 32 and has some well-preserved sculptures. The final temple, the small **Cave 34**, also has interesting sculptures. On the hilltop over the Jain temples, a 5m-high image of Parasnath looks down on Ellora.

Sleeping & Eating

Hotel Kailas
HOTEL $$

(📞 244446; www.hotelkailas.com; d ₹1761, with AC ₹2435, cottages from ₹2935; ❄) The sole decent hotel near the site, this place should be considered only if you can't have enough of Ellora in a single day. The comfy cottages here come with hot showers; those with cave views are pricier. There's a good restaurant (mains ₹100 to ₹250) and a lush lawn tailor-made for an evening drink.

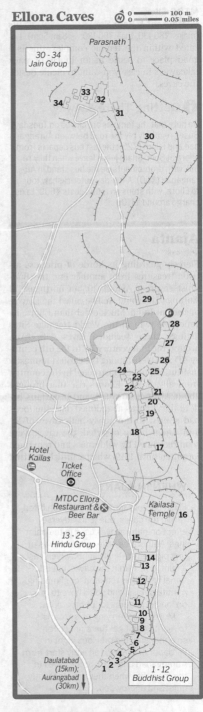

Ellora Caves

0 ——— 100 m
0 ——— 0.05 miles

Parasnath

30 - 34
Jain Group

33
32
34
31
30

29
28
27
26
24 25
23
22
21
20
19
18
17

Hotel
Kailas

Ticket
Office

MTDC Ellora
Restaurant &
Beer Bar

Kailasa
Temple 16

13 - 29
Hindu Group

15
14
13
12
11
10
9
8
7
6
5
4
3
2
1

Daulatabad
(15km);
Aurangabad
(30km)

1 - 12
Buddhist Group

MAHARASHTRA ELLORA

**MTDC Ellora
Restaurant & Beer Bar** INDIAN $
(mains ₹80-130, thali ₹80-130; ⊘8am-5pm) Located within the temple complex, this is a good place to settle in for lunch, or pack takeaways in case you want to picnic beside the caves.

🛈 Getting There & Away

Do note that the temples are closed on Tuesday! Buses regularly ply the road between Aurangabad and Ellora (₹25); the last bus departs from Ellora at 8pm. Share jeeps leave when they're full, with drop-off outside the bus stand in Aurangabad (₹60). A full-day autorickshaw tour to Ellora, with stops en route, costs ₹600; taxis charge around ₹1100.

Ajanta
📱 02438

Fiercely guarding its horde of priceless artistic treasures from another era, the Buddhist caves of Ajanta, 105km northeast of Aurangabad, could well be called the Louvre of ancient India. Much older than Ellora, its venerable twin in the World Heritage Sites listings, these secluded caves date from around the 2nd century BC to the 6th century AD and were among the earliest monastic institutions to be constructed in the country. Ironically, it was Ellora's rise that brought about Ajanta's downfall, and historians believe the site was abandoned once the focus had shifted to the newly built caves of Ellora. Upon being deserted, the caves were soon reclaimed by wilderness and remained forgotten until 1819, when a British hunting

---

WHEN IN AJANTA...

Flash photography is strictly prohibited within the caves, due to its adverse effect on natural dyes used in the paintings. Authorities have installed rows of tiny pigment-friendly lights, which cast a faint glow within the caves, but additional lighting is required for glimpsing minute details, and you'll have to rely on long exposures for photographs.

Most buses ferrying noisy tourists to Ajanta don't get there until noon, so either stay the previous night in Fardapur or push for an early start from Aurangabad and explore the caves in the morning, when they are pleasantly quiet and uncrowded.

---

party led by officer John Smith stumbled upon them purely by chance.

The primary reason to visit Ajanta is to admire its renowned 'frescoes', actually temperas, which adorn many of the caves' interiors. With few other examples from ancient times matching their artistic excellence and fine execution, these paintings are of unfathomable heritage value. It's believed that the natural pigments for these paintings were mixed with animal glue and vegetable gum to bind them to the dry surface. Many caves have small, crater-like holes in their floors, which acted as palettes during paint jobs.

Despite their age, the paintings in most caves remain finely preserved today, and many attribute it to their relative isolation from humanity for centuries. However, it would be a tad optimistic to say that decay hasn't set in.

Authorised guides are available to show you around for ₹600.

⊙ Sights & Activities

★ The Caves CAVE
(Indian/foreigner ₹10/250, video ₹25; ⊘9am-5.30pm Tue-Sun) The 30 caves of Ajanta line the steep face of a horseshoe-shaped gorge bordering the Waghore River. They are sequentially numbered from one end to the other, barring Caves 29 and 30. The numbering has nothing to do with their chronological order; the oldest caves are actually in the middle.

Caves 3, 5, 8, 22 and 28 to 30 remain either closed or inaccessible. Other caves might be closed from time to time due to restoration work. During rush periods, viewers are allotted 15 minutes within the caves, many of which have to be entered barefoot (socks/shoecovers allowed).

Five of the caves are *chaityas* while the other 25 are *viharas*. Caves 8, 9, 10, 12, 13 and part of 15 are early Buddhist caves, while the others date from around the 5th century AD (Mahayana period). In the simpler, more austere early Buddhist school, the Buddha was never represented directly – his presence was always alluded to by a symbol such as the footprint or wheel of law.

Cave 1, a Mahayana *vihara*, was one of the last to be excavated and is the most beautifully decorated. This is where you'll find a rendition of the Bodhisattva Padmapani, the most famous and iconic of the Ajanta artworks. A verandah in front leads to a large congregation hall, housing sculptures and

Ajanta Caves

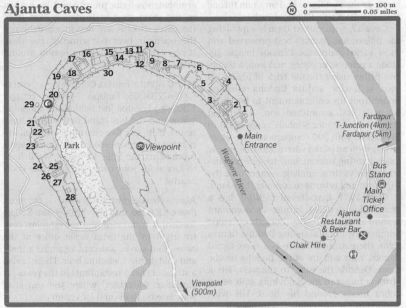

narrative murals known for their splendid perspective and elaborate detailing of dress, daily life and facial expressions. The colours in the paintings were created from local minerals, with the exception of the vibrant blue made from Central Asian lapis lazuli. Look up to the ceiling to see the carving of four deer sharing a common head.

Cave 2 is also a late Mahayana *vihara* with deliriously ornamented columns and capitals, and some fine paintings. The ceiling is decorated with geometric and floral patterns. The murals depict scenes from the Jataka tales, including Buddha's mother's dream of a six-tusked elephant, which heralded his conception.

Cave 4 is the largest *vihara* at Ajanta and is supported by 28 pillars. Although never completed, the cave has some impressive sculptures, including scenes of people fleeing from the 'eight great dangers' to the protection of Avalokitesvara.

Cave 6 is the only two-storey *vihara* at Ajanta, but parts of the lower storey have collapsed. Inside is a seated Buddha figure and an intricately carved door to the shrine. Upstairs the hall is surrounded by cells with fine paintings on the doorways.

Cave 7 has an atypical design, with porches before the verandah leading directly to the four cells and the elaborately sculptured shrine.

Cave 9 is one of the earliest *chaityas* at Ajanta. Although it dates from the early Buddhist period, the two figures flanking the entrance door were probably later Mahayana additions. Columns run down both sides of the cave and around the 3m-high dagoba at the far end.

Cave 10 is thought to be the oldest cave (200 BC) and was the first one to be spotted by the British hunting party. Similar in design to Cave 9, it is the largest *chaitya*. The facade has collapsed and the paintings inside have been damaged, in some cases by graffiti dating from soon after their rediscovery. One of the pillars to the right bears the engraved name of Smith, who left his mark here for posterity.

Cave 16, a *vihara,* contains some of Ajanta's finest paintings and is thought to have been the original entrance to the entire complex. The best known of these paintings is the 'dying princess' – Sundari, wife of the Buddha's half-brother Nanda, who is said to have fainted at the news that her husband was renouncing the material life (and her) in order to become a monk. Carved figures appear to support the ceiling, and there's a statue of the Buddha seated on a lion throne teaching the Noble Eightfold Path.

Cave 17, with carved dwarfs supporting the pillars, has Ajanta's best-preserved and most varied paintings. Famous images include a princess applying make-up, a seductive prince using the old trick of plying his lover with wine, and the Buddha returning home from his enlightenment to beg from his wife and astonished son. A detailed panel tells of Prince Simhala's expedition to Sri Lanka: with 500 companions he is shipwrecked on an island where ogresses appear as enchanting women, only to seize and devour their victims. Simhala escapes on a flying horse and returns to conquer the island.

Cave 19, a magnificent *chaitya,* has a remarkably detailed facade; its dominant feature is an impressive horseshoe-shaped window. Two fine, standing Buddha figures flank the entrance. Inside is a three-tiered dagoba with a figure of the Buddha on the front. Outside the cave, to the west, sits a striking image of the Naga king with seven cobra hoods around his head. His wife, hooded by a single cobra, sits by his side.

Cave 24, had it been finished, would have been the largest *vihara* at Ajanta. You can see how the caves were constructed – long galleries were cut into the rock and then the rock between them was broken through.

Cave 26, a largely ruined *chaitya,* is now dramatically lit, and contains some fine sculptures that shouldn't be missed. On the left wall is a huge figure of the 'reclining Buddha', lying back in preparation for nirvana. Other scenes include a lengthy depiction of the Buddha's temptation by Maya.

Cave 27 is virtually a *vihara* connected to the Cave 26 *chaitya.*

Viewpoints
VIEWPOINT
Two lookouts offer picture-perfect views of the whole horseshoe-shaped gorge. The first is a short walk beyond the river, crossed via a bridge below Cave 8. A further 40-minute uphill walk (not to be attempted during the monsoons) leads to the lookout from where the British party first spotted the caves.

Sleeping & Eating

Accommodation options close to the caves are limited and you're better off using Aurangabad or Jalgaon as a base.

MTDC Holiday Resort
HOTEL $$
(244230; Aurangabad–Jalgaon Rd, Fardapur; d with/without AC ₹1262/1577;) This government hotel sits pretty amid lawns just by the main road in Fardapur, 5km from the caves. Rooms are decent enough, and the open-air beer bar clinches the deal. It's by far the best lodging option around here.

MTDC Ajanta Tourist Complex
HOTEL $$
(09422204325; Fardapur T-junction; cottages ₹2103;) Located just behind the shopping 'plaza' and the bus stand is this mint-fresh resort, featuring five charming and well-appointed cottages nestled amid grassy lawns overlooking the hills. However, you'll have to forage for your own food from the stalls nearby.

Ajanta Restaurant & Beer Bar
FAST FOOD $
(mains ₹100-150, thali from ₹120; 9am-5.30pm Tue-Sun) A restaurant and refreshment centre, right by the main ticket office at the caves, that serves a decent vegetarian thali, and cold drinks including beer. There is also a string of cheap restaurants in the plaza (at Fardapur T-junction) where you can stuff your face on thalis and ice cream etc.

ℹ Information

A cloakroom is available at Fardapur T-junction (but not at the caves), where you can leave gear (₹10 per item for four hours), in case you are visiting Ajanta en route from Aurangabad to Jalgaon or vice versa. The caves are a short, steep climb from the ticket office; the elderly can opt for a chair carried by four sweaty bearers (₹600).

On a rather perplexing note, a new tourist complex near the T-junction is under construction, where they reportedly intended to replicate the major caves alongside restaurants and shops!

ℹ Getting There & Away

Note that the caves are closed on Monday. Buses from Aurangabad or Jalgaon will drop you off at the T-junction (where the highway meets the road to the caves), 4km from the site. From here, after paying an 'amenities' fee (₹10), walk to the departure point for the green-coloured buses (with/without AC ₹20/10), which zoom up to the caves. Buses return on a regular basis (half-hourly, last bus at 5pm) to the T-junction.

All MSRTC buses passing through Fardapur stop at the T-junction. After the caves close you can board buses to either Aurangabad or Jalgaon outside the MTDC Holiday Resort in Fardapur, 1km down the main road towards Jalgaon. Taxis are available in Fardapur; ₹1200 should get you to Jalgaon.

Jalgaon

☏ 0257 / POP 460,468 / ELEV 208M

Apart from being a handy base for exploring Ajanta 60km away, Jalgaon is really nothing more than a convenient transit town. It sits on the main line leading northeast from Mumbai, and has rail connections to all major cities across India.

🛏 Sleeping

★ Hotel Plaza
HOTEL $

(☏ 9370027354, 2227354; hotelplaza_jal@yahoo.com; Station Rd; dm ₹200, s/d ₹500/700, r with AC from ₹1000; ❉ @) Spending a night here is reason enough to halt in Jalgaon. Stepping into this serene hotel with its clean lines and white interior is just the tonic after a long rail journey. And it is only a short walk from the station. The rooms vary in size and layout but all are kept squeaky clean and fresh. The effusive owner is a mine of useful information and can assist with train reservations and taxi hire.

Hotel Royal Palace
HOTEL $$

(☏ 2233555; www.hotelroyalpalace.in; Mahabal Rd, Jai Nagar; s/d incl breakfast from ₹2320/2436; ❉ 🛜) Luxurious by Jalgaon's standards, the Royal Palace has bland business-hotel rooms that are adequately comfortable, but don't quite reach the heights promised by the glitzy lobby. There's also a decent pure-veg, multicuisine restaurant serving north Indian, coastal, Chinese and Continental fare.

🍴 Eating & Drinking

Hotel Arya
INDIAN $

(Navi Peth; mains ₹55-95; ⏰ 8.30am-10.50pm) Vegetarian-only grub on offer but it's delicious; try one of the lip-smacking Punjabi delights. There's also Chinese and South Indian dishes. It's a short walk south along Station Rd, left at MG Rd, and left at the clock tower. You may have to queue for a table.

Silver Palace
BAR

(Station Rd; mains ₹60-190) This restaurant bar's claims of luxury may be stretching things too far. But the beer is cold, and females won't feel like they are trespassing on male-only territory. It is next door to Hotel Plaza.

ℹ Information

You can find a couple of banks, ATMs and internet cafes on Nehru Rd, which runs along the top of Station Rd.

ℹ Getting There & Away

Several express trains connecting Mumbai (sleeper/2AC ₹286/1035, eight hours), Delhi (sleeper/2AC ₹470/1900, 18 hours), Ahmedabad (sleeper/2AC ₹326/1260, 14 hours) and Varanasi (sleeper/2AC ₹450/1870, 21 hours) stop at Jalgaon train station. The Sewagram Express goes to Nagpur (sleeper/2AC ₹282/1015, eight hours, 10pm), while the Nizamuddin Vasco-da-Gama Express goes to Goa (sleeper/2AC ₹465/1880, 23 hours, 7.55am).

Buses to Fardapur (₹45, 1½ hours) depart half-hourly from the bus stand starting at 6am, continuing to Aurangabad (₹160, four hours).

WORTH A TRIP

LONAR METEORITE CRATER

If you like off-beat adventures, travel to Lonar to explore a prehistoric natural wonder. About 50,000 years ago, a meteorite slammed into the earth here, leaving behind a massive crater, 2km across and 170m deep. In scientific jargon, it's the only hyper-velocity natural-impact crater in basaltic rock in the world. In lay terms, it's as tranquil and relaxing a spot as you could hope to find, with a shallow green lake at its base and wilderness all around. The lake water is supposedly alkaline and excellent for the skin. Scientists think that the meteorite is still embedded about 600m below the southeastern rim of the crater.

The crater's edge is home to several Hindu temples as well as wildlife, including langurs, peacocks, deer and numerous birds.

MTDC Tourist Complex (☏ 07260221602; d with/without AC ₹1300/1060; ❉) has a prime location just across the road from the crater, and offers eight rooms of relatively good value, considering the location. There are a couple of buses a day between Lonar and Aurangabad (₹150, 3½ hours). It's also possible to visit Lonar on a day trip from Aurangabad or Jalgaon if you hire a car and driver, and don't mind dishing out about ₹2400.

Jalgaon's train station and bus stand are about 2km apart (₹20 by autorickshaw). Private bus companies on Station Rd offer services to Aurangabad (₹140, 3½ hours), Mumbai (₹350, nine hours) and Pune (₹350, with AC ₹550, nine hours).

Nagpur

☑ 0712 / POP 2.4 MILLION / ELEV 305M

In the heart of India's orange country, Nagpur is located way off the main tourist routes. Apart from being at its festive best during Dussehra, the city – as such – is hopelessly devoid of sites. Nonetheless, it makes a good base for venturing out to the far eastern corner of Maharashtra. First up, it's close to the temples of Ramtek and the ashrams of Sevagram. Besides, Nagpur is also a convenient stop for those looking for tigers in the isolated **Tadoba-Andhari Tiger Reserve**, 150km south of Nagpur, as well as Pench National Park, just across the border in Madyha Pradesh.

If you have some time to kill in the evening, take a stroll in the city's Civil Lines area, dotted with majestic buildings and mansions dating back to the Raj, now used as government offices. Summer is the best time to sample the famed oranges.

🛏 Sleeping & Eating

Nagpur's overpriced hotels cater primarily to business travellers, not tourists. Stay in the Central Ave area if you're on a budget, or have a train to catch in the wee hours. It's a 15-minute walk east of the train station. Otherwise, consider moving to Ramdaspeth, closer to the city centre.

Hotel Blue Diamond   HOTEL $

(☑ 2727461; www.hotelbluediamondnagpur.com; 113 Central Ave; s/d ₹500/700, with AC ₹1350/1500; ❄) The mirrored ceiling in reception is straight out of a 1970s nightclub, and the rooms are pretty much the type you'd expect above a 1970s nightclub. There's a dungeon-like bar on the mezzanine floor. AC rooms have LCD TVs and crumpled linoleum flooring.

Hotel Centre Point   HOTEL $$

(☑ 2420910; www.centrepointgroup.org; 24 Central Bazar Rd, Ramdaspeth; s/d incl breakfast from ₹4345/4932; ❄ 🛜 ⛱) A trusted address that's been setting the standards of luxury in Nagpur for some time now. Rooms are plush, with fluffy beds and high-speed internet

access, and there's a coffee shop and restaurant. It's located in the heart of the business and entertainment district, and airport transfers are complimentary.

Pride Hotel   HOTEL $$$

(☑ 2291102; www.pridehotel.com; Wardha Rd, opposite airport; s/d from ₹5262/5430; ❄ 🛜 ⛱) Located close to the airport and away from the din of the city, this sleek business hotel is a good stopover option for touch-and-go travellers. Royal Lancers, its lobby bar, and Puran Da Dhaba, a dolled-up version of a traditional Punjabi eatery, are good places to settle in for the evening.

Krishnum   SOUTH INDIAN $

(Central Ave; mains ₹50-80) This popular place dishes out South Indian snacks and generous thalis, as well as freshly squeezed fruit juices. There are branches found in other parts of town.

Picadilly Checkers   FAST FOOD $

(VCA Complex, Civil Lines; mains ₹60-80) A favourite eating joint for Nagpur's college brigade. A good range of all-vegetarian quick bites are on offer.

ⓘ Information

Numerous ATMs line Central Ave.

Computrek (18 Central Ave; per hr ₹20; �⌚10am-10pm) Internet access on the main drag.

MTDC (☑2533325; near MLA Hostel, Civil Lines; ☌10am-5.45pm Mon-Sat)

State Bank of India (Kingsway; ☌11am-2pm Mon-Fri) A two-minute walk west of the train station. Deals in foreign exchange.

ⓘ Getting There & Away

AIR

Domestic airlines, including **Indian Airlines** (☑2533962) and **Jet Airways** (☑5617888), fly daily to Delhi (from ₹6000, 1½ hours), Mumbai (from ₹5000, 1½ hours) and Kolkata (from ₹8000, 1½ hours), as well as linking Hyderabad, Ahmedabad, Bengaluru, Chennai and Pune. Taxis/autorickshaws from the airport to the city centre cost ₹400/200.

BUS

The main MSRTC bus stand is 2km south of the train station. Ordinary buses head for Wardha (₹65, three hours) and Ramtek (₹40, 1½ hours). There are two buses to Jalgaon (₹370, 10 hours), and three to Hyderabad (₹358, 12 hours).

TRAIN

From Mumbai's Chhatrapati Shivaji Terminus (CST), the Duronto Express runs daily to Nagpur (sleeper/2AC ₹470/1825, 10 hours, 9:15pm). From Nagpur, it departs at 8.50pm and arrives at 7.50am the following morning. Heading north to Kolkata is the Gitanjali Express (sleeper/2AC ₹475/1920, 17½ hours, 7.05pm). Several expresses bound for Delhi and Mumbai stop at Jalgaon (for Ajanta caves; sleeper/2AC ₹282/1015, eight hours).

Around Nagpur

Ramtek

About 40km northeast of Nagpur, Ramtek is believed to be the place where Lord Rama, of the epic Ramayana, spent some time during his exile with his wife Sita and brother Lakshmana. The place is marked by a cluster of **temples** (◷ 6am-9pm) about 600 years old, which sit atop the Hill of Rama and have their own population of resident monkeys. Autorickshaws will cart you the 5km from the bus stand to the temple complex for ₹80. You can return to town via the 700 steps at the back of the complex. On the road to the temples you'll pass the delightful **Ambala Tank**, lined with small shrines. Boat rides around the lake are available.

Not far from the main temple cluster, **Rajkamal Resort** (☑ 07114202761; d without/with AC ₹1050/1410; ❄) has large, featureless rooms with TVs, and a basic restaurant-bar.

Buses run half-hourly between Ramtek and the MSRTC bus stand in Nagpur (₹41, 1½ hours). The last bus to Nagpur is at 7pm.

Sevagram

☑ 07152

About 85km from Nagpur, Sevagram (Village of Service) was chosen by Mahatma Gandhi as his base during the Indian Independence Movement. Throughout the freedom struggle, the village played host to several nationalist leaders, who would regularly come to visit the Mahatma at his **Sevagram Ashram** (☑ 284753; ◷ 6am-5.30pm). The overseers of this peaceful ashram, built on 40 hectares of farmland, have carefully restored the original huts where Gandhi lived and worked, and which now house some of his personal effects.

Very basic lodging is available in the **Yatri Nivas** (☑ 284753; d ₹100), across the road from the entry gate (booking recommended), and simple vegetarian meals can be served in the ashram's dining hall with prior notice.

Just 3km from Sevagram, Paunar village is home to the **Brahmavidya Mandir Ashram** (☑ 288388; Paunar; ◷ 4am-noon & 2-8pm). Founded by Vinoba Bhave, a nationalist and disciple of Gandhi, the ashram is run almost entirely by women. Modelled on *swaraj* (self-sufficiency), it's operated on a social system of consensus, with no central management.

Sevagram can be reached by taking a Wardha-bound bus from Nagpur (₹55, three hours).

TADOBA-ANDHARI TIGER RESERVE

Under India's Project Tiger directorate, this little-explored national park – with a healthy population of Bengal tigers – lies 150km south of Nagpur. Less visited than most other forests in India, this is a place where you can get up close with wildlife (which also includes gaurs, chitals, nilgais and sloth bears) without having to jostle past truckloads of shutter-happy tourists. The trade-off is that you'll have to make do with basic amenities and low comfort levels. The park remains open through most of the year.

The **MTDC Resort** (☑ 9822713201; d without/with AC ₹1645/1996; ❄) in nearby Moharli has decent rooms and dining facilities, though bring your own mosquito net. The resort can arrange jungle safaris in jeeps and minibuses. Bookings can be made at the MTDC's Nagpur office. If you're travelling in groups of six or more, MTDC can arrange an all-inclusive overnight package out of Nagpur, which takes care of logistical hassles.

Several state buses ply the road between Nagpur and Chandrapur through the day (₹124, 3½ hours).

SOUTHERN MAHARASHTRA

Konkan Coast

Despite being flanked on both ends by two of India's top urban centres, it's laudable how the Konkan Coast manages to latch on to its virginal bounties. A little-developed shoreline running southward from Mumbai all the way to Goa, it is a picturesque strip of land peppered with postcard beaches, vivid green paddy fields, rolling hills and decaying forts. Travelling through this tropical backwater can be sheer bliss. However, remember that accommodation is scant, the cuisine unsophisticated though tasty, and the locals unaccustomed to tour groups, especially foreigners. Since transport is both limited and unreliable, a good option is to rent a taxi in Mumbai and drift slowly down the coast to Goa. What you'll get in return is an experience that money can't buy.

Murud

☑ 02144 / POP 12,700

Even if you don't plan on exploring the whole coast, the sleepy fishing hamlet of Murud – 165km from Mumbai – should be on your itinerary. Once you step on to its lazy beaches and feel the warm surf rush past your feet, you'll be happy you came.

Sight-wise, Murud is home to the magnificent island fortress of **Janjira** (admission free; ☉ 7am-5.30pm), standing about 500m offshore. The citadel was built in 1140 by the Siddis, descendants of sailor-traders from the Horn of Africa, who settled here and allegedly made their living through piracy. No outsider ever made it past the fort's 12m-high walls which, when seen during high tide, seem to rise straight from the sea. Unconquered through history, the fort finally fell to the spoils of nature. Today, its ramparts are slowly turning to rubble as wilderness reclaims its innards.

The only way to reach Janjira is by boat (₹20 return, 15 minutes) from Rajpuri Port. Boats depart from 7am to 5.30pm daily, but require a minimum of 20 passengers. You can also have a boat to yourself (₹600), and most oarsmen will double as guides for a negotiable fee (around ₹350). To get to Rajpuri from Murud, take an autorickshaw (₹70) or hire a bicycle from the Golden Swan Beach Resort.

Back in Murud you can waste away the days on the beach, joining in with karate practice or playing cricket with locals. Alternately, you could peer through the gates of the off-limits Ahmedganj Palace, estate of the Siddi Nawab of Murud, or scramble around the decaying mosque and tombs on the south side of town.

🛏 Sleeping & Eating

Golden Swan Beach Resort　　　HOTEL $$
(☑ 274078; www.goldenswan.com; Darbar Rd; d incl full board from ₹4700; ❄) With only waving palms separating it from the beach, this upscale hotel offers accommodation in cosy rooms and cottages looking out to the sea, with views of the Ahmedganj Palace and Kasa Fort. There are also rooms in a charming old bungalow located five minutes away from the main property. Rates increase by 25% on weekends.

THE LEGEND OF 'BABA' AMTE

The legend of Murlidhar Devidas 'Baba' Amte (1914–2008) is oft-repeated in humanitarian circles around the world. Hailing from an upper-class Brahmin family in Wardha, Amte was snugly ensconced in material riches and on his way to becoming a successful lawyer, when he witnessed a leper die unattended in the streets one night. It was an incident that changed him forever.

Soon after, Amte renounced worldly comforts, embracing an austere life through which he actively worked for the benefit of leprosy patients and those belonging to marginalised communities. In the primitive forested backyards of eastern Maharashtra, he set up his ashram called **Anandwan** (Forest of Joy; anandwan@gmail.com). A true Gandhian, Amte believed in self-sufficiency, and his lifelong efforts saw several awards being conferred upon him, including the Ramon Magsaysay Award in 1985.

Amte's work has been continued by his sons Vikas and Prakash and their wives – the latter couple also won the Magsaysay Award in 2008. The family now runs three ashrams in these remote parts to care for the needy, both humans and animals. Volunteering opportunities are available.

BOUNDLESS BEACHES

Apart from its main sands, the Konkan Coast boasts a string of less-explored but heavenly beaches that host weekend-away-type resorts for stressed-out Mumbai-ites. About 17km north of Murud, well connected by share autorickshaws (₹100), lies **Kashid,** a fantastic beach where you can cosy up with your favourite paperback while sipping on tender coconuts.

South of Murud is **Diveagar**, swarming with colonies of sand bubbler crabs, scenic **Harihareshwar**, famous for its seaside temple, and serene **Vengurla**, 10km from Tarkarli (p796), a place you probably wouldn't mind being shipwrecked. Most of these places are connected by back roads where public transport is scant, so they are best visited in a hired cab.

Sea Shell Resort　　　　HOTEL $$
(📞 274306; www.seashellmurud.com; Darbar Rd; d without/with AC ₹2280/2500; ❄ 🏊) A cheery place with breezy sea facing rooms and a multicuisine restaurant, this understated hotel scores quite well with Mumbai's weekend travellers. The swimming pool at the entrance is a welcome addition, and dolphin safaris can be arranged.

★**New Sea Rock Restaurant**　　INDIAN $
(Rajpuri; mains ₹50-160; ⏱ 7am-8pm) Perched on a cliff overlooking the beach at Rajpuri, this joint has an awesome view of Janjira. A perfect place to steal a million-dollar sunset for the price of a chai (₹10), though you will probably be tempted to try the Indian or Chinese mains. The proprietors also arrange kayak rides and other water sports during the high season.

Hotel Vinayak　　　　　INDIAN $
(Darbar Rd; mains ₹70-190; ⏱ 8am-10pm) A decent place overlooking the beach to tuck into a delicious and fiery Malvani thali, served with pink kokam syrup to smother the spices. Veg and nonveg dishes available.

❶ Getting There & Away

AC catamarans (₹120, two hours) from the Gateway of India in Mumbai cruise to Mandva pier between 6am and 7pm. The ticket includes a free shuttle bus to Alibag (30 minutes), otherwise an autorickshaw will be about ₹200. Rickety local buses from Alibag head down the coast to Murud (₹41, two hours). Alternatively, buses from Mumbai Central bus stand take almost six hours to Murud (ordinary/semideluxe ₹133/180).

Avoid the train. The nearest railhead is at Roha, two hours away and poorly connected.

Ganpatipule

📞 02357

Primarily a temple town, Ganpatipule has been luring a steady stream of sea-lovers over the years with its warm waters and lonely stretches of sand. Located about 375km from Mumbai, it's a village that snoozes through much of the year, except during holidays such as Diwali or Ganesh Chaturthi. These are times when hordes of boisterous 'tourists' turn up to visit the seaside **Ganesha Temple** (⏱ 6am-9pm) housing a monolithic Ganesha (painted a bright orange), supposedly discovered 1600 years ago.

Activities on and off the beach at Ganpatipule include camel (₹50) and boat (₹100) rides. Neither of which are recommended over a long walk on the sand away from the crowd.

About 40km south, **Ratnagiri** is the largest town on the southern Maharashtra coast and the main train station for Ganpatipule (it's on the Konkan Railway). You'll also find several ATMs strung along Ratnagiri's main street. But once you've refilled your wallet and gone shopping for conveniences, the only sight worth checking out – apart from a dirty beach – are the remnants of the **Thibaw Palace** (Thibaw Palace Rd; admission free; ⏱ 10am-5.30pm Tue-Sun), where the last Burmese king, Thibaw, was interned under the British from 1886 until his death in 1916.

🛏 Sleeping & Eating

MTDC Resort　　　　　HOTEL $$
(📞 235248; d without/with AC from ₹1938/2280; ❄) Spread over prime beachfront, this is the best place to stay. It's well kept with a small army of gardeners, and offers an assortment of rooms and cottages. It also packs in a decent restaurant with cold beer. The Konkani

huts, themed on traditional Malvani villages, is an offshoot located well away from the main resort, which offers its own restaurant with beachside dining and a bit more seclusion. The huts themselves are basic concrete blocks, but OK.

Hotel Vihar Deluxe
HOTEL $$

(☑ 02352222944; Main Rd, Ratnagiri; d without/with AC ₹1285/1754; ❈) This gigantic operation is one of a few functional hotels that line the main strip in Ratnagiri. It was undergoing extensive renovations when we visited. Rooms reflect the business traveller mindset and are far from luxurious, while the food – especially the seafood – is commendable. A South Indian breakfast is complimentary.

Tarang Restaurant
INDIAN $

(MTDC Resort; mains ₹80-190) This is just one of several similar places where you can grab a decent, inexpensive meal, such as a thali or Chinese noodles in Ganpatipule.

❶ Getting There & Around

Ordinary buses shuttle between Ganpatipule and Ratnagiri (₹49, 1½ hours). An autorickshaw will cost ₹400. An autorickshaw ride from the MSRTC bus stand to the MTDC Resort will cost ₹25.

One MSRTC bus heads out at 8.45am to Mumbai (₹428, 10 hours), and departs from Mumbai at 8pm. There are three daily buses each to Pune (₹330) and Kohlapur (₹135).

Ratnagiri's train station is 6km out of town on the road to/from Kohlapur. From Ratnagiri, the Mandovi Express goes to Mumbai (2nd class/1st class ₹123/1365, 6½ hours, 2.25pm). The return train heading for Goa (2nd class/1st class ₹105/1125, 3½ hours) is at 1.15pm. From Ratnagiri's old bus stand, semideluxe buses leave for Goa (₹255, seven hours) and Kolhapur (₹150, four hours).

❶ Information

There is a Bank of Maharashtra ATM at the entrance of the Ganesha Temple, and a much more reliable Bank of India ATM in town, about 400m from the MTDC Resort. For internet (₹100 per hour), look for Tapaswi Sandanand Niwas who works in the Spanco office beside the Bank of Maharashtra (not the aforementioned ATM).

Tarkarli & Malvan
☑ 02365

A government tourism promo parades this place as comparable to Tahiti, which may be a bit ambitious! Within striking distance of

Goa, about 200km from Ratnagiri, pristine Tarkarli boasts near-white sands and sparkling waters, but what's lacking is tourist infrastructure and resort-style comforts, but do you care?

The monstrous **Sindhudurg Fort**, built by Shivaji and dating from 1664, lies on an offshore island and can be reached by frequent ferries (₹30) from Malvan. MTDC can arrange snorkelling trips to the clear waters around the fortress.

Of the few hotels and resorts available, the good old **MTDC Holiday Resort** (☑ 252390; d from ₹2280; ❈) is still your most economical bet. Enquire at the resort about backwater tours on its fabulous **houseboats** (☑ 8805389003; standard/luxury incl full board ₹7410/9690).

The closest train station is Kudal, 38km away. Frequent buses (₹28, one hour) cover the route from Malvan bus stand. An autorickshaw from Kudal to Malvan or Tarkarli is about ₹500. Malvan has buses daily to Panaji (₹79, three hours) and a couple of services to Ratnagiri (₹147, five hours).

Matheran
☑ 02148 / POP 5287 / ELEV 803M

Literally 'Jungle Above', Matheran is a tiny patch of peace and quiet capping a craggy Sahyadri summit within spitting distance of Mumbai's heat and grime. Endowed with shady forests criss-crossed with foot trails and breathtaking lookouts, it is easily the most elegant of Maharashtra's hill stations.

The credit for discovering this little gem goes to Hugh Malet, erstwhile collector of Thane district, who chanced upon it during one of his excursions in 1850. Soon it became a hill station patronised by the British and populated by Parsi families.

Getting to Matheran is really half the fun. While speedier options are available by road, nothing beats arriving in town on the narrow-gauge toy train that chugs laboriously along a 21km scenic route to the heart of the settlement. Motor vehicles are banned within Matheran, making it an ideal place to give your ears and lungs a rest and your feet some exercise.

◉ Sights & Activities

You can walk along shady forest paths to most of Matheran's viewpoints in a matter of hours, and it's a place well suited to stress-free ambling. To catch the sunrise, head to **Panorama Point**, while **Porcupine Point** (also known as Sunset Point) is the most popular (read: packed) as the sun drops. **Louisa Point** and **Little Chouk Point** also have stunning views of the Sahyadris, and if you're visiting **Echo Point**, give it a yell. Stop at **Charlotte Lake** on the way back from Echo Point, but don't go for a swim – this is the town's main water supply and stepping in is prohibited. You can reach the valley below One Tree Hill down the path known as **Shivaji's Ladder**, supposedly trod upon by the Maratha leader himself.

A couple of **ropeways** (₹250) have sprung up for those that find the peaceful setting, well, too peaceful. The best of these takes you out between Honeymoon Point and Louisa Point. There's a shorter one at Myra Point that seems to be anchored by a rather wimpy looking tree.

Horses can be hired along MG Rd for rides to the lookout points; they cost about ₹300 per hour (negotiable).

🛏 Sleeping & Eating

Apart from a few exceptions, hotels in Matheran are generally overpriced for what's on offer. Many places have a minimum two-night stay, which makes sense, as there's no point in rushing a trip to a place geared for relaxation. Check-out times vary wildly (as early as 7am), as do high- and low-season rates. Matheran shuts shop during the monsoons.

Hope Hall Hotel   HOTEL **$**
(📞230253; MG Rd; d from ₹1000) 'Since 1875', says a plaque at the entrance, and frankly, the age shows! However, going by the 'thank you' notes left by guests, it must be a cheerful place to stay. Be prepared for mosquitoes (and their multilegged friends and enemies), bucket hot water and the lack of an inhouse restaurant.

Lord's Central Hotel   HERITAGE HOTEL **$$**
(📞230228; www.matheranhotels.com; MG Rd; d incl full board from ₹4600; ❄@⊠) Owned by a gracious Parsi family for over six generations, this charming colonial-style affair is one of Matheran's most reputed establishments, and guarantees a pleasant stay within its old-world portals. The rooms are comfy, the swimming-pool deck offers fabulous views of the valley and distant peaks, and a jumbo chess board out on the lawns is a nice place to down a beer.

Hotel Woodlands   HOTEL **$$**
(📞230271; www.woodlandsmatheran.com; Chinoy Rd; d 1/2-nights ₹3765/5035) Woodlands is a venerable old homestead with historic charm and enough modern comforts thrown in to keep the most fussy guest satisfied. The forested setting is very relaxing and the playground should keep the kids occupied. But it's the verandah that steals the show; a great place to kick back and dine.

⭐**Verandah In The Forest**   HERITAGE HOTEL **$$$**
(📞230296; www.neemranahotels.com; Barr House; d incl breakfast from ₹5883) This deliciously preserved 19th-century bungalow thrives on undiluted nostalgia. Step past the threshold of one of its quaintly luxurious rooms or suites and find yourself reminiscing about bygone times in the company of ornate candelabras, antique teak furniture, Victorian canvases, grandfather clocks and a rush of other memorabilia. The eponymous verandah is probably the most beautiful location from where to admire Matheran's woods, and there's a good selection of food and beverages to keep you company.

Shabbir Bhai   INDIAN **$**
(Merry Rd; mains ₹70-100; ⊙10am-10pm) Known locally as the 'Byrianiwala', this funky joint has a full North Indian menu, but here it's all about the spicy biryanis: chicken, mutton and veg. To find it, take the footpath uphill beside the Jama Masjid on MG Rd and follow your nose.

Rasna   INDIAN **$**
(MG Rd; mains ₹100-150; ⊙9am-11pm) This simple and cheerful restaurant opposite Naoroji Lord Garden serves tasty vegetarian food. Try the popular Punjabi (North Indian) thali.

ℹ Information

Entry to Matheran costs ₹40 (₹20 for children), which you pay on arrival at the train station or the Dasturi car park.

You can buy an entertaining, if not entirely accurate, guidebook and map (₹15) at many of the shops along MG Rd. The **Union Bank of India** (MG Rd; ⊙10am-2pm Mon-Fri, to noon Sat) has an ATM.

ℹ Getting There & Away

TAXI
Buses (₹25) and share taxis (₹70) run from Neral to Matheran's Dasturi car park (30 minutes). You could take the taxi without sharing for ₹350. Horses (₹300) and hand-pulled rickshaws

(₹400) wait here to whisk you (relatively speaking) to Matheran's main bazaar. You can also walk this stretch in a little under an hour and your luggage can be hauled for you for ₹200.

TRAIN

The toy train (2nd class/1st class ₹35/225) chugs between Matheran and Neral Junction five times daily. The service is suspended during monsoons. From Mumbai, Mumbai Suburban Rail (Central), on the Mumbai CST–Khopoli line, departs Mumbai CST at 12.19pm to arrive at Neral Junction (2nd class/1st class ₹19/155) at 2.03pm.

Express trains from Mumbai CST include the 7.10am Deccan Express and the 8.40am Koyna Express (2nd class/chair ₹56/249, 1½ hours), which stop at Neral junction. Other expresses from Mumbai stop at Karjat, down the line from Neral, from where you can backtrack on a local train or catch a bus to Matheran (₹30). From Pune, you can reach Karjat by the Sinhagad Express (2nd class/chair ₹57/249, two hours, 6.05am). Note: trains from Pune don't stop at Neral Junction.

ⓘ Getting Around

Apart from hand-pulled rickshaws and horses, walking is the only other transport option in Matheran.

Lonavla

☏ 02114 / ELEV 625M

Lonavla is an overdeveloped (and overpriced) mercantile town about 106km southeast of Mumbai. It's far from attractive, with its main drag consisting almost exclusively of garishly lit shops flogging *chikki*, the rock-hard, brittle sweet made in the area.

The only reason you'd want to come here is to visit the nearby Karla and Bhaja Caves which, after those at Ellora and Ajanta, are the best in Maharashtra.

Hotels, restaurants and the main road to the caves lie north of the train station (exit from platform 1). Most of the Lonavla township and its markets are located south of the station.

🏃 Activities

Founded in 1924, the **Kaivalyadhama Yoga Hospital** (☏ 273039; www.kdham.com; s/d per week incl full board from ₹4700/8000), set about 2km from Lonavla en route to the Karla and Bhaja Caves, combines yoga courses with naturopathic therapies. Room rates cover accommodation, yoga sessions,

programs and lectures over seven days. Two-, three- and four-week packages are also offered.

Mumbai-based **Nirvana Adventures** (☏ 022-26053724; www.flynirvana.com) offers various paragliding courses (including full board from ₹8000) or 10-minute tandem flights (₹2500) at Kamshet, 25km from Lonavla.

🛏 Sleeping & Eating

Lonavla's hotels suffer from inflated prices and low standards. All hotels listed here have a 10am checkout.

Hotel Adarsh   HOTEL $$

(☏ 272353; near bus stand; d from ₹3248; ❄ ❂) This is clearly the best-value place in town. Centrally located, it has smart rooms and good service, and the terrace pool gives you another good reason to stay.

Hotel Lonavla   HOTEL $$

(☏ 272914; Mumbai–Pune Rd; d from ₹1495, with AC ₹2495) Relatively cheap by Lonavla's standards. Bulk bookings can often leave you without a room, so enquire in advance. They insist that you clear your bills every third day (who stays that long anyway?).

Biso   ITALIAN $$

(Citrus Hotel, DT Shahani Rd; mains ₹220-300) This could be a delightfully redeeming feature of your Lonavla trip. A top-class alfresco restaurant thrown around the lawns of a sleek business hotel about 15 minutes east of the bus stand, Biso serves an excellent selection of pastas, wood-fired pizzas and desserts.

ⓘ Information

The petrol pump opposite Hotel Rama Krishna now has three ATMs dispensing cash. Internet access is available at **Balaji Cyber Café** (1st fl, Khandelwal Bldg, New Bazaar; per hr ₹15; ◷ 12.30-10.30pm), immediately south of the train station.

ⓘ Getting There & Away

Lonavla is serviced by MSRTC buses departing from the bus stand to Dadar in Mumbai (ordinary/semideluxe ₹74/107, two hours) and Pune (ordinary/semideluxe ₹62/91, two hours). Luxury AC buses (₹200) also travel to both cities.

All express trains from Mumbai to Pune stop at Lonavla (2nd class/chair ₹65/273, 2½ hours). From Pune, you can also reach Lonavla by taking an hourly shuttle train (₹15, two hours).

Karla & Bhaja Caves

While they pale in comparison to Ajanta or Ellora, these rock-cut caves (dating from around the 2nd century BC) are among the better examples of Buddhist cave architecture in India. They are also low on commercial tourism, which make them ideal places for a quiet excursion. Karla has the most impressive single cave, but Bhaja is a quieter site to explore.

◉ Sights

Karla Cave
CAVE

(Indian/foreigner ₹5/100; ⊙ 9am-5pm) Karla Cave, the largest early Buddhist *chaitya* in India, is reached by a 20-minute climb from a mini-bazaar at the base of a hill. Completed in 80 BC, the *chaitya* is around 40m long and 15m high, and sports similar architectural motifs as *chaityas* in Ajanta and Ellora. Excluding Ellora's Kailasa Temple, this is probably the most impressive cave temple in the state.

A semicircular 'sun window' filters light in towards a dagoba or stupa (the cave's representation of the Buddha), protected by a carved wooden umbrella, the only remaining example of its kind. The cave's roof also retains ancient teak buttresses. The 37 pillars forming the aisles are topped by kneeling elephants. The carved elephant heads on the sides of the vestibule once had ivory tusks.

There's a **Hindu temple** in front of the cave, thronged by pilgrims whose presence adds colour to the scene.

Bhaja Caves
CAVE

(Indian/foreigner ₹5/100; ⊙ 8am-6pm) Across the expressway, it's a 3km jaunt from the main road to the Bhaja Caves, where the setting is lusher, greener and quieter than at Karla Cave. Thought to date from around 200 BC, 10 of the 18 caves here are *viharas,* while Cave 12 is an open *chaitya,* earlier than that at Karla, containing a simple dagoba. Beyond this is a strange huddle of 14 stupas, five inside and nine outside a smaller cave.

🛏 Sleeping & Eating

MTDC Karla Resort
HOTEL $$

(☎ 02114-282230; d without/with AC from ₹1740/2090; ❄) Set off the highway, close to the Karla–Bhaja access point, this place is much more peaceful than Lonavla. Rooms and cottages are well kept, and there's a good restaurant.

❶ Getting There & Away

Karla and Bhaja can be visited on a local bus (₹15, 30 minutes) to the access point, from where it's about a 6km return walk on each side to the two sites. But that would be exhausting and hot. An autorickshaw should charge about ₹500 from Lonavla for the tour, including waiting time.

Pune

📋 020 / POP 3.1 MILLION / ELEV 535M

Once little more than an army outpost, Pune (also pronounced 'Poona') is a city that epitomises 'New India', with its baffling mix of capitalism, spirituality, ancient and modern. Today, it is a thriving centre of academia and business. Pune is also famous, or notorious, globally for its number-one export: the late guru Bhagwan Shree Rajneesh and his ashram, the Osho International Meditation Resort.

Pune was initially given pride of place by Shivaji and the ruling Peshwas, who made it their capital. The British took the city in 1817 and, thanks to its cool and dry climate, soon made it the Bombay Presidency's monsoon capital. Globalisation knocked on Pune's doors in the 1990s, following which it went in for an image overhaul. However, some colonial-era charm was retained in a few of its old buildings and residential areas, bringing about a pleasant coexistence of the old and new, which (despite the pollution and hectic traffic) makes Pune a worthwhile place to explore. In September Ganesh Chaturthi brings on a tide of festivities across the city, and provides a fantastic window for exploring the city's cultural side. On a more sombre note, the fatal 2010 terrorist attack on the German Bakery, a once favourite haunt for travellers and ashramites alike, remains a painful memory in this peace-loving city.

The city sits at the confluence of the Mutha and Mula rivers. Mahatma Gandhi (MG) Rd, about 1km south of Pune train station, is the main commercial street. Koregaon Park, northeast of the train station, is the destination for backpackers and pilgrims. Here you'll find numerous hotels, restaurants, coffee shops and of course, the Osho Ashram.

Pune

◎ Sights & Activities

Raja Dinkar Kelkar Museum   MUSEUM
(www.rajakelkarmuseum.com; Bajirao Rd, 1377-1378
Natu Baug; Indian/foreigner ₹20/200; ⊙ 9.30am-
5.30pm) This peculiar museum is one of
Pune's true delights, housing only a fraction

of the 20,000-odd objects of Indian daily life
painstakingly collected by Dinkar Kelkar
(who died in 1990). The quirky pan-Indian
collection includes hundreds of hookah
pipes, writing instruments, lamps, textiles,
toys, entire doors and windows, kitchen

Pune

utensils, furniture, puppets, jewellery, betelnut cutters and an amazing gallery of musical instruments.

Tribal Cultural Museum   MUSEUM
(28 Queen's Garden; admission ₹10; ◉10.30am-5.30pm Mon-Sat) About 1.5km east of the train station, near the army cantonment, this small museum showcases artefacts (jewellery, utensils, musical instruments, even black-magic accessories) from remote tribal belts. Don't forget to check out the section featuring ornate papier-mâché festival masks, to the rear of the building.

Aga Khan Palace   PALACE
(Ahmednagar Rd; Indian/foreigner ₹5/100; ◉9am-5.45pm) Set amid a wooded 6.5-hectare plot across the Mula River in Yerwada, the grand Aga Khan Palace (housing the **Gandhi National Memorial**) is easily Pune's biggest crowd-puller. Built in 1892 by Sultan Aga Khan III, this lofty building was where the Mahatma and other prominent nationalist leaders were interned by the British for about two years following Gandhi's Quit India resolution in 1942. Both Kasturba Gandhi, the Mahatma's wife, and Mahadeobhai Desai, his secretary for 35 years, died here in confinement. You'll find their shrines (containing their ashes) in a quiet garden to the rear.

Within the main palace, you can peek into the room where Gandhi used to stay. Photos and paintings exhibit moments in his extraordinary career.

Shaniwar Wada   FORT
(Shivaji Rd; Indian/foreigner ₹5/100; ◉8am-6pm) The remains of this fortressed palace of the Peshwa rulers are located in the old part of the city. Built in 1732, Shaniwar Wada was destroyed in a fire in 1828, but the massive walls and plinths remain, as do the sturdy palace doors with their daunting spikes. In the evenings, there is an hour-long **sound-and-light show** (admission ₹25; ◉8.15pm Thu-Tue).

Pataleshvara Cave Temple   TEMPLE
(Jangali Maharaj Rd; ◉6am-9.30pm) Set across the river is the curious rock-cut Pataleshvara Cave Temple, a small and unfinished (though living) 8th-century temple, similar in style to the grander caves at Elephanta Island. Adjacent is the **Jangali Maharaj**

Temple (☉ 6am-9.30pm), dedicated to a Hindu ascetic who died here in 1818.

★ Osho International
Meditation Resort   MEDITATION
(☎ 66019999; www.osho.com; 17 Koregaon Park) You'll either like it or hate it. A splurge of an institution, this ashram, located in a leafy, upscale northern suburb, has been drawing thousands of *sanyasins* (seekers), many of them Westerners, ever since the death of Osho in 1990. With its placid swimming pool, sauna, 'zennis' and basketball courts, massage and beauty parlour, bookshop and a luxury boutique guesthouse, it is, to some, the ultimate place to indulge in stress-busting meditation. Alternately, there are detractors who point fingers at the ashram's blatant commercialisation and accuse it of marketing a warped version of the mystic East to gullible Westerners.

The main centre for meditation and the nightly white-robed spiritual dance is the Osho Auditorium (no coughing or sneezing, please). The Osho Samadhi, where the guru's ashes are kept, is also open for meditation. The commune's 'Multiversity' runs a plethora of courses in meditation and other esoteric techniques. If you wish to take part, or even just meditate, you'll have to pay ₹1150/1550 (Indian/foreigner), which covers registration, a mandatory on-the-spot HIV test (sterile needles used), introductory sessions and your first day's meditation pass. You'll also need two robes (one maroon and one white, from ₹200 per robe). For subsequent days, a daily meditation pass costs ₹300/700 (Indian/foreigner), and you can come and go as you please. If you want further involvement, you can also sign up for a 'work as meditation' program.

The curious can watch a video presentation at the visitor centre and take a 10-minute silent tour of the facilities (₹10; adults only, cameras and phones prohibited) at 9.15am and 2pm daily. Tickets have to be booked at least a day in advance (9.30am to 1pm and 2pm to 4pm). It's also worth checking out the 5-hectare garden, **Osho Teerth** (admission free; ☉ 6-9am & 3-6pm), behind the commune, and accessible all day for those with a meditation pass.

Ramamani Iyengar
Memorial Yoga Institute   YOGA
(☎ 25656134; www.bksiyengar.com; Model Colony, 1107 B/1 Hare Krishna Mandir Rd) To attend classes at this famous institute, 7km northwest of the train station, you need to have been practising yoga for at least eight years.

🛏 Sleeping

Pune's accommodation hubs are around the train station and Koregaon Park. Most midrange hotels have checkout at noon, and accept credit cards. Many families in

---

OSHO: GURU OF SEX

Ever tried mixing spirituality with primal instincts, and garnishing with oodles of expensive trinkets? Well, Bhagwan Shree Rajneesh (1931–90) certainly did. Osho, as he preferred to be called, was one of India's most flamboyant 'export gurus' to market the mystic East to the world, and undoubtedly the most controversial. Initially based in Pune, he followed no particular religion or philosophy, and outraged many across the world with his advocacy of sex as a path to enlightenment. A darling of the international media, he quickly earned himself the epithet 'sex guru'. In 1981, Rajneesh took his curious blend of Californian pop psychology and Indian mysticism to the USA, where he set up an agricultural commune in Oregon. There, his ashram's notoriety, as well as its fleet of (material and thus valueless!) Rolls Royces grew, until raging local paranoia about its activities moved the authorities to charge Osho with immigration fraud. He was fined US$400,000 and deported. An epic journey then began, during which Osho and his followers, in their search for a new base, were either deported from or denied entry into 21 countries. By 1987, he was back at his Pune ashram, where thousands of foreigners soon flocked for his nightly discourses and meditation sessions.

They still come from across the globe. Such is the demand for the resort's facilities that prices are continually on the rise, with luxury being redefined every day. Interestingly, despite Osho's comments on how nobody should be poor, no money generated by the resort goes into helping the disadvantaged. That, resort authorities maintain, is up to someone else.

Koregaon Park rent out rooms starting at about ₹500. Rickshaw drivers will know where to find homestays.

National Hotel HOTEL $

(☎ 26125054; 14 Sassoon Rd; s/d/q ₹750/850, cottages s/d ₹550/650) What the National can't provide in terms of comfort, it compensates for with antique charm. Housed in a crumbling colonial-era mansion opposite the train station, the spacious, low-end rooms in this hotel may not match your idea of 'clean'. The cottages across the garden are more cramped, but come with tiled sit-outs.

★**Hotel Surya Villa** HOTEL $$

(☎ 26124501; www.hotelsuryavilla.com; 294/2 Koregaon Park; s/d from ₹1490/1761, with AC ₹1761/2348; ✽) A bright and cheerful place with spotless and spacious rooms, this is one of the best of Pune's midrange options. It stands just off the Koregaon Park backpacker hub, so you're always clued in to the coolest developments in town. Decent breakfasts and other meals are available next door at the associated Yogi Tree Cafe.

★**Hotel Sunderban** HOTEL $$

(☎ 26124949; www.tghotels.com; 19 Koregaon Park; s/d incl breakfast from ₹2936/3523; ✽ ⎙) Set around a manicured lawn right next to the Osho Resort, this renovated art-deco bungalow effortlessly combines classy antiquity with boutique appeal. The huge non-AC rooms in the main building sport a variety of dated furniture, and have a generally quaint air. The pricier rooms are across the lawns, in a sleek, glass-fronted building. An additional draw is the in-house fine-dining restaurant, Dario's (p804).

Hotel Lotus HOTEL $$

(☎ 26139701; www.hotelsuryavilla.com; Lane 5, Koregaon Park; s/d ₹1644/2231, with AC ₹2231/2818; ✽) Hotel Lotus is a sibling to Hotel Surya Villa, and really you are paying a bit extra for the quiet Koregaon Park location, as the rooms are not as spacious here. There's also no attached restaurant, although there are plenty of eating options close by.

Hotel Ritz HOTEL $$

(☎ 26122995; fax 26136644; 6 Sadhu Vaswani Path; s/d incl breakfast from ₹2348/2936; ✽) Plush, friendly, atmospheric: three words that best describe the Ritz, a Raj-era building that holds its own in town. There are just three Royal deluxe rooms in the main building, while the cheaper ones are located in an an-

nexe next to the garden restaurant, which serves good Gujarati and Maharashtrian food. There's also safe parking and a helpful travel desk.

Hotel Homeland HOTEL $$

(☎ 26123203; www.hotelhomeland.net; 18 Wilson Garden; s/d ₹1050/1292, with AC from ₹1521/1755; ✽) A surprisingly restful place, Homeland is very convenient to the train station, yet tucked away from the associated din. The labyrinthine corridors lead to rooms with freshly painted walls and clean sheets, and the restaurant downstairs shows movies in the evenings.

Samrat Hotel HOTEL $$

(☎ 26137964; thesamrathotel@vsnl.net; 17 Wilson Garden; s/d incl breakfast from ₹2114/2583; ✽ ⎙) A slick business-traveller hotel with excellent rooms opening around a central, top-lit foyer, this place sure knows how to make you feel special. The staff is courteous and eager to please, and the well-appointed rooms meet every expectation you could have from hotels in this price bracket. Complimentary airport pick-up.

Hotel Srimaan HOTEL $$

(☎ 26136565; srimaan@vsnl.com; 361/5 Bund Garden Rd; s/d ₹2936/3405; ✽ @ ⎙) A central location, free wi-fi, and a very good Italian restaurant, Little Italy La Pizzeria, earn this place plenty of points before you even step into the compact but luxurious rooms. The pricier rooms have lovely windows with soothing green views outside.

Osho Meditation Resort Guesthouse GUESTHOUSE $$$

(☎ 66019900; www.osho.com; Koregaon Park; s/d ₹7397/7985; ✽) This uberchic place will only allow you in if you come to meditate at the Osho International Meditation Resort. The rooms and common spaces are an elegant exercise in modern minimalist aesthetics with several ultra-luxe features, such as purified fresh-air supplied in all rooms! Be sure to book well in advance.

Westin HOTEL $$$

(☎ 67210000; www.starwoodhotels.com; 36/3B Koregaon Park Annexe; d incl breakfast from ₹8983; ✽ ⎙ ⎙) Sprawled out like a giant luxury yacht on Koregaon Park's eastern fringes is this plush international-standard hotel, combining the best of luxury and leisure with impeccable service. The rooms offer lovely views of the river and city.

✗ Eating

★**Kayani Bakery** BAKERY $
(6 East St; cakes & biscuits from per kg ₹200; ⊘7.30am-1pm & 3.30-8pm) A Raj-era institution that seems to be stuck in a time warp, where those in the know queue (in the loose sense of the word) for Shrewsbury biscuits (₹240 per kg), bread and Madeira cake.

Juice World CAFE $
(2436/B East St; snacks ₹60-70; ⊘11am-11.30pm) As well as producing delicious fresh fruit juices and shakes, this casual cafe with outdoor seating serves inexpensive but wholesome snacks such as pizza and *pav bhaji* (spiced vegetables and bread).

Coffee House CAFE $
(Moledina Rd; mains ₹60-130; ⊘8am-11.30pm) A calm and clean, coffee-coloured, almost art-deco retreat with booth seating, a huge inexpensive menu and satisfying filter coffee. Dishes include dosas and other excellent South Indian creations, plus North Indian curries and Chinese.

German Bakery BAKERY $
(North Main Rd; dishes ₹80-150, cakes ₹30-70; ⊘6.30am-11.30pm) Pune's melting pot and once compulsory halt on the Koregaon Park backpacker trail, this long-running cafe has reopened after the fatal terrorist attack in 2010. It is known for its light, healthy snacks and a good range of cakes and puddings.

★**Malaka Spice** ASIAN FUSION $$
(North Main Rd, Lane 5, Koregaon Park; mains ₹275-650; ⊘11.30am-11.30pm) This upscale alfresco restaurant serves mouth-watering Southeast Asian fare that is given a creative tweak or two by its star chefs. There are plenty of seafood dishes, such as the grilled kingfish in banana leaves, or the burnt garlic and shrimp rice, plus vegetarian, chicken, duck and mutton offerings. The air-con section doubles as an art gallery, while outdoor diners are kept cool with an occasional spurt from the mist machine.

Prem's MULTICUISINE $$
(North Main Rd, Koregaon Park; mains ₹140-340; ⊘8am-11.30pm) In a quiet, tree-canopied courtyard tucked away behind a commercial block, Prem's is perfect for a lazy, beer-aided lunch session. Its relaxed ambience attracts droves of loyalists throughout the day, who slouch around the tables and put away countless pints of draught and imported beers before wolfing down their 'usual' orders. The noisy sizzlers are a hit with everyone, so don't leave without trying one.

The Place:
Touche the Sizzler MULTICUISINE $$
(7 Moledina Rd; mains ₹310-440; ⊘11.30am-3.30pm, 7-10.45pm) The perfect old-school eating option. A variety of smoking sizzlers (veg, seafood, beef, chicken), and other assorted Indian fare, is on offer at this Parsi-owned, family-style eatery. The ambience is 'quaint mess hall', but the overall experience more than makes up for it.

★**Dario's** ITALIAN $$$
(www.darios.in; Hotel Sunderban, 19 Koregaon Park, mains ₹310-380; ⊘11.30am-3pm & 7-11pm) This bistro serves only the best of Italian cuisine, made from a selection of local organic produce and hand-picked rations flown straight in from Italy. There's a yummy selection of homemade penne, gnocchi and spaghetti on offer, while dishes such as the *torta di funghi* (mushroom tart with pan-fried mushrooms, garlic, onion and chilli) serenade your palate with delicious flavours. Leave room for the tempting desserts.

♀ Drinking & Entertainment

Pune puts a great deal of effort into its nocturnal activities, yet some pubs tend to shut up shop as quickly as they open, so ask around for the latest hot spots. Most are open from 7pm to around 1.30am.

Café Barista CAFE $
(Sterling Centre, 12 MG Rd; ⊘8am-9pm) A branch of the popular coffee chain that dishes up decent espresso coffee.

1000 Oaks NIGHTCLUB
(2417 East St; ⊘7pm-late) This one is an old favourite among Pune's tipplers, featuring a cosy pub-style bar, a compact dance floor and a charming, foliaged and moodily lit sit-out area for those who prefer it quieter. There's live music on Sundays, to go with your favourite poison.

Mocha CAFE
(North Main Rd, Koregaon Park; ⊘8am-8pm) This popular cafe was undergoing renovations at the time of research, but we expect the friendly staff and brilliant selection of coffees from around the world, from the famed Jamaican Blue Mountain to Indian Peaberry

to return. There are flavoured hookahs on offer, too.

Arc Asia
BAR

(ABC Farms; ☺7.30pm-late) A classy affair, in the ABC Farms compound east of Koregaon Park. A great stock of malts, scotches and beers, with grooves on the PA.

Inox
CINEMA

(Bund Garden Rd) A multiplex where you can take in the latest blockbuster from Hollywood or Mumbai.

🛍 Shopping

Bombay Store
SOUVENIRS

(322 MG Rd; ☺10.30am-8.30pm Mon-Sat) The best spot for quality souvenirs and contemporary furnishings.

Pune Central
CLOTHING

(Bund Garden Rd, Koregaon Park) This glass-fronted mall is full of global labels and premium Indian tags.

Crossword
BOOKS

(Sohrab Hall, RBM Rd, 1st fll; ☺10.30am-9pm) An excellent collection of fiction, nonfiction and magazines. There's a smaller **branch** on East St.

Either Or
CLOTHING

(24/25 Sohrab Hall, 21 Sassoon Rd; ☺10.30am-8pm Fri-Wed) Modern designer Indian garments and accessories are available at this popular boutique.

Fabindia
CLOTHING

(Sassoon Rd, Sakar 10; ☺10am-8pm) For Indian saris, silks and cottons, as well as diverse accessories and handmade products.

ℹ Information

You'll find several internet cafes along Pune's main thoroughfares.

Destination Finder (₹65) provides a great map of the city, along with some key travel information.

There's a Citibank ATM on North Main Rd. HSBC dispenses cash at its main branch on Bund Garden Rd. You'll find ICICI Bank and State Bank of India ATMs at the railway station, an Axis Bank ATM on MG Rd and an HDFC Bank ATM on East St.

DHL (Bund Garden Rd; ☺10am-8pm Mon-Sat)

Internet Cafe (Koregaon Park; per hr ₹20) A short stroll from Hotel Surya Villa.

Main Post Office (Sadhu Vaswani Path; ☺10am-6pm Mon-Sat)

MTDC Tourist Office (☑26126867; I Block, Central Bldg, Dr Annie Besant Rd; ☺10am-5.30pm Mon-Sat, closed 2nd and 4th Sat) Buried in a government complex south of the train station. There's also an **MTDC desk** (☺10am-5.30pm Mon-Sat) at the train station.

Thomas Cook (☑66007903; 2418 G Thimmaya Rd; ☺9.30am-6pm Mon-Sat) Cashes travellers cheques and exchanges foreign currency.

Yatra.com (☑65006748; www.yatra.com; North Main Rd; ☺10am-7pm Mon-Sat) The city office of the reputed internet ticketing site of the same name.

ℹ Getting There & Away

AIR

Airlines listed below fly daily from Pune to Mumbai (from ₹5700, 45 minutes), Delhi (₹6300, two hours), Bengaluru (₹3400, 1½ hours), Nagpur (₹5600, 1½ hours), Goa (₹7500, 1½ hours), Chennai (₹6000, 1½ hours) and hopping flights to Kolkata (₹9000, four hours).

GoAir (☑9223222111; www.goair.in)

Indian Airlines (☑26052147; www.indian-airlines.nic.in; 39 Dr B Ambedkar Rd)

IndiGo (☑9910383838; www.goindigo.in)

Jet Airways (☑02239893333; www.jetair ways.com; 243 Century Arcade, Narangi Baug Rd)

SpiceJet (☑1800 1803333; www.spicejet.com)

MAJOR TRAINS FROM PUNE

Express fares are sleeper/2AC; Deccan Queen fares are 2nd class/chair.

DESTINATION	TRAIN NO & NAME	FARE (₹)	DURATION (HR)	DEPARTURE
Bengaluru	16529 Udyan Express	414/1735	21	11.45am
Chennai	12163 Chennai Express	465/1880	19½	12.10am
Delhi	11077 Jhelum Express	547/2295	27	5.20pm
Hyderabad	17031 Hyderabad Express	321/1320	13½	4.35pm
Mumbai CST	12124 Deccan Queen	86/355	3½	7.15am

BUS

Several private buses head to Panaji (Panjim) in Goa (ordinary/air-con sleeper ₹650/850, 12 hours), Nasik (semideluxe/deluxe ₹290/500, five hours) and Aurangabad (₹200, six hours). Pune has three bus stands:

➡ **Pune train station stand** (✆ 02026126218) For Mumbai, Goa, Belgaum, Kolhapur, Mahabaleshwar and Lonavla. Deluxe buses shuttle from here to Dadar (Mumbai) every hour (₹296, four hours).

➡ **Shivaji Nagar bus stand** (✆ 02025536970) For Aurangabad, Ahmedabad and Nasik.

➡ **Swargate bus stand** (✆ 02024441591) For Sinhagad, Bengaluru and Mangalore.

TAXI

Share taxis (up to four passengers) link Pune with Mumbai airport around the clock. They leave from the **taxi stand** (✆ 02026121090) in front of Pune train station (per seat ₹750, 2½ hours). Several tour operators hire out long-distance taxis over days or even weeks for intrastate travelling. Try **Simran Travels** (✆ 26153222; North Main Rd, Koregaon Park).

ℹ Getting Around

The airport is 8km northeast of the city, and boasts a swanky new building. An autorickshaw there costs about ₹120; a taxi is ₹300.

Autorickshaws can be found everywhere.

A ride from the train station to Koregaon Park costs about ₹40 (₹80 at night).

Turtle-paced city buses leave the **PMT depot** (opposite Pune train station) for Swargate (bus 4) and Shivaji Nagar (bus 5) and Koregaon Park (bus 159).

Around Pune

Sinhagad

The ruined **Sinhagad** (Lion Fort; admission free; ☉ dawn-dusk), about 24km southwest of Pune, was wrested by Maratha leader Shivaji from the Bijapur kings in 1670. In the epic battle (where he lost his son Sambhaji), Shivaji is said to have used monitor lizards yoked with ropes to scale the fort's craggy walls. Today, it's a sad picture of its past, but worth visiting for the sweeping views and opportunity to hike in the hills.

From Sinhagad village, share jeeps (₹50) can cart you 10km to the base of the summit. Bus 50 runs frequently to Sinhagad village from Swargate (₹25, 45 minutes).

Shivneri

Situated 90km northwest of Pune above the village of Junnar, **Shivneri Fort** (admission free; ☉ dawn-dusk) holds the distinction of being the birthplace of Shivaji. Within the ramparts of this ruined fort are the old royal stables, a mosque dating back to the Mughal era and several rock-cut reservoirs. The most important structure is Shivkunj, the pavilion in which Shivaji was born.

About 4km from Shivneri, on the other side of Junnar, is an interesting group of Hinayana Buddhist caves called **Lenyadri** (Indian/foreigner ₹5/100; ☉ dawn-dusk). Of the 30-odd caves, Cave 7 is the most impressive, and interestingly houses an image of the Hindu lord Ganesh.

A bus (₹80, two hours, 7.15am) goes to Junnar from Pune's Shivaji Nagar terminus. A return bus leaves Junnar at 11.30am. A day cab from Pune will cost at least ₹2500.

Mahabaleshwar

✆ 02168 / POP 12,750 / ELEV 1372M

Up in the Western Ghats, Mahabaleshwar – founded in 1828 by British governor Sir John 'Boy' Malcolm – was, at one time, the summer capital of the Bombay presidency. However, what was once a pretty hill station oozing old-world charm is today a jungle of mindless urban construction. Swarms of raucous holiday-makers who throw the place into a complete tizzy only make things worse. Mahabaleshwar's only face-saver is the delightful views it offers, but they're not half as good in practice, given that you'll have to combat the riotous tourists while appreciating them.

The hill station virtually shuts down during the monsoons (June to September), when an unbelievable 6m of rain falls.

The action can be found in the main bazaar (Main Rd, also called Dr Sabane Rd) – a 200m strip of holiday tack. The bus stand is at the western end. You have to cough up a ₹20 'tourist tax' on arrival.

⊙ Sights & Activities

Viewpoints   VIEWPOINT

The hills are alive with music, though it's usually blasted out of car stereos as people race to tick off all the viewpoints. To beat them, start very early in the morning, and you can savour fine views from **Wilson's**

Point (Sunrise Point), within easy walking distance of town, as well as **Elphinstone, Babington, Kate's** and **Lodwick Points**.

The sunset views at **Bombay Point** are stunning; but you won't be the only one thinking so! Much quieter, thanks to being 9km from town, is **Arthur's Seat**, on the edge of a 600m cliff. Attractive waterfalls around Mahabaleshwar include **Chinaman's, Dhobi's** and **Lingmala Falls**. A nice walk out of town is the two-hour stroll to Bombay Point, and then following **Tiger Trail** back in. Maps (₹20 to ₹65) of varying accuracy are available from several shops within the bazaar.

👉 Tours

Leaving the bus stand thrice from 2.15pm, the MSRTC conducts a Mahabaleshwar sightseeing round (₹80, 4½ hours) taking in nine viewpoints plus Old Mahabaleshwar. Alternatively, taxi drivers will give a 15-point, 2½-hour tour for ₹450. Tours are also available to Panchgani (₹500, 2½ hours) and Pratapgad Fort (₹750, three hours).

🛏 Sleeping

Hotel prices soar during weekends and peak holidays (November to June). At other times you might get hefty discounts. Most hotels are around the main bazaar, while dozens of resort-style lodges are scattered around the village. Check out is usually at 8am or 9am. If you're a lone male Indian traveller, be aware that most hotels will be reluctant to rent you a room.

MTDC Resort HOTEL **$**
(☑ 260318; Bombay Point Rd; d from ₹1645) This large-scale operation is situated about 2km southwest from town, and comes with quieter and greener surroundings. Rooms come in various grades but all smack of government aesthetics and suffer from the incredibly damp environment. Taxis can drop you here from the city centre for about ₹50.

Hotel Panorama HOTEL **$$**
(☑ 260404; www.panoramaresorts.net; 28 MG Rd; d without/with AC from ₹4150/4750; ❋ ☒) Business meets leisure at Mahabaleshwar's most reputed midtown address. Professionally managed, it boasts clean, comfy and tastefully appointed rooms, and there's some

BERRY FRESH

Fruity Mahabaleshwar is India's berry-growing hub, producing some of the country's finest strawberries, raspberries and gooseberries. Harvested from November to June, the best crops come around February and can be bought fresh at Mahabaleshwar's bazaar. You can also pick up fruit drinks, sweets, squashes, fudges or jams from reputed farms such as **Mapro Gardens** (☑ 02168240112; ⏱ 10am-1pm & 2-6.30pm), halfway between Mahabaleshwar and Panchgani.

great vegetarian food at the restaurant. There's a good-sized pool, and a water channel where you might want to ride a paddle boat.

Hotel Vyankatesh HOTEL **$$**
(☑ 260575; hotelvkt@yahoo.com; MG Rd; d from ₹2000) A typically overpriced hotel cashing in on Mahabaleshwar's never-ending tourism boom. Located behind a textile store, this place has slightly dreary, boxy rooms, but so have lots of hotels around town.

🍴 Eating & Drinking

Elsie's Dairy & Bakery BAKERY **$**
(MG Rd; ⏱ 7.30am-1pm) Since 1849 says the sign. Great for fresh cakes, biscuits, bread and nostalgia.

Aman Restaurant INDIAN **$**
(MG Rd; mains ₹80-150) Little more than a roadside stall, Aman can pull out some amazing kebabs and other meaty bites.

★ Grapevine MULTICUISINE **$$**
(Masjid Rd; mains ₹130-350; ⏱ 9.30am-3pm & 5-10pm) Skip this place, and you've missed half the fun in town. Tucked away behind the main drag, this tiny restaurant serves a delectable range of Indian, Continental and Thai dishes using organic vegetables and (safe) seafood. Do try the excellent Parsi fare, including the signature *dhansak*, or the cinnamon grilled chicken sticks with harissa. A wrought-iron table set-up at the entrance tastefully lends a Mediterranean air. And the bar boasts cold beer and a smart wine list (which you can purchase by the glass or bottle).

Cafe Coffee Day CAFE
(Masjid Rd; ⏰9am-6pm) Here at Cafe Coffee Day, you may have to tell the staff to turn on the generator first, but a decent espresso is your reward for patience.

ℹ Information

Joshi's Newspaper Agency (Main Rd; per hr ₹50; ⏰9am-9pm) Slow internet access if working at all.

MTDC Tourist Office (✆260318; Bombay Point Rd) At the MTDC Resort south of town.

RB Travels (✆260251; Main Rd) Local tours, ticketing, taxi hire and bus services.

State Bank of India (Main Rd; ⏰11am-5pm Mon-Fri, 11am-1pm Sat) Handles foreign currency. ATM on Masjid Rd.

ℹ Getting There & Away

From the bus stand, state buses leave regularly for Pune (semideluxe ₹150, 3½ hours) via Panchgani (₹25, 30 minutes). There's one ordinary bus to Goa (₹370, eight hours, 8.30am) via Kolhapur (₹150, five hours), while seven buses ramble off to Mumbai Central Station (ordinary/semideluxe ₹210/275, seven hours).

Private agents in the bazaar book luxury Mercedes and Volvo buses to destinations within Maharashtra, and Goa (seat/sleeper ₹1000/1300, 12 hours, with a changeover at Surur). Remember to ask where they intend to drop you. Buses to Mumbai (₹550, 6½ hours) generally don't go beyond Borivali, while those bound for Pune (₹350) will bid you adieu at Swargate.

ℹ Getting Around

Taxis and Maruti vans near the bus stand will take you to the main viewpoints or to Panchgani.

Cycling is also an option, but be careful of speeding traffic, especially on the outskirts. Bikes can be hired from **Vasant Cycle Mart** (Main Rd; per day ₹50; ⏰8am-8pm).

Around Mahabaleshwar

Pratapgad Fort

The windy **Pratapgad Fort** (admission free; ⏰7am-7pm), built by Shivaji in 1656 (and still owned by his descendents), straddles a high mountain ridge 24km northwest of Mahabaleshwar. In 1659, Shivaji agreed to meet Bijapuri General Afzal Khan here, in an attempt to end a stalemate. Despite a no-arms agreement, Shivaji, upon greeting Khan, disembowelled his enemy with a set of iron *baghnakh* (tiger's claws). Khan's tomb (out of bounds) marks the site of this painful encounter at the base of the fort.

Pratapgad is reached by a 500-step climb that affords brilliant views. Guides are available for ₹200 who will take you to 20 points of interest taking nearly two hours. The state bus (₹90 return, one hour, 9.30am) does a daily shuttle from Mahabaleshwar, with a waiting time of around one hour. A return taxi ride (2½ hours' waiting time) is about ₹750.

Raigad Fort

Some 80km from Mahabaleshwar, all alone on a high and remote hilltop, stands the enthralling **Raigad Fort** (Indian/foreigner ₹5/100; ⏰8am-5.30pm). Having served as Shivaji's capital from 1648 until his death in 1680, the fort was later sacked by the British, and some colonial structures added. But monuments such as the royal court, plinths of royal chambers, the main marketplace and Shivaji's tomb still remain, and it's worth a day's excursion.

You can hike a crazy 1475 steps to the top. But for a more 'levitating' experience, take the vertigo-inducing **ropeway** (return ₹175; ⏰8.30am-5.30pm), which zooms up the cliff and offers an eagle-eye view of the deep gorges below. Guides (₹200) are available within the fort complex. **Sarja Restaurant** (snacks ₹30-100), adjoining the ropeway's base terminal, is a good place for lunch or snacks.

Public transport to Raigad is infrequent and the road from Mahabaleshwar is in a terrible state. A return taxi from Mahabaleshwar will cost at least ₹2500.

Kolhapur

✆0231 / POP 549,283 / ELEV 550M

A little-visited town, Kolhapur is the perfect place to get intimate with the flamboyant side of India. Only a few hours from Goa, this historic town boasts an intensely fascinating temple complex. In August, Kolhapur is at its vibrant best, when **Naag Panchami** (⏰Jul/Aug), a snake-worshipping festival, is held in tandem with one at Pune. Gastronomes take note: the town is also the birthplace of the famed, spicy Kolhapuri cuisine, especially chicken and mutton dishes.

The old town around the Mahalaxmi Temple is 3km southwest of the bus and train stations, while the 'new' palace is a similar distance to the north. Rankala Lake, a popular spot for evening strolls, is 5km southwest of the stations.

◉ Sights

★ Shree Chhatrapati Shahu Museum
MUSEUM

(Indian/foreigner ₹18/30; ⊙9.30am-5.30pm) 'Bizarre' takes on a whole new meaning at this 'new' palace, an Indo-Saracenic behemoth designed by British architect 'Mad' Charles Mant for the Kolhapur kings in 1884. The ground floor houses a madcap museum, featuring countless trophies from the eponymous king's trigger-happy jungle safaris, which were put to some ingenious uses, including walking sticks made from leopard vertebrae, and ashtrays fashioned out of tiger skulls and rhino feet. Then, there's an armoury, which houses enough weapons to stage a mini coup. The horror-house effect is brought full circle by the taxidermy section. However, don't forget to visit the ornate durbar hall, where the erstwhile rulers held court sessions. Photography inside is strictly prohibited. A rickshaw from the train station will cost ₹30.

Old Town
AREA

Kolhapur's atmospheric old town is built around the lively and colourful **Mahalaxmi Temple** (⊙5am-10.30pm) dedicated to Amba Bai, or the Mother Goddess. The temple's origins date back to AD 10, and it's one of the most important Amba Bai temples in India. Non-Hindus are welcome. Nearby, past a foyer in the Old Palace, is **Bhavani Mandap** (⊙6am-8pm), dedicated to the goddess Bhavani.

Kolhapur is famed for the calibre of its wrestlers, and at the **Motibag Thalim**, a courtyard reached through a low doorway and passage beside the entrance to Bhavani Mandap (ask for directions), young athletes train in a muddy pit. You are free to walk in and watch, as long as you don't mind the sight of sweaty, semi-naked men and the stench of urine emanating from the loos. Professional matches are held between June and December in the **Kasbagh Maidan**, a red-earth arena a short walk south of Motibag Thalim.

Shopaholics, meanwhile, can browse for the renowned Kolhapuri leather sandals, prized for their intricate needlework. Most designs are priced from ₹300 to ₹500. The break-in blisters on your feet come free of charge.

🛏 Sleeping & Eating

Hotel Tourist
HOTEL $

(☑2650421; www.hoteltourist.co.in; Station Rd; s/d incl breakfast from ₹888/1099, with AC ₹1480/1714; ❄) This is one of the better places on the main street, offering cosy though minimalist rooms. There's an acclaimed restaurant serving great veg food, and welcoming staff.

Hotel Panchshil
$$

(☑2537517; www.hotelpanchshilkolhapur.com; 517 A2 Shivaji Park; s/d incl breakfast ₹1937/2348, with AC ₹2583/3053; ❄🖥) This professionally run business hotel, with a helpful front desk, has an underwhelming plain brown decor. Nevertheless, the spacious, clean rooms with TV and internet are comfortable, there's also a complimentary business centre, and best of all, there's a branch of **Little Italy** (Shivaji Park; mains ₹250-450), the Italian restaurant chain, downstairs.

Hotel Pavillion
HOTEL $$

(☑2652751; www.hotelpavillion.co.in; 392 Assembly Rd; s/d incl breakfast ₹1350/1585, with AC from ₹1761/1996; ❄@) Located at the far end of a leafy park-cum-office area, this Mediterranean-style hotel guarantees a peaceful stay in large, clean rooms with windows that open out to delightful views of seasonal blossoms. It's very close to the MTDC office.

Hotel Pearl
HOTEL $$

(☑6684451; reservation@hotelpearl.biz; New Shahupuri; s/d incl breakfast ₹2583/2936, with AC from ₹3170/3757; ❄@) Modelled on big-city business hotels, this place has good rooms, a spa, a travel desk and a decent, pure veg, multicuisine restaurant.

Surabhi
INDIAN $

(Hotel Sahyadri Bldg; mains ₹70-100) Close to the bustling bus stand, Surabhi is a great place to savour Kolhapur's legendary snacks such as the spicy *misal* (puffed rice tossed with fried rounds of dough, lentils, onions, herbs and chutneys), thalis and lassi. Saawan Dining Hall, located alongside, serves nonveg food.

ℹ️ Information

Axis Bank ATM Twenty-four-hour ATM near Mahalaxmi Temple.

Internet Zone (Station Rd, Kedar Complex; per hr ₹20; ⏰8am-11pm) Internet access.

MTDC Tourist Office (📞2652935; Assembly Rd; ⏰10am-5.30pm Mon-Sat) Opposite the Collector's Office.

State Bank of India (Udyamnagar; ⏰10am-2pm Mon-Sat) A short autorickshaw ride southwest of the train station near Hutatma Park. Handles foreign exchange. There's also a 24-hour **ATM** (Indumati Rd), parallel to Station Rd.

ℹ️ Getting There & Around

Autorickshaws are abundant in Kolhapur and many drivers carry conversion charts to calculate fares from the outdated meters.

From the bus stand, services head regularly to Pune (semideluxe/deluxe ₹262/449, five hours) and Ratnagiri (ordinary/semideluxe ₹115/154, four hours). Most private bus agents are on the western side of the square at Mahalaxmi Chambers, across from the bus stand. Overnight services with AC head to Mumbai (seat/sleeper ₹450/750, nine hours) and non-AC overnighters go to Panaji (₹245, 5½ hours).

The train station, which is known as Chattrapati Shahu Maharaj Terminus, is 10 minutes' walk west of the bus stand. Three daily expresses, including the 10.50pm Sahyadri Express, zoom to Mumbai (sleeper/2AC ₹302/1195, 13 hours) via Pune (sleeper/2AC ₹236/855, eight hours). The Rani Chennama Express makes the long voyage to Bengaluru (sleeper/2AC ₹371/1575, 17½ hours, 2.20pm).

Kolhapur airport was not operational at the time of research.

Goa

Best Places to Eat

- ➡ Upper House (p821)
- ➡ Fiesta (p833)
- ➡ La Plage (p840)
- ➡ Plantain Leaf (p833)
- ➡ Seafood at seasonal beach shacks (all over)

Best Beaches

- ➡ Palolem (p849)
- ➡ Mandrem (p840)
- ➡ Cola Beach (p848)
- ➡ Anjuna (p834)
- ➡ Arambol (p841)

Why Go?

Goa is like no other state in India. It may be the Portuguese colonial influence, the endless beaches, the glorious whitewashed churches or the relaxed culture of *susegad* – a uniquely Goan term that translates loosely to 'laid-backness' and is evident in all aspects of daily life and the Goan people themselves.

But Goa is far more than its old-school reputation as a hippie haven or its relatively new status as a package-holiday beach getaway. Goa is as beautiful and culturally rich as it is tiny and hassle-free, so you can go birdwatching in a butterfly-filled forest, marvel at centuries-old cathedrals, venture out to white-water waterfalls or meander the capital's charming alleyways. Add a dash of Portuguese-influenced food and architecture, infuse with a colourful blend of religious traditions, pepper with parties, and you've got a heady mix that makes Goa easy to enjoy and extremely hard to leave.

When to Go
Goa (Panaji)

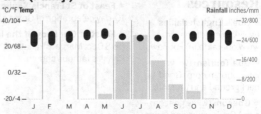

| Early Nov Post-monsoon, the shacks and beach huts are up but the crowds are still down. | Early Dec Festivals, Christmas spirit and great weather, before the peak prices and crowds. | Mar Carnival and Easter celebrations as the season winds down. |

GOA

Fast Facts

➜ **Population:** 1.46 million

➜ **Area:** 3702 sq km

➜ **Capital:** Panaji (Panjim)

➜ **Telephone code:** ☑0832

➜ **Main languages:** Konkani, Marathi, English and Hindi

➜ **Sleeping prices: $** below ₹1200, **$$** ₹1200 to ₹4000, **$$$** above ₹4000

Top Tips

➜ Don't swim wasted!

➜ If you can handle the Christmas and New Year crowds, this is a fun time but book well ahead and expect to pay for the privilege.

Resources

➜ **Goa's English dailies** (www.navhindtimes.in, www.oheraldo.in) For news.

➜ **Goa Tourism** (www.goa-tourism.com) Good background and tour info.

➜ **Goacom** (www.goacom.com) Goa's news and views.

➜ **Lonely Planet** (www.lonelyplanet.com/india/goa) For planning advice, author recommendations, traveller reviews and insider tips.

Food & Drink

Goan cuisine is a tantalising fusion of Portuguese and South Indian flavours. Goans tend to be hearty meat and fish eaters, and fresh seafood is a staple, as is the quintessential Goan lunch 'fish-curry-rice': fried mackerel steeped in coconut, tamarind and chilli sauce. Traditional dishes include vindaloo (fiery dish in a marinade of vinegar and garlic) or *xacuti* (a spicy chicken or meat dish cooked in red coconut sauce). For dessert try the layered bebinca.

The traditional Goan drink is *feni*, a double-distilled fiery liqour made from the cashew fruit or palm toddy.

DON'T MISS

There's little chance of missing the **beach** – much of Goa's 100km of Arabian Sea coastline has some spectacular stretches. Dining on **fresh seafood** at one of the many beach shacks up and down the coast is a must. Goa has a fascinating colonial **history** that also shouldn't be missed: set aside some time to explore evocative Panaji (Panjim), Old Goa, Quepem and Chandor.

Top State Festivals

➜ **Feast of the Three Kings** (☺6 Jan, Chandor, p845, & Reis Magos) Boys re-enact the story of the three kings bearing gifts for Christ.

➜ **Shigmotsav (Shigmo) of Holi** (☺Feb/Mar, statewide) Goa's version of the Hindu festival Holi sees coloured powders thrown about and parades in most towns.

➜ **Sabado Gordo** (☺Feb/Mar, Panaji, p820) A procession of floats and street parties on the Saturday before Lent.

➜ **Carnival** (☺Mar, statewide) A four-day festival kicking off Lent; the party's particularly jubilant in Panaji (p820).

➜ **Fama de Menino Jesus** (☺2nd Mon in Oct, Colva, p846) Colva's Menino Jesus statue is paraded about town.

➜ **Feast of St Francis Xavier** (☺3 Dec, Old Goa, p823) A 10-day celebration of Goa's patron saint.

➜ **Feast of Our Lady of the Immaculate Conception** (☺8 Dec, Margao, Panaji, p817) Fairs and concerts around Panaji's famous church.

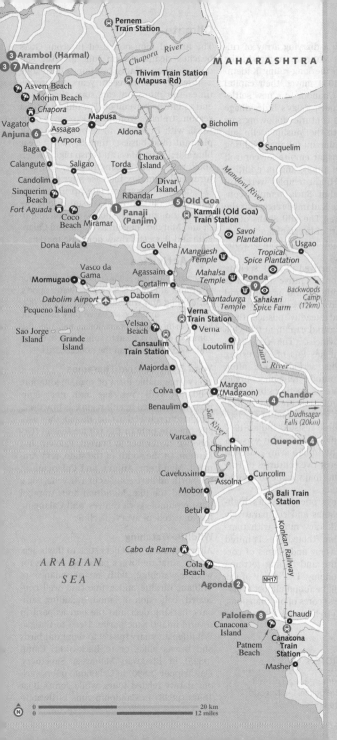

Goa Highlights

1 Wander the Portuguese quarters of **Panaji** (Panjim; p817) and linger over lunch at one of its traditional Goan restaurants

2 Indulge in barefoot luxury on long white-sand **beaches** (p842), like Agonda (p848), in the state's sleepy southern stretches

3 Open up your chakras while doing **yoga** (p814) to the rhythm of ocean waves and swaying palms at Mandrem (p840) and Arambol (p841)

4 Dream of times gone by in the mansions of **Quepem** (p842) and **Chandor** (p845)

5 Bask in the glory of grand cathedrals and observe the countryside from a hilltop chapel in **Old Goa** (p823)

6 Bargain hard at **Anjuna's flea market** (p837) then watch the sunset over a Kingfisher at a beachside bar

7 Worship the sun away from the northern crowds on the beautiful beach at **Mandrem** (p840)

8 Kayak out to see playful dolphins at sunset at **Palolem Beach** (p849)

9 Spend a day learning about the spices that first made Goa famous at a **spice plantation** (p826) near Ponda

History

Goa went through a dizzying array of rulers from Ashoka's Mauryan empire in the 3rd century BC to the long-ruling Kadambas, who in AD 1054 moved their capital from present-day Chandor to a new settlement called Govepuri, today's little village of Goa Velha. The centuries following saw much conflict, with the Muslim Delhi sultanate and then Bahmani sultanate fighting the Hindu Vijayanagar empire for control; these were violent times, and in addition to many deaths, Hindu temples were also razed. (Tiny Tambdi Surla temple, constructed during the Kadamba reign, was the only one to survive.) The Adil Shahs of Bijapur, formerly part of the Bahmani sultanate, created the capital we now call Old Goa in the 15th century.

The Portuguese arrived in 1510, seeking control of the region's lucrative spice routes by way of Goa's wide natural harbours and plentiful waterways. They defeated the Bijapur kings and steadily pushed their power from their grand capital at Old Goa out into the provinces. (The Goa State Museum in Panaji has lots of interesting artefacts from this period.) Soon after, Portuguese rule and religion spread throughout the state – sometimes by force – and the Goan Inquisition brought repression and brutality in the name of Christianity. The Portuguese resisted India's 1947 Independence from Britain and it was not until 1961, when the Indian army marched into Goa, that almost five centuries of Portuguese occupation finally came to an end on the subcontinent.

Today Goa enjoys one of India's highest per-capita incomes and comparatively high health and literacy rates, with tourism, iron-ore mining (though this is mired in political controversy and claims of corruption), agriculture and fishing forming the basis of its economy. The legacy of the Portuguese can still be found almost everywhere, in the state's scores of old mansions, its cuisine, its churches and even in its language.

ⓘ EMERGENCIES

Dial ☏108 in an emergency. This will connect you to the police, fire brigade or medical services.

Climate

The annual monsoon used to scour Goa's beaches clean between June and the end of September reliably, but things have gone a little haywire in recent years, and sometimes the monsoon can start slowly and end as late as November. The official tourist season stretches from mid-October to early April, with December to February the most pleasant (and busiest) time to visit – clear blue skies, warm days and crisp nights when you'll rarely need airconditioning. Temperatures and humidity increase after February. Out of season, between late April and September, you'll find most coastal resorts deserted, though towns such as Panaji, Mapusa and Margao chug on as usual, and Calangute and Baga still draw domestic tourists.

Activities

In season Goa has a whole host of options for yoga and alternative therapies, water sports, paragliding and wildlife-watching. Many outfits change annually, so we've only listed the longer-established operations; for the full gamut of options, head to your beach of choice and ask around or scan the noticeboards.

Yoga & Alternative Therapies

Every imaginable form of yoga, meditation, reiki, ayurvedic massage and other spiritually orientated health regime is practised, taught and relished in Goa, though they usually operate only in the winter season (October or November to March). Palolem and Patnem, in the south of the state, and Arambol, Mandrem, Anjuna and Calangute in the north all have courses in ayurveda, yoga, reiki and the like. Mandrem and Arambol have reputable yoga centres, and Calangute has an excellent ayurveda clinic.

Wildlife-Watching

Although many travellers stick to the beach, Goa is a nature lover's paradise, perfect for wildlife-watching, with an abundance of brilliant birdlife and a fine (but well concealed) collection of fauna, including sambars, barking deer and the odd leopard in several inland sanctuaries. Head to Cotigao Wildlife Sanctuary (p849) to scout out birds and beasts alike, or to Backwoods Camp (p825) in Bhagwan Mahaveer Sanctuary. Day Tripper (p830) in Calangute offers various nature-related tours, while John's Boat Tours (p828) in Candolim runs birdwatch-

THINK LIKE THE LOCALS...

Venture beyond the tourist areas and you're sure to find locals who will sadly shake their heads and say that Goa has changed for the worse. The spread of serious drug use amongst locals, overdevelopment and environmental damage, and Goa's growing reputation within India as a place for bad behaviour are the dark underbelly to its tropical paradise. You can help repair Goa's image by following a few simple steps:

➡ Away from the beaches, adopt the same, more modest dress that you would in other parts of the country. This generally means shoulders and knees covered, and keeping your shirt on. Nude or topless sunbathing is illegal in Goa and can result in fines.

➡ Keep your naughtiest behaviour confined to appropriate venues. Partying into the night with illegal substances at a family guesthouse might disturb the owners, not to mention attracting the authorities.

➡ Women should be cautious when partying; rape, sadly, has been an issue in Goa, and though we don't believe (as many do) that bikinis are to blame, it makes sense to be in control of your surroundings.

ing boat trips, along with crocodile- and dolphin-spotting rides.

Water Sports

Based in Baga, Barracuda Diving (p830), offers scuba diving courses and trips. Parasailing and jet-skiing are readily available on the beaches at Baga, Benaulim and Colva, and you can try paragliding at Anjuna and Arambol. Palolem, with its relatively calm waters, is the best place for kayaking.

ℹ Dangers & Annoyances

One of the most deceptive dangers in Goa is to be found right in front of your beautiful bit of beach: the Arabian Sea, with its strong currents and dangerous undertows, claims dozens of lives each year, many of them foreigners who knew how to swim. All of Goa's popular beaches are now overseen by lifeguards during daylight hours with patrolled swimming areas marked by flags, but it's extremely important to heed local warnings, and don't venture into the water after drinking or taking drugs, especially at night.

Other dangers and annoyances are of the rather more universal kind. Keep your valuables under lock and key, especially if you're renting an easy-to-penetrate coconut, and don't walk along empty stretches of beach alone at night.

One of the pleasures of Goa is being able to get around on a cheaply hired scooter or motorbike, but lots of tourists come unstuck on the road. Traffic can be heavy and unpredictable in tourist areas and around towns: ride with care, don't ride intoxicated and wear a helmet (compulsory in Goa since 2012). Also be sure to carry your licence and the bike's registration papers to avoid unwanted police attention.

DRUGS

Acid, ecstasy, cocaine, charas (hashish), marijuana and all other forms of recreational drugs are illegal in India (though still very much available in Goa), and purchasing or carrying drugs is fraught with danger. Goa's Fort Aguada jail is filled with prisoners, including some foreigners, serving lengthy sentences for drug offences, and being caught in possession of even a small quantity of illegal substances can mean a 10-year stretch in a cockroach-infested cell.

ℹ Information

The **Goa Tourism Development Corporation** (GTDC; www.goa-tourism.com), also known as Goa Tourism, provides maps and information, operates average hotels throughout the state and runs a host of one-day and multiday tours. Its main office is in Panaji, but you can book tours and get a simple map of Goa at any of its hotel branches. Panaji's Indiatourism (p823) office also has information on Goa.

ACCOMMODATION

Accommodation prices in Goa are generally higher than in most other states of India and vary wildly depending on the season. High-season prices, often more than twice the mid-season rates, run from early December to early February, while prices climb higher to a peak rate during the crowded Christmas and New Year period (around 22 December to 3 January). Mid-season runs from the mid-October through November (when most beach shacks are just being built) and from February to April, and low season runs through the rainy season (April to October). All accommodation rates listed are for the high season – *not* the peak Christmas period, when you'll almost certainly have to book ahead anyway. Prices can still fluctuate from year to year, and some hotels may bump up their high-season tariffs more than others depending on demand. Always call ahead for rates. Most accommodation options have a standard noon checkout, except in Panaji, where many hotels cruelly demand you depart at 9am or earlier.

❶ Getting There & Away

AIR

Goa's sole and diminutive airport, Dabolim, is 29km south of Panaji, 30km north of Margao and an easy taxi ride from any of the state's beaches. Few international flights go here directly; those that do are package-holiday charters, mostly from Russia, Europe and Britain. Independent travellers from the UK could check **Thomson** (www.thomsonfly.com), and from Germany, **Condor** (www.condor.com); both offer direct flight-only fares. Generally, the quickest way to reach Goa from anywhere else overseas is to take a flight into Mumbai (Bombay) or Chennai (Madras), and then a one-hour hop by domestic airline to Goa. There are plenty of domestic flights daily through Jet Airways, SpiceJet, Air India and several other budget airlines to most major capitals.

Dabolim Airport has a money-exchange office, a GTDC counter, charter-airline offices, an ATM and two prepaid taxi booths.

BUS

Plenty of long-distance interstate buses – both 'government' and 'private' – operate to and from Panaji, Margao, Mapusa and Chaudi, near Palolem. Fares for private operators are only slightly higher than for Kadamba government buses, and they fluctuate throughout the year. Long-distance buses can be standard, air-conditioned (AC), Volvo (the most comfortable seater buses) and sleeper. Sleeper buses have improved over the years to include sidebars or even fully-reclining seats, but this is not like travelling on a train – be prepared to be thrown out of your bed while hurtling round a corner at 3am! Most interstate buses depart between 6pm and 10pm.

TRAIN

The **Konkan Railway** (www.konkanrailway.com), the main train line running through Goa, runs between Mumbai and Mangalore. The biggest station in Goa is Margao's Madgaon station, from which there are several useful daily services to Mumbai. Other smaller useful stations on the line include Pernem for Arambol, Thivim for Mapusa and the northern beaches, Karmali (Old Goa) for Panaji, and Canacona for Palolem.

Book tickets online; at Madgaon station; at the train reservation office at Panaji's Kadamba bus stand; or at any travel agent vending train tickets (though you'll pay a small commission). Only the stations at Margao and Vasco da Gama (near Dabolim Airport) have foreign-tourist-quota booking counters. Book as far in advance as possible for sleepers, since they fill up very quickly.

❶ Getting Around

TO/FROM THE AIRPORT

Dabolim's two prepaid taxi counters – one in the arrivals hall and the other just outside – make arriving easy; buy your ticket here and you'll be ushered to a cab. Real budgeteers without much luggage can try walking out to the main road and waving down one of the frequent buses heading east from Vasco da Gama to Margao and catch onward transport from there.

BUS

Goa has an extensive network of buses, shuttling to and from almost every town and village. They run frequently and have no numbers, and fares rarely exceed ₹30. Buses are in fairly good condition and tend to be pretty efficient.

CAR & MOTORCYCLE

It's easy in Goa to organise a private car with a driver for long-distance day trips. Prices vary, but you should bank on paying from ₹1000 (if you're lucky) to ₹1500 for a full day out on the road (usually defined as eight hours and 80km). It's also possible, if you have the nerves and the need to feel independent, to procure a self-drive car. A small Maruti will cost from ₹700 to ₹1000 per day and a jeep around ₹1200 to ₹1400, excluding petrol and usually with a kilometre limit. Your best bet for rental is online at sites like www.mygoatour.com or www.goa2u.com. Note the slightly mystifying signposts posted on Goa's major National Highway 17 (NH17), which advise of different speed limits (on the largely single-carriageway road) for different types of vehicles.

You'll rarely go far on a Goan road without seeing a tourist whizzing by on a scooter or motorbike, and renting (if not riding) one is a breeze. You'll likely pay from ₹200 to ₹300 per day for a scooter, ₹400 for a smaller Yamaha motorbike, and ₹500 for a Royal Enfield Bullet. These prices can drop considerably if you're renting for more than a few days or if it's an off-peak period – it's all supply and demand, so bargain if there are lots of machines around. You'll find them hanging around the taxi/bus stand at any beach resort or near the post office in Panaji.

Bear in mind that Goan roads – while better than many Indian roads – can be treacherous, filled with human, bovine, canine, feline, mechanical and avian obstacles, as well as a good sprinkling of potholes and hairpin bends. Take it slowly, try not to drive at night (when black cows can prove dangerous), don't attempt a north–south day trip on a 50CC scooter, and ask for a helmet – a law which has routinely been ignored by Goans and tourists alike over the years but is now compulsory.

TAXI & AUTORICKSHAW

Taxis are widely available for town-hopping, and, as with a chauffeured car, a full day's sightseeing, depending on the distance, will be around ₹1500. Unlike elsewhere in India, autorickshaws are not much cheaper than taxis and are not as common, but they're still good for short trips. Motorcycles, known as 'pilots', are also a licensed form of taxi in Goa. They're cheap, easy to find and can be identified by a yellow front mudguard – and even the heftiest of backpacks seems to be no obstacle.

CENTRAL GOA

Panaji (Panjim)

POP 115,000

One of India's most relaxed state capitals, Panaji (more commonly known as Panjim) sits at the mouth of the broad Mandovi River, where paddle-wheel boats and floating casinos ply the waters and giant neon advertising signs cast reflections in the night. A glorious whitewashed church lords over the city centre and grand colonial buildings rub shoulders with arty boutiques, old-school bookshops and backstreet bars.

But it's the tangle of narrow streets in the old quarter that really steal the show. Nowhere is the Portuguese influence felt more strongly than here, where the late afternoon sun lights up yellow houses with purple doors, and around each corner you'll find crumbling ochre-coloured mansions with wrought-iron balconies and cats lying in front of bicycles parked beneath oyster-shell windows. Panjim is a place for walking, enjoying the peace of the afternoon siesta, eating well and meeting real Goans. It's not to be missed.

⊙ Sights & Activities

One of the pleasures of Panaji is long, leisurely strolls through the sleepy Portuguese-era Sao Tomé, Fontainhas and Altinho districts.

★ Church of Our Lady of the Immaculate Conception   CHURCH

(cnr Emilio Gracia & Jose Falcao Rds; ⊙10am-12.30pm & 3-5.30pm Mon-Sat, 11am-12.30pm & 3.30-5pm Sun) Panaji's spiritual and geographical centre is its gleamingly white and oh-so-photogenic main church, consecrated in 1541. When Panaji was little more than a sleepy fishing village this place was the first port of call for sailors from Lisbon, who would clamber up here to thank their lucky stars for a safe crossing before continuing to Old Goa, the state's capital until the 19th century, further east up the river. It's usually closed in the evening, but the exterior is wonderfully illuminated at night. Mass in English is held at 8am weekdays and 8.15am Sunday.

Goa State Museum   MUSEUM

(☑2438006; www.goamuseum.gov.in; EDC Complex, Patto; ⊙9am-5.30pm Mon-Sat) **FREE** This spacious museum, in the developing Patto area near the bus stand, has a sleepy feel and an intriguing hodgepodge of exhibits. In addition to Hindu and Jain sculptures and bronzes, the museum has a good collection of wooden Christian sculptures, a room devoted to the history of print in Goa (replete with hulking old-school presses), an exhibition on Goa's freedom fighters, and nice examples of Portuguese-era furniture, including an elaborately carved table used during the notoriously brutal Portuguese Inquisition in Goa.

Secretariat Building   HISTORIC BUILDING

(Avenida Dom Joao Castro) This colonial-era building is on the site of Bijapur Sultan Yusef Adil Shah's summer palace. The current structure dates from the 16th century and became the Portuguese viceroy's official residence in 1759. Nowadays it houses less exciting government offices, but as the oldest colonial buildings in town it's worth a gaze. Immediately to the west, the compelling **statue** of a man bearing down upon a supine female form depicts Abbé Faria, a Goan priest, 'father of hypnotism' and friend of Napoleon, in melodramatic throes.

Menezes Braganza Institute   HISTORIC BUILDING

(Malaca Rd) This beautiful early 20th-century affair is worth dropping into to see the pretty blue-and-white *azulejos* (glazed ceramic-tile compositions) in the entrance hall.

Campal   NEIGHBOURHOOD

The Campal neighbourhood, to the west of Panaji, is home to some green spaces that are perfect for whiling away an afternoon. Goa's premier cultural centre, Kala Academy (p822) has a lovely campus, with an art gallery, a lighthouse, pier and benches along

Panaji (Panjim)

GOA PANAJI (PANJIM)

0 400 m
0 0.2 miles

Mandovi Bridge

Betim (2km);
Houses of Goa Museum (4km);
Mario Gallery (4km);
Torda (4km);
Mapusa (13km)

Mandovi River

33
34

New Patto Bridge
Old Patto Bridge
Ouiem Creek

PATTO

Old Goa (9km);
Karmali (12km);
Ponda (34km)

Goa Tourism
Development
Corporation
Indiatourism

Dabolim (29km);
Vasco da Gama (32km);
Margao (34km)

32 31 30

Avenida Dom João Castro

MG Rd

23

24

14 15 26

11
GP Rd
6

19

Emilio Gracia Rd

Footbridge

Ourem Rd

CA Rd

Rua de Natal

St Sebastian Rd

21 5

10

Goa State
Central
Library

Dabolim
(29km);
Margao
(34km)

Fountain

FONTAINHAS

Dr Álvaro
Costa Rd

Steps
SÃO
TOMÉ

8

31st January Rd

José Falcão Rd

4 3

12

7

Church of Our
Lady of the Immaculate
Conception

1

Panaji Jetty

Dr RS Rd

13

29

Municipal
Gardens
(Church
Square)

20

Cunha-Rivara Rd

Cozy
Nook

27

Jama Masjid

Avenida Pe Agnelo

Mahalaxmi
Temple

ALTINHO

MG Rd

Ormuz Rd

Azad
Maidan

Dr Pisurlekar Rd

18
17

Dr P Shirgaonkar Rd

Malaca Rd

2

Ferry to Betim

Dayanand Bandodkar Marg

Thomas
Cook

INOX Cinema (300m);
Campal Gardens (400m);
Kala Academy (800m)

22

16

Swami Vivekanand Rd

Forest
Department

9

Dr Dada Vaidya Rd

Dr Atmaram Borkar Rd

18th June Rd

Gen Costa Alvares Rd

General Bernado Guedes Rd

Heliodoro Salgado Rd

Municipal
Market

25

Vintage
Hospitals
(1.5km)

Panaji (Panjim)

the water, and a library with great books on Indian arts. East of this is **Campal Gardens** (Bhagwan Mahaveer Bal Vihar), a peaceful, expansive park with playgrounds and river views.

Houses of Goa Museum MUSEUM
(☏2410711; www.archgoa.org; Torda; adult/child ₹100/25; ☉10am-7.30pm Tue-Sun) This little museum, about 8km north of Panaji, was created by a well-known local architect, Gerard da Cunha, to illuminate the history of Goan architecture. Interesting displays on building practices and European and local design will change the way you see those old Goan homes. Next door is the **Mario Gallery** (☏2410711; admission free; ☉10am-5.30pm Mon-Fri, to 1pm Sat), with works by one of India's favourite cartoonists, the late Mario Miranda (1926–2011). To get here, take a Mapusa-bound bus and get off at Okukora Circle, also known as Kokeru; an autorickshaw from here and back, including waiting time, costs ₹150. From Panaji, a taxi or autorickshaw will cost you about ₹350 one-way.

 Courses

On the Menu COOKING
(www.holidayonthemenu.com; courses from US$149) This London-based outfit offers a variety of Goan-cooking holidays (at a price), ranging from a Saturday 'Curry Morning' to a one-week program (US$1599) that includes trips to a spice plantation and a local market.

 Tours

The Goa Tourism Development Corporation (GTDC; Goa Tourism) operates a range of popular boat trips along the Mandovi River, including hour-long sunset and evening **cruises** (₹150; ☉6pm & 7.15pm) and two-hour **dinner cruises** (₹500; ☉8.45pm Wed & Sat) aboard the *Santa Monica*. All include a live band and dancers – sometimes lively, sometimes lacklustre – performing Goan folk songs and dances. Cruises depart from the Santa Monica jetty beside the New Patto Bridge, where the **GTDC boat counter** (☏2438754; Santa Monica jetty) also sells tickets.

Three private companies offer similar one-hour **night cruises** (adult/child ₹150/free; ⊙ 6.15pm, 7.30pm & 8.45pm) also departing from Santa Monica jetty. With bars and DJs playing loud music, these tend to be a lot livelier than the GTDC cruises but can get rowdy with groups of local male tourists – avoid on weekends.

GTDC also runs a full-day **backwater cruise** (₹750; ⊙ 9.30am-4pm) to Old Goa, then a bus to a spice farm where lunch is included.

You can take your own free tour aboard the local ferries that depart frequently (whenever full) at the dock next to Quarterdeck; locals have reported seeing dolphins on evening rides. Avoid rush hour, when the boats are crammed.

Heritage walking tours (☎ 9823025748; ajit_sukhija@yahoo.com; per person ₹500, per person ₹250 for five or more), covering the old Portuguese quarter from Tobacco Sq, through Sao Tomé, Fountainhas and the Hindu Mala district, are conducted by experienced local guides on demand.

🎊 Festivals & Events

Sabado Gordo　　　　STREET FESTIVAL
(Panaji; ⊙ Feb/Mar) 'Fat Saturday' is a procession of floats and street parties on the Saturday before Lent.

Carnival　　　　　　　　FESTIVAL
(statewide; ⊙ Mar) This four-day festival kicks off Lent and is particularly jubilant in Panaji where elaborate floats take to the streets.

**International Film
Festival of India**　　　FILM FESTIVAL
(www.iffi.nic.in; Panaji; ⊙ Nov) International film screenings and Bollywood glitterati everywhere.

**Feast of Our Lady of the
Immaculate Conception**　RELIGIOUS FESTIVAL
(Margao, Panaji; ⊙ 8 Dec) Fairs and concerts are held, as is a beautiful church service at Panaji's Church of Our Lady of the Immaculate Conception.

🛏 Sleeping

As in the rest of Goa, prices vary wildly in Panaji depending on supply and demand. Lots of rock-bottom options pepper 31st January Rd, but most consist of a cell-like room, with a 9am or earlier checkout, for ₹500 or less. Inspect a few before you decide.

Pousada Guest House　　GUESTHOUSE $
(☎ 2422618; sabrinateles@yahoo.com; Luis de Menezes Rd; s/d ₹525/630, d with AC ₹750; ❄) The four rooms in this bright-yellow place in the old quarter are simple but clean and come with comfy spring-mattress beds and TV. Owner Sabrina is friendly and no-nonsense, and at this price it's one of the better budget deals.

Republica Hotel　　　　　HOTEL $
(☎ 2224630; Jose Falcao Rd; s/d from ₹400/800, d with AC ₹1000; ❄) The Republica is a story of unexplored potential, an architectural beauty that's been left to fall apart – but still it was booked out when we visited! Ramshackle it may be, but the location is good and the price acceptable for this part of town.

Afonso Guest House　　GUESTHOUSE $$
(☎ 2222359, 9764300165; www.afonsoguesthouse.com; St Sebastian Rd; r ₹1500-2000; ❄) Run by the friendly Jeanette, this place in a pretty Portuguese-era townhouse offers spacious, well-kept rooms with timber ceilings. The little rooftop terrace makes for sunny breakfasting. It's a simple, serene stay in the heart of the most atmospheric part of town; checkout is 9am and bookings are accepted online but not by phone.

Casa Paradiso　　　　　HOTEL $$
(☎ 3290180; www.casaparadisogoa.com; Jose Falcao Rd; r with AC ₹1575-2100; ❄) The location alone makes this place worth a look. It's a little cramped but just steps away from the Church of Our Lady of the Immaculate Conception, with bright, air-con rooms, cable TV and friendly staff.

Mayfair Hotel　　　　　HOTEL $$
(☎ 2223317; manishafernz@yahoo.com; Dr Dada Vaidya Rd; s/d from ₹980/1180, d with AC ₹1500; ❄) The oystershell windows and mosaic murals in the lobby at this corner hotel are promising but the rooms are not quite as bright – ask to see a few as there's old and new wings with rooms of varying quality. Friendly family owners, a potentially nice back garden and noon checkout.

★ Panjim Inn　　　HERITAGE HOTEL $$
(☎ 2226523, 9823025748; www.panjiminn.com; 31st January Rd; s/d incl breakfast from ₹2900/3450, ste ₹5950; ❄@🖧) A longstanding Panaji favourite for its heritage character, this beautiful 19th century hotel has a variety of charismatic original rooms,

along with some newer rooms with more modern touches, but all with four-poster beds, colonial furniture and local artworks. Across the road and run by the same family is the **Panjim Peoples**, with four enormous rooms upstairs and the Gitanjali Gallery downstairs, also across the road is the tranquil nine-room **Panjim Pousada**, in an old Hindu home.

Crown Hotel   HOTEL $$$
(☑ 2400000; www.thecrowngoa.com; off Jose Falcao Rd; d incl breakfast ₹6600-10,450, ste from ₹13,750; ❋ @ 🛜 ☙) Perched on a hill above the Sao Tomé district, with fine views out over the Mandovi, this spa-hotel-casino is a great option for a little bit of luxury in the heart of the city. Refurbished rooms are airy and tastefully done in mustards and whites (some with balconies) and the pool-bar area is incredibly enticing (nonguests ₹250). There's also a day spa and gym.

Casa Nova   GUESTHOUSE $$$
(☑ 9423889181, 7709886212; www.goaholiday accommodation.com; Gomez Pereira Rd; ₹4300; ❋) In a gorgeous old Portuguese-style home (c 1831), Casa Nova consists of just one stylish, exceptionally comfy apartment, accessed via a little alley and complete with arched windows, wood-beam ceilings and mod cons like a kitchenette. Sister property **Casa Morada** (☑ 9822196007, 9881966789; agomes@tbi.in; Gomes Pereira Rd; s/d incl breakfast ₹5000/10,000) is as fancy as Nova is modern. Its two bedrooms and sitting room are full of antique furniture and objets d'art.

✖ Eating

You'll never go hungry in Panaji, where food is enjoyed fully and frequently. A stroll down 18th June or 31st January Rds will turn up a number of great, cheap canteen-style options, as will a quick circuit of the Municipal Gardens.

★ Viva Panjim   GOAN $
(31st January Rd; mains ₹90-120; ⊙ 11.30am-3.30pm & 7-11pm Mon-Sat, 7-11pm Sun) Though well-known to tourists, this little side-street eatery, in an old Portuguese house, still delivers tasty Goan classics at reasonable prices – there's a whole page of the menu devoted to pork dishes, as well as tasty *xacuti* and *cafreal*-style dishes and desserts like bebinca and *serra durra*. Fair drink prices too.

Satkar Vegetarian Restaurant   INDIAN $
(18th June Rd; thalis ₹70-90, mains ₹50-100; ⊙ 7am-10.30pm) Casual, cheap, pretty good pure-veg and tasty thalis.

Legacy of Bombay   INDIAN $
(Hotel Fidalgo, 18th June Rd; mains ₹40-150; ⊙ 7am-11.15pm) One of several restaurants in Hotel Fidalgo, this street level place serves excellent pure-veg food, including veg versions of pizza and burgers.

Hotel Vihar   VEGAN $
(MG Rd; mains ₹40-100; ⊙ 7.30am-10pm) A vast menu of 'pure veg' food, great big thalis and a plethora of fresh juices make this clean, simple canteen a popular place for locals and visitors alike.

Tea Cafe Goa   CAFE $$
(5/218 31st January Rd; cakes from ₹80, meals ₹150-250; ⊙ 10.30am-6.30pm) This cute modern cafe contrasts with some of the older places, serving excellent sandwiches, quiches, cupcakes and other sweet treats in a charmingly restful air-conditioned interior.

★ Upper House   GOAN $$
(☑ 2426475; www.theupperhousegoa.com; Cunha Rivara Rd; mains ₹125-385; ⊙ 11am-10pm) Climbing the stairs to the Upper House is like stepping into a cool European restaurant, with a modern but elegant dining space overlooking the Municipal Gardens at the front, a chic neon-lit cocktail bar next door and more formal restaurant space at the back. But the food is very much Goan – a high standard of regional specialities such as crab *xec xec* (crab cooked in a roasted-coconut gravy), pork vindaloo, and fish-curry-rice done the old-fashioned way. Even the veg adaptations (eg mixed veg and mushroom *xacuti*) are show-stoppers.

Hotel Venite   GOAN $$
(31st January Rd; mains ₹210-280; ⊙ 9am-10.30pm) Atmospheric Venite is a long-time tourist favourite: its tiny, rickety balcony tables make the perfect lunchtime spot. Success may have gone to Venite's head – the Goan food is OK but the prices are exorbitant. We still love the place though – call in for a cold beer or snack and chill out on the balcony before deciding.

Sher-E-Punjab   NORTH INDIAN $$
(18th June Rd; mains ₹80-200; ⊙ 10.30am-11.30pm) Sher-E-Punjab is widely regarded as one of the best North Indian places in

GOA PANAJI (PANJIM)

town, catering to well-dressed locals with its generous, carefully spiced Punjabi dishes. There's a pleasant garden terrace out back. The food at the fancier branch of **Sher-E-Punjab** (Hotel Aroma, Cunha-Rivara Rd; mains ₹120-270; ☺11am-3pm & 7-10.30pm) is equally tasty.

George Bar & Restaurant   GOAN $$
(Church Sq; mains ₹90-170; ☺ 9.30am-10.30pm) Slightly cramped wooden tables and a healthy mix of drunks and families make for a down-to-earth local vibe, and there's an air-con section upstairs. Seafood and Goan classics are the speciality.

Verandah   GOAN $$
(☑ 2226523; 31st January Rd; ₹150-280; ☺11am-11pm) The breezy first-floor restaurant at Panjim Inn is indeed on a balcony with Fountainhas street views. Excellent Goan cuisine is the speciality, but there's also a range of Indian and Continental dishes, and local wines.

🍸 Drinking & Nightlife

Panaji has pick-me-up pit stops aplenty, especially in the Sao Tomé and Fontainhas areas. Mostly simple little bars with a few plastic tables and chairs, they're a great way to get chatting with locals over a glass of feni.

Cafe Mojo   BAR
(www.cafemojo.in; Menenzes Braganza Rd; ☺10am-4am Mon-Thu, to 6am Fri-Sun) Cafe Mojo is cool. The decor is cosy English pub, the clientele young and up for a party, and the hook is the e-beer system. Each table has its own beer tap and LCD screen: you buy a card (₹1000), swipe it at your table and start pouring – it automatically deducts what you drink (you can also use the card for spirits, cocktails or food). Wednesday night is ladies' night and the weekends go till late.

Riverfront & Down the Road   BAR
(cnr MG and Ourem Rd; ☺11am-3am) The balcony of this bar-restaurant overlooking the creek and Old Patto Bridge makes for a great sundowner spot; the ground-floor bar has occasional live music.

☆ Entertainment

Several casino boats sit moored on the Mandovi, offering a surprisingly entertaining night out.

Casino Royale   CASINO
(☑6519471; www.casinoroyalegoa.com; entry Mon-Thu ₹3000, Fri-Sun ₹3500; ☺24hr) The biggest and best of Panaji's three floating casinos, this upscale floating shrine to all things speculative is as much entertainment as gaming. Admission includes unlimited buffet dinner, free drinks, live music and ₹2000 worth of chips. Various age and dress restrictions apply.

Kala Academy   CULTURAL PROGRAMS
(☑2420452; Dayanand Bandodkar Marg) On the west side of the city at Campal is Goa's premier cultural centre, featuring an excellent program of dance, theatre, music and art exhibitions throughout the year. Many plays are in Konkani, but there are occasional English-language productions; call to find out what's on.

INOX Cinema   CINEMA
(☑2420900; www.inoxmovies.com; Old GMC Heritage Precinct; tickets ₹160-200; ☺10.30am-11.30pm) This modern multiplex cinema shows Hollywood and Bollywood blockbusters alike.

🛍 Shopping

Panaji's covered **municipal market** (☺from 7.30am) is a great place for people-watching and buying necessities, while the new **Caculo Mall** (www.caculomall.in; St Inez) is Goa's biggest shopping mall, with designer brands, food courts and gaming arcades.

Singbal's Book House   BOOKS
(Church Sq; ☺ 9.30am-1pm & 3.30-7.30pm Mon-Sat) Lots of books and newspapers and heaps of character at this slightly grumpy establishment that, incidentally, had a cameo role in the *Bourne Supremacy*.

Barefoot Handicrafts   HANDICRAFTS
(31st January Rd; ☺10am-8pm Mon-Sat) Barefoot is part of Panaji's new wave of very high end shops specialising in design of one kind or another. Barefoot, though pricey, has some nice gifts, ranging from traditional Christian paintings on wood to jewellery and beaded coasters.

Khadi Gramodyog Bhavan   HANDICRAFTS
(Dr Atmaram Borkar Rd; ☺9am-noon & 3-7pm Mon-Sat) Goa's only outpost of the government's Khadi & Village Industries Commission has an excellent range of hand-woven cottons, along with oils, soaps, spices and other handmade products that come straight from and directly benefit – regional villages.

ℹ️ Information

A new tourism complex has been established at Patto on the east side of the Ourem Creek, housing the GTDC (Goa Tourism), Indiatourism and various travel agents. ATMs are plentiful, especially on 18th June Rd and around the Thomas Cook office.

Cozy Nook (18th June Rd; per hr ₹45; ☺9am-8.30pm) Welcoming internet joint and travel agent.

Goa State Central Library (Sanskruti Bhavan, Patto; ☺9am-7.30pm Mon-Fri, 9.30am-5.45pm Sat & Sun) Panaji's ultra-modern new state library has six floors of reading material, a bookshop and gallery. Internet access is technically for academic research only.

Goa Tourism Development Corporation (GTDC; ☑2424001; www.goa-tourism.com; Dr Alvaro Costa Rd, Paryatan Bhavan; ☺9.30am-5.45pm Mon-Sat) Pick up maps of Goa and Panaji here and book one of GTDC's host of tours.

Indiatourism (Government of India tourist office; ☑2223412; www.incredibleindia.org; Dr Alvaro Costa Rd, Paryatan Bhavan; ☺9.30am-6pm Mon-Fri, to 2pm Sat) Helpful staff can provide a list of qualified guides for tours and trips in Goa. A half /full day tour for up to five people costs ₹700/875.

Main Post Office (MG Rd; ☺9.30am-5.30pm Mon-Sat)

Thomas Cook (☑2221312; Dayanand Bandodkar Marg, 8 Alcon Chambers; ☺9.30am-6pm Mon-Sat) Changes travellers cheques commission-free and handles currency exchange, wire transfers, cash advances on credit cards, and air bookings.

Vintage Hospitals (☑6644401, ambulance 9764442220; www.vintagehospitals.com; Caculo Enclave, St Inez; ☺24hr) A couple of kilometres southwest of Panaji, Vintage is a reputable hospital with all the fixings.

ℹ️ Getting There & Away

A taxi from Panaji to Dabolim Airport takes about an hour, and costs ₹600.

BUS

All government buses depart from the huge and busy **Kadamba bus stand** (☑interstate enquiries 2438035, local enquiries 2438034; www.goakadamba.com; ☺reservations 8am-8pm), with local services heading out every few minutes. To get to south Goan beaches, take an express bus to Margao and change there; Ponda buses also stop at Old Goa. Kadamba station has an ATM, an internet cafe – and a Ganesh temple.

Calangute (₹15, 45 minutes)
Candolim (₹13, 30 minutes)
Mapusa (₹11, 20 minutes)
Margao (express shuttle; ₹30, 35 minutes)
Old Goa (₹9, 15 minutes)

State-run long-distance services also depart from the Kadamba bus stand. Private operators have booths outside Kadamba, but the buses depart from the interstate bus stand next to New Patto Bridge. One reliable company is **Paulo Travels** (☑2438531; www.paulotravels.com; Kardozo Bldg). Some high-season government and private long-distance fares include the following:

Bengaluru (₹650, 15 hours, five daily)
Bengaluru (private; ₹550 to ₹1000, 14 to 15 hours)
Hampi (private sleeper; ₹700 to ₹800, 10 to 11 hours)
Mumbai (₹650, 12 to 14 hours)
Pune (₹550 to ₹650, 11 hours)
Pune (private; ₹550 to ₹800, 10 to 11 hours)

TRAIN

Panaji's closest train station is Karmali (Old Goa), 12km to the east, where many long-distance services stop (check timetables). A taxi there costs ₹300. Panaji's **Konkan Railway reservation office** (☑2712940; www.konkan railway.com; ☺8am-8pm Mon-Sat) is on the 1st floor of the Kadamba bus stand.

ℹ️ Getting Around

Panaji is generally a pleasure to explore on foot, and it's unlikely you'll even need a pilot or autorickshaw, which is good because they charge a lot for short distances: an autorickshaw from Kadamba to the city centre will cost ₹60. Frequent buses run between Kadamba and the municipal market (₹5).

To Old Goa, a taxi or autorickshaw costs around ₹300. Lots of taxis hang around the Municipal Gardens, while you'll find autorickshaws and pilots in front of the post office, on 18th June Rd, and just south of the church.

Scooters and motorbikes can easily be hired from around the post office from around ₹200/300 per day.

Old Goa

From the 16th to the 18th centuries, when Old Goa's population exceeded that of Lisbon or London, this former capital of Goa was considered the 'Rome of the East'. You can still sense that grandeur as you wander the grounds, with its towering churches and cathedral and majestic convents. Its rise under the Portuguese, from 1510, was meteoric, but cholera and malaria

Old Goa

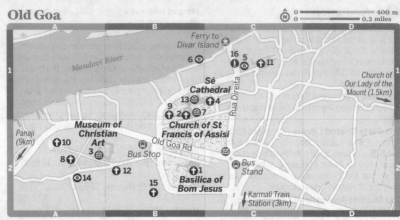

Old Goa

outbreaks forced the abandonment of the city in the 1600s. In 1843 the capital was officially shifted to Panaji.

Some of the most imposing churches, the cathedral and a convent or two are still in use and are remarkably well-preserved, while other historical buildings have become museums or ruined sites. It's a fascinating day trip, but it can get crowded: consider visiting on a weekday morning, when you can take in Mass (in Konkani) at Sé Cathedral or the Basilica of Bom Jesus (remember to cover your shoulders and legs in the churches and cathedral), and definitely stop by if you're around in the 10 days leading up to the **Feast of St Francis Xavier** on 3 December. Once every decade (the next one is 2014), the saint's body is carried through Old Goa's streets.

⊙ Sights

★ Basilica of Bom Jesus   CHURCH
(⊙7.30am-6.30pm; English-language mass 10.15am Sun) Famous throughout the Roman Catholic world for its rather grizzled and grizzly long-term resident, the basilica's vast, gilded interior forms the last resting place of Goa's patron saint, St Francis Xavier (except for his diamond-encrusted fingernail, which sits in Chandor). In 1541, the saint embarked on a mission to put right the sinful, heady lifestyles of Goa's Portuguese colonials. Construction of the imposing red-stone basilica was completed in 1605; St Francis himself is housed in a **mausoleum** to the right, in a glass-sided coffin amid a shower of gilt stars.

Sé Cathedral   CHURCH
(⊙7.30am-6.30pm) The largest church in Old Goa, the Sé de Santa Catarina, is also the largest in Asia, at over 76m long and 55m wide. Construction began in 1562, under orders from Portugal's King Dom Sebastião, and the finishing touches were made 90 years later. Fairly plain all-round, the cathedral has three especially notable features: the first, up in the belfry, is the **Golden Bell**, the largest bell in Asia; the second is in the screened chapel inside to the right, known as the **Chapel of the Cross of Miracles**,

wherein sits a cross said to have miraculously, and vastly, expanded in size after its creation by local shepherds in 1619. The third is the massive gilded reredos (ornamental screen behind the altar), which depicts the life of St Catherine, to whom the cathedral is dedicated and who came to a sticky end in Alexandria, Egypt, where she was beheaded.

Next to the cathedral, in the old archbishop's house, **Kristu Kala Mandir Art Gallery** (admission ₹10; ☺ 9.30am-5.30pm Tue-Sun) has contemporary Christian art and religious objects, including old church confessionals and altar pieces. The decorative wall frescoes may be the gallery's prettiest holdings.

Church of St Francis of Assisi CHURCH
(☺ 8.30am-5.30pm) The gorgeous interior of this 1661 church, built over a 16th-century chapel, is filled with gilded and carved woodwork, murals depicting the life of St Francis, frescoes of decorative flowers and various angels, 16th-century Portuguese tombstones and another stunning reredos.

Just behind the church, the former convent houses the **Archaeological Museum** (admission ₹10; ☺ 9am-5pm), whose small but worthwhile collection includes a portrait gallery of Portuguese viceroys, a couple of bronze statues, fragments of Hindu temple sculpture and some interesting 'hero stones', carved to commemorate Hindu warriors who perished in combat.

★ Museum of Christian Art MUSEUM
(http://christianartmuseum.goa-india.org; adult/child ₹30/free; ☺ 9.30am-5pm) This excellent museum, in a stunning space in the restored 1627 **Convent of St Monica**, has a fine collection of 16th- and 17th-century Christian art from Old Goa and around the state. There are some exquisite pieces here – wooden sculptures glittering with gilt and polychrome, processional lamps, tabernacle doors, polychrome paintings and other religious objects from Old Goa's prime – that are almost, but not quite, outdone by the atmospheric interior. The four-storey-high ceilings, exposed wood-beams and terracotta-work, and all-around beauty of the place are worth a visit in their own right.

Church of St Cajetan CHURCH
(☺ 9am-5.30pm) Modelled on the original design of St Peter's in Rome, the beautiful Church of St Cajetan (1655) was built by Italian friars of the Order of Theatines, who were sent by Pope Urban III to preach Christianity in the kingdom of Golconda (near Hyderabad). The friars were not permitted to work in Golconda, so settled at Old Goa in 1640.

Church of Our Lady of the Mount CHURCH
For a wonderful view of the city, hike up to this hilltop church, also known as **Capela de Monte**, 2km east of Sé Cathedral; it's especially worth the trip for a spectacular sunset. (Locals will warn you not to go solo; the site is a bit remote.) The church is rarely open but was recently restored and, with its exceptional acoustics, now hosts concerts during the Feast of St Francis Xavier in December, the Monte Music Festival in February, and at other times during the year.

Monastery of St Augustine HISTORIC SITE
The melancholy, evocative ruins of this once vast and impressive Augustinian monastery are all that remain of a huge structure founded in 1572 and abandoned in 1835. The building's facade came tumbling down in 1942; all that remains, amid piles of rubble, is the towering skeletal belfry, though the bell itself was rescued and now hangs in Panaji's Church of Our Lady of the Immaculate Conception.

GOA OLD GOA

WORTH A TRIP

BACKWOODS CAMP

In a forest in the Bhagwan Mahaveer Sanctuary full of butterflies and birds, **Backwoods Camp** (☎ 9822139859; www.backwoodsgoa.com; 2-day ₹6000-7000, 3-day ₹8500-10,000) could hardly be in a more magical, serene spot. The resort is about 1km from Tambdi Surla temple in the state's far east, and for birdwatching enthusiasts it offers one of Goa's richest sources of feathered friends, with everything from Ceylon frogmouths and Asian fairy bluebirds to puff-throated babblers and Indian pittas putting in a regular appearance. Accommodation is in comfortable tents on raised platforms, bungalows and farmhouse rooms (all with attached bathroom), and the camp makes valiant attempts to protect this fragile bit of the Goan ecosystem through measures including waste recycling, replanting indigenous tree species and employing local villagers.

Other Sights

There are plenty of other monuments in Old Goa to explore, including the **Viceroy's Arch**, **Adil Shah Palace Gateway**, **Chapel of St Anthony**, **Chapel of St Catherine**, **Albuquerque's Steps**, the **Convent & Church of St John**, **Sisters' Convent** and the **Church of Our Lady of the Rosary**.

ℹ Getting There & Away

Frequent buses from Old Goa head to Panaji's Kadamba bus stand (₹10, 25 minutes) from Old Goa Rd, just beside the Tourist Inn and at the main roundabout to the east.

Ponda & Around

The workaday inland town of Ponda, 29km southeast of Panaji, has two big drawcards in the vicinity – Hindu temples and spice plantations – and is well worth a day away from the beach. Temple aficionados, however, might be a little disappointed; most were built or rebuilt after the originals were destroyed by the Portuguese, so they're not as ancient as those elsewhere in India.

The 18th-century hilltop **Mangueshi Temple** at Priol, 5km northwest of Ponda, is dedicated to Manguesh, a god known only in Goa, while 1km away at Mardol is the **Mahalsa Temple**, also dedicated to a specifically Goan deity. The 1738 **Shantadurga Temple**, meanwhile, just west of Ponda, is dedicated to Shantadurga, the goddess of peace, and is one of the most famous shrines in Goa.

There are regular buses to Ponda from Panaji (₹20, 45 minutes) and Margao, after which you'll need to arrange a taxi to visit the temples or spice farms. Taxis from Panaji charge ₹1200 for a day trip to the area (up to eight hours and 80km).

NORTH GOA

Mapusa

POP 40,100

The pleasantly bustling market town of Mapusa (pronounced 'Mapsa') is the largest town in northern Goa and a transport hub for local and interstate buses. The main reason to visit is for its busy **Friday market** (☺8am-6.30pm), which attracts scores of buyers and sellers from neighbouring towns and villages, and a healthy intake of tourists from the northern beaches. It's a good place to pick up the usual embroidered bedsheets and the like at prices lower than in the beach resorts.

Mapusa is also home to the exceptionally awesome **Other India Bookstore** (☑2263306; www.otherindiabookstore.com; Mapusa Clinic Rd; ☺9am-5pm Mon-Fri, to 1pm Sat), specialising in 'dissenting wisdom' and alternative press – a small but spectacular selection of books on nature, farming, politics, education and natural health. To find it, go up the steps next to the old Mapusa Clinic, and follow the signs.

WORTH A TRIP

SPICE OF LIFE

There are several spice farms in the Ponda area that make an excellent day trip. **Tropical Spice Plantation** (☑2340329; www.tropicalspiceplantation.com; admission incl lunch ₹400; ☺9am-4pm), 5km northeast of Ponda, is one of the most popular with an entertaining 45-minute tour of the 120-acre plantation's 'demo garden' followed by a banana-leaf buffet lunch. Elephant rides (₹600 for 10 minutes) and bathings (₹600) can be fun. **Sahakari Spice Farm** (☑2312394; www.sahakarifarms.com; admission incl lunch ₹400; ☺9am-4pm), 2km from Ponda, offers a similar experience but with a more traditional hut-style restaurant and the added attraction of folk dances and tree-swinging to collect betel nuts.

The 200-year-old family **Savoi Plantation** (☑2340272, 9822133309; www.savoiplantation.com; ☺9am-4.30pm), whose motto is 'Organic Since Origin', is much mellower, less touristed and elephant-free. You'll find a warm welcome from knowledgeable guides keen to walk you through the 100-acre plantation at your own pace. Local crafts are for sale, and you're welcomed with fresh kokum juice, cardamom bananas and other organic treats.

✹ Volunteering

If you're interesting in working with disadvantaged children while staying in Goa, there are a couple of well-established options.

El Shaddai VOLUNTEERING
(📞6513286, 6513287; www.childrescue.net; El Shaddai House, Socol Vaddo, Assagao) Runs daycare, night shelters and homes for street children and orphans. Volunteers are required to give a minimum commitment of four weeks, pay a £500 volunteer donation (includes meals and accommodations), and supply background checks. Apply early. You can also sponsor a child via the website

Mango Tree Goa VOLUNTEERING
(📞9881 261886; www.mangotreegoa.org; 'The Mango House', near Vrundavan Hospital, Karaswada, Mapusa) Based at the Mango House near Mapusa, this is another UK-based charity that seeks to help disadvantaged children with shelter, healthcare and education. Visitors are welcome by prior arrangement. Volunteers with teaching and nursing backgrounds are sometimes required.

🛏 Sleeping & Eating

There's little reason to stay the night in Mapusa when the beaches of the north coast are all so close and most long-distance transport departs at night. If you do, **Hotel Vilena** (📞2263115; Feira Baixa Rd; d/tr ₹600/750, with AC ₹840; ❄) is central and Mapusa's best budget bolt-hole. There are plenty of decent local cafes within the market area. The thalis are excellent at busy **Ashok Snacks & Beverages** (thalis & mains ₹40-70; ⊙6am-10.30pm Mon-Sat, to 4pm Sun), overlooking the market. **Hotel Vrundavan** (thalis ₹50-75; ⊙7am-10pm Wed-Mon), an all-veg place bordering the municipal gardens, is another great joint with good chai and snacks, while the **Pub** (near the market; ⊙9am-10.30pm) is the best spot for a drink and prime people-watching on market day.

ℹ Information

There are plenty of ATMs and a few internet places scattered about the town centre and market area.
Mapusa Clinic (📞2263343; ⊙consultations 10.30am-1.30pm Mon-Sat, 3.30-7pm Mon, Wed & Fri) A well-run medical clinic, with 24-hour emergency services. Be sure to go to the 'new' Mapusa Clinic, behind the 'old' one.

ℹ Getting There & Away

If you're coming to Goa by bus from Mumbai, Mapusa's **Kadamba bus stand** (📞2232161) is the jumping-off point for the northern beaches. Local services run every few minutes; just look for the correct destination on the sign in the bus windscreen and try to get an express. For buses to the southern beaches, take a bus to Panaji, then Margao, and change there.

Local services include the following:
Anjuna (₹15, 20 minutes)
Arambol (₹27, 1½ hours)
Calangute/Candolim (₹10/12, 20/35 minutes)
Panjim (₹15, 20 minutes)
Thivim (₹15, 20 minutes)

Interstate services run out of the same lot, but private operators have their offices next to the bus stand. There's generally little difference in price between private services and the Kadamba buses, but shop around as there are various standards of bus.

Long-distance services include the following:
Bengaluru (private; AC or sleeper ₹1400, 13-14hr)
Mumbai (private; non-AC ₹700, AC ₹1200, 12-15hr)
Pune (private; non-AC from ₹650, AC ₹1200, sleeper ₹1000, 11-13hr)

There's a prepaid taxi stand outside the bus terminal with a list of prices. Cabs to Anjuna or Calangute cost ₹300, Arambol ₹500 and Panaji ₹500; autorickshaws typically charge ₹50 less than taxis.

Thivim, about 12km northeast of town, is the nearest train station on the Konkan Railway. Local buses meet trains; an autorickshaw into Mapusa from Thivim costs around ₹200.

Candolim, Sinquerim & Fort Aguada

POP 8600

Candolim's vast beach, which curves round as far as smaller Sinquerim beach in the south, is largely the preserve of older, slow-roasting package tourists from the UK, Russia and Scandinavia, and is fringed with seasonal beach shacks, all offering sun beds and shade in exchange for your custom.

Candolim's beach is pleasant, the town is mellow, there are some very good hotels hidden among the palms behind the beach and the main drag has a good array of restaurants, but it's somewhat fading and lacks the personality of many other beach towns. The post office, supermarkets, travel agents, internet cafes, pharmacies and plenty of banks with ATMs are all on the main Fort Aguada Rd, which runs parallel to the beach.

◉ Sights & Activities

Fort Aguada
FORT, AREA

(⊙ 8.30am-5.30pm) Guarding the mouth of the Mandovi River and hugely popular with Indian tour groups, Fort Aguada was constructed by the Portuguese in 1612 and is the most impressive of Goa's remaining forts. It's worth braving the crowds and hawkers at the moated ruins on the hilltop for the views; unfortunately, there was no entry at research time to the fort's four-storey **Portuguese lighthouse**, built in 1894 and the oldest of its type in Asia. But just down the road is the peninsula's active **lighthouse** (Indian/foreigner ₹10/50, camera ₹25; ⊙ 3-5.30pm), which you can climb for extraordinary views. It's a pleasant 2km ride along a hilly, sealed road to the fort, or you can walk via a steep, uphill path past Marbella Guest House. Beneath the fort is the **Fort Aguada Jail**, whose cells were originally fort storehouses, and **Johnny's Mansion**, owned by a famously wealthy Goan and often used as a set for Indian films. Neither is open to the public.

Boat Cruises
BOATING

Some of the most popular boat trips around town are run by **John's Boat Tours** (☎ 9822182814, 6520190; www.johnboattrips.com), including dolphin-watching cruises (₹1000), boat trips to Anjuna Market (₹800), a Grand Island snorkelling excursion (₹1400), and even overnight houseboat cruises (₹5500 per person, full board). For something more low-key (read: cheaper), head to the **excursion boat jetty** along the Nerul River where you can haggle with independent local boats to Anjuna (₹400) and dolphin cruises (₹300) that pass by Coco Beach, Fort Aguada Jail, the fort, and 'Johnny's Millionaire House'.

🛏 Sleeping

Candolim has a good range of accommodation, including some of North Goa's top hotels – the southern end is dominated by the Taj hotels. Most of the best-value budget choices are in the lush area in northern Candolim between the road and the beach; wander through the tiny trails off laneways and you're sure to find something.

Beach Nest
GUESTHOUSE $

(☎ 2489866, 9822381853; Monteiro's Rd, Escrivai Vaddo; d ₹900-1200) There are no sea views here but this is a spotless and friendly little place that's just a quick jungle-footpath walk to the beach. The more expensive upstairs rooms have balcony, kitchenettes and fridges, the owners are helpful, and the atmosphere is serene and homey.

Villa Ludovici Tourist Home
GUESTHOUSE $

(☎ 2479684; Fort Aguada Rd; d incl breakfast ₹900) The five well-worn, creaky rooms in this grand old Portuguese-style villa have been sheltering budget travellers for years. Back from the beach but a warm place to stay.

★ Bougainvillea Guest House
GUESTHOUSE $$

(☎ 2479842, 9822151969; www.bougainvilleagoa.com; off Fort Aguada Rd, Sinquerim; r ₹2500, penthouse ₹4500; ❋ ��}) A lush, plant-filled garden leads the way to this gorgeous family-run guesthouse down a quiet lane off the southern end of Fort Aguada Rd. The eight light-filled suite rooms are spacious and spotless, with fridge, flat-screen TV and either balcony or private sit-out – the top floor penthouse has its own rooftop terrace. This is the kind of place guests come back to year after year. Book ahead.

D'Mello's Sea View Home
HOTEL $$

(☎ 2489650; www.dmellos.com; Monteiro's Rd, Escrivao Vaddo; d ₹1200-1700; @) The name says it all – rooms in the sea-facing building at family-run D'Mello's are divine, with only three walls: the fourth is your balcony, with ocean views. Even the back rooms are stylish, with perky colours and chic cotton bedspreads. All rooms are fastidiously clean and have mosquito nets but tiny bathrooms. It's a short clamber to the beach and if this place is full, there's a bunch of others nearby.

Candolim Villa Horizon View
HOTEL $$

(☎ 2489105; www.candolimvilla.com; d with AC ₹2200-2750; ❋ @ � 🌊) Simple air-con rooms are set around a small swimming pool at this friendly, professional midranger.

★ Marbella Guest House
HOTEL $$$

(☎ 2479551, 9822100811; www.marbellagoa.com; off Fort Aguada Rd, Sinquerim; r ₹3200-6100; ❋) This stunning Portuguese-era villa, filled with antiques and backed by a lush, peaceful courtyard garden, is a romantic and sophisticated old-world remnant. Rooms are

GREEN GOA?

Goa's environment has suffered from an onslaught of tourism over the last 40 years, but also from the effects of logging, mining and local customs (rare turtle eggs have traditionally been considered a dining delicacy). Construction proceeds regardless of what the local infrastructure or ecosystem can sustain, while plastic bottles pile up in vast mountains. There are, however, a few easy ways to minimise your impact on Goa's environment:

➡ Take your own bag when shopping and refill water bottles with filtered water wherever possible. The 5L Bisleri water bottles come with a deposit and are returnable to be reused. Better yet, bring a water filter with you.

➡ Rent a bicycle instead of a scooter, for short trips at least, and ask around if you don't find any: bicycle rentals are declining as a result of our scooter infatuation and the bikes are poor quality, but they'll bounce back if the demand is there.

➡ Dispose of cigarette butts, which are nonbiodegradeable, and any plastic litter in bins; birds and sealife may mistake them for food and choke.

Turtles are currently protected by the **Forest Department** (www.goaforest.com), which operates huts on beaches, such as Agonda and Morjim, where turtles arrive to lay eggs. Drop into these or check out the website to find out more about the department's work. Also doing good work is the **Goa Foundation** (☎2256479, 2263305; www.goafoundation. org; St Britto's Apts, G-8 Feira Alta, Mapusa), the state's main environmental pressure group based in Mapusa. It has spearheaded a number of conservation projects since its inauguration in 1986, and its website is a great place to learn more about Goan environmental issues. The group's excellent *Fish Curry & Rice* (₹400), a sourcebook on Goa's environment and lifestyle, is sold at Mapusa's Other India Bookstore (p826). The Foundation occasionally runs volunteer projects; call or swing by for details.

individually themed, including the Moghul, Rajasthani and Bouganvillea. Its kitchen serves up some imaginative dishes, and its penthouse suite is a dream of polished tiles and four-posters. No kids under 12.

🍴 Eating & Drinking

Candolim's plentiful beach shacks are popular places to eat or relax with a beer.

★ **Café Chocolatti** CAFE, BAKERY $$
(409A Fort Aguada Rd; baked goods ₹45-100, mains ₹120-220; ☺9am-7pm Mon-Sat) Treat yourself at this lovely tearoom, set in a green garden on the main road but light years from the bustle of traffic or the beach. The cafe serves great coffee, sandwiches and salads, but the chocolate cake and waffles are the stars.

Stone House STEAKHOUSE, BAR $$
(Fort Aguada Rd; mains ₹150-500; ☺11am-3pm & 7pm-midnight) Surf 'n' turf's the thing at this venerable old Candolim venue, inhabiting a stone house and a leafy front courtyard. 'Swedish Lobster' cooked in beer tops the list, followed by other beefy plates, seafood and Goan dishes. It's run by the affable Chris and there's quality live music most nights of the week in season.

Bob's Inn MULTICUISINE, BAR $$
(Fort Aguada Rd; mains ₹80-300; ☺10.30am-4pm & 6.30pm-midnight) Great fish dishes, relaxed ambience and old dudes – foreigners and locals alike – chillaxing at the communal table. The African wall hangings, thatch everywhere, and terracotta sculptures are a nice backdrop to the *rava* (semolina wheat) fried mussels or 'drunken prawns'.

Chili Hip THAI $$
(☎6650281; www.chilihipgoa.com; Accron Place, Fort Aguada Rd; mains ₹200-380; ☺noon-3pm & 6.30-10.30pm) Savour authentic, spicy Thai dishes prepared by a Bangkok chef in this stylish new restaurant attached to the Centara day spa. Upstairs, Vibes is a chic cocktail bar.

Republic of Noodles ASIAN FUSION $$$
(mains ₹375-450; ☺11.30am-3pm & 7-11pm) For a sophisticated dining experience, this award-winning pan-Asian place delivers with its dark bamboo interior, Buddha heads and floating candles. Delicious, huge noodle plates, wok stir-fries and clay-pot dishes are the order of the day – consider the coconut and turmeric curry of red snapper – and there are some exciting dishes for the veggies.

❶ Getting There & Away

Buses run frequently to Panaji (₹12, 30 minutes) and Mapusa (₹12, 35 minutes) and stop at the turn-off near John's Boat Tours. Calangute buses (₹5, 15 minutes) start at the Fort Aguada bus stop and can be flagged down on Fort Aguada Rd.

Calangute & Baga

POP 15,800

For better or worse, Calangute and Baga are Goa's most popular beaches – a least with the cashed-up domestic tour crowd and European package tourists. Once a refuge of wealthy Goans, and later a 1960s hot spot for naked, revelling hippies, Calangute has adapted its scant charms to extended Indian families, groups of Indian bachelors and partying foreigners. If you want to experience authentic Indian (or Russian) tourism full-on, come to Calangute. The northern beach area can get crowded – including the water, which fills up with people, boats and jet skis – but the southern beach is more relaxed. Baga, to the north, meanwhile, is the place for drinking and dancing, and Northern Baga, across the Baga River, is surprisingly tranquil, with budget accommodation bargains clinging to the coast.

🏃 Activities

Water Sports

You'll find numerous jet-ski and parasailing operators on Calangute and Baga beaches. Parasailing costs around ₹650 per ride, jet-skiing costs ₹1000 per 15 minutes.

Barracuda Diving DIVING
(Map p832; ☑2279409, mobile 9822182402; www.barracudadiving.com; Sun Village Resort, Baga; courses from ₹4500) This long-standing diving school offers a range of dives and courses, from two-day Discover Scuba (₹4500) to four-day PADI open water (₹20,000). It's also exceptional for its 'Project A.W.A.R.E', which undertakes marine-conservation initiatives and annual underwater and beach clean-ups.

Yoga & Ayurveda
Ayurvedic Natural Health Centre AYURVEDA, YOGA
(☑08322409275; www.healthandayurveda.com; Chogm Rd, Saligao; ⏰7.30am-7.30pm) This highly respected centre, 5km inland at Saligao, offers a range of massages and other ayurvedic treatments lasting from one hour to three weeks. Herbal medicines and consulta-

tions with an ayurvedic doctor are also available. Professional courses are given here in ayurveda, yoga and other regimes; enquire well in advance. For the more spontaneous, drop-in yoga classes (₹300) are held daily.

Boat Trips
Local fishers congregate around northern Baga beach, offering dolphin-spotting trips (₹500 per person), visits to Anjuna Market (₹300 per person) and whole-day excursions to Arambol and Mandrem (₹1100 per person).

👉 Tours

Day Tripper (Map p831; ☑2276726; www.daytrippergoa.com; Gaura Vaddo, Calangute; ⏰9am-5.30pm Mon-Sat Nov-Apr) runs a variety of trips around Goa, including two weekly to Dudhsagar Falls (₹1330), overnight houseboat trips (₹5300 per person) aboard a Keralan-style rice barge, and a sailing trip through the mangroves of the Cumbarjua River (₹1650).

GTDC tours can be booked online (www.goa-tourism.com) or at **Calangute Residency** (Map p831; ☑2276024; ⏰24hr), by the main entrance to the beach.

🛏 Sleeping

Calangute and Baga's sleeping options are plentiful, lining the main roads and laneways down to the beach for several kilometres. Generally, the quietest hotels lie in south Calangute, and across the bridge north of Baga.

🛏 Calangute

⭐ **Johnny's Hotel** HOTEL $
(Map p831; ☑2277458; Calangute; d ₹700-900, with AC ₹1100-1300; ❄ 🛜) The 15 simple rooms in this backpacker-popular place make for a sociable stay, with a downstairs restaurant-bar and regular classes available in yoga and reiki. A range of apartments and houses are available for longer-stayers.

Ospy's Shelter GUESTHOUSE $
(Map p831; ☑2279505; oscar_fernandes@sify.com; d ₹700-800) Tucked away in a quiet, lush little area full of palms and sandy paths between the beach and St Anthony's Chapel, are a bunch of family-run guesthouses. Ospy's, just a two-minute walk to the beach, is a good bet. Spotless upstairs rooms have fridges and balconies, and the whole place has a cosy family feel. Check out the

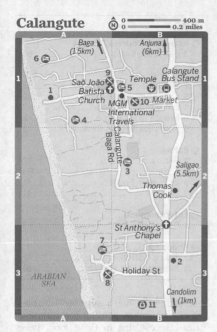

Calangute

a bargain from April to October when rates are less than half. Portuguese-style yellow-ochre buildings orbit a pretty pool courtyard, decor is bright and fresh, and the big, clean rooms have safes, flat-screen TVs and other high-end and thoughtful touches.

gorgeous old floor tiles on the ground floor. Take the road directly west of the chapel but it's tough to find, so call ahead.

Garden Court Resort GUESTHOUSE $
(Map p831; ☏2276054; luarba@dataone.in; r ₹600-1000, with AC ₹700-1200; ❄ 🛜 🏊) Despite being on the busy market road, the rooms here, fronted by a Portuguese-style family home and set amongst pretty gardens, are remarkably quiet. They're not flashy but are reasonable value and come with balconies.

Coco Banana GUESTHOUSE $
(Map p831; ☏2279068; www.cocobananagoa.com; d ₹750-950, with AC ₹1200) Among the palms south of the main entrance to Calangute beach, this tranquil place is run by a friendly Swiss-Goan family who keep the spacious rooms spotless and the vibe mellow. For families or groups it also has an apartment at nearby Casa Leyla, with separate sitting room and kitchen area.

★ Casa de Goa HOTEL $$$
(Map p831; ☏6717777; www.casadegoa.com; Tivai Vaddo; r/ste/villa ₹11,500/14,000/15,400; ❄ @ 🛜 🏊) The beautiful Casa de Goa is popular with Indian families and books up months in advance for weekends and high season – but at these prices it's really only

Baga

Indian Kitchen GUESTHOUSE $
(☏2277555; www.indian-kitchen-goa.com; s/d/chalet ₹770/990/1200; ❄ @ 🛜 🏊) If a colourful stay is what you're after, look no further than this family-run guesthouse, which offers basic rooms with much attempt at individual charm, set around a sparkly central courtyard. There's even a small swimming pool out the back, a small gym and a sauna.

Melissa Guest House GUESTHOUSE $
(Map p832; ☏2279583; d ₹600) Small, neat rooms, all with attached bathrooms and hot-water showers, comprise this quiet, excellent-value little place, pleasantly located in a plant-filled garden near the Baga River with views across to the beach.

Divine Guest House GUESTHOUSE $
(Map p832; ☏2279546, 9370273464; www.indivinehome.com; d from ₹800, with AC ₹1200; ❄ @ 🛜) The Divine welcomes you with a 'Praise the Lord' gatepost and keeps perky reminders throughout the place, so only stay here if you don't mind cheerful proselytising. Rooms are sweet and homey, with bright colours, lots of kitsch and the odd individual touch, all at a quiet riverside location. Two-night minimum.

GOA CALANGUTE & BAGA

Baga

Arpora (2km);
Anjuna (5.5 km)

Baga River

Baga Bus Stand

BAGA

Calangute-Baga Rd

ARABIAN SEA

Tito's Rd

Calangute (1.5km)

Baga

around a garden and a gorgeous Portuguese colonial bungalow housing the restaurant Balcao, specialising in Goan food. Pricey compared with its neighbours but still a good bet.

★ **Nilaya Hermitage**　　　　HOTEL $$$
(☎ 2269793, 2269794; www.nilaya.com; Arpora; d incl breakfast, dinner & spa €350; ✸@🖎🛎) Ultimate Goan luxury, set 5km inland from Baga beach at Arpora, a stay at this hilltop hideaway will see you signing the guestbook with the likes of Giorgio Armani, Sean Connery and Kate Moss. Ten beautiful redstone rooms undulate around a swimming pool, alongside four luxury tents. The food is as dreamy as the surroundings, and the ayurvedic spa (all inclusive) will spoil you rotten.

✕ Eating

Calangute and Baga have everything from fresh fish cooked up on a beach barbecue to the finest Italian proscuitto in homemade pasta. The main beach strip is thick with vendors selling grilled corn, *pav bhaji* (spiced vegetables and bread) and luminescent candyfloss, as well as the usual beach-shack fare. Dining gets more sophisticated to the north and south – some of Baga's best restaurants are along the road north of the Baga River. Calangute's busy market area, meanwhile, is filled with chai-and-thali joints.

Alidia Beach Cottages　　GUESTHOUSE $$
(Map p832; ☎ 2279014; www.alidiabeachcottages.com; Calangute-Baga Rd, Saunta Waddo; d ₹1500, with AC ₹2500-2800, ste ₹3500; ✸🖎🛎) Set back behind a whitewashed church, this convivial place has beautifully kept Mediterranean-style rooms orbiting a gorgeous pool. Cheaper rooms are at the back but all are in good conditon, the staff are keen to please and there's a path directly to the beach.

Cavala Seaside Resort　　　HOTEL $$
(Map p832; ☎ 2276090; www.cavala.com; Calangute-Baga Rd; s/d incl breakfast from ₹1050/2100, d with AC ₹3250-5400, ste ₹3900-4750; ✸🖎🛎) With its laterite-brick, ivy-clad exterior, Cavala has been charming Baga-bound travellers for more than 30 years, and continues to deliver clean, simple, nicely furnished rooms. The bar-restaurant cooks up a storm, with live music most nights in season. There's a second **pool** (nonguests ₹200) across the road at Cavala's Banana Republic bar.

**Nani's Bar &
Rani's Restaurant**　　　GUESTHOUSE $$
(Map p832; ☎ 2276313; www.naniranigoa.com; r without/with AC ₹1400/1600; ✸@) Nani's is as charming as it is well situated, with nine clean, simply furnished rooms (getting a thorough renovation when we visited), set

Calangute

★ Plantain Leaf
INDIAN $

(Map p831; thali ₹100-125, mains ₹80-200; ⊙11am-10pm) On the 1st floor, at a slight remove from the chaos of the market intersection below, is the pure-veg Plantain Leaf. The many Indian families that fill the booths here know a good thing when they see it: cosy, busy and bright, and the veg thali might be the best you'll get in Goa.

Infantaria
BAKERY, ITALIAN $$

(Map p831; Calangute-Baga Rd; pastries ₹80-150, mains ₹180-300; ⊙7.30am-midnight) What started out as Calangute's best little bakery has matured and morphed into a fabulous little two-level Italian restaurant. It's still a great place for breakfast, loaded with homemade croissants, flaky pastries and real coffee, but it's also a fine lunch or dinner spot with Goan and Italian specialities, wine and thoughtful cocktails.

A Reverie
INTERNATIONAL $$$

(Map p831; ✆9823505550; Holiday St; mains ₹340-600; ⊙7pm-late) A gorgeous lounge-bar, all armchairs, cool jazz and sparkling crystals, this is the place to spoil yourself with the likes of Serrano ham, grilled asparagus, French wines and Italian cheeses. Start with tapas plates and move on to a world menu featuring European, Asian and India flavours.

Baga

Lila Café
CAFE $$

(Map p832; mains ₹40-280; ⊙8.30am-6pm) This German-run garden restaurant on the Baga River is a favourite for breakfast with homebaked breads, croissants, perfect, frothy cappuccinos and powerhouse mains like goulash with spaetzle.

Britto's
MULTICUISINE, BAR $$

(Map p832; mains ₹100-380; ⊙8.30am-midnight) Britto's is an arena-sized Baga institution at the north end of the beachfront. It's good for breakfast but gets very busy for lunch and dinner. The drinks list is longer than the food menu and there's live music on most nights in season.

★ Fiesta
CONTINENTAL $$$

(Map p832; www.fiestagoa.in; Tito's Rd; ₹250-600; ⊙7pm till late) Tucked away off noisy Tito's Lane, there's something magical about stepping into Fiesta's candlelit split-level tropical garden. Soft music and exotic furnishings add to an upmarket Mediterranean-style dining experience that starts with homemade pizza and pasta (herb ricotta ravioli or penne with gorgonzola) and extends to French-influenced seafood dishes and some of the finest desserts around. Worth a splurge.

Le Poisson Rouge
FRENCH $$$

(Map p832; mains ₹390-480; ⊙7pm-midnight) This Indo-French garden restaurant just across the river is one of Baga's best fine-dining affairs. Simple local ingredients are combined into winning dishes such as beetroot carpaccio, burgundy chicken stew and calamari and prawn risotto, all served up beneath the stars.

▼ Drinking & Nightlife

Baga's club scene bubbles on long after the parties further north have been locked down. If you're up for a night of decadent drinking or dancing on the tables, you're in the right place. Although Tito's Lane in Baga is the hotspot, there are lots of little bars scattered around, many offering live music on weekends.

Café Mambo
NIGHTCLUB

(Map p832; ✆9822765002; www.titos.in; couple ₹500; ⊙10.30pm-3am) Mambo's is a slightly sophisticated (relative to Baga) late-night club, with DJs pumping out mostly commercial house and hip hop, and the occasional (Western) retro night. It's strictly 'couples-only', though single women should have no trouble getting in (free); single men can forget it. Tito's, just next door, used to be Baga's 'it' club, and is still worth a visit, especially for Bollywood nights. Cover, rules and hours are the same as Mambo's.

⬛ Shopping

Both Mackie's Saturday Nite Bazaar (www.mackiesnitebazaar.com; ⊙from 6pm Sat Nov-Apr), in Baga, and the larger Saturday Night Market (Map p832; www.snmgoa.com; ⊙from 6pm Sat Nov-Apr), in Arpora, about 2km northeast of Baga, set up in season and are fun alternatives to Anjuna's Wednesday market, with food stalls, entertainment and the usual souvenir stalls. They have been cancelled from time to time in recent years for reasons unclear. Ask around to see if they're on.

Karma Collection SOUVENIRS
(Map p832; www.karmacollectiongoa.com; ⊙9.30am-10.30pm) This fixed-price shop near the end of the road to Baga Beach has the usual patchwork wall hangings, but also antiques from across South Asia.

Literati Bookshop & Cafe BOOKS
(Map p831; ☑2277740; www.literati-goa.com; ⊙10am-6.30pm Mon-Sat) A refreshingly different bookstore, this place is in the owners' Calangute home. Ask about readings and other events.

ℹ Information

Currency exchange offices, ATMs, pharmacies and internet cafes cluster around Calangute's main market and bus stand area, with several more (of everything) along the Baga and Candolim roads.

MGM International Travels (☑2276037; www.mgmtravels.com; Umta Vaddo, Calangute; ⊙9.30am-6.30pm Mon-Sat) A long-established and trusted travel agency with competitive prices on domestic and international air tickets.

Thomas Cook (☑2282455; Calangute-Anjuna Rd, Calangute; ⊙9am-6pm Mon-Sat) Currency exchange.

ℹ Getting There & Around

Frequent buses to Panaji (₹15, 45 minutes) and Mapusa (₹10) depart from the Baga and Calangute bus stands, and a local bus (₹5) runs between the Baga and Calangute stands every few minutes; catch it anywhere along the way. Taxis charge a silly ₹100 between Calangute and Baga. A prepaid taxi from Dabolim Airport to Calangute costs ₹750.

Anjuna

Dear old Anjuna. The stalwart of India's hippy scene still drags out the sarongs and sandalwood each Wednesday for its famous – and once infamous – flea market, and still has that floating in-between-town feel that we love. With its long beach, rice paddies and cheap guesthouses huddled in relatively peaceful pockets, it continues to pull in droves of backpackers and long-term hippies, while midrange tourists are also increasingly making their way here. The village itself might be a bit ragged around the edges, but that's all part of its haphazard charm, and Anjuna remains a favourite of long-stayers and first-timers alike.

⊙ Sights & Activities

Anjuna's charismatic **beach** runs for almost 2km from the northern village area to the flea market. The northern end is mostly cliffs lined with cheap cafes and basic guesthouses, but the beach proper (starting just south of San Francisco Restaurant) is a lovely stretch of sand with a bunch of beach bars at the southern end. For more action, **paragliding** (tandem rides ₹1800) sometimes takes place on market days off the headland at the southern end of the beach.

Yoga

There's lots of yoga, reiki and ayurvedic massage offered around Anjuna; look for notices at Café Diogo and the German Bakery. Drop-in classes are organised by **Brahmani Yoga** (☑9370568639; www.brahmaniyoga.com), next to Hotel Bougainvillea, and **Oceanic Yoga** (☑9545112278; www.oceanicyoga.com; Anjuna; ⊙1½ hr classes ₹400), which also offers intensive courses and teacher training.

⊟ Sleeping

Most accommodation and other useful services are sprinkled along the beach cliffs, on the Anjuna–Mapusa Rd leading to the bus stand or down shady inland lanes. Dozens of rooms of the largely concrete cell

Anjuna

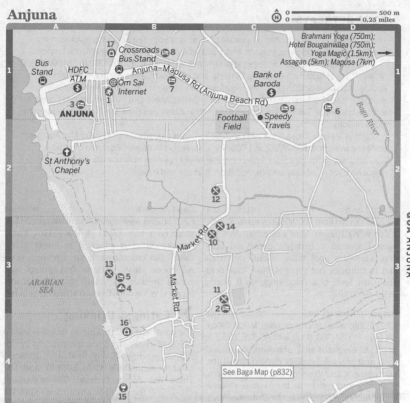

See Baga Map (p832)

variety run along Anjuna's northern clifftop stretch; most come in at ₹500 to ₹700 per night (more during peak season). There are also plenty of small, family-run guesthouses tucked back from the main beach strip, offering nicer double rooms for a similar price; take your pick from the dozens of 'Rooms to Let' signs.

Elephant Art Cafe TENTED CAMP **$**
(☑ 9970668845; elephantartcafe@gmail.com; tents ₹800-1000) The spacious tents here are lined with embroidered fabric, have tile floors and attached bathrooms, and are set in pretty grounds – like a little tent village – with winding, lamp-lit paths. The location, behind the beach shack of the same name, isn't bad either.

Vilanova GUESTHOUSE **$**
(☑ 6450389, 9225904244; mendonca90@rediffmail.com; d without/with AC ₹800/1100; ❄) Big, clean rooms have fridge, TV, 24-hour hot wa-

ter and window screens and are set in three Portuguese-style bungalows in a cute little compound. There are good vibes and a comfortable family atmosphere, with friendly staff and a good-value restaurant.

Florinda's GUESTHOUSE **$**
(☑ 9890216520; r ₹400-700, with AC ₹1200; ❄) One of the better cheapies near the beach, Florinda's has a mixed bag of clean rooms, with 24-hour hot water and window screens, set around a flower-filled garden.

Paradise GUESTHOUSE **$**
(☑ 9922541714; janet_965@hotmail.com; Anjuna-Mapusa Rd; d ₹1000, with AC ₹2000; ❄@☎) The friendly Paradise is fronted by an old Portuguese house, and its clean rooms are set in rustic grounds full of crowing roosters and sleeping cats. Proprietor Janet and her enterprising family also run a general store, restaurant, internet cafe and more.

GOA ANJUNA

YOGA RETREATS

The Anjuna/Vagator area has a number of high-end yoga retreats where you can immerse yourself in courses, classes and a zen vibe during the October–March season.

Yoga Magic (☑ 6523796; www.yogamagic.net; s/d lodge ₹6400/8000, ste ₹8400/10,500; ☎ ⌘) ✿ Solar lighting, vegetable farming and compost toilets are just some of the worthy initiatives practised in this ultraluxurious yoga resort. The lodge features dramatic Rajasthani tents under a thatched shelter. Minimum three-night stay; rates include breakfast. Daily yoga classes cost extra unless you book the inclusive week-long 'yoga holiday'.

Purple Valley Yoga Retreat (☑ 2268364; www.yogagoa.com; 142 Bairo Alto, Assagao; dm/s one week from £580/720; ☎) Popular yoga resort in nearby Assagao offering one- and two-week residential and nonresidential courses in Ashtanga yoga; weekly residential rates include accommodation, classes and meals.

Peace Land GUESTHOUSE $
(☑ 2273700; s/d from ₹600/1000, with AC ₹1500-2000; ⌘ ⌘) Rooms here are small but arranged around a tranquil courtyard garden. There's a pool table, a chill-out area and hammocks, but reports from travellers about the level of service suggests it needs to lift its game.

Palacete Rodrigues HERITAGE HOTEL $$
(☑ 2273358; www.palacetegoa.com; Mazal Vaddo; s/d from ₹1575/2100, d/ste with AC ₹2620/3150; ⌘) This old-fashioned mansion, crammed with antiques, elaborately carved furniture, odd corners and bags of fun, tacky charm, is as cool and quirky as they come. Choose your theme: rooms come in Chinese, Vietnamese, Portuguese and, of course, Goan flavours.

Banyan Soul BOUTIQUE HOTEL $$
(☑ 9820707283; www.thebanyansoul.com; d ₹2200; ⌘) A slinky 12-room option, tucked just behind Anjuna's German Bakery, lovingly conceived and run by a young escapee of the Mumbai technology rat race. Rooms are chic and well equipped with cable TV and air-con. It's certainly among the better midrange choices in town.

Hotel Bougainvillea HERITAGE HOTEL $$$
(Granpa's Inn; ☑ 2273270, 2273271; www.granpasinn.com; Anjuna Beach Rd; d/ste incl breakfast from ₹3950/4450; ⌘ ⌘ ⌘) This old-fashioned hotel in a 200-year-old yellow mansion is ridiculously pretty. Elegant rooms have that rare combination of charm and luxury, and the pool area is gorgeous. The grounds are so lush and shady that it seems a good few degrees cooler than the rest of Anjuna. The downside is that it's a long way back from the beach.

Casa Anjuna HOTEL $$$
(☑ 2274123-5; www.casaboutiquehotels.com; D'Mello Vaddo 66; r from ₹7700; ⌘ ⌘ ⌘) This lovely heritage hotel is enclosed in lovely plant-filled gardens around an inviting pool. All rooms have antique furnishings and period touches; like many upmarket places it's good value out of season when rates halve.

🍴 Eating & Drinking

The southern end of Anjuna beach boasts a string of super-sized semipermanent beach shacks serving all day food and drinks – good ones include Cafe Lilliput and the Shore Bar. At the far end, **Curlie's** (mains ₹90-280; ⊙ 9am-3am) is a notorious spot for an evening sunset drink, with an alternative crowd and the odd impromptu party. While there are plenty of restaurants near the bus stand and along the cliff, Anjuna's best are squirrelled away on the road to the flea market. **Oxford Arcade** (☑ 2273436; ⊙ 8.30am-8pm Mon-Sat), near the Starco Crossroads, is an excellent supermarket where you can stock up on imported goods and cheap alcohol.

Café Diogo CAFE $
(Market Rd; snacks ₹60-140; ⊙ 8.30am-7pm) Probably the best fruit salads in Goa are sliced and diced at Café Diogo, a small locally run cafe on the way to the market. Also worth a munch are the generous toasted avocado, cheese and mushroom sandwiches.

Whole Bean Tofu CAFE $
(Market Rd; mains ₹60-150; ⊙ 8am-5pm) One of the few places in Goa where vegans can eat well, this tofu-filled health-food cafe focuses on all things created from the versatile soya bean.

Martha's Breakfast Home CAFE $$

(meals ₹80-300; ☺7am-2pm) Martha's specialises in all-day breakfasts, served up in a quiet garden on the way down to the flea-market site. The porridge and juice may be mighty tasty, but the star of the breakfast parade is undoubtedly the piping-hot plates of pancakes and waffles, just crying out to be smothered in real maple syrup. There are a few tidy rooms (₹1000) at the side.

German Bakery MULTICUISINE $$

(www.german-bakery.in; bread & pastries ₹40-80, mains ₹80-270; ☺8am-11pm; 🛜) Leafy and filled with prayer flags, jolly lights and atmospheric curtained nooks, this is a local favourite for breakfast, crepes or a relaxed vegetarian lunch or dinner. Innovative tofu dishes are a speciality.

Shore Bar MULTICUISINE $$

(mains ₹120-400) The Shore Bar has been crowded out by the beachfront competition over the years but it's still an Anjuna institution and with the addition of a soundproof upstairs lounge-bar-nightclub, it's back in the good books. The food here is excellent but pricey, and it's always a cool spot for a sunset drink on market day.

❶ Information

Anjuna has three ATMs, clustered together on the main road to the beach.

Speedy Travels (☏2273266; ☺9am-6.30pm Mon-Sat, 10am-1pm Sun) Reliable agency for air and train ticket booking, a range of tours, and credit card advances or currency exchange.

❶ Getting There & Away

Buses to Mapusa (₹15) depart every half-hour or so from the main **bus stand** near the beach; some from Mapusa continue on to Vagator and Chapora. Two daily buses to Calangute depart

from the main **crossroads**. Taxis and pilots gather at both stops, and you can hire scooters and motorcycles easily from the crossroads.

Vagator & Chapora

Vagator's twin beaches are small by Goan standards but the dramatic red-stone cliffs, rolling green hills, patches of forest and a crumbling 17th-century Portuguese fort provide Vagator and its diminutive neighbour Chapora with one of the prettiest settings on the north Goa coast. Once known for their wild trance parties and heady, hippy lifestyles, things have slowed down considerably these days. Vagator is still the place of choice for many backpackers and party-goers, and Chapora – reminiscent of *Star Wars'* Mos Eisley Cantina – remains a fave for smokers, with the scent of charas hanging heavy in the air. Vagator has the bulk of eating and sleeping choices, along with what's left of the party scene.

Hang around long enough in Vagator and you'll likely be handed a flyer for a party (many with international DJs), which can range from divine to dire.

🛌 Sleeping

🛏 Vagator

You'll see lots of signs for 'Rooms to Let' in private homes and guesthouses along Ozran Beach Rd and on side roads too. Most charge around ₹600 per double.

Asterix HOSTEL $

(☏9766267606; www.asterixhostel.com; dm/d incl breakfast ₹500/1300, dm with AC ₹600; ❄ @ 🛜) True backpacker hostels are rare in Goa, but Asterix brings the dorm experience and an international vibe to Vagator. Run by a

---

GOA'S FLEA MARKET EXPERIENCE

Wednesday's weekly **flea market** (☺8am-late Wed, usually late Oct-late Mar) at Anjuna is as much part of the Goan experience as a day on the beach. More than three decades ago it was the sole preserve of hippies smoking jumbo joints and convening to compare experiences on the heady Indian circuit. Nowadays, things are far more mainstream – the stalls carry crafts from Kashmir and Karnataka and Tibetan trinkets – and package tourists seem to beat out independent travellers in both numbers and purchasing power. A couple of hours here and you'll never want to see a mirrored bedspread, brass figurine or floaty Indian cotton dress again in your life. But it's still a good time, a place to meet and mingle, and you can find some interesting one-off souvenirs and clothing in among the tourist tat. Remember to bargain hard and take along equal quantities of patience and stamina, applicable to dealing with local and expat vendors alike.

Vagator & Chapora

Vagator & Chapora

⊚ Sights
1 Chapora Fort B1

🛏 Sleeping
2 Alcove Resort B3
3 Asterix C2
4 Bean Me Up D3
5 Casa de Olga C1
6 Paradise on the Earth B3
7 Shalom B3

⊗ Eating
Bean Me Up Soya Station .... (see 4)
8 Mango Tree C2

9 Sunrise Restaurant C2
10 Thalassa B3
11 Yangkhor Moonlight B3

☕ Drinking & Nightlife
12 Jai Ganesh Fruit Juice Centre C2
13 Scarlet Cold Drinks C2

✪ Entertainment
14 Hilltop C3
15 Nine Bar B3

🛍 Shopping
16 Rainbow Bookshop C3

couple of well-travelled Goans, the six-bed dorms are clean and bright, and things like lockers, wi-fi, communal kitchen and travel advice are free. It's behind the small chapel next to Mango Tree. Bookings via the website only.

Bean Me Up   GUESTHOUSE $
(Enterprise Guest House; ☏ 2273479; www.beanmeup.in; 1639/2 Deulvaddo; d without/with bathrooms ₹475/680; ☏) Each of the rooms around the leafy, parachute-silk covered courtyard are simple but themed with their own exotic decor, mosquito nets and com-

mon verandas. The mellow, yoga-friendly vibe matches the clientele of the popular vegan restaurant here. Excellent value.

Paradise on the Earth   BEACH HUT $
(☏ 2273591; www.moondance.co.nr; huts without bathroom ₹600-700) Simple bamboo cocohuts (not too common in these parts) clinging to the cliff above Little Vagator Beach are great value for the beachside location, though the name might be a little overkill.

Shalom   GUESTHOUSE $$
(☏ 2273166; jul_and@hotmail.com; d ₹800-1200, with AC ₹1500; ❋☏) Arranged around a

placid garden not far from the path down to Little Vagator Beach, this friendly family-run guesthouse has a variety of extremely well-kept rooms, including one with aircon, and a two-bedroom apartment for long-stayers.

Alcove Resort HOTEL $$$
(2274491; www.alcovegoa.com; Little Vagator Beach; d without/with AC from ₹3300/3850, cottages ₹4400/4950; ✳@🛜≋) The location overlooking Little Vagator Beach and a few steps from the popular Nine Bar is hard to beat. Attractively furnished rooms, slightly larger cottages and four suites surrounding a decent pool, bar and restaurant make this a good place for those who want a touch of luxury at reasonable prices.

Chapora

Head down the road to the harbour and you'll find lots of rooms – and whole homes – for rent; check out a few before you commit.

Casa de Olga GUESTHOUSE $
(2274355, 9822157145; eadsouza@yahoo.co.in; r ₹1200, without bathroom ₹600) This welcoming family place has rooms arranged around a pretty garden in a quiet location on the way to Chapora harbour. The cheaper ones are basic (but comfy and clean), while the pricier ones have hot showers, kitchenette with fridge, and balcony.

Eating

Vagator

A few eating options cluster around the entrance to Little Vagator Beach, along with the usual slew of much-of-a-muchness beach shacks down on the sands.

★ **Thalassa** GREEK $$
(9850033537; mains ₹180-400; ⊙4pm-midnight) Thalassa has built a solid reputation for authentic and very good Greek food served on a breezy terrace overlooking Little Vagator Beach. Fresh ingredients, expert preparation and imaginative dishes. Reservations essential.

Yangkhor Moonlight TIBETAN, MULTICUISINE $$
(mains ₹70-200) Superfresh food is glorified in the Tibetan and even the Italian dishes here. The veg *momo* (Tibetan dumpling) soup is outstanding. The chairs and tablecloths are plastic and the walls are lime green, but the food and atmosphere are good.

Mango Tree BAR, CAFE $$
(mains ₹50-170; ⊙9am-4am) With loud reggae, crappy service, dark-wood furniture and mango-coloured walls, a sometimes rambunctious bar scene, draught beer, terracotta lanterns and generally a good vibe, Mango Tree is an ever-popular meeting place for all that and its really good food. Films or sports are screened most nights.

Bean Me Up Soya Station VEGAN $$
(1639/2 Deulvaddo; mains ₹120-250; ⊙8am-11pm) Oh, veggies and vegans, you've had a hard time in Goa. In a mellow garden setting, Bean Me Up specialises in vegan and raw foods, including homemade tofu and tempeh, vegan hot dogs and pizza and an internationally-inspired range of meals. There's also health juices, a bar, and an on-site shop selling tofunaise and soysage.

Chapora

Tiny Chapora's eating scene is not as evolved as Vagator's. Little restaurants pepper the main street, but they're reliable only for caloric intake. **Sunrise Restaurant** (mains ₹70-180; ⊙8.30am-10.30pm) is reliable enough, especially for breakfast, while **Scarlet Cold Drinks** (juices & snacks ₹30-50; ⊙8.30am-midnight) and **Jai Ganesh Fruit Juice Centre** (juices ₹25-60; ⊙8.30am-midnight) are both popular meeting places side by side in close proximity to the thickest gusts of charas smoke. Scarlet has an exceptionally good noticeboard, while Jai Ganesh has cold coffee and avocado lassis.

Drinking & Entertainment

Aside from secretive parties, there's not as much going on in Vagator and Chapora these days; gone are the all-nighters and the beach trance is now turned off promptly at 10pm. Still, Vagator's party scene is hanging on, mainly at **Nine Bar** (⊙6pm-4am), a late-night semi–open air bar overlooking the beach, and **Hilltop** (2273025, 2273665; ⊙sunset-late), where trance parties are still organised, especially over the peak Christmas/New Year period – the Sunday session is legendary. The Russians, having taken the party crown away from the Israelis, seem to create nightlife in various spots around town.

WHERE'S THE PARTY?

Though Goa was long legendary among Western visitors for its all-night, open-air Goan trance parties, a central government 'noise pollution' ban on loud music in open spaces between 10pm and 6am has largely curbed its often notorious, drug-laden party scene: Goa simply does not party the way it used to. With a tourist industry to nurture, however, authorities tend to turn a blind eye to parties during the peak Christmas–New Year period. Late nights are also allowed in interior spaces, which is why clubs carry on without problems. If you're looking for the remainder of the real party scene, though, you'll need to cross your fingers, keep your ear close to the ground, and wait out for word in Vagator or Anjuna.

🛍 Shopping

Rainbow Bookshop   BOOKS
(⏱10am-2pm & 3-7pm) In Vagator, near Primrose Cafe, this lovely little shop stocks a good range of secondhand and new books.

ℹ Information

Vagator's closest ATM is the HDFC at the petrol station on the back road to Anjuna and Mapusa. Plenty of internet places are scattered around town and lots of accommodation places offer wi-fi.

ℹ Getting There & Away

Frequent buses run from Chapora, through Vagator, to Mapusa (₹10) throughout the day, many via Anjuna. The buses start in Chapora village, but there are a couple of other stops in Chapora and Vagator. Scooters/motorbikes can easily be hired for around ₹200/300 per day in high season.

Morjim & Asvem

Morjim and Asvem, a pretty strip of mostly empty sand, are two North Goan beaches where sunbathing doesn't attract hordes of hawkers, dogs and onlookers. The water, though, does suffer from a bit of river run-off pollution and cannot ever be described as crystal clear. Nonetheless, rare olive ridley turtles nest at the beach's southern end from September to February, so this is a protected area, which, in theory at least, means no development and no rubbish. Morjim and Asvem have a handful of low-key beach shacks and several places to stay and eat, including the excellent beachfront **Goan Café & Resort** (✆2244394; www.goancafe.com; apt & cottage from ₹1050, with AC ₹1250, treehouse without/with bathroom from ₹800/1150; ❄🛜), whose friendly three brother-owners have built a fine array of treehouse huts as well as year-round apartments; **Meems' Beach Resort** (✆3290703; www.meemsbeachresort.com; huts ₹1500-2500, r ₹2000, with AC ₹3000; ❄🛜), which has a range of huts and rooms also right on the beach, along with free wi-fi and an atmospheric restaurant; and **La Plage** (mains ₹210-320), perhaps the fanciest beach shack in Goa, renowned for its high-calibre French food.

Mandrem

Peaceful, hidden Mandrem has become a refuge for those seeking a break from the traveller scenes of Arambol and Anjuna – and those who avoided the scene to begin with. The beach is beautiful, and there's little to do but laze on it with a good book. Coco-huts can be had from ₹600 to ₹1000. It's not easy to get here by public transport; hire a scooter or cab in Arambol.

There's lots of yoga around, mostly taught by foreigners each season. **Himalaya Yoga Valley** (✆9922719982; www.yogagoaindia.com) specialises in hatha and ashtanga teacher-training courses, but also has drop-in classes (₹300) twice daily.

🛏 Sleeping & Eating

⭐**Dunes Holiday Village**   BEACH HUTS $
(✆2247219; www.dunesgoa.com; huts ₹900-1100; @🛜) The pretty huts here are peppered around a palm-forest allée leading to the beach, and at night, globe lamps light up the place like a palm-tree dreamland. Dunes also has friendly, helpful staff, and a good restaurant on the beach.

Cuba Retreat   HOTEL $$
(✆2645775; www.cubagoa.com; d without/with AC ₹1650/2200; ❄) One of a number of fine Cuba properties around Goa, this one really scores for its retro white-and-green exterior, clean

rooms with spring mattresses, kind staff and good bar-restaurant in the courtyard.

Villa River Cat GUESTHOUSE $$$
(☎2247928; www.villarivercat.com; 438/1 Junasa-waddo; d ₹3015, with bathroom ₹3770-4800; ❄) Styling itself as a retreat for artists, writers and other bohemian types, this unusual circular Portuguese guesthouse is filled with art, antiques and a lot of pets. The riverside location (close to the beach) is lovely but might not justify this price.

Arambol (Harmal)

Beautiful Arambol, with its craggy cliffs and sweeping beach, first emerged in the 1960s as a mellow paradise for long-haired long-stayers, and ever since, travellers attracted to the hippy atmosphere have been drifting up to this blissed-out corner of Goa. As a result, in the high season the beach and the road leading down to it (known as Glastonbury St) can get pretty crowded with huts, people and nonstop stalls selling the usual tourist stuff. If you're looking for a committed traveller vibe, this is the place to come; if you're seeking laid-back languidness, you might be better off heading down the coast to Mandrem or Morjim.

🏃 Activities

The cliffs north of Arambol beach are a popular spot for **paragliding. Arambol Paragliding School** (☎9822867570) and **Arambol Hammocks** (☎9822389005; www.arambol. com; per 20min ₹1800; ⏰9am-6pm) both offer tandem flights in season from around ₹1800. Several places also offer **yoga** classes and courses.

Follow the cliff path north of Arambol Beach to pretty **Kalacha Beach**, which meets the small 'sweetwater' lake, a great spot for swimming.

Himalayan Iyengar Yoga Centre YOGA
(www.hiyogacentre.com; Madhlo Vaddo; five-day yoga course ₹3000; ⏰Nov-Mar) This is the winter retreat for the popular Dharamsala-based Iyengar yoga centre. Five-day courses (beginning on Fridays, orientation every Tuesday), intensive workshops, children's classes, and teacher training are all available. The centre is a five-minute walk from the beach, off the main road; look for the big banner. HI also has **huts** (s/d without bathroom ₹250/300) for students.

🛏 Sleeping

Arambol is well known for its sea-facing, cliff-hugging budget huts – trawl the cliffside to the north of Arambol's main beach stretch for the best hut options. It's almost impossible to book in advance: simply turn up early in the day to check who's checking out. The area around the Narayan temple (take a left turn off the main road as you enter town), also has several guesthouses of similar quality.

Chilli's HOTEL $
(☎9921882424; d ₹300-450, with AC ₹600; ⏰year-round) The bright yellow house on the main road to the beach, run by the helpful Derick Fernandes, is one of Arambol's best noncliff bargains. Chilli's offers 10 bright, no-frills rooms, all with attached bathroom, fan and hot-water shower, some with fridge and balcony.

Shree Sai Cottages BEACH HUTS $
(☎9420767358, 3262823; shreesai_cottages@ yahoo.com; huts without bathroom ₹500-600) The last set of huts on the cliffs before Kalacha (Sweet Water) Beach, Shree Sai has a calm, easygoing vibe and basic but cute hut-cottages with little balconies and lovely views out over the water.

Om Ganesh BEACH HUTS $
(☎9404436447; r & huts ₹400-800) Popular huts and some more solid rooms on the cliffs overlooking the water, managed by the friendly Sudir. The seaside Om Ganesh Restaurant is also a great place for lunch or dinner. Note that almost everyone in the area will tell you that their place is Om Ganesh.

Famafa Beach Resort HOTEL $$
(☎2242516; www.famafaarambolgoa.com; Glastonbury St; r from ₹1200; ❄@) For a little bit of comfort (including some air-con rooms) close to the beach, Famafa is a staid but clean and reliable midranger.

🍴 Eating & Drinking

Beach shacks with chairs and tables on the sand and parachute-silk canopies line the beach at Arambol. Many change annually, but **21 Coconuts** (for seafood) and **Relax Inn** (for Italian) are mainstays. There are more restaurants and cafes lining the main road from the village to the beach. For simpler fare, head up to Arambol village, by the bus stop, where small local joints will whip you up a thali and a chai for less than ₹50.

GOA ARAMBOL (HARMAL)

Shimon
MIDDLE EASTERN $

(meals ₹70-140; ⊙ 9am-11pm) Just back from the beach and understandably popular with Israeli backpackers, Shimon is the place to fill up on an exceptional falafel (₹110) or other specialities like *sabikh*, aubergine slices stuffed into pita bread with boiled egg, potato, salad and spicy relishes in pita. Follow either up with Turkish coffee or a fruit shake.

German Bakery
BAKERY $

(Welcome Inn; pastries ₹20-70) This rather dim and dingy corner cafe is surprisingly popular, with decent pastries (eg lemon cheese pie, ₹60) and espresso coffee.

Fellini
ITALIAN $$

(mains ₹140-300; ⊙ 11am-11pm) Pizza is the big deal here – the menu has more than 40 different kinds – and they are good. The pastas, calzones and paninis, especially with seafood, are also tasty. The tiramisu will keep you up at night, thinking back on it fondly.

Loeki Café
MULTICUISINE $$

(Glastonbury St; mains ₹50-200; ⊙ 8.30am-late) As much a chill-out and live music joint as a place to eat, Loeki is a very relaxed place with cushions on the floor, regular live music and jam sessions on Thursday and Saturday. Typically extensive world menu, including Goan dishes.

Double Dutch
MULTICUISINE $$

(mains ₹100-290) Longtime popular place for steaks, salads, Thai and Indonesian dishes, and famous for its apple pies, all in a pretty garden setting.

ℹ Information

Internet outfits, travel agents and money changers are as common as monsoon frogs on the road leading down to Arambol's beach. The nearest ATM is in Arambol village near the bus stop.

ℹ Getting There & Around

Buses to Mapusa (₹27, 1½ hours) depart from Arambol village every half-hour. It's only about 1.5km from the main beach area, but you're lucky if you get a cab, or even an autorickshaw, for ₹60. A prepaid taxi to Arambol from Dabolim Airport costs ₹1000; from Mapusa it's ₹400.

Lots of places in Arambol rent scooters/motorbikes, for ₹200/300, respectively, per day.

SOUTH GOA

Margao (Madgaon)

POP 94,400

Margao (also known by its train station name of Madgaon) is the main population centre of south Goa and for travellers is chiefly a transport hub, with the state's major train and bus stations. Although lacking much of Panaji's charm, it's a bustling market town of a manageable size for getting things done, or for simply enjoying the busy energy of urban India without big-city hassles.

◉ Sights

It's worth a walk around the lovely, small **Largo de Igreja** district, home to lots of atmospherically crumbling and gorgeously restored old Portuguese homes, and the quaint and richly decorated 17th-century **Church of the Holy Spirit**, particularly

---

THE FOUNDING FATHER OF QUEPEM

When Father José Paulo de Almeida looked out his oyster-shell doors and windows, he saw the Church of the Holy Cross beyond the palm trees out front, the river that functioned as his road into and out of the forest out back, and below, lush gardens elaborately designed with cruciform patterns. The Portuguese priest and nobleman arrived in Goa in 1779 and set up the town of Quepem not long after. Today the **Palácio do Deão** (☑ 2664029, 9823175639; www.palaciododeao.com; ⊙ 10am-5pm Sat-Thu) may look a lot like it did when he lived there, with original woodwork, furniture, religious effects and even the garden design all lovingly restored in the past few years by Goan couple Ruben and Celia Vasco da Gama. The Vasco da Gamas also host lunches and teatime on the back verandah; call for reservations and prices. All donations to the Palácio are used to continue restoration work and eventually create a cultural centre here.

A taxi from Margao, 14km away, will cost ₹600 round trip, including waiting time, but the bus (₹10, every few minutes) stops just a few minutes' walk down the road.

impressive when a Sunday morning service is taking place. The church also hosts services at 4pm on weekdays but is open erratically at other times.

The city's business district orbits the rectangular **Municipal Gardens**, a mini-oasis. At the southern end the Municipal Building is home to the dusty and awesome **Municipal Library** (⊗8am-8pm Mon-Fri, 9am-noon & 4-7pm Sat & Sun), which has some great books on Goa and a retro reading room where you can read the paper along with lots of gents in button-downs.

🛏 Sleeping

Hotel Tanish HOTEL $
(☑2735656; hoteltanishgoa@gmail.com; Reliance Trade Centre, Valaulikar Rd; s/d ₹650/900, s/d/ste with AC ₹800/1100/1800; ❄) The best budget place to stay in town – incongruously located on the top floor of a mall – has kind staff and tidy, well-equipped rooms with great views of the surrounding countryside. Suites come with a bathtub, big TV and views all the way to Colva. Just make sure to ask for an outside-facing room; some overlook the mall interior.

Om Shiv Hotel HOTEL $$
(☑2710294; www.omshivhotel.com; Cine Lata Rd; d with AC ₹2700-3800, ste ₹4850; ❄) In a bright-yellow building tucked away behind the Bank of India, Om Shiv does a fine line in 'executive' rooms, which all have air-con, balcony and an ordered air. The suites have exceptional views, and it's home to Margao's 'only night hotspot', the Rockon Pub.

🍴 Eating

Swad INDIAN $
(New Market; ₹25-110; ⊗7.30am-8pm) Many regard this family-friendly favourite as having Margao's best pure veg food. The North Indian thalis are reliably good, as are the snacks, South Indian tiffins and dosas.

Café Tato INDIAN $
(Valaulikar Rd; thalis ₹60, mains ₹30-70; ⊗7am-10pm Mon-Sat) A favourite local lunch spot: tasty vegetarian fare and thalis in a bustling backstreet canteen.

★Longhuino's GOAN, MULTICUISINE $$
(Luis Miranda Rd; mains ₹80-160; ⊗8.30am-11pm) Since 1950, quaint old Longhuino's bar and restaurant, with its old wooden chairs, whirring fans and slow service, has been serving up tasty Goan, Indian and Chinese dishes

Margao (Madgaon)

GOA MARGAO (MADGAON)

Margao (Madgaon)

popular with locals and tourists alike. It also does a decent job of desserts like bebinca and tiramasu. Great place to watch the world go by.

🛍 Shopping

MMC New Market   MARKET
(◎8.30am-9pm Mon-Sat) Margao's bustling covered MMC New Market is one of the most colourful in Goa.

Golden Heart Emporium   BOOKS
(Confidant House, Abade Faria Rd; ◎10am-1.30pm & 4-7pm Mon-Sat) One of Goa's best bookstores, crammed with fiction, nonfiction and illustrated books on the state's food, architecture and history.

ℹ Information

Banks offering currency exchange and 24-hour ATMs are all around town, especially near the municipal gardens and along Luis Miranda Rd.

There's a handy HDFC ATM in the Caro Centre near Longuinhos.

Apollo Victor (☎2728888; Station Rd, Malbhat) Reliable medical services.

Cyberlink (Caro Centre; Abade Faria Rd; per hr ₹20; ◎8.30am-7.30pm Mon-Sat)

Main Post Office (◎9am-1.30pm & 2.30-5pm Mon-Sat) North of the Municipal Gardens.

Goa Tourism Desk (Margao Residency; ☎2715096; www.goa-tourism.com; Luis Miranda Rd) Book GTDC trips here.

Grace Cybercafe (Valaulikar Rd, 1st fl, Reliance Trade Centre; per hr ₹30; ◎9.30am-6.30pm) Fastest and friendliest.

ℹ Getting There & Around

BUS

Government and private long-distance buses both depart from Kadamba bus stand, about 2km north of the Municipal Gardens. Shuttle buses (₹30, 35 minutes) run to Panaji every few minutes. For North Goa destinations it's best to head to Panaji and change there. Local buses

MAJOR TRAINS FROM MARGAO (MADGAON)

DESTINATION	TRAIN	FARE (₹)	DURATION (HR)	DEPARTURES
Bangalore	02779 Vasco da Gama-SBC Link	278/779 (D)	15	3.30pm
Chennai (Madras; via Yesvantpur)	17312 Vasco-da-Gama-Chennai Express	343/971/1500 (C)	21	3.20pm Thu
Delhi	12431 Rajdhani Express	2110/3050 (A)	27	10.20am Tue, Thu & Fri
Ernakulam	12618 Lakshadweep Express	325/889/1345 (C)	14½	7.25pm
	16345 Netravati Express	305/858/1315 (C)	15	11.10pm
Hubli	02779 Vasco-da-Gama-SBC Link	144/359 (D)	6½	3.50pm
Mangalore	12133 Mangalore Express	214/564/830 (C)	5½	7.10am
Mumbai (Bombay)	10112 Konkan Kanya Express	288/811/1235 (C)	12	6pm
	10104 Mandovi Express	288/811/1235 (C)	12	9.30am
Mumbai (Dadar)	12052 Jan Shatabdi Express	197/700 (B)	8½	2.30pm
Pune	12779 Goa Express	264/714/1060 (C)	12	3.30pm
Thiruvananthapuram	12432 Rajdhani Express	1405/2005 (A)	19	2.45pm Mon, Wed & Thu
	16345 Netravati Express	347/982/1520 (C)	19½	11.10pm

Fares: (A) 3AC/2AC, (B) 2S/CC, (C) sleeper/3AC/2AC, (D) sleeper/3AC

to Benaulim (₹10, 20 minutes), Colva (₹10, 20 minutes) and Palolem (₹30, one hour) stop at the bus stop on the east side of the Municipal Gardens every 15 minutes or so.

Private buses ply interstate routes several times daily, most departing between 5.30pm and 7.30pm, and can be booked at offices around town; try **Paulo Travel Masters.** (☑2702922; Luis Miranda Rd, 1st fl, Bella Vista Apt; ⊙8am-7pm) The following are sample long-distance high-season fares:

Bengaluru (private; without/with AC ₹600/850, 13 hours)

Hampi (sleeper; ₹750, nine hours)

Mumbai (private; without/with AC ₹700/1000, 14 hours)

Pune (without/with AC ₹500/850, 12 hours)

TAXI

Taxis are plentiful around the Municipal Gardens, train station and Kadamba bus stand, and they'll go anywhere in Goa, including Palolem (₹800), Panaji (₹800), Dabolim airport (₹600), Calangute (₹1100), Anjuna (₹1200) and Arambol (₹1700). Except for the train station, where there's a prepaid booth, you'll have to negotiate the fare with the driver.

TRAIN

Margao's well-organised train station, about 2km south of town, serves the Konkan Railway and other routes. Its **reservation hall** (☑PNR enquiry 2700730, information 2712790,; ⊙8am-2pm & 2.15-8pm Mon-Sat, 8am-2pm Sun) is on the 1st floor. Services to Mumbai, Mangalore, Ernakulum and Thiruvananthapuram are the most frequent. A taxi or autorickshaw to or from the town centre should cost around ₹100.

Chandor

The lush village of Chandor, 15km east of Margao, makes a perfect day away from the beaches, and it's here more than anywhere else in the state that the once opulent lifestyles of Goa's former landowners, who found favour with the Portuguese aristocracy, are still visible in its quietly decaying colonial-era mansions. Chandor hosts the colourful **Feast of the Three Kings** on the 6 January, during which local boys re-enact the arrival of the three kings from the Christmas story.

Braganza House, built in the 17th century, is possibly the best example of what Goa's scores of once grand and glorious mansions have today become. Built on land granted by the King of Portugal, the house was divided from the outset into two wings, to house two

DUDHSAGAR FALLS

On the eastern border with Karnataka, Dudhsagar Falls (603m) are Goa's most impressive waterfalls, and the second highest in India, best seen as soon as possible after the rains. To get here, take the 8.13am train to Colem from Margao (there are only three trains daily in each direction), and from there, catch a jeep for the bumpy 40-minute trip to the falls (₹4000 for the six-passenger jeep). It's then a short but rocky clamber to the edge of the falls themselves. A much easier option is to take a full-day GTDC tour from Panaji, Mapusa or Calangute (₹750, Wednesday and Sunday), or arrange an excursion with travel agencies at any of the beach resorts.

GOA CHANDOR

sides of the same family. The **West Wing** (☑2784201; admission ₹150; ⊙9am-5pm, last admission 4pm) belongs to one set of the family's descendants, the Menezes-Bragança, and is filled with gorgeous chandeliers, Italian marble floors, rosewood furniture, and antique treasures from Macau, Portugal, China and Europe. Despite the passing of the elderly Mrs Aida Menezes-Bragança in 2012, the grand old home, which requires considerable upkeep, remains open to the public. Next door, the **East Wing** (☑2857630; admission ₹100; ⊙9am-5.30pm) is owned by the Braganza-Pereiras, descendants of the other half of the family. It's nowhere near as grand, but it's beautiful in its own lived-in way, and has a small but striking family chapel that contains a carefully hidden fingernail of St Francis Xavier – a relic that's understandably a source of great pride. Both homes are open daily, and there's almost always someone around to let you in.

About 1km east of Chandor's church, the original building of the **Fernandes House** (☑2784245; admission ₹200; ⊙9am-6pm), also known as Casa Grande, dates back more than 500 years, while the Portuguese section was tacked on by the Fernandes family in 1821. The secret basement hideaway, full of gun holes and with an escape tunnel to the river, was used by the family to flee attackers.

The best way to get here is by taxi from Margao (₹350 round trip, including waiting time).

Colva & Benaulim

POP 12,000

Colva and Benaulim boast broad, open beaches, but are no longer the first place backpackers head in south Goa – most tourists here are of the domestic or ageing European varieties. There's no party scene as in north Goa and they lack the beauty and traveller vibe of Palolem. Still, these are the closest beaches to the major transport hubs of Margao and Dabolim airport. Of the two, Benaulim has the greater charm, with only a small strip of shops and a village vibe, though out of high season it sometimes has the sad feel of a deserted seaside town. From here you can explore this part of the southern coast (the beach stretches unbroken as far as Velsao in the north and the mouth of the Sal River at Mobor in the south), which in many parts is empty and gorgeous. The inland road that runs this length is perfect for gentle cycling and scootering, with lots of picturesque Portuguese-era mansions and whitewashed churches along the way.

◉ Sights & Activities

The beach entrances at Colva, and to a lesser extent Benaulim, throng with operators keen to sell you **parasailing** (per ride ₹700), **jet-skiing** (per 15 minutes ₹800), and one-hour **dolphin-watching trips** (per person from ₹400).

★ Goa Chitra   MUSEUM
(☑ 6570877; www.goachitra.com; St John the Baptist Rd, Mondo Vaddo, Benaulim; admission ₹200; ☺ 9am-6pm Tue-Sun) Artist and restorer Victor Hugo Gomes first noticed the slow extinction of traditional objects He created this ethnographic museum from the more than 4000 cast-off objects that he collected from across the state over 20 years. Admission to the museum is via a one-hour guided tour (held on the hour). In addition to the organic traditional farm out back, you'll see tons of tools and household objects, Christian artefacts and some fascinating farming implements. Goa Chitra is 3km east of Maria Hall.

🛏 Sleeping

🛏 Colva

Colva still has quite a few basic budget guesthouses among the palm groves back from the beach; ask around locally.

Sam's Guesthouse   HOTEL **$**
(☑ 2788753; r ₹500) Up away from the fray, about 1km north of Colva's main drag, Sam's is a cheerful place with good value rooms arranged around a garden. It's a short hop across the road to the beach.

La Ben   HOTEL **$**
(☑ 2788040; www.laben.net; Colva Beach Rd; r without/with AC ₹860/1300; ❋ 🛜) Neat, clean and not entirely devoid of atmosphere, La Ben is top value for this central Colva location. The rooftop restaurant is a bonus. Wi-fi is ₹40 per hour.

Skylark Resort   HOTEL **$$**
(☑ 2788052; www.skylarkresortgoa.com; 4th Ward; r without/with AC from ₹2380/2970; ❋ ▦) Easily the pick of Colva's hotels for value, Skylark has colourful, immaculate rooms – the more expensive ones face the large pool. Locally-made teak furniture, block-print bedspreads and giant shower heads add to the charm, and Colva's best bar is next door.

🛏 Benaulim

There are lots of homes around town advertising simple rooms to let. This, combined with a couple of decent budget options,

---

COLVA'S MENINO JESUS

Colva's 18th-century **Our Lady of Mercy Church** has been host to several miracles, it's said. Inside, closely guarded under lock and key, lives a little statue known as the 'Menino' (Baby) Jesus, which is thought to miraculously heal the sick. It only sees the light of day during the **Fama de Menino Jesus festival**, on the second Monday in October, when the little image is paraded about town, dipped in the river, and installed in the church's high altar for pilgrims to pray to. At other times of year you can still visit the church in the early evening, and if you have any afflictions, you might choose to stop on your way in to buy a plastic ex-voto shaped like the body part in question or offering to the Baby Jesus.

PUPPY LOVE

International Animal Rescue (IAR; ☎ 2268328; www.internationalanimalrescue.org; Animal Tracks, Madungo Vaddo, Assagao) runs the Animal Tracks rescue facility is Assagao, North Goa. At Colva's **Goa Animal Welfare Trust Shop** (◷ 9.30am-1pm & 4-7pm Mon-Sat), next to Skylark Resort, you can pick up some gifts, donate clothes and other stuff you don't want, and borrow books from the lending library. You can also learn more about the work of **GAWT** (☎ 2653677; www.gawt.org; Old Police Station, Curchorem; ◷ 9am-5.30pm Mon-Sat, 10am-1pm Sun), which operates a shelter in Curchorem (near Margao). At Chapolim, a few kilometres northeast of Palolem, the **Animal Rescue Centre** (☎ 2644171; arcingoa@gmail.com; Chapolim; ◷ 10am-1pm & 2.30-5pm Mon-Sat) also takes in sick, injured or stray animals. Volunteers are welcome at the shelters, even for a few hours, to walk or play with the dogs.

make Benaulim a better bet for backpackers than Colva.

Rosario's Inn　　　　　　GUESTHOUSE **$**
(☎ 2770636; r without/with AC ₹400/700; ❄) Across a football field flitting with young players and dragonflies, Rosario's is a big family-run place that's been around for a while and is still a steal at this price.

D'Souza Guest House　　　GUESTHOUSE **$**
(☎ 2770583; d ₹700) If you value a homey atmosphere more than proximity to the beach, this traditional blue house is run by a friendly local Goan family but there's just three spacious, clean rooms – book ahead.

Palm Grove Cottages　　　　　HOTEL **$$**
(☎ 2770059, 2771170; www.palmgrovegoa.com; d ₹1450, with AC ₹1730-3100; ❄) Ensconced in the leafiest garden you'll find, Palm Grove Cottages is close to the Benaulim shops but feels a world away. Guest rooms are atmospheric (some have balconies), and the ever-popular Palm Garden Restaurant graces the garden. The deluxe rooms in the new Portuguese-style building are top notch.

Anthy's Guesthouse　　　GUESTHOUSE **$$**
(☎ 0832 2771680; anthysguesthouse@rediffmail.com; Sernabatim Beach; r ₹1400-1950) One of just a handful of places actually on the beach, Anthy's is a firm favourite with travellers (book ahead). Well-kept chalet-style rooms, which stretch back from the beach, are surrounded by a pretty garden and restaurant.

✗ Eating & Drinking

✗ Colva

Colva's beach has a string of shacks offering the standard fare and fresh seafood. At the roundabout near the church, you'll find chai shops and thali places, fruit, vegetable and fish stalls, and, at night, *bhelpuri* vendors. For the less traditional there's even a branch of Subway and Cafe Coffee Day.

Sagar Kinara　　　　　　　INDIAN **$**
(Colva Beach Rd; mains ₹40-160; ◷ 7am-10.30pm) A pure-veg restaurant with tastes to please even committed carnivores, this top-floor place is super-efficient and serves up cheap and delicious North and South Indian cuisine.

Leda Lounge & Restaurant　CONTINENTAL, BAR
(mains ₹200-600; ◷ 7.30am-midnight) The food at stylish Leda – everything from seafood, steaks and Indian standards to pasta – is pricey but the attraction here is the comfy, cosmopolitan bar with live music most nights.

✗ Benaulim

Malibu Restaurant　　　INDIAN, ITALIAN **$$**
(mains ₹100-180; ◷ 8.30am-11pm) With a secluded garden setting full of flowers, cool breezes and butterflies, Malibu is off the beach but still one of Benaulim's tastier and more sophisticated dining experiences, with great renditions of Italian favourites. In season the same owners operate the Malibu beach shack.

Pedro's Bar &
Restaurant　　　　GOAN, MULTICUISINE **$$**
(Vasvaddo Beach Rd; mains ₹110-300; ◷ 7am-midnight) In a large, shady garden just back from the beachfront and popular with local and international tourists alike, Pedro's offers standard Indian, Chinese and Italian dishes, as well as a good line in Goan choices and some super 'sizzlers'.

Johncy Restaurant GOAN, MULTICUISINE $$
(Vasvaddo Beach Rd; mains ₹110-195; ⊘7am-
midnight) At the main entrance to the beach,
Johncy has been around forever, dispensing
standard beach-shack favourites from its
semipermanent location just off the sands.

ⓘ Information

Colva has plenty of banks and ATM machines
strung along the east–west Colva Beach Rd,
and a post office on the lane that runs past the
eastern end of the church. Benaulim has a '24-
hour' Bank of Baroda ATM at Maria Hall and (if
that's locked) a HDFC ATM on the back road to
Colva. Most useful services (pharmacies, super-
markets, internet, travel agents) are clustered
around Benaulim village, which runs along the
east–west Vasvaddo Beach Rd.

ⓘ Getting There & Around

As with other beaches, scooters can be rented at
Colva and Benaulim for around ₹200.

COLVA

Buses run from Colva to Margao every few
minutes (₹10, 20 minutes) until around 7pm. An
autorickshaw/taxi to Margao costs ₹200/250.

BENAULIM

Buses from Benaulim to Margao are also
frequent (₹10, 20 minutes); they stop at the
Maria Hall crossroads, 1.2km east of the beach.
Some from Margao continue south to Varca and
Cavelossim. Autorickshaws and pilots charge
around ₹200 for Margao, and ₹60 for the five-
minute ride to the beach.

Benaulim to Agonda

Immediately south of Benaulim are the
beach resorts of **Varca** and **Cavelossim**,
with wide, pristine sands and a line of flashy
five-star hotels set amid landscaped private
grounds fronting the beach. About 3km
south of Cavelossim, at the end of the penin-
sula, **Mobor** and its beach is one of the pret-
tiest spots along this stretch of coast, with
simple beach shacks serving good food.

If you're here with your own transport,
you can cross the Sal River from Cavelos-
sim to Assolna on the rusting tin-tub **ferry**,
which will run until the nearby bridge (you
can't miss it) is completed in late 2014. Fer-
ries run approximately every 30 minutes
between 6.15am and 8.30pm (free for pedes-
trians and motorbikes). Continuing south,
after about 7km you'll pass the charming
fishing village of **Betul**.

From Betul heading south to Agonda, the
road winds over gorgeous, undulating hills
thick with palm groves. It's worth stopping
off at the bleak old Portuguese fort of **Cabo
da Rama** (look for the green, red and white
signposts leading the way), which has a
small church within the fort walls, stupen-
dous views and several old buildings rapidly
becoming one with the trees.

Back on the main road to Agonda, look
out for the turn-off to the right (west) to
Cola Beach, one of south Goa's most gor-
geous hidden beach gems complete with
emerald-green lagoon. It's reached via a
rough 2km dirt road from the highway, but
it's not totally deserted – a couple of beach
shacks and a tent resort set up in season.
Agonda is only about 2.5km south of the
Cola Beach turnoff.

Agonda

Peaceful Agonda is a small village with a
wide, relatively empty stretch of white-sand
beach on which rare olive ridley turtles
sometimes lay their eggs. Although there's
a string of beach huts and restaurants here
in season, Agonda is low-key compared
with Palolem – strong currents make the
water here unsafe for swimming at times,
which has kept Agonda from getting too
popular.

There's lots of yoga and ayurveda in
Agonda – look out for notices – and a com-
munity feel among the shops and cafes
in the street running parallel to the beach.
There's a HDFC ATM near the church
crossroads.

🛏 Sleeping & Eating

Cocohuts and shack restaurants set up along
the beach from November to May, and there
are a few more permanent places on the
side road running parallel to the beach.

Agonda White Sand BEACH HUTS $$
(☑9823548277; www.agondawhitesand.com; Ago-
nda Beach; huts ₹2800-3500; ☎) Beautifully
designed and constructed cottages with
open-air bathrooms and spring mattresses
surround a central bar and restaurant at this
stylish beachfront place. Less than 100m
away the same owners have a pair of amazing five-star sea-facing **villas** (₹8500) with
enormous beds and cavernous bathrooms
large enough to contain a garden and fish
pond!

Fatima Restaurant   GOAN $

(thalis ₹65-75; ⏱12.30-8pm) Tiny Fatima, with just four tables, is an Agonda institution for its cheap and tasty veg and fish thalis.

Palolem & Around

Palolem has long been 'discovered' but it's still the tropical star of Goa's beaches – a stunning crescent of sand, calm waters and leaning coconut palms lend it a castaway vibe, but it does get crowded in season! It's a backpacker and family-friendly, laid-back sort of place with lots of bamboo-hut budget accommodation along the sands, good places to eat, safe swimming and kayaking in calm seas, and all the yoga, massage and alternative therapies you could wish for. Nightlife is still sleepy here – just beach bars and a couple of 'silent discos'. Many travellers end up staying in Palolem longer than they expected.

If even Palolem's version of action is too much for you, head south, along the small rocky cove named **Colomb Bay**, which hosts several basic places to stay, to **Patnem Beach**, where a fine selection of beach huts, and a less pretty – but infinitely quieter – stretch of sand awaits.

Note that Palolem, even more so than other beach towns, operates seasonally; many places aren't up and running until November.

🏃 Activities

Yoga

Palolem and Patnem are the places to be if you're keen to yoga, belly dance, reiki, t'ai chi or tarot the days away. There are courses and classes on offer all over town, with locations and teachers changing seasonally. Bhakti Kutir offers daily drop-in yoga classes, as well as longer residential courses, but it's just a single yogic drop in the area's ever-changing alternative-therapy ocean. You'll find info on daily yoga classes (₹200) and cooking classes (₹1000) at Butterfly Book Shop (p852).

Beach Activities

Kayaks are available for rent on both Patnem and Palolem beaches; an hour's paddling will cost ₹100 to ₹150, including life jacket. Fishermen and other boat operators hanging around the beach offer dolphin-spotting trips or rides to beautiful **Butterfly Beach**, north of Palolem, for ₹1000 for two

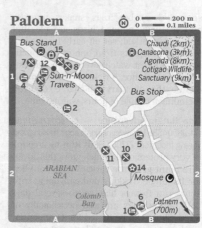

people, including one hour's waiting time. There are so many outrigger boats around that you should be able to bargain them down.

Trekking

Cotigao Wildlife Sanctuary   NATURE RESERVE

(📞2965601; admission/camera ₹5/25; ⏱7am-5.30pm) About 9km south of Palolem is this beautiful, remote-feeling sanctuary. Don't expect to bump into its more exotic residents (including gaurs, sambars, leopards and

GOA PALOLEM & AROUND

spotted deer), but frogs, snakes, monkeys and blazingly plumed birds are plentiful. Trails are marked; set off early for the best sighting prospects from one of the sanctuary's two forest watchtowers, 6km and 9km from the entrance. A rickshaw/taxi from Palolem to the sanctuary will charge ₹600/700, including a couple of hours' waiting time.

Goa Jungle Adventure OUTDOOR ADVENTURE
(☑ 9850485641; www.goajungle.com; trekking/canyoning trips from ₹1700/1900) Run by a couple of very professional French guys, this adventure outfit gets rave reviews from travellers for its jungle trekking and canyoning trips. Tours run from a half-day to several days, and rafting trips are also occasionally offered. Shoes can be rented for ₹190 per day. Book or enquire at Casa Fiesta restaurant.

🛏 Sleeping

🛏 Palolem

Most of Palolem's accommodation is of the simple seasonal beach-hut variety, though there are plenty of old-fashioned guesthouses or family homes to be found back from the beach with decent rooms from ₹500. It's still possible to find a basic palm-thatch hut without bathroom somewhere near the beach for ₹500, but many of the huts these days are made of plywood or timber and come with attached bathrooms and multiple levels. For a quality sea-facing hut in season you can pay more that ₹5000! Since the huts are dismantled and rebuilt each year, standards and ownership can vary – for this reason the places listed here are either permanent guesthouses or well-established hut operations. Popular set-ups include Cozy Nook, Dreamcatcher and Bridge N Tunnel.

My Soulmate GUESTHOUSE $
(☑ 9823785250; mysolmte@gmail.com; off Palolem Beach Rd; d ₹800, with AC ₹1200-2000; ❄ 🌐) This friendly two-storey guesthouse is down a lane (roughly behind Magic Italy) with easy access to the beach. Clean rooms come with TV and hot water and the newest ones have sexy circular beds!

Sevas HUT $
(☑ 2639194; www.sevaspalolemgoa.com; huts ₹500-1500; @) Hidden in the jungle on the Colomb Bay side of Palolem, Sevas comprises a village of well-built and maintained huts and cabanas ranging from basic to stylish. Most have attached bathroom, some are

built on stilts. Yoga classes, ayurvedic massage and a restaurant are on offer.

Bhakti Kutir COTTAGE $
(☑ 2643472; www.bhaktikutir.com; Colomb Bay; cottages ₹1000-1600; @) Ensconced in a thick wooded grove between Palolem and Patnem, Bhakti's rustic cottages are looking a little worn, and you might find yourself sharing with the local wildlife, but they still make for a unique jungle ecoretreat. There are daily drop-in yoga classes and ayurvedic treatments, a relaxing vibe, and the outdoor restaurant serves up imaginative, healthful food.

Palolem Beach Resort RESORT $$
(☑ 2645775, 9764442778; www.cubagoa.com/palolem; r without/with AC ₹1750/2500, cottages ₹2000; ❄ 🌐) You can't beat the location, right at the main beach entrance, and although not flash, Palolem Beach Resort's seasonal cottages are clean and comfortable, and the staff efficient and friendly. It also has some of the only beachfront air-con rooms (which are open year-round). The plywood nonair-com rooms at the back are disappointing for the price.

Palolem Guest House HOTEL $$
(☑ 2644879; www.palolemguesthouse.com; d ₹1200-1800, with AC ₹1750-2800; ❄) If you can't face another hut or the crazy beach scene, this is a good choice a five-minute walk back from the southern end of Palolem Beach. The variety of rooms are simple but clean and comfortable, some with balconies, and the leafy garden restaurant is a good place to hang out.

★ Ciaran's BEACH HUT $$$
(☑ 2643477; www.ciarans.com; huts incl breakfast ₹3500-4000; r with AC ₹3500; ❄ 🌐) Ciaran's has some of the sturdiest and best-designed huts on the beach, with real windows, stone floors, full-length mirrors, wood detailing and nicer bathrooms than you'll find in most hotels, all arranged around peaceful palm-filled gardens and a genuine lawn. It's the perfect balance of rustic and sophisticated. There's also a free library, free breakfast and afternoon tea and two quality restaurants, one of which is Palolem's only tapas bar.

🛏 Patnem

Long-stayers will love Patnem's choice of village homes and apartments available for rent. A very basic house can cost ₹10,000 per month, while a fully equipped apartment can run up to ₹40,000.

Micky Huts & Rooms
BEACH HUT **$**

(✉9850484884; www.mickyhuts.com; Patnem Beach; huts ₹300, r & huts with bathroom ₹1500-3000) If you don't mind huts so basic they don't even have electricity, you can sleep cheap here. Fear not: there are also better (pricier) huts with attached bathroom and power, along with the cruisy bar and restaurant, all set in a thick bamboo and coconut grove at the northern end of Patnem Beach.

Papaya's
COTTAGE **$$**

(✉9923079447; www.papayasgoa.com; huts ₹2500-3500; 🛜) Lovely huts head back into the palm grove from Papaya's popular restaurant. Each is lovingly built, with lots of wood, four-poster beds and floating muslin, as well as a porch, and the staff are incredibly keen to please.

Sea View Resort
HOTEL **$$**

(✉2643110; www.seaviewpatnem.com; cottage ₹500, d ₹1000-2000, with AC ₹3000; ❄@) For year-round accommodation about 100m back from the beach, Sea View is a decent choice with basic cottages, clean rooms – many with balconies, some with kitchens – and a garden setting.

✖ Eating

With limited beach space, restaurant shacks are mercifully banned from the sand at Palolem and Patnem, but there are plenty of beach-facing restaurants on the periphery, all offering all-day dining and fresh seafood. Palolem also has some interesting dining choices back along the main road to the beach.

Shiv Sai
INDIAN **$**

(thalis ₹50-60, mains ₹40-100; ⊗9am-11pm) A local lunch joint knocking out cheap and tasty thalis, including Goan fish and veggie versions.

★ Café Inn
CAFE **$$**

(www.cafeinn.in; meals ₹110-330; ⊗10am-11pm; 🛜) This fun semi-outdoor place has loud music, servers in saris and a cool cafe vibe. The Italian coffee, snacks, shakes, burgers and salads are great, but it's the evening barbecue that stands out: pick your base, toppings, sauces and bread to create a grilled mix-and-match masterpiece.

German Bakery
BAKERY, MULTICUISINE **$$**

(pastries ₹25-80, mains ₹115-180; ⊗8am-10pm) It's worth the trek back from the beach for tasty baked treats, excellent coffee and yak-cheese croissants at the cosy German Bakery. Set breakfasts are good and there's a full menu of Italian, Indian, Chinese and Israeli dishes for dinner.

Fern's By Kate's
GOAN **$$**

(✉9822165261; ₹120-350; ⊗8.30am-10.30pm; 🛜) Back from the beach, this solid timber place with a vague nautical feel serves up excellent authentic Goan food such as local sausages and shark *amok-tik*. Upstairs are two beautifully-finished air-con rooms (₹4000) with large bathrooms, four-poster beds and sea views.

Magic Italy
ITALIAN **$$**

(mains ₹230-380; ⊗3pm-midnight) On the main beach road, Magic Italy has been around for a while but the quality of its pizza and pasta is getting ever better, with imported Italian ingredients like ham, salami and olive oil, imaginative wood-fired pizzas and home-made pasta. The atmosphere is busy but chilled.

Casa Fiesta
MEXICAN **$$**

(mains ₹90-280; ⊗8.30am-midnight) Fiesta serves up a bit of a 'world menu' but its

GOA PALOLEM & AROUND

SILENT PARTIES

Neatly sidestepping the statewide ban on loud music after 10pm, Palolem is home to two hugely popular silent rave parties where guests don a pair of headphones and dance the night away in outward quiet. You usually get the choice of two or three channels featuring inhouse Goan and international DJs playing hip hop, house, electro and funk. The parties generally don't fire up till after midnight. Admission includes headphones. **Silent Noise** (www.silentnoise.in; Neptune's Point, Colomb Bay; admission ₹500; ⊗9am-4am Sat Nov-Apr) is the original Saturday night headphone party, in an awesome location at Neptune Point looking back towards Palolem Beach. On Thursday, **Silent Disco @ Alpha Bar** (admission ₹500; ⊗9pm-4am Thur Nov-Apr) kicks off back among the palms at the southern end of Palolem Beach.

speciality (or point of difference) is Mexican, and it makes a pretty good fist of fajitas, burritos and tacos with most dishes under ₹200. The mellow hut ambience is also working, as are margaritas.

Cheeky Chapati MULTICUISINE **$$**
(mains ₹110-270; ⊙7am-11pm) Expat-run Cheeky Chapati is a rustic, welcoming sort of place offering a full range of Continental and Indian dishes, kebabs and burgers. Sunday is roast night.

★**Home** CONTINENTAL **$$**
(☑2643916; www.homeispatnem.com; Patnem Beach; mains ₹160-260; ⊙8.30am-9.30pm) A hip, relaxed veg restaurant serving up pasta, salads, Mediterranean-style goodies and desserts, this is a Patnem favourite. Home also rents out nicely decorated, bright rooms (singles/doubles ₹1000/3000); call to book or ask at the restaurant.

🛍 Shopping

Butterfly Book Shop BOOKS
(☑9341738801; www.yogavillapalolem.com; ⊙9am-10.30pm) A great bookshop with some neat gifts and a range of books on yoga, meditation and spirituality. You can also arrange yoga and cooking classes here.

ℹ Information

Palolem's main road is lined with travel agencies, internet places and money changers. The nearest ATM is about 1.5km away, where the main highway meets Palolem Beach Rd, or head to nearby Chaudi.

Sun-n-Moon Travels (Palolem Beach Rd; per hr ₹40; ⊙9am-10.30pm; 🖥) One of several travel agencies with fast internet. Also sells SIM cards and mobile phone top-ups.

ℹ Getting There & Around

Scooters and motorbikes can easily be hired along the main road leading to the beach from ₹200. Bicycles (₹100 per day) can be hired from the shop next to Palolem Dental Clinic.

BUS

Services to Margao (₹30, one hour, every 30 minutes) and Chaudi (₹5, every 15 minutes), the nearest town, depart from the bus stand down by the beach and stop at the Patnem turn-off. Chaudi has good bus connections, but for Panaji and north Goa, it's much better to go to Margao and catch an express from there.

Buses from Chaudi include the following services:

Agonda (₹8, half-hourly)

Cabo da Rama (₹20, 9am; return buses depart Cabo da Rama at 3pm)

Gokarna (₹70, 2pm)

Karwar (₹35, half-hourly)

Margao (₹30, every 10 minutes)

Panaji (₹55, three daily)

TAXI & AUTORICKSHAW

An autorickshaw from Palolem to Patnem costs ₹60, as does a rick from Palolem to Chaudi. To Agonda it's ₹200. A prepaid taxi from Dabolim Airport to Palolem costs ₹1100.

TRAIN

Many trains that run north or south out of Margao stop at the **Canacona Train Station** (☑2643644, 2712790).

Karnataka & Bengaluru

Why Go?

Blessed with a diverse geography that takes the highlights from its encompassing states and mixes it in with its own charms, Karnataka is an intoxicating cocktail that is quintessential India. It's a winning blend of palaces, beaches, banana groves, tiger reserves, ancient ruins and legendary hangouts.

At its nerve centre is the silicon-capital Bengaluru (Bangalore), overfed with the good life. Scattered around the epicurean city are rolling hills rife with spice and coffee plantations, the regal splendour of Mysore and jungles teeming with monkeys, tigers and Asia's biggest population of elephants.

If that all sounds too mainstream, head to the countercultural enclave of tranquil Hampi with hammocks, psychedelic sunsets and boulder-strewn ruins. Or the blissful beaches of Gokarna, a beach haven minus the doof doof. Or better yet, leave the tourists behind entirely and take a journey to stunning Islamic ruins of northern Karnataka.

Best Places to Eat

➡ Karavalli (p863)

➡ Koshy's Bar & Restaurant (p863)

➡ Sapphire (p877)

➡ Lalith Bar & Restaurant (p889)

Best Places to Stay

➡ Casa Piccola Cottage (p862)

➡ Green Hotel (p875)

➡ Vivanta (p884)

➡ Dhole's Den (p881)

When to Go
Bengaluru

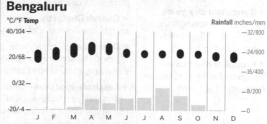

| **Jan** The best season to watch tigers and elephants in Karnataka's pristine national parks. | **Oct** Mysore's Dasara (Dussehra) carnival brings night-long celebrations and a jumbo parade. | **Dec** The coolest time to explore the northern districts' forts, palaces, caves and temples. |

MAIN POINTS OF ENTRY

Many visitors arrive at Bengaluru's shiny modern airport, 40km north of the city. Mangalore on the western coast serves as a transit point for those going north to Goa, or south to Kerala. Hubli in central Karnataka is also a railway hub that links Hampi with Goa and Mumbai.

Fast Facts

➡ **Population:** 61.1 million

➡ **Area:** 191,791 sq km

➡ **Capital:** Bengaluru (Bangalore)

➡ **Main languages:** Kannada, Hindi, English

➡ **Sleeping prices:** $ below ₹1000, $$ ₹1000 to ₹4000, $$$ above ₹4000

Resources

➡ **Karnataka Tourism** (KSTDC; www.karnatakatourism.org) Sleek government site showcasing state highlights.

➡ **Bengaluru city guide** (www.discoverbangalore.com) General travel info on the state's capital.

➡ **Hampi. India!** (www.hampi.in) Excellent resource for everything Hampi.

Food

The diverse and delectable cuisine of Karnataka is perhaps reason enough for you to visit this state. The highest-flying of all local delicacies is the spicy *pandhi* (pork) masala, a flavourful Kodava signature dish. Mangalore, out on the coast, tosses up a train of fiery dishes – mostly seafood. The crunchy prawn *rawa* (semolina) fry and the sinful chicken ghee roast are two of Mangalore's many dishes to have gathered a pan-Indian following. Vegetarians, meanwhile, can head to Udupi to sample its legendary veg thalis. Oh, and did we mention the classic steak-and-beer joints of Bengaluru?

DON'T MISS

The **temples** of Hampi, Pattadakal, Belur and Halebid, and Somnathpur are some of India's best archaeological sites, embellished with sculptures of stellar quality.

Top State Festivals

➡ **Udupi Paryaya** (⊙ Jan, Udupi, p892) Held in even-numbered years, with a procession and ritual marking the handover of swamis at the town's Krishna Temple.

➡ **Classical Dance Festival** (⊙ Jan/Feb, Pattadakal, p907) Some of India's best classical dance performances.

➡ **Vijaya Utsav** (Hampi Festival; ⊙ Jan, Hampi,, p896) A three-day extravaganza of culture, heritage and the arts at the foot of Hampi's Matanga Hill.

➡ **Tibetan New Year** (⊙ Feb, Bylakuppe, p886) Lamas in Tibetan refugee settlements take shifts leading nonstop prayers that span the weeklong celebrations.

➡ **Vairamudi Festival** (⊙ Mar/Apr, Melkote, p880) Lord Vishnu is adorned with jewels at Cheluvanarayana Temple, including a diamond-studded crown belonging to Mysore's former maharajas.

➡ **Ganesh Chaturthi** (⊙ Sep, Gokarna, p894) Families march their Ganesh idols to the sea at sunset.

➡ **Dussehra** (⊙ Oct, Mysore, p875) Also spelt 'Dasara' in Mysore. The Maharaja's Palace is lit up in the evenings and a vibrant procession hits town to the delight of thousands.

➡ **Lakshadeepotsava** (⊙ Nov, Dharmasthala, p892) Thousands and thousands of lamps light up this Jain pilgrimage town, offering spectacular photo ops.

➡ **Huthri** (⊙ Nov/Dec, Madikeri, p882) The Kodava community celebrates the start of the harvesting season with ceremony, music, traditional dances and much feasting for a week.

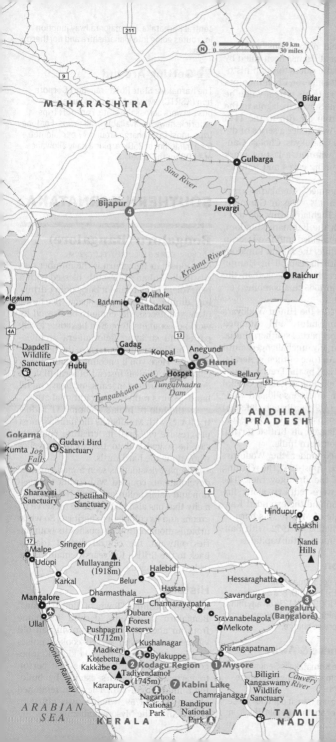

Karnataka & Bengaluru Highlights

1 Be bowled over by the grandiose **royal palace** (p869) in Mysore

2 Savour aromatic coffee while recharging your soul in the cool highlands of the **Kodagu Region** (p882)

3 Drink yourself under the table, or stab into top-notch global cuisine in **Bengaluru** (p863)

4 Stroll peaceful manicured grounds of exquisite 16th-century Islamic architecture in **Bijapur** (p907)

5 Marvel at the gravity-defying boulders, and wander among the melancholic ruins of **Hampi** (p896)

6 Chill the hell out on Om beach in **Gokarna** (p894)

7 Spy on lazy tuskers and listen to exotic birds in the forests bordering the serene **Kabini Lake** (p881)

History

A rambling playfield of religions, cultures and kingdoms, Karnataka has been ruled by a string of charismatic rulers through history. India's first great emperor, Chandragupta Maurya, made the state his retreat when he embraced Jainism at Sravanabelagola in the 3rd century BC. From the 6th to the 14th centuries, the land was under a series of dynasties such as the Chalukyas, Cholas, Gangas and Hoysalas, who left a lasting mark in the form of stunning caves and temples across the state.

In 1327 Mohammed Tughlaq's army sacked Halebid. In 1347 Hasan Gangu, a Persian general in Tughlaq's army, led a rebellion to establish the Bahmani kingdom, which was later subdivided into five Deccan sultanates. Meanwhile, the Hindu kingdom of Vijayanagar, with its capital in Hampi, rose to prominence. Having peaked in the early 1550s, it fell in 1565 to a combined effort of the sultanates.

In subsequent years the Hindu Wodeyars of Mysore grew in stature and extended their rule over a large part of southern India. They remained largely unchallenged until 1761, when Hyder Ali (one of their generals) deposed them. Backed by the French, Hyder Ali and his son Tipu Sultan set up capital in Srirangapatnam and consolidated their rule. However, in 1799 the British defeated Tipu Sultan and reinstated the Wodeyars. Historically, this flagged off British territorial expansion in southern India.

Mysore remained under the Wodeyars until Independence – post-1947, the reigning maharaja became the first governor. The state boundaries were redrawn along linguistic lines in 1956 and the extended Kannada-speaking state of Mysore was born. It was renamed Karnataka in 1972, with Bangalore (now Bengaluru) as the capital.

ⓘ Information

In Karnataka, luxury accommodation tax is 4% on rooms costing ₹151 to ₹400, 8% on those between ₹401 and ₹1000, and 12% on anything over ₹1000. Some midrange and top-end hotels may add a further service charge.

ⓘ Getting There & Away

The main gateway to Karnataka is Bengaluru, serviced by most domestic airlines and some international carriers.

Coastal Mangalore is a transit point for those going north to Goa, or south to Kerala. Hubli, in central Karnataka, is a major railway junction for routes going into Maharashtra and northern India.

ⓘ Getting Around

The Karnataka State Road Transport Corporation (KSRTC; www.ksrtc.in) has a superb bus network across the state. For short trips autorickshaws are available in all towns. For long trips, most taxis charge around ₹7 per kilometre for a minimum of 250km, plus a daily allowance of ₹200 for the driver.

SOUTHERN KARNATAKA

Bengaluru (Bangalore)

🖉 080 / POP 8.5 MILLION / ELEV 920M

Cosmopolitan Bengaluru is the number one city in the Indian deep south, blessed with a benevolent climate and a burgeoning drinking, dining and shopping scene. It's not a place you necessarily come to be wowed by world-class sights (though it has some lovely parks and striking Victorian-era architecture), but instead to experience the new face of India. Here you'll encounter many locals chatting in English instead of local dialects and getting around in jeans and heavy metal band T-shirts rather than traditional attire.

As the hub of India's booming IT industry, it vies with Mumbai as the nation's most progressive city, and its creature comforts can be a godsend to the weary traveller who's done the hard yards.

The past decade has seen a mad surge of development, coupled with traffic congestion and rising pollution levels. However, it's a city that has also taken care to preserve its greens and its colonial-era heritage. So while urbanisation continually pushes its boundaries outward, the central district (dating back to the British Raj years) remains more or less unchanged.

History

Literally meaning 'Town of Boiled Beans', Bengaluru supposedly derived its name from an ancient incident involving an old village woman who served cooked pulses to a lost and hungry Hoysala king. Kempegowda, a feudal lord, was the first person to earmark Bengaluru's extents by building a mud fort in 1537. The town remained obscure until 1759, when it was gifted to Hyder Ali by the Mysore maharaja.

The British arrived in 1809 and made it their regional administrative base in 1831, renaming it Bangalore. During the Raj era the city played host to many a British officer, including Winston Churchill, who enjoyed life here during his greener years and famously left a debt (still on the books) of ₹13 at the Bangalore Club.

Now home to countless software, electronics and business-outsourcing firms, Bengaluru's knack for technology developed early. In 1905 it was the first Indian city to have electric street lighting. Since the 1940s it has been home to Hindustan Aeronautics Ltd (HAL), India's largest aerospace company. And if you can't do without email, you owe it all to a Bangalorean – Sabeer Bhatia, the inventor of Hotmail, grew up here.

The city's name was changed back to Bengaluru in November 2006, though few care to use it in practice.

ℹ Orientation

Finding your way around Bengaluru can be difficult at times. In certain areas, roads are named after their widths (eg 80ft Rd). The city also follows a system of mains and crosses: 3rd cross, 5th main, Residency Rd, for example, refers to the third lane on the fifth street branching off Residency Rd.

◎ Sights

Lalbagh Botanical Gardens   GARDEN
(www.lalbaghgardens.com; admission ₹10; ☉5.30am-7.30pm) Spread over 240 acres of landscaped terrain, the expansive Lalbagh gardens were laid out in 1760 by the famous Mysore ruler, Hyder Ali. As well as amazing centuries-old trees it claims to have the world's most diverse species of plants. You can take a guided tour with Bangalore Walks (p861), in a ecofriendly buggy (per head ₹100), or otherwise just stroll around at your own pace. On weekends you'll see health-conscious locals jogging and playing badminton all over the park.

National Gallery of Modern Art   ART GALLERY
(NGMA; ☑22342338; www.ngmaindia.gov.in/ngma_bangalore.asp; 49 Palace Rd; admission ₹150; ☉10am-5pm Tue-Sun) Housed in a 200 year-old mansion – the former vacation home of the Raja of Mysore – this museum showcases an impressive permanent collection as well as changing exhibitions. The Old Wing exhibits works from pre-Independence, including paintings by Raja Ravi Varma and Abanindranath Tagore (nephew of Rabindranath Tagore, and founder of the avant-garde Bengal School art movement), while the New Wing focuses on post-Independence with works by MF Hussain and FN Souza.

Cubbon Park   GARDEN
In the heart of Bengaluru's business district is Cubbon Park, a sprawling 120-hectare garden named after former British commissioner Sir Mark Cubbon. Under its leafy boughs, groups of Bengaluru's residents converge to steal a moment from the rat race that rages outside. On the fringes of Cubbon Park are the red-painted Gothic-style **State Central Library**, while at the northwestern end of the park are the colossal neo-Dravidian-style **Vidhana Soudha**, built in 1954, and the neoclassical **Attara Kacheri**, that houses the High Court. Both of the latter are closed to the public.

Government Museum   MUSEUM
(Kasturba Rd; admission ₹4; ☉10am-5pm Tue-Sun, closed every 2nd Sat) In a beautiful red colonial-era building dating from 1877, you'll find a dusty collection of 12th-century stone carvings and artefacts excavated from Halebid, Hampi and Attriampakham. Your ticket also gets you into the **Venkatappa Art Gallery** (admission free; ☉10am-5pm Tue-Sun) FREE next door, where you can see works and personal memorabilia of K Venkatappa (1887-1962), court painter to the Wodeyars.

Visvesvaraya Industrial
and Technical Museum   MUSEUM
(Kasturba Rd; adult/child ₹20/free; ☉10am-6pm) This hands-on science museum makes you feel a bit like you're on a school excursion, but there are some cool electrical and engineering displays, plus kitschy fun-house mirrors and a walk-on piano. There's also a replica of the Wright brothers' 1903 flyer.

Bengaluru Palace   PALACE
(Palace Rd; Indian/foreigner ₹210/400, camera/video ₹600/1250; ☉10am-5.30pm) The private residence of the Wodeyars, erstwhile maharajas of the state, Bengaluru Palace preserves a slice of bygone royal splendour. Still the residence of the 20th maharaja, an audioguide provides a detailed explanation of the building, designed to resemble Windsor Castle, and you can marvel at the lavish interiors and galleries featuring hunting trophies (along with grisly photos of expeditions), family photos and a collection of nude portraits.

KARNATAKA & BENGALURU BENGALURU (BANGALORE)

Bengaluru (Bangalore)

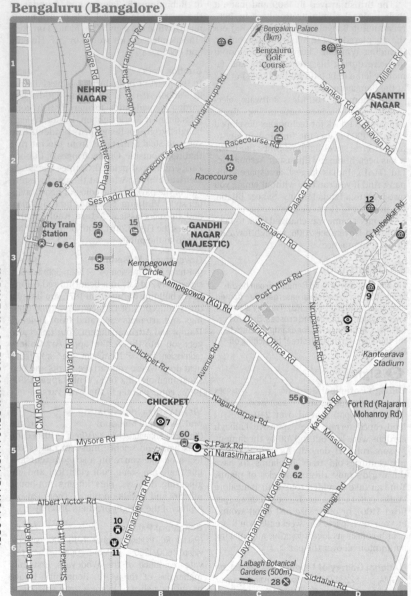

Karnataka Chitrakala Parishath ART GALLERY (www.karnatakachitrakalaparishath.com; Kumarakrupa Rd; admission ₹50; ⏰10am-5.30pm Mon-Sat) One of Bengaluru's premier art institutions, with a wide range of Indian and international contemporary art on show in its galleries, and permanent displays of Mysore-style paintings and folk and tribal art from across Asia. A section is devoted to the works of Russian master Nicholas Roerich, known for his vivid paintings of the Himalayas.

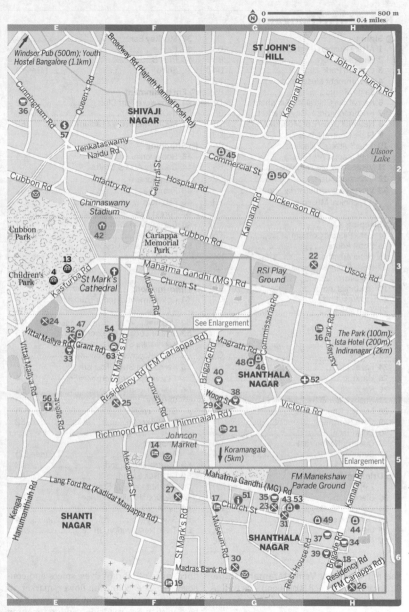

Tipu Sultan's Palace   PALACE

(Albert Victor Rd; Indian/foreigner ₹5/100, video ₹25; ◷8.30am-5.30pm) Close to the vibrant Krishnarajendra (City) Market stands the elegant palace of Tipu Sultan, notable for its teak pillars and ornamental frescoes.

Though not as beautiful (or well maintained) as Tipu's summer palace in Srirangapatnam, it's an interesting monument, and worth an outing when combined with other nearby sights such as the massive **Jama Masjid** (Silver Jubilee (SJ) Park Rd; ◷admission

Bengaluru (Bangalore)

free) and the ornate **Venkataraman Temple** (Krishnarajendra Rd; ⊙ 8.30am-6pm) – as well as the fort and market.

Krishnarajendra (City) Market MARKET
(Silver Jubilee Park Rd; ⊙ 6am-10pm) For a pungent taste of traditional urban India, dive into the bustling Krishnarajendra Market and the dense grid of commercial streets that surround it. Weave your way around this lively colourful market past fresh produce, piles of vibrant dyes, spices and copperware. The colourful flower market in the centre is the highlight. Sundays are the best with more roadside vendors opening up.

Bangalore Fort FORT
FREE The last remnants of this 1761 fort is a peaceful escape from the chaotic surrounds, with its manicured lawn and stone pink walls. There's a small dungeon here, and

Ganesh temple with its Mooshak (ratlike creature) statue.

Bull Temple &
Dodda Ganesha Temple HINDU TEMPLE
(Bull Temple Rd, Basavangudi; ⊙7am-8.30pm) Built by Kempegowda in the 16th-century Dravidian style, the Bull Temple contains a huge granite monolith of Nandi and is one of Bengaluru's most atmospheric temples. Nearby is the **Swee Dodda Ganapathi Temple,** (Bull Temple Rd, Basavangudi; ⊙7am-8.30pm) with an equally enormous Ganesh idol. The temples are about a kilometre south of Tipu Sultan's Palace, down Krishnarajendra Rd.

Iskcon Temple HINDU TEMPLE
(www.iskconbangalore.org; Chord Rd, Hare Krishna Hill; ⊙7am-1pm & 4-8.30pm) Built by the International Society of Krishna Consciousness (Iskcon), also referred to as the Hare Krishnas, this shiny temple, inaugurated in 1997, is lavishly decorated in a mix of ultra-contemporary and traditional styles.

🏃 Activities

Ayurvedagram YOGA
(☑65651090; www.ayurvedagram.com; Hemmandanhalli, Whitefield) Set over 15 acres of tranquil gardens with heritage homes transplanted from Kerala, this centre specialises in specifically tailored Ayurvedic treatments and rejuvenation programs.

Soukya YOGA
(☑28017000; www.soukya.com; Soukya Rd, Samethanahalli, Whitefield; ⊙6am-8.30pm) Soukya offers some fantastic long-term programs in ayurvedic therapy and yoga (seven days from ₹6600) as well as medical and therapeutic skin treatments (₹2750 per hour) at its internationally renowned place set on a picture-perfect 30-acre organic farm.

☞ Tours

In a city lacking in blockbuster sights, the following companies offer fantastic grassroots tours to get under Bengaluru's skin.

Bangalore Walks WALKING
(☑9845523660; www.bangalorewalks.com) Choose between a traditional culture walk, the medieval Old City history walk, garden walk through Lalbagh Gardens or the 19th-century Victorian walk. Held on Saturdays and Sundays (7am to 10am), the walks (adult/child ₹500/300) are all about knowing and loving Bengaluru in a way that many locals have forgotten. There's a delicious breakfast en route. Book in advance.

Art of Bicycle CYCLING
(☑9538973506, 8105289167; www.artofbicycletrips.com; from ₹950 per person) Recommended cycling tours with handcrafted itineraries that explore the city, state and beyond, including Victoria-era tours, challenging routes up to Nandi Hills or 10-day journeys to Gokarna. All equipment is provided, including 21-speed mountain bikes and support vans.

Getoff ur Ass ADVENTURE TOUR
(☑26722750; www.getoffurass.com; 858 1D Main Rd, Giri Nagar 2nd Phase) Getoff ur Ass has perfect recipes for outward-bound adventures, including off-beat cultural trips, rafting and trekking in Karnataka and elsewhere. Also sells and rents outdoor gear.

Bus Tours SIGHTSEEING
The **government tourism department** (☑43344334; www.karnatakaholidays.net) runs city bus tours, all of which begin at Badami House. The basic half-day city tour runs twice daily at 7.30am and 2pm (non AC/AC ₹230/255), while the full-day tour departs at 7.15am (non AC/AC ₹385/485) Wednesday to Sunday.

The day trips are worth considering, particularly the daily departure to the hard to get to Belur, Halebid and Shravanabelagola (non AC/AC ₹910/970). It can also arrange the luxurious **Golden Chariot** (☑11-42866600; www.thegoldenchariot.co.in) rail journeys that head across Karnataka.

🛏 Sleeping

Decent budget rooms are in short supply but a stack of dive lodges line Subedar Chatram (SC) Rd, east of the bus stands and around the train station; convenient if you're in transit.

🛏 MG Road Area

Hotel Ajantha HOTEL $
(☑25584321; www.hotelajantha.in; 22A MG Rd; s/d incl breakfast from ₹988/1541, d incl breakfast with AC from ₹1899; ❄🌐) Stacks of potted foliage welcome you into this oldie located on Ashley Park Rd, with a range of par-for-the-course rooms in a semiquiet compound. Unfortunately they've doubled the prices, so is no longer the steal it once was, but still the best budget option in the Mahatma Gandhi (MG) Rd area.

KARNATAKA & BENGALURU BENGALURU (BANGALORE)

Casa Piccola Cottage
HERITAGE HOTEL $$

(☏ 22270754; www.casapiccola.com; 2 Clapham Rd; r incl breakfast from ₹4300; ❋ 🛜) Located on a quiet back lane, this beautifully renovated heritage building turned into cute cottages is a tranquil sanctuary from the city madness. Its personalised brand of hospitality has garnered it a solid reputation and rooms come with tiled floors, spotless bathrooms and colourful bedspreads. Deluxe rooms offer the best value with their own verandah sitting area with cane furniture in garden surrounds of papaya and avocado trees. Go for Room 1 with its loft-style bedroom and spacious living and kitchen area. The garden gazebo dining room is the perfect place to tuck into breakfast.

St Mark's Inn
HOTEL $$

(☏ 41122783; www.stmarkshotels.com; St Marks Rd; r incl breakfast ₹2500; ❋ 🛜) There are only six smart rooms on offer at this fresh new boutique hotel, so get in fast. Immaculate rooms are decked out with modern decor, big comfy beds, in-room safe and sparkling stainless-steel bathroom fittings, free wi-fi and double-glazed windows.

Hotel Empire International
HOTEL $$

(☏ 42678888; www.hotelempire.in; 36 Church St; s/d incl breakfast from ₹1789/2135; ❋ @ 🛜) Right in the heart of the action and nightlife, Hotel Empire is a sure deal. Rooms vary in size and decency so ask to check a few out before committing. Spacious upstairs rooms are clean, bright and airy, and have good access to wi-fi. The front desk staff are professional and courteous, and there's a busy social restaurant downstairs.

Monarch
HOTEL $$

(☏ 42507000; www.monarchhotels.in; 54 Brigade Rd; s/d incl breakfast from ₹3060/4285; ❋ 🛜) The well-located and good-valued Monarch is a top midrange choice with super-comfy rooms that make the most of their innumerable facilities (free wi-fi, 24-hour currency exchange counter, courier service and a dozen others).

Tom's Hotel
HOTEL $$

(☏ 25575875; 1/5 Hosur Rd; s/d incl breakfast from ₹1632/1924; ❋ 🛜) Long favoured for its low tariffs, bright and cheerful Tom's allows you to stay in the heart of town in spacious clean rooms with friendly staff. Traffic noise is the only fault here so ask for a room away from the main road.

The Park
HOTEL $$$

(☏ 25594666; 14/7 MG Rd; s/d incl breakfast from ₹15,000/16,000) A swanky designer hotel with oodles of glitz and glam. Home to the reputed Italian restaurant, i-t.ALIA.

Ista Hotel
HOTEL $$$

(☏ 25558888; www.istahotels.com; 1/1 Swami Vivekananda Rd, Ulsoor; s/d from ₹8000/8500; ❋ @ 🛜) With its name meaning 'sacred space', Ista delivers accommodation happiness in a cool, business-boutique, minimalist style. The smallish but elegant rooms come with king-sized windows and some offer sweeping vistas across Ulsoor lake. The bar and restaurant open on to the infinity pool, and the spa will pamper you with diverse treatments kicking off at around ₹1200.

🛏 Other Areas

Hotel Adora
HOTEL $

(☏ 22200024; 47 SC Rd; s/d ₹546/780, with AC ₹936/1444; ❋) A largish and popular budget option near the station, with unfussy rooms with clean sheets. Downstairs is a good veg restaurant, Indraprastha.

Youth Hostel Bangalore
HOSTEL $

(☏ 25924040; www.youthhostelbangalore.com; 65/2 Millers Rd; dm/d ₹150/650, d with AC ₹850) One for those watching their pennies, with the very basics on offer, but you can opt in for extras like bucket hot water (₹15), wi-fi (per hour ₹20) and downstairs security lockers (per day ₹15). It's popular with Indian students and discounts are available for YHA members.

★ Villa Pottipati
HERITAGE HOTEL $$

(☏ 23360777; www.neemranahotels.com; 142 8th Cross, 4th Main, Malleswaram; s/d incl breakfast from ₹3000/4000; ❋ @ 🛜) Located a little off-centre, this heritage building was once the garden home of the wealthy expat Andhra family. Needless to say, it's flooded with memories in the form of numerous artefacts scattered within its rooms. Dollops of quaintness are added by features such as antique four-poster beds and arched doorways, while the overall ambience gains from a garden full of ageless trees, seasonal blossoms and a dunk-sized pool.

Taj West End
HERITAGE HOTEL $$$

(☏ 66605660; www.tajhotels.com; Racecourse Rd; s/d incl breakfast from ₹14,000/15,000; ❋ 🛜 🛜) The West End saga flashbacks to 1887, when it was incepted by a British family as a 10-room hostel for passing army officers. Since then, nostalgia has been a permanent resident at this lovely property which – spread over 20 acres of tropical gardens – has evolved as a definitive icon of Indian luxury hospitality.

✖ Eating

Bengaluru's adventurous dining scene keeps pace with the whims and rising standards of its hungry, moneyed locals and IT expats. You'll find high-end dining, gastro pubs and cheap local favourites.

✖ MG Road Area

Queen's Restaurant   INDIAN $
(Church St; mains ₹100-220; ⊙12.30-3.30pm & 7-10.30pm, closed Mon) This reputed joint serves some quick and tasty Indian morsels such as a range of vegetable and dhal preparations, to go with fluffy and hot chapati. The interiors are rustic village-style, with painted motifs adorning earthy walls.

Koshy's Bar & Restaurant   MULTICUISINE $$
(39 St Mark's Rd; mains ₹127-380; ⊙9am-11pm) They say half of Bengaluru's court cases are argued around Koshy's tables, and many hard-hitting newspaper articles written over its steaming coffees. Serving the city's intelligentsia for decades, this buzzy and joyful resto-pub is where you can put away tasty North Indian dishes or the popular fish and chips in between fervent discussions and mugs of beer. The decor is old school with creaky ceiling fans and dusty wooden shuttered windows.

Only Place   STEAKHOUSE $$
(13 Museum Rd; mains ₹260-540; ⊙noon-3pm & 7-11pm) Juicy sirloin steaks, brawny burgers and the classic shepherd's pie – no one serves them better than this time-tested restaurant which has many an expat loyalist in town.

Sunny's   ITALIAN $$
(☑41329366; 34 Vittal Mallya Rd; mains ₹300-700; ⊙noon-11pm; 🛜) A well-established fixture in Bengaluru's restaurant scene, Sunny's is all about authentic charcoal thin-crust pizzas, homemade pastas, imported cheese and some of the best desserts in the city – go the blueberry crème brûlée. There's atmospheric lounge seating upstairs, downstairs modern dining or often buzzing outdoor tables. There's another branch in Indiranagar.

Ebony   MULTICUISINE $$
(☑41783344; 84 MG Rd, 13th fl, Barton Centre; mains ₹200-450) Despite it's salivating-inducing menu of delectable Indian, Thai and French dishes, here it's all about the luxurious views from its heavenly rooftop location. There's a good alcohol selection too, but skip the syrupy cocktails.

★Karavalli   SEAFOOD $$$
(☑66604545; 66 Residency Rd, Gateway Hotel; mains ₹325-1200; ⊙12.30-3pm & 7-11.30pm) The Arabian Sea may be 500km away, but you'll have to come only as far as this superb spot to savour South India's finest coastal cuisines. The decor is a stylish mash of thatched roofs and vintage woodwork, and does superb fiery Mangalorean fish dishes and the signature Lobster Balchao (₹1200).

Fava   MEDITERRANEAN $$$
(UB City; mains ₹350-850; ⊙noon-11pm) Sail away to the Med at Bangalore's stylish newcomer. It may be set in a mall but it serves up a classy atmosphere, whether indoors or al fresco on its canopy-covered decking. Feast on large plates of mezze, hummus and pita, fish kebabs, Greek-style moussaka, zatar sausages or something healthier from the organic menu. End the night with a strong Turkish coffee and blueberry panna cotta. If you're up for it, there's two hours of all-you-can-drink alcohol for ₹1200.

Olive Beach   MEDITERRANEAN $$$
(☑41128400; 16 Wood St, Ashoknagar; mains ₹350-400; ⊙noon-11.30pm) Lodged in upscale Ashoknagar is this white-washed villa straight from the coast of Santorini, with food that evokes wistful memories of sunny Mediterranean getaways. Try the almond-encrusted kingfish or spinach and goat's cheese pizza and request the indulgent chocolate mousse cocktail for dessert. The fairly lit pebbled al fresco area is ridiculously atmospheric while loved-up couples get romantic in the dimly lit dining room among candles and flowers.

✖ Other Areas

★Mavalli Tiffin Rooms   SOUTH INDIAN $
(MTR; Lalbagh Rd; mains ₹40-60; ⊙6.30-11am, 12.30-2.45pm, 3.30-7.30pm & 8-9.30pm) A legendary name in South Indian comfort food, this super-popular eatery has had Bengaluru eating out of its hands since 1924. Head to the dining room upstairs, queue

KARNATAKA & BENGALURU BENGALURU (BANGALORE)

FOOD STREET

For a real local eating experience, head to Harrar St, aka **Food Street**, where a short strip is home to several hole-in-the-wall eateries serving up classic street-food dishes. Things kick off around 5pm when the stalls fire up and people stand around watching rotis being handmade and spun in the air or bhaji dunked into hot oil before being dished up on paper plates to enjoy standing in the street. It's an all-vegetarian affair with a range of dosas, curries, roti and deep-fried goodies. The street packs out on weekends around 9pm.

for a table, and then admire the dated images of southern beauties etched on smoky glass as waiters bring you savoury local fare, capped by frothing filter coffee served in silverware. It's a definitive Bengaluru experience.

Gramin INDIAN $$
(☑41104104; 20, 7th Block Raheja Arcade, Koramangala; mains ₹70-150; ◷12.30-3.30pm & 7-11pm) Translating to 'from the village', Gramin offers a wide choice of flavourful rural North Indian fare at this cosy, eclectic all-veg place popular with locals. Try the excellent range of lentils and curries best had with oven-fresh rotis and sweet rose-flavoured lassi served in a copper vessel.

Harima JAPANESE $$
(☑41325757; Residency Rd, 4th fl, Devatha Plaza; mains ₹250-280; ◷noon-3pm & 6-11pm) Authentic Japanese staples cooked up by the Osakan owner/chef, including flavourful yakitori, tempura, sushi and sashimi. Wash it down with a few cold Asahis before finishing off with green tea ice cream. The decor here is traditional and atmospheric.

Windsor Pub MULTICUISINE $$
(1st Main Vasanthnagar, 7 Kodava Samaja Bldg; mains ₹230-300; ◷11.30am-3pm & 6-11pm) It's dark pub interior may not inspire, but it has a fantastic menu of regional favourites such as flavoursome Mangalorean fish, or the tangy *pandhi* (pork) masala from Kodagu's hills. Otherwise go the awesome fillet steak, accompanied by a draft beer and a soundtrack of blues, jazz and '70s rock.

Caperberry CONTINENTAL $$$
(☑25594567; 121 Dickenson Rd; tapas ₹275-625, mains ₹425-950; ◷12.30-3.30pm & 7-11.30pm) A smart blend of mod Euro decor and glittering South Indian goldwork create a sophisticated ambience at this fancy restaurant specialising mostly in Spanish food. Pick from grilled lamb chops with garlic and rosemary or squid rings with aioli, accompanied with jugs of sangria. There's also tasting menus from ₹1950. It's tucked away at the back of the block.

 Drinking & Nightlife

Bars & Lounges

Despite Bengaluru's rock-steady reputation, local laws require pubs and discos to shut shop at 11.30pm (opening time is usually 7pm). However, given the wide choice of chic watering holes around, you can indulge in a spirited session of pub-hopping in this original beer town of India. The trendiest nightclubs will typically charge you a cover of around ₹1000 per couple, but it's often redeemable against drinks or food.

Monkey Bar PUB
(www.mobar.in; 14/1 Wood St; ◷noon-11pm) From the owners of Olive Beach comes this chic industrial gastro pub with a stylish vintage feel. Affordable cocktails and good pub classics draws a mixed, jovial crowd to knock back drinks around the bar or at wooden booth seating. Ottherwise head down to the basement to join the 'party' crew shooting pool, playing foosball and rocking out to bangin' tunes.

Shiro BAR
(UB City; ◷12.30-11pm) A sophisticated lounge to get sloshed in style, Shiro has elegant interiors complemented by the monumental Buddha busts and Apsara figurines. Its commendable selection of cocktails and drinks draws rave reviews from patrons, who often fight off their Saturday night hangovers by converging again for Sunday brunch sessions (₹2200 all you can eat and drink).

Biere Club PUB
(20/2 Vittal Mallya Rd; ◷11am-11pm) Beer lovers rejoice as South India's first microbrewery serves up handcrafted beers on tap, six of which are brewed onsite. Brewing equipment and large copper boilers sit behind the bar, and renowned DJs and Bollywood stars

are occasional guests. The music pumps in the spacious upstairs room and good pub grub and beer snacks are on the menu. It attracts a good crowd of students, professionals, tourists and IT expats.

Plan B   PUB
(20 Castle St, Ashoknagar; ⊙12pm-11pm) Finish your beer. There are sober kids in India', says a poster adorning this hip pub's industrial interiors. And to aid you in this eminently enjoyable task, ₹1000 will get you a 3.5L beer tower. There's a whole line of awesome bites from 14 kinds of burgers to porky platters, with rock and metal tunes on rotation.

Pecos   BAR
(Rest House Rd; ⊙10.30am-11pm) Hendrix, The Grateful Dead and Frank Zappa posters adorn the walls of this charmingly shabby, narrow tri-level bar. It's a throwback to simpler times where cassettes line the shelves behind the bar, sports are on the TV and the only thing to quench your thirst is one choice of cheap beer on tap. No wonder it's an all-time favourite with students.

13th Floor   BAR
(84 MG Rd, 13th fl, Barton Centre; ⊙5-11pm) Come early to grab a spot on the rooftop terrace, with all of Bengaluru glittering at your feet. It attracts a refined, yet lively crowd, sipping on martinis. Happy hour is 5pm to 7pm, with 30% off drinks.

Cafes & Teahouses

Bengaluru is liberally sprinkled with good chain cafes. Café Coffee Day has several outlets across town, including one on **Brigade Rd** (Brigade Rd; ⊙8am-11.30pm) and another on **MG Rd** (MG Rd; ⊙8am-11.30pm).

★Matteo   CAFE
(Church St; ⊙9am-11pm; 🛜) The coolest rendezvous in the city centre where local hipsters lounge on retro couches sipping first-rate brews while chatting, plugged into free wi-fi, or browsing a great selection of newspapers and mags. Also does comfort food such as toasties.

Infinitea   CAFE
(Cunningham Rd, 2 Shah Sultan Complex; pot of tea from ₹100; ⊙11am-11pm; 🛜) This smart yet homely cafe has an impressive menu of steaming cuppas, including orthodox teas from the best estates, and a few fancy selections such as chocolate-ginger rooibos and blooming flower teas like the peony rosette. Order your pot and team it with a delectable sweet or light lunch.

☆ Entertainment

Cinema

INOX   CINEMA
(☎41128888; www.inoxmovies.com; Magrath Rd, 4th fl, Garuda Mall) Screens new releases from Bollywood and the West.

Sport

For a taste of India's sporting passion up close, attend one of the regular cricket matches at **M Chinnaswamy Stadium** (ksca.co.in; MG Rd); check its website for upcoming matches.

Horse racing is also big, and can make for a fun day out. Bengaluru's horse-racing seasons are from November to February and May to July. Contact the **Bangalore Turf Club** (www.bangaloreraces.com; Racecourse Rd) for details.

Theatre

Ranga Shankara   THEATRE
(☎26592777; www.rangashankara.org; 36/2 8th Cross, JP Nagar) All kinds of interesting theatre (in a variety of languages and spanning various genres) and dance are held at this cultural centre.

🛍 Shopping

Bengaluru's shopping options are abundant, ranging from teeming bazaars to glitzy malls. Some good shopping areas include Commercial St, Vittal Mallya Rd and the MG Rd area. Commercial St is best for clothing and gets packed on weekends.

Some good malls in town include **Garuda Mall** (McGrath Rd), **Forum** (Hosur Rd, Koramangala) and **Leela Galleria** (23 Airport Rd, Kodihalli).

Mysore Saree Udyog   CLOTHING
(www.mysoresareeudyog.com; 316 Kamaraj Rd, 1st fl; ⊙10.30am-11pm) A great choice for top-quality silk blouses and men's shirts, scarves and saris, this busy store has been in business for over 70 years and has something to suit all budgets. Ninety-nine percent of the garments here are made with Mysore silk, and the store also stocks 100% pashmina shawls. All fixed prices.

Cauvery Arts & Crafts Emporium SOUVENIRS
(49 MG Rd; ⊙10am-8pm) Showcases a great collection of sandalwood and rosewood products as well as textiles.

Forest Essentials COSMETICS
(www.forestessentialsindia.com; 4/1 Lavelle Junction Bldg, Vittal Mallya Rd; ⊙11am-8.30pm) Smell the lemongrass as you browse the shelves at this tranquil store selling all-organic beauty products.

Fabindia CLOTHING
(www.fabindia.com; 54 17th Main, Koramangala; ⊙10am-8pm) Commercial St (152 Commercial St; ⊙10am-8.30pm) Garuda mall (McGrath Rd, Garuda mall) These branches contain Fabindia's full range of stylish clothes and homewares in traditional cotton prints and silks.

UB City CLOTHING
(Vittal Mallya Rd; ⊙11am-9pm) Global haute couture (Louis Vuitton, Jimmy Choo, Burberry) and Indian high fashion come to roost at this towering mall in the central district.

Magazines BOOKS
(55 Church St; ⊙10am-10pm) An astounding collection of international magazines. Up to 70% discount on back issues.

Bombay Store SOUVENIRS
(100Ft Rd; ⊙10.30am-8.30pm) For gifts ranging from ecobeauty products to linens.

Bookworm BOOKS
(Shrungar Shopping Complex, MG Rd; ⊙10am-9pm) Great secondhand bookstore filled with contemporary and classic literature as well as travel guidebooks.

Page Turners BOOKS
(☑25595111; www.pageturners.in; 89 Kannan Bldg, MG Rd; ⊙10am-8.30pm Mon-Sat, 11am-8pm Sun) Stocks an excellent range of Penguin books from Indian and international writers, set over three floors.

ℹ️ Information

INTERNET ACCESS
Being an IT city, internet cafes are plentiful in Bengaluru, as is wi-fi access in hotels.

LEFT LUGGAGE
The City train station and Central bus stand have 24-hour cloakrooms (per day ₹10).

MAPS
The tourist offices give out decent city maps and you can find excellent maps at most major bookstores.

MEDIA
Time Out Bengaluru (₹50) is an excellent magazine which covers all the latest events, nightlife, dining and shopping in the city. *080* and *What's Up Bangalore* are great monthly magazines covering the latest in Bengaluru's social life. *Kingfisher Explocity Nights* (₹200) gives the low-down on the best night spots. All titles are available in major bookstores.

MEDICAL SERVICES
Hosmat (☑25593796; www.hosmatnet.com) For critical injuries and other general illnesses.
Mallya Hospital (☑22277979; www.mallya hospital.net; 2 Vittal Mallya Rd) Emergency services and 24-hour pharmacy.

MONEY
ATMs are everywhere, as are moneychangers, including **TT Forex** (☑22254337; 33/1 Cunningham Rd; ⊙9.30am-6.30pm Mon-Fri, 9.30am-1.30pm Sat).

POST
Main Post Office (Cubbon Rd; ⊙10am-7pm Mon-Sat, 10am-1pm Sun)

TOURIST INFORMATION
Government of India Tourist Office
(☑25585417; 48 Church St, 2nd level; ⊙9.30am-6pm Mon-Fri, 9am-1pm Sat) Very helpful for Bengaluru and beyond.
Karnataka State Tourism Development Corporation (KSTDC) Badami House;
☑43344334; Badami House, Kasturba Rd; ⊙10am-7pm Mon-Sat) Karnataka Tourism House (☑41329211; 8 Papanna Lane, St Mark's Rd, Karnataka Tourism House; ⊙10am-7pm Mon-Sat) Mainly about booking tours and accommodation, but has a city map and useful website and can provide a general overview of things to do.

TRAVEL AGENCIES
Jungle Lodges & Resorts Ltd (☑25597944; www.junglelodges.com; MG Rd, Shrungar Shopping Complex, Bengaluru; ⊙10am-5.30pm Mon-Sat) Books government-run lodges across the state, including wildlife parks and reserves; however inflated rates for foreigners means they're not cheap.
Skyway (☑22111401; www.skywaytour.com; St Mark's Rd, 8 Papanna Lane; ⊙9am-6pm Mon-Sat) A thoroughly professional and reliable outfit for booking long-distance taxis and air tickets.
STIC Travels (☑911244595300; www.stic travel.com; 33/1 Cunningham Rd, G5 Imperial

Ct; ⊗9.30am-6pm Mon-Sat) For ticketing, vehicles, hotels and holiday packages.

ⓘ Getting There & Away

AIR

International flights arrive to Bengaluru's airport in Hebbal, and there are direct daily flights to major cities all across India, including Chennai (₹2500, two hours), Mumbai (₹3000, two hours), Hyderabad (₹2500, one hour), Delhi (₹4500, 2½ hours) and Goa (₹2500, one hour).

Air India (⏹22277747; www.airindia.com; JC Rd, Unity Bldg)

GoAir (⏹47406091; www.goair.in; Bengaluru airport)

IndiGo (⏹9910383838; www.goindigo.in)

Jet Airways (⏹39893333; www.jetairways.com; JC Rd, Unity Bldg)

SpiceJet (⏹18001803333; www.spicejet.com)

BUS

Bengaluru's huge, well-organised **Central bus stand** (Gubbi Thotadappa Rd), also known as Majestic, is directly in front of the City train station. **Karnataka State Road Transport Corporation** (KSRTC; ⏹44554422; www.ksrtc.in) buses run throughout Karnataka and to neighbouring states. Other interstate bus operators:

Andhra Pradesh State Road Transport (APSRTC; www.apsrtc.gov.in)

Kadamba Transport Corporation (⏹22351958, 22352922) Services for Goa.

Maharashtra State Road Transport Corporation (MSRTC; www.msrtc.gov.in)

Tamil Nadu State Transport Corporation (SETC; www.tnstc.in)

Computerised advance booking is available for most buses at the station. KSRTC also has convenient booking counters around town. It's wise to book long-distance journeys in advance.

Numerous private bus companies offer comfier and only slightly more expensive services. Private bus operators line the street facing the Central bus stand, or you can book through a travel agency.

TRAIN

Bengaluru's **City train station** (Gubbi Thotadappa Rd) is the main train hub and the place to make reservations. **Cantonment train station** (Station Rd) is a sensible spot to disembark if you're arriving and headed for the MG Rd area, while **Yeshvantpur train station** (Rahman Khan Rd), 8km northwest of downtown, is the starting point for Goa trains.

If a train is booked out, foreign travellers can use the foreign-tourist quota. Buy a wait-listed ticket, then fill out a form at the **Divisional Railway Office** (Gubbi Thotadappa Rd) building immediately north of the City train station. You'll know about 10 hours before departure whether you've got a seat (a good chance); if not, the ticket is refunded. The computerised **train reservation office** (⏹139; ⊗8am-8pm Mon-Sat, 8am-2pm Sun), on the left facing the station, has separate counters for credit-card purchase, women and foreigners. Luggage can be left at the 24-hour cloakroom on Platform 1 at the City train station (₹10 per bag per day).

ⓘ Getting Around

TO/FROM THE AIRPORT

The swish city **airport** (⏹66782251; www.bengaluruairport.com) is in Hebbal, about 40km north from the MG Rd area. Prepaid taxis can take you from the airport to the city centre

MAJOR BUS SERVICES FROM BENGALURU

DESTINATION	FARE (₹)	DURATION (HR)	FREQUENCY
Chennai	363 (R)/650 (V)	7-8	6.35am-11.55pm, every hour
Ernakulam	532 (R)/902 (V)	10-12	7 daily, 4am-9.45pm
Gorkana	517 (R)/650 (V)	12	3 daily
Hampi	444 (R)	8½	1 daily, 11pm
Hospet	411 (R)/381 (V)	8	2pm-11pm, every hour
Hyderabad	640 (R)/904 (V)	11	16 buses daily, from 7.30am-10.30pm
Jog Falls	500 (R)	9	1 daily, 9.50pm
Mangalore	451 (R)/650 (V)	9	every 30min 6.30am-2pm & 7-11.30pm
Mumbai	1200 (V)	19	5 daily, from 3pm
Mysore	180 (R)/290 (V)	3	Every 10min, 24hr
Ooty	360 (R)/600 (V)	8	8 daily, 6.30am-11.15pm
Panaji	602 (R)/847 (V)	15	3 daily, from 5am

R – Rajahamsa Semideluxe, V – Airavath AC Volvo

(₹750). You can also take the hourly shuttle Vayu Vajra AC bus service to Majestic or MG Rd (₹170).

AUTORICKSHAW

The city's autorickshaw drivers are legally required to use their meters; few comply in reality. After 10pm, 50% is added onto the metered rate. Flag fall is ₹20 for the first 2km and then ₹11 for each extra kilometre.

BUS

Bengaluru has a thorough local bus network, operated by the **Bangalore Metropolitan Transport Corporation** (BMTC; www.bmtcinfo .com). Red AC Vajra buses criss-cross the city, while green Big10 deluxe buses connect the suburbs. Ordinary buses run from the **City bus stand**, next to Majestic; a few operate from the **City Market bus stand** further south.

To get from the City train station to the MG Rd area, catch any bus from Platform 17 or 18 at the City bus stand. For the City Market, take bus 31, 31E, 35 or 49 from Platform 8.

METRO

Bengaluru's shiny new AC metro service, known as Namma Metro finally had some lines up and running at the time of research (running from Baiyappanahalli to MG Road) while others are still in development. With trains plying every fifteen minutes and tickets costing marginally more than intra-city buses, upon completion the service will come as a welcome alternative to the city's congested public transport system. For the latest updates on the service, log on to www. bmrc.co.in.

TAXI

Several places around Bengaluru offer taxi rental with driver. Standard rates for a long-haul Tata Indica cab are ₹7 per kilometre for a minimum of 250km, plus a daily allowance of ₹200 for the driver. For an eight-hour day rental, you're looking at around ₹2000. Try **Skyway** (22111401) or **Meru Cabs** (44224422).

Around Bengaluru

Hessaraghatta

Located 30km northwest of Bengaluru, Hessaraghatta is home to **Nrityagram** (080-284 66313; www.nrityagram.org; 10am-2pm Tue-Sun), a leading dance academy established in 1990 to revive and popularise Indian classical dance.

The brainchild and living legacy of celebrated dancer Protima Gauri Bedi (1948–98), the complex was designed like a village by Goa-based architect Gerard da Cunha. Long-term courses in classical dance are offered to deserving students here, while local children are taught for free on Sundays. Self-guided tours cost ₹50 or you can book a tour, lecture and demonstration and vegetarian meal (₹1500 to ₹2000, minimum 10 people).

Opposite the dance village, **Taj Kuteeram** (080-28466326; www.tajhotels.com; d ₹4000;) is a hotel that combines comfort with rustic charm. It also offers ayurveda and yoga sessions.

MAJOR TRAINS FROM BENGALURU

DESTINATION	TRAIN NO & NAME	FARE (₹)	DURATION (HR)	DEPARTURES
Chennai	12658 Chennai Mail	193/735	6½	10.45pm
	12028 Shatabdi	529/1155	5	6am Wed-Mon
Delhi	12627 Karnataka Express	546/2485	39	7.20pm
	12649 Sampark Kranti Express	536/2425	35	10.10pm Mon, Wed, Fri, Sat & Sun
Hospet	16592 Hampi Express	191/785	9½	10pm
Hubli	16589 Rani Chennamma Express	203/840	8	9.15pm
Kolkata	12864 YPR Howrah Express	508/2625	35	7.35pm
Mumbai	16530 Udyan Express	363/1600	24	8.10pm
Mysore	12007 Shatabdi	316/665	2	11am Thu-Tue
	12614 Tippu Express	66/233	2½	3pm
Trivandrum	16526 Kanyakumari Express	307/1320	22	9.40pm

Shatabdi fares are AC chair/AC executive; Express (Exp/Mail) fares are 2nd-class/AC chair for day trains and sleeper/2AC for night trains.

LEPAKSHI

While actually located in Andhra Pradesh, Lepakshi is most easily accessible from Bengaluru, and is the site of the **Veerbhadra Temple** (admission free). The town gets its name from the Ramayana: when demon Ravana kidnapped Rama's wife, Sita, the bird Jatayu fought him and fell, injured, at the temple site. Rama then called him to get up; 'Lepakshi' derives from the Sanskrit for 'Get up, bird'.

Look for the 9m-long monolithic **Nandi** – India's largest – at the town's entrance. From here, you can see the temple's **Naga-lingam** (a phallic representation of Shiva) crowned with a seven-headed cobra. The temple is known for its unfinished **Kalyana Mandapam** (Marriage Hall), depicting the wedding of Parvati and Shiva, and its **Natyamandapa** (Dance Hall), with carvings of dancing gods. The temple's most stunning features, though, are the Natyamandapa's ceiling **frescoes**.

To get here from Bengaluru, take a Hindupur-bound bus (₹70, 1½ hours) or train, from where it's a further 11km to the temple. A private car from Puttaparthi is ₹1000.

Our Native Village (☑9591700577, 080-41140909; www.ournativevillage.com; s/d incl full board & activities ₹5100/7500; ☒), an eco-health retreat situated in the vicinity, is a great place to unwind in style while engaging in yoga, meditation and sound therapies as well as fun activities such as flying kites or riding bullock carts.

From Bengaluru's City Market, buses 266, 253, 253D and 253E run to Hessaraghatta (₹25, one hour), with bus 266 continuing on to Nrityagram. From Hessaraghatta an autorickshaw will cost ₹70.

Nandi Hills

Rising to 1455m, the **Nandi Hills** (www.nandihills.co.in; admission ₹5; ☺6am-6pm), 60km north of Bengaluru, were once the summer retreat of Tipu Sultan (his palace is still here). Today, it's the Bengaluru techie's favourite weekend getaway, and is predictably congested on Saturdays and Sundays. Nonetheless, it's a good place for hiking, with good views and two notable **Chola temples**. Buses head to Nandi Hills (₹50, two hours) from Bengaluru's Central bus stand.

Janapada Loka Folk Arts Museum

Situated 53km south of Bengaluru, this **museum** (adult/child ₹10/5; ☺9am-5.30pm) dedicated to the preservation of rural cultures has a wonderful collection of folk-art objects, including 500-year-old shadow puppets, festival costumes and musical instruments. Departing from Bengaluru, Mysore-bound buses (one hour) can drop you here; get off 3km after Ramnagar.

Mysore

☑0821 / POP 887,500 / ELEV 707M

If you haven't been to Mysore, you just haven't seen South India. Conceited though it may sound, this is not an overstatement. An ancient city with more than 600 glorious years of legacy, Mysore is one of the most flamboyant places in India. Known for its glittering royal heritage, bustling markets, magnificent monuments, cosmopolitan culture and a friendly populace, it is also a thriving centre for the production of premium silk, sandalwood and incense. It also flaunts considerable expertise in yoga and ayurveda, two trades it markets worldwide.

History

Mysore owes its name to the mythical Mahisuru, a place where the demon Mahisasura was slain by the goddess Chamundi. Its regal history began in 1399, when the Wodeyar dynasty of Mysore was founded, though they remained in service of the Vijayanagar empire until the mid-16th century. With the fall of Vijayanagar in 1565, the Wodeyars declared their sovereignty, which – save a brief period of Hyder Ali and Tipu Sultan's supremacy in the late 18th century – remained unscathed until 1947.

◉ Sights

★ **Mysore Palace**   PALACE

(Maharaja's Palace; www.mysorepalace.tv; Indian/foreigner ₹40/200, children under 10 free, Sound & Light show adult/child ₹40/25; ☺10am-5.30pm) Among the grandest of India's royal buildings, this fantastic palace was the former seat of the Wodeyar maharajas. The old

Mysore

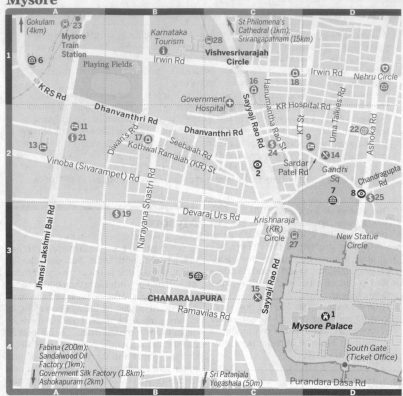

palace was gutted by fire in 1897; the one you see now was completed in 1912 by English architect Henry Irwin at a cost of Rs4.5 million. (See also the illustration, p872.)

The interior of this Indo-Saracenic marvel – a kaleidoscope of stained glass, mirrors and gaudy colours – is undoubtedly over the top. The decor is further embellished by carved wooden doors, mosaic floors and a series of paintings depicting life in Mysore during the Edwardian Raj. The way into the palace takes you past a fine collection of sculptures and artefacts. Don't forget to check out the armoury, with an intriguing collection of 700-plus weapons.

Every weekend, on national holidays, and through the Dasara (Duesshera) celebrations, the palace is illuminated by nearly 100,000 light bulbs that accent its majestic profile against the night.

Entrance to the palace grounds is at the South Gate on Purandara Dasa Rd. While you are allowed to snap the palace's exterior, photography within is strictly prohibited. Cameras must be deposited in lockers at the palace entrance.

Also available within the compound is a multilingual guided audiotour of the palace, the price of which is included in the foreigners' ticket.

A Sound & Light show is held most evenings at 7pm, which narrates the palace's history with effects of illumination; English-language shows were being launched at time of research.

Devaraja Market   MARKET

(Sayyaji Rao Rd; ⊙6am-8.30pm) Dating from Tipu Sultan's reign, this lively bazaar has local traders selling traditional items such as flower garlands, spices and conical piles of *kumkum* (coloured powder used for bindi dots), all of which makes for some great photo-ops. Refresh your bargaining skills before shopping.

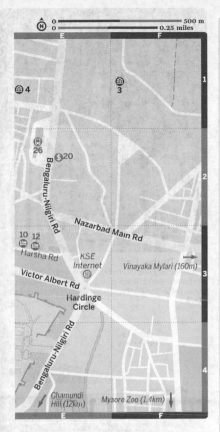

KARNATAKA & BENGALURU MYSORE

Chamundi Hill VIEWPOINT

At a height of 1062m, on the summit of Chamundi Hill, stands the **Sri Chamundeswari Temple** (⊙7am-2pm, 3.30-6pm & 7.30-9pm), dominated by a towering 40m-high *gopuram* (entrance gateway). It's a fine half-day excursion, offering spectacular views of the city below. Queues are long at weekends, so visit during the week. You can take bus 201 (₹23, 30 minutes) that rumbles up the narrow road to the summit. A return autorickshaw trip will cost about ₹400.

Alternatively, you can take the foot trail comprising 1000-plus steps that Hindu pilgrims use to visit the temple. One-third of the way down is a 5m-high statue of **Nandi** (Shiva's bull) that was carved out of solid rock in 1659.

Jayachamarajendra Art Gallery ART GALLERY

(Jaganmohan Palace Rd; adult/child ₹100/50; ⊙8.30am-5pm) Built in 1861 as the royal auditorium, the **Jaganmohan Palace**, just west of the Mysore Palace, houses the Jayachamarajendra Art Gallery. Set over three floors it has a collection of kitsch objects and regal memorabilia of the Mysore royal family including rare musical instruments, Japanese art, and paintings by the noted artist Raja Ravi Varma.

Mysore Palace

The interior of Mysore Palace houses opulent halls, royal paintings, intricate decorative details, as well as sculptures and ceremonial objects. There is a lot of hidden detail and much to take in, so be sure to allow yourself at least a few hours for the experience. A guide can also be invaluable.

After entering the palace the first exhibit is the **Doll's Pavilion 1**, which showcases the maharaja's fine collection of traditional dolls and sculptures acquired from around the world. Opposite the **Elephant Gate 2** you'll see the seven cannons that were used for special occasions, such as the birthdays of the maharajas. Today the cannons are still fired as part of Dasara festivities.

At the end of the Doll's Pavilion you'll find the **Golden Howdah 3**. Note the fly whisks on either side; the bristles are made from fine ivory.

Make sure you check out the paintings depicting the Dasara procession in the halls on your way to the **Marriage Pavilion 4** and look into the courtyard to see what was once the wrestling arena. It's now used during Dasara only. In the Marriage Pavilion, take a few minutes to scan the entire space. You can see the influence of three religions in the design of the hall: the glass ceiling represents Christianity, stone carvings along the hallway ceilings are Hindu design and the top-floor balcony roof (the traditional ladies' gallery) has Islamic-style arches.

When you move through to the **Private Durbar Hall 5**, take note of the intricate ivory inlay motifs depicting Krishna in the rosewood doors. The **Public Durbar Hall 6** is usually the last stop where you can admire the panoramic views of the gardens through the Islamic arches.

Private Durbar Hall
Rosewood doors lead into this hall, which is richly decorated with stained-glass ceilings, steel grill work and chandeliers. It houses the Golden Throne, only on display to the public during Dasara.

Entry to the Palace

Doll's Pavilion
The first exhibit, the Doll's Pavilion, displays the gift collection of 19th- and early-20th-century dolls, statues and Hindu idols that were given to the maharaja by dignitaries from around the world.

Public Durbar Hall

The open-air hall contains a priceless collection of paintings by Raja Ravi Varma and opens into an expansive balcony supported by massive pillars with an ornate painted ceiling of 10 incarnations of Vishnu.

Marriage Pavilion

This lavish hall used for royal weddings features themes of Christianity, Hindu and Islam in its design. The highlight is the octagonal painted glass ceiling featuring peacock motifs, the bronze chandelier and the colonnaded turquoise pillars.

Elephant Gate

Next to the Doll's Pavilion, this brass gate has four bronze elephants inlaid at the bottom, an intricate double-headed eagle up the top and a hybrid lion-elephant creature (the state emblem of Karnataka) in the centre.

Golden Howdah

At the far end of the Doll's Pavilion, a wooden elephant howdah decorated with 80kg of gold was used to carry the maharaja in the Dasara festival. It now carries the idol of goddess Chamundeswari.

Indira Gandhi Rashtriya Manav Sangrahalaya
MUSEUM

(National Museum of Mankind; ☑ 2448231; www.igrms.com; Irwin Rd, Wellington Lodge; 2-week workshops ₹50; ☉ 10am-5.30pm Tue-Sun) As well as excellent rotating exhibitions showcasing arts from rural India, this arts-cultural centre also organises two-week workshops in traditional, folk and tribal art forms, which are open to the public. It could be painting, embroidery, woodwork or paper mâché maskmaking conducted by specialist instructors. You need to book well in advance and commit to full-day workshops over two weeks.

Jayalakshmi Vilas Mansion Museum Complex
MUSEUM

(Mysore University Campus; ☉ 10.15am-5pm Mon-Sat) **FREE** Housed in a grand mansion, this museum specialises in folklore with artefacts, stone tablets and sculptures, including a wooden puppet of the 10-headed demon Ravana, and rural costumes.

Rail Museum
MUSEUM

(KRS Rd; adult/child ₹5/2, camera/video ₹10/25; ☉ 9.30am-6.30pm Tue-Sun) Located behind the train station, this open-air museum's main exhibit is the Mysore maharani's saloon, a wood-panelled beauty dating from 1899 that provides an insight in to the stylish way in which the royals once rode the railways. There are also six steam engines, each with its own story (told effectively through cutesy captions) and memorabilia from the Indian Railways' chequered past. A toy train rides the track around the museum (adult/child ₹5/2).

Mysore Zoo
ZOO

(Indiranagar; adult/child ₹40/20, camera ₹20; ☉ 8.30am-6.30pm Wed-Mon) Unlike many other pitiful zoos in India, Mysore zoo conforms to much higher standards, set in pretty gardens that date from 1892. Highlights include white tigers, lowland gorillas and rhinos.

Colonial Architecture
ARCHITECTURE

For architecture buffs, Mysore has quite a handful of charming buildings. Dating from 1805, **Government House** (Irwin Rd), formerly the British Residency, is a Tuscan Doric building set in 20 hectares of gardens. Facing the north gate of the Maharaja's Palace is the 1927 **Silver Jubilee Clock Tower** (Ashoka Rd); nearby stands the imposing

Rangacharlu Memorial Hall, built in 1884. The beauty of towering **St Philomena's Cathedral** (St Philomena St; ☉ 8am-5pm), built between 1933 and 1941 in neo-Gothic style, is emphasised by beautiful stained-glass windows.

Activities

Royal Mysore Walks
WALKING

(☑ 9632044188; www.royalmysorewalks.com; 2hr walks from ₹600) A walking tour is an excellent way to familiarise yourself with Mysore's epic history and heritage. Techie-turned-historian Vinay and his team organise weekend walks with a specific focus on either the city's royal history, its markets, its old quarters or its handicrafts. Offbeat walks, such as a yoga and spirituality tour or Mysore silk tour, can also be arranged at extra cost. They also conduct cycling and jeep tours.

Emerge Spa
AYURVEDA

(☑ 2522500; www.thewindflower.com; Maharanapratap Rd, Windflower Spa & Resort, Nazarbad; ☉ 7am-9pm) Slick, out-of-town resort offering pampering ayurvedic sessions (try the one-hour Abhayanga massage for ₹1800 which involves two therapists) followed by the steam chamber or a range of Balinese massage, hydrotherapy and beauty treatments. Rates include pick-up and drop off.

Indus Valley Ayurvedic Centre
AYURVEDA

(☑ 2473263; www.ayurindus.com; Lalithadripura) Set on 25 acres of gardens, this classy centre derives its therapies from ancient scriptures and prescriptions. The overnight package (single/double including full board ₹9500/16,900) includes one session each of ayurveda, yoga and beauty therapy.

Swaasthya Ayurveda Centre
AYURVEDA

(☑ 6557557; www.swaasthya.com; No 726/B, 6th Cross, opp Yoganarsimhaswamy Temple; treatments from ₹250) Professional Ayurveda therapists providing traditional treatments and all-inclusive packages that include accommodation and food. Also has a retreat in Coorg.

Karanji Lake Nature Park
NATURE PARK, BIRDWATCHING

(Indiranagar; admission ₹20, camera ₹20; ☉ 8.30am-5.30pm) Next to the zoo, this nature park is the place to spy on various bird species, including cormorants, herons, rose-ringed parakeets, painted storks and many butterflies.

🐘 Courses

Jayashankar, the music teacher at **Shruthi Musical Works** (📞 9845249518; Irwin Rd, 1189 3rd Cross; ⏱ 10.30am-9pm Mon-Sat, 10.30am-2pm Sun), gets good reviews for his tabla instructions (₹300 per hour).

👉 Tours

KSTDC runs a daily Mysore city tour (from ₹725), taking in the entire city, Chamundi Hill, Srirangapatnam and Brindavan Gardens. It starts daily at 6.30am, ends at 11.30pm and is likely to leave you breathless!

Other KSTDC tours include one to Belur, Halebid and Sravanabelagola (₹450) on Tuesday, Wednesday, Friday and Saturday from 7.30am to 9pm. It requires a minimum of 10 people, so call in advance.

All tours leave from the tours office at Hotel Mayura Hoysala (p875). Bookings can be made at the KSTDC Transport Office (located at the hotel) or at travel agencies around town.

🛏 Sleeping

Mysore attracts tourists through the year and can fill up very quickly during Dussehra. Booking early is recommended.

Mysore Youth Hostel　　　HOSTEL **$**
(📞 2544704; www.yhmysore.com; Gangothri Layout; dm/students from ₹100/75) Set against a patch of green lawns 3km west of town, this hostel has clean, well-maintained male and female dorms. OK, there's a 10.30pm curfew, no alcohol allowed, bucket hot water and no towels, but you can't go past these prices. Take a city bus to Maruthi Temple, from where it's a short walk; an autorickshaw costs ₹60.

Hotel Dasaprakash　　　HOTEL **$**
(📞 2442444; www.mysoredasaprakashgroup.com; Gandhi Sq; s/d from ₹400/702; d with AC ₹1732; ❄) Popular with local tourists and pilgrim groups, rooms here are a bit rundown, but the building has character and makes for a decent budget option. It has an inexpensive veg restaurant with good dosas.

Hotel Mayura Hoysala　　　HOTEL **$**
(📞 2426160; 2 Jhansi Lakshmi Bai Rd; s/d incl breakfast from ₹953/1050; ❄) This government-owned hotel continues to offer its blend of mothballed heritage (lace-lined curtains, heavy wooden doors, assorted cane furniture and old photographs lining its corridors) at affordable prices. The bar here is popular with Mysore's tipplers.

★ Green Hotel　　　HERITAGE HOTEL **$$**
(📞 4255000; www.greenhotelindia.com; 2270 Vinoba Rd, Jayalakshmipuram; s/d incl breakfast from ₹3550/4050; 📶) 🍴 Undergoing several fascinating reincarnations over the years, the character-filled Green Hotel was originally built as the Chittaranjan Palace in the 1920s by the maharajah for his three daughters, before becoming a major film studio from the 1950s to 1987. Today its 31-rooms, set among charming gardens, are all run on solar power and those in the Palace building include themes such as a Writers room or kitschy

KARNATAKA & BENGALURU MYSORE

DUSSEHRA JAMBOREE

Mysore is at its carnivalesque best during the 10-day **Dussehra** (Mysore; ⏱ Oct) (locally spelt 'Dasara') festival in October. During this time the Maharaja's Palace is dramatically lit up every evening, while the town is transformed into a gigantic fairground, with concerts, dance performances, sporting demonstrations and cultural events running to packed houses. On the last day the celebrations are capped off in grand style. A dazzling procession of richly costumed elephants, garlanded idols, liveried retainers and cavalry kicks off around 1pm, marching through the streets to the rhythms of clanging brass bands, all the way from the palace to the Bannimantap parade ground. A torchlight parade at Bannimantap and a spectacular session of fireworks then closes the festival for the year.

Mysore is choc-a-bloc with tourists during the festival, especially on the final day. To bypass suffocating crowds, consider buying a Dasara VIP Gold Card (₹7500 for two). Though expensive, it assures you good seats at the final day gala and helps you beat the entry queues at other events and performances, while providing discounts on accommodation, dining and shopping. It's also possible to buy tickets (₹250 to ₹1000) just for entering the palace and Bannimantap for the final day's parades. Contact the the **Dasara Information Centre** (📞 2418888; www.mysoredasara.gov.in) for more details.

MYSORE ASHTANGA YOGA

It's not just the palace that attracts visitors to Mysore; this city is also famous for yoga, attracting thousands of international students each year to learn, practice or become certified in teaching Ashtanga.

Unlike at casual centres, here students are required to be austerely committed to the art, and will need at least a month's commitment. You'll also need to register far in advance, as courses are often booked out. Call or email the centres for details.

Most yoga institutes, as well as local laws, insist that all visitors arriving in Mysore to train in yoga must do so on a student visa, not a casual tourist visa. You are also required to register yourself at the local police station within 14 days of your arrival.

Yoga Centres

Ashtanga Yoga Research (AYRI; ☑ 9880185500; www.kpjayi.org; 235 8th Cross, 3rd Stage, Gokulam; 1 month ₹28,600) Founded by the renowned Ashtanga teacher K Pattabhi Jois, who taught Madonna her yoga moves. He has since passed away and the reigns have been handed over to his son, who is proving very popular. A tourist visa is OK but you need to register two months in advance.

Yoga India (Abhyasa Yoga Shala; www.aananda.in; 7th Main, 3rd Stage, Gokulam) Offers Hatha and Ashtanga yoga with a young guru, Bharath Shetty, who learnt under the legendary BKS Iyengar from Pune.

Atma Vikasa (☑ 2341978; www.atmavikasayoga.com; 18, 80ft Rd, Ramakrishnanagar) 'Backbending expert' Yogacharya Venkatesh offers courses in yoga, Sanskrit and meditation. It has a new location in a peaceful suburb 5km southwest of the palace.

Sri Patanjala Yogashala (Yoga Research Institute; ☑ 2430721, 9986390093; www.bnsiyengar.org; 490 Devamba Agrahara, KR Mohalla; ⊘ 6-8am & 5-7pm) The baby of well-respected Ashtanga practitioner BNS Iyengar (not to be confused with BKS Iyengar, famed exponent of Iyengar yoga). Conveniently located in the city centre.

Sleeping & Eating

No yoga centres offer acccommodation, so you'll need to make own arrangements. Many foreign yoga students congregate stay in the residential suburb of Gokulam, where the following are located.

Anokhi Garden Guest House (☑ 4288923; www.anokhigarden.com; 408 Contour Rd, 3rd stage, Gokulam; s/d from ₹1700/2400; ⊘ cafe 8am-12.30pm Thu-Sun; ☎) Boutique guesthouse with four rooms in leafy propery, and a lovely cafe that does yummy vegetarian meals, vegan breakfasts and brunches.

Urban Oasis (☑ 2410713; www.urbanoasis.co.in; 7 Contour Rd, 3rd Stage, Gokulam; r from ₹1500, monthly from ₹26,000; ✳ ☎) More of a business hotel, but popular with students for its comfortable rooms.

Anu's Bamboo Hut (☑ 9900909428; anugan@gmail.com; 365, 2nd Main, 3rd Stage, Gokulam; lunch buffet ₹250, cooking class ₹450; ⊘ 1-3pm & 5-7pm Fri-Wed) Rooftop shack cafe catering to yoga students with healthy vegetarian lunch buffets, and evening smoothies. A great source of info and offers cooking classes.

Bollywood decor. Best of all, the profits are distributed to charity and environmental projects across India. It's 3km west of town.

Parklane Hotel HOTEL **$$**
(☑ 4003500; www.parklanemysore.com; 2720 Harsha Rd; r from ₹2000; ✳ @ ☎) Travellers' central on Mysore's tourist circuit, the Parklane is over-the-top kitsch but it's hard to dislike with its massive rooms which are immaculate, ultracomfortable and thoughtfully outfitted with mobile-phone chargers and very useful toiletry kits. The restaurant on the 1st is always busy and has a lively atmosphere.

Hotel Maurya Residency HOTEL **$$**
(☑ 2523375; www.hotelmauryaresidency.com; Harsha Rd; d from ₹1400; ✳ ☎) Along with Hotel Maurya Palace, its twin establishment next door, the Maurya Residency remains

a trusted name among the Harsha Rd mid-range gang. It's a friendly place with budget-midrange decent rooms. **Veg Kourt**, the restaurant downstairs, serves a sumptuous all-you-can-eat breakfast for ₹85.

★**Lalitha Mahal Palace** HERITAGE HOTEL $$$
(☑8212526100; turret room incl breakfast ₹4834, heritage classic room incl breakfast ₹12,080; ✳@⍟) A former maharaja's guesthouse built in 1921, this grand majestic heritage building has been operating as a hotel since 1974. Old-world charm comes in bucketloads from the 1920s birdcage elevator to mosaic tiled floors. The 'standard' turret room offers good value with wooden floors and bright bathrooms, but the heritage classic rooms are where you'll feel the history. Spacious four poster beds sit next to antique furniture, claw-foot baths sit on marble bathroom floors and shuttered windows look out to stately landscaped gardens. There's also a gym and tennis courts. Watch out for the cheeky monkeys here.

Royal Orchid Metropole HERITAGE HOTEL $$$
(☑4255566; www.royalorchidhotels.com; 5 Jhansi Lakshmi Bai Rd; s/d incl breakfast from ₹6568/7160; ✳⍟✲) Originally built by the Wodeyars to serve as the residence of the Maharaja's British guests, this is undoubtedly one of Mysore's leading heritage hotels. The charming colonial-era structure has 30 rooms oozing historical character, and there are performances of magic shows, music, dance and snake charming when tour groups pass through.

✗ **Eating & Drinking**

Malgudi Café CAFE $
(Green Hotel; mains ₹60-80; ⍟10am-7pm; ⍟) ✎ Set around an inner courtyard within the Green Hotel, this ambient cafe brews excellent coffees and Himalayan teas to be enjoyed with tasty snacks, cakes or fresh bread baked on the premises daily. Staff here come from underprivileged backgrounds and are mostly women, and profits assist with downtrodden communities, so you can do your bit by ordering a second cuppa. Service can be slow.

Hotel RRR SOUTH INDIAN $
(Gandhi Sq; mains ₹75-102) Classic Andhra-style food is ladled out at this ever-busy eatery, and you may have to queue for a table during lunch. One item to try is the piping-hot veg thali (₹85) served on banana leaves. There's a second branch on Harsha Rd.

Vinayaka Mylari SOUTH INDIAN $
(769 Nazarbad Main Rd; mains ₹30-50; ⍟7.30-11.30am & 4-8pm) Local foodies say this is one of the best eateries in town to try South Indian classics of *masala dosa* (lentil-flour pancake filled with vegetables) and *idlis* (spongy, round, fermented rice cakes). There's a similar branch up the road run by the owner's brother.

Pelican Pub PUB $
(Hunsur Rd; mains ₹75-150; ⍟11am-11pm) A popular watering hole located en route to Green Hotel, this laid-back joint serves beer for ₹65 a mug in the indoor classic pub or al fresco style garden setting out back. Tasty food pairs nicely with a cold beer, try some sinful pork chilli for ₹135 a platter, or spinach balls in a sticky sauce. There's live music Wednesdays.

Hotel Sree Annapoorna SOUTH INDIAN $
(Sayyaji Rao Rd; mains ₹30-80; ⍟7.30am-10pm) ✎ This typically busy South Indian eatery rolls out steaming breakfast platters for Mysore's office-goers, and welcomes them back in the evenings with aromatic filter coffee and a convoy of delicious snacks, including speciality dosa each day of the week.

★**Sapphire** INDIAN $$
(mains ₹180-450; ⍟lunch 12.30-2.45pm, snacks 2.45-7.45pm, dinner 8-11pm) Dine in absolute royal Indian-style in the grand ballroom of the Lalitha Mahal Palace hotel. And grand it is, with high stained-glass ceilings, lace tablecloths and polished teak floors. Order the royal Mysore silver thali which gets you an assortment of vegetables, breads and sweets served on lavish brassware (₹390) while enjoying live Indian sitar performances over lunch and dinner.

Parklane Hotel MULTICUISINE $$
(2720 Harsha Rd, Parklane Hotel; mains ₹100-140) Mysore's most social restaurant with buzzing picnic-style garden tables, lit up moodily by countless lanterns. The food here is stock standard, with the usual Indian dishes, but live traditional music, and a fully stocked bar, make for a great night out.

Tiger Trail INDIAN $$
(5 Jhansi Lakshmi Bai Rd, Royal Orchid Metropole; mains ₹150-300; ⍟12.30-3.30pm & 7-11pm) This sophisticated restaurant works up delectable Indian dishes in a courtyard that twinkles with torches and fairy lights at night

and a menu comprising jungle recipes collected from different tiger reserves across India. Also has a lunch buffet from ₹450.

Shopping

Mysore is a great place to shop for its famed sandalwood products, silk saris and wooden toys. It is also one of India's major incense-manufacturing centres. Look for the butterfly-esque 'Silk Mark' on your purchase; it's an endorsement for quality silk.

Government Silk Factory CLOTHING
(Mananthody Rd, Ashokapuram; ☉10am-6.30pm Mon-Sat, outlet 10.30am-7.30pm Mon-Sat) Given that Mysore's prized silk is made under its very sheds, this is the best and cheapest place to shop for the exclusive textile. Behind the showroom is the factory, where you can drop by to see how the fabric is made.

Sandalwood Oil Factory SOUVENIRS
(Mananthody Rd, Ashokapuram; ☉9.30-1pm & 2-5pm Mon-Sat) A quality-assured place for sandalwood products such as incense, soap, cosmetics and the prohibitively expensive pure sandalwood oil. Guided tours are available to show you around the factory and explain how the products are made.

Cauvery Arts & Crafts Emporium CLOTHING
(Sayyaji Rao Rd; ☉10am-7.30pm) Not the cheapest place, but the selection is extensive, and there's no pressure to buy.

Fabindia CLOTHING
(☑2334451; www.fabindia.com; Jaya Lakshmi Vilas Rd, Chamrajpuram; ☉10.30am-8.30pm) A branch of the ever reliable clothing and homewares shop with North Indian items and fixed prices.

Shruthi Musical Works MUSIC STORE
(Irwin Rd, 1189 3rd Cross; ☉10am-9pm Mon-Sat) Sells a variety of traditional musical instruments including tabla sets and assorted percussion instruments.

Sapna Book House BOOKS
(1433 Narayana Shastri Rd; ☉10.30am-8.30pm) Paperbacks and magazines, as well as guidebooks and yoga books; excellent for maps.

Information

INTERNET ACCESS

Pal Net (per hour ₹40; ☉9am-9pm Mon-Sat, to 2pm Sun)
KSE Internet (BN Rd, Hotel Ramanashree Complex; per hr ₹60; ☉8am-10pm)

LEFT LUGGAGE

The City bus stand's cloakroom, open from 6am to 11pm, costs ₹10 per bag for 12 hours.

MEDICAL SERVICES

Government Hospital (☑4269806; Dhanvanthri Rd) Has a 24-hour pharmacy.

MONEY

HDFC Bank (Devaraj Urs Rd) ATM.
ICICI Bank ATM (BN Rd) ATM at Hotel Pai Vista.
State Bank of Mysore (cnr Irwin & Ashoka Rds; ☉10.30am-2.30pm & 3-4pm Mon-Fri, 10.30am-12.30pm Sat) Changes cash and ATM.
Thomas Cook (☑2420090; 9/2 Ashoka Rd, Silver Tower; ☉9.30am-6pm Mon-Sat) Foreign currency.

POST

Main Post Office (cnr Irwin & Ashoka Rds; ☉10am-6pm Mon-Sat)

TOURIST INFORMATION

Karnataka Tourism (☑2422096; adtourism-mysore@gmail.com; Irwin Rd, Old Exhibition Bldg; ☉10am-5.30pm Mon-Sat) Extremely helpful, and plenty of brochures.
KSTDC Transport Office (☑2423652; 2 Jhansi Lakshmi Bai Rd; ☉8.30am-8.30pm) Offers general tourist information and provides a useful map. Has counters at the train station and Central bus stand, as well as this transport office next to Hotel Mayura Hoysala.

Getting There & Away

AIR

Mysore's airport was not operating any flights at the time of research but discussions were in place about the possibility of resuming commercial flights in future. Check with the tourism office for updates.

BUS

The **Central bus stand** (BN Rd) handles all KSRTC long-distance buses. The **City bus stand** (Sayyaji Rao Rd) is for city, Srirangapatnam and Chamundi Hill buses.

The **Private bus stand** (Sayyaji Rao Rd) also has services to Hubli, Bijapur, Mangalore, Ooty and Ernakulam. You'll find several ticketing agents around the stand.

TRAIN

From Mysore's **railway booking office** (☑131; ☉8am-8pm Mon-Sat, 8am-2pm Sun), buy a ticket on the 6.45am Chamundi Express (₹57/202) or the 11am Tippu Express to Bengaluru (2nd class/AC chair ₹66/233, three hours at 11am). The 2.15 Shatabdi Express also connects Bengaluru (AC chair/AC executive chair ₹285/620, two hours) and Chennai (AC chair/

AC executive chair ₹741/1535, seven hours) daily except Wednesday. Several passenger trains to Bengaluru (₹25, 3½ hours) stop at Srirangapatnam (₹15, 20 minutes). The 10.30pm Mysore Dharwad Express goes to Hubli (sleeper/2AC ₹212/880, 9½ hours).

ℹ Getting Around

Agencies at hotels and around town rent cabs for about ₹7 per kilometre, with a minimum of 250km per day, plus a daily allowance of ₹200 for the driver.

The flagfall on autorickshaws is ₹20, and ₹10 per kilometre is charged thereafter. Count on around ₹800 for a day's sightseeing.

Around Mysore

Srirangapatnam

📞 08236

Steeped in bloody history, the fort town of Srirangapatnam, 16km from Mysore, is built on an island straddling the Cauvery River. The seat of Hyder Ali and Tipu Sultan's power, this town was the de facto capital of much of southern India during the 18th century. Srirangapatnam's glory days ended when the British waged an epic war again Tipu Sultan in 1799, when he was defeated and killed. However, the ramparts, battlements and some of the gates of the fort still stand, as do a clutch of monuments. The island is now linked to the mainland by bridge.

There's no real reason to stay overnight, but **Mayura River View** (📞 252114; d from ₹2300, restaurant mains ₹100-120; ❄) has a nice location on the riverbank and is a good place to lunch.

◉ Sights

Daria Daulat Bagh　　　　　　PALACE
(Indian/foreigner ₹5/100; ◷9am-5pm) Set within lovely manicured grounds, Srirangapatnam's star attraction is Tipu's summer palace, 1km east of the fort. Built largely out of teak, the palace may not look like much from the outside, but the lavish decoration that covers every inch of its interiors is impressive. The ceilings are embellished with floral designs, while the walls bear murals depicting courtly life and Tipu's campaigns against the British. There's a small museum within displaying artefacts and interesting paintings.

Gumbaz　　　　　　MAUSEOLEUM
(admission free; ◷8am-6.30pm) **FREE** Located within a serene garden, the historically significant Gumbaz is the resting place of the legendary Tipu Sultan, his equally famed father, Hyder Ali, and his wife. The interior of the onion-dome mausoleum is painted in tiger-like motif as a tribute to the sultan. Aross from the tomb is the **Masjid-E-Aska** (mosque).

Sri Ranganathaswamy Temple　HINDU TEMPLE
(◷7.30am-1pm & 4-8pm) Constructed in 894 AD, this attractive Vaishnavite temple has a mix of Hoysala and Vijayanagar design. Within are cavernous walkways, pillars and the centerpiece 4.5m long reclining statue of Ranganatha, a manifestation of Vishnu.

Jamia Masjid　　　　　　MOSQUE
This cream-coloured mosque with two minarets was built by the sultan in 1787 and features an interesting blend of Islamic and

KARNATAKA & BENGALURU AROUND MYSORE

KSRTC BUSES FROM MYSORE

DESTINATION	FARE (₹)	DURATION (HR)	FREQUENCY
Bandipur	75 (O)/200 (V)	2	every 30min 6.30am-3.30pm
Bengaluru	110 (O)/162 (R)/270 (V)	3	every 20min
Channarayapatna	70 (O)	2	hourly
Chennai	930 (V)/ 531 (R)	12	4 daily
Ernakulam	593 (V)	11	4 daily
Gokarna	412 (O)	12	1 daily
Hassan	110 (O)	3	hourly
Hospet	372 (O)/491 (R)	10	4 daily
Mangalore	210 (O)/310 (R)/500 (V)	7	hourly
Ooty	127 (O) 191 (R)/300 (V)	5	8 daily

O – Ordinary, R – Rajahamsa Semideluxe, V – Airavath AC Volvo

Hindu architecture. Climb the stairs at the back for panoramic views of the site.

Colonel Bailey's Dungeon
HISTORICAL SITE

FREE North of the island on the banks of the Cauvery is this well-preserved 18th-century white-walled dungeon used to hold British prisoners of war, including Colonel Bailey who died here in 1780. Jutting out from the walls are stone fixtures used to chain prisoners. East from here along the river is **Thomas Inman's Dungeon**, hidden away beneath undulating terrain, with a more undiscovered feel that's fun to explore.

ⓘ Getting There & Away

Take buses 313 or 313a (₹15, 50 minutes) that depart every hour from Mysore's City bus stand. Passenger trains travelling from Mysore to Bengaluru (₹2, 20 minutes) also stop here. Bus 307 (₹18, 30 minutes) heading to Brindavan Gardens is just across from Srirangapatnam's main bus stand.

ⓘ Getting Around

The sights are spread out, so hiring an autorickshaw is the best option (₹250 for three hours) of getting around.

Melkote

Life in the devout Hindu town of Melkote, about 50km north of Mysore, revolves around the atmospheric 12th-century **Cheluvanarayana Temple** (Raja St; ⊙8am-1pm & 5-8pm), with its rose-coloured *gopuram* (gateway tower) and ornately carved pillars. Get a workout on the hike up to the hilltop **Yoganarasimha Temple**, which offers fine views of the surrounding hills. The town really comes alive for the **Vairamudi Festival** (Melkote; ⊙Mar/Apr) in March or April, attracting 400,000 pilgrims for the crowning of the statue of Vishnu.

Three KSRTC buses shuttle daily between Mysore and Melkote (₹60, 1½ hours).

Somnathpur

The astonishingly beautiful **Keshava Temple** (Indian/foreigner ₹5/100; ⊙8.30am-5.30pm) is one of the finest examples of Hoysala architecture, on par with the masterpieces of Belur and Halebid. Built in 1268, this star-shaped temple, 33km from Mysore, is adorned with superb stone sculptures depicting various scenes from the Ramayana,

Mahabharata and Bhagavad Gita, and the life and times of the Hoysala kings.

Somnathpur is 12km south of Bannur and 10km north of Tirumakudal Narsipur. Take one of the half-hourly buses from Mysore to either village (₹35, 30 minutes) and change there. There are also government-run day tours that visit from Mysore

Bandipur National Park

A part of the Nilgiri Biosphere Reserve, **Bandipur National Park** (Indian/foreigner ₹75/1000, video ₹100; ⊙6am-6pm) is one of South India's most famous wildernesses areas. Covering 880 sq km, it was once the Mysore maharajas' private wildlife reserve, and is now a protected zone for over 100 species of mammals, including tiger, elephant, leopard, gaur (Indian bison), chital (spotted deer), sambar, sloth bear and langur. It's also home to an impressive 350 species of bird. Only 80km south of Mysore on the Ooty road, it's very accessible from both Bengaluru and Mysore.

Only government vehicles are permitted to run safaris within the park, and the best option is to go on Bandipur Safari Lodge's (p881) two-hour drives for ₹2000, inclusive of park entry fees. The forest department also arrange **safaris** (2hr jeep safari ₹3000; ⊙6am & 4pm), but its rumbling minibus is simply best avoided.

🛏 Sleeping & Eating

It's also possible to stay at the **forest department bungalows** (☑236021; dc_bandipur@yahoo.com; 20-bed dm ₹1000, bungalow foreigner from ₹3000), but you're likely to pay a ₹1000 entry fee, making it terrible value given it's a 20-bed dorm.

Hotel Bandipur Plaza
HOTEL $$

(☑8547680406; Ooty-Mysore Hwy; r ₹1500) Its highway location may not be what you hope for when visiting a national park, but its rooms are functional and affordable in an otherwise pricey destination. It's close to Bandipur Safari Lodge, so it's easy to book safaris in the park.

Tiger Ranch
LODGE $$

(☑8095408505; www.tigerranch.net; Mangala Village; r incl full board ₹1105) The only place in Bandipur with a genuine outdoorsy feel to it, the *very* basic rooms here blend wonderfully into nature. It has an atmospheric thatched-roof dining hall, and evenings can be enjoyed around the bonfire. Be warned that monkeys are a nuisance here, so don't leave valuables (or food!) lying around your room. There's no alcohol here, but it's fine to bring your own. It's inconveniently located away from the park, so you'll need to call ahead to arrange a pickup (₹300).

★ **Dhole's Den**　　　　　　LODGE $$$
(☎8229-236062; www.dholesden.com; Kaniyanapura Village; s/d incl full board & safari from ₹9000/10,000; ☞) 🍃 With a boutique design that's lifted straight from the pages of an architectural magazine, Dhole's effectively mixes comfort and its lovely pastoral surrounds. Stylish rooms are decked out with art and colourful fabrics, plus couches and deck chairs that look out to the dam. It's environmentally conscious with solar power, tank water and organic veggies. A 20-minute drive from the park headquarters, rates include transfers and safaris, but not park entry (₹1000).

Bandipur Safari Lodge　　CAMPGROUND $$$
(www.junglelodges.com/index.php/resorts/bandipur.html; Mysore-Ooty Rd; r incl full board & safari Indian/foreigner ₹3750/7000; ❄) This sprawling government-owned camp has well-maintained, comfortable cottages, but it lacks character and 'safari' atmosphere. However, it's conveniently located on the fringes of the park, and rates include two safaris per day.

⊙ Getting There & Away

Buses between Mysore and Ooty can drop you at Bandipur (₹65, three hours), an 88km journey. Skyway (p866) can arrange an overnight taxi from Mysore for about ₹2000.

Nagarhole National Park & Around

Blessed with rich wildlife, attractive jungle and a scenic lake, **Nagarhole National Park** (Rajiv Gandhi National Park; Indian/foreigner ₹200/1000, video ₹100; ☺6am-6pm), pronounced nag-ar-hole-eh, is one of Karnataka's best wildlife getaways. Adjoining **Kabini Lake**, it forms an important animal corridor that runs through neighbouring Bandipur National Park – making up a part of the Nilgiri Biosphere Reserve. Despite sharing the same wildlife, it sees much fewer visitors than Bandipur, making it all the more appealing. Set over 643 sq km, Nagarhole features a good blend of dense jungle and open sightlines along the river bank, which makes for fantastic wildlife-watching. Its lush forests are home to tigers, leopards, elephants, gaurs, barking deer, wild dogs, bonnet macaques and common langurs, plus 270 species of birds. The park can remain closed for long stretches between July and October, when the rains transform the forests into a giant slush-pit.

The traditional inhabitants of the land, the hunter-gatherer Jenu Kuruba people, still live in the park, despite government efforts to relocate them.

The best time to view wildlife is during summer (April to May), though winter (November to February) is more comfortable.

Government-run **jeep safaris** (2½hr jeep safari ₹1750) and **boat trips** (₹1750) are conducted from Kabini River Lodge between 6.30am and 9.30am and 4pm and 7pm, which are both good ways to see animals.

🛏 Sleeping & Eating

Since the government banning of private vehicles in the park, most people stay in lodges around Kabini Lake. Unfortunately there's no genuine budget lodging; however, it's worth touching base with Waterwoods Lodge to see if it offers camping on its property.

★ **Bison Wilderness**　　　　LODGE $$$
(☎80-41278708; www.thebisonresort.com; Gundathur Village; s/d incl full board US$250/260; ☀) Inspired by the luxury safari lodges in Africa, Bison succeeds in replicating the classic wilderness experience. It has a stunning location on the waterfront, with luxurious tents and stilted cottages linked by a rickety wooden platform. Each is done out in decadent touches of polished timber floors, throw rugs and clawfoot baths. It has a swimming pool built into a wooden decking, nightly bonfires and expert naturalists for safaris.

Waterwoods Lodge　　GUESTHOUSE $$$
(☎082-28264421; www.waterwoods.in; s/d incl full board ₹5500/7800; ☀) A boutique guesthouse on the grassy embankment of the scenic lake, Waterwoods has a homely atmosphere that makes for a relaxing stay. It's run by two likeable young, environmentally aware owners who are very knowledgeable about the area. It's kid-friendly with trampoline, infinity pool and woodfired pizzas. Each evening there's a bonfire to accompany a screening of wildlife docos.

KARNATAKA & BENGALURU NAGARHOLE NATIONAL PARK & AROUND

BILIGIRI RANGANNA (BR) HILLS

Much less known than Bandipur or Nagarhole, the **Biligiri Ranganna Temple Wildlife Sanctuary** in the BR Hills makes a great alternative to live out your *Jungle Book* fantasies. Set over 570 sq km, it was declared a tiger reserve in 2010 with a population of 36 tigers inhabiting the area – but like most parks, you'll need to be *extremely* lucky to spot one. Elephants, leopards, sloth bears and dholes (wild dogs) also roam the hills here.

The government-owned **K Gudi Wilderness Camp** (www.junglelodges.com; per person tented camp incl full board & activities ₹7000, huts ₹7500) has a fantastic site among the peaceful forest, with grazing warthog and spotted deer. Accommodation is in tented cottages or delightful stilted log cabins, and rates include meals, two safaris and wildlife screenings in the evening.

The wildlife sanctuary is a 4½-hour drive from Bengaluru. It's best to hire a vehicle although it is theoretically possible to get there by public transport. You can either catch a direct 7.45am bus from Mysore to K Gudi, or otherwise a bus to Chamarajanagar and connect to a 1.30pm bus to K Gudi. From Chamarajanagar you can arrange a jeep for ₹700.

Kabini River Lodge　　　　　LODGE **$$$**
(☑ 080-40554055; www.junglelodges.co; per person India/foreigner incl full board & activities from ₹5000/9000; ✿) These attractive government-run bungalows have a prime location beside the lake in the serene, tree-lined grounds of the former Mysore maharaja's hunting lodge. It has large tented cottages and bungalows and an atmospheric colonial-style bar. Rates include safaris, boat rides and entry fees.

❶ Getting There & Away

The park's main entrance is 93km southwest of Mysore. A few buses depart daily from Mysore to Kabini village, but you'll need transport for the last leg to the resorts.

Kodagu (Coorg) Region

Nestled amid ageless hills that line the southernmost edge of Karnataka is the luscious Kodagu (Coorg) region, gifted with emerald landscapes and acres of plantations. A major centre for coffee and spice production, this rural expanse is also home to the unique Kodava race, believed to have descended from migrating Persians and Kurds or perhaps Greeks left behind from Alexander the Great's armies. The uneven terrain and cool climate make it a fantastic area for trekking, birdwatching or lazily ambling down little-trodden paths winding around carpeted hills. All in all, Kodagu is rejuvenation guaranteed.

Kodagu was a state in its own right until 1956, when it merged with Karnataka. The region's chief town and transport hub is Madikeri, but for an authentic Kodagu experience, you have to venture into the plantations. Avoid weekends, when places can quickly get filled up by weekenders from Bengaluru.

Madikeri (Mercara)

☑ 08272 / POP 32,500 / ELEV 1525M

Also known as Mercara, this congested market town is spread out along a series of ridges. The only reason for coming here is to organise treks or sort out the practicalities of travel. A colourful time to visit is around November and December when the Kodava community celebrates **Huthri**, a week-long festival that commemorates the start of the rice harvesting season.

❍ Sights

Madikeri Fort　　　　　HISTORICAL SITE
FREE Originally Tipu Sultan's fort in the 16th century, before Raja Lingarajendra II took over in 1812, today it's the less glamorous site of the municipal headquarters. Within the fort's walls are the hexagonal palace (now the dusty district commissioner's office) and colonial church, which houses a quirky **museum** (⊘ 10am-5.30pm Sun-Fri) **FREE** displaying eclectic exhibits.

Raja's Seat　　　　　VIEWPOINT
(MG Rd; ₹5; ⊘ 6am-7.30pm) The place to come to watch sunset, as the raja himself did, with fantastic outlooks to rolling hills and endless valleys.

Raja's Tombs
HISTORIC BUILDING

FREE Stop off en route to Abbi Falls at the quietly beautiful Raja's Tombs, better known as Gaddige. Built in Indo-Sarcenic style, the domed tombs are the resting place for Kodava royalty and dignitaries. Located 7km from town, an autorickshaw costs ₹200 return.

Abbi Falls
WATERFALLS

A spectacular sight after the rainy season, these 21.3m-high falls can pack a punch. It's ₹250 for a return autorickshaw, including stop off at Raja's Tombs.

🏃 Activities

Coorg is all about enjoying the outdoors, and a novel approach is to head up into the skies via a microlight flight with **Coorg Sky Adventures** (☏9448954384; www.coorgskyadventures.com; 10/30 min ₹2250/4850).

Ayurveda

★**Jiva Spa**
AYURVEDA

(☏0827-2665800; www.tajhotels.com/JivaSpas/index.html; Vivanta, Galibeedu) Surrounded by rainforest, the stunning Vivanta (p884) is *the* place to treat yourself with a range of rejuvenating treatments amid lavish atmosphere. Appointments essential.

Ayurjeevan
AYURVEDA

(☏224466; www.ayurjeevancoorg.com; Kohinoor Rd; 7.30am-7pm) Ayurjeevan, a short walk from ICICI Bank, is an ayurvedic 'hospital' that offers a whole range of intriguing and rejuvenating techniques; refer to its website for details. Hour-long treatments cost ₹900.

Swaasthaya Ayurveda Retreat Village
AYURVEDA

(www.swaasthya.com; Bekkesodlur Village; s/d incl full board & yoga class ₹2500/3500) For an exceptionally peaceful and refreshing ayurvedic vacation, head to south Coorg to soothe your soul among the lush greenery on 4 acres of coffee and spice plantations. To get here from Madikeri, catch a bus to Gonikoppa (1½ hours) from where you'll need to transer to a bus heading to Kutta and disembark at Bekkesodlur Village.

Trekking

Exploring the region by foot is a highlight for many visitors to the area that offers part cultural experience, part nature encounter. The best season for trekking is October to March; there are no treks during monsoon.

The most popular routes are to the peaks of Tadiyendamol (1745m) and Pushpagiri (1712m), and to smaller Kotebetta (1620m). As well as good walking shoes you'll need insect repellant. A trekking guide is essential for navigating the labyrinth of forest tracks.

V-Track
TREKKING

(☏229102, 229974; v_track@rediffmail.com; College Rd, opp Corporation Bank; 10am-2pm & 4.30-8pm Mon-Sat) Veteran guides Raja Shekhar and Ganesh can arrange one- to 10-day treks, which include guide, accommodation and food. Lodging is a mix of village homestays and basic huts. Rates are ₹950 to ₹1250 per person per day, depending upon group size.

Coorg Trails
TREKKING

(☏9886665459; www.coorgtrails.com; Main Rd; 9am-8.30pm) Another recommended outfit, Coorg Trails can arrange day treks around Madikeri for ₹450 per person, and a 16km trek to Kotebetta, including an overnight stay in a village (₹850 per person).

🛏 Sleeping & Eating

With fantastic guesthouses in the surrounding area, there's no real reason to stay in Madikeri; though you may have to a spend a night if you arrive late.

Hotel Chitra
HOTEL $

(☏225372; www.hotelchitra.net; School Rd; dm ₹200, d from ₹728, d with AC ₹1620; ❄) A short walk off Madikeri's main traffic intersection is this austere hotel, providing low-cost, no-frills rooms. The sheets are clean and service is efficient, which – coupled with its midtown location – makes it a good budget option.

Hotel Mayura Valley View
HOTEL $$

(☏228387; d incl breakfast from ₹1600; ❄) On a secluded hilltop past Raja's Seat, this government hotel is one of Madikeri's best, with large bright rooms and fantastic valley views. Its restaurant-bar with terrace overlooking the valley is a great spot for a beer.

★Coorg Cuisine
INDIAN $

(Main Rd; mains ₹70-90; noon-4pm & 7-10pm) Finally a place that makes an effort to serve regional dishes, cooking up unique Kodava specialities such as *pandhi barthadh* (pork dry fry) and *kadambuttu* (rice dumplings). It's above a shop on the 1st floor on the main road.

ℹ SPICE OF LIFE

If you have space in your bag, remember to pick up some local spices and natural produce from Madikeri's main market. There's a whole range of spices on offer at the shops lining the streets, including vanilla, nutmeg, lemongrass, pepper and cardamom, as well as the unbranded aromatic coffee that comes in from plantations. Sickly sweet homemade wines are also widely available.

Hotel Popular Guruprasad SOUTH INDIAN $
(Main Rd; mains ₹30-50; ⊙6.30am-9.30pm) A hearty range of vegie options, including a value-for-money veg thali (₹50) make this a favourite with the locals.

ℹ Information

Travel Coorg (☑ 321009; www.travelcoorg .in; outside KSRTC bus stand; ⊙24hr) provides excellent travel information, and can arrange homestays and guides.

State Bank of India (☑ 229959; College Rd) and **HDFC** (Racecourse Rd) have ATMs. **Cyber Inn** (Kohinoor Rd; per hour ₹20; ⊙9am-9pm) has internet access, opposite from Ayurjeebah.

ℹ Getting There & Away

Seven deluxe buses a day depart from the KSRTC bus stand for Bengaluru (fan/AC ₹315/450 six hours), stopping in Mysore (₹195, 3½ hours) en route. Deluxe buses go to Mangalore (₹169/250, four hours, three daily), while frequent ordinary buses head to Hassan (₹95, four hours) and Shimoga (₹210, eight hours).

The Plantations

Spread around Madikeri are Kodagu's quaint and leafy spice and coffee plantations. Numerous estates here offer 'homestays', which are actually more B&Bs (and normally closed during monsoon). Some high-end resorts have begun to spring up too.

🛏 Sleeping

★**Golden Mist** HOMESTAY $$
(☑ 08272-265629; www.golden-mist.net; Galibeedu; s/d incl full board ₹2500/4000; @) One of Coorg's finest plantation stays, the friendly Indian-German-managed Golden Mist has character-filled loft-style cottages on its lovely 26-acre property of rice paddies and tea-, coffee- and spice-plantations. Meals are tasty rustic veg and nonveg dishes made from the farm's organic produce, including homemade cheese and bread. Rates include nature walks and plantation tours. You'll need to bring your own alcohol. A rickshaw costs ₹150 from Madikeri.

Rainforest Retreat GUESTHOUSE $$
(☑ 08272-265639; www.rainforestours.com; Galibeedu; dm ₹1000; s/d tent ₹1500/2000; r from ₹2000/4000) 🖉 A nature-soaked refuge located on an organic plantation, the Rainforest Retreat is an NGO that devotes itself to exploring organic and ecofriendly ways of life. Organic farming, sustainable agriculture and waste management are catchphrases here; check the website for details. Accommodation is in tents and eco-chic cottages with solar power, and activities include plantation tours, birdwatching and treks. An autorickshaw from Madkeri is ₹200.

Honeypot Homes B&B $$
(☑ 9448720382; www.honeypothomes.com; off Bangalore Rd; d incl breakfast ₹4000; 🖀) Set over 225 acres of dense coffee and spice plantations, this quaint 'homestay' has three red-brick cottages that look out to lush surrounds. Walking tours and explanations of coffee production process is inclusive of rates. It's located 7km from Madikeri.

★**Vivanta** HOTEL $$$
(☑ 0827-665800; www.vivantabytaj.com; Galibeedu; r incl breakfast from ₹17,900; @🖀🏊) Another stunner by the Taj group, built across 180 acres of misty rainforest. Its stylish design incorporates principles of space and minimalism, and effectively blends itself into its environment. Old cattle tracks lead to rooms, with pricier ones featuring private indoor pools, fireplaces and butlers. Meanwhile the 9000 sq ft presidential suite, costing a cool lakh (₹100,000), is the size of a small village. Other highlights are its stunning views from the lobby and infinity pool, the outdoor amphitheatre surrounded by water, ayurvedic spa and Xbox room.

Kakkabe
☑ 08272

About 40km from Madikeri, the village of Kakkabe is an ideal base to plan an assault on Kodagu's highest peak, Tadiyendamol. At the bottom of the summit, 3km from Kakkabe, is the picturesque **Nalakunad Palace** (⊙9am-5pm) FREE, the restored hunting lodge of a Kodagu king dating from 1794. The caretaker will happily show you around; bring a torch.

The **Honey Valley Estate** (☏08272-238 339; www.honeyvalleyindia.in; d from ₹800) has a wonderful location 1250m above sea level where you can wake to a chirpy dawn and cool, fresh air. The owners' friendliness, eco-mindedness and scrumptious organic food make things even better. Run by the same family, **Chingaara** (☏08272-204488; www.chingaara.com; r incl full board from ₹1800) is a delightful farmhouse on the same road, with spacious rooms and roaming donkeys. Both are great bases for treks, and guides are available for ₹400. It's a rough, steep road up here, so you'll need to call ahead to arrange transport from Kabbinakad (inclusive in room rates).

Regular buses run to Kabbinakad from Madikeri (₹35, 1½ hours) and from Virajpet (₹20, one hour).

Belur & Halebid

☏0817 / ELEV 968M

The Hoysala temples at Halebid (also known as Halebeedu) and Belur (also called Beluru) are the apex of one of the most artistically exuberant periods of ancient Hindu cultural development. Architecturally, they are South India's answer to Khajuraho in Madhya Pradesh and Konark near Puri in Odisha (Orissa).

Only 16km lie between Belur and Halebid, they are connected by frequent buses from 6.30am to 7pm (₹20, 40 minutes).

To get here you'll need to pass through the busy transport hub of **Hassan** – easily accesible from Mysore and Bengaluru, with buses departing every half-hour to Mysore (₹96, three hours), Bengaluru (semideluxe/deluxe ₹155/340, four hours) and Mangalore (₹150, 340). From Hassan's well-organised train station, three passenger trains head to Mysore daily (2nd class ₹120, three hours). For Bengaluru, take the 1.30am Yeshvantpur Express (sleeper ₹140, 5½ hours). It's also possible to visit on day trip from Bengaluru with KSTDC (p861) offering tours.

Belur

The **Channakeshava Temple** (Temple Rd; admission free; ⊙7.30am-7.30pm) was commissioned in 1116 to commemorate the Hoysalas' victory over the neighbouring Cholas. It took more than a century to build, and is currently the only one among the three major Hoysala sites still in daily use – try to be there for the ritual *puja* ceremonies at around 8.45am and 6.45pm. Some parts of the temple, such as the exterior lower friezes, were not sculpted to completion and are thus less elaborate than those of the other Hoysala temples. However, the work higher up is unsurpassed in detail and artistry, and is a glowing tribute to human skill. Particularly intriguing are the angled bracket figures depicting women in ritual dancing poses. While the front of the temple is reserved for images depicting erotic sections from the Kama Sutra, the back is strictly for gods. The roof of the inner sanctum is held up by rows of exquisitely sculpted pillars, no two of which are identical in design.

Scattered around the temple complex are other smaller temples, a marriage hall which is still used, and the seven-storey *gopuram*, which has sensual sculptures explicitly portraying the activities of dancing girls.

Guides can be hired for ₹250; they help to bring some of the sculptural detail to life.

Hotel Mayura Velapuri (☏222209; Kempegowda Rd; d ₹950, with AC ₹1200; ❀), a state-run hotel gleaming with postrenovation glory, is located on the way to the temple, and is the best place to camp in Belur. The restaurant-bar serves a variety of Indian dishes and snacks (₹70 to ₹90) to go with beer. The cheaper **Sumukha Residency** (Temple Rd; d with fan/AC ₹500/700) is another option.

There's an Axis ATM on the road leading to the temple.

There are buses to/from Hassan (₹24, one hour), 38km away, every half-hour.

Halebid

Construction of the stunning **Hoysaleswara Temple** (admission free; ⊙dawn-dusk), Halebid's claim to fame, began around 1121 and went on for more than 190 years. It was never completed, but nonetheless stands today as a masterpiece of Hoysala architecture. The interior of its inner sanctum, chiselled out of black stone, is marvellous. On the outside, the temple's richly sculpted walls are covered with a flurry of Hindu deities, sages, stylised animals and friezes depicting the life of the Hoysala rulers. Two statues of Nandi (Shiva's bull) sit to the left of the main temple, facing the inner sanctum. Guides are available to show you around for ₹250.

BYLAKUPPE

Tiny Bylakuppe, 5km southeast of Kushalnagar, was among the first refugee camps set up in South India to house thousands of Tibetans who fled from Tibet following the 1959 Chinese invasion. Over 10,000 Tibetans live here (including some 3300 monks), making it South India's largest Tibetan settlement. The atmosphere is heart-warmingly welcoming, and home to much festivity during the **Tibetan New Year** (Bylakuppe; ⊙Feb) celebrations.

The area's highlight is the atmospheric **Namdroling Monastery** (www.palyul.org), home to the jaw-droppingly spectacular **Golden Temple** (Padmasambhava Buddhist Vihara; ⊙7am-8pm), presided over by three 18m-high gold-plated Buddha statues. The temple is at its dramatic best when prayer is in session and it rings out with gongs, drums and the drone of hundreds of young monks chanting. You're welcome to sit and meditate; look for the small blue guest cushions lying around. The **Zangdogpalri Temple** (⊙7am-8pm), a similarly ornate affair, is next door.

Foreigners are not allowed to stay overnight in Bylakuppe without a Protected Area Permit (PAP) from the Ministry of Home Affairs in Delhi, which can take up to five months to process. Contact the **Tibet Bureau Office** (☑11–26474798; www.tibetbureau.in; New Delhi) for details. Daytrippers are welcome to visit, however, and many base themselves in nearby Kushalnagar. If you have a permit, the simple **Paljor Dhargey Ling Guest House** (☑258686; pdguesthouse@yahoo.com; d from ₹350) is opposite the Golden Temple. There are many hotels in Kushalnagar, including **Iceberg** (☑9880260544; Main Rd; s/d from ₹550/750), with clean functional rooms, and located next door to a good veg restaurant.

For delicious momos or *thukpa* (noodle soup), pop into the Tibetan-run **Malaya Restaurant** (momos ₹60-90; ⊙7am-9pm).

Autorickshaws (shared/solo ₹10/40) run to Bylakuppe from Kushalnagar, 5km away. Buses frequently do the 34km run to Kushalnagar from Madikeri (₹40, 1½ hour) and Hassan (₹98, four hours). Most buses on the Mysore–Madikeri route stop at Kushalnagar.

The temple is set in large, well-tended gardens, adjacent to which is a small **museum** (admission ₹5; ⊙9am-5pm Sat-Thu) with a collection of beautiful sculptures from around Halebid.

Take some time out to visit the nearby, smaller **Kedareswara Temple**, or a little-visited enclosure containing three **Jain** temples about 500m away, which also have fine carvings.

Hotel Mayura Shanthala (☑273224; d ₹850), set around a leafy garden opposite the temple complex, is the best sleeping option.

Regular buses depart for Hassan (₹34, one hour), 33km away.

Sravanabelagola

☑08176

Atop the bald rock of Vindhyagiri Hill, the 17.5m-high statue of the Jain deity Gomateshvara (Bahubali), said to be the world's tallest monolithic statue, is visible long before you reach the pilgrimage town of Sravanabelagola. Viewing the statue close up is the main reason for heading to this sedate town, whose name means 'Monk of the White Pond'.

◉ Sights

Gomateshvara Statue   MONUMENT
(Bahubali; ⊙6.30am-6.30pm) **FREE** A steep climb up 614 steps takes you to the top of Vindhyagiri Hill, the summit of which is lorded over by the towering naked statue of the Jain deity Gomateshvara. Commissioned by a military commander in the service of the Ganga king Rachamalla and carved out of a single piece of granite by the sculptor Aristenemi in AD 981, its serenity and simplicity is in stark contrast to the Hoysala sites at Belur and Halebid.

Bahubali was the son of emperor Vrishabhadeva, who later became the first Jain *tirthankar* (revered teacher) Adinath. Embroiled in fierce competition with his brother Bharatha to succeed his father, Bahubali realised the futility of material gains and renounced his kingdom. As a recluse, he meditated in complete stillness in the forest until he attained enlightenment. His lengthy meditative spell is denoted by vines curling around his legs and an ant hill at his feet.

Leave shoes at the foot of the hill, but it's fine to wear socks.

Every 12 years, millions flock here to attend the **Mastakabhisheka** (☺Feb) ceremony, when the statue is dowsed in holy waters, pastes, powders, precious metals and stones. The next ceremony is slated for 2018.

Jain Temples
JAIN TEMPLES

Apart from the Bahubali statue, there are several interesting Jain temples in town. The **Chandragupta Basti** (Chandragupta Community; ☺6am-6pm), on Chandragiri Hill opposite Vindhyagiri, is believed to have been built by Emperor Ashoka. The **Bhandari Basti** (Bhandari Community; ☺6am-6pm), in the southeast corner of town, is Sravanabelagola's largest temple. Nearby, **Chandranatha Basti** (Chandranatha Community; ☺6am-6pm) has well-preserved paintings depicting Jain tales.

🛏 Sleeping & Eating

The local Jain organisation **SDJMI** (☑257258) handles bookings for its 15 guesthouses (d/tr ₹210/260). The office is behind the Vidyananda Nilaya Dharamsala, past the post office.

Hotel Raghu
HOTEL $

(☑257238; d from ₹500; ☺restaurant 6am-9pm; ❄) The only privately owned hotel around, offering basic but clean rooms. There's a vegetarian restaurant downstairs, which works up an awesome veg thali (₹50).

ⓘ Getting There & Away

There are no direct buses from Sravanabelagola to Hassan or Belur – you must go to Channarayapatna (₹41, 20 minutes) and catch an onward connection there. Three daily buses run direct to Bengaluru (₹120, 3½ hours) and Mysore (₹80 2½ hours). Long-distance buses clear out before 3pm. If you miss these, catch a local bus to Channarayapatna and change there.

A 3pm train heads to Hassan (₹7), 48km from Sravanabelagola, for onward travel to Mysore or Mangalore.

KARNATAKA COAST

Mangalore

📱 0824 / POP 484,785

Alternating from relaxed coastal town to hectic nightmare, Mangalore has a Jekyll and Hyde thing going, but it's a pleasant enough place to break up your trip. While there's not a lot to do here, it has an appealing off-the-beaten-path feel, and the spicy seafood dishes are sensational.

It sits at the estuaries of the picturesque Netravathi and Gurupur Rivers on the Arabian Sea coast and has been a major pit stop on international trade routes since the 6th century AD.

◉ Sights

Ullal Beach
BEACH

While it's no Om Beach, this stretch of golden sand is a good place to escape the city heat. It's best enjoyed from Summer Sands Beach Resort, which also has a pool for swimming (₹300). It's about an hour's drive south of town. An autorickshaw is ₹200 one way, or the frequent bus 44 (₹9) from the City bus stand will drop you right outside the gate.

St Aloysius College Chapel
CHURCH

(Lighthouse Hill; ☺9am-6pm) Catholicism's roots in Mangalore date back to the arrival of the Portuguese in the early 1500s, and one of the most impressive legacies is the 1880 Sistine Chapel–like St Aloysius chapel, with its walls and ceilings painted with brilliant frescoes.

Sultan's Battery
FORT

(Sultan Battery Rd; ☺6am-6pm) The only remnant of Tipu Sultan's fort is this small lookout with views over scenic backwaters. It's 4km from the city centre on the headland of the old port; bus 16 will get you there.

Kadri Manjunatha Temple
HINDU TEMPLE

(Kadri; ☺6am-1pm & 4-8pm) This Kerala-style temple houses a 1000-year-old bronze statue of Lokeshwara.

🛏 Sleeping

Hotel Manorama
HOTEL $

(☑2440306; KS Rao Rd; s/d from ₹530/650, with AC ₹884; ❄) A decent, centrally located budget option, with clean, good-value rooms and a lobby decked out with replicas of artifacts.

Mangalore

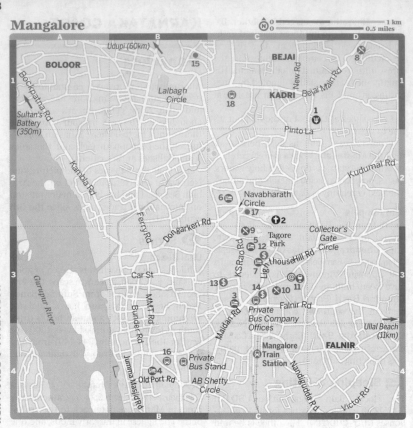

Mangalore

◎ Sights
1 Kadri Manjunatha Temple	D1
2 St Aloysius College Chapel	C2

⌂ Sleeping
3 Adarsh Hotel	C3
4 Gateway Hotel	B4
5 Hotel Manorama	C3
6 Hotel Ocean Pearl	C2
7 Nalapad Residency	C3

✗ Eating
8 Gajalee	D1
9 Janatha Deluxe	C3
Kadal	(see 7)

10 Lalith Bar & Restaurant	C3

◉ Drinking & Nightlife
11 Liquid Lounge	C3

ⓘ Information
12 HDFC	C3
13 ICICI Bank ATM	C3
14 State Bank of Mysore ATM	C3

ⓘ Transport
15 Air India	B1
16 City Bus Stand	B4
17 Jet Airways	C2
18 KSRTC Bus Stand	C1

Adarsh Hotel HOTEL $

(☎2440878; Market Rd; s/d ₹230/330) Long-established cheapie with very basic rooms, but it gets the job done and is well maintained.

Nalapad Residency HOTEL $$

(☎2424757; www.nalapad.com; Lighthouse Hill Rd; s/d incl breakfast from ₹800/1000; ☀) The best midrange option in Mangalore comes with spruce rooms featuring floor-to-ceiling win-

RANI ABBAKKA THE WARRIOR QUEEN

The legendary exploits of Rana Abbakka, one of India's first freedom fighters – who just so happens to be a female – is one that gets surprisingly little attention outside the Mangalore region. An Indian Joan of Arc, her inspiring story is just waiting to be picked up by a Bollywood/Hollywood screenwriter.

As the Portuguese consolidated its power along India's western coastline in the 16th century, seizing towns across Goa and down to Mangalore, their attempts to take Ullal proved more of a challenge. This was thanks to its 'fearless queen' who proved to be a major thorn in its grand plans to control the lucrative spice trade. Her efforts to continually repel their advances is the stuff of local legend.

Well trained in the art of war, both in strategy and combat, she knew how to brandish a sword, and while she was eventually defeated, this was a result of her treacherous ex-husband, who conspired against her in leaking intelligence to the enemy.

Her efforts to rally her people to defeat the powerful Portuguese is not forgotten by locals: she's immortalised in a bronze statue on horseback at the roundabout on the road to Ullal beach, and has an annual festival dedicated to her.

The shore temple that looks over the beautiful Someshwara beach a few kilometres south from Ullal was the former site of her fort, and only sections of its wall remains intact.

dows and heavy red curtains. The rooftop restaurant, **Kadal**, will spice up your stay with fantastic views.

Hotel Ocean Pearl HOTEL $$$
(☎ 2413800; www.theoceanpearl.in; Navabharath Circle; s/d from ₹4300/5280; ❄ @ ⌘) Designer hotel with mint-fresh rooms and all the creature comforts that are paraded by business hotels. Its **Jazz** bar is a good place for a drink.

Gateway Hotel HOTEL $$$
(☎ 6660420; www.tajhotels.com/gateway; Old Port Rd; s/d incl breakfast from ₹6570/7460; ❄ @ ⌘ ☀) From plasma TVs and beds laden with pillows to swimming pool surrounded by lawn and deck chairs, it's high standards across the board at this reliable four-star chain. No need to go beyond the standard rooms.

Summer Sands Beach Resort HOTEL $$$
(☎ 2467690; www.summersands.in; d from ₹5971; ❄ @ ☀) Set amid palm groves on a remote patch along Ullal Beach, Summer Sands offers a series of comfortable bungalows arranged in a tropical-resort-style setup. Its restaurant has a great seafood selection, but nonguests have to pay a ridiculous ₹100 to eat here.

✗ Eating & Drinking

Don't leave town without sampling Mangalorean delights such as masala fish fry smothered in saucy red coconut curry, or scrumptious deep-fried prawn *rawa* fry.

Janatha Deluxe SOUTH INDIAN $
(Hotel Shaan Plaza; mains ₹50-70; ⊙ 7am-11pm) A local favourite that serves tasty veg thali (₹70), and North and South Indian veg dishes in the comfort of air-con and cushioned seating.

Lalith Bar & Restaurant SEAFOOD $$
(Balmatta Rd; mains ₹150-400; ⊙ 11.30am-3.30pm & 6.30-11.30pm) First impressions can be deceiving, so ignore the divey basement decor and order the masala fish fry with a chilled beer and you'll instantly be transported to heaven. The day's special seafood is also a good choice.

Kadal SOUTH INDIAN $$
(Lighthouse Hill Rd, Nalapad Residency; mains ₹150-220; ⊙ 11.30am-3.30pm & 6.30-11pm) This high-rise restaurant has elegant and warmly lit interiors, with sweeping views all around. Try the spicy chicken *uruval* (a coconut coastal curry) or the yummy prawn ghee roast.

Gajalee SEAFOOD $$$
(www.gajalee.com/rest_mangalore.html; Circuit House, Kadri Hills; mains ₹150-1200; ⊙ 11am-3.30pm & 6.30-11pm) In a town famous for seafood, locals often cite this as the best. Its interior is fairly posh, while outdoor tables more low key.

Liquid Lounge PUB
(☎ 4255175; Balmatta Rd; ⊙ 7-11.30pm) A stiff Jack and Coke or a cold Corona will sort you

The Southern Shores

Pretty palm-fringed stretches of sun-warmed sand peering over shimmering waters. Welcome to India's southern peninsula, which is particularly famed for its bounty of beautiful beaches that make ideal spots to swap the hustle and bustle of India's dusty roads for the revivifying bliss of cool ocean waters.

JOHNNY HAGLUND / GETTY IMAGES ©

KIMBERLEY COOLE / GETTY IMAGES ©

1. Varkala's Papanasham beach (p954), Kerala
Stretch of sand framed by red laterite cliffs.

2. Middle Andaman (p1099), Andaman Islands
Island communities dot this isolated Indian outpost

3. Marina Beach (p1010), Chennai
Locals and travellers alike make this beach a colourful spot away from the city's hustle and bustle.

4. Palolem (p849), Goa
This colourful beach is a popular traveller enclave.

CLAUDE RENAULT / GETTY IMAGES ©

out at this trendy pub with funky posters and neon-lit interiors. Also does decent food.

ⓘ Information

State Bank of Mysore, **HDFC** and **ICICI Bank** have ATMs on Balmatta Rd and Lighthouse Hill Rd.

There's cheap internet cafes along **Balmatta Rd** (per hour ₹15) and near KSTRC bus station

ⓘ Getting There & Away

AIR

The airport is precariously perched atop a plateau in Bajpe, about 20km northeast of town. **Air India** (☑ 2451046; Hathill Rd), **Jet Airways** (☑ 2441181; KS Rao Rd, Ram Bhavan Complex) and **SpiceJet** (☑ 18001803333) all operate daily flights to Mumbai, Bengaluru, Hyderabad and Chennai.

BUS

The **KSRTC bus stand** (☑ 2211243; Bejai Main Rd) is on Bejai Main Rd, 3km from the city centre. Several deluxe buses depart every half-hour to Bengaluru (ordinary/semideluxe/deluxe ₹290/451/650, nine hours), via Madikeri (ordinary/semideluxe/deluxe ₹103/190, five hours) and Mysore every half-hour (ordinary/semideluxe/deluxe ₹220/320/396, seven hours). Semideluxe buses go to Hassan (₹175, five hours). A 10.30pm deluxe bus heads to Panaji (semideluxe/deluxe ₹440/586, seven hours).

From opposite the **City bus stand**, private buses connect Udupi (₹75, 1½ hours), Dharmasthala (₹55, 2½ hours) and Jog Falls. Buses to Gokarna (₹130, seven hours) depart at 11am and 1.30pm.

TRAIN

The main train station Mangalore Central is south of the city centre. The 6.25pm Malabar Express heads to Thiruvananthapuram (Trivandrum; sleeper/2AC ₹257/1085, 15 hours). The 9.30pm West Coast Express heads to Chennai (sleeper/2AC ₹317/1370, 18 hours).

Several Konkan Railway trains (to Mumbai, Margao, Ernakulam or Trivandrum) use Mangalore Junction (aka Kankanadi), 5km east of Mangalore. This includes the 12.20am Netravati Express, stopping at Margao in Goa (sleeper/2AC ₹214/800, 5½ hours) and continuing to Mumbai (sleeper/2AC ₹367/1620, 15 hours).

ⓘ Getting Around

To get to the airport, take buses 47B or 47C from the City bus stand, or catch a taxi (₹500).

Flag fall for autorickshaws is ₹20, and ₹13 per kilometre thereafter. For late-night travel, add 50%. An autorickshaw to Kankanadi station costs around ₹60, or take bus 9 or 11B.

Dharmasthala

Inland from Mangalore are a string of Jain temple towns, such as Venur, Mudabidri and Karkal. The most interesting among them is Dharmasthala, 75km east of Mangalore by the Netravathi River. Some 10,000 pilgrims pass through this town every day. During holidays and major festivals such as the five-day pilgrim festival of **Lakshadeepotsava** (Dharmasthala; ☉ Nov), the footfall can go up tenfold.

The **Manjunatha Temple** (☉ 6.30am-2pm & 5-9pm) is Dharmasthala's main shrine, devoted to the Hindu lord Shiva. Men have to enter with legs covered. Simple free meals are available in the temple's **kitchen** (☉ 11.30am-2.15pm & 7.30-10pm), attached to a hall that can seat up to 3000.

Associated sights in town include the 12m-high statue of Bahubali at Ratnagiri Hill, and the **Manjusha Museum** (admission ₹5; ☉ 9am-1pm & 4.30-9pm), which houses an eclectic collection of everything from artefacts to quirky collections of vintage cameras, telephones and typewriters (better than it sounds!). Don't forget to visit the fantastic **Car Museum** (admission ₹3; ☉ 8.30am-1pm & 2-7pm), home to 48 vintage autos, including a 1903 Renault, a 1920s Studebaker President used by Mahatma Gandhi and a 1951 Jaguar.

Should you wish to stay, contact the helpful **temple office** (☑ 08256-277121; www.shridharmasthala.org) for accommodation (per person ₹50) in pilgrim lodges.

There are frequent buses to Dharmasthala from Mangalore (₹55, 2½ hours).

Udupi (Udipi)

☑ 0820

Udupi is a buzzing yet relaxed pilgrim town that's home to the atmospheric 13th-century **Krishna Temple** (Car St; ☉ 3.30am-10pm), which draws thousands of Hindu pilgrims through the year. Surrounded by eight *maths* (monasteries), it's a hive of ritual activity, with musicians playing at the entrance, elephants on hand for *puja*, and pilgrims constantly passing through. Non-Hindus are welcome inside the temple; men must enter bare-chested. Elaborate rituals are also performed in the temple during the **Udupi Paryaya festival** (Udupi; ☉ Jan) (held every even year) in which outgoing swamiji

SURFING SWAMIS

While there's always been a spiritual bond between surfer and Mother ocean, the **Surfing Swamis** (☑9880659130; www.surfingindia.net; 6-64 Kolachikambla, Mulki; s/d incl full board from Rp2500/3000; ☎) at Mulki, 30km north of Mangalore, take things to a whole new plane. At this working ashram, which was established by its American guru who's been surfing since 1963 (and living in India for four decades), devotees follow a daily ritual of puja, chanting, mediation and a pure vegetarian diet in between catching barrels.

The best waves are May to June and September to October. The Swamis can also assist with information on surfing across India. Board hire is ₹500 per day (it also has bodyboards and stand-up paddleboards) and lessons are ₹1500 per day.

Accommodation is pricey , but it has a homely beach-house feel, and rates include meals.

All are welcome to visit, but it's important to be aware it's strictly a place of worship and there are guidelines to abide by, including no alcohol and refraining from sex during their stay. See the website for more details.

of each of the eight *math* transfer duties to new swamiji.

There are several pilgrim hotels near the temple including **Shri Vidyasamuda Choultry** (☑2520820; Car St; r ₹150), but they're often booked out. The smartest choice is **Hotel Sriram Residency** (☑2530761; www.hotelsriramresidency.com; r with fan/AC ₹780/1445) with a fantastic upstairs restaurant bar.

Udupi is famed for its vegetarian food, and recognised across India for its sumptuous thali; it's also the birthplace of the humble dosa. A good place to sample the local fare is the subterranean **Woodlands** (Dr UR Rao Complex; mains ₹60-90; ⊗8am-9.30pm), a short walk south of the temple.

ICICI (Car St) has an ATM near the temple.

Udupi is 58km north of Mangalore along the coast; regular buses ply the route (₹75, 1½ hours). Buses also head to Gokarna (₹170, six hours) and Bengaluru (₹350/500/720, 10 hours). Regular buses head to Malpe (₹7).

Malpe
☑0820

A laid-back fishing harbour on the west coast 4km from Udupi, Malpe has nice beaches ideal for flopping about in the surf. A good place to stay is the **Paradise Isle Beach Resort** (☑2538777; www.thepara diseisle.com; s/d from ₹1300/1500, with AC ₹3000/3500; ❀@☎☒); ask for a room with a sea view. It can also organise **houseboat cruises** (per couple ₹4000; ⊗Oct-Mar) on back-

waters that are similarly scenic to Kerala's, yet untouched by tourism.

From Malpe pier you can take a boat (₹100 return, 45 minutes) every 30 minutes from 9.30am to 5.30pm out to tiny **St Mary's Island**, where Vasco da Gama supposedly landed in 1498. Over weekends the island is busy with locals inspecting the curious hexagonal basalt formations that jut out of the sand; during the week you might have it to yourself. No boats run between June and mid-October.

Buses to Udupi are ₹7, and an autorickshaw ₹70.

Jog Falls
☑08186

Nominally the highest waterfalls in India, the Jog Falls only come to life during the monsoon. At other times, the Linganamakki Dam further up the Sharavati River limits the water flow and spoils the show. The tallest of the four falls is the Raja, which drops 293m.

To get a good view of the falls, bypass the scrappy area close to the bus stand and hike to the foot of the falls down a 1200-plus step path. Watch out for leeches during the wet season.

Jog Falls has buses roughly every hour to Shimoga (₹65, three hours), and three daily to Karwar via Kumta (₹25, three hours), where you can change for Gokarna (₹21, one hour). For Mangalore, change at Shimoga. A return taxi from Gokarna will cost around ₹1800.

FORMULA BUFFALO

Call it an indigenous take on the Grand Prix. Kambla, or traditional buffalo racing, is a hugely popular pastime among villagers along the southern Karnataka coast. Popularised in the early 20th century and born out of local farmers habitually racing their buffaloes home after a day in the fields, the races have now hit the big time. Thousands of spectators attend each edition, and racing buffaloes are pampered and prepared like thoroughbreds.

Kambla events are held between November and March, usually on weekends. Parallel tracks are laid out in a paddy field, along which buffaloes hurtle towards the finish line. In most cases the man rides on a board fixed to a ploughshare, literally surfing his way down the track behind the beasts.

Keep your cameras ready, but don't even think of getting in the buffaloes' way to take that prize-winning photo. The faster creatures can cover the 120m-odd distance through water and mud in around 14 seconds!

Gokarna

☑ 08386

A regular nominee among travellers' favorite beaches in India, Gokarna is a more laid-back and less-commercialised version of Goa. It attracts a crowd for a low-key, chilled-out beach holiday and not full-scale parties. Most accommodation is in thatched bamboo huts set along several stretches of blissful coast.

In actual fact there are two Gokarnas. Foremostly it's a sacred Hindu pilgrim town, full of ancient temples and important festivals such as **Shivaratri** (☺Feb/Mar) and **Ganesh Chaturthi** (Gokarna; ☺Sep). While its lively bazaar is an interesting place to visit, 99% of foreign tourists don't hang around here, instead making a bee-line straight to the adjoining beaches.

◉ Sights & Activities

◉ Temples

Foreigners and non-Hindus are not allowed inside Gokarna's temples. However, there are plenty of colourful rituals to be witnessed around town. At the western end of Car St is the **Mahabaleshwara Temple**, home to a revered lingam (phallic representation of Shiva). Nearby is the **Ganapati Temple**, while at the other end of the street is the **Venkataraman Temple**. About 100m further south is **Koorti Teertha**, the large temple tank (reservoir) where locals, pilgrims and immaculately dressed Brahmins perform their ablutions next to washermen on the ghats (steps or landings).

◉ Beaches

Popular with local tourists, Gokarna's 'town beach' is dirty, and not meant for casual bathing. A short walk north along here will bring you to a nicer stretch of sand with some basic bungalow accommodation. **Co-copelli Surf School** (☑8105764969; www.cocopelli.org) can arrange board rental (₹750) and surf lessons (1½ hour ₹1000).

The best beaches are due south of Gokarana town, with Om Beach and Kudle Beach being the most popular.

Don't walk around the paths after dark, and not alone at any time – it's easy to slip or get lost, and muggings have occurred.

OM BEACH

Gokarna's most famous beach twists and turns over several kilometres in a way that's said to resemble the outline of an Om symbol. It's a great mix of lovely long beach and smaller shady patches of sand, perfect for sunbathing and swimming. There's plenty of guesthouses and beach shack restaurants. It's a 20-minute walk to Kudle Beach, while an autorickhaw to Gokarana town is about ₹150.

KUDLE BEACH

Also lined with rows of restaurants and guesthouses, Kudle Beach has emerged as a popular alternative to Om Beach. It's Gokarna's longest and widest beach, with plenty of room to stretch out on its attractive sands. Unfortunately the odd jet-ski marrs what's an otherwise perfect beach.

It's a 20-minute hike from both Gokarna town or Om Beach along a path that heads atop along the barren headland with expansive sea views. Otherwise it's a ₹60 rickshaw ride to town.

HALF MOON & PARADISE BEACH

Well hidden away south of Om Beach lie the small sandy coves of Half Moon Beach and Paradise Beach. Half Moon is the more attractive of the two, with a lovely sweep of powdery sand, and basic hut accommodation. Paradise Beach is a mix of sand and rocks, and a haven with the long-term 'turn-on-tune-in-drop-out' crowd. However, unfortunate developments at time of research had seen the government destroying all the huts out this way, leaving it in a ramshackle state.

From Om Beach, these beaches are a 30-minute and one-hour walk, respectively. Watch out for snakes along the path and don't walk it after dark. A fishing boat (which can fit 10 people) from Om Beach will cost around ₹700.

🛏 Sleeping & Eating

With a few exceptions, the choice here is basic, but perfectly comfortable, beach shacks. Most close May to August.

There are also rudimentary huts (₹150) at Half Moon and north along Gorkana Beach. In town, there's slightly more comfortable concrete rooms, but they're lacking in atmosphere.

🛏 Om Beach

Om Shree Ganesh　　　BUNGALOWS **$**
(☑8386257310; www.omshreeganesh.com; hut ₹500, without bathroom ₹300) A winning combination of cheap bungalows, friendly management and beachside location makes this place justifiably popular. It's atmospheric double-storey restaurant rocks at night and does tasty dishes such as tandoori prawns, mushroom tikka and *momos*.

Sangham　　　BUNGALOWS **$**
(☑9448101099; r with/without bathroom ₹400/200) A blissful spot overlooking the water, with sandy path leading to the bungalows out the back among banana trees, life's definitely a beach at Sangham.

Dolphin Shanti　　　GUESTHOUSE **$**
(☑973962790; r from ₹150) Occupying the last plot of land on Om Beach, this mellow guesthouse sits perched upon the rocks with fantastic ocean views, and lives up to its name with dolphins often spotted. It's run by a friendly family and rooms are basic yet appealing.

Nirvana Café　　　GUESTHOUSE **$**
(☑329851; d ₹250, cottage ₹400-600; @) Located on the southern end of Om, Nirvana has el cheapo huts and spacious cottages set among a shady garden. Has internet for ₹40 per hour.

Namaste Café　　　GUESTHOUSE **$**
(☑257141; Om Beach; s/d ₹300/936, r with AC ₹2000; ❄@) This well-established guesthouse at the beginning of Om has slightly overpriced rooms, but a good choice for those wanting air-con. Its popular open-air restaurant has cold beer and dreamy sea views.

★SwaSwara　　　HOTEL **$$$**
(☑257132, 0484-3011711; www.swaswara.com; Om Beach; s/d 5 nights €1725/18755; ❄@🛜🏊) One of South India's finest retreats, this health resort offers a holiday based around yoga and ayurveda. No short stays are possible, but once you've set eyes upon its elegant private villas – some with forest views, others with river – you'll be happy to stay put. All have small garden courtyards full of basil and lemongrass, open-air showers and lovely sitting areas. There's an interactive kitchen here, and the artists in residence can help you hone your creative skills. Rates also include transport from Goa, leisure activities and daily yoga sessions.

Dolphin Bay Cafe　　　MULTICUISINE **$**
(mains ₹60-180; ⊗8am-10pm) Literally plonked on the beach. Dolphin Bay is your classic chilled-out shack restaurant that's what makes Gokarna so great.

🛏 Kudle Beach

Sea Rock Cafe　　　GUESTHOUSE **$**
(☑7829486382; r from ₹300) Yet more chilled-out bungalows, but this one with an option of more-comfortable rooms, and a beachside restaurant where the good times roll.

Ganga Guesthouse　　　GUESTHOUSE **$**
(☑08386257195; r from ₹250 ; @🛜) Occupying the last spot on Kudle, relaxed Ganga is a perennial favourite. Has internet and wi-fi (per hour ₹50).

Goutami Prasad　　　GUESTHOUSE **$**
(☑9379481358; huts from ₹150, r ₹500) Relaxed, family-run guesthouse with a prime spot in the centre of Kudle Beach. Choose between basic huts with sandy floors or more comfortable concrete rooms.

KARNATAKA & BENGALURU GOKARNA

Gokarna

Kamat Lodge
GUESTHOUSE $

(📠256035; Main St; s/d/tr ₹275/500/675, s/d with AC ₹1175/1325; ❄) On Gokarna's main drag, Kamat has clean rooms with fresh sheets and large windows. But don't expect room service and other such fluffs.

Shastri Guest House
GUESTHOUSE $

(📠256220; narasimha.shastri@gmail.com; Main St; s/d/tr ₹150/250/350) A hostel-like place with good, airy doubles in the new block out back. The singles are cramped, though.

🛍 Shopping

Shree Radhakrishna Bookstore
BOOKS

(🕐10am-6pm) A good selection of second-hand novels, postcards and maps

ℹ Information

Axis Bank (Main St)

SBI (Main St, Gorkana Town) Has an ATM.

Shama Internet Centre (Car St; per hr ₹40; 🕐10am-11pm) Fast internet connections.

Sub Post Office (1st fl, cnr Car & Main Sts; 🕐10am-4pm Mon-Sat)

ℹ Getting There & Away

Be aware that trains arriving from Mumbai or Goa, and private buses from Hampi/Hospet, may get you into Gokarna at the ungodly hour of 3am, so it might be worth notifying your guesthouse to see if there's someone who can check you in.

BUS

From the KSRTC bus stand, buses roll to Madgaon in Goa (₹100, four hours) at 8.15am or otherwise to Karwar (₹33, 1½ hours), which has connections to Goa. There are buses to Hospet (₹240, nine hours) for Hampi, Bengaluru (from ₹415, 12 hours) and Mangalore (₹200, 6½ hours), to Kunda (₹25) for Jog Falls (₹100) and frequent direct buses run to Hubli (₹134, four hours).

TRAIN

Many express trains stop at Gokarna Rd station, 9km from town; however, double check your ticket as some stop at Ankola, 26km away. Many of the hotels and small travel agencies in Gokarna can book tickets.

The 3am Matsyagandha Express goes to Mangalore (sleeper ₹200, 3½ hours); the return train leaves Kumta around 6pm for Margao (sleeper ₹200, 2½ hours) and Mumbai.

Autorickshaws charge ₹250 to go to Gokarna Rd station (or ₹500 from Ankola); a bus charges ₹35 and leaves every 30 minutes.

CENTRAL KARNATAKA

Hampi

📞 08394

Unreal and bewitching, the forlorn ruins of Hampi dot an unearthly landscape that will leave you spellbound the moment you cast your eyes on it. Heaps of giant boulders perch precariously over miles of undulating terrain, their rusty hues offset by jade-green palm groves, banana plantations and paddy fields. A World Heritage Site, Hampi is a place where you can lose yourself among wistful ruins, or simply be mesmerised by the vagaries of nature.

Hampi is a major pit stop on the traveller circuit; November to March is the high season. While it's possible to see the main sites in a day or two, this goes against Hampi's relaxed grain. Plan on lingering for a while.

The main travellers' ghetto is Hampi Bazaar, a village crammed with budget lodges, shops and restaurants, and towered over by the majestic Virupaksha Temple. Across the river is also popular, a more tranquil setting that's love at first sight for many a traveller.

The Vijaya Utsav (p854) festival in January is a good time to visit, with three day spectacle of dance, music, puppetry and a grand finale procession. The **Virupaksha Car Festival** (🕐Mar/Apr) in March/April is another big event, a colourful procession characterised by a giant wooden chariot (the temple car from Virupaksha Temple) being pulled along the main strip of Hampi bazaar.

History

Hampi and its neighbouring areas find mention in the Hindu epic Ramayana as Kishkinda, the realm of the monkey gods. In 1336 Telugu prince Harihararaya chose Hampi as the site for his new capital Vijayanagar, which – over the next couple of centuries – grew into one of the largest Hindu empires in Indian history. By the 16th century it was a thriving metropolis of about 500,000 people, its busy bazaars dabbling in international commerce, brimming with precious stones and merchants from faraway lands. All this, however, ended in a stroke in 1565, when a confederacy of Deccan sultanates razed Vijayanagar to the ground, striking it a death blow from which it never recovered.

⊙ Sights

Set over 36 sq km, there are some 3700 monuments to explore here, and it would take months if you were to do it justice. The ruins are divided into two main areas: the Sacred Centre, around Hampi Bazaar; and the Royal Centre, towards Kamalapuram.

Be aware that the ₹250 ticket for Vittala Temple entitles you to same-day admission into most of the paid sites across the ruins, so don't lose your ticket.

Virupaksha Temple
HINDU TEMPLE

(Map p900; admission ₹2, camera ₹50; ⊙ dawn-dusk) The focal point of Hampi Bazaar is the Virupaksha Temple, one of the city's oldest structures, and Hampi's only remaining working temple. The main *gopuram,* almost 50m high, was built in 1442, with a smaller one added in 1510. The main shrine is dedicated to Virupaksha, an incarnation of Shiva.

If Lakshmi (the **temple elephant**) and her attendant are around, she'll smooch (bless) you for a coin. The adorable Lakshmi gets her morning bath at 8am, just down the way by the river ghats.

To the south, overlooking Virupaksha Temple, **Hemakuta Hill** has a few early ruins, including monolithic sculptures of Narasimha (Vishnu in his man-lion incarnation) and Ganesha. At the east end of Hampi Bazaar is a monolithic **Nandi statue** (Map p900), around which stand colonnaded blocks of the ancient marketplace. Overlooking the site is Matanga Hill, whose summit affords dramatic views of the terrain at sunrise. The Vijaya Utsav (p854) festival is held at the base of the hill in January.

Vittala Temple
HINDU TEMPLE

(Map p898; Indian/foreigner ₹10/250; ⊙ 8.30am-5.30pm) The undisputed highlight of the Hampi ruins, the 16th-century Vittala Temple stands amid the boulders 2km from Hampi Bazaar. Though a few cement scaffolds have been erected to keep the main structure from collapsing, the site is in relatively good condition.

Work possibly started on the temple during the reign of Krishnadevaraya (r 1509-29). It was never finished or consecrated, yet the temple's incredible sculptural work remains the pinnacle of Vijayanagar art.

The ornate **stone chariot** that stands in the courtyard is the temple's showpiece and represents Vishnu's vehicle with an image of Garuda within. Its wheels were once capable of turning.

The outer 'musical' pillars reverberate when tapped, which supposedly were designed to replicate 81 different Indian instruments, but authorities have placed them out of tourists' bounds for fear of further damage, so no more do-re-mi. As well as the main temple, whose sanctum was illuminated using a design of reflective waters, here you'll find the marriage hall and prayer hall the structures to the left and right upon entry, respectively.

Sule Bazaar
HISTORIC SITE

(Map p898) Halfway along the path from Hampi Bazaar to the Vittala Temple, a track to the right leads over the rocks to deserted Sule Bazaar, one of ancient Hampi's principal centres of commerce and reputedly the red-light district. At the southern end of this area is the atmospheric, deserted Achyutaraya Temple.

Royal Centre
HISTORIC SITE

While it can be accessed by a 2km foot trail from the Achyutaraya Temple, the Royal Centre is best reached via the Hampi–Kamalapuram road. A number of Hampi's major sites stand here.

The **Mahanavami-diiba** (Map p898) is a 12m-high three-tired platform with intricate carvings and panoramic vistas of the walled complex of ruined temples, stepped tanks and the King's audience hall. The platform was used as Royal viewing area for the Dasara festivities, religious ceremonies and processions.

Further along is the **Hazarama Temple** (Map p898), with exquisitive carvings that depict scenes from the Ramayana, and polished black granite pillars.

Northeast from here within the walled ladies' quarters is the **Zenana Enclosure** (Map p898; Indian/foreigner ₹10/250; ⊙ 8.30am-5.30pm). Its peaceful grounds and lush lawns feel like an oasis amid the arid surrounds. Here is the **Lotus Mahal** (Map p898), a delicately designed pavilion which was supposedly the queen's recreational mansion. It overlooks the 11 grand **Elephant Stables** (Map p898; ⊙ 8.30am-5.30pm) with arched entrances and domed chambers. There's also a small museum and army barracks within the high-walled enclosure.

Further south, you'll find various temples and elaborate waterworks, including the **Queen's Bath** (Map p898; ⊙ 8.30am-5.30pm),

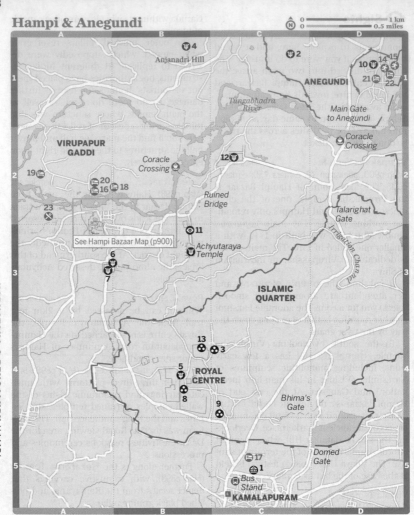

deceptively plain on the outside but amazing within, with its Indo-Islamic architecture.

Other interesting stop offs along the road to the Virupaksha Temple is the 6.7m monolithic statue of the bulging-eyed **Lakshimi Narasmiha** (Map p898) in a cross-legged yoga position and topped by a hood of seven snakes. Nearby is the **Krishna Temple** (Map p898) built in 1513, which is fronted by a D-cupped apsara and 10 incarnations of Vishnu

Archaeological Museum   MUSEUM
(Map p898; Kamalapuram; ⏰10am-5pm Sat-Thu) Worth popping in for its quality collection

of sculptures from local ruins, plus neolithic tools, fascinating coins, 16th-century weaponry and a large floor model of the Vijayanagar ruins.

Hampi Heritage Gallery   GALLERY
(Map p900; ⏰10am-1pm & 3-6pm Tue-Sun) Books and photo albums on Hampi's history and architecture, and can arrange walking tours.

 Activities

Get in touch with Kishkinda Trust (p902) for info on activities in the region.

Hampi & Anegundi

Rock Climbing ROCK CLIMBING
(Around Hampi) Hampi is the undisputed bouldering capital of India. The entire landscape is a climber's adventure playground made of granite crags and boulders, some bearing the marks of ancient stonemasons. **Tom & Jerry** (☏9481093862, 9482746697; luckykoushik1@gmail.com; Virupapur Gaddi; 3hr class ₹350) are two local lads who are doing great work in catering to climbers' needs, providing quality mats, shoes and local knowledge. They can also organise all-inclusive bouldering trips to Badami for ₹1600. Challenging rock faces can also be found in Ramnagar, 40km south of Bengaluru, Savandurga, 50km west of the capital, and Turahalli, on Bengaluru's southern outskirts.

🛏 Sleeping

Most guesthouses are cosy family-run digs, perfect for the budget traveller. A handful of places also have larger, more-comfortable rooms with air-con and TV. If you're needing something more comfortable, Hospet has more upmarket options.

🛏 Hampi Bazaar

★**Padma Guest House** GUESTHOUSE $
(Map p900; ☏241331; padmaguesthouse@gmail.com; d from ₹500-800, with AC from ₹1600; 🛜) In a quiet corner of Hampi Bazaar, the astute and amiable Padma has basic but squeaky-clean rooms and is a pleasant deviation from Hampi's usual offerings. Those on the 1st floor have good views of the Virupaksha Temple, while new rooms have creature comforts of TV and air-con. There's free wi-fi downstairs.

Archana Guest House GUESTHOUSE $
(Map p900; ☏241547; addihampi@yahoo.com; d from ₹500, with AC ₹1200; ❄@🛜) At the end of a lane on the riverfront, quiet and cheerful Archana is another friendly family-run affair, that makes for a fantastic budget choice. Decent rooms are painted in vivid purple and green, and there's a lovely rooftop hangout.

Pushpa Guest House GUESTHOUSE $
(Map p900; ☏9948795120; pushpaguesthouse99@yahoo.in; d from ₹750, with AC from ₹1100; ❄) A top all-round option, Pushpa is a bit pricier than others, but it gets you a comfortable room and an extremely cordial family playing host. It has a lovely sit-out on the 1st floor, and a reliable travel agency.

Gopi Guest House GUESTHOUSE $
(Map p900; ☏241695; www.gopiguesthouse.com; r ₹500-700; @🛜) Centrally located amid the bustle of the bazaar, this pleasant dive continues to provide commendable service to travellers. The new block is quite upscale for Hampi's standards, with ensuite rooms fronted by a sun-kissed terrace. The rooftop cafe – with a lovely view of the Virupaksha Temple – is a nice place to hang out.

Ranjana Guest House GUESTHOUSE $
(Map p900; ☏241696; r from ₹800, with AC ₹1200) Run by a friendly, tight-knit family, Ranjana is slightly overpriced, but it prides itself on well-appointed rooms and killer temple-views from its terrace.

Vicky's GUESTHOUSE $
(Map p900; ☏241694; vikkyhampi@yahoo.co.in; r ₹520; 🛜) An old faithful with decent rooms, rooftop cafe and free wi-fi.

Hampi Bazaar

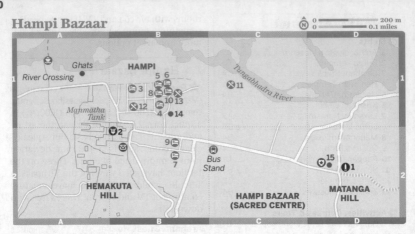

Hampi Bazaar

◎ Sights
1 Nandi Statue..D2
2 Virupaksha Temple B2

🛏 Sleeping
3 Archana Guest House.......................... B1
4 Gopi Guest House................................. B1
5 Kiran Guest House................................. B1
6 Netra Guesthouse................................. B1
7 Padma Guest House.............................B2
8 Pushpa Guest House............................ B1
9 Ranjana Guest House...........................B2
10 Vicky's B1

✕ Eating
11 Garden Paradise C1
12 Prince Restaurant................................. B1
13 Ravi's Rose... B1

ℹ Information
14 Akash Art Gallery & Bookstore........... B1
15 Hampi Heritage Gallery.......................D2
 Internet..(see 10)
 Tourist Office...............................(see 2)

Kiran Guest House   GUESTHOUSE $
(Map p900; ☎9448143906; kiranhampi2012@
gmail.com; r ₹400-600) Chilled-out guesthouse
on the riverfront and banana groves.

Netra Guesthouse   GUESTHOUSE $
(Map p900; ☎9483419731; r from ₹300, without
bathroom from ₹200) Basic but relaxed option
for shoestringers.

🛏 Virupapur Gaddi

Many travellers prefer the tranquil atmosphere of Virupapur Gaddi, across the river
from Hampi Bazaar.

Sunny Guesthouse   GUESTHOUSE $
(Map p898; ☎9448566368; www.sunnyguest-
house.com; r ₹200-750; @🛜) Sunny both in
name and disposition, this popular guesthouse is a hit among backpackers for its
cheap rooms, tropical garden, hammocks
and chilled-out restaurant. It has a good
choice of rooms, all with attached bathroom.

Shanthi   GUESTHOUSE $
(Map p898; ☎9449260162; www.shanthihampi.
com; r without bathroom ₹200, cottage ₹500-1650;
@🛜) Shanthi's earth-themed, thatched
cottages have sublime rice-field, river and
sunset views, with couch swings dangling
on their front porches. The restaurant does
good thalis and pizzas.

Manju's Place   GUESTHOUSE $
(Map p898; ☎9449247712; r ₹300, without bathroom from ₹100) The place for those who like
things quiet, with a bucolic setting among
rice fields and nearby boulders. Its attractive
mud-brick huts are wonderful, and overall a
top spot to chill out.

Durga Huts   GUESTHOUSE $
(Map p898; ☎9482051515; durgahuts@yahoo.com;
huts without bathroom ₹100, r ₹700) Relocating
across the river following Hampi Bazaar
being bulldozed, Durga's new offering is basic thatched huts with hammocks, that are
perfect for those watching their rupees. Its
restaurant gets good reviews.

Kamalapuram

Hotel Mayura Bhuvaneshwari HOTEL **$$**
(Map p898; 241474; s/d from ₹1200/1500; ❈)
This tidy government operation, about 3km
south of the Royal Centre, has well-appoint-
ed rooms, a lovely big garden, a much-ap-
preciated beer bar, and good multicuisine
restaurant.

Eating

Due to Hampi's religious significance, meat
is strictly off the menu in all restaurants,
and alcohol is banned (though some restau-
rants can order it for you).

★ **Garden Paradise** INDIAN, MULTICUISINE **$**
(Map p900; mains from ₹120) Not only does it
have a sublime riverside location, but easily
the best food. Dine on outdoor tables under
shady mango trees or indoors on cushions
and psychedelic murals. It does the best piz-
zas outside Bangalore, while the signature
paneer lavadar in creamy spinach sauce
and cashews is unbelievable. Breakfasts
are good too, with vegemite or marmite on
toast, strong coffee and excellent juices. Also
has accommodation here.

Ravi's Rose MULTICUISINE **$**
(Map p900; mains from ₹70) This slightly
sketchy rooftop-restaurant is the bazaar's
most social hangout, with a good selection
of dosas, but most are here for the, erm,
tasty lassis (cough, cough). It's built into a
rockface, where you can scramble through
under boulders to get incredible sunset
views.

Laughing Buddha MULTICUISINE **$**
(mains from ₹100; ☻8am-10pm) The other side
of the river's equivalent to the Mango Tree,
with serene river views that span beyond to
the temples and ruins. Its menu is curries,
burgers, pizzas, you know the drill...

Mango Tree MULTICUISINE **$$**
(Map p898; mains ₹80-150; ☻7.30am-9.30pm)
Creativity blends with culinary excellence at
this legendary rural-themed chill-out joint,
spread out under the eponymous mango tree
by the river. Once a haven for hippies, now
it's equally popular with Indian families. The
terraced seating is perfect for whiling away a
lazy afternoon, book in hand. Walk through
a banana plantation to get here, and try the
special vegetable curry or the spaghetti with
cashew nuts and cheese (₹100).

OUT OF HARM'S WAY

Hampi Bazaar is an extremely safe
area, but do not wander around the ruins after dark or alone. It's a dangerous
terrain to get lost in; long-time guides
have even sighted sloth bears prowling
around Vittala Temple at night!

Local laws require all foreign travellers to report to the police station (Map
p900) with their passports upon arrival, and notify the authorities about
their proposed duration of stay.

Prince Restaurant MULTICUISINE **$$**
(Map p900; mains ₹70-180; ☻7.30am-10pm)
Food here takes ages to arrive, so thankfully
this atmospheric shady hut is a good place
to chill out with cushioned seating on the
floor. Does *momos*, pizzas etc.

Shopping

Akash Art Gallery & Bookstore BOOKS
(Map p900; ☻6am-9pm) Stocks an excellent
selection of books on Hampi and India, plus
secondhand fiction. It has a free Hampi
map.

Information

There's no ATM in Hampi; the closest is 3km
away in Kamalapuram – a ₹100 autorickshaw
return trip.

Internet (per hour Rs40) is ubiquitous in
Hampi Bazaar; some guesthouses have paid
wi-fi. A good tourist resource for Hampi is www.
hampi.in.

Tourist Office (Map p900; 241339; ☻10am-
5.30pm Sat-Thu) Dingy office inside Virupaskha
Temple has brochures and can arrange guides
for ₹600/1000 for a half-/full day.

Getting There & Away

A semideluxe bus connects Hampi Bazaar to
Bengaluru (₹434, eight hours) leaving at 8pm.
Overnight private sleeper buses ply to/from
Goa and Gokarna occasionally departing from
Hampi, but more likely Hospet. Numerous travel
agents in Hampi Bazaar book onward tickets or
arrange taxis.

The first bus from Hospet (₹15, 30 minutes,
half-hourly) is at 6.30am; the last one back
leaves Hampi Bazaar at 8.30pm. An autorick-
shaw costs ₹150 to ₹200.

Hospet is Hampi's nearest train station.

HAMPI BAZAAR

While in 1865 it was the Deccan sultanates who leveled Vijayanagar, today a different battle rages in Hampi between conservationists bent on protecting Hampi's architectural heritage and the locals who have settled there. In mid-2012 the master plan that had been in the works since mid-2000s, and which aims to classify all of Hampi's ruins as protected monuments, was finally put into action. Overnight many shops, hotels and homes in the bazaar were bulldozed, reducing the main strip to rubble overnight, as villagers who'd made the site a living monument were evicted.

While villagers were compensated with a small plot of land in Kaddirampur, 4km from the bazaar (where there is talk of new guesthouses eventually opening up), many locals remained displaced months later as they awaited their pay out.

So what does this mean for tourism, and are any guesthouses remaining in Hampi Bazaar? For now, thankfully little has changed in terms of tourist infrastructure. While at the time of research rubble from demolished buildings remained, and the main temple road resembled a bombed-out town, all hotels just back from the bazaar remained intact and the owners were confident of continuing to do so. There was talk, however, that height restrictions may be enforced, which would see three-storey buildings having to be cut back to two floors. This would mean a lot Hampi's appealing rooftop restaurants would disappear.

ⓘ Getting Around

Bicycles cost about ₹30 per day in Hampi Bazaar, while mopeds can be hired for around ₹100 to ₹150. Petrol is ₹90 a litre.

A small **boat** (Map p900; person/bicycle/motorbike ₹15/10/20; ⊙7am-6pm) shuttles frequently across the river to Virupapur Gaddi from 7am to 6pm. A large backpack will cost ₹5 extra, while a special trip after 6pm is ₹50 to ₹100 per person depending on how late you cross.

Walking the ruins is recommended too, but expect to cover at least 7km just to see the major sites. Autorickshaws and taxis are available for sightseeing, and will drop you as close to each of the major ruins as they can. Hiring an autorickshaw for the day costs ₹750.

Organised tours depart from Hospet.

Around Hampi

Anegundi

Across the Tungabhadra, about 5km northeast of Hampi Bazaar, sits Anegundi, an ancient fortified village that's part of the Hampi World Heritage Site but predates Hampi by way of human habitation. Gifted with a landscape similar to Hampi, quainter Anegundi has been spared the blight of commercialisation, and thus continues to preserve the local atmosphere minus the touristy vibe.

◉ Sights & Activities

Hindu Temples   HINDU TEMPLES

Mythically referred to as Kishkinda, the kingdom of the monkey gods, Anegundi retains many of its historic monuments, such as sections of its defensive wall and gates, and the **Ranganatha Temple** (Map p898; ⊙dawn-dusk) devoted to Rama. The whitewashed **Hanuman Temple** (Map p898; ⊙dawn-dusk), accessible by a 570-step climb up the Anjanadri Hill, has fine views of the rugged terrain around. Many believe this is the birthplace of the Hindu monkey god Hanuman. On the pleasant hike up, you'll be courted by impish monkeys, and within the temple you'll find a horde of chillum-puffing resident sadhus. Also worth visiting is the **Durga Temple** (Map p898; ⊙dawn-dusk), an ancient shrine closer to the village.

★Kishkinda

Trust   CULTURAL PROGRAMS, OUTDOOR ADVENTURE

(TKT; Map p898; ☑08533-267777; www.thekishkindatrust.org) ⊘ The Kishkinda Trust, an NGO that promotes sustainable tourism in Anegundi, organises activities such as rockclimbing, treks, visits to prehistoric cave paintings, canal tours, birdwatching and other community initiatives such as performing arts sessions. Mountain bikes are available for ₹250 per day. Volunteers are also accepted.

Banana Fibre
Craft Workshop HANDICRAFTS WORKSHOP
(Map p898; admission ₹10, camera ₹100 ; ⊙ 10am-
1pm & 2-5pm Mon-Sat) Watch on at this small
workshop as workers ply their trade making
a range of handicrafts and accesories using
the bark of a banana tree, and recycled materials. Of course they sell it all too.

🛏 Sleeping & Eating

A great place to escape the hippies in Hampi, Anegundi has fantastic homestays in
restored heritage buildings that provide a
lovely experience. The following are managed by Kishkinda Trust.

Peshagar Guest House GUESTHOUSE $
(Map p898; ☑ 09449972230; www.urammaher-
itagehomes.com; s/d ₹450/850) Six simple
rooms done up in rural motifs open around
a pleasant common area in this heritage
house–now–budget guesthouse, with lovely
courtyard garden.

TEMA Guest House GUESTHOUSE $
(Map p898; per person ₹350) The two rooms in
this village heritage house are decked out in
traditional style with plenty of colour and
cow dung floors. Has a full kitchen.

Champa Guest House GUESTHOUSE $
(Map p898; s/d incl breakfast ₹350/650) Champa
offers basic but pleasant accommodation in
two rooms, and is looked after by an affable
village family.

Uramma House GUESTHOUSE $$
(Map p898; www.urammaheritagehomes.com;
house incl full board for 4-persons ₹8000; 🖀) This
4th-century heritage house is a gem, with
traditonal-style rooms featuring boutique
touches throughout. It's a great deal for
groups, and has an attractive dining room,
rooftop area and even a butler!

★ Uramma Cottage COTTAGE $$$
(Map p898; ☑ 08533-267792; www.urammaher-
itagehomes.com; s/d incl full board ₹3700/5500;
❋🖀) Delightful thatched-roof cottages with
rustic farmhouse charm that are both comfortable and attractive. Each has outdoor
seating and hammocks, and there's a library
with good reading material for the relaxed
landscaped garden setting.

Hoova Craft Shop & Café CAFE $
(Map p898; mains ₹40-60; ⊙ 8.30am-9.30pm) A
lovely place for an unhurried flavoursome
local meal.

❶ Getting There & Away
Anegundi can be reached by crossing the river
on a coracle (₹10) from the pier east of the Vittala Temple. By far the most convenient way is to
hire a moped or bicycle (if you're feeling energetic) from Virupapur Gaddi, or get an autorickshaw
here for around ₹200.

Hospet
☑ 08394 / POP 206,159
The busy regional town of Hospet is the
main transport hub for Hampi. Unless
you're wanting to stay in an upmarket hotel,
few choose to linger in Hospet as it's a dusty,
unattractive town with not much going on.

🛏 Sleeping & Eating
Hotel Malligi HOTEL $$
(☑ 228101; www.malligihotels.com; Jabunatha
Rd; r ₹450-2680; ❋@❋) Hospet's premier
luxury option builds its reputation around
clean and well-serviced rooms, an aquamarine swimming pool and a good multicuisine restaurant. Also has some budget
rooms.

Royal Orchid HOTEL $$$
(☑ 300100; www.royalorchidhotels.com; r incl
breakfast ₹6890; ❋@🖀❋) If you're in

DAROJI SLOTH
BEAR SANCTUARY

About 30km south of Hampi, amid
a scrubby undulating terrain, lies
the **Daroji Sloth Bear Sanctuary**
(admission Indian/foreigner ₹50/300;
⊙1.30pm-6pm), which over 83 sq km
nurses a population of around 150 free-
ranging sloth bears. You have a very
good chance of spotting them, as
honey is slathered on the rocks to
coincide with visitors' arrival. However,
you can only see them from afar at the
viewing platform. Bring binoculars, or
basically there's no point turning up.
Generally 4pm to 6pm is the best time
to visit.

The sanctuary is also home to leopards, wild boars, hyenas, jackals and
others animals, but you're unlikely to
see anything other than peacocks. You'll
need to arrange transport to get here,
which should cost around ₹500 for an
autorickshaw and ₹1000 for a car.

Hospet seeking comfort, look no further than Royal Orchid with its plush business-hotel standards of wi-fi, flat-screen TVs, gym, four restaurants and bar. It's popular with package tourists, and staff here are professional.

Udupi Sri Krishna Bhavan   SOUTH INDIAN $
(Bus stand; mains ₹40-80; ⊙6am-11pm) Opposite the bus stand, this clean spot dishes out Indian vegie fare, including thalis for ₹45.

ⓘ Information

There are ATMs along the main drag and Shanbagh Circle. Internet joints are common, costing ₹40 per hour.

ⓘ Getting There & Away

BUS

The bus stand has services to Hampi every half-hour (₹15, 30 minutes). Several express buses run to Bengaluru (ordinary/deluxe ₹290/412, nine hours). Buses for Gokarna (₹315, eight hours) depart at 9.15am, or take a bus to Hubli (₹108, 4½ hours) and change. Two buses head to Badami (₹180, four hours) at 1pm and 1.30pm. There are frequent buses to Bijapur (₹210, six hours) and overnight services to Hyderabad (semideluxe/deluxe ₹435/654, 10 hours) at 8.30pm. For Mangalore or Hassan, take a morning
bus to Shimoga (₹240, five hours) and change there.

For Goa, **Paulo Travels** (☑0832-6637777) has a 7pm bus (₹355, 11 hours) via Gokarna (₹700 to ₹800), but arrives at Gokarana at the inconvenient time of 3am, so it's best to go with the KSTRC bus.

TRAIN

Hospet's train station is a ₹30 autorickshaw journey from town. The 5.30am Rayalaseema Express heads to Hubli (2nd class ₹120, 3½ hours). For Bengaluru, take the 8.40pm Hampi Express (sleeper/2AC ₹191/785, nine hours). Every Monday, Wednesday, Thursday and Saturday, a 6.30am express train heads to Vasco da Gama (sleeper/2AC ₹194/715, 8½ hours).

For Badami, catch a Hubli train to Gadag and change there.

Hubli

☑ 0836 / POP 943,857
Prosperous Hubli is a hub for rail routes for Mumbai, Bengaluru, Goa and northern Karnataka. The train station is a 15-minute walk from the old bus stand. Most hotels sit along this stretch.

🛏 Sleeping & Eating

Ananth Residency   HOTEL $$
(☑2262251; ananthresidencyhubli@yahoo.co.uk; Jayachamaraj Nagar; d from ₹1500; ✱) A comfortable option that sports a sleek business-hotel look and feel. Has good-value rooms and efficient service, and a cheerful restaurant with chilled beer.

Hotel Ajanta   HOTEL $
(☑2362216; Jayachamaraj Nagar; s/d from ₹300/400) This well-run place near the train station has basic, functional rooms. Its popular ground-floor restaurant serves delicious regional-style thalis for ₹35.

ⓘ Information

SBI has an ATM opposite the bus stand. On the same stretch are several internet cafes, charging around ₹30 per hour.

ⓘ Getting There & Away

AIR

From Hubli's basic airport, SpiceJet has daily flights to Bengaluru.

BUS

Buses stop briefly at the old bus stand before moving to the new bus stand 2km away. There are numerous semideluxe services to Bengaluru (semideluxe/AC Volvo/sleeper ₹352/401/600, 10 hours), Bijapur (₹180, six hours) and Hospet (₹164, 4½ hours). There are regular connections to Mangalore (₹300, 10 hours, several daily), Borivali in Mumbai (semideluxe/sleeper ₹515/780, 14 hours, four daily), Mysore (₹320, 10 hours, three daily), Gokarna (₹175, five hours, two daily) and Panaji (₹161, six hours, six daily).

Private deluxe buses to Bengaluru run from opposite the old bus stand.

TRAIN

From the train station, expresses head to Hospet (2nd class ₹120, 3½ hours, six daily), Bengaluru (sleeper/2AC ₹203/910, 11 hours, four daily) and Mumbai (sleeper/2AC ₹285/1215, 14 hours). The 11pm Hubli-Vasco Link Express goes to Goa (sleeper ₹153, six hours).

NORTHERN KARNATAKA

Badami

☑ 08357 / POP 26,000
Once the capital of the mighty Chalukya empire, today Badami is famous for its mag-

WALK ON THE WILD SIDE

Located in the jungles of the Western Ghats about 100km from Goa, emerging **Dandeli** is a wildlife getaway that promises close encounters with diverse exotic wildlife such as elephants, leopards, sloth bears, gaur, wild dogs and flying squirrels. It's a chosen birding destination too, with resident hornbills, golden-backed woodpeckers, serpent eagles and white-breasted kingfishers. Also on offer are a slew of adventure activities ranging from kayaking to bowel-churning white-water rafting on the swirling waters of the Kali River.

Kali Adventure Camp (☑ 08-25597944; www.junglelodges.com/index.php/resorts/kali.html; per person incl full board & activities Indian/foreigner from ₹2500/4000; ❋) offers accommodation in tented cottages and rooms, done up lavishly while adhering to eco-friendly principles.

Frequent buses connect Dandeli to both Hubli (₹50, two hours) and Dharwad (₹42, 1½ hours), with onward connections to Goa, Gokarna, Hospet and Bengaluru.

nificent rock-cut cave temples, and red sandstone cliffs that resemble the Wild West. While the dusty main road is an eyesore that will have you wanting to get the hell out of there, its backstreets are a lovely area to explore with old houses, carved wooden doorways, an occasional Chalukyan ruin and flocks of curious kids.

History

From about AD 540 to 757, Badami was the capital of an enormous kingdom stretching from Kanchipuram in Tamil Nadu to the Narmada River in Gujarat. It eventually fell to the Rashtrakutas, and changed hands several times thereafter, with each dynasty sculpturally embellishing Badami in their own way.

The sculptural legacy left by the Chalukya artisans in Badami includes some of the earliest and finest examples of Dravidian temples and rock-cut caves. During Badami's heydays, Aihole and Pattadakal served as trial grounds for new temple architecture; the latter is now a World Heritage Site.

◉ Sights

Cave Temples   CAVES
(Indian/foreigner ₹5/100, video camera ₹25; ⊙ 6am-6pm) Badami's highlight is its beautiful cave temples. Nonpushy and informed guides ask ₹300 for a tour of the caves. Late afternoon is the best time to visit. Watch out for pesky monkeys and don't carry food on you.

Cave one, just above the entrance to the complex, is dedicated to Shiva. It's the oldest of the four caves, probably carved in the latter half of the 6th century. On the wall to the right of the porch is a captivating image of Nataraja striking 81 dance moves in the one pose. On the right of the porch area is a huge figure of Ardhanarishvara. The right half of the figure shows features of Shiva, while the left half has aspects of his wife Parvati. On the opposite wall is a large image of Harihara; half Shiva and half Vishnu.

Dedicated to Vishnu, **cave two** is simpler in design. As with caves one and three, the front edge of the platform is decorated with images of pot-bellied dwarfs in various poses. Four pillars support the verandah, their tops carved with a bracket in the shape of a *yali* (mythical lion creature). On the left wall of the porch is the bull-headed figure of Varaha, an incarnation of Vishnu and the emblem of the Chalukya empire. To his left is Naga, a snake with a human face. On the right wall is a large sculpture of Trivikrama, another incarnation of Vishnu.

Between the second and third caves are two sets of steps to the right. The first leads to a **natural cave**, where resident monkeys laze around. The eastern wall of this cave contains a small image of Padmapani (an incarnation of the Buddha). The second set of steps – sadly, barred by a gate – leads to the hilltop **South Fort**.

Cave three, carved in AD 578, is the largest and most impressive. On the left wall is a carving of Vishnu, to whom the cave is dedicated, sitting on a snake. Nearby is an image of Varaha with four hands. The pillars have carved brackets in the shape of *yalis*. The ceiling panels contain images, including Indra riding an elephant, Shiva on a bull and Brahma on a swan. Keep an eye out for the image of drunken revellers, in particular one lady being propped up by her husband. There's also original colour on the ceiling;

the divots on the floor at the cave's entrance were used as paint palettes.

Dedicated to Jainism, **cave four** is the smallest of the set and dates between the 7th and 8th centuries. The pillars, with their roaring *yalis*, are similar to the other caves. The right wall has an image of Suparsh-vanatha (the seventh Jain *tirthankar*) surrounded by 24 Jain *tirthankars*. The inner sanctum contains an image of Adinath, the first Jain *tirthankar*.

Other Sights
HISTORIC SITES

Badami's caves overlook the 5th-century **Agastyatirtha Tank** and the waterside **Bhutanatha temples**. On the other side of the tank is an **archaeological museum** (admission ₹5; ⊙9am-5pm Sat-Thu), which houses superb examples of local sculpture, including a remarkably explicit Lajja-Gauri image of a fertility cult that once flourished in the area. The stairway behind the museum climbs through a sandstone chasm and fortified gateways to reach the ruins of the **North Fort**.

🏃 Activities

The bluffs and the horseshoe-shaped red sandstone cliff of Badami offer some great low-altitude climbing. For more information, visit www.indiaclimb.com.

🛏 Sleeping & Eating

Station Rd, Badami's main street, has several hotels and restaurants.

Mookambika Deluxe
HOTEL $

(☏220067; Station Rd; d from ₹750, with AC ₹1650; ❄) Faux antique lampshades hang in the corridors of this friendly hotel, leading to comfy rooms done up in matte orange and green. Staff are a good source of travel info.

Hotel New Satkar
HOTEL $

(☏220417; Station Rd; d with/without AC ₹1000/600; ❄) This once dive hotel now has decent budget rooms, but prices have tripled.

Hotel Mayura Chalukya
HOTEL $$

(☏220046; Ramdurg Rd; d from ₹990, with AC ₹1600; ❄) A government issue buried behind civic offices away from the bustle, this renovated hotel has large and clean (though featureless) rooms. There's a decent restaurant serving Indian staples.

Hotel Badami Court
HOTEL $$$

(☏220231; badamicourt@bsnl.in; Station Rd; d incl breakfast from ₹4403; ❄🏊) This luxury hotel sits amid a pastoral countryside 2km from town. Rooms are more functional than plush. Nonguests can use the pool for ₹150.

Banashree
INDIAN $

(Station Rd; mains ₹60-90; ⊙6.30am-10.30pm) The awesome North Indian thalis (₹80) at this busy and popular eatery in front of Hotel Rajsangam are tasty to the last morsel.

Golden Caves Cuisine
MULTICUISINE $

(Station Rd; mains ₹55-100; ⊙8.30am-5pm & 7.30-11.30pm) A shabby place that produces good North and South Indian fare, and has a pleasant outdoor area that's perfect for a beer on a balmy evening.

ℹ Information

The **KSTDC tourist office** (☏220414; Ramdurg Rd; ⊙10am-5.30pm Mon-Sat), adjoining Hotel Mayura Chalukya, has a brochures on Badami, but otherwise is not useful.

SBI and Axis have ATMs on the main road.

Internet is available at **Hotel Rajsangam** (Station Rd; per hr ₹20) in the town centre.

ℹ Getting There & Away

Buses regularly shuffle off from Badami's bus stand on Station Rd to Kerur (₹20, 45 minutes), which has connections to Bijapur and Hubli. Three buses go direct to Hospet (₹180, six hours).

By train, the 7.30am Bijapur Express runs to Bijapur (sleeper/2nd class ₹120/39, 3½ hours), while the 11am Hubli Express goes to Hubli (2nd class ₹120, 3½ hours). For Bengaluru, take the 8pm Gol Gumbaz Express (2nd class ₹244, 13 hours).

ℹ Getting Around

Frequent, on-time local buses make sightseeing in the area quite affordable. You can visit Aihole and Pattadakal in a day from Badami if you get moving early. Start with Aihole (₹37, one hour) departing at 7.45am, then move to Pattadakal (₹15, 30 minutes), and finally return to Badami (₹18, one hour). The last bus from Pattadakal to Badami is at 5pm. Take food with you.

Taxis/autorickshaws cost around ₹1000/600 for a day trip to Pattadakal, Aihole and nearby Mahakuta. Badami's hotels can arrange taxis.

Around Badami

There's no accommodation or restaurants at either Pattadakal or Aihole.

Pattadakal

A secondary capital of the Badami Chalukyas, Pattadakal is known for its group of **temples** (Indian/foreigner ₹10/250, video camera ₹25; ⊘6am-6pm), which are collectively a World Heritage Site. Barring a few temples that date back to the 3rd century AD, most others in the group were built during the 7th and 8th centuries AD. Historians believe Pattadakal served as an important trial ground for the development of South Indian temple architecture. A guide here costs about ₹250.

Two main types of temple towers were tried out here. Curvilinear towers top the Kadasiddeshwra, Jambulinga and Galaganatha temples, while square roofs and receding tiers are used in the Mallikarjuna, Sangameshwara and Virupaksha temples.

The main **Virupaksha Temple** is a massive structure, its columns covered with intricate carvings depicting episodes from the Ramayana and Mahabharata. A giant stone sculpture of Nandi sits to the temple's east. The **Mallikarjuna Temple**, next to the Virupaksha Temple, is almost identical in design. About 500m south of the main enclosure is the Jain **Papanatha Temple**, its entrance flanked by elephant sculptures. The temple complex also serves as the backdrop to the annual **Classical Dance Festival** (Pattadakal; ⊘Jan/Feb), held between January and February.

Pattadakal is 20km from Badami, with buses (₹18) departing every 30 minutes until about 5pm. There are two buses to Aihole (₹15), 13 km away, at 8am and 2.30pm.

Aihole

Some 100 temples, built between the 4th and 6th centuries AD, speck the ancient Chalukyan regional capital of Aihole (*ay-ho-leh*). Most, however, are either in ruins or engulfed by the modern village. Aihole documents the embryonic stage of South Indian Hindu architecture, from the earliest simple shrines, such as the most ancient Ladkhan Temple, to the later and more complex buildings, such as the Meguti Temple.

The most impressive of them all is the 7th-century **Durga Temple** (Indian/foreigner ₹5/100, camera ₹25; ⊘8am-6pm), notable for its semicircular apse (inspired by Buddhist architecture) and the remains of the curvilinear *sikhara* (temple spire). The interiors house intricate stone carvings. The small **museum** (admission ₹5; ⊘9am-5pm Sat-Thu) behind the temple contains further examples of Chalukyan sculpture.

To the south of the Durga Temple are several other temple clusters, including early examples such as the Gandar, Ladkhan, Kontigudi and Hucchapaya groups – all pavilion type with slightly sloping roofs. About 600m to the southeast, on a low hillock, is the Jain **Meguti Temple**. Watch out for snakes if you're venturing up.

Aihole is about 40km from Badami and 13km from Pattadakal.

Bijapur

☏ 08352 / POP 326,360 / ELEV 593M

A fascinating open-air museum dating back to the Deccan's Islamic era, dusty Bijapur tells a glorious tale dating back some 600 years. Blessed with a heap of mosques, mausoleums, palaces and fortifications, it was the capital of the Adil Shahi kings from 1489 to 1686, and one of the five splinter states formed after the Islamic Bahmani kingdom broke up in 1482. Despite its strong Islamic character, Bijapur is also a centre for the Lingayat brand of Shaivism, which emphasises a single personalised god. The **Lingayat Siddeshwara Festival** runs for eight days in January/February.

⊙ Sights

There's a lot to see here, so you'll need to start early if you're going to cover it in a day.

★**Golgumbaz**   MONUMENT
(Indian/foreigner ₹5/100, camera ₹25; ⊘6am-6pm) Set in tranquil gardens, the magnificent Golgumbaz is big enough to pull an optical illusion on you; despite the perfect engineering, you might just think it's ill-proportioned! Golgumbaz is actually a mausoleum, dating back to 1659, and houses the tombs of emperor Mohammed Adil Shah (r 1627–56), his two wives, his mistress (Rambha), one of his daughters and a grandson.

Octagonal seven-storey towers stand at each corner of the monument, which is capped by an enormous dome. An astounding 38m in diameter, it's said to be the largest dome in the world after St Peter's Basil-

Bijapur

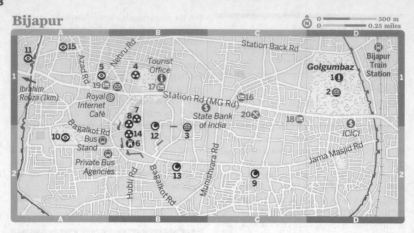

Bijapur

◉ Top Sights
1 Golgumbaz	D1

◉ Sights
2 Archaeological Museum	D1
3 Asar Mahal	B2
4 Bara Kaman	B1
5 Central Market	A1
6 Citadel	B2
7 Gagan Mahal	B1
8 Jala Manzil	B1
9 Jama Masjid	C2
10 Jod Gumbad	A2
11 Malik-e-Maidan	A1
12 Mecca Masjid	B2
13 Mihtar Mahal	B2
14 Sat Manzil	B2
15 Upli Buruj	A1

⊜ Sleeping
Hotel Basava Residency	(see 16)
16 Hotel Madhuvan International	C1
17 Hotel Mayura Adil Shahi Annexe	B1
18 Hotel Pearl	C1
19 Hotel Tourist	A1

⊗ Eating
Hotel Madhuvan International	(see 16)
20 Kamat Restaurant	C1
Swapna Lodge Restaurant	(see 19)

ica in Rome. Climb the steep, narrow stairs up one of the towers to reach the 'whispering gallery' within the dome. An engineering marvel, its acoustics are such that if you whisper into the wall, a person on the opposite side of the gallery can hear you clearly.

Unfortunately people like to test this out by hollering (its unnerving acoustics have the effect of a bad acid trip), so come early while most tourists are still snoozing. Be sure to take the stairs down from the back exit.

Set in the lawns fronting the monument is a fantastic **archaeological museum** (admission ₹5; ☉10am-5pm Sat-Thu), with an excellent collection of artefacts, such as Persian carpets, china crockery, weapons, armours, scrolls and objects of daily use, dating back to Bijapur's heyday.

★**Ibrahim Rouza**　MONUMENT
(Indian/foreigner ₹5/100, video ₹25; ☉6am-6pm)
The beautiful Ibrahim Rouza is among the most elegant and finely proportioned Islamic monuments in India. Its tale is rather poignant: the monument was built by emperor Ibrahim Adil Shah II (r 1580–1627) as a future mausoleum for his queen, Taj Sultana. Ironically, he died before her, and was thus the first person to be rested there. Interred here with Ibrahim Adil Shah and his queen are his daughter, his two sons, and his mother, Haji Badi Sahiba.

Unlike the Golgumbaz, noted for its immense size, the emphasis here is on grace and architectural finery. Its 24m-high minarets are said to have inspired those of the Taj Mahal. For a tip (₹150 is fine), caretakers can show you around the monument, including the dark labyrinth around the catacomb where the actual graves are located.

Citadel　FORT
FREE Surrounded by fortified walls and a wide moat, the citadel once contained

the palaces, pleasure gardens and durbar (royal court) of the Adil Shahi kings. Now mainly in ruins, the most impressive of the remaining fragments is the colossal archway of **Gagan Mahal**, built by Ali Adil Shah I around 1561 as a dual-purpose royal residency and durbar hall. The gates here are locked, but someone will be on hand to let you in.

The ruins of Mohammed Adil Shah's seven-storey palace, the **Sat Manzil**, are nearby. Across the road stands the delicate **Jala Manzil**, once a water pavilion surrounded by secluded courts and gardens. On the other side of Station Rd (MG Rd) are the graceful arches of **Bara Kaman**, the ruined mausoleum of Ali Roza.

Central Market   MARKET
(⊘9am-9pm) A refreshing change in pace from historical ruins, this lively market is an explosion of colour and scents with flowers, spices and fresh produce on sale. It's a great mix of welcoming Muslim and Hindu people.

Jama Masjid   MOSQUE
(Jama Masjid Rd; admission free; ⊘9am-5.30pm) Constructed by Ali Adil Shah I (r 1557–80), the finely proportioned Jama Masjid has graceful arches, a fine dome and a vast inner courtyard with room for more than 2200 worshippers. You can take a silent walk through its assembly hall, which still retains some of the elaborate murals. Women should make sure to cover their heads and not wear revealing clothing.

Asar Mahal   HISTORIC BUILDING
(admission free) Built by Mohammed Adil Shah in about 1646 to serve as a Hall of Justice, the Asar Mahal once housed two hairs from Prophet Mohammed's beard. The rooms on the upper storey are decorated with frescoes and a square tank graces the front. It's out of bounds for women.

Mecca Masjid   MOSQUE
(admission free) On the eastern side of the citadel is the tiny, walled Mecca Masjid, thought to have been built in the early 17th century. Some speculate that this mosque, with high surrounding walls, may have been for women.

Upli Buruj   HISTORIC SITE
(admission free) Upli Buruj is a 16th-century, 24m-high watchtower near the western walls of the city. An external flight of stairs leads to the top, where you'll find two hefty cannons and good views of other monuments around town.

Malik-e-Maidan   HISTORIC SITE
(Monarch of the Plains) FREE Perched upon a platform is this beast of a cannon – over 4m long, almost 1.5m in diameter and estimated to weigh 55 tonnes. Cast in 1549, it was supposedly brought to Bijapur as a war trophy thanks to the efforts of 10 elephants, 400 oxen and hundreds of men!

Jod Gumbad   HISTORIC SITE
FREE In the southwest of the city, off Bagalkot Rd, stand the twin Jod Gumbad tombs with handsome bulbous domes. An Adil Shahi general and his spiritual adviser, Abdul Razzaq Qadiri, are buried here.

🛏 Sleeping

Hotel Tourist   HOTEL $
(☑250655; Station Rd; s/d ₹150/230) Bang in the middle of the bazaar, with scrawny (but clean) rooms. Service is apathetic, so bring that DIY manual along.

Hotel Mayura Adil Shahi Annexe   HOTEL $
(☑250401; Station Rd; s/d from ₹519/577, with AC ₹831/923; ※) One of the better government hotels with massive rooms, balconies and a garden setting that lends an oasis feel. It has an appealing open-air restaurant that's a good place for a beer. Staff here are friendly.

Hotel Pearl   HOTEL $$
(☑256002; www.hotelpearlbijapur.com; Station Rd; d with fan/AC from ₹936/1296; ※) Very good midrange hotel with clean and bright rooms around a central atrium, and conveniently located to Golgumbaz.

Hotel Madhuvan International   HOTEL $$
(☑255571; Station Rd; d with fan/AC ₹988/1326; ※) Hidden down a lane off Station Rd, this pleasant hotel boasts lime-green walls, tinted windows, an amiable management and a lovely outdoor garden restaurant.

Hotel Basava Residency   HOTEL $$
(☑243777; www.hotelbasavaresidency.com; Station Rd, Makund Nagar; s/d incl breakfast from ₹2160/2800; ※ 🛜) The Basava Residency is a new boutique hotel found down a quiet street. It has spacious rooms with plasma TVs and patterned walls. It also has wi-fi in the lobby and a smart vegetarian restaurant.

KARNATAKA & BENGALURU BIJAPUR

✕ Eating & Drinking

Kamat Restaurant   SOUTH INDIAN $
(Station Rd; mains ₹60-80; ⊙7am-10pm) Below
Hotel Kanishka International, this popular
joint serves diverse South Indian snacks and
meals, including an awesome thali bursting
with regional flavours.

Swapna Lodge Restaurant   INDIAN $
(Station Rd; mains ₹90-160; ⊙noon-11pm) It's
two floors up a dingy staircase next to Hotel
Tourist, and has good grub, cold beer and a
1970s lounge feel. Its open-air terrace is a
pleasant lounging spot, albeit a little noisy
with maddening traffic below.

Hotel Madhuvan International   INDIAN $
(Station Rd; mains ₹60-80; ⊙9am-11am, noon-
4pm & 7-11pm) Forget its motel-facade surrounds, this attractive outdoor garden restaurant does fantastic vegetarian dishes including eight different kinds of *dosa* and 14
paneer dishes. The downside is that there is no
alcohol on offer.

ℹ Information

You'll find ATMs about town, including **SBI**
(Station Rd) and **ICICI**. Cheap internet is at
Royal Internet Cafe (Station Rd, below Hotel
Pearl; per hr ₹30; ⊙9.30am-9.30pm) near
Golumbaz.

   The **tourist office** (☑ 250359; Station Rd;
⊙10am-5.30pm Mon-Sat) at Hotel Mayura Adil
Shahi Annexe has a good brochure on Bijapur
with useful map.

ℹ Getting There & Away

BUS

From the **bus stand** (☑ 251344), two evening
buses at 10pm and 11pm head to Bidar (₹250,
seven hours). Ordinary buses head frequently
to Gulbarga (₹125, four hours) and Hubli
(₹160, six hours). There are buses to Bengaluru
(ordinary/sleeper ₹438/650, 12 hours, seven
daily) via Hospet (₹180, five hours), Hyderabad
(₹500, 11 hours, four daily) and Mumbai
(₹500, 12 hours, eight daily) via Pune (₹380,
10 hours).

TRAIN

From Bijapur train station, express trains go to
Sholapur (2nd class ₹80, 2½ hours, three daily),
Bengaluru (sleeper/2AC ₹277/1190, 17 hours,
three daily), 3pm service to Mumbai (2nd class
₹150; 12 hours, four weekly) and Hyderabad
(sleeper ₹150, 14 hours, one daily) at 6pm. There
are three trains to Badami (₹120).

ℹ Getting Around

Given the amount to see and distance to cover,
₹450 is a fair price to hire an autorickshaw for
a day of sightseeing. Expect to pay ₹40 to
get from the train station to the town centre,
and ₹50 between Golgumbaz and Ibrahim
Rouza.

Bidar

☑ 08482 / POP 211,944 / ELEV 664M

Tucked away in Karnataka's far northeastern corner, Bidar is a little gem that most
travellers choose to ignore, and no one
quite knows why. At most an afterthought
on some itineraries, this old walled town –
first the capital of the Bahmani kingdom
(1428–87) and later the capital of the Barid
Shahi dynasty – is drenched in history.
That aside, it's home to some amazing
ruins and monuments, including the colossal Bidar Fort, the largest in South India.
Wallowing in neglect, Bidar sure commands more than the cursory attention it
gets today. The old town has a conservative
Islamic feel to it.

◉ Sights

Bidar Fort   FORT
(⊙9am-5pm) FREE Keep aside a few hours
for peacefully wandering around the remnants of this magnificent 15th-century fort.
Sprawled across rolling hills 2km east of
Udgir Rd, it was once the administrative
capital of much of southern India. Surrounded by a triple moat hewn out of solid
red rock and 5.5km of defensive walls (the
second longest in India), the fort has a fairy-
tale entrance that twists in an elaborate chi-
cane through three gateways.

   While entry to the fort is free, the catch is
you'll need a guide (₹150 to ₹200) to unlock
the gates to the most interesting ruins within the fort. These include the **Rangin Mahal**
(Painted Palace), which sports elaborate tilework, teak pillars and panels with mother-
of-pearl inlay, the **Solah Khamba Mosque**
(Sixteen-Pillared Mosque) and **Tarkash Mahal** with exquisitive Islamic inscriptions and
wonderul roof-top views.

   There's also a small **museum** in the
former royal bath with local artefacts and
crude wooden rifles. Clerks at the **archaeological office** beside the museum often
double as guides.

Bahmani Tombs HISTORIC SITE

(☉ dawn-dusk) The huge domed tombs of the Bahmani kings in Ashtur, 3km east of Bidar, have a desolate, moody beauty that strikes a strange harmony with the rolling hills around them. These impressive mausoleums were built to house the remains of the sultans – their graves are still regularly draped with fresh satin and flowers – and are arranged in a long line along the edge of the road. The painted interior of Ahmad Shah Bahman's tomb is the most impressive, and is regularly prayed in.

About 500m prior to reaching the tombs, to the left of the road, is **Choukhandi** (admission free; ☉ dawn-dusk), the serene mausoleum of Sufi saint Syed Kirmani Baba, who travelled here from Persia during the golden age of the Bahmani empire. An uncanny air of calm hangs within the monument, and its polygonal courtyard houses rows of medieval graves, amid which women in hijab sit quietly and murmur inaudible prayers.

Khwaja Mahmud
Gawan Madrasa RUINS, HISTORIC SITE

(admission free; ☉ dawn-dusk) Dominating the heart of the old town are the ruins of Khwaja Mahmud Gawan Madrasa, a college for advanced learning built in 1472 by Mahmud Gawan, then chief minister of the empire. It was later used as an armoury by Mughal emperor Aurangzeb, when a gunpowder explosion ripped the building in half. To get an idea of its former grandeur, check out the remnants of coloured tiles on the front gate and one of the minarets which still stands intact.

🛏 Sleeping & Eating

Hotel Mayura HOTEL $

(✆ 228142; Udgir Rd; d with fan/AC from ₹500/800; ❄) Smart and friendly, with cheerful and well-appointed rooms (though hard beds),

this is the best hotel to camp at in Bidar. It's bang opposite the bus stand. Look out for its NBC-peacock symbol.

Hotel Mayura Barid Shahi HOTEL $

(✆ 221740; Udgir Rd; s/d ₹350/450, r with AC ₹785; ❄) Otherwise featureless with simple, minimalist rooms (service is OK, though), this place scores due to its central location. The lovely garden bar-restaurant to the rear brims over with joy and merriment every evening.

Jyothi Fort INDIAN $

(Bidar Fort; mains ₹45-90) Delightful outdoor restaurant with peaceful setting at the fort's entry. Tables are set up on the grass under sprawling banyan trees, while the kitchen is in an attractive stone-brick homestead-style building, and cooks up some delicious vegetarian meals. There's also seating in private stone chambers.

ℹ Information

You can find **ATMs** (Udgir Rd) and **internet** (per hr ₹ 20; ☉ 9am-9pm) on the main road and opposite from Hotel Mayura Barid Shahi.

ℹ Getting There & Away

From the bus stand, frequent buses run to Gulbarga (₹110, three hours), which is connected to Mumbai and Bengaluru. Buses also go to Hyderabad (₹112, four hours), Bijapur (₹260, seven hours) and a 6am bus to Bengaluru (semideluxe/AC ₹700/900, 12 hours).

The train station, around 1km southwest of the bus stand, has services to Hyderabad (sleeper ₹120, five hours, three daily) and Bengaluru (sleeper ₹280, 17 hours, one daily).

ℹ Getting Around

Rent a very basic bicycle at **Sami Cycle Taxi** (Basveshwar Circle; per day ₹ 20; ☉ 10am-10pm) against your proof of identity, or arrange a day tour in an autorickshaw for around ₹400.

Andhra Pradesh

Best Places to Eat

➡ Hotel Shadab (p925)

➡ Shah Ghouse Cafe (p925)

➡ So. (p926)

➡ Southern Spice (p926)

➡ Dharani (p934)

Best Off the Beaten Track

➡ Maredumilli (p936)

➡ Guntupalli (p939)

➡ Sankaram (p935)

➡ Moula Ali Dargah (p918)

➡ Bhongir (p933)

Why Go?

Andhra Pradesh won't hit you over the head with its attractions. It doesn't have the flashiness of Rajasthan or the pride of Tamil Nadu; it doesn't brag. So when you come here – to see the ornate palaces, tombs and mosques of Hyderabad's bygone royal families, or to wander the deserted ruins of hilltop monasteries that once housed monks from across Asia – you might be the only traveller around. You might even be the only person around. And if the place is out of the way, as so many of Andhra's sights are, you might just feel like you've discovered it yourself.

So come, but be prepared to dig for the jewels; get ready to wend your way through paddy fields and 500-year-old urban markets, to climb towering smooth-granite hills, and to feel the liberating uncertainty of being off the tourist trail and in a wonderland of forgotten history.

When to Go
Hyderabad

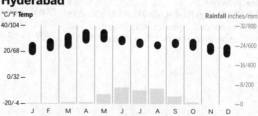

Dec–Jan Explore Hyderabad's sights in perfect 20–25°C weather.

Jun–July Join locals digging into *haleem*, a Ramzan (Ramadan) favourite.

Jun–Sep Rains make travel tough, but they also make for good surfing at Vizag beaches.

Food

Andhra Pradesh is known for its residents' love of good food, and Hyderabadis especially take great pride in their city's offerings. The state's cuisine has two major influences: The Mughals brought tasty biryanis, *haleem* (pounded, spiced wheat with goat or mutton) and kebabs. The Andhra style is vegetarian and famous across India for its delicious spiciness. If you're in Hyderabad during Ramadan (known locally as Ramzan), look out for the clay ovens called *bhattis*. You'll probably hear them before you see them. Men gather around, taking turns to vigorously pound *haleem* inside purpose-built structures. Come nightfall, the serious business of eating begins. The taste is worth the wait. In 2010, this love of the dish was taken a step further when 'Hyderabadi haleem' was given 'Geographical Indication' protection: it cannot be served by that name unless it meets strict quality guidelines.

DON'T MISS

The splendid architecture of **Hyderabad's** royal kingdoms – which ran from the 16th century to Indian independence – is what brings most visitors to the region. The Qutb Shahis produced some masterful architecture, including the stunning **Charminar**, **Golconda Fort** and their final resting place, the opulent **Qutb Shahi tombs**. The lavish nizam lifestyle is on display all over Hyderabad, especially at **Chowmahalla Palace**, **HEH the Nizam's Museum** and **Falaknuma Palace**, now an extravagant hotel. Before any of these wealthy princes came along, another prince held sway: the Buddha. Scenic monastic ruins at **Nagarjunakonda**, **Guntupalli** and **Sankaram** will bring you to a peaceful place.

Top State Festivals

→ **Sankranti** (☺ Jan, statewide) This important Telugu festival marks the end of harvest season. Kite-flying abounds, doorsteps are decorated with colourful *kolams* (rice-flour designs) and men adorn cattle with bells and fresh horn paint.

→ **Brahmotsavam** (☺ Sep/Oct, Tirumala, p938) This nine-day festival sees the Venkateshwara temple adorned in decorations. Special *pujas* and chariot processions are held, and it's an auspicious time for *darshan* (deity-viewing).

→ **Muharram** (☺ Oct/Nov; Hyderabad, p922) Muharram commemorates the martyrdom of Mohammed's grandson. Shiites wear black in mourning, and throngs gather at Badshahi Ashurkhana.

→ **Visakha Utsav** (☺ Dec/Jan, Visakhapatnam, p933) A celebration of all things Visakhapatnam, with classical and folk dance and music performances, some on the beach.

Fast Facts

→ **Population:** 84.7 million

→ **Area:** 276,754 sq km

→ **Capital:** Hyderabad

→ **Main languages:** Telugu, Urdu, Hindi

→ **Sleeping prices: $** below ₹1000, **$$** ₹1000 to ₹3000, **$$$** above ₹3000

Top Tip

Tea's gaining a foothold, but Andhra is traditionally coffee country. Skip the chai here and order the filter coffee when you see it.

Resources

→ **APTDC** (www.aptdc.in)

→ **Deccan Chronicle** (www.deccanchronicle.com)

→ **Full Hyderabad** (www.fullhyderabad.com)

→ **Zomato** (www.zomato.com)

ANDHRA PRADESH

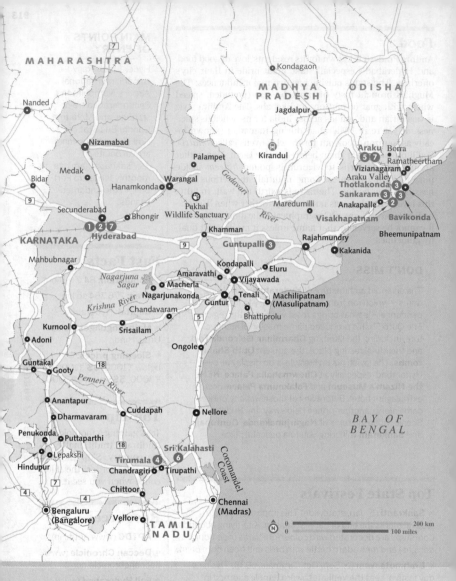

Andhra Pradesh Highlights

1 Imagine a life of riches, pleasure gardens and poetry in **Hyderabad's** many palaces and royal structures (p915)

2 Soak up centuries-old ambience at Hyderabad's colourful **Laad Bazaar** (p917)

3 Absorb the meditative vibrations of monks past at **Sankaram** (p935), **Bavikonda** (p935) and **Thotlakonda** (p935), and **Guntupalli** (p939), destinations on a 2300-year-old monastic trail

4 Find devotion you didn't know you had alongside thousands of Hindu pilgrims at **Tirumala** (p938)

5 Enjoy the views as your train chugs through the spectacular Eastern Ghats to **Araku** (p936)

6 Get hypnotised by the lush intricacy and colours of *kalamkari* paintings in **Sri Kalahasti** (p940)

7 Learn about Andhra's rich ethnic diversity at tribal museums in **Hyderabad** (p919) and **Araku** (p936)

History

From the 3rd century BC the Satavahana empire, also known as the Andhras, reigned throughout the Deccan plateau. It evolved from the Andhra people, whose presence in southern India may date back to 1000 BC. Buddha's teaching took root here early on, and the Andhras fully embraced it, building huge edifices in its honour. In the coming centuries, the Andhras would develop a flourishing civilisation that extended from the west to the east coast of South India.

From the 7th to the 10th century, the Chalukyas ruled the area, establishing their Dravidian style of architecture, especially along the coast. The Chalukya and Chola dynasties merged in the 11th century to be overthrown by the Kakatiyas, who introduced pillared temples into South Indian religious architecture. The Vijayanagars then rose to become one of the most powerful empires in India.

By the 16th century the Islamic Qutb Shahi dynasty held the city of Hyderabad, but in 1687 was supplanted by Aurangzeb's Mughal empire. In the 18th century the post-Mughal rulers in Hyderabad, known as nizams, retained relative control as the British and French vied for trade, though their power gradually weakened. The region reluctantly became part of independent India in 1947, and in 1956 the state of Andhra Pradesh, an amalgamation of Telugu-speaking areas plus the predominantly Urdu-speaking capital, was created.

Telangana, one of the three main regions that combined to become Andhra Pradesh, is still being fought over: a movement to create a separate state got traction in 2009 when the split was approved by the federal government. But the new state's formation was shelved following protests from Andhra's coastal and northeastern regions. The issue is still being viciously debated.

Hyderabad

⚲ 040 / POP 6.81 MILLION

Hyderabad, City of Pearls, is like an elderly, impeccably dressed princess with really faded, really expensive jewellery. Once the seat of the powerful and wealthy Qutb Shahi and Asaf Jahi dynasties, the city has seen centuries of great prosperity and innovation. Today, the 'Old City' is full of centuries-old Islamic monuments and even older charms. In fact, the whole city is laced with architectural gems: ornate tombs, mosques, palaces and homes from the past – some weathered and enchanting, others recently restored and gleaming – are peppered across town.

The 1990s saw the rise of Hyderabad's west side (the aged princess's fun, stylish granddaughter) and the emergence of a new decadence. 'Cyberabad', with Bengaluru (Bangalore) and Pune, is the seat of India's mighty software dynasty and has created a culture of good food and posh lounges for the city's new royalty.

Secunderabad, north of the Hussain Sagar, is the former British cantonment, now useful to travelers mainly for its huge train station.

Traffic is a problem here: keep in mind that even short distances can take a long time to cover.

History

Hyderabad owes its existence to a water shortage at Golconda in the late 16th century, when the reigning Qutb Shahis were forced to abandon Golconda Fort. They relocated to the banks of the Musi River. The new city of Hyderabad was established, with the brand-new Charminar as its centrepiece.

In 1687 the city was overrun by the Mughal emperor Aurangzeb, and subsequent rulers of Hyderabad were viceroys installed by the Mughal administration in Delhi.

In 1724 the Hyderabad viceroy, Asaf Jah, took advantage of waning Mughal power and declared Hyderabad an independent state with himself as leader. The dynasty of the nizams of Hyderabad began, and the traditions of Islam flourished. Hyderabad became a focus for the arts, culture and learning, and the centre of Islamic India. Its abundance of rare gems and minerals – the world-famous Kohinoor diamond is from here – furnished the nizams with enormous wealth. (William Dalrymple's *White Mughals* is a fascinating portrait of the city at this time.)

When Independence came in 1947, the then-nizam of Hyderabad, Osman Ali Khan, considered amalgamation with Pakistan, then opted for sovereignty. Tensions between Muslims and Hindus increased, however, and military intervention saw Hyderabad join the Indian union in 1948.

The city continues to fall victim to tensions and violence: several bombings in 2007, including at Mecca Masjid, killed 55 people, and two bombs in market areas

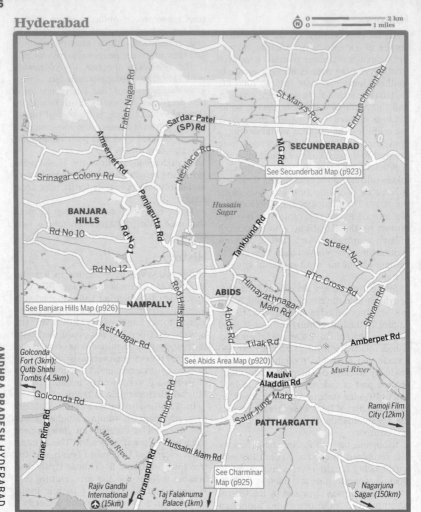

killed at least 16 commuters and shoppers in 2013. Anger over plans to expand a Hindu temple on the side of Charminar, the city's iconic Islamic monument, resulted in injuries, cars set on fire, and a police blockade of the old city for several days in late 2012.

Sights

★ Charminar   MONUMENT, MARKET
(Map p925; Indian/foreigner ₹5/100; ⏲ 9am-5pm) Hyderabad's principal landmark was built by Mohammed Quli Qutb Shah in 1591 to commemorate the founding of Hyderabad and the end of epidemics caused by Golconda's

water shortage. The dramatic four-column, 56m-high structure has four arches facing the cardinal points. Minarets sit atop each column. The 2nd floor, home to Hyderabad's oldest mosque, and upper columns are not open to the public. The structure is illuminated from 7pm to 9pm.

The crowded lanes around the Charminar – the neighbourhood is also known as Charminar – are the perfect place to get lost, with sidewalks full of everything from perfumes to kitchen implements to coconuts. Skilled wanderers may find the bird market, or the workshops where *varakh* (silver foil) is pounded out for use in sweets. **Laad Bazaar** (Map p925), west of the monument, is known across southern India as the last word in wedding saris, jewels and bangles, and the area is also the centre of India's pearl trade: some great deals can be had – if you know your stuff.

★ **Golconda Fort** FORT
(Indian/foreigner ₹5/100, sound-and-light show adult/child ₹50/30; ⊙ 9am-5pm, English-language sound-and-light show 6.30pm Nov-Feb, 7pm Mar-Oct) Although most of this 16th-century fortress dates from the time of the Qutb Shah kings, its origins as a mud fort have been traced to the earlier reigns of the Yadavas and Kakatiyas.

Golconda was the capital of the eponymous independent state for nearly 80 years, in 1590, Sultan Mohammed Quli Qutb Shah abandoned the fort and moved to the new city of Hyderabad.

The citadel is built on a 120m-high granite hill and surrounded by crenellated ramparts constructed from large masonry blocks. Outside the citadel stands another crenellated rampart, with a perimeter of 11km, and yet another wall beyond this. The massive gates were studded with iron spikes to obstruct war elephants.

Survival within the fort was also attributable to water and sound. A series of concealed glazed earthen pipes ensured a reliable water supply, while the ingenious acoustics guaranteed that even the smallest sound from the entrance would echo across the fort complex.

Naya Qila (new fort) is home to a magnificent 400-year-old **baobab tree** (*hatiyan ka jhad*: elephant tree), with a circumference of 27m, said to have been brought from Abyssinia by Arab traders. The crumbling rampart here has great views of the fort and tombs.

Guides charge a whopping ₹600 per 90-minute tour. Small guidebooks to the fort are also available. A **sound-and-light show** is held nightly.

Mornings are best for peace and quiet. The fort is about 12km from Abids; take bus 119 from Nampally station, or 66G or Setwin bus 66 from Charminar (one hour). Autorickshaw drivers charge ₹400 return, including waiting.

Chowmahalla Palace MUSEUM
(Map p925; www.chowmahalla.com; Indian/foreigner ₹40/150, camera ₹50; ⊙ 10am-5pm Sat-Thu) In

their latest act of architectural showmanship, the nizam family has restored this dazzling palace – or, technically, four *(char)* palaces *(mahalla)*. Begun in 1750, it was expanded over the next 100 years, absorbing Persian, Indo-Saracenic, Rajasthani and European styles. The southern courtyard has one *mahal* with period rooms containing the nizams' over-the-top furniture; another *mahal* with an exhibit on life in the *zenana* (women's quarters) that includes bejewelled clothes, carpets and a bride palanquin; antique cars (one nizam allegedly used a Rolls Royce as a garbage can); and curiosities like elephant seats.

In the northern courtyard is the **Khilwat Mubarak**, a magnificent durbar hall where nizams held ceremonies under 19 enormous chandeliers of Belgian crystal. Today the hall houses exhibitions of photos, arms and clothing. Hung with curtains, the balcony over the main hall once served as seating for the women of the family, who attended all durbars in purdah.

Stop by the **Royal Photo Studio** on your way out to dress up like royalty and have your sepia-tone photo taken (₹100).

Qutb Shahi Tombs HISTORIC SITE
(adult/child ₹10/5, camera/video ₹20/100; ⊙ 9.30am-5.30pm) These graceful domed tombs sit serenely in landscaped gardens about 1.5km northwest of the Golconda Fort entrance. Seven of the nine Qutb Shahi rulers were buried here, as well as members of the royal family and respected citizens, from entertainers to doctors. You could easily spend half a day here taking photos and wandering in and out of the mausoleums. The upper level of Mohammed Quli's tomb, reached via a narrow staircase, has good views of the area. The Qutb Shahi Tombs **booklet** (₹20) is available at the ticket counter.

The tombs are an easy walk from the fort; alternatively, take bus 80S or 142K, or an autorickshaw (about ₹30). From town, take bus 142M from Nampally or Setwin bus 66 from Charminar.

Paigah Tombs HISTORIC SITE
(Santoshnagar; ⊙ 10am-5pm) FREE The aristocratic Paigah family, purportedly descendents of the second Caliph of Islam, were fierce loyalists of the nizams, serving as statespeople, philanthropists and generals under and alongside them. The Paigahs' necropolis, in a quiet neighbourhood 4km

STATE OF GOOD KARMA

In its typically understated way, Andhra Pradesh doesn't make much of its vast archaeological – and karmic – wealth. But the state is packed with impressive ruins of its rich Buddhist history. Only a few of Andhra's 150 stupas, monasteries, caves and other sites have been excavated, turning up rare relics of Buddha with offerings such as golden flowers.

They speak of a time when Andhra Pradesh – or Andhradesa – was a hotbed of Buddhist activity, when monks came from around the world to learn from some of the tradition's most renowned teachers, and when Indian monks set off for Sri Lanka and Southeast Asia via the Krishna and Godavari Rivers to spread Buddha's teachings.

Andhradesa's Buddhist culture, in which *sangha* (the community of monks and nuns), laity and statespeople all took part, lasted around 1500 years from the 6th century BC. There's no historical evidence for it, but some even say Buddha himself visited the area.

Andhradesa's first practitioners were likely disciples of Bavari, an ascetic who lived on the banks of the Godavari River and sent his followers north to bring back Buddha's teachings. But the dharma really took off in the 3rd century BC under Ashoka, who dispatched monks across his empire to teach and construct stupas enshrined with relics of the Buddha. (Being near these was thought to help progress on the path to enlightenment.)

Succeeding Ashoka, the Satavahanas and then Ikshvakus were also supportive. At their capital at Amaravathi, the Satavahanas adorned Ashoka's modest stupa with elegant decoration. They built monasteries across the Krishna Valley and exported the dharma through their sophisticated maritime network.

It was also during the Satavahana reign that Nagarjuna lived. Considered the progenitor of Mahayana Buddhism, the monk was equal parts logician, philosopher and meditator, and he wrote several ground-breaking works that shaped contemporary Buddhist thought. Other important monk-philosophers would emerge from the area in the following centuries, making Andhradesa a sort of Buddhist motherland of the South.

Today, the state's many sites are ripe for exploring; even in ruins, you can get a sense of how large some of the stupas were, how expansive the monastic complexes, and how the monks lived, sleeping in caves and fetching rainwater from stone-cut cisterns. Most of the sites have stunning views across seascapes and countryside.

The once-flourishing Buddhist complexes of Nagarjunakonda (p931) and Amaravathi (p938) have good infrastructure and helpful museums on-site. For more ambience and adventure, head to the area around Vijayawada for Guntupalli (p939) or Bhattiprolu, and near Visakhapatnam for Thotlakonda (p935) and Bavikonda (p935), Sankaram (p935), and Ramatheertham.

southeast of Charminar, is a small compound of exquisite mausoleums made of marble and lime stucco. The main complex contains 27 tombs with intricate inlay work, surrounded by delicately carved walls and canopies, stunning filigree screens with geometric patterning and, overhead, tall, graceful turrets. The tombs are down a small lane across from Owasi Hospital. Look for the Preston Junior College sign. *The Paigah Tombs* (₹20) booklet is sold at the AP State Museum, but not here.

Moula Ali Dargah   SACRED SITE

The top of Moula Ali hill has spectacular views of the cityscape, cool breezes and a dargah with an ornate interior covered in thousands of tiny mirrors. The dargah is also filled, it is said, with healing blessings. It all started one night in 1578, when an ill member of the Qutb Shahi court dreamt that Ali, the son-in-law of the Prophet Mohammed, visited the hill. The next day, not only was he cured, but Ali's handprints were found there, and the sultan immediately built a dargah over the prints and a mosque. Today, the hill is a pilgrimage site for the sick as well as one of the city's most dramatic sights, a smooth solid-rock mound towering 600m over the city (via 484 steps – avoid the midday heat).

The hill has an eastern approach, too, adjacent to the recently restored **mausoleum** of Mah Laqa Bai (1768–1824), a poet, courtesan and powerful member of the courts of the second and third nizams.

Moula Ali hill is about 10km northeast of Secunderabad. Frequent buses run from Secunderabad bus stand to the ECIL stop, as does bus 136H from Nampally. ECIL is 2km from the hill.

Salar Jung Museum   MUSEUM

(Map p925; www.salarjungmuseum.in; Salar Jung Marg; Indian/foreigner ₹10/150; ⊙ 10am-5pm Sat-Thu) The huge and varied collection, dating back to the 1st century, was put together by Mir Yusaf Ali Khan (Salar Jung III), the grand vizier of the seventh nizam, Osman Ali Khan (r 1910–49). The 14,000 exhibits from every corner of the world include sculptures, wood carvings, devotional objects, Mughal miniature paintings, illuminated manuscripts, weaponry, toys and textiles. Cameras are not allowed. Avoid Sunday, when it's bedlam. From Abids, take bus 8 or 8A, which stop in front of the museum, or bus 7 to **Afzal Gunj bus stop** on the north side of the nearby Musi River bridge.

Just west of the bridge (on the north side) is the spectacular **Osmania General Hospital**, and, on the south, the **High Court** and **Government City College**, all built under the seventh nizam in the Indo-Saracenic style.

HEH The Nizam's Museum   MUSEUM

(Purani Haveli; Map p925; adult/student ₹70/15, camera ₹150; ⊙ 10am-4.30pm Sat-Thu) The 16th-century Purani Haveli was home of the sixth nizam, Fath Jang Mahbub Ali Khan (r 1869–1911). He was rumoured to have never worn the same thing twice: hence the 72m-long, two-storey Burmese teak wardrobe. In the palace's former servants' quarters are personal effects of the seventh nizam, Osman Ali Khan, and gifts from his Silver Jubilee, lavish pieces that include an art deco silver letterbox collection. The museum's guides do an excellent job putting it all in context.

The rest of Purani Haveli is now a school, but you can wander around the grounds and peek in the administrative building, the nizam's former residence.

Badshahi Ashurkhana   HISTORIC BUILDING

(Map p925) The 1594 Badshahi Ashurkhana (literally 'royal house of mourning') was one of the first structures built by the Qutb Shahs in the new city of Hyderabad. It's easy to miss, set back from the road in a corner of Charminar, but inside its walls are practically glowing with intricate, brightly-coloured tile mosaic. Look closely to see the faux-tile painting at the bottom: a 1908 flood destroyed the first two metres of tile. The Ashurkhana is packed during Muharram, as well as on Thursdays, when local Shiites gather to commemorate the martyrdom of Hussain Ibn Ali. You should remove your shoes and dress modestly (including a head-scarf for women).

Nehru Centenary Tribal Museum   MUSEUM

(Map p926; Masab Tank; Indian/foreigner ₹10/100; ⊙ 10.30am-5pm) Andhra Pradesh's 33 tribal groups, based mostly in the northeastern part of the state, comprise several million people. This museum, run by the government's Tribal Welfare Department, exhibits photographs, dioramas of village life, musical instruments and some exquisite Naikpod masks. It's basic, but you'll get a glimpse into the cultures of these fringe peoples. There's also an excellent **library** (library 1-2pm & 4-5pm).

AP State Museum   MUSEUM

(Map p920; Public Gardens Rd, Nampally; admission ₹10, camera/video ₹100/500; ⊙ 10.30am-4.30pm Sat-Thu) This sprawling museum hosts a collection of important archaeological finds from the area, as well as an exhibit on Andhra's Buddhist history, with relics of Buddha himself. There are also Jain and bronze sculpture galleries, a decorative-arts gallery and a 4500-year-old Egyptian mummy.

The museum is in a fanciful building constructed in 1920 by the seventh nizam as a playhouse for one of his daughters. It, along with the gorgeous **Legislative Assembly** (Map p920) building nearby (also commissioned by the nizam), is floodlit at night.

Buddha Statue & Hussain Sagar   MONUMENT, LAKE

(Map p920; boats adult/child ₹50/25) Set picturesquely on a plinth in the Hussain Sagar, a lake built by the Qutb Shahs, is one of the world's largest free-standing stone Buddha statues. It's an especially magnificent sight when illuminated at night.

Frequent **boats** make the 30-minute return trip to the statue from both **Eat Street** (Map p926; ⊙ launches 2.30-8.15pm) and **Lumbini Park** (Map p920; admission ₹10; ⊙ 9am-9pm). It's a pleasant place to enjoy sunsets and the popular musical fountain and laser show. The Tankbund Rd promenade, on the eastern shore of Hussain Sagar, has great views of the statue.

Abids Area

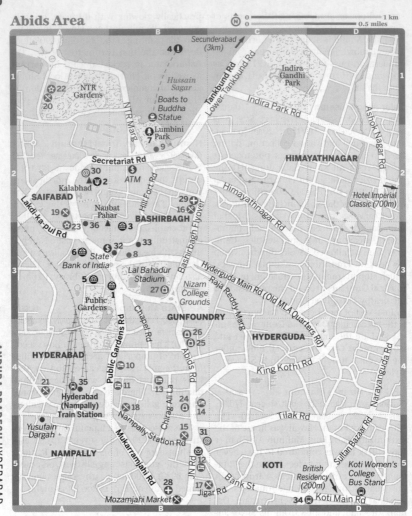

British Residency
HISTORIC BUILDING

(☎24657813) This ornate home, built in 1803 by British Resident James Achilles Kirkpatrick, was featured in William Dalrymple's historical love story *White Mughals*. Kirkpatrick became enchanted by Mughal culture and eventually married Khair-un-Nissa, the teenage granddaughter of Hyderabad's prime minister. The Residency, now part of Koti Women's College, was in disrepair at research time but was about to undergo restoration. With its grand staircases and halls, it's fascinating to see, either way. Contact Principal Seetha for permission to visit.

Taramati Baradari
HISTORIC BUILDING

(Ibrahimbagh; ⊙11.30am-8.30pm) According to legend, this elegant pavilion atop a hill 4km from Golconda Fort was built by Sultan Abdullah Qutb Shah for his courtesan, Taramati, whose singing and dancing performances the sultan watched from a perch at the fort. Autorickshaws charge ₹300 return from Golconda.

Birla Mandir
HINDU TEMPLE

(Map p920; ⊙7am-noon & 2-9pm) The ethereal Birla Mandir, constructed of white Rajasthani marble in 1976, graces Kalabahad

Abids Area

(Black Mountain), one of two rocky hills overlooking the Hussain Sagar. Dedicated to Venkateshwara, the temple is a popular Hindu pilgrimage centre and affords magnificent views over the city, especially at sunset.

Birla Modern Art Gallery   MUSEUM
(Map p920; www.birlasciencecentre.org; admission ₹40; ⊗10.30am-6pm) Formerly a so-so collection of local art, this museum was recently overhauled and now hosts a skilfully curated collection of modern and contemporary works – the best you'll see in South India. Look for paintings by superstars Jogen Chowdhury, Tyeb Mehta, Arpita Singh and Thota Vaikuntam.

Mecca Masjid   MOSQUE
(Map p925; Shah Ali Banda Rd, Charminar; ⊗9am-5pm) This mosque is one of the world's largest, with space for 10,000 worshippers. Women are not allowed inside.

Several bricks embedded above the gate are made with soil from Mecca – hence the name. To the left of the mosque an enclosure contains the tombs of Nizam Ali Khan and his successors. Since the 2007 bomb blasts here, security is tight; no bags are allowed inside.

BM Birla Science Centre   MUSEUM
(Map p920; www.birlasciencecentre.org; science museum/planetarium ₹35/40; ⊗museum 10.30am 8pm, planetarium shows 11.30am, 4pm & 6pm) The fun, retro Birla Science Centre comprises a museum of science, a planetarium, archaeology and fine-art exhibits and a 'dinosaurum'.

🏃 Volunteering

Blue Cross of Hyderabad   VOLUNTEERING
(☑23544355; www.bluecrosshyd.in; Rd No 35, Jubilee Hills) This 2-acre shelter with 1000 animals rescues sick animals, and vaccinates and sterilises stray dogs. Volunteers can help in the shelter (grooming and feeding animals), in the adoption centre (walking and socialising dogs) or in the office.

📚 Courses

Vipassana International Meditation Centre   MEDITATION
(Dhamma Khetta; ☑24240290; www.khetta. dhamma.org; Nagarjuna Sagar Rd, Km12.6) Intensive 10-day meditation courses in peaceful grounds 20km outside the city. The centre is convenient but not as comfortable as the centre at Nagarjuna Sagar (p932). Apply

ANDHRA PRADESH HYDERABAD

online. Bus 277 (from MGBS or Koti Women's College) runs to the centre; it's a 1km walk from the bus stop.

Tours

Andhra Pradesh Tourism
Development Corporation
TOURS

(APTDC; ☑ 24hr info 23450444; www.aptdc.in; ☉ 7am-8pm) APTDC tours the city (₹300), Ramoji Film City (₹900), Nagarjuna Sagar (weekends, ₹500) and destinations across Andhra Pradesh. The Sound & Light tour (₹230) takes in Golconda Fort's sound-and-light show, but you get stuck in traffic. Reserve at the **Bashirbagh** (Map p920; ☑ 66746370; NSF Shakar Bhavan, opposite Police Control Room), **Secunderabad** (Map p923; ☑ 27893100; www.aptdc.in; Yatri Nivas Hotel, SP Rd) or **Tankbund Rd** (Map p920; ☑ 65581555) offices.

Heritage Walks
WALKING TOUR

(☑ 9849728841; www.aptdc.in/heritage_walks; tours per person ₹50) These Sunday-morning tours were designed and are sometimes led by architect Madhu Vottery, whose *A Guide to Heritage of Hyderabad: The Natural and the Built* are part of a movement to preserve and illuminate Hyderabad's rich architectural heritage.

Society To Save Rocks
WALKING TOUR

(☑ 23552923; www.saverocks.org; 1236 Rd No 60, Jubilee Hills) This NGO organises monthly walks through the Andhran landscape and its surreal-looking 2.5-billion-year-old boulders.

Abbas Tyabji
HISTORIC TOUR

(☑ 9391010015; abbastyabji@gmail.com; 8hr tour incl transport ₹3500) Passionate local photojournalist Abbas Tyabji can take you to less touristy sights: historic caravan routes or natural areas in the city's outskirts to see toddy tappers.

✸ Festivals & Events

Muharram
MUSLIM

(☉ Oct/Nov) Muharram is the first month of the Islamic year and commemorates the martyrdom of Mohammed's grandson with mass mourning and all-night sermons. Hyderabad is known for its massive procession on the 10th day. which draws people from around the region.

Sankranti
HINDU

(statewide; ☉ Jan) Hyderabad's skies fill with kites during this important Telugu harvest festival.

🛏 Sleeping

Gents can book a dorm bed (with/without air-con ₹100/60) at Mahatma Gandhi bus station (p930).

Hotel Suhail
HOTEL $

(Map p920; ☑ 24610299; www.hotelsuhail.in; Troop Bazaar; s/d/tr from ₹475/650/945; ❀ @) If all budget hotels were like the Suhail, we'd be much better off. Staff are friendly and there's cheap internet, while rooms are large, quiet and have balconies and hot water. It's tucked away on an alley behind the main post office and the Grand Hotel.

Hotel Rajmata
HOTEL $

(Map p920; ☑ 66665555; royalrajmata@gmail.com; Public Gardens Rd; s/d ₹900/1012; ❀) Rajmata's

---

KITSCHABAD

Mixed in with Hyderabad's world-class sights are some attractions that err on the quirkier side.

Ramoji Film City (www.ramojifilmcity.com; adult/child from ₹600/500; ☉ 9am-10pm) Andhra Pradesh's film industry, Tollywood, is massive, and its primary studio is fittingly huge. The 670-hectare Film City produces films and TV shows in Telugu, Tamil and Hindi, among others. The four-hour bus tour will take you through flimsy film sets and gaudy fountains, stopping for dance routines and stunt shows. Take bus 204A, 205/205A/205B, 206, 207 or 299 from Koti Women's College (one hour, 20km).

Health Museum (Map p920; Public Gardens Rd, Nampally; admission free; ☉ 10.30am-5pm Sat-Thu) A throwback to a 1950s classroom, this place has a bizarre collection of medical and public-health paraphernalia, including a rather terrifying giant model of a crab louse.

Sudha Cars Museum (www.sudhacars.com; Bahadurpura; Indian/foreigner ₹40/150; ☉ 9.30am-6.30pm) The genius work of Sudhakar includes cars in the shape of a computer, cricket bat, hamburger and condom, among other wacky designs. Poke your head into the workshop to see his latest project. The museum is east of Nehru Zoological Park.

Secunderabad

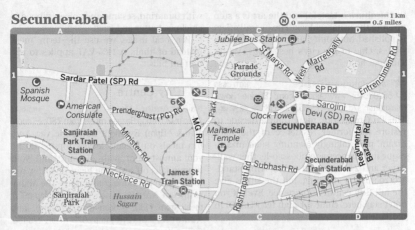

location is prime: across from Nampally station, but set back from the road, keeping things quiet. Standard rooms are aged but good-value; deluxe rooms (singles/doubles ₹2023/2248) are overpriced but fresh and roomy; some have views of the station. Popular with families.

YMCA   HOSTEL **$**
(Map p923; ☑ 27806049; secunderabadymca @yahoo.co.in; SP Rd, Secunderabad; dm/s/d ₹125/500/650, s/d with shared bath ₹350/450; ❄) This cheery hostel in a quiet spot in Secunderabad has no-frills rooms that are clean-ish, some with balcony. It's near the clock tower.

**Secunderabad
Retiring Rooms**   RAILWAY RETIRING ROOM **$**
(Map p923; dm/s/d from ₹75/500/600; ❄) An excellent deal for late arrivals at Secunderabad, even with the 5am check-out.

★ Taj Mahal Hotel   HOTEL **$$**
(Map p920; ☑ 66120606; www.hoteltajmahalindia. com; Abids Rd; s/d with air-con from ₹1349/1855; ❄ 🛜) This 1924 heritage building has a magnificent exterior, plants peppered about and some rooms with character (ie boudoirs, crystal-knobbed armoires and wood-beam ceilings). The hotel recently annexed a modern building next door and renovated, reducing the old-timey feel. It's still the city's best value, with daily room cleaning, super-helpful reception, good wi-fi/broadband (₹100 per day) and a fabulous veg restaurant.

Hotel Imperial Classic   HOTEL **$$**
(☑ 66137698/99; www.imperialclassic.in; RTC Cross Rd, Chikkadpally; s/d from ₹1012/1124; ❄)

In a commercial area removed from the usual tourist hoods, this simple place is keeping it real: friendly staff, reasonable prices, soundproofed windows and plain rooms that go more clean than character.

Golden Glory Guesthouse   GUESTHOUSE **$$**
(Map p926; ☑ 23554765; www.goldengloryguest house.com; off Rd No 3, Banjara Hills; s/d incl breakfast from ₹900/1236, s without bathroom ₹393; ❄ 🛜) This little hotel on a quiet residential street in ritzy Banjara Hills scores big on location. Rooms are modest, but clean and homey, and some have balconies. The downside: the welcome's not the warmest.

Hotel Harsha   HOTEL **$$**
(Map p920; ☑ 23201188; www.hotelharsha.net; Public Gardens Rd; s/d incl breakfast from ₹1798/2023; ❄ 🛜) Rooms don't have tons of character and can be noisy (ask for a rear-facing room) but they're bright, have fridges,

the furniture is tasteful and the art is a step up from the usual schlock. The overall effect is polished but comfy, and the staff are all smiles. One of the city's best deals. Wi-fi's ₹100 per hour.

★ Taj Falaknuma Palace HOTEL $$$
(☎66298585; www.tajhotels.com; Engine Bowli, Falaknuma; s/d from ₹25,852/27,538; ❄@📶🏊) The Taj Group took more than a decade to restore the former residence of the sixth nizam, painstakingly mending such nizam-esque indulgences as embossed-leather wallpaper and 24-karat-gold ceiling trim. Standard rooms are stunning, but the suites give the full 19th-century experience. Even if you don't stay here, come for high tea (₹1500) in the Jade Room.

★ Marigold HOTEL $$$
(Map p926; ☎67363636; www.marigoldhotels.com; Greenlands Rd, Begumpet; s/d incl breakfast from ₹8430/9554; ❄@📶🏊) The new Marigold is as practical as it is stylish. Rooms are smart but not try-hard, with golds, neutrals and fresh flowers, while the lobby has vanishing-edge fountains, artful chandeliers and pod-like reservation counters. The rooftop pool was also a good idea. Rates listed are rack; they're often significantly lower.

GreenPark HOTEL $$$
(Map p926; ☎66515151; www.hotelgreenpark.com; Greenlands Rd, Begumpet; s/d incl breakfast from ₹6744/7868; ❄@📶) Don't bother going beyond the standard rooms here, which are comfy and classy, with sleek desks, bamboo flooring and flower petals in the bathroom. Good taste reigns (as does sensibleness, eg free wi-fi). The lobby, meanwhile, is a paragon of peace and gentle lighting, while smiley staff look on.

Mercure HOTEL $$$
(Map p920; ☎67122000; www.mercure.com; Chirag Ali Lane, Abids; s/d incl breakfast from ₹4496/5058; ❄@📶) The gargantuan black chandelier, mirrored elevators and jazz soundtrack in the Mercure's lobby give off a slight Manhattan vibe, while overlooking a busy (but very convenient) part of Abids. Rooms have stylish textiles and big glass showers. The hotel is veg and alcohol-free.

Eating

In the early evenings, look out for *mirchi bhajji* (chilli fritters), served at street stalls with tea. The Hyderabadi style is famous: chillis are stripped of their seeds, stuffed with tamarind, sesame and spices, dipped in chickpea batter and fried.

Per local usage, we use the term 'meal' instead of 'thali'. A 14% VAT applies to restaurant bills.

City Centre

Kamat Andhra Meals ANDHRA $
(Map p920; Troop Bazaar; meals from ₹80; ⏰noon-4pm & 7-11pm) Excellent authentic veg Andhra meals on banana leaves, topped up till you almost faint with pleasure and your tongue falls off from the heat. Its sister restaurants in the same compound – the Maharashtrian **Kamat Jowar Bhakri** (Map p920; meals from ₹130; ⏰noon-4pm & 7-11pm), and **Kamat Restaurant** (Map p920; meals ₹75-150; ⏰7am-10.30pm) – are also good. No relation to Kamat Hotel.

Kamat Hotel SOUTH INDIAN $
(Map p920; Nampally Station Rd; mains ₹60-120, meals ₹50-135; ⏰7am-11pm) Each Kamat is slightly different, but they're all cheap and good. There's also a **Kamat Hotel** (Map p923; SD Rd; mains ₹80-120; ⏰8am-10pm) near Secunderabad's Paradise Circle, another **Kamat** (Map p923; SD Rd, Secunderabad; mains ₹80-120; ⏰8am-10pm) near the clock tower, and **Kamat Hotel** (Map p920; meals ₹80-150, mains ₹125-175; ⏰8am-10pm) in Saifabad. Meals are reliably delish.

Subhan Bakery BAKERY $
(Map p920; www.subhanbakery.com; Yousufain Dargah Cross Rd, Nampally; baked goods ₹10-150; ⏰7am-11pm) The Osmania biscuit, so named because it was nizam Osman Ali Khan's favourite, is a Hyderabadi classic – a cardamom-inflected shortbread best eaten with tea – and Subhan's is famous. So is its *dil khush* – literally 'happy heart' – a pie filled with dried fruit that really will make your heart happy.

Eat Street FAST FOOD $
(Map p926; Necklace Rd; light meals from ₹40; ⏰7.30am-11pm) This kitschy food court has a Minerva Coffee Shop with excellent tiffins, a Café Coffee Day and fun fast food, as well as kids' rides, boat launches to the Buddha Statue and tables on a waterfront boardwalk.

G Pulla Reddy SWEETS $
(Map p920; www.gpullareddysweets.org; Nampally Station Rd, Abids; sweets from ₹10; ⏰8.30am-10pm) Sweets so good you'll die. Try the

Charminar

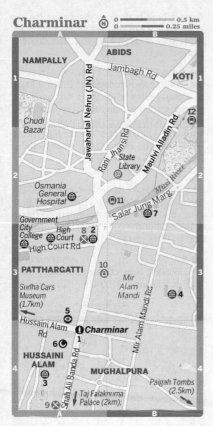

ariselu, a Telugu specialty made with rice flour, ghee and jaggery.

★ Hotel Shadab
HYDERABADI $$

(Map p925; High Court Rd, Charminar; mains ₹120-280; ☉noon-midnight) One meal at Shadab and you'll be forever under its spell. This hopping restaurant is the capital of biryani, kebabs and mutton in all configurations and, during Ramzan (Ramadan), *haleem*. Packed with Old City families and good vibes.

★ Shah Ghouse Cafe
HYDERABADI $$

(Map p925; Shah Ali Banda Rd; mains ₹90-220; ☉5am-midnight) During Ramzan, Hyderabadis line up for Shah Ghouse's famous *haleem*, but unusually, it also serves it outside of Ramzan. The biryani and other dishes are equally revered (and a bargain: 'half' portions feed two). Don't expect ambience: just good, hard-working, traditional food.

Taj Mahal Hotel
ANDHRA $$

(Map p920; Abids Rd; mains ₹120-180, meals from ₹130; ☉7am-10.30pm) The Taj's restaurant is a beloved family spot for Andhra meals. You'll have a hard time finding a table at lunch, when an army of servers will bring you heap after heap of rice and refills of exquisite, burn-your-tongue-off veg dishes.

Paradise
HYDERABADI $$

(Map p920; ☑ 66661138; www.paradisefoodcourt. com; NTR Gardens; mains ₹170-350; ☉11.30am-11pm) Paradise is synonymous with biryani in these parts. **Paradise Secunderabad** (Map p923; cnr SD & MG Rds; mains ₹170-300; ☉11.30am-11pm) is the mother ship, but this new location, part of the NTR Gardens complex with Prasads cinema (p928), is more fun.

Gufaa
NORTH INDIAN $$$

(Map p920; Ohri's, Bashirbagh Rd; mains ₹250-350; ☉12-3.30pm & 7-11pm) Gufaa has faux-rock walls, stars on the ceiling and Bollywood oldies playing in the background. And it serves Peshawari food. But somehow it works, and even the dhal here is special.

Waterfront
MULTICUISINE $$$

(Map p926; ☑65278899; Necklace Rd; mains ₹175-575; ☉noon-3.30pm & 6-11pm) The peaceful waterfront deck here has views of the Buddha Statue, Hussain Sagar and the city's twinkling lights. The tandoori, Chinese and Western food is adequate, but desserts include *qubani ka meetha*, a Hyderabadi speciality of stewed apricots and cream.

🍴 Banjara Hills & Jubilee Hills

24-Letter Mantra
GROCERY **$**

(Map p926; www.24mantra.com; Rd No 12; 🕐9am-9pm) 🍃 This tiny grocery shop has organic produce, snacks and juices, and is an organic-farming pioneer. Pick up spices, traditional soaps, beauty products and news about green happenings.

★ Southern Spice
SOUTH INDIAN **$$**

(Map p926; Rd No 3; mains ₹225-375; 🕐noon-3.30pm & 7-10.30pm) Southern Spice does a fine Andhra meal as well as specialities from all over the south. It's a good place to sample typical Andhra dishes, like *natu kodi iguru* ('country chicken') or *chapa pulusu*, a tasty, coconutty preparation of river fish.

Chutneys
SOUTH INDIAN **$$**

(Map p926; Rd No 3; mains ₹170-215, meals ₹170; 🕐7am-11pm) Chutneys is famous for its South Indian thalis and tiffins. The difference here is that the dishes are low on chilli, so you can get the full 'Andhra meals' experience without the pain. The decor is quasi-classy.

Big Dosa Company
SOUTH INDIAN FUSION **$$**

(Rd No 45, Jubilee Hills; dosas ₹95-250; 🕐8.30am-10.30pm) There's a lot that's big here: the portions, the taste and the very idea of innovating on the dosa. The place itself is tiny, with cool white booths. The cheddar cheese red-chilli-paste dosa (₹250), among others, make the trip worthwhile.

Mocha
CAFE

(Map p926; Rd No 7, Banjara Hills; coffees ₹50-150, light meals ₹90-200; 🕐9am-11pm; 🛜) Slightly dingy and full of too-cool twenty-somethings smoking, but the coffee, breakfasts, paninis and wi-fi are great.

★ So.
MEDITERRANEAN **$$$**

(☏23558004; www.notjustso.com; 550F Aryan's, 4th fl, Rd No 92; mains ₹250-425; 🕐11am-11pm) On

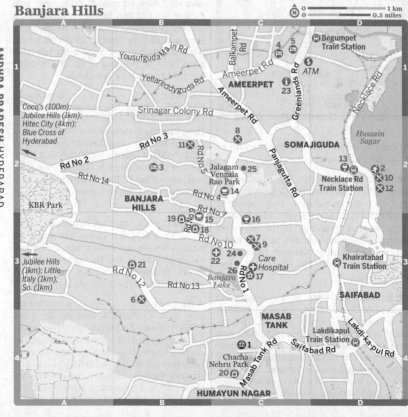

Banjara Hills

a quiet Jubilee Hills rooftop, with candles, loungy playlists and wooden tables surrounded by sugarcane and banana plants, So's the most atmospheric eating and drinking spot in town. *And* the Indian-inflected Mediterranean dishes are exquisite. Downstairs is the very popular **Little Italy** (23558001; www.littleitaly-india.com; Rd No 92, Jubilee Hills; mains ₹245-450; ⏰noon-3pm & 7-11pm), for pasta and wine.

Fusion 9   CONTINENTAL $$$
(Map p926; 65577722; www.fusion9.in; Rd No 1; mains ₹445-555; ⏰12.30-3.30pm & 7-11.30pm) Soft lighting and cosy decor set off Persian lamb kebabs on saffron rice (₹475) or Moroccan paneer steak with harissa-lemon couscous (₹445). One of the best international menus in town. Downstairs, **Deli 9** (Map p926; Rd No 1; snacks ₹35-100; ⏰9am-10.30pm; 🛜) has quiches, cakes and wi-fi.

Barbeque Nation   INDIAN $$$
(Map p926; 64566692; www.barbeque-nation. com; Rd No 1; veg/nonveg lunches ₹425/475, dinners ₹550/650; ⏰noon-3pm & 7-10.30pm) All-you-can-eat BBQ skewers in unpretentious surrounds. The menu changes often, but kebab options might include veg coconut or Goan prawn. Reserve on weekends; dinner discounts for early birds.

🍷 Drinking & Nightlife

Hyderabad's nightlife is limited by an 11.30pm curfew law. Some of the following charge covers (₹500 to ₹2000) on certain nights – for couples, that is: guys usually need a gal to enter.

★Lamakaan   CAFE, THEATRE
(Map p926; www.lamakaan.com; off Rd No 1, Banjara Hills; teas & snacks ₹10-50; ⏰10am-10.30pm Tue-Sun; 🛜) This 'noncommercial collective' is an open centre where artists stage plays, screen films, organize music-appreciation sessions and whatever else inspires. It's also a great cafe, with cheap tea and snacks, free wi-fi, artsy types collaborating on the leafy patio and a bulletin board with all of Hyderabad's most interesting possibilities. It's on a small lane off Rd No 1, north of GVK1 mall.

Beyond Coffee   CAFE
(www.beyondcoffee.in; Rd No 36, Jubilee Hills, near Jubilee Checkpost; coffees ₹55-100, light meals ₹170-300; ⏰7am-10.30pm; 🛜) Hyderabad has a zillion Baristas and Café Coffee Days, but the coffee here is in another league entirely, making it worth the trip. It also has rotating contemporary-art exhibitions, live music on Thursdays and free wi-fi.

Coco's   BAR
(23540600; 217 Rd No 2, opp KBR Park, Banjara Hills; mains ₹145-295) The rooftop setting,

ANDHRA PRADESH HYDERABAD

along with the cosy white-cushion bamboo couches, makes Coco's perfect for a cold drink on a balmy evening. There's live music daily, plus decent Indian and Continental dishes. (Reserve for dinner on weekends.)

Syn
LOUNGE

(Map p926; Taj Deccan, Rd No 1, Banjara Hills; ⏰ Tue-Sun) Syn has sparkly black floors, blue lighting and futuristic white-vinyl seating, but it's still classy, in a space-age way. The outdoor seating is equally atmospheric. But it's the sushi, cocktails and weekend parties that have made it Hyderabad's new favourite scene.

Aqua
BAR

(Map p926; www.theparkhotels.com/hyderabad; The Park, Raj Bhavan Rd, Somajiguda) The live music here goes well with the infinity pool, chaises longues, city views and late-night hookahs. Come in the early evening for a swim, a Thai starter and a sundowner, or on Saturdays, for the DJ pool party.

Kismet
NIGHTCLUB

(Map p926; www.theparkhotels.com/hyderabad; The Park, Raj Bhavan Rd, Somajiguda; ⏰ Wed-Sun) Kismet is expensive and glamorous, but it also has macrame hanging chairs, chimneys leading to the illuminated glass-bottom pool overhead, passageways covered in mirrors and a secret smoking room (favoured by gals maintaining reputations). Friday's Bollywood night.

Liquids Et Cetera
NIGHTCLUB

(Map p926; ☎ 66259907; www.liquidsetc.com; 5th fl, Bhaskar Plaza, Rd No 1, Banjara Hills) Regularly featured in the papers' society pages, Liquids doesn't bother with a sign; enter through the cellar.

☆ Entertainment

Ravindra Bharathi Theatre
THEATRE

(Map p920; ☎ 23210295; www.ravindrabharathi.org; Public Gardens Rd) Regular music, dance and drama performances; check local papers.

Prasads Multiplex
CINEMA

(Map p920; ☎ 23448888, booking 39895050; www.prasadz.com; NTR Gardens; tickets ₹150-250) Six theatres, one a monstrous Imax, plus shopping and food courts.

🛍 Shopping

Charminar's the most exciting place to shop: you'll find exquisite pearls, slippers, gold and fabrics alongside billions of bangles.

Hyderabad Perfumers
PERFUMERY

(Map p925; Patthargatti; ⏰ 10am-8.30pm Mon-Sat) The family-run Hyderabad Perfumers, in business for four generations, can whip something up for you on the spot.

AA Husain & Co
BOOKS

(Map p920; Abids Rd; ⏰ 10.30am-8.30pm Mon-Sat) A superbly curated collection of Indian and foreign authors, magically condensed into a tiny shop.

Malkha
CLOTHING

(Map p926; www.malkha.in; Khadi Bhavan, Humayan Nagar, Masab Tank Rd, opposite NMDC; ⏰ 10.30am-7pm Mon-Sat) 🍃 Unlike industrial cotton, Malkha cloth is made near the cotton fields, by hand and with natural dyes, which reduces strain to the cotton, the environment and on the rural job market. The result is gorgeous; pick up shawls or fabric at reasonable prices. Upstairs is **Gandhi Handmade Papers** (Map p926; Khadi Bhavan, Humayun Nagar; ⏰ 10.30am-7.30pm Mon-Sat), with papers, books and gifts.

Suvasa
CLOTHING

(Map p926; www.suvasa.in; Rd No 12, Banjara Hills) Suvasa's block-printed kurtas (long shirt with a short/no collar), *patialas* (baggy, pleated pants) and *dupattas* are a step up – in styling, cut and prints – from the other mainstream boutiques. A Suvasa kurta plus some leggings equals your new favourite travel outfit.

Sheela's Arts & Crafts
HANDICRAFTS

(Map p920; www.sheelashandicraftindia.com; No 17, Lal Bahadur Stadium; ⏰ 10am-8pm Mon-Sat) Tiny Sheela's is packed with handicrafts and souvenirs: some of it's great, some of it's schlock, but there's enough of it that you'll find stuff you like.

Lepakshi
HANDICRAFTS

(Map p920; www.lepakshihandicrafts.gov.in; Gunfoundry; ⏰ 10am-8pm Mon-Sat) A great selection of Andhra crafts.

Bidri Crafts
HANDICRAFTS

(Map p920; Abids Rd, Gunfoundry; ⏰ 11am-9pm Mon-Sat) Tiny shop selling bidriware at good prices.

Anokhi
CLOTHING

(Map p926; www.anokhi.com; Rd No 10, Banjara Hills; ⏰ 10.30am-7.30pm Mon-Sat) Sophisticated clothes in hand-block prints.

Fabindia CLOTHING
(Map p926; www.fabindia.com; Rd No 9, Banjara Hills; ⊘11am-8.30pm) ✦ Clothes and accessories in traditional artisanal fabrics.

ℹ Information

INTERNET ACCESS

Net World (Map p920; Taramandal Complex, Saifabad; per hr ₹15; ⊘10am-9pm)

Reliance Web World (Map p920; MPM Mall, Abids Circle; per 4hr ₹100; ⊘11am-9pm Mon-Sat, 12-7pm Sun)

State Library (Map p925; Digital Library section, 2nd fl, Maulvi Allaudin Rd; per hr ₹10; ⊘10.30am-5pm Mon-Sat) Check your email where Hyderabad's rare books and manuscripts (from as far back as 1650) are being digitised.

MEDIA

Good 'what's on' guides include **Channel 6** (₹25), *GO Hyderabad* and *City Info*. The juiciest is **Wow! Hyderabad** (www.wowhyderabad.com; ₹35). The *Hindu* is by far the best of the city's papers. The *Hyderabad Chronicle* insert in the *Deccan Chronicle* has info on happenings.

MEDICAL SERVICES

Care Hospital (www.carehospitals.com) Banjara Hills (Map p926; ☑30418888; Rd No 1); Banjara Hills Outpatient (Map p926; ☑39310444, 1800 1086666; 4th Lane); Nampally (Map p920; ☑30417777; Mukarramjahi Rd); Reputable hospital with a 24-hour pharmacy.

Mor Chemists (Map p920; ☑65547111; Bashirbagh Rd; ⊘9.30am-9.30pm Mon-Sat, 10am-2pm Sun) Helpful and well-stocked.

MONEY

The banks offer the best currency-exchange rates here. ATMs are everywhere.

State Bank of India (Map p920; HACA Bhavan, Saifabad; ⊘10.30am-4pm Mon-Fri)

POST

General Post Office (Map p920; Abids Circle; ⊘8am-8pm Mon-Sat, 10am-2pm Sun)

Secunderabad Post Office (Map p923; Rashtrapati Rd; ⊘8am-7pm Mon-Sat)

TOURIST INFORMATION

Indiatourism (Government of India; Map p926; ☑23409199; www.incredibleindia.org; Paryatak Bhavan, Tourism Plaza, Greenlands, Begumpet; ⊘9.30am-6pm Mon-Fri, to 1pm Sat) Very helpful, with information on Hyderabad, Andhra Pradesh and beyond.

ℹ Getting There & Away

AIR

Hyderabad's massive, modern **Rajiv Gandhi International Airport** (☑1800 4192008, 66546370; www.hyderabad.aero) is 22km southwest of the city in Shamshabad.

You'll get the best fares online or with a travel agent. Try **Neo Globe Tours & Travels** (Map p920; ☑66751786; Saifabad; ⊘10am-8pm Mon-Sat).

Most airline offices are open 9.30am to 5.30pm Monday to Friday, with a one-hour lunch break, and to 1.30pm Saturday.

Air India (Map p920; ☑23389744, airport 66605163; HACA Bhavan, Hill Fort Rd)

Emirates (Map p926; ☑33773377; Reliance Classic Building, Rd No 1, Banjara Hills)

Etihad Airways (Map p926; ☑1800 2090808; Rd No 1, Banjara Hills)

IndiGo (☑airport 24255052)

Jet Airways (Map p920; ☑39893333; Hill Fort Rd; ⊘9am-7pm Mon-Sat) Also handles bookings for JetKonnect.

Qatar Airways (Map p926; ☑7930616000, airport 66605121; Rd No 1, Banjara Hills)

Thai Airways (Map p926; ☑23333030, airport 66605022; Rd No 1, Banjara Hills)

ANDHRA PRADESH HYDERABAD

MAJOR BUS ROUTES FROM HYDERABAD & SECUNDERABAD

BUS NO	ROUTE
65G, 66G	Charminar–Golconda, via Abids
87	Charminar–Nampally
2/2V, 8A/8U	Charminar–Secunderabad station
20D	Jubilee station–Nampally
142K	Koti–Golconda
142M	Nampally–Golconda
1P, 25	Secunderabad station–Jubilee station
1K, 1B, 3SS, 40	Secunderabad station–Koti
20P, 20V, 49, 49P	Secunderabad station–Nampally

BUSES FROM HYDERABAD

DESTINATION	FARE (₹)	DURATION (HR)	FREQUENCY (DAILY)
Bengaluru	640-905	10-12	20
Bidar	140	4½	half-hourly
Chennai	645-1010	12-14	4
Hospet	305-650	10	5
Mumbai	1065	15	1
Mysore	1215	14	3
Nagarjuna Sagar (Hill Station)	144	4	hourly
Tirupathi	550-1320	12	23
Vijayawada	265-390	6	half-hourly
Visakhapatnam	630-1500	14	18
Warangal	135	3½	frequent

BUS

Hyderabad's long-distance bus stations are mind-bogglingly efficient, and some of the **AP-SRTC** (Andhra Pradesh State Road Transport Corporation; ☏1800 2004599) air-con services are quite good. Visit www.apsrtc.co.in for time-tables and fares; most long-distance services depart in the evening. When booking ahead, women should request seats up front as these are reserved for women.

Near Abids, **Mahatma Gandhi bus station** (Map p925; ☏23434268) (MGBS), more commonly known as Imlibun, has **advance booking offices** (MGBS; ☏23434269; ◷8am-10pm). For trips to Karnataka, go with **KSRTC** (☏24656430; ◷8am-9pm) near platform 30. See p930 for useful routes.

Secunderabad's **Jubilee bus station** (Map p923; ☏27802203) is smaller. Useful routes include the following:

Bengaluru (Volvo AC ₹895, 10 hours, three daily)

Mumbai ('express' ₹655, 14 hours, 2pm)

Tirupathi (express/Volvo AC ₹650/885, 14 hours, 7.30pm/7pm)

Visakhapatnam (Volvo AC ₹960, 12 hours, 5pm)

Private bus companies are on Nampally High Rd, near the train station.

TRAIN

Secunderabad, Hyderabad (also known as Nampally), and Kacheguda are Hyderabad's three major train stations. Most through trains stop at Kacheguda, which is convenient for Abids and Secunderabad. See p931 for key routes.

The **Nampally** (Map p920; ☏27829999) and **Secunderabad** (Rathifile; Map p923; Regimental Bazaar Rd, Secunderabad) reservation complexes have foreign-tourist-quota counters (bring passport and visa photocopies, along with originals). The Secunderabad reservation complex is around the corner from the station, next to the bus stand. For enquiries and PNR status, phone ☏139.

ⓘ Getting Around

TO/FROM THE AIRPORT

The airport is about a 45-minute drive from town.

Bus

Frequent APSRTC buses (₹15 to ₹20) run from the airport to Jubilee and Imlibun stations.

APSRTC's new **Pushpak** air-conditioned services run to various points in the city, including Rd No 1 in Banjara Hills (₹150, half-hourly), Secretariat (₹200, hourly; convenient for Abids) and Secunderabad (₹200, twice hourly).

All buses stop running between 11pm and 3am.

Taxi

The **prepaid taxi booth** is inside the terminal; cabs to Abids and Banjara Hills cost ₹500.

Meru (☏44224422) and **Sky Cabs** (☏49494949) 'radio taxis' queue up outside arrivals and charge ₹18 per kilometre, ₹22.50 at night. The fare for Abids or Banjara Hills shouldn't exceed ₹700.

AUTORICKSHAW

Flag fall is ₹16 for the first kilometre, ₹9 for each additional kilometre. Between 10pm and 5am a 50% surcharge applies. Meters are often broken or uncalibrated and lots of drivers will not use them: so be prepared to negotiate.

BUS

Many local buses originate at **Koti bus stand** (Map p920; Turrebaz Khan Rd), so if you come here you might get a seat. The 'travel as you like' ticket (₹60), available from conductors, permits unlimited travel anywhere within the city on the day of purchase. *City Bus Route Guide* (₹20) is available at bookshops around Koti.

CAR

Arrange car hire through your hotel or with **Links Travels** (☎ 9348770007). At research time, the going rate for a non-aircon car and driver for sightseeing (eight hours/80km maximum) was ₹950.

TRAIN

MMTS trains (www.mmtstraintimings.in; ₹2-10) are convenient, particularly for the three main stations, but infrequent (every half-hour). There are two main lines: Hyderabad (Nampally) to Lingampalli (northwest of Banjara Hills) stops at Necklace Rd, Begumpet and Hitec City; the Falaknuma (south of Old City) to Begumpet line passes by Kacheguda and Secunderabad stations and joins the Hyderabad–Lingampalli line at Begumpet. Trains are labelled with start and end points, eg HF for Hyderabad–Falaknuma.

Nagarjunakonda

The Hill of Nagarjuna, 150km southeast of Hyderabad, is a peaceful island peppered with ancient Buddhist structures. From the 3rd century BC until the 4th century AD, the Krishna River valley was home to powerful empires that supported the sangha, including the Ikshvakus, whose capital was Nagarjunakonda. This area alone had some 30 monasteries.

The remains here were actually discovered in 1926 in the adjacent valley. In 1953, in anticipation of the new dam, which would flood the area with the **Nagarjuna Sagar** reservoir, an excavation was launched to unearth the area's many ruins: stupas, *viharas* (monasteries), *chaitya-grihas* (assembly halls with stupas) and *mandapas* (pillared pavilions), as well as some outstanding white-marble depictions of the Buddha's life. The finds were reassembled on Nagarjunakonda.

The thoughtfully laid-out **Nagarjunakonda Museum** (Indian/foreigner ₹5/100; ◷8am-5pm, closed Fri) has Buddha statues and beautifully carved limestone slabs that once adorned stupas. The reassembled monuments are arranged around the hilltop outside.

Boats (₹90, one hour) depart for the island from Vijayapuri at 9.30am, 11.30am and 1.30pm, and stay for one hour. You'll want to take the morning launch out and the afternoon one back.

MAJOR TRAINS FROM HYDERABAD & SECUNDERABAD

DESTINATION	TRAIN NO & NAME	FARE (₹)	DURATION (HR)	DEPARTURE TIME & STATION
Bengaluru	12430 Rajdhani	1475/1037 (B)	12	6.50pm Secunderabad (Tue, Wed, Sat & Sun)
	12785 Bangalore Exp	274/742/1105 (A)	11½	7.05pm Kacheguda
Chennai	12604 Hyderabad–Chennai Exp	295/801/1200 (A)	12½	5.20pm Hyderabad
	12760 Charminar Exp	312/854/1285 (A)	14	6.30pm Hyderabad
Delhi	12723 Andhra Pradesh Exp	465/1298/2045 (A)	27	6.25am Hyderabad
	12429 Rajdhani	1789/2595 (B)	22	7.50am Secunderabad (Mon, Tue, Thu, Fri)
Kolkata	12704 Falaknuma Exp	442/1231/1925 (A)	26	4pm Secunderabad
Mumbai	12702 Hussainsagar Exp	313/883/1355 (A)	14½	2.45pm Hyderabad
	12220 Duranto Exp	892/1390 (B)	12	11.05pm Secunderabad (Tue, Fri)
Tirupathi	12734 Narayanadri Exp	284/772/1155 (A)	12	6.05pm Secunderabad
	12797 Venkatadri Exp	277/750/1115 (A)	11½	8.05pm Kacheguda
Visakhapatnam	12728 Godavari Exp	297/808/1210 (A)	13	5.15pm Hyderabad

Fares: (A) sleeper/3AC/2AC, (B) 3AC/2AC

Keeping Buddha's teachings alive in the region, **Dhamma Nagajjuna** (☑ 9440139329, 9348456780; www.nagajjuna.dhamma.org; Hill Colony) meditation centre offers free 10-day courses in charming flower-filled grounds overlooking Nagarjuna Sagar. Apply in advance. If you take a bus from Hyderabad, get down at Buddha Park.

At the convenient **Nagarjuna Resort** (☑ 08642242471; r without/with AC ₹674/1349; ❄), across the road from the boat launch, slightly shabby rooms have geysers and balconies with good views. Two kilometres up the hill from the bus stand is the government **Vijaya Vihar Haritha** (☑ 08680277362/3; r with AC on weekday/weekend from ₹1574/2810; ❄ ☀), with rooms overlooking the lake and APTDC on-site. Both hotels have restaurants.

The easiest way to visit Nagarjunakonda, other than with a private vehicle, is to go with APTDC (p922) (₹500) from Hyderabad; however, tours only run on weekends, when the site can be crowded.

To make your own way there from Hyderabad, take a bus to Hill Station/Nagarjuna Sagar (₹144, four hours, hourly); get down at Pylon and catch a ₹20 shared autorickshaw to Vijayapuri.

Warangal

☑ 0870 / POP 620,000

Warangal was the capital of the Kakatiya kingdom, which covered most of present-day Andhra Pradesh from the late 12th to early 14th centuries. The Hindu Kakatiyas were great builders and patrons of Telugu literature and arts, and during their reign the Chalukyan style of temple architecture reached its pinnacle.

◉ Sights

Fort   FORT

(Indian/foreigner   ₹5/100;   ⊙ 9am-6pm) Warangal's fort was a massive construction with three circular strongholds surrounded by a moat. Four paths with decorative gateways led to the Swayambhava, a huge Shiva temple. The gateways are still obvious, but most of the fort is in ruins. A **pillared hall** can be seen at the children's park across the street. From Warangal, take a bus (four daily) or autorickshaw (₹300 return). Admission includes entry to nearby **Kush Mahal**, a 16th-century royal hall.

1000-Pillared Temple   HINDU TEMPLE

(⊙ 6am-6pm) Built in 1163, the 1000-Pillared Temple, on the slopes of Hanamkonda Hill, is a fine example of Chalukyan architecture in a leafy setting. Dedicated to Shiva, Vishnu and Surya, it has been carefully restored, with intricately carved pillars and an impressive black-granite Nandi (bull; Shiva's mount).

Down the hill and 3km to the right is the small **Siddheshwara Temple**. The lakeside **Bhadrakali Temple**, whose striking deity sits with a weapon in each of her eight hands, is on a hill between Hanamkonda and Warangal.

🛏 Sleeping & Eating

Vijaya Lodge   HOTEL $

(☑ 2501222; Station Rd; s/d from ₹200/350) Close to the train station, the Vijaya is well organised with helpful staff and pin-striped hallways. Rooms are borderline dreary but workable.

Hotel Ashoka   HOTEL $$

(☑ 2578491-94; hotelashoka_wgl@yahoo.co.in; Main Rd, Hanamkonda; r from ₹1349; ❄ @) Good-value rooms near the Hanamkonda bus stand and the 1000-Pillared Temple. Also in the compound are a restaurant, a bar-restaurant, a pub and the veg **Kanishka** (meals ₹90).

Sri Geetha Bhavan   ANDHRA $

(Market Rd, Hanamkonda; mains ₹60-100; ⊙ 7am-11pm) Really good South Indian meals (₹75).

❶ Information

ATMs and internet cafes are plentiful. **APTDC** (☑ 2571339; 1st fl, Hanamkonda-Kazhipet Rd, Hanamkonda; ⊙ 10.30am-5pm Mon-Sat), opposite Indian Oil, is helpful.

❶ Getting There & Around

Frequent buses from **Hanamkonda bus stand** (☑ 9959226056) and hourly buses from **Warangal bus stand** (☑ 9959226057) go to Hyderabad (express/deluxe/luxury ₹120/130/140, four hours).

Warangal is a major rail junction, with several trains daily to the following (fares are sleeper/3AC/2AC) destinations:

Chennai (₹277/750/1115, 11 hours)
Delhi (₹442/1231/1925, 25 hours)
Hyderabad (₹140/292/640, three hours)
Vijayawada (₹144/328/610, four hours)

Shared autorickshaws (₹15) ply fixed routes around Warangal and Hanamkonda.

Around Warangal

Bhongir

Most Hyderabad–Warangal buses and trains stop at Bhongir, 50km from Hyderabad. It's worth jumping down for a couple of hours to climb the fantastical-looking 12th-century Chalukyan hill fort (admission ₹3; ⊙10am-5pm). Looking like a gargantuan stone egg, the smooth hill is mostly ringed by stairs. Legend has it that an (as-yet-undiscovered) underground tunnel leads from the fort to Golconda.

Palampet

About 65km northeast of Warangal, the stunning Ramappa Temple (⊙6am-6.30pm), built in 1234, is an attractive example of Kakatiya architecture. Its pillars are ornately carved and its eaves shelter fine statues of female forms. The Kakatiyas constructed a lake, Ramappa Cheruvu, 1km south, to serve as temple tank. It's popular with migrating birds. APTDC has a guesthouse (☑08715200200; r ₹950) here.

The easiest way to get here is by private car (₹1200), but frequent buses also run from Hanamkonda to Mulugu (₹40), then a further 13km to Palampet (₹15). The temple is about 500m from here.

Visakhapatnam

☑0891 / POP 1.73 MILLION

Visit Visakhapatnam – also called Vizag (vie-zag) – during the holiday season and you'll see domestic tourism in rare form: balloons, fairy floss (cotton candy) and, of course, weddings! But the crowds only enhance the area's kitschy coasts. The rundown boardwalk along Ramakrishna Beach has spunk, and nearby Rushikonda beach is Andhra's best.

The old beach-resort vibe exists despite the fact that Vizag is Andhra Pradesh's second-largest city, famous for shipbuilding and steel. It's big and dusty, but surrounded by little gems: sweet beaches, a gorgeous temple and, further out, the Araku Valley and several ancient Buddhist sites.

If you're here in December or January, seek out Visakha Utsav, the city's annual festival with events on the beach.

Yo! Vizag (₹25), available at bookshops, lists events.

◉ Sights & Activities

Beaches BEACH
The long beaches of Waltair overlook the Bay of Bengal, with its mammoth ships and brightly-painted fishing boats. Its coastal Beach Rd, lined with parks, is great for long walks.

Kailasagiri Hill (Beach Rd; admission ₹5, cable car adult/child ₹60/30; ⊙11am-8.30pm) has a cable car with incredible views, playgrounds, a toy train and a gargantuan Shiva and Parvati. A Telugu-heritage museum is in the works.

Rushikonda, one of the nicest stretches of India's east coast, 10km north of town, is the best beach for swimming. Weekends are busy and festive. Surfers can rent decent boards from local surf pioneer, Melville, at SAAP (Sports Authority of Andhra Pradesh; ☑9848561052; Rushikonda; lessons/board rental ₹300/300). To avoid unwanted attention, gals should go for modest swim attire (T-shirts and shorts).

Submarine Museum MUSEUM
(Beach Rd; adult/child ₹40/20, camera ₹50; ⊙2-8.30pm Tue-Sat, 10am-12.30pm & 2-8.30pm Sun) The 91m-long Indian navy submarine *Kursura* saw battle in 1971 during the Liberation War (when India sided with East Pakistan in its struggle for independence). The museum is a fascinating look inside the vessel and its jumble of knobs, switches, gauges and dials.

Simhachalam Temple HINDU TEMPLE
(⊙6-10am & 4-6pm) Dedicated to Narasimha, an incarnation of Vishnu, this important 11th-century temple is atop Simhachalam (literally 'lion hill') 10km northwest of town. Bus 6A/H goes here.

☞ Tours

The APTDC (www.aptdc.in) operates city tours (from ₹350) and several to Araku Valley from the RTC Complex (p935) and train station (☑2788821; ⊙6am-8.30pm).

🛏 Sleeping

Beach Rd is the place to stay, but it's low on inexpensive hotels.

Hotel Morya HOTEL $
(☑2731112; www.hotelmorya.com; Bowdara Rd; s/d from ₹438/618; ❄) Nothing special, but a good cheapie in town, close to the train station.

Railway

Retiring Rooms   RAILWAY RETIRING ROOM $
(dm/r ₹150/450, with air-con ₹225/750 ; 🔆) Near
the train station.

Haritha Hotel   HOTEL $$
(📞2788824; Beach Rd, Appughar; r incl breakfast
from ₹1236; 🔆) This slightly tired APTDC
hotel is near Kailasagiri Hill and across from
the beach. The lowest-priced rooms (with no
views) are only so-so; bump yourself up if
you can.

Haritha Beach Resort   HOTEL $$
(📞2788826; www.aptdc.in; Rushikonda; r with AC
incl breakfast from ₹2136) The service is iffy,
but the Haritha's location – high on a hill
in Rushikonda – is sublime. Down the hill,
Vihar (Rushikonda; mains ₹100-240; ⊙11am-
10.30pm) is great for a beer or a meal: views
from the terrace are insane.

Sai Priya Resort   HOTEL $$
(📞2790333444; www.saipriyabeachresorts.com;
cottages/r from ₹955/2136; 🔆@🏊) With a
prime Rushikonda beach location, Sai Priya
rests on its laurels. Some rooms have sea
views and bamboo cottages are quaint, but
everything here falls short of its potential –
and checkout's 8am. Nonguests can use the
pool (₹100).

Hotel Supreme   HOTEL $$
(📞278247234;   hotelsupreme@hotmail.co.in;
Beach Rd, near Coastal Battery; s/d from
₹1461/1686; 🔆) The rooms are more budget
than the price would suggest, but the Supreme's spot across the street from the
beach is worth a few bucks. Pricier rooms
have sea views.

Park   HOTEL $$$
(📞3045678; www.theparkhotels.com; Beach Rd;
s/d from ₹7714/9918; 🔆@🏊) Vizag's best
hotel is very elegant, very high-design, but
also warm and inviting, with 6 acres of
beachfront gardens. Rooms are cosy and
sophisticated and have internet connectivity
through the flatscreen TV.

✗ Eating

At night snack stalls on Ramakrishna Beach
are hopping.

Pastry, Coffee n' Conversation   BAKERY $
(PCC; Dutt Island, Siripuram Junction; pastries ₹20-
60, light meals ₹60-200; ⊙11am-10.30pm) This
hangout spot for Vizag's hip young crowd is
the place for coffee, pizza and a ridiculously
good 'lava cake'.

New Andhra Hotel   ANDHRA $
(Sree Kanya Lodge, Bowdara Rd; mains ₹50-125;
⊙11am-4pm & 7-10.30pm) An unassuming
place with decent, spicy Andhra dishes; go
for the meals (from ₹55) or biryani.

★**Dharani**   ANDHRA $$
(Daspalla Hotel, Suryabagh; mains ₹110-135;
⊙7am-3.30pm & 6.30-11.30pm) Words don't
do justice to the super-deliciousness of the
meals (₹98) at this family veg restaurant.
The fabulous Daspalla Hotel has several
other restaurants in the building too. Be
sure to try the South Indian–style coffee: it's
heavenly.

Masala   INDIAN $$
(Signature Towers, 1st fl, Asilmetta; mains ₹100-190;
⊙11.30am-3.30pm & 7-10.30pm) Near Sampath
Vinayaka Temple, Masala does out-of-this-
world Andhra, tandoori and Chinese in a
friendly family setting.

Sea Inn   SEAFOOD $$
(Beach Rd, Rushikonda; mains ₹100-150; ⊙noon-
3.30pm Tue-Sun) The chef here cooks Andhra-
style seafood dishes the way her mom did,
and serves it up in a simple dining room
with bench seating. The restaurant is below
street level and has no sign: look for the
thatch roof and white gate 500m south of
Sai Priya Resort.

Bamboo Bay   ANDHRA $$$
(The Park, Beach Rd; mains ₹300-650; ⊙7-11pm)
Excellent coastal Andhra, Chettinad and
Mughlai food in gardens on the beach,
framed by palms and magnolias. The less
formal **Beach Shack** has drinks and grilled
catches of the day.

🛍 Shopping

Tribes India   HANDICRAFTS
(www.tribesindia.com; GCC, East Point Colony,
Beach Rd; ⊙10.30am-8pm Mon-Sat) Unique tex-
tiles, artwork and crafts from tribal villages
in Andhra and beyond.

Fabindia   CLOTHING
(www.fabindia.com; 1st fl, Dutt Island, Siripuram
Junction;   ⊙11.30am-8.30pm)   Traditional
prints and modern cotton cuts for men and
women.

ⓘ Information

ATMs are everywhere. RTC Complex has several
internet cafes (per hour ₹20).
Apollo Pharmacy (📞2788652; Siripuram
Junction; ⊙24hr)

Thomas Cook (☑2588112; Eswar Plaza, Dwarakanagar; ⊗9am-6pm Mon-Sat) Near ICICI Bank.

ⓘ Getting There & Around

You'll have to negotiate fares with autorickshaw drivers here. Most in-town rides are around ₹40. **Guide Tours & Travels** (☑9866265559, 2754477), reliable for car hire, is opposite the RTC Complex 'out gate'.

AIR

Take an autorickshaw (₹200), taxi (₹270) or bus 38 (₹10, 30 minutes) to Vizag's airport, 12km west of town. The arrivals hall has a prepaid taxi booth.

Nonstop flights run daily to Hyderabad, Chennai, Delhi, Bhubaneswar, Kolkota and Mumbai. **Air India** (☑2746501, airport 2572521; LIC Bldg) The only airline with a town office.

BOAT

Boats depart monthly-ish for Port Blair in the Andaman Islands. Book for the 56-hour journey (₹2000 to ₹8000) at the **Shipping Office** (☑2565597, 9866073407; Av Bhanoji Row; ⊗9am-5pm Mon-Sat) in the port complex. Bring your passport.

BUS

Vizag's well-organised **RTC Complex** (☑9177101947) has frequent services to the following:

Hyderabad ('superluxury'/Volvo ₹629/987, 14/12 hours)

Rajahmundry (₹209, four hours)

Vijayawada ('superluxury'/Volvo ₹373/469, eight/seven hours)

TRAIN

The **train station** is on the western edge of town, near the port. The prepaid autorickshaw stand and cloak room are open 24 hours.

Vizag is on the main Kolkata–Chennai line; the 12841 Coromandel Express is the fastest in both directions.

Chennai (sleeper/3AC/2AC ₹312/854/1285, 12½-16 hours)

Kolkata (via Bhubaneswar; sleeper/3AC/2AC ₹333/914/1385, 14-16 hours)

Vijayawada (via Rajahmundry; sleeper/3AC/2AC ₹190/495/720, seven hours)

On Mondays and Fridays, the 18512 Visakhapatnam–Koraput Intercity Express heads near Chatikona (p615), Onkadelli (p616) and Chandoori Sai (p617) in Odisha.

Around Visakhapatnam

Bheemunipatnam

This former Dutch settlement, 25km north of Vizag, is the oldest municipality in mainland India, with bizarre sculptures on the beach, an 1861 lighthouse, an interesting Dutch cemetery and Bheemli Beach, where local grommets surf on crude homemade boards. Catch bus 999 or 900 (₹22, 40 minutes) or a shared autorickshaw.

Bavikonda & Thotlakonda

The Vizag area's natural harbours have long been conducive to dropping anchor, which helped monks from Sri Lanka, China and Tibet come here to learn meditation. **Bavikonda** (⊗9am-5pm) and **Thotlakonda** (⊗8am-6pm) were popular hilltop monasteries on the coast that hosted up to 150 monks at a time – with the help of massive rainwater tanks and, at Thotlakonda, a natural spring.

The monasteries flourished from around the 3rd century BC to the 3rd century AD, and had votive stupas, congregation halls, *chaitya-grihas*, *viharas* and refectories. Today only the ruins of these monastic compounds remain, but they're impressive nonetheless, with a placid, almost magical, air and sea views to meditate on. Bavikonda and Thotlakonda are 14km and 16km, respectively, from Vizag on Bheemli Beach Rd. Vizag's autorickshaw drivers charge around ₹500 return from RTC Complex to see both.

Sankaram

Forty kilometres southwest of Vizag is this stunning **Buddhist complex** (⊗dawn-dusk), better known by the name of its two hills, Bojjannakonda and Lingalakonda. Used by monks from the 2nd to 9th centuries AD, the hills are covered with rock-cut caves, stupas, ruins of monastery structures and reliefs of Buddha that span the Theravada, Mahayana and Vajrayana periods. Bojjannakonda has a two-storey group of rock-cut caves flanked by *dwarapalakas* (doorkeepers) and containing a stupa and gorgeous carvings of Buddha. Atop the hill sit the ruins of a huge stupa and a monastery; you can still make out the individual cells where monks meditated. Lingalakonda is piled high with stupas, some of them enormous.

A private car from Vizag costs around ₹900. Or, take a frequent bus (₹32, 1½ hours) or train (₹30, one hour) to Anakapalle, 3km away, and then an autorickshaw (₹100 return including waiting).

Araku Valley

🚂 08936 / ELEV 975M

Andhra's best train ride is through the magnificent Eastern Ghats to the Araku Valley, 115km north of Vizag. The area is home to isolated tribal communities and a small **Museum of Habitat** (admission ₹10; ⊙ 8am-8pm) with exhibits on indigenous life.

The coffee from this area is excellent – mostly organic, with hints of berry and chocolate; pick up some at the roadside stands by the **Ananthagiri coffee plantations**, 28km from Araku. You can sample local coffee and chocolate-covered coffee beans at **Araku Valley Coffee House** (⊙ 8am-8pm), next to the tribal museum, which has a tiny coffee museum.

APTDC runs **tours** (from ₹550) from Vizag, which take in a performance of Dhimsa, a tribal dance, and the million-year-old limestone **Borra Caves** (adult/child ₹40/30, camera ₹25; ⊙ 10am-1pm & 2-5pm), 30km from Araku.

The most atmospheric place to stay is **Jungle Bells** (www.aptdc.in; Tyda; cottages incl breakfast from ₹1200; ﹡), 45km from Araku, with cottages tucked away in woods. Book with APTDC (p933).

There are several hotels near the train station, including the unfriendly but well-maintained **Hotel Rajadhani** (🚂 249580; www.hotelrajadhani.com; d/tr from ₹700/900; ﹡). APTDC's **Valley Resort** (🚂 249202; r incl breakfast from ₹1200; ﹡) is closer to the town centre, such as it is. The train station has **retiring rooms** (₹225). The restaurant at **Hill Resort Mayuri** (🚂 249204; meals ₹100, cottages from ₹850; ﹡) serves good Andhra meals.

The Kirandol passenger train (₹22, five hours) leaves Vizag at 6.50am and Araku at 3pm. It's a slow, spectacular ride; sit on the right-hand side coming out of Vizag for best views. For Jungle Bells, get off at Tyda station, 500m from the resort. Frequent buses (₹90, 4½ hours) leave Araku for Vizag every half-hour until 7pm.

Vijayawada

🚂 0866 / POP 1.05 MILLION

Vijayawada is a busy city and an important port, but it's also intersected by canals, lined with ghats and ringed by fields of rice and palm. The surrounding area is intensely lush and green.

Vijayawada is low on sights, but it has an important Durga temple and is considered by many to be the heart of Andhra culture and language. It's a good base for visiting the area's important Buddhist sites.

OFF THE BEATEN TRACK

MAREDUMILLI

A little **nature circuit** (🚂 088642449968; www.vanavihari.com; admission to all sites ₹25, guides per day ₹250, r & cottages ₹562-1124) 🖉 has been set up in the village of Maredumilli by the local tribal community and AP's Forest Department. A guesthouse, with cottages in a woodsy setting and excellent meals (₹50), is at one end of a 16km road lined by eight lush natural sites, including: a 70-hectare coffee plantation with pepper vines, wild mango and orange trees, and great trekking; a medicinal-plant garden; two waterfalls tucked away in the forest; and a 260-hectare medicinal-plant conservation area, with walking trails, 203 plant species and 170 species of birds.

The sites have been developed mindfully, with natural materials, and it's easy to immerse yourself in the forest. Some trails require a guide, which the guesthouse can arrange; it also hires bicycles and can set up autorickshaw day hire (₹450).

The Maredumilli area is known for its 'bamboo chicken' – chicken roasted in a bamboo trunk. October to February is toddy season.

Maredumilli is about 80km from Rajahmundry, which is about halfway between Vijayawada and Visakhapatnam. From Rajahmundry, take any Bhadrachalam bus to Maredumilli (₹63, three hours, every two hours until 4pm). If you need to stay the night in Rajahmundry, **Akanksha Inn** (🚂 0883-2477775/6; akanksha.inn@gmail.com; Alcot Gardens, opp railway station, Rajahmundry; s/d with AC from ₹400/1000; ﹡), across from the train station, will do fine.

☉ Sights

Undavalli Cave Temples HISTORIC SITE, HINDU
(Indian/foreigner ₹5/100; ⊙9am-5pm) Seven kilometres southwest of Vijayawada, these stunning cave temples cut a fine silhouette against the palm trees and rice paddies. Shrines are dedicated to Brahma, Vishnu and Shiva, and one cave on the third level houses a huge reclining Vishnu. The caves, in their Hindu form, date to the 7th century, but they're thought to have been constructed for Buddhist monks 500 years earlier. Bus 301 (₹11, 20 minutes) goes here; autorickshaws ask ₹250 return.

Victoria Jubilee Museum MUSEUM
(MG Rd; Indian/foreigner ₹30/100, camera ₹3; ⊙10.30am-5pm Sat-Thu) The best part of this museum is the building itself, built in 1887 to honour Queen Victoria's coronation jubilee. The museum also has a small collection of art and arms, and a garden with temple sculptures from around the state.

🛏 Sleeping

Hotel Sripada HOTEL $
(☎6644222; hotelsripada@rediffmail.com; Gandhi Nagar; s/d from ₹913/1028; ☒) One of the only budget hotels in Vijayawada authorised to accept foreign guests, the Sripada has small but bright rooms, a decent restaurant and helpful staff. Near the train station.

Railway
Retiring Rooms RAILWAY RETIRING ROOM $
(dm/s/d from ₹75/180/375; ☒) The train station's clean and spacious rooms are a great option.

Alankar Inn HOTEL $$
(www.alankarinn.com; Alankar Circle, Gandhi Nagar; s/d with AC from ₹1686/2248; ☒🛜) The Alankar, new at the time of research, was still working out the kinks. Hopefully, they're sorted now, and the compact, semi-chic rooms and free wi-fi are all fulfilling their potential.

Hotel Golden Way HOTEL $$
(☎2576693; Purnanandapet; s/d incl breakfast from ₹1574/2019; ☒) A good midranger right near the train station.

✕ Eating

★Minerva Coffee Shop INDIAN $
(Museum Rd; mains ₹75-170, meals ₹65-145; ⊙6.30am-11pm) Near Big Bazaar, this outpost of the fabulous Minerva chain has great North and South Indian cuisine, including top-notch dosas. A newer **Minerva** (MG Rd; mains ₹125-185; ⊙7am-11pm) serves similarly excellent food in airy, sophisticated surrounds.

Lotus Food City INDIAN $$
(www.lotusthefoodcity.com; Seethanagaram; mains ₹110-190; ⊙12.30pm-11pm) This APTDC food complex has a lovely spot on the Krishna River (over the Prakasam Barrage) where you can dine in or outdoors looking over the water.

ℹ Information

APTDC (☎2571393; MG Rd, opposite PWD Grounds; ⊙8am-8pm) Good for brochures.
Department of Tourism (☎2578880; train station; ⊙10.30am-5pm)
MagicNet (Swarnalok Complex, Eluru Rd; per hr ₹20; ⊙10am-10pm) Internet access.

ℹ Getting There & Around

BUS
Frequent bus services, most in the evening, run to the following destinations:
Amaravathi (ordinary/express ₹26/36, two hours)
Chennai (superluxury/Venella ₹453/1074, nine hours)
Hyderabad (express/Venella ₹197/630, seven/five hours)
Rajahmundry (express/superluxury ₹114/149, three hours)
Tirupathi (express/Indra ₹312/508, nine hours)
Visakhapatnam (express/Venella ₹281/895, nine hours)

TRAIN
Vijayawada is on the main Chennai–Kolkata and Chennai–Delhi railway lines. The Chennai–Kolkata 12842 Coromandal Express is quick. The **advance-booking office** (☎enquiry 2577775; ⊙8am-8pm Mon-Sat, till 2pm Sun) is in the basement. Fares below are for sleeper/3AC/2AC.
Chennai (₹214/564/830, seven hours)
Hyderabad (₹190/495/720, 6½ hours, 17 daily)
Kolkata (₹395/1093/1690, 20 hours)
Tirupathi (₹178/490/730, seven hours, 11 daily)
Warangal (₹144/359/640, three hours, 20 daily)
 The train station has a prepaid autorickshaw stand.

Around Vijayawada

Eluru

Dhamma Vijaya   MEDITATION
(Vipassana Meditation Centre; ☏9441449044, 08812225522; www.dhamma.org; Eluru-Chintalapudi Rd, Vijayarai) Intensive 10-day *vipassana* meditation courses are offered free of charge (donations are accepted) in lush palm- and cocoa-forested grounds; apply in advance. Buses depart Vijayawada for Eluru (₹50, 1½ hours, half-hourly, 64km), and Eluru for Vijayarai (₹15, 20 minutes, half-hourly). Call for details.

Amaravathi

Amaravathi was once the Andhran capital and a significant Buddhist centre. India's biggest **stupa** (Indian/foreigner ₹5/100; ☉8am-6pm), measuring 30m high and 51m across, was constructed here in the 3rd century BC, when Emperor Ashoka sent monks south to spread Buddha's teaching. All that remains are a mound and some of the stones, but the nearby **museum** (admission ₹5; ☉10am-5pm, closed Fri) has a small replica of the stupa, with its intricately carved pillars, marble-surfaced dome and carvings of scenes from Buddha's life. In the courtyard is a reconstruction of part of the surrounding gateway, which gives you an idea of the stupa's massive scale. It's worth the trip, but many of Amaravathi's best sculptures are in London's British Museum and Chennai's Government Museum.

About 1km down the road is the **Dhyana Buddha**, a 20m-high Buddha on the site where the Dalai Lama spoke in 2006.

Buses run from Vijayawada to Amaravathi half-hourly (ordinary/express ₹26/36, two hours), passing some lovely scenery.

Tirumala & Tirupathi

☏ 0877 / POP 287,000

The holy hill of **Tirumala** is, on any given day, filled with tens of thousands of blissed-out devotees, many of whom have endured long journeys to see the powerful **Lord Venkateshwara** here, at his home. It's one of India's most visited pilgrimage centres: 50,000 pilgrims come each day, and *darshan* runs 24/7. Temple staff alone number 14,000, and the efficient **Tirumala Tirupathi Devasthanams** (TTD; ☏2233333, 2277777; www.tirumala.org) brilliantly administers the crowds. As a result, although the throngs can be overwhelming, a sense of order, serenity and ease mostly prevails, and a trip to the Holy Hill can be fulfilling, even if you're not a pilgrim.

'It is believed that Lord Sri Venkateshwara enjoys festivals', according to the TTD. And so do his devotees: *darshan* queues during September/October's **Brahmotsavam** can run up to several kilometres, with up to 500,000 people visiting a day.

Tirupathi is the service town at the bottom of the hill, with hotels, restaurants and transport; a fleet of buses constantly ferries pilgrims the 18km up and down. You'll find most of your worldly needs around the Tirupathi bus station (TP Area) and, about 500m away, the train station.

◉ Sights

Venkateshwara Temple   HINDU TEMPLE
Devotees flock to Tirumala to see Venkateshwara, an avatar of Vishnu. Among the many powers attributed to him is the granting of any wish made before the idol at Tirumala. Many pilgrims also donate their hair to the deity – in gratitude for a wish fulfilled, or to renounce ego – so hundreds of barbers attend to devotees. Tirumala and Tirupathi are filled with tonsured men, women and children.

Legends about the hill itself and the surrounding area appear in the Puranas, and the temple's history may date back 2000 years. The main temple is an atmospheric place, though you'll be pressed between hundreds of devotees when you see it. The inner sanctum itself is dark and magical; it smells of incense, resonates with chanting and may make you religious. There, Venkateshwara inspires bliss and love among his visitors from the back of the sanctum. You'll have a moment to say a prayer and then you'll be shoved out again. Don't forget to collect your delicious *ladoo* from the counter: Tirumala *ladoos* (sweet ball made with chickpea flour, cardamom and dried fruits) are famous across India.

'Ordinary *darshan*' requires a wait of anywhere from two to eight hours in the claustrophobic metal cages ringing the temple. Several kinds of special-*darshan* tickets (₹300) will get you through the queue faster, though you'll still have to brave the gauntlet of the cage, which is part of the fun, kind of... Head to the Supatham complex or the Seeghra Darshan counters

ANDHRA PRADESH AROUND VIJAYAWADA

GUNTUPALLI

Getting here is a very scenic adventure. The former **monastic compound** (Indian/foreigner ₹5/100; ⊙10am-5pm), high on a hilltop overlooking a vast expanse of forest and paddy fields, is noteworthy for its circular rock-cut *chaitya-griha*. The cave's domed ceiling is carved with 'wooden beams' designed to look like those in a hut. The *chaitya-griha* also has a well-preserved stupa and, like the monk dwellings that line the same cliff, a gorgeous arched facade also designed to look like wood (note the 'rafters'). Also check out the stone 'beds' in the monks' cells, and the compound's 60-plus votive stupas. The monastery was active from the 2nd century BC to the 3rd century AD.

Guntupalli is best reached from Eluru, on the main Vijayawada–Visakhapatnam train line. From Vijayawada, buses run half-hourly to Eluru (₹50, 1½ hours); from here, take another bus to Kamavarapukota (₹30, one hour, half-hourly, 35km). Guntupalli is 10km west of Kamavarapukota; catch a local bus or autorickshaw. A private car from Eluru costs around ₹900 return.

at Vaikuntam Queue Complex 1 for these tickets. There are special hours for special entry; call ahead.

Upon entry, you'll have to sign a form declaring your faith in Lord Vishnu.

Tours

If you're pressed for time, APTDC (p922) runs three-day tours (₹2300) to Tirumala from Hyderabad. KSTDC and TTDC offer the same from Bengaluru and Chennai, respectively. **APTDC** (☑2289126; Sridevi Complex, 2nd fl, Tilak Rd; ⊙8.30am-8pm) also has a full-day tour (₹310) of temples in the Tirupathi area.

🛏 Sleeping & Eating

The TTD runs vast **dormitories** (beds free) and **guesthouses** (r ₹50-6000) around the temple in Tirumala, but these are intended for pilgrims. To stay, check in at the Central Reception Office. Huge **dining halls** (meals free) on the hill feed thousands of pilgrims daily; veg restaurants also serve meals for ₹25.

Small, inexpensive restaurants cluster around Tirupathi's train and bus stations. The following are all in Tirupathi.

Hotel Mamata Lodge   HOTEL $
(☑2225873; 1st fl, 170 TP Area; s/d/tr/q ₹250/300/400/500) A friendly, spick-and-span cheapie. Some of the sheets are stained, but they're tucked in tight and lovingly patched with white squares. Avoid the downstairs lodge of the same name.

Railway
Retiring Rooms   RAILWAY RETIRING ROOM $
(dm/r from ₹75/225, with AC ₹225/450) The station retiring rooms are super value.

Hotel Annapurna   HOTEL $$
(☑2250666; Nethaji Rd; r without/with AC ₹1236/1911; 🌣) Rooms at the convenient and well-organised Annapurna are clean and pink. Since it's on a corner across from the train station, nonair-con front rooms can be noisy, but air-con rooms are not as good-value. Its veg **restaurant** (mains ₹100 to ₹175) has fresh juices and excellent food.

★**Minerva Grand**   ANDHRA $$
(☑6688888; www.minervagrand.com; Renigunta Rd; mains & meals ₹130-185, s/d with AC from ₹3147/3822; ⊙7am-11.30pm; 📶) The dining room here is contemporary and somewhat cold – the Minerva is part of a new generation of sleek properties in town – but it's warmed up by the exquisite meals: dish after dish of Andhra food done good and right. Follow it with the dynamite filter coffee. The rooms here are the best in town.

Maya   INDIAN $$
(Bhimas Deluxe Hotel; ☑2225521; bhimasdeluxe @rediffmail.com; G Car St; meals & mains ₹135-190, r with AC ₹1855-2023; ⊙6am-10pm) Great veg meals in the basement of the Bhimas Deluxe, which also has good-value rooms (some without windows: beware) near the train station. Not to be confused with Bhimas Hotel.

ⓘ Information

Anu Internet Centre (per hr ₹20; ⊙9am-7.30pm) Next to the bus stand, along with several other internet cafes.
Apollo Pharmacy (G Car St; ⊙24hr)

❶ Getting There & Away

It's possible to visit Tirupathi on a (very) long day trip from Chennai. If travelling by bus or train, buy a 'link ticket', which includes transport from Tirupathi to Tirumala.

AIR

Renigunta Airport, 14km outside Tirupathi, was at research time being upgraded to an international airport. **Air India** (☑ 2283992, airport 2283992; Tirumala Bypass Rd; ⊙ 9.30am-5.30pm), with an office 2km from Tirupathi, **SpiceJet** (☑ airport 2275595) and **JetKonnect** (☑ airport 2274155) all fly to Hyderabad daily. You can book with the mobile **Mitta Travels** (☑ 2225981; DR Mahal Rd; ⊙ 11am-11pm).

BUS

Tirupathi's **bus station** (☑ 2289900) is a wonder of logistics. Useful routes include the following destinations:

Bengaluru (express/Volvo/night Volvo ₹201/400/450, four to six hours)

Chennai (express/Volvo ₹110/208, four hours)

Hyderabad (superluxury/Volvo ₹548/896, 10-12 hours)

Vijayawada (express/superluxury/Volvo ₹300/412/600, nine hours)

Private buses depart from TP Area, opposite the bus stand.

TRAIN

Tirupathi station is well served by express trains; the **reservation office** (⊙ 8am-8pm Mon-Sat, 8am-2pm Sun) is across the street. Fares are for sleeper/3AC/2AC.

Bengaluru (₹168/470/665, seven hours)

Chennai (₹140/298/640, three hours)

Hyderabad (₹284/764/1075, 12 hours)

Vijayawada (₹198/502/730, seven hours)

❶ Getting Around

There's a prepaid taxi booth outside the train station.

BUS

Tirumala Link buses have a stand next to the main bus stand and another outside the train station. The scenic 18km trip to Tirumala takes one hour (₹72 return); if you don't mind heights, sit on the left side for views.

WALKING

TTD has constructed probably the best footpath in India for pilgrims to walk up to Tirumala. It's about 15km from Tirupathi and takes four to six hours. Leave your luggage at the toll gate at Alipiri near the Hanuman statue. It will be transported free to the reception centre. There are shady rest points along the way, and a few canteens.

Around Tirumala & Tirupathi

Chandragiri Fort

Only a couple of buildings remain from this 15th-century **fort** (Indian/foreigner ₹10/100; ⊙ 9am-5pm, Sat-Thu), 14km west of Tirupathi. Both the Rani Mahal and the Raja Mahal, which houses a small **museum** (⊙ 9am-5pm Sat-Thu), were constructed under Vijayanagar rule and resemble structures in Hampi's Royal Centre. There's a nightly **sound-and-light show** (admission ₹35; ⊙ 7pm Mar-Sep, 6.30pm Oct-Feb), narrated by Bollywood great Amitabh Bachchan. Buses for Chandragiri (₹14) leave Tirupathi every 15 minutes. Prepaid taxis are ₹450 return.

Sri Kalahasti

Around 36km east of Tirupathi, Sri Kalahasti is known for its important **Sri Kalahasteeswara Temple** and for being, along with Machilipatnam near Vijayawada, a centre for the ancient art of *kalamkari*. These paintings are made with natural ingredients: the cotton is primed with *myrabalam* (resin) and cow's milk; figures are drawn with a pointed bamboo stick dipped in fermented jaggery and water; and the dyes are made from cow dung, ground seeds, plants and flowers. See the artists at work in the Agraharam neighbourhood, 2.5km from the bus stand. **Sri Vijayalakshmi Fine Kalamkari Arts** (☑ 9441138380; door No 15-890) is an old family business with 40 artists.

Buses leave Tirupathi for Sri Kalahasti every 10 minutes (₹30, 45 minutes); a prepaid taxi is ₹700 return.

Kerala

Best Wildlife-Watching

➡ Wayanad Wildlife Sanctuary (p996)

➡ Thattekkad Bird Sanctuary (p990)

➡ Periyar Wildlife Sanctuary (p969)

➡ Neyyar Wildlife Sanctuary (p949)

➡ Parambikulam Wildlife Sanctuary (p976)

Best Homestays

➡ Green Woods Bethlehem (p982)

➡ Cherukara Nest (p964)

➡ Tranquil (p998)

➡ Graceful Homestay (p947)

➡ Reds Residency (p983)

Why Go?

A sliver of a state in India's deep south, Kerala is shaped by its landscape – almost 600km of glorious Arabian Sea coast and beaches, a languid network of backwaters and the spice and tea covered hills of the Western Ghats. As relaxing as an ayurvedic massage, just setting foot on this swath of soul-quenching green will slow your stride to a blissed-out amble. Kerala is a world away from the frenzy of elsewhere, as if India had passed through the Looking Glass and become an altogether more laid-back place.

Besides its famous backwaters, rice paddies, coconut groves, elegant houseboats and delicately spiced, taste-bud-tingling cuisine, Kerala is home to wild elephants, exotic birds and the odd tiger; and crazily vibrant traditions such as Kathakali plays and snake-boat races. Few visitors neglect to put Kerala on a South India itinerary – the biggest problem is choosing where to linger the longest.

When to Go
Thiruvananthapuram

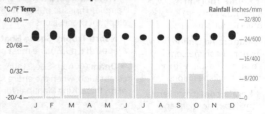

Jan–Feb Perfect beach and backwater weather. Ernakulathappan Utsavam festival in Kochi (Cochin).

Apr Kathakali at Kottayam and Kollam festivals, and the elephant procession in Thrissur.

Aug–Sep End of the monsoon period: Onam festival, snake-boat races.

MAIN POINTS OF ENTRY

Thiruvananthapuram (Trivandrum), Kozhikode (Calicut) and Kochi (Cochin) are Kerala's air and rail transport hubs.

Fast Facts

➡ **Population:** 33.34 million

➡ **Area:** 38,864 sq km

➡ **Capital:** Thiruvananthapuram (Trivandrum)

➡ **Main Language:** Malayalam

➡ **Sleeping Prices:** $ below ₹1000, $$ ₹1000 to ₹3500, $$$ above ₹3500

Planning Your Trip

High season in the backwaters and beach resorts is around November to March; between mid-December and mid-January prices creep up further. There are great deals during the monsoon (June to September).

Resources

➡ **Kerala Tourism** (www.keralatourism.org) Kerala's official tourism site.

➡ **Manorama Online** (www.manoramaonline.com) Local newspaper with an online English edition.

➡ **Kerala.com** (www.kerala.com) News, tourism and loads of links.

➡ **Lonely Planet** (www.lonelyplanet.com/india/kerala) Planning advice, reviews, recommendations and insider tips.

Food

Delicious South Indian breakfast dishes include *puttu* (steamed rice powder and coconut), *idlis* (spongy, round, fermented rice cakes), *sambar* (fragrant vegetable dhal), and dosas with coconut chutney.

Kerala's spice plantations, coconut-palm groves and long coastline shape the local cuisine, with deliciously delicate dishes such as fish *molee* or the spicy Malabar chicken curry. Fresh seafood, such as pomfret, kingfish and prawns, can be bought from fishing boats along the coast.

For dessert, *payasam* is made of brown molasses, coconut milk and spices, garnished with cashew nuts and raisins.

DON'T MISS

Fort Cochin is an extraordinary town, resonant with 500 years of colonial history. There are few more magical experiences than floating along **Kerala's backwaters** on a houseboat, canoe or even a kayak. For a true Keralan family welcome, try spending the night in a **homestay**, where you can eat (and cook) with the family.

Top State Festivals

➡ **Ernakulathappan Utsavam** (☉ Jan/Feb, Shiva Temple, Ernakulam, Kochi, p981) Eight days of festivities culminating in a parade of elephants, music and fireworks.

➡ **Thirunakkara Utsavam** (☉ Mar, Thirunakkara Shiva Temple, Kottayam, p966) All-night Kathakali dancing on the third and fourth nights of this 10-day festival.

➡ **Kollam Pooram** (☉ Apr, Asraman Shri Krishna Swami Temple, Kollam, p959) A 10-day festival with all-night Kathakali performances and a procession of 40 ornamented elephants.

➡ **Thrissur Pooram** (☉ Apr/May, Vadakkunathan Kshetram Temple, Thrissur, p991) The elephant procession to end all elephant processions.

➡ **Nehru Trophy Snake Boat Race** (☉ 2nd Sat in Aug, Alappuzha, p959) The most popular of Kerala's boat races.

➡ **Onam** (☉ Aug/Sep, statewide) Kerala's biggest cultural celebration, when the entire state celebrates the golden age of mythical King Mahabali for 10 days.

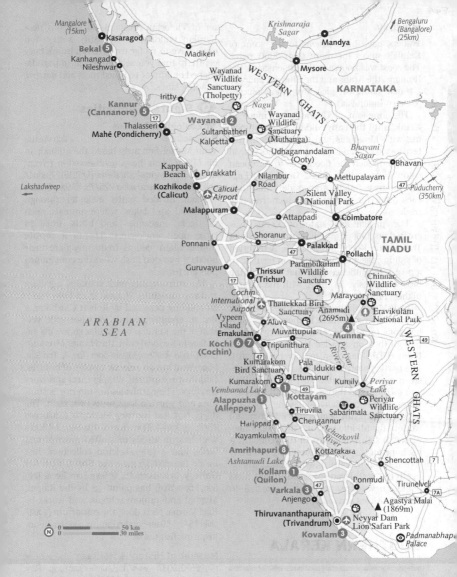

Kerala Highlights

① Take a houseboat or canoe through Kerala's fabled **backwaters** (p966) from Alleppey, Kollam or Kottayam

② Spot wild elephants at **Wayanad** (p996) amid spectacular scenery

③ Amble around the breathtaking beach resort of **Varkala** (p954) and

have some laid-back fun in **Kovalam** (p950)

④ Bed down in a remote resort and trek through emerald tea plantations around **Munnar** (p973)

⑤ Explore the golden-sand beaches and backwaters around **Kannur** (p998) and **Bekal** (p1001)

⑥ Relax in a homestay in **Fort Cochin** (p982) in Kochin

⑦ Experience the ritual of a **Kathakali** performance or martial arts **kalarippayat** in Kochi (p987)

⑧ Take the **cruise** between Kollam and Alleppey, stopping off at Amrithapuri to visit the 'Hugging Mother' (p961)

History

Traders have been drawn to the scent of Kerala's spices for more than 3000 years. The coast was known to the Phoenicians, the Romans, the Arabs and the Chinese, and was a transit point for spices from the Moluccas (eastern Indonesia).

The kingdom of Cheras ruled much of Kerala until the early Middle Ages, competing with kingdoms and small fiefdoms for territory and trade. Vasco da Gama's arrival in 1498 opened the floodgates to European colonialism as Portuguese, Dutch and English interests fought Arab traders, and then each other, for control of the lucrative spice trade.

The present-day state of Kerala was created in 1956 from the former states of Travancore, Kochi and Malabar. A tradition of valuing the arts and education resulted in a post-Independence state that is one of the most progressive in India, with the nation's highest literacy rate.

In 1957 Kerala had the first freely elected communist government in the world, which has gone on to hold power regularly since – though the Congress-led United Democratic Front (UDF) has been in power since 2011. The participatory political system has resulted in a more equitable distribution of land and income, and impressive health and education statistics. Many Malayalis (speakers of Malayalam, the state's official language) work in the Middle East and their remittances play a significant part in the economy. A big hope for the state's future is the relatively recent boom in tourism, with Kerala emerging in the past decade as one of India's most popular new tourist hot spots – more than 10 million visitors arrived in 2011.

SOUTHERN KERALA

Thiruvananthapuram (Trivandrum)

☑ 0471 / POP 752,500

Kerala's capital – for obvious reasons still often referred to by its colonial name, Trivandrum – is an energetic place and an easygoing introduction to city life down south. Most travellers merely springboard from here to the nearby beachside resorts of Kovalam and Varkala, but Trivandrum has enough sights – including its zoo and clus-

ter of Victorian museums in glorious neo-Keralan buildings – to justify a stay. You don't have to go far from Trivandrum's busy centre to find yourself immersed in pagoda-shaped buildings, red-tiled roofs and narrow, winding lanes.

⊙ Sights & Activities

★ Zoological Gardens & Museums   ZOO, MUSEUM

Yann Martel famously based the animals in his *Life of Pi* on those he observed in Trivandrum's **zoological gardens** (☑ 2115122; adult/child ₹10/5, camera/video ₹25/75; ⊙ 9am-5.15pm Tue-Sun). Shaded paths meander through woodland and lakes, where animals, such as tigers, macaques and birds, frolic in large open enclosures. There's a **reptile house** where cobras frequently flare their hoods – just don't ask what the cute guinea pigs are for.

The surrounding park contains a gallery and two museums. Housed in an 1880 wooden building designed by Robert Chisholm, a British architect whose Fair Isle–style version of the Keralan vernacular shows his enthusiasm for local craft, the **Napier Museum** (adult/child ₹5/2; ⊙ 10am-5pm Tue & Thu-Sun, 1-5pm Wed) has an eclectic display of bronzes, Buddhist sculptures, temple carts and ivory carvings. The carnivalesque interior is stunning and worth a look in its own right. The dusty **Natural History Museum** (adult/child ₹5/2; ⊙ 9am-4.30pm Tue & Thu-Sun, 1-4.30pm Wed) has hundreds of stuffed animals and birds, and a fine skeleton collection. Just inside the eastern gate, the **Shri Chitra Art Gallery** (admission ₹5; ⊙ 9am-5pm Tue & Thu-Sun, 1-5pm Wed) has paintings by the Rajput, Mughal and Tanjore schools, and works by Ravi Varma. Next door, the **aquarium** (adult/child ₹5/2; ⊙ 9am-5pm) contains a series of uninspiring fish tanks.

Museum of History & Heritage   MUSEUM

(☑ 9567019037; www.museumkeralam.org; Park View; Indian adult/child ₹20/10, foreigner adult/child ₹200/50, camera ₹25; ⊙ 10am-5.30pm Tue-Sun) In a lovely heritage building within the Kerala Tourism complex, this spacious new museum traces Keralan history and culture through superb static displays and interactive audiovisual presentations. Exhibits range from Iron Age implements to bronze and terracotta sculptures, murals, *dhulichitra* (floor paintings) and recreations of traditional Keralan homes. Admission is steep but it's all beautifully presented.

Shri
Padmanabhaswamy Temple   HINDU TEMPLE
(⊙Hindus only 4am-7.30pm) This 260-year-old temple is Trivandrum's spiritual heart. Its main entrance is the 30m-tall, seven-tier eastern *gopuram* (gateway tower). In the inner sanctum, the deity Padmanabha reclines on the sacred serpent and is made from over 10,000 *salagramam* (sacred stones) that were purportedly transported from Nepal by elephant.

The path around to the right of the gate offers good views of the *gopuram*.

Puthe Maliga Palace Museum   MUSEUM
(Fort; Indian/foreigner ₹15/50, camera/video ₹30/250; ⊙8.30am-1pm & 3-5pm Tue-Sun) The 200-year-old palace of the Travancore maharajas has carved wooden ceilings, marble sculptures and even imported Belgian glass. Inside you'll find Kathakali images, an armoury, portraits of maharajas, ornate thrones and other artefacts. Admission includes a 45-minute guided tour, though you can skip that and just visit the outside of the palace grounds (free), where you'll also find the **Chitrali Museum** (₹50), a newly opened section of the palace containing loads of historical memorabilia, photographs and portraits from the Travancore dynasty.

An annual **classical music festival** is held here in January.

🎓 Courses

Ayushmanbhava
Ayurvedic Centre   AYURVEDA, YOGA
(✍4712556060; www.ayushmanbhava.com; Pothu janam; massage from ₹600; ⊙yoga classes 6.30am) This centre, 3km west of MG Rd, offers massage, daily therapeutic-yoga classes, as well as longer ayurvedic treatments.

Margi Kathakali School   CULTURAL PROGRAM
(✍2478806; www.margitheatre.org; Fort) Conducts courses in Kathakali and *Kootiattam* (traditional Sanskrit drama) for beginner and advanced students. Fees average ₹300 per two-hour class. Visitors can peek at uncostumed practice sessions held from 10am to noon Monday to Friday. It's in an unmarked building behind the Fort School, 200m west of the fort.

CVN Kalari Sangham   MARTIAL ARTS
(✍2474182; www.cvnkalari.in; South Rd; 15-day/1-mth course ₹1000/2000) Offers long-term courses in *kalarippayat* for serious students (aged under 30) with some experience in martial arts. Training sessions are held Monday to Saturday from 7am to 8.30am.

TRADITIONAL KERALAN ARTS

Kathakali
The art form of Kathakali crystallised at around the same time as Shakespeare was scribbling his plays. The Kathakali performance is the dramatised presentation of a play, usually based on the Hindu epics the Ramayana, the Mahabharata and the Puranas. All the great themes are covered – righteousness and evil, frailty and courage, poverty and prosperity, war and peace.

Drummers and singers accompany the actors, who tell the story through their precise movements, particularly *mudras* (hand gestures) and facial expressions.

Preparation for the performance is lengthy and disciplined. Paint, fantastic costumes, ornamental headpieces and meditation transform the actors both physically and mentally into the gods, heroes and demons they are about to play.

Traditional performances can last for many hours, but you can see cut-down performances in tourist hot spots all over the state, and there are Kathakali schools in Trivandrum (p945) and near Thrissur (p993) that encourage visitors.

Kalarippayat
Kalarippayat is an ancient tradition of martial arts training and discipline, still taught throughout Kerala. Some believe it is the forerunner of all martial arts, with roots tracing back to the 12th-century skirmishes among Kerala's feudal principalities.

Masters of *kalarippayat*, called Gurukkal, teach their craft inside a special arena called a *kalari*. You can see often *kalarippayat* performances at the same venues as Kathakali.

Thiruvananthapuram (Trivandrum)

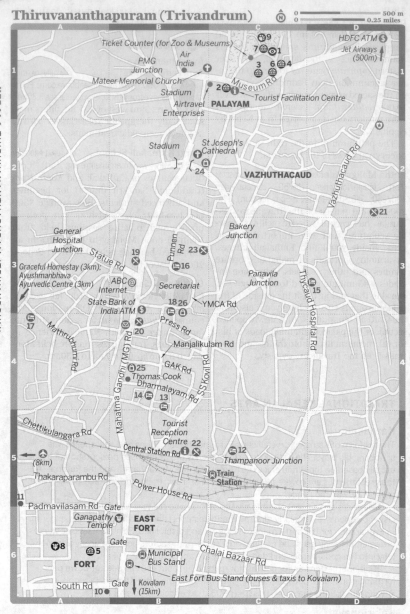

Tours

KTDC (Kerala Tourist Development Corporation) runs several tours, all leaving from the Tourist Reception Centre at the KTDC Hotel Chaithram on Central Station Rd. The City Tour (₹300) includes the zoo and other local sights; the Kanyakumari Day Tour (₹700) visits Padmanabhapuram Palace, Kanyakumari in Tamil Nadu and the nearby Suchindram Temple. Other trips include Neyyar Dam (₹400) and Kovalam (₹200).

Thiruvananthapuram (Trivandrum)

🛏 Sleeping

YMCA International Guesthouse HOSTEL $
(✆2330059; www.ymcatvm.org; YMCA Rd; s/d ₹376/732, with AC ₹788/1125; ❄) Centrally located but down a relatively quiet street, this is one of the best budget deals in town; rooms are spacious, spotless and come with tiled bathrooms and TV. Both men and women accepted.

Princess Inn HOTEL $
(✆2339150, Manjalikulam Rd; s/d ₹350/600, with AC from ₹750/850, ❄) In a glass-fronted building, the Princess Inn promises a relatively quiet sleep in a central sidestreet location. It's clean and comfortable, with satellite TV and immaculate bathrooms; the 'deluxe' rooms are spacious.

Hotel Regency HOTEL $
(✆2330377; www.hotelregency.com; Manjalikulam Cross Rd; s/d ₹600/900, with AC ₹1125/1350; ❄🖥) This tidy, welcoming place offers small but spotless rooms with satellite TV; the deluxe rooms are larger and there's wi-fi available downstairs.

Greenland Lodge HOTEL $
(✆2328114; Thampanoor Junction; s/d ₹435/680, with AC ₹900/1070; ❄) Close to the muted mayhem of the train station and bus stand, Greenland is acceptable for the location with lots of serenity-inducing pastel colours. Rooms are cleanish but variable so ask to see a few. Officious staff demand a hefty two-night advance deposit.

★**Graceful Homestay** HOMESTAY $$
(✆2444358; www.gracefulhomestay.com; Pothujanam Rd, Philip's Hill; downstairs s/d ₹1300/1500, upstairs & ste s/d incl breakfast ₹2000/2500; @🖥) In Trivandrum's leafy western suburbs, this lovely, serene house set in a couple of hectares of garden is owned by Sylvia and run by her brother Giles. The four rooms are all neatly furnished with access to kitchen, living areas and balconies. The pick of the rooms has an amazing covered terrace with views overlooking a sea of palms.

Wild Palms Home Stay HOMESTAY $$
(✆2471175; www.wildpalmsonsea.com; Mathrubhumi Rd; s ₹1095-1495, d ₹1395-1795, ste s/d ₹1795/2195; ❄🖥) A leafy courtyard garden greets you in front of this ornate but cosy family home with plenty of character. The seven rooms are all spacious with enormous bathrooms – the best is the upstairs suite with balcony, reached by a spiral staircase. Breakfast included.

★**Varikatt Heritage** HOMESTAY $$$
(✆2336057; www.varikattheritage.com; Punnen Rd; r incl breakfast ₹3950-5050; 🖥) Trivandrum's most charismatic place to stay is the 250-year-old home of Colonel Roy Kuncheria. It's a wonderful Indo-Saracenic bungalow with four rooms flanked by verandahs facing a pretty garden. Every antique – and the home itself – has a family story attached. Lunch and dinner available (₹300).

Taj Vivanta HOTEL $$$
(✆6612345; www.vivantabytaj.com; Thycaud Hospital Rd; s/d incl breakfast from ₹9500/10,700, ste

THE INDIAN COFFEE HOUSE STORY

The Indian Coffee House is a place stuck in time. Its India-wide branches feature old India prices and waiters dressed in starched white with peacock-style headdresses. It was started by the Coffee Board in the early 1940s, during British rule. In the 1950s the Board began to close down cafes across India, making employees redundant. At this point, the communist leader Ayillyath Kuttiari Gopalan Nambiar began to support the workers and founded with them the India Coffee Board Worker's Co-operative Society. The intention was to provide them with better opportunities and promote the sale of coffee. The Coffee House has remained ever since, always atmospheric, and always offering bargain snacks and drinks such as Indian filter coffee, rose milk and *idlis*. It's still run by its employees, all of whom share ownership.

₹25,500; ✳@🛜🛏) The lobby here is bigger than most hotels in town, so the Taj doesn't disappoint with the wow factor. Rooms are sufficiently plush, the lawn and pool area is well maintained, there's a gym and a couple of good restaurants.

🍴 Eating

For some unusual refreshments with your meal, look out for *karikku* (coconut water) and *sambharam* (buttermilk with ginger and chilli).

★ Indian Coffee House   INDIAN $
(Maveli Cafe; Central Station Rd; snacks ₹10-45; ⊘7am-11pm) The Central Station Rd branch of Indian Coffee House serves its strong coffee and snacks in a crazy red-brick tower that looks like a cross between a lighthouse and a pigeon coop, and has a spiralling interior lined with concrete benches and tables. You have to admire the hard-working waiters. There's another, more run-of-the-mill branch near the zoo.

Ariya Nivaas   INDIAN $
(Manorama Rd; thalis ₹70; ⊘6.45am-10pm) Always busy thanks to its superb all-you-can-eat South Indian veg thalis, Ariya Nivaas is away from the main drag but convenient for the train station.

Ananda Bhavan   INDIAN $
(☎2477646; MG Rd; dishes ₹28-40; ⊘lunch & dinner) A classic sit-down-and-dig-in-with-your-hands-type situation with dosas and veg snacks.

Cherries & Berries   CAFE $$
(www.cherriesandberries.in; Carmel Towers, Cotton Hill; ₹45-130; ⊘9.45am-10pm; 🛜) For serious comfort food, icy air-con and free wi-fi, take a trip east of the centre to Cherries & Berries. Waffles, mini-pizzas, toasties, good coffee and indulgent chocolate-bar milkshakes.

Azad Restaurant   INDIAN $$
(Press Rd; dishes ₹75-145; ⊘noon-11.30pm) A busy family favourite serving up authentic Keralan fish dishes, like fish *molee*, and excellent biryanis and tandoori.

Vibhav   MULTICUISINE $$
(☎4076000; Vanross Junction; mains ₹80-250; ⊘8am-10.30pm) This smart restaurant at Magic Days Hotel offers a terrific buffet for lunch and dinner, as well as à la carte Indian, Chinese and Continental.

🛍 Shopping

Wander around **Connemara Market** (MG Rd) to see vendors selling vegetables, fish, live goats, fabric, clothes, spices and more bananas than you can poke a hungry monkey at.

SMSM Institute   HANDICRAFTS
(www.keralahandicrafts.in; YMCA Rd; ⊘9am-8pm Mon-Sat) Kerala Government–run handicraft emporium with an Aladdin's cave of well-priced goodies.

Sankers Coffee & Tea   FOOD & DRINK
(☎2330469; MG Rd; ⊘9am-9pm Mon-Sat) You'll smell the fresh coffee well before you reach this dainty shop. It sells Nilgiri Export OP Leaf Tea (₹520 per kilo) and a variety of coffees and nuts.

ℹ Information

ABC Internet (MG Rd, Capital Centre; per hr ₹20; ⊘8.30am-9pm) One of several good internet places in this small mall.

KIMS (Kerala Institute of Medical Sciences; ☎3041000, emergency 3041144; www.kims-kerala.com; Kumarapuram; ⊘24hr) Best choice for medical problems; about 3km northwest of Trivandrum.

Main Post Office (☎2473071; MG Rd)

Thomas Cook (☎ 2338140, 2338141; MG Rd; ⊙ 10.30am-6pm Mon-Sat) Changes cash and travellers cheques.

Tourist Facilitation Centre (☎ 2321132; Museum Rd; ⊙ 24hr) Near the zoo; supplies maps and brochures.

Tourist Reception Centre (KTDC Hotel Chaithram; ☎ 2330031; Central Station Rd; ⊙ 7am-9pm) Arranges KTDC-run tours.

ⓘ Getting There & Away

AIR

Between them, **Air India** (☎ 2317341; Mascot Sq), **Jet Airways** (☎ 2728864; Sasthamangalam Junction) and **SpiceJet** (☎ 09871803333; www.spicejet.com; Trivandrum airport) fly from Trivandrum airport to Mumbai (Bombay), Kochi, Bengaluru (Bangalore), Chennai (Madras) and Delhi.

There are also direct flights from Trivandrum to Colombo in Sri Lanka, Male in the Maldives and major Gulf regions such as Dubai, Kuwait and Bahrain.

All airline bookings can be made at the efficient **Airtravel Enterprises** (☎ 3011300; www.ate. travel; MG Rd, New Corporation Bldg).

BUS

For buses operating from the KSRTC bus stand, opposite the train station, see the table.

For Tamil Nadu destinations, State Express Transport Corporation (SETC) buses leave from the eastern end of the KSRTC bus stand.

Buses leave for Kovalam beach (₹15, 30 minutes, every 20 minutes) between 6am and 9pm from the southern end of the East Fort bus stand on MG Rd.

TRAIN

Trains are often heavily booked, so it's worth visiting the **reservation office** (☎ 139; ⊙ 8am-

8pm Mon-Sat, to 2pm Sun) at the main train station. While most major trains arrive and depart at Trivandrum Central Station close to the city centre, some express services terminate at Vikram Sarabhai Station (Kochuveli), about 7km north of the city – check in advance.

Within Kerala there are frequent express trains to Varkala (sleeper/3AC ₹57/175, one hour), Kollam (₹64/175, 1¼ hours) and Ernakulam (₹128/342, 4½ hours), with trains passing through either Alleppey (₹120/267, three hours) or Kottayam (₹120/313, 3½ hours). There are also numerous daily services to Kanyakumari (sleeper/3AC ₹120/218, three hours).

ⓘ Getting Around

The **airport** (☎ 2501424) is 8km from the city and 15km from Kovalam; take local bus 14 from the East Fort and City Bus stand (₹7). Prepaid taxi vouchers from the airport cost ₹350 to the city and ₹500 to Kovalam.

Autorickshaws are the easiest way to get around, with short hops costing ₹20 to ₹30.

Around Trivandrum

Neyyar Wildlife Sanctuary

Surrounding an idyllic lake created by the 1964 Neyyar Dam 35km north of Trivandrum, the main attraction at this sanctuary is the **Lion Safari Park** (☎ 2272182, 9744347582; Indian/foreigner ₹200/300; ⊙ 9am-4pm Tue-Sun). Admission includes a boat ride across the lake, lion safari by bus, a visit to a **deer park** and **Crocodile Production Centre** (named for Australian legend Steve Irwin). The fertile forest lining the shore is home to gaurs,

BUSES LEAVING FROM TRIVANDRUM (KSRTC BUS STAND)

DESTINATION	FARE (₹)	DURATION (HR)	FREQUENCY
Alleppey	100, AC 191	3½	every 15min
Chennai	560	17	10 daily
Ernakulam (Kochi)	135, AC 250	5	every 20min
Kanyakumari	50	2	6 daily
Kollam	43	1½	every 15min
Kumily (for Periyar)	200	8	2 daily
Munnar	250	7	2 daily
Neyyar Dam	30	1½	every 40min
Thrissur	200	7½	every 30min
Ooty (Udhagamandalam)	485	14	1 daily
Varkala	40	1¼	hourly

MAJOR TRAINS FROM TRIVANDRUM

DESTINATION	TRAIN NO & NAME	FARE (₹, SLEEPER/3AC/2AC)	DURATION (HR)	DEPARTURES (DAILY)
Bengaluru	16525 Bangalore Express	307/864/1320	18	1pm
Chennai	12696 Chennai Express	341/936/1425	16½	5.10pm
Coimbatore	17229 Sabari Express	191/524/785	9¼	7.15am
Delhi	12625 Kerala Express	595/1676/2780	50½	11.15am
Mangalore	16347 Mangalore Express	257/719/1085	14½	8.40pm

sambar deer, sloth, elephants, lion-tailed macaques and the occasional tiger.

Get here from Trivandrum's Kerala State Road Transport Corporation (KSRTC) bus stand by frequent bus (₹30, 1½ hours). A taxi is ₹900 return (with two hours' waiting time) from Trivandrum, ₹1300 from Kovalam. The KTDC office in Trivandrum also run tours to Neyyar Dam (₹400).

Sivananda Yoga Vedanta Dhanwantari Ashram

Just before Neyyar Dam, the superbly located **Sivananda Yoga Vedanta Dhanwantari Ashram** (☏0471-2273093; www.sivananda.org/ndam), established in 1978, is renowned for its hatha yoga courses. Courses start on the 1st and 16th of each month, run for a minimum of two weeks and cost ₹800 per day for accommodation in a double room (₹1500 with air-con) and ₹500 in a dormitory (meals are included). Low season (May to September) rates are ₹100 less. There's an exacting schedule (5.30am to 10pm) of yoga practice, meditation and chanting. Bookings are required. Month-long yoga-teacher training and ayurvedic massage courses are also available.

Kovalam

☏0471

Once a calm fishing village clustered around its crescent beaches, these days Kovalam is Kerala's most developed resort. The main stretch, **Lighthouse Beach**, is touristy with hotels and restaurants built up along the shore, while **Hawa Beach** to the north is usually crowded with day-trippers heading straight from the taxi stand to the sand. Neither beach is particularly clean, but at less than 15km from the capital it's a convenient place to have some fun by the sea, there's some promising surf and it makes a good base for ayurvedic treatments and yoga courses.

About 2km further north by road, **Samudra Beach** has several upmarket resorts and a peaceful but steep beach.

ⓘ Dangers & Annoyances

Bikini-clad women are likely to attract male attention, though this is definitely more of an annoyance than a danger. Cover up with a sarong when you're out of the water.

There are strong rips at both ends of Lighthouse Beach that carry away several swimmers every year. Swim only between the flags in the area patrolled by lifeguards and avoid swimming during the monsoon.

Kovalam has frequent blackouts and the paths behind Lighthouse Beach are unlit, so carry a torch (flashlight) after dark.

◉ Sights & Activities

Vizhinjam Lighthouse   LIGHTHOUSE
(Indian/foreigner ₹10/25, camera/video ₹20/25; ⊙10am-5pm) Kovalam's most distinguishing feature is the candy-striped lighthouse at the southern end of the beach. Climb the spiral staircase for endless views along the coast.

Santhigiri   AYURVEDA
(☏2482800; www.santhigiriashram.org; Lighthouse Beach Rd; ⊙9am-8pm) Excellent massages and ayurvedic treatments from ₹1000.

🛏 Sleeping

Kovalam is chock-a-block with hotels, though budget places here cost more than usual and are becoming a dying breed in high season. Beachfront properties are the most expensive, but look out for smaller places tucked away in the labyrinth of paths behind the beach among the palm groves and rice paddies; they're often much better value. All places offer big discounts outside the December–January high season, but call ahead in peak times.

Green Valley Cottages
GUESTHOUSE $

(2480636; indira_ravi@hotmail.com; r ₹500-800) Back amongst the palm trees, this serene complex feels a little faded but it's quiet and good value at this price. Rooms are simple, but the upper rooms have good views from the front terraces.

Hotel Greenland
GUESTHOUSE $

(2486442; hotelgreenlandin@yahoo.com; r ₹600-1200) This friendly family-run place has refurbished rooms in a multilevel complex just back from the beach. It's not flash but rooms have lots of natural light and the larger upstairs rooms have a balcony.

Hotel Sky Palace
GUESTHOUSE $

(9745841222; hotelskypalace@yahoo.com; r ₹500-700) This little two-storey place lies down a small lane; rooms are well kept, brightly painted in greens and blues, some with TV; the ground-floor rooms are cheaper (but the same).

Dwaraka Lodge
GUESTHOUSE $

(2480411; d ₹500) With regular licks of paint helping to cover up the war wounds of this tired old-timer attached to Rock Cafe, friendly Dwaraka is the cheapest and most basic oceanside property.

Kovalam

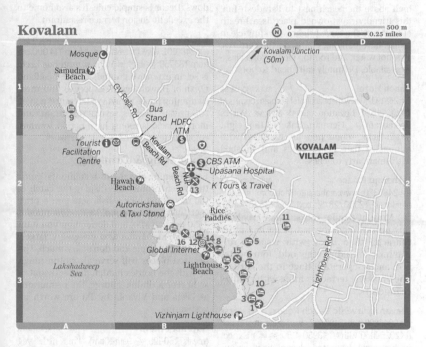

Kovalam

★ **Paradesh Inn** GUESTHOUSE $$
(📞 9995362952; inn.paradesh@yahoo.com; Avaduthura; d incl breakfast ₹1600, ste ₹2500; @) Well back from the beach above the palms, tranquil Italian-run Paradesh Inn resembles a Greek island hideaway – a whitewashed house highlighted in blue. Each of the six fan-cooled rooms has a hanging chair outside, there are sweeping views from the rooftop, fab breakfasts and *satya* cooking ('yoga food') for guests.

Treetops GUESTHOUSE $$
(📞 9847912398, 2481363; treetopsofkovalam@yahoo.in; r ₹1000; @) Indeed in the treetops high above the beach next to Paradesh Inn, this friendly expat-owned place is a breath of fresh air. The three bright, sparkling-clean rooms have hanging chairs on the terraces, TVs, hot water, and rooftop views; yoga classes available. Definitely call ahead to book.

Beach Hotel GUESTHOUSE $$
(📞 2481937; www.thebeachhotel-kovalam.com; s/d ₹1850/2850) Location alert! Below Waves Restaurant & German Bakery, the eight beach-facing rooms here are designed with minimalist flair, ochre tones and finished with smart, arty touches.

Maharaju Palace GUESTHOUSE $$
(📞 2485320; www.maharajupalace.com; s/d incl breakfast ₹2300/2875, cottage ₹3680/4600; ❄) More of a quiet retreat than a palace, this quirky Dutch-owned place has more character than most, with wooden furnishings, including the odd four-poster bed, and a separate cottage in the garden. The breakfast terrace is hung with chintzy chandeliers.

Jeevan Ayurvedic Beach Resort RESORT $$
(📞 9846898498, 2480662; www.jeevanresort.net; d ₹2025-3150, with AC ₹3950-4150; ❄ ☷) Expect inoffensively decorated, decent-sized rooms with bathtubs and an alluring pool – one of the few on the seafront. All but the cheapest ground-floor rooms have sea views and balconies.

Sea Flower HOTEL $$
(📞 2480554; www.seaflowerkovalam.com; d ₹1150-2300, with AC ₹2600; ❄) At the southern end of Lighthouse Beach, this slightly dowdy place is reasonably priced for the beachfront location. Rooms are simple but fresh, with a premium for the upper-floor rooms.

Sea Star Hotel HOTEL $$
(📞 2488088; www.patanjaliresort.com; Lighthouse Beach; r ₹1800-2500, with AC from ₹3000; ❄ @) In a handy location tucked down a laneway at the north end of Lighthouse Beach, Sea Star has spacious and immaculate rooms and a professional attitude. Yoga sessions with a view from the rooftop.

★ **Beach Hotel II** HOTEL $$$
(📞 9400031243, 2481937; www.thebeachhotel-kovalam.com; d ₹4500, with AC ₹5600; ❄) Tucked into the southern end of Lighthouse Beach, this stylish pad has 10 sea-facing rooms all with balcony and large sliding French windows. Decor is simple chic. It's also home to the excellent Fusion terrace restaurant.

Leela HOTEL $$$
(📞 2480101; www.theleela.com; d from ₹14,000, ste from ₹33,750; ❄ @ 🛜 ☷) The sumptuous Leela is set in extensive grounds on the headland north of Hawah beach. Expect to find three swimming pools, an ayurvedic centre, a gym, two private beaches, several restaurants and more. Spacious rooms have period touches, colourful textiles and Keralan artwork.

✖ Eating & Drinking

Each evening dozens of restaurants lining the beach promenade display the catch of the day – just pick a fish, settle on a price (per fillet serve around ₹350, tiger prawns ₹550 per half kilo) and decide how you want it prepared. Menus and prices are largely indistinguishable and don't vary much. Unlicensed places will serve alcohol in mugs, or with the bottles hidden discreetly out of sight. For a dining splurge, the restaurants at Leela and Vivanta by Taj are worth investigating.

Suprabhatham KERALAN $
(meals ₹60-125; ⊙ 9am-10pm) This little veg place hidden back from the beach doesn't look like much, but it dishes up excellent, dirt-cheap Keralan cooking in a rustic setting of dirt floor and plastic chairs.

Devi Garden Restaurant INDIAN $
(NUP Beach Rd; mains ₹30-170; ⊙ 7.30am-11pm) Garden is overstating it, but this tiny, family-run eatery just up the road from the taxi stand whips up great veg and nonveg Indian and Chinese food at refreshingly reasonable prices – most veg dishes are under ₹80.

Waves Restaurant & German Bakery
MULTICUISINE $$

(Beach Hotel; breakfast ₹70-300, mains ₹150-550; ⊘7am-11pm) With its broad, burnt-orange balcony, ambient soundtrack and wide-roaming menu, Waves is always busy with foreigners. It morphs with the German Bakery, a great spot for breakfast with fresh bread, croissants, pastries and decent coffee, while dinner turns up Thai curries, German sausages and seafood. There's a small book-shop attached.

Swiss Cafe
CAFE $$

(mains ₹70-390; ⊘7.30am-11pm) Swiss Cafe stands out for tasty Euro dishes like rosti, schnitzel, pasta and pizza, as well as the usual fresh seafood and Indian staples. The balcony with its wicker chairs is a good place to take in the action.

Malabar Cafe
INDIAN $$

(mains ₹100-450; ⊘8am-11pm) The busy tables tell their own story: with candlelight at night and views through pot plants to the crashing waves, Malabar offers tasty food and good service.

Fusion
MULTICUISINE $$

(mains ₹120-340; ⊘8.30am-10.30pm) The ter-race restaurant at Beach Hotel II is one of the best dining experiences on Lighthouse Beach, with an inventive East-meets-West menu, a range of Continental dishes, Asian fusion and interesting seafood numbers like lobster steamed in vodka. Also serves French press coffee and herbal teas.

☆ Entertainment

During high season, an abridged version of Kathakali is performed most nights – en-quire about locations and times at the Tour-ist Facilitation Centre.

❶ Information

Almost every shop and hotel will change money. Near the hospital is a CBS ATM taking Visa cards. About 500m uphill from the beach are HDFC and Axis ATMs, and there are Federal Bank and ICICI ATMs at Kovalam Junction. There are several small internet cafes charging around ₹30 per hour.

Global Internet (Leo Restaurant; per hr ₹30; ⊘8.30am-11pm; 🛜) Check your email with wi-fi over a cold beer.

Post Office (Kovalam Beach Rd; ⊘9am-1pm Mon-Sat)

Tourist Facilitation Centre (☑2480085; Kovalam Beach Rd; ⊘9.30am-5pm) Helpful; in the entrance to Government Guesthouse near the bus stand and Leela Hotel.

Upasana Hospital (☑2480632) Has English-speaking doctors who can take care of minor injuries.

❶ Getting There & Around

BUS

Buses start and finish at an unofficial stand on the main road outside the entrance to Leela Hotel and all buses pass through Kovalam Junction, about 1.5km north of Lighthouse Beach. Buses connect Kovalam and Trivandrum every 20 minutes between 5.30am and 10.10pm (₹9, 30 minutes). There are two buses daily to Ernakulam (₹200, 5½ hours), stopping at Kallambalam (for Varkala, ₹70, 1½ hours), Kollam (₹80, 2½ hours) and Alleppey (₹120, four hours). There's another 6.30am bus to Ernakulam via Kottayam that bypasses Varkala.

MOTORBIKE HIRE

K Tours & Travel (☑2127003), next door to Devi Garden Restaurant, rents out scooters/Enfields for around ₹400/550 per day.

TAXI

A taxi between Trivandrum and Kovalam beach is around ₹400; an autorickshaw should cost ₹250. From the bus stand to Lighthouse Beach costs around ₹50.

Around Kovalam

Pulinkudi & Chowara

Around 8km south of Kovalam, amid seem-ingly endless swaying palms, colourful village life, and some empty golden-sand beaches, are some ayurvedic resorts that make tantalising high-end alternatives to Kovalam's crowded centre.

Dr Franklin's Panchakarma Institute (☑2480870; www.dr-franklin.com; Chowara; s/d hut €15/20, r from €25/32, with AC €38/55; @🛜) is a reputable and less expensive alternative to the flashier resorts. Daily treatment with full board costs €56. Accommodation is tidy and comfortable but not resort style.

Surya Samudra Private Retreats (☑2480413; www.suryasamudra.com; Pulinkudi; r incl breakfast ₹14,100-22,600; ❄❄) offers A-list-style seclusion, with 22 transplanted tradi-tional Keralan homes, with four-poster beds and open-air bathrooms, set in a palm grove above sparkling seas. There's an infinity pool carved out of a single block of granite, ayurvedic treatments, gym and spectacular outdoor yoga platforms.

Bethsaida Hermitage (☑2267554; www.bethsaidahermitage.com; Pulinkudi; s €80-140, d €140-155; ❋) ✎ is a resort with a difference: this is a charitable organisation that helps support two nearby orphanages and an old people's home. It's also an inviting, somehow old-fashioned beachside escape with sculpted gardens, a friendly welcome and putting-green perfect lawns.

Thapovan Heritage Home (☑2480453; www.thapovan.com; hillside s/d from ₹2700/3480, cottages ₹4500/5700, beachfront s/d cottage ₹4800/6000) has two properties about 100m apart – one has beachfront cottages in Keralan style and the other is on a gorgeous hilltop location, with teak cottages filled with handcrafted furniture and set amidst perfectly manicured grounds with wonderful views to the ocean and swaying palm groves.

Varkala

☑0470 / POP 42,270

Perched almost perilously along the edge of dizzying cliffs, the resort of Varkala has a naturally beautiful setting and the clifftop stretch has steadily grown into Kerala's most popular backpacker hang-out. A strand of golden beach nuzzles Varkala's cliff edge, where restaurants play innocuous trance music and stalls sell T-shirts, baggy trousers and silver jewellery. While this kind of tie-dye commercialism can grate on the nerves – the daily wander along the cliff path is made a little less relaxing by the constant chants of 'come see my shop' – Varkala is still a great place to watch the days slowly turn into weeks, and it's not hard to escape the crowds further north or south.

Despite its backpacker vibe, Varkala is essentially a temple town, and the main Papanasham beach is a holy place where Hindus come to make offerings for passed loved ones, assisted by priests who set up shop beneath the Hindustan Hotel. You can while away days watching the mix of fishermen, Hindu rituals, volleyball-playing visitors, locals gazing at the sea and strolling backpackers that make up the traffic on the beach.

ⓘ Dangers & Annoyances

The beaches at Varkala have strong currents; even experienced swimmers have been swept away here. This is one of the most dangerous beaches in Kerala; swim between the flags or ask locally. During the monsoon the beach all but disappears and the cliffs themselves are slowly being eroded. Take care walking on the cliff path, especially at night – much of it is unfenced and can be slippery in parts.

If women wear bikinis or even swimsuits on the beach at Varkala, they are likely to feel uncomfortably exposed to stares. Wearing a sarong when out of the water will help avoid offending local sensibilities. It pays to dress sensitively, especially if you're going into Varkala town.

◉ Sights

Janardhana Temple   HINDU TEMPLE

Varkala is a temple town and Janardhana Temple is the main event – its technicolour Hindu spectacle sits hovering above Beach Rd. The temple is closed to non-Hindus, but you may be invited into the temple grounds where there is a huge banyan tree and shrines to Ayyappan, Hanuman and other Hindu deities.

Sivagiri Mutt   SACRED SITE

(☑2602807; www.sivagirimutt.org) Sivagiri Mutt is the headquarters of the Shri Narayana Dharma Sanghom Trust, the ashram devoted to Shri Narayana Guru (1855–1928), Kerala's most prominent guru. This is a popular pilgrimage site and the resident swami is happy to talk to visitors.

🏃 Activities

Yoga is offered at several guesthouses for ₹200 to ₹300 per session. **Boogie boards** can be hired from places along the beach for ₹100; plese be wary of strong currents. Many of the resorts and hotels along the north cliff offer ayurvedic treatments and massage.

Laksmi's   MASSAGE

(☑9895948080; Clafouti Beach Resort; manicure/pedicure from ₹400/600, henna ₹300, massage ₹800; ◷9am-7pm) This tiny place offers treatments such as threading and waxing as well as massages (women only).

Haridas Yoga   YOGA

(www.pranayogavidya.com; Hotel Green Palace; classes ₹250; ◷8am & 4.30pm Aug-May) Recommended 1½-hour hatha yoga classes with experienced teachers.

Eden Garden   MASSAGE

(☑2603910; www.eden-garden.net; massage from ₹1000) Offers a more upmarket ayurvedic

Varkala

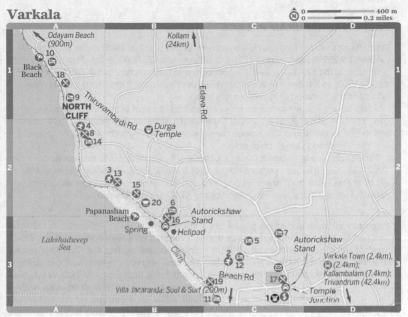

Varkala

◉ Sights
1 Janardhana Temple..............................C3

⏣ Activities, Courses & Tours
2 Eden Garden...C3
3 Haridas Yoga B2
4 Laksmi's A2

🛏 Sleeping
Eden Garden......................................(see 2)
5 Guest House Varkala...........................C3
6 Jicky's...B2
7 Kaiya House...C3
8 Kerala Bamboo House A2
9 Puthooram...A1
10 Sea Breeze..A1
11 Sea Pearl Chalets.................................C3

12 Taj Gateway Hotel................................C3

✦ Eating
13 Café del Mar...B2
14 Hungry Eye Kitchen A2
15 Juice Shack...B2
16 Oottupura Vegetarian Restaurant........B3
17 Sreepadman..C3
18 Trattorias...A1
19 Wait n Watch..C3

● Drinking & Nightlife
20 Coffee Temple......................................B2

✹ Entertainment
Rock n Roll Cafe............................(see 14)

experience, including single treatments and packages.

Soul & Surf SURFING, YOGA
(☏ 9746512584; www.soulandsurf.com; South Cliff; surf guide ₹800, with board rental ₹1200) This UK outfit organises surfing trips and yoga retreats in season, usually through packages with accommodation included, but if there's space, nonguests can join the regular surfing tours.

🛏 Sleeping

Most places to stay are crammed in along the north cliff where backpackers tend to congregate, but there are some nice places down by the southern cliffs; some are only open for the tourist onslaught in November. Less-developed Odayam beach, about 1km further north of Varkala's black beach, is a tranquil alternative.

PADMANABHAPURAM PALACE

With a forest's worth of intricately carved ceilings and polished-teak beams, this **palace** (☎04651250255; Indian/foreigner ₹25/200, camera/video ₹25/1500; ⊙9am-5pm Tue-Sun) is considered the best example of traditional Keralan architecture today. Parts of it date back to 1550; as the egos of successive rulers left their mark, it expanded into the magnificent conglomeration of 14 palaces it is today.

Asia's largest wooden palace complex, it was once the seat of the rulers of Travancore, a princely state taking in parts of Tamil Nadu and Kerala. Constructed of teak and granite, the exquisite interiors include carved rosewood ceilings, Chinese-style screens and floors finished to a high black polish.

Padmanabhapuram is about 60km southeast of Kovalam, just over the border in Tamil Nadu. Catch a local bus from Kovalam (or Trivandrum) towards Kanyakumari and get off at Thuckalay, from where it's a short autorickshaw ride or 15-minute walk. Alternatively, take one of the tours organised by the KTDC from Trivandrum.

Practically all accommodation places can be reached by taxi or autorickshaw via the network of lanes leading to the cliffs, but the commission racket is alive and well – make sure your driver takes you to the place you've asked for.

⭐ **Jicky's** GUESTHOUSE $
(☎2606994; www.jickys.com; s ₹400, d ₹600-1000, cottage ₹1250-1750, r with AC ₹2500) In the palm groves just back from the cliffs and taxi stand, family-run Jicky's remains as friendly as they come and has spread into several buildings offering plenty of choice for travellers. The rooms in the main whitewashed building are lovely and fresh, and nearby are two charming octagonal double cottages, and some larger air-con rooms.

Guest House Varkala GUESTHOUSE $
(☎2602227; d ₹220, with AC ₹440) It would take a true budgeteer to trek to this government-run guesthouse (ironically close to the five-star Taj), but the spartan rooms here are bargain-basement in season if you don't mind the location and basic rooms.

⭐ **Kaiya House** GUESTHOUSE $$
(☎9746126909, 9995187913; www.kaiyahouse.com; s/d incl breakfast ₹1500/2000, d with AC ₹2500; ❋ ☎) Well back from the cliffs, what Kaiya House lacks in sea views it makes up for with charm, welcoming owners and sheer relaxation. Each of the five rooms is thoughtfully furnished and themed (African, Indian, Chinese, Japanese and English) with four-poster beds and artworks on the walls. There's a lovely rooftop terrace and rear courtyard with calming vibe. The cliff-top is 10 minutes' walk away.

Eden Garden RESORT $$
(☎2603910; www.edengarden.in; cottages €16-25, deluxe cottages incl breakfast €83) This recommended ayurvedic resort overlooks peaceful paddy fields back from the main beach. Stylish rooms come with high wooden ceilings and attractive furniture, set around a lush lily pond. There are also bamboo cottages and deluxe organically-shaped cottages like white space-mushrooms with intricate paintwork, round beds, and mosaic circular baths. Ayurvedic packages range from three- to 30-day packages.

Kerala Bamboo House RESORT $$
(☎9895270993; www.keralabamboohouse.com; huts d ₹1500-3000) For that bamboo-hut experience, this popular place squishes together dozens of pretty Balinese-style huts and a neatly maintained garden in a cliff-top compound. Some of the huts are nicer than others, so look at a few. Ayurvedic treatments, yoga and cooking class are on offer.

Puthooram RESORT $$
(☎3202007; www.puthooram.com; r ₹1150-2875, with AC ₹3450-4500; ❋ @) Puthooram's wood-lined bungalows are set around a charming little garden of pot plants. Rooms with sea view are pricier.

Sea Pearl Chalets RESORT $$
(☎2660105; www.seapearlchalets.com; d ₹1500) Perched on Varkala's quieter southern cliff, these basic, pod-like huts have unbeatable views and are surrounded by prim lawns. Worth checking out before they tumble into the ocean.

Sea Breeze GUESTHOUSE $$
(☑ 9746079790; www.seabreezevarkala.in; r ₹1725, with AC ₹2500-3450; ❋ 🐱) The spacious, orderly, if dull rooms at this friendly guesthouse offer sea views and share a large verandah – perfect for nightly sunset adulation.

Villa Jacaranda GUESTHOUSE $$$
(☑ 2610296; www.villa-jacaranda.biz; d incl breakfast ₹5600-7000; 🐱) The ultimate in understated luxury, this romantic retreat has just a handful of huge, bright rooms in a large two-storey house, each with a balcony and decorated with a chic blend of minimalist modern and period touches. The top-floor room has its own rooftop garden with sea views.

Blue Water Beach Resort COTTAGES $$$
(☑ 94468 48534; www.bluewaterstay.com; Odayam Beach; cottages ₹3000-5000) At quiet Odayam Beach, north of Varkala, Blue Water is the pick of the beachfront places with sturdy individual timber cottages with tiled roofs arranged in a pleasant lawn area sloping down to the beach.

Taj Gateway Hotel HOTEL $$$
(☑ 6673300; www.thegatewayhotels.com; d incl breakfast from ₹7700; ❋ @ 🐱 ⊠) Varkala's flashiest hotel is looking hot – refurbished rooms with gleaming linen and mocha cushions overlook the garden, while the more expensive rooms have sea views and private balconies. There's a fantastic pool with bar (nonguests ₹500), tennis court and well-regarded GAD restaurant.

🍴 Eating & Drinking

Most restaurants in Varkala offer the same mishmash of Indian, Asian and Western fare to a soundtrack of easy-listening trance and Bob Marley, but the quality of the cliffside 'shacks' has improved out of sight over the years and most offer free wi-fi. Join in the nightly Varkala saunter till you find a place that suits. Unlicensed places will usually serve alcohol discreetly.

Sreepadman SOUTH INDIAN $
(thali ₹40) To grab dirt-cheap and authentic Keralan fare – think dosas and thalis – where you can rub shoulders with rickshaw drivers rather than tourists, check out hole-in-the-wall Sreepadman opposite the Janardhana temple.

Oottupura Vegetarian Restaurant INDIAN $
(mains ₹35-80) Near the taxi stand, this budget eatery has a respectable range of cheap

---

AYURVEDA

With its roots in Sanskrit, the word ayurveda is from *ayu* (life) and *veda* (knowledge); the knowledge or science of life. Principles of ayurvedic medicine were first documented in the Vedas some 2000 years ago, but may have been practised centuries earlier.

Ayurveda sees the world as having an intrinsic order and balance. It argues that we possess three *doshas* (humours): *vata* (wind or air); *pitta* (fire); and *kapha* (water/earth), known together as the *tridoshas*. Deficiency or excess in any of them can result in disease: an excess of *vata* may result in dizziness and debility; an increase in *pitta* may lead to fever, inflammation and infection. *Kapha* is essential for hydration.

Ayurvedic treatment aims to restore the balance, and hence good health, principally through two methods: panchakarma (internal purification), and herbal massage. Panchakarma is used to treat serious ailments, and is an intense detox regime, a combination of five types of different therapies to rid the body of built-up endotoxins. These include: *vaman* – therapeutic vomiting; *virechan* – purgation; *vasti* – enemas; *nasya* – elimination of toxins through the nose; and *raktamoksha* – detoxification of the blood. Before panchakarma begins, the body is first prepared over several days with a special diet, oil massages (*snehana*) and herbal steam-baths (*swedana*). Although it may sound pretty grim, panchakarma purification might only use a few of these treatments at a time, with therapies like bloodletting and leeches only used in rare cases. Still, this is no spa holiday. The herbs used in ayurveda grow in abundance in Kerala's humid climate – the monsoon is thought to be the best time of year for treatment, when there is less dust in the air, the pores are open and the body is most receptive to treatment – and every village has its own ayurvedic pharmacy.

veg dishes, including breakfast *puttu* (flour with milk, bananas and honey).

Juice Shack

CAFE $

(juices ₹50, snacks ₹30-150; ⊙7am-7pm; ⊚) It's looking a little 'shack-like' next to the fancy new places, but this funky little health-juice bar still turns out great juices, smoothies and snacks such as Mexican wraps.

Café del Mar

MULTICUISINE $

(dishes ₹80-350; ⊚) It doesn't have the big balcony like some of its neighbours, but Café del Mar is always busy thanks to efficient service, good coffee and consistently good food, albeit from a 10-page menu.

Hungry Eye Kitchen

MULTICUISINE $

(meals ₹70-250; ⊙8am-11pm) Hungry Eye is a reliable multilevel cliff-top choice where Tibetan momos meet Thai curries and steaks, along with the usual Indian and Chinese.

Trattorias

MULTICUISINE $$

(meals ₹100-400; ⊙8.30am-11pm) Trattorias aims to specialise in Italian with a decent range of pasta and pizza but also offers Japanese – including sushi – and Thai dishes. This was one of the original places with an Italian coffee machine, and the wicker chairs and sea-facing terrace are cosy.

Wait n Watch

INDIAN $$

(Hindustan Hotel; mains ₹120-280; ⊙11am-10pm) The top-floor restaurant and cocktail bar at this beachfront hotel block offer tasty-enough Indian fare and seafood, but the real reason to come here is the view from the balcony (with just a couple of tables) over the beach action. There's another alfresco restaurant by the pool.

Coffee Temple

CAFE

(⊙from 6am; ⊚) For your early morning coffee fix it's hard to beat this English-run place, where the beans are freshly ground. Also good cakes and fresh bread.

☆ Entertainment

Kathakali performances are organised during high season – look out for notices locally.

Rock n Roll Cafe

LIVE MUSIC

(⊙24hr) Music is the thing at this otherwise unremarkable restaurant-bar. There's live music, DJs or movies on most nights in season, as well as tabla lessons. Cold beer and a good cocktail list.

ⓘ Information

A 24-hour ATM at Temple Junction takes Visa cards, and there are more ATMs in Varkala town. Many of the travel agents lining the cliff do cash advances on credit cards and change travellers cheques. **Internet cafes** (per hr around ₹40) dot the cliff top but most of the restaurants and cafes offer free wi-fi – save emails often, as power cuts are not uncommon.

Post Office (⊙10am-2pm Mon-Sat) North of Temple Junction.

ⓘ Getting There & Away

There are frequent local and express trains to Trivandrum (sleeper/3AC ₹140/249, one hour) and Kollam (₹140/249, 40 minutes), as well as four daily services to Alleppey (2nd-class/chair class ₹50/185, two hours). It's feasible to get to Kollam in time for the morning backwater boat to Alleppey. From Temple Junction, three daily buses pass by on their way to Trivandrum (₹40, 1½ to two hours), with one heading to Kollam (₹30, one hour).

A taxi to Trivandrum costs ₹1100 and to Kollam ₹800.

ⓘ Getting Around

It's about 2.5km from the train station to Varkala beach, with rickshaws going to Temple Junction for ₹60 and north cliff for ₹80. Local buses also travel regularly between the train station and Temple Junction (₹4).

Many places along the cliff hire out scooters/Enfields for ₹250/350 per day.

Around Varkala

Kappil Beach

About 9km north of Varkala, Kappil Beach is a beautiful and, as yet, undeveloped stretch of sand. It's also the start of a mini network of backwaters. The **Kappil Lake Boat Club**, near the bridge, hires out boats for short trips on the lake.

Kappil Paradise Resort

COTTAGES $$

(☑938775509; mohdrafi20@rediffmail.com; r ₹1200) Located just steps from the golden sand of Kappil and with very little around to disturb the peace, this is a pretty basic place with a handful of solid cottage-style rooms among the palms. Meals are available and the owner can help with transport to/from Varkala (around ₹150) and motorbike rental.

Kollam (Quilon)

✆ 0474 / POP 349,000

Untouristy Kollam (Quilon) is the southern approach to Kerala's backwaters and one end of a popular backwater ferry trip to Alleppey. One of the oldest ports in the Arabian Sea, it was once a major commercial hub that saw Roman, Arab, Chinese and later Portuguese, Dutch and British traders jostle into port – eager to get their hands on spices and the region's cashew crops. The centre of town is reasonably hectic, but surrounding it are the calm waterways of Ashtamudi Lake, fringed with coconut palms, cashew plantations and traditional villages – a great place to get a feel for the backwaters without the crowds.

◉ Sights

The best thing to do from Kollam is explore the backwaters around **Munroe Island**. There's a rowdy **fish market** at Kollam Beach where customers and fisherfolk alike pontificate on the value of the day's catch; there's also an evening fish market from 5pm to 9pm. The average **beach** is 2km south of town, a ₹35 rickshaw ride away.

🏃 Activities

Santhigiri Ayurveda Centre 　　 AYURVEDA
(✆ 2763014; http://santhigiriashram.com; Asramam Rd, Kadappakada) An ayurvedic centre with more of an institutional than a spa vibe, popular for its seven- to 21-day treatment packages – accommodation is available for ₹500 a night. You can also just visit for a rejuvenation massage (₹1000).

☞ Tours

★ Canal Cruise 　　 BOATING
(www.dtpckollam.com; per person ₹400; ⊙ 9am-1.30pm & 2-6.30pm) Excellent tours through the canals of Munroe Island and across Ashtamudi Lake are organised by the DTPC (District Tourism Promotion Council) and a few private operators. After a 25km drive to the starting point, you take a three-hour trip via punted canoe. On these guided excursions you can observe daily village life, see *kettuvallam* (rice barge) construction, toddy (palm beer) tapping, coir-making (coconut fibre), prawn and fish farming, and do some birdwatching on spice-garden visits.

Houseboat Cruises 　　 BOATING
(www.dtpckollam.com; 2/4/6 people overnight from ₹3000/4000/5500, Kollam to Alappuzha cruise ₹10,000/12,000/14,000) Kollam has far fewer houseboats than Alleppey, which can mean a less-touristy experience. The DTPC organises various houseboat cruise packages, both locally and to Alleppey and Kochi.

✯ Festivals & Events

Kollam Pooram is a colourful annual temple festival held in April, featuring elephants and mock sword fights. Snakeboat races are common in villages around Kollam. The **President's Trophy Boat Race**, held on Ashtamudi Lake on 1 November, is the largest and most prestigious in the region.

🛏 Sleeping

The DTPC office keeps a list of **homestays** in and around Kollam.

Karuna Residency 　　 GUESTHOUSE $
(✆ 3263240; Main Rd; s/d ₹350/450, r with AC ₹700; ❄) This little budgeteer is starting to show its age and is very basic, but it's still in reasonable condition and the owner is accustomed to travellers.

★ Ashtamudi Villas 　　 GUESTHOUSE $$
(✆ 98471 32449, 2706090 www.ashtamudivillas.com; near Kadavoor Church, Mathilil; d ₹1000-1500; 🛜) These charming brick cottages on the water's edge are easily the best choice for a relaxing, affordable stay in Kollam. Ebullient host Prabhath Joseph offers a warm welcome and pulls out all the stops with thoughtful architectural design, colourful decor, gleaming bathrooms, hammocks swinging between palm trees by the lake and a library of books on Kerala. Access is by road or boat – call ahead for directions.

Nani Hotel 　　 HOTEL $$
(✆ 2751141; www.hotelnani.com; Chinnakada Rd; d incl breakfast ₹1300, with AC ₹2080-3650; ❄ @ 🛜) This boutique business hotel is a surprise in Kollam's busy centre, and very good value. Built by a cashew magnate, it's beautifully designed and mixes traditional Keralan elements and modern lines for a sleek look. Even the cheaper rooms have flat-screen TVs, feathery pillows and sumptuous bathrooms.

Kollam (Quilon)

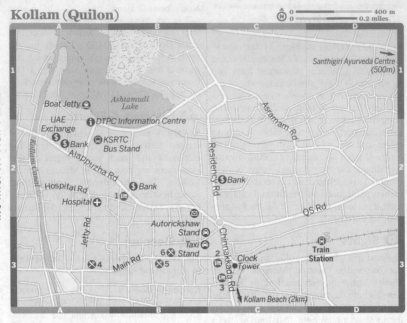

Kollam (Quilon)

🛏 Sleeping

1	Hotel Sudarsan	B2
2	Karuna Residency	C3
3	Nani Hotel	C3

🍴 Eating

4	Fayalwan Hotel	A3
5	Hotel Guru Prasad	B3
6	Indian Coffee House	B3
	Kedar Restaurant	(see 1)
	Prasadam	(see 3)

Hotel Sudarsan   HOTEL $$

(☎ 2744322; www.hotelsudarsan.com; Alappuzha Rd; d ₹1100, s/d with AC from ₹1350/1460, ste ₹2250/2500; ❈ @) Close to the boat jetty, Sudarsan is a decent-value midranger with rooms set around an inner carpark-courtyard. The spacious suites are a bargain at this price. There's a restaurant, bar and coffee shop on site and 24-hour checkout.

🍽 Eating

Indian Coffee House   INDIAN $

(Main Rd; dishes ₹10-40; ⊗7am-10pm) Reliable for a decent breakfast and strong coffee.

Hotel Guru Prasad   INDIAN $

(Main Rd; meals ₹10-25) In a neat colonial building, this busy lunchtime place draws (mostly male) punters with dirt-cheap set meals.

Fayalwan Hotel   INDIAN $

(Main Rd; meals ₹15-50) This is a real Indian working-man's diner, packed to the rafters come lunchtime. There are concrete booths and long benches for sitting and tucking in – try the mutton biryani.

Prasadam   MULTICUISINE $$

(☎ 2751141; Chinnakada Rd, Nani Hotel; mains ₹60-240; ⊗8am-10pm) The restaurant at the Nani Hotel has a slightly formal feel with high-backed chairs amid intricate copper-relief artwork depicting Kollam history. Meals, including Keralan dishes such as Travancore egg masala, as well as tandoori and Chinese, are well prepared and tasty thalis are available at lunchtime.

Kedar Restaurant   INDIAN $$

(Hotel Sudarsan; meals ₹90-150; ⊗7am-11pm) This darkened air-con restaurant is recommended for its tasty veg and nonveg cuisine, thalis and Sunday lunch buffet. There's a less-formal coffee shop for snacks and the Golden Tavern bar in the same hotel complex.

ⓘ Information

DTPC Information Centre (☑2745625; www.
dtpckollam.com; ☺8am-7pm) Helpful and can
organise backwater trips; near the KSRTC bus
stand and boat jetty.

Post Office (☑2746607; Alappuzha Rd)

UAE Exchange (☑2751240; Alappuzha Rd;
☺9.30am-6pm Mon-Fri, to 4pm Sat, to 1.30pm
Sun) For changing cash and travellers cheques.

ⓘ Getting There & Away

BOAT

There are cruises to Alleppey (p966). From the
main boat jetty there are frequent public ferry
services across Ashtamudi Lake to Guhanan-
dapuram (one hour). Fares are around ₹10
return, or ₹3 for a short hop.

BUS

Kollam is on the Trivandrum–Kollam–Alleppey–
Ernakulam bus route, with buses departing every
10 or 20 minutes to Trivandrum (₹50, two hours),
Alleppey (₹55, 2½ hours) and Ernakulam (Kochi,
₹95, 3½ hours). Buses depart from the **KSRTC
bus stand** (☑2752008), conveniently near the
boat jetty.

TAXI

A taxi to Alleppey costs ₹1200 and to Varkala
₹700.

TRAIN

There are frequent trains to Ernakulam
(sleeper/3AC ₹140/308, 3½ hours, six daily) and
Trivandrum (₹140/249, one hour) via Varkala

(₹36/165, 30 minutes). A couple of trains daily
go to Alappuzha (Alleppey; 2nd-class/AC chair
₹45/165, 1½ hours).

Around Kollam

Krishnapuram Palace Museum

Two kilometres south of Kayamkulam (between Kollam and Alleppey), this restored
palace (☑04792441133; admission ₹10, camera/
video ₹25/250; ☺9am-1pm & 2-4.30pm Tue-Sun)
is a fine example of grand Keralan architecture. Now a museum, inside are paintings,
antique furniture, sculptures and a renowned 3m-high mural depicting the Gajendra Moksha (the liberation of Gajendra, chief
of the elephants) as told in the Mahabharata.

Buses (₹26, one hour) leave Kollam every
few minutes for Kayamkulam. Get off at the
bus stand near the temple gate, 2km before
the palace.

Alappuzha (Alleppey)

☑0477 / POP 174,200

Alappuzha – still more romantically known
as Alleppey – is the hub of Kerala's backwaters, home to a vast network of waterways
and more than 1000 houseboats. Wandering around the small but chaotic city centre,
with its modest grid of canals, you'd be hard-
pressed to agree with the 'Venice of the East'

MATHA AMRITHANANDAMAYI MISSION

Well worth a visit if you are doing the backwater cruise (p966) between Kollam and Alleppey is the incongruously pink Matha Amrithanandamayi Mission
(☑04762897578; www.amritapuri.org; Amrithapuri). One of India's few female gurus, Amrithanandamayi is also known as Amma (Mother), or the 'Hugging Mother,' because of the
darshan (audience) she offers, often hugging thousands of people in marathon all-night
sessions. The ashram runs official tours daily – call ahead for times. It's a huge complex,
with about 3000 people living here permanently – monks, nuns, students and families,
both Indian and foreign. It offers food, ayurvedic treatments, yoga and meditation. Amma
travels around for much of the year, so you might be out of luck if in need of a cuddle.

Visitors should dress conservatively and there is a strict code of behaviour. With prior
arrangement – register online – you can stay at the ashram for ₹200 per day (including simple vegetarian meals) and pick up an onward or return cruise a day or two later.
Alternatively, cross to the other side of the canal and grab a rickshaw 10km south to
Karunagappally or 12km north to Kayankulam (around ₹200), from where you can
catch onward buses or trains.

If you're not taking the cruise, catch a train to either Karunagappally or Kayankulam
and take an autorickshaw (around ₹100) to Vallickavu and cross the pedestrian bridge
or take the punt across the canal from there. Alternatively, if you intend to stay a while,
you can book online for an ashram taxi – they pick up from as far away as Kochi or
Trivandrum.

Alappuzha (Alleppey)

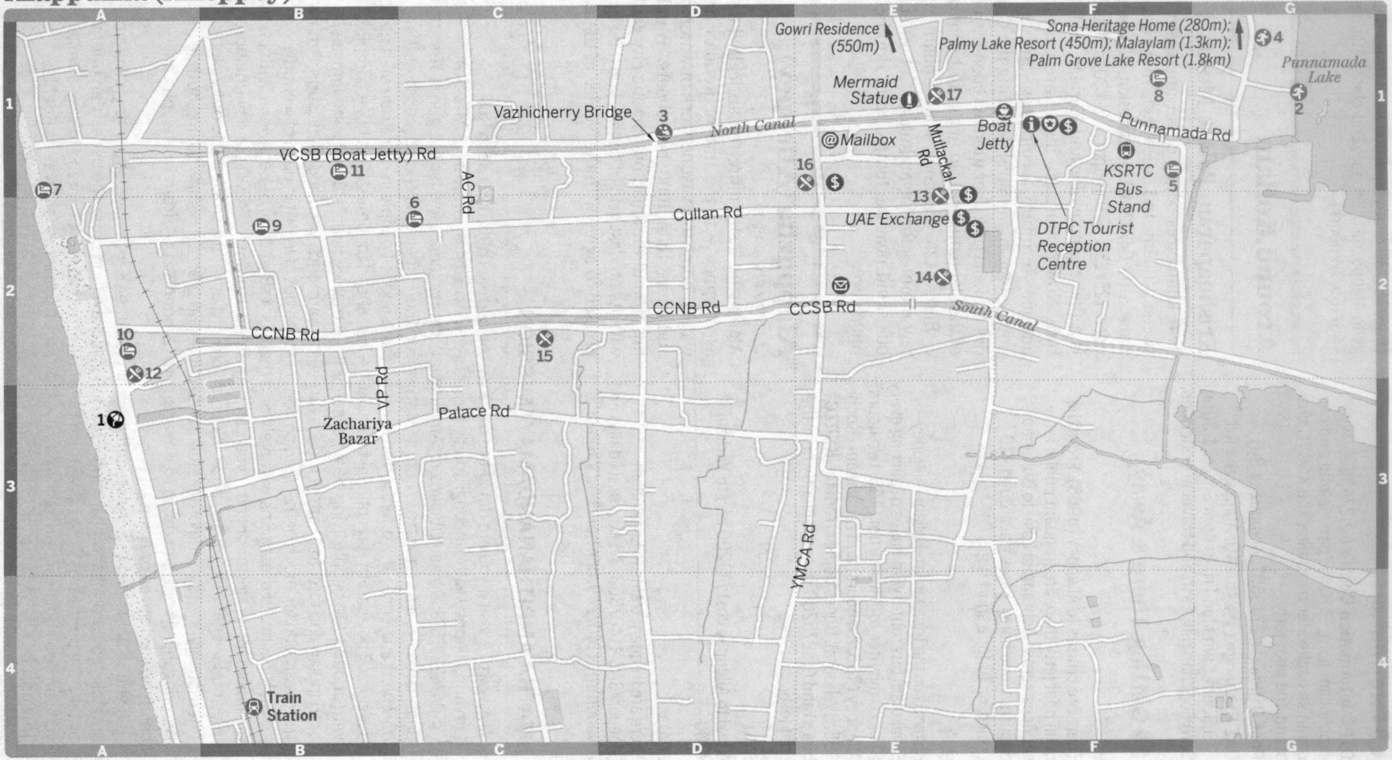

500 m
0.25 miles

Punnamada Lake

Sona Heritage Home (280m); Malayalam (1.3km); Palm Grove Lake Resort (1.8km)

Punnamada Rd

KSRTC Bus Stand

DTPC Tourist Reception Centre

Palmy Lake Resort

Boat Jetty

Mullackal Rd

UAE Exchange

Mermaid Statue

Gowri Residence (550m)

@Mailbox

North Canal

South Canal

CCSB Rd

YMCA Rd

Cullan Rd

CCNB Rd

Vazhicherry Bridge

AC Rd

Palace Rd

VP Rd

Zachariya Bazar

VCSB (Boat Jetty) Rd

CCNB Rd

Train Station

Alappuzha (Alleppey)

tag. But step out of this mini-mayhem and head west to the beach – or in practically any other direction towards the backwaters – and Alleppey is graceful and greenery-fringed, disappearing into a watery world of villages, canoes, toddy shops and, of course, houseboats. Float along and gaze over rice fields of succulent green, curvaceous rice barges and village life along the banks. This is one of Kerala's most mesmerisingly beautiful and relaxing experiences.

◎ Sights & Activities

Alleppey Beach   BEACH
Alleppey's main beach is about 2km west of the city centre; there's no shelter at the beach itself and swimming is fraught, but the sunsets are good and there are a few places to stop for a drink or snack. The beach stretches up and down the coast.

Kerala Kayaking   KAYAKING
(☏ 2245001, 9846585674; www.keralakayaking. com; per person 4-/7-/10-hour ₹1000/3000/4000) The first (and only) kayaking outfit in Alleppey, the young crew here offer excellent guided kayaking trips through narrow backwater canals. Paddles in single or double kayaks include a support boat and motorboat transport to your starting point.

**Shri Krishna
Ayurveda Panchkarma Centre**   AYURVEDA
(☏ 3290728; www.krishnayurveda.com) For ayurvedic treatments; one-hour rejuvenation massages are ₹800, but it specialises in three-, five- and seven-night packages with accommodation and yoga classes. It's near the Nehru race finishing point.

☞ Tours

Any of the dozens of travel agencies in town, guesthouses, hotel, or the KTDC can arrange canoe or houseboat tours of the backwaters.

✺ Festivals & Events

Nehru Trophy Boat Race   BOAT RACE
(http://nehrutrophy.nic.in; tickets from ₹50) Held on the second Saturday in August on Punnamada Lake, this is the most popular and fiercely-contested of Kerala's snake-boat races.

⊨ Sleeping

Even if you're not planning on boarding a houseboat, Alleppey has some of the most charming and best-value accommodation in Kerala, from heritage homes and resorts to family-run homestays with backwater views.

The rickshaw-commission racketeers are at work here, particularly at the train and bus stations; ask to be dropped off at a landmark close to your destination, or if you're booked in, call ahead for a pick-up.

Mathews Palmy Residency   GUESTHOUSE $
(☏ 2235938; www.palmyresidency.com; off Finishing Point Rd; r ₹400-700) One of the better budget deals in town, this place has six spotless rooms with Italian marble floors, three with garden-facing verandahs. The serene location is great too – north of the canal only five minutes' walk from the bus stand but set well back from the road amid lush greenery. Cross over the new Matha footbridge east of the bus station, turn right and take the first laneway to the left.

Mandala Beach House   GUESTHOUSE $
(www.mandalabeachhouse.com; Alleppey Beach; d ₹600-900, cottage ₹750, ste ₹2000) Beachfront accommodation on a budget doesn't get much better than this in Alleppey. Super laid-back Mandala sits on the edge of the sand and has a range of simple rooms – the best being the glass-fronted 'penthouse' with unbeatable sunset views. Impromptu parties are known to crank up here in season.

Johnson's GUESTHOUSE $
([☑] 2245825; www.johnsonskerala.com; d ₹400-750; @ 🛜) This backpacker favourite in a tumble-down mansion is as quirky as its owner, the gregarious Johnson Gilbert. It's a rambling residence with themed rooms filled with funky furniture, loads of plants outside and a canoe-shaped fish tank for a table. Johnson hires out his 'eco-houseboat' (₹6500 to ₹9000) and has a secluded riverside guesthouse in the backwaters.

Palmy Lake Resort HOMESTAY $
([☑] 2235938; www.palmyresorts.com; Punnamada Rd East; cottages d ₹850) With six handsome individual cottages, some bamboo and some concrete, there's loads of charm and peace at this welcoming homestay, 3.5km north of Alleppey. Friendly owners (who also run Mathews Palmy Residency) offer free pick-up from town and home-cooked meals.

Nanni Beach Residence GUESTHOUSE $
([☑] 9895039767; nannitours@gmail.com; Cullan Rd; d ₹250-400) You can't beat the price at this basic guesthouse, a short walk from the beach and 1.5km north of the train station. The young owner Shibu is a good source of local information and works hard at sprucing the place up.

★**Cherukara Nest** HOMESTAY $
([☑] 2251509; www.cherukaranest.com; d/tr incl breakfast ₹750/900, with AC ₹1200, AC cottage ₹1500; ❄ @ 🛜) Set in well-tended gardens, with a pigeon coop at the back, this lovely heritage home has the sort of welcoming family atmosphere that makes you want to stay. In the main house there are four large characterful rooms, with high ceilings, lots of polished wood touches and antediluvian doors with ornate locks – check out the spacious split-level air-con room. Owner Tony also has a good-value houseboat (₹5500 for two people) – one of the few that still uses punting power.

Gowri Residence GUESTHOUSE $
([☑] 2236371; www.gowriresidence.com; SH40; d ₹675-1350, AC cottages ₹1350-2250; ❄ 🛜) This rambling complex about 800m north of North Canal has a startling array of rooms and cottages in a large garden: traditional wood-panelled rooms in the main house, several types of lovely bungalows made from either stone, wood, bamboo or thatch – the best with cathedral ceilings, air-con and flat-screen TV – and a very cool towering tree house. Good food is served, free bicycles and there's an aviary that even includes an emu.

Tharavad HOMESTAY $$
([☑] 242044; www.tharavadheritageresort.com; West of North Police Station; d ₹1200-1500, with AC ₹2000; ❄) In a quiet canalside location between the town centre and beach, this charming ancestral home has lots of glossy teak and antiques, shuttered windows, five characterful rooms and well-maintained gardens.

Sona Heritage Home GUESTHOUSE $
([☑] 2235211; www.sonahome.com; Lakeside, Finishing Point; r ₹800-900, with AC ₹1125; ❄ 🛜) Run by the affable Joseph, this beautiful old heritage home has slightly shabby but high-ceilinged rooms with faded flowered curtains, Christian motifs and four-poster beds overlooking a well-kept garden.

Malayalam RESORT $$
([☑] 2234591; malayalamresorts@yahoo.com; Punnamada; r ₹1200-2500) This little family-run pad has four cute bamboo cottages, tree houses and a big new two-storey four-room house facing the lake near the Nehru Trophy Boat Race starting point. Views from the upstairs rooms with balcony are sweet. It's a bit hard to find: walk past the Keraleeyam resort reception and along the canal bank.

Palm Grove Lake Resort RESORT $$
([☑] 2235004; www.palmgrovelakeresort.com; Punnamada; cottages d ₹1970-2200, with AC ₹3320) Close to the starting point of the Nehru Trophy Boat Race on Punnamada Lake, the stylish individual double cottages here are set in a palm-filled garden with lake views.

★**Raheem Residency** HOTEL $$$
([☑] 2239767; www.raheemresidency.com; Beach Rd; d €112-146; ❄ 🛜 ☀) This thoughtfully renovated 1860s heritage home is a joy to visit, let alone stay in. The 10 rooms have been restored to their former glory and have bathtubs, antique furniture and period fixtures. The common areas are airy and comfortable, there are pretty indoor courtyards, a well-stocked library, a great little pool and an excellent restaurant.

✗ Eating & Drinking

Mushroom ARABIAN, INDIAN $
(near South Police Station; mains ₹40-90; ☺ noon-midnight) Breezy open-air restaurant with wrought-iron chairs specialising in cheap, tasty and spicy halal meals like chicken kali

mirch, fish tandoori and chilli mushrooms. Lots of locals and travellers give it a good vibe.

Kream Korner Art Cafe   MULTICUISINE $
(☎2252781; www.kreamkornerartcafe.com; Mullackal Rd; dishes ₹25-150; ⊙9am-10pm) The most colourful dining space in town, this food-meets-art restaurant greets you with brightly painted tables and contemporary local art on the walls. It's a relaxed, airy place popular with Indian and foreign families for its inexpensive and tasty menu of Indian and Chinese dishes. There's also a pint-sized **Cullan Rd** (veg thalis ₹45) branch of Kream Korner with just a few seats and popular.

Thaff   INDIAN $
(YMCA Rd; meals ₹45-110) A popular hole-in-the-wall that has tasty Indian bites, with some Arabic flavours mixed in. It does succulent spit roast chicken, *shwarma* and brain-freezing ice-cream shakes. There's another location on Punnamada Rd.

Indian Coffee House   CAFE $
(snacks ₹8-40; ⊙8am-9pm) Branches on Mullackal Rd, YMCA Rd and Beach Rd – the latter is a pavilion in a breezy beachside location.

Harbour Restaurant   MULTICUISINE $$
(☎2230767; Beach Rd; meals ₹100-290; ⊙10am-10pm) This enjoyable beachside place is run by the nearby Raheem Residency. It's more casual and budget-conscious than the hotel's restaurant, but promises a range of well-prepared Indian, Chinese and Continental dishes, and some of the coldest beer in town.

Royale Park Hotel   INDIAN $$
(YMCA Rd; meals ₹100-200; ⊙7am-10.30pm, bar 10.30am-10.30pm; ☎) There is an extensive menu at this air-con hotel restaurant, and the food is excellent, including scrumptious veg/fish thalis (₹120/150). You can order from the same menu in the surprisingly nice upstairs bar and wash down your meal with a cold Kingfisher.

Chakara Restaurant   MULTICUISINE $$$
(☎2230767; Beach Rd; mini Kerala meal ₹420, mains from ₹450; ⊙12.30-3pm & 7-10pm) The restaurant at Raheem Residency is Alleppey's finest, with seating on a *bijou* open rooftop, reached via a spiral staircase, with views over to the beach. The menu creatively combines traditional Keralan and European cuisine, specialising in locally-caught fish.

❶ Information

DTPC Tourist Reception Centre (☎2251/96; www.dtpcalappuzha.com; Boat Jetty Rd; ⊙9am-5pm) Close to the bus stand and boat jetty. Staff are helpful and can advise on home-stays and houseboats.

Mailbox (☎2339994; Boat Jetty Rd; per hr ₹20; ⊙9am-8pm) Internet access.

Tourist Police (☎2251161; ⊙24hr) Next door to the DTPC.

UAE Exchange (☎2264407; cnr Cullan & Mullackal Rds; ⊙9.30am-6pm, to 4pm Sat, to 1pm Sun) For changing cash and travellers cheques.

❶ Getting There & Away

BOAT
Ferries run to Kollayam from the boat jetty on VCSB (Boat Jetty) Rd.

WORTH A TRIP

GREEN PALM HOMES

Kerala's backwaters snake in all directions from Alleppey and, while touring on a house-boat is a great experience, taking time to slow down and stay in a village can be just as rewarding.

Just 12km from Alleppey on a backwater island, **Green Palms Homes** (☎9495557675, 0477-2724497; www.greenpalmhomes.com; Chennamkary; r without bathroom incl full board ₹2250, r ₹3250-4000) is a series of homestays that seem a universe away, set in a picturesque village, where you sleep in simple rooms in villagers' homes among rice paddies (though 'premium' rooms with attached bathroom and air-con are available). It's splendidly quiet, there are no roads in sight and you can take a guided walk, hire bicycles (₹50 per hour) and canoes (₹100 per hour) or take cooking classes with your hosts (₹150).

To get here, call ahead and catch one of the hourly ferries from Alleppey to Chennamkary (₹5, 1¼ hours). It's also accessible by autorickshaw (around ₹150) then canoe across to the island. This is a traditional village; dress appropriately.

KERALA'S BACKWATERS

The undisputed highlight of a trip to Kerala is travelling through the 900km network of waterways that fringe the coast and trickle inland. Long before the advent of roads, these waters were the slippery highways of Kerala, and many villagers still use paddle-power as their main form of transport. Trips through the backwaters traverse palm-fringed lakes studded with cantilevered Chinese fishing nets, and wind their way along narrow, shady canals where coir (coconut fibre), copra (dried coconut kernels) and cashews are loaded onto boats. Along the way are isolated villages where farming life continues as it has for eons.

Tourist Cruises

The popular tourist cruise between Kollam and Alleppey (₹400) departs from either end at 10.30am, arriving at 6.30pm, daily from August to March and every second day at other times. Generally, there's a 1pm lunch stop (with a basic lunch provided) and a brief afternoon chai stop. The crew has an ice box full of fruit, soft drinks and beer to sell, but it pays to bring snacks, sunscreen and a hat.

It's a scenic and leisurely way – the journey takes eight hours – to get between the two towns, but the boat travels along only the major canals – you won't have many close-up views of the village life that makes the backwaters so magical. Another option is to take the trip halfway (₹250) and get off at the Matha Amrithanandamayi Mission (p961) and meet one of India's few female gurus.

Houseboats

If the stars align, renting a houseboat designed like a *kettuvallam* (rice barge) could well be one of the highlights of your trip to India. It can be an expensive experience (depending on your budget) but for a couple on a romantic overnight jaunt or split between a group of travellers, it's usually worth every rupee. Drifting through quiet canals lined with coconut palms, eating delicious Keralan food, meeting local villagers and sleeping on the water – it's a world away from the clamour of India.

Houseboats cater for couples (one or two double bedrooms) and groups (up to seven bedrooms!). Food (and an onboard chef to cook it) is generally included in the quoted cost, as is a driver/captain. Houseboats can be chartered through a multitude of private operators in Alleppey, Kollam and Kottayam. This is the biggest business in Kerala: some operators are unscrupulous. The quality of boats varies widely, from rust buckets to floating palaces – try to check out the boat before agreeing on a price. Travel-agency reps will be pushing you to book a boat as soon as you set foot in Kerala, but it's better to wait till you reach a backwater hub: choice is greater in Alleppey (an incredible 1000-plus boats

BUS

From the KSRTC bus stand, frequent buses head to Trivandrum (₹120, 3½ hours, every 20 minutes), Kollam (₹55, 2½ hours) and Ernakulam (Kochi, ₹50, 1½ hours). Buses to Kottayam (₹40, 1¼ hours, every 30 minutes) are much faster than the ferry. One bus daily leaves for Kumily at 6.40am (₹120, 5½ hours). The Varkala bus (₹100, 3½ hours) leaves at 9am and 10.40am daily.

TRAIN

There are several trains to Ernakulam (2nd-class/sleeper/3AC ₹39/120/218, 1½ hours) and Trivandrum (₹59/120/267, three hours) via Kollam (₹66/140/250, 1½ hours). Four trains a day stop at Varkala (2nd-class/AC chair ₹71/218, two hours). The train station is 4km west of town.

Getting Around

An autorickshaw from the train station to the boat jetty and KSRTC bus stand is around ₹60. Several guesthouses around town hire out scooters for ₹200 per day.

Kottayam

☏ 0481 / POP 172,878

Sandwiched between the Western Ghats and the backwaters, Kottayam is renowned for being the centre of Kerala's spice and rubber trade rather than for its aesthetic appeal. For most travellers it's a hub town, well connected to both the mountains and the backwaters, with many travellers taking the

and counting), and you're much more likely to be able to bargain down a price if you turn up and see what's on offer. Most guesthouses and homestays can also book you on a houseboat.

In the high season you're likely to get caught in backwater-gridlock – some travellers are disappointed by the number of boats on the water. It's possible to travel by houseboat between Alleppey and Kollam and all the way to Kochi – the DTPC in Kollam can organise these trips. Expect a boat for two people for 24 hours to cost about ₹5000 to ₹8000 at the budget level; for four people, ₹8000 to to ₹12,000; for larger boats or for air-conditioning expect to pay from ₹12,000 to ₹30,000. Shop around to negotiate a bargain – though this will be harder in the peak season. Prices triple from around 20 December to 5 January.

Village Tours & Canoe Boats

More and more travellers are opting for village tours or canal-boat trips. Village tours usually involve small groups of five to six people, a knowledgable guide and an open canoe or covered *kettuvallam*. The tours (from Kochi, Kollam or Alleppey) last from 2½ to six hours and cost from around ₹400 to ₹800 per person. They include visits to villages to watch coir-making, boat building, toddy tapping and fish farming. The Munroe Island trip from Kollam is an excellent tour of this type; the tourist desk in Ernakulam also organises recommended tours.

In Alleppey, rented canoe boats offer a nonguided laze through the canals on a small, covered canoe for up to four people (two people for two/four hours ₹200/400).

Public Ferries

If you want the local backwater transport experience for just a few rupees, there are State Water Transport (www.swtd.gov.in) boats between Alleppey and Kottayam (₹10 to ₹12, 2½ hours) five times daily starting from Alleppey at 7.30am. The trip crosses Vembanad Lake and has a more varied landscape than the Kollam–Alleppey cruise.

Environmental Issues

Pollution from houseboat motors is becoming a major problem as boat numbers swell every season. The Keralan authorities have introduced an ecofriendly accreditation system for houseboat operators. Among the criteria an operator must meet before being issued with the 'Green Palm Certificate' are the installation of solar panels and sanitary tanks for the disposal of waste – ask operators whether they have the requisite certification. Consider choosing one of the few remaining punting, rather than motorised, boats if possible, though these can only operate in shallow water.

backwater cruise to or from Alleppey. The city itself has a crazy, traffic-clogged centre, but you don't have to go far to be in the villages and waterways.

Kottayam has a bookish history: the first Malayalam-language printing press was established here in 1820, and this was the first district in India to achieve 100% literacy. A place of churches and seminaries, it was a refuge for the Orthodox church when the Portuguese began forcing Keralan Christians to switch to Catholicism in the 16th century.

The **Thirunakkara Utsavam festival** is held in March at the Thirunakkara Shiva Temple.

🛏 Sleeping

The accommodation options are pretty average in Kottayam – you're better off heading to Kumarakom for some great lakeside accommodation.

Ambassador Hotel HOTEL $
(☎ 2563293; ambassadorhotelktm@yahoo.in; KK Rd; d from ₹560, with AC from ₹950) This old-school place gets our vote for best budget hotel in town. Rooms with TV are spartan but fairly clean, spacious and quiet for this price. It has a bar, an adequate restaurant, a pastry counter and a boat-shaped fish tank in the lobby.

Homestead Hotel HOTEL $

(☑2560467; KK Rd; s/d from ₹425/782, d with AC ₹1500; ❀) This has reasonably well maintained rooms – though some are a little musty and come with eye-watering green decor – in a blissfully quiet building off the street.

Pearl Regency HOTEL $$

(☑2561123; www.pearlregency.in; MC Rd, TB Junction; s/d from ₹2430/2950; ❀@) This business-focused multistorey contender is efficient, decent value and a passable stay if you're stuck in Kottayam. Two restaurants and a 24-hour coffee shop mean you won't even need to leave the hotel.

Windsor Castle &
Lake Village Resort HOTEL $$$

(☑2363637; www.thewindsorcastle.net; MC Rd; s/d from ₹3375/4500, cottages ₹6750; ❀🖵🛏) This grandiose white box has some of Kottayam's best hotel rooms, but the more interesting accommodation is in the Lake Village behind the hotel. Deluxe cottages, strewn around the private backwaters and manicured gardens, are pricey but top notch. There's a pleasant restaurant overlooking landscaped waterways.

✖ Eating

Thali SOUTH INDIAN $

(1st fl, KK Rd; meals ₹45-95; ☉8am-8.30pm) A lovely, spotlessly kept 1st-floor dining room with slatted blinds, Thali is a swankier version of the typical Keralan set-meal place. The food here is great, including Malabar fish curry and thalis.

Meenachil MULTICUISINE $

(2nd fl, KK Rd; dishes ₹50-125; ☉noon-3pm & 6-9.30pm) A favourite place in Kottayam to fill up on Indian and Chinese fare. The family atmosphere is friendly, the dining room modern and tidy, and the menu expansive.

★Nalekattu SOUTH INDIAN $$

(MC Rd, Windsor Castle; dishes ₹140-210; ☉noon-3pm & 7-10pm) The traditional Keralan restaurant at the Windsor Castle overlooks some neat backwaters and serves tasty Keralan specialities like *chemeen* (mango curry). The hotel's more upmarket indoor restaurant, **Lake Paradise**, serves a spectacular multicuisine buffet at lunch and dinner for ₹300.

❶ Information

The KSRTC bus stand is 1km south of the centre; the boat jetty is a further 2km (at Kodimatha).

The train station is 1km north of Kottayam. There's a handful of ATMs around.

DTPC Office (☑2560479; www.dtpckottayam. com; ☉10am-5pm Mon-Sat) At the boat jetty. Offers daily backwater trips to Alleppey and Kumarakom for ₹250.

UAE Exchange (☑2303865; 1st fl, MC Rd; ☉9.30am-6pm Mon-Sat, 9.30am-1pm Sun) Changes cash and travellers cheques.

❶ Getting There & Away

BOAT

Daily ferries (p966) run to Alleppey from the boat jetty.

BUS

The **KSRTC bus stand** has buses to Trivandrum (₹98, four hours, every 20 minutes), Alleppey (₹40, 1¼ hours, every 30 minutes) and Ernakulam (Kochi, ₹52, two hours, every 20 minutes). There are also frequent buses to nearby Kumarakom (₹15, 30 minutes, every 15 minutes), Thrissur (₹98, four hours), Calicut (₹190, seven hours, 13 daily), Kumily for Periyar Wildlife Sanctuary (₹71, four hours, every 30 minutes) and Munnar (₹100, five hours, five daily). There are also buses to Kollam (₹65, four daily), where you can change for Varkala.

TRAIN

Kottayam is well served by frequent trains running between Trivandrum (2nd-class/sleeper/3AC ₹82/140/307, 3½ hours) and Ernakulam (₹60/140/225, 1½ hours).

❶ Getting Around

An autorickshaw from the jetty to the KSRTC bus stand is around ₹40, and from the bus stand to the train station about ₹30. Most trips around town cost ₹30.

Around Kottayam

Kumarakom

☑0481

Kumarakom, 16km west of Kottayam and on the shore of Vembanad Lake – Kerala's largest lake – is an unhurried backwater town with a smattering of dazzling top-end sleeping options and a renowned bird sanctuary. You can arrange houseboats through Kumarakom's less-crowded canals, but expect to pay considerably more than in Alleppey.

Arundhati Roy, author of the 1997 Booker Prize–winning *The God of Small Things*, was raised in the nearby Aymanam village.

☉ Sights & Activities

Kumarakom Bird Sanctuary NATURE RESERVE (Indian/foreigner ₹30/100, video ₹1000; ☉6am-5pm) This reserve on the five-hectare site of a former rubber plantation is the haunt of a variety of domestic and migratory birds. October to February is the time for travelling birds like the garganey teal, osprey, marsh harrier and steppe eagle; May to July is the breeding season for local species such as the Indian shag, pond herons, egrets and darters. Early morning is the best viewing time. A guide costs ₹200 for a two-hour tour (₹300 from 6am to 8am).

Buses between Kottayam's KSRTC stand and Kumarakom (₹15, 30 minutes, every 15 minutes) stop at the entrance to the bird sanctuary.

🛏 Sleeping

Cruise 'N Lake RESORT $$
(☎2525804; www.homestaykumarakom.com; Puthenpura Tourist Enclave, Cheepunkal; r ₹1500, with AC ₹2000; ❄) Location, location. Surrounded by backwaters on one side and a lawn of rice paddies on the other, this is the ideal affordable Kumarakom getaway. The three double rooms are plain but have verandahs facing the water. Go a couple of kilometres past the sanctuary to Cheepunkal and take a left; it's then 2km down a rugged dirt road. Management can arrange pick-ups from Kottayam (₹450), and houseboats and all meals are available from here.

Tharavadu Heritage Home GUESTHOUSE $$
(☎2525230; www.tharavaduheritage.com; d ₹1070-2025, bamboo cottage ₹1575, d with AC ₹2475-2800; ❄@) Rooms are either in the superbly restored 1870s teak family mansion or in equally comfortable individual creekside bamboo cottages. All are excellently crafted and come with arty touches. It's 4km before the bird sanctuary.

Santitheeram Heritage Home HOMESTAY $$
(☎048112525122; Pushpalayam, Kavanattinkara; r ₹1200) Just two rooms in this cosy and welcoming traditional family home on the water's edge just a few hundred metres from the KTDC boat jetty.

Ettumanur

The **Shiva Temple** at Ettumanur, 12km north of Kottayam, has inscriptions dating from 1542, but parts of the building may be even older. The temple is noted for its exceptional woodcarvings and murals similar to those at Kochi's Mattancherry Palace. The annual **festival** is held in February/March.

Sree Vallabha Temple

Devotees make offerings at this temple, 2km from Tiruvilla, in the form of traditional, regular all-night **Kathakali** performances that are open to all. Around 10km east of here, the **Aranmula Boat Race**, one of Kerala's biggest snake-boat races, is held during Onam in August/September.

THE WESTERN GHATS

Periyar Wildlife Sanctuary

☎04869
South India's most popular wildlife sanctuary, **Periyar** (☎224571; www.periyartigerreserve.org; Indian/foreigner ₹25/300; ☉6am-6pm, last entry 5pm) encompasses 777 sq km and a 26-sq-km artificial lake created by the British in 1895. The vast region is home to bison, sambar, wild boar, langur, 900 to 1000 elephants and 35 to 40 hard-to-spot tigers. Firmly established on both the Indian and foreigner tourist trails, the place can sometimes feel a bit like Disneyland-in-the-Ghats, but its mountain scenery and jungle walks make for an enjoyable visit. Bring warm and waterproof clothing.

Kumily, 4km from the sanctuary, is the closest town and home to a growing strip of hotels, spice shops, chocolate shops and Kashmiri emporiums. Thekkady is the sanctuary centre with the KTDC hotels and boat jetty. Confusingly, when people refer to the sanctuary they tend to use Kumily, Thekkady and Periyar interchangeably.

☉ Sights & Activities

Various tours and trips access Periyar Wildlife Sanctuary. Most hotels and agencies around town can arrange all-day 4WD **jungle safaris** (per person ₹1600-2000; ☉5am-6.30pm), which cover over 40km of trails in jungle bordering the park, though many travellers complain that at least 30km of the trip is on sealed roads.

You can arrange **elephant rides** (per 30min/1-hr/2- ₹350/750/1000) at most hotels and agents in town. If you want the extended elephant experience, you can pay ₹2500 for a 2½-hour ride that includes elephant feeding and washing. **Cooking classes** (around ₹200-400) are offered by many local homestays.

Periyar Lake Cruise
BOATING

(adult/child ₹150/50; ⊘ departures 7.30am, 9.30am, 11.15am, 1.45pm & 3.30pm) These 1½-hour boat trips around the lake are the main way to tour the sanctuary without taking a guided walk. You might see deer, boar and birdlife but it's generally more of a cruise – often a rowdy one – than a wildlife-spotting experience. Boats are operated by the Forest Department and by KTDC – the **ticket counters** are together in the main building above the boat jetty, and you must buy a ticket before boarding the boat. In high season get to the ticket office 1½ hours before each trip to buy tickets. The first and last departures offer the best prospects for wildlife spotting, and October to March is generally the best time to see animals.

Ecotourism Centre
OUTDOOR ADVENTURE

(☑ 224571; www.periyartigerreserve.org; Thekkady Rd; ⊘ 9am-1pm & 2-5pm) A number of more adventurous explorations of the park can be arranged by the Ecotourism Centre, run by the Forest Department. These include border hikes (₹1000; from 8am to 5pm), 2½-hour nature walks (₹200), full-day bamboo rafting (₹1500) and 'jungle patrols' (₹750), which cover 4km to 5km and are the best way to experience the park close up, accompanied by a trained tribal guide. Trips usually require a minimum of four or five people. There are also overnight 'tiger trail' treks (per person ₹4000, solo ₹6000), which are run by former poachers retrained as guides, and cover 20km to 30km.

Gavi Ecotourism
OUTDOOR ADVENTURE

(☑ 223270, 994792399; http://gavi.kfdcecotourism.com; treks ₹1000, jeep safaris ₹1500; ⊘ 9am-8pm) This Forest Department venture offers jeep safaris, treks and boating to Gavi, a cardamom plantation and jungle area bordering the sanctuary about 45km from Kumily. Hotels can help organise the same trips.

Spice Gardens & Tea Plantation
GARDENS, TEA ESTATE

This part of the ghats is an important spice-growing region – check out the many spice shops in Kumily's bazaar to see what's harvested. Several spice plantations are open to visitors and most hotels can arrange tours (₹450/750 by autorickshaw/taxi for two to

three hours). If you want to see a tea factory in operation, do it from here – working tea-factory visits are not permitted in Munnar.

If you'd rather do a spice tour independently, you can visit a few excellent gardens outside Kumily. The one-hectare **Abraham's Spice Garden** (☑ 222919; www.abrahamspice.com; Spring Valley; tours ₹100; ⊘ 7am-6.30pm) has been going for 56 years. **Highrange Spices** (☑ 222117; tours ₹100; ⊘ 7am-6pm), 3km from Kumily, has 4 hectares where you can see ayurvedic herbs and vegetables growing. A rickshaw/taxi to either spice garden and back will be around ₹200/300. About 13km away from Kumily the working **Connemara Tea Plantation** (Vandiperiyar; tours ₹100; ⊘ 8am-5pm) offers guided tours of the fields and tea-making process. Any bus heading towards Kottayam will stop at the tea factory in Vandiperiyar on request (₹11, every 15 minutes).

Santhigiri Ayurveda
AYURVEDA

(☑ 223979; www.santhigiri.co.in; Munnar Rd, Vandanmedu Junction; ⊘ 8am-8pm) An excellent and authentic place for the ayurvedic experience, offering top-notch massage (₹650 to ₹1500) and long-term treatments lasting seven to 14 days.

🛏 Sleeping

🏕 Inside the Sanctuary

The KTDC runs three steeply priced hotels in the park, including Periyar House, Aranya Nivas and the grand Lake Palace. Make reservations (at any KTDC office), particularly for weekends. Note that there's effectively a curfew at these places – guests are not permitted to roam the sanctuary after 6pm.

The Ecotourism Centre can arrange tented accommodation inside the park at the **Jungle Camp** (d tent ₹5000). Rates include trekking and meals but not the park entry fee. Also ask about **Bamboo Grove** (d ₹1500), a group of basic cottages and tree houses not far from Kumily town.

Lake Palace
HOTEL $$$

(☑ 223887; www.lakepalacethekkady.com; r incl all meals ₹20,000-25,000) There's a faint whiff of royalty at this restored old summer palace, located on an island in the middle of the Periyar Lake. The six charismatic rooms are decorated with flair using antique furnishings and a selection of modern conveniences (like flat-screen TVs). Staying in the midst of the sanctuary gives you a good chance of seeing wildlife from your private terrace, and rates include meals, boat trip and trekking.

🛏 Kumily

Mickey Homestay
GUESTHOUSE $

(📞 223196; www.mickeyhomestay.com; Bypass Rd; r ₹500-850) Mickey is a genuine homestay with just a handful of intimate rooms in a family house and a rear cottage, all with homely touches that make them some of the most comfortable in town. Balconies have rattan furniture and hanging bamboo seats and the whole place is surrounded by greenery.

Coffee Inn
GUESTHOUSE $

(📞 222763; coffeeinn@sancharnet.in; Thekkady Rd; r without bath ₹400, d ₹800-2000, tree house ₹600) This whimsical timber hotel and cafe has a range of neatly furnished and quirky wood-lined rooms, as well as rustic tree houses and cottages in a back garden overlooking a rather urban section of the sanctuary. Decent restaurant.

★ Green View Homestay
HOMESTAY $

(📞 224617; www.sureshgreenview.com; Bypass Rd; r incl breakfast ₹500-1750; 🛜) It has grown from its humble homestay origins but Greenview is a lovely place that manages to retain its personal and friendly family welcome from owners Suresh and Sulekha. The two buildings house several classes of beautifully maintained rooms with private balconies, some overlooking a lovely rear spice garden. Excellent vegetarian meals and cooking lessons (veg/nonveg ₹200/350) are available.

El-Paradiso
HOMESTAY $

(📞 222350; www.goelparadiso.com; Bypass Rd; d ₹750-1250, q ₹1850; @🛜) This immaculate family homestay has fresh rooms with balconies and hanging chairs, or rooms opening onto a terrace overlooking greenery at the back. Cooking classes (₹400 including meal) are a speciality here.

Tranquilou
HOMESTAY $$

(📞 223269; www.tranquilouhomestay.com; off Bypass Rd; r incl breakfast ₹800-1200; @🛜) Another friendly family homestay in a peaceful

Kumily & Periyar Wildlife Sanctuary

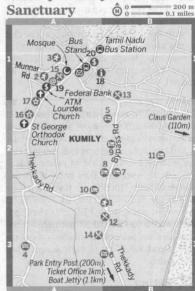

Kumily & Periyar Wildlife Sanctuary

location. Neatly furnished rooms surround a pleasant garden; the two doubles that adjoin a shared sitting room are a good family option.

Claus Garden
HOMESTAY $$

(222320; www.homestay.in; s/d without bathroom ₹800/950, d/tr ₹1500/1600;) Set well away from the hustle and bustle and up a very steep hill, this lovely big building has gently curving balconies, splashes of colour and six rooms around a lush green garden.

Chrissie's Hotel
GUESTHOUSE $$

(9447601304, 224155; www.chrissies.in; Bypass Rd; r ₹1920-2400) This four-storey building behind the popular expat-run restaurant of the same name somehow manages to blend in with the forest-green surrounds. The chic rooms are spacious and bright, with cheery furnishings, lamps and colourful pillows. Yoga, shiatsu and reiki classes can be arranged.

Spice Village
HOTEL $$$

(04843011711; www.cghearth.com; Thekkady Rd; villas ₹14,000-20,000;) This CGH Earth place takes its green credentials very seriously and has captivating, spacious cottages that are smart yet cosily rustic, in pristinely kept grounds. Its restaurant does lavish lunch and dinner buffets (₹1000 each), there's a colonial-style bar and you can find the **Wildlife Interpretation Centre** (222028; 6am-6pm) here, which has a resident naturalist showing slides and answering questions about the park. Good value out of high season when rates halve.

✕ Eating

There are plenty of good cheap veg restaurants in the bazaar area, and some decent traveller-oriented restaurants on the road to the wildlife sanctuary.

Shri Krishna
INDIAN $

(KK Rd; meals ₹60-120) A local favourite in the bazaar, serving up spicy pure veg meals including several takes on thali.

Ebony's Cafe
MULTICUISINE $

(Bypass Rd; meals ₹40-240; 8.30am-9.30pm) This friendly rooftop joint with lots of pot plants, check tablecloths and traveller-friendly tunes serves up a tasty assortment of Indian and Western food from mashed potato to pasta and cold beer (₹150).

French Restaurant & Bakery
CAFE, BAKERY $

(meals ₹40-175; 7.30am-10pm) This family-run shack set back from the main road is a good spot for breakfast or lunch, serving up croissants, pancakes and baguettes, along with decent pasta and noodle dishes.

Chrissie's Cafe
MULTICUISINE $

(Bypass Rd; meals ₹80-200; 8am-9.30pm) A perennially popular haunt, this airy 1st-floor cafe satisfies travellers with cakes and snacks, excellent coffee and well-prepared Western faves like pizza and pasta.

Ambadi Restaurant
INDIAN $

(dishes ₹80-250; 7.30am-9.30pm) At the hotel of the same name, Ambadi has a more formal feel than most with an almost church-like decor, but the broad menu of North and South Indian dishes are reasonably priced.

☆ Entertainment

Mudra Kathakali Centre
CULTURAL PROGRAM

(9446072901; www.mudraculturalcentre.com; Lake Rd; admission ₹200, camera/video free/₹200; shows 4.30pm & 7pm) Twice daily one-hour Kathakali shows at this cultural centre are highly entertaining. Make-up and costume starts 30 minutes before each show; very photogenic. Arrive early for a good seat.

Kadathanadan Kalari Centre
CULTURAL PROGRAM

(www.kalaripayattu.co.in; Thekkady Rd; ₹200; shows 6pm) Hour-long demonstrations of the exciting Keralan martial art of *kalaripayat* are staged here every evening. Tickets are available from the box office throughout the day.

ⓘ Information

There's a Federal Bank ATM at the junction with the road to Kottayam accepting international cards, and several internet cafes in the bazaar area.

DTPC Office (222620; 10am-5pm Mon-Sat) Behind the bus stand, not as useful as the Ecotourism Centre.

Ecotourism Centre (224571; www.periyar tigerreserve.org; 9am-1pm & 2-5pm) For park tours, information and walks.

Mt Sinai Cyber Cafe (222170; Thekkady Junction; per hr ₹20; 9am-10pm)

State Bank of Travancore (10am-3.30pm Mon-Fri, to 12.30pm Sat) Changes travellers cheques and currency; has an ATM accepting foreign cards.

ⓘ Getting There & Away

Kumily's KSRTC bus stand is at the eastern edge of town.

Eleven buses daily operate between Ernakulam (Kochi) and Kumily (₹120, five hours). Buses leave every 30 minutes for Kottayam (₹71, four hours), with two direct buses to Trivandrum at 8.45am and 11am (₹210, eight hours) and one daily bus to Alleppey at 1.10pm (₹120, 5½ hours). Private buses to Munnar (₹75, 4 to 5 hours) also leave from the bus stand at 6am, 6.30am and 9.45am.

Tamil Nadu buses leave every 30 minutes to Madurai (₹80, four hours) from the Tamil Nadu bus stand just over the border.

ⓘ Getting Around

It's only about 1.5km from Kumily bus stand to the main park entrance, but another 3km from there to Periyar Lake; you might catch a bus (almost as rare as the tigers), but will more likely take an autorickshaw from the entry post (₹50) or set off on foot – but bear in mind there's no walking path so you'll have to dodge traffic on the road. Autorickshaws will take you on short hops around town for ₹30. **Bicycle hire** is available from many guesthouses.

Munnar

☑ 04865 / POP 68,200 / ELEV 1524M

South India's largest tea-growing region, the rolling hills around Munnar are carpeted in emerald-green tea plantations, contoured, clipped and sculpted like ornamental hedges. The low mountain scenery is magnificent – you're often up above the clouds watching veils of mist clinging to the mountaintops. Munnar itself is a scruffy administration centre, not unlike a North Indian hill station, but wander just a few kilometres out of town and you'll be engulfed in a sea of a thousand shades of green.

Once known as the High Range of Travancore, today Munnar is the commercial centre of some of the world's highest tea-growing estates. The majority of the plantations are now operated by the Kannan Devan Hills Plantation Company (KDHP), a local cooperative which succeeded corporate giant Tata Tea in 2005.

◉ Sights & Activities

The main reason to visit Munnar is to explore the lush, tea-filled hillocks that surround it. Hotels, homestays, travel agencies, autorickshaw drivers and practically every passerby will want to organise a day of sight-

---

OFF THE BEATEN TRACK

SABARIMALA

Deep in the Western Ghats about 20km west of Gavi and some 50km from the town of Erumeli is a place called Sabarimala, home to the Ayyappan temple. It's said to be one of the world's most visited pilgrimage centres, with anywhere between 40 and 60 million Hindu devotees trekking here each year. Followers believe the god Ayyappan meditated at this spot. Strict rules govern the pilgrimage. For information see www.sabarimala.org.

seeing for you: shop around. The best way to experience the hills is on a **guided trek**, which can range from a few hours' 'soft trekking' around tea plantations to more arduous full-day mountain treks, which open up some stupendous views. Trekking guides can easily be organised through hotels and guesthouses or the DTPC for around ₹100 per person per hour (usually a minimum of four hours).

Tea Museum   MUSEUM
(☑230561; adult/child ₹75/35, camera ₹20; ⏲10am-4pm Tue Sun) About 1.5km northwest of town, this museum is about as close as you'll get to a working tea factory around Munnar. It's a demo model of the real thing, but it still shows the basic process. A collection of old bits and pieces from the colonial era, including photographs and a 1905 tea-roller, are also kept here. A 30-minute video explaining the history of Munnar, its tea estates and the programs put in place for its workers screens hourly. The short walk to or from town follows the road but passes some of the most accessible tea plantations from Munnar town. An autorickshaw charges ₹20 from the bazaar.

☞ Tours

The DTPC (p976) runs three fairly rushed full-day tours to points around Munnar. The **Sandal Valley Tour** (per person ₹350; ⏲9am-6pm) visits Chinnar Wildlife Sanctuary, several viewpoints, waterfalls, plantations, a sandalwood forest and villages. The **Tea Valley tour** (per person ₹300; ⏲10am-6pm) visits Echo Point, Top Station and Rajamalai (for Eravikulam National Park), among other places. The **Village Sightseeing Tour**

Munnar

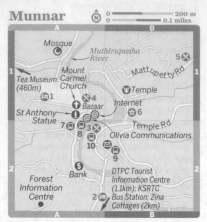

0 — 200 m
0 — 0.1 miles

Mosque

Muthirupuzha River

Mount Carmel Church

Tea Museum (460m)

St Anthony Statue

Bazaar

Temple

Internet

Temple Rd

Olivia Communications

Bank

Forest Information Centre

DTPC Tourist Information Centre (1.1km); KSRTC Bus Station; Zina Cottages (2km)

(₹400; ⏰9.30am-6pm) covers Devikulam, Anayirankal Dam, Ponmudy and a farm tour among others. You can hire a taxi to visit the main local sights for around ₹1200 per day.

🛏 Sleeping

Munnar has plenty of accommodation but the best budget options are just south of the town centre. If you really want to feel the serenity and are willing to pay a bit more, head for the hills.

Around Town

⭐ **JJ Cottage** HOMESTAY $
(☎230104; jjcottagemunnar@sancharnet.in; d ₹350-800; @) The sweet family at this superb purple place a couple of kilometres south of town (but easy walking distance from the main bus stand) will go out of its way to make sure your stay is comfortable. The varied and uncomplicated rooms are ruthlessly clean, bright, great value and have TV and hot water. The one deluxe room on the top floor has a separate sitting room and sweeping views. Free internet but no wi-fi.

Green View GUESTHOUSE $
(☎230940; www.greenviewmunnar.com; d ₹450-700; @🖥) This tidy guesthouse has 10 fresh budget rooms, a friendly welcome and reliable tour advice. The best rooms are on the upper floor and there's a super rooftop garden where you can sample 15 kinds of tea. The young owner organises trekking trips and also runs **Green Woods Anachal** (d incl breakfast ₹750) outside Munnar – a four-room budget option out in the tea and spice plantations.

Zina Cottages HOMESTAY $
(☎230349; r ₹700-900) On the outskirts of town but immersed in lush tea plantations and with fine views, this hospitable homestay is a good deal. Rooms are pretty basic with bucket hot water but the views are sensational. They offer free pick-up from town (an autorickshaw costs about ₹40).

Kaippallil Inn GUESTHOUSE $
(☎9495029259; www.kaippallil.com; r ₹300-800) A stiff walk or rickshaw ride uphill from the bazaar, Kaippallil is a good budget bet in the town centre, thanks mainly to the serene Benoy, who offers free yoga and meditation sessions and plenty of tea. It looks a little tatty from the outside but the rooms are clean and the top ones have little corner balconies with sweeping views.

Royal Retreat HOTEL $$
(☎230240; www.royalretreat.co.in; d ₹2200-2800, ste ₹3900; @) Away from the bustle just south of the main bus stand, Royal Retreat is a reliable midranger with pleasant ground-level rooms facing a pretty garden and others with tea plantation views.

Munnar Hills

Dew Drops GUESTHOUSE $$
(☎04842216455; wilsonhomes2003@yahoo.co.in; Kallar; r incl breakfast ₹1500) Set in thick forest around 20km south of Munnar, this fantastic, remote place lies on 97 hectares of spice

plantation and farmland. The resplendent building has eight bright, simple rooms each with a verandah on which you can sit and enjoy the chirping of birdlife and expansive views. The peace here is zen; call for a pick-up (₹50 per person).

Tea Sanctuary BUNGALOWS $$$
(📞230141; www.theteasanctuary.com; KDHP House; s/d incl breakfast ₹4500/5000) The KDHP operates four charming old heritage bungalows scattered around the Munnar hills under the banner of Tea Sanctuary. The secluded locations are amazing, surrounded by tea plantations. You can book through KDHP House in Munnar town.

★ **Rose Gardens** HOMESTAY $$$
(📞04864278243; www.munnarhomestays.com; NH49 Rd, Karadipara; r incl breakfast ₹4000; @ 🛜) Despite its handy location on the main road to Kochi, around 10km south of Munnar and with good bus connections, this is a peaceful spot overlooking the owner Tomy's idyllic plant nursery, with over 240 types of plants, and his mini spice and fruit plantation. The five rooms are large and comfortable with balconies overlooking the valley, and the family is charming. Cooking lessons are free, including fresh coconut pancakes for breakfast and delicately spiced Keralan dishes for dinner.

Bracknell Forest GUESTHOUSE $$$
(📞9446951963; www.bracknellforestmunnar.com; Bison Valley Rd, Ottamaram; r incl breakfast ₹5000-6000; @ 🛜) A remote-feeling 9.5km southeast of Munnar, this place houses 11 neat, handsome rooms with balconies and lovely views overlooking a lush valley and cardamom plantation. It's surrounded by deep forest on all sides. The small restaurant has wraparound views. A transfer from Munnar costs ₹350.

Windermere Estate RESORT $$$
(📞reservations 04842425237; www.windermere-munnar.com; Pothamedu; d incl breakfast ₹8300-14,000, villa ₹18,500; ❄@🛜) Windermere is a charming boutique-meets-country-retreat 4km southeast of Munnar. There are supremely spacious garden and valley view rooms, but the best are the suite-like 'Plantation Villas' with spectacular views, surrounded by 26 hectares of cardamom and coffee plantations. There's a cosy library above the country-style restaurant. Book ahead at its Kochi office.

✖ Eating

Early-morning food stalls in the bazaar serve breakfast snacks and cheap meals.

Rapsy Restaurant INDIAN $
(Bazaar; dishes ₹30-140; ⏱8am-9pm) This spotless glass-fronted sanctuary from the bazaar is packed at lunchtime, with locals lining up for Rapsy's famous *paratha* or biryani (from ₹50). It also makes a decent stab at fancy international dishes like Spanish omelette, Israeli *shakshuka* (eggs with tomatoes and spices) and Mexican salsa.

SN Restaurant INDIAN $
(AM Rd; meals ₹35-90; ⏱7.30am-10pm) Just south of the DTPC office, SN is a cheery place with an attractive red interior, which seems to be perpetually full of people digging into masala dosas and other Indian veg and non-veg dishes.

Aromas INDIAN $
(www.royalretreat.co.in; Kannan Devan Hills; dishes ₹35-120; ⏱7.30-10am, noon-3pm, 7-9pm) In the Royal Retreat hotel, just south of town, this longstanding favourite has reliably tasty and fresh Indian cooking served in nicely twee rooms with checked tablecloths.

Sree Mahaveer INDIAN $
(Mattupetty Rd; meals ₹85-185; ⏱8.30am-10.30pm) This pure veg restaurant attached to SN Annex Hotel has a nice deep-orange look with slatted blinds on the windows. It's madly popular with families for its great range of thalis: take your pick from Rajasthani, Gujarati, Punjabi and more, plus a dazzling array of veg dishes.

Eastend INDIAN $$
(Temple Rd; dishes ₹110-250; ⏱7.30-10.30am, noon-3.30pm & 6.30-10.30pm) In the slightly fancy hotel of the same name, this brightly lit, smartish place is one of the best in town for nonveg Indian dishes, with Chinese, North and South Indian and Kerala specialities on the menu.

☆ Entertainment

Thirumeny Cultural Centre CULTURAL PROGRAM
(📞9447827696; Temple Rd; shows ₹200; ⏱Kathakali shows 5-6pm & 7-8pm; kalaripayat 6-7pm & 8-9pm) On the road behind the Eastend Hotel, this theatre stages one-hour Kathakali shows and *kalarippayat* martial arts demonstrations twice nightly.

PARAMBIKULAM WILDLIFE SANCTUARY

Possibly the most protected environment in South India – nestled behind three dams in a valley surrounded by Keralan and Tamil Nadu sanctuaries – **Parambikulam Wildlife Sanctuary** (www.parambikulam.org; Indian/foreigner ₹10/100, camera/video ₹25/150; ⊙7am-6pm last entry 4pm) constitutes 285 sq km of Kipling-storybook scenery and wildlife-spotting goodness. Far less touristed than Periyar, it's home to elephants, bison, gaur, sloths, sambar, crocodiles, tigers, panthers and some of the largest teak trees in Asia. The sanctuary is best avoided during monsoon (June to August) and it sometimes closes in March and April.

Contact the **Ecocare Centre** (⌨04253245025) in Anappady to arrange tours of the park, **hikes** (1-/2-day trek from ₹3000/6000, shorter treks from ₹600) and stays on the reservoir's freshwater island (r ₹5000). There are 150 beds in **tree-top huts** (₹2500-3500) throughout the park; book through the Ecocare Centre. Boating or rafting costs ₹600 for one hour.

You have to enter the park from Pollachi (40km from Coimbatore and 49km from Palakkad) in Tamil Nadu. There are two buses in either direction between Pollachi and Parambikulam via Annamalai daily (₹17, 1½ hours).

ⓘ Information

There are ATMs near the bridge, south of the bazaar.

DTPC Tourist Information Office (⌨231516; keralatourismmunnardtpc@gmail.com; Alway-Munnar Rd; ⊙8.30am-7pm) Marginally helpful; operates a number of tours and can arrange trekking guides.

Forest Information Centre (⌨231587; enpmunnar@gmail.com; ⊙10am-5pm) Wildlife Warden's Office, for accommodation bookings in Chinnar Wildlife Sanctuary.

Olivia Communications (per hr ₹35; ⊙9am-9pm) Cramped but surprisingly fast internet in the bazaar.

ⓘ Getting There & Away

Roads around Munnar are in poor condition and can be affected by monsoon rains. The main **KSRTC bus station** (AM Rd) is south of town, but it's best to catch buses from stands in Munnar town (where more frequent private buses also depart). The main stand is in the bazaar.

There are around 13 daily buses to Ernakulam (Kochi, ₹81, 5½ hours), two direct buses to Alleppey (₹110, five hours) at 6.20am and 1.10pm, and five to Trivandrum (₹226, nine hours). Private buses go to Kumily (₹75, four hours) at 11.25am, 12.20pm and 2.25pm.

A taxi to Ernakulam costs around ₹2000, and to Kumily ₹1800.

ⓘ Getting Around

Gokulam Bike Hire (⌨9447237165; per day ₹250-300; ⊙7.30am-7.30pm), in the former bus stand south of town, has motorbikes and scooters for hire. Call ahead.

Autorickshaws ply the hills around Munnar with bone-shuddering efficiency; they charge up to ₹700 for a full day's sightseeing.

Around Munnar

Eravikulam National Park

Sixteen kilometres from Munnar, **Eravikulam National Park** (⌨04865231587; www.eravikulam.org; Indian/foreigner ₹15/200, camera/video ₹25/2000; ⊙8am-5pm Mar-Dec) is home to the endangered, but almost tame, Nilgiri tahr (a type of mountain goat). From Munnar, an autorickshaw/taxi costs around ₹300/500 return; a government bus takes you the final 4km from the checkpoint (₹40).

Chinnar Wildlife Sanctuary

About 10km past Marayoor and 60km northeast of Munnar, this **wildlife sanctuary** (www.chinnar.org; Indian/foreigner ₹100/150, camera/video ₹25/150; ⊙7am-6pm) hosts deer, leopards, elephants and the endangered grizzled giant squirrel. Trekking and **tree house** (s/d ₹1000/1250) or hut accommodation within the sanctuary are available, as well as ecotour programs like river-trekking, cultural visits and waterfall treks (around ₹150). For details contact the Forest Information Centre in Munnar. Buses from Munnar can drop you off at Chinnar (₹35, 1½ hours), or taxi hire for the day will cost ₹1300.

Top Station

High above Kerala's border with Tamil Nadu, Top Station is popular for its spectacular views over the Western Ghats. From Munnar, four daily buses (₹35, from 7.30am, 1½ hours) make the steep 32km climb in around an hour, or you could book a return taxi (₹1000).

CENTRAL KERALA

Kochi (Cochin)

📞 0484 / POP 601,600

Serene Kochi has been drawing traders and explorers to its shores for over 600 years. Nowhere else in India could you find such an intriguing mix: giant fishing nets from China, a 400-year-old synagogue, ancient mosques, Portuguese houses and crumbling remains of the British Raj. The result is an unlikely blend of medieval Portugal, Holland and an English village grafted onto the tropical Malabar Coast. It's a delightful place to spend some time and nap in some of India's finest homestays and heritage accommodation.

Mainland Ernakulam is the hectic transport and cosmopolitan hub of Kochi, while the historical towns of Fort Cochin and Mattancherry, though well-touristed, remain wonderfully serene – thick with the smell of the past. Other islands, including Willingdon and Vypeen, are linked by a network of ferries and bridges.

While you're here, the perfect read is Salman Rushdie's *The Moor's Last Sigh,* which bases much action around Mattancherry and the synagogue.

👁 Sights

👁 Fort Cochin

Fort Cochin has a couple of small, sandy beaches which are only really good for people-watching in the evening and gazing out at the incoming tankers. A popular promenade winds around to the unofficial emblems of Kerala's backwaters: cantilevered **Chinese fishing nets** (Map p978). A legacy of traders from the AD 1400 court of Kublai Khan, these enormous, spiderlike contraptions require at least four people to operate their counterweights at high tide. Unfortunately, modern fishing techniques are making these labour-intensive methods less and less profitable.

Kochi (Cochin)

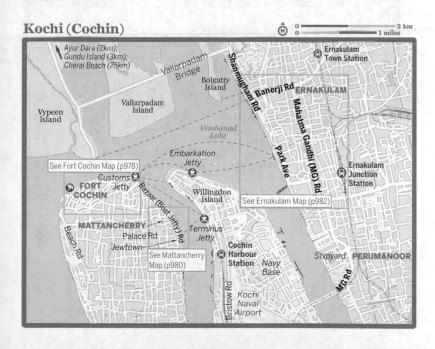

Fort Cochin

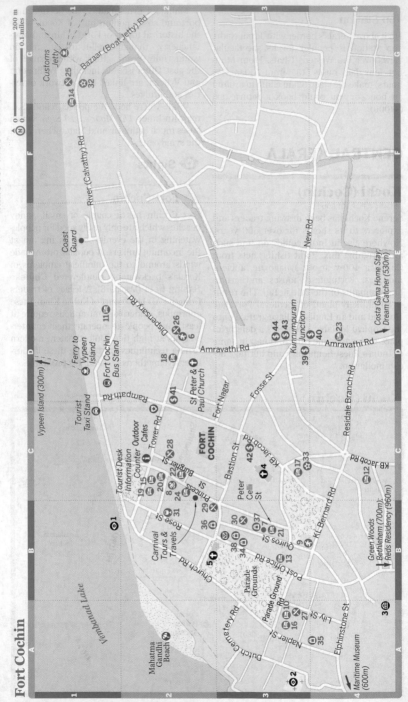

Fort Cochin

Indo-Portuguese Museum MUSEUM
(Map p978; ☎2215400; Indian/foreigner ₹10/25; ◷9am-1pm & 2-6pm Tue-Sun) This museum in the garden of the Bishop's House preserves the heritage of one of India's earliest Catholic communities, including vestments, silver processional crosses and altarpieces from the Cochin diocese. The basement contains remnants of the Portuguese Fort Immanuel.

Maritime Museum MUSEUM
(Beach Rd; admission ₹75, camera/video ₹100/150; ◷9.30am-12.30pm & 2.30-5.30pm) In a pair of former bomb shelters, this museum traces the history of the Indian navy, as well as maritime trade dating back to the Portuguese and Dutch, through a series of relief murals and information panels. There's plenty of naval memorabilia, including a couple of model battleships outside in the garden.

St Francis Church CHURCH
(Map p978; Church Rd; ◷8.30am-5pm) Believed to be India's oldest European-built church, it was originally constructed in 1503 by Por-

tuguese Franciscan friars. The edifice that stands here today was built in the mid-16th century to replace the original wooden structure. Explorer Vasco da Gama, who died in Cochin in 1524, was buried in this spot for 14 years before his remains were taken to Lisbon – you can still visit his tombstone in the church.

Santa Cruz Basilica CHURCH
(Map p978; cnr Bastion St & KB Jacob Rd; ◷7am-8.30pm) The imposing Catholic basilica was originally built on this site in 1506, though the current building dates to 1902. Inside you'll find artefacts from the different eras in Kochi and a striking pastel-coloured interior.

Dutch Cemetery HISTORIC SITE
(Map p978; Beach Rd) Consecrated in 1724, this cemetery near Kochi beach contains the worn and dilapidated graves of Dutch traders and soldiers. Its gates are normally locked but a caretaker might let you in, or ask at St Francis Church.

Mattancherry & Jew Town

About 3km southeast of Fort Cochin, Mattancherry is the old bazaar district and centre of the spice trade. These days it's packed with spice shops and overpriced Kashmiri-run emporiums that autorickshaw drivers will fall over backwards to take you to for a healthy commission. In the midst of this, Jew Town is a bustling port area with a fine synagogue. Scores of small firms huddle together in old, dilapidated buildings and the air is filled with the biting aromas of ginger, cardamom, cumin, turmeric and cloves, though the lanes around the Dutch Palace and synagogue are packed with antique and tourist-curio shops rather than spices. Look out for the Jewish names on some of the buildings.

Mattancherry

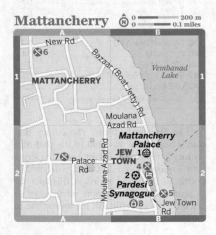

Mattancherry

⊙ Top Sights
1 Mattancherry Palace	B2
2 Pardesi Synagogue	B2

⊜ Sleeping
3 Caza Maria	B2

⊗ Eating
4 Café Jew Town	B2
Caza Maria	(see 3)
5 Ginger House	B2
6 Ramathula Hotel	A1
7 Shri Krishna	A2

⊕ Shopping
8 Niraamaya	B2

★ **Mattancherry Palace**   MUSEUM
(Dutch Palace; Map p980; 2226085; Palace Rd; adult/child ₹5/free; ⊙9am-5pm Sat-Thu) Mattancherry Palace was a generous gift presented to the Raja of Kochi, Veera Kerala Varma (1537–61), as a gesture of goodwill by the Portuguese in 1555. More probably, it was used as a sweetener to securing trading privileges. The Dutch renovated the palace in 1663, hence its alternative name, the Dutch Palace.

The star attractions here are the astonishingly preserved Hindu **murals**, depicting scenes from the Ramayana, Mahabharata and Puranic legends in intricate detail. The central hall on the 1st floor is now a portrait gallery of maharajas from 1864. There's an impressive collection of palanquins (hand-carried carriages), bejewelled outfits and splendidly carved ceilings in every room. Information panels detail the history of the Kochi royal dynasty. Photography is prohibited.

★ **Pardesi Synagogue**   SYNAGOGUE
(Map p980; admission ₹5; ⊙10am-1pm & 3-5pm Sun-Thu, closed Jewish hols) Originally built in 1568, this synagogue was partially destroyed by the Portuguese in 1662, and rebuilt two years later when the Dutch took Kochi. It features an ornate gold pulpit and elaborate hand-painted, willow-pattern floor tiles from Canton, China, which were added in 1762. It's magnificently illuminated by chandeliers (from Belgium) and coloured-glass lamps. The graceful clock tower was built in 1760. There is an upstairs balcony for women who worshipped separately according to Orthodox rites. Note that shorts, sleeveless tops, bags and cameras are not allowed inside.

Ernakulam

Kerala Folklore Museum   MUSEUM
(04842665452; www.folkloremuseum.org; Folklore Junction, Thevara; Indian/foreigner ₹100/200, performances Indian/foreigner ₹100/400; ⊙9.30am-7pm, performances 6-7.30pm Oct-Mar) It's a shame that this interesting place is a bit off the tourist trail on the southeast outskirts of Ernakulam, but it's worthy of the journey. The private museum is created in Keralan style from ancient temples and beautiful old houses collected by its owner, an antique dealer. It includes over 4000 artefacts and covers three architectural

styles: Malabar on the ground floor, Kochi on the 1st, Travancore on the 2nd. Upstairs is a beautiful wood-lined theatre, with a 17th-century wooden ceiling, where nightly performances take place. A rickshaw from Ernakulam should cost ₹80, or you can take any bus to Thevara from where it's a ₹20 rickshaw ride. An autorickshaw from Fort Cochin should cost ₹180.

🏃 Activities

Grande Residencia Hotel   SWIMMING
(Map p978; Princess St, Fort Cochin; ⊘7am-6.30pm) Nonguests can swim at the hotel's small pool for ₹350 per person.

Cherai Beach (Vypeen Island)   SWIMMING
For a dip in the ocean, you can make a day trip out to Cherai Beach (p990), 25km away on Vypeen Island.

Ayur Dara   AYURVEDA
(☑2502362, 9447721041; www.ayurdara.com; Murikkumpadam, Vypeen Island; ⊘9am-5.30pm) Run by third-generation ayurvedic practitioner Dr Subhash, this delightful waterside treatment centre specialises in treatments of one to three weeks (₹9100 per week). By appointment only. It's 3km from the Vypeen Island ferry (autorickshaw ₹35).

Ayush   AYURVEDA
(Map p978; ☑6456566; Amaravathi Rd, Fort Cochin; massage from ₹900; ⊘8am-8pm) Part of an India-wide chain of ayurvedic centres, this place also does long-term treatments.

SVM Ayurveda Centre   AYURVEDA
(Kerala Ayurveda Pharmacy Ltd; Map p978; ☑9847371667; www.svmayurveda.com; Quieros St; massage from ₹600, Hatha yoga ₹400,1½hr; ⊘9.30am-7pm) A small Fort Cochin centre, this offers relaxing massages and Hatha yoga daily at 8am. Longer rejuvenation packages are also available.

📖 Courses

The Kerala Kathakali Centre (p987) has lessons in classical Kathakali dance, music and make-up (short and long-term courses from ₹350 per hour).

For a crash course in the martial art of *kalarippayat*, head out to Ens Kalari (p987), a famed training centre, which offers short intensive courses from one week to one month.

Cook & Eat   COOKING
(Map p978; ☑2215377; www.leelahomestay.com; Quiros St; classes veg/nonveg ₹550; ⊘11am & 6pm)

Mrs Leelu Roy runs popular two-hour cooking classes in her big family kitchen, teaching five dishes to classes of five to 10 people. Several of the homestays in towns are also happy to organise cooking classes for their guests.

🧭 Tours

Most hotels and tourist offices can arrange the popular day trip out to the **Elephant training camp** (⊘7am-6pm) at Kudanadu, 50km from Kochi. Here you can go for a ride (₹200) and even help out with washing the gentle beasts if you arrive at 8am. Entry is free, though the elephant trainers will expect a small tip. A return trip out here in a taxi should cost around ₹1000 to ₹1200.

Tourist Desk Information
Counter   BOAT TOUR, WILDLIFE-WATCHING
(☑2371761; www.touristdesk.in) This private tour agency runs the popular full-day **Water Valley Tour** (₹650) through local backwater canals and lagoons. A canoe trip through smaller canals and villages is included, as is lunch and hotel pick-ups. It also offers a two night **Wayanad Wildlife tour** (₹6000), and an overnight **Munnar Hillstation tour** (₹3000). Prices include accommodation, transport and meals.

KTDC   BOAT TOUR
(☑2353234; backwater tours half-day ₹450, motor-boat tours 2½hr ₹250, houseboat backwater trips day tour ₹650) The KTDC has **backwater tours** at 8.30am and 2pm, and **motor-boat tours** around Fort Cochin at 9am and 2pm. Its full-day **houseboat backwater trips** (⊘8am-6.30pm) visit local weaving factories, spice gardens and toddy tappers.

Kerala Bike Tours   BIKE TOUR
(☑04842356652, 9388476817; www.keralabiketours.com; Kirushupaly Rd, Ravipuram) Organises motorcycle tours in Kerala and the Western Ghats and hires out touring-quality Enfield Bullets (from US$155 per week) with unlimited mileage, full insurance and free recovery/maintenance options.

🎆 Festivals & Events

The eight-day **Ernakulathappan Utsavam festival** (January/February) culminates in a procession of 15 decorated elephants, ecstatic music and fireworks. The **Cochin Carnival** (www.cochincarnival.org; ⊘21-31 Dec) is Fort Cochin's biggest bash, a 10-day festival culminating on New Year's Eve. Street parades,

Ernakulam

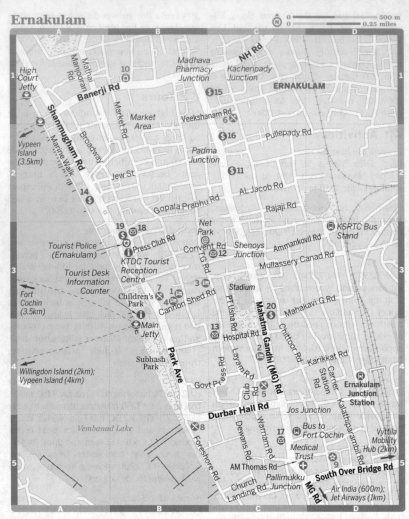

colourful costumes, embellished elephants, music, folk dancing and lots of fun.

🛏 Sleeping

Fort Cochin can feel a bit touristy and crowded in season but it's an ideal place to escape the noise and chaos of the mainland – tranquil and romantic, with some of Kerala's finest accommodation. This could be India's homestay capital, with dozens of family houses offering large and clean budget rooms and a hearty welcome.

Ernakulam is cheaper and more convenient for onward travel, but the ambience and accommodation choices are less inspiring. Regardless of where you stay, book ahead during December and January. At other times you can bargain for a discount.

🛏 Fort Cochin

★ **Green Woods Bethlehem** HOMESTAY $
(☎ 3247791; greenwoodsbethlehem1@vsnl.net; opposite ESI Hospital; s/d incl breakfast ₹800/900) With a smile that brightens weary travellers, welcoming owner Sheeba looks ready to sign your adoption papers the minute you walk through her front door. Down a quiet lane-

Ernakulam

Sleeping
1 Bijus Tourist Home.............................B3
2 Grand Hotel C4
3 John's Residency.................................B3
4 Saas Tower B3

Eating
5 Chillies..C4
6 Frys Village Restaurant......................C1
Grand Pavilion..............................(see 2)
7 Kochin Food Mall B3
8 Subhiksha...B5

Entertainment
9 See India Foundation D5

Shopping
10 DC Books..B1

Information
11 Citibank...C2
12 College Post Office C3
13 Ernakulam Post Office
Branches...C4
14 Federal Bank ATM...............................A2
15 HDFC Bank ATM...................................C1
16 Idbi Bank ATM.......................................C2
17 Post Office C5
18 Post Office B3
19 SBI ATM..B3
20 UAE Exchange..C3

way and with a walled garden thick with plants and palms, this is one of Kochi's most serene homestays. The rooms are humble but cosy; breakfast is served in the fantastic, leafy rooftop cafe, where cooking classes/demonstrations are often held.

Princess Inn GUESTHOUSE $
(Map p978; 2217073; princessinnfortkochi@gmail.com; Princess St; r ₹400-800) Sticking to its budget guns, the friendly Princess Inn spruces up its dull, tiny rooms with cheery bright colours. The comfy communal spaces are a treat, and the three large, front-facing rooms are great value for this location.

Mother Tree HOMESTAY $
(Map p978; 9447464906; www.hotelmothertree.com; off KL Bernard Master Rd; r ₹700, with AC ₹1000; ❄@🖤) There are just a few minuscule rooms in this compact homestay, but the cleanliness and neat rooftop chill-out space make it worth seeking out.

Dream Catcher HOMESTAY $
(2217550; www.dreamcatcherhomestays.com; Vasavan Lane; r ₹800-1000, with AC from ₹2000; ❄) Tucked away on a narrow laneway, this rambling old colonial house has spotless midpriced rooms, an almost gothic sitting room and balconies lined with pot plants: it offers a warm backpacker-friendly welcome from the Portuguese-descended family.

Costa Gama Home Stay HOMESTAY $
(2216122; www.stayincochin.com; Thamaraparambu Rd; r without/with AC ₹800/1200; ❄🖤) With just three rooms, this cosy little place gets good reviews. Across the road are another three rooms in a heritage-style building with a nice terrace.

Royal Grace Tourist Home GUESTHOUSE $
(Map p978; 2216584; Amaravathi Rd; r ₹350-500, with AC ₹1200; ❄) This old-timer is one of the rare budget stalwarts still left in Fort Cochin. There are loads of staid rooms on offer in the off-white four-storey building, each with little more than a bed, four walls and a pint-sized bathroom. The best open onto a balcony.

★**Reds Residency** HOMESTAY $$
(3204060; www.redsresidency.in; 11/372 A, KJ Herschel Rd; d incl breakfast ₹800-1000, with AC ₹1000-1200, AC cottage ₹1500; ❄@🖤) Reds is a relatively new homestay with hotel-quality rooms but a true family welcome from knowledgable hosts Philip and Maryann. The five double rooms are modern and immaculate, and there's a self-contained 'penthouse' cottage with kitchen on the rooftop. It's in a peaceful location near the Maritime Museum.

Noah's Ark HOMESTAY $$
(Map p978; 2215481; www.noahsarkcochin.com; 1/508 Fort Kochi Hospital Rd; r incl breakfast ₹2800-3000; ❄@🖤) This large modern family home comes with a friendly welcome but plenty of privacy. There's a sweeping spiral staircase from the reception room and four immaculate, upmarket rooms – two with a balcony.

Walton's Homestay GUESTHOUSE $$
(Map p978; 2215309; www.waltonshomestay.com; Princess St; r incl breakfast ₹1200-2600; ❄🖤) The fastidious Mr Walton offers big wood-furnished rooms in his lovely old house that's painted a nautical white with blue trim and buried behind a bookshop. Down-

stairs rooms open onto a lush garden while upstairs rooms have a balcony, and there's a nice communal breakfast room.

Raintree Lodge
GUESTHOUSE **$$**

(Map p978; ☑3251489; www.fortcochin.com; Peter Celli St; r ₹2800; ❋) The intimate and elegant rooms at this historic place flirt with boutique-hotel status. Each room has a great blend of contemporary style and heritage carved-wood furniture and the front upstairs rooms have gorgeous vine-covered *Romeo and Juliet* balconies. Good value.

Bernard Bungalow
HOMESTAY **$$**

(Map p978; ☑2216162; www.bernardbungalow.com; Parade Ground Rd; d incl breakfast ₹2000-3000, with AC ₹2500-3500; ❋@☎) This gracious place has the look of a 1940s summer cottage, housed in a fine 350-year-old family home with a collection of interesting rooms. The house has polished floorboards, wooden window shutters, balconies and verandahs, and is filled with lovely period furniture. Top-floor rooms are the best.

Sonnetta Residency
GUESTHOUSE **$$**

(Map p978; ☑2215744; www.sonnettaresidency. com; 1/387 Princess St; s/d/f ₹900/1000/1500, with AC ₹1500-2000; ❋☎) Right in the thick of the Fort Cochin action, the six rooms at this friendly Portuguese-era place are immaculately kept and well-presented, with nice, chintzy touches like curtains, colourful bedspreads and indoor plants. Every room has air-con but you can choose not to use it at the cheaper rate.

Delight Home Stay
GUESTHOUSE **$$**

(Map p978; ☑2217658; www.delightfulhomestay. com; Post Office Rd; r ₹1400-1800, with AC ₹2500; ❋☎) And delightful it is. This grand house's exterior is adorned with frilly white woodwork, and the rooms are spacious and polished. There's a charming little garden, elegant breakfast room and an imposing sitting room covered in wall-to-wall teak. Good food is served and cooking classes are offered in the open kitchen.

Daffodil
GUESTHOUSE **$$**

(Map p978; ☑2218686; Njaliparambu Junction; d incl breakfast without/with AC ₹2000/2500; ❋@☎) Run by a local couple, Daffodil has eight big and brightly painted modern rooms, but the best feature is the carved-wood Keralan balcony upstairs.

★ Malabar House
HOTEL **$$$**

(Map p978; ☑2216666; www.malabarhouse.com; Parade Ground Rd; r ₹230, ste incl breakfast €330-380; ❋@☎) What may just be one of the fanciest boutique hotels in Kerala, Malabar flaunts its über-hip blend of modern colours and period fittings like it's not even trying. While the suites are huge and lavishly appointed, the standard rooms are more snug. The award-winning restaurant and wine bar are top notch.

★ Brunton Boatyard
HOTEL **$$$**

(Map p978; ☑2215461; bruntonboatyard@cghearth. com; River Rd; r ₹21,000, ste ₹28,000; ❋@☎☎) This imposing hotel faithfully reproduces 16th- and 17th-century Dutch and Portuguese architecture in its grand complex. All of the rooms look out over the harbour, and have bathtub and balconies with a refreshing sea breeze that beats air-con any day. It has the excellent History Restaurant and Armoury Bar, along with a couple of open-air cafes.

Tea Bungalow
HOTEL **$$$**

(Map p978; ☑3019200; www.teabungalow.in; 1/1901 Kunumpuram; r US$340; ❋@☎☎) This mustard-coloured colonial building was built in 1912 as headquarters of a UK spice trading company before being taken over by Brooke Bond tea. The 10 graceful boutique rooms – all named after sea ports – are decorated with flashes of strong colour and carved colonial wooden furniture, and have Bassetta-tiled bathrooms. Off-season rates drop by 60%.

Old Harbour Hotel
HOTEL **$$$**

(Map p978; ☑2218006; www.oldharbourhotel.com; Tower Rd; r ₹9250-13,050; ❋@☎) Set around an idyllic garden with lily ponds and a small pool, the dignified Old Harbour is housed in a 300-year-old Dutch/Portuguese heritage building. The elegant mix of period and modern styles lends it a more intimate feel than some of the more grandiose competition. There are 13 rooms, some facing directly onto the garden and some with plant-filled, open-air bathrooms.

Koder House
HOTEL **$$$**

(Map p978; ☑2217988; www.koderhouse.com; Tower Rd; r from ₹8000-9000; ❋☎) A historic 200-year-old mansion overlooking the Chinese fishing nets, this fine heritage property has six characterful suites and an atmospheric, high-ceiling restaurant. Overpriced in season, but worth a splurge at other times.

Fort House Hotel

HOTEL $$$

(Map p978; ☑ 2217103; www.hotelforthouse.com; 2/6A Calvathy Rd; r incl breakfast ₹5520; ✷ @) Close to the ferry point, this is one of the few truly waterfront hotels, though the 16 smart air-con rooms are set back in a lush garden, with the restaurant taking prime waterside position.

Mattancherry & Jew Town

Caza Maria

HOMESTAY $$$

(Map p980; ☑ 9846050901; cazamaria@rediffmail. com; Jew Town Rd, Mattancherry; r incl breakfast ₹4500; ✷) Right in the heart of Jew Town, this unique place has just two enormous, gorgeous heritage rooms overlooking the bazaar. Fit for a maharaja, the rooms feature an idiosyncratic style – with each high-ceilinged room painted in bright colours, filled to the brim with antiques.

Ernakulam

John's Residency

HOTEL $

(Map p982; ☑ 2355395; TD Rd; s/d from ₹450/550, with AC ₹1350; ✷) With a cool yellow foyer featuring interesting clutter such as vintage fans, this is a refreshing backpacker place. Rooms are small (deluxe rooms are bigger) but decorated with flashes of colour that give them a funky feel that's a welcome surprise in this price bracket.

Bijus Tourist Home

HOTEL $

(Map p982; ☑ 2361661; www.bijustouristhome.com; Market Rd; s/d from ₹700/850, with AC ₹1575/1750; ✷ @) This friendly, popular choice is handy for the main jetty and has reasonable, drab but clean rooms and a friendly welcome.

Saas Tower

HOTEL $$

(Map p982; ☑ 2365319; www.saastower.com; Cannon Shed Rd; s/d ₹880/1460, with AC from ₹1755/2100; ✷ @) The flashy lobby is more promising than the rooms in this low-end business hotel but if you're after a step up from the budget hotels near the jetty, this isn't a bad option. Clean rooms filled with wooden furniture. There's a restaurant, business centre and day spa with ayurvedic treatments.

Grand Hotel

HOTEL $$$

(Map p982; ☑ 2382061; www.grandhotelkerala.com; MG Rd; s/d from ₹3000/3600, ste ₹5400; ✷ @ ☏) This 1960s hotel, with its polished original art deco fittings, oozes the sort of retro cool that modern hotels would kill to recreate.

The spacious rooms have gleaming parquet floors and large modern bathrooms, and there's a good restaurant and Ernakulam's most sophisticated bar.

Around Kochi

★ Olavipe

HOMESTAY $$

(☑ 04782522255; www.olavipe.com; Olavipe; s/d incl meals ₹5100/8500) This gorgeous 1890s traditional Syrian-Christian home is on a 16-hectare farm surrounded by backwaters, 28km south of Kochi. A restored mansion of rosewood and glistening teak, it has several large and breezy rooms beautifully decorated in original period decor. There are lots of shady awnings and sitting areas, a fascinating archive with six generations of family history, and the gracious owners will make you feel like a welcome friend rather than a guest.

✕ Eating & Drinking

Some of Fort Cochin's best dining can be found in the homestays, but there are lots of good restaurants and cafes. Covert beer consumption in teapots is de rigueur in many of Fort Cochin's cheaper restaurants, and more expensive in the licensed ones.

✕ Fort Cochin

Behind the Chinese fishing nets are several fishmongers, from whom you can buy fish (or prawns, scampi, lobster), then take your selection to one of the row of simple but popular restaurants on nearby Tower Rd where the folks there will cook it and serve it to you for an additional charge. Market price varies.

Kashi Art Cafe

CAFE $

(Map p978; Burgher St; breakfast & snacks ₹80-110; ⊙ 8.30am-7.30pm) An institution in Fort Cochin, this natural light-filled place has a zen-but-casual vibe and solid wood tables that spread out into a semi-courtyard space. The coffee is as strong as it should be and the daily Western breakfast and lunch specials are excellent. A small gallery shows off local artists.

Teapot

CAFE $

(Map p978; Peter Celli St; mains ₹60-250) This atmospheric cafe is the perfect venue for 'high tea', with 16 types of tea, sandwiches, cake and full meals served in chic, airy rooms. Witty tea-themed accents include loads of antique teapots, tea chests for tables and a gnarled, tea-tree-based glass table.

Loafers Corner
CAFE $

(Map p978; cnr Bastion & Princess Sts; ₹40-90; ☺11am-10pm) If you can grab one of the three window seats there are few better people-watching spots than this corner cafe with a beautiful timber ceiling and earthy tones. The menu is mostly snacks like dosas and kati rolls, as well as shakes, juice and lassis.

★Dal Roti
INDIAN $$

(Map p978; ✆9746459244; 1/293 Lily St; meals ₹100-230; ☺noon-3.30pm & 6.30-10.30pm Wed-Mon) There's a lot to like about busy Dal Roti. Friendly and knowledgable owner Ramesh will hold your hand through his expansive North Indian menu, which even sports its own glossary, and help you dive into his delicious range of vegetarian, eggetarian and nonvegetarian options. From kati rolls to seven types of thali, you won't go hungry. No alcohol.

Arca Nova
SEAFOOD $$

(Map p978; 2/6A Calvathy Rd; mains ₹220-380; ☺7.30am-10.30pm) The waterside restaurant at the Fort House Hotel is a prime choice for a leisurely lunch. It specialises in fish dishes and you can sit out at tables overlooking the water or in the serenely spacious covered garden area.

Casa Linda
MULTICUISINE $

(Map p978; Dispensary Rd; mains ₹95-450; ☺7-10.30pm) This modern dining room above the hotel of the same name might not be much to look at, but it's all about the Indo-European food here. Chef Dipu once trained with a Frenchman and whips up delicious local Keralan dishes alongside French fusion.

★Malabar Junction
INTERNATIONAL $$$

(Map p978; ✆2216666; Parade Ground Rd; mains ₹350-650) Set in an open-sided pavilion, the restaurant at Malabar House is movie-star cool, with white-tableclothed tables in a courtyard close to the small pool. There's a seafood-based, European-style menu – the signature dish is the impressive seafood platter with grilled vegetables. Upstairs, the wine bar serves upmarket snacks such as tapioca-and-cumin fritters in funkily clashing surroundings.

XL Fishnet Bar
BAR

(Map p978; Rose St; ☺10am-10.30pm) This slightly dingy 1st-floor bar-restaurant is a popular place to settle down with a cold Kingfisher, palatable snacks and meals such as beef deep fry. The downstairs restaurant also serves alcohol at slightly higher prices.

✗ Mattancherry & Jew Town

Ramathula Hotel
INDIAN $

(Map p980; Kayees Junction, Mattancherry; biryani ₹40-60; ☺lunch & dinner) This place is legendary among locals for its chicken and mutton biryanis – get here early or miss out. It's better known by the chef's name, Kayikka's.

Shri Krishna
INDIAN $

(Map p980; dishes ₹10-55; ☺7.30am-9.30pm) Simple, busy, basic, but tasty thalis.

Caza Maria
MULTICUISINE $$

(Map p980; Bazaar Rd; mains around ₹150-290; ☺10am-8pm) This enchanting 1st-floor place across from the hotel of the same name is a bright-blue, antique-filled space with funky music and a changing daily menu of North Indian, South Indian and French dishes.

Café Jew Town
CAFE $$

(Map p980; Bazaar Rd; snacks around ₹120-150; ☺9.30am-6pm) Walk through chic antique shops and galleries to reach this sweet Swiss-owned cafe; the few tables proffer good cakes, snacks and Italian coffee.

Ginger House
INDIAN $$$

(Map p980; Bazaar Rd; mains ₹300-700; ☺8.30am-6pm) Hidden behind a massive antique-filled godown (warehouse) is this fantastic waterfront restaurant, where you can feast on Indian dishes and snacks – ginger prawns, ginger ice cream… you get the picture. Less about the pricey food and more about the sculptures – check out the giant snake-boat canoe.

✗ Ernakulam

Frys Village Restaurant
KERALAN $

(Map p982; Veekshanam Rd; dishes ₹75-120; ☺noon-3.30pm & 7-10.30pm) This brightly decorated and breezy place with an arched ceiling is a great family restaurant with authentic Keralan food, especially seafood like *pollichathu* or crab roast. Fish/veg thalis are available for lunch.

Subhiksha
INDIAN $

(Map p982; DH Road, Gandhi Sq; dishes ₹40-120; ☺7.30am-3.30pm & 7-11pm) At Bharat Hotel, this popular pure-veg restaurant is a smart place to dig into tasty thalis.

Kochin Food Mall   MALL **$**

(Map p982; www.cochinfoodmall.com; Park Avenue Rd, Ernakulam; ₹70-170; ⊙10.30am-11pm) Opposite the boat jetty, this super-modern new food mall gives you the choice of 10 food outlets, including North and South Indian, Chinese, pizza and, most interesting of all, Ooru, specialising in tribal foods from Wayanad district.

Chillies   INDIAN **$$**

(Map p982; meals ₹100-210; ⊙11.30am-3.30pm & 7.30-10pm) A dark, buzzing 1st-floor place, serving spicy Andhra cuisine on banana leaves. Try a thali, for all-you-can-eat joy.

★ **Grand Pavilion**   INDIAN **$$$**

(Map p982; MG Rd; meals ₹180-500) The restaurant at the Grand Hotel is as elegant and retro-stylish as the hotel itself, with cream-coloured furniture and stiff tablecloths. It serves a tome of a menu that covers dishes from the West, North India, South India and most of the rest of the Asian continent.

☆ Entertainment

There are several places in Kochi where you can view Kathakali. The performances are certainly made for tourists, but they're a good introduction to this intriguing art form. The standard program starts with the intricate make-up application and costume-fitting, followed by a demonstration and commentary on the dance and then the performance – usually two hours in all. The fast-paced traditional martial art of *kalarippayat* can also be easily seen in Fort Cochin.

☆ Fort Cochin

Kerala Kathakali Centre   CULTURAL PROGRAM

(Map p978; ☑2217552; www.kathakalicentre.com; KB Jacob Rd, Fort Cochin; admission ₹250; ⊙make-up from 5pm, show 6-7.30pm) In an intimate, wood-lined theatre, this place provides a useful introduction to Kathakali, complete with amazing demonstrations of eye movements, plus handy translations of the night's story. The centre also hosts performances of the martial art of *kalarippayat* from 4pm to 5pm daily, traditional music from 8pm to 9pm Sunday to Friday and classical dance at 8pm from 9pm on Saturday.

Greenix Village   CULTURAL PROGRAM

(Map p978; ☑2217000; www.greenix.in; Kalvathy Rd, Fort Cochin; ⊙10am-6pm, shows from 5pm) This touristy 'cultural village' seeks to put the full gamut of Keralan music and arts under one roof with a small cultural museum, performances of Kathakali and *kalarippayat* and other cultural shows in an impressive complex.

☆ Ernakulam

See India Foundation   CULTURAL PROGRAM

(Map p982; ☑2376471; devankathakali@yahoo.com; Kalathiparambil Lane, Ernakulam; admission ₹200; ⊙make-up 6pm, show 7-8pm) One of the oldest Kathakali theatres in Kerala, it has small-scale shows with an emphasis on the religious and philosophical roots of Kathakali.

Ens Kalari   CULTURAL PROGRAM

(☑2700810; www.enskalari.org.in; Nettoor, Ernakulam; admission by donation; ⊙demonstrations 7.15-8.15pm) If you want to see real professionals have a go at *kalarippayat,* it's best to travel out to this renowned *kalarippayat* learning centre, 8km southeast of Ernakulam. There are one-hour demonstrations daily (one day's notice required).

🛍 Shopping

Broadway in Ernakulam is good for local shopping, spice shops and clothing, and around Convent and Market Rds is a huddle of tailors. On Jew Town Rd in Mattancherry there's a plethora of Gujarati-run shops selling genuine antiques mingled with knock-offs and copies. Most of the shops in Fort Cochin are identikit Kashmiri run shops selling a mixed bag of North Indian crafts. Many shops around Fort Cochin and Mattancherry operate lucrative commission rackets, with autorickshaw drivers getting huge kickbacks (added to your price) for dropping tourists at their door. Any driver who offers to take you on a factory tour or to a special viewpoint will be heading straight to a shop.

Niraamaya   CLOTHING

Fort Cochin (Map p978; ☑3263465; Quiros St, Fort Cochin; ⊙10am-5.30pm Mon-Sat); **Mattancherry** (Map p980; VI/217 AB Salam Rd, Jew Town, Mattancherry) Popular throughout Kerala, Niraamaya sells 'ayurvedic' clothing and fabrics – all made of organic cotton, coloured with natural herb dyes, or infused with ayurvedic oils.

DC Books   BOOKS

(Map p982; ☑2391295; Banerji Rd, Ernakulam; ⊙9am-7.30pm Mon-Sat, 11am-6pm Sun) Excellent English-language selection of fiction and nonfiction. Also branches in Fort Cochin and Mattancherry.

MAJOR BUSES FROM ERNAKULAM

The following bus services operate from the KSRTC bus stand and Vyttila Mobility Hub.

DESTINATION	FARE (₹)	DURATION (HR)	FREQUENCY/TIME
Alleppey	41	1½	every 10min
Bengaluru	405-495	14	4 daily
Calicut	133	5	hourly
Chennai	555	16	2pm
Coimbatore	139	4½	hourly
Kannur	210	8	2 daily
Kanyakumari	210	8	2 daily
Kollam	94	3½	every 30min
Kothamangalam	35	2	every 10min
Kottayam	51	2	every 30min
Kumily (for Periyar)	120	5	8 daily
Mangalore	305	12	6.30pm
Munnar	90	4½	every 30min
Thrissur	51	2	every 10min
Trivandrum	138	5	every 30min

Idiom Bookshop BOOKS
(Map p978; ⊙10.30am-9pm Mon-Sat) Huge range of quality new and used books.

Fabindia CLOTHING, HOMEWARES
(Map p978; ☑2217077; www.fabindia.com; Napier St, Fort Cochin; ⊙10.30am-8.30pm) Fine Indian textiles, fabrics, clothes and household linen from this renowned brand.

Cinnamon CLOTHING
(Map p978; Post Office Rd, Fort Cochin; ⊙10am-7pm Mon-Sat) Opposite the parade ground, Cinnamon sells gorgeous Indian-designed clothing, jewellery and homewares in an ultrachic white retail space.

Tribes India HANDICRAFTS
(Map p978; ☑2215077; Head Post Office, Fort Cochin; ⊙10am-6.30pm Mon-Sat) Tucked behind the post office, this TRIFED (Ministry of Tribal Affairs) enterprise sells tribal artefacts, paintings, shawls, figurines etc, at reasonable fixed prices and the profits go towards supporting the artisans.

ⓘ Information

INTERNET ACCESS

There are several internet cafes around Princess St in Fort Cochin charging ₹40 per hour, and a number of homestays offer free wi-fi.

Net Park (Map p982; Convent Rd, Ernakulam; per hr ₹15; ⊙9am-8pm)

MEDICAL SERVICES

Lakeshore Hospital (☑2701032; www.lakeshorehospital.com; NH Bypass, Marudu) Modern hospital 8km southeast of central Ernakulam.

Medical Trust Hospital (Map p982; ☑2358001; www.medicaltrusthospital.com; MG Rd)

MONEY

UAE Exchange (⊙9.30am-6pm Mon-Fri, to 4pm Sat) Ernakulam (☑2383317; MG Rd, Perumpillil Bldg, Ernakulam); Ernakulam (☑3067008; Chettupuzha Towers, PT Usha Rd Junction, Ernakulam); Fort Cochin (Map p978; ☑2216231; Amravathi Rd, Fort Cochin) Foreign exchange and travellers cheques.

POST

College Post Office (Map p982; ☑2369302; Convent Rd, Ernakulam; ⊙9am-5pm Mon-Sat)

Ernakulam Post Office Branches (Map p982; ☑2355467; Hospital Rd; ⊙9am-8pm Mon-Sat, 10am-5pm Sun) Also branches on MG Rd and Broadway.

Main Post Office (Map p978; Post Office Rd, Fort Cochin; ⊙9am-5pm Mon-Fri, to 3pm Sat) Main post office.

TOURIST INFORMATION

There's a tourist information counter at the airport. Many places distribute a free brochure that includes a map and walking tour entitled *Historical Places in Fort Cochin*.

KTDC Tourist Reception Centre (Map p982; ☑2353234; Shanmugham Rd, Ernakulam; ⊙8am-7pm) Also organises tours. There's another office at the jetty at Fort Cochin.

Tourist Desk Information Counter Ernakulam (Map p982; ☑2371761; www.touristdesk.in; Boat Jetty, Ernakulam; ◷8am-6pm); Fort Cochin (Map p978; ☑2216129; Fort Cochin; ◷8am-7pm) A private tour agency that's very knowledgable and helpful about Kochi and beyond. Runs several popular and recommended tours, and its Ernakulam office displays recommended cultural events on in town that day, and has a secondhand book exchange.

Tourist Police Ernakulam (Map p982; ☑2353234; Shanmugham Rd, Ernakulam; ◷8am-6pm); Fort Cochin (Map p978; ☑2215055; Fort Cochin; ◷24hr)

ⓘ Getting There & Away

AIR

Kochi International Airport is a popular hub, with international flights to the Gulf states, Sri Lanka and Singapore. Between them Jet Airways, Air India and Spicejet fly direct daily to Chennai, Mumbai and Bengaluru. Jet Airways and Spicejet also fly to Hyderabad, while IndiGo flies to Trivandrum. Air India flies to Delhi daily and to Agatti in the Lakshadweep islands six times a week. The following airlines have offices in Ernakulam:

Air India (☑2351295; MG Rd)

Jet Airways (☑2359334; MG Rd)

BUS

At the time of writing there were plans afoot for buses to operate directly between Fort Cochin and places like Munnar, Alleppey and Periyar. Until then, all long-distance services operate from Ernakulam. The **KSRTC bus stand** (Map p982; ☑2372033; ◷reservations 6am-10pm) is next to the railway, halfway between the two train stations. There's a separate window for reservations to Tamil Nadu. Government and private buses pull into the massive new **Vyttila Mobility Hub** (☑2306611; www.vyttilamobilityhub.com; ◷24hr), a state-of-the-art transport terminal about 2km east of Ernakulam Junction train station. Numerous private bus companies have super-deluxe, air-con, video and Volvo buses to

long distance destinations such as Bengaluru, Chennai, Mangalore, Trivandrum and Coimbatore; prices vary depending on the standard but the best buses are about 50% higher than government buses. Agents in Ernakulam and Fort Cochin sell tickets. Private buses also use the **Kaloor bus stand**, 1km north of the city.

A prepaid autorickshaw from Vyttila costs ₹67 to the boat jetty, ₹62 to the train station and ₹171 to Fort Cochin.

TRAIN

Ernakulam has two train stations, **Ernakulam Town** and **Ernakulam Junction**. Reservations for both are made at the Ernakulam Junction **reservations office** (☑132; ◷8am-8pm Mon-Sat, 8am-2pm Sun).

There are local and express trains to Trivandrum (2nd-class/AC chair ₹73/264, 4½ hours), via either Alleppey (₹39/171, 1½ hours) or Kottayam (₹39/171, 1½ hours). Trains also run to Thrissur (₹64/205, 1½ hours), Calicut (₹67/237, 4½ hours) and Kannur (₹105/341, 6½ hours).

ⓘ Getting Around

TO/FROM THE AIRPORT

Kochi International Airport (☑2610125; http://cochinairport.com) is at Nedumbassery, 30km northeast of Ernakulam. A new bus services runs between the airport and Fort Cochin (₹70, one hour, eight daily), some going via Ernakulam. Taxis to/from Ernakulam cost around ₹650, and to/from Fort Cochin around ₹900.

BOAT

Ferries are the fastest, most enjoyable form of transport between Fort Cochin and the mainland. The jetty on Willingdon Island's eastern side is called **Embarkation** (Map p977); the west one, opposite Mattancherry, is **Terminus** (Map p977); and Fort Cochin's main stop is **Customs** (Map p978), with another stop at the **Mattancherry Jetty** near the synagogue. One-way fares are ₹2.50 (₹3.50 between Ernakulam and Mattancherry).

MAJOR TRAINS FROM ERNAKULAM

The following are major long-distance trains departing from Ernakulam Town.

DESTINATION	TRAIN NO & NAME	FARE (₹, SLEEPER/ 3AC/2AC)	DURATION (HR)	DEPARTURES (DAILY)
Bengaluru	16525 Bangalore Express	257/719/1085	13	5.55pm
Chennai	12624 Chennai Mail	292/793/1185	12	6.40pm
Delhi	12625 Kerala Express (A)	579/1630/2685	46	3.50pm
Goa	16346 Netravathi Express (A)	305/858/1315	15	2.05pm
Mumbai	16382 Mumbai Express	469/1337/2130	40	1.30pm

(A) Departs from Ernakulam Junction

Ernakulam

There are services to both Fort Cochin jetties (Customs and Mattancherry) every 25 to 50 minutes (⊙ 5.55am to 9.30pm) from Ernakulam's main jetty.

Ferries also run every 20 minutes or so to Willingdon and Vypeen Islands (Map p982; ⊙ 6am to 10pm).

Fort Cochin

Ferries run from Customs Jetty to Ernakulam (⊙ 6.20am to 9.50pm). Ferries also hop between Customs Jetty and Willingdon Island 18 times a day (⊙ 6.40am to 9.30pm, Monday to Saturday).

Car and passenger ferries cross to Vypeen Island from Fort Cochin virtually nonstop (Map p978; ⊙ 6am to 10pm).

LOCAL TRANSPORT

There are no real bus services between Fort Cochin and Mattancherry Palace, but it's an enjoyable 30-minute walk through the busy warehouse area along Bazaar Rd. Autorickshaws should cost around ₹40, much less if you promise to look in a shop. Most autorickshaw trips around Ernakulam shouldn't cost more than ₹35.

To get to Fort Cochin after ferries stop running you'll need to catch a taxi or autorickshaw –

Ernakulam Town train station to Fort Cochin should cost around ₹300; prepaid autorickshaws during the day cost ₹150.

Scooters/Enfields can be hired for ₹250/350-600 per day from a number of agents in Fort Cochin.

Around Kochi

Cherai Beach

On Vypeen Island, 25km from Fort Cochin, Cherai Beach makes a fantastic day trip or getaway from Kochi. It's a lovely stretch of as-yet undeveloped white sand, with miles of lazy backwaters just a few hundred metres from the seafront. Cherai is easily visited on a day trip from Kochi – it's an excellent ride if you hire a scooter or motorbike in Fort Cochin – but a growing number of low-key resorts along the single road running parallel to the beach make it worth hanging out a few days.

Brighton Beach House (☑ 9946565555; www.brightonbeachhouse.org; d ₹1100) has five basic rooms in a small building by the shore. The beach is rocky here, but the place is

THATTEKKAD BIRD SANCTUARY

A serene 25-sq-km park in the foothills of the Western Ghats, cut through by two rivers and two streams, **Thattekkad Bird Sanctuary** (☑ 04852588302; Indian/foreigner ₹10/100, camera/video ₹25/150; ⊙ 6.30am-6pm) is home to over 320 fluttering species – unusual in that they are mostly forest, rather than water birds – including Malabar grey hornbills, Ripley owls, jungle nightjars, grey drongos, darters and rarer species like the Sri Lankan frogmouth. There are kingfishers, flycatchers, warblers, sunbirds and flower peckers (which weigh only 4g). To stay in the **Treetop Machan** (Indian/foreigner dm ₹80/150, d incl meals ₹1500-2500) in the sanctuary, contact the **assistant wildlife warden** (☑ 04852588302) at Kothamangalam. Another option is the **Jungle Bird Homestay** (☑ 08452588143, 9947506188; per person incl meals ₹900), located inside the park and run by the enthusiastic Ms Sudah and son Gireesh, who will meet guests at the gate. Ms Sudah also offers guided birdwatching trips for ₹600.

For more luxury, visit the lovely **Soma Birds Lagoon** (☑ 04712268101; www.somabirdslagoon.com; Palamatton, Thattekkad; s/d incl breakfast €70/85, with AC from €75/90; ✴ ≋). Set deep in the villages near Thattekkad, this low-key resort lies on a seasonal lake among spacious and manicured grounds. The basic rooms here are roomy and the whole place feels refreshingly remote but is just 16km from Kothamangalam. There's also the tented **Hornbill Camp** (☑ 04842092280; www.thehornbillcamp.com; d full board US$110), with accommodation in large permanent tents in a sublimely peaceful location facing the Periyar River. Kayaking, cycling and a spice-garden tour are included in the price. Birdwatching guides cost ₹1500. It's around 8km from Thattekkad by road.

Thattekkad is on the Ernakulam–Munnar road. Take a direct bus from either Ernakulam (₹30, two hours) or Munnar (₹55, three hours) to Kothamangalam, from where a Thattekkad bus travels the final 12km (₹8, 25 minutes), or catch an autorickshaw for around ₹150.

wonderfully secluded, filled with hammocks to loll in, and has a neat, elevated stilt-restaurant overlooking the seawall.

A collection of distinctive cottages lying around a meandering lagoon, **Cherai Beach Resort** (☑04842416949; www.cherai beachresorts.com; Cherai Beach, Vypeen Island; villas from ₹3750, with AC from ₹4500; ✸ @) has the beach on one side and the backwaters on the other. Bungalows are individually designed using natural materials, and there's a bar and restaurant.

Hidden back from the beach but with the backwaters on your doorstep, **Les 3 Elephants** (☑04842480005, 9349174341; www.3elephants.in; Convent St; cottages ₹4000-8000; ✸ ☎) is a superb French-run ecoresort. The 11 beautifully designed boutique cottages are all different but have private sit outs, thoughtful personal touches and lovely backwater views. The restaurant serves home-cooked French-Indian fare. Worth the trip!

For European-style comfort food by the beach – think burgers, pizzas and barbecue – **Chilliout Cafe** (mains ₹180-250; ◷9am-late Oct-May) is a cool hangout with sea breezes and a relaxed vibe.

To get here from Fort Cochin, catch the vehicle-ferry to Vypeen Island (per person ₹2) and either hire an autorickshaw from the jetty (around ₹350) or catch one of the frequent buses (₹15, one hour) and get off at Cherai village, 1km from the beach. Buses also go here direct from Ernakulam via the Vallarpadam bridge.

Tripunithura

At Tripunithura, 16km southeast of Ernakulam, **Hill Palace Museum** (☑04842781113; admission ₹20; ◷9am-12.30pm & 2-4.30pm Tue-Sun) was formerly the residence of the Kochi royal family and is an impressive 49-building palace complex. It now houses the collections of the royal families, as well as 19th-century oil paintings, old coins, sculptures and paintings, and temple models. From Ernakulam catch the bus to Tripunithura from MG Rd or Shanmugham Rd, behind the Tourist Reception Centre (₹5 to ₹10, 45 minutes); an autorickshaw should cost around ₹300 return with one-hour waiting time.

Parur & Chennamangalam

Nowhere is the tightly woven religious cloth that is India more apparent than in **Parur**, 35km north of Kochi. One of the oldest **synagogues** (admission ₹5; ◷9am-5pm Tue-Sun) in Kerala, at **Chennamangalam**, 8km from Parur, has been fastidiously renovated. Inside you can see door and ceiling wood-reliefs in dazzling colours, while just outside lies one of the oldest tombstones in India – inscribed with the Hebrew date corresponding to 1269. The Jesuits first arrived in Chennamangalam in 1577 and there's a **Jesuit church** and the ruins of a Jesuit college nearby. Nearby are a **Hindu temple** on a hill overlooking the Periyar River, a 16th-century **mosque**, and Muslim and Jewish **burial grounds**.

In Parur town, you'll find the **agraharam** (place of Brahmins) – a small street of closely packed and brightly coloured houses originally settled by Tamil Brahmins.

Parur is compact, but Chennamangalam is best visited with a guide. Travel agencies in Fort Cochin can organise tours. **Carnival Tours & Travels** (Map p978; ☑9895224922; www.carnivaltourskochi.com; Princess St) runs a full-day Jewish Heritage Tour to Parur, Chennamangalam and other sites for ₹3000 per person, starting with the ferry to Vypeen Island. A taxi tour for the day can be done for around ₹1000.

Thrissur (Trichur)

☑0487 / POP 315,600

While the rest of Kerala has its fair share of celebrations, untouristy, slightly chaotic Thrissur is the cultural cherry on the festival cake. With a list of energetic festivals as long as a temple-elephant's trunk, the region supports several institutions nursing the dying classical Keralan performing arts back to health. Centred around a large park (known as the 'Round') and temple complex, Thrissur is home to a Nestorian Christian community whose denomination dates to the 3rd century AD. There's not much to see when there's no festivities so plan to arrive during the rambunctious festival season (November to mid-May).

◉ Sights & Activities

Thrissur is renowned for its central temple, as well as for its numerous impressive churches, including the massive **Our Lady of Lourdes Cathedral**, towering, whitewashed **Puttanpalli (New) Church** and the **Chaldian (Nestorian) Church**.

Thrissur (Trichur)

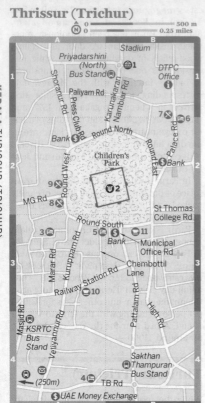

Thrissur (Trichur)

◉ Sights
1 Archaeology Museum B1
2 Vadakkunathan Kshetram Temple B2

⌂ Sleeping
3 Hotel Luciya Palace A3
4 Joys Palace A4
5 Pathans Hotel A3
6 YMCA International Guesthouse B2

✕ Eating
7 India Gate...B1
8 Navaratna Restaurant...........................A2
9 New Ambady Restaurant A2
Pathans Restaurant.....................(see 5)

☕ Drinking & Nightlife
10 Indian Coffee House.............................A3
11 Indian Coffee House.............................B3

Vadakkunathan Kshetram Temple   HINDU TEMPLE

One of the oldest in the state, Vadakkunathan Kshetram Temple crowns the hill at the epicentre of Thrissur. Finished in classic Keralan architecture, only Hindus are allowed inside, though the mound surrounding the temple has sweeping views and is a popular spot to linger.

Archaeology Museum   MUSEUM

(admission ₹10, camera/video ₹25/50; ☺ 9am-1pm & 2-4.30pm Tue-Sun) The Archaeology Museum is housed in the wonderful 200-year-old Sakthan Thampuran Palace. Its mix of artefacts include fragile palm-leaf manuscripts, 12th-century Keralan bronze sculptures and giant earthenware pots. It was closed for renovation at the time of research but should be open by the time you read this.

✨ Festivals & Events

In a state where festivals are a way of life, Thrissur still manages to stand out for temple revelry. Highlights include **Thrissur Pooram** (April/May) – the most colourful and biggest of Kerala's temple festivals with wonderful processions of elephants; **Uthralikavu Pooram** (March/April), whose climactic day sees 20 elephants circling the shrine; and **Thypooya Maholsavam** (January/February), with a *kavadiyattam* (a form of ritualistic dance) procession in which dancers carry tall, ornate structures called *kavadis*.

🛏 Sleeping

Pathans Hotel   HOTEL $
(✉ 2425620;   www.pathansresidentialhotel.com; Round South; ☺ s/d from ₹480/644, with AC ₹840/1200; ❄) No-frills rooms at no-frills prices and the location is unbeatable across from the central park. The basic and cleanish rooms are on the 5th and 6th floors (served by a painfully slow lift) and have TV and occasional hot water.

YMCA International Guesthouse   GUESTHOUSE $
(✉ 2331190; www.ymcathrissur.org; Palace Rd; d ₹650, with AC ₹1000) Clean, comfortable and secure. A good budget choice.

Hotel Luciya Palace   HOTEL $$
(✉ 2424731; www.hotelluciyapalace.com; Marar Rd; s/d with AC ₹1400/1600, ste ₹2600; ❄) In a cream, colonial-themed building, this is one of the few places in town that has some genuine character, and it's great value. Sitting in

a quiet cul-de-sac but close to the temple action, it has comfortable and spacious air-con rooms, a neat lawn garden, a decent restaurant and two of Thrissur's best bars.

Joys Palace HOTEL $$
(☑ 2429999; www.joyshotels.com; TB Rd; s/d incl breakfast from ₹2800/3400, ste ₹6500/7000; ✳@⊛) This ornate 10-storey whitewashed meringue caters to Thrissur's jet set. Rooms have big windows to enjoy the upper floor's sweeping views. There's a 2nd-floor restaurant with an outdoor balcony, a bar and a cool glass-fronted elevator.

🍴 Eating & Drinking

Pathans Restaurant INDIAN $
(1st fl, Round South; dishes ₹30-70; ⊙6.30am-9.30pm) On the first floor of the Pathans Hotel building, this easygoing place opens early for a cheap breakfast and is popular with families for lunch (thali ₹40).

New Ambady Restaurant SOUTH INDIAN $
(Round West; dishes ₹25-70; ⊙8am-9pm) Set back from the main street, this dark-brown place is a huge hit with families tucking into several different varieties of cheap set veg meals.

India Gate INDIAN $
(Palace Rd; dishes ₹55-125; ⊙8am-10pm) In the Kalliyath Royal Square building, this bright, pure-veg place has a vintage feel and an extraordinary range of dosas, including jam, cheese and cashew versions. In the same complex is a Chinese restaurant (China Gate) and a fast food joint (Celebrations).

Navaratna Restaurant MULTICUISINE $
(Round West; dishes ₹80-140; ⊙noon-9.30pm) Cool, dark and intimate, this is one of the classiest dining experiences in town, with seating on raised platforms. Downstairs is veg and upstairs is nonveg, with lots of North Indian specialities, Chinese and a few Keralan dishes.

Indian Coffee House CAFE
(₹25-90; ⊙7.30am-9.30pm) Has branches at Round South and Railway Station Rd.

ℹ Information

There are several ATMs and internet cafes around town.
DTPC Office (☑2320800; Palace Rd; ⊙10am-5pm Mon-Sat)
UAE Money Exchange (TB Rd; ⊙9am-6.30pm Mon-Fri, to 1pm Sat, to 4pm Sun)

ℹ Getting There & Away

BUS
KSRTC buses leave around every 30 minutes from the **KSRTC bus stand** bound for Trivandrum (₹182, 7½ hours), Ernakulam (Kochi, ₹50, two hours), Calicut (₹86, 3½ hours), Palakkad (₹45, 1½ hours) and Kottayam (₹86, four hours). Hourly buses go to Coimbatore (₹79, three hours).

Regular services also chug along to Guruvayur (₹20, one hour), Irinjalakuda (₹22, one hour) and Cheruthuruthy (₹20, 1½ hours). Two private bus stands (**Sakthan Thampuran** and **Priyadarshini**) have more frequent buses to these destinations, though the chaos involved in navigating each station hardly makes using them worthwhile.

TRAIN
Services run regularly to Ernakulam (2nd-class/AC chair ₹64/205, 1½ hours) and Calicut (₹74/220, three hours).

Around Thrissur

The Hindu-only **Shri Krishna Temple** at Guruvayur, 33km northwest of Thrissur, is among the most famous in Kerala. Said to have been created by Guru, preceptor of the gods, and Vayu, god of wind, the temple is believed to date from the 16th century and is renowned for its healing powers. A spectacular annual **Elephant Race** is held here in February or March.

Kerala Kalamandalam (☑04884262418; www.kalamandalam.org; ⊙June-Mar), 32km northeast of Thrissur at Cheruthuruthy, is a champion of Kerala's traditional-art renaissance. Using an ancient Gurukula system of learning, students undergo intensive study in Kathakali, *mohiniyattam* (dance of the enchantress), *Kootiattam,* percussion, voice and violin. **A Day with the Masters** (per person including lunch ₹1000; ⊙9.30am-1pm) is a morning program allowing visitors to tour the theatre and classes and see various art and cultural presentations. Individually tailored **introductory courses** (per month around ₹2500) are offered one subject at a time and last from six to 12 months. The school can help you find local homestay accommodation. For visits, email to book in advance.

Natana Kairali Research & Performing Centre for Traditional Arts (☑04802825559; natanakairali@gmail.com), 20km south of Thrissur near Irinjalakuda, offers training in traditional arts, including rare forms of puppetry and dance. Short **appreciation courses** (per class about ₹400) lasting up to a month are sometimes available to keen foreigners. In December each year, the centre holds five days of *mohiniyattam* **performances.**

River Retreat (☑04884262244; www.riverretreat.in; Palace Rd, Cheruthuruthy; s/d from ₹2600/3300) is only 1km from Kerala Kalamandalam. It's a hotel and ayurvedic resort in the former summer palace of the Maharajas of Cochin.

Regular bus services connect each of these destinations with Thrissur.

NORTHERN KERALA

Kozhikode (Calicut)

☑ 0495 / POP 432,100

Northern Kerala's largest city, Calicut (as it's most commonly known), was always a prosperous trading town and was once the capital of the formidable Zamorin dynasty. Vasco da Gama first landed near here in 1498, on his way to snatch a share of the subcontinent for king and country (Portugal that is). These days, trade depends mostly on exporting Indian labour to the Middle East, while agriculture and the timber industry are economic mainstays. For travellers it's a jumping off point for Wayanad or for the long trip over the ghats to Mysore or Bengaluru.

⊙ Sights

Mananchira Square, a large central park, was the former courtyard of the Zamorins and preserves the original spring-fed tank. South of the centre, the 650-year-old **Kuttichira Mosque** is in an attractive wooden four-storey building that is supported by impressive wooden pillars and painted brilliant aqua, blue and white. The central **Church of South India** was established by Swiss missionaries in 1842 and has unique Euro-Keralan architecture.

About 1km west of Mananchira Square is **Kozhikode Beach** – not much for swimming but good for an evening promenade along the foreshore.

🛏 Sleeping

Alakapuri　　　　　　　　　　　　HOTEL $
(☑2723451; www.alakapurihotels.com; MM Ali Rd; s/d from ₹300/900, with AC ₹750/1000; ❊) Built motel-style around a green lawn (complete with fountain!), this place is set back from a busy road and quieter than most. Various rooms are a little scuffed and dingy, but reasonable value.

Beach Hotel　　　　　　　　　　HOTEL $$
(☑2762055; www.beachheritage.com; Beach Rd; r with seaview or AC ₹3000; ❊@) Built in 1890 to house the Malabar British Club, this is a slightly worn but charming 10-room hotel. Some have bathtubs and secluded sea-facing verandahs; others have original polished wooden floors and private balconies. All are tastefully furnished and drip with character.

Hyson Heritage　　　　　　　　HOTEL $$
(☑4081000; www.hysonheritage.com; Bank Rd; s/d from ₹1300/1700, deluxe ₹2500/3250; ❊☎) You get a fair bit of swank for your rupee at this central business hotel. All rooms are spick and span, while the massive deluxe rooms have views over town. There's a good restaurant and a gym.

★Harivihar　　　　　　　HOMESTAY $$$
(☑2765865; www.harivihar.com; Bilathikulam; s/d incl full board €100/125) In northern Calicut, the ancestral home of the Kadathanadu royal family is as serene as it gets, a traditional Keralan family compound with pristine lawns. The seven rooms are large and beautifully furnished with dark-wood antiques. There's an ayurvedic and yoga centre, with packages available. The pure veg food is delicious and cooking classes are available.

🍴 Eating & Drinking

Paragon Restaurant　　　　　　INDIAN $
(Kannur Rd; dishes ₹50-220; ⊗11.45am-midnight) You might struggle to find a seat at this always-packed restaurant, founded in 1939. The overwhelming menu is famous for fish dishes such as fish in tamarind sauce, and its legendary chicken biryani.

Beach Hotel　　　　　　　　　INDIAN $$
(Beach Rd; ₹85-250; ⊗7am-10.30pm) At the back of the Beach Hotel is a cool open-sided bamboo 'hut' restaurant-bar serving a big range of fish and chicken dishes and Malabari cui-

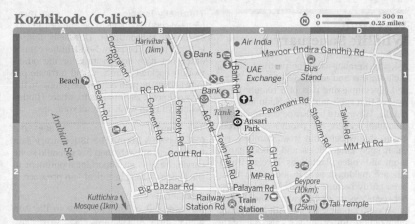

Kozhikode (Calicut)

sine. It's a breezy place for an informal lunch or cold beer.

Indian Coffee House   CAFE
(GH Rd; ₹10-60; ⊙8am-9pm) For tasty snacks and great coffee.

ℹ Information

There are HDFC and State Bank of India ATMs in town, and several internet cafes.

UAE Exchange (☑2762772; Bank Rd; ⊙9.30am-6pm Mon-Fri, to 4pm Sat, to 1pm Sun) Close to the Hyson Heritage hotel.

ℹ Getting There & Away

AIR

Calicut airport is about 25km south of the city in Karipur. It serves major domestic routes as well as international flights to the Gulf. **Air India** (☑2771974; 5/2521 Bank Rd, Eroth Centre) flies daily to Mumbai and Chennai, and twice-weekly to Kochi. **Jet Airways** (☑2712375; Calicut Airport) has one daily flight to Mumbai, while **Spicejet** (www.spicejet.com; Calicut airport) also flies to Chennai and Mumbai.

BUS

The **bus stand** (Mavoor Rd) has government buses to Bengaluru (via Mysore, ordinary/AC ₹256/355, eight hours, 10 daily), Mangalore (₹250, seven hours, three daily) and to Ooty (₹100, 5½ hours, three daily). There are frequent buses to Thrissur (₹70, 3½ hours) and Trivandrum (via Alleppey and Ernakulam; ordinary/express/deluxe ₹270/300/350, 10 hours, eight daily). For Wayanad district, buses leave every 15 minutes heading to Sultanbatheri (₹55, three hours) via Kalpetta (₹35, two hours). Private

Kozhikode (Calicut)

⊙ Sights
  1 Church of South India C1
  2 Mananchira Square C1

⊟ Sleeping
  3 Alakapuri C2
  4 Beach Hotel B2
  5 Hyson Heritage C1

⊗ Eating
     Beach Hotel .... (see 4)
  6 Paragon Restaurant C1

⊙ Drinking & Nightlife
  7 Indian Coffee House C2

buses for various long-distance locations also use this stand.

TRAIN

The train station is 1km south of Mananchira Sq. There are frequent trains to Kannur (2nd-class/sleeper/3AC ₹67/140/250, two hours), Mangalore (sleeper/3AC/2AC ₹147/365/625, five hours), Ernakulam (₹140/343/640, 4½ hours) via Thrissur (₹140/275/625, three hours), and all the way to Trivandrum (₹181/498/745, 11 hours).

Heading southeast, trains go to Coimbatore (sleeper/3AC/2AC ₹120/303/610, 4½ hours), via Palakkad (₹140/278/625, 3½ hours).

ℹ Getting Around

Calicut has a glut of autorickshaws and most are happy to use the meter. It's about ₹30 from the station to the KSRTC bus stand or most hotels.

Wayanad Wildlife Sanctuary

04936 / POP 816,500

Ask any Keralan what the prettiest part of their state is and most will whisper: Wayanad. Encompassing part of a remote forest reserve that spills into Tamil Nadu and Karnataka, Wayanad's landscape combines epic mountain scenery, rice paddies of ludicrous green, skinny betel nut trees, bamboo, red earth, spiky ginger fields, and rubber, cardamom and coffee plantations. Foreign travellers are making it here in increasing numbers, partly because it provides easy access between Mysore or Bengaluru and Kerala, but it's still fantastically unspoilt and satisfyingly remote. Importantly, it's also one of the few places you're almost guaranteed to spot wild elephants.

The 345-sq-km sanctuary has two separate pockets – Muthanga in the east bordering Tamil Nadu, and Tholpetty in the north bordering Karnataka. Three main towns in Wayanad district make good bases and transport hubs for exploring the sanctuary – Kalpetta in the south, Sultanbatheri (Sultan Battery) in the east and Mananthavadi in the northwest – though the best of the accommodation is scattered throughout the region.

Most hotels and homestays can arrange guided jeep tours (7am and 3pm) to various parts of Wayanad.

Sights & Activities

Wayanad Wildlife Sanctuary
NATURE RESERVE

(www.wayanadsanctuary.org; admission to each part Indian/foreigner ₹150/200, camera/video ₹25/150; ☺7-10am & 3-5pm) Entry to both parts of the sanctuary is only permitted as part of a guided trek or jeep safari, both of which can be arranged at the sanctuary entrances. Both Tholpetty and Muthanga close during the June to August monsoon period.

At Tholpetty (04935250853; jeep ₹450, guide ₹300), the two-hour jeep tours can be rough going but are a great way to spot wildlife. Rangers organise guided treks (up to 5 people ₹1500, extra people ₹400) from here.

At Muthanga (271010; jeep ₹450, guide ₹300), similar jeep tours are available in the mornings and afternoons.

Thirunelly Temple
HINDU TEMPLE

(☺dawn-dusk) Thought to be one of the oldest on the subcontinent, Thirunelly Temple is 10km from Tholpetty. Non-Hindus cannot enter, but it's worth visiting for the otherworldly cocktail of ancient and intricate pillars. Follow the path behind the temple to the stream known as Papanasini, where Hindus believe you can wash away all your sins.

Jain Temple
JAIN TEMPLE

(☺8am-noon & 2-6pm) The 13th-century Jain temple near Sultanbatheri has splendid stone carvings and is an important monument to the region's strong historical Jain presence.

Edakal Caves
CAVE

(admission ₹40; ☺9am-5pm) Close to the Jain temple, near Ambalavayal, these caves have petroglyphs thought to date back over 3000 years and views of Wayanad district.

Wayanad Heritage Museum
MUSEUM

(Ambalavayal; admission ₹15; ☺9am-5pm) In the same area as the caves, this museum exhibits headgear, weapons, pottery, carved stone and other artefacts dating back to the 15th century that shed light on Wayanad's significant Adivasi population.

Uravu
HANDICRAFTS CENTRE

(04936231400; www.uravu.net; Thrikkaippetta; ☺8.30am-5pm Mon-Sat) Around 6km southeast of Kalpetta a collective of workers creates all sorts of artefacts from bamboo. You can visit the artists' workshops, where they work on looms, painting and carving, and support their work by buying vases, lampshades, bangles and baskets.

Trekking & Rafting
OUTDOOR ACTIVITY

There are some top opportunities for independent trekking around the district, including a climb to the top of Chembra Peak (2100m), the area's tallest summit; Vellarimala, with great views and lots of wildlife-spotting opportunities; and Pakshipathalam, a seven-hour return mountain trek that takes you to a formation of large boulders high in the forest. Permits are necessary and can be arranged at forest offices in South or North Wayanad. The standard cost for permit and guide is ₹1500 for up to five people – try to arrange a group in advance. The DTPC office in Kalpetta also organises trekking guides and transport, as well as tame rafting excursions on inflatable rafts (half-/full-daytrip ₹2500/5000 for six people).

Wayanad District

Kannur Ayurvedic Centre
AYURVEDA

(☑ 0436203001; www.ayurvedawayanad.com; Kalpetta; massage from ₹500-800, yoga & meditation ₹750; ☺yoga classes 6-7am) For rejuvenation and curative ayurvedic treatments, visit this excellent, small, government-certified and family-run clinic in the leafy backstreets of Kalpetta. Accommodation and yoga classes available.

🛏 Sleeping & Eating

PPS Tourist Home
HOTEL $

(☑ 04936203431; www.ppstouristhome.com; Kalpetta; s/d ₹250/400, d with AC ₹900; ❄) This friendly budget place in the middle of Kalpetta has a variety of reasonably clean rooms in a motel-like compound as well as a popular multicuisine restaurant and a bar. Helpful management can arrange trips around Wayanad.

★ Varnam Homestay
HOMESTAY $$

(☑ 04935215666; www.varnamhomestay.com; Kadungamalayil House, Payyampally; per person incl meals ₹1000; ☎) This oasis of peace and calm is a lovely place to stay only a few kilometres from Katikulam in northern Wayanad. Varghese and Beena will look after you with Wayanad stories, local information and delicious home-cooking. The four rooms in a tradition-al family home are simple but cosy, and the property is surrounded by jungle and spice plantations. Forest drives and trekking to tribal villages can be arranged.

Pachyderm Palace
GUESTHOUSE $$

(☑ reservations 0484237l76l; touristdesk@satyam.net.in; Tholpetty; s/d incl meals ₹1250-2500, tree house ₹2500) This fine old Keralan house lies just outside the gate of Tholpetty Wildlife Sanctuary – handy for early-morning treks, tours and wildlife viewing. The varied rooms include two secluded stilt-bungalow 'tree houses' surrounded by forest and another private cottage. Venu is a stupendous cook, and his son Dilip is a great guide who can organise village and mountain treks.

Ente Veedu
HOMESTAY $$

(☑ 04935220008; www.enteveedu.co.in; Panamaram; r incl breakfast ₹2500-3500; @) Isolated and set in a stunning location overlooking sprawling banana plantations and rice paddies, this homestay halfway between Kalpetta and Mananthavadi is definitely worth seeking out. Several large rooms and two bamboo-lined rooms with private balconies, and hammocks and wicker lounges to enjoy the sensational views. Lunch and dinner are available for ₹200/250 veg/nonveg. Call to arrange a pick-up.

Tamarind HOTEL $$

(☎04935210475; tamarindthirunelly@ktdc.com; Thirunelly; d with AC ₹1400, ste ₹2000; ❊ @) With a lovely setting 750m from the Thirunelly Temple, and forest and mountain views through your window, this remote-feeling KTDC property is looking a bit tired but it's reasonable value and has a restaurant.

Haritagiri HOTEL $$

(☎04936203145; www.hotelharitagiri.com; Kalpetta; s/d incl breakfast ₹1100/1400, with AC from ₹1400/1800; ❊ ☷ ☳) Set back from Kalpetta's busy main streets, this is a comfortable midranger, and some of the rooms, with lively orange, green and blue colour schemes, have good views across the town's greenery from their balconies. There are two good restaurants, a gym, a bar and ayurvedic 'village' found on-site.

Isaac's Hotel Regency HOTEL $$

(☎04936220512; www.issacsregency.com; Sultanbatheri; s/d/tr from ₹1000/1400/1600, with AC from ₹1400/1800/2000; ❊ @ ☳) The pick of Sultanbatheri's motley bunch of hotels, this quiet and no-nonsense place has routine, large and relatively tidy rooms in a U-shaped building. The deluxe rooms differ from the standard ones in price only.

★ **Tranquil** HOMESTAY $$$

(☎04936220244; www.tranquilresort.com; Kuppamudi Estate, Kolagapara; full board s/d from ₹10,101/13,750, tree house ₹13,000/17,900, tree villa ₹14,850/19,500; ☳) This wonderfully serene and exclusive homestay is in the middle of an incredible lush 160 hectares of pepper, coffee, vanilla and cardamom plantations. The elegant house has sweeping verandahs filled with plants and handsome furniture, and there are two tree houses that have to be the finest in the state – the most romantic has sublime views through panoramic windows and a branch growing through the bathroom. A network of marked walking trails meander around the plantation.

❶ Information

The **DTPC office** (☎04936202134; www.dtpc-wayanad.com; Kalpetta; ☉10am-5pm Mon-Sat) at Kalpetta can help organise tours, permits and trekking. There are UAE Exchange offices in Kalpetta and Sultanbatheri, and Federal Bank and Canara Bank ATMs can be found in each of the three main towns, as can a smattering of internet cafes.

❶ Getting There & Away

BUS

Although remote, Wayanad is easily accessible from Calicut and Kannur in Kerala, and from Mysore (Karnataka) and Ooty (Tamil Nadu). Buses brave the winding roads – including a series of nine spectacular hairpin bends – between Calicut and Kalpetta (₹35 to ₹50, two hours) every 15 minutes, with some continuing on to Sultanbatheri (₹55, three hours) and others to Mananthavadi (₹64, three hours). Hourly buses run between Kannur and Mananthavadi hourly (₹55, 2½ hours). From Sultanbatheri, an 8am bus heads out for Ooty (₹76, four hours), with a second one passing through town at around 1pm. Buses for Mysore (₹101 to ₹141, three hours) leave every 30 minutes or so. There are at least two daily buses to Mysore (₹85 to ₹90, three hours) on the alternative northern route from Mananthavadi.

❶ Getting Around

The Wayanad district is quite spread out but plenty of private buses connect Mananthavadi, Kalpetta and Sultanbatheri every 10 to 20 minutes during daylight hours (₹15 to ₹25, 45 minutes to one hour). From Mananthavadi, regular buses also head to Tholpetty (₹15, one hour). You can hire jeeps or taxis to get between towns for ₹500 to ₹700 each way, or hire a vehicle to tour the region for around ₹2000 per day.

There are plenty of autorickshaws and taxis for short hops within the towns.

Kannur & Around

☎0497 / POP 1.6 MILLION

The main draw in this part of coastal Kerala are the undeveloped beaches and the enthralling *theyyam* possession rituals. Under the Kolathiri rajas, Kannur (Cannanore) was a major port bristling with international trade – explorer Marco Polo christened it a 'great emporium of spice trade'. Since then, the usual colonial suspects, including the Portuguese, Dutch and British, have had a go at exerting their influence on the region. Today it is an unexciting, though agreeable, town known mostly for its weaving industry and cashew trade.

Beaches to the south and north of Kannur – some of the nicest in Kerala – and the growing number of family homestays are the big attractions. Bear in mind you can't swim during the monsoon season because of rough seas. This is a predominantly Muslim area, so local sensibilities should be kept in mind: wear a sarong over your bikini on the beach.

THEYYAM

Kerala's most popular ritualistic art form, *theyyam* is believed to pre-date Hinduism, originating from folk dances performed during harvest celebrations. An intensely local ritual, it's often performed in *kavus* (sacred groves) throughout northern Kerala.

Theyyam refers both to the shape of the deity/hero portrayed, and to the actual ritual. There are around 450 different *theyyams*, each with a distinct costume; face paint, bracelets, breastplates, skirts, garlands and especially headdresses are exuberant, intricately crafted and sometimes huge (up to 6m or 7m tall). During performances, each protagonist loses their physical identity and speaks, moves and blesses the devotees as if they were that deity. Frenzied dancing and wild drumming create an atmosphere in which a deity indeed might, if it so desired, manifest itself in human form.

During October to May there are annual rituals at each of the hundreds of *kavus*. *Theyyams* are often held to bring good fortune to important events such as marriages and housewarmings.

The best place for visitors to see *theyyam* is in village temples in the Kannur region of northern Kerala (most frequently between late November and mid-April).

Although tourists are welcome to attend, this is not a dance performance but a religious ritual, and the usual rules of temple behaviour apply: dress appropriately, avoid disturbing participants and villagers; refrain from displays of public affection. Photography is allowed but avoid using a flash.

Sights & Activities

Kannur's main town beach is the 4km-long **Payyambalam Beach**, which starts about 1.5km east of the train station, just past the military cantonment.

St Angelo Fort FORT
(⊙9am-6pm) **FREE** The Portuguese built the St Angelo Fort in 1505 from brilliantly red laterite stone on a promontory a few kilometres south of town.

Loknath Weavers' Co-operative HANDICRAFTS WORKSHOP
(☑2726330; ⊙8.30am-5.30pm Mon-Sat) Established in 1955, this is one of the oldest co-operatives in Kannur and occupies a large building busily clicking with the sound of looms. You can stop by for a quick (free) tour and visit the small shop here that displays the fruits of their labours. It's 4km south of Kannur town.

Kerala Dinesh Beedi Co-Operative HANDICRAFTS WORKSHOP
(☑2835280; www.keraladinesh.com; ⊙8am-6pm Tue-Sat) This region is also known for the manufacture of *beedis*, those tiny Indian cigarettes deftly rolled inside green leaves. This is one of the largest and purportedly best manufacturers, with a factory at Thottada, 7km south of Kannur and about 4km from Thottada beach. A skilled individual can roll up to 1000 a day! An autorickshaw should cost around ₹100 return from Kannur town.

Theyyam Rituals RELIGIOUS
The Kannur region is the best place to see the spirit-possession ritual called *theyyam*; on most nights of the year there should be a *theyyam* ritual on at a village temple somewhere in the vicinity. The easiest way to find out is to contact Kurien at Costa Malabari guesthouse or by asking at your accommodation.

Kerala Folklore Academy ARTS SCHOOL
(☑04972778090; http://keralafolkloreakademy.com; Chirakkal) At this training academy near Chirakkal Pond Valapattanam, about 6km north of Kannur, you can see vibrantly coloured folklore costumes up close and sometimes catch a performance.

Sleeping & Eating

Although there a plenty of hotels in Kannur, the best places to stay are homestays near the beach at Thottada (8km south) and towards Thalassery.

Kannur Town

Hotel Meridian Palace HOTEL $
(☑2761676; www.hotelmeridianpalace.com; Bellard Rd; s from ₹300/400, with AC from ₹900-1000) In the market area opposite the main train station, this is hardly palatial but friendly enough and offers a cornucopia of clean budget rooms and a Punjabi restaurant.

Mascot Beach Resort HOTEL **$$**
(✆2708445; www.mascotresort.com; d ₹1350, with AC from ₹1800, ste ₹4500; 🌢@🛜🏊) All rooms are sea-facing at this compact, midrange hotel looking over the small, rocky Baby Beach. Facilities are good, including a pool and restaurant.

🏖 Thottada Beach & Around

⭐ **Blue Mermaid Homestay** HOMESTAY **$$**
(✆9497300234; www.bluemermaid.in; Thottadda Beach; full board s/d ₹1850/2700, d with AC ₹3200; 🌢) With a prime location in the palms facing Thottada Beach, Blue Mermaid is a charming and immaculate guesthouse with rooms in a traditional home, bright air-con rooms in a lovely new building and a whimsical stilted 'honeymoon cottage'. Friendly young owners cook up Keralan meals.

Costa Malabari GUESTHOUSE **$$**
(✆09447775691, reservations 04842371761; touristdesk@satyam.net.in; Thottada Beach; s/d incl meals ₹1500/2750, d with AC ₹3000 ; 🌢🛜) Surrounded by lush greenery above the beach, Costa Malabari pioneered tourism in this area. Spacious rooms in an old hand-loom factory, a huge communal space and comfy lounging areas outside. Extra rooms are offered in two other buildings. The home-cooked Keralan food is plentiful, varied and delicious. Manager Kurien is an expert on the *theyyam* ritual and can help arrange a visit.

Waves Beach Resort HOMESTAY **$$**
(✆9447173889; s/d incl meals ₹1250/2500; 🛜) If the crashing waves don't lull you to sleep they might just keep you awake at this very cute pair of hexagonal laterite brick huts overlooking a semi-private little crescent beach. There are four rooms here (two up, two down). The welcoming owners also have rooms in two other nearby properties, including cheaper rooms in an old Keralan house.

Kannur Beach House HOMESTAY **$$**
(✆04972708360, 9847184535; www.kannurbeach-house.com; Thottada Beach; s/d ₹2200/3000) The original beachfront homestay, rooms in this traditional Keralan building have handsome wooden shutters, but are looking a little worn. Still, you can enjoy sensational ocean sunset views from your porch or balcony. Breakfast and dinner included.

Ezhara Beach House HOMESTAY **$$**
(✆04972835022; www.ezharabeachhouse.com; 7/347 Ezhara Kadappuram; s/d incl meals ₹1250/2500; 🛜) Beside the unspoilt Kizhunna Ezhara beach, midway between Kannur and Thalassery railway stations (11km from each) the blue Ezhara Beach House is run by no-nonsense Hyacinth. The five rooms are simple and small, but the house has char-

---

OFF THE BEATEN TRACK

VALIYAPARAMBA BACKWATERS

For those seeking to escape the burgeoning commercialism around Alleppey, what are often referred to as the northern backwaters offer an intriguing alternative. This large body of water is fed by five rivers and fringed by ludicrously green lands punctuated by rows of nodding palms. One of the nearest towns is Payyanur, 50km north of Kannur. It's possible to catch the ferry from Kotti, from where KSWTD operates local ferries to the surrounding islands. It's five minutes' walk from Payyanur railway station. The 2½-hour trip (₹10) from Kotti takes you to the Ayitti Jetty, 8km from Payyanur; then catch the return ferry.

You can stay at the tiny Valiyaparamba Retreat (✆2371761; www.touristdesk.in/valiyaparambaretreat.htm; d full board ₹3000), a secluded place 15km north of Payyanur and 3km from Ayitti Jetty. It has two simple rooms and two stilted bungalows, fronted by an empty golden-sand beach. Kochi's Tourist Desk (p989) also runs day trips (🕐per person incl lunch ₹600) for groups of four to 15 people, on a traditional houseboat around the Valiyaparamba Backwaters.

Around 22km south of Bekal, Bekal Boat Stay (✆04672282633, 9447469747; www.bekalboatstay.com; Kottappuram, Nileshwar) is one of the few operators in the region to offer overnight houseboat trips (2/4 people per 24hr ₹8500/10,500) around the Valiyaparamba backwaters. Sunset/day cruises (₹3000/6000 for up to six people) are also available. It's about 2km from Nileshwar – get off any bus between Kannur and Bekal and take an autorickshaw from there (₹20).

acter and there's a terrace where you can sit and gaze out to sea and enjoy home cooking.

ℹ Information

The **DTPC Office** (☎ 2706336; www.dtpckannur.com; ⊙ 10am-5pm Mon-Sat), opposite the KSRTC bus stand, supplies basic maps of Kannur. There are Federal Bank and State Bank of India ATMs adjacent to the bus stand. A **UAE Exchange** (☎ 2709022; Fort Rd, City Centre; ⊙ 9.30am-6pm Mon-Sat, 11am-1pm Sun) office changes travellers cheques and cash; it's located in City Centre mall, five minutes from the train station.

ℹ Getting There & Away

BUS

Kannur has several bus stands but the enormous **central bus stand** – the largest in Kerala – is the place to catch long-distance buses, both private and government. It's about 500m southeast of the train station. Some government buses also use the **KSRTC bus stand** near the Caltex junction, 1km northeast of the train station.

There are daily buses to Mysore (₹190, eight hours, five daily), Mangalore (₹92, four hours, two daily), Madikeri (₹63, 2½ hours, 11am) and Mananthavadi (₹55, 2½ hours, hourly) for Wayanad. There's one daily bus to Ooty (via Wayanad, ₹171, nine hours) at 10pm.

For Thottada Beach, take bus No 29 (₹7) from Plaza Junction opposite the train station and get off at Adikatalayi village.

TRAIN

There are several daily trains to Calicut (2nd-class/AC chair ₹67/205, 1½ hours), Mangalore (sleeper/3AC/2AC ₹140/283/625, three hours) and Ernakulam (₹166/420/625, 6½ hours).

Bekal & Around

☎ 0467

Bekal and nearby Palakunnu and Udma, in Kerala's far north, have some long white-sand beaches begging for DIY exploration. The area is gradually being colonised by glitzy five-star resorts catering to fresh-from-the-Gulf millionaires, but it's still worth the trip for off-the-beaten-track adventurers intent on discovering the beaches before they get swallowed up by developers.

The laterite-brick **Bekal Fort** (Indian/foreigner ₹5/100; ⊙ 8am-5pm), built between 1645 and 1660, sits on Bekal's rocky headland and houses a small Hindu temple and plenty of goats. Next door, **Bekal Beach** (admission ₹5) encompasses a grassy park and a long, beautiful stretch of sand that turns into a circus

on weekends and holidays when local families descend here for rambunctious leisure time. Isolated **Kappil Beach**, 6km north of Bekal, is a beautiful, lonely stretch of fine sand and calm water, but beware of shifting sandbars.

There are lots of cheap, poor quality hotels scattered between Kanhangad (12km south) and Kasaragod (10km north), with a few notable exceptions.

Gitanjali Heritage HOMESTAY $$
(☎ 9447469747, 04672234159; www.gitanjaliheritage.com; s/d full-board ₹3500/5000; @) This lovely place lies surrounded by rice paddies, deep among Kasaragod's inland villages. It is just 5km from Bekal and is an intimate heritage home with three comfortable rooms filled with ancestral furniture and polished wood.

★ **Neeleshwar Hermitage** RESORT $$$
(☎ 04672287510; www.neeleshwarhermitage.com; Ozhinhavalappu, Neeleshwar; s/d cottages from ₹10,600/12,600, seaview ₹16,000/17,300; ☎) This spectacular beachfront ecoresort consists of 16 beautifully designed thatch-roof cottages modelled on Keralan fisherman's huts but with modern comforts like iPod docks and a five-star price tag. Built according to the principles of Kerala Vastu, the resort has an infinity pool that gazes out to sea, nearly 5 hectares of lush gardens fragrant with frangipani, superb organic food and Ayurvedic massage, meditation and yoga programs.

ℹ Getting There & Around

A couple of local trains stop at Fort Bekal station, right on Bekal beach. Kanhangad, 12km south, is a major train stop, while Kasaragod, 10km to the north, is the largest town in the area. Frequent buses run from Bekal to both Kanhangad and Kasaragod (around ₹10, 20 minutes), from where you can pick up major trains to Mangalore or south to Kochi. An auto-rickshaw from Bekal Junction to Kappil beach is around ₹50.

LAKSHADWEEP

POP 64,500

Comprising a string of 36 palm-covered, white-sand-skirted coral islands 300km off the coast of Kerala, Lakshadweep is as stunning as it is isolated. Only 10 of these islands are inhabited, mostly with Sunni Muslim fishermen, and foreigners are only allowed

DIVING

Lakshadweep is a diver's dream, with excellent visibility and an embarrassment of marine life living on undisturbed coral reefs. The best time to dive is between November and mid-May when the seas are calm and visibility is 20m to 40m.

Dive Lakshadweep (☏ 94460 55972; http://divelakshadweep.com; Agatti Island; single dive ₹3000, PADI open water course ₹24,000) is based on Agatti Island and offers a variety of PADI courses and dive packages, including Discover Scuba (₹1700) dives for beginners. Unfortunately, at the time of writing foreigners were not permitted on Agatti Island and not able to use this outfit under a dispute with Lakshadweep administration, but this situation is likely to change.

to stay on a few of these. With fishing and coir production the main sources of income, local life on the islands remains highly traditional, and a caste system divides the islanders between Koya (land owners), Malmi (sailors) and Melachery (farmers).

The real attraction of the islands lies under the water: the 4200 sq km of pristine archipelago lagoons, unspoiled coral reefs and warm waters are a magnet for flipper-toting travellers and divers alike.

Lakshadweep can only be visited on a prearranged package trip. At the time of research, only the resorts on Kadmat and Minicoy islands were open to tourists – most visits to the islands are boat-based packages which include a cruise from Kochi, island visits, watersports, diving and nights spent on board the boat. Packages include permits and meals, and can be arranged through SPORTS.

ℹ️ Information

SPORTS (Society for the Promotion of Recreational Tourism & Sports; ☏ 9495984001, 04842668387; www.lakshadweeptourism.com; IG Rd, Willingdon Island; ⊙ 10am-5pm Mon-Sat) is the main organisation for tourist information and package tours.

PERMITS

At the time of writing, foreigners were only allowed to stay at the government resorts on Kadmat and Minicoy islands, though Agatti (which has a private resort and the only airport), Kavaratti and Bangaram should reopen in the future; enquire at SPORTS. Any visits require a special permit (one month's notice) which can be organised by tour operators or SPORTS in Kochi.

ℹ️ Getting There & Away

Air India flies between Kochi and Agatti Island (from ₹7000 return) daily except Sunday. Boat transport between Agatti and Kadmat is included in the package tours available, and the same goes for transport from Kochi to Kadmat and the Minicoy Islands. See the package section of www.lakshwdeeptourism.com for more details.

Kadmat Island

Kadmat Beach Resort (☏ 04844011134; www.kadmat.com; 4 nights from €512 per person; ❄) has 28 modern cottages, administered by Mint Valley (www.mintvalley.com) and can be reached by overnight boat from Kochi, or by boat transfer from Agatti airport on Tuesday and Saturday.

Minicoy Island

You can stay on the remote island of Minicoy, the second-largest island and the closest to the Maldives, in modern cottages or a 20-room guesthouse at **Minicoy Island Resort** (☏ 04842668387; www.lakshadweeptourism.com; s/d ₹3000/4000, with AC ₹5000/6000; ❄) via SPORTS Swaying Palms and Coral Reef Packages.

Tamil Nadu & Chennai

Best Temples

➡ Meenakshi Amman Temple (p1058)

➡ Brihadishwara Temple (p1048)

➡ Sri Ranganathaswamy Temple (p1053)

➡ Arunachaleshwar Temple (p1034)

➡ Nataraja Temple (p1045)

Best Places to Stay

➡ Visalam (p1057)

➡ Les Hibiscus (p1040)

➡ Bungalow on the Beach (p1046)

➡ 180° McIver (p1075)

Why Go?

Tamil Nadu is the homeland of one of humanity's living classical civilisations, stretching back uninterrupted for two millennia and very much living on today in the Tamils' language, dance, poetry and Hindu religion.

But this state with its age-old trading vocation is as dynamic as it is immersed in tradition. Fire-worshipping devotees who smear tikka on their brows in the famously spectacular Tamil temples may then head off to IT offices to develop new software applications – and afterwards unwind in a stylish nocturnal haunt in rapidly modernising Chennai (Madras).

When the heat and noise of Tamil Nadu's temple towns overwhelm, escape to the very end of India where three seas mingle, or up to the cool, forest-clad, wildlife-prowled Western Ghats. It's all packed into a state that remains proudly distinct from the rest of India, while at the same time being among the most welcoming.

When to Go
Chennai

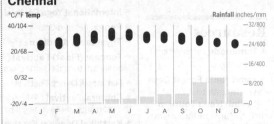

Jan The weather is at its (relative) coolest and Pongal (harvest) celebrations spill into the streets.

Jul–Sep Head to the hill stations after the crowded, expensive 'season', weather is still good.

Nov–Dec The full-moon festival of lights.

MAIN POINTS OF ENTRY

Chennai Airport will be your probable entry point if you're flying into Tamil Nadu from overseas, although Trichy, Madurai and Coimbatore also have (limited) international services. The same four cities are also the state's major train junctions.

Fast Facts

➡ **Population:** 72.1 million

➡ **Area:** 130,058 sq km

➡ **Capital:** Chennai (Madras)

➡ **Main language:** Tamil

➡ **Sleeping prices:**
$ below ₹1000, $$ ₹1000 to ₹5000, $$$ above ₹5000

Top Tip

If you need train tickets in a hurry, the Foreign Tourist Cell at Chennai Central is the most helpful and efficient we've ever come across; tickets for booked-up trains anywhere in India seem to become magically available here.

Resources

➡ **Tamilnadu** (http://tamil nadu.com)

➡ **Tamil Nadu Forest Dept** (www.forests.tn.nic .in) **Tamil Nadu Tourism** (http://tamilnadutourism .org)

➡ **Lonely Planet** (www .lonelyplanet.com.au/ india)

Food

Tamil Nadu's favourite foods are overwhelmingly vegetarian, with lots of coconut and chilli. You'll find dosas, *idlis* (spongy, round fermented rice cakes) and *vadas* (deep-fried lentil-flour doughnuts), all served with coconut chutney and *sambar* (lentil broth). Almost as ubiquitous is the *uttapam*, a thick, savoury rice pancake that typically comes with chopped onions, green chillies and coriander. South Indian 'meals' – thalis based around rice, lentil dishes, *rasam* (hot and sour tamarind soup) and chutneys, often served on a banana leaf – are also good. The main local exception to the all-veg diet is Chettinad food, originating from the Chettinadu region south of Trichy but available at restaurants in bigger towns. The dishes are spicy but not fiery. For a state growing a lot of tea, Tamil Nadu really loves its coffee; filtered coffee (mixed with milk and sugar, of course, and a dash of chicory) is often more readily available than tea. Restaurant prices include the taxes added to menu rates at some places.

DON'T MISS

Few parts of India are as fervent in their worship of the Hindu gods as Tamil Nadu. Great temples stun with their spectacular architecture, the colour of their crowds of worshippers, and their noisy, chaotic festivals. For artistry don't miss the World Heritage–listed trio at **Thanjavur**, **Darasuram** village (near Kumbakonam) and **Gangaikon-dacholapuram**. For spectacle and contemporary fervour, head to **Madurai**, **Chidambaram**, **Srirangam** (Trichy) and **Tiruvannamalai**. Escape from the heat of the plains to the hill stations in the cool, misty **Western Ghats**. The Nilgiri Mountain Railway, alias the 'toy train', snaking its way up nearly 2000m of forest-clothed mountain, makes a trip to **Ooty** (Udhagamandalam) unforgettable; **Kodaikanal** is a smaller, prettier, quirkier alternative to Ooty.

Top State Festivals

➡ **International Yoga Festival** (☺ 4–7 Jan, Puducherry, p1036)

➡ **Pongal** (☺ mid-Jan, statewide) Harvest festival.

➡ **Thyagaraja Aradhana** (☺ Jan, Thiruvaiyaru, p1049)

➡ **Teppam (Float) Festival** (☺ Jan/Feb, Madurai, p1060) Meenakshi temple deities are taken on a tour of the town.

➡ **Natyanjali Dance Festival** (☺ Feb/Mar, Chidambaram, p1045)

➡ **Chithirai Festival** (☺ Apr/May, Madurai, p1060) Celebrates the marriage of Meenakshi to Sundareswarar (Shiva).

➡ **Karthikai Deepam Festival** (☺ Nov/Dec, statewide) Festival of lights.

➡ **Chennai Festival of Music & Dance** (☺ mid-Dec–mid-Jan, Chennai, p1014) Celebrates southern music and dance.

➡ **Mamallapuram Dance Festival** (☺ Dec–Jan, Mamallapuram, p1028) Four-weeks of dance, drama and music.

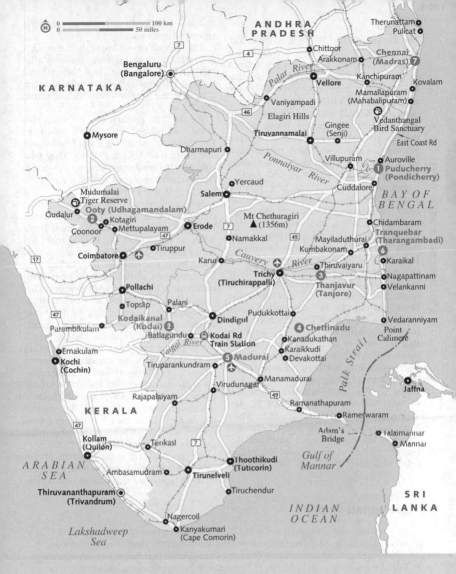

Tamil Nadu Highlights

① Soak up the unique Franco-Indian style of **Puducherry** (Pondicherry, p1036)

② Climb into the cool forests of the Western Ghats at **Kodaikanal** (p1067) or **Ooty** (Udhagamadalam, p1077)

③ Admire the magnificence of Chola architecture at Thanjavur's **Brihadishwara Temple** (p1048)

④ Spend the night in an opulent mansion in **Chettinadu** (p1056)

⑤ Immerse yourself in the colour of Tamil temple life at Madurai's **Meenakshi Amman Temple** (p1058)

⑥ Relax at tranquil **Tranquebar** (p1046), a quirky old Danish colony

⑦ Get acquainted with the many faces of traditional but increasingly cosmopolitan and contemporary **Chennai** (p1007)

History

The Tamils consider themselves the standard bearers of Dravidian – pre-Aryan Indian – civilisation. Dravidians are defined as speakers of languages of the Dravidian family, the four most important of which are all rooted in South India – Tamil, Malayalam (spoken in Kerala), Telugu (Andhra Pradesh) and Kannada (Karnataka). South Indian cultures and history are distinct from Aryan North India, and Tamils' ability to trace their identity back in an unbroken line to classical antiquity is a source of considerable pride.

Despite the Dravidians' long-standing southern location, elements of Dravidian culture – including a meditating god seated in the lotus position, who may be the world's first depiction of the yogi archetype – existed in the early Indus civilisations of northwest India some 4000 years ago. Whether Dravidian culture was widespread around India before Aryan cultures appeared in the north in the 2nd millennium BC, or whether the Dravidians only reached the south because the Aryans drove them from the north, is a matter of debate. But there is no question that the cushion of distance has allowed South Indian cultures to develop with little interruption from northern influences or invasions for over 2000 years.

The Tamil language was well established in Tamil Nadu by the 3rd century BC, the approximate start of the Sangam Age, when Tamil poets produced the body of classical literature known as Sangam literature. Romantic versions of the era have the region ruled by feuding poet-kings; one visitor at the time described the Tamils as favouring rose petals over gold.

The Sangam period lasted until about AD 300, with three main Tamil dynasties arising in different parts of Tamil Nadu ('Tamil Country'): the early Cholas in the centre, the Cheras in the west and the Pandyas in the south.

By the 7th century the Pallavas, also Tamil, established an empire based at Kanchipuram extending from Tamil Nadu and north into Andhra Pradesh. They take credit for the great stone carvings of Mamallapuram and also constructed the region's first free-standing temples.

Next up were the medieval Cholas (whose connection with the early Cholas is hazy). Based in the Cauvery valley of central Tamil Nadu, at their peak the Cholas ruled Sri Lanka and the Maldives as well as much of South India, and extended their influence to Southeast Asia, spreading Tamil ideas of reincarnation, karma and yogic practice. This cross-pollination spawned architectural wonders such as Angkor Wat, the intellectual gestation of Balinese Hinduism and much of the philosophy of classical Buddhism.

The Cholas raised Dravidian architecture to new levels with the magnificent towered temples of Thanjavur and Gangaikondacholapuram, and carried the art of bronze image casting to its peak, especially in their images of Shiva as Nataraja, the cosmic dancer. *Gopurams,* the tall temple gate towers characteristic of Tamil Nadu today, make their appearance in late Chola times.

By the late 14th century much of the Tamil Nadu was under the sway of the Vijayanagar empire based at Hampi in Karnata-

DRAVIDIAN PRIDE

Since before Indian independence in 1947, Tamil politicians have railed against caste (which they see as favouring light-skinned Brahmins) and the Hindi language (seen as North Indian cultural imperialism). The pre-Independence 'Self Respect' movement and Justice Party, influenced by Marxism, mixed South Indian communal values with class-war rhetoric, and spawned Tamil political parties that remain the major powers in Tamil Nadu today. In the early post-Independence decades there was even a movement for an independent Dravida Nadu nation comprising the four main South Indian peoples, but today Dravidian politics is largely restricted to Tamil Nadu, where parties are often led by former film stars.

During the conflict in nearby Sri Lanka, many Indian Tamil politicians loudly defended the Tamil Tigers, the organisation that assassinated Rajiv Gandhi in a village near Chennai in 1991. There is still considerable prejudice among the generally tolerant Tamils towards anything Sinhalese.

Throughout the state, male politicians don a white shirt and white *mundu* (sarong), the official uniform of Tamil pride.

ka. As the Vijayanagar state weakened in the 16th century, some of their local governors, the Nayaks, set up strong independent kingdoms, notably at Madurai and Thanjavur. Vijayanagar and Nayak sculptors carved wonderfully detailed statues and reliefs at many Tamil temples.

Europeans first came sniffing around Tamil shores in the 16th century, when the Portuguese settled at San Thome. The Dutch, British, French and Danes followed in the 17th century, striking deals with local rulers to set up coastal trading colonies. Eventually it came down to a contest between the British, based at Madras (now Chennai), and the French, based at Pondicherry (Puducherry), for supremacy among the colonial rivals. The British won out in the three Carnatic Wars, fought between the two European powers in alliances with various Indian princes, between 1744 and 1763. By the end of the 18th century British dominance over the majority of Tamil lands was assured.

The area governed by the British from Madras, the Madras Presidency, included parts of Andhra Pradesh, Kerala and Karnataka, an arrangement that continued after Indian independence in 1947, until the four existing southern states were created on linguistic lines in the 1950s.

CHENNAI (MADRAS)

♪ 044 / POP 7.7 MILLION

The 'capital of the south' has always been the rather dowdy sibling among India's four biggest cities, with its withering southern heat, roaring traffic, and scarcity of outstanding sights. For many travellers, it is as much a gateway as a destination in itself. If you're just caught here between connections, it's certainly worth poking around one of the museums or taking a sunset stroll along Marina Beach. If you have more time to explore Chennai's varied neighbourhoods and appreciate its role as keeper of South Indian artistic and religious traditions, the odds are this 70-sq-km conglomerate of urban villages will grow on you. Recent years have added a new layer of cosmopolitan glamour in the shape of luxury hotels, shiny boutiques, classy contemporary restaurants and even a smattering of clubs and bars open into the wee hours.

One of Chennai's biggest assets is its people, infectiously enthusiastic about their hometown. They won't hit you with a lot of hustle and hassle, and they will mostly treat you as a guest rather than a commodity.

The old British Fort St George and the jumble of narrow streets and bazaars that is George Town constitute the historic hub of the city. The two main train stations, Egmore and Central, sit inland from the fort. Much of the best eating, shopping and accommodation lies in the leafier southern and southwestern suburbs such as Nungambakkam, T Nagar (Thyagaraya Nagar) and Alwarpet. The major thoroughfare linking northern with southern Chennai is Anna Salai (Mount Rd).

History

The southern neighbourhood of Mylapore existed long before most of the rest of Chennai and there is evidence that it traded with Roman and even Chinese and Greek merchants. The Portuguese established their San Thome settlement on the coast nearby in 1523. Another century passed before the British East India Company, searching for a good southeast Indian trading base, struck a deal with the local Vijayanagar ruler to build a fort-cum-trading post at the fishing village of Madraspatnam. This was Fort St George, erected between 1640 and 1653.

The three Carnatic Wars between 1744 and 1763 saw Britain and its colonialist rival France allying with competing South Indian princes in their efforts to get the upper hand over the locals and each other. The French occupied Fort St George from 1746 to 1749 but the British eventually won out, with the French withdrawing to Pondicherry (now Puducherry).

As capital of the Madras Presidency, one of the four major divisions of British India, Madras grew into an important naval and commercial centre. After Independence, it became capital of Madras state and its successor Tamil Nadu. The city itself was renamed Chennai in 1996. IT and motor-vehicle manufacture are its industrial mainstays today.

ⓘ Dangers & Annoyances

Unless the city's authorities and its autorickshaw drivers manage to strike a deal over fares, convincing a driver to use the meter will remain a Vatican-certified miracle, with fares bordering on the astronomical. Avoid paying upfront, and never get into an autorickshaw before agreeing the fare.

TAMIL NADU & CHENNAI CHENNAI (MADRAS)

Chennai (Madras)

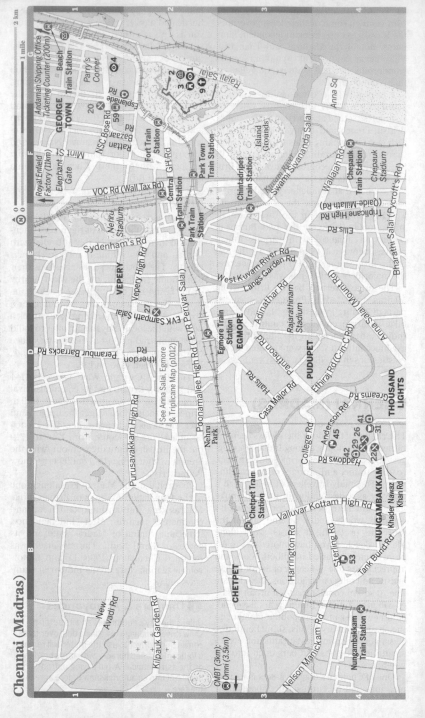

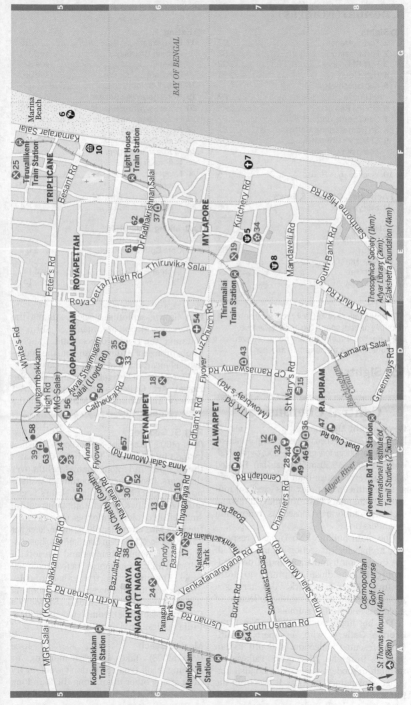

BAY OF BENGAL

Marina Beach

TRIPLICANE

ROYAPETTAH

GOPALAPURAM

MYLAPORE

TEYNAMPET

ALWARPET

RA PURAM

THYAGARAYA NAGAR (T NAGAR)

Panagal Park

Natesan Park

Cosmopolitan Golf Course

Adyar River

Kodambakkam Train Station

Mambalam Train Station

Thirumailai Train Station

Light House Train Station

Tiruvallikeni Train Station

Greenways Rd Train Station

Boat Club Rd

Kamarajar Salai

Kamaraj Salai

Greenways Rd

Santhome High Rd

RK Mutt Rd

South Bank Rd

Mandaveli Rd

Kutchery Rd

St Mary's Rd

CP Ramaswamy Rd

Luz Church Rd

Dr Radhakrishnan Salai

Thiruvika Salai

Roya Pettah High Rd

Peter's Rd

White's Rd

Nungambakkam High Rd (MG Salai)

Avvai Shanmugam Salai (Lloyds Rd)

Cathedral Rd

TTK Rd (Mowbray's Rd)

Eldham's Rd

Anna Salai (Mount Rd)

Cenotaph Rd

Chamiers Rd

Boag Rd

Burkit Rd

Southwest Boag Rd

Venkatanarayana Rd

Thankachalam Rd

Sir Thyagaraya Rd

Usman Rd

North Usman Rd

South Usman Rd

Bazullah Rd

GN Chetty Rd (Gopathy Rd)

Nakeeran Rd

MGR Salai (Kodambakkam High Rd)

Anna Flyover

Flyover

Bazaar

Pondy

Besant Rd

Theosophical Society (1km); Adyar Library (2km); Kalakshetra Foundation (4km)

International Institute of Tamil Studies (2.5km)

St Thomas Mount (8km)

Chennai (Madras)

⊙ Sights

1 Fort Entrance	G2
2 Fort Museum	G2
3 Fort St George	G2
4 High Court	G1
5 Kapaleeshwarar Temple	E7
6 Marina Beach	F5
7 San Thome Cathedral	F7
8 Sri Ramakrishna Math	E7
9 St Mary's Church	G2
Tomb of St Thomas the Apostle	(see 7)
10 Vivekananda House	F5

⊕ Activities, Courses & Tours

11 Storytrails	D6

⊟ Sleeping

12 Footprint B&B	C7
13 Lotus	B6
14 Park Hotel	C5
15 Raintree	D7
16 Residency Towers	C6

⊗ Eating

17 Big Bazaar	B6
Copper Chimney	(see 33)
Dakshin	(see 32)
Eco Cafe	(see 36)
18 Enté Keralam	D6
19 Hotel Saravana Bhavan	E7
20 Hotel Saravana Bhavan	F1
21 Hotel Saravana Bhavan	B6
22 Kryptos by Willi	C4
23 Kumarakom	C5
24 Murugan Idly Shop	B6
25 Natural Fresh	F5
26 Nilgiri's	C4
27 Spencer's	D2
28 Tuscana on Chamiers	C7
29 Tuscana Pizzeria	C4

⊙ Drinking & Nightlife

30 10 Downing Street	C6
31 Café Coffee Day	C4
32 Dublin	C7
Leather Bar	(see 14)
Pasha	(see 14)

Tempting offers of ₹50 'city tours' by auto-rickshaw drivers sound too good to be true. They are. You'll spend the day being dragged from one shop or emporium to another.

⊙ Sights

⊙ Central Chennai

Government Museum
MUSEUM

(Map p1012; www.chennaimuseum.org; Pantheon Rd, Egmore; Indian/foreigner ₹15/250, camera/video ₹200/500; ⊙9.30am-5pm Sat-Thu) Housed across several British-built buildings known as the Pantheon Complex, this excellent museum is Chennai's best. You may find some sections temporarily closed as renovation meanders on.

The main building (No 1) has a respectable archaeological section representing all the major South Indian periods from 2nd-century-BC Buddhist sculptures to 16th-century Vijayanagar work. Also here is a zoology section with a motley collection of skeletons and stuffed animals.

The big highlight is building No 3, the **Bronze Gallery**, with a superb, beautifully presented collection of South Indian bronzes from the 7th-century Pallava era through to modern times, with English-language explanatory material. It was from the 9th to 11th centuries, in the Chola period,

that bronze sculpture peaked. Among the impressive pieces are many of Shiva as Nataraja, the cosmic dancer, and a superb Chola bronze of Ardhanarishvara, the androgynous incarnation of Shiva and Parvati.

The same ticket gets you into the **National Art Gallery**, **Contemporary Art Gallery** and **Children's Museum**, in the same complex.

Fort St George
FORT

(Map p1008; Rajaji Salai; ⊙9am-5pm) Finished in 1653 by the British East India Company, the fort has undergone many facelifts over the years. Inside the vast perimeter walls is now a precinct housing Tamil Nadu's Legislative Assembly & Secretariat, along with a smattering of older buildings. One of these, the **Fort Museum** (Map p1008; Indian/foreigner ₹5/100, video ₹25; ⊙9am-5pm Sat-Thu), has displays on Chennai's origins and the fort itself, and military memorabilia from colonial times. The upstairs portrait gallery of colonial bigwigs includes a very assured-looking Robert Clive (Clive of India). **St Mary's Church** (Map p1008), completed in 1680, is India's oldest surviving British church.

Marina Beach
BEACH

(Map p1008) Take an early-morning or evening stroll (you really don't want to fry here at any other time) along the 3km-long main stretch of Marina Beach and you'll pass cricket matches, flying kites, fortune tellers, fish markets and families enjoying the sea breeze. Try a cob of roast corn with lime and chilli powder from one of the vendors – delicious. Don't swim: strong rips make it dangerous.

Vivekananda House   MUSEUM
(Vivekanandar Illam, Ice House; Map p1008; www. vivekanandahouse.org; Kamarajar Salai; adult/ child ₹10/5; ⊙10am-12.15pm & 3-7.15pm Thu-Tue) The Vivekananda House is interesting not only for its displays on the famous 'wandering monk', Swami Vivekananda, but also for its semicircular form, built in 1842 to store ice imported from the USA. Vivekananda stayed here briefly in 1897 and preached his ascetic Hindu philosophy to adoring crowds. The exhibits include a pictorial overview of Hindu philosophy and sacred literature, a photo exhibition on the swami's life, and the room where Vivekananda stayed, now used for meditation. Free one-hour meditation classes are held on Wednesdays at 7pm.

High Court   NOTABLE BUILDING
(Map p1008; Parry's Corner) Completed in 1892, this imposing red Indo-Saracenic structure is said to be the largest judicial building in the world after the Courts of London. Depending on current regulations, you may or may not be allowed to enter the buildings or even the grounds. If you fancy trying, take your passport.

Southern Chennai

Kalakshetra Foundation   ARTS SCHOOL
(☑24524057; www.kalakshetra.net; Muthulakshmi St, Thiruvanmiyur; admission ₹50; ⊙campus 8.45am-11.15am Mon-Sat late Jun–mid-Mar, craft centre 9am-1pm & 2-5pm Mon-Sat, all closed 2nd & 4th Sat of month) Founded in 1936, Kalakshetra is a leading serious school of Tamil classical dance and music (courses last four to six years), set in beautiful, shady grounds in the far south of the city. During morning class times visitors can walk around the grounds (without interrupting classes), and visit the **Rukmini Devi Museum**. Across the road is the Kalakshetra Craft Centre where you can witness Kanchipuram-style hand-loom weaving, textile block-printing and the fascinating, rare art of Kalamkari (hand-painting on textiles with vegetable dyes). The Thiruvanmiyur bus stand, terminus of many city bus routes, is 500m west of the Kalakshetra entrance.

While here it's also worth visiting the **Book Building** (☑42601033; www.tarabooks. com; Plot 9, CGE Colony, Kuppam Beach Rd, Thiruvanmiyur; ⊙10am-7.30pm Mon-Sat), 700m south

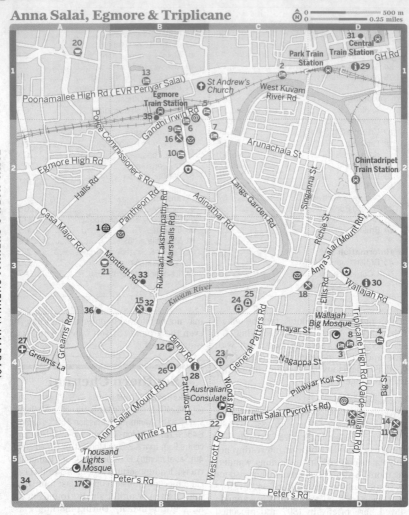

of Kalakshetra, where Tara Books stages exhibitions and events as well as displaying its own highly original, attractive handmade books. With prior notice, you can visit the workshop where the books are created (10 minutes' drive away).

Kapaleeshwarar Temple HINDU TEMPLE
(Map p1008; Ponnambala Vathiar St, Mylapore; ☉5am-noon & 4-9.30pm) The Mylapore neighbourhood is one of Chennai's most characterful and traditional; it predated colonial Madras by several centuries. Kapaleeshwarar Temple is Chennai's most

active and impressive temple. It displays the main architectural elements of many a Tamil Nadu temple – a rainbow-coloured *gopuram* (gateway tower), pillared *mandapas* (pavilions) inside and out, and a huge tank – and it's dedicated to the state's most popular deity, Shiva. Legend tells that in a fit of pique Shiva once turned his consort Parvati into a peacock, and instructed her to worship him here in order to regain her normal form. Parvati supposedly did as instructed at a spot just outside the northeast corner of the temple's central block, where a shrine commemorates the event.

Anna Salai, Egmore & Triplicane

San Thome Cathedral CHURCH
(Map p1008; www.santhomechurch.com; Santhome High Rd) This soaring Roman Catholic cathedral, a stone's throw from the beach, was founded by the Portuguese in the 16th century, then rebuilt in neo-Gothic style in the 1890s. Behind the cathedral is the entrance to the **tomb of St Thomas the Apostle** (Map p1008; admission free; ☉ tomb & museum 6am-8.30pm). It's believed 'Doubting Thomas' brought Christianity to the subcontinent and was killed at St Thomas Mount, Chennai, in AD 72. Although most of his mortal remains are apparently now in Italy, a small cross on the chapel wall containing a tiny bone fragment is marked 'Relic of St Thomas'. A museum above contains various Thomas-related artefacts including the lancehead believed to have killed him.

Sri Ramakrishna Math HINDU TEMPLE
(Map p1008; www.chennaimath.org; 31 RK Mutt Rd; ☉ Universal Temple 5-11.45am & 3.30-9pm, evening prayers 6.30-7.30pm) The tranquil, leafy grounds of the Ramakrishna Math are a world away from the chaos and crazy rickshaw drivers outside. Monks glide around and there's a reverential feel here. The Math is a monastic order following the teachings of the 19th-century sage Sri Ramakrishna, who preached the essential unity of all religions. The Universal Temple here is a handsome modern building incorporating architectural elements from several different religions. It's open to all, to participate in worship or pray or meditate in silence.

Theosophical Society GARDEN
(www.ts-adyar.org; south end of Thiru Vi Ka Bridge, Adyar; admission free; ☉ grounds 8.30-10am & 2-4pm Mon-Sat) Between the Adyar River and the coast, the 100-hectare grounds of the Theosophical Society provide a green and peaceful retreat from the city. A lovely spot just to wander, they contain a church, mosque, Buddhist shrine and Hindu temple as well as a huge variety of native and introduced trees. The **Adyar Library** (1yr reader's card ₹50

(deposit ₹250); ⊘9am-5pm Tue-Sun) here has an immense collection of books on religion and philosophy, some of which are on display, from 1000-year-old Buddhist scrolls to intricate, handmade 19th-century Bibles.

St Thomas Mount
SACRED SITE

(Parangi Malai; off Lawrence Rd) The reputed site of St Thomas' martyrdom rises in the southwest of the city, 2.5km north of St Thomas Mount train station. The St Thomas Shrine, built by the Portuguese in 1523, contains what are supposed to be a fragment of Thomas' bone and a cross he carved; the views across the city are wonderful.

Courses

International Institute of Tamil Studies
LANGUAGE

(☑22542781; www.ulakaththamizh.org; CIT Campus, 2nd Main Rd, Tharamani) Runs intensive three-month and six-month courses in Tamil.

Kalakshetra Foundation
TEXTILE PAINTING

(☑24524057;www.kalakshetra.net;MuthulakshmiSt, Thiruvanmiyur) The crafts centre here offers one- or two-month courses in the old art of Kalamkari – hand-painting of textiles using vegetable inks – which survives in only a handful of places. Courses usually occupy three hours per day for around ₹10,000 a month.

Tours

The Tamil Nadu Tourism Development Corporation (p1020) conducts half-day city tours (non-AC/AC ₹215/235) and day trips to Mamallapuram (₹275/350). Book ahead for weekends and holidays; be ready for cancellations on quiet weekdays. Every full moon there's an overnight pilgrimage trip to Tiruvannamalai (₹650/780).

TRADITIONAL TRADERS

Even as Chennai expands relentlessly to the south, west and north, George Town, the local settlement that grew up near the British Fort St George, remains the city's wholesale centre. Many streets are entirely given over to selling one particular type of merchandise as they have for hundreds of years – paper goods in Anderson St, fireworks in Badrian St, jewellery on NSC Bose Rd and so on. Even if you're not in the market for anything, wander the maze-like streets to see Indian life flowing seamlessly from the past into the present.

Storytrails
WALKING TOURS

(Map p1008; ☑42124214, 9940040215; http://story trails.in; 1, 2nd Cross St, CIT Colony, Mylapore; 3hr tour ₹695-795.) Runs entertaining and informative neighbourhood walking tours based around themes such as dance, temples, jewellery and bazaars, as well as tours specially aimed at children.

Royal Enfield Factory
FACTORY TOUR

(☑42230400; www.royalenfield.com; Tiruvottiyur High Rd, Tiruvottiyur) The classic Enfield Bullet motorcycle has been manufactured since 1955 at the Royal Enfield Factory, in far northern Chennai. Tours (per person ₹600) run on the second and fourth Saturdays of each month for about two hours from 10.30am. It's essential to book.

Festivals & Events

Chennai Festival of Music & Dance
MUSIC, DANCE

(Madras Music & Dance Season; ⊘mid-Dec–mid-Jan) One of the largest of its type in the world, this festival is a celebration of South Indian music and dance.

Sleeping

Hotels in Chennai are pricier than in the rest of Tamil Nadu and don't, as a rule, offer much bang for your buck. The Triplicane High Rd area is best for budget accommodation. There are some cheapies in Egmore, where you'll also find a good number of midrange options. Most top-end hotels are in the more middle-class areas to the south.

It's always a good idea to call ahead; many hotels in Chennai fill up by noon. For the most expensive hotels, check their websites for good discounts.

Egmore & Around

Raj Residency
HOTEL $

(Map p1012; ☑28192219; www.rajresidencyhotel. com; 2/22 Kennet Lane; s ₹675-1315, d ₹785-1555; ❄) The non-AC rooms here are reasonable value, a bit dingy and worn but kept clean enough, in shades of brown.

Regal Lodge
HOTEL $

(Map p1012; ☑28191122; 15 Kennet Lane; s/d ₹380/490) If you're in need of a cheap room near Egmore station, the Regal can give you a small, dingy one with grubby walls. At least they change the sheets and clean the rooms between occupants.

YWCA International Guest House
GUESTHOUSE $$

(Map p1012; ☑ 25324234; ywcaigh@indiainfo.com; 1086 Poonamallee High Rd; s/d incl breakfast ₹785/1045, with AC ₹1300/1500; ❄@⊜) The YWCA guesthouse, set in green and shady grounds, offers a calm atmosphere and exceptionally good value. Very efficiently run by an amiable staff, it provides good-sized, impeccably clean rooms, spacious common areas and good-value meals (₹150/225 for veg/nonveg lunch or dinner). Wi-fi (in the lobby) costs ₹100 per day.

Hotel Park Plaza
HOTEL $$

(Map p1012; ☑ 30777777; www.hotelparkplaza.in; 29 Whannels Rd; s/d incl half-board ₹3238/3837; ❄⊜) With dinner and wi-fi included in rates as well as breakfast, and good, spacious rooms, the Park Plaza is a decent deal.

Hotel Chandra Park
HOTEL $$

(Map p1012; ☑ 28191177; www.hotelchandrapark.com; 9 Gandhi Irwin Rd; s ₹1319-2279, d ₹1499-2578, all incl breakfast; ❄) Chandra Park's prices remain mysteriously lower than most comparable establishments. Standard rooms are small but have air-con, clean towels and tight, white sheets. Throw in a decent bar and a hearty buffet breakfast and this is good value by Chennai standards.

Bell Central
HOTEL $$

(Map p1012; ☑ 40412200; www.bellhotels.in; 47 Poonamallee High Rd; s ₹2399-2999, d ₹2999-3598, all incl breakfast; ❄⊜) The Bell is a welcome relief from the typical dreary midrange decor. Rooms are smallish, but they're cheerfully contemporary, bright and colourful and have tea/coffee makers. The hotel is convenient for Chennai Central station and has a multicuisine restaurant. Wi-fi costs ₹50 per hour.

Vivanta by Taj – Connemara
HERITAGE HOTEL $$$

(Map p1012; ☑ 66000000; www.vivantabytaj.com; Binny Rd; s/d from ₹11,992/13,191; ❄@⊜≋) The top-end Taj group has four hotels in and around Chennai but this is the only one with historical ambience, built in the 1850s as the British governor's residence. There's a beautiful pool in tropical gardens, and even the smallest rooms are large and very comfy, with all mod cons.

Fortel
HOTEL $$$

(Map p1012; ☑ 30242424; www.fortelhotels.com; 3 Gandhi Irwin Rd; s ₹4197-6596, d ₹4797-7195, all incl breakfast; ❄⊜) Conveniently close to Egmore train station, the Fortel is cool and stylish in a wood, mirrors and white walls way, with comfy cushion-laden beds and two good restaurants. Wi-fi costs ₹200/500 per one/24 hours.

Triplicane

Paradise Guest House
HOTEL $

(Map p1012; ☑ 28594252; paradisegh@hotmail.com; 17 Vallabha Agraharam St; s ₹400-500, d ₹500-600; ❄) Paradise offers some of Triplicane's best-value digs – simple rooms with clean tiles, a breezy rooftop, friendly staff and hot water by the steaming bucket.

Broad Lands Lodge
HOTEL $

(Map p1012; ☑ 28545573; broadlandshotel@yahoo.com; 18 Vallabha Agraharam St; s ₹350-400, d ₹400-525; ⊜) In business since 1951, Broad Lands was a hippie-era stalwart and may not have had a fresh coat of pale-blue paint or a good spring clean since. But this colonial-era mansion with three leafy courtyards, and rooms located up several rambling staircases, still has its devotees, who love its laid-back atmosphere and don't seem to mind the bare-bone, idiosyncratic rooms, dank bathrooms, colony of cats or the high-volume muezzins of Wallajah Big Mosque. Wi-fi (a concession to the 21st century) is ₹20 per hour.

Royal City
HOTEL $

(Map p1012; ☑ 28443819; 10 Venkatachalam St; s ₹368-968, d ₹605-1089; ❄) A friendly place on a fairly quiet street with smallish but very clean, marble-floored rooms.

Cristal Guest House
HOTEL $

(Map p1012; ☑ 28513011; 34 CNK Rd; r ₹300, with AC ₹650; ❄) The clean, pink abodes in this modern building are not quite the cheapest rooms in Chennai, but they're only about ₹10 more expensive than many others close by - and that difference means the hotel is more likely to have vacancies.

Southern Chennai

★ Footprint B&B
B&B $$

(Map p1008; ☑ 9840037483; http://chennaibedandbreakfast.com; Gayatri Apartments, 16 South St, Alwarpet (behind Sheraton Park Hotel); r incl breakfast ₹4045; ❄@⊜) This is a wonderfully comfortable and relaxed base for your Chennai explorations, in a quiet street in a leafy neighbourhood. Bowls of pretty flowers and old-Madras drawings set the scene. The nine cosy, spotless rooms have king-size or wide twin beds. Breakfasts (Western or Indian) are generous, wi-fi is free and the hospitable owners can tell you all you need to make the most of your time. Phone or email in advance; walk-ins are discouraged.

★**Lotus** HOTEL **$$**
(Map p1008; ☎28157272; www.thelotus.in; 15 Venkatraman St, T Nagar; s ₹2980-4170, d ₹3930-4470, all incl breakfast; ✳🛜) An absolute gem, the Lotus offers a quiet setting away from the main roads, a good veg restaurant, and fresh, stylish rooms with wood floors and cheerful decor. Wi-fi is free (but doesn't reach all rooms).

★**Residency Towers** HOTEL **$$$**
(Map p1008; ☎28156363; www.theresidency. com; Sir Thyagaraya Rd, T Nagar; s ₹7135-8994, d ₹7675-8994, all incl breakfast; ✳@🛜🏊) Residency Towers combines five-star elegance with personality at very good prices for this level of accommodation. Rooms have sliding doors in front of windows to block out noise, walnut-veneer furniture, weighing scales and other thoughtful touches. Also here are three restaurants, a nice outdoor pool and a 'pub' that becomes a heaving weekend night spot. Wi-fi is free.

★**Park Hotel** BOUTIQUE HOTEL **$$$**
(Map p1008; ☎42676000; www.theparkhotels.com; 601 Anna Salai; s ₹12,592-17,988, d ₹13,791-17,988, ste from ₹19,187; ✳@🛜🏊) We love this super-stylish large boutique hotel, which flaunts design everywhere you look, from the bamboo, steel and gold cushions of the towering lobby to the posters from classic South Indian movies shot in Gemini Studios, the previous incarnation of the hotel site. Rooms have lovely lush bedding, all mod cons and stylish touches including glass-walled bathrooms. It's all pretty swish, and that goes for the three restaurants, large open-air pool, luxurious spa and two night spots too!

Raintree HOTEL **$$$**
(Map p1008; ☎24304050; www.raintreehotels. com; 120 St Mary's Rd, Alwarpet; s ₹10,000-12,500, d ₹11,250-13,750, all incl breakfast; ✳@🛜) 🛥
At this 'ecosensitive' hotel, floors are made of bamboo or rubber, water and electricity conservation hold pride of place, and the heat generated by the AC warms the bathroom water. The sleek, minimalist rooms are stylish and comfortable, and the rooftop supports a sea-view infinity pool (which doubles as insulation) as well as a restaurant.

 Eating

Chennai is packed with inexpensive 'meals' joints, serving thalis for lunch and dinner, and tiffin (snacks) such as *idlis* and dosas for the rest of the day. It's feasible to eat every meal at Chennai's 20 Hotel Saravana Bhavan restaurants, where you can count on quality vegetarian food. In the Muslim area around Triplicane High Rd you'll find great biryani joints every few steps.

Classier and more stylish Indian restaurants are growing in number, and international cuisines have finally taken off in Chennai, so there's a reasonable choice of more upmarket eating. Big top-end hotels always have a variety of reliably good eating options.

Useful supermarkets for picking up your own supplies include **Spencer's** (Map p1008; 15 EVK Sampath Salai, Vepery; ⏰9am-10pm), not too far from Egmore and Central stations, **Big Bazaar** (Map p1008; 34 Sir Thyagaraya Rd; ⏰10.30am-9.30pm) in T Nagar and **Nilgiri's** (Map p1008; 14 Wallace Garden 3rd St, Nungambakkam; ⏰10am-8pm) off Nungambakkam High Rd.

✗ Egmore

★**Hotel Saravana Bhavan** INDIAN **$**
(Map p1012; www.saravanabhavan.com; 21 Kennet Lane; mains ₹60-150; ⏰6am-10pm) Dependably delish, lunchtime and evening South Indian thali 'meals' at the Saravana Bhavans usually run ₹80 to ₹100. This famous Chennai vegetarian chain is also excellent for South Indian breakfasts (*idlis* and *vadas* for ₹49), ice cream, filter coffee and other Indian vegetarian fare including biryanis and pilaus. Branches include **George Town** (Map p1008; 209 NSC Bose Rd; ⏰6am-10.30pm), **Triplicane** (Map p1012; Shanthi Theatre Complex, 44 Anna Salai; ⏰7am-11pm), **Thousand Lights** (Map p1012; 293 Peter's Rd; ⏰11.30am-11pm), **Mylapore** (Map p1008; 70 North Mada St; ⏰6am-11pm) and **T Nagar** (Map p1008; 102 Sir Thyagaraya Rd; ⏰6am-11pm), not to mention London, Paris and New York! The Thousand Lights branch is more upscale than most, with silver cutlery.

Annalakshmi INDIAN **$$**
(Map p1012; ☎28525109; www.annalakshmichennai.co.in; 1st fl, Sigapi Achi Bldg, 18/3 Rukmani Lakshmipathy Rd; mains ₹180-240, set/buffet lunch ₹575/400; ⏰noon-3pm & 7-9pm) Very fine

South and North Indian vegetarian fare in a beautiful dining room adorned with carvings and paintings, inside a high-rise behind the Air India building. The buffet option is served in another part of the same premises. Annalakshmi is run by devotees of Swami Shanthanand Saraswathi; proceeds support medical programs for the poor.

Basil   MULTICUISINE $$
(Map p1012; Fortel, 3 Gandhi Irwin Rd; mains ₹150-250; ⊙7am-11pm) This restaurant at the Fortel hotel has an impressive Western breakfast range, if you're really after hash browns, as well as tasty North Indian and Continental dishes in a pleasant setting.

✕ Triplicane & Around

Ratna Café   SOUTH INDIAN $
(Map p1012; 255 Triplicane High Rd; dishes ₹25-70; ⊙6am-10.30pm) Though often crowded and cramped, Ratna is renowned for its scrumptious *idlis* and the hearty doses of *sambar* that go with it – people sit down to this ₹26.50 dish at all times of day.

A2B   SOUTH INDIAN $
(Map p1012; 47/23 Bharathi Salai; mains ₹75-110; ⊙6am-11.30pm) Sit down to South Indian classics or veg biryani in the clean AC hall upstairs, or get a big choice of sweets downstairs. If you've got any room left, head to nearby **Natural Fresh** (Map p1008; 35 Bharathi Salai; scoop ₹50-60; ⊙11am-11pm) for excellent ice cream.

Express Avenue Garden   MULTICUISINE $$
(Map p1012; Express Avenue Shopping Centre, White's Rd, Royapettah; dishes ₹100-300; ⊙10am-11pm) This food court on the top floor of Chennai's newest shopping mall has about 30 Indian and international outlets. With picture windows and trees in pots it's quite a pleasant place for a bite.

✕ Nungambakkam & Around

Kumarakom   KERALAN $$
(Map p1008; www.kumarakomrestaurant.com; 9 Kodambakkam High Rd; mains ₹75-300; ⊙noon-4pm & 6.30-11pm) You may have to queue for a table at this popular Keralan restaurant with dark-wood furniture, cool AC and busy waiters. The seafood is the standout – try the prawns masala or *karimeen pollichat-*

thu (pearl-spot fish marinated and steamed in a banana leaf) – but everything's fresh and tasty.

★ Tuscana Pizzeria   ITALIAN $$$
(Map p1008; ☑45038008; www.tuscana.in; 19, 3rd St, Wallace Garden; pizzas & pasta ₹315-690; ⊙noon-11.30pm) This, my pizza-loving friends, is the real deal, and Chennai has embraced it enthusiastically. Tuscana serves authentic thin-crust pizzas with toppings such as prosciutto, as well as interesting takes such as hoison chicken pizza. Pasta and desserts are also top-notch. There's another branch, **Tuscana on Chamiers** (Map p1008; ☑45000008; www.tuscanaonchamiers.in; 89 Chamiers Rd, Alwarpet; ⊙12.30-3.15pm & 6.30-11.15pm), in Alwarpet. Reservations are a good idea at both.

Kryptos by Willi   GREEK $$$
(Map p1008; ☑45038001; www.kryptosbywilli.com; Basement, Yafa Tower, Khader Nawaz Khan Rd; mains ₹380-690; ⊙12.30-3.30pm & 6.30-11.30pm) From the same stable as the nearby Tuscana Pizzeria comes another successfully authentic Mediterranean restaurant. There's good seafood as well as Greek favourites such as *spanakopita* (spinach and cheese pastries), souvlaki and baklava.

Raintree   CHETTINAD $$$
(Map p1012; www.vivantabytaj.com; Vivanta by Taj – Connemara, Binny Rd; mains ₹475-700; ⊙12.30-2.45pm & 7.30-11.40pm) This hotel restaurant is probably the best place in Chennai to savour the delicious flavours of Tamil Nadu's Chettinadu region. Chettiar cuisine is superbly spicy without being chilli-laden, and includes a good number of meat dishes. In good weather you can sit out in the leafy courtyard.

✕ South Chennai

Murugan Idly Shop   SOUTH INDIAN $
(Map p1008; 77 GN Chetty Rd, T Nagar; dishes ₹25-75; ⊙7am-11.30pm) Those in the know generally agree this particular branch of the small chain serves some of the best *idlis* and South Indian meals in town. We heartily concur.

★ Eco Cafe   MULTICUISINE $$
(Map p1008; Chamiers, 106 Chamiers Rd, RA Puram; mains ₹250-375, breakfasts ₹175-305; ⊙8.30am-9.30pm) This 1st-floor cafe feels a continent

away from Chennai, except that Chennai-ites love it too. Leafy wallpaper, leaves through the windows, discreetly spaced tables, wonderful banana nut bread and cappuccino, English breakfasts, American pancakes, pasta, quesadillas, waffles, salads...

Enté Keralam   KERALAN $$

(Map p1008; 32216591; www.orientalcuisines.in; 1 Kasturi Estate 1st St, Poes Garden; mains ₹175-475; noon-3pm & 7.30-11.30pm) A calm ambience prevails in the four orange-toned rooms of this Keralan restaurant, holding just three or four tables each. Try the lightly spiced *pachakkari* vegetable stew or *kozhi porichatu* (deep-fried marinated chicken) and wind up with *paal ada payasam*, a kind of sweet rice pudding.

★ Copper Chimney   NORTH INDIAN $$$

(Map p1008; 28115770; 74 Cathedral Rd, Gopalapuram; mains ₹200-575; noon-3pm & 7-11.30pm) The vegetarian dishes aren't the priority here, but meat eaters will drool over the yummy North Indian tandoori dishes served in stylishly minimalist surroundings. The *machchi* tikka – skewers of tandoori-baked fish – is superb.

Dakshin   SOUTH INDIAN $$$

(Map p1008; Sheraton Park Hotel, 132 TTK Rd, Alwarpet; mains ₹550-900; 12.30-2.45pm & 7-11.15pm) Dakshin specialises in the cuisine of the four states of South India. Traditional sculptures set the scene, and flute and tabla musicians play nightly except Monday. Food suggestion: the Andhra Pradesh fish curry.

🍷 Drinking & Nightlife

Cafes

Café Coffee Day (www.cafecoffeeday.com; 9am-11pm) provides a range of reliably good hot and cold coffees and teas for ₹60 to ₹120, and usually some tempting cakes, in pleasant ambience at several locations, including **Egmore** (Map p1012; Alsa Mall, Montieth Rd), **Vepery** (Map p1012; 92 Dr Alagappa Rd), **Nungambakkam** (Map p1008; Khader Nawaz Khan Rd) and **Express Avenue Mall** (Map p1012; 1st, 2nd & 3rd fl, Express Avenue Mall, White's Rd).

Bars & Nightclubs

Chennai has possibly the most liberal licensing laws in India – for five-star hotels. Bars and clubs at these hotels can serve alcohol 24 hours a day, seven days a week, and so that's where most of the jumping joints are found. Other hotel bars mostly close at midnight. There are very few salubrious places to get a drink without loud music after about 6pm. For listings see www.timescity.com/chennai.

Zara the Tapas Bar   BAR

(Map p1008; 28111462; zaratapasbar.in; 71 Cathedral Rd; cocktails ₹400-500, tapas ₹225-375; 12.30-3pm & 6.30pm-midnight) Where else in the world would you find DJs playing club music beneath bullfight posters next to TVs showing cricket? Zara is packed with a happy 20s and 30s crowd most nights. There's a small space to dance but most of the acreage is occupied by tables, and it's a good idea to reserve one. And the tapas? The *jamón serrano* is sacrilegiously minced into a paste, but the *tortilla española* is authentically good.

Leather Bar   BAR

(Map p1008; Park Hotel, 601 Anna Salai; 11am-4am) 'Leather' refers to floor and wall coverings rather than anything kinky. This tiny, modish pad has mixologists serving up fancy drinks and DJs spinning dance tunes from around 9pm. How half of Chennai fits into it on Friday and Saturday nights is a mystery.

Dublin   PUB, NIGHTCLUB

(Map p1008; Sheraton Park Hotel, 132 TTK RD, Alwarpet; nightclub per person ₹1500; from 6pm Wed-Sat) A long-running favourite with 30- and 40-somethings, including a fair sprinkling of expats, this Irish pub and nightclub has three levels of dancing and music from hip hop to Bollywood. Until 10pm it's a pub, then it becomes a club, alive to 2am or 3am on Saturday nights. No unaccompanied men, or 'stags' as they call them.

10 Downing Street   PUB

(10D; Map p1008; North Boag Rd, T Nagar; drinks ₹250-500, food ₹200-650; noon-midnight) An English-themed pub (pictures of Big Ben on the wall, fish fingers on the menu) with a small dance floor, 10D is often packed with a mixed bag of 20s-to-40s professionals and some expats. Wednesday is Ladies' Night (free drinks for women), Friday Retro Night ('70s/'80s) and Saturday Club Night.

Pasha   NIGHTCLUB

(Map p1008; Park Hotel, 601 Anna Salai; men ₹2000 incl ₹500 drink voucher, women free; 9pm-4am Wed-Mon) A fashionable, mostly 20s, even late-teens bunch crowds into this two-level, Moroccan-themed club and tries to get onto the small dance floor.

☆ Entertainment

There's *bharatanatyam* (Tamil classical dance) and/or a Carnatic music concert going on somewhere in Chennai almost every evening. Check listings in the *Hindu* or *Times of India*, or the website www.timescity.com/chennai. The **Music Academy** (Map p1008; ☑ 28112231; www.musicacademymadras.in; 168 (old 306) TTK Rd, Royapettah) is the most popular venue; the Kalakshetra Foundation (p1011) and **Bharatiya Vidya Bhavan** (Map p1008; ☑ 24643420; www.bhavanchennai.org; East Mada St, Mylapore) also stage many events, often free.

🔒 Shopping

Thyagaraya Nagar (aka T Nagar) has great shopping, especially at Pondy Bazaar and around Panagal Park. Nungambakkam's shady Khader Nawaz Khan Rd is a pleasant lane of designer shops, cafes and galleries.

The best shopping malls include **Express Avenue** (Map p1012; White's Rd), **Chennai Citi Centre** (Map p1008; 10 Dr Radhakrishnan Salai, Mylapore) and **Spencer Plaza** (Map p1012; Anna Salai), all full of major international and Indian apparel chains. They normally open from 10am to 9pm. Spencer Plaza is a bit downmarket from the others, and includes many smaller craft and souvenir shops.

Handicrafts

Srushti (Map p1008; www.srushtihandicrafts.com; 86 Chamiers Rd, Alwarpet; ⊙10.30am-8.30pm) is an artisan outlet with some very good (and some less good) bronze and wooden sculptures, and **Shilpi** (Map p1008; 29 CP Ramaswamy Rd, Alwarpet; ⊙10am-8pm) has beautiful saris, salwars and kurtas in silk and cotton.

Fabindia CLOTHING, HANDICRAFTS
(Map p1012; www.fabindia.com; Woods Rd; ⊙10.30am-8.30pm) This nationwide chain sells attractively contemporary, village-made crafts. This branch has ceramics, table and bed linen and personal care products, as well as fabulous clothes. Fabindia is also at **Spencer Plaza** (Map p1012; 2nd fl, Phase 3, Spencer Plaza, Anna Salai; ⊙11am-8.30pm), **Express Avenue** (Map p1012; 1st fl, Express Avenue Mall, White's Rd; ⊙11am-9pm) and **T Nagar** (Map p1008; 84 GN Chetty Rd, T Nagar; ⊙10.30am-8.30pm).

Naturally Auroville HANDICRAFTS
(Map p1008; 8 Khader Nawaz Khan Rd, Nungambakkam; ⊙10am-8pm Mon-Sat, 11.30am-7.30pm Sun) *Objets* (pottery, bedspreads, scented candles) and a few teas, cheeses and pastries, all from Auroville, near Puducherry.

Chamiers CLOTHING, HANDICRAFTS
(Map p1008; 106 Chamiers Rd, RA Puram; ⊙10am-8pm) Upstairs, next to the Eco Cafe, is a shop with some original gifts including witty Chennaigaga T-shirts. Downstairs is **Anokhi** (Map p1008; ☑24311495; 85/47 Chamiers Rd; ⊙10am-8pm), with wonderful and well-priced hand-block-printed and other clothes in light fabrics.

Poompuhar HANDICRAFTS
(Map p1012; 108 Anna Salai; ⊙10am-8pm Mon-Sat, 11am-7pm Sun) This large branch of the fixed-price state-government handicrafts chain is good for everything from cheap technicolor plaster deities to a ₹200,000, 1m-high bronze Nataraja.

Silk

Many of the finest Kanchipuram silks turn up in Chennai, and the streets around Panagal Park are filled with silk shops; if you're lucky enough to be attending an Indian wedding this is where you buy your sari.

Nalli Silks TEXTILES
(Map p1008; www.nalli.com; 9 Nageswaran Rd, T Nagar; ⊙9.30am-9.30pm) The huge, super-colourful granddaddy of silk shops, with a jewellery branch next door.

Kumaran Silks TEXTILES
(Map p1008; 12 Nageswaran Rd, T Nagar; ⊙9.30am-9.30pm) Saris, saris (including 'budget saris') and plenty of Kanchipuram silk.

Bookshops

Higginbothams BOOKS
(Map p1012; higginbothams@vsnl.com; 116 Anna Salai; ⊙9am-8pm Mon-Sat, 10.30am-7.30pm Sun) Open since 1844, this is reckoned to be India's oldest bookshop. It has a decent English-language selection, including Lonely Planet guides, and a good range of maps.

Oxford Bookstore BOOKS
(Map p1008; www.oxfordbookstore.com; 39/12 Haddows Rd, Nungambakkam; ⊙9.30am-9.30pm) A big English-language selection and a nice cafe.

Landmark BOOKS
(Map p1012; www.landmarkonthenet.com; 1st fl, Phase II, Spencer Plaza, Anna Salai; ⊙10.30am-9pm) Landmark has several large shops selling DVDs and CDs as well as lots of English-

TAMIL NADU & CHENNAI CHENNAI (MADRAS)

language books. Also at **Thousand Lights** (Map p1008; Apex Plaza, Nungambakkam High Rd; ◷10.30am-9.30pm) and **Mylapore** (Map p1008; Chennai Citi Centre, Dr Radhakrishnan Rd; ◷10.30am-9pm).

Information

INTERNET ACCESS

'Browsing centres' are dotted all over town.

Cyber Palace (Map p1012; 114 Bharathi Salai; per hr ₹25; ◷8am-10.30pm)

Internet (Map p1012; 6 Gandhi Irwin Rd, Egmore; per hr ₹30; ◷7.30am-10pm) In the Hotel Imperial yard.

LEFT LUGGAGE

Egmore and Central train stations have left-luggage offices (signed 'Cloakroom') for those with journey tickets. The airport also has left-luggage facilities.

MEDICAL SERVICES

Apollo Hospital (Map p1012; ☑28293333, emergency 1066; www.apollohospitals.com; 21 Greams Lane) State-of-the-art, expensive hospital popular with 'medical tourists'.

St Isabel's Hospital (Map p1008; ☑24991081; www.stisabelshospital.in; 49 Oliver Rd, Mylapore) Affordable quality care.

MONEY

ATMs are everywhere, including at Central train station, the airport and the main bus station.

Thomas Cook (Map p1012; Phase I, Spencer Plaza, Anna Salai; ◷10am-6pm Mon-Sat, 10am-4pm Sun) Charges only ₹50 commission on all foreign cash exchanges. Also changes American Express travellers cheques.

POST

DHL (Map p1012; ☑42148886; www.dhl.co.in; 85 VVV Sq, Pantheon Rd, Egmore; ◷8am-11pm Mon-Sat, 9am-6pm Sun) For secure international parcel delivery. There are several branches around town.

Main Post Office (Map p1008; Rajaji Salai, George Town; ◷8am-8.30pm Mon-Sat, 10am-6pm Sun)

TOURIST INFORMATION

Indiatourism (Map p1012; ☑28460285; www. incredibleindia.org; 154 Anna Salai; ◷9am-6pm Mon-Fri) Maps and information on all of India; helpful on Chennai too.

 ATMS

Axis Bank, Canara Bank, HDFC Bank, ICICI Bank and State Bank of India ATMs are the best for withdrawing cash with foreign cards in Tamil Nadu.

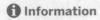 **HOLIDAY TRANSPORT**

All kinds of transport in, to and from Tamil Nadu can get booked up weeks in advance for the periods around major festivals including Pongal, Karthikai Deepam and Diwali. Plan ahead.

Tamil Nadu Tourism Development Corporation (TTDC; Map p1012; ☑25383333; www. tamilnadutourism.org; Tamil Nadu Tourism Complex, 2 Wallajah Rd, Triplicane; ◷24hr) The state tourism body's main office takes bookings for its own bus tours and mediocre hotels, and also answers questions and hands out a few leaflets. In the same building are state tourist offices from all over India, mostly open 9am to 6pm Monday to Friday. The TTDC has 24-hour office (Map p1012; ☑25384356; 4 Poonamallee High Rd; ◷24hr) near Central train station and counters at Central and Egmore stations.

TRAVEL AGENCIES

Milesworth Travel (Map p1008; ☑24320522; http://milesworth.com; RM Towers, 108 Chamiers Rd, Alwarpet; ◷9.30am-6pm Mon-Sat) A very professional and amiable agency that can help with just about any travel need you have.

Getting There & Away

AIR

Chennai Airport (☑22560551) is at Tirusulam in the far southwest of the city. A brand-new domestic terminal was due to open soon, with the international terminal expanding to occupy the whole of the old building.

There are direct flights to over 20 Indian cities, including Trichy, Madurai, Coimbatore and Thoothikudi (Tuticorin) within Tamil Nadu. Internationally, Chennai has plenty of direct flights to/from Colombo, Singapore, Kuala Lumpur and Bangkok, as well as the Gulf states. The best fares from Europe are often on Jet Airways (with connections at Mumbai or Delhi) or Emirates (via Dubai). Cathay Pacific flies to Hong Kong, and Maldivian to Male.

Airlines

Air Asia (Map p1008; ☑33008000; www. airasia.com; Ispahani Centre, 123/12 Nungambakkam High Rd; ◷9.30am-1pm & 2-6pm Mon-Fri, 9.30am-1.30pm Mon-Sat)

Air India (Map p1012; ☑23453301; www. airindia.com; 19 Rukmani Lakshmipathy Rd, Egmore; ◷9.30am-1pm & 2-5.15pm Mon-Sat)

Air India Express (Map p1012; ☑23453375; www.airindiaexpress.in; 19 Rukmani Lakshmipathy Rd, Egmore; ◷9.30am-1pm & 2-5.15pm Mon-Sat)

TAMIL NADU & CHENNAI CHENNAI (MADRAS)

Emirates (Map p1008; ☑33773377; www.
emirates.com; 1st fl, Riaz Garden, 12 & 13 Kodambakkam High Rd; ⊙9am-5.30pm Mon-Sat)

Go Air (☎1800 222111, 22560293; www.goair.in)

IndiGo (☑09910383838; www.goindigo.in)

Jet Airways (Map p1012; ☑39893333; www.
jetairways.com; 43/44 Montieth Rd, Egmore;
⊙10am-6pm Mon-Sat)

JetKonnect (☑39893333; www.jetkonnect.
com)

Malaysia Airlines (Map p1008; ☑42191919;
www.malaysiaairlines.com; 90 Dr Radhakrishnan Salai; ⊙9am-5.30pm Mon-Sat)

Maldivian (Map p1012; ☑45028833; www.mal
divian.aero; Spencer's Travel Services, Lakshmi
Bhavan, Sundaram Ave, 609 Anna Salai)

SilkAir & Singapore Airlines (Map p1008;
☑45921921; www.silkair.com; Westmin-
ster, 108 Dr Radhakrishnan Salai, Mylapore;
⊙9.15am-5.45pm Mon-Fri, 9.15am-1pm Sat)

SpiceJet (☎1800 1803333; cpioojct.com)

SriLankan Airlines (Map p1008; ☑43921241;
www.srilankan.com; 4 Kodambakkam High Rd;
⊙9am-5.30pm Mon-Sat, 9am-1pm Sun)

Thai Airways International (Map p1012;
☑42063311; www.thaiair.com; 4th fl, KGN
Towers, Ethiraj Rd, Egmore; ⊙9.30am-5.30pm
Mon-Fri)

BOAT

Passenger ships sail from the George Town
harbour direct to Port Blair in the Andaman
Islands twice a month. The Andaman Shipping
Office Ticketing Counter (p1087) sells tickets
(₹2160 to ₹8420) for the 60-hour trip. Book
several days ahead to ensure a place, and take
three copies each of your passport data page
and Indian visa. It can be a long process.

BUS

Most government buses operate from the
large but surprisingly orderly CMBT (Chennai

MOVING ON?

For further information, head to shop
.lonelyplanet.com to purchase a downloadable PDF of the West Coast chapter
from Lonely Planet's *Sri Lanka* guide.

Mofussil Bus Terminus; Jawaharlal Nehru Rd,
Koyambedu), 6km west of the centre. The most
comfortable and expensive are the AC buses,
followed by the UD ('Ultra Deluxe'), and these
can generally be reserved in advance. The T
Nagar Bus Terminus (Map p1008; South Usman
Rd) has a few daily departures to Bengaluru,
Madurai, Mysore, Thanjavur and Trichy, plus bus
599 to Mamallapuram (₹27, two hours, about
hourly).

Private buses offer generally greater comfort than non-AC government buses to many
destinations, at up to double the price. Service
information is available at www.redbus.in, and
tickets can be booked at many travel agencies.
Their main terminal is the Omni Bus Stand (off
Kaliamman Koil St, Koyambedu), 500m west of
the CMBT, but some companies also pick up and
drop off elsewhere in the city. Parveen Travels,
for example, has services to Ernakulam (Kochi),
Kodaikanal, Madurai, Puducherry, Trichy and
Trivandrum for which it picks up passengers at
its Egmore office (Map p1012; ☑28193538;
www.parveentravels.com; 11/5 Kennet Lane,
Egmore).

CAR

Renting a car with a driver is the easiest way
of going almost anywhere and is easily arranged through most travel agents, midrange
or top-end hotels, or the airport's prepaid taxi
desks. Sample rates for non-AC/AC cars are
₹1300/1550 to Mamallapuram (Mahabalipuram) and ₹2700/3200 to Puducherry.

TAMIL NADU & CHENNAI CHENNAI (MADRAS)

NONSTOP DOMESTIC FLIGHTS FROM CHENNAI

DESTINATION	AIRLINES	FARE FROM (₹, ONE WAY)	DURATION (HR)	FREQUENCY (DAILY)
Bengaluru	AI, SG, S2, 6E	2668	1	8
Delhi	AI, SG, 6E, 9W	4840	2¾	16
Goa	AI, SG	2668	1¼-2	1-2
Hyderabad	AI, SG, S2, 6E	2668	1-1½	13
Kochi	SG, S2, 9W	2668	1½	6
Kolkata	AI, SG, S2, 6E	4137	2¼	8
Mumbai	AI, G8, SG, 6E, 9W	4136	2	16
Port Blair	AI, G8, SG, 9W	4137	2¼	4
Trivandrum	AI, SG, 6E, 9W	2668	1¼	5

Airline codes: AI – Air India, G8 – Go Air, SG – SpiceJet, S2 – JetKonnect, 6E – IndiGo, 9W – Jet Airways

GOVERNMENT BUSES FROM CMBT

DESTINATION	FARE (₹)	DURATION (HR)	FREQUENCY
Bengaluru	355-650	8	60 daily
Coimbatore	420	11	10 daily (6pm to 10pm)
Ernakulam (Kochi)	565	16	3pm
Kanchipuram	47	2	38 daily
Kodaikanal	495	13	5pm
Madurai	350-420	10	33 daily
Mamallapuram	80	2	every 30min
Mysore	530-900	11	7 daily (7pm to 11.30pm)
Ooty	430	13	4.30pm, 5.45pm, 7.15pm
Puducherry	100	4	every 30min
Thanjavur	260-340	8½	40 daily
Tirupathi	100-180	4	55 daily
Trichy	260-300	7	every 30min
Trivandrum	570	16	hourly, 10am to 9pm
Vellore	81	3½	58 daily

TRAIN

Interstate trains and those heading west generally depart from Central station, while trains heading south mostly leave from Egmore. The **advance reservations office** (Map p1012; 1st fl, Chennai Central local station; ☺ 8am-8pm Mon-Sat, 8am-2pm Sun), with its extremely helpful Foreign Tourist Cell, is in a separate 11-storey building just west of the main Central station building. The **Passenger Reservation Office** (Map p1012; ☑ 28194579) at Egmore station keeps the same hours.

🛈 Getting Around

TO/FROM THE AIRPORT

The Chennai Metro Rail system, expected to open in 2014, will provide a cheap and easy link between the airport and city. Meanwhile, the cheapest option is a suburban train to or from Tirusulam station, connected by a pedestrian underpass to the parking areas outside the international terminal. Trains run several times hourly from 4am to midnight to/from Chennai Beach station (₹7, 42 minutes) with stops including Kodambakkam, Egmore, Chennai Park and Chennai Fort.

Prepaid taxi kiosks at the airport charge ₹380/515 for a non-AC/AC cab to Egmore, and slightly less to T Nagar.

AUTORICKSHAW

The city authorities have been trying to negotiate a deal with autorickshaw drivers for fixed fares of ₹10 per kilometre, with a minimum charge of ₹20. If no deal eventuates, drivers will doubtless continue refusing to use their meters and instead quote astronomical fares for locals and tourists alike: you can expect to pay at least ₹40 for a short trip down the road, around ₹80 for a 3km trip and ₹100 to ₹120 for 5km. Prices are at least 25% higher after 10pm. There are prepaid booths outside the CMBT (₹160 to Egmore) and Central station.

BUS

Chennai's city bus system is worth getting to know, although buses get packed to overflowing at busy times. Fares are between ₹3 and ₹14 (up to double for express and deluxe services, and multiplied by five for AC services). Route information is online at http://busroutes.in/chennai. See also p1024.

METRO RAIL

Chennai Metro Rail, a new, part-underground rapid transit system, is expected to open in 2014 and should make moving around the city significantly easier. Line 1 goes from the airport to Teynampet, Thousand Lights, Central train station, the High Court and Washermanpet in the north of the city, running beneath Anna Salai for several kilometres. Line 2 goes from Central train station west to Egmore and the CMBT then south to St Thomas Mount.

TRAIN

Efficient, cheap suburban trains run from Beach station to Fort, Park (near Central station), Egmore, Chetpet, Nungambakkam, Kodambakkam, Mambalam, Saidapet, Guindy, St Thomas Mount, Tirusulam (for the airport), and on down to Tambaram. At Egmore station, the suburban platforms (10 and 11) and ticket offfice are on the north side of station. A second line branches south after Fort to Parktown, Chepauk, Tiruvallikeni (for Marina Beach), Light House and Thirumailai (near Kapaleeshwarar Temple). Trains run from 4am to midnight, several times hourly; rides cost between ₹4 and ₹7.

NORTHERN TAMIL NADU

Chennai to Mamallapuram

Chennai's sprawl peters out after an hour or so heading south on the East Coast Road (ECR), at which point Tamil Nadu becomes green fields, trees, red dirt, blue skies and not a few towns and villages (or, if you take the 'IT Expressway' inland, huge new buildings).

There's a tropical bohemian groove floating around Injambakkam village, site of the **Cholamandal Artists' Village** (☎044-24490092; Injambakkam; museum ₹20; ⏲museum & galleries 9am-6.30pm), 10km south of the Adyar River. This 3-hectare artists' cooperative – founded in 1966 by artists of

the Madras Movement, pioneers of modern art in South India – is a serene muse away from the world, and the art in its museum and galleries is very much worth inspection. Look especially for work by KCS Paniker, SG Vasudev, M Senathipathi and S Nandagopal. You can have a very good Iranian meal in a lovely garden at **Shiraz** (mains ₹150-300, Sunday lunch buffet ₹600; ⏲11am-11pm Wed-Mon), just along the lane past the museum.

As Cholamandal is to contemporary artistic expression, **DakshinaChitra** (☎044-27472603; www.dakshinachitra.net; East Coast Rd, Muttukadu; Indian adult/student ₹75/30, foreign ₹200/70; ⏲10am-6pm Wed-Mon), 12km further south, is to South India's traditional arts and crafts. This jumble of open-air museum, traditional architecture, artisan workshops (including pottery, silk weaving, puppet building and basket making) and live theatre and dance performances is another stop that's well worth it (including for kids).

Kovalam, a fishing village 4km south of DakshinaChitra, has probably the best surfing waves on the Tamil Nadu coast. Waves get up to 2m and rides of 200m aren't uncommon. For classes or surf companionship,

MAJOR TRAINS FROM CHENNAI

DESTINATION	TRAIN NO & NAME	FARE (₹)	DURATION (HR)	DEPARTURE
Bengaluru	12007 Shatabdi Express*	529/1155	5	6am CC
	12609 Chennai-Bangalore Intercity Express	110/386	6½	1.35pm CC
Coimbatore	12675 Kovai Express	132/488	7½	6.15am CC
	12671 Nilgiri Express	232/616/910	7½	9.15pm CC
Delhi	12621 Tamil Nadu Express	528/1482/2375	33	10pm CC
Goa	17311 Vasco Express (Friday only)	343/971/1500	22	2.10pm CC
Hyderabad	12759 Charminar Express	312/854/1285	14	6.10pm CC
Kochi	16041 Alleppey Express	275/770/955	12¼	8.45pm CC
Kolkata	12842 Coromandel Express	461/1242/1955	27	8.45am CC
Madurai	12635 Vaigai Express	132/488	8	1.20pm CE
	12637 Pandyan Express	232/594/880	9	9.20pm CE
Mumbai	11042 Mumbai Express	383/1085/1700	26	11.55am CC
Mysore	12007 Shatabdi Express*	679/1470	7	6am CC
	16222 Kaveri Express	212/564/850	10¼	9.30pm CC
Tirupathi	16053 Tirupathi Express	60/206	3¼	1.50pm CC
Trichy	12635 Vaigai Express	104/381	5	1.20pm CE
Trivandrum	12623 Trivandrum Mail	337/925/1405	15¾	7.45pm CC

Departure codes: CC – Chennai Central, CE – Chennai Egmore
*Daily except Wednesday
Shatabdi fares: chair/executive; Express and Mail fares are 2nd/chair car for day trains, sleeper/3AC/2AC for overnight trains

look up villager Murthy, Kovalam's original local surf pioneer, who runs the 'social surfing school' **Kovelong Point** (☎9840975916; www.covelongpoint.com).

Madras Crocodile Bank (☎044-27472447; www.madrascrocodilebank.org; Vadanemmeli; adult/child ₹35/10, camera/video ₹20/100; ⏱8.30am-5.30pm Tue-Sun) 🍴, 6km on down the ECR from Kovalam, is a fascinating peep into a world of reptiles, and an incredible conservation and research trust to boot. With 18 of the world's 23 species of crocodilian (crocodiles and similar creatures) now here, the Bank does crucial work in maintaining genetic reserves of these animals, several of which are endangered. There are thousands of reptiles here, including gharials (a rare North Indian river crocodilian with a long, thin snout), Indian muggers (a marsh croc) and saltwater crocs of the Andaman and Nicobar Islands – plus turtles, tortoises and snakes. The Croc Bank has openings for volunteers with an interest in wildlife (minimum two weeks): email volunteer.mcbt@gmail.com for more information if you're interested.

Nine kilometres past the Croc Bank (just 5km short of Mamallapuram), the **Tiger Cave** (Saluvankuppam; admission free; ⏱6am-6pm) is an unfinished but impressive rock-cut shrine, probably dating from the 7th century. What's special is the 'necklace' of 11 monstrous heads framing its central shrine-cavity. At the north end of the parklike grounds is a rock-cut **Shiva shrine** from the same era. Just beyond this, outside the fence, lies the recently excavated **Subrahmanya Temple**, comprising an 8th-century granite shrine built over a Sangam-era brick temple dedicated to Murugan, which is one of the two oldest known temples in Tamil Nadu.

To reach these places, take any bus heading south from Chennai to Mamallapuram and ask to be let off at the appropriate point(s). Another option is the TTDC's Chennai–Mamallapuram round-trip bus tour (₹275, 10 hours), which visits several of the sites as well as Mamallapuram itself. A full-day taxi tour from Chennai costs around ₹3000. It's unwise to swim along the coast because of strong currents and tides.

Mamallapuram (Mahabalipuram)

☎ 044 / POP 17,666

Mamallapuram was the major seaport of the ancient Pallava kingdom based at Kanchipuram, and a wander round the town's great, World Heritage-listed temples and carvings inflames the imagination, especially at sunset.

CHENNAI BUS ROUTES

BUS NO	ROUTE
A1	Central–Anna Salai–Rd (Mylapore) –Theosophical Society–Thiruvanmiyur
1B	Parry's–Central–Anna Salai–Airport
10A	Parry's–Central–Egmore(S)–Pantheon Rd–T Nagar
11	Broadway–Central–Anna Salai–T Nagar
12	TNagar–Pondy Bazaar–Eldham's Rd–Vivekananda House
15B &15F	Broadway–Central–Egmore (N)–CMBT
21H	Broadway–FortSt George–Kamarajar Salai–San Thome Cathedral–Theosophical Society
27B	CMBT–Egmore(N)–Central–Bharathi Salai (Triplicane)
27C	TNagar–CMBT
27D	Egmore(S)–Anna Salai–Cathedral Rd–Dr Radhakrishnan Salai–San Thome Cathedral
32& 32A	Central–Triplicane High Rd–Vivekananda House

Routes operate in both directions.
Broadway – Broadway Bus Terminus, George Town
Central – Central Station
Egmore (N) – Egmore station (north side)
Egmore (S) – Egmore station (south side)
Parry's – Parry's Corner
T Nagar – T Nagar Bus Terminus

And then, in addition to ancient archaeological wonders, there's the traveller ghetto of Othavadai and Othavadai Cross Sts. Restaurants serve pasta, pizza and pancakes, shops sell hand sanitiser and things from Tibet, and you know you have landed, once again, in the Kingdom of Backpackistan.

'Mahabs', as some call it, is only two hours by bus from Chennai, and many travellers make a beeline straight here. The town is small and laid-back, and its sights can be explored on foot or by bicycle.

◉ Sights

You can easily spend a full day exploring Mamallapuram's marvellous temples and rock carvings. Most of them were carved from the rock in the 7th century during the reign of Pallava king Narasimhavarman I, whose nickname Mamalla (Great Wrestler) gave the town its name. Apart from the Shore Temple and Five Rathas, admission is free. Official Archaeological Survey of India guides can be hired at the sites for around ₹50; they're worth the money.

★**Shore Temple**　　　　　HINDU TEMPLE
(combined 1-day ticket with Five Rathas Indian/foreigner ₹10/250, video ₹25; ◉6am-6pm) Standing like a magnificent fist of rock-cut elegance overlooking the sea, the two-towered Shore Temple symbolises the heights of Pallava architecture and the maritime ambitions of the Pallava kings. Its small size belies its excellent proportion and the supreme quality of the carvings, many of which have been eroded into vaguely Impressionist embellishments. Built under Narasimhavarman II in the 8th century, it's the earliest significant free-standing stone temple in Tamil Nadu. The two towers rise above shrines to Shiva and their original linga (phallic symbols of Shiva) captured the sunrise and sunset. Between the Shiva shrines is one to Vishnu, shown sleeping.

★**Five Rathas**　　　　　HINDU TEMPLE
(Pancha Ratha; Five Rathas Rd; combined 1-day ticket with Shore Temple Indian/foreigner ₹10/250, video ₹25; ◉6am-6pm) Huddled together at the south end of Mamallapuram, the Five Rathas look like buildings, but they were, astonishingly, all carved from single large rocks. Each of these 7th-century temples was dedicated to a Hindu god and is now named after one or more of the Pandavas, the five hero-brothers of the epic Mahabharata, or

their common wife, Draupadi. Outside each one is a carving of its god's animal mount.

Ratha is Sanskrit for chariot, and may refer to the temples' form or to their function as vehicles for the gods. The *rathas* were hidden in the sand until excavated by the British 200 years ago. It's thought they didn't originally serve as actual places of worship, but were created as models for structures to be built elsewhere.

The first *ratha* on the left after you enter the gate is the **Draupadi Ratha**, in the form of a stylised South Indian hut. It's dedicated to the demon-fighting goddess Durga, who looks out from inside, standing on a lotus. A huge sculpted lion, Durga's mount, stands guard outside.

Next in line is the 'chariot' of the most important Pandava, the **Arjuna Ratha**, dedicated to Shiva. Its pilasters, miniature roof shrines, and small, octagonal dome make it a precursor of many later temples in South India. A huge Nandi bull, vehicle of Shiva, stands behind. Shiva (with Nandi) and other gods are depicted on the temple's outer walls.

The barrel-roofed **Bhima Ratha** was never completed, as is evidenced by the missing colonnade on its north side. Inside is a shrine to Vishnu. The **Dharmaraja Ratha**, tallest of the temples, is similar in form to the Arjuna Ratha but one storey higher. Large carvings on its outer walls mostly represent gods, including the androgynous Ardhanarishvara (half Shiva, half Parvati) on the east side. King Narasimhavarman I appears at the west end of the south side.

The **Nakula-Sahadeva Ratha** (named after two twin Pandavas) stands aside from the other four and is dedicated to Indra. The life-size stone elephant beside it is one of the most perfectly sculpted elephants in India. Approaching from the gate to the north you see its back end first, hence its nickname Gajaprishthakara (elephant's backside).

★**Arjuna's Penance**　　　HINDU, MONUMENT
(West Raja St) The crowning masterpiece of Mamallapuram's stonework, this giant relief carving is one of the greatest works of ancient art in India. Inscribed on a huge boulder, the Penance bursts with scenes of Hindu myth and everyday vignettes of South Indian life. In the centre *nagas,* or snake-beings, descend a cleft once filled with water, meant to represent the Ganges. To the left Arjuna performs self-mortification (fasting and standing on one leg), so that the

TAMIL NADU & CHENNAI MAMALLAPURAM (MAHABALIPURAM)

Mamallapuram (Mahabalipuram)

See Enlargement

four-armed Shiva will grant him his most powerful weapon, the god-slaying Pasupata. (Some scholars believe the carving shows not Arjuna but the sage Bagiratha, who did severe penance to obtain Shiva's help in bringing the Ganges to earth.) Shiva is attended by dwarves, and celestial beings fly across the upper parts of the carving, including the moon god (above Shiva) and sun god (right of the cleft) with orbs behind their heads. Below Arjuna/Bagiratha appears a temple to Vishnu, mythical ancestor of the Pallava kings. The many wonderfully carved animals include a small herd of elephants and – humour amid the holy – a cat performing penance to a crowd of appreciative mice.

South along the road from Arjuna's Penance are the **Panch Pandava Mandapa** (☉6.30am-6pm), an unfinished cave temple; the **Krishna Mandapa** (☉6.30am-6pm), with a famous carving depicting Krishna lifting Govardhana Hill above villagers and cows to protect them from a storm sent by the god Indra; an **unfinished relief carving** similar in size to Arjuna's Penance; and the **Dharmaraja Cave Temple** (☉6.30am-6pm).

◉ Mamallapuram Hill

Many interesting monuments are scattered over the rock-strewn hill on the west side of the town. It takes an hour or so to walk round the main ones. The hill area is open from 6am to 6pm and has two entrances: a northern one on West Raja St, and a southern one just off Five Rathas Rd.

Straight ahead inside the northern entrance you can't miss the huge boulder that bears the inspired name of **Krishna's Butterball**. Immovable, but apparently balancing precariously, it's a favourite photo opportunity. Pass between some rocks north of here to the **Trimurti Cave Temple**, honouring the Hindu 'trinity', with a shrine for

Mamallapuram (Mahabalipuram)

each deity: Brahma (left), Shiva (centre) and Vishnu (right). Around the back of the same rock is a beautiful group of carved elephants, with a monkey and peacock.

Back south of Krishna's Butterball you reach the **Ganesh Ratha**, carved from a single rock. Once a Shiva temple, it became a shrine to Ganesh (Shiva's elephant-headed son) after the original lingam was removed. Southwest of here, the **Varaha Mandapa** houses some of Mamallapuram's finest carvings. The left panel shows Vishnu's boar avatar, Varaha, lifting the earth out of the oceans. The outward-facing panels show Vishnu's consort Lakshmi (washed by elephants) and Durga, while the right-hand panel has Vishnu in his eight-armed giant form, Trivikrama, overcoming the demon king Bali.

A little further south, then up to the left, is the 16th-century **Raya Gopura** (Olakkanatha Temple), which is probably an unfinished *gopuram* (tall temple entrance tower). The main path continues south to the **Ramanuja Mandapa** and up to Mamallapuram's **lighthouse**, which offers fine panoramas. Just southwest of the lighthouse is the **Mahishamardini Mandapa**, carved from the rock with excellent scenes from the Puranas (Sanskrit stories from the 5th century AD).

The left-side panel shows Vishnu sleeping on the coils of a snake; on the right, Durga bestrides her lion vehicle while killing the demon-buffalo Mahisha. Inside the central shrine, Murugan is depicted sitting between his parents Shiva and Parvati.

🏃 Activities

Beach

The beach fronting the village isn't exactly pristine and gets downright grubby in some spots, but south of the Shore Temple it clears into very fine sand. You'll also be further away from the leers of men who spend their days gawking at tourists. Like most of Tamil Nadu's coast, these beaches are not great for swimming, as there are dangerous rips.

Therapies

Numerous places offer massage, reiki, yoga and ayurvedic practices.

Sri Durga (📞9840288280; sridurgamassageyoga1999@yahoo.com; 35 Othavadai St; 45min massage ₹700-900, 1hr yoga ₹200) offers massages and ayurvedic treatments (with male therapists for men and female for women), as well as yoga sessions at 7am and 7pm. Several other operators in town have similar rates and timings. As always, and especially for such an intimate service, ask fellow travellers, question the therapist carefully and if you have any misgivings, don't proceed.

The Radisson resort has a branch of the popular ayurvedic treatment centre Ayush as well as a spa with a wide range of massages, mud rubs and more – both open to nonguests.

👉 Tours

Hi! Tours
CYCLING, BIRDWATCHING

(☑27443360; www.hi-tours.com; 123 East Raja St; bicycle tours ₹350-400; ⊙9.30am-6pm Mon-Fri, 9.30am-2pm Sat) Runs half-day bicycle tours to nearby villages, observing activities like rice- and masala-grinding and kolam drawing (the 'welcome' patterns outside doorways, also called rangoli). It also organises day trips to places including Kanchipuram and Vedantangal Bird Sanctuary and can put together longer packages with reasonable prices on accommodation and transport.

🎊 Festivals & Events

Mamallapuram Dance Festival
DANCE

(⊙late Dec-late Jan) A four-week dance festival showcasing classical and folk dances from all over India, with many performances on an open-air stage against the imposing backdrop of Arjuna's Penance. Dances include the Bharata Natyam (Tamil Nadu), Kuchipudi (Andhra Pradesh) tribal dance, Kathakali (Kerala drama); there are also puppet shows and classical music performances. Performances are held only from Friday to Sunday.

🛏 Sleeping

Hotel Daphne
HOTEL $

(☑27442811; www.moonrakersrestaurants.com; 17 Othavadai Cross St; r ₹300-1500; ❄) Most of the Daphne's rooms are quite acceptable if nothing special, but the new, top-floor AC rooms 12 and 13 are great value, with four-poster beds, balconies and cane swing chairs. The leafy courtyard is another drawcard.

Tina Blue View
Lodge & Restaurant
GUESTHOUSE $

(☑27442319; 34 Othavadai St; s/d/tr ₹400/500/600) Tina is one of Mamallapuram's originals and kind of looks it, with some frayed and faded edges, but remains deservedly popular for its whitewashed walls, blue accents and tropically pleasant garden, as well as tireless original owner Xavier ('I am same age as Tony Wheeler!').

Sri Harul Guest House
GUESTHOUSE $

(Sea View Guest House; ☑9384620173; 181 Bajanai Koil St, Fishermen's Colony; r ₹500-1000) Surf crashes on to the rocks right below your balcony if you get one of the half-dozen seaview rooms at Sri Harul, one of the best of several seafront cheapies. Rooms are basic, medium-sized and quite clean.

La Vie en Rose
HOTEL $

(☑9444877544; Old College Rd; d without/with AC ₹700/1200; ❄) Simple, decent-sized, clean rooms (though a bit worn), a nice leafy entrance and friendly staff.

Lakshmi Cottage
HOTEL $

(☑27442463; lakshmilodge2002@yahoo.co.in; 5 Othavadai Cross St; r ₹400-800, with AC ₹1200; ❄) One of the better of several backpacker-oriented places along Othavadai Cross St, the Lakshmi has lots of rooms in primary colours, and assorted travel services on the ground floor. Beds range from concrete to carved wood.

Butterball Bed 'n Breakfast
B&B $$

(☑9094792525; suhale2009@gmail.com; 9/26 West Raja St; s/d incl breakfast ₹1600/1800; ❄🗑) There's a great view of the eponymous giant rock from the roof terrace, and a nice lawn. The smallish but clean, pleasant rooms have old English prints, writing desks and blue-tiled bathrooms. Breakfast is a good Western-style affair; also welcome is the civilised 24-hour checkout, rare in Mamallapuram. Free wi-fi throughout.

Hotel Mahabs
HOTEL $$

(☑27442645; www.hotelmahabs.com; 68 East Raja St; r ₹1319, with AC ₹2159-2518; ❄@🗑🗑) Friendly Mahabs is centred on an attractive pool (₹300 for nonguests) surrounded by trees, plants and murals. Rooms are in shades of brown but very clean and comfy. There's a decent in-house restaurant; internet use is ₹50/200 per hour/24 hours.

Hotel Mamalla Heritage
HOTEL $$

(☑27442060; www.hotelmamallaheritage.com; 104 East Raja St; s ₹2136-2611, d ₹2374-3086, all incl breakfast; ❄🗑🗑) Popular with tour groups, the Mamalla has large, comfortable rooms with spotless bathrooms. The pool's a decent size, and there's a quality rooftop restaurant. Wi-fi costs ₹50/200 per hour/24 hours.

⭐Radisson Blu
Resort Temple Bay
RESORT $$$

(☑27443636; http://radissonblu.com/hotel-mamallapuram; 57 Kovalam Rd; s/d incl breakfast

TAMIL NADU TEMPLES

Tamil Nadu is a gold mine for anyone wanting to explore Indian temple culture. Not only does this state have some of the country's most spectacular temple architecture and sculpture, its people are among the most devout and fervent in their Hindu beliefs. Tamil Nadu's 5000-odd temples are constantly busy with worshippers flocking in for *puja* (offering or prayer), and colourful temple festivals abound. Among the plethora of Hindu deities, Shiva probably has most Tamil temples dedicated to him, in a multitude of aspects including Nataraja, the cosmic dancer, who dances in a ring of fire with two of his four hands holding the flame of destruction and the drum of creation, while the third makes the *abhaya mudra* (fear not) gesture and the fourth points to the dwarf of ignorance being trampled beneath Shiva's foot. Tamils also have a soft spot for Shiva's peacock-riding son Murugan (also called Kartikeya or Skanda).

The special significance of many Tamil temples makes them goals of countless Hindu pilgrims from all over India. The Pancha Sabhai Sthalangal are the five temples where Shiva is believed to have performed his cosmic dance (chief among them Chidambaram). Then there's the Pancha Bootha Sthalangal, the five temples where Shiva is worshipped as a manifestation of one of the five elements – land, water, air, sky/space, fire. Each of the nine Navagraha temples in the Kumbakonam area is the abode of one of the nine celestial bodies of Hindu astronomy – key sites given the importance of astrology in Hindu faith.

Typical Tamil temple design features tall stepped entrance towers called *gopurams*, encrusted with often colourfully painted sculptures of gods and demons; halls of richly carved columns called *mandapas*; a sacred water tank; and a ground plan comprising a series of compounds (*prakarams*) of diminishing size, one within the next, with the innermost containing the central sanctum where the temple's main deity resides. The earliest Tamil temples were small shrines sculpted direct from the living rock; the first free-standing temples were built in the 8th century AD; *gopurams* began to appear around the 12th century.

Admission to almost all temples is free, but non-Hindus are often not allowed inside inner sanctums, which can be disappointing for many travellers. At other temples priests may invite you in and in no time you are doing *puja*, having a *tilak* daubed on your forehead and being asked for a donation.

Temple touts are fairly common and can be a nuisance, but there are also many excellent guides who deserve both your time and rupees; use your judgement, talk to other travellers and be on the lookout for badge-wearing official guides, who tend to be excellent resources.

A South Indian Journey by Michael Wood is a great read if you're interested in learning more about Tamil culture. TempleNet (www.templenet.com) is one of the best online resources.

from ₹8934/9893; ❄ @ 🛜 🏊) The Radisson's 144 luxurious chalets, villas and bungalows are spread around manicured gardens stretching 500m to the beach. Somewhere in the midst is India's longest swimming pool, all 220m of it. Rooms range from large to enormous and the most expensive have private pools. The Radisson also offers Mamallapuram's finest (and most expensive) dining and two top-notch spas (one exclusively ayurvedic). It's a popular getaway for well-heeled Chennai-ites. Free wi-fi throughout.

Ideal Beach Resort RESORT $$$
(✆ 27442240; www.idealresort.com; East Coast Rd; s/d from ₹5934/6527; ❄ @ 🏊) With a landscaped garden setting and its own stretch of (pretty nice) beachfront, this laid-back resort, 3km north of town, is popular with families and couples. There's a lovely poolside restaurant where live classical music is sometimes performed. Internet costs ₹100 per 24 hours.

✖ Eating

Eateries on Othavadai and Othavadai Cross Sts provide semi-open-air settings, decent

Western mains and bland Indian curries. Most of them can serve you a beer. For real Indian food, there are a few decent cheap veg and biryani places near the bus stand.

Le Yogi
MULTICUISINE $$

(19 Othavadai St; mains ₹120-350; ☺7.30am-11pm) This is some of the best Western food in town; the steaks, pasta, pizzas and crepes are genuine and tasty (if small); service is good, and the airy setting, with bamboo posts and pretty hanging lamps, has a touch of the romantic.

Gecko Café
MULTICUISINE $$

(www.gecko-web.com; 14 Othavadai Cross St; mains ₹150-290; ☺8am-10.30pm) Two friendly brothers run this cute little spot on a thatch-covered rooftop overlooking a large pond. The offerings and prices aren't that different from other tourist-oriented spots, but there's more love put into the cooking here and it comes out tastier. At research time they were building a second location around the corner.

Freshly 'n Hot
CAFE $$

(Othavadai Cross St; mains ₹60-225; ☺7.30am-9pm) Yes, the name makes no sense, but the ambience is relaxed and the decor clean and fresh. A comparatively small menu of perfectly OK pizza, pasta, sandwiches, egg items and crepes accompanies a long list of coffees. The iced coffees are excellent.

Moonrakers
MULTICUISINE $$

(34 Othavadai St; mains ₹100-300; ☺10am-11.30pm) You're likely to end up here at some stage; it's the sort of place that dominates the backpacker-ghetto streetscape. The food won't win any prizes but it's OK, and the three floors of tables keep pretty busy. For a change of scene try the same owners' Blue Elephant (Othavadai St), opposite, with almost identical food and nicer decor.

Water's Edge Cafe
MULTICUISINE $$$

(Radisson Blu Resort Temple Bay, 57 Kovalam Rd; mains ₹250-700; ☺24hr) Offers everything from American breakfast to lamb goulash and Indian veg dishes. Also in the Radisson is the Wharf (mains ₹550-2000; ☺noon-3pm & 7-11pm), a gourmet multicuisine seaside restaurant.

🛍 Shopping

The roar of electric stone-grinders has replaced the tink-tink of chisels in Mamallapuram's stone-carving workshops, enabling them to turn out ever more granite sculptures of varying quality, from ₹100 pendants to a ₹400,000 Ganesh that needs to be lifted with a crane. There are also some good art galleries, tailors and antique shops here. For clothes, we recommend Ponn Tailoring (Othavadai St; ☺9.30am-10pm). Nice prints, cards and original art can be found at Shriji Art Gallery (14/21 Othavadai St; ☺9am-10pm), and expensive but beautiful curios culled from local homes, along with quality new sculptures, at Southern Arts & Crafts (☎27443675; www.southernarts.in; 72 East Raja St; ☺9am-7.30pm).

Apollo Bookshop (89 Fishermen's Colony; ☺9am-9pm) has a decent range of books in several languages to sell and swap.

🛈 Information

Head to East Raja St for ATMs.

Hi Tech Net-Centre (Othavadai St; internet per hr ₹30; ☺8am-9.30pm) Welcome spacious conditions.

Ruby Forex (East Raja St; ☺9.30am-7pm Mon-Sat) Currency exchange.

Suradeep Hospital (☎27442448; 15 Thirukula St; ☺24hr) Recommended by travellers.

Tourist Office (☎27442232; Kovalam Rd; ☺10am-5.45pm Mon-Fri) Quite helpful and friendly.

🛈 Getting There & Away

From the bus stand (East Raja St), bus 599 heads to Chennai's T Nagar Bus Terminus (₹27, two hours) 24 times daily, and AC bus 568C (588C on Saturday and Sunday) runs to Chennai's CMBT (₹85, two hours) about hourly, 8am to 9pm. For Chennai Airport take bus 515 to Tambaram (every 30 minutes, 6.20am to 9.30pm), then a taxi, autorickshaw or suburban train from there. There are also nine daily buses to Kanchipuram (₹31, two hours) from the bus stand. Buses to Puducherry (₹50, two hours) stop about every half-hour at the junction of Kovalam Rd and the Mamallapuram bypass, 1km north of the town centre.

Taxis are available from the bus stand, travel agents and hotels. It's about ₹1000 to ₹1200 to Chennai, or ₹1500 to Puducherry.

You can make train reservations at the Southern Railway Reservation Centre (32 East Raja St, 1st fl; ☺10am-1pm & 2.30-5pm Mon-Sat, 8am-2pm Sun)

🛈 Getting Around

The easiest way to get around is on foot, though on a hot day it's quite a hike to see all the monuments. Bicycles can be hired at some guesthouses and hotels, and at a few rental stalls, usually for ₹50 per day.

Vedanthangal Bird Sanctuary

About 55km southwest of Mamallapuram, this 30-hectare **sanctuary** (admission ₹5, camera/video ₹25/150; ⊙6am-6pm) is a spectacular breeding ground for many kinds of water birds, which migrate here from October to March. Some years as many as 100,000 birds mass at Vedanthangal Lake and its marshy surrounds. The best viewing times are early morning and late afternoon; head for the watchtower and look down on the noisy nests across the water.

Three basic AC rooms are available at the **Forest Department Resthouse** (r ₹750) 500m before the sanctuary. For these you're supposed to book in advance with the **Wildlife Warden's Office** (Map p1008; ☑044-24321471; DMS Compound, 259 Anna Salai, Teynampet) in Chennai. It's worth phoning the office beforehand, as it may be changing location – or just book through a travel agency such as Hi! Tours (p1028) in Mamallapuram, or Chennai's Milesworth Travel (p1020). If you just turn up the caretaker may just find a room if one's available. You should bring all food and drinks with you.

Visitors often make a day trip by taxi from Mamallapuram; this should cost around ₹1500. To get here by public transport, first get to Chengalpattu, an hour's bus ride from Mamallapuram en route to Kanchipuram. From here you can take a bus to Vedanthangal via Padalam, where you may have to change buses again. Most Vedanthangal buses go to the sanctuary entrance, but some stop at the village bus station, 1km away.

Kanchipuram

☑ 044 / POP 164,225

Kanchipuram, 80km southwest of Chennai, was capital of the Pallava dynasty during the 6th to 8th centuries, when the Pallavas were creating the great stone monuments of Mamallapuram. Today a typically hectic modern Indian town, it's famed for its numerous important and busy temples, some dating from Pallava, Chola or Vijayanagar times, and also for its high-quality silk saris, woven on hand looms by thousands of families in the city and nearby villages. Silk and sari shops are strung along Gandhi Rd, southeast of the centre, though their wares are generally no cheaper than at silk shops in Chennai. Kanchi can easily be visited in a day trip from Mamallapuram or Chennai.

Kanchipuram

◎ Sights
1 Ekambareshwara Temple A1
2 Kamakshi Amman Temple A1
3 Vaikunta Perumal Temple B2

◎ Sleeping
4 GRT Regency B3
5 Sree Sakthi Residency B2

◎ Eating
Dakshin .... (see 4)
6 Sangeetha Restaurant B2
7 Saravana Bhavan A2

◎ Transport
8 Bicycle Hire B2

◎ Sights

All temples are open from 6am to noon and 4pm to 8pm. All have free admission, though you may have to pay small amounts for shoe-keeping and/or cameras.

Kailasanatha Temple
HINDU TEMPLE

Kanchi's oldest temple is its most impressive, not for its size but for its weight of historical presence and the delicacy of its stonework. As much monument as living temple, Kailasanatha is much quieter than other temples in town. Dedicated to Shiva, it was built in the 8th century by the Pallava king Narasimhavarman II, who also gave us Mamallapuram's Shore Temple. The low-slung sandstone compound has fascinating carvings, including many of the half-animal deities in vogue in early Dravidian architecture. The inner sanctum is centred on a large prismatic lingam, which non-Hindus are permitted to view from a distance of about 8m. The tower rising above it is a precursor of the great *vimanas* of later Chola temples. An autorickshaw from the centre is ₹40, but it's a nice walk.

Ekambareshwara Temple   HINDU TEMPLE

(Ekambaranathar Temple; camera/video ₹20/100) Of the five South Indian Shiva temples associated with the five elements, this 12-hectare precinct is the shrine of earth. You'll enter beneath a 59m-high unpainted *gopuram* on the south side, whose lively carvings were chiselled in 1509 under Vijayanagar rule. Inside, a columned hall leads left into the central compound: non-Hindus cannot go into the inner sanctum, which includes a mirror chamber whose central Shiva image is reflected in endless repetition, alluding to his infinite presence.

According to legend, the goddess Kamakshi (She Whose Eyes Awaken Desire; a form of Parvati, Shiva's consort) worshipped Shiva under a mango tree here. The temple's name means 'Lord of the Mango Tree' and in one courtyard behind the inner sanctum you can see a mango tree said to be 3500 years old, with four branches representing the four Vedas (sacred Hindu texts).

Kamakshi Amman Temple   HINDU TEMPLE

This imposing temple, dedicated to Kamakshi/Parvati, is one of India's most important places of *shakti* (female energy/deities) worship. It's thought to have been founded by the Pallavas. The entire main building inside is off-limits to non-Hindus, but the small, square marriage hall, to the right inside the temple's southeast entrance, is worth a good look for its wonderful ornate pillars. Each February/March carriages bearing the temple deities are hauled through the streets; don't miss this procession if you're in the vicinity.

Varadaraja Perumal Temple   HINDU TEMPLE

(Devarajaswami Temple; 100-pillared hall ₹1, camera/video ₹5/100) The enormous Varadaraja Perumal Temple in the southeast of the city is dedicated to Vishnu and was built by the Cholas in the 11th century. The main central compound is off-limits to non-Hindus, but the artistic highlight is the '100-pillared' marriage hall, added in the 16th century just inside the western entrance. Its pillars (actually 96) are superbly carved with countless animals and monsters; at its corners hang four stone chains each carved from a single rock.

Every 40 years the waters of the temple tank are drained, revealing a huge wooden statue of Vishnu that is worshipped for 48 days. Next viewing: 2019. Meantime, very popular processions carrying temple idols through the streets happen several times a year.

Vaikunta Perumal Temple   HINDU TEMPLE

Roughly 1200 years old, this Vishnu temple is a Pallava creation. A passage around the central shrine has lion pillars and a wealth of weathered wall panels, some showing historical scenes. The main shrine, uniquely spread over three levels, contains images of Vishnu standing, sitting, reclining and riding his preferred mount, the garuda (half-eagle, half-man).

🏃 Volunteering

RIDE   VOLUNTEERING

(Rural Institute for Development Education; ☏ 27268223; www.rideindia.org; 48 Periyar Nagar, Little Kanchipuram) Kanchipuram's celebrated silk-weaving industry has traditionally depended heavily on child labour. The NGO RIDE has been a leader in reducing child labour numbers in the industry from over 40,000 in 1997 to less than 1000 by 2010, by its own estimates. RIDE also works to empower the rural poor through education and women's self-help groups. It welcomes volunteers from one week to two years to work in a wide variety of projects. Volunteers pay between ₹1500 and ₹7000 per week (depending how long they are staying) for accommodation, food and other costs.

👉 Tours

RIDE offers original and fascinating **tours** (per person incl lunch half/full day ₹600/900) covering diverse themes from silk weaving and temples to released child labour or an Indian cookery class with market visit.

🛏 Sleeping & Eating

RIDE   GUESTHOUSE $
(Rural Institute for Development Education;
☑ 27268223; www.rideindia.org; 48 Periyar Nagar,
Little Kanchipuram; s/d incl breakfast ₹350/700;
❄) This NGO has several simple but clean
and sizeable rooms for travellers, at its base
in a residential area about 5km southeast of
the city centre (signposted from the main
road about 1km past Varadaraja Perumal
Temple). Contact them a day ahead if possible. Home-cooked lunch and dinner are
available (₹250 each).

GRT Regency   HOTEL $$
(☑ 27225250; www.grthotels.com; 487 Gandhi
Rd; s/d incl breakfast ₹3000/3500; ❄🛜) The
GRT has the cleanest and most comfortable
rooms you'll find in Kanchi, boasting marble
floors and bathroom fittings and tea/coffee
makers. The hotel's **Dakshin** (mains ₹185-
390; ⏰7am-11pm) restaurant is a tad over-
priced but offers a big multicuisine menu
including Western-style breakfast, good sea-
food and tasty tandoori.

Sree Sakthi Residency   HOTEL $$
(☑ 27233799; www.sreesakthiresidency.com; 71
Nellukara St; s ₹1319-1439, d ₹1559; ❄) Simple
blonde-wood furniture and coloured walls
make the rooms fairly modern, and they're
good and clean. The **Sangeetha Restaurant** (mains ₹50-140; ⏰6am-10.30pm) here,
with AC and non-AC sections, does very
good veg food.

Saravana Bhavan   SOUTH INDIAN $$
(66 Nellukara St; meals ₹80-230; ⏰6am-10pm) A
reliable veg restaurant with a welcome AC
dining room.

ℹ Getting There & Away

Suburban trains to Kanchipuram (₹15, 2½
hours) leave Chennai's Egmore station (platform
10) six times daily.

The busy **bus stand** is in the centre of town.
Departures:

Chennai ₹47, two hours, every 15 to 30 minutes
Mamallapuram ₹42, two hours, 10 daily
Puducherry ₹75, three hours, 11 daily
Tiruvannamalai ₹70, three hours, 11 daily
Vellore ₹41, two hours, every 15 minutes

ℹ Getting Around

Bike hire (per hour ₹5) is available at stall
around the bus stand. An autorickshaw for a
half-day tour of the five main temples (around
₹400) will inevitably involve a stop at a silk shop.

Vellore

☑ 0416 / POP 185,895

For a dusty bazaar town, Vellore feels kinda
cosmopolitan, thanks to a couple of terti-
ary institutions and the Christian Medical
College (CMC), one of India's finest hospi-
tals, attracting medical students as well as
patients from all over the country. On the
main Chennai–Bengaluru road, Vellore is
worth a stop mainly for its massive Vijay-
anagar fort.

Central Vellore is bounded on the north
by Ida Scudder Rd (Arcot Rd), home to the
hospital and cheap sleeping and eating op-
tions; and on the west by Officer's Line
(Anna Salai), with Vellore Fort on its west
side. Buses arrive at the New Bus Stand,
1.5km north.

⊙ Sights

Vellore Fort   FORT
A circuit of the moat-surrounded ramparts
(nearly 2km) of the splendid fort is the most
peaceful experience available in Vellore.
The fort was built in the 16th century and
passed through Maratha and Mughal hands
before the British occupied it in 1760. These
days it houses, among other things, govern-
ment offices, two parade grounds (capable
of hosting a dozen simultaneous games of
cricket), a church and a police recruiting
school. Also inside is the **Jalakantesvara
Temple** (⏰6am-1pm & 3-8.30pm), a gem of
late Vijayanagar architecture, built about
1566. Check out the small, detailed sculp-
tures on the walls of the marriage hall in
the southwest corner. The fort contains two
museums: the dusty exhibits in the **Gov-
ernment Museum** (Indian/foreigner ₹5/100;
⏰9.30am-5pm Sat-Thu) have seen better days,
but the **Archaeological Survey Museum**
(admission free; ⏰9am-5pm Sat-Thu) has a good
collection of Pallava, Chola and Nayak stone
sculptures, plus exhibits on the 1806 Vellore
Mutiny, the earliest anti-British uprising by
Indian troops. Next door, pretty **St John's
Church** (1846) is only open for Sunday serv-
ices.

🛏 Sleeping & Eating

Vellore's cheap hotels are concentrated
along Ida Scudder Rd and in the busy, nar-
row streets south of there. The cheapest
are pretty grim, and the better ones fill up
quickly.

Hotel Solai
HOTEL $

(☑ 2222996; hotelsolai@gmail.com; 26 Babu Rao St; s/d ₹315/473, with AC ₹520/825; ※) If you can get a room, this almost-new hotel is probably the best value, near the hospital. It has clean rooms, reasonably airy walkways, and a back-up generator for those power cuts.

Darling Residency
HOTEL $$

(☑ 2213001; www.darlingresidency.com; 11/8 Officer's Line; s ₹1882-2118, d ₹2235-2471, all incl breakfast; ※ @ ⑤) It's not five-star, but rooms are clean and comfortable (if forgettable), staff are friendly and the hotel has four restaurants, including the cool and breezy **Aaranya Roof Garden Restaurant** (mains ₹100-150; ⊙ 6.30-10.45pm). It's 1.5km south of Vellore Fort entrance.

Hotel Palm Tree
HOTEL $$

(☑ 2222960; www.hotelpalmtree.co.in; 10 Thennamaram St; s/d ₹524/770, with AC s ₹1079-1319, d ₹1187-1499; ※) On a narrow street off Officer's Line, 750m south of Vellore Fort entrance, the Palm Tree offers clean, spruce rooms with IKEA-style furniture, and its staff are very helpful.

Hotel Arthy
INDIAN $

(Ida Scudder Rd; dishes ₹20-60, meals ₹45-75; ⊙ 6.30am-10.30pm) A bunch of cheap veg restaurants line Ida Scudder Rd, but this is one of the cleanest, with tasty North and South Indian favourites including good thalis and cheap, yummy biryani.

ⓘ Information

Sri Apollo (Ida Scudder Rd; internet per hr ₹30.; ⊙ 8.30am-9pm)

State Bank of India ATM (Officer's Line) About 700m south of Vellore Fort entrance.

ⓘ Getting There & Away

BUS

Departures from the New Bus Stand:

Bengaluru ₹138, five hours, every 30 minutes

Chennai AC Volvo buses ₹161, 2½ hours, about hourly; other buses ₹81, three hours, every 10 to 20 minutes

Kanchipuram ₹41, two hours, every 15 minutes

Tiruvannamalai ₹47, two hours, every 15 minutes

TRAIN

Vellore's main station is 5km north at Katpadi. There are at least 20 daily superfast or express trains to/from Chennai Central (2nd class/AC chair ₹64/226, 2¼ to 3¾ hours), most with a big choice of classes, and 10 trains to/from Bangalore City station. Bus 192 shuttles between the station and town.

Tiruvannamalai

☑ 04175 / POP 144,683

There are temple towns, there are mountain towns, and there are temple-mountain towns where God appears as a phallus of fire. Welcome to Tiruvannamalai. Set below boulder-strewn Mt Arunachala, this is one of South India's five 'elemental' cities of Shiva; here the god is worshipped in his fire incarnation as Arunachaleshwar. At every full moon 'Tiru' swells with thousands of pilgrims who come to circumnavigate the base of Arunachala in a purifying ritual known as Girivalam, but at any time you'll see Shaivite priests, sadhus (holy people) and devotees gathered around the big Arunachaleshwar Temple. The area's reputation for strong spiritual energies has engendered numerous ashrams, and Tiruvannamalai is attracting growing numbers of spiritual-minded travellers. Around the main cluster of ashrams, on and near Chengam Rd about 2km southwest of the centre, you'll find a few congenial cafes and sleeping options.

◉ Sights & Activities

★ Arunachaleshwar Temple
HINDU TEMPLE

(Annamalaiyar Temple; http://arunachaleswarar.org; ⊙ 5am-12.30pm & 3.30-9.30pm) During festivals the Arunachaleshwar is awash in golden flames and the roasting scent of burning ghee, as befits the fire incarnation of the Destroyer of the Universe. This 10-hectare temple is one of the largest in India. Its oldest parts date back to the 9th century and the site was a place of worship long before that. Four large unpainted *gopurams* mark the entrances, with the main, eastern one rising 13 storeys and an astonishing 66m. Inside the complex are five more *gopurams*, two tanks and a profusion of sub-temples and shrines (the interactive map at www.arunachaleswarar.com/earunastructure.html is a help). To reach the innermost sanctum, with its huge lingam, worshippers must pass through five surrounding *prakarams* (compounds). The temple elephant gives blessings inside the second *gopuram* coming from the east.

Mt Arunachala
MOUNTAIN

This 800m-high extinct volcano dominates Tiruvannamalai and local conceptions of the element of fire, which supposedly finds its sacred abode in Arunachala's heart. Devout barefoot pilgrims, especially on full-moon and festival days, make the 14km circumambulation of the mountain, stopping at eight famous linga along the route. If you're not quite that devoted, buy a Giripradakshina map (₹15) from the bookshop at Sri Ramana Ashram (p1035), hire a bicycle on the roadside nearby, and ride your way around. Or make an autorickshaw circuit for about ₹250 (up to double at busy times).

For a superb view of the Arunachaleshwar Temple and Tiruvannamalai, climb part or all the way up the hill. The hot ascent to the top and back takes five or six hours: start early and take water. A 'Skandasramam & Virupakshi Cave' sign, across the road from the northwest corner of Arunachaleshwar Temple, points the way up past homes and two caves, **Virupaksha** (about 20 minutes up) and **Skandasramam** (30 minutes). Sri Ramana Maharshi lived and meditated in these caves from 1899 to 1922.

Sri Ramana Ashram
(Sri Ramanasramam; ☑ 237200; www.sriramana maharshi.org; Chengam Rd; ⊗ office 7.30am-12.30pm & 2-8pm) This tranquil ashram, in green surrounds 2km southwest of the city centre, draws devotees of Sri Ramana Maharshi, one of the first Hindu gurus to gain an international following, who died here in 1950 after half a century in contemplation. Visitors can meditate or attend daily *pujas* and chantings, mostly in the samadhi hall where the guru's body is enshrined. A limited amount of free accommodation (donations accepted; maximum three days) is available: write at least a month ahead (email is acceptable).

Sri Seshadri Swamigal Ashram   ASHRAM
(☑ 236999; www.tiruvarunaimahan.org; Chengam Rd) Dedicated to a contemporary and helper of Sri Ramana. It has meditation platforms and some accommodation. It is located in the southwest of town near the famous Sri Ramana Ashram.

Other Ashrams   ASHRAMS
Side by side 7km west of town, just off the Krishnagiri road, are two ashrams that are places for retreat rather than permanent communities, both with good Arunachala views and personable young staff accustomed to foreigners. **Sri Anantha Niketan** (☑ 9444862276; gopi.chitra@yahoo.com; Periya Paliyapattu Village; by donations) has tree-shaded

grounds, homey rooms and daily chanting in an attractive meditation hall. **Singing Heart Ashram** (☑ 9443969220; www.cosmicairport. com; Periya Paliyapattu Village; per person per day incl meals from ₹450; ⊗ Oct-Mar) sits on a spacious, open site with simple rooms. You can join organised meditation retreats, or just participate in morning meditation, help with running the place and 'relax in the energy field'.

🛏 Sleeping & Eating

Many visitors prefer to stay in the less hectic Chengam Rd area, but there are also some typical temple-town options near the Arunachaleshwar Temple. During Karthikai Deepam (November/December) prices at some places multiply several times.

Hill View Residency   HOTEL $
(☑ 9442712441; www.hillviewresidency.com; 120 Seshatri Mada St; r from ₹400, with AC from ₹750) Extremely good value, Hill View has large, clean, cool, marble-floored rooms round two small garden patios, up a lane off Chengam Rd. Upstairs under a big palm roof, **Tasty Café** (dishes ₹50-130; ⊗ 7am-10pm; 🖀) does well-prepared Indian and Western food.

Arunachala Ramana Home   HOTEL $
(☑ 236120; www.arunachalaramanahome.co.in; 70 Ramana Nagar; s/d ₹400/600, with AC r ₹1000; 🌐) Basic, clean and friendly, this popular place is down a lane off Chengam Rd. It has a rooftop restaurant.

Hotel Ganesh   HOTEL $
(☑ 226701; lingam100@indiatimes.com; 111A Big St; s/d ₹250/500, with AC d/tr ₹825/1210; 🌐) Set 400m northeast of the Arunachaleshwar Temple's east gate. Some rooms are small and most have squat toilets, but they're clean enough, management is friendly and the inner courtyard balcony is pleasant. The sign atop the building says 'Hotel Kanna'.

Arunachala Inn   HOTEL $$
(Hotel Arunachala; ☑ 228300; www.hotelarunachala.com; 5 Vada Sannathi St; s/d ₹525/770, with AC ₹880/1100, deluxe d ₹1687; 🌐) This place right next to the Arunachaleshwar Temple's east entrance is clean and fine with pretensions to luxury in the marblesque floors and ugly furniture. Many of the slightly faded standard rooms are being upgraded to deluxe. **Hotel Sri Arul Jothi** (dishes ₹35-60; ⊗ 6.30am-10.30pm), the veg restaurant downstairs, has simple, very good, South Indian dishes.

Shanti Café CAFE $
(www.shanticafe.com; 115A Chengam Rd; food items
₹50-100, drinks ₹30-70; ☺8.30am-8.30pm; 🖼)
This relaxed cafe with floor-cushion seating,
up a lane off Chengam Rd, is highly popular among short- and long-term visitors and
serves wonderful croissants, cakes, pies, baguettes, omelettes, pancakes, juices, coffees,
teas and breakfasts. Wi-fi is ₹25 per hour;
there's also an **internet cafe** (☺8.30am-2pm
& 3.30-8pm) downstairs.

🛍 Shopping

**Shantimalai Handicrafts
Development Society** HANDICRAFTS
(www.smhds.org; 83/1 Chengam Rd; ☺8.30am-
7pm Mon-Sat, 9am-2pm Sun) Attractive bedspreads, incense, oils, bangles, scarves and
more, made by local village women.

ℹ Getting There & Around

A taxi to Puducherry with a two- to three-hour
stop at Gingee costs around ₹2000.

The bus stand is in the north of town, 800m
north of Arunachaleshwar Temple, and a ₹50 to
₹60 autorickshaw ride from the main ashram area.

Chennai ₹100 to ₹110, 3½ hours, every 15 minutes

Puducherry ₹63, three hours, about hourly

Trichy ₹120, five to six hours, 12 daily

Vellore ₹47, two hours, every 15 minutes

Gingee (Senji)

With three separate hilltop citadels and a
6km perimeter of cliffs and thick walls, the
ruins of enormous **Gingee Fort** (Indian/for-
eigner ₹5/100; ☺9am-5.30pm) poke out of the
Tamil plain, 37km east of Tiruvannamalai,
like castles misplaced by the *Lord of the
Rings*. It was constructed mainly in the 16th
century by the Vijayanagars and was later
occupied by the Marathas, Mughals, French
and finally the British before being abandoned in the 19th century.

Today the main road from Tiruvannamalai towards Puducherry slices through the
fort, just before Gingee town. Of the three
citadels, the easiest to reach, Krishnagiri,
rises north of the road. To the south are the
highest of the three, Rajagiri, and the most
distant and least interesting, Chakklidurg.

Remains of numerous buildings stand in
the lower parts of the site, especially at the
foot of Rajagiri, where the main landmark
of the old palace area is the white, restored,
seven-storey Kalyana Mahal (Marriage
Hall). Just east of the palace area is an 18th-
century mosque, and southeast of that is the
large, abandoned, 16th-century Venkatara-
mana Temple.

It's a good hike to the top of Krishnagiri
and even more so to the top of Rajagiri
(more than 150m above the plain) and you
need half a day to cover both hills. Start
early and bring water.

Gingee is on the Tiruvannamalai–
Puducherry bus route, with buses from
Tiruvannamalai (₹20, 1½ hours) running
about every half-hour. Get off at the fort to
save a trip back out from Gingee town.

Puducherry (Pondicherry)

📍 0413 / POP 241,773

Let's get something clear: if you came to Puducherry (formerly called Pondicherry and
almost always referred to as 'Pondy') expecting a Provençal village on the Bay of Bengal,
you're in for a disappointment, *mon ami*.
Pondy is South India: honk-roar-haggle-
honk South India. That said, the older part
of this former French colony (where you'll
probably spend most of your time) does

THE LINGAM OF FIRE

Legend has it Shiva appeared as the original lingam of fire on Mt Arunachala to restore
light to the world after his consort Parvati had playfully plunged everything into darkness
by closing Shiva's eyes. Each November/December full moon, the **Karthikai Deepam
Festival** (statewide; ☺Nov/Dec) celebrates this legend throughout India but becomes
particularly significant at Tiruvannamalai. The lighting of a huge fire atop Mt Arunachala
on the full moon night, from a 30m wick immersed in 3 tonnes of ghee, culminates a
10-day festival with nightly processions for which many hundreds of thousands of people
converge on Tiruvannamalai. Huge crowds scale the mountain or circumnavigate its
base. On the upward path, steps quickly give way to jagged, unstable rocks. The sun is
relentless and the journey must be undertaken barefoot – none of which deters the thousands of pilgrims who joyfully make their way to the top and the abode of their deity.

TAMIL NADU & CHENNAI GINGEE (SENJI)

have a lot of quiet, clean, shady, cobbled streets, lined with mustard-yellow colonial townhouses numbered in an almost logical manner. In fact, if you've come from Chennai or some of the inland cities, old Pondy may well seem a sea of tranquillity.

Puducherry was under French rule until 1954 and some people here still speak French (and English with French accents). Hotels, restaurants and 'lifestyle' shops sell a seductive vision of the French-subcontinental aesthetic, enhanced by Gallic creative types whose presence has in turn attracted Indian artists and designers. Thus Pondy's vibe: less faded colonial-era *ville*, more a bohemian-chic, New Age–cum–Old World node on the international travel trail. Part of the vibe stems from the presence of the internationally famous Sri Aurobindo Ashram and its offshoot just out of town, Auroville. These draw large numbers of spiritually minded visitors and are responsible for a lot of the creative artisanry. Enjoy the shopping, the French food (hello steak!), the beer (goodbye Tamil Nadu alcohol taxes – Pondy is a Union Territory), the sea air and, if you like, some yoga and meditation.

Puducherry is split from north to south by a partially covered canal. The more 'French' part of town is on the east side (towards the sea). Nehru (JN) St and Lal Bahadur Shastri St (better known as Rue Bussy) are the main east–west streets; Mahatma Gandhi (MG) Rd and Mission St (Cathedral St) are the chief north–south thoroughfares. Many streets change names as they go along and may also have English, French and Tamil names all at the same time.

◉ Sights

French Quarter
NEIGHBOURHOOD
Pocketed away just behind the seafront is a series of cobbled streets, white and mustard buildings in various states of romantic dishevelment, and a slight sense of Gallic glory gone by, otherwise known as the French Quarter. A do-it-yourself **heritage walk** through this area could start at the French Consulate near the north end of Goubert Ave, the seafront promenade. Head south then turn inland to shady **Bharathi Park**, with the neoclassical governor's residence, **Raj Nivas**, facing its north side. Return to the seafront at the **Gandhi Memorial**, pass the **Hôtel de Ville** (City Hall) and then it's a matter of pottering south through

what's known as the 'white town' – Dumas, Romain Rolland, Suffren and Labourdonnais Sts. Quite a lot of restoration has been going on down here: if you're interested in Pondy's history and architectural heritage check out **INTACH Pondicherry** (www.intachpondicherry.org). The Tourist Info Bureau (p1043) also details heritage walks on its website.

Seafront
PROMENADE
(Goubert Ave) Pondy is a seaside town, but that doesn't make it a beach destination; the city's sand is a thin strip of dirty brown that slurps into a seawall of jagged rocks. But Goubert Ave (Beach Rd) is a killer stroll, especially at dawn and dusk when half the town takes a constitutional or romantic amble there. In a stroke of genius the city council has banned traffic here from 6pm to 7.30am.

There are a few sandy beaches north and south of town, but they're not places for sunbathing due to crowds of men and boys, nor for swimming due to possible undertow or rip tides.

Sri Aurobindo Ashram
ASHRAM
(www.sriaurobindoashram.org; Marine St; ⊙ general visits 8am-noon & 2-6pm) Founded in 1926 by Sri Aurobindo and a French-born woman known as 'the Mother', this spiritual community now has about 1200 members who work in the ashram's many departments including its commercial sections and large education centre. Aurobindo's teachings focus on an 'integral yoga' as the path towards a 'supramental consciousness which will divinise human nature'. Devotees work in the world, rather than retreating from it.

General visits to the main ashram building on Marine St are cursory – you just see the flower-festooned samadhi of Aurobindo and the Mother, then the bookshop, then you leave. People staying in ashram guesthouses have access to other areas and activities. Collective meditation around the samadhi from 7.25pm to 7.50pm Monday, Tuesday, Wednesday and Friday is open to all.

The ashram's **Bureau Central** (☑ 2233604; bureaucentral@sriaurobindoashram.org; Ambour Salai; ⊙ 6am-8pm) has interesting exhibitions on the lives and teachings of Sri Aurobindo and the Mother.

Puducherry Museum
MUSEUM
(St Louis St; Indian/foreigner ₹10/50; ⊙ 10am-1pm & 2-5pm Tue-Sun) Goodness knows how this cute little museum keeps its artefacts from rotting, considering there's a whole floor of

Puducherry (Pondicherry)

French-era furniture and decorations sitting in the South Indian humidity. On the ground floor look especially for the Chola, Vijayanagar and Nayak bronzes, and the pieces of ancient Greek and Spanish pottery and amphorae (storage vessels) excavated from Arikamedu, a once-major trading port a few kilometres south of Puducherry.

Sri Manakula Vinayagar Temple
HINDU TEMPLE

(Manakula Vinayagar Koil St; ⏰5.45am-12.30pm & 4-9.30pm) Pondy may have more churches than most towns, but this is still India, and the Hindu faith still reigns supreme. Don't miss the chance to watch tourists, pilgrims and the curious get a head pat from the temple elephant at this temple dedicated to Ganesh. The temple also contains over 40 skilfully painted friezes.

Churches
CHURCHES

Puducherry has one of the best collections of over-the-top cathedrals in India. *Merci*, French missionaries. **Our Lady of the Immaculate Conception Cathedral** (Mission St), completed in 1791, is a robin's-egg-blue-and-cloud-white typically Jesuit edifice in a

Puducherry (Pondicherry)

Goa like Portuguese style, while the brown-and-white grandiosity of the **Sacred Heart Basilica** (Subbayah Salai) is set off by stained glass and a Gothic sense of proportion. The twin towers and dome of the mellow pink-and-cream **Notre Dame des Anges** (Dumas St), built in the 1850s, look sublime in the late-afternoon light. The smooth limestone interior was made using eggshells in the plaster.

⚐ Activities

Sita ARTS, COOKING
(☑ 9944016128; www.pondicherry-arts.com; 22 Candappa Moudaliar St; single class ₹250-1000) This energetic young Franco-Indian cultural centre runs a host of activities and classes for adults and kids, which visitors are welcome to join. You can try Indian or French cooking, *bharatanatyam* or Bollywood dance, *kolam* making, *mehndi* (henna 'tattoos'), yoga, ayurveda and more. For most activities, it's possible to do a single session.

Temple Adventures DIVING
(☑ 9940219449; www.templeadventures.com; 5 Veeramamunivar St, Colas Nagar; 1-day Discover Scuba Diving ₹7500, 2-dive day for qualified divers ₹5000; ◷ 9am-6.30pm) The waters off Puducherry contain coral reefs and plenty of tropical fish. Experienced, multilingual Temple Adventures offers fun dives for qualified divers and a full range of PADI and NAUI diving courses, from beginners up. Best months: February to April and September to November.

Yoga & Ayurveda

You can practise (and study) yoga at Sri Aurobindo Ashram (p1037) and Auroville. The **Ayurveda Holistic Healing Centre** (☑ 6537651; www.ayurojas.org; 6 Sengeniamman Koil St, Vazhakulam; ◷ 9am-7.30pm) performs ayurvedic and varma-point treatments for all manner of ailments, and offers courses in yoga, ayurveda and varma. The **International Centre for Yoga Education & Research** (Ananda Ashram; ☑ 2241561; www.icyer.com; 16A Mettu St, Chinnamudaliarchavady,

Kottukuppam), 5km north of town, conducts annual six-month yoga-teacher-training courses and three-week introductory courses (₹550 including food and lodging).

☞ Tours

Shanti Travel (p1043) offers recommended two-hour **walking tours** (per person ₹400) of Puducherry with English- or French-speaking guides.

🎊 Festivals & Events

International Yoga Festival YOGA
(⏰4-7 Jan) Puducherry's ashrams and yoga culture are put on show with workshops, demonstrations and music and dance events. The event attracts experts from all over India and beyond.

Bastille Day PARADE
(⏰14 Jul) Street parades and a bit of French pomp and ceremony are part of the fun at this celebration.

🛏 Sleeping

If you've been saving for a special occasion, this is the place for it, because Puducherry's lodgings are as good as South India gets. Local heritage houses manage to combine colonial-era romanticism with comfort and, dare we say, French playfulness; many of these rooms would cost four or five times as much back in Europe. It's smart to book ahead if you're arriving at a weekend.

Sri Aurobindo Ashram (p1037) runs several simple but clean guesthouses. They're primarily intended for ashram visitors, but many accept other guests who are willing to abide by their rules: 10.30pm curfew and no smoking, alcohol or drugs. Only some accept advance bookings. The ashram's Bureau Central (p1037) has a list.

Kailash Guest House HOTEL $
(☎2224485; http://kailashguesthouse.in; 43 Vysial St; s/d ₹600/800, with AC d ₹1000; ✳) The best value for money in this price range; Kailash has simple, super-clean rooms with well mosquito-proofed windows, and friendly management. It's geared to traveller needs, with communal areas, clothes-drying facilities and laundry service.

Park Guest House ASHRAM GUESTHOUSE $
(☎2233644; 1 Goubert Ave; r ₹600, with AC ₹800-900; ✳) The most sought-after ashram guesthouse in town thanks to its wonderful seafront position. All front rooms face the sea and have a porch or balcony, and there's a large garden suitable for yoga or meditation. These are the best-value AC rooms in town. No advance bookings, though.

New Guest House ASHRAM GUESTHOUSE $
(☎2233634; newguesthouse@gmail.com; 64 Romain Rolland St; d/tr ₹300/450, r for 6 ₹850) Sparse, huge and packed with ashram faithful; this is a great spot for those who love the monastery cubicle school of lodging. You can book up to two months ahead.

★Les Hibiscus HERITAGE GUESTHOUSE $$
(☎2227480; www.leshibiscus.in; 49 Suffren St; s/d incl breakfast ₹2200/2500; ✳@🖥) Hibiscus has just four pristine, high-ceilinged rooms with gorgeous antique beds, coffee-makers and a mix of quaint Indian art and old-Pondy photos. The whole place is immaculately tasteful, the breakfast is fabulous, internet is free and management is genuinely friendly and helpful. Well worth booking ahead for.

Gratitude HERITAGE GUESTHOUSE $$
(☎9442065029; www.gratitudeheritage.in; 52 Romain Rolland St; s ₹3335-5448, d ₹3891-6671, all incl breakfast; ✳🖥) A wonderfully tranquil 19th-century house (no TVs, no children) with welcoming staff, Gratitude has been painstakingly restored to a state probably even more charming than the original. The eight good-sized, spotless rooms are set on two floors around a shady courtyard, and there's a lovely roof terrace. Free wi-fi.

Coloniale Heritage Guest House HERITAGE GUESTHOUSE $$
(☎2224720; http://colonialeheritage.com; 54 Romain Rolland St; r incl breakfast ₹2000-4000; ✳🖥) This colonial home with six comfy rooms is chock-full of character thanks to the owner's amazing collection of gem-studded Tanjore paintings, Ravi Varma lithographs and other 19th- and 20th-century South Indian art. Breakfast is served in a sunken patio next to the leafy garden. Free wi-fi.

Hotel de Pondichéry HERITAGE HOTEL $$
(☎2227409; www.hoteldepondicherry.com; 38 Dumas St; s ₹2000, d ₹2800-3800, all incl breakfast; ✳🖥) A heritage spot with comfy, quiet, high-ceilinged, colonial-style rooms and a dash of original modern art. The large front courtyard area houses the good restaurant, Le Club (p1042). Staff are lovely and there's free wi-fi in the lobby.

Meeranjali
HOMESTAY **$$**

(☏2334009; www.meeranjali.com; 9 Capitaine Marius Xavier St; r incl breakfast ₹2500-3000; ❄🛜) This lovely modern town house was designed and built by its welcoming owners, who are full of good ideas on how to spend your time here. Rooms have comfy beds, good blue-tiled bathrooms and fine Burmese teak furniture. Free wi-fi.

Dumas Guest House
HERITAGE GUESTHOUSE **$$**

(☏2225726; www.dumasguesthouse.com; 36 Dumas St; r ₹2400; ❄) All whitewash and dark wood, the antique-filled Dumas has real personality to which the odd patch of flaking paint kind of contributes. Enjoy the carved doors, quiet gardens, slightly quirky decor and friendly multilingual staff. All rooms have three beds.

Sea Side Guest House
ASHRAM GUESTHOUSE **$$**

(☏2231700; seaside@aurosociety.org; 14 Goubert Ave; s ₹1208-1746, d ₹1396-1934, all incl breakfast; ❄🛜) A cut above your typical ashram guesthouse, Sea Side has pristine, neat, freshly decorated rooms, and looks straight across the road to the sea. Sea-facing rooms have balconies. Advance bookings are accepted; wi-fi is ₹300 per 24 hours.

Hotel De L'Orient
HERITAGE HOTEL **$$$**

(☏2343067; www.neemranahotels.com; 17 Romain Rolland St; r incl breakfast ₹3760-8056; ❄🛜) A grand restored colonial mansion with breezy verandahs, charming rooms kitted out with antique furniture and *objets*, and a large, pretty courtyard at its heart. A place to get that old Pondy feel while enjoying polished service and French, Italian or creole (French-Indian) food in the courtyard Carte Blanche Restaurant (mains ₹250-400; ⏱7.15-10.30am, noon-6pm, 7-9.30pm).

Maison Perumal
HERITAGE HOTEL **$$$**

(☏2227519; www.cghearth.com; 44 Perumal Koil St; r incl breakfast ₹9500; ❄) The old Tamil Quarter has almost as many mansions as the French Quarter but is off most tourists' radars. This recently renovated 200-year-old building has cool, pleasant rooms above two lovely pillared patios. The excellent Tamil/French **restaurant** (dinner ₹990, lunch mains ₹300-400) cooks everything to order from fresh ingredients. Staff are charming and wi-fi is free. From March to Christmas rates dip by 30% or more.

✖ Eating

Puducherry is a culinary highlight of Tamil Nadu; you get good South Indian cooking plus several restaurants specialising in well-prepped French and Italian cuisine. If you've been missing cheese or have a hankering for pâté, you're in luck, and *everyone* in the French quarter offers crepes and good brewed coffee.

Baker Street
CAFE **$**

(123 Rue Bussy; items ₹40-130; ⏱7am-10pm) A very popular upmarket, French-style bakery with delectable cakes, croissants and eclairs. Baguettes, brownies and quiches aren't bad either. Eat in or take away.

Surguru
SOUTH INDIAN **$**

(235 (old 99) Mission St; mains ₹65-110; ⏱7.30am-10.30pm) Simple South Indian served in a relatively posh setting. Surguru is the fix for thali and dosa addicts who like their veg accompanied by good strong AC. Thali is available at lunchtime.

Saravana Bhavan
SOUTH INDIAN **$**

(Hotel Pondicherry; Nehru St; dishes ₹30-120; ⏱11am-10.30pm) A clean, AC setting with good, cheap South Indian food – all the thalis, dosas and *vadas* you could want.

★ Satsanga
MULTICUISINE **$$**

(☏2225867; www.satsanga.co.in; 54 Labourdonnais St; mains ₹150-340; ⏱8am-11pm) Deservedly popular for its excellent Continental cuisine, Satsanga, like most places in this genre, offers a full Indian menu as well. It's especially strong on steaks, fish, prawns and pâtés. There are good vegetarian options too, and the homemade bread and butter goes down a treat. Some have complained of slow service, but we found it fine. For a table on the breezy terrace, it's a good idea to book.

Café des Arts
CAFE **$$**

(Labourdonnais St; light dishes ₹100-190; ⏱8.30am-7pm Mon & Wed-Fri, 9am-5pm Sat & Sun; 🛜) Good brekky and coffee, free wi-fi and a nice outdoor/verandah setting outside a small gallery.

Café de Flore
CAFE **$$**

(Maison de Colombani, 37 Dumas St; dishes ₹90-290; ⏱8.30am-7.30pm) In the gallery and building of Pondy's Alliance Française, on an airy verandah overlooking a grassy garden, you'll find mocktails, great coffee, salads, *croques monsieur,* pasta and vegie burgers.

Kasha Ki Aasha
CAFE $$

(23 Rue Surcouf; mains ₹165-295; ☺8am-7pm) You'll get a great pancake breakfast, good lunches and delicious cakes on the pretty rooftop of this colonial-house-cum-craft-shop-cum-cafe. Fusion food includes chips with chutney, 'European-style thali' and 'Indian enchilada'. The heat in some dishes has been dialled back for Western tastes, but it's all tasty.

Le Café
CAFE $$

(Goubert Ave; dishes ₹30-210; ☺24hr) This seafront spot is good for baguettes, croissants, salads, cake and organic South Indian coffee (hot or iced), plus welcome fresh breezes from the Bay of Bengal. It's popular, so sometimes you have to wait for, or share, a table.

La Pasta
ITALIAN $$

(http://lapastapondy.blogspot.com; 55 Vysial St; mains ₹125-350; ☺noon-2pm & 6-9.30pm Tue-Sun) Pasta aficionados, make a little pilgrimage to this spot with just three check-cloth tables, where a real Italian whips up her own yummy sauces and concocts her own perfect pasta in an open kitchen as big as the dining area. No alcohol: it's all about the food, and she even has wholemeal options.

Le Club
CONTINENTAL, INDIAN $$$

(38 Dumas St; mains ₹330-440; ☺8.30am-10.30pm) The steaks (with sauces such as Béarnaise or blue cheese), pizzas and crepes are all top-class at this romantically lit garden restaurant. Tempting local options include creole prawn curry and Malabar-style fish, and there are plenty of cocktails and even wine to go with your meal.

Self-Catering

Nilgiri's
SUPERMARKET

(23 Rangapillai St; ☺9.30am-9pm) A well-stocked place to shop for groceries (and toiletries) in AC comfort.

🍷 Drinking & Nightlife

Although this is one of the better spots in Tamil Nadu to sink a beer, closing time is a decidedly un-Gallic 11pm. Despite low taxes on alcohol, you'll really only find cheap beer in 'liquor shops' or the darkened bars attached to them.

L'e-Space
CAFE, BAR

(2 Labourdonnais St; cocktails ₹200, pancakes ₹100; ☺5-11pm) A quirky little semi-open-air upstairs cafe that serves decent cocktails and where some people may be away on something other than alcohol. Locals and tourists congregate here, and during the season it can be a social traveller spot.

Shopping

With all the yoga yuppies congregating here, Pondy specialises in the boutique-chic-meets-Indian-bazaar school of fashion and souvenirs, and there is some appealing and original stuff, quite a lot of it produced by Sri Aurobindo Ashram or Auroville.

★ Kalki
CLOTHING, ACCESSORIES

(134 Mission St; ☺9.30am-8.30pm) Beautiful, jewel-coloured silk and cotton clothes, as well as incense, essential oils, handmade-paper products and more, nearly all made at Auroville.

Fabindia
TEXTILES

(www.fabindia.com; 59 Suffren St; ☺10am-8pm) This shop has a good variety of silk, cotton and wool clothes in Indian and Western styles, plus quality tablecloths and bags, predominantly made by villagers using traditional craft techniques but with a contemporary feel. The Fabindia chain has been in operation since 1960, and one of its selling points is its emphasis on handmade products and promoting rural employment.

La Boutique d'Auroville
HANDICRAFTS

(38 Nehru St; ☺9.30am-1pm & 3.30-8pm Mon-Sat) It's fun browsing through the crafts here, including jewellery, clothes, slippers and pretty wooden trays.

Hidesign
BAGS

(www.hidesign.com; 69 Nehru St; ☺9am-10pm) Established in Pondy in the 1970s, Hidesign sells beautifully made designer leather bags, briefcases, purses and belts in a range of colours, at very reasonable prices for what you get. It now has outlets in many countries. The top-floor cafe, **Le Hidesign** (69 Nehru St; mains ₹135-170; ☺9.30am-9.30pm; 🛜), serves delicious tapas and excellent coffee.

Auroshikha Agarbathies
INCENSE

(17 Gingee Salai; ☺8.30am-12.30pm & 3-7pm Tue-Sun) A wonderful array of incense, perfumed candles and essential oils, produced by Sri Aurobindo Ashram.

Geethanjali
ANTIQUES

(20 Rue Bussy; ☺9am-8.30pm) The sort of place where Indiana Jones gets the sweats, this antique and curio shop sells sculptures, carved doors, wooden chests, paintings and

furniture culled from Puducherry's colonial and even pre-colonial history. It ships to Europe for ₹12,000 per cubic metre and can obtain export permits for free.

Kasha Ki Aasha   CLOTHING, HANDICRAFTS
(23 Rue Surcouf; ⊙8am-7pm) Fabulous fabrics, gorgeous garments and comfy leather sandals are sourced directly from their makers and sold by an all-female staff in a lovely colonial-era house.

Focus the Book Shop   BOOKS
(204 Mission St; ⊙9.30am-1.30pm & 3.30-9pm Mon-Sat) A great collection of India-related and other books in English (including Lonely Planet guides).

Libraire Kailash   BOOKS
(169 Rue Bussy; ⊙9am-1pm & 3-7.30pm Mon-Sat) Good selection of India and Asia titles in French.

❶ Information

ATMs are plentiful and there are numerous currency-exchange offices on Mission St near the corner of Nehru St.

Rue Bussy between Bharathi St and MG Rd is packed with clinics and pharmacies.

Citibank ATM (22 Rue Bussy) This ATM can dispense ₹30,000 in one go, saving on bank charges.

Coffee.Com (11A Romain Rolland St; per hr ₹80; ⊙9am-10pm) A genuine internet cafe, with good coffee and light food (₹60 to ₹100) to help your browsing.

New Medical Centre (☏2225289; www.nmcpondy.com; 470 MG Rd; ⊙24hr) Recommended private clinic and hospital.

Shanti Travel (☏4210401; www.shantitravel.com; 13 Romain Rolland St; ⊙10am-7pm) Professional agency offering transport ticketing, walking tours, cultural activities, day trips and Chennai airport pick-ups.

Tourist Info Bureau (☏2339497; http://tourism.puducherry.gov.in; 40 Goubert Ave; ⊙9am-6pm) Has enthusiastic staff and the website has some worthwhile maps.

❶ Getting There & Away

BUS

The **bus stand** (Maraimalai Adigal Salai) is in the west of town, 2km from the French Quarter. Private bus companies, running mostly overnight to various destinations, have offices along Maraimalai Adigal Salai west of the bus stand. The only service to Kodaikanal (₹600, eight hours) is an 11pm semisleeper with **Parveen Travels** (www.parveentravels.com; 288 Maraimalai Adigal Salai).

TRAIN

Puducherry station has only a few services. Two daily trains run to Chennai Egmore, with unreserved seating only (₹28 to ₹53, four to five hours). You can connect at Villupuram, 38km west of Puducherry, for many more services north and south. Puducherry station has a computerised booking office for trains throughout India.

❶ Getting Around

One of the best ways to get around Pondy's flat streets is by walking. Autorickshaws are plentiful. Official metered fares are ₹20 for up to 2km and ₹1 for each further 100m, which should mean ₹25 maximum from bus stand to French Quarter. If drivers refuse to use their meters, you'll probably have to pay ₹50 or ₹60 for that trip.

Auroville

☏ 0413 / POP 2249

Auroville is one of those ideas that anyone with idealistic leanings will love: an international community dedicated to peace, harmony, sustainable living and 'divine consciousness', where people from around the globe, ignoring creed, colour and nationality, work together to build a universal, cash-free, non-religious township and realise good old human unity.

BUSES FROM PUDUCHERRY (PONDICHERRY) BUS STAND

DESTINATION	FARE (₹)	DURATION (HR)	FREQUENCY (DAILY)
Bengaluru	188-200 (Volvo AC 500-600)	8	6 (Volvo AC 8.30am, 10.30pm)
Chennai	97 (Volvo AC 190)	4	124 (25 Volvo AC)
Chidambaram	42	2½	40
Kumbakonam	80	4	6
Mamallapuram	50	2	70
Tiruvannamalai	63	3	11
Trichy	138	5	5

Making reality out of such a dream would never be easy. Imagine over 100 small settlements scattered across an area of Tamil countryside, with 2100 residents of more than 40 nationalities. Nearly 60% of Aurovillians are foreign, and most new members require more funds than most Indians are ever likely to have. Outside opinions of Auroville's inhabitants range from admiration to accusations of self-indulgent escapism. But the vibe you will receive on a visit is likely to be positive, and the energy driving the place is palpable.

Some 12km northwest of downtown Puducherry, Auroville was founded in 1968 on the inspiration of 'the Mother', co-founder of Puducherry's Sri Aurobindo Ashram, and her philosophy still guides it. Aurovillians run a huge variety of projects ranging from schools and IT to organic farming, renewable energy and handicrafts production, and they employ at least 4000 people from nearby villages.

The **Auroville website** (www.auroville.org) is an encyclopedic resource.

◉ Sights & Activities

Auroville in general is not geared for tourism – most inhabitants are just busy getting on with their lives – but it does have a good **Visitors Centre** (☑ 2622239; ☺ 9am-6pm) with information services, exhibitions and a few shops selling Auroville products. You can buy a handbook and map here, and after watching a 10-minute video you can get a pass for external viewing of the **Matrimandir** (☺ passes issued 9.30am-12.30pm daily & 2-4pm Mon-Sat), Auroville's 'soul', a 1km walk away through the woodlands.

The large, golden, almost spherical Matrimindir has been likened to a golf ball or a UFO. You might equally feel that its grand simplicity of form, surrounded by pristine green parkland, does indeed evoke the divine consciousness it's intended to represent. The orb's main inner chamber, lined with white marble, houses a large glass crystal that suffuses a beam of sunlight around the chamber. It's conceived as a place for individual silent concentration and if, after viewing the Matrimandir from the gardens, you want to spend time inside, you must make a reservation at least one day ahead at the **Matrimandir access office** (☑ 2622268; Visitors Centre; ☺ 10-11am & 2-3pm Wed-Mon).

Visitors are quite free to wander round Auroville's network of roads and tracks and look at some of the unusual and original buildings. It's a large area, about 20 sq km, but with two million trees planted since Auroville's foundation it has an attractive forested ambience.

If you're interested in getting to know more about Auroville, they recommend you stay at least 10 days and join one of their introduction programs or retreats. To get seriously involved, you normally need to come as a volunteer, in any of a wide variety of programs, usually for two to 12 months. The **Auroville Guest Service** (☑ 2622675; www.aurovilleguestservice.org; Solar Kitchen Bldg, 2km east of Visitors Centre; ☺ 9.30am-12.45am Mon-Sat) provides information and help on active participation.

🛏 Sleeping & Eating

Auroville has over 40 **guesthouses** (per person ₹300-1000) of varying comfort levels, offering from two to 46 beds. You can book them through the **Guest Accommodation Service** (☑ 2622704; www.aurovilleguesthouses.org; Visitors Centre; ☺ 9.30am-12.30pm & 2-5pm) or directly with individual guesthouses. For the peak seasons, December to March and August and September, reservations three or four months ahead are advised.

TYPICALLY TAMIL FESTIVALS

As well as local festivals (often temple-centred) and national ones that are celebrated here, Tamil Nadu has a couple of important state-wide festivals of its own.

Pongal (statewide; ☺ mid-Jan), the harvest festival, is held over four days in mid-January and is one of the year's most important occasions for families to get together. It's named after a Tamil rice-and-lentil dish cooked at this time in new clay pots. For many, the celebrations begin with temple rituals, followed by family gatherings. Later it's the animals, especially cows, that are honoured for their contribution to the harvest.

Held during full moon in November/December, Karthikai Deepam (p1036) is Tamil Nadu's 'festival of lights'. It is celebrated throughout the state with earthenware lamps and firecrackers, but the best place to see it is Tiruvannamalai, where the legend began.

The **Right Path Cafe** (Visitors Centre; mains ₹60-340; ⏱12.15-3pm & 6.30-9pm) serves decent Indian and Western food.

ℹ️ Getting There & Away

The main turning to Auroville from the East Coast Rd is at Periyar Mudaliarchavadi village, 6km north of Puducherry. From there it's about 6km west to the Visitors Centre. An autorickshaw one way from Puducherry is about ₹250, or you could take a Kottukuppam bus northbound on Ambour Salai to the Auroville turnoff (₹6), then an autorickshaw for ₹150. A good way to explore Auroville used to be by rented two-wheeler from outlets on and around northern MG Rd and Mission St in Puducherry, but the Puducherry authorities banned such rentals in 2012. If they relent, expect to pay around ₹50/150/250 per day for a bicycle/scooter/motorbike.

CENTRAL TAMIL NADU

Chidambaram

📞 04144 / POP 82,458

There's basically one reason to visit here: the great temple complex of Nataraja, Shiva as the Dancer of the Universe. One of the holiest of all Shiva sites, this also happens to be a Dravidian architectural highlight.

Of the town's many festivals, the two largest are the 10-day **chariot festivals** in June/July and December/January. In February/March the five-day **Natyanjali Dance Festival** attracts classical dancers from all over India to the Nataraja Temple.

Most accommodation is close to the temple or the bus stand (500m southeast of the temple). The train station is about 1km further southeast.

◉ Sights

★ **Nataraja Temple**   HINDU TEMPLE
(⏱inner compound 6am-noon & 4.30-10pm) The legend goes: one day Shiva and Kali got into a dance-off that was judged by Vishnu. Shiva dropped an earring and picked it up with his foot, a move that Kali could not duplicate, so Shiva won the title Nataraja (Lord of the Dance). It is in this form that he is worshipped at this great temple, which draws an endless stream of pilgrims and worshippers. The temple was erected during Chola times (Chidambaram was a Chola capital), but the shrines at its heart date back to at least the 6th century.

The high-walled 22-hectare complex has four towering *gopurams* decked out in schizophrenic Dravidian stone and stucco work. The main entrance is through the east *gopuram*, off East Car St. In its passageway are carved the 108 sacred positions of classical Tamil dance. To your right through the *gopuram* are the 1000-pillared **Raja Sabha** (King's Hall; ⏱festival days), and the large temple tank, the **Sivaganga**.

The central compound (no cameras allowed) is entered from the east. In its southern part (left from the entrance) is the **Nritta Sabha** (Dance Hall) in the form of a chariot with 56 very fine carved pillars. Some say this is the very spot where Shiva outdanced Kali.

Through a door north of the Nritta Sabha you enter the inner courtyard. In front of you is the **Kanaka Sabha**, a pavilion where many temple rituals are performed. At *puja* times devotees crowd into and around the pavilion to witness the rites performed by the temple's hereditary Brahmin priests, the Dikshithars, who shave off some of their hair but grow the rest of it long and tie it into topknots.

Behind (north of) the Kanaka Sabha is the innermost sanctum, the golden-roofed **Chit Sabha**, which holds the temple's central bronze image of Nataraja – Shiva the cosmic dancer, ending one cycle of creation, beginning another and uniting all opposites.

Priests may offer to guide you around the temple complex. Since they work as a kind of cooperative to fund the temple, you may wish to support this magnificent building by hiring one (for anything between ₹30 and ₹300, depending on their language skills and knowledge).

🛏️ Sleeping & Eating

Many cheap pilgrims' lodges are clustered around the temple, but some of these are pretty dire. If there's anywhere really nice to stay in Chidambaram, we haven't found it yet. There are lots of cheap veg eats in the area surrounding the temple, but the best places to eat are in hotels.

Hotel Saradharam   HOTEL **$$**
(📞 221336; www.hotelsaradharam.co.in; 19 VGP St; r incl breakfast ₹990, with AC ₹2100; 🕯🛜) The busy, friendly Saradharam is as good as it gets, and is conveniently located across from the bus stand. It's a bit worn but comfortable enough, and a welcome respite from the frenzy of the town centre. Breakfast is

TRANQUIL TRANQUEBAR

South of Chidambaram the many-armed delta of the Cauvery River stretches 180km along the coast and deep into the hinterland. The Cauvery is the beating heart of Tamil agriculture and its valley was the heartland of the Chola empire. Today the delta is one of the prettiest, poorest and most traditional parts of Tamil Nadu.

Easily the most appealing base is the little coastal town of Tharangambadi, still mostly known by its old name Tranquebar. A great place to recharge from the sweaty, crowded towns inland, this former Danish colony is quiet, orderly, pretty and set right on a long sandy beach with a few fishing boats and delicious sea breezes. The old part of town inside the 1791 Landporten gate makes an enjoyable stroll, and has seen a lot of restoration since the 2004 tsunami, which killed about 800 people here. INTACH Pondicherry (p1037) has an excellent downloadable map. The old Danish fort, **Dansborg** (Indian/foreigner ₹5/50, camera/video ₹30/100; ⊙10am-1pm & 2-5.30pm Sat-Thu), dates from 1624 and contains an interesting little museum. Other notable buildings include **New Jerusalem Church** (Tamil Evangelical Lutheran Church; King's St), an interesting mix of Indian and European styles built in 1718, and the 14th-century beachside **Masilamani Nathar Temple**, recently repainted in kaleidoscopic colours.

All accommodation is run by the **Bungalow on the Beach** (☑04364-288065; http://neemranahotels.com; 24 King's St; r incl breakfast ₹3600-7195, budget r ₹990; ✴ ⊛), in the former residence of the British administrator (Denmark sold Tranquebar to the British East India Company in 1845). This amounts to 17 lovely heritage-style rooms in the main building and two other locations in town, plus five clean, sizeable, budget rooms in the Hotel Tamil Nadu, opposite the main building. All rooms are AC. The main building has a lovely swimming pool and a good multicuisine **restaurant** (mains ₹150-250; ⊙7.30-9.30am, 12.30-2.30pm, 7.30-9.30pm). For weekends and holidays you should book ahead.

Tranquebar is a good base for exploring the delta area. At Velankanni, 47km south, the **Basilica of Our Lady of Health** stands where a young buttermilk boy glimpsed the Virgin Mary in the 16th century. The Virgin's image supposedly has curative powers and this is a big pilgrimage spot, with some distinctly Hindu styles of worship. A 10-day festival culminates on 8 September. Tamil Nadu's largest temple chariot is hauled around Thiruvarur during the Thyagararaja Temple's 10-day car festival in April/May.

Buses in this region are often extremely crowded, but Tranquebar has regular connections with Chidambaram (₹23, two hours, hourly) and Karaikal (₹11, 30 minutes, half-hourly). From Karaikal there are buses to Kumbakonam (₹26, 2¼ hours, 36 daily), Thanjavur (₹68, 3½ hours, three daily) and Puducherry (₹65, four hours, five daily).

a good buffet, there's free wi-fi in the lobby, and the hotel has three restaurants – two vegetarian places plus the good multicuisine, AC **Anupallavi** (mains ₹145-280; ⊙7-10am, noon-3pm, 6-10.30pm).

Hotel Akshaya
HOTEL $$

(☑220192; www.hotel-akshaya.com; 17-18 East Car St; r incl breakfast ₹1090, with AC ₹2050-2400; ✴) Close to the temple, this hotel has a wide range of rooms in various states of preservation. Some non-AC rooms are in better condition than some AC ones. The **Annapoorani Restaurant** (mains ₹65-90; ⊙7-10am, 11am-3pm, 6-9.30pm) here does an excellent ₹75 South Indian lunch and other good vegetarian fare. Next door, **Dravidian Handicrafts** (www.dravidiansculpturescom; 9 East Sannathi) sells quality reproduction bronzes.

ⓘ Information

ICICI Bank ATM (Hotel Saradharam, VGP St)

ⓘ Getting There & Away

Buses head to Chennai (₹140, six hours) every half-hour, most going via Puducherry (₹42, 2½ hours). Other destinations include Kumbakonam (₹48, 2½ hours, every 20 minutes), Thanjavur (₹90, four hours, every 30 minutes) and Tranquebar (Tharangambadi; ₹23, two hours, hourly). Universal Travels, opposite the bus stand, has three daily comfortable Volvo AC departures to Chennai (₹450).

Three or more daily trains head to Trichy (2nd-class/3AC/2AC ₹61/277/610, 3½ hours) via Kumbakonam and Thanjavur, and five to Chennai (₹78/362/610, 5½ hours).

Kumbakonam

♪ 0435 / POP 140,113

At first glance Kumbakonam is another Indian junction town, but then you notice the dozens of colourful *gopurams* pointing skyward from Kumbakonam's 18 temples, a reminder that this was once a seat of medieval South Indian power. With two World Heritage–listed Chola temples nearby, it's worth staying at least one night.

◎ Sights

Most of the temples are dedicated to Shiva or Vishnu. All are open from 6.30am to 12.30pm and 4.30pm to 8.30pm, with free admission.

The largest Vishnu temple, with a 45m-high eastern *gopuram* as its main entrance, is **Sarangapani Temple** (no photography allowed inside). Past the temple cowshed, another *gopuram* and a pillared hall you reach the inner sanctuary, a 12th-century Chola creation, which is given a chariot appearance by large carved elephants, horses and wheels.

Kumbeshwara Temple, entered via a nine-storey *gopuram,* is the largest Shiva temple. It dates from the 17th and 18th centuries and contains a lingam said to have been made by Shiva himself when he mixed the nectar of immortality with sand.

The **Nageshwara Temple**, founded by the Cholas in 886, is Kumbakonam's oldest temple, and is dedicated to Shiva in the guise of Nagaraja, the serpent king. On three days of the year (in April or May) the sun's rays fall on the lingam..

The huge **Mahamaham Tank**, surrounded by 17 pavilions, is one of Kumbakonam's most sacred sites. It's believed that every 12 years the waters of the Ganges flow into the tank, and at this time a festival is held; the next is due in 2016.

🛏 Sleeping & Eating

Pandian Hotel   HOTEL $
(♪2430397; 52 Sarangapani East Sannathi St; s/d ₹294/473, d with AC ₹990; ❄) It feels a bit institutional, but in general you're getting fair value at this clean-enough budget standby.

Hotel Raya's   HOTEL $$
(♪2423170; www.hotelrayas.com; 18 Head Post Office Rd; r ₹990, with AC ₹1320-2280; ❄) Friendly service and reliably spacious, clean rooms make this your best lodging option in town. They have a convenient car service for out-

of-town trips. **Sathars Restaurant** (mains ₹85-175; ⊙11.30am-11.30pm) here does good veg and nonveg fare in clean surroundings.

Hotel Kanishka   HOTEL $$
(♪2425231; 18/450 Ayekulam Rd; r ₹770-880, AC ₹1100-1238; ❄ 🛜) A cheerful place with smallish, simple but stylish rooms with yellow or pink feature walls. It's owned by a young couple who keep the hotel family-friendly. Free wi-fi in the reception area.

Paradise Resort   RESORT $$$
(♪3291354; www.paradiseresortindia.com; Tanjore Main Rd, Darasuram; s ₹5396-10,193, d ₹5996-10,193; ❄ 🛜 ⊛) Five kilometres west of downtown, this charming resort occupies large, lush grounds that even include a small village. The luxurious rooms have antique doors, carved wood furnishings and lovely big bathrooms. You can enjoy cooking demos, bullock-cart rides, ayurveda and yoga, and the high-class multicuisine restaurant has some great South Indian specialities.

Hotel Sri Venkkatramana   INDIAN $
(TSR Big St; thalis ₹50-65; ⊙5.30am-10pm Mon-Sat) Serves good fresh veg food and is very popular with locals.

Taj Samudra   INDIAN $$
(80 Nageswaran South St; mains ₹100-170; ⊙11am-3pm & 7-11pm) Here you can get tasty veg and nonveg dishes from all over India, in neat, even stylish surroundings – and the pictures on the menu and screen will help if you're not familiar with their names!

ⓘ Information

Speed Systems (Sarangapani East St; internet per hr ₹20; ⊙9.30am-9.30pm) Take your passport.

ⓘ Getting There & Away

Eleven daily trains head to Thanjavur (2nd-class/3AC/2AC ₹35/218/610, 30 minutes to one hour) and Trichy (₹46/218/610, two to 2½ hours). Four daily trains to/from Chennai Egmore include the overnight Rock Fort Express (sleeper/3AC/2AC/1AC ₹191/524/785/1340, 9½ hours), via Thanjavur and Trichy, and the daytime Chennai Express/Trichy Express (₹158/428/635/1075, six to seven hours).

Government buses from the **bus stand**:
Chennai ₹156 to ₹230, seven to eight hours, every 15 minutes
Chidambaram ₹48, 2½ hours, every 20 minutes
Karaikal ₹26, 2¼ hours, every 30 minutes
Thanjavur ₹29, 1½ hours, every 10 minutes

Kumbakonam

N 0 ——— 500 m
0 ——— 0.25 miles

Kumbakonam

◎ Sights
1	Kumbeshwara Temple	A2
2	Mahamaham Tank	C2
3	Nageshwara Temple	B1
4	Sarangapani Temple	B1

⌂ Sleeping
5	Hotel Kanishka	C1
6	Hotel Raya's	C2
7	Pandian Hotel	B1

⊗ Eating
8	Hotel Sri Venkkatramana	B1
	Sathars Restaurant	(see 6)
9	Taj Samudra	C1

ⓘ Information
10	Speed Systems	B1
11	STH Hospital	C1

ⓘ Transport
12	Train Station	D2

Thanjavur (Tanjore)

☏ 04362 / POP 222,619

Here are the ochre foundation blocks of perhaps the most remarkable civilisation of Dravidian history, one of the few kingdoms to expand Hinduism beyond India, a bedrock for aesthetic styles that spread from Madurai to the Mekong. A dizzying historical legacy was forged from Thanjavur, capital of the great Chola Empire during its heyday, which is today...a hectic, crowded, noisy, modern Indian town. But the past is still very much present: every day thousands of people still worship at the Cholas' grand Brihadishwara Temple, and Thanjavur's labyrinthine royal palace preserves memories of other powerful dynasties from later centuries.

◎ Sights

★Brihadishwara Temple   HINDU TEMPLE
(admission free; ◷ 6am-8.30pm) Come here twice: in the morning, when the tawny granite begins to assert its dominance over the white dawn sunshine, and in the evening, when the rocks capture a hot palette of reds, oranges, yellows and pinks on the crowning glory of Chola temple architecture. The World Heritage–listed Brihadishwara Temple was built between 1003 and 1010 by Rajaraja I (whose name means 'king of kings'), a monarch so organised he had the names and addresses of all his dancers, musicians, barbers and poets inscribed into the temple wall. The outer fortifications were put up by Thanjavur's later Nayak and British regimes.

You enter through a Nayak gate, followed by two original *gopurams* with elaborate stucco sculptures. You'll often find the temple elephant below one of the *gopurams,* dispensing good luck with a dab of his trunk to anyone who puts a rupee in it. Several shrines are dotted around the extensive grassy areas of the walled temple compound, including one with one of India's largest statues of Nandi (Shiva's sacred bull) facing the main temple building. Cut from a single rock, this 16th-century Nayak creation is 6m long.

A long, columned assembly hall leads to the central shrine with its 4m-high Shiva lingam, beneath the superb 61m-high *vimana* (tower). The assembly hall's southern steps are flanked by two huge *dvarapalas* (temple guardians). Many lovely, graceful deity images stand in niches around the *vimana's* lower levels, including Shiva emerging from the lingam (beside the southern steps); Shiva as the beggar Bhikshatana (first image, south side); Harihara (half Shiva, half Vishnu) on the west wall; and Ardhanarishvara (Shiva as half-man, half-woman), leaning on Nandi, on the north side. Set between the deity images are panels showing positions of classical dance.

The compound also contains a worthwhile interpretation centre along the south wall and, in the colonnade along the west and north walls, hundreds more linga as well as some good Nayak-era murals. North of the temple compound, but still within the outer fortifications, is a park containing the **Sivaganga tank** and 18th-century **Schwartz's Church**.

★ **Royal Palace**   PALACE
(Indian/foreigner/camera ₹10/50/30; ☉9am-5pm) Thanjavur's royal palace is a mixed bag of decrepitude and renovation, superb art and random royal paraphernalia, with a frequent whiff of dung and decay. The labyrinthine complex was constructed partly by the Nayaks who took over Thanjavur in 1535, and partly by a local Maratha dynasty that ruled from 1676 to 1855.

Seven different sections of the palace can be visited, and you need four separate tickets to see them all! The two don't-miss sections are the Art Gallery and Saraswati Mahal Library Museum. The main entrance is from the north, via a lane off East Main St. On the way in you'll find the ticket office for the Maratha Palace Museum, which comprises three of the seven sections: the Mahratta Dharbar Hall, the bell tower and the Saarjah Madi (this last under reconstruction at research time).

Past this ticket office, a passage to the left leads to, first, the **Royal Palace Museum** (admission ₹1; ☉9am-6pm), a small miscellany of sculptures, weaponry, elephant bells and rajas' headgear; second, the **Maharaja Serfoji Memorial Hall** (admission ₹4; ☉9am-6pm), commemorating the enlightened Maratha scholar-king Serfoji II (1798–1832), with a better miscellany overlooking a once-splendid, now overgrown courtyard; and third, the **Mahratta Dharbar Hall**, where Maratha rulers gave audience in a pavilion adorned with colourful murals, including

their own portraits behind the dais and hunting scenes on the north wall.

As you exit the passage from the above, the **Saraswati Mahal Library Museum** (admission free; ☉10am-1pm & 1.30-5.30pm) (no photos allowed) is on your left. Perhaps Serfoji II's greatest contribution to posterity, this is testimony both to the 19th-century obsession with knowledge accumulation and to an eclectic mind that collected prints of Chinese torture methods, Audubon-style paintings of Indian flora and fauna, and sketches of the London skyline. Serfoji amassed more than 65,000 books and 50,000 palm-leaf and paper manuscripts in Indian and European languages, though these aren't included in the exhibit.

Exiting the library, turn left again for the **Art Gallery** (Indian/foreigner ₹7/60, camera ₹30/100; ☉9am-1pm & 3-6pm). Set around the courtyard of the Nayak palace, this contains a large collection of superb, mainly Chola, bronzes and stone carvings. One of the rooms is the Nayak Durbar Hall, built in 1600, which also contains a statue of Serfoji II. From the courtyard, steps lead about halfway up a large *gopuram*-like tower affording good views over Thanjavur. The Maratha bell tower, outside the Art Gallery entrance, can be climbed with your Palace Museum ticket.

🎭 Festivals & Events

Thyagaraja Aradhana   MUSIC FESTIVAL
(☉Jan) At Thiruvaiyaru, 13km north of Thanjavur, this important eight-day Carnatic music festival honours the saint and composer Thyagaraja.

🛏 Sleeping

Hotel Ramnath   HOTEL $
(☎272567; hotel_ramnath@yahoo.com; 1335 South Rampart; r ₹900, with AC ₹1200; ✴) The best of a bunch of places facing the local bus stand downtown (the attendant noise is not as bad as you might expect), the Ramnath is a decent 'upmarket budget' option with clean, not very big, pine-furnished rooms.

Hotel Valli   HOTEL $
(☎231580; www.hotelvalli.com; 2948 MKM Rd; s ₹504, d ₹605-715, r with AC ₹1463; ✴) Near the train station, green-painted Valli has good-value, spick-and-span rooms. Staff are personable, and the hotel has a decent restaurant. It's in a reasonably peaceful location beyond a bunch of greasy backstreet workshops.

Thanjavur (Tanjore)

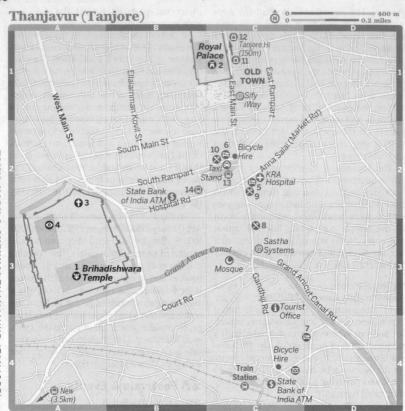

Hotel Gnanam
HOTEL $$

(☎278501; www.hotelgnanam.com; Anna Salai; s/d incl breakfast from ₹2159/2518; ❄️🛜) With the best overall value in town, the Gnanam has stylish, comfy rooms (the more expensive ones with lovely clean bath-tubs) and is perfect for anyone needing wi-fi (in the lobby; free), good meals and other modern amenities while they're plopped in Thanjavur's geographic centre.

Tanjore Hi
BOUTIQUE HOTEL $$$

(☎252111; http://tanjorehihotel.com; 464 East Main St; r incl breakfast from ₹9341; ❄️🛜) A 1926 house revamped by a German architect, Tanjore Hi has lovely, stylish, all-different rooms in blue and white, with solid wood floors, large contemporary art prints and free wi-fi. The bright top-floor **restaurant** (mains ₹200-320; ⊘7.30-10am, 12.30-2.30pm, 7.30-10-30pm) serves appetising international and Indian dishes.

🍴 Eating

Sri Venkata Lodge
SOUTH INDIAN $

(Gandhiji Rd; thalis ₹50; ⊘5.15am-10pm) A friendly, popular, veg-only place near the centre of everything, that does a nice thali.

Vasanta Bhavan
INDIAN $

(1338 South Rampart; mains ₹50-70; ⊘6am-11pm) The most appealing of several veg places facing the local bus stand downtown, Vasanta Bhavan has welcome AC and offers biryani and North Indian curries as well as your usual southern favourites.

Sahana
INDIAN $$

(Anna Salai, Hotel Gnanam; mains ₹95-115; ⊘7am-11pm) This classy hotel restaurant does a very nice line in fresh, tasty, mainly Indian veg dishes. The hotel's pricier nonveg **Diana** (mains ₹140-250; ⊘11am-3pm & 6.30-10pm) is also very good, with a wide range of north-

Thanjavur (Tanjore)

◎ **Top Sights**
 1 Brihadishwara Temple........................A3
 2 Royal Palace..C1

◎ **Sights**
 3 Schwartz's Church A2
 4 Sivaganga Tank......................................A3

🛏 **Sleeping**
 5 Hotel Gnanam C2
 6 Hotel Ramnath C2
 7 Hotel Valli..D4

✖ **Eating**
  Diana...(see 5)
  Sahana ....(see 5)
 8 Sathars...C3
 9 Sri Venkata Lodge C2
 10 Vasanta Bhavan....................................C2

🛍 **Shopping**
 11 Chola Art Galerie................................ C1
 12 Kandiya Heritage C1

ℹ **Transport**
 13 Local Bus Stand....................................C2
 14 SETC Bus Stand....................................B2

ern dishes and local Chettinad fare – and beer too.

Sathars   INDIAN $$
(167 Gandhiji Rd; mains ₹80-160; ⊙ noon 4pm & 6.30-11.30pm) Good service and quality food make this place popular, and the upper floor has a bit of fresh air. You can get biryanis, five types of chicken tikka kebab, good *parathas* (flaky bread stuffed with veg), and mutton, seafood and plenty of veg dishes.

🔒 Shopping

Thanjavur is a good place to shop for handicrafts, especially near the palace, where shops such as **Kandiya Heritage** (634 East Main St; ⊙ 9am-7.30pm Mon-Sat) and **Chola Art Galerie** (78/799 East Main St; ⊙ 10am-7pm) sell antiques, reproduction bronzes, brightly painted wooden horses, old European pottery and more.

ℹ Information

Sify iWay (927 East Main St; internet per hr ₹20; ⊙ 9am-9pm)

Tourist Office (🖉 230984; Gandhiji Rd; ⊙ 10am-5pm Mon-Fri) One of Tamil Nadu's more helpful offices.

ℹ Getting There & Away

BUS
The downtown **SETC bus stand** (⊙ reservation office 7.30am-9.30pm) has AC express buses to Chennai (₹260, eight hours) every 45 minutes from 5.30am to 1pm, and five times between 8pm and 10.45pm. Buses for other cities leave from the New Bus Station, 5km southwest of the centre. Many arriving buses can let you off in the city centre before heading out there. Services from the New Bus Station:

Chidambaram ₹90, four hours, every 30 minutes

Karaikal ₹45, 3½ hours, 11 daily

Kumbakonam ₹29, 1½ hours, every 15 minutes

Madurai ₹90, four hours, every 15 minutes

Trichy ₹31, 1½ hours, every 10 minutes

TRAIN
The station is reasonably central at the end of Gandhiji Rd. Five daily trains head to Chennai Egmore (seven to nine hours) including the 8.30pm Rock Fort Express (sleeper/3AC/2AC/1AC ₹190/490/730/1225). Eighteen trains head to Trichy (2nd-class/3AC/2AC ₹37/218/610, 1½ hours), and 12 to Kumbakonam (2nd-class/3AC/2AC ₹35/218/610, 40 minutes to 1½ hours).

ℹ Getting Around

Bus 74 (₹6) shuttles between the New Bus Station and the local bus stand downtown. An autorickshaw can cost ₹100.

Trichy (Tiruchirappalli)

📞 0431 / POP 846,915

Welcome to (more or less) the geographic centre of Tamil Nadu. Tiruchirappalli, universally known as Trichy or Tiruchi, isn't just a travel junction; it also mixes up a throbbing bazaar with some major mustsee temples. It's a big, crowded, busy city, and the fact that most hotels are grouped around the large bus station isn't exactly a plus point. But Trichy has a strong character and long history and a way of overturning first impressions.

Trichy may have been a capital of the early Cholas in the 3rd century BC. It passed through the hands of the Pallavas, medieval Cholas, Pandyas, Delhi Sultanate and Vijayanagars before the Madurai Nayaks really brought it to prominence, making it a capital in the 17th century and building its famous Rock Fort Temple.

Trichy stretches a long way from north to south, and most of what matters to travellers

DON'T MISS

CHOLA TEMPLES NEAR KUMBAKONAM

Two of the three great monuments of Chola civilisation stand in villages near Kumbakonam. Unlike the also World Heritage–listed Brihadishwara Temple at Thanjavur, these temples receive relatively few worshippers today. They are wonderful both for their overall form (with pyramidal towers rising at the heart of rectangular walled compounds) and for the exquisite detail of their carved stone.

Only 3km west of Kumbakonam in Darasuram village, the **Airavatesvara Temple** (admission free; ⊙ 6.30am-8.30pm), dedicated to Shiva, was constructed by Rajaraja II (1146–63). Guides can explain everything inside for around ₹100. The steps of the Rajagambhira Hall are carved with vivid elephants and horses pulling chariots. This pavilion's 108 all-different pillars have a plethora of detailed carving including dancers, acrobats and the five-in-one beast Yali who has an elephant's head, lion's body, goat's horns, pig's ears and the backside of a cow. On the outside of the main shrine are several fine carved images of Shiva. Inside the **shrine** (⊙ 6am-noon & 4-7pm) you can pay your respects to the central lingam and receive a *tilak* mark for ₹10. The **Nataraja Mandapa** contains a museum of sculptures from the site plus boards of historical information.

The **temple** (admission free; ⊙ 6.30am-8.30pm) at Gangaikondacholapuram ('City of the Chola who Conquered the Ganges'), 35km north of Kumbakonam, is also dedicated to Shiva. It was built by Rajendra I in the 11th century when he moved the Chola capital here from Thanjavur after successful campaigns in northern India. The temple has many similarities to the earlier Brihadishwara at Thanjavur. Its beautiful 49m-tall main tower, however, has a slightly concave curve, in contrast to the mildly convex one at Thanjavur. Gangaikondacholapuram is thus considered the 'feminine' counterpart to the Thanjavur edifice.

A large Nandi bull (Shiva's vehicle) faces the temple from the surrounding grassy lawns. The main shrine, beneath the tower, contains a huge lingam and is approached through a long, gloomy, 17th-century hall. The complex's artistic highlights are the wonderfully graceful sculptures around the tower's exterior. These include Shiva as the beggar Bhikshatana, immediately left of the southern steps; Ardhanarishvara (Shiva as half-man, half-woman), and Shiva as Nataraja, on the south side; and Shiva with Ganga, Shiva emerging from the lingam, and Vishnu with Lakshmi and Bhudevi (the first three images on the west side). Most famous of all is the beatiful panel of Shiva garlanding the head of his follower, Chandesvara, beside the northern steps.

From Kumbakonam bus stand, frequent buses heading to nearby villages will drop you at Darasuram; buses to Gangaikondacholapuram (₹19, 1½ hours) go every half-hour. An autorickshaw to Darasuram costs about ₹120 round trip. A half-day car trip to both temples, through Hotel Raya's (p1047), is ₹950 (₹1100 with AC).

---

is split into three distinct areas. The Trichy Junction, or Cantonment, area in the south has most of the hotels and restaurants and the main bus and train stations. The Rock Fort Temple and main bazaar area is 4km north of here; the other important temples are in Srirangam, a further 4km north again, across the Cauvery River. Fortunately, the whole lot is connected by a good bus service.

◉ Sights

★ **Rock Fort Temple**   HINDU TEMPLE
(Map p1054; admission ₹3, camera/video ₹20/100; ⊙ 6am-8pm) The Rock Fort Temple, perched 83m high on a massive outcrop, lords over Trichy with stony arrogance. The ancient rock was first hewn by the Pallavas and Pandyas, who cut small cave temples on its south side, but it was the war-savvy Nayaks who later made strategic use of the naturally fortified position. There are over 400 stone-cut steps to climb to the top. From NSB Rd on the south side, you pass between small shops and cross a street before entering the temple precinct proper. Then it's 180 steps up to the Thayumanaswamy Temple (Swami Amman Sannathi) on the left (closed to non-Hindus). This is the rock's biggest temple and prominently visible from below and above. A gold-topped tower rises over its sanctum, which houses a 2m-high Shiva lingam. Heading on up, you pass the 6th-century Pallava cave temple on the left – it's often railed off but should you get inside, check

out the famous Gangadhara panel on the left, showing Shiva restraining the waters of the Ganges with a single strand of his hair. From here it's just another 183 steps to the small Uchipillaiyar Temple at the summit, dedicated to Ganesh. The view is wonderful, with eagles wheeling beneath and Trichy sprawling all around.

★ Sri Ranganathaswamy Temple
HINDU TEMPLE

(Map p1054; camera/video ₹50/100; ⊙6am-9pm) All right temple-philes, here's the one you've been waiting for: quite possibly the biggest temple in India – so large, it feels like a self-enclosed city. It has 49 separate shrines, all dedicated to Vishnu, and reaching the inner sanctum from the south, as most worshippers do, requires passing through seven *gopurams*. The first, the **Rajagopuram** (Map p1054), was added to the 20 older ones in 1987, and is claimed to be Asia's tallest temple tower at 73m high. You pass through streets with shops, restaurants and cars until you reach the temple proper at the fourth *gopuram*. Inside here is the ticket desk for the nearby **roof viewpoint** (ticket ₹10; ⊙8am-6pm), which gives a semi-panoramic view of the complex. Non-Hindus cannot pass the sixth *gopuram* so won't see the innermost sanctum whose image shows Vishnu as Lord Ranganatha, lying on a five-headed snake.

Turn right just before the fifth *gopuram* to the small but intriguing **Art Museum** (admission ₹5; ⊙9am-1pm & 2-6pm), with good bronzes, tusks of bygone temple elephants, and a collection of superb 17th-century Nayak ivory figurines depicting gods, demons, kings and queens (some of them erotically engaged) and even a portly Portugese soldier. Continue round to the left past the museum to the **Sesha Mandapa**, a 16th-century pillared hall with magnificent, large but detailed Vijayanagar carvings of rearing horses in battle.

The temple's most important festival is the 21-day Vaikunta Ekadasi (Paradise Festival) in December/January, when the celebrated Vaishnavaite text, Tiruvaimozhi, is recited before an image of Vishnu.

Bus 1 from or to the Central Bus Station or the Rock Fort stops right outside the Rajagopuram.

Sri Jambukeshwara Temple
HINDU TEMPLE

(Tiruvanakoil; camera/video ₹30/200; ⊙6am-8pm) If you're visiting Tamil Nadu's five elemental temples of Shiva, you need to visit Sri Jambukeshwara, dedicated to Shiva, Parvati and the medium of water. The liquid theme is realised in the central shrine (closed to non-Hindus), whose Shiva lingam reputedly issues a nonstop trickle of water. If you're taking bus 1, ask for 'Tiruvanakoil'; the temple is 350m east of the main road.

Lourdes Church
CHURCH

(Map p1054; College Rd) The hush of this 19th-century church makes an interesting contrast to the frenetic activity of Trichy's Hindu temples. In the green, cool campus of Jesuit St Joseph's College next door, an eccentric and dusty **museum** (Map p1054; admission free; ⊙9am-noon & 2-4pm Mon-Sat) contains the natural history collections of the Jesuit priests' excursions to the Western Ghats in the 1870s. Bang on the door and the caretaker will let you in (if he's there).

🛏 Sleeping & Eating

Most hotels are near the Central Bus Station, a short walk north from Trichy Junction train station.

The most enjoyable eateries are in the better hotels, but there are some decent cheaper places too.

Hotel Abbirami
HOTEL $

(Map p1056; ☑2415001; 10 McDonald's Rd; r ₹770-990, with AC ₹1439-2159; ✱) Most appealing are the 1st-floor renovated rooms with light wood and colourful glass panels adding a touch of fun. Older rooms have darker wood and are a bit worn, but all are kept clean. It's a busy place with friendly staff.

Hotel Mathura
HOTEL $

(Map p1056; ☑2414737; www.hotelmathura.com; 1 Rockins Rd; r ₹680, with AC ₹1100; ✱) Rooms are very ordinary but tolerably clean. Those on the 2nd floor, at least, have had a fairly recent coat of paint. Next door, **Hotel Meega** (Map p1056; ☑2414092; 3 Rockins Rd; s ₹446, d ₹605-660, s/d with AC ₹715/880; ✱) is on similar lines.

Hotel Ramyas
HOTEL $$

(Map p1056; ☑2414646; www.ramyas.com; 13-D/2 Williams Rd; r ₹1089, with AC s ₹2039-2518, d ₹2878-3118, all incl breakfast; ✱ @ 🛜) Excellent rooms, service and facilities make this business-oriented hotel a fine choice. 'Business class' singles are small but it's only another ₹200-odd for an excellent executive room. The **Thendral** (Map p1056; mains ₹90-195; ⊙noon-3.30pm & 7-11pm) roof-garden restaurant is lovely, breakfast is an excellent buffet,

TAMIL NADU & CHENNAI TRICHY (TIRUCHIRAPPALLI)

Trichy (Tiruchirappalli)

Trichy (Tiruchirappalli)

◎ **Top Sights**
1 Rock Fort Temple B4
2 Sri Ranganathaswamy Temple.......... A1

◎ **Sights**
3 Lourdes Church A5
4 Rajagopuram.................................A1
5 St Joseph's College Museum.............A5

🛏 **Sleeping**
6 Hotel Royal Sathyam..........................B5
7 Hotel Susee Park B5

✖ **Eating**
8 Banana Leaf.................................A5
9 Vasanta Bhavan.............................B5

🛍 **Shopping**
10 Saratha's......................................B5

ℹ **Information**
11 Canara Bank ATM.............................B5
12 ICICI Bank ATM...............................A5

spacious bar. It's a cut above other midrange hotels, and singles are as big as doubles. Autorickshaws charge ₹40 from the bus station; it's on the top floor of the Reliance supermarket building.

Femina Hotel   HOTEL **$$**
(Map p1056; ☑2414501; www.feminahotels.in; 109 Williams Rd; s ₹1559-2998, d ₹2039-4797, all incl breakfast; 🕸@⊛) The Femina looks 1950s outside but renovations have given the inside quite a contemporary look. Facilities are good and staff helpful. Economy rooms are closest to the busy street, and a bit jaded. Standard rooms are cosier and have a much lower honk factor. There's a nice outdoor **pool** (nonguests per hr ₹100; ⊙7am-7pm Tue-Sun) and eateries include the stylish coffeeshop-cum-veg-restaurant **Round the Clock** (Map p1056; mains ₹90-110; ⊙24hr).

PLA Krishna Inn   HOTEL **$$**
(Map p1056; ☑2406666; www.plakrishnainn.com; 8A Rockins Rd; s ₹2099-2758, d ₹2392-2758, all incl breakfast; 🕸🛜) New in 2012, PLA Krishna has bright, spacious rooms sporting trendy rectangular white washbasins and plus-size shower heads. With two restaurants, a bar, polished service and free in-room wi-fi, you won't go wrong here.

Breeze Residency   HOTEL **$$**
(Map p1056; ☑2414414; www.breezeresidency. com; 3/14 McDonald's Rd; s/d ₹2998/3478, ste

and the **Chola Bar** (Map p1056; ⊙11am-3.30pm & 6.30-11pm) is livelier and less dingy than most hotel bars (though still male-dominated). In-room wi-fi is ₹50 per three hours,

Hotel High Point   BOUTIQUE HOTEL **$$**
(☑2416766; www.hotelhighpoint.in; Manghalam Towers, 9 Reynolds Rd; s ₹2159-3238, d ₹2998-3957, all incl breakfast; 🕸🛜) In a relatively upmarket, leafy neighbourhood, High Point provides very comfy, stylish rooms incorporating pop-art prints, red-and-yellow-striped walls, free wi-fi and glassed-in showers. There's a good multicuisine restaurant and a

₹4197-5996, all incl breakfast; ❖@🛜🌊) The Breeze is enormous, semiluxurious and in a relatively quiet location. The best rooms are on the top floor,s but all are well appointed. Facilities include a gym, the good **Madras Restaurant** (Map p1056; mains ₹100-300; 🕐12.30-3.30pm & 7-11pm) and a bizarre Wild West theme bar.

Hotel Royal Sathyam　　　　HOTEL **$$**
(Map p1054; ☑ 4011414; www.sathyamgrouphotels.com; 42A Singarathope; s ₹1439-1919, d ₹1679-2998, all incl breakfast; ❖🛜) The classiest option if you want to be close to the temple and market action. Rooms are small but stylish, with extra-comfy mattresses and a fresh wood-and-whitewash theme. There's free wi-fi in the lobby. Nearby **Hotel Susee Park** (Map p1054; ☑ 2812345; www.hotelsuseepark.com; 45 Singarathope; r ₹1079, with AC ₹1498-2278) is also fine.

Vasanta Bhavan　　　　INDIAN **$**
(Map p1054; 3 NSB Rd; mains ₹50-80, thalis ₹80-110; 🕐6am-11pm) A good spot for a meal with a view and, with luck, a breeze near the Rock Fort. Tables on the outer gallery overlook the Teppakulam Tank. It's good for North Indian veg food – that of the *paneer* and naan genre – as well as South Indian. It gets very busy at lunchtime when people crowd in for the good thalis. There's another **branch** (Map p1056; Rockins Rd; mains ₹40-55, thalis ₹60-90; 🕐6am-11pm) in the Cantonment.

Banana Leaf　　　　INDIAN **$$**
(Map p1056; McDonald's Rd; mains ₹80-175; 🕐11am-midnight) A big menu of veg and non-veg regional favourites is served in two small AC rooms. The speciality is the fiery, vaguely vinegary cuisine of Andhra Pradesh. Another **branch** (Map p1054; Madurai Rd) is near the Rock Fort.

🛍 Shopping

The main bazaar, immediately south of the Rock Fort, is as chaotic and crowded as you could want; it constantly feels as if all of Trichy is strolling the strip. While you'here, do have a look round **Saratha's** (Map p1054; 45 NSB Rd; 🕐9am-9.30pm), which claims to be (and may indeed be) the 'largest textile showroom in India' and sells men's and women's clothes of every conceivable kind.

ⓘ Information

Indian Panorama (☑ 4226122; www.indian panorama.in; 5 Annai Avenue, Srirangam) Trichy-based and covering all of India, this professional, reliable travel agency/tour operator is run by an Indian–New Zealander couple.
Kauvery Hospital (Map p1056; KMC Speciality Hospital; ☑ 4077777; www.kmcspecialityhospital.in; 6 Royal Rd) A large, well-equipped, private hospital.
Tourist Office (Map p1056; ☑ 2460136; McDonald's Rd; 🕐10am-5.45pm Mon-Fri)

ⓘ Getting There & Away

AIR

Trichy's airport has a few international flights, as well as daily flights to Chennai on **JetKonnect** (www.jetkonnect.com), **Air India Express** (☑ 2341744; www.airindiaexpress.in) and **SpiceJet** (www.spicejet.com), and Bengaluru SpiceJet. To Colombo, **SriLankan Airlines** (Map p1056; ☑ 2460844; 14C Williams Rd; 🕐9am-5.30pm Mon-Fri) flies twice daily, and **Mihin Lanka** (☑ 4200606; www.mihinlanka.com; Reynolds Rd, Translanka Air Travels; 🕐9.30am 6pm Mon-Fri, 9.30am-2pm Sat) four times weekly. **Air Asia** (Map p1056; ☑ 4540393; www.airasia.com; 18/3-5 Ivory Plaza, Royal Rd) flies to Kuala Lumpur, **Tiger Airways** (www.tigerairways.com) to Singapore, and Air India Express to Singapore and Dubai, all daily.

GOVERNMENT BUSES FROM TRICHY

DESTINATION	FARE (₹)	DURATION (HR)	FREQUENCY
Bengaluru	350 Ultra Deluxe (UD)	8	6 UD daily
Chennai	180 regular, 235 UD, 350 AC	6-7	15 UD, 4 AC daily
Coimbatore	140	5-6	every 30min
Kodaikanal	110	5	6.40am, 8.30am, 11.50am
Madurai	80	3	every 15min
Ooty	260 UD	8	10.15pm UD
Rameswaram	180	6½	hourly
Thanjavur	31	1½	every 10min

Trichy Junction Area

BUS

Government buses use the busy **Central Bus Station** (Map p1056; Rockins Rd). The best services for most longer trips are the UD ('ultra deluxe'), which have softer seats than regular buses. There's a booking office for these in the southwest corner of the station. For Kodaikanal, a good option is to take one of the frequent buses to Dindigul (₹30, two hours) and change there.

Several private bus companies have offices near the Central Bus Station, including **Parveen Travels** (Map p1056; www.parveentravels.com; 12 Ashby Complex) which offers AC services to Chennai (₹560 to ₹720, four daily), Coimbatore (₹260, 11.30pm), Bengaluru (₹650, 11pm) and Trivandrum (₹1300 to ₹1400, 12.30am and 1am).

TAXI

Plenty of travel agencies can provide a car and driver. **Femina Travels** (Map p1056; ☑ 2418532; 109 Williams Rd) has an efficient, reasonably priced service. AC cars for up to 10 hours start at ₹1000 plus ₹6 per kilometre.

TRAIN

Trichy Junction station is on the main Chennai–Madurai line. Of 15 daily express or SuperFast services to Chennai, the best daytime option is the Vaigai Express (2nd/chair class ₹104/381, 5¾ hours) departing at 9am. The overnight Rock Fort Express (sleeper/3AC/2AC/1AC ₹164/430/640/1085, seven hours) leaves at 10.20pm. Twelve daily trains to Madurai include the 7.15am Bharathi Express (2nd/chair class ₹71/244, 2¼ hours) and the 1.15pm Guruvaya Express (2nd-class/sleeper/3AC/2AC ₹62/120/282/610, 3¼ hours). Eighteen trains head to Thanjavur (2nd-class/3AC ₹37/218, 40 minutes to 1½ hours).

ⓘ Getting Around

The 5km ride between the airport and Central Bus Station area is about ₹300 by taxi and ₹150 by autorickshaw; there's a prepaid taxi stand at the airport. Or take bus K1.

Bus 1 from Rockins Rd outside the Central Bus Station goes every few minutes to Sri Ranganathaswamy Temple (₹6) and back, stopping close to the Rock Fort Temple and Sri Jambukeshwara Temple en route.

SOUTHERN TAMIL NADU

Chettinadu

The Chettiars, a community of traders based in and around Karaikkudi, 95km south of Trichy, really hit the big time back in the 19th century as financiers and entrepreneurs in colonial Sri Lanka and Southeast Asia. They lavished their fortunes on building at least 10,000, maybe 20,000 opulent mansions in the 90-odd towns and villages of their rural homeland, Chettinadu. No expense was spared on bringing the finest materials to adorn these palatial homes – Burmese teak, Italian marble, Indian rosewood, Belgian chandeliers, English steel, and art and sculpture from everywhere. In the aftermath of WW II, the Chettiars' business networks collapsed and many families had to leave Chettinadu to seek new opportunities. Disused mansions fell into decay and were demolished or sold off piecemeal. Awareness of their value started to revive around the turn of the 21st century, and several have now been turned into gorgeous heritage hotels where, among other things, you can enjoy authentic Chetttinad cuisine, known throughout India for its brilliant use of spices.

◉ Sights & Activities

Hotels can give cooking demos or classes, and provide bicycles or bullock carts for rural rambles. They can also arrange visits to sari-weavers, temples, the Athangudi tileworks (producing the colourful handmade tiles you see in many Chettiar mansions), and shrines of the popular pre-Hindu deity Ayyanar (identifiable by their large terracotta horses, Ayyanar's vehicle). The antique shops in Karaikkudi's Muneeswaran Koil St will give you a feel for how much of the Chettiar heritage is still being sold off.

The nondescript town of Pudukkottai, 51km south of Trichy and 44km north of Karaikkudi, has historical significance in inverse proportion to its current obscurity; it was the capital of the only princely state in Tamil Nadu to remain officially independent throughout British rule.

Vijayalaya Cholisvaram   HINDU TEMPLE
(Narthamalai) **FREE** This small but stunning 8th-century temple stands on a rock slope 1km southwest of Narthamalai village, about 16km north of Pudukkottai. Reminiscent of the Shore Temple at Mamallapuram, without the crowds, it was probably built in late Pallava times. The caretaker, if present, will open two rock-cut Shiva shrines in the adjacent rock face, one with 12 impressively large reliefs of Vishnu. The walk from the village is lovely, with panoramas of fields, water tanks and dramatic rock outcrops unfolding as you go. The Narthamalai turn-off is 7km south of Keeranur on the Trichy–Pudukkottai road; it's 2km west to the village.

Pudukkottai Museum   MUSEUM
(Indian/foreigner ₹5/100; ⊙ 9.30am-5pm Sat-Thu) The relics of bygone days are on display in this wonderful museum, in a renovated palace building in Pudukkottai town. Its eclectic collection includes musical instruments, megalithic burial artefacts, and some remarkable paintings and miniatures.

Thirumayam Fort   FORT
(Indian/foreigner ₹5/100; ⊙ 9am-5.30pm) Simple and imposing, the renovated Thirumayam Fort, about 20km south of Pudukkottai, is worth a climb for the 360-degree views from the battlements over the surrounding countryside. There's a rock-cut Shiva shrine up some metal steps on the west side of the small hill.

🛏 Sleeping & Eating

To get a feel for the palatial life, book a night or two in one of Chettinadu's top-end hotels; they're pricey but they provide a fantastic experience.

★ Visalam   HERITAGE HOTEL $$$
(☎ 04565-273301; www.cghearth.com; Local Fund Rd, Kanadukathan; r incl breakfast ₹9000-15,600; ❄@🛜🏊) 🌊 Stunningly restored and professionally run by a Malayali hotel chain, Visalam is a relatively young Chettiar mansion, done in the fashionable art-deco style of the 1930s. It's still decorated with the original owners' photos, furniture and paintings, and staff can tell you the sad story of the young woman the house was built for. The garden is lovely, the rooms large and stylish, and the pool setting is magical, with a low-key cafe alongside it. There's free in-room wi-fi. Kanadukathan is 9km south of Thirumayam.

★ Bangala   BOUTIQUE HOTEL $$$
(☎ 04565-220221; www.thebangala.com; Devakottai Rd, Karaikkudi; r ₹6400; ❄🛜🏊) This lovingly restored whitewashed 'bungalow' isn't a typical mansion but has all the requisite charm, with quirky decorations, antique furniture and fascinating old family photos. It's famous for its food: the ₹700 set lunch or dinner is actually a Chettiar wedding feast and worth every single paisa (it's available to nonguests from noon to 3pm for ₹1000; call at least two hours ahead). The Bangala has a lovely pool and there's free in-room wi-fi.

Saratha Vilas   BOUTIQUE HOTEL $$$
(☎ 9884203175, 9884936158; www.sarathavilas.com; 832 Main Rd, Kothamangalam; r incl

breakfast ₹6050-7060; ※@☜) A different style of Chettiar charm inhabits this French-run mansion 6km east of Kanadukathan. Rooms combine traditional and contemporary with distinct French panache and the food is an enticing mix of Chettiar and French. The owners are very active in the conservation and promotion of Chettinad heritage through the NGO ArcHeS (www.arche-s.com), which they founded (and which has volunteer openings for the likes of historians, geographers and architects, especially Tamil-speaking ones!).

Chidambara Vilas HERITAGE HOTEL **$$$**
(☏0433-3267070; www.chidambaravilas.com; TSK House, Kadiapatti; s/d incl breakfast ₹11,000/12,000; ※@▨) This mansion in a village 5km east of Thirumayam has been restored into a luxurious hotel with plenty of original Burmese teak, rosewood, stained glass and colourful paintwork. Most rooms are in a new block but still full of Chettiar atmosphere, including punka fans that you can operate yourself from your four-poster bed. A bar, pool and recreation room help you to relax in style. Check for discount offers.

Chettinadu Mansion HERITAGE HOTEL **$$$**
(☏04565-273080; www.chettinadumansion.com; 11 AR St, SARM House, Kanadukathan; s/d incl breakfast ₹5200/7050, half-board ₹5800/8250; ※☜) Slightly shabbier than some other Chettiar joints, but very colourfully decorated, this century-old house is still owned by the original family. Service is top-notch, and all 12 sizeable rooms have private balconies looking over other village mansions. Wi-fi is ₹100 per day. The owners also run **Chettinadu Court** (☏04565-283776; www.deshadan.com; Raja's St, Kanadukathan; s/d incl breakfast ₹3350/3850, half-board ₹3800/4750; ※☜) a few blocks away, with eight pleasant new rooms sporting a few heritage touches, and free wi-fi.

ⓘ Getting There & Away

Car is the best way to get to and around this area. Renting one with a driver from Trichy, Thanjavur or Madurai for two days should cost around ₹3500. Otherwise there are buses about every 10 minutes from Trichy to Pudukkottai (₹31, 1½ hours) and Karaikkudi (₹56, 2½ hours) and you can get off and on along the way. There are also buses from Thanjavur, Madurai and Rameswaram.

Madurai

☑ 0452 / POP 1.02 MILLION

Chennai may be the capital of Tamil Nadu, but Madurai claims its soul. Madurai is Tamil-born and Tamil-rooted, one of the oldest cities in India, a metropolis that traded with ancient Rome and was a great capital long before Chennai was even dreamt of.

Tourists, Indian and foreign, usually come here to see the Meenakshi Amman Temple, a labyrinthine structure ranking among the greatest temples of India. Otherwise, Madurai, perhaps appropriately given her age, captures many of India's glaring dichotomies with a centre dominated by a medieval temple and an economy increasingly driven by IT, all overlaid with the energy and excitement of a large Indian city and slotted into a much more manageable package than Chennai's sprawl.

History

Ancient documents record the existence of Madurai from the 3rd century BC. It was a trading town, especially in spices, and according to legend was the home of the third *sangam* (gathering of Tamil scholars and poets). Over the centuries Madurai came under the sway of the Cholas, Pandyas, local Muslim sultans, Hindu Vijayanagar kings, and the Nayaks, who ruled until 1736. Under Tirumalai Nayak (1623–59) the bulk of the Sri Meenakshi Temple was built, and Madurai became the hub of Tamil culture, playing an important role in the development of the Tamil language.

In 1840 the British East India Company razed Madurai's fort and filled in its moat. The four broad Veli streets were constructed on top of this fill and to this day define the limits of the old city.

⊙ Sights

★**Meenakshi Amman Temple** HINDU TEMPLE
(camera/video ₹50/250; ⊙4am-12.30pm & 4-9.30pm) The abode of the triple-breasted goddess Meenakshi ('fish-eyed' – an epithet for perfect eyes in classical Tamil poetry) is considered by many to be the height of South Indian temple architecture, as vital to the aesthetic heritage of this region as the Taj Mahal is to North India. It's not so much a temple as a 6-hectare complex with 12 tall *gopurams,* all encrusted with a staggering array of gods, goddesses, demons and heroes (1511 of them on the south *gopuram* alone).

Madurai

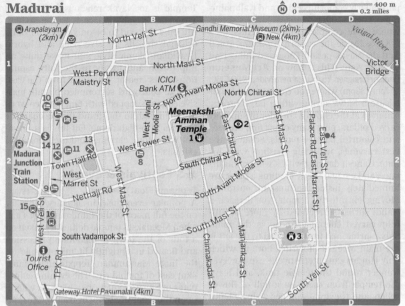

According to legend, the beautiful Meenakshi (a version of Parvati) was born with three breasts and this prophecy: her superfluous breast would melt away when she met her husband. The event came to pass when she met Shiva and took her place as his consort. The existing temple was built during the 17th-century reign of Tirumalai Nayak, but its origins go back 2000 years to when Madurai was a Pandyan capital.

The four streets surrounding the temple are pedestrian-only. The main entrance is by the eastern *gopuram*. First, have a look round the **Pudhu Mandapa** (East Chitrai St), the 100m-long, 16th-century pillared hall facing the *gopuram*. It's filled with colourful textile and craft stalls and tailors at sewing machines, partly hiding some of the lovely pillar sculptures, but it's easy to find the triple-breasted Meenakshi near the southeast corner, and her marriage to Shiva, accompanied by Vishnu, just inside the western entrance. A particularly handsome light-blue Nandi bull (Shiva's vehicle) sits outside the *mandapa's* eastern entrance.

Dress codes are fairly strict for the temple itself: no women's shoulders, or legs of either gender, may be exposed. Despite this the temple has a happier, more joyful atmosphere than some of Tamil Nadu's more solemn shrines, and is adorned with

Madurai

⊙ Top Sights
1	Meenakshi Amman Temple	B2

◎ Sights
	Art Museum	(see 1)
2	Pudhu Mandapa	C2
3	Tirumalai Nayak Palace	C3

✦ Activities, Courses & Tours
4	Foodies Day Out	D2

🛏 Sleeping
5	Hotel Keerthi	A2
6	Hotel Park Plaza	A1
7	Hotel Supreme	A2
8	Hotel West Tower	B2
9	Madurai Residency	A2
10	Royal Court	A1
11	TM Lodge	A2

✕ Eating
12	Anna Meenakshi Restaurant	A2
13	Dhivya Mahal Restaurant	A2
	Surya Restaurant	(see 7)

ⓘ Information
14	State Bank of India	A2
	Supreme Web	(see 7)

ⓘ Transport
	Air India	(see 14)
15	Periyar Bus Stand	A2
16	Shopping Complex Bus Stand	A3

particularly colourful ceiling and wall paintings. There's often classical dance somewhere in the complex at the weekends.

Once inside the eastern *gopuram*, you'll find the Nayak-period Thousand Pillar Hall on your right. This is now an **Art Museum** (Indian/foreigner ₹5/50, camera/video ₹50/250; ⊙ 7am-7.30pm) where you can admire at your leisure a Shiva shrine with a large bronze Nataraja at the end of a corridor of superbly carved pillars, plus many other fine bronzes and colourful painted panels. Some of the best carvings, including Krishna with his flute, Ganesh dancing with a woman on his knee, and a female deity cradling a baby, are immediately inside the museum entrance. Moving on into the temple, you'll reach a Nandi shrine surrounded by more beautifully carved columns. Ahead is the main Shiva shrine, and further ahead to the left is the main Meenakshi shrine, both of which only Hindus can enter. Anyone can however wander round the temple tank, and leave the temple from there via a hall of flower sellers and the arch-ceilinged Ashta Shakti Mandapam, which is actually used as the temple entrance by most worshippers and is lined with relief carvings of the goddess's eight attributes and has perhaps the loveliest of all the temple's brightly painted ceilings.

Gandhi Memorial Museum　　MUSEUM
(Gandhi Museum Rd; camera ₹50; ⊙ 10am-1pm & 2-5.45pm Tue-Sun) FREE Housed in a 17th-century Nayak queen's palace, this excellent museum contains an impressively moving and detailed account of India's struggle for independence from 1757 to 1947, and the English-language text pulls no punches about British rule. Included in the exhibition is the blood-stained dhoti (long loincloth) that Gandhi was wearing when he was assassinated in Delhi in 1948; it's here because it was in Madurai, in 1921, that he first took up wearing the dhoti as a sign of native pride. The small **Madurai Government Museum** (Indian/foreigner ₹5/100, camera ₹20; ⊙ 9.30am-5pm Sat-Thu) is next door, and the **Gandhian Literary Society Bookshop** (⊙ 10am-1pm & 2.30-6.30pm Mon-Sat) behind. Bus 75 from Periyar Bus Stand goes to the Tamukkam bus stop on Alagarkoil Rd, 600m from the museum.

Tirumalai Nayak Palace　　PALACE
(Palace Rd; Indian/foreigner ₹10/50, camera/video ₹30/100; ⊙ 9am-5pm) What the Meenakshi Temple is to Nayak religious architecture, Tirumalai Nayak's palace is to the secular. Although it's said to be only a quarter of its original size, its massive scale and hybrid Dravidian-Islamic style still make quite an impression and testify to the lofty aspirations of its creator. You enter from the east. A large courtyard surrounded by tall, massive columns topped with fancy stucco work leads through to the grand throne chamber with its 25m-high dome. Off this is a museum with stone carvings and archaeological exhibits.

★ Festivals & Events

Teppam (Float) Festival　　TEMPLE FESTIVAL
A popular event held in January/February on the full moon of the Tamil month of Thai, when Meenakshi temple deities are taken on a tour of the town in elaborate procession and floated in a brightly lit 'mini-temple' on the huge Mariamman Teppakkulam tank, 3km east of the old city. The evening culminates in Shiva's seduction of his wife, whereupon the icons are brought back to the temple to make love and, in so doing, regenerate the universe (Meenakshi's diamond nose stud is even removed so it doesn't irritate her lover).

Chithirai Festival　　TEMPLE FESTIVAL
The main event on Madurai's busy festival calendar is this two-week event in April/May celebrating the marriage of Meenakshi to Sundareswarar (Shiva). The deities are wheeled around the Meenakshi Amman Temple in massive chariots that form part of long, colourful processions.

🛏 Sleeping

Budget hotels in the central area are mostly dreary and unloved, but there is a big choice of good and near-identical midrange places along West Perumal Maistry St, not far from the train station. Most of them have rooftop restaurants with temple and sunset views.

Hotel West Tower　　HOTEL $
(☑ 2346908; 42/60 West Tower St; s/d ₹473/825, r with AC ₹1238; ✳) The West Tower's best asset is that it's very near the temple, but it's also acceptably clean and friendly.

TM Lodge　　HOTEL $
(☑ 2341651; http://hellomadurai.in/tmlodge; 50 West Perumal Maistry St; s/d ₹399/605, r with AC ₹1294; ✳) The walls are a bit grubby, but the

sheets are clean. TM is efficiently run, even with a lift operator!

Madurai Residency
HOTEL $$

(📞 438000; www.madurairesidency.com; 15 West Marret St; s ₹2039-2518, d ₹2398-2878, all incl breakfast; ❄ 🛜) The service is stellar and the rooms are comfy and fresh at this winner, which has one of the the highest rooftop restaurants in town. It's very popular, so book at least two days ahead. There's wi-fi in the lobby.

Hotel Park Plaza
HOTEL $$

(📞 3011111; www.hotelparkplaza.net; 114 West Perumal Maistry St; s/d incl half-board ₹2878/3358; ❄ 🛜) The Plaza's rooms are comfortable and simply but attractively furnished, with free wi-fi. Four have temple views. It also boasts a good multicuisine rooftop restaurant and the (inappropriately named) Sky High Bar – on the 1st floor.

Hotel Supreme
HOTEL $$

(📞 2343151; www.hotelsupreme.in; 110 West Perumal Maistry St; s ₹2278-3118, d ₹2578-3298, all incl breakfast; ❄ 🛜) The Supreme is a well-presented hotel with friendly service that is very popular with domestic tourists. Don't miss the chance to walk into Apollo 96, a bar built to look like a spaceship, and wonder if someone laced your lassi last night. There's good food at the inhouse Surya Restaurant, and free in-room wi-fi.

Hotel Keerthi
HOTEL $$

(📞 4377788; http://hellomadurai.in/hotelkeerthi; 40 West Perumal Maistry St; r incl breakfast ₹1379-1918; ❄) This shiny, modern hotel has decent prices, small 'classic' rooms and large 'deluxe'. They're almost stylish thanks to their minimalist lines, funky wall mirrors and feature walls. No wi-fi though.

Royal Court
HOTEL $$$

(📞 4356666; www.royalcourtindia.com; 4 West Veli St; s ₹3957-4917, d ₹4797-5636, all incl breakfast; ❄ @ 🛜) The Royal Court manages to blend a bit of white-sheeted, hardwood-floored colonial elegance with comfort, good eating options, professional service and free in-room wi-fi. It's an excellent, central choice for someone who needs a bit of spoiling.

Gateway Hotel Pasumalai
HOTEL $$$

(📞 6633000; www.thegatewayhotels.com; 40 TPK Rd, Pasumalai; s ₹5996-8394, d ₹7195-9594) A lovely escape from city scramble, the Gateway is spread over hilltop gardens 4km southwest of the centre. The views, outdoor pool and resident peacocks are just great, the rooms are well equipped, very comfy and mostly large, and the panoramic **Garden All Day** (🕒 6.30am-11pm) restaurant does a terrific multicuisine dinner buffet for ₹717.

🍴 Eating

The hotel-rooftop restaurants along West Perumal Maistry St offer breezy night-time dining and temple views (don't forget the mosquito repellent); most of the hotels also have AC restaurants open for breakfast and lunch. For a great evening tasting Madurai specialities with a local food enthusiast, call or email **Foodies Day Out** (📞 9840992340; www.foodiesdayout.com; 2nd fl, 56 East Veli St; tour per person ₹1500). They'll pick you up around 5.30pm and take you to seven or eight restaurants and stalls to sample the signature dish at each. Vegetarian tours are available; at least two people are needed.

Dhivya Mahal Restaurant
MULTICUISINE $

(📞 2342700; 21 Town Hall Rd; mains ₹50-150; 🕒 noon-11pm) One of the better multicuisine restaurants not attached to a hotel, Dhivya Mahal is clean, bright, air-conditioned and friendly. The curries go down a treat, and where else are you going to find roast leg of lamb in Madurai?

Anna Meenakshi Restaurant
INDIAN $

(West Perumal Maistry St; mains ₹60-100; 🕒 6am-11pm) With marginally more attention to decor and ambience than other cheapies along the street, Anna Meenakshi is a busy spot where you can get a decent South Indian thali for ₹60.

Surya Restaurant
MULTICUISINE $$

(110 West Perumal Maistry St; mains ₹70-160; 🕒 4pm-midnight) The rooftop restaurant of Hotel Supreme offers a superb view over the city, stand-out service and good pure-veg food, but the winner here has got to be the iced coffee, which might have been brewed by God when you sip it on a dusty, hot day.

🛍 Shopping

Madurai teems with cloth stalls and tailors' shops, as you may notice upon being approached by tailor touts. A great place for getting clothes made up is the Pudhu Mandapa. Here you'll find rows of tailors busily treadling away and capable of whipping up a good replica of whatever you're wearing in an hour or two. A cotton top or shirt can cost as little as ₹350. Drivers, guides and touts will also be keen to lead you to the Kashmiri craft shops in North Chitrai St, offering to show you the temple view from the rooftop – the views are good, and so is the inevitable sales pitch.

ℹ️ Information

State Bank of India (West Veli St) Has foreign-exchange desks and an ATM.

Supreme Web (110 West Perumal Maistry St; per hr ₹30; ⏰ 7am-11pm) An efficient place with browsing, printing, scanning and photocopying. Take your passport.

Tourist Office (☑ 2334757; 1 West Veli St; ⏰ 10am-5.45pm Mon-Fri) Reasonably helpful.

ℹ️ Getting There & Away

AIR

SpiceJet (www.spicejet.com) flies at least once daily to Bengaluru, Chennai, Colombo, Delhi, Hyderabad and Mumbai. Further Chennai flights are operated by **JetKonnect** (☑ 2690771; www.jetkonnect.com; Airport) three or four time daily, and **Air India** (☑ 2341795; www.airindia.com; 7A West Veli St) once daily.

BUS

Most government buses arrive and depart from the **New Bus Stand** (Melur Rd), 4km northeast of the old city. Services to Coimbatore, Kodaikanal and Ooty go from the **Arapalayam bus stand** (Puttuthoppu Main Rd), 2km northwest of the old city. Tickets for more expensive (and mostly more comfortable) private buses are sold by agencies on the south side of the **Shopping Complex Bus Stand** (btwn West Veli St & TPK Rd). Most travel overnight.

TRAIN

From Madurai Junction station, 13 daily trains head north to Trichy (two to five hours) and nine to Chennai, the fastest being the 6.45am Vaigai Express (Trichy 2nd/chair class ₹71/253, two hours; Chennai ₹132/488, eight hours). A good overnight train for Chennai is the 8.35pm Pandyan Express (sleeper/3AC/2AC/1AC ₹232/730/880/1500, nine hours). To Kanyakumari the only daily train departs at 1.55am (sleeper/3AC/2AC ₹157/398/640, five hours), though there's a later train some days (at varying times). Trivandrum (three trains daily), Coimbatore (two daily) and Bengaluru (one daily) are other destinations.

ℹ️ Getting Around

The airport is 12km south of town and taxis cost ₹300 to the centre. Alternatively, buses 15 and 16 run to/from the **Periyar Bus Stand** (West Veli St). From the New Bus Stand (p1062), bus 5 (₹4) shuttles into the city; an autorickshaw is ₹100.

Rameswaram

☑ 04573 / POP 46,461

Rameswaram was once the southernmost point of sacred India; to leave its boundaries was to abandon caste and fall below the status of the lowliest skinner of sacred cows. Then Rama, incarnation of Vishnu and hero of the Ramayana, led an army of monkeys and bears across a monkey-built bridge to the island of (Sri) Lanka, where he defeated the demon Ravana and rescued his wife, Sita. Afterwards, prince and princess came to this spot to offer thanks to Shiva.

If all this seems like so much folklore, it's absolute truth for millions of Hindus, who flock to the Ramanathaswamy Temple to worship where a god worshipped a god.

GOVERNMENT BUSES FROM MADURAI

DESTINATION	FARE (₹)	DURATION (HR)	FREQUENCY
Chennai	325	9-10	40 daily
Coimbatore	125	6	every 15min
Ernakulam (Kochi)	340	8	9am & 9pm
Kanyakumari	140-150	4	31 daily
Kodaikanal	75	4	14 buses 5am-2pm, & 5.50pm
Mysore	280-360	16	7 buses 4.30-9.45pm
Ooty	170	9	/7.30am & 9.30pm
Puducherry	265	8	8.45pm & 9.30pm
Rameswaram	110	5	every 30min
Trichy	90	3	40 daily

WORTH A TRIP

DHANUSHKODI

The promontory stretching 22km southeast from Rameswaram narrows to a thin strip of sand dunes about halfway along, and near the end stands the ghost town of Dhanush-kodi. Once a thriving port, Dhanushkodi was washed away by the tidal waves of a monster cyclone in 1964. The shells of its train station, church, post office and other ruins still stand among a scattering of fishers' shacks, and Adam's Bridge (or Rama's Bridge), the chain of reefs, sandbanks and islets that almost connects India with Sri Lanka, stretches away to the east.

Autorickshaws charge about ₹400 round trip (including waiting time) to Moonram Chattram, a collection of fishers' huts about 14km from town. From there to Dhanush-kodi it's a hot 4km walk along the beautiful sands, or a ₹100 two-hour round trip in a truck or minibus which will go when it fills up with 12 to 20 customers. It's tempting to swim, but beware of strong rips.

Apart from these pilgrims, Rameswaram is a small fishing town on an island, Pamban, which is connected to the mainland by a 2km-long road and rail bridges. The town smells of drying fish and has a lot of flies, and if you're not a pilgrim, the temple alone would barely merit the journey here. But the eastern point of the island, Dhanushkodi, only 30km from Sri Lanka, has a natural magic that adds considerably to Rameswaram's attractions.

Most hotels and eateries are clustered around the Ramanathaswamy Temple, which is surrounded by North, East, South and West Car Streets. Middle St heads west towards the bus stand (2km). The train station is 1.5km southwest of the temple.

◉ Sights

Ramanathaswamy Temple   HINDU TEMPLE
(camera ₹25; ⊙5am-9.30pm) When Rama decided to worship Shiva, he figured he'd need a lingam to do the thing properly. Being a god, he sent Hanuman to find the biggest lingam around – a Himalayan mountain. But the monkey took too long, so Rama's wife Sita made a simple lingam of sand, which is enshrined today in this temple's inner sanctum (open to Hindus only). Besides housing the world's holiest sand mound, the temple, dating mainly from the 16th to 18th centuries, is notable for its long, long, 1000-pillar halls and 22 *theerthams* (tanks and wells). Pilgrims are expected to bathe in all 22 as well as the sea before visiting the deity. The temple bathing takes the form of attendants tipping pails of water over the (often fully dressed) faithful, who then hurry on to the next *theertham*. All this water sloshing around makes the temple floors pretty wet, and you'll have a less slippery amble round the corridors if you go when the inner sanctum is closed (12.30pm to 4.30pm).

🛏 Sleeping & Eating

Many hotels are geared towards pilgrims, and some cheapies (which are mostly pretty dire) refuse to take in single travellers, but there's a string of reasonable midrange hotels. Book ahead before festivals. Budget travellers can try heading to the **rooms booking office** (East Car St; ⊙24hr), which can score doubles for as low as ₹500 a night.

A number of inexpensive vegetarian restaurants such as **Vasantha Bhavan** (East Car St; dishes ₹28-50; ⊙6am-10.30pm) and **Ananda Bhavan** (West Car St) serve vegetarian thali lunches for around ₹40, and evening dosai and *uttapams* for around ₹30. You might find fish in some restaurants, but other flesh is hard to come by.

Hotel Venkatesh   HOTEL $
(☎221296; SV Koil St; r ₹420-550, with AC ₹770; ❄) The lemon-walled rooms here are reasonably clean and not bad value for the price, and it accepts single travellers. It's on the westward continuation of South Car St.

Hotel Royal Park   HOTEL $$
(☎221680; www.hotelroyalpark.in; Ramnad Hwy; s ₹1919-2638, d ₹2398-3358; ❄@) Away from the temple action, this place on the main road 400m west of the bus stand is one of the most peaceful in town. Rooms are good and clean with some nice artwork, and the AC veg restaurant is good value (mainly South Indian, but the cheese and tomato toastie is perfect too).

Hotel Sri Saravana
HOTEL $$

(📞 223367; http://srisaravanahotel.com; 1/9A South Car St; r ₹1395-2815; ❄) The best of the town-centre hotels, Sri Saravana is friendly and clean with good service and spacious, colourful rooms. Those towards the top have sea views (and higher rates).

Hotel Sunrise View
HOTEL $$

(📞 223434; www.hotelsunriseview.com; 1/3G East Car St; r ₹1463; ❄) This has sparkling wall tiles and wooden furniture that's a tad better quality than at some other spots. It's acceptably clean and some rooms do indeed have sunrise (and sea) views; just try to look at the ocean rather than the rubbish on the ground.

ℹ Information

Siva Net (Middle St; per hr ₹40; ◷8am-9pm Mon-Sat)

State Bank of India ATM (South Car St) Accepts international cards.

ℹ Getting There & Around

Buses run to Madurai (₹110, five hours) every 30 minutes, and to Trichy (₹180, 6½ hours) every hour. 'Ultra Deluxe' (UD) services are scheduled twice daily to Chennai (₹450, 12 hours) and Kanyakumari (₹250, eight hours), but don't always run.

The three daily trains to/from Madurai (₹24, four hours) have unreserved seating only. The Sethu Express departs daily at 8pm for Chennai (sleeper/3AC/2AC ₹246/665/1000, 12½ hours) via Trichy and Thanjavur. The Rameswaram–Kanyakumari Express leaves at 8.45pm Monday, Thursday and Saturday, reaching Kanyakumari (sleeper/3AC ₹204/519) at 4.05am.

Bus 1 (₹4) shuttles between the bus stand and East Car St. Autorickshaws to the centre from the bus stand or train station should be ₹40.

Kanyakumari (Cape Comorin)

📞 04652 / POP 23,844

There's a sense of accomplishment on making it to the point of the subcontinent's 'V', past the final dramatic flourish of the Western Ghats and the green fields, glinting rice paddies and slow-looping wind turbines of India's deep south. Like all edges, there is a sense of the surreal here. At certain times of year you can see the sun set and the moon rise over three seas simultaneously. The Temple of the Virgin Sea Goddess and the 'Land's End' symbolism draw crowds of pilgrims and tourists to Kanyakumari, but it remains a small-scale, refreshing respite from the hectic Indian road.

◉ Sights & Activities

Kumari Amman Temple
HINDU TEMPLE

(◷4.30am-12.30pm & 4-8.15pm) The legends say the *kanya* (virgin) goddess Kumari, a manifestation of the Great Goddess Devi, single-handedly conquered demons and secured freedom for the world. At this temple at the tip of the subcontinent, pilgrims give her thanks in an intimately spaced, beautifully decorated temple, where the crash of waves from three seas can be heard behind the twilight glow of oil fires clutched in vulva-shaped votive candles (a reference to the sacred femininity of the goddess). You're likely to be asked for a donation to enter the inner precinct, where men must remove their shirts, and cameras are forbidden.

The shoreline around the temple has a couple of tiny, sandy beaches, and bathing ghats where some worshippers immerse themselves before visiting the temple. A *mandapa* south of the temple is a highly popular spot for sunset-watching and grabbing a bit of daytime shade. A small bazaar of souvenir shops leads back from here to the main road.

Vivekananda Memorial
MONUMENT

(admission ₹10; ◷8am-5pm) Four hundred metres offshore is the rock where the famous Hindu apostle Swami Vivekananda meditated from 25 to 27 December 1892, and decided to take his moral message beyond India's shores. A two-*mandapa* memorial was built in Vivekananda's memory in 1970, and reflects architectural styles from all over India. With all the tourist crowds this brings, Vivekananda would undoubtedly choose somewhere else to meditate today.

The huge **statue** on the smaller island next door, looking like an Indian Colossus of Rhodes, is of the ancient Tamil poet Thiruvalluvar. The work of more than 5000 sculptors, it was erected in 2000 and honours the poet's 133-chapter work *Thirukural* – hence its height of exactly 133ft (40.5m).

Ferries shuttle out to the Vivekananda island (₹30 return) between 7.45am and 4pm, but there's no regular service to Thiruvalluvar.

Gandhi Memorial
MONUMENT

(admission free; ◷7am-7pm) Appropriately placed at the end of the nation that Gan-

Kanyakumari (Cape Comorin)

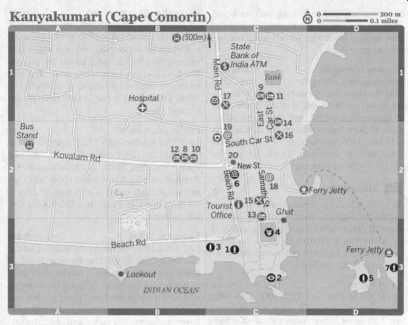

Kanyakumari (Cape Comorin)

⊙ Sights

1 Gandhi Memorial	C3
2 Ghat	C3
3 Kamaraj Memorial	C3
4 Kumari Amman Temple	C3
5 Statue of Thiruvalluvar	D3
6 Swami Vivekananda Wandering Monk Exhibition	C2
7 Vivekananda Memorial	D3

🛏 Sleeping

8 Hotel Narmadha	B2
9 Hotel Sivamurugan	C1
10 Hotel Tri Sea	B2
11 Manickhan Tourist Home	C1
12 Santhi Residency	B2

13 Saravana Lodge	C2
14 Seashore Hotel	C2

⊗ Eating

15 Hotel Saravana	C2
16 Hotel Sea View	C2
17 Sangam Restaurant	C1
Seashore Hotel	(see 14)

ⓘ Information

18 Tony Travels Internet Cafe	C2
19 Xerox, Internet, Fax	C2

ⓘ Transport

20 SETC Booking Office	C2

dhi fathered, this lemon-and-pink memorial is designed in the form of an Odishan temple embellished by Hindu, Christian and Muslim architects. The central plinth was used to store some of the Mahatma's ashes, and each year, on Gandhi's birthday (2 October), the sun's rays fall on the stone. Exhibits are limited to a few uncaptioned photos; the tower is a popular sunset-viewing position.

Swami Vivekananda
Wandering Monk Exhibition   MUSEUM
(Main Rd; admission ₹10; ⊙ 8am-noon & 4-8.15pm) This newly refurbished exhibition details Swami Vivekananda's wisdom, sayings and encounters with the mighty and the lowly during his five years as a wandering monk around India from 1888 to 1893. The spiritual organisation **Vivekananda Kendra** (www. vivekanandakendra.org), devoted to carrying

out Vivekananda's teachings, has its headquarters at Vivekanandapuram, an ashram 1km north of town with some tourist accommodation.

Kamaraj Memorial
MONUMENT

(admission free; ⊗7am-7pm) This memorial near the shoreline commemorates K Kamaraj, known as the 'Gandhi of the South'. One of the most powerful and respected politicians of post-Independence India, Kamaraj held the chief ministership of both Madras State and its successor, Tamil Nadu. The photos inside do have captions.

🛏 Sleeping

As befits a holiday destination, many Kanyakumari hoteliers have gone for bright, cheerful decor; after the bland sameness of midrange hotels around the state, it's quite exciting to find a large neon-coloured tiger painted on your bedhead.

Hotel Narmadha
HOTEL $

(☑246365; Kovalam Rd; r ₹300-500) This long concrete block conceals some friendly staff and a range of cheap rooms, some of which are cleaner and have less dank bathrooms than others; the ₹500 sea-view doubles with spearmint-stripe sheets are decent value.

Saravana Lodge
HOTEL $

(☑246007; Sannathi St; r ₹300-500, with AC ₹1000; ❄) It's basic, but you can get a reasonable deal here, just outside the temple entrance. All rooms have private bathrooms, though there's no hot water. The better rooms are on the upper floors of the new block at the far end from the entrance.

Hotel Tri Sea
HOTEL $$

(☑246586; www.triseahotel.com; Kovalam Rd; d ₹800-1800; ❄⛲) You can't miss the highrise Tri Sea, whose sea-view rooms are huge, spotless and airy, with particularly hectic colour schemes. The top-floor triples are even grander. The rooftop pool is a welcome bonus, though the restaurant is a sad afterthought.

Hotel Sivamurugan
HOTEL $$

(☑246862; www.hotelsivamurugan.com; 2/93 North Car St; r ₹1000-1200, with AC ₹1600-2000; ❄) A welcoming, well-appointed new hotel, with spacious, spotless, marble-floored rooms. The 'super-deluxes' have sea views past a couple of buildings. There's 24-hour hot water, which not all competitors can claim.

Manickhan Tourist Home
HOTEL $$

(☑246387; www.hotelmaadhini.com; North Car St; r ₹800-900, with AC ₹1400-1800; ❄) This friendly hotel is professionally run and a pleasant place to doss in; the large rooms are all outfitted with clean bathrooms, and, if you're willing to shell out a bit, AC and superb sea views. Prices tend to rise in December, January and May.

Santhi Residency
HOTEL $$

(☑247091; Kovalam Rd; r ₹1000, with AC ₹1500; ❄) A smaller, older restored house with two leafy courtyards, Santhi has an unusually restrained style for Kanyakunari (the only decoration in each room is a picture of Jesus). It's quiet and clean with smallish rooms and bathrooms.

Seashore Hotel
HOTEL $$$

(☑246704; http://theseashorehotel.com; East Car St; r ₹4137-7795; ❄📶) The fanciest hotel in town has shiny, spacious rooms with gold curtains and cushions, glassed-in showers, and useful equipment including kettles and hair-dryers. All rooms except the cheapest have panoramic sea views and the 7th-floor restaurant is one of Kanyakumari's best. Free wi-fi in the lobby.

🍴 Eating

Hotel Saravana
INDIAN $

(Sannathi St; mains ₹54-91; ⊗6am-10pm) A clean, very popular spot with plenty of North and South Indian vegetarian dishes, and lunchtime thalis.

Hotel Sea View
MULTICUISINE $$

(East Car St; mains ₹90-250; ⊗6am-11pm) This AC hotel restaurant doesn't have a sea view, but it does do excellent fresh seafood and versions of North and South Indian faves. The vibe is upmarket and the service professional. It's also probably the best breakfast spot in town, with buffet, Continental and American options.

Seashore Hotel
MULTICUISINE $$

(East Car St; mains ₹160-600; ⊗7am-10.45pm) Amazingly, the 7th-floor restaurant here is the only one in Kanyakumari with a sea view. And a fabulous view it is. What's more, the food and service are worthy of it. There's very good grilled fish and plenty of Indian veg and nonveg choices, plus a few Continental options.

Sangam Restaurant INDIAN $$

(Main Rd; mains ₹75-200; ⊘7.30am-11pm) It's as if the Sangam started in Kashmir, trekked the length of India, and stopped here to offer top veg and nonveg picks from every province along the way. The food is good, the seats are soft and the joint is bustling.

ⓘ Information

State Bank of India ATM (Main Rd) Accepts international cards.

Tony Travels Internet Cafe (Sannathi St; per hr ₹60; ⊘7.30am-10pm) Friendly – possibly over-friendly (but not unsafe) for lone women.

Tourist Office (☑246276; Beach Rd; ⊘10am-5.15pm Mon-Fri) Helpful.

Xerox, Internet, Fax (Main Rd; per hr ₹30; ⊘7.30am-11pm Mon-Sat) Staffed by women, and does what its name says.

ⓘ Getting There & Away

BUS

The sedate **bus stand** (Kovalam Rd) is a 10-minute walk west of the centre and there's a handy **SETC booking office** (cnr Main Rd & New St; ⊘7am-9pm) in town. Ordinary buses go about hourly to both Madurai (₹140 to ₹150) and Trivandrum (₹65, 2½ hours). The most comfortable buses are the so-called Ultra Deluxe (UD), which includes the following:

Chennai ₹520, 12 to 15 hours, seven daily
Kodaikanal ₹300, 10 hours, 8.15pm
Madurai ₹210, four hours, seven daily

TAXI

Drivers ask ₹1500 for a ride to Kovalam.

TRAIN

The train station is a walkable distance north of the centre. The one daily northbound train, the Kanyakumari Express, departs at 5.20pm for Chennai (sleeper/3AC/2AC/1AC ₹305/831/1245/2125, 13½ hours) via Madurai (₹157/398/640/1080, 4½ hours) and Trichy (₹204/538/790/1345, 7¼ hours). Two daily express trains depart in the morning for Trivandrum (2nd-class/sleeper/3AC/2AC ₹31/120/218/610, 2¼ hours), both continuing to Kollam and Ernakulam. Several more trains go from Nagercoil Junction, 15km northwest of Kanyakumari.

For real long-haulers or train buffs, the Vivek Express runs all the way to Dibrugarh in Assam, 4241km and 85 hours away – the longest single train ride in India. It departs from Kanyakumari at 2.45pm Saturday (sleeper/3AC/2AC ₹673/1948/3340).

THE WESTERN GHATS

Welcome to the lush Western Ghats, some of the most welcome heat relief in India. Rising like an impassable bulwark of evergreen and deciduous tangle from north of Mumbai to the tip of Tamil Nadu, the Ghats (with an average elevation of 915m) contain 27% of India's flowering plants and an incredible array of endemic wildlife. In Tamil Nadu they rise to 2000m and more in the Palni Hills around Kodaikanal and the Nilgiris around Ooty. British influence lingers a little stronger up in these hills, where the colonists covered the slopes in neatly trimmed tea bushes and created their 'hill stations' to escape the heat of the plains. It's not just the air and (relative) lack of pollution that's refreshing – there's a certain acceptance of quirkiness and eccentricity in the hills that is rarer in the lowlands. Think organic farms, handlebar-moustached trekking guides and tiger-stripe earmuffs for sale in the bazaars.

Kodaikanal (Kodai)

☑ 04542 / POP 41,882 / ELEV 2100M

There are few more refreshing Tamil Nadu moments than boarding a bus in the heat-soaked plains and disembarking in the sharp pinch of a Kodaikanal night or morning. It's not all cold though; during the day the weather is positively pleasant, more reminiscent of deep spring than early winter. This misty hill station, 120km northwest of Madurai in the Palni hills, is more relaxed and more intimate than its big sister Ooty (brochures call Kodai the 'Princess of Hill Stations', while Ooty is the Queen). The renowned Kodaikanal International School provides a bit of cosmopolitan influence, with students from around the globe.

Centred on a very pretty lake, Kodai rambles up and down hillsides with patches of *shola* forest, unique to the Western Ghats in South India, and evergreen broadleaf trees such as magnolia, mahogany, myrtle and rhododendron. Another plant speciality around here (in the grasslands) is the *kurinji* shrub, whose lilac-blue blossoms only appear every 12 years: next due date 2018.

Kodai is popular with honeymooners, who flock to the spectacular lookout points and waterfalls in and around town.

Kodaikanal (Kodai)

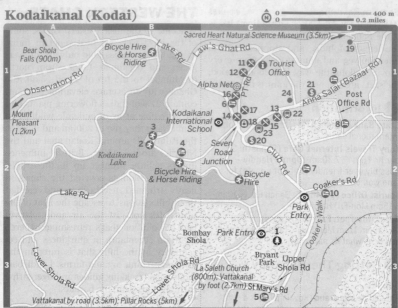

Sights & Activities

Sacred Heart Natural Science Museum
MUSEUM

(Sacred Heart College, Law's Ghat Rd; admission ₹10; ⊙9am-5pm) In the grounds of a former Jesuit seminary about 4km downhill east of town, this museum has a ghoulishly intriguing miscellany of flora and fauna put together over more than 100 years by priests and trainees. Displays range over bottled snakes, human embryos (!), giant moths, stuffed animal carcasses and black-and-white photos of solemn priests with huge snakes draped over them. You can also see some pressed *kurinji* flowers (*Strobilanthes kunthiana*) in case you're not around for their flowering.

Parks & Waterfalls

Bryant Park (adult/child ₹20/10, camera/video ₹30/75; ⊙9am-6.30pm), landscaped and stocked by the British officer after whom it's named, is pretty, and often busy with canoodling couples as well as tourists.

Several beauty spots around Kodai are very popular with Indian tourists and crowded with souvenir and snack stalls too. They're best visited by taxi unless you like walking along busy roads. Taxi drivers offer a tour of eight 'sightseeing places' for

₹500 (₹600 April to June). **Green Valley View** (6km from downtown), **Pillar Rocks** (7km) and less visited **Moir's Point** (13km), all along the same road west of town, have spectacular views to the plains far below. To go beyond Moir's Point to pretty, forest-surrounded **Berijam Lake** requires a Forest Department permit. Taxi drivers can organise this, if asked the day before, and do four-hour 'forest tours' to Berijam, via a couple more lookouts, for ₹1600. Access to the lake is closed on Tuesdays.

The river that empties Kodaikanal Lake tumbles dramatically down **Silver Cascade**, on the Madurai road 7km from town. Compact **Bear Shola Falls** are in a pocket of forest on the northwest edge of town.

Walking

Assuming it's not cloaked in opaque mist, the views from paved **Coaker's Walk** (admission ₹5, camera ₹10; ⊙7am-6.30pm) are magnificent, all the way down to the plains 2000m below. The stroll takes all of five minutes.

Kodai's lake is very pretty and the 5km lake circuit is pleasant in the early morning when you can count the kingfishers before the tourist traffic starts. A walk along Lower Shola Rd will take you through the Bombay

Kodaikanal (Kodai)

Shola, the nearest surviving patch of *shola* to downtown Kodai.

Most serious trekking routes in the Kodai area require Forest Department permits which can only be obtained with considerable time, patience and luck. Contact the **Principal Chief Conservator of Forests** (Map p1008; ☏ 044-24321174; Panagal Maaligai, Anna Salai, Saidapet) office in Chennai, then Kodai's **District Forest Office** (☏ 240287; Muthaliarpuram; ⊙ 10am-5.45pm Mon-Fri). Kodai's tourist office (p1071) and accommodation places such as Greenlands Youth Hostel (p1069) can put you in touch with local guides who may be able to offer interesting off-road local routes for ₹1000 to ₹1500 per full day.

Boating, Cycling & Horse Riding

If you're sappy in love like a bad Bollywood song, the thing to do in Kodai is rent a pedal boat (₹50 per half-hour for two people), rowboat (₹90 including boatman) or Kashmiri *shikara*, aka 'honeymoon boat' (₹260 including boatman) from the **Kodaikanal Boat & Rowing Club** (⊙ 9am-5.30pm) or **Tamil Nadu Tourist Development Corporation** (⊙ 9am-5.30pm); screechy crooning is strictly optional.

Around the lake are a few **bicycle-rental** (₹20/200 per hour/day) and **horse-riding stands** (₹60 per 500m, or ₹300 per hour).

🛏 Sleeping

Some hotel prices rise by up to 100% during the high season (April to June). There are some lovely heritage places, and some good-value midrange options if you can live without colonial-era ambience. Most hotels have a 9am or 10am checkout time in high season, but the rest of the year it's usually 24 hours.

Hotel Cokkers Tower   HOTEL $
(☏ 240374; cokkers.tower@yahoo.com; Woodville Rd; dm/d ₹110/825) A straightforward hotel with simple, very clean, light-coloured rooms (no colonial wood here). The dorm has narrow beds reminiscent of train bunks, and is best avoided during the monsoon when its roof may leak, but its bathroom is sparkling and you can't beat the price.

Snooze Inn   HOTEL $
(☏ 240873; www.jayarajgroup.com; Anna Salai; r ₹770-935; 🖥) The outside has a bit more character than the rooms, but this is a decent-value budget choice with clean bathrooms, plenty of blankets and free wi-fi.

Greenlands Youth Hostel   HOSTEL $
(☏ 240899; www.greenlandskodaikanal.com; St Mary's Rd; dm ₹250, d ₹600-1800) This long-running spot has a nice garden and excellent views, but the accommodation is very bare and basic, hot water is only available from 8am to 10am, and washing in the dorms is by buckets of cold water.

★ Villa Retreat   HOTEL $$
(☏ 243556, 240940; www.villaretreat.com; Club Rd; r incl breakfast ₹2878-4677; 🖥) You can enjoy the awesome Coaker's Walk views from your garden breakfast table at this lovely old stone-built family hotel, right next to the walk's northern end. It's a friendly place

WORTH A TRIP

VATTAKANAL WALK

This is a lovely walk of about 4.5km (each way) from the centre of town, on which you might, if lucky, spot gaur (bison) or giant squirrels in the forested bits. Follow St Mary's Rd west then southwest from the south end of Coaker's Walk, passing La Saleth Church after 1.2km. At a fork 400m after the church, go left downhill on what quickly becomes an unpaved track passing through part of the Pambar Shola forest. After 450m you emerge on a road by a bridge above some falls. Across the bridge you'll find snack stalls selling fruit, tea, coffee, bread omelettes, and roasted corn with lime and masala – all yummy! Follow the road 1km downhill, with panoramas opening up as you go, to Vattakanal village. Take the path down past Altaf's Cafe and in about 15 minutes you'll reach the Dolphin's Nose, a rock lookout overhanging a precipitous drop.

with comfy, good-sized rooms and free wi-fi in the dining room. Checkout time is 9am.

Hilltop Towers HOTEL $$

(☑ 240413; www.hilltopgroup.in; Club Rd; r incl breakfast ₹2160-2700) Although it's bland on the outside, rustic accents like polished teak floors and wooden embellishments, plus friendly staff, in-room coffee-makers and 90-channel TV make the Hilltop a good midrange choice.

Mount Pleasant BOUTIQUE HOTEL $$

(☑ 242023, 9655126023; www.kodaikanalheritage.com; 19/12-20 Observatory Rd; r incl breakfast ₹2278-3718; ☏) A lot of perfectly decent hotels are scattered around the outer reaches of Kodai's spaghetti-like street map. In most cases the inconvenient distance outweighs their appeal, but Mount Pleasant is worth finding for its quiet setting, comfy rooms and the amiable Keralan owner's slightly quirky taste – colourful wall weavings, coconut-wood beds, coir matting. Tasty buffet dinners are available. It's advisable to book.

Hotel Sunrise HOTEL $$

(☑ 241358; www.kodaihotelsunrise.com; 8/62 Post Office Rd; r ₹1438-2877) Cosy red-and-brown rooms, amiable staff, 24-hour hot water and sunrise views from about half the rooms make this a worthy option.

★ Carlton Hotel HOTEL $$$

(☑ 240056; www.krahejahospitality.com; Lake Rd; d/cottages incl half-board ₹9550/14,500; ☏) The cream of Kodai's hotels is a magnificent five-star colonial-era mansion that overlooks the lake. Rooms are bright and spacious and some have private balconies. The common areas and grounds very much succeed at recreating hill-station ambience, with stone walls, housie (bingo) by the fireplace at 6.30pm, billiards, badminton, putting

green and a bar that might make you want to demand a scotch now, dammit, from the eager staff.

🛏 Vattakanal

Little Vattakanal village, about 4.5km southwest of the town centre, is a great rural retreat for budget travellers. It's very popular with, among others, Israeli travellers, and a party atmosphere develops here at busy times. Several village houses have rooms to rent for about ₹400 to ₹600. Altaf's Cafe (p1070) has a few sizeable three-bed rooms accommodating up to five or six people (sometimes more!) with private bathroom for ₹1000.

🍴 Eating

PT Rd is best for cheap restaurants and it's here that most travellers and students from the international school congregate.

Hotel New Punjab NORTH INDIAN $

(PT Rd; mains ₹55-200; ⊙12.30-10pm) For North Indian cuisine, including tandoori (and any nonveg curries in general), this little place is Kodai's favourite. It serves the best tandoori chicken in South India, according to locals.

Tava INDIAN $

(PT Rd; mains ₹40-90; ⊙11am-9pm) A clean, fast and cheap veg option, Tava has a wide menu; try the spicy, cauliflower-stuffed *gobi paratha* or *sev puri* (crisp, puffy fried bread with potato and chutney).

Altaf's Cafe MULTICUISINE $

(☑ 9488569632; Vattakanal; dishes ₹50-150; ⊙7.30am-8pm; ☏) This open-air cafe does Indian and Middle Eastern dishes including *sabich* (Israeli aubergine-and-egg pita sandwiches) and assorted breakfasts, for the hungry travellers at Vattakanal.

Pot Luck
CAFE $

(PT Rd; snacks & light meals ₹30-130; ⊘11am-7pm Wed-Mon) Sandwiches, pancakes, coffee, omelettes and quesadillas (!) served up on a pretty, tiny terrace attached to a pottery shop.

Cloud Street
MULTICUISINE $$

(PT Rd; mains ₹175-300; ⊘8.30am-10.30pm) Why yes, that is a real Italian-style wood-fire pizza oven. And yes, that's hummus, felafel and nachos on the menu, alongside pasta, Spanish omelette and pepper steak – it's all great food in a simple, relaxed setting.

Hotel Astoria
INDIAN $$

(Anna Salai; mains ₹85-135; ⊘7am-10pm) This veg restaurant is always packed with locals and tourists, especially at lunchtime when it serves excellent all-you-can-eat thalis.

★ Carlton Hotel
MULTICUISINE $$$

(buffet lunch/dinner ₹720/810; ⊘7-10am, 1-3pm, 7.30-10.30pm) The buffet meals here provide a big variety of excellent Indian and Continental dishes in limitless quantity. Definitely the place to come for a splash-out fill-up.

Self-Catering

Pastry Corner
BAKERY $

(Anna Salai; ⊘10am-2pm & 3-7pm) Pick up great picnic sandwiches and yummy muffins and croissants at this highly popular bakery, or squeeze onto the benches with a cuppa to watch the world go by.

Eco Nut
ORGANIC $

(PT Rd; ⊘9.30am-5.30pm Mon-Sat) This interesting shop sells a wide range of local organic food – wholewheat bread, muffins, marmalade, spices – and oils, herbs and herb remedies.

Shopping

Shops and stalls all over town sell spices, homemade chocolate and natural oils. Some also reflect a low-key but long-term commitment to social justice.

Re Shop
HANDICRAFTS

(www.bluemangoindia.com; Seven Roads Junction; ⊘10am-7pm Mon-Sat) Stylish jewellery, T-shirts, cards and more, at reasonable prices, made by and benefiting marginalised village women around Tamil Nadu.

Cottage Craft Shop
HANDICRAFTS

(PT Rd; ⊘10am-7.30pm Mon-Sat, 11am-7.30pm Sun) This shop sells hats, incense, embroidery and other goods crafted by disadvantaged groups, with about 80% of the purchase price returned to the makers.

Information

Alpha Net (PT Rd; per hr ₹60; ⊘9am-8.30pm)
Tourist Office (☑241675; PT Rd; ⊘10am-5.45pm Mon-Fri) Doesn't look too promising but they're surprisingly helpful.

Getting There & Away

The nearest train station is Kodai Road, down in the plains about 80km east of Kodaikanal. There are nine daily trains to/from Chennai Egmore including the overnight Pandiyan Express (sleeper/3AC/2AC/1AC ₹220/561/825/1419, eight hours), departing Chennai at 9.20pm and departing Kodai Road northbound at 9.10pm. For most closer destinations, it's quicker and easier to get a bus. Taxis to/from the station cost ₹1100. There are plenty of buses between the station and Batlagundu, which is on the Kodai–Madurai bus route. There's a **train booking office** (off Anna Salai; ⊘8am-noon & 2.30-5pm Mon-Sat, 8am-noon Sun) in town.

Government buses from Kodai's **bus stand** (Anna Salai):

Bengaluru ₹425-450, 11 hours, 5.30pm and 6pm
Chennai ₹380, 11 hours, 6.30pm
Coimbatore ₹120, five hours, 8.30am and 4.30pm
Madurai ₹68, four hours, 15 daily
Trichy ₹111, 5½ hours, four daily

Raja's Tours & Travels (☑242422; Anna Salai) runs 20-seat minibuses with push-back seats to Ooty (₹350, eight hours) at 7.30pm, to Madurai (₹250) at 4pm and to Kochi (₹600, 10 hours) at 6pm. It also sells tickets for overnight AC sleeper buses to Chennai (₹820) and Bengaluru (₹830).

Getting Around

The central part of Kodaikanal is compact and easy to get around on foot. There are no autorickshaws (believe it or not), but plenty of taxis. Trips within town generally cost ₹100.

Around Kodaikanal

One of the better escapes in the area, about three hours' drive below Kodaikanal off the Dindigul–Batlagundu road, is fabulous **Cardamom House** (☑9360691793, 0451-2556765; www.cardamomhouse.com; near Athoor Village; r ₹3300-4000 Apr-Nov, ₹4500-5500 Dec-Mar) 🍃. Created with love and care by a retired Brit, this comfortable guesthouse – at the end of a scenic road beside bird-rich

Lake Kamarajar – runs on solar power, uses water wisely, farms organically, and trains and employs only locals (who produce terrific meals). Book well ahead, hire a driver to take you there, and prepare for some serious relaxation.

Coimbatore

📞 0422 / POP 1.06 MILLION

This large business and junction city – the second largest in Tamil Nadu, sometimes known as the Manchester of India for its textile industry – is friendly enough, but the dearth of interesting sights means that for most travellers it's just a stepping stone towards Ooty or Kerala. It has plenty of accommodation and eating options if you need to spend the night.

🛏 Sleeping

Legend's Inn HOTEL $$
(📞 4350000; legends_inn@yahoo.com; Geetha Hall Rd; r ₹1089-1439, s/d with AC ₹1799/2040; ❄) One of the best-value midrange options, with spacious, clean, comfortable rooms at good prices for what you get. It gets busy, so it's worth booking ahead.

Hotel ESS Grande HOTEL $$
(📞 2230271; www.hotelessgrande.co.in; 358-360 Nehru St; s/d incl breakfast from ₹2159/2518; ❄@) Near a few of the bus stands, the ESS has small but very clean, fresh rooms, and possibly the sparkliest bathrooms in Coimbatore. Free cable internet in rooms. There are several other midrange and budget hotels on this street.

Hotel AP HOTEL $$
(📞 2301773; hotelap@yahoo.com; Geetha Hall Rd; s/d ₹990/1440; ❄) One of at least 10 places on this lane opposite the train station, the AP has renovated all its rooms, which are now all AC, with white paint and light wood,

and reasonable value. If you don't need AC and price is the priority, try **Sree Subbu Hotel** (📞 2300006; Geetha Hall Rd; s/d ₹420/605) a few doors away.

Residency HOTEL $$$
(📞 2241414; www.theresidency.com; 1076 Avinashi Rd; s/d incl breakfast from ₹6596/7075; ❄@🔊❄) The Residency is top choice for, among other things, its friendly staff, attractive and well-equipped rooms, swimming pool, free wi-fi and excellent eating and drinking options: the buffet meals in the **Pavilion** (buffet breakfast/lunch/dinner ₹450/670/670; ⏰24hr) restaurant are very good value. Check the website for discounts.

🍴 Eating

Naalukattu SOUTH INDIAN $
(Nehru St; mains ₹65-140; ⏰11am-11pm) Like a dark-wood-accented Keralan verandah, with Malayalam-inspired food that's all good – especially the seafood.

That's Y On The Go MULTICUISINE $$
(167 Racecourse Rd; mains ₹100-250; ⏰12.30-3pm & 7-11pm) With a clean, contemporary, cheerful ambience, this is a good place to enjoy tasty North Indian dishes and global fare from Italian to Southeast Asian to Middle Eastern. Tempting chocolatey desserts, too.

Hot Chocolate WESTERN $$
(734 Avinashi Rd; mains ₹90-300; ⏰10am-10.30pm) This place is not bad at all if you're hankering after Tex-Mex, pasta, sandwiches or indulgent cakes.

ℹ️ Information

ATMs (State Bank Rd) State Bank of India and Canara Bank, among others, have ATMs outside the train station.
Travel Gate (Geetha Hall Rd; per hr ₹25; ⏰9am-10pm) Cramped and sweaty internet cafe.

MAJOR TRAINS FROM COIMBATORE

DESTINATION	TRAIN NO & NAME	FARE (₹)	DURATION (HR)	DEPARTURE
Bengaluru	16525 Island Express	194/533/800	8	10.55pm
Chennai Central	12676 Kovai Express	132/471*	7½	2.20pm
	12674 Cheran Express	232/594/880	8½	10.20pm
Ernakulam	17230 Sabari Express	122/323/610	5	8.30am
Madurai	16610 Nagercoil Express	155/419/-	5½	8.30pm

*2nd-class/AC chair
All other fares are sleeper/3AC/2AC

ⓘ Getting There & Away

AIR

The airport is 10km east of town, with daily direct flights to domestic destinations including Bengaluru, Chennai, Delhi, Hyderabad and Mumbai on **Air India** (✆ 2303569; www.airindia.com), **IndiGo** (www.goindigo.in), **JetKonnect** (✆ 2243465; www.jetkonnect.com) or **SpiceJet** (www.spicejet.com). **SilkAir** (✆ 4370271; www.silkair.com) flies three times weekly to/from Singapore.

BUS

From the **SETC Bus Stand** (Thiruvalluvar Bus Stand; Bharathiyar Rd), government express buses head to Bengaluru (₹367 to ₹700, nine hours, five daily), Chennai (₹360, 11 hours, nine buses 5.30pm to 10pm), Ernakulam (₹139, 5½ hours, three daily), Mysore (₹147 to ₹300, six hours, 13 daily) and Trivandrum (₹300, 10½ hours, eight daily). The **Ooty Bus Stand** (New Bus Stand; Mettupalayam (MTP) Rd), northwest of the centre, has services to Ooty (₹52, four hours) via Mettupalayam (₹21, one hour) and Coonoor (₹40, three hours) every 20 to 30 minutes from 1.30am to 9pm, plus hourly buses to Kotagiri (₹32, three hours, 5.15am to 7.15pm), 18 daily to Mysore and eight to Bengaluru. Buses to Trichy (₹140, six hours) and Madurai (₹125, six hours), both every 15 minutes from 5.30am to 6.30pm, go from the **Singanallur Bus Stand** (Kamaraj Rd), 6km east of the centre: take city bus 80 from the **Town Bus Stand** (cnr Dr Nanjappa & Bharathiyar Rds).

Ukkadam Bus Station (NH Rd), southwest of the centre, has buses to southern destinations including Pollachi (₹25, 1¼ hours, every 10 minutes), Kodaikanal (₹120, six hours, 10am) and Munnar (₹140, 6½ hours, two daily), plus some services to Madurai and Ernakulam.

Private buses to Bengaluru, Ernakulam, Chennai and Trivandrum start from the **Omni Bus Stand** (Sathy Rd), 500m north of the Town Bus Stand. Many agencies on Sathy Rd sell tickets.

TAXI

A taxi up the hill to Ooty (three hours) costs about ₹1800; Ooty buses are often so crowded that it's an option worth considering.

TRAIN

Coimbatore Junction is on the main line between Chennai and Ernakulam (Kochi, Kerala), with at least 12 daily trains in each direction. The 5.15am Nilgiri Express to Mettupalayam connects with the miniature railway departure from Mettupalayam to Ooty at 7.10am. The whole trip to Ooty takes about seven hours.

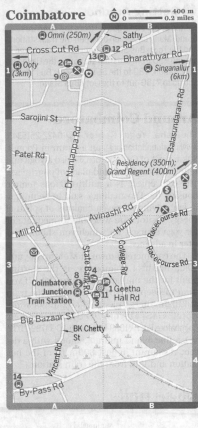

TAMIL NADU & CHENNAI COIMBATORE

Coimbatore

ⓘ Getting Around

For the airport take bus 20 from the Town Bus Stand. Many buses run between the train station and the Town Bus Stand. Autorickshaws charge around ₹50 from the train station to the Ukkadam Bus Station, ₹80 to the SETC or Town Bus Stands, and up to ₹150 out to the Ooty Bus Stand.

Around Coimbatore

The **Isha Yoga Center** (☑ 0422-2515345; www.ishafoundation.org), an ashram in Poondi, 30km west of Coimbatore, is also a yoga and rejuvenation retreat and place of pilgrimage. The centrepiece is a multireligious temple housing the Dhyanalinga, said to be unique in embodying all seven chakras of spiritual energy. Visitors are welcome to meditate or for yoga courses, for which you should register in advance.

The commercial town of **Mettupalayam**, 40km north of Coimbatore, is the starting point for the miniature train to Ooty. If you want to sleep here before catching the train at 7.10am, there's plenty of accommodation. **Hotel EMS Mayura** (☑ 04254-227936; 212 Coimbatore Rd; r ₹1089-1439, with AC ₹1799-2039; ✱), a fine, bland midrange hotel with a decent restaurant, is just 300m from the bus station and 1km from the train station.

Coonoor

☑ 0423 / POP 54,355 / ELEV 1720M

Coonoor is one of the three Nilgiri hill stations – Ooty, Kotagiri and Coonoor – that sit high above the southern plains. Smaller and quieter than Ooty, it has some terrific small hotels and guesthouses, from which you can do just the same kind of things as you would do from bigger, busier Ooty. From upper Coonoor, 1km to 2km above the town centre, you can look down over the sea of red-tile rooftops to the slopes beyond and soak up the peace, cool climate and beautiful scenery. Just note you get none of the above in central Coonoor, which is a bustling, honking mess.

⊙ Sights & Activities

The **Dolphin's Nose viewpoint**, about 10km from town, exposes a vast panorama encompassing Catherine Falls (p1075) across the valley. On the same road, **Lamb's Rock**, a favourite picnic spot in a pretty patch of forest, has amazing views past the hills to the hazy plains. The easiest way to see these sights is a rickshaw tour for around ₹600. If you like, walk the 6km or so back into town from Lamb's Rock (it's mostly downhill).

Nilgiri Hills

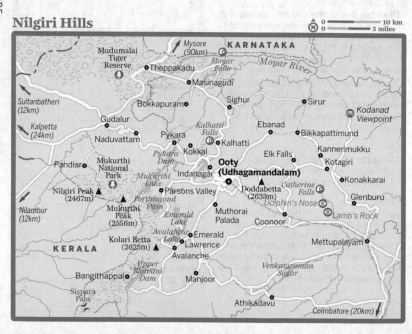

Sim's Park   PARK
(adult/child ₹20/10, camera/video ₹30/75; ⊘8am-6.30pm) Upper Coonoor's 12-hectare Sim's Park, established in 1874, is a peaceful oasis of manicured lawns sloping down to a small lake, with more than 1000 plant species from several continents, including magnolia, tree ferns and camellia. Kotagiri-bound buses can drop you here.

🛏 Sleeping & Eating

You'll need a rickshaw, car or good legs to reach any of these places. If you're self-catering, visit the **Green Shop** (www.lastforest.in; Jograj Bldg, Bedford Circle; ⊘9.30am-7pm Mon-Sat) for fair-trade local tribal products like wild honey, nuts, spices and organic tea (plus attractive tribal crafts). The well-stocked supermarket in **Tulsi Mall** (31 Mount Pleasant Rd) has a range of packaged Western goods.

YWCA Wyoming Guesthouse   HOSTEL $
(☑2234426; ywcacoonoor@gmail.com; Bedford; dm/s/d ₹150/345/810; @) A ramshackle, 150-year-old gem, the Wyoming is ageing and draughty but oozes character with wooden terraces and serene views through trees over the town. Staff are welcoming and the rooms are good and clean, with geysers for hot water. Meals available with two or three hours' notice.

★180° McIver   BOUTIQUE HOTEL $$
(☑2233323; http://serendipityo.com; Orange Grove Rd; r incl breakfast ₹3857-5875; 🛜) A classic 1880s British bungalow at the top of town has been turned into something special with a *soupçon* of French taste. The six lovely, large rooms sport antique furniture, working fireplaces and big fresh bathrooms, and the panoramas from the wraparound front lawn are fabulous. The in-house restaurant, **La Belle Vie** (mains ₹150-450; ⊘noon-2.45pm & 7-10pm), uses organic produce and has guests driving a long way to sample its European-Indian–Southeast Asian menu. There's free wi-fi throughout.

Acres Wild   FARMSTAY $$
(☑9443232621; www.acres-wild.com; Upper Meanjee Estate, Kannimariamman Kovil St; r incl breakfast ₹2398-4797; 🛜) 🐾 This gorgeously situated farm on the southeast edge of town is run on sustainable lines with solar heating, rain harvesting and cheese like you've never tasted in India from the milk of its own cows. Guests can take a two-day cheese-making course. The five rooms, in three cottages, are ample and stylish, with kitchens and fireplaces, and your friendly hosts have lots of ideas for things to do away from tourist crowds. Advance booking advisable.

Tryst   GUESTHOUSE $$$
(☑2207057; http://trystindia.com; Carolina Tea Estate; s/d incl breakfast & dinner ₹5500/6600; ⊘Oct-Apr; @🛜) If you're looking for a gregarious accommodation experience that's quirky and classy, check out the website of this highly original and welcoming guesthouse and book ahead. It's beautifully located in a former tea-plantation manager's bungalow, in a valley about 4km west of town, with lovely local walks.

ℹ Getting There & Away

Coonoor is on the miniature train line between Mettupalayam (27km) and Ooty (19km), with three daily trains just to/from Ooty as well as the daily Mettupalayam–Ooty–Mettupalayam service. Buses to and from Ooty (₹10, one hour) run about every 10 minutes; buses to Kotagiri (₹11, one hour) and Coimbatore (₹40, three hours) go roughly every 20 minutes.

Kotagiri

☑04266 / POP 29,777 / ELEV 1800M

The oldest and smallest of the three Nilgiri hill stations, Kotagiri is a quiet, unassuming place with a forgettable town centre – the appeal is the escape to red dirt tracks in the pines, blue skies and the high green walls of the Nilgiris.

You can visit **Catherine Falls**, 8km south, off the Mettupalayam road (the last 3km is on foot, and the falls only flow after rain), **Elk Falls** (6km) and **Kodanad Viewpoint** (22km), where there's a view over both the Coimbatore Plains and the Mysore Plateau. A half-day taxi tour to all three costs around ₹1000. The scenery on the road to Mettupalayam is gorgeous, too.

If you've any interest in the history of the Nilgiris, do visit the **Sullivan Memorial** (☑9942545085; www.sullivanmemorial.org; Kannerimukku; admission ₹10; ⊘10am-5pm Mon-Sat), 2km north of Kotagiri centre. The house built in 1819 by John Sullivan, founder of Ooty, has been refurbished and filled with fascinating photos and artefacts about local tribal groups, European settlement and icons such as the toy train.

Also here are the offices of the **Keystone Foundation** (☑272277; www.keystone-foundation.org; Groves Hill Rd), an NGO working

THE NILGIRIS & THEIR TRIBES

The forest-clothed, waterfall-threaded walls of the Nilgiris (Blue Mountains) rise abruptly from the surrounding plains, ascended only by winding ghat roads and the famous Nilgiri Mountain Railway which snakes up the relatively less steep eastern slope. The Nilgiris stand between the lowland towns of Mettupalayam to the southeast and Gudalur to the northwest, with the Sispara Pass and Kodanad Viewpoint marking their approximate southwest and northeast extremities. The upland territory, a jumble of valleys and hills with more than 20 peaks above 2000m, is a botanist's dream with 2300 flowering plant species, although a lot of the native *shola* forest and grasslands have been displaced by tea, eucalyptus and cattle.

The Unesco-designated Nilgiri Biosphere Reserve is a larger, 5520-sq-km area that also includes lowland areas and parts of Kerala and Karnataka states. It contains several important tiger reserves, national parks and wildlife sanctuaries, and is rated one of the world's biodiversity hot spots.

The Nilgiris' tribal inhabitants were left pretty much to themselves in their isolated homeland until the British arrived two centuries ago. Today, the effects of colonialism and migration from the lowlands have reduced many tribal cultures to the point of collapse, and some have assimilated to the point of invisibility. Some, however, continue at least a semi-traditional lifestyle, practising small-scale agriculture or herding, or gathering wild forest produce. Organisations such as the Keystone Foundation (p1075) are helping to promote traditional activities and crafts.

Best known of the tribes, thanks to anthropologists' interest and their proximity to Ooty, are the Toda, who now number around 1000. Some still inhabit tiny villages of their traditional barrel-shaped huts made of bamboo, cane and grass. Toda women wear their hair in long, shoulder-length ringlets, and both sexes wear characteristic black-and-red-embroidered shawls of homespun cotton. The water buffalo is at the centre of Toda life. Buffalo milk and ghee are integral to their diet and are also bartered for grain, tools and medical services. The dairy produce also provides offerings to the gods. Traditionally, it is only at funerals that the strictly vegetarian Toda kill a buffalo, not for food but to provide company for the deceased.

The 350,000-strong Badaga are believed to have migrated into the Nilgiris from the north around 1600 AD, and are thus not usually considered truly indigenous. Their traditional dress is of white cloth with a border of narrow coloured stripes. They worship the mother goddess Hetti Amman, to whom their six-day Hettai habba festival in December or January is dedicated.

The Kota live in seven settlements in the Kotagiri area. Cultivators, they still undertake ceremonies in which the gods are beseeched for rains and bountiful harvests. They have adapted relatively well to modernity, with a significant number holding government jobs.

The Kurumba inhabit the thick forests of the south and are traditional gatherers of forest products such as bamboo and wild honey, which they collect from cliffs, rocky crevices and trees.

to improve environmental conditions in the Nilgiris while working with, and creating better living standards for, indigenous communities. It has some openings for volunteers with communications, design and other skills. The foundation's **Green Shop** (Johnstone Sq; ⊙ 9.30am-7pm Mon-Sat) in Coonoor has goodies for picnics (local organic cheese, wild honey and more) plus appealing tribal crafts.

Hope Park (☑ 271229; www.hopeparkhotel. com; Hope Park; r ₹1679-2398) has big, clean rooms, a decent restaurant and friendly staff. French-owned **La Maison** (☑ 273347; Hadatharai; s/d ₹7425/8910; ☎) is a beautifully renovated 1890s Scottish bungalow, in the countryside about 5km southwest of town: the Franco-Indian fusion food is one of the attractions here.

Buses to and from Ooty run half-hourly (₹13, 1½ hours), crossing one of Tamil Nadu's highest passes. Buses to Mettupalayam leave hourly.

Ooty (Ootacamund, Udhagamandalam)

☏ 0423 / POP 111,918 / ELEV 2240M

Ooty may be a bit bustling for some tastes, and the town centre is, frankly, an ugly mess, but it doesn't take long to get up into the greener, quieter areas where tall pines rise above what might almost be mistaken for English country lanes. Ooty combines Indian bustle and Hindu temples with lovely parks and gardens and charming Raj-era bungalows, the latter providing its most memorable (and generally most expensive) places to stay.

The town was established by the British in the early 19th century as the summer headquarters of the Madras government, and memorably nicknamed 'Snooty Ooty'. Development ploughed in a few decades ago, but somehow old Ooty survives. You just have to walk a bit further out from the centre to find it.

The journey up here on the celebrated miniature train is romantic and the scenery stunning. Even the road up from the plains is pretty impressive. From April to June (the *very* busy season) Ooty is a welcome relief from the hot plains, and in the colder months (October to March) you'll need warm clothing, which you can buy cheap here, as overnight temperatures occasionally drop to 0°C.

The train and bus stations are at the west end of Ooty's racecourse, in almost the lowest part of town. To their west is the lake, while the streets of the town snake upwards all around. From the bus station it's a 20-minute walk to Ooty's commercial centre, Charing Cross. Like Kodaikanal, Ooty has an international school whose students can often be seen around town.

◉ Sights

Botanical Gardens
GARDEN

(adult/child ₹20/10, camera/video ₹30/75; ⊙7am-6.30pm) Established in 1848, these lovely gardens are a living gallery of the natural flora of the Nilgiris. Look out for a fossilised tree trunk believed to be around 20 million years old, and on busy days, roughly 20 million Indian tourists.

Doddabetta Lookout
VIEWPOINT

(admission ₹5; ⊙7am-6pm) This is it: the highest point (2633m) of the Nilgiris and one of the best viewpoints around, assuming the day is clear (go early for better chances of a mist-free view). It's about 7km from the town centre: Kotagiri buses will drop you at the Dodabetta junction, then you have a fairly energetic 3km walk or a quick jeep ride. Taxis will do the round trip from Charing Cross for ₹400.

Rose Garden
GARDEN

(Selbourne Rd; admission ₹20, camera/video ₹30/75; ⊙8.30am-6pm) With its terraced lawns and over 20,000 rose bushes of 2200 varieties – best between May and July – the large Rose Garden is a pleasant place for a stroll. There are good views over Ooty from the hilltop location.

Tribal Research Centre Museum
MUSEUM

(Muthorai Palada; ⊙10am-1pm & 2-5pm Sat-Thu) FREE It's hard to say why you should love this museum more: for its decently executed exhibits on Nilgiri and Andaman tribal groups, or the decomposing corpses of badly stuffed local wildlife. Seriously, the artefacts are fantastic – you may never get the chance to hold a Stone Age bow in your life again – and descriptions of the tribes are good, albeit academically anthropological. It's just beyond the village of Muthorai Palada (M Palada), 11km south of Ooty on the way to Emerald and served by frequent buses. A rickshaw costs around ₹350 return. Note that opening times can be a bit fluid.

St Stephen's Church
CHURCH

(⊙10.30am-5pm, services 8am & 11am Sun) Perched above the town centre, the immaculate St Stephen's, built in 1829, is the oldest church in the Nilgiris. It has lovely stained glass, huge wooden beams hauled by elephant from the palace of Tipu Sultan some 120km away, and the sometimes kitschy, sometimes touching, slabs and plaques donated by colonial-era churchgoers. In the quiet, overgrown cemetery you'll find headstones commemorating many an Ooty Brit.

Nilgiri Library
LIBRARY

(Hospital Rd; ⊙reading room 9.30am-1pm & 2.30-6pm Sat-Thu) This quaint little haven in a crumbling 1867 building has more than 60,000 books, including rare titles on the Nilgiris and hill tribes. Visitors can consult books in the reading room in return for a donation (whatever you want to give).

Ooty (Udhagamandalam)

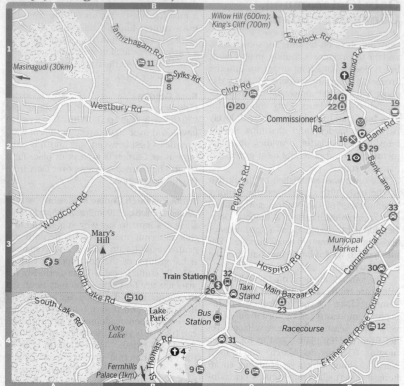

🏃 Activities

Hiking & Trekking

To make the most of Ooty, you should get out into the beautiful Nilgiris. Ooty's tourist office and many accommodation places can put you in touch with local guides who do day trips for ₹400 to ₹450 per person including lunch. You'll normally drive out of town and walk around hills, tribal villages and tea plantations. The tourist office can give basic information about some self-guided hikes but doesn't have any leaflets or decent maps of them.

More serious trekking in the best forest areas with plenty of wildlife – such as beyond Avalanche to the south or Parsons Valley to the west, or in Mukurthi National Park – requires Tamil Nadu Forest Department permits and you will probably need to take a guide from the department. Take a written application and your passport to the **District Forest Office Nilgiris South Division** (☎ 2444083; dfosouth@sancharnet.in; Mount Stuart Hill) or **District Forest Office Nilgiris North Division** (☎ 2443968; dfonlg@tn.nic.in; Mount Stuart Hill): permits, if granted, are normally issued the same day. The department has basic accommodation available in some locations. A great trek of three to five days, if you can organise it, is the 'Silent Valley' route southwest from Bangithappal in Mukurthi National Park, to the Sispara Pass and down to Walakkad and Sairandhri in Kerala's Silent Valley National Park.

The **Nilgiri Wildlife & Environment Association** (☎ 2447167; http://nwea.in; Mount Stuart Hill; ⏰ 10am-1pm & 3-5pm Mon-Fri, 10am-1pm Sat) can be helpful with trekking advice. Its members can act as guides for ₹2000 to ₹3000 per day (including food).

Boating

Rowboats can be rented from the **Boathouse** (admission ₹5, camera/video ₹10/100; ⏰ 9am-6pm) by Ooty's lake. Prices start from

Ooty (Udhagamandalam)

₹100 (with a ₹100 deposit) for a two-seater pedal boat (30 minutes).

Horse Racing

Ooty's racecourse dominates the valley between Charing Cross and the lake. Racing season runs from mid-April to mid-June, and on the two or three race days each week the town is a hive of activity; it's an event you can't miss if you're in town. Racing happens between about 10.30am and 2.30pm.

Tours

Fixed taxi tour rates are ₹800 for four hours tootling around Ooty, ₹950 for Coonoor (four hours), or ₹1600 for Mudumalai Tiger Reserve.

🛏 Sleeping

Ooty has some gorgeous colonial-era residences at the high end and some decent backpacker dosses. There's not much on offer in the lower midrange though. Be warned: it's a sellers' market in the high season (1 April to 15 June), when many hotels hike their rates and checkout time is often 9am.

YWCA Anandagiri
HOSTEL $

(☏2442218; www.ywcaagooty.com; Ettines Rd; dm ₹99-110, s ₹230-960, d ₹345-960) This former brewery and sprawling complex of cottages is dotted with flower gardens; throw in spacious common areas including a restaurant with good-value meals (book ahead for these), and you've got some excellent budget accommodation going on. Rooms are clean and mostly quite spacious, though high ceilings can mean cold nights; ask for extra blankets if you might need them.

Reflections Guest House
GUESTHOUSE $

(☏2443834; reflectionsin@yahoo.co.in; 1B North Lake Rd; s ₹500-600, d ₹550-800) A long-running budget haunt, Reflections sits across the road from Ooty's lake, and most of its 12 clean and decent rooms have lake views. It also serves Indian and Continental food at fair prices (₹60 to ₹180). Hot showers are available for two hours per day; there's a ₹20 charge for toilet paper and towels.

Hotel Sweekar
HOTEL $

(☏2442348; hotelsweekar@gmail.com; 236 Race View Rd; r ₹350-550) The Sweekar hosts guests in small but clean rooms in a traditional Ooty cottage at the end of a flower-lined path. Hot water is limited to 7.30am to 9.30am, but the Sweekar is good value for its prices, and is run by a very helpful Bahai manager.

★Lymond House
HERITAGE HOTEL $$

(☏2223377; http://serendipityo.com; 77 Sylks Rd; r incl breakfast ₹4137-4797; 🛜) What is it about this 1850s British bungalow that gives it the edge over its peers? The cosy cottage ambience with flowers, four-poster beds, fireplaces, white linen and warm lighting? The contemporary fittings and free wi-fi accompanying the old-world style in the spacious rooms and bathrooms? The bright dining room and pretty country garden? All of those, no doubt – plus an informal yet efficient management style that helps you feel right at home.

Hotel Welbeck Residency
HOTEL $$

(☏2223300; www.welbeck.in; Welbeck Circle, Club Rd; r incl breakfast ₹2878-4257; @🛜) An attractive older building that's been thoroughly tarted up with comfortable and cosy rooms, a touch of colonial-era class (a 1920 Austin saloon at the front door!), a decent restaurant and helpful staff.

Mount View Hotel
HOTEL $$

(☏2442077; www.hotelmountviewooty.com; Ettines Rd; r ₹1971-3943; 🛜) Perched on a quiet driveway convenient to the bus and train stations, the nine enormous, wood-lined, high-ceilinged rooms in this elegant old bungalow have recently been renovated to a good standard of comfort. It's a pity they still aren't using the fireplaces, though.

Willow Hill
HOTEL $$

(☏2223123; www.willowhill.in; 58/1 Havelock Rd; s ₹1319-3598, d ₹1559-3957, all incl breakfast) Sitting high above town, Willow Hill's large windows provide great views of Ooty if you're on one of the upper floors. The 10 rooms have a distinct alpine-chalet chic, with the most expensive offering a private garden.

★Savoy Hotel
HERITAGE HOTEL $$$

(☏2225500; www.tajhotels.com; 77 Sylks Rd; s ₹5341-10,088, d ₹5934-12,275, all incl breakfast; @🛜) The Savoy is one of Ooty's oldest hotels, with parts dating back to 1829. Big cottages are arranged around a beautiful garden of flowerbeds, lawns and clipped hedges. The quaint rooms have large bathrooms, log fires and bay windows. Service is very good, and modern facilities include a bar, wi-fi (chargeable), plenty of games for kids and adults, and an excellent multicuisine dining room. During high season, full-board arrangements may be obligatory.

Ferrnhills Palace
HERITAGE HOTEL $$$

(☏2443910; www.welcomheritagehotels.com; Fern Hill; r incl breakfast ₹11,192-33,576; @🛜) The Maharaja of Mysore's splendiferous Anglo-Indian summer palace has been lovingly restored in gorgeous, over-the-top princely colonial style; if you can afford to stay here, you really should. All rooms are large suites, with antique furnishings, fireplaces and Jacuzzis. Play billiards, walk in the huge, forest-surrounded grounds and dine on regal multicuisine fare beneath vivid murals.

King's Cliff
HERITAGE HOTEL $$$

(☏2452888; www.littlearth.in; Havelock Rd; r incl breakfast ₹2129-5966; 🛜) High above Ooty on Strawberry Hill is this classic colonial-era house with wood panelling, antique furnishings and cosy lounge. The cheaper ones don't have quite the same old-world charm as the more expensive ones, however.

✕ Eating & Drinking

Top-end hotels such as the Savoy and Ferrn-hills Palace have atmospheric, multicuisine restaurants that are the best places to go for a classy meal.

Garden Restaurant   SOUTH INDIAN $
(Commercial Rd; mains ₹50-130; ⊙7.30am-9.30pm) Very good South Indian food in a clean setting behind the Nahar Nilgiris Hotel, along with juices, ice creams, snacks and moderate pizza.

Kabab Corner   NORTH INDIAN $$
(Commercial Rd; mains ₹70-300; ⊙1-11pm) This is the place for meat eaters who are tiring of South Indian vegetarian food. It doesn't look much from the outside, but here you can tear apart perfectly grilled and spiced chunks of lamb, chicken and, if you like, paneer, sopping up the juices with pillowy triangles of naan. The ₹640 tandoori platter is exceptionally good for a group; if there are fewer than four of you, it may defeat you.

Shinkow's Chinese Restaurant   CHINESE $$
(38/83 Commissioner's Rd; mains ₹100-250; ⊙noon-3.45pm & 6.30-9.45pm) Shinkow's is an Ooty institution and the simple menu of chicken, pork, beef, fish, noodles and rice dishes is reliably good and quick to arrive at your table.

Willy's Coffee Pub   CAFE $
(KCR Arcade, Walsham Rd; dishes ₹20-80; ⊙10am-9.30pm) Climb the stairs and join international students and local cool kids for board games, a small lending library and very reasonably priced pizzas, fries, toasted sandwiches, cakes and cookies.

Café Coffee Day   CAFE $
(Garden Rd; coffee ₹60-110; ⊙9am-11pm; 🛜) Reliably fine coffee, tea and cakes. There's another branch (Church Hill Rd; ⊙9am-11pm; 🛜) on Church Hill Rd.

Self-Catering
Modern Stores (144 Garden Rd; ⊙9.30am-8.30pm) is a mini-supermarket with all kinds of Western foods from muesli to Seville orange marmalade, as well as Nilgiri-produced bread and cheese. The fair-trade and organic-oriented **Green Shop** (Sargan Villa, off Club Rd; ⊙9.30am-7pm Mon-Sat) has excellent wild honey, plus attractive crafts and also a bee museum. **Virtue Bakes** (Garden Rd; ⊙10.30am-8.30pm) sells excellent cakes, pastries and bread to take away.

🛍 Shopping

The main shopping street is Commercial Rd, where you'll find Kashmiri shops as well as outlets for Keralan crafts and *khadi* (hand-spun cloth). Elsewhere, **K Mahaveer Chand** (291 Main Bazaar Rd; ⊙9.30am-8pm) has been selling particularly attractive Toda tribal and silver jewellery for over 40 years, and **Mohan's** (Commissioner's Rd; ⊙10am-8pm) has a curious assortment of antique telephones, radios and beer tankards as well as warm clothes. Near the botanical gardens entrance, Tibetan refugees sell sweaters and shawls, which you may appreciate on a chilly Ooty evening. **Higginbothams** (📋2443736; Commercial Rd; ⊙9am-1pm & 3.30-7.30pm Mon-Sat) has a good English-language book selection (including Lonely Planet guides), and another **branch** (📋2442546; Commissioner's Rd; ⊙9am-1pm & 2-6pm Mon-Sat) up the hill.

ℹ Information

Cyber Planet (Garden Rd; per hr ₹30; ⊙9.30am-6.30pm)

Global Net (Commercial Rd; per hr ₹30; ⊙9am-9.30pm)

Tourist Office (📋2443977; Wenlock Rd; ⊙10am-5.45pm Mon-Fri; ☎) Good for maps and information.

ℹ Getting There & Away

The fun way to arrive in Ooty is aboard the miniature train from Mettupalayam. Buses also run regularly up and down the mountain from other parts of Tamil Nadu, from Kerala and from Mysore and Bengaluru in Karnataka. Taxis cluster at several stands in town and there are fixed one-way fares to many destinations, including Coonoor (₹600), Kotagiri (₹700), Coimbatore (₹1500) and Mudumalai Tiger Reserve (₹1000).

BUS

For Kochi (Cochin, Kerala) take the 7am or 8am bus to Palakkad (₹80, six hours) and change there. **Royal Tours** (📋2446150), opposite the train station, runs a 9am minibus to Kodaikanal (₹500, eight hours).

The Tamil Nadu, Kerala and Karnataka state bus companies all have reservation offices at the busy **bus station**. Departures include:

Bengaluru ₹350-600, eight hours, 12 daily

Chennai ₹450, 14 hours, three daily

Coimbatore ₹52, four hours, every 30 minutes, 5.30am to 8.30pm

Mysore ₹135, five hours, about every 45 minutes, 6.15am to 5.45pm

TRAIN

The miniature (or 'toy') train from Met-tupalayam to Ooty – one of the Mountain Railways of India given World Heritage status by Unesco – is the best way to get here. Called the Nilgiri Mountain Railway, it requires special cog wheels on the locomotive, meshing with a third, 'toothed' rail on the ground, to manage the exceptionally steep gradients There are marvel-lous views of forest, waterfalls, mountainsides and tea plantations along the way. The section between Mettupalayam and Coonoor uses steam engines, which push, rather than pull, the train up the hill.

For the high season, try to book the train sever-al weeks ahead; at other times a few days ahead is advisable, though not always essential. The train departs Mettupalayam for Ooty at 7.10am daily (1st/2nd class ₹155/23, five hours). From Ooty to Mettupalayam the train leaves at 2pm and takes 3½ hours. Departures and arrivals at Mettupalayam connect with those of the Nilgiri Express to/from Chennai Central. There are also three daily passenger trains each way just be-tween Ooty and Coonoor (₹18, 1¼ hours).

Note that Ooty is usually listed as Udagaman-dalam in train timetables.

❶ Getting Around

There are plenty of autorickshaws and taxis: autorickshaw fare charts are posted outside the bus station and botanical gardens and else-where. An autorickshaw from the train or bus station to Charing Cross costs about ₹60.

There are jeep taxi stands near the bus station and municipal market: expect to pay about 1.5 times local taxi fares.

Mudumalai Tiger Reserve

☑ 0423

In the foothills of the Nilgiris, this 321-sq-km reserve is like a classical Indian landscape painting given life: thin, spindly trees and light-slotted leaves concealing spotted chi-tal deer and grunting wild boar. Also here are around 50 tigers, giving Mudumalai the highest tiger population density in India – though you'll still be very lucky to see one. Overall the reserve is the best place for spot-ting wildlife in Tamil Nadu. The creatures you're most likely to see include deer, pea-cocks, wild boar, langurs and Malabar giant squirrels. There's also a significant chance of sighting wild elephants (the park has several hundred) and gaur (Indian bison).

Along with Karnataka's Bandipur and Nagarhole and Kerala's Wayanad, Mudu-malai forms part of an unbroken chain of protected areas comprising an important wildlife refuge.

Mudumalai sometimes closes for fire risk in April, May or June. Rainy July and August are the least favourable months for visiting.

The reserve's **reception centre** (☑ 2526235; ⊙ 6.30am-6pm), and some gov-ernment-run accommodation, is at Theppa-kadu, on the main road between Ooty and Mysore. The closest village to Theppakadu is Masinagudi, 7km east.

◉ Sights & Activities

Hking in the reserve is not allowed and private vehicles are only allowed on the main Ooty–Gudalur–Theppakadu–Mysore road and the Theppakadu–Masinagudi and Masinagudi–Moyar River roads. Some wildlife can be seen from these roads, but the best way to see the reserve is on the enjoyable official 45-minute **minibus tours** (per person ₹35; ⊙ 7am, 8am, 3pm, 4pm & 5pm), which make a 15km loop in camouflage-striped 26-seat buses. Get to the reception centre 30 minutes beforehand to ensure a seat. Half-hour **elephant rides** (for 4 people ₹460; ⊙ 7-8am & 4-5pm) are also available from the reception centre. At 6pm you can watch the reserve's working elephants being fed at the nearby **elephant camp** (minibus-tour customers free, others ₹15).

Some operators may offer treks in the buffer zone around the reserve, but these are potentially dangerous and the reserve au-thorities advise very strongly against them. Jeep safaris organised through the better re-sorts, with expert guides, are a safer option.

🛏 Sleeping & Eating

The reserve runs some simple accommo-dation along a track just above the Moyar River at Theppakadu. For these it's advis-able to book in advance at the **Office of the Field Director** (Map p1078; ☑ 0423-2444098; fdmtr@tn.nic.in; Mount Stuart Hill, Ooty; ⊙ 10am-6pm Mon-Fri, 10am-1pm Sat) in Ooty, though the reception centre will accept walk-in book-ings if there are vacancies. Best is the well maintained **Theppakadu Log House** (d/q ₹1100/1600), whose comfortable rooms have private bathrooms. **Sylvan Lodge** (d ₹600) is on similar lines though less comfortable. The caretaker can arrange meals at both places (dinner costs ₹40 to ₹50). Also here is the extremely basic, government-run **Hotel Tamil Nadu** (☑ 2526580; htn-mdm@ttdconline. com; dm/d/q ₹125/550/950), with a restaurant.

Better accommodation is provided by numerous lodges and forest resorts outside the park's fringes, many of them family-run businesses with a warm atmosphere, high standards and breathtaking views. Many of the best cluster in Bokkapuram village, 5km from Masinagudi at the foot of the mountains. Don't wander outside your resort at night; leopards, among other wild animals, are present. Meals at the resorts, where not included in room rates, cost between ₹250 and ₹450 each.

★ **The Wilds at Northernhay** LODGE $$
(☎ 9843149490; http://serendipityo.com; Singara; r incl breakfast ₹4035-4747) A wonderful lodge 8km southwest of Masinagudi, in a converted coffee warehouse on a coffee plantation with many tall trees that give it a deep-in-the-forest feel. Cosy rooms (two of them up in the trees) and excellent meals complement the two-hour morning and evening jeep safaris (₹2750), on which you can expect to see a very good variety of wildlife.

Jungle Retreat RESORT $$
(☎ 2526469; www.jungleretreat.com; Bokkapuram; dm ₹524, r ₹2941-4706; ▓) One of the most stylish resorts in the area, with accommodation in sturdy bamboo huts or lovingly built stone cottages or even a high treehouse, all spread out to give a feeling of seclusion. The bar, restaurant and common area are great places to meet fellow travellers, and the owners are knowledgeable and friendly. The beautiful pool has a stunning setting, and elephants and leopards have been known to visit it for a drink.

Forest Hills Guest House RESORT $$
(☎ 2526216; www.foresthillsindia.com; Bokkapuram; d ₹2177-4430) Forest Hills is a family-run, family-sized guesthouse (14 rooms on 5 hectares) with a few cute bamboo huts and treehouses, some clean spacious rooms, and a watchtower room that's great for wildlife-watching and birdwatching. There's a slight colonial-era air here with a gazebo-style bar, games rooms and evening bonfires.

Jungle Hut RESORT $$$
(☎ 2526463; www.junglehut.in; Bokkapuram; full board s ₹3400-5300, d ₹5000-6900; ▓ ⌘ ▓) Along with spacious rooms in cottages scattered around a large property, and a sociable common area, this welcoming resort has probably the best food in Bokkapuram (if you're visiting the restaurant from another resort after dark, don't walk home on your own!). A herd of chital deer grazes the grounds morning and evening, and jeep safaris, treks and birdwatching walks can be organised.

❶ Getting There & Around

You can do a taxi day-trip to Mudumalai from Ooty for around ₹1600. Do go at least one way by the alternative Sighur Ghat road with its spectacular 36-hairpin hill. A one-way taxi from Ooty to Theppakadu should be ₹1000.

Buses between Ooty and Mysore go via Gudalur and stop at Theppakadu (₹45, three hours from Ooty). Smaller buses that can manage the Sighur Ghat road run from Ooty to Masinagudi (₹10, 1½ hours, eight daily). Local buses run every two hours between Masinagudi and Theppakadu (₹5); shared jeeps also ply this route for ₹10 per person if there are enough passengers, or you can have one to yourself for about ₹100. Costs are similar for jeeps between Masinagudi and Bokkapuram.

Andaman Islands

Best Beaches

➡ Radhanagar (p1093)
➡ Merk Bay (p1100)
➡ Ross & Smith Islands (p1101)
➡ Butler Bay (p1102)
➡ Beach 5 (p1095)

Best Places to Stay

➡ Emerald Gecko (p1096)
➡ Aashiaanaa Rest Home (p1091)
➡ Pristine Beach Resort (p1101)
➡ Blue View (p1102)
➡ Blue Planet (p1100)

Why Go?

Long fabled among travellers for its legendary beaches, world-class diving and far-flung location in the middle of nowhere, the Andaman Islands are still the ideal place to get away from it all.

Its lovely opaque emerald waters are surrounded by primeval jungle and mangrove forest, and snow-white beaches that melt under flame-and-purple sunsets. The population is a friendly masala of South and Southeast Asian settlers, as well as Negrito ethnic groups whose arrival here still has anthropologists baffled. Adding to the intrigue is its remote location, some 1370km from the mainland, meaning the islands are geographically more Southeast Asia – 150km from Indonesia and 190km from Myanmar.

While the archipelago comprises some 300 islands, only a dozen or so are open to tourists, Havelock by far being the most popular for its beaches and diving. The Nicobars are strictly off limits to tourists, as are the tribal areas.

When to Go
Port Blair

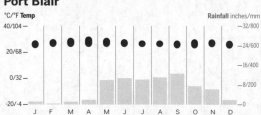

Dec–Mar Perfect sunny days, optimal diving conditions, and turtle nesting.

Oct–Dec & Mar–mid-May Weather's a mixed bag, but fewer tourists and lower costs.

May–Aug Pumping waves on Little Andaman for experienced surfers.

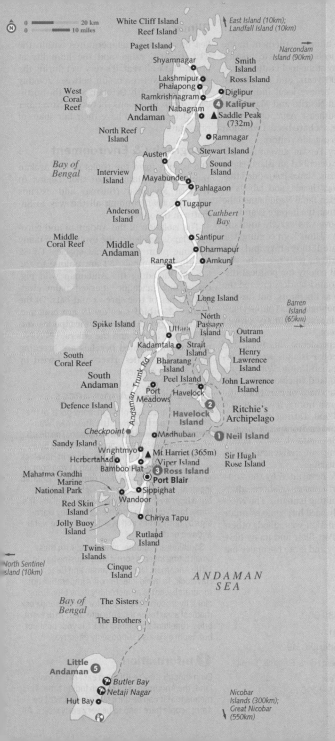

Andaman Islands Highlights

1 Regress to infantile laziness and happiness on **Neil Island** (p1098)

2 Dive, snorkel and socialise on **Havelock Island** (p1093)

3 Glimpse Port Blair's colonial history at **Ross Island** (p1090)

4 Experience the true wilds of Northern Andaman in **Kalipur** (p1101) while island-hopping to pristine beaches and coral reefs

5 Find Butler Bay and paradise on **Little Andaman** (p1101)

History

The date of initial human settlement in the Andamans and Nicobars is lost to history. Anthropologists say stone-tool crafters have lived here for 2000 years, and scholars of human migration believe local indigenous tribes have roots in Negrito and Malay ethnic groups in Southeast Asia. Otherwise, these specks in the sea have been a constant source of legend to outside visitors.

The 10th-century Persian adventurer Buzurg Ibn Shahriyar described an island chain inhabited by cannibals, Marco Polo added that the natives had dogs' heads, and tablets in Thanjavur (Tanjore) in Tamil Nadu named the archipelago Timaittivu: the Impure Islands.

None of the above was exactly tourism-brochure stuff, but visitors kept coming: the Marathas in the late 17th century and, 200 years later, the British, who used the Andamans as a penal colony for political dissidents. In WWII some islanders greeted the invading Japanese as liberators, but despite installing Indian politicians as (puppet) administrators, the Japanese military proved to be harsh occupiers.

Following Independence in 1947, the Andaman and Nicobar Islands were incorporated into the Indian Union. With migration from the mainland (including Bengali refugees fleeing the chaos of partition), the population has grown from a few thousand to more than 350,000. During this influx, tribal land rights and environmental protection were often disregarded; some conditions are improving but indigenous tribes remain largely in decline.

The islands were devastated by the 2004 Indian Ocean earthquake, offshore aftershocks and the resulting tsunami. The Nicobars were especially hard hit; some estimate a fifth of the population was killed; others were relocated to Port Blair and many have yet to return. But by and large normalcy has returned.

FAST FACTS

➡ **Population:** 380,000

➡ **Area:** 8248 sq km

➡ **Telephone code:** ☑ 03192

➡ **Main languages:** Hindi, Bengali, Tamil

➡ **Sleeping prices:**
$ below ₹800, $$ ₹800 to ₹2500,
$$$ above ₹2500

Climate

Sea breezes keep temperatures within the 23°C to 31°C range and the humidity at around 80% all year. It's very wet during the southwest (wet) monsoon between roughly mid-May and early October, while the northeast (dry) monsoons between November and December also have their fair share of rainy days.

Geography & Environment

The islands form the peaks of the Arakan Yoma, a mountain range that begins in Western Myanmar (Burma) and extends into the ocean running all the way to Sumatra in Indonesia.

The isolation of the Andaman and Nicobar Islands has led to the evolution of many endemic plant and animal species. Of 62 identified mammals, 32 are unique to the islands, including the Andaman wild pig, crab-eating macaque, masked palm civet, and species of tree shrews and bats. Of the islands' 250 bird species, 18 are endemic, including ground-dwelling megapodes, *hawabills* (swiftlets) and the emerald Nicobar pigeon. The isolated beaches are breeding grounds for turtles; rivers are prowled by saltwater crocodiles.

ⓘ Dangers & Annoyances

Crocodiles are a way of life in many parts of the Andamans, particularly Little Andaman, Wandoor, Baratang and North Andaman. The death of an American tourist who was attacked by a saltwater crocodile while snorkelling in Havelock in 2010 (at Neils Cove near Beach 7) was considered extremely unusual, and remains an isolated incident. There have been no sightings since, but a high level of vigilance remains in place. It's important you keep informed, heed any warnings by authorities and avoid being in the water at dawn or dusk.

Sandflies are another hindrance, with these small biting insects sometimes causing havoc in Little Andaman, North Andaman and Beach 7 on Havelock. To avoid infection, it's imperative not to scratch what is an incredibly itchy bite. Bring along hydrocortisone cream for the bite and seek medical assistance if it gets infected. To prevent bites, repellant containing DEET is your best bet, but neem oil is also supposedly effective.

ⓘ Information

Even though they're 1000km east of the mainland, the Andamans still run on Indian time. This means that it can be dark by 5pm and light by 4am; people here tend to be very early risers. All telephone numbers must include the 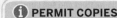 03192 area code, even when dialling locally.

ACCOMMODATION

Prices here are listed for high season (December to March), though be aware tariffs can rise during peak season of mid-December to January. In peak season accommodation on the islands can be stretched, so reservations are a good idea. May to November is low to mid-season, which brings healthy discounts. Camping is not permitted on the islands.

PERMITS

All foreigners need a permit to visit the Andaman Islands; it's issued free on arrival. The 30-day permit allows foreigners to stay in Port Blair, South and Middle Andaman (excluding tribal areas), North Andaman (Diglipur), Long Island, North Passage, Little Andaman (excluding tribal areas), and Havelock and Neil Islands. It's possible to get a 15-day extension from the **Immigration Office** (☑ 03192-239247; ☺ 8.30am-1pm & 2-5.30pm Mon-Fri, to 1pm Sat) in Port Blair, or at police stations elsewhere.

The permit also allows day trips to Jolly Buoy, South Cinque, Red Skin, Ross, Narcondam, Interview and Rutland Islands, as well as the Brothers and the Sisters.

Boat passengers will probably be met by an immigration official on arrival; if not, seek out the immigration office at Haddo Jetty immediately. Keep your permit on you at all times – you won't be able to travel without it. Police frequently ask to see it, especially when you're disembarking on other islands, and hotels will need permit details. Check current regulations regarding permits with the following agencies:

Andaman & Nicobar Tourism (☑ 03192-232694; www.and.nic.in/newtourism; Kamaraj Rd; ☺ 8.30am-12.30pm & 1.30-4.30pm Mon-Fri, 8.30am-noon Sat)

Foreigner's Registration Office (☑ Chennai 044-23454970, Kolkata 033-22470549; www.immihelp.com/nri/protected-restricted-area-permit-india.html)

Additional permits are required to visit some national parks and sanctuaries. The tourism office in Port Blair can tell you whether a permit is needed and how to go about getting it. If you plan to do something complicated, you'll be sent to the **Chief Wildlife Warden** (CWW; ☑ 03192-233321; Haddo Rd, Port Blair; ☺ 8.30am-noon & 1-4pm Mon-Fri).

For most day permits it's not the hassle but the cost. For areas such as Mahatma Gandhi Marine National Park, and Ross and Smith Islands near Diglipur, the permits cost ₹50/500 for Indians/foreigners. For Saddle Peak National Park, also near Diglipur, the cost is ₹25/250. Students with valid ID pay minimal entry fees, so don't forget to bring your card.

ⓘ PERMIT COPIES

At the time of research it was a requirement to produce a photocopy of your permit when booking ferry tickets. While you're not always asked to provide it, to avoid the trauma of having to re-queue, it's worth taking five or so copies before arriving at Port Blair's ferry office: you'll likely need them later in your trip.

The Nicobar Islands are off-limits to all except Indian nationals engaged in research, government business or trade.

ⓘ Getting There & Away

AIR

There are daily flights to Port Blair from Delhi, Kolkata and Chennai, although flights from Delhi and Kolkata are often routed through Chennai. Round-trip fares are between US$250 and US$600 depending on how early you book; some airlines offer one-way flights for as low as US$80, but these need to be booked months in advance. Airlines that head to Port Blair include **SpiceJet** (☑ 1800 1803333; www.spicejet.com), **GoAir** (☑ 1800 222111; www.goair.in), **Air India** (☑ Port Blair 03192-233108; www.airindia.com), **Jet Airways** (☑ 22-39893333; www.jetairways.com) and **JetLite** (☑ 03192-242707; www.jetlite.com). Kingfisher flights were suspended at time of research.

There are no international flights from Port Blair to Southeast Asia.

BOAT

Depending on who you ask, the infamous boat to Port Blair is either 'the only *real* way to get to the Andamans' or a hassle and a half. The truth lies somewhere in between. There are usually three to four sailings a month between Port Blair and Chennai (60 hours) and Kolkata (64 hours), plus a monthly ferry to Vizag (56 hours). All ferries from the mainland arrive at Haddo Jetty.

➜ For Chennai you can book tickets through the **Andaman Shipping Office** (☑ 25226873; www.and.nic.in; 2nd fl, Shipping Corporation of India, Jawahar Bldg, 17 Rajaji Salai, George Town; ☺ 9am-1pm & 2-3pm Mon-Fri, 9am-noon Sat)

➜ Kolkata and Vizag are booked through **Shipping Corporation of India** (☑ in Kolkata 033-22484921, in Vizag 0891-2565597; www.shipindia.com; 13 Strand Rd, Kolkata)

Take sailing times with a large grain of salt – travellers have reported sitting on the boat at Kolkata harbour for up to 12 hours, or waiting to dock near Port Blair for several hours. With hold-ups and variable weather and sea conditions, the trip can take 2½ to five days.

You can organise your return ticket at the ferry booking office (p1092) at Phoenix Bay. Bring two passport photos and a photocopy of your permit. Updated schedules and fares can be found at www.and.nic.in/newtourism or www.shipindia.com.

Classes vary slightly between boats, but the cheapest is bunk (₹2160), followed by 2nd class B (₹4280), 2nd class A (₹5540), 1st class (₹6320) and deluxe cabins (₹7640). The MV *Akbar* also has AC dorm berths (₹3620). Higher-end tickets cost as much as, if not more than, a plane ticket. If you go bunk, prepare for waking up to a chorus of men 'hwwaaaaching' and spitting, little privacy and toilets that tend to get... unpleasant after three days at sea. That said, it's a good way to meet locals, and is one for proponents of slow, adventure travel.

Food (tiffin for breakfast, thalis for lunch and dinner) costs around ₹150/200 per day for bunk/cabin class, though bring something (fruit in particular) to supplement your diet. Some bedding is supplied, but if you're travelling bunk class bring a sleeping sheet. Many travellers take a hammock to string up on deck.

There is no ferry between Port Blair and Thailand, but private yachts can get clearance. You can't legally get from the Andamans to Myanmar (Burma) by sea, although we hear it's been done by those with their own boat. Be aware you risk imprisonment or worse from the Indian and Burmese navies if you give this a go.

ⓘ Getting Around

AIR

Two modes of air transport link Port Blair with the rest of the islands. If your budget allows it, it's worth it for the views.

The new amphibious **Sea Plane** (☏ 03192-244312; andamanseaplane@gmail.com; ⊗ Mon-Sat) links Port Blair with Havelock (₹4100), Little Andaman (₹7170) and Diglipur (₹10,500), landing and taking off on the water, and the runway in Port Blair.

There's also the interisland helicopter service that runs from Port Blair to Little Andaman (₹2625, 35 minutes), Havelock (₹1500, 20 minutes), Diglipur (₹4125, one hour) and Mayabunder (₹3375). Priority is given to government

---

ⓘ FERRY CANCELLATIONS

Bad weather can seriously muck up your itinerary, with ferry services often cancelled if the sea is too rough. Build in a few days' buffer to avoid being marooned and missing your flight.

---

workers and the 5kg baggage limit precludes most tourists from using this service. You can chance your luck by applying at the **Secretariat** (☏ 03192-230093) in Port Blair.

BOAT

Most islands can only be reached by water. While this sounds romantic, ferry ticket offices can be hell: expect hot waits, slow service, queue-jumping and a rugby scrum to the ticket window. To hold your spot and advance you need to be a little aggressive (but don't be a jerk) – or be a woman; ladies' queues are a godsend, but they really only apply in Port Blair. You can buy tickets the day you travel by arriving at the appropriate jetty an hour beforehand, but it's risky, and normally one or two days in advance is recommended. You can't prebook ferry tickets until you've been issued your island permit upon arrival in the Andamans; see p1087.

There are regular boat services to Havelock and Neil Islands, as well as Rangat, Mayabunder, Diglipur and Little Andaman. A schedule of inter-island sailing times can be found at the website www.and.nic.in/spsch/iisailing.htm.

The private ferry **Makruzz** (www.makruzz.com; from ₹775) runs a daily boat to Havelock, which is quicker but triple the cost. At the time of research, **Coastal Cruise** (☏ 03192-241333; www.coastalcruise.in) was another private operator that was set to begin a fast boat service linking Havelock with Neil Island and Port Blair.

CAR & MOTORCYCLE

Hiring a car and driver costs ₹ 550 per 35km, or around ₹10,000 for a return trip to Diglipur from Port Blair (including stopovers along the way). Mopeds can hired from ₹300 per day.

BUS

All roads – and ferries – lead to Port Blair, and you'll inevitably spend a night or two here booking onward travel. The main island group – South, Middle and North Andaman – is connected by road, with ferry crossings and bridges. Cheap state and more expensive private buses run south from Port Blair to Wandoor, and north to Bharatang, Rangat, Mayabunder and finally to Diglipur, 325km north of the capital. The Jarawa reserve closes to most traffic at around 3pm; thus, buses that pass through the reserve leave from around 4am up till 11am.

PORT BLAIR

POP 100,608

Though surrounded by attractive lush forest and rugged coastline, Port Blair itself is a somewhat gritty town that serves as the

Port Blair

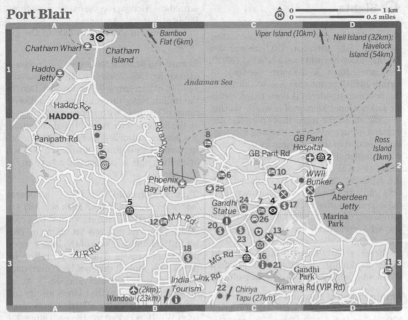

Port Blair

◎ Sights
1 Anthropological Museum	C3
2 Cellular Jail National Memorial	D2
3 Chatham Saw Mill	A1
4 Clock Tower	C2
5 Samudrika Marine Museum	B2

🛏 Sleeping
6 Aashiaanaa Rest Home	C2
Amina Lodge	(see 7)
7 Azad Lodge	C2
8 Fortune Resort – Bay Island	C2
9 Hotel Driftwood	A2
10 Hotel Lalaji Bay View	C2
11 Hotel Sinclairs Bayview	D3
12 TSG Emerald	B3

✕ Eating
13 Annapurna	C3
Bayview	(see 11)
Excel Restaurant	(see 10)
Gagan Restaurant	(see 4)
14 Lighthouse Residency	C2
Mandalay Restaurant	(see 8)
15 New Lighthouse Restaurant	D2

ⓘ Information
16 Andaman & Nicobar Tourism	C3
17 Axis Bank ATM	C2
18 Axis Bank ATM	B3
19 Chief Wildlife Warden	A2
E-Cafe	(see 4)
Green Island Tours	(see 4)
20 ICICI ATM	C3
21 Immigration Office	C3
22 Secretariat	C3
23 State Bank of India	C3

ⓘ Transport
24 Bus Stand	C2
25 Ferry Booking Office	C2
26 Taxi & Autorickshaw Stand	C3

provincial capital of the Andamans. It's a vibrant mix of Indian Ocean inhabitants – Bengalis, Tamils, Telugus, Nicobarese and Burmese. Most travellers don't hang around any longer than necessary (usually one or two days while waiting to book onward trav-

el in the islands, or returning for departure), instead hell-bent on heading straight to the islands. And while 'PB' can't compete with the beaches of Havelock, its fascinating history makes for some outstanding sightseeing that warrants a day or two spent here.

⊙ Sights

Cellular Jail
National Memorial   HISTORIC BUILDING
(GB Pant Rd; admission ₹10, camera/video ₹25/100, sound-and-light show adult/child ₹20/10; ⊘8.45am-12.30pm & 1.30-5pm Tue-Sun) A former British prison that is now a shrine to the political dissidents it once jailed, Cellular Jail National Memorial is worth visiting to understand the important space the Andamans occupy in India's national memory. Construction of the jail began in 1896 and it was completed in 1906 – the original seven wings (several of which were destroyed by the Japanese during WWII) contained 698 cells radiating from a central tower. Like many political prisons, Cellular Jail became something of a university for freedom fighters, who exchanged books, ideas and debates despite walls and wardens.

There's a fairly cheesy **sound-and-light show** in English at 7.15pm on Monday, Wednesday and Friday – weather permitting.

Anthropological Museum   MUSEUM
(⌨03192-232291; MG Rd; admission ₹10, camera ₹20; ⊘9am-1pm & 1.30-4.30pm Tue-Sun) The best museum in Port Blair provides a thorough and sympathetic portrait of the islands' indigenous tribal communities. The glass display cases may be old school, but they don't feel anywhere near as ancient as the simple geometric patterns etched into a Jarawa chest guard, a skull left in a Sentinelese lean-to or the totemic spirits represented by Nicobarese shamanic sculptures. Publications on Andaman and Nicobar's indigenous culture are for sale in the gift shop.

Samudrika Marine Museum   MUSEUM
(Haddo Rd; adult/child ₹20/10, camera/video ₹20/50; ⊘9am-1pm & 2-5pm Tue-Sun) Run by the Indian Navy, this museum has a diverse range of exhibits with informative coverage of the islands' ecosystem, tribal communities, plants, animals and marine life (including a small aquarium). Outside is a skeleton of a young blue whale washed ashore on the Nicobars.

Chatham Saw Mill   HISTORIC SITE
(admission ₹10; ⊘8.30am-2.30pm Mon-Sat) Located on Chatham Island (reached by a road bridge), the saw mill was set up by the British in 1836 and was one of the largest wood processors in Asia. The mill is still operational and, while it may not be to everyone's taste – especially conservationists – it's an interesting insight to the island's history and economy. There's also a large bomb crater from WWII, accessed via the path alongside the forest museum.

Corbyn's Cove   BEACH
No one comes to Port Blair for the beach, but if you need a break from town, Corbyn's Cove has a small curve of sand backed by palms. It's not really a beach you'll want to laze on, but the coastal road here makes for

---

DON'T MISS

ROSS ISLAND

Just a 20-minute boat ride from Port Blair, visiting Ross Island (not to be confused with its namesake island in North Andaman) feels like discovering a jungle-clad Lost City, à la Angkor Wat. Here the ruins happen to be Victorian English rather than ancient Khmer. The former administrative headquarters for the British in the Andamans, Ross Island in its day was fondly called the 'Paris of the East' (along with Pondicherry, Saigon etc etc...). But the cute title, vibrant social scene and tropical gardens were all wiped out by the double whammy of a 1941 earthquake and the invasion of the Japanese (who left behind some machine-gun nests that are great fun to poke around in).

Today the old English architecture is still standing, even as it is swallowed by a green wave of fast-growing jungle. Landscaped paths cross the island and most of the buildings are labelled. There's a small **museum** with historical displays and photos of Ross Island in its heyday, and a small park where resident deer nibble on bushes.

Ferries to Ross Island (₹90, 20 minutes) depart from Aberdeen Jetty behind the aquarium in Port Blair at 8.30am, 10.30am, 12.30pm and 2pm every day other than Wednesday.

You can tack on a visit to **Viper Island** (₹75), where you'll find the ruins of gallows built by the British in 1867, but it's a fairly forgettable excursion.

a scenic journey, and passes several **Japanese WWII bunkers** along the way. Located 7km from town, an autorickshaw here costs ₹200, or you can rent a scooter.

👉 Tours

Andaman & Nicobar Tourism   TOURS
(IP&T; ☑ 03192-232694; www.and.nic.in/newtourism; Kamaraj Rd) Popular with Indian mainland tourists, these tours include day trips to Mt Harriet (₹250), Wandoor via spice and rubber plantations (₹200), Chiriya Tapu (₹200), Baratang limestone caves (₹525) and snorkelling trips to Jolly Buoy or Redskin Islands (₹500).

🛏 Sleeping

⭐ **Aashiaanaa Rest Home**   GUESTHOUSE $
(☑ 09474217008; shads_maria@hotmail.com; Marine Hill; r without bathroom ₹300, with AC from ₹600; ❄ 🛜) Port Blair's most comfortable budget choice has homely rooms decked out in marine, and a convenient location uphill from Phoenix Bay jetty. Most have cable TV and reliable hot water, while pricier rooms get you a balcony and air-con. Staff can help out with booking ferry tickets and takeaway food delivery, though a restaurant was planned at the time of research.

Hotel Lalaji Bay View   GUESTHOUSE $
(☑ 9476005820, 03192-236333; www.lalajibayview.com; RP Rd; s/d ₹300/400, r with AC ₹800; ❄ 🛜) Set among ramshackle colonial buildings, just up from the mosque, this popular budget hotel is run by the friendly Nirman, a young entrepreneur who's an excellent source of travel information. The rooms are small and basic, but good value, and it has a sociable rooftop restaurant with paid wi-fi access.

Amina Lodge   GUESTHOUSE $
(☑ 9933258703; aminalodge@ymail.com; Aberdeen Bazaar; s/d ₹350/450) Run by an entertaining couple, Amina has good-value, clean rooms with TV and a handy, though sometimes noisy, location in the heart of the bazaar. Prices are fixed.

Azad Lodge   GUESTHOUSE $
(☑ 03192-242646; MA Rd, Aberdeen Bazaar; s/d without bathroom ₹200/300, d with bathroom ₹500, r with AC ₹850) An old budget favourite that's popular for its simple and clean rooms; though singles without bathroom are like prison cells.

Hotel Driftwood   HOTEL $$
(☑ 03192-244044; hoteldriftwood@rediffmail.com; JN Rd, Haddo; r from ₹2150; ❄ 🛜) The midrange Driftwood makes a fine choice with sunny, decent-sized rooms; the pricier ones have lovely views of lush jungle. It has smiley staff, a good restaurant with an attached outdoor bar (beware Saturday night karaoke), and wi-fi access in the lobby.

TSG Emerald   HOTEL $$
(☑ 03192-246488; www.andamantsghotels.com; MA Rd, Haddo; r from ₹2470; ❄ 🛜) While a business-chic hotel may not necessarily suit the Andamans, this place is pretty plush with sleek, sparkling, modern rooms. Also has a nautical-themed bar upstairs.

Hotel Sinclairs Bayview   HOTEL $$$
(☑ 03192-227824; www.sinclairshotels.com; South Point; s/d incl breakfast from ₹6900/7520; ❄ 🛜) Located on the road to Corbyn's Cove, 2km outside town, Sinclairs' big comfy rooms have the best views in town, opening right out to the water. It has a nice seaside garden with hammocks to lounge in, and several Japanese WWII bunkers on-site. Airport transfer is free.

Fortune Resort – Bay Island   HOTEL $$$
(☑ 03192-234101; www.fortunehotels.in; Marine Hill; s/d incl breakfast from ₹6445/7300; ❄ 🛜) One of PB's finest, with lovely bay views, tropical garden and modern rooms with polished floors; ask for a sea-facing room.

🍴 Eating & Drinking

Gagan Restaurant   INDIAN $
(Clock tower, Aberdeen Bazaar; mains from ₹30; ⏱ 7am-10pm) Popular with locals, this hole-in-the-wall place serves up great food at good prices, including seafood curries, coconut chicken, and dosas for breakfast. There's also air-con seating upstairs.

Excel Restaurant   INTERNATIONAL, INDIAN $
(RP Rd; meals from ₹60; ⏱ 7am-11pm) Not to be confused with the seedy downstairs bar, the popular Excel rooftop restaurant above Hotel Lalaji Bay brings a 'Havelock' menu to the city. Burgers, grilled seafood, and Israeli dishes are all good, and its fully stocked bar makes it a great place to meet fellow travellers.

Annapurna   INDIAN $
(MG Rd; mains from ₹40) An excellent veg option that looks like a high-school cafeteria

and serves consistently good dosas and rich North Indian–style curries.

★**Lighthouse Residency** INDIAN $$
(MA Rd; mains ₹80-800; ⊙11am-11pm) The best place for seafood in Port Blair, if not the Andamans, where you select from the display of red snapper, crab or tiger prawns to barbecue, grill or cook in the tandoor and served with rice, chips and a cold Kingfisher. There's a cheaper **second branch** (Marina Park; mains ₹80-400) in an outdoor shack near the water.

Bayview MULTICUISINE $$$
(Hotel Sinclairs Bayview; mains ₹110-500; ⊙11am-11pm) Right on the water with a lovely cool sea breeze, the Bayview is a great spot for lunch. While the grilled fish is delicious and the beer cold, this place is much more about the location than the food. Ask the friendly staff to show you the Japanese WWII bunkers on the premises. An autorickshaw here costs ₹40.

Mandalay Restaurant INDIAN, MULTICUISINE $$$
(Marine Hill; mains ₹160-480; ⊙7am-11pm) A good place to while away an afternoon, with sensational sea views from the outdoor deck (the ₹20 note is actually based on this spot). Food is pricey, but it does a tasty Goan prawn curry, plus sandwiches and burgers.

ℹ Information

There are several ATMs around town including SBI and Axis that accept foreign cards. You can find internet cafes in Aberdeen Bazaar, including the air-conditioned **Green Island Tours** (per hour ₹30; ⊙9am-9pm Mon-Sat; 🛜) and **E-Cafe** (internet & wi-fi per hr ₹40; ⊙8am-10pm) near the clock tower; both have wi-fi. Green Island can also book flights.

Aberdeen Police Station (📞03192-232400; MG Rd)

Andaman & Nicobar Tourism (📞03192-232694; www.and.nic.in/newtourism; Kamaraj Rd; ⊙8.30am-12.30pm & 1.30-4.30pm Mon-Fri, 8.30am-noon Sat) The main island tourist office is the place to book permits for areas around Port Blair. It also sells the useful tourist booklet *Emerald Islands* (₹120), which you can also pickup from the airport.

Axis Bank ATM (Netaji Rd, Aberdeen Bazar)

Axis Bank ATM (MG Rd)

GB Pant Hospital (📞emergency 03192-232102, 03192-233473; GB Pant Rd)

Main Post Office (MG Rd; ⊙9am-7pm Mon-Sat)

State Bank of India (MA Rd; ⊙9am-noon & 1-3pm Mon-Fri, 10am-noon Sat) Foreign currency can be changed here.

ℹ Getting There & Away

The airport is about 4km south of town.

BOAT

Most interisland ferries depart from **Phoenix Bay Jetty**. Tickets can be purchased from the **ferry booking office** (⊙9am-1pm & 2-4pm Mon-Sat); inexplicably closed Sundays. Ferries can be prebooked one to three days in advance; if sold out you can chance your luck with a same-day ticket issued an hour before departure from outside the ticket office at the end door.

Most people head straight to Havelock (₹195, 2½ hours), with ferries departing daily at 6.20am, 11.30am and 2pm.

Otherwise there's the privately owned **Makruzz** (www.makruzz.com; from ₹775), departing daily at 8.45am (1½ hours). Tickets are available from the airport or travel agents in Aberdeen Bazaar.

There are also daily services to Neil Island and Little Andaman, which regularly sell out, and several boats a week to Diglipur and Long Island.

Those not wanting to hang around Port Blair should make the jetty their first port of call to book tickets.

BUS

There are buses all day from the **bus stand** at Aberdeen Bazaar to Wandoor (₹18, one hour) and Chiriya Tapu (₹18, one hour). Two buses run at 4am and 4.15am to Diglipur (₹230, 12 hours) and 4.30am for Mayabunder (₹180, 10 hours) via Rangat (₹130, six hours) and Baratang (₹80, three hours). More-comfortable, and pricier, private buses are also available; their 'offices' (a guy with a ticket book) are located across from the main bus stand.

ℹ Getting Around

TO & FROM THE AIRPORT

A taxi or autorickshaw from the airport to Aberdeen Bazaar costs around ₹70. There are also hourly buses (₹10) to/from airport, located 100m outside the complex, to the main bus stand.

AUTORICKSHAW

Aberdeen Bazaar to Phoenix Bay Jetty is about ₹20, and to Haddo Jetty it's around ₹40.

MOTORBIKE

You can hire a scooter from Green Island Tours for ₹400 per day.

AROUND PORT BLAIR & SOUTH ANDAMAN

Wandoor

Wandoor, a tiny speck of a village 29km southwest of Port Blair, has a nice beach (though at the time of research, swimming was prohibited due to crocodiles), and some chilled-out guesthouses. It's better known as a jumping-off point for **Mahatma Gandhi Marine National Park** (Indian/foreigner ₹50/500). Covering 280 sq km it comprises 15 islands of mangrove creeks, tropical rainforest and reefs supporting 50 types of coral. Depending upon the time of year, the marine park's snorkelling sites alternate between Jolly Buoy and Red Skin, allowing the other to regenerate. Both are popular day trips from Wandoor Jetty (₹450; Tuesday to Sunday), That said, if Havelock or Neil Islands are on your Andamans itinerary, it's probably easier and cheaper to wait until you reach them for your underwater experience; particularly due to Red Skin and Jolly Bouy's popularity with package tourists and damage suffered from coral bleaching.

However, for serious divers, **Lacadives** (☑ 9679532104; www.lacadives.com) is well worth checking out to visit more-remote areas of Mahatma Gandhi National Park.

Genuine nature lovers – the kind who like snakes and insects – will want to stay at **ANET** (Andaman & Nicobar Environmental Team; ☑ 03192-280081; www.anetindia.org; North Wandoor; per person incl full board ₹1100; @ 🛜). Led by an inspiring team of dynamic young Indian ecologists, this is the place to gain a true sense of the Andamans' wilderness as you'll learn about the mangroves and intertidal zones, snakes, birds and crocs, and go on night walks. All activities are inclusive, but volunteers are given priority to the bamboo-hut accomodation. Reservations are essential.

Buses run from Port Blair to Wandoor (₹18, one hour).

Chiriya Tapu

Chiriya Tapu, 30km south of Port Blair, is a tiny village fringed by beaches and mangroves, and is famous for celestial sunsets. It also has some of the best **diving** outside Havelock. Lacadives and **Infinity Scuba** (☑ 03192-281183; www.infinityscubandamans. com) are two reputable dive companies that

visit spectacular **Cinque Island, Rutland Island** and a wrecked ship. Snorkelling is also reportedly very good off the beach at sunset point, though like many places coral bleaching has occurred; enquire at the dive shops for more info.

There's also the **biological park** (Indian/foreigner ₹20/50; ⊙ 9am-4pm Tue-Sun), essentially a zoo, but with a pleasant forested setting and natural enclosures for crocodiles, Andaman wild pig, water monitors and spotted deer.

Most visit as a day trip from Port Blair, but **Wild Grass** (☑ 9474204508; r incl breakfast ₹4500; ❄) has double-storey cottages looking out to green surrounds.

There are seven buses a day to Port Blair (₹18, one hour); last bus is 6pm.

HAVELOCK ISLAND

POP 5500

With snow-white beaches, teal shallows, a coast crammed with beach huts and some of the best diving in Asia, Havelock has a well-deserved reputation as a backpacker paradise. For many, Havelock is *the* Andamans, and is what lures most tourists across the Bay of Bengal, many of whom are content to stay here for the entirety of their trip.

👁 Sights & Activities

Most come to Havelock for some serious R and R, whether lazing on the beach, or diving or snorkelling.

Some resorts can organise guided **jungle treks** for keen walkers or birdwatchers, but be warned the forest floor turns to glug after rain. The inside rainforest is a spectacular, emerald cavern, and the **birdwatching** – especially on the forest fringes – is rewarding; look out for the blue-black racket-tailed drongo or golden oriole.

Sport fishing is another option, with **Captain Hook's** (☑ 9434280543; www.andamansportsfishing.com; Beach 3; half-day for 2 people ₹5500) offering the most reasonable rates for its boat trips.

Beaches

The prettiest and most popular stretch of sand is the critically acclaimed **Radhanagar Beach (Beach 7)**. It's a beautiful curve of sugar fronted by perfectly spiraled waves, all backed by native forest. Late afternoon is the best time to visit to avoid the heat and

ISLAND INDIGENES

The Andaman and Nicobar Islands' indigenous peoples constitute 12% of the population and, in most cases, their numbers are decreasing. The Onge, Sentinelese, Andamanese and Jawara are all of Negrito ethnicity, who share a strong resemblance to people from Africa. Tragically, numerous groups have become extinct over the past century. In February 2010 the last survivor of the Bo tribe passed away, bringing an end to both the language and 65,000 years of ancestry.

Onge

Two-thirds of Little Andaman's Onge Island was taken over by the Forest Department and 'settled' in 1977. The 100 or so remaining members of the Onge tribe live in a 25-sq-km reserve covering Dugong Creek and South Bay. Anthropologists say the Onge population has declined due to demoralisation through loss of territory.

Sentinelese

The Sentinelese, unlike the other tribes in these islands, have consistently repelled outside contact. For years, contact parties arrived on the beaches of North Sentinel Island, the last redoubt of the Sentinelese, with gifts of coconuts, bananas, pigs and red plastic buckets, only to be showered with arrows, although some encounters have been a little less hostile. About 150 Sentinelese remain.

Andamanese

As they now number only about 50, it seems impossible the Andamanese can escape extinction. There were around 7000 Andamanese in the mid-19th century, but friendliness to colonisers was their undoing, and by 1971 all but 19 of the population had been swept away by measles, syphilis and influenza epidemics. They've been resettled on tiny Strait Island.

Jarawa

The 350 remaining Jarawa occupy the 639-sq-km reserve on South and Middle Andaman Islands. In 1953 the chief commissioner requested that an armed sea plane bomb Jarawa settlements and their territory has been consistently disrupted by the Andaman Trunk Rd, forest clearance and settler and tourist encroachment. In 2012, a video went viral showing an exchange between Jarawa and tourists, whereby a policeman orders them to dance in exchange for food. This resulted in a government inquest that saw to the end of the so-called 'human safari' tours. Most Jarawa remain hostile to contact.

Shompen

Only about 250 Shompen remain in the forests on Great Nicobar. Semi-nomadic hunter-gatherers who live along the riverbanks, they have resisted integration and avoid areas occupied by Indian immigrants.

Nicobarese

The 30,000 Nicobarese are the only indigenous people whose numbers are not decreasing. The majority have converted to Christianity and been partly assimilated into contemporary Indian society. Living in village units led by a head man, they farm pigs and cultivate coconuts, yams and bananas. The Nicobarese, who probably descended from people of Malaysia and Myanmar, inhabit a number of islands in the Nicobar group, centred on Car Nicobar, the region worst affected by the 2004 tsunami – with an estimated one fifth of the population killed or missing.

crowds, as well as for its sunset. The further you walk from the main entry the more privacy you'll get. **Elephant rides** are possible in high season with work elephants, or, if you have a spare ₹30,000, you can swim with Rajan, Barefoot Resort's elephant. Radhanagar is on the northwestern side of the island about 12km.

Northwest of Radhanagar is the gorgeous 'lagoon' at **Neils Cove**, another gem of sheltered sand and crystalline water. Swimming is prohibited dusk and dawn; and take heed of any warnings regarding crocodiles (p1086).

On the other side of the island from Radhanagar, the palm-ringed **Beach 5** has your more classic tropical vibe, with the bonus of shady patches and less sandflies. However, swimming is very difficult in low tide when water becomes shallow for miles. Most of the island's accommodation is out this way.

About 5km beyond No 5 Village, you'll find the low-key **Kalapathar**, another pristine beach. There's an elephant training camp out this way, but not much action to see at the time of research.

Diving & Snorkelling

Havelock is the premier spot for scuba diving in the Andamans. It's world renowned as much for its relative isolation as for its crystal-clear waters, deep-sea corals, schools of fish, turtles and kaleidoscope of colourful marine life. Diving here is suitable for all levels.

The main dive season is roughly November to April, but trips still occur year-round.

Prices are standardised, so it's a matter of finding a dive operator you feel comfortable with. Recommended operators include **Andaman Bubbles** (☑ 03192-282140; www. andamanbubbles.com; No 5 Village), a quality outfit with professional, personable staff; long-established **Barefoot Scuba** (☑ 9566088560; www.diveandamans.com; No 3 Village), with budget dive-accommodation packages in A-frame huts; **Dive India** (☑ 9932082205; www.diveindia.com; btwn No 3 & 5 Village), the original PADI company in Havelock, and still one of the best; and new operator **Ocean Tribe** (☑ 9531836695; www. ocean-tribe.com; No 3 Village), run by legendary local Karen divers.

All offer fully equipped boat dives, and prices vary depending on the location, number of participants and duration of the course. Diving starts from around ₹4725 for a two-tank dive, with options of discover scuba (one hour ₹4500), PADI open-water (four dives ₹20,000) and a range of advanced courses (three dives ₹12,000).

Popular sites are **Pilot Reef** with its abundance of coral, **South Button** for macro dives and rock formations, **Jackson Bar** for sharks, rays and turtles and **Minerva's Delight** for a bit of everything.

Keep an eye out for trips further afield such as **Barren Island**, home to India's only active volcano whose ash produces an eerie underwater spectacle and regarded as one of the best.

While coral bleaching has been a major issue since 2010, diving remains world-class. The shallows may not have bright corals, but all the colourful fish are still here, and for depths beyond 20m, corals remain as vivid as ever. The Andamans fully recovered from a similar bleaching in 1998, and today things are likewise slowly repairing themselves.

Dive companies can arrange **snorkelling** trips, but it's cheaper to organise a *dunghi* (motorised wooden boat) through your guesthouse. Trips cost ₹1500 to ₹2000, depending on the number of people going, distance involved etc – if you go with a good-sized group you may pay as low as ₹300 per head. Snorkelling gear is widely available on Havelock from resorts and small restaurants, but is generally very low quality.

Most boats head to Elephant Beach for snorkelling, which can also be reached by a 40-minute walk through a muddy elephant logging trail; it's well marked (off the cross-island road), but turns to bog if it's been raining. At high tide it's also impossible to reach – ask locally. Lots of snorkelling charters, and even jet skis, come out this way, so be prepared, it can be bit of a circus.

🛏 Sleeping

Most lodges in Havelock are of the cluster-of-beach-huts genre. They all claim to be 'eco' huts ('eco' apparently meaning 'cheap building material'), but they're great value for money, especially in low season. Hammocks are available from the bazaar at Beach 3 for ₹150.

Orient Legend Resort GUESTHOUSE $
(☑ 03192-282389; Beach 5; huts ₹300, r ₹800-2000, with AC ₹3000) This popular sprawling place on Beach 5 covers most budgets, from doghouse A-frame huts, to concrete rooms and double-storey cottages that give a glimpse of the ocean.

Coconut Grove GUESTHOUSE $
(☑ 9474269977; huts ₹400, without bathroom ₹300; ▣) Popular with Israeli travellers, Coconut Grove has an appealing communal vibe with psychedelic-painted huts

Havelock Island

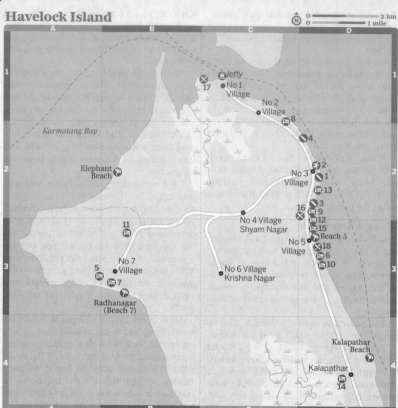

arranged in a circular outlay that directs everyone to the raised, concrete restaurant.

Dreamland Resort   GUESTHOUSE $
(☏9474224164; Beach 7; huts without bathroom ₹400) In a prime location, only 50m from Beach 7, Dreamland is an old backpacker favourite with simple blue thatched bungalows and friendly owners.

Pellicon Beach Resort   BUNGALOWS $
(☏9932081673; www.pelliconbeachresort.com; Beach 5; huts from ₹500) Attractive beach-side bungalows, and Nicobari huts with private porches on a peaceful plot of land close to the beach.

El Dorado   BUNGALOWS $
(☏03192-282451; Beach 5; r from ₹350, with AC ₹3000) Chilled-out budget bamboo huts set in a tropical garden leading to Beach 5. Also has a restaurant-bar and fancier concrete air-con rooms.

Green Land Resort   GUESTHOUSE $
(☏9933220625; huts ₹200-250, without bathroom ₹150-200) A taste of village life, with simple huts 2km from Radhanagar.

★Emerald Gecko   BUNGALOWS $$
(☏03192-282170; www.emerald-gecko.com; huts from ₹1200) On an island where very little thought goes into design, Emerald Gecko stands miles ahead. Comfortable double-storey bungalows have couches on its upper balcony looking to the water, while pricier rooms have sumptuous lighting and outdoor bathrooms that feel like Gilligan's Island. All are lovingly constructed from bamboo rafts drifted ashore from Myanmar. The concrete-floored rooms at the back are much less attractive. Staff are friendly, its restaurant quality and there's free filtered water.

Eco Villa   BUNGALOWS $$
(☏03192-282212; www.havelock.co.in/ecovilla; Beach 2; r from ₹3000) Backpacker turned

Havelock Island

overpriced resort with plush beachfront duplexes.

Wild Orchid
HOTEL $$$

(☎ 03192-282472, www.wildorchidandaman.com; r incl breakfast from ₹5000; ✳ @ 📶) One of the Andamans' premier resorts, with thoughtfully furnished Andamanese-style cottages, or modern rooms with TV and air-con, all set around a fabulous tropical garden a stone's throw from the beach. It has the Red Snapper restaurant.

Barefoot at Havelock
RESORT $$$

(☎ 044-24341001; www.barefootindia.com; Beach 7; tented cottage incl breakfast ₹5050, Nicobari cottages ₹8920, with AC ₹11,820; ✳) Havelock's most luxurious resort, boasting beautifully designed timber and bamboo-thatched cottages just back from the famed Radhanagar Beach. Its romantic restaurant is a good place to splurge. Barefoot also has attractive beachside duplexes at its dive resort on Beach 3.

People Tree
BUNGALOWS, RETREAT $$$

(Kalapathar; r ₹2500-3500) Hidden away on Kalapathar beach, in a pastoral setting of rice paddies and betel palms, this yoga and meditation retreat was just opening its doors at time of research. Its elegant bamboo duplexes are constructed from driftwood and feature outdoor stone-garden bathrooms. A menu of healthy organic food was on the cards. It's a few minutes' walk from the beach.

✕ Eating

There are *dhabas* (snack bars) near the jetty or try the main bazaar (No 3 Village) for local meals.

Anju-coco Resto
INDIAN, CONTINENTAL $

(mains ₹120-250; ⊙ 8am-10.30pm) Having expanded to a much bigger restaurant, Anju-coco is still popular and is run by a friendly owner. There's a varied menu, with standouts being BBQ fish and its big breakfasts (₹60). Its original shack restaurant up the road does tasty Indian dishes.

Welcome Restaurant
INDIAN, SEAFOOD $

(No 3 Village; mains from ₹50; ⊙ 7.30am-9.30pm) Just across from the market, this small eatery does delicious seafood curries and prawn rolls with rolled-up *parathas*.

Rony's
INDIAN $

(Beach 5; mains from ₹40) Popular family-run cheapie serving up inexpensive seafood curries.

Fat Martin's
SOUTH INDIAN $

(Beach 5; mains from ₹60; ⊙ 7.30am-8pm) Squeaky-clean open-air shack serving up a good selection of dosas, including paneer tikka and nutella dosas.

Why Like This?
INDIAN, ISRAELI $

(Beach 5; mains from ₹100) Named as a tribute to the Israeli traveller, with a menu of schnitzels (including a fish version), and BBQ seafood dishes.

★ Red Snapper
SEAFOOD, MULTICUISINE $$

(Wild Orchid; mains ₹200-800; ⊙ breakfast, lunch & dinner) Easily Havelock's best restaurant, with its atmospheric polished-bamboo decor and thatched-roof exuding a romantic island ambience. Pick from lavish seafood platters, BBQ fish and handmade pastas, accompanied by delicious cheese-and-olive naan. The outdoor deck seating is a

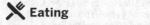

ANDAMAN ISLANDS HAVELOCK ISLAND

good spot to catch a breeze, and watch the glassed-in tandoori kitchen.

B3 – Barefoot Bar & Restaurant   PIZZA **$$**
(No 1 Village; ⊙11am-4pm & 6-9.30pm) Modern decor with classic movie posters on the walls; there's a Western-heavy menu, with the best pizzas in Havelock, and it's a good place to wait for your ferry.

ℹ Information

There are two ATMs side by side in No 3 Village. Internet is insanely pricey (per hour ₹350!), so try to send all your emails in Port Blair.

Havelock Tourist Service (Beach 3) in the bazaar can arrange air tickets and has the schedule for government ferries.

ℹ Getting There & Away

Government ferries run from Havelock to Port Blair two to three times a day (₹195, 2½ hours), and you're best to book tickets from the **port** (⊙9.15am-noon & 2-4pm Mon-Sat, to 2pm Sun) at least a day in advance. Otherwise Makruzz (p1092) has a daily service at 4pm.

One to two ferries a day link Havelock with Neil Island (₹195, one hour 10 minutes), while four boats a week head to Long Island (₹195, two hours) en route to Rangat.

ℹ Getting Around

A local bus (₹10, 40 minutes) connects the jetty, villages and Radar Nagar on a roughly hourly circuit until 6pm. Otherwise you can rent a scooter (per day from ₹300) or bicycle (per day ₹60).

An autorickshaw from the jetty to No 3 Village is ₹40, to No 5 ₹60 and to No 7 ₹200.

NEIL ISLAND

Happy to laze in the shadows of its more famous island neighbour, tranquil Neil is still the place for that added bit of relaxation. Its beaches may not be as luxurious as Havelock's, but they have ample character and are a perfect distance apart to explore by bicycle. There's a lovely unhurried pace of life here; cycling through picturesque villages you'll get many friendly hellos. In Neil Island you're about 40km from Port Blair, a short ferry ride from Havelock and several universes away from life at home

There's no ATM or moneychanging facilities on Neil, so bring plenty of cash. There's pricey satellite **internet** (per 30min ₹150; ⊙8.30am-9pm) and a post office in the bazaar. The main bazaar has a mellow vibe, and is a popular gathering spot in the early evening.

◉ Sights & Activities

Neil Island's five beaches (numbered one to five) all have their unique charms, though they're not necessarily great for swimming.

Beach 1 (Lamanpur) is a long sweep of sandy beach and mangrove, a 40-minute walk west of the jetty and village. The island's best **snorkelling** is around the coral reef at the far (western) end of this beach at high tide. If you're extremely lucky you may spot a dugong feeding in the shallows at high tide. There's a good sunset viewpoint out this way accessed via Pearl Park Resort, which becomes a communal spot in the sand for tourists and locals come early evening.

Beach 2, on the north side of the island, has the **Natural Bridge** rock formation, accessible only at low tide by walking around the rocky cove. To get here by bicycle take the side road that runs through the bazaar, then take a left where the road forks.

Beach 3 (Ram Nagar) is a secluded powdery sand cove, which is best accessed via Blue Sea Restaurant. There's also good snorkelling here.

The best swimming beach is at **Beach 4 (Bharatpur)**, though its proximity to the jetty is a slight turn-off.

Further ahead the more wild and rugged **Beach 5 (Sitapur)**, 5km from the village, and reached via the village road to the eastern side of the island, is a nice place to walk along the beach, with small limestone caves accessible at low tide.

You can dive with **India Scuba Explorers** (☏9474238646; www.indiascubaexplorers.com) or **Dive India** (☏9932082205; www.diveindia.com/neil.html), which both have snorkelling gear for ₹150. Those interested in free diving can contact Sanjay at Gayan Garden. Hiring a fishing boat to go to offshore snorkelling or fishing will costs around ₹1500.

Cooking classes (from ₹200) can be arranged at Gayan Garden Restaurant, where you can learn to cook your favourite Indian dishes; reservations essential.

🛏 Sleeping

Pearl Park Beach Resort   BUNGALOWS **$**
(☏9434260132; www.andamanpearlpark.com; Beach 1; huts with/without bathroom ₹500/250,

Nicobari cottages ₹1500) One of Neil's original bamboo-bungalow 'resorts', with pleasant huts arranged around a flower-filled garden and the best sunset point on the island.

Breakwater Beach Resort BUNGALOWS $
(Beach 3; r ₹400) Family-run bungalows on Beach 3 wins rave reviews for its chilled-out ambience and delicious food.

A-N-D Beach Resort BUNGALOWS $
(☑214722; Beach 4; huts with/without bathroom ₹600/200) Just to the left of the pier, on an attractive stretch of beach, these laid-back thatched bungalows have friendly staff and a good restaurant.

Gayan Garden BUNGALOWS $
(Beach One; r ₹300) 🌿 Attractive bamboo cottages are situated between the bazaar and Beach 1, with a relaxed garden, seafood restaurant and filtered coffee. Also has excellent recycling initiatives and free filtered water.

Tango Beach Resort HOTEL $
(☑9474212842; www.tangobeachandaman.com; Beach 1; huts ₹500, cottages from ₹1000) Famous for its sea breeze, this Beach 1 classic is a bit pricier than most, but its sea-facing rooms are still a fine choice. Has a good map on its website.

Kalapani BUNGALOWS $
(☑9474274991; Beach 3; huts ₹350) Another reason why travellers are heading to Beach 3, with relaxed bungalows run by a friendly couple, a sandy garden, free snorkelling gear and a book exchange.

Seashell RESORT $$$
(☑9933239625; www.seashellneil.com; Beach 1; r incl breakfast ₹5370) It was only a matter of time before a fancy resort arrived at Neil, but thankfully it's nice and unobtrusive, with tented cottages leading down to the mangrove-lined beach.

✖ Eating

Moonshine SEAFOOD, INDIAN $
(mains ₹40-150) On the road to Beach 1, this backpacker favourite has excellent home-made pastas, fish thalis and cold beer.

Blue Sea SEAFOOD, INDIAN $
(Beach 3; mains from ₹90; ☺8.30am-10.30pm) Old-school beach shack with sandy floor and dangling beach curios, and all the usual dishes. The path here leads to arguably Neil's best beach.

Chand Restaurant INDIAN, CONTINENTAL $
(Bazaar; mains ₹50-200; ☺6am-10.30pm) Best place in the market with good mix of international and Indian dishes, strong filtered coffee and delicious seafood.

ℹ Getting There & Around

A ferry heads to Port Blair two or three times a day (₹195, two hours). There's also one or two daily ferries to Havelock (₹195, one hour), and three ferries a week to Long Island (₹260, five hours). There's talk the Makruzz ferry might commence a service to/from Port Blair.

Hiring a bicycle (per day from ₹50) is the best way to get about; roads are flat and distances short. You'll be able to find one in the bazaar, or guesthouses. An autorickshaw will take you to Beach 1 or 3 from the jetty for ₹50 to ₹60.

MIDDLE & NORTH ANDAMAN

The Andamans aren't just sun and sand. They're also jungle that feels as primeval as the Jurassic, a green tangle of ancient forest that could have been birthed in Mother Nature's subconscious. This shaggy, wild side of the islands can be seen on a long, loping bus ride up the Andaman Trunk Rd (ATR), framed by antediluvian trees and roll-on, roll-off ferries that cross red-tannin rivers prowled by saltwater crocodiles.

But there's a negative side to riding the ATR: the road cuts through the homeland of the Jarawa and has brought the tribe into incessant contact with the outside world. Modern India and tribal life do not seem able to coexist – every time Jarawa and settlers interact, misunderstandings have led to friction, confusion and, at worst, violent attacks and death. Indian anthropologists and indigenous rights groups such as Survival International have called for the ATR to be closed; its status continues to be under review at time of writing. At present, vehicles are permitted to travel only in convoys at set times from 6am to 3pm. Photography is strictly prohibited, as is stopping or any other interaction with the Jarawa people – who are becoming increasingly reliant on handouts from passing traffic.

The first place of interest north of Port Blair is the impressive limestone caves (☺closed Mon) at Baratang. It's a 45-minute boat trip (₹300) from the jetty, a scenic trip through mangrove forest. A permit is required, organised at the jetty.

Rangat is the next main town, a transport hub with not much else going for it. If you do get stuck here, **UK Nest** (☑ 9434276356; Rangat; r from ₹400) has clean rooms. There's an ATM nearby. Ferries depart Long Island (₹7) from Yeratta Jetty, 8km from Rangat. Otherwise Rangat Bay, 10km outside town, has ferries to/from Port Blair (₹55, six hours) and Havelock (₹195, two hours). A daily bus goes to Port Blair (₹95, seven hours) and Diglipur (₹90, four hours).

Long Island

With its friendly island community and lovely slow pace of life, Long Island is perfect for those wanting to take the pace down even a few more notches. Other than the odd motorcycle, there's no motorised vehicles on the island, and at times you may be the only tourist here.

A 1½-hour trek in the jungle (not advisable after heavy rain) will lead you to the secluded **Lalaji Bay**, a beautiful white-sand beach with good swimming; follow the red arrows to get here. Hiring a *dunghi* (₹2000 return) makes it much easier – especially if you don't like leeches. There's a closer, OK beach reached via the yellow arrows.

You can also get a *dunghi* to North Passage island for snorkelling at the stunning **Merk Bay** (₹2500) with blinding white sand and translucent waters.

Blue Planet now offers **diving**, charging ₹4000 for two dives, and visits Campbell Shoal for its schools of trevally and barracuda.

There are four ferries a week to Havelock, Neil and Port Blair (₹195). From Yerata, there are two daily boats to Long Island (₹9, one hour) at 9am and 4pm, returning at 7am and 2pm.

🛏 Sleeping

Construction of a luxury hotel at Lalaji Bay was about to commence at the time of research.

★**Blue Planet**   GUESTHOUSE **$**
(☑ 9474212180; www.blueplanetandamans.com; r with/without bathroom from ₹1000/350; @) The only place to stay on the island, so fortunately it's a gem, with thatched-bamboo rooms and hammocks set around a lovely Padauk tree. It sets an excellent example by incorporating bottles washed ashore into its architecture, and provides free filtered water. Follow the blue arrows from the jetty to get here. It also has wonderful double-storey bamboo cottages (from ₹2000) at a nearby location.

Diglipur & Around

Those who make it this far north are well rewarded with some impressive attractions in the area. It's a giant outdoor adventure playground designed for nature lovers: home to Andaman's highest peak, a network of caves, a famous turtle nesting site and crocodile

MAYABUNDER & AROUND

In 'upper' Middle Andaman, Mayabunder is most famous for its villages inhabited by Karen, members of a Burmese hill tribe who were relocated here during the British colonial period. **Sea'n'Sand** (☑ 03192-273454, fax 03192-273455; thanzin_the_great@yahoo.co.in; r from ₹200; ❄) is easily the best place to stay with comfortable rooms, and attractive bamboo restaurant and bar. It's run by Titus and Elizabeth (and their extended Karen family), who are a good source for everything Mayabunder. It's a low-key destination and will appeal to travellers looking for an experience away from the crowds.

You can go on a range of day tours, with the highlight being jungle trekking at creepy **Interview Island** (boat ₹4000 fits eight people), inhabited by a population of 42 wild elephants, released after a logging company closed for business in the 1950s. You'll feel very off the beaten track here. Armed guards accompany you in case of elephant encounters. A permit (₹500) is required, which is best organised by faxing your details to Titus at Sea'n'Sand. Other trips include **Forty One Caves**, where hawabills make their highly prized edible nests, and snorkelling off **Avis Island**.

Mayabunder, 71km north of Rangat, is linked by daily buses from Port Blair (₹180, 10 hours) and by thrice-weekly ferries. There's an unreliable ATM here.

sanctuaries, to go with white-sandy beaches and the best snorkelling in the Andamans.

However, don't expect anything of Diglipur, the northernmost major town in the Andamans, which is a sprawling, gritty bazaar town with an ATM and slow internet connection (per hour ₹40). You should instead head straight for the tranquil coastal village of **Kalipur.**

Ferries arrive at Aerial Bay Jetty, from where it's 11km to Diglipur, and 8km to Kalipur in the other direction.

◉ Sights & Activities

Diglipur has huge tourist potential, and those who hang around will have plenty to discover. Get in touch with Pristine Beach Resort, who are involved with the Darted grassroots tourist initiative to promote Alfred Caves, mud volcanoes and crocodile habitats. It's also possible to visit elephant work camps.

Ross & Smith Islands   BEACH, SNORKELLING
(Indian/foreigner ₹50/500; ◉ Forest Office 6am-2pm Mon-Sat) Like lovely tropical counterweights, the twin islands of Smith and Ross are connected by a narrow sandbar of dazzling white sand, and are up there with the best in the Andamans.

Since this is designated as a marine sanctuary, you need a ₹500 permit from the Forest Office opposite Aerial Bay Jetty. However, at time of research, you could apply in writing to the Forest Office to visit Smith Island for free (which is duly linked to Ross...); Pristine Beach Resort can assist with this process.

You can organise a boat from Aerial Bay for ₹2000, but if you're staying at Pristine Resort it's easier and cheaper to take its *dunghi* for ₹1800, meaning you don't have to travel to Aerial Bay.

Craggy Island, a small island off Kalipur, also has good snorkelling. Strong swimmers can make it across (flippers recommended), otherwise a *dunghi* is available (₹200 return).

Saddle Peak   TREKKING
(Indian/foreigner ₹25/250) At 732m, Saddle Peak is the highest point in the Andamans. You can trek through subtropical forest to the top and back from Kalipur in about six hours; the views from the peaks onto the archipelago are incredible. Again, a permit is required from the Forest Office and a local guide will make sure you don't get

TURTLE NESTING

Reputedly the only beach in the world where leatherback, hawksbill, olive ridley and green turtles all nest along the same coastline, Kalipur is a fantastic place to observe this evening show between mid-December and April. Turtles can be witnessed most nights, and you can assist with collecting eggs, or with the release of hatchlings. Contact Pristine Beach Resort for more information.

There's also turtle breeding grounds at Cuthbert Bay, a 45-minute drive from Rangat.

lost. Otherwise follow the red arrows marked on the trees.

⌂ Sleeping & Eating

A new budget guesthouse in Kalipur was about to open a few doors down from Pristine at time of research.

★ **Pristine Beach Resort**   GUESTHOUSE **$**
(☏9474286787; www.andamanpristineresorts.com; huts ₹300-1000, r ₹2500-3500; ❄@) Huddled among the palms between paddy fields and the beach, this relaxing resort has simple bamboo huts, more romantic bamboo 'tree houses' and upmarket rooms. Its attractive restaurant-bar serves up delicious Nicobari fish and cold beer. Alex, the super-friendly owner, is a top source of information. It also rents bicycles/motorcycles (per day ₹60/250).

❶ Getting There & Around

Diglipur, located about 80km north of Mayabunder, is served by daily buses to/from Port Blair (₹230, 12 hours), as well as buses to Mayabunder (₹50, 2½ hours) and Rangat (₹100, 4½ hours). There are also ferries to Port Blair (seat/bunk ₹110/310, nine hours) three times a week.

Buses run the 18km journey from Diglipur to Kalipur (₹13, 30 mintues) every 45 minutes; an autorickshaw costs ₹200.

LITTLE ANDAMAN

As far south as you can go in the islands, Little Andaman has an appealing end-of-the-world feel. It's a gorgeous fist of mangroves, jungle and teal, ringed by beaches as fresh as bread out of the oven.

Badly hit by the 2004 Boxing Day tsunami, Little Andaman has slowly rebuilt itself. Located about 120km south of Port Blair, the main settlement here is **Hut Bay**, a pleasant small town that primarily produces smiling Bengalis and Tamils.

Sights & Activities

Little Andaman has a coastline of uninterrupted white sandy beach. **Netaji Nagar Beach**, 11km north of Hut Bay, and **Butler Bay** (₹20), a further 3km north, are gorgeous, deserted (apart from the odd cow) and great for surfing.

Inland, the **White Surf** and **Whisper Wave waterfalls** offer a forest experience (the latter involves a 4km jungle trek and a guide is highly recommended); they're pleasant falls and you may be tempted to swim in the rock pools, but beware of local crocodiles.

Little Andaman lighthouse, 14km from Hut Bay, is another worthwhile excursion. Standing 41m high, exactly 200 steps spiral up to magnificent views over the coastline and forest. The easiest way to get here is by motorcycle, or otherwise a sweaty bicycle journey. You could also take an autorickshaw until the road becomes unpassable, and walk for an hour along the blissful stretch of deserted beach.

Kalapathar lagoon is a popular enclosed swimming area with shady patches of sand. Look for the cave in the cliff face that you can scamble through for stunning ocean views. It's just located before Butler Bay, and accessed via a side road that runs past modern housing constructed post-tsunami.

Harbinder Bay and **Dugong Creek** are designated tribal areas for the Nicobarese and Onge, respectively, and are off-limits.

Intrepid surfing travellers have been whispering about Little Andaman since it first opened up to foreigners several years ago. The reef breaks are legendary, but best suited for more experienced surfers. **Surfing Little Andaman** (☑9609688970; www.surfinglittleandaman.com; 2hr lessons ₹1000, board rental half/full day ₹500/900), based in Hut Bay, hire out boards, conduct lessons and have all the info on waves for Little Andaman and around.

Sleeping & Eating

There are plenty of cheap and tasty thali and tiffin places in town. None of the following serve alcohol, but you can stock up from a 'wine shop' in Hut Bay.

★ Blue View   BUNGALOWS $
(☑9734480840; Km11.5; r without bathroom ₹350-500) Prime real estate across the road from Netaji Nagar Beach, Blue View's simple thatched bungalows are run by the lovely Azad and his wife. It has surfboards (per hour/day ₹100/500) and rents out bicycles/motorbikes (per day ₹50/300). The food here is very good.

Jina Resort   BUNGALOWS $
(9476038057; Netaji Nagar 11km; r from ₹150) This newcomer also has chilled-out bungalows sprawled out over a lovely garden, just across from a lovely beach. Also rents out bikes.

Hotel Sea Land   HOTEL $
(☑03192-284525; Hut Bay; s/d ₹250/400, with AC ₹700) In town, Sea Land offers more-comfortable concrete rooms, but lacks atmosphere, though it has a nice gazebo with a sea breeze and hammocks.

Palm Groove   INDIAN $
(Hut Bay; ⊙6am-9pm) Attractive heritage-style bungalow with outdoor garden gazebo serving up a good selection of biriyanis and thalis.

❶ Getting There & Around

Ferries land at Hut Bay Jetty on the east coast; from there the beaches lay to the north. Buses (₹10) to Netaji Nagar usually coincide with ferry arrivals, or otherwise pass by every hour or so. Shared jeeps (₹50) are the other option. Failing that, an autorickshaw from the jetty to Netaji Nagar is ₹250, or ₹50 to town. Motorbikes and bicycles are available from most lodges.

Boats sail to Port Blair daily, alternating between afternoon and evening departures on vessels ranging from big ferries with four-/two-bed rooms (₹220/260, 8½ hours) to faster 5½-hour government boats (₹30); all have air-con. The ferry office is closed Sundays.

There's an ATM in Hut Bay, but no internet.

Understand India

India Today

With so many states, languages, cultures, religions, traditions, opinions and people – so many people! – India always has a lot going on. The political, economic and social systems of the world's largest democracy are complex, and they don't always work. Conflicts with Pakistan have been obstacles to progress, as has violence at home, between religious groups and against women. But Indians are looking for change – and moving ever closer towards it.

Best in Film

Fire (1996), **Earth** (1998) and **Water** (2005) The Deepa Mehta–directed trilogy was popular abroad, but controversial in India.

Pyaasa (Thirst; 1957) and **Kaagaz Ke Phool** (Paper Flowers; 1959) Two bittersweet films directed by and starring film legend Guru Dutt.

Gandhi (1982) The classic.

Best in Print: Fiction

Midnight's Children Salman Rushdie's allegory about Independence and Partition.

The Guide and **The Painter of Signs** Classic RK Narayan novels set in the fictional town of Malgudi.

White Tiger Aravind Adiga's Booker-winning novel about class struggle in globalised India.

Best in Print: Nonfiction

India after Gandhi: The History of the World's Largest Democracy An elegant post-Gandhi history by Ramachandra Guha.

The Nehrus and the Gandhis Tariq Ali's astute portrait-history of these powerful families.

Behind the Beautiful Forevers Katherine Boo's fascinating account of life in one of Mumbai's slums.

The Kashmir Impasse

In January 2013, Indian officials published a notice in newspapers in Kashmir about preparing for nuclear war, with tips on constructing shelters, stockpiling supplies and what to do if caught outside during an explosion. Delhi officials claimed that the notice was a normal public-education announcement – and not a response to recent border skirmishes, the worst in a decade, that killed three Pakistanis and two Indian soldiers, one of whom was beheaded.

This was only the latest in a long series of tragic events here: the predominantly Muslim Kashmir Valley is claimed by India and Pakistan (as well as the much less powerful Kashmiris themselves), and the impasse has plagued relations between the two countries since Partition in 1947.

Three India–Pakistan wars – in 1947, 1965 and 1971 – resolved little, and by 1989 Kashmir had its own Pakistan-backed armed insurgency. Tens of thousands were killed in the conflicts, and India has maintained hundreds of thousands of troops in Indian-administered Kashmir ever since. India–Pakistan relations sunk even lower in 1998 when both governments tested nuclear devices in a muscle-flexing show: nukes were now in the picture.

Talks that might have created an autonomous region were derailed in 2008, when terrorists killed at least 163 people at 10 sites around Mumbai (Bombay) during three days of coordinated bombings and shootings. The one sniper caught alive, a Pakistani, had ties to Lashkar-e-Taiba, a militant group that formed to assist the Pakistani army in Kashmir in the 1990s. Pakistan denied any involvement.

The dust was beginning to settle in 2012, and talks were making headway. But in late 2012, India secretly executed the Pakistani sniper, and then, in early 2013, a Kashmiri man convicted for involvement in a 2001 attack on Parliament was also hanged, heightening – once again – tensions between the countries.

Communal Tension

While Kashmir is the site of India's most persistent conflict, religion-based confrontation further south may be its most insidious. One of the most violent episodes occurred in 1992, when Hindu extremists destroyed a mosque, the Babri Masjid, in Ayodhya, Uttar Pradesh, revered by Hindus as the birthplace of Rama. The Hindu-revivalist BJP, then the main opposition, did little to discourage the acts, and rioting in the north killed thousands.

The BJP grew in popularity and won the elections in 1998 and 1999. Prime Minister Atal Bihari Vajpayee appeared moderate, but many BJP members and supporters took a more belligerent posture. In 2002, when 58 Hindus died in a suspicious train fire, more than 2000 people, mostly Muslims, were killed in subsequent riots; according to the nonprofit Human Rights Watch, some BJP government officials were directly involved.

The year 2008 was one of India's darkest: bomb blasts in Jaipur, Ahmedabad and Delhi each killed dozens of people. Investigations pointed at hardline Islamist groups. Tensions seemed to be cooling in 2010, when a court stated that the Ayodhya site would be split between Hindus and Muslims and the response was peaceful. The ruling was suspended by the Supreme Court in 2011 after appeals by both Hindus and Muslims. But blasts in Mumbai and Delhi in 2011 were reminders that extremism isn't dead.

Congress Today & the Economy

When the Congress Party regained power in 2004, it was under the leadership of Sonia Gandhi – the Italian-born wife of the late Rajiv Gandhi, who served as prime minister from 1984 to 1989. The BJP's planned national agitation campaign against Sonia Gandhi's foreign origins was subverted when she stepped aside to allow Manmohan Singh to be sworn in as prime minister. With a reputation for transparency and intelligence, Singh is reasonably popular among Indians, though many believe that Gandhi still wields considerable influence over the actual decisions.

Under Singh's leadership, India has carried out a program of economic liberalisation along with a number of education, health and other social-reform initiatives. In 1991, Singh, then finance minister, floated the rupee against a basket of 'hard' currencies. State subsidies were phased out and the economy was opened up to foreign investment, with multinationals drawn by India's multitudes of educated professionals and low wages. India became the world's second-fastest growing economy (after China). But in recent years, that growth has dropped off, the rupee has slumped and inflation has soared. Some economists

POPULATION: 1.21 BILLION

GDP: US$1.85 TRILLION (2011)

UNEMPLOYMENT RATE: 9.8%

LITERACY RATE: 65/82% (FEMALE/MALE)

GENDER RATIO: 940/1000 (FEMALE/MALE)

if India were 100 people

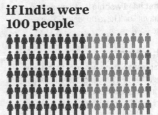

55 would speak one of 21 other official languages
41 would speak Hindi
4 would speak one of 400 other official languages

belief systems
(% of population)

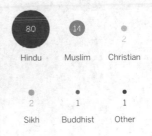

80 Hindu
14 Muslim
2 Christian
2 Sikh
1 Buddhist
1 Other

population per sq km

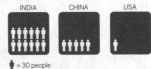

INDIA   CHINA   USA

≈ 30 people

Dos & Don'ts

Dress modestly Avoid tight clothes and keep shoulders and knees covered, especially at holy places.

PDA Public displays of affection – kissing, cuddling or holding hands – is not condoned.

Pure feet Remove shoes before entering people's homes and holy sites.

Photos Always ask before photographing people or holy places.

Bad vibes Avoid pointing the soles of your feet towards people or deities, or touching anyone with your feet.

That head wobble It can mean 'yes', 'maybe' or 'I have no idea'. Go with the flow!

Niceties

Namaste Saying *namaste* with hands together in a prayer gesture is a traditional, respectful Hindu greeting and a universally accepted way to say hello.

Hugs Hugs between strangers are not the norm.

Thanks 'Please' and 'thank you' aren't used much, but they never hurt.

Pure hands Only use your right hand for eating and shaking hands; the left hand is the 'toilet' hand.

see benefits to slower growth: it could slow down inflation and reduce economic disparity. Huge sections of the country's billion-plus population benefited little from the boom, and the gap between the haves and the have-nots continues to be vast.

Singh made international headlines in 2006 by concluding a civilian nuclear agreement with the US, which grants India access to nuclear fuel and technology, but he has more recently been criticised for weak leadership regarding a series of corruption allegations levelled towards his government.

In January 2013, Rahul Gandhi, Sonia's son, assumed the post of Vice President of the Congress Party. The move didn't surprise anyone: the Nehru-Gandhi name has become synonymous with the party. But he's not considered a charismatic or strategic figure, and it's expected to be a struggle to get a Gandhi back in the PM seat in 2014.

Violence Against Women

In December 2012, a 23-year-old paramedic and her male friend boarded a bus on their way home from the movies in Delhi only to find that it was a fake city bus, with blackened windows, where six men awaited them. The men beat the two friends, and raped the woman so brutally that she died 12 days later. The woman became known in India as Nirbhaya, or 'fearless one', and the event set off massive protests and soul-searching nationwide. Within weeks, India passed a package of new but controversial laws to deter violence against women: rape now carries a seven-year minimum sentence, with the death penalty in cases where the victim dies.

But in the months following the murder, more crimes took place, including violent rapes of girls as young as four. And while some Indian politicians condemned the rapists, others made comments that downplayed rape or blamed the victim. Many in India are also now reflecting on other abuses of women (tens of thousands die over dowry disputes alone each year), widespread police and justice-system mishandling of cases (of the more than 600 reported rapes in Delhi in 2012, just one resulted in a conviction), and the larger problems of gender inequality. The situation for women's violence isn't good, but many are hopeful that, now that the issues are out in the open, change will follow.

History

Throughout thousands of years of great civilisations, invasions, the birth of religions and countless cataclysms, India has proved itself to be, in the words of its first prime minister, Jawaharlal Nehru, 'a bundle of contradictions held together by strong but invisible threads'. Indian history has always been a work-in-progress, an evolution that can prove elusive for those seeking to grasp its essence. And yet, a vibrant, diverse nation has emerged, as enduring and grounded as it is dynamic.

Indus Valley Civilisation

The Indus Valley, straddling the modern India–Pakistan border, is the cradle of civilisation on the Indian subcontinent. The first inhabitants of this region were nomadic tribes who cultivated land and kept domestic animals. Over thousands of years, an urban culture began to emerge from these tribes, particularly from 3500 BC. By 2500 BC large cities were well established, the focal points of what became known as the Harappan culture, which would flourish for more than 1000 years.

The great cities of the Mature Harappan period were Moenjodaro and Harappa in present-day Pakistan, and Lothal near Ahmedabad. Lothal can be visited, and from the precise, carefully laid-out street plan, some sense of this sophisticated 4500-year-old civilisation is still evident. Harappan cities often had a separate acropolis, suggesting a religious function, and the great tank at Moenjodaro may have been used for ritual bathing purposes. The major Harappan cities were also notable for their size – estimates put the population of Moenjodaro at as high as 50,000.

By the middle of the 3rd millennium BC the Indus Valley culture was arguably the equal of other great civilisations emerging at the time. The Harappans traded with Mesopotamia, and developed a system of weights and measures, along with a highly developed art in the form of terracotta and bronze figurines. Recovered relics, including models of bullock carts and jewellery, offer the earliest evidence of a distinctive Indian culture. Indeed, many elements of Harappan culture would later become assimilated into Hinduism: clay figurines found at these sites suggest worship of a Mother goddess (later personified as Kali) and a male three-faced

RK Narayan's 1973 *Ramayana* is a condensed and novelistic retelling of the 3rd century BC classic. The renowned novelist took on the *Mahabharata* in 1978.

TIMELINE	10,000 BC	2600–1700 BC	1500 BC
	Stone Age paintings first made in the Bhimbetka rock shelters, in what is now Madhya Pradesh; the art continues here for many centuries. Settlements thought to exist across subcontinent.	The Indus Valley civilisation's heyday. Spanning parts of Rajasthan, Gujarat and Sindh province in present-day Pakistan, it takes shape around metropolises such as Harappa and Moenjodaro.	The Indo-Aryan civilisation takes root in the fertile plains of the Indo-Gangetic basin. Settlers speak an early form of Sanskrit, from which several Indian vernaculars, including Hindi, later evolve.

god sitting in the pose of a yogi (believed to be the historic Shiva) attended by four animals. Black stone pillars (associated with phallic worship of Shiva) and animal figures (the most prominent being the humped bull; later Shiva's mount, Nandi) have also been discovered.

Early Invasions & the Rise of Religions

To learn more about the ancient Indus Valley civilisations, ramble around Harappa (www. harappa.com), which presents an accessible yet scholarly multimedia overview.

The Harappan civilisation fell into decline from the beginning of the 2nd millennium BC. Some historians attribute the end of the empire to floods or decreased rainfall, which threatened the Harappans' agricultural base. The more enduring, if contentious, theory is that an Aryan invasion put paid to the Harappans, despite little archaeological proof or written reports in the ancient Indian texts to that effect. As a result, some nationalist historians argue that the Aryans (from a Sanskrit word for 'noble') were in fact the original inhabitants of India and that the invasion theory was invented by self-serving foreign conquerors. Others say that the arrival of Aryans was more of a gentle migration that gradually subsumed Harappan culture.

Those who defend the invasion theory believe that from around 1500 BC Aryan tribes from Afghanistan and Central Asia began to filter into northwest India. Despite their military superiority, their progress was gradual, with successive tribes fighting over territory and new arrivals pushing further east into the Ganges plain. Eventually these tribes controlled northern India as far as the Vindhya Hills. Many of the original inhabitants of northern India, the Dravidians, the theory goes, were pushed south.

Mauryan Remains

Junagadh (Gujarat)

Allahabad Fort (Uttar Pradesh)

Sarnath (Uttar Pradesh)

Sanchi (Madhya Pradesh)

Bodhgaya (Bihar)

Vaishali (Bihar)

Amaravathi (Andhra Pradesh)

The Hindu sacred scriptures, the Vedas, were written during this period of transition (1500–1200 BC), and the caste system became formalised.

As the Aryan tribes spread across the Ganges plain in the late 7th century BC, many were absorbed into 16 major kingdoms, which were, in turn, amalgamated into four large states. Out of these states arose the Nanda dynasty, which came to power in 364 BC, ruling over huge swathes of North India.

During this period, the Indian heartland narrowly avoided two invasions from the west which, if successful, could have significantly altered Indian history. The first was by the Persian king Darius (521–486 BC), who annexed Punjab and Sindh (on either side of the modern India–Pakistan border). Alexander the Great advanced to India from Greece in 326 BC but turned back without ever extending his power into India itself.

The period is also distinguished by the rise of two of India's most significant religions, Buddhism and Jainism, which arose around 500 BC. Both the Buddha and Jainism's Mahavir questioned the Vedas and were critical of the caste system.

1500–1200 BC	599–528 BC	563–483 BC
The Rig-Veda, the first and longest of Hinduism's canonical texts, the Vedas, is written; three more books follow. Earliest forms of priestly Brahmanical Hinduism emerge.	The life of Mahavir, the 24th and last *tirthankar* (enlightened teacher) who established Jainism. Like the Buddha, he preaches compassion and a path to enlightenment for all castes.	The life of Siddhartha Gautama. The prince is born in modern-day Nepal and attains enlightenment beneath the Bodhi Tree in Bodhgaya (Bihar), thereby transforming into the Buddha (Awakened One).

➜ Bodhi Tree (p524), Bihar

The Mauryan Empire & its Aftermath

If the Harappan culture was the cradle of Indian civilisation, Chandragupta Maurya was the founder of the first great Indian empire. He came to power in 321 BC, having seized the throne from the Nandas, and he soon expanded the empire to include the Indus Valley previously conquered by Alexander.

From its capital at Pataliputra (modern-day Patna), the Mauryan empire encompassed much of North India and reached as far south as modern-day Karnataka. The empire reached its peak under emperor Ashoka. Such was Ashoka's power to lead and unite that after his death in 232 BC, no one could be found to hold the disparate elements of the Mauryan empire together. The empire rapidly disintegrated, collapsing altogether in 184 BC.

None of the empires that immediately followed could match the stability or enduring historical legacy of the Mauryans, although the post-Ashokan era did produce at least one line of royalty whose patronage of the arts and ability to maintain a relatively high degree of social cohesion were substantial. The Satavahanas eventually controlled all of Maharashtra, Madhya Pradesh, Chhattisgarh, Karnataka and Andhra Pradesh.

History Good Reads

A History of India, Romila Thapar (Vol 1) and Percival Spear (Vol 2)

Empires of the Indus, Alice Albinia

India: a History, John Keay

AN ENLIGHTENED EMPEROR

Apart from the Mughals and then the British many centuries later, no other power controlled more Indian territory than the Mauryan empire. It's therefore fitting that it provided India with one of its most important historical figures.

Emperor Ashoka's rule was characterised by flourishing art and sculpture, while his reputation as a philosopher-king was enhanced by the rock-hewn edicts he used to both instruct his people and delineate the enormous span of his territory. Some of these moral teachings can still be seen, particularly the Ashokan Edicts at Junagadh in Gujarat.

Ashoka's reign also represented an undoubted historical high point for Buddhism: he embraced the Buddha's teaching in 262 BC, declaring it the state religion and cutting a radical swathe through the spiritual and social body of Hinduism. The emperor also built thousands of stupas and monasteries across the region, the extant highlights of which are visible at Sarnath in Uttar Pradesh – on the spot where Buddha delivered his first sermon expounding the Noble Eightfold Path, or Middle Way to Enlightenment – and Sanchi in Madhya Pradesh. Ashoka also sent missions abroad, and he is revered in Sri Lanka because he sent his son and daughter to carry the Buddha's teaching to the island.

One of this emperor's many legacies is the Indian national flag: its central design is the Ashoka Chakra, a wheel with 24 spokes.

5th–4th Century BC	326BC	321–185 BC	Mid-3rd Century BC
Nanda dynasty evolves from the wealthy region of Magadha (roughly, today's Bihar) and grows to encompass a huge area, from Bengal to Punjab. It falls to Maurya in 321 BC.	Alexander the Great invades India. He defeats King Porus in Punjab to enter the subcontinent, but a rebellion within his army keeps him from advancing beyond Himachal Pradesh's Beas River.	Rule of the Maurya kings. Founded by Chandragupta Maurya, this pan-Indian empire is ruled from Pataliputra (present-day Patna) and briefly adopts Buddhism during the reign of Emperor Ashoka.	Buddhism spreads across subcontinent and beyond via Ashoka's monastic ambassadors: monks travel to Sri Lanka and Southeast Asia. Amaravathi, Sanchi and other stupas are erected.

Under their rule, between 230 BC and AD 200, the arts, especially literature and philosophy, blossomed; the Buddha's teaching thrived; and the subcontinent enjoyed a period of considerable prosperity. South India may have lacked vast and fertile agricultural plains on the scale of North India, but it compensated by building strategic trade links via the Indian Ocean. Trade across the subcontinent grew during this time, in fact – with the Roman Empire (overland, and by sea through the southern ports) and, overland, with China.

Mahavir and the Buddha were contemporaries, and their teachings overlapped. The Buddha lays out the discrepancies (and his critiques) in the Sankha Sutta and Devadaha Sutta, referring to Mahavir as Nigantha ('free from bonds') Nataputta. Read them at the Theravada resource www. accesstoinsight. com.

The Golden Age of the Guptas

The empires that followed the Mauryans may have claimed large areas of Indian territory as their own, but many secured only nominal power over their realms. Throughout the subcontinent, small tribes and kingdoms effectively controlled territory and dominated local affairs.

In AD 319 Chandragupta I, the third king of one of these tribes, the little-known Guptas, came to prominence by a fortuitous marriage to the daughter of one of the most powerful tribes in the north, the Liccavis. The Gupta empire grew rapidly and under Chandragupta II (r 375–413) achieved its greatest extent. The Chinese pilgrim Fa-hsien, visiting India at the time, described a people 'rich and contented', ruled over by enlightened and just kings.

Poetry, literature and the arts flourished, with some of the finest work done at Ajanta, Ellora, Sanchi and Sarnath. The Guptas were tolerant of, and even supported, Buddhist practice and art. Towards the end of the Gupta period, Hinduism became the dominant religious force, however, and its revival eclipsed Jainism and Buddhism; the latter in particular went into decline in India with the Hun invasion and would never again be India's dominant tradition.

The invasions of the Huns at the beginning of the 6th century signalled the end of this era, and in 510 the Gupta army was defeated by the Hun leader Toramana. Power in North India again devolved to a number of separate Hindu kingdoms.

The concepts of zero and infinity are widely believed to have been devised by eminent Indian mathematicians during the reign of the Guptas.

The Hindu South

Southern India has always laid claim to its own unique history. Insulated by distance from the political developments in the north, a separate set of powerful kingdoms emerged, among them the Satavahanas – who, though predominantly Hindu, probably practiced Buddhist meditation and patronised Buddhist art at Amaravathi and Sanchi – as well as the Kalingas and Vakatakas. But it was from the tribal territories on the fertile coastal plains that the greatest southern empires – the Cholas, Pandyas, Chalukyas, Cheras and Pallavas – came into their own.

Mid-3rd Century BC	c 235 BC	3rd Century BC	AD 52
Bhakti movement emerges in Hinduism, following first mention in the 5th-century-BC Bhagavad Gita. It emphasises individual devotion and union with the Divine, challenging traditional hierarchy of Brahmanism.	Start of Chola reign. The Tamil dynasty, known for the power and territory it accreted in the 9th to 13th centuries, ruled in India's south for more than 1500 years.	The Satavahana empire, of Andhra origin, rules over a huge central Indian area until the 2nd century AD. Their interest in art and maritime trade influences artistic development regionally and in Southeast Asia.	Possible arrival of St Thomas the Apostle on the coast of Kerala. Christianity thought to have been introduced to India with his preaching in Kerala and Tamil Nadu.

The Chalukyas ruled mainly over the Deccan region of south-central India, although their power occasionally extended further north. In the far south, the Pallavas ruled from the 4th to 9th centuries and pioneered Dravidian architecture, with its exuberant, almost baroque, style. The surviving architectural high points of Pallava rule can be found across Tamil Nadu, including in the erstwhile Pallava capital at Kanchipuram.

The south's prosperity was based on long-established trading links with other civilisations, among them the Egyptians and Romans. In return for spices, pearls, ivory and silk, the Indians received Roman gold. Indian merchants also extended their influence to Southeast Asia. In 850 the Cholas rose to power and superseded the Pallavas. They soon set about turning the south's far-reaching trade influence into territorial conquest. Under the reign of Rajaraja Chola I (985–1014) they controlled almost the whole of South India, the Deccan plateau, Sri Lanka, parts of the Malay peninsula and the Sumatran-based Srivijaya kingdom.

Not all of their attention was focused overseas, however, and the Cholas left behind some of the finest examples of Dravidian architecture, most notably the sublime Brihadishwara Temple in Thanjavur and Chidambaram's stunning Nataraja Temple. Both Thanjavur and Chidambaram served as Chola capitals.

Throughout, Hinduism remained the bedrock of South Indian culture.

The Muslim North

While South India guarded its resolutely Hindu character, North India was convulsed by Muslim armies invading from the northwest.

At the vanguard of Islamic expansion was Mahmud of Ghazni. In the early 11th century, Mahmud turned Ghazni (in today's Afghanistan) into one of the world's most glorious capital cities, which he largely funded by plundering his neighbours' territories. From 1001 to 1025, Mahmud conducted 17 raids into India, most infamously on the famous Shiva temple at Somnath in Gujarat. The Hindu force of 70,000 died trying to defend the temple, which eventually fell in early 1026. In the aftermath of his victory, Mahmud transported a massive haul of gold and other booty back to his capital. These raids effectively shattered the balance of power in North India, allowing subsequent invaders to claim the territory for themselves.

Following Mahmud's death in 1033, Ghazni was seized by the Seljuqs and then fell to the Ghurs of western Afghanistan, who similarly had their eyes on the great Indian prize. The Ghur style of warfare was brutal.

In 1191 Mohammed of Ghur advanced into India. Although defeated in a major battle against a confederacy of Hindu rulers, he returned the following year and routed his enemies. One of his generals, Qutb uddin Aibak, captured Delhi and was appointed governor; it was during

A History of South India from Prehistoric Times to the Fall of Vijayanagar by KA Nilakanta Sastri is arguably the most comprehensive (if heavy-going) history of this region.

SOUTH INDIA

1st Century	319–510	4th to 9th Centuries	500–600
International trade booms: the region's elaborate overland trade networks connect with ports linked to maritime routes. Trade to Africa, the Gulf, Socotra, Southeast Asia, China and even Rome thrives.	The golden era of the Gupta dynasty, the second of India's great empires after the Mauryas. The period is marked by a creative surge in literature and the arts.	The Pallavas, known for their temple architecture, enter the shifting landscape of southern power centres, establishing dominance in Andhra Pradesh and northern Tamil Nadu from their base in Kanchipuram.	The emergence of the Rajputs in Rajasthan. Hailing from three principal races supposedly of celestial origin, they form 36 clans which spread across the region to secure their own kingdoms.

his reign that the great Delhi landmark, the Qutb Minar complex, was built. (In its 800-year history, the Qutb Minar has been damaged by two lightning strikes and one earthquake and has been repaired or built up by four sultans, one British major and one governor general.) A separate Islamic empire was established in Bengal, and within a short time almost the whole of North India was under Muslim control.

Following Mohammed's death in 1206, Qutb ud-din Aibak became the first sultan of Delhi. His successor, Iltutmish, brought Bengal back under central control and defended the empire from an attempted Mongol invasion. Ala-ud-din Khilji came to power in 1296 and pushed the borders of the empire inexorably south, while simultaneously fending off further attacks by the Mongols.

North Meets South

Ala-ud-din died in 1320, and Mohammed Tughlaq ascended the throne in 1324. In 1328 Tughlaq took the southern strongholds of the Hoysala empire, which had centres at Belur, Halebid and Somnathpur. However, while the empire of the pre-Mughal Muslims would achieve its greatest extent under Tughlaq's rule, his overreaching ambition also sowed the seeds of its disintegration. Unlike his forebears, Tughlaq dreamed not only of extending his indirect influence over South India, but of controlling it directly as part of his empire.

After a series of successful campaigns Tughlaq decided to move the capital from Delhi to a more central location. The new capital was called Daulatabad and was near Aurangabad in Maharashtra. Tughlaq sought to populate the new capital by forcefully marching the entire population of Delhi 1100km south, resulting in great loss of life. However, he soon realised that this left the north undefended, and so the entire capital was moved north again. The superb hilltop fortress of Daulatabad stands as the last surviving monument to his megalomanic vision.

The days of the Ghur empire were numbered. The last of the great sultans of Delhi, Firoz Shah, died in 1388, and the fate of the sultanate was sealed when Timur (Tamerlane) made a devastating raid from Samarkand (in Central Asia) into India in 1398. Timur's sacking of Delhi was truly merciless; some accounts say his soldiers slaughtered every Hindu inhabitant.

After Tughlaq's withdrawal from the south, several splinter kingdoms arose. The two most significant were the Islamic Bahmani sultanate, which emerged in 1345 with its capital at Gulbarga, and later Bidar, and the Hindu Vijayanagar empire, founded in 1336 with its capital at Hampi. The battles between the two were among the bloodiest communal violence in Indian history and ultimately resolved nothing in the two centuries before the Mughals ushered in a more enlightened age.

Architecture of the Deccan Sultanates

Citadel, Golgumbaz, Ibrahim Rouza, Jama Masjid (Bijapur)

Fort, Bahmani Tombs (Bidar)

Golconda Fort, Qutb Shahi Tombs, Charminar (Hyderabad)

610	12th–19th Centuries	1192	1206
Prophet Mohammed establishes Islam. He soon invites the people of Mecca to adopt the new religion under the command of God, and his call is met with eager response.	Africans are brought to the Konkan Coast as part of trade with the Gulf; the slaves become servants, dock workers and soldiers and are known as Siddis or Habshis.	Prithviraj Chauhan loses Delhi to Mohammed of Ghori. The defeat effectively ends Hindu supremacy in the region, exposing the subcontinent to subsequent Muslim rulers marching in from the northwest.	Ghori is murdered during prayer while returning to Ghazni from Lahore. In the absence of an heir, his kingdom is usurped by his generals. The Delhi Sultanate is born.

The Mughals

Even as Vijayanagar was experiencing its last days, the next great Indian empire was being founded. The Mughal empire was massive, at its height covering almost the entire subcontinent. Its significance, however, lay not only in its size. Mughal emperors presided over a golden age of arts and literature and had a passion for building that resulted in some of the finest architecture in India: Shah Jahan's sublime Taj Mahal ranks as one of the wonders of the world.

The founder of the Mughal line, Babur (r 1526–30), was a descendant of both Genghis Khan and Timur (Tamerlane). In 1525, he marched into Punjab from his capital at Kabul. With technological superiority brought by firearms, and consummate skill in simultaneously employing artillery and cavalry, Babur defeated the larger armies of the sultan of Delhi at the Battle of Panipat in 1526.

THE STRUGGLE FOR THE SOUL OF INDIA

Founded as an alliance of Hindu kingdoms banding together to counter the threat from the Muslims, the Vijayanagar empire rapidly grew into one of India's wealthiest and greatest Hindu empires. Under the rule of Bukka I (c 1343–79), the majority of South India was brought under its control.

The Vijayanagars and the Bahmani sultanate, which was also based in South India, were evenly matched. The Vijayanagar armies occasionally got the upper hand, but generally the Bahmanis inflicted the worst defeats. The atrocities committed by both sides almost defy belief. In 1366 Bukka I responded to a perceived slight by capturing the Muslim stronghold of Mudkal and slaughtering every inhabitant bar one, who managed to escape and carry news of the attack to Mohammad Shah, the sultan. Mohammad swore that he would not rest until he had killed 100,000 Hindus. Instead, according to the Muslim historian Firishtah, 500,000 'infidels' were killed in the ensuing campaign.

Somehow, Vijayanagar survived. In 1484, the Bahmani sultanate began to disintegrate, and five separate kingdoms, based on the major cities – Berar, Ahmadnagar, Bidar, Bijapur and Golconda – were formed. Bijapur and Bidar still bear exceptional traces of this period of Islamic rule. With little opposition from the north, the Hindu empire enjoyed a golden age of almost supreme power in the south. In 1520 the Vijayanagar king Krishnadevaraya even took Bijapur.

Like Bahmani, however, Vijayanagar's fault lines were soon laid bare. A series of uprisings divided the kingdom fatally, just at a time when the Muslim sultanates were beginning to form a new alliance. In 1565 Hampi was destroyed at the Battle of Talikota. Although the last of the Vijayanagar line escaped and the dynasty limped on for several years, real power passed to local Muslim rulers or Hindu chiefs once loyal to the Vijayanagar kings. One of India's grisliest periods came to an end when the Bahmani kingdoms fell to the Mughals.

13th Century	1321	1336	1345
The Pandyas, a Tamil dynasty dating to the 6th century BC, assumes control of Chola territory, expanding into Andhra Pradesh, Kalinga (Odisha [Orissa]) and Sri Lanka from their Madurai capital.	The Tughlaqs come to power in Delhi. Mohammed bin Tughlaq expands his empire but becomes known for inelegant schemes: moving the capital to Daulatabad and creating forgery-prone currency.	Foundation of the mighty Vijayanagar empire, named after its capital city, the ruins of which can be seen today in the vicinity of Hampi (in Karnataka).	Bahmani Sultanate is established in the Deccan following a revolt against the Tughlaqs of Delhi. The capital is set up at Gulbarga, in today's northern Karnataka, later shifting to Bidar.

Despite this initial success, Babur's son, Humayun (r 1530–56) was defeated by a powerful ruler of eastern India, Sher Shah, in 1539 and forced to withdraw to Iran. Following Sher Shah's death in 1545, Humayun returned to claim his kingdom, eventually conquering Delhi in 1555. He died the following year and was succeeded by his young son Akbar (r 1556–1605) who, during his 49-year reign, managed to extend and consolidate the empire until he ruled over a mammoth area.

True to his name, Akbar (which means 'great' in Arabic) was probably the greatest of the Mughals: he not only had the military ability required of a ruler at that time, but was also a just and wise ruler and a man of culture. He saw, as previous Muslim rulers had not, that the number of Hindus in India was too great to subjugate. Although Akbar was no saint – reports of massacres of Hindus at Panipat and Chitrod tarnish his legacy – he remains known for integrating Hindus into his empire and skilfully using them as advisers, generals and administrators. Akbar also had a deep interest in religious matters, and spent many hours in discussion with religious experts of all persuasions, including Christians and Parsis.

Jehangir (r 1605–27) ascended to the throne following Akbar's death. Despite several challenges to Jehangir's authority, the empire remained more or less intact. In periods of stability Jehangir spent time in his beloved Kashmir, eventually dying en route there in 1627. He was succeeded by his son, Shah Jahan (r 1627–58), who secured his position by executing all male relatives who stood in his way. During his reign, some of the most vivid and permanent reminders of the Mughals' glory were constructed; in addition to the Taj Mahal, he oversaw the construction of the mighty Red Fort (Lal Qila) in Delhi and converted the Agra Fort into a palace that would later become his prison.

The last of the great Mughals, Aurangzeb (r 1658–1707), imprisoned his father (Shah Jahan) and succeeded to the throne after a two-year struggle against his brothers. Aurangzeb devoted his resources to extending the empire's boundaries, and thus fell into much the same trap as that of Mohammed Tughlaq some 300 years earlier. A combination of decaying court life and dissatisfaction among the Hindu population at inflated taxes and religious intolerance weakened the Mughal grip.

The empire was also facing serious challenges from the Marathas in central India and, more significantly, the British in Bengal. With Aurangzeb's death in 1707, the empire's fortunes rapidly declined, and Delhi was sacked by Persia's Nadir Shah in 1739. Mughal 'emperors' continued to rule right up until the First War of Independence (Indian Uprising) in 1857, but they were emperors without an empire.

1398	1469	1484	1498
Timur (Tamerlane) invades Delhi, on the pretext that the Delhi Sultans are too tolerant with their Hindu subjects. He executes tens of thousands of Hindus before the battle for Delhi.	Guru Nanak, founder of the Sikh faith, which has millions of followers within and beyond India to the present day, is born in a village near Lahore (in modern-day Pakistan).	Bahmani Sultanate begins to break up following independence movements; Berar is the first to revolt. By 1518 there are five Deccan sultanates: Berar, Ahmadnagar, Bidar, Bijapur and Golconda.	Vasco da Gama discovers the sea route from Europe to India. The first European to reach India by sea, he engages in trade with the local nobility of Kerala.

The Rajputs & the Marathas

Throughout the Mughal period, there remained strong Hindu powers, most notably the Rajputs. Centred in Rajasthan, the Rajputs were a proud warrior caste with a passionate belief in the dictates of chivalry, both in battle and state affairs. The Rajputs opposed every foreign incursion into their territory, but they were never united. When they weren't battling foreign oppression, they squandered their energies fighting one another. This eventually led to their territories becoming vassal states of the Mughal empire. Their prowess in battle, however, was acknowledged, and some of the best military men in the Mughal armies were Rajputs.

The Marathas were less picaresque but ultimately more effective. They first rose to prominence under their great leader Shivaji, also known as Chhatrapati Shivaji, who gathered popular support by championing the Hindu cause against the Muslim rulers. Between 1646 and 1680 Shivaji performed heroic acts in confronting the Mughals across most of central India. Shivaji was captured by the Mughals and taken to Agra, but, naturally, he managed to escape and continue his adventures. Tales of his larger-than-life exploits are still popular with wandering storytellers. He is a particular hero in Maharashtra, where many of his wildest adventures took place. (Today, you'll see Shivaji's name all over Mumbai.) He's also revered for the fact that, as a lower-caste Shudra, he showed that great leaders don't have to be of the Kshatriya (soldier) caste.

Shivaji's son was captured, blinded and executed by Aurangzeb. His grandson wasn't made of the same sturdy stuff, so the Maratha empire continued under the Peshwas, hereditary government ministers who became the real rulers. They gradually took over more of the weakening Mughal empire's powers.

The expansion of Maratha power came to an abrupt halt in 1761 at Panipat. In the town where Babur had won the battle that established the Mughal empire more than 200 years earlier, the Marathas were defeated by Ahmad Shah Durrani from Afghanistan. Maratha expansion to the west was halted, and although they consolidated their control over central India, they were to fall to India's final imperial power – the British.

The Rise of European Power

In 1498 Vasco da Gama arrived on the coast of modern-day Kerala, having sailed around the Cape of Good Hope. Pioneering this route gave the Portuguese a century-long monopoly over Indian and far-Eastern trade with Europe. In 1510 they captured Goa, followed by Diu in 1531, two enclaves the Portuguese controlled until 1961. In its heyday, the trade flowing through 'Golden Goa' was said to rival that passing through Lisbon. However, the Portuguese didn't have the resources to maintain a

NIZAMS

The nizams of Hyderabad ruled over this vast central-Indian state from 1720 until Independence – first under the Mughals and then on their own – and were known for their wealth; their fondness for architecture, poetry and precious gems; and, at Independence, their determination to remain independent.

1510	1526	1542–45	1556
Portuguese forces capture Goa under the command of Alfonso de Albuquerque, whose initial attempt was thwarted by then-ruler, Sultan Adil Shah of Bijapur. He succeeds following Shah's death.	Babur becomes the first Mughal emperor after conquering Delhi. He stuns Rajasthan by routing its confederate force, gaining an edge with the introduction of matchlock muskets in his army.	St Francis Xavier's first mission to India. He preaches Catholicism in Goa, Tamil Nadu and Sri Lanka, returning in 1548–49 and 1552 in between travels in the Far East.	Hemu, a Hindu general in Adil Shah Suri's army, seizes Delhi after Humayun's death. He rules for barely a month before losing to Akbar in the Second Battle of Panipat.

worldwide empire and they were quickly eclipsed and isolated after the arrival of the British and French.

In 1600 Queen Elizabeth I granted a charter to a London trading company that gave it a monopoly on British trade with India. In 1613 representatives of the East India Company established their first trading post at Surat in Gujarat. Further British trading posts, administered and governed by representatives of the company, were established at Madras (Chennai) in 1639, Bombay (Mumbai) in 1661 and Calcutta (Kolkata) in 1690. For nearly 250 years a commercial trading company and not the British government 'ruled' over British India.

By 1672 the French had established themselves at Pondicherry (Puducherry), an enclave they held even after the British departed and where architectural traces of the French era remain. The stage was set for more than a century of rivalry between the British and French for control of Indian trade. At one stage, the French appeared to hold the upper hand, even taking Madras in 1746. But they were outmaneuvered by the British, and by the 1750s were no longer a serious influence on the subcontinent. But serious French aspirations effectively ended in 1750 when the directors of the French East India Company decided that their representatives were playing too much politics and doing too little trading. Key representatives were sacked, and a settlement designed to end all ongoing political disputes was made with the British. The decision effectively removed France as a serious influence on the subcontinent.

Britain's Surge to Power

The transformation of the British from traders to governors began almost by accident. Having been granted a licence to trade in Bengal by the Mughals, and following the establishment of a new trading post at Calcutta (Kolkata) in 1690, business began to expand rapidly. Under the apprehensive gaze of the nawab (local ruler), British trading activities became extensive and the 'factories' took on an increasingly permanent (and fortified) appearance.

Eventually the nawab decided that British power had grown large enough. In June 1756 he attacked Calcutta and, having taken the city, locked his British prisoners in a tiny cell. The space was so cramped and airless that many were dead by the following morning.

Six months later, Robert Clive, an employee in the military service of the East India Company, led an expedition to retake Calcutta and entered into an agreement with one of the nawab's generals to overthrow the nawab himself. He did this in June 1757 at the Battle of Plassey (now called Palashi), and the general who had assisted him was placed on the throne. With the British effectively in control of Bengal, the company's agents engaged in a period of unbridled profiteering. When a subsequent

Plain Tales from the Raj by Charles Allen (ed) is a fascinating series of interviews with people who played a role in British India on both sides of the table.

1560–1812	1600	1631	1672
Portuguese Inquisition in Goa. Trials focus on converted Hindus and Muslims thought to have 'relapsed'. Thousands were tried and several dozen were likely executed before it was abolished in 1812.	Britain's Queen Elizabeth I grants the first trading charter to the East India Company, with the maiden voyage taking place in 1601 under the command of Sir James Lancaster.	Construction of the Taj Mahal begins after Shah Jahan, overcome with grief following the death of his wife Mumtaz Mahal, vows to build the most beautiful mausoleum in the world.	The French East India Company establishes an outpost at Pondicherry (Puducherry), which the French, Dutch and British fight over repeatedly in the coming century.

nawab finally took up arms to protect his own interests, he was defeated at the Battle of Baksar in 1764, a victory that confirmed the British as the paramount power in east India.

In 1771 Warren Hastings was made governor in Bengal. During his tenure the company greatly expanded its control. He was aided by the fact that India was experiencing a power vacuum created by the disintegration of the Mughal empire. The Marathas, the only real Indian power to step into this gap, were divided among themselves. Hastings concluded a series of treaties with local rulers, including one with the main Maratha leader. From 1784 onwards, the British government in London began to take a more direct role in supervising affairs in India, although the territory was still notionally administered by the East India Company until 1858.

In the south, the picture was confused by the strong British–French rivalry, and one ruler was played off against another. This was never clearer than in the series of Mysore wars in which Hyder Ali and his son, Tipu Sultan, waged a brave and determined campaign against the British. In the Fourth Mysore War (1789–99), Tipu Sultan was killed at Srirangapatnam, and British power took another step forward. The long-running struggle with the Marathas was concluded a few years later, leaving only Punjab (held by the Sikhs) outside British control. Punjab finally fell in 1849 after the two Sikh Wars.

By the early 19th century, India was effectively under British control, although there remained a patchwork of states, many nominally independent and governed by their own rulers, the maharajas (or similarly titled princes) and nawabs. While these 'princely states' administered their own territories, a system of central government was developed. British bureaucratic models were replicated in the Indian government and civil service – a legacy that still exists.

Trade and profit continued to be the main focus of British rule in India, with far-reaching effects. Iron and coal mining were developed, and tea, coffee and cotton became key crops. A start was made on the vast rail network that's still in use today, irrigation projects were undertaken, and the Mughal-era zamindar (landowner) system was encouraged, further contributing to the development of an impoverished and landless peasantry.

The British also imposed English as the local language of administration. For them, this was critical in a country with so many different languages, but it also kept the new rulers at arm's length from the Indian populace.

Colonial-era Architecture

Colaba and Kala Ghoda, Mumbai (British)

BBD Bagh and environs, Kolkata (British)

Old Goa and Panjim, Goa (Portuguese)

Puducherry, Tamil Nadu (French)

The Road to Independence

Opposition to the British increased at the turn of the 20th century, spearheaded by the Indian National Congress, the country's oldest political party, also known as the Congress Party and Congress (I).

1674	1707	1757	1801
Shivaji establishes the Maratha kingdom, spanning western India and parts of the Deccan and North India. He assumes the imperial title of Chhatrapati, which means 'Great Protector'.	Death of Aurangzeb, the last of the Mughal greats. His demise triggers the gradual collapse of the Mughal empire, as anarchy and rebellion erupt across the country.	The East India Company registers its first military victory on Indian soil. Siraj-ud-Daulah, nawab of Bengal, is defeated by Robert Clive in the Battle of Plassey.	Ranjit Singh becomes maharaja (Great King) of the newly united Sikhs and forges a powerful new kingdom from his capital in Lahore (in present-day Pakistan).

It met for the first time in 1885 and soon began to push for participation in the government of India. A highly unpopular attempt by the British to partition Bengal in 1905 resulted in mass demonstrations and brought to light Hindu opposition to the division; the Muslim community formed its own league and campaigned for protected rights in any future political settlement. As pressure rose, a split emerged in Hindu circles between moderates and radicals, the latter resorting to violence to publicise their aims.

With the outbreak of WWI, the political situation eased. India contributed hugely to the war: more than one million Indian volunteers were enlisted and sent overseas, suffering more than 100,000 casualties. The contribution was sanctioned by Congress leaders, largely with the expectation that it would be rewarded after the war. No such rewards transpired and disillusion followed. Disturbances were particularly persistent in Punjab, and in April 1919, following riots in Amritsar, a British

THE FIRST WAR OF INDEPENDENCE: THE INDIAN UPRISING

In 1857, half a century after having established firm control of India, the British suffered a serious setback. To this day, the causes of the Indian Uprising are the subject of debate. The key factors included the influx of cheap goods, such as textiles, from Britain that destroyed many livelihoods; the dispossession of territories from many rulers; and taxes imposed on landowners.

The incident that's popularly held to have sparked the Indian Uprising, however, took place at an army barracks in Meerut in Uttar Pradesh on 10 May 1857. A rumour leaked out that a new type of bullet was greased with what Hindus claimed was cow fat, while Muslims maintained that it came from pigs; pigs are considered unclean to Muslims, and cows are sacred to Hindus. Since loading a rifle involved biting the end off the waxed cartridge, these rumours provoked considerable unrest.

In Meerut, the situation was handled with a singular lack of judgment. The commanding officer lined up his soldiers and ordered them to bite off the ends of their issued bullets. Those who refused were immediately marched off to prison. The following morning, the soldiers of the garrison rebelled, shot their officers and marched to Delhi. Of the 74 Indian battalions of the Bengal army, seven (one of them Gurkhas) remained loyal, 20 were disarmed and the other 47 mutinied. The soldiers and peasants rallied around the ageing Mughal emperor in Delhi. They held Delhi for some months and besieged the British residency in Lucknow for five months before they were finally suppressed. The incident left festering scars on both sides.

Almost immediately the East India Company was wound up and direct control of the country was assumed by the British government, which announced its support for the existing rulers of the princely states, claiming they would not interfere in local matters as long as the states remained loyal to the British.

1835–1858	1857	1858	1869
Life of Lakshmi Bai, Rani of Jhansi. The queen of the Maratha state led her army against the British, who seized Jhansi after her husband's death. She died in battle.	The First War of Independence (Indian Uprising) against the British. With no national leader, freedom fighters coerce the Mughal king, Bahadur Shah Zafar, to proclaim himself emperor of India.	British government assumes control over India – with power officially transferred from the East India Company to the Crown – beginning the period known as the British Raj.	Opening of Suez Canal accelerates trade from Europe and makes Bombay (Mumbai) India's first port of call; trip from England goes from three months to three weeks.

army contingent was sent to quell the unrest. Under direct orders of the officer in charge, they ruthlessly fired into a crowd of unarmed protesters. News of the massacre spread rapidly throughout India, turning huge numbers of otherwise apolitical Indians into Congress supporters.

At this time, the Congress movement found a new leader in Mohandas Gandhi. Not everyone involved in the struggle agreed with or followed Gandhi's policy of nonviolence, yet the Congress Party and Gandhi remained at the forefront of the push for independence.

As political power-sharing began to look more likely, and the mass movement led by Gandhi gained momentum, the Muslim reaction was to consider its own immediate future. The large Muslim minority realised that an independent India would be dominated by Hindus and that, while Gandhi's approach was fair-minded, others in the Congress Party might not be so willing to share power. By the 1930s Muslims were raising the possibility of a separate Islamic state.

Political events were partially disrupted by WWII when large numbers of Congress supporters were jailed to prevent disruption to the war effort.

Mahatma Gandhi

One of the great figures of the 20th century, Mohandas Karamchand Gandhi was born on 2 October 1869 in Porbandar, Gujarat. After studying in London (1888–91), he worked as a barrister in South Africa. Here, the young Gandhi became politicised, railing against the discrimination he encountered. He soon became the spokesperson for the Indian community and championed equality for all.

Gandhi returned to India in 1915 with the doctrine of ahimsa (nonviolence) central to his political plans, and committed to a simple and disciplined lifestyle. He set up the Sabarmati Ashram in Ahmedabad, which was innovative for its admission of Untouchables.

Within a year, Gandhi had won his first victory, defending farmers in Bihar from exploitation. This was when it's said he first received the title 'Mahatma' (Great Soul) from an admirer (often said to be Bengali poet Rabindranath Tagore). The passage of the discriminatory Rowlatt Acts, which allowed certain political cases to be tried without juries, in 1919 spurred him to further action, and he organised a national protest. In the days that followed this hartal (strike), feelings ran high throughout the country. After the massacre of unarmed protesters in Amritsar, a deeply shocked Gandhi immediately called off the movement.

By 1920 Gandhi was a key figure in the Indian National Congress, and he coordinated a national campaign of noncooperation or satyagraha (nonviolent protest) to British rule, with the effect of raising nationalist feeling while earning the lasting enmity of the British. In early 1930 Gandhi captured the imagination of the country, and the world, when

Gandhian Sites

Raj Ghat, Delhi

Gandhi Smriti, Delhi

Anand Bhavan, Allahabad

Sabarmati Ashram, Ahmedabad

Kaba Gandhi No Delo, Rajkot

Mani Bhavan, Mumbai

Gandhi National Memorial, Pune

1885	1919	1930	1940
The Indian National Congress, India's first home-grown political organisation, is set up. It brings educated Indians together and plays a key role in India's enduring freedom struggle.	The massacre, on 13 April, of unarmed Indian protesters at Jallianwala Bagh in Amritsar (Punjab). Gandhi responds with his program of civil (nonviolent) disobedience against the British government.	Salt Satyagraha begins on 12 March. Gandhi embarks on a 24-day walk from his Sabarmati Ashram near Ahmedabad to the coastal village of Dandi to protest the British salt tax.	The Muslim League adopts its Lahore Resolution, which champions greater Muslim autonomy in India. Campaigns for the creation of a separate Islamic nation are spearheaded by Mohammed Ali Jinnah.

GANDHI

he led a march of several thousand followers from Ahmedabad to Dandi on the coast of Gujarat. On arrival, Gandhi ceremoniously made salt by evaporating sea water, thus publicly defying the much-hated salt tax; not for the first time, he was imprisoned. Released in 1931 to represent the Indian National Congress at the second Round Table Conference in London, he won the hearts of many British people but failed to gain any real concessions from the government.

Disillusioned with politics, he resigned his parliamentary seat in 1934. He returned spectacularly to the fray in 1942 with the Quit India campaign, in which he urged the British to leave India immediately. His actions were deemed subversive, and he and most of the Congress leadership were imprisoned.

In the frantic Independence bargaining that followed the end of WWII, Gandhi was largely excluded and watched helplessly as plans were made to partition the country – a dire tragedy in his eyes. Gandhi stood almost alone in urging tolerance and the preservation of a single India, and his work on behalf of members of all communities drew resentment from some Hindu hardliners. On his way to a prayer meeting in Delhi on 30 January 1948, he was assassinated by a Hindu zealot, Nathuram Godse.

Independence & the Partition of India

The Labour Party victory in the British elections in July 1945 dramatically altered the political landscape. For the first time, Indian independence was accepted as a legitimate goal. This new goodwill did not, however, translate into any new wisdom as to how to reconcile the divergent wishes of the two major Indian parties. Mohammed Ali Jinnah, the leader of the Muslim League, championed a separate Islamic state, while the Congress Party, led by Jawaharlal Nehru, campaigned for an independent greater India.

A golden oldie, *Gandhi,* directed by Richard Attenborough, is one of the few movies that adeptly captures the grand canvas that is India in tracing the country's rocky road to Independence.

In early 1946 a British mission failed to bring the two sides together, and the country slid closer towards civil war. A 'Direct Action Day', called by the Muslim League in August 1946, led to the slaughter of Hindus in Calcutta, which prompted reprisals against Muslims. In February 1947 the nervous British government made the momentous decision that Independence would come by June 1948. In the meantime, the viceroy, Lord Archibald Wavell, was replaced by Lord Louis Mountbatten.

The new viceroy encouraged the rival factions to agree upon a united India, but to no avail. A decision was made to divide the country, with Gandhi the only staunch opponent. Faced with increasing civil violence, Mountbatten made the precipitous decision to bring forward Independence to 15 August 1947.

Dividing the country into separate Hindu and Muslim territories was immensely tricky; the dividing line proved almost impossible to draw.

1942
Mahatma Gandhi launches the Quit India campaign, demanding that the British leave India without delay and allow the country to get on with the business of self-governance.

1947
India gains independence on 15 August. Pakistan is formed a day earlier. Partition is followed by mass cross-border exodus, as Hindus and Muslims migrate to their respective nations.

→ Bronze statue of Mahatma Gandhi

DALLAS STRIBLEY / GETTY IMAGES ©

Some areas were clearly Hindu or Muslim, but others had evenly mixed populations, and there were 'islands' of communities in areas predominantly settled by other religions. Moreover, the two overwhelmingly Muslim regions were on opposite sides of the country and, therefore, Pakistan would inevitably have an eastern and western half divided by a hostile India. The instability of this arrangement was self-evident, but it was 25 years before the split finally came and East Pakistan became Bangladesh.

An independent British referee was given the odious task of drawing the borders, well aware that the effects would be catastrophic for countless people. The decisions were fraught with impossible dilemmas. Calcutta, with its Hindu majority, port facilities and jute mills, was divided from East Bengal, which had a Muslim majority, large-scale jute production, no mills and no port facilities. One million Bengalis became refugees in the mass movement across the new border.

The problem was worse in Punjab, where intercommunity antagonisms were already running at fever pitch. Punjab, one of the most fertile and affluent regions of the country, had large Muslim, Hindu and Sikh communities. The Sikhs had already campaigned unsuccessfully for their own state and now saw their homeland divided down the middle. The new border ran straight between Punjab's two major cities, Lahore and Amritsar. Prior to Independence, Lahore's population of 1.2 million included approximately 500,000 Hindus and 100,000 Sikhs. When the dust had finally settled, roughly 1000 Hindus and Sikhs remained.

Punjab contained all the ingredients for an epic disaster, but the resulting bloodshed was far worse than anticipated. Huge population exchanges took place. Trains full of Muslims, fleeing westward, were held up and slaughtered by Hindu and Sikh mobs. Hindus and Sikhs fleeing to the east suffered the same fate at Muslim hands. The army that was sent to maintain order proved totally inadequate and, at times, all too ready to join the sectarian carnage. By the time the Punjab chaos had run its course, more than 10 million people had changed sides and at least 500,000 had been killed.

India and Pakistan became sovereign nations under the British Commonwealth in August 1947 as planned, but the violence, migrations and the integration of a few states, especially Kashmir, continued. The Constitution of India was at last adopted in November 1949 and went into effect on 26 January, 1950, and, after untold struggles, independent India officially became a Republic.

PARTITION

Deepa Mehta's 1998 film *Earth* is a dramatic retelling of the violence of Partition through the eyes of a young girl in Lahore.

After Independence

Jawaharlal Nehru tried to steer India towards a policy of nonalignment, balancing cordial relations with Britain and Commonwealth member-

1947–48	1948	1948	1948–56
First war between India and Pakistan takes place after the (procrastinating) maharaja of Kashmir signs the Instrument of Accession that cedes his state to India. Pakistan challenges the document's legality.	Mahatma Gandhi is assassinated in New Delhi by Nathuram Godse on 30 January. Godse and his co-conspirator, Narayan Apte, are later tried, convicted and executed (by hanging).	Asaf Jah VII, Hyderabad's last nizam, surrenders to the Indian government on 17 September. The Muslim dynasty was receiving support from Pakistan but had refused to join either new nation.	Rajasthan takes shape, as the princely states form a beeline to sign the Instrument of Accession, giving up their territories which are incorporated into the newly formed Republic of India.

ship with moves towards the former USSR. The latter was due partly to conflicts with China, and US support for its arch-enemy Pakistan.

The 1960s and 1970s were tumultuous times for India. A border war with China in what was then known as the North-East Frontier Area (NEFA; now the Northeast States) and Ladakh, resulted in the loss of Aksai Chin (Ladakh) and smaller NEFA areas. Wars with Pakistan in 1965 (over Kashmir) and 1971 (over Bangladesh) also contributed to a sense among many Indians of having enemies on all sides.

In the midst of it all, the hugely popular Nehru died in 1964 and his daughter Indira Gandhi (no relation to Mahatma Gandhi) was elected as prime minister in 1966. Indira Gandhi, like Nehru before her, loomed large over the country she governed. Unlike Nehru, however, she was always a profoundly controversial figure whose historical legacy remains hotly disputed.

In 1975, facing serious opposition and unrest, she declared a state of emergency (which later became known as the Emergency). Freed

THE KASHMIR CONFLICT

Kashmir is the most enduring symbol of the turbulent partition of India. In the lead up to Independence, the delicate task of drawing the India–Pakistan border was complicated by the fact that India's 'princely states' were nominally independent. As part of the settlement process, local rulers were asked which country they wished to belong to. Kashmir was a predominantly Muslim state with a Hindu maharaja, Hari Singh, who tried to delay his decision. A ragtag Pashtun (Pakistani) army crossed the border, intent on racing to Srinagar and annexing Kashmir for Pakistan. In the face of this advance, the maharaja panicked and requested armed assistance from India. The Indian army arrived only just in time to prevent the fall of Srinagar, and the maharaja signed the Instrument of Accession, tying Kashmir to India, in October 1947. The legality of the document was immediately disputed by Pakistan, and the two nations went to war, just two months after Independence.

In 1948 the fledgling UN Security Council called for a referendum (which remains a central plank of Pakistani policy) to decide the status of Kashmir. A UN-brokered ceasefire in 1949 kept the countries on either side of a demarcation line, called the Cease-Fire Line (later to become the Line of Control, or LOC), with little else resolved. Two-thirds of Kashmir fell on the Indian side of the LOC, which remains the frontier, but neither side accepts this as the official border. The Indian state of Jammu & Kashmir, as it has stood since that time, incorporates Ladakh (divided between Muslims and Buddhists), Jammu (with a Hindu majority) and the 130km-long, 55km-wide Kashmir Valley (with a Muslim majority and most of the state's inhabitants). On the Pakistani side, over three million Kashmiris live in Azad (Free) Kashmir. Since the frontier was drawn, incursions across the LOC have occurred with dangerous regularity. See p1104 for more information.

1949	1950	1962	1965
The Constitution of India, drafted over two years by a 308-member Constituent Assembly, is adopted. The Assembly is chaired by BR Ambedkar and includes members from scheduled castes.	Constitution goes into effect on 26 January, and India becomes a republic. Date commemorates the Declaration of Independence, put forth by the Indian National Congress in 1930.	Border war (known as the Sino-Indian War) with China over the North-East Frontier Area and Ladakh. China successfully captures the disputed territory and ends the war with a unilateral ceasefire.	Skirmishes in Kashmir and Gujarat's disputed Rann of Kutch flare into the Second India-Pakistan War, which involved the biggest tank battles since WWII. The war ends with a UN-mandated ceasefire.

of parliamentary constraints, Gandhi was able to boost the economy, control inflation remarkably well and decisively increase efficiency. On the negative side, political opponents often found themselves in prison, India's judicial system was turned into a puppet theatre and the press was fettered.

Gandhi's government was bundled out of office in the 1977 elections, but the 1980 election brought Indira Gandhi back to power with a larger majority than ever before, firmly laying the foundation for the Nehru-Gandhi family dynasty that would continue to dominate Indian politics to the present day.

Makers of Modern India, edited by Ramachandra Guha, is a fascinating collection of speeches and writings by 19 of modern India's most influential activists and thinkers.

1966	1971	1972	1975
Indira Gandhi, daughter of Jawaharlal Nehru, becomes prime minister of India, remembered today for her heavy-handed rule. She has been India's only female prime minister.	East Pakistan champions independence from West Pakistan. India gets involved, sparking the Third India-Pakistan War. West Pakistan surrenders, losing sovereignty of East Pakistan, which becomes Bangladesh.	The Simla Agreement between India and Pakistan attempts to normalise relations. The Kashmiri ceasefire line is formalised: the 'Line of Control' remains the de-facto border between the two countries.	In a questionable move, Prime Minister Indira Gandhi declares a state of emergency under Article 352 of the Indian Constitution, in response to growing civil unrest and political opposition.

The Way of Life

Spirituality is the common thread in the richly diverse tapestry that is India. It, along with family, lies at the heart of society – for most Indians, the idea of being unmarried by one's mid-30s is somewhat unpalatable. Despite the rising number of nuclear families – primarily in the more cosmopolitan cities such as Mumbai, Bengaluru and Delhi – the extended family remains a cornerstone in both urban and rural India, with males – usually the breadwinners – generally considered the head of the household.

Matchmaking has embraced the cyber age, with popular sites including www.shaadi.com, www.bharatmatrimony.com and, more recently, www.secondshaadi.com – for those seeking a partner again.

Marriage, Birth & Death

Marriage is an auspicious event for Indians and although 'love marriages' have spiralled upwards in recent times (mainly in urban hubs), most Hindu marriages are still arranged. Discreet enquiries are made within the community. If a suitable match is not found, the help of professional matchmakers may be sought, or advertisements may be placed in newspapers and/or on the internet. The horoscopes of both potential partners are checked and, if propitious, there's a meeting between the families.

Dowry, although illegal, is still a key issue in some arranged marriages (mostly in conservative communities), with some families plunging into debt to raise the required cash and merchandise (from cars and computers to refrigerators and televisions). Health workers claim that India's high rate of abortion of female foetuses (sex identification medical tests being banned in India, but they still clandestinely occur in some clinics) is predominantly due to the financial burden of providing a daughter's dowry.

The Hindu wedding ceremony is officiated over by a priest and the marriage is formalised when the couple walk around a sacred fire seven times. Despite the existence of nuclear families, it's still the norm for a wife to live with her husband's family once married and assume the household duties outlined by her mother-in-law. Not surprisingly, the mother–daughter-in-law relationship can be a thorny one, as portrayed in the various Indian TV soap operas which largely revolve around this theme.

Divorce and remarriage is becoming more common (primarily in India's bigger cities), but divorce is still not granted by courts as a matter of routine and is generally not looked upon very favourably by society. Among the higher castes, widows are traditionally expected not to remarry and are admonished to wear white and live pious, celibate lives.

The birth of a child, in Hindu-majority India, is another momentous occasion, with its own set of special ceremonies, which take place at various auspicious times during the early years of childhood. These include the casting of the child's first horoscope, name-giving, feeding the first solid food, and the first hair cutting.

Hindus cremate their dead, and funeral ceremonies are designed to purify and console both the living and the deceased. An important aspect of the proceedings is the *sharadda,* paying respect to one's ancestors by offering water and rice cakes. It's an observance that's repeated at each anniversary of the death. After the cremation the ashes are collected and, 13 days after the death (when blood relatives are deemed ritually pure), a member of the family usually scatters them in a holy river such as the Ganges or in the ocean.

The Caste System

Although the Indian constitution does not recognise the caste system, caste still wields considerable influence, especially in rural India, where the caste you are born into largely determines your social standing in the community. It can also influence your vocational and marriage prospects. Castes are further divided into thousands of *jati,* groups of 'families' or social communities, which are sometimes but not always linked to occupation. Conservative Hindus will only marry someone of the same *jati.*

According to tradition, caste is the basic social structure of Hindu society. Living a righteous life and fulfilling your dharma (moral duty) raises your chances of being reborn into a higher caste and thus into better circumstances. Hindus are born into one of four varnas (castes): Brahmin (priests and scholars), Kshatriya (soldiers and administrators), Vaishya (merchants) and Shudra (labourers). The Brahmins were said to have emerged from the mouth of Lord Brahma at the moment of creation, Kshatriyas were said to have come from his arms, Vaishyas from his thighs and Shudras from his feet.

Beneath the four main castes are the Dalits (formerly known as Untouchables), who hold menial jobs such as sweepers (lowest caste servants, performing the most menial of tasks) and latrine cleaners. The word 'pariah' is derived from the name of a Tamil Dalit group, the Paraiyars. Some Dalit leaders, such as the renowned Dr BR Ambedkar (1891–1956), sought to change their status by adopting another faith; in his case it was Buddhism. At the bottom of the social heap are the Denotified Tribes. They were known as the Criminal Tribes until 1952, when a reforming law officially recognised 198 tribes and castes. Many are nomadic or seminomadic tribes, forced by the wider community to eke out a living on society's fringes.

To improve the Dalits' position, the government reserves considerable numbers of public-sector jobs, parliamentary seats and university places for them. Today these quotas account for almost 25% of government jobs and university (student) positions. The situation varies regionally, as different political leaders chase caste vote-banks by promising to include them in reservations. The reservation system, while generally regarded in a favourable light, has also been criticised for unfairly blocking tertiary and employment opportunities for those who would have otherwise got positions on merit.

Pilgrimage

Devout Hindus are expected to go on a *yatra* (pilgrimage) at least once a year. Pilgrimages are undertaken to implore the gods or goddesses to grant a wish, to take the ashes of a cremated relative to a holy river, or to gain spiritual merit. India has thousands of holy sites to which pilgrims travel; the elderly often make Varanasi their final one, as it's believed that dying in this sacred city releases a person from the cycle of rebirth.

The Wonder That Was India by AL Basham gives descriptions of Indian civilisations, major religions and social customs – a good thematic approach to weave the disparate strands together.

Based on Rabindranath Tagore's novel, *Chokher Bali* (directed by Rituparno Ghosh) is a poignant film about a young widow living in early-20th-century Bengal who challenges the 'rules of widowhood' – something unthinkable in that era.

RANGOLIS

Rangolis, the striking and breathtakingly intricate chalk, rice-paste or coloured powder designs (also called *kolams*) that adorn thresholds, especially in South India, are both auspicious and symbolic. *Rangolis* are traditionally drawn at sunrise and are sometimes made of rice-flour paste, which may be eaten by little creatures – symbolising a reverence for even the smallest living things. Deities are deemed to be attracted to a beautiful *rangoli,* which may also signal to sadhus (holy people) that they will be offered food at a particular house. Some people believe that *rangolis* protect against the evil eye.

Most festivals in India are rooted in religion and are thus a magnet for throngs of pilgrims. This is something that travellers should keep in mind, even at those festivals that may have a carnivalesque sheen.

Kumbh Mela

If crowds worry you, stay away. This one's big. Very big. Held four times every 12 years at four different locations across central and northern India, the Kumbh Mela is the largest religious congregation on the planet. This vast celebration attracts tens of millions of Hindu pilgrims, including mendicant *nagas* (naked sadhus, or holy people) from radical Hindu monastic orders. The Kumbh Mela doesn't belong to any particular caste or creed – devotees from all branches of Hinduism come together to experience the electrifying sensation of mass belief and to take a ceremonial dip in the sacred Ganges, Shipra or Godavari Rivers.

The origins of the festival go back to the battle for supremacy between good and evil. In the Hindu creation myths, the gods and demons fought a great battle for a *kumbh* (pitcher) containing the nectar of immortality. Vishnu got hold of the container and spirited it away, but in flight four drops spilt on the earth – at Allahabad, Haridwar, Nasik and Ujjain. Celebrations at each of these cities last for around six weeks but are centred on just a handful of auspicious bathing dates, normally six. The Allahabad event, known as the Maha (Great) Kumbh Mela, is even larger with even bigger crowds. Each location also holds an Ardh (Half) Mela every six years and a smaller, annual Magh Mela.

CASTE SYSTEM

If you want to learn more about India's caste system these two books are a good start: *Interrogating Caste*, by Dipankar Gupta and *Translating Caste*, edited by Tapan Basu.

Women in India

According to the most recent census, India's population is comprised of 586 million women, with an estimated 68% of those working (mostly as labourers) in the agricultural sector.

Women in India are entitled to vote and own property. While the percentage of women in politics has risen over the past decade, they're still notably underrepresented in the national parliament, accounting for around 10% of parliamentary members.

Although the professions are male dominated, women are steadily making inroads, especially in urban centres. Kerala was India's first state to break societal norms by recruiting female police officers in 1938. It was also the first state to establish an all-female police station (1973). For village women it's much more difficult to get ahead, but groups such as the Self-Employed Women's Association (SEWA) in Gujarat have shown what's possible. Here, socially disadvantaged women have been organised into unions, offering at least some lobbying power against discriminatory and exploitative work practices.

INDIAN ATTIRE

Widely worn by Indian women, the elegant sari comes in a single piece (between 5m and 9m long and 1m wide) and is tucked and pleated into place without the need for pins or buttons. Worn with the sari is the choli (tight-fitting blouse) and a drawstring petticoat. The *palloo* is the part of the sari draped over the shoulder. Also commonly worn is the *salwar kameez*, a traditional dresslike tunic and trouser combination accompanied by a *dupatta* (long scarf). Saris and *salwar kameez* come in a fantastic range of fabrics, colours and designs. Traditional attire for men includes the dhoti, and in the south the lungi and the *mundu* are also quite often worn. The dhoti is a loose, long loincloth pulled up between the legs. The lungi is more like a sarong, with its end usually sewn up like a tube. The *mundu* is like a lungi but is always white.

There are regional and religious variations in costume – for example, you may see Muslim women wearing the all-enveloping burka.

Local women in colourful attire

In low-income families, especially, girls can be regarded as a serious financial liability because at marriage a dowry must often be supplied.

For the urban middle-class woman, life is materially much more comfortable, but pressures still exist. Broadly speaking, she is far more likely to receive a tertiary education, but once married is still usually expected to 'fit in' with her in-laws and be a homemaker above all else. Like her village counterpart, if she fails to live up to expectations – even if it's just not being able to produce a grandson – the consequences can sometimes be dire, as demonstrated by the extreme practice of 'bride burning', wherein a wife is doused with flammable liquid and set alight. Reliable statistics are unavailable, but some women's groups claim that for every reported case, roughly 300 go unreported, and that less than 10% of the reported cases are pursued through the legal system.

Although the constitution allows for divorcees (and widows) to remarry, relatively few reportedly do so, simply because divorcees are traditionally considered outcasts from society, most evidently so beyond big cities. Divorce rates in India are among the worlds' lowest, despite having risen from around seven in 1000 in 1991, to roughly 12 in 1000 in 2012. Most divorces take place in urban centres and are generally deemed less socially unacceptable among those occupying the upper echelons of society.

In October 2006, following women's civil rights campaigns, the Indian parliament passed a landmark bill (on top of existing legislation) which gives women who are suffering domestic violence increased protection and rights. Prior to this legislation, although women could lodge police complaints against abusive spouses, they weren't automatically entitled to a share of the marital property or to ongoing financial support. The new law purports that any form of physical, sexual (including marital rape), emotional and economic abuse entails not only domestic violence, but also

TRIBAL AFFAIRS

Read more about India's tribal communities at www.tribal.nic.in, a site maintained by the Indian government's Ministry of Tribal Affairs.

CRICKET

human rights violations. Perpetrators face imprisonment and fines. Under this law, abused women are legally permitted to remain in the marital house. In addition, the law prohibits emotional and physical bullying in relation to dowry demands. Critics claim that many women, especially those outside India's larger cities, are still reluctant to seek legal protection because of the social stigma involved. And despite the good intentions of the law reforms, the conviction rate for crimes against women remains relatively low; around 25% in 2011 as compared to 45% in the 1970s.

According to India's National Crime Records Bureau (NCRB), crimes against women have jumped by 7.1% between 2010 and 2011), with an increase in the number of rapes reported too. Human rights analysts say that many sexual assaults go unreported, largely due to family pressure and/or shame, especially if the perpetrator is known to the family. The NCRB reported that 228,650 of the total 256,329 violent crimes recorded in 2011 were against women. Of these, 8618 were dowry-related deaths, 24,206 were rape (an increase of 9% from the previous year) and 42,968 were molestation.

Following the highly publicised brutal gangrape (and subsequent death) of a 23-year-old Indian student in Delhi in December 2012, tens of thousands of people protested in the capital and beyond, demanding swift government action to address the country's escalating gender-based violence. The government was criticised for its slow response to the public outrage and later vowed to deliver harsher punishments (including the death penalty) for sex offenders. Time will tell whether any reforms introduced prove effective.

Sport

Cricket lovers are likely to be bowled over by *The Illustrated History of Indian Cricket* by Boria Majumdar and *The States of Indian Cricket* by Ramachandra Guha.

In India, it's all about cricket! Cutting across all echelons of society, cricket is more than just a national sporting obsession – it's a matter of enormous patriotism, especially evident whenever India plays against Pakistan. Matches between these South Asian neighbours – which have had rocky relations since Independence – attract especially passionate support, and the players of both sides are under immense pressure to do their respective countries proud. The most celebrated contemporary Indian cricketer is Sachin Tendulkar – fondly dubbed the 'Little Master' – who, in 2012, became the world's only player to score 100 international centuries. Tendulkar announced his retirement from one-day international matches in December 2012. India's first recorded cricket match was in 1721. It won its first test series in 1952 in Chennai against England. Today cricket – especially the recently rolled out Twenty20 for-

ADIVASIS

India's Adivasis (tribal communities; Adivasi translates to 'original inhabitant' in Sanskrit) have origins that precede the Vedic Aryans and the Dravidians of the south. Today, they constitute less than 10% of the population and are comprised of more than 400 different tribal groups. The literacy rate for Adivasis falls significantly below the national average. Historically, contact between Adivasis and Hindu villagers on the plains rarely led to friction as there was little or no competition for resources and land. However, in recent decades an increasing number of Adivasis have been dispossessed of their ancestral land and turned into impoverished labourers. Although they still have political representation thanks to a parliamentary quota system, the dispossession and exploitation of Adivasis has reportedly at times been with the connivance of officialdom – an accusation the government denies. Whatever the arguments, unless more is done, the Adivasis' future is an uncertain one.

Read more about Adivasis in *Archaeology and History: Early Settlements in the Andaman Islands* by Zarine Cooper, *The Tribals of India* by Sunil Janah and *Tribes of India: The Struggle for Survival* by Christoph von Fürer-Haimendorf.

HIJRAS

India's most visible nonheterosexual group is the *hijras*, a caste of transvestites and eunuchs who dress in women's clothing. Some are gay, some are hermaphrodites and some were unfortunate enough to be kidnapped and castrated. Since it has long been frowned upon to live openly as a gay man in India, *hijras* get around this by becoming, in effect, a third sex of sorts. They work mainly as uninvited entertainers at weddings and celebrations of the birth of male children, and possibly as prostitutes.

Read more about *hijras* in *The Invisibles* by Zia Jaffrey and *Ardhanarishvara the Androgyne* by Dr Alka Pande.

mat (www.cricket20.com) – is big business in India, attracting lucrative sponsorship deals and celebrity status for its players. The sport has not been without its murky side though, with Indian cricketers among those embroiled in match-fixing scandals over past years. International games are played at various centres – see Indian newspapers or check online for details about matches that coincide with your visit. Keep your finger on the cricketing pulse at www.espncricinfo.com (rated most highly by many cricket aficionados) and www.cricbuzz.com.

While cricket is the overwhelmingly favourite sport of contemporary India, the country is also known for its historical links to horse polo, which intermittently thrived on the subcontinent (especially among nobility) until Independence, after which patronage steeply declined due to dwindling funds. Today there's a renewed interest in polo thanks to beefed-up sponsorship and, although it still remains an elite sport, it's attracting more attention from the country's burgeoning upper middle class. The origins of polo are not completely clear. Believed to have its roots in Persia and China around 2000 years ago, on the subcontinent it's thought to have first been played in Baltistan (in present-day Pakistan). Some say that Emperor Akbar (who reigned in India from 1556 to 1605) first introduced rules to the game , but that polo, as it's played today, was largely influenced by a British cavalry regiment stationed in India during the 1870s. A set of international rules was implemented after WWI. The world's oldest surviving polo club, established in 1862, is in Kolkata – see Calcutta Polo Club (www.calcuttapolo.com). Polo takes place during the cooler winter months in major cities including Delhi, Jaipur, Mumbai and Kolkata. It is also occasionally played in Ladakh and Manipur.

Despite being India's national sport, field hockey no longer enjoys the same fervent following it once did, largely due to the unassailable popularity of cricket, which snatches most of India's sponsorship funding. During its golden era, between 1928 and 1956, India won six consecutive Olympic gold medals in hockey; it later bagged two further Olympic gold medals, one in 1964 and the other in 1980. Recent initiatives to ignite renewed interest in the game have had mixed results. At the time of writing, India's national men's/women's hockey world rankings were 11/12 respectively. Tap into India's hockey scene at Indian Hockey (www.indianhockey.com) and Indian Field Hockey (www.bharatiyahockey.org).

Other sports which are growing in popularity in India include tennis (the country's star performers are Sania Mirza, Leander Paes and Mahesh Bhupathi) – to delve deeper, click www.aitatennis.com; football (soccer), which is particularly strong in the country's east and south – in 2013 India occupied the 166th spot in the FIFA world rankings; and horse racing, which is reasonably popular in the larger cities such as Mumbai, Delhi, Kolkata and Bengaluru.

If you'd like to see a sporting event, check local newspapers (or ask at a tourist office) for current details about dates and venues.

INDIAN DIASPORA

India has one of the world's largest diasporas – over 25 million people – with Indian banks holding upwards of US$50 billion in Non-Resident Indian (NRI) accounts.

Spiritual India

From elaborate city shrines to simple village temples, spirituality suffuses almost every facet of life in India. The nation's major faith, Hinduism, is practised by around 80% of the population and it, along with Buddhism, Jainism and Zoroastrianism, is one of the world's oldest extant religions, with roots extending beyond 1000 BC. The mind-stirring sight of sacred architecture and the soul-warming sound of bhajans and qawwali, are bound to burn bright in your memory long after you've left India.

Hinduism

The Hindu pantheon is said to have a staggering 330 million deities; those worshipped are a matter of personal choice or tradition.

Hinduism has no founder or central authority and it isn't a proselytising religion. Essentially, Hindus believe in Brahman, who is eternal, uncreated and infinite. Everything that exists emanates from Brahman and will ultimately return to it. The multitude of gods and goddesses are merely manifestations – knowable aspects of this formless phenomenon.

Hindus believe that earthly life is cyclical: you are born again and again (a process known as 'samsara'), the quality of these rebirths being dependent upon your karma (conduct or action) in previous lives. Living a righteous life and fulfilling your dharma (moral code of behaviour; social duty) will enhance your chances of being born into a higher caste and better circumstances. Alternatively, if enough bad karma has accumulated, rebirth may take animal form. But it's only as a human that you can gain sufficient self-knowledge to escape the cycle of reincarnation and achieve moksha (liberation).

Gods & Goddesses

All Hindu deities are regarded as a manifestation of Brahman, who is often described as having three main representations, the Trimurti: Brahma, Vishnu and Shiva.

Brahman

The One; the ultimate reality. Brahman is formless, eternal and the source of all existence. Brahman is *nirguna* (without attributes), as opposed to all the other gods and goddesses, which are manifestations of Brahman and therefore *saguna* (with attributes).

Brahma

Only during the creation of the universe does Brahma play an active role. At other times he is in meditation. His consort is Saraswati, the goddess of learning, and his vehicle is a swan. He is sometimes shown sitting on a lotus that rises from Vishnu's navel, symbolising the interdependence of the gods. Brahma is generally depicted with four (crowned and bearded) heads, each turned towards a point of the compass.

Vishnu

The preserver or sustainer, Vishnu is associated with 'right action'. He protects and sustains all that is good in the world. He is usually depicted with four arms, holding a lotus, a conch shell (it can be blown like a trumpet so symbolises the cosmic vibration from which existence emanates), a discus and a mace. His consort is Lakshmi, the goddess of wealth, and his vehicle is Garuda, the man-bird creature. The Ganges is said to flow from his feet.

Shiva

Shiva is the destroyer – to deliver salvation – without whom creation couldn't occur. Shiva's creative role is phallically symbolised by his representation as the frequently worshipped lingam. With 1008 names, Shiva takes many forms, including Nataraja, lord of the *tandava* (cosmic victory dance), who paces out the creation and destruction of the cosmos.

Sometimes Shiva has snakes draped around his neck and is shown holding a trident (representative of the Trimurti) as a weapon while riding Nandi, his bull. Nandi symbolises power and potency, justice and moral order. Shiva's consort, Parvati, is capable of taking many forms.

Shiva is sometimes characterised as the lord of yoga, a Himalaya-dwelling ascetic with matted hair, an ash-smeared body and a third eye symbolising wisdom.

Other Prominent Deities

Elephant-headed Ganesh is the god of good fortune, remover of obstacles, and patron of scribes (the broken tusk he holds was used to write sections of the Mahabharata). His animal vehicle is Mooshak (a ratlike creature). How Ganesh came to have an elephant's head is a story with several variations. One legend says that Ganesh was born to Parvati in the absence of his father Shiva, and so grew up not knowing him. One day, as Ganesh stood guard while his mother bathed, Shiva returned and asked to be let into Parvati's presence. Ganesh, who didn't recognise Shiva, refused. Enraged, Shiva lopped off Ganesh's head, only to later discover, much to his horror, that he had slaughtered his own son. He vowed to replace Ganesh's head with that of the first creature he came across, which happened to be an elephant.

Another prominent deity, Krishna is an incarnation of Vishnu sent to earth to fight for good and combat evil. His alliances with the *gopis* (milkmaids) and his love for Radha have inspired countless paintings and songs. Depicted with blue-hued skin, Krishna is often seen playing the flute.

Hanuman is the hero of the Ramayana and loyal ally of Rama. He embodies the concept of bhakti (devotion). He's the king of the monkeys, but is capable of taking on other forms.

Among the Shaivite (followers of the Shiva movement), Shakti, the goddess as mother and creator, is worshipped as a force in her own right. The concept of *shakti* is embodied in the ancient goddess Devi (divine mother), who is also manifested as Durga and, in a fiercer evil-destroying incarnation, Kali. Other widely worshipped goddesses include Lakshmi, the goddess of wealth, and Saraswati, the goddess of learning.

Did you know that blood-drinking Kali is another form of milk-giving Gauri? *Myth = Mithya: A Handbook of Hindu Mythology* by Devdutt Pattanaik sheds light on this and other fascinating Hindu folklore.

Sacred Texts

Hindu sacred texts fall into two categories: those believed to be the word of god (*shruti,* meaning 'heard') and those produced by people (smriti, meaning 'remembered'). The Vedas are regarded as *shruti* knowledge and are considered the authoritative basis for Hinduism. The oldest of the Vedic texts, the Rig-Veda, was compiled over 3000 years ago. Within its 1028 verses are prayers for prosperity and longevity as well as an explanation of the universe's origins. The Upanishads, the last parts of the Vedas, reflect on the mystery of death and emphasise the oneness of the universe. The oldest of the Vedic texts were written in Vedic Sanskrit (related to Old Persian). Later texts were composed in classical Sanskrit, but many have been translated into the vernacular.

The smriti texts comprise a collection of literature spanning centuries and include expositions on the proper performance of domestic ceremonies as well as the proper pursuit of government, economics and religious law. Among its well-known works are the Ramayana and Mahabharata, as well as the Puranas, which expand on the epics and promote the notion of the Trimurti. Unlike the Vedas, reading the Puranas is not restricted to initiated higher-caste males.

The Mahabharata

Thought to have been composed around 1000 BC, the Mahabharata focuses on the exploits of Krishna. By about 500 BC the Mahabharata had evolved into a far more complex creation with substantial additions, including the Bhagavad Gita (where Krishna proffers advice to Arjuna before a battle).

The story centres on conflict between the heroic gods (Pandavas) and the demons (Kauravas). Overseeing events is Krishna, who has taken on human form. Krishna acts as charioteer for the Pandava hero Arjuna, who eventually triumphs in a great battle against the Kauravas.

The Ramayana

Composed around the 3rd or 2nd century BC, the Ramayana is believed to be largely the work of one person, the poet Valmiki. Like the Mahabharata, it centres on conflict between the gods and the demons.

The story goes that Dasharatha, the childless king of Ayodhya, called upon the gods to provide him with a son. His wife duly gave birth to a boy. But this child, named Rama, was in fact an incarnation of Vishnu, who had assumed human form to overthrow the demon king of Lanka (now Sri Lanka), Ravana.

As an adult, Rama, who won the hand of the princess Sita in a competition, was chosen by his father to inherit his kingdom. At the last minute Rama's stepmother intervened and demanded her son, Barathan, take Rama's place. Rama, Sita and Rama's brother, Lakshmana, were exiled and went off to the forests, where Rama and Lakshmana battled demons and dark forces. Ravana's sister attempted to seduce Rama but she was rejected and, in revenge, Ravana captured Sita and spirited her away to his palace in Lanka.

Rama, assisted by an army of monkeys led by the loyal monkey god Hanuman, eventually found the palace, killed Ravana and rescued Sita. All returned victorious to Ayodhya, where Rama was welcomed by Barathan and crowned king.

Unravelling the basic tenets of Hinduism are two books both called *Hinduism: An Introduction* – one is by Shakunthala Jagannathan, the other by Dharam Vir Singh.

Naturally Sacred

Animals, particularly snakes and cows, have long been worshipped on the subcontinent. For Hindus, the cow represents fertility and nurturing, while snakes (especially cobras) are associated with fertility and welfare.

OM

One of Hinduism's most venerated symbols is 'Om'. Pronounced 'aum', it's a highly propitious mantra (sacred word or syllable). The 'three' shape symbolises the creation, maintenance and destruction of the universe (and thus the holy Trimurti). The inverted *chandra* (crescent or half moon) represents the discursive mind and the *bindu* (dot) within it, Brahman.

Buddhists believe that, if intoned often enough with complete concentration, it will lead to a state of blissful emptiness.

THE SACRED SEVEN

The number seven has special significance in Hinduism. There are seven sacred Indian cities, which are all major pilgrimage centres: Varanasi, associated with Shiva; Haridwar, where the Ganges enters the plains from the Himalaya; Ayodhya, birthplace of Rama; Dwarka, with the legendary capital of Krishna thought to be off the Gujarat coast; Mathura, birthplace of Krishna; Kanchipuram, site of the historic Shiva temples; and Ujjain, venue of the Kumbh Mela every 12 years.

There are also seven sacred rivers: the Ganges (Ganga), Saraswati (thought to be underground), Yamuna, Indus, Narmada, Godavari and Cauvery.

Naga stones (snake stones) serve the dual purpose of protecting humans from snakes and appeasing snake gods.

Plants can also have sacred associations, such as the banyan tree, which symbolises the Trimurti, while mango trees are symbolic of love – Shiva is believed to have married Parvati under one. Meanwhile, the lotus flower is said to have emerged from the primeval waters and is connected to the mythical centre of the earth through its stem. Often found in the most polluted of waters, the lotus has the remarkable ability to blossom above murky depths. The centre of the lotus corresponds to the centre of the universe, the navel of the earth: all is held together by the stem and the eternal waters. The fragile yet resolute lotus is an embodiment of beauty and strength and a reminder to Hindus of how their own lives should be. So revered has the lotus become that today it's India's national flower.

Worship

Worship and ritual play a paramount role in Hinduism. In Hindu homes you'll often find a dedicated worship area, where members of the family pray to the deities of their choice. Beyond the home, Hindus worship at temples. *Puja* is a focal point of worship and ranges from silent prayer to elaborate ceremonies. Devotees leave the temple with a handful of *prasad* (temple-blessed food) which is shared among others. Other forms of worship include *aarti* (the auspicious lighting of lamps or candles) and the playing of bhajans (devotional songs).

Islam

Islam is India's largest minority religion, followed by approximately 13.4% of the population. It's believed that Islam was introduced to northern India by Muslim rulers (in the 16th and 17th centuries the Mughal empire controlled much of North India) and to the south by Arab traders.

Islam was founded in Arabia by the Prophet Mohammed in the 7th century AD. The Arabic term *islam* means to surrender, and believers (Muslims) undertake to surrender to the will of Allah (God), which is revealed in the scriptures, the Quran. In this monotheistic religion, God's word is conveyed through prophets (messengers), of whom Mohammed was the most recent.

Following Mohammed's death, a succession dispute split the movement, and the legacy today is the Sunnis and the Shiites. Most Muslims in India are Sunnis. The Sunnis emphasise the 'well-trodden' path or the orthodox way. Shiites believe that only imams (exemplary leaders) can reveal the true meaning of the Quran.

All Muslims, however, share a belief in the Five Pillars of Islam: the shahada (declaration of faith: 'There is no God but Allah; Mohammed is his prophet'); prayer (ideally five times a day); the zakat (tax), in the form of a charitable donation; fasting (during Ramadan) for all except

A sadhu is someone who has surrendered all material possessions in pursuit of spirituality through meditation, the study of sacred texts, self-mortification and pilgrimage. Explore further in *Sadhus: India's Mystic Holy Men* by Dolf Hartsuiker.

ANATOMY OF A GOMPA

Parts of India, such as Sikkim and Ladakh, are known for their ornate, colourful gompas (Tibetan-style Buddhist monasteries). The focal point of a gompa is the *dukhang* (prayer hall), where monks assemble to chant passages from the sacred scriptures (morning prayers are a particularly atmospheric time to visit gompas). The walls may be covered in vivid murals or *thangkas* (cloth paintings) of bodhisattvas (enlightened beings) and *dharmapalas* (protector deities). By the entrance to the *dukhang* you'll usually find a mural depicting the Wheel of Life, a graphical representation of the core elements of Buddhist philosophy (see www.buddhanet.net/wheel1.htm for an interactive description of the Wheel of Life).

Most gompas hold *chaam* dances (ritual masked dances to celebrate the victory of good over evil) during major festivals. Dances to ward off evil feature masks of Mahakala, the Great Protector, usually dramatically adorned with a headdress of human skulls. The Durdag dance features skull masks depicting the Lords of the Cremation Grounds, while Shawa dancers wear masks of wild-eyed stags. These characters are often depicted with a third eye in the centre of their foreheads, signifying the need for inner reflection.

Another interesting activity at Buddhist monasteries is the production of butter sculptures, elaborate models made from coloured butter and dough. The sculptures are deliberately designed to decay, symbolising the impermanence of human existence. Many gompas also produce exquisite sand mandalas – geometric patterns made from sprinkled coloured sand, then destroyed to symbolise the futility of the physical plane.

the sick, young children, pregnant women, the elderly and those undertaking arduous journeys; and the hajj (pilgrimage) to Mecca, which every Muslim aspires to do at least once.

Sikhism

Sikhism, founded in Punjab by Guru Nanak in the 15th century, began as a reaction against the caste system and Brahmin domination of ritual. Sikhs believe in one god and although they reject the worship of idols, some keep pictures of the 10 gurus as a point of focus. The Sikhs' holy book, the Guru Granth Sahib, contains the teachings of the 10 Sikh gurus, among others. Like Hindus and Buddhists, Sikhs believe in rebirth and karma. In Sikhism, there's no ascetic or monastic tradition ending the cycles of rebirth. Almost 2% of India's citizens are Sikhs, with most living in Punjab.

Born in present-day Pakistan, Guru Nanak (1469–1539) was largely dissatisfied with both Muslim and Hindu religious practices. He believed in family life and the value of hard work – he married, had two sons and worked as a farmer when not travelling around, preaching and singing self-composed *kirtan* (Sikh devotional songs) with his Muslim musician, Mardana. He is said to have performed miracles and he encouraged meditation on God's name as a prime path to enlightenment.

Nanak believed in equality centuries before it became socially fashionable and campaigned against the caste system. He was a practical guru – 'a person who makes an honest living and shares earnings with others recognises the way to God'. He appointed his most talented disciple to be his successor, not one of his sons.

His *kirtan* are still sung in gurdwaras (Sikh temples) today and his picture is kept in millions of homes on and beyond the subcontinent.

To grasp the intricacies of Sikhism read Volume One (1469–1839) or Volume Two (1839–2004) of *A History of the Sikhs* by Khushwant Singh.

Buddhism

India's 2011 census reveals that 0.8% of the country's population is Buddhist. Bodhgaya, in the state of Bihar, is one of Buddhism's most sacred sites, drawing pilgrims from right across the world.

Buddhism arose in the 6th century BC as a reaction against the strictures of Brahminical Hinduism. Buddha (Awakened One) is believed to have lived from about 563 to 483 BC. Formerly a prince (Siddhartha Gautama), the Buddha, at the age of 29, embarked on a quest for emancipation from the world of suffering. He achieved nirvana (the state of full awareness) at Bodhgaya, aged 35. Critical of the caste system and the unthinking worship of gods, the Buddha urged his disciples to seek truth within their own experiences.

The Buddha taught that existence is based on Four Noble Truths: that life is rooted in suffering, that suffering is caused by craving, that one can find release from suffering by eliminating craving, and that the way to eliminate craving is by following the Noble Eightfold Path. This path consists of right understanding, right intention, right speech, right action, right livelihood, right effort, right awareness and right concentration. By successfully complying with these one can attain nirvana.

Buddhism had somewhat waned in parts of India by the turn of the 20th century. However, it saw a revival in the 1950s among intellectuals and Dalits who were disillusioned with the caste system. The number of followers has been further increased with the influx of Tibetan refugees. Both the current Dalai Lama and the 17th Karmapa reside in India.

Two recommended publications containing English translations of holy Hindu texts are *The Bhagavad Gita* by S Radhakrishnan and *The Valmiki Ramayana* by Romesh Dutt.

Jainism

Jainism arose in the 6th century BC as a reaction against the caste restraints and rituals of Hinduism. It was founded by Mahavira, a contemporary of the Buddha.

Jains believe that liberation can be attained by achieving complete purity of the soul. Purity means shedding all *karman,* matter generated by one's actions that binds itself to the soul. By following various austerities (eg fasting and meditation) one can shed *karman* and purify

RELIGIOUS ETIQUETTE

Whenever visiting a sacred site, dress and behave respectfully – don't wear shorts or sleeveless tops (this applies to men and women) – and refrain from smoking. Loud and intrusive behaviour isn't appreciated, and neither are public displays of affection or kidding around.

Before entering a holy place, remove your shoes (tip the shoe-minder a few rupees when retrieving them) and check if photography is allowed. You're permitted to wear socks in most places of worship – often necessary during warmer months, when floors can be uncomfortably hot.

Religious etiquette advises against touching locals on the head, or directing the soles of your feet at a person, religious shrine or image of a deity. Protocol also advises against touching someone with your feet or touching a carving of a deity.

Head cover (for women and sometimes men) is required at some places of worship – especially gurdwaras (Sikh temples) and mosques – so carry a scarf just to be on the safe side. There are some sites that don't admit women and some that deny entry to non-adherents of their faith – enquire in advance. Women may be required to sit apart from men. Jain temples request the removal of leather items you may be wearing or carrying and may also request that menstruating women not enter.

Taking photos inside a shrine, at a funeral, at a religious ceremony or of people taking a holy dip can be offensive – ask first. Flash photography may be prohibited in certain areas of a shrine, or may not be permitted at all.

the soul. Right conduct is essential, and fundamental to this is ahimsa (nonviolence) in thought and deed towards any living thing.

The religious disciplines of followers are less severe than for monks (some Jain monks go naked). The slightly less ascetic maintain a bare minimum of possessions which include a broom to sweep the path before them to avoid stepping on any living creature, and a piece of cloth tied over their mouth to prevent the accidental inhalation of insects.

Today, around 0.4% of India's population is Jain, with the majority living in Gujarat and Mumbai. Some notable Jain holy sites include Sravanabelagola, Palitana, Ranakpur and the temples of Mt Abu.

Christianity

There are various theories circulating about Christ's link to the Indian subcontinent. Some, for instance, believe that Jesus spent his 'lost years' in India, while others say that Christianity came to South India with St Thomas the Apostle in AD 52. However, many scholars attest it's more likely Christianity is traced to around the 4th century with a Syrian merchant, Thomas Cana, who set out for Kerala with around 400 families. India's Christian community today stands at about 2.3% of the population, with the bulk residing in South India.

Catholicism established a strong presence in South India in the wake of Vasco da Gama's visit in 1498, and orders that have been active – not always welcomed – in the region include the Dominicans, Franciscans and Jesuits. Protestant missionaries are believed to have begun arriving – with a conversion agenda – from around the 18th century.

Zoroastrianism

Zoroastrianism, founded by Zoroaster (Zarathustra), had its inception in Persia in the 6th century BC and is based on the concept of dualism, whereby good and evil are locked in a continuous battle. Zoroastrianism isn't quite monotheistic: good and evil entities coexist, although believers are urged to honour only the good. Both body and soul are united in this struggle of good versus evil. Although humanity is mortal it has components that are timeless, such as the soul. On the day of judgement the errant soul is not called to account for every misdemeanour – but a pleasant afterlife does depend on one's deeds, words and thoughts during earthly existence.

Zoroastrianism was eclipsed in Persia by the rise of Islam in the 7th century and its followers, many of whom openly resisted this, suffered persecution. Over the following centuries some immigrated to India, where they became known as Parsis. Historically, Parsis settled in Gujarat and became farmers; however, during British rule they moved into commerce, forming a prosperous community in Mumbai.

In recent decades the Parsi population has been spiralling downward; there are now believed to be only between 40,000 and 45,000 Parsis left in India, with most residing in Mumbai.

TOWERS OF SILENCE

The Zoroastrian funerary ritual involves the 'Towers of Silence' where the corpse is laid out and exposed to vultures that pick the bones clean.

Delicious India

India's culinary terrain – with its especially impressive patchwork of vegetarian cuisine – is not only intensely delectable, it's also richly steeped in history. From the flavoursome meaty preparations, including succulent tandoori (clay oven) fare, of the Mughals and Punjabis to the deep-sea delights of former southern colonies, Indian kitchens continue to churn out traditional favourites, often with inventive contemporary twists. Indeed, it's the sheer diversity of what's on offer that makes eating your way through India so deliciously rewarding.

A Culinary Carnival

India's culinary story is an ancient one. The cuisine that exists today reflects an amalgam of regional and global influences. From the traditional Indian food prepared in simple village kitchens, to the piled-high Italian-style pizzas served in cosmopolitan city restaurants, the carnival of flavours available on the subcontinent is nothing short of spectacular.

Land of Spices

Christopher Columbus was actually searching for the black pepper of Kerala's Malabar Coast when he stumbled upon America. The region still grows the finest quality of the world's favourite spice, and it's integral to most savoury Indian dishes.

Turmeric is the essence of the majority of Indian curries, but coriander seeds are the most widely used spice and lend flavour and body to just about every savoury dish. Indian 'wet' dishes – commonly known as curries in the West – usually begin with the crackle of cumin seeds in hot oil. Tamarind is sometimes known as the 'Indian date' and is a popular souring agent in the south. The green cardamom of Kerala's Western Ghats is regarded as the world's best, and you'll find it in savouries, desserts and warming chai (tea). Saffron, the dried stigmas of crocus flowers grown in Kashmir, is so light it takes more than 1500 hand-plucked flowers to yield just one gram.

Rice Paradise

Rice is a common staple, especially in South India. Long-grain white rice varieties are the most popular, served hot with just about any 'wet' cooked dish. From Assam's sticky rice in the far northeast to Kerala's red grains in the extreme south, you'll find countless regional varieties that locals will claim to be the best in India, though this honour is usually conceded to basmati, a fragrant long-grain variety which is widely exported around the world.

Flippin' Fantastic Bread

While rice is paramount in the south, wheat is the mainstay in the north. Roti, the generic term for Indian-style bread, is a name used interchangeably with chapati to describe the most common variety, the irresistible unleavened round bread made with whole-wheat flour and cooked on a *tawa* (hotplate). It may be smothered with ghee (clarified butter) or oil.

Spotlighting rice, *Finest Rice Recipes* by Sabina Sehgal Saikia shows just how versatile this humble grain is, with classy creations such as rice-crusted crab cakes.

PAAN

Meals are often rounded off with *paan*, a fragrant mixture of betel nut (also called areca nut), lime paste, spices and condiments wrapped in an edible, silky *paan* leaf. Peddled by *paan*-wallahs, who are usually strategically positioned outside busy restaurants, *paan* is eaten as a digestive and mouth-freshener. The betel nut is mildly narcotic and some aficionados eat *paan* the same way heavy smokers consume cigarettes – over the years these people's teeth can become rotted red and black.

There are two basic types of *paan*: *mitha* (sweet) and *saadha* (with tobacco). A parcel of *mitha paan* is a splendid way to finish a meal. Pop the whole parcel in your mouth and chew slowly, allowing the juices to ooooooooze.

In some places, rotis are bigger and thicker than chapatis and possibly cooked in a tandoor.

Dhal-icious!

While the staple of preference divides north and south, the whole of India is united in its love for dhal (curried lentils or pulses). You may encounter up to 60 different pulses: the most common are *channa,* a slightly sweeter version of the yellow split pea; tiny yellow or green ovals called *moong* (mung beans); salmon-coloured *masoor* (red lentils); the ochre-coloured southern favourite, *tuvar* (yellow lentils; also known as *arhar*); *rajma* (kidney beans); *urad* (black gram or lentils); and *lobhia* (black-eyed peas).

Meaty Matters

Although India probably has more vegetarians than the rest of the world combined, it still has an extensive repertoire of carnivorous fare. Chicken, lamb and mutton (sometimes actually goat) are the mainstays; religious taboos make beef forbidden to devout Hindus and pork to Muslims.

In northern India you'll come across meat-dominated Mughlai cuisine, which includes rich curries, kebabs, koftas and biryanis. This spicy cuisine traces its history back to the (Islamic) Mughal empire that once reigned supreme in India.

Tandoori meat dishes are another North Indian favourite. The name is derived from the clay oven, or tandoor, in which the marinated meat is cooked.

Deep-Sea Delights

India has around 7500km of coastline, so it's no surprise that seafood is an important staple, especially on the west coast, from Mumbai down to Kerala. Kerala is the biggest fishing state, while Goa boasts particularly succulent prawns and fiery fish curries, and the fishing communities of the Konkan Coast – sandwiched between these two states – are renowned for their seafood recipes. Few main meals in Odisha (Orissa) exclude fish, and in West Bengal, puddled with ponds and lakes, fish is king.

The Fruits (& Vegetables) of Mother Nature

Vegetables are usually served at each main meal across India, and *sabzi* (vegetables) is a word recognised in every Indian vernacular. They're generally cooked *sukhi* (dry) or *tari* (in a sauce) and within these two categories they can be fried, roasted, curried, stuffed, baked, mashed and combined (made into koftas) or dipped in chickpea-flour batter to make a deep-fried *pakora* (fritter).

Potatoes are ubiquitous and popularly cooked with various masalas (spice mixes), with other vegetables, or mashed and fried for the street

Containing handy tips, including how to best store spices, Monisha Bharadwaj's *The Indian Spice Kitchen* is a slick cookbook with more than 200 traditional recipes.

TRADITIONAL RECIPES

snack *aloo tikki* (mashed-potato patties). Onions are fried with other vegetables, ground into a paste for cooking with meats, and served raw as relishes. Heads of cauliflower are usually cooked dry on their own, with potatoes to make *aloo gobi* (potato-and-cauliflower curry), or with other vegetables such as carrots and beans. Fresh green peas turn up stir-fried with other vegetables in pilaus and biryanis and in one of North India's signature dishes, the magnificent *mattar paneer*. *Baigan* (eggplant/aubergine) can be curried or sliced and deep-fried. Also popular is *saag* (a generic term for leafy greens), which can include mustard, spinach and fenugreek. Something a little more unusual is the bumpy-skinned *karela* (bitter gourd) which, like the delectable *bhindi* (okra), is commonly prepared dry with spices.

India's fruit basket is a bountiful one. Along the southern coast are super-luscious tropical fruits such as pineapples and papayas. Mangoes abound during the summer months (especially April and May), with India offering more than 500 varieties – the pick of the juicy bunch is the sweet Alphonso. Citrus fruit such as oranges (which are often yellow-green in India), tangerines, pink and white grapefruits, cumquats and sweet limes are widely grown. Himachal Pradesh produces crisp apples in autumn, while plump strawberries are especially good in Kashmir during summer. You'll find fruit inventively fashioned into a *chatni* (chutney) or pickle, and also flavouring lassi, *kulfi* and other sweet treats.

The Anger of Aubergines: Stories of Women and Food by Bulbul Sharma is an amusing culinary analysis of social relationships interspersed with enticing recipes.

Vegetarians & Vegans

India is king when it comes to vegetarian fare. There's little understanding of veganism (the term 'pure vegetarian' means without eggs), and animal products such as milk, butter, ghee and curd are included in most Indian dishes. If you are vegan your first problem is likely to be getting the cook to completely understand your requirements.

DELICIOUS INDIA A CULINARY CARNIVAL

PETER ADAMS / GETTY IMAGES ©

Vegetable stall at a market in Pushkar, Rajasthan

FEASTING INDIAN-STYLE

Most people in India eat with their right hand. In the south, they use as much of the hand as is necessary, while elsewhere they use the tips of the fingers. The left hand is reserved for unsanitary actions such as removing shoes. You can use your left hand for holding drinks and serving yourself from a communal bowl, but it shouldn't be used for bringing food to your mouth. Before and after a meal, it's good manners to wash your hands.

Once your meal is served, mix the food with your fingers. If you are having dhal and *sabzi* (vegetables), only mix the dhal into your rice and have the *sabzi* in small scoops with each mouthful. If you are having fish or meat curry, mix the gravy into your rice and take the flesh off the bones from the side of your plate. Scoop up lumps of the mix and, with your knuckles facing the dish, use your thumb to shovel the food into your mouth.

For further information, surf the web – good places to begin include Indian Vegan (www.indianvegan.com) and Vegan World Network (www.vegansworldnetwork.org).

Pickles, Chutneys & Relishes

Pickles, chutneys and relishes are accompaniments that add zing to meals. A relish can be anything from a tiny pickled onion to a delicately crafted fusion of fruit, nuts and spices. One of the most popular side dishes is yoghurt-based raita, which makes a tongue-cooling counter to spicy food. *Chatnis* can come in any number of varieties (sweet or savoury) and can be made from many different vegetables, fruits, herbs and spices. But you should proceed with caution before polishing off that pickled speck sitting on your thali; it may quite possibly be the hottest thing that you've ever tasted.

Sweet at Heart

India has a fabulously colourful kaleidoscope of, often sticky and squishy, *mithai* (Indian sweets), most of them sinfully sugary. The main categories are *barfi* (a fudgelike milk-based sweet), soft *halwa* (made with vegetables, cereals, lentils, nuts or fruit), *ladoos* (sweet balls made with gram flour and semolina), and those made from *chhana* (unpressed paneer), such as *rasgullas*. There are also simpler – but equally scrumptious offerings such as crunchy *jalebis* that you'll see all over the country.

Kheer (called *payasam* in the south) is one of the most popular after-meal desserts. It's a creamy rice pudding with a light, delicate flavour, enhanced with cardamom, saffron, pistachios, flaked almonds, chopped cashews or slivered dried fruit. Other favourites include hot *gulab jamuns* and refreshing *kulfi*.

Each year, an estimated 14 tonnes of pure silver is converted into the edible foil that decorates many Indian sweets, especially during the Diwali festival.

INDIAN CURRY?

Technically speaking, there's no such thing as an Indian 'curry' – the word, an anglicised derivative of the Tamil word *kari* (sauce), was used by the British as a term for any dish including spices.

Where to Fill Up?

India has oodles of restaurants, from ramshackle street eateries to swish five-star hotel offerings. Most midrange restaurants serve one of two basic genres: South Indian (which usually means the vegetarian food of Tamil Nadu and Karnataka) and North Indian (which largely comprises Punjabi/Mughlai fare). You'll also find the cuisines of neighbouring regions and states. Indians frequently migrate in search of work and these restaurants cater to the large communities seeking the familiar tastes of home.

Not to be confused with burger joints and pizzerias, restaurants in the south advertising 'fast food' are some of India's best. They serve the whole gamut of tiffin (snack) items and often have separate sweet counters. Many upmarket hotels have outstanding restaurants, usually with pan-Indian menus so you can explore various regional cuisines. Meanwhile, the independent restaurant dining scene keeps mushrooming in India's larger cities, with menus sporting everything from Mexican and Mediterranean to Japanese and Italian.

Dhabas (basic snack bars) are oases to millions of truck drivers, bus passengers and sundry travellers going anywhere by road. The original *dhabas* dot the North Indian landscape, but you'll find versions of them throughout the country. The rough-and-ready but satisfying food served in these happy-go-lucky shacks has become a genre of its own known as '*dhaba* food'.

The Book of Indian Sweets by Satarupa Banerjee contains a yummy jumble of regional sweet treats, from Bengali rasgullas to Goan bebinca.

Street Food

Whatever the time of day, food vendors are frying, boiling, roasting, peeling, simmering, mixing, juicing or baking some type of food and drink to lure peckish passers-by. Small operations usually have one special that they serve all day, while other vendors have different dishes for breakfast, lunch and dinner. The fare varies as you venture between neighbourhoods, towns and regions; it can be as simple as puffed rice or peanuts roasted in hot sand, as unexpected as a fried-egg sandwich, or as complex as the riot of different flavours known as *chaat* (savoury snack).

Railway Snack Attack

One of the thrills of travelling by rail in India is the culinary circus that greets you at almost every station. Roving vendors accost arriving trains, yelling and scampering up and down the carriages; fruit, *namkin* (savoury nibbles), omelettes, nuts and sweets are offered through the grills on the windows; and platform cooks try to lure you from the train with the sizzle of spicy goodies such as samosas. Frequent rail travellers know

---

STREET FOOD: TIPS

Tucking into street eats is a glowing highlight of travelling in India – here are some tips to help avoid tummy troubles.

➡ Give yourself a few days to adjust to the local cuisine, especially if you're not used to spicy food.

➡ You know the rule about following a crowd – if the locals are avoiding a particular vendor, you should too. Also take notice of the profile of the customers – any place popular with families will probably be your safest bet.

➡ Check how and where the vendor is cleaning the utensils, and how and where the food is covered. If the vendor is cooking in oil, have a peek to check it's clean. If the pots or surfaces are dirty, there are food scraps about or too many buzzing flies, don't be shy to make a hasty retreat.

➡ Don't be put off when you order some deep-fried snack and the cook throws it back into the wok. It's common practice to partly cook the snacks first and then finish them off once they've been ordered. In fact, frying them hot again kills germs.

➡ Unless a place is reputable (and busy), it's best to avoid eating meat from the street.

➡ The hygiene standard at juice stalls varies, so exercise caution. Have the vendor press the juice in front of you and steer clear of anything stored in a jug or served in a glass (unless you're confident with the washing standards).

➡ Don't be tempted by glistening pre-sliced melon and other fruit, which keeps its luscious veneer with regular dousing of (often dubious) water.

Jalebis (coils of deep-fried batter dunked in sugar syrup)

which station is famous for which food item: Lonavla station in Maharashtra is known for *chikki* (rock-hard toffeelike confectionery), Agra for *peitha* (square sweet made from pumpkin and glucose, usually flavoured with rose water, coconut or saffron) and Dhaund near Delhi for biryani.

Daily Dining Habits

Three main meals a day is the norm in India. Breakfast is usually fairly light, maybe *idlis* and *sambar* in the south, and *parathas* in the north. Or simply fruit, cereal and/or eggs. Lunch can be substantial (perhaps the local version of the thali) or light, especially for time-strapped office workers. Dinner is usually the main meal of the day. It's generally comprised of a few different preparations – several curried vegetable (maybe also meat) dishes and dhal, accompanied by rice and/or chapatis. Dishes are served all at once rather than as courses. Desserts are optional and most prevalent during festivals or other special occasions. Fruit may wrap up a meal. In many Indian homes dinner can be a rather late affair (post 9pm) depending on personal preference and possibly the season (eg late dinners during the warmer months). Restaurants usually spring to life after 9pm.

Got the munchies? Grab *Street Foods of India* by Vimla and Deb Kumar Mukerji, which has recipes of much-loved Indian snacks, from samosas and *bhelpuri* to *jalebis* and *kulfi*.

Spiritual Sustenance

For many in India, food is considered just as critical for fine-tuning the spirit as it is for sustaining the body. Broadly speaking, Hindus traditionally avoid foods that are thought to inhibit physical and spiritual development, although there are few hard-and-fast rules. The taboo on eating beef (the cow is holy to Hindus) is the most rigid restriction. Jains avoid foods such as garlic and onions, which, apart from harming insects in their extraction from the ground, are thought to heat the blood and arouse sexual desire. You may come across vegetarian restaurants that make it a point to advertise the absence of onion and garlic in their dishes for this reason. Devout Hindus may also avoid garlic and onions. These items are also banned from many ashrams.

Some foods, such as dairy products, are considered innately pure and are eaten to cleanse the body, mind and spirit. Ayurveda, the ancient science of life, health and longevity, also influences food customs.

Pork is taboo for Muslims and stimulants such as alcohol are avoided by the most devout. Halal is the term for all permitted foods, and haram for those prohibited. Fasting is considered an opportunity to earn the approval of Allah, to wipe the sin-slate clean and to understand the suffering of the poor.

Buddhists and Jains subscribe to the philosophy of ahimsa (nonviolence) and are mostly vegetarian. Jainism's central tenet is ultra-vegetarianism, and rigid restrictions are in place to avoid even potential injury to any living creature – Jains abstain from eating vegetables that grow underground because of the potential to harm insects during cultivation and harvesting.

India's Sikh, Christian and Parsi communities have little or no restrictions on what they can eat.

Food which is first offered to the gods at temples then shared among devotees is known as prasad.

Cooking Courses

You might find yourself so inspired by Indian food that you want to take home a little Indian kitchen know-how, via a cooking course, such as those offered in Delhi (p78), Udaipur (p161) and McLeod Ganj (p325). Some courses are professionally run, others are very informal, and each is of varying duration. Most require at least a few days' advance notice. Use Lonely Planet recommendations or quiz fellow travellers.

Drinks, Anyone?

Gujarat is India's only dry state but there are drinking laws in place all over the country, and each state may have regular dry days when the sale of alcohol from liquor shops is banned. To avoid paying high taxes, head for Goa, where booze isn't subject to the exorbitant levies of other states.

You'll find excellent watering holes in most big cities, especially Mumbai, Bengaluru, Kolkata and Delhi, which are usually at their liveliest on weekends. The more upmarket bars serve an impressive selection of domestic and imported drinks as well as draught beer. Many bars turn into music-thumping nightclubs anytime after 8pm although there are quiet lounge-bars to be found in most large cities. In smaller towns the bar scene can be a seedy, male-dominated affair – not the kind of place thirsty female travellers should venture into alone.

Wine-drinking is steadily on the rise, despite the domestic wine-producing industry still being relatively new. The favourable climate and soil conditions in certain areas – such as parts of Maharashtra and Karnataka – have spawned some commendable Indian wineries including those of the Grover and Sula Vineyards.

Complete Indian Cooking by Mridula Baljekar, Rafi Fernandez, Shehzad Husain and Manisha Kanani has '325 deliciously authentic recipes for the adventurous cook'. They include chicken with green mango and masala mashed potatoes.

DOSA

Savoury dosas (also spelt dosais), a family of large papery rice-flour crêpes, usually served with a bowl of hot *sambar* (soupy lentil dish) and another bowl of cooling coconut *chatni* (chutney), are a South Indian breakfast speciality that can be eaten at any time of day. The most popular is the *masala dosa* (stuffed with spiced potatoes), but there are also other fantastic dosa varieties – the *rava* dosa (batter made with semolina), the Mysore dosa (like *masala dosa* but with more vegetables and chilli in the filling), and the *pessarettu* dosa (batter made with mung-bean dhal) from Andhra Pradesh. Nowadays, dosas are readily found far beyond South India, thanks to their widespread appeal.

LINDSAY BROWN / GETTY IMAGES ©

Locals sipping a cup of hot chai (tea)

Stringent licensing laws discourage drinking in some restaurants but places that depend on the tourist rupee may covertly serve you beer in teapots and disguised glasses – but don't assume anything, at the risk of causing offence.

Very few vegetarian restaurants serve alcohol.

Nonalcoholic Beverages

Chai (tea), the much-loved drink of the masses, is made with copious amounts of milk and sugar. A glass of steaming, frothy chai is the perfect antidote to the vicissitudes of life on the Indian road; the disembodied voice droning 'garam chai, garam chai' (hot tea, hot tea) is likely to become one of the most familiar and welcome sounds of your trip through India.

While chai is the traditional choice of most of the nation, South Indians have long shared their loyalty with coffee. In recent years, though, the number of coffee-drinking North Indians has skyrocketed, with ever-multiplying branches of slick coffee chains, such as Barista and Café Coffee Day, widely found in what were once chai strongholds.

Masala soda is the quintessentially Indian soft drink. It's a freshly opened bottle of fizzy soda, pepped up with lime, spices, salt and sugar. Also refreshing is *jal jeera,* made of lime juice, cumin, mint and rock salt. Sweet and savoury lassi, a yoghurt-based drink, is especially popular nationwide and is another wonderfully rejuvenating beverage.

Falooda is an interesting rose-flavoured drink made with milk, cream, nuts and strands of vermicelli, while *badam* milk (served hot or cold) is flavoured with almonds and saffron.

India has zillions of fresh-fruit juice vendors, but be wary of hygiene standards. Some restaurants think nothing of adding salt or sugar to juice to intensify the flavours; ask the waiter to omit these if you don't want them.

Homegrown Brews

An estimated three-quarters of India's drinking population quaffs 'country liquor' such as the notorious arak (liquor distilled from coconut-palm sap, potatoes or rice) of the south. This is widely known as the poor-man's drink and millions are addicted to the stuff. Each year, many people are blinded or even killed by the methyl alcohol in illegal arak.

An interesting local drink is a clear spirit with a heady pungent flavour called *mahua,* distilled from the flower of the *mahua* tree. It's brewed in makeshift village stalls all over central India during March and April, when the trees bloom. *Mahua* is safe to drink as long as it comes from a trustworthy source. There have been cases of people being blinded after drinking *mahua* adulterated with methyl alcohol.

Rice beer is brewed all over east and northeast India, while in the Himalaya you'll find a grain alcohol called *raksi,* which is strong, has a mild charcoal flavour and tastes vaguely like Scotch whisky.

Toddy, the sap from the palm tree, is drunk in coastal areas, especially Kerala, while feni is the primo Indian spirit, and the preserve of laid-back Goa. Coconut feni is light and rather unexceptional but the more popular cashew feni – made from the fruit of the cashew tree – is worth a try.

Meanwhile, if you fancy sipping booze of the blue-blood ilk, traditional royal liqueurs of Rajasthan (once reserved for private consumption among nobility) are sold at some city liquor shops, especially in Delhi and Jaipur. Ingredients range from aniseed, cardamom and saffron to rose, dates and mint.

> The sub-continent's wine industry is an ever evolving one – take a cyber-sip of Indian wine at www.indianwine.com.

Menu Decoder

achar	pickle
aloo	potato; also *alu*
aloo tikki	mashed-potato patty
appam	South Indian rice pancake
arak	liquor distilled from coconut milk, potatoes or rice
baigan	eggplant/aubergine; also known as *brinjal*
barfi	fudgelike sweet made from milk
bebinca	Goan 16-layer cake
besan	chickpea flour
betel	nut of the betel tree; also called areca nut
bhajia	vegetable fritters
bhang lassi	blend of lassi and bhang (a derivative of marijuana)
bhelpuri	puffed rice tossed with fried rounds of dough, lentils, onions, herbs and chutneys).
bhindi	okra
biryani	fragrant spiced steamed rice with meat or vegetables
bonda	mashed-potato patty
chaat	savoury snack, may be seasoned with *chaat* masala
chach	buttermilk beverage
chai	tea
channa	spiced chickpeas
chapati	round unleavened Indian-style bread; also known as roti
chawal	rice

cheiku	small, sweet brown fruit
dahi	curd/yoghurt
dhal	spiced lentil dish
dhal makhani	black lentils and red kidney beans with cream and butter
dhansak	Parsi dish; meat, usually chicken or lamb, with curried lentils, pumpkin or gourd, and rice
dosa	large South Indian savoury crêpe
falooda	rose-flavoured drink made with milk, cream, nuts and vermicelli
faluda	long chickpea-flour noodles
feni	Goan liquor distilled from coconut milk or cashews
ghee	clarified butter
gobi	cauliflower
gulab jamun	deep-fried balls of dough soaked in rose-flavoured syrup
halwa	soft sweet made with vegetables, lentils, nuts or fruit
idli	South Indian spongy, round, fermented rice cake
imli	tamarind
jaggery	hard, brown, sugarlike sweetener made from palm sap
jalebi	orange-coloured coils of deep-fried batter dunked in sugar syrup; served hot
karela	bitter gourd
keema	spiced minced meat
kheer	creamy rice pudding
khichdi	blend of lightly spiced rice and lentils; also *khichri*
kofta	minced vegetables or meat; often ball-shaped
korma	currylike braised dish
kulcha	soft leavened Indian-style bread
kulfi	flavoured (often with pistachio) firm-textured ice cream
ladoo	sweet ball made with gram flour and semolina; also *ladu*
lassi	yoghurt-and-iced-water drink
masala dosa	large South Indian savoury crêpe (dosa) stuffed with spiced potatoes
mattar paneer	unfermented cheese and pea curry
methi	fenugreek
mishti doi	Bengali sweet; curd sweetened with jaggery
mithai	Indian sweets
momo	savoury Tibetan dumpling
naan	tandoor-cooked flat bread
namak	salt
namkin	savoury nibbles
pakora	bite-sized vegetable pieces in batter
palak paneer	unfermented cheese chunks in a puréed spinach gravy
paneer	soft, unfermented cheese made from milk curd
pani	water
pappadam	thin, crispy lentil or chickpea-flour circle-shaped wafer; also *pappad*
paratha	flaky flatbread (thicker than chapati); often stuffed
phulka	a chapati that puffs up on an open flame

pilau	rice cooked in spiced stock; also *pulau*, *pilao* or *pilaf*
pudina	mint
puri	flat savoury dough that puffs up when deep-fried; also *poori*
raita	mildly spiced yoghurt, often containing shredded cucumber or diced pineapple
rasam	dhal-based broth flavoured with tamarind
rasgulla	cream-cheese balls flavoured with rose-water
rogan josh	rich, spicy lamb curry
saag	leafy greens
sabzi	vegetables
sambar	South Indian soupy lentil dish with cubed vegetables
samosa	deep-fried pastry triangles filled with spiced vegetables
sonf	aniseed; used as a digestive and mouth-freshener; also *saunf*
tandoor	clay oven
tawa	flat hotplate/iron griddle
thali	all-you-can-eat meal; stainless steel (sometimes silver) compartmentalised plate
thukpa	Tibetan noodle soup
tiffin	snack; also refers to meal container often made of stainless steel
tikka	spiced, often marinated, chunks of chicken, paneer etc
toddy	alcoholic drink, tapped from palm trees
tsampa	Tibetan staple of roast-barley flour
upma	*rava* (semolina) cooked with onions, spices, chilli peppers and coconut
uttapam	thick savoury South Indian rice pancake with finely chopped onions, green chillies, coriander and coconut
vada	South Indian doughnut-shaped deep-fried lentil savoury
vindaloo	Goan dish; fiery curry in a marinade of vinegar and garlic
wazwan	traditional Kashmiri banquet

The Great Indian Bazaar

India's bazaars and shops sell a staggering range of goodies: from woodwork to silks, chunky tribal jewellery to finely embroidered shawls, sparkling gemstones to rustic village handicrafts. The array of arts and handicrafts is vast, with every region – sometimes every village – having its own traditions, some of them ancient. Be prepared to encounter – and bring home – some spectacular items. India's shopping opportunities are as inspiring and multifarious as the country itself.

Rajasthan is a treasure trove of handicrafts. Its capital, Jaipur, is known for its blue-glazed pottery with pretty floral and geometric motifs.

Bronze Figures, Pottery, Stone Carving & Terracotta

In southern India and parts of the Himalaya, small images of deities are created by the age-old lost-wax process. A wax figure is made, a mould is formed around it, and the wax is melted, poured out and replaced with molten metal; the mould is then broken open to reveal the figure inside. Figures of Shiva as dancing Nataraja are quite popular, but you can also find images of Buddha and numerous deities from the Hindu pantheon.

The West Bengalese also employ the lost-wax process to make Dokra tribal bell sculptures, while in Chhattisgarh's Bastar region, the Ghadwa Tribe has an interesting twist on the lost-wax process: a fine wax thread covers the metal mould, leaving a lattice-like design on the final product.

In Buddhist areas, you'll find striking bronze statues of Buddha and the Tantric deities, finished off with finely polished and painted faces.

In Mamallapuram in Tamil Nadu, craftsmen using local granite and soapstone have revived the ancient artistry of the Pallava sculptors; souvenirs range from tiny stone elephants to enormous deity statues weighing half a tonne. Tamil Nadu is also known for bronzeware from Thanjavur and Trichy (Tiruchirappalli).

A number of places produce attractive terracotta items, ranging from vases and decorative flowerpots to images of deities, and children's toys.

At temples across India you can buy small clay or plaster effigies of Hindu deities.

Carpets, Carpets, Carpets!

Carpet-making is a living craft in India, with workshops throughout producing fine wool and silkwork. The finest carpets are produced in Kashmir, Ladakh, Himachal Pradesh, Sikkim and West Bengal. Carpet-making is also a major revenue earner for Tibetan refugees; most refugee settlements have cooperative carpet workshops. You can also find reproductions of tribal Turkmen and Afghan designs in states such as Uttar Pradesh. Antique carpets usually aren't antique – unless you buy from an internationally reputable dealer; stick to 'new' carpets.

The price of a carpet is determined by the number and the size of the hand-tied knots, the range of dyes and colours, the intricacy of the design and the material. Silk carpets cost more and look more luxurious, but wool carpets usually last longer. Expect to pay upwards of US$250 for a good quality 90cm by 1.5m (or 90cm by 1.8m, depending on the region) wool carpet, and around US$2000 for a similar-sized carpet in silk. Tibetan carpets are cheaper, reflecting the relative simplicity of the designs; many refugee cooperatives sell the same size for around US$100.

Some people buy carpets thinking that they can be sold for a profit back home, but unless you really know your carpets, you're better off just buying a carpet because you love it. Many places can ship carpets home for a fee – although it may be safest to send things independently to avoid scams (follow your instincts) – or you can carry them in the plane's hold (allow 5kg to 10kg of your baggage allowance for a 90cm by 1.5m carpet).

In Kashmir and Rajasthan you'll find coarsely woven woollen *numdas* (or *namdas*), which are much cheaper than knotted carpets. Various regions manufacture flat-weave *dhurries* (kilim-like cotton rugs), including Kashmir, Himachal Pradesh, Rajasthan and Uttar Pradesh. Kashmiris also produce striking *gabbas* (rugs with appliqué), made from chain-stitched wool or silk.

Children have been employed as carpet weavers in the subcontinent for centuries. The carpets produced by Tibetan refugee cooperatives are almost always made by adults; government emporiums and charitable cooperatives are usually the best places to buy.

Dazzling Jewellery

Virtually every town in India has at least one bangle shop selling an extraordinary variety, ranging from colourful plastic and glass to brass and silver.

Heavy folk-art silver jewellery can be bought in various parts of the country, particularly in Rajasthan: Jaipur, Udaipur and Pushkar are good places to find silver jewellery pitched at foreign tastes. Jaipur is also renowned for its precious and semiprecious gems (and gem scams). Chunky Tibetan jewellery made from silver (or white metal) and semiprecious stones is sold all over India. Many pieces feature Buddhist motifs and text in Tibetan script, including the famous mantra *Om Mani Padme Hum* (Hail to the Jewel in the Lotus). Some of the pieces sold in Tibetan centres such as McLeod Ganj and Leh are genuine antiques, but there's a huge industry in India, Nepal and China making artificially aged souvenirs. For creative types, loose beads of agate, turquoise, carnelian and silver are widely available. Buddhist meditation beaded strings made of gems or wood also make good souvenirs.

Pearls are produced by most Indian seaside states, but they're a particular speciality of Hyderabad. You'll find them at most state emporiums across the country. Prices vary depending on the colour and shape: you pay more for pure white pearls or rare colours like black, and perfectly round pearls are generally more expensive than misshapen or elongated pearls. A single strand of seeded pearls can cost as little as ₹500, but better-quality pearls start at around ₹1000.

Leatherwork

As cows are sacred in India, leatherwork is made from buffalo, camel, goat or some other animal skin. Kanpur in Uttar Pradesh is India's major leatherwork centre. Most large cities offer a smart range of modern leather footwear at very reasonable prices, some stitched with zillions of sparkly sequins – marvellous partywear!

The states of Punjab and Rajasthan (especially Jaipur) are famed for *jootis* (traditional, often pointy-toed slip-on shoes). *Chappals*, wonderful (often curly-toed) leather sandals, are sold throughout India but are particularly good in the cities of Kolhapur, Pune and Matheran.

In Bikaner in Rajasthan, artisans decorate camel hide with gold to produce beautiful mirror frames, boxes and bottles, while in Indore in

Be cautious when buying items that include international delivery, and avoid being led to shops by smooth-talking touts, but don't worry about too much else – except your luggage space

Cuttack in Odisha (Orissa) is famed for its lacelike silver-filigree ornaments known as *tarakasi*. A silver framework is made and then filled in with delicate curls and ribbons of silver.

MIHA PAVLIN / GETTY IMAGES ©

Shelves filled with colourful Indian bangles

Madhya Pradesh, craftspeople stretch leather over wire-and-cloth frameworks to make cute toy animals.

Metal & Marble Masterpieces

You'll find copper and brassware throughout India. Candleholders, trays, bowls, tankards and ashtrays are particularly popular buys. In Rajasthan and Uttar Pradesh, the brass is inlaid with exquisite designs in red, green and blue enamel.

Many Tibetan religious objects are created by inlaying silver in copper; prayer wheels, ceremonial horns and traditional document cases are all inexpensive buys. Resist the urge to buy *kangling* (Tibetan horns) and *kapala* (ceremonial bowls) made from inlaid human leg bones and skulls – they are illegal!

> Throughout India you can find finely crafted gold and silver rings, anklets, earrings, toe rings, necklaces and bangles, and pieces can often be crafted to order.

In all Indian towns you can find *kadhai* (Indian woks, also known as *balti*) and other cookware for incredibly low prices. Beaten-brass pots are particularly attractive, while steel storage vessels, copper-bottomed cooking pans and steel thali trays are also popular souvenirs. Be sure to have your name engraved on them (free of charge)!

The people of Bastar in Chhattisgarh use an iron-smelting technique similar to the one discovered 35,000 years ago to create abstract sculptures of spindly animal and human figures. These are often also made into functional items such as lamp stands and coat racks.

A sizeable cottage industry has sprung up in Agra reproducing the ancient Mughal art form of pietra dura (inlaying marble with semiprecious stones).

Musical Instruments Galore

Quality Indian musical instruments are mostly available in the larger cities, especially Kolkata (Calcutta), Varanasi and Delhi. Prices vary according to the quality and sound of the instrument.

Decent tabla sets (pair of drums) with a wooden tabla (tuned treble drum) and metal *doogri* (bass tone drum) cost upwards of ₹5000. Cheaper sets are generally heavier and often sound inferior.

Sitars range anywhere from ₹5000 to ₹20,000 (possibly even more). The sound of each sitar will vary with the wood used and the shape of the gourd, so try a few. Note that some cheaper sitars can warp in colder or hotter climates. On any sitar, make sure the strings ring clearly and check the gourd carefully for damage. Spare string sets, sitar plectrums and a screw-in 'amplifier' gourd are sensible additions.

Other popular instruments include the *shehnai* (Indian flute), the *sarod* (like an Indian lute), the harmonium and the *esraj* (similar to an upright violin). Conventional violins are great value – prices start at ₹3500, while Kolkata is known for its quality acoustic guitars (from ₹2500).

Exquisite Paintings

India is known for its rich painting history. Reproductions of Indian miniature paintings are widely available, but the quality varies: the cheaper ones have less detail and are made with inferior materials. Udaipur and Bikaner in Rajasthan have a particularly good range of shops specialising in modern reproductions on paper and silk, or you can browse Delhi's numerous state emporiums.

In regions such as Kerala and Tamil Nadu, you'll come across miniature paintings on leaf skeletons that portray domestic life, rural scenes and deities. In Andhra Pradesh, *cheriyal* paintings, in bright, primary colours, were originally made as scrolls for travelling storytellers.

The artists' community of Raghurajpur near Puri (Odisha) preserves the age-old art of *patachitra* painting. Cotton or *tassar* (silk cloth) is covered with a mixture of gum and chalk; it's then polished, and images of deities and scenes from Hindu legends are painted on with exceedingly fine brushes. Odisha also produces *chitra pothi,* where images are etched onto dried palm-leaf sections with a fine stylus.

Bihar's unique folk art is Mithila (or Madhubani) painting, an ancient art form preserved by the women of Madhubani. These captivating paintings are most easily found in Patna but are also sold in big city emporiums. In Khajuraho, the Adivart Tribal & Folk Art Museum sells original Bhili paintings.

Exquisite *thangkas* (rectangular Tibetan paintings on cloth) of Tantric Buddhist deities and ceremonial mandalas are sold in Tibetan Buddhist areas, including Sikkim, parts of Himachal Pradesh and Ladakh. Some perfectly reproduce the glory of the murals in India's medieval gompas (Tibetan Buddhist monasteries); others are simpler. Prices vary, but bank on at least ₹4000 for a decent-quality *thangka* of A3 size, and a lot more for large, intricate *thangkas*. The selling of antique *thangkas* is illegal, and you would be unlikely to find the real thing anyway.

In big cities like Delhi, Mumbai and Kolkata, look out for shops and galleries selling contemporary paintings by local artists.

Sumptuous Shawls, Silk & Saris

Indian shawls are famously warm and lightweight – they're often better than the best down jackets. It's worth buying one to use as a blanket on cold night journeys. Shawls are made from all sorts of wool, and many are embroidered with intricate designs.

The undisputed capital of the Indian shawl is the Kullu Valley in Himachal Pradesh, with dozens of women's cooperatives producing very fine woollen pieces.

Ladakh and Kashmir are major centres for *pashmina* (wool shawl) production – you'll pay at least ₹6000 for the authentic article – however, be aware that many so-called *pashminas* are actually made from a

In Andhra Pradesh, intricately drawn, graphic cloth paintings called *kalamkari* depict deities and historic events.

Bidri, a method of damascening where silver wire is inlaid in gunmetal (a zinc alloy) and rubbed with soil from Bidar, Karnataka, is used to make jewellery, boxes and ornaments.

TRADITIONAL TEXTILES

mixture of yarns. Shawls from the Northeast States are famously warm, with bold geometric designs. In Sikkim and West Bengal, you may also find fantastically embroidered Bhutanese shawls. Gujarat's Kutch region produces some particularly distinctive woollen shawls, patterned with subtle embroidery and mirrorwork. Handmade shawls and tweeds can also be found in Ranikhet and Almora in Uttarakhand.

Saris are a very popular souvenir, especially given that they can be easily adapted to other purposes (from cushion covers to skirts). Real silk saris are the most expensive, and the silk usually needs to be washed before it becomes soft. The 'silk capital' of India is Kanchipuram in Tamil Nadu, but you can also find fine silk saris (and cheaper scarves) in centres including Varanasi, Mysore and Kolkata. Assam is renowned for its *muga*, *endi* and *pat* silks (produced by different species of silkworms), which are widely available in Guwahati. You'll pay upwards of ₹3000 for a quality embroidered silk sari.

Patan in Gujarat is the centre for the ancient and laborious craft of *patola*-making. Every thread in these fine silk saris is individually hand-dyed before weaving, and patterned borders are woven with real gold. Slightly less involved versions are produced in Rajkot. Gold thread is also used in the famous *kota doria* saris of Kota in Rajasthan.

Aurangabad, in Maharashtra, is the traditional centre for the production of *himroo* shawls, sheets and saris, made from a blend of cotton, silk and silver thread. Silk and gold-thread saris produced at Paithan (near Aurangabad) are some of India's finest – prices range from around ₹7000 to a mind-blowing ₹300,000. Other regions famous for sari production include Madhya Pradesh for its cotton Maheshwari saris (from Maheshwar) and silk Chanderi saris (from Chanderi), and West Bengal, for its *baluchari* saris from Bishnupur, which employ a traditional form of weaving with untwisted silk thread.

Traditional Indian Textiles, by John Gillow and Nicholas Barnard, explores India's beautiful regional textiles and includes sections on tie-dye, weaving, bead-work, brocades and even camel girths.

Terrific Textiles

Textile production is India's major industry and around 40% takes place at the village level, where it's known as *khadi* (homespun cloth) – hence the government-backed *khadi* emporiums around the country. These inexpensive superstores sell all sorts of items made from *khadi*, including the popular Nehru jackets and kurta pyjamas (long shirt and loose-fitting trousers), with sales benefiting rural communities.

You'll find a truly amazing variety of weaving and embroidery techniques around India. In tourist centres such as Goa, Rajasthan and Himachal Pradesh, textiles are stitched into popular items such as shoulder bags, wall hangings, cushion covers, bedspreads, clothes and much more. The region of Kutch is known for its embroidery.

PUTTING YOUR MONEY WHERE IT COUNTS

Overall, a comparatively small proportion of the money brought to India by tourism reaches people in rural areas. Travellers can make a greater contribution by shopping at community cooperatives, set up to protect and promote traditional cottage industries and provide education, training and a sustainable livelihood at the grassroots level. Many of these projects focus on refugees, low-caste women, tribal people and others living on society's fringes.

The quality of products sold at cooperatives is high and the prices are usually fixed, which means you won't have to haggle. A share of the sales money is channelled directly into social projects such as schools, healthcare, training and other advocacy programs for socially disadvantaged groups. Shopping at the national network of Khadi and Village Industries Commission emporiums will also contribute to rural communities.

Wherever you travel, keep your eyes peeled for fair-trade cooperatives.

> ## GANDHI'S CLOTH
>
> More than 80 years ago Mahatma Gandhi urged Indians to support the freedom movement by ditching their foreign-made clothing and turning to *khadi* – homespun cloth. *Khadi* became a symbol of Indian independence, and the fabric is still closely associated with politics. The government-run, nonprofit group Khadi and Village Industries Commission (www.kvic.org.in) serves to promote *khadi*, which is usually cotton, but can also be silk or wool.
>
> *Khadi* outlets are simple, no-nonsense places where you can pick up genuine Indian clothing such as kurta pyjamas, headscarves, saris and, at some branches, assorted handicrafts – you'll find them all over India. Prices are reasonable and are often discounted in the period around Gandhi's birthday (2 October). A number of outlets also have a tailoring service.

Appliqué is an ancient art in India, with most states producing their own version, often featuring abstract or anthropomorphic patterns. The traditional lampshades and *pandals* (tents) used in weddings and festivals are usually produced using the same technique.

In Adivasi (tribal) areas of Gujarat and Rajasthan, small pieces of mirrored glass are embroidered onto fabric, creating eye-catching bags, cushion covers and wall hangings. Gujarat has a diversity of textile traditions: Jamnagar is famous for its vibrant *bandhani* (tie-dye work) used for saris and scarves, among other things, and Vadodara is renowned for block-printed fabrics, used for bedspreads and clothing. Ahmedabad is a good place to buy Gujarati textiles.

Block-printed and woven textiles are sold by fabric shops all over India: each region has its own speciality. The India-wide retail chain-store Fabindia (www.fabindia.com) is striving to preserve traditional patterns and fabrics, transforming them into home-decor items and Indian- and Western-style fashions.

Odisha has a reputation for bright appliqué and *ikat* (a Southeast Asian technique where thread is tie-dyed before weaving). The town of Pipli, between Bhubaneswar and Puri, produces striking appliqué work. The techniques used to create *kalamkari* cloth paintings in Andhra Pradesh (a centre for this ancient art is Sri Kalahasti) and Gujarat are also used to make lovely wall hangings and lampshades.

Lucknow, in Uttar Pradesh, is noted for hand-woven embroidered *chikan* cloth, which has intricate floral motifs. Punjab is famous for the attractively folksy *phulkari* embroidery (flowerwork with stitches in diagonal, vertical and horizontal directions), while women in West Bengal use chain stitches to make complex figurative designs called *kantha*. A similar technique is used to make *gabba,* women's kurtas (long shirts) and men's wedding jackets in Kashmir.

Batik can be found throughout India. It's often used for saris and *salwar kameez* (traditional dresslike tunic and trouser combination for women). City boutiques flaunt trendy *salwar kameez* in a staggering array of fabrics and styles. Pick up haute couture by Indian designers, as well as moderately priced Western fashions, in Mumbai, Bengaluru, Hyderabad and Delhi.

Crafts aren't necessarily confined to their region of origin; artists migrate and are sometimes influenced by regional aesthetics, resulting in some interesting stylistic combinations.

Beautiful Woodcarving

Woodcarving is an ancient art form throughout India. In Kashmir, walnut wood is used to make finely carved wooden screens, tables, jewellery boxes and trays, inspired by the decorative trim of houseboats. Willow cricket bats are another Kashmiri speciality.

Wood inlay is one of Bihar's oldest crafts – you'll find lovely wooden wall hangings, tabletops, trays and boxes inlaid with metals and bone.

Sandalwood carvings of Hindu deities are one of Karnataka's specialities, but you'll pay a king's ransom for the real thing – a 10cm-high Ganesh costs around ₹3000 in sandalwood, compared to roughly ₹300 in kadamb wood. However, the sandalwood will release fragrance for years.

In Udaipur in Rajasthan, you can buy brightly painted figures of Hindu deities carved from mango wood. In many parts of Rajasthan you can also find fabric printing blocks carved from teak wood.

Buddhist woodcarvings are a speciality of Sikkim, Ladakh, Arunachal Pradesh and all Tibetan refugee areas. You'll find wall plaques of the eight lucky signs, dragons and *chaam* masks, used for ritual dances. Most masks are cheap reproductions; you can sometimes find genuine *chaam* masks made from lightweight whitewood or papier mâché from ₹3000.

Other Great Finds

It's little surprise that Indian spices are snapped up by tourists. Virtually all towns have shops and bazaars selling locally made spices at great prices. Karnataka, Kerala, Uttar Pradesh, Rajasthan and Tamil Nadu produce most of the spices that go into garam masala (the 'hot mix' used to flavour Indian dishes), while the Northeast States and Sikkim are known for black cardamom and cinnamon bark. Note that some countries, such as Australia, have stringent rules regarding the import of animal and plant products. Check with your country's embassy for details.

Shops selling attar (essential oil, mostly made from flowers and used as a base for perfumes) can be found around the country. Mysore in Karnataka is famous for its sandalwood oil, while Mumbai is a major centre for the trade of traditional fragrances, including valuable *oud,* made from a rare mould that grows on the bark of the agarwood tree. In Tamil Nadu, Ooty and Kodaikanal produce aromatic and medicinal oils from herbs, flowers and eucalyptus.

Indian incense is exported worldwide, with Bengaluru and Mysore, both in Karnataka, being major producers. Incense from Auroville in Tamil Nadu is also well regarded.

A speciality of Goa is feni (liquor distilled from coconut milk or cashews) – a head-spinning spirit that often comes in decorative bottles.

Quality Indian tea is sold in Darjeeling and Kalimpong (West Bengal), Assam and Sikkim, as well as parts of South India, such as Munnar in Kerala. There are also good tea retailers in Delhi and other urban hubs.

In Bhopal in Madhya Pradesh, colourful *jari* shoulder bags, embroidered with beads, are a speciality. Also on the portables front, the Northeast States are noted for their beautiful hand-woven baskets and wickerwork – each tribe has its own unique basket shape.

Jodhpur in Rajasthan, among other places, is famed for its antiques (though be aware that exporting antiques is prohibited).

Artisans in Jammu and Kashmir have been producing lacquered papier mâché for centuries, and papier-mâché bowls, boxes, letter holders, coasters, trays and Christmas decorations are now sold across India. In Rajasthan, look for colourful papier-mâché puppets, typically sold as a pair and often depicting a husband and wife.

Fine-quality handmade paper – often fashioned into cards, boxes and notebooks – is worth seeking out. Puducherry in Tamil Nadu, Delhi and Mumbai are good places to start.

Hats are also popular: the Assamese make decorated reed-pith sun hats, and Tibetan refugees produce woollen hats, gloves and scarves, sold nationwide. Traditional caps worn by men and women of Himalayan tribes are available in many Himachal Pradesh towns.

India has a phenomenal range of books at very competitive prices, including leather-bound titles. Asian Educational Services publishes old (from the 17th century) and out-of-stock titles in original typefacc.

Be aware that it's illegal to buy shahtoosh shawls, as rare Tibetan antelopes are slaughtered to provide the wool. If you come across anyone selling these shawls, inform local authorities.

In towns with Buddhist communities, such as McLeod Ganj, Leh, Manali, Gangtok, Kalimpong and Darjeeling, keep an eye out for 'Buddha shops' selling prayer flags, singing bowls and prayer wheels.

The Arts

Over the millennia India's many ethnic groups have spawned a rich artistic heritage, and today, you'll experience art both lofty and humble around every corner: from intricately painted trucks on dusty roads to harmonic chanting from an ancient temple to wedding-season hands adorned with mehndi (henna). The wealth of creative expression is a highlight of travelling here, and today's artists fuse ancient and modern influences to create art, dance, literature and music that are as evocative as they are beautiful.

Dance

The ancient Indian art of dance is traditionally linked to mythology and classical literature. Dance can be divided into two main forms: classical and folk.

Classical dance is essentially based on well-defined traditional disciplines. Some classical dance styles:

➡ Bharata Natyam (also spelt *bharatanatyam*), which originated in Tamil Nadu, has been embraced throughout India.

➡ Kathak has Hindu and Islamic influences and was particularly popular with the Mughals. Kathak suffered a period of notoriety when it moved from the courts into houses where nautch (dancing) girls tantalised audiences with renditions of the Krishna-and-Radha love story. It was restored as a serious art form in the early 20th century.

➡ Kathakali, which has its roots in Kerala, is sometimes referred to as 'dance' but essentially is not.

➡ Kuchipudi is a 17th-century dance-drama that originated in the Andhra Pradesh village from which it takes its name. The story centres on the envious wife of Krishna.

➡ Odissi, from Odisha (Orissa), is thought to be India's oldest classical dance form. It was originally a temple art, and was later also performed at royal courts.

➡ Manipuri, which has a delicate, lyrical flavour, hails from Manipur. It attracted a wider audience in the 1920s when acclaimed Bengali writer Rabindranath Tagore invited one of its most revered exponents to teach at Shantiniketan (West Bengal).

India's second major dance form, folk, is widespread and varied. It ranges from the high-spirited bhangra dance of Punjab to the theatrical dummy-horse dances of Karnataka and Tamil Nadu, and the graceful fishers' dance of Odisha. In Gujarat, the colourful group dance known as garba is performed during Navratri (Hindu festival held in September or October).

Pioneers of modern dance forms in India include Uday Shankar (older brother of the late sitar master Ravi), who once partnered with Russian ballerina Anna Pavlova. Rabindranath Tagore was another innovator; in 1901 he set up a school at Shantiniketan in West Bengal that promoted the arts, including dance.

The dance you'll most commonly see, though, is in films. Dance has featured in Indian movies since the dawn of 'talkies' and often combines traditional, folk, modern and contemporary choreography.

Indian Classical Dance by Leela Venkataraman and Avinash Pasricha is a lavishly illustrated book covering various Indian dance forms, including Bharata Natyam, Odissi, Kuchipudi and Kathakali.

Music

Indian classical music traces its roots back to Vedic times, when religious poems chanted by priests were first collated in an anthology called the Rig-Veda. Over the millennia classical music has been shaped by many influences, and the legacy today is Carnatic (characteristic of South India) and Hindustani (the classical style of North India) music. With common origins, they share a number of features. Both use the raga (the melodic shape of the music) and *tala* (the rhythmic meter characterised by the number of beats); *tintal,* for example, has a *tala* of 16 beats. The audience follows the *tala* by clapping at the appropriate beat, which in *tintal* is at beats one, five and 13. There's no clap at the beat of nine; that's the *khali* (empty section), which is indicated by a wave of the hand. Both the raga and the *tala* are used as a basis for composition and improvisation.

Both Carnatic and Hindustani music are performed by small ensembles, generally comprising three to six musicians, and both have many instruments in common. There's no fixed pitch, but there are differences between the two styles. Hindustani has been more heavily influenced by Persian musical conventions (a result of Mughal rule); Carnatic music, as it developed in South India, cleaves more closely to theory. The most striking difference, at least for those unfamiliar with India's classical forms, is Carnatic's greater use of voice.

One of the best-known Indian instruments is the sitar (large stringed instrument), with which the soloist plays the raga. Other stringed instruments include the sarod (which is plucked) and the sarangi (which is played with a bow). Also popular is the tabla (twin drums), which provides the *tala*. The drone, which runs on two basic notes, is provided by the oboelike *shehnai* or the stringed *tampura* (also spelt tamboura). The hand-pumped keyboard harmonium is used as a secondary melody instrument for vocal music.

Indian regional folk music is widespread and varied. Wandering musicians, magicians, snake charmers and storytellers often use song to entertain their audiences; the storyteller usually sings the tales from the great epics.

In North India you may come across *qawwali* (Sufi devotional singing), performed in mosques or at musical concerts. *Qawwali* concerts usually take the form of a *mehfil* (gathering) with a lead singer, a second singer, harmonium and tabla players, and a thunderous chorus of junior singers and clappers, all sitting cross-legged on the floor. The singers whip up the audience with lines of poetry, dramatic hand gestures and religious phrases as the two voices weave in and out, bouncing off each other to create an improvised, surging sound. On command the chorus dives in with a hypnotic and rhythmic refrain. Members of the audience often sway and shout out in ecstatic appreciation.

A completely different genre altogether, filmi (music from films) includes modern, slower-paced love serenades along with hyperactive dance songs. To ascertain the latest filmi favourites, as well as in-vogue Indian pop singers, enquire at music stores, or invest in a portable radio.

RAGA

To tune into the melodious world of Hindustani classical music, including a glossary of musical terms, get a copy of *Nad: Understanding Raga Music* by Sandeep Bagchee.

Painting

Around 1500 years ago artists covered the walls and ceilings of the Ajanta caves in Maharashtra, western India, with scenes from the Buddha's past lives. The figures are endowed with an unusual freedom and grace, and contrast with the next major style that emerged from this part of India in the 11th century.

India's Jain community created some particularly lavish temple art. However, after the conquest of Gujarat by the Delhi Sultanate in 1299, the Jains turned their attention to illustrated manuscripts, which could be hidden away. These manuscripts are the only known form of Indian painting that survived the Islamic conquest of North India.

The Indo-Persian style – characterised by geometric design coupled with flowing form – developed from Islamic royal courts, although the depiction of the elongated eye is one convention that seems to have been retained from indigenous sources. The Persian influence blossomed when artisans fled to India following the 1507 Uzbek attack on Herat (in present-day Afghanistan), and with trade and gift-swapping between the Persian city of Shiraz, an established centre for miniature production, and Indian provincial sultans.

The 1526 victory by Babur at the Battle of Panipat ushered in the era of the Mughals in India. Although Babur and his son Humayun were both patrons of the arts, it's Humayun's son Akbar who is generally credited with developing the characteristic Mughal style. This painting style, often in colourful miniature form, largely depicts court life, architecture, battle and hunting scenes, as well as detailed portraits. Akbar recruited artists from far and wide, and artistic endeavour first centred on the production of illustrated manuscripts (topics varied from history to mythology), but later broadened into portraiture and the glorification of everyday events. European painting styles influenced some artists, and this influence occasionally reveals itself in experiments with motifs and perspective.

Akbar's son Jehangir also patronised painting, but he preferred portraiture, and his fascination with natural science resulted in a vibrant legacy of paintings of flowers and animals. Under Jehangir's son Shah Jahan, the Mughal style became less fluid and, although the bright colouring was eye-catching, the paintings lacked the vigour of before.

Various schools of miniature painting (small paintings crammed with detail) emerged in Rajasthan from around the 17th century. The subject matter ranged from royal processions to shikar (hunting expeditions), with many artists influenced by Mughal styles. The intense colours, still evident today in miniatures and frescoes in some Indian palaces, were often derived from crushed semiprecious stones, while the gold and silver colouring is finely pounded pure gold and silver leaf.

By the 19th century, painting in North India was notably influenced by Western styles (especially English watercolours), giving rise to what has been dubbed the Company School, which had its centre in Delhi.

In 21st-century India, paintings by modern and contemporary Indian artists have been selling at record numbers (and prices) around the world. One very successful online art auction house is the Mumbai-based Saffronart (www.saffronart.com). Delhi and Mumbai are currently India's contemporary-art centres.

Get arty with Indian Art *by Roy C Craven,* Contemporary Indian Art: Other Realities *edited by Yashodhara Dalmia, and* Indian Miniature Painting *by Dr Daljeet and Professor PC Jain.*

Cinema

India's film industry was born in the late 19th century – the first major Indian-made motion picture, *Panorama of Calcutta,* was screened in 1899. India's first real feature film, *Raja Harishchandra,* was made during the silent era in 1913 and it's ultimately from this film that Indian cinema traces its vibrant lineage.

Today, India's film industry is the biggest in the world – twice as big as Hollywood. Mumbai (Bombay), the Hindi-language film capital, aka 'Bollywood', is the biggest producer, but India's other major film-producing cities – Chennai (Kollywood), Hyderabad (Tollywood) and Bengaluru (Sandalwood) – also have a huge output. A number of other centres produce films in their own regional vernaculars too. Big-budget films are often partly or entirely shot abroad, with some countries vigorously

Encyclopedia of Indian Cinema by Ashish Rajadhyaksha and Paul Willemen chronicles India's dynamic cinematic history, spanning from 1897 to the 21st century.

MAGICAL MEHNDI

Mehndi is the traditional art of painting a woman's hands (and sometimes feet) with intricate henna designs for auspicious ceremonies, such as marriage. If quality henna is used, the design, which is orange-brown, can last up to one month.

In touristy areas, *mehndi*-wallahs are adept at applying henna tattoo 'bands' on the arms, legs and lower back. If you get *mehndi* applied, allow at least a few hours for the design process and required drying time (during drying you can't use your hennaed hands).

It's always wise to request the artist to do a 'test' spot on your arm before proceeding: nowadays some dyes contain chemicals that can cause allergies. (Avoid 'black henna', which is mixed with some chemicals that may be harmful.) If good-quality henna is used, you should not feel any pain during or after the application.

wooing Indian production companies because of the potential spin-off tourism revenue these films generate.

An average of 1000 feature films are produced annually in India. Apart from hundreds of millions of local Bolly-, Tolly- and Kollywood buffs, there are also millions of Non-Resident Indian (NRI) fans, who have played a significant role in catapulting Indian cinema onto the international stage.

Broadly speaking, there are two categories of Indian films. Most prominent is the mainstream 'masala' movie – named for its 'spice mix' of elements. Designed to have something for every member of the family, the films tend to have a mix of romance, action, slapstick humour and moral themes. Three hours and still running, these blockbusters are often tear-jerkers and are packed with dramatic twists interspersed with numerous song-and-dance performances. There is no explicit sex, or even kissing (although smooching is creeping into some Bollywood movies) in Indian films made for the local market; however, lack of nudity is often compensated for by heroines dressed in skimpy or body-hugging attire, and lack of overt eroticism is more than made up for with heaps of intense flirting and loaded innuendoes.

The second Indian film genre is art house, which adopts Indian 'reality' as its base. Generally speaking they are, or at least are supposed to be, socially and politically relevant. Usually made on infinitely smaller budgets than their commercial cousins, these films are the ones that win kudos at global film festivals and award ceremonies. The late Bengali director Satyajit Ray, most famous for his 1950s work, is the father of Indian art films.

Literature

India has a long tradition of Sanskrit literature, although works in the vernacular have contributed to a particularly rich legacy. In fact, it's claimed there are as many literary traditions as there are written languages.

The brilliant and prolific writer and artist Rabindranath Tagore won the Nobel Prize in Literature in 1913 for *Gitanjali*. For a taste of Tagore's work, read *Selected Short Stories*.

Bengalis are traditionally credited with producing some of India's most celebrated literature, a movement often referred to as the Indian or Bengal Renaissance, which flourished from the 19th century with works by Bankim Chandra Chatterjee. But the man who to this day is mostly credited with first propelling India's cultural richness onto the world stage is the Bengali Rabindranath Tagore.

One of the earliest Indian authors writing in English to receive an international audience, in the 1930s, was RK Narayan, whose deceptively simple writing about small-town life is subtly hilarious. Keralan Kamala Das (aka Kamala Suraiyya) wrote poetry and memoir in English; her frank approach to love and sexuality, especially in the 1960s and '70s, broke ground for women writers.

India has an ever-growing list of internationally acclaimed contemporary authors. Particularly prominent writers include Vikram Seth, best known for his epic novel *A Suitable Boy,* and Amitav Ghosh, who has won a number of accolades; his *Sea of Poppies* was shortlisted for the 2008 Man Booker Prize. Indeed, recent years have seen a number of Indian-born authors win the prestigious Man Booker Prize, the most recent being Aravind Adiga, who won in 2008 for his debut novel, *The White Tiger*. The prize went to Kiran Desai in 2006 for *The Inheritance of Loss;* Kiran Desai is the daughter of the award-winning Indian novelist Anita Desai, who has thrice been a Booker Prize nominee. In 1997 Arundhati Roy won the Booker Prize for her novel *The God of Small Things,* while Salman Rushdie took this coveted award in 1981 for *Midnight's Children.*

Hobnob with acclaimed local and international writers at Asia's biggest literary event, the Jaipur Literature Festival (www.jaipurliteraturefestival.org), held in late January in Jaipur (Rajasthan).

Sacred Architecture

India has a remarkable assortment of historic and contemporary sacred architecture that draws inspiration from a variety of religious denominations. Although few of the wooden and occasionally brick temples built in early times have weathered the vagaries of nature, by the advent of the Guptas (4th to 6th centuries AD) of North India, sacred structures of a new type – better engineered to withstand the elements – were being constructed, and these largely set the standard for temples for several hundred years.

For Hindus, the square is a perfect shape, and complex rules govern the location, design and building of each temple, based on numerology, astrology, astronomy and religious principles. Essentially, a temple represents a map of the universe. At the centre is an unadorned space, the *garbhagriha* (inner sanctum), which is symbolic of the 'womb-cave'

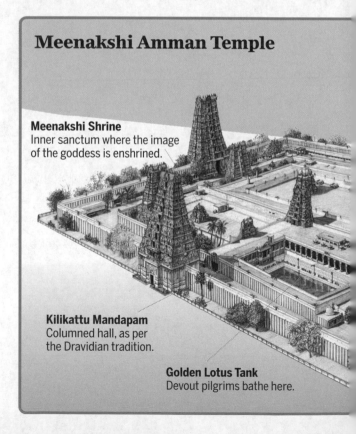

Meenakshi Amman Temple

Meenakshi Shrine
Inner sanctum where the image of the goddess is enshrined.

Kilikattu Mandapam
Columned hall, as per the Dravidian tradition.

Golden Lotus Tank
Devout pilgrims bathe here.

from which the universe is believed to have emerged. This provides a residence for the deity to which the temple is dedicated.

Above a Hindu temple's shrine rises a tower superstructure known as a *vimana* in South India, and a *sikhara* in North India. The *sikhara* is curvilinear and topped with a grooved disk, on which sits a pot-shaped finial, while the *vimana* is stepped, with the grooved disk being replaced by a solid dome. Some temples have a *mandapa* (forechamber) connected to the sanctum by vestibules. The *mandapa* may also contain *vimanas* or *sikharas*.

A *gopuram* is a soaring pyramidal gateway tower of a Dravidian temple. The towering *gopurams* of various South Indian temple complexes, such as the nine-storey *gopurams* of Madurai's Meenakshi Amman Temple, took ornamentation and monumentalism to new levels.

Commonly used for ritual bathing and religious ceremonies, as well as adding aesthetic appeal, temple tanks have long been a focal point of temple activity. These often-vast, angular, engineered reservoirs of water, sometimes fed by rain, sometimes fed – via a complicated drainage system – by rivers, serve both sacred and secular purposes. The waters of some temple tanks are believed to have healing properties, while others are said to have the power to wash away sins. Devotees (as well as travellers) may be required to wash their feet in a temple tank before entering a place of worship.

Masterpieces of Traditional Indian Architecture by Satish Grover and *The History of Architecture in India* by Christopher Tadgell proffer interesting insights into temple architecture.

Gopurams
Nine-storey gateway towers decorated with thousands of figures.

Ashta Shakti Mandapam
Most people enter the temple through this pillared pavilion.

SACRED ARCHITECTURE

Golden Temple

Pilgrim accommodation

Main entrance
Clock tower and Sikh museum.

GOMPA

The focal point of a gompa is the *dukhang* (prayer hall), where monks assemble to chant passages from sacred scriptures.

From the outside, Jain temples can resemble Hindu ones, but inside they're often a riot of sculptural ornamentation, the very opposite of ascetic austerity.

Buddhist shrines have their own unique features. Stupas, composed of a solid hemisphere topped by a spire, characterise Buddhist places of worship and essentially evolved from burial mounds. They served as repositories for relics of the Buddha and, later, other venerated souls. A further innovation is the addition of a *chaitya* (assembly hall) leading up to the stupa itself. Bodhgaya, where Siddhartha Gautama attained enlightenment and became the Buddha, has a collection of notable Buddhist monasteries and temples. The gompas (Tibetan Buddhist monasteries) found in places such as Ladakh and Sikkim are characterised by distinctly Tibetan motifs.

In 262 BC the Mauryan emperor Ashoka embraced Buddhism, and as a penance built the Great Stupa at Sanchi, in the central Indian state of Madhya Pradesh. It is among the oldest surviving Buddhist structures in the subcontinent.

India also has a rich collection of Islamic sacred sites, as its Muslim rulers contributed their own architectural conventions, including arched cloisters and domes. The Mughals uniquely melded Persian, Indian and provincial styles. Renowned examples include Humayun's Tomb in Delhi, Agra Fort, and the ancient fortified city of Fatehpur Sikri. Emperor Shah

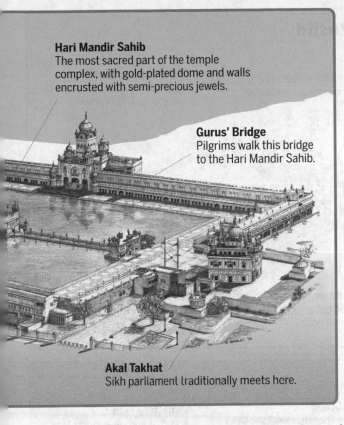

Hari Mandir Sahib
The most sacred part of the temple complex, with gold-plated dome and walls encrusted with semi-precious jewels.

Gurus' Bridge
Pilgrims walk this bridge to the Hari Mandir Sahib.

Akal Takhat
Sikh parliament traditionally meets here.

Jahan was responsible for some of India's most spectacular architectural creations, most notably the milky white Taj Mahal.

Islamic art eschews any hint of idolatry or portrayal of God, and it has evolved a vibrant heritage of calligraphic and decorative designs. In terms of mosque architecture, the basic design elements are similar worldwide. A large hall is dedicated to communal prayer and within the hall is a mihrab (niche) indicating the direction of Mecca. The faithful are called to prayer from minarets, placed at cardinal points. Delhi's formidable 17th-century Jama Masjid is India's biggest mosque, its courtyard able to hold 25,000 people.

The Sikh faith was founded by Guru Nanak, the first of 10 gurus, in the 15th century. Sikh temples, called gurdwaras, can usually be identified by a *nishan sahib* (a flagpole flying a triangular flag with the Sikh insignia). Amritsar's stunning Golden Temple is Sikhism's holiest shrine.

Discover more about India's diverse temple architecture (in addition to other temple-related information) at Temple Net (www.templenet.com).

Jama Masjid

Minaret
Tower from which the muezzin (crier) calls the faithful to worship.

Central Courtyard
Holds up to 25,000 people for Friday prayers.

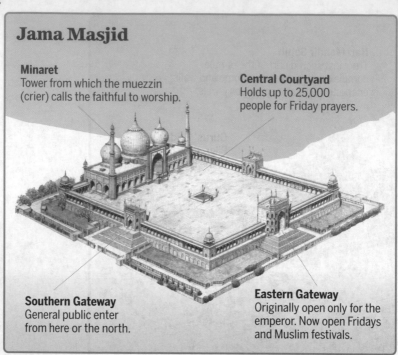

Southern Gateway
General public enter from here or the north.

Eastern Gateway
Originally open only for the emperor. Now open Fridays and Muslim festivals.

Sanchi

Great Stupa
Built by the emperor Ashoka in the 2nd century BC to enshrine relics of the Buddha.

Monastery Ruins
Accommodation surrounding a central courtyard.

Stupa Three
Contained the relics of two important disciples of the Buddha.

Processional path
Pilgrims circumambulated the stupa along this path.

India's Wildlife & Parks

The wildlife of India comprises a fascinating melting pot of animals from Europe, Asia and ancient Gondwanaland all swirled together in a bewildering mix of habitats ranging from steamy mangrove forests and jungles to sandy deserts and icy alpine meadows. India is celebrated for its big, bold, exalted species – tigers, elephants, rhinos, leopards, bears and monkeys. But there is much much more, including a mesmerising collection of colourful birds and some of India's most endangered and intriguing wildlife, such as the Ganges river dolphin and Asiatic lion.

Signature Species

If you had to pick India's most charismatic species, the list would inevitably include tigers, elephants and rhinos, all of which are scarce and in need of stringent protection.

Asian elephants – a thoroughly different species to the larger African elephant – are revered in Hindu custom and were able to be domesticated and put to work; fortunately they've not been hunted into extinction (as they were in neighbouring China). It's true that many Indian elephants still survive in the wild, however, because elephants migrate long distances in search of food, these 3000kg animals require huge parks and run into predictable conflict when herds of them attempt to follow ancestral paths that are now occupied by villages and farms. Some of the best parks for elephant viewing are Corbett Tiger Reserve in Uttarakhand and Nagarhole National Park in Karnataka.

There are far fewer one-horned rhinos left and two-thirds (just shy of 2000) of the world's total population can be found in Kaziranga National Park, where they serenely wander the park's lush alluvial grasslands at the base of the Himalaya. They may look sedate but rhinos are unpredictably dangerous, built like battering rams, covered in plates of armour-like skin and use their sharp teeth to tear off chunks of flesh when they attack, so let's just say that it's safest to watch rhinos from the back of an elephant.

India's national animal is the tiger, its national bird is the peacock and its national flower is the lotus. The national emblem of India is a column topped by three Asiatic lions.

Their Future in Our Hands

Understandably, wildlife-watching has become one of the country's prime tourist activities and there are hundreds of national parks and wildlife sanctuaries offering opportunities to spot rare and unusual wildlife. Even better, your visit helps notify the government that protecting parks and wildlife is important and of economic value.

Most of the semitropical lowland and hill forests that once dominated central and southern India have been cut down, lost to the human competition for land and water, but this region is still home to the majority of India's most intriguing animals, especially where the remaining forests have been protected. So take some time to track down a rhino or spot a tiger on safari.

Cool for Cats

Resources

Wildlife, conservation and environment awareness-raising at www.sanctuary asia.com

The Wildlife Trust of India news at www.wti.org.in

Top birdwatching information and photo galleries at www.birding.in

India is justifiably famous for its tigers, and just admit it – you secretly hope to see one. But India is also home to 14 other species of cats, so don't miss any opportunities to see one of the other gorgeous felines.

It could be said that the global effort to protect tigers started in India, and many experts agree that India's sizeable population of tigers is the species' last great stronghold.

Unfortunately, despite a massive and well-funded conservation effort, the black market in tigers remains an irresistible temptation for both wildlife-poaching gangs and impoverished villagers, so tiger numbers continue to fall at a precipitous rate, even in supposedly secure sanctuaries.

Protection efforts have been successfully made on behalf of the Asiatic lion, a close relative of the more familiar African lion. A hundred years ago there were only 20 of these lions left in the world, but their population of 300 now seems to be doing fairly well in Gujarat's Sasan Gir Wildlife Sanctuary, where it's also possible to see 300 or so leopards, another of India's famous big cats.

Closely related but much paler in colour is the much celebrated snow leopard, an animal so elusive that many locals claim it can appear and disappear at will. A unknown number of snow leopards survive in Ladakh, Sikkim, Uttarakhand, Himachal Pradesh and Arunachal Pradesh. Other furred felines include the clouded leopard and its smaller cousin the marbled cat, both of which lurk in the jungles of northeast India. These cats are strikingly marbled with rosettes and rings of colour for camouflage in the dappled light of their forest homes.

Adaptation the Key to Success

By far the most abundant forms of wildlife you'll see in India are deer (nine species), antelope (six species), goats and sheep (10 species), and primates (15 species). In the open grasslands of many parks look for the stocky nilgai, India's largest antelope, or elegantly horned blackbucks. If you're heading for the mountains, keep your eyes open in the Himalaya for blue sheep with their partially curled horns or the rare argali with its fully curled horns that can be found in Ladakh. The deserts of Rajasthan and Gujarat are home to desert-adapted species such as chinkaras (Indian gazelles); while the mangrove swamps of the Sundarban Delta

PROJECT TIGER

When naturalist Jim Corbett first raised the alarm in the 1930s no one believed that tigers would ever be threatened. At the time it was believed there were 40,000 tigers in India, although no one had ever conducted a census. Then came Independence, which put guns into the hands of villagers who pushed into formerly off-limits hunting reserves to hunt for highly profitable tiger skins. By the time an official census was conducted in 1972, there were only 1800 tigers left, and the international outcry prompted Indira Gandhi to make the tiger the national symbol of India and set up **Project Tiger** (http://projecttiger.nic.in). It has since established 39 tiger reserves totalling over 32,000 sq km that not only protect this top predator but all animals that live in the same habitat. After an initial round of successes (perhaps owing to counting anomalies), tiger numbers have continuously plummeted from 3600 in 2002 to around 1700 due to relentless poaching. And although numbers were supposedly up in the 2011 census and countless rupees and high-tech equipment continue to be devoted to the effort, the slide towards extinction in the wild appears inevitable as available tiger habitat continues to shrink.

The decline has lead to Project Tiger cutting safari numbers to try and minimise the impact of the ever-growing tourist trade (p677).

A CONTROVERSIAL CHEETAH

India's last wild cheetahs were likely shot by the Maharaja of Surguja in 1947, and they have been absent for so long that few people think of cheetahs and India in the same sentence. In 2009, in a headline-catching statement, India's former minister for the environment, Jairam Ramesh, announced that cheetahs would be brought from Iran, Namibia and South Africa and released in the Kuno-Palpur Wildlife Sanctuary, the Nauradehi Wildlife Sanctuary in Madhya Pradesh and an area in the desert near Jaisalmer in Rajasthan. Although a successful political stunt, there remains considerable disagreement about whether these releases are a good idea. Official studies concluded that most of the potential cheetah habitat was severely overgrazed by livestock and subject to poaching. Lastly, Iran has refused to send any of its Asiatic cheetahs to India or allow Indian scientists to clone them. And in 2012, the Supreme Court of India put on hold plans to introduce African cheetahs.

have chitals (spotted deer), who cope with their brackish environment by excreting salt from their nasal glands. Chitals are also the most abundant deer in central India's high-profile tiger reserves.

India's primates range from the extremely rare hoolock gibbon and golden langur of the northeast to species that are so common as to be a pest – most notably the stocky and aggressive rhesus macaque and the elegant grey (Hanuman) langur. In the south, the pesky monkeys that loiter around temples and tourist sites are bonnet macaques.

Endangered Species

Despite having amazing biodiversity, India faces a growing challenge from its exploding human population. Wildlife is severely threatened by poaching and habitat loss. A recent count suggested India had over 500 threatened species, including 247 species of plants, 53 species of mammals, 78 species of birds, 22 species of reptiles, 68 species of amphibians, 35 species of fish and 22 species of invertebrates. In 2012, the International Union for Conservation of Nature released a list of the 100 most threatened species in the world. It included four Indian species; a spider, a turtle and two birds, the great Indian bustard and white-bellied heron.

Although much touted as a success story, even the well-resourced Project Tiger faces an uphill battle every day. And every good news story seems to be followed by yet another story involving poor villagers and corrupt officials. All of India's wild cats, from leopards to snow leopards, panthers and jungle cats, are facing extinction from habitat loss and poaching for the lucrative trade in skins and body parts for Chinese medicine (a whole tiger carcass can fetch upwards of UK£32,000). Government estimates suggest that India is losing 1% of its tigers every year to poachers.

Even highly protected rhinos are poached for the medicine trade – rhino horn is highly valued as an aphrodisiac in China and as a material for making handles for daggers in the Gulf. Elephants are regularly poached for ivory, and 320 elephants were poached from 2000 to 2008 – we implore you not to support this trade by buying ivory souvenirs. Various species of deer are threatened by hunting for food and trophies, and the chiru, or Tibetan antelope, is nearly extinct because its hair is woven into wool for expensive shahtoosh shawls.

India's bear species remain under threat, although sloth bears will experience a reprieve with the official demise of the dancing bear industry. In the rivers, India's famous freshwater dolphins are in dire straits from pollution, habitat alteration and direct human competition. The

India has 238 species of snake, of which about 50 are poisonous. Of the various species of cobra, the king cobra is the world's largest venomous snake, attaining a length of 5m.

Top Parks – North

Corbett Tiger Reserve

Kaziranga National Park

Keoladeo Ghana National Park

Ranthambhore National Park

sea-turtle populations that nest on the Odisha (Orissa) coast also face environmental challenges.

Threatened primate species clinging on in rainforests in the south include lion-tailed macaques, glossy black Nilgiri langurs and the slender loris, an adept insect-catcher with huge eyes for nocturnal hunting.

Birds

With well over 1000 species of birds, India is a birdwatcher's dream. Many birds are thinly spread over this vast country, but wherever critical habitat has been preserved in the midst of dense human activity you might see phenomenal numbers of birds in one location. Winter can be a particularly good time, as wetlands throughout the country host northern migrants arriving to kick back in the lush subtropical warmth of the Indian peninsula. Keoladeo Ghana National Park in Rajasthan is rightly famous for its migratory visitors. Throughout the year, wherever you may be travelling look for colourful kingfishers, barbets, sunbirds, parakeets and magpies, or the blue flash of an Indian roller. Keen types will take a special trip into the Himalaya in search of one of India's (and the world's) mostly highly sought-after birds, the enigmatic ibisbill.

Once considered the premier duck-hunting destination in the British Empire when royal hunting parties would shoot 4000 ducks in a single day, the seasonal wetlands of Keoladeo Ghana were elevated to national park status in 1982. Now whittled down to a relatively small pocket of habitat amid a sea of villages and agricultural fields, this is still one of the finest birdwatching destinations in the world. Even better, Keoladeo Ghana and its abundant birdlife are ridiculously easy to explore, just hop on a bike at the gate and toodle around the flat tracks that weave amongst the park's clearly defined ponds and marshes. In the winter there are so many ducks, herons, storks, cranes, egrets and raptors packing themselves into the park that your foremost problem will be trying to identify individual animals amid the chaos.

Top Parks – Central

Bandhavgarh National Park

Kanha National Park

Panna National Park

Sunderbans Tiger Reserve

Plants

Once upon a time India was almost entirely covered in forest; now its total forest cover is estimated to be around 20%, although the Forest Survey of India has set an optimistic target of returning to 33% cover. Despite widespread clearing of native habitats, the country still boasts 49,219 plant species, of which some 5200 are endemic. Species on the southern peninsula show Malaysian ancestry, while desert plants in Rajasthan are more clearly allied with the Middle East, and the conifer forests of the Himalaya derive from European and Siberian origins.

Outside of the mountain forests found in the Himalaya, nearly all the lowland forests of India are subtypes of tropical forest, with native sal forests forming the mainstay of the timber industry. Some of these tropical forests are true rainforest, staying green year-round, such as in the Western Ghats and in the Northeast States, but most forests are deciduous, for example, the teak forests of central India can look surprisingly

---

UNBEARABLY GOOD NEWS

In 2012 the Indian government announced that the dancing bear industry was extinct. After several centuries, the cultural tradition had finally ended with few lamenting its demise. In fact, the practice was bought out when the few remaining bear-handling communities, known as Kalandars, were redirected into more profitable enterprises. Although the dancing bear entertainment was outlawed in 1972, it took a couple of decades for the tradition to die out.

dusty and forlorn in the dry season. Fortunately, the leaf fall and dry vegetation makes wildlife viewing easier in otherwise dense woodlands.

High-value trees such as Indian rosewood, Malabar kino and teak have been virtually cleared from the Western Ghats, and sandalwood is endangered across India due to illegal logging for the incense and wood-carving industries. A bigger threat to forested lands is firewood harvesting, often carried out by landless peasants who squat on gazetted government land.

Several trees have significant religious value in India, including the silk-cotton tree, a huge tree with spiny bark and large red flowers under which Pitamaha (Brahma), the god of creation, sat after his labours. Two well-known figs, the banyan and peepal, grow to immense size by dangling roots from their branches and fusing into massive multitrunked jungles of trunks and stems – one giant is nearly 200m across. It is said that Buddha achieved enlightenment while sitting under a peepal (also known as the Bodhi tree).

The foothills and slopes of the Himalaya preserve classic montane species, including blue pine and deodar (Himalayan cedar) and deciduous forests of apple, chestnut, birch, plum and cinnamon. Above the snowline, hardy plants such as anemones, edelweiss and gentians can be prolific, and one fabulous place to see such flowers is at the Valley of Flowers National Park.

India's hot deserts have their own unique species – the khejri tree and various strains of scrub acacia. The hardy sea-buckthorn bush is the main fruiting shrub in the high-altitude deserts of the Himalaya.

Also worth noting is that around 2000 plant species are described in Ayurveda (traditional Indian herbal medicine) texts.

National Parks & Wildlife Sanctuaries

Prior to 1972 India only had five national parks, so the Wildlife Protection Act was introduced that year to set aside land for parks and stem the abuse of wildlife. The Act was followed by a string of similar pieces of legislation with bold ambitions but few teeth with which to enforce them.

India now has about 100 national parks and 500 wildlife sanctuaries, which constitute around 5% of India's territory. An additional 70 parks have been authorised on paper but not yet implemented on the ground or only implemented to varying degrees. There are also 14 biosphere reserves, overlapping many of the national parks and sanctuaries, providing safe migration channels for wildlife and allowing scientists to monitor biodiversity.

We strongly recommend visiting at least one national park or sanctuary on your travels – the experience of coming face-to-face with a wild elephant, rhino or tiger will stay with you for a lifetime, while your visit adds momentum to efforts to protect India's natural resources. Wildlife reserves tend to be off the beaten track and infrastructure can be limited – book transport and accommodation in advance, and check opening times, permit requirements and entry fees before you visit. Many parks close to conduct a census of wildlife in the low season, and monsoon rains can make wildlife-viewing tracks inaccessible.

Almost all parks offer jeep/van tours, but you can also search for wildlife on guided treks, boat trips and elephant safaris. New rules introduced in 2012 put an end to 'tiger shows', whereby resting tigers became sitting ducks for tourists that were radioed in, taken off their jeep and put on elephants to get close to the, presumably peeved, resting tiger. Also, in many reserves, safari vehicle visits have been cut and for one day in the week, some tiger sanctuaries will be closed to safaris. These new rules are in flux, so do find out the latest situation before booking your safari.

Top Parks – South

Mahatma Gandhi Marine National Park

Nagarhole National Park

Periyar Wildlife Sanctuary

INDIA'S WILDLIFE & PARKS NATIONAL PARKS & WILDLIFE SANCTUARIES

Located almost perfectly in the centre of the country, Bandhavgarh National Park is one dynamic example of what the original Indian landscape might have been like. Here you can explore meadows, forests and rocky ridges in a thrilling search for tigers, leopards and other big fauna.

The Landscape

India is an incredibly diverse country with everything from steamy jungles and tropical beaches to arid deserts and the soaring icy peaks of the Himalaya. At 3,287,263 sq km, it is the second-largest Asian country after China, and forms the vast bulk of the South Asian subcontinent – an ancient block of earth crust that carried a wealth of unique plants and animals like a lifeboat across a prehistoric ocean before slamming into Asia about 40 million years ago. India is home to 18% of the world's population, crowded together on 2.5% of the world's landmass.

The Lie of The Land

It is estimated that India's population will reach 1.26 billion people by 2016.

Look for the three major geographic features that define modern-day India: Himalayan peaks and hills along the northern borders, the alluvial floodplains of the Indus and Ganges Rivers in the north, and the elevated Deccan Plateau that forms the core of India's triangular southern peninsula.

The Himalaya

As the world's highest mountains – with the highest peak in India (Khangchendzonga) reaching 8598m – the Himalaya create an almost impregnable boundary separating India from its neighbours to the north. These mountains formed when the Indian subcontinent broke away from Gondwanaland, a supercontinent in the Southern Hemisphere that included Africa, Antarctica, Australia and South America. All by itself, India drifted north and finally slammed slowly, but with immense force, into the Eurasian continent about 40 million years ago, buckling the ancient seafloor upward to form the Himalaya and many lesser ranges that stretch 2500km from Afghanistan to Myanmar (Burma).

When the Himalaya reached its great heights during the Pleistocene (less than 150,000 years ago), it blocked and altered weather systems, creating the monsoon climate that dominates India today, as well as forming a dry rainshadow to the north.

Although it looks like a continuous range on a map, the Himalaya is actually a series of interlocking ridges, separated by countless valleys. Until technology enabled the building of roads through the Himalaya, many of these valleys were virtually isolated, creating a diverse series of mountain cultures.

The Indo-Gangetic Plain

Covering most of northern India, the vast alluvial plains of the sacred Ganges River are so flat that they drop a mere 200m between Delhi and the waterlogged wetlands of West Bengal, where the river joins forces with the Brahmaputra River from India's northeast, before dumping into the sea in Bangladesh. Vast quantities of eroded sediments from the neighbouring highlands accumulate on the plains to a depth of nearly 2km, creating fertile, well-watered agricultural land. This densely populated region was once extensively forested and rich in wildlife.

Gujarat in the far west of India is separated from Sindh (Pakistan) by the Rann of Kutch, a brackish marshland that becomes a huge inland sea during the wet season; the waters recede in the dry season, leaving isolated islands perched on an expansive plain.

The Deccan Plateau

South of the Indo-Gangetic (northern) plain, the land rises to the Deccan Plateau, marking the divide between the Mughal heartlands of North India and the Dravidian civilisations of the south. The Deccan is bound on either side by the Western and Eastern Ghats, which come together in their southern reaches to form the Nilgiri Hills in Tamil Nadu.

On the Deccan's western border, the Western Ghats drop sharply down to a narrow coastal lowland, forming a luxuriant slope of rainforest.

The Islands

Offshore from India are a series of island groups, politically part of India but geographically linked to the landmasses of Southeast Asia and islands of the Indian Ocean. The Andaman and Nicobar Islands sit far out in the Bay of Bengal, while the coral atolls of Lakshadweep (300km west of Kerala) are a northerly extension of the Maldives islands, with a land area of just 32 sq km.

The Andaman and Nicobar Islands comprise 572 islands and are the peaks of a vast submerged mountain range extending almost 1000km between Myanmar (Burma) and Sumatra (Indonesia).

Environmental Issues

With well over a billion people, ever-expanding industrial and urban centres, and growth in chemical-intensive farming, India's environment is under tremendous pressure. An estimated 65% of the land is degraded in some way, most of it seriously, and the government has been consistently falling short of the majority of its environmental protection goals. Many current problems are a direct result of the Green Revolution of the 1960s when chemical fertilisers and pesticides enabled huge growth in agricultural output but at enormous cost to the environment.

Despite numerous environmental laws, corruption continues to exacerbate environmental degradation – exemplified by the flagrant flouting of laws by companies involved in hydroelectricity and mining. Usually, the people most affected are low-caste rural farmers and Adivasis (tribal people) who have limited political representation and few resources to fight big businesses.

Agricultural production has been reduced by soil degradation from over-farming, rising soil salinity, loss of tree cover and poor irrigation. The human cost is heart-rending, and lurking behind all these problems is a basic Malthusian truth: there are far too many people for India to support.

As anywhere, tourists tread a fine line between providing an incentive for change and making the problem worse. For example, many of

Get the inside track on Indian environmental issues at Down to Earth (www.downtoearth.org.in), an online magazine that delves into stories overlooked by mainstream media.

A DAM TOO FAR?

The most controversial of India's many hydroelectric schemes is the Narmada Valley Development, a US$6-billion scheme to build 30 hydroelectric dams along the Narmada River in Madhya Pradesh and Gujarat. Despite bringing benefits in terms of irrigation to thousands of villages and reducing desert encroachment into rural areas, the project will flood the tribal homelands of some 40,000 Adivasi villagers, many of whom worship the waters as a deity. The government has promised to provide alternative accommodation, but so far only 10% of the displaced people have found adequate farmland as compensation. The World Bank refused to fund the ongoing development, but Britain's Barclays Bank stepped in with loans and the Indian government has overruled every legal challenge to the development. Despite active protests for over 25 years and some high-profile names joining the anti–Narmada Dam movement – including Booker Prize–winner Arundhati Roy – the fight has started to lose momentum.

the environmental problems in Goa are a direct result of years of irresponsible development for tourism. Always consider your environmental impact while travelling in India.

Climate Change

Changing climate patterns – linked to global carbon emissions – have been creating dangerous extremes of weather in India. While India's per-capita carbon emissions still rank far behind that of the USA, Australia and Europe, the sheer size of its population makes it a major polluter.

It has been estimated that by 2030 India will see a 30% increase in the severity of its floods and droughts. In the mountain deserts of Ladakh, increased rainfall is changing time-honoured farming patterns, while glaciers on nearby peaks are melting at alarming rates. Conversely, other areas are experiencing reduced rainfall, causing drought and riots over access to water. Islands in the Lakshadweep group as well as the low-lying plains of the Ganges delta are being inundated by rising sea levels.

Deforestation

Since Independence, over 50,000 sq km of India's forests have been cleared for logging and farming, or destroyed by urban expansion, mining, industrialisation and river dams. Even in the well-funded, highly protected Project Tiger parks, the amount of forest cover classified as 'degraded' has tripled due to illegal logging. The number of mangrove forests has halved since the early 1990s, reducing the nursery grounds for the fish that stock the Indian Ocean and Bay of Bengal.

India's first Five Year Plan in 1951 recognised the importance of forests for soil conservation, and various policies have been introduced to increase forest cover. Almost all have been flouted by officials or criminals and by ordinary people clearing forests for firewood and grazing in forest areas. What can you do? Try to minimise the use of wood-burning stoves while you travel. Further, you could support the numerous charities working with rural communities to encourage tree planting.

Water Resources

Arguably the biggest threat to public health in India is inadequate access to clean drinking water and proper sanitation. With the population set to double by 2050, agricultural, industrial and domestic water usage are all expected to spiral, despite government policies designed to control water use. The World Health Organization estimates that, out of more than 3000 cities and towns in India, only eight have adequate waste-water treatment facilities. Many cities dump untreated sewage and partially cremated bodies directly into rivers, while open defecation is a simple fact of life in most rural (and many urban) areas.

Rivers are also affected by run-off, industrial pollution and sewage contamination – the Sabarmati, Yamuna and Ganges are amongst the most polluted rivers on earth (downstream of Varanasi the Ganges River is a black, septic mess with 3000 times the acceptable limit of faecal coliform bacteria). At least 70% of the freshwater sources in India are now polluted in some way. In recent years, drought has devastated parts of the subcontinent (particularly Rajasthan and Gujarat) and has been a driving force for rural-to-urban migration.

Water distribution is another volatile issue. Since 1947 an estimated 35 million people in India have been displaced by major dams, mostly built to provide hydroelectricity for this increasingly power-hungry nation. While hydroelectricity is one of the greener power sources, valleys across India are being sacrificed to create new power plants, and displaced people rarely receive adequate compensation.

Noise pollution in major cities has been measured at over 90 decibels – more than 1½ times the recognised 'safe' limit. Bring earplugs!

Air pollution in many Indian cities has been measured at more than double the maximum safe level recommended by the World Health Organization.

Survival Guide

Scams

Scams, both classic and newfangled, are known to exist in India. Of course, most can be avoided with a little bit of common sense and an appropriate amount of caution. Chat with fellow travellers to keep abreast of the latest cons. Look at the India branch of Lonely Planet's Thorn Tree Travel Forum (www.lonelyplanet.com/thorntree), where travellers often post timely warnings about problems they've encountered on the road.

Contaminated Food & Drink

The late 1990s saw a scam in North India where travellers died after consuming food laced with dangerous bacteria from restaurants linked to dodgy medical clinics. In unrelated incidents, some clinics have also given more treatment than necessary to procure larger payments from insurance companies.

While in transit, try to carry packed food if possible. If you must eat at bus or train stations, follow the crowd and buy food only from fast-moving places.

Most bottled water is legit, but ensure the seal is intact and the bottom of the bottle hasn't been tampered with.

Credit-Card Con

Be careful when paying for souvenirs with a credit card. While government shops are usually legitimate, private souvenir shops have been known to surreptitiously run off extra copies of the credit-card imprint slip and use them for phoney transactions later. Ask the trader to process the transaction in front of you. Memorising the CVV/CVC2 number and scratching it off the card is also a good idea, to avoid misuse.

Druggings

Occasionally, tourists (especially those travelling solo) are drugged and robbed during train or bus journeys. A spiked drink is the most commonly used method for sending them off to sleep – chocolates, chai from a co-conspiring vendor and 'homemade' Indian food are also known to be used. Use your instincts, and if you're unsure, politely decline drinks or food offered by strangers.

Gem Scams

This classic scam involves charming con artists who promise foolproof 'get rich quick' schemes. Travellers are asked to carry or mail gems home and then sell them to the trader's (non-existent) overseas representatives at a profit. Without exception, the goods – if they arrive at all – are worth a fraction of what you paid, and the 'representatives' never materialise.

KEEPING SAFE

➡ A good travel-insurance policy is essential.

➡ Email copies of your passport identity page, visa and airline tickets to yourself, and keep copies on you.

➡ Keep your money and passport in a concealed money belt or secure place under your shirt.

➡ Store at least US$100 separately from your main stash.

➡ Don't publicly display large wads of cash when paying for services or checking into hotels.

➡ Consider using your own padlock at cheaper hotels.

➡ If you can't lock your hotel room securely from the inside, stay somewhere else.

Don't believe hard-luck stories about an inability to obtain an export licence, and don't believe the (fake traveller) testimonials they show you. Travellers have reported this con happening in Agra, Delhi, and Jaisalmer among other places, but it's particularly prevalent in Jaipur. Carpets, curios and *pashmina* woollens are other favourites for this con.

Overpricing

Always agree on prices beforehand while availing services that don't have regulated tariffs. This particularly applies to friendly neighbourhood guides, snack bars at places of touristy interest, and autorickshaws and taxis without meters.

Photography

Use your instincts (better still, ask for permission) while photographing people. The common argument – voiced only after you've snapped your photos – is you're going to sell them to glossy international magazines, so it's only fair that you pay a posing fee.

Theft

Theft is a risk in India, as anywhere else. Keep luggage locked and chained on buses and trains. Remember that snatchings often occur when a train is pulling out of the station, as it's too late for you to give chase.

Take extra care in dormitories and never leave your valuables unattended. Use safe deposit boxes where possible.

Touts & Commission Agents

Touts come in many avatars and operate in mysterious

ways. Cabbies and autorickshaw drivers often coerce you to stay at a budget hotel of their choice, only to collect a commission (included within your room tariff) from the receptionists afterward.

Wherever possible, arrange hotel bookings (if only for the first night), and request a hotel pick-up. You'll often hear stories about hotels of your choice being 'full' or 'closed' – check things out yourself.

Be very sceptical of phrases like 'my brother's shop' and 'special deal at my friend's place'. Many fraudsters operate in collusion with souvenir stalls, so be careful while making expensive purchases in private stores.

Avoid friendly people in train and bus stations who offer unsolicited help. Look confident, and if anyone asks if this is your first trip to India, say you've been here several times, even if you haven't. Telling touts that you have already prepaid your transfer/tour/onward journey can help dissuade them.

Touts can be particularly bothersome in major tourist centres like Delhi, Jaipur, Agra and Varanasi.

Transport Scams

Upon arriving at train stations and airports, always book transport from government-approved booths. All major airports now have radio cab, prepaid taxi and airport shuttle bus counters within the arrival lounge. Never go with a loitering cabbie who offers you a cheap ride into town, especially at night.

While booking multiday sightseeing tours, stick to itineraries offered by tourism departments, or those that come recommended either in this guidebook or by friends who've personally used them. Be extremely wary of anyone in Delhi offering houseboat tours to Kashmir – we've received many complaints over the years about dodgy deals.

When buying a bus, train or plane ticket anywhere other than the registered office of the transport company, make sure you're getting the ticket class you paid for. Use online booking facilities where possible.

Some tricksters pose as Indian Railways officials and insist you pay to have your e-ticket validated on the platform; ignore them.

Women & Solo Travellers

Women and solo travellers may encounter a few extra hurdles when visiting India – from cost (for those travelling alone) to maintaining appropriate dress codes (women). As with anywhere else in the world, it pays to be prepared.

Women Travellers

Although Bollywood might suggest otherwise, India remains a largely conservative society. Female travellers should be aware that their behaviour and attire choice are likely to be under constant scrutiny, particularly away from tourist centres.

Attention

➡ Be prepared to be stared at; it's something you'll simply have to live with so don't allow it to get the better of you.

➡ Refrain from returning male stares; this can be considered a come-on.

➡ Dark glasses, phones, books or electronic devices are useful for averting unwanted conversations.

Clothing

Avoiding culturally inappropriate clothing will help avert undesirable attention.

➡ Steer clear of sleeveless tops, shorts, miniskirts (ankle-length skirts are recommended) and anything else that's skimpy, see-through or tight-fitting.

➡ Wearing Indian-style clothes is viewed favourably and can help deflect harassment.

➡ Draping a dupatta (long scarf) over T-shirts is another good way to avoid stares – it's also handy if you visit a shrine that requires your head to be covered.

➡ Wearing a *salwar kameez* (traditional dresslike tunic and trousers) will help you blend in.

➡ If you're not keen on wearing a *salwar kameez*, a smart alternative is a kurta (long shirt) worn over jeans or trousers.

➡ Avoid going out in public wearing a choli (sari blouse) or a sari petticoat (which some foreign women mistake for a skirt); it's like strutting around half-dressed.

➡ Aside from at pools, many Indian women wear long shorts and a T-shirt when swimming in public view; it's wise to wear a sarong from the beach to your hotel.

Health & Hygiene

➡ Sanitary pads are widely available but tampons are usually restricted to pharmacies in big cities and tourist towns (even then, the choice may be limited). Carry additional stocks for travel off the beaten track.

Sexual Harassment

Many female travellers have reported some form of sexual harassment while in India.

➡ Most cases are reported in urban centres of North India and prominent tourist towns elsewhere, and have involved lewd comments, invasion of privacy and groping.

➡ Other cases have included provocative gestures, jeering, getting 'accidentally' bumped into on the street and being followed.

➡ Incidents are particularly common at exuberant (and crowded) public events such as the Holi festival.

➡ Women travelling with a male partner are less likely to be hassled.

Staying Safe

The following tips will hopefully help you avoid uncomfortable situations during your journey:

➡ Keep conversations with unknown men short – getting involved in an inane conversation with someone you barely know can be misinterpreted as a sign of sexual interest.

➡ Questions and comments such as 'Do you have a boyfriend?' or 'You're very beautiful' are indicators that the conversation may be taking a steamy tangent.

➡ Some women wear a pseudo wedding ring, or announce early on in the conversation that they're married or engaged (regardless of the reality).

➤ If you feel that a guy is encroaching on your space, he probably is. A firm request to keep away usually does the trick, especially if your tone is loud and curt enough to draw the attention of passers-by.

➤ The silent treatment can also be very effective.

➤ Follow local women's cues and instead of shaking hands say *namaste* – the traditional, respectful Hindu greeting.

➤ Avoid wearing expensive-looking jewellery and carrying flashy accessories.

➤ Check the reputation of any teacher or therapist before going to a solo session (get recommendations from travellers). Some women have reported being molested by masseurs and other therapists. If you feel uneasy at any time, leave.

➤ Female filmgoers may attract less attention and lessen the chances of harassment by going to the cinema with a companion.

➤ At hotels keep your door locked, as staff (particularly at budget and midrange places) can knock and automatically walk in without waiting for your permission.

➤ Arrive in towns before dark. Don't walk alone at night and avoid wandering alone in isolated areas even during daylight.

➤ Act confidently in public; to avoid looking lost (and thus more vulnerable) consult maps at your hotel (or at a restaurant indoors) rather than on the street.

Taxis & Public Transport

Being female has some advantages; women can usually queue-jump for buses and trains without consequence and on trains there are special ladies-only carriages.

➤ Solo women should prearrange an airport pick-up from their hotel, especially if their flight is scheduled to arrive after dark.

➤ Delhi and some other cities have prepaid radio cab services such as Easycabs – they're more expensive than the regular prepaid taxis, but promote themselves as being safe, with drivers who have been vetted as part of their recruitment.

➤ If you do catch a regular prepaid taxi, make a point of writing down the car registration and driver's name – in front of the driver – and giving it to one of the airport police.

➤ Avoid taking taxis alone late at night and never agree to have more than one man (the driver) in the car – ignore claims that this is 'just my brother' etc.

➤ Solo women have reported less hassle by opting for the more expensive classes on trains.

➤ If you're travelling overnight in a three-tier carriage, try to get the uppermost berth, which will give you more privacy (and distance from potential gropers).

➤ On public transport, don't hesitate to return any errant limbs, put luggage between you and others, be vocal (attracting attention, thus shaming the pest), or simply find a new spot.

Solo Travellers

One of the joys of travelling solo in India is that you're more likely to be 'adopted' by families, especially if you're commuting together on a long rail journey. It's a great opportunity to make friends and get a deeper understanding of local culture. If you're keen to hook up with fellow travellers, tourist hubs such as Goa, Rajasthan, Kerala, Manali, McLeod Ganj, Leh, Agra and Varanasi are

some popular places to do so. You may also be able to find travel companions on Lonely Planet's Thorn Tree Travel Forum (www.lonelyplanet.com/thorntree).

Cost
The most significant issue facing solo travellers is cost.

➤ Single-room accommodation rates are sometimes not much lower than double rates.

➤ Some midrange and top-end places don't even offer a single tariff.

➤ It's always worth trying to negotiate a lower rate for single occupancy.

Safety
Most solo travellers experience no major problems in India but, like anywhere else, it's wise to stay on your toes in unfamiliar surroundings.

➤ Some less honourable souls (locals and travellers alike) view lone tourists as an easy target for theft and sexual assault.

➤ Single men wandering around isolated areas have been mugged, even during the day.

Transport
➤ You'll save money if you find others to share taxis and autorickshaws, as well as when hiring a car for longer trips.

➤ Solo bus travellers may be able to get the 'co-pilot' seat (near the driver) on buses, which not only has a good view out front, but is also handy if you've got a big bag.

Directory A–Z

Accommodation

Accommodation in India ranges from grungy backpacker hostels with concrete floors and cold 'bucket' showers to opulent palaces converted into beautiful five-star hotels. We've listed reviews by author preference within price categories; standout options are indicated by ★.

Categories

As a general rule, budget (₹) covers everything from basic hostels, hotels and guesthouses in urban areas to traditional homestays in villages. Midrange hotels (₹₹) tend to be modern concrete and glass affairs that usually offer extras such as cable/satellite TV and air-conditioning (although some just have noisy 'air-coolers' that cool air by blowing it over cold water). Top-end places (₹₹₹) stretch from luxury five-star chains to gorgeous heritage palaces and resorts.

Costs

Given that the cost of budget, midrange and top-end hotels varies so much across India,

BOOK YOUR STAY ONLINE

For more accommodation reviews by Lonely Planet authors, check out http://lonelyplanet.com/india/hotels. You'll find independent reviews, as well as recommendations on the best places to stay. Best of all, you can book online.

it would be misleading for us to provide a 'national' price range for each category. Keep in mind that most establishments raise tariffs annually, so the prices may have risen by the time you read this. Prices are highest in large cities (eg Delhi, Mumbai), lowest in rural areas (eg Bihar, Andhra Pradesh). Costs are also highly seasonal – hotel prices can drop by 20% to 50% outside of peak season.

Note, while usually the internet or pre-booking rate is expected to be cheaper than the rack rate, in India, however, the reverse is common. Travellers may find that the rack rate is often significantly higher when booking ahead than the walk-in rate. The rack rate is the price that usually appears on the ubiquitous tariff list card.

Price Icons

Lonely Planet price indicators refer to the cost of a double room, including private bathroom, unless otherwise noted.

The table below is based on price indicators for Bihar, Tamil Nadu and Rajasthan and gives an example of the differences in accommodation costs across India.

Reservations

The majority of top-end and some midrange hotels require a deposit at the time of booking. The figure can range from a day's tariff to the full amount. This can usually be done with a credit card.

Some midrange places may ask for a cheque or cash deposit into a bank account to secure a reservation. This is usually more hassle than it's worth. Some places honour phone reservations – call to reconfirm the day before you arrive, especially during high tourist seasons.

Some budget options won't take reservations as they don't know when people are going to check-out; call

SAMPLE ACCOMMODATION COSTS

CATEGORY	BIHAR	TAMIL NADU	RAJASTHAN
₹ budget	<₹1000	<₹1000	<₹500
₹₹ midrange	₹1000-2500	₹1000-5000	₹500-1500
₹₹₹ top end	>₹2500	>₹5000	>₹1500

ahead to check or just turn up around check-in time.

Other places will want a deposit at check-in – ask for a receipt and be wary of any request to sign a blank impression of your credit card. If the hotel insists, consider going to the nearest ATM and paying cash.

Verify the check-out time when you check-in – some hotels have a fixed check-out time (usually 10am or noon), while others offer 24-hour check-out. In some places, check-out can be as early as 9am.

Seasons

Rates given are full price in high season. High season usually coincides with the best weather for the area's sights and activities – normally spring and autumn in the mountains (March to May and September to November), and the cooler months in the plains (around November to mid-February).

In areas popular with foreign tourists, there's an additional peak period over Christmas and New Year; make reservations well in advance.

At other times you may find significant discounts; if the hotel seems quiet, ask for one.

Some hotels in places like Goa shut during the monsoon period. Certain hill stations like Manali close down during winter.

Many temple towns have additional peak seasons around major festivals and pilgrimages.

Taxes & Service Charges

State governments slap a variety of taxes on hotel accommodation (except at the cheaper hotels), and these are added to the cost of your room.

Taxes vary from state to state. Even within a state prices can vary, with more expensive hotels levying higher taxes.

Many upmarket hotels also add an additional 'service charge' (usually around 10%).

Rates quoted in this book include taxes.

Some upscale restaurants may add a service charge (between 10% and 13%) on meals.

Budget & Midrange Hotels

Apart from some traditional wood or stone guesthouses in remote mountain areas, most budget and midrange hotels are modern-style concrete blocks with requisite creature comforts. Some are charming, clean and good value; others less so.

Room quality can vary considerably within a hotel so try to inspect a few rooms first; avoid carpeted rooms at cheaper hotels unless you like the smell of mouldy socks.

Shared bathrooms (often with squat toilets) are usually only found at the cheapest lodgings.

Most rooms have ceiling fans and better rooms have electric mosquito killers and/or window nets, though cheaper rooms may lack windows altogether.

If you're mostly staying in budget places, bring your own sheet or sleeping-bag liner. Sheets and bedclothes at cheap hotels can be stained, well worn and in need of a wash.

An insect repellent and a torch (flashlight) are essential accessories for survival in many budget hotels.

Sound pollution can be irksome (especially in urban hubs); pack good-quality earplugs and request a room that doesn't face a busy road.

It's wise to keep your door locked at all times, as some staff (particularly in budget hotels) may knock and automatically walk in without awaiting your permission.

PRACTICALITIES

➡ **Newspapers & Magazines** Major English-language dailies include the *Hindustan Times, Times of India, Indian Express, Hindu, Statesman, Telegraph, Daily News & Analysis (DNA)* and *Economic Times*. Regional English-language and local-vernacular publications are found nationwide. Incisive current-affairs magazines include *Frontline, India Today, Week, Open, Tehelka* and *Outlook*.

➡ **Radio** Government-controlled All India Radio (AIR), India's national broadcaster, has over 220 stations broadcasting local and international news. Private FM channels broadcast music, current affairs, talkback and more.

➡ **TV & Video** The national (government) TV broadcaster is Doordarshan. More people watch satellite and cable TV; English-language channels include BBC, CNN, Star World, HBO, National Geographic and Discovery.

➡ **Weights & Measures** Officially India is metric. Terms you're likely to hear are lakhs (one lakh = 100,000) and crores (one crore = 10 million).

Blackouts are common (especially during summer and the monsoon) so double-check that the hotel has a back-up generator if you're paying for electric 'extras' such as air-conditioners, TVs and wi-fi.

Note that some hotels lock their doors at night. Members of staff might sleep in the lobby but waking them up can be a challenge. Let the hotel know in advance if you'll be arriving late at night or leaving early in the morning.

Away from tourist areas, cheaper hotels may not take foreigners because they don't have the necessary foreigner-registration forms.

Camping

There are few official camping sites in India. On the other hand, wild camping is often the only accommodation option on trekking routes.

In some mountain areas you'll also find summer-only tented camps, with accommodation in semipermanent 'Swiss tents' with attached bathrooms.

Dormitory Accommodation

A number of hotels have cheap dormitories, though these may be mixed gender and, in less touristy places, full of drunken males – not ideal conditions for women.

More traveller-friendly dorms are found at the handful of hostels run by the YMCA, YWCA and Salvation Army as well as at those associated with HI or YHAI (Youth Hostels Association of India).

Government Accommodation & Tourist Bungalows

The Indian government maintains a network of guesthouses for travelling officials and public workers, known variously as rest houses, dak bungalows, circuit houses, PWD (Public Works Depart-

ment) bungalows and forest rest houses.

These places may accept travellers if no government employees need the rooms, but permission is sometimes required from local officials and you'll probably have to find the chowkidar (caretaker) to open the doors. Besides, there's always the risk of being thrown out if officials suddenly arrive during your stay!

'Tourist bungalows' are run by state governments – rooms are usually midpriced (some with cheap dorms) and have varying standards of cleanliness and service.

Some state governments also run chains of more expensive hotels, including some lovely heritage properties. Details are normally available through the state tourism offices.

Homestays & B&Bs

These family-run guesthouses will appeal to those seeking a small-scale, uncommercial setting with home-cooked meals.

Standards range from mud-and-stone village huts with hole-in-the-floor toilets to comfortable middle-class homes in cities.

In places like Ladakh, homestays are increasingly the way to go but standards are fairly simple.

Be aware that some hotels market themselves as 'homestays' but are run like hotels with little (or no) interaction with the family.

Contact local tourist offices for full lists of participating families.

Railway Retiring Rooms

Most large train stations have basic rooms for travellers holding an ongoing train ticket or Indrail Pass. Some are grim, others are surprisingly pleasant but suffer from the noise of passengers and trains.

They're useful for early-morning departures and there's usually a choice of dormitories or private rooms (24-hour check-out) depending on the class you're travelling in.

Some smaller stations may have waiting rooms instead of retiring rooms. These are large halls with rows of chairs (similar to an airport lounge but with substantially lower degrees of comfort and cleanliness) and are usually located in the vicinity of toilets and cafeterias. Once again, there may be different waiting rooms for passengers travelling in different classes.

Temples & Pilgrims' Rest Houses

Accommodation is available at some ashrams (spiritual retreats), gurdwaras (temples) and dharamsalas (pilgrims' guesthouses) for a donation or a nominal fee. Vegetarian meals are usually available at the refectories.

These places have been established for genuine pilgrims so please exercise judgement about the appropriateness of staying.

Always abide by any protocols. Smoking and drinking within the premises are a complete no-no.

Top-End & Heritage Hotels

India has plenty of top-end properties, from modern five-star chain hotels to glorious palaces and unique heritage abodes.

Most top-end hotels have rupee rates for Indian guests and US dollar rates for foreigners, including Non-Resident Indians (NRIs).

Officially, you're supposed to pay the dollar rates in foreign currency or by credit card, but many places will accept rupees adding up to the dollar rate (verify this when checking in).

The Government of India tourism website, **Incredible India** (www.incredibleindia. org), has a useful list of palaces, forts and other erstwhile royal retreats that accept paying guests – go to the 'Travel' page and click on the 'Royal Retreats' link.

In recent times, India has also seen a mushrooming of luxury eco- and forest resorts in and around several national parks.

Customs Regulations

Technically you're supposed to declare any amount of cash/travellers cheques over US$5000/10,000 on arrival.

Indian rupees shouldn't be taken out of India; however, this is rarely policed.

Officials very occasionally ask tourists to enter expensive items such as video cameras and laptop computers on a 'Tourist Baggage Re-export' form to ensure they're taken out of India at the time of departure.

Electricity

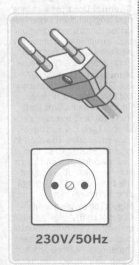

230V/50Hz

230V/50Hz

Embassies & Consulates

Most foreign diplomatic missions are based in Delhi, but several nations operate consulates in other Indian cities (see websites, where provided, for more details). Many missions have certain timings for visa applications, usually mornings: phone for details. The following are just some of the many foreign missions found in India.

Australian (www.india.high-commission.gov.au); Chennai (☎044-45921300; 9th fl, Express Chambers, Whites Rd, Royapettah); Delhi (☎011-41399900 1/50G Shantipath, Chanakyapuri); Mumbai (☎022-67574900; 10th fl, A Wing, Crescenzo Bldg, G Block, Plot C 38-39, Bandra Kurla Complex)

Bangladeshi Delhi (☎011-24121394; www.bhcdelhi.org; EP39 Dr Radakrishnan Marg, Chanakyapuri); Kolkata (☎033-40127500; 9 Bangabandhu Sheikh Mujib Sarani)

Bhutanese (☎011-2688 9230; www.bhutan.gov.bt; Chandragupta Marg, Chanakyapuri, Delhi)

Canadian (www.canada international.gc.ca/india-inde/); Chennai (☎044-28330888;

18, 3rd fl YAFA Tower, Khader Nawaz Khan Rd); Delhi (☎011-41782000; 7/8 Shantipath, Chanakyapuri); Mumbai (☎022-67574900; 10th fl, A Wing, Crescenzo Bldg, G Block, Plot C 38-39, Bandra Kurla Complex)

Chinese (www. in.chineseembassy.org); Delhi (☎011-26112345; 50D, Shantipath, Chanakyapuri); Kolkata (☎033-40048169; EC72, Sector I Salt Lake); Mumbai (☎022-56324303; Hoechst House, 193 Backbay Reclamation, Nariman Point)

French (http://ambafrance -in.org); Delhi (☎011-24196100; 2/50E Shantipath, Chanakyapuri); Mumbai (☎022-56694000; Wockhardt Towers, East Wing, 5th fl, Bandra Kurla Complex); Puducherry (☎0413-2231000; 2 Marine St)

German (www.new-delhi.diplo. de); Chennai (☎044-24301600; 9 Boat Club Rd, RA Puram); Delhi (☎011-44199199; 6/50G Shantipath, Chanakyapuri); Kolkata (☎033-24791141; 1 Hastings Park Rd, Alipore); Mumbai (☎022-22832422; 10th fl, Hoechst House, Nariman Point)

Israeli (http://delhi.mfa.gov. il); Delhi (☎011-30414500; 3 Aurangzeb Rd); Mumbai (☎022-22819994; Earnest House, 16th fl, NCPA Marg, 194 Nariman Point)

Japanese (www.in.emb-japan.go.jp); Chennai (☎044-24323860; 12/1 Cenotaph Rd, 1st St Teynampet); Delhi (☎011-26876581; 50G Shantipath, Chanakyapuri); Kolkata (☎033-2421-1970; 55 MN Sen Lane, Tollygunge); Mumbai (☎022-23517101; 1 ML Dahanukar Marg, Cumballa Hill)

Malaysian (☎011-26111291/97; www.kln.gov.my/ web/ind_new-delhi/home; 50M Satya Marg, Chanakyapuri, Delhi)

Myanmar (www.mofa.gov. mm/myanmarmissions/india. html); Delhi (☎011-24678822; 3/50F Nyaya Marg); Kolkata (☎033-24851658; 57K Ballygunge Circular Rd)

Nepali Delhi (☎011-23327361; Mandi House, Barakhamba Rd); Kolkata (☎033-24561224; 1 National Library Ave, Alipore)

Netherlands (www.holland-india.org); *Chennai* (☏044-42112770; 8B Adyar Club Gate Rd, RA Puram); *Delhi* (☏011-24197600; 6/50F Shantipath, Chanakyapuri); *Mumbai* (☏022-22194200; Forbes Bldg, Charanjit Rai Marg, Fort)

New Zealand (www.nzembassy.com/india); *Chennai* (☏044-28112472; Rane Engine Valves Ltd, Maithri, 132 Cathedral Rd); *Delhi* (☏011-46883170; Sir Edmund Hillary Marg, Chanakyapuri); *Mumbai* (☏022-61316666; Level 2, Maker Maxity, 3 North Ave, Bandra Kurla Complex)

Pakistani (☏011-26110601; www.mofa.gov.pk/india; 2/50G Shantipath, Chanakyapuri, Delhi)

Singaporean (www.mfa.gov.sg/newdelhi); *Chennai* (☏044-28158207; 17A North Boag Rd, T Nagar); *Delhi* (☏011-46000915; E6 Chandragupta Marg, Chanakyapuri); *Mumbai* (☏022-22043205; 152, Maker Chambers IV, 14th fl, 222 Jamnalal Bajaj Rd, Nariman Point)

Sri Lankan (www.newdelhi.mission.gov.lk); *Chennai* (☏044-24987896; 196 TTK Rd, Alwarpet); *Delhi* (☏011-23010201; 27 Kautilya Marg, Chanakyapuri); *Mumbai* (☏022-22045861; Mulla House, 34 Homi Modi St, Fort)

Thai (www.thaiemb.org.in); *Chennai* (☏044-42300730; 3 First Main Rd, Vidyodaya Colony, T Nagar); *Delhi* (☏011-26150130; 4/5 Vasant Vihar); *Kolkata* (☏033-24407836; 18B Mandeville Gardens, Ballygunge); *Mumbai* (☏022-22823535; 1st fl, Dalamal House, Jamnalal Bajaj Marg, Nariman Point)

UK (http://ukinindia.fco.gov.uk); *Chennai* (☏044-42192151; 20 Anderson Rd); *Delhi* (☏011-24192100; Shantipath, Chanakyapuri); *Kolkata* (☏033-22885172; 1A Ho Chi Minh Sarani); *Mumbai* (☏022-66502222; Naman Chambers, C/32 G Block, Bandra Kurla Complex)

US (http://newdelhi.usembassy.gov); *Chennai* (☏044-28574000; Gemini Circle, 220 Anna Salai); *Delhi* (☏011-24198000; Shantipath, Chanakyapuri); *Kolkata* (☏033-39842400; 5/1 Ho Chi Minh Sarani); *Mumbai* (☏022-2672 4000; C49, G Block, Bandra Kurla Complex)

Gay & Lesbian Travellers

Homosexuality is legal in India, although the country remains largely conservative. Public displays of affection are generally frowned upon for both homosexual and heterosexual couples.

There are gay scenes in a number of cities including Mumbai, Delhi, Kolkata, Chennai and Bengaluru (Bangalore) – Gay Pride marches are held annually at some of these centres.

Publications

Time Out Delhi (www.timeoutdelhi.net) Includes fortnightly listings of gay events in Delhi.

Time Out Mumbai (www.timeoutmumbai.net) Gay events in Mumbai.

Websites

Delhi Frontrunners & Walkers (www.delhifrontrunners.org) Weekly running and walking club for Delhi's LGBT crowd.

Gay Bombay (www.gaybombay.org) Lists gay events as well as offers support and advice.

Gay Delhi (www.gaydelhi.org) LGBT support group, organising social events in Delhi. Register for more details.

Gaysi (http://gaysifamily.com) Started as a forum for LGBTQ South Asians, it has excellent news, reviews and features.

Indian Dost (www.indiandost.com/gay.php) News and information including contact groups in India.

Indja Pink (www.indjapink.co.in) India's first 'gay travel boutique' founded by a well-known Indian fashion designer.

Queer Azaadi Mumbai (http://queerazaadi.wordpress.com) Mumbai's queer pride blog, with news.

Queer Ink (www.queer-ink.com) Online bookshop specialising in gay- and lesbian-interest books from the subcontinent, including the story collection *Out!*, which it published.

Support Groups

Chennai Dost (www.chennaidost.blogspot.com) Organises varied events, including parties, exhibitions, campaigns and the Chennai Rainbow Pride march every June.

Humsafar Trust (☏022-26673800; www.humsafar.org; Old BMC Bldg, 1st fl, Nehru Rd, Vakola, Santa Cruz East) Runs gay and transgender support groups and advocacy programs. The drop-in centre in Santa Cruz East hosts workshops and has a library – pick up a copy of the pioneering LGBT magazine *Bombay Dost*.

Nigah (http://nigahdelhi.blogspot.com) Autonomous collective that holds monthly queer events and organises the annual Nigah Queerfest.

Sangama (www.sangama.org) Deals with crisis intervention and provides a community

EATING PRICE RANGES

Prices in this book reflect the cost of a standard main meal (unless otherwise indicated). Reviews are listed by author preference within price categories.

CATEGORY	COSTS
₹ budget	₹100
₹₹ midrange	₹100-300
₹₹₹ top end	>₹300

outreach service for gay and bisexual men and women, transgenders and *hijras* (transvestites and eunuchs).

Sappho (www.sapphokolkata. org) Operates as a support organisation for lesbian, bisexual and transgender women.

Wajood Society (www. wajoodsociety.com) Hyderabad's budding queersupport group organises get-togethers.

Insurance

Comprehensive travel insurance to cover theft, loss and medical problems (as well as air evacuation) is strongly recommended.

Some policies specifically exclude potentially dangerous activities such as scuba diving, skiing, motorcycling, paragliding and even trekking: read the fine print.

Some trekking agents may only accept customers who have cover for emergency helicopter evacuation.

If you plan to hire a motorcycle in India, make sure the rental policy includes at least third-party insurance.

Check in advance whether your insurance policy will pay doctors and hospitals directly or reimburse you later for overseas health expenditure (keep all documentation for your claim).

It's crucial to get a police report in India if you've had anything stolen; insurance companies may refuse to reimburse you without one.

Worldwide travel insurance is available at www.lonelyplanet.com/travel_services. You can buy, extend and claim online anytime – even if you're already on the road.

Internet Access

Internet cafes are widespread and connections are usually reasonably fast, except in more remote areas. Wireless (wi-fi) access is available in an increasing number of ho-

tels and some coffee shops in larger cities. Note that wi-fi services may be either free or chargeable; each establishment sets its own rules. Hotels offering internet access are marked by @.

Practicalities

Internet charges vary regionally; charges fall anywhere between ₹15 and ₹100 per hour and often with a 15- to 30-minute minimum.

Power cuts are not uncommon; avoid losing your email by writing and saving messages in a text application before pasting them into your browser.

Bandwidth load tends to be lowest in the early morning and early afternoon.

Some internet cafes may ask to see your passport.

Security

Be wary of sending sensitive financial information from internet cafes; some places are able to use keystroke-capturing technology to access passwords and emails.

Avoid sending credit-card details or other personal data over a wireless connection; using online banking on any nonsecure system is generally unwise.

If you must use public peripherals to carry out financial transactions during your trip, be sure to change all passwords (email, netbanking, credit card 3-D Secure code etc) the moment you get back home.

Laptops

Many internet cafes can supply laptop users with internet access over a LAN Ethernet cable; alternatively take out an account with a local Internet Service Provider (ISP).

Companies that offer prepaid wireless 2G and 3G modem sticks (called dongles) include Reliance, Airtel, Tata Docomo and Vodafone. Just plug one into the USB port of your laptop and you can access the internet. To organise a connection you have to submit your identity

proof and address in India – usually a letter or receipt from your hotel will suffice. A nonrefundable activation fee (around ₹1200) has to be paid, which includes the price of the dongle.

Tariffs for broadband internet start from ₹150 per month for 4GB up to ₹1000 per month for 11GB.

Make sure the areas you will be travelling to are covered by your service provider.

Consider purchasing a fuse-protected universal AC adaptor to protect your circuit board from power surges.

Plug adaptors are widely available throughout India, but bring spare plug fuses from home.

Language Courses

The following places offer language courses, some requiring a minimum time commitment.

Delhi Hindi classes at Delhi's **Central Hindi Directorate** (Map p78; 26178454; http://hindinideshalaya.nic. in; West Block VII, RK Puram; 60hr course ₹6000). Hindi, Urdu and Sanskrit classes at Zabaan.

Himachal Pradesh Long and short courses in Tibetan at the **Library of Tibetan Works & Archives** (Map p319; 222467; www.ltwa.net; Secretariat Complex; 9am-1pm & 2-5pm Mon-Sat, closed 2nd & 4th Sat of month), in McLeod Ganj.

Mumbai Beginners' courses in Hindi, Marathi and Sanskrit at **Bharatiya Vidya Bhavan** (Map p746; 23871860; 2nd fl, cnr KM Munshi Marg & Ramabai Rd, Girgaum; per hr ₹500; 4-8pm).

Tamil Nadu Tamil courses at **International Institute of Tamil Studies** (22542781; www.ulakaththamizh.org; CIT Campus, 2nd Main Rd, Tharamani), in Chennai.

Uttar Pradesh Hindi courses at **Pragati Hindi** (Map p394; 9335376488;

www.pragatihindi.com; B-7/176 Harar Bagh), in Varanasi.

Uttarakhand Hindi courses at the **Landour Language School** (✆2631487; www. landourlanguageschool.com; Landour; group per hr ₹175, private per hr ₹275; ⊘Feb-Dec), in Mussoorie (p417).

West Bengal Tibetan courses at the **Manjushree Centre of Tibetan Culture** (Map p496;✆2252977; www. manjushreetibcentre.org; 12 Ghandi Rd; 2-/3-/6-month courses US$180/260/380, plus registration US$30; ⊘mid-Mar–mid-Dec), in Darjeeling.

Legal Matters

If you're in a sticky legal situation, contact your embassy as quickly as possible. However, be aware that all your embassy may be able to do is monitor your treatment in custody and arrange a lawyer. In the Indian justice system, the burden of proof can often be on the accused and stints in prison before trial are not unheard of.

Antisocial Behaviour

Smoking in public places is illegal throughout India but this is very rarely enforced; if caught you'll be fined ₹200.

People can smoke inside their homes and in most open spaces such as streets (heed any signs stating otherwise).

A number of Indian cities have banned spitting and littering, but this is also enforced irregularly.

Drugs

Indian law does not distinguish between 'hard' and 'soft' drugs; possession of any illegal drug is regarded as a criminal offence.

If convicted, the *minimum* sentence is 10 years, with very little chance of remission or parole.

Cases can take months, even several years, to appear before a court while the accused may have to wait in prison. There's also usually a hefty monetary fine on top of any custodial sentence.

Be aware that travellers have been targeted in sting operations in Manali, Goa and other backpacker enclaves.

Marijuana grows wild in various parts of India, but consuming it is still an offence, except in towns where bhang is legally sold for religious rituals.

Police are getting particularly tough on foreigners who use drugs, so you should take this risk very seriously.

Police

You should always carry your passport; police are entitled to ask you for identification at any time.

If you're arrested for an alleged offence and asked for a bribe, note: it is illegal to pay a bribe in India. Many people deal with an on-the-spot fine by just paying it to avoid trumped-up charges. Corruption is rife so the less you have to do with local police the better; try to avoid all potentially risky situations.

Maps

Maps available inside India are of variable quality. Throughout India, most state-government tourist offices stock basic local maps. These are some of the better map series, which should be available at good bookshops:

Eicher (http://maps.eicherworld.com/)

Nelles (www.nelles-verlag.de)

Nest & Wings (www.nestwings.in)

Survey of India (www.surveyofindia.gov.in)

TTK (www.ttkmaps.com)

Money

The Indian rupee (₹) is divided into 100 paise (p), but paise coins are becoming increasingly rare. Coins come in denominations of ₹1, ₹2, ₹5 and ₹10 (the 1s and 2s look almost identical); notes come in ₹5, ₹10, ₹20, ₹50, ₹100, ₹500 and ₹1000 (the last is handy for paying large bills but can pose problems

---

PROHIBITED EXPORTS

To protect India's cultural heritage, the export of certain antiques is prohibited, especially those which are verifiably more than 100 years old. Reputable antique dealers know the laws and can make arrangements for an export-clearance certificate for old items that are OK to export. Detailed information on prohibited items can be found on the government webpage www.asi.nic.in/pdf_data/8.pdf. The rules may seem stringent but the loss of ancient artworks and sculptures in places such as Ladakh, Himachal Pradesh, Gujarat and Rajasthan, due to the international trade in antiques, has been alarming. Look for quality reproductions instead.

The Indian Wildlife Protection Act bans any form of wildlife trade. Don't buy any product that endangers threatened species and habitats – doing so can result in heavy fines and even imprisonment. This includes ivory, shahtoosh shawls (made from the down of chirus or rare Tibetan antelopes) and anything made from the fur, skin, horns or shell of any endangered species. Products made from certain rare plants are also banned.

when getting change for small services). The Indian rupee is linked to a basket of currencies and has been subject to fluctuations in recent years.

ATMs

ATMs are found in most urban centres.

Visa, MasterCard, Cirrus, Maestro and Plus are the most commonly accepted cards.

ATMs at the following banks recognise foreign cards: Axis Bank, Citibank, HDFC, HSBC, ICICI and State Bank of India. Other banks may accept major cards (Visa, MasterCard etc) but not necessarily all types of cards.

Before your trip, check whether your card can reliably access banking networks in India and ask for details of charges.

Notify your bank that you'll be using your card in India (provide dates) to avoid having your card blocked; take along your bank's phone number just in case.

Always keep the emergency lost-and-stolen numbers for your credit cards in a safe place, separate from your cards, and report any loss or theft immediately.

Away from major towns, always carry cash (including a stock of rupees) or travellers cheques as back-up.

Black Market

Black-market moneychangers exist but legal moneychangers are so common that there's no reason to use illegal services, except perhaps to change small amounts of cash at land border crossings. If someone approaches you on the street and offers to change money, you're probably being set up for a scam.

Cash

Major currencies such as US dollars, pounds sterling and euros are easy to change throughout India, although some bank branches insist on travellers cheques only.

Some banks also accept other currencies such as Australian and Canadian dollars, and Swiss francs.

Private moneychangers deal with a wider range of currencies, but Pakistani, Nepali and Bangladeshi currency can be harder to change away from the border.

When travelling off the beaten track, always carry an adequate stock of rupees.

Whenever changing money, check every note. Don't accept any filthy, ripped or disintegrating notes, as these may be difficult to use.

It can be tough getting change in India so keep a stock of smaller currency; ₹10, ₹20 and ₹50 notes are helpful.

Officially you cannot take rupees out of India, but this is laxly enforced. You can change any leftover rupees back into foreign currency most easily at the airport (some banks have a ₹1000 minimum). You may have to present encashment certificates or credit card/ATM receipts, and show your passport and airline ticket.

Credit Cards

Credit cards are accepted at a growing number of shops, upmarket restaurants, and midrange and top-end hotels, and they can usually be used to pay for flights and train tickets.

Cash advances on major credit cards are also possible at some banks.

MasterCard and Visa are the most widely accepted cards.

Encashment Certificates

Indian law states that all foreign currency must be changed at official moneychangers or banks.

For every (official) foreign-exchange transaction, you'll receive an encashment certificate (receipt), which will allow you to change rupees back into foreign currency when departing India.

Encashment certificates should cover the amount of rupees you intend to change back to foreign currency.

Printed receipts from ATMs are also accepted as evidence of an international transaction at most banks.

International Transfers

If you run out of money, someone back home can wire you cash via moneychangers affiliated with **Moneygram** (www.moneygram.com) or **Western Union** (www.westernunion.com). A fee is added to the transaction.

To collect cash, bring your passport and the name and reference number of the person who sent the funds.

Moneychangers

Private moneychangers are usually open for longer hours than banks and are found almost everywhere (many also double as internet cafes and travel agents).

Upmarket hotels may also change money, but their rates are usually not as competitive.

Tipping, Baksheesh & Bargaining

In tourist restaurants or hotels, a service fee is usually added to your bill and tipping is optional. Elsewhere, a tip is appreciated.

Hotel bellboys and train/airport porters appreciate anything around ₹50; hotel staff should be given similar gratuities for services above and beyond the call of duty.

It's not mandatory to tip taxi or rickshaw drivers, but it's good to tip drivers who are honest about the fare.

If you hire a car with driver for more than a couple of days, a tip is recommended for good service.

Baksheesh can loosely be defined as a 'tip'; it covers everything from alms for beggars to bribes.

Many Indians implore tourists not to hand out sweets, pens or money to children, as it encourages them to beg. To make a lasting difference, donate to a reputable school or charitable organisation.

Except in fixed-price shops (such as government emporiums and fair-trade cooperatives), bargaining is the norm.

Travellers Cheques

All major brands are accepted, but some banks may only accept cheques from American Express (Amex) and Thomas Cook.

Euros, pounds sterling and US dollars are the safest currencies, especially in smaller towns.

Keep a record of the cheques' serial numbers separate from your cheques, along with the proof-of-purchase slips, encashment certificates and photocopied passport details. If you lose your cheques, contact the Amex or Thomas Cook office in Delhi.

To replace lost travellers cheques, you need the proof-of-purchase slip and the numbers of the missing cheques (some places require a photocopy of the police report and a passport photo). If you don't have the numbers of your missing cheques, the issuing company (eg Amex) will contact the place where you bought them.

Opening Hours

Official business hours are from 10am to 5pm Monday to Friday but many offices open later and close earlier.

Most offices have an official lunch hour from around 1pm.

Bank opening hours vary from town to town, so check locally; foreign-exchange offices may open longer and operate daily.

Some larger post offices are open a full day on Saturday and a half-day on Sunday.

In some places with six-day weeks, establishments may be closed on the second and fourth Saturdays of the month.

Due to sporadic bouts of volatility curfews can sometimes apply in certain areas, notably parts of Kashmir and the Northeast Region.

Business hours do vary wildly from state to state. Also, in remote areas like the Northeast Region, shops may open and close depending on the weather, local political situation or the proprietor's mood.

Permits

Access to certain parts of India – particularly disputed border areas – is controlled by an often-complicated permit system.

A permit known as an Inner-Line Permit (ILP) or a Restricted Area Permit (RAP) is required to visit Arunachal Pradesh, Sikkim and certain parts of Himachal Pradesh, Ladakh and Uttarakhand that lie close to the disputed border with China/Tibet. Permits are also necessary for travel to the Andaman and Lakshadweep Islands.

Obtaining the ILP/RAP is basically a formality, but travel agents must apply on your behalf for certain areas, including many trekking routes passing close to the border.

Permits are issued by regional magistrates and district commissioners, either directly to travellers (for free) or through travel agents (for a fee).

We recommend that you double-check with tourism officials to see if permit requirements have undergone any changes before you head out to these areas.

Photography

For useful tips and techniques on travel photography, read Lonely Planet's guide to *Travel Photography*.

Digital

Memory cards for digital cameras are available from photographic shops in most large cities and towns. However, the quality of memory cards is variable – some don't carry the advertised amount of data.

Expect to pay upwards of ₹500 for a 4GB card.

To be safe, regularly back up your memory card to CD; internet cafes may offer this

STANDARD HOURS

We've only listed business hours where they differ from the following standards.

BUSINESS	OPENING HOURS
Airline office	9.30am-5.30pm Mon-Sat
Government office	9.30am-1pm & 2-5.30pm Mon-Fri, closed 2nd and 4th Sat in some places
Museum	10am-5pm Tue-Sun
Nationalised bank	10am-2pm or 4pm Mon-Fri, to noon or 1pm Sat
Post office	10am-4pm Mon-Fri, to noon Sat
Restaurant	lunch noon-3pm, dinner 7-10pm or 11pm
Shop	10am-7pm or 8pm, some closed Sun
Sight	10am-5pm or dawn-dusk

service for ₹60 to ₹120 per disc.

Some photographic shops make prints from digital photographs for roughly the standard print-and-processing charge.

Restrictions

India is touchy about anyone taking photographs of military installations – this can include train stations, bridges, airports, military sites and sensitive border regions.

Photography from the air is mostly OK, unless you're taking off from (or landing in) airports actively shared by defence forces.

Many places of worship – such as monasteries, temples and mosques – also prohibit photography. Taking photos inside a shrine, at a funeral, at a religious ceremony or of people publicly bathing (including rivers) can also be offensive – ask first.

Flash photography may be prohibited in certain areas of a shrine or historical monument, or may not be permitted at all.

Exercise sensitivity when taking photos of people, especially women, who may find it offensive – obtain permission in advance.

It is not uncommon these days for people in touristy areas to demand a posing fee in return for being photographed. Exercise your discretion in these situations: if you think the money would make a positive difference in the lives of your subjects and their families, then go ahead and donate by all means. Alternately, if it looks like a scam to earn a quick buck, refrain. In any case, ask first to avoid misunderstandings later.

Post

India has the biggest postal network on earth, with over 155,500 post offices. Mail and poste-restante services are generally good, although the speed of delivery will depend on the efficiency of any given office. Airmail is faster and more reliable than sea mail, although it's best to use courier services (such as DHL and TNT) to send and receive items of value – expect to pay around ₹3000 per kilogram to Europe, Australia or the USA. Smaller private couriers are often cheaper, but goods may be repacked into large packages to cut costs and things sometimes go missing.

Receiving Mail

To claim mail you'll need to show your passport.

Ask senders to address letters to you with your surname in capital letters and underlined, followed by poste restante, GPO (main post office), and the city or town in question.

Many 'lost' letters are simply misfiled under given/first names, so check under both your names and ask senders to provide a return address.

Letters sent via poste restante are generally held for around one to two months before being returned.

It's best to have any parcels sent to you by registered post.

Sending Mail

LETTERS

Posting letters/aerogrammes to anywhere overseas costs ₹20/15.

International postcards cost around ₹7.

For postcards, stick on the stamps *before* writing on them, as post offices can give you as many as four stamps per card.

Sending a letter overseas by registered post costs an extra ₹15.

PARCELS

Posting parcels can either be relatively straightforward or involve multiple counters and lots of queuing; get to the post office in the morning.

Prices depend on weight (including packing material).

Packing the article safely is your responsibility.

A small package (unregistered) costs ₹40 (up to 100g) to any country and ₹30 per additional 100g (up to a maximum of 2000g; different charges apply for higher weights).

Parcel post has a maximum of 20kg to 30kg depending on the destination.

Airmail takes one to three weeks, sea mail two to four months and Surface Air-Lifted (SAL) – a curious hybrid where parcels travel by both air and sea – around one month.

Express mail service (EMS; delivery within three days) costs around 30% more than the normal airmail price.

All parcels sent through the government postal service must be packed up in white linen and the seams sealed with wax – agents outside the post office usually offer this service for a small fee.

Customs declaration forms, available from the post office, must be stitched or pasted to the parcel. No duty is payable by the recipient for gifts under the value of ₹1000.

Carry a permanent marker to write on the parcel any information requested by the desk.

Books or printed matter can go by international book post for ₹350 (maximum 5kg), but the package must be wrapped with a hole that reveals the contents for inspection by customs – tailors can do this in such a way that nothing falls out.

India Post (www.indiapost.gov.in) has an online calculator for domestic and international postal tariffs.

Public Holidays

There are officially three national public holidays. Every state celebrates its own official holidays, which cover bank holidays for government workers as well as major religious festivals. Most businesses (offices, shops etc) and tourist sites close on public holidays, but transport is usually unaffected. It's wise to make transport and hotel reservations well in advance if you intend to visit during major festivals.

Republic Day 26 January

Mahavir Jayanti (Jain) February

Holi (Hindu) March

Easter (Christian) March/April

Buddha Jayanti (Buddhist) April/May

Independence Day 15 August

Eid al-Fitr (Muslim) August/September

Dussehra (Hindu) September/October

Gandhi Jayanti 2 October

Diwali (Hindu) October/November

Guru Nanak Jayanti (Sikh) November

Christmas (Christian) 25 December

Safe Travel

Travellers to India's major cities may fall prey to petty and opportunistic crime, but most problems can be avoided with a bit of common sense and an appropriate amount of caution. Women and solo travellers should read p1176; for scams, see p1174. Also have a look at the India branch of Lonely Planet's **Thorn Tree Travel Forum** (www.lonelyplanet.com/thorntree), where travellers often post timely warnings about problems they've encountered on the road. Always check your government's travel advisory warnings.

Rebel Violence

India has a number of (sometimes armed) dissident groups championing various causes, who have employed the same tried and tested techniques of rebel groups everywhere: assassinations and bomb attacks on government infrastructure, public transport, religious centres, tourist sites and markets.

Certain areas are particularly prone to insurgent violence – specifically Kashmir, states in the Northeast Region such as Assam, Manipur and Nagaland, remote tribal regions in Bihar, Jharkhand, Chhattisgarh and, less frequently, parts of West Bengal.

Curfews and strikes can close the roads (as well as banks, shops etc) for days on end in sensitive regions like Kashmir or Assam.

International terrorism is as much of a risk in Europe or the US, so this is no reason not to go to India, but it makes sense to check the local security situation carefully before travelling (especially if visiting high-risk areas).

Telephone

There are few payphones in India (apart from in airports), but private STD/ISD/PCO call booths do the same job, offering inexpensive local, interstate and international calls at lower prices than calls made from hotel rooms.

These booths are found around the country. A digital meter displays how much the call is costing and usually provides a printed receipt when the call is finished.

Costs vary depending on the operator and destination but can be from ₹1 per minute for local calls and between ₹5 and ₹10 for international calls.

Some booths also offer a 'call-back' service – you ring home, provide the phone number of the booth and wait for people at home to call you back, for a fee of around ₹20 on top of the cost of the preliminary call.

Getting a line can be difficult in remote country and mountain areas – an engaged signal may just mean that the exchange is overloaded or broken, so keep trying.

Useful online resources include the **Yellow Pages** (www.indiayellowpages.com) and **Justdial** (www.justdial.com).

Mobile Phones

Indian mobile phone numbers usually have 10 digits,

USEFUL GOVERNMENT RESOURCES

The following government websites offer travel advice and information on current hotspots.

➡ **Australian Department of Foreign Affairs** (www.smarttraveller.gov.au)

➡ **British Foreign Office** (www.gov.uk/fco)

➡ **Canadian Department of Foreign Affairs** (www.voyage.gc.ca)

➡ **German Foreign Office** (www.auswaertiges-amt.de)

➡ **Japan Ministry of Foreign Affairs** (www.mofa.go.jp)

➡ **Netherlands Ministry of Foreign Affairs** (www.government.nl)

➡ **Swiss Department of Foreign Affairs** (www.eda.admin.ch)

➡ **US State Department** (http://travel.state.gov)

mostly beginning with 9 (but sometimes also with 7 or 8).

There's roaming coverage for international GSM phones in most cities and large towns.

To avoid expensive roaming costs (often highest for incoming calls), get hooked up to the local mobile-phone network by applying for a local prepaid SIM card.

Mobiles bought in some countries may be locked to a particular network; you'll have to get the phone unlocked or buy a local phone (available from ₹2000) to use an Indian SIM card.

Getting Connected

Getting connected is inexpensive but complicated, owing to security concerns, and involves some amount of paperwork.

Foreigners must supply between one and five passport photos, their passport and photocopies of their passport identity and visa pages.

You must also supply a residential address, which can be the address of your hotel (ask the management for a letter confirming this).

Some phone companies send representatives to the listed address; others call to verify that you are actually staying there.

Some travellers have reported their SIM cards being 'blocked' once the company realised they had moved from the hotel where they registered their phone. Others have been luckier for the duration of their travels.

Another option is to get a friendly local to obtain a connection in their name.

Prepaid mobile phone kits (SIM card and phone number, plus an allocation of calls) are available in most towns for about ₹200 from a phone shop, local STD/ISD/PCO booth or grocery store.

You must then purchase more credit, sold as direct credit. You pay the vendor and the credit is deposited

straight into your account, minus some taxes and a service charge.

Charges

Calls made within the state or city where you bought the SIM card are less than ₹1 a minute. You can call internationally for less than ₹10 a minute.

SMS messaging is even cheaper. International outgoing messages cost ₹5. Incoming calls and messages are free.

Most SIM cards are state-specific. If you use them in another state, you have to pay (nominal) roaming charges for both incoming and outgoing communications.

The government could do away with roaming charges altogether in the near future, making calls on the move cheaper.

Unreliable signals and problems with international texting (messages or replies not coming through or being delayed) are not uncommon.

The leading service providers are Airtel, Vodafone, Reliance, Idea and BSNL.

As the mobile-phone industry continues to evolve, rates, coverage and suppliers are all likely to develop during the life of this book.

Jammu & Kashmir & Assam

Due to ongoing terrorist threats, mobile phone use in Jammu and Kashmir, as well

as Assam, is more strictly controlled.

Roaming on foreign mobiles won't work here, nor will pay-as-you-go SIM cards purchased elsewhere in India.

To purchase a SIM card you'll need a photocopy of your passport and visa, four or five passport photos and a reference from a local who has known you for at least one month.

You may be able to tip a local to apply for a SIM in their name and sell it on to you.

An additional stumbling block is that your ID is supposed to provide proof of your father's name – if this detail isn't in your passport (as is the case for many Western nationals) you might not get the SIM at all.

During times of tension, networks may be jammed.

Phone Codes

When calling India from abroad dial your country's international access code, then ♫91 (India's country code), then the area code (without the initial zero), then the local number. For mobile phones, the area code and initial zero are not required.

If calling internationally from India dial ♫00 (the international access code), then the country code of the country you're calling, then the area code (without the initial zero) and the local number.

Land-phone numbers have an area code followed by up to eight digits.

Toll-free numbers begin with ☏1800.

To make interstate calls to a mobile phone, add 0 before the 10-digit number.

To call a land phone from a mobile phone, you always have to add the area code (with the initial zero).

Some call centre numbers might require the initial zero (eg calling an airline ticketing service based in Delhi from Karnataka).

A Home Country Direct service, which gives you access to the international operator in your home country, exists for the US (☏000 117) and the UK (☏000 4417).

To access an international operator elsewhere, dial ☏000 127. The operator can place a call to anywhere in the world and allow you to make collect calls.

Time

India uses the 12-hour clock and the local standard time is known as Indian Standard Time (IST). IST is 5½ hours ahead of GMT/UTC. The floating half-hour was added to maximise daylight hours over such a vast country.

Toilets

Public toilets are most easily found in major cities and tourist sites; the cleanest (usually with sit-down and squat choices) are often at modern restaurants, shopping complexes and cinemas.

Beyond urban centres, toilets are of the squat variety and locals may use the 'hand-and-water' technique, which involves carrying out ablutions with a small jug of water and the left hand. It's always a good idea to carry your own toilet paper and hand sanitiser, just in case.

Tourist Information

In addition to Government of India tourist offices (also known as 'India Tourism'), each state maintains its own network of tourist offices.

These vary in their efficiency and usefulness – some are run by enthusiastic souls who go out of their way to help, others are little more than a means of drumming up business for State Tourism Development Corporation tours.

The first stop for information should be the tourism website of the Government of India, **Incredible India** (www.incredibleindia.org); for details of its regional offices around India, click on the 'Help Desk' tab at the top of the homepage.

Travellers with Disabilities

India's crowded public transport, crush of humanity and variable infrastructure can test even the hardiest able-bodied traveller. If you have a physical disability or are vision impaired, these can pose even more of a challenge. If your mobility is considerably restricted, you may like to ease the stress by travelling with an able-bodied companion.

Accommodation Wheelchair-friendly hotels are almost exclusively top-end. Make pretrip enquiries and book ground-floor rooms at hotels that lack adequate facilities.

Accessibility Some restaurants and offices have ramps but most tend to have at least one step. Staircases are often steep; lifts frequently stop at mezzanines between floors.

Footpaths Where pavements exist, they can be riddled with holes, littered with debris and packed with pedestrians. If using crutches, bring along spare rubber caps.

Transport Hiring a car with driver will make moving around a lot easier; if you use a wheelchair, make sure the car-hire company can provide an appropriate vehicle to carry it.

GET TO KNOW YOUR BATHROOM

Most Indian midrange hotels and all top-end ones have sit-down toilets with toilet paper and soap supplied. In ultracheap hotels, and in places off the tourist trail, squat toilets (described as 'Indian style', as opposed to 'Western style') are the norm and toilet paper is rarely provided.

Terminology for hotel bathrooms varies across India. 'Attached bath' or 'private bath' means the room has its own en suite bathroom. 'Common bath' or 'shared bath' means communal bathroom facilities.

Not all rooms have hot water. 'Running', '24-hour' or 'constant' water means hot water is available round-the-clock (not always the case in reality). 'Bucket' hot water is only available in buckets (sometimes for a small charge).

Many places use wall-mounted electric geysers (water heaters) that need to be switched on up to an hour before use. The geyser's switch can sometimes be located outside the bathroom.

The hotel rooms we have listed have their own private bathroom unless otherwise indicated.

For further advice pertaining to your specific requirements, consult your doctor before heading to India.

The following organisations may be able to proffer further information or at least point you in the right direction.

Accessible Journeys (www.disabilitytravel.com)

Access-Able Travel Source (www.access-able.com)

Global Access News (www.globalaccessnews.com)

Mobility International USA (MIUSA; www.miusa.org)

Royal Association for Disability & Rehabilitation (RADAR; www.radar.org.uk)

Visas

Citizens of Finland, Japan, Luxembourg, New Zealand, Singapore, Cambodia, Vietnam, the Philippines, Laos, Myanmar (Burma) and Indonesia are currently granted a 30-day single-entry visa on arrival at Mumbai, Chennai, Kolkata and New Delhi airports. All other nationals – except Nepali and Bhutanese – must get a visa *before* arriving in India. These are available at Indian missions worldwide. Note that your passport needs to be valid for at least six months beyond your intended stay in India, with at least two blank pages.

Entry Requirements

In 2009 a large number of foreigners were found to be working in India on tourist visas, so regulations surrounding who can get a visa and for how long have been tightened.

Most people travel on the standard six-month tourist visa.

Student and business visas have strict conditions

(consult the Indian embassy for details).

Tourist visas are valid from the date of issue, not the date you arrive in India. You can spend a total of 180 days in the country.

Five- and 10-year tourist visas are available to US citizens *only* under a bilateral arrangement; however, you can still only stay in the country for up to 180 days continuously.

Currently you are required to submit two passport photographs with your visa application; these must be in colour and must be 5.08cm by 5.08 cm (2in by 2in).

An onward travel ticket is a requirement for most visas, but this isn't always enforced (check in advance).

Additional restrictions apply to travellers from Bangladesh and Pakistan, as well as certain eastern European, African and central Asian countries. Check any special conditions for your nationality with the Indian embassy in your country.

Visas are priced in the local currency and may have an added service fee (contact your country's Indian embassy for current prices).

Extended visas are possible for people of Indian origin (excluding those in Pakistan and Bangladesh) who hold a non-Indian passport and live abroad.

For visas lasting more than six months, you're supposed to register at the **Foreigners' Regional Registration Office** (FRRO; ☎011-26711443; frrodil@nic.in; Level 2, East Block 8, Sector 1, Rama Krishna (RK) Puram, Delhi; ☺9.30am-3pm Mon-Fri) in Delhi within 14 days of arriving in India; enquire about these special conditions when you apply for your visa.

Re-Entry Requirements

A law barring re-entry of foreigners into India within two months of the date of their previous exit was scrapped in late 2012, allowing tourists on subcontinental or South Asian itineraries to transit freely between India and its neighbouring countries. However, the 60-day-gap law still applies to citizens of China, Pakistan, Iraq, Iran, Afghanistan, Bangladesh and Sudan.

Visa Extensions

India has traditionally been very stringent with visa extensions. At the time of writing, the government was granting extensions only in circumstances such as medical emergencies or theft of passport just before the applicant planned to leave the country (at the end of their visa).

If you do need to extend your visa due to any such exigency, you should contact the Foreigners' Regional Registration Office in Delhi. This is also the place to come for a replacement visa, and if you need your lost/stolen passport replaced (required before you can leave the country). Regional FRROs are even less likely to grant an extension.

Assuming you meet the stringent criteria, the FRRO is permitted to issue an extension of 14 days (free for nationals of most countries; enquire on application). You must bring your confirmed air ticket, one passport photo (take two, just in case) and a photocopy of your passport identity and visa pages. Note that this system is designed to get you out of the country promptly with the correct official stamps, not to give you two extra weeks of travel and leisure.

Transport

GETTING THERE & AWAY

Getting to India is supremely easy. Plenty of international airlines service the country, and overland routes to and from Nepal, Bangladesh, Bhutan and Pakistan are all currently open. Flights, tours and other tickets can be booked online at www.lonely-planet.com/bookings.

Entering India

Entering India by air or land is relatively straightforward, with standard immigration and customs procedures. A frustrating law barring re-entry into India within two months of the previous date of departure has now been done away with (except for citizens of some Asian countries), thus allowing travellers to freely combine their India tour with side trips to neighbouring countries.

Passport

To enter India you need a valid passport, visa and an onward/return ticket. Your passport should be valid for at least six months beyond your intended stay in India. If your passport is lost or stolen, immediately contact your country's representative. Keep photocopies of your airline ticket and the identity and visa pages of your passport in case of emergency. Better yet, scan and email copies to yourself. Check with the Indian embassy in your home country for any special conditions that may exist for your nationality.

Air

Airports & Airlines

As India is a big country, it makes sense to fly into the airport that's nearest to the area you'll be visiting. India has six main gateways for international flights (see the following list); however, a number of other cities such as Goa, Kochi (Cochin), Lucknow and Trivandrum also service international carriers. For detailed information, log on to www.aai.aero.

India's national carrier is **Air India** (☑1800 1801407; www.airindia.com), of which the former state-owned domestic carrier, Indian Airlines, is now a part. Air travel in India has had a relatively decent safety record in recent years.

Bengaluru (Bangalore; BLR; ☑1800 4254425; www.bengaluruairport.com; Bengaluru International Airport)

Chennai (Madras; MAA; ☑044-22560551; www.chennaiairportguide.com; Anna International Airport)

Delhi (New Delhi; DEL; ☑0124-3376000; www.newdelhiairport.in; Indira Gandhi International Airport)

Hyderabad (HYD; www.hyderabad.aero; Rajiv Gandhi International Airport)

Kolkata (Calcutta; CCU; ☑033-39874987; Netaji Subhash Chandra Bose International Airport)

Mumbai (Bombay; BOM; ☑022-26264000; www.csia.in; Chhatrapati Shivaji International Airport)

Tickets

An onward or return air ticket is usually a condition of the Indian tourist visa, so few visitors buy international tickets inside India. For side trips to neighbouring countries, only designated travel agencies book international flights, or you can book directly with the airline. Departure tax and other charges are usually included in airline tickets. You are required to show a copy of your ticket and your passport in order to enter the airport, whether flying internationally or within India.

Land

Border Crossings

Although most visitors fly into India, it is possible to travel overland between India and Bangladesh, Bhutan, Nepal and Pakistan. The overland route from Nepal is the most popular. For more on these routes, consult Lonely Planet's *Istanbul to Kathmandu*, or see the 'Europe to India overland' section on www.seat61.com/India.htm.

If you enter India by bus or train, you'll be required to disembark at the border for standard immigration and customs checks.

You *must* have a valid Indian visa in advance, as no visas are available at the border.

Drivers of cars and motorbikes will need the vehicle's registration papers, liability insurance and an international drivers' permit in addition to their domestic licence. You'll also need a *Carnet de Passage en Douane*, which acts as a temporary waiver of import duty on the vehicle.

For travellers wishing to visit Tibet from India, the only way to do so is to exit to Nepal and then enter Tibet through the border crossing at Kodari as part of an organised tour. Alternately, you could fly to Lhasa from Kathmandu.

To find out the latest requirements for the paperwork and other important driving information, contact your local automobile association.

Bangladesh
Foreigners can use four land crossings between Bangladesh and India, all in West Bengal or the Northeast States.

Heading from India to Bangladesh, tourist visas should be obtained in advance from a Bangladeshi mission. Visas are not available at the border.

Heading from Bangladesh to India, you have to prepay

the exit tax, this can be done at a Sonali Bank branch (either in Dhaka, another big city or at the closest branch to the border).

Exiting Bangladesh overland is complicated by red tape – if you enter by air, you require a road permit (or 'change of route' permit) to leave by land.

To apply for visa extensions and change of route permits you will need to visit the **Immigration and Passport Office** (📞 00-88-2-8159525; www.dip.gov.bd; Agargaon Rd; 🕑 Sat-Thu) in Dhaka.

Some travellers have reported problems exiting Bangladesh overland with the visa issued on arrival at Dhaka airport.

Bhutan
Phuentsholing is the main entry and exit point between India and Bhutan, although the eastern checkpost at Samdrup Jongkhar is also used.

All non-Indian nationals need a Bhutanese visa to enter the country and are required to book a tour with a registered tour operator in Bhutan; this can be done directly through an affiliated travel agency abroad.

As entry requirements need advance planning and are subject to change, we recommend you consult a travel agent or Bhutanese embassy for up-to-the-minute details. Also see www.tourism.gov.bt and Lonely Planet's *Bhutan*.

Nepal
Political and weather conditions permitting, there are five land border crossings between India and Nepal. Check the current security status before crossing into Nepal; local newspapers and websites are good sources of information.

Travellers entering Nepal may purchase 15-day (US$25), one-month (US$40) or three-month (US$100) multiple-entry visas at the border. Payment is in US dollars and you need two recent passport photos. Alternatively, obtain a visa in advance from a Nepal mission.

Travellers have reported being harassed crossing into India at the Sunauli border and having to pay inflated prices for bus and train tickets. Consider taking a taxi to Gorakpur and getting a train or bus from there.

Pakistan
Given the rocky relationship between India and Pakistan, crossing by land depends on the current state of relations between the two countries – check locally.

If the crossings are open, you can reach Pakistan from Delhi, Amritsar (Punjab) and Rajasthan by bus or train. The bus route from Srinagar to Pakistan-administered Kashmir is currently only open to Indian citizens.

You must have a visa to enter Pakistan. It's easiest to obtain this from the Pakistan mission in your home country. At the time of writing,

CLIMATE CHANGE & TRAVEL

Every form of transport that relies on carbon-based fuel generates CO_2, the main cause of human-induced climate change. Modern travel is dependent on aeroplanes, which might use less fuel per kilometre per person than most cars but travel much greater distances. The altitude at which aircraft emit gases (including CO_2) and particles also contributes to their climate change impact. Many websites offer 'carbon calculators' that allow people to estimate the carbon emissions generated by their journey and, for those who wish to do so, to offset the impact of the greenhouse gases emitted with contributions to portfolios of climate-friendly initiatives throughout the world. Lonely Planet offsets the carbon footprint of all staff and author travel.

BORDER CROSSINGS

Overland to/from Bangladesh

ROUTE/BORDER TOWNS	TRANSPORT	VISAS	MORE INFORMATION
Kolkata–Dhaka/ Petrapole (India) & Benapole (Bangladesh)	Regular daily buses run from Kolkata to Dhaka; twice-weekly train via Darsana border post.	Must be obtained in advance. To buy a train ticket, Darsana must be marked on your Bangladesh visa.	p479
Siliguri–Chengra-bandha/Chengra-bandha (India) & Burimari (Bangladesh)	Regular direct buses run from Siliguri to Chengrabandha; then bus to Rangpur, Bogra & Dhaka.	Must be obtained prior to travel.	p492
Shillong–Sylhet/ Dawki (India) & Tamabil (Bangladesh)	Jeeps run from Shillong to Dawki. From Dawki walk (1.5km) or take a taxi to Tamabil bus station for regular buses to Sylhet.	Must be obtained prior to travel.	p586
Agartala–Dhaka/ Agartala, 3km from border along Akhaura Rd (India) & Akhaura, 5km from border (Bangladesh)	Akhaura is on Dhaka–Comilla train line. Dhaka–Sylhet trains run from Ajampur train station, 3km further north.	Must be obtained prior to travel.	p586

Overland to/from Bhutan

ROUTE/BORDER TOWNS	TRANSPORT	VISAS	MORE INFORMATION
Siliguri–Kolkata–Phuentsholing/Jaigon (India) & Phuentshol-ing (Bhutan)	From Kolkata, direct bus at 7pm. From Siliguri daily buses and possibly shared jeeps to Jaigon/ Phuentsholing.	Non-Indian nationals need visa & tour booking.	p479, p492

Overland to/from Pakistan

ROUTE/BORDER TOWNS	TRANSPORT	MORE INFORMATION
From Delhi and Amritsar to Lahore/ Attari (India) & Wagah (Pakistan)	Direct bus & train from Delhi to Lahore. Lahore Bus Service departs Delhi 6am daily for Lahore (12hr). Advance bookings essential. Sami-jhauta Express train leaves twice weekly from Old Delhi train station to Lahore; customs & immigration stop at Attari (Indian border).	Security on this route tightened but is still a concern after the 2007 bomb attack on the Delhi-Lahore train. Border formalities can be quicker for independent travellers.
Jodhpur-Karachi/ Munabao (India) & Khokrapar (Pakistan)	Weekly Thar Express train between Jodhpur and Karachi (schedule is erratic).	

Overland to/from Nepal

ROUTE/BORDER TOWNS	TRANSPORT	VISAS	MORE INFORMATION
Delhi, Varanasi–Kathmandu/Sunauli (India) & Bhairawa (Nepal)	Trains from Delhi to Gorakhpur, half-hourly buses to border. Buses from Varanasi to Sunauli leave early morning & eve (uncomfortable ride). Buses & jeeps from Bhairawa to Kathmandu.	Nepali available at border. Indian must be acquired in advance.	p402
Kolkata (Patna & the eastern plains)–Kathmandu & Pokhara/Raxaul (India) & Birganj (Nepal)	Daily buses from Patna & Kolkata to Raxaul. Mithila Express train daily from Kolkata. Regular day/night buses from Birganj to Kathmandu & Pokhara.	As above.	p523
West Bengal–Eastern Nepal/Panitanki (India) & Kakarbhitta (Nepal)	Regular buses from Kakarbhitta to Kathmandu (17hr) & other destinations. Bhadrapur airport (23km away) flights to Kathmandu.	Nepali available at border (7am-7pm).	p505, p492
Jamunaha, Uttar Pradesh–Nepalganj, Western Nepal/Rupaidiha (India) & Nepalganj (Nepal)	Good gateway for Nepal's Royal Bardia National Park. Flights to Kathmandu.	Nepali available at border. Indian must be acquired in advance.	
Uttarakhand–Western Nepal/Banbassa (India) & Mahendranagar (Nepal)	Border is 5km from Banbassa, then an autorickshaw to Mahendranagar. From there, buses to Kathmadu & Pokhara (1 daily).	Border open 9am-5pm.	p449

the **Pakistan Embassy** (011-26110601; www.mofa.gov.pk; 2/50G Shantipath, Chanakyapuri) in Delhi was not issuing tourist visas for most nationalities, but this may well change.

Sea

There are several sea routes between India and surrounding islands but none leave Indian sovereign territory. After a 28-year hiatus, a ferry service between southern India and Sri Lanka began again in 2011, linking Thoothikudi (Tuticorin) in Tamil Nadu with Colombo. However, it was suspended after five months. A new service between the same ports, or on the old route between Rameswaram and Ta-

laimannar, may start; check the internet for updates.

GETTING AROUND

Air

Airlines in India

India has a very competitive domestic airline industry. Well-established players are Air India (which now includes Indian Airlines), Go Air, IndiGo, Jet Airways and Spicejet.

Airline seats can be booked cheaply over the internet, through travel agencies or over the telephone. In fact, private operators – in a bid to reduce operational costs – are slowly doing away with city offices in favour of

online or phone bookings. Several authorised agents, however, still continue to book tickets on their behalf. Domestic airlines set rupee fares for Indian citizens, while foreigners may be charged US dollar fares (usually payable in rupees).

Apart from airline sites, bookings can be made through reliable ticketing portals such as **Cleartrip** (www.cleartrip.com), **Make My Trip** (www.makemytrip.com) and **Yatra** (www.yatra.com).

Security norms require you to produce your ticket and your passport at the time of entering an airport. Airline counters at airports can issue you a printed copy of your ticket (if you don't have one) for ₹50.

At the time of writing, the following airlines were

operating across various destinations in India. Keep in mind, however, that the competitive nature of the aviation industry means that fares fluctuate dramatically. Holidays, festivals and seasons also have a serious effect on ticket prices so check for the latest fares online.

Security at airports is generally stringent. In smaller airports, all hold baggage must be x-rayed prior to check-in (major airports now have in-line baggage screening facilities). Every item of cabin baggage needs a label, which must be stamped as part of the security check (don't forget to collect tags at the check-in counter). Flights to sensitive destinations, such as Srinagar and Ladakh, have extra security restrictions. You may also have to allow for a spot-check of your cabin baggage on the tarmac before you board.

Keeping peak hour congestion in mind, the recommended check-in time for domestic flights is two hours before departure – the deadline is 45 minutes. The usual baggage allowance is 20kg (10kg for smaller aircraft) in economy class.

Air India (☑1800 1801407; www.airindia.com) India's national carrier operates many domestic and international flights.

GoAir (☑1800 222111; www.goair.in) Reliable low-cost carrier servicing Goa, Kochi, Jaipur, Delhi and Bagdogra, among other destinations.

IndiGo (☑099-10383838; www.goindigo.in) The best and trendiest of the lot, with plenty of flights across India and to select overseas destinations. Has a reputation for always being on time.

Jet Airways (☑1800 225522; www.jetairways.com) Operates flights across India and to select overseas destinations.

JetKonnect (☑1800 223020; www.jetkonnect.com) Jet Airways' budget carrier flies to numerous destinations including Amritsar, Dehradun, Chennai and Jodhpur.

Spicejet (☑1800 1803333; www.spicejet.com) Destinations include Bengaluru, Varanasi, Srinagar, Colombo (Sri Lanka) and Kathmandu (Nepal).

Bicycle

There are no restrictions on bringing a bicycle into the country. However, bicycles sent by sea can take a few weeks to clear customs in India, so it's better to fly them in. It may actually be cheaper – and less hassle – to hire or buy a bicycle in India itself. Read up on bicycle touring before you travel: Rob Van Der Plas' *Bicycle Touring Manual* and Stephen Lord's *Adventure Cycle-Touring Handbook* are good places to start. Consult local cycling magazines and clubs for useful information and advice. The **Cycling Federation of India** (www.cyclingfederationofindia.org) can provide local information.

Hire

Tourist centres and traveller hang-outs are the easiest spots to find bicycles for hire – simply enquire locally.

Prices vary: between ₹40 and ₹100 per day for a roadworthy, Indian-made bicycle; mountain bikes, where available, are usually upwards of ₹350 per day.

Hire places may require a cash security deposit (avoid leaving your airline ticket or passport).

Practicalities

Mountain bikes with off-road tyres give the best protection against India's puncture-inducing roads.

Roadside cycle mechanics abound but you should still bring spare tyres, brake cables, lubricating oil, chain repair kit and plenty of puncture-repair patches.

Bikes can often be carried for free, or for a small luggage fee, on the roof of public buses – handy for uphill stretches.

Contact your airline for information about transporting your bike and customs formalities in your home country.

Purchase

Delhi's **Jhandewalan Cycle Market** (Map p64) has imported and domestic, new and second-hand bikes, and spare parts.

Mountain bikes with reputable brands that include Hero (www.herocycles.com) and Atlas (www.atlascycles

---

RIDING THE RAILS WITH YOUR BIKE

For long hauls, transporting your bike by train can be a convenient option. Buy a standard train ticket for the journey, then take your bike to the station parcel office with your passport, registration papers, driver's licence and insurance documents. Packing-wallahs will wrap your bike in protective sacking for around ₹200 to ₹500 and you must fill out various forms and pay the shipping fee – around ₹2500 to ₹3500 (charges are less on an ordinary train) – plus an insurance fee of 1% of the declared value of the bike. Bring the same paperwork to collect your bike from the goods office at the other end. If the bike is left waiting at the destination for more than 24 hours, you'll pay a storage fee of around ₹100 per day.

onepat.com) generally start at around ₹5000.

Reselling is usually fairly easy – ask at local cycle or hire shops or put up an advert on travel noticeboards. If you purchased a new bike and it's still in reasonably good condition, you should be able to recoup around 50% of what you originally paid.

Road Rules

Vehicles are driven on the left-hand side in India but otherwise road rules are virtually nonexistent.

Cities and national highways can be hazardous places to cycle so, where possible, stick to back roads.

Be conservative about the distance you expect to cover – an experienced cyclist can manage around 60km to 100km a day on the plains, 40km to 60km on all-weather mountain roads and 40km or less on dirt roads.

Boat

Scheduled ferries connect mainland India to Port Blair in the Andaman Islands.

There are sporadic ferries from Visakhapatnam (Andhra Pradesh) to the Andaman Islands.

Between October and May there are boat services from Kochi (Kerala) to the Lakshadweep islands.

There are also numerous shorter ferry services across rivers, from chain pontoons to coracles and various boat cruises.

Bus

Buses go almost everywhere in India and are the only way to get around many mountainous areas. They tend to be the cheapest way to travel. Services are fast and frequent.

Roads in mountainous or curvy terrain can be especially perilous; buses are often driven with wilful

abandon, and accidents are always a risk.

Avoid night buses unless there's no alternative: driving conditions are more hazardous and drivers may be inebriated or suffering from lack of sleep.

All buses make snack and toilet stops (some more frequently than others), providing a break but possibly adding hours to journey times.

Shared jeeps complement the bus service in many mountain areas.

Classes

State-owned and private bus companies both offer several types of buses, graded loosely as 'ordinary', 'semi-deluxe', 'deluxe' or 'super deluxe'. These are usually open to interpretation, and the exact grade of luxury offered in a particular class can vary from place to place.

In general, ordinary buses tend to be ageing rattletraps while the deluxe grades range from less decrepit versions of ordinary buses to flashy Volvo buses with air-con and reclining (locally called 'push-back') two-by-two seating.

Buses run by the state government are usually the more reliable option (if there's a breakdown, another bus will be sent to pick up passengers), and seats can usually be booked up to a month in advance. Many state governments now operate super-deluxe buses.

Private buses are either more expensive (but more comfortable), or cheaper but with kamikaze drivers and conductors who cram on as many passengers as possible to maximise profits.

Travel agencies in many tourist towns offer relatively expensive private two-by-two buses, which tend to leave and terminate at conveniently central stops.

Take earplugs on long-distance buses to muffle the often deafening music

or movies played in some buses.

On any bus, try to sit upfront to minimise the bumpy effect of potholes. Avoid sitting directly above the wheels.

Costs

The cheapest buses are 'ordinary' government buses, but prices vary from state to state.

Add around 50% to the ordinary fare for deluxe services, double the fare for air-conditioning, and triple or quadruple the fare for a two-by-two super-deluxe service.

Luggage

Luggage is stored in compartments underneath the bus (sometimes for a small fee) or carried on the roof.

Arrive at least an hour before departure time – some buses cover roof-stored bags with a canvas sheet, making last-minute additions inconvenient/impossible.

If your bags go on the roof, make sure they're securely locked, and tied to the metal baggage rack – unsecured bags can fall off on rough roads.

Theft is a (minor) risk: watch your bags at snack and toilet stops. Never leave day-packs or valuables unattended inside the bus.

Reservations

Most deluxe buses can be booked in advance – government buses up to a month ahead – at the bus station or local travel agencies.

Online bookings are now possible in select states such as Karnataka and Rajasthan, or at the excellent portal **Redbus** (☑1800 30010101; www.redbus.in).

Reservations are rarely possible on 'ordinary' buses; travellers can be left behind in the mad rush for a seat.

To secure a seat, send a travelling companion ahead to claim some space, or pass a book or article of clothing through an open window and place it on an empty seat.

THE BRAVE BRO

In Ladakh, Arunachal Pradesh and Sikkim, the Border Roads Organisation (BRO) builds 'roads in the sky', including some of the world's highest passes accessible by car. Risking life and limb to keep the roads open, the BRO has a wicked sense of humour when it comes to driver warnings:

➡ Overtaker beware of Undertaker

➡ Better to be Mister Late than a late Mister

➡ Go easy on my curves

➡ Love thy neighbour, but not while driving

This 'reservation' method rarely fails.

If you board a bus midway through its journey, you may have to stand until a seat becomes free.

Many buses only depart when full – passengers might suddenly leave yours to join one that looks nearer to departing.

Many bus stations have a separate women's queue (not always obvious when signs are in Hindi and men join the melee).

Women have an unspoken right to elbow their way to the front of any bus queue in India, so don't be shy, ladies!

Car

Few people bother with self-drive car hire – not only because of the hair-raising driving conditions, but also because hiring a car with driver is wonderfully affordable in India, particularly if several people share the cost. Seatbelts are either nonexistent or of variable quality. **Hertz** (www.hertz. com) is one of the few international companies with representatives in India.

Hiring a Car & Driver

Most towns have taxi stands or car-hire companies where you can arrange short or long tours.

Not all hire cars are licensed to travel beyond their home state. Those that are

will pay extra state taxes, which are added to the hire charge.

Ask for a driver who speaks some English and knows the region you intend visiting. Try to see the car and meet the driver before paying anything.

A wide range of cars now ply as taxis. From a proletarian Tata Indica hatchback to a comfy Toyota Innova SUV, there's a model to suit every pocket.

Hire charges for multiday trips cover the driver's meals and accommodation, and drivers should make their own sleeping and eating arrangements.

It is essential to set the ground rules from day one; politely but firmly let the driver know that you're boss in order to avoid anguish later.

Costs

Car hire costs depend on the distance and the terrain (driving on mountain roads uses more petrol, hence the higher cost).

One-way trips usually cost the same as return ones (to cover the petrol and driver charges for getting back).

Hire charges vary from state to state. Some taxi unions set a time limit or a maximum kilometre distance for day trips – if you go over, you'll have to pay extra. Prices also vary according to the make and model of the taxi; luxury cabs and SUVs

cost more than ordinary hatchbacks.

To avoid potential misunderstandings, get in writing what you've been promised (quotes should include petrol, sightseeing stops, all your chosen destinations, and meals and accommodation for the driver). If a driver asks you for money for petrol en route because he is short of cash, get receipts for reimbursement later. If you're travelling by the kilometre, always check the odometer reading before you set out so as to avoid confusions while paying up.

For sightseeing day trips around a single city, expect to pay upwards of ₹1000/1200 for a non-aircon/air-con car with an eight-hour, 80km limit per day (extra charges apply). For multiday trips, operators usually peg a 250km maximum running distance per day and charge around ₹8/10 per km for a non-air-con/air-con car. If you overshoot, you pay extra.

A tip is customary at the end of your journey; ₹100 per day is fair (more if you're really pleased with the driver's service).

Hitching

Hitching is never entirely safe, and we don't recommend it. Travellers who hitch should understand that they are taking a small but potentially serious risk. However, for a negotiable fee, truck drivers supplement the bus service in some remote areas. As drivers rarely speak English, you may have difficulty explaining where you wish to go, and working out a fair price to pay. Be aware that truck drivers have a reputation for driving under the influence of alcohol. As anywhere, women are strongly advised against hitching alone or even in pairs. Always use your instincts.

Local Transport

Buses, cycle-rickshaws, auto-rickshaws, taxis, boats and urban trains provide transport around India's cities.

Costs for public transport vary from town to town.

For any transport without a fixed fare, agree on the price *before* you start your journey and make sure that it covers your luggage and every passenger.

Even where meters exist, drivers may refuse to use them, demanding an elevated 'fixed' fare. Insist on the meter; if that fails, find another vehicle. Or just bargain hard.

Fares usually increase at night (by up to 100%) and some drivers charge a few rupees extra for luggage.

Carry plenty of small bills for taxi and rickshaw fares as drivers rarely have change.

In some places, taxi/auto-rickshaw drivers are involved in the commission racket.

Autorickshaw, Tempo & Vikram

Similar to the tuk-tuks of Southeast Asia, the Indian autorickshaw is a three-wheeled motorised contraption with a tin or canvas roof and sides, with room for two passengers (although you'll often see many more squeezed in) and limited luggage.

They are also referred to as autos, scooters and riks.

They are mostly cheaper than taxis and usually have a meter, although getting it turned on can be a challenge.

Travelling by auto is great fun but, thanks to the open windows, can be noisy and hot (or severely cold!).

Tempos and *vikrams* (large tempos) are outsized autorickshaws with room for more passengers, shuttling on fixed routes for a fixed fare.

In country areas, you may also see the fearsome-looking 'three-wheeler' – a crude tractor-like tempo with a front wheel on an articulated arm – or the Magic, a cute minivan that can take up to a dozen passengers.

Boat

Various kinds of local boats offer transport across and down rivers in India, from big car ferries to wooden canoes and wicker coracles. Most of the larger boats carry bicycles and motorcycles for a fee.

Bus

Urban buses range from fume-belching, human-stuffed mechanical monsters that travel at breakneck speed to sanitised air-conditioned vehicles with comfortable seating and smoother ride quality. In any case, it's usually far more convenient to opt for an autorickshaw or taxi, as they are quicker and more frequent.

Cycle-Rickshaw

A cycle-rickshaw is a pedal cycle with two rear wheels, supporting a bench seat for passengers. Most have a canopy that can be raised in wet weather or lowered to provide extra space for luggage.

Fares must be agreed upon in advance – speak to locals to get an idea of what is a fair price for the distance you intend to travel.

Kolkata is the last bastion of the hand-pulled rickshaw, known as the *tana* rickshaw. This is a hand-cart on two wheels pulled directly by the rickshaw-wallah.

Taxi

Most towns have taxis, and these are usually metered, however, getting drivers to use the meter can be a hassle. To avoid fare-setting shenanigans, use prepaid taxis where possible.

Prepaid Taxis & Radio Cabs

Most major Indian airports and train stations now incorporate prepaid-taxi and radio-cab booths. Here, you can book a taxi for a fixed price (which will include baggage) and thus avoid commission scams. Hold onto your receipt until you reach your destination, as proof of payment.

Radio cabs cost marginally more than prepaid taxis, but are air-conditioned and manned by the company's chauffeurs. Cabs have electronic, receipt-generating fare meters and are fitted with GPS units, so the company can monitor the vehicle's movement around town. These minimise chances of errant driving or unreasonable demands for extra cash by the driver afterward.

Smaller airports and stations may have prepaid autorickshaw booths instead.

Other Local Transport

In some towns, tongas (horse-drawn two-wheelers) and *victorias* (horse-drawn carriages) still operate. Kolkata has a tram network, and both Delhi and Kolkata have efficient underground train systems (with Bengaluru set to join them). Mumbai, Delhi, Kolkata and Chennai, among other centres, have suburban trains that leave from ordinary train stations.

MANNING THE METER

Getting a metered ride is only half the battle. Meters are almost always outdated, so fares are calculated using a combination of the meter reading and a complicated 'fare adjustment card'. Predictably, this system is open to abuse. To get a rough estimate of fares in advance, try the portal www.taxiautofare.com.

Motorcycle

Despite traffic challenges, India is an amazing country for long-distance motorcycle touring. However, it can be quite an undertaking; there are some popular motorcycle tours for those who don't want the rigmarole of going it alone.

The most preferred starting point for motorcycle tours is Delhi, and popular destinations include Rajasthan, South India and Ladakh. Weather is an important factor and you should check for the best times to visit different areas. To cross from neighbouring countries, check the latest regulations and paperwork requirements from the relevant diplomatic mission.

Driving Licence

To hire a motorcycle in India, technically you're required to have a valid international drivers' permit in addition to your domestic licence. In tourist areas, some places may rent out a motorcycle without asking for a driving permit/licence, but you won't be covered by insurance in the event of an accident, and may also face a fine.

Hire

The classic way to motorcycle around India is on a Royal Enfield, built to both vintage and modern specs. As well as making a satisfying chugging sound, these bikes are fully manual, making them easy to repair (parts can be found almost everywhere in India). On the other hand, Enfields are often less reliable than many of the newer, Japanese-designed bikes.

Plenty of places rent out motorcycles for local trips and longer tours. Japanese- and Indian-made bikes in the 100–150cc range are cheaper than the big 350–500cc Enfields.

As security, you'll need to leave a large cash deposit (ensure you get a receipt that stipulates the refundable amount) or your passport/air ticket. We strongly advise not leaving these documents, in particular your passport, which you need for hotel check-ins and if stopped by the police.

For three weeks' hire, a 500cc Enfield costs from ₹22,000; a 350cc costs ₹15,000. The price includes excellent advice and an invaluable crash course in Enfield mechanics and repairs.

As for accessories, helmets are available for ₹500 to ₹2000; extras (panniers, luggage racks, protection bars, rear-view mirrors, lockable fuel caps, petrol filters, extra tools) are also easy to come by.

A useful website for Enfield models is www.royalenfield.com.

The following dealers come recommended:

Delhi Run by the knowledgable Lalli Singh, **Lalli Motorbike Exports** (☎011-28750869; www.lallisingh.com; 1740-A/55 (basement), Hari Singh Nalwa St, Abdul Aziz Rd, Karol Bagh) sells and rents out Enfields and parts, and buyers get a crash course in running and maintaining these lovable but temperamental machines. He can also recommend other reputable dealers in the area.

Mumbai With a buy-back option, **Allibhai Premji Tyrewalla** (☎022-23099313; www.premjis.com; 205 Dr D Bhadkamkar (Lamington) Rd) sells new and second-hand motorcycles.

Jaipur Recommended as a place for hiring, fixing or purchasing a motorcycle is **Rajasthan Auto Centre** (☎9829188064; Sanjay Bazaar, Sanganeri Gate). To hire a 350cc Bullet costs ₹500 to ₹600 per day (including helmet).

Purchase

For longer tours, purchasing a new motorcycle may sound like a great idea. However, sales of motor vehicles to foreigners comes with reams of complicated paperwork, and in many situations, procuring a motorcycle might not be possible or feasible at all.

Second-hand bikes are widely available though (and paperwork is simpler than for a new machine).

To find a second-hand motorcycle, check travellers' noticeboards and ask motorcycle mechanics and other bikers.

A well-looked-after second-hand 350cc Enfield costs ₹40,000 to ₹50,000. The 500cc model ranges between ₹50,000 and ₹65,000. You will also have to pay for insurance.

Ownership Papers

There's plenty of paperwork associated with owning a motorcycle. The process is complicated and time-consuming, so it's wise to seek advice from the agent selling the bike.

Registration papers are signed by the local registration authority when the bike is first sold; you need these when you buy a second-hand bike.

Foreign nationals cannot change the name on the registration but you must fill out forms for change of ownership and transfer of insurance.

Registration must be renewed every 15 years (for around ₹5000); make absolutely sure that it states the 'road-worthiness' of the vehicle, and that there are no outstanding debts or criminal proceedings associated with the bike.

Insurance

Only hire a bike that has third-party insurance – if you hit someone without insurance the consequences can be very costly. Reputable companies will include third-party cover in their policies; those that don't probably aren't trustworthy.

You must also arrange insurance if you buy a motorcycle (usually you can organise this through the person selling the bike).

The minimum level of cover is third-party insurance – available for around ₹600 per year. This will cover repair and medical costs for any other vehicles, people or property you might hit, but not cover you for your own machine. Comprehensive insurance (recommended) costs upwards of ₹1200 per year.

Fuel, Spare Parts & Extras

Petrol and engine oil are widely available in the plains, but petrol stations are fewer in the mountains. If travelling to remote regions, carry enough extra fuel (seek local advice about fuel availability before setting off). At the time of writing, petrol cost around ₹70 to ₹75 per litre in different states.

If you're going to remote regions it's also important to carry basic spares (valves, fuel lines, piston rings etc). Parts for Indian and Japanese machines are widely available in cities and larger towns; Delhi's Karol Bagh is a good place to find parts for all Indian and imported bikes.

Get your machine serviced regularly (particularly older ones). Indian roads and engine vibration work things loose quite quickly.

Check the engine and gearbox oil level regularly (at least every 500km) and clean the oil filter every few thousand kilometres.

Given the road conditions, the chances are you'll make at least a couple of visits to a puncture-wallah – start your trip with new tyres and carry spanners to remove your own wheels.

It's a good idea to bring your own protective equipment (jackets, gloves etc).

Road Conditions

Given the varied road conditions, India can be challenging for novice riders. Hazards range from cows and chickens crossing the carriageway to broken-down trucks, unruly traffic, pedestrians on the road, and ubiquitous potholes and unmarked speed humps. Rural roads sometimes have grain crops strewn across them to be threshed by passing vehicles – a serious sliding hazard for bikers.

Try not to cover too much territory in one day and never ride in the dark – many vehicles drive without lights, and dynamo-powered motorcycle headlamps are useless at low revs while negotiating around potholes.

On busy national highways, expect to average 40 to 50km/h without stops; on winding back roads and dirt tracks this can drop to 10km/h.

Organised Motorcycle Tours

Dozens of companies offer organised motorcycle tours around India with a support vehicle, mechanic and guide. Below are some reputable outfits (see websites for contact details, itineraries and prices).

Blazing Trails (www.blazingtrailstours.com)

Classic Bike Adventure (www.classic-bike-india.com)

Ferris Wheels (www.ferriswheels.com.au)

H-C Travel (www.hctravel.com)

Himalayan Roadrunners (www.ridehigh.com)

Lalli Singh Tours (www.lallisingh.com)

Moto Discovery (www.motodiscovery.com)

Royal Expeditions (www.royalexpeditions.com)

Saffron Road Motorcycle Tours (www.saffronroad.com)

Wheel of India (www.wheelofindia.com)

Shared Jeeps

In mountain areas shared jeeps supplement the bus services, charging similar fixed fares.

Although nominally designed for five to six passengers, most shared jeeps squeeze in more. The seats beside and immediately behind the driver are more expensive than the cramped bench seats at the rear.

Jeeps only leave when full; people often bail out of a half-full jeep and pile into one with more passengers that's ready to depart. Drivers will leave immediately if you pay for all the empty seats and 'reserve' a vehicle for yourself.

Jeeps run from jeep stands and 'passenger stations' at the junctions of major roads; ask locals to point you in the right direction.

In some states, jeeps are known as 'sumos' after the Tata Sumo, a popular vehicle.

Travel sickness, particularly on winding mountain roads, may mean you'll be asked to give up your window seat to queasy fellow passengers.

Tours

Tours are available all over India, run by tourist offices, local transport companies and travel agencies. Organised tours can be an inexpensive way to see several places on one trip, although you rarely get much time at each place. If you arrange a tailor-made tour, you'll have more freedom about where you go and how long you stay.

Drivers may double as guides, or you can hire a qualified local guide for a fee. In tourist towns, be wary of touts claiming to be professional guides.

International Tour Agencies

Many international companies offer tours to India, from straightforward sightseeing trips to adventure tours and activity-based holidays. To find current tours that match your interests, quiz travel agents and surf the web.

Some good places to start your tour hunt:

Dragoman (www.dragoman. com) One of several reputable overland tour companies offering trips in customised vehicles.

Exodus (www.exodus.co.uk) A wide array of specialist trips, including tours with a holistic, wildlife and adventure focus.

India Wildlife Tours (www. india-wildlife-tours.com) All sorts of wildlife tours, plus jeep, horse or camel safaris and birdwatching.

Indian Encounter (www.in-dianencounters.com) Special-interest tours that include wildlife-spotting, river-rafting and ayurvedic treatments.

Intrepid Travel (www. intrepidtravel.com) Endless possibilities, from wildlife tours to sacred rambles.

Peregrine Adventures (www.peregrineadventures. com) Popular cultural and trekking tours.

Sacred India Tours (www. sacredindiatours.com) Includes tours with a holistic focus such as yoga and ayurveda, as well as architectural and cultural tours.

Shanti Travel (www.shanti travel.com/en) A range of tours including family and adventure tours run by a Franco-Indian team.

World Expeditions (www. worldexpeditions.com) An array of options that includes trekking and cycling tours.

Train

Travelling by train is a quint-essential Indian experience. Trains offer a smoother ride than buses and are especially recommended for long journeys that include overnight travel. India's rail network is one of the largest and busiest in the world and Indian Railways is the largest utility employer on earth, with roughly 1.5 million workers. There are around 6900 train stations scattered across the country.

We've listed useful trains in this book but there are hundreds more. The best way of sourcing updated railway information is to use relevant internet sites such as **Indian Railways** (www.indianrail.gov. in) and the excellent **India Rail Info** (www.indiarail-info.com), with added offline browsing support. There's also *Trains at a Glance* (₹45), available at many train station bookstands and better bookshops/newsstands, however, it's published annually so it's not as up to date as websites. Nevertheless, it offers comprehensive timetables covering all the main lines.

Booking Tickets in India

You can either book tickets through a travel agency or hotel (for a commission), or in person at the train station. You can also book online through **IRCTC** (www.irctc. co.in), the e-ticketing division of Indian Railways, or portals such as **Make My Trip** (www. makemytrip.com) and **Yatra** (www.yatra.com). Remember, however, that online booking of train tickets has its share of glitches: travellers have reported problems with registering themselves on some portals and using certain overseas credit cards. Big stations often have English-speaking staff who can help with reservations. At smaller stations, the stationmaster and his deputy usually speak English. It's also worth approaching tourist-office staff if you need advice.

At the Station

Get a reservation slip from the information window, fill in the name of the departure station, destination station, the class you want to travel and the name and number of the train. Join the long queue for the ticket window where your ticket will be printed. Women should take advantage of the separate women's queue – if there isn't one, go to the front of the regular queue.

Tourist Reservation Bureau

Larger cities and major tourist centres have an International Tourist Bureau, which allows you to book tickets in relative peace – check www. indianrail.gov.in for a list of these stations.

EXPRESS TRAIN FARES (₹)

DISTANCE (KM)	1AC	2AC	3AC	EXECUTIVE CHAIR	CHAIR CAR (CC)	SECOND (II)
100	848	500	155	353	120	90
200	848	500	251	559	196	90
300	848	500	342	755	266	122
400	1064	627	425	937	331	151
500	1279	754	509	1121	396	182
1000	2140	1255	829	1853	644	295
1500	2780	1624	1049	Not Applicable	816	374
2000	3420	1993	1270	Not Applicable	987	452

Reservations

Bookings open 120 days before departure and you must make a reservation for chaircar, sleeper, 1AC, 2AC and 3AC carriages. No reservations are required for general (2nd-class) compartments; you have to grab seats here the moment the train pulls in.

Trains are always busy so it's wise to book as far in advance as possible, especially for overnight journeys. There may be additional services to certain destinations during major festivals but it's still worth booking well in advance.

Reserved tickets show your seat/berth and carriage number. Carriage numbers are written on the side of the train (station staff and porters can point you in the right direction). A list of names and berths is posted on the side of each reserved carriage.

Refunds are available on any ticket, even after departure, with a penalty – rules are complicated, check when you book.

Trains can be delayed at any stage of the journey; to avoid stress, factor some leeway into your plans.

Be mindful of potential drugging and theft.

If the train you want to travel on is sold out, enquire about other options.

Tourist Quota

A special (albeit small) tourist quota is set aside for foreign tourists travelling between popular stations. These seats can only be booked at dedicated reserva-

tion offices in major cities, and you need to show your passport and visa as ID. Tickets can be paid for in rupees (some offices may ask to see foreign exchange certificates – ATM receipts will suffice), British pounds, US dollars, euros, or Thomas Cook and American Express travellers cheques.

Taktal Tickets

Indian Railways holds back a small number of tickets on key trains and releases them at 10am one day before the train is due to depart. A charge of ₹10 to ₹300 is added to each ticket price. First AC tickets are excluded from the scheme.

Reservation Against Cancellation (RAC)

Even when a train is fully booked, Indian Railways sells a handful of seats in each class as 'Reservation Against Cancellation' (RAC). This means that if you have an RAC ticket and someone cancels before the departure date, you will get his or her seat (or berth). You'll have to check the reservation list at the station on the day of travel to see if you've been allocated a confirmed seat/berth. Even if no one cancels,

you can still board the train as an RAC ticket holder and travel without a seat.

Waitlist (WL)

If the RAC quota is maxed out as well, you will be handed a waitlisted ticket. This means that if there are enough cancellations, you may eventually move up the order to land a confirmed berth, or at least an RAC seat. Check your booking status at www.indianrail.gov. in/pnr_stat.html by entering your ticket's PNR number. You can't board the train on a waitlisted ticket, but a refund is available – ask the ticket office about your chances.

Costs

Fares are calculated by distance and class of travel; Rajdhani and Shatabdi trains are slightly more expensive, but the price includes meals. Most air-conditioned carriages have a catering service (meals are brought to your seat). In unreserved classes it's a good idea to carry portable snacks. Seniors (those over 60) get 30% off all fares in all classes on all types of trains. Children below the age of five travel free, those aged between five and 12 are charged half price.

Health

There is huge geographical variation in India, so environmental issues like heat, cold and altitude can cause health problems. Hygiene is generally poor in most regions so food and water-borne illnesses are fairly common. A number of insect-borne diseases are present, particularly in tropical areas. Medical care is basic in various areas (especially beyond the larger cities) so it's essential to be well prepared.

Pre-existing medical conditions and accidental injury (especially traffic accidents) account for most life-threatening problems. Becoming ill in some way, however, is common. Fortunately, most travellers' illnesses can be prevented with some common-sense behaviour or treated with a well-stocked travellers' medical kit – however, never hesitate to consult a doctor while on the road as self-diagnosis can be hazardous.

The following information is a general guide only and certainly does not replace the advice of a doctor trained in travel medicine.

BEFORE YOU GO

You can buy many medications over the counter in India without a doctor's prescription, but it can be difficult to find some of the newer drugs, particularly the latest antidepressant drugs, blood-pressure medications and contraceptive pills. Bring the following:

➡ Medications in their original, labelled containers

➡ A signed, dated letter from your physician describing your medical conditions and medications, including generic names

➡ A physician's letter documenting the medical necessity of any syringes you bring

➡ If you have a heart condition, a copy of your ECG taken just prior to travelling

➡ Any regular medication (double your ordinary needs)

Insurance

Don't travel without health insurance. Emergency evacuation is expensive. Consider the following when buying insurance:

➡ You may require extra cover for adventure activities such as rock climbing and scuba diving.

➡ In India, doctors usually require immediate payment in cash. Your insurance plan may make payments directly to providers or it will reimburse you later for overseas health expenditures. If you do have to claim later, make sure you keep all relevant documentation.

➡ Some policies ask that you telephone back (reverse charges) to a centre in your home country where an immediate assessment of your problem will be made.

Vaccinations

Specialised travel-medicine clinics are your best source of up-to-date information; they stock all available vaccines and can give specific recommendations for your trip. Most vaccines don't give immunity until *at least* two weeks after they're given, so visit a doctor well before departure. Ask your doctor for an International Certificate of Vaccination (sometimes known as the 'yellow booklet'), which will list all the vaccinations you've received.

Medical Checklist

Recommended items for a personal medical kit:

➡ Antifungal cream, eg Clotrimazole

➡ Antibacterial cream, eg Mupirocin

➡ Antibiotic for skin infections, eg Amoxicillin/ Clavulanate or Cephalexin

➡ Antihistamine – there are many options, eg Cetrizine for daytime and Promethazine for night

➡ Antiseptic, eg Betadine

REQUIRED & RECOMMENDED VACCINATIONS

The only vaccine required by international regulations is **yellow fever**. Proof of vaccination will only be required if you have visited a country in the yellow-fever zone within the six days prior to entering India. If you are travelling to India from Africa or South America, you should check to see if you require proof of vaccination.

The World Health Organization (WHO) recommends the following vaccinations for travellers going to India (as well as being up to date with measles, mumps and rubella vaccinations):

Adult diphtheria & tetanus Single booster recommended if none in the previous 10 years. Side effects include sore arm and fever.

Hepatitis A Provides almost 100% protection for up to a year; a booster after 12 months provides at least another 20 years' protection. Mild side effects such as headache and sore arm occur in 5% to 10% of people.

Hepatitis B Now considered routine for most travellers. Given as three shots over six months. A rapid schedule is also available, as is a combined vaccination with Hepatitis A. Side effects are mild and uncommon, usually headache and sore arm. In 95% of people lifetime protection results.

Polio Only one booster is required as an adult for lifetime protection. Inactivated polio vaccine is safe during pregnancy.

Typhoid Recommended for all travellers to India, even those only visiting urban areas. The vaccine offers around 70% protection, lasts for two to three years and comes as a single shot. Tablets are also available, but the injection is usually recommended as it has fewer side effects. Sore arm and fever may occur.

Varicella If you haven't had chickenpox, discuss this vaccination with your doctor.

These immunisations are recommended for long-term travellers (more than one month) or those at special risk (seek further advice from your doctor):

Japanese B Encephalitis Three injections in all. Booster recommended after two years. Sore arm and headache are the most common side effects. In rare cases, an allergic reaction comprising hives and swelling can occur up to 10 days after any of the three doses.

Meningitis Single injection. There are two types of vaccination: the quadravalent vaccine gives two to three years' protection; meningitis group C vaccine gives around 10 years' protection. Recommended for long-term backpackers aged under 25.

Rabies Three injections in all. A booster after one year will then provide 10 years' protection. Side effects are rare – occasionally headache and sore arm.

Tuberculosis (TB) A complex issue. Adult long-term travellers are usually recommended to have a TB skin test before and after travel, rather than vaccination. Only one vaccine given in a lifetime.

➡ Antispasmodic for stomach cramps, eg Buscopam

➡ Contraceptive

➡ Decongestant, eg Pseudoephedrine

➡ DEET-based insect repellent

➡ Diarrhoea medication – consider an oral rehydration solution (eg Gastrolyte), diarrhoea 'stopper' (eg Loperamide) and antinausea medication (eg Prochlorperazine). Antibiotics for diarrhoea include Ciprofloxacin; for bacterial diarrhoea Azithromycin; for giardia or amoebic dysentery Tinidazole

➡ First-aid items such as scissors, elastoplasts, bandages, gauze, thermometer (but not mercury), sterile needles and syringes, safety pins and tweezers

➡ Ibuprofen or another anti-inflammatory

➡ Iodine tablets (unless you are pregnant or have a thyroid problem) to purify water

➡ Migraine medication if you suffer from migraines

➡ Paracetamol

➡ Pyrethrin to impregnate clothing and mosquito nets

➡ Steroid cream for allergic or itchy rashes, eg 1% to 2% hydrocortisone

➡ High-factor sunscreen

➡ Throat lozenges

➡ Thrush (vaginal yeast infection) treatment, eg Clotrimazole pessaries or Diflucan tablet

➡ Ural or equivalent if prone to urine infections

Websites

There is a wealth of travel-health advice on the internet – www.lonelyplanet.com is a good place to start. Some other suggestions:

Centers for Disease Control and Prevention (CDC; www.cdc.gov) Good general information.

MD Travel Health (www.mdtravelhealth.com) Provides complete travel-health recommendations for every country, updated daily.

World Health Organization (WHO; www.who.int/ith) Its helpful book *International Travel & Health* is revised annually and is available online.

Further Reading

Lonely Planet's *Healthy Travel – Asia & India* is a handy pocket size and packed with useful information, including pre-trip planning, emergency first aid, immunisation and disease information, and what to do if you get sick on the road. Other

recommended references include *Travellers' Health* by Dr Richard Dawood and *Travelling Well* by Dr Deborah Mills – check out the website of **Travelling Well** (www.travellingwell.com.au).

IN INDIA

Availability of Health Care

Medical care is hugely variable in India. Some cities now have clinics catering specifically to travellers and expatriates; these clinics are usually more expensive than local medical facilities, and offer a higher standard of care. Additionally, they know the local system, including reputable local hospitals and specialists. They may also liaise with insurance companies should you require evacuation. It is usually difficult to find reliable medical care in rural areas.

Self-treatment may be appropriate if your problem is minor (eg traveller's diarrhoea), you are carrying the relevant medication and you cannot attend a recommended clinic. If you suspect a serious disease, especially malaria, travel to the nearest quality facility.

Before buying medication over the counter, check the use-by date, and ensure the packet is sealed and properly stored (eg not exposed to the sunshine).

Infectious Diseases

Malaria

This is a serious and potentially deadly disease. Before you travel, seek expert advice according to your itinerary (rural areas are especially risky) and on medication and side effects.

Malaria is caused by a parasite transmitted by the bite of an infected mosquito. The key symptom of malaria is fever, but general symptoms, such as headache, diarrhoea, cough or chills, may also occur. Diagnosis can only be properly made by taking a blood sample.

Two strategies should be combined to prevent malaria: mosquito avoidance and antimalarial medications. Most people who catch malaria are taking inadequate or no antimalarial medication.

Travellers are advised to prevent mosquito bites by taking these steps:

➡ Use a DEET-based insect repellent on exposed skin. Wash this off at night – as long as you are sleeping under a mosquito net. Natural repellents such as citronella can be effective, but must be applied more frequently than products containing DEET.

➡ Sleep under a mosquito net impregnated with pyrethrin.

➡ Choose accommodation with proper screens and fans (if not air-conditioned).

➡ Impregnate clothing with pyrethrin in high-risk areas.

➡ Wear long sleeves and trousers in light colours.

➡ Use mosquito coils.

➡ Spray your room with insect repellent before going out for your evening meal.

There are a variety of medications available:

Chloroquine & Paludrine combination Limited effectiveness in many parts of South Asia. Common side effects include nausea (40% of people) and mouth ulcers.

Doxycycline (daily tablet) A broad-spectrum antibiotic that helps prevent a variety of tropical diseases, including leptospirosis, tick-borne disease and typhus. Potential side effects include photosensitivity (a tendency to sunburn), thrush (in women), indigestion, heartburn, nausea and interference with the contraceptive pill. More serious side effects include ulceration of the oesophagus – take your tablet with a meal and a large glass of water, and never lie down within half an hour of taking it. It must be taken for four weeks after leaving the risk area.

Lariam (mefloquine) This weekly tablet suits many people. Serious side effects are rare but include depression, anxiety, psychosis and seizures. Anyone with a history of depression, anxiety, other psychological disorders or epilepsy should not take Lariam. It is considered safe in the second and third trimesters of pregnancy. Tablets must be taken for four weeks after leaving the risk area.

Malarone A combination of atovaquone and proguanil. Side effects are uncommon and mild, most commonly nausea and headache. It is the best tablet for scuba divers and for those on short trips to high-risk areas. It must be taken for one week after leaving the risk area.

Other Diseases

Avian Flu 'Bird flu' or Influenza A (H5N1) is a subtype of the type A influenza virus. Contact with dead or sick birds is the principal source of infection and bird-to-human transmission does not easily occur. Symptoms include high fever and flu-like symptoms with rapid deterioration, leading to respiratory failure and death in many cases. Immediate

medical care should be sought if bird flu is suspected. Check www.who.int/en/ or www.avianinfluenza.com.au.

Dengue Fever This mosquito-borne disease is becomingly increasingly problematic, especially in the cities. As there is no vaccine available it can only be prevented by avoiding mosquito bites at all times. Symptoms include high fever, severe headache and body ache and sometimes a rash and diarrhoea. Treatment is rest and paracetamol – do not take aspirin or ibuprofen as it increases the likelihood of haemorrhaging. Make sure you see a doctor to be diagnosed and monitored.

Hepatitis A This food- and water-borne virus infects the liver, causing jaundice (yellow skin and eyes), nausea and lethargy. There is no specific treatment for hepatitis A, you just need to allow time for the liver to heal. All travellers to India should be vaccinated against hepatitis A.

Hepatitis B This sexually transmitted disease is spread by body fluids and can be prevented by vaccination. The long-term consequences can include liver cancer and cirrhosis.

Hepatitis E Transmitted through contaminated food and water, hepatitis E has similar symptoms to hepatitis A, but is far less common. It is a severe problem in pregnant women and can result in the death of both mother and baby. There is no commercially available vaccine, and prevention is by following safe eating and drinking guidelines.

HIV Spread via contaminated body fluids. Avoid unsafe sex, unsterile needles (including in medical facilities) and procedures such as tattoos. The growth rate of HIV in India is one of the highest in the world.

Influenza Present year-round in the tropics, influenza (flu) symptoms include fever, muscle aches, a runny nose, cough and sore throat. It can be severe in people over the age of 65 or in those with medical conditions such as heart disease or diabetes – vaccination is recommended for these individuals. There is no specific treatment, just rest and paracetamol.

Japanese B Encephalitis This viral disease is transmitted by mosquitoes and is rare in travellers. Most cases occur in rural areas and vaccination is recommended for travellers spending more than one month outside of cities. There is no treatment, and it may result in permanent brain damage or death. Ask your doctor for further details.

Rabies This fatal disease is spread by the bite or possibly even the lick of an infected animal – most commonly a dog or monkey. You should seek medical advice immediately after any animal bite and commence postexposure treatment. Having pretravel vaccination means the postbite treatment is greatly simplified. If an animal bites you, gently wash the wound with soap and water, and apply iodine-based antiseptic. If you are not prevaccinated you will need to receive rabies immunoglobulin as soon as possible, and this is very difficult to obtain in much of India.

Tuberculosis While TB is rare in travellers, those who have significant contact with the local population (such as medical and aid workers and long-term travellers) should take precautions. Vaccination is usually only given to children under the age of five, but adults at risk are recommended to have pre- and post-travel TB testing. The main symptoms are fever, cough, weight loss, night sweats and fatigue.

Typhoid This serious bacterial infection is spread via food and water. It gives a high and slowly progressive fever and headache, and may be accompanied by a dry cough and stomach pain. It is diagnosed by blood tests and treated with antibiotics. Vaccination is recommended for all travellers who are spending more than a week in India. Be aware that vaccination is not 100% effective, so you must still be careful with what you eat and drink.

Travellers' Diarrhoea

This is by far the most common problem affecting travellers in India – between 30% and 70% of people will suffer from it within two weeks of starting their trip. It's usually caused by a bacteria, and thus responds promptly to treatment with antibiotics.

Travellers' diarrhoea is defined as the passage of more than three watery bowel actions within 24 hours, plus at least one other symptom, such as fever, cramps, nausea, vomiting or feeling generally unwell.

Treatment consists of staying well hydrated; rehydration solutions like Gastrolyte are the best for this. Antibiotics such as Ciprofloxacin or Azithromycin should kill the bacteria quickly. Seek medical attention quickly if you do not respond to an appropriate antibiotic.

Loperamide is just a 'stopper' and doesn't get to the cause of the problem. It can be helpful, though (eg if you have to go on a long bus ride). Don't take Loperamide if you have a fever or blood in your stools.

Amoebic Dysentery Amoebic dysentery is very rare in travellers but is quite often misdiagnosed by poor-quality labs. Symptoms are similar to bacterial diarrhoea: fever, bloody diarrhoea and generally feeling unwell. You should always seek reliable medical care if you have blood in your diarrhoea. Treatment involves two drugs: Tinidazole or Metronidazole to kill the parasite in your gut and then a second drug to kill the cysts. If left untreated complications such as liver or gut abscesses can occur.

Giardiasis Giardia is a parasite that is relatively common in travellers. Symptoms include nausea, bloating, excess gas, fatigue and intermittent diarrhoea. The parasite will eventually go away if left untreated but this can take months; the best advice is to seek medical treatment. The treatment of choice is Tinidazole, with Metronidazole being a second-line option.

Environmental Hazards

Air Pollution

Air pollution, particularly vehicle pollution, is an increasing problem in most of India's urban hubs. If you have severe respiratory problems, speak with your doctor before travelling to India.

Diving & Surfing

Divers and surfers should seek specialised advice before they travel to ensure their medical kit contains treatment for coral cuts and tropical ear infections. Divers should ensure their insurance covers them for decompression illness – get specialised dive insurance through an organisation such as **Divers Alert Network** (DAN; www.danasiapacific.org) Certain medical conditions are incompatible with diving: check with your doctor.

Food

Dining out brings with it the possibility of contracting diarrhoea. Ways to help avoid food-related illness:

➜ Eating only freshly cooked food

➜ Avoiding shellfish and buffets

➜ Peeling fruit

➜ Cooking vegetables

➜ Soaking salads in iodine water for at least 20 minutes

➜ Eating in busy restaurants with a high turnover of customers

Heat

Many parts of India, especially down south, are hot and humid throughout the year. For most visitors it takes around two weeks to comfortably adapt to the hot climate. Swelling of the feet and ankles is common, as are muscle cramps caused by excessive sweating. Prevent these by avoiding dehydration and excessive activity in the heat. Don't eat salt tablets (they aggravate the gut); drinking rehydration solution or eating salty food helps. Treat cramps by resting, rehydrating with double-strength rehydration solution and gently stretching.

Dehydration This is the main contributor to heat exhaustion. Recovery is usually rapid and it is common to feel weak for some days afterwards. Symptoms include:

➜ Feeling weak

CARBON-MONOXIDE POISONING

Some mountain areas rely on charcoal burners for warmth, but these should be avoided due to the risk of fatal carbon-monoxide poisoning. The thick, mattress-like blankets used in many mountain areas are amazingly warm once you get beneath the covers. If you're still cold, improvise a hot-water bottle by filling your drinking-water bottle with boiled water and covering it with a sock.

→ Headache

→ Irritability

→ Nausea or vomiting

→ Sweaty skin

→ A fast, weak pulse

→ Normal or slightly elevated body temperature.

Treatment:

→ Get out of the heat

→ Fan the sufferer

→ Apply cool, wet cloths to the skin

→ Lay the sufferer flat with their legs raised

→ Rehydrate with water containing one-quarter teaspoon of salt per litre.

Heat stroke Symptoms of this serious medical emergency:

→ Weakness

→ Nausea

→ A hot dry body

→ Temperature of over 41°C

→ Dizziness

→ Confusion

→ Loss of coordination

→ Seizures

→ Eventual collapse.

Treatment:

→ Get out of the heat

→ Fan the sufferer

→ Apply cool, wet cloths to the skin or ice to the body, especially to the groin and armpits.

Prickly heat This is a common skin rash in the tropics, caused by sweat trapped under the skin. Treat it by moving out of the heat for a few hours and by having cool showers. Creams and ointments clog the skin so they should be avoided. Locally bought prickly-heat powder can be helpful.

Altitude Sickness

If you are going to altitudes above 3000m, Acute Mountain Sickness (AMS) is an issue. The biggest risk factor is going too high too quickly – follow a conservative accli-

DRINKING WATER

→ Never drink tap water.

→ Bottled water is generally safe – check the seal is intact at purchase.

→ Avoid ice unless you know it has been made hygienically.

→ Be careful of fresh juices served at street stalls in particular – they may have been watered down or may be served in unhygienic jugs/glasses.

→ Boiling water is usually the most efficient method of purifying it.

→ The best chemical purifier is iodine. It should not be used by pregnant women or those with thyroid problems.

→ Water filters should also filter out most viruses. Ensure your filter has a chemical barrier such as iodine and a small pore size (less than four microns).

matisation schedule found in good trekking guides, and *never* go to a higher altitude when you have any symptoms that could be altitude related. There is no way to predict who will get altitude sickness and it is quite often the younger, fitter members of a group who succumb.

Symptoms usually develop during the first 24 hours at altitude but may be delayed up to three weeks. Mild symptoms:

→ Headache

→ Lethargy

→ Dizziness

→ Difficulty sleeping

→ Loss of appetite

AMS may become more severe without warning and can be fatal. Severe symptoms:

→ Breathlessness

→ A dry, irritative cough (which may progress to the production of pink, frothy sputum)

→ Severe headache

→ Lack of coordination and balance

→ Confusion

→ Irrational behaviour

→ Vomiting

→ Drowsiness

→ Unconsciousness

Treat mild symptoms by resting at the same altitude until recovery, which usually takes a day or two. Paracetamol or aspirin can be taken for headaches. If symptoms persist or become worse, immediate descent is necessary; even 500m can help. Drug treatments should never be used to avoid descent or to enable further ascent.

The drugs Acetazolamide and Dexamethasone are recommended by some doctors for the prevention of AMS; however, their use is controversial. They can reduce the symptoms, but they may also mask warning signs; severe and fatal AMS has occurred in people taking these drugs.

To prevent acute mountain sickness:

→ Ascend slowly – have frequent rest days, spending two to three nights at each rise of 1000m

→ Sleep at a lower altitude than the greatest height reached during the day, if possible. Above 3000m, don't increase sleeping altitude by more than 300m daily

→ Drink extra fluids

→ Eat light, high-carbohydrate meals

→ Avoid alcohol and sedatives

Insect Bites & Stings

Bedbugs They don't carry disease but their bites can be very itchy. They usually live in furniture and walls and then migrate to the bed at night. You can treat the itch with an antihistamine.

Lice Most commonly appear on the head and pubic areas. You may need numerous applications of an antilice shampoo such as pyrethrin. Pubic lice are usually contracted from sexual contact.

Ticks Contracted walking in rural areas. Ticks are commonly found behind the ears, on the belly and in armpits. If you have had a tick bite and have a rash at the site of the bite or elsewhere, or fever or muscle aches, you should see a doctor. Doxycycline prevents tick-borne diseases.

Leeches Found in humid rainforest areas. They do not transmit any disease but their bites are often intensely itchy for weeks and can easily become infected.

Apply an iodine-based antiseptic to any leech bite to help prevent infection.

Bee and wasp stings Anyone with a serious bee or wasp allergy should carry an injection of adrenalin (eg an Epipen). For others pain is the main problem – apply ice to the sting and take painkillers.

Skin Problems

Fungal rashes There are two common fungal rashes that affect travellers. The first occurs in moist areas, such as the groin, armpits and between the toes. It starts as a red patch that slowly spreads and is usually itchy. Treatment involves keeping the skin dry, avoiding chafing and using an antifungal cream such as Clotrimazole or Lamisil. The second, *Tinea versicolor*, causes light-coloured patches, most commonly on the back, chest and shoulders. Consult a doctor.

Cuts and scratches These become easily infected in humid climates. Immediately wash all wounds in clean water and apply antiseptic. If you develop signs of infection (increasing pain and redness), see a doctor.

Women's Health

For gynaecological health issues, seek out a female doctor.

Birth control Bring adequate supplies of your own form of contraception.

Sanitary products Pads, rarely tampons, are readily available.

Thrush Heat, humidity and antibiotics can all contribute to thrush. Treatment is with antifungal creams and pessaries such as Clotrimazole. A practical alternative is a single tablet of Fluconazole (Diflucan).

Urinary-tract infections These can be precipitated by dehydration or long bus journeys without toilet stops; bring suitable antibiotics.

Language

The number of languages spoken in India helps explain why English is still widely spoken here, and why it's still in official use. Another 22 languages are recognised in the constitution, and more than 1600 minor languages are spoken throughout the country.

Major efforts have been made to promote Hindi as the national language of India and to gradually phase out English. However, English remains popular, and while Hindi is the predominant language in the north, it bears little relation to the Dravidian languages of the south such as Tamil. Consequently, very few people in the south speak Hindi.

Many educated Indians speak English as virtually their first language and for a large number of Indians it's their second tongue. Although you'll find it easy to get around India with English, it's always good to know a little of the local language.

HINDI

Hindi has about 600 million speakers worldwide, of which 180 million are in India. It developed from Classical Sanskrit, and is written in the Devanagari script. In 1947 it was granted official status along with English.

Most Hindi sounds are similar to their English counterparts. The main difference is that Hindi has both 'aspirated' consonants (pronounced with a puff of air, like saying 'h' after the sound) and unaspirated ones, as well as 'retroflex' (pronounced with the tongue bent backwards) and nonretroflex consonants. Our simplified pronunciation guides don't include these distinctions – read them as if they were English and you'll be understood.

Pronouncing the vowels correctly is important, especially their length (eg a and aa). The consonant combination ng after a vowel indicates nasalisation (ie the vowel is pronounced 'through the nose'). Note also that au is pronounced as the 'ow' in 'how'. Word stress is very light – we've indicated the stressed syllables with italics.

Basics

Hindi verbs change form depending on the gender of the speaker (or the subject of the sentence in general), so it's the verbs, not the pronouns 'he' or 'she' (as is the case in English) which show whether the subject of the sentence is masculine or feminine. In these phrases we include the options for male and female speakers, marked 'm' and 'f' respectively.

Hello./Goodbye.	नमस्ते ।	na·ma·ste
Yes.	जी हाँ ।	jee haang
No.	जी नहीं ।	jee na·heeng
Excuse me.	सुनिये ।	su·ni·ye
Sorry.	माफ़ कीजिये ।	maaf kee·ji·ye
Please ...	कृपया ...	kri·pa·yaa ...
Thank you.	थैंक्यू ।	thayn·kyoo
You're welcome.	कोई बात नहीं ।	ko·ee baat na·heeng

How are you?
आप कैसे/कैसी हैं? | aap kay·se/kay·see hayng (m/f)

Fine. And you?
मैं ठीक हूँ । | mayng teek hoong
आप सुनाइये । | aap su·naa·i·ye

WANT MORE?

For in-depth language information and handy phrases, check out Lonely Planet's *Hindi, Urdu & Bengali Phrasebook* and *India Phrasebook*. You'll find them at **shop.lonelyplanet.com**, or you can buy Lonely Planet's iPhone phrasebooks at the Apple App Store.

What's your name?
आप का नाम क्या है?   aap kaa naam kyaa hay

My name is ...
मेरा नाम ... है।   *me*·raa naam ... hay

Do you speak English?
क्या आपको अंग्रेज़ी   kyaa aap ko an·*gre*·zee
आती है?   *aa*·tee hay

I don't understand.
मैं नहीं समझा/   mayng na·*heeng sam*·jaa/
समझी।   *sam*·jee (m/f)

Accommodation

Where's a ...?   ... कहाँ है?   ... ka·*haang* hay

   guesthouse   गेस्ट हाउस   gest *haa*·us
   hotel   होटल   *ho*·tal
   youth hostel   यूथ हास्टल   yoot *haas*·tal

Do you have   क्या ... कमरा   kyaa ... *kam*·raa
a ... room?   है?   hay

   single   सिंगल   *sin*·gal
   double   डबल   da·*bal*

How much is   ... के लिये   ... ke li·ye
it per ...?   कितने पैसे   *kit*·ne pay·se
   लगते हैं?   *lag*·te hayng

   night   एक रात   ek raat
   person   हर व्यक्ति   har *vyak*·ti

   air-con   ए० सी०   e see
   bathroom   बाथरूम   *baat*·room
   hot water   गर्म पानी   garm *paa*·nee
   mosquito net   मसहरी   *mas*·ha·ree
   washerman   धोबी   do·*bee*
   window   खिड़की   *kir*·kee

Directions

Where's ...?
... कहाँ है?   ... ka·*haang* hay

How far is it?
वह कितनी दूर है?   voh *kit*·nee door hay

What's the address?
पता क्या है?   pa·*taa* kyaa hay

Can you show me (on the map)?
(नक्शे में) दिखा   (*nak*·she meng) di·*kaa*
सकते है?   *sak*·te hayng

Turn left/right.
लेफ्ट/राइट मुड़िये।   left/*raa*·it mu·ri·ye

Numbers – Hindi			
1	१	एक	ek
2	२	दो	do
3	३	तीन	teen
4	४	चार	chaar
5	५	पाँच	paanch
6	६	छह	chay
7	७	सात	saat
8	८	आठ	aat
9	९	नौ	nau
10	१०	दस	das
20	२०	बीस	bees
30	३०	तीस	tees
40	४०	चालीस	*chaa*·lees
50	५०	पचास	pa·*chaas*
60	६०	साठ	saat
70	७०	सत्तर	*sat*·tar
80	८०	अस्सी	*as*·see
90	९०	नब्बे	*nab*·be
100	१००	सौ	sau
1000	१०००	एक हज़ार	ek ha·*zaar*

at the corner   कोने पर   *ko*·ne par
at the traffic   सिगनल पर   *sig*·nal par
   lights
behind ...   ... के पीछे   ... ke *pee*·che
in front of ...   ... के सामन   ... ke *saam*·ne
near ...   ... के पास   ... ke paas
opposite ...   ... के सामने   ... ke *saam*·ne
straight ahead   सीधे   *see*·de

Eating & Drinking

What would you recommend?
आपके ख़्याल में   aap ke kyaal meng
क्या अच्छा होगा?   kyaa *ach*·chaa *ho*·gaa

Do you have vegetarian food?
क्या आप का खाना   kyaa aap kaa *kaa*·naa
शाकाहारी है?   shaa·kaa·*haa*·ree hay

I don't eat (meat).
मैं (गोश्त) नहीं   mayng (gosht) na·*heeng*
खाता/खाती।   *kaa*·taa/*kaa*·tee (m/f)

I'll have ...
मुझे ... दीजिये।   mu·*je* ... *dee*·ji·ye

That was delicious.
बहुत मज़ेदार हुआ।   ba·*hut* ma·ze·*daar* hu·aa

Please bring the menu/bill.
मेन्यू/बिल लाइये।   *men*·yoo/bil *laa*·i·ye

Key Words

bottle	बोतल	bo·tal
bowl	कटोरी	ka·to·ree
breakfast	नाश्ता	naash·taa
dessert	मीठा	mee·taa
dinner	रात का खाना	raat kaa kaa·naa
drinks	पीने की चीज़ें	pee·ne kee chee·zeng
food	खाना	kaa·naa
fork	काँटा	kaan·taa
glass	गिलास	glaas
knife	चाकू	chaa·koo
local eatery	ढाबा	daa·baa
lunch	दिन का खाना	din kaa kaa·naa
market	बाज़ार	baa·zaar
plate	प्लेट	plet
restaurant	रेस्टोरेंट	res·to·rent
set meal	थाली	taa·lee
snack	नाश्ता	naash·taa
spoon	चम्मच	cham·mach

Meat & Fish

beef	गाय का गोश्त	gaai kaa gosht
chicken	मुर्गी	mur·gee
duck	बतख़	ba·tak
fish	मछली	mach·lee
goat	बकरा	bak·raa
lobster	बड़ी झींगा	ba·ree jeeng·gaa
meat	गोश्त	gosht
meatballs	कोफ़्ता	kof·taa
pork	सुअर का गोश्त	su·ar kaa gosht
prawn	झींगी मछली	jeeng·gee mach·lee
seafood	मछली	mach·lee

Fruit & Vegetables

apple	सेब	seb
apricot	खुबानी	ku·baa·nee
banana	केला	ke·laa
capsicum	मिर्च	mirch
carrot	गाजर	gaa·jar
cauliflower	फूल गोभी	pool go·bee
corn	मक्का	mak·kaa
cucumber	ककड़ी	kak·ree
date	खजूर	ka·joor
eggplant	बैंगन	bayng·gan
fruit	फल	pal
garlic	लहसुन	leh·sun
grape	अंगूर	an·goor
grapefruit	चकोतरा	cha·kot·raa

lemon	निम्बू	nim·boo
lentils	दाल	daal
mandarin	सन्तरा	san·ta·raa
mango	आम	aam
mushroom	खुम्भी	kum·bee
nuts	मेवे	me·ve
orange	नारंगी	naa·ran·gee
papaya	पपीता	pa·pee·taa
peach	आड़ू	aa·roo
peas	मटर	ma·tar
pineapple	अनन्नास	a·nan·naas
potato	आलू	aa·loo
pumpkin	कद्दू	kad·doo
spinach	पालक	paa·lak
vegetables	सब्ज़ी	sab·zee
watermelon	तरबूज़	tar·booz

Other

bread	चपाती/ नान/रोटी	cha·paa·tee/ naan/ro·tee
butter	मक्खन	mak·kan
chilli	मिर्च	mirch
chutney	चटनी	chat·nee
egg	अण्डे	an·de
honey	मधु	ma·dhu
ice	बर्फ़	barf
ice cream	कुल्फ़ी	kul·fee
pappadams	पपड़	pa·par
pepper	काली मिर्च	kaa·lee mirch
relish	अचार	a·chaar
rice	चावल	chaa·val
salt	नमक	na·mak
spices	मिर्च मसाला	mirch ma·saa·laa
sugar	चीनी	chee·nee
tofu	टोफू	to·foo

Drinks

beer	बियर	bi·yar
coffee	काॅफ़ी	kaa·fee
(sugarcane) juice	(गन्ने का) रस	(gan·ne kaa) ras
milk	दूध	dood
red wine	लाल शराब	laal sha·raab
sweet fruit drink	शरबत	shar·bat
tea	चाय	chaai
water	पानी	paa·nee
white wine	सफ़ेद शराब	sa·fed sha·raab
yoghurt	लस्सी	las·see

Emergencies

Help!
मदद कीजिये!   ma·dad kee·ji·ye

Go away!
जाओ!   jaa·o

I'm lost.
मैं रास्ता भूल   mayng raas·taa bool
गया/गयी हूँ।   ga·yaa/ga·yee hoong (m/f)

Call a doctor!
डॉक्टर को बुलाओ!   daak·tar ko bu·laa·o

Call the police!
पुलिस को बुलाओ!   pu·lis ko bu·laa·o

I'm ill.
मैं बीमार हूँ।   mayng bee·maar hoong

Where is the toilet?
टॉइलेट कहाँ है?   taa·i·let ka·haang hay

Shopping & Services

I'd like to buy ...
मुझे ... चाहिये।   mu·je ... chaa·hi·ye

I'm just looking.
सिर्फ़ देखने आया/   sirf dek·ne aa·yaa/
आयी हूँ।   aa·yee hoong (m/f)

Can I look at it?
दिखाइये।   di·kaa·i·ye

How much is it?
कितने का है?   kit·ne kaa hay

It's too expensive.
यह बहुत महँगा/   yeh ba·hut ma·han·gaa/
महँगी है।   ma·han·gee hay (m/f)

There's a mistake in the bill.
बिल में गलती है।   bil meng gal·tee hay

bank	बैंक	baynk
post office	डाक ख़ाना	daak kaa·naa
public phone	सार्वजनिक फ़ोन	saar·va·ja·nik fon
tourist office	पर्यटन ऑफ़िस	par·ya·tan aa·fis

Time & Dates

What time is it?
टाइम क्या है?   taa·im kyaa hay

It's (10) o'clock.
(दस) बजे हैं।   (das) ba·je hayng

Half past (10).
साढ़े (दस)।   saa·re (das)

morning	सुबह	su·bah
afternoon	दोपहर	do·pa·har
evening	शाम	shaam
Monday	सोमवार	som·vaar
Tuesday	मंगलवार	man·gal·vaar
Wednesday	बुधवार	bud·vaar
Thursday	गुरुवार	gu·ru·vaar
Friday	शुक्रवार	shuk·ra·vaar
Saturday	शनिवार	sha·ni·vaar
Sunday	रविवार	ra·vi·vaar

Transport

When's the ... (bus)?   ... (बस) कब जाती है?   ... (bas) kab jaa·tee hay
  first   पहली   peh·lee
  last   आख़िरी   aa·ki·ree

bicycle	साइकिल	saa·i·kil
rickshaw	रिक्शा	rik·shaa
boat	जहाज़	ja·haaz
bus	बस	bas
plane	हवाई जहाज़	ha·vaa·ee ja·haaz
train	ट्रेन	tren

a ... ticket   के लिये ... टिकट दीजिये।   ke li·ye ... ti·kat dee·ji·ye
  one-way   एक तरफ़ा   ek ta·ra·faa
  return   आने जाने का   aa·ne jaa·ne kaa

bus stop	बस स्टॉप	bas is·taap
ticket office	टिकटघर	ti·kat·gar
timetable	समय सारणी	sa·mai saa·ra·nee
train station	स्टेशन	ste·shan

Does it stop at ...?
क्या ... में रुकती है? kyaa ... meng ruk·tee hay

Please tell me when we get to ...
जब ... आता है,   jab ... aa·taa hay
मुझे बताइये।   mu·je ba·taa·i·ye

Please go straight to this address.
इसी जगह को   is·ee ja·gah ko
फ़ौरन जाइए।   fau·ran jaa·i·ye

Please stop here.
यहाँ रुकिये।   ya·haang ru·ki·ye

TAMIL

Tamil is the official language in the South Indian state of Tamil Nadu. It's one of the major Dravidian languages of South India, with records of its existence going back more than 2000 years. Tamil has about 62 million speakers in India.

Like Hindi, the Tamil sound system includes a number of 'retroflex' consonants (pronounced with the tongue bent backwards). Unlike Hindi, however, Tamil has no 'aspirated' sounds (pronounced with a puff of air). Our simplified pronunciation guides don't distinguish the retroflex consonants from their nonretroflex counterparts – just read the guides as if they were English and you'll be understood. Note that aw is pronounced as in 'law' and ow as in 'how'. The stressed syllables are indicated with italics.

Numbers – Tamil

1	ஒன்று	on·*dru*
2	இரண்டு	i·*ran*·tu
3	மூன்று	*moon*·dru
4	நான்கு	naan·*ku*
5	ஐந்து	ain·*tu*
6	ஆறு	*aa*·ru
7	ஏழு	*ey*·zu
8	எட்டு	et·*tu*
9	ஒன்பது	on·pa·*tu*
10	பத்து	pat·*tu*
20	இருபது	i·ru·pa·*tu*
30	முப்பது	mup·pa·*tu*
40	நாற்பது	naar·pa·*tu*
50	ஐம்பது	aim·pa·*tu*
60	அறுபது	a·ru·pa·*tu*
70	எழுபது	e·zu·pa·*tu*
80	எண்பது	en·pa·*tu*
90	தொன்னூறு	ton·noo·*ru*
100	நூறு	noo·*ru*
1000	ஓராயிரம்	aw·raa·yi·ram

Basics

Hello.	வணக்கம்.	va·*nak*·kam
Goodbye.	போய் வருகிறேன்.	*po*·i va·*ru*·ki·reyn
Yes./No.	ஆமாம்./இல்லை.	aa·maam/*il*·lai
Excuse me.	தயவு செய்து	ta·ya·vu sei·*du*
Sorry.	மன்னிக்கவும.	man·nik·ka·vum
Please.	தயவு செய்து.	ta·ya·vu chey·*tu*
Thank you.	நன்றி.	nan·dri

Do you speak English?

நீங்கள் ஆங்கிலம் பேசுவீர்களா?	*neeng*·kal aang·ki·lam pey·chu·*veer*·ka·la

I don't understand.

எனக்கு விளங்கவில்லை.	e·*nak*·ku vi·*lang*·ka·vil·*lai*

Accommodation

Where's a ... nearby?	அருகே ஒரு ... எங்கே உள்ளது?	a·ru·*ke* o·ru ... eng·ke *ul*·la·tu
guesthouse	விருந்தினர் இல்லம	vi·*run*·ti·nar *il*·lam
hotel	ஹோட்டல	hot·tal
Do you have a ... room?	உங்களிடம் ஓர் ... அறை உள்ளதா?	ung·ka·li·tam awr ... a·*rai* *ul*·la·taa
single	தன	ta·ni
double	இரட்டை	i·rat·*tai*
How much is it per ...?	ஓர் ... என்னவிலை?	awr ... en·na·vi·lai
night	இரவுக்கு	i·ra·*vuk*·ku
person	ஒருவருக்கு	o·ru·va·*ruk*·ku

air-conditioned	குளிர்சாதன வசதியுடையது	ku·*lir*·chaa·ta·na va·*cha*·ti·yu·*tai*·ya·tu
bathroom	குளியலறை	ku·li·*ya*·la·rai
bed	படுக்கை	pa·*tuk*·kai
window	சன்னல	*chan*·nal

Eating & Drinking

Can you recommend a ...?	நீங்கள் ஒரு ... பரிந்துரைக்க முடியுமா?	*neeng*·kal o·ru ... pa·rin·tu·*raik*·ka mu·ti·yu·maa
bar	பார்	paar
dish	உணவு வகை	u·na·vu va·*kai*
place to eat	உணவகம்	u·na·va·ham
I'd like (a/the) ..., please.	எனக்கு தயவு செய்து ... கொடுங்கள்.	e·*nak*·ku ta·ya·vu chey·*tu* ... ko·*tung*·kal
bill	விலைச்சீட்டு	vi·*laich*·cheet·tu
menu	உணவுப்– பட்டியல்	u·na·*vup*· pat·ti·yal
that dish	அந்த உணவு வகை	an·ta u·na·*vu* va·hai

Do you have vegetarian food?

உங்களிடம சைவ உணவு உள்ளதா?	ung·ka·li·tam chai·va u·na·*vu* *ul*·la·taa

LANGUAGE TAMIL

Emergencies

| Help! | உதவு! | u·ta·vi |
| Go away! | போய் விடு! | pow·i vi·tu |

Call a doctor!
ஐ அழைக்கவும்   i a·zai·ka·vum
ஒரு மருத்துவர்!   o·ru ma·rut·tu·var

Call the police!
ஐ அழைக்கவும்   i a·zai·ka·vum
போலீஸ்!   pow·lees

I'm lost.
நான் வழி தவறி   naan va·zi ta·va·ri
போய்விட்டேன்.   pow·i·vit·teyn

Where are the toilets?
கழிவறைகள் எங்கே?   ka·zi·va·rai·kal eng·key

Shopping & Services

Where's the market?
எங்கே சந்தை   eng·key chan·tai
இருக்கிறது?   i·ruk·ki·ra·tu

Can I look at it?
நான் இதைப்   naan i·taip
பார்க்கலாமா?   paark·ka·laa·maa

How much is it?
இது என்ன விலை?   i·tu en·na vi·lai

That's too expensive.
அது அதிக விலையாக   a·tu a·ti·ka vi·lai·yaa·ka
இருக்கிறது.   i·ruk·ki·ra·tu

bank	வங்கி	vang·ki
internet	இணையம்	i·nai·yam
post office	தபால்	ta·paal
	நிலையம்	ni·lai·yam
tourist office	சுற்றுப்பயண	chut·rup·pa·ya·na
	அலுவலகம்	a·lu·va·la·kam

Time & Dates

What time is it?
மணி என்ன?   ma·ni en·na

It's (two) o'clock.
மணி (இரண்டு).   ma·ni (i·ran·tu)

Half past (two).
(இரண்டு) முப்பது.   (i·ran·tu) mup·pa·tu

yesterday	நேற்று	neyt·tru
today	இன்று	in·dru
tomorrow	நாளை	naa·lai
morning	காலை	kaa·lai
evening	மாலை	maa·lai
night	இரவு	i·ra·vu

Monday	திங்கள்	ting·kal
Tuesday	செவ்வாய்	chev·vai
Wednesday	புதன்	pu·tan
Thursday	வியாழன்	vi·yaa·zan
Friday	வெள்ளி	vel·li
Saturday	சனி	cha·ni
Sunday	ஞாயிறு	nyaa·yi·ru

Transport & Directions

Where's the ...?
... எங்கே இருக்கிறது?   ... eng·key i·ruk·ki·ra·tu

What's the address?
வீலாசம் என்ன?   vi·laa·cham en·na

Can you show me (on the map)?
எனக்கு (வரைபடத்தில்)   e·nak·ku (va·rai·pa·tat·til)
காட்ட முடியுமா?   kaat·ta mu·ti·yu·maa

Is this the ... to (New Delhi)?
இது தானா   i·tu taa·naa
(புது–   (pu·tu
டில்லிக்குப்)   til·lik·kup)
புறப்படும் ...?   pu·rap·pa·tum ...

bus	பஸ்	pas
plane	வீமானம்	vi·maa·nam
train	இரயில்	i·ra·yil

One ... ticket (to Madurai), please.
(மதுரைக்கு)   (ma·tu·raik·ku)
தயவு செய்து   ta·ya·vu chey·tu
... டிக்கட்   ... tik·kat
கொடுங்கள்.   ko·tung·kal

one-way	ஒரு	o·ru
	வழிப்பயண	va·zip·pa·ya·na
return	இரு	i·ru
	வழிப்பயண	va·zip·pa·ya·na
bicycle	சைக்கிள்	chaik·kil
boat	படகு	pa·ta·ku
bus stop	பஸ்	pas
	நிறுத்தும்	ni·rut·tum
economy class	சிக்கன	chik·ka·na
	வகுப்பு	va·kup·pu
first class	முதல்	mu·tal
	வகுப்பு	va·kup·pu
motorcycle	மோட்டார்	mowt·taar
	சைக்கிள்	chaik·kil
train station	நிலையம்	ni·lai·yam

What time's the first/last bus?
எத்தனை மணிக்கு   et·ta·nai ma·nik·ku
முதல்/இறுதி   mu·tal/i·ru·ti
பஸ் வரும்?   pas va·rum

How long does the trip take?
பயணம் எவ்வளவு   pa·ya·nam ev·va·la·vu
நேரம் எடுக்கும்?   ney·ram e·tuk·kum

GLOSSARY

Adivasis – tribal people

Ardhanarishvara – *Shiva's* half-male, half-female form

Arjuna – Mahabharata hero and military commander; he had the *Bhagavad Gita* related to him by *Krishna*.

Aryan – Sanskrit for 'noble'; those who migrated from Persia and settled in northern India

ashram – spiritual community or retreat

ASI – Archaeological Survey of India; an organisation involved in monument preservation

autorickshaw – noisy, three-wheeled, motorised contraption for transporting passengers, livestock etc for short distances; found throughout the country, they are cheaper than taxis

Avalokitesvara – in Mahayana Buddhism, the *bodhisattva* of compassion

avatar – incarnation, usually of a deity

ayurveda – ancient and complex science of Indian herbal medicine and holistic healing

azad – Urdu for 'free', as in Azad Jammu and Kashmir

Baba – religious master or father; term of respect

bagh – garden

bahadur – brave or chivalrous; an honorific title

baksheesh – tip, donation (alms) or bribe

banyan – Indian fig tree; spiritual to many Indians

baoli – see *baori*

baori – well, particularly a step-well with landings and galleries; in Gujarat it is more commonly referred to as a *baoli*

barasingha – deer

basti – slum

bearer – like a butler

Bhagavad Gita – Hindu Song of the Divine One; Krishna's lessons to *Arjuna*, the main thrust of which was to emphasise the philosophy of *bhakti*; it is part of the Mahabharata

bhajan – devotional song

bhakti – surrendering to the gods; faith, devotion

bhang – dried leaves and flowering shoots of the marijuana plant

bhangra – rhythmic Punjabi music/dance

Bharat – Hindi for India

bhavan – house, building; also spelt bhawan

Bhima – Mahabharata hero; the brother of Hanuman, husband of Hadimba, father of Ghatotkach, and renowned for his great strength

bindi – forehead mark (often dot-shaped) made from *kumkum*, worn by women

BJP – Bharatiya Janata Party

Bodhi Tree – tree under which *Buddha* sat when he attained enlightenment

bodhisattva – enlightened beings

Bollywood – India's answer to Hollywood; the film industry of Mumbai (Bombay)

Brahma – Hindu god; worshipped as the creator in the Trimurti

Brahmanism – early form of Hinduism that evolved from Vedism (see *Vedas*); named after *Brahmin* priests and *Brahma*

Brahmin – member of the priest/scholar caste, the highest Hindu caste

Buddha – Awakened One; the originator of *Buddhism*; also regarded by Hindus as the ninth incarnation of *Vishnu*

Buddhism – see *Early Buddhism*

cantonment – administrative and military area of a Raj-era town

Carnatic music – classical music of South India

caste – a Hindu's hereditary station (social standing) in life; there are four main castes: Brahmin, Kshatriya, Vaishya and Shudra

chaam – ritual masked dance performed by some Buddhist monks in gompas to celebrate the victory of good over evil and of Buddhism over preexisting religions

chaitya – prayer room; assembly hall

chakra – focus of one's spiritual power; disc-like weapon of *Vishnu*

Chamunda – form of Durga; armed with a scimitar, noose and mace, and clothed in elephant hide, her mission was to kill the demons Chanda and Munda

chandra – moon, or the moon as a god

Chandragupta – Indian ruler in the 3rd century BC

chappals – sandals or leather thonglike footwear; flip-flops

char dham – four pilgrimage destinations of Badrinath, Kedarnath, Yamunotri and Gangotri

charas – resin of the marijuana plant; also referred to as hashish

charbagh – formal Persian garden, divided into quarters (literally 'four gardens')

chedi – see *chaitya*

chhatri – cenotaph (literally 'umbrella'),or pavilion

chikan – embroidered cloth (speciality of Lucknow)

chillum – pipe of a hookah; commonly used to describe the pipes used for smoking ganja (marijuana)

chinkara – gazelle

chital – spotted deer

chogyal – king

choli – sari blouse

chorten – Tibetan for stupa

choultry – pilgrim's rest house; also called dharamsala

chowk – town square, intersection or marketplace

Cong (I) – Congress Party of India; also known as Congress (I)

coracle – a small, traditional keel-less boat, often round or oval in shape, comprising a wickerwork or lath frame over which greased cloth or hide is stretched

dagoba – see *stupa*

Dalit – preferred term for India's Untouchable caste; see also *Harijan*

dargah – shrine or place of burial of a Muslim saint

darshan – offering or audience with a deity

deul – temple sanctuary

Devi – *Shiva*'s wife; goddess

dhaba – basic restaurant or snack bar

dham – holiest pilgrimage places of India

dharamsala – pilgrim's rest house

dharma – for Hindus, the moral code of behaviour or social duty; for Buddhists, following the law of nature, or path, as taught by Buddha

dhobi – person who washes clothes; commonly referred to as dhobi-wallah

dhobi ghat – place where clothes are washed

dhoti – long loincloth worn by men; like a lungi, but the ankle-length cloth is then pulled up between the legs

Digambara – 'Sky-Clad'; Jain group that demonstrates disdain for worldly goods by going naked

diwan – principal officer in a princely state; royal court or council

Diwan-i-Am – hall of public audience

Diwan-i-Khas – hall of private audience

dowry – money and/or goods given by a bride's parents to their son-in-law's family; it's illegal but still widely exists in many arranged marriages

Draupadi – wife of the five Pandava princes in the Mahabharata

Dravidian – general term for the cultures and languages of the deep south of India, including Tamil, Malayalam, Telugu and Kannada

dukhang – Tibetan prayer hall

dun – valley

dupatta – long scarf for women often worn with the *salwar kameez*

durbar – royal court; also a government

Durga – the Inaccessible; a form of *Shiva*'s wife, Devi, a beautiful, fierce woman riding a tiger/lion; a major goddess of the *Shakti* order

Early Buddhism – any of the schools of Buddhism established directly after Buddha's death and before the advent of Mahayana; a modern form is the Theravada (Teaching of the Elders) practised in Sri Lanka and Southeast Asia; Early Buddhism differed from the Mahayana in that it did not teach the *bodhisattva* ideal

gabba – appliquéd Kashmiri rug

gali – lane or alleyway

Ganesh – Hindu god of good fortune; elephant-headed son of *Shiva* and Parvati, he is also known as Ganpati and his vehicle is Mooshak (a ratlike creature)

Ganga – Hindu goddess representing the sacred Ganges River; said to flow from *Vishnu*'s toe

ganj – market

gaon – village

garh – fort

Garuda – man-bird vehicle of *Vishnu*

gaur – Indian bison

Gayatri – sacred verse of Rig-Veda repeated mentally by Brahmins twice a day

geyser – hot-water unit found in many bathrooms

ghat – steps or landing on a river; a range of hills or a road up hills

giri – hill

gompa – Tibetan Buddhist monastery

Gopala – see *Govinda*

gopi – milkmaid; Krishna was fond of them

gopuram – soaring pyramidal gateway tower of Dravidian temples

Govinda – Krishna as a cowherd; also just cowherd

gumbad – dome on an Islamic tomb or mosque

gurdwara – Sikh temple

guru – holy teacher; in Sanskrit literally 'goe' (darkness) and 'roe' (to dispel)

Guru Granth Sahib – Sikh holy book

haat – village market

haj – Muslim pilgrimage to Mecca

haji – Muslim who has made the haj

hammam – Turkish bath; public bathhouse

Hanuman – Hindu monkey god, prominent in the Ramayana, and a follower of Rama

Hari – another name for *Vishnu*

Harijan – name (no longer considered acceptable) given by Mahatma Gandhi to India's Untouchable caste, meaning 'children of god'

hashish – see *charas*

hathi – elephant

haveli – traditional, often ornately decorated, residences, particularly those found in Rajasthan and Gujarat

hijab – headscarf used by Muslim women

hijra – eunuch, transvestite

hookah – water pipe used for smoking marijuana or strong tobacco

howdah – seat for carrying people on an elephant's back

ikat – fabric made with thread which is tie-dyed before weaving

imam – Muslim religious leader

imambara – tomb dedicated to a Shiite Muslim holy man

Indo-Saracenic – style of colonial architecture that integrated Western designs with Islamic, Hindu and Jain influences

Indra – significant and prestigious Vedic god; god of rain, thunder, lightning and war

jagamohan – assembly hall

Jagannath – Lord of the Universe; a form of Krishna

jali – carved lattice (often marble) screen; also refers to the holes or spaces produced through carving timber or stone

Jataka – tale from Buddha's various lives

jauhar – ritual mass suicide by immolation, traditionally performed by Rajput women at times of military defeat to avoid being dishonoured by their captors

jhula – bridge

ji – honorific that can be added to the end of almost anything as a form of respect; thus 'Babaji', 'Gandhiji'

jooti – traditional, often pointy-toed, slip-in shoes; commonly found in North India

juggernaut – huge, extravagantly decorated temple 'car' dragged through the streets during certain Hindu festivals

yoti linga – naturally occurring lingam believed to derive currents of *Shakti*

kabaddi – traditional game (similar to tag)

Kailasa – sacred Himalayan mountain; home of *Shiva*

Kali – ominous-looking evil-destroying form of Devi; commonly depicted with dark skin, dripping with blood, and wearing a necklace of skulls

Kama – Hindu god of love

Kama Sutra – ancient Sanskrit text largely covering the subjects of love and sexuality

kameez – woman's shirtlike tunic; see also *salwar kameez*

karma – Hindu, Buddhist and Sikh principle of retributive justice for past deeds

khadi – homespun cloth; Mahatma Gandhi encouraged people to spin this rather than buy English cloth

Khalsa – Sikh brotherhood

Khan – Muslim honorific title

khur – Asiatic wild ass

kirtan – Sikh devotional singing

koil – Hindu temple

kolam – see *rangoli*

kot – fort

kothi – residence or mansion

kotwali – police station

Krishna – *Vishnu*'s eighth incarnation, often coloured blue; he revealed the *Bhagavad Gita* to *Arjuna*

kumkum – coloured powder used for *bindi* dots

kund – lake or tank; Toda village

kurta – long shirt with either short collar or no collar

Lakshmana – half-brother and aide of Rama in the Ramayana

Lakshmi – *Vishnu*'s consort, Hindu goddess of wealth; she sprang forth from the ocean holding a lotus

lama – Tibetan Buddhist priest or monk

Laxmi – see *Lakshmi*

lingam – phallic symbol; auspicious symbol of *Shiva*; plural 'linga'

lok – people

Lok Sabha – lower house in the Indian parliament (House of the People)

Losar – Tibetan New Year

lungi – worn by men, this loose, coloured garment (similar to a sarong) is pleated by the wearer at the waist to fit

madrasa – Islamic seminary

maha – prefix meaning 'great'

Mahabharata – Great Hindu Vedic epic poem of the Bharata dynasty; containing approximately 10,000 verses describing the battle between the Pandavas and the Kauravas

Mahakala – Great Time; *Shiva* and one of 12 jyoti linga (sacred shrines)

mahal – house or palace

maharaja – literally 'great king'; princely ruler

maharana – see *maharaja*

maharani – wife of a princely ruler or a ruler in her own right

maharao – see *maharaja*

maharawal – see *maharaja*

mahatma – literally 'great soul'

Mahavir – last tirthankar

Mahayana – the 'greater-vehicle' of Buddhism; a later adaptation of the teaching that lays emphasis on the *bodhisattva* ideal, teaching the renunciation of nirvana in order to help other beings along the way to enlightenment

maidan – open (often grassed) area; parade ground

Maitreya – future Buddha

mandal – shrine

mandala – circle; symbol used in Hindu and Buddhist art to symbolise the universe

mandapa – pillared pavilion, temple forechamber

mandi – market

mandir – temple

mani stone – stone carved with the Tibetan-Buddhist mantra 'Om mani padme hum' ('Hail the jewel in the lotus')

mani walls – Tibetan stone walls with sacred inscriptions

mantra – sacred word or syllable used by Buddhists and Hindus to aid concentration; metrical psalms of praise found in the *Vedas*

Maratha – central Indian people who controlled much of India at various times and fought the Mughals and Rajputs

marg – road

masjid – mosque

mata – mother

math – monastery

maya – illusion

mehndi – henna; ornate henna designs on women's hands (and often feet), traditionally for certain festivals or ceremonies (eg marriage)

mela – fair or festival

mithuna – pairs of men and women; often seen in temple sculpture

Moghul – see *Mughal*

monsoon – rainy season

muezzin – one who calls Muslims to prayer, traditionally from the minaret of a mosque

Mughal – Muslim dynasty of subcontinental emperors from Babur to Aurangzeb

Mumbaikar – resident of Mumbai (Bombay)

namaste – traditional Hindu greeting (hello or goodbye), often accompanied by a respectful small bow with the hands together at the chest or head level

Nanda – cowherd who raised Krishna

Nandi – bull, vehicle of *Shiva*

Narayan – incarnation of *Vishnu* the creator

Nataraja – *Shiva* as the cosmic dancer

nawab – Muslim ruling prince or powerful landowner

Naxalites – ultra-leftist political movement begun in West Bengal as a peasant rebellion; characterised by violence

nilgai – antelope

nirvana – ultimate aim of Buddhists and the final release from the cycle of existence

niwas – house, building

nizam – hereditary title of the rulers of Hyderabad

nullah – ditch or small stream

Om – sacred invocation representing the essence of the divine principle; for Buddhists, if repeated often enough with complete concentration, it leads to a state of emptiness

Osho – the late Bhagwan Shree Rajneesh, a popular, controversial guru

paan – mixture of betel nut and leaves for chewing

padma – lotus; another name for the Hindu goddess Lakshmi

pagoda – see *stupa*

paise – the Indian rupee is divided into 100 paise

palanquin – boxlike enclosure carried on poles on four bearer's shoulders; the occupant sits inside on a seat

Pali – the language, related to Sanskrit, in which the Buddhist scriptures were recorded; scholars still refer to the original Pali texts

pandal – marquee; temple shrine

Parsi – adherent of the Zoroastrian faith

Partition – formal division of British India in 1947 into two separate countries, India and Pakistan

Parvati – another form of Devi

pashmina – fine woollen shawl

PCO – Public Call Office, from where you can make local, interstate and international phone calls

peepul – fig tree, especially a bo tree

peon – lowest-grade clerical worker

pietra dura – marble inlay work characteristic of the Taj Mahal

pradesh – state

pranayama – study of breath control; meditative practice

prasad – temple-blessed food offering

puja – literally 'respect'; offering or prayers

pukka – proper; a Raj-era term

punka – cloth fan, swung by pulling a cord

Puranas – set of 18 encyclopaedic Sanskrit stories, written in verse, relating to the three gods, dating from the 5th century AD

purdah – custom among some conservative Muslims (also adopted by some Hindus, especially the Rajputs) of keeping women in seclusion; veiled

Purnima – full moon; considered to be an auspicious time

qawwali – Islamic devotional singing

qila – fort

Quran – the holy book of Islam, also spelt Koran

Radha – favourite mistress of Krishna when he lived as a cowherd

raga – any of several conventional patterns of melody and rhythm that form the basis for freely interpreted compositions

railhead – station or town at the end of a railway line; termination point

raj – rule or sovereignty; British Raj (sometimes just Raj) refers to British rule

raja – king; sometimes rana

rajkumar – prince

Rajput – Hindu warrior caste, former rulers of northwestern India

Rama – seventh incarnation of *Vishnu*

Ramadan – Islamic holy month of sunrise-to-sunset fasting (no eating, drinking or smoking); also referred to as Ramazan

Ramayana – story of Rama and Sita and their conflict with Ravana; one of India's best-known epics

rana – king; sometimes raja

rangoli – elaborate chalk, rice-paste or coloured powder design; also known as kolam

rani – female ruler or wife of a king

ranns – deserts

rath – temple chariot or car used in religious festivals

rathas – rock-cut Dravidian temples

Ravana – demon king of Lanka who abducted Sita; the titanic battle between him and Rama is told in the Ramayana

rickshaw – small, two- or three-wheeled passenger vehicle

Rig-Veda – original and longest of the four main *Vedas*

rishi – any poet, philosopher, saint or sage; originally a sage to whom the hymns of the *Vedas* were revealed

Road – railway town that serves as a communication point to a larger town off the line, eg Mt Abu and Abu Road

Rukmani – wife of Krishna; died on his funeral pyre

sadar – main

sadhu – ascetic, holy person, one who is trying to achieve enlightenment; often addressed as 'swamiji' or 'babaji'

sagar – lake, reservoir

sahib – respectful title applied to a gentleman

salai – road

salwar – trousers usually worn with a kameez

salwar kameez – traditional dresslike tunic and trouser combination for women

samadhi – in Hinduism, ecstatic state, sometimes defined as 'ecstasy, trance, communion with God'; in Buddhism, concentration; also a place where a holy man has been cremated/buried, usually venerated as a shrine

sambar – deer

samsara – Buddhists, Hindus and Sikhs believe earthly life is cyclical; you are born again and again, the quality of these rebirths being dependent upon your karma in previous lives

sangha – community of Buddhist monks and nuns

Saraswati – wife of Brahma, goddess of learning; sits on a white swan, holding a veena (a type of string instrument)

Sat Sri Akal – Sikh greeting

Sati – wife of *Shiva*; became a sati ('honourable woman') by

**immolating herself; although
banned more than a century
ago, the act of sati is still (very)
occasionally performed

satra** – Hindu Vaishnavaite
monastery and centre for art

satyagraha – nonviolent
protest involving a hunger strike,
popularised by Mahatma Gandhi;
from Sanskrit, literally meaning
'insistence on truth'

Scheduled Castes – official
term used for the Untouchable
or Dalit caste

Shaivism – worship of *Shiva*

Shaivite – follower of *Shiva*

shakti – creative energies
perceived as female deities;
devotees follow Shaktism order

sheesha – see *hookah*

shikara – gondola-like boat used
on lakes in Srinagar (Kashmir)

shikhar – hunting expedition

Shiva – Destroyer; also the
Creator, in which form he is
worshipped as a lingam

shola – virgin forest

shree – see *shri*

shri – honorific male prefix;
Indian equivalent of 'Respected
Sir'

Shudra – caste of labourers

sikhara – Hindu temple-spire
or temple

Singh – literally 'lion'; a surname
adopted by Sikhs

Sita – Hindu goddess of agriculture; more commonly associated
with the Ramayana

sitar – Indian stringed
instrument

Siva – see *Shiva*

sree – see *shri*

sri – see *shri*

stupa – Buddhist religious
monument composed of a solid
hemisphere topped by a spire,
containing relics of Buddha; also
known as a *dagoba* or *pagoda*

Subhadra – Krishna's
incestuous sister

Sufi – Muslim mystic

Sufism – Islamic mysticism

Surya – the sun; a major deity
in the *Vedas*

sutra – string; list of rules
expressed in verse

swami – title of respect meaning
'lord of the self'; given to initiated Hindu monks

tabla – twin drums

tal – lake

tank – reservoir; pool or large
receptacle of holy water found at
some temples

tantric Buddhism – Tibetan
Buddhism with strong sexual and
occult overtones

tempo – noisy three-wheeler
public transport vehicle, bigger
than an *autorickshaw*; see *Vikram*

thakur – nobleman

thangka – Tibetan cloth painting

theertham – temple tank

Theravada – orthodox form of
Buddhism practised in Sri Lanka
and Southeast Asia that is characterised by its adherence to the
Pali canon; literally 'dwelling'

tikka – mark Hindus put on their
foreheads

tirthankars – the 24 great Jain
teachers

tonga – two-wheeled horse or
pony carriage

torana – architrave over a
temple entrance

trekkers – jeeps; hikers

Trimurti – triple form or three-
faced; the Hindu triad of *Brahma,
Shiva* and *Vishnu*

Untouchable – lowest caste or
'casteless', for whom the most
menial tasks are reserved; the
name derives from the belief that
higher castes risk defilement if
they touch one; formerly known
as *Harijan,* now *Dalit*

Upanishads – esoteric doctrine;
ancient texts forming part of
the *Vedas*; delving into weighty
matters such as the nature of
the universe and soul

urs – death anniversary of a revered Muslim; festival in memory
of a Muslim saint

Valmiki – author of the
Ramayana

Vedas – Hindu sacred books;
collection of hymns composed
in preclassical Sanskrit during
the second millennium BC and
divided into four books: Rig-
Veda, Yajur-Veda, Sama-Veda and
Atharva-Veda

vihara – Buddhist monastery,
generally with central court or
hall off which open residential
cells, usually with a Buddha
shrine at one end; resting place

vikram – tempo or a larger version of the standard tempo

vimana – principal part of
Hindu temple; a tower over the
sanctum

vipassana – insight meditation
technique of Theravada
Buddhism in which mind and
body are closely examined as
changing phenomena

Vishnu – part of the Trimurti;
Vishnu is the Preserver and
Restorer who so far has nine
avatars: the fish Matsya; the
tortoise Kurma; the wild boar
Naraha; Narasimha; Vamana;
Parasurama; Rama; Krishna; and
Buddha

wallah – man; added onto almost anything, eg dhobi-wallah,
chai-wallah, taxi-wallah

yakshi – maiden

yali – mythical lion creature

yatra – pilgrimage

yatri – pilgrim

yogini – female goddess attendants

yoni – female fertility symbol;
female genitalia

zenana – area of an upperclass
home where women are
secluded; women's quarters

Behind the Scenes

SEND US YOUR FEEDBACK

We love to hear from travellers – your comments keep us on our toes and help make our books better. Our well-travelled team reads every word on what you loved or loathed about this book. Although we cannot reply individually to postal submissions, we always guarantee that your feedback goes straight to the appropriate authors, in time for the next edition. Each person who sends us information is thanked in the next edition – the most useful submissions are rewarded with a selection of digital PDF chapters.

Visit **lonelyplanet.com/contact** to submit your updates and suggestions or to ask for help. Our award-winning website also features inspirational travel stories, news and discussions.

Note: We may edit, reproduce and incorporate your comments in Lonely Planet products such as guidebooks, websites and digital products, so let us know if you don't want your comments reproduced or your name acknowledged. For a copy of our privacy policy visit lonelyplanet.com/privacy.

OUR READERS

Many thanks to the travellers who used the last edition and wrote to us with helpful hints, useful advice and interesting anecdotes:

A Claire Ahern, Frey Albert, Earl Almeida, Ruben Alonso, Naama Anabell, Margaret Andrews, Jeevan Asad **B** Miriam Baigorri, Harriet Ball, Joanna Balon, Gaia Barbato, Jean-luc Bargetzi, Vaskor Basak, Silvia Beccacece, Sophie Beckwith, Barbara Beun, Jennifer Black, Wendy Braak, Angela Bracegirdle, Roy Bradford, Mark Brennan, Jason Brewer, Gemma Briggs, Allen Brown, Katherine Brown, Marcia Browne, Bill Burdett, Paul Buxton **C** Richard Cabeza, Mette Cecilie Norholm, Ruff Cecillia, David Chambers, Nigel Chin, Samantha Choma, Neeraj Chowdhary, Sam Crisp, Ulrich Christensen, Mark Clifton, Nicola Cole, Valeria Corridori, Fiorenza Corte, Kirsty Cunningham **D** Sockhy Da Silva, Fiona Darcy, Robin De Ruiter & Inge Klaver, Vincenzo Del Re, Paulo Derela, Desset family, Abhishek Dhoot, Brett Dixon, Anne Dobson, Maegan Dobson, Emma Dayan **E** Bat El Nir, Ed Elberfeld, Robert Elliott, Maya Enabell, Pascal Endstra **F** Lisa Feldman, Leslie Fernandez, Grand Florence, Jon Foreman, Markus Franke, Toby & Inbal Frankenstein, Sarah Fulham **G** Eve Gage, Ewa Gembicka, Johannes Gergely, Debjit Ghosh, Adam Green, Kim Grossman, Matthew Grove, Pala Gulamnabi

H Peter Halford, Sarah Hallas-møller, Lis Hammer, Emma Harding, Luke Harding, Roy Hartling, Alisha Hawrylyszyn, Brian Heatley, Gerard Helmink, Murielle Henri, Rüdiger Hess, Shanny Hill, Suzan Hughes, Andre Huguet **I** Ben Ireland, Alicia Irwin, Caro Iuel **J** Ajay Jain, Mike Johnson **K** Yoshihiro Kaburagi, Birgit Kaider, Bram Kampschreur, Farah Karachiwala, Ewa & Magda Kaszynska, Nina Kenny, Ursula Krebs, Eva Kuijer, Pratik Kulkarni, Karthik Kumar, Parveen Kumar **L** Jan Lampe, Kristin Larkin, Todd Larue, Bill Lennox, Chantelle L'Heureux, Samuel Lickiss, Óscar López, Pam E Low, Melanie Luangsay, Marit Lucas **M** Jernej Markelj, Brian Mathias, Michael McKay, Michiel Meijs, Janneke Mekken, Liza Mendal, Marcos Mendonca, Sheila Miller, Ben Misterka, Tapabrata Mitra, Sandeep Moonka, Kate Morgan, Julie & Cameron Muir, Hannah Musisi **N** Lise Nadai, Shoaban Nair, Malcolm Noden **O** Redmond O' Shea, Ilona ÒBeirne, Roderick O'Brien, Nikos Oikonomou, Josu Ozkaritz **P** Kevin Paige, Hitesh Pant, Martina Parizkova, Pintu Patel, Mike Pearson, Garry Pedder, Marisa Pettit, Kevin Pitter, Martin Platter, Colburne Poapst **R** ME Rademaker, Radha Rajan, Shashi Ranjan, Clair Ricketts, Liz Rideal, Gulsah Robertson, Andrea Roessler, Jessica Rose, Christopher Rowland **S** Greg Sandford, Kalle Sankala, Anna Sauer, Wendy Saunders, Astrid Schaap-Vermolen, Werner Schmid, Ivri Schneider, Uwe Scholz, Hannah Shanks, Mahendra Singh,

Mannu Singh, Rajendra Singh, Sandeep Singh, Vijendra Singh, Lisa Smeets, John P Smith, Pooja Somaia, Josefine Stare, Robert Stirling, Salila Sukumaran, Jaewon Sun, Mahaveer Swami **T** Subash Tamang, Virág Tarnai, Finn Teylor, Heather Thoreau, Hannah Timmis, Anniger Tosse, Maureen Traughber **U** Johanna Unger, Scott Urbach **V** Bas Van Der Heide, Niki Van Turenhout, Veronique Verlinden, Simon Paul Vernon, Tom Verschraege, K Vijayakrishnan, Swami Vishwananda **W** Katherien Walker, Sarah J Walsh, Robert Wenzel, Rob Wiemer, Suzie Williams, Emma Worsham, Rolf Wrelf, Sarah Wursthorn **Y** Sue Yarrow, Emily Young, Tina Yu **Z** Adam Zbiejczuk, Scott Zinski

AUTHOR THANKS

Sarina Singh
A big thank you to everyone at Lonely Planet – with special mention to Suzannah and Brigitte – who worked so hard on this book. Gratitude, also, to the many readers across the world who took the time to write to us. Finally, warm thanks to the fantastic team of authors – you made this edition a delight for me to coordinate.

Michael Benanav
Huge thanks go to Lalji, Neeta, Sonal, Ashwin and their families, for their hospitality and insights into all things Gujarati. In Uttarakhand, I'd like to thank Debopam and Manto for helping me get beneath the surface of the state. My time in Kachchh wouldn't have been nearly as fun without my 'sister' Jessica. And my deepest gratitude goes to Kelly and Luke, who gracefully dealt with a number of challenges back home while I was on the road.

Joe Bindloss
Thanks firstly to Linda and Tyler for tagging along for the ride and putting up with the time I was away from home. In Delhi, thanks to the hospitable Sadia Dehlvi for providing a home away from home, and for offering the inside track on life as a Delhi-ite. Thanks also to Mayank Austen Soofi for invaluable tips and insights.

Lindsay Brown
I am very grateful for the assistance of various hotel managers, travel desks and tourism centres for putting up with all my questions. I would particularly like to thank Homi in Mumbai, coordinating author Sarina Singh, fellow traveller and Kingfisher fancier Stephen Nicholson, and Jenny, Pat and Sinead at home.

Mark Elliott
Many thanks to Rajesh, Mowgli and the gang, Rouf, Namgyal and family, Jai, Bunny and family, Mohd-Ali and Selim, Sharif, Abbas, Mirza, Sunny, Kaga and Amid the stone-savers, Jeannie and Yuruzu, Anirban, Shahdid and Lehaj, Yuka, Dave Davies, Harald Schaffer, Eitan and Inbar, Hossein in Turtuk, Grant Winter for fixing my neck, Barbara, Bijoo, Nawang; and not forgetting inspiring fellow travellers Birgit, Pika, Steve, Brenbo and sister Jane. Eternal thanks as ever to my beloved parents.

Paul Harding
Thanks to the many lovely people in Kerala and Goa who helped with tips, advice and a drink or two. In particular Debra, Johnson, Shibu, Niaz, Philip and Maryann, Suresh, Varghese and Beena, Walter, Ajit, Jack and family. But mostly thanks to Hannah and my beautiful daughter, Layla, who made Goa so much more enjoyable.

Trent Holden & Kate Morgan
First up thanks to Suzannah and Glenn for commissioning us to work on our dream book again. Cheers also to Sarina for her great work in piecing this together. In the Andamans, a massive thanks to all who helped out with tips and assistance in organising ferry schedules etc. Big sing out to Steve, too, for his trailblazing efforts. While in Karnataka we're also indebted to those who helped us get around and for all the leads and feedback.

Amy Karafin
I'm deeply grateful to the people of Andhra Pradesh and Bombay for all their help and for making such interesting places. Special thanks to Sandhya Kanneganti, Ram Babu, Jayasri Anand and Gayatri, Taps and Devi Vasireddy, Dr Kishore and Sandeep Kishore, Asif Husain Arastu, Saaz Aggarwal, Malini and Hari Hariharan, Akash Bhartiya, Surekha and Manik Bhartiya, Naresh Fernandes, Mujju, Satish Asi, Sarina Singh, Suzannah Shwer, Brigitte Ellemor, and everyone at Dhamma Khetta, Dhamma Vijaya and the Global Pagoda. *Bhavatu sabba mangalam*!

Anirban Mahapatra
Sincerest thanks to CEs Suzannah Shwer and Glenn van der Knijff for allowing me – once again – the privilege of exploring this crazy, quirky and wonderful country on assignment. To the entire team at Lonely Planet, for their unfailing support and encouragement through thick and thin. To Sarina Singh and all my fellow authors – together we stand! To Oken, Sange, Katu, Dr Kano, Raj, Neil, Suzanne, Rintu, Boo, Monjit, Jyoti, Lee, Babul, Krishna and Sang for their help, support and hospitality along the way. And finally, to my family and friends for standing by me. Beers for all!

Bradley Mayhew

Many thanks to Rajah Bannerjee and Ravindra Kang in Kurseong; to Norbu-la and Sangay-la in Darjeeling; and to Norden in Kalimpong for taking me on some wonderful day hikes in the region. In Chamba thanks to Prakash Dhami for some fascinating conversations, and in Jiri thanks to the Negi brothers for trekking information. Many thanks to fellow scribe Virginia Jealous for her generous help and tips in Shimla and around. Cheers as always to Andre for yet another great trek through Zanskar and to Mervyn Mitchell for joining us through Spiti. Most of all thanks to Kelli, for everything.

Daniel McCrohan

Thanks to colleagues Abigail Hole and John Noble for great tips. In Jaipur, Mr and Mrs Singh were fabulous hosts. I'm indebted to Sunny Gaur and his trusty moped for saving me from the Jodhpur touts, and to Gouri for his enthusiasm in Bikaner. Thanks also to Lois Mason and Veronica Gledhill Hall for help in Jaisalmer. Mostly, though, thank you to my wonderful mum, my darling wife and our incredible children for being brave enough to join me on this latest adventure.

John Noble

Extra special thanks to super-efficient research assistant and perfect travelling companion Isabella Noble; Ashish Gupta and colleagues; V Rangaraj Pillai; the Chennai autorickshaw driver who insisted on a fare lower than I offered; and, during write-up, to Coley, Hilary, Josh and Nala for the witty conversation, and to Jack for meals in the home stretch.

Kevin Raub

First and foremost, thanks to my wife, Adriana Schmidt Raub, who doesn't appreciate the subcontinent with quite the same fervour as hubby, but does love a tandoor. At Lonely Planet, thanks to Glenn van der Knijff, Suzannah Shwer, Sarina Singh and Daniel Mc-Crohan. On the road, thank you Mini-Google, Ramesh and Anil Wadhwa, Sanghamitra Jena, Bubu Yugabrata, Pankaj Bhatnagar, Michael Schmid, Nicole Seregni, Naheed Varma, Guatam Kumar Singh, Kamalakanta Samal, Claudia Günther and Prasanna Kumar Sahoo.

ACKNOWLEDGMENTS

Climate map data adapted from Peel MC, Finlayson BL & McMahon TA (2007) 'Updated World Map of the Köppen-Geiger Climate Classification', Hydrology and Earth System Sciences, 11, 1633-44.

Cover photograph: Women drying saris with views of the Taj Mahal, Agra, Uttar Pradesh/ Gavin Hellier/AWL.

Illustrations p1160, p1162, p1164 by Kelli Hamblet; p370, p872 by Michael Weldon; p62, p356, p636 by Javier Zarracina.

THIS BOOK

This 15th edition of Lonely Planet's *India* guidebook was researched and written by Sarina Singh (coordinating author), Michael Benanav, Joe Bindloss, Lindsay Brown, Mark Elliott, Paul Harding, Trent Holden, Amy Karafin, Anirban Mahapatra, Bradley Mayhew, Daniel McCrohan, Kate Morgan, John Noble and Kevin Raub.

This guidebook was commissioned in Lonely Planet's Melbourne office, and produced by the following:

Commissioning Editors Glenn Van der Knijff, Suzannah Shwer

Coordinating Editor Gina Tsarouhas

Senior Cartographer David Kemp

Coordinating Layout Designer Mazzy Prinsep

Managing Editors Brigitte Ellemor, Annelies Mertens

Managing Cartographer Adrian Persoglia

Managing Layout Designer Jane Hart

Assisting Editors Nigel Chin, Adrienne Costanzo, Andrea Dobbin, Carly Hall, Kate James, Elizabeth Jones, Helen Koehne, Shawn Low, Susan Paterson, Ross Taylor, Jeanette Wall

Assisting Cartographers Enes Basic, Jeff Cameron, Xavier Di Toro, Julie Dodkins

Assisting Layout Designer Wibowo Rusli

Cover Research Naomi Parker

Internal Image Research Kylie McLaughlin

Language Content Branislava Vladisavljevic

Thanks to Anita Banh, Ryan Evans, Larissa Frost, Errol Hunt, Genesys India, Laura Jane, Andi Jones, Jouve India, Stephen Palmer, Trent Paton, Kerrianne Southway, Gerard Walker, Amanda Williamson

Index

Map Pages **000**
Photo Pages **000**

Map Legend

Sights
- Beach
- Buddhist
- Castle
- Christian
- Hindu
- Islamic
- Jewish
- Monument
- Museum/Gallery
- Ruin
- Winery/Vineyard
- Zoo
- Other Sight

Activities, Courses & Tours
- Diving/Snorkelling
- Canoeing/Kayaking
- Skiing
- Surfing
- Swimming/Pool
- Walking
- Windsurfing
- Other Activity/Course/Tour

Sleeping
- Sleeping
- Camping

Eating
- Eating

Drinking
- Drinking
- Cafe

Entertainment
- Entertainment

Shopping
- Shopping

Information
- Bank
- Embassy/Consulate
- Hospital/Medical
- Internet
- Police
- Post Office
- Telephone
- Toilet
- Tourist Information
- Other Information

Transport
- Airport
- Border Crossing
- Bus
- Cable Car/Funicular
- Cycling
- Ferry
- Monorail
- Parking
- Petrol Station
- Taxi
- Train/Railway
- Tram
- Underground Train Station
- Other Transport

Routes
- Tollway
- Freeway
- Primary
- Secondary
- Tertiary
- Lane
- Unsealed Road
- Plaza/Mall
- Steps
- Tunnel
- Pedestrian Overpass
- Walking Tour
- Walking Tour Detour
- Path

Geographic
- Hut/Shelter
- Lighthouse
- Lookout
- Mountain/Volcano
- Oasis
- Park
- Pass
- Picnic Area
- Waterfall

Population
- Capital (National)
- Capital (State/Province)
- City/Large Town
- Town/Village

Boundaries
- International
- State/Province
- Disputed
- Regional/Suburb
- Marine Park
- Cliff
- Wall

Hydrography
- River, Creek
- Intermittent River
- Swamp/Mangrove
- Reef
- Canal
- Water
- Dry/Salt/Intermittent Lake
- Glacier

Areas
- Beach/Desert
- Cemetery (Christian)
- Cemetery (Other)
- Park/Forest
- Sportsground
- Sight (Building)
- Top Sight (Building)

Bradley Mayhew

Himachal Pradesh, West Bengal & Darjeeling (West Bengal Hills) A self-professed mountain junkie, Bradley has been travelling to the Indian Himalaya for almost 20 years. For this edition he spent a month trekking across Zanskar, jeeped through Spiti and spent a week testing hikes around Kalimpong. Bradley is the coordinating author of Lonely Planet guides to *Tibet*, *Bhutan* and *Nepal* and recently completed a five-part Arte TV documentary retracing the route of Marco Polo. See what he's up to at www.bradleymayhew.blogspot.com.

Daniel McCrohan

Rajasthan Daniel has written 15 books for Lonely Planet, including six *India* titles, and this latest research trip was as incident-packed as any. He survived a sleeper-train bed collapsing on his shins, a man throwing up over him on a packed bus and a genuinely scary road chase, in which he was chased by crazy hotel touts before being saved by a guardian angel with a fast moped. When he's not risking his life in India, Daniel can usually be found in Beijing, or on Twitter (@danielmccrohan).

John Noble

Tamil Nadu & Chennai John, from England, lives in Spain and has written about 20-odd countries for Lonely Planet. He first experienced Tamil Nadu in the 1980s when Chennai's Triplicane High Rd was clogged with bullock carts and families milked their buffaloes beside it. Autorickshaws have replaced bullock carts now, but the bustle of Tamil cities remains as exhilarating and exhausting as ever, and the thrill of reaching cool, green Kodaikanal will never pall. Best discovery of the trip: the tranquillity of Tranquebar.

Kevin Raub

Uttar Pradesh & the Taj Mahal, Odisha Kevin grew up in Atlanta, USA, and started his career as a music journalist in New York, working for *Men's Journal* and *Rolling Stone* magazines. He ditched the rock 'n' roll lifestyle for travel writing and moved to Brazil. On his seventh trip to India, a cow threw sand at him and he was nearly attacked by a monkey – but he persevered. This is Kevin's 23rd Lonely Planet guide. Find him at www.kevinraub.net.

Lindsay Brown

Madhya Pradesh & Chhattisgarh, Maharashtra Lindsay, a former conservation biologist and Publishing Manager at Lonely Planet, has been a frequent visitor to India for more than 25 years. Lindsay has trekked, jeeped, ridden and stumbled across many a mountain pass and contributed to Lonely Planet's *Bhutan*, *Nepal*, *South India*, *Rajasthan*, *Delhi & Agra* and *Pakistan & the Karakoram Highway* guides, among others. Lindsay also wrote the Travel with Children, India's Wildlife & Parks and The Landscape chapters.

Mark Elliott

Jammu & Kashmir (including Ladakh), Kolkata (Calcutta) Mark has been making forays to the subcontinent since a 1984 adventure that lined his stomach for all eventualities. For this edition he was delighted to find Srinagar curfew-free and to see how well Ladakh had recovered from the flash floods that had caused such devastation during his last visit. When not writing guidebooks Mark is studying geopolitics in Sussex while rediscovering the England of his birth after living abroad for more than 20 years.

Paul Harding

Goa, Kerala Paul has explored India and all its mayhem many times over the past 15 years, frequently writing about it. He still has a soft spot for the south, where the pace of life is that little bit slower. For this trip he investigated Kerala's backwaters at close range, was charged by wild elephants in Wayanad, and carefully inspected all of Goa's beautiful beaches while taste-testing fresh seafood. Tough life! This was Paul's seventh assignment on Lonely Planet *India*; he has also authored the *Goa* guidebook.

Trent Holden & Kate Morgan

Karnataka & Bengaluru, Andaman Islands Having worked together on books from Zimbabwe to Japan, Trent and Kate were thrilled to be assigned to India again for Lonely Planet, this time working as coauthors. In Karnataka they had the not-so-shabby task of testing Bengaluru's countless bars and classy restaurants, spotting leopards on safari and taking in Hampi's famous ruins. Trent also returned to the Andamans for more sun, surf and sand. Based in Melbourne, in between travels they write about food and music.

Amy Karafin

Mumbai (Bombay), Andhra Pradesh Indian in several former lives, Amy first fell for the country in 1996, when she discovered *idlis* (spongy, round, fermented rice cakes), meditation and endless train rides. In many visits since, she has written about everything from Bollywood to *mithai* (Indian sweets), contemporary art to ancient religions, and yoga ghettoes to nizams' palaces; read more at www.amykarafin.com. When not on the road, she can be found watching Guru Dutt movies or singing filmi in Brooklyn, where she mostly lives. This is Amy's fifth time coauthoring *India*. Amy also wrote the India's Top 17, If You Like, Month by Month, India Today, History, The Great Indian Bazaar and The Arts chapters.

> Read more about Amy at:
> lonelyplanet.com/members/amykarafin

Anirban Mahapatra

West Bengal & Darjeeling (South of Kolkata, North of Kolkata), Bihar & Jharkhand, Sikkim, Northeast States Anirban threw away a career in newspaper journalism and hit the road as a travel writer in 2007, not long after realising that good food, great music and that awesome experience called life all existed outside the confines of a sanitised office cubicle. On this assignment, he retraced his oft-travelled routes through east and northeast India, meditating in Bodhgaya, befriending rhinos in Kaziranga's grasslands, quaffing *chhang* (barley beer) with Sikkimese villagers, trundling through Arunachal's primordial forests, gorging on Nagaland's porky delights, grooving to the blues in Meghalaya and feasting his eyes on southern Bengal's gold-and-green rice fields. Anirban also wrote the Scams, Directory A–Z and Transport chapters. To know more about his escapades, log onto www.anirbanmahapatra.in.

OUR STORY

A beat-up old car, a few dollars in the pocket and a sense of adventure. In 1972 that's all Tony and Maureen Wheeler needed for the trip of a lifetime – across Europe and Asia overland to Australia. It took several months, and at the end – broke but inspired – they sat at their kitchen table writing and stapling together their first travel guide, *Across Asia on the Cheap*. Within a week they'd sold 1500 copies. Lonely Planet was born.

Today, Lonely Planet has offices in Melbourne, London and Oakland, with more than 600 staff and writers. We share Tony's belief that 'a great guidebook should do three things: inform, educate and amuse'.

OUR WRITERS

Sarina Singh

Coordinating Author After finishing a business degree in Melbourne, Sarina travelled to India where she pursued a hotel corporate traineeship before working as a journalist. After five years she returned to Australia and completed postgraduate journalism qualifications before coauthoring Lonely Planet's first edition of *Rajasthan*. Apart from numerous Lonely Planet books, she has written for a raft of newspapers and magazines, and has been a high-profile travel columnist. Sarina is also the author of two prestigious books – *Polo in India* and *India: Essential Encounters*. Her award-nominated documentary film premiered at the Melbourne International Film Festival before being screened internationally. Sarina wrote the Welcome to India, The Way of Life, Spiritual India, Delicious India, Sacred Architecture and Women & Solo Travellers chapters.

Michael Benanav

Uttarakhand, Gujarat As a writer and photojournalist who covers issues affecting traditional cultures, Michael knew he hit the mother lode when he first visited Gujarat, criss-crossing the state on his way to remote tribal villages. In Uttarakhand, he's migrated with nomadic water buffalo herders into the Himalaya and joined religious worshippers on mountainous pilgrimage trails. The abundance of fascinating stories in these states – and the friendships he's formed in these places – keep drawing him back. Michael also wrote the Trekking chapter.

Joe Bindloss

Delhi, Haryana & Punjab Joe has been writing about India for more than a decade, covering everywhere from Delhi to the high Himalaya. He has written more than 40 guides for Lonely Planet, trotting the globe from Australia and Asia to Africa and Europe. If pushed, he would say his favourite spot in the world was somewhere in India, ideally with a clear mountain view. Between projects, Joe is based in London, with his growing collection of Indian instruments. Joe also wrote the Need to Know, Itineraries, Booking Trains, Yoga, Spas & Spiritual Pursuits, Volunteering and Regions at a Glance chapters.

OVER PAGE
MORE WRITERS

Published by Lonely Planet Publications Pty Ltd
ABN 36 005 607 983
15th edition – October 2013
ISBN 978 1 74220 412 3
© Lonely Planet 2013   Photographs © as indicated 2013
10 9 8 7 6 5 4 3 2 1
Printed in Singapore

Although the authors and Lonely Planet have taken all reasonable care in preparing this book, we make no warranty about the accuracy or completeness of its content and, to the maximum extent permitted, disclaim all liability arising from its use.